Albanian-English Dictionary

EDITED BY LEONARD NEWMARK

OXFORD UNIVERSITY PRESS

OXFORD
UNIVERSITY PRESS

Great Clarendon Street, Oxford OX2 6DP

Oxford University Press is a department of the University of Oxford.
It furthers the University's objective of excellence in research, scholarship,
and education by publishing worldwide in

Oxford New York

Athens Auckland Bangkok Bogotá Buenos Aires Calcutta
Cape Town Chennai Dar es Salaam Delhi Florence Hong Kong Istanbul
Karachi Kuala Lumpur Madrid Melbourne Mexico City Mumbai
Nairobi Paris São Paulo Singapore Taipei Tokyo Toronto Warsaw

with associated companies in Berlin Ibadan

Oxford is a registered trade mark of Oxford University Press
in the UK and in certain other countries

Published in the United States
by Oxford University Press Inc., New York

British Library Cataloguing in Publication Data

Data available

Library of Congress Cataloging in Publication Data

Data available

ISBN 0-19-864340-3 (Hbk)
ISBN 0-19-860322-3 (Pbk)

Printed in Great Britain by
Cox & Wyman Ltd, Reading, Berkshire

Albanian letter	Technical Description	Approximate English equivalent
q	voiceless palatal stop	like *c* in *cute*
r	apical flap	like *d* in American pronunciation of *modest*
rr	apical trill	like *tter* in fast American pronunciation of *butter*
s	voiceless apical sibilant	like *s* in *soup*
sh	voiceless palatal sibilant	like *sh* in *shine*
t	voiceless apical stop	= *t*
th	voiceless interdental fricative	like *th* in *thing*
u	back rounded high vowel	like *oo* in *roof*
v	voiced interdental fricative	= *v*
x	voiced apical affricate	like *dz* in *adz*
xh	voiceless palatal affricate	like *j* in *jar*
y	high front rounded vowel	like Southern American pronunciation of *uu* in *vacuum*
z	voiceless apical sibilant	= *z*
zh	voiceless palatal sibilant	like *z* in *azure* (like French *j* in *je*)

Albanian pronunciation is reflected rather directly by standard spelling, with a few notable exceptions:

    Unstressed *ë* is pronounced very lightly or not at all by. At the ends of morphemes and words, voiced obstruents (**b, d, g, dh, v, xh, zh**) are usually devoiced by Tosk speakers, so that they sound respectively like **p, t, k, th, f, ç, sh** in those positions.

    Gheg speakers use nasalized vowels and long vowels. Nasalized vowels are marked by a circumflex ^ over the vowel: **â, ê, î, ô, û.** Long vowels are distinctive in Gheg but are not represented in normal orthography.

    Through the years, many printers have lacked fonts containing the special characters used in printing standard Albanian orthography, and there is a substantial amount of published material that fails to distinguish e from ë, c from ç, and nasalized vowels from their oral counterparts: a from â, e from ê, etc. Albanians have little difficulty recognizing words in context even when these clues are missing, but the foreign reader will have to struggle with the problem until words and phrases become familiar enough to be recognized despite the reduced information in the printed word.

VARIABLE FORMS

Many stems and affixes are variable in form. This dictionary includes irregularly formed or used stem alternants, but in general, it does not include regularly formed ones. If the reader does not recognize a form in the text, the **Reverse List of Possible Word Terminations** beginning on p. xlix may help identify it.

VARIABLE LETTERS

To help the reader recognize text forms related to, but not identical to those listed in the dictionary, lightface and boldface italics have special values in this dictionary not found in normal Albanian orthography.

The evanescent letter *ë* at the end of a citation form disappears before any suffix beginning in a vowel, and evanescent *ë* at the beginning of a suffix disappears after any stem ending in a vowel. For example, the citation form **rru'gë** reflects the inflected forms **rruga, rruge, rrugat, rrugash,** and **rrugave,** [12] which lack the final **ë** of the citation form, as well as the forms **rrugë, rrugën,** and **rrugës,** [13] which have it.

In standard Albanian orthography, when two nouns differ only in the presence or absence of **ë** at the end, the one with **ë** is feminine *(nf),* and the one without is *nm.*

    lug *nm* trough
    lugë *nf* spoon
    breshk *nm* tortoise (male)
    breshkë *nf* tortoise (female)

In other positions, *ë* is an evanescent letter, indicating that it may be absent in other forms of the word; in other varieties of the language, it may be totally absent or may appear as *e* or *i.* For example, **trashëgim** is **trashgim** in some varieties of Albanian, in others, **trashigim;** m*ë*ko•N is mko•N in some varieties of Albanian.

---

[12] **rruga** and **rruge** are the nominative definite and ablative/dative indefinite case forms of the noun; **rrugat, rrugash** and **rrugave** are case forms of its plural derivative **rruga.**

[13] **rrugë** serves as the nominative and accusative indefinite, **rrugën** as the accusative definite, and **rrugës** as the ablative/dative definite.

The evanescent letter *e* at the end of a noun citation form is replaced by *j* before the *nf* nominative definite suffix -**a** and optionally before the *nf* dative indefinite suffix -**e**: for example, the *nf* stem **lu'le**, has the nominative definite case form **lulja** and in the colloquial dative indefinite case form **lulje**.

There is considerable dialectal variation between *e* and *ë* as terminal vowels; one person or one dialect will have a final *ë* rather than *e* in a particular stem and vice versa. For example, while the standard form is **lu'le**, a common form in some varieties of Albanian in **lu'lë**, and that form even finds its way into the standard language in the many compound words with the latter form, alongside other compounds with the former.

The evanescent letters *het* (or *et*, if the verb stem ends in a consonant) mark the end of a citation form for a verb in the passive voice (including all *vpr* stems). The letters *he* appear in all on the present and imperfect inflected forms of the verb, while the final letter *t* appears only in t the present tense 3sg form. All other passive voice forms of the verb are identical to those of the active voice, except that the presence of the clitic reflexive marker **u** marks them as passive. For example, the *vpr* stem **la'·het**, has the imperfect 1sg form **la'hesha**, but the past definite 1sg form **u lava**.

Letters in boldface italics generally indicate that other forms of that stem have other letters in place of the italicized ones. For example, a final *t* in a verb citation form represents a variable letter which may appears as either **t** or **s** in various forms of the same verb:

citation form	2 & 3 sg pres	1sg pdef	2 & 3 sg pres	1sg pres	pl pres	subj	impf
py'et·	**py'et**	**py'eta**	**py'etni** or **py'esni**	**py'es**	**py'esim**	**py'esë**	**py'esnim**

The variable letter *e* designates a vowel which is **e** in the citation form, but may be absent altogether or may appear as a different vowel (**e** or **i** or **o** or **a**) in other forms of the word:

     jep· is represented in various inflected forms as **jep**, **jap**, or **jip**

     sheh· is represented in various inflected forms as **sheh**, **shoh**, or **shih**

The variable letter *ë* in the citation forms **vë'·** and **zë'·** is a reminder that the verb **vë'** is not to be ruled out when one encounters such inflected forms as **vija**, **vihet**, **vura**, and **vumë**, as well as in more transparent forms such as **vë**, **vënë**, **vëntë**, and **vënka**.

For entries whose stem has alternate forms, the symbol "~" after a grammatical label stands for the part of the stem that precedes the italicized letters in the head entry, and the letters after the ~ indicate the addition or replacement of the italicized letters:

     budalla' *adj, nm (pl ~e'nj)*…means that the plural stem for **budalla** is **budalle'nj**

Variable diphthongs are regularly replaced in certain grammatical forms:

     u'a is replaced by **o'**   in *oblique* forms of *nm* stems   **potku'a**   **potko'i**
     u'a is replaced by **o'**   in *sg pdef* and *opt* of *v* stems   **blu'a·**   **blo'ftë**
     u'a is replaced by **u'**   in *general passive* forms of *v* stems   **blu'a·**   **blu'het**
     u'e is replaced by **o'**   in *oblique* forms of *nm* stems   **llëku'e**   **llëko'i**
     y'e is replaced by **e'**   in *pdef* forms of *v* stems   **ngjy'e·N** **ngje'va**
     ï'e is replaced by **i'**   in *general passive* forms of *v* stems **ndï'e·N**   **ndi'het**

USE OF BRACKETS AND PARENTHESES

In general, brackets in this dictionary stand for components essential to the sense being defined. Square brackets [] are used if the bracketed component is in the accusative case; angle brackets ◇ if it is in the ablative/dative case; curly brackets or braces {} if it is in the nominative case:

     abon|o'·n *vt* to subscribe to [a periodical]

     lakm|o'·het *vpr* to get a sudden craving for ◇

     te *prep (nom)* at/to the location of {}: at/to {}'s place, at {}

Boldface parentheses () enclose optional components of the Albanian part of an entry, components that may or may not be present without affecting the sense. Italicized parentheses *()* enclose special information in the grammatical part of an entry, such as the case required for the object of a preposition or the indicated proclitic article for an articulated entry; they are also used to enclose usage labels (see **dërnok** *nm* [Bot] hedge hyssop *Gratiola officinalis*

     kërp *nm* hemp *(Cannabis sativa)*

Usage Labels, p. xxi). In definitional parts of an entry, plain parentheses () enclose hints or additional information in English to help the reader understand the entry.

     vra'p|thi(t) *adv* in haste, hastily

     dëgj|u'ar|it *nn (të)* (sense of) hearing

xixe̸|**r**|**i'me** *nf* crackling sound (of wood giving off sparks)

SAMPLE ENTRIES

Each sample entry below is composed of components—numbered below the example—distinguished by their format. The table following the examples lists the components, in the order in which they are most likely to appear in a given entry:

ABD a-bë-dë' *abbreviation* < **artileria bregdetare** *[Mil]* coastal artillery
  1   2   3   4   6   8

afio'n I§ *nm* opium II§ *adj* (*Fig*) pale
  1   3a   8   3a 5   8

aj I§ *interj* **1** hey! **2**= **haj** II§ *pron* * = ai'
  1   3a   7 8   7   4b   3a   4b

tri'shull *nm* (*np ~j*) *[Bot]* bladdernut (*Staphylea*)
  1 12   3   3 13 5 8   9

bam *onomat* (*Colloq*) sound of a gunshot or loud collision: wham!, bam!, bang!
  1   3   5   8

○ **bam e bum** attempt by any means, try by might and main
    10 8

○ **ia bë· bam 1** to shoot, fire a gun **2** to have the daring to fight **3** to strike
  10 7   8   7 8   7 8

        out of anger **4** to finish a project **5** to do something unusually dashing or brave
             7   8   7   8

○ **bar argjendi** *[Bot]* "silvergrass" horsetail (*Equisetum*)
    10   6   11 8   9

Component	Format Form
1. Headword of an entry	*hanging and in boldface*
2. Pronunciation aid	*roman characters before grammatical label*
3. Grammatical label	italics
a) if multiple within an entry	preceded by a roman numeral followed by §
4. Cross-reference	
a) to the source entry[14]	boldface characters after <
b) to a synonymous entry	boldface characters after =
5. Usage label	initially capitalized italics between parentheses
a) if applicable to all definitions	appears before number in definition
b) if applicable to single definition	appears after number in definition
6. Domain label	initially capitalized italics between square brackets
a) if applicable to all definitions	appears before number in definition
b) if applicable to single definition	appears after number in definition
7. Sense number	boldface number (only if there are more-than-one senses)
8. Definition	roman characters
9. Technical identification	italics (scientific term: *Genus species*)
	italics in parenthesis (technical name for a common term)
10. Phrasal entry	boldface characters after ○
11. Literal translation	between quotation marks
12. Variable letters	boldface italics
13. Replacement letters	~ followed by the replacement of the variable letters

---

[14]That is, the entry which provides the sense(s) of the stem from which this form is derived.

OVERVIEW OF THE FORM AND CONTENT OF ENTRIES

This dictionary contains three kinds of entries: main entries, phrasal entries, and cross-references, each with a heading in boldface letters.

The dictionary assumes that its user has some knowledge of regular Albanian grammar, but can use help with unknown stems and compounds, as well as with the hundreds of irregular (unpredictable from general rules) stem forms in the language. The initial aim of this dictionary was to list in their own proper alphabetical position all Albanian stem forms whose citation form is not automatically recognizable by the general rules for generation of forms given in the grammatical sketch. That aim has been narrowed by exigencies of time: in order to make a useful dictionary available in print within the twentieth century, I have limited the lexicon to words and phrases that have appeared in print since Albanian independence, and further, to such items as have been recognized in lexical sources available to me. The full Albanian vocabulary, including thousands more dialectal forms from speakers in and outside of Albania, recent borrowings into the language since 1991, and specialized vocabulary in all aspects of Albanian life, would require tens of years in addition to those I have dedicated to the task.

Albanian stems may be bare, thematic, or compound. A bare stem, or BASE, consists of a single MORPHEME, a sound/letter or sequence of sounds/letters that function as a single unit. A COMPOUND stem contains more than one base. A thematic stem, or THEME, consists at least one base and at least one derivational suffix or extension. A DERIVATIONAL SUFFIX contributes a grammatical function to the word; for example, it may indicate that the stem is a plural noun, that it is a gerund, that it is a passive verb, that it is a diminutive noun of feminine gender, that it is a participle, etc. An extension does not itself contribute a grammatical function to the word, but it may 1) reflect a historically earlier pronunciation; 2) help mark the tense of a verb; 3) suggest a semantic nuance that might be absent without the extension; 4) serve the "euphonic" purpose of breaking up sequences of sounds that speakers of a particular variety of Albanian find difficult to pronounce.

Most stems may appear as words in their own right. In texts, verbs and nouns appear in an inflected form from which their syntactic role in the clause may be inferred. This inflected form may end in an overt INFLECTIONAL SUFFIX. When that suffix is covert, that is, when it is not represented by any sound/letter, it is termed Ø ("zero"). The imperative form of many verbs has such a Ø, and all nominative and accusative indefinite nouns have it.

Where helpful for clarification, a pair of square brackets [] is used to stand for any pronoun in the accusative case, which in turn may stand for any accusative referent; a pair of angle brackets ◇ stands for any pronoun in the dative/ablative case, which in turn may stand for any dative or ablative referent. The brackets may be filled to indicate the scope or nature of the object.

> **hij|**o·**·n** *vt* to turn [] to ashes: incinerate
>
> **kalpët|**o·**·n** *vt* to plug [a leaky wooden container] up
>
> **për|ngja**·*n vi* to be very much like ◇, resemble ◇ strongly
>
> **taks** *vt* (*Colloq*) to promise [something] to ◇someone◇

To indicate a stem that appears mainly as part of larger constructions rather than as an independent word, the morpheme-division symbol | is placed at the end of that stem. For example:

> **mba|jt|** *stem for pd, opt, adm, part* < **mba·**n

indicates that the form **mba|jt|** is part of such constructions as **mbajta, mbajtëm, mbajtka,** and **u mbajt,** all of which are inflectional forms of **mba·**n.

Senses and collocations that apply only to a particular paradigmatic form are entered under the entry for that form and not under the main entry. This policy is unlike that of most other dictionaries, and the reader must be prepared for it. For example, if a phrasal entry requires the plural form **duar** *hands* rather than its singular form **dorë** *hand,* the entry will be found under **du'ar** and not under **do'rë.**

MAIN ENTRIES

Main entries provide the principal information a reader needs to recognize and interpret the individual words encountered in texts. Each main entry is headed by a citation form. In order to clarify the structure of the form and help the reader relate it to other forms, morphemic divisions are indicated by a vertical mark |:

> **bashkë|li'dh|ur** *joined together, united*

which consists of the morphemes **bashkë** *together,* **lidh** *join,* and **-ur** *participial suffix.*

Sequences of letters that are the same except for differences in morphemic division are treated as separate entries.

> **pish|i'n**ë *nf* **1** pine grove **2** alburnum/sapwood of the pine tree
>
> **pishi'n**ë *nf* swimming pool

CITATION FORMS

The main entry for INFLECTED words, whose form changes to mark grammatical function, is headed by a CITATION FORM, as indicated in the following table:

Abbreviation	Grammatical Category	Citation Form
adj	Adjective	masculine singular stem
adj (i)	Articulated	indicates that an attributive article appropriate for the gender of the referent precedes the adjective stem
adv (së)	Gerundial adverb	indicates that the proclitic **së** precedes the adverb
n	Noun	Nominative indefinite (the traditional citation form)
n (i)	Articulated	indicates that an attributive article appropriate for the gender precedes the noun stem
nf	Feminine	singular if a singular form of the noun exists
nf (e)	Articulated	indicates that an attributive article appropriate for feminine gender precedes the noun stem
nm	Masculine	singular if a singular form of the noun exists
nn	Neuter	singular if a singular form of the noun exists
nn (të)	Articulated	indicates that the attributive article **të** precedes the noun stem
np	Plural	plural
np (të)	Articulated	indicates that the attributive article **të** precedes the plural noun stem
part	Participle	Regularly formed participles are not listed as entries unless they also have special uses as adjectives.
pron	Pronoun	Nominative case
v	Verb	The 3rd person singular present tense form of the verb, with the symbol · marking the end of the stem. In phrasal entries, this identifying mark enables the reader to recognize that other forms of the verb, in any tense, person, and number, share the same collocational sense.
vi	Intransitive	active form
vpr	Reflexive	passive form (ending in ·*et* or ·*het*)
vt	Transitive	active form

In general, single-word Albanian proper nouns are cited in their nominative indefinite form; the English form may give them in their more usual definite form:

    Tira'në *nf* Tirana (capital city of Albania)

Some common Albanian personal names have been included, particularly those that 1) have non-obvious English equivalents: **Gjon** = John, **Skënder** = Alexander; 2) designate males, but are nouns with feminine declension, 3) are homonymous with common nouns that might present interpretation problems in an actual text—for example, it might confuse the reader not to know that **Dritë** and **Liri** are popular names for females and not just capitalized versions of **dritë** *light* and **liri** *freedom*, and that **Yll** is a popular name for males and not just capitalized **yll** *star*.

Entries for prefixes are followed by a hyphen: **para-**. Suffixes are included in the Reverse List of Possible Word Terminations, beginning on p. xlix.

PRONUNCIATION

Since normal Albanian orthography is quite regular, the only special symbol needed to indicate pronunciation is the ' mark after the stressed vowel of a word.

    ATSH at-të-shë < **Agjencia Telegrafike Shqiptare** *nf* Albanian Telegraphic Agency (the Albanian news service)

GRAMMATICAL LABELS

A reader can sometimes determine the grammatical category of a puzzling word, even though its meaning is not known. In such cases the dictionary can be helpful by providing information about which GRAMMATICAL FUNCTIONS its main entries may serve: in this dictionary, these functions are indicated by abbreviated grammatical labels in italics.

When the citation form at the head of the entry has multiple grammatical functions for which a single definition suffices, these functions may follow one another, separated by a comma.

    gjerma'n *adj, n* German

When the citation form at the head of the entry has multiple grammatical functions for which a single English definition does not suffice, the grammatical label is preceded by a Roman numeral followed by the symbol §.

mënda'fsh I§ *nm* silk II§ *adj* silken

treg|t|u'e|s I§ *adj.* commercial II§ *n* merchant, dealer

VERB ENTRIES

The main entry for a verb is headed by its citation form: the stem for the 3rd person singular present tense form *(3sg pres)*. The symbol **·** indicates the end of the verb stem and the attachment point for inflectional suffixes. The English infinitive marker "to" marks the beginning of the definition of each separate sense of the verb, but it is not repeated for each subsense.[15]

mat· *vt* to measure

ngurr|o'·n *vi* to hesitate

ngro'h·et *vpr* to get warm; warm up

TRANSITIVE VERBS

TRANSITIVE VERBS, whose stems are labeled *vt* in the dictionary, take objects in the accusative case and have both ACTIVE and PASSIVE forms. In the English part of the definition, square brackets [] may be used to indicate the place of a pronominal direct object in the accusative case.

llom|i't· *vt* to make [] muddy

is understood to imply all inflected forms, including, for example, both active forms like **më llomiti** *he made me muddy* and passive forms like the past definite **u llomita** *I was made muddy*. Note that passive forms of transitive verbs are systematically ambiguous if a corresponding reflexive verb exists; thus **u llomita** can also mean *I got muddy*, since the reflexive verb exists:

llom|i't·et *vpr* to get muddy

INTRANSITIVE VERBS

INTRANSITIVE VERB stems, labeled *vi* in the dictionary, do not take objects in the accusative case. In an active form, the grammatical subject of an intransitive verb is the agent of the action represented by the verb.

rrym|o'·n *vi* to flow in a current/stream

dësht|o'·n *vi* to abort, miscarry; go wrong; fail

REFLEXIVE VERBS

Entries marked *vpr* are REFLEXIVE VERBS with passive voice inflection but middle voice uses and senses (see Voice, p. xxx). The passive voice forms that the reader sees in texts may be forms of these *vpr* verbs, but they may also be passive forms of a *vt* stem, with passive, reciprocal, or reflexive senses. These straightforward passive, reciprocal, and reflexive senses are not separately enumerated in this dictionary, since the entry for every transitive verb would be needlessly tripled in size thereby.[16]

For many *vpr* verbs there is no corresponding active verb:[17]

stër|qi't·et *vpr* to be a constant nuisance to ◇, constantly annoy ◇

ke'q·et *vpr* **1** to get worse **2** to speak/answer harshly to ◇; threaten ◇ **3** to have a falling out, be on bad terms

IMPERSONAL VERBS

Verbs marked *impers* have a vague 3rd person singular grammatical subject, sometimes corresponding to a grammatical subject "it" (in *it's raining*) or "there" (in *there's no convincing some people*) in English. In many expressions, the experiencer of an impersonal verb is expressed as a dative referent.

e'rr·et *vpr impers* it grows dark, night falls

te'k·et *vpr impers* ◇ *feels* like having/doing something: ◇ *has* a whim/hankering, ◇ *gets* an urge

PRONOMINAL ENTRIES

The labels *pron* and *pronominal* are generic terms for words and stems that function like nouns or noun phrases (e.g., they can be the objects of prepositions or verbs), but that indicate grammatical categories rather than substantive entities. Thus **unë** *I* is the nominative case form of the pronoun that refers to a 1st person singular,

---

[15] So-called Albanian "infinitives"—**për të** +*participle*, e.g., **për të shkuar** *(in order) to go*, do not serve most of the functions of English infinitives.

[16] For the same reason, for many verbs, the gerund formed regularly by suffixing -**i'm** (for verb stems ending in **o'**, **u'a**, **y'**, or **y'e**) or by suffixing -**je** (for verb stems ending in a consonant) are not provided, if a reader can be expected to arrive at their identity and meaning easily.

[17] For a linguistically sophisticated account of syntax and semantics of passive voice forms, see Philip Hubbard, *The Syntax of the Albanian Verb Complex*, New York, Garland Publishing, Inc., 1985.

and is not the name of the person speaking; **asnjeri** *no one, nobody* denies the involvement of any entity in the category of persons. Some pronominal stems (e.g., **cil**) are declined for gender, case, and number, as if they were nominalized adjectives; some (e.g., **kush**) are declined only for case; some (e.g., **gjëkafshë**) are invariable in form; some are clitics (e.g., **ç'**); some (e.g., 1st and 2nd person personal pronouns) reflect differences in person, number, and case; some (e.g., the 3rd person determiners that serve as the 3rd person pronouns for Albanian) reflect differences in gender, number, and case.

NOUN ENTRIES

The citation form of a noun is its uninflected, nominative indefinite stem form.

Noun stem labels start with *n*, usually followed by a gender/number indicator *m, f, n, p*, (*masculine, feminine, neuter*, and *plural*, respectively).

A stem labeled simply *n* is an *nm* stem when it designates a male. When it designates a female, it adds a derivational suffix *-e* or *-ë* and becomes an *nf* stem. When it designates males, it adds a derivational suffix **-ë** or *-Ø* and becomes an *np* stem. When it designates females, it adds a derivational suffix **-a** or *-Ø* (if the derivational suffix is *-e*) and becomes an *np* stem.

In Early Albanian, a number of *nm* stems ended in **n**. When that **n** was immediately followed by a vowel in the same word, it became **r** in Tosk dialects but remained **n** in Gheg. If there was no immediately following vowel, the vowel preceding the **n** became nasalized, and then the **n** dropped. Such nasalized vowels continued to be spoken in Gheg dialects (and are often represented by ^ in standard orthographies), but lost their nasalization in Tosk dialects.

As a result, in this dictionary a number of descendants of these stems have two forms: the BARE STEM form (which serves as the nominative/accusative indefinite case of the noun), and the OBLIQUE form, which appears when a suffix beginning in a vowel immediately follows. If the 20th century form is descended from a Tosk form, it will have the extension **r** in the oblique form and end in a plain vowel in the citation form; if it is a Gheg descendent, it may have the extension **n** in both stems or may have **n** only in the oblique stem. Such citation forms are listed in the alphabetical position of the bare stem form, followed by the extension italicized between parentheses *(r)* or *(n)*. If the oblique form, with the -i suffix that invariably follows it, would not immediately follow the bare stem alphabetically in the list, it appears as a separate entry and cross-refers to the citation form.

> **blet|o're** *nf* apiary
>
> **bli'|** *stem for 2nd pl pres, impf, imper, vp* **ble'• n**
>
> **bli**(n) *nm* sturgeon
>
> **bli**(r) *nm* linden
>
> **bli|ba'rdh** *nm* Adriatic sturgeon *Acipenser naccarii*
>
> ...
>
> **blin||i** obl < **bli**(n)
>
> ...
>
> **blir||i** obl < **bli**(r)

There are other noun stems whose bare stem and oblique stem differ in the way they end. For these, if part of the bare stem form is missing in the oblique form, that part is italicized. The extension or replacement of letters for the oblique stem is indicated between parentheses following the grammatical label. This same method is often used for nouns whose corresponding plural stem *(np)* is formed in some way other than by the usual suffixation of **-a, -e, -ë, −ra,** or *-Ø.*

> **she'ku*ll*** *nm* (*np ~j*) century

(that is, the plural of the masculine noun **she'kull** *century* is **she'kuj** *centuries*)

Again, if the two forms, stem and oblique, are not alphabetically contiguous, the oblique form (with its appropriate suffix) appears as a separate entry and cross-refers to the citation form.

ARTICULATED NOUNS

The label *n (i)* indicates a noun stem that must be used with a proclitic attributive article. In the words based on this stem, the proclitic form of the attributive article (**i, e, të,** or **së**), as well as the inflection of the stem itself, reflects the gender, number, and case of the referent of the noun:

> **rri'tur** *n (i)* adult, grownup
>
> > **i rrituri** *the adult* (male)
> >
> > **e rritura** *the adult* (female)
> >
> > **të rriturat** *the adults* (females)
> >
> > **i së rriturës** *of the adult* (female)

The label *nf (e)* indicates an *nf* noun stem that must be preceded by an attributive article form (**e, të,** or **së**):

shfryrë *n (e)* emotional outburst

    e shfryra *the emotional outburst*

    të shfryrat *the emotional outbursts*

The label *np (të)* and *nn (të)* indicate *np* and *nn* noun stems, respectively, that must be used with the proclitic attributive article form **të**. Noun stems labeled *nn (të)* are typically derived from participles and normally appear with the *definite* suffix **-t**; a vowel **-i** appears before the **-t** suffix if the stem ends in **-r** at the end of an unstressed syllable.

vo'n|a *np (të) fem* late crops harvested in late autumn

    të vonat *the late fall crops*

shiju'ar *nn (të)* sense of taste

    të shijuarit *the sense of taste*

GERUND ENTRIES

Entries labeled *ger* are verbal nouns, GERUNDS, that substantivize the verb stems to which they are cross-referred and designate processes, actions, or acts implied by those verb stems. Corresponding English nouns may also end in *-ing*. The same noun may also designate results or states, usually corresponding to English nouns ending in *-(a)tion*, *-ment*, *-ance*, or *ence*. For some entries, it is assumed that the meaning can be easily deduced from the main definitions of the cross-referred verb or verbs, and no other definition is added; for others, specific definitions may be supplied:

magje'ps|je *nf ger* 1 > magje'ps·, magje'ps·*et* 2 enchantment, bewitchment

In its first sense, since both **magje'ps·** and **magje'ps·***et* are cross-referred, **magje'ps|je** may designate either the active process, act, or action of enchanting or bewitching, or else the passive process, act, or action of being enchanted or bewitched. In its second sense, it designates the state of enchantment or bewitchment.

ADJECTIVE ENTRIES

A stem labeled *adj (i)* is always used with a proclitic attributive article; one labeled *adj* is used without such an article. By convention, the citation form of an adjective is the masculine singular form, but the stem is used with a full range of referents (masculine, feminine, plural, or neuter), and the attributive article (i) stands for any of the possible forms **i**, **e**, **të** or **së**.

- Adjective stems whose citation form ends in **-ur**, **-uar**, **-un**, **-ër**, **-ël**, **-ët**, and *-ë* are identical for masculine and feminine singular and masculine plural; for feminine plural a derivational suffix **-a** is added and the evanescent *ë* disappears.

- Adjective stems whose citation form ends in **-an**, **-al**, **-ar**, **-or**, **-ëm**, **-më**, **-ç**, **-q** and **-ës** typically add the derivational suffix **-e** to form a feminine singular and feminine plural stem; the evanescent *ë* disappears.[18]

- Adjective stems whose citation form ends in **-e** are invariable in form.

- Feminine and plural adjectival stems that are not derived regularly from the citation form in the dictionary (usually by the addition of a derivational suffix **-e** for the feminine singular and plural, or **-a** for the masculine plural) are generally listed under their own heading.

DEFINITION

How can a dictionary give the "MEANING" of an Albanian word to a reader? A moment's reflection suffices to show that the task is in fact impossible: the meaning of **mollë** is no more giveable than its meaning "apple" is eatable: it is the apple that one can eat, not its meaning, and it is the apple that can be given, not its meaning. This dictionary must adopt a variety of strategies to help its user "get" a meaning that it cannot give.

SENSE DESCRIPTION AND DIFFERENTIATION

Preceding the definition of a sense there may be an indication of the USAGE *(in italics between round brackets)* and/or SEMANTIC DOMAIN *[in italics between square brackets]*, which may enrich or clarify the interpretation of the definition. In numbered definitions, bracketed information following the number applies only to the sense with that number; preceding the number, the bracketed information applies to all the senses for that grammatical function.

The main definition attempts to find English expressions corresponding to the Albanian ones, but quite often the correspondence can only hint at the sense conveyed by the Albanian entry. Especially for phrasal entries, a more literal definition, between parentheses and quotation marks, precedes the main definition, in order to provide greater insight into the underlying structure and sense of the Albanian entry.

---

[18]The *-ë* of **-ës** is retained in spelling the feminine stem, although in normal speech it is usually not pronounced.

For some senses, a set of possible English translations for the targeted Albanian item may be offered in the attempt to suggest the meaning of the Albanian item for the reader. Commas separate different suggested translations that are all aimed at conveying aspects of the same sense; semicolons separate closely related, but somewhat different sub-senses. Boldface numbers (**1**, **2**,…) separate senses that are substantially or completely different from each other.

In order to offer the reader an appreciation of what is being conveyed in Albanian and thus free the reader to consider translation possibilities better suited to a given context than those suggested in a proposed list of general translation equivalents, more discursive paraphrases or explanations of senses are often given in addition to or instead of the translations. In such definitions, the translation is separated from the paraphrase/explanation by a colon (:).

In some cases, encyclopedic information may be provided to supply a context that may be missing in the passage being read.

For items whose standard scientific identification is known, that identification is given in italics. If a term is widely used, and not just by specialists, the scientific label may be placed between parentheses.

> **dërnok** *nm* [*Bot*] hedge hyssop *Gratiola officinalis*
>
> **kërp** *nm* hemp *(Cannabis sativa)*

USAGE LABELS

Usage labels indicate some connotations that an Albanian reader is likely to attach to a word or sense. A capitalized usage label is indicated in italics between parentheses (round brackets). If a usage label follows the number in a definition containing several senses, it applies only to that particular sense; otherwise, it applies to all senses of the term in that grammatical category.

The following labels appear, some in abbreviated form:

LABEL	MEANING
(Bookish)	contrived and formal in tone
(Child)	children's language, baby talk
(Colloq)	colloquial
(Collec)	collective
(Contempt)	contemptuous, scornful
(Crude)	vulgar, rude, coarse
(Disparaging)	disparaging, derogatory
(Curse)	curse, imprecation
(Dimin)	diminutive
(Elevated)	elevated style
(Familial)	used among family members
(Folk)	folk customs, folklore
(Euph)	euphemism
(Felic)	felicitation, well-wishing, congratulation
(Hist)	historical
(HistPK)	during the Communist period in Albania (1946-91)
(Impolite)	impolite, discourteous
(Insult)	insulting, offensive
(Intens)	intensive degree
(Iron)	ironic
(Joc)	jocular
(Npc)	not politically condoned during the period 1946-91
(Oath)	oath, swearing, prayer
(Obscene)	obscene
(Old)	archaic or obsolete or obsolescent
(Onomat)	onomatopoetic
(Pejorative)	disparaging in tone, reflecting speaker's negative attitude
(Derog)	derogatory
(Pet)	affectionate, endearing
(Poet)	poetic
(Proverb)	proverb, adage, saying
(Pur)	purist attempt to replace a borrowing
(Regional)	regional in tone or use
(Reg Arb)	arbërisht (spoken in Italy or Greece)
(Reg Calab)	spoken in Calabria

LABEL	MEANING
(Reg Gheg)	characteristic of Gheg (northern) speech
(Reg Gk)	regional Greek borrowing
(Reg Kos)	spoken in Kosovo
(Reg Mont)	regional Montenegrin borrowing
(Reg Tir)	spoken in Tirana
(Reg Tosk)	characteristic of Tosk (southern) speech
(Scorn)	scornful, contemptuous

DOMAIN LABELS

Domain (field) labels provide a frame of reference for interpreting the definition. A capitalized domain label is indicated by italics enclosed between square brackets. If a domain label follows the number in a definition containing several senses, it applies only to that particular sense; otherwise, it applies to all senses of the term in that grammatical category.

The following labels appear, some in abbreviated form:

LABEL	MEANING
[Agr]	agriculture, farming
[Anat]	anatomy
[Anth]	anthropology
[Archeology]	archeology
[Architecture]	architecture
[Art]	the visual arts
[Astron]	astronomy
[Aviation]	aviation, aeronautics
[Bacteriology]	bacteriology
[Biol]	biology
[Bot]	botany
[Broadcasting]	radio/television
[Chem]	chemistry
[Chess]	chess
[Choreography]	choreography, dance
[Cine]	cinema, film, movies
[Commerce]	business, commerce
[Constr]	building construction
[Dairy]	dairy processes or products
[Diplomacy]	diplomacy
[Econ]	economics
[Electr]	electronics, electrical work
[Entom]	entomology
[Famil]	familial
[Fin]	finance
[Fish]	fishing
[Folklore]	folk stories and beliefs
[Food]	food, food preparation, cooking
[Forestry]	forestry
[Geod]	geodesy, cartography
[Geog]	geography
[Geol]	geology
[Geom]	geometry
[Hist]	history
[Hort]	horticulture, gardening
[Hunting]	hunting
[Hydrol]	hydrology and hydrotechnology
[Ichth]	ichthyology
[Invert]	invertebrate
[Law]	law
[Ling]	linguistics, grammar

LABEL	MEANING
[*Lit*]	literature
[*Logic*]	logic
[*Naut*]	nautical
[*Math*]	mathematics
[*Medic*]	medicine, medical
[*Meteor*]	meteorology
[*Milit*]	military
[*Min*]	mineralogy or mining
[*Music*]	music
[*Mythology*]	mythology
[*Offic*]	official, government
[*Optics*]	optics
[*Ornit*]	ornithology, birds
[*Paleo*]	paleontology
[*Pedag*]	pedagogy
[*Pharm*]	pharmaceutics, pharmacy, pharmacology
[*Philosophy*]	philosophy
[*Photography*]	photography
[*Physics*]	physics
[*Physiol*]	physiology
[*Poet*]	poetry
[*Politics*]	politics
[*Post*]	postal, post-telegraph
[*Psychol*]	psychology
[*Publ*]	publishing, printing, press
[*Relig*]	religion
[*Rr*]	railroad
[*Spec*]	term used in multiple specialized fields
[*Sport*]	sports
[*Tech*]	engineering, technology
[*Textil*]	textile industry, textiles
[*Theat*]	theater
[*Veterinary*]	veterinary medicine
[*Zool*]	zoology, animal

TECHNICAL TERMS

Technical terms are generally italicized in this dictionary. The italicized scientific labels provided for flora and fauna often identify the species and varieties with which Albanians are most likely to be familiar, even when the English name in the definition has a more general reference (e.g., *eagle*). To indicate that the Albanian term is the every-day one, the italicized technical label is put inside parentheses. In this way, useful information is given to both specialist and non-specialist readers. It is even possible for a same term to have one sense to the specialists and another to the general public, as in the following example. Note that the non-specialist sense is indicated by the parentheses around its technical label:

> **lop**ë **deti   1** [*Zool*] walrus **2** [*Ichth*] common eagle ray *Myliobatis aquila* = **shqiponjë deti**
> **3** [*Ichth*] devil ray *(Mobula mobular)*

EXAMPLES

Illustrative examples are included in this dictionary only to help the user interpret schematic definitions. While illustrative examples would be indispensable for a dictionary aimed at writers or speakers, who need models to use the word properly, they are generally not needed in this dictionary, which is designed for readers who come to the dictionary with examples of their own, namely those encountered in the texts that sent them to the dictionary in the first place.

PHRASAL ENTRIES

This dictionary includes more than 16,000 phrasal entries whose Albanian uses are unlikely to be inferred by an English reader from the defined senses of the component parts. These entries, preceded by a raised circle °, generally appear under the entry for the first verb, if there is one, in the phrase; if there is no verb, the phrase appears under the main entry of the first salient component of the phrase. Phrasal entries include multi-word entries called by various names: collocations, idioms and figurative idioms, idiomatic expressions, locutions, fixed phrases, phrasal expressions, phrased senses, phrasal terms, sayings, proverbs, curses, and felicitations. If the meaning is easily inferable by a reader who knows English, an expression is *not* listed:

aeroplani ulet *the airplane lands*

Instead, the dictionary includes enough information under each component to make the inferences possible.: e.g., the entry **u'l·***et*, includes the sense *set down, come to earth*, from which the reader can infer the specific English word *lands* in the context of airplanes.

VARIABLE SEGMENTS

In order to extend the reader's understanding of a collocation and make it possible to recognize other instances of the collocation in a form somewhat different from that listed in the dictionary, several devices are used. First, a rather literal translation (between quotation marks) is often provided before the rest of the definition. Second, because it is often not obvious to a foreign reader what parts of a collocation may be different without affecting the integrity of the collocation, variable components are indicated in special ways:

To save space, a slash / (= *or*) separates alternatives that yield the same sense in the idiom.

fle'·/pre·*het* **mbi dafi'na** "sleep/relax on laurels" to rest on one's laurels

For entries with variable constituents, several devices are used to indicate the range of variation:

In phrases with a finite verb constituent, the Albanian constituent represented by the citation form of the verb—indicated by · after the verb stem—represents any of the conjugated forms of the verb. For *vt* (transitive) verbs, the conjugation includes all *vp* forms; those forms are used to express passive, reflexive, and reciprocal corresponding meanings for each of the senses defined in the main entry. For *vi* (intransitive) verbs, the only *vp* forms that occur regularly are 3rd sg forms with impersonal senses corresponding to English expressions like *peshkohet* **mirë atje** *there is good fishing there*, **s'pihej duhan** *there was no smoking permitted*. The citation form of a passive verb constituent ends in ·*et* or ·*het*.

The variability of the English constituent that corresponds to a variable Albanian verb constituent is indicated either by an infinitive (introduced by *to* or *not*) or by a verb in italics. If the variability is limited to certain tenses, persons, or numbers, that limitation may be indicated by an italicized superscript in Albanian with corresponding italicization in the English definition.

◇ **ha·** *3sg pres/imperf* **gjuha** "◇'s tongue *eats* ◇" ◇ *cannot* keep from talking

USE OF BRACKETS

As noted above, brackets stand for essential parts of an entry required for the sense being defined. Matching brackets, square [], angle ◇, or curly {} in the Albanian phrase and its English definition indicate corresponding reference between them. Square brackets are used if the bracketed component in Albanian is in the accusative case, ◇ if it is in the ablative/dative case, {} if it is in the nominative case.

[] **ka·** **për nder** to consider [] an honor

◇ **jep·** **pazar** to propose a price to ◇, enter into bargaining/haggling with ◇

s'merr· **erë nga** {} to be completely ignorant about {}; not suspect a thing about {}

In the English definition, the form of the bracket matches that of the Albanian, although Albanian cases do not match English ones. If the English variable would be in the possessive (genitive) case, that is indicated by 's after the brackets.

◇ **shko·** *n* **pas bishtit** "go behind ◇'s tail" to support and encourage ◇

◇ **rrjedh·** *3pl* **sytë** ◇'s eyes *flow* with tears

The brackets may be filled to indicate the scope or nature of the indirect object:

◇ **vë·** **ballu'k***e* to put a cuckold's horns on <one's husband>: make ◇ a cuckold

The corresponding parts often function differently in the two languages. In the Albanian expression, ◇ goes with the verb to indicate the dative indirect object of the verb, while in English the corresponding expression indicates the genitive possessor of the subject, a correspondence that occurs frequently between the two languages (◇'s indicates a genitive possessor). Filling in the variable represented by ◇ with some examples:

më rridhnin sytë my eyes were flowing with tears (literally: "to me were flowing the eyes")

na rrjedhin sytë our eyes are flowing with tears

ju rridhnin sytë your eyes were flowing with tears

i rrjedhin sytë asaj her eyes are flowing with tears

i rrjedhin sytë Agimit Agim's eyes are flowing with tears

u rridhnin sytë atyre their eyes were flowing with tears

Before a verb, a pair of angle brackets ◇ indicates that a dative indirect object is essential for the sense being defined. The pronominal proclitics that may fill this slot are:

më	*1st sg*
të	*2nd sg*
i	*3rd sg*
na	*1st pl*
ju	*2nd pl*
u	*3rd pl* or *specific passive* [19]

Immediately following such a pair of angle brackets ⬦, the variable *a* stands for a 3rd sg direct object which has the form **a** when the ⬦ slot is filled by **më, të, ju, i,** or **u,** but the form **e** when it is filled by **na.** For example, for

⬦*a* **humb·** **derën** "lose ⬦'s door" to stop visiting ⬦

the *a* will be realized as **a** if ⬦ is filled by **më:**

ma humbi derën "lost my door" he stopped visiting me

but the *a* will be realized as **e** if ⬦ is filled by **na:**

na e humbi derën "lost my door" he stopped visiting us

Similarly, immediately following a pair of angle brackets ⬦, the variable *i* stands for a 3rd pl object that has the form **i** when the ⬦ slot is filled by **më, të,** or **na,** but stands for the form **a** when the ⬦ slot is filled by any other pronominal clitic. For example, for

⬦*i* **di·** **kryqet** "know ⬦'s tail bones" to know <someone> intimately

the *i* will be realized as **i** if ⬦ is filled by **më:**

m'i dinte kryqet "knew ⬦'s tail bones" he knew me intimately

but the *i* will be realized as **a** if ⬦ is filled by **i:**

ia dinte kryqet he knew her intimately

USE OF SUPERSCRIPT

In many idioms, a verb is constrained in person and number; that constraint is indicated in superscript after the ·. Frequently, the constraint is that the verb is found only in a 3rd sg form with an impersonal grammatical subject, while the dative indirect object matches the subject in the equivalent English expression:

◦⬦ **shko·** n^{3sg}/**ik·** εn^{3sg} **bizgë** ("it *goes* diarrhea for ⬦") ⬦ *has* diarrhea

◦ [] **ha** ^{3sg} **ana** ("the side *eats* []") [] *leans* badly

USE OF SLASH MARKS

Single-word alternates are simply separated by /, but multi-word alternates are separated by // and are italicized to indicate the scope of the alternation.

◦ **e ka·** **kokën** *e fortë//shkëmb.* to be hard-headed/obstinate

The italics in the Albanian expression show that the alternation extends to **e,** so that the alternation is between **e fortë** and **shkëmb** rather than between **fortë** and **shkëmb,** say, or between **kokën e fortë** and **shkëmb.** The single-word alternation of <u>hard-headed</u> with <u>obstinate</u> in the definition is marked simply by the single slash "/".

CROSS-REFERENCES

Cross-reference serves as a shorthand device to obviate the necessity of repeating full definitions.

CROSS-REFERENCE WITH <

Some entries provide grammatical identification of a form, followed by the symbol < and the citation form for the main entry:[20]

lango'|nj *np* < **langu'a**

The cross-reference here indicates that **lango'|nj** is the plural (*np*) stem of **langu'a.** No further definition is supplied, implying that its definition can be inferred from that of the main entry to which it is cross-referred.

Irregular stems are separately listed, especially if their own alphabetic position would not be immediately adjacent to the main entry:

vëlle'zër *np* < **vëlla'**

meh| *stem for pdef, opt, adm, part* < **me·** n

The form **vëlle'zër** is the plural of **vëlla',** and **meh|** is the stem that is used to form the past definite, optative, admirative, and participle forms of the verb **me·** *n.*

The symbol < is also used to cross-refer verbal nouns (gerunds)—indicated by the label *ger* —to the main verb entry that provides the underlying definition. Unless otherwise indicated, a gerund in Albanian may function like

---

[19] The specific tenses of the passive voice are formed by preceding the active tense form by the proclitic **u.**

[20] That is, the entry which provides the sense(s) of the stem from which this form is derived.

a gerund in English with the ending *-ing* in designating the process embodied in the verb; for this function, the definition in English is usually not provided. For many verbs, the corresponding gerund also designates the action or result of the verb, often corresponding to a derived noun in English ending in *-(at)ion* or *-ment*; these correspondences are not always spelled out in the gerund entry, but the reader should be ready to give such an interpretation to any gerund.

CROSS-REFERENCE WITH =

Some cross-references, in boldface characters after an equal sign "=", identify a non-standard form (marked by an asterisk *) with the more standard one cited after the equal sign:

*këmi' = kumi'

Less often, a cross-reference may indicate that another entry expresses a sense or set of senses in a less ambiguous or more favored way than does the cross-referring item:

dobi|pru'r|ës *adj* = **dobi'shëm**

mardha' *nf* **1** hidden defect **2** hidden locus of a disease/illness **3**= **hile'**

The reader who encounters forms such as **ap, apim, apin, apësh** will find the entry

ap| = jap|

which cross-refers to the entry **jap|**, the stem for the corresponding forms **jap, japim, japin, japësh**. The dictionary entry

kundra|= kundër|

is expected to direct the reader puzzled by a text word like **kundravajtës**, to the dictionary entry **kundër|vajt|ës**. Similarly, if the text has **manevrimit, manevruan,** or **manovrueshme,**

manevr| = manovr|

is intended to send the reader to look at the entries **manovr|im, manovr|o·n,** and **manovr|ue|shëm.**

Occasionally, cross-reference is made even for items that are quite equivalent:

ha'p|t|azi *adv* = **haptas**

GRAMMATICAL SKETCH FOR READERS OF ALBANIAN

INTRODUCTION

A reader needs a certain amount of grammatical knowledge of a language in order to understand texts in that language and in order to understand the entries in a dictionary. To understand Albanian, the reader must at least distinguish between the STEM of a word—the part which is listed and defined in the dictionary—and its INFLECTIONS—the part which indicates or reflects the grammatical function of the word, and which is normally described in a grammatical description of the language. In addition, in any extensive reading of the language, the reader will encounter new Albanian words not listed in the dictionary; some of these will be borrowed from other languages (the lucky reader may be able to guess their meaning), some will be compounds of stems that are listed in the dictionary, and some will be formed by derivation (most usually, by adding a derivational suffix) from listed stems. No dictionary of Albanian could be large enough to include every possible inflected and derived form of Albanian words.[21]

This sketch is intended to provide a minimum of grammatical information that a reader might find useful in arriving at a reasonable reading of a text in hand; it is not intended to be a general grammar of Albanian.

For a more detailed description of Albanian grammatical forms, particularly inflectional morphology and problematic syntactic constructions, see Leonard Newmark, Philip Hubbard, and Peter Prifti, *Standard Albanian: A Reference Grammar for Students*, Stanford University Press, 1982.

GRAMMATICAL CATEGORIES IN ALBANIAN

PERSON, the distinctive reference to participants in a communication, applies to certain verb, pronoun, and adjective forms: *1st* person specifically includes the speaker (*singular I, me, my*; *plural we, us, our*); *2nd* person specifically includes the addressee (*you, your*); *3rd* person includes neither the speaker nor the addressee specifically (*singular he, him, his; she, her; it, its*; *plural they, them, their*). Nouns all act as *3rd* person referents.

NUMBER, the distinction between singular and plural, is a complex category with values that transcend various grammatical classes in Albanian.

1. A FINITE VERB has an inflection that reflects the person and number of its subject: *1sg* = *I*; *1pl* = *we*; *2sg* = *you* [individual or generic]; *2pl* = *you* [individuals or polite individual]; *3sg* = *he, she,* or *it*; *3pl* = *they*.

2. A singular noun may function as a *3sg* subject of a verb, and a plural noun may function as a *3pl* subject.

3. There are different pronouns for singular and plural referents.

4. The form of an adjective depends on the gender and number of its referent.

5. The form of a proclitic attributive article depends on the case, gender and number of its referent.

6. The form of certain determiners and pronouns reflects the number of a referent.

GENDER, the distinction between MASCULINE and FEMININE, is a category that is reflected in the form of adjectives, certain determiners, and pronouns. Nouns that denote males are *masculine*, and nouns that denote females are *feminine*; the gender of all other nouns is determined by their inflectional class: nouns with *nm* stems are *masculine*, and nouns with *nf* stems are *feminine*. Nouns with *n* stems are *masculine* and take *nm* inflection when they designate males, but add a feminine suffix *-e* or *-ë* to become *feminine* and take *nf* inflection. Nouns with *np* stems are more variable in gender: those that designate males and those irregularly formed from other *nm* stems are masculine; all others are generally feminine, although great variation is apparent in spoken and written Albanian. The gender of nouns with *nn* stems not only varies from speaker to speaker, but may vary from time to time for the same speaker.

CLITICS

Clitics are unstressed particles that are usually written as separate words, but function as part of an adjacent word.

---

[21]Existing dictionaries differ in the degree to which they include stem variants. One common practice is to list a single citation form for any inflected stem and to list few dialectal variants, if any. For the foreign reader, this practices presents grave difficulties: in order to be able to use the dictionary—something necessary especially in early stages of study—he must already know the language well, a peculiarity that seems either to escape the notice of the guilty lexicographers or to be answered by, "If words are too easy to find, the reader will never gain the discipline necessary to learn more." I reject such arguments as a dodge of the lexicographer's responsibility to produce the maximally usefully tool for the intended users of the particular dictionary, and have tried here to make the dictionary as easy for the foreign reader to use as I can, recognizing that the task of reading a foreign language is difficult enough without putting artificial roadblocks in the way.

User's Guide

VERB CLITICS

The most common PROCLITIC (a clitic that precedes the word to which it is attached) in Albanian is the conjunctive **të**, which marks the following present or imperfect tense verb as subjunctive.

> **të shkojë** *that (he) go, that (he) be going, to go*
> **të shkonte** *that (he) went, that (he) were going, that (he) would go, to go*
> **shpreson të shkojë** *he hopes to go*
> **do të shkojë** *he will go*
> **do të shkonte** *he would go*

Other common verb clitics are the negative proclitics **s'** (actually written as part of the following word), **nuk, mos,** and **para** (only after one of the other negative clitics):

> **s' do të shkojë** *he won't go*
> **nuk do të shkojë** *he won't go*
> **mos të shkojë** *he shouldn't go, lest he go, if he doesn't go*
> **mos shkoni** *don't go*
> **s'para shkoni** *you hardly go*

Pronominal Clitics

One or two pronominal clitics are attached to verbs to indicate the person and number of an identifiable indirect object and/or direct object of the verb, whether or not that object is otherwise present in the sentence. Preceding the verb, any of the following forms may occur.

Person	Number	English equivalent	Direct Object	Indirect Object
1st				
	Singular	*me*	**më**	**më**
	Plural	*us*	**na**	**na**
2nd				
	Singular	*you*	**të**	**të**
	Plural	*you*	**ju**	**ju**
3rd				
	Singular	*him, her, it*	**e**	**i**
	Plural	*them, 'em*	**i**	**u**

When the 3rd person object pronominal clitic **e** occurs in combination with any of the dative pronominal clitics (except **na**) or after the conjunctive proclitic **të**, its form is **a**; it is now non-standard to include an apostrophe in those combinations, but one can still find combinations written **m'a, t'a, i'a**, instead of the standard forms written as one word, as illustrated below. The combination of pronominal clitics **i + a** is pronounced **ja** and is sometimes found that way in non-standard spelling, instead of as standard **ia**. The pronominal clitic combination **i + i** sometimes appears as **ia** (non-standardly **ja**) and sometimes as simply **i**. It should be pointed out also that Albanians are not consistent in forming pronominal clitic combinations with the plural indirect objects **ju** and **u**, especially in combinations with the plural 3rd person object pronominal clitic; in actual texts the forms **jua, ja,** and **ua,** and in some dialects **jau,** may not conform to the following formulas:

Indirect Object	Direct Object	Combination	Example	Meaning
më	**e**	= **ma**	**ma dha Agimi**	*Agim gave it to me*
më	**i**	= **m'i**	**m'i dha Agimi**	*Agim gave them to me*
të	**e**	= **ta**	**ta dha Agimi**	*Agim gave it to you*
			ta japë Agimi	*that Agim give it*
të	**i**	= **t'i**	**t'i dha Agimi**	*Agim gave them to you*
			t'i japë Agimi	*that Agim give them*
na	**e**	= **na e**	**na e dha Agimi**	*Agim gave it to us*
na	**i**	= **na i**	**na i dha Agimi**	*Agim gave them to us*
ju	**e**	= **jua**	**jua dha Agimi**	*Agim gave it to you*
ju	**i**	= **jua**	**jua dha Agimi**	*Agim gave them to you*
i	**e**	= **ia**	**ia dha Agimi**	*Agim gave it to him/her*
i	**i**	= **ia**	**ia dha Agimi**	*Agim gave them to him/her*
u	**e**	= **ua**	**ua dha Agimi**	*Agim gave it to them*
u	**i**	= **ua**	**ua dha Agimi**	*Agim gave them to them*

In positive imperative verb forms, the pronominal clitic forms, including reflexive clitic **u**, may be suffixed to the stem, coming before the inflectional 2nd pl suffix **-ni** if it is present: **silli** *bring them!* **sillmani** *bring it to me!* **mblidhini** *gather them together!* **mblidhuni** *gather yourselves together!*

THE ATTRIBUTIVE ARTICLE

The form of the proclitic attributive article (**i**, **e**, **të**, or **së**) reflects the gender, number, case, definiteness and position of the referent of the articulated word. The articulated word may be:

- an attributive adjective
  shtëpi e madhe *big house*
  rroba të reja *new clothes*

- a pronominal adjective
  burri i saj *her husband*
  librat e tij *his books*
  nëna e tyre *their mother*

- a noun that indicates a close (inalienable) social relationship to a third person:
  e ëma *his/her/their mother*
  i kunati *his/her/their brother-in-law*
  i zoti *his/her/their master/lord* a nominalized adjective (see p.xlv or articulated noun (see p. xix)

If the article is **i**:   the referent is masculine and in the nominative case.

If the article is **së**:   the referent is feminine and in the dative or ablative case.

If the article is **e**:   the referent is either feminine and in the nominative case;

or the referent is definite, either nominative or accusative,

and immediately precedes the articulated word.

If the article is **të**:   the referent is something other than these.

In summary:

	masculine	feminine	plural
nominative	i	e	të or e[22]
accusative	të or e[23]	të or e[24]	të or e[25]
dative/ablative	të	të or së[26]	të

FULL WORDS

VERBS

Tense

Every verb has a paradigm of finite forms, also termed its "conjugation", consisting of three sets of tenses: GENERAL, SPECIAL, and PERFECT. A TENSE is a set of finite verb forms identical in every way except for their marking of person and number of the subject of the verb.

Many verbs have slightly different stems for their General tense forms than for their Special tense forms. All verbs form their Perfect tenses with their participle, preceded by a form of an auxiliary verb: for active verb forms, the auxiliary verb is **ka·**; for passive verb forms, the auxiliary verb is **ësh·te**.

General Tenses

---

[22]**e** appears only after an immediately preceding noun referent ending in the definite accusative suffix **të**.

[23]**e** appears only after an immediately preceding noun referent ending in the definite accusative suffix **në**.

[24]**e** appears only after an immediately preceding noun referent ending in the definite accusative suffix **në**.

[25]**e** appears only after an immediately preceding noun referent ending in the definite accusative suffix **të**.

[26]**së** appears after an immediately preceding noun referent ending in the definite ablative/dative suffix **së** and before nominalized adjectives in the definite ablative/dative case

The GENERAL tenses have quite general uses, depicting events or situations in relation to time that is dependent on the linguistic and real world context in which the verb is embedded. The General tenses are PRESENT and IMPERFECT. The IMPERATIVE mood of most verbs uses the same stem as the GENERAL tenses and is included here for that reason.

> The PRESENT tense may be used to make generic statements of present validity, as well as to depict ongoing, continuing, or habitual events or situations in the present time. In a narrative context, it may vividly represent events or situations in the past. After the conjunctive clitic **të**, present tense forms become subjunctive. Present tense subjunctive forms in turn may be used as suggestive ("shall we go?"), or may follow the particle **do** to form a volitional future ("we will go"), the particle **le** to form a jussive mood ("let's go!"), or the particle **po** to form a simple hypothetical ("if we go").

> The IMPERFECT tense may be used to make generic statements of past validity, as well as to depict ongoing, continuing, or habitual events or situations in the past time. In a narrative context, it may represent events or situations continuing over a period in the past. After the conjunctive clitic **të**, present tense forms become past subjunctive. IMPERFECT subjunctive forms in turn may be used as a contrary-to-fact hypothetical ("if we went"), or may follow the particle **do** to form the conditional ("we would go [if …]!"), or the particle **po** to form a contrary-to-expectation hypothetical ("if we would go").

> IMPERATIVE mood forms express orders and commands. For all verbs, the formal imperative—addressed to one or more individuals—is the same as the informal one, with the suffix **-ni** tacked on at the end. For most verbs, the informal imperative form—addressed to an individual—is identical with its citation form. For verbs with a variable stem vowel *e* in the citation form, the informal imperative has the stem vowel **i**. Some *V*-stem verbs add a suffix **-j** after the vowel

Special Tenses

The SPECIAL TENSEs are PAST DEFINITE, OPTATIVE, and ADMIRATIVE, which have quite specific uses.

> The PAST DEFINITE tense implies that the event or situation it depicts is anterior to a sharp boundary between present and past. While in its usual use is as a simple past tense, it may also be used in announcements of a projected past:
> ("Haven't you left yet?") **Tani shkova.** *I'm leaving right now! I've already left.*
> **Largohu se të shtypa.** *Scram or I'll run you over!*

> OPTATIVE mood forms express wishes, whether for something good (as in felicitations) or something bad (as in curses); after the particle **në** for contrary-to-fact conditionals ("if we were to go").

> ADMIRATIVE tenses (present and past) make contrary-to-expectation statements; they typically express surprise or amazement.

Perfect Tenses

The PERFECT tenses are PRESENT PERFECT (called PERFECT for short), PAST PERFECT, and PLUPERFECT, which all depict events or situations previous to a reference point in time.

> The PRESENT PERFECT implies that the event or situation it depicts is previous to a reference point in the present ("we have gone"). There is overlap between the scope of the past definite and present perfect, and speakers vary in whether they use the one or the other to express the same idea in the same situation.

> The PAST PERFECT implies that the event or situation it depicts is previous to a reference point in the past ("we had gone").

> The PLUPERFECT implies that the event or situation it depicts is previous to a reference point prior to another reference point in the past ("we had gone"). This tense is quite rare in actual texts.

Voice

For each tense there are two subsets of VOICE forms: ACTIVE and PASSIVE. A VOICE is a set of verb forms that reflect the role of the grammatical subject of a verb with respect to the agent and object (if any) of the verb. ACTIVE forms indicate that the effect of the verb is external to the subject. PASSIVE forms indicate that the effect of the verb is on the subject itself. .In a passive form the verb may express PASSIVE, RECIPROCAL, or REFLEXIVE senses.

> PASSIVE senses are those for which the subject of a verb is the object of the action of the verb.

la'hen *they are washed*

RECIPROCAL senses are those for which the subjects of a verb indiscriminately serve as agents and objects of the action of the verb.

la'hen *they wash each another*

REFLEXIVE senses are those for which the subject of a verb is simultaneously both the agent and the object of the action of the verb.

la'hen *they wash themselves*

MIDDLE senses are those in which the subject of a verb is depicted as engaging or becoming engaged in the action without necessarily being its active agent or passive object

la'hen *they bathe/wash; they get exonerated; they clear up; they have diarrhea; they spawn*

IMPERSONAL senses express the general possibility (permissibility or capability) of the action represented by a verb in a *3rd sg passive* form with an unexpressed subject.

la'het *washing is possible (permitted/feasible)*

Verb Stems

Every verb form in Albanian contains a stem and one or more suffixes. Many suffixes have different forms that depend on the form of the verb. In general, verb stems that end in a consonant are referred to as *C*-stems, those ending in a vowel, as *V*-stems.

Regular Stems

Regularly formed variants of stems are generally not listed in this dictionary. For the vast majority of verbs, those variants are regularly determinable from the citation form alone.

Every *V*-stem regularly has an extension **-v-** before the *1st* and *2nd sg pdef* suffixes **-a** and **-e**, respectively, and **-f-** before the *optative* extension **-sh-**:

Citation form	forc|o'·*n*	gënj|e'·*n*	la'·*n*	shkru'a·*n*	zhy'e·*n*
1st sg pdef	forc|o'|v|a	gënj|e'|v|a	la'|v|a	shkr|o'|v|a	zh|e'|v|a
2nd sg pdef	forc|o'|v|e	gënj|e'|v|e	la'|v|e	shkr|o'|v|e	zh|e'|v|e
1st sg opt	forc|o'|f|sh|a	gënj|e'|f|sha	la'|f|sh|a	shkr|o'|f|sh|a	zh|e'|f|sh|a
1st pl opt	forc|o'|f|sh|im	gënj|e'|f|sh|im	la'|f|sh|i	shkr|o'|f|sh|im	zh|e'|f|sh|i

Every verb whose citation form ends in **t·** has an unlisted alternant stem with **s** rather than **t** in the *3rd sg active impf* form:

Citation form	stërvi't·	diha't·
3rd sg active impf	stërvi'ste	diha'ste

Thematic Verb Stems

Large numbers of verb stems, including both those in this dictionary as well as freshly formed ones, are formed by adding a THEMATIC suffix to a base or stem: **-o'·** or **-e'·** produces *V*-stems; **-e't·**, **-i't·**, or **-o's·** produces *C*-stems.

In particular, every verb whose citation form stem ends in thematic **o'·** (the largest class of verbs in Albanian) or thematic **e'·**, has an unlisted, but regular alternate stem with **u'a** or **y'e**, respectively, instead of the thematic vowel in the *participle*, the *1st pl pdef, 2nd pl pdef, 3rd pl pdef, 3rd sg passive pdef, 3rd sg passive pdef,* and (optionally) any *admirative* form:

Citation form	forc|o'·*n*	gënj|e'·*n*
participle	forc|u'a|r	gënj|y'e|r
1st pl pdef	forc|u'a|m	gënj|y'e|m
2nd pl pdef	forc|u'a|t	gënj|y'e|t
3rd pl pdef	forc|u'a|n	gënj|y'e|n
3rd sg passive pdef	u forc|u'a	u gënj|y'e

3rd sg admirative	forc|u'a|ka	gënj|y'e|ka

If the stem of the citation form of the verb ends in a two-vowel sequence **u'a** or **y'e**, only the first vowel of the sequence remains before the passive voice marker **-he-**; the stem vowel becomes **o'** or **e'**, respectively, before the **v** and **f** extensions:

Citation form	shkru'a·n	zhy'e·n
3rd sg pres	shkr|u'|het	zh|y'|het
3rd pl impf	shkr|u'|heshin	zh|y'|heshin
1st sg pdef	shkr|o'|va	zh|e'|va
2nd sg pdef	shkr|o'|ve	zh|e'|ve
1st sg opt	shkr|o'|fsha	zh|e'|fsha
1st pl opt	shkr|o'|fshim	zh|e'|fshim

Irregular Stems

Variants of verb stems that are not determinable from the citation form are listed in their own alphabetically placed entry and cross-referred to the main entry for the verb:

vde'k\| *stem for part, opt, adm* < **vdes·**

...

vde'k\|ur *part* < **vdes·**

...

vdes· *vi* ...

...

vdi'q\| *stem for pdef* < **vdes·**

...

vdi's\| *stem for 2nd pl pres, impf, imper, vp* < **vdes·**

IMPORTANT NOTE: Since the uses of *passive* forms for transitive and intransitive verbs are quite general and automatic, they are not generally listed as separate senses in the main entries of those verbs. In interpreting a particular passive form, the reader of Albanian must keep in mind the possibility that that form may represent a passive, reciprocal, reflexive, or impersonal sense of a transitive or intransitive verb not specifically listed in the dictionary, as well as one of the listed senses of a reflexive verb.

Formation of Tenses

General Considerations

The particular combination of stem form with suffixes signals the cluster of grammatical categories expressed by the verb, in addition to the senses of the verb stem as described in the dictionary. Verbs are traditionally classified into conjugation classes according to the pattern exhibited by their stem and suffix alternants. The problem with this classification is that so many verbs exhibit parts of different patterns as to necessitate sub-classes within subclasses, and exception upon exception. Instead, this dictionary simply lists most stem alternants in ordinary alphabetical order.

The form of a verb in a text reflects the PERSON and NUMBER of its subject and simultaneously its VOICE, MOOD, TENSE, and ASPECT; in the imperative mood the verb form may also reflect the person and number of its direct and/or indirect object.

In the Reverse List of Possible Word Endings in Albanian, p. xlix, a list of possible terminations of Albanian words is given in reverse alphabetical order, to permit a reader to identify most of the possible interpretations of any final sequence of letters in a word found in an Albanian text.

A transitive verb (*vt*) potentially has 58 different inflected forms: 3 persons (1st, 2nd, 3rd) times 2 numbers (sg, pl) times 3 primary tenses (pres, impf, pdef) times 2 voices (active, reflexive); plus 2 present subjunctive forms (2nd sg, 3rd sg); plus 3 persons times 2 numbers times 2 tenses (present, past) times 1 mood (admirative); plus 3 persons times 2 numbers (optative); plus 2 imperative forms (2nd sg, 2nd pl). In addition, the participle derived from the verb may be used in "perfect" constructions with any of 48 forms of 2 auxiliary verbs (**ka·**, **ësh·***ıë*) for a total of 154 forms, not even counting the syntactic constructions of the particle **do** + subjunctive forms that serve as future tense and conditional mood functions, constructions of the particle **mund** + subjunctive forms that serve as a possibilitive mood, constructions of the auxiliary verb **ësh·***ıë* + **duke** + participle that serve to form progressive tenses, constructions of particles **s'**, **nuk**, or

mos + any of the other forms to form negative expressions, use of the prepositions **me** or **për** to form an infinitive-like construction, the preposition **pa** + participle to form a privative construction, or the preposition **para** with negative present and imperfect constructions that parallel English expressions with "hardly ever".

A verb labeled *vi* or *vp* has something more than half this number of forms.

Formation Rules

While this rich array of forms looks very complicated at first sight, for most verbs only a few, quite consistent elements and rules determine each form, given the stem. Irregular verb forms that deviate from these rules are listed separately in the dictionary, identified, and cross-referred to their main entry:

> **ha·|më** *1st pl pres* < **ha·**

Sound/Letter combination rules

- An initial evanescent *ë* in a suffix drops if a vowel precedes; a final evanescent *ë* in a suffix appears only if the vowel in the preceding syllable is stressed.
- The unstressed vowel **-i** becomes **-j** between a vowel and a following consonant.
- The combination **tsh** may be spelled **ç** or **tç** or **tsh**.
- **sh** may become **ç** when it follows **n, r, rr, l,** or **ll**.

Person-number rules

Present tense

The marker of *2pl* forms *(active, passive,* and *imperative)* is the ending *-ni*

- For most *V*-stems, the person-number ending **-j** (**-nj** in Tosk) marks the *1sg pres*, and the person-number ending **-n** marks both the *2sg pres* and *3sg pres* forms.
  > The verbs **pi·, ha·, di·, do·, bi'e·, shpi'e·, shti'e·, ve·** *te*, and for some speakers, **ble·** *n* have no person-number ending for *pres 1sg, 2sg,* and *3sg,* and have no plural extension **-i** before in their *pres pl* forms.
- For most *C*-stem verbs, the *pres 1sg, 2sg,* and *3sg* forms have no person-number ending.
- *C*-stem verbs that have the variable vowel *e* all have **i** instead in their *pres 2pl* form.
- *C*-stem verbs that end in the variable consonant *t* have **s** instead in their *pres 1sg, pres 1pl, pres 3pl, pres subjunctive 2sg* and *pres subjunctive 3sg* forms.
- Some *C*-stem verbs that have the variable vowel *e* have the vowel **a** or **o** instead in those forms as well. These stem forms are separately listed in the body of the dictionary.

Non-present tense

- The marker of *1sg* forms is the ending **-a**.
- The marker of *2sg* forms is the ending **-e**.
- The marker of *1pl* forms is the ending **- ëmë**.
- The marker of *2pl* forms is the ending **- ëtë**.
- The marker of *3pl* forms is the ending **- ënë**.

Subjunctive

- The marker of *pres subjunctive 2sg* is the ending **-(ë)sh**.
  > The *ë* appears only after *C*-stems.
- The marker of *pres subjunctive 3sg* is the ending **-(j)ë**.
  > The **j** appears only after *V*-stems.
- All other forms of the *subjunctive* following the subjunctive particle **të** (*pres* and *impf* only) are the same as the *pres* and *impf* forms of the verb.

Miscellaneous

- The marker of *1pl* forms for *passive pres* forms, as well as for the verbs **tho·** *të*, **ka·**, **ësh·** *të*, and for some speakers, **ve·** *te*, is the ending **-mi**.

Extension rules

- Except in *pdef* forms, *2pl* forms with **-ni**, and *1pl* forms with **-mi**, an unstressed extension **-i** appears immediately before *plural* person-number endings.
- Following the passive extension, the marker for *passive impf* forms is the extension **-sh-**, which was formerly the marker of all *impf* forms.

Active

- The marker of *sg impf* forms is the extension **-j-**.
- The marker of *pl impf* forms is the extension **-n-**.

Passive

- The marker of *passive* forms in General tenses, is the extension **-(h)e-**.
  > The *h* appears only after *V*-stems.
- In all Special tenses, the *passive* is marked by the reflexive proclitic **u** preceding the active form.

Optative

- The marker for most *optative* forms is the extension -(f)sh-.
  f appears only after *V*-stems.
- The marker of *optative 3sg* is the ending -(f)të
  f appears only after *V*-stems.

Admirative

The marker for *admirative* forms is the extension -k- and the endings are those of the auxiliary verb ka•.

The greatest deviation from these generalizations is shown in the singular tense forms of the present tense, and in the markers of *3sg*. As for *present tense* forms:

Third person singular

The markers of *3sg* are different for each tense.

- The marker of *impf 3sg* is the ending -(n)te.
  The n appears only after *V*-stems.
  C-stem verbs that end in t or r have s instead before the -te.
- The marker of *passive pres 3sg* is the ending -t.
- The marker of *passive impf 3sg* is the ending -j.
- The marker of *pdef 3sg* is the ending -i after o' or any consonant except g, k, or h.
- The marker of *pdef 3sg* is the ending -u after a stem ending in one of the vowels a, e, i, or y, or a consonants g, k, or h
- The marker of *passive pdef 3sg* is the proclitic u followed by the bare Special stem of the verb with no person-number ending: **mblodhi** *he gathered []* (active form) vs. **u mblodh** *he huddled up* (passive form)

Person-Number Endings

The following tables show the interplay among stem types and tense

	After thematic V				After athematic V			
	present		past definite		present		past definite	
person	singular	plural	singular	plural	singular	plural	singular	plural
1st	-j	-jmë	-va	-më	-Ø	-më	-a	-më
2nd	-n	-ni	-ve	-të	-Ø	-ni	-e	-të
3rd	-n	-jnë	-u or -i (after o')	-në	-Ø	-në	-u	-në

Table showing the most common inflectional endings that mark the person/number of the subject of a verb:

	present				other	
	singular		plural		singular	plural
	after most V-stems	after most C-stems	after most V-stems	after most C-stems		
1st person	-j	-Ø	-jmë	-im	-a	-(ë)m(ë)
2nd person	-n	-Ø	-ni	-ni	-e	-(ë)t(ë)
3rd person	-n	-Ø	-jnë	-in	-i/-u/-Ø	-(ë)n(ë)

Regular Verbs: Inflectional Endings

ACTIVE	REGULAR *V*-STEMS					REGULAR *C*-STEMS			
	o'-stems	*u'a-stems*	*e'-stems*	*y'e -stems*	other *V*-stems	most *C*-stems	*Vt-stems*	*Vt-stems*	*eC-stems*
pres									
sg									
1	o'j	u'aj	e'j	y'ej	*V*'j	*C*	*V*t	*V*s	e*C*
2	o'n	u'an	e'n	y'en	*V*'n	*C*	*V*t	*V*t	e*C*
3	o'n	u'an	e'n	y'en	*V*'n	*C*	*V*t	*V*t	e*C*
pl									
1	o'jmë	u'ajmë	e'jmë	y'ejmë	*V*'jmë	*C*im	*V*tim	*V*sim	e*C*im
2	o'ni	u'ani	i'ni or e'ni	y'eni	*V*'ni	*C*ni	*V*tni	*V*tni	i*C*ni
3	o'jnë	u'ajnë	e'jnë	y'ejnë	*V*'jnë	*C*in	*V*tin	*V*sin	e*C*in
pres subjunctive									
sg									
2	o'sh	u'ash	e'sh	y'esh	*V*'sh	*C*ësh	*V*tësh	*V*sësh	e*C*ësh
3	o'jë	u'ajë	e'jë	y'ejë	*V*'jë	*C*ë	*V*të	*V*së	e*C*ë
impf									
sg									
1	o'ja	u'aja	e'ja	y'eja	*V*'ja	*C*ja	*V*tja	*V*tja	i*C*ja
2	o'je	u'aje	e'je	y'eje	*V*'je	*C*je	*V*tje	*V*tje	i*C*je
3	o'nte	u'ante	e'nte	y'ente	*V*'nte	*C*te	*V*ste	*V*ste	i*C*te
pl									
1	o'nim	u'anim	e'nim	y'enim	*V*'nim	*C*nim	*V*tnim	*V*tnim	i*C*nim
2	o'nit	u'anit	e'nit	y'enit	*V*'nit	*C*nit	*V*tnit	*V*tnit	i*C*nit
3	o'nin	u'anin	e'nin	y'enin	*V*'nin	*C*nin	*V*tnin	*V*tnin	i*C*nin
pdef									
sg									
1	o'va	o'va	e'va	e'va	*V*'va	*C*a	*V*ta	*V*ta	i*C*a
2	o've	o've	e've	e've	*V*'ve	*C*e	*V*te	*V*te	i*C*e
3	o'i	o'i	e'u	e'u	*V*'u	*C*i[27]	*V*ti	*V*ti	i*C*i
pl									
1	u'am	u'am	y'em	y'em	*V*'më	*C*ëm	*V*tëm	*V*tëm	i*C*ëm
2	u'at	u'at	y'et	y'et	*V*'të	*C*ët	*V*tët	*V*tët	i*C*ët
3	u'an	u'an	y'en	y'en	*V*'në	*C*ën	*V*tën	*V*tën	i*C*ën
optative									
sg									
1	o'fsha	o'fsha	e'fsha	e'fsha	*V*'fsha	*C*sha	*V*tsha	*V*tsha	i*C*sha
2	o'fsh	o'fsh	e'fsh	e'fsh	*V*'fsh	*C*sh	*V*tsh	*V*tsh	i*C*sh
3	o'ftë	o'ftë	e'ftë	e'ftë	*V*'ftë	*C*të	*V*ttë	*V*ttë	i*C*të
pl									
1	o'fshim	o'fshim	e'fshim	e'fshim	*V*'fshim	*C*shim	*V*tshim	*V*tshim	i*C*shim
2	o'fshit	o'fshit	e'fshit	e'fshit	*V*'fshit	*C*shit	*V*tshit	*V*tshit	i*C*shit
3	o'fshin	o'fshin	e'fshin	e'fshin	*V*'fshin	*C*shin	*V*tshin	*V*tshin	i*C*shin
imperative									
sg									
2	o'	u'aj	e'	y'ej	*V*'j	*C*	*V*t	*V*t	i*C*
pl									
2	o'ni	u'ani	e'ni	y'eni	*V*'ni	*C*ni	*V*tni	*V*tni	i*C*ni
participle	u'ar	u'ar	y'er	y'er	*V*'rë	*C*ur	*V*tur	*V*tur	i*C*ur

---

[27] If C = g, k, or h, then the *3sg pdef* suffix is u, rather than i.

| PASSIVE[28] | | REGULAR *V*-STEMS | | | | REGULAR *C*-STEMS | | |
	o'-stems	*u'a*-stems	*e'*-stems	*y'e*-stems	other *V*-stems	most *C*-stems	*Vt*-stems & *Vt*-stems	*eC*-stems
pres								
sg								
1	o'hem	u'hem	e'hem	y'hem	*V*hem	*C*em	*V*tem	i*C*em
2	o'hesh	u'hesh	e'hesh	y'hesh	*V*hesh	*C*esh	*V*tesh	i*C*esh
3	o'het	u'het	e'het	y'het	*V*het	*C*et	*V*tet	i*C*et
pl								
1	o'hemi	u'hemi	e'hemi	y'hemi	*V*hemi	*C*emi	*V*temi	i*C*emi
2	o'heni	u'heni	e'heni	y'heni	*V*heni	*C*eni	*V*teni	i*C*eni
3	o'hen	u'hen	e'hen	y'hen	*V*hen	*C*en	*V*ten	i*C*en
impf								
sg								
1	o'hesha	u'hesha	e'hesha	y'hesha	*V*hesha	*C*esha	*V*tesha	i*C*esha
2	o'heshe	u'heshe	e'heshe	y'heshe	*V*heshe	*C*eshe	*V*teshe	i*C*eshe
3	o'hej	u'hej	e'hej	y'hej	*V*hej	*C*ej	*V*tej	i*C*ej
pl								
1	o'heshim	u'heshim	e'heshim	y'heshim	*V*heshim	*C*eshim	*V*teshim	i*C*eshim
2	o'heshit	u'heshit	e'heshit	y'heshit	*V*heshit	*C*eshit	*V*teshit	i*C*eshit
3	o'heshin	u'heshin	e'heshin	y'heshin	*V*heshin	*C*eshin	*V*teshin	i*C*eshin
imperative								
sg								
2	o'hu	u'hu	e'hu	y'hu	*V*hu	*C*u	*V*tu	i*C*u
pl								
2	o'huni	u'huni	e'huni	y'huni	*V*huni	*C*uni	*V*tuni	i*C*uni

---

[28] With the exception of the *3 rd sg pdef* noted above, all passive forms in Special tenses are identical to their corresponding active forms, except that the reflexive dative clitic **u** precedes the verb.

Irregular Verbs

	di·	do·	flet·	ha·	ik·	jep·
pres						
sg						
1	di′	du'a	flas	ha′	i'ki	jap
2	di′	do	flet	ha′	i'kën	jep
3	di′	do	flet	ha′	i'kën	jep
pl						
1	di'më	du'am	fla'sim	ha'më	i'kim	ja'pim
2	di'ni	do'ni	fli'tni or fli'sni	ha'ni	i'kni	je'pni or ji'pni or i'pni
3	di'në	du'an	fla'sin	ha'në	i'kin	ja'pin
pres subjunctive						
sg						
2	di'sh	du'ash	fla'sësh	ha'sh	i'kësh	ja'pësh
3	di'jë	do'jë	fla'së	ha'jë	i'kë	ja'pë
impf						
sg						
1	di'ja	doja	fli'tja or fli'sja	ha'ja	i'kja	je'pja or ji'pja or i'pja
2	di'je	doje	fli'tje or fli'sje	ha'je	i'kje	je'pje or ji'pje or i'pje
3	di'nte	donte	fli'ste	ha'nte	i'kte	je'pte or ji'pte or i'pte
pl						
1	di'nim	donim	fli'tnim or fli'snim	ha'nim	i'knim	je'pnim or ji'pnim or i'pnim
2	di'nit	donit	fli'tnit or fli'snit	ha'nit	i'knit	je'pnit or ji'pnit or i'pnit
3	di'nin	donin	fli'tnin or fli'snin	ha'nin	i'knin	je'pnin or ji'pnin or i'pnin
pdef						
sg						
1	di'ta	de'sha	fo'la	hë'ngra	i'ka	dha'shë
2	di'te	de'she	fo'le	hë'ngre	i'ke	dhe
3	di'ti	de'shi	fo'li	hë'ngri	i'ku	dha
pl						
1	di'tëm	de'shëm	fo'lëm	hë'ngrëm	i'këm	dha'më
2	di'tët	de'shët	fo'lën	hë'ngrët	i'kët	dha'të
3	di'tën	de'shën	fo'lën	hë'ngrën	i'kën	dha'në
optative						
sg						
1	di'tsha	da'ça	fo'lsha	ngrë'nsha	i'ksha	dhë'nça
2	ditsh	daç	fo'lsh	ngrënsh	i'ksh	dhë'nç
3	di'ttë	da'shtë	fo'ltë	ngrë'ntë	i'ktë	dhë'ntë
pl						
1	di'tshim	da'çim	fo'lshim	ngrë'nshim	i'kshim	dhë'nçim
2	di'tshit	da'çi	fo'lshit	ngrë'nshit	i'kshit	dhë'nçit
3	di'tshin	da'çin	fo'lshin	ngrë'nshin	i'kshin	dhë'nçin
imperative						
sg						
2	di'	du'aj	fo'l	ha'	ik	jep or jip or nëm
pl						
2	di'ni	do'ni	fli'tni or fli'sni	ha'ni	i'kni	jepni or jipni or nëmni

	pi•	tho'•të	ve•te	vj•en	vjedh•	vret•	zë'•
pres							
sg							
1	pi'	them	ve'te	vij	vjedh	vras	zë'
2	pi'	thu'a	ve'te	vjen	vjedh	vret	zë'
	pi'	tho'të	ve'te	vjen	vjedh	vret	zë'
pl							
1	pi'më	the'mi	ve'më or ve'mi	vi'jmë	vje'dhim	vra'sim	zë'më
2	pi'ni	tho'ni	vi'ni		vi'dhni	vri'tni or vri'sni	zi'ni
3	pi'në	tho'në	ve'në	vi'jnë	vje'dhin	vra'sin	zë'në
pres subjunctive							
sg							
2	pi'sh	thu'ash	ve'sh	vi'sh	vje'dhësh	vra'sësh	zë'sh
3	pi'jë	tho'të	ve'jë	vi'jë	vje'dhë	vra'së	zë'rë
impf							
sg							
1	pi'ja	tho'sha or tho'ja	vi'ja		vi'dhja	vri'tja or vri'sja	zi'ja
2	pi'je	tho'she or tho'je	vi'je		vi'dhje	vri'tje or vri'sje	zi'je
3	pi'nte	tho'shte or tho'nte	vi'nte		vi'dhte	vri'ste	zi'nte
pl							
1	pi'nim	tho'shnim or tho'nim	vi'nim		vi'dhnim	vri'tnim or vri'snim	zi'nim
2	pi'nit	tho'shnit or tho'nit	vi'nit		vi'dhnit	vri'tnit or vri'snit	zi'nit
3	pi'nin	tho'shnin or tho'nin	vi'nin		vi'dhnin	vri'tnin or vri'snin	zi'nin
pdef							
sg							
1	pi'va	tha'shë	va'jta	e'rdha	vo'dha	vri'ta	zu'ra
2	pi've	the	va'jte	e'rdhe	vo'dhe	vri'te	zu're
3	pi'u	tha	va'jti	e'rdhi	vo'dhi	vri'ti	zu'ri
pl							
1	pi'më	tha'më	va'jtëm	e'rdhëm	vo'dhëm	vri'tëm	zu'më
2	pi'të	tha'të	va'jtët	e'rdhët	vo'dhët	vri'tën	zu'të
3	pi'në	tha'në	va'jtën	e'rdhën	vo'dhën	vri'tën	zu'në
optative							
sg							
1	pi'fsha	thë'nça	va'fsha	a'rdhsha	vo'dhsha	vra'fsha	zë'nça
2	pifsh	thë'nç	vafsh	a'rdhsh	vo'dhsh	vra'fsh	zënç
3	pi'ftë	thë'ntë	va'ftë	a'rdhtë	vo'dhtë	vra'ftë	zë'ntë
pl							
1	pi'fshim	thë'nçim	va'fshim	a'rdhshim	vo'dhshim	vra'fshim	zë'nçim
2	pi'fshit	thë'nçit	va'fshit	a'rdhshit	vo'dhshit	vra'fshit	zë'nçit
3	pi'fshin	thë'nçin	va'fshin	a'rdhshin	vo'dhshin	vra'fshin	zë'nçin
imperative							
sg							
2	pi'	thu'aj		e'ja	vi'dh	vri't	zë'rë
pl							
2	pi'ni	tho'ni		e'jani	vi'dhni	vri'tni	zi'ni

	bi'e·₁	bi'e·₂	shpi'e·	shti'e·
pres				
sg				
1	bi'e		shpi'e	shti'e
2	bi'e		shpi'e	shti'e
3	bi'e		shpi'e	shti'e
pl				
1	bi'em		shpi'em	shti'em
2	bi'ni		shpi'ni	shti'ni
3	bi'en		shpi'en	shti'en
pres subjunctive				
sg				
2	bi'esh		shpi'esh	shti'esh
3	bje'rë		shpje'rë	shtje'rë
impf				
sg				
1	bi'ja		shpi'ja	shti'ja
2	bi'je		shpi'je	shti'je
3	bi'nte		shpi'nte	shti'nte
pl				
1	bi'nim		shpi'nim	shti'nim
2	bi'nit		shpi'nit	shti'nit
3	bi'nin		shpi'nin	shti'nin
pdef				
sg				
1	ra'shë	pru'ra	shpu'ra	shti'va
2	re	pru're	shpu're	shti've
3	ra	pru'ri	shpu'ri	shti'u
pl				
1	ra'më	pru'më	shpu'më	shti'më
2	ra'të	pru'të	shpu'të	shti'të
3	ra'në	pru'në	shpu'në	shti'në
optative				
sg				
1	rë'nça	pru'fsha	shpë'nça	shtë'nsha
2	rënç	prufsh	shpënç	shtënsh
3	rë'ntë	pru'ftë	shpë'ntë	shtë'ntë
pl				
1	rë'nçim	pru'fshim	shpë'nçim	shtë'nshim
2	rë'nçit	pru'fshit	shpë'nçit	shtë'nshit
3	rë'nçin	pru'fshin	shpë'nçin	shtë'nshin
imperative				
sg				
2	bje'rë	bje'rë	shpjer	shtjer
pl				
2	bi'ni	bi'ni	shpi'ni	shti'ni

Participles

The typical marker of a participle is **-r** (**-n** or **-m** or **-∅** in Gheg). After a regular verb stem ending in a consonant, the participial ending is **-ur** (**-un** in Gheg) ; after a regular verb stem ending in an unstressed vowel, the participial ending is **-r** (**-më**, **-m** or **-∅** in Gheg); after a regular verb stem ending in a stressed vowel,[29] the participial ending is **-r** (**-∅** in Gheg); after a verb stem ending in a stressed *variable ë*, the participial ending is **-në** (no such verb stems in Gheg); after a verb stem ending in **err** (and for some verb stems, **jell** or **edh**) the participial ending in Gheg may be *-ë*.

Verb stem ends in:	Stem	Participle	(in Gheg)
a consonant	var, prit|, hekuro's	va'rur, pri'tur, hekuro'sur	va'run, pri'tun, hekuro'sun
an unstressed vowel	kuptu'a, ly'e	kuptu'ar, ly'er	kuptu'em, ly'em or kuptu'e, ly'e or kuptu', ly'
a stressed vowel	bë (bâ in Gheg) ça, lëpi'	bë'rë ça'rë, lëpi'rë	bamë, bam, bâ çâ, lëpî
stressed variable ë	vë', parathë'	vë'në, parathë'në	vë'në, parathë'në
err	cjerr shqerr	cje'rrur shqe'rrur	çje'rrë or cje'rrun, shqe'rrë or shqe'rrun
jell	mbjell	mbjellur	mbjellë or mbjellun
edh	mbledh	mbledhur	mbledhë or mbledhun

NOUNS

Noun Stems

A noun stem is labeled *nm, nf, np, n,* or *nn,* according to which set of case suffixes it takes, its DECLENSION.

For most nouns, the grammatical label following a noun stem (*nm, nf, np, nn* —masculine, feminine, plural, neuter, respectively) is sufficient to indicate its declension and its gender agreement—that is, the form of variable pronouns, adjectives, adjectival articles, and determiners that have that noun as referent. For exceptional words, its declension and its gender are both listed:

> **gë'rxho** *nf with masculine agreement* **1** old man suffering from senility **2** uncultivated person, boor

Nouns that have *nm* stems serve as *masculine* referents, and unless otherwise specified, nouns that have *nf* stems serve as *feminine* referents.

For an *nm* stem, there are four distinct case forms: the uninflected form, which serves as the nominative/accusative indefinite case of the noun; the oblique form with the inflectional suffix **-i** or **-u** (after stems that end in a stressed vowel, **g, k,** or **h**), which serves as both the nominative definite and the ablative/dative indefinite case of the noun; the oblique form plus the inflectional suffix **-n,** which serves as the accusative definite case of the noun;[30] and the oblique form plus the inflectional suffix **-t,** which serves as the ablative/dative indefinite case of the noun.

For an *nf* stem, there are five distinct case forms: the uninflected form, which serves as the nominative/accusative indefinite case of the noun; the nominative definite form with the inflectional suffix **-a** or **-ja** (after stems ending in any vowel other than **ë**); the accusative definite form with the inflectional suffix **-n** or **-në** (after stems that end in a stressed vowel); the ablative/dative definite form with the inflectional suffix **-s** or **-së** (after stems that end in a stressed vowel); and the ablative/dative indefinite form with the inflectional suffix **-e** or **-je** (after stems ending in any vowel other than **ë**). If the *nf* stem ends in the unstressed vowel *e,* that vowel drops when the **-ja** suffix is added, and it may or may not drop when the **-je** suffix is added:[31] *nf* **lule** *flower,* **lulja** (nominative definite), **lulje** or **luleje** (ablative/dative indefinite)

---

[29]Throughout this dictionary, the term "stressed vowel" includes both the single vowel in monosyllabic stems with a single syllable, as well as the vowels marked with a stress mark ' in stems with more than one vowel.

[30]The reader may encounter alternate accusative definite case forms with the inflectional suffix **-në** directly added to bare *nm* stems ending in a stressed vowel: the accusative definite form of the *nm* noun **dhe** *earth* may be either **dheun** or **dhenë**.

[31]There is considerable vacillation as to which variant is chosen; the choice is not entirely determined by regional variation.

For an *np* stem, there are four distinct case forms: the uninflected form, which serves as the nominative/accusative indefinite case of the noun; the nominative definite form with the inflectional suffix **-t**, the ablative/dative—indefinite or definite— form with the inflectional suffix **-ve**;[32] and the ablative indefinite form with the inflectional suffix **-sh**.

For most nouns, the plural stem *(np)* is derived from a singular *(nm, nf, n)* stem by adding a suffix *-∅*,[33]**-a**, **-e**, **-ë**, or **-ra**. Stems so formed are listed in this dictionary only when the *np* stem has different or more limited senses or uses than the singular form. Readers must be open to the possibility that a stem with any of these suffixes may have an interpretation as a plural, since there is in fact great variability in noun-plural formation in both spoken and written Albanian. The senses of such plural nouns are just the plural of the senses of the underlying *nm* or *nf* stem. Nouns with *np* stems, plural determiners and pronouns, and compound phrases composed of nouns and/or pronouns may all serve as *plural* referents.

The plurals of *nf* stems are all *feminine plural*. The plurals of *nm* stems that designate males are all *masculine plural*; but the plurals of other *nm* stems may be *masculine plural* or *feminine plural*.

Nouns that have *n* stems are listed in the form that takes *nm* inflectional endings and serves as a *masculine* referent. For every such noun, an *nf* stem can, in principle,[34] be derived with the same senses except that it has a feminine referent rather than a masculine one. The *nf* stem is not listed in the dictionary, since it is regularly formed from the *n* stem—for most *n* stems, especially those ending in **-a'r**, **-ës**, **-a'n**, or **-as**, simply by adding the feminine suffix **-e**.

Stems that serve both as nouns and adjectives (e.g. **afrika'n**) may be marked either *n, adj* or *adj, n*; the definition may provide a generic noun between parentheses to indicate the meaning when used as a noun:

> **labër|qa'r** *adj n (Pej)* (person) wanting something for nothing, parasitic on others

Nouns with *nn* stems may take adjectives that are either *masculine* or *feminine*. Nominalized participles preceded by a proclitic attributive article **të** all have *nn* stems. Otherwise, there is considerable variation among Albanians as to which nouns are "neuter"—i.e., have *nn* stems.

If a proclitic attributive article is required for a particular noun or noun sense, the grammatical label is followed by the nominative form of the appropriate article between parentheses: *nm (i) , nf (e), np (të), nn (të)* . The label *n (i)* indicates a nominalized adjective which will take either *nm* or *nf* (or *np*) inflectional endings depending on whether the referent is male, female, or plural.

---

[32]According to the prescriptive standard. There are varieties of Albanian that distinguish the dative indefinite **-ve** from the dative definite **-vet** for the plural.

[33]Thus the singular and plural stems for many nouns are identical in form, distinguishable formally only by the inflectional suffixes they take and syntactically by their grammatical agreement with other forms. Nouns that typically have identical singular and plural stems are *nf* stems that end in any vowel except **ë**. Without exception, *nf* stems formed with the agentive derivational suffix **-ës** or with a derivational suffix that ends in r (in particular, the participial suffix) are identical their singular forms, except that they add i before the single-consonant plural suffixes **-t** and **-sh**.

[34]Albanian society traditionally divided male and female roles sharply, so that for many such nouns only the *nm* stem was used and used exclusively for *masculine* referents. As the role of women shifts in Albania society, a number of new *nf* stems (derived with the suffix **-e**) serving as *feminine* referents have come into use, and the potential for new ones is, in principle, unlimited.

Case Suffixes

The form of the suffixes which mark the case of a noun or nominalized adjectives (see p. xlv) depends on two factors: 1) the function of the suffix in marking case, gender, number, and definiteness; and 2) the terminal letters of the stem.

	Singular				Plural	
	Masculine		Feminine			
	Indef	Def	Indef	Def	Indef	Def
Nominative						
		-i		-a		-t
after ĕr or ĕs		-i		-a		-it
after k, g, h		-u				
after *V'*		-j or -u		-ja		-tĕ
after o'				-ja		-t
after o				-ua		-t
Accusative						
		-in or -n		-n		-t
after ĕr or ĕs		-in		ĕn		-it
after k, g, h		-un				
after *V'*		-jnĕ or -un		-nĕ		-tĕ
after o		-n		-n		-t
Dative						
	-i	-it	-e	-s	-ve	-ve(t)
after ĕr or ĕs	-i	-it	-e	-ĕs	-ve	-ve(t)
after k, g, h	-ut	-u				
after *V'*	-j or -u	-jt or -ut	-je	-sĕ	-ve	-ve(t)
after unstressed *V*			-je	-s	-ve	-ve(t)
Ablative						
	-i		-e		-sh	
after ĕr or ĕs	-i		-e	-ĕs	-ĕsh	
after k, g, h	-u					
after *V'*	-j or -u		-je	-sĕ	-sh	
after unstressed *V*			-je	-s	-sh	

Leaving out the details:

	singular				plural	
	indefinite		definite		indefinite	definite
	nm	nf	nm	nf	np	np
nominative	-Ø	-Ø	-i/-u[35]	-a/-ja[36]	-Ø	-tĕ/-it
accusative	-Ø	-Ø	-in/-un	-nĕ	-Ø	-tĕ/-it
dative[37]	-i/-u	-e	-it/-ut	-sĕ	-ve	-ve/-vet
ablative	-i/-u	-e	-it/-ut	-sĕ	-sh	-ve/-vet

Gerunds

Gerunds are nouns that are formed regularly from verb stems:

1. by dropping a stressed thematic vowel *o'* or *e'* and suffixing **-i'm** to form an *nm* stem
2. by suffixing **-mĕ** after the stem-final stressed vowel **i'** to form an *nf* stem
3. by suffixing **-je** after the stem-final consonant to form an *nf* stem
4. by suffixing **-rje** or **-jtje** after a stem-final stressed vowel **a'** or **e'** to form an *nf* stem
5. by suffixing **-jtje** after a stem-final stressed vowel **u'** to form an *nf* stem

---

[35]In all endings in which **i** and **u** alternate, **u** is the alternant that appears immediately after **g, k** or **h**.

[36]If the target word has **ja** after a vowel, the citation form of the stem ends in that vowel; if **ja** appears after a consonant, the citation form of the stem ends in the unstressed vowel **e**.

[37]The so-called genitive form is just the dative form preceded by a proclitic attributive article.

In addition to these, a gerundial construction may always be formed by creating a nominalized adjective from the participle of the verb, designating the process conveyed by the verb. The nominalized adjective so created has *nn*-stem characteristics, but restricted in use and forms. As a nominative or accusative noun it ends in the suffix **-it** and is preceded by the proclitic article **të: të ngji'turit** *the ascension*

PRONOMINALS
Pronominals are words that may function as noun phrases.

Personal Pronouns
Pronominal subjects of verbs are normally indicated by inflectional endings, while pronominal direct and indirect objects are indicated by pronominal clitics. A personal pronoun is used when the pronoun is isolated or emphasized, or when it serves as object of a preposition.

First and second person personal pronouns distinguish four cases, though no pronoun has distinct forms for the same four. To complicate matters, in practice some Albanians use the form **ne've** and **ju've** throughout their respective declensions, a practice opposed but not altogether eliminated by the proponents of standard Albanian. The ablative forms are used exclusively as objects of prepositions.

	English equivalent	Nominative	Accusative	Dative	Ablative
1st person					
Singular	I, me	**u'në**	**mu'a**	**mu'a**	**me'je**
Plural	we, us	**ne**	**ne**	**ne've**	**nesh**
2nd person					
Singular	you	**ti**	**ty**	**ty**	**te'je**
Plural	you	**ju**	**ju**	**ju've**	**jush**

As stressed forms of 3rd person personal pronouns, Albanian uses deictic determiners whose form conveys the distance—actual or felt—of the referent.

	English equivalent	Nominative		Accusative		Dative		Ablative	
3rd person		*Far*	*Near*	*Far*	*Near*	*Far*	*Near*	*Far*	*Near*
Singular									
Masculine	that one: he, it, him	**ai'**	**ky**	**atë'**	**këtë'**	**ati'j**	**ati'j**	**ati'j**	**ati'j**
Feminine	that one: she, it, her	**ajo'**	**kjo**	**atë'**	**këtë'**	**asa'j**	**kësa'j**	**asa'j**	**kësa'j**
Plural									
Masculine	they, them	**ata'**	**ky**	**ata'**	**këta'**	**aty're**	**këty're**	**aso'sh**	**këso'sh**
Feminine	they, them	**ato'**	**kjo'**	**ato'**	**këto'**	**aty're**	**këty're**	**aso'sh**	**këso'sh**

Relative Pronouns
With definite noun suffixes, **cil** *which* is used as an interrogative pronoun, translated as 'which (one)' or 'who' in English, depending on whether the referent is considered human or not. Preceded by a proclitic attributive article (indicated between parentheses below), these same forms serve as relative pronouns.

	English equivalent	Nominative	Accusative	Dative
Singular				
Masculine	which (one), who; whom	**(i) ci'li**	**(të) ci'lin**	**(të) ci'lit**
Feminine	which (one), who; whom	**(e) ci'la**	**(të) ci'lën**	**(së) ci'lës**
Plural				
Masculine	which (one), who; whom	**(të) ci'lët**	**(të) ci'lët**	**(të) ci'lëve**
Feminine	which (one), who; whom	**(të) ci'lat**	**(të) ci'lat**	**(të) ci'lave**

Like **cil** *which* is **seci'l**, used as a determiner 'each' or as a nominalized adjective 'each one'.

ATTRIBUTIVE AND PREDICATIVE MODIFIERS

Modifiers may be used attributively or predicatively. Used attributively, a modifier generally implies an inherent characteristic of the referent. In Albanian, attributive modifiers typically follow nouns; predicative modifiers typically follow verbs.

A referent may precede the modifier in the discourse, come after it, or merely be understood by the participants in the discourse.

> **ka trup të lidhur** *he [unexpressed overtly] has a strong build*
> **është i mirë** *he is good*
> **i ati** *his/her/their father*
> **i ati i Agronit** *Agron's father*
> **e fejuara** *his fiancée*
> **e fejuara e Agronit** *Agron's fiancée*

Used predicatively, a modifier implies a temporary characteristic of the referent:

> **e çuan lidhur** *they conducted him bound*
> **është mirë** *he is well*

Adjectives

Articulated adjectives consist of the proclitic attributive article, followed by the base, or adjective proper. In **i mirë** *good*, the base is **mirë** and the article is **i** and the form of both parts may reflect the gender and number of the referent of the adjective. Like articulated adjectives, unarticulated adjectives may have different endings for feminine and/or plural forms.

Adjective Stem Forms

In addition to the masculine singular base form listed in the dictionary, adjectives have feminine and/or plural forms that are used for feminine and/or plural referents. A few common adjectives have special feminine or plural forms, which are listed in their proper alphabetical order in this dictionary and cross-referred after the symbol < to the main entry for the adjective.

> **mëdha'** *fem pl* < **madh**
> **mëdhe'nj** *masc pl* < **madh**

Adjective stems that end in **-ë** or formerly ended in **-ë**, such as participles (whose stems now end in **-ur**, **-uar**, **-yer**, or **-un**) and stems ending in **-ër**, **-ërr**, **-ël**, **-ëll**, *-ull*, have the same form for the feminine singular.

Many other adjective stems whose base form ends in a consonant have an easily recognizable feminine form derived from that base. In particular, many feminine adjectives are regularly derived by adding unstressed *-e* to the dictionary base form, including all articulated adjectives whose base form ends in *ë*m or *më*. The *ë* of the base form disappears, of course, before the ending *-e*. The derived form also serves as the feminine plural form of the adjective.

> **goj|u'sh** *adj (i)* garrulous
> **gru'a e goju'shme** *garrulous woman*
> **gra të goju'shme** *garrulous women*

> **i a'fërm** *(masc)*, **e a'fërme** *(fem)*, **të a'fërm** *(masc pl)*, **të a'fërm** *(fem pl)*
> **i vle'fshëm** *(masc)*, **e vle'fshme** *(fem)*, **të vle'fshëm** *(masc pl)*, **të vle'fshme** *(fem pl)*
> **i so'tëm** *(masc)*, **e so'tme** *(fem)*, **të so'tëm** *(masc pl)*, **të so'tme** *(fem pl)*

Similarly, unarticulated adjectives whose base form ends in **-a'k**, **-a'n**, **-a'r**, **-e'z**, **-i'st**, **-ësh**, **-ta'r**, **-to'r**, **-as**, **-ës**, or **-u'es** all add a suffix *-e* to form a feminine singular and plural. Of these, **-ak**, **-a'n**, **-a'r**, **-e'z**, **-i'st**, **ësh**, **-ta'r**, **-to'r** also form a masculine plural form by adding the suffix **-ë**:

> **shqipta'r** *(masc)*, **shqipta're** *(fem)*, **shqipta'rë** *(masc pl)* **shqipta're** *(fem pl)*
> **tira'nas** *(masc)*, **tira'nase** *(fem)*, **tira'nas** *(masc pl)*, **tira'nase** *(fem pl)*

Most adjectives whose feminine singular form does not end in a stressed vowel or *-e* have a derived feminine plural form ending in *-a*.

> **ngro'h|të** *adj (i)* warm

duar të ngrohta warm hands

The following table summarizes the relationships among various adjective forms:

| | ENDING OF STEM | | EXAMPLES | | |
	masculine	feminine	masculine	feminine	MAIN SENSE
singular	-ë	-ë	i mi'rë	e mi'rë	good
plural	-ë	-a	të mi'rë	të mi'ra	
singular	-C	-e	amfi'b	amfi'be	amphibian
plural	-Cë	-e	amfi'bë	amfi'be	
singular	-ëm	-me	i e'pshëm	e e'pshme	flexible
plural	-ëm	-me	të e'pshëm	të e'pshme	
singular	-ër	-ër	i va'rfër	e va'rfër	poor
plural	-ër	-ra	të va'rfër	të va'rfra	
singular	-C	-C	i pa'fund	e pa'fund	endless
plural	-C	-C	të pa'fund	të pa'fund	
singular	-ur	-ur	i di'tur	e di'tur	knowledgeable
plural	-ur	-ura	të di'tur	të di'tura	
singular	-uar	-uar	i shku'ar	e shku'ar	past
plural	-uar	-uara	të shku'ar	të shku'ara	
singular	-ët	-ët	i la'gët	e la'gët	wet
plural	-ët	-ëta	të la'gët	të la'gëta	
singular	-ël	-ël	i vo'gël	e vo'gël	small
plural	-ël	-la	të ve'gjël	të vo'gla	
singular			i zi'	e ze'zë	black
plural			të zi'nj	të ze'za	
singular			i ri'	e re'	new
plural			të ri'nj	të re'ja	
singular			i ma'dh	e ma'dhe	big
plural			të mëdhe'nj	të mëdha'	
singular			i ke'q	e ke'qe	bad
plural			të këqi'(n)j	të ke'qe	

Feminine Plurals of Masculine Singulars

When the referent of an adjective is a plural noun whose singular form is grammatically masculine but semantically inanimate, the adjective typically has its feminine plural form. For example, all gerunds ending in **-im** are masculine nouns in the singular and have corresponding plurals ending in **-ime**; an adjective with such a plural as referent will have its feminine plural form: **mësime të mëdha** *great teachings*

Relation of Adjectives to other Parts of Speech

Adjectives are regularly formed from participles, adverbs, and certain classes of nouns, and vice versa. Knowing a few simple correspondences will greatly enhance the reader's vocabulary.

Formation from Participles

A participle preceded by an attributive article serves as an adjective: **shkruar** *written*—**fjala e shkruar** *the written word.*

Relation to Adverbs

The difference between an adjective and an adverb may be simply the presence or absence of an attributive article: **i mirë** *good*—**mirë** *well*, **i keq** *bad*—**keq** *badly.*

Relation to Nouns

As in English, a number of forms, especially those ending in **-a'k, -a'n, -a'r, -e'z, -i'st, -ësh, -ta'r, -to'r, -as, -ës,** or **-u'es** may be used either as nouns or as unarticulated adjectives: **amerika'n** *American* (person)— **gaze'të amerika'ne** *American newspaper.*

Nominalized Adjectives

An adjective in Albanian is nominalized when it either precedes the noun it modifies, or is used in place of the noun altogether (as in English "The big must protect the small."). In either case, the adjective takes the endings for case, gender, number and definiteness that a noun would take in the same place. A nominalized adjective is articulated if its underlying adjective is articulated.

>i pasho'qi *the peerless one* (from the adjective **i pasho'q** *peerless*)
>
>i bu'kuri *the handsome one* (masc)
>
>e bu'kura *the beautiful one* (fem)
>
>një i bu'kur *a good one* (masc)
>
>një e bu'kur *a good one* (fem)
>
>ca të bu'kurave *to some beautiful ones*

Adjectives generally follow their referent noun in Albanian, but that order may be inverted to put emphasis on the adjective. If the adjective precedes the noun, the adjective takes its nominalized form, while the noun has its bare stem (singular or plural, masculine or feminine) form.

>i bu'kuri dja'lë *the handsome boy*
>
>afër të bu'kurave va'jza *near the beautiful girls*
>
>i bu'kuri gjerma'n *the handsome German (male)*
>
>e bu'kura gjerma'ne *the beautiful German (female)*

In principle, any stem labeled *adj* (including articulated adjectives) may be NOMINALIZED and used as a noun stem with the meaning "one with the characteristic of the adjective". Such a noun stem will be masculine, feminine, or plural to reflect the gender of the intended referent and will take *nm*, *nf*, or *np* case suffixes, respectively. An attributive article stays with an articulated adjective if that adjective is nominalized, the form of the article reflecting the gender and case of the nominalized adjective. For example, **i fejuar** is an adjective (itself derived from the participle **fejuar** *engaged to be married*) that means *engaged to be married, affianced*, from which the nominalized nominative definite nouns meaning literally "one engaged to be married," **i fejuari** *the fiancé* and **e fejuara**, *the fiancée* are derived.

Since such a nominalized adjective can function as a noun, in genitive constructions, a second article whose form reflects the gender and case of the referent would be preposed:

>kunati i së fejuarës *the fiancées brother-in law*
>
>me vëllanë e së fejuarës *with the fiancées brother*
>
>kunati i të fejuarit *the fiancés brother-in law*

Note that the form of the article in all these examples reflects the GENDER and GRAMMATICAL FUNCTION of the word to which the article is attached, rather than the properties of the referent.

For some adjectives, the adjective and its nominalization have the same English correspondent. For example, many ethnic adjectives have this characteristic: e.g., **amerika'n** as adjective or noun both correspond to English *American*. To eliminate unnecessary repetition, this fact is indicated by simply putting both grammatical labels after the form:

>amerik|a'n *adj, n* American

For other nominalized adjectives, English syntax requires a noun after the adjective to express the nominalized sense. In such cases, an English noun is put between parentheses to indicate the scope of the nominalization:

>dy|grre'mç *adj, nm* (pitchfork) with two prongs

This entry means that there is an adjective **dygrre'mç** conveying the quality of being two-pronged, and that its nominalization **dygrre'mç** takes *nm* inflectional endings and has the specific sense: pitchfork with two prongs.

The nominalization of adjectives is a living, productive process in Albanian, and a reader must be open to words listed as adjectives in the dictionary being used as nouns, as just described. In addition, there are many fossilized nominalizations: earlier adjectives (many themselves formed from participles, sometimes from varieties of Albanian that are no longer in regular use) that have lost their adjectival function, but still are used in their nominalized form. Such nominalizations are listed in this dictionary as articulated nouns (see p. xix).

Genitive Case Modifiers

Attributive modifiers may consist of a proclitic attributive article (**i, e, të**, or **së**) followed by a noun in the dative case. In traditional Albanian grammars such a modifier is called the "genitive case" of the noun, since in other languages the same function may be served by a separate *genitive* case form of the noun. The functions served by genitive case modifiers in Albanian are very similar to those served by *of* phrases, nouns used as modifiers, and *'s* words in English:

>për shkak të zhurmës *because of the noise*
>
>e dini emrin e fshatit *you know the name of the town*
>
>shtëpia e Zotit *the house of the Lord*

turigjati i luleve *flower weevil*
shtëpia e Agimit *Agim's house*

Predicatives

In contrast with adverbs, predicatives modify nouns. In contrast with attributive adjectives, they convey states into which the noun is brought, rather than characteristic attributes of the noun. As an attributive adjective **li'r|shëm**, preceded by a proclitic attributive article means *loose-fitting, loose*. As an adverb, **li'r|shëm** it means *in a loose/easygoing manner*. Contrast the predicative "he attached the rope loosely" with the adverb "he attached the rope quickly". The predicative, defined as *loosely*, characterizes not the verb action itself, but its effect on the noun "rope".

Many adjectives in Albanian are preceded by a proclitic attributive article when they are used attributively or are nominalized. In this dictionary, such adjectives are indicated by the label *adj (i)*:

> **i'mët** *adj (I)* fine, thin

When used predicatively, adjectives do not have this article. Absence of the article leads many scholars to label them "adverb" in this use:

> **e bluan grurin të imët** *he is grinding the fine grain*
> **e bluan grurin imët** *he is grinding the grain fine*

Adverbs

The label *adv* is used in this dictionary, as in most others, to designate a wide variety of uninflected words with adverbial functions. Most of the subtypes are not specifically identified by label; the English definition usually makes their specific function evident.

DETERMINERS

A determiner characterizes the scope of the noun that follows it in a noun phrase.

With definite noun suffixes, **secil** *each (one)* is used as both determiner and pronoun.

	English equivalent	Nominative	Accusative	Dative
Singular				
Masculine	each (one)	secili	secilin	secilit
Feminine	each (one)	secila	secilën	secilës
Plural				
Masculine	each (one)	secilët	secilët	secilëve
Feminine	each (one)	secilat	secilat	secilave

With definite noun suffixes added before the final suffix **-do'**, **secil-do** *every (one)* is used as both determiner and pronoun.

	English equivalent	Nominative	Accusative	Dative
Singular				
Masculine	each (one)	secilido	secilindo	secilitdo
Feminine	each (one)	secilado	secilëndo	secilësdo
Plural				
Masculine	each (one)	secilëtdo	secilëtdo	secilëvedo
Feminine	each (one)	secilatdo	secilatdo	secilavedo

NUMBERS

0	zero	10	dhjetë					
1	një	11	njëmbëdhjetë			100	njëqind	1000 një mijë
2	dy	12	dymbëdhjetë	20	njëzet	200	dyqind	2000 dy mijë
3	tre/tri	13	trembëdhjetë	30	tridhjetë	300	treqind	3000 tre mijë
4	katër	14	katërmbëdhjetë	40	dyzet	400	katërqind	4000 katër mijë
5	pesë	15	pesëmbëdhjetë	50	pesëdhjetë	500	pesëqind	5000 pesë mijë
6	gjashtë	16	gjashtëmbëdhjetë	60	gjashtëdhjetë	600	gjashtëqind	6000 gjashtë mijë
7	shtatë	17	shtatëmbëdhjetë	70	shtatëdhjetë	700	shtatëqind	7000 shtatë mijë
8	tetë	18	tetëmbëdhjetë	80	tetëdhjetë	800	tetëqind	8000 tetë mijë
9	nëntë	19	nëntëmbëdhjetë	90	nëntëdhjetë	900	nëntëqind	9000 nëntë mijë

Joining these numbers with the conjunction **e** creates the rest of the numbers. For example:

21	**njëzet e një**	101	**njëqind e një**
22	**njëzet e dy**	220	**dyqind e njëzet**
142	**njeqind e dyzet e dy**		

Contrary to English practice, written out large numbers in Albanian use periods, rather than commas, to separate groups of three digits, whereas decimal numbers are written with a comma (**presje**) rather than a period as the decimal point.

1,000,000		**një milion**
2,000,000		**dy milion**
3,000,000		**tri milion**
10,000,000		**dhjetë milion**
1,000,001	1.000.001	**një milion e një**
12.027	12,027	**dymbëdhjetë presje zero njëzet e shtatë**
.04	,04	**presje zero katër**
	23.516.798	**njëzet e tri milion e pesëqind e gjashtëmbëdhjetë mijë e shtatë qind e nëntëdhjetë e tetë**

PREPOSITIONS

Dictionary entries for prepositions are marked *prep* followed by an indication between parentheses of the case of the object of the preposition. The majority of prepositions in Albanian have ablative case objects, but a few very frequent prepositions **me, pa, në, më, për, mbi, nën, ndër, nëpër**, as well as phrasal prepositions ending in one of these (e.g., **për në. brenda në, tok me, bashkë me**), have objects in the accusative case. The prepositions **nga** and **tek** (or **te**) and their dialectal variants (**ka** and **ne**, respectively) have objects in the nominative case.

INTERROGATIVES

Interrogatives are uninflected words used to introduce direct and indirect questions. Their further classification as adjectives, pronouns, adverbs, or conjunctions depends on their further grammatical role in the clause.

PARTICLES

Particles are uninflected words with some of the functions in language that gestures have in face-to-face communication. The expression on your face can tell someone you are talking to directly whether you really mean what you are saying; head, hand, and arm gestures can emphasize particular parts of what you are saying, can express different kinds of negativity, and in various ways can help express speaker attitudes in ways that are difficult to define. Many of those gestural functions can be performed in Albanian by particles; the definitions of particles in this dictionary attempt to characterize these particles to help the reader understand them, but as with gesture, the differences between one particle and another can sometimes only be hinted at.

FINDING YOUR WORD IN THE DICTIONARY

Since foreign readers of Albanian cannot be expected to know all the intricate details of Albanian grammar thoroughly, this dictionary presents extensive aids for recognizing forms encountered in texts which are not identical to the citation forms in the dictionary.

WORKING BACKWARDS

Most text words in Albanian differ from a dictionary form only in their last part; that is, the first part of the text word matches the first part of some dictionary form, but the last part does not match. The usual source of this mismatch is in the ending of the word, since suffixes are so frequently added to indicate the grammatical and syntactic functions of words, as described in the section GRAMMATICAL SKETCH FOR READERS OF ALBANIAN.

Depending on the date and provenance of its author and/or editor, a text word may also differ from a corresponding dictionary form in other parts of the word, and a frequent source for such differences is the dialectal variation so common in spoken and written Albanian. Many of these differences are tabulated in the section Dialectal Variation & Standard Albanian.

REVERSE LIST OF POSSIBLE WORD TERMINATIONS

The following list provides information that the reader can use to interpret the structure of a puzzling text form not listed as such in the body of the dictionary. The list makes use of the fact that a word can end in only very limited ways, and that particular terminal sequences of letters have limited possible analyses.

> Column 1, *Terminations*, lists possible ways words in Albanian texts may end; the terminal sequences are listed in alphabetical order, working from the end of the word towards the beginning. For most terminal sequences in the list, more than one interpretation is available.

> Column 2, *Analysis*, indicates the composition of these sequences in terms of morpheme divisions: a single | precedes a derivational suffix, a double || precedes an inflectional suffix. This enables the user to see where the stem, which may be listed in the dictionary, breaks off and the suffix begins.

> If the word ends in a derivational suffix, Column 3, *Derivational Category*, identifies the category of the word created by that suffix. If the word ends in an inflectional suffix, that column is blank.

> Column 4, *Grammatical Function*, indicates the grammatical function that may be served by a word with this termination.

> Column 5, *End of Dictionary Entry*, indicates the likely termination of the dictionary entry under which the definition may be found that matches the puzzling form.

> Column 6, *Stem Label*, indicates the grammatical label that would precede that definition; the abbreviations are those used in the body of the dictionary to label the grammatical functions of stems.

> Column 7, *Examples*, provides examples of forms with the termination in question.

> For some entries, Column 8, *Clarification*, may make the example clearer by presenting a standard Albanian equivalent—for a termination marked *—or by giving a short English gloss of the example.

Termination	Analysis	Derivational Category	Grammatical Function	End of Dictionary Entry	Stem Label of Dictionary Entry	Examples	Clarification
ba	b|a	*pl fem*	*nom/acc*	bë	*nf*	këmba	
ba	b|a	*pl masc*	*nom/acc*	b	*nm*	krimba	
ba	b|a	*pl fem*		b or bë	*adj*	kokëshkëmba kokëzhgaba	
ba	b||a		*1st sg pdef*	b·	*v*	gjerba	
ca	c|a		*nom def*	cë	*nf*	hardhuca	
ca	c|a	*pl fem*	*nom acc*	cë	*nf*	hardhuca	
ca	c|a	*pl fem*	*nom acc*	c	*nm*	beca	
ca	c|a		*pl fem*	cë	*adj*	sygaca	
ca	c||a		*1st sg pdef*	c·	*v*	bëltuca	

Termination	Analysis	Derivational Category	Grammatical Function	End of Dictionary Entry	Stem Label of Dictionary Entry	Examples	Clarification
ça	ç‖a		nom def	çë	nf	brumça	
ça	ç‖a	pl fem	nom acc	çë	nf	brumça	
ça	ç|a	pl fem	nom acc	ç	nm	viça	
ça	ç‖a		1st sg pdef	ç·	v	shkyça	
da	d‖a		nom def	dë	nf	parmenda	
da	d|a	pl fem	nom acc	dë	nf	parmenda	
da	d|a	pl fem	nom acc	d	nm	kinda	
da	d|a		pl fem	d or dë	adj	të rënda	
da	d‖a		1st sg pdef	d·	v	shkunda	
dha	dh‖a		nom def	dhë	nf	udha	
dha	dh|a	pl fem	nom acc	dhë	nf	udha	
dha	dh|a	pl fem	nom acc	dh	nm	kudha	
dha	dh|a		pl fem	dh or dhë	adj	të verdha	
dha	dh‖a		1st sg pdef	dh·	v	zbardha	
fa	f‖a		nom def	fë	nf	gufa	
fa	f|a	pl fem	nom acc	fë	nf	gufa	
fa	f|a	pl fem	nom acc	f	nm	pefa	
fa	f|a		pl fem	f	adj	të paqejfa	
fa	f‖a		1st sg pdef	f·	v	brofa	
ga	g‖a		nom def	gë	nf	paga	
ga	g|a	pl fem	nom acc	gë	nf	paga	
ga	g|a		pl fem	g or gë	adj	zhunga	
ga	g‖a		1st sg pdef	g·	v	croga	
gja	gj‖a		nom def	gjë	nf	vegja	
gja	gj|a	pl fem	nom acc	gjë	nf	vegja	
gja	gj|a	pl fem	nom acc	gj	nm	qengja	
gja	gj‖a		1st sg pdef	gj·	v	gjegja	
ha	h‖a		nom def	hë	nf	koha	
ha	h|a	pl fem	nom acc	hë	nf	koha	
ha	h|a	pl fem	nom acc	h	nm	*mëteha	
ha	h|a		pl fem	hë	adj	të pagjuha	
ha	h‖a		1st sg pdef	h·	v	njoha	
ia	i|a		nom def	i	nf	shtëpia	
ia	|i‖a		imper sg | 3rd ind.obj | 3rd dir.obj	C	v	sillia	
gia	g‖ia		1st sg impf	g·	v	crogia	
ja	e‖a		nom def	e	nf	lulja	
ja	j|a	pl fem	nom acc	jë	nf	akullnaja	
ja	i‖e		imper sg ‖ 3rd ind.obj | 3rd dir.obj	V	v	drejtoja	
ja	j|a		pl fem	j or jë	adj	të huaja	
ja	j|a		1st sg pdef	j·	v	uja	
ja	‖ja		1st sg impf	Any (except g)	v	gudulisja	
ka	k‖a		nom def	kë	nf	pika	
ka	k|a	pl fem	nom acc	kë	nf	pika	
ka	k|a	pl fem	nom acc	k	nm	petka	
ka	k|a		pl fem	kë	adj	mendjelaraska	
ka	k|a		1st sg pdef	k·	v	fika	
ka	‖ka		3rd sg pres adm	Any	v	paska	
*kërka	|kër|ka		3rd sg pres adm	Any	v	*qënkërka	

Termination	Analysis	Derivational Category	Grammatical Function	End of Dictionary Entry	Stem Label of Dictionary Entry	Examples	Clarification
uaka	o'‖ka‖		3rd sg pres adm	o'	v	mbaruaka	
yeka	e'‖ka‖		3rd sg pres adm	e'	v	kërcyeka	
la	l‖a		nom def	lë	nf	pula	
la	l‖a	pl fem	nom acc	lë	nf	pula	
la	l‖a	pl fem	nom acc	l	nm	tela	
la	l‖a		pl fem	lë	adj	lela	
la	l‖a		1st sg pdef	l·	v	ngula	
lla	ll‖a		nom def	llë	nf	njolla	
lla	ll‖a	pl fem	nom acc	llë	nf	njolla	
lla	ll‖a	pl fem	nom acc	ll	nm	këshilla	
lla	ll‖a		pl fem	llë	adj	të gjalla	
lla	ll‖a		1st sg pdef	ll·	v	kalla	
ma	m‖a		nom def	më	nf	dhoma	
ma	m‖a	pl fem	nom acc	më	nf	dhoma	
ma	m‖a	pl fem	nom acc	m	nm	qilima	
ma	m‖a		1st sg pdef	m·	v	njoma	
ma	‖m‖a		imper sg ‖ 1st sg ind.obj ‖ 3rd sg dir.obj	Any	v	sillma	bring it to me
na	n‖a		nom def	në	nf	pishina	
na	n‖a	pl fem	nom acc	në	nf	pishina	
na	n‖a	pl fem	nom acc	n	nm	çuna	
na	n‖a		pl fem	në	adj	të vona	
na	‖na		imper sg ‖ 1st pl ind.obj/dir.obj	Any	v	sillna	
nja	nj‖a		nom def	një	nf	rrëfenja	
nja	nj‖a	pl fem	nom acc	një	nf	rrëfenja	
nja	nj‖a	pl fem	nom acc	nj	nm	kunja	
nja	nj‖a		pl fem	një	adj	të denja	
*nja	nj‖a		1st sg impf	Any	v	*shkonja	
pa	p‖a		nom def	pë	nf	gropa	
pa	p‖a	pl fem	nom acc	pë	nf	gropa	
pa	p‖a	pl fem	nom acc	p	nm	xhepa	
pa	p‖a		1st sg pdef	p·	v	hapa	
pa	p‖a		pl fem	pë	adj	të prapa	
qa	q‖a		nom def	që	nf	heqa	
qa	q‖a		1st sg pdef	q·	v	shfaqa	
ra	r‖a		nom def	rë	nf	ara	
ra	r‖a	pl fem	nom acc	rë	nf	ara	
ra	r‖a	pl fem	nom acc	r	nm	hekura	
ra	r‖a	pl fem	nom acc	ër	nm	emra	
ra	r‖a	pl fem	nom acc	ër	nf	qendra	
ra	‖ra	pl fem	nom acc	Any	nm	shira, fshatra	
ra	‖ra	pl fem	nom acc	Any	nf	ujëra	
ra	r‖a		pl fem	r	adj	të prejardhura	
ra	r‖a		pl fem	rë	adj	të mira	
ra	r‖a		1st sg pdef	r·	v	përdora	
rra	rr‖a		nom def	rrë	nf	arra	
rra	rr‖a	pl fem	nom acc	rrë	nf	arra	
rra	rr‖a	pl fem	nom acc	rrë	nm	burra	
rra	rr‖a	pl fem	nom acc	rr	nm	derra	

Termination	Analysis	Derivational Category	Grammatical Function	End of Dictionary Entry	Stem Label of Dictionary Entry	Examples	Clarification
rra	rr‖a		pl fem	rr or rrë	adj	të marra	
rra	rr‖a		pl fem	rr or rrë	adj	feckëderra	
rra	rr‖a		1st sg pdef	rr·	v	shporra	
sa	s‖a		nom def	së	nf	banesa	
sa	s‖a	pl fem	nom acc	së	nf	banesa	
sa	s‖a	pl fem	nom acc	s	nm	lisa	
sa	s‖a		pl fem	së	adj	gresa	
sa	s‖a		1st sg pdef	s·	v	zmbrapsa	
sha	sh‖a		nom def	shë	nf	kisha	
sha	sh‖a	pl fem	nom acc	shë	nf	kisha	
sha	sh‖a	pl fem	nom acc	sh	nm	tetëfaqësha	
sha	sh‖a		1st sg pdef	sh·	v	prisha	
sha	‖sh‖a		1st sg impf	ish kish thosh	v	isha kisha thosha	
esha	e‖sh‖a		1st sg impf	C	vp	tërhiqesha	
hesha	he‖sh‖a		1st sg impf	V	vp	lahesha	
fsha	fsh‖a		nom def	fshë	nf	kafsha	
fsha	fsh‖a	pl fem	nom acc	fshë	nf	kafsha	
fsha	‖fsh‖a		1st sg opt	V	v	mbarofsha	
ta	t‖a		nom def	të	nf	drita	
ta	t‖a	pl fem	nom acc	të	nf	drita	
ta	t‖a	pl fem	nom acc	t	nm	pleshta	
ta	t‖a		pl fem	t or të	adj	të gjata	
ta	t‖a		1st sg pdef	t·	v	mata	
tha	th‖a		nom def	thë	nf	vatha	
tha	th‖a	pl fem	nom acc	thë	nf	vatha	
tha	th‖a	pl fem	nom acc	th	nm	katha	
tha	th‖a		pl fem	thë	adj	të gjitha	
tha	th‖a		1st sg pdef	th·	v	mbatha	
*ua	o‖a		nom def	o	nm	vito	
ua	ua		3rd sg pdef non-active (and the verb is preceded by the reflexive pronominal clitic u)	o'·het	vp	u kuptua	
va	v‖a		nom def	vë	nf	brava	
va	v‖a	pl fem	nom acc	vë	nf	brava	
va	v‖a	pl fem	nom acc	v	nm	nerva	
va	‖v‖a		1st sg pdef	o'/e'	v	mbarova mbërtheva	
va	v‖a		1st sg pdef	v·	v	hova	
xa	x‖a		nom def	xë	nf	xixa	
xa	x‖a	pl fem	nom acc	xë	nf	xixa	
xha	xh‖a		nom def	xhë	nf	kanxha	
xha	xh‖a	pl fem	nom acc	xhë	nf	kanxha	
za	z‖a		nom def	zë	nf	driza	
za	z‖a	pl fem	nom acc	zë	nf	driza	
za	z‖a	pl fem	nom acc	z	nm	breza	
za	z‖a		pl fem	zë	adj	symiza	
za	z‖a		1st sg pdef	z·	v	lëviza	
zha	zh‖a		nom def	zhë	nf	grezha	

Termination	Analysis	Derivational Category	Grammatical Function	End of Dictionary Entry	Stem Label of Dictionary Entry	Examples	Clarification
zha	zh|a	*pl fem*	*nom acc*	zhë	*nf*	grezha	
zha	zh|a		*pl fem*	zhë	*adj*	mazha	
b				bë		*shtalbë	
b				p		*shtalp	
alec	|alec	*(pejorative) noun or adjective*	*nom/acc*	C	*n/adj*	bardhalec	
avec	|avec	*(pejorative) noun or adjective*	*nom/acc*	C	*n/adj*	jargavec	
aluc	|aluc	*(pejorative) noun or adjective*	*nom/acc*	C	*n/adj*	ngrehaluc	
*c							cë
*d						*mënd	dë; t
*Vdh							dhë; th
be	b||e		*abl indef*	bë	*nf*	këmbe	
be	b|e	*pl fem*	*nom acc*	b	*nm*	umbe	
be	b|e		*fem sg/pl*	b	*adj*	arabe	
be	b||e		*2nd sg pdef*	b·	*v*	gjerbe; hurbe	
be	b||e		*imper sg || 3rd dir.obj*	b·	*v*	gjerbe; hurbe	
ce	c||e		*abl indef*	cë	*nf*	hardhuce	
ce	c|e	*pl fem*	*nom acc*	c	*nm*	kotece	
ce	c|e		*fem sg/pl*	c	*adj*	kurnace	
ce	c||e		*2nd sg pdef*	c·	*v*	kice	
ce	c||e		*imper sg || 3rd dir.obj*	c·	*v*	kice	
çe	ç||e		*abl indef*	çë	*nf*	brumçe	
çe	ç|e	*pl fem*	*nom acc*	ç	*nm*	taçe	
çe	ç|e		*fem sg/pl*	ç	*adj*	trazovaçe	
çe	ç||e		*2nd sg pdef*	ç·	*v*	shkyçe	
çe	ç||e		*imper sg || 3rd dir.obj*	ç·	*v*	shkyçe	
de	d||e		*abl indef*	dë	*nf*	parmende	
de	d|e	*pl fem*	*nom acc*	d	*nm*	okside	
de	d|e		*fem sg/pl*	d	*adj*	bojargjende	
de	d||e		*2nd sg pdef*	d·	*v*	shkunde	
de	d||e		*imper sg || 3rd dir.obj*	d·	*v*	shkunde	
dhe	dh||e		*abl indef*	dhë	*nf*	udhe	
dhe	dh|e	*pl fem*	*nom acc*	dh	*nm*	gardhe	
dhe	dh|e		*fem sg/pl*	dh	*adj*	e madhe	
dhe	dh||e		*2nd sg pdef*	dh·	*v*	zbardhe	
dhe	dh||e		*imper sg || 3rd dir.obj*	dh·	*v*	zbardhe	
fe	f||e		*abl indef*	fë	*nf*	gufe	
fe	f|e	*pl fem*	*nom acc*	f	*nm*	zarfe	
fe	f|e		*fem sg/pl*	f	*adj*	tuhafe	
fe	f||e		*2nd sg pdef*	f·	*v*	brofe; qafe	
fe	f||e		*imper sg || 3rd dir.obj*	f·	*v*	brofe; qafe	
ge	g||e		*abl indef*	gë	*nf*	page	
ge	g|e	*pl fem*	*nom acc*	g	*nm*	zigzage	

Termination	Analysis	Derivational Category	Grammatical Function	End of Dictionary Entry	Stem Label of Dictionary Entry	Examples	Clarification
ge	g|e		fem sg/pl	g	adj	bishtcunge	
ge	g|e		2nd sg pdef	g·	v	croge	
ge	g|e		imper sg || 3rd dir.obj	g·	v	croge	
gje	gj|e		abl indef	gjë	nf	vegje	
gje	gj|e	pl fem	nom acc	gj	nm	ligje	
gje	gj|e		fem sg/pl	gj	adj	*karravagje	
gje	gj|e		2nd sg pdef	gj·	v	gjegje	
gje	gj|e		imper sg || 3rd dir.obj	gj·	v	gjegje	
he	h||e		abl indef	hë	nf	kohe	
he	h|e	pl fem	nom acc	h	nm	tehe	
he	h||e		2nd sg pdef	h·	v	njohe	
he	h||e		imper sg || 3rd dir.obj	h·	v	krihe	
ie	i||e		abl indef	i	nf	shtëpie	
*ie			bare stem	je	any		
je	|je	gerund	nom/acc indef	C	nf	tërheqje	
je	j||e		abl indef	jë	nf	akullnaje	
je	j|e	pl fem	nom acc	j	nm	faje	
je	j||e		2nd sg pdef	j·	v	uje	
je	j||e		imper sg || 3rd dir.obj	j·	v	uje	
ke	k||e		abl indef	kë	nf	pike	
ke	k|e	pl fem	nom acc	k	nm	bronke	
ke	k|e		fem sg/pl	k	adj	petullake	
ke	k||e		2nd sg pdef	k·	v	fike	
ke	k||e		imper sg || 3rd dir.obj	k·	v	fike	
ke	||ke		2nd sg pres adm	Any	v	paske	
*kërke	|kër||ke		2nd sg pres adm	Any	v	*qënkërke	
uake	o'||ke		2nd sg pres adm	o'	v	mbaruake	
yeke	e'||ke		2nd sg pres adm	e'	v	kërcyeke	
le	l||e		abl indef	lë	nf	pule	
le	l|e	pl fem	nom acc	l	nm	male	
le	l|e		fem sg/pl	l	adj	jeshile	
le	l||e	~	2nd sg pdef	l·	v	ngule	
le	l||e		imper sg || 3rd dir.obj	l·	v	ngule	
lle	ll||e		abl indef	llë	nf	njolle	
lle	ll|e	pl fem	nom acc	l	nm	kavalle	
lle	ll|e		fem sg/pl	ll	adj	katrasyll	
lle	ll||e		2nd sg pdef	ll·	v	kalle	
lle	ll||e		imper sg || 3rd dir.obj	ll·	v	kalle	
me	m||e		abl indef	më	nf	dhome	
me	m|e	pl fem	nom acc	m	nm	gabime	
me	m|e		fem sg/pl	m	adj	e sipërme	
me	m|e		fem sg/pl	ëm, më	adj	e vetme	
shme	shm|e		fem sg/pl	shëm	adj	e vajshme	

Termination	Analysis	Derivational Category	Grammatical Function	End of Dictionary Entry	Stem Label of Dictionary Entry	Examples	Clarification
me	m‖e		2nd sg pdef	m·	v	njome	
me	m‖e		imper sg ‖ 3rd dir.obj	m·	v	njome	
ne	n|e		abl indef	në	nf	pishine	
ne	n|e	pl fem	nom acc	n	nm	zakone	
ne	n|e		fem sg/pl	n	adj	arushane	
nje	nj‖e		abl indef	një	nf	rrëfenje	
nje	nj‖e		2nd sg pdef	nj·	v	thinje	
nje	nj‖e		imper sg ‖ 3rd dir.obj	nj·	v	thinje	
*nje	nj‖e		2nd sg impf	Any	v	*shkonje	
pe	p‖e		abl indef	pë	nf	grope	
pe	p‖e	pl fem	nom acc	p	nm	djepe	
pe	p‖e		fem sg/pl	p	adj	shterpe	
pe	p‖e		2nd sg pdef	p·	v	hape	
pe	p‖e		imper sg ‖ 3rd dir.obj	p·	v	hape	
qe	q‖e		abl indef	që	nf	heqe	
qe	q|e	pl fem	nom acc	q	nm	kryqe	
qe	q|e	pl fem	nom acc	k	nm	caqe gomarllëqe	
qe	q|e		fem sg/pl	q	adj	e kuqe	
qe	q‖e		2nd sg pdef	q·	v	shfaqe	
qe	q‖e		imper sg ‖ 3rd dir.obj	q·	v	shfaqe	
re	r|e		abl indef	rë	nf	are	
re	r|e	pl fem	nom acc	r	nm	pazare	
re	r|e	fem	nf nom/acc indef	r	n	tregtare	
re	r|e	fem	fem sg/pl	r	adj	tregtare	
re	r‖e		2nd sg pdef	r·	v	përdore	
re	r‖e		imper sg ‖ 3rd dir.obj	r·	v	përdore	
rre	rr‖e		abl indef	rrë	nf	arre	
rre	rr|e	pl fem	nom acc	rr	nm	zjarre	
rre	rr|e	fem	fem sg/pl	rr	adj	qorre	
rre	rr‖e		2nd sg pdef	rr·	v	shporre	
rre	rr‖e		imper sg ‖ 3rd dir.obj	rr·	v	shporre	
se	s‖e		abl indef	së	nf	banese	
se	s|e	fem	nf nom/acc indef	s	n	nxënëse	
se	s|e	fem	pl fem nom/acc indef	s	n	nxënëse	
se	s|e	fem	fem sg/pl	s	adj	shkëlqyese	
se	s‖e		2nd sg pdef	s·	v	zmbrapse	
se	s‖e		imper sg ‖ 3rd dir.obj	s·	v	zmbrapse	
she	sh‖e		abl indef	shë	nf	kishe	
she	sh|e	pl fem	nom acc	s	nm	tallashe	
she	sh|e	fem	fem sg/pl	sh	adj	thartoshe	
she	sh‖e		2nd sg pdef	sh·	v	prishe	
she	sh‖e		imper sg ‖ 3rd dir.obj	sh·	v	prishe	

Termination	Analysis	Derivational Category	Grammatical Function	End of Dictionary Entry	Stem Label of Dictionary Entry	Examples	Clarification
eshe	|e||she		2nd sg impf	C	vp	tërhiqeshe	
heshe	|he||she		2nd sg impf	V	vp	laheshe	
she	||sh||e		2nd sg impf	ish kish thosh	v	ishe kishe thoshe	
*she	||sh||e		1st or 2nd sg impf	C	v	*falshe	
*she	||sh||e		1st or 2nd sg impf	ble·*n* di· do· ha· pi·	v	*bleshe *dishe *doshe *hashe *pishe	
*jshe	||jsh||e		1st or 2nd sg impf	o'	v	*punojshe	
*jshe	||jsh||e		1st or 2nd sg impf	e'	v	*kërcejshe	
fshe	||fsh||e		1st sg opt	V	v	mbarofshe	
fshe	fsh|e	pl fem	nom acc	fsh	nm	afshe	
fshe	fsh||e		abl indef	fshë	nf	kafshe	
te	t||e		abl indef	të	nf	drite	
te	t|e	pl fem	nom acc	t	nm	grushte	
te	t|e		fem sg/pl	t	adj	delikate	
te	t||e		2nd sg pdef	t·	v	mate	
te	t||e		imper sg || 3rd dir.obj	t·	v	mate	
te	||te		3rd sg impf	Any	v	hapte	
nte	||n||te		3rd sg impf	V	v	shkonte	
ste	||te		3rd sg impf	t·	v	kulloste preste	
the	th||e		abl indef	thë	nf	vathe	
the	th|e	pl fem	nom acc	t	nm	gypthe	
the	th||e		2nd sg pdef	th·	v	mbathe	
the	th||e		imper sg || 3rd dir.obj	th·	v	mbathe	
*ue	|ue		participle	uar	v	shikuar	
*ue	ue		nom/acc sg indef	ua	nm	*thue	
*ue	ue		nom/acc sg indef	ua	nf	*grue	
*ue	|ue		participle	o'	v	*me shkue	
ve	v||e		abl indef	vë	nf	brave	
ve	v|e	pl fem	nom acc	v	nm	hove	
ve	v|e		fem sg/pl	v	adj	pozitive	
ve	||v|e		2nd sg pdef	o'	v	mbarove	
ve	||v|e		2nd sg pdef	e'	v	mbërtheve	
ve	v||e		2nd sg pdef	v·	v	hove	
ve	||(ë)ve		abl/dat	Any	np	grave nxënësve netëve	
xe	x||e		abl indef	xë	nf	xixe	
xhe	xh||e		abl indef	xhë	nf	kanxhe	
xhe	xh|e	pl fem	nom acc	xh	nm	borxhe	
ze	z||e		abl indef	zë	nf	drize	
ze	z||e		abl indef	ëz	nf	arëze	

Termination	Analysis	Derivational Category	Grammatical Function	End of Dictionary Entry	Stem Label of Dictionary Entry	Examples	Clarification
ze	z‖e	pl fem	nom acc	z	nm	buzagaze	
ze	z‖e		fem sg/pl	z	adj	angleze	
ze	z‖e		2nd sg pdef	z•	v	lëvize	
ze	z‖e		imper sg ‖ 3rd dir.obj	z•	v	lëvize	
zhe	zh‖e		abl indef	zhë	nf	grezhe	
zhe	zh‖e	pl fem	nom acc	zh	nm	drenazhe	
bë	b‖ë		3rd sg subj	b•	v	të dhembë	
bë	b‖ë	pl fem	nom acc	b	nm	humbë	
bë	b‖ë		pl masc	b	adj	amfibë	
cë	c‖ë		3rd sg subj	c•	v	të ngucë	
cë	c‖ë	pl fem	nom acc	c	nm	memecë	
cë	c‖ë		pl masc	c	adj	përtacë	
çë	ç‖ë		3rd sg subj	ç•	v	të kyçë	
çë	ç‖ë	pl fem	nom acc	ç	nm	gagaçë	
çë	ç‖ë		pl masc	ç	adj	gungaçë	
dë	d‖ë		3rd sg subj	d•	v	të bindë	
dë	d‖ë	pl fem	nom acc	d	nm	invalidë	
dë	d‖ë		pl masc	d	adj	solidë	
dhë	dh‖ë		3rd sg subj	dh•	v	të lidhë	
dhë	dh‖ë	pl fem	nom acc	dh	nm	gjedhë	
dhë	dh‖ë		pl masc	dh	adj	aguridhë	
fë	f‖ë		3rd sg subj	f•	v	të qafë	
fë	f‖ë	pl fem	nom acc	f	nm	fotografë	
fë	f‖ë		pl masc	f	adj	tuhafë	
gë	g‖ë		3rd sg subj	g•	v	të shmangë	
gjë	gj‖ë		3rd sg subj	gj•	v	të gjegjë	
*gjë	gj‖ë		pl masc	gj	adj	*karravagjë	
hë	h‖ë		3rd sg subj	h•	v	të njohë	
hë	h‖ë	pl fem	nom acc	h	nm	krahë	
jë	j‖ë		3rd sg subj	j•	v	të ujë	
jë	j‖ë	pl fem	nom acc	j	nm	samurajë	
jë	j‖ë		pl masc	j	adj	të pafajë	
ejë	e‖jë		3rd sg subj	e•·n	v	të pëlcejë	
yejë	ye‖jë		3rd sg subj	y'e•n	v	të lyejë	
ojë	o‖jë		3rd sg subj	o'·n	v	të shkojë	
uajë	ua‖jë		3rd sg subj	u'a•n	v	të luajë	
yjë	y‖jë		3rd sg subj	y•n	v	të hyjë	
kë	k‖ë		3rd sg subj	k•	v	të zhdukë	
kë	k‖ë	pl fem	nom acc	k	nm	abakë	
kë	k‖ë		pl masc	k	adj	besnikë	
lë	l‖ë		3rd sg subj	l•	v	të ngulë	
lë	l‖ë	pl fem	nom acc	l	nm	gjeneral	
lë	l‖ë		pl masc	l	adj	aktualë	
llë	ll‖ë		3rd sg subj	ll•	v	të kallë	
llë	ll‖ë	pl fem	nom acc	ll	nm	kaptellë	
llë	ll‖ë		pl masc	ll	adj	fodullë	
më	m‖ë		3rd sg subj	m•	v	të njomë	
më	m‖ë		pl masc	m	adj	legjitimë	
më	‖më		1st pl pd	V•	v	lamë	

Termination	Analysis	Derivational Category	Grammatical Function	End of Dictionary Entry	Stem Label of Dictionary Entry	Examples	Clarification
më	|më		1st pl pres	di· fle· ha· lë· pi· rri· vë· zë·	v	dimë flemë hamë lëmë pimë rrimë vëmë zëmë	
jmë	|jmë		1st pl pres	ble'·n mbaro'·n ru'a·n	v	blejmë mbarojmë ruajmë	
në	n|ë	pl fem	nom acc	n	nm	timonë	
në	n|ë		pl masc	n	adj	amerikanë	
në	|në		3rd pl pd	V'	v	lanë	
në	|në		3rd pl pres	di· fle· ha· lë· pi· rri· vë· zë·	v	dinë flenë hanë lënë pinë rrinë vënë zënë	
inë	|inë	noun denoting an area	nom/acc indef	C	nf	gurinë	
jnë	|jnë		3rd pl pres	V	v	blejnë mbarojnë ruajnë	
një	nj||ë		3rd sg subj	nj·	v	të thinjë	
pë	p||ë		3rd sg subj	p·	v	të hapë	
pë	p|ë	pl fem	nom acc	p(ë)	nm	dollapë	
pë	p|ë		pl masc	p(ë)	adj	kallpë	
që	q||ë		3rd sg subj	q·	v	të heqë	
që	q|ë	pl fem	nom acc	q	nm	hutaqë	
që	q|ë		pl masc	q	adj	lakuriqë	
rë	r||ë		3rd sg subj	r·	v	të përdorë	
rë	r|ë	pl fem	nom acc	r	nm	berberë	
rë	r|ë		pl masc	r	adj	fillestarë	
rrë	rr|ë	pl fem	nom acc	rr	nm	picorrë	
rrë	rr|ë		pl masc	rr	adj	qorrë	
së	s||ë		3rd sg subj	s·	v	të zmbrapsë	
së	s|ë	pl fem	nom acc	s	nm	qerosë	
së	s|ë		pl masc	s	adj	jetosë	
shë	sh||ë		3rd sg subj	sh·	v	të prishë	
shë	sh|ë	pl fem	nom acc	sh	nm	kataroshë	
shë	sh|ë		pl masc	sh	adj	murrmashë	
shë	||shë		1st sg pdef	jep· lë· ësh·të bie·₁ tho·të	v	dha||shë la||shë qe||shë ra||shë tha||shë	
të	|të		2nd pl pd	V'	v	latë	
të	t||ë		3rd sg subj	t·	v	të matë	
të	||të		pl nom/acc def	V'	nf	shtëpitë	
të	t|ë	pl fem	nom acc	t	nm	aspirantë	
të	t|ë		pl masc	t	adj	delikatë	

Termination	Analysis	Derivational Category	Grammatical Function	End of Dictionary Entry	Stem Label of Dictionary Entry	Examples	Clarification
të	‖të		3rd sg opt	C	v	lidhtë	
ftë	‖ftë		3rd sg opt	V^	v	mbaroftë	
ishtë	‖ishtë	noun denoting an area	nf	Any	v	kurpnishtë	
thë	th‖ë		3rd sg subj	th·	v	të mbathë	
thë	th‖ë	pl fem	nom acc	th	nm	urithë	
thë	th‖ë		pl masc	th	adj	skithë	
vë	v‖ë		3rd sg subj	v·	v	të hovë	
vë	v‖ë	pl fem	nom acc	v	nm	detektivë	
vë	v‖ë		pl masc	v	adj	sportivë	
xhë	xh‖ë	pl fem	nom acc	xh	nm	xhuxhë	
zë	z‖ë		3rd sg subj	z·	v	të lëvizë	
zë	z‖ë	pl fem	nom acc	z	nm	marangozë	
zë	z‖ë		pl masc	z	adj	kanadezë	
zë	‖zë	diminutive	nf	V^(C)		rrufezë	
*f							fë; v
*g							gë; k
*Vh						ngreh	Vhë; V
ai	a‖i		nom def	a	nm	babai	
bi	b‖i		nom def	b	nm	elbi	
bi	b‖i		indef abl	b	nm	elbi	
bi	b‖i		3rd sg pdef	b·	v	humbi	
bi	b‖i		imper sg ‖ 3rd ind.obj	b·	v	humbi	
bi	b‖i		imper sg ‖ 3rd pl dir.obj	b·	v	humbi	
ci	c‖i		nom def	c	nm	keci	
ci	c‖i		indef abl	c	nm	keci	
ci	c‖i		3rd sg pdef	c·	v	nguci	
ci	c‖i		imper sg ‖ 3rd ind.obj	c·	v	nguci	
ci	c‖i		imper sg ‖ 3rd pl dir.obj	c·	v	nguci	
çi	ç‖i		nom def	ç	nm	kyçi	
çi	ç‖i		indef abl	ç	nm	kyçi	
çi	ç‖i		3rd sg pdef	ç·	v	kyçi	
çi	ç‖i		imper sg ‖ 3rd ind.obj	ç·	v	kyçi	
çi	ç‖i		imper sg ‖ 3rd pl dir.obj	ç·	v	kyçi	
di	d‖i		nom def	d	nm	vendi	
di	d‖i		indef abl	d	nm	vendi	
di	d‖i		3rd sg pdef	d·	v	bindi	
di	d‖i		imper sg ‖ 3rd ind.obj	d·	v	bindi	
di	d‖i		imper sg ‖ 3rd pl dir.obj	d·	v	bindi	
dhi	dh‖i		nom def	dh	nm	gardhi	
dhi	dh‖i		indef abl	dh	nm	gardhi	
dhi	dh‖i		3rd sg pdef	dh·	v	lidhi	
dhi	dh‖i		imper sg ‖ 3rd ind.obj	dh·	v	lidhi	
dhi	dh‖i		imper sg ‖ 3rd pl dir.obj	dh·	v	lidhi	

Termination	Analysis	Derivational Category	Grammatical Function	End of Dictionary Entry	Stem Label of Dictionary Entry	Examples	Clarification
fi	f‖i		nom def	f	nm	qejfi	
fi	f‖i		indef abl	f	nm	qejfi	
fi	f‖i		3rd sg pdef	f·	v	qafi	
fi	f‖i		imper sg ‖ 3rd ind.obj	f·	v	qafi	
fi	f‖i		imper sg ‖ 3rd pl dir.obj	f·	v	qafi	
gi	g‖i		imper sg ‖ 3rd ind.obj	g·	v	shmangi	
gi	g‖i		imper sg ‖ 3rd pl dir.obj	g·	v	shmangi	
gji	gj‖i		nom def	gj	nm	ligji	
gji	gj‖i		indef abl	gj	nm	ligji	
gji	gj‖i		3rd sg pdef	gj·	v	gjegji	
gji	gj‖i		imper sg ‖ 3rd ind.obj	gj·	v	gjegji	
gji	gj‖i		imper sg ‖ 3rd pl.dir.obj	gj·	v	gjegji	
hi	h‖i		imper sg ‖ 3rd ind.obj	h·	v	krihi	
hi	h‖i		imper sg ‖ 3rd pl dir.obj	h·	v	krihi	
ji	j‖i		nom def	j	nm	faji	
ji	j‖i		indef abl	j	nm	faji	
ji	j‖i		3rd sg pdef	j·	v	uji	
ji	|j|i		imper sg	3rd ind.obj	j·	v	laji	
ji	|j|i		imper sg ‖ 3rd pl.dir.obj	j·	v	laji	
ki	k‖i		imper sg ‖ 3rd ind.obj	k·	v	zhduki	
ki	k‖i		imper sg ‖ 3rd pl dir.obj	k·	v	zhduki	
li	l‖i		nom def	l	nm	mali	
li	l‖i		indef abl	l	nm	mali	
li	l‖i		3rd sg pdef	l·	v	nguli	
li	l‖i		imper sg ‖ 3rd ind.obj	l·	v	nguli	
li	l‖i		imper sg ‖ 3rd pl dir.obj	l·	v	nguli	
lli	ll‖i		nom def	ll	nm	kavalli	
lli	ll‖i		indef abl	ll	nm	kavalli	
lli	ll‖i		3rd sg pdef	ll·	v	kalli	
lli	ll‖i		imper sg ‖ 3rd ind.obj	ll·	v	kalli	
lli	ll‖i		imper sg ‖ 3rd pl dir.obj	ll·	v	kalli	
mi	m‖i		nom def	m	nm	gabimi	
mi	m‖i		indef abl	m	nm	gabimi	
mi	m‖i		3rd sg pdef	m·	v	njomi	he wet them
mi	m‖i		imper sg ‖ 3rd ind.obj	m·	v	bëlldumi	splash down in it!
mi	m‖i		imper sg ‖ 3rd pl dir.obj	m·	v	njomi	wet them!

Termination	Analysis	Derivational Category	Grammatical Function	End of Dictionary Entry	Stem Label of Dictionary Entry	Examples	Clarification
mi	|m|i		*imper sg | 1st sg ind.obj | 3rd pl dir.obj*	Any	*v*	**sillmi** **tregomi**	*bring me them! show them to me!*
emi	|e|mi		*1st pl pres*	*C*	*vp*	**tërhiqemi**	
hemi	|he|mi		*1st pl pres*	*V*	*vp*	**lahemi**	
kemi	||ke|mi		*1st pl pres adm*	*V*	*vp*	**lakemi**	
uakemi	*o'*||ke|mi		*1st pl pres adm*	*o'*	*v*	**mbaruakemi**	
yekemi	*e'*||ke|mi		*1st pl pres adm*	*e'*	*v*	**kërcyekemi**	
ni	n||i		*nom def*	**n**	*nm*	**zakoni**	
ni	n||i		*indef abl*	**n**	*nm*	**zakoni**	
ni	ni		*2nd pl pres*	Any	*v*	**shkoni**	
ni	ni		*imper pl*	Any	*v*	**shkoni**	
eni	|e|ni		*1st pl pres*	*C*	*vp*	**tërhiqeni**	
heni	|he|ni		*1st pl pres*	*V*	*vp*	**laheni**	
keni	||ke|ni		*2nd pl pres adm*	*V*	*vp*	**lakeni**	
uakeni	*o'*||ke|ni		*2nd pl pres adm*	*o'*	*v*	**mbaruakeni**	
yekeni	*e'*||ke|ni		*2nd pl pres adm*	*e'*	*v*	**kërcyekeni**	
nji	nj||i		*3rd sg pdef*	**nj·**	*v*	**thinji**	
nji	nj||i		*imper sg || 3rd ind.obj*	**nj·**	*v*	**thinji**	
nji	nj||i		*imper sg || 3rd pl dir.obj*	**nj·**	*v*	**thinji**	
oi	o||i		*nom def*	**ua**	*nm*	**thoi**	
oi	o||i		*3rd sg pdef*	*o'·n*	*v*	**shkoi** **shkroi**	
oi	o||i		*3rd sg pdef*	*u'a·n*	*v*	**shkoi** **shkroi**	
pi	p||i		*nom def*	**p**	*nm*	**djepi**	
pi	p||i		*indef abl*	**p**	*nm*	**djepi**	
pi	p||i		*3rd sg pdef*	**p·**	*v*	**hapi**	
pi	p||i		*imper sg || 3rd ind.obj*	**p·**	*v*	**hapi**	
pi	p||i		*imper sg || 3rd pl dir.obj*	**p·**	*v*	**hapi**	
qi	q||i		*nom def*	**q**	*nm*	**kryqi**	
qi	q||i		*indef abl*	**q**	*nm*	**kryqi**	
qi	q||i		*3rd sg pdef*	**q·**	*v*	**heqi**	
qi	q||i		*imper sg || 3rd ind.obj*	**q·**	*v*	**heqi**	
qi	q||i		*imper sg || 3rd pl dir.obj*	**q·**	*v*	**heqi**	
ri	r||i		*nom def*	**r**	*nm*	**pazari**	
ri	r||i		*indef abl*	**r**	*nm*	**pazari**	
ri	r||i		*3rd sg pdef*	**r·**	*v*	**përdori**	
ri	r||i		*imper sg || 3rd ind.obj*	**r·**	*v*	**përdori**	
ri	r||i		*imper sg || 3rd pl dir.obj*	**r·**	*v*	**përdori**	
rri	rr||i		*nom def*	**rr**	*nm*	**zjarri**	
rri	rr||i		*indef abl*	**rr**	*nm*	**zjarri**	

Termination	Analysis	Derivational Category	Grammatical Function	End of Dictionary Entry	Stem Label of Dictionary Entry	Examples	Clarification
rri	rr‖i		3rd sg pdef	rr·	v	shporri	
rri	rr‖i		imper sg ‖ 3rd ind.obj	rr·	v	shporri	
rri	rr‖i		imper sg ‖ 3rd pl dir.obj	rr·	v	shporri	
si	s‖i		nom def	s	nm	nxënësi	
si	s‖i		indef abl	s	nm	nxënësi	
si	s‖i		3rd sg pdef	s·	v	zmbrapsi	
si	s‖i		imper sg ‖ 3rd ind.obj	s·	v	zmbrapsi	
si	s‖i		imper sg ‖ 3rd pl dir.obj	s·	v	zmbrapsi	
shi	sh‖i		nom def	sh	nm	gjyshi	
shi	sh‖i		indef abl	sh	nm	gjyshi	
shi	sh‖i		3rd sg pdef	sh·	v	prishi	
shi	sh‖i		imper sg ‖ 3rd ind.obj	sh·	v	prishi	
shi	sh‖i		imper sg ‖ 3rd pl dir.obj	sh·	v	prishi	
shi	‖sh‖i		2nd pl opt	C	v	gjetshi	
fshi	‖fsh‖i		2nd pl opt	V	v	mbarofshi	
ti	t‖i		nom def	t	nm	grushti	
ti	t‖i		indef abl	t	nm	grushti	
ti	t‖i		3rd sg pdef	t·	v	mati	
ti	t‖i		imper sg ‖ 3rd ind.obj	t·	v	mati	
ti	t‖i		imper sg ‖ 3rd pl dir.obj	t·	v	mati	
thi	th‖i		nom def	th	nm	gypthi	
thi	th‖i		indef abl	th	nm	gypthi	
thi	th‖i		3rd sg pdef	th·	v	mbathi	
thi	th‖i		imper sg ‖ 3rd ind.obj	th·	v	mbathi	
thi	th‖i		imper sg ‖ 3rd pl dir.obj	th·	v	mbathi	
thi	‖thi	adv		Any		mbrapthi	
vi	v‖i		nom def	v	nm	hovi	
vi	v‖i		indef abl	v	nm	hovi	
vi	v‖i		3rd sg pdef	v·	v	hovi	
vi	v‖i		imper sg ‖ 3rd ind.obj	v·	v	hovi	
vi	v‖i		imper sg ‖ 3rd pl dir.obj	v·	v	hovi	
xi	x‖i		nom def	x	nm	*thinxi	
xi	x‖i		indef abl	x	nm	*thinxi	
xhi	xh‖i		nom def	xh	nm	borxhi	
xhi	xh‖i		indef abl	xh	nm	borxhi	
zi	z‖i		nom def	z	nm	breza	
zi	z‖i		indef abl	z	nm	breza	
zi	z‖i		3rd sg pdef	z·	v	lëvizi	
zi	z‖i		imper sg ‖ 3rd ind.obj	z·	v	lëvizi	
zi	z‖i		imper sg ‖ 3rd pl dir.obj	z·	v	lëvizi	

Termination	Analysis	Derivational Category	Grammatical Function	End of Dictionary Entry	Stem Label of Dictionary Entry	Examples	Clarification
azi	|azi	*adv*	adverb	*C(ë)*		**mëbarkazi**	
zhi	zh||i		*nom def*	**zh**	*nm*	**drenazhi**	
zhi	zh||i		*indef abl*	**zh**	*nm*	**drenazhi**	
*j				**jë**			
aj	a|j		*imper sg*	**a'•n**	*v*	**mbaj**	
aj	a||j		*1st sg pres*	**a'•n**	*v*	**mbaj**	
ej	e|j		*imper sg*	**e'•n**	*v*	**brej**	
ej	e||j		*1st sg pres*	**e'•n**	*v*	**pëlqej**	
ej	e||j		*3rd sg impf*	*C*	*vp*	**tërhiqej**	
hej	he||j		*3rd sg impf*	*V*	*vp*	**lahej**	
ëj	ë|j		*imper sg*	**ë'•n**	*v*	**bëj**	
ëj	ë||j		*1st sg pres*	**ë•n**	*v*	**bëj**	
ij	i||j		*1st sg pres*	**i•n**	*v*	**prij**	
*kj				**q**			
oj	o||j		*1st sg pres*	**o'**	*v*	**mbaroj**	
uj	u|j		*imper sg*	**u'•n**	*v*	**mbruj**	
uj	u||j		*1st sg pres*	**u'•n**	*v*	**mbruj**	
yj	y||j		*1st sg pres*	**y•n**	*v*	**shtyj**	
*k					*nm*	***brekë**	**kë**
*k					*nm*	***brek**	**g**
*k	kë	*diminutive*				***brethk, *bushk**	**kë**
ak	|ak	*diminutive; augmentative*		*C(ë)*	*nm*	**qafak**	
ak	|ak	*diminutive; augmentative*		*C(ë)*	*adj*	**qafak**	
*ak	|ak	*ethnonym: -ese, -an, -ian, -man*		*C(ë)*	*nm*	***bosnjak**	**an**
*ak	|ak	*ethnonym: -ese, -an, -ian, -man*		*C(ë)*	*adj*	***bosnjak**	**an**
ek	|ek	*diminutive; augmentative*		*C(ë)*	*nm*	**tymek**	
ek	|ek	*diminutive; augmentative*		*C(ë)*	*adj*	**tymek**	
ik	|ik	*-ic*	*masc sg indef*	*C(ë)*	*adj*	**barbarik**	
ok	|ok	*diminutive; augmentative*		*C(ë)*	*n*	**capok**	
ok	|ok	*diminutive; augmentative*		*C(ë)*	*adj*	**capok**	
uk	|uk	*diminutive; augmentative*		*C(ë)*	*nm*	**bishtuk**	
uk	|uk	*diminutive; augmentative*		*C(ë)*	*adj*	**bishtuk**	
*ḷ				**lë**		***djal**	
*l				**ll**			
al	|al						
el	|el						
ol	|ol						
ul	|ul						
ll				**llë**			
ll				**l**			
ll				**dh**			
ll				**dhë**			
ell							

Termination	Analysis	Derivational Category	Grammatical Function	End of Dictionary Entry	Stem Label of Dictionary Entry	Examples	Clarification
ëll	|ull			ull			
ill							
ull	|ull			ëll			
oll							
*m				më			
*m				mb			
kam	||ka||m		1st sg pres adm	Any	v	qënkam	
uakam	o'||ka||m		1st sg pres adm	o'	v	mbaruakam	
yekam	e'||ka||m		1st sg pres adm	e'	v	kërcyekam	
uam	o'||m		1st pl pd	o'	v	mbaruam	
hem	|he||m		1st sg pres	V	vp	lahem	
yem	e'||m		1st pl pd	e'	v	kërcyem	
*ëm				më		dasëm	
shëm	|shëm	derivational suffix	masc sg	Any	adj (i)	i vajshëm	
im	||im		1st pl pres	C	v	ngulim	
im	|im	gerund	nom/acc indef	o' or e'		shtizim	
nim	||n||im		1st pl impf	Any	v	mbaronim	
shim	||sh||im		1st pl impf	ish kish thosh	v	ishim kishim thoshim	
eshim	|e||sh||im		1st pl impf	C	vp	tërhiqeshim	
heshim	|he||sh||im		1st pl impf	V	vp	laheshim	
këshim	||kë||sh||im		1st pl impf adm	Any	v	qënkëshim	
fshim	||fsh||im		1st pl opt	V	v	mbarofshim	
sm				smë			
sm				sëm			
shm				shmë			
shm				shëm			
zm				zmë			
zm				zëm			
zhm				zhmë			
zhm				zhëm			
*n				në			
*n				nd			
kan	||ka||n		3rd pl pres adm	Any	v	qënkan	
uakan	o'||ka||n		3rd pl pres adm	o'	v	mbaruakan	
uan	o'||n		3rd pl pd	o'	v	mbaruan	
hen	|he||n		3rd sg pres	V	vp	lahen	
yen	e'||n		3rd pl pd	e'	v	kërcyen	
yekan	e'||ka||n		3rd pl pres adm	e'	v	kërcyekan	
en	|e||n		3rd pl pres	C	vp	tërhiqen	
hen	|he||n		3rd pl pres	V	vp	lahen	
*ën				në		cikën	
*ën				r		*shkurtën	
in	||i||n		def acc	C except g, h, k	nm	malin	
nin	||n||in		3rd pl impf	Any	v	mbaronin	
shin	||sh||in		3rd pl impf	ish kish thosh	v	ishin kishin thoshin	

Termination	Analysis	Derivational Category	Grammatical Function	End of Dictionary Entry	Stem Label of Dictionary Entry	Examples	Clarification
eshin	|e||sh||in		3rd pl impf	C	vp	tërhiqeshin	
heshin	|he||sh||in		3rd pl impf	V	vp	laheshin	
këshin	||kë||sh||in		3rd pl impf adm	Any	v	qënkëshin	
fshin	||fsh||in		3rd pl opt	V	v	mbarofshin	
sn							
shn							
*un			participle	ur		*ditun	
zn							
zhn							
*anj	a||nj		1st sg pres	a•n	v	*lanj	
*enj	e||nj		1st sg pres	e'•n	v	*pëlqenj	
*inj	i||nj		1st sg pres	i•n	v	*prinj	
*onj	o||nj		1st sg pres	o•n	v	*kuptonj	
*unj	u||nj		1st sg pres	u•n	v	*zbrunj	
*ynj	y||nj		1st sg pres	y•n	v	*ndërhynj	
o	|o'	thematic suffix	imper sg	C(ë)	v	*retifiko	
*o	|o'		imper sg	e', i'	v	*fishkëllo	
*o	o		nom/acc indef	ua	nm	*drago	
*o			imper sg	u'a•n	v	*shkro	
uo				ua, o			
p				pë		*prap	
p				b		*tharp	
aq	|aq	diminutive augmentative		C(ë)	nm	ngordhaq	
aq	|aq	diminutive augmentative		C(ë)	adj	ngordhaq	
alaq	|alaq	diminutive augmentative		C(ë)	nm	ngordhalaq	
alaq	|alaq	diminutive augmentative		C(ë)	adj	ngordhalaq	
iq	|iq	diminutive augmentative		C(ë)	nm	bubuliq	
iq	|iq	diminutive augmentative		C(ë)	adj	bubuliq	
uq	|uq	diminutive augmentative		C(ë)	nm	nanuq	
uq	|uq	diminutive augmentative		C(ë)	adj	nanuq	
*r							rë; rr; n
ar	|ar	agent		C(ë)	nm	shular	
ar	|ar	agent		C(ë)	adj	shular	
(ë)tar	t|ar	agent		Any	nm	treg(ë)tar	
(ë)tar	t|ar	agent		Any	adj	treg(ë)tar	
uar	ua|r	participle		o'	v		
uar	ua|r	adj (i)		o'	v		
ër	|ër	adj (i)		C	v		
or	|or	agent		C(ë)	nm	koreanojugor	
or	|or	agent		C(ë)	adj	koreanojugor	
ator	|ator	agent		C(ë)	nm	racator	
ator	|ator	agent		C(ë)	adj	racator	
ur	|ur	participle		C	v		
ur	|ur	adj (i)		C	v		
yer	ye|r	participle		e'•n	v		

Termination	Analysis	Derivational Category	Grammatical Function	End of Dictionary Entry	Stem Label of Dictionary Entry	Examples	Clarification
yer	ye|r	*adj (i)*		*e'•n*	*v*		
*rr				rrë			
*rr				r			
*s						*oris	së; z
as	|as	*adv*	*adverb*	*C(ë)*		lehtas	
ës	|ës	agent	*adj*	*C*	*v*		
ës	|ës	agent	*n*	*C*	*v*		
is	|is	*v*	*1st sg pres*	*C*			
os	|is	*v*	*1st/2nd/3rd sg pres*	*C*		hekuros	
ps		borrowing from Greek					
ts							c
ues	ue|s	agent	*adj*	*o'*	*v*		
ues	ue|s	agent	*n*	*o'*	*v*		
yes	ye|s	agent	*adj*	*e'*	*v*		
yes	ye|s	agent	*n*	*e'*	*v*		
*us	u|s	agent	*adj*	*o'*	*v*		ues
*us	u|s	agent	*n*	*o'*	*v*		ues
*ys							yes
sh	||sh		*2nd sg subj*	*V*	*v*	mbarosh	
sh	||sh		*2nd sg opt*	*C*	*v*	lidhsh	
*sh							shë; ç
esh	e||sh		*2nd sg impf*	*C*	*vp*	tërhiqesh	
hesh	he||sh		*2nd sg impf*	*V*	*vp*	lahesh	
ësh	|ësh		*2nd sg subj*	*C*	*v*	lidhësh	
fsh	||fsh		*2nd sg opt*	*V*	*nf*	mbarofsh	
osh	|osh	*diminutive augmentative*		*C(ë)*	*nm*	mjekërrosh	
osh	|osh	*diminutive augmentative*		*C(ë)*	*adj*	mjekërrosh	
*mpsh							msh
*tsh							ç
ush	|ush	*diminutive augmentative*		*C(ë)*	*nm*	gjatush	
ush	|ush	*diminutive augmentative*		*C(ë)*	*adj*	gjatush	
*t							të; d
at	|a||t		*pl nom/acc def*	*ë*	*nf*	këmbat	
at	|a||t		*pl nom/acc def*	*C*	*nm*	krimbat	
uat	o'||t		*2nd pl pd*	*o'*	*v*	mbaruat	
et	e||t		*pl nom/acc def*	*C*	*nm*	gardhet	
et	e||t		*1st sg pres*	*C*	*vp*	tërhiqet	
Vhet	|he||t		*1st sg pres*	*V*	*vp*	lahet	
yet	e'||t		*2nd pl pd*	*e'*	*v*	kërcyet	
Cët	Cë||t		*pl nom/acc def*	*C(ë)*	*np*	amerikanët kafshët	
*Cët				*të*		*i imët	
shët	sh||ët		*2nd pl pdef*	*sh•*	*v*	prishët	
it	||i||t		*def abl*	*C except g, h, k*	*nm*	malit	
it	||i||t		*def abl*	*V*	*nm*	babait	
nit	||n||it		*2nd pl impf*	*Any*	*v*	mbaronit	
ërit	ër|i||t		*nom/acc def*	*ër*	*np*	prindërit	

Termination	Analysis	Derivational Category	Grammatical Function	End of Dictionary Entry	Stem Label of Dictionary Entry	Examples	Clarification
sit	s‖i‖t		pl nom/acc def	s	nm	nxënësit	
shit	‖sh‖it		2nd pl impf	ish kish thosh	v	ishit kishit thoshit	
shit	‖sh‖it		2nd pl opt	C	v	gjetshit	
eshit	e‖sh‖it		2nd pl impf	C	vp	tërhiqeshit	
heshit	he‖sh‖it		2nd pl impf	V	vp	laheshit	
këshit	‖kë‖sh‖it		2nd pl impf adm	Any	v	qënkëshit	
fshit	‖fsh‖it		2nd pl opt	V	v	mbarofshit	
*ft	‖ft		3rd sg opt	V	v	*mbroft	ftë
*ht						*ftoht	htë
*jt	‖jt	extension	3rd sg pdef	V	vp		
*njt					adj (i)	*i shtrënjt	njtë
ot	o‖t		pl nom/acc def	o	nf	balot	
*rt					adj (i)	*i lart	rtë
*sht					adj (i)	*i gjasht	shtë
ut	‖u‖t		def abl	g, h, k	nm	bregut	
*th						*gjith	thë
*th	‖th	diminutive				*birth	
u	C‖u		imper sg	C·et	vp	krimbu	
au	a‖u		3rd sg pdef	a'	v	lau	
*au	a‖u		nom def	a'	nm	*vëllau	
bu	b‖u		imper sg	b·et	vp	krimbu	
bu	b‖u		imper sg | 3rd pl ind.obj	b·	v	krimbu	
cu	c‖u		imper sg	c·et	vp	ngucu	
cu	c‖u		imper sg ‖3rd pl ind.obj	c·	v	ngeci	
çu	ç‖u		imper sg	ç·et	vp	përlloçu	
du	d‖u		imper sg	d·et	vp	bindu	
du	d‖u		imper sg ‖3rd pl ind.obj	d·	v	rendu	
dhu	dh‖u		imper sg	dh·et	vp	hidhu	
dhu	dh‖u		imper sg ‖3rd pl ind.obj	dh·	v	bridhu	
eu	e‖u		nom def	e'	nm	atdheu	
eu	e‖u		3rd sg pdef	e'	v	bleu	
fu	f‖u		imper sg	f·et	vp	plafu	
fu	f‖u		imper sg |3rd pl ind.obj	f·	v	brofu	
gu	g‖u		nom def	g	nm	bregu	
gu	g‖u		3rd sg pdef	g·	v	shtangu	
gju	gj‖u		imper sg	gj·et	vp	përligju	
gju	gj‖u		imper sg ‖3rd pl ind.obj	gj·	v	gjegju	
hu	h‖u		imper sg	·het	vp	mbahu	
hu	h‖u		3rd sg pdef	h·	v	fshehu	
hu	h‖u		nom def	h	nm	krahu	
iu	a‖i		nom def	i'	nm	bariu	
ju	j‖u		imper sg ‖3rd pl ind.obj	V	v	mbaju	
ku	k‖u		imper sg	k·et	vp	duku	
ku	k‖u		nom def	k	nm	miku	

Termination	Analysis	Derivational Category	Grammatical Function	End of Dictionary Entry	Stem Label of Dictionary Entry	Examples	Clarification
ku	k‖u		*3rd sg pdef*	k•	*v*	iku	
lu	l‖u		*imper sg*	l•*et*	*vp*	ulu	
lu	l‖u		*imper sg ‖3rd pl ind.obj*	l•	*v*	falu	
llu	ll‖u		*imper sg*	ll•*et*	*vp*	çmallu	
llu	ll‖u		*imper sg ‖3rd pl ind.obj*	ll•	*v*	mbyllu	
mu	m‖u		*imper sg*	m•*et*	*vp*	shpërgjumu	
mu	m‖u		*imper sg ‖3rd pl ind.obj*	m•	*v*	grymu	
nju	nj‖u		*imper sg*	nj•*et*	*vp*	përgjunju	
nju	nj‖u		*imper sg ‖3rd pl ind.obj*	nj•	*v*	kaçkinju	
nu	n‖u		*imper sg*	n•*et*	*vp*	mënjanu	
pu	p‖u		*imper sg*	p•*et*	*vp*	zhdëpu	
pu	p‖u		*imper sg ‖3rd pl ind.obj*	p•	*v*	hapu	
qu	q‖u		*imper sg*	q•*et*	*vp*	ndrequ	
qu	q‖u		*imper sg ‖3rd pl ind.obj*	q•	*v*	fëlliqu	
ru	r‖u		*imper sg*	r•*et*	*vp*	dëliru	
ru	r‖u		*imper sg ‖3rd pl ind.obj*	r•	*v*	lëbyru	
rru	rr‖u		*imper sg*	rr•*et*	*vp*	pirru	
rru	rr‖u		*imper sg ‖3rd pl ind.obj*	rr•	*v*	shperru	
su	s‖u		*imper sg*	s•*et*	*vp*	kujdesu	
su	s‖u		*imper sg ‖3rd pl ind.obj*	s•	*v*	kujdesu	
shu	sh‖u		*imper sg*	sh•*et*	*vp*	vishu	
shu	sh‖u		*imper sg ‖3rd pl ind.obj*	sh•	*v*	buzëqeshu	
tu	t‖u		*imper sg*	t•*et*	*vp*	çmorritu	
tu	t‖u		*imper sg ‖3rd pl ind.obj*	t•	*v*	bërtitu	
thu	th‖u		*imper sg*	th•*et*	*vp*	mbathu	
thu	th‖u		*imper sg ‖3rd pl ind.obj*	th•	*v*	zbathu	
vu	v‖u		*imper sg ‖3rd pl ind.obj*	v•	*v*	hovu	
zu	z‖u		*imper sg*	z•*et*	*vp*	zbrazu	
zu	z‖u		*imper sg ‖3rd pl ind.obj*	z•	*v*	lëvizu	
iv	‖iv	*adjectival*	*-ive*		*adj*	alternativ	
*z	z‖ë	*diminutive*				*thupërz	
Cez	‖ez	*ethnonym*	*-ese, -an, -ian, -man*	C(ë)	*n*	eskimez anglez	*Eskimo Englishman*
Cez	e‖z	*diminutive*		Ce	*nf*	fijez	
Cëz	‖ëz	*diminutive*		C(ë)	*nf*	gurëz gushëz	
oz	‖oz	*adjectival*	*-ous*		*adj*	melodioz	

DIALECTAL VARIATION & STANDARD ALBANIAN

"STANDARD LITERARY ALBANIAN"

Albanians are used to considerable variability in form of words, both in terms of inflection and in terms of dialectal variation; foreign readers whose own language shows greater standardization of forms must be prepared to be quite flexible in reading Albanian texts. There have been several attempts to establish a standard set of forms for Albanian that would be the same for all writers, irrespective of their regional provenance. The most effective of these attempts, promulgated as a set of orthographic rules in the 1968 publication of *Rregullat e drejtshkrimit të shqipes* (*The Rules of Albanian Orthography*) in Tirana and supported in Kosovo by the Linguistic Conference of Prishtinë in 1968 (at the expense of their own regional standard Gheg), was enforced by the full power of the government in Albania and embodied in the two large dictionaries *Fjalor i shqipes së sotme* (*Dictionary of present-day Albanian*) and *Fjalor i gjuhës së sotme shqipe* (*Dictionary of the present-day Albanian language*) published in 1980 and 1984, respectively, in Tirana by the Instituti i Gjuhësisë dhe i Letërsisë of the Akademia e Shkencave (Institute of Linguistics and Literature of the Academy of Sciences of the People's Republic of Albania). It would be impossible to discuss the way in which decisions were made as to the principles on which this "Standard Literary Albanian" was based without a lengthy discussion of Albanian politics and political personalities, discussion which would lead us far afield of the use of this dictionary. Suffice it to say here that for a period of over 40 years, Albanian children were taught this standard in schools, publications in Albania were strictly forced to conform to this standard, radio and television broadcasts, plays and films shown in Albanian were required to adhere to this standard, so that by the end of the period of official enforcement of the standard, it had become natural for large numbers of people all over the Albanian-speaking world to understand and use the forms promulgated to fit that standard.

More than half of the entries in this dictionary are based on forms and senses sanctioned by inclusion in those 1980 and 1984 Tirana dictionaries. The spellings and senses without an asterisk in this dictionary reflect these attempts over a half century to standardize the spelling of Albanian words, attempts that have succeeded in some respects and failed in others. Dialectal, stylistic, and personal variation continue to characterize Albanian speech and continue to be reflected in different degrees in print. However, readers of Albanian need to be aware that in actual documents, particularly those published before and after the great normalization efforts from 1968 to 1989, many words appear in forms different from the present-day standard ones. In this dictionary, words and senses that have not been judged to conform to that standard are preceded by an asterisk: *. Such marking does not imply any kind of value judgement "wrong" vs. "right", "bad" vs. "good", "unacceptable" vs. "acceptable". The asterisk is provided only to inform the reader that the word or sense that follows is likely to be viewed by many present-day educated Albanians as aberrant in some way from the standard. Such knowledge may be useful, for example, in understanding intended nuances in modern literary works, or in judging the provenance or age of older non-literary publications. But the sensitive reader must be aware that linguistic variation is rampant in Albanian texts and must be flexible in dealing with word forms and senses that are not matched by those chosen for inclusion here.

DIALECT VARIANTS

Readers must be especially aware that unstressed *ë* and *e* are particularly unstable in Albanian: *ë* is often not pronounced and is often omitted in writing, even when the official orthography would require its presence. In modern standard literary Albanian, there have been valiant attempts to control spellings in regard to ë, but dialectal, stylistic, and personal variation continues to resist standardization. For nouns, presence of *ë* or *e* in final position in writing the nominative singular indefinite form (the usual citation form) reflects the treatment of the noun as feminine (with inflectional endings -**a** (or -**ja**), -**e** (or -**je**), -**s**, -**n**, while their absence indicates that the noun is treated as masculine (with inflectional endings -**i** (or -**u**), -**it** (or -**un**), -**in** (or -**un**). For example, some Albanians (and some dictionaries) would insist that the correct form of the word for *millipede* is **dyzetkëmbëshe**, a feminine noun in declension and agreement, while others insist that it is **dyzetkëmbësh**, a masculine noun in declension and agreement (still others think that the word is **shumëkëmbësh**).

Variable ë

Because unstressed ë is pronounced very lightly, if at all, in most spoken varieties of Albanian, the appearance of the letter ë is highly variable in print, even when the official orthography would require its presence. Readers must be especially flexible in recognizing that a form found in a text with ë may be found in the dictionary without that letter, and vice versa; a text form that ends in a consonant plus ë plus l—which can be represented schematically as *C*ël—may be found in the dictionary with the ë at the end rather than in the middle of the sequence—represented schematically as *C*lë. The same is true for the letters **ll, r, rr, m, n, k, t, s, z** around ë. The same word may end in *C*ë in one dialect of Albanian, *C*e in another, and just *C* in a third.

At the end of a stem, unstressed *ë* always drops out before a suffix that begins in a vowel. In other positions, the appearance of ë in print continues to reflect dialectal, stylistic, and personal variation. For example, between two consonants, an unstressed *ë* may drop out before a vowel, but only if the sequence of consonants left by its disappearance is pronounceable in the variety of Albanian in which the text is written; but that implies that speakers of different varieties of Albanian will differ in whether they say (and write) that ë in a particular word.

The implication for the Albanian dictionary user is that the possibility must be kept open that a form found in a text with an ё may be found in the dictionary without that letter, and vice versa. Since there would be room for little else if every possible variant with and without ё were separately listed, for the most part this dictionary follows the choice of the 1980 *Fjalor i gjuhës së sotme shqipe* for its primary entries, but for certain sub-entries—e.g., the feminine forms of adjectives that drop the stem ё when the suffix -e is added—including those forms would needlessly pad the dictionary with easily interpretable forms.

In modern standard Albanian, suffixes with an underlying form consisting of a single consonant followed by ё— schematically -Cё—typically lose the ё if the vowel in the preceding syllable is unstressed:

> qen + -tё = qentё
> shtёpi' + -tё = shtёpi'tё
> lume'nj + -tё = lume'njtё
> armi'q + -tё = armi'qtё
> *but*
> lu'le + -tё = lu'let
> bu'rra + -tё = bu'rrat
> du'ar + -tё = duart
> nje'rёz + -tё = nje'rёzit

> shtёpi' + -sё = shtёpi'sё
> *but*
> lu'le + -sё = lu'les

It is common to lengthen (in pronunciation) a stressed vowel in a syllable preceding a final ё. In varieties of Albanian that have dropped the final ё (e.g., most northern dialects), that lengthening may have been preserved. Just as an English speaker used a different vowel to distinguish *bit* from *bite*, even though the final written *e* is no longer pronounced, so an Albanian who does not pronounce the final unstressed ё may still distinguish between **bishtu'k** and **bishtu'kё**, on the basis of the length of the **u'**. However, for many speakers of Albanian, the unstressed ё seems quite arbitrary in the orthography, and many variations appear in print.

TABLE OF DIALECTAL VARIANTS

The following Table of Dialectal Variants includes many of the possible ways in which text forms differ from dictionary forms. For words found in work published outside of Albania or before 1969 inside Albania, the reader may find it necessary to try out several possibilities listed in the table in order to find the proper match— "proper" meaning that the match enables the reader to make sense of the passage in which the troublesome word is found. Because this dictionary is so large, and because it is not the usual case that a single word will be crucial for the needs of a reader, this cryptoanalytic technique should not be required often; the tools here are provided for those rare cases when it is so required.

In Text[38]	Standard Form	Pre-standard	Function	Example	Standard
∅	ё		spelling difference	djal	djalё
∅	e		grammatical difference	angjinar	angjinare
CC	CёC	Northern	spelling difference	fajsi ancak	fajёsi anёcak
CёCV'	CCV'	Older	spelling difference	shndёrit	shndrit
CёC#	CC#	Older	spelling difference	lapёs	laps
Cs	Cёs	Older	pronunciation difference	hiths	hithёs
CRV	CёRV	Older	spelling difference	ndrron	ndёrron

---

[38]In this chart:

> *V* stands for any vowel.
> *V* stands for any stressed vowel.
> *V·* stands for any unstressed vowel.
> *C* stands for any consonant.
> *C_O* stands for any voiceless consonant.
> *C_V* stands for any voiceless consonant.
> *N* stands for any nasal consonant—n, m, or nj
> *R* stands for any liquid consonant—r, rr, l, or ll
> # stands for the end of a word
> ø stands for nothing, that is, null, the absence of anything

In Text[38]	Standard Form	Pre-standard	Function	Example	Standard
VV	VjV	Older	spelling difference	bia	bija
VV	VhV	Older	pronunciation difference	tuaf	tuhaf
â	ë'	Northern	pronunciation difference	âsht bâ hângra	është bë hëngra
â	Vn	Northern	pronunciation difference	dumâ	duman
âj	ënj	Northern	pronunciation difference	âjtun	ënjtur
am	ëm	Northern	pronunciation difference	bamë	bëmë
ân	Vn	Northern	pronunciation difference	dângë	dangë
an	ën	Northern	2nd sg pres of verbs	ban	bën
anV	ërV	Northern	pronunciation difference	banë	bëre
-ar	-or	Older	derivational suffix	cikalar ndërqytetar	cikalor ndërqytetor
ardh|	erdh|	Northern	verb stem	ardha	erdha
c	ç	Older	pronunciation difference	kacamill	kaçamill
c	s	Older	pronunciation difference	cfurk frakcion	sfurk fraksion
c	x	Older	pronunciation difference	gucim kapërcej	guxim kapërxej
cb	zb	Older	spelling difference	cbardh cbath	zbardh zbath
cd	zd	Older	pronunciation difference	cdrukth	zdrukth
cf	sf	Older	pronunciation difference	cfurk	sfurk
cg	zg	Older	pronunciation difference	cfurk	sfurk
-ci	-si	Northern	derivational suffix	egërci	egërsi
ck	sk	Older	pronunciation difference	ckallua	skallua
cm	sm	Older	pronunciation difference	cmag	smag
-co	-so	Northern	derivational suffix	egërcoj	egërsoj
cp	sp	Older	pronunciation difference	cpërkas	spërkas
cq	sq	Older	pronunciation difference	cqufur	squfur
crr	cër	Older	pronunciation difference	crrule	cërule
cv	zv	Older	pronunciation difference	cverk	zverk
ç	q	Northern	pronunciation difference	çarkim	qarkim
ç	c		pronunciation difference	çikël	cikël
ç#	xh	Southern	pronunciation difference	borç	borxh
çb	zhb	Southern	pronunciation difference	çbalancim	zhbalancim
çd	zhd	Southern	pronunciation difference	çdëfrim çduk	zhdëfrim zhduk
çf	sf	Southern	pronunciation difference	çfilit	sfilit
çf	shf	Southern	pronunciation difference	çfaq	shfaq
çg	zhg	Southern	pronunciation difference	çgënjim	zhgënjim
çgj	zhgj	Southern	pronunciation difference	çgjaksim	zhgjakësim
çk	shk	Southern	pronunciation difference	çkëput çkishëroj	shkëput shkishëroj
çp	shp	Southern	pronunciation difference	çporr	shporr
çq	shq	Southern	pronunciation difference	çqis	cqis
çt	shth	Southern	pronunciation difference	çthur	shthur
çth	sht	Southern	pronunciation difference	çtillem	shtillem
çv	zhv	Southern	pronunciation difference	çvarros	zhvarros
d	nd	Mountain	pronunciation difference	dal	ndal
dh	ll	Mountain	pronunciation difference	modhë	mollë
dh	gdh	Northern	pronunciation difference	drudhëndës	drugdhendës
e	ë	Variable	pronunciation difference	atëhere	atëherë

In Text[38]	Standard Form	Pre-standard	Function	Example	Standard
e	ej	Northern	pronunciation difference	çartaqefas	çartaqejfas
ê	e	Northern	pronunciation difference	frê pê	fre pe
ê	ë	Older	pronunciation difference	mêngë	mëngë
ên	ën	Northern	pronunciation difference	krênd	krënd
-esha#	-ej#	Southern	*1st sg impf vpr*	nderohesh	nderohej
ë	Ø	Older or Regional	gender difference	frenë	fren
ë	Ø	Older	older spelling	mollëzë	mollëz
ëll	ull	Older	spelling difference	gargëll rrotëll	gargull rrotull
ëm	më	Older	spelling difference	dogëm murrëm	dogmë murrmë
ën	en	Older	pronunciation difference	dëndur mëndje	dendur mendje
ëni	ëri	Northern	pronunciation difference	dëndur	dendur
ër	ur	Older	pronunciation difference	fërtunë bukër	furtunë bukur
ërV	rV	Variable	spelling difference	afërisht	afrisht
-ët	-të	Older	spelling difference	cemët	cemtë
-ëz	-zë	Older	spelling difference	fejëz	fejzë
f	th	Regional	pronunciation difference	fellë	thellë
f#	v#	Southern	spelling difference	dif administratif	div administrativ
f#	h#	Northern	pronunciation difference	shof	shoh
g	gj	Regional	pronunciation difference	legendë	legjendë
g	ng	Older	pronunciation difference	gastër	ngastër
g#	k#	Older	spelling difference	dyfeg	dyfek
ØV	hV	Older	pronunciation difference[39]	alë duet	halë duhet
i	e	Southern	pronunciation difference	çil	cel
i	ë	Older	pronunciation difference	diftesë	dëftesë
i	y	Dialectal	pronunciation difference	diqan kacafit lip	dyqan kacafyt lyp
î	i'	Northern	pronunciation difference	brî ullî	bri ulli
î	i'n	Northern	pronunciation difference	kofî	kofin
iV	jV	Older	spelling difference	diamant	djamant
ie	je	Older	spelling difference	çierr viell	çjerr vjell
ie	ije	Older	spelling difference	dietar	dijetar
îj	inj	Northern	pronunciation difference	kërthîjtë	kërthinjtë
-im	-imë	Older	derivational suffix	bulurim	bulurimë
-inë	-imë		derivational suffix	bubullinë	bubullimë
-inë	-irë		derivational suffix	butësinë	butësirë
-ismë	-izëm	Older	derivational suffix	komunismë	komunizëm
Vj	Vî	Older	spelling difference	hajr	hair
Vj	Vnj	Northern	pronunciation difference	kuj lumej	kunj lumenj

---

[39] Most present-day speakers of Albanian pronounce **h** very weakly, if at all, in ordinary speech, especially if the vowel following the **h** is unstressed. However, for many educated speakers, failure to write the letter in words that have a standard spelling would be evidence of poor education.

In Text[38]	Standard Form	Pre-standard	Function	Example	Standard
j*V*	i*V*	Older	spelling difference	dhjatë	dhiatë
je	ie	Older	spelling difference	kantjer	kantier
je	ie	Southern	spelling difference	djell	diell
je	e	Regional	pronunciation difference	aguridhje	aguridhe
k	g	Southern	spelling difference	akzot	agzot
k#	g#		spelling difference	prak ahenk	prag aheng
kc	ks	Older	pronunciation difference	injekcion	injeksion
kt	gt	Southern	spelling difference	dhoktë	dhogtë
l	ll	Older	pronunciation difference	portokal abdhelë	portokall abdhellë
ll	dh	Mountain	pronunciation difference	brell	bredh
ll	l	Older	pronunciation difference	billanc formulloj	bilanc formuloj
llzë	llëz	Older	spelling difference	mollzë	mollëz
m	mb	Northern	pronunciation difference	pamuk mesë plum	pambuk mbesë plumb
mâ	më	Northern	pronunciation difference	mâparë	mëparë
mb	m	Southern	pronunciation difference	damblla	damlla
më	rë	Northern	pronunciation difference	buzëqamë	buzëqarë
më	rë	Northern	participle	lamë	larë
ml	mbl	Northern	pronunciation difference	mlodha	mblodha
mll	mbll	Northern	pronunciation difference	mllaçis	mbllaçis
mr	mbr	Northern	pronunciation difference	mres	mbres
msh	fsh	Older	pronunciation difference	msheh	fsheh
mësh	fsh	Older	pronunciation difference	mësheh	fsheh
mësh	mbësh	Older	pronunciation difference	mështjell	mbështjell
mpsh	msh	Older	pronunciation difference	lëmpsh	lëmsh
n	nd	Northern	pronunciation difference	kanil nër askun	kandil ndër askund
*V*n*V*	*V*r*V*	Northern	pronunciation difference	atyne dreni pruni	atyre dreri pruri
*C*n	ën	Northern	pronunciation difference	dnes	dënes
*C*n	ër	Northern	pronunciation difference	kafshnore	kafshërore
*C*ën #	ër#	Northern	pronunciation difference	dimën emën	dimër emër
*C*n*V*	*C*r*V*	Northern	pronunciation difference	emni	emri
-na	-ra	Northern	noun plural suffix	shina	shira
nd	n	Southern	pronunciation difference	ndofull	nofull
ndr	dr	Older	pronunciation difference	ndrejt	drejt
ni	ëri	Northern	derivational suffix	pleqni	pleqëri
ns	nc	Older	spelling difference	agjensi	agjenci
nsh	nç		pronunciation difference (especially for optative)	vënshin	vënçin
nj	j	Southern	pronunciation difference	kuptonj bënj	kuptoj bëj
nj	ngj	Northern	pronunciation difference	njall njyrë	ngjall ngjyrë
-njës	-ues	Southern	pronunciation difference	pushtonjës mësonjës	pushtues mësues

In Text[38]	Standard Form	Pre-standard	Function	Example	Standard
o'	u'a	Non-standard	theme vowel	loj pagoj	luaj paguaj
vo	va	Northern	pronunciation difference	votër	vatër
p	b	Older	pronunciation difference	kupël	kupël
p#	b#	Southern	pronunciation difference	thelp korp	thelb korb
p#	b#	Southern	pronunciation difference	lap elp komp korp	lab elb komb korb
prë	për	Older	spelling difference	prëçartë	përçartë
psh	fsh	Older	pronunciation difference	pshat	fshat
psh	mbësh	Older	pronunciation difference	pshtjellje	mbështjellje
psht	shpët	Older	pronunciation difference	pshtoj	shpëtoj
pt	bët	Older	pronunciation difference	dopta	dobëta
pth	bth	Older	spelling difference	elpth	elbth
q	gj	Southern	pronunciation difference	qenq	qengj
q	k	Older	pronunciation difference	kanisq	kanisk
r	rr	Southern	pronunciation difference	mar rotë tmer	marr rrotë tmerr
ri	si	Arbitrary	abstract noun formative	miqëri	miqësi
rr	r	Northern	pronunciation difference	bythkrromë rradhë	bythkromë radhë
s#	z#	Southern	spelling difference	çapras oris	çapraz oriz
-së	-ës	Older	spelling difference	gryksë	grykës
sg	zg	Older	spelling difference	sgafullon	zgafullon
sgj	zgj	Older	spelling difference	sgjebe	zgjebe
sj	sq	Older	pronunciation difference	sjoll	sqoll
skj	sq	Older	spelling difference	skjep	sqep
sh	ç	Older	pronunciation difference	dishka shradhit	diçka çradhit
sh	zh	Southern	pronunciation difference	proshëm	prozhëm
sh#	zh#	Southern	pronunciation difference	garash	garazh
-sh-	-n-	Northern	pl impf	hapshim	hapnim
-shëm	-ja	Northern	1st sg impf	hapshëm	hapja
shm	çm	Older	pronunciation difference	përshmoj	përçmoj
t	d	Older	spelling difference	tefter	defter
t#	d#	Southern	spelling difference	murtat ment	murtad mend
-tçëm-	-tshëm-	Older	spelling difference	barabitçëm	barabitshëm
ts	c	Older	spelling difference	tsar	car
ts	t	Older	pronunciation difference	fajtsoj	fajtoj
th#	dh#	Older	spelling difference	i math kukuth	i madh kukudh
u	y	Older	pronunciation difference	burek musafir	byrek mysafir
u'	u'a	Northern	pronunciation difference	rruj	rruaj
û	u	Northern	pronunciation difference	drû kërcû	dru kërcu
u'a	o	Older Southern	theme vowel	rruaj	rroj
u'ame	u'ar	Northern	feminine adjective	e kaluame	e kaluar

In Text[38]	Standard Form	Pre-standard	Function	Example	Standard
u'ar	o'r	Southern	adjectival suffix	lakruar	lakror
u'arshëm	u'eshëm	Southern	adjectival suffix	afru'arshëm	afru'eshëm
u'e	u'a	Northern	theme vowel	çapue	çapua
u'e	u'a	Northern	pronunciation difference	grue	grua
u'e	u'ar	Northern	participles, adjectives	takue	takuar
-u'em	-o'r	Northern	adjectives	botuem	botor
-u'em	-u'ar	Northern	participles, adjectives	buem punuem	buar punuar
-u'eme	-u'ar	Northern	feminine adjective	e kalueme	e kaluar
-u'er	-o'r	Northern	qualitative nouns, adjectives	balluer aeruer	ballor aeror
-u'es	-u's	Northern	agentive nouns, adjectives	shkues	shkus
-un	-ur	Northern	participles, adjectives	pjekun pritun	pjekur pritur
ull	ëll	Northern	spelling difference	esull	esëll
x	z	Older	pronunciation difference	horixont xbavit xylyfe	horizont zbavit zylyfe
xh	zh	Older	pronunciation difference	grixhël kuxhinë xhvesh	grizhël kuzhinë zhvesh
xh	gj	Northern	pronunciation difference	xherdek	gjerdek
y	i	Northern	pronunciation difference	bylbyl krymb	bilbil krimb
y	u	Regional	pronunciation difference	dyke	duke
y'	y'e	Older	theme vowel	rryshëm pys	rryeshëm pyes
ye	e	Older	theme vowel	kaptyell	kaptell
ye	e	Older	theme vowel	bërdyell	bërdilë
-yem	-yer	Northern	participles, adjectives	pashlyem	pashlyer
z	x	Older	pronunciation difference	zamare	xamare
zë	ëz	Older	diminutive suffix	gjuhzë	gjuhëz

SOURCE REFERENCE

In addition to the published works listed below, a number of specialists have contributed their expertise to this dictionary. Thanks to their efforts, hundreds of words previously unknown to me have been added, and thousands of entries found elsewhere with only general or seriously inaccurate definitions have been amended and included here. The names of those specialists consulted personally, preceded by an asterisk and followed by their fields of expertise (in upper case letters) are included in the list below. The assistance of the specialists in Albania was obtained through the extraordinary efforts of Vladimir Dervishi. I wish to express here my deepest appreciation to them all for their valuable and unselfish help. Specialists whose work was used, but who were not consulted personally, are listed without an asterisk.

SOURCES CONSULTED

*Bajza, Emin: MUSHROOMS
*Basho, Frank: CINEMATOGRAPHY
Bregu, Ferdinand: ZOOLOGY
*Broka, Alexander: VETERINARY SCIENCE
*Bucholz, Oda: LEXICOGRAPHY
Bucholz, Oda, Wilfried Fiedler & Gerda Uhlisch. *Wörterbuch Albanisch-Deutsch,* Leipzig: VEB Verlag Enzyklopädie Leipzig, 1977.
Buda, A. & Sh. Lloshi, eds. *Fjalori enciklopedik shqiptar,* Tirana: Akademia e Shkencave e RPSSH, 1985.
Cipo et al., K. *Fjalor i gjuhës shqipe,* 1954.
Çekrezi, C.A. *Chekrezi's English-Albanian Dictionary,* Boston: Ilia Chapullari, 1923.
*Çipuri, Hasan: MILITARY SCIENCE
Cordignano, Fulvio, S.J. *Dizionario Albanese-Italiano,* Milan: Ulrico Hoepli, 1934.
*Demiraj, Mustafa: BOTANICAL TERMS
Demiri, Mustafa. *Flora Ekskursioniste e Shqipërisë,* Tirana: Shtëpia Botuese e Librit Shkollor, 1983.
Demiraj, Shaban. *Gjuha Shqipe dhe Historia e Saj,* Tirana: Shtëpia Botuese e Librit Universitar, 1988.
Demiraj, Shaban. "Rreth apofonisë në gjuhën shqipe", *Studime Filologjike,* 40:160, 1986.
Dervishi, Vladimir, personal correspondence
Domi, M. & Sh. Demiraj, eds. *Fonetika dhe gramatika e gjuhës së sotme letrare shqipe: Morfologjia,* Tirana: Akademia e Shkencave e RPSSH, 1976.
Drizari, Nelo. *Albanian-English and English-Albanian Dictionary,* 2nd edition, New York: Frederick Ungar, 1957.
Duro, Ilo & Ramazan Hysa. *Fjalor shqip-anglisht: Albanian-English Dictionary,* 1981.
*Fiedler, Wilfried: LEXICOGRAPHY
Filipi, Ndoc & Ndoc Rakaj. "Glosar Iktiologjik," *Buletini i Studimeve Shkencore të Peshkimit,* 1959.
Instituti i Fizkulturës: SPORTS
Gazulli, Nikollë. *Fjalorth i ri,* Tirana: Shtypshkroja "Gurakuqi," 1941.
Goci, Sadik. *Zooteknika për Teknikumet Bujqësore,* Tirana: Shtëpia Botuese e Librit Shkollor, 1968.
Godin, Marie Amelie Freiin von. *Wörterbuch der albanischen und deutschen Sprache,* Leipzig: Otto Harrassowitz, 1930.
Gozmány, László. *Vocabularium Nominum Animalum Europae: Septem Linguis Reductum,* Budapest: Akadémiai Kiadá, 1979.
Gjergji, Andromaqi. *Veshjet shqiptare në shekuj,* Tirana: Instituti i Kulturës Popullore, 1987.
Gjevori, Mehmet. *Frazeologjizma të gjuhës shqip,* Prishtina: Rilindja, 1972.
*Gjika, Rahim: MEDICAL TERMS
*Gjiknuri, Lek: BIOLOGICAL TERMS
*Haxhialushi, Estref: BOTANICAL TERMS
*Haxhiu, Idriz: ZOOLOGY
Haxhiymeri, Tahir. *Katalog i ilustruar për mekanikën,* Tirana: Shtëpia Botuese "8 Nëntori," 1988.
Haznedari, Ismail & Sami Repishti. *Albanian: Language Competencies for Peace Corps Volunteers in Albania,* Washington: Peace Corps, 1992.
*Henegar, Sue: TEXTILE TERMS
Hetzer, Armin. *Lehrbuch der vereinheitlichten albanischen Schriftsprache,* Hamburg: Helmut Buske Verlag, 1978.
Hetzer, Armin & Zuzana Finger. *Lehrbuch der verinheitlichten albanischen Schriftsprache,* 3rd edition, Hamburg: Helmut Buske Verlag, 1989.
Hysa, Ramazan. *Fjalor i astronomisë,* Tirana: Shtëpia Botuese "8 Nëntori," 1978.

Kacori, Thoma. *A Handbook of Albanian,* Sofia: Sofia University "Kliment Ohridski," 1979.

Kadare, Ismail. *Kronikë në Gur,* 2nd ed., reprinted in Prishtina, Yugoslavia: Rilindja, 1976.

Kapo, M., P. Geço, V. Naço & V. Kristo. *Fjalor i termave të gjeografisë: shqip-rusisht-frëngjisht,* Tirana: Mihal Duri, 1975.

Katundi, Mihallaq: POST-TELEGRAPH

Kiçi, Gaspar. *Albanian-English Dictionary,* 1976.

Kiçi, Gaspar & Hysni Aliko. *English-Albanian Dictionary,* 1969.

Koçi, R., A. Kostallari & Dh. Skendi. *Fjalor i shkurtër shqip-rusisht,* 2nd edition, Moscow: National Publisher of Foreign and Ethnic Dictionaries, 1951.

Kokona, Vedat. *Fjalor shqip-frengjisht,* Tirana: Shtëpia Botuese "8 Nëntori", 1981.

Kostallari, Androkli, ed. *Fjalor i gjuhës së sotme shqipe,* Akademia e Shkencave e RPS të Shqipërisë: Instituti i Gjuhësisë dhe i Letërsisë, Tiranë, 1980.

Kostallari, Androkli, ed. *Fjalor i shqipes së sotme,* Akademia e Shkencave e RPS të Shqipërisë: Instituti i Gjuhësisë dhe i Letërsisë, Tiranë, 1984.

Kostallari, Androkli, personal correspondence

Lako, Nikolla: BOTANICAL TERMS

Lama, Skënder & Muharrem Seseri. *Fjalor i termave të gjeodezisë: shqip-anglisht-frëngjisht-rusisht,* Tirana: University of Tirana, 1982.

*Lamani, Fotaq: ORNITHOLOGY

Lambertz, Max. *Lehrgang des Albanischen,* Halle: VEB Max Niemeyer Verlag, 1959.

Leka, F., F. Podgorica, & S. Hoxha. *Fjalor shpjegues i termave të letërsisë,* Tirana: Mihal Duri, 1984.

Leka, Ferdinand & Zef Simoni. *Fjalor Italisht-Shqip,* Tirana: 8 Nëntori, 1986.

Leotti, Angelo. *Dizionario Albanese-Italiano,* Roma: Istituto per L'Europa orientale, 1937.

Lloshi, Xhevat, personal correspondence

Macura, P. *Elsevier's Dictionary of Botany: I. Plant Names,* Amsterdam: Elsevier Scientific Publishing Company, 1979.

Mann, Stuart E. *An Historical Albanian-English,* London: Longmans, Green, 1948.

Mborja, Dhimitër & Rrok Zoizi. *Arti Popullor në Shqipëri,* Tirana: Universiteti Shtetëror i Tiranës, 1959.

Misja, Kristaq: ENTOMOLOGY

Mitrushi, Ilia. *Drurët e shkurret e Shqipërisë,* Tirana: Instituti i Shkencave, 1955.

__. *Dendroflora e Shqipërisë,* Tirana: Universiteti Shtetëror i Tiranës, 1966.

*Murraj, Xhelo: ENTOMOLOGY

Newmark, L., P. Prifti & P. Hubbard. *Reader in Albanian,* Washington, D.C.: ERIC, 1981.

Newmark, Leonard. *Standard Albanian,* Stanford: Stanford University Press, 1982.

__. *Spoken Albanian,* Ithaca, New York: Spoken Language Services, 1980.

*Papa, Asti: GEOLOGY

Paparisto, K., M. Demiri, I. Mitrushi & Xh. Qosja. *Flora e Shqipërisë,* 1988.

Paparisto, K., Xh. Qosja, & M. Demiri. *Flora e Tiranës,* Tirana: Universiteti Shtetëror i Tiranës, 1961.

Permanent Committee of Geographical names for British Official Use. *Albanian (Glossaries: 3),* London: House of the Royal Geographical Society, 1943.

Polunin, Oleg. *Flowers of Greece and the Balkans: A Field Guide,* Oxford: Oxford University Press, 1980.

Qafezezi, Niko: BOTANICAL TERMS

Qafzezi, Ndoc. *Fjalor i bujqësisë: shqip, latinisht, italisht, rusisht,* Tirana: Shtëpia Botuese "8 Nëntori," 1978.

Qarri, Mehmet, Koço Adami & Vilhelm Sima. *Fjalor i terminologjisë së gjeometrisë deskriptive dhe i izatimit teknik,* Tirana: University of Tirana, 1989.

*Qosja, Xhevdet: BOTANICAL TERMS

Rakaj, Ndoc. "Emërtime popullore të peshqve të bregdetit të Shqipërisë," *Studime Filologjike XXVI,* no. 2, 1989.

Rakaj, Ndoc. "Emrat e peshqëve dhe organizmave të ujit: Emrat shqip të disa peshqvet, ernave dhe veglavet ë peshkimit," *Buletini i Shkencave Natyrore,* 1970.

Reineck, Janet. *The Past as Refuge: Gender, Migration, and Ideology Among the Kosova Albanians,* Doctoral Dissertation, 1991.

Ressuli, Namik. *Albanian Literature,* ed. by Eduard Liço, Boston: Vatra, 1987.

*Robinson, Phillip T.: VETERINARY TERMS IN ENGLISH

*Rrakaj, Ndoc: ICHTHYOLOGY

Sejdia, Shefki: BOTANICAL TERMS

Selenica, Myslym: VETERINARY SCIENCE

Shkupi, Dëfrim N. *Fjalor i gjeologjisë,* Tirana: Shtëpia Botuese "8 Nëntori," 1984.

Sholjan, Tonko. *Fishes of the Adriatic,* Zagreb: Nakladni Zavod Hrvatske, 1948.
Sokoli, Ramadan. *Veglat muzikore të popullit shqiptar,* Tirana: Botim i Shtëpisë Qendrore të Krijimtarisë Popullore, 1966.
Stefanllari, Ilo. *Fjalor Anglisht-Shqip,* [ed., Xh Lloshi & F. Idrizi] Tirana: Shtepia Botuese "8 Nëntori," 1986.
Sugarman, Jane. "The Nightingale and the Partridge: Singing and Gender among Prespa Albanians." *Ethnomusicology,* 33:191-215, 1989.
Whitehead, P.J.P. et al., ed. *Fishes of the North-eastern Atlantic and the Mediterranean,* Paris: Unesco, 1984.
Xhuvani, Aleksandër. "Fjalë dhe shprehje të gjuhës shqipe," *Studime Filologjike,* 1971-1987.
Fjalor i terminologjisë tekniko-shkencore, Tirana: Akademia e shkencave e RPSSH., reprinted in Prishtina: Enti i Botimeve Shkollore i Republikës Socialiste të Sërbisë.

> *Fjalor anglisht-shqip i mjekësisë,* 1978.
> *Fjalor i mikrobiologjisë,* 1980.
> *Fjalor i termave të anatomisë,* 1985.
> *Fjalor i termave të bibliotekës dhe të bibliografisë,* 1982.
> *Fjalor i termave të ekonomisë politike,* 1983.
> *Fjalor i termave të financës e të kontabilitetit,* 1985.
> *Fjalor i termave të gjeologisë,* 1988.
> *Fjalor i termave të gjuhësisë,* 1975.
> *Fjalor i termave të histologjisë dhe të embriologjisë,* 1986.
> *Fjalor i termave të obstetrikës dhe gjinekologjisë,* 1987.
> *Fjalor i termave të së drejtës,* 1986.
> *Fjalor i termave të tregtisë së jashtme,* 1976.
> *Terminologjia e akustikës,* 1963.
> *Terminologjia e arkitekturës,* 1964.
> *Terminologjia e botanikës,* 1963.
> *Terminologjia e elektromagnetizmit,* 1963.
> *Terminologjia e elektroteknikës,* 1963.
> *Terminologjia e energisë atomike,* 1963.
> *Terminologjia e kimisë,* 1963.
> *Terminologjia e letërsisë,* 1970.
> *Terminologjia e matematikës dhe e mekanikës teorike,* 1967.
> *Terminologjia e mekanikës,* 1963.
> *Terminologjia e optikës,* 1963.
> *Terminologjia e së drejtës ndërkombëtare,* 1970.
> *Terminologjia e termodinamikës,* 1963.

Also consulted occasionally were articles or portitons of the following:
Dizionario Italiano-Albanese Scutari, 1938. (Reprinted by Forni Editore in Bologna, 1968)
"Emrat shqip të disa peshqeve, organizmave të ujit dhe veglave të peshkimit," *Buletini i shkencave natyrës,* Tirana, 1970.
Gjuha Jonë (various)
Gjuha Letrare Kombëtare Shqipe dhe Epoka Jonë, Tirana: Instituti i Gjuhësisë dhe i Letërsisë, 1988.
"Glosar Iktiologjik," *Buletini i studimeve shkencore të peshkimit,* Tirana, 1959.
Albanian-English Dictionary, First Edition, Washington, D. C.: Armed Forces Security Agency, 1950.
Gjurmime Albanologjike (various)
Iktiofauna e Shqiperisë
Kartoteka e Institutit të Gjuhësisë, (checked by Vladimir Dervishi, 1991).
Studia Albanica (various).
Studime Filologjike (various).
The Albanians and Their Territories, Tirana: The "8 Nëntori" Publishing House, 1985.

a

I § nf first letter of the alphabet; the vowel or letter "a"

II § interj = ah

III § conj **1** or (exclusive), either, whether **2** (before a verb phrase, signals a yes/no question)

∘ **a ⁀ apo ⁀** whether ⁀ or ⁀

∘ **A je, si je?** *(Reg Gheg)* So how are you? (a greeting)

∘ **a thua se ⁀** just as if ⁀

*â· *vi (Reg Gheg)* = **ë·njt·**

*â·*het vpr (Reg Gheg)* = **ë·njt·***et*

aba *nf (Old)* thin felt (usually white or gray)

abaci *nf* **1** *[Rel]* abbacy, jurisdiction of an abbot **2** abbey

abak *nm* abacus

*abakë *nf* ash-tray

abanos *nm* = **abanoz**

abanoz *nm* *[Bot]* ebony

abat *nm* *[Rel]* abbot; Catholic clergyman

abazhur *nm* **1** lamp shade **2** lamp (support together with the shade)

ABC *[a-bë-cë]* *abbreviation* = **abëcë**

ABD *[a-bë-dë]* *abbreviation* < **artileria bregdetare** *[Mil]* coastal artillery

*abdes *nm* = **avdes**

*abdesanë *nf* = **avdeshanë**

*abdest *nm* = **avdes**

abdikim *nm ger (Book)* **1** < **abdiko·**·*n* **2** abdication

abdiko··*n vi (Book)* to abdicate

*abdhellë *nf* = **abdhellë**

*abdhellë *nf (Reg Gk)* leech, bloodsucker = **avgellë**

abe *nf (Reg)* **1** spectre, phantasm **2** gracefulness ***3** *(Reg Colloq)* alphabet

abece *nf* = **abëcë**

*abetar *nm* = **abetare**

abetare *nf* reading primer

*abë *nf* frieze

abëcë *nf* ABC's, alphabet

abis *nm (Book)* abyss

abisin *nm* = **abisinas**

abisinas *adj, n* Abyssinian, Ethiopian

Abisini *nf* Abyssinia, Ethiopia

ablativ *nm [Ling]* ablative = **rrjedhore**

abnegacion *nm* abnegation = **vetëmohim**

*abolla *conj (Reg Old)* so that, in order that

abonim *nm ger* **1** < **abono·**·*n*, **abono·**·*het* **2** subscription

abono··*het vpr* to be a subscriber

abono··*n vt* to subscribe to [a periodical]

abonuar

I § adj (i) subscribing

II § n (i) subscriber

abordazh *nm [Naut]* attack by boarding (at sea)

abort *nm [Med]* abortion

abortar *nm [Med]* maternity ward section for miscarriages and abortions

abortues *nm [Med]* abortive

abrash

I § adj (Colloq) **1** having blond hair/eyebrows; flecked/streaked with light spots; dappled; speckled **2** *(Fig)* rude, unruly, mischievous **3** *(Fig)* bringing bad luck; ill-boding

II § nm [Entom] cockroach *(Blatta orientalis)*

abrashe *nf (Colloq)* freckle; pockmark

abrashkë *nf* **1** = **abrashe 2** (any) bird with a black head

abraziv *adj, nm [Tech]* abrasive (material)

abrazh *adj* = **abrash**

abresh *adj* (of fruit) dark-skinned

abrogim *nm ger* **1** < **abrogo·**·*n* **2** abrogation

abrogo··*n vt* to abrogate

absces *nm [Med]* abscess

absent

I § adj absent

II § nm * = **absint**

abses *s* = **absces**

absidë *nf* **1** *[Archit]* apse **2** chancel of a church, sanctuary

absint *nm* absinthe, wormwood

absolut *adj* absolute

absolutësi *nf (Book)* absoluteness

absolutisht *adv* absolutely

absolutizëm *nm (Book)* absolutism

absolutizim *nm ger (Book)* < **absolutizo·**·*n*, **absolutizo·**·*het*

absolutizo··*n vt (Book)* to take [] as an absolute, take [] as given, consider [] to be indisputable; esteem [] beyond measure

*absolvent *nm (Old)* one who has graduated from a school, graduate

absorbim *nm ger* **1** < **absorbo·**·*n* **2** absorption

absorbo··*n vt* to absorb

abstenim *nm ger* **1** < **absteno·**·*n* **2** abstention

absteno··*n vi* to vote neither yes nor no: abstain

abstenues *nm* abstainer

abstragim *nm ger* < **abstrago·**·*n*

abstrago··*n vt* = **abstrakto·**·*n*

abstraksion *nm (Book)* abstraction

abstraksionist *adj, n [Art]* abstractionist

abstraksionizëm *nm* abstractionism

abstrakt *adj* abstract

abstraktësi *nf (Book)* abstractness

abstraktim *nm ger (Book)* < **abstrakto·**·*n*

abstrakto··*het vpr (Book)* to think in abstract general terms

abstrakto··*n*

I § vt (Book) to abstract

II § vi **1** to think in abstract general terms **2** *(Colloq)* to ignore

absurd *adj (Book)* absurd

absurditet *nm (Book)* absurdity, nonsense

abshisë *nf [Math]* abscissa

*****abubu** *interj* = **ububu**

abutilon *nm [Bot]* button weed, butter print *Abutilon avicennae*

abuz *nm (Reg)* dark place in dense underbrush; suitable place for hiding or for waiting in ambush

abuzim *nm ger* 1 <**abuzo**·*n* 2 abuse

abuzo·*n vt* to abuse

○ **abuzo**·*n* **në** [] 1 to overindulge in [] 2 to abuse one's position in []

abuzues *nm* abuser

*****acal** *nm (Old)* steel = **çelik**

acar

I § *adj* 1 bitterly cold 2 *(Fig)* rough, cruel, nasty 3 icy pure, limpid; clean and neat (especially in dress) 4 *(Fig)* acute, sharp-witted

II § *nm* 1 bitter cold, frosty cold; wintry season, frosty period 2 *(Fig)* enervating fear 3 severity, roughness; anger 4 *(Old)* steel = **çelik**

III § *adv* 1 purely; neatly 2 roughly, gruffly, harshly 3 tightly

acare *nf* tiny bell

acari *nf* 1 dry and freezing cold 2 *(Fig)* cruelty; anger 3 *(Fig)* roughness, severity 4 harsh constraint 5 particular cleanliness and neatness in dress

○ **acari në veshje** excessive fastidiousness in dress and appearance

acarim *nm ger* 1 <**acaro**·*n* 2 irritation 3 coercion 4 spiteful stubbornness

acaro·*het vpr* 1 to become extremely cold 2 to become tense, irritated, aggravated; have a falling out in relations 3 to get worse, become inflamed, fester; get chapped 4 *(Fig)* to be threatening or intimidating

acaro·*n vt* 1 to make [] worse: exacerbate 2 to irritate, chafe; make [] more irritating 3 to increase the tension on []: tighten

○ **acaro**·*n* **për** [] to be in dire need of []

acartë *adj (i)* 1 extremely cold, icy, frosty 2 *(Fig)* cruel, nasty

acaruar *adj (i)* 1 strained to the bursting point 2 cruel and embittered 3 inflamed (of wounds), irritated, made sore, in serious condition

acetat *nm [Chem]* acetate

acetik *adj [Chem]* acetic, vinegary

acetilen *nm [Chem]* acetylene

aceton *nm [Chem]* acetone

*****acër** = **acar**

acid

I § *nm [Chem]* acid

II § *adj* acidic

○ **acid azot** nitric acid

acidedashës *adj [Biol]* acidophilic

aciddurues *adj* acid-resistant

acidik *adj* acidic

acidim *nm ger [Chem]* <**acido**·*n*

aciditet *nm* acidity

acido·*het vpr [Chem]* to turn acidic

acido·*n vt [Chem]* to acidify; treat with acid; make sour

aç

I § *adv (Reg)* with an empty stomach, hungry

II § *nm* *[Bot]* dill

açik

I § *adj (Colloq)* 1 light-colored 2 shameless, insolent

II § *adv (Colloq)* 1 clearly; openly, frankly 2 in plain words

açuge *nf [Ichth]* anchovy = **ancuje**

adalet

I § *adv (Crude)* very much, intensely: to beat the band

II § *adj (Colloq)* great big

adaptim *nm ger (Book)* 1 <**adapto**·*n* 2 adaptation

adapto·*n vt (Book)* to adapt, remodel

adaptueshëm *adj (i)* adaptable, adjustable

adaptueshmëri *nf* adaptability

adash *nm* namesake

adaxhio *adv, nf [Mus]* adagio

*****addunar** *nm* meeting place

*****addunar**·*et vpr* to meet, assemble

adekuat *adj (Book)* adequate

aderim *nm ger* 1 <**adero**·*n* 2 adherence; membership

adero·*n vi* to join a group sharing a common interest, become an adherent/member

adet *nm (Colloq)* habit, custom

adezion *nm* adhesion

adër *nm (Reg)* twaddle, chatter, nonsense; joke, kidding; pack of lies

adërtar *n (Reg)* jokester, kidder; one who talks nonsense

adiabatë *nf [Phys]* adiabatic line

adiabatik *adj [Phys]* adiabatic

Adil *nm* Adil (male name)

*****adjektiv** *nm* adjective = **mbiemër**

*****adjudikatë** *nf* contractual offer

adjutant *nm [Mil]* adjutant

adjutanturë *nf [Mil]* duty or office of an adjutant

administratë *nf* administration, administrative offices

administrativ *adj* administrative

administrativisht *adv* administratively

administrativo-tokësor *adj [Law]* regionally administered

administrator *n* manager (of another's interests): administrator, steward

administrim *nm ger* 1 <**administro**·*n* 2 administration

administro·*n vt* to administer

administrues *nm* administrative staff member

admiracion *nf* admiration

admiral *nm [Mil]* admiral

admiraliat *nm [Mil]* admiralty

admiratë *nf* admiration

admirativ *adj [Ling]* = **habitore**

admirim *nm ger* 1 <**admiro**·*n* 2 admiration

admiro·*n vt* to admire

admiruar *adj (i)* admired

admirues *nm* admirer

admirueshëm *adj (i)* admirable

ADN *abbrev (German, East Germany)* <**Allgemeine Deutscher Nachrichtendienst** German News Service

adonik *adj (Book Poet)* Adonic

adoptim *nm ger (Book)* 1 <**adopto**·*n* 2 adoption

adoptiv *adj* adoptive

adopto· -*n vt* to adopt
adoptuar *adj (i)* adopted
adoptues *nm* adopter
adoptueshëm *adj (i)* adoptable
adra *np* <**adër**
adrenalinë *nf* adrenalin
adresë *nf* address
adreso· -*n vt* to address [a letter]
Adrianopojë *nf* Adrianople
Adriatik *adj* **1** Adriatic **2** Adriatik (male name)
adsorbim *nm* [*Chem*] adsorption
adsorbo· -*n vt* [*Chem*] to adsorb
adverb *nm* adverb = **ndajfolje**
*****adyqar** *nm* proconsul
*****adha** *adv* therefore, so
*****adham** *nm (Old)* diamond
*****adhër** = **adhur**
*****adhiqi** *nf (Old Regional Gk)* injustice = **padrejtësi**
*****adhjase**· -*n vt (Old)* to sweep [ ] away
*****adhr** = **adhur**
*****adhrues** *adj (Old)* of or pertaining to a plea, pleading
*****adhurësë** *nf* = **adhurim**
adhurim *nm ger* **1** <**adhuro**· -*n* **2** adoration *****3** *(Old)* entreaty, plea, petition
adhurimtar *n* = **adhurues**
adhuro· -*n vt* **1** to adore **2** to worship *****3** *(Old)* to entreat, beseech, implore
adhuruarshëm *adj (i)* = **adhurueshëm**
adhurues
   I § *nm* **1** admirer; adorer; devotee **2** worshipper; idolator *****3** *(Old)* supplicant, petitioner
   II § *adj* adoring, idolizing
adhurueshëm *adj(i)* worthy of adoration: adorable, adored
aed *nm* [*Lit*] minstrel, bard
aerator *nm* [*Tech*] aerator
aero *formative prefix* aero-, air-
aeroanie *nf (Old)* = **aeroplan**
aerob *nm* [*Biol*] aerobe
aerobi *nf* [*Bot*] = **aerob**
aerodetar *adj* air-and-sea
aerodinamik *adj* aerodynamic
aerodinamikë *nf* aerodynamics
aerodrom *nm* airport, airfield
   ○ **aerodrom i rremë** [*Mil*] dummy airfield
aerolit *nm* aerolite, meteorite
aeromekanikë *nf* [*Tech*] aeromechanics
aeromodelist *nm* model airplane enthusiast
aeromodelizëm *nm* model airplane flying
*****aeronaftë** *nf* = **aerostat**
aeronaut *nm* aeronaut
aeronautik *adj* aeronautical
aeronautikë *nf* aeronautics
aeropankë *nf* [*Ichth*] butterfly ray *Gymnura altavela* = **peshk-laraskë**
aeroplan *nm* airplane
   ○ **aeroplan bombardues** bomber
   ○ **aeroplan gjuajtës** fighter plane
   ○ **aeroplan ndjekës** pursuit plane
   ○ **aeroplan reaktiv** jet plane
   ○ **aeroplan udhëtarësh** passenger plane
   ○ **aeroplan vëzhgimi** reconnaissance plane

   ○ **aeroplan zbulues** reconnaissance plane
aeroplanmbajtës *nm* aircraft carrier
*****aeroplanmbart**ës *nm* = **aeroplanmbajtës**
aeroport *nm* airport
*****aeror** *adj* = **ajror**
aerostat *nm* aerostat
   ○ **aerostat pengimi** barrage balloon
af *nm* sheen
afarist
   I § *n* **1** businessman **2** *(Pej)* profiteer
   II § *adj* commercial, of or pertaining to business
afarizëm *nm* **1** business, trade **2** *(Pej)* profiteering
afat *nm* time limit: deadline, due date
afatgjatë *adj* long-term
afatshkurtër *adj* short-term
afazi *nf* aphasia
afçë *nf* [*Ornit*] golden oriole *(Oriolus oriolus L)* = **beng**
afekt *nm (Book)* emotional affect
afektuar *adj (i)* [*Lit*] affected, unnatural
afel *nm* [*Astron*] aphelion
afendiko *nm (Colloq Old)* **1** Mister, rich man (used as a title for wealthy Orthodox men) **2** *(Pej)* pretentious or conceited person
aferezë *nf* [*Ling*] aphaeresis
aferim *interj (Colloq)* bravo!
*****aferin** *interj* = **aferim**
afetar *n* **1** non-religious, non-believing **2** non-believer
afetari *nf* non-belief (in a religion), lack of faith
afetarizëm *nm* = **afetari**
afër
   I § *adv* **1** near, nearby; close **2** not very different **3** related (by family) **4** approximately, about **5** *(Fig)* intimately
   II § *prep (abl)* near, by, close to; around (in expressions of time)
   III § *adj (i)* = **afërm**
   IV § *nm (i) (Old)* neighbor
   ○ **afër e afër** very close/near
   ○ **ësh-të**^{3sg} **afër mendsh/mendjes** it *goes* without saying
   ○ **afër mendsh** = **afërmendsh**
   ○ **afër mënç** obvious = **afërmendsh**
afërdet *nm (Old)* seashore
Afërdita *nf* Afërdita (female name)
*****afërditë** *nf* **1** daybreak, dawn **2** Venus, morning star
afërina *np* environs, vicinity
*****Afërlindje** *nf* Near East
afërm
   I § *adj (i)* **1** close, near **2** next, adjacent **3** closely related **4** = **afërt**
   II § *n (i)* close family member; close colleague
*****afërmas** *adv* nearby
afërme *nf (e)* that which is near at hand
*****afërmënç** *adv (Reg)* = **afërmendsh**
afërmendësi *nf* obviousness
afërmendsh *pred* obvious, self-evident, clear
afërmendshëm *adj (i)* **1** obvious, self-evident, clear **2** reasonable
*****afërmeni** *nf* nearness, closeness; kinship
*****afërmënç** *adv (Reg)* = **afërmendsh**
afërmëndshëm *adj (i)* = **afërmendshëm**

a·fër·m·i *adv (së)* **1** at close hand; from close up, close up ; close at hand **2** in a while, soon; a while ago

afër·nde·nj·ës *adj (Book)* **1** [*Geom*] adjacent **2** neighboring

afërsí
 I § *nf* **1** proximity, nearness **2** kinship, family relationship **3** affinity **4** *(Fig)* intimacy **5** approximation = **përafërsí**
 II § *np* environs, vicinity; suburbs

afërsí·na *np fem* = **fërsíra**

afërsí·në *nf* = **afërsírë**

afërsipërfaqësor *adj* [*Spec*] very near the surface

afërsíra *np* environs, vicinity; suburbs

afërsírë *nf(Reg)* **1** neighborhood, proximity **2** contour line

afërsí·shëm *adj (i)* = **përafërt**

afërsísht *adv, pcl* approximately

a·fërt *adj (i)* **1** proximate in terms of space or time: adjacent, contiguous; recent or approaching time **2** = **afërm 3** on close terms **4** similar **5** [*Ling*] genetically related

afërtí·në *nf* neighborhood

afëruar·shëm *adj (i)* = **afrueshëm**

affrai *nf* fear

afgán *adj, n* Afghan

Afganistán *nm* Afghanistan

afganistán·as *adj, n* Afghan

afíde *np* [*Biol*] aphids, plant lice *Aphidoidea*

afíf *adj* = **hafíf**

afinitét *nm (Book)* affinity

afión
 I § *nm* **1** [*Bot*] opium poppy **2** opium
 II § *adj (Fig)* pale

afirmím *nm ger* **1** <**afirmo·n 2** affirmation

afirmó·n *vt* to assert; affirm

afirmúar *adj (i)* established, confirmed; acknowledged

afíshe *nf* poster, posted notice, placard

afishím *nm ger* <**afisho·n**

afishó·n *vt* to post [a notice]

afjón = **afíon**

afjóntë *adj (i)* opiate

afoní *nf* [*Med*] aphonia

aforfé *nf* [*Sport*] forfeit

aforistík *adj* aphoristic

aforizëm *nm* aphorism

aforós *nm* excommunication

AFP *abbrev (French)* <**Agencie France Presse** French News Service

áfras *adv* closely

afratë
 I § *nf* facial bleaching lotion (usually made of bitter mercury chloride) used by women
 II § *adj* very bitter

afrází *adv* = **afras**

afresë *nf (Reg)* likeness

afrésk *nm* [*Art*] fresco

afrí *nf* **1** kinship, kindred **2** affinity, close similarity **3** kinfolk, kin

afrikán *adj, n* African

afrikáns *n* Afrikaans

afrikáte *nf* [*Ling*] affricate

Afríkë *nf* Africa

afrím *nm ger* **1** <**afro·n, afro·het 2** bringing near, approach, contact, association, mutual understanding **3** access; affinity **4** [*Cine*] dollying-in
 ∘ **afrim optik** [*Cine*] zoom-in

Afrím *nm* Afrim (male name)

afrí·shëm *adj (i) (Elev)* **1** affined **2** [*Ling*] related **3** [*Math*] affine; similar

afrísht *adv* approximately

afrítje *nf (Reg)* coming near, approaching

afró *OR* **áfro** *pcl* about; nearly, almost

afró·het *vpr* **1** to get closer: approach **2** *(Fig)* to become close to someone; endear oneself **3** to resemble, become similar **4** to agree
 ∘ **Afrohu!** [*Mil*] Close ranks! Close up!
 ∘ **nuk <> afro·het as te gishti i këmbës** doesn't hold a candle to <>

afró·n
 I § *vt* **1** to bring [ ] near/nearer/together; hand [ ] over **2** to attract
 II § *vi* = **afro·het**

afro-amerikán *adj, n* Afro-American

afro-aziatík *adj* Afro-Asiatic

Afrovítii *nm with fem agreement* Aphrodite

afruar *adj (i)* **1** brought near, standing near, bunched, adjacent = **afërt 2** approachable, affable = **afrueshëm 3** approximate = **përafërt**

afrués
 I § *adj* **1** converging, convergent **2** approachable, affable
 II § *n* person or thing that conveys an object closer to the point of work

afrue·shëm *adj(i)* **1** approachable, affable **2** *(Colloq)* (of a beverage) pleasant

afrueshmëri *nf (Book)* friendliness, sociability

afsh *nm* **1** vapor; haze **2** strong aroma **3** *(Fig)* inner fire, ardor, passion (including sexual passion) **4** readiness for impregnation or seeding **5** fumes, smoke

afshët *adj (i)* giving off an aroma

afshí *nf* current of air given off by something hot or cold, vapor, haze

afshó·het *vpr* to become hot to the point of giving off heat/vapor

afshó·n *vi* to give off heat/vapor

áfta *np* [*Veter*] foot-and-mouth disease

áftë
 I § *adj (i)* capable, able, fit, qualified, sufficient
 II § *nf* [*Med*] oral blister or lesion

áftër *nf (Old)* wick-holder in an oil lamp

aftësí *nf* capability, competence, ability; aptitude
 ∘ **aftësi prodhuese** productive capacity

aftësím *nm* **1** <**aftëso·n, aftëso·het 2** training, qualification

aftësísht *adv* skillfully, capably

aftësó·het *vpr* to gain proficiency/mastery

aftësó·n *vt* to train, make [ ] capable

aftëzím *nm* [*Veter*] vaccination to control epidemic of foot-and-mouth disease

aftím *nm* humid weather

aftós *adj* afflicted by oral blisters

aftós·et *vpr* to become afflicted with oral blisters

ag *nm* **1** pre-dawn light, daybreak: dawn **2** half-darkness, mistiness **3** *(Fig)* dawning, beginning *4 (Reg)* black mark around the eyes of the dead
 ∘ **agu i syrit** the pupil of the eye

aga nm **1** Ottoman nobleman (ranking below bey) with a landed estate **2** rich man; honorary title held by such a man; title of respect for a man **3** (Old) clan chief **4** (Pej) pretentious or officious person **5** small landlord, gentleman

agalla·r nm **1** [Bot] herbaceous perennial with a long stem and long fuzzy leaves; it grows in meadows or gravelly soil and blooms in the summer ***2** any grassy meadow plant taller than the others

agalla·rë np < aga

agallari nf collec agas taken as a whole

agalle·shë nf = ageshë

agallëk nm (np ~ qe) **1** the state of being or living like an aga **2** (Pej) aga-like behavior

***aga·t** I § nm OR **aga·të** II § nf agate

aga·ve nf [Bot] agave
  ○ **agave amerikane** [Bot] century plant *Agave americana*

agdë nf depilatory made of sugar syrup and eggwhite

***agenci** nf (Old) = agjenci

***agenoj** nm = agjerim

AGERPRESS abbrev (Rumanian) < **Agentia Romana de Presa** Romanian Press Agency

age·shë nf wife of an aga

agë
  I § nf with masc agreement **1** = aga **2** [Folklore] brave and valiant battlemate
  II § adj *dusky, dark

agërsha·k nm (Reg) weight at the end of a drop spindle to add inertia: whorl

***agëzotllë·k** nm (np ~ qe) = agzotës

agim nm ger **1** = ago·n **2** dawn; daybreak
  ○ **agim polar** aurora borealis

Agim nm Agim (popular male name)

agimo·r adj (Poet) of or pertaining to dawn

agim·pru·rës adj (Poet) dawn-bringing

agim·ta·r adj (Poet) happening at dawn

AGIP abbrev (Italian) < **Azienda Generale Italiana Petroli** [Hist] Italian petroleum enterprise

aglomera·t nm (mineral) agglomerate

aglomerim nm ger < aglomero·n

aglomero··n vt to form a mineral agglomerate by volcanic action

agmi
  I § nf pre-dawn light; glow
  II § adj (Fig) kind, generous, compassionate
  ○ **agmi njeri** kind and generous person, wonderful person

agnosticizëm nm [Phil] agnosticism

agnu·she nf [Bot] yellow gentian (Gentiana lutea)

aglo··n vi to become morning/daylight: dawn

agoni nf death agony, death throes; agony

ago·r nm facial expression

agr. abbrev < **agronom** agronomist

agra·r adj agrarian; farming

agra·re nf (Colloq) agrarian reform

agraro-industria·l adj = bujqësor-industria·l

agrega·t nm **1** [Tech] aggregate **2** aggregation of mechanical or administrative components with a common purpose **3** mineral aggregate; soil aggregate

agreme·nt nm [Dipl] diplomatic accreditation

***agre·p** nm **1** = akre·p **2** fish hook **3** crusty person

agresio·n nm aggression

agresi·iv adj **1** aggressive **2** [Spec] corrosive; erosive

agreso·r
  I § n aggressor, attacker
  II § adj aggressor

agrikulturë nf agriculture

agro formative prefix agro-, agri-

agro·biologji nf agrobiology

AGROEKSPORT [agro-export] abbrev agency for the export of agricultural and food products

agro·fond nm [Agr] agricultural methods that determine the productivity of an area

agro·kimi nf agrochemistry, soil chemistry

agro·kimik adj agrochemical

agro·komple·ks nm complex of services dedicated to improving crop production

agro·logji nf agrology

agro·mekanikë nf agricultural mechanics, technology dealing with farm machinery

Agro·n nm Agron (popular male name)

agro·no·m n agronomist

agro·nomi nf agronomy

agro·nomik adj agronomic, agronomical

agro·r nm roof rafter

agro·rregullo·re nf set of technical guidelines for the cultivation of crops

agro·teknik adj agrotechnical

agro·teknikë nf agricultural technology

agro·zootekni nf the science and technology of agriculture and animal husbandry

agru·me np citrus, citrus fruit

agrume·rri·tës n citrus grower

agrume·shte nf citrus grove

agrumi·shtë nf = agrumi·shte

agrumo·r adj suitable for citrus growing; planted with citrus

agrumo·re nf = agrumi·shte

agsho·l nm break of dawn

agu·em·it nn (të) (Reg Gheg) dawning

aguli·çe nf [Bot] primrose (Primula vulgaris)

aguli·çore np [Bot] primrose family (Primulaceae)

agull nm **1** pre-dawn light, twilight **2** half-darkness, mistiness

agull·a·ç adj (Reg) unripe, immature

agull·im nm dawn, daybreak

agull·imë nf pale light of dawn

agullo··het vpr to become dim/clouded/veiled

agullo··n vi to dawn

agullo·r adj (Poet) of dawn, auroral

***aguri·çkë** nf (Colloq) vegetable

aguri·dh adj unripe; immature

aguri·dh·e nf **1** unripe grape **2** (Fig) immature person

***agusti·mje** nf defense, justification

***agusto·n·et** vpr to justify/excuse oneself

agushi nf = zagushi

agu·shtë adj (i) hot and humid, sultry, oppressively warm

agzo·t
  I § nm (Old) fine gunpowder used with old flintrock weapons: priming powder, tinder match
  II § adj (Fig) **1** quick as a flash **2** brave

agzo·tës nm powder chamber in a gun

***agzo·zë** nf blindworm, slowworm = bollëve·rbët

*agjapis· *vt* to love

agjenci *nf* agency

agjensi *nf* agency

agje·nt *nm* 1 agent 2 *(Pej)* foreign spy; foreign collaborator 3 *[Spec]* factor; chemical reagent

agjenturë *nf* spy agency; network of spies; espionage forces

agjenturo·r *adj* agential

*agje·r *nm* donkey, ass

agjeru·arshëm *adj (i)* pertaining to fasting

agjëre·së *nf [Relig]* = agjërim

agjërim *nm ger* 1 < agjëro·n 2 *[Relig]* fast, fasting

agjëro·n *vi [Relig]* to fast
  ◦ **agjëro·n ditën e vjedh· natën** "fast during the day and steal at night" *(Pej)* to be a hypocrite

agjëronjë *nf(Reg) [Ornit]* common heron = gatë

*agjin = agjër

agjiro·n *vi* = agjëro·n

*agjironjë *nf [Ornit]* = agjëronjë

agjitacio·n *nm* 1 political agitation 2 *(Colloq)* attempt to persuade

agjitativ *adj* 1 politically agitative 2 *(Pej)* attempting to persuade with empty words 3 agitative

agjitato·r *n* political agitator

agjito·n *vt* to galvanize [ ] into political activity: agitate

agjitpro·p *nm* short for "agitation-propaganda"

*agjivonjë *nf* = agjëronjë

*agjo·sh *nm* gutter = ago·sh

ah· *vi* to sigh "ah" as an expression of emotion

*ah·et *vpr* < ah·

ah

  I § *interj* 1 expresses pain/grief/disappointment: oh no! 2 expresses anger or fright: oh! 3 expresses rejection: eah! 4 expresses pleased surprise/delight: ah!

  II § *nm* 1 soulful cry to express unhappiness/surprise/joy 2 curse, damnation

ah *nm* 1 *[Bot]* beech *(Fagus sylvatica L.)* 2 = hak 3 reverberation, echo
  ◦ **ah i bardhë** *[Bot]* white hornbeam

aha *interj* 1 expresses sudden discovery, aha! 2 expresses ironic disbelief, yeah sure! 3 expression confirming one's belief in the impossibility of some action, oh yeah?!

aha *onomat* sound of yawning

*ahçi *nm* = akçi

*ahçillëk *nm (np ~ qe)* = akçillëk

aheng *nm (np ~ gje) (Colloq)* 1 musical revelry, including singing, dancing, and instrumental music; party with musical fun 2 *(Pej)* unrestrained revelry with excessive drinking and disorderly conduct 3 folk band that plays the music for a party 4 urban folk music (as opposed to traditional folk music of rural areas and to epic and ritual songs), popular music

ahengxhi *nm (np ~ nj) (Colloq)* 1 performer in a folk band 2 participant in folk revelry

*ahe·nk *nm* = aheng

ahe·re *adv (Colloq)* = atëhe·re

*ahe·rshëm *adj (i)* contemporary, of that time

*ah·ër *nm* = ahur

*ahie·ra *adv (Reg)* = atëhe·rë

ahime *interj (Book)* alas!

ahishte *nf* = ahishtë

ahishtë *nf* beech forest

ahisho·r *nm* beech grove

*ahma·k *nm* stupid fool

*ahma·rr = hakma·rr

*ahme·rr·et *vt* = hakme·rr·et

ahmë *nf* soulful cry expressing suffering/surprise/joy

*ahmo·r = hakmor

aho··n *vi* 1 to express suffering by sighing "ah"; groan; suffer *2 to grieve, mourn

aho·re *np [Bot]* beech family *Fagaceae*

ahra *np* < ahër

aht *nm* 1 sigh, deep moan; swearing arising out of spiritual suffering 2 final gasp before dying 3 sorrow, misery *4 = afsh

ah·të *adj (i)* of beechwood: beechen

ahu *interj* expresses indifference or contempt: pooh!

*ahullim *nm ger* < ahullo·n

*ahullo·n *vi* to rumble/rage (said of storms)

ahur *nm* 1 ground floor of house where livestock and their feed are kept 2 ground floor storage for dairy products as well as tools and firewood 3 cellar 4 stable, barn, shed
  ◦ **ahur derrash** pigsty

ai

  I § distal 3rd sg masc determiner that
  II § distal 3rd sg masc pron that one, he, it
  ◦ **ai i hurdhës** *(Colloq Euph)* Satan, the Devil
  ◦ **ai i lumit** *(Euph)* the Devil, Satan
  ◦ **Ai mulli s'e bluan dot atë misër.** "That mill cannot grind that corn at all." { }'s day is over. { } *is* over the hill. { } *has run* out of gas.
  ◦ **ai i rripave** *(Euph)* the devil
  ◦ **Ai stan atë bulmet ka.** "That herdsman's camp has that dairy product." What would you expect from people at a place like that?!

*Aidin *nm* Aidin (male name)

*aikugjë *nf (Reg Arb) [Ornit]* eagle

AIPA *abbrev (Italian)* < **Azienda Italiana Petroli Albania** *[Hist]* Italian Agency for Petroleum in Albania

aj

  I § *interj* 1 hey! 2 = haj
  II § *pron* *= ai

aj *nm* 1 biting, bite 2 mouthful, bite

*aja·n *nm* local town official under the Ottoman Empire: mayor

aja·r

  I § *mn (Old)* 1 large basket for holding or measuring grain 2 *(Colloq)* equalization of weight
  II § *adv* in balance, balanced

aja·smë *nf* mumps

aja·zmë *nf* 1 *[Relig]* holy water 2 ritual of preparing or sprinkling holy water 3 *[Bot]* = mendër 4 excursion destination

a·jdës *nm [Bot]* laburnum, Scotch laburnum *(Laburnum alpinum, Cytisus alpinus)*

*aje *nf* swelling

aje·r *nm* air
  ◦ **Ajri!** Air raid!
  ◦ **aje·r i pastër** open air; pure air
  ◦ **aje·r i prishur** foul air
  ◦ **aje·r i rëndë** stale air

aje·rfry·r·ës *nm* inflator

aje·rfto·h·ës

  I § *adj* air cooling; air-conditioning
  II § *nm* air cooler; air conditioner

ajërmatës
I § *nm* aerometer, air gauge
II § *adj* aerometric

ajërngrohës
I § *nm* air heater
II § *adj* air-heating

ajërngjeshës *nm* air compressor

ajërnxjerrës
I § *nm* device for extracting air: air pump, air exhauster
II § *adj* of or pertaining to the extraction of air

ajërpastrues *nm* air filter

ajërshpërndarëse *nf* [*Agr*] air blower (for drying hay): air manifold

ajërt *adj (i)* airy

ajërtransportueshëm *adj (i)* transportable by air

ajërthithëse *nf* intake fan

ajëz *nm* = ajth

ajgeto·n *vt* to espy, discern, descry

*****aji** = ai

ajkë
I § *nf* 1 fat-rich top layer that forms on a boiled or fermented liquid: cream *2 *(Reg)* [*Dairy*] curds resulting from churning fermented milk: clotted cream 3 *(Fig)* best part: cream, elite 4 hair/wool grease
II § *adj* greasy

ajkëmatës *nm* [*Dairy*] instrument for measuring butterfat content of milk: creamometer

ajkësinë *nf* swamp, swampland

ajkët *adj (i)* creamy thick

ajkëto·het *vpr* to become thickened

ajkëto·n
I § *vt* to thicken [a liquid], make [] thicker and more dense
II § *vi* 1 to secrete skin oil 2 to drip in thick drops

ajkëtor *nm* [*Food*] cream roll

ajkëtore *nf* [*Dairy*] 1 apparatus for separating cream from milk: cream separator, creamer 2 vat for collecting cream 3 *(Old)* dairy, creamery

ajkëtyrë *nf* = ajkësinë

ajko·het *vpr* to become greasy (said of hair or wool)

ajko·n *vt* to make [leather/hair] greasy; make [] dirty, soil

ajkore *nf* = ajkëtor

ajkos·et *vpr* to become creamy thick and sweet; become mushy

ajkosur *adj (i)* creamy thick and sweet; mushy

ajnik *nm* *(Reg)* gentle sea breeze

ajo *distal 3rd sg fem determiner* 1 that, that one, she, it 2 *(Euph)* (used to avoid mentioning a taboo referent) That One
 ○ **Ajo baltë për atë mur është.** *(Pejor)* The devil has found the right mate.
 ○ **ajo botë** *(Euph)* life after death: the next world
 ○ **ajo e fëmijëve** *(Euph)* epilepsy
 ○ **ajo jetë** *(Euph)* life after death: the next life, the afterlife
 ○ **ajo e kalit** *(Euph)* sty (in the eye)
 ○ **Ajo kokë, atë feste do** "That head wants that fez." *(Prov)* You get what you deserve.
 ○ **ajo punë** *(Euph)* epilepsy
 ○ **ajo e tokës** *(Euph Colloq)* [*Med*] epilepsy

ajo·het *vpr* to swell up with water

ajo·n *vt* to swell wood with water (in order to seal it against leakage)

ajodhímë *nf* [*Relig*] apse of an Orthodox church

*****Ajodhímë** *nf* [*Relig*] Holy Sacrament

*****ajraní** *nf* = aeroplan

*****ajraníe** *nf* = aeroplan

*****ajrët** *adj (i)* = ajërt

ajrí *nf (Poet)* = ajër

ajrím *nm ger* 1 <ajro·n, ajro·het 2 aeration; ventilation

ajris· *vt* = ajro·n

ajrísje *nf ger* = ajrím

ajro·het *vpr* to air out; become well-ventilated

ajro·n *vt* 1 to air, air out []; ventilate; aerate 2 [*Publ*] to space out [type/words] (in order to improve legibility): lead out [], space (in typing)

*****ajroaníje** *nf* = aeroplan

ajrolundrues *nm (Old)* = aeronaut

*****ajrom** *adv* = avrom

*****ajropllan** *nm* = aeroplan

ajror
I § *adj* of air, air, aerial; airborne
II § *nm (Book)* airplane

ajrore *nf* ventilator

ajros· *vt* = ajro·n

ajros·et *vpr* = ajro·het

ajrosje *nf ger* = ajrím

ajrosur *adj (i)* = ajruar

*****ajrshëm** *adj (i)* = ajërt

ajruar *adj (i)* aerated, airy, having clean air

ajrues
I § *adj* serving to ventilate/aerate
II § *nm* ventilator, aerator

ajsberg *nm* iceberg

ajth *nm* 1 core of a kernel of grain; flour that has been sifted through the finest sieve 2 *(Fig)* core, essence, quintessence

*****ajthët** *adj (i)* = hajthëm

ajugë *nf* [*Bot*] bugle *(Ajuga)*
 ○ **ajugë e lindjes** [*Bot*] eastern bugle *Ajuga orientalis*
 ○ **ajugë zvarranike** [*Bot*] bugle *Ajuga reptans*

ajzberg *nm* = ajsberg

AKA *abbrev* <Artileria kundërajrore [*Mil*] antiaircraft artillery

akacie *nf* [*Bot*] 1 acacia *(Acacia)* 2 locust (tree) *Robinia pseudoacacia* L.

akacje *nf* = akacie

akad. *abbrev* <akademik academic (as a title)

akademi *nf* academy

akademik
I § *nm* member of an academy; academician
II § *adj* academic; in an academic style

akademikisht *adv* academically

akademist *nm* 1 academy student 2 one who adopts or acts in an academic style

akademizëm *nm* academicism

akantë *nf* [*Bot*] acanthus *Acanthus* = dashtër

akantore *nf* [*Bot*] acanthus family *Acanthaceae*

akaparim *nm ger (Pej)* <akaparo·n

akaparo·n *vt (Pej)* to hoard; monopolize

akaparues *nm (Pej)* hoarder; monopolizer

akare *nf* [*Invert*] mite

*****akari** *nf* = akare

*****akatastasí** *nf* disorder

*akc- = aks-

akçe'she nf (Colloq Old) female cook

akçi' nm (Colloq Old) cook

*akçia'ne nf = akçiha'ne

akçia'sh nm [Food] sweet made of rice, beans, walnuts and dried figs

akçiha'ne nf (Colloq Obs) small and informal restaurant; kitchen

*akçillëk nm kitchen, cooking (as a trade or occupation)

ake'n nm [Bot] achene

akë formative prefix indicates vagueness of reference

akëci'l n determiner (definite case forms only) some _ or other, a certain _

akëku' adv somewhere or other, here and there

akëku'sh pron someone or other, so and so, a certain _

a'kël nm alcove

akëqy'sh adv in some way or other, somehow or other

a'kër nf acre

*akëro'·n vt = hakrro'·n

a'kës nm [Bot] strawflower (Helichrysum)

akëseci'l n determiner (definite case forms only) one or another, one _ or the other

akëseku' adv = akëku'

akëseku'sh pron = akëku'sh

*akështo'·n vi to be worthy

*akështua'r adj (i) worthy

a'kët adj (i) 1 thick (said of liquids) *2 dense, compact

*akika't adj = hakika't

*akile'gë nf [Bot] = akuile'gjë

akin'xhi' nm (np ~ nj) [Hist] soldier in the shock troops of the Ottoman Empire: mounted scout

*akki'r adv somewhere

aklimatizi'm nm ger (Book) 1 <aklimatizo'·n, aklimatizo'·het 2 acclimatization

aklimatizo'·het vpr to become acclimated

aklimatizo'·n vt to acclimatize

akllaç nm slab of ice

*akllai' nf = okllai'

*akllaje nf = okllai'

akllaji' nf = okllai'

*aklle'k nm rouge

*akllo'j nm = okllai'

*ako'lle nf circle, turning/spinning around; hoop

ako'ma adv still, yet; even; still more
   ○ akoma edhe pak a little more
   ○ akoma ti?! 1 are you still at it?; are you still harping on that? 2 you bet your life!

*akompanji'm nm ger 1 <akompanjo'·n [Mus] 2 accompaniment = shoqëri'm

*akompanjo'·n vt [Mus] to accompany [] (on a musical instrument) = shoqëro'·n

akompji'm nm [Spec] connection, coupling

akoni't nm [Bot] monkshood Aconitum

akopju'ar adj (i) [Spec] coupled

ako'rd nm 1 [Mus] accord, consonance; chord 2 [Econ] business contract, business deal 3 (Book) agreement, accord

akordi'm nm ger 1 <akordo'·n 2 [Ling] grammatical agreement = përshta'tje

akordo'·het vpr to enter into accord, become consonant

akordo'·n vt 1 to tune; tune [] in 2 to give, grant: accord 3 (Book) to bring [] into accord, make [] consonant, bring [] into harmony
   ○ i akordo·n telat me [] "bring one's strings in tune with []" (Pej) to make a deal with []

akordu'es nm tuner

akraba' nf (Colloq Old) 1 kith and kin 2 (Pej) go-between who obtains favors for one through friendship with someone else

akraballe'k nm (np ~ qe) (Pej) favoritism towards family and friends, nepotism; unwholesome friendship

*akra'pje nf = akro'pje

akrediti'm nm ger [Dipl] <akredito'·n

akrediti'v nm [Fin] (commercial) letter of credit

akredito'·n vt [Dipl] to accredit as a diplomat

akre'p nm 1 [Invert] scorpion 2 indicator needle (in measuring instruments); clock/watch hand 3 (Pej) stingy person 4 (Pej) sneaky and treacherous person

akrepta'r nm [Hist] billman, soldier armed with a bill

A'krë nf Acre

akrili'k
   I § adj acrylic
   II § nm acrylic fiber

*akri'm nm ger = hakërri'm

akrinjo'lle nf [Bot] bittersweet, woody nightshade (Solanum dulcamara)

*akro'·n vt = akrro'·n

akrobaci' nf acrobatics

akrobaci'ra np <akrobaci' deceptive tricks: swindling, cheating

akroba't nm acrobat

akrobati'k adj 1 acrobatic 2 (Fig Pej) deceptively clever

*akro'pje nf thriving state, prosperity

akro'pol nm acropolis

*akro'sur adj (i) = hakërru'ar

*akrua'r adj (i) = hakërru'ar

*akrr = hakërr'

aks nm 1 axis 2 axle 3 metal shaft (in a machine)
   ○ aks me brigje camshaft
   ○ aks me gunga camshaft
   ○ aks i pasmë rear axle
   ○ aks i përparmë front axle

*aksa'fna adv suddenly, unexpectedly

akseleri'm nm ger 1 [Spec] <akselero'·n 2 acceleration

akselero'·n vt [Spec] to accelerate

akselero'gra'f nm [Spec] accelerograph

akseleru'es
   I § adj [Spec] accelerating
   II § nm [Spec] accelerator

akse'nt = akce'nt

aksepto'r nm [Phys] acceptor

akseso'r nm (Book) accessory

*aksë
   I § adj (i) worthy, apt, able, fit
   II § nf * = aks

*aksëm adj (i) deft, agile; swift, speedy; bold, confident

*aksi' nf worth, value; capability, capacity

aksia'l adj axial

aks·ial·isht *adv* axially

aks·ial·ite't *nm* axiality

***aksid** *nm (Old)* = acid

akside'nt *nm* accident

akside'ntal *adj* accidental

aksidental·isht *adv* accidentally

aksiom·atik *adj* axiomatic

aksiome *nf* axiom

aksio'n *nm* **1** group work project carried out by volunteers **2** [*Mil*] military action **3** [*Sport*] (tactical) play **4** action, undertaking **5** [*Fin*] share of stock

aksion·ar
  I § *adj* [*Fin*] pertaining to stocks
  II § *nm* [*Fin*] stockholder

aksion·ist
  I § *n* **1** volunteer in a work project **2** [*Fin*] stockholder, shareholder
  II § *adj* pertaining to volunteer work projects

***akso** *nf* = aks

aks·or *adj* axial

***aksua** *nm* = aks

aksh *nm* [*Bot*] lesser centaury

ak·sh *determiner* a certain __, some __

aksha'm *nm (Old)* **1** = mbrëmje **2** [*Relig*] Moslem evening prayer

***akshëm** *adj (i)* = aksëm

akt *nm* **1** [*Theat*] act (of a play) **2** (*Book*) act, action **3** [*Offic*] official decision/act; official document; certificate ***4** (*Reg*) [*Art*] nude

akt·akuzë *nf* **1** [*Law*] indictment, charge; information **2** (*Fig*) accusation

akt·bes·im *nm* (*Book*) declaration of faith or doctrine

akt·da'lje *nf* [*Offic*] receipt for goods from a storehouse, warehouse receipt

akt·deleg·im *nm* [*Law*] proof of delegated authority

akt·detyr·im *nm* [*Law*] official statement of duties, charge

akt·dën·im *nm* [*Law*] sentence by a court

akt·dëshm·i *nf* [*Law*] transcript of testimony

akt·dorëzan·i *nf (Old)* [*Law*] surety bond

akt·dorëz·im *nm* report of transfer; transfer deed

***akterma** *nf* transshipment

***akte** *adj (i)* = aket

akt·gjyk·im *nm* [*Law*] document containing court decision, judgment

akt·het·im [*akt-he-tim*] *nm* [*Law*] document containing the findings of a judicial investigation

***akti** *nf (Reg)* density, compactness

***aktif** *adj* = aktiv

***akt·im** *nm (Reg)* compression

akt·in *nm* [*Invert*] sea anemone *Actinia*

aktiv
  I § *adj* **1** active, energetic **2** executive **3** [*Fin*] showing a profit, in the black
  II § *nm* **1** assembly of representative delegates of interest groups **2** [*Fin*] assets
  ○ **aktivi e pasivi** credit and debit

aktiv·im *nm ger* **1** < aktivo'·n **2** [*Spec*] (chemical) activation

aktiv·ist *n* activist; active participant in an organization; elected delegate of an interest group to a representative assembly

aktiv·isht *adv* actively, energetically

aktiv·ite't *nm* activity

aktiv·iz·im *nm ger* < aktivizo'·n, aktivizo·het

aktiv·izo'·het *vpr* to take active part; become activated/energized

aktiv·izo'·n *vt* to activate, energize; arouse [] to activism; put [] to work, put [] into play

aktiv·o'·n *vt* [*Spec*] to activate chemically

akt·jetërs·im *nm (Old)* [*Law*] transfer deed

akt·kontroll *nm* [*Offic*] record of an official investigation

akt·lidhje *nf* [*Offic*] certificate of association

akt·lindje *nf* [*Offic*] birth certificate

akt·lir·im *nm* [*Hist*] bill of manumission

akt·martes·ë *nf* [*Offic*] marriage certificate

akt·marrëveshje *nf (Offic)* contract certificate

akt·ndarje *nf* [*Offic*] divorce certificate; legal separation papers

akt·njoftim *nm* [*Offic*] affidavit

***akto'·n** *vt (Reg)* = ajketo'·n

aktor *n* [*Theat*] actor
  ○ **aktor kryesor** [*Cine*] actor in a leading role

***aktoreshë** *nf* = aktore

akt·padi *nf* [*Law*] legal complaint

akt·pajt·im *nm* [*Law*] legal settlement

akt·peshim *nm* [*Offic*] weight certificate (used to keep track of monthly weights of calves, pigs, etc.)

akt·përfaqës·im *nm* [*Law*] power of attorney, certification of legal representation

akt·pronës·i *nf (Old)* [*Offic*] seizin, certificate of ownership, title deed

akt·pun·im *nm* [*Offic*] certificate of completion of work

akt·shitje *nf* [*Offic*] bill of sale

akt·shtojcë *nf* [*Offic*] legal addendum, legal supplement

aktual *adj* current, contemporary; of current relevance

aktual·isht *adv* at present, presently, currently

aktual·ite't *nm* **1** present-day situation, present circumstances **2** relevance to the present day

***aktue·shëm** *adj (i)* compressible

akt·vdekje *nf* [*Offic*] death certificate

akt·vendim *nm* [*Offic*] written resolution

akt·vërtetim *nm* [*Offic*] certificate

akt·zotër·im *nm* [*Offic*] deed of title

akth *nm (Reg)* [*Bot*] = makth

akuarel *nm* [*Art*] water color (referring to the paints, the method, or the resulting picture)

akuarel·ist *n* [*Art*] painter in water colors: watercolorist

akuarium *nm* aquarium

akuile·gj *nf* [*Bot*] columbine *Aquilegia*

***akul** *nm (Reg)* hunter's trap, snare

akull
  I § *nm (np ~ j)* ice
  II § *adj* ice cold, cold, frozen; cold (in feeling); spotlessly clean, spick-and-span
  III § *adv, pcl* very, quite, very nicely, very beautifully, purely
  ○ **qiri akulli** icicle

akull·aç *nm* ice floe

akull·çar·ës *nm* ice axe

akull·emë *adj (i)* **1** extremely cold, quite cold **2** (*Fig*) dull (said of a cutting edge), not very sharp

akullim *nm ger* **1** <akullo·*n*, akullo·*het* **2** = akullimë **3** [*Geol*] glaciation

akullimë *nf* extreme cold, frost

akullirë *nf* = akullimë

akullishtë *nf* **1** area covered by ice **2** piece of ice; icicle; ice floe

akullmbajtëse *nf* icebox

akullnajë *nf* glacier

akullnajor *adj* glacial

akullo·het *vpr* **1** to become frozen; get very cold **2** to ice up

akullo·n
  I § *vt* **1** to freeze, make [ ] into ice, chill **2** (*Fig*) to petrify, stun
  II § *vi* to freeze up, become ice

akullor *adj* **1** (*Book*) icy, extremely cold; glacial *2* (*Old*) = akullnajë

akullore *nf* [*Dairy*] ice cream

akulloreshitës *nf* [*Dairy*] ice cream peddler

akullsi *nf* (*Book*) extreme cold; something cold as ice

*akullsinë *nf* hoarfrost

akullt *adj (i)* of ice, icy, frigid

akullthyes *adj* ice-breaking

akullthyese *nf* ice-breaking ship, ice-breaker

akulluar *adj (i)* **1** frozen; numb **2** (*Fig*) in a state of emotional shock

akullues *adj* freezing

akullzim *nm ger* = akullim

akumulator *nm* storage battery; accumulator

akumulim *nm ger* **1** <akumulo·*n*, akumulo·*het* **2** (*Book*) accumulation

akumulo·het *vpr* (*Book*) to increase gradually: accumulate

akumulo·n *vt* (*Book*) to accumulate

akupunkturë *nf* [*Med*] acupuncture

akustik *adj* **1** acoustic **2** acoustical **3** resounding

akustikë *nf* acoustics

akut *adj* [*Med*] acute (illness)

*akuzatë *nf* accusation

akuzativ *adj, nm* [*Ling*] accusative

akuzë *nf* **1** [*Law*] indictment **2** complainant **3** accusation

akuzo·n *vt* [*Law*] to accuse

akuzuar *nm (i)* [*Law*] the accused, defendant

akuzues
  I § *nm* [*Law*] accuser, complainant, complaining party
  II § *adj* accusing

*akzot *nm* = agzot

*ala *conj* still, yet = hala

Alabamë *nf* Alabama

alabastër *nm* alabaster

alamet
  I § *nm* (*Colloq*) **1** personal calamity **2** impolite insult
  II § *adj* emphasizes the praiseworthy quality of the following noun: what a wonderful _ **Alamet burri ka qenë!** What a wonderful man he was!
  ○ **alamet dasme** a fantastic wedding
  ○ **alamet djali** that's some boy!
  ○ **alamet shtëpie** a honey of a house

*alamidh *nm* [*Ichth*] Atlantic bonito (*Sarda sarda*) = palamid

*alanit·et *vt* to become worn out from crying; become faint from terror

alarm *nm* alarm

alarmant *adj* alarming

alarmist *n* alarmist

alarmo·het *vpr* to become alarmed

alarmo·n *vt* to alarm

alarmuar *adj (i)* troubled, anxious, uneasy

alarmues
  I § *adj* alarming, disturbing, unsettling
  II § *n* = alarmist

Alaskë *nf* Alaska

Alban *nm* Alban (male name)

albanë *np* [*Hist*] an Illyrian tribe located in central Albania

albanolog *n* Albanologist, student of Albanology

albanologji *nf* scholarly field concerned with Albanians, their language, literature, and culture

albanologjik *adj* Albanological, of or pertaining to Albanology

Albanopolis *nm* [*Hist*] Albanopolis

albatros *nm* [*Ornit*] albatross

albër *nf* **1** thin sliver or chip, wood splinter **2** piece of detached skin **3** thin membrane covering newborn: caul

albërishtë *nf* wood-chopping place where wood chips collect; pile of wood chips on the ground

albicie *nf* **1** [*Bot*] albizzia, silk tree *Albizzia* **2** silk-tree albizzia, silk tree *Albizzia julibrissin*

ALBIMPORT *abbrev* Albanian import agency

ALBKONTROLL *abbrev* agency that regulates Albanian export and import

ALBTRANSPORT *abbrev* Albanian air transport agency

ALBTURIZEM *abbrev* Albanian tourism agency

album *nm* album

albuminë *nf* albumin, albumen

albuminoz *adj* albuminous

alburë *nf* ship mast

alç *nm* [*Zool*] elk, moose (*Alces alces, Alces palmatus*)

aleancë *nf* alliance

aleat
  I § *nm* ally
  II § *adj* allied; of or pertaining to an alliance

alebardë *nf* [*Hist*] halberd

alegori *nf* allegory

alegorik *adj* allegorical

alegro
  I § *adv* [*Mus*] allegro
  II § *nf* [*Mus*] allegro piece or movement

Aleks *nm* male name

Aleksandri *nf* Alexandria

alem *nm* (*Old Colloq*) world; mankind
  ○ **alemi e polemi** the whole world; all mankind

*aleman = alleman

*Alemanjë = Allemanjë

alergji *nf* allergy

alergjik *nf* allergic

alet *nm* (*Colloq Old*) **1** tool **2** weapon, arm

alezator *nm* [*Tech*] reamer

alezim *nm ger* [*Tech*] <alezo·*n*

alezo·n *vt* [*Tech*] to ream

*alë *nf* = halë

*alëçis· *vi* = allestis·

*alëm *nm* 1 unction, ointment 2 union

*alës *nm* chain

*alësivë *nf* = alisivë

alfa *indecl fem* the Greek letter alpha

alfabet *nm* alphabet
 ○ alfabeti telegrafik Morse code

*alfabetar *adj* = alfabetik

alfabetik *adj* alphabetical, in alphabetical order

alfabetikisht *adv* alphabetically, in alphabetical order

alfabetor *adj* alphabetic, of or pertaining to the alphabet

alfë *nf (Book)* 1 alpha (the Greek letter) 2 *(Fig)* the beginning, starting point

algë *nf* 1 *[Bot]* alga 2 pine cone

algë-furçë *nf* *[Bot]* kind of brown alga *Cladostephus hirsutus*

algë-gur *nm* *[Bot]* an incrusting calcareous red alga *Lithophyllum papillosa*

algoritëm *nm* algorithm

algjebër *nf* algebra

algjebrik *adj* algebraic

Algjer *nm* Algiers

Algjeri *nf* Algeria

algjerian *adj, n* Algerian

Ali *nm* Ali (male name)

*aliancë *nf* = aleancë

*aliat *nm* = aleat

aliazh *nm* *[Tech]* alloy

alibi *nf* *[Law]* alibi

aligator *nm* *[Zool]* alligator

*alijer = halijer

aliluja *interj, nf* hallelujah

alimente *np* alimony

alimurg *nm* liquid squeezed from olive mash

*aliq *nm* = haliç

alisivë *nf* lye

alismatore *np* *[Bot]* alisma family *Alismataceae*

aliteracion *nm* *[Lit]* alliteration

alitirim *nm* *[Tech]* < alitiro·n

alitiro·n *vt* *[Tech]* to calorize

alivan *nm* faint, swoon = fikët

alivanos·et *vpr* to faint

alivanosur *adj (i)* in a faint, fainted

aliver *nm* 1 *(Anat)* reticulum (of ruminant animals) = nanuq *2 rainbow

*alivert *nm* elevator = ashensor

alizarinë *nf* alizarin

alk *nm* *(Old)* = krijesë

*alkolizinë *nf* = alkoolizëm

alkool *nm* alcohol

alkoolik *adj* of or pertaining to alcohol, alcoholic

alkoolist *n* alcohol addict, alcoholic

alkoolizëm *nm* alcoholism

alkoolizim *nm ger* < alkoolizo·n, alkoolizo·het

alkoolizo·het *vpr* 1 to become an alcoholic 2 to turn into alcohol, become alcoholic

alkoolizo·n *vt* to mix [] with [] alcohol, add alcohol to [a liquid]

alkoolmatës *nm* instrument for measuring the amount of alcohol in a liquid

Alma *nf* Alma

almanak *nm* 1 annual (usually) collection of creative literary or scientific writing 2 *(Old)* almanac

*almicë *nf* = almise

almise *nf* 1 tool, implement; farm implement 2 part of a tool or mechanism 3 *(Old)* wooden siege engine used for attacking castles

*almistër *nf* = almise

*almishti *nm* demon, goblin

*almizhda *np* works, mechanism

alo *interj* hello (only for telephone use)

aloklinë *nf* *[Bot]* = voshtër

alpakë *nf* alpaca

alpe *np* range of alpine mountains

Alpe *np fem* Alps

alpin *adj* alpine

alpinist *n* *[Sport]* alpinist

alpinizëm *nm* *[Sport]* alpinism

*alqimi = alkimi

*alqimist *n* = alkimist

Alsasë *nf* Alsace

altar *nm* altar

alternativ *adj* alternate, alternative

alternativë *nf* alternative

alternator *nm* *[Elec]* alternator

alternim *nm* 1 < alterno·n 2 alternation; interchange

alterno·n *vt* to alternate

alternuar *adj (i)* alternating

*altëro·n *vi impers* to dawn

Altin *nm* Altin (male name)

alto *nf* 1 *[Mus]* alto 2 viola 3 alto horn

altoparlant *nm* 1 megaphone; loudspeaker 2 *(Fig Pej)* spokesman for someone else: mouthpiece

altorelievë *nm* *[Archit]* high relief

altruist
 I § *nm (Book)* altruist
 II § *adj* altruistic

altruizëm *nm (Book)* altruism

aludo·n *vi (Book)* to allude; hint

alumin *nm* aluminum

aluminë *nf (Colloq)* vessel/plate made of aluminum

alumintë *adj (i)* *(Colloq)* made of aluminum

*alun *nm* student

*aluri·n *vi* = ulëri·n

*alurim *nm* = ulërimë

*alurinjës *nm* = ulërak

*aluris| *stem for 1st sg pres, pl pres, 2nd & 3rd sg subj, imperf* < bubit·

*alurit· *vi* = ulëri·n

*aluritje *nf ger* = ulërimë

aluvion *nm* *[Geol]* alluvium

aluzion *nm (Book)* allusion

alveo'lë *nf* [*Anat*] alveolus: tooth socket in the jaw-bone; air sac in the lungs

all *adj* bright red, scarlet

alla *adverb-forming prefix (Colloq)* a là, like

***allaba'nd**ë *adv* in bulk, wholesale

***alladis**| *stem for 1st sg pres, pl pres, 2nd & 3rd sg subj, imperf* <**alladi**t·

***alladi**t· *vt* to refresh, cool [ ] off

***allafra'ng**a *adv* = **allafrënga**

allafrënga *adv, adj (Colloq)* in West-European style (as opposed to allaturka)

alla'h
 I § nm Allah
 II § interj expresses wonder or fright, oh my god!

***allaim**ë *adv* separately, individually

***allaj** *nm* regiment

allaj'be *nm* [*Hist*] regional commander of military or police forces during the Turkish occupation

***alla'je** *nf* = **allaj**

***allajk**ë *nf* black slave

***allaka**t·*et vpr* = **hallaka**t·*et*

Allama'një *nf (Old)* Germany

***alla'rm**ë *nf* = **ala'rm**

alla'shqip'ta'rçe *adv (Colloq)* Albanian-style

***alla't** *nm* = **hallat**

***allatis**· *vt* to fan, cool

***alla'tk**ë *nf* (cooling)fan

***allaturi'n**ë *nf* instrument, tool

alla'turka *adv, adj (Colloq)* Turkish-style; oriental (as opposed to allafrënga)

***allavit**·*et vpr (Reg)* to grope

allaxha| *nf* **1** shiny cotton-and-silk flowered-print fabric; clothing made of such material **2** [*Agr*] disease causing spotting on tobacco leaves **3** corn with kernels of variegated color

***allba'n** *nm* = **nallban**

allc *nm* [*Spec*] insole

allç *nm* sorrel horse

allça'k
 I § nm (Colloq) half-wit, idiot
 II § adj half-witted, idiotic

***allça'm** *adj* squinting

allçi *nf* **1** plaster of paris **2** cast for a broken/sprained limb

a'lle *nf* **1** deep red color **2** goat with deep-red hair

***allema'n** *adj, n (Old)* German

***Allema'nj**ë *nf (Old)* Germany = **Allamanjë**

***alle's** *nm* habit, custom

***alles'tis**· *vi* to be accustomed to, have the habit of, be used to

***alfjer** *nm* = **alfjer**

allishveri'sh *nm* **1** *(Colloq Old)* business deal, commerce, business **2** *(Pej)* dirty business, fraud

a'llkë *nf* raised dividing strip between fields

a'llme *nf* [*Bot*] Jerusalem artichoke *(Helianthus tuberosus)*

***allmi'** *nf* exhaustion

***allmi'o**·*n vt* = **shkallmo**·*n*

allo'e *nf* aloe

***allona'r** *nm* July = **korri'k**

allo're *nf* [*Ichth*] gilt-head *Chrysophrus auratus*

***alta'r** *nm* = **altar**

***alltenba'sh** *nm* plaster for removing hair from the skin

alltë'n *nm (Old)* gold

allti *nf (Old)* six-shooter, revolver

ama'
 I § conj but
 II § interj expresses amazement (often sardonic): boy!
  ◦ **Ama ç'e paske tharë!** *(Iron)* (mock praise) Boy, you sure have that down cold!
  ◦ **Ama na kandise!** *(Iron)* Boy, did you convince us! (We don't believe a word of it.)

amalga'më *nf* amalgam

ama'n *interj (Colloq)* **1** expresses a request **2** requests pardon or mercy: oh please! **3** intensifies a following expression of unhappiness: ah me!

Ama'n *nm* Amman

amane't *nm (Colloq)* **1** pledge, deposit, custody, something entrusted to another **2** last wishes before death

amare'të *nf* [*Food*] amaretto cookie (made with crushed walnuts or almonds); macaroon

amarilido're *nf* [*Bot*] amaryllis family *Amaryllidaceae*

amarili's *nm* [*Bot*] amaryllis

***amarti'** *nf* fault, guilt

***amashi'r**ë *nf* bowl, dish

amato'r
 I § adj involving amateurs, of or pertaining to amateurs
 II § n **1** enthusiast, __-lover, fan **2** amateur
  ◦ **amator i kinemasë** film buff
  ◦ **amator i muzikës** music-lover

amazo'në *nf (Book)* amazon

Amazo'në *nf* Amazon

ambala'zh *nm* **1** packaging, wrapping **2** *(Fig Pej)* deceptive cover for true intentions

ambalazh'im *nm ger* **1** <**ambalazho**·*n* **2** = **ambalazh**

ambalazho'·*n vt* to pack for shipment or marketing, make a package

***amba'r** *nm* = **hambar**

***ambarrëz**ë *nf* wooden bar/peg

ambasa'dë *nf* embassy

ambasado'r *n* ambassador

ambasadoria'l *nm* ambassadorial

***ambasa't**ë *nf* = **ambasa'd**ë

***amberi'k** *nm* **1** ring, brooch ***2** liqueur

***amberi'nk** *nm* ring, brooch

***a'mb**ël = **ëmb**ël

ambi'cie *nf* **1** ambition, ambitiousness **2** *(Pej)* unprincipled ambitiousness

***ambicio'n** *nm* = **ambi'cie**

ambicio'z
 I § adj ambitious
 II § nm ambitious person

ambie'nt *nm* **1** ambiance, environment **2** site of a particular kind of activity **3** *(Fig)* social atmosphere

ambiento'·*het vpr* to become acclimatized, get used to

ambiento'·*n vt* to adapt someone to an environment, get someone used to certain conditions

ambi'gue *adj* ambiguous

ambiguite't *nm* ambiguity

***ambo'n**ë *nm* [*Archit*] = **amvon**ë

ambrazu'rë *nf* [*Spec*] aperture, opening

ambro'zë = **ambrozi'**

ambrozì *nf* [*Bot*] ambrosia

ambula'ncë *nf* **1** clinic for ambulatory patients, infirmary, emergency room **2** (*Colloq*) ambulance

ambula'nt *adj* ambulant; ambulatory

ambulato'r *adj* [*Med*] first-aid, infirmary

ambulla'kër *nf* tentacle

a'me *nf* [*Ichth*] **1** meagre (*Argyrosomus regius*) **2** pompano (*Lichia amia*) = **lojbë**

ame'bë *nf* amoeba

ame'l *nm* (*Colloq*) **1** laxative, purgative **2** diarrhea **3** (*Fig*) mood, emotional state

amendame'nt *nm* [*Law*] amendment

amerika'n *adj, n* American

amerika'n atë *nf* (*Pej*) **1** American-like behavior **2** music with those characteristics

amerikan izi'm *nm ger* **1** < **amerikanizo'·n**, **amerikanizo'·het** **2** Americanization

amerikan izo'·het *vpr* to become Americanized

amerikan izo'·n *vt* to Americanize

Ameri'kë *nf* America

  ◦ **Amerika Latine** Latin America

ameti'st *nm* amethyst

a'më *nf* **1** headwater, source, spring; stream bed **2** individual from which a set of animals/plants are descended: mother, queen (bee) **3** [*Anat Bot*] ovary **4** metal plate from which copies are made: stereotype **5** metal casting used to make copies: die **6** stub from which a ticket/check/invoice/coupon is torn off **7** [*Constr*] short wooden strut **8** large marine fish with good-tasting flesh

  ◦ **a'më e çatisë** rafter, joist

  ◦ **a'më e vegjës** [*Text*] roller of a loom

â'më *nf* (*Reg Gheg*) **1** = **ë'më 2** taste, flavor; scent, fragrance **3** river channel, riverbed **4** (*Reg Gheg*) sediment, dregs

amë no'r *adj* (*Book*) **1** maternal, of mothers, motherly **2** (*Geol*) indigenous, autochthonous, original

amë si' ** *nf* **1 motherhood; maternity **2** [*Law*] maternity; maternal rights **3** maternal descent

amë si'm *nm* [*Poet*] pleasant wind

amë si'sht *adv* motherly, maternally, tenderly

amë so'r *adj* **1** [*Agr*] saved for seed or for propagation **2** = **amë nor**

a'më sht *adj* (*i*) without flavor, flavorless; bland; insipid

amë shti' *nf* flavorlessness; blandness; insipidity

amë shti'q *adj* somewhat bland/flavorless; musty

amë shu'ar *adj* (*i*) = **amshu'ar**

amë shu'e shëm *adj* (*i*) = **amshu'ar**

a'mët *adj* (*i*) **1** damp, moist, humid **2** = **a'mullt 3** = **a'mësht**

â'mët *adj* (*i*) (*Reg Gheg*) foolish, foppish

amë ta'r *adj* = **amta'r**

amë ti' *nf* **1** sediment, dregs **2** (*Fig*) stagnancy, sluggishness

amë to'·het *vpr* to take on an odor

amë vras ës

  I § *n* mother-killer, matricide

  II § *adj* matricidal

amë vras je *nf* matricide

a'mëz *nf* **1** food odor **2** smell given off by freshly ploughed ground; smell of a fire **3** = **a'më 4** = **a'mzë**

amfi'b *adj, n* amphibian

amfib ë *np* amphibian (*Amphibia*)

  ◦ **amfibët pa bisht** [*Invert*] anurans *Salientia*

amfibra'k *nm* [*Lit*] amphibrach

amfitea'tër *nm* amphitheater

ami' *nm* [*Bot*] ammi, bishop's weed *Ammi majus*

amia'nt *nm* [*Spec*] amianthus, asbestos

ami'cë *nf* head of a tapeworm

amido'n *nm* [*Chem*] starch

ami'n *interj* [*Relig*] amen

  ◦ **amin, o hoxhë** (*Crude*) whatever you say, boss (said of an ass-licker)

amino pla'st *nm* [*Chem*] amino plastic

amira'l *nm* = **admira'l**

ami's *stem for 1st sg pres, pl pres, 2nd & 3rd sg subj, imperf* < **ami't·**

ami't· *vt* to caress, cajole, coax

amnezi' *nf* amnesia

amni' *nf* = **amësi'**

amnisti' *nf* [*Law*] reduction of criminal sentence; amnesty

amnisto'·n *vt* [*Law*] to reduce criminal sentence; grant amnesty

amnistu'ar *nm* (*i*) [*Law*] one who has received amnesty

âmno'·n *vt* (*Reg Gheg*) to become a mother, give birth

amo'n *nm* [*Chem*] ammonium

amo'në *nf* coppersmith's anvil

amonia'k *nm* [*Chem*] ammoniac; liquid ammonia

amoniako'r *adj* [*Chem*] ammoniacal

amo'r *nm* estrus, rutting, heat, mating season

amora'l *adj* (*Book*) **1** amoral **2** immoral

amora'l shëm *adj* (*i*) (*Book*) immoral

amo'rf *adj* (*Book*) amorphous; of indeterminate character

amortiz ato'r *nm* [*Tech*] shock absorber

amortiz i'm *nm ger* **1** < **amortizo'·n**, **amortizo'·het** **2** [*Econ*] amortization

amortizo'·het *vpr* **1** [*Econ*] to become amortized **2** [*Tech*] to become attenuated: damp

amortizo'·n *vt* **1** [*Econ*] to amortize **2** [*Tech*] to damp, attenuate

amortizu'ar *adj* (*i*) **1** [*Econ*] amortized **2** buffered, mitigated, attenuated, damped **3** [*Tech*] worn, shabby

amortizu'es *adj* **1** [*Econ*] amortizing **2** [*Tech*] shock-absorbing; muffling

ampe'r *nm* ampere

amper me'tër *nm* [*Phys*] ammeter

amplifikato'r *nm* [*Tech*] amplifier

ampu'lë *nf* [*Pharm*] ampule, vial

amputacio'n *nm* [*Med*] amputation

amsi'm *nm* smell, fragrance, scent

amshi' *nf* = **amshi'në**

amshi'm *nm ger* **1** < **amsho'·n**, **amsho'·het** **2** immortalization; perpetuation **3** eternity

amshi'në *nf* perpetuity, permanence

amsho'·het *vpr* (*Book*) to become immortal, go on forever

amsho'·n *vt* (*Book*) to perpetuate, make eternal, immortalize

a'mshtë *adj* (*i*) = **a'mësht**

âmsht i'k

  I § *adj* (*Reg Gheg*) **1** = **a'mësht 2** musty

  II § *nm* mustiness

âmsht i'm *nm* (*Reg Gheg*) insipidness, blandness

amshu'ar *adj (i)* eternal

amshu'e'shëm *adj (i)* *(Book)* = **amshu'ar**

amshu'e'shm|ëri *nf* *(Book)* existence throughout eternity: everlastingness

am'ta'r *adj* **1** ancestral **2** maternal = **amëno'r**

*__a'mte__ *nf* = **a'mtë**

a'm|të *adj (i)* **1** tasteless, bland *__2__ stagnant *__3__ dense *__4__ sultry

amt|o'·n *vi* to sedimentize, settle to the bottom

*__am'ty'rë__ *nf* = **naty'rë**

*__amu'j|ë__ *nf* stream, brook, spring

a'mull

  I § *nm (np ˜ j)* motionless pool of water: stagnant pond

  II § *adv* without movement, at a standstill

  III § *adj* = **a'mullt**

   ○ **të daltë amulli** *(Curse)* I hope you rot!

amull|i *nf* **1** stagnancy, stagnation; standstill **2** [*Med*] stasis

amull|i'm *nm* = **amulli'**

amull|o'·het *vpr* to come to a standstill, stagnate

amull|o'r *adj* = **a'mullt**

a'mull|t *adj (i)* stagnant, motionless

amu'r *nm* [*Ichth*]

  ○ **amur i bardhë** *Ctenopharyngodon idellus Valenciennes*

Amu'r *nm* Amur

*__amvi's__ *n* head of a household

amvi's· *vt* to manage a household

amvi's|ë *nf* housekeeper, home manager: housewife

amvis|ëri' *nf* the art of managing a household, home management, home economics, house keeping

*__amvis|i'm__ *nm ger* **1** <**amviso'·n 2** = **amvisëri'**

amvi's|je *nf ger* **1** <**amvis· 2** housekeeping, home management

*__amvis|o'·n__ *vi* to keep house, manage a household

amvo'në *nf* [*Archit*] church pulpit; tribune, gallery

a'mzë *nf* **1** official register, registry **2** enrollment list **3** stub (of a ticket/check/invoice/coupon) **4** headwater, source, spring; stream bed **5** individual from which a set of animals/plants are descended: mother, queen (bee)

*__amz|o'r__ *adj* matrimonial

.__ **an** *nm* **1** [*Anat*] womb; caul **2** joint (between bones) *__3__ room, vessel

an|a'ç *adj (Pej)* malingering, deceitful

*__ana|de't__ *nm* = **anëde't**

ana|de'tas *n* = **bregde'tas**

Anado'll *nm* Anatolia

anadoll|a'k OR **anado'll|as** *adj, n* **1** [*Hist*] Anatolian **2** *(Pej)* old-fashioned and reactionary

*__Anadoll|i'__ *nf* = **Anatoli'**

anadoll|i'zëm *nm* *(Pej)* a manner that is oldfashioned and reactionary

anagji'r *nm* [*Bot*] Mediterranean stinkbush *(Anagyris foetida)*

*__anahori't__ *nm* anchorite

an|a'k *nm* **1** = **anëca'k** *__2__ garland, wreath; necklace

*__ana'ke__ *nf* circle

*__ana|ko'hë__ *nf* armistice, time-out

anakolu't *nm* [*Lit*] anacoluthon

anakron|i'k *adj* anachronistic

anakron|i'zëm *nm* anachronism

ana'le *np* annals

analfabe't *adj, n* illiterate

analfabet|i'zëm *nm* illiteracy

anali'st *nm* analyst

analiti'k *adj* analytic

anali'zë *nf* analysis

analiz|i'm *nm ger* **1** <**analizo'·n 2** act, action, or result of analysis

analiz|o'·n *vt* to analyze

analiz|u'e|s

  I § *adj* analytical

  II § *n* analyst, analyzer

analiz|u'e'shëm *adj (i)* analyzable

analo'g *nm* analogue

analogji' *nf* analogy

analogji'k *adj* analogical

an|alu'mas *n* = **bregalu'mas**

*__analy'zë__ *nf* = **anali'zë**

an|ama'l|as *n* mountain dweller

aname'nd *adv* = **aname'ndas**

aname'nd|as *adv* absent-mindedly, bemusedly, absently

ana'me|s

  I § *adv (Reg)* **1** in the middle **2** through, across, athwart

  II § *prep (abl)* among

*__an|amë'nd__ *adv* = **aname'ndas**

*__an|amë'nd|as__ *adv* = **aname'ndas**

anana's *nm* pineapple *(Ananas comosus)*

an|anga's· *vt (Reg)* to provoke, stir up; urge on, excite, incite

*__an|anga's·et__ *vpr (Reg)* to hurry up, hustle

*__ananka's·__ *vt (Reg)* = **ananga's·**

anape'st *nm* [*Lit*] anapest

an|apra'pt|as *adv* backwards, from the back

an|apra'pt|ë *adj (i)* backward

anarki' *nf* anarchy

anark|i'k *adj* anarchic

anark|i'st *n* anarchist

anark|i'zëm *nm* anarchism

anarko|sindikal|i'st *n* anarchosyndicalist

anarko|sindikal|i'zëm *nm* anarchosyndicalism

*__anarqi'__ *nf* = **anarki'**

a'na|s

  I § *n* resident, indigenous resident

  II § *adj* indigenous

  III § *adv* = **a'nash**

ana'sje II· *vt* **1** to turn [] around, turn [] in a different/ opposite direction **2** to reverse/upset the order of []

an|a'sje'll|as *adv* **1** inversely, conversely, vice versa; looking at it from the other side, on the other hand *__2__ alternately

an|a'sje'llë

  I § *adj (i)* **1** inverse, in opposite order; alternate **2** [*Math*] (multiplicative) inverse, reciprocal

  II § *nf* = **anasje'llje**

ana'sje'll|ët *adj (i)* = **anasje'llë**

ana'sje'll|je *nf ger* **1** <**anasje II· 2** inversion; reversal

*__ana'sje'll|shëm__ *adj (i)* alternate

ana'sje'll|tas *adv* = **anasje'llas**

ana'sje'll|të *adj (i)* inverse; in reverse order; contrary, opposite

*__anaso'n__ *nm* **1** anise *(Pimpinella anisum)* **2** aniseed

a'nash adv alongside, beside; to the side, sidelong, sideways

*anash'kalo·n vt 1 to try to avoid [], skirt around [] 2 to bypass

anate'më nf anathema

Anatolí nf Anatolia

anatomí nf anatomy

anatomík nf anatomic

anatomíst n anatomist

*anathe'më nf = anate'më

a'nazí adv = a'nash

*a'ncë nf = a'nzë

*ancuje nf [Ichth] anchovy Engraulis encrasicholus L.

ançín ë nf (Pej) barren slope

andaj conj (Colloq) = prandaj

Andaluzí nf Andalusia

*andame'ndas adv = aname'ndas

anda'nte
  I § adv [Mus] andante
  II § nf andante piece or movement

anda'rt adj, n [Hist] 1 Greek guerrilla *2 bandit

*ânde nf (Reg Gheg) = ë'ndë

A'nde np Andes (mountains)

andej
  I § adv 1 that way, in that direction, around there, along about there; over that way, over there 2 about then, along about there; since about then, from about then 3 (Colloq Fig) concerning that, about that
  II § prep (abl) there by that; beyond, towards beyond
    ○ andej këha (Reg) over here, over on this side
    ○ andej (e) këtej back and forth; all over the place
    ○ andej pari over that way, around over there

andej-këndej adv hither and thither, here and there

*andejm adv = andejmi

andejm ë adj (i) = andejsh ë m

andejm i adv (së) from around there, from there

*andej na adv right around there

andej pari adv somewhere around there, somewhere in that direction

andej sh ë m adj (i) of/from over there, of the far side, on that side, (located) around there

*andejt ím nm ger 1 <andejto·n 2 transmission, transportation

*andejto·n vt to transmit, transport

andej za adv = andej

*anderi nf = anteri

*ande'se adv although

*ande'zaj adv = andej

*a'ndë nf = ë'ndë

*ande'prue's
  I § nm appetizer
  II § adj appetizing

*a'ndër nm, nf = a'rnë

*andëro·n vt = arno·n

*a'ndërr adv = ë'ndërr

*a'ndësh ë m adj (i) pleasant, likable

*andik ë nf = antik ë

*andiko's· vt to age; beat down, depress

*andik tar nm = antiku'ar

*andíl ë nf glint of the sun on a pole

*andín ë nf yard (of a mast)

*andi prosopík nm anti-personnel weapon

*andís prep instead of, in place of

*a'ndje nf = ë'ndë

*ando·n vt = ë'nd·et

Ando'rrë nf Andorra

andra'llë nf (Colloq) worry, trouble, problem; headache

andrallë'ma'dh
  I § adj (Colloq) in deep trouble, with lots of problems
  II § n someone with a great many problems

andrallë'ta'r n one with many headaches/problems

andrallís· vt = andrallo's·

andrallo's· vt (Colloq) to cause headaches/problems, bother

andrallo's·et vpr 1 to be drowned in trouble; have one's mind set spinning with problems 2 to get dizzy, be dazed, be out of one's mind

andrallo'su'r adj (i) (Colloq) beset by problems; dazed, out of one's mind

Andre'a nm Andrew

*andre's ë nf 1 = a'rnë 2 = arnes'ë

*a'ndrë nf = a'rnë

andrí nf 1 equipment used for plowing and for managing the plowing team *2 plowing team

*andrím nm ger = arním

*andro·n vt = arno·n

*andrr = ë'ndërr

*andrra'mênd adv (Reg Gheg) = aname'ndas

*a'ndshëm adj (i) = ë'ndshëm

*Andu'n nm Anthony

*andy'shtje adv however

ane nf (Reg) mother

anekdo'të nf anecdote

anekdotík adj anecdotal

ane kë'nd
  I § adv 1 in all parts, everywhere, all over 2 in all directions
  II § prep (abl) throughout

ane'ks nm 1 annex; addition 2 kitchenette 3 appendix (to a document)

*aneks a'të nf annexation

aneks ím nm ger 1 <a_nekso·n 2 annexation

aneks ít nm [Med] annexitis, annexitis

aneks o·n vt 1 to annex [] by force 2 to append

aneks ua'r adj (i) 1 annexed by force 2 appended

*aneku·et vpr to mourn, grieve; make one's condolences

*anelín nm = anilín ë

ane mba'në
  I § adv throughout, everywhere, all over, on all sides
  II § prep (abl) throughout

anemí nf 1 anemia *2 = enemí
  ○ anemi e Mesdheut "Mediterranean anemia" [Med] Cooley's anemia

anemík adj anemic

ane përqa'rk adv all around, from one end to the other

ane qa'rk adv all around, all over

ane's ë nf partiality, favoritism

anestetík adj anesthetic

anestetík ë nf [Med] anesthesiology

anestezí nf [Med] anesthesia

a'në nf 1 side 2 edge 3 region, portion 4 direction 5 aspect, phase; facet, face 6 point of view 7 partiality, favoritism 8 behalf, side, part 9 side (of the

family), family line **10** means *11 extremity, end; limb **12** [*Text*] silk or cotton thread used as edging **13** [*Anat*] uterus, womb
∘ **anë e borës** north side
∘ **anë e cekë** in all parts, everywhere, all over; in all directions
∘ **ana e detit** west side
∘ **ana e diellit** east side
∘ **nuk do·t'ia di·nga ajo anë** not be afraid of that, not worry about that
∘ **ana e keqe** (*Euph*) the devil
∘ **anë e kënd** on every side, in all parts, everywhere, all over; in all directions; exactly, in every detail
∘ **ana e mbarë** side (of textile material) that shows: right side, face
∘ **ana e mesditës** (*Colloq*) the south side
∘ **anë (e) më anë** throughout = **anembanë**
∘ **më një anë = mënjanë**
∘ **anë për anë 1** throughout, everywhere **2** up to the brim, chock-full
∘ **anë e përqark** round about
∘ **anë e qark** round about
∘ **anë e rrobës** hem
∘ **anë e skaj** in all parts, everywhere, all over; in all directions
∘ **anë e shiut** south side
∘ **anët e trupit** the parts of the body
∘ **anë e zgeq** anywhere

anëcak
I § *adj* biased, partial, partisan, one-sided
II § *nm* **1** stone ledge jutting out of a wall **2** [*Archit*] cantilever, console; corbel; cornice

anëdet *nm* seashore, seacoast

anëdetas
I § *adj* (*Old*) coastal = **bregdetar**
II § *n* shore-dweller

anëdetës = anëdetas

anëdetje *nf* coast

anëje *nf* fabric cover for a bench

anëkalesë I § *nf OR* **anëkalim** II § *nm* bypass

anëliqen *nm* lakeside

anëlumë *nm* river bank, riverside; river walk

anëmal *nm* mountainside

anëmalas *n* = anamalas

anëmarrje *nf* **1** [*Mil*] taking the flanks **2** roundabout maneuver **3** partiality, bias

anëmbajtës
I § *n* defender, defense attorney
II § *adj* partisan, partial

anëmbana *np* accessories, gadgets

anëmbanë *adv* = anembanë

anëmbythje *nf* hindquarters

anëngrënë *adj* worn out on the sides, with worn/ eroded edges

anëpëranë *adv* on all sides, all over, from one end to the other, everywhere, all around

anër *nf* = arnë

anëro·n *nf* = arno·n

anërojë *nf* [*Mil*] flank guard

anërrugë *nf* sidewalk

anës
I § *adv* **1** at the side, on the side, alongside, around **2** indirectly, in a roundabout way
II § *prep* (*abl*) along, beside, by

∘ **anës e anës 1** keeping to the side, staying to one side **2** in a circumspect way: cautiously

anëse *nf* **1** side plank of a cart/wagon bed **2** = **anie**

anësi *nf* **1** partiality, favoritism **2** [*Anat*] body limb
∘ **anësi e poshtme** leg
∘ **anësi e sipërme** arm

anësim *nm ger* = **anim**

anësisht *adv* **1** laterally; obliquely; indirectly **2** with partiality, exhibiting favoritism

anëso·het *vpr* to take sides, be inclined toward one side, be partial to one party

anëso·n *vt* = ano·n

anësor
I § *nm* **1** [*Sports*] referee on the sideline: linesman **2** [*Sports*] player in the right or left wing position: winger, flanker, outside player **3** lateral/cross member of a constructed object **4** [*Mil*] flank
II § *adj* **1** lateral, side **2** (*Fig*) secondary, incidental **3** [*Mil*] on the flank: flanking

anësore *nf* **1** [*Agr*] moldboard of a plow **2** safety fence along the side of a highway **3** side-alley **4** siding (along the sides of a truck/lorry bed) **5** wheel rim

anësujë *nf* (*Old*) island

anëshëm *adj* (i) = **anshëm**

anëshkrim *nm* marginal notation

anëshkrimisht *adv* with marginal notation

anëshkruar *adj* (i) [*Math*] adjacent (in respect to sides or angles)

anëtar *n* member
∘ **anëtar nderi** honorary member

anëtarësi *nf* membership

anëtari *nf* = anëtarësi

ang *nm* nightmare

angari
I § *nf* **1** [*Hist*] forced labor, corvée **2** (*Fig*) drudgery, unpleasant chore; fruitless work
II § *adv* **1** under coercion and for no pay **2** (*Fig*) unwillingly and in a slipshod manner

angazhim *nm ger* **1** < **angazho·n**, angazho·het **2** = **zotim 3** [*Mil*] engagement to battle, commitment of troops

angazho·het *vpr* **1** to be engaged in, enter into **2** = **zoto·het 3** [*Mil*] to be committed (to battle) **4** to accept a responsibility, take charge

angazho·n *vt* **1** to hire, rent **2** [*Mil*] to commit [troops] **3** (*Book*) to engage; charge [ ] with a responsibility

angër *nf* = angërr

angërduf *nm* (*Reg*) cocky and pompous swaggerer

angërduf·et *vpr* (*Reg*) to puff oneself up (like a turkeycock); strut and swagger; show off

angërr *nf* **1** membrane surrounding a body organ **2** interior cavity *3** hinge

angërra *np* < angërr entrails, guts
∘ **angrra e zorrëve** (*Colloq*) peritoneum

angështa
I § *adj* (i) (*Reg*) **1** narrow, tight **2** (*Fig*) stingy, tight **3** (*Fig*) taciturn *4** rough, gruff, harsh
II § *adv* (*Reg*) **1** tightly, narrowly, closely **2** (*Fig*) maliciously, malevolently *3** roughly, gruffly, harshly

angështi *nf* **1** (*Reg*) stinginess, tight-fistedness **2** anxiety, emotional tenseness **3** sultry weather, sultriness

angështím *nm ger* 1 <**angështo'·n**, **angështo'·het** 2 feeling anxious; anxiety

angështo'·het *vpr* 1 to become constricted/restricted 2 to feel anxious/distressed

angështo'·n *vt (Reg)* to constrict, restrict

angështua'r *adj (i)* suffering anxiety, anxious, distressed

anglez
   I § *nm* Englishman
   II § *adj* of or pertaining to England, English

Anglí *nf* England

anglicizëm *nm* Anglicism

anglicizo'·n *vt* to Anglicize

anglika'n *adj, n* Anglican

anglísht *adv* in English (language)

anglíshte *nf* English language

anglo-amerika'n *adj, n* Anglo-American

anglofíl *adj* Anglophile

anglofo'b *adj* Anglophobe

anglomaní *nf* Anglomania

anglosakso'n *adj* Anglo-Saxon

***angllatís·** *vt* to explain, inform

ango'las OR **angole'z** *adj, n* Angolan

Angolë *nf* Angola

***ango'në** *nf (Reg Gk)* corner

***ango'rë** *nf* = **spira'ncë**

***angth** = **ankth**

***angulíçe** = **agulíçe**

angullí·n *vi* to whine, whimper; squeal, squeak

angullímë *nf ger* 1 <**angullí·n** 2 whine, whimper; squeal, squeak

angullít· *vi* = **angullí·n**

angullítje *nf ger* <**angullít·**

***angu're** *nf* 1 entrails 2 = **spira'ncë**

***angu'rrë** = **angu're**

***angurro'·n** = **ankoro'·n**

***angusë** *nf* anguish, sorrow

***angushí** *nf* compunction, sense of guilt

***angushtím** = **angështím**

***angushto'·n** = **angështo'·n**

***angutësi** *nf* caste

***angjelíkë** *nf* [*Bot*] angelica

***angjëc** *adv* even

***angjín** *nm* hook, grappling iron

angjina're *nf* [*Bot*] 1 artichoke (*Cynara*) 2 globe artichoke (*Cynara scolymus*) 3 cardoon (*Cynara cardunculus*)
   ○ **angjinare e egër** [*Bot*] cardoon *Cynara cardunculus*

angjínë *nf* [*Med*] 1 tonsillitis, quinsy 2 angina
   ○ **angjina e kraharorit/gjoksit** anginal syndrome *angina pectoris*

***angjinídhe** *nf* [*Bot*] Greek camelthorn (*Alhagi graecorum*)

angjístër *nf* fishhook

anhidríd *nm* [*Chem*] anhydride

anhidrít *nm* [*Min*] anhydrite

ani
   I § *adv (Colloq)* 1 later, afterward 2 no matter, never mind; well anyway, so then
   II § *interj* hey! well now! (used as a term of address or as a line filler at the beginning of a verse in a folk song)

III § *nf* = **aníje**
   ○ **ani kush** *(Iron)* oh sure!, that's certainly someone to talk!
   ○ **ani më** oh sure!
   ○ **ani qysh** *(Iron)* oh sure!, that's certainly how to do it!

anie *nf* 1 side strip, long narrow piece 2 broad strip of colored material decorating a bench/chair; rug beside a hearth or on the side of a room 3 unploughed strip along the side of a field 4 flitch (of lumber); roof beam, rafter 5 felloe (of a wheel)

***aníe** *nf* = **aníje**

***anie'sí** *nf* 1 seamanship, navigation 2 navy, fleet

***anie'sor** *adj* = **anijesor**

***anieta'r** *adj* = **anijetar**

***anie'tor** *nm* = **anijetor**

***anie'tore** *nf* = **anijetore**

anija'të *nf* [*Archit*] church nave

aníje *nf* 1 ship, boat; air ship 2 [*Archit*] church nave
   ○ **anije balenagjuajtëse** whaling ship, whaler
   ○ **anije dëfrimi** pleasure boat
   ○ **anije flamurtare** flagship
   ○ **anije kabotazhi** [*Naut*] vessel engaged in coastal sea commerce: coaster
   ○ **anije kozmike** spaceship
   ○ **anije lufte** warship
   ○ **anije me pëlhurë** sailing vessel
   ○ **anije me vela** sailing vessel
   ○ **anije tregtare** merchant ship
   ○ **anije vajgurmbajtëse** oil tanker

anijedrejtue's *nm* ship pilot

anijendërtue's
   I § *nm* shipbuilder
   II § *adj* shipbuilding

anije'rí *nf (Old)* seamanship

anije'sí *nf (Old)* navy, fleet

anije'sor *adj (Old)* naval, marine, nautical

anijeta'r
   I § *nm (Old)* seaman, sailor, boatman
   II § *adj* nautical, naval

***anije'tor** *nm* sailor

***anije'tore** *nf* navy yard, naval arsenal

anije'thy'erje *nf (Book)* shipwreck

anilínë *nf* [*Chem*] aniline

aním *nm ger* 1 <**ano'·n**, **ano'·het** 2 inclination, slant, tendency, propensity; bias; drift

***animâ** *adv (Reg Gheg)* then, afterwards; well then, and so

animírë *adv* however

animíst *adj* animist

animízëm *nm* animism

anio'n *nm* anion

anís *nm* [*Bot*] anise *Pimpinella anisum*

***ankala's·** *vt* to hug, embrace in one's arms

anka'nd *nm* auction

***anka'ndë** *nf* = **ankand**

anke'së *nf* 1 complaint, grievance *2 lament

anke'të *nf* 1 inquiry, investigation 2 questionnaire, survey, poll

anketím *nm ger* <**anketo'·n**

anketo'·n *vi* to conduct an inquiry; investigate

anketue's *nm* investigator

ankím *nm ger* 1 <**anko'·n** 2 = **ankesë**

ankimo'r *adj* [*Law*] containing a legal complaint, complaining

ankim|ta'r n (Book) = anku'es

anko'·het vpr to make/register a complaint, complain

anko'·n
I § vi to complain; moan and groan
II § vt to tell [one's troubles] to ◇

ankoj'ë nf (Pej) constant complainer

*****ankonj'ës** adj, n = anku'es

ankori'm nm ger 1 <ankoro'·n, ankoro'·het 2 anchorage

ankoro'·het vpr to let out the anchor, dock, cast anchor, make anchorage

ankoro'·n
I § vt to anchor
II § vi = ankoro'·het

*****ankra'n** nm pal, buddy

ankth nm 1 nightmare 2 anxiety, emotional strain, anguish

a'nkth|shëm adj (i) 1 causing anxiety 2 full of anxiety, anxious

anku'es
I § nm [Offic] complainant, plaintiff; complainer
II § adj 1 complaining; whining; plaintive, grieving
2 [Offic] presenting a complaint, complaining

anku'e|shëm adv complainingly, plaintively

*****anku'rë** nf = spiran'cë

*****anmi'k** nm (np ~ q) (Reg Gheg) = armi'k

*****anmik|su'e|shëm** adj (i) (Reg Gheg) = armiqe'so'r

*****anmi'q** np (Reg Gheg) = armi'q

ano'·het vpr to lean, sag to one side, tilt

ano'·n
I § vt to tilt, lean
II § vi 1 = ano'·het 2 (Fig) to side (with [ ]), have a bias, take sides, be inclined toward one side, be partial to one party 3 to resemble
◦ ano·n^{3sg} kali the load on the packhorse leans to one side

ano'dë nf [Phys] anode

anofe'le nf [Entom] anopheles mosquito

anomali' nf anomaly

anoni'm
I § nm 1 anonymous author 2 corporation
II § adj anonymous

ano'r adj showing partiality/favoritism: biased, partisan

ano're nf 1 hearth rug, scatter rug 2 roof beam

anorma'l adj abnormal

ano's· vt 1 to tilt 2 (in sewing) to hem, seam

ano's·et vpr = ano'·het

ANSA abbrev (Italian) <Agenzia Nazionale Stampa Associata Italian National Press Association

ansa'mbël nm ensemble, company

*****ansu'jezë** nf = anësu'jë

a'n|shëm adj (i) 1 lateral, of the side, side 2 (Fig) showing partiality/favoritism: biased, partisan

an|shm'ëri nf favoritism, partiality

antagoni'st
I § n (Book) antagonist
II § adj antagonistic

antagoni'zëm nm antagonism

anta'ntë nf entente

Antarkti'dë nf South Polar Region

antarkti'k adj Antarctic

Antarkti'kë nf Antarctica

antena|gja'të nm "long-antenna" [Entom] (Plagionotus floralis)
◦ **antenagjati i fikut** [Entom] Pogonochaerus (Pityophilus) hispidus

antena'rie nf [Bot] pussytoes, cat's-foot Antennaria

antena|shku'rtër adj [Invert] brachycerous

ante'në nf antenna

ante'nëz nf [Invert] antennule

anteri' nf (Old) 1 long-sleeved tunic worn by men or women 2 long gown or nightgown for women

anti formative prefix anti-, against = ku'ndër

anti|ajro'r
I § adj antiaircraft
II § nm antiaircraft gun

anti|alkooli'k nm opposed to the use of alcohol, dry, prohibitionist, anti-alcoholic

anti|artisti'k nm inartistic

anti|bioti'k nm antibiotic

anti|ciklo'n nm anticyclone

anti|demokrati'k adj antidemocratic

anti|dialekti'k adj opposed to dialectic principles, anti-dialectic

anti|fashi'st adj, n anti-fascist

anti|fe'ta'r adj, n anti-religious

anti|feuda'l adj anti-feudalistic

anti|fri'zë nf [Spec] antifreeze

anti|ga'z nm = ku'ndërga'z

Antigone'|la nf [Hist] Antigone

anti|gri'mcë nf [Phys] antiparticle

anti|higjeni'k adj = johigjeni'k

anti|histori'k adj antihistorical

anti|imperiali'st adj antiimperialistic

anti'k adj 1 belonging to antiquity (Greco-Roman times) 2 of olden times, antique 3 (Colloq) anti-quated, out-of-date, behind the times; amusingly old-fashioned, funny old

anti|kapitali'st adj anti-capitalist

anti'kë nf (Colloq) 1 antique 2 eccentric, old codger

anti|kishta'r adj anti-church

anti|ki'te't nm antiquity

anti|klerika'l adj anticlerical

anti|klerikali'zëm nm anticlericalism

anti|koloniali'st adj anti-colonialist

anti|koloniali'zëm nm anti-colonialism

anti|kombëta'r adj anti-national

anti|komuni'st adj, n anticommunist

anti|komuni'zëm nm anticommunism

*****anti|ko's** vt = andiko's

anti|kri'sht adj, n antichrist

*****anti|kta'r** n = antiku'ar

anti|ku'a'r nm antiquary, antiquarian

anti|kushtetu'e's adj unconstitutional

anti'l nm [Bot] = antili'dë

Anti'le np fem Antilles
◦ **Antilet e Vogla** Lesser Antilles

anti|lë'ndë nf [Phys] antimatter

antili'dë nf [Bot] anthyllis Anthyllis
◦ **antilidë shë'ruese** [Bot] kidney vetch, wound-wort Anthyllis vulneraria

anti|ligjo'r adj = kundërligjo'r

antilo'pë nf [Zool] antelope

anti|malari'k adj = kundërmalari'k

anti|marks|îst *adj* anti-Marxist

anti|mate|rie *nf* [*Phys*] antimatter = **antilë**nd*ë*

anti|militar|îst *adj* anti-militarist

anti|militar|îzëm *nm* anti-militarism

antimo|n *nm* antimony *Sb*

anti|monark|îk *adj* antimonarchial

antimoni *nf* = **antimo**n

anti|nevralgj|îk *adj, n* anti-neuralgic

antinomî *nf* [*Phil*] antinomy

anti|njer|ëz|o|r *adj* inhumane; misanthropic

anti|parti *adj* anti-party

anti|pa|stë *nf* antipasto

anti|patî *nf* antipathy

anti|patî
 I § *adj* unlikable, unpleasant, creating a feeling of antipathy
 II § *n* unpleasant person

anti|patriot|îk *adj* unpatriotic

antipo|d *nm* [*Geog*] antipode

anti|popull|o|r *adj* inimical to the people, antagonistic to the interests of the people, unpopular

anti|pun|ë|to|r *adj* against the working class: antilabor

anti|pushte|t *adj* opposed to government authority

anti|qeveri|ta|r *adj* anti-government

anti|revizion|îst *adj* anti-revisionist

anti|semî|t
 I § *adj* anti-Semitic
 II § *nm* anti-Semite

anti|semit|îzëm *nm* anti-Semitism

anti|septîk *nm, adj* antiseptic

anti|sizm|îk *adj* protecting against earthquakes: aseismic

anti|social|îst *adj* anti-socialist

anti|soviet|îk *adj* anti-Soviet

anti|sportî|v *adj* unsportsmanlike

anti|shkenc|o|r *adj* antiscientific

anti|shoq|ër|o|r *adj* antisocial

anti|shqip|ta|r *adj* anti-Albanian

anti|shtet|ër|o|r *adj* against the state, anti-state

anti|ta|nk *adj* antitank = **kundërta**nk

anti|te|zë *nf* antithesis

anti|tru|p *adj* antibody = **kundërtru**p

anti|tuberkul|a|r *adj* anti-tubercular

anti|thërr|mî|jë *nf* [*Phys*] anti-particle = **kundër-grî**mc*ë*

anti|velu|es *adj* [*Cine*] antifogging compound/device

anti|veneria|n *adj* anti-venereal

anti|zog|îst *adj* anti-Zogist, opposed to former King Zog

antologjî *nf* anthology

antonî|m *nm* antonym

antonimî *nf* antonymy

antozoa|r *nm* [*Invert*] anthozoan *Anthozoa*

antraci|t *nm* anthracite

antra|kt *nm* [*Theat*] entr'acte, intermission

antri|sk *nm* [*Bot*] beaked chervil, anthriscus *Anthriscus*
 ◦ **antrisk gjethedyllî** chervil *Anthriscus cerfolium*
 ◦ **antrisk pyjor** wild chervil, cow parsley *Anthriscus sylvestris*

antropo|gjeografî *nf* anthropogeography

antropo|î|d *adj, n* anthropoid

antropo|lo|g *n* anthropologist

antropo|logj|î *nf* anthropology

antropo|logj|îk *adj* anthropological

antropo|mo|rf *adj* anthropomorphic

antropo|nî|m *nm* [*Ling*] anthroponym, human name

antropo|nomî *nf* 1 [*Ling*] anthroponomy 2 the set of names of people used by a language or a people

*anti|u|e|m** *nm* = anua|r

*ant|hropo|** = antropo|

anua|r *nm* annual = vjeta|r

an|ua|r *adj* (i) leaning/sagging to one side, tilted

anul|î|m *nm ger* 1 <anulo|•n 2 annulment; recision

anul|o|•n *vt* to annul; rescind

anul|o|•n *vt* = anulo|•n

an|ur|î|në *nf* narrow strip of ground at an edge or corner of a field

anu|rk|ë *nf* variety of sweet, red apple that matures late and lasts long

Anver|së *nf* Antwerp

anxhi|k *nm* 1 small leather pouch usually worn at the belt by shepherds and used to carry food 2 leather pouch

*a|nz|ë** *nf* 1 wasp 2 aniseed 3 lintel 4 womb, uterus

*anj** *interj* hey! = aj

a|njëz *nf* [*Entom*] nit, young louse = e|rgjëz

aorî|st *nm* [*Ling*] aorist

ao|rtë *nf* [*Anat*] aorta

AP *abbrev* (*American*) <**Shtypi i Bashkuar** Associated Press

ap = jap|

APA *abbrev* (*German*) <**Austria Presse Agentur** Austrian Press Agency

Apala|she *np* Appalachians

*apalla|dhe** *nf* = apΙla|dhe

apansëz *adv* (*Colloq*) all of a sudden, unexpectedly

apara|t *nm* 1 apparatus 2 operational system/staff of a social organization
 ◦ **aparat blici** photoflash
 ◦ **aparat druri** [*Cine*] wooden camera
 ◦ **aparat i ekspresit** espresso machine
 ◦ **aparat fotografik** camera; still camera
 ◦ **aparati i frymëmarrjes** respiratory apparatus
 ◦ **aparat kinematografik** [*Cine*] movie camera
 ◦ **aparat kopjimi** photocopying machine
 ◦ **aparat marrës** [*Cine*] = aparat kinematografik
 ◦ **aparat multi** [*Cine*] trick camera
 ◦ **aparat radiomarrës** radio receiving set: radio receiver
 ◦ **aparat reportazhi** [*Cine*] press camera
 ◦ **aparat transmetues** transmitter
 ◦ **aparat xhirimi** [*Cine*] = aparat kinematografik

aparatu|rë *nf* equipment, physical fixtures or apparatus, device

apare|ncë *nf* outward show, semblance, appearance

*aparia|t** *vi* = aparja|t•

*aparj|as** stem for *1st sg pres, pl pres, 2nd & 3rd sg subj, pind* <aparja|t•

*aparja|t** *vi* to lose hope/confidence; withdraw, retire

apartame|nt *nm* apartment

apasionu|a|r *adj* (i) passionate, emotional

apatî *nf* apathy

apat|îk *adj* apathetic

*apathî** *nf* = apati

ape'l nm 1 roll call 2 (Old) [Law] appeal for judicial review 3 appeal for support

apeli'm nm ger 1 [Law] <apelo' ·n 2 appeal brief

apelo' ·n vt 1 to appeal [a decision] 2 [Law] to appeal a lower court's judgment to a higher court

apendici't OR apendisi't nm [Med] appendicitis

Apeni'ne np Appennines

aperiti'v nm aperitif

*ape't adv = përsëri

a'pë nf with masc agreement (Reg) 1 elder brother 2 pet name used by children for their father

*apika's· vt to notice, perceive; suppose, conjecture

apikulture'rë nf apiculture

*api'stje nf [Bot] wormwood (Artemisia absinthium)

*aplika'të nf = aplikim

apliki'm nm ger 1 <apliko' ·n 2 application 3 appliqué

apliko' ·n vt to apply, carry out [] = zbato' ·n

apliku'ar adj (i) = zbatu'ar

aplla'dhe nf 1 platter, usually made of copper 2 large wooden or clay platter

apo'
   I § conj (expresses exclusive or) or, or else, or rather = a
   II § pcl 1 (introduces a yes/no question with a suggested answer) well maybe _? 2 (negates a following negative in order to express strong support of what has preceded)
   ○ apo jo (tag question that asks for confirmation) is that so? isn't that so? right?

apocino're nf [Bot] dogbane family Apocynaceae

*apofasi' nf resolution, intent, purpose; conclusion

*apofasi's· vi to resolve, decide, conclude

apogje' nm [Astron] apogee

apokali'ps nm [Rel] apocalypse

apokalipti'k adj [Rel] apocolyptic

a'politi'k adj apolitical

a'politi'zëm nm apoliticism, refusal to take a political position

apologje't nm (Book) apologist

apologji' nf (Book) argument defending a position or person, apology

Apoloni' nf [Hist] Apollonia

*apomoni' nf patience

*apople'ks nf = apopleksi'

apopleksi' nf apoplexy

apostafa't adv (Colloq) on purpose, deliberately

*aposti'më nf abscess

apostola'të nf apostolate, mission

apostoli' nf apostleship

apostoli'k adj [Relig] apostolic; papal

*apostolu'er adj (Old) = apostoli'k

*apo'stoll nm = apo'stull

apostrof' nm the apostrophe mark ': apostrophe

apostro'fë nf [Lit] exclamatory passage: apostrophe

apostrofi'm nm ger 1 [Lit] <apostrofo' ·n 2 apostrophe

apostrofo' ·n vt 1 [Lit] to apostrophize 2 to substitute an apostrophe mark for a vowel or syllable

*apostua'l nm = apo'stull

*apostue'shëm adj (i) = apostoli'k

apostula'të nf holy mission, apostolate

apo'stull nm (np ˜ j) apostle

apoteo'zë nf apotheosis

*apo'th nm breeze

aproksimati'v adj (i) approximate = përa'fërt

aprovi'm nm ger 1 <aprovo' ·n 2 approval

aprovo' ·n vt to approve

*apsi'nth nm = absi'nt

*apsi'th nm = absi'nt

*apusti' nf shelter, lee

aq
   I § adv 1 to such a degree/extent, so, so much 2 as much as could be imagined 3 to some extent but not much 4 (before a verb) not so much, not very much
   II § quant 1 so much/many 2 not all that much/many, only that much/many
   III § pcl (at the end of a clause after a conjunction) that's that, only that
   ○ aq <> arrijnë shkallët to the extent of <>'s abilities
   ○ aq <> bën <> doesn't really care, it doesn't bother <>
   ○ aq dua! that's exactly what I need, I don't need anything more
   ○ aq gjë so little/few (as that)
   ○ {number} herë aq {} times as much/many
   ○ aq e kaq such and such an amount
   ○ aq kish· gajle now (that [he] got what [he] wanted) [he] doesn't care anymore
   ○ aq mend ka·! that's how much sense {} has!
   ○ aq më shumë and in particular, especially, particularly
   ○ aq më fort especially, even more
   ○ aq më tepër and in particular, especially, particularly
   ○ aq më tepër që/se _ the more so since _, especially because _
   ○ aq mund· aq shkund· to perform to the limit of one's capabilities
   ○ aq e pati! well that's the end of that
   ○ aq sa <> peshon djersa "as much as <>'s sweat weighs" as much as justified by one's own hard work, by the sweat of one's brow
   ○ aq sa arri·n to the extent of one's mental ability
   ○ aq sa _ so much that _
   ○ aq _ sa _ to the same degree/extent _ as, as many/much _ as _; so many/much _ that _
   ○ aq tepër so much

*aqa'nshëm adj (i) equilateral

a'që adv = aq

*aqë'he'ra conj = aqhe'rë

*aqë'vle'rës adj equivalent

aqhe'rë adv while, during the time that

*aqpeshi'm nm equipoise, balance

*aqrëndi'm nm equilibrium

*aqsi'm nm 1 <aqso' ·n 2 equation

*aqso' ·n vt to equalise; equate

AQSh abbrev <Arkivi Qendror i Shtetit Central State Archive

*aqto'r nm equator

ar
   I § nm gold; gilt
   II § nm are (area equal to 100 square meters)

ara'b
   I § nm Arab
   II § adj 1 Arabian, Arabic (numerals) 2 [Ornit] = ara'pës

araba' *nf (Old)* open four-wheel carriage drawn by horses: coach, buggy

*****araba'ck**ë *nf dimin* baby carriage/buggy

*****araba'shnje** *nf* rubbish

araba|xhi' *nm (np ~ nj) (Old)* carriage driver, coachman

arab'çe *adv (Colloq)* **1** in Arabic **2** *(Fig)* unintelligibly, confused; backwards

*****arabe'l** *nm* = harabe'l

*****arabe'ske** *np* arabesques

arab'ës *nm* [*Bot*] rock-cress *(Arabis)*

Arabi' *nf* Arabia
  ◦ **Arabia Saudite** Saudi Arabia

arabido'pës *nm* [*Bot*] arabidopsis

arabi'k *adj* Arabic, of or pertaining to Arabia

arabi'sht *adv* in Arabic (language)

arabi'sht|e *nf* Arabic (the language)

aradhe' *nf* **1** *(Old)* [*Mil*] battalion **2** *(Fig)* advance guard, armada

Arago'në *nf* Aragon

arago'st|e *nf* [*Invert*] lobster, spiny lobster, crawfish *(Homarus vulgaris)*

*****ara'k** *nm* expert

*****araka't** *nm* = arraka't

*****araki'dh** *nm* **1** [*Bot*] peanut **2** earthquake

arakni'|dë *nf* arachnid

*****arakno' ·n** *vt* to master [a skill]

arali' *nf* [*Bot*] aralia *Aralia*

*****arali'k** *adj* withered, blighted

arali'o're *np masc* [*Bot*] ivy family *Araliaceae*

aral|ë'k *nm (np ~ qe) (Old)* **1** intervening space, distance; chasm **2** hallway between rooms **3** lobby, vestibule **4** free time, leisure time; work break
  ◦ **s'bë·n arallëk** not take breaks from work

a'ra-ma'ra *adv* harum-scarum, helter-skelter

*****ara'më** *nf* copper

*****arami'** *nm* **1** yellowhammer *(Emberiza citrinella)* **2** goldfinch *(Carduelis elegans)*

arança't|e *nf* orangeade

*****aranki|mbre't** *nm (Reg)* empire, realm

ara'p
  I § *n* **1** *(Colloq)* someone with dark complexion, swarthy person **2** frightening big, dark and powerful character in Balkan folktales **3** common name for dark-colored domestic animals **4** [*Zool*] tadpole
  II § *adj* very dark in color
  ◦ **arap i zi** very dark

arapa'sh *nm* a thick corn mush (prepared in some regions with finely minced liver and intestines of sheep or goats or with cabbage)

arapa'shk|ë *nf* variety of apple with red spots that is sweet, good tasting and long lasting

arape' *nf (Colloq)* **1** female with dark complexion, swarthy woman **2** name for dark-colored female domestic animals

arape'shë *nf (Colloq)* **1** negress, black female, swarthy woman **2** Arab woman

*****arape'shk|ë** *nf* = arape'shë

arap'ës *nm* [*Ornit*] house sparrow *(Passer domesticus)*

*****arapi'shte** *adv* = arabi'sht|e

*****arap'kë** *nf* = ara'pe

arapli' *nm (Reg)* [*Bot*] = bar delli

ara'qe
  I § *nf (Reg)* loosely tied noose, bowknot, slipknot
  II § *adv* loosely (tied)

ar'a'r *n* = arto'r

*****araro't** *nm* arrowroot

a'ras *adv* out in the fields, in the countryside

ara'shk|e *nf (Reg)* turnip *Brassica rapa*

*****arati'** *nf* = arrati'

arati'm *nm ger* **1** *(Old)* <arato' ·n **2** tillage, cultivation

*****arati's|** *nf* = arrati's

arato' ·n *vt (Old)* to cultivate

arauhij|ë *nf* [*Bot*] bladder flower, araujia *Araujia*

*****arave'l** *nm* = harabe'l

a'razi *adv*

*****Arbani'** *nf* = Arbëri'

Arbe'n *nm* Arben (male name)

a'rb'ër
  I § *nm collec* **1** [*Hist*] Albanians in the Middle Ages taken as a whole; Albanian; Italo-Albanian, Greco-Albanian **2** *(Reg)* local Albanian (as distinct from newcomers or foreigners) **3** *(Reg)* lowland **4** lowlander (especially those of coastal Labëria) *****5** *(Reg)* little boy
  II § *adj* [*Hist Poet*] of or pertaining to Arbër people

A'rb'ër *nm* Arbër (male name)

arbëre'sh
  I § *n* **1** Albanian of southern Italy, Greece, or Dalmatia descended from emigrés from Albania in the Middle Ages **2** *(Old)* Albanian in the Middle Ages **3** *(Reg)* lowlander (especially those of coastal Labëria)
  II § *adj* **1** [*Hist Poet*] of or pertaining to or inhabited by Albanians transplanted to southern Italy, Greece, or Dalmatia **2** *(Old)* Albanian **3** *(Reg)* of or pertaining to Labëria, or to their inhabitants

Arbëri' *nf* [*Hist*] Albania (in medieval times)

arbëri'sht *adv* **1** in the variety of Albanian spoken in southern Italy, Greece, or Dalmatia **2** *(Reg)* following the custom or life-style of the lowlanders of Labëria

arbëri'sht|e *nf* **1** [*Hist*] Albanian language (in medieval times) **2** the speech of the Albanian settlements in southern Italy or Greece

arbëri'o'r *adj, n* [*Poet*] Albanian

arbit'ër *nm* **1** arbiter, arbitrator **2** [*Sport*] referee, umpire

arbitra'r *adj* arbitrary

arbitrari'sht *adv* arbitrarily

arbitrari'te't *nm (Book)* arbitrariness

arbitrari'zëm *nm (Book)* = arbitrarite't

arbitra'zh *nm* [*Offic*] **1** arbitration **2** the body charged with carrying out arbitration procedures

arbitri'm *nm ger* **1** <arbitro' ·n **2** arbitration

arbitro' ·n
  I § *vt (Book)* to arbitrate
  II § *vi* [*Sport*] to act as referee

arbitro'r *adj* [*Law*] of or pertaining to or composed of arbiters

arceuto'bë *nf* [*Bot*] dwarf mistletoe *Arceuthobium*

*****arç** *nm* = arrç

*****arç'** stem for opt <vje·n

arça're *nf (Reg)* small hole

*****arderdho'r** *nm* goldsmith

ardian
I § n [Hist] member of one of the Illyrian tribes that formerly inhabited territory between Lake Scutari and Dalmatia
II § adj of or pertaining to the Ardians

*ardiç nm = hardhiç

ardh
I § stem for adm, opt, part <vje·n
II § stem for pdef (Reg)

ardhacak nm immigrant, newcomer

*ardhânës adj (Reg Gheg) = armbajtës

ardhang· vt to refresh, invigorate; revive

ardhang·et vpr to be invigorated; gain strength, be refreshed

ardhangësi nf vitality

ardhangët adj (i) robust and vigorous

ardhangie nf 1 robustness; freshness, vigor 2 [Spec] swollenness of cells and tissues of an organism

ardhëm adj (i) = ardhshëm

ardhën nm [Bot] = arne

*ardhëngët adj (i) = ardhangët

ardhës
I § nm 1 newcomer 2 child who accompanies a widowed or divorced mother into her new marriage
II § adj newly arrived
∘ **Ardh** opt **si vera!** "May {} come like summer!" (Felic) May {} come back with success!

*ardhëshëm adj (i) = ardhshëm

*ardhi nf [Bot] = hardhi

ardhishkë nf = hardhje

ardhje nf ger 1 <vje·n 2 arrival 3 (Old) income *4 future

ardhkish stem of admirative pind forms <vje·n

ardhme nf (e) 1 future 2 better future 3 [Ling] future tense

ardhmëni nf [Poet] 1 future 2 better future

*ardhmës nm descendant

ardhsh stem for opt <vje·n

ardhshëm adj (i) 1 future; coming, next (in date designations) 2 (Reg Colloq) having a well-built body 3 (Reg Colloq) sociable, charming, amiable *4 handy, useful, suitable

ardhshme nf (e) = ardhme

ardhshmëri nf (Book) the future world, the future

ardht ë 3sg opt <vje·n
∘ <> **ardhtë pas veshit/qafës!** "May it fall on <>'s ears/neck!" (Curse) May misfortune/death fall suddenly on <>!

*ardhun = ardhur

ardhur
I § part <vje·n
II § adj (i) 1 newly arrived, that which has come/arrived 2 imported 3 [Biol Geol] invasive 4 having reached the proper condition: (of bread dough) risen, (of soil) plowed and ready for planting; ripe 5 (Fig Colloq) having a well-developed body, physically mature 6 (Fig Colloq) courteous and charming: real nice

ardhura np (të) income, revenues, proceeds, earnings

*arenc nm steel = çelik

arendë nf [Econ] land lease

arene nf arena

arenikolë n [Invert] lugworm Arenicola marina

*arenz nm = arenc

areometër nf [Phys] areometer, hydrometer

*arest = arrest

arë nf arable soil, farmland, field, piece of ground

arëbërës n (Colloq) one who clears new land

*arëmatje nf surveying

*arësimore nf educational institution

*arësimtarkë nf (Reg Tosk) female teacher, instructress

*arëso·n vt 1 to chase/drive [] away *2 = arsimo·n

*arësuar adj (i) = arsimuar

arëz nf 1 [Entom] wasp, hornet, yellow-jacket 2 (Fig) person who is a nuisance to others

*arfaje adj ancient, biblical

*argali nf loom

*argalis· vt, vi to weave

argalis·et vpr (Colloq) to have a hilarious time; be amusing, tease one another

argan nm [Bot] bush with twisted stems, very small, dense, lanceolate leaves, and violet-colored flowers used to make a clothing dye

arganist n winch operator

argano nf [Tech] winch

argas· vt = regj·

argas·et vpr = regj·et

argasje nf ger = regjje

argasur adj (i) = regjur

argat nm 1 hired hand, farm hand; peon 2 (Old) day laborer, farmer who comes to give free help to another farmer 3 (Old) the amount of land (about a quarter of an acre) that a single person could plough in one day

argateshë nf = argate

argatëri nf [Hist] 1 hired hands as a class 2 day labor in farming; the condition of being a hired hand

argati nf = argatëri

argavan nm [Bot] = jargavan

argëlidh nm [Bot] wild olive = ullastër

argëllëk nm (Ethnog Old) bride price, money paid by the groom to the bride for her to prepare a trousseau

*argësh nm = argsh

argëtim nm ger 1 <argëto·n 2 enjoyment, amusement, entertainment

argëto·het vpr to enjoy oneself, have fun

argëto·n
I § vt 1 to entertain, amuse 2 to soothe, caress
II § vi = argëto·het

argëtues adj amusing, entertaining

*argim nm 1 <argo·n 2 drizzle 3 flattery

*argo nm termination, end

*argo·n vt 1 to drizzle 2 to flatter, entertain

*argomaz nm = argomë

*argomë nf fallow field

argon nm argon

Argos nm Argos

argosh·et vpr to get a skin rash

argoshë nf skin rash, heat rash, rash

argsh nm crude pontoon raft or bridge made of wickerwork and inflated bladders

*argti nf entertainment, amusement

*argtueshëm adj = argëtues

argull nm (np ~ j) nit, young louse

argument nm argument

argumentïm *nm ger* **1** <**argumento·n 2** argumentation, reasoning

argumento·n *vt* to advance arguments, argue for, bring proof, reason

argumentua·r *adj (i)* based on argument or reason

*argjandsïna *np (Reg Gheg)* = argjendurïna

argje·nd
I § *nm* **1** silver **2** silver thread
II § *adj* = argje·ndtë
○ argjend i trashë nickel silver, German silver

argjenda·r *n* silversmith, silver worker

argjenda·rï *nf* **1** silversmithery, the craft of the silversmith **2** silversmithy, workshop devoted to silver

argjend|da·sh|ës *n (Old)* miser

argje·nd|e *np* things made of silver = argjendurïna

argje·nd|ë *adj (i)* = argje·ndtë

argjend|ïm *nm ger* <argjendo·n, argjend|o·het

argjendo··het *vpr* to gleam like silver; turn grey or white

argjendo·n
I § *vt* **1** to coat [ ] with silver, silverplate, silver **2** to make silvery or white in color
II § *vi* to gleam like silver

argjendo·r *adj [Poet]* = argje·ndtë

argje·nd|pun|ue·s *adj* = argjenda·r

argje·ndt|ë *adj (i)* **1** made of silver; silverplated, silvered **2** silvery, gleaming like silver

argjendua·r *adj (i)* **1** silver-coated, silverplated, silvered **2** silvery, gleaming like silver

argjend|urïna *np* things made of silver

argjentïnas
I § *nm* Argentinian
II § *adj* Argentine, of or pertaining to Argentina

Argjentïnë *nf* Argentina

*argjentja·n *adj, n* = argjentïnas

*argjë·nt *nm* = argje·nd

*argjë·ntë *adj (i)* = argje·ndtë

*argjë·nttë *adj (i)* = argje·ndtë

argjï·l *nm* = argjï·lë

argjï·lë *nf* argil = deltï·në

argjï·lo·r *adj* argillaceous = deltïno·r

argjina·re *nf [Bot]* = angjina·re

argjinatu·rë *nf* river levee, flood-control embankment: check dam, flood wall

*argjipe·shk *nm* = argjipe·shkëv

argjipe·shkëv *nm* archbishop

argjipeshk|no·r *adj* archiepiscopal

argjipeshkvï· *nf* archbishopric, jurisdiction of an archbishop

*argjï·të *nf* = arqï·të

Arhange·lsk *nm* Archangel (the city)

*arhï· *nf* authority

*arhï|mandrï·t *nm* = arkimandrï·t

*arhï|mandrïto·r *adj* archimandritic

*arhond|e·shë *nf* = arko·ndeshë

*arho·nt = arko·nd

arï *nm* bear
○ ari i bardhë "white gold" *(Book)* cotton
○ ari i gjelbër *(Book)* timber forest
○ ari i zi *(Book)* petroleum; coal

aria·n *n* Aryan

Arianï·t *nm* Arianit (male name)

arï·çkë *nf* pullet

a·rie *nf* aria

*Arï·f *nm* Arif (male name)

*arï·lë *nf* silk worm cocoon/chrysalis

*arï·ng *nm* = harï·ng

arï·ngë *nf [Bot]* tree of heaven *Ailanthus glandulosa*

arï·nj *np* <arï·

aristokracï· *nf* aristocracy
○ aristokraci punëtore "working-class aristocracy" *(Pej)* proletariat that has sold out to bourgeois values

aristokra·t
I § *nm* aristocrat
II § *adj* aristocratic

*aristokratï· *nf* = aristokracï·

aristokratï·k *adj* aristocratic

aristolokio·re *nf [Bot]* birthwort family *Aristolochiaceae*

arï·shtë *nf* **1** field left fallow for a few years **2** small field of farmland **3** farmland

aritmetï·k *adj* arithmetic(al)

aritmetï·kë *nf* arithmetic

aritmetik|ïsht *adv* arithmetically

aritmetiko·r *adj* = aritmetï·k

aritmï· *nf* **1** *[Med]* arhythmia **2** *[Mus]* irregularity of rhythm

aritmï·k *nf* **1** *[Med]* arhythmic **2** *[Mus Lit]* without regular rhythm, lacking rhythm

arï·th *nm [Bot]* horsetail *(Equisetum telmateja)*

arï·the *nf (Reg) [Bot]* tragacanth, goat's thorn = urï·the

arï·thi *adv* bear-fashion, on hind legs like a bear, rearing (like a horse)

arithmetï·kë *nf* = aritmetï·kë

arixhe·shkë *nf female* <arixhï·

arï·xhï *nm (np ⁻ nj)* Gypsy, Rom

arixho·fkë *nf* = arixhe·shkë

*ark *nm (np ⁻ qe)* = hark

arka· *nf* saw-blade

*arka·de *nf* arcade

*arka·fo·rte *nf* safe, vault

arka·ïk *adj* archaic

arka·ïzëm *nm* archaism

arkapï· *nf (Reg)* small door (especially, the door in a backyard wall between neighbors)

arka|pun|ue·s *nm (Old)* carpenter who makes bride's hope chest

a·rk|as *adv* box-like, in the form of a box (e. g., said of tables set up in a U-shaped arrangement)

arkebu·z *nm [Hist]* harquebus

arkeo·lo·g *n* archeologist

arkeo·logjï· *nf* archeology

arkeo·logjï·k *adj* archeological

a·rkë *nf* **1** storage chest; crate, box **2** strongbox, cashbox **3** cashier's desk/office/register **4** treasury **5** *[Fin]* savings institution, depository **6** *(Colloq)* coffin **7** chest for a bride's trousseau **8* ark **9** *[Mollusc]* kind of ark shell *Anadara diluvii*
○ arkë e dry never apart, inseparable
○ ësh·të arkë e mbyllur "be a closed storage chest" **1** to be a very private person **2** to be a sealed book, be a mystery

arkë-ko·sh *nm [Mollusk]* kind of ark shell *Anadara corbuloides*

○ **arkë-kosh e Noes** [*Invert*] Noah's ark shell *Arca noae*

***arkël** *nf* small cashbox

arkërkue·s *nm* gold prospector

arkëtar *n* cashier; treasurer

arkëtim *nm ger* 1 <**arkëto**·*n* 2 bank deposit

arkëto·*n vt* to deposit [funds] in a bank or treasury

arkëtue·s *adj* [*Fin*] of or pertaining to banking of money

arkëz *nf* small box for keeping valuables, jewel box, cashbox; storage case

arki *formative prefix* 1 (*Book*) indicates high degree or title, arch-/archi- 2 (*Pej*) indicates extreme degree

arkidioqezë *nf* archdiocese

arkidukë *nf with masc reference* archduke

arkimandrit *nm* archimandrite

arkioportunist *n* opportunist of the worst kind

arkipelag *nm* archipelago

***arkipellg** = arkipelag

arkitekt *n* architect

arkitektonik *adj* 1 architectonic 2 = arkitektural

arkitektonikë *nf* architectonics

arkitektural *adj* architectural

arkitekturë *nf* architecture

arkitra *nf* [*Archit*] architrave; lintel, crossbeam

arkitrav *nm* = arkitra

arkiv *nm* archive

arkival *adj* = arkivor

***arkivë** *nf* = arkiv

arkivim *nm ger* [*Offic*] <**arkivo**·*n*

arkivist *n* archivist

arkivo·*n vt* to put [] into archives

arkivol *nm* coffin, bier

arkivolpunue·s *nm* coffinmaker

arkivor *adj* archival

arkond *nm* [*Hist*] 1 archon 2 baron

arkondeshë *nf* baroness

arkondi *nf* barony

arktik *adj* arctic

***arktor** *nm* = harkëtar

***arktuar** *nm* = harkëtar

***arktuer** *nm* = harkëtar

armaç *nm* 1 (*Ethnog*) piece of brocade sewn on the front of harem pants or men's trousers or underpants ***2** flyflap on men's trousers 3 (*Old*) [*Text*] brocade

***armakolë** *nf* armory; gun barrel

***armakollë** *nf* = armakolë

armatesë *nf* 1 armature 2 [*Min*] reinforced lining of a mine tunnel: timbering, shoring

armatë *nf* 1 [*Mil*] large military unit consisting of two or more army corps: corps, army 2 (*Fig*) large mass of people working together towards a common goal 3 (*Fig*) large mass of technological equipment 4 gold necklace

armatim *nm* 1 [*Mil*] arms provisioning 2 [*Mil*] armament 3 [*Min*] arming (with explosives)

armatis· *vt* = armatos·

***armatollos** *nm* warrior, man-at-arms

armator *nm* 1 owner or operator of a ship who equips and uses it commercially 2 = armatue·s

armatos· *vt* 1 to provide [] with arms: arm 2 [*Mil*] to prepare [a weapon] for firing: arm, load 3 to shore up [a mine]

armatos·et *vpr* to be armed; prepared for a task

***armatosi** *nf* decoration, ornament; the rigging on a ship

armatosje *nf ger* 1 <armatos·, armatos·et 2 armament

armatosur *adj (i)* armed, having weapons

***armatuer** *nm (Old)* armorer; arms manufacturer

armatue·s *nm* miner who constructs the tunnel framework

armaturë *nf* 1 armature 2 [*Tech*] (pipe) fittings 3 frame (for glasses, mirror, etc.); case, cabinet (for radio, etc.) 4 storage cabinet (for guns, tools, etc.) 5 [*Hist*] military provisions for ancient and medieval armies 6 [*Mus*] key signature 7 [*Constr*] reinforced concrete

armbajtës *adj* [*Geol*] gold-bearing

armë *nf* 1 pickled cabbage, sauerkraut 2 (*Reg*) [*Dairy*] salted yogurt or milk stored in leather bottles for winter

armegane *np (Ethnog Old)* gift (usually sweets and fruits) from groom to bride one day before the wedding

armen *adj, n* Armenian

***armena** *np* rigging, tackle

armenas *adj, n* Armenian

Armeni *nf* Armenia

***armenis**· *vi* 1 to disembark, land 2 to tack (sailing maneuver), change course ***3** (*Reg Gk*) to rig, equip, fit out; sail with sails set

***armenisurë** *nf (e)* boarding (a ship); landing

armenisht *adv* in Armenian (language)

armenishte *nf* the Armenian language

***armeri** *nf* = armëri

armë

　I § *nf* 1 weapon, arm 2 branch of military forces

　II § *np* 1 military forces 2 munitions

　○ **armë e bardhë** bladed weapon

　○ **armë brezi** weapon carried in the belt sash

　○ **arma e këmbësorisë** the infantry (branch)

　○ **armë me zjarr** firearm

　○ **armë zjarri** firearm

armëlarë *nf* 1 [*Poet*] with armor/arms bathed in gold/silver; in shining armor 2 glorious in battle, victorious

armëmbajtës *nm* 1 [*Hist*] armsbearer for a knight, squire 2 (*Fig*) lackey 3 (*Book*) arms bearer

armëmbajtje *nf* [*Law*] arms possession

armëndreqës *nm* craftsman who repairs armor/arms

armëngrirë *nf (Poet)* with armor/arms bathed in gold/silver; in shining armor

armëngjeshur *adj* with arms girded on, armed and ready for battle

armëpathyer *adj (Poet)* undaunted, undefeated in battle; dauntless

armëpishë *nf (Poet)* arms-at-the-ready, ever ready for battle

armëpunue·s *nm (Old)* armorer

armëpushim *nm* cease-fire, armistice; truce

***armëqitje** *nf* target shooting, target practice

***armërëndë** *np* heavily armed soldiers

armëri *nf (Old)* 1 [*Mil*] armory ***2** heraldry; coat of arms

armëshitës *nm* armsmonger, arms dealer

armëtar *nm* **1** [*Mil*] weapons specialist; person in charge of military weapons **2** *(Old)* armorer, gunsmith ***3** infantryman

armëtari *nf (Old)* the craft of the armorer; arms manufacture

armëtore *nf* [*Mil*] armory

*armi·n *vt* = gërmo·*n*

*armih· *vt* = rrëmih·

armik *nm, adj* enemy
  ○ **armik i padeklaruar** person who works in secret against one: undeclared/secret enemy

*armikëri *nf(Old)* = armiqëri

armim *nm ger* [*Constr*] <armo·*n*

armiq *np masc* <armik

armiqëri *nf collec (Colloq)* one's enemies taken as a whole, the enemy

armiqësi *nf* enmity, hostility, antagonism

armiqësim *nm ger* <armiqëso·*n*, armiqëso·*het*

armiqësisht *adv* antagonistically, hostilely

armiqëso·het *vpr* to get hostile, become antagonistic

armiqëso·n *vt* to create enmity/hostility between [], antagonize

armiqësor
  I § *adj* hostile, antagonistic, inimical; opposed
  II § *n* antagonist

armiqësuar *adj (i)* antagonized, made hostile, angered

armirë *nf* [*Bot*] bastard toadflax (*Thesium*)

*armishtë *nf* armory, ammunition factory

armo·n *vt* **1** [*Constr*] to reinforce with metal bars ***2** to arm

armoçiment *nm* = armaturë

*armoni *nf* = harmoni

*armonium *nm* harmonium

*armonizo·n *vt* = harmonizo·*n*

armor *nm (Old)* armor

*armtar *nm* = armatuer

*armtore *nf* = arsenal

*armubulicë *nf* churn

arna-arna *adj* **1** all in patches **2** stained, spotted, patchy

arnaje *nf* farmland, plowed land

*arnar *nm* lime (calcium oxide)

arnatar *n* patcher, repairer

arnaut *nm, adj (Old)* Albanian (so called by the Turks)

arne(n) *nm (np ~ nj)* [*Bot*] Heldreich pine (*Pinus heldreichii*)
  ○ **arne i bardhë** [*Bot*] Macedonian pine *Pinus peuce*

arnesar *nm (Old)* = arnues

arnesë *nf* patched part: patch

arnë *nf* patch, piece of material used to make a patch
  ○ **U ndesh arna me thesin.** The devil has found his mate.

arni *nf collec (Reg)* farmland taken as a whole; farmland

arnicë *nf dimin* little patch

arnim *nm ger* **1** <arno·*n*, arno·*het* **2** = arnesë

*arnis· *vt* to refuse, deny

arnishtë *nf* **1** old piece of material used as a patch **2** something old with patches **3** pine forest

arno·het *vpr* **1** to patch clothes **2** *(Fig)* to make do with what one has

arno·n *vt* to patch, mend, restore, repair

arnojse *nf (Reg)* needle

arnuar *adj (i)* patched, mended, with patches

arnues *n* person who mends clothes or shoes

*arogant *adj* = arrogant

aromatik *adj* aromatic

aromë *nf* aroma

*aroplan *nm* = aeroplan

aror *adj* of or pertaining to farmland/fields

aros· *vt (Old)* to gild

arosur *adj (i) (Old)* gilded, gold-plated

*arpë *nf* harp = harpë

arpion *nm* [*Tech*] ratchet

*arprues *adj* gold-bearing, auriferous

arpunuar *adj (Poet)* made of or decorated with gold, golden, gilt

arpunues *nm* = argjendar

*arq *nm* superiority, priority

*arqe *np* = harqe

*arqeolog *n* = arkeolog

*arqeologji *nf* = arkeologji

*arqeologjik *adj* = arkeologjik

*arqi *nf* = hark

*arqiduk *nm* = arkidukë

arqidukë = arkidukë

*arqif *nm* = arkiv

arqimandrit = arkimandrit

arqiomarksist *adj, n* [*Hist*] archeo-Marxist: (person) belonging to a political group founded in Greece in 1920

*arqipel *nm* = arkipelag

*arqipelag *nm* = arkipelag

*arqipeshk *nm* = argjipeshkëv

*arqipeshkv *nm* = argjipeshkëv

*arqipeshkvi *nf* = argjipeshkvi

*arqitekt *nm* = arkitekt

*arqitekturë *nf* = arkitekturë

*arqitektyrë *nf* = arkitekturë

arqitë *nf (Reg)* **1** osier **2** thin willow twig used for wickerwork

*arqivë *nf* = arkiv

*arqivol *nm* = arkivol

arse·het *vpr* **1** to learn, be instructed, gain knowledge, become educated **2** to learn how to behave

arse·n *vt* **1** to instruct, educate, train, advise **2** to give [] a lesson in how to behave: scold, reprove **3** *(Reg)* to oust [an animal] **4** *(Reg Fig)* to complete one's work on []

arsenal *nm* arsenal

arsenik *nm* arsenic

arsenikor *adj* arsenic(al)

*arsëzë
  I § *adj* audacious, impudent, recklessly bold
  II § *adv* courageously, audaciously, resolutely

arsim *nm* instruction, education, teaching
  ○ **arsim i mesëm** secondary school education

arsimdashës
  I § *adj* eager to learn; supportive of education
  II § *n* eager learner; promoter of education

arsimo·het *vpr* to be instructed, go to school, get an education

arsimo·n *vt* to instruct, educate

arsimo̱r *adj* pertaining to education, educational, instructional, pedagogical, academic, scholastic

*__arsi̱mshëm__ *adj (i)* didactic; rational

arsimta̱r
   I § *n* educator, pedagogue, instructor
   II § *adj* *educational

arsimua̱r *adj (i)* having a formal education, educated

*__arsi̱tës__ *n, adj* renegade, turncoat, rebel

arsye̱ *nf* reason

arsye̱ *stem for part, adm, 3rd sg pdef, pl pdef, 3rd sg vp* <arse·n

arsye̱shëm
   I § *adj (i)* reasonable
   II § *adv* reasonably, thoughtfully

arsyeti̱m *nm ger* <arsyeto·n, **arsyeto̱·het**

*__arsyeti̱sht__ *adv* rationally, reasonably

arsyeto̱·het *vpr* to explain oneself; present an excuse

arsyeto̱·n
   I § *vi* to reason, reason out; judge on the basis of reason; argue
   II § *vt* to advance arguments for [ ], argue for [ ]; justify, explain

arsyetua̱r *adj (i)* **1** explanatory **2** annotated

arsyetue̱s
   I § *n (Book)* one skillful in arguing/explaining; rational person; reasoner, arguer
   II § *adj* **1** *(Book)* rational **2** explanatory **3** skillful in arguing/explaining

arsyetue̱shëm *adj (i)* rational

*__arshaje̱__ *np* military cramp

*__arshidu̱k__ *nm* = arkidu̱kë

*__arshi̱k__ *nm* sweetheart, suitor = ashi̱k

*__arshi̱n__ *nm* = rrëshi̱rë

*__arshiqi̱__ *nf* = ashikëri̱

*__arshi̱vë__ *nf* = arki̱v

art *nm* art
   ○ **artet e bukura** the fine arts
   ○ **artet e lira** *(Book)* the liberal arts
   ○ **arti për art** art for art's sake

Arṯa *nf* Arta (female name)

*__arta̱b__ *nm* Turkish measure equal to 140 or 150 kilograms

Arta̱n *nm* Artan (male name)

*__arta̱r__ *nm* goldsmith

artdasẖës
   I § *n* art lover
   II § *adj* art-loving

arte̱l *nm* artel

arte̱r *nm* = arte̱rie

*__arteri̱__ *nm* = arte̱rie

arte̱rie *nf* artery

arteriosklero̱zë *nf* [Med] arteriosclerosis

arteri̱t *nm* [Med] arteritis

*__arterue̱r__ *adj (Old)* arterial

artezia̱n *adj* artesian

a̱rtë *adj (i)* made of gold, of gold; golden

arti̱(r) *nm (np ⁓ nj)* [Bot] Heldreich pine *(Pinus heldreichi)*
   ○ **arti i bardhë** = arne̱

artiço̱k *nm* artichoke, globe artichoke *(Cynara scolymus)*

artificia̱l *nm* artificial; false

artificiali̱sht *adv* artificially

arti̱kull *nm (np ⁓j)* article produced by manufacturing or processing
   ○ **artikuj kancelarie** stationery items

artikullo̱·n *vt* to articulate

artikullshkrue̱s *nm* article writer, author of an article

artileri̱ *nf* artillery

*__artileri̱k__ *adj* of artillery

artileri̱st *nm* = artilje̱r

artilje̱r *nm* artilleryman

arti̱nj *np* <arti̱(r)

*__artiqo̱k__ *nm* = artiço̱k

arti̱ṟi *obl* <arti̱(r)

arti̱s· *vt* [Agr] to transplant [a seedling]

arti̱sës *nm* [Agr] garden trowel

arti̱sëse *nf* [Agr] seedling planter

arti̱sje *nf ger* [Agr] <arti̱s·

arti̱st *n* artist

*__arti̱stë__ *nf* <arti̱st

artisti̱k *adj* artistic

artistiki̱sht *adv* artistically

arti̱sur *adj (i)* [Agr] (of a seedling) transplanted

arti̱shtë *nf* pine forest

artito̱re *nf* [Agr] = shpërngulto̱re

artiza̱n *n* artisan

artizana̱l *adj* **1** made by artisans, crafted, handcrafted **2** pertaining to the crafts **3** *(Pej)* old-fashioned

artizana̱t *nm* **1** handicraft **2** handcrafted product

*__arto̱·n__ *vt* = harto̱·n

arto̱r *n (Old)* farmworker who works in the fields

artri̱s *stem for 1st sg pres, pl pres, 2nd & 3rd sg subj, pind* <artri̱t·

artri̱t *nm* [Med] arthritis

artri̱t· *vt* to transplant

artropo̱d *nm* arthropod

arturi̱në *nf* gold ornament

*__a̱rth__ = a̱rdh

*__a̱rthç__ *stem for opt* <vje·n

*__a̱rthëm__ *adj (i)* = a̱rdhshëm

arthi-goma̱rthi *adv (Reg)* leapfrog

*__a̱rthme__ *nf (e)* = a̱rdhme

*__a̱rthmë__ *adj (i)* = a̱rdhshëm

*__a̱rthsh__ *stem for opt* <vje·n

arumani̱sht *adv* in Arumanian/Wallachian

arumani̱shte *nf* the Arumanian/Wallachian language

arumu̱n *nm* Arumanian/Wallachian

arusha̱n *adj* **1** having a strong and good-looking body, well-built and handsome: built like a bear **2** tireless and skillful at heavy work **3** *(Fig)* brave and strong

arushë̱ *nf* **1** she-bear **2** *(Colloq)* tireless, powerful and brave person; powerful tool
   ○ **Arusha e Madhe** [Astron] the Big Dipper *(Ursa Major)*
   ○ **Arusha e Vogël** [Astron] the Little Dipper *(Ursa Minor)*

arushkë̱ *nf* **1** bear cub, small bear **2** *(Reg)* honeyed breadpudding made on New Year's Eve

*__arva̱t·et__ *vpr* = orva̱t·et

*__arxhevi̱s__ *nm* [Bot] = arrë hindi̱

*arxh|o·*n vt* = harxho·*n*
*ary|e·rë *adv* = atëhe·rë
*a·rzë *nf* = arëz
*arzua·l *nm* = arzuha·ll
*arzual|xhi *nm (np ~ nj)* petitioner
arzuha·ll *nm (Old)* request in writing, written petition
*arraba·shnj|ë *nf* rubbish, sweepings
arraka·çe *nf (Reg) [Bot]* = luleka·çe
arraka·t *adj, n* vagrant; stray
arraka·t· *vt* to scatter, disperse
arraka·t·*et vpr* **1** to stray from the flock; scatter, disperse **2** to wander around separately
*arrasi|xha·rrasi *adv* boisterously, roughly and noisily
arrati *nf* **1** = arrati·sje **2** exile to escape pursuit
*arrati·a|k *adj* errant
arrati·|s· *vt* **1** to expel, banish, send [] into exile, deport, drive [] out **2** to disperse, scatter; force [] into hasty retreat
arrati·s·*et vpr* **1** to flee; take refuge **2** to go away, make oneself scarce, desert **3** to become dispersed **4** to wander all around **5** *(Reg)* to collapse, collapse violently
arrati·s|je *nf ger* **1** <arrati·s·, arrati·s·*et* **2** flight, escape; desertion; dispersal
arrati·s|ur
  I § *adj (i)* **1** escaped, in refuge **2** exiled, banished
  II § *nm* **1** escapee, refugee **2** fugitive from justice **3** *(Fig)* wanderer, exile
*arravonja·s· *vt* to betroth
arrç *nm* **1** *[Bot]* buckthorn *(Rhamnus)* **2** *[Entom]* mole cricket, house cricket *(Gryllus grullotalpa)* ***3** *[Entom]* cockchafer *Melolontha vulgaris* **4** *[Anat]* Adam's apple ***5** *[Anat]* first cervical vertebra
  ◦ arrç i egër *[Bot]* Alpine buckthorn *Rhamnus alpinus ssp. fallax*
  ◦ arrç i zi glossy buckthorn, alder buckthorn *Rhamnus frangula*
arrço·re *np [Bot]* buckthorn family *Rhamnaceae*
arre·st *nm* arrest
arrest|i·m *nm ger* <arresto·*n*
arresto·*n vt* to arrest
arrestu·a|r
  I § *adj (i)* arrested, under arrest
  II § *n (i)* arrested person
a·rrë
  I § *nf* **1** walnut *(Juglans regia L.)* **2** *[Anat]* tonsil
  II § *adj* nut-like: (of bread) hard outside and soft inside
  ◦ arrë bukje walnut with a large kernel that comes out easily
  ◦ arrë dheu *[Bot]* leguminous root tubers
  ◦ arrë e egër *[Bot]* = a·rrë hindi
  ◦ arrë fyçkë "empty walnut" *(Pej)* empty-headed fool
  ◦ arra e fytit Adam's apple
  ◦ arrë hindi *[Bot]* tree of heaven *(Ailanthus glandulosa)*
  ◦ arrë mishje walnut whose kernel is hard to get out
  ◦ arrë myshku = arrëmy·shk
  ◦ arrë në gojë a hard nut to swallow
  ◦ arra pa thelb "walnuts without nutmeat" castles in the air
  ◦ arrë pjeshke walnut whose kernel comes out easily

  ◦ arrë pufkë hollow walnut
  ◦ arrë pufte hollow walnut
  ◦ arrë e qelbët *[Bot]* *= a·rrë hindi
arrë|my·shk *nm* nutmeg
a·rrës *nm [Bot]* cat thyme *Teucrium marum*
  ◦ arrës i verdhë *[Bot]* yellow germander *Teucrium flavum*
*arrë·si·në *nf* persecution
arrë·thy·ese *nf* nutcracker
a·rrëz *nf* **1** *[Anat]* first cervical vertebra *(Atlas)* **2** Adam's apple **3** walnut grove **4** *[Bot]* woodland angelica, wild angelica *Angelica sylvestris* **5** *[Bot]* Scotch laburnum *Laburnum alpinum*
  ◦ thyej/këput arrëzën! scram! get ere!
arri·*het*
  I § *vpr* **1** to ripen **2** to swell up with pus to the bursting point **3** to reach a goal
  II § *vpr* to be reached/attained
arri·*n*
  I § *vi* **1** to arrive **2** to suffice, be sufficient; survive **3** to come to a desirable state of affairs
  II § *vt* **1** to reach; attain **2** to manage to do [something], succeed in doing [] **3** to catch up with [] **4** to reach, arrive at []
  ◦ s'‹› arrin dora "‹›'s arm *doesn't* reach (that far)" ‹›'s capacities do not permit
  ◦ [] arri·*n* me dy a tri pupa to get to [] quickly: get to [] in a couple of hops
  ◦ ‹› arri·*n*³*pl* sytë gjer te maja e hundës *(Pej)* ‹› sees only to the end of ‹›'s nose
*arri·|j = arri·|
arri·j|shëm *adj (i)* **1** = arri·shëm ***2** = arri·rë
*arri·jt|ës
  I § *adj* arriving, reaching; adequate
  II § *n* newcomer, arrival
arri·rë *adj (i)* **1** having reached the proper condition: (of bread dough) risen, (of soil) plowed and ready for planting; ripe **2** *(Fig)* mature **3** accomplished
arri·sh|ëm *adj (i)* capable of being achieved: realizable
arri·sht|ë *nf* walnut grove
arri·t stem for pdef, opt, adm, part <arri·*n*
*arri·t|ë *adj (i)* mature, ripe
*arri·t|ësi *nf* maturity, ripeness
arri·t|je *nf ger* **1** <arri·*n*, arri·*het* **2** arrival; attainment **3** accomplishment, success **4** *[Sport]* finish line
arri·t|shëm *adj (i)* **1** attainable, possible; feasible **2** understandable, comprehensible
arri·t|ur
  I § *part* <arri·*n*
  II § *adj (i)* **1** accomplished **2** *(Old) [Fin]* cumulative
*arri·v| stem for 1st & 2nd sg pdef <arri·*n*
arrivi·st
  I § *n (Book)* opportunist, social-climber
  II § *adj (Book)* opportunistic, social-climbing
arrivi·z|ëm *nm (Book)* social climbing, opportunism
*arrmi·zë *nf* = arrëmy·shk
*arrni·s·*et vpr* to make a denial
*arrni·sht|ë *nf* scrap, old piece
arr|nje·t *nm* walnut grove
arroga·nc|ë *nf* arrogance, contempt
arroga·nt *adj n* arrogant/contemptuous (person)

arro·r *adj* [*Agr*] having walnut-sized lumps (said of soil)

arro·re *np* [*Bot*] walnut family *Juglandaceae*

arrs *nm* [*Bot*] germander *(Teucrium)*

a·rrtë *adj (i)* made of walnut, of walnut

as

I § *conj* and not, neither, nor

II § *pcl* **1** not even, no; nary **2** expresses a mild request or suggestion

III § *nm* skirt pleat

∘ **as ballë as bisht** neither first nor last, neither best nor worst

∘ **as cing, as ming** without making a peep

∘ **as ciu as miu/viu** not a peep

∘ **as gjallë as vdekur 1** at death's door **2** terribly frightened

∘ **as jep·, as merr· 1** to give no sign of life; not move a muscle; be stuck/frozen; get stuck **2** [*Ethnog*] not engage in intermarriage

∘ **as kullo·n, as turbullo·n** to keep to oneself, not get involved; count neither as friend nor as foe

∘ **as lidh·et as zgjidh·et** to be stubbornly set in one's ways

∘ **as ma jep!** how about just giving it to me! why don't you just give it to me!

∘ **as mbarë as prapë** neither well nor badly, not good not bad

∘ **as me buaj, as me qe** unable to decide: on the fence

∘ **as mish as peshk** neither fish nor fowl

∘ **as nam, as nishan** without leaving a trace

∘ **as ndez·, as shua·n 1** to be very pedestrian **2** to always take a neutral position

∘ **as në thes as në torbë** fickle

∘ **as në thembër s'<>a arri·n** "not even reach <>'s heel" to be far inferior to <>: not be comparable to <> at all, not begin to compare, not come up to <>'s toenail

∘ **as në ujë, as për ujë** as bad as it could be, it couldn't be worse

∘ **as në han, as në va** *(Fig Pej)* of indeterminite status, neither here nor there; hanging in air, indefinite

∘ **as nuk të pri·n as nuk të ndjek·** "neither lead you nor follow you" *(Impol)* to be incapable of being of any help

∘ **as një morr qorr** "not a single blind louse" not even a tiny bit, none

∘ **as prish·, as ndreq·** to be incapable of being of any help

∘ **as qan, as qesh** "neither cries, nor laughs." doesn't say yes, doesn't say no

∘ **as që** _ not even _

∘ **as rob as korb** no one, not a single person

∘ **as sot as mot** never never

∘ **as të ngroh·, as të ftoh· 1** to be neither a help nor a hindrance **2** to make no particular impression on you one way or another, not be exciting one way or another **3** to be feckless

∘ **as të fal as të vret** "neither forgives you nor kills you" won't say yes, won't say no; keeps you hanging

∘ **as turbullo·n, as kthjello·n** "neither cloud up nor clear up" be of neither help nor hindrance

as *nm* **1** ace (in cards) **2** expert **3** *(Hist)* small Roman coin made of copper

as| *formative prefix* (negative of the following stem) no-, non-

a·saj

I § *dat/abl* <**ajo**'

*a·sajt *OR* **a·sajta** *adv* yonder, over there; from there

asamble *nf* (legislative) assembly

asamblïst *n* assemblyman, member of the assembly

asbe·st *nm* asbestos

as·diku·sh = **asku·sh**

Asdre·n *nm* Asdren (male name)

a·se *conj* = **o·se**

aseptïk *adj* aseptic

***ases
í** *adv* = **assesí**

*ase·t *nm* = **hase·t**

*asevï *nf* impiety, irreligiousness

*a·së = **nu·ku**

a·sëll *pcl* *(Crude)* well really/basically/essentially

∘ **asëll-asëll** well when you get right down to it

*a·së·soj = **asiso·j**

asfa·lt *nm* **1** asphalt; asphalt pavement/street **2** [*Min*] pitch

asfa·lt-beto·n *nm* material used to make asphalt pavement: asphalt concrete

asfaltïm *nm ger* <**asfalto·n**

asfalto·n *vt* to pave [] with asphalt

asfaltua·r *adj (i)* paved with asphalt

asfaltue·s *nm* worker who does asphalt paving

*asfa·lltë *nf* = **asfa·lt**

asfa·re *adv* *(Colloq)* not at all, not a bit, nothing at all = **aspak**

asfa·re·gjë *pron* *(Colloq)* nothing at all = **asgjë·fare**

asfiksï *nf* [*Med*] asphyxia, suffocation

*asga·n *adj* = **azga·n**

*asgjâ *pron* *(Reg Gheg)* = **asgjë**

*asgja·ma·ngut *conj* = **asgjë·ma·ngut**

asgjë

I § *pron* **1** nothing; never **2** nothing important **3** you're welcome (after a thank you)

II § *nf* *(Book)* nothingness

asgjë·ka·fshë *pron* nothing, not a thing

asgjë·ku·nd *adv* = **asgjëku·ndi**

asgjë·ku·ndi *adv* nowhere, not anyplace

∘ **s'ësh-të asgjëku·ndi** not be getting anywhere, not be making the slightest progress

*asgjëku·nt *adv* = **asgjëku·ndi**

asgjë·ma·ngut *conj* *(Book)* nevertheless, however; although

asgjë·se·nd *pron* = **asgjë·se·ndi**

asgjë·se·ndi *pron* nothing, none

asgjë·sï *nf* *(Book)* nonexistence, nothingness; total emptiness

asgjë·sïm *nm ger* **1** <**asgjëso·n 2** annihilation, destruction

asgjëso·n *vt* **1** to reduce [] to nothing: annihilate, totally destroy **2** [*Mil*] to strike [] on target

asgjë·sue·s *adj* **1** annihilating **2** brutal, devastating

asgjë·shëm *adj (i)* *(Book)* of no importance/value, inconsequential

*a·sì·ko·he *OR* **a·sì·ko·het** *adv* = **asoko·he**

*asïl *nm* exile = **azïl**

a·si·lloj

I § *determiner (Colloq)* of that kind

II § *adv (Colloq)* in that way, thus

asimetrï *nf* asymmetry

asimetrïk *adj* asymmetric(al)

asimilīm *nm ger* 1 <asimilo'·*n* 2 assimilation

asimilo'·n *vt* to assimilate; digest, ingest

asimilua'r *adj (i)* assimilated

asimilue's
I § *adj* assimilative, assimilating
II § *n (Book)* assimilator, one who attempts to ingest another country or people

asimilue'shëm *adj (i)* 1 ingestive 2 *(Fig)* good at assimilating something

asimpto'të *nf* asymptote

asinkro'n *adj* [*Phys*] asynchronous

asi' *(Old)*
I § *abl* <ai'lata'
II § *determiner* such as that/those

Asiri' *nf* Assyria

asiria'n *adj, n* Assyrian

asi'so'j
I § *determiner (Colloq)* of that sort, such, that sort of
II § *adv (Colloq)* in that way, in such a way; like that, in the same way, thus

asiste'ncë *nf (Book)* assistance

asiste'nt *n (Book)* 1 professional assistant to a professional person (as to a doctor/engineer/professor) 2 title of a teaching assistant in higher education; one who holds that title

asisto'·n *vt* to assist

*****a'si'sh** *abl* <ata'

*****a'si'shmëny'ra'sh** *adv* that way, in that way, in such a way

*****asja't** *adj, n* = aziatik

*****asja'tër** *adj* neuter, neutral

*****asja'tëro'r** *adj* = asja'tër

*****asja'tërsi'** *nf* neutrality

*****asja'tërso'r** *adj* = asja'tër

aska'th *nm* 1 sty, eye inflammation 2 dried fig 3 overripe fig *4 barleycorn

*****aska'thi'ër** *nm* sty, eye inflammation

aske't *nm* ascetic, hermit, recluse

asketi'k *nm* ascetic, pertaining to asceticism

asketi'zëm *nm* ascetism

askë'nd *acc* <asku'sh

aski' *np* suspenders for holding up pants or skirts

asklepiado're *nf* [*Bot*] milkweed family *Asclepi-adaceae*

asku'jt *dat/abl* <asku'sh

asku'nd *adv* not anywhere, nowhere, no place

asku'ndi = asku'nd

*****asku'r** = asku'rrë

asku'rrë *adv* at no time, never, never again

asku'rrfa're *quant* no kind of, none of them, not even a little bit

asku'rrgjë' *pron* nothing at all, nothing in the slightest

asku'rrka'h *adv (Reg)* not anywhere, nowhere, not anyplace

*****asku'rrkë'** *acc* <asku'sh

*****asku'rrku'jt** *dat* <asku'sh

asku'rrku'nd *adv* = asgjëku'nd

asku'rrku'sh *pron* = asku'sh

asku'sh *pron* 1 no one, nobody, not a single person 2 *(Colloq)* person of no value: a nobody
  ○ **askush tjetër veç** <> none other than <>

*****asku'va'së** = askuva'zë

*****asku'va'zë** *nf* toad

*****asla'n** *nm* = asllan

aslla'n *nm (Old)* lion

*****as'ndo'kë'nd** = askë'nd

*****as'ndo'ku'j** = asku'j

*****as'ndo'ku'jt** = asku'jt

*****as'ndo'ku'sh** = asku'sh

as'ndo'një' *quant* not a single, not one

as'ndo'një'he'rë *adv* at no time, not ever, never at all

as'ndo'një'r *nm, nf (definite case forms only)* = asnjë'r

as'ndo'një'se'nd *pron* nothing whatever

as'nja'nës
I § *adj* 1 neutral 2 [*Ling*] neuter
II § *n* 1 *(Book)* neutral country or person 2 [*Ling*] neuter gender 3 [*Phys*] non-conductor

as'nja'nësi' *nf* neutrality
  ○ **asnjanësi e armatosur** neutrality while remaining well prepared for battle: armed neutrality

as'nja'nësi'm *nm ger* 1 *(Book)* <asnjanëso'·*n*, as-njanëso'·*het* 2 neutralization

as'nja'nësi'sht *adv (Book)* neutrally

as'nja'nëso'·het *vpr (Book)* to become neutral

as'nja'nëso'·n *vt (Book)* 1 to neutralize 2 to counterbalance

as'nja'nësue's *adj* neutralizing

*****as'nja'nsi'** *nf(Reg Gheg)* = asnjanësi'

*****as'nja'nso'·n** *vt (Reg Gheg)* = asnjanëso'·*n*

as'nja'nshëm *adj (i) (Book)* unbiased, unprejudiced, neutral

*****as'njê'ni** *(Reg Gheg)* = asnjeri'

as'njeri' *pron* no one, nobody

as'një' *quant* not (even) one, not any, none, not a single one, not a, no
  ○ **asnjë ashkël nuk** <> **hiq·**et^{3sg} <> doesn't give a damn, <> doesn't care one bit
  ○ **asnjë çikë** not a bit, not at all
  ○ **asnjë fije** "not a hair" not one little bit, not even a little bit
  ○ **asnjë fije floku** not a one, not at all, not even a little bit
  ○ **asnjë grimë** not even a little bit, none at all
  ○ **asnjë majë gjilpëre** not a bit, not even a little
  ○ **asnjë për be** not even one
  ○ **asnjë për derman** not a one, absolutely none
  ○ **asnjë për farë** not even one, not a single one
  ○ **asnjë qime** "not a hair" not one little bit
  ○ **Asnjë s'të kruan si dora jote.** "No one scratches you like your own hand" *(Prov)* No one can deal with your problems better than you can.
  ○ **asnjë tehri** not one little bit
  ○ **asnjë thërrime** none at all, not even a little bit

*****as'një'a'nës** *adj* = asnja'nës

as'një'fa'rë *pron, quant* none of that kind; not a single one

as'një'fa'rëllo'j *pron, quant* = asnjëfa'rë

as'një'he'rë *adv* not once, at no time, never; under no circumstances, in no case

as'një'r *nm, nf (definite case forms only)* not one: neither, none

*****as'nji'** = asnjë'

*****a'so-a'so'sh** *adj* such, like, similar

a'so'bo'te *adv (Reg)* at that time, in those days, then

asociacio'n *nm* association

a'socia'l *adj* asocial

a'sodo're *determiner (Reg)* of that kind, such

a|so|he're *adv* at that time, then
a|so|her'shëm *adj (i)* = atëhershëm
a|so|ko'h|e *adv* at that time, then, in those days
a|so|ko'shëm *adj (i)* = atëhershëm
asona'ncë *nf* [Lit Ling] assonance
asortime'nt *nm* 1 assortment 2 the amount and nature of diversity in an assortment 3 the assortment of goods produced by an enterprise 4 production specifications
a|so'sh *abl fem pl* <ato' (Old) those
as|pa'k *adv* not at all, not in the least bit, not in the slightest; in no way
as|pa'k|të *adj (i) (Book)* 1 totally missing; totally unknown; quite worthless 2 null, non-existent
aspara'g *nm* asparagus = shparg
aspe'kt *nm* 1 aspect, partial view, perspective 2 point of view; facet 3 [Ling] aspect
  ∘ aspekti i kryer [Ling] perfect aspect
asperu'gë *nf* [Bot] madwort Asperugo
a'spër *nf (Old)* small low-valued silver coin formerly used in Albania: denier
aspira'nt *nm* 1 [Mil] sergeant major, top sergeant, warrant officer 2 (Old) candidate for a high academic degree, postgraduate
aspirantu'rë *nf* high academic degree, master's
aspira'të *nf (Book)* aspiration
aspirato'r *nm* [Tech] aspirator
aspiri'në *nf* aspirin
aspiro'·n
  I § *vt (Book)* to aspire to, have high hopes for, wish for
  II § *vi* to have aspirations, have high hopes
aspo' *pcl (Colloq)* 1 expresses disappointment 2 added on to a statement as a tag question requiring an answer of yes or no
*a'sprë *nf* = a'spër
asqe'r *nm* 1 (Old) soldier 2 (Pej) irregular soldier 3 army
asqeri'e *nf* [Hist] fee paid to substitute for military service during the Turkish occupation
as|sesi *adv* in no way, by no means, not at all
astaku'a *nm (obl ⁓ o'i, np ⁓ o'nj) (Reg Gk)* [Ichth] crayfish (Palinurus vulgaris)
*astani'k *nm* 1 architrave 2 capital of pillar
asta'r *nm* lining, casing
astaro'·n *vt* to line [] (with material), insert/sew/provide/install a lining
aste'r *nm* [Bot] aster Aster
*aste'rë *nf* = a'spër
astero're *nf* [Bot] aster family Asteraceae
a'stë *nf* [Spec] rod; shaft
astma'ti'k *adj* asthmatic
a'stmë *nf* asthma
astraga'ç *nm* rolling pin = qehën
astraga'n *nm* 1 astrakhan *2 rolling pin
*astraka'n *nm* = astraga'n
Astraka'n *nm* Astrakhan
astri't *nm* 1 [Zool] green whip snake (Coluber jugularis) 2 (Fig) agile and intrepid person *3 snake; dragon
Astri't *nm* Astrit (male name)
astro' *formative prefix* astro-
astro|fizi'kë *nf* astrophysics
astro|lo'g *n* astrologist

astro|lo'gi'k *adj* astrological
astro|logji *nf* astrology
*astro|llo'g *n* = astrolo'g
astro|nau't *nm* 1 astronaut 2 specialist in astronautics
astro|nau'ti'kë *nf* astronautics
astro|no'm *nm* astronomer
astro|nomi *nf* astronomy
astro|nomi'k *adj* astronomic
Asturi *nf* Asturia
Asua'n *nm* Aswan
*a'su'll *nm (np ⁓ j)* = ha'sëll
asha'r *nm* [Hist] tithe
*ashari *nf* lust, concupiscence
*asha'sh *nm* = hasha'sh
a'she *nf* [Bot] holly (Ilex aquifolium)
ashe'f *nm (Reg)* food preparation area, kitchen area
ashenso'r *nm* elevator, lift (British)
ashensori'st *n* elevator/lift operator
a'shër
  I § *nf* 1 wood split up for fire: firewood; wood sliver/splinter/chip/chunk 2 wood slat used in wall lath or roof sheathing 3 [Bot] buckeye, horse chestnut Aesculus, Pavia
  II § *nm* 1 cartilage in the rear part of the horse's hoof 2 [Veter] crippling/laming of a horse; windgall
  ∘ bë·het³ᵖˡ ashër duart one's hands get chapped
  ∘ ashër e pisë (i zi) very dark, (pitch) black
ashëri'më *nf* wattle; wattle roof; wattle fence
ashëro'·n *vt* 1 to chop/split [wood] 2 to apply sheathing to [a roof]
ashi'k *nm* 1 anklebone 2 knucklebone of sheep/goat; dice game using knucklebones 3 (Reg) tuning peg in a stringed instrument 4 (Old) lover, suitor 5 (Pej) good-time Charlie, confirmed hedonist
ashik|ëri *nf (Old)* dalliance, courting, gallantry; being in love
*ashiko'r *adj* amorous
ashiqa're *adv (Crude)* openly, publicly
ashk *nm* 1 warmth of freshly plowed soil; condition of soil prepared for sowing 2 (Fig) fervor, passion, enthusiasm
a'shkë *nf* 1 = a'shkël 2 (Reg) eyelash, eyelid
  ∘ s'merr· ashkë not be open to reason
a'shkël *nf* 1 splinter, sliver; chip; shaving *2 shard, shell fragment 3 [Bot] Scotch laburnum Laburnum alpinum
  ∘ s'lesho·n ashkël not be open to reason
ashkëli'm *nm ger* < ashkëlo'·n
*a'shkëlje *nf* bark, skin, peel, shell, membrane
ashkëlo'·n
  I § *vt* to chop up [], chip, split, splinter
  II § *vi* to create wood or metal chips/splinters
ashkë'ti *nm* = aske't
*ashkë'to're *nf* hermitage
a'shkla-a'shkla *adv* in small pieces, one by one
ashkth *nm* [Med] children's disease whose symptom is a blister in the mouth (palatum phthisis)
ash|o're *nf* [Bot] holly family Aquifoliaceae
a'shpër
  I § *adj (i)* harsh, rough, rugged; unrefined, crude, coarse; severe, acute, sharp, unrelenting, stern, strict
  II § *adv* 1 roughly, coarsely 2 (Fig) harshly, brutally, crudely, sternly; abruptly, strictly

ashpëra'k *adj* shaggy

ashpërí *nf* 1 harshness, roughness, coarseness, crudeness, cruelty, severity, sternness 2 bitterly cold weather

ashpërím *nm ger* 1 <ashpëro´·n, ashpëro´·het 2 = ashpërsí

ashpërínë *nf* soil that is dry and trampled down

ashpërísht *adv* = ashpërsísht

ashpëro'·het *vpr* = ashpërso´·het

ashpëro'·n *vt* 1 to harshen; roughen 2 *(Fig)* to harden [one's heart], embitter; aggravate

ashpërsí *nf* 1 harshness, crudeness, cruelty, severity 2 bitterly cold weather 3 harsh countryside; rough surface

ashpërsím *nm ger* <ashpërso´·n, ashpërso´·het

ashpërsísht *adv* harshly, bitterly

ashpërso'·het *vpr* 1 to intensify in severity 2 to become acerbated; get savage; become bitterly angry

ashpërso'·n *vt* 1 to increase the intensity or severity of [] 2 = ashpëro´·n

ashpërsua'r *adj (i)* 1 intensified; strained 2 acerbated

***a'shpërt** *adj (i)* = a'shpër

***ashpërtí** *nf (Reg)* stunted seedling

ashpërtíre *nf* [*Bot*] type of oak with rough-textured leaves

ashpërua'r *adj (i)* 1 roughened, cracked 2 bitterly angry, brutal, cruel 3 intensified

***ashpre'së** *nf* = ashpërím

***ashprí** *nf* = ashpërím

***ashprísht** *adv* = ashpërísht

***ashpro'·n** *vt* = ashpëro´·n

asht *nm* 1 bone 2 *(Reg)* small button made of bone 3 [*Bot*] herbaceous prairie annual with small, sparse ovate leaves, violet-colored flowers and a branching stalk which exudes a white liquid when broken off
  ∘ **asht e lëkurë** skin and bones, emaciated

***âsht** *(Reg Gheg)* = ë'shtë

a'shtër = eshtër

***a'shtët** *adj (i)* = ashttë

***ashtní** *nf* = eshtërí

***ashtním** *nm* = eshtërím

***ashtno'·het** *vpr* = eshtëro´·het

***ashtno'·n** *vt* to ossify

***ashtno're**
  I *§ nf* = eshtëro're
  II *§ adj fem* <ashtnuer

***ashtnue'r** *adj (Old)* = eshtëro'r

***ashtnue's** *adj* = eshtërue's

***a'shttë** *adj (i)* = e'shtërt

ashtth *nm* [*Veter*] disease of horses that affects their leg bones

ashtu *adv* 1 in that way, that way, thus, like that 2 so-so 3 somewhat; so-so; somehow; about the same 4 aimlessly
  ∘ **Ashtu i do mushka drutë.** "That is how the mule wants the logs." *(Pej)* That's what {} deserves. {} is just getting the punishment {} deserves.
  ∘ **dhe/edhe ashtu** even so, even as it is
  ∘ **ashtu e ka·** {} it's in {}'s nature/character to act that way
  ∘ **ashtu qoftë** so be it, let's hope so
  ∘ **ashtu si _ ashtu edhe _** just as _ so _

  ∘ **ashtu siç** just as, as

ashtu-ashtu *adv* 1 so-so, neither well nor badly 2 in the same way; equally, just like that

ashtu-kështu *adv* = ashtu-ashtu

ashtuqua'jtur *adj (i)* so-called

***ashtuque'jtun** *adj (i) (Reg Gheg)* = ashtuqua'jtur

***ashu'ng** *nm* kidney fat

ashu're *nf* 1 *(Old)* a holiday celebrated by Bektashi Moslems, the fast of Ashura 2 [*Food*] sweet dish made of beans and hulled barley (eaten after the fast of Ashura)

at *nm* 1 saddle horse 2 *(Fig)* hard-working strong and agile man 3 stallion, steed 4 = a'të

a'ta *distal 3rd pers pl masc determiner* they, those

***ata'k** *nm* [*Med*] attack

atako'·n *vt* to attack

atashe' *nm* [*Diplomacy*] attaché

atasho'·n *vt* 1 to 2 *(Book)* to assign to a duty attached to a particular individual, agency, or institution

atavík *adj (Book)* atavistic

atavízëm *nm* atavism

***atça'st** *adv* <atë çast at that moment

a'tdhe' *nm* 1 fatherland, homeland, one's native land, land of birth 2 place of origin, native habitat; habitat

atdhe'da'sh'ës
  I *§ adj* patriotic
  II *§ n* patriot

atdhe'da'sh'je *nf* = atdhedashurí

***a'tdhe'dasht'ni** *nf* = atdhedashurí

***a'tdhe'dashun'í** *nf* = atdhedashurí

atdhe'dashurí *nf* love of country/homeland, patriotism

atdhe'moho'njës *n* = atdhemohue's

atdhe'mohue's
  I *§ nm (Book)* one who renounces his fatherland, traitor
  II *§ adj* treasonous, unpatriotic

atdhe'sí *nf (Old)* [*Poet*] = atdhetarí

atdhe'so'r *adj* = atdheta'r

***a'tdhe'she'm** *adj (i)* = atdheta'r

atdhe'shití'es *n (Book Old)* traitor, one who sells out his country

atdhe'ta'r
  I *§ adj (Book)* patriotic
  II *§ n* patriot

atdhe'tarí *nf* patriotism, love of country

atdhe'tarísht *adv* patriotically

atdhe'tarízëm *nm (Book)* = atdhetarí

ateíst
  I *§ adj* atheistic
  II *§ n* atheist

ateízëm *nm* atheism

***a'tej** *adv* 1 = atje *2 = andejmi

***a'teje** *adv* = andejmi

atelié *nf* 1 studio, atelier 2 *(Old)* master workshop; special department of a factory

atelie'r *nm* = atelie

atenta't *nm* 1 assassination attempt 2 *(Fig)* attack attempt

atentato'r *n* attempted assassin

aterínë *nf* [*Ichth*] Atherina hepsetus
  ∘ **aterínë symadhe** [*Ichth*] Atherina boyeri

atestím *nm ger* 1 *(Offic)* <atesto´·n 2 certification, attestation

atesto·*n* *vt* (*Offic*) to certify attainment of a title or degree of accomplishment

a'të *acc* <aí, ajo
  ○ **atë çast** right then, at that very moment
  ○ **atë çka** all that, that which, what
  ○ **Atë kokë ka, atë feste do** "One has that head, one wants that fez." (*Prov*) You get what you deserve.
  ○ **Atë që ul qafën, e dhjesin pulat.** "Whoever bows his neck, the chickens crap on." (*Prov Crude*) If you let others order you around, you get the abuse you deserve. People will walk all over you if you let them.

a'të *nm* **1** father, sire **2** (term of address to a priest) father
  ○ **i ati** his/her/its/their father
  ○ **atë i gjetur** stepfather
  ○ **atë pas ati** generation after generation

atëbotë *adv* = atëherë

*****atëça's** *adv* = atëherë

*****atëça'st** *adv* = atëherë

atëça'stshëm *adj* (*i*) (*Book*) momentary, immediate, right then

atëdi'tshëm *adj* (*i*) (*Book*) of that day, for that day

atëgjy'sh *nm* (*Old*) grandfather

*****atëhe're** = atëherë

atëhe'rë *adv* **1** then, at that time **2** in that case, so, then **3** therefore, as a result
  ○ **atëherë kur** __ while __

atëhe'rshëm *adj* (*i*) then, of that time; of those times, of those days

atëko'hë *adv* then, at that time

atëko'hshëm *adj* (*i*) **1** simultaneous, contemporary **2** = atëhershëm

atëlo'sh *nm* (*Colloq*) term of respect for addressing grandfather or other old man

atëri' *nf* = atësi

atëri'sht *adv* (*Book*) fatherly, paternally, in a fatherly fashion

atëro'r *adj* (*Book*) **1** belonging to or deriving from the father: from the father: paternal **2** fatherly, paternal

atësi' *nf* (*Offic*) **1** paternity **2** father's name, paternal name, family name **3** fatherhood

atëso'r *adj* (*Old*) = atëror

atëvra'sës *n* (*Book*) one who commits patricide

atëvra'sje *nf* patricide

*****atgjy'sh** *nm* ancestor

a'tij *dat/abl* <aí

*****a'tija** *fem pl* <atíllë

Ati'kë *nf* Attica

a'tillë *adj* (*i*) **1** such as that, like that **2** such
  ○ **i atillë e i këtillë** "such and such" all kinds of bad things (used to avoid saying specific bad words)

*****ati'llët** *adj* (*i*) valiant

atinta'n
  I § *n* [*Hist*] member of one of the Illyrian peoples that lived between the Vjosë and Osum rivers
  II § *adj* of or pertaining to the Atintan people

atje' *adv* at that place; there, over there, yonder
  ○ **Atje ku bëhet dasmë e madhe, merr lugë të vogël.** "Where there is a big wedding, take a small spoon (because there won't be much to eat)." **1** (*Prov*) When they make it sound too good to you, don't expect much from it. **2** A lot of smoke, but no fire. Don't get fooled by a lot of razzle-dazzle.

○ **atje tej** over there/yonder

atje'shëm *adj* (*i*) of that place, there

*****atje'tej** *adv* yonder

atki'në *nf* **1** saddle mare **2** (*Fig*) hard-working strong and adept girl or young woman

*****atko'hë** *adv* = atëkohë

atla'nt *nm* = atlas

atlanti'k *adj* of or pertaining to the Atlantic Ocean

Atlanti'k *nm* Atlantic

atla's *nm* atlas

atle't *n* athlete

atleti'k *adj* athletic

atleti'kë *nf* [*Sport*] athletics (not including ball games)
  ○ **atletikë e lehtë** [*Sport*] track and field sports
  ○ **atletikë e rëndë** [*Sport*] weightlifting and contact sports

atleti'zëm *nm* **1** athleticism; development of athletic bodies through training and practice **2** (*Old*) = atletikë

atllanti'k *adj* = atlantik

atlla'rë *np* <at

atlla's *nm* **1** satin, sateen **2** = atlas

atlla'stë *adj* (*i*) of satin/sateen

a'tme *nf* (*Poet*) = atdhe
  ○ **atme deti** [*Bot*] hollyhock *Althaea rosea*

atmosfe'rë *nf* atmosphere

atmosferi'k *adj* atmospheric

*****atni'sht** *adv* = atërisht

a'to *distal 3rd pers pl fem determiner* those, they
  ○ **ato (të grave)** (*Euph*) menstrual period, menstruation: monthlies, period
  ○ **ato të muajit** (*Euph*) menstruation: monthlies, period

ato'l *nm* atoll

ato'm *nm* atom

atomi'k *adj* atomic

atomi'st *n* **1** specialist in atomic energy **2** (*Pej*) one who supports atomic armament or who produced atomic weapons

ato'n *adj* [*Ling*] unstressed, unaccented

*****atpo'** *adv* just as

*****atra'gë** *nf* marking (of horses)

atraksio'n *nm* **1** [*Phys*] = tërheqje **2** something that attracts: attraction; side show

atrecati'm *nm* [*Tech*] equipping, setting up

atrecatu'rë *nf* [*Tech*] equipment, set-up, fittings

atribuo'·*n* *vt* to attribute

atribu't *nm* (*Book*) **1** essential attribute **2** attribute, permanent characteristic **3** (*Offic*) privilege and prerogative that goes with an official position: perquisite of office

atrofi' *nf* atrophy

atrofizi'm *nm ger* **1** <atrofizo·*n*, atrofizo·*het* **2** atrophy

atrofizo'·*het* *vpr* to atrophy

atrofizo'·*n* *vt* to cause [] to atrophy

*****atso'** = aso

ATSh [*a-të-shë*] <**Agjencia Telegrafike Shqiptare** *nf* Albanian Telegraphic Agency (the Albanian news service)

atu' *nf* (*Book*) trump card

*****atvra'sësi** *nf* patricide

aty *adv* **1** near there (in relation to the position in space or time of one or both of the participants in the speech act or to another position immediately identifiable by them), there by you, there by me, right there, there **2** at the same time, while
◦ **aty afër** approximately, about, almost
◦ **aty edhe** __ including even __
◦ **aty e ka• (fjalën)** that's what { } *is driving* at, here is what { } *is trying* to say
◦ **aty ta ka• (fjalën)** that's what { } *is driving* at, here is what { } *is trying* to say
◦ **aty e kam** that's precisely it! that's the point!
◦ **aty më rri** (*Colloq*) stop right there!, that's what we want!
◦ **aty pari** in that general neighborhood, around there
◦ **aty për aty** immediately, on the spot, right then and there, right there
◦ **aty përpara** shortly before that, a little while earlier
◦ **s'përpjek• aty** not succeed there, not get past that one
◦ **aty pranë** somewhere nearby; right near there
◦ **aty e prapa** from that time on
◦ **aty shpejti** shortly before that, a little while earlier
aty-aty *adv* (*Colloq*) **1** soon, shortly, in a second, right away **2** thereabout, almost equal
*****atydej** *adv* recently
aty-këtu *adv* **1** here and there, not everywhere **2** from time to time, now and then, sporadically
*****atylashti** *adv* formerly
*****atyne** = **atyre**
*****atyne** *nf* [*Relig*] paternoster, the Lord's Prayer
atypari *adv* **1** near a known place, somewhere around there, somewhere close by **2** around that time, about then; a little bit earlier **3** about that much, almost that much
atyperatyshëm *adj* (*i*) immediate, spontaneous, of the moment
atyre *dat/abl* <**ato, ata**
atyshëm *adj* (*i*) of that place, near there (in relation to the position in space of one or both of the participants in the speech act or to another position immediately identifiable by them), there by you, there by me, right there, there.
*****atyshpejt** OR **atyshpejti** *adv* very recently, just a short time ago, lately
ath• *vt* to benumb, make numb; embitter
ath-et *vpr* to become numb, become embittered
*****athësi** *nf* = **athtësi**
athët
I § *adj* (*i*) **1** tart **2** bitter; pungent **3** bitterly cold **4** (*Fig*) harsh, unpleasantly sour **5** (*Fig*) testy, peevish, touchy
II § *adv* nastily, tartly, bitterly; somewhat harshly
athëti *nf* = **athtësi**
athëtim *nm ger* **1** <**athëto•n, athëto•het 2** = **athëtim**
athëtimë *nf* **1** bitter and dry piercing cold; icy wind, penetrating bitter frost **2** sourness, acidity, bitterness, harshness
athëtirë *nf* **1** something that tastes tart/bitter **2** tart/sour taste **3** = **athtësi**
athëto•het *vpr* **1** to become tart/bitter **2** to have a bitter taste in one's mouth
athëto•n *vt* to make tart, embitter, sour; pickle
athëtor *adj* = **athët**

athëtuar *adj* (*i*) **1** soured, made tart **2** (*Fig*) embittered
athinas *adj, n* Athenian
Athinë *nf* Athens
athinian *adj* Athenian
athje *nf* [*Bot*] = **athjez**
athjez *nf* [*Bot*] spiny restharrow (*Ononis spinosa*)
*****athletikë** *nf* athletics
athtësi *nf* **1** sourness, tartness, acidity; degree of sourness *****2** sharpness, roughness, harshness
athtësim *nm* = **athëtim**
athtëso•het *vpr* = **athëto•het**
athtëso•n *vt* = **athëto•n**
athtësuar *adj* = **athëtuar**
*****athua** = **a thua** *pcl* (*in questions*) = **thua**
audiencë *nf* (*Offic*) a formal hearing with the head of state or other high official, audience
auditor *nm* **1** lecture hall, auditorium **2** audience, auditor
*****augur** *nm* augury = **ogur**
*****augurtar** *n* augurer, seer
*****auktor** *n* = **autor**
aukubë *nf* [*Bot*] aucuba *Aucuba*
aulli•n *vi* to whimper, yelp; howl, whine
aullimë *nf* whimpering, yelping; howling, whining
*****aullis** *stem for 1st sg pres, pl pres, 2nd & 3rd sg subj, imperf* <**aullit•**
*****aullit•** *vi* to bellow, roar
*****aullitje** *nf ger* **1** <**aullit• 2** bellow, roar
aureolë *nf* aureole
aurorë *nf* (*Book*) pre-dawn light; dawn
◦ **aurora boreale** aurora borealis
*****aus** *nm* cistern
Austerlic *nm* Austerlitz
Australi *nf* Australia
australian *adj, n* Australian
Austri *nf* Austria
austriak *adj, n* Austrian
austro-hungarez *adj* Austro-Hungarian
autarki *nm* autarky
autarkik *nm* autarkic
autenticitet *nm* (*Book*) authenticity
autentik *adj* (*Book*) authentic
*****auto** *nf* automobile
auto|*formative prefix* **1** automatic **2** having to do with automobiles **3** self
autoambulancë *nf* ambulance
autobetoniere *nf* transit mix truck, concrete delivery mixer
autobiografi *nf* autobiography
autobiografik *adj* autobiographical
autobitumatriçe *nf* [*Tech*] bitumen paving machine: bitumen sprayer
autoblindë *nf* [*Mil*] armored car
autobot *nm* tanker truck
autobus *nm* motor bus, bus
autocisternë *nf* = **autobot**
autodidakt
I § *adj* (*Book*) autodidactic, self-taught
II § *nm* autodidact, self-taught person
autodrom *nm* field used for automobile sports and for testing cars and training drivers

auto|dyqa·n *nm* vehicle equipped to sell goods in villages, travelling store

auto|frigorife·r *nm* refrigerator van

auto|gara·zh *nm* automobile garage

auto|go·l *nm* [*Soccer*] goal scored accidentally by a player against his own team: own goal

auto|gra·f *nm* autograph

auto|grejder *nm* grading machine, motor grader, road grader

auto|inspektora·t *nm* state agency in charge of automobile and traffic regulation and control

auto|kaza·n *nm* gas tank in an automobile

auto|kinema *nf* vehicle equipped with film projector for showing movies in public places

auto|kla·vë *nf* autoclave

auto|kolo·në *nf* motorcade

auto|komba·jnë *nf* self-propelled harvester: combine

auto|kraci *nf (Book)* autocracy

auto|kra·t *nm (Book)* autocrat

auto|krat·ik *adj* autocratic

auto|krit·ik *adj* self-critical

auto|krit·ikë *nf* self-criticism

auto|kto·n
  I § *nm (Book)* autochthon
  II § *adj (Book)* autochthonous

auto|kton·i *nf (Book)* autochthony

auto|ma·t
  I § *adj* automatic
  II § *nm* **1** [*Tech*] automatic device/machine/tool **2** *(Fig)* person who behaves like a robot

auto|mat·ik
  I § *nm* **1** [*Mil*] submachine gun, automatic rifle **2** [*Tech*] robot **3** *(Colloq)* telephone exchange, telephone central
  II § *adj* automatic

auto|mat·ikë·s
  I § *adj* [*Mil*] armed with an automatic weapon
  II § *n* [*Mil*] submachine gunner

auto|mat·ik·isht *adv* automatically

auto|mat·izëm *nm (Book)* automatism

auto|mat·izi·m *nm ger* **1** <**automatizo··n**, **automatizo··het 2** automation

auto|mat·izo··het *vpr* to become automated

auto|mat·izo··n *vt* to automate

auto|mje·t *nm* motor vehicle

auto|mobi·l *nm* automotive vehicle: bus, truck (lorry), car

auto|mobil·i·st *n* **1** [*Sport*] participant in motor racing **2** *(Old)* chauffeur, driver, truck (lorry) driver

auto|mobil·ist·ik *adj* pertaining to automobiles

auto|mobil·izëm *nm* competitive sports with automobiles

auto|mobil·nga·s·ës *n* chauffeur, driver

auto|no·m *adj* autonomous

auto|nom·i *nf* autonomy

auto|nom·i·st
  I § *n (Book)* one who strives for the autonomy of his country, autonomist
  II § *adj* striving for autonomy, autonomistic

auto|ofiçi·në *nf* small mechanical workshop set up in a van

auto|pa·rk *nm (np ~ qe)* [*Tech*] place where vehicles are kept and repaired: garage, motor pool; parking lot

auto|portre·t *nm* self-portrait

autopsi *nf* autopsy

auto|qefa·l *adj* **1** independent **2** autocephalous, independent of the Patriarchy of Istanbul

auto|qefal·i *nf* autocephaly

auto·r *n* author

autor·ësi *nf* authorship

autor·ita·r *adj* authoritarian

autor·ite·t *nm* **1** authority **2** official

autor·itet·shëm *adj (i) (Book)* authoritative

autor·izi·m *nm ger* **1** <**autorizo··n 2** authorization, warrant, order

autor·izo··n *vt* to authorize

auto|so·ndë *nf* [*Tech*] self-propelled drilling machine

auto|stra·dë *nf* motor highway

auto|sugjestio·n *nm* autosuggestion

auto|transpo·rt *nm* motor vehicle transportation

auto|vi·nç *nm* [*Tech*] motorized crane, crane lorry

auto|vinç·ier *n* [*Tech*] operator/driver of a motorized crane: *(crane rigger)*

auto|zjarr·fik·ëse *nf* fire engine, fire truck

authent·ik *adj* = **autent·ik**

au·z *nm (Reg)* = **kërri·ç**

av. *abbrev* <**avokat** attorney

avalla·ngë *nf* avalanche; mass attack

avallo··het *vpr* to lust (for)

avanbe·g *nf* [*Tech*] girder launching device

avan·cë *nf (Colloq)* **1** wages paid in advance **2** *(Fig)* initial advantage

avanc·i·m *nm ger (Book)* **1** <**avanco··n 2** headway, progress, advancement **3** accomplishment in advance of expectation

avanco··n
  I § *vi (Book)* to make progress, progress, advance, go forward
  II § *vt* to move up the due date for [ ]

avanga·rdë *nf* [*Lit*] avant-garde, vanguard

avangard·i·st *n* [*Lit*] avant-gardist

avanta·zh *nm* advantage

avan·të *nf* advantage

ava·r *nm* seed corn hung up from the rafters to dry

ava·rdë *nf* small fishing net

avari
  I § *nf* [*Tech*] breakdown, damage
  II § *adv (Old)* together, all together

ava·s *nm* = **ava·z**

ava·sh *adv (Colloq)* **1** slowly, unhurriedly **2** softly, with a soft voice, making little sound, imperceptibly

ava·sh-ava·sh *adv (Colloq)* little by little, very slowly

ava·shëm *adj (i) (Colloq)* slow

ava·shtë *adj (i) (Colloq)* **1** slow-moving, slow-acting, unhurried, slow **2** spoken softly, soft (in sound)

ava·z *nm (Colloq)* **1** refrain, tune, melody, song **2** *(Fig)* something that is repeated over and over in the same way; something annoyingly repeated **3** tedious nuisance **4** *(Pej)* annoying mannerism; defect, fault

○ **i bie**₁· **(po) një avazi** *(Pej)* to keep playing the same old tune, harp on the same old theme
○ **avazi i Mukës** the same old refrain
○ **avaz i vjetër** same old story

avda·ll
  I § adj (Crude) **1** big, unattractive and clumsy; lumbering **2** thick-witted, stupid
  II § nm big lummox, big oaf

avda·ll·çe *adv (Crude)* **1** clumsily, awkwardly; ploddingly, sluggishly **2** stupidly, bumblingly, crazily

avde·s *nm [Relig]* Moslem ablution rite: washing hands, face, and feet before prayer

avdes·a·në = **avdesha·në**

avdesha·në [*av-des-ha·n*] *nf (Old)* **1** ritual washing place **2** wash basin, sink, lavatory **3** toilet

avdo·s *nm [Ornit]* chaffinch (*Fringilla coelebs*) = **bo·rës**

*****avdo·sk** *nm* = **avdo·s**

*****avdo·skë** *nf* = **avdo·s**

aveni·r *nm* future

aventu·rë *nf* adventure

aventuri·er
  I § nm **1** adventurer *****2** swindler, scoundrel
  II § adj adventurous, dangerous

aventur·izëm *nm* adventurism

*****ave·rmë** *nf (Reg)* leather thong on a moccasin

*****avermo·** ·*n vt* to secure [ ] with a thong

a·vër
  I § nf **1** current of warm air; hot breeze; warm vapor **2** sweltering heat, heat from a fire; sultry weather **3** biting-cold wind, icy wind **4** field of ice, glacier *****5** synagogue
  II § nm open space, expanse; expanse of uncultivated ground

*****avge·llë** *nf* leech, bloodsucker = **abdhe·llë**

*****avgullo·n** *nm (Reg)* ointment, salve

aviacio·n *nm* **1** aviation **2** air fleet; air force
  ○ **aviacioni sulmues** [*Mil*] tactical air force

*****aviasio·n** *nm* = **aviacio·n**

aviato·r *n* aviator

avi·kulturë *nf* poultry farming

avio·mode·l *nm* model airplane

avio·mode·list *n* airplane modelist

avio·model·izëm *nm* model airplane building and flying

avio·n *nm* airplane

*****avi·s** *nm* = **abi·s**

avi·s *stem for 1st sg pres, pl pres, 2nd & 3rd sg subj, pind* <**avi·t**·

*****Avisini** *nf* = **Abisini**

avi·t· *vt (Colloq)* = **afro·**·*n*

avi·t·et *vpr (Colloq)* = **afro·**·*het*

*****avi·t·ës** *adj* approaching

avi·tje *nf ger (Colloq)* <**avi·t·**, **avi·t·et**

avi·tshëm *adj (i) (Colloq)* = **afru·eshëm**

avi·tur *adj (i) (Colloq)* = **afru·ar**

*****avi·z** *nm* news

avle·me·nd *nm* loom, hand-loom

*****avle·mend·ëri** *nf* weaving

*****avlime·n** OR **avlime·nt** *nm* = **avle·me·nd**

avlli *nf* **1** garden wall, wall around a yard **2** walled garden, courtyard *****3** hall, porch, vestibule

avoka·t *nm* **1** lawyer, attorney **2** *(Pej)* one who acts as advocate for another person whether or not that person is right or wrong

avokati· *nf (Old)* **1** area of law providing right to legal counsel **2** advocacy

avokat·llë·k *nm (np ~qe) (Colloq)* lawyering, acting as advocate for another person whether or not that person is right or wrong

avokato·r *adj (Old)* pertaining to lawyers or to their duties

avokato·re *nf (Old)* lawyer's office

*****avokat·si·** *nf* = **avokatu·rë**

avokatu·rë *nf* legal profession, the Bar

avo·re *nf* vapor coming out of the ground

*****avra·m** *nm* **1** mass, crowding throng **2** cluster, clump

avra·pë *nf (Reg)* hairy mole on the skin

*****avre·t** *nm (Reg)* devil

*****a·vrë** *nf* synagogue

*****avri·** *nm* wind

*****avri·m** *nm* **1** <**avro·**·*het* **2** swelling caused by cold

avro··het *vpr* to swell up and become flushed from the intense cold

*****avro·**·*n vi* = **avro·**·*het*

avro·m *adv (Reg)* without being selective, randomly

*****avuka·t** *nm* = **avoka·t**

a·vull
  I § nm (np ~j) **1** vapor, steam **2** current of hot, humid air, hot vapor **3** *(Colloq)* ardor, fervor
  II § adj hot, very warm
  ○ **ësh·të avull kungulli** to be lazy and inept

*****avullani·** *nf* steamship

*****avulli·** = **avlli**

avulli·m *nm ger* **1** <**avullo·**·*n*, **avullo·**·*het* **2** steam-treatment **3** vaporization; evaporation

avull·ma·t·ës *nm* apparatus that measures the amount of steam passing through ducts

avullo··het *vpr* **1** to turn into steam, vaporize; evaporate **2** to be misted over: steam up **3** to get very hot and sweaty

avullo··*n*
  I § vt **1** to make [ ] into steam: vaporize **2** to treat [ ] with steam **3** *(Reg)* to prepare a [clearing] for planting by burning the vegetation and pulling out the roots
  II § vi **1** to turn into steam, evaporate, vaporize **2** to give off vapor/steam *****3** *(Fig)* to cloud, darken (a face) *****4** to fly into a passion
  ○ <> **avullo·**·*n*³ˢᵍ **koka** <> *is* in a predicament
  ○ <> **avullo·**·*het*³ˢᵍ **gjaku** <>'s blood *boils*, <> *steams* with anger

avullo·re *nf* steamship, steamboat

avullo·sh *adj* warm and giving off vapor/steam

*****avull·qe·rre** *nf* steam engine (on a railroad); railroad car

avull·sje·ll·ës *nm* steam ducting, steam line

*****avull·so·**·*n vt* to dim, cloud over

avull·shëm *adj (i)* volatile, vaporous

a·vull·t *adj (i)* **1** vaporous, steamy **2** misty; light as vapor

avull·u·ar *adj (i)* **1** vaporized, turned into steam, made gaseous **2** steamy; sweaty **3** misted **4** steam-treated

avull·u·es *adj* giving off vapor/steam from the heat, steaming; pertaining to steaming or steam-treatment

*****avullu·eshëm** *adj (i)* vaporizable; volatile

avullueshmëri *nf* vaporizability; degree of vaporization

avullzim *nm ger* 1 [*Phys*] <**avullzo'·n** 2 vaporization

avullzo·n *vt* [*Phys*] to vaporize

*****avushë** *nf* abyss = **abis**

*****avys** *nm* = **abis**

*****axima** *np* Passover

axhami
I § *nm (Colloq)* 1 child 2 person inexperienced and untrained for a job
II § *adj* 1 naive 2 *(Pej)* inexperienced and untrained

axhamillëk *nm (np~qe) (Colloq)* immaturity, childish matter; naiveté

axhele *nf (Colloq)* urgency

*****Axhemistan** *nm* Persia

axhë *nf (np ~ allar) with masculine agreement (Reg)* uncle *collateral male relative in ego's patriline ascending from father's brother* = **xhaxha**

*****axhudikatë** *nf* = **adjudikatë**

axhustator *n* repairman; fitter

axhusteri *nf* 1 [*Tech*] machine fitting, adjustment 2 fitting shop

axhustim *nm* [*Tech*] bench work

*****ay** = **ai**

azat *adj (Old)* freed, unrestrained, out of control, free

azbest *nm* = **asbest**

azdis· *vt (Colloq)* 1 to stimulate extraordinary growth or development 2 *(Fig)* (of children) to allow to run wild, leave uncontrolled

azdis·et *vpr* 1 to become frisky/uncontrollable, run wild 2 to go on a spree, have a fling *3 to prance, rear (said of a horse)

azdisur *adj (i)* 1 developed/grown to an extraordinary degree 2 *(Fig)* frisky; uncontrollable, rabid 3 loose, unrestrained, uncontrolled

Azerbajxhan *nm* Azerbaijan

azerbajxhanas *adj, n* Azerbaijani

azër *adv (Old)* ready = **hazër**

azgan *adj, n (Colloq)* 1 (person) who is tall and well-built 2 audacious/daring/bold (person); adept 3 unruly (person/animal)

azgën *adj* = **azgan**

*****azglan** *adj* audacious, impudent, bold

Azi *nf* Asia
○ **Azia e Vogël** Asia Minor

aziatik *adj, n* Asiatic

azil *nm (Old)* 1 old-age asylum, old people's home 2 *(Fig)* refuge, shelter 3 exile

azimut *nm* 1 [*Astron*] azimuth 2 [*Mil Geod*] angle of azimuth

*****azine** *nf* = **hazine**

azmatik *adj* = **astmatik**

azmë *nf* = **astmë**

Azore *np fem* Azores
○ **Ishujt Azore** the Azore Islands

azot *nm* [*Chem*] nitrogen

azotemi *nf* [*Med*] azotemia, uremia

azotik *adj* [*Chem*] azotic

azotim *nm* [*Tech*] nitriding

azoto·n *vt* [*Tech*] to harden [ ] by nitriding

azotuar *adj (i)* nitrogenous, nitrogenated

azhdë *nf (Reg)* 1 honeycomb 2 grape stem

azhur *nm* embroidered or knitted eyelet

azhurnim *nm ger* <**azhurno'·n, azhurno'·het**

azhurno·het *vpr* 1 to become updated, get up to date 2 to be adjourned, postponed, deferred

azhurno·n *vt (Book)* 1 to adjourn, postpone, put/break off until later, defer 2 to update, bring up to date

Bb

b [bë] nf **1** the consonant letter "b" **2** the voiced bilabial stop represented by the letter "b"

***bâ·het** vpr = bë·het

***ba·n** vt (Reg Gheg) = mba·n

***bâ** (Reg Gheg) = bë

baba nm **1** father; dad; pops; founder **2** [Relig] religious head of a Bektashi congregation
○ **baba qafor** stepfather

ba·ba·ba! interj expresses a negative reaction to a suggestion: unthinkable! absolutely not! not on your life!

baba|cke nf (Pet Colloq Reg) daddy

baba|gjysh n endearing and respectful family term for one's grandparent or other elderly person

baba|gjysh|ër np <babagjysh

baba|lar|ë np <baba **1** fathers; ancestors, earlier generation **2** (Old) the reactionary members in the Albanian parliament during Zog's regime **3** (Iron) nobles, those who consider themselves the social elite
○ **baballarët e kombit** (Hist) men in positions of national power, national leaders

baba|llëk
I § nm (np ~qe) **1** [Constr] broach post, central post, king post **2** (Colloq) nice old guy; kindly, good-natured person
II § adj good-natured, kindly, innocent

baba|madh nm (Reg) paternal grandfather

baba|nace nf coarse/soggy cornbread

baba|nik nm [Bot] live-forever, orpine (used in folk medicine to treat wounds) (Sedum telephium)

baba|plak nm = babagjysh

baba|pleq np = babagjysh

baba|raqe nf (Reg) **1** extreme cold; cold wind, chill **2** terror, dread, terrible fear

***babasor** n native of the village of Baba

***babauk** nm [Zool] spider

babaxhan
I § adj (Colloq) **1** good-natured, kind, likable **2** strong and healthy; capable and daring, enterprising
II § nm **1** kind/friendly person **2** (intimate term for a friend) old friend, buddy **3** (intimate term for one's father) daddy

baba|zi nm (Colloq) poor/unfortunate/wretched father; father inept in his paternal role

baba|zot nm **1** grandfather = gjysh, babagjysh **2** [Ethnog] property-owning patriarchal head of a large family

bab|ë nf with masculine agreement (np ~allarë) **1** = baba **2** [Bot] plant that supplies the pollen for cross breeding ***3** (Reg Gheg) [Anat] rectum, colon
○ **babë pas babe e djalë pas djali** generation after generation

bab|ëlok
I § n (Colloq) **1** endearing and respectful family term for parent or grandparent **2** affectionate conversational term of address **3** strong/healthy/capable person **4** good mixer, very friendly person

II § adj (Colloq) = babaxhan

bab|ëlosh nm = babëlok

***bab|ësjell|ë** nf [Veter] a cattle disease, a form of pyroplasm

bab|ëzi nf **1** greed, avarice, gluttony, insatiability, greediness **2** wretched poverty, terrible misfortune/bad luck **3** (Colloq) glutton, insatiable/avaricious person

bab|ëzi|ar adj (Colloq) = babëzitur

bab|ëzi|sht adv greedily, ravenously, insatiably

bab|ëzit·et vpr to get greedy, become insatiable

bab|ëzi|tur adj (i) **1** gluttonous, insatiable **2** (Fig) insatiably greedy: avaricious

bab|i children's word for their father (Child) daddy

babil nm [Ornit] European bee-eater (Merops apiaster L.)
○ **babil uji** [Ornit] kingfisher (Alcedo atthis L.)

babilon|as adj, n Babylonian

Babiloni nf Babylonia

***bab|it·et** vpr to be stunned/dizzy (from a blow)

***bab|it|ës** n assistant at a birth

bab|lok
I § nm **1** (intimate term for a friend) old friend, buddy **2** (intimate term for one's father) daddy
II § adj **1** good-natured; guileless, artless **2** naive; simpleminded

bab|o nf (Old) midwife

babu|in nm [Zool] baboon

babu|ne nf [Agr] round wooden bucket used as a measure (approximately 10 kilograms): peck = karro|çe

babu|sh nm (Child) **1** children's name for their father, grandfather, or other elderly man; daddy, grandpa **2** affectionate conversational term of address

***bac** nm **1** = bace **2** companion, mate; partner

***bâc** I § nm OR **bâcë** II § nf (Reg Gheg) clod of earth, lump, ball

bacarak nm [Food] pie made of corn meal and filled with leeks, onions, or other vegetables

ba|ce
I § nf with masc agreement (Reg Gheg) term for one's eldest brother, father, or father's brother; also used as an honorific title before the name of one of these persons or of another older person
II § nf = dackë

bacil nm [Biol] bacillus; bacterium

bacil|mba|rt|ës
I § adj [Med Veter] germ carrying
II § nm germ carrier

bac|kë nf **1** = dackë **2** concavity behind the knee, pit of the knee

bac|kos· vt (Colloq) to slap

***bactkoçe** nf = bretkosë

baç nm (Reg) **1** broad woolen strap used to keep a baby in a cradle or to carry a heavy load; woolen cord used to decorate clothes **2** belt-cord **3** cowherd, dairyman *baça' *nf* = ba'hçe

*ba'çe *nf* = ba'hçe

baçkallo'më *nf* *(Colloq)* something that cannot be used because it is too old or in disrepair; dilapidated hovel, ruin

baçkallo's· *vt* *(Colloq)* to destroy; bring into ruin

*ba'çkë *nf* slap, smack = da'ckë

*badakçi *nm* crook, scoundrel, rogue; swindler

*badakçi'llëk *nm* roguery

*bada'në *nf* whitewash

*badbadba'd *adv(Reg)*

*bade'më *nf* kind of pastry, almond tart

ba'dër *nf* 1 [*Bot*] common iris *(Iris germanica)* 2 [*Bot*] white asphodel *Asphodelus albus* 3 wild leek *Allium tricoccum* 4 child's kite made of stalks of wild leek

  ○ bad'ër e bardhë [*Bot*] white asphodel *Asphodelus albus*

  ○ bad'ër fyle [*Bot*] hollow-stemmed asphodel *Asphodelus fistulosus*

  ○ bad'ër uji [*Bot*] yellow flag iris *(Iris pseudocorus)*

badiava' = badihava'

badifo'kë *nf* leather pouch for keeping flint and tinder

badihava'

  I § *adv (Colloq)* 1 gratis, for nothing, for a song; very cheap, practically for nothing 2 *(Fig)* fruitlessly, ineffectually *3 for fun, in fun

  II § *adj* low-cost, quite cheap; practically free

badjava' = badihava'

ba'dhër *nf* [*Bot*] = ba'dër

*bae' OR bahe *nf* = ba'he

ba'fë *nf* *(Ichth)* female of the bass

ba'fër *nf* *(Bot)* terebinth, turpentine tree *(Pistacia terebinthus)* = qe'lbës

baft *nm(Colloq Old)* fate; luck

baft'ma'dh *adj* lucky; successful

baft'zi *adj* unlucky; unsuccessful

*baga *nf(Reg)* large tray for serving alcohol

*bagana'ce *nf(Reg)* 1 coarse cornbread 2 *(Fig)* girl, woman

*bagara'çe *nf* trash can

baga'zh *nm* baggage

Bagda'd *nm* Baghdad

ba'gë *nf* 1 [*Veter*] disability in horses caused by overloading, resulting in swelling of pasterns and fetlock, bowed tendon 2 = bajgë

ba'gël *nm* = bajgë

ba'gëm *nm* 1 [*Relig*] unction 2 = pogani'k

bagëti *nf* 1 livestock 2 *(Insult)* crude and uneducated person: dumb animal, dummy; ignoramus

  ○ bagëti e imët/hollë small livestock: sheep and goats

  ○ bagëti e leshtë livestock that are sheared for their wool/hair: sheep and goats

  ○ bagëti e trashë cattle: cows, oxen, domestic buffalo

bagllo'·n *vt* to spread manure on []: dung

*baglladi *nf* [*Mil*] camouflage netting

bagoli'në *nf* = thuapu'lë

*bagra'c *nm* gasoline can

bagre'n *nm* [*Bot*] false acacia *(Robinia pseudacacia)*

bah *interj* *(Colloq)* expresses disagreement or disbelief; expresses surprise

ba'hçe *nf(Colloq)* 1 kitchen garden planted with fruit trees, vegetables, or flowers 2 *(Old)* flower bed

  ○ bahçe me lule "flower garden" wonderful place, heavenly paradise

bahçeva'n *nm* *(Colloq)* gardener

ba'he *nf* = hobe

bahe'ta'r *nm (Old)* = hobeta'r

*ba'hëra = ba'rëra

*ba'hre *nf* pond, pool; well with water for drinking

Bahre'jn *nm* Bahrein

*baht = baft

bajagi *adv* *(Colloq Reg)* rather, quite, to some extent

bajalldi' *nf* *(Colloq)* nausea by exhaustion or overeating or eating spoiled food

bajalldi's· *vi* to faint, swoon

*baja'm *nm* = baja'me

baja'me *nf* 1 [*Bot*] almond *(Prunus dulcis Mill)* 2 [*Anat Med*] tonsils

  ○ bajame e egër [*Bot*] = gjipi'shtë

Baja'me *nf* Bajame (female name)

bajame'shi't'ës *n* roasted-almond seller

bajami'shtë *nf* almond grove

bajamo'r *adj* [*Med*] tonsillar

bajam'të *adj (i)* made with almonds

baja't *adj (Colloq)* 1 stale, lacking freshness 2 *(Fig)* trite

*baja'zë OR baje'zë *nf* = ba'jzë

*ba'jë *nf* 1 = ba'një *2 scarecrow

ba'jgë *nf* 1 horse/cow manure; dung 2 *(Folk Pej)* dirty son of a bitch

bajgo're *nf* *(Old)* large basket plastered inside and out with mud and dung, used to carry grain

bajgo's· *vt, vi* to soil with dung, defecate (said of large farm animals)

bajgo's·et *vpr* to become soiled by dung; have diarrhea (said of farm animals)

bajgo'sur *adj (i)* soiled by dung; having diarrhea (said of farm animals)

bajgu'sh *nm* [*Entom*] dung beetle

baji'shtë *nf* spawning area for mountain trout

bajlo'z *nm* 1 *(Old)* emissary, legate 2 [*Folklore*] evil giant who comes out of the sea and wreaks havoc

bajma'k *adj(Colloq)* having crooked legs and a sidewise gait, bandy-legged; lop-sided, crooked, awry

bajma'k'thi *adv* *(Colloq)* with a gait pulling to the side

bajone'të *nf* 1 bayonet 2 foot soldier (in counting units of military force) 3 *(Fig)* armed force, military force 4 [*Constr*] clout nail

bajpa's *nm* [*Spec*] bypass

bajra'k

  I § *nm* 1 banner 2 clan group, tribe 3 [*Hist*] territorial unit created by the Ottomans as a military (and later administrative) entity 4 [*Ethnog*] red banner adorned with flowers and tassels and carried by the wedding party on their way to deliver the bride to the groom 5 *(Fig)* handsome person with erect bearing; one who stands out above the rest

  II § *adj* tall and handsome

  ○ ësh·të me bajrak *(Pejor)* to have a bad reputation, be notorious

bajra'k'as *adv* like a banner

bajrakta'r *nm* 1 *(Old)* standard bearer 2 chief of the bajrak: chieftain; administrator of the patriarchal laws of the bajrak 3 *(Pejor)* one who behaves with arrogant cruelty, martinet, dictator; boss who uses old-fashioned, authoritarian methods **4** member of the wedding party who carries the wedding banner; best man at a wedding

bajraktarizëm nm **1** [Hist] system of territorial and military organization along patriarchal clan lines; realm of the bajraktar **2** (Pejor) old-fashioned, authoritarian way of ruling; attitude and behavior of a bajraktar; trying to act like a bajraktar

Bajram nm [Relig] name of two of the main Moslem religious holidays celebrated after Ramadan: Bairam
 ○ **Bajram i madh** greater Bairam (end of fasting)
 ○ **Bajram i vogël** lesser Bairam

bajramcurras n native or resident of Bajram Curri, a city in northeastern Albania

*__**bajt** = mbajt__ (Colloq)

*__**bajtë** = baltë__

bajth nm = baqth

bajukë nf **1** [Ornit] coot (Fulica atra) **2** spotted cow

bajun nm early-ripening, large, sweet white fig = fik llopës

bajzë nf **1** [Ornit] coot (Fulica atra L.) = pulëzezë *__**2** = hobe__

bakaje nf groceries bought on credit rather than with cash

*__**bakal** nm (Reg) chamber pot__

*__**bakala** = bakalaro__

bakalaro
 I § nf [Ichth] salt cod, bakalao
 II § adj (Colloq) skinny

bakall nm (Old) grocer

bakallaro nf = bakalaro

bakallëk nm (Old) **1** grocery item **2** grocery business

bakallëqe np < bakallëk groceries

*__**bakara** nf baccarat__

*__**bakardar** nm porridge__

bakej np < bakall

bakelit nm bakelite

bakeq nm (np ˜ i) (Reg) wrong-doer, miscreant, villain, hoodlum = keqbërës

bakeqës n = bakeq

bakeqësi nf crime, evil

bakeqësi nf (Reg) the game of tag

bakëm nm **1** [Bot] logwood, brazilwood (Haematoxylon campechianum) **2** slivers of logwood used for dying; logwood red

bakëqij np < bakeq

bakër nm **1** [Chem] copper ((Cu)) **2** (Colloq) poisonous salt formed in untinned copper utensils **3** (Fig Pej) something of little value; something valued below its real worth

bakëre np copper goods/items, copper utensils

bakërim nm ger [Tech] < bakëro•n, bakërohet

bakërishte nf **1** = bakëre **2** copper artifacts, pieces of copper, copper remnants **3** infertile land, poor soil

bakërizëm nm = bakërim

bakërmbajtës adj cupriferous, copper-bearing, containing copper

bakëro•n vt [Tech] to plate with copper

bakëror adj (Book) containing copper, made of copper

bakërore nf copper utensil, copper pot

bakëros•et vpr **1** to get copper poisoning (from eating out of an untinned copper utensil) **2** to lose tinning and expose the copper; develop poisonous salts by losing the tinning that protects the copper

bakërosur adj (i) **1** with bare copper exposed; having poisonous copper salts **2** poisoned by eating out of an untinned copper utensil

bakërpunues nm coppersmith

bakërt adj (i) **1** made of copper **2** copper-colored

bakërta np (të) = bakëre

bakërxhi nm (np ˜ nj) = bakërpunues

bakllama nf **1** (Old) hinge **2** [Mus] guitar-like instrument with three strings

bakllava nf baklava
 ○ **nuk bëhet bakllava me miell thekre** "baklava can't be made with rye flour" you can't do it right if you don't have the right ingredients
 ○ **bakllava me dy iça** baklava with two nut layers

bakra np **1** < bakër **2** = bakëre

bakraç nm (Old) small copper pot for preparing food or holding water

bakshish nm **1** tip for service rendered, gratuity *__**2** bribe *3 charity__

bakter nm [Biol] bacterium

bakteriolog n bacteriologist

bakteriologji adj bacteriology

bakteriologjik nf bacteriological

*__**bakterje** nf = bakter__

baktermbartës adj = bacilmbartës

baktermbytës
 I § adj bactericidic
 II § nm bactericide

bakteror adj (Book) bacterial; containing bacteria

*__**baktí** = bagëti__

bakthi adv (Reg) with feet together = pupthi

bakull adj (Colloq) having a strong and healthy body, robust

bal nm dog with white spots; sheepdog

baladë nf [Lit Mus] ballad

balalaikë nf balalaika

balan nm [Invert] barnacle

balancë nf (Book) balance = peshore
 ○ **ësh-të në balancë** to urgently need to be decided

balancim nm ger (Book) < balanco•n = baraspeshim

balanco•n vt, vi to balance = baraspesho•n

balanoglos nm [Invert] acorn worm (Enteropneusta)

balast nm **1** ballast (on a ship) **2** ballast under railroad tracks **3** (Fig) excessively heavy weight

balash adj **1** (said of a domestic animal, usually a horse or ox) with blazed face or spotted body; roan **2** (Pejor) shameless **3** (said of hair or beard) dappled, black and white; completely white **4** (Fig Pej) motley, variegated

*__**balcam** nm = balsam__

balci•n vi to bound, jump

*__**balco•n** vi = balci•n__

balç nm **1** [Bot] common St. John's wort, klamath weed (Hypericum perforatum) **2** extract/balm of St. John's wort **3** waistband for trousers

*__**balça** np braces, suspenders__

balçak nm [Ichth] = kryegjatë

balçëm nm = balsam

baldo'së nf [Zool] 1 badger 2 (Reg) mole cricket

balena'gjua'jt ës adj whale-hunting

bale'në nf 1 [Zool] whale 2 (Colloq) whalebone, whalebone stay
  ○ **balena kokëmadhe** [Zool] common rorqual Balaenoptera physalus
  ○ **balena me mustaqe** [Zool] baleen whale Mystacoceti
  ○ **balena me sqep** [Zool] goosebeak whale, Cuvier's beaked whale Ziphius cavirostris

baleri'n nm ballet dancer

baleri'në nf ballerina

bale'stër nf [Tech] leaf spring, coil spring

bale't nm 1 ballet 2 ballet company 3 (Colloq) ballet school; ballet hall

balet'mae'stër nm balletmaster, artistic director of a ballet

bale'
  I § nf 1 white blaze on the face or body of a domestic animal 2 an animal (usually a goat, ewe, or cow) with a white blaze on the face or body 3 (Fig) stain/stamp of dishonor 4 (Reg) = **baldo'së**
  II § adj (i) = **bale'r**

bale'dre'një nf goat with long, straight horns and a white blaze on the forehead

bale'mushkë nf goat with dun-colored hair (like a mule) and a white blaze on the forehead

bale'r adj (i) 1 having a white blaze on the face/muzzle 2 (Fig) stained/stamped by dishonor/shame

bale'so'rrë nf black ewe with a white blaze on the forehead

*_**ba'lgë** nf = **bajgë**_

balgo're nf (Reg Tosk) large mud-coated basket for carrying grain

bali'cë = **balli'cë**

bali'k nm = **ba'lo**

bali'skë nf 1 patch of white on the face or body of a domestic animal 2 an animal (usually a goat, ewe, or cow) with a white blaze on the face or body 3 the middle of the forehead 4 ornamental hame strap

balisti'k adj ballistics

balisti'kë nf ballistics

balli'shë nf 1 bangs (of hair) 2 white blaze on the face or body of a domestic animal 3 an animal (usually a goat, ewe, or cow) with a white blaze on the face or body

balkro'cë nf [Bot] evergreen rose (Rosa sempervirens)

*_**balku'e** nm (obl ˜ oni) (Reg Gheg) = **ballko'n**_

balmu'q nm leaf fat, unmelted lard

ba'lo nf with masc agreement 1 dog/ox with white-spotted face or body 2 (Colloq) albino 3 notorious rogue, shameless person

ba'loj nm white-blazed steer

ba'lok adj, nm (horse/dog) with patches of white on the face/muzzle/paws

balo'në nf 1 balloon 2 toy kite 3 (Reg Kos Old Colloq) airplane 4 [Spec] glass or metal bulb used to hold liquid or gas
  ○ **balonë prove** (Book) trial balloon

ba'los• vt 1 to make a white mark on [a surface]: blaze 2 (Fig) to mark with dishonor

ba'losh adj = **bala'sh**

ba'losha'n adj = **bala'sh**

ba'lo'she nf 1 white-blazed or spotted animal 2 [Bot] white birch

baloti'm nm [Med] ballottement

balo'z nm very wealthy person

balsa'm nm 1 balsam 2 medicinal extract of St. John's wort = **balç** 3 balm, salve
  ○ **balsam bredhi** [Bot] balsam fir (Abies balsamea)

balsama're nf clay flask used to hold balm or perfume

balsam'im nm ger < **balsamo'•n**

balsamino're np [Bot] balsam family Balsaminaceae

balsamo'•n
  I § vt to embalm; preserve [] by taxidermy
  II § vi, vt (Fig) to comfort, console, alleviate suffering, salve

balsamo's vt = **balsamo'•n**

balsamo'sje nf ger < **balsamo's•**

balsamo'sur adj (i) = **balsamu'ar**

balsa'mtë adj (i) 1 containing or pertaining to balsam 2 oleoresinous

balsamu'ar adj (i) 1 embalmed 2 having a pleasantly smell

balsamu'es nm taxidermist, embalmer

*_**balsu'ke** nf (Reg) = **ballu'ke**_

ba'lt•et vpr to become mushy, get the consistency of mud

balta'k
  I § adj = **baltani'k**
  II § nm mud puddle, muddy place = **bata'k**

baltani'k adj muddy

balta'r n person who prepares the mud to make tile or brick

ba'ltas adv in the mud, with mud

balta've'c
  I § adj 1 of the consistency of mud 2 (Fig Pej) mushy; sluggish, lazy, clumsy
  II § nm (Pejor) lazybones

balte'më adj (i) 1 mushy, of the consistency of soft mud 2 unappetizing, tasteless, vapid, bland

ba'ltë
  I § nf 1 mud, soil; muddy place, slush; clay; silt, sediment, sludge 2 ground, earth, soil 3 substance of which something is made 4 dregs, sediment, lees, grounds, refuse, alluvium, filth, dross 5 (Fig Pej) cheap thing; worthless thing; dirty thing; disgraceful thing 6 (Fig) difficult situation, trouble, bad mess 7 (Poet) homeland
  II § adj (i) = **ba'ltërt**
  ○ **baltë e dobët** 1 weak person, weakling 2 (Pejor) person of weak character
  ○ **baltë e ngjitur** (Pej) annoying person who won't leave one alone, persistent nuisance: sticky pest
  ○ **baltë xhamash** putty

baltë'go're nf large pot made of a clay and ash mixture

baltë'ke'qe nf muddy, unworkable soil; swampland

baltë'pu'nue's nm laborer who prepares the mud in a cement or pottery plant

ba'ltë'ra np < **ba'ltë**

ba'ltërro'k nm [Bot] buckthorn shrub that reaches a meter in height and has yellow flowers and yellowish or reddish berries that yield a yellow dye (Rhamnus oleoides)

ba'ltërt adj (i) made of clay/mud, earthen

ba'ltëz nf [Zool] **1** tadpole *2 = **baldo'së**

***baltice** nf = **balti'shtë**

baltik adj muddy, marshy

baltim nm ger **1** <**balto'**·n, **balto'**·het **2** bad taste in the mouth

baltinë nf muddy ground

baltishtë nf ground that gets muddy quickly; ground with water that doesn't run off

balto'·het vpr to get a bad taste in one's mouth

balto'·n vt to daub/cover [] with mud

balto'k nm baked clay or stone support placed under a cooking pan

***baltome** nf mud, filth

baltore nf **1** eathenware pot **2** = **balti'shtë**

baltos· vt **1** to soil/spatter [] with mud **2** to create mud by trampling [wet soil]

baltos·et vpr to be muddied; turn to mud

baltovec nm [Zool] = **baltu'k**

baltovicë nf muddy place/path

baltovinë nf muddy ground, mud puddle; mire, quagmire, fen, morass, slough

baltuk nm [Ichth] southern barbel (found in muddy water) (Barbus meridionalis petenyi Heck.) = **mustak**

***baltuke** nf mudbed

ba'ltur adj (i) wet and of the consistency of mud

balturinë nf **1** pieces of mud/earth/clay **2** clay utensils, earthenware; clay products

balthu'kë nf [Bot] large shrub with flexible branches, small, longish leaves, and bad-smelling yellow flowers

***balu'(n)** nm bale (of cloth)

baluke nf [Ornit] = **bajzë**

balu'n nm (Old) big sack used to carry material like wool

balusha'n nm ram with a white patch on the forehead

balushë nf **1** white patch on the face or body of an animal = **balë 2** patch of light in a dark place **3** = **bajzë**

balla np half-soles (in shoe repair)

ballaballas adv head to head, face to face; facing, opposite

ballaballë adv = **ballaballas**

balladër nf (Reg) **1** cataract, waterfall, cascade **2** ravine, precipice, abyss

ballafaqas adv = **ballafaqe**

ballafaqe adv face to face, eye to eye; openly, publicly, frankly

***ballafaqes** adv = **ballafaqe**

ballafaqim nm ger <**ballafaqo'**·n, **ballafaqo'**·het

ballafaqo'·het vpr **1** to confront **2** [Law] to conduct an examination (of a witness/defendant) **3** to have a face-to-face conference **4** to face up to an opponent

ballafaqo'·n vt **1** to face, confront; defy **2** to compare [] face to face **3** (Reg) to butt [objects] together

ballaku'me nf dessert made of eggs, flour, sugar, and butter

ballama'r nm [Naut] **1** hawser, mooring line **2** thick rope for securing a load

***ballanc** = **bala'nc**

ballandër nf waterfall

ballanik nm **1** forehead **2** facia of a building

ballanike nf shingle

ballanxhë nf (Reg) pond, pool of water

ballargje'nd adj (Poet) bright-eyed, beaming, radiant, handsome, beautiful

ballas adv **1** in front, facing, opposite; face to face **2** right out in the open

ballastama' nf [Naut] stem of a boat, beam extending the keel of a boat and projecting upward at the bow or stern

***ballato'**·n vt to face

ballave'sh adj (Colloq) having a high, unbecoming forehead; balding

ballazi adv = **ballas**

***ballbreshkë** OR **ballbreshtëz** nf [Bot] common goat's rue, French lilac (Galega officinalis)

ballcë nf (Old) headband or cap, usually embroidered, worn by women low over the forehead

***ballcor** nm outpost

ballça'k nm (Reg) wattled gate for a sheep pen; wattled fence surrounding a sheep fold = **trinë**

balle' nf gable

ballë

I § nm **1** forehead, brow **2** front; forefront, front line; forepart; bow (of a ship) **3** choice/best part, elite; early part **4** building facade **5** cartridge clip containing five or six rounds of ammunition **6** [Spec] measure of the energy released by an earthquake: magnitude **7** [Meteor] weather front *8 kerchief

II § prep (abl) in front of, facing, opposite

III § adv, interj * (Colloq) great, swell

○ **i ballët** frontal

○ **ballët e arkës** either of the narrow sides of a rectangular box/chest

○ **ballët e dhomës** either of the narrow sides of a room

○ **ballë e fund** completely: head to toe, front to back, top to bottom

○ **balli i kazanit** first and strongest raki from the still

○ **Balli Kombëtar** [Hist] anticommunist nationalist organization in Albania near the end of World War II

○ **ballët e krevatit** headboard (or tailboard) of a bed(stead)

○ **balli i oxhakut** cosy nook by the hearth

○ **ballë për ballë** face to face, facing

○ **ballë qorr** [Min] tunnel unconnected to ventilation and with only one exit: blind drift

○ **ballë i tunelit** [Tech] tunnel heading

○ **ballët e vozës** flat ends of the barrel

ballëbardhë adj white-faced (bird or animal)

ballëbreshtëz nf [Bot] sainfoin, esparcette (Onobrychis viciifolia)

ballëçelik adj (Poet) strong and unbending as steel

ballëçelur adv **1** smilingly **2** proudly

ballëdalë adj having a protuberant forehead

ballëfshehur adj bashful, timid

ballëgështenjë adj (Poet) handsome, beautiful

ballëgrep adj (Poet) with furrowed brow

ballëgjerë

I § adj having a broad forehead

II § nm [Ichth] large broad-headed fresh-water fish (Aristichthys nobilis)

○ **ballëgjerë i bardhë** [Ichth] silver carp Hypophthalmichthys molitrix

○ **ballëgjerë larosh** [Ichth] Aristichthys nobilis = **ballëgjerë**

ballëhapët

I § adv = **ballëha'pur**

II § adj sincere, frank

ballëhapur *adv, adj* with a clear conscience: sincere(ly); with head erect: courageous(ly); proud(ly)

ballëhark *adj (Poet)* = **ballëgrep**

ballëhёnë *nf* 1 animal (usually a cow) with a moon-shaped white patch on the forehead 2 *(Poet)* radiantly beautiful woman

ballëkrenar

  I § *adv (Poet)* proudly, with head held high

  II § *adj* proud

ballëkuq *adj* having a patch of red on the forehead; (animal) with a red forehead

ballëlarë *adj, adv* unstained by guilt, completely innocent

ballëlart *adv* with head held high, undaunted; proud of accomplishment

ballëlartë *adj* 1 having a high forehead 2 proud; resolute, fearless, undismayed

ballëlmadh *adj* having a broad/high forehead

ballëndritur *adj (Poet)* 1 with a shining face, bright-eyed, beaming, radiant, handsome, beautiful 2 *(Fig)* successful

ballëngrysur *adj* with darkened visage, frowning, depressed, gloomy, saddened

ballëngushtë *adj* having a narrow forehead

ballënxirë *adj* = **ballëngrysur**

ballëplot *adv* full face, head-on

ballëpruar *adj (Poet)* = **ballëndritur**

ballërrudhur *adj* submerged in thought, thinking; worried, concerned

ballёs *nm* 1 back of the hand 2 stick that holds up the slate slab in a birdtrap 3 handhold at the head end of a cradle

ballёso·n *vt (Old)* to face up to [ ]; confront

ballёsor

  I § *adj* on a broad scale: comprehensive, thorough

  II § *nm* 1 on a saddle or packsaddle, the saddlebow or pommel; the front part of a cradle 2 principal rafter of a roof 3 breast collar on a draft animal

ballёsore *nf* 1 a level spot on a mountain slope; a sunny spot 2 flat end of a barrel, barrel bottom

ballёstolisur *adj (i) (Poet)* with brow adorned

ballëtar *nm* leader, bellwether

ballёtor *nm* 1 bellwether, leading ram 2 pommel of a saddle

ballёvenetik *adj (Poet)* "Venetian-browed" with a beautiful high forehead; handsome, beautiful

ballёverdhё *nf* [*Ornit*] small bird with red forehead flecked with yellow

ballёvrenjtur *adj* gloomy-faced

ballёz *nf* one of the two runners – curved up at the front end – on which a sled/sleigh is mounted

ballёzi *adj, n (fem sg ~ez, masc pl ~inj, fem pl ~eza)* (fowl) with a black spot on the forehead; (fowl) with a black forehead

ballgam *nm* phlegm

  ∘ **ballgam në zemёr** regret deep in one's heart: deep regret, heartfelt regret

ballgёm = **ballgam**

ballgun *nm (Reg)* [*Bot*] = **shpardh**

ballgunishtё *nf (Reg)* grove of Italian oaks

balli *nm* pigeon with a rufous patch on the head

ballicё *nf* kerchief worn over the forehead

balliç *adj (Pejor)* having a prominent forehead

ballik *nm* [*Hist*] visor, vizor

ballinë *nf* 1 [*Archit*] main facade of a building; ornamented area above a door or window of a house: frontispiece 2 [*Publ*] frontispiece of a book; title page

ballist *adj* of or pertaining to the Balli Kombёtar political party which opposed the communist Fronti Nacionalçlirimtar during and after World War II

ballje *nf* [*Ethnog*] piece of white cloth or black satin worn over the forehead by women as a sign of mourning

ballkan *n* Balkan (person)

ballkanas

  I § *adj, n* of or pertaining to the Balkan people

  II § *n* native of the Balkans

ballkanik *adj* of or pertaining to the Balkans: Balkan

ballkanolog *n (Book)* Balkanologist, one who studies the Balkans

ballkanologji *nf (Book)* Balkanology, the study of the history, languages, and cultures of the Balkan peoples

ballkanologjik *nm (Book)* Balkanological, pertaining to the Balkans or to Balkanology

ballkё *nf* a reddish squash with a large head

ballkon *nm* balcony

ballkot *nm* [*Bot*] 1 Aaron's rod, great mullein *(Verbascum thapsus)* = **bar peshku** 2 mullein powder (used to daze fish) 3 a variety of long-bearded wheat with white grains

ballnik *nm* 1 flat end of a barrel/keg/cask 2 *(Old)* the part of the helmet that protects the warrior's forehead 3 the groin at the bottom of the abdomen 4 *(Old)* vanguard, advance guard 5 head end (of a bed)

ballo *nf* dancing party: ball, dance

ballok *nm* the part of the forehead between the eyebrows

ballomatar OR **ballomaxhi** *nm (Old)* cobbler, shoe-repairman, patcher

ballomё *nf* 1 = **mballomё** 2 large pie pan = **tepsi bakllavaje**

ballon *nm* = **balonё**

ballor

  I § *nm* 1 [*Anat*] frontal bone of the skull 2 *(Fig)* elite, choice/best part, cream

  II § *adj* 1 [*Anat*] frontal, cranial, of the forehead 2 located at the front, frontal, advance; directly, face to face; having a broad front

ballore *nf* 1 wicker basket attached to the front or back of a cart 2 front (of a house, saddle, cradle, etc.), fore part 3 = **ballcё** 4 [*Ichth*] crowned dentex *(Dentex gibbosus)* = **kocё pendёgjatё**

ballosh *adj* = **ballёgjerё**

ballotё *nf* 1 [*Bot*] ballota, horehound *Ballota* *2 popgun, peashooter *3 package

*ballpris *nm* leader

ballsam = **balsam**

*ballsamo·s *vt* = **balsamo·n**

*ballsamosje *nf ger* < **ballsamos·**

*ballsim *nm ger (Old)* < **ballso·n**

*ballso·n *vt (Old)* to face, confront; be a match for [ ]

ballsor *n* 1 leader 2 member of the nobility 3 facade 4 = **ballshtor**

Ballsh *nm* town in western Albania: Ballsh

Ballshak

  I § *adj* of or pertaining to Ballsh

  II § *n* native of Ballsh

ballshtor nm front part of a packsaddle

balltinë nf = ballinë

balltje nf large narrow-necked axe used to trim tree trunks; hatchet

balltuke nf 1 axe with a narrow heel 2 wide-bladed hoe

balluk nm 1 front part of a packsaddle/cradle = kaptell 2 billy-goat with forelocks hanging over his forehead

balluke nf 1 hair hanging over the forehead: forelock, bangs; lock, tress 2 ewe or cow with forelocks *3 wide-bladed hoe = balltuke

ballukecjap adj (Tease) having straight, long forelocks

ballukedredhur adj, n having twisted forelocks

ballukemadh
I § adj having long forelocks
II § n person/animal with long locks of hair

ballukemënjanë
I § adj having forelocks on one side of the head
II § n person/animal with long locks of hair hanging on one side

ballukepërpjetë adj having forelocks standing straight up

ballukeprerë adj, n having short forelocks

ballukeverdhë adj, n having blond forelocks; blond

ballukezi adj, n (fem sg ~ ez, masc pl ~ inj, fem pl ~ eza) (one) with black/dark forelocks; dark-haired, brunette

ballulur adv 1 with head held low, shamefacedly; sadly 2 humbly, modestly

ballungë nf = bullungë

bam
I § onomat (Colloq) sound of a gunshot or loud collision: wham! bam! bang!
II § adv in a sudden rush, with a bang
III § nm (Reg) offspring
∘ **bam __, bam __** suddenly going from __ to __
∘ **bam e bum** (Colloq) by every means possible: by might and by main
∘ **bam këtej, bam andej** (Colloq) by every means possible: by might and by main
∘ **bam këtu, bam atje** (Colloq) by every means possible: by might and by main

bambë nf = bambu

bambu nf [Bot] bamboo

bamë nf (Reg Old) large clay jug for water or olive oil

bâmës n (Reg Gheg) = bërës

bamirës adj = mirëbërës

bamirësi nf = mirëbërësi

bamje nf ger [Bot] okra (Abelmoschus esculentus L.)

banak nm 1 serving counter (for food or drinks): bar 2 workbench

banakier n counter attendant, bartender

banal adj 1 trite, hackneyed 2 banal, mundane, lacking in high ideals 3 (Pejor) indecent, tasteless, dirty (said of words), in poor taste

banalitet nm (Book) banality; triteness; tastelessness, indecency

banalizim nm ger <banalizo·n

banalizo·n vt to reduce [] to banality; debase, vulgarize

banane nf [Bot] banana

bananishte nf banana grove

bandazh nm 1 [Med] bandage = fashë 2 [Tech] drive belt, fan-belt

bandazhist n [Tech] maker of drive belts

banderolë nf 1 banderole 2 packing tape 3 band around a cigar

bandë nf 1 group of musicians playing instruments: band; wind band; brass band 2 (Pejor) band of criminals, gang 3 [Med] bandage 4 piece of fabric, embroidered or woven, hung on the wall as decoration

bandil nm small spade/hoe, weed chopper

bandill nm (Colloq) 1 handsome young boy; nice, amiable boy 2 (Tease Pej) lover boy, gallant, philanderer

bandit nm bandit, criminal, evil-doer, merciless killer and robber

banditizëm nm robbery, banditry; action of a band of criminals

bandra np = pranga

Bandung nm Bandung

banesë nf residential building, residence, lodgings; apartment, flat
∘ **banesa e fundit** (Euph) final resting place: the grave

banë nf 1 shepherd's hut 2 house, home, dwelling

bangë OR bango nf (Reg Gk) bench, schoolbench, schooldesk = bankë
∘ **bangë e dëshmitarit** witness box

bângë nf (Reg Gheg) package; paper bag

Bangkok nm Bangkok

Bangladesh nm Bangladesh

bangladeshas
I § adj of or pertaining to Bangladesh
II § n native of Bangladesh

bango nf table

banik adj worn every day; much used, worn out

banike nf (Euph) buttocks, rump, bottom

banim nm ger 1 <bano·n, bano·het 2 residence, dwelling, domicile

banishtë nf site on which shepherd's huts are built

bankar adj banking, of or pertaining to banks or bank business

banket nm banquet

bankë nf 1 bench, schoolbench, schooldesk 2 workbench 3 bank (of earth) 4 bank (financial institution)

bankënotë nf banknote, paper money

bankëprovë nf [Tech] test bench

bankier n owner of a bank, banker

bankinë nf 1 pier, dock, wharf 2 [Sport] shelter for non-playing participants: dug-out

bano·het vp impers there is habitation; it is habitable

bano·n vi to reside, dwell, live

banonjës = banues

banor n inhabitant, resident
∘ **banorët e pyllit** denizens of the forest

banqer nm = bankier

banuar adj (i) inhabited, populated

banues nm = banor

banueshëm adj (i) habitable

banjar n = banjtar

banjë nf 1 bath 2 bath-room; bathhouse 3 spa 4 bathing, swimming 5 (Euph) bathroom, toilet
∘ **banjë deti** bathing/swimming in the ocean
∘ **banjë dielli** sunbathing
∘ **banjë dobësimi** [Cine] reducing bath

○ **banjë me avull** steam bath
○ **banjë ndënjur** [Med] sitz bath
○ **banjë ngjyrash** [Cine] chromatic bath
○ **banjë popullore** public baths, public bathhouse
○ **banjë qetësuese** [Med] sedative bath
○ **banjë turke** [Med] Turkish bath, sweat bath

banjëmari nf 1 [Spec] heating in a double boiler 2 double boiler, bain marie

banjëzim nm ger <banjëzo·n

banjëzo·n vt to bathe, immerse

banjo nf (Colloq) = banjë

banjore nf small bathroom

*banjtar nm 1 bath steward/attendant 2 bather

baobab nm [Bot] baobab (Adansonia digitata)

*baq nm = baqth

baqth nm lower belly (from the navel to the anus), below the belt

bar nm (np ~ëra) 1 [Bot] grass; grassy plot, lawn 2 (Fig) bland/tasteless food 3 herb, herbaceous plant 4 (Colloq) spice, food additive 5 medicinal plant, medicament, medication 6 (Fig Colloq) palliative, cure, solution, way out of a difficulty 7 chemical substance used to repel or eliminate noxious insects or animals 8 [Phys] unit of atmospheric pressure 9 bar (for drinking): pub, coffeehouse
○ **bar argjendi** "silver-grass" [Bot] horsetail (Equisetum)
○ **bar i ariut** "bear-grass" [Bot] = krahnjerr
○ **bar balsami** "balm-grass" [Bot] = balç
○ **bar i bardhë** "whitegrass" [Bot] hyssop (Hyssopus officinalis)
○ **bar beronje** "infertility-grass" [Bot] European holly (used in folk medicine as a fertility drug) = ashe
○ **bar bibe** "turkey-grass" [Bot] knotgrass (used to treat jaundice in waterfowl/turkeys) (Polygonum aviculare)
○ **bar blete** "bee-grass" [Bot] = barblete
○ **bar bostani** [Bot] Greek camelthorn (Sanguisorba minor)
○ **bar brenge** [Bot] "worry-grass" used in folk medicine, is a herbaceous plant with willow-like leaves and thin, rose-colored flowers
○ **bar breshën** "hail-grass" [Bot] *= halmucë
○ **bar breshke** "turtle-grass" [Bot] German clover = halmucë
○ **bar bubash** [Bot] large dodder, greater dodder (Cuscuta europaea)
○ **bar buçi** [Bot] = bar gjarpri
○ **bar capoj** scarlet pimpernel (Anagallis arvensis)
○ **bar i çikës** "crumb-grass" [Bot] herbaceous medicinal with basil-like leaves used in folk medicine as a treatment for conjunctivitis
○ **bar dalëgjaje** nodding navelwort (Umbilicus pendulinus, Cotyledon umbilicus)
○ **bar i dalës** "emergent-grass" [Bot] *= bar plasjeje
○ **bar dallëndysheje** "swallow-grass" [Bot] herbaceous annual with small roundish leaves marked in the middle with a black spot
○ **bar delli** "sinew-grass" [Bot] great plantain (Plantago major L.)
○ **bar derri** "pig-grass" [Bot] yellow foxtail (Setaria glauca)
○ **bar djathi** "cheese-grass" 1 [Bot] globe artichoke (used to turn milk into cheese) (Cynara scolymus) 2 [Dairy] starter for cheese
○ **bar dlirës** "purging-grass" purgative

○ **bar dreqi** "devil-grass" [Bot] dodder (Cuscuta) = helmëz
○ **bar dreri** "deer-grass" [Bot] joint pine (Ephedra fragilis Desf. ssp. campylopoda)
○ **bar drëni** [Bot] field cow-wheat (Melampyrum arvense)
○ **bar i drithit** "grain-grass" [Bot] herbaceous plant with white flowers clustered at the top, spread in grain bins to keep vermin away
○ **bar i dytë** second-growth crop, rowen, aftermath
○ **bar dhëmballe** "molargrass" [Bot] yellow germander (Teucrium flavum) *= arrës
○ **bar i egër** "wild-grass" weed
○ **bar ere** [Bot] tansy (Tanacetum vulgare)
○ **bar ethesh** "fever-grass" [Bot] centaury, drug centaurium (Centaurium umbellatum) *= trikë
○ **bar fare** "seed-grass" [Bot] herbaceous annual with long narrow leaves and darnel-like stalk whose seeds are used in folk medicine
○ **bar gardelinash** [Bot] common groundsel (Senecio vulgaris)
○ **bar gomari** "donkey-grass" [Bot] = gjembaç
○ **bar griskle** "fishscale-grass" [Bot] toothwort (Lathraea squamaria)
○ **bar gryke** "throat-grass" [Bot] herbaceous perennial with a straight, velvety stem and laterally cleft leaves
○ **bar guri** "stone-grass" [Bot] joint-fir, ephedra (Ephedra) = gjunjëz
○ **bar gjaku** [Bot] = bargjak
○ **bar gjalpi** "butter-grass" [Bot] a variety of grass that gives off the odor of a dairy
○ **bar gjani** [Bot] horsetail (Equisetum arvense)
○ **bar gjarpri** "snake-grass" [Bot] scale fern (used in folk medicine to treak snakebite in livestock) (Ceterach officinarum)
○ **bar gjedheni** "cattle-grass" [Bot] horsetail (Equisetum)
○ **bar gjergji** moneywort (Lysimachia nummularia)
○ **bar i gjësë** "thing-grass" [Bot] = bar plasjeje
○ **bar gjumi** 1 [Bot] opium poppy (Papaver somniferum) 2 [Bot] = qimnon
○ **bar havlle** blue hound's-tongue (Cynoglossum creticum)
○ **bar helmi** "poison-grass." [Bot] poisonous (to animals) type of micromeria (Micromeria juliana)
○ **bar helmues** "poisonous drug" ideological poison; carrier of such poison
○ **bar hënëze** "moon-grass" [Bot] honesty Lunaria = barhënë
○ **bar i hidhët** "bitter-grass" [Bot] butcher's broom (Ruscus aculeatus) = rrushkull
○ **bar hikrraqi** "sheep-rot-grass" [Bot] = syka
○ **bar hirre** "whey-grass" 1 [Bot] burning bush (used to give flavor to dry, salted cottage cheese and used in folk medicine to cure a disease of sheep and goats that thins their milk and blinds them) (Dictamnus albus) 2 = bar përdhesi
○ **bar hirrëze** "whey-grass" [Bot] = bar hirre
○ **bar hudhre** "garlic-grass" [Bot] = barhudhër
○ **bar i imët** "thin-grass" [Bot] bent grass, fiorin, redtop, white bent (Agrostis alba L., Agrostis vulgaris, Agrostis byzantina) = barimëz
○ **bar italiani** "Italian-grass" [Bot] Italian rye grass Lolium italicum

○ **bar jeli** [*Bot*] **1** common four-o'-clock, marvel-of Peru (*Mirabilis jalapa*) ***2** bladder campion, cowbell silene (*Silene latifolia (vulgaris)*)

○ **bar i jetës** "life-grass" [*Bot*] herbaceous annual growing in both planted fields and stubble land, the juice of whose seeds causes vomiting and loss of consciousness

○ **bar jodi** "iodine-grass" [*Bot*] greater celandine (*Chelidonium majus*)

○ **bar kallkë** bulbous barley (*Hordeum bulbosum; Hordeum murinum*)

○ **bar i keq** "bad grass" ***1** noxious weed **2** socially harmful defect; person with such a defect

○ **bar kimik** chemical; drug

○ **bar kolaneci** "sausage-grass" [*Bot*] = **bar përdhe·si**

○ **bar krend** [*Bot*] mistletoe (*Viscum album*)

○ **bar krimbi** "worm-grass" [*Bot*] felty germander (*Teucrium polium*)

○ **bar kripi** "salt-grass" [*Bot*] = **përçu·k**

○ **bar kryezi** "brunette-grass" [*Bot*] = **bar i së paemrës**

○ **bar kukunjëze** "pimple-grass" [*Bot*] herbaceous annual with narrow leaves like the musk thistle and with yellow flowers like fenugreek (used in folk medicine to treat pimples)

○ **bar kulurxhi** [*Bot*] milk vetch (*Astragalus glycyphyllos*)

○ **bari i të kuqit të madh** [*Bot*] ***=** **shikaku·q**

○ **bar i lebërit** common groundsel (*Senecio vulgaris*)

○ **bar lebre** "curdler-grass" [*Bot*] common groundsel (used in folk medicine to treat a problem in the milk of nursing women) (*Senecio vulgaris*)

○ **bar lepuri** "rabbit-grass" [*Bot*] herbaceous annual used as feed for animals: hare's foot clover (*Trifolium arvense*)

○ **bar lëkure** "leather-grass" insecticide

○ **bar lëngose** "wasting-away-grass" [*Bot*] = **bar përdhe·si**

○ **bar lëngjyre** "typhoid-grass" [*Bot*] herbaceous plant with long leaves and violet-colored, strongly scented flowers (used in folk medicine as a treatment for typhoid fever)

○ **bar lëshec** [*Bot*] common velvet grass, Yorkshire fog (*Holcus lanatus*)

○ **bar i lotzonjës** [*Bot*] lily of the valley = **dre·këz**

○ **bar lugati** [*Bot*] sharp-leaved asparagus (*Asparagus acutifolius*)

○ **bar lunge** "carbuncle-grass" [*Bot*] sylvan violet, hooded blue violet (*Viola sylvestris*)

○ **bar i llazesë** [*Bot*] leadbush glasswort (*Salicornia fruticosa*)

○ **bar macesh** [*Bot*] catnip (*Nepeta cataria*)

○ **bar i madh** "big-grass" [*Bot*] = **shpe·ndër**

○ **bar majasëlli** "hemorrhoid-grass" [*Bot*] felty germander (used in folk medicine as a treatment for piles) (*Teucrium polium*)

○ **bar mastiku** [*Bot*] burning bush, gas-plant dittany, fraxinella *Dictamnus albus* ***=** **di·shull**

○ **bar me kokë** "headed-grass" (*Reg*) [*Bot*] = **tërfi·l**

○ **bar mëndafshi** "silk-grass" [*Bot*] poisonous herbaceous perennial with twining stem, cordate leaves, clusters of lilac-colored flowers, and seeds encased in a leaf covered by thick down (*Asclepia vincetoxicum*)

○ **bar i minurit** [*Bot*] Jerusalem oak, Jerusalem oak goosefoot (*Chenopodium botrys*)

○ **bar mish** rat poison

○ **bar miu** "mouse-grass" [*Bot*] sharp-leaved asparagus (*Asparagus acutifolius*)

○ **bar mjalti** "honey-grass" [*Bot*] = **lule blete**

○ **bar mjekimi** medicinal herb

○ **bar mole** "moth-grass" insecticide

○ **bar morri** "louse-grass" [*Bot*] stavesacre (used against lice) (*Delphinium staphysagria*)

○ **bar muri** nodding navelwort (*Umbilicus pendulinus (Cotyledon umbilicus)*)

○ **bar ndërgishteje** "whitlow-grass" [*Bot*] creeping cinquefoil, fivefinger, five-leaf grass (used in folk medicine as a treatment for whitlow) (*Potentilla reptans*)

○ **bar nepërke** "viper-grass" [*Bot*] bugloss (*Echium vulgare*)

○ **bar ngalose** "sheep-rot-grass" [*Bot*] = **gurgulle·shë**

○ **bar ngjitës** "sticky-grass" [*Bot*] joint-fir ephedra; sea grape (*Ephedra distachya*)

○ **bar nozëll** [*Bot*] yarrow, milfoil (*Achillea millefolium*)

○ **bar i njomë** green/fresh hay/grass

○ **bar pa rrënjë** [*Bot*] common dodder (*Cuscuta epithymum*)

○ **bar paresh** "money grass" [*Bot*] field horsetail (*Equisetum arvense*)

○ **bar pasrregulli** "swooning-grass" [*Bot*] used as a restorative in folk medicine to treat someone feeling faint, is a herbaceous plant with round, red flowers and leaves shaped like a duck's foot

○ **bar pate** "goose-grass" [*Bot*] prostrate knotweed, knotgrass (which yields small seeds eaten by fowl, especially geese) (*Polygonum aviculare*)

○ **bar peshku** "fish-grass" ***1** [*Bot*] Aaron's rod, great mullein (used to catch fish by dazing them) (*Verbascum thapsus*) **2** longleaf mullein (*Verbascum longifolium*)

○ **bar pezmi** "sore-grass" [*Bot*] yarrow, milfoil (used in folk medicine to treat festering wounds) (*Achillea millefolium*)

○ **bar pezul** [*Bot*] saxifrage (*Saxifraga*)

○ **bar përdhesi** "gout-grass" [*Bot*] yarrow (used as folk medicine to treat arthritic disease in cattle) (*Achillea*)

○ **bar plakash** "oldwomen-grass" [*Bot*] common autumn crocus, meadow saffron (*Colchium autumnale*)

○ **bar plasjeje** "anthrax-grass" [*Bot*] figwort with clusters of white flowers, oval leaves (used in folk medicine as a treatment for anthrax) (*Scrophularia romosissima*)

○ **bar plehu** "dung-grass" [*Bot*] herbaceous plant that grows in dungheaps and blooms in midsummer with nettle-like leaves, rose-colored flowers, and reddish seeds like those of flax

○ **bar pleshtash** "flea-grass" [*Bot*] tansy whose seeds are used as a folk insecticide against fleas (*Tanacetum cinerariaefolium*)

○ **bar pleshti** pale alyssum (*Alyssum alyssoides*)

○ **bar prisi** bladder campion, cowbell silene (*Silene latifolia (vulgaris)*)

○ **bar pulash** "hen-grass" [*Bot*] prostrate knotweed, knotgrass (used for food or as a folk medicine) (*Polygonum aviculare*)

○ **bar pushi** "fuzz grass" [*Bot*] bulbous bluegrass (*Poa bulbosa*)

○ **bar qelbës** "stink-grass" [*Bot*] madder (*Putoria calabrica*)

○ **bar i qelbur** "rotten-grass" [*Bot*] *= **bar qe'lbës**

○ **bar qeni** [*Bot*] "dog-grass" **1** horehound *(Marrubium peregrinum L.)* **2** European plumbago, leadwort *(Plumbago europaea)*

○ **bar qerose** "ringworm-grass" [*Bot*] black nightshade (used in folk medicine as a treatment for ringworm) *(Solanum nigrum)*

○ **bar qime femën** fragrant orchid *Gymnadenia conopsea*

○ **bar qimesh** pink convolvulus *(Convolvulus cantabricus)*

○ **bar qumështi** "milk-grass" [*Bot*] common dandelion (fed to cows to increase their milk yield) *(Taraxacum officinale)*

○ **bar rakije** [*Bot*] burning bush, gas-plant dittany, fraxinella *(Dictamnus albus)* *= **di'shull**

○ **bar rresh** "roundworm-grass" [*Bot*] large dodder (used in folk medicine as a treatment for roundworm) *(Cuscuta europaea)*

○ **bar sahati** "clock-grass" [*Bot*] herbaceous plant with hyacinth-like flower buds that put out fibers resembling the hands of a clock

○ **bar sapuni** "soap-grass" [*Bot*] soapwort, bouncing Bet/Bess *(Saponaria officinalis)*

○ **bar i së paemrës** [*Bot*] "shingles-grass" **1** lycopod, clubmoss *(Lycopodium clavatum)* **2** star thistle *(Centaurea calcitrapa)* **3** scarlet pimpernel *(Anagallis arvensis)*

○ **bar së premi** *1 mugwort *(Artemisia vulgaris)* **2** common St. John's wort *(Hypericum perforatum)*

○ **bar squfuri** "sulfur-grass" [*Bot*] clubmoss, lycopodium

○ **bar syri** [*Bot*] "eye-grass" *1 daisy *(Bellis perennis)* **2** scarlet pimpernel *(Anagallis arvensis)*

○ **bar shëllire** "brine-grass" [*Bot*] herbaceous plant used in cheese vats against cheese mites and bearing small leaves and velvety white flowers

○ **bar shëngjergji** "St.-George-grass" *1 [*Bot*] crosswort *(Galium cruciatum)* **2** moneywort *(Lysimachia nummularia)*

○ **bar shëngjini** [*Bot*] wormwood, artemisia

○ **bar shkëndije** "spark-grass" [*Bot*] herbaceous plant with nettle-like leaves marked with a white stripe (used in folk medicine as an eye treatment)

○ **bar shkumëz** bouncing Bet/Bess, soapwort *(Saponaria officinalis)*

○ **bar shpatëz** "sword-grass" [*Bot*] cinquefoil

○ **bar shpërgëtie** "shingles-grass" [*Bot*] *= **bar i së paemrës**

○ **bar shpirre** "asthma-grass" [*Bot*] = **bar i dreqit**

○ **bar shpretke** "spleen-grass" **1** [*Bot*] rue *(Ruta graveolens)* **2** vervain *(Verbena officinalis)*

○ **bar shqiponje** "eagle-grass" [*Bot*] yellow foxglove *(Digitalis ambigua)*

○ **bar i shtërgjisë** [*Bot*] bishop's goutweed *(Aegopodium podagraria)*

○ **bar shurrëgjakeje** "badblood-grass" [*Bot*] chrysoplene, alternate-leaved golden saxifrage (used in folk medicine to treat a blood disease in livestock) *(Chrysosplenium alternifolium)*

○ **bar tambli** **1** [*Bot*] common dandelion *(Taraxacum officinale)* **2** = **tridhëbo'të** **3** spurge, euphorbia *(Euphorbia)*

○ **bar tamli** [*Bot*] *= **bar tambli**

○ **bar teli** [*Bot*] = **teli'sh**

○ **bar telishi** "filigree-grass" **1** [*Bot*] = **teli'sh** *2 silvery sedge, whitish sedge *(Carex canescens)*

○ **bar teshi** "shingles-grass" **1** [*Bot*] knapweed with pinnate leaves and purple flowers (used to treat herpes-caused conditions such as shingles) *(Centaurea alba)* **2** common St. John's wort *(Hypericum perforatum)*

○ **bar të hasmi** *= **bar i të hasurit**

○ **bar i të hasurit** "hex-grass" [*Bot*] type of micromeria used as a folk antidote to curses or spells *(Micromeria juliana)*

○ **bar të preri** "cutting-grass" [*Bot*] common St. John's wort, klamath weed *(Hypericum perforatum)*

○ **bar të thekmit/thekuri** knotgrass, prostrate knotweed *(Polygonum aviculare)*

○ **bar i trashë** "thick-grass" [*Bot*] henbane, hogbean *= **madërgo'në**

○ **bar i thatë** "dry-grass" hay

○ **bar theku** [*Bot*] *= **barthe'k**

○ **bar thëllëze** "partridge-grass" **1** [*Bot*] mercury *(Mercurialis)* **2** = **xerxe'le**

○ **bar thiu** "swine-grass" [*Bot*] = **tri'kë**

○ **bar udhe** "road-grass" [*Bot*] stonecrop, goldmoss stonecrop, gold moss *(Sedum acre)* *= **rrushqy'qe**

○ **bar ujcë** tubular water dropwort *(Oenanthe fistulosa)*

○ **bar uji** "water-grass" [*Bot*] water fennel *(Oenanthe aquatica)* *= **mara'skë**

○ **bar ujithi** **1** [*Bot*] gromwell *(Lithospermum officinale)* = **kokërru'jë** **2** castor-oil plant, castor bean *(Ricinus communis)*

○ **bar urdheje** [*Bot*] goldmoss stonecrop, goldmoss = **rrushqy'qe**

○ **bar urithi** "mole-grass" [*Bot*] herbaceous field plant that has hyacinth-like stem and leaves and is much favored by bees, is a

○ **bar i uzos** [*Bot*] burning bush *(Dictamnus albus)* *= **di'shull**

○ **bar vedre** "bucket-grass" [*Bot*] a herbaceous plant with blue flowers, leaves lined up on two sides of the stem and a pleasant smell like that of rosemary

○ **bar venetiku** [*Bot*] reed canary grass *(Phalaris arundinacea)* *= **kokëma'dhe**

○ **bar verdhçi** [*Bot*] *= **bar verdhëze**

○ **bar i verdhë** "yellow-grass" [*Bot*] = **kusku'të**

○ **bar verdhëze** "jaundice-grass" [*Bot*] lesser meadow rue (used in folk medicine to treat jaundice) *(Thalictrum minus)*

○ **bar vese** "dew-grass" [*Bot*] herbaceous annual that grows hand-high and has blue flowers and that is used in folk medicine to treat skin problems

○ **bar veshi** "ear-grass" [*Bot*] roof houseleek, hen-and-chickens (used in folk medicine to treat ear problems) *(Sempervivum tectorum)*

○ **bar vneri** [*Bot*] electuary

○ **bar zemre** "heart-grass" *1 [*Bot*] yellow gentian *(Gentiana lutea)* = **sa'nëz** **2** round-leaved birthwort *(Aristolochia rotunda)*

○ **bar zgjebeje** "itch-grass" [*Bot*] scabious (used in folk medicine to treat itching) *(Scabiosa)*

○ **bar i zgjebëz** [*Bot*] = **bar zgjebeje**

○ **bar zogu** "bird-grass" [*Bot*] chickweed *(Stellaria media)*

○ **bar zonje** [*Bot*] felty germander *(Teucrium polium)*

baraba'n *nm* [*Tech*] drum (of a machine)

bara|ba'r *adv* equally, evenly, equal, alike, even

bara|bardh nm [Bot] a kind of long, white grass with red tassels

bara|bar|ësi nf equality = **barazí**

bara|bartë adj (i) equal

bara|bís stem for 1st sg pres, pl pres, 2nd & 3rd sg subj, pind (Reg) < **barabít**•

bara|bít• vt (Reg) to give [] equal value, consider [] equal: compare, equate

barabít•et vpr
  ∘ **barabit**•et me [] to be comparable to [someone], be on the same level as []

*****bara|bít|çëm** adj (i) = **barabítshëm**

*****bara|bít|ës** adj comparative

bara|bít|je nf ger 1 < **barabít**•, **barabít**•et 2 comparison

bara|bít|shëm adj (i) (Reg) comparable

bara|brínj|ës nm [Geom] equilateral

*****baraka'n** nm cloak, burnoose

bara'kë nf simple structure providing space for storage, sleeping, or selling: barrack, hut, booth, shed

bara|krah|ës adj (Old) [Geom] isosceles

bara'ngë nf (Colloq) = **barakë**

bara'|s pred 1 at the same time/level, in the same amount, even 2 (in mathematical operations) equal

*****baras|í** nf egalitarianism, equality

*****baras|ím** nm ger = **barazím**

baras|larg|ësí nf equidistance

baras|larg|ua'r adj (i) [Geom] equidistant

baras|lart|ësí nf height/altitude equal to one under comparison

baras|na'të nf equinox

baras|o'•n vt, vi = **barazo'**•n

baras|pe'shë nf [Spec] equilibrium, static equilibrium

baras|peshím nm ger 1 < **baraspesho'**•n 2 equilibrium; equalization of forces

baras|pesho'•n vt to put [] into equilibrium, balance [forces]; counterpose

baras|tíngull nm [Mus] unison

baras|vle'rë nf equivalence

baras|vle'r|ës nm something of equivalent value, equivalent

baras|ve'r|shëm adj (i) equivalent

bara'sh nm (Reg Pej) person who likes to spend time running around

bara|shto'•n vt to bring [] into even balance; equalize, make [] level

ba'r|az adv = **ba'ras**

ba'ra|zi adv = **ba'ras**

barazí nf equality

barazím
  I § nm ger 1 < **barazo'**•n, **barazo'**•het 2 [Sport] tie, draw 3 equality 4 [Math] equation 5 [Electr] compensation
  II § adv in a tie

bara|zím|ta'r adj (Book) egalitarian

bara|zím|tarí nf (Book) equalization

bara|zím|tar|izëm nm egalitarianism

bara|zí|sht adv (Book) on the same terms/level: equally, evenly

barazo'•het vpr 1 to become equal 2 [Sport] (of a score) become tied, (of a game) be drawn

∘ **barazo'**•het me [] to be comparable to [someone], be on the same level as []

barazo'•n
  I § vt 1 to equalize, even up, balance 2 to consider [] equal: equate 3 [Fin] to balance [a budget], bring [] into balance; settle [an account]
  II § vi to tie the score, tie, draw

bara|zu'a'r adj (i) 1 equated, compared 2 [Fin] brought into balance: balanced; settled 3 [Sport] (of a score) tied, (of a game) drawn

bara|zu'e|s adj 1 serving to equalize or balance 2 (Old) comparative, by comparison

bara|zu'e|shëm adj (i) comparable

bara'zh nm 1 dike, dam 2 [Mil] barrage 3 (Fig) protective barrier

*****bara'zhgë** nf difficult situation, quandary; trouble, anxiety

barba'ç adj, n (Colloq) Albanian of Greece

Barbado's nm Barbados

barbaga'm nm [Fish] thick beam placed across the poles of a fish weir

*****barbal|ís** stem for 1st sg pres, pl pres, 2nd & 3rd sg subj, pind < **barbalít**•

*****barbal|ít**• vi to play the buffoon

barbal|ít•et vpr to mutter

barbalu'sh nm (Reg) corn mush = **mëmëlí'gë**

*****barbaník** nm [Bot] = **babaník**

barba'r
  I § adj barbarous
  II § n barbarian

barbar|í nf barbarity; barbarism

Barbar|í nf Barbary

barbar|ísht adv barbarically, barbarously

barbar|izëm nm barbarianism; barbarity; barbarism

*****barbaro'z** nm 1 pet lamb 2 [Bot] = **barbaro'zë**

barbaro'zë nf [Bot] rose-leaf geranium, rose pelargonium (Pelargonium roseum, Pelargonium graveolens)

*****barba'rtë** adj (i) = **barba'r**

*****barberha'në** nf barbershop = **berberha'në**

*****ba'rbë** nf with masculine reference uncle

*****bar|bëla'c** nm [Bot] snakeroot, bistort (Polygonum bistorta)

*****barbër|ës** n = **barnata'r**

barble'te nf [Bot] common balm, lemon balm (Melissa officinalis) = **mílcë**

*****barbole'c** nm = **borbole'c**

*****barbo'në** nf [Veter] a poultry disease

*****barbû(n)** nm (Reg Gheg) [Ichth] = **barbu'n**

bar-bufe' nf pub/bar with stand-up service for food and drink

*****barbulíq** nm 1 corncob 2 [Ichth] = **barburíq**

ba'rbull nm (np ˉ j) 1 = **ça'pëz** 2 ball of the foot next to the big toe, ball of the hand next to the thumb

barbu'n nm [Ichth] red mullet (Mullus barbatus)
  ∘ **barbun balte** [Ichth] = **barbu'n**
  ∘ **barbun guri** striped mullet, long-snouted mullet Mullus surmuletus L.

barbu'nj np < **barbu'n**

barbu'një nf [Bot] kidney bean (Phaseolus vulgaris var. romanus Savi)

barburíq nm [Ichth] butterfly blenny (Blennius ocellaris L.B)
  ∘ **barburiq bari** zebra blenny Blennius basiliscus

○ **barburiq deti** red-speckled blenny *Parablennius sanguinolentus*

○ **barburiq guri** rock blenny, tompot blenny *Parablennius gattorugine*

○ **barburiq lumi** fresh-water blenny *Blennius fluviatilis Pollini*

***barbu·sh** *nm* [*Bot*] field pepperweed (*Lepidium campestre*)

***barbu·t** *nm* dice

***barbu·tk**ë *nf* game of dice

Barcelo·në *nf* Barcelona

barda·k *nm* = **bardha·k**

bardali·ke *adj*

bar·dre·dh *nm* [*Bot*] = **dre·dhkë**

bardh· *vt, vi (Reg)* = **zbardh·**

Bardh *nm* Bardh (male name)

ba·rdh·a *np (të)* **1** white clothes; linen **2** [*Med*] discharge of amniotic fluid or vaginal mucous: leukorrhea **3** dairy products **4** cereals, crops **5** (*Euph*) imaginary mountain-dwelling or subterranean creatures in folklore who appear in the form of girls and do terrible things when angered

bardh·a·ç *adj* = **bardhe·m**ë

bardh·a·jkë *nf* **1** rotten wood of a whitish color **2** white sheep, goat, or cow

bardha·k
 I § *adj* = **bardho·k**
 II § *nm* **1** large water glass, usually with a handle; brandy glass **2** tall clay pot with a spout

bardha·le·c *adj* ashy white, sickly pale

bardha·n *adj* = **bardho·k**

bardha·në *nf* white sheep, goat, or cow

bardh·a·qe·n *nm* [*Bot*] Alps honeysuckle (*Lonicera alpigena*)

bardha·sh
 I § *adj* = **bardho·sh**
 II § *nm* white billy goat; white dove, white horse

bardh·ave·l *adj* whitish pink, light pink; blond, fair

bardhe·c
 I § *adj* = **bardho·k**
 II § *n* white goat

bardhe·më *adj (i)* whitish

bar·dhe·së *nf* = **bar përdhesi**

bardhe·zi *adv* in black and white

ba·rdhë
 I § *adj (i)* **1** white **2** light-colored **3** illuminated by a white light **4** blank (piece of paper) **5** counter-revolutionary (as opposed to red) **6** (*Fig*) fortunate, lucky **7** mild (said of certain diseases) **8** pure, clean, fresh
 II § *nf* white sheep or goat; fair-skinned girl
 III § *nf (e)* **1** the color white; white paint; something white **2** (*Fig*) good deed, something nice
 IV § *nn (të)* **1** white facial cleansing cream **2** = **bardh**ë**si 3** egg white
 V § *adv* whitish, in white
 ○ **E bardhë është edhe bora në mal, por po ta prekësh mërdhin.** "The snow in the mountain is indeed white, but if you touch it you freeze." (*Prov*) All that glitters is not gold.
 ○ **i bardhë si qefin** white as a sheet
 ○ **e bardha//të bardhët e syrit** the white of the eye
 ○ **i bardhë shkum**ë white as foam, milk white
 ○ **e bardha//të bardhët e vezës** the white of the egg, eggwhite?

○ **bardhë e zi** in black and white; in simple terms

bardh·ë**ku·q**
 I § *adj* red and white, partly red and partly white
 II § *nf* [*Bot*] common mushroom agaric, common field mushroom, common mushroom (*Agaricus campestris*)

ba·rdhë**·l** *nf* variety of whitish pear

bardhë**lle·m**ë *adj (i)* = **bardhe·m**ë

bardhë**lli·m**ë *nf* = **zbardh**ë**lli·m**

bardhë**llo·r** *adj* (*Poet*) white; shining

bardhë**llo·sh** *adj* (*Poet*) = **bardho·sh**

ba·rdhë**m** *adj (i)* whitish

bardhë**re·m**ë *adj (i)* = **bardhe·m**ë

***ba·rdh**ë**·s** *nm* [*Ornit*] hobby (*Falco subbuteo*)

bardhë**si** *nf* **1** whiteness, the color white, white **2** (*Fig*) purity of thought and feeling

bardhë**si·r**ë *nf* **1** = **bardh**ë**si 2** dawning

bardhi·lë *nf* white cow

bardhi·skë *nf (Reg)* white sheep or goat

bardhi·she *nf* white goat

ba·rdhje *adj* light or pale in color

ba·rdh·kë *nf* [*Bot*] daisy (*Bellis*)

***bardh·ni** *nf* (*Reg*) = **bardh**ë**si**

ba·rdh·o *nf* with masc agreement **1** white dog, horse, or ox **2** person with white hair

bardho·i *obl* < **bardhu·a**

bardho·k
 I § *adj* fair-haired; white-haired; white
 II § *nm* white ram

Bardho·k *nm* Bardhok (male name)

bardho·l *nm* white bull/steer/ox

bardho·nj *np* < **bardhu·a**

bardho·një *nf* **1** white or whitish animal (usually a cow, goat, mare, or mule) **2** blond girl

bardho·r *adj* (*Poet*) = **bardh**ë**llo·r**

bardho·sh
 I § *adj* **1** pallid, pale **2** blond or gray-haired **3** whitish
 II § *nm* white bull/steer/ox

bardho·she *nf* white cow/goat

***bardho·shin**ë *nf* **1** chalk **2** [*Med*] leukorrhea

bardho·vinë *nf* barren, light-colored soil

bardhu·a *nm* (*obl* ˜*o·i, np* ˜*o·nj*) white ox

***bardhu·c**ë *nf (Old)* [*Med*] diphtheria; quinsy

bardhu·k *nm* = **bardhe·m**ë

bardhu·l *adj* = **bardho·sh**

bardhuli·n *adj* (person) born with white hair

***bardhu·ll·er** *adj* (˜*o·re*) (*Old*) whitish, pale white, pale

bardhu·sh *adj* = **bardho·sh**

bardhusha·n *adj* (*Pet*) = **bardho·sh**

bardhu·shë *nf* = **bardho·she**

bardhushi·në *nf* barren, light-colored soil

bardhu·shkë *nf* **1** [*Bot*] herbaceous plant with reddish flowers and comestible tubers **2** white cow/sheep/goat

Bardhy·l *nm* Bardhyl (male name)

bare·lë *nf* stretcher (for carrying the sick)

bareni·m *nm ger* [*Tech*] < **bareno··n**

bareno··n *vt* [*Tech*] to make a boring in [ ]: bore

bare·s stem for 1st sg pres, pl pres, 2nd & 3rd sg subj, imperf < **bare·t·**

bare's | *stem for 1st sg pres, pl pres, 2nd & 3rd sg subj, pind* <bare·t·

bare'shë *nf* <barí shepherdess

baret·
I § *vi (Colloq)* 1 to wander up and down, hike along, stroll along, amble 2 to hurry; walk fast, run
II § *vt (Colloq)* to wander all over []

barëra *np* <bar grasses, herbs, medicines

*****bargatonjës** *nm* = barnatár

bargja'k *nm* [*Bot*] 1 loosestrife (Lythrum) 2 Turkish micromeria (Micromeria) = **bishtmí** 3 = halmu'cë

bargja'n *nm* [*Bot*] giant horsetail (Equisetum telmateja)

bargje'rgj *nm* [*Bot*] moneywort (Lysimachia numularia)

barhë'në *nf* [*Bot*] honesty (Lunaria)

barhu'dhër *nf* [*Bot*] garlic mustard, hedge garlic (Alliaria officinalis)

barí
I § *nm* 1 herdsman, shepherd, goatherd 2 (Old) [Relig] pastor 3 [Ornit] marsh-dwelling waterfowl with brown plumage and a chicken-like beak that feeds on small fish
II § *nf* livestock herding
○ **barí derra'sh** swineherd
○ **barí dhísh** goatherd
○ **barí lopësh** cowherd

baribo'jë *nf* [*Ornit*] song-thrush

barí'k *adj* [*Meteor*] pertaining to atmospheric pressure

*****barika'dë** *nf* barricade

*****barí'lë** *nf* barrel, cask

barí'më·z *nf* [*Bot*] redtop, redtop grass, bonnet grass, white bent grass (Agrostis alba)

barí'na *np (Colloq)* weeds

barí'nj *np* <barí

*****barí's** | *stem for 1st sg pres, pl pres, 2nd & 3rd sg subj, pind* <bare·t·

barisfe'rë *nf* [*Geol*] barysphere

barí'ste *3rd sg pind* <bare·t·

barishta'k *adj* having dense grass, grassy

barí'shte *nf* herbaceous plants, the grasses, herbage; green leafy vegetables, greens, herbage
○ **barishte truske** [*Bot*] = tru'skë

barishto're
I § *nm* [*Entom*] small reddish-brown insect that does damage to grassy plants
II § *adj* 1 herbaceous, like grasses; lacking a tree-like trunk 2 grassy, having grasslands
○ **barishtori jeshil** [*Entom*] shorthorned grasshopper Omocestus viridulus L.
○ **barishtori larash** [*Entom*] kind of grasshopper Stenobothrus nigromaculatus

barishto're *nf* vegetable

barí't *nm* [*Geol*] barite, heavy spar

barí't | *stem for part, pdef, pind, 2nd pl pres, imper, vp* <bare·t·

barí'tje *nf ger (Colloq)* <bare·t

barito'n *nm* [*Mus*] baritone voice/singer/instrument

barito'r *adj* pastoral

barí'tur
I § *adj (i)* 1 tasteless, bland, flat 2 (Colloq) who's been around, knowledgeable, well-traveled
II § *nf (e)* walk, walking

bariu'm *nm* [*Chem*] barium (Ba)

*****barja'k** *nm* = bajra'k

bark *nm (np ˉ qe)* 1 belly; abdomen; paunch 2 convex surface; concavity, interior space 3 midsection 4 (Colloq) middle part of a period of time 5 innards, entrails 6 (Fig Colloq) heart, spirit 7 womb 8 litter, brood; the offspring of a man and woman taken as a collective whole; members of a lineal kin group, clan 9 (Fig Colloq) generation 10 [Med] diarrhea
○ **bark i fryrë** 1 bloated belly 2 [Med] distended abdomen
○ **bark i harkut** [*Archery*] face of the bow
○ **bark i keq/lig** [*Med*] dysentery
○ **bark e kurriz** completely: from head to toe, from top to bottom
○ **bark i lëshuar** [*Med*] pendulous abdomen
○ **bark lundrak** [*Med*] carinate abdomen
○ **bark më bark** 1 full to the brim 2 in a friendly and informal manner, on a personal level
○ **bark i ngurtë** [*Med*] bound belly
○ **Barkun petë, por shpatullat/kurrizin drejt!** "Empty stomach, but back straight." Hungry, but not without pride!
○ **ësh·të³ᵖˡ bark e shpinë** to be inseparable, be like the fingers of one hand
○ **bark i valës** [*Phys*] antinode
○ **bark i verës** [*Med*] cholera infantum

barkace'l *adj (Pej)* = barkale'c

barka'ç *adj* 1 swollen bellied, big-bellied, obese 2 (Pej) glutton

barka'çe *nf* = barkasho're

*****barka'ço'r** *n* glutton; sponger, parasite

barkafe' *nf* pub which serves both coffee and alcoholic beverages

barkala'q *adj (Pej)* = barkale'c

barkala'rtas *adv* belly up; lying down belly up

barkale'c *adj, n (Pej)* (person/thing) with a bulging middle: potbellied (person/thing)

barkalí'q *adj (Pej)* = barkale'c

barkanjo'z *adj (Pej)* = barkma'dh

barkaposhta's *adv* belly down, prone; lying belly down

barka'r *n* = barkëtar

barkarí's· *vt (Reg)* 1 to load [] on a boat; carry [] on boat 2 (Fig Pej) to send [] far away

barkarí's·et *vpr (Reg Pej)* to go far away

barka'rtë *nf* [*Entom*] brown-tail moth (Euproctis chrysorrhoea L.)

ba'rkas *adv* prone, belly down, on all fours

barkasho'r *adj, n* 1 (person/thing) with a bulging middle: potbellied (person/thing) 2 (Pej) gluttonous (person)

barkasho're *nf* potbellied clay or metal pot

*****barka'tar** *nm* = barkëtar

*****barka'xhi** *nm* = barkëtar

ba'rkazi *adv* = ba'rkas

barkba'rdhë *adj, n* white-bellied (animal)

barkbo'sh *adj* = barkzbra'zur

barkbu'all *adj, n (Insult)* "buffalobelly" (person) who is obese/insatiable/gluttonous

barkcalí'k *adj* = barkfry'rë

barkculla'k *adj* = barkja'shtë

barkda'lë *adj* having a prominent belly

barkde'rr *adj (Insult)* = barkma'dh

barkdërra'së *adj (Colloq)* flat-bellied, hollow-bellied, thin (from not eating)

bark'do'së *adj (Insult)* = barkma'dh

bark'dre'q *nm (Insult)* one who lives off others, glutton: parasite, sponge

ba'rke *nf* = nënbarkëz

ba'rkë *nf* boat, barge

ba'rkë**s** *nm* 1 woolen vest worn by women 2 take-up roller on a loom

bark'ë**se** *nf* 1 bellyband, girth, cinch (on a pack animal) 2 thick piece of material tied around a baby's belly

bark'ë**s'o** •*n* *vi* 1 to bulge out at the belly 2 to bulge; sag

bark'ë**so're** *nf* something made of or stuffed with belly wool

bark'ë**ta'r** *nm* boatman

ba'rk'ë**z** *nf* short, lower-quality wool cut from the belly of sheep or goats

ba'rkë'z *nf* small boat

****ba'rk'**ë**zaj** *adv* = ba'rkas

bark'fry're *adj* having an inflated belly: potbellied

bark'fu'tur *adj* having a hollow belly

bark'gja'të *adj, nm* [Invert] macruran

bark'gje'rë *nf, adj* 1 wide or fat in the midsection 2 (Fig Colloq) tolerant; generous; big-hearted 3 [Ichth] Lake Ohrid schneider (Alburnoides bipunctatus ohridanus Kar.)

bark'iç *adj, n (Pej)* = barkale'c

bark'ja'shtë *adj* 1 with belly exposed, undressed 2 (Fig) very poor, broke; tattered

ba'rkje *nf* 1 bellyband, girth, cinch (on a pack animal) 2 thick piece of material tied around a baby's belly 3 fatty part of a pig above the intestines

bark'kace'k *adj* = barkfry're

bark'kalb'ur *adj (Colloq Pej)* = barkke'q

bark'ke'q *adj (Colloq Pej)* 1 malicious, evil, wicked, malevolent, spiteful *2 greedy, gluttonous

bark'ku'q *adj* red-bellied

bark'ku'qe *nf* 1 [Bot] a variety of edible mushroom whose cap has a reddish underside 2 [Zool] a variety of frog with a reddish underside

bark'le'dh *adj (Folk Pej)* 1 paunchy, big-bellied 2 (Pej) piggish, gluttonous

bark'le'pur *nm* ear of corn with few kernels

bark'le'sh *adj, nm* 1 hairy-bellied 2 (Insult) dimwitted, dimwit

bark'lëshu'a'r *adj* having a sagging belly

bark'lubi *adj (Colloq Pej)* gluttonous, greedy, insatiable

bark'ma'ce *adj (Colloq)* having a small appetite, little-bellied

bark'ma'dh *adj, n* 1 paunchy/big-bellied (one) 2 (Pej) piggish/gluttonous (one) 3 (Fig) (one) who is exploitative, (one) who gets rich at the expense of others

bark'mbu'sh'ur *adj* = barkplo't

bark'ngim'ë *adj (Reg)* satiated, stuffed

bark'ngo'pur *adj* 1 satiated, stuffed 2 rich, wealthy

bark'ngu'shtë *adj (Colloq)* stingy, ungenerous, narrow-minded

bark'onj'ë *nf* 1 = ba'rkje 2 (Euph) child's excrement

bark'o'r *adj* 1 [Anat] abdominal, located in or pertaining to the belly portion 2 convex, humped *3 gastric

bark'o're *nf* 1 woman's woolen apron or weskit 2 woman's belly 3 bellyband, girth, cinch (on a pack animal) 4 thick piece of material tied around a baby's belly 5 potbellied clay or metal pot *6 reptile

bark'o's• *vt (Colloq)* 1 to gorge [ ] with food 2 to shear the underside of [a sheep/goat]

bark'o's•*et* *vpr (Colloq)* 1 to gorge oneself 2 [Tech] to become flexible

bark'o'sh *adj, n* = barkasho'r

bark'pango'pur

I § *adj* insatiable with food, with a bottomless belly

II § *nm* one who is poor and broken, down-and-outer

bark'përpje'të *adv* belly up

bark'plo't

I § *adj* gorged, satiated

II § *nm* person with plenty to eat; rich man

bark'rënë *adj* hanging belly down; fallen belly down

****bark'so**•*n*

I § *vi* to cause [ ] to bulge

II § *vt* *to bulge out

bark'stihi *adj (Reg)* = barklubi

bark'shku'rtë**r**

I § *adj* [Invert] brachyurous

II § *nm* brachyura

bark'shpu'a'r *adj (Colloq)* = barkpango'pur

bark'shty'pur *adj* flat-bellied

bark'shu'ar *adj* barren, sterile (in women)

bark'th *nm* = barkës

bark'tha'rë *adj* = barktha't**ë**

bark'tha'të

I § *adj* 1 (Colloq) (of a woman) barren, sterile 2 unfed, unwatered, left hungry/thirsty

II § *nm* one who is poor and broken, down-and-outer

bark'the's *adj (Colloq)* insatiable

bark'u'c *adj* = barkale'c

bark'ule'c *nm* [Ichth] gambusia, top minnow, mosquitofish (Gambusia affins)

○ **barkulec pikalosh** [Ichth] speckled mosquitofish Gambusia affins holbrocki

bark'uli'q [Ichth] = barkule'c

****bark'u'qe** *nf* meadow mushroom

bark'u'sh *adj* [Sport] belly-forward, leading with the belly (e. g., in high-jumping)

bark'u'she *nf* [Anat] ventricle

bark'vo'zë *adj (Crude)* = barkma'dh

bark'zbra'zur

I § *adj* having an empty stomach, hungry

II § *nm* pauper, one who is poor

bark'z'bulu'a'r *adj (i)* = barkja'asht**ë**

bark'z'gro'p'ur *adj (Colloq)* = barkzbra'zur

bark'zha'bë *adj (Colloq Pej)* with a big, sagging belly

bar-lul'i'shte *nf* an outdoor summer cafe serving food and drink, usually located in a flower garden and providing a place for dancing

Barma'l *nm* Barmal (male name)

ba'rmë *nf* [Bot] cambium

ba'r'na *np* <ba'r 1 medicinal plants, medicaments, medications 2 insecticides, animal repellents/poisons 3 (Colloq) spices

****bar'na'ri** *nf* = barnato're

bar'na'shit'ë**s** *n* = barnata'r

bar'na'ta'r *n* pharmacist = farmaci'st

bar'na'to're *nf* drugstore, pharmacy = farmaci'

barn'grënë**s**

I § *adj* [Biol] herbivorous

II § *n* herbivore

barˈni *nf* vegetation

baˈroˈ·n
I § *vi* to wear a covering of grass
II § *vt* *to cover [ ] with grass

baroˈgraˈf *nm* [*Meteor*] barograph

baˈrojˈë *nf* weed

baˈroˈk *nm, adj* [*Art*] baroque

***baˈrokˈë**
I § *adj* raw, crude
II § *nf* coffee canister

baroˈmeˈtër *nm* barometer

baroˈmetriˈk *adj* barometric

baroˈmˈë *nf* cud

baromiˈnë *nf* [*Tech*] = **barramiˈnë**

baroˈn *nm* baron

baroneˈshˈë *nf* baroness

***baronjaˈk** *adj* baronial

baroˈr *adj* = **barishtoˈr**

baroˈs· *vt* to treat [ ] with medication

baroˈskˈë *nf* [*Ornit*] speckled bird with a thrush-like body

***baroˈsˈun** *adj (i)* grass-covered

baroˈt = **baruˈt**

baˈrqe *np* 1 <**barˈk** 2 generation (as a measure time)

***barsˈeˈri** *nf* = **barrsëˈri**

barˈshkuˈmbˈës *nf* [*Zool*] = **shkuˈmëz**

barˈt· *vt* 1 to bear, carry, transport = **mbarˈt·** 2 *(Old)* to hold = **mbaˈ·n**

baˈrt·et *vpr* to take one's belongings and change residence: move = **mbaˈrt·et**
○ **S'barˈtet çorba me kaçile**. "Soup is not carried in a basket." *(Prov)* It can't be done. You can't carry water in a sieve.

***barteˈl** *nm* honeysuckle, woodbine

baˈrtˈë *adj (i)* 1 made of grass or reed 2 flavorless, bland

baˈrtˈës
I § *adj* carrying
II § *n* carrier = **mbaˈrtës**

bartiˈm *nm* transportation, move

baˈrtje *nf ger* = **mbaˈrtje**

bartoˈre *nf* barrow = **shkalˈc**

barth *nm* 1 porridge made of shortening, flour, and sheep/goat intestines or blood *2 tonsil

barˈtheˈk *nm* [*Bot*] brome, brome-grass *(Bromus)*

baruˈjcˈë *nf* [*Bot*] fine-leaved water dropwort, water fennel *(Oenanthe aquatica)*

baruˈn *nm (Reg)* dark-haired dog

baruˈrina *np* various grasses or herbs, herbaceous plants

baruˈt
I § *nm* 1 gunpowder 2 *(Old)* the black seeds of the onion
II § *adj (Fig)* explosive in temperament; fiery
○ **barut pambuku** guncotton

***barutˈçoˈre** *nf* powder mill

***barutˈhaˈnˈe** *nf (Old)* powder magazine

baˈrxhˈë
I § *nf* goat with mottled white and black coat
II § *adj* grayish, ashen in color

barxhuˈl *nm* billy goat with mottled coat

***barˈraˈbaˈjtˈës** *adj*

barraˈmiˈnˈë *nf* [*Tech*] drill steel/rod (to make holes for inserting explosives): drill jib, drill steel

baˈrre *nf* fence-post rammer, piledriver; battering ram

barˈre *nf* ramming tool; mallet

baˈrrˈë *nf* 1 burden; load 2 large quantity/amount 3 *(Fig)* heavy responsibility 4 [*Law*] burden on property, encumbrance 5 fetus 6 *(Old)* = **paˈjˈë**
○ **barrˈë e lagˈët** evil person
○ **barra e nuses** *(Old)* hope chest, trousseau
○ **barrˈë plumbi** 1 very heavy burden 2 person who is difficult to bear
○ **barrˈë e shkuar** miscarriage
○ **barrˈë e vrarˈë (në bark të nënës)** "dead weight (in one's mother's belly)" 1 shiftless and worthless person who is a terrible burden 2 unfortunate wretch

barrˈëndaluˈes *adj* [*Med*] contraceptive

barrˈësiˈ *nf* pregnancy

barrˈësiˈm *nm ger* = **mbaˈrsje**

barrˈësoˈ·het *vpr* = **mbarsˈ·et**

barrˈësoˈ·n *vt* = **mbarsˈ·**

barrˈëtoˈr *nm (Old)* 1 porter, stevedore 2 person in charge of draft animals taking grain to the mill; hostler 3 person charged with responsibility; culprit

baˈrrˈëz *nf dimin* small load

barrikaˈdˈë *nf* 1 barricade 2 [*Sport*] wall (in soccer)

***barriroˈ·n** *vi* to roar, bellow

***barrmaˈsˈë** *nf (Old)* barometer

barroˈ·het *vpr* = **barros·et**

barroˈ·n *vt* = **barros·**

***barroˈre** *nf* packsaddle

barroˈs· *vt* to load; impose a burden on

barroˈs·et *vpr (Colloq)* to take on a responsibility, take on a load

baˈrrsˈë *adj (Old)* (said of animals) pregnant, carrying

barrsˈeˈri *nf (Book)* pregnancy

barrsoˈ·n *vt* = **mbars·**

baˈrrshˈëm *adj (i)* 1 heavy, burdensome 2 important, weighty

***barrtaˈr** *nm* porter, stevedore

***barrvraˈme** *nf* miscarriage

bas *nm* 1 [*Mus*] bass voice, bass singer, bass instrument *2 = **bast**

***bàˈs** *nm (Reg Gheg)* = **bëˈrës**

basamaˈk *nm* 1 stair railing, handrail; stair step 2 border of reinforcing rocks along both sides of a cobblestone street

baseˈn *nm* 1 reservoir to hold water or other liquids, basin 2 the drop-off into the ocean near a harbor

***baˈsˈëm** *nf* = **basmˈë**

bask *adj, n* Basque

bask *adj, n* Basque

basketboˈll *nm* the game of basketball

basketbollˈiˈst *n* basketball player

***baskiˈ** *nf (Reg)* 1 big nail, spike; peg in a wall to hang things on 2 = **ballaniˈke** 3 blacksmith's hammer with a sharp tip and flattened heel
○ **ëshˈ-të baski** to be very adept

Baskiˈ *nf* region of the Basques (in France and Spain)

baskiˈshte *nf* Basque language

baskoˈre *nf (Reg)* wood slat

basma = **basmˈë**

***basmˈara** *nf* cotton print

baˈsmˈë *nf* cotton fabric, calico

basorelieˈv *nm* bas-relief

*ba'sso nf [Mus] bass = bas

bast nm bet, wager

basta'r nm small hut used by shepherds

basta'rd
I § adj 1 [Biol] crossbred (with loss of the desirable qualities of the original strains) 2 (Insult) degenerate, perverted, corrupt
II § n (Insult) bastard

bastardim nm ger 1 <bastardo'·n, bastardo'·het 2 bastardization

bastardo'·het vpr to become bastardized

bastardo'·n vt to bastardize

*bastardh = bastard

ba'stër nf (Reg) 1 [Bot] = vrug 2 hot southern wind that dries out crops

bastëro's·et vpr (Reg) [Agr] (of plants) to be afflicted by mildew blight

basti nf surprise raid and search

bastis· vt to make a surprise raid and search [ ]

bastis je nf ger <bastis·

*bastu'er = balluk

bastu'n nm 1 walking cane, stick 2 [Veter] graduated stick for measuring an animal's height 3 (Old) long, thin loaf of bread

bastvën ës n (Book) bettor, wagerer

bash
I § nm 1 [Naut] forward part of a ship: bow, stem 2 (Colloq) choice/best part, cream, elite 3 coziest part of a room, cozy nook
II § adv (Colloq) exactly, smack in the __, right in the

*bâshëm adj (i) (Reg Gheg) = bështëm

bashibozu'k nm 1 [Hist] auxilliary irregular soldier in the Ottoman Empire 2 (Pej) member of a band of irregular troops who kill and plunder a populace; undisciplined, irregular soldier

bashk. shk. abbrev <bashkëpunëtor shkencor Scientific Associate

bashk. vjet .shk. abbrev <bashkëpunëtor i vjetër shkencor Senior Scientific Associate

bashka'lesh nm a whole shorn fleece

bashkanëta'r n fellow member

bashkangjis stem for 1st sg pres, pl pres, 2nd & 3rd sg subj, pind <bashkangjit·

bashkangjit· = bashkëngjit·

bashkari nf = bashkëri

bashkari'sht adv = bashkëri'sht

ba'shkas adv = bashkë

bashkatdheta'r n person with the same fatherland as another: compatriot, fellow countryman

bashkatdhetari nf compatriotism

bashkauto'r n co-author, joint author

bashkautor ësi nf co-authorship, joint authorship

ba'shkazi adv = bashkë

*bashkderdhje nf assimilation

*bashkdi'je nf complicity, connivance

bashkekzistencë nf (Book) coexistence

bashkekzisto'·n vi (Book) to coexist

ba'shkë adv 1 together; jointly 2 simultaneously, during the same time period
○ s'ka·pl gjë bashkë not have anything in common; not come to an agreement

ba'shkë nf 1 a whole shorn fleece 2 (Fig) something fleecy: white, soft, and puffy

bashkë formative prefix indicating shared or joint activity or characteristic co-, con-, fellow-, syn-, joint

bashkëbanim nm ger (Book) 1 <bashkëbano·n 2 cohabitation

bashkëbano'·n vi (Book) to cohabit

bashkëbano'r n (Book) cohabitant

bashkëbanu'es n (Book) = bashkëbanor

bashkëbisede'i nf (Book) colloquy, discussion

bashkëbisedim nm ger 1 <bashkëbisedo·n 2 colloquy; conference; general discussion; conversation 3 final oral examination

bashkëbisedo'·n vi to have a joint discussion; have a mutual exchange of views

bashkëbisedu'es nm conversational partner; discussant

bashkëbosht ësi nf [Tech] coaxiality, concentricity

bashkëfaj ësi nf [Law] complicity

bashkëfajto'r n [Law] accomplice

bashkëfeta'r n coreligionist

bashkëfis as n (Book) person of the same lineage/clan: kinsman

bashkëfjalim nm ger (Book) colloquy; conference; general discussion; conversation

bashkëfjalo's·et vpr (Book) to converse

bashkëfol ës n (Book) = bashkëbisedues

bashkëfshata'r n person from the same village/town as another: fellow villager/townsman

bashkëgodi'tje nf (Book) simultaneous strike/hit; collision

bashkëgjak ësi nf 1 [Veter] inbreeding 2 blood relationship, descent from a common ancestor

bashkëjete'së nf cohabitation; coexistence
○ bashkëjetes e paligjshme/ndaluar [Law] concubinage

bashkëjetim nm ger 1 <bashkëjeto·n 2 cohabitation

bashkëjeto'·n vi to live together, live in cohabitation

bashkëkatunda'r n (Old) person from the same village as another, fellow villager

*bashkëkoh as = bashkëkohës

bashkëkoh ës adj contemporary, coeval

bashkëkoh ësi nf [Ling] contemporaneity, simultaneity, synchrony

bashkëkohëta'r n 1 person living today: contemporary 2 person living at the same time: contemporary

bashkëkoho'r adj 1 contemporary, present-day 2 synchronous, synchronic, concurrent

bashkëkomb as adj from the same country/nation, compatriot

bashkëkomb ës adj = bashkëkombas

bashkëkryeta'r n (Offic) joint chief, co-chairman, co-director

bashkëlidh· vt (Book) 1 to tie/bind/join together 2 to correlate

bashkëlidhje nf (Book) 1 <bashkëlidh· 2 interconnection, interrelationship, union; association, coalition, alliance 3 correlation

bashkëlidh ur adv (Offic) in connection with; jointly

bashkëlind· vi (Book) to come into being together, arise jointly

bashkëlind·**ur** *adj (i) (Book)* congenital, innate

bashkëlojta·**r** *n* partner in a game

bashkëlufteta·**r** *n* **1** comrade-in-arms, war buddy **2** *(Elev)* fellow combatant, companion-in-battle, comrade-in-arms

bashkëlufto·**n** *vi (Book)* to fight side by side

bashkëluftu·**e**·**s** *adj (Book)* allied in war/battle

bashkëmarrëdhënie *nf (Book)* interrelationship

bashkëmatshëm *adj (i)* [Math] commensurable

bashkëmba·**rt**· *vt (Book)* to include, contain as well

bashkëmbështet·**ur** *adj (i)* [Geom] adjacent (said of angles), sharing a common side

bashkëmby·**ll**· *vt (Book)* to enclose (in a letter or package)

bashkëmby·**ll**·**ur** *adv (Book)* enclosed in a letter or package

bashkëmendimta·**r** *n* person with the same opinions or point of view ·

bashkëmosha·**ta**·**r** *adj* age-mate, of the same age

bashkëndënjës *n* roommate

bashkëngjis *stem for 1st sg pres, pl pres, 2nd & 3rd sg subj, pind* <**bashkëngjit**·

bashkëngji·**t**· *vt* **1** to attach **2** *(Offic)* to enclose something in writing as an appendix

bashkëngjitje *nf ger* **1** <**bashkëngjit**·, **2** [Med] conglutination

bashkëngji·**t**·**ur** *adj (i), adv* **1** attached **2** *(Offic)* enclosed (as an attachment to a document) **3** [Ling] = **përngjitur**

bashkënxënës *n* classmate, schoolmate

bashkëpajtim *nm* = **bashkëpërkim**

bashkëpatrio·**t** *nm* = **bashkatdhetar**

bashkëpërgjegjës *adj (Book)* jointly responsible

bashkëpërgjegjësi *nf (Book)* joint responsibility

bashkëpërkim *nm ger* [Ling] correspondence, matching, congruence

bashkëpërpjekje *nf (Book)* joint effort

bashkëpërpu·**th**·**et**· *vpr* [Ling] to merge, converge

bashkëpërpu·**th**·**je** *nf ger* **1** [Ling] <**bashkëpërpu**·**th**·**et** **2** [Ling] merger

bashkëpjesëmarrës *n (Book)* joint participant

bashkëpjesëmarrje *nf (Book)* joint participation

bashkëpjesëta·**r** *n (Book)* participant, associate

bashkëprodhim *nm (Book)* joint production

bashkëprona·**r** *n (Book)* joint owner, co-owner

bashkëpron·**ësi** *nf* [Law] joint ownership

bashkëpron·**ëso**·**n** *vt* [Law] to have joint ownership

bashkëpun·**ëto**·**r** *n* **1** co-worker, colleague; associate **2** collaborator, stringer (for a newspaper or magazine) **3** contributor (to a research study), participant

○ **bashkëpunëtor shkencor i vjetër** (research rank just below doctor) senior researcher (discontinued in 1993)

bashkëpunim *nm ger* **1** <**bashkëpuno**·**n 2** cooperation, collaboration, joint contribution

bashkëpuno·**n** *vi* **1** to cooperate **2** to collaborate **3** to make a research contribution, act as a stringer for a newspaper or magazine

bashkëqendro·**r** *adj* [Geom] **1** concentric **2** centripetal

bashkëqendror·**ësi** *nf* [Geom] concentricity

bashkëqen·**ie** *nf* **1** coexistence, contemporaneity **2** symbiosis

bashkëqyteta·**r** *n* person from the same city as another, fellow citizen, fellow townsman

bashkëqyteta·**s** *n* = **bashkëqytetar**

bashkërefera·**t** *nm (Book)* main discussion paper of the theme paper at a public forum

bashkëreferu·**e**·**s** *n (Book)* main discussant of the lead-off paper at a public forum

bashkërendim *nm ger* **1** <**bashkërendo**·**n 2** coordination

bashkërendis *stem for 1st sg pres, pl pres, 2nd & 3rd sg subj, pind* <**bashkërendit**·

bashkërendi·**t**· *vt* **1** to coordinate **2** [Ling] to join into a coordinative construction

bashkërendi·**t**·**et** *vpr* **1** to be coordinated **2** [Ling] to be joined into a coordinative construction

bashkërendit·**ës** *adj* [Ling] coordinating, coordinative

bashkërenditje *nf ger* **1** <**bashkërendit**·, **bashkërendit**·**et 2** coordination

bashkërendi·**t**·**ur** *adj (i)* coordinating, coordinative

bashkërendo·**n** *vt* to coordinate

bashkërendu·**a**·**r** *adj (i)* coordinated

bashkërendu·**e**·**s** *adj* coordinative

bashkëri *nf* **1** shared characteristic, common portion: commonality, similarity **2** one's friends and companions taken as a collective whole, society **3** [Hist] primitive commune **4** *(Old)* community **5** *(Old)* organization **6** [Hist] primitive commune

bashkërisht *adv* **1** in common, jointly, conjointly; by joint endeavor; simultaneously, in unison: together **2** [Hist] communally

bashkërritje *nf (Book)* growing up together, development in common

bashkërrjedh·**ës** *adj* confluent

bashkërrjedhje *nf* confluence

bashkësi *nf* **1** having something in common: commonality, affinity **2** community **3** simple communal society, commune **4** [Math] set, collection **5** [Geol] assemblage ***6** co-ownership

bashkësundim *nm ger (Book)* **1** <**bashkësundo**·**n 2** joint rule; joint reign, joint rulership, joint sovereignty

bashkësundimta·**r** *n (Book)* joint ruler

bashkësundo·**n** *vi (Book)* to rule/reign jointly

bashkëshkolla·**r** *n* fellow pupil

bashkëshkri·**het** *vpr (Book)* to become fused together

bashkëshkri·**n** *vt (Book)* to fuse [] together

bashkëshoqërim *nm ger (Book)* **1** <**bashkëshoqëro**·**n**, **bashkëshoqëro**·**het 2** association **3** [Agr] plant consociation/association

bashkëshoqëro·**het** *vpr (Book)* to be accompanied, be coupled

bashkëshoqëro·**n** *vt* **1** *(Book)* to accompany, accouple, couple, combine **2** [Agr] to consociate, associate

bashkëshoqëru·**a**·**r** *adj (i)* [Agr] sown together (with another plant in a certain association)

bashkëshoqëru·**e**·**s** *adj (Book)* accompanying, complementary

bashkësho·**rt** *n (Offic)* spouse

bashkëshort·**ësi** *nf (Offic)* conjugal/marital life; marriage

bashkë·short·or adj (Offic) conjugal, marital

bashkë·shtet·as n (Book) person from the same country as another, fellow citizen, compatriot

bashkëting·ëll·im nm ger [Mus] 1 <bashkëting-ëllo·n 2 harmonious sound, harmony

bashkëting·ëllo·n vi 1 to sound in harmony 2 (Fig) to be fitting, be appropriate, be agreeable, fit in

bashkëting·ëll·or adj [Ling] consonantal

bashkëting·ëll·ore nf [Ling] consonant sound: consonant

bashkëtrash·ëg·im·tar n [Law] joint heir, coheir

bashkëtheme·lu·es nm co-founder

bashkëvajtje nf [Ling] syntactic connection

bashkëvar·ësi nf (Book) mutual dependence, interdependence

bashkëvend·ës n fellow from the same place/ country: fellow countryman, compatriot

bashkëveprim nm ger 1 <bashkëvepro·n 2 joint action, cooperation, collaboration, synergy 3 interaction

bashkëvepro·n vi 1 to cooperate, collaborate, act in concert with, act jointly 2 to interact

bashkëvepr·u·es
I § adj (Book) collaborative
II § n collaborator

bashkëvëlla nm close comrade, colleague and friend, buddy

***bashkëzim** nm union

bashkëzot·ër·im nm ger [Law Old] = bashkëpron·ësi

bashkëzot·ër·o·n vt [Law Old] = bashkëpronëso·n

bashkëzot·ër·u·es adj [Law Old] = bashkëpronar

***bashkfetar** n coreligionist

***bashkfjal·o·n** vi = bashkëfjalos·et

***bashkfjal·o·s·** vi = bashkëfjalos·et

***bashkgodis** stem for 1st sg pres, pl pres, 2nd & 3rd sg subj, pind <bashkgodit·

***bashkgodit·** vt (Book) to combine

bashki nf city hall

bashki·ak adj pertaining to city hall, municipal

***bashki·ak** = bashkiak

bashkim nm ger 1 <bashko·n, bashko·het 2 unity, unification 3 association, union, confederation, organization 4 [Chem] compounding
◦ **Bashkimi Sovjetik** The Soviet Union

Bashkim nm Bashkim (male name)

***bashkim·tar** n confederate

bashkinteres·u·ar adj (i) having a joint interest

***bashkkomb·tar** = bashkëkombas

bashkkrij·u·es nm coauthor

***bashkkuvend·im** nm talk, chat

***bashkndihm·ës** n helper; ally

***bashkngjarje** nf coincidence

bashko·het vpr 1 to unite with, join up, join the ranks, enter into association; ally oneself with; combine with 2 (Colloq) to get married

bashko·n vt 1 to join, join together, unite, combine
◦ **bashko·n armët** to join forces
◦ **bashko·n** pl **besën** to pledge mutual allegiance
◦ **bashko·n zërin me** [ ] to express one's support for [ ]

***bashkradh·im** nm (Reg Tosk) parallelism, coordination

***bashkshort·ës** n = bashkëshort

bashku adv (së) 1 together, jointly 2 simultaneously, during the same time period

bashku·ar adj (i) joined, united

bashkudhë·tar n travel companion, fellow traveler

bashkudhë·to·n vi 1 to travel together 2 (Fig) to accompany a phenomenon

bashk·u·es
I § adj combinatory, unifying; linking
II § nm [Tech] device for coupling parts of a mechanism: connector, coupling

***bashkvu·em** adj (i) (Reg Gheg) composite, synthetic

***bashkxa·n·ës** adj (Reg Gheg) fellow pupil

***bashkzân·ore** OR **bashkzân·tore** nf (Reg Gheg Old) consonant

***bashlin** nf pin

bashllëk nm (np ˜ qe) (Old) 1 large rock, usually engraved, that supports a chimney or arch 2 headstone at a gravesite

***bashmeni** nf sturdiness, stoutness

***bashtë** nf = kopsht

bashtinar n [Hist] owner of a family fief

bashtinë nf 1 [Hist] family fief 2 garden

***bashtull** adj, n = bastard

bat
I § nm dead-fall trap for birds, trap
II § adj low; ruined, destroyed

batak nm mire, slush; mud pond, slough

batakçe·shë nf <batakçi

batakçi nm (Colloq) one who tries to put one over on someone else: swindler, crook, con-artist, fraud

batakçillëk nm (np ˜ qe) (Colloq) swindle, scam, fraud; swindling, crookedness

batakovinë nf big mud pond, area with mud ponds

***batalinë** nf fright, terror

batalion nm battalion

batall
I § adj 1 (Colloq) useless, unusable; worthless, barren 2 (Fig) ungainly, clumsy
II § adv (Colloq) idly, uselessly
◦ **batall i madh (fort)!** (Iron) big deal!

batall·inë nf fallow land

batall·is· vt = batallo·n

batall·is·et vpr = batallo·het.

batall·ishtë nf (Colloq) fallow land; barren land, wasteland

batall·o·het vpr (Colloq) to go out of commission/ use

batall·o·n vt (Colloq) to leave fallow; take out of commission/use

***Batame** nm Bartholomew

batanije nf fluffy blanket made of cotton or thin wool, bed blanket

batare nf simultaneous firing of firearms: salvo, volley, battery

batate nf [Bot] sweet potato, batata Ipomoea batata

batbat adv

batec nm early-bearing fig with large, light-colored fruit

batentë nf [Tech] collar ring

bateri nf 1 [Mil] artillery battery 2 [Electr] storage battery 3 [Sport] subset of a team, squad 4 [Mus] percussion section of an orchestra

***batë** nf stitch, mesh

batërdï nf (Colloq) **1** ruin, destruction, shambles; carnage, havoc, slaughter **2** tumultuous noise: din, clamor

batërdï s· vt to ruin, destroy, reduce to a shambles; crush, squash, crumble

batërdï s·et vpr to be ruined, destroyed, reduced to a shambles; be crushed, squashed

batërdï sur adj (i) ruined, destroyed, reduced to shambles; crushed, squashed

*__batërr__ adv disorderly

batic̈e nf **1** high tide, flood tide, flow (as opposed to ebb) **2** (Fig) periodic surge

batico̓r adj (Book) of or pertaining to flood tide

batïm nm ger <bato̓·n, bato̓·het

batïnas adv

batïnë nf **1** slate slab in a dead-fall trap for birds **2** large stone used to mark a path or a boundary

*__batipa̓l__ nm ram, piledriver

batïs·

   I § vt (Colloq) **1** = batërdïs· **2** to knock down, bring down, pull down; overturn, upset **3** (Fig) to weigh heavily on, upset **4** (Fig) to send far away **5** (Colloq) to propagate vegetatively by covering tendrils or runners with soil
   II § vi **1** to capsize **2** to spring up or disappear suddenly and unexpectedly

batïs·et vpr **1** to sink; capsize; collapse, fall down ·**2** (Colloq) = batërdïs·et

batïsje nf ger <batïs·, batïs·et

batiska̓f nm bathyscaph

batïskë nf a kind of basket used to catch fish in shallow waters

batïst nm [Text] batiste

batïsur adj (i) in shambles, in ruin, fallen down, collapsed

bato̓·het vpr to list heavily; capsize

bato̓·n vt to tip [a boat] to the point of capsizing: capsize

Ba̓to nf with masc agreement Bato (male name)

bato̓q nm bell clapper/tongue

*__bato̓r__ nm **1** [Math] factor **2** [Optics] coefficient

batra̓ç nm tobacco that ripens in autumn

batu̓k nm yearling male kid, young billy-goat

ba̓tull nf shallows, shallow area in a body of water

*__batu̓n__ adj netted, meshed

*__batu̓ta__ np (Reg Tosk) [Mus] chords

bathë nf [Bot] **1** fava bean, broad bean (Vicia faba L.) **2** (Reg) string bean
   ○ **Bathë, bathë, po një kokërr** "Beans, beans, but the same bean." Always harping on the same old thing. Always playing the same old tune.
   ○ **bathë deti** [Bot] = çiçibano̓z
   ○ **bathë e egër** "wild bean" [Bot] poisonous herbaceous annual found in mountainous areas with pods and seeds resembling the domestic bean
   ○ **Bathë ka· parë e bathë tregon.** (Contempt) to speak without knowing much, have little experience of life
   ○ **janë një bathë e një kokër** they're like two peas in a pod
   ○ **bathë e mbirë në udhë** "bean that has sprouted in the road" orphan; person alone
   ○ **ësh·të³ᵖˡ bathët të numëruara** "all the beans counted" every penny counts, times are hard

bathër nf **1** [Bot] poet's narcissus, pheasant's-eye (Narcissus poeticus) **2** white asphodel (Asphodelus albus)

bathëz nf **1** [Bot] small horse bean (used chiefly as fodder for animals) (Vicia faba L. var. minor Beck) **2** pea-sized swelling caused by an insect sting

bathïshtë nf bean field

bathje nf (said of certain fruit) broad and flat like a bean

batho̓re nf **1** = bathïshtë **2** broad bean **3** wild leek, asphodel **4** dry beanstalk; dry, thin stalk

*__bauksït__ nm bauxite

*__bau̓l__ nm = bau̓le

bau̓le nf = bau̓lle

bau̓lle nf small trunk with a curved lid: storage chest, steamer trunk

bavare̓z adj, n Bavarian

Bava̓ri nf Bavaria

bavroje̓ nf [Zool] Montpellier snake (Malpolon monspessulanus)

*__baxë__ nf darling

baxha nf = baxhë

baxha̓na̓k nm husband of one's wife's sister: brother-in-law

baxha̓xhi nm (np ~ nj) [Hist] municipal sales tax collector

baxhë nf **1** attic; trap door into the attic **2** dormer window; skylight; smokehole in roof **3** = frëngjï **4** [Hist] during the Turkish occupation, a municipal tax; in later times, a sales tax
   ○ **baxhë e tunelit** tunnel hatchway

baxhï nf (Old) **1** (Colloq) respectful appellation for an old woman **2** among Moslems, an old woman who washes female corpses
   ○ [] **laftë baxhia.** "May the old woman wash []!" (Curse) I hope [] drops dead!

baxho̓ nf **1** (small) workroom near herdsman's mountain camp where milk is collected and processed **2** = baxhoxhï

baxho̓xhï nm (np ~ nj) dairyman

baxhu̓le nf sawtoothed embroidery at the bottom of linen blouse

*__baxhulïdhe__ np fem sweepings, rubbish

baza̓l adj (Book) basic = themelo̓r

baza̓lt nm basalt

bazame̓nt nm **1** foundation **2** basement

bazdravi̓cë nf (Reg) wart

Baze̓l nm Basel

baze̓n nm basin
   ○ **bazen i mbyllur** [Swimming] indoor swimming pool

*__bazerja̓n__ nm merchant

bazë nf **1** basis, foundation **2** base **3** field site (as opposed to the home office)
   ○ **baza ushqimore** [Agr] forage, fodder

bazënisje nf starting point, point of departure, cornerstone

bazïk adj [Chem] pertaining to or characteristic of bases: basic, alkaline

bazilikë nf basilica

bazïm nm ger **1** <bazo̓·n, bazo̓·het **2** basis; base

bazo̓·het vpr **1** to base oneself (on); rest on, take as a basis **2** [Mil] to be based, have as base

bazo̓·n vt to base [] on; argue on the basis of [], ground [] on; assume

bazu'ar *adj (i)* principled, grounded firmly

bazu'kë *nf [Mil]* bazooka

bazhda'r *nm [Hist]* public weighmaster, man who collects a fee for weighing goods at a market

bazhdar'i *nf [Hist]* **1** weighing fee **2** public scales, weigh station **3** occupation of the public weighmaster

bazhga're *nf* **1** piece of chaff; chaff; trash **2** corn-husk; bean pod **3** weed

*****ba'zhnje** *nf* weeds; brushwood used as a windbreak; sweepings

*****bazhu're** *nf [Bot]* corn poppy, field poppy, red poppy *(Papaver rhoeas)*

BBC *abbrev* BBC = British Broadcasting Corporation

be *nf* **1** oath; vow, pledge, swearing **2** testimony
  ○ **be në rrenë** false oath
  ○ **be pastruese** *[Ethnog]* exculpatory testimony (at a trial held by a council of elders)
  ○ **be për derë** *[Ethnog]* family representative (at a trial held by a council of elders)

be'be *nf* **1** baby, infant **2** pupil of the eye

be'b'ëz *nf* pupil of the eye

*****be'bkë** = **be'bëz**

bec *nm* **1** small lamb **2** *(Fig)* quiet and gentle child, little angel

Beçuanale'nd *nm* Bechuanaland (now Botswana)

beda' *nf* misfortune, mishap

bede'l
  I § *nm* **1** *[Hist]* payment paid to a substitute to satisfy one's required military or other duty **2** *[Hist]* person paid as substitute for military or other duty **3** *(Pej)* one who does another person's work
  II § *adv* in vain, for nothing

bede'n *nm* **1** bulwark, crenelated battlement **2** dentate lace or ribbon serving as decorative edging on clothing **3** *(Colloq)* row of teeth; saw-toothed edge

*****bedevi'** *nm (np ~nj)* bedouin

bed'is *stem for 1st sg pres, pl pres, 2nd & 3rd sg subj, pind* <**bedi't·**

bed'i't· *vt* to attack

bedi't·et *vpr (Old)* **1** to make a sudden appearance **2** to pester, stick to one persistently

bedunic'ë *nf [Bot]* **1** rockrose *(Cistus)* **2** *(Reg)* = **sherbe'lë**

bedh'o·n *vt (Reg)* to treat courteously

bef *invar*

*****bef·** *vi* = **beh·**

befa' *nf (Old)* collateral, pawned object

be'fas *adv* suddenly, unexpectedly, unawares, by surprise

befas'i *nf* suddenness; sudden chance/accident

befas'i'm *nm ger* **1** <**befaso'·n, befaso'·het** **2** surprise

befas'i'shëm *adj (i)* sudden, surprising; unpredictable, unexpected

befas'i'sht *adv* = **be'fas**

befas'o'·het *vpr* to be surprised; be taken by surprise

befas'o'·n *vt* **1** to surprise, take [] by surprise **2** to attack/capture [] by surprise

befas'u'ar *adj (i)* surprised; taken by surprise

*****be'fët** *adj (i)* sudden, unexpected

*****be'fme** *nf (e) (Old)* adventure

beft *nm* = **beh**

be'ftë *adj (i)* sudden, unexpected

be'fti *vi impers 3rd sg pdef*
  ○ **<> befti** it happened to <> unexpectedly

beg *nm* **1** = **bej 2** *[Tech]* input valve for oil

bega't· *vt* = **begato'·n**

bega't·et *vpr* = **begato'·het**

bega't'ë *adj (i)* = **bega'tshëm**

begati' *nf* wealth, prosperity; richness, abundance

begati'm *nm ger* **1** *(Book)* <**begato'·n, begato'·het** **2** enrichment
  ○ **begatim pa shkak** *[Law]* unjust enrichment

begati'shumë *adj* = **bega'tshëm**

begato'·het *vpr* to get enriched; get rich, grow in wealth, become wealthy

begato'·n *vt* to enrich

begato'r *adj (Poet)* = **bega'tshëm**

bega'tshëm *adj (i)* rich, wealthy, prosperous; fertile, fruitful, abundant

be'ge *nf* variety of white grape with round fruit and thin skin

begen'i *nf (Colloq)* polite consideration

begen'i's·
  I § *vt (Colloq)* to welcome/treat [] with condescension
  II § *vi (Iron)* to deign, condescend: stoop

begen'i'sje *nf ger (Colloq)* **1** <**begenis· 2** = **begeni'**

begen'i'sur *adj (i) (Colloq)* courteous towards those of inferior station, gracious: nice to everybody

begen'i'shëm *adj (i) (Colloq)* = **begeni'sur**

bego'nie *nf* begonia

begu'n *nm (Reg)* **1** young rabbit/hare, leveret, cony **2** *(Fig)* cowardly person

beh *nm (Colloq)* **1** vigilance to prevent being caught off guard, wariness **2** = **befasi'**

beh· *vi (Colloq)* to happen suddenly/unexpectedly, pop up
  ○ **ia beh·** to appear out of the blue

beha'r
  I § *nm (Colloq)* summertime, warm months; summer
  II § *adj (Fig)* cheerful; happy

beha're *np (Colloq)* spices, condiments

behar'i'sht
  I § *adv (Colloq)* in summery fashion, in a way suitable for summer
  II § *adj* = **beharo'r**

beha'rna *np fem* spices

beharo'·n *vi (Colloq)* to spend the summer (somewhere)

beharo'r *adj (Colloq)* summery, suitable for summer = **vero'r**

bej *nm* **1** *[Hist]* landowner in the feudal system, bey; Ottoman title of the nobleman (lower in ranked than a pasha) heading the government of a district, count **2** *(Old)* used after a man's name as a sign of respect

bejbisi'ter *n* babysitter

be'jçe *nf (Old)* **1** *(Scorn)* son of a bey; minor bey **2** *(Pet)* youngest son in a family; boy about to become a bridegroom

*****bej'endi's** = **begeni's**

bejk
  I § *adj* white-haired (said of sheep)
  II § *nm* white ram

bejkë' *nf* **1** white ewe **2** *(Pet)* pretty young blond girl

bejku'sh *nm* = **bejk**

bejle'g *nm (np ~gje)* **1** *(Old)* duel **2** *(Reg)* corn tassel; hank of hair, bangs, lock of hair **3** *(Reg)* runt kid or lamb **4** *(Fig)* person with a distinguishing mark or defect; strong little runt

bejle·ge *nf* **1** sheep or goat with a forelock hanging over the eyes **2** chicken egg, especially one that is small and hard, as from a pullet **3** strong and nimble young girl

bejlegtar *nm* duellist

bejlereshë *nf* [*Hist*] wife/daughter of a bey

bejlerë *np* < bej

bejlurçinë *nf (Contempt)* small-time bey, down-at-the-heels bey

bejllëk *nm collec* **1** [*Hist*] position/title of a bey; beys taken as a whole **2** *(Pej)* the easy life of a bey at the expense of others; behavior of a bey

Bejrut *nm* Beirut

*****bejt** *nm* = bejte

bejtar *n* composer of extemporary verse

bejte *nf* **1** oriental verse composed of couplets that was prevalent in Albania in the 17th and 18th centuries **2** *(Pej)* extemporary verse: doggerel
  ○ **bejte në shkop** doggerel verses ad libbed back and forth between versifiers

bejtexhi *nm (np ~ nj)* = bejtar

bekacë *nf* [*Ornit*] European woodcock *(Scolopax rusticola)*

bekacinë *nf* [*Ornit*] snipe *(Gallinago gallinago)*

bekçi *nm (Old)* rural police, ranger; watchman appointed to guard crops, field patrol

bekim *nm* **1** < beko·n, beko·het **2** blessing, benediction **3** expression of gratitude

Bekim *nm* Bekim (male name)

beko·het *vpr (Relig)* to be blessed

beko·n *vt* **1** *(Relig)* to bless, pronounce a benediction **2** *(Colloq)* to wish well, bless; express gratitude

bekri *nm* drunk

bektashi *nm* [*Relig*] member of the Bektashi sect

bektashian *adj* [*Relig*] of the Bektashi sect, Bektashian

bektashizëm *nm* [*Relig*] Bektashi sect, a Sufi order of Islam founded by Hunqar Hajji Bektash in the 13th century, spreading during and after the 15th century to North Africa, the Balkans, and the Middle East, and gaining particular importance in Albania in the 19th and 20th centuries; a Moslem sect characterized by religious and doctrinal liberalism and by personal commitment to pantheistic mysticism: Bektashiism

bekuar
  I § *adj (i) (Colloq)* blessed, consecrated
  II § *n (i) (Colloq Euph)* blessed one: darn thing/animal/guy
  III § *nf (e) (Euph)* smallpox

bel *nm* **1** waist, middle (of the body); small of the back, lower back **2** (garden) spade; the depth a spade reaches in digging
  ○ **bel çatall** spade with two thick prongs at the end
  ○ **Beli ka (edhe) bisht.** "The spade (even) has a handle." *(Prov)* Every action has its consequences.
  ○ **bel ulluk** spade with a curved blade

bela *nf (Colloq)* **1** trouble **2** annoyance, nuisance

belaçor *adj (Colloq)* = belaqar

belamadh *nm (Colloq)* **1** person who is a constant nuisance, pain-in-the-neck, pest **2** *(Curse)* person upon whom we wish calamities to fall

belaqar *adj, n (Colloq)* bothersome/obnoxious/pestering (person)

belara *np* < bela

belas *adv* by the waist, by the middle

belaxhi *nm (np ~ nj)* **1** = beltar **2** *(Old)* = belshak

belb *adv* = belbër

belb·et *vpr* to begin to stammer/stutter

belbacak *adj, n (Contempt)* (person) with a stammer/stutter: mushmouth = belbër

belbacuk *adj (Contempt)* = belbët

belban *adj* = belbët

belbaq *adj (Contempt)* = belbacak

belbaraq *adj (Contempt)* = belbacak

belbe *nf* [*Ornit*] bean goose *(Anser fabalis)*

belbër
  I § *adv, adj (i)* with a speech impediment: stammering, stuttering
  II § *nm* person with a speech impediment: stutterer, stammerer

belbëri *nf* speech impediment: stammering, stuttering

*****belbërim** *nm* **1** = belbëri **2** whirr, hum

belbëro·n *vi* = belbëzo·n

belbët *adj (i)* having a speech impediment: stammering, stuttering

belbëzak *adj* muttered, spoken indistinctly

belbëzim *nm ger* < belbëzo·n

belbëzo·n *vi, vt* **1** to pronounce [words] indistinctly, stammer, stutter; mutter, murmur, speak under one's breath **2** *(Pej)* to babble, chatter

belbëzonjës
  I § *adj* = belbëzues
  II § *n* stutterer, stammerer

belbëzues *adj* spoken indistinctly, proceeding by fits and starts: muttered, stammered

belbicë *nf* [*Ichth*] = belushkë

belbit·et *vpr* to vacillate; grow faint; flicker

*****belbuq** *adj, n (Insult)* = belbacak

belcë *nf* thick hearthrug; thick saddle blanket

*****belçetë** *nf* rabble, populace

belçik *nm* iron ring placed around or through the nose of an animal for attachment to a chain

beledie *nf* [*hist*] town hall during the Ottoman empire

*****beleg** *nm* = bejleg

*****belegji** *nf (Old)* mischief, misdeed

*****belesh** *adv* in vain, for nothing

belexhik *nm* bracelet, bangle

*****belezik** *nm* = belexhik

Belfast *nm* Belfast

belg *nm* = belgjian

belgjian *adj, n* Belgian

belgjik *nm (Colloq)* pre-World-War-II Belgian-produced gun

Belgjikë *nf* Belgium

belhollë *adj* slim-waisted

beli *adv (Old Colloq)* **1** obviously; out in the open **2** (used parenthetically) as you see

belicar
  I § *adj* of or pertaining to Belize
  II § *n* native of Belize

belicë
  I § *nf* **1** variety of cherry or pear with large, pale yellow or white fruit; large-grained pale yellow or white corn **2** *(Reg)* white ewe
  II § *adj* having blond fruit

Belicë *nf* Belize

****Beligrad** *nm* Belgrade = **Beograd**

belik *adj (Old)* state-owned, belonging to the state

****beline** *nf* [*Bot*] = **bezgë**

belishë *nf* [*Bot*] German velvet grass *(Holcus mollis)* = **pungacë**
  ○ **belishë leshatake 1** [*Bot*] common velvet grass, Yorkshire fog **2** Holcus lanatus = **pungacë**

belizmë *nf* [*Bot*] kind of grass *(Andropogon pubescens)*
  ○ **belizmë e zezë** [*Bot*] cricket rhaphis *Chrysopogon gryllus, Rhaphis gryllus*

bel këputur *adj* slim-waisted, slender, slim

****belkua** *nm* [*Bot*] white water-lily *(Nymphaea alba)*

belo·n *vt* to work/cultivate [soil] with a spade

belor *adj* of or pertaining to the waist; waisted

belore *nf* woman's blouse worn over a chemise and reaching only to the waist

belot *nm* [*Bot*] evergreen shrub whose berries are used to make a dye: Mediterranean buckthorn *(Rhamnus alaternus)*

belqim *pcl (Old)* perhaps, maybe

belshak *nm (Old)* poor farmer who hires out to work with a spade

beltar *n* one who works with a spade

Beluçistan *nm* Baluchistan

belunazë *adj (Poet)* = **belkëputur**

belush *nm* [*Bot*] whortleberry *(Vaccinium myrtillus)*
  ○ **belush i kuq** [*Bot*] grouse whortleberry *Vaccinium scoparicum*

belushkë *nf* [*Ichth*] a variety of small, silver trout found in Lake Ohrid *(Salmothymus ohridanus Steindachner)*

****beluz** = **beluz**

belvedere *nf* observation tower

****bellogardist** = **bjellogardist**

belluz *nm* [*Text*] smooth and shiny woolen fabric with a long float

bemak *nm* [*Ichth*] Italian roach *(Rutilus rubilio Ohridanus)*

bemol *nm* [*Mus*] flat: the sign affixed to a note to indicate the semitone below the value of the unaffixed note

****bena** *np* < **be** *(Reg Gheg)*

bend *nm* **1** cistern, small water reservoir **2** *(Pej)* snoop, conniver, spy **3** mocking/waspish word **4** idle word or argument, twaddle

benediktin *nm* Benedictine

Beneluks *nm* Benelux

BENELUX *abbrev* Benelux (economic union of Belgium, the Netherlands, and Luxembourg

benevrekë *np* wide-cut white trousers; long underwear made of cotton and wool

bene *nf* north side; northerly exposure, side open to the north wind

beng *nm (np ~ gje) (Ornit)* **1** golden oriole *(Oriolus oriolus L.)* **2** *(Reg)* necklace made of precious stones or gold **3** *(Reg)* mole (on the face or body)

Bengal *nm* Bengal

Beni *nm* Beni (male name, nickname for Arben)

beniamin *nm (Book)* one given specially favored treatment, pet, favorite, protégé

Benin *nm* Benin

beninj *adj* [*Med*] benign

benzen *nm* [*Chem*] benzene

benzinatë *nf* motorboat

benzine *nf* benzine; gasoline, petrol

benzol *nm* benzol, benzene

Beograd *nm* Belgrade

Beograd *nm* Belgrade

beqar *adj, n* bachelor

beqari *nf* **1** bachelorhood, celibacy **2** *(Collec)* bachelors taken as a collective whole

beqarllëk *nm (np ~ qe) (Colloq)* = **beqari**

ber *nm* **1** bow; arc, arch, curve **2** [*Bot*] thorny herbaceous plant with a long, tufted stalk; dart made from the stalk of this plant **3** [*Zool*] = **shigjetull**

Berat *nm* city in south-central Albania: Berat

beratas
  I § *n* native of Berat
  II § *adj* of or pertaining to Berat or its natives

beratçe *nf* folk dance characteristic of Berat

berbecul *adj (Colloq)* poor, needy, raggedy; belonging to the most scorned social class

berber *nm* barber

berbereshë *nf* = **berber**

berberhanë *nf* barbershop; hairdresser salon, beauty shop

berdankë *nf (Old)* old cartridge-loading gun

bereqet *nm (Colloq)* **1** grain **2** crop, harvest **3** *(Fig)* fruitful result, blessing

bereqetshëm *adj (i) (Colloq)* fruitful, successful, valuable, profitable

beretë *nf* **1** round cap, beret **2** Beretta (small Italian revolver)

berëz *nf* **1** = **ber 2** spool made of reed **3** *(Ornit)* gray wagtail *(Motacilla cinerea)*

beribat
  I § *adj (Old)* **1** messy, in great disorder ***2** loose with money
  II § *n* maniac; vandal

beriha *nf (Colloq)* cry of alarm; alarm

****berihaj** *nm* = **beriha**

berilium *nm* beryllium

berk *nm (np ~ qe)* [*Bot*] **1** alburnum, sapwood ***2** bark

****berki** *nm* [*Bot*] wild service tree *(Sorbus torminalis)*

berlinez
  I § *adj* of or pertaining to Berlin
  II § *n* Berliner

Bermude *np fem* Bermuda

Bernë *nf* Bern

Bernë *nf* Berne

beronjë *nf* **1** barren female; barren soil **2** [*Zool*] sidewinder *(Malpolon monspessulanus Herns)* **3** [*Bot*] English holly *(Ilex aquifolium aquifolium)*

****beronjësi** *nf* sterility, barrenness

****beronjësh** *adj* sterile, barren

****berq** *nm* heap, pile

bersalake [*Ichth*] female fish with ventral parts enlarged by maturing sexual organs

bersalier *nm* [*Hist*] Italian infantryman in World War II

berunzë *nf* [*Bot*] teasel *(Dipsacus)*

berunzore *nf* [*Bot*] scabious family *Dipsacaceae*

berr *nm* small livestock (sheep or goat)

****berrak** *nm* = **bërrakë**

berrejshëm *adj* perjuring, swearing falsely

berrgatë *nf* foam formed by the action of acid

be'sa *pcl (Colloq)* really, to tell the truth, in fact

Be'sa *nf* Besa (female name)

be'sa-be'së *nf* solemn promise, sacred pledge, word of honor

Besa'rt *nm* Besart (male name)

besata'r *n (Old)* **1** = besimta'r **2** = besë'lidhës

besati'm *nm ger* **1** *(Old)* <**besato'** ·*het* **2** allegiance

besato' ·*het vpr (Old)* to swear allegiance

***besdi'le** = bëzhdi'lё

bes'ё *nf* **1** pledge, word of honor **2** oath **3** *(Old)* pledge taken by a family to take revenge on the murderer of a member of that family within a particular period of time; truce between the two parties to a blood-feud; truce period; the protection enjoyed by a guest during his stay with the host; protection, custody, aegis **4** *(Colloq)* religious faith, faith **5** alliance; faithfulness **6** trust, belief

◦ **nuk ka**·*past* **besё** {} did not have patience: {} couldn't stand to wait

besё'ke'q *adj* untrustworthy/perfidious (person)

besё'kotё *adj* superstitious

besё'kotё'si *nf (Book)* superstition

besё'li'dhёs

I § *adj* allied

II § *n* ally

besё'li'dhje *nf* alliance

besё'mi'rë

I § *adj* having unquestioning religious belief, deeply religious

II § *n* believer

besё'pa'kё *adj* distrustful, incredulous, disbelieving, of little faith

besё'plo'të *adj* full of faith, trusting

besё'pre'rё *adj, n (Pej)* (person) who goes back on his word: traitor

besё'qe'n *adj* = besё'ke'q

besё'qe'ni *nf* <breach of honor/trust, bad faith, perfidy

besё'shka'lё *adj* dishonorable, faithless, traitorous, untrustworthy

besё'ta'r *n (Old)* **1** = besni'k **2** = besimta'r **3** mediator in a blood feud

besё'ty'të *adj* superstitious

besё'ty'tni *nf* superstition

besё'tytno'r *adj (Book)* superstitious

besё'thy'e'r *adj* = besё'shka'lё

besё'thy'e'rje *nf (Book)* breach of honor/trust, perfidiousness

besё'thy'e's *adj* = besё'shka'lё

besi'm *nm* belief, conviction; faith; trust

◦ **i besimit** worthy of trust

◦ **besim në vetvete** self-confidence, self-assurance

Besi'm *nm* Besim (male name)

besi'mplo'të *adj* confident

besimta'r

I § *n* believing, religious/pious

II § *n* believer, religious/pious person

***be'sk**ё *nf* braid, cording

***besni** *nf (Reg)* = besnikёri

besni'k

I § *adj* **1** true to one's word, faithful, trustworthy, loyal, honorable **2** faithful (to), accurate, accurately reflecting

II § *nm* **1** man of his word, faithful/loyal person **2** religious/pious person

Besni'k *nm* Besnik (male name)

besni'ke'ri *nf* fidelity, faithfulness, loyalty, trustworthiness, honesty

besni'ke'risht *adv* faithfully, loyally, honestly

***besni'ki** = besnikёri

beso' ·*het vpr* to be believed in; be thought/supposed

beso' ·*n*

I § *vt, vi* **1** to believe; be of the opinion that, suppose, think **2** to entrust <> with [ ]; entrust [ ] to <>

II § *vi* to be/become a (religious) believer

◦ **s'u beso**·*n* **as syve, as veshёve tё vet** "not even believe one's own eyes nor ears" to insist too much on confirmation with one's own eyes

***beso'jm**ё *nf* credo

***besty't** *nf* = besё'tyt

besua'r *adj (i)* trusted, believed; loyal, faithful

besu'e'shёm *adj (i)* believable, plausible; trustworthy, reliable

besu'e'shmё'ri *nf (Book)* believability, plausibility

beshame'l *nm [Food]* bechamel sauce

be'shte *nf (Reg)* humbug, nonsense, bunk, baloney

beshte'ma'dh

I § *adj (Reg)* quite fanciful, mendacious

II § *nm* big liar

be'shtё *nf (Reg) [Bot]* **1** dodder *(Cuscuta)* = he'lmёz **2** danewort *(Sambucus ebulus)* = qi'ngёl

***bet·** *vt* to displease

be'ta *indecl fem* the Greek letter beta

beta'r *n [Ethnog]* one who swears to the innocence of another

bete'c *nm* variety of large, sweet, early-ripening fig

bete'jё *nf* battle

bete'r

I § *adj (Old Colloq)* the very worst, horrible

II § *adv (Old Colloq)* very, terribly, horribly

***bete're** *nf* oddment, trifle

beti'm *nm ger* **1** <**beto'** ·*n*, beto' ·*het* **2** pledge, oath

Beti'm *nm* Betim (male name)

Beti'me *nf* Betime (female name)

beti'ne *nf* wooden bird-trap

beto' ·*het vpr* to take an oath, swear; pledge

◦ **beto**·*het* **e pёrbeto**·*het* to swear up and down, swear by all that's holy

beto' ·*n vt (Book)* **1** to swear [ ] in, administer an oath/pledge to [ ] **2** to swear to [ ]

beto'n *nm* concrete

beton'arme *nf* reinforced concrete

betonie'r *nm* cement worker

betonie'rё *nf* cement/concrete mixer

betoni'm *nm ger* **1** <**betono'** ·*n* **2** pavement

betono' ·*n vt* to line/pave/fill [ ] with concrete, reinforce [ ] with concrete

beton'shku'mё *nf [Constr]* foam concrete

beton'shpu'es *adj [Mil]* concrete piercing

beto'ntё *adj (i)* **1** made of concrete, of concrete **2** solid as concrete

betonu'es *nm* person who mixes or lays concrete, concrete worker

betua'r

I § *adj (i)* sworn; committed; loyal, faithful

II § *nm [Law]* sworn witness

***beth** *nm* flyblow

be'xgё *nf [Bot]* = be'zgё

***bez** *nm (Reg)* island of scum floating on a pond

bezdi' *nf (Colloq)* bother, annoyance

bezdí s· *vt (Colloq)* to bother, annoy, trouble
  ○ **bezdis· gur e dru** to be very annoying

bezdí s·*et vpr* to worry, be concerned

bezdí sje *nf ger (Colloq)* bothering, bother, annoyance, trouble

bezdí sshëm *adj (i) (Colloq)* annoying, troublesome, bothersome

bezdí sur *adj (i) (Colloq)* = **bezdíssh**ëm

be ze *nf* 1 [*Text*] strong cotton/linen fabric: cotton baize, fustian, buckram 2 piece of cloth, banner

*****beze le** *nf* = **bize**le

*****beze le** *nf (Old)* sand dune

be zgë *nf* [*Bot*] Jerusalem sage *(Phlomis fruticosa)*

bezista n *nm (Old)* partly covered, enclosed part of an Oriental bazaar

bez të *adj (i)* made of cotton baize

*****bezha·***n* = **bëza·**n

*****bezhdí le** *nf* = **bëzhdí**l**ë

bezhë *nf, adj* beige

*****bezho rr**ë *nf* [*Ornit*] pelican = **bozho**r

bë·*het vpr* 1 to become: turn into, turn; get; acquire the characteristics of 2 to ripen 3 to appear 4 to happen, occur 5 (of a quantity of time) to pass
  ○ **bë·***het* {*adjective*} 1 to become {} 2 *(Colloq)* to pretend to be {} **u bë i sëmurë** he pretended to be ill **bëhen të rritur** they are pretending to be grown up
  ○ **bë·***het* **abanoz** to live a long time
  ○ **bë·***het* **ahur** to turn into a shambles
  ○ <> **bë·***het* **akrep** <> *is a thorn in* <>'s side
  ○ **bë·***het* **akull** to become cold as an icicle
  ○ **bë·***het* **arak në** [] to become expert in []
  ○ **bë·***het* **ashër** to begin quarreling, split apart
  ○ **bë·***het*[3pl] **ashkla-ashkla** to be split apart by dissension: split up
  ○ <> **bë·***het*[3sg] **balta flori** "mud *turns into* gold for <>" <> *has* a golden touch
  ○ <> **bë·***het* **baltë** to humiliate oneself before <>, bow down to <>
  ○ **bë·***het* **baltë (në fytyrë)** "become mud in the face" to grow pale
  ○ **bë·***het* **baltë para** <> to humiliate oneself before <>, bow down before <>
  ○ **bë·***het* **baltë e pluhur** 1 to bow down in complete submission; let others walk all over one 2 to be brought low
  ○ <> **bë·***het* **baltë në opingë** "stick like mud on <>'s clog" *(Pej)* to stick to <> like a leech
  ○ **bë·***het* **bark e shpinë** to waste away, get very weak
  ○ **bë·***het* **bark e shpinë me** [] to become very close with [], become good friends with []
  ○ <> **bë·***het*[3sg] **barku daulle** "<>'s belly *becomes* a drum" *(Impol)* <> gets stuffed (with food) to the gills
  ○ <> **bë·***het*[3sg] **barku dërrasë** *(Colloq)* <>'s stomach is empty, <> *is starving*
  ○ <> **bë·***het*[3sg] **barku gropë** *(Colloq)* <>'s stomach is empty, <> *is starving*
  ○ <> **bë·***het*[3sg] **barku kacek** "<>'s belly *becomes* a skinbag" *(Impol)* <> gets stuffed (with food) to the gills
  ○ <> **bë·***het* **barku kaçup** <> becomes bloated from excessive eating/drinking
  ○ <> **bë·***het*[3sg] **barku lodër** "<>'s belly *becomes* a drum" *(Impol)* <> gets stuffed (with food) to the gills

  ○ <> **bë·***het*[3sg] **barku palë-palë** "<>'s belly *becomes* pleated" <> gets too fat
  ○ <> **bë·***het*[3sg] **barku petë** "<>'s belly *becomes* flat" *(Colloq)* <>'s stomach *is empty*, <> *is* very hungry
  ○ <> **bë·***het*[3sg] **barku petë-petë** "<>'s belly *becomes* pleated" <> gets too fat
  ○ <> **bë·***het*[3sg] **barku tupan** "<>'s belly *becomes* a drum" *(Impol)* <> gets stuffed (with food) to the gills
  ○ <> **bë·***het*[3sg] **barku** {*voluminous round object*} <>'s stomach *swells* up like a {} from overeating
  ○ **bë·***het* **barut** to become so dry that {} crumbles
  ○ **bë·***het* **begun** to grow weak and thin
  ○ **bë·***het* **behar** to light up with happiness
  ○ **bë·***het* **beja e dheut** to become an object of public scorn
  ○ <> **bë·***het* **bela** to become burdensome to <>
  ○ **bë·***het* **berber në kokën e tjetrit** to learn something at someone else's expense
  ○ **bë·***het* **bërllok** to get reduced to chaff, get cut to pieces, be destroyed 2 to get dead drunk
  ○ **bë·***het* **bërryl** to become dead drunk
  ○ **bë·***het* **bëzhdila** to crumble
  ○ **bë·***het* **bic** to gorge oneself, become sated, become bloated from eating
  ○ **bë·***het* **bigorr** to become stone-hard
  ○ **bë·***het* **bilbil** to become better behaved, straighten up
  ○ **bë·***het* **bishë** to get ferociously angry
  ○ **bë·***het* **bisht** to become a mere tool in someone else's hands
  ○ **bë·***het* **bishtajë** 1 to get devastated 2 to get weak and emaciated
  ○ **bë·***het* **bludë** to lose strength
  ○ **bë·***het* **bllacë *1** to get soaked 2 to be still mushy
  ○ **bë·***het*[3rd] **bollë** to stretch on and on without result
  ○ **bë·***het* **bozë** 1 to become monotonous 2 to go down in price, get cheaper
  ○ **bë·***het* **brumë** to get very soft
  ○ **bë·***het* **buburrec** to cringe in fear
  ○ **bë·***het* **buhasi** to get red in the face
  ○ <> **bë·***het*[3sg] **buka gjemb/gorricë** (because of bad news) the food stuck in <>'s throat, <> *is* unable to eat
  ○ <> **bë·***het*[3sg] **buka shirit** 1 <> *loses* <>'s appetite 2 it *takes* <> forever to eat
  ○ <> **bë·***het*[3sg] **buka shkarpë** "food seems like brushwood to <>" the food *tastes* like cotton in <>'s mouth
  ○ **bë·***het* **bunacë** 1 to have the belly get larger during pregnancy 2 to swell up from eating
  ○ <> **bë·***het* **(si) burri i nënës** "become like <>'s mother's new husband to <>" to become an intolerable nag to <>: get on <>'s back
  ○ **bë·***het* **burrë** to grow up, become an adult
  ○ **bë·***het* **burrë me mustaqe** "*becomes* a man with a mustache" <> *becomes* a man, <> *is* no longer a child
  ○ **bë·***het*[3sg] **buzë gjyshi** *(Crude)* it's colder than a witch's tit
  ○ <> **bë·***het*[3pl] **buzët shkrumb** <>'s lips *are burning* (with thirst/fever/heat)
  ○ **bë·***het* **byk** 1 to become dead tired, be wiped out 2 to be destroyed, be ruined 3 to be wiped out spiritually, be mentally exhausted

◦ <> bë·_het_ **cergë** to become a nuisance to <> (by always being around)

◦ bë·_het_ **cingaridhe** to become weak and frail; wither away

◦ bë·_het_ **cironkë** to become emaciated

◦ <> bë·_het_^{3sg} **cjepurr** to go badly for <>, turn out badly for <>

◦ bë·_het_^{3pl} **cokla** 1 to become scattered like straw 2 (of people) to be thoroughly routed/defeated

◦ bë·_het_ **copë** 1 to be wounded/hurt/damaged badly 2 to do by might and main, try with all one's strength, knock oneself out to do, die trying

◦ bë·_het_ **copë e gojë** to try one's best, try hard

◦ bë·_het_ **currubabë** to swell up

◦ <> bë·_het_ **çandër** to stand up to <>, stand up firmly against <>

◦ bë·_het_ **çarçaf** to get white as a sheet from fright

◦ bë·_het_ **çengel** to get very weak, wither away

◦ bë·_het_ **çivit në fytyrë** to get blue in the face

◦ bë·_het_ **çull** to dress in black as a sign of mourning

◦ **S'bëhet dasma me një fyell.** "A wedding isn't made with one shepherd's pipe." _(Prov)_ A big undertaking requires more than one person.

◦ bë·_het_ **daulle** 1 to swell up like a drum 2 to become overwrought 3 _(Impol)_ to drop dead

◦ **S'bëhet deng me rrush.** "A full sack isn't made with a grape." _(Prov)_ It can't be done.

◦ bë·_het_ **derr** 1 to get bored 2 to get fed up

◦ bë·_het_ **det** 1 to become inundated; get completely wet 2 to become gorged/sated (with food)

◦ bë·_het_ **dërrmak** to become exhausted, get very tired

◦ bë·_het_ **ding** to get overfilled, get crammed in

◦ bë·_het_^{3sg} **djali dhëndër** the boy grows into a man (ready to be married)

◦ **S'bëhet dora topanxhë.** "The hand isn't made into a pistol." 1 _(Prov)_ You need the right tool for the job 2 It simply can't be done.

◦ **nuk bë·**_het_ **dot katër/katërsh** "{} cannot be divided into four parts" to be too busy to take on more work

◦ bë·_het_ **dru** 1 to become hard, congeal 2 to get numb; get stone drunk 3 to get thin as a rail

◦ <> bë·_het_^{3pl} **duart mish** <>'s hands/feet _are_ worn to a bloody pulp (from hard work/walking)

◦ <> bë·_het_^{3pl} **duart thela-thela** <>'s hands _get_ all cracked and wrinkled

◦ bë·_het_ **dushk** to dry up; burn to cinders

◦ bë·_het_ **dyllë në fytyrë** to become very pale in the face

◦ bë·_het_ **dyman** 1 to vanish suddenly, vanish like smoke 2 to get very drunk: get plastered/smashed 3 to fume with rage

◦ bë·_het_ **dhé** to become very pale

◦ bë·_het_ **dhé** {} **(në fytyrë)** "become earth in the face" to grow pale

◦ bë·_het_ **edhe (një herë) kaq/aq** to be very glad, be delighted

◦ bë·_het_ **erë** to vanish into thin air; run out of sight in a flash

◦ <> bë·_het_^{3pl} **faqet gjak** <> gets red in the face

◦ <> bë·_het_^{3sg} **faqia shollë** 1 <>'s face/skin _gets_ tough as leather 2 <> _gets_ become hardened and indifferent; <> _gets_ thick-skinned

◦ <> bë·_het_^{3sg} **faqja rrogoz** "<>'s face _becomes_ a floor mat" <> _becomes_ absolutely shameless, _loses_ all sense of shame

◦ <> bë·_het_^{3sg} **ferra Brahim** <> _becomes_ afraid of his own shadow

◦ bë·_het_ **ferrë** to stick to <> like a burr

◦ bë·_het_ **fill** to become thin as a rail

◦ bë·_het_ **finjë me** [ ] to have it out with [ ]

◦ bë·_het_ **finjë** _(Colloq)_ 1 to become all skin and bones 2 (of soil) to become worn out, lose fertility

◦ bë·_het_ **firë** _(Colloq)_ to disappear; die out

◦ <> bë·_het_^{3sg} **fjala lak** <> _gets_ tongue-tied

◦ bë·_het_^{3sg} **fjalë për** [ ] _it is_ about [ ], it _refers_ to [ ], it _is_ a matter of [ ]

◦ bë·_het_ **flakë në fytyrë** to get red in the face: blush

◦ bë·_het_ **flakë** to blush deeply

◦ bë·_het_ **flluskë** to become a mere shadow of oneself

◦ bë·_het_ **fshikull** to become thin as a rail

◦ bë·_het_ **fuçi** "becomea barrel" 1 to become gorged with food or drink 2 to swell up

◦ bë·_het_ **furkë** to become nothing but skin and bones

◦ bë·_het_ **furtunë** 1 to disappear suddenly 2 to get blind drunk 3 to go into a rage

◦ bë·_het_ **furrë** to become enraged

◦ bë·_het_ **futë në faqe** {}'s face _gets_ black (with dirt/smoke); {}'s face _gets_ all black and blue

◦ bë·_het_ **futë** to get all black; get all black and blue

◦ bë·_het_ **fyell** to become naked as a jay bird

◦ <> bë·_het_^{3sg} **fytyra dhé** <> _turns_ pale (from distress), <> _turns_ blue (from cold)

◦ <> bë·_het_^{3sg} **fytyra lëvere** <> _turns_ very pale in the face

◦ bë·_het_ **gacë** to blush deeply

◦ <> bë·_het_ **gapërr** to stick to <> like a leech

◦ bë·_het_ **gazi i botës/dheut** to become a public laughingstock

◦ bë·_het_ **gëlqere në fytyrë** to grow very pale

◦ bë·_het_ **gogël** to shrivel/contract out of cold, fear, etc.

◦ <> bë·_het_^{3sg} **goja hanxhar** "<>'s mouth became a sharp knife" <> _is_ very cruel with words

◦ <> bë·_het_^{3sg} **goja për arapash** "<>'s mouth is fit for soft corn mush" <> _loses_ all <>'s teeth

◦ <> bë·_het_ **goja shkrumb** "<>'s mouth is burning up" <> _feels_ very thirsty/hot; <> _has_ a fever

◦ <> bë·_het_^{3sg} **goja shkrumb** <>'s mouth _is burning_ (with thirst/fever/heat)

◦ bë·_het_ **gorricë** to shrink/ shrivel up

◦ bë·_het_ **grep** to become skin and bones

◦ bë·_het_ **gribë** 1 to become parched 2 to fall into ruin

◦ <> bë·_het_ **gur në opingë** to be a thorn in <>'s side

◦ bë·_het_ **gjak** to become very close, become like brothers

◦ <> bë·_het_^{3sg} **gjaku bozë** <> _becomes_ very disturbed/upset

◦ bë·_het_^{3sg} **gjaku bozë** <>'s blood _turns_ to water: <> _gets_ terribly scared/upset/angry

◦ <> bë·_het_^{3sg} **gjaku lëng** "<>'s blood _becomes_ liquid" 1 <> _gets_ badly frightened: <>'s blood runs cold 2 <> _becomes_ badly upset/annoyed, <> _gets_ angry

◦ <> bë·_het_^{3sg} **gjaku mavi** <> _turns_ blue with fear, <> _is_ scared pink

◦ <> bë·_het_^{3sg} **gjaku ujë** "<>'s blood _turns_ to water" 1 <> _gets_ badly frightened: <>'s blood runs cold 2 <> _becomes_ badly upset/annoyed, <> _gets_ angry

◦ **S'bëhet gjaku ujë.** "Blood doesn't turn to water." _(Prov)_ Blood is thicker than water.

◦ **bë·**_het_ **gjalmë** to get thin/slim; get weaker/feeble

◦ **bë·**_het_ **gjethe plepi** to become all skin and bones; turn pale

◦ **nuk bë·**_het_^{3sg} **gjë** nothing _comes_ of it

◦ **s'ësh·të**^{3sg} **gjë që bëhet** it _is_ simply impossible; it _is_ simply not done

◦ **bë·**_het_^{3sg} **gjë?** (in questions) _does_ it hurt anything?

◦ <> **bë·**_het_^{3sg} **gjol e përrua** many obstacles _confront_ <>; <> _is having_ a lot of trouble

◦ **bë·**_het_ **gjysmë njeriu** (of a person) to become shrunken, become all skin and bones

◦ <> **bë·**_het_ **gjysh në vatër** to become a burden to <>

◦ <> **bë·**_het_^{3sg} **halli** <> _finds_ a solution for a problem

◦ **bë·**_het_ **hambar** to eat till stuffed

◦ **bë·**_het_ **hamull** to flare up, burst into rage

◦ **bë·**_het_ **harbi** to become stiff with rage, seethe with anger

◦ <> **bë·**_het_ **harrje** to pester <> constantly

◦ <> **bë·**_het_ **havale** to bother <> terribly; be a big nuisance to <>

◦ **bë·**_het_^{3sg} **helm gjella** the food _is_ too salty

◦ **bë·**_het_ **hell 1** to become thin as a rail **2** to be stunned (by a surprise)

◦ **bë·**_het_ **hi** to get burned up completely

◦ **bë·**_het_ **hija e vetvetes** to become a mere shadow of one's former self

◦ <> **bë·**_het_ **hije 1** to stick to <>; serve <> loyally **2** to protect/defend <>

◦ **bë·**_het_ **hije nga sëmundja** to be emaciated by a disease

◦ **i bë·**_het_ **hije** to stick closely behind

◦ **bë·**_het_ **hime** to become useless/worthless

◦ **bë·**_het_ **histori 1** _(Pej)_ (of a incident reported to one's disfavor) to be spread widely, get all over town **2** (of a story) to get endlessly repeated

◦ **bë·**_het_ **hut** to run away fast

◦ **bë·**_het_ **i madh 1** to grow up, become an adult **2** to become a big shot

◦ **bë·**_het_ **i shtëpisë** to become one of the family

◦ **bë·**_het_ **i hairit** to become successful

◦ **bë·**_het_ **ibret** to look a mess, get all dirty; look terrible

◦ **bë·**_het_ **jeshil (në fytyrë)** to become pale; turn black and blue

◦ <> **bë·**_het_ **jeta burg** "life _becomes_ prison for <>" <>'s life _becomes_ a living Hell

◦ <> **bë·**_het_ **jorgan** to defend <>, support <>

◦ **bë·**_het_ **kacek** to swell up; get bloated from eating

◦ **bë·**_het_ **kaçak** to disappear mysteriously, drop out of sight; not have been seen for a long time

◦ **bë·**_het_ **kaçup 1** to swell up, become swollen; become bloated **2** to bloat up from drowning

◦ **bë·**_het_ **kaike** _(Impol)_ to get completely drunk: get loaded

◦ **bë·**_het_ **kallkan 1** to become frostbitten **2** _(Fig)_ to feel very cold; feel numb with cold **3** to solidify/harden; freeze up; be covered with ice

◦ **bë·**_het_ **karabojë** to look black as thunder; steam with rage

◦ **bë·**_het_^{3pl} **kashtë e koqe 1** to become scattered like straw **2** (of people) to be thoroughly routed/defeated

◦ **bë·**_het_ **kashtë e kokërr 1** to become scattered all over **2** to suffer a rout, be badly defeated

◦ **bë·**_het_ **katërsh** "do the work of four" **1** to overwork oneself **2** to become divided into four parts

◦ **bë·**_het_ **keq** to become ill

◦ **bë·**_het_ **këmbë e dorë** to get married and have children: start a family

◦ **bë·**_het_ **këmbë e krye** to become a confusing mess

◦ <> **bë·**_het_^{3pl} **këmbët mish** <>'s hands/feet _are_ worn to a bloody pulp (from hard work/walking)

◦ **bë·**_het_ **kërcu** to become numb

◦ **bë·**_het_ **kërrabë 1** to get a hump on one's back **2** to become all skin and bones

◦ **s'bë·**_het_^{3sg} **kiameti** it's no big deal

◦ **bë·**_het_ **kockë e lëkurë 1** to become all skin and bones **2** to be down to one's last penny, become poor

◦ **bë·**_het_^{3sg} **koha pihar** the weather _clears_ up completely

◦ <> **bë·**_het_^{3sg} **koka barut** "<>'s head becomes gunpowder" <> _gets_ hot under the collar

◦ <> **bë·**_het_^{3sg} **koka finjë** <>'s mind _feels_ drained, <>'s head _feels_ exhausted

◦ **bë·**_het_ **kokërr** to stand firm, stand eyeball to eyeball

◦ <> **bë·**_het_ **komb** to prick <>'s conscience, weigh on <>'s heart

◦ <> **bë·**_het_ **konak** to give <> shelter

◦ **Bë·**_het_^{3sg} **kopshti pyll.** the garden _gets_ overgrown with too many trees/bushes

◦ <> **bë·**_het_ **kripë** to turn out badly/wrong for <>

◦ <> **bë·**_het_^{3sg} **kurrizi qymyr** <>'s back/body gets black and blue (from heavy beating)

◦ **bë·**_het_ **labot 1** to turn deathly pale **2** to become all skin and bones

◦ <> **bë·**_het_^{3sg} **lak në fyt/grykë** <> _gets_ a lump in <>'s throat

◦ **bë·**_het_ **lakër** (because of fatigue/heat/illness) to collapse

◦ **bë·**_het_ **lapër** to become all skin and bone, become emaciated

◦ **bë·**_het_ **lapotë** to get skinny

◦ **bë·**_het_^{3sg} **leku gur mulliri** "the lek _becomes_ a mill stone" it _is_ almost impossible to earn any money

◦ <> **bë·**_het_ **lepitkë 1** _(Pej)_ to stick to <> like a flea **2** to pester <> **3** to come crawling to <>

◦ **bë·**_het_ **lesë** to get thoroughly drunk: get plastered/smashed

◦ **bë·**_het_ **lesh** to become limp with fatigue, get completely worn out

◦ **bë·**_het_ **lesh e mish me** [] _(Colloq)_ to get into a terrible tangle with [], have a bad quarrel/fight with []

◦ <> **bë·**_het_^{3sg} **lëkura rrogoz** "<>'s skin becomes a floor mat" **1** _(Scorn)_ <>'s skin _becomes_ rough and tough **2** <> _becomes_ inured to criticism: _becomes_ thick-skinned

◦ <> **bë·**_het_^{3sg} **lëkura shollë 1** <>'s face/skin _gets_ tough as leather **2** <> _gets_ become hardened and indifferent; <> _gets_ thick-skinned

◦ **bë·**_het_^{3sg} **lëmë** (of a liquid) to form a big puddle

◦ <> **bë·**_het_^{3sg} **lëmsh (në grykë)** to get a knot/lump in <>'s throat

◦ **bë·**_het_ **lëmsh** to be bungled

◦ **bë·**_het_^{3sg} **lëmsh** {_something_} _gets_ all mixed up

◦ **bë·**_het_ **lëng** to get very wet, get soaked

○ **bë**·*het* **lëvere** to become all skin and bones
○ **bë**·*het* **liktyrë** to become a bag of bones, become all skin and bones
○ **bë**·*het* **limë** to be left bare and empty
○ **bë**·*het* **limon** to become very pale
○ **bë**·*het* **lipsan** to look like a corpse
○ **bë**·*het* **lis** to grow tall and strong
○ **bë**·*het* **livadh** *(Tease)* to get rip-roaring drunk
○ **bë**·*het* **log** to come out in the open, become public
○ **bë**·*het* **lojë e <>** to be made a laughingstock by <>, be the butt of <>'s ridicule
○ **bë**·*het* **lopë** to get big as a cow
○ **bë**·*het* **lug** to double over (with pain); bend over
○ **bë**·*het* **lule 1** to get completely well, recover completely **2** to become well-behaved: come to one's senses, straighten out
○ **bë**·*het* **lule kungulli** "become like a squash flower" to become shocked and pale in the face; become thin and drawn
○ **bë**·*het* **lul*ë*kuqe** to blush deep red, turn red as a beet
○ **bë**·*het* **lumë** *(Impol)* to get drunk as a skunk
○ **bë**·*het* **(si) lundër** to get fat (as an otter)
○ **bë**·*het* **lundër** *(Impol)* to get so drunk that one staggers: get falling-over drunk
○ **S'bëhet lundra me dru marene.** "No boat is isn't made of lilac chaste wood." *(Prov)* You can't make a silk purse out of a sow's ear.
○ **<> bë**·*het* **lungë në zemër** to be very sad, grieve deeply
○ **bë**·*het* **llum 1** to get all dirty, become filthy **2** to be bungled
○ **bë**·*het* **makut** to be greedy
○ **bë**·*het* **mavi në fytyrë** to turn blue in the face: be in a rage
○ **<> bë**·*het* **mbarë** <> *gets* the (right) opportunity
○ **bë**·*het* **me cen** to get scarred for life, get an infirmity; develop a paranoia
○ **bë**·*het* **me fletë** "get wings" to jump with joy, become very happy
○ **bë**·*het* **me rrashta zogjsh** "be made of bird bones" to be built of straw; be about to collapse
○ **bë**·*het* **me turp** to become ashamed
○ **bë**·*het* **me [ ] 1** to get all covered with [ ] **2** to acquire [ ]
○ **bë**·*het* **mel** to cringe, cower
○ **<> bë**·*het*^{3sg} **mendja çorbë** <>'s mind *gets* completely confused
○ **<> bë**·*het*^{3sg} **mendja havale 1** <> *loses* <>'s mind **2** <> is in a constant state of worry; <>'s mind is stuck, <> *has* an idée fixe
○ **<> bë**·*het*^{3sg} **mendja ujë** <> *gets* thoroughly confused; <>'s mind *is beginning* to change, <> *is wavering*; <> *is getting* confused
○ **<> bë**·*het*^{3sg} **mendja veri** "<>'s mind *becomes* the north wind" <>'s mind *is possessed* by an obsession
○ **<> bë**·*het* **merak** "become the object of <>'s devotion" <> *falls* in love with { }
○ **bë**·*het* **merak** to get worried
○ **bë**·*het* **mermer 1** to turn to stone, become hard as marble; become stone dead, die **2** *(Joke)* to become memorialized in stone, become a martyr
○ **bë**·*het* **më vete** to become separated, get isolated
○ **bë**·*het* **mish e gjak** to become very close, become like brothers
○ **bë**·*het* **mish e kocka me [ ]** to become part and parcel of [ ]

○ **<> bë**·*het*^{3rd} **miza-miza** { } to feel pins and needles in { }
○ **<> bë**·*het*^{3sg} **mjekra** <>'s beard grows out, <> needs a shave
○ **<> bë**·*het* **morr** to become a real pest to <>
○ **bë**·*het* **mukajet** to show solicitude, get involved out of concern, take an active interest
○ **<> bë**·*het* **mullë në bark** to become a real nuisance/pest/burden to <>
○ **<> bë**·*het* **në gjumë** to appear to <> in a dream
○ **bë**·*het* **nuse** to get dressed and adorned as a bride on her wedding day
○ **<> bë**·*het* **njerk** "become <>'s stepfather" to get to be an unbearable nag to <>: get on <>'s back
○ **bë**·*het* **një be** to become an object of public scorn
○ **bë**·*het* **një dorë** to shrink up
○ **bë**·*het* **një dorë njeri** to curl into a fetal position; (of a very sick person) shrivel up
○ **bë**·*het* **një grusht** to shrink up
○ **bë**·*het* **një me tokën** "become one with the earth" to go six feet under: die
○ **bë**·*het* **një me tokën** to lie flat on the ground
○ **<> bë**·*het* **një nyjë në grykë/fyt** <> *gets* an emotional lump in <>'s throat
○ **bë**·*het* **njësh me tokën** "become one with the earth" to go six feet under: die
○ **<> bë**·*het* **ombrellë** "become <>'s umbrella" to take <> under one's protection
○ **bë**·*het* **paçamur** to become a mess
○ **<> bë**·*het*^{3rd} **pajë** to become the cause of permanent shame for <>
○ **bë**·*het* **pastërma** to get deeply tanned in the face by the sun; become old and withered up
○ **bë**·*het* **pe** "become thread" to get very thin and weak
○ **bë**·*het* **pelte i butë** to become very meek and subdued
○ **bë**·*het* **pellg në ujë/djersë** "become a pond of water/sweat" to be wet to the skin
○ **bë**·*het* **petë përtokë** to lie flat on the ground
○ **bë**·*het* **petë** to become all skin and bones
○ **bë**·*het* **për çudë** to fall into a loathsome condition; be inspired to fear and loathing of others
○ **bë**·*het*^{3rdpast} **për djall** "became ready for the devil" *(Impol)* { } *has* really gone downhill; { } *is* ready for the junk heap
○ **bë**·*het* **për gaz** to be made an object of ridicule
○ **bë**·*het* **për hekura** to go crazy/mad
○ **bë**·*het* **për i/e/të** {*adjective*} *(Colloq)* to claim/pretend to be { } **bëhej për i sëmurë** he was pretending to be ill **bëhet për e sëmurë** she is pretending to be ill **bëhen për të zgjuar** they claim/pretend to be smart
○ **bë**·*het* **për medet** to have fallen into a woeful state
○ **bë**·*het* **për në plasë të derës** "fit into a door crack" to become thin as a rail
○ **bë**·*het* **për oturak** to be very old and sick
○ **bë**·*het* **për prush** "become fit for burning" to be ready for the trash heap
○ **bë**·*het* **për shkop** "be fit for a cane" to get so old that one needs a cane in order to walk
○ **bë**·*het*^{3sg} **për t'i rënë me dyfek** "become ready to hit with a gun" (of bread or other food) to get so hard you have to cut it with an axe
○ **bë**·*het* **për t'u çarë katërsh** to get too fat; get really big
○ **bë**·*het*^{3rd} **për ta/t'u hedhur në pleh/plehra** to become utterly worthless: be ready for the dungheap

○ **bë**·*het* **për të çarë me sharrë** "be fit for cutting up with a saw" to put on a lot of weight, get fat

○ **bë**·*het*^{past} **për të pirë helmin** "became ready to take poison" *became* very depressed/sad

○ **bë**·*het* **për të pirë miza** "be ready to drink flies" to be about ready to take poison, be very sad

○ **bë**·*het* **për të qarë me lot** "become ready to mourn with tears" to get into a sorrowful condition

○ **bë**·*het* **për të vënë rubën e zezë** "be about to put on one's black kerchief (mourning clothes)" to be on the brink of disaster

○ **bë**·*het* **për thikë 1** (of livestock) to be ready for slaughter **2** (of people) to be getting ready to kill one another

○ **bë**·*het* **për vig** "become ready for the bier/stretcher" to become so wasted by illness that one cannot walk; be on the brink of death; have one foot in the grave

○ **bë**·*het* **për zjarr** "become fit for burning" to be ready for the trash heap

○ **bë**·*het*^{pl} **përshesh (me njëri-tjetrin)** to have a real free-for-all

○ **bë**·*het* **përshesh me** [] to be in a brawl with []: mix it up with []

○ **bë**·*het* **përralla e botës** "become a public story" to get a bad reputation

○ **bë**·*het* **përrallë** to sound like the same old story

○ **bë**·*het* **pikë e pesë** to become widely scattered: scatter like flies, become scattered like straw

○ **bë**·*het* **pile** to intrude

○ **bë**·*het* **piper** to fly into a rage, suddenly get very angry

○ <> **bë**·*het* **plagë në sy** to become hateful to <>

○ <> **bë**·*het* **plesht (në vesh)** to stick to <> like a flea

○ **bë**·*het* **pluhur** to go to hell, be completely destroyed

○ **bë**·*het* **plumb** "become lead" to become heavy, take on a lot of weight

○ **bë**·*het* **presh** (of a plant) to dry up, wither

○ **bë**·*het* **prush *1** to blush deeply **2** to get a feverish temperature

○ **bë**·*het* **prush në fytyrë 1** to get red in the face **2** to get very angry

○ **bë**·*het* **prushërimë** to break out in a rash

○ <> **bë**·*het* **pullë (poste)** "become like a (postage) stamp to <>" to follow <> closely: stick to <> like glue, not let <> out of one's sight

○ <> **bë**·*het*^{3sg} **puna shirit** <> *takes* forever to finish the job

○ <> **bë**·*het* **pus** to go wrong for <>

○ **bë**·*het* **pus 1** to get very sad in the face, look dismal **2** to get red in the face: get very angry

○ **bë**·*het* **pus pa fund** "become a bottomless well" to become a sea of blood

○ **S'bëhet pusi me gjilpëra.** "A well isn't made with a needle." *(Prov)* You need the right tools to do an important task.

○ <> **bë**·*het*^{3sg} **qafa palë-palë/me pala** "<>'s neck becomes ringed in folds" <> *gets* very fat; <> *gets* very rich

○ **bë**·*het* **qefin** to become white as a sheet, get pale in the face, blanch visibly

○ <> **bë**·*het*^{3sg} **qejfi** <> *is* very pleased; <> *benefits*

○ <> **bë**·*het*^{3sg} **qejfi pushkë** <> *is* enormously pleased, <> *is* very glad

○ **bë**·*het* **qengj** to become quiet and well-behaved: become a little lamb

○ **bë**·*het* **qepaze** to become disgraced

○ **bë**·*het*^{3sg} **qielli pus** the sky *becomes* very dark

○ **bë**·*het* **qiri** to become thin as a rail

○ **bë**·*het* **qumësht** to calm down; become quiet and subdued

○ **bë**·*het* **qyqe** to become completely drunk: get stewed

○ **bë**·*het* **re** to disappear/vanish like a cloud

○ **bë**·*het* **rehat** to be sitting pretty

○ <> **bë**·*het* **retër** <> *gets* constantly pestered

○ **bë**·*het* **retra** to get worn to rags/pieces

○ **bë**·*het* **rrafsh me tokën** to lie flat on the ground

○ **bë**·*het*^{past} **rrap e rrënjë** to have lived a long time; have seen and heard a lot (in one's day)

○ **bë**·*het* **rreth oxhaku** to get old and become a recluse

○ <> **bë**·*het* **rrëqebull** "hang on to <> like a wildcat" to pester <> constantly

○ **bë**·*het* **rricë** to curl up in fear, cower in fear

○ **bë**·*het* **rrip daulleje** "become a drumhead" to get very drunk: get tighter than a drum

○ <> **bë**·*het* **rriqër** *(Pej)* to stick around <> so much as to become a nuisance; pester <> incessantly; stick to <> like a burr

○ <> **bë**·*het* **rrodhe** *(Pej)* to stick around <> so much as to become a nuisance; pester <> incessantly; stick to <> like a burr

○ **bë**·*het* **rrogoz 1** (of plants) to be knocked flat to the ground **2** to become carpeted with fallen fruit

○ **bë**·*het* **rrumbull** to get dead drunk

○ **S'bëhet rrushi deng.** "A grape does not become a full sack." *(Prov)* It can't be done.

○ **bë**·*het* **rrushkull** to become dirt poor

○ **bë**·*het* **sa nuk** [] **nxë·**^{3sg} **dera** to get very fat ("so fat that [] *doesn't fit* in the doorway"), get as big as a house

○ **bë**·*het* **sa një plep** *(Colloq)* to grow up big and tall: become a grown-up adult

○ <> **bë**·*het*^{3sg} **sahati mot** "the hour *becomes* a year for <>" time *drags* for <>, <> *grows* impatient because of the long wait

○ **bë**·*het* **(si) sardele** to be packed in like sardines

○ **bë**·*het* **sëpatë** to become a mere tool in someone else's hands

○ **bë**·*het* **si bisht luge** "be getting to look like a spoon handle" to be getting to look very skinny

○ **bë**·*het* **si boja** to go pale (from shock, anger, fright)

○ **bë**·*het* **si bundër** (of a person) to shrivel up with old age

○ **bë**·*het* **si e ëma e zjarrit** to become unkempt and sloppy in appearance

○ **bë**·*het* **si fiçor** to become disheveled (with unkempt hair and a scraggly beard)

○ **bë**·*het* **si gjuha në gojë** to get completely wet, get soaked to the skin

○ **bë**·*het*^{pl} **si këmbët e dhisë** "become like the feet of a goat" to become confused about who's boss

○ **bë**·*het* **si lafsha e gjelit** to get red in the face with anger

○ **bë**·*het* **si lakër e bujtur** to become dull and boring; lose importance/interest

○ **bë**·*het* **si lepur** to become thin as a rail, get skinny

∘ **bë·het si lëkurë maceje** "become like cat skin" (of livestock) to get very skinny, become all skin and bones

∘ **bë·het si lugë çervishi** to stick one's nose into everything, get mixed up in everything

∘ **bë·het si pelte** to get soft and mushy

∘ **bë·het si plak bostani** to become ugly as sin

∘ **bë·het si prift** "become like a priest" to need a shave

∘ **bë·het si qyqe** to become very thin and drawn

∘ **bë·het si qyqe në degë** "become like a cuckoo on a branch" to be in a miserable situation

∘ **bë·het si re e bardhë** "become like a white cloud" to become hard to make out, become indistinct

∘ **bë·het si rrunëz** to fill out nicely, become nice and plump

∘ **bë·het si shejtani** (Pej) to get covered with filth

∘ **bë·het si thes me lesh** "become like a sack of wool" to get as fat as pig

∘ **bë·het^{3rd} si veza/veja surbull** to become soft and sloppy

∘ **bë·het^{3rd} si xanë** (of a woven material) to get frazzled with age, get old and frayed

∘ **bë·het si** {adjective} to pretend to be { } **u bë si i vdekur** he pretended to be dead

∘ <> **bë·het si** { } to look to <> like { }

∘ <> **bë·het sikur __** to seem to <> as if __

∘ **bë·het skra** to get thin and weak, become emaciated

∘ **bë·het spec (i kuq)** to get red in the face

∘ **bë·het spec** to blush deeply, get beet red; fly into a rage, suddenly get very angry

∘ **bë·het spol** to get dead drunk: get tanked

∘ **S'bëhet stan me lepuj.** "It is not possible to make a dairy with rabbits." (Prov) There's nothing that can be done if you have the wrong people.

∘ **bë·het^{3sg} syri bakër për** [] to be burning with desire to have [], burn with desire for []

∘ <> **bë·het^{3pl} sytë ujë** <>'s eyes are exhausted from overwork

∘ <> **bë·het^{3pl} sytë ujë për** [] <>'s eyes are longing to see [] again

∘ **bë·het (fare) shirit** to become nothing but skin and bones

∘ **bë·het shirk** to get bloated from eating

∘ **bë·het shkarpë 1** to become thin as a rail **2** to become destitute, be left dirt poor

∘ **bë·het shkrumb** to get burned up completely

∘ **bë·het shollondur** to suffer many injuries, get badly torn up (by injuries)

∘ <> **bë·het^{3sg} shpirti derr** (Colloq) <> is getting exasperated; <> is getting fed up

∘ <> **bë·het^{3sg} shpirti gomar** <> gets fed up

∘ <> **bë·het^{3sg} shpirti helm** <> becomes bitterly sad

∘ <> **bë·het^{3sg} shpirti vrer** <> becomes bitterly sad

∘ **bë·het shporiz** to spread like a weed

∘ **bë·het shportë** (of a container) to become full of holes

∘ **bë·het (një) shtëpi** to become allied as a single family (by a marriage)

∘ **bë·het^{3sg} shtëpi me themel** to become economically sound

∘ <> **bë·het shtëpia hithërishtë** <>'s family line comes to an end

∘ <> **bë·het^{3sg} shtëpia rrasë (e gjallë)** <>'s house is left bare, there is absolutely nothing left in <>'s house

∘ <> **bë·het shtrat** to become <>'s backer; become <>'s basis of support

∘ **bë·het shuall** (of fruit fallen from trees) to form a veritable carpet on the ground

∘ **bë·het telef** to get dead tired: got pooped (out)

∘ **bë·het top** to become frozen solid

∘ **bë·het topil** to get soaked, get soaking wet

∘ **bë·het trëndelinë** to become weak and scrawny

∘ **bë·het trinë** (Colloq) to get blind drunk

∘ **bë·het^{3rd} tru** to boil too long and become mushy

∘ **bë·het trung** to get numb from cold; get dead drunk

∘ <> **bë·het^{3sg} trupi qymyr** <>'s back/body gets black and blue (from heavy beating)

∘ <> **bë·het^{3pl} trutë çorbë** <>'s mind gets completely confused

∘ **bë·het tufan 1** to disappear suddenly **2** to get blind drunk **3** to go into a rage

∘ **bë·het turrë 1** to become hunched up **2** to become deaf

∘ **bë·het tym 1** to vanish suddenly, vanish like smoke **2** to get very drunk: get plastered/smashed **3** to fume with rage

∘ **bë·het tym e flakë** to fume with rage

∘ **bë·het tym e mjegull** to fume with rage

∘ **bë·het tyrbe pas** <> "be a mausoleum over <>'s grave" to be constantly at <>'s elbow

∘ **bë·het thelë e copë** "become slices and chunks" to engage in mutual slaughter, cut each other to ribbons

∘ **bë·het thëngjill** to burn to a crisp, burn up completely

∘ **bë·het thërrime** to crumble into little pieces

∘ **bë·het (si) thuk** (of a man) to get round and plump

∘ <> **bë·het ujk** to become a hateful nag to <>

∘ **bë·het ujk** to get very angry

∘ <> **bë·het urë (e vig)** "become <>'s bridge" let <> walk all over one

∘ **bë·het urë e gurë** to slave away, work like a horse, break one's back

∘ **bë·het urë e zezë** "become a black ember" **1** to get black as coal **2** to get deeply saddened

∘ **S'bëhet urë me gëzhdalla.** "A bridge is not made of splinters." (Prov) You need the right materials and equipment for the job.

∘ **bë·het uthull** to get very angry

∘ **bë·het valë** to become nice and warm; get too hot

∘ <> **bë·het vath në vesh** "become an earring in <>'s ear" to hang around <> all the time; keep pestering <>

∘ <> **bë·het velenxë** "become <>'s protective covering" to cover up <>'s mistakes/faults, protect <> by hiding <>'s dirty linen

∘ **bë·het^{3sg} vendi zjarr** the place gets too uncomfortable for <> to stay any longer

∘ **bë·het verem 1** to get deeply sad **2** to come to the end of one's patience, become unable to take it anymore

∘ **bë·het veri** "become the north wind" to leave/vanish suddenly

∘ <> **bë·het ves** to become addictive to <>: <> becomes addicted to { }

∘ **s'<> bëhet vonë për** [] <> feels no concern about []: [] is no big deal for <>; is not worried about []

○ **bë·***het* **vozë** "becomea barrel" **1** to become gorged with food or drink **2** to swell up

○ **bë·***het*^{3sg} **vrasje e madhe** there *is* massive carnage

○ **bë·***het* **zeher** to get very sad

○ **<> bë·***het*^{3sg} **zemra behar** <> *gets* a big kick, <> *is* delighted

○ **<> bë·***het*^{3sg} **zemra borë** "<>'s heart becomes snow" <>'s heart *stops* with fright?

○ **<> bë·***het*^{3sg} **zemra bukë** "<>'s heart becomes like bread" **1** <>'s heart *swells* (with delight/pride) **2** <> *is* deeply touched/moved

○ **<> bë·***het*^{3sg} **zemra copë** <> *gets* deeply hurt/grieved/sorrowed

○ **<> bë·***het*^{3sg} **zemra çyrek** *(Colloq)* <>'s heart *swells* with happiness: <> *gets* a happy feeling

○ **<> bë·***het*^{3sg} **zemra gropë** <> *becomes* heartbroken

○ **<> bë·***het*^{3sg} **zemra helm** <> *becomes* bitterly sad

○ **<> bë·***het*^{3sg} **zemra hon** <> *is* deeply saddened; <> *gets* very angry

○ **<> bë·***het*^{3sg} **zemra kala** "{}'s heart becomes like a castle" {}'s heart *swells* (with delight/pride)

○ **<> bë·***het*^{3sg} **zemra mal (e bjeshkë)** "<>'s heart becomes like a mountain" <>'s heart *swells* (with delight/pride)

○ **<> bë·***het*^{3sg} **zemra plagë** <> *gets* deeply hurt/grieved/sorrowed

○ **<> bë·***het*^{3sg} **zemra pus** "<>'s heart *becomes* a well" <> *gets* deeply sad

○ **<> bë·***het*^{3sg} **zemra shpellë** "<>'s heart *becomes* a deep cave" <> *is* deeply grieved, <> *feels* desolated

○ **<> bë·***het*^{3sg} **zemra shtupë** all the heart goes out of <>, <> *becomes* demoralized

○ **<> bë·***het*^{3sg} **zemra vrer** <> *becomes* bitterly sad

○ **<> bë·***het*^{3sg} **zemra zhur** <>'s heart has a longing; <> suffers with longing

○ **bë·***het* **zjarr** to get very angry, fly into a rage

○ **bë·***het* **zot i vetes** "become one's own master" **1** to grow up, become mature **2** to take charge of one's own affairs

○ **bë·***het* **zot në shtëpi të huaj** to act like the boss on somebody else's turf

bë·*n*

I § vt **1** to make; cause; produce, create **2** to do, engage in [an activity] **3** to make [] ready, prepare **4** to earn **5** to spend [a period of time] **6** to constitute **7** [*Math*] to equal

II § vi **1** to do something, act, behave **2** to cost, come to [] **3** to be adequate/appropriate, make it: fit **4** to be (of weather or climate) **5** to mature, ripen; be readied/prepared **6** to take place **7** (of an agricultural subject) to have a good yield **8** to become one of, join up with **9** to pass (said of periods of time) **10** *(Colloq)* to pretend to be, act as if **11** *(Colloq)* to get stuck with **12** *(Colloq)* to comprise **13** *(Colloq)* to go off somewhere **14** (in negative constructions only) not to feel like, be disinclined/indisposed to **15** to seem/appear to be

III § vi impers 3rd sg it is permitted/okay

○ **ia bë·***n* to get along, manage

○ **bë·***n* **aheng 1** to have a loud musical celebration **2** *(Reg)* to have fun

○ **bë·***n* **ajar sahatin** to regulate the clock/watch

○ **bë·***n* **ajar ujët** to get the water to the right temperature

○ [] **bë·***n* **alarm** to make a big stew about []

○ **bë·***n* **amin** to be a yes-man; accept anything someone else says

○ [] **bë·***n* **ar***ë* **e hamull** to spread wild rumors about []

○ **s'<>a bë·***n* **as një as dy** not prolong matters with <>, not waste time with <>

○ **s'bë·***n*^{3rd} **asnjë pare** to be no value, be worthless

○ [] **bë·***n* **ashure** to make a confused mess of []

○ **bë·***n* **autobiografinë** *(Colloq)* to give a short autobiographical summary: prepare one's curriculum vitae

○ **Bëmë baba, të të ngjaj/përngjaj!** "Make me, father, so I will be like you!" (said when a child is just like its father) His father's spitting image!

○ **bë·***n* **badër** to demolish, destroy

○ **<> bë·***n* **bajgën** *(Crude)* to leave <> in the lurch

○ **bë·***n* **Bajram** to be living in a fool's paradise

○ **bë·***n* **bakallëk me** [] t.· treat [] as an object of haggling

○ **bë·***n* **baltë** *(Tease)* to waste one's time idly, stand around doing nothing

○ **e bë·***n* **baltë** to wear out one's welcome

○ [] **bë·***n* **baltë** to completely destroy []: devastate/demolish []

○ [] **bë·***n* **ballafaqe** to put [] face to face, make [] face each other

○ **<> bë·***n* **ballë 1** to face up to <>; face <>, confront <>; resist <> **2** to achieve <>, reach <>, attain <>

○ **bë·***n* **ballë** to loom into view

○ **ia bë·***n* **bam** *(Colloq)* **1** to shoot, fire a gun **2** to have the experience of firing a gun **3** to get it done **4** to explode with frustration/anger

○ **bë·***n* **banjë** to bathe: take a bath, go for a swim

○ [] **bë·***n* **bar** to devastate [], reduce [] to dust

○ **bë·***n* **bark** to eat a lot

○ **e bë·***n* **barkun hambar** to take a lot of abuse without reacting, be very tolerant/patient about annoying things

○ **e bë·***n* **barkun katua 1** to fill one's belly full, eat one's fill **2** to take a lot of abuse without reacting, be very tolerant/patient about annoying things

○ **e bë·***n* **barkun lerë** to swell one's belly with drinking, drink a lot

○ **e bë·***n* **barkun pallaskë** to cram food into one's belly: get stuffed absolutely full

○ **<>a bë·***n* **barkun ujë** to touch <> to the quick, affect <> deeply

○ **e bë·***n* **barkun** {*voluminous round object*} to swell up like a {} from overeating

○ [] **bë·***n* **barut** to spend [] wastefully: spend [money] like water, throw [one's money] away

○ **bë·***n* **bashkë** to get along together

○ [] **bë·***n* **batall** to break [], put [] out of commission

○ **<>a bë·***n* **be** to swear revenge on <>

○ **bë·***n* **be** to take an oath, swear

○ **bë·***n* **be e rrufe** to keep swearing

○ **bë·***n* **be për** [] ***1** to have great respect for [] ***2** to swear by []

○ **bë·***n* **be se** _ to swear that _; could swear that _

○ **bë·***n*^{3sg} **beh** to happen suddenly

∘ e **bë**·*n* **beh 1** to be cautious, pay close attention **2** to suppose, think, imagine

∘ s'<> **bë**·*n* **beh** to be unintimidated by <>, unafraid of <>

∘ <> **bë**·*n* **bela** to become burdensome to <>

∘ <>[] **bë**·*n* **bela** to saddle <> with [a responsibility]

∘ **bë**·*n*^{3sg} **beli** *(Old Colloq)* it *is* completely clear/obvious

∘ e **bë**·*n* **beli** *(Old Colloq)* to show just who one is, come out into the open

∘ **bë**·*n* **belin e parë** to start the first row of digging with a spade

∘ <> **bë**·*n* **benzinën** to put <> to the torch; destroy <> completely

∘ [] **bë**·*n* **beribat** *(Old)* to make a mess of [], foul [] up; ruin []

∘ <> **bë**·*n* **berra** to break <> up into small pieces: mince <>, pound <> up

∘ [] **bë**·*n* **bërllok** to reduce [] to chaff, cut [] to pieces, destroy []; make a mess of []

∘ [] **bë**·*n* **bërryl** *(Old)* to support []

∘ <> **bë**·*n* **bisht** *1 to avoid facing <> 2** to evade <>

∘ **bë**·*n* **bisht 1** to turn tail **2** to be evasive

∘ e **bë**·*n* **bishtin palë** *(Scorn)* **1** to fold one's tail between one's legs and die: kick off **2** to be brought down from one's high horse

∘ [] **bë**·*n* **bjeshkë** to exaggerate []

∘ ia **bë**·*n* **bof** to explode with frustration/anger

∘ [] **bë**·*n* **bokë** to ignore [] as worthless

∘ <>a **bë**·*n* **borxh** to have to pay <> back; deserve retribution from <> for bad behavior

∘ [] **bë**·*n* **borzilok** to make [] look very neat

∘ [] **bë**·*n* **bosh** *(Old)* to get rid of []: oust, eject

∘ [] **bë**·*n* **brashnjë** to lambaste [] in strong language: cuss [] out

∘ [] **bë**·*n* **buall** to exaggerate [], blow [] out of reasonable proportion

∘ [] **bë**·*n* **bujë** to make too big a thing of []; make a great stir and clamor about []

∘ [] **bë**·*n* **burnot** to pulverize []; break/destroy []

∘ <> **bë**·*n* **buzë** to show one's dislike of <>: make a face at <>

∘ **bë**·*n* **buzën në gaz** "put one's lips into a smile" to smile

∘ [] **bë**·*n* **byk 1** to destroy []; obliterate [] **2** *(Impol)* to beat [] badly, soundly trounce [], win overwhelmingly over [], smash [], wipe [] out

∘ **bë**·*n* **caq** to score a goal

∘ <> **bë**·*n* **cepa** to try to put one over on <>, try to fool <>

∘ [] **bë**·*n* **copë** to fracture/injure/wound [] badly, seriously damage/hurt/harm []; decimate []

∘ **bë**·*n*^{3sg} **ç'bë**·*n*^{3sg} **dhe** __ *1 do as one may, __ **2** whatever else one *does*, still __

∘ **bë**·*n* **çabulle** to make a big mess, turn topsy-turvy

∘ **bë**·*n*^{3sg} **çak** to be a dud, not fire

∘ **nuk bë**·*n* **çak** not fire a shot, not fight

∘ **bë**·*n* **çak pushka** to click empty (on a gun)

∘ **bë**·*n* **çap e jakë 1** to walk back and forth **2** *(Fig)* to keep busy doing nothing

∘ **nuk bë**·*n* **çap 1** not make a move, not move **2** to get nowhere

∘ [] **bë**·*n* **çarçaf** to rip [] to pieces

∘ [] **bë**·*n* **çeçe** to destroy [] utterly, make [] into mincemeat

∘ e **bë**·*n* **çështje të përbashkët** to make common cause with

∘ [] **bë**·*n* **çështje** to make a big thing out of []; keep at [], draw everyone's attention to []

∘ [] **bë**·*n* **çift** *(Colloq)* to marry off []

∘ [] **bë**·*n* **çikë** to grind [] fine, break [] into tiny pieces

∘ [] **bë**·*n* **çirak** (sometimes said ironically) to put [] on []'s feet

∘ **bë**·*n* **çmos** to do one's utmos

∘ s'po **bë**·*n* **çorap** to make no progress, not go well

∘ [] **bë**·*n* **çorap** to make a mess of []

∘ [] **bë**·*n* **çorbë** to make a complete mess of []

∘ **bë**·*n* **çudi** to marvel, be surprised

∘ **bë**·*n*^{pl} **dajre** "play the tambourine" to play musical instruments and have a good time

∘ [] **bë**·*n* **dalje 1** [*Fin*] to ship [] out **2** *(Colloq)* to kick [] out; give [] the sack, fire []

∘ <> **bë**·*n* **dasmën** "arrange a wedding for <>" *(Iron Crude)* to kill <>: take <> for a ride

∘ **bë**·*n* **dashuri** to engage in lovemaking; make love

∘ [] **bë**·*n* **def** to get rid of []

∘ **bë**·*n*^{3sg} **det** there *is* a heavy sea, there *are* heavy waves

∘ **bë**·*n* **dëm** to do harm

∘ [] **bë**·*n* **dëm** to kill [], do [] in

∘ **bë**·*n* **dëng** to burst with envy/jealousy

∘ [] **bë**·*n* **dërrmake** to destroy []; make [] very tired

∘ [] **bë**·*n* **ditë** to make [] as bright as day

∘ s'<> **bë**·*n* **dora (të _)** <> can't bring oneself to (do) it: <> just can't/won't do it

∘ **bë**·*n* **dorë** to get down to work

∘ **nuk bë**·*n* **dot dy fjalë (bashkë)** "be totally unable to join two words (together)" to be incapable of expressing oneself clearly

∘ <> **bë**·*n* **dredha** to dodge <>

∘ **bë**·*n* **dredha 1** to make turns, spin **2** to be a malingerer; be evasive

∘ i **bë**·*n* **dredha plumbit** "dodge the bullet" *(Impol)* to be cowardly

∘ e **bë**·*n* **drithë e mjell** *(Impol)* to make a big mess, ruin everything

∘ s'i **bë**·*n* **drutë të gjata** "not make the logs long" to be sparing with words; be brusque

∘ **bë**·*n* **dua** *(Colloq Old)* to pray

∘ i **bë**·*n* **duart me gjak** to stain one's hands with blood: participate in murder

∘ **bë**·*n* **durim** to have patience

∘ s'<> **bë**·*n* **dy bashkë** <> *is* incapable of accomplishing anything

∘ s'i **bë**·*n* **dy bashkë** to be incapable of chewing gum and walking at the same time, be totally inept

∘ [] **bë**·*n* **dy uj**ë **e një oriz** to dilute [] beyond recognition, ruin/spoil {}

∘ e **bë**·*n* **dhespotin me barrë** *(Joke)* to make up something totally unreal and impossible

∘ e **bë**·*n* **dheun breg** *(Crude)* to die: kick off

∘ <>i **bë**·*n* **dhëmbët misër** "make <>'s teeth into corn" to knock <>'s teeth out

∘ <> **bë**·*n*^{3sg} **edhe gjeli vezë** "Even the rooster is laying eggs." Everything *is going* well for <>.

∘ **bë**·*n* **efekt** to take effect

∘ **bë**·*n* **emër** to become famous

∘ **bë**·*n* **fallco** to sing off-key, play out of tune

∘ [] **bë**·*n* **fani** to obliterate []

∘ <> **bë**·*n* **faqet gur** to make <> chubby-cheeked

∘ e **bë**·*n* **ferrën pëllë** "make a bramble bush into a nanny goat" to present something bad in a good light, make something bad seem good, make a misrepresentation

◦ [] bë·n fetë 1 to reduce [] to crumbs: crumble [] 2 to ruin [], destroy []

◦ bë·n firë to suffer a loss of weight

◦ bë·n^{3sg} fishek (of a fire or a person in difficult circumstances) to manage to burst through, find a way to break out/through

◦ bë·n fjalë me [] to argue with [], have an argument with []

◦ bë·n^{3rd} fjalë për [] to talk about [], be about []

◦ s'bë·n fjalë 1 not say a word, be amenable: not complain, not argue 2 to be easy-going, be easy to get along with

◦ bë·n fjalë 1 to speak 2 to gossip, talk about 3 to argue 4 to make an agreement

◦ i bë·n fjalët gërshetë to speak at great length, go on and on

◦ bë·n flluska në erë to build castles in the air

◦ bë·n fole 1 to settle down 2 to appear, take shape

◦ ia bë·n fora 1 to display extraordinary daring; do something amazing; make a name for oneself 2 to run up terrible expenses

◦ <> bë·n fresk to cool <> off

◦ bë·n^{3sg} fresk (of weather/climate) to be cool

◦ bë·n^{3sg} freskët to be cool

◦ [] bë·n frugull to scorch []; burn [] down, reduce [] to ashes

◦ bë·n fshat më vete "make a village by oneself" 1 to live on one's own 2 to act independently, follow one's own opinions

◦ [] bë·n fshesë to treat [] like dirt

◦ bë·n^{3sg} ftohtë (of weather/climate) to be cold

◦ [] bë·n fugë to burn [] to ashes, destroy [] completey

◦ bë·n furtunë to wreak havoc

◦ [] bë·n furrë to burn [] to a crisp, burn [] to cinders

◦ [] bë·n fushë to make off with all of []

◦ [] bë·n fyt 1 to eat [] all up 2 to utterly destroy []

◦ bë·n gargarë to gargle

◦ bë·n gati to make ready, prepare

◦ bë·n gaz to have fun

◦ bë·n gazepin to be a constant grumbler/whiner

◦ [] bë·n gërshet to make a mess of []

◦ <> bë·n gilivili 1 to stroke <>'s throat caressingly with the fingers, tickle <> under the chin 2 to be unstable and untrustworthy

◦ u bë·n gisht to have become thin as a rail

◦ <> bë·n glasën "leave <> birdshit" (Crudelm-polite) to leave <> unexpectedly; leave <> high and dry

◦ <>a bë·n gogël to make <> do what one wants, force <> to do something

◦ e bë·n gojën çorap "make/open the mouth like a stocking" to talk a lot, talk too much

◦ e bë·n gropë vendin to stay too long in one place

◦ <>a bë·n gropën 1 to dig <>'s grave: kill <> 2 to cause <> great harm, do a terrible thing to <>

◦ e bë·n groshin kacidhe "treat every dime like a dollar" to make one's money stretch; pinch pennies, be miserly

◦ bë·n guga to prattle

◦ [] bë·n gur e hi to demolish [] completely

◦ bë·n gurët e zez accomplished nothing (in past tenses only)

◦ <> bë·n gurin e gjakut to wear <> out, exhaust

◦ bë·n gurin e gjakut to cause a disaster, create havoc

◦ bë·n gjah to do one's utmost, do one's best

◦ bë·n gjak to butcher (an animal)

◦ [] bë·n gjak to master [] thoroughly

◦ e bë·n gjalmë to talk interminably, go on and on

◦ <> bë·n gjeth to grind <> to dust, completely destroy <>

◦ bë·n gjëmë to wail, lament loudly

◦ <> bë·n gjëmën to cause terrible calamity to fall on <>

◦ bë·n gjumë të lehtë/rëndë to sleep lightly/deeply

◦ bë·n gjyq me [] 1 to quarrel with [] 2 to be in a legal suit against []

◦ bë·n haber to send word

◦ bë·n hair to succeed in life, do well, prosper

◦ bë·n hajmedet to mourn a loss loudly, make a public lament; complain noisily

◦ [] bë·n hak to deserve []

◦ e bë·n halën tra "make a roof beam out of a hair" to make a mountain out of a molehill

◦ <>a bë·n hallall 1 to give [] to <> with all one's heart 2 to forgive <> for [a wrong]

◦ bë·n një hap to take a step, step

◦ bë·n hapa to make progress

◦ bë·n hapa në vend to mark time (in one place); stay in place, not change; lag behind

◦ bë·n hapa përpara to take forward steps, advance

◦ bë·n hapa prapa to take backward steps, go backward

◦ e bë·n hapin kilometër to walk in huge steps, go fast; advance at a giant's pace

◦ [] bë·n haps to put [] in jail/prison

◦ <>[] bë·n haram to spoil <>'s enjoyment of [], spoil [] for <>

◦ [] bë·n hasha to deny having ever said []

◦ bë·n hatanë 1 (Crude) to wreak havoc 2 to make a terrible fuss

◦ [] bë·n helaq (Crude) to insult [] publicly with all stops pulled out: cuss [] out

◦ bë·n heqësi to be evasive

◦ i bë·n hesapet pa hanxhinë "make calculations without the innkeeper" to make a decision without adequate thought

◦ [] bë·n hi (e pluhur) 1 to burn [] down; wipe [] out completely 2 to finish [] all up, polish [] off

◦ <> bë·n hije 1 to serve <> blindly 2 to shelter <> 3 to hang around <a person> doing nothing

◦ bë·n hije (mbi dhé) (Pej) to be doing nothing useful in life, just occupy space

◦ nuk <> bë·n hije (as) vetes to be incapable even of looking after oneself

◦ nuk bë·n hije në diell to be absolutely worthless, of no account

◦ <> bë·n hile to deceive <>, cheat <>

◦ bë·n hov 1 to move forward forcefully: leap, spring, lunge 2 to rush, mount an assault, attack

◦ e bë·n hoxhën me barrë (Joke) to make up something totally unreal and impossible

◦ [] bë·n hundë me buzë to do very quickly

◦ <>[] bë·n hundët përshesh to smash <> in the face, break/bloody <>'s nose

◦ [] bë·n hyrje [Fin] to enter [] into the inventory, record the receipt of []: receive [merchandise]

◦ <> bë·n hyzmet to look after <>, take care of <>

◦ <>a bë·n hyzmetin (Colloq) to take good care of <> (as essential to one's livelihood)

◦ <> bë·n jehonë to make [] widely known, promote [], publicize

◦ bë·n jetë (Colloq) to live a life of comfort

○ <>*a* **bë·***n* **jetën pus** to make <>'s life a living hell
○ [] **bë·***n* **kabull 1** to agree to do [], accept [something] **2** to forgive [someone]
○ [] **bë·***n* **kail** to persuade []
○ [] **bë·***n* **kallame** to leave nothing standing in []: destroy [] completely
○ [] **bë·***n* **kalldrëm** to pave [] with cobblestone
○ [] **bë·***n* **kalli** to leave nothing standing in []: destroy [] completely
○ **e bë·***n* **kaun me viç** "make an ox out of a calf" to make up things that are quite untrue, make it up out of whole cloth
○ <> **bë·***n* **keq** to do harm to <>, hurt <>
○ **bë·***n* **keq** to cause harm
○ **s'**<> **bë·***n*^{3pl} **(më) këllqet** <>'s old bones just won't carry <> any more
○ **bë·**^{past} **këmbë** "it has grown legs" *(Iron)* it must have gotten up and walked away: it was stolen, it has disappeared
○ **i bë·***n* **këmbët bigë** *(Crude)* to keel over and die, kick the bucket
○ **nuk** <> **bë·***n*^{3pl} **këmbët 1** <> *does* not have the strength to walk (any more): <>'s legs *won't* make it **2** <> *does* not dare to go
○ **i bë·***n* **këmbët baras/kizë/çift** *(Impol)* to kick the bucket, turn up one's toes (and die)
○ <>*i* **bë·***n* **këmbët bërdila** to beat <> hard and repeatedly on the legs
○ **i bë·***n* **këmbët të lehta** to walk/run quickly; run away quickly
○ **bë·***n* **kërdinë** to wreak havoc
○ **bë·***n* **kiametin** to make a big clamor, raise Cain; wreak havoc
○ <>*a* **bë·***n* **kobën** to do <> in, kill <>
○ <>*a* **bë·***n*^{3sg} **koka** <>'s suffering is of <>'s own making
○ <> **bë·***n*^{3sg} **koka miza** "<>'s head *makes* flies: <>'s head *is* all abuzz" <> *has* a lot to worry/think about
○ **bë·***n* **kokë nga bishti** to leave no stone unturned
○ <>*a* **bë·***n* **kokën çorbë/dhallë** to make <> thoroughly confused
○ **e bë·***n* **kokën tullë** to cut one's hair very short; shave one's head
○ <>*a* **bë·***n* **kokën daulle** to confuse <> with words; tire <> by too much talk
○ <>*a* **bë·***n* **kokën petë** to beat [] badly: beat [] to a pulp
○ <>*a* **bë·***n* **kokën sallatë** to confuse <> thoroughly
○ **e bë·***n* **kokën tullë** to clip/shave off all the hair on the head, make the head look like a billiard ball
○ **bë·***n* **konak** to take shelter; stay over (at someone's house)
○ **bë·***n* **kontroll** to inspect, check
○ [] **bë·***n* **kopan 1** to beat [] up badly, beat [] to death **2** to leave [] dead
○ **bë·***n* **krahasim** to make a comparison, compare
○ **bë·***n* **kryq** to make the sign of a cross, cross oneself
○ **bë·***n* **kthesë** to make a big change in one's life: turn over a new leaf
○ **bë·***n* **kulaç në hi** to have unrealistic plans/hopes: build castles in the air, have pipedreams
○ **bë·***n* **kursim** to economize, make savings
○ <>*a* **bë·***n* **kurrizin më të butë se barkun** "make <>'s back as soft as <>'s belly" to beat <> to a pulp
○ <>*a* **bë·***n* **kurrizin qull** to beat <> to a pulp
○ <> **bë·***n* **lak** to dodge/evade *<an obligation>*

○ [] **bë·***n* **lakër** to make [] into small pieces
○ [] **bë·***n* **lakror 1** to beat [someone] to a pulp **2** to make a confused mess of []
○ [] **bë·***n* **lanet** to curse/damn and abandon []: say to hell with [] and leave []
○ **bë·***n* **lart 1** to go uphill **2** to get higher, grow
○ [] **bë·***n* **lavër** to make a mess of [], completely wreck []
○ **bë·***n* **lec** (of fruit trees) to have abundant fruit
○ [] **bë·***n* **leckë** to lambaste [] in strong language: cuss [] out
○ <> **bë·***n* **ledha** to flatter; cajole, coax
○ [] **bë·***n* **legjendë** to weave a whole legend around []
○ [] **bë·***n* **lepur** to make [] frightened/afraid
○ **bë·***n* **lerë** to stain []'s honor, shame []
○ **nuk** <> **bë·***n*^{3sg} **lëkura një para** "<>'s skin *is* not worth a farthing" <> *is* unable to anything useful, <> *is* a good-for-nothing
○ [] **bë·***n* **lëkurë** *(Crude)* to beat [] up badly, beat [] to a pulp, beat [] to within an inch of []'s life
○ <>*a* **bë·***n* **lëkurën për pesë para** "make <>'s skin look like two cents" to cuss [] out in public
○ <>*a* **bë·***n* **lëkurën postiqe** to flay <>, slaughter<>; kill <>
○ <>[] **bë·***n* **lëmë** to depict [] to <> as being a paradise
○ **bë·***n* **lëmë (në ajër)** to circle around (in the air)
○ [] **bë·***n* **lëmë** to level [] to the ground, destroy [] completely
○ [] **bë·***n* **lëm***e* **më lëmë e hënë më hënë** to have fashioned [] perfectly
○ [] **bë·***n* **lëndinë 1** to level [] to the ground, destroy [] completely **2** to depict [] as a paradise, make [] sound like paradise
○ **bë·***n* **lëshime** to be lenient; make concessions
○ [] **bë·***n* **lëvere** to rip/tear [] to pieces
○ **bë·***n* **lidhje** to make a connection: connect, link
○ **bë·***n* **ligjin** *(Fig)* to make one's own rules
○ [] **bë·***n* **limë** to level [] to the ground, destroy [] completely
○ <> **bë·***n*^{3pl} **liqtë gojë** "the harnesses in the loom make an opening for <>" a path *has been* opened for <> (to get something previously forbidden)
○ **bë·***n* **litani** to make an long entreaty, plead
○ [] **bë·***n* **litar** to drag [] out needlessly, go too slowly with []
○ [] **bë·***n* **livadh** to make [] sound wonderful, make [] sound like paradise
○ [] **bë·***n* **log** to pound/press [] flat
○ **bë·***n* **lojë të dyfishtë** to play a double game
○ **bë·***n* **lojën e** <> **1** to make a deceptive pretense of being <>: play the <> **2** to play up to <>
○ **bë·***n* **lojën e strucit** *(Book)* to hide one's head in the sand; refuse to face reality
○ **bë·***n* **llafe me** [] to have an argument with [], have words with []: have a tiff with []
○ **bë·***n* **llaka-llaka** *(Colloq)* to chatter
○ **bë·***n* **llogari 1** to make a calculation: calculate, compute **2** to make plans
○ [] **bë·***n* **llogari** to think [] through
○ **i bë·***n* **llogaritë gabim** to act without careful consideration
○ **i bë·***n* **llogaritë pa hanxhinë** "make calculations without the innkeeper" to make a decision without adequate thought

◦ [] **bë·**n **llum 1** to bungle [], do [] all wrong **2** to confuse [] totally

◦ **S'bën macja mullar.** "A cat doesn't build haystacks." *(Prov)* You can't expect an incompetent person to do this job.

◦ **bë·**n^{3sg} **majë anija** the ship comes into view (on the horizon)

◦ **i bë·**n **malet fushë** to do the impossible, accomplish miracles

◦ **s'**[] **bë·**n **mall** to give no consideration to [], not consider [], ignore []

◦ **bë·**n **masë** [*Electr*] to short out

◦ [] **bë·**n **maskara** to make [] out to be a scoundrel; cuss [] out, call [] bad names

◦ [] **bë·**n **mat 1** to checkmate [] **2** to put [] in a tight position, put [] with []'s back against the wall

◦ **bë·**n **matje** to take measurements: measure

◦ **bë·**n **mbi udh**ë **e nën udhë** to operate in both legal and extralegal ways

◦ **e bë·**n **me be** to swear to it

◦ [] **bë·**n **me beriha** to make a big to-do out of doing []

◦ [] **bë·**n **me cen** to give [] a permanent scar/infirmity; make [] paranoid

◦ **<>**a **bë·**n **me çelëz** to try to trick <>

◦ [] **bë·**n **me çika** to sprinkle [], spatter []

◦ [] **bë·**n **me detyrim** to do [] under coercion

◦ **e bë·**n **me fjalë** to agree on it in advance

◦ **ia bë·**n **me gisht** to make a gesture with the finger

◦ [] **bë·**n **me gjyq** to do [] but only with certain conditions

◦ **<>**a **bë·**n **me kokë** to make a head gesture to <>

◦ [] **bë·**n **me majë** to put a point on []: sharpen []

◦ [] **bë·**n **me marre** to cause disgrace to fall on []: disgrace []

◦ [] **bë·**n **me nerva** to put []'s nerves on edge; do [] while one's nerves are on edge

◦ [] **bë·**n **me porosi** to make [] to order

◦ **<>**a **bë·**n **me sy 1** to give <> the eye, wink at <> **2** *(Joke)* (of something) to be just begging <> to be bought/taken

◦ [] **bë·**n **me sherr** to cause [] to quarrel

◦ [] **bë·**n **me shëndet** to eat the first of the season's [produce]

◦ [] **bë·**n **me të tekur** to do [] only when one feels like it

◦ [] **bë·**n **me turp** to shame []; put [] to shame

◦ **bë·**n **me udhë/rrugë** to act/speak/work in accordance with accepted procedure, act/speak/work with propriety

◦ [] **bë·**n **me vete** to win [] over

◦ **e bë·**n **me inat me** [] to do it to spite []; do it in response to a challenge by []

◦ [] **bë·**n **me mend** to rehearse [] in one's mind

◦ **i bë·**n **me thagme (gjërat)** to make things seem wonderful, exaggerate things

◦ **bë·**n **medet** to be in mourning

◦ **bë·**n **mend** to have the intention, intend; make up one's mind

◦ **bë·**n **mend me** [] to exchange opinions/ideas with []: talk things over with []

◦ **<>**a **bë·**n **mendjen çapraz** to make <> all confused, put <> into a dilemma

◦ **<>**a **bë·**n **mendjen çarçaf** to dazzle <> with words, beguile <> with talk

◦ **<> bë·**n **mendjen çorap** to confuse <> utterly

◦ **<>**a **bë·**n **mendjen çorbë** to confuse <> utterly

◦ **<>**a **bë·**n **mendjen livadh** to dazzle <>

◦ **<>**a **bë·**n **mendjen pordhë** "make <>'s mind into a fart" (*Crude*) to fill <>'s mind with a lot of hot air, convince <> with a lot of hot air

◦ [] **bë·**n **mendjen pupa** to set one's mind on []

◦ **<>**a **bë·**n **mendjen sallatë** to confuse <> thoroughly

◦ **e bë·**n **mendjen top** to make up one's mind once and for all

◦ **<>**a **bë·**n **mendjen ujem** "make <>'s mind a hodgepodge" to lead [] into confusion, confuse []

◦ **<> bë·**n **mes (punës)** "bend one's back (to the task)" to get down to *<work>*

◦ **<> bë·**n **metani** to implore <>

◦ **bë·**n **mënjanë** to move out of the way; make room

◦ **ia bë·**n **minushë** to scamper away, run like mice

◦ **<> bë·**n **mirë** to do <> some good, be good for <>; treat <> nice

◦ **bë·**n **miskël** to put on makeup

◦ [] **bë·**n **mish e gjak** to master [] thoroughly

◦ [] **bë·**n **mish për hell** to torture []; beat [] up badly

◦ **<>**a **bë·**n **mishin paçavure të zezë** to beat <> black and blue

◦ **e bë·**n **mizën buall/ka** "make the flea/fly into a buffalo/ox" to make a mountain out of a molehill

◦ **bë·**n^{3sg} **moti** to be good weather

◦ **bë·**n^{3sg} **mu** *(Colloq)* it *is* completely clear/obvious, it *strikes* you immediately

◦ **bë·**n **muckë** to pout

◦ **bë·**n **muhabet** to have a pleasant talk: chat

◦ [] **bë·**n **muhabet pazari** to tell [] to absolutely everyone, make [] public knowledge

◦ **e bë·**n **muhabetin fjollë** to be good at small talk; be a good talker

◦ **e bë·**n **murrizin hardhi** "make a hawthorn into a grapevine" to depict something bad to be good

◦ **<> bë·**n **namin** *(Colloq)* to unleash a tirade on <> for a minor transgression: tear into <> over nothing

◦ **bë·**n **namin** *(Colloq)* to do much more than could possibly be expected

◦ [] **bë·**n **natë** to make [] dark as night

◦ **e bë·**n **natën ditë** to work day and night

◦ **<> bë·**n **nder *1** to honor <> **2** to do <> a favor

◦ **<> bë·**n **(një) nder** to do <> a favor

◦ **bë·**n **nder me** [] to make a present of [], offer [] as gift

◦ **bë·**n **ndryshime** to make changes/modifications

◦ **bë·**n **nevojën** *(Euph)* to defecate

◦ **bë·**n **në katër liq** *(Colloq)* **1** to have the freedom to do as one chooses **2** to be capable of carrying things through

◦ **<>**[] **bë·**n **në ngarkim** to charge <> for (the damage to) []

◦ [] **bë·**n **në sedije** *(Colloq)* to ignore []

◦ **bë·**n **në vend-numëro** to make no progress: spin one's wheels

◦ **s'**[] **bën (më) nëna** "mothers will not make another []" []'s like will never be seen again: [] is wonderful

◦ **Bëmë nënë, të të ngjaj/përngjaj!** "Make me, mother, so I will be like you!" (said when a child is just like its fmother) His mother's spitting image!

◦ [] **bë·**n **nga halli jo nga malli** to do [] out of necessity and not by choice

◦ **bë·**n^{3sg} **ngrohtë** (of weather/climate) to be warm

◦ **bë·**n **nijet** to have in mind (to do something)

◦ **bë·**n **not** to swim

○ [] **bë·*n* nuse me tel** "make [] into a new bride (with her metal adornments)" *(Impol)* to make [] behave properly; tame []

○ **bë·*n* një dush** to take a shower (bath)

○ **bë·*n* një gjilpërë** to make an injection

○ [] **bë·*n* një me tokën** "make [] even with the earth" to level [] to the ground, demolish []

○ **bë·*n* një porosi** to make a request, put in an order

○ **bë·*n* një qark** to circle around, make a circular tour

○ <> **bë·*n* një rreng** to play a dirty trick on <>, do <> an ill turn

○ **bë·*n* një sy gjumë** to have a short nap

○ **bë·*n* një vesh të shurdhër e një sy qorr para** <> to act as if one does not see or hear <>, pretend not to notice <>

○ [] **bë·*n* një sy të verbër/qorr** to turn a blind eye to []

○ [] **bë·*n* një vesh *të shurdhër/shurdh*** "make a deaf ear" to pretend not to hear; be lenient

○ **bë·*n* një vrimë në qiell/ujë** to have no effect

○ **bë·*n* një vrimë në ujë** "make a hole in water" to do useless work, waste effort

○ **bë·*n* një vrimë në ujë** to do work of no value, do useless work

○ **bë·*n* një xhiro** *(Colloq)* to take a stroll

○ **bë·*n* njërën 1** to try by hook or by crook to get what one wants, try every which way to get what one wants **2** to make a noisy complaint: make a big fuss

○ [] **bë·*n* njësh me tokën** "make [] even with the earth" to level [] to the ground, demolish []

○ **bë·*n* ofsh** to make sounds of suffering

○ **bë·*n* ojna 1** to make a pretense of dislike, be coy *2* to revel

○ <>*a* **bë·*n* oroqen** *(Old)* to do as <> says

○ <>*a* **bë·*n* pa rrugë** to treat <> unfairly

○ **bë·*n* pa udhë/rrugë** to act/speak/work in disregard of accepted procedure

○ **e bë·*n* paçariz** ([]) to make a mess (of [])

○ [] **bë·*n* paçavure** to lambaste [] in strong language: cuss [] out

○ **ia bë·*n* pajë dreqit/shejtanit** "make a trousseau for the devil" to get rid of someone/something: send the devil packing

○ [] **bë·*n* palaço 1** to call [] every name in the book, cuss [] up and down **2** to make [] a laughingstock

○ [] **bë·*n* palë** to press [] flat

○ [] **bë·*n* pallamar** to drag [] out needlessly, go too slowly with []

○ **bë·*n* pallë** to have a rollicking good time, waste time having fun

○ [] **bë·*n* pambuk** to beat [] to a pulp, beat [] up badly

○ **bë·*n* paraqitje** to make a presentation

○ **bë·*n* pas** <> to be devoted to <>

○ [] **bë·*n* pas vetes** to win [] over

○ [] **bë·*n* pasqyrë** to make [] sparkle like a mirror

○ [] **bë·*n* patështinë** to squash [] completely; beat [] to a bloody pulp

○ **bë·*n* pazar 1** to engage in bargaining in the market: bargain, haggle **2** to shop

○ **bë·*n* pazarin** to do one's shopping

○ **bë·*n* pazarllëqe 1** to haggle/bargain **2** to engage in dirty business

○ <>*a* **bë·*n* pe** "make thread of <>" to teach <> a good lesson

○ [] **bë·*n* pelte** to beat [] to a pulp

○ **e bë·*n* perin tra** "make a roof beam out of a hair" to make a mountain out of a molehill

○ **nuk bë·*n* pesë para** "not worth five farthings" not be worth a nickel

○ [] **bë·*n* pestil** to beat [] to a pulp

○ [] **bë·*n* peshk** *(Crude)* to beat [] to a pulp

○ [] **bë·*n* petë** to press [] flat; flatten [] out

○ **i bë·*n* petullat me ujë** "make pancakes out of water" to be unrealistic in one's thinking, build castles in the air; make unrealistic promises

○ **i bë·*n* petullat pa vaj** "make pancakes without oil" to be unrealistic in one's thinking, build castles in the air; make unrealistic promises

○ [] **bë·*n* për asgjë** to treat [] like dirt

○ **s'**[] **bë·*n* për burrë** to have no respect for []

○ [] **bë·*n* për dyshek** to beat [] to a pulp

○ **s'**[] **bë·*n* për fjalë** not talk about [], be close-mouthed about []

○ [] **bë·*n* për lemzë** to beat [] up badly, beat [] to a pulp

○ [] **bë·*n* për lesë** to beat [] to a pulp, beat [] to within an inch of []'s life

○ [] **bë·*n* për merak** to do/make [] to perfection, do [] beautifully

○ [] **bë·*n* për një lek** to lambaste [] in strong terms: blast []

○ **s'<>** **bë·*n* për osh** *(Colloq)* to ignore <>, disregard <>

○ [] **bë·*n* për pesë para** to make [] look like two cents by cussing [] out in public

○ [] **bë·*n* për shkalc** to beat the living daylights out of [], beat the stuffing out of []

○ [] **bë·*n* për turp** to cast shame on []; shame []

○ [] **bë·*n* për ujë *me kripë/të kripur*** "make [] ready for salt water" to give [] a severe beating

○ [] **bë·*n* për ujë në zemër 1** to scare [] to death **2** to make [] feel terrible by severe criticism: rake [] over the coals

○ [] **bë·*n* për ujë të ftohtë** "make [] ready for cold water" to give [] a severe tongue-lashing; give [] a severe beating

○ [] **bë·*n* për vaj e për uthull** "make [] ready for oil and vinegar" **1** to beat [] to a pulp **2** to give [] a thorough tongue-lashing

○ [] **bë·*n* për vete** to win []'s heart, gain []'s favor; win [] over, win [] over to one's side

○ [] **bë·*n* për vig** "make [] ready for the bier/stretcher" to beat [] to a pulp, beat [] to within an inch of []'s life

○ **bë·*n* përpara** to make progress, get somewhere

○ **bë·*n* përpjekje** to make attempts, try

○ **bë·*n* përpjetë** to grow bigger and better, make good progress

○ **bë·*n* përshesh** to make a mess of []

○ [] **bë·*n* pistil** <[] **bë·*n* pestil** to beat [] to a pulp

○ <>*a* **bë·*n* pishë** to show oneself to be better than <> (in ability)

○ **bë·*n* pjesë** to be a member/participant; be a part/constituent

○ **bë·*n* plaçkë (të madhe) 1** to amass (a lot of) material objects **2** *(Colloq)* to loot/plunder/pillage (heavily)

○ [] **bë·*n* pleh** to beat [] to a pulp

○ **bë·*n* pleqëri 1** to spend one's old age {*adverbial/adjectival complement*}; spend one's old age as a {*nominal complement*} **2** *(Old)* to hold a council of elders

○ **bë·*n* pleqësi** to give careful consideration to a matter

○ **e bë·*n* pleshtin buall/ka** "make the flea/fly into a buffalo/ox" to make a mountain out of a molehill

∘ [] **bë·**n **porotë** to expose [] to public shame

∘ [] **bë·**n **postek** to flay []; flog []

∘ **bë·**n **poshtë** to take a downward direction: descend, go down

∘ **bë·**n **prapa** to back up/away/back off; move backward

∘ **bë·**n **prapë** to be/act naughty

∘ [] **bë·**n **prapë** to dissuade []

∘ [] **bë·**n **pre** to cause devastation on [the enemy]

∘ **bë·**n **prenë** to create havoc, cause devastation

∘ **bë·**n **presion** to bring pressure to bear, bear down

∘ e **bë·**n **priftin me barrë** (Joke) to make up something totally unreal and impossible

∘ [] **bë·**n **problem** to make a lot of trouble about []

∘ **bë·**n **provim** to take a test

∘ **<>a bë·**n **puc** to put <> under strict discipline

∘ [] **bë·**n **pulë** to make [] behave; put [] down, squelch []

∘ **bë·**n **punë** to be useful

∘ **<> bë·**n **punë të madhe//shumë punë** to be of great help to <>

∘ **<>a bë·**n **pus** to depict <> as utterly dismal

∘ [] **bë·**n **pus** to ruin []

∘ **<> bë·**n **pusi** to lie in wait/ambush for <>

∘ **bë·**n **pushkë me** [] to have a gun battle with []; have a fight with []

∘ **bë·**n **qejf** to have fun, have a good time, enjoy oneself

∘ **<> bë·**n **qejfin** to do as <> wants; agree with whatever <> says

∘ **<>a bë·**n **qejfin** to do as <> wants; agree with whatever <> says

∘ **bë·**n **qejfin e <vet>** to do as one likes

∘ **s'e bë·**n **qejfin qeder** not give a damn, couldn't care less

∘ [] **bë·**n **qepaze** to humiliate []; cover with shame

∘ [] **bë·**n **që të mos tund·***et* **nga vendi** to beat [] till [] *cannot* move

∘ e **bë·**n **qimen tra** "make a roof beam out of a hair" to make a mountain out of a molehill

∘ **bë·**n **qitje** to fire at targets

∘ [] **bë·**n **qorr** "treat [] as blind" (Pej) to try to put something over on []

∘ **<> bë·**n **radhë** to give way to <>, let <> go first; let [] have []'s way

∘ **bë·**n **rehat** to sleep well; rest easy

∘ **bë·**n **rezistencë** to put up resistence: resist

∘ **bë·**n **rojë** to stand guard, be on guard

∘ [] **bë·**n **rrafsh (me tokën)** to level [] to the ground

∘ [] **bë·**n **rreckë** to lambaste [] in strong language: cuss [] out

∘ [] **bë·**n **rregzinë** to rake [] over the coals, cuss [] out

∘ **<> bë·**n **rrethin 1** to encircle; surround **2** to hit on the way to put the screws to ruin <>

∘ **<>a bë·**n **rrethin** to find the way to get to <someone>

∘ **i bë·**n **rrëke shtëpisë së vjet** "make the flood its own home" to keep evil away from one's door; take precautions to protect oneself against a disaster

∘ **<>a bë·**n **rricë** to teach <> a (good) lesson, administer discipline to <>

∘ [] **bë·**n **rrip daullje** to let [] go to ruin; leave [] destitute

∘ **<> bë·**n **rrugë** to give way to <>, step aside for <>, step out of the way of <>

∘ **bë·**n **rrugë me** [] to travel by []

∘ **bë·**n **rrugë** to make [] into an (annoying) habit

∘ [] **bë·**n **rrush e prush** "turn [] into grapes and embers" to do a sloppy job with []

∘ **<>a bë·**n **samarin copë** "break <>'s packsaddle into pieces" **1** to beat <> badly, thoroughly defeat <> **2** to scold <> severely

∘ [] **bë·**n **sefte 1** to start [] **2** to have one's first taste of []

∘ **bë·**n **sehir 1** to look around just to pass the time, watch idly **2** (Pej) to look on without helping or taking part, sit comfortably on the sidelines **3** (Reg) to be very surprised

∘ **bë·**n **si bebe** to act like a baby

∘ **bë·**n **si bë·**n to manage somehow

∘ **bë·**n **si pula kur i vjen veza** "act like the hen about to lay an egg" to be very restive, keep moving around from place to place

∘ **bë·**n **si zorra/veza në prush** "act like an intestine/egg on a bed of hot coals" to be very uneasy, have ants in one's pants, be very antsy

∘ **bë·**n **sikur __** to act as if __, pretend

∘ **bë·**n **sipas kokës** to do as one likes

∘ [] **bë·**n **skllop** to make [] into a soft mush

∘ [] **bë·**n **stavë** to place [] in a stack: stack []

∘ [] **bë·**n **sukull 1** to have [] eating out of one's hand **2** to lambaste [] in strong language: cuss [] out

∘ [] **bë·**n **sus** to quiet [] down, make [] behave

∘ [] **bë·**n **syrgjyn** to send [] into exile

∘ **<> bë·**n^{3sg} **syri rehat** <> experiences deep pleasure, <> *is* greatly pleased

∘ **bë·**n **syrin gjyveç** to be watchful

∘ **<> bë·**n^{3pl} **sytë agull** <>'s eyes get misty

∘ **i bë·**n **sytë katër** to watch carefully/attentively; stay alert

∘ **<> bë·**n^{3pl} **sytë shkëndija/çika/xixa** "<>'s eyes make sparks of light" (when <> is hit in the head <>'s vision goes dark) <> *sees* stars

∘ **<> bë·**n^{3pl} **sytë tre e tre** "<>'s eyes *make* three and three" <>'s eyes are playing tricks on <>, <> is not seeing things clearly

∘ **<>i bë·**n **sytë vet***e***timë** "make <>'s eyes like lightning" to make <> see stars (by smacking <> hard in the face)

∘ **bë·**n **shaka** to be kidding/joking

∘ **bë·**n **shaka me** [] to be kidding [], kid []

∘ **bë·**n **shamatë për** [] to object loudly to [], make a big fuss about []

∘ **nuk <> bë·**n **shamatë** not raise a hue and cry against <>

∘ [} **bë·**n **shamatë** to make a big fuss about []·

∘ **bë·**n **shëtitje** to go for a stroll

∘ **bë·**n **shiun e diellin** "make the rain and the sun" to do as one likes without consulting anyone

∘ [] **bë·**n **shkrumb e hi** to reduce [] to ashes, destroy [] utterly

∘ **bë·**n **shkumë** to foam

∘ [] **bë·**n **shoshë** to fill [] full of holes

∘ **<>a bë·**n **shpinën më të butë se barkun** "make <>'s back as soft as <>'s belly" to beat <> to a pulp

∘ **<> bë·**n^{3sg} **shpirti rehat** <> experiences deep pleasure, <> *is* greatly pleased

∘ **<>a bë·**n **shpirtin derr** to exasperate <>

∘ **<> bë·**n **shteg** to open a path for <>

∘ **bë·**n **shtëpi në mes të udhës** to be very capable, be extremely able

∘ [] **bë·**n **shtupë enësh** "treat [] like a washrag for pots" to treat [] like a dog

○ **bë·**n **shyqyr** *(Colloq)* to have a good time, have a ball

○ [] **bë·**n **tabelë qitjeje** *(Book)* to make [] a target of criticism

○ **bë·**n **tamah** to be greedy

○ **<>**i **bë·**n **tarbë** to take all <>'s [money]: break <>, clean <> out

○ [] **bë·**n **tarbë** to make [] behave properly; tame []

○ [] **bë·**n **tepsi** to make [] flat, level [] out

○ **<>**a **bë·**n **tetë me dy** *(Crude)* to teach <> a good lesson, make <> toe the mark

○ **bë·**n **tijën 1** to do his best **2** to do his duty, do what is expected of him **3** to act on his own without regard to others, be headstrong **4** to make [] his own

○ **bë·**n **tuajën 1** to do your best **2** to do your duty, do what is expected of you **3** to act on your own without regard to others, be headstrong **4** to make [] your own

○ **bë·**n **tyren 1** to do their best **2** to do their duty, do what is expected of them **3** to act on their own without regard to others, be headstrong **4** to make [] their own

○ **<> bë·**n **të fala** to give regards to <>!

○ [] **bë·**n **të ha· bar** to administer a humiliating to [], make [] say uncle

○ [] **bë·**n **të kërce·**n^{subj}**/lua·**n^{subj}**/hedh·**^{subj} **valle në tepsi** "make [] dance on a baking tray" to make [] dance to one's tune, make [] eat dirt, make [] knuckle under

○ [] **bë·**n **të madhe** to make a big thing of []; make [] sound big

○ **bë·**n **të mundshmen e të pamundshmen** to do absolutely everything possible

○ **bë·**n **të pamundurën** to do one's utmost

○ [] **bë·**n **të përmjerr·**^{subj}**/vjell·**^{subj} **gjak** "make [] piss blood" *(Crude)* to make [the bastard] suffer; get one's revenge against [the bastard]

○ **s'<>**a **bë·**n **të gjatë** not show leniency to <>, not be patient with <>

○ **s'e bë·**n **të gjatë** to act quickly, not take long

○ **bë·**n **të sajën 1** to do her best **2** to do her duty, do what is expected of her **3** to act on her own without regard to others, be headstrong **4** to make [] her own

○ **bë·**n^{3sg} **të sajën** to run its course

○ [] **bë·**n **të skuq·**et to make [] blush with shame

○ **e bë·**n **të bardhën të zezë** "make white black" to make a misrepresentation, distort the truth

○ **bë·**n **të** {*verb*^{subj}} to begin/start to {}

○ **bë·**n **të vetën 1** to do all one can, do one's best **2** to act on one's own without regard to others, be headstrong **3** to make [] one's own

○ **bë·**n **tënden 1** to do your best **2** to do your duty, do what is expected of you **3** to act on your own without regard to others, be headstrong **4** to make [] your own

○ [] **bë·**n **tërkuzë** to drag [] out needlessly, go too slowly with []

○ **e bë·**n **tërkuzë** to talk interminably, go on and on

○ **bë·**n **timen 1** to do my best **2** to do my duty, do what is expected of me **3** to act on my own without regard to others, be headstrong **4** to make [] my's own

○ [] **bë·**n **tjegull** "make [] into roof tile" to dry [] out too much; overbake [], bake [] too hard

○ **bë·**n **tobe** to repent and promise not to do it again

○ **bë·**n **toka** to shake hands

○ **bë·**n **tonën 1** to do our best **2** to do our duty, do what is expected of us **3** to act on our own without regard to others, be headstrong **4** to make [] our own

○ **bë·**n **trashë** to have a plentiful yield

○ **<>**a **bë·**n **trutë sallatë** to confuse <> thoroughly

○ **bë·**n **tufan** to wreak havoc

○ [] **bë·**n **tul** to beat [] to a pulp

○ **<>**[] **bë·**n **turinjtë përshesh** to smash <> in the face, break/bloody <>'s nose

○ **<>**i **bë·**n **turinjtë plloçë** *(Crude)* to smash <>'s nose/face in

○ [] **bë·**n **turshi** to pickle []

○ [] **bë·**n **tym e flakë** "make [] smoke and flame" to burn [] up: turn [] to ashes, utterly destroy []

○ [] **bë·**n **tym** to spend [] wastefully: spend [money] like water, throw [one's money] away

○ [] **bë·**n **thela-thela** to slice [] up

○ [] **bë·**n **thepla** to splinter/fragment []

○ **<> bë·**n **thirravajë** to bring a legal complaint against <>

○ **<> bë·**n **thirrje ndërgjegjes/arsyes** to appeal to <>'s conscience/reason

○ **nuk <> bë·**n^{3sg} **udha shteg** "<>'s road *does* not become a path" <> *cannot* manage to get underway, <> *is* prevented from getting started

○ **nuk bë·**n **udhë** not make a start; not make a move to leave

○ [] **bë·**n **udhë** to make [] into an (annoying) habit

○ **<>**[] **bë·**n **udhën burg** to fail to provide any guidance for []

○ **bë·**n **ugar** to bring a fallow field back into cultivation

○ [] **bë·**n **ugar** to make sure that [] is done right, arrange [] properly

○ [] **bë·**n **ujem** to lead [] into confusion, confuse []

○ **bë·**n **ujët** *(Colloq)* to make water, urinate

○ **e bë·**n **ujin mullar** "make (sea)water into dunes (of salt)" to pile salt (that has been evaporated from sea water) into dunes

○ **bë·**n **ujkun bari** "make the wolf a shepherd" to put the fox to guard the chickencoop

○ **bë·**n **urdhër** *(Colloq)* to give an order, give orders

○ [] **bë·**n **urdhër** *(Colloq)* to take [] as an order

○ **bë·**n **vaj** "make a lament" to make a complaint, complain

○ **bë·**n^{3sg} **vaki** *(Colloq)* to happen

○ [] **bë·**n **valë** to make [] nice and warm; make [] too hot

○ **bë·**n **valixhet** to pack one's bags

○ **bë·**n **valle** to assemble a group of people in one place

○ **bë·**n **vapën** to rest in the shade during hot weather

○ **e bë·**n **vdekjen si të lindë** "treat death as if it were birth" to be utterly fearless, have no fear of death

○ **bë·**n **vegshin e s'i vë· vjegën/vegjën.** "{} *makes* the pot and *does* not put the handle on it." {} *leaves* a task not quite finished.

○ **bë·**n **vek** to weave (at a loom)

○ **<> bë·**n **vend** to make room for <>

○ **bë·**n **vend** to become firmly established, get entrenched

○ **bë·**n **vend në zemrën e <>** *(Elev)* to earn/win a place in <>'s heart

○ **<>**[] **bë·**n^{3sg} **verë (me gojë)** "{} *makes* [] summer for <> (by talking)" {} *paints* a rosy picture of [] for <>, {} *lures* <> with a false description of []

∘ **i bë**·*n* **vesh bigë** *(Impol)* to prick up one's ears, pay close attention

∘ **<> bë**·*n*[3pl] **veshët** <>'s ears *are playing* tricks on <>: <> *is hearing* things (that aren't there)

∘ **i bë**·*n* **veshët katër** to listen (in) attentively; keep one's ears wide open, listen for the slightest sound

∘ **i bë**·*n* **veshët pipëz/bigë/curr/çift/gërshërë/katër** to listen attentively: listen with all ears, be all ears

∘ **bë**·*n* **veshin të shurdhër//shurdh** "make one's ear deaf" to pretend not to hear; turn a deaf ear

∘ **s'e bë**·*n* **veten** not to give public expression to one's ideas or feelings, be reticent

∘ **e bë**·*n* **vezën deve** to make a mountain out of a molehill

∘ [] **bë**·*n* **vëng** to put [] on a tight tether, rein [] in, make [] toe the line

∘ [] **bë**·*n* **vërzomë** to make a mess of []

∘ **bë**·*n* **vrasje** to commit murder

∘ **bë**·*n* **vrima në shoshë** to do work of no value, do useless work

∘ **bë**·*n* **xing** to pick up the card discarded by one's opponent

∘ [] **bë**·*n* **xhan** *(Child)* to kiss and fondle []: love [] up, make nice to []

∘ **bë**·*n*[3sg] **xhiro makina** the (vehicle's) wheels *are* spinning

∘ **<> bë**·*n* **xhumbë në grykë/bark** "become a lump in <>'s throat/belly" to get a knot/lump in <>'s throat

∘ **bë**·*n* **yrysh mbi** [] to make an assault on [], attack []

∘ [] **bë**·*n* **zabun** *(Colloq)* to defeat [], prostrate []: lay [] low

∘ [] **bë**·*n* **zap 1** to teach <> a (good) lesson, administer discipline to <> **2** to get [] under control, keep [] under restraint: curb **3** to break []'s will (to resist): break []

∘ **bë**·*n* **zarar** to cause harm, do damage

∘ **<>a bë**·*n* **zavë** to tighten the reins

∘ **nuk <> bë**·*n*[3sg] **zemra lak** <>'s heart *does* not waver, <> *is* undaunted

∘ **bë**·*n* **zemrën e botës** to (suffer a mishap and so) give pleasure to people who have resented one's success: gladden people's spiteful hearts

∘ **e bë**·*n* **zemrën gur** to put aside one's feelings, harden one's heart

∘ **<>a bë**·*n* **zemrën mal (e bjeshkë)** "make <>'s heart big as the mountains" to swell <>'s heart (with delight/pride): gladden <>'s heart

∘ **<>a bë**·*n* **zemrën thëngjill** to grieve <> deeply

∘ **<>a bë**·*n* **zemrën ujë 1** to move <> to tears, touch <>'s heart deeply **2** to turn <>'s blood cold

∘ **<> bë**·*n* **zë 1** to cry out to <>, call to <>, yell at <> **2** to tell <> in a loud voice, tell <>, let <> know

∘ **nuk bë**·*n* **zë 1** not say anything **2** not make a sound

∘ **bë**·*n* **zustra** to do as one likes

∘ **bë**·*n* **zhegun** to rest in the shade during hot weather; take a siesta during the heat of the day

∘ [] **bë**·*n* **zhele** to humiliate [] by cussing [] out in public

∘ [] **bë**·*n* **zhubël 1** to humiliate [] by cussing [] out in public **2** to beat [] badly (in a game): demolish []

***bëça'kë** *nf* = biça'k

bëçi'të *nf(Reg)* pool springing out of the ground

***bëga'të** *adj (i)* = bega'tshëm

***bëha'rna** *np* = beha'rna

***bëha's** *stem for 1st sg pres, pl pres, 2nd & 3rd sg subj, pind* <bëha't·

***bëha't·** *vt* to amaze, stupefy

bë'j *1st sg pres, sg imper* <bë·n

∘ **Bëju fshesë shtëpisë sate!** *(Prov)* Clean up your own house (before you criticize others)!

∘ **Bëje vrapin sa ke hapin!** "Make your speed match your stride!" *(Prov)* Adjust your wants in accordance with your abilities!

∘ **Bëje zap gjuhën!** Hold your tongue! Watch what you say!

***bëjkë** *nf* = bejkë

***bë'jt** *stem for pdef, opt, adm, part, vp* <bë·n *(Old)*

bëlta'cë *nf* **1** *(Reg)* = bëltajë **2** sediment layer that forms in stagnant vinegar

bëlta'jë *nf* the inner pulp of a melon or squash

***bëlto'·n** *vt* to plant

bëltu'c· *vt* to squeeze [] to a pulp

bëltu'c·et *vpr* to get soft or mushy from the application of pressure

bëlldu'm *onomat (Colloq)* kerplash! splash!

bëlldu'm· *vi* to fall with a splash; come suddenly and unexpectedly

bëlldu'ngë *nf* bump on the forehead

bëmë *nf* deed; distinguished action

***bën**·*et vpr* <bë·*n* *(Reg Tosk)* = bë·*het*

bë'r *stem for sg pdef, part* <bë·*n*

***bërba(n)** *nm* = brumbu'll

***bërbëli's** *stem for 1st sg pres, pl pres, 2nd & 3rd sg subj, pind* <bërbëli't·

bërbëli't· *vt* to pronounce [] softly and indistinctly; stammer, stutter; mutter, murmur

bërbëli'tje *nf* **1** words pronounced indistinctly, muttering **2** stammering, stuttering

bërbje'k *nm (Reg)* **1** melon that remains small and unripe **2** *(Fig)* underaged child, juvenile

bërca'k *nm* small/young fish, fry

bërca'n *nm* big olive with little oil

bërce'k *nm* male bee; drone

bërce'l *nm [Bot]* einkorn, a hardy variety of wheat *(Triticum monococcum)*

bërçi'k *nm* span between the stretched thumb and forefinger

bërçu'k *nm* **1** ear of corn that remains small; corncob **2** *(Fig)* dwarf

***bërda'këll** *nf (Reg)* = bërdo'kull

bërdale'c *nm (Reg)* syphilis = sifili'z

***bërda'll** *nm [Bot]* purslane *(Portulaca oleracea)*

***bërda's** *stem for 1st sg pres, 1st & 3rd pl pres, 2nd & 3rd sg subj* <bërde't·

***bërde't·** *vt* = bërte't·

bërdi'lë *nf [Text]* upper or lower bar of the beater frame on a loom

***bërdi's** *stem for 2nd pl pres, pind* <bërde't·

***bërdi't** *stem for pdef, opt, adm, part, pind, 2nd pl pres, imper, vp* <bërde't·

bërdo'kull *nf* **1** bump, lump **2** *(Fig)* prattle, chatter, nonsense, gossip

***bërdye'll** *nm* **1** pivot, swivel, hinge **2** = bërdi'lë

bërdha'c *nm (Euph)* louse

***bërdha'më** *adj* pale, yellowish

***bërdhëlle'më** *adj* = bardhe'më

bë·rë
I § *part* <**bë·**n
II § *adj (i)* **1** ripe, finished, done, made **2** *(Colloq)* crafted; artificial, synthetic; ready-made
III § *nf (e)* **1** product, result **2** heroic act, deed
IV § *nn (të)* **1** fact, action **2** *(Reg)* yogurt starter
○ **ёs̄·h·të bёrё për pushkё 1** to be old enough for a gun, old enough to fight **2** to deserve to be killed

bё·rёs *nm (Old)* doer, maker, author, creator

Bё·rёtё *nn (të) (Old)* Genesis

bёrha·pё *nf* [*Bot*] dogtooth violet, Ravenna-grass (*Erianthus ravennae*)

bёrho·z *nm* chaff from hay

bёrhu·kё *nf* **1** [*Bot*] wild dill, fennel **2** thin, dry twig

bё·rje *nf ger* <**bё·**n, **bё·**het

*bёrki *nf* sorb apple = **va·dh**ё

*bёrko·q *nm* suckling pig, piglet

bёrlu·t *vt* to crush into rubble

bёrlu·të *nf* = **bёrllo·k**

bёrly·k·et *vpr* to wallow on the ground and bellow (said of big livestock)

bёrllo·k
I § *nm* small and worthless debris: chaff; dust; rubbish
II § *adj (Pej)* dirty; worthless

Bё·rno *nf* Brno

bёrnja·k *adj* youngling under 6 months; suckling (lamb or kid)

bёrsi· *nf* residual mash: marc, pomace; dregs, lees
○ **bёrsi e butё** mash from which all the oil is not yet extracted
○ **bёrsi e egёr** second squeezings, mash squeezed for the second time
○ **bёrsi pambuku** residue from making cottonseed oil, cottonseed mash (fed to livestock)

bёrsi··n *vt* to crush, mash

*bёrsko·t *nm* speck, fragment

*bёrshaj *nm* *(Old)* vagabondage

*bёrsha·n *nf* gun of the type made in Brescia

*bёrshe·(n) *nm* [*Bot*] = **bёrshe·n**

bёrshe·n *nm* [*Bot*] English yew *(Taxus baccata)*

bёrshi·m *nm* = **ibёrshi·m**

*bёrsho·të *nf* unsociable, aloof, stiff

*bёrta·jё *nf* *(Reg Gheg)* call for help, distress call

bёrta·s *stem for 1st sg pres, 1st & 3rd pl pres, 2nd & 3rd sg subj* <**bёrte·**t·

bёrte·t· *vi* **1** to call out loudly: yell, shout **2** to yell at [ ]; scold **3** *(Pej)* to make a lot of noise in order to attract attention: make a big hullabaloo **4** *(Pej)* to whimper, whine
○ **bёrte·t· me njё zё** to cry/call out in unison, yell simultaneously
○ **bёrte·t· me sa ka· nё kokё** to bellow/yell with all one's might, cry out at the top of one's
○ **bёrte·t· nё kupё tё qiellit** "yell to the dome of the sky" to yell at the top of one's voice; cry out to the high heavens
○ **bёrte·t· nё tё gjitha udhёkryqet** to make a hullabaloo so that the whole world knows about it; let the whole world in on it

*bёrti·mё *nf* = **bri·tm**ё

bёrti·s *stem for 2nd pl pres, pind* <**bёrte·**t·

bёrti·t *stem for 2nd pl pres, imper, vp* <**bёrte·**t·

bёrti·tёs *n* shouter, crier

bёrti·tje *nf ger* **1** <**bёrte·**t· **2** yell, cry **3** shouted insult, lambasting

bёrti·tur *nf (e)* **1** yell, cry **2** shouted insult, lambasting

bёrtha·më *nf* fruit pit, stone, kernel, seed; nucleus, core

bёrtha·mёz *nf* [*Biol*] nucleole

bёrtha·mje
I § *nf* [*Bot*] drupe
II § *adj* [*Bot*] drupaceous

bёrtha·mo·r *adj* **1** related to the atomic nucleus or to the energy released from it: nuclear **2** [*Bot*] having a pit or stone **3** [*Biol*] pertaining to the cell nucleus

bёrtha·mo·re *np* [*Bot*] drupaceous trees

bёrtha·nёz *np* [*Bot*] = **thanu·k**ё

bёrtho·kёl *np* **1** fruit pit **2** [*Bot*] fruit with a big pit **3** *(Reg)* [*Bot*] squill, sea onion *(Scilla maritima)* **4** *(Reg)* = **bersi·B**

bёrtho·kёlo·r *adj* [*Bot*] having fruit with pits

*bёrthu·c *nm* *(Pet)* little boy: laddie

bёrxo·llё *nf* = **bёrzo·ll**ё

bёrxhi·k *nm* measure equal to the distance from the tip of the index finger to the tip of the spread thumb

*bёrxho·llё *nf* = **bёrzo·ll**ё

bёrxhy·ke *np* door staples through which a padlock is attached

bёrza·nё *nf* *(Reg)* female animal that has just been pregnant; female animal that gets pregnant or gives birth quickly

bёrzo·llё *nf* [*Food*] cut of meat containing a bone: (veal or pork) cutlet, (lamb or mutton) chop; grilled meat

bёrr *onomat* sound of shivering (as from cold): brr!

bё·rra·kё *nf* pond; marsh

bё·rra·ko·re *nf* wetlands; marshland

bё·rro·re *nf (Reg)* packsaddle

bё·rru·c *nm* men's wool cloak, usually black and covered with long tassels

bёrry·l *nm* **1** elbow; elbow joint **2** sharp turn/bend
○ **bёrryl hekuri** iron bracket
○ **bёrryl me bёrryl** elbow to elbow, shoulder to shoulder
○ **bёrryl sobe** elbow joint in a stovepipe
○ **bёrryl stufe** elbow joint in a stovepipe

bёrry·lak *nm* bend in the road, bend in the river

bёrry·la·s *adv* alongside, beside

bё·shё·m *adj (i)* **1** robust, hale **2** plump, full-bodied **3** productive, fertile (of land)

bёshnja·k·et *vpr (Reg)* to become very weak or sickly

bёshta·jё *nf* copse of slender oak

bёshti·nё *nf* flock of sheep or goats without a shepherd

*bёshty· = **pёshty·**

bёta·jё *nf (Reg)* **1** dread, terror **2** row, din, commotion **3** *(Euph)* epilepsy

*bёte·re *nf* ill-timed jest

bёti·kё *nf (Reg)* skin bag

bёz *nm* **1** dune **2** large clod of earth **3** clump of marshgrass or thick weeds in a swamp; islet in a swamp

bёza··n *vi* **1** to scream, call out; call, call to, speak to **2* to ejaculate

bёza·jt *stem for pdef, part, opt, adm* <**bёza··**n

bёzbё·ze *nf* whispering in one's ear, whispering; gossip, rumor, hearsay

bëzz *onomat* sound of buzzing

bëzhdílë *nf* **1** sweepings; dust, rubbish **2** small splinter **3** weeds (particularly in planted fields)

b.f. *abbrev* <**bie fjalë** for instance, for example *e. g.*

BFSSh *abbrev* <**Bashkimi i Fizkulturistëve dhe i Sportistëve të Shqipërisë** Union for Physical Culture and Sports

BGASh *abbrev* <**Bashkimi i Grave Antifashiste Shqiptare** [*Hist*] Union of Anti-fascist Albanian Women

BGSh *abbrev* **1** Union of Women of Albania <**Bashkimi i Grave të Shqipërisë 2** Union of Journalists of Albania <**Bashkimi i Gazetarëve të Shqipërisë**

BGT *abbrev* <**Baza grosiste e tregëtisë** wholesale storehouse

*****bíe₁·** *het vp* <**bíe₁·**
  ◦ **s'i bihet malit me kokë** "there's no hitting one's head against the mountain" you can't fight city hall
  ◦ **s'bihet murit me kokë.** "there's no hitting one's head against the wall" *(Prov)* you can't fight city hall.

*****bi·n** *vi* = **mbi·n**

bi *stem for 2nd pl ind, imper, pind* <**bíe·**

*****bíba(n)** *nm* = **bíban**

bíban *nm* turkey, tom turkey

*****bíber** *nm* = **píper**

biberón *nm* baby bottle with nipple; rubber nipple, pacifier

bíbë *nf* **1** young waterfowl, duckling, gosling; turkey chick; turkey hen **2** *(Fig Pej)* stupid girl/woman

bíbël *nf* Bible

bíbëz *nf dimin* = **bíbë**

bibilúsh *nm* *(Child)* (child's word for penis) weenie

bibísh *nm* [*Food*] dish prepared with tomatos, rice and fried onion; a kind of pastry

bibizáne *nf* shawm-like folk instrument

bibl ík *adj* biblical

bibliofíl *nm* bibliophile

bibliográf *nm* bibliographer

bibliografí *nf* bibliography

bibliografík *adj* bibliographical

bibliotekár *n* librarian

bibliotékë *nf* library
  ◦ **bibliotekë ambulante** traveling library
  ◦ **bibliotekë e gjallë** walking library, erudite person

*****bibliothékë** = **bibliotékë**

bic
  I § *nm* **1** piglet, suckling pig, young pig **2** dog or other animal with a small body
  II § *adj* *chubby, robust
  III § *interj* * (*Old Child*) (exclamation to arouse jealousy) see what I've got!

bíce *nf* **1** indentation in the ground made by heel and defended as a goal by players in a children's game **2** *(Fig)* worn path/place: home base, comfortable niche/corner

bícë *nf* **1** mother pig: sow *2 defiance

*****bicíklëtë** = **bicíklétë**

bicúlë *nf* double flute

bicún *nm* piglet, suckling pig, young pig

biçák *nm* **1** pocketknife, penknife, jackknife **2** [*Invert*] curved variety of razor shell mollusk *(Ensis ensis)*

*****bíçës**
  I § *n* *(Reg Tosk)* settled gypsy

II § *adj* *(Reg Tosk)* of or characteristic of settled gypsies

biçikletár *n* bicycle repairman

biçikletarí *nf* bicycle repair shop

biçíkletë *nf* bicycle

biçím *nm (Crude)* **1** sort, similar sort **2** face; appearance **3** *(Pej)* bad sort

bíçki *nf* leatherworker's knife with a curved blade

bidákthi *adv*

*****bidát** *nm* novelty, innovation

bidón *nm* large metal or plastic can with lid and handle, used to carry liquids (water, milk, oil)

bíe₁· *vi* **1** to fall; fall down/off/away **2** to drop; sink **3** to diminish: lose force, abate, weaken, soften; decrease, lessen **4** to land up **5** to fall victim **6** to move in for the night, stay overnight **7** to strike (<>); strike (<>) suddenly, hit <>; descend with force (on <>); knock on <> **8** to come down hard on <>: reprimand <>, scold <> **9** to cause <>to vibrate; play <*a musical instrument>* **10** *(Colloq)* to do something quickly <*with a tool*> **11** to happen (to <>); come about by chance **12** to happen upon <>, come upon by chance <>, run into <> **13** to get through <>, pass over, traverse **14** to fall to <>, become <*one's>* charge, be <*one's>* business **15** to tell <> outright **16** *(Colloq)* to get deeply interested in <>, be caught up in <> **17** *(Fig)* to get tired of doing something repetitiously **18** *(Fig)* to fit <>, suit <> **19** *(Fig Colloq)* to cost (dear/cheap)

  ◦ <> **bie₁·** {*kinship relation*} "fall into the classification of {} to <>" to be a {} of <> **Agimi më bie kushëri** Agim is a cousin of mine

  ◦ <*food>* **bie₁·** *(Colloq)* to start polishing off <>

  ◦ <> **bie₁· alivan** <> falls into a swoon: <> *faints*

  ◦ <> **bie₁· ashri** <> *falls lame*

  ◦ **s'i bie₁· atij krah** to pretend not to see the point

  ◦ **i bie₁· ballit me dorë** "strike one's forehead with one's hand" to display strong emotion (surprise/repentance/anger)

  ◦ **bie₁· barkas** to lie flat on the belly

  ◦ <> **bie₁·**³ˢᵍ **barku në bela** "<>'s belly falls into trouble" *(Joke)* <> *eats* a lot of good food

  ◦ <> **bie₁· bela** to become burdensome to <>

  ◦ **bie₁·**³ˢᵍ **borë** it *snows*

  ◦ **bie₁· borë me thekë** to snow in large fleecy flakes

  ◦ **bie₁· boria** the bugle/horn/whistle *sounds*

  ◦ **i bie₁· breg pas bregu** to beat around the bush

  ◦ **bie₁· brenda (me këmbët e <>)** "fall in (with one's own two feet)" **1** *(Colloq)* to land up in jail **2** to fall for it (hook, line, and sinker) **3** to fall (head over heels) in love

  ◦ **bie₁·**³ˢᵍ **breshër** it *hails*

  ◦ <> **bie₁·**³ˢᵍ **bretku 1** <> *suffers* from lumbago **2** <> *becomes* exhausted (from backbreaking work)

  ◦ <> **bie₁·**³ᵖˡ **brinjët** <> *gets* bone-weary, <> *becomes* utterly exhausted

  ◦ <> **bie₁·**³ˢᵍ **bruzi** <> *gets* offended, <> *gets* sore

  ◦ **bie₁·**³ˢᵍ **brymë** it *frosts* up, it *falls* below freezing, hoarfrost *forms*

  ◦ **bie₁· bujtës tek** {} to stay overnight as {}'s guest

  ◦ **bie₁· butë** *1 to fall softly **2** to get comfortable **3** to have it easy; find a cushy life

  ◦ **i bie₁· buzukut** "play the buzuk" *(Joke)* to spout nonsense, talk gibberish

○ <> **bie₁· copë** <>'s {} *is peeling/coming* off in pieces

○ **bie₁· copë** to give one's all, do one's utmost, work to the point of exhaustion: knock oneself out

○ **i bie₁· cyles** to speak in vain, talk to the wind

○ <> **bie₁·**^{3sg} **çehrja e vdekjes** "the pallor of death *falls* on <>" <> *gets* a death pallor on <>'s face

○ **i bie₁· çekanit** to insist forcefully; draw attention

○ **i bie₁· çokut** to speak in vain, talk to the air

○ **i bie₁· daulles në një vend** "beat the drum in the same spot" *(Pej)* to keep playing the same old tune, harp on the same old theme

○ **i bie₁· daulles së** <> *(Pej)* to be <>'s tool

○ **i bie₁· daulles** to sound the alarm

○ **bie₁·**^{3sg} **dëbora roga-roga** the snow *falls* in uneven patches

○ **bie₁· dëborë** to snow

○ **bie₁· dëshmor** to fall on the field of honor, become a martyr

○ <> **bie₁·**^{3pl} **djersë të ftohta** <> *breaks* out in a cold sweat

○ **bie₁· drapri** "the sickle falls" it *is* harvest season

○ **i bie₁· drejt** to speak directly/bluntly, not beat around the bush

○ <> **bie₁·**^{3pl} **duart në tokë** "<>'s hands fell to the ground" **1** <>'s hands are numb from cold/exhaustion **2** <> *is* exhausted from working so hard

○ <> **bie₁·**^{3pl} **dhëmbët** "<>'s teeth fell out" **1** <> got old **2** <> *is* a little long in the tooth, <> *has* been there too long

○ **bie₁·**^{3sg} **e drejta në shesh** justice *applies* equally to all

○ **bie₁·**^{3sg} **erë barut** "it *smells* of gunpowder" there *is* a smell of war/battle in the air

○ **bie₁· erë 1** to smell, give off an odor; stink **2** to be in the wind: something's up

○ **bie₁· erë myk 1** to smell musty **2** to have old-fashioned ideas

○ **bie₁· fashë** to calm down, quiet down, come to a rest, pause

○ **bie fjala** for instance, for example, let's say, such as

○ **bie₁·**^{3sg} **fjala** the subject *comes* up, the topic *arises*

○ **s'<> bie₁·**^{3sg} **fjala në/për tokë** "<>'s word *does not fall* on the ground" <> *is* a person worth listening to

○ <> **a bie₁· fjalën rrotull** to speak in roundabout terms to <>, beat around the bush with <>

○ **bie₁· fjalës** to misspeak, make a slip

○ <> **bie₁·**^{3pl} **fletët 1** <>'s feathers fall off **2** *(Impol Fig)* <> *loses* <>'s former power/influence; <> *comes* down off <>'s high horse

○ **bie₁· fli** to sacrifice oneself; fall sacrifice

○ <> **bie₁·**^{3sg} **fshesa** <> *gets* laid off

○ **i bie₁· fyellit** to talk to the wall, talk in vain

○ <> **bie₁· fyellit në një vrimë** "play the flute on one hole" to keep repeating the same thing monotonously: keep harping on the same thing

○ **bie₁· gaca më vezme** "the live coal *falls* on <>'s gunpowder box" <> *is sitting* on a powder keg

○ <> **bie₁·**^{3sg} **goja** <> *talks* with no one listening; <> gets tired of saying the same thing, <> *seems* to be talking to the wall; <> *speaks* endlessly about something

○ **bie₁· goma** the tire *goes* flat

○ **i bie₁· gur më gur** to get it done at low cost

○ <> **bie₁· gurë në lug** <> has obstacles to overcome

○ <> **bie₁·**^{3pl} **gurë në lug** "rocks fall into <>'s trough" <> *encounters* impediments: problems *come* up for <>

○ **bie₁·**^{3sg} **guri në opingë** a terrible thing *happens* to <>

○ **i bie₁· gurit e drurit** to beat one's brains out

○ <> **bie₁·**^{3sg} **gurthi** *<a girl>* begins to form breasts (signalling puberty)

○ <> **bie₁·**^{3sg} **gjaku në sy/lëkurë** <> *gets* very tired

○ <> **bie₁·**^{3sg} **gjaku te këmbët/në fund të këmbëve 1** <> *gets* numb (from too much walking/standing) **2** <> *gets* terrified

○ **bie₁· gjallë e ngushtë** to be in difficult circumstances: be in a tight spot

○ <> **bie₁· gjatë** to deal with <> in a lengthy way: do <> the long way, treat <> at length

○ **i bie₁· gjoksit me grushte** "beat one's breast with one's fists" to announce one's guilt publicly, bare one's breast in public; repent vociferously

○ <> **bie₁· gjuha** "<>'s tongue *is falling*" <> *is getting* tired of saying the same thing over and over again

○ <> **bie₁· gjuha e këmborës 1** <> never *talks* any more **2** no one listens to <> any more, no one pays any attention to <> any more

○ <> **bie₁· hasha** to deny having ever said <>

○ <> **bie₁· hera** "opportunity *falls* to <>" <> *has* the chance/opportunity

○ **i bie₁· hilesë** to see through the deceit/trickery

○ <> **bie₁·**^{3sg} **hunda** *(Tease)* **1** <> *has* <>'s nose out of joint, <> *is* offended **2** <> *comes* down from <>'s high horse

○ <> **bie₁·**^{3sg} **hunda në dhé** *(Iron)* <> *gets* very angry/indignant

○ **nuk** <> **bie₁· hunda në shesh** <> *is* never at <>'s wits' end, <> *is* never totally discomfited

○ <> **bie₁·**^{3sg} **hunda përdhe** *(Iron)* <> *gets* very angry/indignant

○ <> **bie₁·**^{3sg} **i lehti** *(Colloq)* <> has an epileptic seizure

○ **bie₁· jashtë** *(Old)* to be contrary to, not agree with

○ <> **bie₁·**^{3pl} **kacabunjtë** <> *cools* off, <> *calms* down

○ **bie₁·**^{3sg} **kambana** the (big) bell *peals/rings*

○ **bie₁·**^{3sg} **kambana e vdekjes (për [ ])** "the bell of death *tolls* (for [ ])" the fatal hour *approaches* (for [ ]), the end (of [ ]) is in sight

○ **i bie₁· kambanës 1** to ring the (big) bell **2** to give the alarm

○ **i bie₁· kambanës së rrezikut** *(Book)* to sound the alarm, give warning of imminent danger

○ **i bie₁· kashtës përmbi kallinj** to be a braggart, brag, boast

○ **i bie₁· kavallit** to talk to the wall, talk in vain

○ <> **bie₁·**^{3pl} **këllqet** <>'s very bones ache (from so much exertion)

○ **i bie₁· këmbës 1** to strive in vain **2** *(Impol)* to kick the bucket: die

○ <> **bie₁·**^{3pl} **këmbët** <> *walks* <>'s feet off (looking all over for something)

∘ <> **bie₁·**^{3pl} **këmbët (copë)** "<>'s feet *fall* in pieces" <>'s feet *get worn* out; ∘ *wears* out <>'s feet searching

∘ **u bie₁· këmbëve** to run away as fast as possible, take to one's heels

∘ **bie₁· këmisha** <> *is* shocked, <>'s jaw *drops*

∘ <> **bie₁· kërbishtet** <>'s back hurts (at the waist), <> *has* lumbago

∘ <> **bie₁·**^{3pl} **kockat** to get bone tired

∘ <> **bie₁·**^{3pl} **kokës 1** to hit <> in the head **2** to criticize/rebuke <> **3** to punish <> **4** to let <> all go to waste, use <> up recklessly

∘ **i bie₁· kokës me grushta 1** to beat one's head with sorrow **2** to keep beating oneself over the head: regret deeply

∘ <> **bie₁·**^{3pl} **krahët** <> *breaks* <>'s bones working, <> *works* <>'s tail off

∘ <> **bie₁· krahëve** to coddle/mollycoddle <>

∘ <> **bie₁· kryq e tërthor** to crisscross <>, cross <> in all directions, traverse <> from one end to the other

∘ <> **bie₁·**^{3pl} **kryqet** <> *becomes* physically exhausted: <> *gets* bone tired

∘ **bie₁· kur këndojnë gjelat** to go to bed very late

∘ <> **bie₁·**^{3sg} **kurrizi** <>'s back *is breaking* from overwork

∘ **i bie₁· lapsit** to make a careful calculation

∘ <> **bie₁· legenit 1** (*Crude*) to beat one's gums for nothing; talk gibberish, blather away **2** to waste time doing something of no value: just twiddle one's thumbs

∘ **i bie₁· legenit** to be talking to the four winds

∘ <> **bie₁·**^{3pl} **letrat në ujë** "<>'s letters fall into water" no one *pays attention* to <> anymore, <> no longer *has* any influence

∘ <> **bie₁· lëkura (në punë)** to wear oneself out (working)

∘ <> **bie₁·**^{3rd} **lirë** to cost <> very little, be very cheap for <>

∘ <> **bie₁·**^{3sg} **lotaria** the lot *falls* to <>, chance has picked []

∘ <> **bie₁·**^{3sg} **luga në mjaltë** to luck into something good

∘ <> **bie₁·**^{3sg} **luga në qumësht** "<>'s spoon *falls* into milk" <> *lives* in comfort

∘ **i bie₁· maces me lugë** "hit the cat with a spoon" to be still wet behind the ears; act like a child

∘ **bie₁· mbi** [] to be located just above []

∘ <> **bie₁· me gisht të madh** "hit <> with the thumb" to do <> carelessly, do <> with the left hand

∘ <> **bie₁· me hanxhar** "hit <> with a cleaver" to do a great deal of damage to <>: damage <> badly

∘ <> **bie₁· me havan në kokë** to rebuke <> severely, reprimand <>

∘ <> **bie₁· me lugë të madhe** "start polishing off <> with a big spoon" to give <> away profligately, spend <> extravagantly

∘ **bie₁· me pulat** to go to bed with the chickens, go to bed early

∘ **i bie₁· me sëpatë** to cut the matter off without further discussion

∘ <> **bie₁· me sy** to cast an eye at <>, glance at <>

∘ **bie₁· me shpullë** to slap

∘ <> **bie₁· me shuplakë** to slap <>

∘ <> **bie₁· me top 1** (*Colloq*) to waste <> all quickly; ruin <> completely: blow <> away **2** to solve <> in an audacious way

∘ <> **bie₁· me** [] to hit <> with [ ]

∘ *i* **bie₁· me limë** to use careful thought to <what one is saying>; choose <one's words> carefully; put <the matter> delicately

∘ <> **bie₁·**^{3sg} **mekthi (në** [])** <> *becomes* utterly exhausted (from []): *gets* completely worn out (by [])

∘ **i bie₁· mendjes (prapa)** to see the error of one's ways, change for the better: reform

∘ **bie₁·**^{3sg} **mesdita** "noon *falls*" it *is* already noon

∘ **bie₁·**^{3sg} **mesnata** "midnight *falls*" it *is* already midnight

∘ <> **bie₁· më qafë 1** to be a big bother to <>, annoy <> **2** to falsely accuse <>, unfairly scold <> **3** to place a burden on <>

∘ <> **bie₁·**^{3sg} **mielli** "the flour *falls* on <>" <>'s hair *turns* silver with age

∘ <> **bie₁· mirë** to be to <>'s advantage

∘ <> **bie₁·**^{3sg} **mirë** <> *comes* out all right

∘ <> **bie₁·**^{3sg} **mishi për truall** <> *is coming* apart from terrible suffering

∘ **bie miu e thye kokën** "the mouse falls and breaks his head" the cupboard is bare

∘ **1bien miu e thyen kokën** "the mouse would fall and break its neck (because the place is so empty)" there is absolutely nothing there (to eat)

∘ **bie₁·**^{3sg} **mjegull** it gets foggy

∘ <> **bie₁· moh** to deny having ever said <>

∘ **bie₁·**^{3sg} **muhabeti** the subject has come up, (it) has been mentioned

∘ **i bie₁· muzikës** to play music

∘ <> **bie₁· ndesh** to be in conflict with <>

∘ <> **bie₁· ndër këmbë 1** to kneel (in submission/supplication) **2** to plead with <>

∘ <> **bie₁·**^{3sg} **ndër mend** it occurs to <>

∘ **bie₁· ndër pleq** to come up for consideration by the village elders

∘ <> **bie₁· ndore** (*Old*) to ask for <>'s protection; enter into <>'s good hands, come under <>'s protection

∘ **nuk bie₁· ndore** not capitulate/surrender

∘ <> **bie₁· nenit të këmbës** to strike <> at <>'s weak point: hit <> in <>'s Achilles' heel

∘ **i bie₁· në atë krah** to touch that subject, bring up that subject

∘ **bie₁· në baltë** to get into trouble

∘ **bie₁· në bark** to bow down, submit

∘ **bie₁· në batak** to get into trouble; get mixed up with some bad people, fall in with a bad lot

∘ **bie₁· në bela** (*Colloq*) to get into trouble

∘ **bie₁· në bisht** to give up, admit defeat

∘ **bie₁· në brazdë *1** to come to an agreement **2** to get back on the right track; see the light

∘ **i bie₁· në bri** to get it, grasp it thoroughly; get the point

∘ **bie₁·**^{past} **në bylyk** (*Old*) {} achieved adulthood: {} came of age, {} became a man

∘ **bie₁· në çanakun e** <> (*Pej*) **1** to make oneself right at home at <>'s place **2** to fall in with <>

∘ <> **bie₁· në dorë 1** <> *happens* to get {}, <> *comes* across {} **2** to come into <>'s power, <> has {} in <>'s power

∘ <> **bie₁· në erë 1** to get wind of <> **2** to pick up <>'s scent **3** to sense <>'s presence; sense <>

∘ **i bie₁· në fije** to make some sense of it

∘ **bie₁· në fill me** [] to come to an agreement with []

∘ <> **bie₁· në fjalë** to interrupt <>, break in on <>

∘ **bie₁· në fjalë 1** to reach agreement **2** to have a quarrel

∘ **bie₁· në gojë të qenit** to place oneself in danger

∘ **bie₁· në gojë të** [] "fall into []'s mouth" to be gossiped about by []

∘ **bie₁· në grep** to take the bait

∘ **bie₁· në grindje** to come to have an unfriendly relationship: get on bad terms

∘ **bie₁· në gjak pa gjak** to make an enemy even without actually killing anybody

∘ **bie₁· në gjumë** to fall asleep

∘ **bie₁· në gjunjë** to kneel, rest on one's knees; kneel (in submission/supplication): fall on one's knees

∘ **bie₁· në gjurmë** to pick up the scent/trail

∘ **bie₁· në hall** to fall into a predicament

∘ <> **bie₁· në hundë** <> *gets* an inkling (about {})

∘ <> **bie₁· në kokë *1** to hit <> in the head **2** to criticize/rebuke <> **3** to punish <> **4** to let <> all go to waste, use <> up recklessly **5** to make <>'s head swim **6** to entice/charm <>

∘ **bie₁· në krahët e** <> *(Pej)* to collaborate with <>

∘ **bie₁· në kundërshtim me** [] to be contrary to []

∘ **bie₁· në kurriz** "fall on one's back" to fall over laughing, die laughing

∘ **bie₁· në kuvend** to join in with the group agreement

∘ **bie₁· në llum** to get into trouble; get mixed up with some bad people, fall in with a bad lot

∘ **bie₁· në marrëveshje** to come to an agreement

∘ <> **bie₁· në mend/mendje** to come back into <>'s mind, <> *is* reminded of {}

∘ **bie₁· në mendje** to come to, come to one's senses

∘ **bie₁·**³ˢᵍ **në mendje për** [] **1** [] *is* constantly in <>'s mind, <> cannot get [] out of <>'s mind **2** <> *remembers* to think about []

∘ **bie₁· në mes dy zjarresh** "fall between two fires" to be between the devil and the deep blue sea

∘ **bie₁· në mjaltë** to get all one's needs satisfied, come into a comfortable life

∘ **bie₁· në mosmarrëveshje** to come to a disagreement

∘ **bie₁· në pazar** to come to an agreement after haggling: strike a bargain

∘ <> **bie₁·**³ˢᵍ **në pjesë** <> *suffers* a piece of bad luck

∘ **bie₁· në prush** to fall into deep trouble

∘ <> **bie₁· në qafë 1** to be a big bother to <>, annoy <>; provoke **2** to falsely accuse <>, unfairly scold <> **3** to place a burden on <>

∘ <> **bie₁· në qokë** to hit the nail on the head, hit the mark, get it just right

∘ **nuk** <> **bie₁· në sqep** <> *doesn't* have a chance of getting {}

∘ <> **bie₁· në sy** to catch <>'s attention, <> notices {}

∘ **bie₁· në sy** to stand out immediately (from the rest); catch the eye

∘ **bie₁· në sherr** to come to have an unfriendly relationship: get on bad terms

∘ **i bie₁· në teste** to get the point right away, guess it right

∘ **i bie₁· në të** to get the point right away, guess it right

∘ **bie₁· në tokë** *(Colloq)* (of a child) to be born, come out (of the womb), see the light of day

∘ <> **bie₁· në tru *1** to go to <>'s head, make <> dizzy **2** to obsess <>

∘ <> **bie₁· në tru** to stick in <>'s mind

∘ **bie₁· në thekër** to become thoroughly confused

∘ **bie₁· në thundër** (of a hoofed animal) to stumble badly and almost fall

∘ **bie₁· në ujdi (me** []) to reach agreement (with [])

∘ **bie₁· në ujdi** to come to an agreement

∘ **bie₁· në usta** to meet one's master, lose to a better opponent

∘ **nuk bie₁· në va** not come to an agreement, not reach an accord; not hit it off, not get along well

∘ **bie₁· në vesh të shurdhër** "go into a deaf ear" to fall on deaf ears

∘ **bie₁· në zi** to begin a period of mourning

∘ <*i/u*> **bie₁· nëpër të** to scan <> quickly, not go deeply into <>

∘ **bie₁· nga fiku** *(Iron)* to lose one's high position

∘ **bie₁· nga fuqia 1** to fall from power, lose power/authority **2** to lose legal force

∘ **bie₁· nga gjendje** to fall on hard times

∘ **bie₁· nga kali 1** to be unable to finish what one has started: get stuck in the middle **2** to fall from a high rank, lose one's high position

∘ **bie₁· nga pesha** to go down in weight, lose weight

∘ **bie₁· nga shiu në breshër** "fall from the rain into hail" out of the frying pan into the fire

∘ **bie₁· nga shkallët** to suffer a terrible fall: suffer a catastrophe; topple from one's high position

∘ **i bie₁· një çakallje me** [] *(Pej)* to fall in with []'s desires every time in order to curry favor with []

∘ <> **bie₁· një çember** <>'s face *goes* white, *turns* pale

∘ <> **bie₁· një hije** <> *takes* on a beautiful appearance

∘ <> **bie₁· një valë mbi kokë/krye 1** <> *is* consumed by passion; <> *is* obsessed with an idea **2** <> *is* overwhelmed by problems

∘ <> **bie₁· okoll** to go around the outside periphery of <>: go around <>

∘ **bie₁·**³ˢᵍ **ora e vdekjes (për** []) "the clock of death *strikes* (for [])" the fatal hour *approaches* (for []), the end (of []) is in sight

∘ <> **bie₁·**³ˢᵍ **ora gjithnjë dymbëdhjetë/shtatë/tetë** "<>'s clock always *strikes* twelve/seven/eight o'clock" <> is aloof and indifferent to what is going on

∘ **bie₁·**³ˢᵍ **ora për** [] the time *has come* for []

∘ <> **bie₁·**³ᵖˡ **orët** <>'s anger *abates*: <> *calms* down

∘ <> **bie₁· pas** to take care of <>, see to <>; take an interest in <>'s welfare

∘ <> **bie₁· pash më pash** to travel through <*a place*> inch by inch, cover <> from one end to another

∘ **bie₁·**³ˢᵍ **pazari** the price *falls*

∘ <> **bie₁·**³ˢᵍ **pelikori** <> *falls* into a faint

∘ <> **bie₁·**³ˢᵍ **pelikori i vdekjes** <> *takes* on the pallor of death

∘ <> **bie₁·**³ᵖˡ **pendët 1** <>'s feathers fall off **2** *(Impol Fig)* <> *loses* <>'s former power/influence; <> *comes* down off <>'s high horse

∘ **<> bie₁· për hise** to be <>'s lot, fall on <>

∘ **<> bie₁·³ˢᵍ për pjesë** to fall to <>'s lot

∘ **<> bie₁· për shtat 1** to suit/serve <> well **2** (of clothes) to fit <> well

∘ **<> bie₁· për thonjsh** <>gets numb with cold in <>'s hands/feet

∘ **<> bie₁· përpara** to take another route in order to get somewhere before <>: cut <> off (at some place)

∘ **<> bie₁· përqark** to take a tour around <>, have a look around <>

∘ **<> bie₁·³ˢᵍ pika 1** <> has a stroke **2** <> is suddenly moved (by emotion)

∘ **bie₁· pikë gjallë** to fall dead

∘ **i bie₁· pikës** to hit it exactly on the mark, get it exactly right

∘ **bie₁· plëndës** (ColloqImpolite) to fall with a thud, fall in a dead heap

∘ **i bie₁· po asaj gozhde** "hit the very same nail" to keep playing the same old tune

∘ **i bie₁·³ˢᵍ po atij avazi** (Colloq) to keep harping on <>, keep playing the same tune

∘ **i bie₁· po atij teli** to keep playing the same old tune

∘ **bie₁· poshtë 1** to lie down to sleep **2** to go down in value; get worse **3** to fall from power **4** to get depressed

∘ **i bie₁· pragut të dëgjo·ⁿ³ˢᵍˢᵘᵇʲ dera** "hit the doorsill so that the door will hear" to say something to someone with the intention that someone else will overhear it

∘ **<> bie₁· prapa 1** to look after <>, see to <> **2** to show concern for <>'s welfare; take constant care of <>; take good care of <> (as essential to one's livelihood)

∘ **bie₁· prapët** to fall on one's back

∘ **bie₁· pre** to be taken prisoner (in war)

∘ **bie₁·³ˢᵍ pula klloçkë** the hen begins sitting on a brood of eggs

∘ **i bie₁· punës prapa** to attend to one's work until it gets done

∘ **<> bie₁·³ᵖˡ puplat 1** <>'s feathers fall off **2** (Impol Fig) <> loses <>'s former power/influence; <> comes down off <>'s high horse

∘ **bie₁· pykë** to get into trouble, get into a tight spot

∘ **i bie₁· qarit** (Colloq) to get a benefit one does not deserve

∘ **bie₁·³ˢᵍ qielli dhe** [] **zë·³ˢᵍ** "the sky comes down and gets []" the sky falls in on []

∘ **<> bie₁·³ᵖˡ qipujt** "the goblins descend from <>" <> calms down, <>'s rage abates

∘ **<> bie₁· qylit** (Crude Pej) to be always looking for a free hand-out, be a moocher

∘ **<> bie₁·³ˢᵍ radha** it is <>'s turn

∘ **<> bie₁·³ˢᵍ rasti __** <> has the occasion/opportunity to __; <> chances/happens to {}

∘ **bie₁· rehat** {} to find it comfortable {somewhere}

∘ **Nuk bie reja në hithra.** "No cloud falls on nettles" (ProvImpolite) Nothing bad happens to bad people. The devil looks after his own.

∘ **<> bie₁· rëndë** to hurt <> deeply, make <> feel very bad

∘ **bie₁· rrafsh me tokën** to fall flat to the ground

∘ **i bie₁· rrangalles** to talk in vain

∘ **<> bie₁· rreth e rrotull/qark** to go all over <>; go travel over every part of <>

∘ **<> bie₁· rrotull** to go over every part of <>

∘ **Nuk bie rrufeja në hithra.** "Lightning doesn't strike nettles" (ProvImpolite) Nothing bad happens to bad people. The devil looks after his own.

∘ **[] bie₁· rrufull *1** to lead [] all around the mulberry bush **2** to cause a mess for [], make things a mess for []

∘ **<> bie₁·³ˢᵍ sahati gjithnjë dymbëdhjetë/shtatë/tetë** "<>'s clock always strikes twelve/seven/eight o'clock" <> is aloof and indifferent to what is going on

∘ **<> bie₁· sepata në gur** <> hit a stone wall

∘ **<> bie₁·³ˢᵍ sëpata në mjaltë** to luck into something good

∘ **bie₁·³ᵖˡ sëpatat në një vend** "the axes strike at the same place" agreement is reached, everyone agrees

∘ **bie₁· si miu në poç** "fall like the mouse in the flagon" to fall into the trap (like a rat)

∘ **bie₁· si pula/gjeli në thekër** "fall like a hen/rooster into rye" to have plenty of food to eat

∘ **<> bie₁·³ˢᵍ si rrufe** "hit <> like a lightning bolt" to hit <> out of the blue, it strikes <> suddenly

∘ **bie₁· si sëpata pa bisht** "fall like an axe with no handle" to fall down heavily as if dead

∘ **bie₁· si ujku/zagari në thekër** "fall like a wolf/hound in rye" to be stuck in a hopeless situation

∘ **<> bie₁·³ˢᵍ sqepi në mjaltë** to luck into something good

∘ **<> bie₁· supeve** to pat <> on the back

∘ **<> bie₁· sharra** <> has epileptic fits; <> has lockjaw

∘ **<> bie₁·³ˢᵍ sharra në gozhdë** "<>'s saw hits a nail" <>'s plan hits a snag; <> runs into a dead end

∘ **<> bie₁· sherrit prapa** to ask for trouble

∘ **bie₁·³ˢᵍ shi** it rains

∘ **bie₁·³ˢᵍ shi gjerbë qiejsh** to rain in buckets, rain hard

∘ **bie₁·³ˢᵍ shi me fërtomë** to rain heavily: come down in buckets

∘ **bie₁·³ˢᵍ shi me grykë gjymi/pusi/shtambe** it rains in buckets, it rains cats and dogs

∘ **bie₁·³ˢᵍ shi me gjyma/ibrikë/kova/legenë/shtamba** it rains in buckets, it rains cats and dogs

∘ **bie₁· shi me kaçupë** to rain in buckets, rain heavily

∘ **bie₁·³ˢᵍ shi me kënaçe** to rain in buckets, rain heavily

∘ **bie₁· shi me litarë** to rain heavily: rain cats and dogs, come down in buckets

∘ **bie₁· shi me rrëshek** to rain in buckets

∘ **bie₁·³ˢᵍ shi në vedra** to rain in buckets, rain in torrents

∘ **po bie₁·³ˢᵍ shi si më shtambë** to be raining in buckets

∘ **<> bie₁·³ˢᵍ shiu në lakra** Fortune smiles on <>. <> has it made.

∘ **<> bie₁· shkurt 1** to do the job on <> in a quick and dirty way, find a shortcut to do the work on <> **2** to finish <> off quickly, cut <> short

∘ **<> bie₁·³ˢᵍ shpata në mjaltë** to luck into something good

∘ **<> bie₁·³ˢᵍ shpina** <>'s back is breaking from overwork

○ <> **bie**₁·^{3sg} **shtëpia mbi kokë** responsibility for supporting the family *falls* on <>; <> becomes head of the household

○ <> **bie**₁·^{3rd} **shtrenjtë** to cost <> too much, be very expensive for <>

○ **bie**₁· **shuall** (of fruit fallen from trees) to form a veritable carpet on the ground

○ <> **bie**₁· **telit** (*Colloq*) to send a wire to <>, telegraph <>

○ <> **bie**₁· **teneqesë** (*Impol*) to beat one's gums for nothing

○ <> **bie**₁· **të fikët** <> *faints*, <> *falls* into a faint

○ **bie**₁· **të fle·** to go to bed, go to sleep

○ <> **bie**₁· **të rëndët** <> *falls* into a dead faint, <> *faints*

○ <> **bie**₁· **të verdhë** <> *faints*, <> *falls* into a faint

○ <> **bie**₁· **të zhagitun** <> *faints*, <> *falls* into a faint

○ **bie**₁·^{3sg} **tërmet** there *is* an earthquake

○ **bie**₁· **trashë me** [] to get into trouble with []; not be able to get along with []

○ <> **bie**₁· **trup e trup** to cross and recross the entire <*area*>, traverse <> thoroughly

○ <> **bie**₁·^{3sg} **thika në mjaltë** to luck into something good

. **bie**₁· **thikas** to be very steep/sheer

○ <> **bie**₁· **thikë në zemër** to cause <> deep emotional anguish: strike <> to the heart

○ **bie**₁· **thikë më thikë** "gall knife to knife" to come into direct conflict

○ <> **bie**₁·^{3pl} **thonjtë 1** <>'s hands/feet *get* numb with cold **2** <> *gets* numb from fatigue **3** (*Impol*) <> *loses* <>'s former power/wealth; <> *loses* <>'s touch **4** (*Impol*) <> *kicks* the bucket: <> *dies*

○ <> **bie**₁· **thopërçit** <> *gets* edgy/nervous

○ **i bie**₁· **thumbit e potkoit** "hit both the nail and the horseshoe" (*Colloq*) to knock oneself out trying

○ <> **bie**₁·^{3sg} **uji i valë** <> *has a* scare

○ <> **bie**₁· **vaut** to cross <> at a ford

○ **bie**₁· **vesë** to drizzle; be dewy

○ <> **bie**₁·^{3pl} **veshët** "<>'s ears *fall*" <> *has a* comeuppance, <> *comes* down from <>'s high horse

○ <> **bie**₁·^{3pl} **veshët rehat** "<>'s ears find comfort" <>'s ears get a rest

○ **i bie**₁· **veshit** "hit the ear" to think seriously, think it over

○ <> **bie**₁· **vetja** <> *gets* a hernia

○ <> **bie**₁·^{3pl} **vetullat** "<>'s eyebrows *fall*" to get a sullen expression on one's face; take on a gloomy look; look offended

○ <> **bie**₁· **vula** to lose one's position of authority; lose one's reputation

○ <> **bie**₁·^{3pl} **xhindet** "the jinni *descend* from <>" <> *calms* down, <>'s rage *abates*

○ <> **bie**₁·^{3sg} **zemra te thembra** "<>'s heart *falls* to <>'s heels" <>'s heart sinks (to <>'s toes): <> *gets* fearful; <> *gets* demoralized/disappointed

○ **i bie**₁· **ziles** to ring the (little) bell

○ **bie**₁·^{3sg} **zjarr** a fire *breaks* out

○ <> **bie**₁·^{3sg} **zjarri** fire completely *destroys* <>, <> *goes* up in smoke

○ **bie**₁· **(në) zhyt** to dive/plunge in

bie₂· *vt* **1** to bring **2** (*Fig*) to bring about [], cause

○ [] **bie**₂· **anepërqark** to give [] the runaround

○ <> **a bie**₂· **fjalën rrotull/vërdallë//larg e larg** to beat around the bush with <>

○ **e bie**₂· **kokën/kryet** (*Impol*) (expressing displeasure at an arrival) to get one's damn self here: arrive

○ [] **bie**₂· **në dyzen** to tune [a stringed musical instrument]

○ **i bie**₂· **rreth 1** to approach a matter indirectly; speak indirectly **2** to go at things by a circuitous route

○ **i bie**₂· **rrotull 1** to approach a matter indirectly; speak indirectly **2** to go at things by a circuitous route

○ [] **bie**₂· **rrotull** to give [] the runaround

○ [] **bie**₂·^{3sg} **rruga** "the road *brings* [] {*somewhere*}" chance *takes* [] {*somewhere*}, [] *happens* to be {*somewhere*}

○ <> **a bie**₂· **shpirtin në fyt//ndër dhëmb** "bring <>'s soul in <>'s throat//between <>'s teeth" to cause <> torment, be a pain in the neck to <>

○ [] **bie**₂·^{3sg} **udha** "the road *brings* [] {*somewhere*}" chance *takes* [] {*somewhere*}, [] *happens* to be {*somewhere*}

○ <> **bie**₂· **vërdallë** to go over every part of <>

○ **i bie**₂· **vërdallë 1** to approach a matter indirectly; speak indirectly **2** to go at things by a circuitous route

○ [] **bie**₂· **vërdallë** to give [] the runaround

bie·llë *nf* [*Tech*] connecting rod

bi·f *nf* [*Bot*] chard, Swiss chard (*Beta cicla*) = **pazi**

bi·fke *nf* **1** young plant, sprig; sprout, shoot **2** small tassel on a cap **3** leg feather on poultry

bifk·o·n *vi* to sprout

bifte·k *nm* [*Food*] beef/veal steak

biga·ç *adj* (*Reg Tosk*) forked, two-pronged

biga·çe *nf* forked stick

bigami *nf* bigamy

***biga·në** *nf* (*Reg Gheg*) tongs; vice, clamp

bi·gë

  I § *nf* **1** bifurcated object: fork, tree fork; branch **2** large, two-armed hoisting crane **3** (*Reg*) tongs **4** double-peaked mountain; peaked crag; space between adjacent crags **5** bouquet of flowers tied to the top of a forked stick; bouquet composed of several kinds of flowers

  II § *adv* sticking straight up/out on both sides

bi·gël *nf* **1** bifurcated object, prong **2** tongs **3** double-peaked mountain; peaked crag; space between adjacent crags **4** land with rocks and debris: rocky landscape; scree

bi·gët *adj* (*i*) forked, branching, pronged

bi·gëz *nf* forked pole on which fodder is left for livestock

big·ëzi·m *nm ger* <**bigëzo·n**, **bigëzo·het 1** branching **2** fork (in a tree/road)

bigëzo·het *vpr* to branch into a fork: bifurcate

bigëzo·n *vt* to create a fork at the end of []: bifurcate

***big·nu·em** *adj* (*i*) (*Reg Gheg*) = **biga·ç**

bigo·het *vpr* = **bigëzo·het**

bigo·n *vi* = **bigëzo·n**

bigo·në *nf* [*Mus*] a folk double flute made of bone, with a single mouthpiece branching into two fingering tubes

bigoni *nf* (*Old*) malicious gossip: slander, defamation

***bigoni·s** *nf* (*Old*) to vilify, slander, defame

bigo·r *nm* [*Bot*] kind of heather

bigo·rr *nm* **1** porous limestone **2** calcified residue left by water: scale **3** (*Fig*) dregs, scum **4** (*Fig*) vileness

bigudi *nf* hair curler, hair roller

bij *np* <**bir** sons; children

bijë nf **1** daughter **2** piece of paper detachable from a stub: coupon, check, ticket
◦ **bijë e gjetur** stepdaughter
◦ **bijë në shpirt** adopted daughter
◦ **bijë e qasur** (Colloq) foster daughter, adopted daughter

bijëri nf **1** someone's sons and daughters, progeny **2** = **bijësi**

bijësi nf(Book) filiation

bijim nm ger **1** <**bijo·n 2** (Collec) progeny; generation

bijo·n vt to procreate, beget [a child]

bijor adj (Book) filial = **birnor**

*__bijsë__ nf (Reg Tosk) twig

*__bijzë__ nf (Old) piece of paper detachable from a stub: coupon, check, ticket

bikarbonat nm [Chem] bicarbonate; baking soda

*__bikë__ nf kiss

bikër nf[Zool] tadpole = **bishtfultere**

bikme nf silk embroidery thread

bikonkav adj [Optics] biconcave

bikonveks adj [Optics] biconvex

bikutina np curlers, rollers (for curling hair)

bilan nm (Reg) **1** martingale **2** ornamental necklace or headband made of metal coins and worn by women

bilanc nm **1** financial balance **2** balance statement
◦ **bilanc aktiv 1** [Fin] credit balance, positive balance **2** (Book) good condition, comfortable situation
◦ **bilanc pasiv** [Fin] negative balance

*__bilanç__ = **bilanc**

bilardo nf **1** billiards **2** billiard table

bilashnjok nm shoot/sprout growing out of the stump of a felled oak tree

bilateral adj bilateral

bilbicë nf **1** [Ichth] Lake Ohrid Adriatic trout (Salmothymus ohridanus Stein) *__2__ marble used as a shooter: taw

bilbil
I § nm [Ornit] **1** nightingale (Luscinia megarhynchos Brehm.) **2** small whistle **3** pintle and socket hinge on a window
II § adj having the voice of a nightingale (beautiful and fast)
◦ **ësh-të bilbil** to have nothing left, be flat broke
◦ **bilbil gjyzari** [Folklore] miracle-working nightingale with a beautiful voice
◦ **bilbil i kënetave** [Ornit] Cetti's warbler Cettia cetti Temm.
◦ **bilbil i ujit** [Ornit] kingfisher Alcedinidae

Bilbil nm Bilbil (male name)

bilbilbardhë nf [Bot] summer snowflake (Leucolum aestivum)

bilbileshë nf female nightingale

bilbilth nm [Ornit] Savi's warbler (Locustella luscinoides Savi.B)
◦ **bilbilthi i kallameve** [Ornit] reed warbler Acrocephalus scirpaceus
◦ **bilbilthi këngëtar** [Ornit] Orphean warbler Sylvia hortensis Gm.
◦ **bilbilthi kokëzi** [Ornit] blackcap Sylvia atricapilla
◦ **bilbilthi i kopshtit** [Ornit] garden warbler Sylvia borin Bodd.
◦ **bilbilthi me mustaqe** [Ornit] mustached warbler Acrocephalus melanopogon

◦ **bilbilthi i përhimë** [Ornit] whitethroat Sylvia communis Latham
◦ **bilbilthi i ujit** [Ornit] aquatic warbler Acrocephalus paludicola Vieillot.
◦ **bilbilthi i zhukave** [Ornit] sedge warbler Acrocephalus schoenobaenus

bile pcl (Colloq) in fact; even, indeed; especially; furthermore
◦ **bile bile** as a matter of fact

bile nf (Child) (child's word for penis) weenie

biletari nf place where tickets are sold

biletashitës n ticket seller

biletë nf **1** ticket **2** [Fin] banknote **3** piece of paper containing examination questions
◦ **biletë vajtje ardhje** round-trip ticket

bilë nf billiard ball; metal sphere

bilke nf tall vessel, normally made of tin, with a narrow spout; oil can, watering pot (to give water to babies)

bilion nm [Math] billion; trillion

*__bilog__ nm stack, heap

bilonjë nf **1** straight sapling growing from a tree stump **2** (Fig) tall, slender woman or girl

bilur
I § nm (Colloq) **1** porcelain, china **2** crystal, clear glass
II § adj extremely clean and clear; completely white
III § adv (extremely) crystal
◦ **bilur i pastër** pure as crystal

bilurtë adj (i) (Colloq) **1** made of crystal or porcelain **2** (Fig) white as porcelain

*__bim__ nm piglet

Bim nm short form of Ibrahim

bimbaq nm [Ornit] sea-gull

bimbash nm [Hist] major (military officer) in the Ottoman Empire

*__bimcë__ nf storage cellar

*__bimco·n__ vt to store

bimë nf **1** plant **2** crop **3** (Fig Colloq) progeny, descendants
◦ **bimë grunore** grains
◦ **bimë kultivuese** cultivated/agricultural crops
◦ **bimë njëvjeçare** annuals
◦ **bimë shumëvjeçare** perennials
◦ **bimë të buta** domestic plants

bimël nf piece of chaff, sliver, mote

bimëngrënës
I § adj [Biol] phytophagous
II § nm [Biol] phytophaga

bimësi nf vegetation; flora

bimët adj (i) = **bimor**

bimëtore nf(Book) herbarium

bimëz nf small/young plant: seedling, sprout

bimishtë nf place with dense vegetation

*__bimni__ nf (Reg Gheg Old) botany = **botanikë**

bimor adj botanical, vegetable

bimore nf agricultural land; fertile soil; vegetable garden

*__bimrâjë__ nf (Reg Gheg Old) taproot

bimsë nf cellar, basement

*__bimtar__ n botanist, herbalist

*__bimte__ nf coarse thread

bina nf (Colloq) **1** building; building foundation **2** (Fig) someone/something with a big body **3** (Collec) progeny

○ **U shof**^{opt} **me bina** *(Curse)* May { }'s tribe vanish from the earth! May { } be alone and miserable!

bina·da·lë *adj (Colloq)* = **binashuar**

***bina·k** *n* twin = **binjak**

bina·ma·dh *adj (Colloq)* huge in size

bina·r *nm* **1** thick board, beam; rafter **2** metal rail, track (of a railway) **3** *(Fig)* proper track/path/road
○ **binar hekurudhe** railroad track

bina·shu·ar *adj* **1** without issue/heirs/seed, with no posterity, ending a lineage **2** *(Curse)* may his tribe vanish from the earth!; may he be alone and miserable!

bind *nm* something that elicits astonishment/fear: wonder, marvel; horror, monster

bind· *vt* **1** to convince, persuade **2** *(Colloq)* to astonish

bind·et *vpr* **1** to be convinced, be persuaded, be assured **2** to obey **3** to be astonished

bi·nde *nf(Reg)* demijohn

***bindedër** *nf (Old)* marvel, wonder

***bindedërshëm** *adj (i) (Old)* marvelous, wonderful

bindë *nf* **1** [*Tech*] lifting gear, hoister *****2** amazement, astonishment

binderme
I § *nf* **1** groove in the edge of a board to permit a smooth fitting **2** edge-routing tool, trenching plane
II § *adv* fitting together closely one atop the other

bind·ës *adj* persuasive, convincing

bindje *nf ger* **1** < **bind·**, **bind·et 2** total belief in the truth of something: conviction **3** obedience; acquiescence; docility, submission

bindshëm
I § *adj (i)* **1** obedient; docile **2** *(Old)* astonishing, surprising
II § *adv* persuasively, convincingly, assuringly

bindur *adj* **1** convinced **2** obedient

binek *nm* [*Bot*] **1** a parasitic herbaceous plant which appears in rice fields and has a short, thin stem and small sorghum-like grain *****2** saddle horse

binish *nm (Old)* **1** cassock worn by Moslem clergymen; long, men's coat made of good material **2** long, hooded, cotton cloak worn by Moslem women

binokël *nm (Book)* binoculars

binom *nm* [*Math*] **1** binomial **2** *(Fig Book)* dyad

binoshe *nf* tree or stick with two branches, fork

bintë *nf* bandage, band, binding

binjak
I § *adj* **1** composed of twin components; twinned, dual **2** *(Fig)* duplicate, highly similar
II § *nm* **1** twin brother; twin **2** *(Fig)* double **3** ear of corn composed of several small ears joined together

binjake *nf* twin sister

***binjarak** *nm* = **binjak**

***binjok** *nm* = **binjak**

***binjor** *nm (Reg Tosk)* prong

binjore *nf* forked branch; fork

bio *formative prefix* bio-

biofizikë *nf* biophysics

biograf *nm* biographer

biografi *nf* **1** biography **2** personal information of a political nature

biografik *adj* biographical

biokimi *nf* biochemistry

***biokimik** *adj* biochemical

biokimist *n* biochemist

***bioksid** *nm* dioxide

biolog *n* biologist

biologji *nf* biology

biologjik *adj* biological

*****biond** = **bjond**

biorrymë *nf* [*Spec*] electric current generated by cells in living tissue

biosferë *nf* [*Spec*] biosphere

biplan *nm* [*Av*] airplane with two wings, biplane

BIPM *abbrev (French)* < **Bureau International des Poids et Mesures** International Bureau of Weights and Measurements

bir
I § *nm* son
II § *nm (i)* his, her, or their son
○ **bir i ftohtë** foster/adopted son
○ **bir i gjetur** stepson
○ **i biri i botës** "outsider's son" **1** boy who does not belong to one's family circle, stranger **2** *(Contempt)* this/some (damn) guy
○ **i biri i njerkës** child given especially nice treatment; pampered/spoiled child
○ **i biri i vashës** "the son of the maiden" *(Poet)* great hero, bravest of the brave
○ **bir në shpirt** adopted son
○ **bir pas biri** generation after generation
○ **bir i qasur** *(Colloq)* foster son, adopted son
○ **bir i vetëm** only son

*****bir·et** *vp* < **bie₂**·

bira-bira *adv* full of holes

biraç *nm* wall niche next to the hearth

biraçok *nm* small hole

*****birak** *adj* filial

biralec *nm* round, unleavened bun with a hole in the middle

bira·lie *nf* perforated spoon for ladling out food, perforated ladle

biramel
I § *adj (Reg)* nosy, inquisitive, prying
II § *n* snoop

*****birastjel** *nm (Old)* = **frëngji**

birbo *nf (Pej)* frivolous person with no possessions who leads a disorganized life: bum

birçe *nf with masc agreement (Colloq)* **1** *(Pet Dimin)* sonny boy, little boy **2** *(Impol)* lazy boy; someone else's son

birë *nf* hole, opening
○ **birat e hundës** nostrils

birëri *nf (Book)* = **bijësi**

birëse *nf* hammer or chisel used to make holes

birësi *nf (Book)* = **bijësi**

birësim *nm ger (Book)* **1** [*Law*] < **birëso·n 2** adoption

birëso·n *vt (Book)* [*Law*] to adopt (a child)

birësuar *adj (i)* [*Law*] adopted

birësues *adj* [*Law*] person who adopts, adopter

birëveshe *nf* [*Entom*] earwig = **gërshërëz**

birëz *nf* small hole
○ **birëzat e lëkurës** skin pores

birim *nm ger* < **biro**·*n*

birinxhi
I § *adv (Colloq)* very well, marvelously, like a pro
II § *adj* really fine, swell, terrific, super

birko
I § *nf with masc agreement (Impol)* = **birçe**

II § *adv* excellent, splendid

*__birko'kë__ *nf* apricot

birma'n *adj, n* Burmese

birmane'z *adj, n* Burmese

Birmani' *nf* Burma

Birminge'm *nm* Birmingham

*__bir'ni__ *nf* (*Reg*) = bir**ë'ri'**
  ○ **birni në shpirt** adoption

bir'no'r *adj* filial, characteristic of sons

bi'ro! *vocative case* <**bir** hey son!

biro'·n *vt* to perforate, pierce, bore
  ○ <>**a biro·n jetën** to ruin <>'s life
  ○ <>**a biro·n shpirtin/zëmrën** <> make <>'s heart bleed

biro'çe *nf* two-wheeled horse cart

biro'jë *nf* [*Zool*] Montpellier snake (*Malpolon monspessulanus*)

*__biro's·__ *vt* = biro'·n

*__birq__ *nm* 1 bung, tap 2 = pirg

*__birth__ *nm dimin* 1 little son *2 pimple

*__birth__ *nm* carbuncle, boil

biru'cë *nf* 1 small hole 2 small cell in prison; solitary; prison 3 (*Fig*) small, narrow, unlit room

biru'es
  I § *adj* hole-making
  II § *nm* 1 [*Entom*] borer, hole-boring insect 2 (*Pej*) busybody
  ○ **biruesi i hardhisë** "vine borer" [*Entom*] *Sinoxylon sexdentatum*
  ○ **biruesi i ullirit** "olive borer" [*Entom*] olive bark beetle, olive beetle *Phloeotribus scarabaeoides*

birra'r *n* beer seller, barman

birra'ri' *nf* pub that serves beer, beer parlor, saloon

birre'
  I § *stem for pres, pind* <bjerr·
  II § *vpr* 1 to get lost; disappear, vanish 2 to be infatuated with 3 to die; be sacrificed; come to nothing, go for naught

birrë *nf* beer, ale

birrë'shit'ës *n* = birra'r

*__birrëta'r__ *nm* = birra'r

bis
  I § *interj* encore!
  II § *adj* (*Book*) marks a second occurrence

bisbi'q *nm* 1 small weakling sheep that keeps straying from the flock 2 (*Pej*) troublesome brat; talkative troublemaker 3 [*Food*] corn biscuit

biseda'r
  I § *adj* eloquent
  II § *n* orator

bise'dë *nf* conversation, discussion; discourse
  ○ **bisedë pa kokë** talk/discussion that fails to come to a point
  ○ **bisedë pas bisede** after discussing matters

bisedi'm *nm ger* 1 <bisedo'·n 2 conversation, talk

bisedi'me *np* (*Book*) negotiations

bisedo'·n
  I § *vi* to carry on a conversation/discussion; exchange ideas: converse; negotiate
  II § *vt* to discuss
  ○ **bisedo·n rrafsh me** [] to sit down and talk things over with [] personally
  ○ **bisedo·n**³ᵖˡ **vesh më vesh** "talk ear to ear" to talk confidentially with one another so as not to be overheard

bisedo'r *adj* [*Ling*] conversational, colloquial

bisedu'es *nm* participant in discussion; discussant

bisekstil *adj* bissextile

bisk
  I § *nm (np ˜ qe)* 1 straight young twig; sprig, sprout, shoot 2 small stream, rill 3 twist of hair 4 a kind of hand embroidery
  II § *adj, adv* in a continuous straight line

biska'jë *nf* = bisko'një

biska'r
  I § *adj* long, thin, and straight; slender
  II § *nm* (*Reg*) [*Zool*] = astri't

bi'skë *nf* [*Ornit*] blue-billed pintail (duck) (*Anas acuta*)

bisko'·n *vi* to sprout; sprout a new branch

bisko'një
  I § *nf* 1 long, straight twig; young sprout 2 (*Fig*) tall, slender girl/woman; pretty girl/woman
  II § *adj* tall and slender, long and slender

*__bisko'rrë__ *nf* new twig; young sprout

bisko'të *nf* twice-baked sweet biscuit, cookie

bi'skull *nm* twig

bismu't *nm* [*Chem*] bismuth (*Bi*)

*__biso'n__ *nm* [*Zool*] bison = bizo'n

bi'sqe *np* <bis**k**

bista'k *nm* bunch of grapes, grape cluster

bi'stër
  I § *adj* 1 having a sharp taste: very sour, bitter, tart 2 (*Fig*) caustic, shrewish 3 very cold and crystal clear, limpid = ce'mtë 4 (*Fig*) fast and efficient
  II § *nf* 1 [*Ichth*] broad-nosed pipefish = gjilpë'rëz 2 [*Ornit*] bar-tailed godwit *Limosa lapponica* *3 crystal, quartz, cut glass *4 bitter, unripe fruit

bistë'ro'k *adj* (*Reg*) having a sharp taste: strong (of alcohol/vinegar), bitter, tart, sour, unripe

Bistri'cë *nf* small river in southeastern Albania: Bistrica

bistric'o't *adj, n* person who lives along the Bistrica river

*__bistu'r__ *nm* = bisturi'

bisturi' *nf* [*Surgery*] bistoury

*__bish'ana'k__ *adj* (*Reg Tosk*) bestial

bish'a'r *n* (*Pej*) bestial person, brute

*__bish'bile'c__ *nm* (*Reg*) mountain tea

bi'she *nf* 1 savage beast, wild animal 2 (*Colloq*) wolf 3 (*Fig*) bestial or bloodthirsty person, brute 4 [*Ichth*] armless snake eel (*Dalophis imberbis*)
  ○ **bishë deti** [*Ichth*] spotted snake eel *Ophisurus serpens*

bishi'një *nf* strip of land between two rows of grapevines

bishko'rr *nf* mare whose tail was cropped when her master died

bishma'ku'q'ës *n* [*Ornit*] = bishtku'q

*__bishni'cë__ *nf* bagpipe

*__bish'no'r__ = bisho'r

bish'o'r *adj* (*Book*) savage, ferocious, wild, bestial

bisht *nm* 1 tail 2 tail end; butt, residual part 3 stem (of a flower/fruit/leaf) 4 handle, (broom)stick 5 (*Fig Pej*) unexpected and excessive addition: stinger, gimmick 6 (*Fig*) unfinished piece of business, loose end 7 (*Old Fig*) lower class person; insignificant and worthless person 8 (*Fig Pej*) person who hounds another 9 [*Geog*] piece of land jutting out into a body of water: cape 10 (*Colloq*) twist or braid of hair

11 *(Colloq)* (in counting or judging amounts) a head of livestock; an unsatisfactorily small amount
○ **s'lidh·*et* as për bisht as për krye** "can be tied neither by the tail nor by the head" to be stubbornly set in one's ways
○ **bisht bilardoje** cue stick
○ **bisht daci** "tomcat tail" [*Bot*] = **bishtda'c**
○ **bishti i flokëve** ponytail
○ **bishti i fshesës** "broom handle" person whose opinion is ignored
○ **bisht gomari** "donkey tail" [*Bot*] field horsetail *Equisetum arvense*
○ **bishti i lumit** source of the river
○ **bisht mëllenje** [*Ichth*] turbot *Psetta maxima*
○ **bisht miu** [*Bot*] = **bishtmi'**
○ **Bishti i Pallës** hilly cape on the Adriatic north of Durazzo: Sword Handle
○ **bisht pas bishti** inseparable
○ **bisht pene** penholder
○ **bishti i syrit** corner of the eye

bishta'dhi'zë *nf* [*Bot*] European glorybind (*Convolvulus arvensis*)

bishta'fu'rkë *nf* [*Zool*] weasel (*Mustela nivalis*)

bishta'ga'n *nf* [*Entom*] dragonfly = **pilive's**ë

bishta'gy'p *nf* (*Colloq*) "tube tail" penholder

bishta'gja'të *nf* [*Ornit*] long-tailed titmouse (*Parus caudatus L.*)

bishta'gjel *nf* **1** [*Ornit*] pintail (*Anas acuta*) **2** a kind of yellow corn with small kernels **3** (*Reg*) [*Bot*] lily

bishta'jë *nf* **1** seed pod, legume **2** snap bean, string bean **3** (*Reg*) corn husk

bishta'jo'·*n* *vi* to bear pods

bishta'jo'r *adj* pod-bearing, having pods

bishta'jo're *np collec* [*Bot*] pea family (*Leguminosae*)

bishta'k
I § *adj* **1** long-stemmed **2** having a tail-like appendage; having a handle
II § *nm* **1** yearling colt **2** (*Fig*) little child not yet able to walk **3** watering can with a spout; long-handled spoon, ladle **4** end part of a plow handle **5** [*Bot*] petiole ***6** cup with a handle ***7** = **bista'k**

bishta'k'e *nf* cow with a long tail

bishta'kre'p *nm* [*Bot*] scorpion's-tail (*Scorpiurus*)

bishta'ku'q *nm* **1** [*Ornit*] = **bishtku'q 2** [*Ichth*] roach (*Rutilus rutilus*) **3** long-stemmed red fig shaped like an eggplant

bishta'le'c *nm* braid of hair, pigtail
○ **<> kanë dalë mendtë mbi bishtaleca** "<>'s brains have spilled out over <>'s pigtails" (*Pej*) <> has lost her good sense

bishta'lu'g *nm* (*Reg*) corn mush

*bishtallukçi' *nf* (*Old*) [*Ethnog*] party of men conducting the bride to the groom's house

*bishta'mi'th *nm* [*Bot*] yarrow, milfoil (*Achillea millefolium*)

bishta'n *adj* long-stemmed

bishta'nja'k *adj* = **bishta'k**

bishta'nja'ke *nf* [*Ichth*] **1** common stingray (*Trygon pastinaca, Dasyatis pastinaca*) **2** roughtail stingray (*Dasyatis centroura*)

bishta'qe'n *nm* [*Bot*] = **bishtqe'n**

bishta'r *adj* **1** having a tail **2** (*Fig Pej*) avoiding one's responsibilities

bishta'ra'k *nm* **1** narrow strip of land extending from a field like a tail; tail like extension hanging down from something **2** plow handle **3** type of long-stemmed fig **4** = **bishtara'ke**

bishta'ra'ke *nf* small, long-handled pot for brewing Turkish coffee

bishta'rtë
I § *nf* [*Entom*] a variety of yellow-tailed butterfly (*Euproctis chrysorrhoea*)
II § *adj* golden-tailed

bishta's *adv* **1** asquat, squatting **2** dragging one's hind end on the ground

bishta'tu'nd = **bishtatu'nd**ës

bishta'tu'ndës *nm* [*Ornit*] wagtail (*Motocilla*)
○ **bishtatundës i bardhë** [*Ornit*] white/pied wagtail *Motacilla alba L.* = **zogu i deles**
○ **bishtatundës i malit** [*Ornit*] gray wagtail *Motacilla cinerea L.*
○ **bishtatundës i verdhë** [*Ornit*] yellow wagtail *Motacilla flava*

bishtba'rdhë
I § *nf* [*Ornit*] wheatear (*Oenanthe oenanthe L.*)
II § *adj* white-tailed
○ **bishtbardha e gurit** [*Ornit*] = **bishtba'rdh**ë
○ **bishtbardha gushëzezë** [*Ornit*] black-eared wheatear *Oenanthe hispanica L.*

bisht'ca'kër *adj* tail-erect

bisht'cu'b *adj* = **bishtcu'ng**

bisht'cube'l *adj* = **bishtcu'ng**

bisht'cu'ng *adj* **1** bobtailed, with a short tail, docked **2** [*Zool*] sand viper, nose-horned viper (*Vipera ammodytes*)

bisht'çata'll *adj* = **bishtgërshë'r**ë

bisht'da'c *nm* [*Bot*] larger horsetail (*Equisetum maximum*)

bisht'dallëndy'she *nf* [*Ichth*] pompano, derbio (*Trachinotus ovatus*)

bisht'dre'dh'ur *adj* (*Pej*) having loose morals, immoral

bisht'du'ng *nm* [*Zool*] sand viper, nose-horned viper (*Vipera ammodytes*)

bisht'du'ngë
I § *nf* herbaceous annual found in wet meadows, with a wheat-like stalk and narrow leaves, and clusters of long, soft-bearded seeds
II § *adj* having a tufted tail

bisht'du'rd *adj* (*Reg*) = **bishtcung**

bisht'dhe'lpër *nf* [*Bot*] **1** meadow foxtail (*Alopecurus pratensis*) **2** a variety of white, oblong grape with fruit clusters shaped like fox tails

bishte' *nf* = **nënbi'shte**

bishte'c = **bishtale'c**

bishte'n *nm* (*Old*) tax on grain that farmers used to pay landlords for irrigation of fields, water tax

*bishte'shufra'bu'kurë *nf* [*Zool*] = **fishnja'r**

bishte'zë
I § *nf* = **nënbi'shte**
II § *adj* * = **bishta'n**

bi'sht'ëm *adj* (*i*) at/on the tail end: hindmost, last, final

bi'sht'ërr *nf* [*Zool*] = **bishtfulte're**

bi'sht'ës *adj* (of fruit) long-stemmed

bi'sht'ëz *nf* **1** short tail **2** plow handle ***3** crupper; cantle of a saddle

bisht'fëlte're = **bishtfulte're**

bisht·fryrë adj having a tufted tail

bisht·fulte·re nf [Zool] tadpole, polliwog

bisht·furka·bu·kur nf(Reg) [Zool] stoat

bisht·gërshërë nf[Ornit] "scissor-tail" **1** (Colloq) swallow **2** pintail duck (Anas acuta)

*****bisht·gyp** nm (Old) penholder

bisht·gjatë
  I § nf **1** (Euph) fox **2** [Ornit] magpie (Pica pica L.) **3** [Ornit] wagtail = **bishtatundës**
  II § adj long-tailed, long-stemmed

bisht·gjele nf "rooster-tail" [Ornit] pintail duck (Anas acuta)

bisht·hollë [bisht-holl` `] nf "thin-tail" [Bot] herbaceous plant with ovate leaves and thin, single spikelets that grows in nonarable coastal soil Lepturus cylindricus Willd., Rottboellica cylindrica Willd.

*****bisht·inë** nf trick, stratagem

bisht·je
  I § nf **1** cooking pot with a long handle **2** a variety of long-stemmed, small, yellow pear
  II § np stumps of branches that remain after pruning
  III § adj (of fruit) long-stemmed

bisht·kali adv (Colloq) ponytailed, with hair tied into a single clump

bisht·këputur adj (Colloq) "broken-tailed" left without family, deprived of kinfolk

bisht·korrë nf horse whose tail has been docked as a sign of grief for the death of his master

bisht·kuq nm [Ornit] redstart (Phoenicurus phoenicurus L.B)
  ∘ **bishtkuq i mureve = bishtkuq**
  ∘ **bishtkuq zeshkan** [Ornit] black redstart Phoenicurus ochruros Gmelin L.

bisht·kuqe nf [Ichth] = **bishtakuq**

bisht·lagur adj (Colloq) "wet-tailed" humbled and shamed; defeated

bisht·lepur nm **1** [Bot] rabbit-tail grass (Lagurus) **2** wheat with empty husks

bisht·lëkundës nm [Ornit] = **bishtatundës**

bisht·lëshuar adj (Colloq Pej) = **bishtluajtur**

bisht·lëvizur adj (Colloq Pej) = **bishtluajtur**

bisht·lopatë nf [Zool] = **bishtfulte·re**

bisht·luajtur adj (Colloq Pej) loose in morals, licentious

bisht·luan nm [Bot] motherwort (Leonurus)

*****bisht·meno·n** vi (Old) to play truant

bisht·mëllenjëz nf [Ichth] brill (Bothus rhombus, Rhombus laevis)

bisht·mi nf **1** [Bot] Turkish micromeria (Micromeria) **2** [Ichth] rabbitfish (Chimaera monstruosa) = **kokënjëso·re 3** [Ichth] common stingray (Trygon pastinaca, Dasyatis pastinaca)

bisht·mushkë nf **1** [Bot] field horsetail (Equisetum arvense) **2** larger horsetail (Equisetum maximum)

bisht·ni nf evasiveness, avoidance; trickiness, shiftiness

bisht·nïcë nf [Mus] a double-tubed, folk musical instrument made from a single piece of wood

bisht·nïm nm ger <**bishtno·n**

bisht·no·n vi **1** to avoid contact with unwelcome person/thing, be evasive; sneak away, escape by subterfuge **2** (Fig) to try to avoid work/responsibility; shirk; equivocate

bisht·nues adj evasive, shirking, alibiing

*****bisht·o·n = bishtno·n**

bisht·ok
  I § adj short-tailed
  II § nm **1** watering can with a spout; long-handled spoon, ladle **2** meat cut from the tail, oxtail

bisht·or
  I § nm simple oil lamp held by a tail-like handle = **bishtuk**
  II § adj [Anat] **1** caudal **2** long-stemmed **3** [Tech] consisting of a single part and an appendage **4** [Tech] consisting of a single part and an appendage

bisht·o·re nf **1** long-handled spoon, ladle **2** pot with a long handle; small, long-handled pot for brewing Turkish coffee **3** piece of ground bordering a field **4 = nënbishte**

bisht·o·s· vt to shear [a sheep/goat] around the tail

bisht·o·sje nf ger <**bishto·s·**

*****bisht·pallua** nm (obl ~ oi) [Entom] fan-shaped brown alga (Padina pavonia)

bisht·pelëz nf[Bot] sheep's fescue, tall fescue, fescue (Festuca)

bisht·penë nf penholder

bisht·përdredhur adj **1** having a twisted tail **2** (Fig Pej) = **bishtdredhur**

bisht·përpjetë adj **1** having an erect tail **2** (Fig Pej) conceited, haughty, pretentious, snobbish, arrogant

bisht·pllakare nf flat-handled wooden spoon

bisht·prerë adj **1** bobtailed, having a cut-off tail **2** (Fig) having no support from others; unable to wield any influence on others

bisht·qen nm [Bot] crested dog's-tail (Cynosurus cristatus)

bishtra-bishtra adv completely scattered

bisht·rrudhët adj corkscrew-tailed

bisht·shkundës nm = **bishtatundës**

bisht·shkurtër adj short-tailed

bisht·shufra·bukurë nf [Zool] = **fishnjar**

bisht·tundëse nf = **bishtatundës**

bisht·th nm stem of a leaf or fruit, petiole

*****bisht·ues** adj unstable

bisht·uk
  I § adj long-stemmed
  II § nm **1** simple oil lamp held by a tail-like handle **2** board for carrying mortar: mortarboard **3** fire log; torch

bisht·uke nf black or red cow with a white tail

bisht·urina np (Colloq) dregs, lees, grounds

*****bite·m** nm [Entom] sheep parasite Melophagus ovinus

bit·evi
  I § adv (Colloq) completely, wholly; continuously, in one piece
  II § adj whole, one-piece, full, complete, solid

bit·ërr nf **1** small corn plant pulled up to thin out the crop *****2** (Old) cattle-fattening fodder

bit·is·
  I § vt (Colloq) **1** to complete, finish, fulfill **2** to destroy completely, ruin
  II § vi to come to an end; be decided, be resolved

bit·is·et vpr to come to an end; be destroyed, be ruined

bit·me nf seedling, sprout, scion, shoot

bito·një nf = **bitme**

*****bit·ulë** nf [Agr] = **betulë**

bit·um nm [Min] bitumen

bitum·atrïçe nf = **autobitumatrïçe**

bitum|ino·z *adj* bituminous

bitum|mba·jtës *adj* [*Min*] containing/bearing bitumen

bitum|o· ·n *vt* to cover [] with bitumen/asphalt; spread asphalt over []: tar

***bitha·sh** *nm* **1** child not yet able to walk; crawler **2** paralytic

biu·le *nf* **1** drinking straw, drinking tube **2** double reed for musical instruments

bixa·n *nm* olive with small elongated fruit that yields much oil; oil olive

bi·xhas *adv*

bi·xhë *nf* flat pebbles or metal chips used in children's games

***bixho·xhi·** *nm (np ¯ nj)* = **bixhozçi·**

bixho·z *nm* gambling game, especially one played with cards

bixho·zçi *nm* gambler, especially card gambler

biz *nm* *awl = **bi·z**ë

Biza·nt *nm* [*Hist*] Byzantium, the Byzantine Empire

bizanti·n *adj (Book)* Byzantine

bize·le

I § *nf* **1** [*Bot*] pea (*Pisum L.*) ***2** green beans

II § *adj* pea green in color

Bize·rtë *nf* Bizerte

bi·zë *nf* **1** awl **2** embroidery needle; crochet hook ***3** sole, plaice

bizgë *nf* loose stool passed in diarrhea

bizg|o·s·et *vpr* to get diarrhea, suffer from diarrhea

bizg|o·s|ur *adj (i)* **1** diarrheal **2** *(Fig Pej)* disheveled, slack, dissolute

bizne·s *nm* business, commercial enterprise

bizo·n *nm* [*Zool*] bison

***bi·zhg**ë *nf* [*Bot*] sharp-leaved asparagus (*Asparagus acutifolius*)

***bizho·z** = **bixho·z**

bizhuteri· *nf* jewelry

***bjâ·** *vt (Reg Gheg)* to stain

bjeli·shë *nf* [*Bot*] melic grass, onion grass *(Melica)*

bje·llë *nf* [*Tech*] connecting rod

bjellogardi·st *adj, n* **1** (person) belonging to the "White Guard" in the Russian Revolution **2** counterrevolutionary

bjellorus *adj, n* Byelorussian

Bjellorusi· *nf* Byelorussia

bje·r *sg imper* <**bie**₁·, **bie**₂·

○ **Bjeri daulles!** *(Impol)* Go ahead and yammer! (because no one is paying attention)

○ **bjer e çohu/ngrehu!** "get down and get up!" **1** just the same thing over and over again **2** you just keep striving and suffering

○ **bjer shi në arën time** "let it rain only on my field" (said of someone completely selfish) just looking out for number one, not bothering about anyone else: as long as I get mine!

○ **bjeri t'i biem** (this is what is called) doing something just to be doing something (said of disorganized/pointless work)

bjerr· *vt* to lose, forfeit

bjerra|di·të *nf* = **bjerradi·t**ës

bjerra|di·tës *n* loafer, time waster

bjerra|fa·t *adj* unfortunate

bjerra|mo·t *adj* loafer, time waster

bjerr|je *nf ger* **1** <**bjerr·**, **bi·rr·et 2** loss

bjeshka·ta·r

I § *n* mountaineer; mountain livestock husbandman, mountain shepherd

II § *adj (Poet)* mountain pastoral

bje·shkë *nf* **1** high mountain with summer pasture; highland pasture, mountain pasture **2** rocky and infertile land in rugged country

bjeshki· *nf* dairy husbandry in summer pastures

bjeshk|i·m *nm ger* <**bjeshko· ·n**

bjeshko· ·n

I § *vi* **1** to take livestock to a highland pasture, tend livestock in a highland pasture **2** to live in the mountains

II § *vt* to pasture [livestock] in the mountains in summer

bjeshk|o·r

I § *adj* alpine

II § *nm* = **bjeshkata·r**

bje·zgë *nf* splinter of wood

bjond *adj, n* blond (person)

BKSh *abbrev* <**Banka Kombëtare e Shqypnis** [*Hist*] National Bank of Albania

bla·cë *nf* place made impassable by dense thorny undergrowth; bramble thicket

blând|ës *nm (Old Regional Gheg)* = **plënd|**ës

***bla·ne** *nf* small stick, twig; tinder

bla·në *nf* **1** bruise, scar **2** blemish, stain, splotch **3** [*Bot*] plant disease in which dark spots appear on leaves and fruit **4** [*Bot*] sapwood = **urr**ë

***blano·z** *nm* [*Ornit*] golden oriole (*Oriolus oriolus*)

bla·një *nf* piece that has been separated or cut off from something larger

***blaq** *nm* silly person, fool

blasfemi· *nf (Book)* blasphemy

bla·të *nf (Old)* **1** [*Relig*] bread offered in the eucharist: oblate; the wooden seal used to mark that bread = **mblatë(s) 2** seal, stamp **3** gift, offering

blat|i·m *nm ger* **1** <**blato· ·n, blato··het 2** oblation, offering to a deity **3** a gift of honor, sacrificial gift, sacrifice

***blati·sht**ë *nf* swamp, marsh

blato··het *vpr (Elev)* to dedicate oneself, be dedicated

blato· ·n *vt* **1** *(Relig)* to make an oblation **2** *(Elev)* to give [] to <> to show one's gratitude; dedicate

***blato·r** *adj* as an offering/oblation

blatu·e·s *nm (Old)* offerer, gift giver

ble *nm* **1** book volume, tome **2** *(Reg)* fleece; tuft of wool or of fibers **3** *(Reg)* outer cabbage leaves **4** chip cut, but not detached, from wood

ble·n *vt* **1** to buy **2** *(Pej)* to bribe [] **3** *(Colloq Fig)* to comprehend, grasp, understand, catch **4** *(Colloq Fig)* to learn [] from others

○ [] **ble·n** *{a quantity of money}* to pay {} for [], buy [] for {}

○ **e ble·n belanë me para** "buy trouble for money" to ask for trouble

○ <>**a ble·n mendimin** to figure out <>'s motives

○ <> **ble·n mendjen** to find out what <> thinks; read <>'s thoughts

○ <> **ble·n mendjen** to figure out what <> thinks; read <>'s mind; read <>'s mind, figure out <>'s intentions

○ [] **ble·n më/në këmbë** to buy [] on the hoof, buy [] live

○ <> **ble·n neshtrashen** to see what <> is up to

ble·*n* **nga nënbanaku** *(Pej)* to buy/sell under the counter (unofficially and as a personal favor)

[ ] **ble**·*n* **për pesë para** "buy [ ] for five cents" to sell/buy [ ] at a very low price: sell/buy [ ] for a song

ble·*n* **qen dhe <> del**·*3sg* **këlysh** to get less than <> bargained for

blec *adj (Reg)* undressed, naked

bleci *nf* nakedness

bleco·*n vt* to undress, denude

blegë *nf* shepherdess

blegëri·*n vi* **1** to bleat **2** *(Fig)* to wail, sob

blegërimë *nf ger* <**blegëri**·*n*

blegëro·*n vi* = **blegëri**·*n*

***blegras** *stem for 1st sg pres, 1st & 3rd pl pres, 2nd & 3rd sg subj* <**blegret**·

***blegret**· *vt* to bleat; moo, low; neigh

***blegris**
  I § *stem for 2nd pl pres, pind* <**blegret**·
  II § *stem for 1st sg pres, pl pres, 2nd & 3rd sg subj, pind* <**blegrit**·

blegrit· *vt* = **blegret**·

***blegrit** *stem for pdef, opt, adm, part, pind, 2nd pl pres, imper, vp* <**blegret**·

blegtor
  I § *n* stock farmer, herdsman
  II § *adj* = **blegtoral**

blegtoral *adj* pertaining to stock farming; pastoral

***blegtorar** = **blegtoral**

blegtoreshë
  I § *nf* <**blegtor**
  II § *adj fem* pastoral

blegtori *nf* **1** stock farming, animal husbandry **2** livestock
  blegtori e imët 1 animal husbandry for sheep and goats **2** *(Collec)* sheep and goats

***blejë** *nf* = **blerje**

blejzë *nf* hemp fiber

***blem** *nm (Reg Gheg)* market

***blemje** *nf ger (Reg Gheg)* = **blerje**

blendë *nf* [Geol] zinc blende, sphalerite

Blendi *nm* Blendi (male name)

***bleno**·*n vt* to sew [ ] together

***blerak** *adj* greenish

blerë
  I § *participle* <**ble**·*n*
  II § *adj (i)* **1** purchased; store-bought (in contrast with homemade) **2** *(Pej)* achieved by bribery, bought and paid for; corrupt

blerës
  I § *adj* purchasing, buying
  II § *n* buyer: customer

blerim *nm ger* **1** <**blero**·*n*, **blero**·*het* **2** greenery, verdure

Blerim *nm* Blerim (male name)

blerime *np* <**blerim** = **blerinë**

blerinë *nf* verdant countryside, green meadowland/ pasture

blerje *nf ger* <**ble**·*n*, **bli**·*het*

***blerkë** *nf* purchase

blero·*n vi* **1** to become verdant, sprout; be covered by green plants, be clothed in greenery, turn green **2** *(Reg)* to proliferate, increase quickly

blerosh *adj (Poet)* = **blertë**

blertë *adj (i)* green, grassy green; verdant

blertësi *nf (Book)* verdant green; greenery

bleruar *adj* verdant; green

***blerueshëm** *adj (i)* verdant

***bletakeqas** *adv* painfully, terribly

bletar *n* beekeeper

***bletar** *nm* = **bletërritës**

bletari *nf* apiculture, beekeeping

bletas *adv*

bletë
  I § *nf* **1** [Zool] honeybee *(Apis mellifica L.)* **2** bee colony, hive of bees
  II § *adj (Fig)* quick and adroit
  bletë e vulosur person who is economically secure: well-fixed person

bletëkapëse *nf* wire cage for capturing swarming bees

bletëngrënës *adj* bee-eating

***bletëri** *nf* beekeeping, apiculture

bletërritës *n* beekeeper

bletëz *nf* [Bot] **1** = bar blete **2** = lëpjetë

bletore *nf* apiary

bli(*n*) *nm* [Ichth] sturgeon *(Acipenser sturio L.)*
  bli i bardhë [Ichth] Adriatic sturgeon *Acipenser naccarii*
  bli Drini [Ichth] = **bli i bardhë**
  bli i llirisë [Ichth] star sturgeon *Acipenser stellatus*
  bli turigjatë [Ichth] sturgeon *Acipenser sturio*
  bli turishkurtër [Ichth] shortnose sturgeon, beluga *Huso huso L.*

bli(*r*) *nm* [Bot] **1** linden, lime tree *(Tilia)* **2** linden flower (used to make linden tea) **3** [Ichth] sturgeon *(Acipenser sturio)*

bli *stem for 2nd pl pres, pind, imper, vp* <**ble**·*n*
  bli ditë e shko wasting time

blibardh *nm* [Ichth] Adriatic sturgeon *(Acipenser naccarii)*

blic *nm* [Photo] flashbulb

blidë *nf* feed-bucket that attaches to a horse's head

***bligë** *nf* **1** aspergillum **2** piece of wood used to shuck corn

***bligo**·*n vt* to sprinkle, moisten

bligje *nf* **1** wooden stylus or scraper used by potter **2** knobbed wooden spool used to hold thread

***blikë** *nf* = **bligë**

***blim** *nm ger* <**blua**·*n*

***blime** *np* <**blem**

blinajë *nf* = **blinishtë**

blindazh *nm* [Mil] structure reinforced by armor; armored bunker

blindë *nf* [Mil] armorplate, armor; cuirass; protective skin

blindëshpues
  I § *adj* [Mil] armor-piercing
  II § *n* [Mil] soldier armed with armor-piercing weapon

blindim *nm ger* <**blindo**·*n*

blindo·*n vt* to dress [ ] in armor, provide [ ] with armorplate; provide [ ] with armed protection

blinduar *adj (i)* **1** armored **2** clothed in armor

blini *obl* <**bli**(*n*)

blinishtë *nf* forest of linden trees

blinore *np* linden family *Tiliaceae*

blinorë *np fem* [Zool] chondrostei

blinth *nm* [Bot] thick-stalked herbaceous plant with spear-like blades that grows in wetlands

bliqin nm [Bot] flowering rush (Butomus umbellatus)

blir|i obl <**bli**(r)

blirim nm ger **1** <**bliro**·n **2** tide

bliro·n vi **1** to overspill a channel, overflow, flood **2** (Reg) to go mad, lose one's mind

blirojë nf inundation, flood, overflow

blister adj [Spec] blistered (caused by impurities in metal smelting)

blo| stem for pdef <**blua**·n
  ○ **Bloftë bathë në mokër!** "May he grind beans on a millstone!" (Curse) May he suffer from hunger!

blo|çkë nf **1** corncob **2** pinecone *3 [Bot] cone of the female hop plant: (strobile)

blof nm (Book) **1** bluff (in card playing) **2** (Fig) bluffing, artifice

blofo·n vi (Book) to bluff

blogu|rë nf (Reg) the outer surface of a plant or plant part: tree bark, husk, peel, rind

blojë nf **1** pulverization of seed kernels by milling or grinding: milling **2** milled flour **3** sawdust

blojt|ës nm miller, grinder

*__blok__ nm (np ~ qe) = **bllok**

*__blokadë__ nf blockade

blokëra np dust left over from threshing, rubbish; sweepings

*__blokim__ nm ger <**bloko**·n

*__bloko__·n vt to blockade

*__blond__ adj blond = **bjond**

*__blore__ nf = **vlore**

*__bloshkë__ = **bloçkë**

blozak adj covered with soot, sooty; soot-colored

blozar nm beam above a fireplace to which is attached the chain holding a pothook

blozë nf **1** soot **2** [Chem] carbon dust **3** fungus disease in plants that results in the formation of masses of black, powdery spores in the parts affected: smut **4** a shelf on the wall for dishes, pots, and pans

blozëri nf dirty rubbish

*__blozët__ adj (i) charred

*__blozhë__ nf **1** moth **2** = **blozhëm**

blozhëm nf sawdust

blozhët adj (i) like sawdust, in a coarse powder

*__blozhitun__ adj (i) (Reg Gheg) moth-eaten; rotten, decayed

*__blozhurinë__ nf = **blozhëm**

blu adj, nf blue

blua·n
  I § vt **1** to grind, mill **2** to digest [food]; chew **3** (Fig) to assimilate [] by constant repetition or rehearsal **4** (Fig) to chew over [a problem] in one's head; scrutinize [a matter] from every angle **5** (Fig) to cause [] continuous/deep suffering
  II § vi (Colloq) to yak away, babble on, chatter away
  ○ **blua**·n **egjër** to be reduced to eating sawdust, be very poor
  ○ **blua**·n **imët** to have a keen mind, be smart/shrewd
  ○ **blua**·n **me mend** to think hard
  ○ **blua**·n **mendime të zymta në kokë** to have the blues, be in low spirits
  ○ **S'bluan më ai mulli.** "That mill no longer grinds." {}'s day is over. {} is over the hill.
  ○ **blua**·n **miell të hollë** "grind fine flour" to say wise/smart things
  ○ **blua**·n **në të thatë** to prattle on, talk to the wind

  ○ [] **blua**·n **nën lëkurë** to keep [] secret for a painfully long time
  ○ **blua**·n **si mulliri pa kokrra/ujë** to talk and talk without saying anything
  ○ **blua**·n **të trasha** to say stupid things, talk nonsense
  ○ **blua**·n **trashë** to say stupid things, talk nonsense

bluar adj (i) milled, pulverized, made into dust/powder/flour; ground up, broken into small pieces

bluarje nf ger <**blua**·n, **blu**·het

bluashkë nf wood chip/shaving

bludë nf wooden dish/bowl

bludë nf moldy growth that forms on wine allowed to stand too long

blum nm [Tech] bloom (of metal)

blumim nm [Spec] the process of forming metal blooms from ingots

blumues|e nf [Spec] blooming mill

*__blurinë__ nf crockery, china, glassware

*__blush__ nm plush, velvet

bluzë nf **1** blouse, tunic **2** smock
  ○ **bluzë tutash** sweatshirt

bluzhdë nf **1** small particle **2** = **bluzhdër**

bluzhdër nf minced and boiled cabbage

bluzhdo·n vt to break [] into small particles: pulverize

bllacaro·n vt to press [] into a mush

bllacë nf **1** swamp **2** = **bllacore**

bllacore nf [Food] corn-flour pasty filled with spinach or cabbage and with egg, butter, and milk on top

*__bllaçis__ stem for 1st sg pres, pl pres, 2nd & 3rd sg subj, pind <**bllaçit**·

*__bllaçit__· vt to chew

*__bllaçthën|ësi__ nf blasphemy

bllamburit· vi (Colloq) to mumble; prattle, babble

bllaskë nf thin piece of lumber, strip of lumber

*__bllatë__ nf (Old) [Relig] = **blatë**

*__bllatim__ nm = **blatim**

blloçkëlo|pë nf (Reg) [Zool] = **thithëlopë**

bllok nm (np ~ qe) **1** large, heavy block of a strong, solid material **2** concrete block **3** concrete pipe used to line water wells **4** cluster of structures **5** residential block serving as a neighborhood unit for organized social activities; city/town ward **6** (HistPK) reserved residential compound occupied by the political elite **7** orchard plot **8** thick notepad; notebook **9** political bloc **10** a group of components forming a unit of a more complex entity **11** [Sport] blocking a volleyball from getting over the net
  ○ **ësh·të**[3pl] **bllok** to be strongly and inseparably united
  ○ **bllok individual** [Volleyball] one-man block
  ○ **bllok zëri** [Cine] sound pick-up

bllokadë nf blockade

bllokha|us nm [Mil] blockhouse

bllokierë nf [Constr] mold for making cement blocks

bllokim nm ger **1** <**bloko**·n **2** blockade, blockage
  ○ **bllokim me trup** [Soccer] body check

bllokist nm = **bllokmen**

bllokmen nm (HistPK) member of the Communist elite living in a reserved residential compound

blloko'·*het vpr* to get blocked up/off; get stuck, block up

blloko'·*n vt* **1** to block; block [] off; blockade; block off [] **2** to prevent, interrupt, suspend **3** [*Soccer*] to check

blloku'ar *adj (i)* **1** blockaded **2** blocked off, interrupted **3** not working, stuck

bllokue's *nm* **1** [*Sport*] blocker (in volleyball) **2** [*Tech*] block, lock

bllo'qe *np* <**bllok**

bllo're *nf* **1** tree bark **2** corn husk

bllo'shkë *nf* **1** = **bluashkë** **2* = **barmë**

****bllu'shtër** *nf* salamander

****bllu'zë** *nf* blouse, sport jersey

BNA *abbrev (Italian)* <**Banco nazionale d'Albania** [*Hist*] National Bank of Albania = **BKSh**

****bo** *nf* = **boa**

bo'·*het vpr* (of animals) to copulate

bo'·*n vt* (of animals) to copulate with [ ]

bo'a *nf* [*Zool*] boa (snake)

bobe'l *nf* **1** [*Invert*] snail that appears in spring, usually after a rain, edible snail *Helix pomatia* **2** [*Invert*] tun shell *Tonna galea* **3** [*Mus*] wind instrument made of horn or from a large sea shell and used for signalling **4* = **bobo'l**ë

bobe'z *nf (Reg)* **1** [*Entom*] tick (parasite) **2** beam supporting the waterwheel of a mill

bobi'në *nf* **1** [*Tech*] bobbin; reel, spool **2** induction coil

○ **bobi'në dhë'nëse** [*Cine*] feed reel

○ **bobi'në filmi** [*Cine*] film spool, reel of film

○ **bobi'në marrëse** [*Cine*] taking reel

bo'bo *interj* **1** expresses regret, sorrow, pain or suffering about some misfortune; alas! = **bubu 2** expresses surprise at something unexpected or unusual; oh boy! **3** expresses misgivings or fear about some unpleasant eventuality; oh-oh! = **obobo 4** expresses reluctance or annoyance about doing something; aw! = **obobo**

bobo'ku'qe *nf* the flower of the Judas tree or of butcher's-broom

bobo'l *nm* **1** [*Bot*] European hackberry, nettle tree *(Celtis australis)* = **carac 2** [*Entom*] scarab beetle **3** seed; pulse

bobola'k *adj* rounded and plumped-up

bobo'le *nf* **1** a swollen kernel of a seed food, such as corn, beans, or wheat, when it has been boiled in water **2** boiled macaroni or lentils **3** *(Fig)* short, pudgy woman **4* [*Bot*] European hackberry, nettle tree *(Celtis australis)* **5** hackberry

bobole'sh *nm (Reg)* a large, round cucumber

bobore'shë *nf* [*Entom*] ant

bobori'cë *nf* [*Entom*] cockroach

bobo'shtar

I § *adj* of or pertaining to Boboshtica

II § *n* native of Boboshtica

Bobo'shtica *nf* historic village in southeastern Albania: Boboshtica

bobo'te *nf* corn mush; mushy corn bread

boboti'·*n vi (Colloq)* to sob uncontrollably, cry mournfully (while saying "bobo")

****boca'r** *nm* bottle maker

boce'l *nm* = **boce**

bo'cë *nf* **1** table flask, bottle; vial, small bottle **2** [*Publ*] proofsheet

bocma'n *nm* [*Naut*] boatswain

****bocû** *nm (Reg Gheg)* = **bocu'n**

bocu'n *nm (Reg)* big-bellied bottle; small demijohn

boç *nm* large, round, oleaginous olive

bo'çe *nf* **1** flower bud **2** round or conical husk-covered fruit of certain plants: cotton boll, pine cone **3** corncob **4** fleshy outer rind like that of walnuts or chestnuts **5** round object about the size of a fist; small, round purse **6** wooden spool holding wool fiber to be spun into yarn **7** egg yolk; egg fried without breaking the yolk **8** embroidered decoration, such as a flower, on clothing

boçe'thye's *nm* [*Ornit*] nutcracker *(Nucifraga caryocatactes L.)*

bo'çë *nf* = **boçe**

○ **bo'ça e fytit** [*Anat*] Adam's apple

boçe'bo'rë *nf* [*Bot*] common snowdrop *(Galanthus nivalis)*

bo'çkë

I § *nf* **1** small, globular fruit, such as that of chestnuts or cherries **2** [*Bot*] a poisonous medicinal plant: squill, sea onion *(Scilla maritima L.)*

II § *adj* plump

bode'c *nf* **1** metal tip of a goad **2** metal tool for dehusking corn

bode'ce *nf* small auger or drill bit used to start nail or screw holes

****bodi'le** *nf (Reg)* bottle

bodru'm *nm* **1** basement, storage cellar = **qila'r 2** dark, wet, subterranean hole **3** *(Old)* dungeon

****Boe'mi** *nf* Bohemia = **Bohemi**

boe'në *nf* flood, inundation, deluge; overflow

bof *onomat (Colloq)* expresses a sudden, unexpected event, in the way that English speakers might say "just like that!", accompanied by a snap of the fingers = **brof**

bo'fkë *nf* whole walnut/chestnut in its husk

****boga'ni'k** = **poganik**

****boga'ri's** *stem for 1st sg pres, pl pres, 2nd & 3rd sg subj, pind* <**bogari't·**

****bogari't·** *vt* to dry, shrivel

boga'z *nm (Old)* deep gorge in rugged mountain pass, dense with underbrush

Bogda'n *nm* Bogdan (male name)

boge'l *nf* small, unripe fruit

****bo'gëz** *nf* salt mine

****bogo'rr** *nm* tufa stone

bohi'asi *nf (Old)* **1** thin, bright red material used to wrap bundles for traveling, to make bedsheets, or to line clothes **2** the thread used to make this material

bohi'çalle'k *nm (np ˜ qe) (Old)* **1** gift of clothing brought by a bride or by the bride's parents when a child is born **2** = **bo'hçe**

bo'hçe *nf* **1** square piece of cloth in which items are wrapped for traveling or storage; bundle wrapped in a kerchief **2** decorated long apron of cotton or wool

bohe'më *nf (Book Pej)* bohemian

Bohe'mi *nf* Bohemia

bohorri't-*et vpr* to behave silly

boj *nm* stature, height

****boja'k** *adj* stale

boja'lle'shë *adj* = **bojalli**

boja'lli *adj* **1** varicolored, multicolored; beautifully colored **2** *(Colloq)* tall and handsome, tall and pretty

boja'rgje'nd *adj* silver (in color)

bojatis· *vt* **1** to paint **2** *(Old)* to dye, color **3** *(Colloq Pej)* to paint [one's face] with| cosmetics **4** *(Colloq Fig)* to adorn with color, give a sheen; decorate

bojatis je *nf ger* < **bojatis·**

boja xhi *nm (np ~ nj)* **1** painter (of houses, furniture, metalware, etc.) **2** dyer; dyeworker

bojë *nf (np ~ ra)* **1** paint; pigment; dye **2** color, tint **3** names or attributes the color of the noun (in the indefinite ablative case) that follows: the color of **4** *(Colloq)* complexion, facial color **5** *(Pej)* face **6** *(Reg)* mildew **7** *(Colloq)* (of a person) body, build, stature **8** approximate measure of height roughly equal to that of an average person, body-length
  ○ **bojë deti** light blue
  ○ **bojë festje** dark red
  ○ **bojë hall** scarlet, vermillion
  ○ **bojë hiri** color of ash: light gray
  ○ **bojë jargavani** mauve
  ○ **bojë kafe** dark brown
  ○ **bojë këpucash** shoe cream
  ○ **bojë qeramike** terra cotta
  ○ **bojë qielli** sky-blue
  ○ **bojë simpatike** sympathetic ink, invisible ink
  ○ **bojë smalti** enamel paint
  ○ **bojë shkrimi** ink
  ○ **bojë vaji** oil paint

bojë bize le *adj* pea green in color

bojë çeli k *adj* steel gray in color

bojë fi një *adj* lye-colored, dishwater gray

bojë gështe një *adj* chestnut brown

bojë gru rë *adj* wheat-colored, dark tan

bojë gja k *adj* blood-red, dark red, crimson

bojë gja ke *nf* reddish brown animal (usually cow or goat)

bojë hu rmë *adj* persimmon in color, reddish yellow

bojë jeshi l *adj* green-colored

bojë kafe *adj* coffee-colored, brown

bojë ka shtë *adj* straw-colored, light tan, blond

bojë limo n *adj* lemon-colored, yellow

bojë ma dh *adj (Colloq)* large-bodied, tall

bojë manusha qe *adj* violet-colored, violet

bojë mi sh *adj* "meat color" vinegar-red in color

bojë mja ltë *adj* honey-colored, brownish yellow

bojë portoka ll *adj* orange-colored

bojë ra *np* < **bojë**

bojë she gë *adj* pomegranate-colored, bright red

bojë shi t es *nm (Old)* merchant selling clothing dyes

bojë shku rtër *adj (Colloq)* small-bodied, short

bojë shpa tëz *adj* cornflower-colored, light blue

bojë tje gull *adj* tile-colored, dark red

bojë trëndafi l *adj* pink, rose-colored

bojë tu llë *adj* brick red

bojë ve rë *adj* wine-colored

bojë vi shnje *adj* cherry-colored

bojë vjo llcë *adj* purple, violet

*****boji m** *nm ger* = **bojatis je**

bojko t *nm* boycott

bojkoti m *nm ger* **1** < **bojkoto ·n 2** boycott

bojkoto ·n *vt* **1** to boycott **2** to ostracize

bojkotu a r *adj (i)* boycotted

bojkotu e s *adj* boycotter

bojle r *nm* [*Spec*] boiler

boji i *nf* big-fruited, June-ripening, dark-red cherry

*****boj na** *(Reg Gheg)* = **boj ëra**

bojska ut *nm* boy scout

boju thull *adj* vinegar-red in color

*****bok** *nm* dandruff = **zbokth**

bo kë
  I § *nf* **1** barren and rocky slope; rocky land **2** *(Fig)* dull-witted person, moron
  II § *adj* barren and rocky
  ○ **nuk ësh·të në bokë** not be in one's right mind

bo kël *nf* **1** corncob **2** small wooden bobbin for wool thread

*****bokë ri** *OR* **bok rri** *nf* = **bokëri më**

bokë ri më *nf* **1** dry and bare land; rocky soil **2** = **bokë 3** reef, shoal

bokë ri m të *adj (i)* lacking vegetation, barren, bare; craggy

bokë ri në = **bokëri më**

bokë ri shtë *nf* barren area with rocky slopes

bokë rr *nf* [*Zool*] rust-colored field mouse that is destructive to crops

boko l *nm* [*Tech*] bushing; sleeve (on a machine part)

*****bokoli n** *adj* puny; paltry; disreputable, unsightly

*****bokrri më** *OR* **bok rri në** *nf* = **bokëri më**

boks *nm* **1** [*Sport*] boxing **2** boxing match **3** *(Colloq)* blow with the fist **4** strong and smooth leather, calfskin **5** small pen for keeping new-born livestock **6** crib for storing grain or cotton

bo ks *nf* container for salt and pepper

boks ie r *nm* boxer, fighter in a boxing match

boksi t *nm* [*Min*] bauxite

*****bo kshë** *nf* = **bo hçe**

bo lbe *nf (Colloq)* mishap, accident, blunder; disorder, confusion, trouble

bolc *nm* [*Agr*] sole of a plow

Bolivi *nf* Bolivia

bolivia n *adj, n* Bolivian

bolivia n *adj, n* Bolivia

bolshevi k *nm* Bolshevik; bolshevik

bolshevi zëm *nm* Bolshevism

boll *adv (Colloq)* **1** adequately, enough **2** a great deal, much, plenty

bo llë *nf* **1** [*Zool*] Aesculapian snake (*Elaphe longissima*) **2** [*Invert*] glowworm *Lampyris noctiluca*
  ○ **bollë laramane** [*Zool*] leopard snake *Elaphe situla*
  ○ **bollë shtëpie** [*Zool*] Aesculapian snake (*Elaphe longissima*)
  ○ **bollë uji** [*Zool*] grass snake, ringed snake (*Natrix natrix*)
  ○ **bollë varrezash** [*Zool*] chicken-snake, four-lined rat snake *Elaphe quatuorlineata*

bo llëk *nm (Colloq)* **1** a large amount, a great deal, plenty **2** abundance, plentifulness, profusion **3** wealth, prosperity

bollë si sht *adv* in abundance, profusely

bollë sha rde *nf* **1** *(Folklore)* huge many-headed snake **2** *(Fig Insult)* fierce and evil woman **3** [*Zool*] long snake with a thick, splotchy gray skin

bollë ve rbë *nf* [*Zool*] blindworm, slowworm (*Anguis fragilis*)

bollë z *nf* **1** plowshare **2** sled/sleigh runner

bollgu r *nm* bulgur, cracked grain, groats
  ○ **bollgur tërshëre** oatmeal

bo llka *np (Reg)* baggy pants

*****bo llkë** *nf (Reg)* little shirt; bodice

bollobo'çkë
 I § _adj_ (Reg) **1** plump (said of fruits and vegetables) **2** plump-faced, healthy, robust
 II § _nf_ robust girl

*bollshevík _adj_ = bolshevík

*bollshevízëm _nm_ = bolshevízëm

bollshëm _adj_ (i) **1** quite sufficient **2** bountiful, abundant, plentiful **3** roomy, spacious

bollujce = bollujëse

bolluj·ëse _nf_ [Zool] grass snake, ringed snake (Natrix natrix)

*bomb _nm_ bowler hat: derby

bombahe'dh·ës
 I § _nm_ [Mil] grenade launcher
 II § _adj_ [Mil] grenade-launching

bombardë _nf_ **1** [Hist] medieval catapult/cannon *2 destroyer (warship)

bombardím _nm ger_ **1** <bombardo'·n **2** bombardment

*bombardís· _vt_ = bombardo'·n

*bombardísje _nf ger_ = bombardís· bombardment

bombardo'·n _vt_ to bombard, bomb

bombardue's
 I § _nm_ bomber (airplane)
 II § _adj_ used for bombing

bombastík _adj_ bombastic

Bombe'i _nm_ Bombay

bombë _nf_ bomb; grenade
 ◦ bombë me veprim të ngadalshëm delayed-action bomb
 ◦ bombë nxehtësimatëse [Tech] caliometric bomb
 ◦ bombë vullkanike [Geol] volcanic bomb

*bombík _nm_ silkworm

bombolë _nf_ cylinder for storing a gas

*bomkë _nf_ bombast, pomp

*bomkët _adj_ (i) bombastic

*bomp _adj_ worthless

Bon _nm_ Bonn

bonbo'ne _nf_ bonbon

bonbone'ri _nf_ confectioner's shop, bonbonnière

*bondullë _nf_ bundle

bonifikím _nm ger_ **1** <bonifiko'·n **2** land reclamation

bonifiko'·n _vt_ to reclaim land, convert land to productive use

bonifikua'r _adj_ (i) reclaimed, improved

bonifikue's
 I § _adj_ pertaining to land reclamation
 II § _n_ reclamation worker

bono _nf_ coupon; ticket

bonz _nm_ **1** [Relig] bonze **2** (Book Pejor) autocrat

bonja'k
 I § _adj_ orphaned
 II § _nm_ orphan

bonja'ke _nf_ **1** orphan girl **2** (Reg) swampland

bonjakëri _nf_ **1** orphanhood **2** (Fig) the poor **3** orphanage

bonja'r
 I § _n_ **1** orphan **2** poor person; beggar
 II § _adj_ *orphaned

bo'një
 I § _nf_ worker bee
 II § _adj_ (Fig) (said of women) industrious, tireless

bonjëri _nf_ **1** [Food] something delicious; sweet **2** craving for sweets, sweet tooth

*bo'që _nf_ (Reg Kos) ear of corn with few kernels

bor _nm_ [Chem] boron (Bo)

bo'r _stem for pdef_ <bjerr·

*bora'çe _nf_ = bora'ks

boragjino're _np_ [Bot] borage family Boraginaceae

bora'k _nm_ **1** (Reg) [Ornit] = bo'rës *2 = bora'ks

bora'ks _nm_ [Chem] borax

borani _nf_ [Food] spinach cooked with rice

*bora'shk _nm_ whirlwind

Borba'rdh|a _nf_ Borbardha (female name)

borbo'çine'zë _nf_ oyster

borbole'c _nm_ [Zool] (Reg) sheep botfly, botfly maggot, botfly (Hypoderma bovis, Oestrus ovis)

borbo'll _nm_ [Entom] dung beetle (Goetrupes stercorarius)

bo'rbull _nm_ [Bot] cotoneaster (Cotoneaster)

borç _nm_ **1** [Ornit] siskin (Carduelis spinus) *2 = borxh
 ◦ borç i kuq [Ornit] red poll Carduelis flammea
 ◦ borç lini [Ornit] linnet Carduelis cannabina

*borç|le'shë _nf_ = debtor (female)

*borçlítur _adj_ (i) in debt

bord _nm_ **1** [Naut] ship's side **2** [Naut] deck of a boat/ship **3** [Tech] the interior part of an aircraft or other vessel of transport **4** [Spec] = bordurë

bordatríçe _nf_ [Spec] flanging/beading machine

bo'rde _nf_ opening/hole (in a wall/roof)

borde'l _nm_ bordello, brothel

bordero' _nf_ **1** [Fin] payroll list **2** inventory list, consignment inventory

Bordo' _nf_ Bordeaux

bordulla'k _nm_ [Bot] purslane (Portulaca oleracea)

bordullako're _np_ [Bot] Portulacaceae

bordu're _nf_ rim, edging, border

bo're _nf_ snow-white goat

boreal _adj_ [Geog] boreal

bo'rë
 I § _nf_ snow
 II § _adv_ snowy (used as intensifier with adjectives for whiteness or cleanliness)
 III § _adj_ very cold, ice-cold
 ◦ borë i bardhë snow white, milk-white
 ◦ bora lëmoçe snowdrift, snow pile
 ◦ bora e pleqërisë "the snow of old age" (Poet) the snowy hair of old age: gray hair, white hair

Borë|ba'rdhë _nf_ [Folklore] Snow White (girl made of snow)

borë|ma't|ës _nm_ [Spec] device for measuring snowfall: snow gauge

borë|pastrue's
 I § _adj_ snow-cleaning
 II § _nm_ snow-cleaning machine

bo'rës _nm_ [Ornit] chaffinch (Fringilla coelebs)

borgu'll _nm_ **1** = bollgu'r **2** [Ornit] chaffinch (Fringilla coelebs)

borgje'z _adj, n_ bourgeois
 ◦ borgjez i vogël petit bourgeois.

borgjezí _nf_ bourgeoisie
 ◦ borgjezia kompradore (Book) class of intermediaries who arrange trade of foreign capital for domestic products
 ◦ borgjezi e vogël petite bourgeoisie

borgjezím _nm ger_ <borgjezo'·het

borgjezo'·het _vpr_ to turn bourgeois

borgjezo·*n vt (Pejor)* to endow with bourgeois characteristics

bori *nf* **1** bugle; trumpet **2** signal horn **3** fluted whistle made by children out of a leaf of a willow or Judas tree **4** *(Colloq)* stovepipe **5** *(Colloq)* chimney pot
  ○ **bori automobili** automobile horn

bori'ce *nf* **1** light snow accompanied by a very cold wind **2** cold northerly, snow-carrying wind

bori'gë *nf* [*Bot*] black pine/spruce, Austrian pine *(Pinus negra)*

***bori'gëz** *nf* chip, splinter

bori'k *adj* [*Chem*] boric

bori'më *nf* **1** fine snow mixed with rain; powdery snow **2** unplowed narrow strip of ground at the edge of a field

bori'shtë *nf* poor soil, stripped land

bori't· *vt* to work [the border strips of a field]

bori'za'n *nm* person who blows the bugle/trumpet: bugler, trumpeter

***borlo'g** *nm (Reg Kos)* garbage, trash

bo'rmë *nf* fruit-bearing cutting from the olive tree, olive scion

bor'najë *nf* heavy snowfall; broad expanse of ground covered by snow; snowfield

bo'rnë *nf* [*Electr*] binding post, screw terminal

boro' *nf (Reg)* bureau, chest of drawers

***boroçis**| *stem for 1st sg pres, pl pres, 2nd & 3rd sg subj, pind* <**boroçit**·

***boroçi't**· *vt* to bung up [], stop

***borola'c** *adj* bright, cheerful

***borola'r** *adj* jocular

***boroli'** *nf* fooling around, jesting, tomfoolery

***boroni'** *nf* pan

boroni'cë *nf* [*Bot*] whortleberry, bilberry *(Vaccinum myrtillus)*

***boro'ta'r** *nm* comedian

bors *nm* [*Ornit*] chaffinch *(Fringilla coelebs)*

borsali'në *nf* narrow-brimmed soft felt hat with a decorative ribbon: Borsalino hat

borse'te *nf* handbag, purse

bo'rsë *nf* **1** handbag, purse **2** hot-water bottle

***borsilo'k** *nm* [*Bot*] = **borzilo'k**

bor'shta'ngë *nf* [*Spec*] boring bar

borxh *nm* **1** loan **2** debt
  ○ **ta paça borxh!** *(Felic)* I owe you one!

borxh|li' *nm (Colloq)* **1** borrower, debtor **2** *(Fig)* person who owes a favor

borxh|pa|la'rë *adj* having unpaid debts: deadbeat

borzilo'k *nm* [*Bot*] basil, sweet basil *(Ocimum basilicum)*
  ○ **borzilok i egër** wild basil *Satureja bulgaris*

borro'çit·*et vpr* to wrestle (with each other), scuffle

borro'hit·*et vpr* to groan, cry without tears, sigh

borro'ko'c *nm* **1** bull calf; small-bodied bull **2** *(Fig)* young boy with a sturdy body

borro'vi'q *nm* [*Ornit*] curlew *(Numenius arquata)*

bos *nm* **1** boss, chief **2** *(Colloq)* big shot

Bosfo'r *nm* Bosphorus

bosk *n* hornless goat

***bo'skë** *nf* saltcellar

***bosnja'k** *adj, n* Bosnian

***bo'snj**ë *nf* [*Bot*] crab apple *(Malus sylvestris)*

Bo'snjë *nf* Bosnia

Bo'snjë *nf* Bosnia

bosta'n *nm* **1** melon **2** melon patch; vegetable garden
  ○ **bostan i egër** [*Bot*] squirting cucumber *Ecballium elaterium*

bosta'n|çe *adv* [*Hort*] cultivating the soil separately for each plant

bostan|i'shte *nf* melon patch, field of melons

bostan|o'r *adj* [*Hort*] of or pertaining to melon or gourd-like plants

bostan|o're
  I § *nf* [*Hort*] = **bostani'sht**e
  II § *np* [*Bot*] gourd family *Cucurbitaceae*

bostan|xhi' *nm (np ~ nj) (Colloq)* **1** vegetable/melon gardener **2** vegetable/melon seller

bosti' *nf* long pole used to knock down nuts from a tree

bosh
  I § *adj (Colloq)* **1** empty, blank; unoccupied, free, vacant **2** vacuous, hollow, worthless, meaningless **3** futile, in vain
  II § *adv (Colloq)* **1** emptily, without accomplishing anything **2** *(Fig)* futilely, in vain, for nothing, gratuitously, worthlessly, uselessly, meaninglessly

bosh|ati's· *vt (Colloq)* to empty out, evacuate

bosh|ati's·*et vpr* **1** to be vacant, be empty **2** to remain with nothing

boshati's|je *nf ger (Colloq)* <**boshati's**·

bo'sh|je *nf* empty pod (of peas or beans)

bosh|lle'k *nm (Colloq)* **1** empty/open space/place; emptiness **2** vacancy **3** *(Fig)* deficiency **4** *(Fig)* vacuum **5** *(Fig)* spiritual vacuum, empty feeling

boshnja|'k = **bosnja'k**

bosht
  I § *nm* **1** spindle; bobbin; bobbinful of yarn **2** axle; main shaft of a machine, tool, or implement **3** axis **4** longitudinal core **5** *(Fig)* essence, crux, heart, main direction, basic path **6** *(Fig)* part that bears the major weight of something: pillar
  II § *adj* central, chief; crucial, determining
  ○ **bosht kardanik** [*Tech*] Cardan shaft
  ○ **boshti i këmbës** [*Anat*] fibula
  ○ **boshti i kurrizit** [*Anat*] backbone, spine
  ○ **bosht i plakës** [*Bot*] hoary pepperwort, hoary cress *Lepidium draba*

bosht|a'k *adj* spindle-shaped

bo'sht|ër *nf* [*Bot*] forsythia *(Forsythia europea)*

***bo'sht|ërr** = **bo'sht|ër**

***bosht|i'në** *nf* crochet hook, pin

***bosht|i'n|ëz** *nf dimin* <**bosht|i'në**

bosht-ingrana'zh *nm* [*Tech*] pinion shaft

***bosht|i'nj** *np* <**bosht** *(Reg Tosk)*

bosht|iva'n *nm* diagonal strut/brace, cross-beam

bosht|o'r *adj* **1** [*Spec*] axial, along an axis **2** [*Anat*] spinal, vertebrate

bot
  I § *adv (Colloq)* without let-up, relentlessly
  II § *nm (Colloq)* **1** a certain person, Mr. So and So, someone *2* cistern
  ○ **bot e bir/bot/qyt** with strenuous effort, by struggling hard

botani'k *adj* botanical

botani'kë *nf* botany

botani'st *n* botanist

bo'te *nf* narrow-necked clay jug for liquids

bo'të nf 1 world; earth; the universe 2 people taken as a collective whole 3 someone else, a stranger 4 kind of light-gray clay 5 (Euph) epilepsy

∘ **e bija e botës** 1 girl who does not belong to one's family circle, stranger 2 (Contempt) this/some (damn) girl

∘ **gruaja e botës** 1 girl/woman who does not belong to one's family circle, stranger 2 (Contempt) this/some (damn) girl

∘ **bota e gjallë** living things/beings

∘ **s'ësh·të në këtë botë** not understand what's going on; be cut off from reality

∘ **bota e përtejme** life after death: the next world, the world beyond the grave; afterworld

bo'të bardhë nf a kind of light-gray clay

bo'të gjinato're nf 1 clay rolled into balls by the clay wasp 2 [Entom] long-legged yellow wasp that gathers clay into little balls, clay wasp

bo'të kuptim nm worldview, general outlook, general attitude

bo'të kuptim o'r adj having to do with one's worldview

bo'të ku'qe nf red clay

bo'tëm adj (i) pale, pallid

bo'të ndij i'm nm (Book) world view

bo'të ri'sht adv publicly, openly, right out in the open

bo'të ro'r adj worldwide, global, of the whole world

***bo'të rt** adj (i) of clay, earthen

bo'ti ce nf clay soil

***bo'ti le** nf bottle, flask

bo'tim nm ger 1 <boto·n, boto he 2 publication 3 the set of copies printed from a single setting of type: edition, printing 4 (Old) declaration, notification

bo'ti në nf wetlands, mudhole, swampland

***bo'tna** np <bo'të (Reg Gheg)

***bo'tni sht** adv (Reg Gheg) = bo'të ri'sht

boto·n vt to publish

bo'to nje s = botu'es

bo'to'r adj (Old) 1 entire, general; public 2 civic, communal

bo'to're nf (Colloq Old) office dealing with civil engineering projects

***bo'tra** np <bo'të (Reg Tosk)

***bo'tsi'm** nm publicity

Botsva'në nf Botswana

***bo'tsh ëm** adj (i) = boto'r

botu'es

I § nm publisher

II § adj of or pertaining to publishing

botu'e sh ëm adj (i) publishable, worthy of publication

bo've nf [Naut] buoy

boza'xhi nm (np ~ nj) brewer of grain cider

bo'zë nf tart cider made of corn or millet

***bozi'lo'k** nm [Bot] = borzilo'k

bozoga'ne nf [Bot] 1 wild pear (Pyrus pyraster) = dardhu'ka 2 almond pear, almond-shaped pear tree (Pyrus amygdaliformis) = gorri'cë

***bozu'k** = buzu'k

bo'zhë nf = bozho'r

bozho'r n [Ornit] pelican

bozhu're

I § nf 1 [Bot] peony (Paeonia) 2 animal (cow, mare, or nanny goat) with reddish hair

II § adj barren, infertile, poor (said of land with reddish soil)

BP abbrev <**Bashkimet Profesionale** Trade Unions

BPSh abbrev <**Bashkimet Profesionale të Shqipërisë** Trade Unions of Albania

BQKA abbrev <**Bashkimi Qendror i Kooperativave të Artizanatit** (Old) Central Union of Artisan Cooperatives

brac nm (Colloq) 1 petty thief *2 hook, hanger

bracana're np (Reg) [Geol] stalactites

***bra'ca'r** n (Reg Kos) = brac

***bra'cë** nf 1 upper arm 2 fathom

braci nf (Colloq) 1 petty larceny, petty theft 2

braco·n vi vt 1 to filch, pilfer, swipe 2 to swindle, cheat

***bra'çi në** nf pond, pool

brahma'n nm Brahman

brahma'n i'zëm nm Brahmanism

braho'm nm (Reg) 1 clay baking dish *2 trusted friend; henchman

bra'jë nf a protuberance under a surface: lump, bump, hump

brak nm large, white, short-haired watchdog with big ears and dark body patches

brake'sh a np white woolen trousers

***bra'kë** nf = bërra'kë

***braki** nf [Bot] wild service tree (Sorbus torminalis)

brakicefa'l adj [Anthro] brachycephalic

brakiqefa'l = brakicefa'l

brakti's· vt 1 to abandon [a place], leave 2 to quit, leave off, break off with 3 to desert, turn one's back on

brakti's·et vpr to fall into disuse

brakti'sje nf ger 1 <brakti's·, brakti's·et 2 abandonment

brakti's ur adj abandoned, deserted

bram nm 1 wax drippings; residue left by a melting process, slag 2 wool grease, grime from wool *3 iron filings

brambu'll

I § nm (np ~ j) = buri'sht ë

II § adv in roaring flame

brambu'lli·n vi 1 = brambu'llo·n 2 (Fig) to make a lot of noise 3 (Pej fig) to chatter, chatter away

brambu'lli m ë nf ger <brambu'lli·n

brambu'llo·n vi to make the crackling sound of a roaring fire; make a pitter-pattering sound on the roof

bramc *I §* nm OR **bra'mc** *II §* nf slag, dross

bramsh nm 1 small globular object, little ball 2 unripe fig 3 small unripe melon used for pickling 4 (Fig) immature child, tot, toddler

bran

I § adv = zva'rrë

II § nm *trouble, nuisance

brana'r adj slovenly

brandspo'jt nm [Spec] fire-hose nozzle

bra'n ë

I § nf 1 harrow, rake 2 [Text] forked device on a loom that is weighted down to maintain tension on the warp 3 (Reg) snow avalanche

II § adv adrag, draggingly, along the ground

bran i'm nm ger <brano'·n

branis· vt 1 = brano'·n 2 to drag, drag [] along 3 to slow [] down, prolong *4 to break [] into small pieces by rolling *5 to harass, annoy, bother

bran|**o·**·*n vt* to harrow, rake

branov|**is** *stem for 1st sg pres, pl pres, 2nd & 3rd sg subj, pind* <**branovi·t**·

*****branovi·t**· *vt* to harrow

brash *nm* runt melon

BRASh *abbrev* <**Bashkimi i Rinisë Antifashiste Shqiptare** [*Hist*] Union of Albanian Anti-Fascist Youth

brash|**ani·ke** *nf* premature baby

brashnj|**a·r** *n* **1** shoe repairman **2** poor man, pauper **3** *(Pej)* person who takes bribes, corrupt person; person overly concerned with material goods

bra·shnj|**ë** *nf* **1** old shoe; worn out shoe **2** sweepings, trash **3** *(Pej)* bribe

Bratisla·vë *nf* Bratislava

brav|**ana·k** *nm* bracket into which the door bolt fits

brav|**andreq**|**ë·s** *nm* lock repairman

brav|**apun**|**u**|**e·s** *nm* locksmith

brav|**a·r** *n* herdsman for dairy goats/sheep

brav|**a·re**
    I § *nf* **1** dairy goat/sheep *****2** pet lamb
    II § *np* flock of dairy goat/sheep under the care of a village herdsman
    III § *adj fem* kept in the house as a dairy animal (applied to goat or sheep)

brav|**axhi·** *nm (np ˉ nj)* = **bravapunu·es**

brav|**ë** *nf* **1** keyed lock **2** *(Reg)* door bar, door bolt

*****bravi·c**|**ë** *nf* [*Ichth*] = **llo·sk**ë

bra·vo *interj* bravo! good for you!

*****bravo·**·*n vi* = **brohori·t**·

bravo·s· *vt(Colloq)* to lock with a key, lock up

bra·zd|**ë** *nf* **1** furrow **2** crease, groove **3** *(Fig)* track, trace; impression, scar

brazd|**ë**|**hap**|**ë·s** *nm* [*Agr*] cultivator (farm implement), furrower

brazd|**o·** *vt* to open up furrows in the ground; cultivate soil

*****bra·z**|**ë** *nf* = **brazd·**ë

bra·z|**ëm** *nm* = **kri·sm**ë

brazi·li|**a·n** *adj, n* Brazilian

brazi·m|**ë** *nf* **1** = **bry·m**ë **2** hoarfrost

*****brazh·**|**ëll**|**i·m**|**ë** *nf* babble, din

*****brazh·**|**ëll**|**o·**·*n vi* to make a babble, make noise

*****bra·zh**|**ëm** *nf* = **bra·z**ëm

bre
    I § *interj (Colloq)* **1** vocative particle used to call out to someone, hey! **2** expresses shock/surprise: wow! oh boy!
    II § *nm* [*Bot*] <**bredh**

bre··*het vpr* to quarrel; have an argument/fight; suffer inside

bre·*n*
    I § *vt* **1** to gnaw, nibble **2** to eat away at [ ], corrode, erode
    II § *vi* **1** to itch **2** *(Fig)* to gnaw at one's insides constantly, cause remorse/regret
    ◦ **bre·**·*n* **hekur me** [ ] to be badly at odds with [ ]; quarrel with [ ]
    ◦ [ ] **bre·**·*n*^{3sg} **krimbi** something *keeps* eating/gnawing at [ ]
    ◦ ◇ **bre·**·*n*^{3sg} **miu pallën** "the mouse *gnaws* at ◇'s sword" ◇ *is* a spineless and inactive good-for-nothing
    ◦ ◇ **bre·**·*n*^{3sg} **zemra** ◇ *has* a gnawing suspicion?

◦ ◇ **bre·**·*n* **zemrën** (of a problem) to gnaw at ◇, not let ◇ rest until ◇ finds a solution

bredru·r|**ë** *nf* [*Ornit*] woodpecker = **qukapi·k**

bredh *nm* [*Bot*] fir *(Abies L.)*
    ◦ **bredh i zi** [*Bot*] Norway spruce *Picea abies*

bredh·
    I § *vi* **1** to roam, wander, stroll **2** to run, go fast **3** to frolic, caper, leap/hop about **4** to skip; ricochet **5** *(Pej)* to live frivolously; chase women
    II § *vt* **1** *(Colloq)* to stroll around, circumambulate, wander around **2** to skip, flit over **3** *(Colloq)* to take around to various parts of **4** [*Phys*] to reflect (of sonic or electromagnetic waves)
    ◦ **bredh·** **hu më hu 1** to keep moving around; (of a woman) sleep around (be promiscuous) **2** to wander around, roam
    ◦ **bredh·** **lule me lule** "go from flower to flower" *(Pej)* to run around with one girlfriend after another (but have no permanent attachment to any)

    ◦ ◇ **bredh·**^{3sg} **mendja** ◇'s mind *wanders,* ◇ thoughts *are* elsewhere

bredh|**aca·k**
    I § *adj (Pej)* gadding about, wanderering aimlessly
    II § *nm* vagabond, hobo, drifter

bredh|**ara·k**
    I § *adj* **1** wandering, roaming, itinerant, peripatetic; grazing **2** nomadic
    II § *nm* nomad, wanderer, vagabond

bredh|**ë** *nf* **1** ricochet **2** leap, bound

bredh|**ëri**·*n vi* to roam around

bredh|**ë·s**
    I § *adj* **1** in constant motion: moving, restless; wandering, nomadic, drifting **2** running around, desultory, inconstant **3** [*Phys*] reflective (of sonic or electromagnetic waves)
    II § *n* vagabond, hobo, drifter

*****bredh**|**i·** *nf* ramble, outing

bredh|**i·sht**|**ë** *nf* forest of fir trees, fir copse

bre·dhj|**e** *nf ger* **1** <**bredh·** **2** [*Phys*] reflection

bredh|**o·**·*n vi* = **bre·dh·**

*****bre·dh**|**shëm** *adj (i)* leaping, hopping; running
    ◦ **së bredhshmi** *(Reg Tosk)* suddenly

bre·dht|**ë** *adj (i)* made of fir, of fir

bre·dh|**ur** *adj (i)* much-traveled; very experienced

brefotro·f *nm (Book Old)* children's home, orphanage

breg
    I § *nm* **1** land bordering a body of water, coast, shore **2** dune, hill, hillock, pile of soil **3** edge, rim **4** lump (of some foodstuff)
    II § *np* coastal areas
    ◦ **breg më breg** from one bank (of a body of water) to the other

breg|**abu·n**|**as** *n* person who lives near the Bunë river

*****breg**|**a·det**|**as** *adj* = **bregdeta·r**

breg|**a·le** *nf* = **brego·re**

breg|**al**|**o·**·*n vt* to tumble down from a small height

breg|**al**|**u·m**|**as** *n* person who lives along a river

breg|**a·mat**|**as** *n* person who lives near the Mat river

breg|**a·s** *n* = **bregdeta·r**

breg|**c**|**ë** *nf* [*Ornit*] bee-eater *(Merops apiaster L.)*

breg|**de·t** *nm* seashore, seacoast

breg|**deta·r**
    I § *adj* coastal, littoral
    II § *n* **1** coast dweller **2** [*Mil*] coast guardsman

bregdetas
I § n 1 seacoast inhabitant 2 inhabitant of the coast of the Ionian Sea
II § adj coastal, littoral

bregë nf piece

bregël nf hummock, slight elevation

bregëzim nm ger [Naut] <bregëzo·n

bregëzo·n vt [Naut] to bring a boat or ship to a land mooring, land a boat or ship

breginjë nf hilly area

bregishtë nf 1 area full of hills; area with steep, dry, barren hills *2 border area

breglumas = bregalumas

breglumë nm river bank

bregole nf low rise, hummock, small hillock/knoll

bregor adj 1 hilly 2 = bregdetar

bregore nf 1 low hill, hillock, knoll *2 hilly country

bregosun adj (i) (Reg Gheg) hilly

bregujor adj (Book) dwelling at the edge of a lake or ocean

brejcë nf small knife with no handle

brejë nf 1 cellulitis, festering of tissue around a wound, gangrene *2 touchwood

brejt stem for pdef, part, opt, adm <bre·n

brejtar nm [Zool] = brejtës

brejtës
I § nm [Zool] rodent
II § adj 1 [Zool] of or pertaining to rodents 2 gnawing, nibbling

brejtje nf ger 1 <bre·n, bre·het 2 erosion

brejtur adj (i) gnawed

brekazi nf [Entom] stag beetle (Lucanus cervus)

brekdetas = bregdetas

breke np 1 (Crude) underpants; shorts 2 (Colloq) thick plumage on the legs of certain fowl
○ **breke banje** swimming trunks

brekëcjerrë adj (Colloq) = brekëgrisur

brekëgrisur adj (Colloq) in worn-out underwear; with clothes in tatters

brekëzi nm (np ~ nj) (Colloq) = brekushezi

brekore nf woolen swaddling cloth

brekushe np breeches, pantaloons, Turkish trousers

brekushecjerrë adj (Colloq) = brekëgrisur

brekushegrisur adj (Colloq) = brekëgrisur

brekushezi nm (np ~ nj) (Colloq) person wearing black pantaloons

brelise nf woodpecker = qukapík

bremë part <bre·n

brenaveke np = benevreke

brenc nm knife for scraping off burnt crust from baked loaves

brenda
I § adv prep (abl) inside; within
II § formative prefix intra-, endo-, inner
○ **ësh·të brenda 1** to fall within the law 2 (Pej) to be by the book 3 to be personally knowledgeable, have first-hand expertise
○ **brenda këtyre ditëve** within a few days
○ **brenda në** [ ] inside [ ]
○ **brenda për brenda 1** in private 2 down deep, deep inside

brendafisnor adj within the clan, familial

brendapërbrenda
I § adv 1 in private 2 down deep, deep inside

II § prep (abl) within, within the confines of <>

brendaqelizor adj [Med] intracellular

brendashkrua·n vt [Geom] to inscribe one geometric figure inside another

brendashkruar adj (i) [Geom] inscribed

brendatajitës adj [Med] endocrine, incretory

brendazi adv internally; from within; towards the interior

brendës nm 1 = brendshëm 2 = brendësi

brendësi nf 1 interior 2 insides, contents; core

brendësirë nf = brendësi

brendi nf 1 contents; core 2 content, substance 3 interior

brendior adj (Book) internal; interior, inner

brendshëm
I § adj (i) 1 interior, inside, internal 2 inherent, basic
II § n (i) insider; blood relative
○ **nxënës i brendshëm** student who lives on campus: resident student
○ **student i brendshëm** student who lives on campus: resident student

brendshme nf 1 interior 2 internal organs, entrails 3 underwear

brendshmi adv (së) from the inside, from inside

brenë nf 1 big stick/rod/shaft/pole; fence post, lock bar 2 boatpole 3 [Tech] connecting rod = bjellë

breng·et vpr to break out (in swellings or bumps); bear many scars

brengë nf 1 greatly troublesome thing: bad problem, serious trouble, constant worry 2 scar 3 (Old) [Med] diphtheria
○ **brengë thiu** [Bot] sharp-leaved asparagus Asparagus acutifolius

brengëmadh adj, n (Colloq) 1 (person) afflicted by misery 2 (Curse) may he be miserable!

brengëshumë adj = brengëmadh

brengëzënë adj (Colloq) 1 accursed, laden with trouble 2 (Curse) curse you! damn you!

brengos· vt to trouble, grieve, afflict

brengos·et vpr to be deeply worried, be miserable, grieve; be deeply disturbed, be afflicted

brengosje nf ger <brengos·, brengos·et

brengosur adj (i) deeply grieved; careworn; afflicted

brengshëm adj (i) sad, sorrowful

brenguar adj (i) broken out (in bumps or swellings); scarred, heavily scarred

breno·n vt = brano·n

breqe nf [Zool] green/water frog (Rana ridibunda)

brerëz nf disease of olives that causes the fruit to dry out and fall to the ground

brerimë nf 1 heavy downpour of rain, heavy shower 2 continual patter of rain or similar sound 3 bitter cold rain and wind 4 = shkarëzimë

brero·n vi to drizzle heavily and constantly; drum monotonously (like raindrops on a roof)

brerore nf halo

bresë nf [Bot] = radhiqe

breskë nf white/gray goat

breshanë nf [Hist] muzzle-loading flintlock rifle originally made in Brescia

bresharak nm = breshnizë

breshëllirë nf something minced into hail-size pieces

bre·shë̈r

I § *nm* hail, fall of hail

II § *adv* thick and fast, like hail

○ **breshë̈r i imë̈t** sleet

○ **Breshë̈ri e rreh e hunda me majë.** "The hail beats him and his nose turned up" *(Iron)* (said of a person with low means but high pretensions)

breshë̈ri̇́ *nf* [*Mil*] simultaneous discharge of a battery of guns: hail of fire, salvo, volley

breshë̈ri̇́më̈

I § *nf* **1** = **breshni̇́zë̈** **2** hailstorm **3** *(Fig)* volley of gunfire **4** = **shkarë̈zi̇́më̈**

II § *adj* broken into pieces the size of hailstones

breshë̈ri̇́tje *nf* = **shkarë̈zi̇́më̈**

breshë̈ro·n

I § *vt* to pelt [] with hail

II § *vi* to hail (with hailstones)

○ **<> breshë̈ro·n**^{3sg} **gjuha para mendjes** <>'s tongue runs before <>'s wit, <> speaks without thinking

breshk *nm* male turtle

breshkalë̈kuro·rë̈ *np fem* [*Zool*] the genus of the leatherback turtle *Dermochelys*

breshkamȧ́dh *adj* **1** scrofulous **2** *(Curse)* may-he-be-afflicted-with-scrofula! **3** *(Contempt)* member of the Italian occupational forces during World War II

breshkamȧ́n *nm (Contempt)* = **breshkamȧ́dh**

breshkȧ́n *nm* = **breshk**

breshkȧ́q *nm* **1** = **breshk** **2** = **breshkaqė́n**

breshkaqė́n *nm (Contempt)* **1** = **breshkamȧ́dh** **2** person with boils on the face and body

bre·shkȧ́zi *adv*

bre·shkë̈ *nf* **1** [*Zool*] turtle, tortoise **2** [*Zool*] leopard tortoise *(Testudo hermani)* **3** [*Entom*] plant louse **4** [*Bot*] swelling of an olive tree that may be broken off and planted as a sapling **5** *(Reg)* hard nutshell

○ **breshkë̈ druri** knot in wood, knurl

○ **breshkë̈ lë̈kurore** [*Zool*] leatherback turtle *Dermochelys coriacea*

○ **breshkë̈ malore** [*Zool*] marginated tortoise *Testudo marginata*

○ **breshkë̈ me pllaka** [*Zool*] loggerhead turtle *Caretta caretta*

○ **breshkë̈ toke** [*Zool*] leopard tortoise *Testudo hermani*

○ **breshkë̈ e ugareve** [*Zool*] leopard tortoise *Testudo hermani*

○ **breshkë̈ uji/uj**ë̈se [*Zool*] = **breshkuj**ë̈s*e*

○ **breshkë̈ e zezë̈** [*Zool*] leatherback turtle *Dermochelys coriacea*

bre·shkë̈z *nf (Dimin)* **1** [*Zool*] little turtle **2** [*Entom*] plant louse **3** [*Med*] scrofula **4** [*Bot*] swelling of an olive tree that may be broken off and planted as a sapling **5** popular wedding dance in which the dance leader makes several turtle-like movements *6 [Bot]* diseased growth in figs

○ **breshkë̈za e drithë̈rave** [*Entom*] cereal pest *Aelia rostrata Boh.*

○ **breshkë̈za e fikut** [*Entom*] scale parasite on fig trees *Ceroplastes rusci L.*

○ **breshkë̈za e manit** [*Entom*] armored scale *Diaspis pentagona Targ.*

○ **breshkë̈za e panxharit** [*Entom*] beet tortoise beetle *Cassida nebulosa L.*

○ **breshkë̈za e ullirit** [*Entom*] Mediterranean black scale *Saissetia oleae Bern*

bre·shkë̈za *np* [*Entom*] **1** armored scale insects *(Diaspididae)* **2** soft scale insects *(Coccidae)*

breshko·re *nf* [*Hist*] large, turtle-shaped, battle shield

breshko·rë̈ *np fem* [*Zool*] family of turtles and tortoises *Testudinata*

breshko·sun *adj (i) (Reg Gheg)* knurled, knotted

breshkujcë̈ *nf* [*Zool*] = **breshkuj**ë̈se

breshkujë̈se *nf* **1** [*Zool*] European swamp turtle *(Emys orbicularis)* **2** Caspian terrapin *(Clemmys caspica)*

breshkujzë̈ *nf* = **breshkuj**ë̈se

breshni̇́ *nf* fine, dense hail

○ **breshni̇́ bore** fine particles of frozen snow: sleet

breshni̇́s· *vt* to crumble, break up into small particles

breshni̇́s·et *vpr* to crumble into small particles

breshni̇́z· *vi* to hail (with fine particles of hail)

breshni̇́zë̈ *nf* fine particles of hail; fall of fine hail preceding a snowfall; layer of snow

breshno·het *vpr* **1** to freeze up, become ice; crystallize, petrify, become solid **2** *(Fig)* to become frozen in form

breshno·n *vt* to crystalize

breshnuar *adj (i)* crystallized; solidified

bresht *nm* lens

bresht·et *vpr* **1** to become wild, get furious **2** to freeze, become ice

breshtak *adj* = **bresht**ë̈

breshtë̈

I § *nf* = **bredhi̇́sht**ë̈

II § *adj (i)* wild; rough, rugged; uncivilized, rude, crude; uncultured

*bresht**ë̈ni̇́** *nf* wilderness; wilds

*bresht**ë̈t** *adj (i)* wooded, woody

breshtno·het *vpr* = **bresht·**et

breshtno·n *vt* to make [] rough, roughen; make [] wild

Bretani̇́ *nf* = **Britani̇́**

Bretȧ́një̈ *nf* Brittany

bretk *nm (np ~ q)* **1** [*Zool*] male frog **2** [*Zool*] European tree frog *(Hyla arborea)* **3** [*Anat*] sacrum = **kry̆qe**

bretko·n *vi* to croak

bretkȯ́cë̈ *nf* frog = **bretkos**ë̈

bretkȯ́r *adj* of frogs

bretkȯ́rë̈ *nf* [*Zool*] *Ranidae*

bretkȯ́së̈ *nf* [*Zool*] frog; toad

○ **bretkosa barkverdhë̈** [*Zool*] yellow-bellied toad *Bombina variegata*

○ **bretkosa e dejeve** [*Zool*] edible green/water frog *Rana esculeuta*

○ **bretkosa e drurë̈ve/pemë̈ve** [*Zool*] European tree frog *Hyla arborea*

○ **bretkosa jeshile** [*Zool*] European tree frog *Hyla arborea*

○ **bretkosa kë̈rcimtare** [*Zool*] Dalmatian frog *Rana dalmatina*

○ **bretkosa e leshterikut** [*Zool*] common European water frog, pond frog *Rana lessonae*

○ **bretkosa e pë̈rrenjve** [*Zool*] Grecian frog *Rana graeca*

bretȯ́në̈ *nm* Breton

bretq *np* < **bretk**

brethi̇́shte *nf* **1** [*Bot*] bugle *(Ajuga)* *2* Eastern bugle *(Ajuga orientalis)* *breth|k nf [Bot] = bredh

*bre'thk|ël nf [Bot] silver fir (Abies alba)

bre've nf [Zool] European whip snake (Coluber jugularis)

*breviar nm breviary

brez nm 1 belt; waistband; sash; girdle 2 sash used to bind a baby to the cradle, cradle cloth; swaddling cloth 3 waist, middle 4 band, strip; zone; layer 5 (Collec) the members of a generation, age mates; generation 6 support or reinforcing beam 7 [Bot] inner bark of tree = ba'rmë 8 [Anat] cingulum (in the brain) *9 = bërsí
  ○ brez drite beam of light
  ○ brezat e gjakut [Anthro] patrilineal descendents
  ○ brezat e gjinive [Anthro] matrilineal descendents
  ○ brez pas brezi generation after generation
  ○ brezi i Perëndisë "God's belt" rainbow
  ○ brezi i qiellit "heaven's waist-sash" (Poet) rainbow
  ○ brezi i sulmit [Mil] *1 obstacle course for military training 2 attack zone
  ○ brezi shpatullor [Anat] cingulum membri superioris
  ○ brez shpëtimi lifebelt

breza|hyp'thi adv

brez|a'r
  I § nm 1 waist, middle 2 hill or mountain terrace used for agriculture 3 clothes tree 4 strip of land growing crops different from those of the two adjacent plots of land
  II § adj 1 striped 2 wooden beam running through mud brick walls *3 maker of belts/sashes

brez|a're nf 1 rock bed cutting across a slope 2 agricultural terrace

brez|argj|end adj (Poet) silver-waisted

brez|a'rkë nf large spike used to fasten support beams

brez|aro' •n vt = brezo' •n

brez|aro'jas adv = brezahyp'thi

brez|u'ar adj (i) terraced

brez|a'tar adj of or pertaining to a generation; of the same generation, of the same age

brez|ba'rdhë adj having a white midsection

brez'ë nf harrow = bra'në

brez|ë'mbre'k nm waistband used to tie up underpants = ushku'r

brez|hu'mb|ur [brez-hu-mbur]
  I § adj (Colloq Pej) completely incompetent, good for nothing
  II § nm dolt

brez|í'm nm ger <brezo' •n

bre'z|kë nf black goat with a band of white hair

brez|lësh|u'ar adj ready for a fight

brez|ní nf collec 1 generation, age mates, the members of a generation taken as a whole 2 [Biol] descendants of a generational line: F, F, etc. *3 brooch, ornament

*brez|no' •n vt = bran|ís•

brez|o' •n vt to create agricultural terraces in a hillside or mountainside

brez|o'r adj [Min] terraced, in terraces; stratified

brez|o're nf 1 hand gun, revolver 2 shirtwaist, shirt 3 terraced side of a slope

brez|vën'ë nf wretched/unfortunate/poor woman

*bre'zh|ël nf viscid tumor, boil

*brën'd|a = bre'nda

*brën'd|ësm = bre'ndsh|ëm

*brën'g|aca'k adj freckled

*brën'g|ë nf freckle = pre'kë

*brën'g|ë'z nf = brën'g|ë

*brën'shm|i adv (së) = bre'ndshmi

*brën'j|a'k nm abortion

*bri• vi (Reg Gheg) to tip, tilt

bri prep (abl) 1 beside, alongside, along, by 2 along with, together with
  ○ bri për bri right next to one another

bri(n) nm (np ̄ rë) 1 horn (of a horned animal) 2 [Zool] feeler/antenna; nose-horn of a sand viper 3 (Colloq) thin, elongated part protruding in front of certain objects 4 horn (musical instrument); signal horn
  ○ bri thekre [Bot] ergot, ergot claviceps Claviceps purpurea

bri|a'rtë adj (Poet) golden-horned

bri|bu'alle nf large, red, hot pepper shaped like the horn of a domestic buffalo

bri'c|ë nf flintstone, flint

bri|cja'p
  I § adj "goat-horned" having long straight horns angled backward like those of a billy goat
  II § nm [Entom] apedal wood-eating larva with a broad, triangle-shaped thorax and cone-shaped abdomen

bric|o're nf [Hist] flintlock rifle

bri'çe adj broken-horned, with a broken horn

bri|da'she adj ramshorn

bri|dre'dh|ur adj having twisted horns

bri|dre'jtë adj having horns that point straight up

bri|du'llë nf pocketknife with a curved horn handle

bri'dh| stem for 2nd pl pres, pind, imper, vp <bre'dh•

*bri'e nf [Med] caries

*bri'g nm hard clod

briga'd|ë nf brigade

brigadie'r n brigadier, commander of a brigade, brigade leader

*brigati'në nf brigantine

*brig|ím nm ger 1 <brigo' •n 2 reprimand, rebuke, censure

*brig|o' •n vt to reprimand, rebuke, censure

bri|gre'p adj having hook-shaped horns

bri|gja'të adj long-horned

bri'gje np <breg

bri'gje-bri'gje adj hilly, rugged

bri'gj|ër nm [Bot] holly (Ilex) = a'she

*brig|jo' •n vt to trouble, worry, haunt

bri|ha'lë adj having long pointed horns

bri|ha'pët adj having horns spaced wide apart

bri|he'll adj pronghorned

bri|he'lle nf long, thin, hot pepper with a prong

bri|he'shtë adj having straight, long horns

bri|ho'llë adj having straight, thin horns, prong-horned

bri|jana'c nm (Euph Old) horned devil

*brij|a'r nm (Reg Gheg) cuckold

*brij|e'she nf (Reg Gheg) horned sheep

*bri'jët adj (i) (Reg Gheg) horned

brij|o' -het vpr to get ready to charge (with one's horns)

brij|o'r adj (Book) keratinous, made of horn

bri|kapro'lle adj having pronged horns like a roe deer

brike'qe nf goat with crooked horns

brike't nm briquet

briketi'm nm ger <**briketo'·n**

briketo'·n vt to compress into briquets

brikërra'bë nf hook-horned cow

briko'c adj <**bri'çe**

brikula'ç adj having bent horns pointing forward like a bread roll

brikuro'rë adj having horns bent up and around like a crown

brila'nt nm brilliant (diamond)

brilanti'në nf brilliantine

brilopa'të nf big-horned ((said of deer))

brima'dh adj 1 having big horns 2 (Fig) having loose morals; adulterous 3 = brina'r

brima'jë nf (Reg) cobweb, spiderweb

*∘ **bri'me** nf ger (e) <**bre'·n** gnawing
  ∘ **brime ndërgjegjeje** gnawing conscience, sense of guilt; compunction

brim'ë nf 1 = vri'më *2 (Reg Gheg) = bri'tm**ë

*∘**bri'm'ëz** nf dimin (Reg Gheg) small hole; eyelet

brimo'·n vt 1 to make holes in [ ]: pierce, puncture; drill, bore; perforate 2 (Fig) to search, search out

brimo're nf 1 perforated spoon, ladle with holes used as a strainer 2 [Text] perforated paddle through which threads are passed and twisted together to form a single strand

brimos· vt = brimo'·n

*∘**bri'm'shëm** adj (i) porous

*∘**brimta'r** nm (Reg Gheg) crier

brinaj'ë nf uncultivated strip along the side of a field

brina'r adj (Impol) cuckolded

brinata'k nm = brino'ç

brin'ce nf side board of a chest or cradle

*∘**brindi'll** nm cutting (from a tree)

Brindis nm Brindisi

brino'ç
  I § adj having horns, horned
  II § nm the Horned One, the Devil

*∘**brino'k** adj horned

brino'ke nf horned ewe, ewe with horns

brino'r adj 1 having horns, corniculate 2 = bri'rtë

*∘**brino're** nf cornea

brinja'r
  I § adj having horns, horned
  II § nm 1 cuckold 2 street-sweeper

bri'njas OR **bri'njazi** adv 1 towards the edge, to the side, alongside, beside; on the flanks 2 sideways, sidewise; sidelong 3 (Fig) slightly; superficially, barely 4 = ci'ngëlthi

bri'një nf 1 rib bone; rib 2 chest wall; flank; rib steak 3 steep side of a cliff or mountain; slope 4 narrow edge, lip; flank, side, lateral surface 5 [Geom] side 6 (Reg) water cask
  ∘ **brinjë më brinjë** throughout; completely, entirely; thoroughly, very much
  ∘ **brinj**ë **e verbër** false rib

brinjë'da'lë adj weak and sickly, thin and weak; emaciated, skinny

brinjë'dre'jtë adj straight-sided

brinjë'ja'shtë adj = brinjëda'lë

brinjë'ka' nm [Bot] thoroughwax, thorowax, hare's ear (Bupleurum)

brinjë'ndry'sh'ëm adj [Geom] having sides of unequal length; scalene

brinjë'një'sh'ëm adj [Geom] equilateral

bri'nj'ëse nf 1 rib meat, rib steak 2 rib of a packsaddle frame; saddletree; side board of a chest or cradle

brinjo'·het vpr to turn to one side; lean to one side, sag

brinjo'ke nf hillside, mountainside

brinjo'r adj (Book) 1 costal 2 rib-like, narrow and bowed

brinjo're nf hilly mountainside, hilly countryside, rugged hills

bripërdre'dh'ur
  I § adj (of sheep or goats) having twisted horns
  II § nm (Fig) stubborn person

bripërpje'të adj (of sheep or goats) having horns pointing straight up

bripra'pë adj having horns bent backward ((said of sheep or goats))

briqe'n nm [Folklore] one-horned beast

bri'rë np <**bri(r)**
  ∘ **nuk do·**[3sg] **brirë** "doesn't need horns" one doesn't need a sign, it is perfectly obvious
  ∘ **<> hanë briret** <> is itching to make trouble; <> is spoiling for a fight

brir'ëzu'ar adj (i) hardened into a horny substance

bri'ri sg def, sg abl indef <**bri(r)**

bri'rtë adj (i) made of horn, horn-like: corneous

bri'rth nm horn-like sensory appendage: antenna, feeler

bri'rrëzu'ar adj having horns that curl down

brisë nf [Med Veter] 1 anthrax 2 cellulitis, festering of tissue around a wound, gangrene 3 cornea

brisk
  I § nm 1 razor blade; razor 2 pocketknife; penknife; pruning knife
  II § adj razor-sharp; biting cold
  III § adv extraordinarily, extremely
  ∘ **ësh·të brisk** to have nothing left, be flat broke
  ∘ **Më rrove, të rrova, brisku (qe) i berberit** "You shaved me, I shaved you, the razor (remained) the barber's" We came out even. No one won.
  ∘ **brisk rroje/rrues** razor (for shaving)
  ∘ **s'ka· shkuar brisk në faqe** to be still immature: be still wet behind the ears

bris'kë adj having long, thin and straight horns

brisk'punu'es nm (Old) knife-smith, one who makes or repairs knives or razors

brisorka'dhe adj deer-horned ((said of sheep))

brisqa'p nm [Entom] horned beetle (Cerambyx scopolii L.)

brisqe np <**brisk**

brishtë adj (i) 1 brittle, breakable, friable, frangible 2 frail, fragile; delicate

brishtë'si nf (Book) brittleness, fragility; frangibility, friability

*∘**brishti'** OR **brishtni'** nf brittleness, fragility

*∘**brishtni'o·het** vpr = brishto'·het

*∘**brishtni'o·n** vt = brishto'·n

brishto'·het vpr to become brittle

brishto'·n vt to break into pieces: crumble, shatter; break [ ] apart, dig up [soil]

brishu'l adj "rod-horned" having thick and widely spaced horns ((said of cattle))

*∘**brit·et** = bre·het

brit *stem for pdef, opt, adm, part, pind, 2nd pl pres, imper, vp* <**bërte·t·**

Britani *nf* Britain
∘ **Britania e Madhe** Great Britain

britan·ik *adj* British

brita·r *nm* = **briza·n**

*brit·ës *nm* = **bërtitës**

*brit·je *nf ger* = **bërti·tje**

brit·m *nm (Old)* autumn
∘ **britmi i dytë** October
∘ **britmi i parë** September
∘ **britmi i tretë** November

brit·më *nf* **1** yell, shout; cry, wail **2** cheer **3** clamor, shouting

brit·më·qa·re *nf (Old)* female keener

brith *nm* = **çiba·n**

brithye·r *adj* broken-horned

brivetm·i *nm* unicorn

briza·n *nm [Hist]* horn-blower in medieval battle

bri·zbraz·ës *np [Zool]* bovoidea

bri·zë *nf* **1** sheep's horn used to hackle flax **2** *[Bot]* quaking grass *(Briza)* **3** *[Optics]* cornea

brizo·n *vt* **1** to hackle [flax], separate [flax fibers] from the hards **2** to separate an undesired from a desired part: peel, shell, clean

*brizhdo·n *vt* = **brishto·** *·n*

*brobol *adj* stunted, dwarfed

*brobol·e *nf* dwarfed woman

*brobol·eç *adj* = **brobol**

bro·bull *nf [Food]* sweet fritter made of flour, eggs, and yogurt, and served in syrup

bro·çkull *nf* nonsense, twaddle

Brodue·i *nm* Broadway

bro·dh *stem for pdef* <**bre·dh·**

brof *interj* up quickly!

brof·
I § *vi* **1** to leap to one's feet, stand up quickly, leap up; jump up **2** to rush at, dash
II § *adv* **1** right away, all at once, immediately **2** suddenly, unexpectedly

*bro·gëz *nf* = **brogs·ë**

brogs·ë *nf* tassel

brohora·s *stem for 1st sg pres, 1st & 3rd pl pres, 2nd & 3rd sg subj* <**brohori·t·**

brohor·i *nf* **1** = **brohori·tje 2** ovation

brohori·s *stem for 1st sg pres, 1st & 3rd pl pres, 2nd & 3rd sg subj* = **brohori·t·**

brohori·t·
I § *vi* to applaud and cheer enthusiastically
II § *vt* to applaud [] with enthusiastical cheers, acclaim [] loudly

brohori·tje *nf ger* **1** <**brohori·t· 2** acclaim, acclamation

brojc·ë *nf* **1** one-handled water pitcher of metal or clay **2** wooden measure for grain holding about a pound

broka·ta·re *nf* = **bro·kë**

*bro·ke *nf [Bot]* garlic mustard *(Alliaria officinalis)*

bro·kë *nf* **1** round wooden measure for grain holding about 25 kilograms **2** one-handled pitcher for liquids **3** swelling, lump, knot (in wood) **4** blotch, spot **5* *(Reg Gheg)* grain measure of about half a kilogram

bro·kër *nm [Bot]* sea rocket *(Cakile)*

*bro·kull *nm* oath, curse

bro·lle *nf* **1** corncob **2** skin, rind, husk

brom *nm [Chem]* bromine *(Br)*

brom·ik *adj [Chem]* bromic

bro·mkëz *nf* honeycomb

bromp *interj* informal toast: here's to you! cheers!

*bronc = **bronz**

bronk *nm [Anat]* bronchial tube, bronchus

bro·nk·ëz *nm [Anat]* bronchiole

bronk·ial *adj [Anat]* bronchial

bronk·it *nm [Med]* bronchitis

*bronqi·t = **bronki·t**

brontoza·ur *nm [Paleo]* brontosaur

bronx = **bronz**

bronz *nm* **1** bronze **2** *(Colloq)* brass (as a color)

bronzo· *·n* *vt* to bronze

bronzt·ë *adj (i)* **1** made of bronze, of bronze **2** bronzed

*brosta·r *nm* fireproof wall, chimney wall

brosht *nm [Bot]* = **cërmëde·ll**

broshur·ë *nf* booklet

BRPSH *abbrev* <**Bashkimi i Rinisë së Punës të Shqipërisë** Union of Labor Youth of Albania

BRSS *abbrev* <**Bashkimi i Republikave Socialiste Sovjetike** USSR

bru·c *nm* = **bërru·c**

brucelo·zë *nf [Veter Med]* brucellosis, Bang's disease, undulant fever

*bru·cë *nf* = **bërru·c**

bruç *nm [Entom]* May beetle, cockchafer *(Melolontha vulgaris)*

bru·full *nm (np ~ j) [Ichth]* the young of the mullet

brufull·ak
I § *adj* swollen full, robust, bursting
II § *nm* healthy, robust child

brufull·o· *·n* *vi* **1** to increase quickly in quantity; burst, explode, swarm; sprout **2* to howl

bruhaj·ë *nf* loose soil that is easy to work

bru·kë *nf [Bot]* **1** tamarisk *(Tamarix parviflora)* **2** bush, shrub

Bruksel *nm* Brussels

bru·kth *nm [Bot]* plant with black fibrous tubers

*brul OR **brull** *nm* = **bërry·l**

bruma·ç *nm [Zool]* = **bruç**

*bruma·ll *nm* **1** *[Entom]* cockroach *(Blatta orientalis)* **2** = **brumbu·ll**

*brumall·ak *nm [Entom]* scarab beetle *(Scarabaeus)*

bruma·nik *nm [Food]* pastry made with eggs, cheese, and milk

bru·mbull
I § *nm (np ~ j)* **1** dung beetle **2** *[Entom]* longhorn beetle *(Cerambycidae)* **3** drone (bee)
II § *adv* full, full up, full to the brim
∘ **brumbull i majit** *[Entom]* cockchafer *Melolontha melolontha*
∘ **brumbull i plehut** *[Entom]* dung beetle *(Goetrupes stercorarius)*

*brumbull·ak I § *nm* OR **brumbull·ake** II § *nf* sphere, ball III § *adj* = **rrumbulla·kët**

*brumbull·ak·zo· *·het* *vpr* to leap forward: pounce

*brumbull·ak·zo· *·n* *vt* to round [] off

brumbull·i· *·n* *vi* to buzz

brumbull·o· *·n*
I § *vi* = **brumbulli·** *·n*
II § *vt* to amass, amass [] into a ball or wad; fill [] full

bru·mç *adj (Reg)* robust, healthy

bru'mçë *nf* wad of dough, dumpling

bru'më *nm* **1** dough; leavened dough, pastry dough; sourdough **2** starter dough, leavening **3** viscous mash or pulp (such as molten glass, wood or paper pulp, concrete, rubber, plaster); soggy material **4** basic substance; content (in contrast with vacuousness or lack of real substance) **5** *(Fig Insult)* submissive weakling, milquetoast, good-for-nothing
○ **brum**ë **i ardhur** dough that has risen
○ **brum**ë **i shurdhuar** "deafened dough" dough that fails to rise
○ **brum**ë **i tbartë** starter dough

brumë**gatu'ese** *nf* mixer (for preparing mashes like cement or bread dough)

bru'më'ra *np* <bru'më foods prepared from kneaded dough: baked goods: breads, pastries, pasta

bru'më's *adj* soft and loose, not hard and compact

brumë**'ta'r** *n* worker who operates a mixing machine for preparing mashes like cement or bread dough

brumë**'to're** *nf* **1** large kneading trough for preparation of dough **2** = brumë**gatu'ese**

brumë**'zi'm** *nm ger* <brum**ë**zo·*n*

brumë**zo'·*n* *vt* **1** to prepare [a mash/pulp] **2** to mash [] into a pulp, make [] into a kind of dough *3 to leaven

bru'mje *adj* doughy in texture

**brum'o·*n* *vt* to make [] into dough, knead

brum'o'r *adj (i) (Book)* **1** containing dough, consisting of dough **2** soft as dough; easy to work

brum'o's· *vt* **1** to prepare [dough]; knead [dough] **2** *(Fig)* to mold the character of [] **3** *(Fig)* to prepare, establish [] as a base; reinforce, stiffen, make [] substantial

brum'o's·*et* *vpr* **1 to soften during preparation, become doughy **2** *(Fig)* to become molded in character or form

brum'o'sje *nf ger* <brum**o's·**, brum**o's·***et

brum'o's'ur *adj (i)* well-formed in character

bru'm'shëm *adj (i)* soft as dough, plastic; mashed

bru'm'të *adj (i)* **1** made of leavened dough; leavened **2** doughy **3** *(Fig)* pasty

*brum'to're *nf* = brumë**'to're**

*brumule's *stem for 1st sg pres, 1st & 3rd pl pres, 2nd & 3rd sg subj* <brumulet·

*brum'ul'et· *vt* to add shortening/fat to [] = përmblet·

*brum'ul'is *stem for pind, 2nd pl pres, imper* <brumulet·

*brum'ul'it *stem for part, pdef, pind, 2nd pl pres, imper, vp* <brumulet·

*brumulla'k *nm* lees of wax

brun *adj, n* brunette

*brunc *OR* brunç = bronz

*brunc'o'·*n* *vt* = bronzo'·*n*

*brunx *OR* brunz = bronz

brus *adv* **1** full, brimming, full to the brim **2** successfully, prosperously, with good fortune

brus· *vt* to fill up, fill full

*bru's'ëm *adj (i)* steep, sheer

brus'ni *nf* abundance, plenty, copiousness, affluence

*bruste'm *adj* purple, violet

bru'sht'ë *adj (i)* = bru'ztë

bru'shë *nf* **1** brush = furçë *2* tart, harsh, rough

brush'im *nm ger* <brusho'·*n*

bru'sh'më *adj (i)* **1** tart, slightly sour and slightly bitter **2** nasty, bad-tempered, surly

**brush'o'·*n* *vt* to brush, clean with a brush

*bru'shtë *nf* [Electr] brush = bru'shë

brushtova'te *nf* [Bot] dewberry *(Rubus caesius)*

bru'shtull
 I § *nm, nf* [Food] **1** a kind of heavily beaten sweet pastry made with wheat flour and butter **2** [Food] a kind of turnover made of corn flour and filled with vegetables
 II § *nf* [Bot] ivy *(Hedera helix)*

brushtullu'k *nm* [Ethnog] member of the bride's wedding party who arrives at the groom's house to herald the arriving bride

bruta'l *adj* brutal, savage; bestial, beastly, brutish

brutali'sht *adv* brutally

brutali'te't *nm (Book)* brutality, brutishness

bru'to *adj* **1** [Spec] gross (weight) **2** gross (income or earnings) **3** unrefined, crude, raw (products) **4** rough, crude (data)

bruth *nm* [Entom] June beetle, cockchafer *(Melolontha melolontha)*

bruz *nm* aquamarine (precious stone)

*bru'zët *adj (i)* **1** = bru'ztë **2** abundant

*bruz'ni *nf* abundance

bru'z'të *adj (i)* **1** greenish blue, aquamarine **2** dark blue, indigo, azure

*bruzhdi'lla *np* = bëzhdi'lë

*bryc *nm* = byc

brydh· *vt* to tenderize, make soft, ripen; crumble

**bry'dh·*et* *vpr* to become tender, become soft, ripen (of fruit)

bry'dh'ët *adj (i)* **1** tender, soft, ripe; loose and easy to work (of soil) **2** soft and tender; delicate **3** *(FigImpolite)* flabby, clumsy, awkward

*bryl *nm* = bërry'l

*bryll *nm* = bërry'l

bryma'k *adj* fall-ripening, maturing in autumn (said of tobacco)

*brymç *adj, n = bryms

bry'me *nf* **1** deep-gray goat **2** woman whose hair is almost completely gray

bry'më *nf* frost; hoarfrost
 ○ **brym**ë **e madhe** heavy frost
 ○ **Bryma 's'është dëborë.** "Frost is not snow." *(Prov)* (said of someone with only a superficial similarity to someone else) The resemblance is purely superficial.

bry'mës
 I § *nm* = nëntor
 II § *adj* sorrel or chestnut in color ((said of horses))

brymë**zo'·*het* *vpr* to freeze, become frosted over, turn to frost

brymo'r *nm (Old)* November

brymo'sur *adj (i)* frosted; frosty

*bryms *adj, n* chestnut (horse)

bry'm'të *adj (i)* deep gray

*bryn'ata'k = brino'ç

bryth *nm* [Zool] mole = uri'th

*brra'kë *nf* = bërrakë

*brrakno'·*n* *vt* to stanch

*brraknu'em *adj (i) (Reg Gheg)* stagnant

*brrul = bërry'l

*brru'zhë *nf* mane (of a horse)

*brryc *nm* = byc

*brry'lkë *nf* arm of a chair

***brryltírë** nf bend in a road, hairpin curve
BS abbrev <**Bashkimi Sovjetik** Soviet Union
BShSh abbrev <**Banka e Shtetit Shqiptar** Albanian State Bank
BTA abbrev (Bulgarian) <**Balgarska Telegrafna Agencija** Bulgarian News Agency
bu
 I § onomat **1** expresses the sound of the muffled roar of a river or sea **2** expresses the forceful character of an event: whoosh!
 II § interj expresses surprise, disquiet, or disagreement with something unexpected
bu·n
 I § vi **1** to stay overnight as a guest, lodge **2** [Ethnog] to visit one's family for a few days (usually after a wedding)
 II § vt to put up [] for the night, give overnight lodgings to []
buacë nf = buallícë
buaj np <buall
buall nm (np ˜ j) **1** domestic buffalo, water buffalo, Indian buffalo (bos bubalus arnee bubalis) **2** (Fig pej) big oaf **3** [Zool] = kacadre
 ○ **më sa hyn bualli në veshin e gjilpërës** when Hell freezes over: never; impossible
buallës adj having dark big fruit, jumbo.(said of a kind of fig or a kind of sweet grape)
buallícë nf **1** domestic buffalo cow **2** (Fig Pej) big, heavy, slow-witted and clumsy woman: old cow
buar part <bo·n
***buavís** stem for 1st sg pres, pl pres, 2nd & 3rd sg subj, pind <buavít·
***buavít·** vt = buhavít·
***buavít·et** vpr = buhavít·et
***buavítun** adj (i) (Reg Gheg) = buhavítur
***buback** nm [Invert] = bubas
bubas nm [Invert] maw-worm (ascaris lumbricoides)
***bubash** nm [Invert] = bubas
bubazhel nm **1** boogieman, hobgoblin **2** = bubuzhel
bubcë nf [Invert] roundworm (Ascaride lombricoide)
bubë nf **1** [Invert] larva at an advanced stage; silkworm **2** [Invert] roundworm Ascaride lombricoide **3** [Entom] young louse: nit **4** reptile that bites **5** imaginary monster (sometimes in snake form) used to frighten little children; bugaboo **6** scarecrow **7** (Reg) plush (of wool fabric)
 ○ **bubë mishi** [Entom] gray flesh fly (Sarcophaga carnaria)
 ○ **bubë veshi** [Entom] earwig
bubël nf **1** small lump (knot, nub) in yarn or wool *2 (Old) = bori
***bubëltar** nm (Old) = borizan
bubërri nf trivia
bubërrim nm ger **1** <bubëro·n, bubërohe **2** trivial pursuit/activity **3** trivia
bubërro·n
 I § vi **1** to pick lice, delouse **2** to search all around for something **3** to browse; browse around **4** to rummage/potter about; buzz about **5** to murmur, speak indistinctly **6** (Fig) to busy oneself with trivia in order to pass the time; dawdle **7** to browse on single blades of grass (when there is little pasturage left for cattle)
 *8 to crawl around on all fours

 II § vt (Fig) **1** to annoy, irritate *2 to doll [] up **3** = bubít·
bubës nm = bubas
bubëz nf (Old) touchhole (of a musket)
***bubëzo·n** vi to doll [] up, dress up []
***bubëzuem** adj (i) (Reg Gheg) dolled up, dressed up
bubi nm (Pet) puppy dog
***bubís** stem for 1st sg pres, pl pres, 2nd & 3rd sg subj, pind <bubít·
bubít· vt to delouse; pick lice off of []
***bublar** nm (Old) = borizan
bublishtë nf a bunch of kindling wood; sweepings
bubrek nm [Anat] (Old) kidney
bubrecë nf = buburezë
***bubrreq** nm = bubrek
bubrri nf twaddle, nonsense
bubrrim nm ger <bubrro·n, bubrro·het
bubrrimë nf fuss
bubrrinar n person who quibbles over details
bubrrís stem for 1st sg pres, pl pres, 2nd & 3rd sg subj, pind <bubrrít·
bubrrít· = buburít·
bubu interj expresses worry, misery, or disappointment: alas, oh my, ah me!
bubulak
 I § adj fiercely burning, characterized by large dancing flames
 II § nm fire with large dancing flames
 III § adv burning fiercely, with large dancing flames
***bubulan** nm = bubular
***bubular** nm fireworks
bubulesh adj **1** wooly; having thick wool; downy, with thick down **2** (FigImpolite) wooly-minded, dense, dull-witted, slow
bubullim nm muffled roaring sound of fire
bubulo·n vi to burn with roaring flames
bubullí·n vi **1** to thunder with a crash, emit a clap of thunder, thunder long and loud after a lightning flash: thunder **2** to rumble/roar loudly
bubullim nm ger <bubullo·n
bubullimë nf ger **1** <bubullí·n **2** thunder; thunder clap, peal of thunder, roll of thunder **3** rumble; long, thundering roar; deafening roar
bubullís stem for 1st sg pres, pl pres, 2nd & 3rd sg subj, pind <bubullít·
bubullít· vi = bubullí·n
bubullo·n vi **1** = bubullí·n **2** to emit a loud reverberating sound; make a thundering sound: thunder; echo, peal, rumble
bubunjëz nf wart, mole, callus, corn
***bubuqe** nf = burbuqe
buburezë nf (Reg) [Entom] **1** ladybug, ladybird = mollëkuqe **2** firefly, glowworm
buburíckë = buburezë
***buburís** stem for 1st sg pres, pl pres, 2nd & 3rd sg subj, pind <buburít·
buburískë nf **1** bubble (in a boiling liquid) **2** [Dairy] curd of butter that rises to the top in the churning process **3** firefly
buburít· vi **1** to cook at a low boil: simmer **2** to bubble up **3** to rumble; roar

buburi'zë *nf* **1** curd of butter that rises to the top in the churning process **2** bubble (in a boiling liquid) **3** [*Entom*] ladybug **4** aphid

**bubur'o·n *vi* = bubrro·n

buburre'c *nm* **1** [*Entom*] cockchafer; any small insect harmful to plants, bug **2** [*Entom*] ant **3** [*Zool*] tadpole **4** *(FigImpolite)* person with a small body, runt **5** [*Entom*] roach, cockroach
  ∘ **buburreci i bizeles** [*Entom*] pea weevil *Bruchus pisorum L.*
  ∘ **buburreci i çepallave** [*Entom*] dried-fruit beetle, fruit beetle, corn sap beetle *Carpophilus hemipterus*
  ∘ **buburreci drubirues** [*Entom*] peach capnodis *Capnodis tenebrionis?*
  ∘ **buburreci i fasules** [*Entom*] bean weevil *Acanthoscelides obsoletus Say.*
  ∘ **buburreci i luleve** [*Entom*] *Omophlus lepturoides*
  ∘ **buburreci me kryq** [*Entom*] kind of scarab beetle *Anisoplia agricola*
  ∘ **buburreci i patates** [*Entom*] Colorado potato beetle *Leptinotarsa decemlineata Say.*

**buburri'qe *nf* = bubrek

buburru'qe *nf* [*Bot*] common groundsel *(Senecio vulgaris)*

bubuti·n *vi* **1** to cry "bubu" loudly; wail loudly from pain or suffering **2** to roar, rumble, thunder

bubuzhe'l *nm* [*Entom*] sacred scarab, dung beetle *(Scarabaeus sacer)*

bubuzhe'l·et *vpr* to get dirty, get one's face dirty

bubuzhe'në = bubuzhingë

**bubuzhi·n *vi* to rumble

bubuzhi'më *nf* **1** [*Entom*] = bubuzhingë **2 rumble, roar

bubuzhi'ngë *nf* [*Entom*] = vizhë

bubuzhi'nkë = bubuzhingë

**bubuzhi'rë *nf* [*Entom*] whirligig beetle *(Dytiscus latissimus)*

bu'c·et *vpr* to go head to head in a fight: clash
  ∘ **buc·**et **me** [] to butt heads with []

buca'k *nm* wooden jug, small wooden pail, pitcher

bucela'bërës *n* jug maker

bucela'r *n* = bucelabërës

bucel'e *nf* **1** wooden jug for water **2** clay vessel with a spout, flat on one side and round on the other, used to carry water **3** hub (of a wheel)

**bucel'eri *nf* barrel making, coopering

bucelo're *nf* large drill bit used to make the hole in a wooden hub

bu'cë *nf* **1** soil turned up by a plow: clod; sod **2** snowball

**bûci'shte *nf* *(Reg Gheg)* place full of clods

buç
  I § *adj* round-cheeked, chubby
  II § *nm* *(Reg)* **1** lump, bump, swelling, knot (in wood) **2** *(Reg)* [*Zool*] sand viper, nose-horned viper *(Vipera ammodytes)*

bu'ç·et *vpr* (of female dogs) to be in heat

buça'llë *nf* drone pipe on a bagpipe

buça's *stem for 1st sg pres, 1st & 3rd pl pres* <buçet·

buça't·et *vpr* to swell up in one's face or body

bu'çe *nf* **1** bitch (dog); she-wolf **2** *(Pejor)* mouth

buçet· *vi* **1** to make a powerful prolonged low-pitched sound: boom **2** to boom out, resound, reverberate **3** to explode with a boom: spread suddenly with force, break out; reach a climax, boil up

4 to boom up, spill out, overflow, flood, gush over; gush up, gush forth, well up, spring up
  ∘ <> **buçet.**^{3sg} **gjaku** <> *is* very eager to act, <> *can* hardly contain <>self
  ∘ <> **buçet.**^{3sg} **koka** "<>'s head *is booming*" to have serious problems on one's mind; be beset by headaches
  ∘ <> **buçet.**^{3pl} **veshët 1** <> has a ringing in <>'s ears **2** <> *is* sick and tired of listening to the same old thing

bu'çë *nf* bitch

**buçi'lë *nf* drinking-trough, water spring

buçi'm *nm ger* <buço·n

buçi'më *nf* **1** boom, bang, explosive and reverberating sound; stentorian voice; yelling of many voices; roar, rumbling sound **2** *(Fig)* powerful reverberations of an important event **3** muffled noise in the head, ringing in the ear

**buçi'n [*Bot*] = bungëbu'të

**buçi's *stem for 1st sg pres, pl pres, 2nd & 3rd sg subj, pind* <buçit·

buçi't
  I § *stem for part, pind, imper, opt, adm, pdef* <buçet·
  II § *vi* = buçet·

buçit'ës *adj* reverberating; booming

buçi'tje *nf* **1** = buçi'më **2** burst, explosion, blast, eruption

buçka'ma'dh *adj* having a plump face

buçka'n *adj (Pet)* chubby-cheeked; plump, chubby

buçka'ra'n *adj* = buçkan

buçka'rit· *vt (Colloq)* **1** to scrape the ground with the hoof, paw at the ground **2** to beat someone until the body swells up, beat black and blue

buçka'rit·et *vpr* to puff up, show off, brag, boast

bu'çkë *adj* **1** pudgy **2** roundfaced and healthy, robust; plump **3** (of fruit) filled-out and ripe, plump

bu'çko *nf with masc agreement* **1** *(Pet)* chubby-faced little person (normally a child) **2** *(Pet)* = buçkan **3** *(Colloq)* robust and healthy

buçko·n
  I § *vt* **1** to cause [] to bloom or blossom **2** to cause [] to open
  II § *vi* **1** to blossom, bloom **2** to sprout, bud **3** to flower

buço·n *vi* = buçet·

buçu'k *nm* large round wooden container for measuring grain

buda'll *adj (Reg)* foolish, crazy

budalla' *adj, nm (pl ~ e'nj) (Colloq)* foolish/crazy (person)
  ∘ **budalla me brirë** a real fool, prize idiot

budalla'çkë *nf (Colloq)* = budalla'qe

budalla'llëk *nm (np ~ qe) (Colloq)* foolishness, idiocy, stupidity, nonsense; insanity, craziness
  ∘ **budallallëk me brirë** plain foolishness, out and out nonsense

budalla'llëqe *np (Colloq)* <budallalllëk

budalla'llo's· *vt (Colloq)* to cause someone lose the ability to think normally, make stupid; drive crazy, annoy greatly with stupidities

budalla'llo's·et *vpr* **1** to lose one's mind, go crazy **2** to be driven crazy

budalla'qe *adj fem nf (Colloq)* <budalla'

budalle·nj *np (Colloq)* <budalla·

budall·e·psje *nf [Med]* hebetude

budall·i·cë *nf (Colloq)* = budalla·qe

budall·o·një *nf (Colloq)* = budalla·qe

budi·ng *nm [Food]* pudding

budi·st *adj, n [Relig]* Buddhist

budi·zëm *nm [Relig]* Buddhism

***budru·m** = bodru·m

buduna·r *nm* large log, big timber; floor joist, beam supporting a floor

bue·në *nf* = buja·në

buf

I § nm **1** *[Ornit]* owl *(Strigiformes)* **2** *[Ornit]* eagle owl *Bubo bubo L.* **3** *(Pej)* man or boy with unkempt hair; man with several days' growth of beard **4** *(Colloq)* dolt, dunce; dotard

II § adj (Colloq) **1** something round and plump **2** (of children) chubby **3** (of figs) ripe **4** *(Colloq Pejorative Fig)* slow-witted, simple-minded; dotty **5** *(Fig)* disheveled, unkempt

○ **bufi i dëborës** *[Ornit]* snowy owl *Nyctea scandiaca L.*

○ **bufi i ngordhur** children's game in which one player sits on the ground and the others put their hands on his head

○ **bufi veshgjatë** *[Ornit]* long-eared owl *Asio otus L.*

○ **bufi veshshkurtër** *[Ornit]* short-eared owl *Asio flammeus L.*

bufa·l *nm* rooster with a large head feathered like an owl

bufala·q *adj (Colloq)* **1** fat and clumsy; chubby **2** (said of ticks and mosquitoes) bloated with blood **3** having unkempt hair

bufana·r *nm (Pej)* man with unshaven beard and uncut and unkempt hair

bufa·r *nm* low shed or enclosure in a mountain corral in which small lambs or kids are kept when they are separated from their mothers

***bufa·s|** *stem for 1st sg pres, pl pres, 2nd & 3rd sg subj, pind* <bufa·t·

bufa·t· *vt* = buhavi·t·

bufa·t·et *vpr (Colloq)* to swell/puff up; become swollen

***bufa·tje** = buhavi·tje

bufe *nf* **1** buffet, china cabinet, sideboard; pantry cupboard **2** buffet counter; snack bar, stand-up cafe/pub serving light food and drink **3** buffet reception serving food and drink **4** buffet table laden with food and drink

bu·fer *nm [Tech]* buffer, bumper

bufetie·r *n* counter attendant, bartender

bu·fë *nf* **1** *[Bot]* woodland European grape *(Vitis vinifera sylvestris)* **2** *[Ornit]* buzzard *(Buteo buteo)*

***bufi·c** *adj* **1** *(Old)* swollen, inflated **2** plump, chubby

bufi·t· *vt* to spray [] with water from one's mouth

bufke

I § nf **1** *[Bot]* = xhufkë **2** round and fluffy ball: pompom, boll **3** woman's collarless blouse with long sleeves and puffed shoulders **4** *[Bot]* = lulebufkë = lulebufkë **5** sheep with a wooly muzzle

II § adj **1** puffy **2** (of chickens) having tufts over the ears and feathered feet **3** unripe fig

buflo·n *vi* **1** to burst, burst out **2** *(Fig)* to swell with anger, burst out in anger

***bufnajë** *adj, nf* = bufnjak

bufnja·k

I § adj (said of soil or snow) soft and loose

II § nm **1** soft powdery snow; loose snow **2** loose, uncompacted soil

bufo·n *nm* **1** *(Old)* buffoon, jester, fool **2** *[Theat]* comic actor, comedian; clown

bu·fthi *adv*

bugari *nf [Mus]* four-stringed lute

***buga·z** *nm* = boga·z

bugra· *nf [Text]* fine canvas used to make tapestry, linen sackcloth

***bugrele·** *nf* apple sauce

***bugje·r** *nm (Old)* = ku·pë

buha·r *nm* **1** passageway between rooms, hall, corridor **2** dark and narrow alley **3** = buhari

buhari *nf* fireplace mantel; chimney; fireplace

***buha·s|** *stem for 1st sg pres, pl pres, 2nd & 3rd sg subj, pind* <buha·t·

buhas| *nf [Text]* red material used for lining clothes

buha·t· *vt* = buhavi·t·

buha·tje *nf* hoot of an owl

buhavi·cë *nf [Bot]* yellow flowered reedy plant that grows in clumps and has long ovate downy leaves that emit a sticky liquid

buhavi·s| *stem for 1st sg pres, pl pres, 2nd & 3rd sg subj, imperf* <buhavi·t·

buhavi·t· *vt (Colloq)* **1** to inflate, swell **2** *(Fig Pej)* to bore, vex

buhavi·t·et *vpr (Colloq)* **1** to swell/puff up; become swollen **2** *(Fig Pej)* to get bored, be fed up

buhavi·tje *nf ger (Colloq)* **1** <buhavi·t·, buhavit·et **2** swollen (body) part **3** swelling; lump **4** <buhavi·t·, buhavit·et

buhavi·tur *adj (i) (Colloq)* swollen

***bu·hërt** *adj (i)* sensual

buhi *nf* banquet, feast; fun and joy

buhi·shëm *adj (i)* rich, wealthy; joyful and fun, happy

buhi·t· *vt* to nauseate, make sick

buhi·t·et *vpr* to become nauseated, feel sick

buhu·r *nm (Old)* incense

bui·s· *vi* **1** to ooze; drip **2** to well up, gush forth **3** to appear in a sudden mass: swarm; teem; burst out in all its glory **4** (of a limb) to feel like pins and needles: tingle, feel numb **5** to resound, roar, rumble **6** = buluro·n

***bui·t|** *stem for 2nd & 3rd sg pres, 2nd pl pres, pdef, opt, adm, part, pind, imper, vp* <bui·s·

***bui·tje** *nf ger* <bui·s·

buja·në *nf* **1** deep spot in a river **2** large pool of stagnant water

buja·r

I § nm **1** *[Hist]* boyar, nobleman; large land owner in a feudal society **2** generous person; noble person

II § adj generous, hospitable; noble

Buja·r *nm* Bujar (male name)

bujare·shë *nf* **1** noblewoman, lady **2** generous woman

***bujar·e·ri** = bujarësi

bujar·ë·si *nf* = bujari

bujari *nf* **1** generosity, hospitableness; nobleness, nobility **2** nobility, the upper class

bujari·sht *adv* nobly; generously, unstintingly; hospitably

bujaro·*n vt* to ennoble

bujarso·n = bujaro·*n*

bujashkë *nf* wood chip, splinter; wood shaving

bujë *nf* **1** sensation, stir and clamor, notoriety, splash; fame **2** *(Pej)* ado, commotion, to-do **3** roar, boom, roaring

bujëmadh *adj* **1** sensational, notorious; famous **2** *(Pej)* flashy, sensationalistic

bujgër *nm* [*Bot*] Macedonian oak (*Quercus macedonica, Quercus trojana*)

bujis· = buís·

bujit *stem for 2nd & 3rd sg pres, 2nd pl pres, pdef, opt, adm, part, pind, imper, vp* <buis·

bujitje *nf ger* <buis·

bujk *nm (np ~ q)* **1** farmer, peasant; tenant farmer, sharecropper **2** [*Entom*] = bulk

bujkeshë *nf* <bujk

bujkrob *nm* serf

bujkrobëri *nf* serfdom

bujkrobëro·*het vpr* to become a serf

bujkrobëro·*n vt* to make [] into a serf

bujkrobëror *adj* pertaining to serfdom, of serfdom

bujkrobërues *adj* **1** having dominion over serfs **2** = bujkrobëror

bujq *np* <bujk

bujqëri *nf collec* farmers taken as a whole

bujqësi *nf* **1** agriculture **2** agronomy

bujqësor *adj* **1** agricultural **2** agronomic **3** agrarian

bujqësoro-industrial *adj* agro-industrial

bujrëm *interj (Colloq)* (invitation to a guest to do something): please come in! please sit down! have some food!

bujshëm *adj (i)* **1** impressive, sensational **2** clamorous, noisy, splashy **3** hustling and bustling, booming **4** flourishing

bujt *stem for pdef, opt, adm, part, vp* <bu·n

bujtar *I § n* **1** overnight guest, lodger **2** person who has guests: host **3** innkeeper *II § adj* hospitable

bujtari *nf* hospitality

bujtës *I § n* **1** overnight guest, lodger **2** [*Spec*] host (of a parasite), carrier *II § adj* serving as host (of a parasite)

bujtësi *nf* hospitality

bujti *nf* dwelling place, habitat, lair

bujtinar *n* innkeeper, rooming-house keeper

bujtinë *nf* **1** small hotel, lodgings **2** dormitory; barracks

bujtje *nf ger* **1** <bu·n **2** overnight visit/stay, lodgings

bujto·*n vt* to put up [] for the night, give overnight lodgings to []

bujtore *nf* = bujtinë

bujtshëm *adj (i)* hospitable

bujtur *I § part* <bu·n < *II § adj (i)* **1** left standing for a period of time, allowed to settle **2** left standing out for a period of time: stale

bukafec *nm* [*Food*] pie made with leavened dough

bukagjellë *adv*

bukamel *nm* skinny child

***bukanec** *nm (Reg Gheg)* allocated holding: plot

bukanik *adj* productive, fertile

bukapjekës *nm* = bukëpjekës

bukare *nf (Reg)* firefly

bukas *adv*

bukatar *n (Old)* baker

bukatare *nf (Old)* **1** <bukatar **2** woman who delivers food to men working in fields or pastures

bukator *I § n* **1** person who feeds the grain sheaves into the threshing machine **2** measuring vessel that holds enough flour to make a single loaf of bread *II § adj* (of soil) with a large yield of grain: highly productive

Bukenvald *nm* Buchenwald

bukë *I § nf* **1** bread **2** loaf of bread **3** grain from which flour is made; a year's harvest; a year's production of grain **4** kernel of grain; meaty/fleshy part of a fruit or vegetable, pith; pulp **5** food **6** meal (breakfast, lunch, dinner) **7** *(Fig)* useful/valuable content, worthwhile value at the core **8** *(Fig)* necessities of life, a living, livelihood **9** *(Fig)* employment, job; place of employment **10** *(Fig)* essential material in an industry **11** something in the shape of a round loaf *II § np* **1** loaves **2** *(Colloq Fig)* years (of age)

○ **bukë arëzash** hornet's nest, hive of wasps

○ **bukë blete** round honeycomb

○ **bukë derri** [*Bot*] autumn-blooming herbaceous perennial with ovate leaves and rose-colored flowers that grows in the underbrush

○ **bukë dheu** clump of soil clinging to roots

○ **(me) bukë e pa bukë** sometimes full and sometimes hungry

○ **bukë e ftohtë** stale bread

○ **bukë gruri** wheat bread

○ **bukë kalojeri** red-topped sage *Salvia viridis*

○ **buka e kripa** the most essential things

○ **bukë e lashtë** sourdough bread

○ **na e lë³ʳᵈᵖᵈᵉᶠ bukën** *(Crude)* {} died: {} kicked the bucket

○ **buka e lulediellit** the head of a sunflower with its seeds

○ **bukë mali** [*Bot*] a type of sweet cabbage

○ **bukë e mbrume** leavened bread

○ **bukë e ndorme** unleavened bread

○ **buka e një mielli** *(Pej)* one is no better than the other, they are cut from the same bad cloth

○ **ësh-të pa bukë** not have eaten anything

○ **Buka pa gëlltitur nuk kapërcehet.** "Food doesn't go down without swallowing." It takes time and energy to achieve something.

○ **Buka pa përtypur nuk kapërcehet.** "Without chewing bread cannot be swallowed" *(Prov)* You can't solve anything without working on it.

○ **për (këtë) bukë!** (used as an ordinary oath) On my word of honor! I swear! cross my heart! by God!

○ **bukë qeni** person with whom there can be no conversation

○ **Buka që thyhet, s'ngjitet më.** "A loaf of bread that is broken is not to be put together anymore" *1 (Prov)* A broken friendship cannot be patched up. **2** There's no use crying over spilt milk.

○ **Buka s'ka turp/marre.** "Food has no shame." There is no shame in being hungry (and getting food however you can).

○ **bukë Shëngjini** common grape hyacinth, small grape-hyacinth *Muscari botryoides*

○ **buka e verës** rainbow

○ **bukë e vjetër** "old bread" long-time friend: old friend/pal

○ **nuk e zë· bukën** not manage to assure one's supply of food

bukë·bár *nm* sod, lawn sod, turf

bukë·bárdhë *adj* **1** white-kerneled, white at the core **2** *(Fig)* hospitable; generous

bukë·bërës *nm* breadmaker, baker

bukë·dérr *nm* [*Bot*] sowbread *(Cyclamen neapolitanum)*

****bukë·dhánë** = bukë·dhënë

bukë·dhënë *adj* = bukë·dhënës

bukë·dhënës *adj* hospitable

bukë·fíke *nf* = bukë·fíqe

bukë·fíqe *nf* a small round loaf made of dried figs ground up and pressed together: fig loaf; fig bread

bukë·hárám *nm (Pej)* person who does not work for a living, loafer

bukë·kúq *adj* red-centered, reddish or reddish brown at the core (said of fruit like melons or figs)

bukël *nf* **1** curly lock of hair **2** [*Zool*] weasel *(Mustela nivalis)* **3** [*Bot*] edible mushroom with sweet reddish flesh

○ **bukla e detit** [*Ichth*] fiatolon, pomfret *Stromateus fiatola*

bukë·lépe *nf* [*Bot*] winter-blooming fodder grass that grows in littoral fields

bukë·mísh *nm* [*Food*] rissole

bukë·përmbýs *n* ingrate, ungrateful person

bukë·përmbýsët *OR* **bukë·përmýsët** *adj* ungrateful

bukë·pjekës *nm* baker

bukë·plótë *adj* full of kernels or fruit; having meaty kernels or fruit

bukë·qýqe *nf* red fruit of the cochineal oak

bukë·ra
I § *np* breads, different kinds of bread
II § *np* < bukë crumbs

bukë·rríme *np* residue left by a melting candle

bukë·s *adj* producing plump round fruit; (of fruits like plums and apricots) having ample flesh and a small pit

bukë·sheqére *nf* [*Food*] sweet cake, spongecake; pound cake

bukë·shítës *n* salesclerk in a bakery

bukë·shkálë *OR* **bukë·shkélës** *adj* ungrateful

bukë·shkélje *nf* ingratitude

bukë·tár *nm (Old)* **1** = bukë·pjekës **2** = bujk

bukë·táre *nf (Old)* girl or woman who brings bread to the men in the fields or mountain corrals

bukë·tóre *nf (Old)* bakery, place where bread is baked and sold

bukë·valë
I § *nf* **1** [*Food*] bread boiled to a pulp in water, mixed with oil/butter and cheese: panada **2** [*Ethnog*] sweet made with boiled crackercrumbs, sugar and butter, customarily prepared a few days after the birth of a baby
II § *adj* (of soil) soft and loose, soggy

bukë·z *nf* **1** *(Dimin)* < bukë **2** honey comb or wasp nest that takes on a round shape **3** the seed at the core of a nut or piece of fruit, fruit pit, nut (the meaty part)

bukë·zí *adj (fem sg ⁓ ézȳ, masc pl ⁓ínj, fem pl ⁓eza)* inhospitable; stingy, ungenerous

bukë·zó·het *vpr* = bukó·n

búkje
I § *nf* [*Bot*] broadleafed bulrush, great reed mace *(Typha latifolia)*
II § *adj* (of fruits, nuts, grain, or vegetables) fleshy, meaty

búkla *np* < bukël curls

búklëz *nf* [*Zool*] weasel *(Mustela nivalis)*

buklí *nf* small water pitcher

buklídhë *nf* linchpin on a plowbeam

buklóre *adj (Poet)* beautiful, curly-headed, curly-haired

bukó·het *vpr* to have a meal, eat

bukó·n
I § *vi* **1** to eat bread, eat a meal **2** *(Fig)* to get along well
II § *vt* to feed

bukolík *adj* bucolic

bukolíke *np* bucolic poetry

bukós· *vt* to plug up a hole/crack in [ ]

bukós·et *vpr* to get plugged up

buks *nm* [*Tech*] axle box (in railway)

buksím *nm* [*Tech*] wheel slippage/spinning

bukshëm *adj (i)* **1** having plump full ears/heads of grain **2** *(Fig)* valuable, productive, fruitful

búkthi *adv*

bukulére *nf* oak apple, oak gall

búkur
I § *adj (i)* **1** beautiful; pretty, handsome **2** nice, wonderful
II § *adv* **1** beautifully; fine, well; swell **2** very well, pretty much **3** *(Colloq)* quite, very: pretty
III § *nf (e)* [*Phil*] that which is beautiful
IV § *nm (i)* handsome fellow
V § *np (të) (Euph)* tonsillitis

○ **e Bukura e Dheut** [*Folklore*] beautiful heroine in folktales

○ **e bukura e dheut** [*Zool*] European fire salamander *(Salamandra salamandra)*

○ **i Bukuri i Dheut** [*Folklore*] handsome hero in folktales

○ **Bukur për dhëndër!** *(Felic)* Wear it in the best of health! May he be so good looking when he marries!

bukurázi *adv* very well, beautifully

bukúre *nf* firefly, glowworm

Bukurésht *nm* Bucharest

bukurézë *nf* = bukure

bukurí
I § *nf* beauty
II § *adv (Colloq)* very well, excellently

○ **bukuri në shekull** most beautiful thing/person in the world

****bukuríshtë** *nf* [*Bot*] daisy, garden daisy, English daisy *(Bellis perennis)*

bukurízë *nf* [*Entom*] firefly

bukuró·n *vt* to make [ ] pretty: beautify, adorn, polish

bukurósh
I § *adj (Pet Poet)* **1** good-looking, handsome, pretty **2** *(Iron)* worthless, empty; displeasing, unpleasant
II § *nm* **1** = bishtatúndës **2** rogue, swindler

Bukurósh *n* Bukurosh (male name)

Bukuróshe *nf* Bukuroshe (female name)

bukur·shkrím nm **1** nice handwriting; calligraphy **2** handwriting, penmanship

bukur·shqiptím nm [Ling] **1** good pronunciation, enunciation **2** orthoepy; elocution

bukurtingëllím nm [Ling] euphony

bukurtingëllúe·s adj [Ling] **1** euphonious **2** epenthetic

*__bukuru'sh__ = bukuro'sh

bukurzaní nf [Ling] = bukurtingëllím

bukurzanór adj [Ling] = bukurtingëllúe·s

bulárc = bularës

bulárës nm **1** silversmith's punch for hammering metal into a concave shape *__2__ (Old) bell-clapper; drumstick

*__bularís__ stem for 1st sg pres, pl pres, 2nd & 3rd sg subj, pind <bularít·

*__bularít·__ vi = buluro'·n

bulás· vt to graft [olive trees]

bulb nm bulb; corm
  ○ **bulbi i syrit** eyeball
  ○ **bulbi i trurit** [Anat] medulla oblongata

bulbe adj bulbous

bulbërí nf abundance, wealth

bulbërím nm = bulbërí

bulbëro'·n vi to abound; swarm, teem

bulbërt adj (i) abundant, in abundance; rich

bulbor adj **1** [Bot] having or generated by bulbs **2** bulbous

*__bulcíq__ adj overripe

*__bulcíq·et__ vpr to become overripe

*__bulcíqët__ adj (i) = bulcíq

bulçí nf **1** cheek lining, cheek **2** (Colloq) half a mouthful of food

bulçím nm stifling heat; sultry heat

buldoekskavator nm [Constr] dozer excavator

buldozér nm bulldozer

buldozeríst n bulldozer driver

*__buleder__ nf ox-tongue fungus growing on trees; touchwood

*__buletë__ = biletë

buletín nm **1** bulletin **2** (Old) ballot

bulevárd nm **1** boulevard **2** (Pej) trashy place, source of sleaze

bulé nf **1** bud **2** drop of liquid **3** small bubble **4** [Anat] round, fleshy part of an organ: lobule, lobulus **5** swollen abscess; large pustule **6** for fruits that divide into sections, one such section; nutmeat
  ○ **ësh-të**[3rd] **bulë e flori** "be a drop of gold" (of rain) to be worth its weight in gold
  ○ **bulë e gishtit** finger tip
  ○ **bulë shege** pomegranate section containing a cluster of seeds
  ○ **bulë e veshit** earlobe

bulevéshë nf fish gill

bulëz nf **1** (Dimin) <bulë **2** [Mus] measure; rhythmic/melodic unit

bulëzím nm ger **1** <bulëzo'·n **2** germination

bulëzo'·het vpr **1** to sprout, germinate, bud **2** to be germinated

bulëzo'·n
  I § vi **1** to sprout, germinate, form buds, bud **2** to drip, emerge in droplets; bubble **3** to pout
  II § vt [Agr] to let sprout, allow budding, germinate

bulgë nf (Reg Old) = gjerdek

bulgër = bujgër

bulí (n) nm (np ~ nj) [Bot] fluttering elm, water elm (Ulmus laevis)

bulím nm ger = bulëzím

buliním nm ger [Tech] <bulino'·n

bulíno nf [Tech] graving tool, burin, graver

bulíno··n vt [Tech] to engrave, chisel

bulírë nf (Reg) = buçelë

buljerë nf wooden keg for water

bulk nm [Entom] house cricket (Acheta domesticus)

*__bulkrak__ nm [Bot] = bujgër

bulkth nm **1** [Invert] cricket **2** field cricket (Gryllus campestris)
  ○ **bulkthi ballëlarmë** [Entom] Acheta (Gryllus) frontalis
  ○ **bulkthi ballëverdhë** [Entom] species of cricket Gryllus burdigalensis
  ○ **bulkthi i fushave** [Entom] desert cricket Acheta deserta
  ○ **bulkthi i fushës** [Invert] = bulkth
  ○ **bulkthi i madh** [Entom] field cricket Gryllus campestris
  ○ **bulkthi i shtëpisë** [Invert] = bulk

bulmét nm **1** dairy product **2** (Fig) useful product/result, fruit, harvest, welcome outcome **3** shop that sells dairy products
  ○ **bulmet hudhrash** "dairy product made with garlic" (Iron) something of no conceivable value: garlic toothpaste

bulmét·et vpr to eat a very small amount, take a small bite; have a little taste, taste

bulmetor
  I § adj **1** dairy, pertaining to dairy work or products **2** = bulmetshëm
  II § n dairyman

bulmetóre nf **1** shop selling dairy products: dairy store **2** (Old) [Dairy] dairy where milk products are produced

bulmétra np <bulmet dairy products

bulmetshëm adj (i) **1** giving a lot of milk, productive of milk **2** [Dairy] rich in milk, laden with milk; having a high butterfat content **3** (Fig colloq) fruitful, productive

bulmo'·n vt to add dairy fat to [food]; enrich [] with a dairy product

buló'·n vi **1** = bulëzo'·n **2** to bubble, effervesce **3** (Fig) to barely emerge; barely sprout

*__bulók__ nm rampart; buffer

bulón nm [Tech] bolt (used with a nut)

*__buló·s·__ vt to ward off [], repel

bulqí
  I § nf **1** = bujqësí *__2__ = bulçí
  II § np grain not yet harvested

bulqizák
  I § adj of or pertaining to Bulqiza
  II § n native of Bulqiza

Bulqízë nf town in east-central Albania known for its production of chrome: Bulqiza

bultís· vt to put one's seal on []: approve

*__bulth__ = bulkth

bulurí·n vi = buluro'·n

bulurímë nf mooing, lowing, bellowing; braying

*__bulurís__ stem for 1st sg pres, pl pres, 2nd & 3rd sg subj, pind <bulurít·

bulurít· vi = buluro'·n

bulur o·-*n vi* to bawl: moo; bellow; bray; roar

***bulzu e s** *adj* full, plump; chubby

bullafi q *adj* plump, fleshy; unpleasantly fat, bloated

bullafi q· *vt* to make plump, swell, make obese

bullafi q·-*et vpr* to become obese, swell up, become plump

bullafi q er *adj pl* <**bullafi q**

bullama ç
   I § *nm (Reg)* **1** = **qull 2** feedmash, mash fed to domestic animals
   II § *adj* soggy

***bulla nd er** *nf (Reg Gheg)* = **bullë nd er**

bulla r
   I § *n* **1** [*Zool*] snake characterized by a thick body and sluggish movements: European glass lizard, sheltopusik (*Ophisaurus apodus*) **2** [*Zool*] = **burra ll 3** (*Fig Pej*) chubby or clumsy person
   II § *adj* *vulgar, coarse

bulle d er *nf* [*Bot*] tinder fungus (*Fomes fomentarius, Polyporus fomentarius*) **2** (*Fig Pej*) fat woman ***3** (*Old Regional Gheg*) Moslem woman

bulle t er
   I § *nf* strong vinegar
   II § *adj* very sour, vinegary

bu lle *nf (Old)* **1** [*Ethnog*] woman who adorns the bride for the wedding and accompanies her to the house of the bridegroom **2** Moslem woman ***3** (papal) bull

bullë nd er *nf* **1** hot and salty water used to bathe feet after a tiring journey; dishwater **2** oily dregs; lees; filthy scum

bullga r *adj* Bulgarian

bullgar i *nf* four-stringed lute-like instrument

Bullgar i *nf* Bulgaria

bullgar i sht *adv* in Bulgarian (language)

bullgar i sht e *nf* Bulgarian (language)

bullgu r *nm* hulled kernels of barley

bull i c e *nf* **1** fat woman ***2** = **bualli c e**

bullo g *nm* [*Myth*] dragon's lair

bullo n = **bulo n**

bullu bre shk e *nf (Impol)* overdressed and overmadeup woman

***bullufi** *nf* swelling

***bullufi q** *adj* inflated, swollen, distended

***bullufi q·** *vi* to inflate, swell

bullu ng e *nf* **1** bump/swelling caused by trauma or illness **2** knot/gnarl on a tree trunk **3** dent in a metal vessel

bullu r *nm (Reg)* misfortune, trouble

bullu t *nm* weak and low grade raki, bottom of the barrel

bum
   I § *nm* **1** boom; sudden rise in success **2** [*Naut*] boom (of a sailing ship)
   II § *onomat* **1** deeply resonant percussive/explosive sound: boom! bam! **2** dull sound made upon impact: thud!

buma ll e *nf* [*Entom*] = **furrta re**

***buma rdh e** *nf (Old)* trench mortar

bumba ll e = **buma ll e**

bumba r *nm* [*Food*] [*Food*] **1** = **kukure c 2** minced liver, rice and raisins wrapped in tripe and roasted

***bumbe·**-*het vpr* to swell, swell up

***bumbe·**-*n vt* to inflate, swell

bumbe sk e *nf* new sprout; partially open flower bud

bu mb e *nf* = **bumbe sk e**

bumbë zo·-*het vpr* to be budding

bumbë zo·-*n vi* to have new buds, be budding

***bumbi l** *nm* [*Ornit*] nightingale (*Luscinia megarhynchos*) = **bilbi l**

***bu mbje** *nf* boom, roar

bumb o·-*n vi* **1** = **bumbëzo·**-*n* **2** to burst out; gush up, spring forth

bumb o s· *vt* to stifle, suffocate

bumbre k *nm* = **bubre k**

***bumbull a k** *adj* humming, buzzing

***bumbulli·**-*n vi* = **bubulli·**-*n*

***bumbulli m e** = **bubulli m e**

***bumbull o·**-*n vi* = **bubulli·**-*n*

bumera ng *nm* boomerang

***bu me** *nf* boom (of a sailing ship); brigantine sail

bu mje *nf* **1** (*Colloq*) bomb ***2** = **bu mbje**

bun *nm* **1** shepherd's hut; lean-to **2** dwelling place **3** insect nest ***4** upland pasture

buna c e
   I § *nf* **1** [*Naut*] calm sea; calm, dead calm (no wind) **2** stagnant pool of water; swamp **3** oppressive darkness **4** (*Fig*) calm; stagnation
   II § *adj* extremely dark

buna r *nm (Old)* **1** well (for water), fountain **2** spring, pool around a spring, cistern

bu nd e *nf* **1** strong, wet wind **2** cold caught in wet climates; bad flu **3** mildew-like disease of plants caused by excessive wetness

bu nd er *nf* [*Zool*] polecat

***bundo z** *nm* = **bunda r**

***bune ll e** *nf (Reg Tosk)* table fork

Bu n e *nf* river in northwestern Albania: Buna, Boyana

bung *nm* (*np* ˜ **gje**) [*Bot*] durmast oak (*Quercus petraea*)

bungaj e *nf* **1** forest of durmast oak **2** (*Fig*) confusing and obscure problem or situation

bu ng e *nf* **1** = **xhu ng e 2** [*Bot*] = **bung 3** (*Fig*) lump or knot in one's throat caused by anger or anguish
   ○ **bung e e bute** [*Bot*] = **bung ebu t e**

bung ëbu t e *nf* [*Bot*] pubescent oak, white oak (*Quercus pubescens*)

bung ë ke qe *nf* [*Bot*] **1** Hungarian oak = **shpardh 2** durmast oak = **bung**

bung ë ku qe *nf* [*Bot*] Macedonian oak (*Quercus trojana*)

bu ng ë l *nf* [*Bot*] = **shpardh**

bung ë le she *nf* [*Bot*] = **bung ëbu t e**

bung i sht e *nf* = **bunga j e**

***bung o·**-*n vt* to raise a lump on [ ]

bu ngje *np* **bung**

***bun i m** *nm (Reg Gheg)* = **buri m**

bun i sht e *nf* winter pasture area where shepherds have their huts

bunit·-*et vpr* to swell/puff up; become swollen

bunke r *nm* **1** [*Mil*] pillbox; bunker **2** [*Tech*] funnel-shaped dispensing bin: hopper

***bun o·**-*n vt (Reg Gheg)* = **buro·**-*n*

bunje t e *nf* clump of reeds; piece of marshland whose reed stalks are unharvested

buq
   I § *nm* = **do çe**
   II § *adv (Reg)* for nothing, in vain, up in smoke

buqa'r nm (Old) **1** farmer; city farmer, farmer who travels to his fields from his home in the city **2** absentee landowner; rich man

bu'qe nf = **byp**e

buqe'të nf bouquet of flowers, nosegay

buqi'cë nf **1** padlock = **dry 2** [Ornit] sparrow-sized grayish-green bird that builds swallow-like nests in caves and hollows

*__buqis__· vt to spit [ ] out

bu'qme nf thin cord-like ribbon used to decorate ethnic costumes

burani' nf **1** [Food] dish made with rice and minced greens **2** [Ichth] river gudgeon (Gobio gobio fluviatilis Kessler)

bu'rbuj np < **bu'rbull** (Colloq)

burbu'jë nf hubbub, tumult, clamor

burbule' nf (Old) food containing meat or dairy product forbidden during a fast

burbule'c nm [Entom] larva of the warble fly (Hypoderma bovis)

burbule't· vt (Old) **1** to give someone food containing meat or dairy product forbidden during a fast **2** (Colloq) to give someone a taste of something good; whet someone's appetite

burbule't·et vpr **1** to break one's fast, eat meat or dairy product forbidden during a fast **2** to taste, taste for the first time; have one's mouth water from something delicious

burbule'tur adj (i) (Old) **1** containing meat or dairy product forbidden during a fast **2** (Colloq) guilty of eating meat or dairy product forbidden during a fast

bu'rbull nm (np ~ j) [Bot] European cotoneaster (Cotoneaster integerrima)

burbunjo's·et vpr (Reg) **1** to sprout, germinate, bud **2** to huddle/hunch up (from cold or illness)

*__burbu'q__ adj **1** short **2** dapper **3** good-natured, cheerful

burbu'q·et vpr to sprout, germinate, bud

burbu'qe nf bud; flower bud

burbuqo'·n vi = **burbu'q**·et

*__burde'l__ nm bordello = **borde'l**

burdulla'k nm **1** [Ichth] Bucchich's goby (Gobius bucchichi) **2** [Ichth] rock goby (Gobius paganellus) **3** [Bot] common purslane (Portulaca oleracea)
∘ **burdullak bari** [Ichth] grass goby Zosterisessor ophiocephalus
∘ **burdullak gojëkuq** [Ichth] bloody-mouthed goby Gobius cruentatus
∘ **burdullak guri** [Ichth] giant goby Gobius cobitis
∘ **burdullak i kuq** [Ichth] transparent goby Aphia minuta mediterranea
∘ **burdullak lumi** [Ichth] monkey goby Neogobius fluviatilis fluviatilis
∘ **burdullak i zi** [Ichth] Atlantic black goby Gobius niger jozo

bu'rdhë nf thickly woven cotton sackcloth; sack

*__bure'k__ nm = **byre'k**

bu'rë nf [Naut] rough weather at sea, rough seas, stormy weather; heavy seas; flood tide
∘ **burë deti** billow, surge

burg nm (np ~ gje) **1** prison, jail **2** imprisonment **3** (Reg) food cellar; stable/stall for livestock **4** pitch darkness **5** small, rocky hill detached from a mountain; rocky mountain summit, steep crag

*__burgale'm__ nm [Bot] sowbread = **burth**

burga'ma'dh nm jailbird

burg|ёto'·het vpr **1** to be shut up at home for a long time **2** to have life made a prison, have life made intolerable

burg|ёto'·n vt to make [ ]'s life a prison, make life intolerable for [ ]

*__burgi'__ nf iron post

burgi'm nm ger **1** < **burgo'**·n **2** imprisonment
∘ **burgim i rëndë** heavy prison term

burgo'·n vt = **burgo's**

burgo'një nf Burgundy wine

burgo's· vt to imprison

burgo'sur adj (i) imprisoned

*__burgta'r__ OR **burgt'uer** nm (Old) prisoner

burgth nm [Entom] = **bulk**

bu'rgull nm [Bot] houseleek (Sempervivum)

bu'rgje np < **burg**

burgji' nm **1** screw = **vi'dh**ë **2** worm gear **3** (Reg) auger, gimlet, corkscrew

buri' nf **1** = **bori' 2** large amount/number, multitude **3** water jug

buri'm
I § nm **1** spring, fountainhead **2** head/source of a river or stream **3** source **4** origin **5** resource
II § adv in a trickle, in a stream
∘ **burim force** power source, energy source

burimo'r adj original

buri'shtë nf area with many small springs; wetland, marshland, swampland

*__buri'ta'r__ nm (Old) = **boriza'n**

buriza'n nm = **boriza'n**

burkth = **bu'lkth**

bu'rmë nf **1** small screw **2** worm gear **3** overripe fig **4** dimple; pockmark; small hole or cavity that holds something

burmo'·n vt to secure [ ] with a small screw, screw in

burno't
I § nm snuff (tobacco used for sniffing)
II § adj (Fig pej) worthless, useless; ignorant, mentally retarded

buro'·n vi **1** (of water) to spring up out of the ground, bubble up: well up **2** to originate **3** to flow profusely and continuously **4** to leak, seep
∘ <> **buro**·n[3sg] **goja mjaltë** "<>'s mouth flows with honey" <> speaks pleasantly; <> speaks beautifully

burokraci' nf bureaucracy

burokra't
I § nm bureaucrat
II § adj behaving bureaucratically

burokrati'k adj bureaucratic

burokrati'zëm nm bureaucratism

burokratizi'm nm ger < **burokratizo'**·n, **burokratizo'**·het

burokratizo'·het vpr **1** to behave bureaucratically **2** to become a bureaucrat

burokratizo'·n vt to bureaucratize

buro'më nf **1** spring, fountainhead **2** (Reg) spittle, saliva, slobber

*__buro'nt__ nm snuff

buro'një nf **1** = **buri'm 2** = **buri'sht**ë

bu'rsë nf **1** scholarship award, stipend **2** stock market, commodities exchange, financial market

bursi'st n **1** student on a scholarship, scholarship holder **2** stock market trader

bursor *adj* 1 of or pertaining to scholarships 2 of or pertaining to the stock market

burth *nm* 1 [*Bot*] sowbread (*Cyclamen neapolitanum*) 2 (*Veter*) equine disease symptomized by blood blisters on the roof of the mouth

burues *nm (Book)* source of heat or light energy

burulluk *nm* 1 thin, wispy cloth; veil, cheesecloth 2 head kerchief made of thin white cloth

burumli *nf* silversmith's tweezers

*****burxhak** *nm* animal fodder

burra *np* <burrë

burrac *nm (Colloq)* 1 short ugly man: gnome, homely dwarf 2 *(Impol)* timid, cowardly person

burracak
  I § *adj (Pej)* timid; timorous, cowardly, chicken
  II § *nm* coward; timid person

burracakëri *nf* cowardice; timidity

burrak *nm* = burrac

*****burrakoç** *nm (Old)* superman

*****burrakoçe** *nf (Old)* virile woman

burrall *nm* [*Zool*] slowworm, blindworm = bollëverbët

burran *nm* large man

burras *adv* in a manly way, like a man; boldly, courageously

burrath *nm* little man

burravec *nm (Impol)* 1 timid, cowardly person 2 wimp, chicken, worthless person

burravegjël *np* <burravogël

burravogël *nm* dwarf, midget

*****burre** *nf* = burrëreshë

burrec *nm (Impol)* 1 timid, cowardly person 2 wimp, chicken, worthless person 3 short, homely man

Burrel *nm* Burrel (city in north central Albania)

burrelas *adj, n* Burrelian

burrë
  I § *nm* 1 male person; man 2 husband 3 real man: brave/courageous person, man of his word, loyal person 4 distinguished person
  II § *adj* courageous, brave, loyal, trustworthy
  ○ **A je burrë!** *(Reg)* (greeting between two men) Howdy!
  ○ **burri i dheut** man of strong character
  ○ **Burrin e prishin huqet.** *(Prov)* Vices can destroy even the best man.
  ○ **burrë e gjysmë** bravest of the brave
  ○ **i burri i botës** "outsider's man" 1 man who does not belong to one's family circle, stranger 2 (*Contempt*) this/some (damn) guy
  ○ **burrë katërqind dërhemë** man of the world; courageous man of strong character
  ○ **burrë me (një barrë) mustaqe** 1 man of his word 2 man who follows old customs 3 man of great personal dignity/pride
  ○ **burrë në qokë** man who makes sense
  ○ **Burri në shkallë, po shkalla në mur.** "The man on the ladder, but the ladder on the wall!" *(Prov)* One should proceed, but always with caution. Go ahead, but with care.
  ○ **burrë zakoni** (old) man who keeps to the old customs

burrëreshë *nf* = burrneshë

burrëri *nf* 1 manhood; manliness, virility 2 adulthood, maturity 3 courage, pluck; bravery, valor 4 steadfastness, loyalty

burrërim *nm ger* 1 <burrëro·n, burrëro·het 2 manhood

burrërisht *adv* courageously, bravely; like a man

burrërishte *adj* appropriate for men

burrëro·het *vpr* to become mature, reach manhood

burrëro·n *vt* to make [] into a man, raise to manhood; give a manly appearance

burrëror *adj* appropriate for men: manly; virile; courageous

burrëzi *nm (ColloqImpolite)* incompetent man; wretched/miserable man; worthless man

*****burrëzim** = burrërim

*****burrëzo·het** = burrëro·het

burri *nf* [*Naut*] mild northwind

burrneshë *nf* courageous woman

burrni *nf* = burrëri
  ○ **burrni për burrni** as one man to another, like (brave) men

burrnim *nm* = burrëri

burrno·het *vpr* to attain manhood, become a man

burrno·n *vt* to make a man of []

burrnor *adj* = burrëror

burrnot *nm* = burnot

buso·n *vt* to exude, ooze out []

*****busolë** *nf* = busull

bust *nm [Art]* 1 sculpture of the head and upper body: bust *2 corset

*****busto** *nf* = bust

busull *nf* compass (for pointing north)

bush *nm* [*Bot*] 1 boxwood (*Buxus sempervirens*) 2 mythological swamp-dwelling animal that causes rain by howling

bushak *nm* 1 small and weak lamb with little wool *2 (Old)* flower pot

bushakë *nf* large vessel for oil

*****bushat** *nm (Reg)* estate, property, farm

Bushat *nm* town in north-central Albania: Bushat

bushatas
  I § *adj* of or pertaining to Bushat
  II § *n* native of Bushat

bushenj *np* <bush mythological swamp-dwelling animals

*****bushë** *nf* 1 buttress 2 cantilever of a bridge

*****bushicë** *nf* cornhusk

bushigëz *nf* = fshikëz

*****bushikë** *nf* = fshikë

bushiq
  I § *adj* plump
  II § *nm* bladder

bushk *nm* [*Bot*] boxwood

bushliqe *nf* 1 heat blister 2 cocoon *3 knurl on a tree trunk

bushllizë *nf* [*Bot*] bellbind, hedge bindweed, wild morning glory (*Convolvulus sepium, Calystegia sepium*)

bushnjesh *nm* boxwood grove

bushore *np* [*Bot*] box family *Buxacaea*

bushqan *nm* [*Bot*] *(Reg)* ivy, English ivy (*Hedera helix*)

bushtë *adj* (i) made of boxwood, of boxwood

bushtër *nf* 1 she-dog, bitch 2 *(Crude Insult)* woman of loose morals: tramp, slut, whore; woman who is a troublesome gossip 3 [*Myth*] dragon that spews fire and lightning 4 [*Zool*] = dosëz

bushtërz nf [Entom.] = **dosëz**

*bushtresë nf [Entom.] = **dosëz**

*bushtri nf indecency, baseness; outrage

bushtricas
I § adj of or pertaining to Bushtrica
II § n native of Bushtrica

Bushtricë nf town in northeastern Albania: Bushtrica

bushtrik nm corn plant producing no ears; corn with small ears and little grain

*bushtro·n vt to exasperate, rage

bushurdis· vt to sprinkle [ ] by spitting water out of the mouth

but nm 1 large barrel, hogshead 2 [Anat.] soft spot on top of an infant's head: fontanel 3 rump steak, steak fillet

butac nm (Reg) wooden bowl

butafori nf 1 [Theat.] stage prop 2 (Fig Book) false conditions created for purposes of deception, smoke-screen

butak
I § nm [Invert] mollusk
II § adj 1 soft and mushy; overripe and mushy 2 (Fig) namby-pamby, of weak character

*butarak = **butak**

butazi adv = **butësisht**

bute nf large barrel, hogshead = **but**

butebërës nm tenderizer

*butekë nf (Old) = **dyqan**

butexhi nm (np ˜ nj) = **butebërës**

butë
I § adv softly, gently, tenderly, mildly, moderately
II § adj (i) 1 soft, gentle, mild; smooth; mellow 2 tender; sensitive 3 tame; domesticated; cultivated 4 moderate; mild 5 damp
III § nn (të) gentleness, tenderness, softness
IV § nf earlobe
∘ **i butë shkumë** soft as foam

butëlosh adj = **butë**

butër nm 1 [Veter] glanders, strangles; an acutely contagious disease mainly affecting young colts (Coryza contagiosa equorum) 2 [Med] = **rrufë**

*butërisht adv = **butësisht**

butësi nf 1 softness, tenderness; gentleness, mildness 2 kindness, courtesy, politeness

butësirë nf 1 warm and humid weather; Indian summer 2 soft and damp place 3 fertile field

butësisht adv softly, tenderly; gently, mildly

butëso·het vpr = **zbut·et**

butëso·n vt = **zbut·**

*butëz nf [Bot] = **bungëbutë**

buti adv (së) when there is mild and moist weather, during the mild weather

*butilar n bottle maker

*butile OR **butilë** nf bottle, flask = **bocë**

butinë nf [Bot] viburnum, snowball (Viburnum)
∘ **butinë e butë** [Bot] wayfaring tree Viburnum lanata
∘ **butinë fletëlarë** [Bot] laurustinus viburnum Viburnum tinus
∘ **butinë e kuqe** [Bot] European cranberry bush, guelder rose Viburnum opulus

butishtë nf [Bot] = **bungëbutë**

buto·n
I § vt to saturate [a wooden vessel] with water so that it expands and seals against leakage
II § vi to get drenched with water

Butrint nm archeological site of an ancient city in southwestern Albania

butsim nm = **butësi**

*butsinë nf (Reg) fertile field = **butësirë**

butuk nm yearling billy goat

*butur = **butër**

buthtim nm ger < **buthto·n, buthto·het**

buthto·het vpr to appear, come to light

buthto·n
I § vi to bud; come out into the open
II § vt to bring [ ] out into view: express, show; reveal, expose

buvesh nm blockhead, dope, dolt, dullard

buxhak nm 1 fireside nook; hearth 2 small clearing in a forest 3 [Bot] vetch used as cattle fodder: common vetch, tare (Vicia sativa)

*buxhal nm flowerbed

*buxhek nm [Entom] = **dosëz**

*buxhel nm chubby (like a child)

buxhet nm [Fin] budget

buxhetor adj [Fin] budgetary

buza np (rocky) cliffs; boulders

buzaç adj (Impol) having thick, ugly lips: blubber-lipped

buzagaz
I § nm smile
II § adj ever-smiling, cheerful; amiable
III § adv with a smile on the lips, cheerfully

buzagazni nf cheerfulness; affability

buzak nm 1 wooden water pitcher 2 [Ichth] southern barbel (Barbus meridionalis Risso)

buzake nf [Bot] juicy, thin-skinned lemon

*buzangaz (Reg) = **buzagaz**

buzas adv = **buzëvarur**

buzel adj 1 (Pej) = **buzaç** 2 having a mark on the muzzle (said of domestic animals)

buzë
I § nf 1 lip 2 muzzle (area of an animal's face) 3 edge, rim, brink; boundary line, boundary 4 shore 5 (Fig) beginning 6 (rocky) cliff; boulder
II § prep (abl) 1 along/at the edge of 2 on the threshold of, at the beginning of
∘ **ësh-të buzë brisku** to be razor-thin
∘ **Fshiji buzët për murrizi** (Iron) to get all ready for nothing
∘ **buzë lepuri** [Med] harelip
∘ **ësh-të buzë më buzë (me [ ])** to be friendly (with [ ]), be very close (to [ ])
∘ **buzë më buzë 1** up to the brim, chock-full 2 on the lips, mouth to mouth
∘ **buzë më gaz** smiling, amiable
∘ **buzë nuseje** [Bot] musk thistle with yellow flowers
∘ **buzë për buzë** up to the very edge, to the brink

buzëbardhë adj white-lipped, white-muzzled

buzëburbuqe adj having pretty little red ("rosebud") lips

buzëçarë
I § adj 1 split-lipped 2 (Fig) = **buzëplasur**
II § nm name of a hare in children's stories

buzëdele nf [Bot] = **luleshqerrë**

buzëde'rr adj "pig-lipped" (Insult) hare-lipped

buzëde't nm seacoast, seashore

buzëdje'gur adj 1 having burned/scorched lips 2 (Fig) burned-up about, displeased

buzëdre'dhur adj having lips twisted (by emotion)

buzëflo'ri adj (Poet) having very beautiful ("golden") lips

buzëfry'rë adj swollen-lipped

*****buzëga'z** adj = buzaga'z

buzëho'llë adj 1 thin-lipped, wry-faced 2 (Fig) finicky, fussy; affected

buzëja'shtë adj having lips thrust forward = buzëpërve'shur

buzëkarafi'l adj (Poet) having carnation-red lips, with a beautiful mouth

buzëku'q adj red-lipped, beautiful

buzëku'qe nf 1 [Entom] bedbug 2 [Entom] = mollëku'qe *3 [Invert] rock shell (snail) from which a purple dye was formerly extracted (Thais haemastoma)

buzëkuti adj having small box-like lips

buzëky'çur adj, adv 1 close-mouthed 2 (Fig) sad-faced

buzë'l nf 1 labiate corolla of a flower; labium 2 thin half-veil worn over a woman's face

buzële'pur nm [Med] harelip

buzëleza'k nm [Ichth] = buzëma'dh

buzëlëshu'ar adj = buzëva'rur

buzëlidhur

I § nm (Euph) dead

II § adj = gojëky'çur

buzëlu'le adj 1 having spotted lips (said of domesticated animals) 2 = buzëburbu'qe

buzëma'dh nm [Ichth] boxlip mullet (Oedalechilus labeo)

buzëma'dhe nf [Bot] broad-leafed herbaceous weed with white, violet-shaped flowers

buzëmbrë'mje nf beginning of evening, early evening, dusk

buzëmu'shkë adj "mule-lipped" having wide, brown lips (said mainly of goats)

buzënxi'rë adj 1 dark-lipped, black-lipped 2 (Fig) having suffered much in life

buzëpagëzu'ar adj without having experienced happiness; unfortunate, unhappy

buzëpalo'sur adj having thin, tightly pressed together lips

buzëpaqe'shur adj having unsmiling lips; having suffered much in life

buzëpërdre'dhur adj (Pej) scornful, sneering

buzëpërthy'er adj = buzëpërve'shur

buzëpërve'shur adj having thick, turned-out lips

buzëpërvëlu'ar adj having suffered much = buzëpje'kur

buzëpje'kur adj 1 having dry, chapped lips 2 (Fig) having suffered much, embittered by experience; dejected, downcast

buzëpla'sje nf 1 big headache; severe problem *2 dejectedness

buzëpla'sur adj 1 embittered by life, depressed, unhappy, downcast 2 (Curse) damn you! (with a split lip)

buzëpre'rë adj = buzëça'rë

buzëqa'rë adj 1 pouting, with lips ready to cry, whimpering 2 gloomy, sad

buzëqershi adj (Poet) cherry-lipped, with beautiful red lips

buzëqe'sh· vi 1 to smile 2 to appear with a pleasant, happy countenance 3 to be auspicious

buzëqe'shje nf ger 1 <buzëqe'sh· 2 smile

buzëqe'shur adj, adv smiling, with a smile on the lips

buzëqu'mësht adj immature, still wet behind the ears

buzërri'pë nf face of a hill or cliff, sharp drop-off; cliff

buzësu'mbull nf (Reg Arb) round, narrow-necked bottle for keeping beverages

buzëshe'gë adj "pomegranate-lipped" having beautiful red lips

buzësheqe'r adj "sugar-lipped" = gojëmbël

buzëshkru'mb adj "cinder-lipped" = buzëpje'kur

buzështre'mbër adj having crooked/lopsided lips; lip-wrenching

buzëta'k nm [Ichth] Lake Ohrid nase (Chondrostoma nasus ohridanus) = skobu'z

buzëtra'shë adj thick-lipped

buzëtrëndafi'l adj (Poet) "rose-lipped" having lips like rosebuds, with cute little lips

buzëtha'rë adj 1 having parched lips (from fever or hot weather) 2 = buzëpje'kur

buzëtha'të adj 1 having dry lips 2 poor, without a bite to eat; wretched

buzëthy'er adj broken-lipped (said of pottery or glass vessels)

*****buzëva'jë** nf (Old) sneak

buzëva'rë nf = buzëva'rur

buzëva'rur adj 1 annoyed and angry: pouting, sulking, disgruntled, sullen 2 glum, downcast

*****buzëva'rrët** adj (i) = buzëva'rur

buzëvi'ç adj (Impol) having big, thick lips like a calf

buzëvre'r adj 1 embittered 2 sarcastic, venomous, bitter, acerbic

bu'zëz nf [Veter] 1 disease (mostly of sheep and goats) that causes lip blisters; lip blister resulting from that disease 2 rope muzzle used on draft animals 3 = hu'ndëz

buzëzi adj, n (fem sg ~ ez, masc pl ~ inj, fem pl ~ eza) 1 black-lipped (animal) 2 (Fig) unfortunate (person)

buzi'k nm dog with a black muzzle

buzi'në nf = bordu'rë

bu'zje adj wide-mouthed

buzm nm 1 large firelog 2 [Ethnog] yule log 3 hearthstone
  ○ **buzmi bujar!** Merry Christmas!

bu'zo nf with masc agreement 1 (Pej) person with ugly, thick, pendulant lips 2 male animal with a black or white splotch on the muzzle

buzo'ç nm 1 [Ichth] (Chelon labrosus) = vijo'sh 2 (Pej) = buzaçB
  ○ **buzoç bari** [Ichth] rainbow wrasse Coris julis = peshk bari
  ○ **buzoç i gjelbër** [Ichth] green wrasse Labrus viridis
  ○ **buzoç i hirtë** [Ichth] gray wrasse Symphodus (Crenilabrus) cinereus
  ○ **buzoç i kuqërremtë** [Ichth] gray wrasse Crenilabrus cinereus

○ **buzoç pikalosh** [*Ichth*] striped wrasse, red wrasse, cuckoo wrasse, bimaculated wrasse *Labrus bimaculatus*

○ **buzoç rëre** [*Ichth*] scale-rayed wrasse *Acantholabrus palloni*

○ **buzoç i zi** [*Ichth*] *Crenilabrus quinquemaculatus Risso*

buz·o·qiellzo'r *adj* [*Ling*] labiovelar

buz·o'r *adj* [*Ling*] labial

buz·o're

I § *nf* [*Ling*] labial sound
II § *np* [*Bot*] mint family *Labiatae*

buzu'k *nm* [*Mus*] buzuk, six-stringed lute-like instrument with a short neck and large body

buzhe'l *adj* plump, chubby

buzhe'l·ë *nf* **1** blister on the lips caused by fever or burning **2** large hand drill for boring holes in wood

buzho'l *nm* [*Ichth*] = **krap**

by·n³ʳᵈ *vi* (for animals) to make the sound "by": moo

byc *nm* [*Med*] sty = **elbth**

by'g·ë *nf* circular string of tobacco leaves

byk

I § *nm* **1** chaff **2** wood dust, sawdust **3** (*FigImpolite*) worthless person or thing; dregs, worthless residue
II § *adj* pulverized, broken into small pieces

○ **Byk i Kumbarës** (*Reg*) [*Astron*] Milky Way

byk·ël·i'na *np* straw remnants from threshing = **by'këra**

by'k·ëra *np* < **byk**

byk·ëz·i'm *nm ger* [*Agr*] < **bykëzo'·**n

byk·ëz·o'·n *vt* [*Agr*] to mulch with chaff

***bylby'l** *nm* = **bilbi'l**

***bylbyr·o'·**n *vi* to croon

Byli's *nm* [*Hist*] ancient Illyrian city in southwestern Albania: Bylis

by'lme *nf* **1** [*Constr*] partition, dividing wall **2** saddlecloth, saddle blanket

bylme't = **bulme't**

***bylm·u·a·**n *vt* = **mëlko'·**n

byly'k *nm* **1** [*Hist*] military unit in the Ottoman Empire consisting of some 100-250 mercenary soldiers **2** (*Old*) crowd (of people), flock (of animals), pile (of things)

bylyk·ba'sh *nm* [*Hist*] **1** commander of a bylyk **2** Ottoman military officer responsible for maintaining public order

byly'zy·k *nm* bracelet

byme·het *vpr* **1** to expand; swell, swell up; become full **2** to swell to overflowing: reach flood stage

byme·n *vt* **1** to cause [] to expand: make [] swell **2** to inflate; dilate

bym·e's·ë *nf* expansion; swelling

bym·i'm *nm ger* **1** < **byme·**n, **byme·**het **2** expansion

bym·y'er *adj* (*i*) **1** expanded in physical volume **2** inflated; swollen in ripeness

bym·y'e·s *adj* creating pressure to expand in physical volume, causing expansion

bym·y'e·shëm *adj* (*i*) expandable in physical volume

bym·y'e·shm·ër'i *nf* expansibility in physical volume

by'pe *nf* large bell attached to a ram or a billy-goat

byr *nm* [*Zool*] = **urith**

byr· *vt* (*Reg*) to accomplish, finish up

by'r *stem for 3rd sg pdef, part* < **by·**n

byraze'r *nm* (*Colloq*) = **vëlla**

byraze'r·kë *nf* (*Colloq*) = **mo'tër**

by'rde *nf* (*Reg*) **1** saddle blanket = **paravi'the 2** (*Old*) = **perçe**

*__byrdi'__ *nf* order, command

byre'çk·ë *nf* [*Food*] small triangular or rectangular byrek

byre'k *nm* [*Food*] multi-layered pasty filled with meat, eggs, vegetables or cheese

○ **ta pjek·**³ʳᵈ **byrekun** {} could kill you without blinking an eye

byrek·sheqe'r *nm* [*Food*] baked dessert made with cornmeal, butter and sugar

byrek·shit·ë's *n* seller of pasties and pastry

byrek·to're *nf* shop in which pasties and pastry are made and sold

byre'qe *np* < **byrek** (*Reg*)

byro' *nf* bureau (of an institution)

*__byrokraci'__ = **burokraci'**

*__byrokra't__ = **burokra't**

*__byru'm__ *interj* = **bu'jrëm**

byrynxhy'k *nm* **1** thin silk thread **2** sheer silk cloth

byry't·et *vpr* = **bërly'k·**et

*__by't__ = **mbyt**

byt·ër'i·n *vi* = **bërly'k·**et

byty'nt·ë *adj* (*i*) (*Old*) **1** flat, smooth **2** made of a single piece, single **3** (*Fig*) thickheaded, stupid

*__bytha'ç__ *nm* tobacco cannister

bytha'k *nm* tree stump, log

bytha·kre'j *adv* head over heels, headlong

bytha'n·ë *nf* shoot growing out of the roots of a tree stump

bytha'r *nm* sodomite, pederast

○ **bythar i duhanit** inferior tobacco leaf near the stalk

bythara'k *adj* having large buttocks

by'th·as *adv* (*Colloq*) **1** backwards **2** (scooting) with buttocks dragging along the ground

*__by'th·c·ë__ *nf* cigarette butt

byth·ça'k *nm* trouser seat

by'th·çe *nf* **1** inferior tobacco leaf near the bottom of the plant **2** base and roots of a plant **3** cigarette butt

bythe' *nf* blanket covering the hindquarters of a horse

bythe'c *nm* (*Old*) male brought along to a wedding by one of the guests

bythe'ce *nf* **1** blanket covering the hindquarters of a horse **2** wool cloth placed over a baby's diaper or swaddling to absorb overflow *__3__ patch on the seat of trousers *__4__ apron worn behind

byth·e'z·ë = **bythe'**

by'th·ë

I § *nf* (*Colloq*) **1** hind end, bottom; butt, ass; buttocks, rump **2** outside bottom of a container (bottle, barrel, etc.) **3** stump, base **4** = **by'thçe**

II § *pred* (*Colloq*) blind drunk

III § *prep* (*abl*) (*Crude*) at the base of

○ **ësh·të bythë e brekë** (*Crude Pej*) to be too close to, be too closely associated with

○ **bytha e kusisë** "black as the bottom of a kettle" (*Insult*) black as the ace of spades, black as tar

byth·ë·çje·rr·ë *adj* (*Crude*) **1** raggedy, in tatters **2** (*Fig*) very poor, completely broke

byth·ë·gri's·ur *adj* (*Crude*) = **byth·ë·çje·rr·ë**

byth·ë·gje·r·ë *adj* (*Crude*) extravagant

bythëja·shtë *adj (Crude)* **1** naked, unclothed, bare **2** *(Fig)* out in the open, having no secrets, for all to see

bythëkro·më *nf* [*Bot*] **1** dog rose *(Rosa canina)* **2** smilax, greenbrier *(Smilax aspera)*

bythëma·dh *adj* big-assed

*****bythëmëngjër** *nf* cross, irascible; moody

bythëpërpje·të *adv (Colloq)* upside-down, topsy-turvy, overturned

bythëpra·pa *adv* = pra·ptazi

bythëpra·ps·*et* *vpr* to draw back, go backwards, retreat

bythëpra·pt·as *adv* = pra·ptazi

bythëpra·pt·azi *adv* = pra·ptazi

bythëpra·pt·hi *adv* **1** = pra·ptazi **2** overturned, upside-down; in reverse, backwards

bythëpu·lë *nf* [*Med*] shingles, tetter, herpes

bythëqiqër *nf* [*Bot*] round-leaved birthwort *(Aristolochia rotunda)*

bythëqy·qe *nf* [*Bot*] = bythëqiqër

bythërë·në *adj* droopy-assed

bythëtra·shë *adj* fat-assed

bythëtu·rtull *adj (Crude)* constantly moving ("one's ass") around

bythëz *nf (Colloq)* **1** small stool, seat **2** tail slice of a fowl usually given to a guest as an honor **3** diaper cloth made of wool = bythe·ce

bythëzbulua·r *adj (Crude)* = bythëja·shtë

bythkë *nf (Reg)* thickest part of combed flax or hemp

bythlë *nf* short-staple wool shorn from around the tail of sheep

byzyly·k *nm* **1** bracelet **2** wrist; ankle

byzyly·kë *np* **1** = byzyly·k **2** *(Colloq Iron)* = pra·nga

*****bzhingë** *nf (Old)* = fshikë

Cc

c [tsë] *nf* **1** the consonant letter "c" **2** the voiceless apico-alveolar sibilant affricate represented by the letter "c" **3** symbol of a group of vitamins

ca
  I § *quant, pron* some
  II § *adv* to some degree/extent, in some amount: somewhat; a bit; a little (while)
  III § *pcl* quite some
  ○ {*a number*} **e ca** {} and more, {} or so, {} plus, {} and then some
  ○ **ca nga ca 1** little by little, gradually **2** piece by piece
  ○ **Ca të babait/nënës, ca të njerkut/njerkës.** "Some belong to the father/mother, some to the step-father/mother." Some people unfairly get better treatment than others.

cabík *nm (Reg)* = **pëtës**

cabók *nm (Reg)* **1** = **stom 2** piece of earth, clod; chunk of rock; piece of wood, small log

cac·
  I § *vt* [*Famil*] to teach a child to walk, induce to begin walking
  II § *vi* to walk with difficulty by leaning on something

cacër *nm* large comb used by women; carding comb, card

cafullím *nm ger* < **cafullo·n**

cafullo·n *vi* to yelp (especially said for a hunting hound announcing the spoor)

*__cagë__ *nf* den, lair; nest

caherë *adv (Reg)* toward dark, toward nightfall

cajkë *nf* **1** woven wool cloth prior to treatment by fulling **2** coarse scarf for the head

cak *nm* **1** boundary: boundary line, border marker **2** boundary limit **3** *(Fig)* tolerance amount, permissible degree **4** *(Fig)* goal, destination **5** permanent resting place, permanent position **6** [*Sport*] finish line **7** [*Math*] mathematical limit **8** deadline **9** goal defended by players with bats in a children's game = **bíce 10** line beyond which an opposing player can be touched in certain children's games **11** *(Colloq)* angle, corner, edge

cakë *nf* **1** cloth pouch or small sack for carrying flour, cheese, etc. **2** *(Fin Old)* fixed interest payment

*__cakël__ *nf dimin* = **çakël**

cakëllo·n *vt, vi* to make small rapid tapping movements: gnash/chatter (teeth), clink (glass), tap (fingers)

cakërrán *adj (Colloq)* snooty, arrogant, conceited; frivolous

cakërrí *nf* cold rain mixed with snow, sleet

cakërrím *nm ger* < **cakërro·n**

cakërro·het
  I § *vpr* to have an argument, dispute
  II § *vpr* to emit a sound from being tapped

cakërro·n
  I § *vt* **1** to tap [] lightly **2** *(Fig)* to knock []; put [] into play
  II § *vi* *(Fig)* to extract a soft sound by tapping []: clink

cakësor *adj* at the boundary: limiting, at the limit, boundary

caklasë *nf* long pleated dress worn by women in certain provinces

cakllo·n *vt* to gnash [teeth]

cakorre *nf* **1** hatchet **2** [*Ichth*] small gilthead

cakos·
  I § *vt (Reg)* **1** to use force to fill to capacity: cram into, jam in, squeeze into **2** *(Fig)* to gather bit by bit, amass by saving up little by little, save up gradually
  II § *vt (Colloq)* to nab red-handed, catch with the goods

cakrrí *nf* = **çikërrimë**

caktím *nm ger* **1** < **cakto·n 2** determination, definition, designation, specification **3** *(Colloq)* designated amount, decided time; settled deadline; settled limit **4** *(Old)* [*Law*] decision; legal definition made by an article or clause of a law or regulation

cakto·n *vt* **1** to determine, decide, define, specify; set/fix [a particular value]; set a deadline for []; determine the time required for [] **2** to charge [] with a duty: encharge, commission **3** to put [] aside for a particular purpose

caktúar *adj (i)* **1** designated, determined, defined, established, specified; clearly determined, well-determined, well-defined **2** well-known, well-established, accepted; assumed **3** settled, unchangeable, fixed **4** *(Old)* [*Ling*] definite = **shqúar**

caktúeshëm *adj (i)* determinable; delimitable

cakthi *adv*

*__cakúl__ *nm* = **cakúle**

cakúle *nf* **1** small cloth sack/pouch **2** blister raised by burning or a sting **3** swelling, bump

cakúlthi *adv* in a crouched position, bent over

calík *nm* **1** bottle/bag made of hide, leather bottle **2** small leather pouch **3** [*Min*] circular space in underground mines that serves to join two tunnels or a tunnel to a shaft

calínë *nf (Old)* flintlock pistol

*__callako·n__ *vt* to crush, crumple

callangúr *nm* small unripe melon

*__cambínë__ *nf* bagpipe

*__cambúr__ *nm* small bunch of grapes

*__cambúrë__ *adj* **1** tattered, ragged **2** badly equipped

camërdhók
  I § *nm* small child, urchin, little whippersnapper
  II § *adj* small, little

camërr
  I § *adv (Colloq)* **1** in a vertical position: vertical, perpendicular, erect, plumb, straight up and down; on end **2** with erect posture, proudly
  II § *adj (Fig)* empty; frivolous

camíl *nm* [*Ornit*] = **cinxami**

camúnzë *nf* flexible bark taken off of thin branches of certain trees and used by children to make musical pipes; pipe made of this material

canga'dhe
I § *nf* ewe or nanny goat left without offspring but kept for milking
II § *np* small flock of ewes or nanny goats kept near the house for milking

cangadhj'ar *n* shepherd in charge of the village milk goats and ewes

cang'ë
I § *nf (Reg)* hard, unripened fruit
II § *adj* **1** (of fruit) hard and unripened **2** *(Fig)* immature

cang'ël
I § *nf (Reg)* small hook used to fasten clothes or to hang something on; metal clasp or hook
II § *np* tatters hanging down from worn-out clothes
III § *adv (Reg)* **1** hanging in the air, dangling in the air **2** up in the air, undecided

cang'ëlo·n *vt (Reg)* to raise/carry/hold aloft, hold dangling

cang'ër *adj (Reg)* stale

cang'ërmi *nm [Ornit]* goldfinch (*Carduelis carduelis*)

cang'ëro·het *vpr (Reg)* to become stale

cangla-ca'ngla *adj (Reg)* in tatters, in rags, tattered

cangule'të *nf* small knapsack

***canoke'th** *nm [Bot]* spiny restharrow (*Ononis spinosa*)

***cap** *nm* = cjap

cap'ë *nf* **1** short-handled cultivating tool with two claws on one side and a hoe blade on the other: cultivator **2** hard layer of ground under the topsoil

cap'ërlo·het
I § *vp recip (Colloq)* to tear one another apart in fighting
II § *vpr (Colloq)* to get broken, be badly damaged

cap'ërlo·n *vt (Colloq)* to break/tear into small pieces; devastate, badly damage

cap'ërlu'ar *adj (i)* **1** in small pieces, minced; all torn/broken up **2** *(Fig)* very tired, all in, knocked out

cap'ëtor *nm* = çap'ëtor

cap'ëto're *nf* = çap'ëto're

cap'ím *nm ger* < capo'·n

cap'ín'ë *nf* **1** long-handled tool with a curved iron blade used for dragging and rolling logs, log-roller **2** *[Tech]* long tongs for moving hot pieces of metal **3** hard layer of ground lying under the soft layer being cultivated

cap'ít· *vt* to break up [clods of soil] with a short-handled cultivator, cultivate = çap'ít·

cap'ítje *nf ger* < capít·

cap'ítur *adj (i)* = çap'ítur

cap'o·n *vt* **1** = capít· **2** *(Reg)* to tease [wool] by hand **3** *(Fig)* to get the better of [ ]

cap'ok *nm* = cjap'ok

***capo'n** *nm [Bot]* spiny shrub (*Acantholimon androsaceum, Acantholimon echinus*)

***capo'nj'ë** *nf* horned goat

capo're *nf* = cjapo're

***capo'rre** = cjapo're

***capri·het** *vpr* to be troubled/confused

capu'ar *adj (i)* = çap'ítur

***caq** *nm* **1** *(Reg Gheg)* = cak **2** *(Old)* score, goal **3** *(Old)* position, post

ca'qe *np* < cak

car *nm* czar

***carabu'jk** *nm [Bot]* sharp-leaved asparagus (*Asparagus acutifolius*)

cara'c *nm [Bot]* European hackberry, nettle tree (*Celtis australis*)

cara'c'ë *nf* = cara'c

caradu'ng *adj (Reg)* = shkurtab'íq

***cara'g'ë** *nf [Ichth]* = cera'g'ë

cara'n
I § *nm* **1** stone firedog; hearthstone **2** position near the fireplace **3** gravestone **4** boundary marker **5** large rock
II § *adj* hard as rock, stone-hard
◦ **ësh-të brenda caranit të vatrës** to be on the topic

cara'ngth *nm [Bot]* bristle thistle (*Carduus arvensis*)

cara'ngth'të *adj (i) (Colloq)* prickly, bristling

***carb'ë** *nf* = zarb'ë

ca'rde *nf* **1** small load, part of a load ***2** item

care'qe *nf (Reg)* basket

care'sh'ë *nf* czarina

cari'n'ë *nf* customs tax or property tax in feudal times

car'íst *n* czarist

cariz'ëm *nm* form of absolute monarchy headed by a czar: czarism

***cark** *nm* hunting dog, pen dog

***carky'fte** *nf* clod, lump

caru'qe
I § *nf* leather moccasin with ornamental straps and thin turned-up toe
II § *np* kind of trousers

***carrani'qe** *np* larders, pantries

carro'i *obl* < carru'a

carro'k *nm (Reg)* = camërdho'k

carro'ke *nf (Reg)* = camërdho'ke

carro'nj *np* < carru'a

carru'a *nm (obl ˜o'i, np ˜o'nj)* = camërdho'k

ca'zë *adv (Colloq)* **1** just a little, a little bit **2** a little while, in a short time, for a little while

***caz'ís** *stem for 1st sg pres, pl pres, 2nd & 3rd sg subj, pind* < caz'ít·

***caz'ít·** *vt* to fondle, caress

ce'ce *nf* tsetse

ce'cull *nm (np ˜'j)* blacksmith's hammer with a bladed head used to cut heated metal

ce'dër *nm [Bot]* cedar (*Cedrus L.*)

cedr'ísht'ë *nf* cedar forest

cefalopo'd'ë *np [Invert]* cephalapod

ce'fël *nf* **1** covering layer over a food: rind, shell, husk, eggshell, peel (grape/onion), pod (bean/pea) **2** small fragment of a hard object/surface

ce'fla-ce'fla *adv* in small pieces, in flakes

cefl'ís· *vt* **1** to remove the covering layer from [a food]: peel, husk, shell **2** = ciflo·n

cefl'ís·et *vpr* **1** to lose pieces of its covering layer **2** to fall off in chips/flakes, flake/scale off = ciflo's·et

ceflo'·het *vpr* = ciflo'·het

ceflo'·n *vt* = ciflo'·n

***ce'g'ë**
I § *nf (Reg Gheg)* bitter cold, frost
II § *adj* frigid

ce'g'ëm *nm (Reg)* frosty weather

Cejlo'n *nm* Ceylon

cejlo'ne'z *adj, n* Ceylonese

cek· *vt* **1** to touch [] lightly **2** *(Fig)* to treat [a subject] shallowly, treat superficially, touch on

ce'k·*et vpr* to make light contact

ceka'preka *adv* at odds, at sword's point, contentiously, pugnaciously

ce'kash *adv*

ce'kazi *adv* shallowly

ce'ke *nf* **1** shallow pan **2** small coffeepot for brewing a single cup

ce'kë *nf* **1** = cekëti'në **2** best/choice part: cream, pick of the crop, cream of the crop **3** goal, object **4** the game of tag ***5** decision, intention, determination
  ∘ ceka e qumështit cream

cekëli'në *nf* = cekëti'në

*ce'këm = ce'gëm

ce'kët
  I § *adj (i)* **1** shallow, near the surface; superficial; thin **2** *(Fig)* lacking in depth, superficial, shallow
  II § *nf(e)* shallow place, shallows, shallow end, shallow part
  III § *adv* superficially, shallowly; weakly

cekëti'në *nf* **1** shallow part of a body of water: shallows, shallow end **2** *(Fig Book)* superficiality in thinking, shallowness in judgment and action

ceki'm *nm ger* <ceko'·n, ceko'·het

cekli'në = cekëti'në

ce'kje *nf ger* <cek·, ce'k·et

ceko'·het *vpr* = cektëso'·het

ceko'·n
  I § *vt* **1** = cek· **2** to keep [the plow] shallow **3** to bail [water/fish] out of (a boat), unload [a boat]
  II § *vi* to hit bottom (in a body of water); hit ground, run aground

cekoj'ëse *nf* long-handled fishnet used to catch fish in shallow water or to collect them into larger nets

cektës'i *nf* **1** shallowness **2** shallows, shallow place, ford **3** *(Fig)* superficiality

cektës'im *nm ger* <cektëso'·het

cektësi'rë *nf* = cekëti'në

cektëso'·het *vpr* **1** to become more shallow **2** *(Fig)* to become more superficial, lose profundity

cekth *nm* iron cap on top of the shaft of a grinding mill

ceku're *nf* [*Ichth*] gilt-head sea bream (*Sparus aurata*)

celasto're *np* [*Bot*] spindle-tree family *Celastraceae*

celebri'm *nm ger* <celebro'·n **2** celebration
  ∘ celebrim martese civil marriage ceremony

celebro'·n *vt* to celebrate
  ∘ celebro·n martesën to have a civil marriage

celentera'të *nf* [*Invert*] coelenterate *Coelenterata*

ce'lfë = ce'fel

celfi's· *vt* = cefli's·

celfi's·*et vpr* = cefli's·*et*

*celi'k *nm* [*Ichth*] = barkule'c

celofa'n *nm* cellophane

celofani'm *nm ger* [*Tech*] <celofano'·n

celofano'·n *vt* [*Tech*] to wrap in cellophane

celofanu'ar *adj (i)* [*Tech*] wrapped in cellophane

celu'le *nf* **1** [*Biol*] cell = qeli'zë **2** cell (of a Communist party) **3** [*Mus*] measure, unit of rhythm or melody

celuloi'd *nm* celluloid

celulo'zë *nf* cellulose

cem *nm* **1** cool and clear mountain brook ***2** = cermo'k

*cem· *vt* to warn

*cemërli'kë *nf* [*Bot*] kind of buckthorn (*Rhamnus fallax*)

*ce'mje *nf ger* <cem·

ce'mtë *adj (i)* very cold and clear

cen *nm* **1** physical defect, fault; deformity **2** weakness, defect, flaw **3** *(Fig)* vice, bad habit

Cen *nm* Cen (male name)

cena'k *adj* finicky in eating

*cena'kuq *nf* [*Ornit*] red-spotted dentirostral warbler

*ce'ne *nf(Old)* St. Vitus' dance

ce'në *nf* diligence; enthusiasm

ce'nët *adj (i)* **1** = ce'nshëm **2** defective **3** *(Fig)* touched in the head: demented

ce'ngë *nf* **1** piece of cloth used to tie up the jaws of a corpse ***2** small pot

ceni'm *nm ger* **1** <ceno'·n, ceno'·het **2** violation; injury

ceno'·het *vpr* to feel offended/insulted

ceno'·n *vt* **1** to take a small bite of [] **2** *(Fig)* to cause injury to [] by contact: scratch; injure, damage; violate; offend

ceno's· *vt* **1** to leave [] with a deformity/disfigurement, disfigure **2** *(Old)* = ceno'·n

ceno's·*et vpr* to be left with a deformity/disfigurement

ceno'sur *adj (i)* **1** left with a deformity/disfigurement; afflicted **2** deformed, disfigured **3** *(Fig)* blemished in reputation, tainted; in disrepute

cens *nm* census

censo'r *nm* censor

censu'rë *nf* **1** censorship **2** censure

censuri'm *nm ger* <censuro'·n

censuro'·n *vt* to censor

censuru'ar *adj (i)* censored

cent *nm* cent

centa'ur *nm* centaur

centigra'de *nf* centigrade

centigra'm *nm* centigram

centili'tër *nm* centiliter

centime'tër *nm* centimeter

centra'l
  I § *nm* **1** telephone central **2** power center, power plant
  II § *adj* central

centrali'st *n* telephone switchboard operator, central, operator

centrali'zëm *nm* *(Book)* centralism

centrali'zim *nm ger* **1** [*Offic*] <centralizo'·n **2** centralization **3** *(Book)* concentration

centralizo'·n *vt* *(Book)* **1** <përqendro'·n **2** [*Offic*] to concentrate under a central government: centralize

centralizu'ar *adj (i)* **1** centralized, concentrated **2** [*Offic*] brought under the control of a central government

centrifu'g *adj* centrifugal = qendëri'kës

centrifuga'l *adj* = centrifu'g

centrifu'gë *nf* [*Tech*] centrifuge

centrifugi'm *nm ger* [*Spec*] <centrifugo'·n

centrifugo'·n *vt* [*Spec*] to centrifuge, separate by using a centrifuge

centrifugu'ar *adj (i)* [*Spec*] centrifuged

centri'm *nm ger* [*Sport Tech*] <centro'·n

centripe't *adj* centripetal = qendërsynu'es

centripetal *adj* = centripetal

centrist *adj, n* centrist

centrizëm *nm* centrism

centro·n *vt* **1** [*Tech*] to center, place in the center; bring into balance **2** [*Sport*] to center (the ball)

centroidë *nf* [*Spec*] centroid

centruar *adj (i)* [*Tech*] centered; balanced

centrues

I § *nm* [*Tech*] centering device

II § *adj* [*Tech*] centering

centurie *nf* [*Hist*] subdivision of a Roman legion consisting of 100 soldiers, century

centurion *nm* commander of a Roman century, centurion

cenuar *adj (i)* **1** slightly injured; scratched; nibbled on, with a bite taken out **2** defective; impaired; deformed, disfigured **3** (*Fig*) wounded in pride, insulted; dishonored, shamed, besmirched

cenues

I § *adj* defamatory, derogatory, insulting

II § *n (Book)* defamer, insulter

cenueshëm *adj (i)* **1** vulnerable **2** [*Law*] voidable

cenueshmëri *nf* [*Law*] voidability

cenzurë = censurë

cep *nm* **1** corner; angle **2** extreme end: edge, tip **3** out-of-the-way corner, unfrequented place **4** (*Fig*) border area **5** [*Geom*] external angle **6** [*Geog*] cape (of land) **7** small bunch of grapes **8** type of white grape with fruit clustered in end bunches

○ **cep më cep** all over, everywhere, in every part, from one end to the other

ceparak *nm* **1** small corner of a piece of ground **2** short wooden brace supporting a roof rafter

ceparakthi *adv* from one corner to the opposite corner, diagonally; crossways, crosswise

cepatare *nf* triangular shelf set in the corner of a room

cepazi *adv* moving from one corner to another, all around

cepë = cefël

cepik *nm* icicle

cepinj *np* <cap

ceragë *nf* [*Ichth*] bleak (*Alburnus albidus alborella Filip.C*)

cerast *nm* [*Bot*] chickweed *Cerastium*

ceratofilore *np* [*Bot*] hornwort family *Ceratophyllaceae*

Cerber *nm* **1** Cerberus **2** (*Fig*) fierce and merciless guardian

**cerbotanë *nf* conduit for water: water pipe

cerebral *adj* [*Anat*] **1** cerebral **2** (*Fig Book*) intellectual, cerebral

ceremoní *nf* **1** ceremony **2** (*Colloq*) excessive ceremony

ceremonial *adj, nm* ceremonial

**cerengë *nf* chunk of bread

**cerenik *nm* pantry

**cerfuq *nm* saucepan

cergar *nm* = cergatar

cergatar

I § *n* **1** nomad **2 rug-maker, tent dweller

II § *adj* nomadic

cergë *nf* **1** spiderweb, cobweb **2** thin skin: membrane, film, scum; thin fabric: veil, curtain, tissue **3** old rag, tattered clothing **4** rug or blanket woven of

coarse goat hair **5** (*Old*) lean-to or tent made of coarse fabric such as goat hair

○ **cergë e re** person who has just formed his own family

**cergo·n *vt* to cover [] with cobwebs

cergos· *vt* to cover [] with a coarse blanket

cergos·et *vpr* to be covered with cobwebs

cergosur *adj (i)* covered with cobwebs

cergurinë *nf* (*Colloq*) worn-through old clothes

cerimangë *nf* (*Reg*) spiderweb, cobweb

cerint *nm* [*Bot*] honeywort *Cerinthe*

cerium *nm* [*Chem*] cerium

cerk· *vt* **1** to bump into [], meet **2 to wound

**cerkë *nf* mark, blemish; mole

cerlak *nm* [*Ichth*] young mullet weighing 5-15 kilograms

cermë

I § *nf* **1** [*Med*] arthritis; gout **2** muscle cramp/spasm **3** best part: cream **4** first and strongest raki from the still

II § *adj (i)* cold, cool

**cermëz *nf* cold, catarrh

cermit· *vt* to gnash/grind [teeth]

**cermok *nm* tufa

cernik *adj* (*Reg*) = karvariq

**cerpek *adj* nimble, agile

certifikatë *nf* [*Offic*] certificate; attestation, proof

**cerrak *nm* [*Zool*] bat

**cerrë *nf* = cerrak

**cesnis *stem for pl pres, 3rd sg subj, pind* <cesnit·

**cesnit· *vi* to bubble out; spurt, spring

cetace *np* **1** [*Invert*] Cetacea **2** cetaceans

cezarian *adj, n* Caesarian

cezë *nf* (*Reg*) bobbin (in the shuttle of a loom) = gjep

○ **të dhëncin ujë me cezë** (*Curse*) I hope you fall sick and never get well!

cezium *nm* [*Chem*] cesium

cezurë *nf* [*Lit Mus*] caesura

**cëk = çok

**cëkas *stem for 1st sg pres, 1st & 3rd pl pres, 2nd & 3rd sg subj* <cëkat·

**cëkat· *vt* to hunt for [lice]

cëke *nf* = cëqe

cëmo·n *vi*

○ <> **cëmo·n**[3rd] <> feels a sharp pain in <>'s {}

**cëngël = cëngthi

**cëngër-mëngër *adv* spick and span, neat and tidy

**cëngthi *adv* askew, awry

cënim *nm ger* = cenim

cëno·n *vt* = ceno·n

cënos· *vt* = ceno·n

cëpëz *nf* [*Ornit*] dun-colored bird of the thrush family found in marshlands and rubbish heaps

cëqe *nf* **1** pipette fitting into the plug of a bottle **2** small bottle fitted with a pipette **3** toy squirt gun = stërlages **4** [*Ornit*] continental song thrush, whistling thrush, throstle, mavis (*Turdus philomelos (musicus)*)

cër *nm* sizzling heat, heat of the day

cërcër *nm* [*Entom*] cricket

cërcëret· *vi* to sizzle with heat

cërcëri·n *vi* = cërcëret·

cërcërim = cicërim

cërcëris· = cicëro´·*n*

cërcërit· *vi* = cicëro´·*n*

cërcëritje *nf ger* **1** <cërcëret· **2** sizzling sound; crackling **3** twittering = cicërim

cërcëro´·n = cicëro´·*n*

**cëre *nf* [*Ornit*] missel thrush (*Turdus viscivorus L.*) = tushë mali

cëri·n *vt (Reg)* = cërit·

**cëric *nm* castor oil

cëril *nm* [*Ornit*] = círlë

cërit·
I § *vt* **1** to heat [fat/oil] in a pan; sauté; fry **2** to inflict a sharp pain on []: goad, spur; prick, sting **3** (*Fig*) to hurt [] deeply
II § *vi* to sizzle
III § *vi impers* to distress/trouble <>

cërit· *et vpr* to sizzle
   ○ cërit·*et* si petulla në tigan "wiggle like a pancake on the frying pan" to have an insatiable burning desire; have an agonizing problem: be like a cat on a hot tin roof

cëritje *nf ger* **1** <cërit· **2** sizzle **3** squeal

cëritur *adj (i)* set a-sizzle, browned (in fat), fried

cërkakeq *nm* = cinxami

cërkalarmë *adj* dappled, spotted, dotted

cërkalor *adj* having spots on the face or body, dappled, freckled, mottled

cërkan *nm* grinding mill powered by small stream of water

cërkatë *nf* = cirkatë

cërkazi *adj, n (fem sg ˜ez, masc pl ˜inj, fem pl ˜eza)* (animal/bird) mottled with dark spots

cërkë *nf* = církë

cërko´·n *vt, vi* = cirko´·*n*

**cërlek = curlek

cërlë *nf* [*Ornit*] bunting
   ○ cërla e malit [*Ornit*] rock bunting *Emberiza cia L.*
   ○ cërla verdhashe [*Ornit*] yellowhammer *Emberiza citrinella L.*
   ○ cërla e zakonshme [*Ornit*] corn bunting *Emberiza calandra L.*

**cërlua *nm (obl ˜oi, np ˜onj)* [*Ornit*] starling (*Sturnus vulgaris L.*) = shturë

cërmë *nf* **1** cramp, spasm *2 ceramic baking pan

cërmëdell *nm* [*Bot*] wig tree, smoke tree (used to make a tanning agent) (*Cotinus coggyria*)

cërmëli *nm (np ˜nj)* = cinxami

**cërmo´·n *vt* to provoke, stir up []

cërmok *nm* tuff, pumice

cërulak *adj (Reg)* = culan

cërule *nf (Reg)* **1** bedding **2** rags, old clothes = cule

cërr *nm* **1** tiny chick **2** [*Ornit*] wren (*Troglodytes troglodytes L.*) = çerr

cërran *nm* rivulet, streamlet

cërre *nf* [*Zool*] = círlë

cërrfat· *vt (Reg)* to poke a fire

cërrik *nm* wood lath on which strings of tobacco or other agricultural products such as corn or onions are hung to dry

Cërrik *nm* industrial town in mid-central Albania

cërrikas
I § *adj* of or pertaining to Cërrik
II § *n* native of Cërrik

**cërris *stem for 1st sg pres, pl pres, 2nd & 3rd sg subj, pind* <cërrit·

**cërrit· *vt* = cicëro´·*n*

cërrlë *nf (Colloq)* diarrhea, dysentery

cërro´·n *vi* to spurt or flow slightly (said of a spring or fountain)

**cërrule = cërule

cfagë *nf* **1 [*Bot*] = sfakë *2 cobweb

cfilit = sfilit

**cfinar *adj, n* (person) involved in an intrigue

**cfing *nm* [*Ornit*] kingfisher (*Alcedo atthis*)

**cforis *stem for 1st sg pres, pl pres, 2nd & 3rd sg subj, pind* <cforit·

**cforit· *vt* to cool

**cfrat = sfrat

**cfrato´·n *vt* to dam up []

**cfrë(n) *nm (Reg Gheg)* snowdrift

**cfrete *np* <cfrat

**cfurk = sfurk

**cfyno´s· *vt* to insert a wedge/peg into []

cfytës *nm* **1 blowpipe **2** sprinkler

CGT *abbrev (French)* <**Confederacion Generale du Travail** General Labor Confederation

**ci·n *vi (Reg)* = cijar·

CIA *abbrev (American)* CIA = Central Intelligence Agency

cianizim *nm ger* [*Tech*] <cianizo´·*n*

cianizo´·n *vt* [*Tech*] to harden [] by cyaniding

**cias| = cijas|

ciat· *vi* = cijat·

cibël *nf* shallow well filled by rainwater; cistern

cibun *I §* *nm* OR **cibune** *II §* *nf* knee-length cape made of thick white flannel

cicami *nf* [*Ornit*] = cinxami

ciceron *n* (museum) guide, docent; tour guide

cicë = sisë

cicëri·n *vi* = cicëro´·*n*

cicërim *nm ger* <cicëro´·*n*

cicërimë *nf* twitter, chirping, warble

cicëro´·n *vt, vi* to twitter, chirp, warble

cicërues *adj* twittering, chirping, warbling

**ciciridhe *np* waste from whale blubber

cicmic *nm* **1** game played by two people moving counters on a board or on the ground: morris, ninepenny morris, nine men's morris, five penny morris **2** arrangement in rows

**cidër *nf* cider

cifël *nf* small, thin or pointed piece broken off of a hard object: splinter, chip, sliver

ciflim *nm ger* **1** <ciflo´·*n*, ciflo´·*het* **2** chipped surface

ciflo´·het *vpr* to be chipped

ciflo´·n *vt* **1** to chip, make a chip in, damage [] by chipping **2** to chip [] to pieces, reduce [] to splinters

ciflo´s· = ciflo´·*n*

ciflo´s·et *vpr* = ciflo´·*het*

ciflosje *nf ger* = ciflim

ciflosur *adj (i)* = cifluar

cifluar *adj (i)* chipped, missing one or more chips, damaged by chipping

cifund *nm* metal or wooden duct placed in millrace to increase water force

cifundo´·n *vt* to place a metal or wooden duct in [a millrace of a watermill] in order to increase the force of the water

cifur *nm* [*Bot*] ox-tongue (*Picris*)

cigan

I § *adj, n* Gypsy, Rom

II § *nm* [*Ichth*] minnow *(Phoxinus phoxinus L.)*

cigare *nf* cigarette

∘ **cigare me kapuç** *(Colloq)* filter cigarette

cigarepërdredh*ës* *n* [*Entom*] = **cigarto*r***

cigareshit*ës* *n* tobacconist

*****cigaris** = **cingaris**

cigarishte *nf* cigarette holder

cigarto*r* *nm* [*Entom*] pear leaf roller, hazel leaf-roller weevil *(Byctiscus betulae)*

cigo*në* = **cingo*në***

cija*m*ë *nf* squeaking/chirping sound: squeak, chirp

*****cija*s*** *stem for 1st sg pres, pl pres, 2nd & 3rd sg subj, pind* < **cija*t*** ·

cija*t* · *vi* (of wheels/mice/children) to squeal, squeak; (of crickets/birds) chirp; (of birds) squawk

cija*tje* *nf ger* < **cija*t*** ·

cik *nm (np ˇ qe)* **1** upper part of the side of a container: brim, rim, lip **2** *(Fig)* highest point of development: height, acme, peak, bloom, pinnacle, fullness **3** whey **4** lees, dregs, sediment

∘ **cik më cik** full to the brim, completely full, full up

∘ **cik për cik** no more and no less, just as much as is necessary; equally, in equal amounts, to the same degree

cik· *vt* to touch lightly, brush against; touch, make light contact with

cik·*et* *vpr* to be touched lightly; touch together lightly, make light contact

*****ci*k*a** *np* bed of boulders

cikado*re* *np* [*Bot*] cycad family *Cycadaceae*

*****cikala*r*** = **pikala*r***

*****cikali** *nf* sculpture

*****cikali*s*** *stem for 1st sg pres, pl pres, 2nd & 3rd sg subj, pind* < **cikali*t*** ·

*****cikali*t*** · *vt* to sculpt, carve

*****cikali*t*ës** *n* sculptor

cikalo*r* *adj* speckled, spotted, dotted

cikalo*s*ur *adj* = **cikalo*r***

cikas *adv* = **cekash**

cikatrizi*m* *nm* [*Med*] cicatrization

cika*t*ur *adj (i)* *(Reg)* harebrained, tetched, cracked in the head, nutty, crazy, crackpot

cik*ë* *nf* **1** [*Ornit*] yellow wagtail *(Motacilla flava)* **2** [*Bot*] cycad *(Cycas)*

cik*ël*

I § *nm* **1** cycle **2** grade school level

II § *nf* = **çik*ël***

∘ **cikli i lart*ë*** last four years of elementary school: upper grades

∘ **cikli i ul*ët*** first four years of elementary school: primary grades

*****ci*k*ëm** *nf* **1** bitter cold, frost; crust of ice on a road **2** burnt smell

*****ci*k*ërr** = **çik*ë*rr**

ci*k*ërr *nf* = **çik*ë*rr**

cik*ë*rri·*n* *vi* = **çik*ë*rro·*n***

cik*ë*rri*m*ë *nf* = **çik*ë*rri*m*ë**

cik*ë*rro·*n* *vt, vi* = **çik*ë*rro·*n***

cik*ë*to·*het* *vpr* [*Dairy*] (in making cheese or yogurt) to form whey; extract whey

cikje *nf ger* < **cik·**

ciklami*n*

I § *nm* [*Bot*] cyclamen *(Cyclamen)*

II § *adj* having the pinkish violet color of a cyclamen

*****cikla*q*** *adj* speech impediment: lisp, stammer

cikla*sh* *adj* dappled, spotted

cikli*k* *adj* **1** cyclical **2** [*Chem*] cyclic

*****ciklo·*n*** *vi* to lisp, stammer

cikloid*ë* *nf* [*Math*] cycloid

ciklo*n* *nm* [*Meteor*] cyclone

ciklona*r* *adj* **1** [*Meteor*] cyclonic **2** [*Spec*] using blasts of air in a process

ciklo*p* *nm* **1** Cyclops **2** [*Invert*] Cyclops crab

ciklopi*k* *adj* **1** cyclopean **2** gigantic

ciklosti*l* *nm* [*Publ*] cyclostyle

ci*k*me *nf (e)* touch, contact

ci*k*me *nf* frost; frosty weather

cikn*ë* *nf* **1** frost; frosty weather **2** scorched residue of food stuck to the bottom of a pot

cikno·s· *vt* to overcook [food] so that it sticks to the bottom of the pot: burn

cikno·s·*et* *vpr* to stick to the bottom of the pan and give off a burnt smell as a result of overcooking

cikno·s·ur *adj (i)* scorched to the point of smelling burnt and sticking to the bottom of the pot

ciko·*n* *vi* *(Reg)* to extract juice (of fruits)

cikofu*a* *nm (obl ˇ o*i*, np ˇ o*nj*)* [*Ornit*] = **beng**

ciko*l* *nm (Reg)* tip of a mountain or tree, small mountain peak; peaked hill

ciko*m*ë *nf(Reg)* **1** = **spango** **2** thin flaxen cord (used as packsaddle ties)

*****cikrrina*r*** *n (Reg Gheg)* seller of small wares, shopkeeper

cikrri*n*ë *nf (Reg Gheg)* = **çik*ë*rri*m*ë**

*****cikrro*m*ë** *nf* icicle

∘ **cikrromë akulli** icicle

ci*k*sh*ё*m *adj (i)* **1** *(Reg)* juicy *****2** touchable, tangible

ci*k*th *nm* **1** [*Dairy*] whey formed in the making of cheese or yogurt **2** thin summer mist formed in lowlands

ciku*t*ë *nf* [*Bot*] European waterhemlock *(Cicuta virosa)*

*****cil·** *vi* to eat breakfast = **sillo·*n***

cil

I § *n (definite case forms only) functioning as interrogative pronoun* which, which of, who, which one, which one of, which ones

II § *n (i) (definite case forms only) functioning as relative pronoun* (which), who

cila*do* *fem sg nom* < **cili*do***

cila*t*do *fem plur nom/acc* < **cili*do***

cil*ё*

I § *nf (definite case forms only) functioning as interrogative pronoun* < **cil**

II § *relative pronoun (e) (definite case forms only)* which, who

III § *nf* breakfast = **si*l*lë**

cil*ё*n*do* *masc sg acc* < **cili*do***

cil*ё*s*do* *fem sg dat* < **cili*do***

cil*ё*si *nf* **1** quality; characteristic, feature **2** high quality **3** [*Law*] temporary duty, function, role: capacity **4** [*Chess*] advantage of a major piece over a minor piece: exchange: quality

cil*ё*si*m* *nm ger* [*Book*] < **cil*ё*so·*n***

cil*ё*si*sht* *adv* in terms of quality, qualitatively

cil|ës|o'·n *vt (Book)* **1** to evaluate the quality, distinguish by quality; characterize according to distinguishing features or characteristics: classify; designate, label as, name, call, consider to be **2** to distinguish from others, call by name

cil'ëso'r
I § *adj* **1** qualitative, distinctive **2** [*Ling*] qualifying, qualitative
II § *nm* [*Ling*] = përcakto'r

cil'ësor|'sht *adv (Book)* qualitatively

cil'ës|u'a'r *adj (i) (Book)* **1** qualified, most appropriate; of the highest qualities **2** [*Law*] justifiable **3** [*Law*] legally qualified **4** professionally qualified

cil'ës|u'e's *adj* **1** [*Law*] legally qualifying **2** [*Ling*] qualitative, qualifying

cil'ët *masc plur* <cil

cil'ët'do' *masc plur* <cili'do'

cil'i'do' *n (definite case forms only), determiner, pron* any, anyone

cili'k *nm (Reg)* small creek, brook

***cili|li'ngë** *n* [*Ornit*] = ciripu'pe

cil'in'dër *nm* **1** [*Geom*] cylinder **2** [*Tech*] roller **3** (*Colloq*) steamroller **4** [*Bot*] trunk, branch, or root of a tree with the bark removed **5** top hat

cil'in'do' *masc sg acc* <cili'do'

cilindra'të *nf* [*Tech*] cubic capacity (of a cylinder)

cilindri'k *adj* [*Spec*] cylindrical

cilindri'm *nm ger* [*Tech*] <cilindro'·n

cilindro'·n *vt* [*Tech*] to roll out, flatten with a roller

cilindru'a'r *adj (i)* [*Tech*] rolled out, flattened by a roller

cilindru'e's *nm* [*Tech*] operator of a (steam-) roller

cil'i'n *nf* (*Reg Arb*) silk apron embroidered in gold

cil'i'qe *np (Reg)* = cili'k

cil'it'do' *masc sg dat* <cili'do'

cilivi' *nf* seesaw, teeter-totter

cilivi'le *nf (Reg)* **1** firefly, glowworm **2** (*Fig*) clever, bright girl **3** type of late-ripening, small red apple eaten in winter

***cilo'në** *nf* lacy chaplet; hood

cilo're *nf* tablecloth

***cill** = cil

cille'stër *nf* colter (of a plow)

***cill's** = cil'ës

cima'k *nm* **1** = smag **2** sprout

cima'r *nm* stretcher comb on a loom

cima'rte *nf* [*Bot*] myrtle (*Myrtus communis*)

cimb *nm* **1** = picki'm **2** small hook used for embroidering **3** = sqep
  ○ cimb më cimb = majë më majë

cimb· *vt* = picko'·n

cimba'l *nm* [*Mus*] cymbal

cimbali'st *n* [*Mus*] cymbalist

cimb'i'dh *nf* **1** small and thin particle: sliver, speck, mote **2** tiny leaf on the side of a tobacco plant **3** tender bud of a new twig **4** = cen **5** [*Bot*] herbaceous plant growing along the coastal cliffs, with small smooth clustered leaves boiled and eaten as salad

cimb'i'dh *nm* **1** fire tongs **2** small wide-mouthed pincers **3** barrette **4** tweezers = piskato're **5** roofing shears

cimb'i'dh·
I § *vt* **1** to pinch [ ] (with the fingers) **2** to take a pinch of [food], break/nip off a small piece of [ ]; pluck hair with tweezers
II § *vi* to experience a pricking feeling, hurt = sëmbo'·n

cimb'i'dh·et *vp recip* to pinch each other

cimb'i'dhje *nf ger* <cimb'i'dh·

cimb'i'dh|ur *adj (i)* **1** nibbled-on, missing small fragments; plucked **2** irritated

cimb'i'l *nm (Reg)* **1** sharp goad, spur **2** awl

cimb'i's· *vt* = cimb'i'dh·

cimb'i's·et *vp recip* = cimb'i'dh·et

cimb'i'sje *nf ger* = cimb'i'dhje

cimb'i's|ur *adj (i)* = cimb'i'dhur

***cimb'o'·n** *vt* = cimb'i'dh·

cimbo's'ë *nf* = çimbo'skë

cimb'thi *adv* tightly, tight, in a tight grasp

cimbu'r *nm (Reg)* [*Zool*] = këpu'shë

ci'me *nf (Reg)* [*Ichth*] river bleak

ci'më *nf* **1** [*Naut*] mooring line; rope **2** [*Bot*] cyme

cimëri'kë *nf* [*Bot*] arnica (*Arnica*)

***cimka's** *stem for 1st sg pres, 1st & 3rd pl pres, 2nd & 3rd sg subj* <cimket·

***cimk'et·** *vt* to peck

***cimk'e** *nf* pinch, tweak

***cimk'i's** *stem for 2nd pl pres, pind* <cimket·

***cimk'i't** *stem for pdef, opt, adm, part, pind, 2nd pl pres, imper, vp* <cimket·

ci'm'le *nm* [*Bot*] Russian thistle (*Salsola kali*)

cimo'cë OR **cimo's'ë** *nf* = çimbo'skë

cina'nk *nm* [*Bot*] stranglewort (*Cynanchum*)

***cina'r** *nm* [*Entom*] = do'sëz

cinci'r *nm* [*Zool*] cricket

***ci'ndër** *nf* [*Ornit*] wagtail

***cinema** *nf* cinema

cing *onomat* ding

***cingafu'a** *nm* (obl ~o'i, np ~o'nj) [*Ornit*] golden oriole (*Oriolus oriolus*)

cingali *nf (Reg)* gun trigger

cinga'n *nm* = ciga'n

cingare *nf* **1** small bell hung around the neck of livestock **2** = ciga're

cinga're *nf (Reg)* = ciga're

cinga'ri'dhe *nf* **1** crisp residue of rendered fat: crackling **2** dried out ripe fruit left on the tree

***cingari'm'ë** = cingëri'm'ë

cinga'ri's· *vt* to fry [ ] till brown and crisp

cinga'ri's·et *vpr* to get brown and crisp from frying
  ○ cingaris·et me dhjamin e {*pronominal adj*} to do everything on {*one's*} own, get by on {*one's*} own

cinga'ri's|je *nf ger* <cingari's·

cinga'ri's|ur *adj (i)* fried till brown and crisp

***cingari'shte** *nf* cigarette holder; cigarette case

ci'ng'ë *nf* small clay pot with a handle, pipkin

ci'ng'il *nm* **1** tapered peg used in the game of tipcat; the game of tipcat **2** short stick used to prop up the slab in a birdtrap **3** peg used making wool braid **4** small piece of ornamental jewelry: trinket, spangle, charm

cingëla'n'e *nf* bespangled woman, flashy woman, dandified woman

cingëla'r *n (Reg)* = çikërrimta'r

cingëlatore *nf* woman who adorns brides with spangles

cingëlimë *nf* = **cingare**

cingëliqe *nf* tiny bell hung around the neck of livestock

cingëlo·n *vt* to adorn [ ] with spangles, adorn, beautify

cingëlore *nf* shop which sells spangles and other small objects

cingëlthi *adv*

cingëllimë *nf* faint sound of a small bell; tinkling, jingling

cingëllo·n *vi* to tinkle, jingle

*__cingër__ *nf* bitter cold, frost

cingëri *nf (Colloq)* argument about trivia: spat, quarrel

cingërim *nm* shrill yelping

cingërimë *nf* 1 very cold and dry weather, bitter cold 2 cold shivers 3 clinking or clanking sound 4 ringing sound in the ear 5 chirping/twittering sound made by crickets/katydids/locusts 6 animal's drawn-out whine; howl, bellow

cingërimtë *adj (i)* extremely cold, frozen; icy cold and clear

cingëris· *vt* 1 to poke; goad, spur [ ] on 2 to poke/blow [embers] into flame, stir up [a fire] 3 *(Fig)* to provoke, rouse; heckle
  ○ **<> cingëris· plagën** to open <>'s sore wound, provoke <> in a sensitive area, strike a nerve in <>

cingëris·et *vpr* to become angry about trivia, get mad about nothing, be irritated

cingërisje *nf ger* < **cingëris·**, **cingëris·et**

cingërisur *adj (i)* irritated, provoked

cingërjar
  I § *adj (Colloq)* irritating
  II § *n* irritating person, nuisance, pest

cingëro·n *vi* 1 to feel very cold, be freezing 2 to squeal 3 *(Fig)* to complain, whine 4 to hear a ringing sound in the ear

cingëruar *adj (i)* 1 = **cingërimtë** 2 shivering with cold, frozen by cold

cingërues *adj* 1 making a prolonged distressful sound: squealing 2 *(Fig)* complaining, whining

cinglapjekthi *adv* = **cingëlthi**

cinglash *adv* = **cingëlthi**

cinglazi *adv* = **cingëlthi**

*__cingllo·n__ *vi* to whine; whinny

cingo *nf (Colloq)* 1 enameled sheet metal used to make utensils 2 enameled plate or other utensil; water pitcher

cingone *nf [Mus]* bagpipe; double-reed pipe; shawm

cingor *nm* 1 harsh cold, piercing cold weather, bitter cold 2 thin film of ice floating on water; icicle; ice

cingore *nf (Colloq)* deep enameled plate; enameled dish

cingortë *adj (i)* frozen, iced up, icy cold

cingra-mingra *np* 1 = **çikla-mikla** 2 *(Fig)* trivia

*__cingri__ *nf* squabble, row

cingrim *nm* = **cingërimë**

cingro·n *vi* 1 to howl *2 to hesitate, waver; dally

*__cingruem__ *adj (i) (Reg Gheg)* hesitant

*__cingrues__ *adj, n* hesitant (person)

cingth *nm* 1 tapered peg used in the game of tipcat; the game of tipcat = **cingël** 2 millshaft iron cap bearing the millstone

cingthi *adv* hopping, on one foot

cingull *nm (np ˜ j)* late-ripening white fig with small and sweet long-stemmed fruit

cingun
  I § *adj* stingy, niggardly
  II § *nm* miser, stingy person: skinflint

cingush *nm [Ornit]* small-bodied, large-headed, varicolored, woodland bird that feeds on grasshoppers

cinik
  I § *adj* cynical
  II § *n* cynic

cinizëm *nm* cynicism

*__cink__
  ○ **cink për cink** just right, exactly

cinkë *nf (Reg) [Ornit]* = **trishtil**

cinkograf *nm [Publ]* zincographer

cinkografi *nf [Publ]* 1 zincography 2 photoengraving department

*__cino·n__ = **ceno·n**

cinxakuq *nm [Ornit]* tit/wren with a red patch

cinxami *nm [Ornit]* wren (*Troglodytes troglodytes* L.) = **çerr**

cinxër *nm* 1 *[Entom]* cicada (*Tibicen plebejus*) 2 *(Reg) [Entom]* house cricket 3 *(Fig Iron)* person who is constantly yakking
  ○ **cinxër, minxër, ficër** *(Old)* nonsense formula in children's verse

cinxëreshë *nf* < **cinxër**

cinxërimë *nf* chirping of cricket/cicada/katydid

cinxërit· *vi* = **cinxëro·n**

cinxëritje *nf ger* = **cinxërimë**

cinxëro·n *vi* to chirp, sing (said of the cricket/locust/katydid)

cinj *nf [Ornit]* lapwing (*Vanellus vanellus*)

CIO *abbrev (French)* < **Comite International Olympique** International Olympic Committee

cip *nm* extreme end: tip, corner, edge = **cep**
  ○ **cip më cip** 1 very crowded, packed tightly together 2 very full, full to the brim, packed to the top

cipal
  I § *nm* sliver of wood, splinter; sliver (of soap, meat, etc.)
  II § *adj* very thin and fragile, emaciated

*__cipallë__ *nf* = **cipal**

cipe *adj* small-uddered, with small teats (said of livestock)

ciperore *np [Bot]* sedge family *Cyperaceae*

cipë *nf* 1 thin layer covering a surface: thin skin, coating, film, veneer, crust 2 *[Anat]* membrane 3 *(Colloq)* scum formed over a liquid 4 *(Fig Colloq)* the layer of morality, dignity, and personal character that covers and protects a person's honor: sense of shame, sense of decency, sense of honor, cloak of honor, conscience 5 *(Colloq)* thin cotton fabric 6 *(Colloq)* women's headscarf 7 *(Fig)* something that covers or hides: veil, cover 8 *(Reg)* thin layer of pastry dough
  ○ **cipë e bardheme** *[Med]* sclerotic coat
  ○ **cipë e butë** *[Med]* pia mater (of brain)
  ○ **cipë e kockë** emaciated, skin and bones
  ○ **cipë e lëkurës** thin outer part of a covering layer
  ○ **cipë e merimangës** spiderweb
  ○ **cipë notuese** web (on the feet of amphibians and water birds)
  ○ **cipë e veshit** eardrum

○ **cipë e virgjërisë** [Med] hymen

cipëbardhë adj white-skinned

cipëdal̇ë adj **1** easy to peel, loose-skinned **2** (Fig) shameless

cipëhol̇lë adj **1** having thin skin **2** (Fig) thin-skinned, sensitive *3 cowardly

cipëkuq adj having red skin, reddish-skinned

cipëngrënë adj = cipëplasur

cipëplasur adj shameless, without any sense of shame/honor

***cipër**

　I § adj short-eared

　II § prep = sipër

cipëro·het vpr to be veiled; be misted by clouds, be misty

cipëruar adj (i) veiled; covered by mist

cipëtrashë adj **1** having thick skin **2** (Fig) thick-skinned, insensitive, of little shame, lacking in conscience, without much sense of honor

cipëthatë adj covered by a dry outer layer

cipëz nf **1** (Dimin) < cipë **2** membrane **3** women's headscarf **4** [Anat] membranelle

cipje adj thin-shelled (of nuts)

***ciplidhe** nf chip

cipull nm (np ~ j) [Ethnog] **1** thin bridal veil; veil **2** reddish fig with large fruit that bursts its skin when ripe

cipura np (Reg) = bërsi

ciqe nf woodcock (Scolopax rusticola)

ciqe np = cik

ciqër adj (i) inedible and wild (of figs)

ciragë nf [Ichth] = cironkë

cirë nf (Reg) **1** tree bark **2** bare tree trunk with all branches removed

***ciric** = cëric

cirikokë nf [Ornit] **1** = stërqokë **2** starling = shturë

cirilik adj Cyrillic

ciripupe nf **1** [Ornit] gray wagtail (Motacilla cinerea) **2** (Fig) irresolute and irresponsible person

***ciris** stem for 1st sg pres, pl pres, 2nd & 3rd sg subj, pind < cirit·

***cirit·** vt to urge; vex, irritate

cirk nm (np ~ qe) **1** circus **2** [Geol] cirque, cwm

cirka-cirka

　I § adj having little spots, flecked, spotted, dotted

　II § adv in drops, sprinkling, spattering, dripping, drop by drop, drip by drip

***cirkas** stem for 1st sg pres, 1st & 3rd pl pres, 2nd & 3rd sg subj < cirket·

cirkat· vi, vt = cirko·n

cirkat·et vpr = cirko·het

cirkatë

　I § nf **1** spraying jet of liquid, liquid spray, fountain **2** sleet

　II § adv in a spray

***cirket·** vt = cirko·n

cirkë nf **1** drop of liquid, droplet **2** fleck, dot, polka dot, small spot **3** spotted fowl or sheep **4** [Bot] enchanter's nightshade (Circaea)

○ **Cirka shpon gurin.** "The drop pierces the stone." (Prov) Little strokes fell great oaks. Constant dripping wears away the stone. Little by little and bit by bit.

cirkël nf **1** drop of liquid, droplet **2** fleck, dot, polka dot, small spot

cirkëlo·n vi, vt to spatter, sprinkle, splatter

cirkim nm ger < cirko·n, cirko·het

***cirkis** stem for 2nd pl pres, pind < cirket·

***cirkit** stem for pdef, opt, adm, part, pind, 2nd pl pres, imper, vp < cirket·

***cirklas** stem for 1st sg pres, 1st & 3rd pl pres, 2nd & 3rd sg subj < cirklet·

***cirklet·** vt = cirko·n

***cirklim** nm ger < cirklo·n

***cirklis** stem for 2nd pl pres, pind < cirklet·

***cirklit** stem for pdef, opt, adm, part, pind, 2nd pl pres, imper, vp < cirklet·

***cirklo·n** vi, vt = cirko·n

cirko·het vpr to become bespattered

cirko·n

　I § vt **1** to spatter, sprinkle, spray **2** to strip the udders of [a milk animal]: milk [] to the last drop

　II § vi to fall in drops, drip, splatter

***cirkofaj** nm [Ornit] golden oriole (Oriolus oriolus)

cirkojë nf = cirkatë

cirkuit nm **1** [Spec] circuit **2** [Sport] raceway, circular racecourse for car racing

cirkus nm (Elev) circus = cirk

cirlë nf [Ornit] blackbird (Turdus merula)

○ **cirlë dimërake** [Ornit] = borç

○ **cirlë fushe** [Ornit] song thrush, throstle, mavis (Turdus ericetorum)

cirlua nm (obl ~ oi, np ~ onj) [Ornit] = shturë

ciro nf lost game, defeat

ciroli obl = cirua

***cironak** nm (Reg Tosk) [Ornit] flamingo

***cironi** sg def = cirua

cironkë nf [Ichth] **1** bleak (Alburnus albidus alborella) = gjuhcë **2** small young fish

cironj np = cirua

***cirotë** nf oilcloth

cirqe np = cirk

cirua nm (obl ~ oi, np ~ onj) **1** [Ichth] = cironkë **2** icicle hanging from eaves of a roof **3** (Reg) stunted/shriveled ear of corn

***cirzë** nf [Bot] thistle (Cirsium)

***cirris** stem for 1st sg pres, pl pres, 2nd & 3rd sg subj, pind < cirrit·

cirrit· vt to prick, sting; provoke, incite

cirrozë nf [Med] excessive growth of connective tissue resulting in congestion and malfunctioning of an organ; cirrhosis

***cisk** nm back of a knife

cist nm [Med] cyst

cisternë nf **1** [Tech] large cylindrical metal reservoir: tank, cistern **2** tanker, tank car **3** [Anat] space in the breast where milk accumulates

cistit nm [Med Veter] cystitis

cit nm upper part of the side of a container: brim, rim, lip

○ **cit më cit** up to the brim, chock-full

cit· vt **1** to use force to insert []: force/drive/push/cram [] in **2** to stuff [] with food, satiate

cit·et vpr to become satiated, get stuffed, be stuffed full

citadele nf [Hist] citadel

citanik nm crochet thread

○ **ësh·të në citanik** to be about to give birth

citat nm citation, quotation

cïtazi *adv* using force to insert: by cramming, by stuffing

*****cïter** *nm (Reg Gheg)* zither, harp

cïtë
I § *nf* **1** small wedge **2** wooden pin, peg **3** crochet hook, crochet needle; knitting needle
II § *adv* completely full, chock-full
○ **citë mend** extremely smart, very bright, very intelligent

citïm *nm ger* **1** <**cito**'•*n* **2** citation, quotation

cito'•*n vt* **1** to cite **2** to quote

citologjï *nf* cytology

cito's• *vt* **1** to fasten [] with a pin; stick a pin into [] **2** to stuff/fill [] full, fill [] to the brim **3** to wrap [] up in clothes, tuck [] in

cito's•*et vpr* **1** to pin securely to oneself **2** to be fastened with a pin

*****cïto'sur** *adj (i)* crammed, stuffed

citrïk *adj [Chem]* citric

citrïn *nm (Reg Gheg) [Min]* citrine

cïtur *adv* (of a table) loaded with things to eat

cïu OR **cïu-cïu** *onomat* sound like that made by small birds: peep, cheep, cheep-cheep

cïve *nf [Food]* spicy fried onions **2** fried porridge made with garlic or nuts

civïl
I § *nm* civilian
II § *adj* **1** [Law] pertaining to civil law: civil **2** (Book) characteristic of civilized life: civil, civilized **3** civilian (as opposed to military), civil **4** secular, lay, laic, civil

civïlïsht *adv [Law]* civilly

*****cja'mpë** *nf* frog

cjap *nm* male goat, billy goat
○ **cjap i egër** [Zool] wild goat (Rupicapra rupicapra)
○ **cjapi mish e dhia tavë** it's all the same, it makes no difference
○ **s'ësh-të cjap për atë zile** "not be the billy goat for that bell" not be the right person for the job, not be up to that task

cja'pe *nf* female kid; female goat, nanny goat

cjapo'dhi *nf* hermaphroditic goat

cjapo'k *nm* small billy goat, male kid

cjapo'një *nf* billy goat or bull with large horns sticking straight up

cjapo'r *adj* having large horns sticking straight up

cjapo're *nf* nanny goat or cow with large horns sticking straight up

cjapo's• *vt (Pej)* to cause to be in poor condition and poor appearance: impair, damage and blemish, injure and disfigure, enfeeble and mar

cjapo's•*et vpr* to be impaired in condition and appearance

cjapo'sur *adj (i)* impaired in condition and appearance

cja'pthi *adv* rearing up on two front legs like a billy goat

cjep *np* <**cjap**

cjepu'rr *nm (Reg)* = **shakulïnë**

cjepurr'ak *adj* unfortunate, unsuccessful, wrong

*****cjuka's** *stem for 1st sg pres, 1st & 3rd pl pres, 2nd & 3rd sg subj* <**cjuka'**•

*****cjuka't**• *vt* to peck

*****ckallo'**•*n vi* to sprout, bud

*****ckallu'a** *nm (obl ˜o'i, np ˜o'nj)* sprout, bud = **skallu'a**

*****ckëlfi't** = **skërfi't**

*****ckërf** = **skërf**

*****ckërkë** = **skërkë**

*****ckërm** = **skërm**

*****ckïnj**•*et vpr* to ache

*****cllaqe** *nf* enema

cmag *nm* = **smag**

*****cmato's**• = **smato's**•

*****cmilar** = **smilar**

cmir = **smir**

cof• *vi* = **ngordh**•

cofët
I § *adj (i)* lifeless, dead (of animals); emaciated, practically dead
II § *adv* already dead meat, as carrion; lifelessly

cofëti'në *nf* carrion, animal carcass

*****cofïnë** *nf* = **cofëti'në**

cofje *nf ger* <**cof**•

cohë *nf* **1** [Text] soft, finely-woven wool fabric: serge **2** long embroidered woolen cloak for women
○ **coha e gjelbër** (Old) table around which diplomatic discussions were conducted

cohtë *adj (i)* made of soft finely woven woolen cloth

cok
I § *adv (Reg)* really, for sure, truly; precisely, exactly; straight out, right out, bluntly, clearly
II § *nm* protruding part of a bone joint

cok• *vt* to touch lightly

coka'qe *np* equipment used for sharpening scythes

*****coka's** *stem for 1st sg pres, pl pres, 2nd & 3rd sg subj, pind* <**coka'**•

coka't• *vt* **1** to sharpen [a cutting surface] with a hammer: whet, hone (a scythe), shape (a millstone) **2** to cut lightly into: nick; make an indentation: dent **3** (Fig) to drive insane, drive out of one's mind *****4** (Reg) <**çoka't**•

coka't•*et vpr* to go out of one's mind, go crazy, become insane

*****coka'tës**
I § *adj* knocking
II § *nm* knocker

coka'tje *nf ger* **1** <**coka't**• **2** mark left by a cut or collision: nick, cut, dent

coka'tur *adj (i)* **1** nicked **2** (Fig) crazy, insane, nuts

cokë *nf* [Naut] fluke of an anchor

cok'ël *nf* **1** small piece of wood: chip, splinter; wood shaving **2** small piece of rock: rock chip; pebble

cok'ëlo'•*n vt* to break [] into small pieces/chips, splinter

cok'ëllo'•*n vt* to clack [one's teeth]

*****co'kërr** *nf* wooden clog

coklla's *stem for 1st sg pres, pl pres, 2nd & 3rd sg subj, pind* <**cokllo'**•

cokllo't• *vt* to whine, whimper; moan

Col *nm* Col (generic name for a naughty boy)

colë *nf [Veter]* disease of sheep

*****copacïka** *adv* = **copa-copa**

copa-copa *adv* **1** = **copë-copë 2** piecemeal, piece by piece, in bits; fragmented, in bits and pieces **3** (Fig Colloq) sometimes good and sometimes bad: up and down, so-so

copama'dh *nm (Pej Colloq)* greedy person: greedy pig

copa|ra|k

I § *n* person reared in poverty, person dependent on charity; person who works for others in order to make a living

II § *adj* in pieces, fragmented; ragged, worn to pieces

co|p|ash *adv* in fragments, in bits and pieces, in many pieces

copa|ta|r *n* = coparak

*cop|ç *adv* = copësh

copë *nf* **1** piece broken off from a larger part: fragment, crumb **2** piece, bit, part **3** piece of fabric large enough to sew or patch something: patch, remnant **4** individual entity enumerated in counting instances: exemplar, unit, item, piece **5** piece of a plant used for artificial propagation: cutting, grafting shoot **6** *(Crude Colloq)* sexual reference to a good-looking girl/woman: nice piece of ass, real babe

○ copë e çikë **1** in little bits **2** in total rags, completely worn out

○ copë mishi me dy sy "a piece of meat with two eyes" **1** *(Impol)* imbecile, moron: dodo **2** person with no sense of morality, shameless person

○ copë prove [*Cine*] test strip

○ Copë të bëhesh! Do it anyway (I don't care what happens to you)!

○ Copë të bëhet! Come what may!

cop|ë-co|pë

I § *adv* in little pieces, into fragments

II § *adj* separated into many pieces: shattered, fragmented; tattered, in rags

cop|e|he|rë

cop|ë|la|n *n (Insult)* = leckaman

cop|ë|l|i|m *nm ger* = copëtim

cop|ë|lo·het *vpr* = copëto·het

cop|ë|lo·n *vt* = copëto·n

cop|e|ma|dh *adj* composed/consisting of large pieces

cop|ë|ri|na *np* residual pieces

*co|p|ësh *adv* into small pieces

cop|ë|t|i|m *nm ger* < copëto·n = copëzim

cop|ë|to·het

I § *vpr* to break into pieces: fragment

II § *vp recip* to tear into each other: fight tooth and nail, tear each other up in fighting, cut each other up

○ copëto·het të __ to make every effort to __

cop|ë|to·n *vt* **1** to break/cut/crush/tear [ ] into pieces, reduce [ ] to fragments: fragment, shred; decimate, devastate **2** to damage [ ] seriously: fracture/injure/wound; hurt/harm [ ] badly **3** *(Fig)* to divide [ ] up into parts to be shared with others: divvy up, split up into shares

○ <>a copëto·n zemrën to break <>'s heart

○ <> copëto·het[3sg] zemra <> is deeply touched/moved, it breaks <>'s heart

cop|ë|to|re *nf* place for rooting and nurturing cuttings: tree nursery

cop|ë|t|ua|r *adj (i)* **1** divided/separated into pieces, broken/cut/crushed/torn into pieces **2** fragmented, fragmentary

cop|ë|t|ue|s *adj* [*Tech*] for crushing/dicing/tearing/breaking into small pieces

cop|ë|t|ue|s|e *nf* machine for crushing/dicing/tearing/breaking material into small pieces: crusher, dicer

co|p|ëz *nf* < copë *(Dimin)* bit, fragment

cop|ë|z|i|m *nm ger* < copëzo·n

cop|ë|zo·het *vpr* to be fragmented

cop|ë|zo·n *vt* to divide/separate [ ] into small pieces: fragment

cop|ë|zo|r *adj* [*Geol*] fragmentary

cop|ë|z|ua|r *adj (i)* fragmented

cop|i|në *nf* < copë *(Dimin)* = copëz

cop|i|t· *vi (Colloq)* to eat ravenously

cop|kani|k *nm (Reg)* [*Food*] = përvëlak

co|p|kë *nf* < copë *(Reg Tosk Dimin)* = copëz

cop|t|ue|s *adj* reducing to fragments/pieces

*co|p|thi *adv* piecemeal

co|r|kë *nf* **1** pullet *2 girl

*corkll|i|m|ë *nf* = sokëllimë

*cpo|kë|s *nm* popgun

*cpo|rdhë|s *nm* gullet, esophagus

*cpu|e *nm (obl ˉoˉi, np ˉoˉnj) (Reg Gheg)* = çapua

*cputh *nm* [*Anat*] upper-arm bone: humerus

*cq [*cëq*] *interj (Colloq)* (ingressive voiceless dental affricate (alveolar click) accompanied by a small upward gesture of the head) negative comment expressing mild disappointment/disagreement: tsk; unh-unh, nope

*cqap *nm* = cjap

*cqo|të *nf* = shqotë

*crankth *nm* [*Bot*] sharp-leaved asparagus *(Asparagus acutifolius)*

crog· *vt* **1** to strip/clear [land] of trees **2** to defeather [fowl]

cro|gë *nf* forest clearing, deforested area

cro|gët *adj (i)* **1** (of land) cleared, deforested; stripped **2** (of fowl) plucked

crul|ak *adj* tatterdemalion

cru|le *nf* tatter, rag

cub

I § *nm* **1** mountain bandit, brigand **2** *(Fig)* crazy hero, crazy fool

II § *adj* **1** bobtailed, with a docked tail **2** awnless (of grain)

cub|ak

I § *nm* stubble

II § *adj (Reg)* **1** bobtailed, docked; beardless (of grain) **2** *(Fig)* unwed (of girls)

cub|an *adj (Reg)* **1** = cub **2** *(FigImpolite)* wearing clothes cut short: in short pants

cub|a|r *nm* ladies' man, womanizer

cu|be *nf(Pet)* proud and courageous girl

cub|e|l

I § *adj* **1** = cub **2** cut-off, cut short, shortened

II § *nm* **1** *(Reg)* = cub **2** stump of the tail

cub|ë *nf* **1** bobtailed animal, bobtail **2** short-barreled gun; children's gun loaded with matchheads

cub|n|i *nf* armed robbery, banditry, brigandage

cub|n|isht *adv* in robberlike fashion, like a bandit, piratically, treacherously

cub|no·n *vt (Reg)* to rob

cub|o·n *vt* to cut [ ] off at the end: bob, dock, shorten

cu|cë *nf* **1** *(Reg)* girl = vajzë *2 breast, teat

cu|cëll *nf(Reg)* pacifier for babies, artificial nipple

cu|ce|ni *nf* = vajzëri

cu|cërr *adv (Reg)* forming a concentrated mass: lumped together, all huddled/hunched up, cringing, clenching

cucërrak *adv (Reg)* in a squatting position = galiç

cucërran *adj* crouching and hunched up from fright; cringing in fear

cucërro·het *vpr (Reg)* **1** to hunch up **2** to crouch **3** to cringe

cucërrosh *n (Reg Pej)* person who acts fearful, fraidy-cat

cuckë
I § *adj (Reg)* ripe and juicy
II § *nf dimin* * *(Reg Gheg)* little girl

*__cucni__ *nf (Reg Gheg)* girlhood

cucufendë *nf* [*Bot*] = **fendosë**

*__cufë__ *nf* tuft, crest

cufël
I § *nf* **1** thick snowflake; tiny flake **2** small fibrous tuft
II § *adv* light as a feather, floating on air

*__cugim__ *nm* = **cukni**

*__cuk__ *nm* hound, dog

cuk· *vt (Reg)* **1** to sting, prick = **quk·** **2** to provoke; irritate *__*3__ to press, squeeze *__*4__ to transfix; stab

*__cukacuk__ = **cuka-cuka**

cuka-cuka *adv* piece by piece, little by little

cukë *nf* small part separated from a whole: small piece, fragment, particle

cukël *nf* **1** small residual clumps left over from combing wool, flax, silk, or cotton **2** remnant left over from cutting out a piece of clothing **3** rag *__*4__ small load, bundle; goods and chattels

cukëllan *adj* whose fleece/coat has bare patches

cukëllo·het *vpr* to lose patches of hair, wool, or skin

cukëllo·n *vt* **1** to divide [] into small clumps **2** to fragment, shatter; split

*__cukni__ *nf* pressure; compression

cuks· *vi, vt* to burn, char, scorch, singe, parch

cukumillë *nf* [*Bot*] nettle (*Urtica diodica*)

cukunidhe *nf* [*Bot*] common mallow (*Malva neglecta*)

*__cul__ = **çun**

culan *adj (Reg)* poverty-stricken; poor, in rags

*__culare__ *nf* platter

cule *nf* **1** bedding; swaddling clothes **2** old clothes; rags **3** tibia; shepherd's pipe *__*4__ *(Reg Gheg)* tambourine *__*5__ = **çetë**

cull
I § *adv* *(Reg)* = **lakuriq**
II § *nm* small boy, tot

cullak
I § *adj, adv* = **lakuriq**
II § *nm (Reg)* = **cullë**

cullako·n *vt* to make [] bare/naked: strip, bare

cullan *adj (Reg)* having a swollen belly, with a big stomach

cullë *nf (Reg)* belly, stomach, abdomen

cullnisht *adv (Reg)* childishly, youthfully

cullo·het *vpr* to swell up in the belly

cullufe *nf* **1** hair hanging down over the temple or forehead; lock of hair, tress, plait **2** tuft of hair **3** hair

cullufedredhëz *adj (Colloq)* having long cord-like braids

cullufedredhur *adj* having braided hair

cullufeprerë *adj* **1** having braids cut short **2** having hair cut short

cullufetumbë *nf* having braided hair gathered in clusters

cullufeverdhë *adj* **1** having blond braids **2** having blond hair, blond

cullufezi *adj, n (fem sg ~ ez, masc pl ~ inj, fem pl ~ eza)* (one) with dark braids/hair

*__cum__ *adj* strange, curious

*__cumb__ *nm* idler, good-for-nothing

cumër
I § *nm, nf* **1** short log used as a seat or shelf **2** *(Reg)* = **bucelë**
II § *nm* [*Ichth*] common gray mullet (*Mugilidae cephalus L.*)

cumrak *nm* **1** short log/stump **2** stump of an arm or leg **3** *(Fig)* dwarf; small child yet to grow up **4** [*Ichth*] young summer mullet

cundër *nf (Reg)* big piece: chunk

*__cundro·n__ *vt (Reg)* to chop [] into chunks

cung
I § *nm (np ~ gje)* **1** part of a plant/tree that remains in the ground after cutting: stump, stubble **2** bare grapevine; grapevine root **3** stump of an arm or leg **4** [*Geom*] truncated geometrical figure
II § *adj* **1** missing a limb **2** missing a tail, horn, or wing

cungaje *nf* = **cungishtë**

cungal
I § *nm* **1** king post = **baballëk** **2** short stick used to prop up the slab in a birdtrap = **cingël** **3** *(Old)* sharpened piece of wood used as a weight on an arrowhead; metal arrowhead
II § *adj* truncated, stumped

cungel *adj* = **cung**

cungë *nf* **1** sheep or goat with bobbed tail or short horns **2** child's gums before the emergence of the milk teeth

cungët *adj (i)* **1** truncated, cut off **2** *(Fig)* maimed, amputated, disabled, crippled; defective

cungim *nm ger* **1** < **cungo·n**, **cungo·het** **2** stump remaining of a cut-off part; crippled part **3** truncation, abridgment; amputation

cungishtë *nf* land with tree stumps

cungo·het *vpr* **1** to be missing a limb, become crippled **2** to be abridged, truncated

cungo·n *vt* **1** to lop the branches off [a tree]; reduce [a tree] to a trunk/stump **2** to decrease in size or value by removing a part: shorten, truncate, abridge; dock, bob, cripple **3** [*Med*] to amputate

cunguar *adj (i)* **1** trimmed of branches; having only the trunk left **2** cut off; maimed, crippled **3** abridged, truncated

cungull *adj (Reg)* missing a limb: maimed, crippled

cungullim *nm ger* **1** *(Reg)* < **cungullo·n** **2** removal of limbs, amputation

cungullo·n *vt (Reg)* **1** to trim branches from a tree trunk **2** to amputate; maim

cungulluar *adj (i)* *(Reg)* = **cunguar**

*__cungurit·et__ *vpr* to grow together; accrue

cungje *np* < **cung**

*__cunjo·n__ *vt* = **cus·**

cup
I § *adv* odd (as opposed to even) = **tek**
II § *nm* * *(Solecism)* = **sup**

cupe *nf* *(Old)* small flintlock pistol; small single-barreled pistol

cupërrelë *nf* sharp peak of a hill, cliff

*__cupije__ *nf* [*Ichth*] = **sepje**

cupíl nm 1 roof strut 2 [Min] bracing beam to reinforce the ceiling of a mine gallery: strut, cross-bar 3 thin stick, switch, withe

*****cuq = cq**

*****curak** adj (Reg) = currak

curkë nf trickling spring, fountain

*****curlar** nm kettledrum stick

curle nf [Mus] = surle

*****curlek** nm icicle

curufujkë nf (Reg) small skillet

*****curulat·et** vpr to swing; seesaw

*****curuna** nf (of a fountain) bubbling

*****curunar** nm = curuna

curr
 I § adj having small ears or ears clipped short
 II § nm high cliff, tall crag
 ○ **curr me curr** making no sense, without making sense

curr· vt (Reg) = curro·n

currak adj bare, naked

curran adj 1 having small or clipped ears 2 trimmed of branches; with trees cut down

*****curras** stem for 1st sg pres, 1st & 3rd pl pres, 2nd & 3rd sg subj < curret·

curre nf mare with sparse hair on the forehead

currel nm [Bot] canaliculus = hullízё

*****curret·** vt to eat/drink [] greedily

currë nf 1 sheep or goat with small ears or ears clipped short *2 snow-filled mountain crevice; crag, peak

*****currëm** adj lopped off, truncated; (of horses) docked

curril
 I § nm 1 thin stream of liquid moving with force: jet, spurt, spout 2 spout for water 3 trickling spring
 II § adv 1 moving in a thin hard stream 2 straight, directly *3 in driblets

Currila np fem sandy shore stretching north of Durazzo

*****curris** stem for 2nd pl pres, pind < curret·

*****currit** stem for pdef, opt, adm, part, pind, 2nd pl pres, imper, vp < curret·

*****currli** nm [Ornit] crested lark (Galerida cristata)

curro·n vt 1 to crop [the ears/tail] *2 to wear away, erode
 ○ **curro·n veshët** to prick up the ears, pay close attention; listen in carefully

currubabë nf 1 thin piece of bark or straw inserted in a whistle to make the sound when blown 2 toy whistle 3 [Bot] wild oat (Avena fatua)

currufjas·et vpr (Reg) = matufos·et

currufjasur adj (i) (Reg) = matufosur

currunar nm trickling/dripping spring, rivulet

*****cus·** vt to feel out []: probe

*****cuzgal** nm prop, shoring post

*****cvarr·** vt = zvarrit·

*****cvarros·** vt 1 = zvarrit· 2 to follow [a trail]: track

*****cvjerdh·** vt = zvjerdh·

*****cvjerdhës** adj = cvjerdhshëm

*****cvjerdhshëm** adj (i) disgusting, distasteful, revolting

*****cvordh** stem for pdef < cvjerdh·

*****cvordhit·et** vpr = zvirdh·et

*****cvordhun** nf (e) weaning

cylaq nm penis of male livestock

cyle nf 1 [Mus] short, single- or double-barreled double-reed instrument with eight fingerholes: aulos, tibia; chanter (of a bagpipe) 2 tibia, shinbone 3 pig's snout
 ○ **cyle diare** double flute

cylek nm [Zool] = këllinzë

cyletar n [Mus] player of the cyle

*****cyllë** nf (Old) 1 tube, pipe 2 syringe 3 injection

cyrle nf chanter (of a bagpipe)

*****cys** stem for 1st sg pres, pl pres, 2nd & 3rd sg subj, pind < cyt·

cyt· vt 1 to poke; prod, goad 2 (Fig) to spur [] on, incite, rouse, excite 3 (Fig) to stir up, agitate, irritate, instigate

cyt·et vpr to provoke one another, stir each other up, get excited

cytanik adj (Pej) provocative, inciting, instigative

cytë nf small scratch; small pit in a surface, pockmark

cytës adj 1 annoying; irritating to the nerves 2 rousing, stimulating, provocative, exciting

cytje nf ger < cyt·, cyt·et

cytur adj (i) prodded, urged on, incited, provoked

cyth· vt (Reg) 1 = thumbo·n 2 to pierce []'s skin (for inoculation purposes)

Çç

ç *nf* **1** the consonant or letter "ç" **2** the voiceless palatal affricate represented by the letter "ç"

ç'
I § proclitic **1** what **2** (in exclamations) what a ‿! what ‿! **ç'gomarllëk** what a piece of stupidity! what foolishness! **ç'njeri bujar!** what a generous person! *(Colloq)* (in rhetorical questions) what for **ç'të duhet?** what do you need it for (suggesting that you don't really need it)?
II § conjunctional, proclitic (between repeated verbs) whatever **bën ç'bën** he does whatever it is that he does as much as, whatever, however much
III § exclamatory pcl how ‿! **ç'u lodha** How tired I was! Boy, was I tired!
○ **ç'i bën dhia shqemes, shqemja ia bën lëkurës.** "What the goat does to the sumac, the sumac does to the leather." *(Prov)* What you do unto others will be done unto you.
○ **Ç'bën në det, e gjen në kripë.** "What you do in the sea, you find in the salt." *(Prov)* If you do something bad, it will come back to haunt you. Bad deeds come back to you.
○ **ç'u bëre?** where have you been? what ever became of you?
○ **ç'je/jeni bërë në këtë ditë!** how did you get in such a mess!
○ **ç'bretkun ke?** *(Crude)* what the hell is wrong with you?
○ **ç'e do** what's the use, what for, what good is it
○ **Ç'do dhelpra në pazar?** "What does the fox want in the market?" (said of someone deemed responsible for {}'s own bad fortune): What business does {} have being involved in the first place?
○ **ç'<> du·**het³ˢᵍ what business *is* it of <>'s
○ **ç'është e vërteta/drejta** "what the truth is" (parenthetical remark) as a matter of fact
○ **ç'[']** **gjeti!** oh my god, poor []!
○ **ç'[']** **ka gjetur kështu?** what has gotten [] into such a state?
○ **ç'je bëre?** where have you been?
○ **Ç'ka barku e nxjerr bardhaku.** "What the belly has the brandy glass reveals." *(Prov)* Alcohol loosens the tongue.
○ **ç'ke?** what's wrong with you?
○ **ç'kemi?** "what do we have" what's new?
○ **ç'<> këllet brirët/bretkun/flamën/plasjen!** what's the use of worrying about it <>? <> is not worth the trouble!
○ **Ç'len prej maces gjuan minj.** "What the cat gives birth to chases mice." *(Prov)* Like father, like son.
○ **Ç'mba·**n³ˢᵍ **lëkura** {noun in genitive case}! What (bad secrets/intentions) *is* {noun} hiding!
○ **Ç'pështyn në mëngjes, e lëpin në darkë.** "What {} spits out in the morning, {} licks up in the evening." (said of a shameless and unprincipled liar)
○ **Ç'pjell macja gjuan minj.** "What the cat gives birth to chases mice." *(Prov)* Like father, like son.

○ **Ç'sjell sahati nuk sjell moti.** "What the hour brings is not what the year brings." *(Prov)* You can never tell what the next moment will bring
○ **Ç'sjell minuta, s'e sjell ora/moti** "What a minute brings, an hour/year does not bring." *(Prov)* It doesn't take much time for things to change dramatically.
○ **ç'i sheh/zë syri, ia bën/zë dora** "what the eye takes, the hand does/takes" {} has a knack for everything, {} does everything well
○ **ç'sheh· lëkura** {noun in genitive case} how {noun} suffers!, what suffering {noun} knows
○ **ç'i shtie bar!** Don't bother with it!
○ **Ç'tha i pari, e zëntë behari.** I hope it happens like he/she said.
○ **ç'<> tho·të³ˢᵍ mendja?** what *is* <>'s intention?
○ **ç'vend** what place/country; where

ç
I § formative prefix indicating the opposite or reverse of the meaning of the stem to which it is attached un-, dis-
II § causative formative prefix en-

*ça = ç'

ça·het *vpr* **1** to burst open, split, open up **2** to split apart, become divided; become disunited = **përça·**het **3** *(Fig Colloq)* to spend all one's effort/energy doing something: bust a gut
○ **ça·**het **e nda·**het to do everything possible, try everything to succeed
○ <> **ça·**het³ˢᵍ **hunda (për duhan)** <> *is dying* for a smoke
○ <> **ça·**het³ᵖˡ **hundët (për duhan)** <> *is dying* for a smoke
○ <> **ça·**het³ˢᵍ **koka** <> *has* a splitting headache
○ **ça·**het **nën lëkurë** to be chafing at the bit, be very eager; be ready to explode with anger, not be able to take it any longer
○ <> **ça·**het³ˢᵍ **zemra** <> *is* heartbroken

ça·n
I § vt **1** to split [] lengthwise; chop **2** to cut deeply into [], cut through [] **3** *(Colloq)* to perform surgery on [], operate on [] **4** to tear [] to pieces with the teeth; kill [] by biting **5** to open up [something new]: open up [new territory, the frontier, cut through/overcome [obstacles/opposition], blaze [a trail] **6** to cut across [] **7** *(Colloq)* to disunite
II § vi **1** to cut through quickly, depart quickly **2** to lead the way **3** to cause pronged pain **4** *(Colloq)* to be particularly apt in, ace **5** *(Fig Colloq)* to cut loose, have a wonderful time
○ **ça·**n **akull** **1** to break the ice **2** to blaze the way
○ **ça·**n **akullin** *(Book)* to break the ice
○ **ça·**n **baltërat për** [] to work hard for [], sweat blood for []
○ **ça·**n **dërrasa pa pykë** "chop logs without a wedge" to try and try without achieving anything, tire oneself out for nothing
○ **ça·**n **dërrasa** to talk nonsense; be busy doing nothing

○ **ça·**n **dokrra** to talk nonsense; be concerned about nothing

○ **ça·**n **dushkun** to cut a path out of there fast

○ **ça·**n **dynjanë** to look everywhere: beat the bushes looking

○ **ça·**n **dhenë 1** to do the impossible **2** to travel everywhere

○ **ça·**n **dheun** to look everywhere: beat the bushes looking, leave no stone unturned

○ **ça·**n **ferrën** to run away fast: skedaddle

○ **ça·**n **gur e dru** to do the utmost, do everything possible, leave no stone unturned

○ **nuk e ça·**n **kokën (për** [ ]) **1** not have much concern (for [ ]), not give much thought (to [ ]) **2** not give a damn (about [ ]); not worry much about ([ ]), not care one bit (about [ ])

○ <>**a ça·**n **kokën** to nag <>

○ <> **ça·**n **kokën/kryet** (Colloq) to annoy <> badly by a displeasing repeated action: give <> a splitting headache, drive <> crazy with that stuff

○ **ça·**n **kopalla** to talk nonsense; be busy doing nothing

○ **ça·**n **llafe** to talk twaddle/nonsense

○ **ça·**n **me bërryl** to elbow ahead

○ **ça·**n **me gjoks** to push ahead boldly

○ **ça·**n **përpara** to make progress, forge ahead

○ **ça·**n³ᵖˡ **qiejt** "the skies are *cut open//pierced*" there *is* a cloudburst, it *begins* to rain in buckets, it *is raining* cats and dogs

○ **ça·**n **qimen (më) katërsh/dysh** "divide the hair in four/two" **1** to be extremely skillful/clever **2** (Pej) to be very stingy/miserly **3** to disagree about trivial details: quibble

○ **ça·**n **rrugën 1** to blaze the trail, lead the way **2** to make progress, get somewhere

○ **ça·**n **shtigjet** blaze the trail, lead the way

○ **ça·**n **tokën** to break new ground, work soil for the first time

○ <> **ça·**n **trutë** to annoy <> past endurance

○ **ça·**n **udhën 1** blaze the trail, lead the way **2** to make progress, get somewhere

○ **ça·**n **vendin** to look everywhere: beat the bushes looking

○ <> **ça·**n **veshët** (Colloq) to disturb <> terribly by continual displeasing noise/talk: drive <> off one's rocker, drive <> crazy

çabulle nf **1** banquet **2** crowd of banquet guests

çaçanik nm **1** [Bot] walnut tree **2** fruit of the walnut tree **3** green outer husk of the walnut fruit used for staining

çaçë nf **1** (Child) = **kokodash** *2 soot = **blozë**
○ **çaçë mbi bukë** one good thing on top of another, icing to top the cake, egg in one's beer

çaçkë nf **1** crown of the head, pate **2** crest/comb (on the head of a bird) **3** worn-out or broken utensil

Çad nm Chad

*çadëm nf (Old) partition, division

çadër nf **1** umbrella **2** tent **3** protective shelter; shield, aegis, special protection
○ **çadër dielli** parasol, sunshade
○ **çadër katërshe** four-paneled tent

çadjan
I § adj of or pertaining to Chad
II § n native of Chad

çadrandreqës nm umbrella repairman

çaf nm (Reg) **1** frozen dew, rime, hoarfrost **2** thin layer of ice, ice coating

*çafe nf = çafkë
*çafel nf = çafkel

çafer nm **1** [Ichth] European seabass (Dicentrarchus labrax) **2** clever, quick-witted child **3** [Bot] variety of wheat with large round grains (Triticum vulgare)

*çaferlis stem for 1st sg pres, pl pres, 2nd & 3rd sg subj, pind <çaferit·

*çaferlit· vt **1** to throw [ ] into disorder, disarrange **2** to rend, tear

*çaferlitje nf disorder, mess

çafkë nf **1** cup with a handle, coffee cup; contents of such a cup **2** crown of the head, pate **3** crest/comb (on the head of a bird) **4** (Fig) skinny woman **5** [Ornit] common heron (Ardea cinerea) = gatë

çafkëbardhë nf [Ornit] little egret (Egretta garzetta)

çafkëlore nf [Ornit] **1** crested lark (Galerida cristata) **2** chicken with a crest of head feathers
○ **çafkëlore bishtverdhë** [Ornit] waxwing Bombycilla garrulus L.

çafkëthime nf [Ornit] gray heron

çafkore nf [Ornit] crested lark = çafkëlore
○ **çafkore deti** curlew; snipe

çafkulla r adj crested, tufted

*çagj nf soot = blozë
○ **Nuk çahet pisha me gjilpëra** "The pine tree is not chopped down with a needle." You can't do the job with the wrong tools.

çahje adj freestone (as opposed to clingstone): dehiscent

çair nm grass pasture, grassy meadow

çaj nm **1** mountain tea, tea **2** afternoon tea, tea party
○ **çaji i malit** [Bot] mountain thyme (Sideritis raeseri Boiss. et Heldr.)

çajme nf **1** crown of the head, pate **2** [Ornit] red-backed shrike
○ **çajme e kuqe** [Ornit] squacco heron Ardeola ralloides
○ **çajme rrushi** [Ornit] type of shrike that feeds on wild grapes

çajnik nm tea urn; tea kettle

çajore nf large cup or glass for drinking tea

çajre nf = çair

çajtore nf teahouse

çak
I § onomat clack, bang, clap
II § nm [Cine] clapper

çakaçuke nf **1** door-knocker **2** piece of wood place over the upper millstone to regulate the flow of grain to the grinding surfaces = **çakalle 3** [Ornit] woodpecker = qukapík

çakaçukthi adv

çakall nm **1** [Zool] jackal **2** (Fig) scoundrel
○ **Çakalli bëri kërdinë, ujkut i doli nami.** "The jackal wrought the havoc, the wolf got the blame." (Prov) We blame the one with the bad reputation and miss the real culprit..

çakalle nf **1** wooden clapper activated by the upper millstone to regulate the flow of grain from the hopper to the grinding surfaces **2** (Fig Pej) chatterbox

çakallos·et vpr (Colloq) to become infuriated and bawl out at the top of one's voice, howl with rage

çakalloz
I § *nm* 1 person who talks and acts crazy: nut, madcap, crackpot 2 [*Folklore*] madcap hero of popular folktales who vanquishes ogres or dragons
II § *adj* foolhardy

***çakan**
I § *nm* = çekan
II § *np* = çakall

çakarit = çakërrit

çakçak *adv* with nicks

çakçirë *np* white felt trousers with narrow legs

çakej *np* < çakall

çakë *nf* 1 place at which a field channel branches off from an irrigation canal; irrigation ditch 2 small bell worn by cattle

çakël *nf* 1 small and insignificant piece: crumb, chip; trifle, worthless object 2 (*Fig*) trifle, trivial thing, nonsense
∘ **s'bë·n një çakël** to be worthless, not be worth a red cent

çakëll *nm* 1 crushed stone, ballast 2 rock wall, stone wall constructed without mortar 3 [*Constr*] fill, filler *4 underground passage, tunnel

çakëllimë *nf* gravelly soil, rocky ground

çakëllo·n *vt* to shape [ ] with an adze

çakër *nf* = çakël

çakërdis
I § *vt* (*Colloq*) 1 to scatter [ ] 2 (*Fig*) to bewilder, confuse 3 (*Fig*) to mess [ ] up, get [ ] mixed up
II § *vi* to become bewildered/confused

çakërdis·et *vpr* (*Colloq*) 1 to scatter about 2 to become bewildered/confused
∘ <> **çakërdis·et**[3sg] **gjumi** sleep escapes <>, <> can't get back to sleep

çakërdisur *adj* (*i*) (*Colloq*) 1 scattered about; in disorder, in disarray 2 (*Fig*) bewildered, confused

***çakërrit·** *vt* (*Reg*) = çakërrit·

çakërr *adj* (*Colloq*) 1 having eyes affected by strabismus: cross-eyed, squint-eyed, squinty 2 having varicolored or light-colored eyes 3 (*Fig*) somewhat irregular in behavior; naughty

çakërris stem for 1st sg pres, pl pres, 2nd & 3rd sg subj, pind (*Colloq*) < çakërrit·

çakërrit· *vt* (*Colloq*) 1 to stretch apart, spread apart, open wide 2 to stretch into a strained/irregular/awkward position

çakërrit·et *vpr* (*Colloq*) 1 to open (one's eyes) wide, go pop-eyed; squint 2 to sprawl out, stretch out 3 (*Fig*) to threaten with beady eyes

çakërritur *adj* (*i*) in an unusually awkward/stretched position: (of eyes) squinting, pop-eyed; (of legs) sprawling

çakërrqejf *adv* (*Colloq*) in a pleasantly half-drunk condition: tipsy, tipsily

çaki *nf* (*Old*) penknife

çakist *nm* [*Cine*] beatman

çakllaz *nm* 1 [*Bot*] = halmucë 2 stiff beard of wheat or rye

çakmak *nm* 1 cigarette lighter 2 (*Reg*) = uror

çakmash *nm* herdsman in a herdsman's camp for dairy animals

çakordim *nm ger* 1 < çakordo·n, çakordo·het 2 discord; discordance

çakordo·het *vpr* 1 to be out of tune 2 [*Tech*] to have parts not meshing, have unmatched parts, be out of sync

çakordo·n *vt* 1 [*Mus*] to cause to be out of tune 2 [*Tech*] to cause to be out of sync, cause parts not to mesh correctly

çakorduar *adj* (*i*) 1 out of tune 2 [*Tech*] to have unmatched parts, be out of sync

***çakraman** *nm* rascal, scoundrel; homeless vagabond

***çakrrar** *n* pettifogger

***çakrri** *nf* = çikërrimë

***çakrro·n** *vi* to squint

çakthi *adv* with teeth bared in defense

***çakulis·** *vt* to roll/flatten [ ] out

çal *nm* cripple, lame one

çalakëmbëzi *adv* limping, with a limp; on one leg

çalaman *adj* (*Pej*) 1 lame, crippled 2 (*Fig*) defective

çalas *adv* (*Pej*) = çalthi

çalash *adj* (*Pej*) crippled, lame, gimpy

çalë
I § *adj* (*i*) 1 crippled, lame 2 wrinkled, crumpled 3 defective, deficient
II § *nf* 1 wrinkle (in clothing) 2 [*Veter*] foot-rot
III § *adv* 1 = çalthi 2 defectively; haltingly
∘ **çalë e nguc** hunched over and limping, walking with great difficulty

çalë-çalë *adv* 1 hobbling along 2 (*Fig*) very slowly and with many mistakes: haltingly

çalësi *nf* lameness; limp

çalët *adj* (*i*) lame

çalëz *nf* cuff area of sleeve or pants-leg

çalim *nm ger* 1 < çalo·n 2 lameness 3 (*Fig*) crippling defect, infirmity

çalkë *nf* crippled/limping woman

çalo·n
I § *vi* 1 to limp; limp along, hobble along 2 (*Fig*) to go badly; make poor progress, do poorly, perform with faults/omissions
II § *vt* (*Fig*) to cause to go badly: foul up, impede
∘ **S'çalon gomari nga veshët.** "A donkey does not limp on its ears." (*Prov*) A trivial and irrelevant defect does not matter.
∘ **çalo·n nga të dyja këmbët** to have very serious defects/deficiencies

çalok *adj* (*Pej*) = çalaman

çalosh *adj* (*Impol*) lame, gimpy; limping

çalthi *adv* with a limp, limpingly, crippled, lamely; haltingly, in a hobbling manner

çaluk *adj* (*Pej*) = çalaman

***çallabojkë** *nf* slattern, slut

çallapatis· *vt* to wrinkle, crease

çallatë
I § *nf* 1 deep impression produced in a hard substance by force: nick, dent, gouge mark, chip mark, crack 2 thin, cut-off piece: chip (of wood/metal), chop (of meat) *3 helmet
II § *adv* with a gouging blow

çallato·het *vpr* to get nicked/dented/gouged/chipped/cracked/notched; be ruined (in the blade) by nicks

çallato·n *vt* to nick, notch, gouge, chip, dent

çallë
I § *nf* 1 = çallatë 2 unripe fruit
II § *adj* unripe

çallësti·a·r *adj (Colloq)* hard-working, energetic; enterprising; eager, lively

çallësti·s· *vi, vt* to manage by dint of great effort to arrange matters; manage [] by dint of great effort
  ○ çallëstis· për [] to knock oneself out for []

çallësti·sje *nf ger* 1 <çallëstis· 2 exertion, endeavor

çallësti·s·ur *adj (i)* energetic; painstaking, attentive

çallë·z *nf* unripe fruit

çallma·re *nf[Bot]* herbaceous ornamental plant with a long stem and odorless flowers with overlapping petals

çallmë *nf* 1 turban (green, white, or black) worn by certain religious Moslems 2 crest/tuft on a bird's head 3 [Food] dessert made by pouring boiling sugar syrup over a mixture of flour and eggs shaped in the form of little caps 4 popcorn 5 (Fig Colloq) appearance, look, mien

çallmëbardhë *nm (Impol)* white-turbaned Turk

çallmëjeshi·l *nm (Impol)* green-turbaned Dervish

çallmëmadh
  I § *adj (Impol)* big-turbaned
  II § *nm* turbaned Turk

çallo· *n vt* = çallato·

çallti·s· *vt (Colloq)* = çallëstis·

çallti·sje *nf ger (Colloq)* = çallëstisje

çallti·s·ur *adj (i) (Colloq)* = çallëstiar

çalltor *adj* = çallëstiar

çam
  I § *n* native of Cham (Çaméri)
  II § *adj* of or pertaining to Cham
  III § *nm* 1 [Bot] silver fir (Abies alba) 2 [Bot] Scotch pine (Pinus sylvestris)

*çamaro·k
  I § *nm (Colloq)* = çamarro·k
  II § *adj (Colloq)* = çamaro·k, çamaro·két

çamaro·két *adj (i) (Colloq)* mischievous

çamarro·k
  I § *adj (Colloq)* mischievous
  II § *nm* 1 little rascal, little scoundrel 2 simpleton, fool

*çambella·n *nm (Old)* chamberlain

*çamça·ke *nf* clapper

çamça·kéz *nm* 1 rosin, colophony 2 chewing gum

*ça·me *nf* wooden pot

ça·m|ér *nf* 1 crumb 2 native of Cham

Çam|éri *nf* ethnographic region in the extreme south of Albania bordering the Ionian Sea: Cham

çam|éri·sht *adv* in the dialect of Cham

çam|éri·sht|e *nf* the dialect of Cham

çam|i·shte *nf* = bredhi·shtë

*ça·m|je *nf* 1 cleft, split 2 [Zool] titmouse (Parus)

çam|të *adj (i)* = bredhtë

çana·k *nm* deep bowl for food
  ○ janë të një çanaku me [] (Pej) to share []'s evil objectives and interests, be in on it together with []; act in collusion with []

çanaklëpi·rës *n (Pej)* = sahanlëpi·rës

çand·ër *nf* forked support for a wall or fence: prop

çanësi·m *nm ger (Book)* = përkufizi·m

çanëso··het *vpr (Book)* = përkufizo··het

çanëso··n *vt (Book)* = përkufizo··n

çange *nf* gong; signal bell

çante *nf* carrying case: handbag, briefcase

○ çantë shpine knapsack

*çanj|és *adj* incisive

çap *nm* 1 (Colloq Fig) step, pace; sound of a step 2 (Colloq Fig) manner of action, step taken toward a goal 3 hunting dog, hound 4 gait
  ○ kaq e ka· çapin that is as much as {} can do, this is {}'s limit
  ○ çap pas çapi 1 at every step 2 step by step, little by little, gradually

çap·
  I § *vi (Colloq)* 1 to go somewhere: set off, go 2 to walk with difficulty, walk labordely 3 to stride, pace, step
  II § *vt* 1 to extend [one's leg] for walking: get a move on 2 (Reg) to chew, chew on [] = përçap·

çap·et *vpr (Colloq)* 1 to go somewhere: set off, go 2 = çapit·et 3 (Colloq) to chew, masticate 4 to stride, pace, step

çapaçu·l
  I § *adj (Colloq Pej)* slovenly and incompetent; contemptible
  II § *nm* a nobody

çapali·s *stem for 1st sg pres, pl pres, 2nd & 3rd sg subj, imperf* <çapali·t·

çapali·t· *vt* to cut through [] with the teeth, bite through

çapaqo·rr|as *adv* walking/proceeding with one's eyes shut

çapa·r *nm* 1 ribbon with gold or silver threads used to decorate clothes; decorative silken cord 2 bright line marking on an animal's skin 3 snake with a bright line marking

çapa·re *np* [Mus] cymbals; finger cymbals

çapa·rkë *nf* ribbon

çapa·roz *nm* [Bot] type of wheat with robust, reddish grains and dark awns

ça·pe *nf* large wooden spoon

çapeja·k *nm (Colloq)* = eceja·k

*çape·le *nf* bullfrog

*çape·ll = qape·ll

çapë *nf* 1 = cape 2 wrinkle in clothing 3 triangular metal scraper attached to the end of a plowman's goad to break up sod and remove soil stuck to the plowshare 4 (Reg) = kafsha·të 5

çapëlajkë *nf* piece of lumber securing two others to which it is nailed: crosspiece

çapële·het *vpr* = çapëlo··het

çapële·n *vpr* = çapëlo··n

çapëlo··het *vpr* 1 to be torn to pieces, be quartered 2 to be spread open/apart with force 3 to sit astraddle; sprawl out 4 (Fig) to try very hard, knock oneself out trying

çapëlo··n *vt* 1 to tear [] to pieces, quarter 2 to spread open/apart with force 3 to hurdle
  ○ çapëlo··n sytë to open one's eyes wide

çapëlua·r *adj (i)* 1 torn apart 2 spread wide open/apart, wide open

çapëlye·r *adj (i)* = çapëlua·r

çapën *2nd & 3rd sg pres* <çap·

*çapërdi·s· *vt* to perplex, muddle

çapërfla·k· *vt* to hurl

*çapëri·n *vt* to rile

*çapërtis· = çapërdis·

çapërtis·*et vpr* to become mentally deranged: lose one's reason, go insane

ça'përr *nf* goatskin container for dairy products

çapë'tor *n* person who uses a short-handled cultivator; cultivator

ça'pëz *nf* **1** triangular metal scraper attached to the end of a plowman's goad to break up sod and remove soil stuck to the plowshare **2** [*Bot*] Virginia pokeberry, pokeweed (*Phytolacca decandra*)

capëzo're *np* [*Bot*] pokeweed family *Phytolaccaceae*

ça'pi *1st sg pres* <**cap·**

çapi *nm* [*Zool*] green lizard = **zhapi**

çapik

I § *adj* impudent, saucy, cheeky; boorish, rude; naughty

II § *nm* brat; insolent fellow, lout, boor; rascal

çapis *stem for 1st sg pres, pl pres, 2nd & 3rd sg subj, pind* <**çapit·**

*****çapisht***ë** *nf* [*Ornit*] crane (*Grus grus*) = **krillë**

çapit·

I § *vt* to break up soil

II § *vi* (*Colloq*) = **çapit·***et*

çapit·*et vpr*(*Colloq*) **1** to take one's first steps: toddle, begin walking **2** to walk with difficulty: trudge, plod, walk laboredly, walk heavily **3** to stride, pace, step

çapitje *nf ger* **1** <**çapit·**, **çapit·***et* **2** gait

çapitur *adj (i)* broken up by action of a short-handled cultivator

*****ça'pje** *nf* **1** [*Ornit*] = **ça'pkë** **2** step, pace, stride

ça'pkë *nf* [*Ornit*] common heron (*Ardea cinerea*) = **gatë**

○ **çapkë nate** [*Ornit*] black-crowned night heron (*Nycticorax nycticorax* L., *Ardea nycticorax* L.)

○ **çapkë e përhime** [*Ornit*] = **ça'pkë**

○ **çapkë rrushi** [*Ornit*] purple heron (*Ardea purpurea* L.)

○ **çapkë sqeplugë** [*Ornit*] spoonbill *Platalea leucorodia* L.

○ **çapkë e verdhë** [*Ornit*] Squacco heron *Ardeola ralloides Scop.*

çapkën

I § *adj* full of mischief: mischievous, naughty

II § *n* merry but slightly naughty child: little rascal, mischief-maker

çapkën|çe *adv* (*Colloq*) **1** mischievously **2** lowered to the side over one eye: rakishly, roguishly

çapkën|ëri *nf* **1** mischievousness **2** mischief

çapkën|llëk *nm* = **çapkënëri**

çapko're *np fem* [*Ornit*] *Ardeae*

çaple·*n* = **çaplo·***n*

*****çapli** *nf* buttress, pier

çaplim *nm ger* <**çaplo·***n*

çaplo·*n*

I § *vi* **1** to stride, pace, step **2** to open one's legs; straddle

II § *vt* to open [] wide; split

*****çapluem** *adj (i)* (*Reg Gheg*) straddle-legged

*****çapllo·***n vi* to eat noisily

*****çapo'·***n vi* **1** = **çap·** **2** = **capo'·***n*

çapo'|i *obl* <**ça'pua**

çapok *nm* **1** [*Anat*] hipbone, hip; haunch **2** thighbone; thigh **3** shin; tibia, shinbone = **ça'pua**

çapoko'r *adj* [*Med*] iliac

çapo'|nj *np* <**çapu'a**

*****çapo'rr** *nm* = **ça'pua**

çaprashis *stem for 1st sg pres, pl pres, 2nd & 3rd sg subj, pind* <**çaprashit·** (*Colloq*)

çaprashit·

I § *vt* (*Colloq*) = **ngatërro'·***n*

II § *vi* **1** to walk clumsily, stumble **2** (*Fig*) to prattle, chatter nonsense

çaprashit·*et vpr* (*Colloq*) **1** = **ngatërro'·***het* **2** to walk clumsily, stumble

çapraz

I § *adv* **1** intertwined in an irregular/undisciplined way, convoluted **2** (*Fig Colloq*) in a undesirably irregular or indirect way: sneaky, in a convoluted manner **3** (*Fig Colloq*) all mixed-up, backwards, in a contrary way

II § *nm* **1** crosscut saw with staggered teeth **2** tool for bending saw teeth *****3** ornamental braid on jacket collar **4** (*Fig*) gibberish

III § *adj* **1** (*Colloq*) irregular, odd, peculiar **2** contrary in behavior: ornery, difficult

çapraze *np* <**çapraz 1** cross-strung ornamental chain of raw metal disks hung around neck or waist; cross-hung object **2** (*Fig*) coy airs/manners, affectations

çaprazim *nm ger* **1** <**çaprazo'·***n* **2** saw setting

çaprazo'·*n vt* **1** to set [saw teeth] (alternately left and right) **2** (*Fig Colloq*) to mistake one for another, confuse

çaprazues *nm* person who sets the teeth of a saw: sawsetter

*****çapre·***n vt* to disunite, divide

*****çaprok** *adj* potbellied

çapshpejtë

I § *adj* fast-moving, speedy, rapid, fast

II § *adv* rapidly, quickly

ça'pthi *adv* (usually said of a horse) step by step, not in a hurry

çapu'a *nm (obl ˜o'i, np ˜o'nj)* **1** foot spur on poultry **2** talon, claw **3** claw-shaped object

○ **çaponjtë e misrit** corn roots that stick up out of the ground

*****ça'pull** *nm (np ˜j)* interest

*****çaqe** *nf* [*Invert*] garden spider (*Aranea diademata*)

*****çar** *interrog pron* (*Colloq*) = **çfarë**

çara'p = **çora'p**

ça'razi *adv* deeply in the ground, in deeply plowed soil

çarça'f *nm* **1** bedsheet, sheet **2** (*Old*) black sheet worn over the head by Moslem women outside of the home to cover all but the eyes **3** (*ColloqImpolite*) overlong piece of writing **4** shroud

○ **Të mbledhshin në çarçaf!** "May they wind you in a sheet!" (*Curse*) I hope you die!

çarda'k *nm* **1** wood-floored open balcony of old houses that was used as a summer parlor or for entertaining guests, summer veranda; upstairs corridor one end of which was used for receiving guests **2** (*Reg*) wood floor **3** (*Reg*) cairn **4** game in which the object is for one team to upend crouched members of the other team

ça'rdash *nm* czardas

çardha'k *nm* = **çarda'k**

çare *nf* (*Colloq*) means to solution of a problem or escape from difficulty: remedy, way out, solution

*ça're = çfarë

çarë
I§ part <ça·n
II§ adj (i) **1** having a lengthwise opening produced by a blow or cut: slit; split, cracked **2** lacerated **3** deeply plowed for the first time **4** *(Colloq)* split by disagreement
III§ nf(e) **1** lengthwise opening produced by a blow or cut: fissure, crack, split, rift, crevice; slit, incision **2** *(Fig)* weak point, chink, gap, flaw, fault **3** *(Fig)* division caused by disagreement: rift, split, gap

ça're̱s adj making a cut: cutting, chopping, splitting

ça're̱se nf[Agr] budding knife

ça'rje nf ger **1** <ça·n, ça·het **2** = çarë **3** *(Old)* = përçarje

çark
I§ nm **1** trap (snare) **2** reel; drivewheel; potter's wheel **3** flintlock; firing mechanism of a gun, gun hammer **4** tobacco shredder **5** frame/framework made of wood **6** *(Reg)* bloodletting device **7** *(Colloq)* [Anat] bone joint; jointed bones **8** *(Colloq)* row of teeth in the mouth
II§ adv arched
o **i çarkut** brand-new, just made
o **ësh·të çark më çark me** [] to have a very strained relationship with [], be in tense relations with []; be at loggerheads with []
o **e solli çarku** as luck would have it

çarki nf large metal tray used for food

*çarllata'n nm charlatan, quack = **sharlata'n**

*çarllatano·n vi to practice quackery

çarmati'm nm ger **1** <çarmato·n, çarmato·het **2** disarmament

*çarmati's· = çarmatos·

çarmato·het vpr = **çarmatos·et**

çarmato·n vt **1** = çarmatos· **2** [Min] to remove the supporting framework from a mine tunnel, take out the shoring pillars

çarmatos· vt to disarm []

çarmatos·et vpr **1** to disarm **2** *(Fig)* to remain defenseless

çarmato'sje nf ger **1** <çarmatos·, çarmatos·et **2** disarmament

çarmato'sur adj (i) **1** disarmed **2** *(Fig)* defenseless

*çaro'k adj fresh, young

ça'rqe np <çark

*çars stem for 1st sg pres, pl pres, 2nd & 3rd sg subj, pind <çart·

çarshi nf *(Old)* covered market; street with rows of shops along both sides

çart nm *(Reg)* delirium

çart· vt **1** = prish· **2** = shkel·
o **i çart· pipëzat** "break the flutes" *(Colloq)* to break off a friendship
o **<>a çart· zemrën** to break <>'s heart

ça'rt·et vpr = prish·et

çarta'be̱se nf breaking one's word, betraying ones' honor; disloyalty

çartabu'kas
I§ adj malingering, given to loafing
II§ n loafer, malingerer

*çarta'gaz nm displeasure

*çarta'gaze̱s adj ill-humored, peevish

*çarta'ka'ndas adv *(Reg Gheg)* = çartaqejfas

çarta'kënd·as adv = çartaqejfas

çarta'pre'ras adv badly

çarta'qe̱jf
I§ nm lethargy, apathy
II§ adv = **çartaqejfas**

çarta'qe̱jfas adv *(Colloq)* **1** with broken spirit: lethargically, apathetically **2** with a disagreeable mood: unwillingly, ill-humoredly

çarta'ujk nm *(Colloq)* foolhardy hero

ça'rtë nf disagreement/quarrel due to a misunderstanding

çartje nf ger <çarto·n, çarto·het

çarto·het vpr *(Reg)* **1** = prish·et **2** to go crazy **3** to speak deliriously, rave

çarto·n
I§ vt *(Reg)* **1** = prish· **2** to drive crazy
II§ vi to go crazy

ça'rtur adj (i) **1** = prishur **2** raving mad, crazy (of humans), rabid (of animals) **3** *(Fig)* foolhardy

çarranik nm **1** storage place for keeping food cold: larder; dairy cellar **2** chicken coop

çarrava'lle np *(Reg)* weeds

*çarravame̱ nf scuffle

çarravi nf **1** hindrance, obstacle **2** wrangle over trivia, concern with irrelevant detail; big to-do, tumult, hubbub

*çarravi's stem for 1st sg pres, pl pres, 2nd & 3rd sg subj, pind <çarravi't·

*çarravi't· vt **1** to upbraid, scold **2** to whirr

ças = çast

çast nm brief period of time: moment, instant
o **i çastit** prepared on the spot, made fresh right in front of you **2** of brief duration; fleeting in appearance or value

çast ë adj (i) immediate

çaste̱si nf *(Book)* momentariness, fugacity, transientness

çast'she̱m adj (i) *(Book)* momentary; transitory

ça'she̱m adj (i) splittable, fissile

ça'shme̱ri nf [Spec] fissibility

çâshtje nf *(Reg Gheg)* = çështje

çata'll
I§ nm (np ~ j) **1** fork, branch **2** snaggle tooth; buck tooth; fang **3** double pronged thing: scorpion, hay fork **4** bifurcation **5** *(Colloq)* object with prongs **6** moldboard of a wooden plow **7** one who walks with legs spread crookedly
II§ adj **1** forking, branching **2** growing fork-shaped: forked, with forked branches or roots **3** growing out of alignment, snaggled **4** having divergent strabismus: walleyed **5** confused, bewildered
III§ adv **1** forking out, branching to the side **2** walking crookedly from side to side, with a waddling gait
o **çatall për flokë** hairpin
o **çatall për të ngrënë** dining fork
o **Të prufshin me çatalle!** *(Curse)* may you drop dead!

çata'lle nf **1** forking branch, forked piece of wood **2** wooden stretcher/litter/bier for carrying the sick or dead **3** wooden splint

çata'llë nm notch, indentation

çata'llo·het vpr *(Colloq)* **1** to branch out, branch, open out to the sides; form a fork **2** *(Fig)* to be damaged by a divisive force, be driven apart **3** *(Fig)* to quarrel

çata'llo·n vt *(Colloq)* **1** to create a forking, cause to branch out; bend the ends apart **2** to force apart

3 *(Fig)* to damage [] by creating dissension, drive apart **4** = çaprazo·∙n **5** = çakërrit· **6** to arrange with the ends pointing in opposite directions

çatdhesïm *nm ger* [*Law*] <çatdheso·n, çatdheso·het

çatdheso·het *vpr* [*Law*] to go into exile

çatdheso·n *vt* [*Law*] to expatriate, exile

çatdhesuar *adj (i)* [*Law*] expatriated, in exile

çati *nf* **1** roof **2** shelter, domicile

çatiprishur *adj (Colloq)* **1** messed up at home, having a messed-up home life, domestically in ruins **2** economically ruined, bankrupt, impoverished

çatis· *vi (Colloq)* to pop up, appear suddenly

çatma *nf* [*Constr*] **1** thin partition, thin wall of plaster or wattling **2** lath, plasterboard

çatme *nf* = çatma

çatmo·n *vt* to partition [] off by a thin wall

çatrafilo·het *vpr (Colloq)* **1** to get all mixed up, fall into complete disorder, become chaotic **2** to become utterly confused, lose one's way **3** to be confused with one another, be mistaken for

çatrafilo·n *vt (Colloq)* to create a mix-up, cause confusion, create chaos, confuse

*çatrapilë *nf* confusion, disorder, chaos

*çatrapilo·n *vt* **1** *(Colloq)* to misshape, twist, bend **2** = çatrafilo·n

çaturre *nf* long loose pleated shirt worn by men of the Myzeqe district

çaul *nm* [*Anat*] jaw

çaush *nm* [*Hist*] **1** army corporal in the Ottoman empire **2** adjutant **3** (in pre-Liberation Albania) municipal policeman **4** (in pre-Liberation Albania) administrator of public works **5** [*Ornit*] hoopoe (*Upupa epops*)

çav *stem for 1st & 2nd sg pdef* <ça·n

çavalïs· *vt* to disfigure, deform, mutilate; garble [a message/report]

*çavalïs *stem for 1st sg pres, pl pres, 2nd & 3rd sg subj, pind* <çavalit·

*çavalït· *vt* **1** to struggle, fight *2 *(Fig)* to mutilate [a language]

*çavë [*Ornit*] raven (*Corvus corax* L.) = korbë

*çavullïm *nm ger* <çavullo·n

*çavullo·n *vt* to evaporate

*çbarkïm *nm ger* <çbarko·n

*çbarko·n *vt* to disembark

*çbashkïm *nm ger* <çbashko·n

*çbashko·n *vt* to disunite, sunder

*çbë-n = zhbë-n

çbind· *vt* to dissuade

çbïndje *nf ger* <çbind·

çbllokïm = zhbllokïm

çblloko·n = zhblloko·n

çbojatïs· *vt* to discolor

çbojatïsje *nf ger* <çbojatïs·

*çdëmïm *nm ger* = zhdëmtïm

çdo *determiner* any; all, every, each
  ◦ **Çdo berr varet nga këmbët e veta.** **1** Everyone is responsible for his own deeds. **2** Everyone must be treated on his own merits.
  ◦ **çdo gjë** everything
  ◦ **Çdo mish/berr varet *nga këmbët e veta/në çengelin e vet.*** "Every carcass hangs from its own legs/hook." *(Prov)* Everyone is responsible for his

own work/problems. Everyone must be judged (individually) on his own merits.
  ◦ **Çdo mizë nuk bën mjaltë.** "Not every bee makes honey." *(Prov)* Not everyone is at the same level.

çdoditshëm *adj (i)* everyday, daily

çdofarë *determiner* = çdolloj

çdofarëshëm *adj (i)* = çdollojshëm

*çdofargjâje *pron (Reg Gheg)* everything whatsoever, anything at all

*çdogjâ *pron (Reg Gheg)* everything, anything

çdoherë *adv* at any time, always

çdokënd *acc* <çdokush

çdokujt *dat/abl* <çdokush

çdokush *pron* anyone, whoever it may be, anybody, everybody

çdolloj *determiner* any kind/type of, every kind/type of, all sorts of

çdollojshëm *adj (i)* of all kinds, of various kinds, of any kind/type/sort

çdollojtë *adj (i)* = çdollojshëm

*çdonjâni *(Reg Gheg)* = çdonjëri

çdonjër *nm, nf (definite case forms only)* every one, each one, everyone, anyone

*çdredh· = zhdredh·

*çdrejtë *adj (i)* *(Reg)* = zhdrejtë

*çduk *(Reg)* = zhduk

*çeç *nm* miser

çeçe *nf (Colloq)* **1** soft food for babies: pap; sop **2** = papare

çeço *nf with masc agreement (Colloq)* **1** name by which the father or eldest brother is called by little children **2** *(Pej)* person not right in the head, slightly crazy person, person with a screw loose, nut

*çedër *nf* = cedër

çedukïm *nm ger* <çeduko·n, çeduko·het

çeduko·n *vt* to miseducate, educate poorly/badly

*çefas *adv (Reg)* = fshehtas

*çefi *(Reg)* = çepi

çefkë *nf* **1** hood of a cloak *2* bract of the corn plant

çehre *nf (Colloq)* **1** facial appearance, look, countenance, mien; facial color, complexion, pallor; facial expression **2** kindly facial expression, smiling face **3** gloomy facial expression, downcast look **4** healthy appearance of a plant, robust look of a plant

çehrengrysur
  I § *adj (Colloq)* having an ever gloomy facial expression: always frowning, sullen
  II § *adv* with a gloomy countenance; angrily, harshly

çehreprishur *adj (Colloq)* = fytyrëprishur

çehreverdhë *adj (Colloq)* pale, wan

çehrevarë *adj (Colloq)* suffering look, sad look; pale and wan; darkened mien

çehrevrenjtrë *adj (Colloq)* = çehrengrysur

*çejz *nm (Reg Gheg)* bride's trousseau

çek
  I § *nm* **1** [*Fin*] check **2** food taken along by a shepherd to eat during the day
  II § *adj, n* Czech

çek *adj, n* Czech
  ◦ **çek kokëzi** [*Ornit*] stonechat *Saxicola torquata* L.
  ◦ **çek vetullbardhë** [*Ornit*] whinchat *Saxicola rubetra* L.

çek· *vt* **1** to touch, touch [] lightly, tap, peck; touch on [], touch lightly on [] *2* to cite, quote
  ◦ [] **çek· në kalli** to touch []'s most sensitive spot

ÇEKA *abbrev (Russian)* [*Hist*] Cheka = Soviet secret police

çeka'n *nm* **1** large hammer, sledge hammer, hammer **2** [*Tech*] machine hammer **3** door knocker

çekane'ç *nm* [*Ichth*] the young of carp

çekani'm *nm ger* [*Tech*] <**çekano'**·*n*

çekani's· *vt* **1** to chisel [] out with a hammer; work into shape with a hammer **2** (*Fig Colloq*) to chastise by beating

çekano'·*n vt* [*Tech*] to hammer metal at a forge

çe'ke *nf* **1** (*Reg*) = **cep, skaj 2** chisel edge of a pickax; blade of a tool

*****çekër'k** = **çikrik**

çeki *nf (Old)* **1** measure of weight slightly less than one okë e vogël **2** weighing machine = **pesho're**
  ○ **çeki nga mendtë** lacking in brains

Çeki *nf* territory of the Czechs

çeki'ç *nm* **1** spalling mallet, mallet **2** [*Tech*] machine hammer **3** [*Anat*] hammer bone of middle ear: malleus **4** [*Sport*] object thrown in the hammer throw
  ○ **çekiç druri** heaver, setting hammer
  ○ **çekiç pikës** soldering iron
  ○ **çekiç i shkresës** metalsmith's mallet used to incise lines in copper or tin

çeki'sht *adv* in Czech

çeki'shte *nf* Czech language

çe'kje *nf ger* <**çek**·, **çek**·*et*

çekmexhe' *nf* (*Colloq*) drawer in a table or in other furniture

çekosllova'k *adj* of or pertaining to Czechoslovakia

çekosllova'k *adj, n* Czechoslovakian

Çekosllovaki *nf* Czechoslovakia

Çekosllovaki' *nf* Czechoslovakia

çek'th *nm (Reg)* = **çe'ke**

çekuili'bër *nm (Book)* disequilibrium; disproportion

çekuilibri'm *nm ger (Book)* <**çekuilibro'**·*n*, **çekuilibro'**·*het*

çekuilibro'·*het vpr (Book)* to lose equilibrium, lose balance; lose one's sense of proportion

çekuilibro'·*n vt (Book)* to cause to lose equilibrium, unbalance; destroy the balance or proportion

çekuilibru'ar *adj (i) (Book)* **1** unbalanced, out of equilibrium, out of proportion **2** mentally/spiritually unbalanced

çel·
  I § *vt* **1** to open [] up **2** to uncover, unwrap **3** to unlock **4** to open [] out, unfold **5** to open passage **6** to dig [] up, dig [] out **7** to start [] up, open [something new] **8** (*Fig*) to unloose, unleash **9** to put [] into action, turn on [a lamp/radio, water] **10** [*Fin*] to open [an account] **11** (*Fig*) to break out in a smile **12** (*Fig Colloq*) to open [] up to knowledge and culture, open []'s eyes **13** to hatch [eggs] **14** (*Colloq*) to set livestock out to pasture **15** (*Reg*) to light up [a fire/candle/lamp] **16** (*Reg*) to welcome [a guest]
  II § *vi* **1** to blossom, bloom **2** to begin to get light, dawn **3** (of weather) to clear up **4** to emerge from the egg
  ○ **çel· dyert** "open the doors" to lead the way
  ○ **çel· e s'mbyll** (*Pej*) not stop talking, never to stop yammering
  ○ <> **çel· gojën** "open <>'s mouth" **1** to give <> an undesirable opening to say or ask for something; give undue cause for <> to speak out, give <> an excuse to open <>'s trap **2** to lead <> into making excessive demands

  ○ **iu çel gryka thesit** "untie/open the neck of the sack" to disclose everything
  ○ **Çele gur gojën!** (addressed to someone who is too quiet) Open your mouth and say something!
  ○ **çel· konak 1** to build a new house **2** to get married and start one's own family
  ○ **çel e mbyll** in an open and shut way
  ○ **çel· një hendek** to create a deep division between the parties, cause dissension
  ○ <> **çel· një jaki (të keqe)** to open a (sore) wound for <>
  ○ **çel· njëqind dyer në ditë** (*Pej*) to spend the whole day going from one person to another
  ○ <> **çel· oreksin** to increase <>'s appetite/greed
  ○ **Çeli sytë!** Keep your eyes open! Stay alert!
  ○ **çel· shtëpi më vete** to set up a separate household
  ○ **çel· shtëpi të re** to set up one's own place/household
  ○ **çel· tokën** to break new ground
  ○ **çel· zogj** "hatch chicks" **1** (*Iron*) to lie in bed with a long debilitating illness **2** to remain idly in one place, hang around not doing anything

çel·*et vpr* **1** to become open, open up, be opened **2** to get uncovered, get unwrapped, be uncorked/uncapped **3** to get unfolded, unfold, be opened out **4** to have passage opened **5** to be started up, opened up **6** to recover from an illness, come to life again **7** to break out in a smile **8** (*Fig*) to become more lively and involved with others **9** (*Fig*) to discover new ideas and feelings from within **10** (of weather, sky, throat, voice) to clear up **11** (of skin) to develop deep cracks, become chapped **12** (of eggs) to hatch
  ○ <> **çel·***et*[3*sg*] **dera** <>'s family line now will be continued (said when the first son is born)
  ○ <> **çel·***et*[3*sg*] **goja** <> *starts* speaking without timidity/bashfulness
  ○ **çel·***et* **ndër vete** to rupture
  ○ <> **çel·***et*[3*sg*] **oreksi 1** <> *has* an increase of appetite **2** <> *gets* greedy
  ○ <> **çel·***et*[3*sg*] **qimja** "<>'s hair brightens" <> *is* overjoyed/elated, <> *is* pleased as punch

çela'mbyll'as *adv* = **çelembyll**

çele'g *nm* [*Bot*] fox grape (*Vitis labrusca*)

çele'mbyll *adv*

*****çele'ngër** *nf* [*Ornit*] small hawk

çelë *nf* **1** (in several children's games) starting line **2** best part of something: choice part, best of the best, the cream, the flower **3** worn-out old shoe *****4** (*Colloq*) jail cell

çelë's *nm* **1** key **2** [*Tech*] wrench, spanner **3** knob used for tightening **4** opener: can/bottle opener **5** switch for interrupting and releasing the flow of a current: light switch, gas switch, radio knob **6** [*Mus*] key signature, key **7** [*Constr*] keystone **8** [*Reg*] [*Anat*] bone joint
  ○ **çelës anglez** [*Tech*] monkey wrench
  ○ **çelës i artë** "golden key" (*Book*) magic wand
  ○ **çelës automatik** [*Tech*] automatic lock
  ○ **çelës kopil** skeleton key; master key
  ○ **çelës papagall** lock wrench
  ○ **çelës qemeri** keystone of an arch
  ○ **çelës i rremë** skeleton key; master key

çelë'sabër'ës *nm* locksmith

çelë'sambajt'ës *nm* keeper of the keys, keymaster, watchman in charge of keys

çelë't *adj (i)* clear/light in color, sound, or mood

çelëz *nf* situation arising when a player tries to move several stones simultaneously in the game of nëntësh

***çelfis** *stem for 1st sg pres, pl pres, 2nd & 3rd sg subj, pind* <çelfit·

***çelfit·** *vt* to scar, scarify, scratch

***çelfitje** *nf ger* <çelfit·

çelik
  I § *nm* **1** steel **2** [*Ichth*] mosquitofish *(Gambusia affinis)* = **barkulec**
  II § *adj (Fig)* strong as steel, of steel
  ○ **çelik instrumental** [*Tech*] tool steel

çelikos· *vt* to make [] as strong as steel, temper; make durable and unbreakable, strengthen

çelikos·*et vpr* <çelikos·

çelikosje *nf ger* <çelikos·, çelikos·*et*

çelikran *nm* pruning hook

çelikshkrirës *nm* steel foundryman

çeliktë *adj (i)* **1** made of steel, of steel; steely **2** *(Fig)* very strong and durable; indestructible, unbreakable

çeling *nm* chief herdsman

***çelinok** *nm* [*Bot*] common balm, lemon balm *(Melissa officinalis)* = **milcë**

çeliqe *np* <çelik

çelit··*et* to bloom again, open up to life: recuperate, be reinvigorated; take on a happy face; become livelier and more sociable

çelitur *adj (i)* lively and sociable, open to other people

çelje *nf ger* <çel·, çel·*et*

çelnik *nm (Old)* **1** big livestock-owner; chief herdsman **2** dairyman working in a mountain camp of herdsmen **3** = **çelik**

çelnikatë *nf* [*Hist*] **1** confederation of herdsmen responsible for pasturing large herds of livestock and working together in a dairy **2** grazing tax paid by herdsmen to big landowners

çelnikore *nf (Old)* dairywoman

çelnikos· *vt* to steel, harden

çelnikos··*et vpr* to steel oneself; grow stronger

çelniktë *adj (i)* = **çeliktë**

çeltas *adv* openly, frankly, plainly

çeltazi *adv* = **çeltas**

çeltik *adj* (of cotton or rice) in an unprocessed state: raw, uncleaned, brown, unpolished

çeltinë = **çeltirë**

çeltirë *nf* **1** treeless area in a forest: clearing **2** [*Constr*] aperture, opening

çelulojd *nm* celluloid = **celuloid**

çelur
  I § *adj (i)* **1** open, opened **2** (for colors) unsaturated, light, pale **3** (of a voice) clear, pure **4** ever gay, jolly, joyful **5** of an open nature, sociable **6** open in a particular area, cut-out **7** blooming **8** hatched
  II § *adv* **1** open, opened **2** in operation, open **3** openly, frankly

çelurazi *adv* = **çiltas**

***çellëngri** *nf (Old)* dairy farm

çem *nm (Reg)* fork, branch = **çatall**

çem· *vt* **1** to bring [] up, mention *2* to disclose, reveal, unearth

çember *nm (Old)* **1** kerchief of a meshed, usually white, embroidered fabric, worn over the forehead by women **2** fatty membrane covering the entrails of a farm animal

çemberbardhë *adj (Old)* wearing a short white veil

çemberkuqe *adj (Old)* wearing a short red veil

çembrionizim *nm ger* <çembrionizo·*n*

çembrionizo··*het vpr* <çembrionizo·*n*

çembrionizo·*n* *vt* to remove the embryo from [a seed] (in order to prevent sprouting)

***çement** *nm* = **çimento**

çemento *nf* = **çimento**

çemërim *nm ger* [*Offic*] <çemëro·*n*, çemëro·*het*

*°**çemëro·**·*het vpr* [*Offic*] <çemëro·*n*

çemëro·*n* *vt* [*Offic*] to remove from office, discharge from a position

çend· *vt* to unweave, unravel

çend··*et vpr* <çend·

*°**çendelli·*n*** *vt* to drive [] mad

*°**çendellis** *stem for 1st sg pres, pl pres, 2nd & 3rd sg subj, pind* <çendellit·

*°**çendellit·** *vt* to embitter

çendje *nf ger* <çend·, çend·*et*

çenë *nf* [*Anat*] jaw

çengel
  I § *nm* **1** large iron hook used for hanging things **2** gaff, harpoon **3** iron ring with hooks attached for extracting things immersed in water **4** fireplace chain holding the pothook **5** hinged hook for securing doors, windows or shutters **6** (ship or boat) anchor **7** *(Old)* torture instrument with hooks **8** *(Fig Colloq)* miser, very stingy person
  II § *adj (Fig)* very strong, indefatigable

çengi *nf* **1** female dancer in a folk band **2** *(Pej)* immoral woman, slut, tramp

çep *nm* **1** = **cep 2** spout (as on a tea pot); nozzle *3* stopper, bung; tap *4* gas burner
  ○ **çepi i kroit** gutter leading from a spring

*°**çepallë** *nf* dip net, brail net, brailer

*°**çepallkë** OR **çepellkë** *nf (Reg Tosk)* bottle gourd; gourd bottle

çepe *nf* **1** tuft of hair on an otherwise clean-shaven head *2* wig

çepele *nf* knife blade

çepelit· *vt (Colloq)* to whittle

çepellë *nf* **1** string of dried figs **2** type of fleshy fig dried and hung together in strings

***çepi** *nf* custody, care

çepirok *nm* = **bërçik**

çepka *np* dry kindling gathered from here and there

çepkas *stem for 1st sg pres, pl pres, 2nd & 3rd sg subj, pind* <çepkat·

çepkat· *vt* **1** to disentangle [fibers] by hand **2** to pick/poke at [] superficially; touch/brush [] superficially/lightly, graze **3** to dig around in [] in order to find something; rifle *4* tousle, dishevel

çepkatje *nf ger* <çepkat·

çepojë *nf (Reg)* = **borde**

çeptirë *nf* puddle; area with many puddles: wetlands

***çepue** *nm (obl ~ oi, np ~ onj) (Reg Gheg)* = **çapua**

çeqe *np* <çek

çerçem *nm (Reg)* [*Bot*] = **carac**

çerçive *nf* **1** door/window sash, door/window frame **2** = **menteshë** *3* casement window

çerdhe *nf* **1** bird nest **2** day nursery; nursery school **3** *(Fig)* family home **4** *(Pej)* lair **5** [*Mil*] gun emplacement, gunners' nest **6** [*Ling*] word family, words

based on a common root **7** group of offspring of domestic animals born and raised together: litter, brood
◦ **çerdhe zjarri** [*Mil*] foxhole

çerdhu'kël *nf* [*Ornit*] shore lark *(Eremophila alpestris)*

*__çerdhu'kull__ = çerdhu'kël

*__çe're__ *nf* = çehre

çere'k *nm* **1** quarter, fourth **2** *(Old)* = çere'kje

çerek'çí *nm* *(Old)* impoverished small-time artisan, two-bit tinker

çere'k|e *nf* *(Old)* dry measure of grain equal to a quarter of a shinik

çerek'finale *nf* [*Sport*] quarterfinal

çere'kje *nf* *(Old)* small coin worth a fourth of the silver Turkish mexhite

çerek'kil'ësh *adj* weighing a quarter of a kilogram

çerek'litër'sh *adj* containing a quarter of a liter

çerek'o're *nf* container for grain with a capacity of a çereke

çere'ksh *adj* a quarter of something in value

çere'kshe *nf* **1** container with a capacity of a quarter of a kilogram/liter **2** something equal to a quarter of the whole

çerek'she'kull *nm* quarter of a century

çerek'shekull'o'r *adj* lasting a quarter of a century, twenty-five year old

çere'p *nm* **1** deep earthenware pan for baking bread = saç **2** *(Fig Pej)* person with an extremely ugly face ***3** [*Bot*] mistletoe *(Viscum album)* ***4** waffle iron

çerep'o're *nf* bread baked in a çerep

çeresni'cë *nf* [*Ichth*] nase *(Chondrostama nasus)*

*__çerfo's__ *nm* camphor

*__çeri'ç__ *nm* cobbler's glue

*__çerje'p__ = çere'p

çermeni'k|as
   I § *adj* of or pertaining to Çermenika
   II § *n* native of Çermenika

Çermeni'kë *nf* easternmost region of central Albania: Çermenika

Çermeni'kë *nf* province east of Elbasan

*__çermo'k__ *nm* tufa stone

çernie're. *nf* [*Tech*] articulated mechanism, mechanical hinge

*__çerni'k__ *nm* knapsack, game bag

*__çerola'kë__ *nf* sealing wax

*__çerp__ *nm* **1** topknot, tuft of hair **2** halo

*__çerpa'ckë__ *nf* slatternly woman, slut

*__çe'rpe__ *nf* = përçe

*__çerpe'k__ *adj* deft, nimble

çerq|e *np* < çark

çe'rte
   I § *nf* *(Old)* small shop or pushcart for selling notions/sundries
   II § *np* *(Old)* notions, sundries

çerte'xhi *nm (np ~ nj) (Old)* sundries merchant; pushcart merchant

çertu'ri'na *np* sundries, notions

çerve' *nf* = çevre'

çervi'sh *nm (Old)* **1** [*Food*] dish made with fried mush, garlic, and gravy **2** *(Fig)* mess, mélange, mixture

çerr *nm* [*Ornit*] **1** wren *(Troglodytes troglodytes)* **2** runt chick usually kept apart from other chickens

çerr'ësi'm *nm* [*Cine*] fade in

çerri'k *nm* fishing net on the end of a forked pole

*__çe'sa__ *quant* quite a few, a fair number of

çe'sme *OR* çe'smë *nf* = çezmë

*__çe'ste__ *nf* = qeste

çeshi't *nm (Old)* **1** (of merchandise, wares, goods) sample **2** sort, kind **3** *(Pej)* bad example
◦ **çeshit më vete** peculiar person

çeshti·n *vi* to sneeze

çeta'ni'k *nm* = çeta'r

çeta'r *n (Old)* **1** member of a group of raiders **2** leader of a group of raiders

*__çe'tas__ *adv* = çe'tash

çe'tash *adv*

ÇETEKA *abbrev (Czechoslovakian)* < Cekoslovenska Tiskove Kancelar Czech Press Bureau

çete'le *nf (Old)* **1** stick used to keep account of sales and purchases: tally rod, counting stick **2** piece of wood divided into two parts, one of which is kept with an item to be stored, the other kept by the owner of the item as a receipt: check, tab **3** small identifying mark on an object: tick
◦ **Janë puthitur çetelja me çetelen.** *(Pej)* The devil has found his mate.

çe'të *nf* **1** band of guerrillas; partisan unit **2** [*Hist*] military squadron **3** troop of young pioneers in a school or camp **4** *(Old)* [*Ethnog*] tribe, brotherhood, kin group **5** flock of people, group **6** *(Reg)* < la'gje **7** game of tag between two groups of opponents; tag (the touch)
◦ **çetë vullnetare** local quasi-military civil defense group composed of volunteer women and senior citizens

çe'të'z *nf* game in which each player throws a stick and attempts to hit the sticks thrown by others; a hit in such a game

çeti'm *nm ger* **1** < çeto'·n **2** sortie, raid

çetin'a'k *nm* [*Bot*] Swiss mountain pine *(Pinus mugo, Pinus montano)*

çeti'në
   I § *nf* [*Bot*] black pine/spruce *(Pinus negra)*
   II § *np* *(Fig)* unruly hair standing on end
◦ **çetinë e zezë** stone pine *Pinus pinea*

*__çetni'__ *nm (Reg Gheg)* group, band, company

çeto'·n *vi (Old)* to make a sortie, go out on a raid

çetu'r *nm* cup-shaped eating utensil with a handle, usually used for dairy products; wooden cup

çevre' *nf (Old)* white cloth edged with gold/silver embroidery and used as a hand towel or as a head kerchief

çezma'xhi' *nm (np ~ nj) (Old)* person who installs and repairs a town water supply/fountain

çe'zmë *nf* water spring; water fountain
◦ **çezmë e njomë** spring that always yields water
◦ **çezmë e thatë** water spring that dries up in summer

*__çë__ = ç', që

çëfu't *nm* = çifu't

*__çëmër'ma'dh__ *adj* gluttonous

çë'njt· *vt* to reduce the swelling of [ ]

çë'njt·et *vpr* to become less swollen, go down in swelling

çë'njtje *nf ger* < çë'njt·et

çë'njt'ur *adj (i)* reduced in swelling

çë'shtje *nf* **1** matter at hand: issue; matter of discussion: subject, topic, theme; situation requiring a solution: problem **2** object of support by a group or movement: cause **3** *(Offic)* (legal) case/matter

○ **çështje jete (a vdekjeje)** vital matter, matter of life or death

○ **çështje kohe** a matter of time, something requiring time for completion

***çfajësim** *nm* = shfajësim

***çfajëso·n** *vt* = shfajëso·n

***çfaq** = shfaq

***çfaqësinë** *nf (Reg Gheg)* performance, display

***çfaqët** *adj (i)* explicit, obvious

çfarë
I § *pron* what
II § *determiner (followed by ablative case)* **1** what; what kind; which **2** what a __! what __!
○ **çfarë i del përpara** anything that happens/shows up, anything whatever
○ **Çfarë të bësh ta bëjnë dhe ta teprojnë.** *(Prov)* What you do to others they will do to you, but even worse. Do something bad and it will come back to you in spades.

çfarëdo
I § *determiner (followed by ablative case)* whatever
II § *pron* anything whatever, anything
○ **një** {*noun*} **çfarëdo** any {} whatever

çfarëdolloj *determiner (followed by ablative case)* whatever kind of, whichever kind of, any kind of

çfarëdollojshëm *adj (i)* of any kind whatever, of any sort

çfarëdollojtë *adj (i)* = çfarëdollojshëm

çfarëdoshëm *adj (i)* **1** of any kind whatever, of any sort **2** ordinary, unnotable

çfarësi *nf (Book)* quality, essence

***çfaros** *(Reg)* = shfaros

***çfejo·het** OR **çfejos·et** *vpr* to break off one's engagement = shfejo·et

***çfejo·n** *vt* to cause/make [] break off []'s engagement = shfejo·n

çfëlliq· *vt (Colloq)* to disinfect

***çfoshk·** *vi* = zhvoshk·

çfrê(n) *nm (Reg Gheg)* snowdrift

***çfronëso·n** *vt (Reg)* to dethrone = shfronëso·n

çfryrë *nf* **1** explosion, outburst **2** nostril

çfryrje *nf* gust of wind

***çfrytës** OR **çfrytëz** *(Old)* = shfrytëz

***çfryto·n** *vt (Old)* = shfrytëzo·n

***çfuqizim** *nm ger* <çfuqizo·n, çfuqizo·het

***çfuqizo·n** *vt* **1** to weaken, sap, undermine **2** [*Law*] = shfuqizo·n

***çgjymtyrim** *nm ger* <çgjymtyro·n

***çgjymtyro·n** *vt* = zhgjymto·n

çhundorëzim *nm* [*Ling*] denasalization

çiban *nm* boil, furuncle

çibuk *nm* **1** pipe (for smoking tobacco); long-stemmed cigarette-holder **2** [*Agr*] stem cutting taken from a fruit tree for planting

çibukçi *nm* **1** *(Old)* person who makes and/or sells pipes **2** servant whose duty was to light his wealthy master's pipe **3** *(Fig Pej)* personal servant

çibukpunues *nm* pipemaker

çiçë *nf (Child)* peepee, number one (urine)

çiçëllo·het *vpr (Child)* to go peepee, pee, go tinkle: urinate

çiçërr *nf* sprout growing straight up out of a tree stump

çiçibanoz *nm* [*Bot*] **1** carob tree, carob, locust tree *(Ceratonia siliqua)* **2** carob bean, St. John's bread, locust bean

çiçibune *nf* = çiçibanoz

***çiçirrim** *nm ger* = cicërim

***çiçirritje** *nf ger* = cicërim

çiçkë *nf dimin* little bit; trifle

çiçok *nm* [*Bot*] groundnut pea vine *(Lathyrus tuberosus)*

çidikë *np* white-flannel trousers, wide at the top and narrow in the legs, and decorated with black ribbon down the sides; tight britches

çifçi *nm* [*Hist*] sharecropper on a baronial estate, tenant farmer

çiflig *nm (np ~ gje)* [*Hist*] **1** hereditary quasi-private estate in the later Ottoman Empire: baronial estate, manor; manor house, buildings, and surrounding land **2** *(Colloq)* field on a farm

çifligar
I § *n* [*Hist*] **1** land baron **2** *(Pej)* arrogant and ruthless profiteer
II § *adj* **1** of or pertaining to the manor system, manorial **2** *(Pej)* baronial, ruthlessly exploitative, arrogant

çifligaro-borgjez *adj* based on the dominance of the land barons and the bourgeoisie

çifligsahibi *nm (Old)* owner of large baronial estates

çiflik = çiflig

***çifliktar** = çifligar

çift
I § *adv* in two's, in groups of two; pairwise
II § *nm* **1** pair, couple **2** wedding couple; dance couple **3** breeding pair **4** *(Colloq)* one member of a matched pair: mate, twin
III § *adj* **1** composed of two identical units: twin, double, dual; having two parts: coupled, paired **2** [*Math*] evenly divisible by two: even **3** even-numbered
○ **çift e çift** in couples

çiftar *adj* **1** twinned, of a set of twins **2** having a breeding partner: mated

çiftas *adv* as a couple/pair/duo, two by two

çifte
I § *nf* **1** double-barreled gun **2** tweezers **3** pair of joined containers for ground coffee and sugar
II § *np* < çift pair of hinges

çifteli
I § *nf* two-stringed mandolin with a long neck
II § *adj (Colloq)* **1** double crowned, marked by two patches of different colored hair, piebald **2** *(Fig)* testy, cross, surly, short-tempered, irascible

çiftelist *n* two-stringed mandolinist

çiftësi *nf (Book)* binarity

çiftëz *nf* two garlands or ribbons on the head

çiftëzim *nm ger* = çiftim

çiftëzo·het *vpr* = çifto·het

çiftëzo·n *vt* = çifto·n

çiftim *nm ger* <çifto·n, çifto·het

çifto·het *vpr* to pair up; mate

çifto·n *vt* **1** to join [] together into a pair: pair, yoke [] together, match up **2** to couple [] for insemination: mate

çiftos· *vt.* to couple [] for insemination: mate

çiftos·et *vpr* to take a mate

çiftpendo're *adj* [*Bot*] paripinnate

çifu't
I § *nm* 1 Jew 2 (*Fig Colloq Pej*) miserly and selfish person *3 (*Old*) coward
II § *adj* Jewish

çifutëri *nf* (*Colloq*) Jewry

çifutërisht *adv* (*Colloq*) in Jewish fashion

*ç**ihu'r** *nm* [*Bot*] ox-tongue (*Picris*)

çik *nm* inflammatory word, cause of quarrel

çik·
I § *vt* 1 to touch [] lightly: tap, graze 2 (*Fig*) to touch lightly on [], mention [] briefly 3 to tease [] (with words), provoke
II § *vt* to separate/break [] into very small pieces: shred, mince, chop, grind, grate, crumble
III § *vi* 1 to make light contact 2 to drip, leak water

çik·et *vp recip* to come into light contact: touch (one another), bump; meet

çika *np* 1 <çikë 2 (*Reg*) kindling, tinder

çika-çika *adv* 1 in tiny pieces, into many pieces 2 little by little, one part at a time

Çika'go *nf* Chicago

çika'la'rmë *adj* dappled, spotted, dotted

çika'lo'r *adj* having spots on the face or body, dappled, freckled, mottled

*ç**ika'r** *nm* [*Entom*] great green bushcricket (*Tettigonia viridissima*)

çik'ash *adv* in tiny pieces, into many small pieces

çikë
I § *nf* 1 little bit 2 tiny spot, dot 3 girl 4 (*Fig*) the best part: cream, elite, pick, prime 5 inflammation of the eye, conjunctivitis 6 (*Reg*) spark 7 (*Reg*) drop of water falling from the roof; rain gutter; eaves of a roof 8 (*Reg*) [*Zool*] = xixëllo'një 9 [*Ornit*] chiffchaff *Phylloscopus collybita* 10 [*Ornit*] kinglet warbler *Phylloscopus proregulus*
II § *adv* into tiny pieces
III § *determiner* 1 outstanding (person), prince of a __ 2 (*Impol*) measly little bit of
∘ **ai/ajo/ky/kjo çikë** {*kinship term*} that/this wonderful {} **ky çikë vëlla** this wonderful brother
∘ **(një) çikë e nga një çikë** little by little
∘ **çikën e pikën** every single thing
∘ **çikë e vogël** [*Ornit*] goldcrest *Regulus regulus*

çik'ël *nf* 1 tiny piece broken/torn off of something solid: chip, crumb, splinter, sliver, bit, grain, scrap 2 tiny drop of liquid, droplet
∘ **çikël e pikël** (in/into) little fragments

çik'ëllim *nm ger* <çikëlo'·n, çikëlo'·het

çik'ëllo'·het *vpr* to spray, sprinkle; splatter, spatter

çik'ëllo'·n
I § *vt* 1 to make small pieces out of []: mince, tear up, crush, grind up 2 to spray, sprinkle; spatter 3 (*Reg*) to light [a fire] with tinder
II § *vi* 1 to sprinkle lightly 2 to drip slightly, leak

çik'ëllo're *nf* 1 firefly = xixëllo'një 2 (*Fig*) flighty woman

çik'ërr
I § *nf* 1 tiny piece broken/torn off of something solid: chip, crumb, splinter, sliver, bit, scrap 2 tiny thing 3 thin stream of liquid moving with force: spurt, spout, jet; spring with water spurting out in a jet 4 spark
II § *determiner* (*Impol*) measly little bit of
III § *nm* = karkale'c

çik'ërra'n *nm* small spring with a thin jet of water

çik'ërri *np* trivia, trifles

çik'ërrima *np* 1 <çik'ërrimë 2 small inexpensive item in everyday household use: notions 3 trivial matters, trivia; bric-a-brac, trinkets

çik'ërrimë *nf* 1 small inexpensive item in everyday household use 2 (*Fig*) trifle, knickknack, trinket

çik'ërrimta'r *n* 1 (*Old*) notions merchant, peddler 2 (*Fig*) person who gets involved with trivia

çik'ërro'·n
I § *vi* 1 to drip; sprinkle 2 to give off sparks
II § *vt* 1 to spray, spatter *2 (*Reg Gheg*) to whisk, beat [eggs]

çik'et *adj* (*i*) tiny

çik'ëto'·n *vt* to divide [] into many tiny pieces; grind; tear into shreds

çik'eve're *nf* [*Entom*] (*Reg*) firefly = xixëllo'një

çik'ëz *nf* 1 double-handled net used for fishing in narrows; square net, attached at the corners by two wooden bows, used for river fishing 2 white discharge that appears in a diseased eye; conjunctivitis 3 (*Dimin*) <çikë

çik'je *nf ger* <çik, çik·et

çik'la-mikla *np* (*Colloq*) 1 tiny bits and pieces, specks, grains, crumbs 2 (*Fig*) trivial matters, trivia

çik'lë *nf* [*Bot*] onosmodium (*Onosma*)

çik'list *n* 1 [*Sport*] cyclist, bicycle racer 2 (*Old*) bicycle repairman

çik'listik *adj* [*Sport*] of or pertaining to bicycle racing

çik'lizëm *nm* [*Sport*] bicycle racing

*ç**ik'lo're** *nf* (*Reg*) [*Entom*] firefly

çikma *nf* (*Old*) [*Archit*] fortified bay with embrasures of a highlander's house: battlement parapet

çik'o'·het *vpr* to spray, sprinkle; splatter, spatter

çik'o'·n
I § *vt* to spray; spatter
II § *vi* to drip slightly, leak; drip with moisture, be very damp; sprinkle

çik'o're *nf* chicory = radhi'qe

çikrik *nm* 1 winding reel; winch, windlass, capstan 2 water wheel; turbine 3 small spool (of thread)

*ç**ik'shëm** *adj* (*i*) touchable, tangible

*ç**ik'to'·n** *vt* to dissect

çiku'l *nm* snowshoes woven out of willow withes

çil
I § *adj* 1 having a gray coat of hair 2 white-haired; gray-haired, grizzled 3 made of gray wool; gray in color
II § *vt* * = cël·

çil·et *vpr* to lose its color: fade, grow gray with age

çila'k *adj* 1 having a gray coat of hair 2 white-haired; gray-haired, grizzled

çila'sh *adj* white-haired, gray-haired

çila't·et *vpr* (of a tight cover) to start to come loose, loosen up

çile *nf* 1 gray hair 2 cloak of gray goat-hair 3 skein of yarn

*Ç**ile** *nf* (*Old*) Chile

çile'k *nm* [*Bot*] wild strawberry (*Fragaria vesca*)

*ç**il'ë** *adj* (*i*) 1 = çe'lur 2 (of horses) gray-brown

çilili'ngë *nf* [*Ornit*] = çirpu'pe

çilimi *nm* (*Colloq*) 1 kid, child 2 (*Fig*) childish/immature person

çilimi·llëk *nm (np ˉ qe) (Colloq)* **1** immaturity, childishness **2** *(Pej)* childish characteristic or behavior: prank

çíl·tas *adv* **1** out in the open, openly **2** = **çiltërísht**

çíltazi *adv* = **çíltas**

çíltër *adj (i)* straightforward, frank; sincere, honest

çíltërí *nf* straightforwardness, frankness; sincerity, honesty

çíltërísht *adv* straightforwardly, frankly; sincerely, honestly

çíltërsí *nf* = **çiltëri**

çíltërsísht *adv* = **çiltërísht**

çíl·ur *adj (i)* **1** bleached, whitened **2** hoary, grizzled

*****çill** *nm* roan horse

çimbo·skë *nf* **1** long woolen band (used to secure baby in a cradle) **2** *[Ornit]* coot *(Fulica atra)*

çimçakíz *nm* **1** rosin **2** = **çamçakëz**

çimentím *nm ger* < **çimento·n**, **çimento·het**

çime·nto *nf* **1** *[Constr]* cement, concrete **2** *(Fig)* strong and permanent binding agent **3** *[Anat]* tooth enamel

çimento·het *vpr* *[Geol]* to become cemented into an aggregate of particles of clastic rock

çimento·n *vt* **1** to put a concrete surface on []; cover [] with concrete, pour cement on [] **2** *[Tech]* to reinforce [] with concrete **3** *(Fig)* to set [] in concrete, make [] permanent, cement; strengthen **4** *[Tech]* to harden [steel] (by high-temperature treatment with carbon): carburize

çimentue·s *nm* cement-worker

çímërr *nf* *(Reg)* *[Entom]* = **çimkë, tartabíqe**
○ **çimërr druri** *[Invert]* forest bug *(Pentatoma rufipes)*

*****çimín** *nm* = **çimnon**

çímkë *nf [Entom]* **1** bug **2** bedbug *Cimex lectularius* = **tartabíqe 3** *[Entom]* alfalfa plant bug *Adelphocoris lineolatus* **4** *[Entom]* general designation for small parasitic insects that infest fruit and grains *Eurygaster; Aelia* **5** *[Bot]* common jujube *Ziziphus jujuba*
○ **çimkë bimësh** *[Invert]* shield bug, stink bug *Pentatomidae*
○ **çimka e dardhës** *[Entom]* lace bug *Stephanitis pyri Geoff.*
○ **çimka e drithërave** "grain bug" *[Entom]* *Eurygaster; Aelia*
○ **çimka e fikut** *[Entom]* fig psyllid *Homotoma ficus*
○ **çimka e frutave** *[Entom]* sloe bug *Dolycoris baccarum*
○ **çimka e fushave** "leafhopper of the fields" *[Entom]* *Lagus pratensis*
○ **çimka e gjelbër** *[Entom]* green soldier bug *Palomena viridissima*
○ **çimka e lakrës** "cabbage bug" *[Entom]* *Eurydema ornata*
○ **çimka e mollës** *[Entom]* apple sucker *Psylla mali Schmb.*
○ **çimkë uji** *[Invert]* water boatman, boat bug *Coroxidae*

*****çinaçínë** *nf* quinine

çina·r *nm* *[Bot]* = **rrap**

*****çínas** OR **çíne·z** *adj, n (Old)* Chinese = **kíne·z**

çinërr *nf* *[Ornit]* marsh tit *(Parus palustris)*

çinge·l *nm* = **çenge·l**

çinge·rre *np* corn roots that emerge above ground

*****çíngo** *nf (Colloq)* zinc

çíng·të *adj (i)* of zinc

çiní *nf* **1** *(Colloq)* dish, plate **2** water pitcher *****3** china, crockery

çíno·n *vt* **1** to imitate, copy, mimic **2** *(Pej)* to mock [] by mimicking

çintegrím *nm ger* **1** *(Book)* < **çintegro·n**, **çintegro·het 2** disintegration

çintegro·het *vpr* *(Book)* to fall into separate parts: disintegrate, dissolve; come apart

çintegro·n *vt* *(Book)* to take [] apart, disassemble; break apart [an integrated whole]: dissolve

çinteresím *nm ger* **1** < **çintereso·het 2** absence of interest and concern; coolness of attitude

çintereso·het *vpr* to lose interest and concern

çinteresua·r *adj (i)* **1** uninterested **2** disinterested, not based on personal profit or self-interest

çip

I § *nm* **1** piece located at the extreme limit: corner, edge, tip, extreme end **2** place far off the beaten track, far-away corner **3** *(Colloq)* *[Geog]* small strip of land with a narrow tip jutting into the sea: cape, promontory

II § *adv* with the tip bent upwards
○ **çip më çip 1** in every part, from one to another, everywhere **2** completely full, up to the brim

*****çipa·r** *nm* sleuth

çipëro·n *vt* to prick up [one's ears]

çip·ës *adj, nm* (variety of fig) with long fruit tapering to a point

*****Çípro** *nf (obl ˉ ua) (Old)* Cyprus

*****çipull** *nm (np ˉ j) (Colloq)* inflamed sore

*****çír·et** *(Reg)* = **çírr·et**

çira·k *nm* **1** apprentice; shopkeeper's apprentice **2** *(Fig Contempt)* lackey, blind follower **3** lamp, candle **4** candle-holder, torch-holder

çira·kë *np* **1** < **çira·k 2** fireplace trivet composed of three rocks or tiles

*****çiriljan** *adj (Old)* Cyrillic

*****çirísh** *(Reg)* = **qíríç**

çírr·et *vpr* < **çjerr· 1** (said of clothes) to get ripped, get torn; get snagged **2** to get scratched (by something sharp) **3** *(Fig)* to scream, scream out **4** *(Fig)* to yell, yell at; screech; scold **5** to get hoarse from yelling **6** *(Fig)* to feel/be subjected to piercing pain **7** *(Fig)* to go back on, renege on an agreement **8** *(Reg)* to spring a leak
○ **çírr·et e nduk·et** to scream and carry on (in order to attract attention)
○ **çírr·et në kupë të qiellit** "scream to the dome of the sky" to yell at the top of one's voice; cry out to the high heavens
○ **çírr·et në të gjitha udhëkryqet** to make a hullabaloo so that the whole world knows about it; let the whole world in on it

çirr *stem for 2nd pl pres, pind, imper, vp* < **çjerr·**

çírr·ës *adj* = **çjerrës**

çírrma *np* < **çírrmë** shrill threats/insults

çírrmë *nf* loud scream, shrill yell

çit *interj* **1** (addressed to an animal) shoo, scram *****2** = **cíte·r**

çita·r *nm* narrow casting mold used by goldsmiths

çitja·ne *np (Old)* billowing pantaloons that narrow at the ankles

*****çive·të** *nf [Zool]* civet cat

çiví *nf* hingepin; hinge

çivít *nm* indigo, indigo blue

çízel *nm* [*Agr*] tractor drawn chisel: subsoiler

çízme *nf* **1** boot, high shoe **2** (*Fig*) cruel oppression, foreign yoke
   ○ **kusar/hajdut me çizme** gentleman thief

çizme|bër|ës *nm* bootmaker

çjerr·
   I § *vt* **1** to rip, tear **2** to scratch **3** (*Fig*) to go back on [], renege on [an agreement] **4** (*Fig*) to rip off [a mask] **5** (*Fig*) to cause/subject [] to piercing pain **6** (*Euph*) to castrate **7** (*Reg*) to make a hole in [a cooking vessel]
   II § *vi* to feel a piercing pain
   ○ **<>a çjerr· cipën** to help <> get over <>'s shyness
   ○ [] **çjerr· ku s'arnohet** to damage [] beyond repair
   ○ **<>i çjerr· veshët** to annoy/bother <> by saying something unpleasant
   ○ **<> çjerr· zemrën** to break <>'s heart
   ○ **çjerr· zërin** to scream to the point of hoarseness, screech

çje·rrë
   I § *part* <**çjerr·**
   II § *adj* (*i*) **1** torn, ripped, lacerated **2** scratched **3** screaming; screeching, shrill **4** (*Euph*) castrated **5** (*Reg*) having holes, perforated, leaking
   III § *nf (e)* **1** gash, rip, tear **2** scratch **3** (*Fig*) screech, shrill voice **4** scream

çje·rr|ës *adj* shrill

çje·rr|je *nf ger* <**çjerr·**, **çirr·**et

çje·rr|më *nf* opening created by forcible/violent action: rip, tear, hole, gash, gap

çka
   I § *interrog pron* what
   II § *conj* **1** who, which, that **2** that which, (he/she) who
   III § *adv (Colloq)* so-so, neither well nor badly
   IV § *pcl* indicates equanimity: it's OK, it doesn't matter, what's the difference

*ç**ka·fët** *adj* (*i*) = shka·thët

çkal|ís *stem for 1st sg pres, pl pres, 2nd & 3rd sg subj, pind* <**çkalí·**

çkalí·t *vt* **1** to cultivate [soil] with a short hoe **2** to soothe by rubbing []'s head; fondle

çkal|ít|ar *adj, n* pampered/spoiled (one)

çkal|ít|je *nf ger* <**çkalí·**

çkal|ít|ur *adj* (*i*) foolish, childish; spoiled

*ç**kall|m** (*Reg*) = shkall|m

*ç**kall|** (*Reg*) = shkall|

*ç**kallú|a** *nm* (*obl ̃ói, np ̃ónj*) graft, shoot

*ç**kano·s·** = kano·s·

*ç**kapërxí|m** = shkapërcí|m

*ç**kark|** (*Reg*) = shkark|

*ç**katërr|aq** (*Reg*) = shkatarra|q

*ç**katërr|** (*Reg*) = shkatërr|

*ç**këlq|** (*Reg*) = shkëlq|

*ç**këmb|** (*Reg*) = shkëmb|

*ç**kënaqsí** *nf (Old)* = pakënaqësí

*ç**këpus|** (*Reg*) = shkëpus|

*ç**këput|** (*Reg*) = shkëput|

*ç**kërfí|t** (*Reg*) = skërfí|t

*ç**kilifí** *nf* [*Ornit*] goldfinch (*Carduelis carduelis*)

*ç**kishë|r** (*Reg*) = shkishë|r

*ç**komb|ëtariz|** (*Reg*) = shkomb|ëtariz|

*ç**komb|sí|m** = shkombëtarizí|m

*ç**komb|só·n** = shkombëtarizo·n

*ç**kops|ís** *stem for 1st sg pres, pl pres, 2nd & 3rd sg subj, imperf* <**çkopsí·t**

*ç**kopsí·t·** (*Reg*) = shkopsí·t·

*ç**koq|** (*Reg*) = shkoq|

*ç**kreh|** (*Reg*) = shkreh|

*ç**krep|ët** (*Reg*) = shkrept|

*ç**krep|** (*Reg*) = shkrep|

*ç**krí·n** (*Reg*) = shkrí·n

*ç**krídh|** (*Reg*) = shkrídh|

*ç**kríf|** (*Reg*) = shkrif|

*ç**krift|** (*Reg*) = shkrift|

*ç**krimb·** *OR* **çkrymp·** (*Reg*) = shkrimb·

*ç**krí|r** (*Reg*) = shkrí|r

*ç**krí|shë|m** *adj* (*i*) (*Reg*) = shkrí|shë|m

*ç**kujde|s** (*Reg*) = shkujde|s

*ç**kul·** (*Reg*) = shkul·

*ç**kundërm|o·n** (*Reg*) = shkundërm|o·n

*ç**kurdí·s·** (*Reg*) = shkurdí·s·

*ç**kuror|ëz** (*Reg*) = shkuror|ëz

*ç**kyç·** (*Reg*) = shkyç·

*ç**lëvor|o·n** *vt* to remove the outer covering of [something]: peel, husk, shell

çlidh· *vt* to untie, undo, unfasten; disconnect; unleash; open up

çlídh·et *vpr* <**çlidh·** = zgjídh·et

çlírë *adj* (*i*) = çlírët

çlírët
   I § *adj* (*i*) **1** tied/bound loosely; hanging loose, loose **2** without constraint, unrestrained; loose and relaxed, unforced **3** (*Fig*) natural and uninhibited in behavior
   II § *adv* **1** loosely, unconstrainedly **2** in a relaxed manner **3** (*Fig*) uninhibitedly, naturally

çlirím *nm ger* **1** <**çliro·n, çliro·het 2** liberation

Çlirím *nm* Çlirim (male name)

çlirimta·r
   I § *n* (*Elev*) emancipator
   II § *adj* liberating

çliro·het *vpr* **1** to gain liberty **2** to gain release, escape **3** to be relieved of something tight **4** [*Fin*] to be made available for other purposes, be released

çliro·n
   I § *vt* **1** to set [] free: liberate, free, emancipate **2** to release; unleash **3** to unloose [something tight]: loosen, undo, take off [] **4** [*Chem Phys*] to give off []: emit
   II § *vi* (said of a festering sore with pus) to burst

çliru|ar *adj* (*i*) **1** liberated, freed **2** relieved of something burdensome **3** loosened, undone, released **4** out of joint **5** [*Chem Phys*] emitted, given off, released **6** [*Fin*] available for other purposes, released

çliru|es
   I § *adj* liberating = çlirimta·r
   II § *n* liberator

çlodh· *vt* to relieve [] of fatigue: rest, refresh, revive
   ○ **çlodh· trutë** to rest one's mind

çlódh·et *vpr* **1** to rest, be refreshed, revive, become reinvigorated, feel rested, regain energy, relax **2** to spend one's vacation (somewhere), take a vacation **3** (*Book*) to gain repose, come to permanent rest (die)

çlódh|ës *adj* restful, refreshing, relaxing

çlódh|je *nf ger* **1** <**çlodh·, çlódh·et 2** rest, recreation

çlódh|ur *adj* (*i*) rested, refreshed

çlul|ëzí|m *nm* **1** <**çlulëzo·n 2** defloration

çlul|ëzo·n *vt* to deflower

çluspïm *nm* [*Med*]peeling

çlyrësïm *nm ger* <çlyrëso·n, çlyrëso·het

çlyrëso·het *vpr* to become free of grease/fat, get clean

çlyrëso·n *vt* to clean away grease from [], remove fat from [], cleanse

çlyrësues *adj* detergent

çlyros· *vt* = çlyrëso·n

çlyros·et *vpr* = çlyrëso·het

çmagnetizïm *nm ger* **1** <çmagnetizo·n, çmagnetizo·het **2** demagnetization

çmagnetizo·het *vpr* to lose magnetic quality

çmagnetizo·n *vt* to demagnetize

çmagjeps· *vt* to release [] from a spell

çmagjeps·et *vpr* to wake out of a magic spell

çmah·et *vpr* to live carefree, not worry about anything

çmall· *vt* to satisfy []'s nostalgia/longing; cheer [] up

çmall·et *vpr* to satisfy nostalgic feelings; give vent to one's feelings; catch up for time lost (with those one has missed); exchange reminiscences

*****çmarko·n** *vt* [*Sport*]to stop covering/guarding [an opponent]: stop marking []

çmarto·het *vpr* to get divorced

çmas *stem for 1st sg pres, pl pres, 2nd & 3rd sg subj, pind* <çmat·

çmashkullïm *nm ger* **1** <çmashkullo·n **2** emasculation

çmashkullo·n *vt* to emasculate

çmat· *vt (Colloq)*

çmat·et *vpr* (*Colloq*) to be irresolute: vacillate, shilly-shally

çmaterializo·het *vpr (Book)* to dematerialize

çmbështïll·et *vpr* <çmbësht*je* II· **1** to become unwound: unwind, uncurl, unroll, unfurl **2** to take off one's clothes, undress; become unwrapped, be revealed, be discovered

○ **po <> çmbështill·***et*[3sg] **lëmshi** "<>'s ball of yarn *is unravelling*" <> *is nearing death*

çmbështje II· *vt* **1** to unwind [], straighten [] out, roll [] out: uncurl, unroll, unfurl **2** to unwrap, uncover; discover, reveal, unclothe

çmbështjellje *nf ger* <çmbësht*je* II·, çmbësht*je* II·*et*

çmbështo II *stem for pdef* <çmbësht*je* II·

çmbledh· *vt* = çmbësht*je* II·

çmblidh *stem for 2nd pl pres, imper, pind, vp* <çmble dh·

çmblodh *stem for pdef* <çmble dh·

çmbreh· *vt* to unyoke [a draft animal]

çmbreh·et *vpr* <çmbreh·

çmbre hje *nf ger* <çmbreh·, çmbre·het

çmbush· *vt* to empty

çmek·et *vpr* to get very short of breath, feel very faint; practically faint, almost pass out

*****çmençuri** *nf* = çmenduri

çmend·

I § *vt* to drive [] crazy/mad; annoy greatly

II § *vi* (*Fig*) to be crazy about, be much attracted to, like very much

çmend·et *vpr* **1** to lose one's mind, go crazy **2** to act crazy, behaving wildly **3** (*Fig*) to feel extraordinary happiness, be crazy about; like/love beyond bounds, adore

çmendarak *adj (Colloq)* loony

çmend esï *nf(Old)* = çmenduri

çmendïnë *nf(Colloq)* **1** loony bin, psychiatric hospital **2** lunacy

çmendje *nf ger* <çmend·, çmend·*et*

çmendo·het *vpr*

çmendo·n *vt, vi*

*****çmendore** *nf(Old)* lunatic asylum, madhouse

çmendur

I § *adj (i)* **1** demented, crazy, mad, psychotic **2** crazy, unreasonable **3** (*Fig*) crazy, idiotic

II § *n (i)* person who has lost his mind: crazy person, lunatic, psychotic; idiot

çmenduri *nf* dementia, insanity, lunacy, craziness, madness

çmendurïsht *adv* madly, crazily, beyond reason

çmerïm *nm* something astonishing; horror; monster

çmerïs *stem for 1st sg pres, pl pres, 2nd & 3rd sg subj, pind* <merit·

çmerit· *vt* to astonish, astound, awe, amaze

çmerit·et *vpr* to be astonished, astounded, awed, amazed

*****çmerit ës** *adj* astonishing, amazing

çmeritje *nf ger* **1** <çmerit·, çmerit·*et* **2** amazement, astonishment

*****çmeritshëm** *adj (i)* = çmeritës

*****çmerïtun** *adj (i) (Reg Gheg)* astonished, amazed; bewildered, perplexed

*****çmers** = çmërs

çmese *nf(Old)* **1** = çmim **2** (*Fig*) evaluation

çmesëtar *nm [Hist]* **1** reckoner of damages, person who judged the value of a damage **2** estimator = çmues

çmërs *nm* **1** porous limestone **2** calcification left in a vessel by boiling water **3** calcified deposit on teeth; calcification **4** incrustation **5** moss; residual layer left by decaying moss **6** (*Reg*) pus that forms in a wound

*****çmërsïrë** *nf* porosity

çmërstë *adj (i)* **1** made of porous limestone **2** covered with moss, mossy

çmërzïs *stem for 1st sg pres, pl pres, 2nd & 3rd sg subj, pind* <mërzit·

çmërzit· *vt* to relieve [] of boredom, amuse, distract

çmërzit·et *vpr* to entertain oneself, kill time, distract oneself

çmësïm *nm ger* <çmëso·n, çmëso·het

çmëso·het *vpr* to discontinue a customary usage, wean oneself of a habit, give up something one is used to

çmëso·n *vt* to break off [a habit], cast off [a custom], give up [something one is used to], discontinue

çmësy sh· *vt* to rid [] of the evil eye: break the jinx on [], release [] from a curse

*****çmëz** = çmërs

çmilitarizïm *nm ger* **1** <çmilitarizo·n, çmilitarizo·het **2** demilitarization

çmilitarizo·n *vt* to demilitarize

çmilitarizuar *adj (i)* demilitarized

*****çmilo·n** *vt* to carve, sculpt

çmïm *nm ger* **1** <çmo·n, çmo·het **2** evaluation, value; estimation, esteem, rating **3** [*Econ*] price, value **4** cost, expense, amount to be paid, charge **5** prize, award

○ **çmime të prera** fixed prices

çmimtar *nm* assessor, evaluator

çmimzïm *nm ger* <çmimzo·n

çmim**zo**·*n vt* to set a price on []; assess, evaluate

çmin**im** *nm ger* <çmino·*n*, çmino·*het*

çmin**o**·*n vt* to clear [] of mines (explosives), remove mines from [], minesweep

çmir**ëzo**·*het vpr* to deteriorate in health; waste away, become emaciated

çml**o**·*n vt* 1 to appraise, evaluate 2 to value, appreciate

çmobiliz**im** *nm ger* 1 <çmobilizo·*n*, çmobilizo·*het* 2 demobilization 3 *(Fig)* loss of energy and enthusiasm, demoralization

çmobiliz**o**·*het vpr* to give up trying

çmobiliz**o**·*n vt* 1 to release [] from military service: demobilize 2 *(Fig)* to relax [efforts]

çmobiliz**u**a**r** *adj* 1 [Mil] demobilized, released from military service 2 *(Fig)* having lost the spirit, will, and power to carry something through: impotent and dispirited

çmobiliz**ue**|s *adj* dispiriting, immobilizing

çmont**im** *nm ger* [Tech] <çmonto·*n*, çmonto·*het*

çmont**o**·*n vt* [Tech] to dismantle, take apart, disassemble, dismount

çmorr**is** *stem for 1st sg pres, pl pres, 2nd & 3rd sg subj, imperf* <çmorrit·

çmorr**it**· *vt* 1 to delouse 2 *(Fig)* to scratch lightly, itch; prick lightly

çmorr**it**·*et vpr* to delouse oneself, pick off lice

çmorr**it**je *nf ger* <çmorrit·, çmorrit·*et*

çmos
  I § *determiner (Colloq)* every possible
  II § *pron (Colloq)* everything possible, everything
  ○ çmos kurrë as at no other time, as never before

çmos**ku**|shi *pron* just anybody

çmpi·*et vpr* = shpi·*het*

çmpi·*n vt* = shpi·*n*

çmpleks· *vt* to untwine, unbraid; disentangle, untwist

çmpreh· *vt* to blunt, dull

çmpre**hje** *nf ger* <çmpreh·, çmpri·*het*

çmpri**h**·*et vpr* 1 to lose sharpness, become blunt/dull 2 to lose its cutting edge, weaken in acuity/tension 3 *(Fig)* to lose interest in, withdraw from something previously desired

çmu**a**r *adj (i)* 1 highly valued, of high value, expensive, valuable 2 precious 3 = çmueshëm

çmu**a**rje *nf ger* <çmo·*n*, çmo·*het*

çmu**e**|s *nm* 1 price estimator: appraiser; damage evaluator 2 *(Old)* = çmesëtar 3 *(Fig)* person who highly appreciates the worth of something: connoisseur

çmu**eshëm** *adj (i)* 1 important, highly esteemed, valuable 2 = çmuar

çmund**o**·*n vt* to cause [] constant suffering, keep punishing [], keep bothering []

çnatyr**im** *nm ger* [Spec] <çnatyro·*n*, çnatyro·*het*

çnatyr**o**·*het vpr* 1 [Spec] to lose natural characteristics; become denatured 2 *(Fig Book)* to lose good, natural characteristics: become deformed/distorted

çnatyr**o**·*n vt* 1 [Spec] to cause to lose natural characteristics, denature 2 *(Fig Book)* to cause the loss of good, natural characteristics: deform, distort

çnatyr**u**a**r** *adj (i)* 1 [Spec] denatured 2 *(Fig Book)* having lost good, natural characteristics: deformed, distorted, unnatural

çnder**im** *nm ger* <çndero·*n*, çndero·*het*

çnder**o**·*het vpr* to lose one's honor, lose face, lose one's good name

çnder**o**·*n vt* 1 to dishonor, bring shame upon [], stain the honor of [], blemish []'s reputation; insult, humiliate 2 to rape

çnder**shëm** *adj (i)* dishonorable, disgraceful

çnder**u**a**r** *adj (i)* 1 dishonored, disgraced 2 raped, violated

çnder**ue**|s
  I § *adj* dishonoring, shameful
  II § *n* rapist

çndërr = shndërr|

çndjeshm**ërizim** *nm ger* [Cine] 1 <çndjeshmërizo·*n* 2 desensitization of photographic film

çndjeshm**ërizo**·*n vt* [Cine] to desensitize [film]

çndot· *vt* to cleanse [] of harmful impurities: decontaminate, purify

çndot**je** *nf ger* 1 <çndot· 2 decontamination, clean-up

*çndrint = shndrit·

çndryshk· *vt* 1 to remove the rust from [] 2 *(Fig)* to refresh, enliven, shake [] out of lethargy, restore []'s vitality/skill

çndryshk·*et vpr* 1 to be cleansed of rust 2 *(Fig)* to feel refreshed, liven up; snap out of lethargy, regain vitality and skill

çndryshk**je** *nf ger* <çndryshk·, çndryshk·*et*

çnduk· *vt* to keep pinching/nipping/nibbling/tugging/wrinkling []

çne *pcl (Colloq)* emphasizes surprise and disagreement at the implication of something just said: how can you say that!? come on now! you can't mean that! what are you talking about!
  ○ çne të {+ *verb*}^{subj} why should {}!?

*çnêjkë *nf (Reg Gheg)* fir-cone

*çnervos· *vt* to unnerve

*çnervos·*et vpr* to become unnerved

*çnervo**sje** *nf* hysteria

çngjis| *stem for 1st sg pres, pl pres, 2nd & 3rd sg subj, pind* <çngjit·

çngji**t**· *vt* to detach, unstick

çngji**t**·*et vpr* 1 to become detached, become unstuck, fall off, come off 2 *(Fig)* to leave someone, stop hanging around, stop hanging onto

çngji**t**je *nf ger* <çngjit·, çngjit·*et*

*çngjy·*n vt* = çngjyro·*n*

çngjyr**im** *nm ger* <çngjyro·*n*, çngjyro·*het*

çngjyr**o**·*het vpr* to lose color, fade

çngjyr**o**·*n vt* to cause [] to lose color, cause [] to fade: bleach, discolor

çngjyr**os**· *vt* = çngjyro·*n*

çngjyr**os**·*et vpr* = çngjyro·*het*

çngjyr**os**|ës *nm* = çngjyrue|s

çngjyr**os**je *nf ger* <çngjyro·*n*, çngjyro·*het*

çngjyr**os**ur *adj (i)* = çngjyruar

çngjyr**u**a**r** *adj (i)* faded, bleached, discolored

çngjyr**ue**|s *nm* bleach

çnuk *pcl (Colloq)* what all, anything whatever

çnjeh· *vt* [Law] to disavow [a relationship], disown; withdraw recognition of []

çnjerëz**im** *nm ger* 1 <çnjerëzo·*n*, çnjerëzo·*het* 2 inhumanity

çnjerëz**isht** *adv* inhumanely, barbarously

çnjerëzo·het *vpr* **1** to become dehumanized, lose human characteristics, turn into a beast **2** to become ferocious, become bestial

çnjerëzo·n *vt* to dehumanize: corrupt, spoil, deprave

çnjerëzor *adj* inhuman, cruel

çnjih *stem for 2nd pl pres, pind, imper, vp* <**çnjeh·**

çnjoh· *stem for 1st sg pres, pl pres, 2nd & 3rd sg subj, pind* [*Law*] <**çnjeh·**

çnjo·hje *nf ger* **1** [*Law*] <**çnjeh·** **2** disavowal

ço·het *vpr* <**ço·n** **1** to rise **2** to stand up; get to one's feet **3** to awake, get up **4** to lift (said of clouds), lift off, take off (said of airplanes) **5** *(Fig)* to rise up (politically); create an uprising **6** to arise; loom up **7** to be inseminated/impregnated

∘ **ço·het fluturimthi** to take off into the air: take off

∘ **ço·het gavole** to expand

∘ **ço·het me pupa** *(Colloq)* to hop along

∘ **ço·het peshë** to spring to one's feet, get up quickly; spring into action

∘ <> **ço·het**^{3sg} **pluhuri nga prapa** "<> *raises* dust in back" <> *is* talked about everywhere, <> *creates* a stir wherever <> *goes*

∘ **ço·het praf në këmbë** to spring to one's feet

∘ <> **ço·het**^{3sg} **të rëndët** <> *feels* like throwing up, <> *feels* like vomiting

ço·n

I § *vt* **1** to take [] somewhere, take [] along; deliver **2** to convey, carry **3** to send **4** to direct [] towards a target: cast, shoot **5** to lead **6** *(Fig)* to lead [] forward, help [] make progress, help [] to develop **7** to lead [] to a conclusion **8** to increase [an amount] **9** to spend/pass [a period of time], live **10** *(Colloq)* to last for [a certain time] **11** *(Colloq)* to manage to get [] down the throat: swallow **12** *(Colloq)* to drive [an animal/vehicle]

II § *vt* **1** to move [] to a higher physical or social position: raise, lift [] up **2** to raise/lift/bring [] to an erect position **3** to stimulate [] into activity: awaken, arouse; flush [prey] from a hiding place **4** to increase [] in amount/degree/force **5** to turn over [the soil], plow **6** *(Colloq)* to gather [] together, collect, raise [an army] **7** *(Colloq)* to move

∘ **ia ço·n** *(Colloq)* to get along, manage, make out

∘ [] **ço·n batbat** to put [] off until later

∘ [] **ço·n dëm** to damage [], ruin []

∘ <>**a ço·n dëshirën në vend** to fulfil <>'s wish, make <>'s wish come true

∘ **ço·n dollinë** to raise a glass in proposing a toast: propose a toast

∘ **ço·n dorë/dorën kundër** <> to raise one's hand against; take up battle against <>

∘ **ço·n dorën në silah** *(Old)* to get ready to draw one's weapon, put one's hand on one's holster

∘ **ço·n duart lart/përpjetë** to raise one's hands (in surrender), give up; give up (on a difficult task)

∘ **e ço·n fjalën për** [] to bring up the subject of []

∘ **ço·n gotën** to raise a glass in proposing a toast: propose a toast

∘ **nuk e ço·n më gjatë 1** not last much longer, be almost gone; not have long to live **2** not go on; go no further

∘ **ço·n gjurunti** to raise a hue and cry

∘ **ço·n hundën (përpjetë)** to get conceited

∘ **ço·n hundën** to keep sniffling

∘ **ço·n jetë** to live well

∘ **nuk ço·n kandar** to be of no value/importance, not matter, not count; have no effect on the outcome

∘ **i ço·n këmbët bigë** *(Crude)* to keel over and die, kick the bucket

∘ **ço·n kokë/krye 1** to rise up; revolt, rebel **2** to raise one's head: make an appearance

∘ **e ço·n kokën 1** to get better, improve in economic condition or health **2** to rise up; revolt, rebel

∘ **s'e ço·n kokën nga** {} to work on [] without stopping

∘ **ço·n kupën** to raise a glass in proposing a toast: propose a toast

∘ **Nuk ço·n lepur nga strofulla.** "{} can't even get a hare out of its hole" {} *can't* do anything right

∘ [] **ço·n lidhur** to conduct [] in handcuffs

∘ **e ço·n mendjen** "take one's mind" to focus one's mind, turn one's thoughts

∘ [] **ço·n më/në këmbë 1** to raise [a child] until [] can stand on []'s own two feet; help [someone ill] to recover, put [someone ill] back on []'s feet; put [] (back) into working order; get [a building] up **2** to get [] to stand up (in rebellion); get [] to become active **3** to get [] organized, arrange []

∘ [] **ço·n më andej** to take [] to a further/higher level

∘ <>**a ço·n muq** to get in <>'s way, hinder <>

∘ [] **ço·n në fluturim** to put [] into the air, take off in []

∘ [] **ço·n në litarë** to send [] to the gallows

∘ [] **ço·n në qiell** to praise [] to the skies; brag about []

∘ [] **ço·n në varr/dhé për së gjalli/të gjallë** "put [] in the grave alive: bury [] alive" to bring [] to an early grave

∘ **e ço·n në vend të vetën** to insist on having one's way, be stubborn about having one's own way

∘ [] **ço·n në vend** to comply with [], fulfil []

∘ **e ço·n në vend të** {timen/tënden/tonën/tuajën/tijën/sajën/tyren/vetën} to go {my/ your/ our/ your/ his/ her/ their, one's} own way, do {my/ your/ our/ your/ his/ her/ their, one's} own thing

∘ **Çon një pelë e ha një thelë.** "You bring a mare (as a gift) and get one slice of meat to eat." *(Prov)* You expect to get a lot (because it is so expensive), but you actually get very little.

∘ **ço·n peshë (mendjen/zemrën)** to lift (people's) spirits, be uplifting

∘ **ço·n peshë** to be influential, wield influence, carry weight

∘ **nuk ço·n peshë** to be of no value/importance, not matter, not count; have no effect on the outcome

∘ [] **ço·n peshë** to lift [] up

∘ [] **ço·n për veshi** "take [] by the ear" to drag [] kicking and screaming, pull [] by the ear

∘ **ço·n pluhur** to stir up dust

∘ **ço·n pluhur në llaç** "raise dust in mortar" to be/get involved in useless work, busy oneself in an impossible task

∘ [] **ço·n poshtë** to bring [] to a bad state; pull [] down

∘ **s'<> ço·n**^{3sg} **puna atje** there *is* nothing there of of interest to <>

∘ [] **ço·n**^{3sg} **rruga** "the road brings [] {somewhere}" chance *takes* [] {somewhere}, [] *happens* to be {somewhere}

∘ **ço·n supet 1** to shrug one's shoulders **2** to answer with a shrug of the shoulders: how should I know!?

∘ [] **ço·n syrgjyn** to send [] into exile

∘ **ço·n sytë** to cast an eye

∘ **ço·n shëndetin** to raise a glass in proposing a toast: propose a toast

∘ i **ço•**n **të gjithë të pinë ujë** "get everyone to drink water" to be cleverer than others

∘ e **ço•**n **trashë** to be economically well off

∘ **ço•**n **tryezën** to clear the table of food and dishes

∘ [] **ço•**n^{3sg} **udha** "the road brings [] {somewhere}" chance takes [] {somewhere}, [] happens to be {somewhere}

∘ **ço•**n **ujë në mullirin e <>** "carry water to <>'s mill" to be beneficial to <one's opponent>

∘ ta **ço•**n^{3sg} **ujët/ujin nën rrogoz/hasër/vete** "put water under your floor mat" to always be doing things behind your back

∘ **ço•**n **velat** to hoist the sails

∘ **ço•**n **veshët** to prick up one's ears, pay close attention

∘ <> **ço•**n^{3sg} **zemra avull** "<>'s heart steams up" <> has a longing/yearning

∘ **ço•**n **zërin (në qiell)** to raise one's voice (to the high heavens); make one's voice heard (all the way to the top)

çoba'n nDF person who tends livestock, herdsman: shepherd, cowherd, goatherd **1** (Colloq) Vlach **2** Vlach shepherd **3** (Reg) [Ornit] = **çafkëlore**

çoban'a'k nm = **stana'r**

çoban'ço adv (Colloq) **1** in shepherd-style = **çobani'sht 2** (Colloq) in the language of the Vlachs

çoba'n'e nf = **çobane'sh**ë

çoban'e'shë nf = **çoba'n** shepherdess

çoban'e'rï nf **1** (Collec) all the livestock herders; pastoral life **2** (Collec) Vlachs **3** livestock herding

çoban'ë'sï nf livestock herding

çoban'i'

I § nf the job/profession of herding livestock

II § nf collec the world of livestock herders, livestock herders; pastoral life

çoban'i'sht adv in the manner of shepherds

çoban'i'kë nf **1** = **çobane'sh**ë **2** (Reg) [Ornit] = **bish-tatu'ndës**

çoban'o•n vi **1** to tend livestock **2** (Fig) to wander around idly, hang around

****çobe'j** OR **çobâj** <**çobe'në**np <**çoba'n**

****çoben'e'rï** (Reg) = **çoban'e'rï**

çoç

I § pron (Colloq) a little something, something, a bit

II § pcl (Colloq) (introduces a sentence to express speaker's lack of certainty) apparently

ço'çër nf **1** [Ornit] = **cinxami' 2** (Fig) short person **3** (Colloq) = **kacami'c**

****çoçobanu'z**ë nf = **çiçibano'z**

∘ **Ço•**het^{3pl} **këmbët e i bie**$_1$•^{3pl} **kokës.** "The legs rise up and hit the head." The servant thinks he can get away with beating the master.

ço'je nf movement of livestock to summer pasture in the highlands; livestock so moved

****ço'jkë** nf queen bee at swarming time = **rro'jk**ë

çok nm **1** hammer for breaking rock: rock hammer **2** door knocker **3** bell clapper, tongue of a bell **4** part of a press that moves to hit the object: stamping part of a tobacco mill; pestle, pounder, hammer, mallet **5** protruding part of a bone joint; knuckle **6** beak **7** walnut-shaped stone used in children's game; cue ball (in billiards) **8** [Ornit] Scops owl Otus scops L. = **qok 9** [Entom] firefly ****10** fetter, shackle

∘ **çoku i bërrylit** tip of the elbow

∘ **çoku i dorës** hard upper part of the wrist

∘ **çoku i gishtit** knuckle

∘ **çoku i këmbës** ankle; hip bone

∘ **çoku i krahut** shoulder bone

çoka'le nf small and noisy bell worn by livestock

çoka'ne nf **1** small bell pressed in on two sides **2** door knocker

çokani•s•

I § vi **1** to chop up into small pieces: mince, dice, hash **2** (Fig) to hit hard; scold severely **3** to chisel stone with a rock hammer

II § vi to knock with a door knocker

çoka's stem for 1st sg pres, 1st & 3rd pl pres, 2nd & 3rd sg subj <**çoke't•**

çoket•

I § vi **1** to knock with a door knocker; knock at a door **2** vt **1** to knock, tap **2** to peck [] with a beak, peck at []

ço'kë nf **1** kitchen cleaver; butcher's cleaver **2** slight knock with a knuckle

ço'këz adv = **guraçokthi**

çoki's

I § stem for 1st sg pres, pl pres, 2nd & 3rd sg subj, pind <**çoki't**

II § stem for pl pres, 2nd & 3rd sg subj, pind <**çoke't•**

çoki't• vt, vi **1** = **çoke't• 2** to crack [], crack [] open

çoki't stem for pdef, opt, adm, part, pind, 2nd pl pres, imper, vp <**çoke't•**

çoki'tje nf ger **1** <**çoki't•**, **çoki't•**et **2** cracking sound

çoko'•n vi, vt **1** to hammer **2** to knock with the knuckles

çokolla'të

I § nf chocolate

II § adj chocolate-colored, dark reddish-brown

çoksidi'm nm ger <**çoksido'•**n

çoksido'•n vt [Tech] to remove rust from; remove layer of oxide from, deoxidize = **çndryshk•**

çoksidu'e's

I § adj [Tech] deoxidizing; rust-removing

II § nm deoxidizer; rust remover

****çokth** = **qokth**

ço'ku adv (Colloq) **1** somewhere, someplace **2** sometimes

ço'ku'sh pron (Colloq) somebody

çol nm **1** (Reg) muddy pond, mire; marsh **2** [Bot] marsh plant eaten by draft animals

****ço'le** nf [Ornit] shore lark (Eremophila alpestris) = **çerdhu'k**ël

****ço'lët** adj (i) marshy

çoma'ge OR **çoma'g**ë <**çoma'ng**ë nf = **çoma'ng**e

çoma'nge nf **1** club with a knob at one end: cudgel, drumstick (for beating a drum) **2** (Fig) oaf **3** (Old) mace **4** shepherd's staff

çomle'k nm [Food] stew made of meat, onions, garlic, spices, and a little vinegar

****ço'nge** nf small lump; pimple

****ço'nje's**

I § adj sending, transmitting

II § n commander

çopa'rka np odds and ends, household junk, miscellaneous household stuff

****çops** nm [Bot] Macedonian oak (Quercus trojana)

ço'qe np <**çok**

ço'r stem for pdef <**çjerr•**

çora'p *nm* **1** stocking, sock **2** foreleg (of a domestic animal) with hair of a different color than the rest of the leg
  ○ **çorapë të shkurtër** socks

çorap·ebër·ese *nf* = **çorapepunu·ese**

çorap·epun·ues·e *nf* **1** female operator of a machine for knitting stockings **2** *(Old)* woman who knits and sells stockings

çorap·to·re *nf* = **çorapebërëse**

çorb·ë *nf* **1** soup made with innards and thickened with rice or noodles **2** sourdough mixed with yogurt or milk, dried in the sun, and then crumbled into small pieces; porridge **3** vegetable soup **4** *(Fig Pej)* disorderly and tasteless mixture; confused mélange, big mess
  ○ **çorbë derri** "pig's porridge" **1** bad food **2** disorderly and displeasing mixture, unbearable mess

****çorco'r** *nf* [*Ornit*] wren (*Troglodytes troglodyte*) = çerr

çorganizi'm *nm ger* <**çorganizo'·n**

çorganizo'·het *vpr* to become disorganized/disordered

çorganizo'·n *vt* **1** to disorganize **2** to disorder

çorganizu'ar *adj (i)* **1** disorganized **2** disordered

çorganizu'es *adj* **1** disorganizing **2** creating disorder

çorientim *nm ger* **1** <**çoriento'·n**, **çoriento'·het 2** misdirection; disorientation

çoriento'·het *vpr* **1** to be misled, be misdirected **2** *(Fig)* to be disoriented, get lost

çoriento'·n *vt* **1** to mislead, misdirect **2** *(Fig)* to disorient

çorientu'ar *adj (i)* **1** misled, misdirected **2** *(Fig)* disoriented, lost

çorientu'es *adj* **1** misleading **2** *(Fig)* disorienting

çorodi' *nf* degeneracy; confusion, bewilderment

çorodi's *stem for 1st sg pres, pl pres, 2nd & 3rd sg subj, pind* <**çorodi't·**

çorodi't· *vt* **1** to impair [] in basic character, cause [] to become degenerate: pervert, deprave, corrupt, vitiate **2** to confuse, disconcert

çorodi't·et *vpr* **1** to lose inherent good qualities: degenerate **2** to lose all sense of direction, become confused/perverted

çorodi't·ës *adj* **1** degenerative, corrupting **2** disconcerting, confusing

çorodi'tje *nf ger* **1** <**çorodi't·**, **çorodi't·et 2** [*Med*] perversion

çorodi'tur *adj (i)* **1** perverted, degenerate, corrupt **2** disconcerted, confused

****çorodhu'kull** *nf* [*Ornit*] shore lark (*Eremophila alpestris*)

çorovo'das
  I § adj of or pertaining to Çorovoda
  II § n native of Çorovoda

Çorovo'dë *nf* industrial town erected in south-central Albania: Çorovoda

****çort** = **qort**

****çorv**ë = **çorb**ë

****çorre** *nf* club

ço'sa *quant (Colloq)* several

****çote'l**ë *nf* grindstone

ço'të *nf* **1** [*Ornit*] = **grifsh**ë **2** [*Ornit*] female of the Scops owl **3** *(Fig)* silly girl or woman who is constantly bickering with others

○ **ësh·të çotë nga goja** to have a sharp tongue

****ço'tër** = **çutërr**

çoti'llë *nf* plunger on a butter churn

****çpabe's·et** *(Reg)* = **shpabes·et**

****çpalo's·** *(Reg)* = **shpalos·**

****çpall** *(Reg)* = **shpall**

****çpengo'·n** *(Reg)* = **shpengo'·n**

****çpengu'ar** *adj (i) (Reg)* = **shpengu'ar**

****çpenko'·n** *(Reg)* = **shpenko'·n**

****çpërbl** *(Reg)* = **shpërbl**

****çpërfi'llje** = **shpërfi'llje**

****çpërka's** *(Reg)* = **spërka's**

****çpërka't·** *OR* **çpërk·et·** *(Reg)* = **spërka't·**

çpështi'll = **çmbështi'll**

çpështje'll· = **çmbështje'll·**

çpështo'll = **çmbështo'll**

****çpi'·het** *(Reg)* = **shpi·het**

****çpif** *(Reg)* = **shpif**

****çpik** *(Reg)* = **shpik**

****çpim** *(Reg)* = **shpim**

****çpla·n** *(Reg)* = **shpla·n**

****çpo'·n** *(Reg)* = **shpo'·n**

****çpo'nj**ës
  I § nm = **shpu'es·e**
  II § adj = **shpu'es**

****çporr·** *(Reg)* = **shporr·**

****çpra'llc**ë *nf* gossipy woman

****çpra'llis** *stem for 1st sg pres, pl pres, 2nd & 3rd sg subj, pind* <**çpra'llit·**

****çpra'lli't·** *vt* to defame, slander

****çpra'ps·et** = **spra'ps·et**

****çprofk**ë *nf* blockhead, imbecile

****çpro'n**ës *(Reg)* = **shpro'n**ës

****çpu'e** *(Reg Gheg)* = **çapu'a**

****çpyll'ëz** *(Reg)* = **shpyll'ëz**

çqendërsi'm *nm ger* **1** <**çqendërso'·n 2** decentralization

çqendërso'·n *vt* to decentralize

****çqep·** *(Reg)* = **shqep·**

****çqe's** *stem for 1st sg pres, 1st & 3rd pl pres, 2nd & 3rd sg subj* <**çqe't·**

****çqet·** *vt (Reg)* = **shqi't·**

****çqet'ësi** *nf* disquiet

****çqet'ëso'·n** = **shqet'ëso'·n**

****çqet'ës** *(Reg)* = **shqet'ës**

****çqet'ës'onjës** *adj* = **shqet'ës'ues**

****çqi's** *stem for pind, 2nd pl pres, imper* <**çqe't·**

****çqit** *stem for part, pdef, pind, 2nd pl pres, imper, vp (Reg)(Reg)* <**çqe't·**

****çqua'nj**ës
  I § adj (Old) = **shqu'es**
  II § nm comma

****çqua'njës'o'r** *adj (Old)* outstanding, distinguishing

****çqu'a** *(Old)* = **shqu'a**

****çqy'e·n** *(Reg)* = **shqy'e·n**

****çra'do'·n** *vt* to render invalid, annul

çradhi's *stem for 1st sg pres, pl pres, 2nd & 3rd sg subj, pind* [*Publ*] <**çradhi't·**

çradhi't· *vt* [*Publ*] to break up rows of type after printing

çradhi't·ës *nm* [*Publ*] person who breaks up rows of type after printing

çradhi'tje *nf ger* [*Publ*] <**çradhi't·**, **çradhi't·et**

çregjistrím *nm ger* <çregjistro'·n, çregjistro'·het

çregjistro'·het
  I § *vpr* to remove one's (own) name from the register/records
  II § *vpr* to go out of alignment

çregjistro'·n *vt* 1 to delete/strike [] from the register; erase [] from a recording 2 to remove [a name] from the rolls; expel [] from membership 3 to put [] out of alignment

çregjistru'a'r *adj (i)* 1 deleted from the register 2 out of alignment

*çrranjo's· *(Reg Gheg)* = çrrënjo's·

çrras· *vt* to loosen

çrra's·et *vpr* 1 to loosen up 2 (of a crowd) to disperse

çrra'së't *adj (i)* loose

çrregullím *nm ger* 1 <çrregullo'·n, çrregullo'·het 2 irregularity, disorder; disturbance; disruption

çrregullíme *np* <çrregullim public disturbances

çrregullo'·het *vpr* 1 to begin to work badly, get out of order, get out of kilter; become irregular 2 to get out of order, break down; become disordered, become chaotic

çrregullo'·n *vt* 1 to create disorder in [], move out of place: disturb, disarrange 2 to put [] out of working condition, break 3 to disrupt 4 [*Med*] to cause [] to break down

çrregullshëm *adj (i)* irregular; disorderly

çrregullt *adj (i)* 1 irregular, disarranged; in disarray, messy, disordered 2 irregular in shape, out of proportion 3 intermittent, irregular 4 against the rules, foul 5 disorderly

çrregullu'a'r *adj (i)* 1 out of kilter, beginning to work badly 2 not functioning properly: disturbed, irregular 3 [*Med*] abnormal

çrregullu'e's *adj* disruptive, disturbing

çrrethím *nm ger* <çrretho'·n, çrretho'·het

çrretho'·n *vt* to break through [a surrounding wall, an encirclement]; lift [a siege]; remove [encircling rings]

çrrënjím *nm ger* = çrrënjo'sje

çrrënjo'·n = çrrënjo's·

çrrënjo's· *vt* 1 to uproot 2 to eradicate, wipe out

çrrënjo'sje *nf ger* 1 <çrrënjo's·, çrrënjo's·et 2 eradication

*çrrod· = çorod·

*çrrodo'·n = çorodí't·

çrrotullo'·het *vpr* <çrrotullo'·n

çrrotullo'·n *vt* 1 to turn/roll [] in the opposite direction; turn [] back, reverse 2 to unroll, unfold

çrrudh· *vt* 1 to rid [] of wrinkles: unwrinkle, uncrease; smooth/iron [] out 2 to clear [one's tongue/mouth] of a bitter taste

çrru'dh·et *vpr* 1 to stop frowning, brighten up 2 to lose the bitter taste (in one's mouth)

*çtërví's *stem for 1st sg pres, pl pres, 2nd & 3rd sg subj, pind* <çtërví't·

*çtërví't· *vt* to free [] of a habit, disaccustom: wean []

*çtír·et *vpr* to disappear

*çtíto're *nf (Old)* school

*çtítra'k *adj (Old)* instructional

*çtitrím *nm ger (Old)* <çtitro'·n

*çtitro'·n *vt (Old)* to instruct, teach

*çtitu'er *nm (obl ˜ o'ri) (Old)* instructor, teacher

*çthur· *(Reg)* = shthur·

*çu·het = ço'·het

çu'a'r
  I § *adj (i)* 1 which has been cut, plowed 2 having reached an appropriate stage of development: ready to walk, ready to work
  II § *adv* 1 standing up, upright 2 awake, not asleep

çu'a'rje *nf ger* <ço'·n, ço'·het

çuba'rdh *adj* white-haired, albino

çu'be' *nf* 1 = kaçu'be' 2 tuft 3 *(Reg)* shock of corn

çub'ísht'e' *nf* underbrush

çuç *nm* chick
  ○ çuç gomari [*Ornit*] hawfinch *(Coccothraustes coccothraustes)*

*çu'çe' *nf (Colloq)* 1 little girl 2 vulva

çuçle·*n* = çuçlo'·n

çuçlím *nm ger* <çuçlo'·n

çuçlo'·n *vi* to gurgle softly, make a small rippling sound, whisper

*çuçll = çuçull

çuçullím *nm ger* <çuçullo'·n

*çuçullo'·n *vt* to warble, croon; murmur, lisp

*çuçu'm *nm [Bot]* nettle tree *(Celtis australis)* = cara'c

*çuçu'ra's = çuçuri's

çuçur·et = çuçurí't·

çuçurí·*n* *vi* = çuçurí't·

çuçurímë *nf ger* 1 <çuçuri·*n* 2 *(Pej)* gossip

çuçurí's *stem for 1st sg pres, pl pres, 2nd & 3rd sg subj, pind* <çuçurí't·

çuçurí't· *vi* 1 to speak in a low voice to someone near, whisper 2 <cicëro'·n 3 to emit a susurrant sound as from fire or flowing water

çuçurí'tje *nf ger* 1 <çuçurí't· 2 low murmur

çuçurja'r *n (Pej)* person who spreads rumors, gossip

çuda'n *adj* ugly

çu'de' *nf (Reg)* 1 = cudí 2 something that inspires fear and disgust
  ○ Të gjettë çuda! *(Curse)* May the worst evil find you!
  ○ ësh·të për çudë to be in a loathsome condition

çudí
  I § *nf* 1 surprise, amazement, astonishment 2 marvel, marvelous occurrence 3 wonder, marvel 4 *(Old)* miracle
  II § *interj* expresses amazement: I'm amazed
  ○ çudi e madhe! what a surprise! incredible!
  ○ (si) për çudi surprisingly
  ○ çudi si ... it's a wonder that ...

çudíbërës
  I § *adj* miracle-working, miraculous, magical
  II § *n* miracle worker

çudí's *stem for 1st sg pres, pl pres & 2nd & 3rd sg subj, pind* <çudít·

çudít· *vt* 1 to amaze, surprise 2 to strike awe in []: astound, astonish

çudít·et *vpr* 1 to be amazed, surprised; find strange 2 to be struck by awe, be astounded, be astonished

çudítëri *nf* amazing thing, wonder

çudítërísht *adv (Book)* 1 surprisingly, strangely, amazingly, miraculously 2 extraordinarily, very

çudítës *adj* 1 astonishing, surprising 2 [*Ling*] admirative

çudítje *nf ger* 1 <çudít·, çudít·et 2 amazement

*çudítní *nf (Reg Gheg)* = çudítëri

çud·it·shëm *adj (i)* **1** surprising, amazing **2** miraculous, wonderful; awesome **3** strange, odd, peculiar **4** extraordinary, very unusual

çud·it·ur *adj (i)* awe-stricken, amazed; surprised and somewhat dubious

***çud·na·r** *n* conjuror, magician

çud·o·n *vt* **1** to damage [] in exterior appearance: make [] ugly, deface, disfigure, deform **2** *(Fig Reg)* to rape

çu·es *nm* **1** sender **2** wooden beam that raises and lowers the upper millstone to regulate the fineness of the grind **3** person on a hunt who raises game from cover: beater

çu·es·e *nf* piece of wool used to pick up a hot baking pan

çu·e·shëm
  I § *adj (i)* transmissible
  II § *nn (të)* transmission

çu·fër *nf* **1** thicket, bush with clustered branches **2** cluster

***çu·fkë** *nf* = xhu·fke

çu·fr·aje *nf* underbrush, area with scrub undergrowth

çu·fr·a·k *adj* **1** tufted, in tufts **2** having thick and curly hair **3** short (in body), dwarfish

***çuhâ(n)** *nm (Reg Gheg)* wooden vessel for preparing/serving food or liquid

çuk *nm (Reg)* **1** = mëz **2** *[Ornit]* owl ***3** mop of hair, topknot ***4** hog

çuk· *vt* **1** to strike [] with a tool; poke, poke at [] **2** = çukit· **3** to try, try [out] **4** to waylay
  ○ **çuk· baltën** to prepare clay by pounding and mixing.
  ○ **çuk· gëlqeren** to prepare lime by pounding and mixing
  ○ **çuk· misrin** to beat the kernels off of dry ears of corn
  ○ [] **çuk· në kalli** to touch []'s most sensitive spot
  ○ **çuk· pemën** to shake fruit down with a pole

çuk·a·le *nf* bare top of a mountain or hill; small hill with a sharp peak

***çuk·a·s** *nm* *[Ornit]* woodpecker = qukapík

çu·k·et· = çukit·

çu·k·ë *nf* **1** high barren peak; mountain peak, hill top, summit **2** top of a tree or plant ***3** mound, hillock ***4** tuft; mons veneris ***5** lop-eared sheep
  ○ **çuka e misrit** corn tassel

çu·k·ë *nf (Reg)* = guraço·k

***çuk·ël·a·r** *nm* *[Ornit]* shore lark *(Eremophila alpestris)*

çukërm·ím *nm ger* **1** <çukërmo·•n **2** sound made by a hoofed animal pawing the ground

çukërm·o··n
  I § *vi* to stamp hooves/feet impatiently on the ground
  II § *vt* to paw/scratch at [the ground]

çu·k·ëz *nf (Reg)* filly = mëze

çuk·is *stem for 1st sg pres, pl pres, 2nd & 3rd sg subj, pind* <çukit·

çuk·it· *vt* **1** to peck, peck at [] **2** (of insects/snakes) to bite **3** to break up [soil] with a tool **4** to knock [] **5** to scratch; wound [] slightly, graze **6** *(Fig)* to scold [] lightly, criticize [] gently

çukit·et *vpr* to get scratched; get slightly wounded

çukit·je *nf ger* **1** <çukit·, çukit·et **2** sound of pecking, tapping sound **3** light scratch, slight wound

***çukurm·o·•n** *vt* to stamp on [], pound

***çule·shë** *nf* = qele·she

çu·lze *nf (Reg)* snout of the pig: snout

çull *nm* **1** coarse, often tasseled, thick blanket made of goat hair **2** thick woolen horseblanket **3** *(Pej)* filthy blanket/clothes **4** *(Old)* black wool rug laid out when someone dies

çulle *adj, nf* short-eared (ewe)

***çull·ufe** *OR* **çull·uf**e *nf* = cullu·fe

çu·mbër *nm* kettle spout

çume *nf* **1** pail, bucket **2** tub of lye used for soaking clothes

çun *nm* **1** *(Colloq)* boy, lad **2** *(Pet)* little boy, son, sonny boy **3** *(Old)* boy hired to help with various odd jobs **4** fishing boat
  ○ **çunat e malit** *(Pet)* partisans, patriotic guerrillas

çun·a·k *nm (Colloq)* **1** young boy, little boy, kid **2** *(Tease)* immature/inexperienced person who behaves childishly

çun·ëri *nf (Colloq)* **1** boyhood **2** boys taken collectively: the world of boys

***çungur·is** *stem for 1st sg pres, pl pres, 2nd & 3rd sg subj, pind* <çunguri·t·

***çungur·i·t·** *vt* **1** to couple, join, tie ***2** to clink, tap ***3** to open

çup *adj* **1** short-eared **2** hornless, without horns **3** with a tail or limb cut short: cropped, docked, bobbed **4** without awns or tassels

çup·ejke *nf* end of an ear of corn broken off to serve as fodder

çupe *nf* **1** girl, lass **2** *(Pet)* little girl, daughter **3** unmarried woman; maiden **4** queen (in a deck of playing cards)
  ○ **çup**e **e ftohtë** *(Colloq)* foster daughter

çup·ël·íne *nf (Colloq)* **1** young girl, little girl **2** *(Tease)* young and foolish girls

çup·ëri *nf* **1** girlhood, maidenhood **2** girls taken collectively: the world of girls

çup·ër·isht *adv (Colloq)* girlishly

çup·ëz *nf dimin* <çup·e

çup·is *stem for 1st sg pres, pl pres, 2nd & 3rd sg subj, pind* <çupit·

çup·it· *vt* to bite/snap at [], peck; nibble at [], eat away at []

çupit·je *nf ger* <çupit·

çu·pkë *nf dimin (Reg)* <çu·pe

***çup·lo·•n** *vt* **1** to bundle/heap [] up; bunch/crumple [] up **2** to pound, beat

çup·ul·íne
  I §
  II § *nf dimin* <çu·pe

***çupur·is** *stem for 1st sg pres, pl pres, 2nd & 3rd sg subj, pind* <çupuri·t·

***çupur·i·t·** *vt* to rummage around for [], search for []

***çur·a·k** *nm* = mburoje

çur·a·n *nm* turkey cock, tom turkey

***çur·a·p** *OR* **çure·p**e = çorap

***çur·ë** *nf [Ornit]* turkey hen

çur·g
  I § *nm (np ~ gje)* **1** trickle of water; stream **2** spring, rill
  II § *adv* spouting, in a jet, in a big stream

çurg·o·•n *vi* to spurt, flow profusely, pour out

çurk *adv* profusely, in a sudden stream

çurk·aje *nf* heavy stream; fast creek

çu'rkë *nf* 1 = çurg *2 *(Reg Tosk)* [*Ornit*] small lake-bird

çurlik|o' ·*n* *vi* to twirp, twitter

çurudhu'kull *nf* [*Ornit*] = çorodhu'kull

*çuruffit·*et* *vpr* (of birds) to mate

*çurukt|i's| *stem for 1st sg pres, pl pres, 2nd & 3rd sg subj, pind* <çurukti't·

*çurukti't· *vt* = çorodi't·

*çurre'l *OR* çurri'l = curri'l

*çu't·ë = çive't·ë

*çu't·ërr

  I § *nm* brook, stream

  II § *nf* wooden pot/flask; wine cask

*çutja'ne = çitja'ne

*çutr|o' ·*het* *vpr* = çudi't·et

*çvat· *(Reg)* = zhvat·

*ç|vend|o' ·*n* = zhvendo's·

*ç|veshk· *(Reg)* = zhvesh·

*ç|vërgjër = zhvirgjër|

*ç|vështj|e'll· = çmbështje'll·

*ç|vidh|o's· *(Reg)* = zhvidho's·

*ç|vill| *(Reg)* = zhvill|

*ç|vje'll· *vt* 1 = zhvje'll· 2 to disclose, reveal 3 to disgorge

*ç|vjerdh| = zvjerdh|

*ç|vle'ft|ës| *(Reg)* = zhvleft'ës|

*ç|volt|o' ·*n* *vt* to unbutton

*ç|voshk· *(Reg)* = zhvoshk·

ç|vul|o's· *(Reg)* = zhvulo's·

*çyç *adj* 1 huddled up; squatting; hunchbacked 2 snubnosed

*çyçebino's *nm* = çiçibano'z

çy'ç|ë *nf (Colloq)* 1 spout from which water flows or through which a liquid is poured = lëfy't 2 long and narrow front part; tip of the foot, shoe tip

*çyçybano'z *nm* = çiçibano'z

*çyla'f = qyla'f

*çyp = qyp

çy'r *nm* [*Mus*] *(Old)* type of mandolin with eight to twelve strings: oud, crwth

çyre'k *nm* round loaf of leavened wheat bread

çyre'q|e *np* <çyre'k

çyry'k *adj* 1 broken, damaged, spoiled, rotted; leaky 2 *(Colloq)* crippled; injured, diseased

çy'sht· *vt* to break [a spell] by an incantation

Dd

d [*dë*] *nf* **1** the consonant letter "d" **2** the voiced post-dental or alveolar apical stop represented by the letter "d"

*da·n *vi, vt* = nda·n

dac
  I § *nm* **1** male cat, tomcat **2** *(Crude)* child born out of wedlock: bastard, illegitimate child
  II § *adv* naked, nude; bare, lacking furnishings
    ∘ **dac deti** [*Ichth*] larger spotted dogfish (*Scyliorhinus stelaris L.*)
    ∘ **dac i egër** [*Zool*] = rrëqe**bull

*dack**anar** *nm* idler, vagabond

dackë *nf* slap in the face

dackos· *vt (Colloq)* to slap, smack

daç *stem for opt* <do·n
  ∘ **daç _ daç** *(Colloq)* either _ or _
  ∘ **(në) daç** *(Colloq)* if you like

*dadaru**q** *nm (Joke)* rogue

dadë *nf* **1** wetnurse = **dado 2** pet name in baby talk for the baby's female caretaker: grandma, mommy, big sister **3** *(Old)* woman who dresses the bride for the wedding; bridesmaid who accompanies the bride to the bridegroom's house

dado *nf* **1** wetnurse (may be human or animal who breast feeds another's offspring) **2** servant who takes care of babies: nanny, baby nurse; maid **3** [*Tech*] nut (for a bolt)

dafinë *nf* **1** [*Bot*] bay, laurel (*Laurus nobilis L.*) **2** laurel branch; bay leaf
  ∘ **dafinë deti** [*Bot*] oleander *Nerium oleander L.* = la**ndër

dafinor *adj* [*Bot*] **1** belonging to the laurel family **2** made of laurel

dafinore
  I § *nf* [*Bot*] grove of bay trees; field of laurel
  II § *nf fem* laurel family *Lauraceae*

dafintë *adj (i)* made of laurel, of laurel

dafnie *nf* [*Entom*] water flea *Daphnia*

dafnje·het *vpr* <**dafnje·n** *(Colloq)* to be exhausted, tired out

dafnje·n *vt* **1** *(Reg)* to tear to bits by tooth and nail **2** *(Colloq)* to beat [ ] up, beat [ ] to a pulp

dafrungë
  I § *nf* ostentatious/elaborate party: fete; excessive luxury, ostentation
  II § *adv* fun and entertaining; very well, couldn't be better

dafurro·n *vt (Reg)* **1** to rummage through; make a mess of **2** to poke (a fire), stir with a poker

*dagëndi**s** = davari**t·

dahuk
  I § *nm (Colloq)* **1** long and pointed tip; tip of something long **2** cap with a long tip **3** farm animal with straight vertical horns
  II § *adj* having a long and pointed tip

dai *nm* **1** generous and brave (man) **2** *(Reg)* = **dajë**

*daire** = da**jre

---

dajak *adj, nm* **1** long heavy stick; club, cudgel; fencepost, supporting pole **2** *(Fig Colloq)* beating with a club **3** *(Fig Colloq)* heavy scolding, strong criticism

dajan *nm* **1** post supporting a wall or roof **2** kingpost; pillar

dajandis·
  I § *vi (Colloq)* **1** to endure, stand **2** to last a long time
  II § *vt* to stand up to [ ], stand up against [ ]

dajeshë *nf* wife of mother's brother: aunt

dajë *nf with masc agreement* **1** mother's brother: uncle *(collateral male relative ascending or descending in ego's matriline)* **2** *(Colloq)* respectful term of familiar address to an older man ***3** = nda**rje

dajëmadh *nm* mother's oldest brother

dajëvogël *nm* mother's youngest brother

*dajk** *adj* = mi**shët

dajke *nf (Reg)* = daje**shë

dajkë *nf* **1** [*Ornit*] = dejke **2** *(Reg)* = daje**shë

dajko *nf with masc agreement (Reg Pet)* uncle

dajlan *nm* **1** weir, fishtrap made of wickerwork **2** *(Old)* = shila**rës

dajo *nf with masc agreement* = da**jë

dajre *nf* tambourine

dajrexhi *nm (np ˜ nj)* tambourine player

*dajri** *nf (Reg)* bride's trousseau

Daj-Sam *nm (Colloq)* Uncle Sam (symbol of the United States of America)

dak *nm, adj* Dacian

*dakë** *nf* **1** = rreng *(Old)* **2** time, era

*dakikë** *nf* = deki**kë

dako *nf (Reg)* butcher's block, wooden block for chopping up meat

dakol
  I § *nm (Pet)* strong and daring man
  II § *adj* strong and daring

dakord *adv* in agreement, agreed

dakort *adv* = dakord

daktil *nm* [*Lit*] dactyl

daktilik *adj* [*Lit*] dactylic, dactyl

daktilim *nm (Book)* communication by hand signals used by the deaf, signing

daktilograf *n* = daktilografi**st

daktilografi *nf* **1** the profession of typewriting; typing skill **2** *(Colloq)* typing room, workroom for typists

daktilografim *nm ger* <daktilografo·**n

daktilografist *n* typist

daktilografo·n *vt* to type [ ] (with a typewriter)

daktilografuar *adj (i)* typewritten, typed

dakull *adv* **1** collapsed and lifeless on the ground; in a state of shock **2** naked, undressed; empty, bare

*dal·** = ndal·

dal *stem for 1st sg pres, 1st & 3rd pl pres, 2nd & 3rd sg subj, part* <de**l·
  ∘ **<> dalshin të dalat!** *(Curse)* May <> break out in boils!

○ **S'dalin dy lëkurë nga një dele/berr.** "You can't get two hides from one sheep." *(Prov)* You can't make a silk purse out of a sow's ear.

○ <> **daltë hithra në vatër!** "May nettles grow in <>'s fireplace!" *(Curse)* May <>'s family line come to an end!

○ <> **dalshin sytë** "May <>'s eyes go out of his head!" *(Curse)* May <> go blind!

○ <> **dalshin trutë** *(Curse)* May <> go insane!

○ <> **daltë vigu!** "May the bier come out for <>!" *(Curse)* I hope <> dies!

da·le *interj (Colloq)* wait a while! just a moment! wait a second!

da·le·ni *interj pl* <**da·le** *(Colloq)*

da·lë
I § *part* <**del·**
II § *adj (i)* **1** protruding, bulging, jutting up/out, protuberant, sticking up/out **2** who has been around, worldly, well-traveled **3** *(Colloq)* (of girls) who has been married
III § *nn (të)* **1** rising, appearance **2** exit, point of egress **3** terminal part of a period of time, termination, end
IV § *nf* boil, carbuncle
V § *nf (e)* **1** protrusion, bump **2** piece of land jutting out into a body of water **3** exit, point of egress **4** [*Fin*] expenditure, outgo
VI § *adv* **1** back to the starting point, back again **2** in the middle, unfinished, hanging

○ **dala e gjësë** [*Veter*] anthrax = **pla·sje**
○ **të dalat jashtë 1** defecation **2** excrement
○ **Të dalë ku të dalë!** However it turns out! Whatever happens! Let's take a chance!

da·lë-da·lë *adv* slowly

da·lëngadalë *adv* **1** unhurriedly, slowly; quietly **2** little by little: gradually

da·l'ës *adj* **1** rising above the surface: protruding, bulging, jutting/sticking up, jutting/sticking out **2** [*Spec*] issuing forth from a source **3** serving as outlet, exhaust

Da·lëtë *nn (të)* Exodus

da·lie *nf* [*Bot*] dahlia *(Dahlia)*

dalipbe·bçe *nf (Old)* argot used by groups of itinerant laborers in several central Albanian districts

da·lje *nf ger* <**del·** **1** emergence, appearance **3** exit **4** [*Fin*] expenditure

*****dal·ka·da·lë** *adv* = **dalngadalë**

Dalmaci *nf* Dalmatia

dalma·t *adj, n* Dalmatian

*****Dalmat·i** = **Dalmaci**

dalmatin = **dalmat**

da·lme *nf (e)* = **da·lje**

daltari *nf* **1** sculpture **2** set of chisels

da·ltë *nf* chisel; graver, stylus, burin
○ **daltë si daltë** no matter how it turns out, no matter what happens
○ **daltë trefletëshe** [*Tech*] self-coring mortising chisel

da·ltëz *nf* **1** small chisel *****2** crowbar

dalti·m *nm ger* <**dalto··n**

dalto··n *vt* to use a chiselling tool on [ ]: chisel, sculpt, grave, engrave

dalton·izëm *nm* [*Med*] daltonism

daltua·r *adj (i)* chiseled, sculpted

daltue·s *nm* one who works with a chiselling tool; sculptor, engraver, wood-carver

*****da·l·un** *(Reg Gheg)* = **da·lë**

*****dal·zo·t** *nm (Old)* surety

dal·zo·t·ës *nm* person who takes on responsibility for someone or something: guarantor, guardian

*****dalla·k** *nm* litharge

*****dalla·më** *nf* = **dolloma**

dallandy·she = **dallëndy·she**

dalla·sh *adv* amiss, wrong

dallavera·xhi *nm (np ~ nj) (Colloq)* swindler, cheat, cheater, deceiver, crook

dallave·re *nf (Colloq)* crafty deception or trickery: skullduggery, swindle

dalldi *nf* rapture, extasy

dalldi·s· *vi* **1** to fall into an extasy **2** to become enraptured, be overwhelmed; get totally caught up, become infatuated **3** to burst up/out, erupt **4** to suddenly make a courageous decision

○ <> **dalldis·**[3sg] **plaga** <>'s wound *becomes* badly inflamed

dalldi·s·et *vpr* **1** to be totally caught up, become infatuated **2** to expand/grow rapidly, be bursting; burst out, erupt

dalldi·sje *nf ger* <**dalldi·s·**, **dalldi·s·et**

dalldi·sur *adj (i)* **1** ecstatic; enraptured, infatuated **2** daring, venturesome

dallëndy·she *nf* **1** swallow *(Hirundinidae)* **2** [*Text*] forked part of the loom framework from which the heddles are suspended: castle **3** wooden linchpin securing the handle to the beam of a plow = **rrogëz** **4** soft part of a horse's hoof

○ **dallëndyshe bishtbardhë** [*Ornit*] house martin *Delichon urbica L.*
○ **dallëndyshe bishtgërshërë** [*Ornit*] barn swallow *Hirundo rustica L.*
○ **dallëndyshe e brigjeve** [*Ornit*] bank swallow *Riparia riparia L.*
○ **dallëndyshe deti 1** [*Ornit*] tern, sea swallow *Sterna hirundo L.* **2** [*Ornit*] collared pratincole *Glareola pratincola* **3** [*Ichth*] blue flying-fish *Exocoetus volitans*
○ **dallëndyshe deti e zezë** [*Ornit*] black tern *Chlidonias niger*
○ **dallëndyshe kërbishtebardha** [*Ornit*] house martin *Delichon urbica L.*
○ **dallëndyshe kërbishtkuqe** [*Ornit*] red-rumped swallow *Hirundu daurica*
○ **dallëndyshe nate** [*Ornit*] nightjar, goat sucker *Caprimulgus europaeus*
○ **dallëndyshe e parë** harbinger of things to come

Dallëndy·she *nf* Dallëndyshe (female name)

dallëndysh·o·rë *np fem* [*Ornit*] Hirundinidae

dallfe·s *nm* bride's fez adorned with gold disks

da·llgë *nf* **1** wave (in a body of water) **2** *(Reg)* strong wind and rain

○ **ësh-të me dallgë** to be in an angry/testy mood

da·llgë-da·llgë *adv* wavy, in waves

dallgëpri·tëse *nf* breakwater, sea wall

dallgëthye·se *nf* = **dallgëpri·tëse**

dallgëzi·m *nm ger* <**dallgëzo··n**, **dallgëzo··het**

dallgëzo··het *vpr* **1** to get wavy **2** to spread/move in waves

dallgëzo··n
I § *vi* to make waves; be wavy
II § *vt* to make [ ] wavy

dallgëzu·ar *adj (i)* wavy, waved

dallgë|zu|es *adj* wavy

dallg|o|re *nf* wave-washed cliff

dall|im *nm ger* 1 <dallo'•*n*, dallo'•*het* 2 differentiating characteristic

dall|im|o|r *adj* discriminatory

dall|im|ta|r *n* = dallu|es

dallkau|k *adj, n (Colloq Pej)* 1 treacherous and two-faced (person) 2 brown-nosing (person)

dallkauk|llë|k *nm (np ˜ qe) (Colloq Pej)* 1 two-faced treachery 2 brown-nosing

dall|o'•het *vpr* to stand out
  ○ **dallo•het si paraja e kuqe** "stand out like red money" *(Impol)* to be immediately recognizable; be notorious, be in the public eye

dall|o'•n
  I § vt 1 to distinguish, discern 2 to differentiate, discriminate 3 to be discriminatory toward [] 4 *(Colloq)* to give recognition to []
  II § vi to be distinctive

dall|oj|e *nf* distinctive characteristic

dall|u|a|r *adj (i)* distinguished

dall|u|e|s *adj* 1 distinctive 2 discriminatory

dall|u|e|shëm *adj (i)* discernible, visible; evident, perceptible; distinguishable

dall|ue|shm|ëri *nf (Book)* distinctiveness

dam *nm* the game of checkers/draughts

*****dam|a|dam** *adv*

damahu|sh• *vt (Colloq•)* = dërrmëha|s•

damahu|sh•et *vpr* = dërrmëha•s•et

damalu|g *nm [Agr]* two-handled steel plow with a large plowshare

dama|r *nm* 1 *[Anat]* blood vessel 2 *[Geol Bot]* vein 3 *[Bot]* duct 4 *[Tech]* strand of wire 5 *(Colloq)* sign of splitting in a surface 6 *(Fig)* connection by blood: family tie 7 *(Colloq)* source, cause 8 *(Fig)* mood, humor, vein 9 *(Fig)* knack, innate talent *****10** water spring

dam|as *adv* separately, apart

dama|sk *nm [Text]* damask

Dama|sk *nm* Damascus

dama|z *nm* male animal selected for breeding: stud

damaz|llë|k *nm (np ˜ qe) (Colloq)* breeding of animals

dambërdu|mb *adv* bumpety-bump

*****dam|bllä** = damlla

*****dam|ço|r** *adj, n* = dëmtu|es

*****da|m|e** *nf (e) (Reg Gheg)* divorced (woman)

da|m|ë *nf* 1 *(Old)* dame, lady, madam 2 (in games) queen 3 the game of checkers/draughts

damixha|n|ë *nf* demijohn

*****da|m|je** *nf (Reg Gheg)* = nda|rje

da|m|kë *nf* 1 scar; mark, brand, stamp 2 branding iron, stamping tool 3 *(Fig)* stigma

dam|kim *nm ger* = damko|sje

dam|ko'•het *vpr* = damko·s•et

dam|ko'•n *vt* = damko·s•

dam|ko·s• *vt* 1 to mark, brand, stamp 2 *(Fig)* to brand [] with shame

dam|ko·s•et *vpr* <damko·s•

dam|ko|s|je *nf ger* <damko·s•, damko·s•et

dam|ko|s|ur *adj (i)* 1 marked, branded, stamped 2 *(Fig)* stigmatized

dam|ku|e|s *nm* branding tool

damlla' *nf* 1 *(Colloq)* stroke, apoplexy 2 *(Colloq Fig)* misfortune, catastrophe 3 *[Med]* apoplectic ictus
  ○ **damllaja e qumështit** *[Veter]* paresis puerperalis, coma puerperalis

damlla|ma|dh *nm (Colloq Curse)* may-he-suffer-great-misfortune!

damlla|rë|n|ë *nm (Colloq Curse)* may-he-suffer-a-stroke

damllo|s• *vt (Colloq)* 1 to paralyze, stun 2 to beat senseless

damllo|s•et *vpr (Colloq)* 1 to suffer a stroke 2 to fall down in a faint

damllo|s|ur
  I § *adj (i) (Colloq)* suffering from stroke
  II § *n (i) (Curse)* person who should suffer a stroke

*****dam|o'•n** = dëmto'•n

*****dâm** *(Reg Gheg)* = dëm|

*****dâm|qa|r** *adj (Reg Gheg) (Reg Gheg)* = dëmta|r

damsa|n|ë *nf* = damixha|n|ë

*****da|m|shëm** *adj (i) (Reg Gheg)* = dëmsh|ëm

*****dam|shpërbli|m** *(Reg Gheg)* = dëmshpërbli|m

*****dam|t** *(Reg Gheg)* = dëmt|

*****dam|to|r** *(Reg Gheg) adj* = dëmta|r

*****da|m|un** *adj (i) (Reg Gheg n(i))* divorced (person)

*****damxha|n** *nm* = damixha|n|ë

danc *nm* = dans

danc|o'•n *vi, vt* to dance

danda|lle *nf (Old)* obstacle, difficulty, trouble

*****Danema|rkë** = Danima|rkë

dan|e|z
  I § *nm* Dane
  II § *adj* Danish, of or pertaining to Denmark

*****da'n|ë** *nf (Reg Gheg)* = dar|ë

dang *onomat* ding
  ○ **dang-dang** ding dong!

danga|ll *adj, n (Colloq)* 1 potbellied/fat (person) 2 *(Contempt)* stupid (oaf)

dangara|q *nm* = danga|ll

da|ng|e *nf (Reg)* 1 = da|mkë 2 paunch, potbelly

*****dani** *nf* dose

dan|ik *nm (Reg)* special purpose room in a house

Danima|rkë *nf* Denmark

dan|i|sht *adv* in Danish

dan|i|sht|e *nf* Danish language

dans *nm* dance

dans|im *nm* <dans|o·•n

dans|o·•n *vi* to dance

dant|e|ll|ë *nf* lace

Danu|b *nm* Danube (River)

danub|ia|n *adj* Danubian

*****dar•** *vt* to disperse

*****da|r·et** *vpr* to become dispersed

darabu|k *nm [Mus]* drum shaped like an hourglass, held between the legs, and beaten with the hands: darabukka

*****da|rçi|n** *nm (Reg)* cinnamon

darda|ll|ë *nf* fishing apparatus consisting of a net hanging from a pole loosely attached to an upright post on a river bank

darda|n *nm [Hist]* northeastern Illyrian tribe

Darda|n *nm* Dardan (male name)

Dardane|le *np fem* Dardanelles

dardh|a|k *adj* pear-shaped

dardh|a|r *n* native of Dardha

da|rdh|ë *nf* pear, pear tree *(Pyrus communis)*

◦ **dardhë bulbe** pear with large, elongated fruit
◦ **dardhë e egër** [*Bot*] = dardhukël
◦ **dardhë elbje** bergamot pear (type of pear with small elongated yellow fruit that ripens in July at the same time as barley)
◦ **dardhë elbore** *= dardhë elbje
◦ **dardhë gomari** large variety of pear
◦ **dardhë gramje** summer-ripening pear with elongated fruit
◦ **dardhë gjembje** [*Bot*] prickly pear
◦ **do ta ha· dardhën** { } will suffer for what ◇ has done
◦ **Dardha e ka bishtin prapa.** "The pear has a stem at the end." (*Prov*) Every action has its consequences.
◦ **dardhë leshje** late-maturing pear with large slightly fuzzy fruit
◦ **dardhë thermometri** bulb of a thermometer
Dardhë *nf* town in the district of Korça: Dardha
dardhëz *nf* [*Bot*] kind of wild pear (*Pyrus sativa*)
*dardhíçkë *nf* (*Reg*) = dardhukël
dardhíshte *nf* 1 pear orchard 2 (*Reg*) [*Bot*] = dardhukël 3 thorn of the wild pear tree
dardhore *nf* young wild pear tree
dardhukël *nf* [*Bot*] wild pear (*Pyrus pyraster*)
dare *nf* [*Commerc*] tare (weight)
darë *nf* 1 pincers; tongs 2 [*Mil*] pincer movement 3 (*Fig*) merciless grip
◦ **darë me majë** silversmith's metal hole-punch
darëprerëse *nf* wire nippers
darí *nf* [*Ethnog*] = darovë
*darís· *stem for 1st sg pres, pl pres, 2nd & 3rd sg subj, pind* <darít·
*darít· *vt* = nda·n
*darje *nf* = ndarje
dark·et *vpr* = darko·het
darka-darkës *adv* at every dinner(time); every evening
darkajkë *nf* [*Bot*] beetroot
darkë *nf* 1 evening meal: supper 2 evening banquet, dinner 3 evening time 4 eve of a religious celebration
◦ **s'kishte as një darkë bukë** there was almost nothing left to eat
darkëçikë *nf* [*Ethnog*] supper to celebrate bride and bridegroom's first visit to her parents
darkëherë *nf* time of the evening meal, suppertime, evening time
darkim *nm ger* <darko·n
darko·het *vpr* to sup; be a guest at a supper/banquet
darko·n
I § *vi* to eat the evening meal, sup
II § *vt* to invite [] for supper, feed [] supper
darovë *nf* [*Ethnog*] gift to the bride/groom from the future in-laws: wedding present
◦ **Darova e armikut o helm, o thikë.** "The wedding gift of the enemy, either poison or the sword." (*Prov*) Beware Greeks bearing gifts.
daroví *nf* [*Ethnog*] = darovë
darovís *stem for 1st sg pres, pl pres, 2nd & 3rd sg subj, pind* <darovít· (*Old*)
darovísht *adv* (*Colloq*) as a gift: gratis
darovít· *vt* [*Ethnog*] to make a present
darovítës *nm* [*Ethnog*] man who presents the wedding gift
darovítje *nf ger* <darovít·

*darsëm *nf* = dasmë
*darsmor *nf* = dasmor
*darsmorísht *adv* as a member of the bridal party
Darvín *nm* Darwin
darviníst *n* Darwinist
darvinízëm *nm* Darwinism
dasaret *nm* [*Hist*] southeastern Illyrian tribe
dasëm *nf* = dasmë
dasí = ndasí
dasík *nm* small piece, small amount, small fragment
daskull *nf* stone slab, flagstone
dasmë *nf* wedding
◦ **dasma e argjendtë** silver wedding anniversary
◦ **dasmë minjsh** "wedding of mice" big commotion/hubbub
◦ **dasmë pa aheng** "wedding without a band" something dull/boring
◦ **Dasmë pa mish nuk ka** "There is no wedding without meat." (*Prov*) Nothing comes without some sacrifice.
dasmo·n *vi* 1 to have a wedding, make a wedding 2 (*Fig*) to be happy and gay
dasmor *nm* wedding celebrant; member of the bridal party
dasmoreshë *nf* bridesmaid
*dasuer *nm* (obl ˜ori) (*Old*) [*Math*] divisor
dash *nm* 1 ram 2 (*Fig*) healthy and good-looking person
◦ **dash deti** [*Ornit*] pelican
◦ **dash hidraulik** [*Tech*] hydraulic ram
◦ **dash i këmborës** ram that leads a flock of sheep: bellwether
◦ **dash i kurbanit** scapegoat
◦ **dash me flokë** "ram with hair" most eminent person
◦ **dash me këmborë** 1 person with leadership abilities 2 head of the family; chief
◦ **mish dashi** mutton
◦ **dash i tredhur** wether
dash *stem for opt, adm, part* <do·n
dashakeq
I § *adj* malevolent, hostile = keqdashës
II § *n* ill-wisher; enemy
dashakeqës *adj, n* = keqdashës
dashakeqësí *nf* = keqdashje
dashaligës *adj* malevolent, hostile = keqdashës
dashaligësí *nf* malevolence, hostility = keqdashje
dashamir OR **dashamirë**
I § *adj* well-wishing, benevolent; kind, friendly, affectionate
II § *n* well-wisher; friend, patron
Dashamir *nm* Dashamir (male name)
dashamirës *adj, n* = dashamir
dashamirësí *nf* good will, benevolence, kindness, friendliness
dashamirësísht *adv* (*Book*) with kindness, affectionately
dashas *adv* intentionally; willingly
dashatar *n* admirer; lover, sweetheart
dashe *nf* 1 pincushion 2 popcorn 3 tame goat
dashez *nf* [*Bot*] bear's breech, soft acanthus (*Acanthus mollis*)
*dashë *adj (i) (Old)* = dashur
*dashëm *adj (i)* = dashur
*dashëm *adj (i)* = ndashëm

*da·sh|ës
 I § adj liking, loving
 II § n lover, adherent
da·shje *nf ger <do·n* 1 willingness; will; intention
 *2 liking, preference
*dash·ke·q = dashake·q
dash·no·r *n* lover, sweetheart
*da·sht·azi *adv* on purpose
dasht·ë *3sg opt <do·n*
da·sht·ër *nf* 1 [*Bot*] acanthus *(Acanthus)* 2 [*Bot*] spiny
 bear's breech *(Acanthus spinosus)* 3 [*Archit*] acanthus
*da·sht·un *OR* da·sh|un *(Reg Gheg)* = da·shur
da·sh|ur
 I § part <do·n
 II § adj (i) wanted, desired; liked, loved, beloved;
 lovable, dear, endearing, friendly
 III § n (i) 1 dear; sweetheart, darling 2 lover
 ◦ dashur pa dashur like it or not
dashur|i *nf* 1 love, affection 2 love, enthusiasm
dashur|i·çkë *nf(Disparaging)* dalliance, superficial
 love
dashur|o·het *vpr* to be in love, fall in love
dashur|o·n *vt* to love
dashur|o·r *adj (Poet)* of or pertaining to love
dashur|ua·r *adj (i)* 1 in love, beloved 2 expressing
 love: loving
dashur|ue·s
 I § adj expressing love: loving
 II § n one who loves something: lover, fan
dat·a·re *adj (Offic)*
da·të *nf* 1 (calendar) date 2 *(Colloq)* dread, anxiety;
 terror 3 *(Colloq)* disgust, nausea
dat·ë·lind·je *nf* 1 birthday 2 [*Mil*] age cohort
dat·im *nm ger <dato·n, dato·het*
dat·iv *nm* [*Ling*] dative = dhano·re
dat·o·het *vpr* to belong to a particular date: be dat-
 able, be dated
dat·o·n
 I § vt to attach a date to [ ]: date
 II § vi = dato·het
dat·ua·r *adj (i)* belonging to a particular date: dated
dat·ue·s *adj* dater, dating
dat·ue·sh|ëm *adj (i)* datable
*dath· *vt (Reg Gheg Old)* = zbath·
*da·th·ë *adj (i) (Reg Gheg Old)* = zba·thur
daul·i·në *nf* [*Ethnog*] torch made of bundled straw and
 used by children at a summer festival
dau·lle *nf* 1 drum; big drum, bass drum 2 *(Reg)* fireplace mantle; chimney
 ◦ ësh·të daulle to be empty-headed
 ◦ Daullja bie për ata që kanë veshë. "The drum
 beats for those who have ears." *(Prov)* There is music
 for those who have ears to hear it.
 ◦ daulle e çarë *(Pej)* something that has become
 worthless, something no longer of any value
 ◦ ësh·të[3sg] daulle për derë "it is a drum for a
 family" it *can* happen to any family
 ◦ daulle e shpuar "leaky drum" *(Pej)* intolerable
 prattler/blabbermouth
 ◦ daulle e veshit [*Anat*] eardrum
daulle·xhi *nm (np ~ nj) (Colloq)* drummer
daull·ta·r *n* drummer
dava· *nf(Colloq)* 1 argument, dispute 2 matter; trouble 3 *(Old)* lawsuit, litigation, trial, case

 ◦ dava e vjetër *(Fig)* an all-too-familiar story
davar·is *stem for 1st sg pres, pl pres, 2nd & 3rd sg
 subj, pind <davari·t·*
davar·i·t· *vt* 1 to disperse, scatter 2 to dispel, alleviate
davar·i·t·et *vpr* 1 to become dispersed/scattered; dissipate 2 to busy oneself with trivia 3 to act scatterbrained
*davar·i·t·ës *adj, n* (one) that disperses/scatters/dissi-
 pates
davar·i·t·je *nf ger <davari·t·, davari·t·et*
davil·ni·k *nm* [*Tech*] forming bar in a metal spinning
 process
DDT *abbrev* DDT (insecticide)
de fa·kto *adv* de facto
de ju·re *adv* de jure
de
 I § pcl (Colloq) expresses intensity after an imperative verb
 II § interj 1 call to a horse to speed up: giddyup!
 2 expresses dissatisfaction or surprise
*de·n *vt = deh·
deba·t *nm (Book)* debate, discussion, controversy
DEBATIK *abbrev <Djemtë e Bashkuar Anëtarë të
 Ideve Komuniste* [*Hist*] Boys United in Support of
 Communist Ideas (youth organization in Albania during World War II)
debatik·as *adj, n* [*Hist*] <Djemtë e Bashkuar
 Anëtarë të Idesë Komuniste belonging to an organization of young Communists active during World
 War II
debat·o·n *vt (Book)* to debate
*de·bël *adj = de·bull
debi· *nf* [*Fin*] debit
debi·në *nf* kind of sweet round grape
debi·t *nm (Book)* quantity (per unit of time) of water,
 oil, or gas issuing from a well; yield
debit·im *nm ger* [*Fin*] 1 <debito·n, debito·het 2 =
 debi·
debit·o·n *vt* [*Fin*] 1 to debit 2 to put into debt
debit·o·r *adj, n* [*Fin*] debtor
*debli· *nf* pastry
*deboja· *np <deboj·ë barracks
deboj·ë *nf* arsenal, armory
*de·bull *adj* faint, weak
debut·im *nm ger (Book)* 1 <debuto·n 2 debut
debut·o·n *vi (Book)* to make a debut, make a first
 appearance on the artistic or sports scene
debut·ue·s
 I § adj (Book) making a debut, making a first appearance
 II § n (Book) person making a debut
*dec *nm (Old)* stratagem, tactic
decentral·iz·ëm *nm (Book)* decentralism
decentraliz·im *nm ger* 1 *(Offic)* <decentralizo·n
 2 decentralization 3 dispersal
decentraliz·o·n *vt (Offic)* to decentralize
deci·gra·dë
 I § adj in tenths of a degree
 II § nf tenth of a degree
deci·gra·m *nm* decigram
deci·li·tër *nm* deciliter
decima·l *adj* [*Math*] decimal = dhjeto·r
deci·me·tër *nm* decimeter
deci·ziv *adj* decisive
*deç *2nd & 3rd sg subj <do·n*

dede adj (Colloq) naive; wishy-washy; fool

Dedë nf with masc agreement Dedë (male name)

dedikim nm ger <dediko'·n

dediko'·het vp reflex (Book) to dedicate oneself, devote oneself = kushto'·het

dediko'·n vt (Book) to dedicate, devote = kushto'·n

*****dedukcio'n** = deduksio'n

deduksio'n nm [Log] deduction

deduktim nm ger [Log] 1 <dedukto'·n 2 deduction

deduktiv adj [Log] deductive

dedukto'·n vt [Log] to deduce

def nm 1 tambourine 2 (Colloq) beat it! get out of here!

∘ **nuk <> bën koka def** "<>'s head makes a tambourine" 1 <> doesn't give a damn 2 <> is hard-headed

defato're nf tambourine player (usually female)

defe'kt nm defect

defensi'v adj defensive

defensi'vë nf defensive position, defensive

*****defën** nf = dafinë

deficit nm deficit

deficita'r adj 1 (Book) [Fin] showing a deficit, having a debit balance, in the red 2 in deficiency: insufficient

definicio'n nm (Book) definition

definiti'v adj (Book) definitive

definitivi'sht adv (Book) definitive

deflegmato'r nm [Spec] dephlegmator

deflekto'r nm [Spec] deflector

*****de'fme** nf [Bot] bay, laurel (Laurus nobilis)

deformim nm ger (Book) 1 <deformo'·n, deformo'·het 2 deformation; distortion

deformo'·het vpr (Book) to warp, become deformed/distorted

deformo'·n vt (Book) to deform, distort, disfigure, deface, warp

deformu'ar adj (i) 1 deformed, distorted, disfigured, defaced 2 effaced

defte'r nm 1 (Old) notebook, copybook; register 2 [Hist] official land registry kept by Ottomans for tax purposes 3 (Colloq) bundle (fifty sheets) of cigarette paper

∘ **defter bakalli** (Pej) torn and dirty sales ledger, messy record-book; sloppy notebook

dega'me nf noisy argument/quarrel: row; uproar

dega'n nm bewildered fool

*****degarim** nm ger <degaro'·n

*****degaro'·n** vt to sunder, scatter

*****de'gas** adv branching out

degat·et vpr 1 to have a loud argument *2 = degëzo'·het

degazim nm ger [Chem] <degazo'·n

degazo'·n vt [Chem] 1 to degas, degasify 2 to clean up gas pollution

de'gazu'es nm [Spec] degasifier

degdi's· vt (Colloq) 1 to send far away, deport *2 to pass/hand along

degdi's·et vpr 1 to go far away (to a forlorn place); end up (somewhere) *2 to crop up, turn up

degdi'sje nf ger (Colloq) <degdi's·, degdi's·et

*****degermi** nf (Reg Gheg) woman's face veil; veil worn by women in mourning

degë

I § nf 1 branch, bough 2 branch 3 [Med] ramus

II § adv erect, straight; stiffly

∘ **Nuk ka degë pa rrënjë.** "There is no branch without roots." (Prov) Nothing and no one can stand without a solid foundation

degë'dend'ur adj having dense branches

degë'gje're adj having spreading branches, wide on top

degë'ha'pur adj having spreading branches

degë'ho'llë adj having thin branches

degë'lë'shu'ar adj having weeping branches

degë'ma'dh adj having long, thick branches

degë'pa'kë adj having few branches

degë'plo'të adj having many branches

degë'pre'rë adj having trimmed branches

degë'rra'llë adj having few branches

degë'shtri'rë adj having low spreading branches

degë'shu'më adj having many branches

*****degë't** adj (i) in branches, ramate

degë'te'ndë adj having tent-like foliage

degë'tra'shë adj having thick branches

degë'tha'të adj having dry branches

degë'va'rur adj having weeping branches

degë'z nf dimin <degë small branch; twig

degë'zim nm ger 1 <degëzo'·n 2 small branch

degë'zo'·het vpr to branch; sprout a branch; branch out; bifurcate, ramify

degë'zo'·n

I § vt to divide [ ] into branches

II § vi = degëzo'·het

degë'zu'ar adj (i) branched, with branches: ramate

degë'zu'es adj giving off branches

*****dego'su'r** adj (i) branched; ramified

degradim nm ger 1 (Book) <degrado'·n = zhgradim 2 demotion 3 deterioration, decline

degrado'·het vpr (Book) to deteriorate, decline (in value)

degrado'·n vt 1 (Book) to demote 2 to degrade

degradu'ar adj (i) degraded, downgraded

*****degsim** nm ger 1 <degso'·n 2 inflorescence

*****degso'·n** vi = degëzo'·n

*****degsu'er** adj (i) (Reg Gheg) = degëzu'ar

*****degtu'em** adj (i) (Reg Gheg) = degëzu'ar

degurina np brushwood, faggots

degjenerim nm ger 1 <degjenero'·n 2 degeneration

degjenero'·het vpr 1 to degenerate, deteriorate 2 to become degenerate/corrupt

degjenero'·n vt to cause [ ] to degenerate; cause [ ] to become degenerate: corrupt

degjeneru'ar adj (i) degenerate, degenerated; corrupt, corrupted

degjeneru'es adj degenerative; corruptive

deh· vt to make [ ] intoxicated: get [ ] drunk, intoxicate

deh·et vpr 1 to become intoxicated, get drunk 2 (of snow) to thaw in patches; (of land) become free of snow; (of bad weather) clear up 3 (of a stream of water) to go down in level, abate 4 (Fig) to get wizened

deh'ës adj intoxicating; heady

deh'je nf ger 1 <deh· 2 intoxication, drunkenness

deh'shëm adj (i) = dehës

de'hur adj (i) intoxicated, drunk

de·íst *adj, n* [*Phil*] deist

de·ízëm *nm* [*Phil*] deism

dej
  I § *np* <**dell** nerves
  II § *adv* *on the day after tomorrow; in the near future
  ○ **dej nesër** tomorrow or the day after; in the near future, soon

***dêj·**et *vpr* (*Reg Gheg*) = **de·h·**et

dejçë *nf* [*Bot*] great plantain (*Plantago major*)

dejë *nf* **1** area where snow has thawed **2** shallows in a river or stream

dejëz *nf* [*Bot*] = **bar delli**

dejkë *nf* [*Ornit*] swift (*Apus apus L.D*)
  ○ **dejka gjoksbardhë** [*Ornit*] alpine swift *Apus melba L.*

dejmarak
  I § *nm* drunkard, dipsomaniac
  II § *adj* given to drunkenness, addicted to drinking, dipsomaniac

***dejmeni** *nf* drunkenness, intoxication

***dejmë**
  I § *adj (i)* drunk, intoxicated
  II § *nn (të)* drunkenness, intoxication

dejshëm *adv* in an intoxicated manner, drunkenly

***dek** = **vdek**

dekadencë *nf (Book)* = **dekadentizëm**

dekadent *adj (Book)* decadent

dekadentizëm *nm* decadence

dekadë *nf (Book)* decade

dekaedër *nm* decahedron

dekagram *nm* decagram

dekalitër *nm* decaliter

dekametër *nm* decameter

dekan *nm* **1** dean **2** chief of a diplomatic mission **3** [*Hist*] commander of 10 men in a Roman legion

dekanat *nm* dean's office, deanery

dekantues *nm* [*Spec*] settler, decanter, settling tank

dekapirim *nm* [*Tech*] pickling (of metal)

***dekë** *nf (Reg)* = **vdekje**

***dekëprues** = **vdekjeprurës**

dekikë *nf (Reg North)* brief period of time: moment, instant

deklamim *nm ger* **1** <**deklamo·**n **2** elocution

deklamo·n *vt* to recite; declaim

deklamues *adj, n* elocutionist

deklaratë *nf* declaration

deklaro·n *vt* to declare, state; speak out, speak up, proclaim

deklaruar *adj (i)* (*Book*) declared, out and out

deklarues *adj* declaratory

deklasim *nm ger* <**deklaso·**n, **deklaso·**het

deklaso·het *vpr* (*Npc*) to become a political and social outcast: become declassé

deklaso·n *vt* (*Npc*) to make [] a political and social outcast; ostracize

deklasuar
  I § *adj (i)* declassé
  II § *n (i)* political and social outcast

deklinacion *nm* [*Ling*] declension

dekolte
  I § *nf* dress or blouse with a low-cut neckline; low-cut neckline
  II § *adj* decolleté

dekompozim *nm ger* **1** <**dekompozo·**n **2** decomposition

dekompozo·het *vpr* to become decomposed, decompose

dekompozo·n *vt* to decompose

dekompozuar *adj (i)* decomposed

dekonspirim *nm ger* <**dekonspiro·**n, **dekonspiro·**het

dekonspiro·het *vpr* to become exposed/unmasked/revealed

dekonspiro·n *vt, vi* to expose, unmask, reveal

dekor *nm* **1** [*Theat*] scenery **2** [*Cine*] set, scenery **3** (*Book*) decor

dekoracion *nm* decoration, ornamentation

dekoratë *nf* decoration, medal

dekorativ *adj (Book)* decorative

dekorator *n (Book)* designer (in theater), decorator

dekore *nf* decoration; decor

dekorim *nm ger* **1** <**dekoro·**n, **dekoro·**het **2** decoration

dekoro·n *vt* to decorate

dekoruar *adj (i)* decorated

dekorues *adj* designer (in theater), decorator

dekovil *nm* [*Rr*] narrow-gauge railway

dekret *nm* decree

dekretim *nm ger* <**dekreto·**n

dekretligj *nm (Old)* legal decree in force for a specified period

dekreto·n *vt* to decree, institute

dekretues *nm* person who makes a decree

***dekshëm** *adj (i)* = **vdekshëm**

dekurajim *nm ger* **1** <**dekurajo·**n, **dekurajo·**het **2** discouragement

dekurajo·het *vpr* to become discouraged

dekurajo·n *vt* to discourage

del·
  I § *vi* **1** to change from inside to outside: exit; go/come outside **2** to go/come to some place: go/come out; open out **3** to come out as a result; eventuate as **4** to make an appearance: appear; emerge; come up, show up, rise, arise **5** to be emitted, issue out, issue forth **6** to issue (from), flow (from); stem (from), come (from), come as a result (of), originate (from), originate (in) **7** to be produced (from), be formed (of) **8** to break off, come off **9** to protrude beyond a normal limit: jut/stick/pop out; curve outward: bulge **10** to pass beyond a usual limit: escape, burst through, leave the track/road, exceed, overflow **11** to grow up, begin to show; sprout **12** to come to an end, finish, be over; get out **13** to leave, quit **14** to become separate, break away **15** to wear off, disappear **16** to get out of trouble: escape **17** to be issued/published, be put into circulation **18** to be solved, come out right **19** to be successful, come out well **20** to succeed in becoming, graduate as **21** to take on a role **22** to become reality: prove to be, turn out to be; come true, come through **23** to suffice **24** to look out (on), lead out (to), be adjacent (to) **25** to head for, intend to go to **26** to be awarded
  II § *vt* to pass beyond [], pass over [], cross
  ○ **s'<> del· as në vesh** "not even get to <>'s ear (let alone <>'s stomach)" not be enough food to fill <> up
  ○ **<> del·**³ˢᵍ **asi** "<>'s ace comes out (of the hole)" <> *gets lucky and wins out*

○ <> **del·**^{3sg} **avull nga koka** <> *is* in a terrible predicament

○ <> **del·**^{3sg} **bakri** *(Pejor)* <>'s true colors *come out*, <> true nature *is* revealed

○ **del· bark** to have diarrhea

○ <> **del·**^{3sg} **boja 1** <>'s true colors *appear*, the truth *comes* out about <> **2** <> *loses* value, <> *goes* out of style; <> *suffers* from too much repetition **3** <> *loses* all sense of shame, <> *goes* beyond all bounds

○ **del·**^{3rd} **bollë** to stretch on and on without result

○ **del· borxhit** to give <> fair warning

○ <> **del·**^{3sg} **cifundi** <> *gets* damaged beyond repair

○ **del· çirak** to improve one's lot, come out okay

○ **del· deficit** to show a deficit

○ **del· dëshmitar** to appear as a witness

○ <> **del·**^{3sg} **djersa në lug** "<>'s sweat is running down the hollow of <>'s back" <> *toils* hard and long

○ <> **del·**^{3pl} **djersë të ftohta** <> *breaks* out in a cold sweat

○ <> **del·**^{3pl} **djersët e mortjes/vdekjes** "death's sweat *flows* from <>" <> *is* dead tired

○ <> **del·**^{3sg} **emri për mirë/keq** <> *gets* a good/bad reputation

○ <> **del· era** the dirty secret about <*something*> *is* revealed

○ <> **del·**^{3sg} **era 1** the dirty secret about <*something*> *is* revealed **2** <> *is* wiped out completely, <> *goes* bankrupt: <> *goes* up in smoke

○ **del· fare** to disappear completely

○ <> **del·**^{3sg} **fati** <*an unmarried girl*> finds a husband

○ **del· fitues** to emerge victorious: win

○ **del·**^{3sg} **fjala në pazar** the news *spreads* all around town

○ <> **del·**^{3sg} **flaka** "flame comes out of <>" **1** <> *goes* up in smoke, <> *is* utterly destroyed **2** <> *comes* to light, <> *is* revealed

○ <> **del·**^{3sg} **flakë nga koka** <>'s head is absolutely spinning with all the things <> has to worry about

○ <> **del·**^{3pl} **fletët** <> *sprouts* wings

○ <> **del·**^{3sg} **fryma** "the spirit goes out of <>" **1** <> *exerts* <>self to the point of exhaustion **2** <> passes away, <> *dies*

○ <> **del·**^{3sg} **fundi** <> *comes* to an end, there *is* almost no <> left

○ <> **del·**^{3sg} **fundi i shpuar** <> *ends* up with nothing

○ <> **del·**^{3sg} **goja prapa** to get tired of saying the same thing over and over, get tired of repeating oneself

○ <> **del·**^{3sg} **gurmazi** "<>'s throat gets torn" <> *gets* hoarse from yelling

○ <> **del· gjel kaproll** to take <*a task*> on boldly, face up to <*a task*>

○ **s'del gjë nga guri** like getting blood from a turnip (expect something from a stingy person)

○ **nuk del·**^{3sg} **gjë 1** nothing *comes* of it **2** not *come* out well, not *work* out

○ **s'<> del· gjë prej thonjve** <> *is* very tightfisted/stingy

○ <> **del·**^{3sg} **gjë? 1** (in questions) *does* any good come of it? **2** *does* it ever come out?

○ <> **del·**^{3sg} **gjuha (një pëllëmbë/pash)** "<>'s tongue *is sticking out* (an inch/six feet)" **1** <>'s tongue *is hanging* out (a mile) from exhaustion **2** <> *is getting* tired of talking so much

○ <> **del·**^{3sg} **gjuha prapa** to get tired of saying the same thing over and over, get tired of repeating oneself

○ <> **del·**^{3sg} **gjumi** <> *awakens*

○ **del· hardall** to come to nothing, turn out to be useless; be all for nothing

○ <> **del·**^{3sg} **hesapi** "<>'s account *comes* out all right" <> *has* sufficient economic means

○ <> **del·**^{3rd} **huq** it *doesn't* work out for <>, it *doesn't* do <> any good; <>'s {} *go* for naught; <>'s {} *miss*

○ **del· huq** to (take aim and) miss

○ <> **del·**^{3sg} **huri në majë të kokës** <> *loses* all sense of shame

○ <> **del·**^{3sg} **içi** the secret about <>, the cat is out of the bag about <>

○ **del· jashtë 1** to go abroad **2** *(Colloq Euph)* to move one's bowels

○ <> **del·**^{3sg} **kafka 1** <> *gets* skinny, <>'s bones begin to stick out **2** <> *gets* bald

○ <> **del· kapuç me mëngë** to turn out to be different from what <> supposed

○ <> **del·**^{3sg} **keq** things turn out bad for <>

○ <> **del·**^{3pl} **këmbët** <> *walks* <>'s feet off (looking all over for something)

○ <> **del·**^{3sg} **kësmeti** "fate emerges for <*a woman*>" <> finds a husband

○ **del· krah** to stand by <>, come out in support of <>

○ <> **del·**^{3pl} **krahët** <> *sprouts* wings

○ <> **del·**^{3sg} **kripa** <> *loses* <>'s appeal, <> *becomes* boring; all the zing *goes out* of <>, <> *gets* boring/dull

○ **i del·**^{3pl} **lakrat lakrorit** "the vegetables emerge from the vegetable pie" the hidden truth *comes* out: the cat is out of the bag

○ <> **del·**^{3sg} **lepuri në shteg** "the hare *appears* right in <>'s path" <> *gets* lucky

○ <> **del·**^{3sg} **lezeti** <> *stops* being enjoyable, <> *is* not pleasurable/enjoyable anymore

○ <> **del·**^{3sg} **lëngu** <> *loses* <>'s charm/attractiveness

○ **del· linjës** *(Colloq)* to be flabbergasted

○ <> **del·**^{3sg} **lotaria** <> *meets* with luck, <> *gets* lucky

○ **del· lugë e larë** to emerge unstained by guilt: come out of it clean as a whistle

○ **del·**^{3sg} **lumi nga shtrati** the river *overflows* its banks

○ <> **del·**^{3rd} **lyç** <>'s {} *ends* up in a muddle/mess

○ <> **del·**^{3sg} **lyra** <> *loses* <>'s appeal/charm

○ <> **del· llapa** <>'s tongue *is hanging* out, <> *is* very tired; <> *toils* very hard

○ **del· mbi të tjerët** to come out ahead of all the others, come out on top

○ **del· mbi ujë** "bob up out of the water" **1** to escape danger; survive difficulties **2** to come out on top **3** *(Pej)* to come to light, get discovered

○ **del· me faqe të bardhë 1** to emerge with honor **2** to be successful

○ <> **del· me flamur** to be completely straightforward/frank with <>

○ **del· me flamur të hapur** to come out with a public proclamation, reveal one's thoughts in public

○ **del· me këpucë të kuqe** to come out of it with a big loss

○ **del· me këpucë të kuqe** *(Iron)* to come out with a loss (on a deal)

○ **del· me nder** to come out okay; be successful

○ **del· mendje mbi mendje** *(Iron)* to think one is so much smarter than everyone else

○ <> **del·**^{3sg} **mendsh** to slip <>'s mind

○ **del· mendsh** to go out of one's mind; go crazy

○ **del· më vete** to become separated, get isolated

○ **del· mirë** to come out well

○ <> **del·**^{3sg} **mishi** <>'s bare skin *is showing*

○ <> **del·**^{3sg} **mjekra duke pritur** "<>'s beard *sprouts* while waiting" <> *gets* impatient waiting so long

○ **s'të del·**^{3sg} **mundimi** it doesn't pay, it's not worth the effort

○ <> **del· nami** to gain a reputation

○ **del· në breg 1** to accomplish something difficult: come through **2** to come to a conclusion; reach agreement

○ **del·**^{pl} **në breg** to reach a final agreement

○ **del· në anë** to get out of a tough spot

○ **del· në dritë 1** to come out, become known **2** to see the light of day; appear in print **3** to improve one's lot, come out okay

○ <> **del·**^{3sg} **në faqe** things *go* well for <>

○ **del· në faqe 1** to make an appearance, appear **2** to achieve a goal

○ <> **del· në frymë** to confront <>; stand up to <>

○ <> **del· në fund** to finish <> successfully

○ **del· në fushë** to be open to view

○ **del· në jetë** to be able to stand on one's own two feet, be on one's own

○ <>*a* **del· në krye** to finish <> successfully, bring <> to successful completion: see/get <> through

○ **nuk** <> **del·**^{3sg} **në kut** it *doesn't* work/come out the way that <> *expects*

○ **del· në lirim** to be released from military service

○ **del· në mal** *(Colloq)* to take refuge in the mountains; become a partisan (guerilla fighter)

○ **del· në mejdan** to come out in the open, become known/clear

○ **del· në mish** to go naked

○ **del· në orbitë 1** *(Book)* to go into orbit **2** to start out on the right path **3** to attain great success (far beyond any possible competitor)

○ **del· në pah** to come into clear view: appear distinctly; come into notice

○ **del· në pension** to retire (from work) on a pension

○ **del· në reliev 1** to become salient, become noticeable; stand out **2** to come out in the open

○ **del· në selamet** to come out all right from a bad situation

○ **del· në sipërfaqe** to come to light, come out in the open

○ **nuk** <> **del· në sy** not bear to look <> in the eye (because of guilt/shame)

○ **del· në shesh** to come out in the open, become known/clear

○ <> **del· në shteg** "appear in <>'s path" to fall into <>'s hands/power

○ **i del· në skaj punës** to manage to accomplish the task successfully

○ **del· në hënëz 1** to lose out **2** to remain poor

○ **del· nëpër vrimë të gjilpërës** to be very adept

○ **del· nga ama** to exceed the permissible limits

○ **del· nga binarët 1** to get off track, be derailed; go astray **2** to lose one's mind, go crazy

○ **del· nga faza** *(Colloq)* to go out of one's mind, go crazy

○ <> **del· nga fjala** to break one's word to <>

○ <> **del· nga hatëri** to lose favor with <>, not appeal to <> any more

○ <> **del· nga hiri** to lose the support and confidence of <>: go out of favor with <>

○ <> **del· nga hundët** <> *pays* through the nose

○ <> **del· nga mendja** to disappear from <>'s mind, escape <>'s mind

○ <> **del·**^{3sg} **nga mendtë** to slip <>'s mind

○ **del· nga meseleja** to break one's word/promise, go back on one's word

○ **del· nga mosha** to exceed the age limit; be too old

○ **s'del· nga pragu** not leave the house, stay inside the house

○ <> **del· nga qejfi** to be out of <>'s good graces, lose favor with <>

○ **del· nga rruga** to stray from the path, take a wrong turn, go wrong

○ **del· nga xhehenemi në xhenet** "go out of Hell and into Heaven" to go from abject misery to utter joy

○ <> **del· nga zemra** "go out of <>'s heart" to go out of favor with <>, no longer be liked/loved by <>

○ **del· nuse** (of a girl) to get married, become a bride

○ **s'<>*a* del·**^{3sg} **njeri për** [] "no one comes out ahead of <> in regard to []" no one *beats* <> at []

○ **nuk del· pa gjë** to get something out of it, not come out of it with nothing

○ <> **del·**^{3pl} **pendët 1** to be grown up enough to be on one's own **2** to recover economically, get back in the black

○ **del· për fushe** to be open to view

○ **del· për hava** to go outside to get some fresh air

○ <> **del· për hundësh** <> *pays* through the nose

○ **del· për kësmet** to go away in order to seek one's fortune

○ <> **del· përpara 1** to appear in front of <> **2** to take measures in advance to avoid <*something bad*> **3** to welcome and support <>'s request **4** to take another route in order to get somewhere before <>: cut <> off (at some place)

○ **del· po në atë/një qafë** to come to the same conclusion

○ **del· prej dini e prej imani** (of a Moslem) to leave the faith

○ **del· prej vllajës e bie**$_1$ **në prush** "get out of the furrow and fall into a bed of hot coals" to fall out of the frying pan and into the fire

○ **del· puplash** *(Colloq)* to lose one's mind: lose one's marbles

○ <> **del·**^{3pl} **puplat 1** to be grown up enough to be on one's own **2** to recover economically, get back in the black

○ **del· pushkë** "turn out to be just a rifle" to be a dud

∘ **del· pushkë e lagur** to turn out to be good for nothing

∘ **del· qemerit** to become dissolute, go bad

∘ <> **del·***3pl* **qime të bardha** "<>'s hairs grow out white." **1** <> *is* getting gray hair **2** <> *grows* old waiting, <> *gets* good and tired of waiting so long

∘ <> **del·***3sg* **qumështi i nënës** "the milk of <>'s mother *comes* out" **1** <> *is* tired to the bone **2** <> *is* totally worn down by suffering

∘ <> **del·***3sg* **qumështi mbi përshesh** "the milk *seeps* out of <>'s bread pudding" <> *lives* in comfort

∘ **del·***3sg* **rakia** <> *becomes* sober, <> *sobers* up

∘ **nuk** <> **del· rend** <> has absolutely no time, <> is much too busy

∘ **del·***3sg* **rrezmit (toka)** the land (soil) *loses* its fertility

∘ <> **del·***3sg* **rruaza** <> *becomes* humpbacked

∘ **del· rruge** to stray from the path, take a wrong turn, go wrong

∘ **del· si boshti para furkës** "go in front like the hand before the pitchfork" to violate the proper status order, not observe one's proper place

∘ **del· si fanti spathi** "come out like the jack of clubs" to appear suddenly

∘ **del· si mëzi para pelës** *(Pej)* to be unable to control oneself; speak out of turn

∘ **del· si rruar, qethur** "emerge as if shaved" to come out of it with barely the shirt on one's back

∘ **del· si vaji mbi ujë** "come out like oil on water" to be totally exonerated: be cleared completely

∘ <> **del·***3pl* **sytë** <>'s eyes *are coming* out of <>'s head: <>'s eyes *are* overworked

∘ <> **del·***3pl* **sytë** *jashtë//nga vendi* <>'s eyes *pop* out of their sockets

∘ **del· sheshit** to come to light, come out in the open

∘ **del·***3sg* **shkumë nga goja 1** <> *is* foaming at the mouth, <> *is* in a foaming rage **2** <> *gets* tired to the bone

∘ **del·***3sg* **shpirti** "the spirit goes out of <>" **1** <> exerts <>self to the point of exhaustion **2** <> passes away, <> *dies*

∘ <> **del·***3sg* **shterp** to turn out badly for <>

∘ <> **del·***3sg* **(puna) shtupë** (the thing/affair/business) *doesn't* work out for <>

∘ **del· shyt** to get nothing for one's pains

∘ **del· ters** to turn out badly

∘ <> **del·***3pl* **trutë** <> *gets* exhausted from thinking so much, <>'s brains *are exploding* from so much thinking/work; <> *is going* out of <>'s head in exasperation, <> *gets* completely exasperated

∘ <> **del·***3sg* **tym nga koka** <>'s head is absolutely spinning with all the things <> has to worry about

∘ <> **del·***3sg* **tymi 1** the dirty secret about <*something*> is revealed **2** <> is wiped out completely, <> *goes* bankrupt: <> *goes* up in smoke

∘ <> **del·***3pl* **thinjat duke pritur** "<> *gets* gray hair while waiting" <> *gets* impatient waiting so long

∘ <> **del·***3sg* **ujë i zi** <> *gets* completely demolished

∘ **del· va pa va 1** to go out without any particular destination **2** to come out all right despite the problems

∘ **S'del vaj nga guri.** "Oil doesn't come out of a rock." *(Prov)* (expresses the unlikelihood of getting

someone to do a favor) Fat chance of getting { } to do a favor!

∘ **del·***3sg* **vetvetiu/vetiu** to become self-evident, become obvious

∘ <> **del· xhani 1** to die **2** to suffer greatly

∘ <> **del·***3sg* **xhani** "the spirit goes out of <>" **1** <> exerts <>self to the point of exhaustion **2** <> passes away, <> *dies*

∘ **s'del·***3sg* **yndyrë nga** { } "no fat *comes* from { }" {*someone*} is not going to be of any help (in using { }'s influence

∘ <> **del·***3sg* **zëri** "<>'s voice gets torn" <> *gets* hoarse from yelling

∘ **del·***3sg* **zjarr nga koka** <>'s head is absolutely spinning with all the things <> has to worry about

∘ <> **del·***3pl* **zorrët (përjashta)** "<>'s guts *come* out(side)" to vomit up one's whole insides; feel very nauseous, want to throw up

∘ <> **del· (për) zot 1** to assume responsibility for <*a task*>: take <> on **2** to assume responsibility for <*a person*>: take <> under one's wing

del·et vpr* <**del·** to extricate oneself

dela'ujë *nf* water source, spring

de'le *nf* **1** sheep *(Ovis aries)* **2** ewe **3** *(Fig Colloq)* person who is very quiet and obedient **4** *(Colloq)* fleece

∘ **dele pikëlore** sheep with a speckled muzzle

dele'da'sh *nm* hermaphrodite

dele'du'k *nm*

delegacio'n *nm* delegation

delega't *nm* delegate

delegi'm *nm ger* **1** <**delego** ·**n** [*Law*] **2** power of attorney, delegation of power

delego ·**n** *vt* to delegate

delegua'r *nm (i)* delegate

delendi's· *vt* **1** to slander, libel **2** to pervert, corrupt

delendi's·et vpr* to grow corrupt

dele'n xhi *nm (np ˆ nj) (Insult)* **1** bad person: bastard, rascal, knave **2** slanderer

dele'sh *nm* sheepskin cape

De'lfi *nm* Delphi

delfi'n *nm* [*Zool*] dolphin *(Delphinus delphis)*

∘ **delfini i madh** [*Zool*] bottle-nose dolphin *Tursiops truncatus*

deli

I § *adj (Colloq)* **1** indicates a high degree of the characteristic quality of the following noun; a real __, super-__ **2** wild and crazy

II § *nm* daring hero

delika't *adj* **1** delicate **2** *(Fig)* well-mannered

delikate'së *nf (Book)* **1** delicacy, daintiness **2** good manners

deli'kt *nm* delict

deli'l *nm* [*Ichth*] painted comber *(Serranus scriba)*

Deli'n||a *nf* Delina (female name)

deli'nj *np* <**deli**

deli'r *nm* delirium

∘ **delir i madhështisë** [*Med*] delusion of grandeur

∘ **delir i mohimit** [*Med*] nihilistic delusion

∘ **delir i persekutimit** [*Med*] persecutory delusion

***Delmaci** *nf* Dalmatia

de'lme *nf (Reg)* = **de'le**

delme'r *nm* shepherd

delmere *nf* [*Ornit*] wagtail = **bishtatundes**

delmeri *nf collec* shepherds taken as a whole

***delmuth** *nm* [*Bot*] spiny restharrow (*Ononis spinosa*)

deltë *nf* [*Geog*] river delta

deltinar *n* potter

deltinë *nf* clay, potter's earth

deltinor *adj* of clay; clayey; argillaceous

deluzion *nm* disillusionment, disenchantment

Delvinë *nf* town in southwestern Albania: Delvina

delvinjot
  I § *adj* of or pertaining to Delvina
  II § *n* native of Delvina

dell *nm* (*np* ˜ *j*) **1** (*Colloq*) blood vessel; nerve **2** (*Colloq*) small stream, rivulet **3** [*Anat*] tendon, sinew **4** [*Tech*] strand of wire in a cable; bare wire **5** (*Fig*) connection by blood: family tie **6** (*Colloq*) source, cause **7** (*Fig*) mood, humor, vein **8** (*Fig*) knack, innate talent
  ○ **dell i priftit** Spanish oyster plant *Scolymus hispanicus*
  ○ **dell i thembrës** [*Med*] Achilles tendon

***dellëngethi** *adv* deliberately, on purpose

dellëzim *nm* venation

dellëzuar *adj* (i) richly veined, venous

dellor *adj* having veins: veined; venous

delltë *adj* (i) (said of some meat) with many veins

***delluer** *adj* (i) (*Old*) = **dellëzuar**

dem *nm* **1** bull **2** main bearing beam in a floor **3** (*Fig*) strong and well-built young man
  ○ **Demin e shtron zgjedha.** "The yoke makes the bull docile." (*Prov*) Hard work makes the tough guy gentle.
  ○ **dem me brirë** stubborn/headstrong person
  ○ **dem ndërzimi** stud bull

demagog *nm* demagogue

demagogji *nf* demagogy

demagogjik *adj* demagogical, demagogic

demaluk *nm* = **damaluk**

demarkacion *nm* (*Book*) demarcation

demaskim *nm ger* < **demasko** • *n*, **demasko** • *het*

demasko • *het vpr* (*Book Fig*) to become unmasked, be exposed, reveal one's true colors

demasko • *n vt* **1** to unmask **2** (*Mil*) to expose/discover [something camouflaged]

demaskuar *adj* (i) unmasked, exposed, revealed

demaskues *adj* unmasking, exposing, revealing

dembel
  I § *adj* lazy
  II § *nm* lazy person
  ○ **dembel Stambolli** (*Impol*) lazybones
  ○ **Dembeli zihet me veglat e punës.** "The lazy person argues with his work tools." (*Prov*) The poor workman blames his tools.

dembeli *nf* laziness

dembelizëm *nm* = **dembeli**

dembelos • *vt* to make [] lazy

dembelos • *et vpr* to get lazy

dembelosje *nf ger* < **dembelos** •, **dembelos** • *et*

dembelosur *adj* (i) having gotten lazy

dembellëk *nm* (*np* ˜ *qe*) (*Colloq*) laziness, lazy behavior

demek *pcl* (*Colloq*) **1** expresses disparaging doubt with irony or surprise: oh, really?; oh, sure! **2** parenthetical expression referring to something previous: okay then, so

demet *nm* **1** sheaf of grain **2** bundle of corn or oak leaves used as rain cover for a haystack

demiroxhak *nm* firedog

demobilizim *nm ger* **1** < **demobilizo** • *n* **2** demobilization

demobilizo • *n vt* to demobilize

demodé *OR* **demoduar** *adj* out of fashion, passé

demografi *nf* demography

demografik *adj* demographic

demokraci *nf* democracy

demokrat *n* democrat

demokratik *adj* democratic

demokratïsht *adv* democratically

demokratizëm *nm* spirit of democracy, the practice of democracy

demokratizim *nm ger* **1** < **demokratizo**, **demokratizo** • *het* **2** democratization

demokratizo • *het vpr* to become more democratic

demokratizo • *n vt* to democratize

demon *nm* (*Book*) demon

demonstratë *nf* demonstration

demonstratim *nm ger* **1** (*Book*) < **demonstro** • *het*, **demonstro** • *het* **2** demonstration

demonstrativ *adj* (*Book*) **1** done deliberately to draw attention, making a public show **2** serving illustrative purposes, demonstrative

demonstratues *adj*, *n* political demonstrator

demonstro • *het vpr* (*Book*) to become apparent

demonstro • *n*
  I § *vt* **1** (*Book*) to show off **2** to demonstrate
  II § *vi* to take part in a (political) demonstration

demoralizim *nm ger* **1** < **demoralizo** • *n*, **demoralizo** • *het* **2** demoralization

demoralizo • *het vpr* to become demoralized, lose heart

demoralizo • *n vt* to demoralize

demoralizuar *adj* (i) demoralized

demoralizues *adj* demoralizing

demostratë = **demostratë**

demostrativë = **demonstrativ**

***denar** *nm* **1** money ***2** (*Old*) diamond (playing card)

denbabaden *adv* (*Colloq*) since ancient times, forever

dend • *vt* **1** to compress; cram **2** (*Colloq*) to force [someone] inside **3** (*Colloq*) to gorge, satiate **4** (*Colloq*) to beat [] up **5** (*Colloq Pej*) to fill [] with false promises
  ○ **dend• brenda** (*Colloq*) to put in jail

dend • *et vpr* **1** to become dense **2** (*Colloq*) to get filled up **3** (*Colloq*) to crowd together
  ○ **dend• et (me gënjeshtra)** (*Colloq Pej*) to get sated [] with lies

dendëro • *n* = **dendëso** • *n*

dendësi *nf* density; frequency

dendësim *nm ger* < **dendëso** • *n*, **dendëso** • *het*

dendësimatës *nm* [*Phys*] **1** ammeter **2** densimeter

dendësirë *nf* **1** density, frequency **2** place with dense vegetation

dendësïsht *adv* densely, frequently

dendëso·het vpr to increase in intensity: thicken, become more dense; become more frequent

dendëso·n vt 1 to intensify: thicken; make [] more frequent 2 to increase one's use of []

dendësuar adj (i) increased in density or frequency: compressed, condensed, frequent

dendëshor adj 1 having thick foliage and a broad crown 2 fat and clumsy

dendur
I § adj (i) 1 dense, compact, thick 2 frequent; numerous
II § adv 1 densely 2 frequently, often

dendurazi adv = **dendur**

denduri nf 1 density 2 [Spec] frequency (of wave motion)

dendurimatës nm [Spec] frequency meter

deng
I § nm (np ̄ gje) 1 full sack 2 bundle, bale 3 (Fig) large amount: whole bundle, pile
II § adv 1 cram-full 2 at the same level, equal

dengëza adv (Colloq) cram-full

dengje np < **deng**

denigrim nm ger 1 < **denigro·n** 2 denigration

denigro·n vt to denigrate

denik nm stormy weather; storm coming from the sea

***Denmarkë** nf Denmark = **Danimarkë**

denoncim nm ger 1 < **denonco·n** 2 denunciation

denonco·n vt to denounce; disavow

denoncues
I § nm denouncer
II § adj denunciatory

densitet nm [Phys] density

dental nm 1 [Ling] dental (sound) 2 [Ichth] common dentex Dentex dentex
  ○ **dental symadh** [Ichth] large-eyed dentex Dentex macrophthalmus

dentar adj dental

dentist n dentist

denjë adj (i) worthy, deserving

denjësi nf worthiness

denjësisht adv worthily, deservingly

denjo·n vt (Book) to deign, condescend

***denjur** adj (i) = **denjë**

departament nm administrative department

depërtim nm ger 1 < **depërto·n** 2 penetration

depërto·n vi vt to penetrate; permeate

depërtues adj penetrating

depërtueshëm adj (i) penetrable; permeable

depërtueshmëri nf penetrability; permeability

depo nf depot, storehouse, warehouse

depolitizim nmact 1 < **depolitizo·n** 2 depoliticization

depolitizo·n vt to depoliticize

deponim nm ger 1 < **depono·n** 2 deposition

depono·n vt [Law] to testify, give a deposition

deponues nm [Law] deponent

deportim nm ger 1 < **deporto·n** 2 deportation

deporto·n vt to deport

depozitar n depository agent
  ○ **depozitar gazetash** newsagent

depozitë nf deposit

depozitim nm ger 1 < **depozito·n**, **depozito·het** 2 deposit, sediment

depozito·het vpr [Chem] to form a deposit, settle, leave a sediment

depozito·n vt 1 to deposit 2 to store

depozitues nm 1 depositor 2 [Fin] bank depositor

depresion nm [Geog] depression

depsëz nm (Colloq) unmannerly boor

deputet nm deputy, parliamentary representative

***deq** nm cunning, trickery

***Deqembër** nm (Old) December = **dhjetor**

deraç nm (Pej) person who goes door-to-door to borrow things or trade gossip

***deratar** nm = **deretar**

***deratëhershëm** adj (i) up to that time, until then, previous

derazi adv right next door

derdimen nm (Impol) stupid

derdyl nm [Ichth] sea bass (Dicentranchus labrax L.) = **levrek**

derdh· vt 1 to pour [] (out), spill 2 (Colloq) to spend [money] lavishly: pour out [money] 3 [Fin] to deposit [money]; pay [] in; contribute 4 [Tech] to cast [metal] 5 (Reg) to survive [a children's disease]
  ○ <> **derdh· balsam** to soothe <>; console <>
  ○ **derdh· gjak/lot** to shed blood/tears
  ○ **derdh· jargët** to drool
  ○ **derdh· jargët për** [] (Colloq Pej) to crave []
  ○ **e derdh· kupën** "spill the bowl" to do too many bad things: go too far
  ○ **derdh· mendtë/trutë** (Pej) to have a restless mind, go woolgathering, { }'s mind keeps wandering
  ○ **derdh· mjaltë/sheqer nga goja** "pour honey/sugar from one's mouth" to speak pleasantly/beautifully
  ○ <> **derdh· plumb në gojë/grykë** "pour lead down <>'s throat" (Colloq) to kill <> viciously
  ○ **e derdh· tokën** to break up the ground

derdh·et
I § vpr 1 to flow, stream out; spill out, pour; spill over, overflow 2 (Colloq) to crumble
II § vpr to hurl oneself, pour down
  ○ <> **derdh·et³ˢᵍ kupa** "<>'s bowl spills over" <> does too many bad things: <> goes too far
  ○ <> **derdh·et si shirit** to attack <> like a flash
  ○ **derdh·et³ˢᵍ vaji (e bie₁) në uthull** "the oil spills (and falls) into the vinegar" there's no harm done

derdhazë nf flood, inundation

derdhës nm 1 [Tech] metal caster 2 [Fin] depositor

derdhje nf ger 1 < **derdh·**, **derdh·et** 2 mouth (of a stream) 3 [Tech] metal-casting (process) 4 ejaculation (of sperm)
  ○ **derdhje mujore** 1 monthly deposit (Old) *2 menses
  ○ **derdhjet mujore** menses

derdhshëm adj (i) (of metals) castable

derdhtore nf foundry

derdhur adj (i) 1 [Tech] cast 2 (Colloq Fig) scattered, spread out 3 (Fig) well-formed 4 (Colloq) crumbled 5 [Fin] deposited (in a bank)

derebe nm [Hist] during Ottoman rule, the official charged with the security of mountain roads

derë nf 1 door; gate 2 family 3 (Fig) solution, way out
  ○ <>**u haptë dera!** (Colloq) (among friends) good luck to <>!

○ <>a lë· (peshqesh) në derë "leave a present at <>'s door" to lay blame on <>; put unwanted responsibility on <>

○ **derë e madhe** *(Colloq)* prominent family

○ **matu në derë** *(Impol)* beat it! get out of here!

○ **derë më derë** right next door

○ **derë pa mandall** door/area open to the public

○ **derë e vogël** *(Euph)* toilet

derë·ba'bë *nf* the home of her parents (for married women)

derë|babë·shu'a|r *adj* (used for married women) left without close family

derë·ba'rdhë *adj* prosperous, lucky

derë·çe'lë = derëçe'lur

derë·çe'l·ur *adj* = derëhapur

*__derë·drita're__ *nf* French window

derë·ha'p·ur *adj* hospitable

derë·ky'ç·ur *adj* = derëmbyllur

derë·ma'dh *adj* highly regarded; noble

derë·mbajt·ës *nm* = derëta'r

derë·mby'll·ët *adj (i)* = derëmby'llur

derë·mby'll·ur *adj* **1** inhospitable **2** left completely alone in the world, without close family

derë·pri'sh·ur *adj* extravagant

de'rë·s *nm* **1** concierge, doorman, house porter **2** beggar

derë·ste'rrë *adj* unfortunate

derë·shu'a|r *adj* left completely alone in the world, without close family

derë·ta'r *n* concierge, doorman, house porter

de'rë·z *nf* **1** *(Dimin)* = de'rë **2** latch for a small door

derë·zi *adj, n (fem sg ˜ ez, masc pl ˜ inj, fem pl ˜ eza)* ill-fated/unfortunate/accursed (one)

de'rgj·et *vpr* **1** to waste away in bed: be bedridden; lie ill; lie helpless; stay in bed **2** to languish

*__de'rgj e__ *nf* disabling illness; lying ill, lying abed

de'rgjë *nf* **1** long and serious illness **2** *(Reg)* tuberculosis, consumption

dergjë·ne'shë *nf* woman lying in for childbirth = lehonë

de'rgj·je *nf ger* **1** < de'rgj·et **2** = de'rgjë

de'rgj·ur *adj (i)* suffering from a wasting illness

deri

I § prep (acc) until, up to, up until, till, to

II § *pcl* **1** (precedes other prepositions or conjunctions to form complex prepositions or conjunctions) **2** (implies an unexpectedly high degree, amount or grade) even

○ **deri diku** to a certain extent, up to a point

○ **deri ku <> arrin çapi** to the extent of <>'s ability

○ **deri ku të arri·** n^{3sg} **syri** as far as the eye *can* see

○ **deri më një** up to the last detail, in every single way

○ **deri në asht** to the bone, very deeply

○ **deri në frymën e fundit** "until the final breath" up to the very end

○ **deri në fund** in full detail

○ **deri në fyt** up to the ears

○ **deri në kockë** to the very bone, to the core

○ **deri në një kokërr** every single one/piece, to the very last one

○ **deri në një qime** down to the smallest detail

○ **deri në palcë të qafës** from head to toe, to one's very core

○ **deri në themel** with complete thoroughness: to the very foundation, to the very roots

○ **deri në thonj** to the highest degree

○ **deri në vdekje 1** for life; forever **2** to the death

○ **deri sa të <> bie** $_1$· ^{3pl} **kockat** as long as <> *lives*

deri|ate'her|shëm *adj (i)* of the time up until then: up to that moment, until then

deri|'çkë *nf* small door; backdoor, way out

*__deri|di'ku__ *adv* somewhat, to some extent

deri|dje'|shëm *adj (i)* until yesterday

deri|këtu'|shëm *adj (i)* up to here

deri|sa *conj* **1** up to a limit: until, as long as, so far as **2** inasmuch as, being that

deri|so't|ëm *adj (i)* until today, so far; up-to-date

deri|so't|shëm *adj (i)* = derisotëm

deri|tani'|shëm *adj (i)* up to now

deri|ta'sh|ëm *adj (i)* = deritani'shëm

deriva't *nm* derivative

derivi'm *nm ger [Math]* **1** < derivo'·n **2** derivation

derivo'·n *vt [Math]* to derive

derivu'a|r *adj (i) [Math]* derived

derk *OR* **de'rku·c** *nm* = derrku'c

derma'n *nm (Colloq)* remedy; solution

dermato'lo'g *n [Med]* dermatologist

dermato|logji' *nf [Med]* dermatology

dermato|logji'k *adj [Med]* dermatological

dermat|o'zë *nf [Med]* dermatosis

de'rmë *nf [Med]* derma, dermis

*__de'rpt__ = depërt

dert *nm (Colloq)* complaint, worry; sorrow

○ **s'ka· dert për fytyrë** to be absolutely shameless, {} has a lot of nerve/gall/brass

dert|i'm *nm ger* **1** < derto'·n **2** complaint, trouble

derto'·n *vi (Colloq)* to talk about one's troubles: complain

derve'n *nm (Old)* **1** mountain gorge **2** wide road, main road **3** *(Reg)* roller that holds the cloth at the back of a loom

dervi'sh *nm* **1** *[Relig]* dervish **2** *(Reg)* scarecrow **3** *[Bot]* bad-smelling long-stemmed mushroom with a white cap: stinkhorn *Phallus impudicus L.* **4** *[Bot]* broadleafed bulrush, great reed mace *Typha latifolia* **5** *(Reg) [Ornit]* = çafkëlorë **6** *(Reg)* corn with heavy tassels

dervish|le're *np* < dervi'sh

derr *nm* **1** *[Zool]* pig, hog, swine *(Sus scrofa)* **2** pork **3** *(Fig Colloq Pej)* person with any or all of the following qualities: fat, dirty, stubborn, stupid, corrupt

○ **derr** {$noun^{abl}$} *(Colloq)* a humongous {}

○ **derr deti** "sea pig" *[Zool]* porpoise

○ **Derri do plumb.** "The pig wants a bullet." *(Prov)* A tough person must be dealt with toughly. Tough people need tough treatment

○ **derr i egër** *[Zool]* wild boar *(Sus scrofa L.)*

○ **Të gjithë derrat një turi kanë.** "All pigs have the same snout." *(Prov)* They are all bad.

○ **derr me zile** "pig with a bell" *(Insult)* crude and coarse, uncouth, uncultured; disobedient, ill-behaved

○ **mish derri** pork

○ **derr në thes** *(Pej)* pig in a poke

○ **pëlcet· (edhe) derrin** "burst even the pig" to be unbearably annoying; {} would try the patience of a saint

○ **pëlcet·** ^{3sg} **(edhe) derri** "even the pig *bursts*" it *is* so hot that you could fry an egg on the sidewalk

derr|a'r *n* swineherd

de'rr|çe *adv (Colloq)* stubbornly, with might and main; bravely; severely, badly

*****derr|da'sh** *nm* mongrel

de'rr|e *nf (Colloq)* **1** stouthearted/brave and tireless woman: doughty woman **2** *(Pej)* stubborn woman **3** fat woman

derr|ëri' *nf collec* **1** swine taken as a whole **2** stubbornness

derr|ëri'sht *adv* = **de'rrçe**

derr|ku'c *nm* suckling pig
  ○ **derrkuc indie** [*Zool*] guinea pig

derr|ne'k *nm* crazy idea; whim

*****derr|ni'** = **derrëri'**

*****derr|ni'sht** *adv* = **de'rrçe**

derr|o|dja'lë *nm* *(Colloq)* really fine young man: some boy!

*****derr|o|gru'e** *nf (Reg Gheg)* shrewish woman

derr|o|pla'k *nm* *(Colloq)* tough old man: tough old geezer!

*****des-** = **vde's·**

desa'nt *nm* [*Mil*] assault landing force: commando unit, marine unit

deskripti'v *adj* descriptive

despo't *nm* despot

despota't *nm* domain governed by a despot

despoti'k *adj* despotic

despoti'zëm *nm* despotism

desteme'l *nm (Reg)* **1** scarf **2** handkerchief

destili'm *nm* distillation

destin|i'm *nm ger* **1** < **destino'·n 2** destination

destin|o'·n *vt* to destine, determine

*****desut|u'a|r** *adj (i)* = **pavde'kshëm**

desh
  I § *stem for pdef* < **do·n**
  II § *pcl* nearly, almost
  III § *np* **1** rams < **dash 2** projecting stones at the sides of a fireplace
  ○ **Deshi ta kafshonte dhe e puthi.** "He tried to bite him and instead kissed him." One intends to hurt someone but instead helps him.

deshifr|i'm *nm ger* **1** < **deshifro'·n 2** decipherment

deshifr|o'·n *vt* to decipher

deshifr|u'e|s
  I § *adj* deciphering
  II § *n* cipher clerk

deshifr|u'e|shëm *adj (i)* decipherable

*****deshm|** = **dëshm**

*****deshpëri'** = **dëshpëri'm**

*****desht** *stem for pdef* < **do·n**

*****de'sht-|et** *vpr* = **dështo'·n**

de'sht|as *adv* intentionally, on purpose

det *nm* sea
  ○ **deti Egje** Aegean Sea
  ○ **deti Jon** Ionian Sea
  ○ **u bë deti kos** "the sea became yogurt" it was there for the taking, there was a ton of the stuff
  ○ **det i lirë** open sea
  ○ **det mbi det** everywhere

deta'j *nm* **1** detail, particular **2** = **deta'l**

deta'l *nm* [*Tech*] machine part, part of a mechanism

deta'r
  I § *adj* of or pertaining to the sea, marine; nautical; maritime; naval; seafaring, seagoing
  II § *n* seaman

det|ari' *nf* seamanship

detashme'nt *nm* [*Mil*] detachment

detekti'v *nm* detective

determin|i'm *nm ger* **1** < **determino'·n 2** determination

determin|i'st
  I § *n* determinist
  II § *adj* deterministic

determin|i'zëm *nm* determinism

determin|o'·n *vt* to determine

de'të *3rd sg subj* < **do·n**

*****det|i'm** *nm ger* **1** < **deto'·n 2** voyage

*****de't|kë** *nf (Reg Tosk)* marble ball (a toy)

*****de'tn|u'e|r** *adj (fem ~ore) (Old)* = **deta'r**

*****det|o'·n** *vi* **1** to sail **2** to dictate

deto'r|ës *n (Old)* = **detyr|ës**

*****de't|ra** *np* < **det**

*****de'ts|u'e|r** *(Old)* = **de'tnu'e|r**

*****det|u'e|r** *(Old)* = **de'tnu'e|r**

detyrë *nf* **1** duty **2** assigned work: task; homework **3** obligation **4** assigned responsibility: charge, mission, post **5** *(Old)* debt
  ○ **detyra shtëpie** homework

detyr|ës *n (Old)* debtor

detyr|i'm *nm ger* **1** < **detyro'·het, detyro'·het 2** obligation **3** coercion **4** moral responsibility **5** debt
  ○ **detyrim ushtarak** compulsory military service

detyr|i'm|i'sht *adv (Book)* obligatorily, compulsorily

detyr|o'·het *vpr* **1** to be compelled, be required, be obliged **2** *(Book)* to be obligated, owe

detyr|o'·n *vt* **1** to compel, require **2** *(Book)* to put [] in one's debt: obligate

*****detyr|ta'r**
  I § *n* debtor
  II § *adj* indebted, in debt

detyr|u'a|r *adj (i)* = **detyru'eshëm**

detyr|u'e|s *adj* compelling, forcible

detyr|u'e|shëm *adj (i)* compulsory, obligatory, required; forced

deve *nf* **1** [*Zool*] camel **2** *(Colloq)* camel hair

deve|di'sh *adj* having large fruit/grain of high quality

*****deve'r** *nm* boy who leads the bride's horse (by the bridle)

devia|cio'n *nm* deviation

devia|to'r *nm* deviator

devij|i'm *nm ger* **1** < **devijo'·n 2** deviation; diversion, detour, divagation; digression **3** [*Biol Med*] deformity

devij|o'·n *vt* **1** to deviate **2** to divert

devi'le *nf* chicanery

*****devi'te** *nf* balcony

devi'zë *nf* **1** [*Fin*] foreign currency **2** *(Book)* motto, slogan

devocio'n *nm* devotion

devoll|i' *nm* native of Devoll

devoll|i'|çe
  I § *nf (Colloq)* folk dance of Devoll
  II § *adv* in the manner of Devoll
  III § *adj* of or pertaining to Devoll

devoll|i't *adj* of or pertaining to Devoll

devo't|shëm *adj (i)* **1** pious **2** devoted, dedicated

devot|shm|ëri' *nf (Book)* devotion

dezert|i'm *nm ger* **1** < **dezerto'·n 2** desertion

dezerto'o·*n vi* to desert

dezertor *n* deserter

dezertue's *nm* = **dezerto'r**

dezine'nce *nf* [*Ling*] desinence, grammatical ending

dezinfekta'nt *nm* disinfectant

dezinfekti'm *nm ger* **1** <**dezinfekto'**·*n* **2** decontamination

dezinfekto'·*n vt* to disinfect, decontaminate

dezinfektua'r *adj (i)* disinfected, decontaminated

dezinfektue's *adj, nm* disinfectant, decontaminant

dezhu'r *nm* building receptionist

dëbi'm *nm ger* <**dëbo'**·*n*

dëbo'o·*n vt* to force [] out/away: expel, deport; chase [] away/out, rout; get rid of [], dispel

dëbo're *nf* snow = **bo're**

dëbore'pastrue's *adj* = **bore'pastrue's**

dëbu'·*het vpr* (of a female animal) to be sexually receptive

dëbu'a'r *adj (i)* forced out/away, kicked out: expelled

dëbue's
　I § nm one who forces another out/away, expeller
　II § adj *expelling

dëfre'·*het vpr* to enjoy oneself

dëfre'·*n*
　I § vi to have fun
　II § vt **1** to entertain, amuse **2** to make [] glad: gladden

dëfri'm *nm ger* **1** <**dëfre'**·*n* **2** amusement, entertainment

Dëfri'm *nm* Dëfrim (male name)

dëfri'mta'r *adj* festive

dëfry'e *stem for pdef, adm, part* <**dëfre'**·*het*

dëfry'e's *adj* amusing, entertaining

dëfry'e'shëm *adj (i)* = **dëfry'es**

dëfte'·*het vpr* to reveal oneself; prove to be

dëfte'·*n vt* **1** to tell **2** to show, indicate **3** to point to/at/out []
　∘ <> **dëfte'**·*n* **dhëmbët** "show <> one's teeth" **1** to threaten <> **2** to reveal one's evil intentions

dëfte'nje's *nm* = **dëftue's**

dëfte'se *nf* **1** receipt; ticket **2** transcript of school record; certificate

dëfti'm *nm ger* <**dëfto'**·*n*, **dëfto'**·*het*

dëfto'o·*het*
　I § vpr to reveal oneself
　II § vpr **1** to confess **2** to prove to be, turn out to be

dëfto'o·*n vt* **1** to indicate, reveal **2** to point to/at [] **3** to tell

*****dëfto'js** *nm* table of contents

dëfto'r
　I § adj [*Ling*] **1** indicative **2** demonstrative
　II § nm [*Ling*] demonstrative pronoun

dëfto're *nf* [*Ling*] indicative mood (of verbs)

dëftue's
　I § adj **1** indicating, indicative **2** evidentiary
　II § nm **1** indicator **2** index finger

*****dëgje'**·*n* = **dëgjo'**·*n*

dëgje'se *nf* **1** obedience **2** (*Old*) <**dëgji'm**

dëgji'm *nm ger* **1** <**dëgjo'**·*n* **2** (sense of) hearing
　∘ **dëgjim me stetoskop** [*Med*] auscultation

dëgji'mo'r *adj* (*Book*) auditory

dëgjo'·*het vpr* to be audible <**dëgjo'**·*n*

∘ **nuk dëgjo'**·*het* [3sg] **as miza** not even a fly *can* be heard: you *can* hear a pin drop, there *is* complete silence

∘ <> **dëgjo'**·*het* [3sg] **fjala** "<>'s word is listened to" <> *is* influential, what <> says *has* a lot of weight

∘ **dëgjo'**·*het* [3sg] **nëpër botë** to be rumored

∘ **dëgjo'**·*het* [3sg] **vetëm kambana e** <> "only <>'s bell is listened to" (*Pej*) <> *is* the only one whose orders are obeyed: <> *is* the only one with any say

∘ **s'**<> **dëgjo'**·*het* [3sg] **zëri (fare)** "<>'s voice is not heard (at all)" <> *is* very quiet; <> *doesn't* say anything

∘ <> **dëgjo'**·*het* [3sg] **zëri** "<>'s voice is heard" **1** <>'s voice carries weight **2** <> *keeps* very quiet **3** <> *is* discovered

dëgjo'·*n*
　I § vt vi **1** to hear **2** to obey **3** to understand
　II § vt **1** to listen to [] **2** to heed, pay attention to [], take notice of [] **3** (with negatives only) won't hear of [], reject
　∘ **nuk dëgjo'**·*n* **nga ajo anë** not be afraid of that, not worry about that

dëgjo'nje's *n* = **dëgjue's**

dëgjua'r *adj (i)* **1** heard **2** obedient **3** renowned, famous

dëgjua'rit *nn (të)* (sense of) hearing

dëgjue's *n* listener; auditor

dëgjue'shëm *adj (i)* **1** audible **2** receptive to advice; obedient

dëgjue'shmëri *nf* (*Book*) **1** audibility **2** hearing ability

dëki'm *nm ger* (*Colloq*) <**dëko'**·*n*, **dëko'**·*het*

dëko'·*het vpr* **1** to fall into ruin **2** to get a hernia

dëko'·*n vt* **1** to beat, thrash **2** to knock [] down: destroy, ruin **3** to give [] a hernia *****4** to pour, spill

dëkua'r *adj (i)* (*Reg*) **1** fallen into ruin **2** herniated

dëli'r·*vt* **1** to clean, clean [] up/out; clear, clear [] up; cleanse **2** to trim **3** (*Euph*) to castrate **4** (*Fig Reg*) to liberate

dëli'r·*et vpr* **1** to get cleaned up **2** to be cleansed **3** to be released (from a burden or obligation) **4** (*Euph*) to give birth **5** (*Fig Regional Pej*) to scram

dëli're
　I § adj (i) **1** clean; pure, chaste **2** cleansed, innocent; honest; open **3** (*Euph*) delivered, relieved (said of a female who has just given birth) **4** (*Old*) liberated
　II § nn (të) cleanliness

dëli'rës
　I § adj cleansing
　II § n *cleaner

dëli're'si *nf* **1** cleanliness **2** purity, chastity; honesty, openness

dëli'rje *nf ger* <**dëli'r**·, **dëli'r**·*et*

*****dëli'rtas** *adv* purely, clearly

*****dëli'rtë** *adj (i)* pure, clear, clean

*****dëllëndy'she** = **dallëndy'she**

dëllë'ng'thi *adv* (*Reg*) with a purpose, deliberately

*****dëllë'nje** = **dëllinje**

dëllinje *nf* [*Bot*] juniper (*Juniperus L.D*)
　∘ **dëllinje e kuqe** [*Bot*] prickly juniper *Juniperus oxycedrus*
　∘ **dëllinje e zezë** [*Bot*] common juniper *Juniperus communis*

dëllinjtë *adj (i)* of or with juniper or juniper berries

dëm

I § *nm* **1** damage, harm **2** loss **3** detriment, disadvantage

II § *adv* for nothing, in vain

dëm|çpërbl|ím = dëmshpërblím

dëm|ës *adj, n (Colloq)* (person) capable of doing damage

dëm|prur|ës

I § *adj* harmful, noxious, damaging

II § *nm* harmful agent

dëm|sjell|ës *adj* = dëmprurës

dëm|sjell|ës *adj* = dëmprurës

dëm|shëm *adj (i)* (of something) capable of doing harm: damaging, harmful, injurious

dëm|shpërbl|e·n *vt* to indemnify, redress, recompensate

dëm|shpërbl|ím *nm ger* **1** <dëmshpërblo'·n **2** compensation, reparation

dëm|ta|r *adj, n* = dëmtues

dëm|t|ím *nm ger* **1** <dëmto·n, dëmto·het **2** damage, injury

dëm|t|o·het *vpr* to deteriorate

dëm|t|o·n *vt* to damage, injure, impair, harm, hurt

dëm|tu|ar *adj (i)* damaged, injured

dëm|tu|es

I § *adj* harmful, noxious, damaging

II § *nm* harmful agent

dëm|tu|e|shëm *adj (i)* perishable, vulnerable

*****dënë|(n)** *nm (Reg Gheg)* post, stake; pillar

dënd| = dend

*****dënd|ët** *adj (i)* = dendur

dënd|ur = dendur

dëne·s· *vi* to whimper; sob

dëne·s·et *vpr* = dënes·

dëne·s|ë *nf* whimper, whimpering; sob, sobbing

dëne·s|o·n *vi* = dënes·

dëng *adv (Colloq)* up to the brim, completely full

dëng|a *adv* = dengëza

dëng|ëza *adv* = dengëza

dëng|la *np (Colloq)* pompous praise; prattle, nonsense

dëng|la|ma|dh *adj (Colloq Pej)* pompous talker, prattler

dëng|je *np* <deng

*****dën|í** *nf* shrinkage, loss, dwindling

dën|ím *nm ger* <dëno·n

  ○ **dënim në mungesë** [*Law*] sentence in absentia

*****dën|im|ta|r** *adj* disciplinary, penal

dën|o·n *vt* **1** to condemn; convict; sentence **2** to punish, chastise, penalize

dën|u|ar *adj (i)* punished, penalized; convicted

dën|u|es *adj* condemnatory, punishing

dën|u|e|shëm *adj (i)* punishable; deserving of censure: reprehensible

dërçíkth *nm* [*Anat*] uvula

*****dërd|ëll|ís|** = dërdëllís

*****dërd|ëll|ít|** = dërdëllít

dërd|ëll|ís *stem for 1st sg pres, pl pres, 2nd & 3rd sg subj, pind* <dërdëllí·*(Old)*

dërd|ëll|ít· *vi vt (Colloq)* to prattle, talk twaddle

dërd|ëll|ít|je *nf ger (Colloq)* **1** <dërdëllít· **2** twaddle, nonsense

dërd|ë·ng *adj (ColloqImpolite)* fat = zdërdë·ng

dër-dër *onomat (Colloq Pej)* sound of pompous prattling: yatata-yatata

*****dërd|ëri|s|** = dërdëllís|

*****dërd|ëri|t|** = dërdëllít

dërdy|l *nm (Old)* **1** [*Folklore*] a big, powerful horse **2** *(Fig)* a big, powerful man

dërg|a|të *nf (Old)* delegation = delegacio'n

dërg|e|së *nf* **1** something sent: dispatch, shipment **2** *(Old)* <dërgím

*****dërg|es|ta|r** *n (Reg)* sender, dispatcher = dërgues

dërg|ím *nm ger* <dërgo·n

dërg|im|ta|r *n* **1** = dërgues *****2** *(Old)* envoy, delegate; apostle

dërg|o·n *vt* **1** to send, dispatch; transmit, forward **2** to mail, send by post; remit **3** to convey, carry, transport

  ○ [] **dërgo·n në djall** "send [] to the devil" to send [] to a living Hell

  ○ [] **dërgo·n në litarë** to send [] to the gallows

  ○ [] **dërgo·n prapa diellit** to send [] into the hinterlands; get rid of [] forever

dërg|u|ar

I § *adj (i)* heard

II § *nm (i)* envoy, delegate; (newspaper) correspondent

dërg|u|es

I § *nm* **1** sender, dispatcher **2** conveyor *****3** errand boy, deliveryman **4** transmitter

II § *adj* sending; transmitting

dërhe'm *nm* **1** *(Old)* former measure of weight equal to a little more than 3 grams **2** *(Colloq)* small metal weights for a balance scale **3** *(Fig Colloq)* tiny amount

dërko|re *nf* restaurant, inn

*****dërku·n** *vi* = dreko·n

dërma|ke *nf* = dërrmake

dërm|ë *nf* = dërrmë

*****dërm|ëhas·** = dërrmëhas·

dërm|í *nf* = dërrmí

dërm|ím *nm ger* <dërrmím

dër|mísh· *vt* **1** to scratch [a part of the body] deeply; tear []'s flesh, lacerate **2** to torture

dër|mishe *nf* torture, agony

*****dërm|ít·** *vi* = dremít·

dërm|o·n *vt* **1** *(Reg)* to sift with a coarse sieve *****2** = dërrmo·n

dërmo|n

I § *nm (Reg)* coarse sieve, riddle = sitac

II § *adv* full of holes

dërm|onjës = dërrmues

*****dërm|ore** = dërrmore

dërm|ue|s = dërrmues

*****dërm|ue|shëm** *adj (i)* crumbly, friable

dërno|k *nm* [*Bot*] hedge hyssop *(Gratiola officinalis)*

*****dër|o·n** = duro·n

dërpë'nj *np* <drapër

dërsi·het *vpr* = djersít·et

dërsi·n *vi vt* = djersít·

*****dërsi|f·** = djersít·

dërsi|rë *adj (i)* = djersitur

*****dërsi|s** = djersís|

*****dërsí·t·** = djersít·

dërsi|tje = djersítje

dërstíl· *vt* = dërstílo·n

dërstíl·et *vpr* = dërstílo·het

dërstila'r n 1 [Text] person who fulls cloth: fuller 2 owner of a fulling machine

dërstili' nf 1 [Text] fulling mill 2 = dërstili'm 3 (Colloq) fulled woolen cloth, felt
  ○ s'[] lan (dot) as dërstila "not even a fulling mill can clean []" 1 [] is deeply soiled 2 all the waters of the world cannot wash out []'s guilt

dërstili'm nm ger [Text] <dërstilo'·n, dërstilo'·het

dërstili'je nf ger [Text] = dërstili'm

dërstilo'·het vpr [Text] to acquire the characteristics of fulled cloth

dërstilo'·n vt [Text] to full [cloth]

*****dërstila'r** = dërstilar

dërstilua'r adj (i) [Text] having the characteristics of fulled cloth

dërstilu'r adj (i) = dërstilua'r

*****dërteje'** OR dërtele' = ndërtese'

dërti' nf (Old) make-up for women = ndërti'

*****dërvllo'sh·** vt to abrade; tear/rip up []; lacerate

dërzhe'kë nf pole used to raise and lower a lift net into the water

dërra'se
  I § nf 1 board, plank 2 stone tile 3 (Colloq) mold-board of a wooden plow
  II § adj 1 (Fig Colloq Pej) smooth and flat as a board; flat-chested 2 (Fig Colloq Pej) stupid; totally ignorant
  ○ ësh-të dërrasë to have nothing left, be flat broke
  ○ dërrasa e dritares window shutter
  ○ dërrasë dyshe board 2 centimeters thick
  ○ dërrasë gjashtëshe six-centimeter thick board
  ○ dërrasë katërshe four-centimeter thick board
  ○ dërrasë e krahërorit [Med] sternum, breastbone
  ○ dërrasë (prej) tallashi particleboard
  ○ dërrasë vizatimi easel
  ○ dërrasë e zezë (school) blackboard

dërra'së'z nf 1 roof board, roof sheathing 2 (Dimin) = dërrasë

dërrasi'm nm [Constr] strip flooring

dërra'skë nf [Constr] wood slat

dërra'stë adj (i) 1 made of wood, wooden 2 flat and smooth

dërrma'ç adj 1 = dërrma'sh *2 fragment, crumb, speck

dërrma'k
  I § adj 1 finely ground = dërrma'ke 2 very small and hunched up; tiny (for the whole body)
  II § adv 1 in a clump/huddle 2 in an incomplete mess, not finished

dërrma'ke nf 1 fragment; crumb 2 baked corn mush

dërrma'sh nm 1 [Dairy] fresh cheese eaten as finger food 2 [Food] warm baked or boiled dish made of soft ground cheese and butter mixed with bread or corn flour

dërrm'ë nf 1 rocky mountain cliff with few trees; chasm *2 inaccessible abyss full of loose stone rubble

dërrmë'ha's· vt (Colloq·) to scatter

dërrmë'ha's·et vpr (Colloq) to become scattered: scatter

dërrmi' nf crushed or crumbled piece: fragment, crumb, shard

dërrmi'm nm ger <dërrmo'·n, dërrmo'·het

dërrmi'sh· vt to scratch (skin) [] deeply

dërrmi'shje nf ger <dërrmi'sh·

dërrmo'·het vpr 1 to crumble to pieces 2 (Fig) to be badly hurt; suffer a terrible shock 3 (Fig) to be utterly worn out

dërrmo'·n vt 1 to break [] into small pieces: crush, squash, shatter 2 (Colloq) to shell [grain] 3 (Fig) to overstrain: wear out, exhaust 4 (Fig) to defeat: crush, overwhelm 5 (Fig) to shock
  ○ <> dërrmo·n dhëmbët/hundët/brinjët/turinjtë/nofullat/fulqinjtë (Scorn) to beat <> to a pulp; teach <> a good lesson; make <> swallow <>'s boasts; make <> eat <>'s words

*****dërrmo're** nf crowd, swarm

dërrmua'r adj (i) 1 fragmented into small pieces, shattered 2 (Colloq) shelled 3 badly hurt/wounded 4 (Fig) badly hurt; suffering a terrible shock 5 (Fig) utterly worn out

dërrmue's adj 1 crushing, shattering 2 (Fig) destructive 3 (Fig) overwhelming

Dëshi'ra nf Dëshira (female name)

*****dëshira'të** nf (Old) object of desire

dëshi'rë nf desire, wish, will

dëshirë'ma'dh adj having a strong desire, desirous

dëshirë'plo'të adj = dëshirë'ma'dh

dëshiri'm nm ger 1 <dëshiro'·n, dëshiro'·het 2 yen, strong desire; yearning, longing

dëshiro'·het vpr 1 to have a strong desire 2 to have a yearning/longing, yearn/long

dëshiro'·n vt 1 to desire, wish, want 2 to yearn/long for []; have a yen for []
  ○ Dëshiron të të puthë e të ha me dhëmbë. "He intends to kiss you and bites you instead." One intends to help you but hurts you instead.

dëshiro'r adj 1 expressing a desire or wish 2 [Ling] optative (mood of verbs), desiderative

dëshiro're nf [Ling] optative

dëshirua'r adj (i) 1 desired; suitable; desirable; necessary 2 desirous, eager 3 expressing desire: appealing

dëshirue's adj expressing strong desire: hungry, covetous

dëshirue'shëm adj (i) desirable; suitable; pleasing

dëshmi' nf 1 testimony, attestation; evidence 2 certificate, affidavit
  ○ dëshmi karantinore certificate of quarantine; quarantine notice

dëshmi'm nm ger 1 <dëshmo'·n, dëshmo'·het 2 testimony

dëshmi'tar n 1 witness 2 (Old) martyr
  ○ dëshmitar pamor eye witness

dëshmo'·het vpr to be attested, be manifested

dëshmo'·n vt to testify, attest, bear witness to

dëshmo'r n martyr

*****dëshmo'rkë** nf (Reg) <dëshmo'r

dëshmue's
  I § adj attesting, evidentiary
  II § nm 1 testimonial, evidence 2 (Old) witness

dëshpëri'm nm ger 1 <dëshpëro'·n, dëshpëro'·het 2 despair, desperation, despondency, discouragement
  ○ dëshpërim i madh deep despair

dëshpëro'·het vpr to despair

dëshpëro'·n vt 1 to cause [] despair: dishearten, demoralize 2 to make [] very sad: sadden

dëshpëru'ar adj (i) 1 in despair, disheartened, disappointed 2 saddened 3 desperate

dëshpër·u·e·s *adj* causing despair

dëshpër·u·e·shëm *adj (i)* **1** desperate **2** saddening, depressing

*dëshprim·ta·r
I § *adj* despairing, pessimistic
II § *n* pessimist

dështa·k *adj* **1** aborted, miscarried **2** *(Reg)* born prematurely **3** *(Pej)* runty **4** *(Fig)* abortive

dështi *nf* **1** miscarriage **2** *(Fig)* failure

dështim *nm ger* **1** < **dështo·** *n* **2** failure; miscarriage **3** premature birth

dështim·o·re *nf* maternity ward section for miscarriages and abortions

dështim·sje·ll·ës *adj* [*Med*] abortifacient

dështo· *n vi* to abort, miscarry; go wrong; fail

dështu·ar *adj (i)* **1** [*Med*] stillborn, aborted, miscarried **2** *(Fig)* failed **3** born prematurely **4** *(Pej)* runty

dështu·e·s *adj* **1** causing abortion; causing failure **2** abortive

dështy·rë *nf (Colloq)* premature child, abortion

*dëvo·rë = dëbo·rë

*dëvo·rr *nm* broad plain

di· *vt* **1** to know **2** to know how to do **3** to consider to be, take for **4** = **gdhi·**n
  ○ **s'<>a di· anën** not *know* where <> *comes* from: not know what *causes* <>
  ○ **ia di· burmat** to find the key, figure out
  ○ **nuk di· ç'është ika** to run away from nothing
  ○ **e di· ç'ke ti?!** (said parenthetically) let me tell you something
  ○ **<>a di· çarkun** to know <> inside out, know <> to <>'s core
  ○ **nuk di· fjalë** not speak in a roundabout way, speak straightforwardly
  ○ **<>a di· fundin e barkut** to know <> to the very depths of <>'s heart
  ○ **s'di gomari ç'është bari** "the donkey doesn't know what grass is" *(Impol)* (said of someone who does not know what good is)
  ○ **E di (vetë) gomari ku e vret samari.** "The donkey (himself) knows where the saddle hurts him." *(Prov)* Everyone knows his own problems best. Who knows best where the shoe pinches.
  ○ **E di Gjoni çfarë ka në trastë/thes.** "John knows what there is in his bag." *(Prov)* Each person know his own situation best.
  ○ **<>a di· gjuhën** to know <>'s intentions, know <> very well
  ○ **<>i di· huqet** to know <>'s habits and ways; know how to deal with <>
  ○ **Nuk di· kë të zë·**^*subj* **e kë të lë·**^*subj* "{} *doesn't* know which to take and which to leave" {} *doesn't* know where even to begin.
  ○ **<>i di· kryqet** "know <>'s tail bones" to know *<someone>* intimately
  ○ **e di· ku <> dhemb dhëmbi** "know where the tooth hurts" to know what <>'s needs are; know where <>'s weaknesses lie
  ○ **e di· ku i ka morri sytë** "*know* where the louse has its eyes" to know everything, be very smart/ shrewd
  ○ **e di· ku pjell pula** "know where the chicken lays eggs" to know what good is
  ○ **di· ku shkel·** "know where one is stepping" to be prudent/cautious

  ○ **s'di· të lidhë as dy fjalë (bashkë)** not know how to put two words together: be incapable of expressing oneself clearly
  ○ **E di luga se ç'ka vorba/vegshi/poçja.** "The spoon knows what the pot contains." *(Prov)* Who knows your problems better than you do?
  ○ **<>i di· lugët e pirunët** "know <>'s spoons and forks" to know *<someone>* inside out, know <> in intimate detail
  ○ **<>i di· lugët në kaçile** "know the spoons in <>'s basket" to know all <>'s secrets, know <> in intimate detail
  ○ **nuk di· llafe** {} does not go for long stories, {} is a person of few words
  ○ **s'i di· majë vetes** "not find one's own hilltop" not know how to get out of a predicament
  ○ **[] di· me rrënjë e me degë** "know [] by root and by branch" to know [] backwards and forwards, know [] inside out?
  ○ **[] di· me pëllëmbë** to know every inch of [the place]
  ○ **E di·**^*3sg* **mesi se ç'ka thesi.** "One's waist knows what the sack contains." *(Prov)* Only the wearer knows where the shoe pinches.
  ○ **<>a di· mirë shtegun/shtigjet** to know (well) the ins and outs of <>
  ○ **nuk di· mort** to be very durable
  ○ **[] di· në majë të gishtrinjve** "know [] to the fingertips" to know [] down to the last detail, know [] backwards and forwards
  ○ **[] di· në thumb e në potkua** to know [] in detail, know [] backwards and forwards
  ○ **s'di· nga kapet** to have no idea how to go about it
  ○ **s'di· nga lidh·**et^*3sg* **gomari** "not know how // from which end a donkey is tied" *(Impol)* not know (how to do) even the simplest thing, be totally incapable
  ○ **nuk di· nga ta zë· fillin** "not know from where to take the thread" not know how to begin, not know what to do (first), not know how to get a handle on it
  ○ **nuk <>a di· optin 1** not even know what <> looks like **2** not have seen <> for a long time, have forgotten what <> looks like; have no idea where <> is
  ○ **[] di· pëllëmbë për pëllëmbë** to know every inch of [the place]
  ○ **[] di· për fije** to know [] in detail
  ○ **<>a di· për nder** to acknowledge <> with gratitude, be grateful to <>
  ○ **E di· qyp!** {} *knows* it perfectly well!
  ○ **<>i di· sa lugë ka· në shtëpi** "know how many spoons one *has* at home" to know *<someone>* inside out, know <> in intimate detail
  ○ **E di se ku [] vret·**^*3sg* **barra.** "[] *knows* where the load *rubs*." [] knows best what []'s problems/ weaknesses are.
  ○ **s'di· si lidh·**et^*3sg* **gomari** "not know how // from which end a donkey is tied" *(Impol)* not know (how to do) even the simplest thing, be totally incapable
  ○ **s'di· si lidhen poturet** "not know how to tie up one's own pants" *(Impol)* not know (how to do) even the simplest thing, be totally incapable
  ○ **<>a di· shtegun/shtigjet** to know (well) the ins and outs of <>
  ○ **<>a di· shyqyrin** to know how valuable <> is
  ○ **s'di· t'i japë ujë as gomarit** "he doesn't know how to give water to the donkey" *(Impol)* {} *is* very

foolish: {} *doesn't* know enough to come in out of the rain

○ **di· t'i rreshto·**n **fjalët** to know how to put things (when one speaks): speak well

○ **nuk di· t'ia zhgrap·** *(Colloq)* not know how to write at all, not even know how to scribble

○ **nuk di· të fshi· hundët** "not know how to wipe one's own nose" *(Impol)* to be incompetent to live on one's own

○ **di· të gdhendë fjalë** "know how shape words" to be able to express oneself beautifully

○ **s'di të lidhë ushkurin/ushkurët** "not know how to tie up one's own waistband" *(Impol)* to be totally incompetent

○ **s'di· të mbath·**^{subj} **as brekët** "can't even put on one's own underpants" *(Impol Crude)* {} *is* totally incompetent, {} can't even do the simplest things

○ **<>i di· të mbërthyerat 1** to be on to <>'s tricks **2** to know how <> is put together

○ **<>i di· të larat e të palarat** to know both the good and the bad about <*someone*>, know <> down to the dirtiest detail

○ **di· të qepë me dyzet gjilpëra** to be very adept/capable

○ **la di trari e carani. 1** Everyone knows his own problems best. You know best where your own shoe pinches **2** The person who works most closely with something knows best where its problems lie.

○ [] **di·**^{pres} **vetë** "*know* [] {}self" {} knows perfectly well how to do []

○ **di· zhurin e detit** "know the sand of the sea" to know all kinds of things, be very knowledgeable

di··*het vpr* <**di·** = **gdhi**·*het*

○ **S'di·**het^{3sg}! You never *know* (what *can* happen)!

diabe't *nm* [*Med*] diabetes

diabetík *adj, n* diabetic

diade'me *nf* diadem

diafi'lm *nm* film strip; set of slides

diafra'gmë *nf* **1** diaphragm **2** [*Cine*] stop; aperture

diagno'zë *nf* diagnosis

diagona'l *adj* diagonal

diagona'le *nf* **1** diagonal line **2** [*Soccer*] diagonal pass

diagra'm *nm* diagram

diako'n *nm* [*Relig*] deacon

diakritík *adj* diacritic, diacritical

diakroni' *nf* [*Ling*] diachrony

diale'kt *nm* [*Ling*] dialect, speech variety

dialektá'l *adj* = **dialekto'r**

dialektík *nm* [*Phil*] dialectic, pertaining to dialectics

dialektíkë *nf* **1** [*Phil*] dialectics **2** dialectical development

dialektikí'sht *adv* dialectically

dialektíz'ëm *nm* [*Ling*] dialectal expression

dialektolo'g *n* dialectologist

dialektologjí *nf* dialectology

dialektologjík *adj* dialectological

dialekto'r *adj* dialectal

dialo'g *nm* dialogue

diama'nt *nm* diamond

diame'tër *nm* diameter

diametra'l *adj* diametric

diametralí'sht *adv* diametrically

diapazo'n *nm* **1** [*Mus*] diapason; tuning fork **2** [*Mus*] pitch **3** *(Fig)* range

diapozitív *nm* (projection) slide, diapositive

diaprojekto'r *nm* [*Cine*] slide projector

diarre' *nf* [*Med*] diarrhea

○ **diarre tropikale** [*Med*] sprue

dia'spër *nm* [*Min*] jasper

diate'zë *nf* [*Ling*] voice, the relationship that a verb form expresses with its subject and object

di'bël

I § *nf* **1** baklava with two layers of nuts **2* weakness, feeling faint

II § *adj* *** = **de'bull**

Di'bër *nf* the city of Dibra

*****diblo·**·*het vpr (Old)* to faint, lose consciousness

*****diblo·**·n *vt (Old)* to cause [] to feel faint; enfeeble

*****diblu'em** *adj (i) (Old)* feeling faint, exhausted

dibra'n

I § *adj* of/from Dibra

II § *n* **1** native of Dibra **2** bricklayer, mason

dibra'nçe *adv* Dibra-style; in the dialect of Dibra

*****di'ca** = **disa**

*****dici'li** = **diku'sh**

diç *pron* = **di'çka**

○ **diç luan këtu/në këtë mes!** something fishy is going on here!

*****di'çëm** *adj (i)* = **di'jshëm**

di'çka

I § *pron* some definite but indeterminate thing: something

II § *adv* somewhat

○ **diçka e atillë** something of that kind

○ **diçka lëviz·**^{3sg} something (fishy) *is* going on

○ **diçka luan këtu/në këtë mes!** something fishy is going on here!

○ **diçka po zien këtu** something is in the works; something fishy is going on here

di'çka'je *abl dat* <**di'çka**

didaktík *adj* didactic

didaktíkë *nf* didactics

didaskalík *adj* pedagogical

di'el *nf (e)* Sunday

dielektrík *adj* [*Phys*] dielectric

di'ell *nm (np* ̃ *j)* sun

○ **Dielli duket që në mëngjes.** "The sun starts appearing in the morning." *(Prov)* You can tell right from the start if something will go well. You can tell right from the start if someone will do well.

○ **Dielli lind për të gjithë.** "The sun rises for all." *(Prov)* There's room for everyone. The world is big enough for everyone.

○ **diell më diell** from sunup to sundown **2** the whole day

○ **Dielli i mëngjesit të ngroh më mirë se i pasdrekës.** "The morning sun warms you better than the afternoon sun does." *(Prov)* One needs to start early when one is still fresh/young.

○ **Mos pa**^{opt} **diell me sy!** *(Curse)* May {} never see daylight again!

○ **gënjeshtra/rrena në diell** patent lies

○ **Diell e paç!** "May you have sun!" *(Felic)* Good luck!

dielldri'dhës *nm* [*Bot*] heliotrope *(Heliotropium europaeum)*

diellishtë *nf* sunny place

diello·r *adj* **1** solar **2** solar

***diellshëm** *adj (i)* sunny

diellzi·m *nm ger* <diellzo`·n`, diellzo`he·t

diellzo`·het *vpr* to lie in the sunshine, be exposed to the sun

diellzo`·n *vt* **1** to bathe [] in sunlight **2** to put/ripen [] in the sun; let [] lie in the sunshine

***diersue·r** *adj (fem ˜ore) (Old)* = djersi`tur

***di·err** = djerr·

***di·es** OR **diesta·r** *n* wizard, sorcerer: seer, sage

die·të *nf* **1** diet regimen: diet **2** payment for per diem expenses

die·z *nm, adj* [Mus] sharp

dif-dragu·a *nm (obl ˜ o`i, np ˜ o`nj)* giant dragon

dife·kt *nm* defect

defensi·v = defensi·v·

difere·ncë *nf (Book)* difference

diferencia·l *nm* differential

diferenci·m *nm ger (Book)* <diferenco`·n, diferenco`·het

diferenco`·het *vpr (Book)* to become differentiated

diferenco`·n *vt (Book)* to differentiate

diferencua·r *adj (i) (Book)* differentiated

***dift** = dëft

***difte·r** = defte·r

difteri· *nf* [Med Veter] diphtheria

***difteri·t** *nm* = difteri·

difto·ng *nm (np ˜ gje)* [Ling] diphthong

   ◦ **diftong ngjitës** [Ling] rising diphthong

   ◦ **diftong zbritës** [Ling] falling diphthong

diftongi·m *nm ger* [Ling] <diftongo`·n

diftongo`·n *vt* to diphthongize

di`gë *nf* **1** dike; dam **2** [Cine] sun arc, sun lamp

digra·m *nm* [Ling] digraph

di`gj·et *vpr* **1** to burn, burn up; get burned **2** to burn out **3** (Fig) to feel a burning sensation; have a yen **4** (Fig Colloq) to lose/quit a game

   ◦ **nuk <> digj·et**^{3sg} **barku për** [] (Scorn) <> doesn't give a damn about [], <> doesn't lose any sleep over []

   ◦ **digj·et**^{3sg} **edhe i njomi (bashkë) me të thatin** "the wet *burns* (together) with the dry" the innocent *pay* (together) with the guilty

   ◦ **<> digj·et**^{3sg} **hasra nën vete** "<>'s floor mat *is burning* under <>" <> *has* a lot to worry about

   ◦ **digj·et**^{3sg} **i njomi për të thatin** "the wet *burns* in place of the dry" the innocent *pay* for the sins of the guilty

   ◦ **<> digj·et**^{3pl} **kartat ndër duar** <>'s plans *go up* in smoke

   ◦ **<> digj·et**^{3sg} **koka** "<>'s head *is burning*" **1** <>'s head *is burning* (with fever **2** <> *is* at wit's end trying to figure a way out of <>'s terrible situation

   ◦ **<> digj·et**^{3pl} **letrat ndër duar** <>'s plans *go up* in smoke

   ◦ **<> digj·et**^{3sg} **mjekra** "<>'s chin *is burning*" <> *is* at wit's end trying to figure a way out of <>'s terrible situation

   ◦ **digj·et ndër vete** to be suffering inside

   ◦ **digj·et në prush për** [] to willing to die for []

   ◦ **<> digj·et**^{3sg} **rrogozi nën vete** "<>'s floor mat *is burning* under <>" <> *has* a lot to worry about

   ◦ **<> digj·et**^{3sg} **shpirti (për** []) "<>'s soul *burns* (for [])" **1** <> *is yearning* (for []), <> has <>'s heart set (on []) **2** <>'s heart *is suffering*

   ◦ **<> digj·et**^{3sg} **toka/trualli nën këmbë** "the ground *burns* under <>'s feet" nowhere *is* there safety for <>, there is no respite for <> there

   ◦ **<> digj·et**^{3sg} **zemra (për** []) "<>'s heart *burns* (for [])" **1** <> *is yearning* (for []), <> has <>'s heart set (on []) **2** <>'s heart *is suffering*

   ◦ **<> digj·et**^{3sg} **zemra horë** <> *has* a burning desire

   ◦ **<> digj·et**^{3sg} **zemra prush për** [] <>'s heart is yearning for []

di`gj *stem for imper, pind, vn, 2nd plur pres* <dje·g·

digje·piq *indecl masc (Old)* time in December when there is no agricultural work to be done in the mountains

***digjo`·n** = dëgjo`·n

diha·s *stem for 1st sg pres, pl pres, 2nd & 3rd sg subj, pind* <diha·t·

diha·t·

  I § *vi* to gasp for air after physical exertion: pant

  II § *vt* to inhale [] deeply

diha·tje *nf ger* <diha·t·

di·je *nf* **1** knowledge, learning **2** (Reg) news, information

dijeda·shës *adj* knowledge-loving

dijeke·q *adj* evil-intentioned, sly

dijekeqësi· *nf* evilness, slyness

dijekeqi· = dijekeqësi·

dije·ni· *nf* knowledge, awareness

dijeplo`të *adj* knowledgeable

dijeta·r *n* (Book) erudite person: savant

di·jë *nf* = di·je

di·jës *n (Old)* **1** savant **2** seer, fortune-teller

dijshëm *adj (i)* knowledgeable, learned, educated

***di·jt** = di·t

***dika·h** = diku·

dikaste·r *nm* government agency/ministry

dikasteria·l *adj* **1** at the level of the governmental agency, ministerial **2** (Pej) bureaucratic

di·kë *nf (Reg)* strong desire, lust

di·kë *acc* <diku·sh

diko`·n

  I § *vi* **1** to flow **2** to trickle out slowly; drip

  II § *vt* to trickle [] out

dikotiledo`n *adj* [Bot] dicotyledonous

dikotiledo`ne *np* [Bot] dicotyledonous plants, dicotyledons

diksio·n *nm (Book)* diction

dikta·t *nm* [Law Book] dictate; dictation

diktato·r *n* dictator

diktatoria·l *adj (Book)* dictatorial

diktatu·rë *nf* dictatorship

diktimi·m *nm ger* **1** <diktimo`·n, dikto`·het **2** dictation

diktimi·m *nm ger* <diktimo`·n

diktimo`·n *vt* [Law] (Old) to appeal a case to a higher court

diktimo·r *adj* [Law] (Old) appellate

dikto`·n *vt* **1** to dictate **2** to detect; figure out []

diktu·es

  I § *nm* **1** person who dictates **2** detector

  II § *adj* detecting

diktu·e·shëm *adj (i) (Old)* [*Law*] subject to appeal: appealable

di·ku *adverb* **1** somewhere, anywhere **2** once in a while
 ○ **diku rrotull** around here somewhere, somewhere around here

diku-diku *adv* here and there

di·ku·jt *dat* <**dikush**

di·ku·nd *adverb* somewhere = **diku**

di·ku·r *adverb* **1** sometime in the past: in the old days, long ago **2** sometime in the future: someday **3** *(Colloq)* finally

di·ku·r·shëm *adj (i)* of former times: old-time, bygone, ancient

di·ku·sh *pron* someone, somebody
 ○ **dikush haj-haj, dikush vaj-vaj** some win, some lose
 ○ **dikush përpjetë e dikush tatëpjetë** some (people) do well, some/others don't

di·ku·te·k *adv* someplace or other, far off somewhere

dil *stem for 2nd pl pres, pind, imper, vn* <**de·l·**

dile·më *nf* dilemma

dileta·nt *nm* **1** *(Pej)* dilettante **2** amateur

diletant·íz·ëm *nm (Pej)* dilettantism

dilu·v *nm* deluge, flood

dimensio·n *nm* dimension

di·më *1st plur pres* <**di·**

di·mër *nm* winter
 ○ **Dimri ha gozhdë/gurë/kashtë.** "Winter eats nails/rocks/straw." *(Prov)* When times are hard, you do with whatever you have.
 ○ **Dimri ha beharin.** "Winter eats the summer." *(Prov)* Summer harvest for winter food. One must plan ahead.
 ○ **dimër i madh** severe winter
 ○ **dimër i rëndë** hard winter

dimëra·k
 I § *adj* wintry
 II § *nm* [*Ornit*] chaffinch (*Fringilla coelebs*) = **borës**

dimër·ím *nm ger* <**dimëro·n, dimëro·het**

dimër·ísht·e *nf* **1** winter pasture **2** winter fodder **3** wild cabbage eaten in winter

dimëro·n
 I § *vi* **1** to spend/survive the winter (somewhere): winter **2** to hibernate
 II § *vt* to arrange winter protection for [animals]

dimëro·r
 I § *adj* wintry, hibernal
 II § *nm (Old)* December

dimëru·e·s *adj* spending the winter, wintering; hibernating

dimí *nf (Colloq)* billowing white satin pantaloons that narrow at the ankles = **çitja·ne**

diminutí·v *nm* [*Ling*] diminutive

dimiski *nf (Old)* two edged sword of ornamented Damascus steel

*****dimisqí** = **dimiski**

*****dimít**ë *nf* = **çitja·ne**

*****dimn**| *(Reg Gheg)* = **dim**ër|

dimr·it *adv* in wintertime, during the winter

din *nm* [*Relig*] *(Old)* faith
 ○ **s'ka· din e iman** to be merciless/hard-hearted

dina·k
 I § *adj* sly, cunning, crafty, wily; tricky

 II § *n* sly fox; tricky person

dinak·ërí *nf* slyness, cunning, craftiness, wiliness; trickery

dinak·ërí·sht *adv* cunningly, craftily, slyly, artfully; using trickery

dinam·ík *adj* dynamic

dinam·ík·ë *nf* dynamics

dinam·ít *nm* dynamite

dinam·íz·ëm *nm* dynamism

dinamo *nf* [*Tech*] dynamo, generator

dinamo·me·tër *nm* [*Tech*] dynamometer

dina·r *nm* **1** dinar (monetary unit used in many countries that were formerly in the Ottoman empire) **2** *(Old)* = **marce·l**

Dinaríkë *np fem* Dinaric Alps

dinastí *nf* dynasty

di·nd·et *vpr* to shake suddenly, quake; jump with a start

di·ndje *nf ger* <**di·nd·et**

di·në *nf* [*Phys*] dyne

di·në *3rd plur pres* <**di·**

*****ding** = **dëng**

di·ngë *nf (Old)* crude workshop for making gunpowder

*****di·ngo·s·et** *vpr* to get crammed in

dinoza·ur *nm* [*Paleo*] dinosaur

dinjita·r *n (Old)* dignitary

dinjite·t *nm* dignity

dinjito·z *adj* dignified

dio·dë *nf* [*Electr*] diode

dioptrí *nf* [*Phys Med*] diopter

dioqe·zë *nf* [*Relig*] diocese

diplomací *nf* diplomacy
 ○ **diplomaci e strucit** policy based on hiding one's head in the sand

diploma·nt *nm* graduating student

diploma·t *nm* diplomat

diplom·atík *adj* diplomatic

diplo·më *nf* **1** diploma **2** diploma project or thesis prepared by a senior in college

diplom·ím *nm ger* <**diplomo··het**

diplomo··het *vpr* to receive a diploma; graduate

diplom·ua·r *adj (i)* having an academic degree or diploma, graduate; having a certificate of participation in a competition

dipo·l *nm* dipole

dipte·rë *np* [*Zool*] diptera

*****di·q** = **vdi·q**

*****diqe·l** = **dhiqe·l**

di·qy·sh *adv* somehow, somehow or other

dirdh *sg imper* <**derdh·**

dire·k *nm* **1** support post made of wood or metal: mast; door jamb, window-post **2** *(Fig)* person of greatest importance or responsibility
 ○ **direku i përparmë** foremast

dire·kt *adj* direct

direktí·vë *nf* directive, instruction

di·rë *nf (Reg)* spoor = **fërke·m**

di·rgj·et *vpr* **1** to melt **2** to come down, go down = **zdirgj·et**

dirigje·nt *n* **1** [*Mus*] conductor **2** *(Fig Book)* director

dirigj·ím *nm ger* <**dirigjo··n**

dirigjo·*n vt* **1** to direct/conduct [musicians] **2** *(Fig Book)* to direct/lead [an organization]

dirigjue̱s *nm* **1** [*Mus*] conductor **2** *(Fig Book)* director

dirk *nm (np ~ q)* = **derk**

dirs· *vi (Reg)* = **djersi̱t**·

di̱rs·*et vpr* = **djersi̱t**·*et*

di̱rsë = **djers**ë

*****di̱rr** *stem for 2nd pl pres, pind, imper, vn* <**djerr**·

disa̱
  I § *quant* several
  II § *pcl* quite some
  ○ **Disa jashtë valles dinë shumë këngë.** "Several of those not dancing know many songs." *(Prov)* It's easy to criticize when you are not doing it yourself.

disaba̱llësh *adj* = **disafa̱qësh**

disadi̱tësh *adj* **1** several days old **2** lasting several days

disadi̱tor *adj* **1** lasting several days **2** several days old

disafa̱qësh *adj* multi-faceted

disahe̱rshëm *adj (i)* repetitive

disaja̱vësh *adj* lasting several weeks

disaka̱tësh *adj* multi-storied

disallo̱jësh *adj* various, varied, of several kinds

disamua̱jësh *adj* **1** several months old **2** several months long, every several months

disamu̱jor *adj* **1** lasting several months **2** several months old

disangjy̱rësh *adj* variegated in color

disavaria̱ntësh *adj* having multiple versions/variants

disavje̱ҫar *adj* **1** lasting several years **2** several years old

disenja̱tor *n* **1** draftsman **2** clothes designer

dise̱njo *nf* design

disertacio̱n *nm* dissertation

disfa̱të *nf* **1** defeat **2** failure

disfati̱st *n* defeatist

disfati̱zëm *nm* defeatism

disfavo̱r *nm* disfavor

disfavo̱rshëm *adj (i)* disfavorable, unfavorable

di̱si *adv* **1** somehow, in some manner; somewhat **2** somewhat, to some degree

diside̱ncë *nf* dissidence

disimili̱m *nm ger* **1** [*Biol*] = **shpërveti̱m** **2** [*Ling*] dissimilation

disipli̱në *nf* discipline

disiplini̱m *nm ger* <**disiplino̱**·*n*, **disiplino̱**·*het*

disiplino̱·*het vpr* to undergo discipline, become disciplined

disiplino̱·*n vt* to discipline

disipli̱nor *adj* disciplinary

disiplinua̱r *adj (i)* well-disciplined, obedient

disiplinue̱s *adj* serving to discipline: disciplinary

disk *nm* **1** disk **2** [*Sport*] discus **3** tray **4** wheel rim
  ○ **disk gome** [*Hockey*] puck
  ○ **disk numrash telefoni** telephone dial
  ○ **disk thirrjeje** telephone dial

diskhe̱dhës *n* [*Sport*] discus-thrower

diski̱m *nm ger* <**disko̱**·*n*

disko̱·*n vt* [*Agr*] to cultivate [] with a disk harrow: disk

disko̱r *adj* disk-shaped

diskote̱kë *nf* **1** collection of phonograph records **2** discotheque

diskrediti̱m *nm ger (Book)* <**diskredito̱**·*n*, **diskredito̱**·*het*

diskredito̱·*het vpr* to fall into discredit

diskredito̱·*n vt (Book)* to bring discredit upon [], ruin the reputation of []

diskreditua̱r *adj (i) (Book)* discredited

diskreditue̱s *adj (Book)* discrediting

diskriminacio̱n *nm (Book)* discrimination

diskrimini̱m *nm ger (Book)* <**diskrimino̱**·*n*

diskrimino̱·*n vt (Book)* to discriminate

diskriminue̱s *adj (Book)* discriminatory

diskuta̱nt *nm* discussant = **diskutue̱s**

diskuti̱m *nm ger* <**diskuto̱**·*n*, **diskuto̱**·*het*

diskuto̱·*het vpr* to be under discussion

diskuto̱·*n vt* **1** to discuss, debate **2** to dispute, argue

diskutue̱s *n* discussant

diskutue̱shëm *adj (i)* debatable, disputable

disloki̱m *nm ger* [*Mil*] <**disloko̱**·*n*

disloko̱·*n vt* [*Mil*] to deploy

disnive̱l *nm (Book)* difference in level, inequality

disona̱ncë *nf* dissonance

dispanseri̱ *nf* [*Med*] medical dispensary, clinic

dispe̱ҫer *nm* dispatcher

*****dispenseri̱** *nf* = **dispanseri̱**

dispe̱nsë *nf* mimeographed textbook

dispepsi̱ *nf* dyspepsia

*****dispje̱k** *nm* anger

disponi̱bël *adj* at one's disposal, available

dispono̱·*n vt* to have [] at one's disposal, have [] available

dispozicio̱n *nm (Book)* **1** disposition, disposal **2** in an unassigned position

dispozi̱të *nf* [*Law*] **1** section of a legal pronouncement: provision; regulation; finding **2** [*Mil*] disposition, placement

dispr = **dëshpe̱r**

disproporcio̱n *nm (Book)* disproportion

dista̱ncë *nf (Book)* **1** distance **2** difference

distanci̱m *nm ger* <**distanco̱**·*he*·*t*

distanco̱·*het vnr* to distance oneself, keep oneself at a distance

DISTAPTUR *abbrev (Italian)* <**Direzione Stampa Propaganda Turismo** [*Hist*] Director of Information and Tourism (during the Italian occupation of Albania, 1940-1944)

disti̱k
  I § *adj* [*Bot*] distichous
  II § *nm* [*Lit*] distich

distila̱t *nm* distillate

distila̱tor *nm* apparatus for distillation of liquids: still, retort

distileri̱ *nf* [*Tech*] distillery

distili̱m *nm ger* [*Tech*] <**distilo̱**·*n*

distilo̱·*n vt* [*Tech*] to distill

distilua̱r *adj (i)* [*Tech*] distilled

distilue̱s
  I § *adj* [*Tech*] used or involved with distilling
  II § *nm* **1** distilling apparatus: still **2** distiller

distinkti̱v *nm* medal (awarded as an honor)

disto̱më *nf* [*Zool*] liver fluke

distributo'r nm [Tech] distributor (device)

distri'kt nm district, region

distrofi' nf [Med Veter] dystrophy

distrofi'k
I § adj [Med Veter] dystrophic
II § nm center for treatment of dystrophic patients

dish adv almost

disharmoni' nm [dis-harmoni'] disharmony

dishe'pull nm (np ~ j) disciple

*di'shël nf [Bot] = di'shull

*di'shëll nf [Bot] 1 = di'shull 2 European mistletoe, white mistletoe (Viscum album)

*di'shfar'soj (Reg Gheg) = çfarëdollo'j

*di'shfa't (Old) = fatzi'

*dishiplin' = disiplin'

*dishiplina'r = disiplino'r

*dishir' = dëshir'

*dishm' (Old) = dëshm'

*dishm u'er adj (fem ~ ore) (Old) = dëshmu'es

*di'shpr = dëshpër

dishra'k adj greedy, gluttonous; voracious; eager

*dishro'·n vt (Reg Gheg) = dëshiro'·n

di'shtë nf bottom opening of the flour hopper in a mill

*di'shull nf [Bot] gas-plant dittany, fraxinella, burning bush, dittany (Dictamnus albus)

di't stem for pdef, adm, opt, participle < di·

dit stem for pdef, adm, opt, participle < di·

di'ta-di'tës adv 1 day after day; continually, always; forever and ever 2 every day, daily 3 any day now, one of these days, soon

dita'r nm 1 diary, journal; grade book 2 measure of land equal to what a yoke of oxen can plow in a single day: juger

dita're nf diary, journal

dite'm dre'kë adv long after sundown: very late

di'të nf 1 day 2 daytime; daylight
∘ T'u bëftë dita një mijë! "May each of your days become a thousand!" (Felic) May you live to be a hundred!
∘ ditë brue autumn days: period of time September 21-25
∘ dita e brumit [Ethnog] the Thursday when the dough for the wedding feast is fermented
∘ Ditën e mirë! Good day! Goodbye! Have a nice day!
∘ Dita e Gjyqit/Gjykimit [Relig] The Day of Judgment
∘ dita e kryqit [Relig] Orthodox holiday (January 6) in which the baptism of Christ is commemorated by throwing a cross into water: Epiphany
∘ ditë e lëvruar (Old) working day
∘ dita e luleve (Old) engagement day
∘ dita me ditë daily, day by day
∘ ditë e mirë holy day, religious holiday
∘ Dita e mirë duket që në mëngjes. "Nice weather is evident by morning." (Prov) You can tell right from the start if something will go well. You can tell right from the start if someone will do well.
∘ dita e moskurrit doomsday
∘ ditën për diell right out in public, out in the open, openly
∘ ditë për ditë daily, day after day, every day
∘ ditë polare polar day: time of the midnight sun
∘ ditë pune workday
∘ ditë pushimi day of vacation
∘ ditë e rrogave payday

∘ Ditën të lëpin këmbët, natën të ngul dhëmbët. "He licks your feet during the day, but at night sticks his teeth into you." (said of a treacherous flatterer)
∘ dita e verës March 1 celebration of the arrival of spring

di'të bardhë adj fortunate, lucky

di'të gja'të adj long-lived

di'të li'ndje nf birthday

di'tën adv in the daytime, during the day

di'të na'të nf a day and a night, 24-hour day

di'të-nje'ri nf man-day (unit of measurement of work)

di'të për di'tshëm adj (i) every day, daily (without fail)

di'të pre're adj 1 short-lived 2 (Curse) may-his-life-be-cut-short!

di'të-pu'në nf work-day (unit of measurement of work)

di'të rrëfe'njës nm (Old) calendar

*di't e's n savant; wise guy

di'të so'sur adj 1 = di'tëshku'rtër *2 weary of life

di'të shku'rtër adj 1 short-lived, short-lasting 2 (Curse) may-he-have-a-short-life!

di'të vdekje nf dying day, day of death; commemoration of the day of death

di'të zaj adv day-before-yesterday

di'të zi adj, n (fem sg ~ ez, masc pl ~ i nj, fem pl ~ eza) unlucky/unfortunate (one)

ditira'mb nm 1 dithyramb 2 (Book Fig) overblown praise

di'tje nf awareness, knowledge

di'to·n
I § vi to spend the day (somewhere)
II § vt to pasture [animals] during the day

di'tor
I § adj 1 pertaining to a day or to daytime: daily, the day's 2 of a day's length: daylong, for the day 3 everyday, everyday's 4 only during the daytime, only for a day; daytime
II § nm 1 [Ethnog Relig] festive day after a holiday *2 name-day *3 diary, journal = dita'r

di't shëm adj (i) = di'tur

di'tur
I § adj (i) 1 knowledgeable, erudite, learned 2 well-known
II § n (i) knowledgeable/erudite/learned person

di'tur a'k adj = dituro'r

dituri' nf knowledge, wisdom

dituro'r adj (Book) of or pertaining to knowledge

div nm 1 [Myth] monster, giant 2 (Colloq) stalwart

diva'n nm 1 divan, couch 2 house corridor wide enough to serve as a room of many uses 3 covered balcony 4 collection of poetry

divan-kreva't nm couch which may also serve as a bed

divergje'ncë nf divergence

divergje'nt adj divergent

diversa'nt nm enemy engaged in subversive activities: diversionist

diversio'n nm subversive activity

divide'nd nm [Econ] dividend

divi't nm (Old) writing equipment; bottle of ink

divi'zë nf 1 uniform 2 motto

divizio'n nm [Mil] division

divo'rc *nm (Book)* divorce

dizajne'r *nm* designer, draftsman = **disenjato'r**

di'zel *nm* diesel, diesel gas

dizenteri' *nf[Med Veter]* dysentery

dizenjato'r *n* designer, draftsman = **disenjato'r**

di'zë *nf [Tech]* nozzle

*****dizëba'q** *nm* garter

di'zgë *nf* strap for fastening something to a human body: hair ribbon, moccasin thong; long band used to keep baby in the cradle: cradle band

dizgio're *nf* **1** knee tendon of animals *****2** hollow of the knee

dizgji'n *nm* bridle strap; bridle

*****dizinfekto'·n = dezinfekto'·n**

*****djafnje'·het** *vpr* to overstrain/overexert oneself

djaj *np* <**djall**

dja'lë *nm* **1** boy, lad **2** son
- **djalë i barkut** natural son, own son
- **djalë burri** "husband's son" stepson
- **djalë i ftohtë** foster son
- **djalë i gjetur** stepson
- **djali i madh** eldest son
- **djalë mamaje/quməshti** *(Impol)* mama's boy
- **djalë shkandull** ill-bred boy
- **djalë në/për shpirt** adopted son/daughter
- **djalë tigani** *(Impol)* pampered/spoiled boy

djalëri' *nf* **1** boyhood, youth **2** *(Collec)* boys taken as a collective whole: youth, young men

djalëri'sht
I § *adj* **1** for boys **2** composed of boys **3** boyish
II § *adv* boyishly

djalëro'r *adj (Book)* boyish

djalo'sh *nm* adolescent boy, youth, juvenile

djalosha'r *adj* youthful, juvenile

djal'th *nm dimin* little boy

djalurçi'në *nf (Impol)* **1** immature/inexperienced boy, little twerp **2** boy who behaves childishly

djall *nm (np ~ j)* devil, demon
- **djalli i detit** *[Ichth]* common weever, greater weever *(Trachinus draco)*
- **djalli e di** *(Impol)* the devil only knows, God knows!
- [] **hëngri djalli** "the devil ate []" [] ended up badly, [] came to a bad end
- **djall me brirë** *(Crude)* evil person: real bastard
- **djalli me të birin** *(Impol)* anyone without distinction: anybody and his brother, just anyone
- [] **mori djalli** "the devil took []" [] ended up badly, came to a bad end
- **Djalli nuk është aq i zi sa duket.** "The devil is not as black as he seems." **1** He/She may not be so bad as he/she seems. **2** The situation is not as bad as it may seem.
- **djall o punë!** damnation! damn it!
- **Djalli s'ka dele dhe shet lesh.** "The devil has no sheep and sells wool." (said of a deceptive person who is always up to something bad) He's a clever snake.
- **djalli ta marrë!** devil take him! damn him!

dja'lle *nf* devilwoman; wily/deceitful woman

djall ëzi' *nf* **1** deceit; deception **2** deviltry

djall ëzi'sht *adv* **1** deceptively **2** diabolically

djall ëzo'·het *vpr* to get to be devilish in behavior, start to act bad

djall ëzo'·n
I § *vt* to inspire deviltry, corrupt

II § *vi* to practice deception, act deceptively

djall ëzo'r *adj* (of persons or things) deceptive, fraudulent; diabolic

djall ëzu'a'r *adj (i)* intentionally deceptive; insidious, diabolic

djallo's· *vt* **1** *(Crude)* to screw [] up, bungle [] *****2** to bedevil

djallo's·et *vpr (Crude)* to screw up, become ruined

djallu'cë *nf(Colloq)* = **djallu'shë**

djallu'sh
I § *nm* devil child; imp; little demon/devil
II § *adj (Colloq)* devilish

djallu'shë *nf(Colloq)* **1** <**djallu'sh** **2** she-devil; real hellcat, clever broad

djatha'ç *nm [Ethnog]* best man at a wedding

djatha'ni'k *nm [Cook]* cheese pie

djatha'r *n* cheesemaker

djatha'xhi *nm (np ~ nj)* cheese merchant = **djathshi'tës**

dja'thë *nm [Dairy]* cheese
- **djathë i bardhë** cheese made from sheep's milk
- **djathë baxhoje** skimmed milk cheese (with holes formed during ripening)
- **djathë i marrë/rrahun** *[Dairy]* cheese made from skimmed milk
- **djathë i mirë në lëkurën të qenit** "good cheese on the skin of a dog" a waste of a good thing/characteristic
- **djathë i pamarrë/parrahun** *[Dairy]* cheese made from whole milk
- **djathë peshe** *[Dairy]* hard cheese (that can be sliced)

*****dja'thna** *np* cheese market

djatho'r *nm [Food]* cornmush made with cheese

djatho're *nf* = **baxho**

djathpunu'es *nm [Dairy]* cheesemaker

djathshi't'ës *n [Dairy]* cheese merchant

djathta'k *adj* right-handed

djathtas *OR* **djahta'zi** *adv* rightwards, on the right, to the right

dja'thtë
I § *adj (i)* **1** right, right-side **2** *(Old)* skillful
II § *nf (e)* the right (as opposed to the left)

djahtësi' *nf(Old)* **1** manual skill, dexterity **2** skill **3** practical arts (subjects taught in school: included home economics and drawing)

djahti'st *adj* right-wing

djahti'zëm *nm* right-wing ideology

dje *adv* yesterday

djeg·
I § *vt* **1** to burn; scorch; singe; scald **2** to burn [] up; cremate **3** to cause [ ]'s ruin **4** to cauterize **5** to render [] invalid **6** *(Colloq)* to light [a cigarette/pipe] **7** to light [an oven]; bake
II § *vi* **1** to smart, sting **2** *(Fig)* to cut to the quick, hurt
- **S'[] djeg as xhehenemi.** "Even Hell won't burn []." {} is so evil that burning in Hell would be too good for [].
- **djeg· e pjek·** to wreak havoc wherever one goes
- **për një plesht djeg· jorganin** "burn the bedquilt because of one flea" to scrap something valuable because of a trivial defect
- **<>a djeg· kartat në dorë** to prevent <> from carrying out <>'s wicked plan

∘ <>a *djeg*· **lëkurën** "burn <>'s skin" to do <> a great injury (deceptively)

∘ *djeg*· **me/në zjarr** to cause devastation

∘ <> *djeg*·^{3sg} **miza** <>'s conscience is bothering <>

∘ *djeg*· **raki** to distill raki

∘ <> *djeg*· **stomaku** <> has heartburn

∘ *djeg*· **shaminë** "burn the handkerchief (at a wedding)" to celebrate gaily

∘ <> *djeg*· **shpirtin** to cause <> deep grief: break <>'s heart, make <> very sad

∘ <> *djeg*· **shpirtin** to make <> very sad

∘ <> *djeg*·^{3pl} **veshët** "<>'s ears *are burning*" <> *is* terribly ashamed

djega gur *nm* peak of summer, hottest period of the year

dje gë *nf*[*Bot*] hedgehog mushroom (with a red stem and white cap with a burning taste) *(Hydnum repandum)*

dje gë s
I § adj **1** burning, incendiary **2** inflammable, combustible **3** piquant, hot (to the taste); caustic, painful, stinging
II § n **1** worker who fires the kiln **2** incendiary, arsonist **3**[*Bot*] garden cress, pepperwort, pepper grass *Lepidium sativum* **4**[*Bot*] upright mignonette *Reseda alba*

djeg ësi *nf* = djegësirë

djeg ësi rë *nf* **1** pungent taste or odor: spiciness, hotness **2** food with a pungent taste (such as garlic, onion, pepper, chili pepper) **3** heartburn; burning sensation **4** scorchingly hot weather

djeg ëso ·het *vpr* **1** to take on a pungent flavor **2** to turn sour

djeg ëso ·n *vt* to add spice to []

djeg ie *nf ger* **1** <*djeg*·, di gj·*et* **2** burning; combustion **3** wound caused by burning **4** cremation

∘ **djegie e brendshme** [*Tech*] internal combustion

∘ **djegie e gjuhës** [*Med*] glossopyrosis

∘ **djegie e kufomave** cremation

∘ **djegie e stomakut** heartburn

*****djeg je** *nf* **1** = dje gie **2**[*Bot*] = dje gë

djeg ore *nf*[*Mil*] fuse mechanism, fuse

djeg qer rës *nm (Old)* coldest month of the year, January

*****djeg sin ë** *nf*(*Old*) combustible material, fuel

dje gshëm *adj (i)* combustible, inflammable

djeg shm ëri *nf (Book)* inflammability, combustibility

*****djeg tar** *n* incendiary

dje gur
I § adj (i) **1** burned **2** burned up; burned out **3** scorched, scalded, parched, sunburned **4** overcooked **5** *(Fig)* burning (with desire longing); consumed with grief, consumed by sadness **6** void, invalid **7** lighted (as for an oven) **8** kiln-baked
II § nf (e) **1** wound made by burning or scalding **2** burn mark/scar **3** heartburn; burning sensation

djeg urin ë *nf* combustible material, fuel

djeg uri shtë *nf* **1** land cleared by burning **2** arid, barren land **3** brushwood used as tinder

dje lë *nf (e)* = di el

∘ **e djela e dafinave** *(Old)* [*Relig*] Palm Sunday

djelm = djem

djelm ëri = djemuri

djelm oshe *np* <djalo sh

djem *np* <dja lë

∘ **Djemtë hanë kumbulla/thana, pleqve u mpihen dhëmbët** "The boys eat plums, the old people's teeth get numb." *(Iron)* (Someone does something, and someone else worries about it.) Stop worrying about other people's problems.

djem ëri shte = djemuri shte

djem nu shë *nf* **1** *(Old)* girl or woman possessed by evil spirits: demoniac **2** *(Fig)* hot-tempered and difficult girl or woman

djemuri *nf collec* youth, boys taken as a whole

djemuri sht
I § adj **1** for boys **2** composed of boys **3** boyish
II § adv boyishly

djep *nm* cradle

∘ **djep pas djepi** generation after generation

∘ **Djepi plot e këmbët jashtë.** "Cradle full and feet outside." *(Iron)* Fully grown, but still acting like a child

dje pe *nf* = djep

dje p ës *n* baby in a cradle

djep ëso r *nm* **1** = dje p ës **2** *(Myth)* baby dragonslayer who fights with his cradle still on

djep ferro s ur *adj (Colloq)* **1** childless **2** *(Curse)* may his cradle be fenced up forever!

djep o ·n *vt* to rock [] (in a cradle)

djep pa tund ur *adj* **1** childless **2** *(Curse)* may his cradle never rock!

djep shkret u ar *adj* **1** childless **2** whose child has died **3** *(Curse)* may his cradle be empty!

djerg·
I § vt **1** *(Reg)* to bring [] down, remove **2** to drop [] socially: snub **3** [*Folklore*] to send
II § vi to descend

djerg ·et *vpr* **1** *(Reg)* to descend en masse: pour down **2** = de rgj·*et*

djerg sore *nf* = dergjëne shë, leho në

dje rs ·et *vpr* = djersi t·*et*

dje rsë *nf* **1** sweat **2** condensation of water on a surface

djers i ·het *vpr* = djersi t·*et*

djersi ·n *vi* = djersi t·

djersi rë *adj (i)* = djersi tur

djersi s *stem for 1st sg pres, pl pres, 2nd & 3rd sg subj, pind* <djersi t·

djersi t·
I § vi **1** to sweat **2** *(Fig)* to expend great effort **3** to drip **4** to fog up **5** to grow out, sprout
II § vt to cause [] to sweat; exhaust, tire [] out

djersi t ·et *vpr* **1** to perspire **2** to form condensation **3** to work hard

djersi tje *nf ger* **1** <djersi t·, djersi t·*et* **2** [*Med*] sudation

djersi tur *adj (i)* **1** covered with sweat **2** (of a cold surface) steamed up

djerr
I § nm **1** fallow land **2** plain undecorated fabric
II § adj adv **1** left fallow **2** *(Fig)* unexplored, uninvestigated
III § nf (e) poor woman, unfortunate woman

djerr·
I § vt **1** to waste; ruin *****2** to condemn
II § vi **1** to get lost **2** = b jerr·

djerr ·et *vpr* **1** to become fallow **2** *(Fig)* to die out; faint

djerr a ditë *nf* = bjerradit ës

djerra|díẗës *nm* **1** = bjerradíẗës **2** [*Entom*] drone bee **3** (*Impol*) loafer, useless person

djerra|díẗëz *nf* (*Impol*) = djerradíẗës

djer̃r|ë *adj (i)* = djerr

djer̃r|ë *part* <djerr·

djer̃r|ín̈ë *nf* fallow land; empty lot; wilderness, moor

djer̃r|íshtë *nf* = djer̃r|n̈ë

djer̃r|o·n *vi vt* **1** to waste time thinking (about [ ]) **2** to make schemes (against [ ]); make up false stories (about [ ])

dje|shëm *adj (i)* of or pertaining to yesterday, yesterday's

dje|shme *nf (e)* **1** the day before, the preceding day **2** not long ago

*****dje|thi|naj** OR **dje|thi|në** *adv* yesterday

*****djoqe|z** *nm* [*Relig*] diocese = dioqe·zë

*****djo|r̈e** *nf* (*Reg Tosk*) = gjo·r̈e

DMRr *abbrev* <Drejtoria e Mirëmbajtjes së Rrugëve Director of Road Maintenance

d.m.th *abbreviation* = domethë·në that is, in other words: i. e.

do· *vt* **1** to want, need **2** to want, wish **3** to like, love **4** to mean, intend

　∘ **do· bukë mbi pogaçe 1** to want/expect too much **2** to want the impossible: want one's cake and eat it too

　∘ **<a do·³ˢᵍ buza, por s'e lë·³ˢᵍ hunda** "the lip wants it, but the nose won't allow it" <>'s desires exceed <>'s means

　∘ **s'do· t'ia di·** to be indifferent: not care

　∘ **i do· drutë të shkurtra** "want one's logs short" to like things to be put concisely and in a direct and honest manner: want straight talk

　∘ **Do dhe Muço|a kafe.** "Even Muço wants coffee." (*Tease*) (said when someone has indicated a desire for something inappropriate, perhaps because the desirer is too young)

　∘ **s'do fjalë** it goes without saying, of course

　∘ **<>[ ] do·³ˢᵍ hunda** <> likes [ ] very much

　∘ **e do· me dru (kokës)** "want it (a blow) (to one's head) with a thick stick" to be asking for severe punishment

　∘ **e do· me kobure/patllake/revole (kokës)** "need a gun at one's head" to need to be shown force (not respond to nice treatment)

　∘ **[ ] do· me kokë** to be crazy in love with [ ], love [ ] to distraction

　∘ **e do· me mykë (kokës)** "want it (a blow) (to one's head) with a blunt instrument" to be asking for severe punishment

　∘ **[ ] do· me thumb** to need [ ] some outside push

　∘ **s'do mend 1** there's no question; of course **2** to be self-evident/obvious

　∘ **<> do· në gojë** (*Pej*) <> wants everything on a silver platter

　∘ **e do·³ˢᵍ puna** the situation requires it, that is what is necessary

　∘ **<> do·³ˢᵍ qethur mishi me gërshërë** "the flesh *needs* to be shorn with scissors" <> *deserves* to be cut up into little pieces

　∘ **[ ] do· qofte** "want [ ] like a meatball" to want to have [ ] without expending any effort: want [ ] on a silver platter

　∘ **do· s'do·** like it or not

　∘ **e do· si breshka gozhdën** to be looking for trouble

　∘ **[ ] do· si djalin e shemrës** "love [ ] like the son of one's second wife" (*Iron*) to despise/hate [ ]

　∘ **[ ] do· si dritë e syve** "love [ ] like one's eyesight" to hold [ ] as precious: treasure [ ]

　∘ **[ ] do· si kripa në sy** "like [ ] as much as salt in one's eye" (*Iron*) to dislike [ ] intensely, hate [ ] like poison

　∘ **[ ] do· si macja ciruan/peshkun** "like [ ] as a cat likes fish" to like [ ] very much, be crazy about [a particular food]

　∘ **[ ] do· si prushin në gji** "love [ ] like a hot ember at one's breast" (*Iron*) to hate [ ] with a passion, dislike [ ] intensely

　∘ **[ ] do· si sytë e ballit** "love [ ] like the eyes in one's face" to hold [ ] very precious: treasure [ ]

　∘ **[ ] do· si zjarrin në gji** "like [ ] like fire on one's breast" to detest [ ], *cannot stand* [ ]

　∘ **<>[ ] do·³ˢᵍ shpirti** "<>'s heart wants [ ]" <> wants [ ] badly, <> really *wants* [ ]

　∘ **do· vrarë me bukë në gojë** "need to be killed even with bread in one's mouth" **1** (*Pej*) to deserve the worst possible punishment: { } should be strung up to die **2** (*Joke*) to be fantastically clever, be incredibly ingenious

do *pcl* **1** used with subj pres verb forms to create future or presumptive tense: will, shall; must **2** used with subj imperf verb forms to create conditional tense: would, should **3** used with subj perf verb forms to create past conditional or past presumptive tense: would have, should have; must have

　∘ **do të thotë** it means

　∘ **do të vejë në fis** (*Pej*) family character will eventually show through: blood will tell

do *quant* (*Reg*) some; several

do *nf* [*Mus*] do (the musical note)

dobare *adv* (*Colloq*) at least

*****dobc̈** = dob̈ës

*****dobedo|le** *nf* = dordole·c

*****dob̈ë** *adj (i)* = do|bët

*****dobërda|c** *nm* tramp, vagabond; brigand

*****dobërdo|le** *nf* = dordole·c

dob̈ës|í *nf* **1** weakness, deficiency, defect **2** feebleness, fragility; skinniness

dob̈ës|ím *nm ger* <dob̈ëso·n, dob̈ëso·het

*****dob̈ësi|në** OR **dob̈ës|i|rë** *nf* debility

dob̈ëso·het *vpr* **1** to grow weaker, weaken; (of light or sound) become dim **2** to grow thin/weak, become emaciated **3** to lose weight, reduce

dob̈ëso·n *vt* to make [ ] weak: weaken; enfeeble, debilitate

dob̈ës|ua|r *adj (i)* weaker and weaker, progressively weaker

dob̈ës|ues *nm* [*Cine*] attenuator

do|bët
　I § *adj (i)* **1** weak; feeble **2** skinny, thin **3** fragile, frail **4** of poor degree or quality **5** ineffective; ineffectual **6** of low moral character, base
　II § *adv* **1** weakly **2** loosely **3** barely, hardly

*****dob̈ët|i** = dob̈ës|í

dob̈ët|o·n = dob̈ëso·n

dobí *nf* benefit, gain, profit, fruit, good, advantage, usefulness

dobiç *nm* (*Crude*) **1** illegitimate child: bastard **2** (*Fig*) lively and smart person

*****dobi|dhán̈ës** *adj* (*Reg Gheg*) = dobí|shëm

dobi|prur̈ës *adj* = dobí|shëm

dobi'shëm _adj (i)_ beneficial, advantageous, useful, profitable, fruitful

dobi'shm'eri _nf (Book)_ usefulness; benefit, profit

*__dobi'tës__ _adj_ victorious, conquering

doc. _abbrev_ <**docent** University Lecturer, Professor

*__do'ca__ = disa

do'ce _nf_ corncob

docent _n_ university lecturer (title awarded for achievement in teaching and research)

do'ckë _nf_ corncob used as a cork

doç _nm (Crude)_ = dobiç

doç'arre'kash _adv_ = doçash

do'çash _adv_

do'ce _nf_ 1 hockey-like game using a corncob (or piece of wood) as a puck 2 corncob (or piece of wood) used in this game 3 clay water jug

do'çkë _nf_ 1 = doçe 2 (Pet dimin) little bitty hand

doe'mos _adv_ 1 no matter what, in any case 2 obviously, certainly, of course, without doubt

*__doga'nar__ = doganier

doga'nçe _nf_ argot spoken by craftsmen in certain parts of southern Albania

doga'në _nf_ 1 customs; customs office 2 tariff, import tax

doganier _n_ customs officer

dogani'm _nm ger_ <**dogano'·n**

*__doga'nishte__ _nf_ thieves' argot = doga'nçe

dogano'·n _vt_ to put [] through customs inspection

dogano'r _adj_ of or pertaining to customs matters

*__dogëndis·__ _vi (Reg Gheg)_ = shëtis

dogm'atik _adj_ dogmatic

dogm'atikë _nf_ dogmatics

dogm'atist _n_ dogmatic person

dogm'atizëm _nm_ dogmatism

do'gmë _nf_ dogma

dogra _nf_ old single-barrel, single-fire rifle

dograma _adj, nf_ (board) prepared for use in an interconnected joint

do'gj _stem for pdef_ <dje'g·

*__dojda'she__ _nf_ mongrel, bastard

do'jë
I § _3rd sg pres_ <do'·n
II § _nf_ desire; wish; will

do'jkë _nf_ 1 wetnurse *2 = do'çe

dok _nm [Text]_ 1 thick cotton twill fabric: duck, canvas 2 clod of soil 3 [Naut] dock
∘ **dok diagonal** twill

do'ke _np_ mores, customs, habits

doke'r _nm_ stevedore

doke'sor _adj [Law]_ customary, habitual

*__do'kë__ = do'çe

do'këdo' _acc_ <dokushdo

*__do'kël__ _nf_ snare, pitfall; trick, trap, stratagem

dokëndis· _vt (Colloq)_ 1 to damage [] (in health), be bad (unhealthful) for [], ruin 2 to offend, insult; annoy 3 to touch deeply

dokëndis·et _vpr_ to be deeply touched

do'kërr _nf_ 1 limb bone ending in a large joint; part of the bone containing the joint 2 strong fist-shaped object 3 = do'çe 4 (Colloq) poppycock, nonsense
∘ **dokrra e gurmazit** (Colloq) Adam's apple

dokleat _adj [Hist]_ of or pertaining to a northern Illyrian tribe

*__doko'l__
I § _adj_ coarse, vulgar
II § _nm_ crude person

do'krras _adv_ 1 = do'çash 2 rolling over and over

dokto'r _nm (Colloq)_ 1 physician 2 doctor (holder of a doctorate degree)

doktor'atë _nf_ 1 doctorate 2 (Colloq) doctoral dissertation

doktore'shë _nf_ female doctor

doktrina'r _adj (Book)_ doctrinaire

doktrin'arizëm _nm_ ideology of the doctrinaire

doktri'në _nf_ doctrine

do'kthi _adv_ 1 = do'çash 2 (Fig) openly, frankly 3 (Reg) limpingly

doku'do'
I § _adv_ 1 just anywhere, just any old place 2 any way whatever, just any old way
II § _adj_ of just any old kind, ordinary

doku'jtdo' _dat_ <dokushdo

dokume'nt _nm_ document
∘ **dokumentet e shoqërimit të automjetit** vehicle registration papers (kept in the vehicle)

dokument'acio'n _nm_ documentation

dokumenta'r _adj (Colloq)_ documentary

dokumenti'm _nm ger_ <dokumento'·n

dokumento'·n _vt_ to document

dokument'ue's _adj_ documentary

dokument'ue'shëm _adj (i)_ documentable

*__dokundis·__ _vi (Reg Gheg)_ = shëtis

do'kurdo' _adv_ at just any old time, just any time

*__do'kush__ = dokushdo

do'kush'do' _pron_ just anybody

do'l _stem for pdef_ <de'l·
∘ **doli çika** <>'s secret is revealed, <> is exposed
∘ <> **doli gorricë** turned out badly for <>, went badly for <>

dolikocefa'l _adj [Anthro]_ dolichocephalic

*__dolikoqefa'l__ = dolikocefal

doli'në _nf_ valley; tapering groove

dolomi't _nm [Geol Min]_ dolomite

dolla'k _nm_ woolen cloth wrapped around the lower leg or knee: puttee

dolla'më _nf_ = dolloma

dolla'p _nm_ 1 piece of furniture used for storage: wardrobe; pantry 2 (Reg) window 3 (Reg) coffee roaster
∘ **dollap librash** bookcase
∘ **dollap i përpunimit** [Postal] sorting case

dolla'pçe _adv (Colloq)_ = dolla'pthi

dollaplie _nf (Old)_ old breech-loaded rifle

dolla'pthi _adv (Colloq)_ 1 upside down 2 rolling over and over

dolla'r _nm_ dollar

dolli' _nf_ a drink to honor someone: toast

dolliba'sh _nm [Ethnog]_ = kryegje'tës

dollma _nf [Cook]_ 1 stuffed cabbage or grape leaf 2 (Reg) food made of sheep or goat offal and bread

dollmallie _adj_ one-storey house with a basement

dolloma' _nf_ knee-length smock worn by men or women as part of their ethnic costume

Dom _nm (Old Relig)_ title prefixed to the name of a Roman Catholic priest

domaçu'ng _nm_ drum mallet

domate *nf* [*Bot*] tomato *(Lycopersicon esulentum Mill, Solanum lycopersicon L.D)*
　◦ **domate e egër** [*Bot*] black nightshade *Solanum nigrum*
　◦ **domate e zezë** [*Bot*] eggplant
domen *nm* [*Hist*] demesne
domethënë *conj* that is to say, that is, which means
domethënës *adj* meaningful
domethënie *nf* meaning, significance
domër *np* <**dom**
dominion *nm (Book)* British dominion
domino *nf* the game of dominos
domino ·n *vt* to dominate
dominues *adj* **1** dominant, prevalent **2** overbearing
domkë *nf* **1** lump, swelling, bump **2** hard and unripe fig **3* flue
domna *np*
****domnjon** *nm* a game played with kernels of grain as objects to be won
domosdo *adv* **1** no matter what, in any case, certainly, of course **2** however, nevertheless
domosdo *nf (Book)* = **domosdoshmëri**
domosdoshëm *adj(i)* **1** indispensable, necessary, essential **2** mandatory, obligatory, compulsory **3** inevitable
domosdoshmëri *nf (Book)* indispensability, necessity
don *nm* [*Bot*] maple *(Acer L.)*
donati *nf* ornament
donatis· *vt* to adorn, adorn [] with ornaments
done *np* long underwear
****dongareq** *adj* stout, plump
donkishot *nm (Book Pej)* Don Quixote
donkishotesk *adj(Book Pej)* quixotic
donzhuan *nm (Book Pej)* Don Juan
****dopak** *adv* a little, somewhat
****dor** *stem for pdef* <**djerr**·
dorac
　I §　nm person missing or having the use of only one hand/arm
　II §　adj **1** one-handed **2* single-handed **3* handcrafted
doracak
　I §　adj portable by hand
　II §　nm manual, handbook
dora-dore *adv* by the hand
dora-dorën *adv* = **dora-dorës**
dora-dorës *adv* **1** hand in hand, by the hand **2** for the time being **3** gradually, little by little **4** occasionally, from time to time
dorak
　I §　nm **1** handle/grip of a tool/instrument: plowhandle, pan handle, crank (handle) **2** cane handle, cane **3** [*Sport*] dumbbell; hand weight
　II §　adj having a handle
dorake *nf* **1** glove **2** cooking vessel with a handle **3** handkerchief **4** sleeve cuff
dorartë *adj* = **duarartë**
doras *adv* **1** left incomplete **2** postponed **3** draggingly, creeping **4** = **dorazi 5** with both hands
doras *nm (Old)* **1** killer, avenger **2** guilty party: culprit
****dorasak** *adj* handy

dorashkë *nf* **1** glove **2** plowhandle; pan handle
　◦ **dorashkë njëgishtëshe** mitten
dorashtë *nf* hank of yarn: skein
dorazi *adv* in hand; hand-delivered, by hand
****dordogan** *n, adj* giant
dordolec *nm* **1** *(Fig)* laughingstock **2** scarecrow **3** [*Ethnog*] = **peperune**
dordololinë *nf* [*Bot*] red clover *(Trifolium pratense)*
dore *nf* **1** embroidered cuff of a sleeve **2** handle on a knife/tool
dorezë *nf* **1** glove **2** handle **3** = **dorëz 4** [*Sport*] pommel on a side horse
　◦ **dorezë havani** pestle
　◦ **dorezë me një gisht** mitten
dorë *nf* **1** hand **2** arm **3** handful; small group **4** handle **5** *(Colloq)* hand signal **6** social level; quality level **7** power **8** *(Colloq)* note of authorization
　◦ **dorë e havanit** pestle
　◦ **dorë më dorë** hand in hand, by the hand
　◦ **dorë pas dore** from hand to hand
　◦ **dorë për dorë** **1** hand in hand, by the hand **2** for right now
　◦ **<u praroftë dora!** "May <>'s hand be gilded!" *(Felic)* Congratulations to <>! Good luck, <>!
　◦ **i dorës së dytë** **1** second-rate **2** of secondary importance
　◦ **i dorës së fundit** of the lowest quality
　◦ **i dorës së parë** **1** first-rate **2** of primary importance
　◦ **dora vetë** **1** signed personally, signed (by his own hand) **2** in person
dorëbardhë *adj* having lily-white hands
dorëborë *adj(Poet)* having hands as white as snow
dorëbutë *adj* **1** having soft hands **2** *(Fig)* pretending to be nice in order to achieve some end
dorëcore *adj* skillful in handwork (usually needlework)
dorëcub *adj* = **dorac**
dorëcung *adj* missing a hand/arm; one-handed, one-armed
dorëçele = **dorëçelur**
dorëçelur *adj* open-handed, generous
dorëdjathtë *adj* **1** right-handed **2** *(Fig)* skillful in handwork; masterful
dorëdredhur *adj* **1** half-hearted in giving something **2** stingy
****dorëdhânë** *(Reg Gheg)* = **dorëdhënë**
dorëdhënë *adj* generous
dorëdhënës *adj* **1** generous **2** giving surety, guaranteeing
dorëdhënie *nf* **1** generosity **2** surety, guarantee
dorëfëlliqur *adj* having dirty hands: guilty of wrongdoing
dorëflori *adj* = **duarflori**
dorëfortë *adj(Book)* = **dorëhekurt**
dorëgrisur *adj(i)* = **dorëlëshuar**
****dorëgjânë** *adj (Reg Gheg)* = **dorëdhënë**
dorëgjatë *adj* **1** brutal, violent **2** powerful and influential **3** thievish; high-handed
dorëgjerë *adj(Book)* generous
dorëgjerësi *nf(Book)* generosity
dorëhapësi *nf (Book)* open-handedness, generosity
dorëhapët *adj(i)* lavish, extravagant

dorë·ha·pur *adj* open-handed, generous

dorë·hartuem *adj (i)* artificial

dorë·hekur *adj* = dorëhekurt

dorë·hekurt *adj* **1** having powerful hands **2** firm in leadership qualities

dorë·heq·ës *adj* resigning, retiring

dorë·heqje *nf* resignation, retirement; abdication
  ∘ **dorëheqje nga ushtria** military discharge

dorë·hollë *adj* **1** poor, needy ***2** adroit, skillful

dorë·jashtë *adj* uninvolved

dorë·keq *adj* **1** = dorëprapë **2** guilty of bad actions: malfeasor

dorë·këput·ur *nm (Curse)* person who should have his hand cut off

*dorë·lartë *adj* noble

dorë·lehtë *adj* light-handed, deft

dorë·lëshuar *adj* **1** free-spending, (too) free with money **2** too easy-going in supervision: lax in discipline

*dorë·lëvizje *nf* gesticulation

dorë·lidh·ur *adj* tight-fisted, stingy, miserly

dorë·lirë *adj* **1** generous **2** free-spending, extravagant = dorëlëshuar

dorë·madh *adj* having big hands

dorë·mbarë *adj* lucky, fortunate

dorë·mbledh·ur *adj* tight-fisted, stingy, miserly

dorë·mbyllur *adj* tight-fisted, stingy, miserly

dorë·me·një *adv* **1** *(Colloq)* at once, right away **2** for sure, beyond doubt

*dorë·me·nji *(Reg Gheg)* = dorëmenjë

dorë·mirë *adj* = dorëmbarë

dorë·ngathët *adj* all thumbs, inept

dorë·ngushtë *adj* = dorështrënguar

dorë·nuse *nf (Reg)* engagement (to be married) = fejesë

dorë·përdorë *adv* for the time being, in the meantime, meanwhile

dorë·përdorshëm *adj (i)* of the present, of right now, present-day

dorë·piper *adj (Colloq)* who gets into and upsets everything

dorë·plot *adv* **1** with hands full **2** liberally, generously

*dorë·plotë *adj* liberal, generous

dorë·prapë *adj* unlucky, unfortunate

dorë·prerë *adj* one-handed

dorë·rëndë *adj* having a heavy touch, heavy-fisted

*dorë·rrudhë OR **dorë·rrudhje** *nf* stinginess, miserliness

dorë·rrudh·ur *adj* stingy, tight-fisted

dorës *nm* **1** = bishtak **2** *[Mus]* bow (for a bowed lute)

dorë·shkathët *adj* skillful in work, good with the hands, handy

dorë·shkresë *nf* manuscript

dorë·shkrim *nm* **1** handwriting **2** manuscript

*dorë·shkronjë *nf (Old)* handwriting

dorë·shkrues *nm* writer; author of a manuscript

dorë·shpuar *adj* extravagant

dorë·shtrenjtë *adj* = dorështrënguar

dorë·shtrëngim *nm* tight-fistedness, stinginess

dorë·shtrënguar
  I § *adj* stingy, miserly: tight-fisted

  II § *nm* skinflint

*dorë·shtrënguet *adj* stingy, miserly: tight-fisted

dorë·trokas *stem for 1st sg pres, 1st & 3rd pl pres, 2nd & 3rd sg subj* < dorëtroket·

*dorë·troket· *vi* to clap (hands)

*dorë·trokis *stem for 2nd pl pres, pind* < dorëtroket·

*dorë·trokit *stem for pdef, opt, adm, part, pind, 2nd pl pres, imper, vn* < dorëtroket·

*dorë·thalmë *(Reg Gheg)* = dorëthatë

dorë·tharë *adj* **1** clumsy, awkward, unskillful = duartharë **2** *(Curse)* be damned by hands grown clumsy!

dorë·thatë *adj* **1** = duarthatë **2** = dorështrënguar

dorë·vatë *nf [Bot]* thorny burnet *(Sarcopoterium spinosum)*

dorë·vogël *adj* having small hands

dorëz *nf* **1** glove **2** handle, haft **3** handful **4** cuff of a sleeve **5** *[Dairy]* round of fresh cheese **6** pestle ***7** sheaf

dorëzane *nf* guarantor

dorëzanë *nm* guarantor

dorëzanës *n* = dorëzanë

dorëzani *nf* guarantee, bail

dorëzano·het *vpr* to act as guarantor

dorëzano·n *vt* to stand behind [] as a guarantor

dorëzë *nf adj* **1** capable, handy, good with the hands **2** = dorështrënguar

dorëzënës *n* = dorëzane

dorëzënie *nf* = dorëzani

dorëzgjidh·ur *adj* loose-spending, extravagant

dorëzim *nm ger* **1** < dorëzo·n, dorëzo·het **2** delivery; consignment **3** surrender; capitulation **4** extradition

dorëzo·het *vpr* **1** to surrender, give up **2** *[Relig]* to be consecrated

dorëzo·n *vt* **1** to hand [] over; deliver **2** to come through on []: deliver [], produce [] (for the use of others) **3** to leave [] in safekeeping: consign **4** to surrender []; surrender [] over **5** to ordain [] (as priest)
  ∘ **dorëzo·n armët** to give up one's arms: stop fighting, stop resisting, surrender
  ∘ **dorëzo·n çelësat 1** to resign from duty, offer one's resignation **2** to fail, throw in the towel
  ∘ **dorëzo·n uniformën** to quit the (military) service

dorëzonjë *nf [Bot]* honeysuckle *(Lonicera)*
  ∘ **dorëzonjë e ëmbël** *[Bot]* sweet honeysuckle *Lonicera caprifolium*

dorëzonjore *np [Bot]* honeysuckle family *Caprifoliaceae*

dorëzues *adj* serving to deliver: delivering, delivery

dorëzueshëm *adj (i)* deliverable; extraditable

dorfolinë *nf [Bot]* = dordolinë

dorgj *stem for pdef* < djerg·et

dori
  I § *adj, n* (horse color) sorrel, bay
  II § *n* pot with two handles, stewpot

dorik *adj* Doric

*dorjashtë *prep (acc)* outside, beyond

dorje *nf* **1** copper pot with handle and attached lid **2** single-handled clay water pitcher **3** *[Text]* bobbin for collecting spun yarn

dorje *nf* = dori

*dor-me-nji *adv (Reg Gheg)* = dorëmenjë

doronik *nm* [*Bot*] leopard's bane *Doronicum*

*dortnall *adv* at a gallop

Doruntína *nf* Doruntina (female name)

dosar *nm* = dosje

dosare *nf* 1 big fat sow *2 proud girl

dosë *nf* 1 [*Zool*] (of swine) sow 2 *(FigImpolite)* fat woman; stubborn woman; slut

dosëbalë *nf* [*Zool*] = baldosë

*dosëbalëz *nf* [*Zool*]
  ∘ dosëbalëz Hindi civet cat

*dosëgrua *nf (np ˉa)* whore

dosëz *nf* [*Entom*] European mole cricket *(Gryllotalpa gryllotalpa)*
  ∘ dosëza e dheut [*Entom*] European mole cricket *(Gryllotalpa gryllotalpa L.)*

dosido
  I § *adv* 1 somehow or other, in some way or another 2 by any which way, in just any old way
  II § *adj* = dosidoshëm

dosidoshëm *adj (i)* 1 done in a careless way: slovenly 2 quite ordinary, nothing special

dosinë *nf* [*Invert*] cow shell, coo shell, rayed artemis *Dosinia exoleta*

dosje *nf* dossier, file

doskë *nf (Reg Tosk)* = dosëz
  ∘ doska e dheut [*Entom*] = dosëza e dheut

doshkado *pron* anyone at all

dot *pcl* expresses impossibility: not at all (possible), (cannot) at all

dovlet *nm (Old)* state, country

*dozar = dosar

dozë *nf* [*Med*] dose

dozim *nm ger* 1 <dozo·n 2 dosage

dozimetër *nm* [*Cine*] dosimeter

dozo·n *vt* [*Spec*] to divide [] into doses; specify the dosage of []

dozuar *adj (i)* [*Spec*] divided into doses; in a specified dosage

*dozhdole *nf* [*Ethnog*] child adorned with leaves and flowers in a cermony to bring rain = dordolec

DPA *abbrev (German)* <Deutsche Presse Agentur German Press Agency

DPCE *abbrev* <Drejtoria e Përgjithshme e Centraleve Elektrike General Administration of Electric Power Plants

dr. shk. *abbrev* <doktor i shkencave Doctor of Science: D.Sc., Ph.D.

dr. *abbrev* <doktor Doctor

dra *nm* 1 [*Dairy*] waste residue left from melting butter 2 dregs, lees, sediment

dragaminë *nf* [*Mil*] mine-sweeper

*dragat *nm* watchman over a field/vineyard

dragë *nf* 1 dredge (boat) 2 avalanche *3 barren ground covered with rocks

drago i *obl* <dragua

dragoman *nm (Old Pej)* dragoman, interpreter

dragonj *stem for pl forms* <dragua

dragua
  I § *nm (obl ˉoi, np ˉonj)* [*Myth*] dragon
  II § *adj* *nm* 1 [*Myth*] dragonslayer; good dragon 2 *(Fig)* bravest of the brave
  ∘ dragua i detit [*Ichth*] common weever, greater weever *(Trachinus draco)*

drahmi *nf* = dhrahmi

*drakëm *nf (Old)* = dhrahmi

drakonian *adj (Book)* Draconian

dramatik *adj* dramatic

dramatikë *nf* dramatic art, drama

dramatizëm *nm* dramatics, dramatic style

dramatizim *nm ger* 1 <dramatizo·n 2 dramatization

dramatizo·n *vt* to dramatize

dramaturg *nm* dramaturge

dramaturgji *nf* dramaturgy

dramaturgjik *adj* dramaturgical

dramë *nf* drama

*drandofille *nf (Reg)* = trëndafil

Drane *nf* Drane (female name)

drang *nm (np ˉ gje) (Reg)* 1 young of an animal: cub, kitten 2 *(Fig Insult)* spawn (of something evil) 3 *(Reg)* wooden bar; bar used to lock a gate 4 pole for propelling a boat in shallow water
  ∘ drang mullari bar pushed round and round by a horse to drive a mill

drangë *nf* [*Ichth*] red-eye, rudd *(Scardinius erythrophthalmus scardafa, Leuciscus scardafa)* = lloskë
  ∘ drangë sykuqe [*Ichth*] Italian roach *(Rutilus rutilus rubilo Bonaparte)*

drango·n *vt (Reg)* to bar (the gate), lock with a bar

drangoneshë *nf* she-dragon

drangua = dragua

*drângjër *adj (Reg Gheg)* bister

dranjash *nm* especially large young drake

drap *nm* = dajak

drapër *nm* sickle
  ∘ drapër lejlek long-handled sickle
  ∘ drapri në thes e maja jashtë "sickle in a bag and its point outside" anyone can see through that dodge, a leopard can't hide his spots, like a wolf trying to hide in sheep's clothing

drapërinj *np* <drapër

drapëro·n *vt* to reap [] with a sickle

drapinj *np* <drapër

draskë *nf* = dra

draskëz *nf* = dra

drasht *vi vt (Reg Gheg)* = drua·n

dre(r)
  I § *nm* 1 stag; deer 2 *(Fig)* lad with the quickness of a stag 3 = drojë
  II § *interj (Reg)* expresses surprise
  ∘ dre i veriut reindeer, caribou

dredh·
  I § *vt* 1 to twist, spin; curl 2 to cause [] to tremble; cause [a current] to oscillate 3 *(Colloq Fig)* to shake [] up, frighten, shock 4 *(Fig Pejorative Colloq)* to beat around the bush about [], vacillate about []
  II § *vi* to change course, make a turn
  ∘ dredh· bishtin "waggle one's tail" 1 *(Pej)* to have loose sexual morals: be a slut 2 to waver in loyalty, be untrustworthy; be unreliable
  ∘ e dredh· gjuhën to take back one's words; break one's word
  ∘ e dredh·[past] këmbën *(Crude)* {} died: {} kicked off, {} cashed it in
  ∘ e dredh· këngën to sing the song beautifully
  ∘ <>a dredh· litarin/konopin "twist <>'s rope" to ruin and make a mess of everything for <>

○ **dredh· pet*ë*** to roll up dough

○ **e dredh· qaf*ë*n** *(Scorn)* to die: kick the bucket

○ **dredh· tespihet** "twist the beads" to waste time idly, twiddle one's thumbs

○ **<>i dredh· turiçkat** to slap <> in the face

○ **e dredh· vallen** to lead a line dance beautifully

○ **e dredh· zërin** "twist the voice" to sing with vibrato

○ **dredh· zinxhirin** "twist the chain" to waste time idly, twiddle one's thumbs

dredh·aca'k *adj* = **dredhara'k**

dre'dh·a-dre'dh·a

I § *adj* having many twists: twisty, curvy, curly

II § *adv* in a twisting manner; in curves: sinuously, meanderingly

dredh·a'k *adj* = **dredhara'k**

dredh·ak*ë*ri OR **dredh·ak*ë*si** = **dredhi'**

dredh·aki *adj* not reliable, undependable

dredh·ale'sh *nm* *(Old)* wool-spinning craftsman: wool spinner

dredh·ani'k

I § *nm* *[Food]* pastry snail

II § *adj* = **dredhara'k**

dredh·ara'k *adj* 1 twisting, twining, curling 2 *(Fig Pej)* wily, sly, crafty, cunning

dre'dh·as *adv* in a twisting manner; in curves: sinuously, meanderingly

dredh·ato'r

I § *adj* = **dredhara'k**

II § *n* equivocator, word-twister

dredh·azi = **dredhas**

dre'dh·e *nf[Bot]* 1 = **dredhk*ë*** 2 vine

○ **dredhja e ar*ë*s** *[Bot]* European glorybind *Convolvulus arvensis*

dre'dh·ë *nf* 1 twist, curl, curve 2 twisted or curved implement: whipcord, whip; flail; curved wire used to comb wool 3 thong 4 winding road 5 weather phenomenon with twisting motion: whirlwind, windspout; whirlpool, waterspout 6 *(Fig)* = **dredhi'** 7 *[Bot]* bindweed *(Convolvulus)* 8 *(Reg)* wrinkle *9 (Reg)* welt/scar/streak on the skin *10 (Reg)* swivel, pivot; key turn

○ **dredha e djallit** *(Pej)* very tricky person

dre'dh·*ë*l *nm* *[Bot]* bellflower *(Campanula)*

dre'dh·*ë*s

I § *adj* 1 rotating on an axis: twisting, spinning 2 *[Bot]* twining (around another plant)

II § *n* 1 worker engaged in a spinning/twisting process 2 machine/device for spinning/twisting: spinning wheel, spindle; spinning rod in a coffee mill 3 adjustment or control knob 4 *[Zool]* stag with branching antlers

dre'dh·ët *adj (i)* twisting, twisted

dre'dh·*ë*z *nf* 1 *[Bot]* wild strawberry *(Fragaria vesca)* 2 *[Bot]* ivy, English ivy *(Hedera helix)* 3 *[Bot]* tendril 4 embroidered decoration 5 twine, string, cord 6 = **mje'd*ë*r**

○ **dredh·*ë*z thiu** *[Bot]* European cyclamen *(Cyclamen europaeum)*

dredh·i' *nf* 1 wiliness, slyness 2 cheating, deceit, chicanery, trickery

dredh·i'm *nm ger* 1 <**dredho'·n** 2 winding course: curve in a road or stream 3 = **dredhi'**

dredh·i'sht *adv* slyly, cunningly; by cheating, using trickery

dre'dh·je *nf ger* 1 <**dredh·**, **dri'dh·et** 2 twist, curl, curve 3 twisted or curved implement: whipcord, whip; flail; curved wire used to comb wool 4 thong 5 winding road 6 eddy 7 voice vibrato 8 *[Bot]* bindweed *(Convolvulus)*

dre'dh·k*ë* *nf[Bot]* bindweed *(Convolvulus)*

○ **dredhka e ar*ë*s** *[Bot]* European glorybind *Convolvulus arvensis*

dre'dh·k*ë*l *nf* *[Bot]* = **dor*ë*zonj*ë***

dredho'·n *vi vt* 1 to twist 2 to make a turn; change course 3 to dodge, spin away 4 *(Fig)* to lie deceptively, equivocate

dredho'r *adj* having many twists: twisty, curvy, curly; spiral

dredho're *np* *[Bot]* convolvulus family *Convolvulaceae*

dredhu'e's *adj* sinuous

○ **dredhuesi i alpeve** *[Ornit]* alpine accentor *Prunella collaris Scop.*

○ **dredhuesi gush*ë*p*ë*rhim*ë*** *[Ornit]* hedgesparrow, dunnock *Prunella modularis L.*

dredhu'le *nf* 1 eddy 2 vibrato

dre'dh·ur *adj (i)* 1 rotated around an axis: twisted 2 spun 3 (of hair) wavy, curled 4 rolled 5 curved, sinuous 6 with vibrato 7 *[Veter]* = **tre'dhur**

dre'dh·ur *nf (e)* 1 bend in a road or river 2 *[Food]* twisted pastry 3 shiver, shudder

dreg·ama'n *adj (Insult)* having many scars from sores: scabrous

dre'g·ce *nf* = **dre'g·ez**

dre'g·ë *nf* = **dre'g·ëz**

dre'g·ëz *nf* 1 scab (formed over a sore) 2 pus-filled sore 3 *[Veter]* disease characterized by pus-filled sores over the body

dreg·ëzama'dh *adj (Pej)* having many scars from sores: scabrous

dreg·ëz·i'm *nm ger* <**dreg·ëzo'·het**

dreg·ëzo'·het *vpr* 1 to get sores 2 to form scabs

drejt

I § *adv* 1 straight, straight ahead; straight up, erect 2 direct 3 correct, right

II § *prep (abl)* toward, towards

○ **drejt e në thela** *(Colloq)* (said critically of someone who wants too much too soon)

○ **e drejta ndërkombëtare** *[Law]* international law

drejt *formativ* <**drejt**

drejt·a's *adv* 1 in a straight direction 2 *(Fig)* on good terms, in agreement

drejt·boshto'r *adj [Spec]* along the axis; rectilinear

drejt·ë *adj (i)* 1 straight 2 having a flat surface 3 at a 90 degree angle: perpendicular, orthogonal, right 4 regular, with regular features 5 direct, straightforward 6 true, right, correct 7 honest, upright, just

dre'jt·ë *nf (e)* 1 right (privilege); legal right 2 justice 3 law, jurisprudence 4 truth 5 correct position; good reason, good justification

○ **e drejta e autorit** author's copyright

○ **e drejta e zgjedhjes** the right to vote

○ **i drejtë si laku** "straight as a curve" *(Iron)* thoroughly dishonest: about as honest as a used car salesman

*****drejt·ëni** *(Reg Gheg)* = **drejt·ësi'**

drejt·ësi' *nf* 1 justice; correctness 2 law, jurisprudence 3 judicial system

drejt·ësida'sh·ës *adj (Book)* justice-loving

drejtë**s**ï**sht** *adv (Book)* justly, rightfully, rightly; legitimately

drejtë**z** *nf* [*Geom*] straight line

drejtfla**to**r**ë** *np* [*Entom*] order of straight-winged insects *Orthoptera*

drejtï *nf* rectitude, righteousness

*****drejt**ï *adv (së)* straight

drejtï**m** *nm ger* **1** <**drejto**ʹ·*n*, **drejto**ʹ·*het* **2** direction, course, path **3** position **4** governing body, directorship **5** postal address

drejtkë**nd**ë**sh**
I § *nm* [*Geom*] rectangle
II § *adj* right-angled

drejtkënd**o**r *adj* right-angled

drejto·*het* *vpr* **1** to straighten up/out, get straight **2** to address/direct oneself **3** to become oriented, find one's way; take on a direction

drejto·*n* *vt* **1** to direct: steer, drive; manage; lead; provide orientation for [] **2** to straighten **3** to repair; rectify **4** to address/send/direct [a message]
○ <> **drejto**·*n* **bërrylin** "show <> one's elbow" to turn <> down
○ **drejto gojën**! be careful with your words! mind your language!
○ **drejto**·*n* **gojën** to mind/watch one's language
○ **Nuk drejtohet konopi/litari/tërkuza në thes.** "A rope does not straighten out in a sack." *(Prov)* It just can't be done.

drejto**r** *nm* director, manager, supervisor, principal (of a school)
○ **drejtor filmi** [*Cine*] (film) producer

drejtor**e**sh**ë** *nf* <**drejto**r

drejtor**i** *nf* **1** directorate, directorship **2** office of the director

drejtor**u**c *nm (Pej)* smalltime/incompetent director/manager

drejtpesh**ï**m *nm ger* **1** <**drejtpesho**ʹ·*n* **2** equilibrium, balance

drejtpesh**o·***n* *vt* to balance

drejtpër**drejt** *adv* directly, straight; straightforwardly

drejtpër**drejt**ë *adj (i)* direct, straight; straightforward

drejtpër**së drejt**ï *adv* = **drejtpërdrejtë**

drejtqë**ndr**ï**m** *nm* [*Mil*] attention

drejtrresht**ï**m *nm ger* [*Spec*] **1** <**drejtrreshto**ʹ·*n* **2** alignment

drejtrresht**o·***n* *vt* to put [] in a straight line

drejts**o**r *adj* pertaining to law, juridical

drejtshkr**ï**m *nm* orthography

drejtshkrim**o**r *adj* orthographic, orthographical

drejtshqipt**ï**m *nm* correct pronunciation

drejtshqipt**im**o**r *adj* correctly pronounced, orthoepic

drejtu**a**r *adj (i)* straightened up/out

drejtu**e**s
I § *adj* **1** managing, directive **2** levelling **3** [*Med*] arrector
II § *nm* **1** director, leader, conductor, head **2** driver; navigator **3** [*Electr*] rectifier **4** sender of a message/letter

drejtu**e**sh**ë**m *adj (i)* **1** able to be straightened **2** manageable; steerable

drejtvendo**s·** *vt* to install [] properly, position [] correctly

drejtvendo**s**je *nf ger* [*Spec*] <**drejtvendos·**

drejtviz**o**r *adj* [*Spec*] rectilinear

drejtviz**o**r**ite**t *nm (Book)* [*Tech*] rectilinearity

drek·*et* *vpr* to eat the midday meal, have dinner, eat lunch, lunch

drek**ë** *nf* **1** midday meal: lunch, dinner, luncheon **2** lunchtime, dinnertime (at midday), midday

drekë**he**r**ë**
I § *nf* lunchtime, dinnertime (at midday), noontime, midday
II § *adv* in the early afternoon

drekë**he**r**sh**ë**m** *adj (i)* of lunchtime/dinnertime, of noontime

drek**ë**z *nf* [*Bot*] lily-of-the-valley *(Convallaria majalis)*

dreko**·***het* *vpr* to have lunch

dreko**·***n*
I § *vi* to eat the midday meal: lunch
II § *vt* to feed [] lunch, treat [] to lunch

drek**o**re *nf* restaurant, lunch-room

drek**o**s·*et* = **dreko**ʹ·*het*

drek**o**s·*et* = **dreko**ʹ·*het*

*****dre**k**s**ë *nf* = **dre**gë**z**

*****dre**m**ï** = **drem**ï·

drem**ï**s *stem for 1st sg pres, pl pres, 2nd & 3rd sg subj, pind* <**dremí·**

drem**ï**t· *vi* **1** to feel sleepy/drowsy; doze, snooze **2** *(Fig)* to become apathetic **3** *(Fig)* to be peaceful, be at rest, be calm

drem**ï**tje *nf ger* **1** <**dremí·**t· **2** drowsiness

drem**ï**tur *adj (i)* drowsy

drem**k**ë *nf* **1** short nap, snooze *****2** dram *****3** *(Fig)* grain, bit

*****dre**n**a**k *adj* cervine

dren**a**zh *nm* **1** drainage system **2** drainage of a wound

dren**azh**ï**m *nm ger* **1** <**drenazho**ʹ·*n* **2** drainage

dren**azh**o**·***n* *vt* = **dreno**ʹ·*n*

dren**azh**o**·***n* *vt* = **dreno**ʹ·*n*

dren**azh**u**a**r *adj (i)* = **drenu**ar

dren**e** *nf* goat with long horns

dren**ë** *nf* drainage pipe

dren**ï**m *nm ger* **1** <**dreno**ʹ·*n* **2** drainage

dren**o**·***n* *vt* **1** to construct a drainage system in []: drain **2** to drain [a wound]

dren**u**a**r *adj (i)* **1** provided with a drainage system **2** drained

dren**u**sh**ë**
I § *nf* doe, hind <**dre**
II § *adj* (of girls) doe-like, tender and gentle like a deer

dren**jë** *nf* **1** [*Ornit*] quail *(Coturnix coturnix)* **2** [*Ornit*] woodlark *(Lullula arborea)* **3** [*Zool*] doe
○ **drenja gushëkuqe** [*Ornit*] red-throated pipit *Anthus cervinus*
○ **drenja e luadhit** [*Ornit*] meadow pipit *Anthus pratensis*
○ **drenja e malit** [*Ornit*] water pipit; rock pipit *Anthus spinoletta*
○ **drenja e përhime** [*Ornit*] short-tored lark *Calandrella cinerea Gm.*
○ **drenja e pyllit** [*Ornit*] tree pipit *Anthus trivialis*

○ **drenja qaf**ëˈzezë [Ornit] calandra lark Melanocorypha calandra L.

dreˈpër np <drap

drepˈinj np <drap

dreq nm devil, demon = djall

○ **dreqi i detit** [Ichth] common weever, greater weever Trachinus draco

○ **u bind dreqi** (Colloq) all hell broke loose

dreˈqe nf she-devil

dreqˈësi nf = djallëzi

dreqˈësiˈsht adv in a devilish way, devilishly

dreqˈni nf (Reg Gheg) devilry

dreqˈnoˈ·het vpr = djallzoˈ·het

dreqˈnoˈ·n

I § vt = djallzoˈ·n

II § vi to curse like the devil

dreqˈnuˈshë nf (Colloq) = djalluˈshë

dreqˈoˈs· vt (Colloq) = djalloˈs·

dreqˈoˈs·et vpr (Colloq) = djalloˈs·et

dreqˈoˈsˈur adj (i) (Colloq) **1** gone to the devil, in terrible shape, down and out, in a bad way, badly off **2** damned, heartbreaking

*__dreˈre__ nf = drenuˈshë

dreˈrë np <dre(r)

dreˈrˈi obl <dre(r)

dreth nm dimin <dre [Zool] fawn

dreˈthˈkëz nf [Bot] vetch; creeper

drë(r) nm (np ˜ rë) stag; deer = dre

drëmˈkë nf little nap, snooze

drëˈnjë nf dark-colored she-goat

*__drëpˈinj__ np <draˈpër

*__Driˈ(n)__ nm (Reg Gheg Old) = Drin

driblˈuˈes nm [Basketball] dribbler

*__driˈcë__ nf skylight, fanlight

dridhˈ· vt to set [] atremble, cause [] to shiver

driˈdhˈ·et vpr **1** to spin/twist/turn around; (of yarn/thread/rope) to get rolled up **2** (of hair) to become wavy, get curly **3** (Colloq) to change direction, change course, turn; turn around, return **4** to shiver, shudder, tremble, quiver **5** to flicker, twinkle

○ **Nuk <> dridh·**et³ˢᵍ **(as) bebja e syrit.** "Not even the pupil of <>'s eye wavers." <> is fearless/intrepid.

○ **dridh·**et³ˢᵍ **barra në bark të/barkun e nënës** "even the babe in the mother's womb is trembling" terror is rampant, fear runs riot

○ **<> dridh·**et **e buza** <>'s lips tremble with emotion

○ **dridh·**et **e përdridh·**et **1** to twist and turn in order to avoid giving a direct answer **2** to slip out of a difficult situation **3** to vacillate in attitude

○ **dridh·**et³ˢᵍ **fëmija/foshnja në barkun a nënës** "even the babe in the mother's womb is trembling" terror is rampant, fear runs riot

○ **<> dridh·**et³ᵖˡ **flokët** <>'s hair stands on end; <> trembles with fear

○ **<> dridhet gjuha** <>'s voice trembles

○ **<> dridh·**et³ᵖˡ **këllqet** <> shivers with fear

○ **<> dridh·**et³ˢᵍ **këmisha në shtat/trup** <> is terror-stricken: <> is trembling in <>'s boots

○ **<> dridh·**et **leqet e këmbëve 1** <> is very tired, <> cannot stay on <>'s feet **2** <> trembles with fear

○ **<> dridh·**et³ˢᵍ **mishtë** "<>'s flesh crawls/shivers" **1** <>'s flesh crawls; <> shakes with fright **2** <> is deeply touched/moved

○ **<> dridheshin plaçkat e barkut** "<>'s belly entrails were shaking" <>'s guts were turning over with fear

○ **<> dridh·**et³ˢᵍ **pushka** "<>'s gun trembles" **1** <> is a coward **2** <> lacks resolve, <> is indecisive

○ **dridh·**et **si gjethe lofate/plepi** to tremble with fear

○ **dridh·**et **si purteka në ujë** "shiver like a withe in water" to shudder with fear

○ **dridh·**et **si thupra në ujë** to shake with fright

○ **<> dridh·**et³ˢᵍ **shpirti 1** <>'s heart trembles with fear/worry/anxiety **2** to wrench <>'s heart

○ **<> dridh·**et³ᵖˡ **telat e zemrës** "<>'s heart wires twist" (Iron) (of a hypocrite pretending to show deep feelings) <> sure can put it on

○ **<> dridh·**et³ˢᵍ **zemra 1** <>'s heart trembles with fear/worry/anxiety **2** to wrench <>'s heart

dridhˈ stem for 2nd pl pres, pind, imper, vn <dreˈdhˈ·

driˈdhë nf = driˈdhmë

dridhˈërˈiˈmë nf = driˈdhmë

driˈdhˈës

I § adj **1** trembling, quavering, throbbing, shivering, shuddering **2** [Ling] trilled

II § nm [Electr] vibrator

driˈdhˈje nf ger **1** <driˈdhˈ·et **2** oscillation, vibration; vibrato, quaver; trembling, shiver, shudder; flicker, twinkle

dridhˈjeˈmaˈtˈës nm [Phys] vibrometer

driˈdhˈmë nf **1** shiver, tremor; shudder **2** (Fig) strong emotion

dridhˈmoˈ·het vpr to shudder, shiver

driˈdhˈmoˈ·n vt to cause [] to shiver, make [] tremble

driˈdhˈshëm adj (i) **1** tremulous, quavering, quaking; shivering **2** flickering, twinkling

dridhˈtiˈm nm ger = drithˈëˈrˈim

dridhˈtoˈ·het vpr = drithˈëroˈ·het

dridhˈtoˈ·n vi = drithˈëroˈ·n

driˈdhˈur adj (i) **1** shivering, shuddering **2** trembling

driˈdhˈur nf (e) **1** shiver, shudder **2** trembling, flickering, twinkling

drill nm [Text] striped twill-woven duck: ticking

driˈllˈtë adj (i) made of twill-woven duck

Drin nm the river Drin

Driˈnˈi nm Drini (male name)

Drinuˈsh nm Drinush (male name)

driˈnjë nf brushwood

Drit nm Drit (male name)

Driˈtˈa nf Drita (popular female name)

Driˈtaˈn nm Dritan (popular male name)

driˈtaˈre nf **1** window **2** opening that provides access **3** (Colloq) open period in a schedule: break (during work), recess (during school)

○ **dritare dyfletëshe** double window

○ **dritare e kuadrit** [Cine] film gate, film trap

○ **dritare e projektimit** [Cine] projection booth window

driˈtaˈrez nf small window; serving window, pass-through; ticket window

driˈtˈargˈjendˈtë adj (Poet) having silvery light

driˈtˈarˈtë adj (Poet) having golden light

driˈtë nf **1** light **2** daylight **3** sparkling clean **4** (Reg) mirror

○ **dritë e egër** [Cine] hard light

○ **dritë fotoflud** [Cine] floodlight

◦ **dritë e keqe** [*Cine*] unfavorable light
◦ **dritë parazite** [*Cine*] stray light
◦ **drita e syrit 1** eyesight **2** the pupil of the eye; the eyes **3** the apple of one's eye
◦ **ësh·të t'<> shkelësh në dritë të syrit** "be able to take your stepping on the light in <>'s eye" to be unflappable
◦ **drita të shkurtra** low beams (on headlights)

dritë|ba'rdh|ë *adj* emitting white light
dritë|da'sh|ës *adj* [*Bot*] photophilic
dritë|dhën|ës *adj (Book)* light-giving, illuminating; luminous
dritë|gja't|ë *adj* [*Med*] far-sighted, hyperopic
dritë|gja'tësi *nf* [*Med*] far-sightedness, hyperopia
dritë|he'dh|ës
  I § *adj* [*Mil*] emitting a strong far-reaching light
  II § *nm* searchlight
dritë|hi'je *nf* **1** [*Art*] chiaroscuro **2** penumbra
dritë|larg|ësi *nf* [*Med*] = **dritëgjatësi**
dritë|la'rgët *adj* [*Med*] = **dritëgjatë**
dritë|lëshu'es *adj (Book)* emitting light
dritë|ma'dh *adj (Book)* emitting strong light: bright
dritë|mekët *adj* giving off a weak light: faint
dritë|ndje'sh|ëm *adj (i)* sensitive to light: photosensitive
dritë|pa'kë *adj* giving off little light: faint
dritë|përshku'e|shëm *adj (Book)* translucent; transparent
dritë|plo't|ë *adj (Book)* brightly shining, sunshiny
dritë|pri't|ëse *nf* lightshade, lampshade
dritë|rrezatu'es *adj (Book)* radiant, shining
*__**dritë|s** *adj* luminous
dritë|si *nf* [*Phys*] light magnitude
dritë|si'm *nm ger (Book)* **1** <**dritëso'·n**, **dritëso'·het 2** illumination
dritë|sje'll|ës *adj (Book)* **1** light-bearing **2** *(Fig)* enlightening
dritë|so'·het *vpr (Book)* to be enlightened
dritë|so'·n *vt (Book)* **1** to illuminate **2** to enlighten
dritë|so'r *adj* [*Forest*] serving to admit more sunlight
dritë|so're *nf (Old)* window
*__**dritë|shëm** *adj (i)* bright, shiny; glossy
dritë|shku'rt|ër *adj* **1** short-sighted **2** nearsighted, myopic **3** *(Book)* short-lasting or short-reaching light **4** shortlived
dritë|shkurtërsi *nf (Book)* [*Med*] near-sightedness, myopia
dritë|shu'ar *adj* blinded, blind
dritë|shu'më *adj (Book)* brightly lit, brightly shining
dritë|veni'tur *adj (Book)* with waning light
dritë|z *nf* **1** hole in the top of the chimney **2** weak light, faint illumination, candlelight **3** *(Reg)* mirror
dritë|zbe'htë *adj (Book)* weakly shining, faintly lit
drit|i'm *nm ger* **1** <**drito'·n 2** illumination
drito'·n *vt* to illuminate
drito're *nf* = **dritare**
drithanik = **drithnik**
dritha'r *n* grain merchant
drithato're *nf* woman who gets the grain ready for milling
drithë *nf* cereal grain, cereal, grain
drithë|ngrën|ës *adj* [*Zool*] grain-eating

---

drithëri'm *nm ger* **1** <**drithëro'·n**, **drithëro'·het 2** = **dridhmë**
drithëri'më *nf* = **dridhmë**
drithëri'shtë *nf* field of grain
drithëro'·het *vpr* to tremble, shiver, shudder, quake
drithëro'·n
  I § *vi* = **drithëro'·het**
  II § *vt* to cause [] to tremble, upset [] greatly
drithëru'ar *adj (i)* trembling, atremble
drithëru'es *adj* causing shivering
drithë|shit|ës *nm (Old)* grain dealer
*__**drith|mara'k** *adj* terrifying, horrible
drithmë *nf* **1** = **dridhje 2** [*Med*] shaking chill
*__**drith|me'ta|r** *adj* trembling, tremulous, vibrant
drithmo'·n
  I § *vt* to cause [] to tremble: intimidate, terrify
  II § *vi* *__to tremble; (of light) flicker
*__**drith|mu'a|r** *adj (i)* = **dridhshëm**
*__**drith|na** *np (Reg)* market area where grain is sold
drithnaj|ë *nf* **1** = **drithërishtë 2** cereals, grain crops
drithni'k *nm* granary; grain hopper
*__**dritho'·n** *vt vi* to shake
drith|o'r *adj* of or pertaining to grains or their production: cereal
*__**drithtëri'm** *nm ger* <**drithtëro'·n**
*__**drithtëro'·n** *vt vi* = **drithëro'·n**
drithti'm *nm ger* <**drithto'·n**, **drithto'·het**
drithto'·het *vpr* to tremble with fear, get a fright
*__**drithto'·n** *vt vi* = **drithëro'·n**
driza're *nf* [*Bot*] **1** Alps honeysuckle (*Lonicera alpigena*) **2** [*Bot*] Christ's-thorn (*Paliurus spina-christi*)
◦ **drizë e butë** [*Bot*] honey locust, false acacia, black locust *Robinia pseudoacacia*
◦ **drizë gjemcë** [*Bot*] Christ's-thorn
driz|ëri *nf* = **drizërishtë**
drizëri'shtë *nf* bramble thicket
drizo'r *adj (Old)* briery, dumose
drizo're *nf* = **drizërishtë**
dro| = **drua**
drobi's *stem for 1st sg pres, pl pres, 2nd & 3rd sg subj, pind* <**drobi't·**
drobi't· *vt (Reg)* to break [] down, exhaust; debilitate
drobi't·et *vpr (Reg)* to become worn out (from overwork, illness, or aging); become debilitated
drobi'tje *nf* exhaustion; debilitation
drobi'tur *adj (i)* exhausted, worn out; debilitated
droboli *nf* entrails, intestines
*__**droboli'k** *adj* intestinal
droboli's *stem for 1st sg pres, pl pres, 2nd & 3rd sg subj, pind* <**droboli't·**
droboli't· *vt* **1** to turn []'s stomach: nauseate **2** to shake [] up, jolt **3** to weaken
droboli't·et *vpr* **1** to grow weary **2** to suffer shock, be shaken up
*__**drobolu'e|r** *adj (fem ˜ ore) (Old)* = **drobolik**
dro'çk|ë *nf* granule of hardened substance: crumb
◦ **droçkë gjaku** [*Med*] embolus
dro'dh| *stem for pdef* <**dredh·**, **dridh·**
*__**dro'e** *nf (Reg Gheg)* = **drojë**
drogama'n *nm* drug addict

dro·gë nf narcotic drug

drogo ·het vpr to take/use a narcotic drug

drogu·a·r adj (i) drugged

dro·jë nf timidity; hesitancy; anxiety; fear

*__drojshëm__ adj (i) terrible, horrible

dro·jt·et vpr = **dru··**het.

dro·jt = **dru·ajt**

drokth nm [Bot] 1 bladder senna (Colutea arborescens) 2 = **vje·gjës**
  ○ **drokth i egër** spike broom Cytisus nigricans
  ○ **drokth lepuri** spike broom Cytisus nigricans

*__drom__ nm (Reg) = **drum**

*__droma·de__ nf = **dromeda·r**

drom·a·k nm wooden piece connected to the breeching of a packsaddle

*__droma·te__ nf = **dromeda·r**

dro·m·cë nf crumb

drom·co ·het vpr to fall into small fragments: crumble apart, shatter

drom·co ·n vt to reduce [ ] to small fragments: crumble, shatter

*__dromeda·r__ nm dromedary

*__drom·is__ stem for 1st sg pres, pl pres, 2nd & 3rd sg subj, pind <**dromit**·

*__dromi·t__· vi 1 to open a path 2 to ramble

dromi·ta·r n traveller

dro·mka np dried and crumbled mixture of yogurt and flour

dromoni·s· vt to winnow/sift [grain]

drop nm (Reg) dessert made with bread crumbs

*__dropk__ nm 1 pus; decay, rot *2 infamy

*__dro·pkët__ adj (i) 1 full of pus, mattery; decayed *2 infamous, despicable

*__dropol__ = **drobol**

Dro·pull nm ethnographic region of Albania south of Gjirokastra

dropull·i·t adj of or pertaining to Dropulli

dropulli·tçe adv Dropulli-style

dropulli·tçe nf characteristic dance of Dropulli

dro·qe np (Reg Arb) homemade macaroni cut in short thick pieces; macaroni shaped in various forms other than the usual rod-shaped one

dro·qkë nf clotted blood, blood clot

dro·sel nm [Tech] throttle

drosht nm [Bot] canary clover (Dorycnium)

dru(r)
  I § nm (np ~rë)
  II § nf (np ~nj) 1 tree 2 wood, lumber, timber 3 tree stump, tree branch 4 log 5 firewood 6 (Colloq) piece of wood 7 (Fig) blockhead, oaf, dolt 8 (Fig) drubbing, beating, thrashing

*__drû(n)__ nm (Reg Gheg) = **dru(r)**

dru··het vpr 1 to be timid, be hesitant 2 to be afraid 3 to be suspicious
  ○ **dru anije** ship's mast
  ○ **dru boje** common smoke tree, Aaron's-beard Cotinus coggygria
  ○ **dru gjethor** deciduous tree
  ○ **dru i kalbur** 1 sickly person; old 2 rotten apple, corrupt person; something growing rotten
  ○ **Druri ndreqet sa/kur është e njomë.** (Prov) "The tree is shaped when it is young and tender." The tree grows as the sapling is bent. Training should begin at a young age.
  ○ **druri i piperit** [Bot] pepper-tree Schinus molle

○ **dru e shtrëmbër** "crooked board" (Fig) rotten apple, bad egg

○ **dru i vjetër** "old wood" hardy/tough person; hardy race

drua··n
  I § vt to be afraid of [ ]
  II § vi = **dru·**·het
  ○ **<>a drua·n sherrin** to fear trouble from <>

dru·ajtje nf timidity; faintheartedness, cold feet

dru·ajtur adj (i) anxious; timid, wary

dru·a·r n = **druva·r**

drubiru·es nm [Entom] bark beetle (Scolytidae)

dru·brejt·ës nm [Entom] carpenter bee (Xylocopidae)

*__dru·cë__ nf [Ornit] = **kukuva·jkë**

*__dru·det__ nm [Bot] oak (Quercus)

drudh· vt to make crumbs out of [ ]: crumble

dru·dh·et vpr 1 to turn to crumbs 2 to be friable

dru·dhe nf 1 crumb; small particle 2 (Reg) single grape 3 (Old) atom

dru·dhë nf curly hair; haircurl

dru·dhëz nf 1 crumb 2 (Reg) residue left by from melting lard

dru·ese adv (Reg) maybe, perhaps

dru·fruto·r adj of or pertaining to fruit trees

drugdhe·nd·ës nm 1 wood-carver *2 carpenter; woodman

dru·gë nf 1 wooden bobbin (onto which yarn is spun) 2 shuttle (of a loom) 3 forked distaff holding skeins to be spun into wool or cotton yarn 4 (Reg) forked part of a slingshot

dru·gëz nf (Dimin) small bobbin; small shuttle; small forked distaff

dru·ju·bë nf [Bot] European glorybind (Lavatera arborea)

*__drum__ nm (Reg) highway, road

*__drum·ta·r__ n (Reg) traveler

dru·naba·rdh·e nf [Bot] European spindle-tree (Euonymus europaeus) = **fshikaku·q**

*__drûn·a·k__ adj (Reg Gheg) = **druno·r**

dru·naku·q nm [Bot] alder buckthorn (Frangula alnus)

dru·ngrën·ës adj [Entom] wood-eating, wood-boring

*__drûn·i__ sg stem (Reg Gheg) = **drû**

dru·ni·shtë nf area with trees

dru·no ·het vpr 1 to turn to wood 2 to grow numb

dru·no·r adj 1 woody, ligneous 2 wooden, of wood

drunj np fem < **dru(r)**

drunjëzi·m nm ger < **drunjëzo** ·het

dru·njëzo ·het vpr 1 to turn to wood; take on the form of a tree; become like wood 2 [Bot] to become lignified: lignify

dru·njëzo ·n vt [Bot] to turn [ ] into wood: lignify

dru·njëzu·a·r adj (i) turned to wood; having the form of a tree; like wood

dru·njtë adj (i) made of wood, wooden

dru·pre·r·ës nm (Book) woodcutter

dru·punu·es nm woodworker

dru·rë np < **dru(r)**

dru·r·i obl < **dru(r)**

dru·rry·ell nm (np ~ j) [Bot] tree spurge (Euphorbia dendroides)

dru·si·m nm = **drunjëzi·m**

dru|**so**·*het vpr* = **drunjëzo**·*het*

dru|**sor** *adj* 1 wooden 2 woody

dru|**su**|**ar** *adj (i)* = **drunjëzu**ar

***drú**|**shëm** *adj (i) (Reg Gheg)* = **druso**r

dru|**shit**|**ës** *nm (Old)* wood merchant

dru|**shtë** *nf* 1 wooden support pole; arbor 2 tree stump

  ∘ **drushtë e telegrafit** telegraph pole

dru|**th** *nm* [*Text*] metal spool holder

***druth** *nm* anger, bitterness

dru|**va**|**r** *n* woodchopper, woodcutter

dry(n) *nm (np ˜na)* 1 padlock; lock 2 *(Reg)* door bar 3 *(Fig)* close-mouthed person

***dry**|**dhe** *nf* flirt

***dry**|**dhë** *nf* = **dru**|**dhe**

dry|**dhë**t *adj (i)* (said of soft wood) easy to work

***dry**|**dh**|**shëm** *adj (i)* crumbly, old

***dryj** *I § nm OR* **dryj**ë *II § nf* yoke for carrying pails

dry|**na** *np* <**dry(n)**

dryn|**a**|**r** *n* locksmith

dryn|**i** *obl* <**dry(n)**

dryn|**i** *obl* <**dry(n)**

dryn|**o**·*het vpr* to be secured by a lock, be locked up

dryn|**o**·*n vt* to use a lock to secure []: lock up []

dry|**shk** = **ndryshk**

***drrudh** = **drudh**

DS. *abbrev* <**Durrës Special** brand of filter-tip cigarettes

dsh. *abbrev* <**dorëshkrim** manuscript

du·*het vpr* <**do**·*n* 1 to be needed 2 to be necessary, must, should, ought 3 to be/fall in love

dua *nf* Moslem prayer said by a priest; curative prayer; prayer written inside an amulet

du|**a** *1st sg pres, stem for 1st and 3rd plur pres, 2nd sg subj* <**do**·*n*

du|**aj** *np* sheaves of grain

duaj|**lidh**|**ës** *adj* pertaining to the binding of sheaves

duaj|**lidh**|**ëse** *nf* binder (machine for binding sheaves)

dua|**k** *nm* saddlebag

dual|**ist** *adj, n* [*Phil*] dualist

dual|**izëm** *nm* dualism

du|**all** *stem for pl pdef* <**de**|**l**·

du|**ar** *np* hands <**do**rë

  ∘ **Duart nga mielli, sytë nga qielli.** "One's hands toward the flour, one's eyes toward the sky." (said to someone not paying attention) Your head is in the clouds.

  ∘ **<>u prenë duart** "<>'s hands went numb" 1 <> is numb from shock 2 <> is left with no one to be of help

duar|**a**|**rtë** *adj* having a golden hand/touch

duar|**bo**|**sh** *adv* without a gift in hand: empty-handed

du|**ar-du**|**ar** *adv* 1 over a period of time, not all at once 2 one bunch after another 3 unevenly, in different ways

duar|**flori** *adj* = **duara**|**rtë**

duar|**kry**|**q** *adv* 1 with arms crossed 2 *(Fig)* sitting on one's hands, doing nothing

duar|**la**|**rë** *adj* guiltless, innocent, clean

duar|**la**|**rë**|**se** *nf* washbasin, washbowl

duar|**lidh**|**ur** *adv* 1 = **duarkry**|**q** 2 handcuffed, with hands tied

duar|**mpi**|**rë** *adj* inactive, not participating, disengaged

duar|**ngri**|**rë** *adj* clumsy

duar|**nxi**|**rë** *adj* having hands blue from the cold

duar|**plo**|**t** *adv* 1 with armloads of good things 2 *(Fig)* full of success

duar|**shka**|**thët** *adj* adroit

duar|**trok**|**a**|**s** *stem for 1st sg pres, pl pres, 2nd & 3rd sg subj, pind* <**duartroki**|**t**·

duar|**trok**|**i**|**t**· *vt vi* to clap hands; applaud

duar|**trok**|**i**|**tje** *nf ger* 1 <**duartroki**|**t**· 2 handclapping; applause

duar|**tha**|**rë** *adj* 1 clumsy, awkward 2 *(Curse)* may-his-hand-atrophy!

duar|**tha**|**të**

  I § adj = **duartha**|**rë**

  II § adv = **duarbo**|**sh**

duar|**zbra**|**z**|**ët** *adv* = **duarbo**|**sh**

duar|**zbra**|**z**|**ur** *adv* = **duarbo**|**sh**

dua|**xhi** *nm (np ˜nj)* 1 adherent, member, follower 2 patron

du|**bël** *nm* [*Cine*] duplicate, dupe

dubla|**nt** *nm* = **dublu**|**es**

dubla|**zh** *nm*

  ∘ **dublazh zëri** voice dubbing

duble|**r** *nm* 1 [*Cine*] actor's double, stand-in 2 [*Theat*] understudy

dublika|**të** *nf* [*Offic*] duplicate copy legally equivalent to the original

dubl|**im** *nm ger (Book)* <**dublo**·*n*

dubl|**o**·*n vt (Book)* 1 to repeat 2 to act as a double: substitute for, stand in for, understudy 3 to dub in [voices] in a film

dublu|**es** *nm (Book)* double: understudy, stand-in, substitute, voice dubber

duc *nm (Colloq Crude)* cunt

du|**dë** *nf* 1 [*Anat*] tissue in which the teeth are embedded: gum *(gingiva)* 2 [*Bot*] black mulberry *(Morus nigra)*

  ∘ **dud**ë **e bardhë** white mulberry *Morus alba*

du|**dësh**

  I § adj toothless

  II § n *toothless old person

dudi *nf* 1 [*Ornit*] = **kumri** 2 *(Fig Colloq)* beautiful girl or woman 3 *(Old)* term of respectful address to an older Moslem woman

dudu|**k** *nm* 1 [*Mus*] reed flute with a single or double pipe made of willow bark or onion stalk 2 onion stalk 3 *(Insult)* stupid person

dudu|**m** *nm* 1 *(Contempt Old)* Ottoman invader; Ottoman lackey 2 *(Colloq)* onion stalk 3 *(Insult)* moron, dumb dodo

due|**l** *nm* duel = **dyluft**|**im**

due|**q** *np* <**dua**|**k**

***du**|**er** *(Reg Gheg)* = **du**|**ar**

due|**t**

  I § nm duet

  II § adv in duet

duf *nm* 1 great anger, rage: huff *2 *(Old)* breath, vapor, atmosphere, spirit

***dufarra**|**k** *adj* tufted; in tufts

***dufe**|**k** *nm (np ˜ qe)* = **dyfe**|**k**

duf|**o**·*het vpr* to get enraged, get in a huff

***dufshk**|**o**·*het vpr* to get bruised; get wrinkled

*dugajë *nf (Reg)* = dyqa·n

*du·gme *nf* ratchet, catch

***dugulis· ** *vt* = gudulis·

duha·ç *nm (Reg)* **1** big storm **2** *[Myth]* long-tailed, smoke-spewing dragon

duha·n *nm* **1** tobacco *(Nicotiana tabacum L.)* **2** *(Colloq)* cigarette
○ **duhan i egër** *[Bot]* = madërgo·në
○ **nuk e nget· duhanin** "not touch tobacco" not be a (habitual) smoker

duhangrir·ës *nm* tobacco shredder

duhanishte *nf* **1** tobacco field **2** stripped tobacco stalk

duhano·r *adj* appropriate for growing tobacco

duhano·re *nf* field of tobacco, row of tobacco

duhanpir·ës *n* tobacco smoker

duhanpunue·s *nm* tobacco worker

duhanshit·ës *n* tobacconist

duhanto·re *nf* **1** *(Old)* tobacco shop **2** *(Colloq)* tobacco mill

duhanxhi· *nm (np ~nj)* **1** *(Old)* tobacconist **2** *(Colloq)* person who smokes: smoker

*du·h|ëm *nf* = du·hmë

duhi·
I § *nf* **1** windstorm **2** powerful burst of activity
II § *adj (Fig)* strong, powerful

duhi·shëm *adj (i)* violently stormy

*du·hme *nf* = du·hmë

du·hmë *nf* oppressive atmosphere: (smell) stink; (hot weather) sultry heat, mugginess; (wind) blustering storm

*du·hshëm *adj (i)* necessary

*du·hunisht *adv (Old)* compulsorily

du·hur
I § *part* <do·n
II § *adj (i)* **1** necessary, required **2** due, owing, owed **3** due, proper

dujkë *nf* fruit that has become ripe and very soft after picking

duk *nm (Colloq)* effect

du·k·et *vpr* **1** to appear; make an appearance **2** to seem **3** to look like, appear to be **4** to show off, put on airs **5** to be obvious/evident
○ **s'<> duk·et binaja** <> *dies* without issue, <> *disappears* without a trace
○ **nuk <> duk·et**[3sg] **boja** there *is* not a trace of <>
○ **duk·et**[3sg] **breshka** "(so level that) the turtle can be seen" it *is* completely level; there *are* no obstacles in the line of sight: the view *is* completely open
○ **<> duk·et**[3sg] **hunda dyfek** "<> thinks <>'s nose is a rifle" *(Pej)* <> *brags* about <>'s bravery; <> *thinks* <> is a big shot
○ **<> duk·et**[3pl] **malet shesh** "the mountains look flat to <>" <> *is* overoptimistic because <> *is* unaware of the difficulties, <> *thinks* everything is so easy
○ **duk·et si kukuvajkë** to look like an old bat
○ **duk·et**[3rd] **si në pëllëmbë të dorës** to be as easily seen as if { } were in the palm of one's hand

dukagjin *nm* grape must at early stage of souring into wine

Dukagjin *nm* mountainous region in north-central Albania

dukagjin|**as** *adj, n* of/from Dukagjin, native of Dukagjin

dukagjin|**e** *nf* grape must that has been fermented with mustard seed

duka·l *adj* ducal

duka·t *nm [Hist]* **1** ducat **2** *(Old)* gold

duka·të *nf[Hist]* dukedom, duchy

du·ke *pcl (always followed by a participle)* indicates an attendant action or state: while {verb}ing, by {verb}ing
○ **ësh·të duke** {VERB PARTICIPLE} to be in the process of {VERB-ing}: be {VERB-ing} **jam duke shkuar** I am (in the process of) going EXishim duke folur me Agimin (while) we were (in the midst of) talking with Agim (when something happened)
○ **Duke parë e duke bërë.** "Seeing and doing." As one sees how it is going, one decides how to proceed.
○ **duke pasë** {verb} having { }ed
○ **duke qenë se (që)** it being the case that: since
○ **duke qenë** {verb} (while) being { }ed

duke·l = dyqe·l

duke·shë *nf [Hist]* duchess

du·kë
I § *nf* = dukje
II § *nf with masculine reference [Hist]* duke

du·kje *nf ger* **1** <du·k·et **2** appearance; look **3** scene **4** outward display **5** obviousness **6** *(Old)* event, phenomenon

*du·kme *nf (e) (Old)* phenomenon

*dukni *nf(Old)* aspect, phase; scene, view

du·kshëm
I § *adj (i)* **1** apparent, evident **2** obvious, conspicuous **3** visible, ostensible **4** *(Old)* superficial **5** *(Colloq)* good-looking
II § *adv* evidently, apparently

dukshm|**ëri** *nf(Book)* visibility

du·kur *adj (i) (Colloq)* good-looking

dukuri· *nf [Phil]* phenomenon

*dulfi(n) *nm (np ~ j) (Reg Gheg)* = delfi·n

*dulti·në *nf* = delti·në

*dultin|**ue·r** *adj (fem ~ ore) (Old)* = deltino·r

*dulla·k = dolla·k

*dulla·p = dolla·p

*du·llë *nf with masc agreement,UICrude* rube, goof-off; jerk; fruit (homosexual)

dum *invar*

dumale·k *nm [Mus]* bowl-shaped drum beaten with hands or sticks

duma·n *nm (Old)* thick cloud of dust/smoke/fog; smoke

dumara·c *adj* short and stout

dumb *nm* mortar (for mashing)

dumbaralle·k *nm (np ~ qe)* cheating

dumbre· *nf* = dushkaj·ë

dumbushe·re *nf* **1** any umbrella-shaped tree with thick foliage; bush-like tree **2** copse of such trees

dumdu·m *nm [Mil]* dumdum bullet

dum-du·m *nm* kind of tractor

du·me *nf* **1** wooden measuring pan holding about six kilograms of grain **2** wooden box for keeping foodstuffs **3** chubby child

dume·n *nm* **1** fire with tall flames; tall flames **2** *[Ethnog]* big bonfire lit at certain festivals

*du·më *adj* chubby, plump

du'mkë
  I § *nf(Reg)* **1** fist ***2** labia of the vulva
  II § *adj* full; quite fat

dumpi'ng *nm* [*Econ*] selling large quantities of a product at low prices to drive out competition: price dumping

dumrej|as *adj* of or pertaining to natives of Dumre

du'në *nf* [*Geog*] dune

du'ngë
  I § *adj* bobtailed (of goats)
  II § *nf(Old)* small single-barreled, flintlock pistol

duni'cë *nf* [*Bot*] Jerusalem sage *(Phlomis fruticosa)*
  ○ **dunicë mali** garden sage *Salvia officinalis*

*dunk *adj* one-handed

duode'n *nm* [*Anat*] duodenum = **dymbëdhjetëgisht-o're**

*dup *nm* medallion, pendant

du'pje *nf(Old)* old gold coin worth two napoleons

duplika'të *nf* duplicate, copy

duq *nm* **1** barrel tap; bung **2** cigarette butt

*duqa'n = **dyqa'n**

du'qe *np* = **hejbe'**

duralumi'n *nm* [*Tech*] duralumin

*durbi' = **dylbi'**

dure's|ë *nf* **1** = **durim 2** [*Tech*] set of permissible deviation from a prescribed standard: tolerance = **tol-era'ncë**

duri'm *nm* *ger* **1** < **duro'·n**, **duro'·het 2** endurance, perseverance **3** patience **4** sense of restraint, tolerance

Duri'm *nm* Durim (male name)

duri'm|ma'dh *adj* very patient

duri'm|plo'të *adj* full of patience, very patient

duri'm|shu'më *adj* remarkably patient

duri'm|ta'r *adj (Book)* patient; hardy

duro'·het *vpr*
  ○ **s'/nuk ◇ duro·het**^{3sg} _ ◇ can't stand/bear/take/endure not _ing, be impatient to _
  ○ **s'/nuk duro·het**^{3sg} _ _ is intolerable

duro'·n
  I § *vt* **1** to endure, bear/stand up under [] **2** to tolerate; stand, bear **3** to resist damage from []
  II § *vi* **1** to be patient **2** to last; resist damage **3** to be postponable: can wait
  ○ **s'[] duro·n**^{3sg} **as qielli, as dheu/toka** "neither the sky nor the earth can bear [the affront]" [it] *is* too much to put up with, [it] *is* too much to take: that *is* just too much!
  ○ **nuk e duro·n litarin në fyt** "not endure the rope on the throat" not submit to anyone
  ○ **Duro të durojmë!** Let's be patient!
  ○ **Duro zemër e mos plas!** Bear up and don't go to pieces! Keep your chin up!

duru'a|r *adj (i)* = **duru'eshëm**

duru'e|s *n* patient person

duru'e|shëm *adj (i)* **1** able to resist hardship/pain: tough, patient **2** durable **3** endurable, tolerable, bearable

duru'e|shm|ëri' *nf(Book)* durability

Du'rrës *nm* the city of Durrës: Durazzo

durrsa'k *adj, n* (native) of Durazzo

DUS *abbrev* < **Drejtoria e Ujërave dhe e Sistemimeve** Director of Water and Soil Management

dush *nm* **1** cleansing spray: shower; shower bath **2** shower room **3** *(Fig)* action/activity that arouses or invigorates

dushk
  I § *nm* (*np* ~ **qe**) **1** [*Bot*] oak *(Quercus L.)* **2** acorn **3** *(Collec)* winter fodder consisting of small leafy oak branches **4** *(Reg)* tender tobacco leaves that ripen in autumn
  II § *np (Reg)* cornhusks
  ○ **dushk i butë** [*Bot*] = **bungëbu'të**
  ○ **dushk i egër** [*Bot*] = **a'she**
  ○ **dushk gurësh** [*Bot*] durmast oak *Quercus petraea*

dushkaj|ë *nf* oak forest, oak glen

dushka'tar *n* person who carries oak branches down from the mountains to serve as winter fodder for livestock

dushk|ërkë *nf* dwarf oak, young oak tree

dushk|isht|ë *nf* = **dushkajë**

dushko'·het *vpr* **1** to get covered with new leaves **2** to get covered by oak trees

dushko'·n *vi* **1** to bear/sprout new leaves **2** to get covered by oak trees **3** to cut small leafy oak branches for use as winter fodder for farm animals

dushko'nja *np* oak logs for the fire

dushko're *nf* = **dushkajë**

du'shk|të *adj* of oak, oaken

du'shk|ull *nm* (*np* ~ **j**) [*Bot*] **1** mastic tree, lentisc *(Pistacia lentiscus)* **2** burning bush, dittany *(Dictamnus albus)*

dushma'n *nm (Colloq)* enemy, occupier, conqueror, invader

dushne'zë *nf* = **shku'rre**

dushni'cë *nf* young copse of oaks

dush|ni'k *nm* = **dushkajë**

dushnje'rre *nf* **1** = **dushkërkë 2** = **dushkajë**

du'shqe *np* < **dushk**

dushqe're *nf* = **dushkajë**

duva'k *nm* [*Ethnog*] **1** bridal veil **2** *(Old)* banner

duzi'në *nf* dozen

duzhi'në = **duzi'në**

d.v. *abbrev* < **dora vetë** signed (by his own hand); personally, in person

dvi'er· *vt* = **degjenero'·n**

dvo'r| *stem for pdef* < **dvier·**

dy
  I § *num* two; number two
  II § *nf* the number two
  ○ **Dy duar për një kokë janë.** "Two hands are needed for one head." You have to protect yourself.
  ○ **dy fjalë** a few words
  ○ **Dy gishta fytyrë ka njeriu.** "A person has a face of only two finger's breadth." A person should have some sense of honor.
  ○ **dy grosh oka** *(Impol)* dirt cheap
  ○ **dy Kamberë në një derë** *(Pej)* two of a kind: tweedledum and tweedledee
  ○ **dy kufomë e një shpirt** two people who like each other very much, two people who are very close to one another
  ○ **ësh·të dy mendjesh** to be of two minds
  ○ **ësh·të dy para burrë/njeri** "be a nickel's worth of man" to be small and scrawny, not be much of a man; be a person of no importance
  ○ **dy pëllëmbë mbi tokë** little guy
  ○ **dy pika** colon (punctuation mark)

○ **të dy** both

dyaktësh *adj* in two acts, two-act

dyanësi *nf (Book)* bilaterality, duality

dyanësisht *adv (Book)* bilaterally, mutually; conversely

dyanësor *adj* 1 double-sided 2 bilateral <**dyanshëm**

dyanësh *adj* = dyanshëm

dyanshëm *adj (i)* 1 two-sided, double-sided 2 on both sides, from both sides, from both points of view: bilateral; mutual 3 alternating; vacillating

dyanshmëri *nf (Book)* bilaterality, duality

dyatomik *adj [Chem]* diatomic

dyballor *adj [Archit]* having a double facade

dybarkor *adj* 1 double-bellied 2 *[Optics]* biconcave

dybarqësh *adj* double-bellied

*****dybe** *nf* doubt, suspicion

dybek *nm* 1 large wooden mortar/pestle used to husk grain 2 *[Dairy]* milk churn 3 *(Reg)* large wooden mallet used to break up clods

dybërthamësh *adj* having two seeds, double-pitted

dyboshtor *adj [Spec]* biaxial

dybrinjështëm *adj [Geom]* isosceles

dybukësh *adj (Reg)* two-year-old; used for plowing for two years in a row (said of oxen)

dybuzor *adj* 1 *[Ling]* bilabial 2 *[Bot]* bilabiate, two-lipped

dyceplësh *adj* having two corners

dycilindërsh *adj [Tech]* having two cylinders

*****dyç** *I §* *nm* OR **dyçkë** *II §* *nf* deuce (in cards)

dydegësh *adj* having two branches: bifurcated

dydirekësh *adj* having two masts: twin-masted

dyditësh *adj* 1 prepared two days in advance 2 = dyditor

dyditor *adj* lasting two days; two-day long

dydynym *adj (Colloq)* measuring two dynyms

dydhëmbësh

I § *adj* having two teeth/tines/prongs

II § *nm [Bot]* bur marigold *Bidens*

dyer *np* <derë

○ [] **pafsha në dyert e botës!** "May I see [] at the doors of strangers!" *(Curse)* I'd like to see [] have to live like a beggar!

dyfaqe *nf* = dyfaqësi

dyfaqësi *nf (Book)* 1 double-facedness 2 two-facedness: hypocrisy, duplicity

dyfaqësh *adj* 1 *[Geom]* double-faced, double-sided: dihedral 2 *(Fig)* duplicitous

dyfaqshëm *adj (i)* duplicitous

dyfarësh *adj* 1 having two seeds 2 of two sorts/kinds

dyfarshëm *adj (i)* = dyfarësh = dyllojshëm

dyfazësh *adj* 1 in/of two phases 2 diphasic

dyfazor *adj [Electr]* diphasic

dyfek *nm (np ~ qe)* gun (one that is a personal weapon)

○ **ësh·të i dyfekut** "be of the gun" 1 to know how to handle a gun 2 to be a real fighter

○ **dyfek i palosur** "folded shotgun" *(Impol)* person unable to work because of a physical or mental handicap

○ **ësh·të dyfek i plasur** to be too old to work; be broken down, be unsafe

○ **dyfek i shtogtë** "wooden gun" 1 *(Impol)* person unable to carry things through 2 inept person

dyfekçi *nm* 1 gunsmith 2 sharpshooter 3 *[Ethnog]* armed member of the bridegroom's party who comes to fetch the bride

dyfekmbajtës *nm [Hist]* rifleman

dyfeko·het *vn recip (Reg)* to exchange gunshots

dyfekshuar *adj* incapable of self-defense, gun-shy

dyfektar *nm* rifleman

dyfeqe *np* <dyfek

dyfeqis·et *vpr* to shoot at one another

dyfilmsh *nm [Cine]* bipack film

dyfish

I § *nm* double the amount, twice as much

II § *adj* double, two-fold

III § *adv* twice as, double the amount

dyfishim *nm ger* <dyfisho·n, dyfisho·het

dyfisho·het *vpr* to increase twofold, double

dyfisho·n *vt* to double, redouble

dyfishtë *adj (i)* 1 twofold 2 double 3 alternate 4 duplicitous

dyfishuar *adj (i)* 1 doubled 2 greatly increased

dyflatrorë *np fem [Entom]* diptera

dyflegërsh *adj* having double doors

dyfletësh *adj* 1 in two panels: two-paneled; double-leafed; two-page 2 having double doors

*****dyfolje** *nf (Old)* dialogue

dyformatsh *adj [Cine]* in double format

dyformësh *adj (Book)* dimorphic

dyfytyrësi *nf (Book)* 1 two-facedness 2 double-facedness 3 duplicity, hypocrisy

dyfytyrësh *adj* duplicity, hypocrisy

dyfytyrshëm *adj (i)* = dyfytyrësh

dygeç *nm* 1 pestle 2 flail

dygrykësh *adj* double-throated, double-barreled

dygrremç *adj, nm* (pitchfork) with two prongs

dygungësh *adj* double-humped

dygjinish *adj (i) [Ling]* having two genders

dygjinor *adj [Zool]* bisexual

dygjuhësi *nf [Ling]* bilingualism

dygjuhësor *adj [Ling]* bilingual

dygjuhësh *adj [Ling]* bilingual

dygjymtyrësh

I § *adj [Ling]* bipartite

II § *nm [Math]* binomial

dyherë *adv* twice

dyherësh *adj* 1 done twice: two-time, twice over 2 bearing fruit twice a year

dyhershëm *adj (i)* done twice: two-time, twice over

dyjar

I § *adj* 1 double, dual, two-fold, twin, paired 2 born as twin lambs/kids in the same litter 3 giving birth to twin lambs/kids: biparous 4 growing double/twinned/paired 5 *[Math]* binary

II § *nm* 1 twin (in a litter of two) 2 lamb that nurses two ewes

dyjare *nf* 1 double flute; double bell 2 two-year-old sheep or goat

dyjavësh

I § *adj* 1 two-week old 2 two-week long 3 biweekly

II § *nm* two-week period, two weeks' time

dyjavor

I § *adj* 1 two-week long 2 biweekly

II § *nm* two-week period, two weeks' time
dy·ja'vshëm *adj* (i) two-week
dy·kal'im·sh *nm* [*Soccer*] indirect free kick
dy·kana't·ësh *adj* having two doors: double-doored
dy·kat'ësh *adj* two-storied, of two floors
*****dy'ke** *pcl* (*always followed by a participle*) **= du'ke**
dy·këmb'ësh
  I § *adj* two-legged, bipedal
  II § *nm* **1** [*Mil*] bipod **2** [*Lit*] dipody, dimeter
dy·kil'ësh *adj* (*Colloq*) weighing two kilograms
*****dykme'** I § *nf* OR **dykme'n** II § *nm* (*Old*) former
  gold coin
dy·ko'h·ësh *adj* two-cycle (engine)
dy·krah'ësh *adj* two-winged
dy·kren'o·r *adj* two-headed, bicephalous
dy·kre'r·ësh *adj* **= dykreno'r**
dy·krye·gymty'r·ësh *adj* [*Ling*]
dy·kuptim'ësi *nf* (*Book*) ambiguity
dy·kuptim'sh·ëm *adj* (i) ambiguous
dy·kuptim·shm'ëri *nf* (*Book*) **= dykuptimësi**
dy·kuptim't·ë *adj* (i) **= dykuptim·shëm**
dy·kuro'r·ësh *adj* (family) of double lineage
dy·kurriz'o·r *adj* [*Optics*] **= dymy'stë**
*****dy·ky'ç** *nm* (*Old*) valve
dylbe'n *nm* (*Old*) thin kerchief; thin veil; thin tissue
dylbi' *nf* binoculars, fieldglasses, opera glasses
  ○ **ta shikosh me dylbi** "when you see it with binoculars" (*Iron*) any day now! (never)
dy·lek'ësh *nm* (*Colloq*) two-lek coin
dy·lit'ër·sh *adj* measuring two liters
*****dylme're** *nf* [*Ornit*] **= bishtatu'ndës**
*****dylmer'** (*Reg*) **= delmer'**
dy·luft'im *nm* duel
dy·luft'o·n *vi* **1** to duel; fight man-to-man **2** [*Sport*]
  to battle one on one
dy·lu'g·ët *adj* (i) concave on both sides: biconcave
*****dyly'm** (*Reg*) **= dyny'm**
dy'llë *nm* wax
  ○ **dyllë druri** resin, rosin
  ○ **dyllë i kuq** red sealing wax
  ○ **dyllë parketi** floor wax
dyllë·çit·et *vpr* to get soft as wax
dyllë·çit'ur *adj* (i) (of bread) still doughy
dyllë·shkri'r·ëse *nf* metal-lined wooden box for
  melting beeswax
dy·ll'im *nm ger* <**dyllo'·n**
dyllo'·n *vt* **= dyllo's·**
dy·llo'j·ësh *adj* **= dyllo'jshëm**
dy·lloj'o·r *adj* [*Spec*] dimorphic
dy·lloj'sh·ëm *adj* (i) of two sorts/kinds
dy·lloj·shm'ëri *nf* (*Book*) dimorphism
dy·lloj't·ë *adj* (i) of two kinds
dy·llo'r *adj* waxen, of wax
dyllo's· *vt* **1** to apply wax to [ ]: wax; rub [ ] with wax
  and polish **2** to seal [ ] with wax
dyllo'sje *nf ger* <**dyllo's·**
dy·llo's·ur *adj* (i) **1** waxed **2** sealed with wax
dy·llt'ë *adj* (i) **1** made of wax, of wax; waxen **2** waxy
dymbe'k *nm* churn
*****dymbele'k** *nm* [*Mus*] **= dumale'k**
dy·mbë'dhjet'ë
  I § *num* twelve; number twelve

II § *nf* the number twelve
III § *adj* (i) n (i) twelfth
dy·mbë'dhjetë·ba'll·ësh *adj* [*Spec*] (of earthquakes) with a magnitude of twelve
dy·mbë'dhjetë·fa'q·ësh *nm* [*Math*] dodecahedron
dy·mbë'dhjetë·gi'sht·ëz *nf* [*Anat*] **= dymbëdhjetë-
  gishto're**
dy·mbë'dhjetë·gisht'o're *nf* [*Anat*] duodenum
dy·mbë'dhjetë·kë'nd·ësh
  I § *nm* [*Geom*] dodecagon
  II § *adj* [*Geom*] dodecagonal
dy·mbë'dhjetë·rro'k·ësh
  I § *adj* [*Lit*] dodecasyllabic
  II § *nm* dodecasyllable
dy·mbë'dhjet'ësh *adj* holding/having twelve bullets: twelve-shot
dy·mbë'dhjetë·vjeça'r *adj* **1** twelve-year old
  2 lasting twelve years
*****dyme'n** *nm* (*Reg*) **= timo'n**
dy·me'ndje *nf* **1** ambivalence, hesitation **2** disagreement
dy·më'ndje·sh *adv* of two minds, ambivalent, with
  hesitation
dy·m'ëz·aj *adv* **1** twofold, twice as much, double
  2 hesitatingly
dy·m'ëz·im *nm ger* <**dymëzo'·n, dymëzo'·het**
dy·m'ëzo'·het *vpr* to increase twofold, double
dy·m'ëzo'·n *vt* to double, redouble
dy·mota'k *adj* two-year old
dy·moto'r·ësh *adj* bimotor
dy·mo't·sh·ëm *adj* (i) **= dyvjeça'r**
dy·mu'aj·sh
  I § *adj* two months old/long; bimonthly
  II § *nm* two-month period
dy·muj'o'r
  I § *adj* bimonthly; two months long
  II § *nm* two-month period
dy·my'sët *adj* (i) [*Optics*] convex on both sides: biconvex
dynd· *vt* (*Colloq*) **1** to move [ ] in a massive way, shake
  from the very foundation: rock, jolt **2** to move [ ]
  forcibly en masse; convey [ ] en masse; stir [masses]
  into action
dynd·et *vpr* **1** to tremble from the very foundation:
  rock quake **2** to move/migrate in massive numbers
  from one place to another; move in hordes **3** (*Colloq*)
  to change residence: move **4** (*Fig*) to make a sudden
  massive invasion: surge forth, converge
dynda'llë *nf* inundation, flood
dynd'ës *n* migrant, emigrant; invader, inundator
dyn'dje *nf ger* **1** <**dynd·, dynd·et 2** concourse,
  great crowd, throng
dy·ngjy'r·ësh *adj* bicolored, of two colors
dyny'm *nm* measure of land equal to about a thousand
  square meters
dynja' *nf* (*Colloq*) **1** world **2** the world of reality, real
  world **3** mankind **4** a massive amount
  ○ **Nuk u shemb dynjaja!** "The world did not collapse!" (*Impol*) So what! So big deal! It's not so
  serious!
dynja'll·ëk *nm* (*Colloq*) **1** whole world, everyone
  2 one's economic situation
dy·oksi'd *nm* [*Chem*] dioxide
dy·palë·dhëmbo'r *adj, n* [*Zool*] diphyodont

dy|pa'l|ësh *adj* between two parties: bilateral, bipartite

*****dy|pi'kë** *nf* = **dypi'kës**

dy|pi'kë|s *nm* colon

dy|pist|ë'sh *adj* [*Cine*] double-tracked

dy|pje'së|sh *adj* having two parts: two-part, bipartite

dy|pola'r *adj* [*Electr*] dipolar

dy|polar|ë'si *nf* [*Electr*] dipolarity

dy|pushte't *nm* rule by two powers: dual sovereignty

*****dyq** *nm* rut, track

dyqa'n *nm* 1 shop, store 2 (*Colloq*) craftsman's workshop 3 (*Old*) craftsman's workshop and store 4 (*Colloq*) fly opening (in trousers)
- **dyqan-shtëpi** village store
- **dyqan hekurishtesh** hardware store, ironmonger

dyqan|xhi' *nm (np ~ nj) (Colloq)* shopkeeper; store owner

dy|qe'l *nm* two-pronged mattock

dy|qeliz'o'r *adj* double-celled

dy|qi'nd
   I § *num* two hundred; number two hundred
   II § *nf* the number two hundred

dy|qind|të *adj (i)* two hundredth

dy|qind|vjeto'r *nm* bicentennial

dy|ra'dh|ësh *adj* = **dyrreshto'r**

*****dyrbi'** = **dylbi'**

*****dyre'k** = **dire'k**

dy|rresht|o'r *adj* having components in double rows: double-rowed

dy|rrok|ësh
   I § *adj* [*Ling*] disyllabic, of two syllables
   II § *nm* [*Ling*] disyllable

*****dy|rro'k|shëm** *adj (i)* = **dyrro'kësh**

dyseks|o'r *adj* [*Spec*] hermaphroditic

dy|si' *nf (Book)* duality

dy|so'r
   I § *nm* [*Ling*] doublet
   II § *adj* 1 composed of two parts: binary, double, paired 2 of two kinds: binary, dual

*****dy|so're** *nf (Old)* airgun

dyst *adv (Colloq)* 1 level, smooth 2 flat on the ground 3 right up to the brim

dyst|aba'n *adj (Colloq)* 1 having flat feet: flat-footed 2 flat-soled

dy'st|ë *adj (i) (Colloq)* 1 level, smooth 2 (cloth) of a single color

dyst|i'm *nm ger (Colloq)* < **dysto'·n**, **dysto'·het**

dyst|i'në *nf* level area: plain

dyst|o'·het *vpr (Colloq)* to become level/smooth, flatten out

dyst|o'·n *vt (Colloq)* 1 to make level/even: level, smooth 2 (*Fig*) to put in order, fix

dy|strof|ësh *adj* [*Lit*] distrophic, two-stanza

dy'|sh *adj (Colloq)* having two parts: double

dy'sh *adv* 1 in two pieces 2 twice, double

dy'sh *nm* 1 playing card with the number two: deuce 2 the number two as an identifying label 3 having a measure of 2 units 4 (*Old*) the grade 2 in a grading system in which 5 is the highest grade 5 (*Old*) ancient Turkish coin worth two para
- **më dysh** 1 of two minds, undecided, uncertain 2 in two parts/pieces
- **dyshi i mirë** deuce of clubs

dy|sh|as *adv* 1 in two pieces, in half 2 of two minds: undecided, uncertain = **mëdy'shas**

dy|she *nf* 1 group of two: pair, couple 2 large square kerchief folded double into a triangle and worn as head covering by women 3 a dance performed by two people

dyshe'k *nm* mattress; padded mat

dyshek|punu'e|s *n* mattress maker

dysheme' *nf* 1 floor; floorboard, floor covering 2 [*Geol Min*] mineral-bearing stratum: floor, sole 3 large woven shawl

dysheme|ti's· *vt (Colloq)* to lay flooring

dyshe'q|e *np* < **dyshe'k**

*****dy|shëm** *adj (i)* 1 dual 2 ambiguous 3 mutual

dy|shifro'r *adj* [*Math*] consisting of two numerals: binary

dysh|i'm *nm* 1 uncertainty, hesitation; doubting, doubt 2 suspicion

dysh|imo'r *adj* [*Ling*] expressing/containing uncertainty or doubt: dubitive

dysh|im|ta'r *n* = **dyshu'es**

dysh|im|tas *adv* irresolutely, indecisively, hesitatingly, uncertainly; suspiciously

dysh|i'm|të
   I § *adj (i)* 1 uncertain, doubtful 2 suspicious, suspected 3 [*Med*] amphibolic
   II § *nf* suspect

dy|shka'll|ësh *adj* having two steps; in two steps/stages

dy|shkë *nf (Colloq)* small coin: cent, sou

dy|sh|kolo'në *nf* [*Mil*] double column, double file

*****dy|shkro'nj|ë** = **dyshkro'njësh**

dy|shkro'nj|ësh *nm* [*Ling*] digraph = **digra'm**

dyshmo'·n = **dysho'·n**

dysho'·het *vpr* to have suspicions

dysho'·n *vi* 1 to be doubtful; be dubious 2 to be suspicious: suspect 3 to be indecisive/irresolute/uncertain

dy|shte'ta|s *n* person with dual citizenship

dy|shtet|ë'si' *nf* dual citizenship

dy|sht|o'·n *vt* to divide [ ] into two parts

dy|shtre's|ësh *adj* having two layers/levels, double-coated

dyshu'a|r *adj (i)* giving cause for suspicion: doubtful, dubious

dyshu'e|s *adj* 1 having doubts, doubting: distrustful, dubious 2 having suspicions, suspecting: suspicious

dy|taki'm|sh *nm* [*Soccer*] indirect free kick

*****dy|te'f|ës** = **dyte'hësh**

dy|te'h|ësh *adj* two-edged, double-bladed

dy|te'h|të *adj* = **dyte'hësh**

dy|të
   I § *adj (i)* 1 (ordinal number) second 2 second (in quality or rank)
   II § *nf (e)* 1 half 2 second course (of a meal) 3 second grade (in elementary school); second grade class/classroom
- **nuk e pa/shihte i pari të dytin** "the first did not see the second" they stumbled all over one another in their panic to escape

dy|t|ëso'r *adj* 1 second (in order), next 2 secondary, second-order

dy|t|ësho'r *n* person bearing a striking resemblance to someone else: double, perfect double, twin

dy·ti *adv (së)* **1** secondly, in the second place **2** again, another time, once more

dy·trajt·ësh *adj* having two forms/shapes: dimorphic

dy·thelb·o·r *adj* [*Bot*] double-kerneled: dicotyledonous

*****dy·thëngjill·a·të** *nf (Old)* [*Chem*] bicarbonate

dy·thundr·ak *adj* [*Zool*] double-hoofed, bifid

dy·thundr·a·kë *np* [*Zool*] double-hoofed animals: even-toed ungulates *(Artiodactyla)*

dy·uj·ë·se *adj* (roof) double-sloped so that water runs down both sides

*****dyva·k = duva·k**

dy·vale·nt *adj* [*Chem*] bivalent

dy·varg·ësh *nm* [*Lit*] distich

dy·ve·gj·ëshe *nf* two-handled clay pot

dy·velëz·o·rë *np fem* [*Zool*] dibranchiata

dy·ve·nd·as *n* person with dual citizenship = **dyshte-tas**

dy·venduz·o·rë *np fem* [*Zool*] digenea

dy·ver·a·k [*Ichth*] young fish less than two years old

dy·vëllim·ësh *adj* in two volumes

dy·vënd·ësh *adj* seating two: two-seater

dy·viz·o·r *adj* bilinear

dy·vjeç·a·r *adj* **1** biennial **2** two-year-old

dy·vjet·o·r
I § *adj* **1** biennial **2** two-year-old
II § *nm* second anniversary

dy·vle·r·shëm *adj (i)* two-valued

dy·zan·o·r
I § *nm* [*Ling*] diphthong

II § *adj* [*Ling*] diphthongal

dy·zash *adv* = **mëdy·sh**

dyze·n *nm (Colloq)* **1** = **aheng 2** *(Reg)* = **çifteli**

dy·ze·t *num* forty; number forty

dy·ze·t·ë *adj (i)* fortieth
◦ **të dyzetat 1** fortieth year of life **2** commemoration of the dead after forty days; meal served at that commemoration

dy·zet·këmb·ësh *nm* [*Invert*] = **shumëkëmbësh**

dy·zet·vjeç·a·r
I § *adj* **1** lasting forty years; accomplished within forty years **2** forty years old
II § *n* forty-year old person

dy·zet·vjet·o·r *nm* fortieth anniversary

*****dy·zgë = di·zgë**

dy·zi·m *nm ger* **1** <**dyzo·n, dyzo··het 2** vacillation between two possibilities **3** acceptance of two mutual incompatibles **4** division/dividing into two parts, duplication, replication

dy·zo··het *vpr* **1** to become twice as large, double **2** to recur, repeat

dy·zo··n
I § *vi* to be of two minds, vacillate between two possibilities: hesitate, waver, be indecisive/irresolute/uncertain
II § *vt* **1** to couple [] **2** to double (in amount); multiply by two; duplicate **3** [*Phil*] to advocate dualism **4** to divide/cut/split in two *****5** to fold, fold [] over

dy·zu·a·r *adj (i)* formed by joining two identical things: doubled; repeated

DHdh

dh [*dhë*] *nf* **1** the digraph "dh" considered to be a single letter in the Albanian alphabet **2** the voiced interdental fricative consonant represented by that letter

dha *conj* thus, so, therefore

dha| *stem for pdef* <**je p**·

dhall|aní'k *nm* [*Food*] pie made of corn meal and buttermilk or yogurt

dha'll|ë *nf* [*Dairy*] buttermilk

dhall|ë'shit|ës *n* [*Dairy*] buttermilk peddler/seller

dhall|ë'to'r *nm* [*Food*] corn bread made with buttermilk or yogurt

***dhama'k** *nm* public

***dhamak|ër|o'·n** *vt* to publish

***dhamak|ësí'** *nf* public

***dhamb|** (*Reg Gheg*) = **dhëmb|**

***dha'm|ë** *nf* (*Reg*) = **dho'm|ë**

***dhâm|** (*Reg Gheg*) = **dhëmb|**

***dhampa'll|ë** *nf* = **dhëmba'll|ë**

***dhampi'r** *nm* child of a ghostly monster, vampire

dhamsu'të *nf* **1** [*Folklore*] mythical deaf mare **2** small white shell

***dhan|** (*Reg Gheg*) = **dhën|**

***dhand|ërr|** (*Reg Gheg*) = **dhëndër|**

***dhan|í'** *nf* (*Old*) dose

dhan|o're
  I § *nf* [*Ling*] dative case
  II § *adj* [*Ling*] dative

***dhan|tí'** *nf* (*Reg Gheg*) = **dhur|ëtí'**

***dhân|un** *adj* (i) (*Reg Gheg*) **1** = **dhë'n|ë** **2** gifted, talented

***dhap|ër|o'·n** *vt* to consume, use

***dhart** *nm* beater used to beat corn kernels off the cob

***dha'rt|ë** *nf* catastrophe

dhaska'j *np* <**dhaska'l** (*Old*)

dhaska'l *nm* **1** (*Old*) teacher **2** (*Pej*) pedant; incompetent, nasty teacher

dhaskal|e'sh|ë *nf* <**dhaska'l** (*Old*)

dhaskal|í'c|ë *nf* = **dhaskale'shë** (*Old*)

dhaske'nj *np* <**dhaska'l**

dha'sh|ë *1st sg pdef* <**je p**·

dha'shk|ë *nf* (*Reg*) prematurely pregnant heifer

dhè OR **dhe** *nf* (*np ˜ ra*) **1** earth **2** ground; soil **3** land **4** world **5** (*Euph*) snake

dhe
  I § *coordinate conj* and
  II § *adv* even
  III § *2nd sg pdef* <**je p**·
  ◦ **dhe _ dhe _** both _ and _
  ◦ **dhe {} {}** too/also, {} as well
  ◦ **dhe ca'zë** a little while longer
  ◦ **dhe pastaj** and furthermore
  ◦ <> **ardhtë era dhe!** "May the smell of earth come to <>!" (*Curse*) May <> be dead and buried!
  ◦ <>**u haptë varri/dheu nën këmbë!** (*Curse*) May the ground open up under <>! May <>'s grave open under <>'s feet! I hope <> dies!

  ◦ **i rëndo·n/rënde·n dheut** (*Impol*) (of a bad/useless person) to just be taking up valuable space, be a burden on the world, the world would be better off without one

dhe'as *adv* = **dhe'ras**

dhe|ba'rdh|ë *nf* = **botëba'rdhë**

***dhe|dhë'n|ie** *nf* (*Old*) land produce/yield

dhe|gërm|u'e|s *adj* for digging up earth: earth-digging

dhe|í'sht|ë *nf* area covered with piles of earth

dhe|ku'qe *nf* red clay = **botëku'qe**

dhel· *vt* to caress, fondle, pet, stroke

dhe|la'të'r
  I § *adj* **1** used to being caressed/petted/fondled/stroked; treated as the pet/favorite **2** flattering
  II § *nm* an only son; pampered child

dhe|la'to'·n *vt* to pamper, coddle

dhe'le *np* fondling caresses

***dhe'l|ë** OR **dhe'l|je** *nf* lure

dhe|lëku'nd|je *nf* (*Book*) earthquake

***dhelfí'n** *nm* [*Zool*] dolphin = **delfí'n**

dhelí'n|ë *nf* [*Bot*] deodar (*Cedrus deodara*)

dhe'l|ke *nf* fondling caress

dhelp|ara'k *adj* foxy, cunning, sly, crafty

dhe'lp|ër *nf* vixen, fox (*Vulpes vulpes L.*)
  ◦ **dhelpër deti** [*Ichth*] thornback ray, roker (*Raja clavata*)

dhelp|ërí' *nf* act/action performed with wiliness, cunning, slyness, craftiness: trick, ruse

dhelp|ërí'sht *adv* slyly, cunningly, craftily

dhelp|ër|o'·n *vi* to use cunning/trickery/deceit, act slyly/craftily

dhelp|ër|o'r *adj* tricky, crafty, cunning; deceitful

dhelp|ër|u'sh *nm* fox pup

***dhelp|na'k** *adj* = **dhelpara'k**

***dhelp|ní'** *nf* = **dhelpërí'**

dhella'k *nm* [*Entom*] cochineal insect (*Dactylopius coccus*)

dhe|ma't|ës
  I § *adj* (*Old*) **1** used for surveying land; of or pertaining to surveying **2** geometrical
  II § *n* (*Old*) land surveyor = **gjeome'të'r**

***dhe|ma'tje** *nf* (*Old*) surveying; geometry

***dhe|mat|s|u'e'r** *adj* (*fem ˜ ore*) (*Old*) = **dhemate's**

dhemb· *vi* **1** to hurt, ache, pain **2** to cause pity/sorrow
  ◦ <> **dhemb·**^{3pl} **sytë (kur [] sheh)** "<>'s eyes *hurt* (when <> *sees* [])" <> *can't bear* the sight (of []), <> *can't stand* []
  ◦ <> **dhemb·**^{3sg} **shpirti** (*Impol*) <> *is scared of* dying
  ◦ <> **dhemb·**^{3sg} **shpirti për** [] <> *feels* very sorry for []
  ◦ <> **dhemb·**^{3sg} **zemra/shpirti (për [])** "<>'s heart *hurts* (for [])" <> *feels* very sad (about [])

dhëmb·et *vpr* to inspire/arouse pity/compassion/ sympathy in ‹›
  ◦ ‹› **dhemb·et** to be a cause of concern to ‹›, ‹› *is* solicitous about ‹›
***dhëmb|** = **dhëmb|**
dhëmb|je *nf* **1** ache, pain; pricking feeling: regret **2** pity, compassion, deep sympathy
  ◦ **dhëmbje e papritur** sudden pang; paroxysm
dhembje|ma'dh *adj* **1** long-suffering, deeply suffering **2** causing pain: painful, aching **3** compassionate, devoted
dhembje|plo't *adj (Poet)* full of love, bounteous with compassion
dhembje|pru'r|ës *adj (Book)* painful
dhembje|qet|ë'su|es *adj* causing reduction of pain: pain-killing, analgesic
dhëmb|kë *nf (Reg)* = **dhe'mbje**
dhëmb|shëm
  I § *adj (i)* **1** painful **2** = **dhëmbshur**
  II § *adv* **1** painfully **2** compassionately, affectionately, tenderly, warm-heartedly
dhëmb|shur *adj (i)* **1** affectionate, tender, warm-hearted **2** compassionate, devoted **3** evoking or deserving compassion/affection: pitiful, sympathetic
dhëmb|shur|i *nf* pity, compassion; affectionateness, tenderness, fondness
dhëmb|shur|isht *adv* fondly, affectionately, tenderly
dhëmb|ur *adj (i)* affectionate, loving; sympathetic, empathetic
dhëmb|ur|a *np (të)* aches, pains; regrets
dhëmb|ur|i *nf* = **dhembshuri**
dhemb|ys·et *vpr* = **dhe'mb·et**
dhe|mi'h|ës *n* laborer who digs up the ground: ditch-digger
dhe|mi'z|ë *nf* **1** maggot, grub; caterpillar **2** blowfly
dhe'|mje *nf* = **dhemi'z|ë**
***dhe'm|shëm** *adj (i)* = **dhe'mbshëm**
dhem|shur = **dhe'mbshur**
dhem|shur|i = **dhembshuri**
dhen *np fem* **1** sheep **2** = **dhe'n|ël**
  ◦ **Dhentë e dhitë e Zeres, nami i Kapllan Qeres.** "Zere's sheep and goats, but Kapllan Qere's credit." One person does all the work, but someone else gets all the credit.
  ◦ **Dhentë pa bari i ha ujku një nga një.** *(Prov)* Sheep without a shepherd are eaten by the wolf one by one
***dhen·** *vt (Reg)* = **gdhend·**
dhen|a'r *n* shepherd, sheep-herder
dhe|n'ël *nf* splinter, chip, shaving
dhe|n'ëz *nf* **1** hangnail **2** bark beetle **3** = **dhe'n|ël**
***dhe|ngri't|ës** *nm (Old)* ore, mineral
dhen|o'r *adj, n* (goat) that sticks with a flock of sheep
dhen|rri't|ës *n* one who raises sheep: sheep breeder
dhe'n|t|ë *adj (i)* **1** ovine **2** woolen
dhe|nxje'rr|ëse *nf* river/canal/harbor dredge; dredge for recovering silt
dhe'|ra *np* ‹**dhe'**›
dhe'|ras *adv* flat on the ground
dhe'|razi *adv* = **dhe'ras**
dher|i'shte *nf* mixture of earth and manure: organic soil
***dhe'r|t|ë** *adj (i) (Old)* of land, terrestrial

dhe|rru'sh *nm [Food]* lime (calcium oxide) used to neutralize the acids in grape jam = **vape'm**
dhes *nm (Colloq)* channel of a stream of water: river bed
dhesk *nm (np ˜ q) [Invert]* horsefly, botfly, gadfly
***dhesk·** *vt* to attract, charm
***dhe'sk|ës** *adj* charming, attractive
dhespo't *nm* bishop in the Orthodox church
dhespot|i *nf* episcopal see, bishopric
dhe|shëm *adj (i)* earthly, of earth
***dheshk** = **dhesk**
***dhe|shkre's|ë** *nf (Old)* geography
***dhe|shkre's|ës**
  I § *n (Old)* geographer
  II § *adj (Old)* geographical
***dhe|shkrim|tar** *n, adj (Old)* = **dheshkre'sës**
***dhe|ta'r**
  I § *adj (Old)* geographical
  II § *nm (Old)* tithe-payer: tither
***dhe't** *(Reg Gheg)* = **dhje't|**
dhe|to'k|ës *nm* snake
***dhet|sh** *nm (Reg Gheg)* = **dhjet|ësh**
dhe|ul *nf* ant
dhe|vështru'es *nm (Folklore)* figure in folktales able to hear and understand far-off sounds by putting an ear to the ground
dhez = **ndez|**
***dhëm|** = **dhëmb**
dhëmb *nm* **1** tooth **2** prong, tine **3** cog; notch
  ◦ **dhëmb çatall** fang, tusk
  ◦ **dhëmb elefanti** elephant tusk
  ◦ **dhëmb fili** ivory
  ◦ **dhëmb kali** maize, Indian corn, corn *(Zea mays)*
  ◦ **dhëmb katarosh** snaggletooth
  ◦ **dhëmb për dhëmb** tooth and nail
  ◦ **dhëmb i përparmë** front tooth, incisor
  ◦ **dhëmb i pjekurisë** wisdom tooth
  ◦ **dhëmb prerës** incisor
  ◦ **dhëmb i prishur** rotten tooth
  ◦ **dhëmbi i qenit** eyetooth, canine
  ◦ **dhëmbi i syrit** eyetooth, canine (tooth)
  ◦ **dhëmb i vënë 1** false tooth **2** *[Tech]* inserted tooth
dhëmb· *vi* = **dhemb·**
dhëmba'c
  I § *adj* **1** *(Insult)* having irregular teeth, gap-toothed, peg-toothed **2** lisping
  II § *n* lisper
dhëmb|ajkë *nf (Reg Tosk)* cog
dhëmb|a'k *adj* **1** indented **2** tooth-like, dentate
dhëmb|a'llë *nf* molar (tooth)
  ◦ **dhëmballë e diturisë/pjekurisë/syrit/urtësisë/ veshit** wisdom tooth
dhëmb|a'n *adj* having large teeth
***dhëmb|a'r** *n (Old)* dentist
dhëmb|ara'sh *adj* having irregular teeth
dhëmb|çi'm *nm ger* ‹**dhëmbço'·n**›
dhëmb|ço'·n *vt* to bite, bite down on [], bite into []
dhëmb|ec *nm* reed (of a loom)
dhëmb|ec|ër *nm* comb with a double set of small teeth for combing wool
dhëmb|ë'ba'rdhë *adj* white-toothed, with pearly white teeth
dhëmb|ë'bri'sk *adj* having razor-sharp teeth
dhëmb|ë'çata'll *adj (Insult)* having irregular teeth: snaggletoothed

dhëmbëdalë adj (Insult) bucktoothed

dhëmbë-dhëmbë adj 1 shaped like teeth, zigzagged; toothed, dentate; sawtoothed, serrate 2 tooth-marked

dhëmbëfildishtë adj ivory-toothed, with sparkling teeth

dhëmbëflorinjtë adj golden-toothed

dhëmbëgjatë adj (Insult) long-toothed

dhëmbëjashtë
  I § adj (Insult) bucktoothed; showing one's teeth in a silly grin
  II § adj, n silly/flippant person

dhëmbëkalë nf [Bot] variety of corn/maize with long ears and large white kernels; white corn (Zea mays alba Haller)

dhëmbëkatarosh adj (Insult) snaggletoothed

dhëmbëkrimbur adj (Insult) having rotten/broken teeth

dhëmbëkruese nf toothpick

dhëmbëluan nm [Bot] hawkbit (Leontodon)

dhëmbëmadh nm big-toothed

dhëmbëmprehtë adj sharp-toothed

dhëmbëprerës
  I § adj [Tech] gear-cutting
  II § nm [Tech] hob (for generating gear teeth)

dhëmbëprishur adj (Insult) having rotten/broken teeth

dhëmbëqelibar adj amber-toothed, having beautiful shiny teeth

dhëmbëqen adj (Insult) 1 dog-toothed 2 snarling

dhëmbëqëruese nf toothpick

dhëmbëqitur adj (Insult) 1 having a constantly curled lip, teeth always bared 2 ever ready to eat: voracious

dhëmbërënë adj whose teeth have fallen out: toothless

dhëmbërruazë adj having small beautiful teeth (like beads of glass)

dhëmbës nm 1 rake, harrow 2 small two-pronged hammer used to chisel rock

*__dhëmbës__ = dhëmbëz

*__dhëmbësi__ nf dentition

*__dhëmbësore__ nf cogwheel

*__dhëmbësori__ nf gear system, gearing

dhëmbësqepar adj (Insult) having teeth that are big and sharp

dhëmbëstrall adj having teeth strong as flint

dhëmbësutë nf 1 [Folklore] a magical deaf mare one can ride to escape from danger 2 [Ichth] small mollusk whose strong white shell is shaped like a doe's tooth

dhëmbësharrë adj having saw-shaped lower teeth; sawtoothed; having sharp teeth

dhëmbështë adj (Insult) having big, long teeth (like a pick)

dhëmbëshkulur adj whose teeth have fallen out: toothless

dhëmbëtar n dentist

dhëmbëtari nf dentistry

dhëmbëto·n vt to bite [] with the teeth, chew on []

dhëmbëthyer adj (Insult) broken-toothed

dhëmbëz nf 1 one of a series of toothlike projections in a tool or machine: tooth, cog 2 notch
  ○ **dhëmbëza dhëmbëza** jagged, serrate, dentate
  ○ **dhëmbëz e ngrënë** indentation

dhëmbëzak nm small chisel with a toothed blade for fine carving

dhëmbëzezë adj fem black-toothed witch

dhëmbëzi adj, n (fem sg ˜ ez, masc pl ˜ inj, fem pl ˜ eza) dark-toothed (one)

dhëmbëzim nm ger 1 <dhëmbëzo·n, dhëmbëzo·het 2 serration 3 serrated/cogged part of a tool/machine

dhëmbëzo·het vpr to be jagged, be toothed

dhëmbëzo·n vt 1 to make tooth-like indentations/notches in [], serrate 2 to make [] jagged

dhëmbëzore nf [Geod] graduated measuring rod: level rod, leveling staff

dhëmbëzuar adj (i) 1 toothed, serrated, cogged, dentate; notched; spiked 2 jagged

dhëmbinxhi adj having regular teeth set like small bright pearls

dhëmbje = dhëmbje

dhëmbo nf with masc agreement (Insult) person with bad/crooked teeth

dhëmbor adj dental

dhëmbore nf 1 rake, harrow 2 [Ling] dental sound

dhëmbur = dhëmbur

*__dhëmbys·__
  I § vt to pity; deplore
  II § vi (Reg Gheg) to grieve

*__dhëmbysshëm__ adj (i) pitiable, deplorable

*__dhëmçuri__ = dhembshuri

*__dhëmkë__ nf (Reg Tosk) pang, pain, ache

*__dhëmp__ = dhëmb

*__dhëmptje__ nf 1 indentation 2 pain

*__dhëmpto·n__ vt to indent

*__dhëmshur__ adj (i) compassionate = dhembshur

dhëmshuri = dhembshuri

*__dhëmshuri__ nf compassion = dhembshuri

dhën
  I § stem for adm, part forms <je p·
  II § np = dhen

dhëna np (të) 1 the givens: data, facts, information 2 specifications; features; capabilities; talent 3 (Old) taxes

dhënar = dhenar

dhënç stem for opt <je p·
  ○ <> **dhënça ujë me lugë!** "May I give water to <> with a spoon!" (Curse) May <> become fatally ill!

dhëndër nm 1 bridegroom; husband 2 son-in-law; brother-in-law
  ○ **dhëndër brenda** (Pej) man who lives in the home of his in-laws
  ○ **dhëndri rruhet në fund** "the bridegroom gets shaved at the end (of the wedding)" the time is not yet ripe, it's still a bit early

dhëndëri nf 1 the state/stage of being a bridegroom 2 (Collec) the husbands in an extended family

dhëndërisht adv in bridegroom style, like a bridegroom

dhëndërishte adj for bridegrooms; during the bridegroom period; performed by bridegrooms

dhëndëro·n vi 1 (of a man) to get married, become a bridegroom; become a brother-in-law/son-in-law 2 to behave like a bridegroom: stand unmoving and erect, act bashful

dhëndër·u·sh *nm (Impol)* man proposed insistently as husband to a reluctant girl (by a matchmaker); man who wants to marry someone against her will

dhë·ndërr = dhëndër

dhëndu·rë *np* <dhëndër

dhëndu·rrë *np* <dhëndërr

dhë·në
I § part <je p·
II § adj (i) **1** given, offered, donated **2** established as a given: set, given; entrusted, encharged; settled, paid; finished, accomplished **3** (of women only) given in marriage: promised, married **4** (Reg) generous, open-handed
III § nf (e) a given: datum, fact, given amount/quantity
IV § nf (Colloq) gift, present; donation
V § nn (të) = dhënie
  ○ **i dhënë pas** <> given to <>: devoted to <>; doting on <>; crazy about <>; addicted to <>
  ○ **S'është me të thënë, por me të dhënë.** "It's not by what is said (to one), but by what (talent) one is given." (Prov) If the talent isn't there, no amount of talking will put it there.

dhë·n|ës
I § adj **1** giving, offering; dealing **2** generous, open-handed **3** [Spec] (for a piece of apparatus) transmitting, sending
II § n **1** donor, giver, offerer **2** generous person
III § nm apparatus for sending electromagnetic signals: transmitter

dhë·n|ëse *nf* [Dairy] animal with a good milk yield

****dhë·n|ëz** *nf* fin

****dhën|gjizë** *nf (Old)* wetnurse

dhë·n|ie *nf ger* **1** <je p· **2** the act or action of giving: bestowal, conferring, rendering

dhi *nf* goat (Capra hircus)
  ○ **dhi e egër** [Zool] chamois (Rupicapra rupicapra L.)
  ○ **Dhia në malësi, delja në vërri.** "The goat in the high ground, the sheep in the low ground." (Prov) People should stay where they belong.
  ○ **dhia e shëllirës** poor man's only wretched milk-goat
  ○ **dhi e zgjebosur/zgjebur/ngordhur e bishtin përpjetë/cakërr** (Tease) person with meager resources but fancy desires

dhi|a'k = dhia'r

****dhiake|shë** *nf* deaconess

****dhia|kë** *nf with masc agreement* deacon = dhjak

****dhiak|oni|** *nf* deaconship = dhjakoni

dhia'r *n* goatherd

dhia're *nf* goat trail

dhia'të *nf* testament

dhia'tës *n (Old)* testator

****dhiato· · n** *vt* to bequeath

****dhiç** *OR* **dhie'ç** *nm* = dhjetësh

dhie| *stem for part, adm* <dhjet·

dhi'mb·et *vpr* to feel compassion, have pity, be sympathetic

dhi'mbë *nf* = dhembje

dhi'mbje *nf* = dhembje

dhi'mb·s·et *vpr* **1** to arouse compassion/pity/sympathy in <> **2** to make <> sorry **3** to be cherished
  ○ **i dhimbs·et edhe qyqes** "even the cuckoo feels sorry for {}" to be in a sorrowful/miserable state

  ○ **i dhimbset gurit e drurit** everyone feels bad about it
  ○ **<> dhimbs·et**^{3sg} **jeta** (Impol) <> worries too much about <>'s health
  ○ **<> dhimbs·et**^{3sg} **lëkura** (Pej) <> wants to save <>'s own skin

dhi'mbs|ur *adj (i)* = dhembshur

dhi'mbsh|ëm
I § adj (i) causing pain: painful
II § adv = dhembshëm

dhimisqi *nf* blade of Damascus steel

****dhi'ms·et** *vpr* = dhimbs·et

****dhi'ms|un** *adj (i) (Reg Gheg)* compassionate = dhembshur

****dhi'ms|uni** *nf (Reg Gheg)* compassion = dhembshuri

****dhi'msh|ëm** *adj (i)* **1** painful = dhimbshëm **2** compassionate = dhëmshur

****dhi'n|të** *adj (i) (Reg Gheg)* = dhi'rtë

****dhioqe'zë** *nf* diocese = dioqezë

dhio'zmë *nm* [Bot] peppermint (Mentha piperita L.)
  ○ **dhiozmë e egër** [Bot] horsemint, water mint (Mentha longifolia)

dhiqe'l *nm* double-pronged hoe, dibble

dhi'ri *nf* flock of goats

dhi'rtë
I § adj (i) **1** of goats **2** of goat hair: mohair
II § nf (e) collec goats, the goat (in a generic sense)

dhis| *stem for 1st sg pres, pl pres, 2nd & 3rd sg subj, pind* <dhjet·

dhisk *nm (nom~qe)* **1** tray, platter **2** (Old) collection plate, salver **3** (Fig Old) charitable help for someone in need **4** = disk

dhi'shkë *nf* dark gray goat

dhi'shtë *nf* = dhi'rtë

dhi'·t·et *vpr* <dhjet· **1** to defecate, move one's bowels **2** (usually said of babies) to go in one's pants **3** (Fig Crude Scorn) to shit it one's pants from fright **4** (Fig Crude Scorn) to suffer total defeat: be shit out of luck **5** (Fig Crude Scorn) to suffer total ruin: be worth shit

dhi't| *stem for 2nd pl pres, pind, imper, vp* <dhjet·

dhiz| = ndiz

dhi'zë *nf* offspring of goats: kid

dhjak *nm* [Relig] deacon

dhjak|ona'r *nm (Contempt)* **1** lazy person who expects to live off the charity of others **2** sly and malevolent scoundrel

****dhjak|oni'** *nf* deaconship

dhjam· *vt* to fatten, fatten [] up

dhja'm·et *vpr* **1** to become fat, get fattened up **2** (Fig Pej) to get filthy rich

****dhjama'nt** *nm* diamond = diama'nt

dhja'më *nm, nn* **1** animal fat, tallow **2** fatty hernia
  ○ **dhjamë cjapi** something that yields no financial benefit, profitless venture: total bust
  ○ **dhjamë në lëkurë të qenit** "perfectly good fat on the skin of a dog" a waste of a good thing/characteristic
  ○ **dhjamë nga pleshti** blood from a turnip
  ○ **dhjamë qeni** "dog fat" worthless object

dhjamësi *nf* corpulence

dhjam|ëzi'm *nm (Book)* increase in fatness; fattening up

dhjamo'r *adj* **1** containing fat: fatty **2** composed of fat **3** [Med] sebaceous

dhjamo's·_et vpr_ = **dhjam·**_et_

dhjamo'sje _nf_ **1** putting on fat: getting fat, fattening up **2** [_Med_] obesity, adiposis

dhjamo'sh _adj_ plump, fleshy

dhjam'shëm _adj (i)_ = **dhja'mur**

dhja'mtë _adj (i)_ **1** made of tallow **2** = **dhja'mur**

dhjam'th _nm_ fatty hernia

dhja'mur _adj (i)_ fattened, fat; thick

dhjamu'she _nf_ piece of raw tallow; piece of fatty meat

dhjat = **dhiat**

dhje _stem for pdef, opt, adm, part_ <**dhjet·**

dhjes _stem for 1st sg pres, pl pres, 2nd & 3rd sg subj, pind_ <**dhjet·**

dhjet·
  _I_ § _vi_ to move the bowels: shit
  _II_ § _vt_ **1** to shit on [] **2** _(Fig)_ to ruin [] completely, make a mess of []

dhjeta'r _n (Old)_ person who collects tithes

dhjetë
  _I_ § _num_ ten; number ten
  _II_ § _adj (i), n (i)_ tenth
  III § _nf_ **1** the number or numeral ten **2** the grade ten (where ten is the highest possible grade) **3** _(Old)_ tithe
  _IV_ § _nf(e)_ **1** tenth grade **2** _(Old)_ tithe of grain or other produce exacted from farmers
  _V_ § _np (të)_ a group of ten, ten at one time; all ten
  ∘ **dhjetë me yll** "ten with a star" ten plus (highest grade in school plus recognition for especially distinguished performance)
  ∘ **dhjeta e mirë** ten of diamonds

dhjetë ba'llësh _adj_ [_Spec_] (of earthquakes) with a magnitude of ten

dhjetë di'tësh _adj_ = **dhjetë ditor**

dhjetë dito'r
  _I_ § _adj_ lasting ten days, for/in ten days
  _II_ § _nm_ ten-day period; ten days from some point in time

dhjetë fi'sh _nm_ tenfold, ten times the amount

dhjetë fish i'm _nm ger_ **1** <**dhjetë fisho'·**_n_ **2** tenfold increase

dhjetë fisho'·het _vpr_ **1** <**dhjetë fisho'·**_n_ **2** to grow/increase greatly

dhjetë fisho'·_n vt_ to increase [] tenfold, multiply [] ten times

dhjetë fish te' _adj (i)_ **1** tenfold, ten times greater **2** _(Fig)_ increased or reinforced greatly

dhjetë ga'rësh _adj, n_ [_Sport_] decathlon

dhjetë gari'st _n_ [_Sport_] decathlon athlete: decathlonist, decathlete

dhjetë ka'tësh _adj_ ten-storey

dhjetë këmbësh
  _I_ § _adj_ [_Invert_] ten-legged
  _II_ § _nm_ decapod

dhjetë këndësh
  _I_ § _adj_ [_Geom_] decagonal
  _II_ § _nm_ decagon

dhjetë kilësh _adj_ weighing ten kilograms

dhjetë le'kësh
  _I_ § _adj (Offic)_ worth ten leks, costing ten leks
  _II_ § _adj, nm (Colloq)_ (coin) worth one lek

dhjetë lite'rsh _adj_ having a capacity/volume of ten liters

dhjetë minu'tësh _adj_ short meeting of about 10 minutes to make a quick decision

dhjetë mu'ajsh
  _I_ § _adj_ **1** ten months old **2** ten-months long; every ten months
  _II_ § _nm_ ten-month period

dhjetë mujo'r
  _I_ § _adj_ ten-months long; every ten months
  _II_ § _nm_ ten-month period

dhjetë qinda'rkësh _adj_ worth ten Albanian cents, priced at ten cents

dhjetë ra _np_ <**dhjetë** many

dhjetë rro'kësh _adj_ [_Lit_] decasyllabic

***dhjetë s** _nm_ commander of a squad of ten

dhjetë sh
  _I_ § _adj_ **1** having ten parts/units **2** ten units in size/worth
  _II_ § _adv_ into ten parts
  III § _nm (Old)_ coin of little value, 10-para coin: dime, farthing

dhjetë sh e
  _I_ § _nf_ **1** pistol with a ten-cartridge clip **2** set/unit of ten; number/numeral in the tens column
  _II_ § _np_ [_Publ_] ten-point type

dhjetë va'rgësh _adj_ [_Lit_] ten-line stanza

dhjetë vjeça'r
  _I_ § _adj_ **1** lasting ten months **2** ten-year-old
  _II_ § _nm_ ten-year period; ten years from some point in time

dhjetë vje'tësh _adj, n_ = **dhjetë vjeça'r**

dhjetë vjeto'r _nm_ tenth anniversary; decennial

dhjetë za'j _adv_ = **dhjetë fi'sh**

dhjeti'm _nm ger_ **1** <**dhjeto'·**_n_ **2** decimation

***dhjeti'n**ë _nf(Old)_ decade

dhjeto'·_n vt_ **1** to decimate **2** to deplete [] greatly; eat a big piece of [] **3** to belittle/denigrate [] greatly **4** _(Old)_ to tithe

dhjeto'r
  _I_ § _nm_ December
  _II_ § _adj_ [_Math_] decimal

dhoga'ç _nm (Impol)_ extremely tall and thin person: beanpole

dho'gë _nf_ = **dërra'së**

***dhogë puno'nj**ës _nm_ board maker

***dhoge'r**ï _nf_ woodwork, timbering

***dho'g**ët _adj (i)_ = **dho'gt**ë

dhogi'ç _adj_ flat

dho'gtë _adj (i)_ made of wooden boards/planks: planked

dhoka'n _nm_ trap, snare; lobster pot, oyster basket

dhokani'k _nm (np ~ qe)_ crutch; crosier

***dhokima's·** _vi_ = **përpíq·**_et_

dho'më _nf_ **1** room (in a building) **2** chamber **3** room furnishings
  ∘ **dhomë buke** dining room; food preparation room
  ∘ **dhomë e dhëndërisë** bridal chamber
  ∘ **dhomë gjumi** sleeping chamber: bedroom
  ∘ **dhomë e madhe** living room
  ∘ **dhomë e miqve** guest room
  ∘ **dhoma e mirë** the room for entertaining guests: the guest parlor
  ∘ **dhomë pritjeje** room in which guests are entertained; guest parlor
  ∘ **dhomë e provës** room for trying on clothes: dressing room
  ∘ **dhoma verzore** [_Ichth_] gill cavity

○ **dhoma e zjarrit 1** cookroom **2** living room with a fireplace

dho'më-muze' *nf* room preserved as a museum for historical purposes: museum room

dho'më|z *nf* small chamber (in an apparatus)

***dhonati'** *nf* ornament, brooch; finery

Dho'rë *nf* Dhora (female name)

dhrahmi' *nf* drachma

dhri' *nf* vine; vine arbor = **hardhi'**

dhri'm *nm* [*Ethnog*] the first and last three days of March during which women do not do regular housework **2** the first twelve days of August (predictive of next year's weather)

dhrom *nm* highway

dhropiki' *nf* [*Med*] dropsy

***dhrosi's·** *vt* to refresh

***dhume'z** *nm (Old)* coat of arms

***dhum|i's** *stem for 1st sg pres, pl pres, 2nd & 3rd sg subj, pind* <**dhumi't·**

***dhum|i't·** *vt* = **thërrmo'·n**

dhu'n|as *adv* by violent force

dhu'n|ë *nf* **1** use of force; violence **2** violation **3** terrible shame/dishonor/insult **4** *(Colloq)* damage, harm

***dhunë|ba'm|ës** *(Reg Gheg)* = **dhunëbë'rës**

***dhunë|bë'r|ës** *n* one who uses violence

dhunë|ta'r *n* = **dhunu'es**

***dhun|i'** *nf* = **dhu'në**

dhun|i'm *nm ger* **1** <**dhuno'·n**, **dhuno'·het 2** rape; violation

○ **dhunim banese** [*Law*] house breaking, illegal entry

dhun|o'·n *vt* **1** to use violence on [] **2** to violate; break into; trespass on; rape, ravish **3** to inflict terrible dishonor on: humiliate, shame

dhu'n|shëm *adj (i)* **1** violent **2** inflicting dishonor: violating, dishonoring, profaning

dhun|ti' *nf* gift, talent, flair = **dhurëti'**

dhun|u'e|s
I § *nm* perpetrator of violence, inflicter of shame: violator, rapist, desecrater, profaner
II § *adj* violent, damaging, dishonoring

Dhura't|a *nf* Dhurata (female name)

dhura't|ë *nf* gift, present

○ **dhuratë kujtimi** keepsake

***dhur|at|i'sht** *adv* gratis, free

dhur|ë'ti' *nf* **1** = **dhura'të 2** *(Old)* [*Ethnog*] bridal gift; livestock brought to a wedding **3** virtue, good trait, talent, gift

dhur|i'm *nm ger* **1** <**dhuro'·n 2** offering, donation

Dhuri'me *nf* Dhurime (female name)

dhur|o'·n *vt* to make a present of [], offer [] as gift: donate, present, bestow

○ <> **dhuro·n jetën** to give <> life

dhur|u'e|s *adj* giver, donor

***dhymy's|** = **dhëmby's**

Ee

e *nf* **1** the letter "e" **2** the unrounded front mid vowel represented by that letter

e *proclitic attributive article* **1** marks nominative singular feminine agreement for the following element **2** marks agreement with an immediately preceding word in a definite nominative/accusative form

e *3rd sg object pronominal clitic preceding a transitive verb, or suffixed to a transitive verb stem in the imper* indicates that the verb has an identifiable 3rd sg direct object: him/her/it

e *conj* **1** and **2** plus

e *interj (Colloq)* **1** used to draw attention to a question about to be asked, hey, well **2** expresses approval of a suggestion, yeah **3** expresses sudden surprise, pleasure, or displeasure; hey

EAM *abbrev (Greek)* <Ethnikon Apeleuterotikon Metopon *[Hist]* National Freedom Front (in Greece during World War II)

ebani't *nm [Spec]* ebonite

*****ebano'z** *nm* ebony = abano'z

eboni't = ebani't

ebrai'sht *adv* in Hebrew (language)

ebrajkë *nf (Reg Tosk)* Jewess

ebre *nm* Hebrew, Jew

*****e'bur** *nm* **1** ivory = fildi'sh **2** piano key

*****ec**·*et vpr* (of roads) to be passable

ec·ën *vi* **1** to move under internal power: go, walk, move; flow; float along (in a liquid) **2** to go forward: go on, proceed; go well, go successfully **3** to be in working condition: work, operate

- <> **ec**·ën³ˢᵍ **bafti** <> *gets lucky*
- **ec**·ën **çap e jak**ë **1** to walk back and forth **2** *(Fig)* to keep busy doing nothing
- **ec drejt hundës tënde!** keep your nose out of it! mind your own business!
- **ec e __** (with a following verb phrase) go try __!, just try __!
- **ec e ec** (used in tales to indicate a prolonged period of walking) continuing on and on
- <> **ec**·ën³ˢᵍ **fati** <> *is lucky*
- **nuk** <> **ec**·ën³ˢᵍ **kali në vijë** "<>'s horse *doesn't* walk straight" <> *isn't having* much luck, things *aren't going* very well for <>
- **ec**·ën **kundër rrymës** to go against the flow; go counter to the crowd
- <> **ec**·ën³ˢᵍ **kungulli mbi ujë** "<>'s squash *goes* on water" things are going very well for <>
- **ec**·ën **mbi driza** to do something difficult and dangerous
- **ec**·ën **mbi thonj** to walk on tiptoe
- **ec**·ën **me këmbë plumbi** "walk with leaden foot" to walk slowly and cautiously
- **ec**·ën **me këmbët e veta** to go one's own way; stand on one's own two legs
- **ec**·ën **në hulli të drejtë** to follow the right path, live a proper life
- **ec**·ën **në majë të gishtave** to walk on tiptoe, walk softly

- **ec**·ën **në tym** to walk aimlessly; proceed without a clear plan
- **ec**·ën **në udhë të drejtë** to take the right path, behave correctly
- **ec**·ën **pa prekur në tokë** to go very fast: run without touching the ground, practically fly
- **ec**·ën **pash më pash** to walk with a swagger
- <> **ec**·ën³ˢᵍ **puna** <> *is lucky*
- <> **ec**·ën³ˢᵍ **puna fjollë** things *are going* very well for <>, <> *is doing* fine
- <> **ec**·ën³ˢᵍ **rroga** <> *continues* to be paid
- <> **ec**·ën³ˢᵍ **(puna) sahat** to go like clockwork, work perfectly
- **ec**·ën **si breshkë** to walk too slowly
- **ec**·ën **si çapëtore** to walk slowly
- **ec**·ën **si mbi vezë** "walk as if on eggs" **1** to walk on eggs, walk gingerly **2** to walk clumsily
- **ec**·ën **si mëqik** to walk with quick steps
- **ec**·ën **si në vaj** to go very smoothly
- **ec**·ën **si patë** to waddle like a goose
- **ec**·ën **tingthi** to hop on one foot

ec'ara'k *adj* (of an animal) capable of walking; able to walk long distances (without loss of value)

eceja'k *nm* frequent coming and going

ec'ës *adj [Tech]* mobile; moving

ec'i *1st sg pres* <ec·ën

ec'je *nf ger* **1** <ec·ën **2** gait **3** sound of steps, noise made by someone walking

*****ecuni** *nf (Reg Gheg)* = ecuri

ecur
I § *nf (e)* **1** = ecje **2** one's manner of walking, step, gait
II § *nn ger (të)* = ecje

ecuri *nf* progression through an action, manner in which something develops: course, process

edepsëz *adj, n (Impol Insult)* low-down, shameless, dirty, contemptible (person)

edepsëz'ke *nf (Impol Insult)* (of a woman) little bitch

Edrene *nf* Adrianople

edukate *nf* **1** upbringing, training **2** civilized behavior: good manners

edukati'v *adj* = eduku'es

edukato'r *n* educator

edukato're *nf* kindergarten teacher

eduki'm *nm ger* **1** <eduko'·n, eduko'·het **2** = edukat**ë**

eduko'·het *vpr* to gain proper training; learn civilized behavior

eduko'·n *vt* to provide [ ]'s early training: rear, bring [ ] up

edukua'r *adj (i)* properly brought up, well-bred; well-behaved, polite

eduku'es
I § *adj* educational
II § *n* teacher, educator

edh *n* goat kid less than a year old

e¦dhe¹ OR ǀe¦dhe

I § conj **1** and also; and; also **2** plus
II § adv **1** yet, still **2** even
III § nf plus sign
○ **edhe** {} {} too/also, {} as well
○ **Edhe dielli ka njolla.** "Even the sun has spots." (Book) Nothing/nobody is perfect.
○ **edhe do·, edhe s'do·** <> wants to but can't
○ **edhe ... edhe ...** both ... and ...
○ **edhe** <> **ha·**^{3sg}**, edhe** <> **djeg·**^{3sg} **1** it itches <> but <> can't scratch it **2** (Crude Iron) <> wants it but can't have it; <> wants to but can't
○ **edhe me një këmbë (bile)** like it or not, by force if necessary
○ **edhe në qoftë se** _ even if _
○ **edhe një herë** once again, again, and once more
○ **edhe një i vetëm** even if only one alone, even singlehandedly, even by oneself
○ **edhe pse/sepse** _ even though _, despite the fact that _, although _
○ **edhe sikur bota të përmbyset!** no matter what else happens
○ **edhe sikur të** <>**a shtro·**n^{subj} **me flori** not even if {} paid <> a million dollars!
○ **edhe sikur** _ even if ..., even though _
○ **Edhe vau të mbyt.** "Even a shallow ford can drown you." (Prov) A small problem can still do you great harm.

efe¦kt nm **1** effect **2** (Offic) purpose *****3** bill of exchange

*****efe¦kt¦e** np <efe¦kt funds, stocks

efekti¦v
I § adj (Book) **1** effective **2** actual **3** [Offic] acting, temporary, in effect **4** [Mil] attached to a military unit
II § nm **1** [Mil] complement of a military unit, military complement **2** (Book) number of personnel/members/participants in an institution/organization/enterprise

efekt¦iv¦i¦sht adv effectively

efekt¦sh¦ëm adj (i) having the desired effect: effective

efendi¦ nm [Hist] **1** title of respect for an educated person in the Ottoman empire: sir **2** (Iron) gentleman

efendi¦le¦rë np <efendi¦

efika¦s adj efficacious

efikas¦ite¦t nm (Book) efficacy

efqeli¦ nf [Relig] holy oil/ointment, unction

efsh nm disgust, nausea

efsho¦·het vpr to feel disgust/nausea

efsho¦·n vt to disgust, nauseate

efsh¦të adj (i) disgusting, nauseating

*****efsh¦ue¦sh¦ëm** adj (i) horrible

e¦gër
I § adj (i) **1** wild; savage **2** fierce, ferocious **3** rough, coarse, raw **4** uncivilized; uncultivated **5** (of land) not easily arable
II § nn (të) savagery, roughness, coarseness
III § adv **1** savagely, brutally, roughly **2** coarsely

egërca¦k
I § adj savage, mean, ferocious
II § nm weedy ground

egër¦le¦ nf [Bot] wild olive = ulla¦stër

egër¦si¦ nf **1** savagery **2** ferocity **3** savage act **4** bitterly cold weather

egër¦si¦m nm ger <egërso¦·n, egërso¦·het

egër¦si¦rë nf **1** wild beast, predatory beast; beast; brute **2** (Fig) brutal, bloodthirsty person

egër¦si¦sht adv **1** wildly, fiercely, ferociously **2** brutally, savagely, mercilessly, cruelly

egër¦so¦·het vpr **1** to go wild; become wilder **2** to get rough **3** to grow furious; become infuriated

egër¦so¦·n vt **1** to drive [] wild **2** (of weather) to increase the rawness/fury of [] **3** to infuriate

egër¦su¦ar adj (i) **1** wild, made wilder **2** (of weather) rough, ferocious **3** infuriated; furious

egër¦sha¦n adj, n fierce; harsh; wild (person)

egër¦ti¦ nf collec **1** wild animals taken as a whole **2** framing of a building, raw walls **3** first coat of whitewash on a wall

eglendi¦s·et vpr (Colloq) to spend time in relaxed enjoyment: just fool around

e¦go nf (Book) ego

ego¦i¦st adj, n egotist, selfish

ego¦i¦zëm nm egotism, selfishness

e¦gras adv **1** savagely **2** ferociously

*****egzist¦** = ekzist¦

Egje¦ nf Aegean

egjë¦r nf **1** [Bot] tare, darnel (Lolium temelentum) **2** (Fig) worthless thing found together with others of value: chaff; good-for-nothing
○ **egjër e egër** Italian rye grass (Lolium multiflorum)
○ **Egjra prish edhe grurin.** "Darnel ruins even wheat." Even the best can be ruined by something really bad.

egjër¦i¦shte = egjërisht¦ënf land with wild animals rampant

*****egjidë¦** nf (Book) aegis

Egji¦pt nm Egypt

egjip¦t¦as = egjiptia¦n

egjiptia¦n adj, n Egyptian

Egjy¦pt = Egji¦pt

eh· vt to sharpen [a blade]: hone

eh interj expresses pain/sadness, surprise/fear, anger, request/desire, pleasure
○ **Eh më!** (Reg) Stop it, I can't take any more!

eh nm metal blade

ehe interj **1** unhunh, yes, sure **2** expresses negative feelings of unhappiness: Oh no! **3** expresses scornful doubt/disagreement: Oh sure!

*****ehëng** (Reg Gheg) = aheng

*****e¦hë** nf (Old) **1** horizon **2** knife blade

*****ehi¦** interj hello!

ehu¦ interj **1** expresses negative feelings of doubt, disagreement, contempt, or anger: Oh sure! Jesus! *****2** alas!

e¦hull nm (np ˜ j) **1** frost, hoarfrost; icicle **2** morning frost **3** acorn **4** [Bot] loranthus (Loranthus europaeus)

ej interj (Colloq) hey!

e¦ja
I § imper <vje·n come!
II § hortative interj come on!
○ **Eja në radhë!** "Come into rows!" [Mil] Line up!

e¦jani
I § pl imper <vje·n
II § hortative interj come on you all!

ejekt¦i¦m nm ger **1** (Spec) <ejekto¦·n **2** ejection

ejekto¦·n vt (Spec) to eject

ejekto¦r nm (Spec) ejector

ejulim nm wailing, lament

ekidnë nf [Zool] echidna

ekinoderme np echinoderm

ekip nm team

ekipazh nm = ekuipazh

eklektik adj, n (Book) eclectic

eklektizëm nm (Book) eclecticism

eklips nm [Astron] eclipse

eklipsо·het vpr 1 to become eclipsed 2 (Fig Book) to disappear temporarily

eklipsо·n vt to eclipse

eklogе nf [Lit] eclogue

ekologji nf ecology

ekologjik adj ecological

ekonom nm manager/employee of the housekeeping office of an enterprise

ekonomajzer nm [Tech] (fuel) economizer

ekonomat nm department that provides required food, clothing, and maintenance services for an enterprise: housekeeping office

ekonomi nf 1 economy 2 economics 3 thrift, thriftiness, saving
  ○ ekonomi shumësektorëshe 1 economy with both socialist and capitalist sectors 2 diversified economy
  ○ ekonomia ujore water resources

ekonomik adj 1 economic 2 economical

ekonomikisht adv economically

ekonomiko-shoqëror adj socio-economic

ekonomiqar adj (Colloq) economical, thrifty

ekonomist n economist

ekonomizëm nm overreliance on economic, rather than political change

ekonomizim nm ger <ekonomizо·n

ekonomizо·n vt to economize on, save

ekran nm 1 display screen 2 [Cine] movie screen
  ○ ekran mat [Cine] screen with a matte surface

ekranizim nm ger <ekranizо·n

ekranizо·n vt to bring [] to the screen, make a movie of []: film; adapt [] for the screen, turn [] into a film

eks = ekz

eksartim nm furniture

ekscentricitet nm [Tech] eccentricity

ekscentrik adj, nm [Tech] eccentric, cam

eksekut = ekzekut

Ekselencë nf with masc agreement Excellency

ekses nm excess, extreme, immoderation

eksiq adv, adj (Colloq) = mangët

eksistо·n vi = egzistо·n

ekskavator nm power shovel, excavator

ekskavatorist n driver of a power shovel, excavator operator

ekskluziv adj exclusive

ekskluzivisht adv exclusively

ekskursion nm excursion

ekskursionist n participant in an excursion

eksod nm exodus

ekspansion nm expansion

ekspansionist n expansionist

ekspansionizëm nm expansionism

ekspeditë nf expedition

eksperiencë nf experience = përvojë

eksperiment nm experiment

eksperimental adj (Book) experimental

eksperimentim nm ger 1 <eksperimentо·n 2 experimentation

eksperimentо·n vt to experiment with, test

eksperimentues nm experimenter

ekspert nm, adj (Book) expert

ekspertim nm ger 1 [Law] <ekspertо·n 2 expert opinion/appraisal

ekspertizë nf [Law] expert investigation; report/ testimony of experts

ekspertо·n vt [Law] to examine [a matter] as an expert; give an expert opinion/appraisal of []; verify [] as an expert

eksploatim nm ger 1 <eksploatо·n 2 exploitation

eksploatо·n vt to exploit

eksploatues
  I § adj exploitative, exploitational
  II § n exploiter

eksplodim nm ger 1 <eksplodо·n 2 explosion

eksplodо·n vi to explode

eksplorator nm explorer

eksplorim nm ger 1 <eksplorо·n 2 exploration

eksplorо·n vt to explore

eksplorues nm explorer

eksplozion nm explosion

eksploziv nm, adj explosive

eksponent nm 1 [Math] exponent 2 (Book) principal representative: exponent

eksport nm export

eksportim nm ger 1 <eksportо·n 2 exportation 3 exported goods

eksportо·n vt 1 to export 2 (Fig) to spread abroad, disseminate

eksportues nm 1 exporter 2 (Fig) disseminator

ekspozim nm ger 1 <ekspozо·n 2 exhibition, display 3 exposure

ekspozimetër nm [Cine] exposure meter

ekspozitë nf exhibition, display, show

ekspozо·n vt 1 to exhibit, display, show 2 to expose 3 (Book) to present an orderly exposition of []

ekspozues nm exhibitor

ekspres
  I § adj transported quickly: express
  II § n 1 espresso 2 fast train; express

ekspresion nm expression

ekspresionist adj [Art Lit] expressionistic

ekspresionizëm nm expressionism

ekstazë nf (Book) ecstasy, rapture

ekstensiv adj (Book) extensive

eksterritorial adj [Law] extraterritorial

eksterritorialitet nm [Law] extraterritoriality

ekstirpator nm [Agr] root extractor

ekstra adj extra

ekstrakt nm (Book) extract

ekstrakttanin nm [Chem] tannin extract

ekstrateritorial adj extraterritorial

ekstravagancë nf extravagance

ekstravagant adj extravagant

ekstrem adj, n extreme

ekstremist adj extremist

ekstremizëm nm (Book) extremism

ekstruder nm [Tech] extruder

ekuacion *nm* [*Math*] equation

ekuator *nm* 1 [*Geog*] equator 2 equatorial countries

ekuatorial *adj* equatorial

ekuilibër *nm* 1 equilibrium, balance 2 *(Fig)* normalcy; sobriety

ekuilibrist *n* equilibrist, tightrope walker

ekuilibro •het *vpr* *(Book)* to maintain equilibrium/balance; come into equilibrium/balance

ekuilibro •n *vt* *(Book)* to put into equilibrium: balance, equilibrate, bring into balance

ekuilibruar *adj (i)* 1 in a state of equilibrium: in balance, balanced 2 sober and mature in thought and deed; in a normal state

ekuinoks *nm* equinox

ekuipazh *nm* crew (of a ship)

ekuivalencë *nf* equivalence

ekuivalent *adj, nm (Book)* equivalent

*****ekujnatë** *nf* equinox

ekzagjerim *nm* 1 <**ekzagjero •n** 2 exaggeration

ekzagjero •n *vt* to exaggerate

ekzagjeruar *adj (i)* exaggerated

ekzakt
I § *adj* exact, accurate, correct, precise
II § *adv* = **ekzaktërisht**

ekzaktërisht *adv* with exactitude/precision: exactly, precisely

ekzaltim *nm ger* 1 <**ekzalto •n, ekzalto •het** 2 exaltation

ekzalto •het *vpr* <**ekzalto •n** 1 to be exalted 2 to be elatedto get carried away (by emotion)

ekzalto •n *vt* to exalt

ekzaltuar *adj (i)* 1 elated, enraptured 2 fanatical

ekzaminim *nm ger (Book)* 1 <**ekzamino •n** 2 examination, inspection

ekzamino •n *vt (Book)* to examine, inspect

ekzekutim *nm ger (Book)* 1 <**ekzekuto •n** 2 execution

ekzekutiv *adj* executive

ekzekuto •n *vt (Book)* to execute

ekzekutues
I § *nm* 1 executor 2 [*Law*] executioner
II § *adj* [*Offic*] executive, effective

ekzemë *nf* [*Med*] eczema, tetter

ekzemplar *nm* exemplar, copy

ekzistencë *nf* existence

ekzistencialist *adj* existentialist

ekzistencializëm *nm* existentialism

ekzisto •n *vi (Book)* to exist

ekzistues *adj* existing

ekzocentrik *adj (Book)* exocentric

ekzoftalmi *nf* [*Med*] exophthalmia

ekzogami *nf* [*Ethnog*] exogamy

ekzotik *adj (Book)* exotic

ELAS *abbrev (Greek)* <**Ellinikos Laikos Apeleuterotikos Stratos** [*Hist*] Greek People's Army for National Liberation

elasticitet *nm* elasticity

elastik *adj* elastic

elastikësi *nf* elasticity

elb *nm* [*Bot*] barley (*Hordeum vulgare L.*)
  ○ **elb distik** [*Bot*] (*two-rowed barley*) (*Hordeum vulgare var. distichum*)

elbarozë *nf* [*Bot*] = **barbarozë**

Elbasan *nm* city and district in central Albania: Elbasan

elbasanas *adj, n* native of Elbasan

elbasançe
I § *adv (Colloq)* Elbasan-style
II § *adj* (of houses) built low and one-storied

elbasanishte *nf* [*Ling*] the dialect of Elbasan and vicinity
  ○ **elbasanishtja letrare** the quasi-standard language of Albania between the two World Wars

elbaze *nf (Old)* fan = **erashkë**

Elbë *nf* Elba (River)

elbëra *np* 1 <**elb** 2 unharvested barley

elbërishte *OR* **elbërishtë** *nf* = **elbore**

elbëse *adj* = **elbje**

elbëz *nf* barleycorn

elbishte *nf* barley hay/straw

elbje *adj, nf* (pasta) of the size and shape of a grain of barley

*****elbna** *np* 1 <**elb** 2 market area where barley is sold

elbnajë *nf* field of barley

elbore
I § *nf* field of barley
II § *adj* planted in barley, growing barley

elbtë *adj (i)* made of barley, of barley

elbth *nm* [*Med*] sty (in eye)

elefant *nm* [*Zool*] elephant
  ○ **elefant deti** elephant seal, sea elephant

elegancë *nf* elegance

elegant *adj* elegant

elegji *nf* [*Lit Mus*] elegy

elegjiak *adj* elegiac

*****elejmosinë** *nf* alms = **lëmoshë**

elektoral *adj (Book)* electoral

elektorat *nm* electorate

elektricist *n* electrician

elektricitet *nm* electricity; electric charge

elektriçist = **elektricist**

elektrifikim *nm ger* 1 <**elektrifiko •n** 2 electrification

elektrifiko •n *vt* to electrify

elektrifikuar *adj (i)* electrified; powered by electricity

elektrik
I § *adj* electric, electrical
II § *nm* 1 *(Colloq)* electrical energy, electric current; electric light 2 flashlight

*****elektrikan** *nm* electrician

elektrizim *nm ger* 1 <**elektrizo •n, elektrizo •het** 2 electrification

elektrizo •het *vpr (Book)* to become electrified with enthusiasm

elektrizo •n *vt* to electrify

elektro *formative prefix* electro-

elektrodë *nf* [*Phys*] electrode

elektrodinamik *adj* electrodynamic

elektrohavi *nf* electric welder

elektrokardiogram *nm* [*Med*] electrocardiogram

elektrokarro *nf* [*Tech*] battery-driven truck

elektrokimi *nf* [*Chem Phys*] electrochemistry

elektrokimik *adj* [*Chem Phys*] electrochemical

elektrolit *nm* [*Spec*] electrolyte

elektrolizë *nf* [*Spec*] electrolysis

elektro magnet nm [Phys] electromagnet

elektro magnetik adj [Phys] electromagnetic

elektro magnetizëm nm [Phys] electromagnetism

elektro mekanik adj [Chem Phys] electromechanical

elektro metalurgji nf [Chem Phys] electrometallurgy

elektro metër nm [Chem Phys] electrometer

elektro motor nm electric motor

elektron nm [Phys] electron

elektro ndez ës nm electric igniter/primer

elektronik adj [Spec] electronic

elektronikë nf [Spec] electronics

elektro saldatriçe nf electric welder

elektro statik adj [Phys] electrostatic

elektro sharrë nf electric saw

elektro shok nm [Med] electric shock

elektro teknik adj having to do with the generation and utilization of electric power: electrotechnological

elektro teknikë nf electrotechnology

elektro teleferik nm [Tech] monorail motor hoist

elektro terapi nf [Med] electrotherapy

elektro turjelë nf [Constr] electric drill

element nm element

elementar adj [Spec] elementary

*****eleminë** nf = enemí

elevator nm elevator

Elez nm Elez (male name)

*****elikë** nf = helikë

eliminator adj [Sport] = eliminues

eliminatore nf [Sport] eliminatory heat/match/trial/race: preliminary

eliminim nm ger 1 <elimino·n, elimino·het 2 elimination

elimino·het vpr 1 [Sport] to get eliminated (from competition) 2 to disappear

elimino·n vt to eliminate

eliminues adj [Sport] eliminatory (heat/match/trial/race): preliminary

Elion a nf Eliona (female name)

elips nm [Geom] ellipse

elipsë nf [Lit Ling] ellipsis

eliptik adj [Geom] elliptical, elliptical

elitë nf (Book) (as a class) elite

elmaz nm 1 diamond 2 glass-cutter

elokuencë nf eloquence

elokuent adj eloquent

elozh nm (Book) excessive praise

elpazë nf (Old) = era shkë

*****ell** nm icicle = e hull

*****Ella dhë** nf(Old) Greece = Greqí

emal nm enamel

emalim nm ger <emalo·n

emalo·n vt [Tech] to coat with enamel: enamel

emal uar adj (i) enameled

emancipim nm ger 1 <emancipo·n, emancipo·het 2 emancipation

emancipo·het vpr to become emancipated

emancipo·n vt to emancipate

emancip uar adj (i) emancipated

embargo nf [Law] embargo

emblemë nf emblem

emboli nf [Med] embolism

embriologji nf [Med] embryology

embrion nm embryo

embrional adj (Book) embryonic

emetim nm ger 1 <emeto·n, emeto·het 2 emission 3 issuance

emeto·het vpr to issue forth, be emitted

emeto·n vt 1 to emit 2 [Fin] to issue

*****êmën** nm (Reg Gheg) = emër

emër nm 1 name 2 reputation 3 [Ling] noun

○ **emër foljor** verbal noun

○ **emër i përgjithshëm** [Ling] common noun

○ **emër përkëdhelës** pet name

○ **emër i përveçëm** [Ling] proper name

○ **emër i rremë** pseudonym

emër harru ar adj whose name has been forgotten

emërim nm ger 1 <emëro·n, emëro·het 2 designation; nomination, appointment

emër ma dh adj of great fame

emër ndritur adj (Elev) illustrious

emëro·n vt to name, nominate, appoint, designate

emëror adj 1 nominal 2 [Ling] nominative

emërore

I § nf[Ling] nominative case

II § adj nominative

emër shu ar adj, n (also used as a curse) (person) whose name will nevermore be mentioned

emër tesë nf 1 nomenclature 2 list of goods or services required to be produced by an enterprise 3 set of positions under a superior administrative unit; position/person in a hierarchic organization

emërtim nm ger 1 <emërto·n 2 designation, denomination

emërto·n vt to designate, denominate, name

emërtues adj [Ling] designative

emërues nm 1 [Math] denominator 2 [Ling] = emërtues

○ **emërues i përbashkët** [Math] common denominator

emërzim nm ger [Ling] 1 <emërzo·n, emërzo·het 2 nominalization

emërzo·het vpr to become nominalized; be used as a noun

emërzo·n vt [Ling] to nominalize; use as a noun

emërz uar adj (i) [Ling] nominalized; used as a noun

*****êmët** (Reg Gheg) = âmët

emfazë nf (Book) emphasis

emigracion nm 1 emigration 2 (Collec) emigrants

emigrant nm emigrant, colonist

emigrim nm ger 1 <emigro·n, emigro·het 2 emigration

emigro·n vi to emigrate

emisar n 1 emissary 2 [Tech] drainage canal

emision nm 1 emission 2 (television or radio) program, broadcast 3 [Fin] issue (of printed money, stamps, or other paper of value)

emiter nm [Phys] emitter

*****emn** = emër

emn ak nm namesake

emnesë nf 1 not-to-be-forgotten event *2 (Reg Gheg) = emërtesë

*emnu'esh**ë**m *adj (i) (Reg Gheg)* **1** famous **2** potentially a candidate

emocio'n *nm* emotion

emocion'al *adj (Book)* emotional

emocion'ant *adj* = emociona'l

emociono·*het vpr* to feel emotional; be moved/ touched/affected; be troubled, become disquieted; get excited

emociono·*n vt* to stir [ ]'s emotions: move, touch, affect, excite

emocionu'ar *adj (i)* stirred by emotion: moved, touched, affected; excited; troubled, disquieted

emocionu'es *adj* stirring the emotions: exciting; moving, touching; disturbing

*em| *(Reg Gheg)* = im|

empiri'k

   I § *adj (Book)* empiric, empirical

   II § *n* [*Phil*] empiricist = empiri'st

empiri'okritici'z**ë**m *nm* [*Phil*] empiriocriticism

empiri'st *n* empiricist

empiri'z**ë**m *nm (Book)* empiricism

e'mra *np* <e'm**ë**r

e'mri *sg def, sg abl indef* <e'm**ë**r

e'mt**ë** *nf* father's sister: paternal aunt

emulacio'n *nm* emulation

emulsio'n *nm* emulsion

*Emzo't *nm* my Lord = Imzo't

enciklopedi' *nf* encyclopedia

enciklopedi'k *adj* encyclopedic

enciklopedi'st *n* encyclopedist

end *nm* [*Bot*] pollen

end·

   I § *vt* **1** to weave **2** to emit, cast, radiate **3** to flyblow

   II § *vi* to bloom, blossom

   ○ end· si merimanga "weave like a spider" to be a scheming person

e'nd·*et vpr* to wander, roam; be a wanderer; wander around, move (around) frequently

endaca'k

   I § *nm* wanderer, nomad, vagabond

   II § *adj* **1** nomadic, wandering, roving **2** migratory **3** loitering

enda'to're *nf* female weaver

e'nde *nf* = e'nd**ë**

ende' *adv* **1** still, yet **2** even more, still more **3** again

endemi'k *adj* endemic

e'nd**ë** *nf* [*Bot*] pollen **2** fine flour; flour dust **3** dust

e'nd|**ë**s

   I § *adj* **1** for weaving **2** errant, wandering, roving

   II § *n* **1** weaver **2** [*Text*] spindle that holds the bobbin ***3** woof **4** [*Bot*] plant sprout: bud, shoot

e'nd|**ë**z *nf* **1** spiderweb **2** *(Old)* measure of cloth length equal to the circumference of the head **3** = e'nd**ë** **4** flyblow **5** [*Entom*] type of tiny butterfly that flies in swarms that feed on flower nectar

   ○ end**ë**z pishe processionary caterpillar *Thaumetopoea pityocampa*

end|**ë**zi'm *nm ger* **1** <end**ë**zo'·*n* **2** pollinization

end|**ë**zo'·*n*

   I § *vi* **1** to give off pollen: pollinize **2** (of a fruit tree) to blossom

   II § *vt* to fertilize [ ] with pollen: pollinate

*endi'r**ë** *nf* yearning, longing, desire

e'ndje *nf ger* <e'nd·, e'nd·*et*

*e'ndme *nf (e)* [*Text*] warp

endo'gami *nf* [*Ethnog*] endogamy

endosko'p *nm* [*Spec*] endoscope

endi'th *nm* fine flour; flour dust

e'ndur *adj (i)* **1** woven **2** flyblown

enduri'n**ë** *nf* something woven: weaving, textile

enemi' *nf* [*Text*] barrel-like reel for winding yarn or thread into skeins

energj'eti'k *adj* of or pertaining to energy

energj'eti'k**ë** *nf* energetics

energji' *nf* energy

energji'k *adj* **1** energetic, active, enterprising **2** vigorous, strong; rough

energjiki'sht *adv* energetically

e'n**ë** *nf* **1** vessel for holding or carrying liquids **2** dish; pot

   ○ en**ë** gjaku [*Anat*] blood vessel

   ○ en**ë** kuzhine **1** kitchenware **2** shop that sells kitchenware

en**ë**la'r**ë**s *n* dishwasher

en**ë**la'rëse *nf* dishwashing machine, dishwasher

en**ë**ngushtu'es *nm* [*Med*] vasoconstrictor

en**ë**zgjeru'es *nm* [*Med*] vasodilator

en**ë**zo'r *adj* vascular

eng *nm* deafmute

engledi's·*et vpr* = egledi's·*et*

*engle'z *adj, n* = angle'z

e'ngj**ë**ll *nm (np ˜j)* angel

   ○ engj**ë**ll deti Angelshark *Squatina squatina* = skadhi'n**ë**

engj**ë**llo'r *adj* angelic

engj**ë**llu'sh *nm (Pet)* good boy; sweet boy, pretty boy

engj**ë**llu'she *nf (Pet)* good girl; sweet girl, pretty girl

Engj**ë**llushe *nf* Engj**ë**llushe (female name)

engj**ë**rdhi' *nf (Colloq)* **1** quicksilver, mercury **2** *(Fig)* lively and adept person

engj**ë**rdhi'shte *nf* [*Bot*] shrub whose long, lithe branches are used to bind sheaves, tie off grapevines, etc.

*engjina'r *nm* [*Bot*] artichoke = angjina're

*engjine'r *nm* = inxhinie'r

*engjullu'er = engj**ë**llo'r

e'ni = e'jani

enigma'tik *adj* enigmatic

eni'gm**ë** *nf* **1** puzzle **2** *(Book)* enigma

e'nkas *adv (Colloq)* deliberately, intentionally, on purpose

enkele'as *adj* [*Hist*] of or pertaining to an Illyrian tribe that lived in the plain of Korça and around Lake Ohrid

enkliti'k *adj* enclitic

E'no *nf with masc agreement* Eno (male name)

eno'r *adj* [*Anat Bot*] vascular = en**ë**zo'r

*enqefa'l *nm* [*Anat*] encephalon

*enqiklopedi' *nf* encyclopedia

ent *nm* established organization with a public function: institution, corporation

entropi' *nf* [*Phys*] entropy

entuzia'st *adj* enthusiastic

entuzia'z**ë**m *nm* enthusiasm

entuzia'zmo·*het vpr* to become enthusiastic

entuzia'zmo·*n vt* to make [ ] enthusiastic, enthrall

Enver *nm* Enver (male name)

enjë *nf* **1** farm animal that continues to be milked after the stillbirth or death of its young **2** [*Bot*] yew (*Juniperus foetidissi*)

*****enjt| = ënjt|

enjte *nf(e)* Thursday

ep *nm* epic (poem)

ep· *vt* to bend; bend into a loop

ep·et *vpr* **1** to be flexible **2** to bend, curve around; bend down, bend over **3** to become submissive, submit

*****ep| = jep|

epër *adj (i)* = **epërm**

epërm *adj (i)* upper, higher; superior; extreme, uppermost = **sipërm**

epërsi *nf* superiority, upper hand; preponderance

epidemi *nf* [*Med*] epidemic

epidemik *adj* epidemic

epidermë *nf* [*Anat Bot*] epidermis

epifani *nf* [*Relig*] Epiphany

*****epifonem** *nm (Old)* [*Ling*] interjection

epigraf *nf* epigraph

epigrafi *nf* epigraphy

epigram *nm* epigram

epik
  I § *adj* [*Lit*] epic, epical
  II § *nm* epic writer/creator

epikë *nf* [*Lit*] epic

epiko-lirik *adj* [*Lit*] having both lyrical and epical qualities

epikureizëm *nm* epicureanism

epikurian *nm* epicurean

epilepsi *nf* [*Med*] epilepsy

epileptik *nm, adj* [*Med*] epileptic

epilog *nm* [*Lit*] epilogue

epiqendër *nf* [*Spec*] epicenter

epirot *adj* of or pertaining to Epirus or to its ancient Illyrian people

epirotas *adj, n* [*Hist*] = **epirot**

episkopatë *nf* diocese, bishopric

episod *nm (Book)* episode

episodik *adj* episodic

epitaf *nm* epitaph

epitet *nm (Book)* epithet

epitrop *nm* [*Relig*] **1** administrator or caretaker of an Orthodox church **2** [*Hist*] administrator or caretaker of Christian guilds

epje *nf ger* **1** <ep·, ep·et *(Old)* **2** tendency, bent, leaning, inclination, preference **3** [*Tech*] pliability

epo *interj* <e po *(Colloq)* (expresses resignation to a disagreeable reality) what can one do? that's how it is

epo·het *vpr* to bend down, bend over

epo·n *vt* to bend

epokë *nf* epoch

epope *nf* [*Lit*] epopee

epos *nm* **1** epic tradition **2** [*Lit*] epos

epror *adj, n* superior (in rank/status)

epruvetë *nf* [*Chem*] test-tube

epsh *nm* lust

epsharak *adj* = **epshor**

epshëm
  I § *adj (i)* **1** flexible, pliable, supple **2** *(Fig)* submissive, weak, compliant
  II § *adj (i)* lustful, lascivious, lecherous

epshndjellës *adj* arousing lechery: prurient, obscene

epshor *adj* lustful, lecherous, lascivious, concupiscent; salacious, prurient, obscene

epshshmëri *nf* flexibility, pliancy, suppleness

eptë *adj (i)* = **epur**

eptim *nm* [*Ling*] inflection

eptueshëm *adj (i)* [*Ling*] inflectional

epur *adj (i)* bent, curved; bent over/down

epyrë *nf* [*Tech*] (in mechanics) diagram, curve

e.r. *abbrev* <era e re "new era" A.D.

eracak *adj* having a good sense of smell, with a keen nose

erak *nm* [*Ornit*] kestrel (*Falco tinnunculus*)

Erand *nm* Erand (male name)

*****erândët** *adj (i) (Reg Gheg)* = **erëkëndshëm**

*****erandshëm** *adj (i)* = **erëkëndshëm**

*****eranije** *nf(Old)* airship

erar *nm* windy place

*****erashi** *nf(Old)* = **erashkë**

erashkë *nf* fan, hand fan

*****eratis·** *stem for 1st sg pres, pl pres, 2nd & 3rd sg subj, pind (Old)* <**eratit·**

*****eratit·** *vt (Old)* to perfume

*****erato·n** *vt (Old)* = **eratit·**

*****erbarozë** *nf* [*Bot*] = **barbarozë**

erdh| *stem for pdef, opt, adm, part forms* <**vje·n**
  ○ <> **erdhi fryma** <> sighed with relief
  ○ **erdhi muhabeti** the subject has come up, (it) has been mentioned

*****erdha·het** *vpr* to eat one's fill, fill up on food, gorge oneself

*****erdhi| = hardhi|

eremi *nf* wasteland, desert

*****eremiqë** *nf* coarse bran

eremit *nm* [*Relig*] eremite, hermit

*****ereni** *nf* **1** winnowing fan *****2** system

*****erethis·** *vt (Reg Tosk)* to irritate

erë *nf* **1** wind **2** *(Colloq)* air = **ajer** **3** odor, smell, scent, perfume, aroma **4** era
  ○ **era e gjethit** leaf-rustling spring breeze
  ○ **erë e keqe** stench, stink
  ○ **erë kërmë** carrion smell
  ○ **erë e kundërt** headwind
  ○ **erë e marrë** squall, whirlwind, gale
  ○ **erë më erë** everywhere
  ○ **erë në favor** tail wind, following wind
  ○ **erë nga goja** [*Med*] halitosis
  ○ **ësh·të**^past **erë e vesë** "{} *was* wind and dew" *(Elev)* {} had a very short life
  ○ **era e zezë** cold winter wind (injurious to plants)

erëdredhë *nf (Colloq)* whirlwind, tornado: twister

erëdhënës *adj* odorous, redolent

erëkeq *adj* bad-smelling, foul-smelling: smelly, stinking

erëkeqe *nf* [*Veter*] anthrax

erëkëndshëm *adj (i)* pleasant-smelling: fragrant, aromatic

erëkuqe *nf* [*Veter*] anthrax

erëmatës *nm* [*Meteor*] anemometer

erëmïrë *adj* nice-smelling: fragrant

erëmïo·n *vi* to emit a fragrance, smell (nice)

erëndshëm *adj (i)* = er**ë**kë**ndsh**ë**m

erëprïtës *nm* windshield

erëra *np* 1 <erë 2 spices = erëza

erërëndë *adj* having a heavy smell: strong-smelling

erëto·n *vt* to fill [] with an (unleasant) odor: smell up []

erëtregueles *nm [Meteor]* vane, weathervane

erëza *np fem* 1 spices 2 *(Euph Reg)* dry manure

erëzo·n *vi* to give off a fragrance; smell good

erg *nm [Phys]* erg

*****ergalïs·** *vt =* stolïs·

*****ergat** = argat

*****ergavan** *nm [Bot]* = jargavan

*****ergjo·n** *vt* to cause, make

ergjend <ergjend = argjend

ergjëz *np* newly hatched louse

*****ergjit** *nm (Old)* bachelor

*****eritrin** *nm [Ichth]* pandora *Pagellus erythrinus*

*****erka** *np* shallows

Ermal *nm* Ermal (male name)

*****ermen** *nm [Bot]* common yarrow, milfoil *(Achillea millefolium)*

*****ermen** = armen

*****ermenkë** *nf (Reg Tosk)* Armenian woman/girl

*****ermer** *nm* armoire, cupboard

ermë *adj (i)* fragrant = mermë

ermik *nm* 1 coarsely ground flour *2 farina made of rice

*****ermo·n** *vt* to rummage around

ero·n *vt (Colloq)* to air out [], ventilate

*****erode** *nf [Bot]* storksbill *Erodium*

*****erodhios** *nm [Ornit]* plover *(Charadrius)*

erore *nf* fan = erashkë

erotïk *adj [Lit]* erotic

erozïon *nm [Geol]* erosion

*****ers** *I § nm OR* ers**ë** *II § nf* fan

*****erso·n** *vt =* ero·*n*, erati*t·*

ershëm *adj (i)* fragrant; odorous

*****erto·n** *vt* to cause [] to smell

*****erth** = erdh

erudicion *nm (Book)* erudition

erudit *adj (Book)* erudite

erupsion *nm [Geol]* eruption

eruptïv *adj [Geol]* eruptive

erurïna *np* spices = erëza

erz *nm (Old)* = nder

Erzen *nm* Erzen (male name)

*****erzim** = rëzimë

erzinë *nf* perfumed liquid: perfume, cologne

err *nm* darkness

err· *vt* 1 to delay/keep [] until dark 2 to blind []'s eyes 3 *(Fig)* to make [] miserable

  ∘ **i err· sytë** to die

err·et

I § *vpr impers* to grow dark, become night
II § *vpr* 1 to be caught by nightfall 2 *(Fig)* (of the countenance) to cloud over, darken, frown

  ∘ **err·et**[3sg] **pa gdhïrë** "get dark without getting dusky" to be over before it starts

  ∘ **<> err·et**[3pl] **sytë 1** <>'s eyes *become* clouded (by illness or emotion) **2** *(Fig)* <> *loses* control over <>'s emotions **3** *(Fig)* <> *closes* <>'s eyes for the last time, <> *dies*

  ∘ **<> err·et**[3sg] **zemra** "<>'s heart *darkens*" <> *gets* heartsick

errësïm *nm ger* 1 <errëso·*n*, errëso·*het* 2 darkening, dimming

  ∘ **errësim detyruar** (obligatory) blackout

errësïrë *nf* darkness, dimness, obscurity

errëso·het *vpr* 1 to be caught by nightfall 2 to turn/ go/get dark 3 to fade out 4 *(Fig)* to frown

  ∘ **<> errëso·het vendi/bota** "the world *goes* dark for <>" <> *loses* temporary control of one's mind, <> *does* not know for a moment what <> *is* doing: <>'s mind goes blank

errëso·n *vt* 1 to darken; dim, obscure 2 to keep [] in the dark, hide 3 *(Fig)* to surpass in accomplishment: leave in the dust, leave standing

errësuar *adj (i)* darkened, in the dark

errësues *adj* serving to reduce glare: glare-reducing

errët

I § *adj (i)* 1 dark, dim, murky 2 (for colors) deep, dark 3 *(Fig)* obscure, vague, unclear 4 *(Fig)* suspicious, shady, of dubious character 5 *(Fig)* unenlightened 6 *(Fig)* frowning

II § *adv* 1 in the dark 2 in an unclear way: murkily

errtas *adv* in an unclear way: murkily

errur *nm (të)* dusk, early evening

ese *nf[Lit]* essay

*****esej** *nm =* ese

esello·het *vpr (Colloq)* 1 to get hungry 2 *(Colloq)* to sober up

esencë *nf* essence

esencïal *adj* essential; basic

esencialïsht *adv* essentially, mainly

esëll *adv* 1 on an empty stomach 2 *(Colloq)* sober (not drunk)

  ∘ **ësh·të esëll në** [] to be completely ignorant about []

esëllt *adj (i)* 1 having an empty stomach 2 sober, sobered-up

*****eskavator** = ekskavator

eskimez *adj, n* Eskimo

eskursïon *nm* excursion, outing

esmer = ezmer

esnaf

I § *nm* 1 guild 2 guildsman
II § *adj (Colloq)* honest

esnafor *adj (Book)* of or pertaining to guilds

*****esofag** *nm [Anat]* esophagus

esparsetë *nf [Bot]* esparcette herb *Onobrychis*

esperanto *nf* Esperanto

este *nm* aesthete

estetïk *adj* aesthetic

estetïkë *nf* 1 aesthetics 2 *(Colloq)* textbook on aesthetics

*****Estnï** = Estonï

eston *adj, n* Estonian

estonez *nm* Estonian = eston

Estonï *nf* Estonia

estonïan = eston

estonïsht *adv* in Estonian (language)

estonïshte *nf* Estonian language

estra·dë *nf* **1** variety show, vaudeville **2** vaudeville troupe; vaudeville hall **3** open air stage; podium

*****esthet** = estet

*****Esthoní** = Estoní

e·sull = e·sëll

esh *nm (Reg)* **1** [*Zool*] hedgehog, porcupine **2** *(FigImpolite)* person who resembles another in a noticeable way: look-alike, carbon copy

esh·a·k *nm* thorn apple

eshk *nm (Colloq)* strong thirst

*****e·shke** *nf* kidney = ve·shkë

e·shkë

I § *nf* **1** wood fungus used in dried form to light a fire: punk **2** [*Bot*] tinder fungus *Fomes fomentarius, Polyporus fomentarius* **3** charcoal (usually of heather wood) used in blacksmith's forge *****4** slag **5** kidney = ve·shkë

II § *pred* very dry, parched; dried up and wrinkled

e·shkë·t *adj (i)* **1** suitable to make charcoal **2** *(Fig)* dried up and wrinkled

eshkë·to·re *nf* = eshko·re

*****e·shk·na** *np* <ve·shkë *(Reg Gheg)* loins, lumbar region

eshko·re *nf* small sack for carrying tinder, flintstone, and piece of steel for striking sparks

eshko·s·et *vpr* **1** to dry up completely, go dry **2** to become parched with thirst or fever

eshko·s·ur *adj (i)* dry (as charcoal), dried up; parched

esht·a·k *adj* **1** made of bone: osseous **2** having bones sticking out: skinny, bony

esht·e·k *nm* metal mold used by craftsmen to shape gold plate into small cupped forms

e·shtë *nf* [*Anat*] fiber, muscle fiber

e·shtër *nf* [*Anat*] bone

eshtër·a·k *adj* big-boned = eshtërma·dh

eshtër·gje·rë *adj* having long bones: long-boned = kockëgje·rë

eshtër·í *nf collec* framework formed by the bones of a body: skeleton

eshtër·ím *nm ger* **1** <eshtëro··het **2** ossification

eshtër·ma·dh *nm* having large bones: big-boned = kockëma·dh

eshtëro··het *vpr* to become ossified

eshtër·o·r *adj* **1** of or pertaining to bone: bony; osseous **2** having bones: bony **3** having bones sticking out: skinny, bony

eshtër·o·re *nf* **1** [*Relig*] ossuary **2** bone-house

e·shtë·rt *adj (i)* made of bone

eshtër·tra·shë *adj* thick-boned

*****esht·n·uem** *adj (i)* *(Reg Gheg)* ossified; osseous

eshto·r *adj* of bone: bony, osseous

e·shtra *np* <asht, e·shtër **1** bones **2** *(Reg)* teeth

*****et** *nm* = e·tje

e·t·et *vpr* **1** to get/be thirsty **2** *(Fig)* to have a craving

eta·pë *nf* **1** stage, phase, step **2** [*Sport*] component stage of a long race: leg

ete·r *nm* ether

eternít *nm* [*Constr*] composition material made with asbestos and used to make drainpipes and corrugated roofing

eter·o·vaj·o·r *adj* containing oil of ether; having the characteristics of oil of ether

e·t·ër *np* **1** <a·të **2** forefathers

*****et·s·u·a·r** *adj (i)* thirsty

e·t||i *gen/dat/abl* <a·të

etík *adj* ethical

etike·të *nf* **1** label, ticket **2** *(Fig)* distinctive mark/characteristic **3** *(Book)* etiquette
  ○ etiketë "e porositur" [*Postal*] label marked "registered mail"
  ○ etiketë e varur [*Postal*] tie-on label, fly-tag

etiket·ím *nm ger* [*Postal*] <etiketo··n

etiketo··n *vt* to attach a label to []: label

etí·kë *nf* ethics

etimo·lo·g *n* etymologist

etimo||logj·í *nf* etymology

etimo||logj·ík *adj* [*Ling*] etymological

etio·p||as *adj, n* Ethiopian

Etiopí *nf* Ethiopia

etj. *abbrev* <e të tjerë, e të tjera etc.

e·tje *nf* **1** thirst **2** longing, yearning, craving

etník *adj* ethnic

etno·gra·f *nm* ethnographer

etno·graf·í *nf* ethnography

etno·graf·ík *adj* ethnographic

etno·gjen·e·zë *nf* ethnogenesis, origin of a people

eto··het *vpr* = e·t·et

Etrít *nm* Etrit (male name)

etru·sk *adj, n* [*Hist*] Etruscan

etrusk·íshte *nf* Etruscan language

e·t·shëm

I § *adj (i)* **1** thirsty **2** eager

II § *adv* thirstily

et·sho··het *vpr* = e·t·et

et·sho··n *vi* to thirst = e·t·et

et·u·a·r *adj (i)* = e·tur

e·tur *adj (i)* thirsty, eager

ety·dë *nf* [*Mus*] étude

eth· *vt* to service [a cow] (with a bull), mate [a heifer]

e·th·et *vpr* (of a cow or sow) to be in heat: rut

eth·a·ck *nm* [*Bot*] herb used against fever and chills: bird's-nest orchid *(Neotica nidus-avis)*

eth·a·to·r *nm* two-year old stud bull/horse

eth·a·to·re *nf* **1** female animal being bred/serviced **2** young female goat

e·the *nf* fever and chills; wave of fever and chills
  ○ ethe e butë "slight fever" wolf in sheep's clothing
  ○ ethet e moçalit *(Colloq)* swamp fever: malaria
  ○ ethet e kënetës malaria
  ○ ethe Malte [*Med Veter*] undulant fever *(brucelosis)*
  ○ ethe të rrasëta debilitating fever and chills

ethe·pru·r·ës *adj* fever-causing

*****e·th·ëz** *nf collec (Old)* [*Entom*] small moths as a class *(Microlepidoptera)*

e·th·je *nf ger* **1** <eth·, e·th·et **2** fever infection/condition

e·th·shëm *adj (i)* **1** with great emotion: heated, feverish **2** urgent **3** expressing great disquiet: distraught

eufemíz·ëm *nm (Book)* euphemism

eufoní *nf* euphony = bukurtingëllím

eufon·ík *adj* euphonic = bukurtingëllu·es

euforbiac·e *nf* [*Bot*] Euphorbia

eufor·í *nf* euphoria

eufor·ík *adj* euphoric

eukalïpt *nm* [*Bot*] eucalyptus *Eucaliptus*

eunuk *nm* eunuch
europ| = evrop|
evakuïm *nm* evacuation
evari *nf(Old)* = mirënjohje
evari|shëm *adj (i) (Old)* = mirënjohës
eventual *adj* eventual
eventual|isht *adv* eventually
eventual|itet *nm (Book)* eventuality
evgjit *adj, n* settled gypsy
evgjit|ëri *nf collec* gypsies
evgjit|kë *nf* [Zool] tadpole
evidencë *nf* [Offic] evidence
evidenc|o •n *vt* to evidence
evident *adj* evident
evitïm *nm ger* 1 <**evito •n** 2 avoidance
evit|o •n *vt* to avoid, avert
evlat *nm (Colloq)* offspring, child: kid
evlet|ër *np* <**evlat** offspring, children: kids

evolent *adj* [Tech] involute
evolucion *nm* evolution
evoluïm *nm ger* 1 <**evoluo •n** 2 evolution
evolu|o •n *vi (Book)* to evolve
evolventë *nf* [Math] involute
*****evrej** *nm (Old)* = ebre
*****evrop|as** *n* European
Evropë *nf* Europe
evrop|ian *adj, n* European
evullë *nf* [Bot] loranthus *(Loranthus europaeus)*
evullore *np* [Bot] mistletoe family *Loranthaceae*
ezmer *adj* of dark complexion, brunette
ezofag *nm* [Anat] esophagus
ezhderha *nf* 1 [Folklore] big dragon 2 *(Fig)* big, strong man; big hero
ezhektïm *nm ger* 1 [Tech] <**ezhekto •n** 2 ejection
ezhekt|o •n *vt* [Spec] to eject
ezhektor *nm* [Spec] ejector

ë [*ë*]
I § nf **1** the letter "ë" **2** the front or central mid vowel represented by that letter
II § interj **1** used to confirm that a preceding clause is a question, hunh? **2** (*Colloq*) used in conversation to request a repetition of a poorly understood utterance **3** expresses pleasure or surprise; hey **4** expresses a sudden remembering

ëh *interj* (*Colloq*) **1** represents the sound of groaning **2** expresses regret

ëh·et = **ënjt·**et

ëhë
I § interj (*Colloq*) **1** expresses distrust, ill will, contempt, or displeased surprise: aw-oh! **2** expresses sadness or regret: ah me!
II § pcl (*Colloq*) expresses tentative approval or agreement: oh sure, all right

ëjtje = **ënjtje**

ëmbël
I § adj (i) **1** sweet **2** pleasing to the senses: sweet, melodious, pretty **3** mild, easy; pleasant, friendly **4** gentle, smooth; soft **5** (of soil composition) without harmful salts
II § nf (e) **1** = **ëmbëlsírë 2** sweetness **3** (*Euph*) used as euphemism for any serious childhood disease
III § nn (të) sweet tenderness, gentleness
IV § adv **1** pleasing to the ear: sweetly **2** gently and tenderly **3** without making noise: quietly, softly

ëmbël|ak *adj* (*Pet*) sweet little

ëmbël|o|sh *adj* slightly sweet, sweetish

ëmbël|sí *nf* **1** sweetness **2** mildness, softness **3** pleasantness, pleasurableness; melodiousness, euphony

ëmbël|s|ím *nm ger* <**ëmbëlso·**n, **ëmbëlso·**het

ëmbël|sìq *adj* not sweet enough; sweetish but without much flavor; unpalatable

ëmbël|sìqe *nf* pastry with insufficient sweetness or flavor

ëmbël|si|ra|shít|ës *nm* (*Old*) pastryman

ëmbël|sírë *nf* [*Food*] sweet: pastry, cookie, cake, candy

ëmbël|sí|sht *adv* gently, tenderly, softly

ëmbël|so·het *vpr* **1** to increase in sweetness, become sweeter **2** to taste the sweetness **3** to eat something sweet to take away a sour taste **4** to become more mild: soften, get better; quiet down

ëmbël|so·n *vt* **1** to sweeten, make [] sweet **2** to reduce the salt content of [soil] **3** (*Fig*) to ameliorate **4** (*Fig Pej*) to put a sweet face on []
  ∘ [] **ëmbëlso·**n me sheqerka "sweeten [] up with candy" to sweet-talk [], inveigle [], cajole []
  ∘ <> **ëmbëlso·**n në [] (*Reg Euph*) it hurts <> in <>'s []

ëmbël|su|ar *adj (i)* **1** sweetened **2** (*Fig Pej*) honeyed, deceptively sweet

ëmbël|tí *nf* = **ëmbëlsí**

ëmbël|t|ím *nm ger* = **ëmbëlsím**

ëmbël|to·het *vpr* = **ëmbëlso·**het

ëmbël|to·n *vt* = **ëmbëlso·**n

ëmbël|to|r *n* pastry cook

ëmbël|to|re *nf* sweet shop, pastry/candy store: confectionary

ëmbl|as *adv* sweetly, tenderly

ëm|ë *nf* **1** mom **2** mother; dam
  ∘ e ëma his/her/their mother

ënd·et *vpr* **1** to be enjoyable for: please **2** to be attractive

ëndë *nf* **1** something to one's liking: pleasure, desire **2** = endë

*∗***ëndër** = **ëndërr**

ëndërr *nf* **1** dream **2** illusion
  ∘ **ëndrra në diell** daydreams
  ∘ **ëndërr (me) sy hapur** daydream, reverie

ëndërr|ím *nm ger* <**ëndërro·**n **2** illusion, imagination **3** dream; reverie, daydream, musing

ëndërr|im|ta|r *n* dreamer = **ëndërru|es**

ëndërr|ít· *vi* = **ëndërro·**n

ëndërr|ít|ës *adj* = **ëndërru|es**

ëndërr|ít|je *nf ger* = **ëndërrím**

ëndërr|o·n
I § vi **1** to dream **2** to engage in reverie: muse
II § vt **1** to dream of [], hope deeply for [] **2** to foresee; see [] in the imagination **3** to remember [] fondly, think of [] with nostalgia

ëndërr|shpjegu|es *nm* **1** seer, fortune-teller **2** book that explains dreams

ëndërr|t *adj (i)* dreamy, dreamlike, fantastic; very pleasant

ëndërr|ta|r *adj, n* (*Poet*) = **ëndërru|es**

ëndërr|u|ar *adj (i)* dreamed-for; dreamed-about

ëndërr|u|es
I § adj **1** dreaming **2** fanciful **3** dreamlike, dreamy
II § n dreamer

ënd|je *nf* **1** enjoyment; delight, pleasure **2** appetite (for food/drink); desire

ëndrr|a|ko|t|ë *adj* with false dreams, dreaming in vain

ëndrr|a|shu|m|ë *adj* full of dreams

ënd|sh|ëm *adj (i)* enjoyable, pleasant = këndshëm

ëngjëll = engjëll

*∗***ënote|r** *nf* [*Bot*] evening primrose Oenothera biennis

ënjt· *vt* **1** to cause [] to swell/bloat **2** to beat [] up **3** (*Colloq Fig*) to cause [] boredom, make [] tired (of something); exasperate
  ∘ [] **ënjt· në dru** to beat [] black and blue

ënjt·et *vpr* **1** to swell up, become bloated **2** (*Colloq Fig*) to be greatly annoyed/angered: be fed up, be exasperated **3** (*Colloq Fig*) to be greatly fatigued: feel beat, be all in

ënjt|je *nf ger* **1** <**ënjt·**, **ënjt·**et **2** swelling; bump **3** [*Med*] edema

ënjt|ur
I § adj (i) swollen
II § nf (e) swelling; bump

*∗***ërce|k** *nm* cad, scoundrel

*ë**rgjë**nt = argjënd

ë**sh·të** *copular and auxiliary verb* to be
  ○ ë**sh·të i/e/të** {*name of a tool in the genitive definite singular case*} to be good at using/wielding a {*tool*} **janë të pushkës** they are good with (shooting) a rifle **ishte e petës** she was good with a rolling pin **është i thikës** he's good with a knife
  ○ ë**sh·të** {*participle form of a VERB*} to have been {*VERB-ed*}
  ○ ë**sh·të gur mulliri** to be very heavy/durable/strong
  ○ ë**sh·të në hava 1** to hover **2** to be wavering, be undecided **3** to be in uncertain circumstances: be hanging in air
  ○ ë**sh·të havadan 1** to hover **2** to be wavering, be undecided **3** to be in uncertain circumstances: be hanging in air
  ○ ë**sh·të i shtëpisë** to be right at home, be in one's own bailiwick
  ○ ë**sh·të jashtë valles** "stay/be out of the dance" not participate and share responsibility

  ○ ë**sh·të kokë më vete** to insist on doing things one's own way, be headstrong
  ○ ë**sh·të ndër grepa** to be in big trouble; be on pins and needles
  ○ ë**sh·të në grepa** to be in big trouble; be on pins and needles
  ○ ë**sh·të në kundërshtim me** [ ] to be contrary to [ ]
  ○ ë**sh·të në mes dy zjarresh** "be between two fires" to be between the devil and the deep blue sea
  ○ ë**sh·të në shenjë** to be easily distinguishable
  ○ ë**sh·të në teh/presë të thikës/briskut/shpatës** to be at the crucial point, be right on the edge; hang in the balance
  ○ ë**sh·të për oturak** to be very old and sick
  ○ ë**sh·të si kukuvajkë** to look like an old bat
  ○ ë**sh·të si farë e hithrës/sinapit/lirit** to multiply like rabbits, grow like weeds
  ○ ë**sh·të shkuar në fije** to become all skin and bones; become exhausted

ë**sh**|t*ë 3rd sg pres* <ë**sh·të** is

Ff

f [fë] *nf* **1** the consonant letter "f" **2** the voiceless labio-dental fricative represented by the letter "f"

f. *abbrev* <**faqe** p. = page

F.V *abbrev* <**Forcat Vullnetare** Volunteer Forces

fa *nf* [*Mus*] the note "fa" on a musical scale

*fâ· *vt (Reg Gheg)* = **ngop·**

*fâ·het *vpr (Reg Gheg)* = **ngop·et**

*fabrika'n = **fabrika'nt**

fabrika'nt *nm* **1** manufacturer, factory owner **2** (*Pej*) capitalist exploiter

*fabrika't *nm* manufactured product; product brand/make

fabri'kë *nf* place where a product is manufactured: factory, mill, plant
  ○ **fabrikë birre** beer brewery
  ○ **fabrikë filature** spinning mill
  ○ **fabrikë letre** paper mill
  ○ **fabrikë mielli** flour mill
  ○ **fabrikë sheqeri** sugar mill
  ○ **fabrikë tekstili** textile mill

fabriki'm *nm ger* **1** <**fabriko'·n, fabriko'·het 2** fabrication

fabriko'·n *vt* **1** to manufacture, produce **2** to fabricate, concoct, make up [], cook [] up

fabriku'e's *nm* manufacturer, inventor

fa'bul *nf* [*Lit*] fable (in verse or prose)

fabuli'st *n* writer of fables

*facole'të *nf (Reg Gheg)* kerchief, handkerchief

*facule'të = **facole'të**

*fafi's *stem for 1st sg pres, pl pres, 2nd & 3rd sg subj, pind* <**fafi't**

*fafi't· *vt* = **farfuri't**

fafi't·et *vpr* = **farfuri't·**

fafi'tje *nf ger* **1** <**fafit, fafit·et 2** flickering light, flicker

fago't *nm* [*Mus*] bassoon

fagu'rë *nf* skin itch, itching

fagu's *nf* [*Med*] cancer

Fai'k *nm* Faik (male name)

fai'z *nm (Old)* usury

*faiz'çi *nf (Old)* usurer

faj *nm* **1** guilt, crime, wrong **2** fault; blame
  ○ **Faji është jetim.** "Guilt is an orphan." (*Prov Pej*) No one wants to take the blame. No one likes to admit guilt..

faja'ncë *nf* faience, majolica, crockery

fajde' *nf* **1** (*Old*) usury **2** (*Colloq*) = **dobi'**

*fajde'dha'në's *OR* **fajde'ta'r** (*Reg*) = **fajdexhi'**

fajde'xhi' *nm* (*np* ˜ *nj*) (*Old*) usurer, money-lender, pawnbroker

faje'si' *nf* [*Law*] culpability, guilt

faje'si'm *nm ger* **1** <**fajëso'·n, fajëso'·het 2** guilt

faje'so'·het *vpr* to admit guilt; accept the blame

faje'so'·n *vt* **1** to accuse [] of guilt, charge [] with a crime: blame, indict **2** to declare [] guilty

faje'su'e's *nm* accusatory

*faj'fa'llë's
  I § *adj* pardoning
  II § *n* pardoner

faj'kë *nf* gunwale

fajko'·n *vt* to polish [] (by rubbing)

fajko'||i *obl* <**fajku'a**

fajk'ore *nf* **1** [*Ornit*] female falcon/hawk **2** large boat; small ship

fajku'a *nm* (*obl* ˜ *o'i, np* ˜ *o'nj*) [*Ornit*] = **skifte'r**

faj'shëm *adj (i)* guilty, to blame

fajto'·n
  I § *vt* = **fajëso'·n**
  II § *vi* to do wrong; commit a crime

fajto'r
  I § *adj* guilty, to blame
  II § *n* guilty person, the one to blame

*faj'ts = **fajt**

*faju'rë *nf* failure

fa'jze *nf* bundle of cotton

fa'kë *nf* mousetrap

fakfu'n *nm* German silver, nickel silver

faki'r *nm* **1** fakir **2** (*Colloq*) poor man, poor wretch

fakir'fukara' *nm collec* (*Colloq*) **1** poor people taken as a whole: the poor **2** poor man, poor wretch

faksi'mile *nf* [*Book*] facsimile

fakt *nm* fact
  ○ **fakt i kryer** accomplished fact, fait accompli

fakto'·n *vt* to prove; give evidence to support an argument: document

fakto'r *nm* factor, component

faktori'zi'm *nm ger* **1** <**faktorizo'·n 2** factorization

faktori'zo'·n *vt* [*Math*] to factor

*faktu'rë *nf* invoice, bill

fakultati'v *adj* **1** facultative, optional **2** permissive

fakulte't *nm* **1** division of an institution of higher education: faculty, college **2** building housing that division **3** (*Colloq*) students and employees of that division

*fakurgji' *nf* = **smi'rë**

fal·
  I § *vt* **1** to offer; give [] (for free), present **2** to forgive, pardon, excuse **3** [*Relig*] to perform the [prayer]: pray **4** to bow/bend [] down (in prayer) **5** to extinguish [a light/fire] **6** = **përshënde't·**
  II § *vi* to go down: set
  ○ **fal· gjakun** to forgive a blood debt, give up a bloodfeud
  ○ **më fal/falni** pardon me! I beg your pardon! excuse me
  ○ **nuk të fal· (as) qimen** "not forgive you (even) a hair" to be very demanding, be a stickler for detail
  ○ **i fal· sytë** to be unable to keep one's eyes open

fal·et *vpr* **1** to make a request, beseech **2** to pray **3** to exchange expressions of respect with: exchange greetings, toast/congratulate one another **4** (*Colloq*) to thank **5** (*Colloq*) to surrender, give up
  ○ <> **fal·et me shëndet** to send <> regards and salutations

○ **falem nderit** thanks, thank you

fal|a *np (të)* greetings sent by one person to another: regards

fal|anik *n (Old)* person who gives free help

fal|as *adv* **1** gratis, free of charge **2** *(Colloq)* for a very low price: cheap

fal|eminderit *interj* thank you!

fal|ë
   I § *nf* **1** [*Anat*] joint **2** = **falëz 3** [*Ethnog*] gift brought by bride for close relatives of groom
   II § *prep (abl)* **1** thanks to, owing to **2** for the sake of
   III § *adv* gratis, free of charge

****fal|ëm** = **falëz**

fal|ëmeshëndet *interj* expresses respect for someone far away: Here's to __!

fal|ënderim *nm ger* **1** < **falëndero 2** thanks

fal|ëndero •*n vt* to thank

fal|ënderonjës *adj* thankful, grateful; expressing gratitude

fal|ës
   I § *adj* generous, magnanimous; merciful, forgiving
   II § *n* *worshipper; pilgrim

fal|ëz *nf* touch-hole in old guns, priming pan

****fal|iment** *nm* bankruptcy

fal|imentim *nm ger* **1** < **falimento** •*n* **2** bankruptcy

****fal|imento** *nf* bankruptcy

fal|imento •*n vi* to go bankrupt

fal|imentuar *adj (i)* bankrupt

****fal|is·et** *vpr* to rave

fal|is *stem for 1st sg pres, pl pres, 2nd & 3rd sg subj, pind* < **falit·**

****fal|isur** *adj (i)* raving mad, crazy

fal|it·
   I § *vi* = **falit·et**
   II § *vt* to drive [ ] crazy

fal|it·et *vpr* to lose one's head, go crazy

fal|je *nf ger* **1** < **fal·**, **fal·et 2** forgiveness, pardon

fal|më *nf* plank forming the base of the side of a cart

fals *adj (Book)* false, fake; counterfeit

fals|ifikator *n* = **falsifikues**

fals|ifikim *nm ger* **1** < **falsifiko** •*n* **2** falsification

fals|ifiko •*n vt* to falsify; misrepresent; counterfeit; forge

fals|ifikuar *adj (i)* falsified, counterfeit

fals|ifikues *nm* person who falsifies: faker, counterfeiter, forger

fals|itet *nm (Book)* falsehood, falsity

fal|so = **fals**

fal|shëm *adj (i)* pardonable; venial

fal|tar *n* [*Relig*] **1** person conducting a religious service: celebrant **2** *(Hist)* templar

fal|tore *nf* prayer chapel, sanctuary, temple

fal|ur
   I § *adj (i)* **1** forgiven, excused, pardoned **2** [*Law*] absolved **3** given for free: donated, bestowed **4** bent down, sloping **5** (of fire or light) gradually damped down, faded; extinguished **6** [*Relig*] = **shpresëtar**
   II § *nn (të)* pardon

fall *nm* fortune-telling, divination

fall|aka *nf (Old)* form of torture in which a person is tied to a post and beaten on the soles of his feet with a club: bastinado

fall|co *adj* false

****fall|çor** *nm* = **falltar**

fall|tar *n* fortuneteller, soothsayer = **fallxhor**

fall|to· *n vi* to cast/tell fortunes, soothsay

****fall|tore** = **fallxheshë**

fall|xheshë *nf* (woman) fortune-teller, soothsayer

fall|xhi *nm (np ˜ nj)* = **falltar**

fall|xhor *nm* fortuneteller, soothsayer

****fambrikë** = **fabrikë**

famë *nf* fame, reputation, renown, good name

famë|dashës *adj* hungry/eager for fame, fame-seeking

famë|keq *adj* of ill repute, notorious

famë|madh *adj* famous, renowned

famë|zi *adj (fem sg ˜ ez, masc pl ˜ inj, fem pl ˜ eza)* = **famëkeq**

famë|zo· *n vt* to make [ ] known

****famil|isht** = **familjarisht**

famil|jar
   I § *adj* < **familje 1** of, for, or pertaining to a family: familiar, domestic **2** having a family; responsible for a family; with warm family relations
   II § *nm* **1** family man **2** family member

famil|jarisht *adv* **1** with the whole family **2** as if with a member of one's own family: familiarly

famil|jaritet *nm (Book)* **1** familiarity **2** favoritism, nepotism

****famil|jarizëm** *nm (Book Regional Kos)* favoritism, nepotism

famil|jarizim *nm ger* **1** < **familjarizo** •*n*, **familjarizo** •*het* **2** familiarization

famil|jarizo •*het vpr* **1** to gain familiarity (with), become familiar (with) **2** to get to be like one of the family, get well acquainted

famil|jarizo •*n vt* to make [ ] feel at home; make friends with [ ] **2** to familiarize

famil|je *nf* family
   ○ **familje e dorës së mesme** middle-class family
   ○ **familje e ngushtë** *(Reg Gheg)* nuclear family
   ○ **familje njëkurorëshe** family consisting of parents and their children: nuclear family
   ○ **familje shumëkurorëshe** family living together in which there is more than one head of household

****fam|os·** *vt* to make [ ] loudly known, proclaim

fam|shëm *adj (i)* famous

fa|mull *nm (np ˜ j)* **1** *(Old)* godchild **2** *(Reg)* small child, baby

famull|eshë *nf* = **famull**

famull|i *nf* [*Relig*] parish

famull|itar
   I § *adj* [*Relig*] of or pertaining to a parish
   II § *nm* [*Relig*] parish priest: parson

famull|or *adj* [*Relig*] = **famullitar**

****famull|tar** = **famullitar**

Fan *nm* Fan (male name)

fanar *nm* **1** beacon = **fener 2** lantern, ship's lantern

fanat|ik
   I § *adj, n* fanatical
   II § *nm* fanatic

fanat|izëm *nm* fanaticism

****fand** = **fant**

****fand|as·** *vt* to imagine, suppose

fanel|latë *nf* flannel, flannelet

fane|llë *nf* **1** undershirt, T-shirt **2** sports jersey **3** sweater

○ **fanell**ë **mishi** woolen undershirt
○ **fanell**ë **pa mëngë** vest-like undergarment, bodice
fane'ps·et *vpr* = **fani't·***et*
fanerogá'me *np fem* [*Bot*] spermatophytes
fanfa'rë *nf* **1** fanfare **2** brass trumpet **3** band composed entirely of wind instruments: wind band; brass band
fang *nm (np ˜ gje)* **1** = **fëng 2** = **fëngi'sht**ë **3** sod; piece of turf
○ **fang i egër** blue moor grass *Sesleria coerulea*
*****fangi** *nf* collapse, breakdown; dilapidation
fang'i'shtë *nf* = **fëngi'sht**ë
fani *nf* **1** phantasm, apparition *****2** *(Old)* catastrophe; ruin
fani't·*et* *vpr* to appear in a phantasmagoric vision
fant *nm* jack (in cards)
fantas'ti'k *adj (Book)* **1** created by the imagination **2** of pure fantasy: only in the mind, impossible **3** fantastic, wonderful; unbelievable, incredible
fantazi' *nf* **1** creative imagination, creative ability **2** fantasy, pure fantasy **3** musical fantasy
fanta'zmë *nf* **1** phantasm, phantom: ghost, apparition **2** *(Fig)* ill omen
fantazo'·n *vt* to fantasize
*****fanteri'** *nf* [*Mil*] infantry
*****fanto'ç** *adj* comic, funny
fanto'më *nf* = **fanta'zm**ë
fap *onomat (Colloq)* **1** sudden percussive noise: pop, crack, bang **2** represents a sudden action: bam, wham, whoosh
*****fa'q'as** *adv* openly; obviously; right out in front
fa'qe
I § *nf* **1** cheek **2** face **3** planar surface: plane, side, facade, facet **4** page of paper **5** outward appearance **6** layer (of pastry, etc.) **7** pillow slip, mattress cover **8** *(Colloq)* page of time: a year's time; a lifetime; a generation **9** *(Fig)* honor
II § *prep (abl)* in the presence of ◇, right in front of ◇
○ **faqja e bardhë** person who brings honor to his name, person who does himself proud
○ **faqe e gjallë** [*Publ*] title page
○ **faqe e jastëkut** pillowcase
○ **faqe këpucësh** uppers of shoes
○ **faqe mbrojtëse** [*Publ*] endpaper
○ **faqe më faqe** face to face, close together
○ **faqe për faqe** **1** facing each other **2** page by page, every single page
○ **faqja e zezë** "dark face" great shame, terrible disgrace
faqe'ba'rdhë *adj (Fig)* with honor and success: successful, fortunate
faqe'butë *adj* **1** having soft cheeks, smooth-faced; still young **2** *(Fig Pej)* pampered
faqe'cje'rrë *adj* **1** having scratch marks on the cheeks **2** showing the scratched face of one in mourning
faqe'dje'gur *adj* **1** with a face scarred by burning **2** *(Fig Pej)* shameless, vile, disgraced
faqe'e'shkë *adj* whose face is dried up and wrinkled
faqe'fi'shkur *adj* having withered and wrinkled cheeks
faqe'furr'a'sh *nm* thin round unleavened bread that bakes quickly
faqe'gro'pkë *adj* hollow-cheeked
faqe'gje'rë *adj* broad-faced; having wide cheeks

faqe'hë'në
I § *nf* girl or woman with a beautiful round face
II § *adj (Poet)* **1** with face resplendent **2** *(Fig)* bright-looking, bright, smart
faqe'ku'q
I § *adj* **1** rosy-cheeked; red-faced; red-tinged **2** blooming with health
II § *nm* [*Ornit*] goldfinch = **kryea'rtëz**
faqe'la'rë *adj* **1** clean-faced **2** *(Fig)* having unblemished honor
faqe'll *nm (Reg)* cambric
faqe'ma'l *adj* mountain face/slope
faqe'mbu'sh'ur *adj* having full-fleshed cheeks; healthy
faqe'me'nde'r *prep (abl) (Colloq)* used before saying an impolite word or insult: no discourtesy intended to = **mender**
faqe'mo'llë
I § *adj* **1** rosy-cheeked; red-faced; red-tinged **2** blooming with health
II § *nf* beautiful girl or woman brimming with health
faqe'nde'zur *adj* with cheeks aflame; red-cheeked
faqe'ndri't'ur *adj* **1** bright and shining: glorious **2** *(Fig Poet)* ever victorious; covered with glory, highly honored
faqe'nxi'rë *adj* **1** having dark cheeks: dirty-faced **2** *(Fig)* covered with shame: shameful **3** *(Fig)* brazen, shameless
faqe'pru'sh *adj* = **faqe'nde'zur**
faqe'rrje'pur *adj* **1** having a face peeling from disease **2** beardless; with a spotty beard
faqe'rrogo'z *adj (Insult)* **1** shameless, cheeky, impudent *****2** foolhardy
faqe'rru'dh'ur *adj* having wrinkled cheeks: wrinkle-faced
faqe'rrumbulla'k *adj* round-faced: robust-looking
*****faqe'si'** *nf (Old)* exterior, appearance, aspect
faqe'she'gë
I § *adj* having cheeks as rosy as pomegranates
II § *nf* rosy-cheeked girl or woman
faqe'të *nf (Reg)* **1** cartridge clip **2** hairpin
faqe'trëndafi'l *adj* rosy-cheeked; healthy
faqe'tu'l *adj (Impol)* fleshy-faced, plump-faced
faqe've'rdhë *adj* sallow-faced, pale
fa'qe'za
I § *adv* **1** face to face **2** publicly, openly; frankly **3** clearly, plainly **4** *(Reg)* as plain as the nose on your face
II § *prep (abl)* in the presence of, right in front of
*****fa'qe'zaj** = **fa'qeza**
faqe'zbe'htë *adj* having pale cheeks: pale-faced
*****fa'qe'zë** *nf* facet
faqe'zi' *adj, n (fem sg ˜ e'z, masc pl ˜ i'nj, fem pl ˜ e'za)* shameless/contemptible/vile (one)
faqe'zja'rr *adj* with cheeks aflame; red-faced
fa'që'z *nf* **1** veil used to cover the face of a sleeping child **2** skein of cotton yarn
faqo'·het *vpr* to come right out, appear face to face
faqo'·n *vt* **1** to create flat surfaces in [ ] by carving or chiseling **2** to flatten [ ] out, make [ ] flat
faqo'l *nm* **1** [*Tech*] molasses **2** head scarf
faqo'll *adj* having one side of different color from the other; having a muzzle of different color from the rest of the body
faqo'r *adj* **1** facial; frontal **2** planar, flat **3** = **faqo'll**

faqo·re *nf* **1** small, flat flask for raki **2** protective cover for bed clothes: pillow case, quilt cover, mattress cover; bedsheet **3** top layer of a prepared dish **4** side board of a cradle **5** cotton apron **6** small rug used as wall decoration **7** veil used to cover the face of a sleeping child **8** cambric

faqos· *vt* **1** to create flat surfaces in [] by carving/chiseling **2** [*Publ*] to divide [] up and arrange into a page: page [] up, paginate

faqos·ës *n* person who does the page make-up: pagemaker

faqos·je *nf ger* **1** < faqos· **2** page make-up, setting up pages

faqo·sh *adj* round and flat-bottomed, squat-shaped

*****faqti·m** *nm (Old)* parade

far *nm* **1** lighthouse **2** [*Cine*] floodlight

*****faragjo·s** *nm* pencil

fara·n *nm* **1** seed corn **2** *(Fig)* brave man with a strong and robust body

farani·k *adj* **1** having many seeds, full of seeds **2** having a small seed; bearing small fruit **3** for sowing
  ○ **drithëra faranike** seed grain, seed grains

farao·n *nm* [*Hist*] pharaoh

fara·shë *nf* **1** dustpan **2** spoon rack, spice rack **3** *(Old)* quiver (for arrows)

fara·shkë *nf* **1** = **fara·shë** **2** seedbox used in sowing **3** [*Bot*] sorghum, sweet sorghum, great millet *(Sorghum vulgare)*

*****fara·sht** *nm* = **fara·shë**

fara·shu·k *adj* **1** full of seeds **2** *(Fig Insult)* pumpkin-headed, crazy, nutty

*****fa·rcë** *nf* seed grain

fare *adv* **1** quite, very, absolutely; (with negatives) at all **2** entirely
  ○ **ësh·të fare 1** to be very stupid **2** to be utterly devastated (emotionally or physically)
  ○ **fare pak** very little

fare·c *nm* **1** seed corn **2** *(Colloq)* sperm

fare·fis *nm* kin, kinfolk; family relative

fare·fis·ni *nf* **1** kinship **2** kinfolk **3** *(Pej)* nepotism

fare·fis·no·r *adj* pertaining to kinfolk, kin-related

fare·gjë *pron* = **farëgjëje**

fa·rë *nf* **1** seed **2** sperm **3** progeny; kin group **4** sort, ilk; race, breed **5** starter in a fermentation process **6** [*Zool*] egg of insect or cold-blooded animal **7** [*Bot*] fertilized ovary **8** *(Iron)* when preceded by a demonstrative and followed by a noun in the ablative case, indicates a judgment of the person indicated by that noun that may be disparaging or praising, depending on the context, much like English "that little so and so"
  ○ **farë buke** yeast
  ○ **farë e fis** = **farefis**
  ○ **farë e kalbur** *(Pej)* corrupt person: rotten apple
  ○ **farë e ligë 1** *(Insult)* bad person; person from a bad family: bad seed **2** bad family
  ○ **farë e keqe 1** *(Insult)* bad person; person from a bad family: bad seed **2** bad family
  ○ **farë kosi** starter for yogurt
  ○ **farë e shëndoshë** very good person, person of fine character
  ○ **fara të imëta** grass seed

farë·ba·rdhë *adj* white-grained

farë·fry·r *nm* [*Bot*] a genus of Apiaceae that produces bladder-like pods *(Physospermum)*

*****farë·gjâ·je** *pron (Reg Gheg)* = **farëgjëje**

farë·gja·të
  I § *adj* long-grained, large-grained
  II § *nm* large-grained corn

farë·gjë·je *pron* not even a little bit

farë·he·dh·ës
  I § *adj* for sowing: sowing
  II § *n* sower

farë·he·dh·ëse *nf* sowing machine, mechanical sower

farë·hu·mb·ur *adj (Colloq)* crazy; totally incompetent

farë·ku·q *adj* red-grained; with a reddish pulp

farë·ku·qe *nf* [*Bot*] firethorn *(Pyracantha coccinea Roem.)*

farë·ma·dh *nm, adj* (corn) with large heads of grain; large-grained

farë·ngrën·ës *nm* **1** [*Entom*] grain/granary weevil, corn weevil *(Calandra granaria)* **2** rice weevil *(Calandra oryzae)*

farë·palë·në *adj (Colloq)* **1** childless, barren **2** *(Curse)* be damned to die childless!

fa·rës *adj* **1** having many seeds, full of seeds **2** used for sowing, serving as seed grain **3** rich in seeds: productive, fruitful

farë·se·ndi *pron* not even a little bit

farë·si *nf collec* progeny of a line of descent: kin

farë·sje·ll·ës *adj* [*Med*] seminiferous

*****farë·soj** *nm* kind, sort

farë·shku·rtër *nm, adj* (corn) with short-ears that ripen in August

farë·shu·ar *adj (Colloq)* whose seed is dead: infertile **2** *(Colloq)* childless, barren **3** *(Curse)* may his seed be extinguished!

farë·to·r *nm* = **farëhedhës**

farë·to·re *nf* sowing machine, mechanical sower

farë·ve·shu·r *adj* **1** [*Bot*] (of fruit) with seeds, with pits **2** having seeds enclosed in an ovary: angiospermous

farë·vo·gël *adj* short-eared (of corn); small-grained

fa·rëz *nf* **1** queen bee < **fa·rë 2** *(Dimin)* tiny seed **3** [*Zool*] tiny egg of insect or cold-blooded animal
  ○ **farëzat e kokës** *(Joke)* one's mental faculties: one's mind

farë·zi *adj, n (fem sg ˜ez, masc pl ˜inj, fem pl ˜eza)* (fruit) with dark-colored/black seeds

farë·zi·m *nm ger* **1** < **farëzo··n 2** [*Med*] semination

farë·zo··n *vi* to form seeds, go to seed

farë·zh·ve·shu·r *adj* having naked seeds: gymnospermous

farfa·llë *nf* [*Tech*] throttle (valve)

*****farfara·n**
  I § *adj* swaggering
  II § *nm* swaggerer

farfuri
  I § *nf* **1** porcelain ***2** = **furfuri**
  II § *np* porcelain objects
  III § *adj* glistening white

farfuri·njtë *adj (i)* **1** of porcelain **2** glistening white

farfuri·s *stem for 1st sg pres, pl pres, 2nd & 3rd sg subj, pind* < **farfurit·**

*****farfuri·sh·ëm** *adj (i)* resplendent

farfuri·t· *vi* to flicker; glisten

farfuri·t·ës *adj* flickering; glistening

farfuri·tje *nf ger* **1** <**farfuri**t· **2** flicker; glisten

farim *nm ger* <**faro**·*n*

faring *nm* [*Anat*] pharynx

faringjit *nm* [*Med*] pharyngitis

farishte
  I § *nf* = **farishtë**
  II § *np* seeds planted in a seedbed, vegetable seeds; sprouts, seedlings

farishtë *nf* **1** seedbed; plant nursery **2** fish hatchery **3** onion sprout; seedling

farishtore *nf* garden plot for growing seedlings: seedbed, nursery

farje *nf, adj* **1** [*Bot*] pulpy (fruit or vegetable) with many seeds **2** [*Entom*] queen (bee)

farkac *nm (Euph)* [*Zool*] snake

*__farkar__ *n* = **farkëtar**

farkë *nf* **1** (blacksmith's) forge; blacksmith's workshop, smithy **2** *(Fig)* people cast at the same forge: type, race, clan **3** characteristic external appearance: cast, physique

farkëtar *nm* smith, blacksmith

farkëtari *nf* **1** blacksmith shop **2** the profession of being a smith: blacksmithing

farkëtim *nm ger* <**farkëto**·*n*, **farkëto**·*het*

farkëto·*het vpr* <**farkëto**·*n* to become forged into shape; become strengthened

farkëto·*n vt* **1** [*Tech*] to forge [metal] **2** *(Fig)* to mold, shape
  ○ **farkëto**·*n* **vargonjtë/zinxhirët** to forge the chains: prepare to enslave, enslave

farkëtuar *adj (i)* **1** forged into shape **2** *(Fig)* morally and physically hardened and tempered

farkëtues *nm* **1** ironworker, blacksmith **2** *(Fig)* tempering agent

farkëtueshëm *adj (i)* capable of being shaped at a forge: malleable

farkëtueshmëri *nf* malleability

farkim *nm ger* **1** <**farko**·*n*, **farko**·*het* **2** slab of concrete or stone, paving

farko·*het vpr* to become morally and physically hardened and tempered

farko·*n vt* **1** =**farkëto**·*n* **2** to chisel out [a millstone]; chisel out [a stone slab/column] **3** to cover [] with a slab of concrete or stone **4** to shoe [a horse/mule] **5** to attach [] strongly **6** *(Fig)* to sculpt **7** *(Fig)* to shut [] up, not allow [] to speak

farkore *nf* **1** swaddling cloth **2** cheesecloth

farkuar *adj (i)* **1** chiseled out of stone **2** covered by a slab of concrete or stone

farmaceutik *adj* [*Med*] pharmaceutic(al)

farmaceutikë *nf* [*Med*] pharmacology

farmaci *nf* **1** drugstore, pharmacy **2** first-aid chest

farmacist *n* pharmacist; pharmacologist

farmak
  I § *nm (np ~ qe) (Colloq)* poison
  II § *adj* too bitter; too salty; poisonous

farmakologji *nf* = **farmaci**, **farmaceutikë**

farmakos·
  I § *vt* to poison
  II § *vi* **1** to eat under trying circumstances: choke down **2** (of someone disliked) to guzzle

*__farmaq__ = **farmak**

*__farmason__ *nm* freemason

farmatore *nf* pharmacy

*__farmë__ = **mbrumë**

faro·*het vpr* **1** to take root, settle in **2** *(Colloq)* to be very hungry

faro·*n*
  I § *vt (Colloq)* **1** to wipe out, finish off, cancel **2** to demolish on a broad scale: exterminate, devastate, eradicate **3** to eat up **4** to take the seeds out of
  II § *vi* = **faro**·*het*

faroç *adj* good for use as seed; rich in seeds

faroke
  I § *nf* onion allowed to go to seed in a seedbed; onion sprout; round fringe on top of an onion in seed
  II § *np* seeds

faror
  I § *nm* fruit or vegetable with small seeds
  II § *adj* **1** bearing fruit with seeds **2** [*Bot*] grown to produce seed

faros· *vt (Colloq)* = **faro**·*n*

faros·*et vpr (Colloq)* = **faro**·*het*

farosje *nf ger* <**faros**·, **faros**·*et*

farosh *adj* **1** having many seeds, full of seeds **2** grown to produce seed

*__farsej__ *adv* altogether, completely

farsë *nf* farce

*__farsoj__ = **farësoj**

farurina *np collec* seeds, seed

*__farraç__ *nm* [*Bot*] virginia pokeberry, pokeweed *(Phytolacca decandra)*

fasadë *nf* facade

*__fasan__ *nm* = **fazan**

*__fasë__ *nf* [*Ornit*] = **fazan**

*__faskomile__ *nf* [*Bot*] three-lobed sage *(Salvia triloba)*

fasonal *adj* [*Tech*] (used for) shaping, forming

*__fastori__ *nf* sect

fasule *nf* [*Bot*] white bean, haricot *(Phaseolus vulgaris L.)*
  ○ **nuk <> ftohen fasulet** "<>'s beans don't get cold" *(Colloq)* <> shows no concern; it's no skin off <>'s nose
  ○ **fasule syskë** black-eyed pea

fasulishtë = **fasulishte** *nf* **1** dried bean pod; crushed bean plant **2** bean field, bean patch

fashetë *nf* [*Tech*] clamp

fashë
  I § *nf* **1** strip, swath; band **2** bandage **3** strip of material: strip, swath **4** such a strip used to bind something: band **5** such a strip used to bind a wound: bandage **6** repose, serenity, quiet, calm
  II § *adv* at rest, at a pause

fashikull *nm (np ~ j)* fascicle

fashinë *nf* [*Constr*] fascine

fashis *stem for 1st sg pres, pl pres, 2nd & 3rd sg subj, pind* <**fashit**·

fashist *adj, n* fascist

fashistizim *nm ger* <**fashistizo**·*n*

fashistizo·*n vt* to establish a fascist regime in []; introduce a fascist spirit into []

fashit· *vt* to bring [] to rest, bring [] to a gradual stop; calm/quiet [] down; gradually extinguish [], fade [] down/out; assuage: soothe, soften

fashit·*et vpr* **1** to calm down **2** to fade out/away, dwindle

fashitës *adj, nm* palliative

fashitje *nf ger* <**fashit**

fashitur adj (i) **1** brought to rest, brought to a gradual stop; quieted down, calmed down **2** faded down/out

fashizëm nm fascism

fashkë
I § nf
II § nf **1** flat rock *2 (Reg Tosk)* bandage, band

*****fashkëro**•n vt to charm, fascinate

fasho nf = **fashë**
∘ **fasho pistoni** [Tech] piston ring

fasho•n vt to bandage, dress; swathe

fashoj np <**fashuall**

fashqe nf swaddling band

fashuall nm honeycomb

fat nm **1** fate, destiny **2** luck, fortune; good luck, success **3** (Old) mate (bride or groom) arranged by a matchmaker

*****fatakeq** adj = **fatkeq**

fatal adj fatal

fatalist n fatalist

fatalitet nm fatality

fatalizëm nm fatalism

fatalumas = **fatlum**

fatamjerë adj melancholy, sad

Fatbardh nm Fatbardh (male name)

Fatbardha nf Fatbardha (female name)

fatbardhë adj **1** lucky, fortunate, born lucky **2** bringing good fortune: propitious, lucky

fatbardhësi nf good luck, success, happiness

fatbardhësisht adv fortunately, luckily, happily

fati nf [Folklore] each of the three Fates that gather around a three-day-old baby to determine its fortune

*****fatim** nm ger **1** <**fato**•n **2** congratulation

fatkeq adj **1** unfortunate, ill-fated, unlucky, hapless **2** unhappy

fatkeqësi nf **1** unhappiness **2** misfortune, adversity **3** mishap, accident

fatkeqësisht adv unfortunately, unluckily

fatkob adj = **fatkeq**

fatlig adj = **fatkeq**

fatlum adj **1** lucky, fortunate **2** bringing happiness; happy

fatlumas = **fatlum**

*****fatlumtëri** nf happiness

fatlumtur adj = **fatbardhë, fatlum**

fatmadh
I § adj lucky
II § nm with a great future: lucky

*****fatmashall** adj (Old) domineering

fatmbarë adj with a successful future: lucky

fatmbarësi nf success; good fortune, good luck

Fatmir nm Fatmir (male name)

Fatmir nm Fatmir (male name)

fatmirë adj = **fatbardhë**

fatmirësi nf **1** luckiness, good luck **2** success; happiness

fatmirësisht adv luckily, fortunately

fatmjerë adj = **fatkeq**

*****fatndjekës** n (Old) vagabond

*****fatnuer** adj (fem ~ ore) (Old Regional Gheg) of or pertaining to fate

fato•n vt to wish [] luck/success, congratulate

fatorino = **faturino**

fatos nm **1** brave, valiant **2** school child in the primary grades **3** [Hist] member of the Young Pioneers

Fatos nm Fatos (male name)

fatpadalë
I § adj not yet blessed by marriage
II § nf still unmarried girl

fatprerë adj = **fatpadalë**

fatprurës adj = **fatsjellës**

fatrrëfyes
I § adj fortune-telling
II § n fortune-teller

fatsjellës adj bringing good fortune: propitious

*****fatshëm** adj (i) fortunate

fatshkretë adj cursed with bad luck, always unlucky, born unlucky: hapless

fatthënë nf **1** [Relig] pulpit **2** soothsayer **3** destiny, fortune, forecast

fatthënës
I § adj fortune-telling, foreboding
II § n soothsayer, fortune-teller

faturë nf bill (for service or merchandise): invoice, shipping receipt

faturim nm ger <**faturo**•n, **faturo**•het

faturino nf with masc agreement ticket collector on a bus/train: conductor

faturist n invoice clerk

faturo•het vpr to record an invoice

faturo•n vt to invoice, make an invoice for []

faturues nm person who makes an invoice

*****fatzezi** nf (Old) misfortune

fatzi adj (fem sg ~ ez, masc pl ~ inj, fem pl ~ eza) terribly unfortunate, ill-fated, very unlucky

faunë nf fauna

favor nm **1** special help/service: favor **2** (Pej) favoritism

favorizim nm ger **1** <**favorizo**•n **2** showing favoritism, favoritism

favorizo•n vt **1** to do a favor for [] **2** (Pej) to show favoritism towards [] **3** to be of advantage to []: favor, help

favorshëm adj (i) favorable

fazan nm [Ornit] pheasant (Phasianus)

fazë nf **1** phase, stage **2** [Sport] time period
∘ **faza e qumështit** period during which the kernels of corn and other grains fill out

*****fazëm** nf phantom

FBI abbrev (English) Federal Bureau of Investigation

FBS abbrev <**Federata Botërore e Sindikatave** World Federation of Trade Unions

FDSh abbrev <**Fronti Demokratik i Shqipërisë** Democratic Front of Albania

fe nf religion; religious belief; faith

feçe nf feces, excrement

feçkë nf **1** snout, trunk (of an elephant), proboscis **2** snout-like projection on a machine; insect palp **3** (Insult) dogface!

feçkëderr adj (Insult) pig-faced, pig, ugly-snout

feçkor nm [Entom] insect with a snout-like head that gnaws on plant shoots and makes holes in fruit: snout beetle, weevil

*****fedak** adj fanatical, excessively religious

federal
I § adj federal; belonging to a federation
II § nm head of the fascist party at the prefecture level during the Italian occupation of Albania

federa'të *nf* federation

federati'v *adj* federative, federal

***fej** *np* <**fye'll**

fe'je *np* <**fye'll 1** narrow ducts in plant/animal bodies **2** nostrils, nares

feje'së *nf* engagement (to be married), betrothal

fejo' ·het *vpr* to get engaged to be married; announce one's engagement

fejo' ·n *vt* to agree to an engagement of marriage for []: betroth, affiance, engage

fejto'n *nm* [*Lit*] satirical article, feuilleton

fejua'r

 I § adj (i) engaged, betrothed

 II § nm (i) fiancé

 III § nf (e) fiancée

***fejue's** *nm* fiancé

fejzë *nf* narrow duct in the body of a plant/animal
 ○ **fejzat e hundës** nostrils

feka'le *np (Book)* human feces, excrement

fekondi'm *nm ger* **1** *(Biol)* <**fekondo' ·n 2** fertilization, fecundation

fekondo' ·n *vt (Biol)* to fertilize, fecundate

feks·

 I § vi, vt **1** to shine **2** *(Colloq)* to slap

 II § vi impers it *dawns*

 III § vt to polish

feksi'm *nm ger* <**fekso' ·n**

fekso' ·n *vt* = **feks·**

***fekto' ·n** *vi* to barely stick one's head out

***feku'l** = **fequl**

***fel** *nm* good mood/humor

feldmaresha'l *nm* field marshal

feldspa't *nm* [*Min*] feldspar

fe'le *OR* **fe'lë** *nf* slice, rasher

***felemo' ·n** *vt* to slice [] up

felëshue's *nm* apostate; infidel; turncoat

felgri'm *nm ger* <**fërgëlli'm**

felgro' ·n *vt* **1** = **fërgëllo' ·n** ***2** to dilate one's nostrils

***feli(n)** *nm (Reg Gheg)* = **fëli**

***felmarsha'l** *nm* field-marshal = **feldmaresha'l**

felmëzo' ·n *vt* to slice [] up

***felti'në** *nf* [*Hist*] harquebus = **arkebu'z**

***fell** *nm (Reg Gheg)* = **fye'll**

***fell** = **thell**

femc *nm* stinger (of a bee/wasp)

fe'me *nf (Reg)* awl = **fëndye'll**

fe'mër *nf, adj* **1** female **2** [*Bot*] ovary in a flower **3** [*Tech*] female part of a composite: mortise (for a tenon), groove (for a tongue), eye (for a hook)

femëri' *nf* **1** femininity **2** females taken as a collective whole: female population

femëro' ·n *vt* (of animals) to give birth to female offspring

femëro'r *ad* **1** pertaining to or consisting of females: female **2** exclusively for females

femëro're *nf* **1** [*Ling*] feminine gender **2** [*Bot*] ovary in a flower

femërzi'm *nm* [*Med*] effeminization

femini' *nf* = **fëmijëri'**

femini'st

 I § adj, n feminist

 II § nm (Colloq) man who is successful sexually; womanizer

femini'zëm *nm* feminism

feminizi'm *nm* [*Med*] feminization

***femno' ·n** = **femëro' ·n**

femohue's *adj, n* infidel; apostate

***fe'na** *np (Reg Gheg)* <**fe'**

fend· *vi* to break wind noiselessly: fart quietly

fe'ndë *nf* soft fart

fendo'së *nf* [*Bot*] puffball fungus (*Lycoperdon plumbeum*)

fene'r *nm* **1** lantern **2** headlight; flashlight **3** lighthouse; beacon **4** *(Fig)* guiding light

feni'kas *adj, n* [*Hist*] Phoenician

Feniki' *nf* [*Hist*] Phoenicia

feni'ks *nm (Book)* **1** phoenix **2** *(Fig)* highly intelligent person with extraordinary abilities in his field

fenome'n *nm (Book)* **1** phenomenon **2** *(Fig)* person with extraordinary talents and abilities

fenomena'l *adj* phenomenal

fenopla'st *nm* [*Chem*] phenolic plastic

***fenu'k** = **fëndu'k**

***fenje'rë** *nf (Reg Gheg)* = **fene'r**

***feoda'l** = **feuda'l**

***fequl** *nm* starch = **niseshte'**

***fequlue'r** *adj (fem ~ ore) (Old)* starchy

***fere'm** = **vere'm**

ferexhe' *nf (Old)* yashmak; veil

***feri'ç** = **ferri'ç**

***feri'g** *nm* east wind

feri'shte *nf* tot, baby

***ferk** = **fark**

ferma'n *nm* firman; edict

fermele' *nf (Old)* long vest embroidered with gold or silver thread worn mainly by women

ferme'nt *nm* fermentation agent = **tharm**

fermenti'm *nm ger* **1** <**fermento' ·n**, **fermento' ·het 2** fermentation

fermento' ·het *vpr* to be fermented

fermento' ·n *vt* to ferment

fermentua'r *adj (i)* fermented

ferme'r *nm* farmer; farm owner

fe'rmë *nf* **1** farm **2** *(HistPK)* state agricultural enterprise

fe'rmo *nf* [*Tech*] (on a machine) catch, lock, stop

fero'dë *nf* [*Tech*] Ferod (brand name of a brake lining): brake lining

***ferte'le** = **fërte'le**

ferr *nm* Hell

ferra'c *nm* [*Bot*] **1** greenbrier (*Smilax aspera*) **2** [*Ornit*] wren = **cinxami'**

ferraca'k

 I § nm **1** [*Ichth*] small spiny fish; small young carp **2** [*Ornit*] = **cinxami'**

 II § adj **1** having thorns, thorny, spiny **2** *(Fig Pej)* (like a burr) sticky

ferra'k

 I § nm [*Ornit*] = **cinxami'**

 II § adj having thorns, thorny, spiny

***ferra'të** *nf (Old)* railroad = **hekuru'dhë**

ferri'c

 I § nm

 II § adj **1** thorny, spiny **2** [*Ornit*] wren

ferrica'k [*Ornit*] wren = **cinxami'**

ferri'çe *nf* **1** [*Bot*] brier; thistle **2** *(Fig)* intrigue, plot **3** *(Reg)* fish bone

ferrëckë *nf* [*Bot*] **1** brier; thistle **2** *(Reg)* = **akaci'e**

fërrë nf **1** general term for a bush that grows wild and has thorny branches: brier **2** thorn **3** thorny branch; thorn **4** = **gjembaç 5** [Bot] blackberry, bramble bush *Rubus L.* **6** (Fig) something that causes us difficulties: impediment, trouble **7** (Fig) someone who is a pain in the neck
  ○ **fërrë e bardhë** [Bot] = **fërrëbardhë**
  ○ **fërrë e butë** [Bot] = **fërrëbutë**
  ○ **fërrë deti** [Bot] = **fërrëdet**
  ○ **fërrë gomari** [Bot] thistle
  ○ **fërrë e jashtme** [Bot] locust Robinia
  ○ **fërrë e keqe** [Bot] **1** bramble bush **2** Christ thorn, Jerusalem tree (*Paliurus spina-christi (aculeatus)*)
  ○ **fërrë krisht** common honey locust, three-thorned acacia (*Gleditsia triacanthos*)
  ○ **fërrë e kuqe** [Bot] *= **fërrëkuqe**
  ○ **fërrë në sy** speck in the eye
  ○ **Ferra e nisi, ferra e grisi.** "Began as a thorn, ended up as a thorn." {He/She} was trouble from beginning to end.
  ○ **fërrë rrodhe** [Bot] spiny clotbur, spiny cocklebur (*Xanthium spinosum*)
  ○ **fërrë shejtani** [Bot] sharp-leaved asparagus (*Asparagus acutifolius*)

fërrëbardhë nf [Bot] dog rose, dog hip (*Rosa canina*)

fërrëbutë nf [Bot] **1** asparagus (*Asperagus officinalis*) **2** iris-like plant (*Rubus tomentosus Borkth.*)

fërrëdet nm [Bot] = **akacie**

fërrëgjatë nf [Zool] porcupine

fërrëkace nf [Bot] dog rose, dog hip (*Rosa canina*)

fërrëkapëse nf [Bot] burdock (*Arctium*) = **rrodhe**

fërrëkuqe nf [Bot] Christ's thorn = **drizë**

fërrëlagëse nf [Bot] elm-leaved blackberry (*Rubus ulmifolius*)

fërrëmanzë nf [Bot] = **manafërrë**

fërrëmi nm [Bot] sharp-leaved asparagus (*Asparagus acutifolius*)

fërrënuse nf [Bot] spiny restharrow, thorny ononis (*Ononis spinosa*)

fërrëpatë nf [Bot] sow-thistle (*Sonchus*)

fërrës
  I § nm [Ornit] = **cinxami**
  II § adj thorny, prickly

ferribot nm ferry boat

ferribujkë nf [Bot] spiny restharrow (*Ononis spinosa*)

*__ferriç__ nm **1** = **filiç 2** ramrod; drumstick

ferrishte nf = **ferrishtë**

ferrishtë nf brier patch, bramble thicket

*__fërrkë__ nf (Reg Tosk) thistle

ferrnajë nf [Bot] = **ferrishtë**

ferro·het vpr to get all scratched up and torn; be pricked by a thorn

ferro·n vt **1** to enclose/line [] with a bramble fence **2** to scratch and tear [] with brambles; prick/scratch [] with something sharp

ferrok nm **1** iron pitchfork with long tines used to handle brambles, hay, straw, etc. **2** (Old) long stick ending in a point; goad

ferrolidhje nf [Tech] ferroalloy

ferromagnetizëm nm ferromagnetism

ferros· vt (Colloq·) **1** to enclose with a bramble fence **2** (Fig) to close permanently

  ○ <> **ferros· shtëpinë** to devastate <> and <>'s family

*__ferruc__ nm [Bot] sharp-leaved asparagus (*Asparagus acutifolius*)

*__ferruer__ adj (fem ~ore) (Old Regional Gheg) hellish, infernal

ferrzë nf [Ichth] starry ray (*Raja asterias*)

fes nm = **feste**

*__fesat__ nm intrigue

festar
  I § adj festive
  II § nm festival participant

feste nf **1** red fez **2** white woolen fez characteristically worn by Albanian men

festebardhë adj **1** wearing a white fez **2** (Fig) snow-peaked

festekuq adj wearing a red fez

festemënjanë adj wearing a fez askew

festë nf **1** holiday **2** holiday celebration, festival

festim nm ger **1** < **festo·n 2** celebration

Festim nm Festim (male name)

festival nm festival

festivalist n person involved with a festival

festo·n vt to celebrate; put on a celebration for

festonjës nm participant in a holiday celebration, celebrator

festueshëm adj (i) festive

*__fetak__ adj **1** religious **2**

fetar
  I § adj **1** religious **2** pious
  II § n believer; member of a religious faith

fetari nf religious devotion: piety

*__fetarisht__ adv (Old) in a religious manner, religiously

fetë nf **1** slice **2** flat pebble

fetish nm (Book) **1** object worshipped for its believed magical/spiritual power: idol, fetish **2** (Fig) something worshipped blindly

fetishizëm nm (Book) idolatry, fetishism

fetishizim nm ger (Book) < **fetishizo·n**

fetishizo·n vt (Book) to make [] into an object of blind worship; worship [] blindly; fetishize

*__feto·n__ vt (Old) to worship

*__fetuer__ adj (fem ~ore) (Old Regional Gheg) religious

feud nm [Hist] feudal land

feudal
  I § adj feudal
  II § nm feudal lord; feudal oppressor

feudalizëm nm feudalism

feudalo-borgjez adj feudal bourgeois

feudo-borgjez adj = **feudalo-borgjez**

fëdigë nf toil, drudgery, hardship

*__fëje·n__ vi to do wrong; sin

*__fëldish__ = **fildish**

*__fëlgro·n__ vi (of a horse) to shy; balk

*__fëli__ n **1** [Ethnog] crumbled white bread soaked in syrup and baked **2** = **poganik** *__3__ dough

*__fëltere__ nf (Reg) frying pan = **tigan**

*__fëllanzë__ nf (Reg) [Ornit] = **thëllëzë**

*__fëllegë__ = **fëlligë**

*__fëllezë__ nf (Reg) [Ornit] = **thëllëzë**

*__fëllënzë__ nf (Reg) = **thëllëzë**

fëlligë nf **1** slovenly woman: slattern, sloven **2** (Fig) = **fëlligështi**

fëlligë∙shti *nf* filthy work/business/matter/thing

fëllím *nm* gentle breeze

fëlliq∙
 I § *vt* **1** to make [] dirty: soil, sully, foul, smear, pollute **2** *(Fig)* to disgrace
 II § *vi* to defecate in an inappropriate place (in one's clothes, in the street, etc.), go in one's pants: make dirty, soil oneself
 ○ **e fëlliq∙ gojën 1** to use foul language **2** to argue using foul language

fëlliq∙et *vpr* **1** to get covered with dirt: get dirty **2** to fall into disgrace, be covered with shame; get a bad name
 ○ **fëlliq∙et vesh më vesh** "get dirty ear to ear" to get one's face all dirty

fëlliqash *adj, n* filthy (wretch)

fëlliqëm *adj (i)* = fëlliqur

fëlliqësí *nf* **1** filthiness; filth **2** filthy thing; dirty residue **3** dishonorable activity: dirty work

fëlliqësírë *nf* **1** = fëlliqështi **2** despicable person

fëlliqët *adj (i)* filthy, dirty

fëlliqur *nf ger* <fëlliq∙, fëlliq∙et

fëlliqur *adj (i)* **1** filthy; foul, putrid **2** sinful, disgraceful **3** obscene, dirty

*__fëmí__ = fëmijë

fëmíjë *nf with masc agreement* **1** child **2** *(Old)* family **3** *(Reg)* wife
 ○ **fëmijë djepi** infant, baby
 ○ **fëmijë gjiri** nursling
 ○ **Fëmijtë hanë kumbulla/thana, pleqve u mpihen dhëmbët** "The children eat plums, the old people's teeth get numb." *(Iron)* (Someone does something, and someone else worries about it.) Stop worrying about other people's problems.
 ○ **fëmijë i lindur jashtë kurore** child born out of wedlock
 ○ **fëmijë rrugësh** *(Pej)* ill-bred and ill-behaved child, foul-mouthed child; juvenile delinquent
 ○ **fëmijë vajc** crybaby

fëmijërí *nf* **1** childhood **2** *(Collec)* children

fëmijërísht *adv* **1** childishly **2** *(Old)* with the whole family

fëmijëror *adj* **1** of, for, or pertaining to children, children's; childlike **2** *(Pej)* childish

fëmijëvrasës *n* *(Book)* child murderer, infanticide

fëmijëvrasje *nf* *(Book)* infanticide

*__fëmíni__ = fëmijëri

*__fënd__ = fend

fëndosh *adj* = fënduk

fënduk *adj* cowardly; timid

fëndyell *nm (np ˜ j)* awl

*__fëner__ = fanar

fëng *nm (np ˜ gje)* **1** *[Bot]* cricket rhaphis *(Chrysopogon gryllus)* **2** = fëngíshtë

fëngíshtë *nf* **1** land full of cricket rhaphis **2** hard-to-work and infertile land

fërfëllí∙n *vi* = fërfëllo∙n

fërfëllím *nm ger* <fërfëllo∙n

fërfëllímë *nf ger* **1** <fërfëllí∙n **2** sound made by wings beating the air: fluttering, rustling

fërfëllízë *nf* flurry of cold wind and fine snow

fërfëllo∙het *vpr* = dridh∙et

fërfëllo∙n
 I § *vi* **1** to make the sound and movement of wings beating the air: flutter, flap; rustle **2** to tremble

 II § *vt* **1** to flap **2** to toss [] far away; expel **3** *(Fig)* (of an emotion) to stir/move <>

fërfërë *nf* *[Bot]* European privet *(Ligustrum vulgare)*

fërfërí∙n *vi* **1** to make a fluttering sound/movement **2** = dridh∙et **3** = end∙et

fërfërímë *nf ger* **1** <fërfërí∙n **2** fluttering or rustling sound

fërfërít∙ *vi* = fërfërí∙n

fërfërítje *nf ger* **1** <fërfërít∙ **2** = fërfërímë

*__fërfllazë__ *nf* snowdrift = mjellazë

fërfllízë *nf* snowstorm, snow flurry

fërg *nm (np ˜ gje)* frying pan

fërgesë *nf* fried food

*__fërgë__ *nf* spavin

fërgëllí *nf* shiver, quiver

fërgëllímë *nf ger* **1** <fërgëllo∙n, fërgëllo∙het **2** shiver, quiver, flutter **3** snort

fërgëllo∙n *vi* **1** to shiver, quiver, flutter **2** to snort

fërgícë *nf* omelette; fried food

fërgím *nm ger* <fërgo∙n, fërgo∙het

fërgo∙het *vpr* to get uncomfortably hot

fërgo∙n *vt* to fry [] (in a pan), sauté
 ○ **fërgo∙het me dhjamin e** {*pronominal adj*} to do everything on {*one's*} own, get by on {*one's*} own

fërguar *adj (i)* pan fried

*__fërgjyze__ *nf* *(Reg)* syphilis = frëngjyzë

fërkas *stem for 1st sg pres, pl pres, 2nd & 3rd sg subj, pind* <fërkat∙

fërkat∙ *vt* **1** to eat [] all up, feast; gobble [] up, swallow [] up; splurge **2** to squander, waste

fërkem *nm* tracks of a wild animal: spoor

fërkim *nm ger* **1** <fërko∙n, fërko∙het **2** friction

fërkimor *adj* **1** *[Ling]* fricative **2** *[Tech]* frictional

fërkíshtë *nf* substance used to rub/scrub/erase

fërko∙het *vpr* **1** to rub oneself **2** *(Fig)* to rub each other the wrong way: be on bad terms, have a misunderstanding, be at odds **3** to get worn out from constant rubbing/chafing **4** *(Fig Pej)* to use flattery to get on good terms: play up to, suck up to

fërko∙n *vt* **1** to rub; wipe; scuff **2** to massage **3** to stroke, pet, smooth
 ○ **fërko∙n krahët/kurrizin/shpatullat/shpinën/zverkun 1** *(Pej)* to butter <> up, curry favor with <> **2** to coddle/mollycoddle <>

*__fërkojcë__ *nf* **1** = fërkojse **2** cleaning tool

*__fërkojse__ *nf* woman's masseuse

fërkues *nm* one that rubs: masseur, eraser

*__fërlaçkë__ *nf* *(Reg)* slingshot, sling = hobe

fërlí *nf[Food]* **1** dish made by frying grated squash, eggs and milk **2** dish made of crumbled unleavened bread covered with syrup or honey **3** type of layered pastry made with eggs = palaník

fërlík *nm* lamb/kid/pig roasted on a spit

fërllazë *nf* sleet

*__fërmo∙n__ *vt* to shatter

fërnelë *nf* blasthole (of a mine)

fërnet *nm* dark-brown herb-flavored brandy

*__fërnetë__ *nf* = frëngji

*__fërngjyz__ *nm* *(Reg)* syphilis = frëngjyzë

fërshëlle∙n *vi* = fishkëlle∙n

fërshëllí *vi* = fishkëlle∙n

fërshëllímë *nf ger* **1** <fërshëlle∙n **2** = fishkëllímë

fërshëllore *nf[Ling]* sibilant

fërshëllye|s _adj_ = fishkëllyes

*__fërshti'z__ë _nf_ softly iterative noise: twittering (of birds); bleating (of sheep); rustling (of leaves)

fërte'le
  _I §_ _nf_ tattered piece of cloth: rag
  _II §_ _adv_ in tatters

*__fërtër__ _nm_ fan = fresko're

*__fërtëri'm__ _nm ger_ < fërtëro'·n

*__fërtëro'·n__ _vt_ to fan

fërto'më _nf_ **1** strong rope for tying down loads **2** (_Fig_) hindrance, obstacle

fërty'më
  _I §_ _nf (Reg)_ **1** great force, push; rush; sudden force, fury **2** strong wind; storm
  _II §_ _adv_ in a great rush

fërra'të _nf_ **1** coarse flour **2** = bollgu'r

*__fërrl__ë _nf_ spinning top

fërro'·n _vt_ **1** to grind away at [something hard] **2** to grind [] coarsely; grind [] up

fërru'e|s _nm_ rasp, grater

*__fësta'n__ = fusta'n

fëstëk _nm_ [_Bot_] = fisti'k

*__fëshfër|ësh__ _nm_ = fëshfë'she

fëshfëri·n _vi_ to make a rustling sound, swish

fëshfëri'më _nf_ rustling sound, swishing

*__fëshfëri't__| _stem for 1st sg pres, pl pres, 2nd & 3rd sg subj, pind_ < fëshfëri't·

fëshfëri't· _vt_ **1** to cause a rustling sound in []: rustle **2** = fëshfëri·n

fëshfëri'tje _nf ger_ = fëshfëri'më

fëshfë'sh
  _I §_ _nm_ = fëshfë'she
  _II §_ _onomat_ imitates a rustling sound
  III § _adv_ *in a whisper

fëshfë'she _nf (Colloq)_ light nylon raincoat

*__fëshkëll__| = fishkëll|

*__fëshllenj__ës
  _I §_ _adj_ sibilant
  _II §_ _n_ whistler

fët _adv (Colloq)_ right away, quickly
  ○ **fët e fët** in a very short time, very quickly, quick as a bunny

*__fët__| = ft|

fëti'gë _nf_ (_Reg_) epilepsy

*__fi__ _nm (Reg Gheg)_ = fi'një

fia'sko _nf_ fiasco

fi'bër _nf_ fiber

fibri'në _nf_ fibrin

fic· _vt_ to make [] soft and mushy

fic·et _vpr_ to get soft and mushy, become overripe

fi'ce _adj_ overripe, soft and mushy

*__fi'ckë__
  _I §_ _nf_ [_Ornit_] golden oriole (_Oriolus oriolus_)
  _II §_ _adj_ = fiç

fi'cur _adj (i)_ = fi'ce

fiç _adj_ soft and mushy, overripe

fiço'r _nm_ **1** pebble; cobblestone **2** (_Fig_) short little boy; short person **3** (_Old_) apprentice

fida'n
  _I §_ _nm_ seedling, sapling, shoot; scion, slip
  _II §_ _adj_ tall and straight

fidan|i'shte _nf_ plant nursery, seedling nursery

fide|i'zëm _nm_ [_Phil_] fideism

fidhe _np_ vermicelli (noodles)

fi'dh|ës _nm_ [_Bot_] Phoenician juniper (_Juniperus phoenicea_)

fier _nm_ [_Bot_] fern
  ○ **fier guri** stone cress _Asplenium_
  ○ **fier hënë** [_Bot_] moonwort _Botrychium lunaria_
  ○ **fier i krojeve** [_Bot_] maidenhair fern _Adianthum capillus-veneris_
  ○ **fier mashkull** [_Bot_] malefern _Dryopteris (Nephrodium) filixmas_
  ○ **fier i murit** [_Bot_] wall rue _Asplenium ruta muralis_

Fier _nm_ city and district in southwestern Albania: Fieri

Fier _nm_ town in southwest Albania

fier|a|jë _nf_ = fieri'shtë

fier|a'k _adj, n_ of/from Fieri

*__fier__ë _nf_ lentil = thje'rrëz

fier|fshi'kë _nf_ [_Bot_] bladder fern (_Cystopteris_)

fier|gu'r _nm_ [_Bot_] spleenwort (_Asplenium_)

fier|i'shte _nf_ **1** land covered with ferns **2** dried fern (used as thatch) **3** poor, unproductive land

fier|ku'qe _nf_ [_Zool_] large poisonous snake found in fern brakes

fier|o're
  _I §_ _nf_ = fieri'shtë
  _II §_ _np_ [_Bot_] the family of ferns _Polypodiaceae_

FIFA _abbrev_ (_French_) < Fédération Internationale Football Association International Football (Soccer) Association

*__figo'n__ _nm_ bellows

figura'nt _n_ [_Theat Cine_] walk-on character, supernumerary, extra

figurati'v _adj_ **1** figurative **2** figural

figu'rë _nf_ figure
  ○ **figurë e lehtë** (_Chess_) minor piece

figuri'në _nf_ figurine, figure

figuro'·n _vi_ to turn up, appear

figur|shëm _adj (i)_ figurative

*__fij__ _np_ < fill

*__fija'n__ _n_ godchild

fij|ata'k _adj_ in fibers; fibrous

fije
  _I §_ _nf_ **1** filament, strand, thread, yarn, staple **2** fiber **3** piece/scrap of fibrous material **4** thin piece; leaf **5** small amount: little bit **6** sheet **7** narrow islet in water **8** matchstick, match
  _II §_ _np_ < fill
  ○ **fije bari** blade of grass
  ○ **fije dëbore** snowflake
  ○ **fije fshese** bristle of a broom
  ○ **fije kashte** piece of straw
  ○ **fije letre** sheet of paper; scrap of paper
  ○ **fijet e majës** warp (in weaving)
  ○ **ësh-të në fije** to be fine, be doing well
  ○ **fije shkrepëse** match, matchstick

fije|de'nd|ur _adj_ densely woven

fije-fije _adv_ in strands, in threads

fije|gja'të _adj_ having long filaments: long-staple

fije|ho'llë _adj_ having fine fibers; (of grass) having thin blades

fije|i'mët _adj_ = fijeho'llë

fije|rra'llë _adj_ loosely woven, wide-meshed

fije|shku'rtër _adj_ having short filaments: short-staple; (of grass) having short stalks, short-bladed

fije|shpe'shtë _adj_ tightly woven, narrow-meshed = fijede'ndur

fije|to·*het vpr* = fijezo·*het*

fije|to·*n vt* = fijezo·*n*

fije|tra'shë *adj* having thick fibers; (of grass) having thick stalks

fi|jez *nf* short, thin fiber; wisp
  ◦ **fijez ndiesash** *(Old)* sensory nerve
  ◦ **fijez nervore** nerve fiber

fije|zi'm *nm ger* <fijezo·*n*, fijezo·*het*

fije|zo·*het vpr* to separate into strands: fray; unravel, ravel

fije|zo·*n*
  I § *vt* to divide [] into separate fibers; separate [] into strands
  II § *vi* = fijezo·*het*

fije|zo'r *adj* fibrous; threadlike, in threads

fi|jë'z *OR* **fije|zë** = fijez

fi|jo·*n*
  I § *vt* to make [] thin and weak; tire [] out, weaken
  II § *vi* (of snow) to fall in thin flakes
  ◦ **e fijo·*n* muhabetin** to be good at making conversation

fijo'r *adj* 1 = fijezo'r *2 (Old)* capillary

fij|u'k *nm [Bot]* plant with thread-like leaves: tall oat grass, tall meadow oat *(Arrhenatherum elatius)*

fik *nm (np ~ q) [Bot]* fig *(Ficus carica L.)*
  ◦ **fik arap** type of small black fig
  ◦ **fik deti/frengu** *[Bot]* Indian fig, prickly pear *(Opuntia ficus-indica Mill.)*
  ◦ **fik deti** prickly pear, Barbary fig, Indian fig *(Opuntia ficus-indica)*
  ◦ **fik rrenës** fig tree whose fruit drops off without ripening
  ◦ **fik shëngjinës** large-fruited fig that ripens in May or June; earliest-ripening fig

fik· *vt* 1 to extinguish, douse, quench, put/blow [] out, turn/switch [] off, wipe [] out 2 *(Fig)* to cause [] great harm, demolish, hurt [] badly
  ◦ <> **fik· derën** "extinguish <>'s family" **1** to do <> great harm, ruin <> **2** to leave <> all alone in the world

fik·*et *vpr* 1 to lose power gradually, get weak: get dim, fade out 2 to stop functioning: go dead, die out, go out 3 *(Fig)* to suffer badly, feel demolished; be finished, come to the end of one's rope 4 *(Reg)* to dry out a little, get partially dry
  ◦ **fik·*et gazit** *(Colloq)* to fall down laughing, laugh so hard as to get weak
  ◦ **fik·*et për gjumë** *(Colloq)* to be badly in need of sleep
  ◦ **s'<> fik·*et^{3sg} syri** <> *is* not fazed for a moment, <> *does* not blink an eye

fik|a|de'rë *adj* profligate = shtëpiprishës

fik|a'n *adj, n* 1 very poor (person), destitute (person) 2 (person) who is totally inept/confused

fik|a|na'k *adj* = fikade'rë

fik|a|plë'ng *nm* spendthrift, prodigal = plëngprishës

fik|a's *stem for 1st sg pres, pl pres, 2nd & 3rd sg subj, pind* <fika't·

fik|a't·
  I § *vt* 1 to dry [] out a bit; dry [] 2 = fik·
  II § *vi* to die down, fade out

fik|a't·*et *vpr* 1 = fik·*et 2 to dry out a little, get somewhat dry = fik·*et 3 to die down/out, damp down, fade out; get deadened

fik|a't|ës *nm* shock absorber

fik|a'tje *nf [Phys]* (wave) dampening

*fi'k|cë *nf [Ornit]* = beng

fi'kë *nf (Colloq)* destruction, eradication; terrible misfortune

fi'k|ës *nm* 1 extinguisher 2 *[Ornit]* = beng

fi'k|ët *nn (të)* sudden weakness, brief loss of consciousness: faint, swoon

fi'k|je *nf ger* <fik·, fi'k·*et

fik|o're *nf* strip of land planted in fig trees

fiks
  I § *adj (Book)* fixed, established, regular
  II § *adv* punctually, sharp, exactly, precisely

fiks|i'm *nm ger* 1 <fikso·*n* 2 fastening 3 fixation

fiks|o·*n vt* to fix [] in place: fasten, affix

fiks|u'es *nm [Chem]* 1 fixative = ngulitës 2 *[Tech]* lock pin

fi'k|të *adj (i)* of fig

fikti'v *adj* fictitious, fictional, fictive, imaginary

fik|th *nm* 1 *[Anat]* Adam's apple 2 unripe fig

fi'k|ur *adj (i)* 1 (of something that was previously lit) gone out, extinguished 2 no longer in working order: not working, dead 3 exhausted, dead tired 4 *(Fig)* very poor: broke

fi'kus *nm [Bot]* India rubber tree *(Ficus elastica)*

fil *nm* 1 *[Zool]* elephant 2 *[Chess]* bishop; minor piece 3 *[Naut]* gunwale

fila'n
  I § *n* someone whose name is not to be mentioned: a certain person
  II § *determiner* a certain __, some unnamed __

filantro'p
  I § *nm (Book)* philanthrope
  II § *adj* philanthropic

filantropi' *nf (Book)* philanthropy

filantropi'k *adj (Book)* philanthropic

*fila'qe *nf (Old)* water outlet

*fila're *adj* in a crisscrossed pattern

filarmoni' *nf* institution that presents symphony concerts, philharmonic

filateli' *nf* philately

filateli'st *n* philatelist

filatu'rë *nf* spinning mill

*filda'n = fidan

fildiko's *nm* strong cotton thread

fildispa'një *nf* plastic filament: fishline, plastic thread

fildi'sh *nm* ivory

fildi'sh|të *adj (i)* of or like ivory; ivory-colored

*filende'rë *nf (Old)* gun, rifle

filet|atri'çe *nf [Tech]* thread-cutting machine

filetatu'rë *nf [Tech]* threading, thread (on a screw/bolt)

file'të *nf* 1 filet 2 *[Bot]* Judas tree *(Cercis siliquastrum)* 3 screw thread

filet|i'm *nm* threading, screw thread

file'to *nf* screw thread

fileto·*n* to form a screw thread on []: thread []

*fili' *nf* family relationship, affiliation; type, race

filia'l *nm* affiliate

fili'ç *nm [Dairy]* plunger in a milk churn

filie'rë *nf [Tech]* drawing die

filigra'n *nm* 1 filigree 2 *[Postal]* watermark

fili'k *nm* 1 the young of a wild pig 2 = fili'qe

Fili'p *nm* Philip (male name)

filipïn|as
I § *adj* Philippine
II § *n* Filipino

Filipïn|e *np* Philippines

filïqe *nf* **1** buttonhole **2** woven loop

*__*__***filïstër** *nm* = filïz

filistïn
I § *nm (Book)* **1** Philistine **2** narrow-minded hypocrite
II § *adj* philistine

filïz
I § *nm* **1** [*Bot*] straight young shoot, tender offshoot: sprout, sprig, twig **2** seedling, sapling; slip **3** *(Fig)* promising young person; promising beginning **4** *(Fig)* heir, descendant, scion; family future
II § *adj (Fig)* **1** straight and tall **2** very young and tender

filiz·ëri *nf collec (Book)* young sprouts taken as a whole

filiz·o'·n *vi* to sprout

film *nm* **1** film **2** movie, film presentation
∘ **film i bardhë** [*Cine*] blank film
∘ **film me zë** "film with voice" talkie
∘ **film multiplikativ** animated film, cartoon
∘ **film rakord** [*Cine*] leader

filmïk *adj* [*Cine*] filmic, cinematographic

filmïm *nm ger* <filmo·n

film·o'·n *vt* to film

filmologjï *nf* [*Cine*] the art and science of motion picture making; cinematography

filmostat *nm* [*Cine*] reel container

filmotekë *nf* [*Cine*] film library

filo *formative prefix* love of ___: philo-

filogjenezë *nf* phylogenesis

filokserë *nf* [*Entom*] phylloxera

filollog *n* philologist

filollogjï *nf* philology

filollogjïk *adj* philological

*__*__***filosof** = filozof

*__*__***filosofïs·** *vi* to philosophize

filoshqiptar *adj* albanophilic

filozof *nm* philosopher

filozofï *nf* philosophy

filozofïk *adj* philosophical

filozofo'·n *vi* to philosophize

filtër *nm* filter

filtrïm *nm ger* **1** <filtro·n **2** filtration

filtr·o'·het *vpr* to filter through, pass through a filter

filtr·o'·n *vt* to filter

filtruar *adj (i)* filtered, clear

filtrues
I § *adj* used for filtering
II § *nm* filtering apparatus

filu'z *adj* penniless, flat broke

filxhan *nm* **1** small drinking cup: demitasse cup, teacup **2** ceramic insulator joining telephone or power lines: feed-through insulator **3** [*Bot*] foxglove (*Digitalis*)

filxhanash *adv*

filxhanthi *adv* = filxhanash

filzigen *nm (Reg)* [*Bot*] = borzilok

fill *nm (np ˜je)* **1** thread **2** filament of any kind: fiber, yarn; wire; hair **3** *(Fig)* connective element: strand, tie **4** *(Fig)* source, cause

∘ **nuk i gjend·et³ˢᵍ filli** it's a real mess
∘ **fill e gjilpërë** in full detail
∘ **fill e nga një fill** little by little
∘ **fill për fill 1** in exactly that way, in every detail, just so **2** single-handedly, entirely alone
∘ **fill e për pe** down to the slightest detail, thoroughly; to the very end, omitting nothing
∘ **fill e rend** each in turn
∘ **fill (i) vetëm** all alone, quite alone

fill *adv* **1** right away, immediately **2** directly **3** alone, single-handed

*__*__***filladhe** *nf* **1** notebook **2** newspaper circulation

fillak
I § *adj* grown tall and straight
II § *nm* **1** tall and straight tree **2** sapling **3** woolen bed covering for a baby

fillak·o'·het *vpr* to take off one's coat, be in shirtsleeves

fillak·o'·n *vt* to take off []'s coat, leave [] in shirtsleeves

fillar
I § *nm* long strand; strand
II § *adv* in a long strand

fillçë *nf* loosely woven cloth

*__*__***fille** *nf* = fije

filles·ë *nf* **1** = fillïm **2** initial form, origin **3** [*Tech*] threaded part of a screw/nut/bolt: thread, threading

fillestar
I § *adj* **1** elementary, beginning, rudimentary **2** initial **3** original, aboriginal
II § *n* beginner; novice, tyro

*__*__***fillëm** *adj (i)* = fillestar

fillër *adv* alone, single-handedly

fillër·o'·n *vi* to live alone, stay by oneself; live on one's own

fillikat *adv* all alone, by oneself; on one's own

fillikate *nf* [*Bot*] anemone (*Anemone*)

fillïm *nm ger* **1** <fillo·n, fillo·het **2** beginning, source, start, genesis, onset **3** original/initial form
∘ **fillim e mbarim** "beginning and ending" **1** everyone, everything **2** during the whole time, all the time

fillïme *np* **1** <fillïm **2** rudiments; elementary/basic knowledge

fillimïsht *adv (Book)* originally, in the beginning, at first, at the start

*__*__***fillimtar** *adj* inaugural; elementary

fillmirë *adj* honest, forthright, honorable

fill·o'·n
I § *vt* to begin, start, commence
II § *vi* **1** to show first signs **2** to originate
∘ **fillo·n radhë të re** "start a new row" to begin a whole new page

fillor *adj* elementary, beginning, primary

fillore *nf* **1** *(Colloq)* (first four years of) elementary school: primary grades **2** wool covering, wool rug **3** wooden shuttle on a loom *__*__***4** ramrod, rod

fillorïst
I § *n (Old)* pupil in elementary school
II § *adj (Old)* attending or teaching in elementary school

*__*__***fillosof** = filozof

fillpres·ë *nf* shears for cutting metal rods

fillrojt·ës *nm* maintenance man for telephone lines: lineman, linesman

fillshtru·es *nm* man who strings telephone lines

filltar *n* **1** pioneer, inaugurator **2** beginner, neophyte

fillthi adv all alone, all by oneself

fillue̱s nm beginner

fillzi adj (fem sg ˜ ez, masc pl ˜ inj, fem pl ˜ eza) ill-intentioned, malicious, nasty, spiteful

****fina̱k** adj, nm (pl ˜ q) = fino̱k

fina̱le nf finale

****finali̱st** nm [Sport] finalist

fina̱ncë nf finance

financia̱r adj financial

financie̱r nm financier

financi̱m nm ger <financo̱ ·n

financo̱ ·n vt to finance

financue̱s
I § adj providing the finances: financing
II § n financier

fine̱së nf finesse, delicacy, refinement

fi̱në np Finnish people, Finns

****fi̱ng** nm 1 ace (in cards) 2 deuce (in dice)

****fi̱n‖i** obl (Reg Gheg) <fi

****Fini** nf (Old) = Finla̱ndë

fini̱k nm [Bot] date palm (Phoenix dactylifera)

fi̱nk nm [Ornit] chaffinch (Fringilla coelebs)

finlande̱z
I § adj Finnish
II § n Finn

Finla̱ndë nf Finland

finlandi̱sht adv in Finnish (language)

finlandi̱shte nf Finnish language

fino̱k
I § adj wily, crafty; clever
II § nm 1 wily villain 2 [Bot] fennel

finoke̱ri
I § adj wily, crafty
II § nf [Bot] fennel (Foeniculum vulgare)

****fino̱q** np <fino̱k

fi̱nte nf [Soccer] feint, fake
  ∘ finte me goditje [Soccer] false kick
  ∘ finte me trup [Basketball] body fake

fi̱një nf lye, alkaline solution

finjëzo̱ ·n vt [Spec] to rinse away the unwanted parts from [something solid]

finjo̱s· vt to wash [] in lye; soak [] in lye

finjo̱s·et vpr 1 to become emaciated; become very pale 2 (of soil) to lose fertility, become worn out

fiore̱t nm [Fencing] foil

fi̱q np <fi̱k
  ∘ fiq rrotullarë long round figs (suitable for hanging in a string)
  ∘ fiq vejuk variety of small dark fig

fiqfi̱q nm [Ornit] small bird with a thin chirp

fiqi̱r nm (Colloq) mind = me̱ndje

Fiqiri nm Fiqiri (male name)

fira̱jkë adj (Reg) hollow = fyl

****fira̱s·** vt to plug

****firaû̱(n)** nm (Reg Gheg) 1 pharaoh 2 gypsy

firaû̱n nm (Crude Insult) malicious and dishonest person: rotten bastard

Fire̱nce nf Florence (Italy)

fi̱rë
I § nf 1 loss in quantity (due to shrinkage, spillage, evaporation) 2 waste
II § adv empty

****fi̱rëz = thje̱rrëz**

firifi̱u adj (ColloqImpolite) immature and empty-headed: silly, batty

firika̱c nm mattock

firi̱m nm ger 1 <firo̱ ·n 2 loss in quantity (due to shrinkage, spillage, evaporation) 3 waste

****firllî̱k** nm [Invert] beetle

fi̱rmë nf 1 signature 2 name of an author 3 [Commerc] industrial/business firm

firmo̱ ·n vt to affix a signature to []: sign = nënshkrua̱ ·n

firmonje̱s n signatory, signer

firmo̱s· vt = firmo̱ ·n

fi̱ro nf = fi̱rë

firo̱ ·n
I § vi 1 to undergo a loss/reduction: dwindle, shrink, spill, evaporate, lose weight; get weak, languish, wane; become empty 2 to disappear without a trace
II § vt to decrease [] in amount; cause [] to disappear

firo̱më nf (Colloq) = fry̱më

firo̱s· = firo̱ ·n

firua̱n nm good-for-nothing

fi̱ruk adj 1 base, cowardly **2 hollow, empty

****fi̱rzë** nf [Bot] fern

fis nm 1 clan, tribe 2 (Colloq) ethnic group, nation, nationality 3 family relationship; family relation, relative 4 (Old) family of nobles, noble family 5 genus
  ∘ do të vejë në fis (Pej) family character will eventually show through: blood will tell

fisana̱k adj related by blood

****fisarmoni̱kë = fizarmoni̱kë**

fi̱sëm adj (i) of good family; of superior stock, well-bred; noble

fise̱ri nf 1 nobility 2 kinship

fiska̱jë
I § nf 1 young seedling: sprout, shoot; sprig, twig 2 thin stick/rod: withe, switch 3 jetting liquid: spurt
II § adj straight and thin as a twig

fiska̱l adj [Fin] fiscal

fi̱skël nf 1 young branch 2 thin withe

fiski̱ nf jetting liquid: spurt

fis kultur‖ = fizkultur‖

fisni̱k
I § adj noble
II § nm 1 person of high moral character: noble person; generous person 2 [Hist] nobleman, gentleman

Fisni̱k nm Fisnik (male name)

fisni̱ke nf 1 (Old) noblewoman 2 (Reg) bride; lady of the house (as a term of respectful address)

fisnike̱ri nf nobility, nobleness
  ∘ fisnikëria juaj (Old) your honor (as a term of respectful address)

fisnikëri̱m nm ger <fisnikëro̱ ·n, fisnikëro̱ ·n

fisnikëri̱sht adv nobly

fisnikëro̱·het vpr 1 to gain in nobility, improve in moral character 2 [Spec] to improve in breed 3 to become purified and improved

fisnikëro̱ ·n vt 1 to ennoble 2 [Spec] to improve the breed of [] 3 to purify and improve []

fisniko̱ ·n = fisnikëro̱ ·n

fisno̱r adj of or pertaining to the kin group: tribal, kin-related

fi̱sshëm adj (i) 1 from a good family 2 noble 3 of superior stock, well-bred

****fista̱k** nm cornhusk

****fista̱n = fusta̱n**

fistik *nm* **1** [*Bot*] stone pine *(Pinus pinea)* **2** pine nut of the stone pine

fistul *nf* [*Med*] fistula

fishe *nf* [*Electr*] jack (connector)

fishek
I § nm **1** cartridge (for a gun); bullet **2** cone-shaped paper cup/container **3** small, tube-shaped object
II § adv (Colloq) fast as a bullet
○ **ësh·të fishek 1** *(Colloq)* to have nothing left, be flat broke **2** to be a babe in the woods
○ **fisheku i fundit** "last cartridge" the last possibility, last chance
○ **ësh·të fishek i lagur** "be a wet cartridge" to be a paper tiger, have a bark worse than one's bite
○ **fishek në pajë** "cartridge in the dowry" (given by the bride's family for her husband to shoot her with if she is ever unfaithful to him)
○ **fishek pa barut** "cartridge without powder" worthless person: good-for-nothing
○ **ësh·të fishek që s'shkrep·**[3sg] "be a cartridge that *doesn't* fire" **1** to be of no help **2** to be cowardly

fishekore *nf* cartridge belt; cartridge case

*****fishekzar** *(Reg)* = **fishekzjarr**

fishekzjarr *nm* (fireworks) rocket; (fireworks) rocket-launcher; light from fireworks

fishë *nf* **1** fiche, filecard **2** [*Electr*] = **fishe**

fishk· *vt* **1** to cause [] to wither, dry out **2** *(Fig)* to weaken the force of []: soften, lessen

fishk·et *vpr* **1** to wither, shrivel up; fade away; become wrinkled **2** *(Fig)* to become listless/apathetic; flag, droop; become numb **3** *(Fig)* to wane, fade; become pale

fishkaraq *adj* **1** all wrinkled/shriveled up **2** sluggish, clumsy

*****fishkë** *nf* = **ferriç**

fishkëlle·n
I § vi **1** to whistle **2** to hiss; whoosh; (of a siren) wail
II § vt to express disapproval by whistling/hissing at []: hiss
○ <> **fishkëlle·n në vesh** "blow/whisper/sing in <>'s ear" to egg <> on

fishkëllenjës *nm* [*Ornit*] willow warbler *(Phylloscopus trochillus)*
○ **fishkëllenjësi gushëbardhë** [*Ornit*] Bonelli's warbler *Phylloscopus bonelli Viell.*
○ **fishkëllenjësi gushëverdhë** [*Ornit*] = **fishkëllenjës**

fishkëllim *nm ger* **1** <**fishkëlle 2** = **fishkëllimë**

fishkëllimë
I § nf ger **1** <**fishkëlle 2** whistling sound
II § adv at great speed, with a great rush

fishkëllo·n = **fishkëlle·n**

fishkëllor *adj* [*Ling*] sibilant

fishkëllyes *adj* **1** whistling **2** [*Ling*] sibilant

*****fishkëri** *nf* dessication, withering; triteness

fishkët *adj (i)* = **fishkur**

fishkje *nf ger* <**fishk·**, **fishk·et**

*****fishkull** *nm* [*Ornit*] finch *(Fringilla)*

fishkur *adj (i)* **1** withered, shriveled up; faded; wrinkled **2** *(Fig)* listless, apathetic; numb **3** *(Fig)* weakened; faded; pale

*****fishlle·n** = **fishkëlle·n·**

fishnjar *nm* **1** [*Zool*] stone marten, beech marten *(Mustela foina, Martes foina)* **2** harpoon

*****fishnjollë** *nf (Old)* craftiness, wiliness

fit
I § adv (Colloq) with no advantage to either party: even Steven, all even
II § nm **1** wedge **2** *(Fig)* provoking action: provocation, incitement

fitesë *nf* profit, gain; net income

fitëz *nf (Dimin)* **1** small wedge **2** wedge-shaped metal bobbin (in the flying shuttle of a loom)

fitil *nm* **1** wick **2** fuse (used to set off explosives) **3** [*Text*] raw cotton yarn **4** thin and resistant yarn used as warp

fitilvënës *nm* person trained to set the fuse of an explosive device

fitim *nm ger* **1** <**fito·n**, **fito·n 2** profit; win **3** *(Old)* victory

fitimdhënës *adj* **1** profitable **2** advantageous

*****fitimmët** *adj (i)* = **fitimprurës**

fitimprurës *adj* profitable, remunerative, gainful; successful, valuable; productive, useful

fitimshëm *adj (i)* = **fitimprurës**

fitimtar
I § adj **1** winning, victorious **2** successful, profitable
II § n winner, victor; achiever

fitme *np* provoking actions, provocations, incitements

fito·het *vpr* [*Spec*] to be generated from a process or from combination of substances

fito·n
I § vt **1** to get [something good]: gain **2** to get for one's efforts: earn **3** to achieve, acquire **4** to win **5** to produce, generate **6** *(Colloq)* to get [something bad]: suffer
II § vi to profit, gain benefit
○ **fito·n bukën e gojës** to make one's living, earn one's livelihood
○ **fito·n flamurin** "win the flag" *(Book)* to get the prize, be victorious, win
○ **fitoi kush fitoi** some people really did well
○ **fito·n me grushte** "gain by handfuls" to make a lot of money
○ **fito·n me lopatë** "earn by the shovelful" *(Colloq)* to do really well for oneself, earn a lot: *be making* a pile
○ **fito·n pafajësinë** [*Law*] to win on appeal, be exonerated
○ **fito·n pesë e ha· gjashtë** "earn five and spend six" to spend more than one earns
○ **fito·n pesë e prish· gjashtë** "earn five and spend six" to spend more than one earns
○ **fito·n pikë** to make points, gain favor
○ **fito·n truall** to gain territory: spread out, extend one's activities, extend one's space
○ **fito·n thellë** to win by a large margin: win big
○ <> **fito·n zemrën** to gain/win <>'s heart

fitore *nf* win, victory
○ **i fitores** bringing victory: winning
○ **fitore me tuç** [*Wrestling*] win by a fall

Fitore *nf* Fitore (female name)

fituar *adj (i)* **1** won, gained **2** victorious **3** achieved by experience (rather than innate): acquired

fitues
I § nm winner, victor
II § adj winning, victorious

fitueshëm *adj (i)* **1** winning, victorious **2** profitable

fïu *adv (Colloq)* in a flash, with a swish, quickly

fizarmon|ic|ïst *n* accordionist
fizarmon|ik|ë *nf* accordion
*****fïz|ë** *nf* seedling
fiz|k
  I § *adj* physical
  II § *nm* physique
fizik|a'n *n* physicist
fizik|a'nt = fizika'n
fizik|ë *nf* **1** physics **2** (*Colloq*) textbook on physics
fizik|ïsht *adv* **1** physically **2** in terms of physics
fizik|oushtar|a'k *adj* pertaining to military physical training
fizio|lo'g *n* physiologist
fizio|logj|i *nf* physiology
fizio|logj|ik *adj* physiological
fizio|nom|i *nf* physiognomy
fizio|terap|i *nf* physiotherapy
fiz|kultur|a'l *adj* = fizkulturo'r
fiz|kultu'r|ë *nf* physical culture
fiz|kultur|ïst *n* physical culturist
fiz|kultur|o'r *adj* of or pertaining to physical culture
*****fja'k|ë** = fla'kë
fjal|ama'n *adj, n* talkative, chattering (person)
*****fjal|âmb|ël** *adj (Reg Gheg)* = fjalëmb'ël
*****fjal|âmb|ël|si** *nf(Reg Gheg)* = fjalëmb'ël|si
fjal|amujt|a's *adv* in a word battle
fjal|a'shp|ër *adj* = fjalëvra'zhdë
fjal|ë *nf* **1** word **2** something said: words **3** speech **4** talk, conversation **5** word of honor, promise **6** matter under discussion, matter at hand: question at hand, subject, topic **7** skill with verbal expression: a way with words
  ○ **fjalë ari** "words of gold" *(Book)* wise saying
  ○ **Fjala e burrit, pesha e gurit.** "The word of a man, the weight of a stone." *(Prov)* A man's word is his bond.
  ○ **Fjala fjalë e puna punë.** "Words are one thing and work is another." Talk must be complemented by action.
  ○ **fjal|ë fluturake** "flying words" adage
  ○ **fjala e fundit 1** most recent development: the latest word **2** authoritative pronouncement: the final word **3** final thought/opinion
  ○ **fjal|ë e halë** gossip, rumors; chitter-chatter
  ○ **fjalë e huajtur** [*Ling*] loanword
  ○ **Fjala ka këmbë.** "The word has legs." News gets around fast.
  ○ **fjalë kryq** crossword
  ○ **fjalë e kundërt** [*Ling*] antonym
  ○ **fjalë e lashtë** old saying, adage
  ○ **fjalë e mbrëmë** last and final word
  ○ **fjal|ë me jastëk** reasonable words, sensible talk
  ○ **fjal|ë me kripë** apt/wise words
  ○ **fjalë me qokë** thoughtful words
  ○ **fjal|ë me vend** witty remark
  ○ **Fjalët i merr era.** "The wind takes words." *(Prov)* Spoken words don't last (they should be down on paper).
  ○ **fjalë në erë** empty words
  ○ **fjalë në hava** silly talk
  ○ **fjala nxjerr fjalën** one topic leads to another: one thing leads to another
  ○ **fjalë pas fjalë** word for word: verbatim, literally
  ○ **fjal|ë petake** appropriate language/words
  ○ **fjalë për fjalë** word for word: verbatim, literally
  ○ **fjal|ë e përbërë** [*Ling*] compound word

  ○ **fjalë pleqsh** sage words
  ○ **fjal|ë e rëndë** offensive language/word
  ○ **fjalë rrug|ësh 1** indecent word, dirty word **2** common gossip, rumor
  ○ **fjal|ë rrumbullake 1** inappropriate words **2** words without influence, words that cut no ice
  ○ **fjalë sokaku** common gossip, rumor
  ○ **Fjalën të gjatë, punën të thatë.** *(Prov)* Too much talk and too little action.
  ○ **Fjalët të ëmbëla, punët të tharta.** Sweet talk with little substance. Big words, but not much action.
  ○ **fjal|ë turpi** bad language, dirty word
  ○ **fjal|ë e urtë** wise saying, proverb, maxim
  ○ **fjala vjen** for instance, for example
  ○ **fjal|ë e vjetër** old saying
fjalë|bu't|ë *adj* soft-spoken
fjal|ë|form|ïm *nm* word formation
fjal|ë|form|u|e|s *adj* [*Ling*] pertaining to word formation: derivational
fjal|ë|gja't|ë *adj, n* long-winded (person)
fjal|ë|ke'q *adj* that speaks ill of others
fjal|ë|ko't|ë *adj* speaking aimless nonsense: nonsensical; rambling
fjal|ë|kry'q *nm* crossword
fjal|ë|kurs|y'er *adj* talking sparingly: of few words; laconic
fjal|ë|ma'dh *adj* **1** garrulous **2** using flowery language: grandiloquent, bombastic
fjal|ë|ma'tur *adj* reflective in speech
fjal|ë|mb'ël *adj* **1** sweet-talking, honey-tongued; soft-spoken, smooth-talking **2** affable
fjal|ë|mb'ël|si *nf* **1** honeyed speech; gentle speech **2** affability
fjal|ë|mi'r|ë *adj* speaking kindly of others, complimentary; supporting
fjal|ë|mpre'ht|ë *adj* sharp as a tack, quick-witted = gojëmpre'ht|ë
fjal|ë|ndrysh|u|e|s *adj* [*Ling*] inflectional, paradigmatic
fjal|ë|pa'k|ë *adj* taciturn; of few words
fjal|ë|pa'k|të *adj* = fjalëpa'kë
fjal|ë|përfja'l|shëm *adj* (i) word-for-word
fjal|ë|plu'mb *adj* offensive in speech
fjal|ë|pre'|r|ë *adj* peremptory, curt; concise, terse
fjal|ë|rëndë *adj* offensive in speech; gruff, rude
*****fjal|ë|rondoko'p** *nm* swaggerer
fja'l|ë|s *nm* [*Ling*] the word list in a dictionary: vocabulary, lexicon
fjal|ë|so'r *adj (Book)* lexical
fjal|ë|shku'rtër *adj* taciturn; concise, terse
fjal|ë|shpa't|ë *adj* bold in speech, sharp-tongued
fjal|ë|shpe'jt|ë *nf* game the object of which is to repeat tongue twisters quickly and without mistakes
fjal|ë|shtr'u|a'r *adj* calm-voiced
fjal|ë|shu'm|ë *adj* talkative, garrulous, loquacious
fjal|ë|ta'r *adj, n* eloquent (person) = gojëta'r
fjal|ë|tërku'z|ë *adj* needlessly drawing out the conversation: long-winded, talkative
fjal|ë|to'·het *vpr* = fjalo's·et
fjal|ë|to'·n *vi* to have words: argue, quarrel, wrangle
fjal|ë|to'r *n* [*Ethnog*] **1** herald **2** go-between
fjal|ë|thy'e|r *adj* = besëthy'er
fjalë|vra'zhd|ë *adj* speaking in a rough tone, offensive in speech, nasty-tongued

fjalëz nf(Dimin) 1 <fjalë 2 [Ling] particle

fjalëzjarrtë adj (Poet) speaking inspiringly: inspirational

fjali nf 1 [Ling] sentence; clause *2 proposition
○ **fjali dykryegymtyrëshe** clause/sentence with a complete subject and a complete predicate
○ **fjali njëkryegymtyrëshe** sentence with either a complete subject or a complete predicate but not both
○ **fjali rrjedhore** [Ling] result clause

fjalim nm 1 speech, lecture *2 (Old) chat, talk
○ **fjalim kauçuk** rambling speech full of ambiguity
○ **fjalim i përmortshëm** funeral oration

*__fjalis__ stem for 1st sg pres, pl pres, 2nd & 3rd sg subj, pind <fjalit·

*__fjalit·__ vt = fjalëto·n

fjalo·het vpr = fjalos·et

fjalo·n vi to speak; converse

fjalor nm 1 dictionary 2 lexicon

fjalorth nm 1 pocket dictionary 2 vocabulary list, glossary

fjalos·
I § vi 1 to converse, carry on conversation 2 to speak, talk; tell
II § vt to say

fjalos·et vpr 1 to carry on conversation, converse 2 to have an argument: quarrel

fjalosës n talker

*__fjalti__ nf(Old) talkativeness, loquacity

*__fjarim__ nm ger <fjaro·n

*__fjaro·n__ vt to fling [] upwards, send [] flying

*__fje·n__ = fëje·n

*__fjerë__ nf [Zool] = nepërkë

*__fjerëz__ nf [Bot] = thjerrëz

*__fjesë__ = fshesë

*__fjeshtë__ = thjeshtë

fjet stem for pdef, opt, adm, part <fl·et
○ **Fjettë të mirën!** "Let {} sleep the good sleep!" (Curse) I hope {} dies!, {} can go to hell!

fjetës
I § adj sleeping, dormant
II § n sleeper

fjetësi nf lethargy; sleepiness

*__fjetgjer__ nm [Bot] Balkan maple (Acer obtusatum)

fjetje nf ger <fl·et, fli·het

fjetore nf large room used for sleeping a large group of people: dormitory, barracks

fjetur
I § part <fle·, fli·het
II § adj (i) 1 sleeping; sleepy 2 stagnant, standing 3 (Fig) sluggish, listless 4 latent
III § adv 1 asleep 2 (Fig) sluggishly, listlessly; not alert, half asleep 3 (Euph) lifeless
○ **paska**^(opt) **fjetur zbuluar** (Iron) "{} must have slept uncovered" 1 {} is sure in one fine mood!, {} is in a terrible mood 2 {} must be dreaming!

fjolla-fjolla adv in thick strands one after another

fjollë
I § nf 1 skein of flax yarn 2 long, loose mass of substance: strand, wisp, thread
II § adv in strands

*__fjongë__ = fjongo

fjongo
I § nf 1 hair ribbon (usually silk) 2 ribbon
II § adv loosely tied

fjord nm [Geog] fjord

*__fjoretë__ nf rapier, foil

*__fjû__ adv (Reg Gheg Colloq) = flu

*__fjuro·n__ vi (Reg Gheg) to flee

*__fkinj__ = fqinj

*__fku·l__ = fequl

*__flaç__ 2nd sg subj <flet·

flagrancë nf(Book) flagrant error (flagrante delicto)

flagrant adj (Book) flagrant

*__flags__ = flakër

*__flagsim__ nm ger 1 <flagso·n 2 inflammation

*__flagso·n__ vt to inflame

*__flagsuer__ adj (fem ~ ore) (Old) inflammatory

*__flagsueshëm__ adj (i) inflammable

*__flâjkë__ nf(Reg Gheg) wine must

flak· vt 1 to throw, hurl, fling; throw away; toss 2 to smack 3 (Fig) to reject, renounce, cast off, eject
○ [] **flak· në mes të rrugës/katër rrugëve** to abandon [] completely
○ [] **flak· në rrugë (të madhe)** to abandon [] completely
○ [] **flak· në udhë/mes të udhës/udhë të madhe/mes të katër udhëve** to kick [] out into the street
○ [] **flak· tej/tutje** to reject [] completely; cast [] out

flak·et vpr 1 to attack suddenly and violently *2 to hop/run away: bolt

flakadan
I § nm 1 blazing fire; large flame 2 [Ethnog] ritual bonfire 3 (Fig Poet) torchbearer
II § adv flaming, ablaze

flakar nm quick-baking thin bread

flakaresh nm slap, slap in the face, box on the ear

flakë
I § nf 1 flame, burning flame; blazing fire 2 (Fig) flash
II § adj, adv blazing, flaming
III § adv completely; immediately: in a flash
○ **flakë e flakë** everywhere, entirely, completely
○ **flakë kashte** short-lived burst of energy, momentary enthusiasm
○ **flakë për flakë** with immediate retorts back and forth, with an immediate retort; blow for blow
○ **ësh·të flakë pushke** to be light on her feet, be very quick
○ **Flaka të djeg, prushi të ngroh.** "A flame burns you, an ember warms you." (Prov) Better stick with what is stable and constant, rather than chase after what looks good for the moment.
○ **ësh·të flakë e zjarr** "be flame and fire" 1 to be very lively and adept 2 to be harsh and cruel

flakëhedhës nm [Mil] soldier armed with flame-thrower

flakëhedhëse nf [Mil] 1 flamethrower 2 fire-starting apparatus

flakëkuq nm (Colloq) large fire, bonfire

flakëri·n
I § vi 1 to flame 2 to blaze brightly 3 to flash; glisten 4 to flash explosively, fulminate
II § vt to fling, hurl

flakërim nm ger 1 <flakëro·n, flakëro·het 2 = flakërimë

flakërimë
I § nf ger 1 <flakëri·n 2 bright flash, flash of dazzling light 3 high fever; hot flashes 4 slap
II § adj 1 lightning fast, extremely fast 2 blushing

III § *adv* quick as a flash, instantly

flak·ëri·s *stem for 1st sg pres, pl pres, 2nd & 3rd sg subj, pind* <flak·ëri·t·

flak·ërishta *np* tinder, dry kindling

flak·ëri·t
I § *vt* to fling, hurl
II § *vi* to give off flames

flak·ëri·t·et *vpr* <flak·ëro·het

flak·ëri·tje *nf ger* <flak·ëri·t·, flak·ëri·t·et

flak·ëro·het *vpr* to flare, flare up; glow red

flak·ëro·n
I § *vi* **1** to give off flames **2** to blaze, burn bright **3** to flare up **4** to give off a red glow **5** to shine bright **6** *(Fig)* to feel on fire **7** to rush; rush away
II § *vt* **1** to scorch, singe, char **2** *(Fig)* to inflame with feeling **3** to throw, hurl, fling; hurl oneself **4** to slap

flak·ëru·ar *adj (i)* **1** flaming, blazing **2** extremely hot **3** reddened

flak·ëru·es *adj* **1** flaming, blazing **2** scorching **3** sparkling

flak·ëru·eshëm *adj (i)* ardent, flaming, passionate

flak·ëso·het *vpr* = flak·ëro·het

flak·ëso·n *vt* = flak·ëro·n

flak·ëshu·es·e *nf[Mil]* flash hider (on a gun)

flak·ëvën·es *adj[Mil]* incendiary

fla·kje *nf ger* <flak·, flak·et

flako·n *vi* to give off flames: blaze

flako·n *nm [Med]* medicine bottle

flako·re *nf* fire with dry tinder, burning tinder, flare-up

***flakta·r** *nm (Old)* lamplighter

flak·të *adj (i)* **1** blazing, flaming, burning **2** fiery; passionate; fervent, ardent

***flak·ue·shëm** *adj (i) (Old)* blazing

fla·kur *adj (i)* discarded, rejected

flak·uri·më *nf* = flakare·sh

flak·uro·n *vi* = flak·ëro·n

fla·më
I § *nf* **1** cholera **2** *[Med]* epilepsy **3** *[Med]* chronic influenza, bad flu **4** *(Reg)* catarrh, cold **5** *[Bot]* disease that ruins grapes/wine **6** *[Folklore]* figure who causes epilepsy or other bad diseases
II § *adj (positioned before a noun)* terrible, awful; annoying

flamë·ma·dh *adj* **1** flaming, in flames **2** *(Curse)* be damned! (with a terrible pox)

flamë·nga·rë *adj, n* epileptic

flam·os·et *vpr* to catch the flu; get a bad cold

flam·os·ur
I § *adj (i)* **1** having a serious disease **2** cursed
II § *nf (e)* serious disease, pox

fla·muj *np* <fla·mur

flamu·r OR **fla·mur** *nm* **1** flag **2** pennant, standard, banner **3** *(Fig)* inspirational symbol **4** children's game played by two opposing teams: capture-the-flag **5** *[Hist]* a territorial unit created by the Ottomans as a military and later administrative entity to take the place of the patriarchal clan organization of certain regions of Albania = bajra·k **6** *(Reg)* peritoneum = ri·zë **7** *[Bot]* large upper posterior petal of legume flowers: standard, banner, vexillum
    ◦ **flamuri kuq e zi** red-and-black flag: Albanian national flag
    ◦ **flamur me gjysmë shtize** flag at half mast

◦ **flamur tranzitor** flag (awarded for merit) which passes from one winner to the next

flamu·ras *adv*

flamur·mbajt·ës *n* = flamurta·r

flamurta·r
I § *nm* **1** flag-bearer, standard bearer **2** chief of a bajrak = bajrakta·r **3** bearer of the banner carried by the wedding party = bajrakta·r
II § *adj* flag-bearing

fland *nm [Publ]* type matrix

flani·kth *nm* **1** chicken coop; poultry pen *2 (Old)* case, crate; cage *3 (Old)* framework

fla·nxhë *nf [Tech]* flange

fla·s *stem for 1st sg pres, 1st & 3rd pl pres, 2nd & 3rd sg subj* <fle·t·
    ◦ **Flas ndryshe me të!** *(Threat)* I'll fix him!

fla·shk·et *vpr* **1** to wither, shrivel up; get wrinkled **2** to wiry get soft and mushy

***fla·shk·azi** *adv* askew, awry

fla·shkë *nf* **1** grain chaff **2** sliver, splinter **3** spurt; trickle

flashkë·si *nf* softness, sluggishness

fla·shkët *adj (i)* **1** lacking firmness: soft and mushy; limp, flabby, flaccid **2** lacking vigor: sluggish, listless **3** lacking strength: feeble, pale

***flashko·n** *vt* to weaken, debilitate

fla·tër *nf* wing

flatra|drejtë *np [Entom] (Orthoptera)*

flatra|fo·rtë *np [Entom]* order of beetles *(Coleoptera)*
    ◦ **flatrafortë shumëpikësh** *[Entom]* cochineal insects *Coccinellidae*

flatra|lëkur·o·rë *np [Entom]* earwigs *Dermaptera*

flatro·n *vi* **1** to flap wings; flutter **2** to fly

flatro·re *np [Entom]* pterygota

flauri
I § *nf* flurry of dust
II § *adv* in a flurry

***flauri·s** *stem for 1st sg pres, pl pres, 2nd & 3rd sg subj, pind* <flauri·t·

***flauri·t** *vt* to put [] into a pother

fla·ut *nm [Mus]* (transverse) flute

flauti·st *n [Mus]* flautist, flute-player

fla·uto *nf [Mus]* transverse flute

FLD *abbrev* <Flota Luftarake Detare Naval Air Fleet

fle·
I § *vi* to sleep
II § *vt* to take [animal/person] (somewhere) to spend the night, leave [animal/person] overnight
    ◦ **fle· gjumin e madh** "sleep the big sleep" **1** *(Euph)* to go to one's eternal rest: die **2** *(Impol)* to be lazy and shiftless
    ◦ **fle· gjumin e shtjerrave** to sleep like a lamb
    ◦ **fle· gjumin e vdekjes** "sleep the sleep of death" **1** *(Euph)* to go to one's eternal rest: die **2** *(Impol)* to be lazy and shiftless
    ◦ **s'<> fle·**^{3sg} **karari** <> *is* unable to make up <>'s mind
    ◦ **fle· kur këndojnë gjelat** to go to bed very late
    ◦ **fle· mbi dafina** to rest on one's laurels
    ◦ **fle· me gretha** to toss and turn while sleeping
    ◦ **fle· me një sy** to sleep with one eye open: be on guard
    ◦ **fle· me pulat** "sleep with the chickens" to go to bed very early

○ **nuk <> fle·**^{3sg} **mendja (te { })** <> *is* unable make up <>'s mind (about { }); <> *doesn't* quite know what to think (about <>); <> *doesn't* quite trust { }

○ **s'<> fle·**^{3sg} **mendja** <> *is* unable to make up <>'s mind

○ **e fle· mendjen** to put one's mind to rest, rest assured

○ **fle· në këmbë** to be asleep on one's feet: be physically and mentally very slow, be totally lost

○ **fle· në një krahë** to be able to rest easy, have nothing to worry about

○ **<> fle· në zemër** to occupy a soft spot in <>'s heart

○ **fle· rëndë** to sleep soundly; sleep deeply

○ **fle· rrasët** to sleep soundly, sleep well

○ **fle· si buall** to sleep deeply

○ **fle· të madhin** "sleep the big one" **1** *(Euph)* to go to one's eternal rest: die **2** *(Impol)* to be lazy and shiftless

○ **nuk <> fle·**^{3sg} **trimëria** "<>'s bravery *does not* sleep in <>" *(Elev)* <> *is* extremely brave

○ **fle· zbathur** "sleep barefooted" to sleep soundly

flegë *nf* = fle**gër**

flegër *nf* **1** each wing of a double door/window/shutter **2** [*Bot*] fruit pod; valve (of a pod) **3** slice **4** [*Anat*] nostril ***5** gill of a fish

flegmatík *adj* phlegmatic

flegro·*n vt* to divide [ ] into slices: slice, slice [ ] up

fleksion *nm* [*Ling*] grammatical inflection, accidence

flet·

I § *vi* **1** to speak; talk; converse; discuss **2** *(Colloq)* to argue

II § *vt* **1** to say; speak, tell **2** *(Colloq)* to scold **3** *(Colloq)* to call, summon; invite **4** *(Colloq)* to console **5** *(Reg)* to promise

○ **flet· çapër** to speak disconnectedly

○ **flet· çatra-patra** to talk claptrap

○ **flet· çelembyll** to beat around the bush, not say exactly what one means

○ **i flet· derës të dëgjojë qilari** "tell the door so that the cellar may hear" to say something intended for someone other than the person spoken to

○ **flet· dokrra në hi** to talk complete nonsense

○ **flet· e shflet·** "says and unsays" (said of someone who doesn't keep his word) { } says things one minute and takes them back the next

○ **flet· fjalë të majme** to use big words, speak in inflated language

○ **flet· hardhje e zhapinj** to talk nonsense

○ **flet· hudhër në kungull** to talk nonsense, speak without thinking

○ **flet· jerm** to speak deliriously, be raving

○ **flet· kodër më kodër** to talk without making sense

○ **flet· kuturu** to ramble on, talk nonsense

○ **flet· larë e pa larë** to use all kinds of language (foul and fair)

○ **flet· mbarë e prapë 1** to talk about everything and everybody **2** to say whatever comes into one's mind, talk without thinking

○ **flet· me bërryl** to be shifty, diabolic, cunning

○ **flet· me buzë** to speak with a lot of smirking

○ **flet· me cep** to make provocative/sarcastic remarks

○ **flet· me qime** to say exactly the right thing

○ **<> flet· me fyt** to speak to <> angrily

○ **flet· me gjemba** to make provocative/sarcastic remarks

○ **flet· me hinkë** *(Colloq)* to speak with a megaphone

○ **flet· me hundë 1** to talk through the nose **2** to speak angrily

○ **flet· me pizëri** to speak with innuendo: make insinuations

○ **flet· me rrugë** to act/speak/work in accordance with accepted procedure, act/speak/work with propriety

○ **flet· me sëpatë** to speak freely

○ **flet· me spica** to make provocative/sarcastic remarks

○ **flet· me tel** *(Colloq)* to speak by telephone

○ **flet· me udhë** to act/speak/work in accordance with accepted procedure, act/speak/work with propriety

○ **flet· me sy e me vetulla** "speak with eyes and eyebrows" to move one's eyes and eyebrows a great deal when one talks; use a lot of facial expression when speaking

○ **flet· në erë** to blather away

○ **flet· në hava** to talk nonsense, say silly things

○ **flet· në mulli** *(Impol)* it's like (one *is*) talking to the wall.

○ **flet· në të gjitha udhëkryqet** to make a hullabaloo so that the whole world knows about it; let the whole world in on it

○ **flet· në tym** to be talking in the air, talk foolishness

○ **<> flet· në vesh** to speak to <> in a low voice: whisper in <>'s ear; gossip to <> with malicious intent

○ **flet· në arë e në vreshtë** to be talking in the air, talk foolishness

○ **flet· nën/nëpër hundë** to mutter under one's breath

○ **flet· nën zë 1** to speak timidly **2** to speak in a low voice (so as not to be overheard); talk in private

○ **flet· nëpër dhëmbë** "talk through one's teeth" **1** to mumble **2** to grumble, mutter with discontent

○ **flet· pa doganë** to talk without thinking

○ **<> flet· pa lesh në bark** *(Colloq)* to talk to <> without hiding anything, give <> the straight scoop

○ **flet· pa shtrak** to speak straightforwardly

○ **flet· pa udhë/rrugë** to act/speak/work in disregard of accepted procedure

○ **flet· pas krahëve 1** to talk/whisper behind people's back **2** to speak (up) unexpectedly

○ **flet· për pasnesër** to talk unrealistically

○ **Flet· për uthullën e kapërce·**n **te qumështi.** "{ } *talks* about vinegar and *jumps* over to milk." { } *is* always changing the subject. { } keeps changing the subject.

○ **flet· prapa krahëve 1** to be a backbiter **2** to speak (up) unexpectedly

○ **flet· prapa shpine** to talk behind someone's back, backbite; be a backbiter

○ **flet·**^{3sg} **puna vetë** the matter speaks for itself, it's obvious

○ **flet· qosheve e skutave** to gossip

○ **flet·**^{3sg} **rakia** it *is* the liquor talking ({ } *does not* mean what { } *says*)

○ **flet· rrafsh me** [ ] to sit down and talk things over with [ ] personally

○ **flet· si cinxër** to talk incessantly

○ **flet· si çakalle mulliri** to keep talking and talking: be a chatterbox

○ **flet· si e ëma e Zeqos majë thanës** "talk like Zeqo's mother on top of the cornel tree" *(Colloq)* to talk utter nonsense

○ **flet· si miza në qyp** to speak in a muffled voice

○ **flet· si pasnesër** to talk unrealistically

○ **flet· të trasha** to talk nonsense

○ **flet· udhë e përmbi udhë** to say whatever comes into one's mouth

○ **flet· va e pa va** to speak without thinking; talk in the air

○ **flet·** *pl* **vesh më vesh** "talk ear to ear" to talk confidentially with one another so as not to be overheard

fleta k *adj* winged

flet anë tar ësi *nf* list of members, membership roll

flet anke të *nf* questionnaire

flet ar *nm* 1 upper millstone 2 wooden lever used to stop the rotation of the wheel in a water mill

flet artë *adj (Poet)* having leaves shining like gold: golden-leaved

flet arrest im *nm [Offic]* arrest warrant

flet emër im *nm [Offic]* document verifying appointment to a job: commission, letter of appointment, official charge

fle të *nf* 1 wing 2 fin 3 leaf 4 sheet; page 5 certificate 6 leaf of a double door/window/shutter; panel of a weaving/tent/carpet 7 husk, pod 8 *(Colloq)* petal

○ **fletë delli** *[Bot]* = **bar delli**

○ **fletë dylli** *[Publ]* mimeograph paper

○ **Fletët i ka të bukura, po t'i shohim pemlat.** "It has beautiful flowers/leaves, but let's see the berries." It looks all right now, but we have to see how it turns out.

○ **fletë kampi** document verifying permission to attend a vacation camp

○ **fletë misri** "cornleaf" *[Bot]* common aspidistra *Aspidistra elatior*

○ **fletë sharre** *[Bot]* bird's-foot serradella *Ornithopus compressus*

○ **fletë shitjeje** bill of sale

○ **fletë tipografike** *[Publ]* 16-page fascicle

fletë bardhë *adj* white-winged; white-leaved

fletë biru ese *nf* plant disease characterized by many holes in the leaves

fletë da lje *nf* release document

fletë den dur *adj* having dense foliage

fletë-fletë

I § *adj* having many leaves/petals

II § *adv* in sheet form

fletë garanci *nf* certificate of warranty: guarantee

fletë gjerë *adj* broad-leaved

fletë ha pët *adj* big-leaved, broad-leaved

fletë ho llë *adj* having thin (not thick) leaves: thin-leaved

fletë hy rje *nf* check-in certificate

fletë kërke së *nf[Offic]* request form, certificate of order

fletë kujte së *nf [Postal]* reference slip

fletë lavdër im *nm* certificate of praise: commendation

fletë le je *nf* furlough document, leave permit

fletë li dh je *nf (Book)* membership certificate

fletë ma dh *adj* large-leaved

fletë mba jt ës *adj* evergreen

fletë ngarke së *nf [Offic]* bill of lading

fletë ngu shtë *adj* narrow-leaved, needle-leaved

fletë page s ë *nf* 1 *[Offic]* invoice 2 payment receipt

fletë pajt im *nm* receipt for a subscription

fletë palo sje *nf* brochure, pamphlet

fletë për dredh ëse *nf* plant disease characterized by twisted leaves

fletë porosi *nf[Offic]* order document

fletë pran im *nm [Offic]* document certifying the right of the bearer to stay in vacation housing

fletë rën ës *adj* deciduous

fletë rrufe *nf* critical opinion expressed on a public wall

fletë s *nm* third chamber of the stomach of a ruminant: manyplies, omasum

fletë së mund je *nf* (hospital) document certifying one's illness

fletë sha rrë *nf* saw blade

fletë shërb im *nm [Offic]* document certifying that a person has been assigned to work outside of his usual place of employment

fletë shoq ër im *nm* packing slip; invoice

fletë shpër ngu lje *nf* 1 *(Old)* document certifying a change of residence 2 *(Colloq)* permit to leave

fletë shtr im *nm* document authorizing hospitalization, hospital permit

fletë tra shë *adj* thick-leaved

fletë thi rrje *nf (Offic)* official call to duty: draft notice, court summons, subpoena

fletë vo gël *adj* small-leaved

fletë vot im *nm* ballot

fletë z *nf dimin* < **fletë** 1 slip of paper 2 thin cheesecloth placed over face of a sleeping baby 3 leaflet 4 feather of an arrow

fletë za *np fem* < **fletë z** old rags or swaddling clothes used as diapers for a baby

flet im ët *adj* = **gjeth i mët**

flet i shtë *nf* = **gjeth i shtë**

fleto· ·n *vi* to sprout leaves

fleto r

I § *nm (Book)* leafy

II § *nm* broad-leafed tree

fletora r *n (Old)* journalist = **gazeta r**

fleto re *nf* 1 notebook 2 *(Old)* newspaper

****flet oriz ëm** *nm (Old)* journalism

fletos· *vt* to stack the leaves of [ ]

fletra c *nm* 1 *[Zool]* bat 2 *[Anat]* = **fle tës**

flet udhë tim *nm [Offic]* travel document

flet ushë *nf [Bot]* bract

flet ushkë *nf* 1 scrap of paper; small sheet of paper 2 *(Scorn)* worthless newspaper: yellow ragleaflet

fle vë *nf* = **fyzë**

****fle xë** *nf* swaddling cloth

****flë· =** **fle·**

fli *nf* sacrifice

fli· ·het

I § *vpr* to get sleepy; fall asleep

II § *vi* to be conducive to sleeping

fli *stem for imper, 2nd pl pres, pind, vp* < **fle·**

****fli çe** *nf* 1 foot of a stocking **2 toecap

****fli gati shëm** *adj* (i) ready for sacrifice: resigned

fli j im *nm ger* 1 < **flijo· ·n, flijo· ·het** 2 object of sacrifice

flijo· ·het *vpr* to make a self sacrifice; become a martyr

flijo· ·n *vt* to sacrifice

flint *nm [Optics]* flint glass

fliq nm (Colloq) tip of the foot, shoe tip

flirt nm non-serious romantic relationship: flirtation

flirto·n vi to flirt

flis| stem for 2nd pl pres, 3rd sg pind <**flet·**

flit nm liquid insecticide

flit·et vp impers **1** there's talk, people are talking **2** one can discuss, one can have a discussion: discussion is possible

flit| stem for 2nd pl pres, pind, vp <**flet·**

flo·çkë nf **1** [Folklore] nymph = **gërshetëz** *2 whistle, pipe

flojere nf [Mus] = **fyell**

flok
  I § nm **1** hair **2** beard of grain; corn tassel **3** snowflake
  II § np fringe on a textile
  ○ **flokë arapi** tangled-up mess
  ○ **flokë bishtek** braid of hair, pigtail *= **bishtalec**
  ○ **flokë të çelët** blond hair

flok|are nf = **flokëse**

flok|argje'nd nm (Poet) **1** silver-haired **2** gray-haired

flok|a'rtë adj, nf (Poet) golden-haired, blond (girl)

flok|aru'shë adj long-haired; with unshorn locks; hairy, hirsute

flok|a'shpër adj coarse-haired

flok|a't adj fringed

flok|ata'r adj hairy

flok|a'të nf = **flokje**

flo·ke nf = **flokje**

flok|e'n|e np [Tech] metal flakes, hairline cracks (in metal)

flok|ëba'rdhë adj, n **1** white-haired (person) **2** gray-haired, grizzled (person)

flok|ëbu'të adj soft-haired

flok|ëdre'dh|ur adj, n curly-haired (person)

flok|ëdri'zë adj having strong, coarse hair

flok|ë-flok|ë adv in large, fleecy flakes

flok|ëgështe'një adj having chestnut-colored hair, auburn, brown-haired

flok|ëgja'të adj long-haired

flok|ëkaçurre'l adj curly-haired

flok|ëkuçe'dër adj having long messy hair

flok|ëku'q adj, n redheaded (person)

flok|ëlëshu'a'r adj **1** having long hair worn loose **2** (Fig Poet) (of trees) whose branches hang down like hair: weeping

flok|ëpa|kre'h|ur adj having uncombed hair: unkempt

flok|ëpre'rë adj (of girls) with bobbed hair, with hair cut short

flok|ërë'në adj whose hair has fallen out: bald

flok|ërru'dh|ët adj = **flokëdredhur**

flo'k|es nm [Bot] bluegrass (Poa)

flo·ke'se nf fringed woolen blanket

flo·ke'sh nm long-haired person

flok|ëshku'rtër adj short-haired

flok|ëshpri'sh|ur adj having mussed up hair

flok|ështri'gë nf **1** (Insult) woman with long and wild hair **2** [Bot] dodder = **kuskute**

flo·kë't adj (i) lazy

flok|ëthi'nj|ur adj grizzled, gray-haired, hoary

flok|ëve'rdhë adj blond, fair-haired

flokë·z nf **1** [Folklore] = **floçkë 2** [Bot] bluegrass (Poa)

flokë·zba'rdh|ur adj having white-tinged hair; grizzled

flokë·zbërdhy'l|ur adj having bleached/faded hair

flokë·zi adj, n (fem sg ~e'z, masc pl ~i'nj, fem pl ~eza) black-haired (person)

flo'kje nf **1** fringed woolen blanket **2** tasseled vest worn by women worn over a knee-length dress

flok|na'jë nf thick crown of hair

flok|o'r adj (Book) **1** tufted. *2 hairy; fibrous; capillary

flo'k|sh nm sequin

flo'kshë = **floçkë**

flok|ta'r
  I § n hairdresser, barber
  II § adj (Old) * = **flokue'r**
  ○ **floktar permanenti** hairdresser

flok|ta'ri' nf = **floktore**

flok|to're nf hairdresser's shop

flo'q|e = **flokje**

flor nm **1** caisson for working under water; diving bell **2** partition in a hope chest; drawer **3** [Chem] = **fluo'r**

Flor|a nf Flora (female name)

flo're nf **1** = **zbokth 2** (onion/rice) husk **3** hope chest

flo're' nf [Bot] flora

flori(r)
  I § nm (np ~nj) **1** gold **2** gold coin, florin **3** golden thread **4** (Fig Pet) (term of affectionate address to a child) dear, honey
  II § adj **1** of gold, golden **2** (Fig) very good, marvelous; extremely valuable
  ○ <> **bëhet balta flori** "mud becomes gold for <>" <> has the golden touch, <> is capable of doing anything well
  ○ **flori i egër** figroot buttercup, buttercup ficaria Ficaria verna
  ○ **flori i kulluar** crystal clear
  ○ **flori në baltë/pleh** (said of something or someone of great intrinsic value but unappreciated in its present circumstances) pearl among swine
  ○ **ësh·të flori në mushama 1** to be pure and of high quality **2** to be a person of great esteem
  ○ **flori në mushama** very good, pure gold
  ○ **flori i pastër** sparkling clean
  ○ **flori i verdhë** golden yellow

Floria'n nm Florian (male name)

flor|i'c nm variety of rye with thin grains

flori'm|të = **florinjtë**

flori'nj np <**flori** gold coins

flori'njt|ë adj (i) **1** of gold; golden **2** bathed in gold: gilded **3** embroidered in gold

flori'r||i obl <**flori**

flo'skë nf horizontal stratum of material: layer

flo'shkë nf homely woman

flo'të nf **1** group that travels together in the sea: fleet (of ships), flotilla; school (of swimming animals) **2** fleet of ships/airplanes under a single command

flu·n vi (Reg Gheg) = **fluturo·n**

flu'ckë = **flluskë**

flu'er nm (obl ~o'ri) (Old) **1** partition in a hope chest; drawer *2 square (on a chessboard)

flug nm = **vrull**

flu'gë nf shingle (of a roof)

flu'gër nf weathercock

flu'gëz *nf* [*Constr*] slat

flug'ta'r *adj* adroit

fluïd *nm* [*Tech*] fluid

fluks *nm* [*Phys*] flux

fluktua'cio'n *nm* [*Spec*] fluctuation

fluo'r *nm* [*Chem*] fluorine

fluoreshe'ncë *nf* fluorescence

flur *nm* [*Constr*] flight (of stairs)

***flura'c**

  I § *nm* **1** small bird **2** (*Fig*) simpleton

  II § *np* poultry

flur'i'm *nm ger* <**fluro'·n**

flur'i'me *np* **1** <**fluri'm· 2** sprayed particles: spray

fluro'·n *vi* **1** to disperse into the air: spray ***2** = **fluturo'·n**

fluro'më *nf* whiff

fluro'r *adj* [*Chem Phys*] volatile

fluru'dhë *nf* [*Mil*] trajectory

flus *nm* [*Tech*] flux

flus'i'm *nm* [*Tech*] fluxing

flu'tur

  I § *nf* **1** [*Entom*] butterfly, moth (*Lepidoptera*) **2** [*Invert*] liver fluke causing liver rot in sheep (*Fasciola hepatica*) **3** butterfly-shaped design or object

  II § *adj* fast and agile; moving lightly

  III § *adv* quickly

  ○ **flutur bajrake** [*Entom*] swallow-tail butterfly

  ○ **flutura e bardhë** [*Entom*] black-veined white *Aporia crataegi* L.

  ○ **flutura e detit** [*Ichth*] sea butterfly *Callionymus risso*

  ○ **flutura e gëlbazës** [*Entom*] liver butterfly

  ○ **ësh·të flutur e gjallë** to be lively and sprightly

  ○ **flutura e hambareve** [*Entom*] Indian meal moth *Plodia interpunctella* Hb.

  ○ **flutura krahëgjelbër** [*Entom*] type of butterfly *Euchloe daplidicae* L.

  ○ **flutura e lakrës** [*Entom*] the cabbage white butterfly *Pieris brassicae* L.

  ○ **flutur i lehtë** light as a butterfly

  ○ **flutura e miellit** [*Entom*] meal moth *Pyralis farinalis* L.

  ○ **flutura e mullinjve** [*Entom*] Mediterranean flour moth *Ephestia kuhniella* Zell.

  ○ **flutur nate** moth

  ○ **flutur pikaloshe** [*Ichth*] dragonet *Callionymus lyra*

  ○ **flutura e rrepës** [*Entom*] the imported cabbageworm *Pieris rapae* L.

  ○ **flutur sypallua** [*Entom*] flea beetle *Saturnia*

  ○ **flutur i shpejtë** very fast

Flu'tur'|a *nf* Flutura (female name)

flutur'a'k

  I § *adj* **1** flying **2** (*Fig*) fast and agile **3** (*Fig*) fleeting

  II § *nm* **1** flying bird/insect **2** (*Reg*) chicken

flutur'a'k|e *nf* **1** butterfly **2** lively girl/woman

flutur'a'shkë *nf* **1** (*Dimin*) <**flu'tur 2** flittering object **3** [*Ichth*] eagle ray (*Myliobatis aquila*) = **shqipo'një deti**

flutur'i'm

  I § *nm ger* **1** <**fluturo'·n**, **fluturo'·het 2** flight, flying

  II § *adv* = **fluturi'mthi**

flutur'i'm|thi *adv* **1** in flight, in mid-air, on the fly **2** quickly **3** (*Fig*) like a shot

fluturo'·n

  I § *vi* **1** to fly **2** to go fast **3** to go by airplane **4** (*Fig Colloq*) to fantasize, imagine things **5** (*Fig*) to spread fast, get around quickly **6** (*Fig*) (of money) to slip through one's fingers

  II § *vt* to toss away/out

  ○ **fluturo·n andej-këtej** to flitter about

  ○ <> **fluturo·n**³ˢᵍ **koka** "<>'s head *flies* off" <> *loses* <>'s neck, <> *gets* killed

  ○ **fluturo·n me një fije bar** "fly on a blade of grass" (*Disparaging*) **1** to be easily pleased with oneself, feel proud of a small accomplishment **2** to be testy

  ○ <> **fluturo·n**³ˢᵍ **mendja** "<>'s mind *flies* away" **1** <>'s mind *is* off somewhere else **2** <> *goes* into a daze **3** <> *goes* out of <>'s mind, <> *goes* crazy

  ○ **fluturo·n nga gazi** to jump for joy

  ○ <> **fluturo·n**³ᵖˡ **trutë** "<>'s brains *fly* off" <> *loses* <>'s neck, <> *gets* killed

fluturo're *np* [*Bot*] family of legumes with paired butterfly-like flowers *Papilionaceae*

flutur'u'es

  I § *adj* **1** in flight, able to fly: flying **2** of or pertaining to flying

  II § *n* flier

flutur'u'shë *nf* toy balloon

***flla'çkë** *nf* = **pllo'skë**

flla'd

  I § *nm* **1** breeze, light wind **2** fresh air

  II § *adv* = **fre'skët**

flladi's| *stem for 1st sg pres, pl pres, 2nd & 3rd sg subj, pind* <**flladi't·**

flladi't· *vt* **1** to make [] cool: cool **2** to refresh, freshen

flladi't·et *vpr* **1** to get cooler: cool off **2** to become refreshed

flladi't'ës *adj* **1** cooling **2** refreshing

flladi't|je *nf ger* **1** <**flladi't·**, **flladi't·et 2** = **freski'**

***flladi't'shëm** = **flla'dshëm**

flla'd'shëm *adj* (i) cool, refreshing

***fllakro'·n** = **flatro'·n**

***flla'shk|azi** *adv* crosswise

***flla'shkë** = **fla'shkë**

flla'shk|ët *adj* (i) flat on both sides

***flli'ç** = **fili'ç**

***flli'g** = **fëlli'q·**

***fllig|aca'r** *n* filthy wretch

***fllig|ët** = **fëlli'qët**

***fllig|shti** = **fëllig'ështi**

***fllu'dë** *nf* (Old) die for minting coins

filug *nm* torch, flare

***flluga'r** *n* boatman, bargeman

fllug'a'r *nf* **1** towed boat: barge, lighter **2** felucca ***3** roof shingle

fllu'skë *nf* **1** bubble **2** blister, burn blister; vesicle; pustule **3** [*Anat*] sac; bladder **4** [*Bot*] plant disease which causes vesicles to form on the leaves **5** (*Colloq*) toy balloon

fllusk|o'·n

  I § *vi* **1** to form bubbles: bubble **2** to emerge in bubbles: bubble out **3** to float

  II § *vt* = **fllusko's·**

fllusk|o's· *vt* **1** to create bubbles, aerate **2** to cause blisters **3** (*Fig*) to dispirit and cause great weariness: beat down **4** to inflate

flluskoˈsˈ·et *vpr* **1** to swell up like a blister **2** to get covered with blisters **3** *(Fig)* to become tired and dispirited: get beaten down

flluskoˈsˈje *nf ger* <**flluskoˈsˈ·**, **flluskoˈsˈ·et**

*****fllyˈem** *adj* dirty

*****fllyˈemˈe** *nf (e)* dirt

FMN *abbrev* <**Fondi Monetar Ndërkombëtar** IMF = International Monetary Fund

*****fnaˈzë** *nf* light fall of snow

|**fobˈi** *formativ (Book)* |phobia

foduˈll
  I § *adj, n (Colloq)* stuck-up/conceited (person); arrogant (person)
  II § *nm* *****brooch, clasp; buckle

fodullˈëk *nm (Colloq)* conceit; arrogance

fodullˈoˈsˈ·et *vpr* to get conceited; attitudinize, swagger

fojleˈtë *nf [Bot]* = **caraˈcë**

fokˈë *nf* **1** *[Zool]* seal *(Monachus monachus)* **2** *(Colloq\Impolite)* ungainly fat man who has trouble moving **3** *[Med]* erysipelas **4** *[Veter]* red murrain

fokˈist *n* stoker, fireman

foks *nm* foxtrot

fokstroˈt *nm* = **foks**

fol *stem for imper, pdef, opt, adm, part* <**fleˈt·**
  ○ **fol o gur, fol o mur!** (addressed to someone who is too quiet) say something!

*****folaˈgë** *nf* *[Ornit]* coot *(Fulica atra)*

fole *nf* **1** nest; aerie **2** *(Fig)* family home **3** *[Mil]* = **çerdhe** **4** group of offspring of domestic animals born and raised together: litter, brood **5** *[Min]* layer or block of a mineral **6** *[Tech]* groove for sliding something into **7** *[Mil]* breech of a gun
  ○ **fole arëzash/grerëzash** "hornet's nest" *(Pej)* group of schemers/plotters; group of squabbling people
  ○ **fole e fishekut** *[Mil]* cartridge chamber
  ○ **fole merimange** spiderweb; cobweb
  ○ **fole pëllumbash** pigeon loft, dove cote
  ○ **fole e predhës** *[Mil]* projectile chamber

foleqeˈsh *adj (Colloq)* fun to be with: affable

folˈës
  I § *adj* speaking, talking
  II § *n* speaker, talker
  III § *nm* *[Geog]* (map) marked with symbols and labels

*****folˈësi** *nf* talkativeness, loquacity

*****foˈlie** *nf (Reg Kos)* foil, tinfoil = **varaˈk**

foˈlje *nf [Ling]* verb

foljeziˈm *nm [Ling]* derivation of verbs: verbalization

foljoˈr *adj [Ling]* **1** verbal **2** deverbal

folkloˈr *nm* folklore

folkloˈrik *adj* folkloric

folkloriˈst *n* folklorist, folklore scholar

folkloristiˈk *adj* folkloristic

folkloristiˈkë *nf* study of folklore

foˈlme *nf (e)* *[Ling]* local variety of a language: local dialect

foltaˈr *nm* = **fjalëtaˈr**

foˈlur
  I § *part* <**fleˈt, fliˈt·et**
  II § *adj (i)* spoken; oral
  III § *nn (të)* **1** speech ability: speech **2** speech manner; speaking style

*****folladhë** *nf [Invert]* small mussel *(Lithodomus)*

follë *nf* **1** metal button **2** *[Ethnog]* small silver or silvered disks used to ornament costumes **3** scale of a fish or reptile **4** body blemish, beauty mark

folloˈsh *nm* animal's home: lair, nest

fom *nm [Bot]* common fumitory *(Fumaria officinalis)*

fond
  I § *nm* **1** fund **2** totality of things of value: wealth, inventory, stock
  II § *np* paper money: currency

fonderˈi *nf* foundry

fonditoˈr *n* foundry worker, foundryman

fonemˈë *nf [Ling]* phoneme

fonetiˈk *adj [Ling]* phonetic

fonetikaˈn *nm [Ling]* phonetician

fonetiˈkë *nf [Ling]* **1** phonetics **2** *(Colloq)* textbook on phonetics

fonograˈf *nm* = **gramafon**

fonograˈm *nm* message sent by telephone or radio

fonologjˈi *nf [Ling]* phonology

fonologjiˈk *nm [Ling]* phonological

fonˈotekë *nf [Cine]* sound library

foˈra *adv (Colloq)* daringly, bravely

foragjeˈr *adj [Agr]* sown or used to provide fodder for animals

foragjeˈre *np [Agr]* forage crops

*****forazheˈre** = **foragjeˈre**

foˈrbël *nf* discarded portion of fruit: rind, pulp, pits

foˈrca *imper interj* use your force: heave-ho!

*****forcaˈde** *nf* = **forcë**

*****forcaˈtë** *nf* = **forcë**

*****forceˈr** *nm* chest, box

forcë *nf* **1** force **2** power; strength
  ○ **forcat e gjalla** men and animals employed (as opposed to equipment)
  ○ **forca e rendit** forces/guardians of law and order

forcëdhëˈnˈës *adj* force-giving: invigorating

forcëˈmaˈtˈës *nm* force meter

forciˈm *nm ger* **1** <**forcoˈ·n**, **forcoˈ·het** **2** reinforcement, strengthening

forcoˈ·het *vpr* **1** to become stronger, increase in strength **2** to harden

forcoˈ·n *vt* **1** to strengthen; reinforce; fortify; temper **2** to harden

*****forcuaˈr** *adj (i)* reinforced; strengthened; hardened

forcuˈes *nm* reinforcing; strengthening; hardening

foreˈ *nf* hope

foˈrë *nf* **1** impetus; dash, élan **2** haughtiness, arrogance

forinˈtë *nf* Hungarian monetary unit: forint

formacioˈn *nm* **1** formation **2** *[Mil]* order of battle, combat formation

formaˈl *adj* formal

formaliˈst *adj* formalist

formaliˈsht *adv* formally

formaliteˈt *nm (Book)* **1** formality **2** mere formality

formaliˈzëm *nm* formalism

formaˈt *nm* format; blank form

foˈrmë *nf* **1** form, shape **2** mold, casting form **3** political/ideological seminar
  ○ **i formës së prerë** *(Offic)* definitively settled, finally disposed, not subject to review

formˈësiˈm *nm ger* **1** <**formësoˈ·n**, **formësoˈ·het** **2** formation

form|ës'o·het *vpr* [*Ling*] to undergo derivation or compounding

form|ës'o·n *vt* [*Tech*] to mold

form|im *nm ger* 1 <**formo'·n, formo'·het** 2 formation 3 upbringing/training to provide fundamental character: grounding 4 [*Ling*] construct formed by derivation or compounding

form|o'·het *vpr* 1 to form; arise; grow 2 to develop basic character through training and upbringing: become well-grounded

form|o'·n *vt* 1 to form 2 to provide fundamental character: train, bring up, ground

form|u'a'r *adj (i)* 1 formed, fleshed-out 2 well-developed, well brought-up, well-trained 3 of strong character: solid

form|u'e's

I § *adj* 1 forming 2 formative

II § *nm* [*Tech*] small metal-working hammer: forming hammer

formul|a'r *nm* [*Tech*] document with blanks to be filled out with information: blank form, form

form|u'lë *nf* formula

formul|im *nm ger* 1 <**formulo'·n** 2 formulation

formul|o'·n *vt* to formulate

***for'o'·n** *vt* to egg [] on, incite; speed [] on

forsa't *nm (Reg)* = **almise**

fort

I § *adv* 1 with great force, strongly 2 tightly 3 loudly 4 to a high degree: very, highly

II § *pcl* to the highest degree: extremely

∘ **fort e më fort** 1 ever so much 2 ever stronger, stronger and stronger

fo'rte *adv* [*Mus*] in a very loud manner: forte

forte's'ë *nf* 1 fortress; bulwark 2 reinforcing material for clothes or shoes

∘ **fortes'ë ajrore** flying fortress

fo'rt|ë *adj (i)* 1 able to withstand force: strong, tough 2 unyielding and inflexible: hard, stiff, tough; severe, stern 3 forming an abrupt angle: steep, sharp 4 in high degree: intense, loud (sound), bright (light), bitter (cold) 5 able to exert force: strong, powerful 6 harsh 7 containing a concentrated amount of a caustic substance (such as acid, alcohol, coffee, nicotine, poison) 8 skillful, able, talented

∘ **i fortë si bugra** very strong

fort|ësi *nf* strength, hardness, harshness

fortifik|a'të *nf* [*Mil*] fortified place: fortification

fortifik|im *nm ger* [*Mil*] 1 <**fortifiko'·n, fortifiko'·het** 2 fortification

fortifik|o'·het *vpr* [*Mil*] to construct protective fortifications

fortifik|o'·n *vt* [*Mil*] to fortify

fortifik|u'a'r *adj (i)* [*Mil*] fortified

fort|i'në *nf* fort

fort|i'ssimo *adv* [*Mus*] in a very loud manner: fortissimo

fort|o'·n *vt* to harden, stiffen

***for'u'e's** *adj* threatening, menacing

for|u'm *nm* 1 (*Book*) forum; discussion meeting, conference 2 (*Reg*) chimney, flue; heating stove *3 (*Reg Gheg*) funnel; retort

forr|a's· *vt* to have a maximum capacity of []

***fo'rr|azi** *adv* at full speed, in a rush

***fo'rr|ë** *nf* = **fo'rë**

fosfa't *nm* [*Chem*] phosphate

fosfat|ik *adj* [*Chem*] phosphatic

fosfo'r *nm* [*Chem*] phosphorus

fosfor|eshe'ncë *nf* phosphorescence

fosfor|ik *adj* [*Chem*] 1 phosphoric, phosphorous 2 phosphorescent

fosfor|it *nm* [*Chem*] phosphorite

fosil *nm* fossil

fosil|iz|im *nm ger* 1 <**fosilizo'·het** 2 fossilization

fosil|iz|o'·het *vpr* to become fossilized

***foshnj|a'r** = **foshnjo'r**

foshnj|ar|a'k *adj* 1 = **foshnjo'r** 2 (*Pej*) infantile

fo'shnj|ë *nf* 1 baby, infant 2 (*Impol*) person still wet behind the ears

∘ **foshnjë gjiri** suckling, nursing child

foshnj|ëri *nf* 1 infancy 2 (*Collec*) infants 3 (*ColloqImpolite*) infantile behavior

foshnj|ëri'sht *adv* in an infantile manner, like a baby

foshnj|o'r *adj* 1 of, pertaining to, or characteristic of infants: infantile 2 pertaining to preschool education: nursery 3 in its infancy: early, beginning

foshnj|o're *nf (Old)* kindergarten

***fo'ti** *nf* oil lamp

foto *formativ (Book)* photo|

foto|apara't *nm* [*Cine*] still camera

foto|efe'kt *nm* [*Phys Cine*] photoelectric effect

foto|ekspozi'të *nf* photography exhibition

foto|eleme'nt *nm* [*Phys*] photocell

foto|fini'sh *nm* [*Track*] photo finish; photo-finish camera; photograph taken of a photo finish

foto|gazet|a'ri *nf* [*Cine*] photojournalism

foto|gra'f *nm* 1 photographer 2 photograph

foto|grafi *nf* 1 photograph 2 photography 3 (*Fig*) exact copy; mere copy, carbon copy

foto|grafik *adj* photographic

foto|graf|im *nm ger* 1 <**fotografo'·n, fotografo'·het** 2 photography

***foto|grafi's·** *vt* = **fotografo'·n**

foto|grafi'st *n* photographer

foto|grafo'·het *vpr* to have one's picture taken, get photographed

foto|grafo'·n *vt* 1 to photograph 2 (*Fig*) to depict/reproduce [] exactly 3 to observe [] in measured detail

foto|graf|u'e's *adj* photographic

foto|gravu'rë *nf* [*Postal Cine*] photogravure

foto|gjen|ik *adj* [*Cine*] photogenic

foto|ko'pje *nf* photocopy

foto|kopj|o'·n *vt* to photocopy

foto'n *nm* [*Phys*] photon

foto|objekti'v *nm* [*Cine*] photographic lens

foto|qeli'zë *nf* [*Cine*] photocell

foto|reporte'r *nm* photo journalist

foto|stu'dio *nf* [*Cine*] photographic studio

foto|te'kë *nf* [*Cine*] library of photographs

foto|zhen|ik *adj* photogenic

***fove'ri** *nf* terror = **tmerr**

***fove'ri's·** *vt* to terrify = **tmerro'·n**

***fo'zhnje** = **fo'shnj**ë

***fqi** *nm (Reg Gheg)* fqinj

fqinj

I § *n* neighbor

II § *adj* neighboring, next-door, adjacent

fqinj|ëri *nf collec* 1 neighborhood 2 = **fqinjësi**

fqinjëro·n *vi* **1** to live nearby, be a neighbor **2** to have friendly relations with one's neighbors

fqinjësi *nf* **1** being neighbors, adjacency **2** relationships with neighbors

fqinjësisht *adv* in a neighborly way

fqinjësor *adj* of or pertaining to relationships with neighbors

*****fqinjëzim** *nm* neighborhood, vicinity

*****fqisí** = fqinjësi

fqollë *nf* = fjollë

*****fraç** *nm* = frrac

fragment *nm* **1** fragment **2** excerpt

fragmentar *adj (Book)* fragmentary

*****fragullo·n** *vt* to reduce [] to ashes; char

fragjo·het *vpr* to become tanned/toasted

fragjo·n *vt* to toast [bread]

frak *nm* frock coat, tails

*****fraksion** = fraksion

fraksion *nm* political/social faction

fraksionist *adj, n (Book)* factionalist

fraksionizëm *nm (Book)* factionalism

frakturë *nf* fracture

francez
  I § *adj* French
  II § *nm* Frenchman

Francë *nf* France

françeskan *adj, nm [Relig]* Franciscan

frang *nm* franc

*****frangji** *nf* = frëngji

*****frangjis·** *vt* to make [] feel numb

*****frangjis·et** *vpr* to feel numb

*****franis·** *vt* = frangjis·

franko *adv* postal/transportation charges prepaid

frantojë *nf [Tech]* crushing machine, crusher

franxholllë *nf* long loaf of white bread, French bread

fraq *nm* bitter cold; cold, dry winter wind

fraqo·het *vpr* **1** to get terribly cold **2** to get dry, dry out **3** (of weather) to be cold and dry **4** to get chapped skin

fraqo·n *vt* **1** to dry [] out; dry [] in the sun/air **2** to toast

frashër *nm [Bot]* ash *(Fraxinus excelsior)*
  ∘ **frashër i egër** *[Bot]* terebinth *(Pistacia terebinthus)* = qelbës
  ∘ **frashër uji** *[Bot]* narrow-leaved ash *Fraxinus angustifolia*

Frashër *nm* village in southeast of Albania

frashërishtë *nf* ash grove

frashërt *adj (i)* made of ash wood

frashi *nf* hot wind from the south

frashnajë *nf* = frashërishtë

*****frashnje** *nf (Reg) [Bot]* = frashër

frashtë *adj (i)* = frashërt

frat *nm* brother in a monastic order: Franciscan monk; friar

frazeologji *nf* **1** *[Ling]* phraseology **2** *(Pej)* persiflage intended to obfuscate

frazeologjik *adj* **1** *[Ling]* pertaining to phrases, phraseological **2** *(Pej)* obfuscating by persiflage

frazë *nf* **1** phrase **2** *(Pej)* cliché **3** *[Ling]* sentence **4** *[Mus]* musical phrase

fre(r) *nm (np ~ rë)* **1** bridle **2** muzzle to prevent an animal from eating or drinking **3** *(Fig)* impediment

to progress; impediment to development **4** stem (of a fruit or melon)
  ∘ **s'ka· fre** to be out of control; be wild

fregatë *nf* **1** frigate **2** *[Ornit]* man-o'-war bird *(Fregata magnificens)*

fregull *nf* **1** long flexible shoot: withe; tall and straight seedling; switch, stick, rod **2** wing/lobe of the nose

frekëputur *adj* **1** with broken bridle: unbridled **2** *(Fig)* unrestrained, uncontrollable; uninhibited

frekuencë *nf [Spec]* frequency = denduri

frekuentim *nm ger (Book)* <frekuento·n

frekuento·n *vt (Book)* to attend [] regularly; frequent

frelëshuar *adj* **1** unbridled **2** *(Fig)* unrestrained, uninhibited

fren *nm* **1** braking mechanism: brake **2** *(Fig)* control device: rein

freng *adj, n* French(man)

frengjisht = frëngjisht

freni *sg* <fre *(Reg Gheg)*

frenim *nm ger* **1** <freno·n, freno·het **2** *[Physiol]* inhibition

freno·het *vp reflex* to hold oneself back, restrain oneself

freno·n *vt* **1** to apply the brakes to []: brake **2** *(Fig)* to put constraints on []; restrain, curb

frenues
  I § *nm* **1** brakeman **2** braking device **3** inhibitor
  II § *adj* **1** serving as a brake: braking **2** *(Fig)* inhibiting; restraining

frenjë *nf* **1** grape stem **2** *(Fig)* worthless part

frenjëz *nf* = frenjë

frerë *np* <fre(r)

frerëz *nf* grape stem

freri *obl* <fre(r)

fresk *nm* **1** coolness (in weather/temperature) **2** cool place **3** cool breeze **4** (cooling) fan

*****freskanë** *nf (Old)* = freskore

freskë *nf [Art]* fresco = afresk

*****freskëri** *nf* = freski

freskët
  I § *adj (i)* **1** cool **2** fresh
  II § *nm (i)* proofreader on a newspaper
  III § *adv* cool

freski *nf* **1** coolness **2** freshness **3** cool breeze

freskim *nm ger* **1** <fresko·n, fresko·het **2** refrigeration; refreshment

*****freskinë** *nf* freshness

*****fresko** *nf [Art]* fresco = afresk

fresko·het *vpr* to become cool, cool off; become refreshed

fresko·n *vt* **1** to cool, cool off **2** to keep [] cool and fresh: refrigerate **3** to refresh, freshen, freshen [] up; revive, renew; refresh [] in one's mind
  ∘ <> **fresko·n zemrën 1** to calm <> down **2** to make <> very pleased

freskograf *n* painter of frescoes

freskor *nm [Ichth]* grayling *(Thymallus thymallus)* = losëF

freskore *nf* (cooling) fan; fan-shaped object
  ∘ **freskore këmbëlundërz** *[Invert]* kind of scallop *Pseudamussium clavatum*
  ∘ **freskore putërmace** *[Invert]* cat's paw *Manupecten pesfelis*

freskʹuʹes *adj* cooling; refreshing

***freshkʹ** = fresk

***freshkʹsi** = freskiʹ

freʹshkullʹ *nm (np ˜j)* [*Bot*] thistle *(Carduus)*

freʹtʹër *np* <frat

***fretniʹ** *nf (Reg Gheg)* friary; monastic order, brotherhood

freth *nm* [*Veter Med*] **1** a pulmonary disease causing breathing difficulties in horses and, less commonly, in children: heaves = peth ***2** grape stalk

frezaʹtoʹr *n* milling-machine operator

freʹzë *nf* **1** [*Tech*] milling machine, mill **2** [*Agr*] disk harrow

 ◦ **frezë bishtore** [*Tech*] end mill, shank cutter

 ◦ **frezë dhëmbëpreʹrëse** [*Tech*] gear cutter, hobber

 ◦ **frezë kreatoʹr** [*Tech*] rotary cutting tool used for generating gear teeth: hob

freziʹm *nm ger* [*Tech*] <frezoʹ•n

frezoʹ•n *vt* **1** [*Tech*] to mill (a piece of metal or wood) **2** to cultivate soil with a disk harrow

***frëʹ(r)** *nm* = fre*(r)*

frëng *nm (np ˜gj) (Colloq)* **1** Frenchman = franceʹz **2** West European

frëngëlloʹ•n *vt* **1** to throw [] without regard to where it lands: heave, toss, fling, sling **2** to whip

frëngjiʹ *nf* **1** *(Old)* embrasure, loophole **2** [*Mil*] gunport

frëngjiʹsht *adv* in French (language)

frëngjiʹshtʹe *nf* French language

***frëngjoʹllë** = franxhoʹllë

***frëngjuʹz** = frëngjyz

frëngjyzaʹk *adj (Colloq)* syphilitic

frëngjyzë *nf (Colloq)* syphilis

***frëniʹs•** *vi* (of body parts) to feel tingly = mizëroʹ•n

***frënxhoʹllë** = franxhoʹllë

***frëʹqe** *nf* mouthful, gulp

***frëtëlloʹ•n** *vi* to snuffle

friʹg•et *vpr* = frikëʹsoʹhe

friʹgas *n* Phrygian

***frigëlloʹ•n** = frikësoʹ•n

frigoriʹfeʹr *nm* refrigerator

friguʹeʹshëm *adj (i)* **1** horrible **2** timid

frikʹ• *vt* to frighten

friʹk•et *vpr* to get scared, become frightened; get jittery/anxious

frikaʹc *adj (Impol)* = frikacaʹk

frikacaʹk

 I § *adj* easily frightened, timorous, cowardly; timid, jittery

 II § *nm* coward, scaredy-cat

frikʹakeʹq *adj (Impol)* = frikacaʹk

frikʹamaʹn *adj (Impol)* = frikacaʹk

frikʹanaʹk *adj, n* = frikacaʹk

frikʹanjoʹs *adj (Impol)* = frikacaʹk

frikʹaʹsh *adj (Impol)* = frikacaʹk

frikʹëʹ *nf* **1** fear, fright; anxiety **2** doubt, worry, uncertainty

 ◦ **Frika i ruan vreshtat.** "Fear guards the grapevines." *(Prov)* Fear of being caught keeps people honest.

frikʹëʹloʹre *nf* walker/go-cart for a baby learning to stand up

frikʹëʹs *adj* = frikacaʹk

frikëʹsiʹm *nm ger* **1** <frikësoʹ•n, frikësoʹ•het **2** intimidation

frikëʹsoʹ•het *vpr* to be frightened, be afraid

 ◦ **frikëso•het nga hija e** {*pronominal adj*} to be afraid of {*one's*} own shadow

frikëʹsoʹ•n *vt* to make [] afraid: frighten, scare; intimidate

frikëʹsuaʹr *adj (i)* frightened, afraid

frikëʹsuʹes *adj* frightening

frikoʹ•het *vpr (Colloq)* = frikësoʹ•het

frikoʹ•n *vt (Colloq)* = frikësoʹ•n

frikʹshëm *adj (i)* **1** frightening, scary **2** easily frightened, cowardly

fringʹëlliʹ•n *vi* to whiz, whir, swish

friʹngo

 I § *adj (Colloq)* brand-new

 II § *adv* in new clothes; all decked out in nice clean clothes

***frinjaʹr** *n* near horse in a team

***frishulloʹ•n** *vt* to season [meat]

***frishulluʹeʹm** *adj (i) (Reg Gheg)* (of meat) strong-tasting

friʹzer *nm* freezer

friʹzë *nf* frieze

frizonʹiʹshte *nf* Frisian (language)

***froʹgʹët** *adj (i)* unruly

***frok** = froʹgët

fron *nm* **1** throne **2** stool; chair **3** pedestal of a cup or other vessel **4** high heel on a woman's shoe **5** funeral bier

fronʹëziʹm *nm ger* **1** <fronëzoʹ•n **2** enthronement

fronʹëzoʹ•n *vt* to enthrone

front *nm* **1** front **2** forefront **3** [*Mil*] front line; battle front **4** [*Meteor*] weather front

frontaʹl *adj (Book)* **1** frontal **2** over a broad range/front

frontaʹliʹsht *adv (Book)* frontally

frontespiʹc *nm* [*Spec*] frontispiece

fror *nm (Old)* February

***frot**

 I § *nm* rat poison, poison

 II § *adj* bitter

***frotoʹs•et** *vpr* to take poison

***fruc** *adj* foolish

***Fruʹer** *nm (obl ˜oʹri) (Old)* February = shkurt

frug *nm* fish bladder

***fruʹgë** *nf* roof shingle

***frugëlliʹm** *nm* wavy line, wave

***frugëlluʹes** *adj* wavy

fruʹgull *nm* fungus disease in plants

frugulloʹ•het *vpr* = vrugoʹ•het

frugulloʹ•n *vt* **1** = vrugoʹ•het **2** to scorch; burn down, reduce to ashes

fruktoʹzë *nf* [*Med*] fructose

***fruleʹtëʹ** *nf* scarecrow

fruljeʹtëʹ *nf* spinning-top

fruʹlliʹ *nf* = fërfëlliʹzë

fruʹlliʹzë *nf* snowflake; snow flurry = fërfëlliʹzë

frulloʹ•n *vi impers* it *is* storming in flurries of fine snow and cold wind

fruq *nm (Reg)* **1** heart of a kernel of grain **2** *(Fig)* value, profit, virtue **3** *(Fig)* heart of the matter, essence **4** *(Fig)* physical strength

***fruʹshʹëz** *nf* riding whip

*fru'shk|ë *nf* dagger

fru'shk|ull *nm (np ~ j) nf* = fshi'kull

frushk|ull|im *nm ger* 1 <frushkullo'·n 2 = frushkulli'më

frushk|ull|i'më *nf* swishing sound made by a whip

frushk|ull|o'·n *vt* 1 to hit [] with a whip: whip 2 *(Fig)* to lambaste, scold strongly, criticize in rough language, rake over the coals

frushk|ull|u'e|s *adj* flagellatory: blistering, harsh, severe, castigating

*fru'sht|ull|ë *nf* whip

fru'sh|ull *nf* = frushulli'më

frush|ull|i'më *nf* 1 whistling of the wind 2 rustling of leaves

frush|ull|o'·n *vi* to make the sound of rushing air: swish, rustle

frut|ari *nf* 1 fruit shop 2 fruit growing

frut|dhë'n|ës *adj* fruit-bearing, fructiferous

fru'të *nf* fruit (from a fruit tree)

frut|ie'r|ë *nf* fruit bowl, fruit dish

frut|i|kultu'r|ë *nf* [*Agr*] = pemëtari

frut|o'·n *vi* (of a fruit tree) to bear fruit

frut|o'r
I § *adj* fruit-bearing, fructiferous
II § *nm* fruit trees

frut|o're *nf* 1 fruit bowl, fruit dish 2 orchard

frut|pru'r|ës *adj* fruitful, profitable

frut|sje'll|ës = frutprurës

fruth *nm* [*Med*] measles, morbilli
  ○ fruthi i keq/zi scarlet fever

*fry *nf* wind, gust of air

fry·*het vpr* 1 to swell, swell up; become swollen; become bloated 2 *(Colloq)* to gorge oneself on food, eat until sated: pig out 3 to get fat 4 to be inflated, billow out 5 *(Fig)* to get a swell head: strut like a peacock 6 to swell with anger; become exasperated
  ○ <> fry·*het*³ᵖˡ ijët "<>'s flanks *swell* out" <> *eats* too much
  ○ <> fry·*het*³ˢᵍ koka 1 <>'s head *gets* exhausted from mental effort 2 <> *gets* swell-headed
  ○ fry·*het* si qumësht "swell up like (boiling) milk" to swell up with rage
  ○ <> fry·*het*³ᵖˡ tëmthat "<>'s temples *are bulging*" <> *gets* very angry
  ○ <> fry·*het*³ˢᵍ zemra <>'s heart *grows* heavy
  ○ <> fry·*het*³ˢᵍ zemra nga gëzimi <>'s heart *swells* with happiness

fry·*n*
I § *vt* 1 to blow; blow on [] 2 to blow up []: inflate 3 to cause [] to swell 4 *(Colloq)* to stuff/gorge [] with food; fatten [] up 5 *(Fig Pej)* to exaggerate 6 *(Fig)* to exasperate 7 *(Fig)* to incite; incite [] to anger
II § *vi* 1 to blow 2 *(Colloq)* to run away: blow, scamper off 3 to breathe a spell into <>'s ear
  ○ fry·*n*³ˢᵍ erë *it is* windy, there's a wind blowing
  ○ fry·*n* hundët to blow one's nose
  ○ i fry·*n* lugës <së vet> to mind <one's> own business
  ○ <> fry·*n* murrani në qese "the north wind *blows* through his purse" <>'s pockets are completely empty, <> is dead broke
  ○ nuk të fry·*n*³ᵖˡ në sy "not breathe in your eye" never be there to help you

  ○ <> fry·*n* në vesh "blow/whisper/sing in <>'s ear" to egg <> on
  ○ fryji/fryjini sytë! cry your eyes out (because you'll never see it again)!
  ○ <a fry·*n* zemrën to break <>'s heart
  ○ i fry·*n* zjarrit to blow on the fire, stir the pot: make the situation even worse

*fry|a'q *adj* windy, breezy

*fry'|ce *nf* bellows

fry'|ça'k *adj, n (Contempt)* fat/obese (person)

*fry'|e·*n* = fry·*n*

*fry'|e|s *nm* blower, fan; sprayer

fry'jë *nf* 1 gale, strong wind 2 snowdrift

fry'më
I § *nf* 1 breath; breathing 2 expelled air 3 wind; gale 4 *(Colloq)* odor, fragrance 5 spirit; soul 6 basic principle; essence, essential 7 *(Fig Old)* life 8 living inhabitant
II § *quant (Colloq)* not a, not a single
  ○ frymë më frymë very close together
  ○ të nxjerrët frymë exhaling
  ○ s'ka· frymë to feel exhausted/weak

frymë|he'qje *nf* inhalation

frymë|këpu'tur *adj* ready-to-drop from exhaustion, out of breath

frymë|ma'rr|ës *adj* 1 respiratory, breathing 2 inhaling, inhalant

frymë|ma'rr|je *nf* 1 respiration, breathing 2 inhalation

frymë|nxje'rr|ës *adj (Book)* exhalatory, expiratory

frymë|nxje'rr|je *nf* exhalation, expiration

frymë|qen *adj (Impol)* dog's breath: camel-breath, bad-breath

frymë|qit|ës *adj* [*Ling*] expiratory

frymë|qit|je *nf* (Book) 1 exhalation 2 [*Ling*] expiration

*frymë|s = frymëz

frymë|so's|ur *adj* 1 very tired, exhausted, out of breath 2 *(Curse)* be damned! (by running out of breath), I hope you choke!

frymë|shu'ar *adj* = frymësosur

frymë|shu'më *adj, n* 1 long-lived (one) 2 *(Felic)* may he continue to breathe for a long time!

frymë|to'·*n* *vt* = ysht

frymë|to're *nf* = y'shtëse

frymë|thi'th|ës *adj* = frymëmarrës

frymë|thi'th|je *nf* 1 = frymëmarrje 2 [*Med*] aspiration

fry'më|z *nf* [*Med*] asthma

frymë|zë'n|ë *adj* 1 out of breath from exhaustion, dead tired 2 *(Curse)* be damned! (by running out of breath), I hope you choke!

frymë|zi'm *nm ger* 1 <frymëzo'·n, frymëo'·*het* 2 inspiration 3 person or thing that is inspired

frymë|zo'·*het vpr* to get inspired

frymë|zo'·*n* *vt* to inspire

frymë|zu'ar *adj (i)* inspired

frymë|zu'e|s *adj* inspirational, inspiring

frym|o'·*het vpr* to become filled with anger
  ○ frymo·*het* në [] to become angry at []

frym|o'·*n* *vt* to fill [] with breath: blow [] up

frymo'r
I § *adj* 1 breathing, alive 2 blown, wind (musical instrument or group) 3 [*Ling*] animate 4 respiratory
II § *nm* animate being

frym|o·s· *vi* to breathe

*****fry|në** *nf(Old)* horn

*****fry|nëz** *nf(Old)* flute

*****fryq** *nm (Old)* essence

fry|rë
  I § *adj (i)* **1** inflated **2** swollen, puffed up **3** bloated **4** distended **5** stuffed with food, gorged, sated **6** overlarge, overgrown **7** *(Fig)* overblown, pompous, bombastic **8** *(FigImpolite)* boastful **9** *(Fig)* swollen with anger: angry **10** *(Old)* under a spell
  II § *nf (e)* swelling
  ○ **i fryrë nga të tjerë** incited by others

fry|r|ës *nm* **1** blowpipe **2** glassblower **3** bellows (at a forge) **4** caster of spells

fry|r|ese *nf* **1** blowpipe **2** instrument used to fan a fire

fry|rje *nf ger* **1** <**fry·n**, **fry·het 2** swelling, turgidity, bloatedness
  ○ **fryrje e barkut** [*Med*] flatulence

*****frys** *stem for 1st sg pres, pl pres, 2nd & 3rd sg subj, pind* <**fryt·**

fry|së *nf* bellows (at a forge) = **fry·rës**

fry|sha·n *adj* stout, corpulent, fat

fry|shëm *adv* swelling with anger

fryt *nm* **1** fruit **2** product, result, fruit **3** [*Biol*] embryo of a mammal

*****fryt·** *vt* = **fry·n**

*****fry|ta** *np* <**fryt**

*****fry|tas** *n* shirker

frytdhë|n|ës *adj* fruitful, productive·

*****fry|të** *adj (i)* = **fry·rë**
  ○ **fryta me pala** pleated frill

fryt|ësi *nf (Book)* = **frytshm|ëri**

*****fryt|ësim** = **frytëzim**

fryt|ëzim *nm ger (Book)* **1** <**frytëzo·n**, **frytëzo·het 2** fructification

fryt|ëzo·n
  I § *vt (Book)* **1** to fructify, make [] fruitful **2** to use to advantage, make productive use of **3** *(Old)* [*Bot*] to fertilize, impregnate = **plleno·n**
  II § *vi* to bear fruit

fryt|fry·r *nm* [*Bot*] *(Physocarpus opulifolus)*

fry|tje
  I § *adj* [*Bot*] swollen
  II § *nf* **1** [*Bot*] = **fry·zë 2** penny whistle

fryt|mba·rt|ës *adj* [*Bot*] fruit-bearing

*****fryt|o·r** *adj* = **frytmba·rtës**

fryt|pru·r|ës *adj* fruitful, profitable

fryt|sje·ll|ës = **frytpru·rës**

*****fryt|s|o·n** *vt* = **frytëzo·n**

fryt|shëm *adj (i)* fruitful; fertile

fryt|shm|ëri *nf* fruitfulness; fertility

*****fryt|yll|o·n** *vi* to faint

*****fry|xë** *nf* = **fry|në**

fry|zë *nf* **1** [*Bot*] great reedmace *(Typha latifolia)* **2** whistle used for signalling
  ○ **fryzë e kuqe** [*Bot*] = **fryzëku·qe**

fryzë|ku·q|e *nf* [*Bot*] red cane

*****frra|c** *nm* box for breadcrumbs; spoon rack

*****frre·ckë** *nf* thistle, briar

*****frri** *nf* = **thërrmij|ë**

*****frri(n)** *nm (Old)* = **çikri·k**

*****frrok** *OR* **frruk** *adj* unruly, wild

FShA *abbrev* <**Federata Shqiptare e Atletikës** Albanian Federation of Athletics

fsha = **ofsha**

FShAÇ *abbrev* <**Federata Shqiptare e Alpinizimt dhe e Çiklizmit** Albanian Federation of Alpinism and Cycling

fsha|çe *adv* = **fshatçe**

fshat *nm* **1** rural population group/center: village **2** rural area
  ○ **Fshati digjet e kurva krihet** "The village burns and the whore combs her hair." Nero fiddles while Rome burns.
  ○ **Fshat e zanat, derë e tabiat.** "Village and customs, family and usage." *(Prov)* Different places and different families have different customs. Other countries, other customs.
  ○ **fshat i paktë** small village: hamlet
  ○ **Fshati që duket s'do kallauz.** "A village that one can see doesn't require a guide." *(Prov)* I don't need anyone to point that out. That's very obvious.

fshat|a·r
  I § *adj* rural, rustic
  II § *n* rural inhabitant; villager; peasant

fshat|ara·k *adj (Colloq)* rustic

fshat|ar|çe *adv (Colloq)* **1** country-style, rustically **2** together with the whole village

fshat|ar|ësi *nf* **1** countryfolk; rural populace **2** peasantry

fshat|ar|kë *nf(Reg)* country girl, village woman

fsha|tçe *adv (Colloq)* **1** by the whole village, with the whole village; in front of the whole village: out in the open **2** country-style

*****fshat|o·n**
  I § *vt* to settle [a place], populate
  II § *vi* to live in a village

fsha|tor *nm* [*Ornit*] gray heron *(Ardea cinerea)*

fsha|tra *np* <**fshat**

fsheh·
  I § *vt* **1** to hide, conceal **2** to contain deep inside
  II § *vi* to dissemble, dissimulate
  ○ **i fsheh· brirët** *(Pej)* to be a wolf in sheep's clothing
  ○ **i fsheh· këmbët** to act slyly, be tricky; act secretively; act in secret
  ○ **i fsheh· letrat** to hide a secret; hold back, not speak openly
  ○ **e fsheh· llafin** to be reserved in speaking, be hard to draw out, be taciturn
  ○ **fsheh· në gjirin e** {*pronominal adj*} to contain in {*one's*} midst: harbor in {*one's*} bosom
  ○ [] **fsheh· nën lëkurë** to keep [] secret for a painfully long time
  ○ **fsheh· sëpatën nën gunë** to be capable of stabbing one in back, not to be trusted

fsheh|a|lo·g|as *adv*

fsheh|ara·k
  I § *adj (Pej)* hidden, secret; secretive, sneaky
  II § *nm (Pej)* dissembler, fraud, hypocrite

fsheh·|ës *n* concealer, fraud, dissembler

fsheh|ësi·rë *nf* hiding place, secret place

fsheh·|ëz *nf* place for lying in wait for ambush; hunting blind

fsheh|je *nf ger* **1** <**fsheh·**, **fshi·het 2** concealment

fsheh|tas *OR* **fsheh|tazi** *adv* secretly, surreptitiously

fshehtë
I § *adj (i)* **1** hidden, concealed, covert **2** secret; clandestine **3** private **4** mysterious **5** *(Fig)* secretive
II § *nf (e)* secret

fshehtësi *nf* **1** secrecy, secretiveness **2** secret

fshehtësirë *nf* **1** secret **2** secret place

fshehur
I § *part* <**fsheh**·
II § *adj (i)* **1** hidden; concealed, covert **2** kept secret: secret **3** secretive **4** latent
III § *adv* in secret, covertly

fshehura *adv* = **fshehtas**

fshehurazi *adv* secretly, surreptitiously

fshehuri *nf* **1** secret matter **2** secrecy

fshehurisht *adv* secretly, surreptitiously = **fshehtas**

***fshere** *nf* wheel-shaped block of wax

***fsheretí·n** = **psheretí·n**

fshesabërës *n* broom maker

fshesar *n* street-cleaner, street-sweeper

fshesaxhi *nm (np ~ nj)* = **fshesar**

fshesë *nf* **1** broom **2** *[Bot]* sorghum **3** *[Bot]* general designation of plants whose stems and branches are used to make brooms: broomcorn **4** sweeping with a broom **5** *[Bot]* sea lavender *(Limonium)*
    ∘ **fshesë deti**. *[Bot]* kind of brown alga, brown seaweed *Stypocaulon scoparium*
    ∘ **fshesë e egër** *[Bot]* kidney-vetch *(Anthyllis hermanniae)*
    ∘ **fshesë elektrike** vacuum cleaner
    ∘ **fshesë me korrent** vacuum cleaner
    ∘ **fshesa e qershisë** *[Agr]* dense clump of branches growing abnormally out of the trunk of a cherry tree
    ∘ **ësh·të (ende) fshesë e re** to be (still) new on the job

fshesëtar *n* **1** broom maker = **fshesabërës 2** = **fshesar**

fshesurina *np* sweepings

FShF *abbrev* <**Federata Shqiptare e Futbollit** Albanian Federation of Football (Soccer)

FShGj *abbrev* <**Federata Shqiptare e Gjimnastikës** Albanian Federation of Gymnastics

fshi·n *vt* **1** to clean off [] with a sweeping motion: sweep, sweep [] away; brush off []; wipe [] off, wipe away [] **2** to wipe [] dry **3** to erase **4** to destroy [] completely; liquidate, eradicate
    ∘ **fshi·n buzët** to be a finicky eater
    ∘ **i fshi·n buzët nga** {} to give up all hope of {}

fshih· *stem for 2nd pl pres, pind, imper, vp* <**fsheh**·

fshihe· *vpr* <**fsheh**· **1** to lie hidden **2** (of the sun) to set **3** to hide oneself
    ∘ **Nuk fshihet drapri/minarja/hosteni në thes.** *(Prov)* It is impossible to hide such an obvious thing. It's too big to sweep under the rug.
    ∘ **fshi·het pas/prapa (hijes së) gishtit** to try in vain to hide something bad, try in vain to hide a defect
    ∘ **fshi·het pas bregut** to try to hide one's actions
    ∘ **fshi·het pas gjuhës së** {*pronominal adjective*} to mask one's real thoughts in speaking

fshihe· *vpr* <**fshi·n 1** to wipe oneself **2** to brush or wipe away spots from one's own body or clothes **3** *(Fig)* to get wiped out; vanish

fshijshëm *adj (i)* effaceable, eraseable

fshik· *vt* **1** to raise small blisters on [] **2** to cause a slight wound: bruise, scratch, graze **3** to touch lightly, brush **4** to whip with a switch: flog, thrash

fshik·et *vpr* to break out in fever blisters on the lip

fshika-fshika *adj* covered with little blisters

fshikakuq *nm* *[Bot]* European spindle tree *(Euonymus europaeus)*

fshikartë *nf* common bladder senna *(Colutea arborescens)*

fshikatar *n* grabber

fshikë *nf* **1** *[Med]* small blister, vesicle; swelling, bump **2** *[Anat]* bladder **3** cocoon
    ∘ **fshikë mëndafshi** silk cocoon

fshikët *adj (i)* **1** *[Bot]* vesiculate **2** *(Fig)* wretched, miserable

fshikëz *nf* **1** *(Dimin)* <**fshikë 2** *[Bot]* = **fshikartë 3** *[Med]* vesicle
    ∘ **fshikëza e mirë** *(Euph)* *[Med]* anthrax
    ∘ **fshikëz e mirë** *(Euph)* *[Veter]* anthrax

fshikëzeze *nf* **1** *[Med]* malignant pustule *(pustula maligna anthrax)* **2** carbuncle, boil

***fshikim** *nm ger* <**fshiko**·**n**

fshikje *nf ger* **1** <**fshik·, fshik·et 2** slight wound, scratch, or bump caused by disease or trauma

***fshiko·het** *vpr* to turn into a chrysalis

***fshiko·n** *vt* to flog

fshikor *adj* *[Med]* vesicular

fshikull *nm (np ~ j)* *nf* **1** thin, long, and flexible stick: switch **2** blow from a switch: lashing **3** *(Fig)* strong blow; bitter scolding, strong criticism

fshikullim *nm ger* **1** <**fshikullo·n 2** whipping noise

fshikullimë *nf* **1** strong blow with a stick: bastinado **2** whipping noise **3** sound of a strongly blowing wind

fshikullo·n *vt* **1** to beat [] with a switch; whip, lash, flagellate **2** to hit hard at []; scold [] bitterly, criticize [] roughly, chastise ***3** to blister

fshikullues *adj* hitting hard, bitterly scolding, roughly criticizing

fshikur
I § *adj (i)* **1** blistered **2** scratched, slightly wounded **3** slightly touched by disease
II § *nf (e)* slight wound, scratch, or bump caused by disease or trauma

fshikurazi *adv* touching slightly: brushing

fshiqe *nf* epidemic of a serious disease

fshira *np (të)* sweepings, rubbish

fshirë
I § *part* <**fshi·n**
II § *adj (i)* **1** swept/brushed/wiped clean **2** wiped dry

fshires
I § *n* person or thing that cleans with a sweeping motion: chimney-sweep; street-cleaner; eraser; swab
II § *adj* used for sweeping/brushing/wiping

fshirëse *nf* **1** eraser **2** shoe-cleaning mat: welcome mat **3** device used for removing dust: dustcloth, feather duster, swab **4** windshield wiper **5** dishcloth

fshirje *nf ger* <**fshi·n, fshi·het**

***fshisë** *nf* wiper, duster; mat

***fshitar** *n (Old)* sweeper

***fshkâ** *nf (Reg Gheg)* elflock

FShL *abbrev* <**Federata Shqiptare e Lojërave** Albanian Federation of Games (for games played with rackets or hands)

FShSR *abbrev* <**Federata Shqiptare e Sporteve të Rënda** Albanian Federation of Heavy Sports (weight lifting, wrestling, shot-putting)

*fshtiell = mbështjell

*fshtir = vështir

*ftek· *vt (Old)* to think [] over, consider

*ftek·et *vpr* to reminisce; have an idea
  ∘ <> **ftek·et** to occur to <>, come to <>'s mind; <> remembers

ftes *nm* = fteses

ftese *nf* invitation
  ∘ **ftese gjyqi** legal summons

ftes·ës *nm* wedding host

*ftige *nf* epilepsy

*ftik· *vt* 1 to stop the flow of []: stanch ***2** to dry [] up

*ftik·et *vpr* to run dry, dry up

*ftikes *adj* stanching

ftillëzim *nm ger* = ftillim

ftillëzo·het *vpr* = ftillo·het

ftillëzo·n *vt* = ftillo·n

ftillëzues *adj [Ling]* = ftillues

ftillim *nm ger* 1 <ftillo·n, ftillo·het 2 disentanglement

*ftillk *nm* explanation, explication

*ftillko·n = ftillo·n

*ftillkuem *adj (i) (Reg Gheg)* reasonable, logical, clear

*ftillkueshëm *adj (i)* well-proportioned, well-built

ftillo·het *vpr* to become clear in one's own mind, get clear

ftillo·n *vt* 1 to disentangle 2 to straighten [] out, put [] in order 3 to explain; clarify, resolve

ftillues *adj* explicative, explicatory, explanatory

ftillzo·n = ftillo·n

ftim *nm ger* 1 <fto·n 2 invitation

fto·n *vt* 1 to issue an invitation to []: invite 2 to issue a summons to []: summon
  ∘ **fto·n në duel** to challenge (to a duel)

*ftofësine *(Reg Gheg)* = ftohtesire

*ftof *(Reg Gheg)* = ftoh

*ftofto·n *vi (Reg Gheg)* to grow cool

ftoh· *vt* 1 to cool, chill, cool off 2 to temper metal by cooling quickly 3 *(Colloq)* to extinguish, douse, quench, turn off 4 to plow land for a third time
  ∘ <> **ftoh· kryet/kokën** to take a big load off <>'s mind

ftoh·et *vpr* 1 to grow cool, cool off 2 to get chilly 3 to catch cold 4 to stop functioning: go dead, die out, go out 5 *(Euph)* to die 6 *(Fig Colloq)* to grow calm
  ∘ **ftoh·et³ᵖˡ gjakrat** tempers *cool*
  ∘ <> **ftoh·et³ˢᵍ gjaku** <> *calms* down, <>'s anger *cools*
  ∘ **nuk** <> **ftoh·et³ˢᵍ pilafi/byreku** "<>'s food doesn't get cold" *(Crude)* it's no skin off <>'s nose
  ∘ <> **ftoh·et³ˢᵍ zemra 1** <>'s enthusiasm *cools* (<>'s heart *is* not in it anymore 2 <>'s friendship *cools*

ftoh·ës
  I § *nm* 1 cooling mechanism: cooler, chiller 2 refrigerant
  II § *adj* for cooling/freezing, for refrigeration

ftohësire *nf* cold, coldness (weather/relationship)

ftohje *nf ger* 1 <ftoh·, fto·het *(Colloq)* 2 cold (the illness)

ftohme *nf (Colloq)* 1 cold weather 2 cold (the illness)

ftohtas *adv* coldly = ftohte

ftohte
  I § *adj (i)* cold; cool, chilly
  II § *nf (e)* 1 cold weather, frost 2 cold (the illness)
  III § *nn (të)* 1 cold weather/temperature; coldness; frigidity 2 chill 3 cold (the illness)
  IV § *adv* coldly
  ∘ [] **pafsha të ftohtë** *(Curse)* May I see [] dead!

ftohtesi *nf* coolness, chilliness, coldness; the cold

ftohtesire *nf* 1 cold weather, frost 2 cold place 3 = ftohtesi

ftohur
  I § *adj (i)* 1 chilled 2 having a cold 3 plowed for a third time 4 *(Euph)* stone cold, dead
  II § *nf (e)* common cold
  III § *nn (të)* 1 = ftohje 2 common cold 3 coldness, coolness

ftolli *obl* <ftua quince

*ftollo·n *vt* = hollo·n

*ftome = ftohme

ftonj *np* <ftua

*ftorit· *vt* = ftoh-

ftorr· *vi* to make a snorting sound: snort

*ftri·n *vi impers* to snow

ftua *nm (obl ˜ oi, np ˜ onj)* quince *(Cydoia oblonga Mill)*
  ∘ **ftua i egër** *[Bot]* 1 European cow-lily, European cotoneaster *(Cotoneaster integerrima)* 2 Judas tree *(Cercis siliquastrum)*

ftua *stem for adm, part, pl pdef* <fto·n

ftuar
  I § *adj (i)* 1 invited 2 *[Law]* summoned
  II § *nm (i)* 1 invitee, guest 2 *[Law]* person under a summons

ftues *nm (Old)* 1 wedding host 2 *[Law]* summons server

ftujak *nm* 1 yearling male goat, male kid 2 *(Fig Pet)* frisky little boy

ftuje *nf* 1 yearling female goat, female kid 2 *(Fig Pet)* frisky little girl

*fturze *nf* crutch

fucak *nm* nosy/inquisitive person

*fuce *nf* hollow walnut

fucka *np [Food]* cookies made of flour and beaten eggs and covered with syrup

fucke *nf* pimple, blister, pustule

fuco·n *vi* to pilfer, filch

fuçi *nf* 1 tun, barrel 2 barrelful 3 *(FigImpolite)* person with a big belly: fatty
  ∘ **fuçi e madhe** hogshead
  ∘ **fuçi e vogël** keg

fuçibërës *nm* barrel maker

fuçipunues *nm* = fuçibërës

FUD *abbrev* <Forcat ushtarako-detare Naval Forces

FUD *nm* abbreviation for Forcat Ushtarako-detare

*fudull = fodull

fufu *nf (Book)* = fufule

fufule *nf* small charcoal grill: charcoal brazier

fug· *vt* 1 to throw/toss [] away 2 *(Fig)* to abandon, leave in the lurch
  ∘ **e fug· festen/kësulën/qeleshen/kapelën/takijen mbi sy/mënjanë** "put one's cap over the eyes (and rest)" to have nothing more to worry about, be free of care

fug·et *vpr* 1 to jump, leap 2 *(Fig)* to grow fast, spring up 3 *(Fig)* (of livestock) to miscarry, have a stillbirth

fugare *nf (Reg)* bonfire

fu'g|as *adv* by throwing

***fuga'të** *nf* [*Ornit*] = **fu'gë**

fu'gë
I § *nf* 1 flame, fire 2 oppressive heat 3 *(Fig Colloq)* burst of energy 4 *(Reg)* hurried gait; big hurry 5 eddy, whirlpool 6 [*Tech*] centrifuge 7 whirling children's toy: top; toy gyroscope/whirligig; rattle 8 [*Ornit*] female of the golden oriole 9 *(Fig)* short, plump, dumpy-looking girl 10 fugue
II § *adv* very quickly

fug|i'm *nm ger* 1 <**fugo'·n**, **fugo'·het** 2 fast running, hurry

fug|i'm|thi *adv* in a hurry, quickly

fug|o'·n *vt* to leave quickly, run away fast

***fugu're** *nf* = **figu're**

fukadru'gë *nf* [*Entom*] moth, clothes moth

fukara'
I § *adj* poor, in poverty
II § *nm* poor man, poor person
III § *nf collec* the poor, poor people

fukara|llë'k *nm (Colloq)* poverty

fukar|e'nj *np* <**fukara'**

***fukël|bu'kur** *nf* [*Zool*] = **nusela'le**

***ful** *adj* = **fyl**

***fu'le** *nf* [*Bot*] pheasant's-eye narcissus (*Narcissus poeticus*)

***fule'të** *nf* [*Bot*] nettle tree (*Celtis australis*) = **cara'c**

fu'li *nf* [*Bot*] wild jasmine (*Jasminum fruticans*)

***fuli'** *nf* unleavened wheat bread made to celebrate the birth of a child

***fulika're** *adv* hastily, suddenly, swiftly

***fu'lpë** *nf* candle, nightlight

fulqi'(r) *nm (Colloq)* 1 jaw 2 = **bërdi'lë**

fulqi|o'r *adj* [*Med*] maxillary

fulte're *nf* skillet, pan, frying pan = **tiga'n**
∘ **më dha saçin, i jap fulteren** one good turn deserves another

fulte'rëz *nf* [*Zool*] tadpole, pollywog

***fulliqi'ni** *nf (Reg Gheg)* = **fëllig|ë'shti**

***full|o'·n** *vi* to blow

full|ta'k *nm* = **fullta'kë**

full|ta'k|a-fullta'k|a
I § *adj* full of blisters caused by burning or stinging
II § *adv* broken out in blisters

full|te'|qe *np* <**fullta'k**

fumig|u'es|e *nf* [*Tech*] fumigating device, fumigator

fund *nm* 1 bottom; bottom part/residue; aft part of a boat 2 end, conclusion 3 lower part of a woman's outer clothing: skirt
∘ **fundi i arkës** "the bottom of the (clothes) chest" best clothes
∘ **fundi i fjalës** __ so at the end of it all __, so to bring the story to an end __
∘ **fundi i fundit** and finally, in the final analysis, in any case
∘ **fundi i kazanit** residual food remaining on bottom of the cooking vat
∘ **fund e krye** from top to bottom; completely
∘ **fundi i kusisë** "bottom of the pot" *(Tease)* (of a person) very dark
∘ **më në fund** at last, finally; in the final analysis

∘ **i fundit o qesh o qan.** "The last one either laughs or cries." *(Prov)* The last in line stands to get a lot or to get nothing.
∘ **fund rripi** common coltsfoot *Tussilago farfara*
∘ **fundi i tiganit** "bottom of the pan" *(Tease)* (of a person) very dark

fund|a'jë *nf* 1 tail-like corner of a field 2 mountain spur 3 part remaining: residue

fund|a'k *nm* fruit tree sprout growing near the trunk of the tree

fund|a'kë *nf* roof lath

fundame'nt *nm* foundation, basis: fundament

***fundane'llë** *nf* fontanelle

fund|a'q *nm* dreg, residue, lees

fund|a'r *nm* bottom of a body of water

fu'nd|azi *adv (Colloq)* finally

fu'nd|ce *nf* 1 bottom leaf of a plant 2 cigarette butt 3 part remaining: residue

***fu'nde** *nf* = **fund**

fund|ë'rr|e'së *nf* 1 [*Chem*] precipitate 2 dregs, leftover

fund|ë'rr|i *nf* residue, dregs, lees

fund|ë'rr|i'm *nm ger* <**fundë'rro'·n**

fund|ë'rr|i'në *nf* 1 worthless residue: dregs 2 = **fundë'rri** 3 *(Fig)* completely worthless person: human filth

fund|ë'rr|o'·n *vi* [*Chem*] to leave a sediment: precipitate

fund|ë'se *nf* bottom leaf of a tobacco plant

fu'nd|i *adv (së)* 1 recently 2 lastly
∘ **fundi-fundit** after all

***fu'nd|i-fu'nd|i** *adv* in the end, finally

fund|i'm *nm ger* <**fundo'·n**

fund|i'në *nf* abyss, depth

fu'nd|it *adj (i)* final, terminal; last, hindmost; utmost

fu'nd|ja *adv* in the end, after all, anyway

fu'nd|ja-fu'nd|jes *adv* in the end, when all is said and done

fu'nd|je *nf (Colloq)* 1 finish, ending 2 end/back section 3 bottom leaf of a plant 4 half-sole (in shoe repair)

fu'nd|më *adj (i)* 1 finite 2 time-limited

fund|o'·het *vpr* = **fundo's·et**

fund|o'·n *vt* = **fundo's·**

fund|o'r *adj (Book)* located in the end/back/bottom portion: final, terminal, end, bottom

fund|o're
I § *nf* [*Ling*] last part of a word: final syllable/sound: coda
II § *nf (Old)* [*Ling*] suffix, ending = **prapashte'së**

fund|o's· *vt* 1 to sink, immerse, plunge 2 *(Fig)* to bring [ ] down; overthrow, dash

fund|o's·et *vpr* 1 to sink, sink down, plunge to the bottom; submerge 2 to sink low; (of ground) subside 3 *(Fig)* to hit/reach bottom, fall low

fund|o'sje *nf ger* <**fundo's·**, **fundo's·et**

fund|o'sur *adj (i)* deeply immersed: sunk, sunken; in subsidence

fu'nd|ra *np* <**fund** remains, residue, left-overs

fund|ri'në *nf* = **fundë'rri**

fu'nd|shëm *adj (i)* uttermost; last; lowest, bottom

fund|shkro'jë *nf* last letter (in a word)

fund|tï'ngull *nm (Old)* final/terminal sound (in a sequence) *fundues* adj conclusive, final

funeral nm funeral

*funkcion = funksion

funksion nm function

funksional adj (Book) functional

funksionar n functionary, official

funksionim nm ger <funksiono•n, funksiono•het

funksiono•n vi to function, work, run, operate

funt nm 1 pound (of weight) 2 pound (of money)

fuq adv (Reg) in vain, for nothing, to no avail

fuqi nf 1 power 2 force 3 strength; ability, capability, capacity 4 [Law] authority, right, power 5 [Phys] power
  ○ fuqi avitëse (Old) centripetal force
  ○ fuqi motorike 1 output capacity of the motorized equipment of a factory: machine power 2 [Med] motor ability
  ○ fuqi sjellse (Old) electrical current

fuqidhënës adj (Book) power-giving; restorative, envigorating, tonic

fuqimadh
  I § adj (Book) powerful, potent; omnipotent, all-powerful
  II § nm [Relig] the Almighty

fuqimisht adv (Book) powerfully, forcefully; vigorously

fuqipaktë adj (Book) powerless, weak

fuqiplotë
  I § adj (Book) plenipotentiary, having full power
  II § nm [Relig] Omnipotent One, the Almighty

*fuqis = fuqiz

*fuqisjellës adj (Old) power-supplying, current-bearing

fuqishëm
  I § adj (i) 1 powerful, strong; mighty 2 forceful, energetic 3 with great force: powerful, vigorous; violent
  II § adv with great force

fuqizim nm ger <fuqizo•n, fuqizo•het

fuqizo•het vpr 1 to gain strength 2 (Old) [Law] to become empowered; (of a law) go into force, take effect

fuqizo•n vt 1 to strengthen: invigorate, reinforce 2 (Old) [Law] to empower; put [a law] into effect, activate

fur-
  I § vt 1 to strangle 2 (Fig) to have a stranglehold on []; compel [] by use of great force 3 to stifle
  II § vi to make an uninvited, surreptitious entrance

fur•et vpr 1 to be caught in a stranglehold; hang from a rope 2 to enter by force: burst right in, rush in 3 to attack with great force
  ○ <> fur•et³ˢᵍ shpirti <> comes to the end of <>'s endurance, <> loses all patience

furacak
  I § adj 1 uninvited: trespassing, crashing 2 (Fig) meddling
  II § nm trespasser, uninvited crasher

furan adj enterprising, energetic

furatë nf wooden rod/stake; stick used to shake fruit out of a tree

*furcatë nf (Old) force, reinforcement; strength, power

*furcë = furçë

furçë nf brush

furços• vt to brush

furçosje nf ger <furços•, furços•et

furde
  I § nf 1 shingle 2 small thing of no importance: oddment, trinket 3 (Fig) slut
  II § adj worthless

*furetë nf [Zool] ferret

furfule
  I § nf (Colloq) 1 = murrlan 2 (Fig) deranged person
  II § np wood shavings

furfullac nm (Joke) = murrlan

furfulli nf light breeze

furfullim nm ger <furfullo•n

furfullo•n vi = fërfëllo•n

*furfuri nf potpourri

furfurit• vi to shimmer, glisten, glitter

*furgëro•n vi
  ○ furgëro•n me [] to buzz/hum/swarm with []

furgon nm (motor) van: delivery van, police van, mail van

furi nf 1 sudden violent, long-lasting storm: tempest 2 (Fig) fury; rage; frenzy

furishëm
  I § adj (i) 1 furious, raging; frantic 2 uncontrollable
  II § adv furiously; frantically, in a frenzy

furkaçe nf 1 large supporting prop forked at one end 2 small forked distaff

furkatore nf spinstress who uses a forked distaff

furkë nf 1 forked stick 2 large supporting prop forked at one end 3 forked distaff 4 (Reg) pitchfork 5 [Invert] furca

furkëz nf (Dimin) 1 <furkë 2 [Mil] distance between the landing sites of bracketing artillery shells used to adjust the gunsight: bracket

*furko•n vt to fork, fork up []

furkulice nf table fork = pirun

*furllazë nf [Bot] common lavender (Lavandula spica)

furmaçe nf unit of length approximately equal to six inches: span = bërxhik

furmaçkë nf = furmaçe

*furneçkë = flegër

furnelë nf oil/gas burner

furnellë nf = furnelë

furnitor nm = furnizues

furnizim nm ger 1 <furnizo•n, furnizo•het 2 (Colloq) business equipment; store fixtures

furnizo•het vpr to get needed supplies

furnizo•n vt to furnish, supply, provide; equip

furnizues
  I § nm 1 supplier, delivery man 2 [Tech] delivery mechanism or device
  II § adj used for or involved in delivery or supply

furqetë nf 1 hairpin 2 knitting needle

furtunë
  I § nf severe storm
  II § adj very fast and adroit

furtunëshëm adj (i) stormy

furuvejkë nf [Ornit] owl = kukuvajkë

furrac nm water mill

furracë nf 1 long-handled tongs used to distribute burning coals in an oven 2 wheat bread prepared in boiling water: dumpling

furrare nf large loaf of baked bread

fu'rrë
I § nf **1** bakery **2** oven **3** kiln **4** industrial furnace **5** *(Colloq)* amount that can be baked at one time: ovenload
II § adj very hot; having a high fever

furrë·bu'bëz *nf* [*Zool*] weasel

furr|i'k *nm (np ˜qe)* **1** brood nest for poultry: hen roost **2** egg in a brood nest **3** *(Fig)* cosy nook **4** very small area, inch

furr|na'ltë *nf* [*Tech*] blast furnace

furro'·n *vt* **1** to bake [] in an oven/kiln/furnace **2** *(Fig)* to spur [] on to do something bad: incite

furro's· *vt* = furro'·n

furr|ta'r *n* **1** baker = bukëpje'kës **2** [*Tech*] furnaceman

furr|ta're *nf* [*Entom*] cockroach (*Blatta orientalis*)

furr|xhi' *nm (np ˜nj)* baker = furrta'r

fus| *stem for 1st sg pres, pl pres, 2nd & 3rd sg subj, pind* <fut·

fu'skë *nf* = fshi'kë

fusta'n *nm* **1** one-piece outer garment with a skirt and a bodice worn by women and girls: dress *(Reg)* **2** skirt **3** *(Fig Colloq)* woman or girl **4** = fustane'llë

fustane'llë *nf* [*Ethnog*] white pleated kilt that forms part of the Tosk ethnic costume for men

fu'stë *nf* **1** wide skirt; skirt **2** chemise **3** *(Old)* battle skiff

fusha'k *nm (Reg)* **1** doorbolt = shul *2 transom

fusha|lo'g *nm (np ˜gje)* flat, open area

fusha|mi'rë *nf (Reg Arb)* grass for sheep

fusha'r *n* = fushara'k

fushara'k
I § adj of or characteristic of plains or of people inhabiting plains, plain-dwelling
II § nm plainsman

fush|ara'ke *nf* plain

fusha'të *nf* **1** campaign **2** military expedition

fush|ati'zëm *nm (Book Pej)* precipitous use of massive means to attack problems

fu'shë *nf* **1** field **2** level ground: plain **3** area of activity or interest **4** [*Mus*] space on a music staff **5** area onto which cards or counters are placed in certain table games; the set of cards remaining in that area during a game
○ **Fusha ka sy e mali/pylli/gardhi/muri ka veshë.** "The plain has eyes and the mountain/forest/fence/wall has ears." *(Prov)* Don't think for a minute that you can keep things secret.
○ **fushë lufte** field of battle, battlefield
○ **fush**ë **me lule** something made to appear rosier than it is
○ **fushë me mina** (veritable) minefield
○ **ësh·të fush**ë **nga mendtë/koka** to be utterly brainless
○ **fushë sahati** dial of a watch/clock
○ **fush**ë **shikimi** [*Mil*] field of vision

fushë**|gro'pë** *nf* **1** basin of land surrounded by hills or mountains **2** lowlands

Fushë**-Kru'j|a** *nf* town north of Tirana

fushë**|pa'mje** *nf (Book)* field of vision

fushë**|py'll** *nm* flat clearing in a forest

fushë**ta'r** *n* fieldworker on a farm

fushë**ti're** *nf* **1** small plain in a hilly or mountainous area **2** valley

fush|i'm *nm ger* **1** <fusho'·n **2** [*Mil*] encampment

fushk *nm* pith of a tree

○ **fushk në dushk** nonsense

fu'shk|ët *adj (i)* flexible, pliant

fushk|ëti' *nf* flexibility, pliancy

fushki' *nf* = fushnji'

fush|na'jë *nf* large open field

fushnji' *nf* **1** manure of sheep or goat **2** area covered with sheep or goat manure

fusho'·n *vi* **1** [*Mil*] to encamp, make bivouac **2** to camp out, make camp

fusho'r *adj* **1** in or of open and flat country: lowland **2** [*Mil*] field-

fusho're *nf* level ground; small clearing

fush|qeta'r *n (Old)* person who sets off rocket flares

fush|qe'të *nf (Old)* rocket flare

fushta'ge *nf* = shtage

fush|u'jë *nf* field that retains moisture: moist ground

fu'shul *nf* [*Invert*] leech

*fushull|i'm *nm ger* <fushullo'·n

*fushull|o'·n = frushullo'·n

fut *nm* foot (12 inches)

fut·
I § vt **1** to put [] inside: insert; thrust/plant [] deep, drive [] in, stick [] in; immerse, plunge; introduce, add **2** *(Colloq)* to patch **3** to put [] aside for safekeeping **4** to install **5** *(Fig)* to include **6** *(Fig)* to involve **7** *(Colloq)* to give [] a quick treatment (with/by) **8** *(Colloq)* to hit ◇ (hard) **9** *(Fig Colloq)* to get [] started (in); start
II § vi (Colloq) to fall/blow/pour hard
○ <>a fut· "stuff it in to<>" *(Colloq)* to hit ◇ (hard), get ◇ ia futa me shkelm I kicked him/her/it hard na e futi me sa fuqi kishte he struck us as hard as he could **Afrohu dhe futja mu në ballë!** Get close and shoot him right through the forehead!
○ **ia fut·** *(Colloq)* to talk off the top of one's head
○ **i**[] **fut·** *(Colloq)* to indulge oneself in []
○ <> **fut· bërrylin** to give <> the elbow; force ◇ away/out
○ [] **fut· brenda** *(Colloq)* to put [] in jail
○ <> **fut· cita** to stir <> up; sow discord among/between <>, provoke dissension among/between <>
○ **e fut· djallin në shishe** "stick the devil in the bottle" *(Joke)* to be devilishly clever
○ **fut· dorën/duart në zjarr/prush** "put one's hand/hands in the fire/coals" to be willing to swear to it, be absolutely certain
○ **e fut· dreqin në shishe** "stick the devil in the bottle" *(Joke)* to be devilishly clever
○ **fut· duart 1** *(Pej)* to get involved in something that is not of one's business: butt in, interfere **2** *(Crude)* to cop a feel
○ **ia fut dushk** *(Impol)* **1** to miss by a mile **2** to mindlessly get way off the subject (of conversation) **3** to make a foolish mistake
○ <> **fut· dyfekun shtëpisë** to incite dissension in the family
○ **fut· farë** to plant a seed (of suspicion)
○ <> **fut· fite** to stir <> up; sow discord among/between <>, provoke dissension among/between <>
○ **fut· fite** "insert wedges" to sow discord, provoke a quarrel
○ <> **fut· fitilin/flakën** to stir <> up, stir the pot in <>; sow discord among/between <>, provoke dissension among/between <>
○ **fut· fitila** to fan the flame; stir up a quarrel
○ <> **fut· flamën 1** *(Crude)* not give a damn about <>, let <> go to hell **2** to scare <> to death, terrify <>

○ <> **fut· gërshërën** to apply the scissors to <>: cut/trim/shear <>, shorten/abridge <>

○ **fut· gishtin** to stick one's fingers into someone else's business

○ **fut· gjemba** to sow discord, provoke a quarrel

○ **nuk fut· gjë në thes** not get a thing out of it for oneself

○ <> **fut· gjilpërat 1** to touch <>'s sore spot, give <> the needle **2** to plant a seed of discord, provoke a quarrel

○ **fut· hundën** to stick one's nose into someone else's business

○ <> **fut· kalla** to provoke <> to do something (wrong); cause <> to quarrel

○ **ia fut· katundit** (*Impol*) **1** to miss by a mile **2** to mindlessly get way off the subject (of conversation) **3** to make a foolish mistake

○ **fut· këmbën/këmbët** {*somewhere*} **1** to set foot in/on {} **2** to poke one's nose into {}

○ <>**i fut· (të dy) këmbët në një këpucë/opingë 1** to put <> into a difficult position **2** to make <> do one's bidding **3** to give <> a good lesson (in proper behavior)

○ **fut· kokën/kryet në strajcën e tjetrit** to stick one's nose into other people's business

○ **fut· kokën në gërshërë** to put one's head on the line

○ <> **fut· krimbin** to give <> a cause for disquiet, plant a seed of suspicion in <>

○ <> **fut· kunja** to stir <> up; sow discord among/between <>, provoke dissension among/between <>

○ **i fut· lugët në kosh** "put the spoons back in the spoonbox" to have to be satisfied with nothing, not get anything at all

○ <> **fut· mizat** to stir <> up; sow discord among/between <>, provoke dissension among/between <>

○ <> **fut· murtajën 1** (*Crude*) not give a damn about <>, let <> go to hell **2** to scare <> to death, terrify <>

○ <>**a fut·**[3sg] **ndër mend/mendje** to call [] to <>'s mind

○ [] **fut· në arkiv** (*Book*) to relegate [] to oblivion, file [] away forever

○ [] **fut· në bigë** to put [] into a difficult position

○ [] **fut· në dollap** to deceive []; entrap []

○ [] **fut· në fre** to bring [] under control

○ **nuk e fut dot në grykën e pushkës** he is brave and cunning

○ <>[] **fut· në gjak 1** to make [] a part of <>'s very essence **2** to cause <> to have a love of []

○ [] **fut· në kallëpe** to preach at [] dogmatically

○ [] **fut· në katror** (*Book*) to get [someone] into a hopeless predicament; get [someone] hopelessly entangled

○ [] **fut· në kornizë** to put limits on [], restrict []

○ [] **fut· në lesë** to lead [] into a trap

○ <>**a fut·**[3sg] **në mend/mendje** to call [] to <>'s mind

○ **fut· në mes** to intercede, intervene

○ s'[] **fut· në numër** not (even) count [], not consider []

○ [] **fut· në një thes me** [] "put [] in the same bag with []" to wrongly put [] in the same category with []

○ [] **fut· në pushkën** "put [] on a gun" to shoot [] down

○ s'[] **fut· në rabush** not give [] the slightest consideration; not bother to take [] into consideration

○ [] **fut· në rreth 1** to encircle; surround **2** to find a plan to exert pressure on []: hit on the way to put the screws to []

○ [] **fut· në sirtar** "put [] into a drawer" (*Pej*) to file [] away instead of taking care of it

○ [] **fut· në shënjestër/shenjë** to target [] for criticism; keep [] under constant attack

○ [] **fut· në shtrungë 1** to put [] into a tight spot **2** to force [] into compliance, force [] to comply

○ [] **fut· në torbë/trastë** "put [] into a sack" to have [] in the palm of one's hand, have [] where one wants []

○ [] **fut· në thekër** to get [] into a quarrel

○ [] **fut· në thes/grackë/kurth/lak/kllapë** "put [] into a trap" **1** to play [] for a sucker, lure [] in, inveigle [] into a trap: sucker [] **2** to succeed in catching [] **3** to have [] in the palm of one's hand, have [] where one wants []

○ [] **fut· në varr/dhé për së gjalli/të gjallë** "put [] in the grave alive: bury [] alive" to bring [] to an early grave

○ [] **fut· në vathë 1** to get [] under complete control **2** to spring a trap on []

○ <>[] **fut· në vesh** "put [] into <>'s ear" to tell [] to <>; whisper [] into <>'s ear; plant [] in <>'s ear

○ **të fut· në vrimë të gjilpërës** "put you through the eye of a needle" to be extraordinarily adept

○ [] **fut· në vrimë të gjilpërës 1** to reprimand [] severely **2** to make [] do something, force [] to **3** to examine [] carefully and in detail

○ [] **fut· në xhep 1** to have [] in the palm of one's hand, have [] where one wants [] **2** to keep [] in mind **3** to try never to forget []; make a reminder of [] for future revenge

○ [] **fut· në zdrukth** "use a plane on []" (*Colloq*) to give [] a real going-over, put [] through the mill, lambaste []

○ [] **fut· nëpër xibërrishta** to put [] through needless suffering, make [] jump through hoops

○ **fut· një grusht miza** "introduce a handful of ants" to cause a quarrel

○ <> **fut· një gur në këpucë** to plant a seed of doubt/hatred in <>

○ <> **fut· një gur në opingë** to plant a seed of doubt/hatred in <>

○ <> **fut· një gur në shollë** to plant a seed of doubt/hatred in <>

○ <> **fut· një mik** to use an influential friend to intercede in <>, use a friend with pull to help with <>

○ **i fut· një tegel** (*Crude Colloq*) to take a pee

○ <>**i fut· pleshtat në vesh** "put fleas into <>'s ear" to make an innuendo: put a bug in <>'s ear, put a bee in <>'s bonnet

○ **fut· qafën** {*somewhere*} to find a temporary place to live {}: find a place to hang one's hat

○ **fut· qafën në zgjedhë** "put one's own neck in the yoke" to take on a very hard task willingly

○ **fut·**[3sg] **rruaza në pe** "string beads on a thread" **1** to work slowly and painstakingly **2** to do wasted work

○ <> **fut· spica** to stir <> up; sow discord among/between <>, provoke dissension among/between <>

○ **fut· spica** to sow discord, provoke a quarrel

○ **e fut· shejtanin në shishe** "stick the devil in the bottle" (*Joke*) to be devilishly clever

○ <> **fut· shkopinj në rrota** "put sticks into <>'s wheels" to deliberately cause <> problems, sabotage <>

○ **fut· turinjtë** to stick one's big nose into someone's else's business

○ <> **fut· thikën prapa kurrizit/shpinës** to stick a knife in <>'s back, betray <>

○ **ta fut·**^{3sg} **ujët/ujin nën rrogoz/hasër/vete** "put water under your floor mat" to always be doing things behind your back

○ **fut· ujkun në vathë** "put the wolf in the sheep-fold" to put a fox in the chicken coop

○ <> **fut· veremin** to drive <> to despair; make <> despondent

○ <> **fut· veshët në tul** "stick the ears in soft flesh" to pretend not to hear; be lenient

○ <> **fut· vijë/vizë 1** to draw a line through <>, line <> out **2** to wash one's hands of <>, have nothing more to do with <>

○ <> **fut· xixat** to stir <> up; sow discord among/between <>, provoke dissension among/between <>

○ **fut· zinë** *(Colloq)* to create a shortage

○ **fut· zjarrin (në shtëpi)** to introduce discord/dissension into the family

○ <> **fut· zjarrin** to stir <> up; sow discord among/between <>, provoke dissension among/between <>

○ **fut· zjarrin në kashtë** to deliberately incite trouble in a sensitive situation: stir the pot, add fuel to the fire

fut·et *vpr* **1** to get inside: enter; penetrate; intrude **2** to sink lower, drop **3** to get involved **4** to shrink **5** *(Colloq)* to get a quick treatment (with/by) **6** *(Colloq)* to start to strike a blow **7** *(Colloq)* (of a heavenly body) to set, go down

○ <> **fut·et** *(Colloq)* to get down to work on <>, get busy with <>; attack <> vigorously

○ <> **fut·et brenda** to get the meaning of <>; come to know <> thoroughly

○ **i fut·et detit me këmbë** to start something that is impossible to finish

○ **Nuk futet drapri/minarja/hosteni në thes.** *(Prov)* It is impossible to hide such an obvious thing. It's too big to sweep under the rug.

○ **fut·et dhëndër** *(Pej)* to move in with one's bride's parents

○ <> **fut·et megjithë opinga** "get down to work on <> even with one's clogs" to become totally committed to working on <>, devote all one's energies to <>

○ **fut·et mirë rolit** *(Book)* **1** to master the new role/responsibility/assignment well **2** to adjust well to the new situation

○ **fut·et në bri të buallit/kaut** to go into hiding, hole up

○ **fut·et në flakë** "plunge into the fire" to plunge right in, act without fear of the dangers

○ **fut·et në gojë të qenit** to place oneself in danger

○ <> **fut·et në gjak** to get into <>'s blood, become part of <>'s body

○ <> **fut·et në taban** to investigate <> to the very core, delve into <> deeply

○ **fut·et në vrimë të miut** "plunge into the mouse hole" to scamper into hiding, be so afraid that one doesn't know where to hide

○ **fut·et në [ ]** to get down to work on/at [ ]

○ **fut·et pesë para në grosh** "enters like five pennies in a pound" to stick one's nose where it doesn't belong

○ **S'futen pleshtat në thes.** "Fleas won't be put into a sack." *(Prov)* It's like catching fish with your hands. It can't be done. There's no way.

○ **fut·et si luga në pilaf** "enter like the spoon in the rice" *(Pej)* to intrude without invitation; stick one's big nose in

○ **fut·et si pykë** to stick one's nose in where it doesn't belong

○ **fut·et si qimja në qull** "intrude like a hair in porridge" to ruin things by sticking one's nose in where it doesn't belong

○ **fut·et si xhol** "plunge in like a joker" to poke one's nose into everything, intrude in matters that are none of one's business

○ **fut·et thellë** to penetrate (too) deeply, go too far

futazh *nm* [*Cine*] footage

futboll *nm* [*Sport*] soccer, football

futbollíst *n* [*Sport*] soccer/football player, footballer

futë
 I § *nf* **1** cotton apron **2** black kerchief worn on the head by women in mourning
 II § *adj* very dark
 ○ **ësh·të në futë** to be in mourning
 ○ **futë i zi/errët** pitch dark

*****fut'ëm** *adj (i)* lodged, caught, snagged

fut'ës *nm* **1** worker who puts tiles in the kiln **2** [*Tech*] insertion device **3** [*Ornit*] great crested grebe (*Podiceps cristatus*) = **kredhara·k**

futësa·k
 I § *adj* meddling
 II § *nm* busybody, meddler

futës·o·n *vi* *(Colloq)* to steal small things: pilfer

futëzezë *adj (Old)* **1** wearing a black kerchief as a symbol of mourning **2** in mourning

futizë *nf* bottom of a fish creel

futje *nf ger* <**fut, fut·et**

futore *nf* cotton apron

*****futrolë** *nf* tool bag/holder

futshëm *adj (i)* easy to get along with: affable, friendly, sociable

futur
 I § *adj (i)* **1** deep-sunk, sunken **2** hidden away; protected from the wind by surrounding hills **3** *(Fig)* enterprising and sociable
 II § *nf (e)* **1** small indentation **2** *(Colloq)* inlet **3** = **futje**
 ○ **ësh·të futur në borxh deri në grykë** to be in hock up to the neck

futuríst *n* [*Lit Art*] futurist

futurizëm *nm* [*Lit Art*] futurism

fuzhnjar *n* person who uses a harpoon to catch fish

fuzhnjë *nf* long-handled fishing harpoon with multiple barbed pronged barbs

f.v. = **fjala vjen** *abbrev* for instance, for example

f.v. *abbrev* <**fjala vjen** e.g. = for example

fy·het *vpr* to take offense, feel insulted

*****fyci** = **fuçi**

fyçkë *adj* **1** having an empty kernel, with content of no value: hollow, empty **2** *(Fig)* empty-headed

fye·n *vt* to insult, offend; dishonor, degrade

fyell
 I § *nm (np ~ j)* **1** flute, fife, shepherd's pipe **2** *(Colloq)* [*Anat*] long articulated human or animal bone **3** *(Colloq)* [*Anat*] body duct/vessel; canal-shaped body opening
 II § *adj* **1** *(Colloq)* straight as a pipe **2** *(Colloq)* hollow, empty

○ **fyell i çibukut** pipe stem
○ **fyell i dorës/krahut** [Anat] armbone, humerus
○ **fyell i gjakut** (Colloq) [Anat] blood vessel
○ **fyell i hundës** [Anat] nostril, nare
○ **fyell i këmbës** [Anat] shin, shinbone *tibia*
○ **fyell pa vrima** "flute without holes" (Impol) worthless person, good-for-nothing; stupid person, fool
○ **fyell i pushkës** gun barrel
○ **fyell i sobës** (Colloq) stovepipe
○ **fyell i veshit** [Anat] ear canal
○ **fyell i zjarrit** fireworks rocket

fyelltar *n* flute-player, piper

*__fyemje__ nf (Reg Gheg) = **fyerje**

fyer adj (i) offended, insulted

fyerje nf ger 1 <**fye·n, fy·het** 2 affront, offense, insult, humiliation

fyes
 I § adj offensive, insulting
 II § n offender

*__fyk__ nm (np ~ qe) [Bot] seaweed

fyl
 I § adj 1 having content of no value: hollow, empty 2 (Fig) empty-headed
 II § adv in vain, for nothing; to no good

*__fyll__ nm (of a cow) udder, teat

fyrbë
 I § adj = **fyl**
 II § nf hollow walnut

fyrle nf tiny hole, pore

fyryfyçkë nf 1 strong and cold wind 2 (Pej) foolish female

*__fyshek__ = **fishek**

*__fyshk__ vt = **fishk·**

fyshtë adj (i) loose, uncompacted = **shkrifët**

fyshtër nf [Bot] forsythia (Forsythia europea) = **boshtër**

fyt
 I § nm 1 throat; gullet 2 (Colloq) pipe, duct 3 (Colloq) spout, tap 4 closed collar (of a piece of clothing) 5 (Colloq) the amount of liquid that can be downed in one swallow: gulp, slug
 II § adj, adv (Colloq) hollow, empty
○ **Fyti është vëllai i detit.** "The throat is the brother of the sea." (Prov) Unbridled eating and drinking can swallow up all that you have.
○ **fyti i keq** [Med] diphtheria
○ **fyt më/për fyt** by the throat

fytafyt adv = **fytas**

fytafyt·et vp recip to be at one another's throat, wrestle

fytafytas adv = **fytas**

fytafytazi adv = **fytas**

fytak nm 1 small wooden jug with a spout 2 glutton

fytaqafë adv 1 slung crosswise over the shoulder = **krahaqafë** 2 in a warm and friendly manner, with warm friendship

fytas adv 1 at each other's throat; hand to hand 2 up to one's ears, full up

fytazi adv = **fytas**

fyte np [Med] mumps = **shyta**

fytës adj gluttonous, greedy

fytëz nf 1 [Bot] = **fryzë** 2 bobbin (in the shuttle of a loom) 3 in a water mill, the narrow part of the bottom

of the water trough through which the water comes with force

fytje adj 1 = **frytje** 2 made of dried cane

fytmadh adj gluttonous, greedy

*__fytme__ nf (e) swallowing

fytore nf 1 clasp holding a bell and fastened to a strap around the neck of a sheep or goat 2 (Old) [Ling] guttural sound, guttural

fytrrec nm larynx

fytthi adv = **fytas**

fytyrë nf 1 face 2 countenance 3 external appearance; surface appearance, surface 4 (Fig) good reputation; honor, sense of honor 5 (Old) [Spec] figure, personage
○ **fytyrë luani** [Med] leontiasis
○ **fytyrë e ndyrë/félliqur** disgusting/despicable/vile person
○ **s'ka· fytyrë** { } has no sense of shame, { } has a lot of nerve/gall/brass
○ **s'<> ësh·të terur kurrë fytyra** "<>'s face has never dried" <> has suffered all <>'s life

fytyrëcelë = **fytyrëçelur**

fytyrëcelur adj having a cheerful face

fytyrëgjatë adj having a long face

fytyrëgjerë adj having a broad face

fytyrëhequr adj having a drawn, thin face; pale-faced

fytyrëhënë adj, nf (Poet) (woman/girl) with a beautiful round face radiant as the moon

fytyrëmadh adj having a big wide face

fytyrëmbushur adj having a full plump face

fytyrëmprehtë adj having sharp features

fytyrëngrysur adj having a gloomy face

fytyrëprishur adj having a shattered expression

fytyrëqeshur adj having a smiling face

fytyrërrudhur adj having a wrinkled face

fytyrërrumbullak adj having a round face

fytyrërrumbullakët adj = **fytyrërrumbullak**

fytyrëtretur adj having a drawn face

fytyrëthatë adj having a shriveled-up face

fytyrëverdhë adj having a pale yellow face

fytyrëvarë adj having a face bearing the wounds of battle or illness

fytyrëvrazhdë adj having a cruel face

fytyrëvrenjtur adj having a frowning face

fytyrëz nf 1 traditional thin black veil worn over the face by women 2 protective faceplate: visor

fytyrëzbehtë adj having a pale face

fytyrëzymtë adj having a gloomy frowning face

fytyrim nm ger 1 <**fytyro·n, fytyro·het** 2 figure, drawing, picture 3 image

fytyro·het vpr 1 to take shape 2 to be imagined

fytyro·n
 I § vt (Old) 1 to picture, draw 2 to imagine
 II § vi to be written down somewhere, appear in writing

fytyruar adj (i) (Old) 1 of definite shape, having a particular form: designed, pictured 2 figurative 3 imagined

fyzë nf 1 tube 2 [Anat] vessel; vein; duct
○ **fyzat e gjakut** [Anat] blood vessels
○ **fyzat e frymës** [Anat] bronchial tubes

Gg

g [gë] *nf* **1** the consonant letter "g" **2** the voiced velar stop represented by the letter "g"

gabardinë *nf* **1** gabardine **2** light topcoat made of gabardine

gabarite *np* [*Tech*] overall dimensions, size

gabel *n, adj* (*Colloq*) nomadic Gypsy/Rom

gabelic̈e *nf* Gypsy girl/woman

gaberr *adj* (*Insult*) stupid, doltish; uncouth, boorish

gabë *nf* **1** (*Reg*) gaffe = **ga**ẗe **2** (*Reg*) [*Ornit*] = **shka**b̈e

gabim
  I § *nm* mistake; error
  II § *adv* by mistake
  ○ **gabim personal/vetiak 1** [*Sport*] personal foul **2** penalty for personal foul
  ○ **gabim i trashë** bad mistake; serious blunder

gabim**isht** *adv* by mistake, mistakenly, erroneously

gabim**ta**r *adj* = **gabues**

gabo·**het** *vpr* **1** to be mistaken, make a mistake, err **2** to do something wrong; fall into error

gabo·**n**
  I § *vi* **1** to make a mistake, err **2** to do something wrong
  II § *vt* **1** to mistake, confuse; miss, get [] wrong **2** to mislead, deceive
  ○ **gabo·n rrugën** to take the wrong road

gabonj̈e *nf* (*Reg*) [*Ornit*] = **shka**b̈e

gaborre *nf* (*Reg*) large pine log with several hollows in it

*__gabrie__ç *nm* [*Invert*] hornet

gabrreç *adj* (of trees) hollowed out

*__gabrro__llë *nf* [*Ornit*] skylark (*Alauda arvensis*)

gabua̧r *adj* (*i*) **1** incorrect, erroneous; wrong, in error **2** mistaken; misled, deceived

*__gabues__
  I § *adj* given to making mistakes
  II § *n* person who often makes mistakes

gabue**shëm** *adj* (*i*) **1** capable of making mistakes: fallible **2** wrong (in direction)

gabue**shm**ëri *nf* **1** fallibility **2** being mistaken

*__gabzhe__r *nm* corncob

gabzherr *nm* [*Anat*] **1** windpipe, trachea **2** larynx **3** Adam's apple. *__4__ gullet

*__gac__ *nm* [*Ornit*] gray heron (*Ardea cinerea*)

gacatore *nf* flintlock rifle

gac̈e
  I § *nf* **1** live coal, burning ember **2** spark **3** (*Reg*) oil lamp
  II § *adj* (*Fig*) sparkling
  ○ **gac̈e e mbuluar** "covered burning ember" (*Pej*) sneaky person, wolf in sheep's clothing
  ○ **gac̈e në para** in the chips, loaded (with money)

gacgavis stem for 1st sg pres, pl pres, 2nd & 3rd sg subj, pind < **gacgavi**t·

gacgavit· *vt* to egg on, agitate

gacgaviẗes
  I § *n* agitator
  II § *adj* agitating; urging, impelling

*__gacm__ = **ngacm**

gaco·**n** *vi* to glisten, shine

gacull**in**ë *nf* (*Reg*) [*Entom*] firefly, glowworm = **xixëllo**nj̈e

gacull**o**·**n** *vi* to glow, twinkle, sparkle

gaç *nm* donkey colt = **kërri**ç

gaç̈e *nf* **1** cow, sheep, or goat that gives birth at an unusually early age = **lla**shk̈e **2** woman who gives birth at an unusually early age **3** [*Bot*] meadow saffron = **ka**ç̈e

*__gaç__ëm = **ga**tshëm

gaç̈kë *nf* [*Bot*] Savoy cabbage (*Brassica oleracea var. capitata*)

*__gada__l = **ngada**l

*__gade__ *nf* [*Ornit*] = **ga**ẗe
  ○ **gade lane** [*Ornit*] night heron *Nycticorax nycticorax*

*__gadi__ = **ga**ti

gadishull *nm* (*np* ~ *j*) [*Geog*] peninsula

gadishull**o**r *adj* [*Geog*] peninsular

*__gado__sh *nm* = **kodo**sh

gaẗe *nf* **1** (*Colloq*) gaffe; gross blunder; clumsy mistake *__2__ obscenity, filthy joke **3** [*Ichth*] greater amberjack (*Seriola dumerili Risso*)

gafërr *nf* big rock, boulder

gafil *adv* (*Colloq*) by surprise

gaforre *nf* [*Invert*] crab, lobster
  ○ **gaforre bregu** [*Invert*] estuary crab *Carcinus aestuarii*
  ○ **gaforre lythore** [*Invert*]   *Erriphia verrucosa*

gaforre-sheg̈e *nf* [*Invert*] coconut crab *Calappa granulata*

gafrro·**het** *vpr* **1** to get rumpled, tousled **2** to puff up/fan out feathers (like a turkey)

gafrro·**n** *vt* to rumple [hair/feathers], dishevel

gafrrua̧r *adj* (*i*) rumpled, tousled, disheveled

gagaç
  I § *nm* stammerer
  II § *adj* stammering

ga-ga-ga *onomat* sound made by a duck: quack-quack

gagarimë *nf* quacking/honking sound

gagaris *stem for 1st sg pres, pl pres, 2nd & 3rd sg subj, pind* < **gagari**t·

gagarit· *vi* **1** to quack, honk **2** (*Fig ColloqImpolite*) to prattle on and on

gagaritje *nf ger* < **gagari**t·

*__gagjari__ *nf* (*Old*) prop for shoring up vines

*__gaja__f *nm* pocket

gajas·
  I § *vt* to tire [] out; make [] weak from laughing or crying
  II § *vi* **1** = **gaja**s·**et 2** to feel dry in the mouth

gaja's·*et vpr* to get tired out, become exhausted; grow weak (from laughing/crying)

gaja's ur
I § *adj (i)* **1** extremely tired, exhausted; feeling weak (from much laughing/crying) **2** bewildered = **hutu a**r
II § *nf (e)* weak sob/giggle

ga'jde *nf*[*Mus*] bagpipe

gajde xhi *nm (np ˜ nj)* [*Mus*] bagpipe player, piper

*****gajdhe'r** *nm* scaffold

*****gajdhu'r** *nm* [*Zool*] donkey, ass

ga'j ës *n* child who urinates a lot

gajgana *nf*[*Food*] **1** eggs fried with peppers, tomatoes, and spices **2** sweet pastry made of eggs, flour, milk, and butter, and covered with syrup

ga'jgë
I § *nf* **1** soft-shelled walnut **2** [*Ornit*] magpie (*Pica pica*)
II § *adj* soft-shelled, easy-to-crack

ga'jle *nf* (*Colloq*) worry, trouble
○ **gajle e madhe!** so what! big deal!

gajre't *nm* (*Colloq*) **1** pluck: guts, grit **2** patience; forbearance

gajre't shëm *adj (i)* (*Colloq*) **1** plucky **2** patient; forbearing

gajta n
I § *nm* **1** braided piping used to finish off or decorate clothing seams **2** decorative braid
II § *adj* (of eyebrows) delicately shaped

gaju'shë *nf* dense underbrush in marshland; dense thicket

gakth *nm* [*Ornit*] bittern (*Botaurus stellaris*)
○ **gakthi i vogël** [*Ornit*] little bittern *Ixobrychus minutus*

gal *adj* **1** Welsh **2** = **gala'n**

galabu'n *nm* [*Entom*] worm larva with an unfinished cocoon

*****galaci'llë** *nf* [*Bot*] Aaron's rod, great mullein (*Verbascum thapsus*)

galaco·*het vpr* to be paralyzed, be unable to walk

galacu (n)
I § *nm (np ˜ nj)* paralytic, invalid = **ulo'k**
II § *adv* **1** all hunched up, in a wad **2** sitting on one leg with the other bent and with its heel on the ground

galakti'kë *nf* [*Astron*] galaxy

galaku'q *adj, n* (person) in a dazed state

gala'msh
I § *nm* completely paralyzed person: total invalid, paralytic
II § *adv* curled/folded up, in a heap

gala'n *adj, n* black (livestock animal)

galanteri *nf* **1** small objects used as personal accessories (such as gloves, belts, watchstraps, combs, brushes, purses, brooches) **2** workshop that makes personal accessories; shop that sells personal accessories

*****galave'le** *nf* flower in full bloom: bloom

gala'vër *nf* **1** ironwood (hornbeam) withe looped around a tree trunk in order to drag it downhill **2** iron or wooden collar placed around a dog's neck

*****galavi'zhdë** *nf* smear, daub

galc *nm (Reg)* **1** short rope; belt **2** (*Fig*) people of the same age: generation

*****galdi** *nf* jollity

galdi'm *nm ger* **1** <**galdo**·*n*, **galdo**·*het* **2** joy, delight, rejoicing; exultation

galdo'·*het vpr* to exult, rejoice

galdo'·*n vi* to rejoice, feel great joy

*****gale** = **gale'rë**

ga'le *nf* [*Bot*] oak-gall, oak-apple = **go'gë**'**ga'le** = **gajle**

gale'dër *nf* = **bili'ke**

gale'në *nf* [*Min*] galena

gale'rë *nf* [*Naut*] many-oared ship: galley

galeri *nf* **1** gallery (of art) **2** mine gallery **3** tunnel **4** theater balcony

gale'të *nf* zwieback, hardtack

galexha'nt *nm* [*Tech*] float (in a flush toilet tank)

gale'z *adj* Welsh

ga'lë
I § *nf* **1** [*Ornit*] jackdaw (*Corvus monedula L.*) **2** black sheep; black cow
II § *nm* (the) Welsh
III § *adj* black-haired

Gali *nf* Wales

gali'cë *nf* [*Ornit*] alpine chough (*Pyrrhocorax graculus*)

gali'ç *adv* in a squatting position, in a squat

galinace *np* [*Ornit*] (*Gallinae*)

gali'në *nf* **1** big clod of earth **2** piece of broken-off rock **3** = **zall 4** = **zalli'shtë**

galiu'm *nm* gallium *Ga*

*****galko'**·*n vi* to ride on horseback

ga'lme *nf* (of livestock) dun-colored, dark gray

galmi'qe *np (Reg)* twigs and small branches used for kindling

*****galo'një** *nf* (*Reg Tosk*) mansion, palace

galo'p
I § *nm* gallop
II § *adv* at a gallop
○ **galop i thatë** [*Riding*] extended canter
○ **galop i vogël** [*Riding*] canter

galopie'r *nm* [*Riding*] galloper

galti'në *nf* debris from a fallen wall

galu'ç *adv* = **gali'ç**

galvaniz i'm *nm ger* <**galvanizo**·*n*

galvani zo'·*n vt* **1** to electroplate **2** to galvanize [ ] into action

galvan ome'tër *nm* galvanometer

galvan oplasti'kë *nf* [*Phys*] galvanoplasty, electroplating

gallabe're
I § *adj* spread open too far
II § *nf* overblown flower

gallaga'n *nm* (*Impol*) unattractive person who is too tall and thin: beanpole

gallahu'të *nf* (*Impol*) unattractive girl/woman who is too tall and thin: beanpole

galla'të *nf* (*Colloq*) uproar created by loud conversation and joking: hubbub

gallëzo'·*n vi* to rejoice = **galdo'**·*n*

*****Galli** *nf* = **Gali**

*****gallm** *I §* *nm* OR **gallmi** *II §* *nf* impetus, inducement, cause

*****gallmo'**·*n vt* to urge, induce, cause

*****gallo'çe** = **gallo'she**

gallo'f *nm* **1** [*Ornit*] hooded crow (*Corvus corone cornix*) **2** male jackdaw **3** (*Fig Insult*) big clumsy oaf; blinking idiot *gallonjë nf gallery, corridor

gallore nf [Bot] herbaceous broad bush injurious to early summer grain crops

galloshe nf 1 galoshes 2 (Colloq) rubber/plastic boots for women

gallustër nf dormer window

gama indecl nf the Greek letter gamma

gametë nf [Med] gamete

gamë nf [Mus] musical scale: gamut

gamërr nf 1 (Reg) fishing bait; baited hook *2 (Old) bacillus

gam-gam onomat sound of a barking dog: woof-woof

gamillar n camel driver

gamile nf [Zool] camel = deve

*gamile|pardale nf (Old) giraffe = gjirafë

gamit· vi to bark

*gamthet·et vpr 1 = gapthet·et 2 to cling

*gamthet|un adj (i) (Reg Gheg) clinging

gamuç nm donkey colt = gaç

gamule nf heap, pile

gamull nm (np ~ j) small waterfall/cascade

gand
   I § nm defect
   II § adv accidentally; unintentionally

gandall nm (np ~ j) (Reg) puddle

gandim nm ger < gando·n, gando·het

gando·het vpr to suffer a body blow/injury, get hurt; get maimed/bruised

gando·n vt 1 to hit [] in the body; injure/hurt [] by hitting; maim, bruise 2 (Fig) to hurt, offend, insult; defame

ganec
   I § nm 1 (Folklore) weak man who acts as guide and aide to witches; warlock 2 (Pej) pimp
   II § adj *of loose morals, immoral

*ganeci nf pimping, procuring

ganez adj, n of/from Ghana, native of Ghana: Ghanian

ganë nf 1 wood chisel *2 filth

Ganë nf Ghana

Gang nf Ganges

*gangër nf [Invert] tadpole

gangrenë nf gangrene

gangrenizim nm ger [Med] < gangreno·het

gangrenizo·het vpr [Med] to become gangrenous

gangrenor adj gangrenous

gangrenoz adj [Med] gangrenous

gangster nm gangster

gangsterizëm nm gangsterism

gangull adv intact, whole, undivided

*gani nf fertility, productivity

*ganishëm adj (i) fertile, productive

ganos· vt 1 to tin [a vessel] 2 to glaze [ceramics]

ganxhe nf = kanxhe

gapërr adv 1 (of eyes) agape and staring 2 frenetically, frantically; greedily

gapërro·n vt to stare at

gapthet·et vpr to wrestle, fight hand-to-hand, scuffle

gaqe np loose blue trousers made of heavy wool worn in some northern areas of Albania

*garaç = garraç

garagaçkë nf [Ornit] magpie (Pica pica)

garamet nm difficulty, problem; worry, trouble

garanci nf 1 guarantee; affidavit 2 [Law] warranty 3 surety, collateral, bail

garant nm 1 guarantor 2 sponsor

*garanti nf = garanci

garantim nm ger < garanto·n, garanto·het

garanto·het vpr to stand as guarantor

garanto·n
   I § vt 1 to guarantee 2 to assure 3 to vouch for [], sponsor 4 (Old) to insure
   II § vi to stand as guarantor

garantuar adj (i) 1 guaranteed 2 (Old) rationed

garantues nm guarantor

garaqe nf snail shell = garroqe

*garavaq adj stiff

*garaz nm spite

garazh nm garage

garbe nf 1 pot or jug with a broken neck; flowerpot 2 bedpan

garbë
   I § nf 1 nick in a blade 2 = garbe
   II § adj hoarse, rasping

garbi nf strong rain-bearing wind from the west or southwest

garbull nm (np ~ j) insect repellent

gardalinë nf 1 [Ornit] goldfinch = kryeartëz 2 [Sport] line referee, linesman (in soccer)

gardë nf military detachment selected for special duty: guard

garderobë nf 1 wardrobe closet/cabinet 2 wardrobe 3 checkroom for leaving coats

garderobist n checkroom attendant

gardian n prison guard, jailer

gardist adj, nm (of or pertaining to) a member of a military guard

gardh nm 1 wicker fence; fence 2 wattled partition 3 barricade 4 (Fig) barrier, obstacle, hindrance
   ○ gardh i gjallë 1 hedge fence 2 human fence
   ○ gardhi ka sy the wall has ears, you can't hide secrets
   ○ qe gardh e u bë shteg "it was a fence and it became a path" no harm done
   ○ gardh i shkulur "uprooted fence" person who has lost his value and importance

gardhec nm round corncrib made of wicker

gardhë nf 1 groove made in the inside wall of a barrel upon with the barrel head rests: croze 2 wood joint

gardhën nf = gardhë

gardhënim nm ger < gardhëno·n

gardhëno·n vt to make grooves in [wood] with a croze: rout

gardhënojcë nf drive wheel

gardhënor nm 1 coopers' sickle-shaped tool used to create a croze for a barrelhead: croze, router 2 railing around the deck of a ship

gardhëtar n 1 person who is skillful at making wattled partitions 2 (Colloq) close neighbor

gardhim nm ger 1 < gardho·n 2 enclosure

gardhiqe nf small protective wicker fence surrounding a fruit tree or sapling

gardhishte nf small fence

gardhnajë nf collec 1 fences taken as a whole: fencing 2 open space bordered by fences

gardh|o'·*n vt* **1** to surround [ ] by a fence: fence in [ ] **2** to gather around, surround

gardh|o'le *nf* **1** small fenced enclosure to separate lambs or kids from the rest of the flock **2** hotbed (for germinating and protecting seedlings) surrounded by a fence **3** wicker cage for trapping animals

gardh|o're *nf* **1** bottle with a covering of woven straw or thin wicker **2** small protective wicker fence surrounding a fruit tree or sapling **3** small fence serving as a retaining wall for soil **4** fenced enclosure

gardh|o's· = **gardho'·***n*

ga're *nf* **1** contest **2** [*Sport*] match, game, race **3** competition

gargali'q *nm* [*Zool*] European tree frog *(Hyla arborea)*

gargali's· *vt* to tickle

garga're *nf* **1** gargling **2** [*Med*] medicinal liquid used for gargling: mouthwash, gargle, collutory

gargar|i's *stem for 1st sg pres, pl pres, 2nd & 3rd sg subj, pind* < **gargari't·**

gargar|i't· *vi* **1** to gargle **2** to emit a croaking sound: croak **3** to prattle, talk twaddle

gargar|i'tje *nf ger* **1** < **gargari't·** **2** croaking sound made by frogs

gargar|i'zëm *nm* gurgle; gargling

garga|'s = **gargari's**

garga|'t· = **gargari't·**

ga'rge *nf* **1** [*Ornit*] bee-eater = **bre'gçe** **2** *(Reg)* bullet cartridge **3** *(Fig)* old, broken-down, and worthless person or thing

*****gargi'** *nf* = **harbi'**

ga'rgull *adv* up to the very brim, brimful

ga'rgull *nm (np ~j)* **1** [*Ornit*] bee-eater *(Merops apiaster)* = **bre'gçe** **2** [*Ornit*] starling = **shtu're**

*****gargj|i's·** *vi* to beam, shine

*****gari't-***et vpr (Reg Tosk)* to trip along

garnitu're *nf* **1** [*Food*] cooked vegetable garnish **2** trimming on clothing

garnizo'n *nm* garrison

garso'n *nm* waiter

*****ga'rth|je** = **gafo're**

*****garu'c** = **garru'c**

garu'zhd|ë *nf* **1** ladle **2** *(Fig Pej)* troublemaker, nuisance

ga'rzë *nf* [*Pharm*] gauze; bandage made with gauze

garra'ç *nm* pot/jug with a broken neck; flowerpot; potsherd

*****garrame't** *nm* = **garame't**

*****garra'n** *nm* gorge, abyss

garrava'ç *adj (Colloq)* bent over from old age or illness: stooped

garrava'rre *nf* rake for gathering in ashes, manure, etc.

garrave'l *nm* large basket for collecting leaves, manure, etc.

garrave'sh *nm* *(Reg)* large supporting prop forked at one end

*****garravi'tëm** *nf* **1** bother, nuisance **2** uproar

*****ga'rre** *nf* ditch; ravine

garri|'s *stem for 1st sg pres, pl pres, 2nd & 3rd sg subj, pind* < **garri't·**

garri|'t· *vi (Reg)* (of a donkey) to bray

garro'q *nm* = **garro'qe**

garro'qe
   I § *nf* **1** hollow place: cave, hole in a tree trunk, pit, hole in the ground **2** hollowed out block of wood used to hold salt and spoons **3** shell of a tortoise or snail **4** sound box of a mandolin **5** *(Fig)* old man stooped by age or illness *****6** porcelain bowl
   II § *adj* *****hollowed out; broken, ruined

*****garru'c** *nm* troublemaker, nuisance

*****garru'mbull** *nm (np ~j) adv* = **gru'mbull**

*****ga's|cëm** = **gazmo'r**

gasta're
   I § *nf* **1** glass, piece of glass **2** glass container **3** farm animal with shiny or whitish hair
   II § *adj* clear and shiny as glass

gastari'na *np (Colloq)* glassware = **qelquri'na**

gasta'rtë *adj (i)* made of glass

*****ga'stër** *nf* = **ngastër**

gasto'r *nm* [*Ichth*] = **gastu'r**

gastrik *adj* gastric

gastri't *nm* [*Med*] gastritis

gastu'r *nm* [*Ichth*] leaping gray mullet *(Liza saliens)*

*****gas|u'er** *adj (fem ~ore) (Old)* gaseous

gashte'lle *nf* kneecap

*****gashtell|o'r** *adj* patellar, rotular

ga'shtë *nf* **1** whetstone; touchstone **2** = **gashte'll**ë

ga't-*et vpr* to get ready

gate'së *nf* specially prepared food: pastry

ga'te *nf* [*Ornit*] common heron *(Ardea cinerea)*

ga'tër *nf* **1** saw mill *****2** bunch of dry leaves

ga'ti
   I § *adv* **1** ready **2** [*Track*] set!, get set!
   II § *pcl* **1** almost, practically, for the most part. **2** about to, on the point of
   ○ **gati sa s'/nuk** {*verb*} nearly {}, almost {}

ga'ti *np* preparations

ga'ti-ga'ti *pcl* **1** almost completely, very nearly **2** just about to

gati'm *nm ger* **1** < **gatu'a·***n*, **gatu·***het* **2** manner of preparation **3** = **gate's**ë

gati'm|e *np* < **gati'm** *(Old)* [*Ethnog*] sweets taken by a bride to her father's home or to her husband upon her return to his home

gati'|s *stem for 1st sg pres, pl pres, 2nd & 3rd sg subj, pind* < **gati't·**

*****gati'|shëm** *adj (i)* = **ga'tshëm**

gati'shm|eri' *nf* readiness

*****gati'|shull** = **gadi'shull**

gati't· *vt* **1** to prepare; get [ ] ready **2** to prepare [ ] for eating: cook

gati't-*et vpr* **1** to make preparations: get ready **2** to take a position and not mover: get set

gati'tje *nf ger* **1** < **gati't·** **2** preparation

gati'to'r *adj* preparatory

gati'to're *nf (Old)* nursery school

*****gati't|shëm** = **ga'tshëm**

gati'tu
   I § *interj* [*Mil*] attention!
   II § *adv* [*Mil*] at attention

*****gati't|un** *(Reg Gheg)* = **ga'tshëm**

gato'| *stem for sg pdef, opt, alternative adm* < **gatu'a·***n*

gato'jcë *nf* female cook; woman who helps prepare the food for a wedding = **gatu'ese**

*****gato'js**ë = **gato'jc**ë

gatrist *n* operator of a gang mill

gatshëm *adj (i)* **1** ready **2** ever ready **3** prepared in advance **4** ready-made

gatu·het *vpr* to be formed, shaped, educated

gatua·n *vt* **1** to prepare [food]; knead [bread] **2** to cook **3** *(Fig Pej)* to cook up, be up to [] **4** *(Fig)* to form, shape, educate **5** *(Fig Colloq)* to fix, put right ◦ <>a gatua·nn kulaçin to cook up something bad for <>, pull a dirty trick on <>

gatuar *adj (i)* **1** prepared for eating: cooked **2** softened by marinating or boiling

*****gatuc** *nm* [*Ichth*] small-spotted catshark (*Scyliorhinus canicula*) = **mace deti**

gatues
I § *n* dough kneader, cook
II § *adj* kneading

gatuese *nf* **1** female cook **2** tool for mixing and kneading dough

gath *nm* **1** [*Bot*] catkin, ament **2** goat's dewlap

gavej *np* <**gavyell**

gavetë *nf* metal bowl (in a mess kit)

gavër *nf (Reg)* **1** = **zgavër 2** hole

gavërz *nf* little hole in skin: pore

gavërr *nf* [*Ichth*] anchovy (*Engraulis encrasicholus*)

gaviç *nm* **1** wooden vat; winepress; milk vat **2** *(Reg)* granary **3** *(Reg)* chimney flue

*****gaviçuer** *nm (obl ~ori) (Old)* **1** tub **2** cooper

*****gavigj** *nm* barrel-shaped fireplace

gavole *nf* **1** bubble **2** blister **3** *(Reg)* shell (of an egg, nut, etc.)

*****gavricë** *nf* = **gavërz**

*****gavro** *nf* [*Ichth*] = **gavërr**

gavrosh *nm* plucky boy

*****gavrucë** *nf* small hole

gavyell *nm (np ~ j)* wooden rim of a cart/wagon wheel; one section of such a rim: felly

*****gaxulline** = **gacullinë**

gaxhahut·et *vpr (Reg)* to be bewildered; be surprised

gaxharronjë *nf (Reg)* wooden hook left by cutting or breaking off a branch above its angle with the stem

gaxhe = **gashtellë**

gaxhi *nf (Colloq)* **1** joke **2** joking **3** mocking, jeering

*****gaxhis** *stem for 1st sg pres, pl pres, 2nd & 3rd sg subj, pind* <**gaxhit·**

gaxhit· *vi (Colloq)* to joke
◦ **gaxhit· me** [] to mock/jeer at []

gaxhit·et *vpr (Colloq)* = **gaxhit·**

*****gaxho·het** *vpr* to kneel on one knee

gaxhole *nf (Reg)* **1** wall of rocks placed near a stream of water to serve to lay out dirty clothes for soaking **2** playhouse for children made with things like piled-up rocks, sticks, and roof tiles

gaxhorr *nm* scarecrow = **gogol**

gaxhullan *nm (Reg)* blazing/flaming fire

*****gaxhup** = **gozhup**

gaxhvile *nf* [*Ornit*] lapwing (*Vanellus vanellus*)

gaz
I § *nm* **1** joy **2** laughter **3** joyful occasion; merriment **4** *(Colloq)* source of joy **5** *(Old)* pleasure, amusement, fun **6** *(Colloq)* wedding couple
II § *nm* **1** gas **2** *(Colloq Old)* oil **3** *(Reg)* oil lamp with a long handle
◦ **gaz fisnik** rare gas

◦ **gaz lotsjellës** tear gas
◦ **gaz mbytës** suffocating gas
◦ **gaz i tokës** natural gas

gazanik *nm* **1** oil lamp with a long handle **2** tin container for oil

gazavaj *nm* mixed joy and sadness

gazel *nm* [*Lit*] in Oriental folk literature a short lyric verse consisting of rhymed couplets: ghazel

gazele *nf (Colloq)* joke = **shaka**

gazelë *nf* [*Zool*] gazelle

gazep
I § *nm (Colloq)* **1** deep trouble; woe **2** troublemaker; very bad person
II § *adv* extremely, to a high degree; too

gazepqar
I § *adj (Colloq)* **1** causing suffering and sadness **2** pessimistic; constantly complaining
II § *n* unlucky person

gazepshëm *adj (i) (Colloq)* **1** painful; exhausting **2** terrible, disastrous

gazetar *n* journalist; newspaperman

gazetari *nf* newspaper journalism

gazetashitës *n* newspaper dealer, newsboy

gazetashpërndarës *n* person who delivers newspapers: newspaper boy

gazetë *nf* newspaper

*****gazë** = **garzë**

*****gazëll** = **ngazëll**

gazët *adj (i)* = **gazor**

gazhedhës [*gaz-he dh-ës*] *adj* gas discharging/dispersing

gazhedhëse [*gaz-he dh-se*] *nf* gas-dispersing weapon

gazifikim *nm ger* <**gazifiko·n, gazifiko·het**

gazifiko·het *vpr* to become gasified

gazifiko·n *vt* **1** to gasify **2** to install a system for delivering natural gas

gazim *nm ger* <**gazo·n** carbonation

*****gazit·et** *vpr* **1** to jest, joke **2** to cheer up, be cheerful

*****gazitës** *adj* **1** cheerful **2** funny, humorous

gazmatës
I § *adj* gas-measuring
II § *nm* **1** gas meter **2** laboratory gasometer
III § *n* person responsible for measuring noxious gas in mines

gazmbajtës *adj* [*Geol*] gasiferous, gas-bearing

gazmend *nm* great joy, elation

Gazmend *nm* Gazmend (male name)

gazmendshëm *adj (i)* **1** enjoyable **2** merry, joyful

gazmim *nm* elation

gazmo·het *vpr* to feel great joy, be elated, be full of joy

gazmo·n
I § *vt* to fill [] with joy, make [] happy, elate
II § *vi* **1** to be full of joy **2** to burst with joy

gazmor *adj* **1** causing joy: enjoyable, delightful **2** expressing joy: joyful, gay **3** spent enjoyably: enjoyable, pleasant **4** jolly, cheerful; convivial

gazmore *nf* light anecdote, amusing little story: joke

*****gazmori** *nf* cheerfulness

gazo·n *vt* **1** to carbonate [a liquid] **2** to make fun of [someone]

gazobeton *nm* [*Spec*] aerated concrete

gazogjen *nm* gas generator, gas producer

gazoline *nf* gasoline

gazometer *nm* **1** laboratory gasometer **2** gas meter

gazor *adj* **1** gaseous **2** gas-bearing

gazozë *nf* carbonated soft drink; bottle of pop

gazplotë *adj (Poet)* **1** joyous **2** joyful; merry

gazra *np* < **gaz 2** stomach/intestinal gas

gazsjellës *adj* **1** pertaining to delivery of gas **2** system of pipes and associated equipment for delivering gas

*****gazshëm** *adj (i)* = **gëzueshëm**

gaztar = **gaztor**

gaztë *adj (i)* gaseous

gaztor

I § *n* **1** *(Old)* buffoon, jester, fool **2** *[Theat]* comic actor; clown **3** funny person, comedian

II § *adj* funny, comical, witty

gazuar *adj (i)* carbonated

gazhdare *nf* corncrib, corn granary

gazhel *nm (Reg)* = **gomar**

gazhinë *nf (Reg)* = **thertore**

gazhup *nm* **1** fur **2** = **gozhup**

*****gdhâ(n)** *nm (Reg Gheg)* = **gdhe(r)**

gdhe(r) *nm* **1** knot (in timber), gnarl **2** *[Bot]* black pine *(Pinus nigra)* **3** *(Fig Colloq)* blockhead

gdheisht *nf* = **pishnajë**

gdhend· *vt* **1** to form [] with a bladed tool: chisel, carve, whittle, sculpt **2** to engrave; etch **3** to make [] smooth with a bladed tool: plane, trim **4** *(Fig)* to polish; refine; educate, civilize **5** *(Fig Colloq)* to hit, smack

  ○ **i gdhend· fjalët** to choose one's words carefully, carefully hone one's words

gdhend·et *vpr (Colloq)* to become more docile/civilized: tame down; become more cultivated, get better educated

  ○ **nuk <> gdhend·et**[3sg] **koka** "<>'s head is too hard to chisel/smooth" nothing gets into <>'s head: <> *is* incapable of learning; <> *is* hard-headed and intransigent; you might as well talk to the wall as to <>

gdhendari *nf* **1** mastery of carving: sculpture **2** sculpture workshop

gdhendë *nf* = **gdhendël**

gdhendël *nf* **1** wood chip **2** small chip

gdhendës

I § *adj* used for carving/sculpting/engraving

II § *n* carver, whittler; sculptor; engraver

gdhendje *nf ger* **1** <**gdhend·**, **gdhend·et 2** sculpture, carving, engraving

  ○ **gdhendje me mjete kimike** etching

gdhendshëm *adj (i)* capable of being incised; suitable for carving or engraving

gdhendur *adj (i)* **1** carved, chiseled **2** incised: engraved, etched **3** *(Fig)* polished; refined **4** *(Fig Colloq)* cultivated, cultured, well educated

gdhenj *np* <**gdhe(r)**

gdheri *obl* <**gdhe(r)**

gdhë(r) *nm (np ~ nj)* = **gdhe(r)**

*****gdhënd** = **gdhend**

gdhi·het

I § *vpr* **1** to spend the night awake **2** to be found by the dawn, awaken in the morning

II § *vp impers* it *becomes* dawn, it *dawns*

  ○ **gdhi·het kallkan** to die in the night and be already cold by dawn: be (found) dead in the morning

gdhi·n

I § *vi impers* it *grows* light, it *dawns*

II § *vi* to stay awake until daybreak

III § *vt* to spend [the night] without sleeping

gdhirë

I § *adj (i)* left over from the previous evening; still unchurned from the previous evening's milking

II § *nn (të)* daybreak, dawn

gegë

I § *adj [Ethnog]* native to Gegëria

II § *n* Albanian from Gegëria: Gheg

Gegëri *nf* ethnographic region including central and northern Albania

gegërisht *adv [Ling]* in Gheg dialect

gegërishte *nf [Ling]* Gheg dialect

gegizëm *nm [Ling]* language feature belonging to the Gheg dialect

gejzer *nm [Geog]* geyser

*****gekue** *nm (obl ~ oni) [Zool]* gecko

gem *nm* young twig/branch: sprig, shoot

gem·et *vpr* to get cross-eyed

geman *adj* cross-eyed = **vëngër**

gemtas *adv* in a crooked line, with zigzags, crooked

gemtë *adj (i)* **1** crooked (in appearance) **2** cross-eyed

gemto·n

I § *vt* to make [] crooked; cross [one's eyes] = **shtrëmbëro·n**

II § *vi* **1** to go in a non-straight line: walk crooked, zigzag, meander **2** *(Fig)* to be devious in behavior

*****gemth** *nm dimin* <**gem**

Genc *nm* Genc (male name)

gencianë *nf [Bot]* yellow gentian *Gentiana lutea* = **sanëz**

giancianëzë *nf [Bot]* gentianella *Gentianella*

genocid *nm* = **gjenocid**

Gent *nm* Gent (male name)

Gentian *nm* Gentian (male name)

*****geologji** *nf* geology

*****gep** *nm* shirtfront

ger *nm [Zool]* = **ketër**

geraniore *np [Bot]* geranium family *Geraniaceae*

*****gerdhet** *nm* storage cellar

germanium *nm [Min]* germanium

germë *nf* letter (of an alphabet), character = **shkronjë**

gerrlë *nf (Reg)* **1** water-eroded rock; rock with a hollow made by water **2** crevasse in rock eroded by water

GESTAPO *abbrev (German)* <**Geheime Staats Polizei** *[Hist]* Gestapo

geta *np* **1** panty-hose **2** *[Sports]* knee-length stockings without heels: football socks

gete *np* = **geta**

geto *nf* ghetto

*****gethletar**

I § *n (Old)* flatterer

II § *adj (Old)* flattering

*****gethletim** *nm (Old)* flattery

*****gethleto·n** *vt (Old)* to flatter; fondle

gëdhirë *adj* = **gdhirë**

*****gëgëri** *nf* giggle

*****gëgëris·** *vi* to giggle

gëk *onomat (Colloq)*

○ **s'bë·n gëk** to be very quiet, not say boo
○ **(s'bë·n) as gëk as mëk** not make a sound; not say boo
gëlbaz *vt* = këlbaz·
gëlbaz·et *vpr* = këlbaz·et
gëlbazë *nf* phlegm, sputum = këlbazë
gëlbazur *adj (i)* = këlbazur
gëlboqe *nf* = këlboqe
gëlçomë *nf(Reg)* cork, stopper, bung
*__gëlkos·__ = këlkos·
gëlo·n *vi* 1 to appear suddenly and noisily in a multitude: teem, swarm 2 to bloom suddenly 3 to gush forth, well up 4 to burn fiercely and noisily: crackle 5 *(Fig)* to bubble with liveliness or intensity
gëlqerar *n* lime slaker
gëlqere *nf* lime (calcium oxide)
○ **gëlqere e gjallë/pashuar** quicklime, burnt lime
○ **gëlqere e shuar** slaked lime
○ **gëlqere e shurdhuar** air-slacked lime
gëlqerebërës *nm* producer of lime
gëlqereshitës *nm* seller of lime
gëlqerexhi *nm (np ˜ nj)* seller of lime; limeburner
gëlqerëz**ím** *nm ger* <gëlqerëzo·n, gëlqerëzo·het
gëlqerëz**o·het** *vt* 1 to calcify, become calcified 2 *[Agr]* to fertilize with lime
gëlqerëz**o·n** *vt* 1 to cause [] to calcify 2 *[Agr]* to fertilize with lime: lime 3 *[Tech]* to calcine
gëlqerëz**uar** *adj (i)* 1 calcified 2 fertilized with lime
gëlqerim *nm ger [Agr]* <gëlqero·n, gëlqero·het
gëlqerinë *nf* peeled-off flake of whitewash
gëlqerishtë *nf* 1 land rich in lime 2 lime pit
gëlqero·n *vt [Agr]* to fertilize [] with lime: lime
gëlqeror
I § *adj* lime-bearing, calcareous
II § *nm [Min]* limestone, calcareous rock
gëlqeros· *vt* 1 to whitewash 2 to treat [hides] with slaked lime: lime
gëlqerosje *nf ger* <gëlqeros·
gëlqerosur *adj (i)* 1 whitewashed 2 limed 3 soaked in lime
gëlqertë *adj (i)* = gëlqeror
gëlqeruar *adj (i)* fertilized with lime
gëlues *adj* moving quickly and noisily in a swarming mass: astir and abuzz
*__gëlvoshë__ OR gëlvozhë = gollovezhgë
*__gëlvozhd__ë OR gëlvozhgë *nf* = gollovezhgë
*__gëllqis·__ *vt* to plunge [] into water
gëlltimë *nf* gulp, sip
gëlltis stem for 1st sg pres, pl pres, 2nd & 3rd sg subj, pind <gëlltit·
gëlltit· *vt* 1 to swallow; swallow [] up; gulp [] down 2 *(Fig)* to endure [something unpleasant] without resistance 3 *(Fig)* to keep [an emotion] bottled up inside 4 *(Fig Colloq)* to be gullible about [ ]: swallow 5 *(Fig Colloq)* to be able to stand [someone] 6 *(Fig Colloq)* to spend/cost a large amount of [ ]: eat up [ ], use [ ] up 7 *(Fig)* to be captivated by [ ]
○ **i gëlltit· fjalët** 1 to mumble 2 to deny having said what one has said
gëlltit·et *vpr (Colloq)* 1 to swallow, gulp 2 *(Fig)* to be unable to get the words out of one's mouth, have one's tongue stuck in one's throat 3 *(Fig)* to be bearable, be possible to take/accept/stand

gëlltitje *nf ger* 1 <gëlltit·, gëlltit·et 2 swallow, gulp
gëlltitur *nf (e)* = gëlltitje
gëmush·et *vpr* to get bushy-haired; get one's hair rumpled
gëmushë *nf* bush
gëmushor *adj* bushy
*__gëndall__ *nm* pond, marsh
*__gënuq__
I § *nm* twig, stick
II § *adj* bony, shrunken
gënje·het *vpr* 1 to be deceived, be wrong 2 to be gullible 3 to beguile oneself 4 to nourish false hopes, lie to oneself
gënje·n
I § *vt* 1 to deceive, delude; fool 2 to beguile 3 *[Sport]* to fake [] out
II § *vi* to lie, tell a lie; tell lies
○ [] **gënje·n³ˢᵍ shpresa se** _ [] has the false hope that _
○ **gënje·n shtruar/përtokë** to be a clever and convincing liar
○ <> **gënje·n³ᵖˡ veshët** <>'s ears *are playing* tricks on <>: <> *is hearing* things (that aren't there)
gënjeshtar
I § *adj* 1 lying; deceitful; deceptive 2 nourishing false hopes: illusory
II § *n* liar
gënjeshtër *nf* 1 lie, fib 2 deception 3 false promise, false hope 4 illusion, delusion
○ **Gënjeshtra e bën vegshin, por nuk ia vë kapakun.** "Deception makes the pot, but does not put the lid on it." *(Prov)* You may succeed in cheating, but you won't succeed in covering it up.
○ **Gënjeshtra i ka këmbët të shkurtra.** "Lies have short legs." *(Prov)* Lies will soon be found out.
○ **gënjeshtra në diell** patent lies
gënjeshtërmadh
I § *adj* lying badly
II § *nm* big liar
gënjeshtërt *adj (i)* 1 fake, false; erroneous 2 lying; insincere, deceptive
gënjeshtrazi *adv* deceitfully, falsely
gënjeshtro·n *vt* to belie
gënjim *nm ger* <gënje·n, gënje·het
gënjyer *adj (i)* 1 wrong, mistaken 2 deceived, fooled 3 disappointed, disillusioned
gënjyes *adj* deceptive, fraudulent
*__gëq__ *onomat* = gëk
gërb *nm (Reg) [Anat]* pelvis; hipbone
*__gërbaç__ *nm* = kërbaç
*__gërball·et__ *vpr* to live a riotous life
*__gërball__ë *nf* high life
gërbegjerë *adj* big-hipped
gërbej *np [Anat]* <gërbyell
gërbellë *nf(Reg)* rock crevice; cave
gërbë *nf [Anat]* hump (on a person's back)
gërbul· *vt* 1 to infect [] with leprosy 2 to make filthy: befoul
gërbul·et *vpr* 1 to become infected with leprosy 2 to get dirty 3 *(Fig)* to get fully satiated, become completely full *4 to decompose
gërbulaç *adj* = gërbulaq
gërbulaq *adj* 1 leprous; purulent 2 filthy

gërbulë *nf* 1 [*Med*] leprosy 2 (*Colloq*) nonsense, poppycock

gërbulët *adj (i)* 1 = gërbulur *2 putrid, rotten

gërbullur *adj (i)* infected with leprosy: leprous

gërbuz·et *vpr* to make a face: grimace

gërbyell *nm* [*Anat*] one of the three pelvic bones on which we sit

gërç *nm* muscle spasm, cramp

gërdallë *adj, nf (Colloq)* scrawny horse/person; worthless old thing

gërdec
  I § *nm* [*Med*] 1 syphilis 2 [*Bot*] small shrub used in folk medicine for treatment of bladder and kidney problems: bearberry (*Arctostaphylos uva ursi L.*)
  II § *adj* 1 solid and hard 2 not cooked enough: rare

*gërdetshëm = gërditshëm

gërdi *nf* nausea = krupë

gërdit· *vt* to nauseate

gërdit·et *vpr* to feel sick, become nauseate, feel like throwing up

gërditshëm *adj (i)* causing nausea: nauseating; disgusting

*gërduk· *vi* to gripe

gërdhajë *nf* 1 discarded part of fruit, fruit residues 2 (*Old Pej*) ignorant masses

gërdham *nm* 1 aggregate of coarse sand and pebbles; gravel 2 limestone concrete 3 trash, waste, rubbish, garbage

gërdhatë *nf* barren area with impassable rocky crags, rugged mountain country

gërdhele *nf* plowed land with many unbroken clods of soil, inadequately plowed field

*gërdhesh·et *vt* = zgërdhi·het

gërdheshtër *nf (Reg)* discarded part of grapes, grape residues

*gërdhisht = gërvisht

gërdhitë *nf* chip mark; physical defect

gërdhomë *nf* 1 residue left after threshing: straw and chaff 2 straw stubble 3 residue, leaving, remnant, waste

gërdhu *np fem* = gërdhushta

gërdhuc· *vt (Reg·)* = gërvisht·

gërdhuc·et *vpr* = gërvisht·et

gërdhuckë *nf* 1 unripe fruit 2 (*Fig*) small child

gërdhuq *nm (Insult)* very old man with a weak and shriveled up body

gërdhushta *np fem* residue left by sifting grain and used as feed for fowl: chaff, bran, chickenfeed

gërdhuz *nm (Colloq)* 1 immature child, baby 2 small-bodied person, midget

gërdhuz·et *vpr* = ngërdhuc·et

gërdhuzë *nf* abnormally small female; female midget

gërëvëra *np (Colloq)* bickering; petty gossip

gërfej *np* < gërfyell

gërfyell
  I § *nm* tunnel
  II § *adj (Fig)* empty-headed, stupid

gërga *stem for pdef, opt, adm, part, imper* < gërget·

*gërgalec OR gërgalaq *nm* [*Invert*] = gargaliq

gërgalle *nf, adj* 1 barren, rocky (soil) 2 (*FigImpolite*) skinny (woman or girl)

gërgalline *nf* piece of barren and rocky ground

gërgamë *nf ger* 1 < gërget· 2 dissension sown by an outside agitator

gërgarë *part* < gërget·

gërgas *n* = gërgasës

gërgas| *stem for 1st sg pres, 1st & 3rd pl pres, 2nd & 3rd sg subj* < gërget·

gërgasë *nf* = gërgamë

gërgasës *n* 1 heckler 2 agitator, inciter; troublemaker

gërgat *stem for part, adm* < gërget·

gërget· *vt* 1 to poke; prick, sting 2 (*Fig*) to pester, annoy 3 (*Fig*) to incite, egg [] on

gërgëlac *nm (Reg)* [*Anat*] = gabzherr

gërgëlak *nm (Reg)* [*Anat*] = gabzherr

gërgëlis| *stem for 1st sg pres, pl pres, 2nd & 3rd sg subj, pind* < gërgëli·

gërgëlit· *vt* = gërgëllo·n

gërgëllo·n *vi* [*Ornit*] to make the distinctive call of a bee-eater: warble, burble

gërgëras| *stem for 1st sg pres, 1st & 3rd pl pres, 2nd & 3rd sg subj* < gërgëret·

gërgërat *stem for part, adm* < gërgëret·

gërgëre *nf* spinning rattle

gërgëret· *vt* to simmer, bubble

gërgërimë *nf* 1 gurgling sound: gurgle, burbling 2 growling, rumbling

gërgëris| *stem for 2nd pl pres, pind* < gërgëret·

gërgërit· *vi* 1 to make a gurgling rattle: gurgle, growl 2 (*Fig*) to prattle

gërgërit| *stem for pdef, opt, adm, part, pind, 2nd pl pres, imper, vp* < gërgëret·

gërgëritje *nf ger* 1 < gërgërit· 2 = gërgërimë

gërgis| *stem for 2nd pl pres, pind* < gërget·

gërgit| *stem for pdef, opt, adm, part, pind, 2nd pl pres, imper, vp* < gërget·

gërgo·n *vt* = gërga·s·

*gërgulë *nf* nightmare

*gërgyle *nf* scuffle

gërhaç *nm* 1 [*Veter*] contagious disease of poultry characterized by a thick mucous discharge in the throat: pip 2 [*Med*] whooping cough 3 snorer

gërhal·et *vpr* 1 to get pockmarks on the face 2 to get rough and flaky skin from the sun

gërhalë
  I § *nf* sharp pointed rock; rock with a rough surface; ground covered by jagged rocks
  II § *adj* deeply furrowed; rough

gërhamë = gërhimë

gërhanë *nf* 1 [*Text*] carding comb for wool; hackle board for flax 2 (*Colloq*) coarse comb

gërhanëtore *nf* woman/girl who uses a carding comb or hackle board

gërhanim *nm ger* < gërhano·n

gërhano·n *vt* to disentangle [fibers] with a coarse comb: card [wool], hackle/comb [flax]

gërhas· *vt* to snore

gërhat *stem for part, adm* < gërhet

gërheq· *vi* to be in the throes of death, be dying

gërhet· *vt* to snore
  ∘ <> **gërhet·**[3pl] **zorrët** <>'s stomach is growling/rumbling (from hunger)

gërhi·n *vi* to make a snoring-like sound: snore; purr, growl, rumble; grunt; rattle; wheeze; sniffle

gërhimë *nf* sound of snoring, snoring sound, snore

gërhis _stem for 2nd pl pres, pind_ < **gërhet**

gërhit _for pdef, opt, adm, part, pind, 2nd pl pres, imper, vp_ < **gërhet**

gërhitës _adj_ 1 snoring, purring 2 [_Med_] stertorous

gërhitje _nf ger_ < **gërhet·**, **gërhi·**n

gërje _nf_ 1 snoring sound 2 last breath, death rattle

gërjezhdë _nf_ ground covered with plants: green land

gërlac _nm_ windpipe

gërlan _nm_ = **gurmaz**

gërlas _stem for 1st sg pres, 1st & 3rd pl pres, 2nd & 3rd sg subj_ < **gërlat·**

gërlat· _vt_ to bend

gërlat·et _vpr_ to bend, bow, sag

*_**gërmac**_ _nm_ glottis

gërmadhë
  I § _nf_ 1 ruins of an old structure: ruin 2 (_Colloq_) dilapidated old building 3 (_Colloq FigImpolite_) person with an emaciated body
  II § _adj_ 1 abandonded, wretched 2 (_Colloq_) dilapidated; emaciated
  ○ [] qau gërmadha "the ruins mourn []" [] has met with a great disaster

gërmadho·n _OR_ **gërmadhos·** _vt_ to ruin

gërmajë
  I § _nf_ 1 hole dug in the ground 2 (_Reg_) = **grumbull** 3 (_Reg_) crowd, throng
  II § _adv_ crowded with, in large numbers, in droves

*_**gërmaz**_ = **gurmaz**

gërmazor _adj_ [_Med_] laryngeal

gërmesë _nf_ digging tool

gërmë _nf_ = **germë**

*_**gërmic·**_ _vt_ = **gërvisht·**

gërmicë _nf_ 1 [_Veter_] = **gërmitë** 2 (_Reg_) = **zverk**

gërmih· _vt, vi_ 1 to dig [] (in the ground) 2 to hoe

gërmim _nm ger_ 1 < **gërmo·**n 2 digging; excavation 3 dug-up ground
  ○ **gërmime dheu** earthworks

gërmime _np_ < **gërmim** [_Archeol_] archeological excavations

gërmis _stem for 1st sg pres, pl pres, 2nd & 3rd sg subj, pind_ < **gërmit·**

gërmit· _vt_ 1 to scratch, rasp, grate 2 to gnaw at [] 3 to poke [a fire], stir up

*_**gërmit·et**_ _vpr_ to clear out, scram

gërmitë _nf_ [_Veter_] hog cholera

gërmo·het _vpr_ 1 to threaten, menace 2 to become stooped over 3 (_Reg_) to try very hard

gërmo·n _vt, vi_ 1 to dig, dig up []; excavate 2 to delve deeply into []; search thoroughly through [] 3 (_Fig_) to make [] stooped-over and weak 4 to poke, spur [] on; poke into []
  ○ **gërmo·n dhé** to dig up earth

gërmuar _adj (i)_ 1 dug up, tilled, furrowed 2 (_Reg_) having ups and downs that make passage difficult 3 (_Reg_) stooped-over, bent

*_**gërmuç**_ _adj_ = **gërmuq**

*_**gërmuçuem**_ _adj (i) (Reg Gheg)_ cringing, cowering

gërmues
  I § _adj_ digging
  II § _nm_ digger; excavator

gërmuq
  I § _adj (Colloq)_ hunched-over; hunchbacked
  II § _nm_ [_Ichth_] = **drangë**

gërmuq· _vt_ to cause [] to hunch over

gërmuq·et _vpr_ 1 to hunch over; become hunchbacked 2 to cringe, cower; huddle up

gërmuqas _adv_ with back bowed: hunched over

gërmuqët _adj (i)_ hunched-over, bent

*_**gërmush·**_ _vt_ to intimidate

gërmush·et _vpr_ to be threatening/menacing: threaten/menace <>

gërnetë _nf_ [_Mus_] clarinet used in folk music

*_**gërnis**_ _stem for 1st sg pres, pl pres, 2nd & 3rd sg subj, pind_ < **gërnit·**

*_**gërnit·**_ _vt_ to melt, dissolve
  ○ **gërnit· qyrrën** to loosen phlegm

gërnjar _adj_ cantankerous, crabby, cranky; quarrelsome, pugnacious

*_**gërnjat·et**_ _vpr_ = **gërnjit·et**

gërnjë _nf_ constant squabbling

gërnji·het _vpr_ = **gërnjit·et**

gërnjit·et _vpr_ 1 to quarrel constantly: squabble 2 to behave like a crybaby 3 to whine, whimper

gërnjitës _adj_ quarrelsome, pugnacious

gërnjollë _nf_ rainy wind from the northwest

*_**gërq**_ = **greq**

*_**Gërqi**_ _nf_ Greece = **Greqi**

gërqinjë
  I § _adj_ yielding elongated fruit
  II § _nf_ 1 plum with elongated fruit *2 = **gërkinë**

*_**gërqisht**_ _adv_ = **greqisht**

*_**gërqishte**_ _nf_ = **greqishte**

gërsenicë _nf_ [_Entom_] caterpillar

*_**gërsi**_ _nf_ = **kërci**

*_**gërsis**_ _stem for 1st sg pres, pl pres, 2nd & 3rd sg subj, pind_ < **gërsit·**

*_**gërsit·**_ _vt_ to knock

*_**gërshânë**_ _(Reg Gheg)_ = **gërshërë**

*_**gërshânëza**_ _(Reg Gheg)_ = **gërshërëza**

gërshani _nf (Old)_ 1 [_Ethnog_] ritual cutting of a child's hair by the godfather; close relationship established by this ritual 2 = **kumbari**

*_**gërshas**_ _stem for 1st sg pres, 1st & 3rd pl pres, 2nd & 3rd sg subj_ < **gërshet·**

gërshet
  I § _nm_ 1 hairbraid 2 braid
  II § _adv_ in a braid
  ○ <> **kanë dalë mendtë mbi gërsheta** "<>'s brains have spilled out over her hairbraids" she has no brains

*_**gërshet·**_ _vt_ to invite = **grish·**

gërshetartë _adj (Poet)_ golden-braided

gërshetdegë _adj_ having braids that stand out from the head

gërshetë _nf_ 1 = **gërshet** 2 [_Folklore_] = **gërshetëz**

gërshetëz _nf_ [_Folklore_] long-haired nymph of rivers/lakes

gërshetgjatë _adj_ long-braided

gërshetim _nm ger_ 1 < **gërsheto·**n, **gërsheto·het** 2 interrelationship

gërsheto·het _vpr_ to become intertwined

gërsheto·n _vt_ 1 to braid, plait, twine 2 (_Fig_) to entwine, enlace

gërshetuar _adj (i)_ 1 braided 2 (_Fig_) intertwined, interwoven, interlaced; interrelated

gërshetues _adj_ braiding

gërshet|vèrdhë *adj* blond-braided

gërshet|zezë *adj (Poet)* dark-braided

gërshër|ë *nf* **1** scissors, shears, clippers **2** shearing; quantity sheared **3** roof rafter

gërshër|ëz *nf* **1** roof rafter **2** [*Entom*] common earwig *(Forficula auricularia L.)* **3** back part of a packsaddle **4** scissor-shaped decoration on cloth; apron with scissor-shaped decorations **5** [*Agr*] = **veshëz**

gërshër|ëza *np* <**gërshërëz 1** forked tongue of a snake ***2** skullbone serrations

***gërsh|is|** *stem for 2nd pl pres, pind* <**gërshet·**

***gërsh|it|** *stem for pind, 2nd pl pres, imper, vp* <**gërshet·**

gërtuk *nm* corn with yellow kernels

***gërty|l|** = **kërtyl|**

gërtha|c *nm* **1** [*Zool*] = **greth 2** [*Bot*] = **ullastër**

gërtha|p *nm* **1** pruning shears **2** [*Entom*] stag beetle *(Lucanus cervus)*

gërth|as| *stem for 1st sg pres, 1st & 3rd pl pres, 2nd & 3rd sg subj* <**gërthet·**

gërthe|(n) *nm (Reg)* [*Bot*] wild strawberry *(Fragaria vesca L.)*

gërthet·
I § *vi* **1** to yell, shout **2** to scream **3** (of certain animals) to call loudly: screech, shriek, bellow
II § *vt* **1** to shout/scream at [], scold [] loudly **2** to invite

gërthël *nf* [*Invert*] = **gaforre**

gërth|is| *stem for 2nd pl pres, pind* <**gërthet·**

gërth|it| *stem for pdef, opt, adm, part, pind, 2nd pl pres, imper, vp* <**gërthet·**

gërth|itje *nf ger* **1** <**gërthet· 2** loud yell, shout, scream **3** loud call of certain animals: screech, shriek, bellow

gërth|itur *nf (e)* **1** yelling, screaming, shouting **2** screeching, shrieking, bellowing

gërthiu|lë *nf* [*Ornit*] = **pupëz**

gërth|je *nf (Reg)* **1** [*Invert*] = **gaforre 2** *(Fig)* annoying person who won't leave you alone: terrible pest

gërv|all·et *vpr* **1** to screech **2** to sing with a raspy voice **3** to bray

gërv|ël|is· *vt* **1** to pester; annoy **2** to rasp against [], scratch, scrape

gërv|i·n *vi* to generate the rasping sound made by hard objects scraping against each other: rasp, squeak, squeal

gërv|imë *nf* rasping sound made by hard objects scraping against each other, metallic squealing, squeak

gërv|ish| = **gërvisht|**

gërv|isht· *vt* **1** to scratch; claw; scrape **2** *(Fig)* to grate on [someone's ears]; deeply disturb []

gërv|isht·et *vpr* to scratch/scrape one's skin: get scratched

gërv|isht|ës
I § *adj* **1** used for scratching **2** *(Fig)* grating [on the ears/nerves]
II § *n* *scribbler

gërv|isht|je *nf ger* **1** <**gërvisht·, gërvisht·et 2** scratch; scratching

gërv|isht|ur
I § *adj (i)* **1** scratched **2** *(Fig)* scratchy
II § *nf (e)* scratch; scratch mark

gërxh *nm* **1** jagged rock; land area covered by jagged rock, rugged and rocky country **2** *(Fig Insult)* = **gërxho**

gërxha|ll *nm* harsh tobacco

gërxha|re *nf* tub for holding cheese or pickles

gërxh|e-gërxh|e *adj* covered by jagged rock

gërxhe|l *nm* **1** tree stump; stump with attached roots used for burning **2** corn stubble **3** round wooden stopper placed in the hole of the lower grist stone to prevent loss of flour **4** corncob **5** *(Fig Insult)* = **gërxho**

gërxhe|li *nf (Colloq)* daring, audacious; foolhardy, reckless; crazy

gërxhe|lo·het *vpr (Colloq)* to show off, brag, boast; strut, swagger; bluff

gërxhe|p *nm* = **kërçep**

***gërxh|ëllo·het** = **gërxhelo·het**

gërxho *nf with masc agreement (Insult)* **1** senile old man **2** crude person, boor

***gërxho|llë** *nf* [*Ornit*] teal *(Anas crecca)*

gërxho|r *adj* full of jagged rock, rugged and rocky: craggy

***gëry|s|un** *adj (i)* = **kërrusur**

gërz|it· *vt* to eat away at [], gnaw at [], munch on []

gërz|it·et *vpr* to munch, ruminate

gërzh|im *nm* **1** dry hay **2** dryness, dessication **3** coarse flour

gërzh|im|të *adj (i)* parched and brittle: dessicated

gërzh|is| *stem for 1st sg pres, pl pres, 2nd & 3rd sg subj, pind* <**gërzhit·**

gërzh|it· *vt* to dry [plants] to the point of brittleness: parch, dessicate

gërzh|it·et *vpr* **1** to become parched **2** to crumble from dryness

gërzh|itje *nf ger* <**gërzhit·, gërzhit·et**

gërzh|itur *adj (i)* dessicated; crumbling, crumbled

***gërzhmetë** *nf* wasteland covered with briars

***gërzho|llë** *nf* = **gërxhollë**

gërr
I § *onomat (Colloq)* rasping sound made by hard objects scraping against each other, metallic squeal
II § *adv* all of a sudden; profusely, in a sudden stream
III § *invar* went fast: whoosh!

gërra|ckë *adj* (of goats) having horns bent backwards

gërra|ç *nm* hooked stick

gërra|në *nf* **1** hollow created by water erosion, river cave **2** sudden stream that creates its own bed: freshet **3** ground that becomes a water channel when the water supply is heavy: wash, arroyo

***gërra|s|** *stem for 1st sg pres, 1st & 3rd pl pres, 2nd & 3rd sg subj* <**gërret·**

gërre|c *nm (Reg)* cavity, small hole, socket

gërre|ç *nm* **1** water gourd **2** sound box of the tambara

gërre|fsh|ë *nf* **1** bundle of coarse bristles sticking out of a turkey's breast **2** hook in a tree formed by the remaining part of a broken or cut-off branch

gërre|llë *nf* **1** cavity eroded out by water; cave in a river bank, river cave **2** rock cave; cave

gërre|së *nf* **1** rasp with a wooden handle **2** scouring tool; scouring **3** place eroded by water **4** burnt crust of food stuck to the bottom of a pan

***gërret·** *vi* **1** = **gërhet· 2** = **gërthet**

gërri|c *nm* **1** persistent pesterer **2** *(Reg)* petty thief, pickpocket

gërric· *vt* = gërvisht·

gërric·*et vpr* = gërvisht·*et*

gërricash *adv* = guraçokthi

gërricë *nf* scratch; scratching

gërricje *nf ger* = gërvishtje

***gërris** *stem for 2nd pl pres, pind* <gërret·

***gërrit** *stem for pdef, opt, adm, part, pind, 2nd pl pres, imper, vp* <gërret·

***gërritje** *nf* shout, scream

***gërrmicë** *nf* [*Veter*] = gërmitë

gërroj *np* <gërruall

gërrolli *sg def, abl indef* <gërruall

gërrqe *nf* gulp, swallow

gërruall *nm* **1** wooden tub carved out of an oak stump **2** pen for small livestock enclosed by a wattle fence **3** forked stick used to carry a prickly load on the shoulder

gërrudhë *nf* deep facial furrow: deep wrinkle

***gërrue·n** = gërrye·n

gërry·*het vpr* to get eaten away gradually: get worn away by erosion; develop ruts/pits

   ○ <> **gërry·het**^{3pl} **sytë** <>'s eyes *become* hollow (from illness, lack of sleep, hunger)

gërrye·n *vt* **1** to eat away at [a surface] gradually **2** to nibble at [], gnaw at []; scrape, grate **3** to erode **4** [*Chem*] to corrode, eat into [] **5** to make [] clean by removing an unwanted surface: scour; dredge **6** (*Fig*) to eat [] up completely: scrape the bottom of [a pan] **7** (*Fig*) to disquiet []: cause to fret

   ○ [] **gërrye·n**^{3sg} **barku për bukë** []'s stomach *is rumbling* out of hunger

   ○ [] **gërrye·n nga lekët** to spend all of []'s money

   ○ **gërrye·n para me lopatë** to make a lot of money without much effort

   ○ **të gërrye·n**^{3sg} **era** "the wind *bites* into you" the wind *is* very strong

   ○ [] **gërrye·n**^{3pl} **zorrët për bukë** []'s insides *are rumbling* out of hunger

gërryer *adj* (*i*) **1** having hollows formed by gradual eating away: eroded, corroded, pitted, scooped out **2** in piles formed by frictional removal of material

gërryerje *nf ger* **1** <gërrye·n, gërry·het **2** erosion; corrosion **3** concavity (hollow/furrow/hole/pit) formed by frictional or corrosive removal of surface material **4** [*Med*] curettage, curettement

gërryes

   I § *adj* **1** corrosive; erosive; gnawing, rasping **2** [*Chem*] caustic

   II § *nm* **1** = gërryese **2** (*Fig*) = zhvatës

   ○ **gërryesi i farave** [*Entom*] lesser grain borer *Rhizopertha dominica F.*

   ○ **gërryes kungulli** = rende

gërryese *nf* tool for removing a surface by abrasive action: scraper, scouring tool, rasp, grater, dredge

gërryeshëm *adj* (*i*) easy to wear away, subject to erosion: corrosible, erodable

gëstall *nm* (*np* ~ *j*) shot glass, liqueur glass

gësterrë *nf* pitch-dark; pitch-black object

gështill *nm* [*Bot*] wild herbaceous plant eaten commonly by livestock; has tender leaves and a stem which exudes a milky sap

gështallë *nf* [*Bot*] bindweed (*Calystegia*)

gështenjapjekës *n* person who roasts chestnuts for sale

gështenjashitës *n* person who sells chestnuts

gështenjë

   I § *nf* [*Bot*] chestnut (*Castanea sativa Mill*)

   II § *adj* (*Colloq*) dark brown with a reddish tinge: auburn

   ○ **gështenjë e egër/kalit** common horse chestnut *Aesculus hippocastanum L.*

gështenjishtë *nf* chestnut grove

gështenjore *nf* = gështenjishtë

gështenjtë *adj* (*i*) **1** made of chestnut (wood) **2** having the color of a chestnut

gëthap *np* <gëthep

gëthep *nm* **1** branch stump jutting out of a tree trunk; peg/hook for hanging things up **2** stubble **3** door bolt, door bar **4** talon, claw **5** tine of a pitchfork **6** battlement of a tower

***gëthlas** *stem for 1st sg pres, 1st & 3rd pl pres, 2nd & 3rd sg subj* <gëthlet·

***gëthlet·** *vt* = përkdhel

***gëthlis** *stem for 2nd pl pres, pind* <gëthlet·

***gëthlit** *stem for pdef, opt, adm, part, pind, 2nd pl pres, imper, vp* <gëthlet·

gëthuq *nm* **1** sharp-pointed stake, peg **2** thorn

gëvezhëz *nf* [*Bot*] birdsfoot-trefoil (*Lotus corniculatus*)

***gëvoshkë** = gollovezhgë

***gëzatës** *n* (*Old*) mischief maker, agitator

gëzim *nm* **1** feeling of joy: joy, happiness, elation **2** enjoyable event/thing, enjoyment **3** person or thing that causes joy

   ○ **gëzim për derë** "door-to-door happiness" (*Iron*) don't gloat over my bad luck today because it may be yours tomorrow, it could happen to you, too, you know!

Gëzim *nm* Gëzim (male name)

gëzimdhënës *adj* (*Book*) joy-giving, pleasurable

gëzimplotë *adj* (*Poet*) bounteous in joy: joyful, joyous

gëzimprurës *adj* (*Book*) joy-bringing, pleasant

gëzimsjellës *adj* = gëzimprurës

gëzimzi *adj, n* (*fem sg* ~ *ez, masc pl* ~ *inj, fem pl* ~ *eza*) **1** (one) who never experiences joy, joyless **2** (*Curse*) may he never experience joy!

gëzo·*het vpr* **1** to get enjoyment; enjoy oneself **2** to be glad; feel happy **3** to rejoice

   ○ **gëzo·het së tepërmi** to be overjoyed

gëzo·n

   I § *vt* **1** to bring/give happiness/pleasure to []: gladden, delight **2** to enjoy the benefit/use of []: enjoy **3** to caress, pet

   II § *vi* to feel glad

gëzof *nm* **1** fur **2** fur pelt

   ○ **janë pe për një gëzof** "they both can be used as thread for the same fur" they are birds of a feather

   ○ <>**a prenë gëzofin** "they cut <>'s fur" they punished <>; <> got what <> deserved

gëzofçi *nm* (*np* ~ *nj*) = gëzoftar

gëzofpunues *nm* furrier

gëzoftar *n* **1** = gëzofpunues **2** fur merchant

gëzoftë *adj* (*i*) made of fur

gëzoftore *nf* **1** furrier's workshop **2** fur shop

gëzuar

   I § *adj* (*i*) **1** cheerful; glad **2** joyous, happy

II § *interj* expresses good wishes for happiness (Good luck!); used as blessing at celebrations, as a toast (Cheers!)
  ○ **Gëzuar Vitin e Ri!** Happy New Year!

gëzu'eshëm
  I § *adj (i)* **1** causing joy: joyous **2** feeling joy: happy, glad, merry **3** of joyful disposition: jolly, cheery, cheerful **4** spent happily: joyful, enjoyable **5** expressing joy: cheerful, smiling
  II § *adv* joyfully, happily

gëzhda'l|a *np* **1** < gëzhda'll*ë* **2** nonsense

gëzhda'll*ë* *nf* **1** splint **2** splinter, sliver **3** dent, gouge mark, chip mark **4** prong of a pitchfork *5 rung (of a ladder) **6** uneven haircut *7 spur of an antler *8 radius bone (of the arm)

gëzhda'p *nm* cudgel, club

gëzhda'p· *vt* to cudgel, club

*****Gëzhdri'j|a** *np (Old)* Ash Wednesday

gëzhi'le *nf* green outer husk surrounding the hard shell of a chestnut

gëzhi'·s *stem for 1st sg pres, pl pres, 2nd & 3rd sg subj, pind* < gëzhit·

gëzhi't· *vt (Reg)* to incite [] against: egg on

gëzhi'tje *nf ger (Reg)* < gëzhit·

gëzhoj'ë *nf* **1** shell **2** shell/jacket/casing of a cartridge

gëzho'lle
  I § *nf* **1** leaf of corn; husk **2** poultry too skinny to be worth butchering
  II § *np* chaff

gëzho'll·ët *adj (i)* empty inside: hollow

gëzhu'të
  I § *nf* grain husk
  II § *np* chaff

gëzhy'tër *nf (Reg)* shell, husk, rind

*****Gibilte're** *nf (Old)* Gibraltar = **Gjibralta'r**

gibo'n *nm* [Zool] gibbon

gic
  I § *nm* **1** suckling pig, pigling **2** *(Fig Pet)* chubby child **3** round pebble **4** heel indentation made in the ground to mark home in a children's game
  II § *adv* completely full, up to the brim

gi'c|a *np (Colloq)* baby teeth, milk teeth

gica'n *nm* ram with a white muzzle dotted with reddish marks

gic'ë *nf* = **gica'n**

gicil'i'm *nm ger* = **guduli'sje**

gicilo'·het *vpr* to be = **guduli's·***et*

gicilo'·n *vt* = **guduli's·**

gicilu'es *nm* = **guduli'sës**

*****gicm|** = **ngacm|**

gi'c|thi *adv* = **do'çash**

gijoti'në *nf* guillotine

gi'lc|ë *nf* [Anat] sinew; tendon; ligament

*****gilic|i's** *stem for 1st sg pres, pl pres, 2nd & 3rd sg subj, pind* < gilici't·

*****gilici't·** *vt* = **guduli's·**

*****gili|gi's** *stem for 1st sg pres, pl pres, 2nd & 3rd sg subj, pind* < giligi't·

*****giligi't·** *vt* = **guduli's·**

gilivi'li *invar (Colloq)* kitchy-koo

gilo'giç *nm* wooden cup used by shepherds to keep salt

gi'në *nf* soft mud: muck

gi'ngë
  I § *nf* = **gollogu'ngë**
  II § *np (Fig)* barbs; barbed words

*****ginja'k** *nm* eggshell

*****gips** = **gjips**

*****gira'fë** *nf* giraffe = **gjira'fë**

*****girgila'c** *nm (Reg Gheg)* [Anat] = **gabzhe'rr**

*****giric'o're** *nf (Old)* place where veterinary surgery is performed

*****giro'll** *nm* [Bot] horse mushroom *(Agaricus arvensis)*

gisht *nm (np ˜ëri'nj)* **1** finger; toe **2** [Tech] pawl (for a ratchet wheel) **3** *(Colloq)* fingerwidth; small amount **4** *(Fig Colloq Contempt)* mere tool, tool
  ○ **ësh·të gisht** to have nothing left, be flat broke
  ○ **ësh·të i gishtit** "be (trigger-)fingered" to be a real man
  ○ **gisht dëftues** index finger
  ○ **gisht i dytë** index finger
  ○ **gishti i pushkës** "gun finger" trigger finger; index finger
  ○ **gishti i këmbës** toe
  ○ **gishti i madh i dorës** thumb
  ○ **gishti i mesit** middle finger
  ○ **gisht pas gishtit** in a series, one after another
  ○ **gisht i shllinës** *(Reg Gheg)* index finger
  ○ **gisht tregues** forefinger, index finger
  ○ **u vranë me gisht** they had a bloody fight, fought tooth and nail
  ○ **gishti i unazës** the ring finger
  ○ **gishti i vogël** little finger, pinkie

gi'sht|a *np* = **gisht'ëri'nj**

gi'sht|a'q *nm* person with six fingers or toes

gi'sht|as *adv* with the fingers; finger by finger

gi'sht|azi *adv* = **gi'shtas**

gisht'cu'ng *adj* = **gishtpre're**

gi'sht|e *nf* thimble

gi'sht|ez *nf (Reg)* glove = **dore'zë**

gisht'ëri'nj *np* **1** < gisht **2** [Text] thin colorful stripes interwoven in a piece of cloth
  ○ **s'janë të gjithë gishtërinjtë njësoj** "not all fingers are the same" not all people are alike
  ○ **mbi majat e gishtërinjve** on tiptoe
  ○ **në majë të gishtërinjve** on tiptoe

gi'sht|ës *nm* spoke (of a wheel)

gi'sht|ëz *nf* **1** *(Reg)* thimble **2** trigger of a weapon

gisht'ëzo'·het *vpr* [Bot] to become digitate

gi'sht|je *nf* **1** [Bot] cupule **2** thimble

gi'sht|o *nf with masc agreement* [Folklore] clever little man or child who appears as a character in folktales: Tom Thumb

gisht'o'r *adj* [Anat] of or pertaining to fingers or toes: digital

gisht'o're *nf* glove

gisht'pre're *adj* missing one or more fingers

*****gishtso'·n** *vt* to point [] out, indicate

*****gi't·et** *vpr (Old)* to seem

*****gixil|** = **guduli's·**

*****gixhvi'le** *nf* [Ornit] = **gaxhvi'le**

gi'z|ë *nf* cast iron
  ○ **gizë e zbardhur** [Tech] chilled cast iron

*****gla'c|ë** *nf* = **gla'së**

gladiato'r *nm* gladiator

gladio'l|ë *nf* [Bot] gladiolus *(Gladiolus)* = **shpa'tëz**

glas· *vi* (of birds) to defecate

gla·s*ë* *nf* **1** bird dropping, guano **2** [*Veter*] wasting disease of chickens in which they produce more droppings **3** flyblow

gla·st*ër* *nf* flowerpot, vase

glazu·r*ë* *nf* glaze, glazing

gle·b*ë* *nf(Reg)* = **skle·pë**

*****gledh**| = **ledh**|

gle·p*ë* *nf* rheum in the eyes = **skle·pë**

glep·o·s·et *vpr* (of the eyes) to be rheumy

gle·t*ë* *nf* sharp chisel for incising stone or wood

gliceri·n*ë* *nf* glycerine, glycerol

glika·nxo *nf* **1** [*Bot*] anise *(Pimpinella anisum)* **2** aniseed

gliko· *nf* fruit preserves (served to guests)

glin *nm* [*Bot*] a genus of Molluginaceae *(Glinus lotoides)*

*****Gli·na** *nf* bottled water from Glina: soda water

gli·n*ë* *nf* white or red potter's clay

gli·qe *np* hamstrings, knee tendons

gli·st*ër* *nf* **1** [*Invert*] earthworm, angleworm **2** [*Invert*] intestinal parasitic worm *(helminth)*

glob *nm* globe

globa·l

   I § *adj (Book)* **1** global **2** *(Pej)* overly concerned with quantity at the expense of quality

   II § *nm* **1** grand total **2** *(Pej)* achievement of a quantitative result at the expense of qualitative concerns

globali·sht *adv* globally

globali·z*ëm* *nm* **1** globalism **2** *(Pej)* overconcern with quantity at the expense of quality

globu·l*ë* *nf* [*Physiol*] blood corpuscle

*****glo·m***ë* *nf* = **gllo·mkë**

gloq *nm (Reg)* = **gle·pë**

*****gloqa·n** *adj* bleary-eyed

*****gloque·m** *adj (i) (Reg Gheg)* = **gloqa·n**

gluko·z*ë* *nf* [*Chem*] glucose

*****gluti·n** *nm* gluten

glyr·*ë* *nf (Reg)* = **bibiza·ne**

gly·t*ër* *nf* **1** the thick, knobby fiber unwound from the first or last parts of a silk cocoon **2** upper closure of a silk cocoon from which unwinding the fiber is begun

gllab·*ëri·m* *nm ger* < **gllabëro·**·n, **gllabëro·**·het

gllab·*ëro·*·het *vpr* to be enraptured/absorbed/engrossed/preoccupied

gllab·*ëro·*·n *vt* **1** to swallow [ ] greedily: devour, gobble [ ] up, gulp [ ] down, drink [ ] down in one gulp **2** to engulf **3** *(Fig)* to regard [ ] covetously **4** *(Fig)* to enrapture, absorb, engross

gllab·*ëru·e*s

   I § *adj* **1** voracious **2** conquering

   II § *n* conqueror

gllab·*ï·s*| *stem for 1st sg pres, pl pres, 2nd & 3rd sg subj, pind* < **gllabi·t**·

gllab·*ï·t·* *vt* = **gllabëro·**·n

gllani·k *nm* **1** hearthstone **2** stepping stone to help a rider mount a horse **3** rock slab used to shut off a canal **4** clod of earth **5** deep hole in the ground; abyss

*****gllap·***ï·s*| *stem for 1st sg pres, pl pres, 2nd & 3rd sg subj, pind* < **gllapi·t**·

*****gllap·***ï·t·* *vt* = **gllabëro·**·n

*****glla·ro** *nf* [*Ornit*] seagull

gllavi·n*ë* *nf* hub/nave of a wheel

*****glle·nj***ë* *nf* [*Bot*] black pine *(Pinus nigra)*

*****gllë·nqk***ë* = **gllë·njkë**

gllë·njk*ë* *nf* quantity of liquid drunk in one swallow: gulp, swig

*****glli·**·n *vi* to turn green, sprout

*****gllo·**·n = **glli·**·n

*****gllo·fët** *adj (i) (Old)* concave, hollow

*****gllofi·s**| *stem for 1st sg pres, pl pres, 2nd & 3rd sg subj, pind* < **gllofi·t**·

*****gllofi·t**| *vt* = **gllabëro·**·n

gllo·fk*ë* *nf* **1** large cave: cavern **2** hollow, hole *****3** window bay

gllo·mk*ë* *nf* knot

glluguri·m*ë* *nf* **1** gulping sound **2** gobbling sound of a turkey

gllugur·o··n *vi* to make a gulping/gobbling sound: gulp, gobble

gllup *nm (Reg)* **1** mouth; throat **2** gun barrel

gne·is *nm* [*Min*] gneiss

gnoseologj·*ï* *nf* [*Phil*] gnoseology

gnoseologj·*ï·k* *adj* [*Phil*] gnoseological

gnosti·k *adj* Gnostic

go·be *nf* gudgeon *(Gobio gobio)*

*****gobe·ll** *nm* single-handled wooden bucket used for milking sheep

gobe·ll*ë* *nf* **1** deep pool in a body of water, drop-off **2** large water vat

gobe·t*ë* *nf* **1** mountain hollow **2** [*Folklore*] deep hole

*****gob·***ësi* = **gope·si**

*****goc** *nm (Reg Gheg)* teenaged boy

*****goca·** *nm* = **goca·n**

goca·n *nm* pumice rock

goca·r *nm* pebble

go·c*ë* *nf* **1** teenage girl **2** shell; seashell **3** [*Invert*] oyster, cockle **4** [*Invert*] common European oyster *(Ostrea edulis)*

go·çe *nf* [*Ichth*] *(Anguilla latirostris)*

god·*as*| *stem for 1st sg pres, 1st & 3rd pl pres, 2nd & 3rd sg subj* < **gode·t**·

god·e·t

   I § *vt* **1** to deliver a blow to [ ]: hit; strike, strike at [ ] **2** to shoot **3** *(Fig)* to criticize [ ] sharply **4** *(Fig)* to destroy [ ] entirely: wipe [ ] out

   II § *vi* **1** to pulsate, beat, throb **2** (of a clock) to strike **3** to direct one's intentions: be driving at

   III § *vi impers* it *happens* (by chance)

   ∘ **godet·** me një çokë to knock

   ∘ **godet·** me pëllëmbë to slap

god·*ï* *nf(Colloq)* **1** agreement, understanding: deal **2** *(Colloq)* ornament, bauble: gewgaw *****3** = **godi·në**

godi·n*ë* *nf* building

god·*ï·s*| *stem for 2nd pl pres, pind* < **gode·t**·

god·*ï·t·* *vt* **1** = **gode·t**· **2** to build **3** to fix, repair, mend **4** to arrange [ ] properly, put [ ] in order **5** to make [ ] pretty, adorn **6** to add flavor to [ ] **7** to create, compose

   ∘ **godit·** në shenjë "strike the target" to be right on target

   ∘ [ ] **godit·**³*ˢᵍ* në zemër [ ] *dies* of a heart attack

   ∘ [ ] **godit·** prapa krahëve to attack [ ] treacherously; make a sneak attack on [ ]

god·*ï·t·*et *vpr* **1** to fight, come to blows **2** to come to an agreement, make a deal **3** to get prettied up, be adorned

godit·ës
I § adj 1 destructive, fatal 2 [*Tech*] penetrating by striking action 3 (*Fig*) striking, remarkable
II § nm 1 repairman; builder 2 [*Tech*] part of a machine that delivers hammering blows: striker, hammer, ram

godi·tje nf ger 1 <godít·, godet·, godít·et 2 strike, hit, knock, blow; thrust 3 percussive sound; percussion 4 construction, building
○ **goditje (nga) këndi** [*Sport*] corner kick (in soccer)
○ **goditje me pushkë** gun shooting, gunshot
○ **goditje nga dielli** [*Med*] sunstroke (*heliosis*)

godit·ur adj (i) 1 marked by a blow 2 (*Fig*) appropriate, proper; well-chosen, apt 3 (*Fig*) astonished: struck 4 built, constructed 5 fixed, repaired 6 fixed up, made pretty, made up; flavored

gof nm fever

go'fe nf (*Reg*) = ijë

go'fë nf 1 [*Ichth*] amber jack (*Seriola dumerili*) 2 bluefish (*Pomatomus saltator*)

goge'sh nm [*Ornit*] wild pigeon, rock pigeon, rock dove (*Columba livia Gm.*)

*****goge'shë** nf Vlach woman

*****go'gë**
I § nf with masc agreement 1 Vlach 2 mason, bricklayer 3 (*Fig*) idler, loafer
II § adj (*Fig*) boorish, crude
III § np *hot temper, fury

go'gël nf 1 hard globular seed or cone of a tree: acorn, cone 2 dark hair dye extracted from acorns/cones 3 small round object: ball of cheese, meatball, abacus bead, berry 4 (*Fig*) small and worthless thing
○ **gogël mbi ujë** silly, foolish

gogë'la·c adj, n short (person): midget

gogë'le·c nm early-ripening round white fig

gogë'lu·qe nf small round meatball

gogë'lu·she nf = gogëlu'qe

*****gogë'ni** nf collec 1 Vlachs as a collective whole 2 Wallachia

*****gogë'ni·sht** adv in the manner of Vlachs; in Vlach

*****gogë'ni·shte** nf Vlach (language)

*****go'gë·s** nm [*Ornit*] = goge'sh

gogë'si·n· vi 1 to yawn, gape 2 to belch

gogë'si·më nf ger 1 <gogësí·n· 2 belch

gogë'si·re nf yawn

gogë'si·t· vi = gogësí·n

gogë'si·tje nf ger = gogësi'më

gogi'shte adj

gogli'q nm [*Bot*] small acorn or globular cone

gogli'u·qe nf small round meatball

*****gogme'l** = gogo'l

gogo'l nm 1 imaginary person invoked to frighten children: boogieman 2 scarecrow

gogole'sh
I § nm scarecrow
II § adj 1 = leshto'r 2 unkempt and unshaven

gogolli'në nf [*Bot*] = gollogu'ngë

*****gogo'sh** nm 1 ringdove 2 idler, loafer 3 silk cocoon = kuku'le

gogo'shë nf leaf sprout, leaf bud

gogozha're nf kind of round and fleshy pepper used for roasting or pickling

gogozhe'l nm 1 = gogo'l 2 badly clothed person, person dressed in rags 3 [*Zool*] = bubuzhe'l

goja'c nm = goja'ç

goja'ç nf (*Insult*) 1 person with a large or crooked mouth 2 stammerer, stutterer 3 (*Pej*) person who talks a lot; person who speaks ill of others, slanderer: bigmouth

goja-goja's adv out of one's very mouth, directly; in private

goja-gojës adv 1 person-to-person; privately 2 from mouth to mouth, by word of mouth, orally

goja'k adj having a crooked mouth, wry-mouthed

*****gojambël** adj (*Reg Gheg*) = gojëmbël

*****goja'r** n (*Elev*) eloquent speaker, orator

*****gojari** nm [*Bot*] = gojaslla'n

gojari'sht adv 1 orally, verbally 2 = goja-gojës

goja'rtë adj (*Poet*) golden-tongued, eloquent

goja's adv 1 orally 2 from mouth to mouth, by word of mouth

gojaslla'n nm [*Bot*] snapdragon = lulego'jë
○ **gojasllan i egër** common toadflax (*Linaria vulgaris*)

goja'sh nm (*Insult*) = goja'ç

goja'shpër adj sharp-tongued, sarcastic, rude

gojavi's stem for 1st sg pres, pl pres, 2nd & 3rd sg subj, pind <gojavít·

gojaví·t· vt 1 to repeat [] word for word 2 to gossip about [], speak ill of []

gojazi adv orally, verbally

goj·c nf 1 knitted stitch, crochet loop; button hole 2 end of a crochet hook that catches the yarn

*****gojç·thu'r·un** = gojështhu'rur

*****gojdhân·ë** (*Reg Gheg*) = gojëdhë'në

gojë nf 1 mouth 2 mouthful; bite 3 (*Fig Colloq*) daily food; eating and drinking 4 talking, speech; local speech variety, dialect 5 receptacle, groove 6 loop; buttonhole 7 space between warp courses in a loom: shed 8 (*Colloq*) member of one's household: mouth to feed 9 muzzle (of a gun)
○ **gojë ariu** [*Bot*] = lulego'jë
○ **gojë asllani** [*Bot*] = gojaslla'n
○ **ësh·të gojë e bark** "is mouth and stomach" to be a big eater, think only about eating
○ **i gojës dhe i shpatës** "of the mouth and of the sword" good both in speaking and in fighting
○ **gojët e liga** scandalmongers
○ **s'ka· gojë të flet·^{subj}/tho·të^{subj}** (*Pej*) to have no right to say anything about other people
○ **s'ka· gojë të kërko·n^{subj}** (*Pej*) to have no right to ask for anything
○ **<>a lag gojën** "wet <>'s mouth" to give<> just a small amount/taste
○ **[] lë· me gojë hapur** "leave [] with mouth open" to surprise/amaze []
○ **<> mbërthe·het^{3sg} goja** "<>'s mouth/tongue is stuck tight" <> is unable to speak
○ **gojë më gojë 1** from mouth to mouth, by word of mouth 2 privately, in privacy 3 end to end, abutting
○ **gojë pas goje** by word of mouth
○ **goja e popullit** (oral) folk literature
○ **gojë e sumbullës** buttonhole
○ **Goja tret edhe malet.** "The mouth dissolves even the mountains." (*Prov*) Too much eating and drinking can use up even a large fortune. Riotous living will take all that you have.

◦ **gojë ujku** [*Bot*] *= gojujk

◦ **gojë ujku** [*Bot*] **= gojaslla'n**

◦ **s'<> ve·te**[3sg] **goja** "<>'s mouth doesn't go" <> *is* unwilling to say something

gojë'bilbí'l *adj (Poet)* speaking beautifully: golden-tongued; speaking sweetly: honey-tongued

gojë'brí'sk *adj* keen-witted in speech: articulate; eloquent; quick on the response

gojë'bu'all *adj (Insult)* **1** large-mouthed **2** *(Fig)* talkative, garrulous

gojë'çora'p *adj (Insult)* **1** large-mouthed **2** *(Fig)* having a big mouth, talkative in an irresponsible way; uninhibited in speech

*gojë'çorb'ë *adj (Insult)* talkative

gojë'dhë'në *adj* legend

gojë'dhë'no'r *adj* legendary

gojë'farma'k *adj* = gojë'he'lm

*gojë'fa've *adj (Insult) (Reg Tosk)* talkative

gojë'fëllí'qur *adj* foul-mouthed

gojë'gja'rpër *adj* hurtful in tone, venomous (in language), biting, acerb

gojë'hale' *adj (Colloq)* foulmouthed

gojë'ha'pës'e *nf* [*Med*] mouth opener, oral screw

gojë'ha'pur *adv* open-mouthed: agape, astonished

gojë'he'lm *adj* having a poisonous tongue

gojë'kama're *adj (Insult)* **1** having a very large mouth **2** *(Fig)* having a big mouth, endlessly talkative, garrulous

gojë'ke'q
 I § *adj* **1** slanderous; blasphemous **2** vulgar, obscene
 II § *n* slanderer; blasphemer

gojë'kra'pe *nf* [*Bot*] = lulego'jë

gojë'kutí' *adj (Poet)* having a beautiful, small mouth: little button mouth

gojë'kutí'zë [*Ichth*] nase *(Chondrostama nasus)* = njí'lë

gojë'ky'çur
 I § *adj, n* = gojë'lí'dhur
 II § *adv* reticently

gojë'la'sh'të *adj* = gojë'ndy're

gojë'lëshu'a'r *adj* **1** irresponsible in speech, running off at the mouth; insolent **2** indecent in speech: foulmouthed

gojë'lí'dhur
 I § *adj* taciturn: close-mouthed; able to keep a secret: tightmouthed
 II § *nm (Euph)* unmentionable animal: wolf; bear; snake

gojë'lí'g *adj* = gojë'ke'q

gojë'lopa'të *adj (Insult)* gabby

gojë'lo'pë *adj* **1** having a mouth big as a cow: largemouthed **2** *(Fig)* talkative and unthinking

gojë'lua'n *adj* [*Bot*] = gojaslla'n

gojë'lubí'
 I § *adj (Pej)* gluttonous
 II § *nm* glutton

gojë'ma'ce *nf* rest-harrow, goatroot ononis *(Ononis arvensis)*

gojë'ma'dh *adj* **1** having a large mouth: largemouthed **2** garrulous **3** gluttonous

gojë'marr'a'q *adj* **1** faltering in speech, mumbling **2** having a speech impediment: stammering, stuttering

gojë'mba'jt'ur *adj* having a speech impediment: stammering

gojë'mbël *adj* "sweetmouthed" **1** gentle/kind/pleasant in speech; having a mellifluous voice *2 eloquent

gojë'mbërth'y'er
 I § *nm (Euph)* = ujk
 II § *nf (Euph)* = milingo'në
 III § *adj* = gojë'ky'çur

gojë'mby'll'ur
 I § *adj* close-mouthed
 II § *adv* with mouth shut, silent

gojë'mí'rë *adj* kind and generous in speaking of others

gojë'mja'ltë *adj, n* (person) of sweet disposition, honey-mouthed

gojë'mpre'h'të *adj* clever on the uptake, sharp as a tack, quick-witted

gojë'ndy'rë *adj* foul-mouthed, obscene

*gojë'ndy'të *= gojë'ndy'rë

gojë'nepë'rkë *adj (Pej)* poisonous in tone, venomous (in language), biting, acerb

gojë'pala'rë *adj* indecent in speech, foul-mouthed

gojë'pashma'gje *adj* = gojë'çora'p

gojë'pipe'rkë *adj (Insult)* = gojë'spe'c

gojë'prí'sh'ur *adj* profane, blasphemous; ribald, vulgar

gojë'qe'p'ur
 I § *adj* close-mouthed
 II § *nm (Euph)* serpent

gojë'qershí' *adj (Poet)* having a beautiful, small mouth with red lips: cherry-lipped

*gojë'ra'ndë *adj (Reg Gheg)* = gojë'rë'ndë

gojë'rë'ndë *adj* speaking harshly: gruff

gojë'rru'dh'ur *adj* **1** taciturn, quiet, silent **2** temperate in speech

gojë'spe'c *adj* inflammatory in tone, provocative in language

gojë'sheqe'r *adj* speaking sweetly

gojë'shpa'të *adj* = gjuhë'shpa'të

gojë'shpe'llë *adj* having a very large mouth

gojë'shpu'a'r *adj* incapable of keeping a secret, unreserved, artless

gojë'shtrë'mbër *adj* having a crooked mouth, wry-faced

gojë'sh'thu'r'ur *adj* = gojë'lëshu'a'r

gojë'ta'r
 I § *n* **1** eloquent speaker **2** *(Elev)* orator
 II § *adj* eloquent; glib

gojë'tarí' *nf (Book)* eloquence, rhetoric, oratory

gojë'te'rs *nm* jinx who attracts bad luck by mentioning it

gojë'tha'r
 I § *adj* = gojë'tha'të
 II § *nm (Curse)* may-his-mouth-be-dry-and-famished!

gojë'tha'të *adj* famished

gojë'vo'gël *adj* small-mouthed

gojë'vra'rë *adj* hurtful in tone, gruff

gojë'vra'zhd *adj* harsh/savage in tone, gruff

gojë'z *nf* **1** *(Dimin)* <go'jë **2** [*Bot*] leaf pore: stoma **3** knitted stitch, crochet loop; button hole **4** end of a crochet hook that catches the yarn **5** muzzle (to prevent eating or biting) **6** bridle bit made of rope or metal **7** groove into which something fits **8** space

between warp courses in a loom: shed **9** sluice in a canal opening onto a small channel; quantity of water entering that channel **10** small skein of yarn, hank of wool **11** [*Veter*] illness of sheep or goat characterized by drooling from the mouth **12** [*Mus*] mouthpiece

*goj**ë**zbra**z**ët *adj* nonsensical, silly

goj**ë**z**ë**n·**e** *adj* **1** tongue-tied; stammering **2** *(Curse)* be damned! (by being struck dumb)

goj**ë**z**i** *nm* [*Ichth*] blackmouth catshark *(Galeus melastomus)*

goj**ë**zo·**n** = gojo·**n**

*goj**k**ë *nf (Reg Tosk)* mouth of a river

gojo·**n** *vt* **1** [*Constr*] to butt [pieces of lumber] together **2** to rout [a piece of lumber]

goj**o**r *adj* **1** spoken, oral, verbal ***2** glib; eloquent

gojo**s·** *vt* to speak ill of [], disparage

gojo**s**je *nf ger <*gojo**s·**

gojo**s**ur *adj (i)* slandered, defamed

*goj**s**ue**r** *(Old)* = gojo**r**

goj**u**jk *nm* [*Bot*] snapdragon = lulego**j**ë

goj**u**sh *adj* gabby

goj**u**thull *adj* hurtful/nasty (in speech)

gol *nm* [*Sport*] scored goal: goal
  ○ gol i barazimit tying goal

gola**sh** *nm* [*Invert*] slug

gola**sh**ën**ue**s *nm* [*Sport*] person who scores a goal

golf *nm* [*Sport*] golf

*goli**ç** *nm* = lla**ç**

*golu**c** *nm* [*Anat*] ilium

*goluga**ç**k**ë** *nf* [*Zool*] bat = gollome**s**h

*goll *adj (i)* bare, naked

golla**k** *nm* **1** purebred rooster with long legs, large body, and featherness neck that crows with a hoarse cry **2** *(Fig)* person with a hoarse voice **3** *(Fig)* crazy person

*golla**sh** = gollave**s**h

*golla**ve**sh *nm* [*Invert*] slug

*golla**xhe**re *nf* whirlpool = gjir

gol**le**
  I § *nf* **1** large hole or cavity inside a solid object **2** *(Fig)* emptiness, void **3** prominent cheek hollow
  II § *adj* hollow, empty

gollga**n** *I §* *nm* OR gollga**n**e *II §* *nf* [*Anat*] = k**ë**rdho**k**ull

golloborda**s** *n* inhabitant of Golloborda (known as being good construction workers)

Golloborda**ë** *nf* Macedonian-speaking region of northeastern Albania: Golloborda

gollogun**g**ë *nf* **1** juniper *(Juniperus)* **2** juniper berry

*gollogu**s**h *nm* nestling, fledgling

gollome**s**h
  I § *nm* [*Zool*] bat
  II § *adj* naked, nude; bare

*gollo**sh** *nm* bare height

*gollo**ve**sh = gollave**s**h

gollo**ve**zhg**ë** *nf* outer covering of a vegetable or fruit: rind, skin, hull, husk, peel, pod, shell

*gom *nm* **1** burden **2** donkey = gomar

goma**r** *nm* **1** donkey, ass *(Equus asinus)* **2** quantity that can be carried by a donkey: donkeyload **3** *(Fig Insult)* stupid person, idiot, ass

○ prit gomar të mbijë bar! "wait, you ass, for the grass to grow!" it's silly just to stand around waiting for something to happen
○ gomar me veshë "donkey with ears" *(Crude Pej)* stupid ass
○ presin të ngordhë gomari që t'i marrin potkonjtë "they wait for the donkey to die to get the horseshoes" *(Disparaging)* (said of lazy people who wait for left-overs from others)
○ gomar i tëri downright ass

gomar**a**zi *adv* **1** = gomar**thi** **2** *(Fig)* neither side winning: even, tied, equal

goma**r**e *nf* **1** she-donkey, donkey mare **2** *(Fig Crude)* stupid girl/woman, idiot **3** [*Bot*] juicy August-ripening pear with large yellow fruit tinged with red **4** forked wooden post

goma**r**ez *nf* **1** sawhorse **2** [*Text*] forked device on a loom that is weighted down to maintain tension on the warp **3** *(Reg)* [*Zool*] = bru**m**bull

goma**r**i *nf (Crude)* mindless/stupid action

gomar**i**c**ë** *nf* **1** she-donkey, donkey mare **2** *(Crude Insult)* (said to a woman) silly ass

*gomar**i**na *np* horseplay, silly pranks

gomar**i**sht *adv (Colloq)* silly, foolishly

gomar**j**ar *n* person who tends or works donkeys: donkey driver, donkeymaster

gomar**ll**ëk *nm (np ˜ qe) (Crude)* piece of stupidity: dumb-ass thing

goma**r**th *nm dimin <*goma**r** [*Bot*] = gjemba**ç**

gomar**thi** *adv* "donkey-fashion" **1** on their sides on the ground (ending in a draw in wrestling since neither wrestler can make the other's shoulders touch the ground) **2** = kaladibra**n**ce

*gome**ll**ë *nf* cave

*gome**r**ë
  I § *nf* lobster
  II § *np* *<gomar

*gome**s**hë *nf (Reg Tosk) <*gomar she-ass

go**m**ë *nf* **1** rubber **2** rubber tire **3** rubber eraser
  ○ gom**ë** peshku neoprene

gom**ë**n *nf* **1** deep spot in water; gulf **2** *(Reg)* headwater, source, spring

*gomi**ç** *nm* dolt, blockhead

gomi**l**ë *nf* cairn

gom**i**m *nm ger <*gomo·**n**

gom**i**st *n* person who makes or repairs rubber objects; tire repairman

gomiste**r**i *nf* workshop for making or repairing rubber objects; tire repair shop

*gomlu**ç** *adv* in a heap; head over heels

*gomne**r**e = humne**r**e

gomo·**n** *vt* **1** to coat [] with rubber: rubberize ***2** = ngarko·**n**

*gom**s**i *nf* resinous juice from diseased fruit

go**m**të *adj (i)* made of rubber

gom**ua**r *adj (i)* rubberized

gomura**j**ë *nf* rocky slope

go**n**dol**ë** *nf (Book)* gondola

gone **r** *nf* [*Tech*] carpenter's square

gong *nm* gong

Go**n**i *nm* Goni (male name, nickname for Agron)

gonio**met**ër *nm* [*Tech*] = k**ë**ndmat**ë**s

go**n**xhe *nf* [*Bot*] flower bud
  ○ gonxhe e pambukut cotton boll

gonxhe'ma'dh *adj* having large flower buds

gonxh'im *nm ger* <gonxho'•*n*

gonxho'•*n* *vi* [*Agr*] to develop flower buds: bud

*****gonjo'me'tër** *nm (Colloq)* = gonio'me'tër

gop *nm (Obscene)* [*Anat*] cunt, hole

gop'ç *n, adj (Colloq)* = gopça'r

gopça'r

  I § *adj (Colloq)* gluttonous, greedy

  II § *n (Colloq)* terrible glutton, pig

gope'de'r *nf (Old)* [*Mil*] muzzle-loading cannon that fires round cannonballs

gop'ësi *nf* **1** gluttony **2** avarice, greed

*****gop'sho'r** OR **gop'to'r** *adj, n* = gopça'r

*****gopze'r** OR **gopzhe'rr** *nm* = gabzhe'rr

gora'r *adj, n* of/from Gora

gora'rçe *nf (Colloq)* folk dance of Gora in which both men and women dance to the music of drum and bagpipe

gordia'n *adj (Book)*

go're *nf* = bu'shtër

gore'c *nm* spout in the hopper through which grain is fed to the millstone

gore'n *nm* north wind; snow blizzard

Go're *nf* mountainous ethnographic region in the district of Korça: Gora

go'rgë *nf* **1** hole in a tree trunk **2** cave **3** hole in the ground, pit; pitted ground **4** deep pool; deep spot in body of water **5** hardened clod of earth

gorgoli'në *nf* barren, rocky soil

go'rgull *nf* container for dry, loose materials, shaped like an inverted pyramid with a wood plug on the bottom: sand hopper

gori'cë *nf* = gorri'cë

gori'llë *nf* [*Zool*] gorilla

*****gormi's** *vt* = ndërro'•*n*

goru'c *nm (Impol)* old man worn-out and stooped by age

gorre' *nf* **1** deep pool (off a river bank) **2** small stream

gorri'ca *np (Fig)* nonsense, poppycock

gorri'cë

  I § *nf* [*Bot*] almond pear (the fruit of which becomes soft and sweet when ripened) *(Pyrus amygdaliformis)*

  II § *adj (Colloq) (Fig)* immature, inexperienced

  ○ **gorrica fice** nonsense

  ○ **gorrica pikla** a bunch of nonsense, claptrap

gorri'c'të *adj (i)* **1** made of wild pear wood **2** *(Fig)* strong

gorri'k *nm* clay loaf pan for baking bread

gorri'shtë *nf* grove of wild pear trees

gorroçe'l *nm (Reg)* large dark September-ripening grape

gorromi's• *vt (Reg Arb)* = gremi's•

gorromi's•*et* *vpr (Reg Arb)* = gremi's•*et*

*****gorroshu'ngë** *nf* bluebottle fly

gorrovi *nf* coarsely ground substance

go'së *nf* pond, pool; wetlands

*****go'skë** = go'cë

gosta'r *n* = gostia'r

*****go'st'ë** *nf* = gosti'

gosti' *nf* **1** feast served to guests; celebration banquet, banquet; dinner party **2** banquet food brought as gifts to a celebration feast

gostia'r *n* **1** host of a banquet celebration **2** guest at a banquet feast

gosti's *stem for 1st sg pres, pl pres, 2nd & 3rd sg subj, pind* <gosti't•

gosti't• *vt* to regale [] with food and drink; treat [] with something to eat or drink, treat [] as a guest

gosti't'je *nf ger* **1** <gosti't• **2** = gosti'

go'shë *nf* ewe with horns

go'të

  I § *nf* **1** drinking glass; liqueur glass, shot glass **2** glassful, shot **3** *(Colloq)* light bulb **4** *(Colloq)* hard drink

  II § *np* [*Med*] glass cups used in treatment of illness by cupping

  ○ **go'të laboratori** beaker

go'të *np* [*Hist*] Goths

goti'k *adj* [*Art*] Gothic, in Gothic style

goti'shte *nf* language of the Goths: Gothic

go'tull *nf* [*Geog*] small inlet from the sea: creek; round bay formed near a river mouth

*****govada'r** *n* cowherd = lopa'r

gova'të *nf* **1** trough *****2** wheelbarrow

  ○ **govatë për ushqimin e kafshëve** manger

goxha

  I § *adv (Colloq)* a lot, quite a bit; fairly, rather

  II § *adj* great, tremendous

goxha'mishe *nf* [*Bot*] = cara'cë

*****gozo'f** = gëzo'f

gozhda'k *nm* ram with a thin dark line above his brow

gozhda'r *nm* **1** iron tool for making nails: nail-trimmer **2** awl **3** thin latch **4** linchpin securing a yoke to the tongue of a cart/wagon or the beam of a plow = qa'jkë

go'zhdë *nf* **1** nail, spike; tack **2** *(Fig)* emotional distress

  ○ **gozhdë dyshe** nail 2 centimeters long

  ○ **gozhdë gjashtëshe** six-centimeter long nail

  ○ **gozhdë katërshe** [*Lit*] four-centimeter long nail

  ○ **gozhdë në zemër** regret deep in one's heart: deep regret, heartfelt regret

  ○ **gozhdë pesëmbëdhjetëshe** nail that is fifteen centimeters long

  ○ **preu gozhdë** "it cut like a nail" it was freezing cold

gozhd'im *nm ger* <gozhdo'•*n*, gozhdo'•*het*

gozhdo'•*het* *vpr* to be required to stay in one place for a long time

gozhdo'•*n* *vt* **1** to affix [] with a nail: nail **2** *(Fig)* to fix in place, prevent from moving: fasten **3** *(Fig)* to overwhelm by convincing arguments, leave dumbfounded by the force of argument *****4** to shoe [a horse]

  ○ [] **gozhdo•***n* **në vend** "nail [] in place" to hold [] in place, keep [] from moving; not allow [] to get ahead, hold [] back

gozhdua'r *adj (i)* **1** nailed tight/shut **2** *(Fig)* fixed in place, required to stay in one place for a long time

gozhu'p *nm* **1** sleeveless coat made of fleece: sheepskin cloak **2** leather or twill jacket with cotton padding *****3** corn husk

GPU [*gë-pu'*] *abbrev (Russian)* <Gosudarstvennoe Politiçeskoe Upravlenie [*Hist*] GPU = state secret police in the Soviet Union

gra *np* <gru'a

gra'b'ë *nf* = rrosho'një

gra'b'ës *adj (Colloq)* predatory; robbing, pillaging, plundering

grabi' *nf* forcible seizure: robbery, pillage, plunder

grabis *stem for 1st sg pres, pl pres, 2nd & 3rd sg subj, pind* <**grabit·**

grabit· *vt* **1** to take/capture [] by violence: seize, snatch, plunder, pillage **2** *(Fig)* to captivate

grabitas *adv* by forcible seizure

***grabitçar** = grabitqar

grabities

I § *adj* = grabitqar

II § *n* predator; robber; pillager, plunderer

grabitje *nf ger* **1** <**grabit·** **2** forcible seizure: robbery, pillage, plunder

grabitqar

I § *nm* predator; raptor

II § *adj* **1** predatory, raptorial **2** predaceous

grabofç *nm* [*Folklore*] two-headed dragon

grabujë *nf* long-handled rake

grabulo· *vi* to rake

grabullor *nm* = grabujë

***grac** *nm* trough

gracë *nf* decorative lace (on clothes)

grackë *nf* **1** trap consisting of a heavy slab held up by a short stick: deadfall **2** *(Fig)* sly trap, snare

***graç** *nm* potsherd

***graçëm** = gratshëm

***graçkë** *nf* [*Bot*] Savoy cabbage *(Brassica oleracea var. capitata)*

graço· *vi* **1** to sink into mud **2** (of ground) to give way, sink **3** *(Fig)* to fall into difficulty, get into trouble

gradaçielë *nf* skyscraper

gradë *nf* **1** (unit of measurement or level) degree **2** degree of strength: proof (of an alcoholic beverage) **3** *(Colloq)* thermometer **4** level on a scale: rank, level **5** [*Mus*] degree on a musical scale **6** insignia indicating military rank **7** academic degree **8** *(Reg)* bird's nest (in a tree) **9** *(Reg)* circular wattled grating used for starting the reeling of silk from cocoons

gradient *nm* [*Phys*] gradient

gradim *nm ger* **1** <**grado·n**, **grado·het** **2** promotion (in rank) **3** *(Colloq)* certificate of promotion **4** graduated scale of an instrument or weapon (as on a gunsight)

gradinë *nf* garden around a house: kitchen garden

gradishtë *nf* [*Archeol Hist*] citadel; ruins of a citadel

grado·het *vpr* to rise/advance in rank

grado·n *vt* **1** to promote [] in rank **2** to line up the sights of [a gun] **3** to set up [an instrument] for a specific task **4** to determine the proper settings of [a device/instrument]

gradosh *nm* variety of grape with large dark fruit

gradual *adj (Book)* gradual

gradualisht *adv* gradually

graduat *nm* **1** *(Book)* (university) graduate **2** *(Old)* [*Mil*] rank attained after initial military training

gradues *nm* **1** [*Tech*] flowmeter **2** [*Mil*] soldier trained to adjust the sights of artillery weapons: setter
  ◦ **gradues i djegores** [*Mil*] fuse puncher
  ◦ **gradues i shënjestrës** [*Mil*] elevation setter

***gradhë** = gradë

grafi *nf* [*Ling*] **1** spelling system, orthography **2** medical x-ray

grafik *adj* graphic; graphical

grafikë *nf* graphics

grafikisht *adv* graphically

grafit *nm* [*Min*] **1** graphite **2** (in a pencil) lead

grafmë *nf* bad smell, stench; bad breath

grafomë *nf* chasm, abyss

***grafull** *adj* bloated, bulging, crowded

grafullim *nm ger* <**grafullo·n**

grafullo· *vi* **1** to boil over **2** *(Fig)* to yell with anger, blow up ***3** to surge, swell, seethe

***gragis** *stem for 1st sg pres, pl pres, 2nd & 3rd sg subj, pind* <**gragit·**

***gragit·** *vt* (of a goose) to hiss

grah-

I § *vt* **1** to drive/make [] go faster, spur [] on **2** *(Fig Colloq)* to do [] with great energy and enthusiasm

II § *vi* **1** to go suddenly, go quickly **2** to surge

***grah·et** *vpr* to croak; caw

grahe *nf* single-barreled shotgun

grahës *nm* drover

grahje *nf ger* <**grah·**

grahmë *nf* **1** last breath, death rattle; death struggle **2** stink **3** cry, howl

grahmëz *nf* [*Med*] apoplexy, stroke

grahuq *adj* bulging, protuberant, humpedconvex

gram *nm* **1** gram **2** *(Fig)* tiny quantity, little bit **3** [*Bot*] couch grass, quack grass *(Agropyron repens)* **4** [*Bot*] bermuda grass *(Cynodon dactylon)* **5** grief, sorrow

gramafon *nm* phonograph

gramar *nm* *(Book)* metal weight used in a computing scale

***gramasis** *stem for 1st sg pres, pl pres, 2nd & 3rd sg subj, pind* <**gramasit·**

***gramasit·** *vt* to gnaw at [], chew, bite

***gramati** *nf (Old)* literacy

gramatikan *n* [*Ling*] grammarian

gramatikë *nf* [*Ling*] **1** grammar **2** grammar book

gramatikisht *adv* [*Ling*] grammatically

gramatikor *adj* [*Ling*] grammatical

gramaturë *nf* weight as expressed in grams: weight in grams

***grambull** *nm (np ~ j)* = grumbull

gramë *nf (Old)* **1** reading and writing; schooling **2** letter (of an alphabet) = shkronjë

graminace *np* [*Bot*] = gramore

graminore *np* [*Bot*] = gramore

gramishtë *nf* land with much quack grass

gramje *adj*

***gramofon** = gramafon
  ◦ **gramofon i prishur** person who constantly blabbers nonsense

gramor *adj* [*Bot*] gramineous

gramore *np* [*Bot*] grass family *Gramineae*

Gramsh *nm* district and city in central Albania: Gramsh

gramshak *adj, n* of/from Gramsh, native of Gramsh

gramshalesh *adv* **1** in a state of constant bickering **2** in a completely confusing way

gramshalesh· *vt* **1** to make a confusing mess of [], create disorder and confusion in [], foul [] up **2** to start up trouble among/between []

gramshalesh·et *vpr* to quarrel; fight, wrestle

gramujë *nf* [*Bot*] coco-grass, nut grass *(Cyperus rotundus)*

granat *nm* [*Min*] garnet

granat|a|he'dh|ës
 I § *nm* 1 [*Mil*] soldier armed with a grenade-launcher
 2 = **granatahe'dhës**e
 II § *adj* grenade-launching

granat|a|he'dh|ëse *nf* [*Mil*] (weapon) grenade-launcher

grana'të *nf* 1 [*Mil*] grenade 2 [*Sport*] grenade-shaped object thrown from a distance in an athletic contest

grani'l *nm* aggregate of granulated stone and cement used to make strong construction slabs: grit

*****gra|ni' *(Reg Gheg)* = **gran'**

grani't
 I § *nm* [*Min*] granite
 II § *adj* (*Fig*) solid/hard as a rock

granul|i'm *nm ger* <**granulo'**•n [*Tech*] granulation

granulo'•n *vt* [*Tech*] to granulate

gra'p|cë *nf* 1 very small and thin chip/shaving 2 mark left by a chiseling tool: nibble mark

grap|c|o'•n *vt (Reg)* 1 to snap at [], nibble away at [] 2 to chip away at []

*****gra'p|ës *adj* thieving, thievish

*****gra'p|sh|ëm *adj* (i) voracious, snapping, grasping

gra|ri' *nf collec* womenfolk, women; womankind

gra|ri'sht *adv* in a womanly way

gra|ri'shte *adj* for/by women: women's; appropriate for women: womanly

grasat|i'm *nm ger* = **grasi'm**

grasat|o'•n *vt* = **graso'**•n

gras|i'm *nm ger* 1 <**graso'**•n 2 moderation/self-restraint in eating and drinking

gra'so *nf* grease (lubricant)

gras|o'•n
 I § *vt* to grease
 II § *vi* to practice moderation/self-restraint in eating and drinking

grashi'në *nf* [*Bot*] vetch (*Vicia*)

*****gra'sht = **grazhd'**

grat *nm (Colloq)* 1 benefit, value; evident result; yield 2 *(Old)* pleasure, enjoyment

grat|ço'r *adj* fertile, productive

gra'të *nf* wattled enclosure
 ◦ **gra't**ë **e parzmi't** *(Old)* chest, thorax

gra'tis *adv* gratis, for free

gra't|sh|ëm *adj* (i) 1 worthwhile; of lasting value 2 productive, fruitful 3 fertile

grath *nm* 1 jagged tooth 2 saw tooth 3 bristle, hard sliver 4 flax straw

gratha'të *nf* [*Bot*] spring heather (*Erica carnea*)

gratha't|ël *nf* [*Bot*] = **gratha't**ë

gra'thë-**gra'th**ë *adj* saw-toothed; serrate

gra'th|ël *nf (Old)* [*Bot*] = **gjë'mba**ç
 ◦ <> **bë**•*het* **grathël** to become a thorn in <>'s side

gra'th|ët *adj* (i) bristly, bristle-like; rough, shaggy

grath|o'•n *vt* to scutch [flax]

gratho're *nf* [*Relig Old*] hairshirt worn by Catholic penitents: cilice; thick knotted sash worn during penitential period

*****gra'th|sh** *nm (Old)* hair shirt

grathte'l *nm* [*Bot*] = **gratha't**ë

grava'të *nf* = **krava't**ë

gra'vë *nf* burrow, hole; den, lair

gravitacio'n *nm* [*Phys*] gravitation

gravite't *nm* [*Phys*] gravity

gravu'rë *nf* [*Art*] engraving, etching

*****gravy'r**ë** = **gravu'r**ë**

grazhd *nm* 1 manger, crib for fodder 2 fodder 3 stall (for cattle/horses/pigs); stable 4 *(Fig Colloq)* source of income 5 dike

grazhd|a'r
 I § *nm* 1 stableman, groom, stable boy 2 saddle horse
 II § *adj* fed and cared for in a stable: stable-bred

*****grazhda're = **gazhda're**

grazhd|i'm *nm ger* 1 <**grazhdo'**•n, **grazhdo'**•het *2 pit in a bog

grazhd|o'•het *vpr (Crude)* to gorge oneself with food: pig out

grazhd|o'•n *vt* to put fodder in the stable for [], give fodder to [animals]

grazhdo're *nf* grain crib, granary

greb|a'sh *nm* rake = **grabu'j**ë

*****grebi's**•** *vt* to rake, scratch

greb|o'•n *vt* to rake; rake [] up/off/together

grebu'sh *nm* = **zga'rb**ë

*****grec** *nm* bunch of unripe grapes

*****greç = **grreç**

*****gre'fsh**ë** *nf* tuft, crest = **kre'sht**ë

grehu'll *nm (np ~ j)* thicket

grejder *nm* [*Constr*] grader

grejfer *nm* part of the mechanism that engages perforations in film: claw

grejpfru't *nm* [*Bot*] grapefruit

grek *adj, n* Greek

*****greki'nj**ë** *nf* = **greqi'nj**ë

*****Greki'ni** *nf (Old)* Greece = **Greqi'**

grek|ofo'n *adj* speaker of Greek: grecophone

*****grek|ojk**ë *nf (Old)* = **greqi'nj**ë

grek|o|ma'dh *adj* committed to or supportive of the territorial expansion of Greece

grek|o|ma'n *adj, n* 1 [*Hist*] pro-Greek *2 [*Scorn*] Greek; pseudo-Greek

*****grek|o's**•** *vt (Old)* to hellenize

greko-tu'rk *adj* Greco-Turkish

gre'llë *nf* deep pool (off a river bank)

gremç = **grremç

gre'më *nf* = **gremi'n**ë

gremi'në *nf* 1 ravine; chasm 2 downfall, collapse, disaster

*****gremin|o'r** *adj* 1 abyssal 2 disastrous

gremi's•** *vt* 1 to make [] fall from a high place; trip; cause the downfall of []; drop, throw down 2 *(Colloq)* to destroy [] completely, utterly ruin 3 *(Fig Colloq)* to force [] to leave, kick [] out, expel

gremi's•*et* *vpr* 1 to fall from a high place, tumble down; trip and fall down; fall down 2 *(Fig Colloq)* to be driven out, forced to leave

gremi's|je *nf ger* 1 <**gremi's**•, **gremi's**•*et* 2 downfall, fall

gre'mshe *nf* [*Ornit*] golden oriole (*Oriolus oriolus*)

gren *nm* egg of the silkworm

gre'nzë *nf* = **gre'r**ë

grep *nm* 1 fishhook 2 crochet hook; barb 3 storage hook 4 *(Colloq)* [*Naut*] ship's anchor 5 manure fork 6 *(Reg Arb)* table fork 7 hairpin 8 latch 9 young sprout newly emerged from the soil 10 [*Zool Reg*] = **zhuzha'k** 11 *(Fig Pejorative Crude)* petty thief: two-bit crook; swindler 12 *(Fig Pejorative Crude)* person you can't get rid of: clinging pest, constant nuisance 13 *(Fig Pejorative Crude)* skinflint

○ **ësh·të grep** *(Reg Arb Pej)* to be a glutton

○ **nuk <> kap grepi** "<>'s hook does not catch" it is more than <> can do, is beyond <>'s capability

○ **grep i sahatit** clock/watch hand

grep· *vt (Crude)* **1** to steal small objects: pinch **2** to swindle: rip off

grepç *nm (Reg) [Invert]* scorpion = **akrep**

grepo·n *vt* **1** to hook [a fish] **2** to extract [] out of a narrow place by using a hook: fish [] out **3** to lance [a snake bite] in order to make the blood flow

greptë *adj (i)* hook-shaped, hooked

grepth *nm dimin* little hook, clasp

grepthikë *nf* hooked knife for cutting and pulling threads in a loom

****Greqëri** *nf(Old)* Greece = **Greqi**

Greqi *nf* Greece

****greqinjë** *nf(Old)* Greek girl/woman

greqisht *adv* in Greek (language)

greqishte *nf* Greek (language)

greqizëm *nm* word borrowed from Greek: Grecism

grerak *nm [Entom]* giant hornet *(Vespa crabro germana)*

grerë *nf [Entom]* = **grerëz**

grerëz *nf* **1** *[Entom]* wasp, hornet **2** *(Fig)* troublemaker

○ **grerëz e madhe** *[Invert]* = **grerak**

○ **grerëz e mollës** *[Entom]* European apple sawfly *Hoplocampa testudinea Klug.*

gresë

  I § *adj, nf* unripe (grape)

  II § *adj* (of land) unsuitable for seasonal planting

****gresm** *nf* = **krezm**

grestë *adj (i)* unripe

greth

  I § *nm [Entom]* **1** hornet **2** *(Fig Pejorative Colloq)* dirty spy **3** broken flax

  II § *adv* completely full, jampacked

○ **greth dardhë** *[Entom]* = **grerak**

grethac *nm* kind of olive that stays green and has little oil; olive that does not ripen well

****grethatel** *nm [Bot]* large dodder *(Cuscuta europaea)*

****grëthëz** *nm (Reg Gheg)* male bee, drone

****grevar** *n (Old)* = **grevist**

grevë *nf* work stoppage by laborers: strike

grevëthyes

  I § *nm* **1** strike-breaker **2** *(Pej)* scab

  II § *adj* strikebreaking

grevist

  I § *n* striker (in a labor dispute)

  II § *adj* pertaining to strikes

****grevues** *nm (Old)* = **grevist**

****grezdë** = **gresë**

grezhë *nf* bristling hair in the beard

****grëmis·et** *vpr* = **gremis·et** to burrow

****grëmshe** *nf [Ornit]* fig-eater

****grëndël** *nf* scrofula

****Grënlandë** *nf* Greenland = **Groenlandë**

gri

  I § *adj* gray

  II § *nf* the color gray

gri·n

  I § *vt* **1** to cut [] into small fragments: mince, chop; grate **2** to eat away at []; gnaw at/on [] **3** *(Colloq)* to kill a large number of [] quickly one after another, wipe [] out completely **4** *(Fig)* to cause [] discomfort/

disquiet: bother **5** *(Fig Colloq)* to cause [] great expense **6** *(Fig Colloq)* to earn/make a lot of [money] **7** *(Fig Crude)* to know [a subject] thoroughly: know [it] cold, have [it] aced

  II § *vi* *(Fig Colloq Pej)* to emit a flow of nonsense: yammer, prattle away

○ **gri·n lakër/sallatë** to talk a lot; talk nonsense/rubbish; waste time talking, talk to the air

○ [] **gri·n si këmbët e mizës** to grind [] very fine

○ <> **gri·n³ᵖˡ zorrët** <>'s stomach ("intestines") *is rumbling*, <> *is hungry*

gribë *nf(Reg)* **1** comb with widely spaced teeth **2** currycomb **3** long-handled rake **4** *[Fish]* = **plumbçë**

grifë *nf* **1** griffin **2** *[Ornit]* griffon vulture *(Gyps fulvus)*

grifshë *nf* **1** *[Ornit]* common jay *(Garrulus glandarius)* **2** *(Insult)* shrewish woman **3** mottled goat

○ **grifshë e detit** *[Ornit]* roller *Coracias garulus L.*

grigjë

  I § *nf* flock (of sheep/goats)

  II § *adv* in hordes; in abundance

****grigjo·het** *vpr* to herd together

****grigjo·n** *vt* to round [] up into a herd

grih· *vt* to sharpen [] with a whetstone: hone, whet

grih·et *vpr* **1** to quarrel badly: tear each other apart, fight **2** to suffer great losses (in men or material): lose badly, be crushed **3** to work hard at, labor at

grihë *nf* **1** whetstone, grindstone **2** = **qostër**

grihës

  I § *nm* **1** blade-sharpener **2** whetstone

  II § *adj* for sharpening/honing blades

grihje *nf ger* <**grih**-

griho·n *vt* to make [] sharp: sharpen; whet, hone

grikëll *nf [Zool]* = **bregcë**

****gril** *nf [Ornit]* = **grillë**

grilë *nf* **1** louvered window shutter; window blind, venetian blind **2** grillwork serving as a gate or screen **3** grill/grid in an oven

grill *nm* **1** shale **2** barren soil **3** *[Bot]* ornamental shrub growing up to six feet in height, with trifoliate leaves, dense yellow flower clusters, and long seed pods *(Petteria ramentacea (Sieber) C. Presl)*

grillë *nf [Ornit]* **1** small wild duck **2** bee-eater *(Merops apiaster)*

grillishtë *nf* ground containing or covered with shale; non-porous soil, barren ground

grillo·n *vt* to file [] down (into powder)

○ <> **grillo·n kokën** to annoy <> by talking a lot of nonsense

grillor *adj* consisting or containing large amounts of shale: non-porous, unproductive

grim *nm* **1** theatrical makeup **2** the art of maquillage

grimasë *nf (Book)* grimace

grimca-grimca *adv* in very small pieces

grimcë *nf* **1** crumb of food **2** small bit: particle, bit, speck, mote **3** *[Spec]* molecule; atom; atomic particle **4** *(Old) [Ling]* particle = **pjesëz**

grimcim *nm ger* <**grimco·n**, **grimco·het**

grimco·het *vpr* to fall into crumbs/particles: crumble

grimco·n *vt* to fragment [] into crumbs/particles: crumble, shatter, powder

grimë *nf* crumb, particle

grimo·het *vpr* to get made up for a theatrical role

grim|**o**·*n* *vt* to apply theatrical makeup to [ ]: make [ ] up

grind· *vt* to harass, pester; cause to fight, egg on

grind·*et* *vpr* **1** to quarrel, bicker **2** (of children) to bawl; carry on, caterwaul **3** (of animals) to howl; snarl

    ○ **grind·***et* **për të bardhat e laraskës** *(Pej)* to argue about nothing, fight over trifles

    ○ <> **grind·***et*³*pl* **trutë** <>'s mind *is* in a whirl, <> *doesn't know* what to do

grind|**a**|**c** *adj, n =* **grindave**|**c**

grind|**ama**|**n** *adj, n =* **grindave**|**c**

grind|**anja**|**r** *adj, n =* **grindave**|**c**

grind|**anjo**|**z** *adj, n =* **grindave**|**c**

grind|**a**|**r** *adj, n =* **grindave**|**c**

grind|**ave**|**c** *adj, n* quarrelsome/contentious (person); faultfinding (person); disagreeable (crank)

grind|**avi**|**k** *adj, n =* **grindave**|**c**

grind|**ë**|**s** *adj =* **grindave**|**c**

grind|**je** *nf ger* **1** < **grind·**, **grind·***et* **2** verbal quarrel: argument

grind|**jembje**|**ll**|**ës** *adj (Book)* quarrel-provoking

grip *nm* **1** [*Med*] influenza, flu: grippe **2** dark-spotted white pigeon

grip|**a**|**l** *adj* of or pertaining to grippe

grip|**o**|**r** *adj =* **gripa**|**l**

gri|**r**|**ë** *adj (i)* **1** cut/chopped up into small pieces: minced, shredded, chopped; grated **2** (of clothes) worn out

gri|**r**|**ë**|**s**

    I § *adj* cutting/chopping up into small pieces: mincing, shredding, chopping; grating

    II § *n* cutter, chopper; operator of a machine for mincing/chopping

gri|**r**|**ëse** *nf* **1** chopping machine: chopper **2** knife with a sharp, curved blade for mincing **3** grater, shredder = **re**|*nde*

gri|**r**|**je** *nf ger* < **gri·**|*n*, **gri·**|*het*

*grir **gris** *nm* food grater for squash

gris· *vt* **1** to tear, rip; tear [ ] up; rip [ ] off **2** to wear [ ] out **3** to scratch, claw **4** [*Poet*] to dispel [ ] suddenly **5** *(Fig Colloq)* to pass through [ ], get over [ ]; finish with [ ] forever

    ○ **Gris gjirin, arno pëqirin.** "Tear from the breast to patch the lap" *(Prov)* Ruin something important to save something unimportant

    ○ <> **gris· zemrën/shpirtin** to break <>'s heart, hurt <> deeply

gris·*et* *vpr* **1** to get torn **2** to get scratched **3** to wear out *4 to fret, worry

gris|**ë** *nf* **1** scratch, claw mark **2** tear, laceration **3** (Old) pocket **4** (Reg) intrigue, machination, plot **5** = **grindje**

*grir **gris**|**ëm** *adj* in tatters = **gri**|**sur**

*grir **gris**|**ët** *adj (i) =* **gri**|**sur**

gris|**je** *nf ger* **1** < **gris·**, **gris·***et* **2** tear, laceration

gris|**kël** *nf* scale of a fish: fish scale

gris|**ur**

    I § *adj (i)* **1** torn, tattered **2** tattered by wear: worn through/away **3** in/with tattered clothes: raggedy

    II § *nf (e)* ripped/torn spot; worn-through hole

grish· *vt* to invite; beckon to come; beckon

grish|**ës**

    I § *n* inviter

    II § *adj* inviting, beckoning

*grir **grish**|**ëz** *nf* [*Ornit*] = **lara**|**skë**

*grir **grish**|**im** *nm ger =* **grish**|**je**

grish|**je** *nf ger* **1** < **grish·** **2** invitation

grish|**ta**|**r** *n, adj =* **gri**|**shës**

grish|**ur** *n (i)* invitee = **ftu**|**ar**

*grir **grit** *stem for pdef* < **gërthet·**

grith·

    I § *vt* to tear, scratch

    II § *vi* to emit a rasping sound

griv· *vpr* to have graying hair, be getting gray

*grir **grive**|**llë** *nf* sieve = **si**|**të**

*grir **grivello**·*n* *vt* to sift = **shosh·**

gri|**v**|**ë** *adj, n* dun-coated (animal); (person) just beginning to turn gray: graying, getting gray

*grir **gri**|**v**|**en** *nf (Old)* [*Tech*] collar of a crankshaft

*grir **gri**|**v**|**ër** = **gri**|**v**|**ë**

griv|**o**|**l** *nm* **1** dun/gray horse **2** *(Joke)* graying man, middle-aged man

grivo|**r** *nm* [*Bot*] thistle *(Cirsium)*

griza|**t**·*et* *vpr* to develop cracks, become cracked/chapped

grizga *np (Reg)* **1** chaff **2** grape marc/mash

gri|**zh**|**ël** *nf* [*Ornit*] = **lara**|**skë**

*grir **gri**|**zh**|**ëm** *adj (i)* dapple-gray

grizh|**le**|**mz**|**ë** *nf* [*Ornit*] jay = **gri**|**fshë**

grizh|**t**|**ë** *adj (i)* grayish

gro|**bull** *nf* [*Bot*] vetch = **ko**|**çkull**

Groenla|**nd**|**ë** *nf* Greenland

grofolo|**k** *nm (Reg)* low place with plenty of sun and no wind

gro|**ll** *adj* curved like a shepherd's crook

gro|**lle** *nf* curved part of a shepherd's crook

*grir **gro**|**më** *nf* nausea

*grir **grom**|**ë**|**si** *nf* belching; nausea; disgust

grom|**ë**|**si**·*n* *vi* **1** to belch **2** *(Fig)* to rumble

grom|**ë**|**si**|**më** *nf =* **grom**|**ë**|**si**|**rë**

*grir **grom**|**ë**|**si**|**n**|**ë** *nf (Reg Gheg) =* **grom**|**ë**|**si**|**rë**

*grir **grom**|**ë**|**si**|**r**|**ë** *nf* **1** belch, belching **2** *(Fig Pej)* sordid activity: dirty business **3** *(Fig Insult)* loathsome person *4 nausea *5 vulgarity

grom|**ë**|**si**|**s** *stem for 1st sg pres, pl pres, 2nd & 3rd sg subj, pind* < **grom**|**ë**|**si**|**t**·

grom|**ë**|**si**|**t**· *vt* **1** to belch **2** to nauseate, disgust

grom|**ë**|**si**|**t**|**ës** *adj* **1** belching **2** nauseating, disgusting

grom|**ë**|**si**|**t**|**je** *nf ger* < **grom**|**ë**|**si**|**t**· belch

gro|**pa**-**gro**|**pa** *adj* full of holes: pitted

gro|**pas** *OR* **gro**|**pazi** *adv*

grop|**e**|**re** *nf* small hole in the ground, shallow pit

grop|**ë**

    I § *nf* **1** hole in the ground: pit, ditch **2** burial hole: grave **3** hollow; cavity; body cavity; dimple **4** [*Geog*] basin of land surrounded by hills or mountains

    II § *adj* hollow

    ○ **grop**|**ë** **ajrore** air pocket

    ○ **ta bë·***n* **gropën** { } could kill you without blinking an eye

    ○ **gropa e syrit** [*Anat*] orbit of the eye, eye socket

    ○ **gropa e ujit** [*Track*] water jump

grop|**ë**|**çe**|**le** *nf* **1** shallow hole in a horizontal surface **2** dimple

gropëqiqër *nf* children's game whose object is to get a small ball into an opponent's hole

*gropësinë *nf (Reg Gheg)* = gropësirë

gropësirë *nf* **1** land pitted with holes **2** puddle; stagnant pool **3** [*Geog*] basin of land surrounded by hills or mountains

gropëz *nf dim* **1** <gropë **2** = gropëqiqër **3** [*Med*] foveola, fossula
   ◦ **gropëz në faqe** dimple (in the cheek)

gropëzim *nm ger* <gropëzo•*n*, gropëzo•*het*

gropëzo•het *vpr* to become pitted with holes

gropëzo•n *vt* to pit [] with holes

gropim *nm ger* **1** <gropo•*n*, gropo•*het* **2** hollowed-out place, hole

gropishtë *nf* land with many hollows

gropkë *nf* shallow hole, indentation, dimple

gropo•het *vpr* = gropos•*et*

gropo•n
   I § *vt* **1** to excavate; pit [] with holes **2** to hollow [] out **3** to bury, inter
   II § *vi* to dig a hole, excavate

gropor *adj* **1** like a hole: hollow, concave **2** having holes: pitted

gropore *nf* **1** land pitted with holes **2** [*Geog*] depression in the ground; small valley: dale, hollow

gropos• *vt* **1** to bury; bury [] in the ground: inter **2** *(Fig)* to overwhelm; put an end to []; knock [] out **3** *(Fig)* to expunge [] from memory **4** = gropo•*n*

gropos•et *vpr* **1** to become sunken **2** to die **3** [*Mil*] to dig in

groposje *nf ger* <gropos•, gropos•*et*

groposur *adj (i)* **1** buried; interred **2** [*Mil*] entrenched, dug in **3** deeply set into a body cavity: deep-set; hollowed-out

gropshar *n (Pej)* person who deliberately destroys or tries to destroy another

groptë *adj (i)* in the form of a hole: hollowed-out, hole-like; with holes, pitted

gropuar *adj (i)* **1** made into a hole: dug out, hollowed out **2** having holes: deeply pitted **3** deeply set into a body cavity: deep-set

grosist
   I § *n* wholesale dealer: wholesaler
   II § *adj* **1** wholesaling **2** sold in wholesale lots

grosh *nm (Old)* **1** Turkish money worth a hundredth of a lira: piaster ***2** = groshë

grosh•et *vpr* **1** to get a skin rash **2** to grow hoarse

groshanicë *nf (Reg Kos)* string bean

groshar *nm (Old)* **1** silver coin worth one grosh **2** silver coin worn by women as jewelry

groshare *nf, nm (Old)* **1** = groshar **2** spotted ewe; ewe with red or brown patches on the muzzle **3** = groshore

groshatar *nm (Old)* = groshar

groshë *nf* **1** white bean, haricot *(Phaseolus vulgaris L.)* **2** lentil = thjerrëz
   ◦ **groshë kuqe** [*Bot*] scarlet runner bean *Phaseolus coccineus*
   ◦ **groshë mishi** *(Colloq)* [*Bot*] = mashurka
   ◦ **groshë qeni** *(Colloq)* [*Bot*] kidney, haricot bean *Phaseolus vulgaris*
   ◦ **groshë qorre** [*Bot*] *(Dolichos melanophthalmus)*

groshëm *adj (i)* (of sheep and goats) having a spotted muzzle, spotted

groshëz *nf* [*Bot*] **1** bird's-foot trefoil *(Lotus corniculatus)* **2** common lentil *(Lens culinaris)* = thjerrëz

groshilë *nf* [*Bot*] vetchling = modhull

*groshinë = grashinë

groshnajë *nf* bean patch

groshore *nf* **1** bean patch **2** wide-bellied clay pot for boiling beans

grotesk *nm, adj (Book)* [*Art Lit*] grotesque

groviqe *nf* [*Food*] foremilk (from a milk animal) mixed with flour and cooked in a pan

grozhël *nf* [*Bot*] bush vetch *(Vicia sepium)*

grua *nf* **1** woman **2** wife **3** womankind
   ◦ **grua e dergjur** = lehonë
   ◦ **grua me fëdigë** pregnant woman
   ◦ **grua natare** woman with a particular knack for domestic tasks
   ◦ **grua pa kurore** mistress, concubine
   ◦ **grua rrugësh** slut

gruar *nm* womanizer; ladies' man

*gruc• *vt* to gobble [] up, devour

gruç *nm (Reg)* corncob

*grudë *nf* clod of earth; sod, turf

*grudinë = rudinë

*grue *nf (Reg Gheg)* = grua

*grueno•het *vpr (Reg Gheg)* (of a girl) to grow into a woman

*grufa-grufa *adv* = gulfa-gulfa

gruhas *stem for 1st sg pres, pl pres, 2nd & 3rd sg subj, pind* <gruha•

gruhat• *vt* to winnow

*grukë = grykë

grumbuj-grumbuj *adv* in piles, in several heaps, in groups

grumbull
   I § *nm (np ˉj)* **1** heap, pile **2** crowd, throng
   II § *adv* in a crowd, in a heap
   ◦ **grumbull dheu** mound

grumbullas *adv* **1** *(Old)* = grumbuj-grumbuj ***2** *(Old)* wholesale

grumbullim *nm ger* **1** <grumbullo•*n*, grumbullo•*het* **2** agglomeration, conglomeration **3** accumulation; stockpiling; collection

grumbullo•het *vpr* **1** to come together in one place: gather **2** to congregate, assemble, get together **3** [*Sport*] to take part in a team warm-up before a game **4** to pile up on <>, get to be too much for <>

grumbullo•n *vt* **1** to pile up [], amass, gather up []; accumulate **2** to gather [] into one place: concentrate, stockpile **3** to store [] up

grumbullor *adj* **1** rounded out, spherical **2** *(Old)* cumulative **3** [*Bot*] bushy

grumbullore
   I § *nf* spherical object, round thing
   II § *np* [*Bot*] bushy trees; plants with flowers growing in clusters

grumbullues
   I § *adj* **1** cumulative, additive **2** *(Old)* stockpiling
   II § *n* **1** collector **2** *(Old)* stockpiler **3** hoarder
   III § *nm* [*Spec*] cumulator

*grumçukë *nf* = dromcë

grunabardh *nm* common wheat (with large spikes and awns and whitish kernels) *(Triticum vulgare)*

grunajë *nf* field planted with wheat; grain, wheat

grunamadh *nm* [*Bot*] common melilot, yellow sweet clover *(Melilotus officinalis)*

grunar *nm* granary

grunc *nm* [*Ichth*] *(Paraphoxinus minutus Kar.)*

***grundë** *nf* hair
○ **grundë ylli** tail of a comet

gruneshë *nf* [*Bot*] herbaceous annual growing on rocky ground or in hedgerows of fields, with violet flowers and thick downy leaves that are used in folk medicine to treat damaged parts of the body

***grunë** *nf (Reg Gheg)* = **grurë**

***grungus** stem for 1st sg pres, pl pres, 2nd & 3rd sg subj, pind < **grungut·**

***grungut·** *vi* to coo, croon

***grunis·** *vi* to creak, squeak

grunishtë *nf* field planted with wheat

gruno·het *vpr* to grow into womanhood

grunor *adj* 1 sown with wheat 2 [*Bot*] cereal

grunore
I § *nf* wheat field
II § *np* 1 [*Bot*] cereal grain plants: cereal grains 2 [*Bot*] variety of pear that matures at the same time as wheat

grunjëra *np* 1 varieties of wheat 2 wheat fields 3 [*Bot*] cereal grain plants: cereal grains

grunjështë *nf* wheat plant before the spike is formed; wheat plant before the kernels are formed; wheat straw

grunjta *np (të)* fields of wheat

grunjtë *adj (i)* 1 wheaten, of wheat 2 of the color of wheat

grup
I § *nm* 1 group 2 [*Mil*] military unit consisting of several batteries: (artillery) battalion/group
II § *adv* in/as a group

grup-armatë *nf* [*Mil*] military unit consisting of several armies: army group

grupash
I § *nm (Pej)* factionalist
II § *adj* factional

grupazh *nm* faction

grupe-grupe *adv* in groups

grupim *nm ger* 1 < **grupo·n, grupo·het** 2 temporary group, grouping

grup-moshë *nf* age-group

grupo·het *vpr* to form into a group; enter a group; gather in groups

grupo·n *vt* to group

grupor *adj* of or pertaining to a group

grup-organizatë *nf* branch of an organization

grurë *nf* [*Bot*] wheat *(Triticum L.G)*
○ **grurë bolle** mouse barley *Hordeum murinum*
○ **grurë breshke** [*Bot*] wall barley, mouse barley *Hordeum murium*
○ **grurë i egër** mouse barley *Hordeum murinum*
○ **grurë lepuri** bulbous barley *Hordeum bulbosum*
○ **grurë i vermë** summer wheat
○ **grurë vjeshtë** wheat sown in fall/autumn

grurëkuq *nm* [*Bot*] red wheat

grurth *nm* 1 [*Bot*] wall barley, mouse barley *(Hordeum murium)* 2 eyelid sty

***grushmaq** *nm (Colloq)* larynx = **gurmaz**

grusht
I § *nm* 1 fist 2 blow of a fist, force of such a blow; punch, blow; strike 3 *(Fig)* fistful; handful 4 something small and clenched together 5 small amount
II § *adv* clenched together, curled/hunched up
○ **grusht i blinduar** iron fist
○ **grusht hidraulik** *(Tech)* water hammer
○ **grusht për grusht** courageously
○ **grusht shteti** coup d'état, coup

***grushtar** *nm (Old)* boxer

grushtim *nm ger* 1 < **grushto·n** 2 punch (with the fist)

grushto·n *vt* to hit [ ] with the fist, punch

gruzë *nf* 1 [*Bot*] = **buhavicë** 2 dyer's weed *(Reseda lutea)*

***gry·n** *vt* = **gërrye·n**

***gryet** *adj (i)* pimply; blotchy

***grykë** *nm* = **grryk**

gryk·et *vpr* to fight by grabbing by the throat; wrestle, fight hand-to-hand, scuffle

grykafytas *adv* = **fytafyt**

gryka-grykas *adv* at each other's throats

gryka-grykazi *adv* = **gryka-grykas**

gryka-grykës = **gryka-grykas**

grykajë *nf* [*Geog*] mouth of a river

grykakuq *nm* [*Ornit*] = **gushëkuq**

grykalarmë *nf* [*Ornit*] bluethroat *(Erithacus svecicus)*

grykargjende *adj (Poet)* having a beautiful, light-skinned throat

grykargjendtë *adj (Poet)* = **grykargjende**

grykas *adv* 1 up to the neck, up to the brim 2 by the neck, around the neck 3 at each other's throats 4 mumps

grykashkë *nf* 1 baby's bib 2 smock worn by children in kindergarten or school 3 [*Agr*] place at which the moldboard is attached to the beam of a two-handled steel plow: frog 4 metal collar that secures the joint of two pieces of wood; metal collar that reinforces each narrow end of the wooden hub of a cartwheel

grykazi *adv* = **grykas**

grykele *nf* narrow mountain pass: gorge

grykë
I § *nf* 1 front part of the neck: throat 2 narrow opening at or near one end of a cavity space: neck, bottle neck 3 muzzle of a gun; barrel of a gun 4 *(Colloq)* mouth 5 [*Geog*] (of a mountain) pass, gorge; (of a river or bay) mouth 6 *(Colloq)* quantity of liquid that can be wallowed in one gulp: slug, swallow 7 collar band 8 shirt with loose sleeves and closed collar 9 curved part of the plow beam to which the plowshare is attached; plow beam 10 *(Fig)* creamiest part of a liquid food that rises to the top: cream 11 *(Fig Colloq)* beginning part of a time period; start of an event
II § *adv* at each other's throat; in constant quarrel
○ **grykë e bardhë/ligë/keqe** *(Colloq)* diphtheria
○ **grykët e bardha** *(Euph)* diphtheria
○ **grykët e mira** mumps *Parotitis epidemica* = **shyta**
○ [ ] **gënjeu gryka** "the throat deceived [ ]" [ ] was deceived by appearances
○ **grykë golf** turtle-neck collar
○ **grykë lumi** river mouth
○ **grykë mali** mountain gorge

○ **grykë më/për grykë** at each other's throat
○ **grykë pusi** neck of a well
○ **grykë pushke** muzzle of a gun
○ **grykë shisheje** neck of a bottle

grykëderdhje *nf* [*Geog*] mouth of a river
grykëgjatë *adj* **1** long-necked **2** long-barreled
grykëgjerë *adj* **1** wide-necked **2** wide-barreled
grykëhollë *nf(Euph)* gun, rifle = **pushkë**
grykëkalbët *adj (Reg Arb)* **1** speaking disparagingly of others: backbiting, malicious **2** foulmouthed
grykëlarik *adj* having spots on the underside of the neck: spotted-throated
grykëngushtë
 I § *adj* **1** narrow-necked **2** narrow-barreled
 II § *nf(Euph)* gun, rifle = **pushkë**
grykëpërpjetë *adj, adv* neck-end (of a container) up, barrel-end (of a gun) up
grykëposhtë *adj, adv* neck-end (of a container) down, barrel-end (of a gun) down
grykës
 I § *adj* gluttonous, greedy
 II § *n* glutton, gourmand
 III § *nm* **1** curved part of the plow beam to which the plowshare is attached; plow beam **2** metal collar that reinforces each narrow end of the wooden hub of a cartwheel *3 (Old)* [*Tech*] = **griven**
grykëse *nf* **1** smock worn over other clothing **2** man's embroidered shirt with a closed neck and no collar **3** woman's embroidered vest **4** collar of a dress that fastens at the neck **5** stocking top
grykësi *nf* = **gopësi**
grykësor *adj* = **grykës**
*grykëtinë *nf* = **grykele**
grykëtharë *adj* "dry-throated" **1** not having eaten or drunk anything for some time: having fasted **2** *(Curse)* (said of someone who has eaten or drunk something without permission) be damned! (by starving to death)
grykëz *nf* **1** *(Pet Dimin)* <**grykë 2** embroidered collar on a woman's dress **3** man's embroidered shirt with a closed neck and no collar **4** woman's embroidered vest **5** baby's bib **6** curved part of the plow beam to which the plowshare is attached; plow beam **7** breast collar attached to a packsaddle **8** [*Dairy*] the cream that forms in the neck of a container
grykëzënë *adj* **1** hoarse **2** close-mouthed and silent **3** *(Curse)* be damned! (by having one's breath taken away), I hope he chokes
grykje
 I § *nf* **1** man's embroidered shirt with a closed neck and no collar **2** woman's embroidered vest **3** shirtcollar **4** water vessel with a long narrow neck
 II § *adj* having a long narrow neck
grykole *nf* **1** women's sleeveless vest **2** women's dickey consisting of a blouse front and an embroidered collar **3** baby's bib
grykor *adj* **1** [*Ling*] guttural **2** sounding hoarse and muffled **3** located in the throat; coming from the throat
grykore *nf* **1** [*Ling*] guttural/velar sound **2** baby's bib **3** women's dickey consisting of a blouse front and an embroidered collar **4** apron **5** *(Old)* frilled collar: ruff *6** (in a suit of armor) chin-piece, beaver
grykos· *vt* **1** to stuff [] with food *2** to choke

grykos·et *vpr* **1** to be at each other's throat, constantly argue; wrestle, fight hand-to-hand, scuffle **2** to embrace (each other)
gryksë *nf* bib (worn by women or children)
*gryksó·het *vpr* to gorge oneself, overeat
*grykzuem *adj (i) (Reg Gheg)* gluttonous
grym· *vt* to curse
grym·et *vpr* **1** to rot, decay; get wormy *2** to be cursed/damned
grymaç *nm (Reg)* feeling of longing for someone far away: yearning
*gryme *nf (e)* banishment
grymë
 I § *adj (i)* = **grymët**
 II § *nf* *rumpus, row, scene
grymët *adj (i)* **1** accursed **2** rotten, decayed, wormeaten; filthy
grymos· *vt* **1** to curse = **malko·** ·n **2** to cause [] to become thin and weak
grymos·et *vpr* to rot, decay; get wormy
grymosur *adj (i)* frail, weak; ailing
*grynjë *adj (i)* of wheat, wheaten
*grynjëra *np* wheat fields; seed wheat
*grynjtë *adj (i)* = **grynjë**
*grraç = **garraç**
*grre *nf with masc agreement (Old)* heavy drinker, boozer
*greç *nm* gourd-bottle
*grrelle *nf* quarry, mine
gremç
 I § *nm* **1** angled hook left by the chopped-off branch of a tree; hook for hanging things up **2** long pole with hooked prongs at one end; boat hook **3** *(Impol Old)* cross **4** *(Colloq)* special means used to accomplish a goal: trick **5** *(Fig ColloqImpolite)* very thin and bent old man
 II § *pred* into a hook
gremçak *adj* **1** hook-shaped **2** having many hooks
gremçe *nf* nanny-goat with hook-shaped horns
gremço· ·n *vt* to form [] into a hook
gremtas *adv* hunched over in order to hide
gremtë *adj (i)* *(Colloq)* hunched/bent over; curved like a hook
*grro·n = **germo·** ·n
*grroç *nm* tortoise shell
grroçe *nf* woven basket for tableware; basket for spoons
*grrona *np* holes/hollows created by water erosion
grror *nm* forked timber driven into the ground to hold hay or leaves to be eaten by livestock
*grrufe *nf* = **gulfe**
grryk *nm (np ~ qe)* cool gust of wind, breeze
*gthapë *nf(Old)* **1** miser **2** = **gëthep**
*gthetër *nf* = **kthetër**
guace *nf* [*Invert*] oyster
guackë *nf* [*Zool*] = **guaskë**
guak *nm* [*Ornit*] woodpigeon *(Columba palumbus L.)* = **pëllumb gugashi**
guall *nm (np ~ j)* **1** hard protective covering of certain animals: shell **2** tough outer covering: husk, dry pod; nutshell, eggshell; crust, scab; incrustation
 ○ **guall hundor** [*Med*] nasal concha
 ○ **guall veshor** [*Med*] concha auriculae
guarnicion *nm* [*Tech*] gasket

gua'skë *nf* **1** [*Invert*] mollusk, oyster, cockle **2** shell; seashell **3** husk; nutshell, eggshell; crust **4** *(Reg)* = **bërtha'më 5** *(Fig)* ivory tower

guaskë'ho'llë *adj* paper-shelled, thin-shelled

guaskë'tra'shë *adj* hard-shelled, thick-shelled

guask'o'r *adj* **1** made of shell **2** containing fossilized shells

*****gua'sh** *nm* [*Ornit*] woodpigeon *(Columba palumbus)*

guatema'l|as *adj, n* Guatemalan

Guatema'lë *nf* Guatemala

gua'zë *nf* hard protective covering: shell

gu'be *nf* *(Reg)* = **grïbë**

gube're *nf* **1** *(Old)* knee-length cape **2** *(Reg)* heavy knee-length woolen jacket

gu'b|ez *nf* [*Veter*] sheep mange

gu'b|ëz *nf* [*Med*] = **bre'shkëz**

gu'cë *nf* puppy

guci|ma'c *nf* **1** caterpillar **2** larva, maggot, grub

*****guc'is** *stem for 1st sg pres, pl pres, 2nd & 3rd sg subj, pind* <**gucï't·**

*****guc'ït·** *vt* to arouse

gu'ckë *nf* [*Entom*] grub of the cabbage white butterfly *(Pieris brassicae)*

guç *nm* horse bite

*****guda'll** *nm* kettledrum

*****gudu|la'c** OR **gudu|la'k** *adj* ticklish

guduli *nf* tickled feeling

gudul'is· *vt* **1** to tickle **2** to give pleasure to [ ]: please

gudul'is·*-et vpr* to be ticklish

  ○ **Nuk gudulis·***et³sg* **me pupël zogu.** "A bird is not tickled with a feather." (said of someone who is completely self-possessed and unflappable) {} is cool as a cucumber.

gudul'is'ës *adj* tickling

gudul'is'je *nf ger* **1** <**gudul'is·**, **gudul'is·***et* **2** tickle **3** tickling feeling

gudu|ve're *nf* *(Old)* [*Ethnog*] = **vero're**

gueri'l *adj* guerilla

gueri'lje *nf* **1** guerilla warfare **2** guerilla band/unit

guf· *vi* = **gufo'·n**

guf·*-et vpr* **1** = **mbufa't·***et*, **gufo'·n 2** *(Fig)* to brag, show off

gu'fa *adv* = **gu'lfa-gu'lfa**

gufa'c *adj* **1** puffed up, billowing; swollen, bulging **2** *(Fig)* bragging, showing off

gufac|a'k *adj* = **gufa'c**

gufa'llë *nf* **1** hole in a tree trunk; hollowed-out trunk **2** *(Fig)* skinny old person, person who is all skin and bones

gufa'r *nm* **1** hollow of the throat *****2** [*Ichth*] plaice, sole

gufa's· *vt* **1** = **mbufa'·***et*, **gufo'·n *****2** to grunt (like a pig)

gufa't·*et vpr* = **mbufa't·***et*, **gufo'·***het*

gufa't *stem for pdef, opt, adm, part, vp* <**gufa's·**

gu'fe

  I § *nf* **1** women's jerkin with puffed sleeves **2** puffed sleeve **3** *(Impol)* plump girl/woman

  II § *adj* having a tuft of feathers

gu'fë *nf* **1** something puffed up: puff, puffed sleeve **2** = **zga'rbë 3** effusion, surge, swell; flood; spring, fountain

gu'fër *nf* *(Reg Arb)* mouth of a volcano; crater

guf|ïm *nm ger* **1** <**gufo'·***n*, **gufo'·***het* **2** swelling, swollen part

gu'fkë

  I § *nf* **1** = **xhu'fkë 2** hen with a tuft of feathers on the head **3** *(Fig)* plump girl/woman

  II § *adj* having a tuft of feathers on the head

guf|llo'·*n vi* to overflow, boil over

guf|mo'·*het vpr* = **gufo'·***het*

*****guf|mo'·***n vt* to swell, inflate

gufo'·*het vpr* **1** to swell up, billow **2** to gush; erupt

gufo'·*n*

  I § *vi* **1** to gush/spurt out, spout **2** to erupt; boil over **3** to sprout **4** to swell, bulge out; overflow **5** *(Fig)* to grow up suddenly and become good-looking **6** to gasp/pant, breathe hard *****7** to grunt

  II § *vt* to inflate [ ] with air; cause [ ] to billow

  ○ <> **gufo·***n³sg* **zemra/shpirti** <>'s heart swells with joy

*****gufo'|më** = **kufo'më**

gufo'skë *nf* *(Reg)* small cave

gufu'ar *adj* (*i*) swollen

gufu'e|s *adj* emerging with force: gushing out/forth, erupting

gu'ga *np* baby's cries; babbling; goo-goo

guga'ç *nm* stammerer

*****gug|ale'c** *nm* scarecrow

guga's· = **guga'***t·*

guga'sh *nm* **1** [*Ornit*] = **guha'k 2** [*Ornit*] = **kumri 3** *(Pet)* clean-cut and good-looking boy **4** [*Mus*] bow for the bowed lute

guga't· *vi* to coo; say goo-goo, babble

guga'tje *nf ger* **1** <**guga'***t·* **2** cooing sound, coo **3** baby's babbling sound, goo-goo, babble; bawling sound, bawl

guge'shë *np* = **guga'sh**

gu'gë *nf* baby's chemise

*****gu'gës** *nm* [*Ornit*] wood pigeon *(Columba palumbus)*

gugo'·*n vi* = **guga'***t·*

gugu'çe *nf* **1** [*Ornit*] female of the collared turtledove = **kumri 2** *(Fig Affectionate Poet)* wholesome and beautiful girl: pretty little turtledove

guguftu' *nf* = **gugu'çe**

gu-gu-gu' *onomat* cooing voice of a turtledove: coo-coo-coo

gugurï'më *nf* cooing, coo

guguro'·*n vi* = **guga'***t·*

gugu'sh *nm* [*Ornit*] = **kumri**

gugusha're *nf* **1** *(Reg)* [*Bot*] = **luleshtry'dhe 2** = **mare**

gugu'she *nf* **1** [*Ornit*] female ringdove **2** [*Bot*] flower of the redbud/Judas tree

*****gug|z** = **gog'ës**

guha'k

  I § *nm* **1** [*Ornit*] ringdove, woodpigeon *(Columba palumbus L.)* **2** *(Fig)* simpleton, gawker

  II § *adj* gawking stupidly, in a daze; stupid

guha's *stem for 1st sg pres, pl pres, 2nd & 3rd sg subj, pind* <**guha't·**

*****guha'sh** *nm* [*Ornit*] = **guha'k**

guha't· *vi* **1** to breathe hard, pant; gasp **2** to yawn

guha'tje *nf ger* **1** <**guha't·** **2** sound of panting

Guine' *nf* Guinea

guís | *stem for 1st sg pres, pl pres, 2nd & 3rd sg subj, pind* <**guít**·

guít· *vi* = gugát·

guítje *nf ger* = gugátje

***gujashkë** *nf* = guall

gujatë *nf* = guall

gujavë *nf* = guall

gujerm *nm (Reg)* sultry weather, mugginess

guksó·*n* *vi (Reg)* **1** to belch **2** to vomit, throw up *3 to yawn

gulash *nm* goulash

gulatë *nf* [*Bot*] winter rape (*Brassica napus*)

gulç *nm* **1** asthma **2** gasp, wheeze **3** air current, draft; beam of light **4** *(Fig)* grief, sorrow; trouble **5** *(Fig)* burning desire: craving, avarice

gulçí *nf* **1** sore throat during a cold **2** serious discomfort/grief, distress

gulçím *nm ger* **1** <gulçó·*n*, gulço·́*het* **2** gasp; wheeze **3** *(Fig)* distress **4** *(Fig)* grief, sorrow

gulçímë *nf* asthmatic coughing, wheezing, wheeze

gulçítje *nf ger* **1** = gulçím **2** suffocation, asphyxia

gulço·*het* *vpr* **1** to be afflicted by great discomfort/worry/sorrow **2** to gush forth; erupt **3** to get a sore throat **4** to feel disgusted

gulço·*n*
  I § *vi* **1** to breathe hard; pant; gasp for air; wheeze **2** *(Fig)* to be afflicted by great discomfort/worry/sorrow **3** *(Fig)* to desire greatly, crave **4** to gush forth; erupt
  II § *vt* *(Fig)* to disquiet, upset, cause worry

gulçues *adj* short of breath: panting, gasping

gulë *nf* [*Bot*] kohlrabi (*Brassica oleracea*)

gulfa-gulfa *adv* in spurts

gulfë *nf* **1** spurt, effusion **2** *(Fig)* outburst of anger, rage **3** quantity of liquid drunk in one swallow: gulp, sip, swig

gulfím *nm ger* **1** <gulfó·*n*, gulfo·́*het* **2** noise made by a spurting liquid

gulfo·*n* *vi* **1** to spurt out **2** to sprout suddenly, burst forth **3** *(Fig)* to have an emotional outburst

gulm *nm* **1** troubled mood; worry **2** noisy commotion; clamor, hubbub *3 death rattle

gulmë *nf* = gulm

gulo·*n* = gëlo·*n*

***guish** = gulç

gultím *nm ger* <gulto·*n*

gulto·*n* *vt* **1** to take/move [ ] from one place to another **2** to take livestock to pasture **3** to drive [prey] from its lair

gullmë *nf* fate, destiny; bad luck, misfortune

gullmëbardhë *adj* lucky, fortunate = fatbardhë

gullmëmadh *adj* lucky, successful = fatmadh

gullmëzi *adj (fem sg ˜ez, masc pl ˜inj, fem pl ˜eza)* unlucky, unfortunate = fatzi

gumallak *nm* shellac

gumanë *nf* [*Entom*] large hornet that makes a very loud noise when it flies

***gumbët** *adj (i)* potbellied

***gumçar** *n (Old)* wag, joker, jester

***gumçi** *nf(Old)* joke, farce; nonsense

***gumen** *n* **1** = igumen **2** fat man *3 gray sheepdog with a large head; shaggy dog

***gumenë** *nf* mooring cable

gumë *nf* reef, shoal

gumëratë *nf* **1** pile of rocks **2** dry creek with a rocky bed of rocks **3** ruins of an old house

gumëzhí·*n* *vi* **1** to make a continuous rapidly vibrating noise, as of flying insects: buzz; hum **2** to make a deafening roar
  ∘ <> **gumëzhi**·*n*[3pl] **veshët 1** <> has a ringing in <>'s ears **2** <> *is* sick and tired of listening to the same old thing

gumëzhím *nm ger* = gumëzhítje

gumëzhímë *nf* **1** a continuous rapidly vibrating noise, as of flying insects: buzz, hum **2** loud roar

gumëzhít· *vi* = gumëzhi·*n*

gumëzhítës *adj* **1** buzzing, humming **2** roaring

gumëzhítje *nf ger* **1** <gumëzhít· **2** = gumëzhímë

***gumo**·*n* *vi* to boom out, resound; rumble, thunder

***gumtar** *n* simpleton

***gumushë** *nf* = gëmushë

gumzhí·*n* *vi* = gumëzhi·*n*

gunar *n* person who makes shepherds' cloaks

*g**uncë** *nf(Old)* bodice

*g**unevgjiTCë** *nf* "gypsy cloak" [*Bot*] corn cockle, corn-campion, crown-of-the-field (*Agrostemma githago, Lychnis githago*)

gunezë *nf* [*Bot*] common garden balm (*Melissa officinalis*) = bar blete

gunë *nf* **1** cloak (especially the knee-length hooded goathair cloak typically worn by herdsmen) **2** knee-length white flannel cape for women **3** [*Ethnog*] wool or linen dress with an open bodice worn by both men and women as part of their ethnic costume **4** *(Fig)* cloak that hides one's true nature

gunëbardhë *adj* wearing a white cloak

gunëçjerrë *adj (Fig)* worn to rags: poor

gunëdhírë
  I § *adj* wearing a goat fleece as a cloak
  II § *nm* *(Impol.Jocular)* goatherd (wearing a goat fleece as a cloak)

gunëgrísur *adj* = gunëçjerrë

gunëgjatë *adj* having a long cloak

gunëkuq *adj* wearing a red cloak

gunëtrashë *adj* having a thick cloak

gunëz *nf* **1** small cloak for young children **2** woman's knee-length tunic **3** neck of the cloak

gunëzí *adj masc sg* black-cloaked (person)

*g**ung** *adj* sexually impotent

gungaç *adj, n* humpbacked (person)

gunga-gunga *adj* having a bumpy/lumpy surface; hilly

gungalec
  I § *nm* hair gathered into a bun and worn at the back of the head: hairbun
  II § *adv* in a round bun

*g**ungallë** *nf* [*Entom*] cicada = gjinkallë

gungar *nm* principal rafter of a roof

gungash *adj* **1** = gungaç **2** having a nasal voice

gungat· *vi* to coo

gungaz *adv* = doçesh

gungë
  I § *nf* **1** lump, swelling, bump **2** hump **3** knot (in wood); bulge **4** small hillock **5** [*Med*] scrofula **6** [*Archit*] = kungë **7** [*Tech*] cam

II § *adj* **1** having a difficult-to-break outer covering: hard-shelled **2** (of livestock) having small tough nipples that give little milk **3** *(Fig)* strong-willed, not a pushover **4** *(Fig Pej)* stubborn **5** *(Fig)* hard of hearing

gu'ng**ë**s *adj* **1** having a difficult-to-break outer covering: hard-shelled **2** *(Fig)* tough

gu'ng**ë**t *adj (i)* **1** humped, bulging **2** lumpy, bump; knotty *3 potbellied *4 sexually impotent; unproductive

gung**ë**zi'm *nm* [*Med*] tuberosity

gung**ë**o' **·***het* *vpr* to develop a hump/lump/knot/swelling

gung**ë**o' **·***n* *vt* to raise a lump on []

gung**ë**o'r *adj* [*Bot*] tuberous: *gibbous*

*gung**ë**ue'm *adj (i) (Reg Gheg)* humped; domed; bulging out

gun**ë**i'shte *nf* **1** small lightweight cloak; children's cloak **2** [*Bot*] herbaceous plant with violet-colored flowers and small downy leaves shaped like olive leaves

gu'p**e** *nf* wide-sleeved woolen jacket worn by women

gur

I § *nm* **1** stone; rock **2** [*Med*] calculus (calcium buildup) **3** hard object used in a game: (chess) piece, domino, (billiard) ball **4** precious stone, gem **5** *(Colloq)* metal weight used in a balance = **grama**'r **6** *(Fig)* deep vexation, heaviness in one's heart **7** quantity of water needed to turn a pair of millstones; quantity of olives fed to an oil press at one time

II § *adj* very heavy; very sturdy

III § *adv* **1** very **2** *(Colloq)* hard fruit seed: pit
- **gur ari** chrysolite
- **guri i bes**ë**s** [*Ethnog*] rock on which one puts one's hand to swear (at a trial held by a council of elders)
- **gur bilardoje** billiard ball
- **gur bronkial** [*Med*] broncholith
- **gur çakmaku** flint
- **gur i çmuar** precious stone, gem
- [] **din**ë **edhe gur**ë**t e rrug**ë**s/sokak**ë**ve** everyone knows about [], it's all over town
- **gur dominoje** domino (tile)
- **gur eshke** flint
- **gur fekal** [*Med*] coprolith
- **gur fem**ë**r** stone that can be broken and formed into a slab
- **guri filozofik** philosopher's stone
- **gur i fundit** last chance
- **gur g**ë**lqereje** limestone
- **gur grilli** schist
- **Gur, gur b**ë**het kala/mur.** *(Prov)* A wall is built stone by stone. Little by little and bit by bit.
- **gur gjaku** [*Min*] hematite, bloodstone
- **gur i gjall**ë barren rock
- **ka· (n**ë **dor**ë**) edhe gurin edhe arr**ë**n** to be able to do whatever one wants, have everything needed
- **ka· (n**ë **dor**ë**) t**ë **gjith**ë **gur**ë**t** to have all the necessary resources
- **gur kafeje** hollowed-out rock used as a mortar to grind coffee
- **gur kali** blue vitriol, copper sulphate
- **gur i kalt**ë**r** blue vitriol, copper sulphate
- **gur kilometrazhi** milestone indicating distance in kilometers
- **gur kufiri 1** boundary marker **2** impediment; person who moves/works so slowly as to impede other people
- **gur kulise** [*Tech*] sliding block

- **gur i kushtues**h**ë**m precious stone
- **gur leshi** asbestos
- **s'l**ë**· gur pa l**ë**vizur/luajtur/trazuar/kthyer** to leave no stone unturned
- **gur liri** asbestos
- **gur mbi gur** little by little
- **gur m**ë**lçije** bezoar
- **gur m**ë**ndafshi** asbestos
- **gur i mir**ë *(Colloq)* precious stone, gem
- [] **mor**ë**n vesh edhe gur**ë**t e rrug**ë**s/sokak**ë**ve** everyone knows about [], it's all over town
- **gur mpreh*s**ë*** whetstone, grindstone
- **ë**sh·t**ë **gur mulliri *1** to be very heavy **2** to be very strong
- **gur mulliri** millstone
- **gur ndez**ë**s** flint
- **gur n**ë **rrokullim**ë in great peril, on the brink of disaster
- **gur i orollit** flint
- **gur i paçmuar** precious stone
- **gur pambuku** asbestos
- **guri i pendes**ë**s** *(Old)* [*Relig*] heavy rock that must be carried around the church as a penance
- **gur peshe** bottle-shaped metal weight in a computing scale
- **gur p**ë**shtyme** [*Med*] ptyalolith
- **gur prove** *(Book)* true test; touchstone
- **qajn**ë **edhe gur**ë**t** (said when a very kind person has suffered terrible misfortune) even the rocks shed tears
- **Guri q**ë **punon shtruar, b**ë**n miell t**ë **but**ë**.** "The millstone that works at a leisurely pace makes fine flour." *(Prov)* The best worker is one who works calmly but steadily.
- **gur qoku** stone marker
- **gur qum**ë**shti** galactite
- **gur sahati** ruby
- **gur smerili** grindstone
- **gur shahu 1** [*Chess*] pawn; chessman **2** *(Impol)* pawn, cat's-paw, stooge
- **gur shkrep**ë**s** flint
- **gur shurre** *(Colloq)* sandstone
- **gur tavile** dice
- **gur t**ë**mthi** [*Med*] gallstone
- **gur themeli** cornerstone, foundation stone
- **guri themeltar** *(Book)* cornerstone, foundation stone
- **gur thoi** agate
- **u b**ë**f**^opt **gur** *(Curse)* May {} die!
- **jan**ë **gur e uror** they mix like oil and water, they don't get along
- **gur vatre** each of the two stones across which wood is placed to burn in a fireplace; hearthstone
- **gur veshi** [*Med*] otolith
- **gur xixash** flintstone
- **gur i xhevahir**ë gemstone
- **gur i zgjebur** pumice stone; tufa
- **gur zjarri** flintstone, flint

gurabi'je *nf* cookie; shortcake

gur**ac**a'k

I § *adj* **1** rocky; craggy **2** at home among the mountain crags, sure-footed **3** brawny

II § *nm* year-round dweller in rocky mountains: mountain man, mountain animal

gur**a**ço'k

I § *nm* round pebble

II § *adv* = guraço'kthi

guraço'kthi *adv*

gura'jë *nf* rocky ground = **guri'shtë**

gurale'c *nm* pebble, small smooth rock; gravel

gurale'c'ash *adv* = **guraço'kthi**

gurame'l *adj* having a small hard pit/seed

gurape'c *adv* = **guraço'kthi**

gurape'sh I § *nm* OR **gurape'shë** II § *nf* folk contest to see who can throw a heavy stone the furthest

gura'she'nj'ash *adv*

*****gura'zi** *nm* [*Min*] basalt

*****gurbe't** = **kurbe't**

gurç *adj* = **gu'rës**

gurë'co'·het *vpr* 1 to get hard as rock: harden 2 to get as strong as a rock: become strong

gurë'c'o'·n *vt* 1 to make [] hard: harden 2 to make [] as strong as a rock: strengthen

gurë'he'dh'ës *nm* [*Hist*] stone catapult

gu'rës *adj* 1 rock-hard: hard-shelled, hard-fleshed; very strong 2 (*Fig Pej*) tightfisted, stingy

gurë'shpu'ese *nf* [*Invert*] date-shell, rock-eater (*Lithodomus (Lithophagus) lithophagus*)

gu'rëz *nf dimin* small pebble; small calcareous deposit at the root of the teeth

gurë'zi'm *nm ger* <**gurëzo'·n**, **gurëzo'·het**

gurë'zo'·het *vpr* 1 to get hard as rock: harden, solidify 2 to get as strong as a rock: become strong

gurë'zo'·n *vt* 1 to make [] hard: harden 2 to make [] as strong as a rock: strengthen

gurga'c I § *nm* OR **gurga'cë** II § *nf* flintstone, flint

gur'gdhe'nd'ës *nm* stone carver, stone cutter

gurgule' *nf* 1 tumult, hubbub, commotion 2 noisy mob of people, throng

gu'rgull *nm (np ˜j)* (*Colloq*) [*Anat*] windpipe, throat

gurgulle'shë *nf* [*Bot*] herbaceous plant with big leaves and tuberous roots, used as a folk treatment for sheep rot

gurgulli'm *nm ger* <**gurgullo'·n**

gurgulli'më *nf* gurgle; gurgling sound

gurgullo'·n

 I § *vi* 1 to gurgle 2 to bubble, boil

 II § *vt* [*Chem*] to introduce a gas into a liquid or molten mass: aerate

gurgullu'es *adj* gurgling, bubbling

gurgu'r *nm* [*Text*] = **masu'r**

gurgja'k *nm* [*Min*] hematite, bloodstone

Gu'ri *nm* Guri (male name)

*****guri'cë** *nf* = **guri'në**

guri'çkë *nf* small rock; pebble

guri'na *np* <**guri'në** pieces of rock, rocks

guri'në *nf* rocky ground/land, stony place

gu'riq *nm* = **guri'çkë**

guri'shtë *nf* land with many small stones, gravelly soil

guri'shto'r *adj* having many small stones: gravelly, stony

gu'rje *adj* (of fruits) hard-fleshed

gurka'lë

 I § *nm* [*Chem*] copper sulfate, blue vitriol

 II § *adj* blue-green

gu'rkë *nf* 1 = **guri'çkë** *****2 cart track, rut; rail track, rail

gur'ky'ç *nm* [*Arch*] keystone of an arch

gur'latu'e's *nm* stonecarver

gur'ma'c

 I § *nm*

 II § *adv* small and smooth round stone: pebble

gur'ma'c'thi *adv* = **guraço'kthi**

gurma'z *nm* 1 [*Anat*] esophagus, gullet; pharynx, throat 2 (*Colloq*) windpipe, larynx 3 = **gllë'nj'kë** 4 maw

gurmaz'tha'të *adj* 1 having nothing to eat or drink 2 (*Fig*) very poor

gur'mi'cë *nf* alabaster

gur'mpre'h'ës *nm* whetstone, grindstone = **gri'hë**

gur'na'jë *nf* = **guri'shtë**

gurne'c *nm* [*Ichth*] white roach (*Rutilus rubilio ohridanus Kar.*)

gurne'c'kë *nf* [*Ichth*] = **gurne'c**

guro'·het *vpr* 1 to turn to stone, become petrified 2 to become like a rock: become strong; harden

guro'·n *vt* 1 to turn [] to stone: petrify 2 to make [] like rock: strengthen; harden, solidify

guro'r *adj* 1 of stone/rock; stony, rocky 2 [*Med*] calculous

guro're *nf* 1 rock quarry, stone pit 2 scree

guro's· *vt* = **nguro's·**

guro's·et *vpr* = **nguro's·et**

guro'sje *nf ger* = **nguro'sje**

gur'punu'e's *nm* = **gur'latu'e's**

*****gur's** = **gurëz**

gur'skali't'ës *nm* = **gurgdhe'ndës**

gur'shkre'p'ës *nm* flintstone, flint

*****gur'ta'r** *nm* stonebreaker, quarryman

gu'rtë *adj (i)* 1 of stone 2 hard, solid 3 (*Fig*) strong 4 (*Fig*) stonelike, stony; stone cold, lifeless

*****gur'to'·n** *vt* = **nguro's·**

*****gur'ts'o'·n** *vt* = **guro'·n**

gur'th *nm* 1 (*Dimin*) <**gur** 2 [*Med*] calculus in a body organ: kidney stone, gallstone; dental calculus 3 fiber-plaiting tool consisting of two crossed strips of wood

gur'theme'l *nm* foundation stone

gur'thërrm'u'e's

 I § *adj* rock-crushing

 II § *nm* rock crusher (person or machine)

gu'r'thi *adv*

gur'thi'mu'r'thi *adv*

gur'thy'e's

 I § *adj* rock-breaking

 II § *nm* worker who breaks large rocks into small pieces: rock breaker

gur'thy'es'e *nf* [*Constr*] 1 <**gurthy'es** 2 rock-crushing machine, stone crusher: (*alligator*)

*****gur'ugu'c** *adj* 1 unsightly 2 ailing

*****gur'ugu'çkë** *nf* berry

gur'zja'rr *nm* flintstone, flint

gu'rrë

 I § *nf* 1 spring issuing out of rock: rock spring; source of a stream; fountainhead; stone drinking trough 2 (*Fig*) fountainhead, source 3 stream, spate

 II § *adv* in a stream, in floods, streaming out

gurrë'shte'rpë *nf* dried up spring

gu'rrëz *nf* small spring; trickling spring

*****gurri'ç** *nm* gravel

*****gurrne'c**

 I § *nm* miser

 II § *adj* miserly

gurrni nf whirlpool, eddy = **vorbull**

gurro·n vi to flow in abundance: stream out/down, pour out/down, gush out
 ◦ **gurro·n nga** {} to originate/come from []

*****gurros** = **guro·n**

gusto nf (good) taste

gush· vt (Child Pet) to hug around the neck

gush·et vp recip (Child Pet) to hug each other around the neck

gushacak adj = **gushëdalë**

gushafarfuri adj (Poet) having a throat like fine white porcelain

gushakadh adj 1 double-chinned 2 = **gushëdal**ë

*****gushakuq** = **gushëkuq**

gushal nm [Ornit] = **gushëkuq**

gushan nm (Pej) = **gushak**

gushana np fem old-fashioned baggy pants that are pegged at the legs

gushar
 I § nm [Ornit] = **gushëkuq**
 II § adj = **gushak**

gusharak adj = **gushak**

gusharake nf hen with prominent wattles

gushas adv by the neck/throat; intimately close together

gushë nf 1 neck area under the jaw: throat, underchin 2 (bird's) crop; neck feathers 3 pendulous part under or behind the jaw: dewlap, wattle 4 [Med] goiter 5 [Mil] magazine of a gun 6 lower collar portion of an ox yoke

gushëbardhë
 I § adj (Poet) white-necked, white-throated
 II § nm [Ornit] sparrow-like dun-colored bird with a white throat often seen in Albania in winter snow

gushëdalë adj 1 having a bulging or swollen throat 2 [Med] suffering from a goiter; strumous 3 (of fowl) crop-full, plump-necked

gushëfryrë adj plump-necked

gushëkuq
 I § adj ruby-throated, red-breasted
 II § nm [Ornit] 1 robin, redbreast (Erithacus rubecula L.) 2 (Old Scorn) red-scarfed policeman (in King Zog's regime)

gushëlëshuar adj double-chinned

*****gushëm** nf wisp of straw

gushëmadh adj 1 thick-necked; having a bulging throat 2 having a bottomless craw: gluttonous

gushëmermer adj (Poet) (of a girl or woman) "marble-throated", with a smooth white throat

gushëpëllumb adj "pigeon-throated" light violet in color

gushëspec adj ruby-throated

gushëshpuar adj (Insult) having a bottomless craw: gluttonous

*****gushëtericë** OR **gushëterikë** nf [Zool] lizard = **hardhje**

gushëvarur adj having hanging dewlaps

gushëverdhë adj yellow-breasted

gushëz nf (Dimin Pet) < **gushë**

gushi stem for 1st sg pres, pl pres, 2nd & 3rd sg subj, pind < **gushit·**

gushiq nm person with a goiter

gushis stem for 1st sg pres, pl pres, 2nd & 3rd sg subj, imperf < **gushit·**

gushit· vt to slit [] in the throat; eviscerate

gusho·n vt to shear the neck fleece of []

gushore nf 1 necklace 2 baby's bib = **grykashkë** 3 leather collar or strap around the neck of an animal 4 fatty part of the neck of a fowl

gushosh adj = **gushëdalë**

gushpëllumb = **gushëpëllumbi**

gushpor adj, n = **hamës**

gusht nm August
 ◦ **Gusht e gunë.** "August and warm clothes" Summer is about over, get ready for winter.

gushtak
 I § adj ripening in August: August-maturing
 II § nm [Ichth] common gray mullet (Mugilidae cephalus L.) = **cumër**

gushtakore nf field sown in August-ripening corn

gushtar adj = **gushtak**

gushtarak adj 1 = **gushtak** 2 hatching in August: August-hatching

gushtavkë nf [Ichth] = **koran**

gushter nm [Zool] lizard
 ◦ **gushteri i verdhë** [Zool] green lizard Lacerta viridis
 ◦ **gushteri i vogël** [Zool] wall lizard Lacerta muralis

*****gushtericë** nf 1 [Bot] mastic tree, lentisc (Pistacia lentiscus) 2 [Zool] wall lizard (Lacerta muralis)

gushtje adj = **gushtak**

gushtor adj = **gushtarak**

gushtore nf [Ichth] = **koran**

gushtovjeshtë nf time period from late August to early September: late summer

gutaperkë nf gutta-percha

gute nf [Med] gout

gutural nm [Ling] guttural/velar sound

*****guvernarë** nf (Old) government

*****guvernar** (Old) = **guvernator**

guvernator n state/colonial governor

guverno·n vt to govern

*****guvernor** = **guvernator**

*****guvertë** nf = **kuvertë**

guvë nf 1 hollow, grotto, cave 2 hollow in a tree = **zgarbë**

guvor nm [Ichth] weatherfish (Misgurnus fossilis)

guxim nm ger 1 < **guxo·n** 2 daring, boldness, courage; initiative; audacity
 ◦ **guxim prej të marri** foolhardiness

guximdhënës adj encouraging, inspiring; courage-building

guximadh adj very daring, venturesome

guximplotë adj (Poet) valiant, audacious

guximshëm adj (i) daring, brave, courageous

guximtar
 I § adj brave, daring, heroic
 II § n 1 brave person, hero 2 person who exhibits initiative: go-getter 3 (Old) [Law] culprit; thief, killer

guximtë adj (i) = **guximshëm**

guxis stem for 1st sg pres, pl pres, 2nd & 3rd sg subj, pind < **guxit·**

guxit· vt (Reg) to annoy, irritate

guxo·n vi to dare, show daring, exhibit initiative; act bravely

gu·xh|as *adv (Reg)* = **do·cash**

guxhuma·r *nm (Reg)* gullet; throat

guxhuvër|ë *nf (Reg)* secret hole, secret hiding place

gu·z|ël *nf [Ornit]* coot *(Fulica atra)*

***gu·z|ël** *nf [Mus]* gusla

***guzí·n|ë** = **guzhí·n|ë**

***guzhí·n|ë** *nf* kitchen = **kuzhí·n|ë**

guzhin|ie·r *n* cook = **kuzhinie·r**

gu·zhm|ë *nf* **1** plaited withe loop used to fasten a yoke to a plow or to a cart tongue; ring fastener, rowlock, oarlock **2** snowshoe made of plaited withes

guzhmo··het *vpr* to have one's affairs all tied up in knots, be all fouled up, have matters brought to a standstill

guzhmo··n *vt* **1** to attach/close [] with a ring fastener; attach [] to a ring **2** *(Fig)* to coerce, force

***gve** *nf [Bot]* black pine *(Pinus nigra)*

***gve·rr|ë** *nf* family dispute

***gvesh** *nm* support pole, prop

***gvo·sk|ë** *OR* **gvo·zhd|ë** = **lëvo·zhg|ë**

gyp *nm* **1** tube; duct, pipe, hose **2** small cylindrical container: pillbox **3** *[Anat Biol]* duct, tract, vas, tube

◦ **gypi i koshës** *(Old)* thighbone, femur

◦ **gypi i llambës** *(Colloq)* lightbulb

gyp|ëz|í·m *nm* pipe/conduit system, tubing

gyp|o·r *adj* tubular

gyp|th *nm* **1** small thin tube **2** *[Med]* ductule

***gyrbet|xhí** *nm (np ~ nj)* = **kurbetçí**

***gzilirí** *nf* delight

***gzhall** *adj* arid

***gzhep** = **g|ëthe·p**

***gzhî·** *vi (Reg Gheg Old)* to eject empty cartridges from a gun

gj [gjë] *nf* **1** the consonant digraph "gj" **2** the voiced palatal stop represented by the digraph "gj"

*****gja** *nf* = gjah

gja·n *vi* = ngja·n

gja *stem for pdef, opt, adm, part, imper* <gja·s·

*****gjâç** *pron (Reg Gheg Old)* what; anything

gjah *nm* **1** hunting: the hunt, the chase **2** object of the hunt: game animal or bird: game **3** *(Fig)* fugitive

◦ **Gjahu në breg e qëllon në kodër.** "The game is in the mountain and {} *shoots* at the hill." {} *is* wide of the mark. {} *is* off on a tangent.

◦ **gjah i trashë** big game

gjaheng *nm* women's coarse woolen overcoat with long sleeves

gjahtar *n* hunter; chaser

*****gjahtarkë** *nf (Reg Tosk)* huntress

gjahto·n

I § *vi* to go hunting

II § *vt* to hunt

gjahtor *n* **1** hunting dog, hound **2** = gjahtar

*****gjajë** OR **gjajkë** *nf* hunt, chase

*****gjajtas** *adv* likewise; analogously

*****gjajtë** *nf (Reg)* event = ngjarje

gjak

I § *nm* **1** blood **2** *(Fig)* relationship by blood: close kinship; close kin, relatives; common descent, peoplehood **3** [*Ethnog*] kin related by patrilineal descent **4** blood feud, blood vengeance **5** [*Veter*] = gjakëz

II § *adj* **1** covered with blood, bloody **2** blood-red, dark red

◦ <>**u avullua gjaku** <>'s blood boiled, <> became very angry

◦ **gjak i bardhë** [*Physiol*] lymph = limfë

◦ <>**u bëftë gjak e dhjamë** "may it become <>'s blood and fat" *(Felic)* may <> enjoy <> the food! bon appetit!

◦ <>**u bëftë gjaku ujë!** *(Curse)* May <>'s blood turn to water! Death to <>!

◦ **ësh·të gjak e gjini (me** []**)** to be related by blood (to []), be blood relatives (of [])

◦ **gjak i kuq** deep red

◦ **të merr gjak në vetull** "{} can find blood in your eyebrows" {} is very brave; {} is shrewd/astute

◦ **gjak në sy** speck in the eye

◦ **gjak qumështi** [*Bot*] = tamblagjak

◦ **gjaku shko·n³ˢᵍ për gisht** (according to the Canon of Mountains) a blood debt can be avenged only by a person with a (trigger) finger

gjaka'shpër *adj* having a harsh attitude toward other people

gjakatar

I § *adj* bloodthirsty, murderous, cruel

II § *n* bloodthirsty person

*****gjakbâmë** *nm (Reg Gheg)* = gjakbërës

gjakbërës

I § *adj* = gjakderdhës

II § *n* person who has killed someone; person who has taken blood vengeance

gjakbutë *adj* **1** having an even temperament: cool-headed, cool-blooded **2** easy to get along with, easy-going, amiable

gjakbutësi *nf* **1** cool-headedness, cool-bloodedness **2** amiability

gjakderdhës

I § *adj* causing much bloodshed; bloodthirsty

II § *n* spiller of blood, killer, murderer

gjakderdhje *nf* bloodshed, spilling of blood; bloodbath

gjakdhënës *n* blood donor

gjake *nf* blood sausage, blood/black pudding

gjakëmbël *adj* easy to get along with, easy-going, amiable

gjakës *nm* **1** person who takes blood vengeance **2** killer, culprit

gjakësi *nf* **1** blood vengeance **2** bloodshed, murder, killing **3** blood relationship, kinship by blood

gjakësim *nm ger* <gjakëso·n, gjakëso·het

gjakësisht *adv* murderously

gjakëso·het *vpr* **1** = gjakos·et **2** to become subject to blood vengeance

gjakëso·n *vt* **1** = gjakos· **2** to cause a blood feud

gjakësor

I § *adj* bloodthirsty, cruel

II § *n* **1** spiller of blood, killer **2** bloodthirsty/cruel person **3** foolhardy hero

gjakëto·het *vpr* to get wounded/bloodied/killed

gjakëto·n *vt* to inflict a bleeding wound on []: bloody

gjakëz *nf* [*Veter*] dietary intoxication in sheep/goats caused by eating certain grasses (treated by letting blood from the ear)

gjakfalur *nm, adj* (person) excused from being killed in a blood feud

gjakformues *adj* [*Med*] sanguifacient

gjakftohtë *adj* **1** having an even temperament: cool-headed, cool-blooded **2** cool, temperate, calm, quiet, sober **3** [*Zool*] cold-blooded

gjakftohtësi *nf* cool-headedness, equanimity, presence of mind, composure

gjakftohtësisht *adv* cool-headedly

gjakhidhur *adj* **1** unsociable, aloof, standoffish **2** hot-tempered, quick to anger

gjakhumbur *adj* = gjakhupës

gjakhupës *nm* **1** person whose killing cannot be avenged because the killer is unknown or because no one in the family is left to take revenge: unavenged person **2** *(Old)* person who was killed by a group as punishment for breaking the code of honor and is therefore not eligible for blood revenge

gjakhupët *adj (i)* unavenged

gjakidhët *adj (i)* hot-blooded, passionate; hot-tempered, hot-headed, irascible

gjakim *nm ger* **1** <gjako·n **2** burning desire: craving, greed, cupidity, lust

gjakkeq *adj* = gjakhidhur

gjak·le'pur adj chicken-hearted = **frikaca'k**

gjak·ma'rr·ës nm killer taking vengeance in a blood feud: avenger

gjak·ma'rr·je nf blood vengeance

*__gjak'marr·si__ nf bloodthirstiness

gjak·mbaj'të·s adj [Med] sanguiferous

gjak·ndal'ë·s adj [Med] stanching the flow of blood: hemostatic

*__gjak·nde'z·ë·s__ adj inflammatory; seditious; exasperating

gjak·nde'z·je nf = gjaknxeht**ë**sí

gjak·nde'z·ur adj = gjaknxe'htë

gjak·ngro·h'të np 1 [Zool] warm-blooded: homeothermic () 2 = gjaknxe'htë

gjak·nxe'htë adj hot-blooded, quick-tempered, irascible

gjak·nxeht'ë·si nf hot-bloodedness, hot temper

gjak·o'·n vt to crave, have a burning desire for []

gjak·o's· vt 1 to inflict bloody wounds on []; beat [] up badly 2 to get blood on [], make [] all bloody; bloody

gjak·o's·et vpr 1 to get wounded/bloodied/killed 2 to become bloodstained 3 to engage in bloody battle

gjak·o's·je nf < gjako's·, gjako's·et

gjak·o's·ur adj (i) 1 bloodied, bloody 2 bloodstained 3 suffering heavy casualties

gjak·osh·a'r adj [Bot] with a reddish pulp

gjak·osh·a're nf [Bot] blood orange (popularly believed to be the fruit of a pomegranate branch grafted onto an orange tree)

gjakova'r

I § adj of or pertaining to Gjakova

II § n native of Gjakova

Gjako've nf Albanian city in southwestern Yugoslavia: Gjakova, Dakovica

gjak·pa'stër adj purebred, thoroughbred

gjak·për'ly·er adj (Book) bloodstained; covered with blood

gjak·pi'r·ës

I § adj 1 bloodsucking; bloodthirsty 2 [Zool] feeding on blood: hematophagous ()

II § n bloodsucker

gjak·pri'sh·ur adj upset, perturbed, disquieted, disturbed

gja'k·ra np < gjak 1 bloodstains, drops of blood 2 (Colloq) menstruation: monthlies

gjak·rrje'dh·je nf bleeding; hemorrhage

gjak·sje'll·ës adj [Med] sanguiferous

gja'k·shëm adj (i) = përgja'kshëm

gjak·shu'a·r adj 1 completely wiped out as a family 2 (Curse) be damned! (by having one's whole family disappear from the face of the earth)

gjak·traz'i'm nm 1 emotional agitation 2 incest

gjak·traz'ue's adj 1 emotionally agitating 2 incestuous

gjak·tha'r·të adj surly, cantankerous; unsociable, disagreeable

gjali'c·ë nf [Ornit] jackdaw (Corvus monedula)

gjalm·ato're nf moccasin with upper of woven thongs

gja'lm·ë nm 1 leather/wool thong; strong cord 2 yarn
  ○ **gjalma nëpër këmbë** troubling obstacles or problems; hampering difficulties

gjalm·ë·ze'z·ë nf 1 woman of Labëria (who ties her moccasins in back with a black thong) 2 (Fig) brave woman who fights side by side with men

gjalm·o'·n vt to weave [] with thongs

gjalp·ani'k nm [Food] 1 kind of two-layered pasty made by folding in butter and rolling out the dough several times 2 pastry made of cornflour and butter

gja'lp·ë nf [Dairy] butter
  ○ **gjalpë brumë** soft butter
  ○ **gjalpi i kakaos** cocoa butter
  ○ **gjalpë i kalbur** well-salted butter
  ○ **gjalpë në lëkurën e qenit** "butter on the skin of a dog" a waste of a good thing/characteristic
  ○ **si (thika) në gjalpë** smoothly, with no trouble
  ○ **gjalpë e vaj me** [] on good terms with [], in good favor with []

gjalpë·to're

I § nf [Bot] buttercup (Ranunculus acris)

II § adj [Dairy] rich in butterfat

gjall·e'se nf 1 life 2 living being: living creature

gja'll·ë

I § adj (i) 1 alive, live, living 2 (Fig) lively, vivacious 3 in a natural state: raw, uncooked, unrefined, untreated 4 real; actual, pure

II § nm (i) living being, living creature, living one; the living

III § nn (të) the period of time during which one is alive: life

IV § adv alive

V § prep (nom) (Fig) just like, exactly like
  ○ **gjallë a vdekur** at all costs, whatever the cost
  ○ **gjallë i ati** just like his/her/their father
  ○ **s'bë·het i gjallë** 1 to remain silent, not move 2 to get lost, never be heard of again
  ○ **gjallë me krye nuk** [] **dorëzo·n** not give [] up as long as {} is still alive
  ○ **gjallë me krye nuk** [] **jep·** not give [] up as long as {} is still alive
  ○ **gjallë e në zall** in terrible poverty, in dire need
  ○ **gjallë e ngushtë/keq** in terrible poverty, in dire need
  ○ **ësh·të gjallë e ngushtë** to be in difficult circumstances: be in a tight spot
  ○ **gjallë e për gazep** in very bad and tough circumstances
  ○ **re e gjallë** very capable person

gjall·ë'ri nf 1 liveliness, vivacity; vitality; vividness 2 being alive: life; time during which one is alive: life

gjall·ë'ri'm nm ger 1 < gjallëro'·n, gjallëro'·het 2 (Reg) life, being, existence 3 [Med] vivification

gjall·ë'ri'sht adv 1 in lively/animated fashion: vivaciously, vigorously 2 just as in real life

gjall·ë'ro'·het vpr to become lively, come to life

gjall·ë'ro'·n

I § vt 1 to bring [] back to life, revive 2 to animate, enliven; energize, arouse

II § vi to live, be alive

gjall·ë'rue's adj invigorating, enlivening, bracing

gjall·ë's = gjallër

gjall·ë'si nf 1 = gjallëri 2 (Collec) living things

gjalli adv (së) while alive; for life
  ○ **(për) së gjalli** while alive

gjall·i'm nm ger 1 < gjallo'·n 2 (Old) life, living

*__gjall·i's__ stem for 1st sg pres, pl pres, 2nd & 3rd sg subj, pind < gjallí·t·

*gjallît· *vt* = **ngjall·**

gja'lije *nf* **1** being alive; time during which one is alive **2** *(Old)* life, living

*gjall'ni'm *nm (Reg Gheg)* life

*gjall'no·n *vi (Reg Gheg)* = **gjallëro·n**

*gjall'no'r *adj* vital; vigorous, lively; brisk

gjall'o·n *vi* **1** to stay alive, be alive **2** (of plants or animals) to flourish, grow

gja'll'shëm *adj (i)* **1** full of vitality, vivacious; full of life, very much alive **2** lively and industrious: hustling and bustling **3** plump; fatty

*gjallu'stër *nf* skylight; window, peephole; shutter, flap

gjam *nm* rocky and treeless patch of land at water's edge: rocky coast/shore/bank

gjam'ato're *nf [Ethnog]* = **vajto're**

*gjam'ëni *nf* large number, whole bunch

*gjam'o·n *vt* to wail in lamentation for the dead: keen

*gjân'as *adv (Reg Gheg)* = **gje'razi**

*gjând'ër OR **gjând'ërr** *nf (Reg Gheg)* = **gjë'ndër**

*gjândr'ëz *nf dimin (Reg Gheg)* glandule

gja'në *nf* mud deposit left by water flow: silt; alluvial land, alluvium

gja'në *nf* alluvial deposit, wash; alluvial land

*gjânë *adj (i) (Reg Gheg)* = **gje're**

gja'n'ës <**gja'nëz** *nf [Ichth]* braize, Couch's sea bream *(Pagrus vulgaris, Pagrus pagrus)*

*gjan'ësi *nf (Reg Gheg)* = **gjer'ësi**

gjani *nf [Phys]* amplitude

*gjân'i *adv (së) (Reg Gheg)* = **gje'ri**

gjan'ishte *nf* land covered with alluvial deposits: silty soil

*gjan'isht *(Reg Gheg) adv* = **gjer'ësi'sht**

*gjan'o·n *(Reg Gheg) vt* = **zgjero·n**

*gjân *(Reg Gheg)* = **gje're**

*gjan'osh *(Reg Gheg) adj* = **gjeru'sh**

*gjân'si'në *nf (Reg Gheg)* (broad) expanse of land, tract

*gjân'si'sht *adv (Reg Gheg)* = **gjer'ësi'sht**

gja'nzë *nf [Ichth]* (Megalobrana amblycephala)

*gjâ *(Reg Gheg)* = **gjë**

*gjapi *nf* = **zhapi**

gja'qe *np* <**gjak** blood feuds, blood vengeances

*gjarda'n *nm* = **gjerda'n**

gja're

I§ *part* <**gja·**n, **gja's·**

II§ *nn (të)*

gja'rkëz *np [Anat]* membrane surrounding the intestines, peritoneum: gut sac

gja'rpër *nm* **1** snake **2** *(Fig Scorn Insult)* treacherous person: snake-in-the-grass **3** *(Fig)* clever and lively person

○ **gjarpër i bokës** *[Zool]* sand viper, nose-horned viper *Vipera ammodytes*

○ **gjarpër i bukur** *[Zool]* leopard snake *Elaphe situla*

○ **gjarpër deti** **1** *[Ichth]* marbled moray *Muraena helena* **2** conger eel *Conger conger*

○ **gjarpër gjuetar** *[Zool]* Montpellier snake *Malpolon monspessulanus*

○ **gjarpër laraman** *[Zool]* smooth snake *Coronella austriaca*

○ **gjarpër larisk** *[Zool]* sand viper, nose-horned viper *Vipera ammodytes*

○ **gjarpër leopard** *[Zool]* leopard snake *Elaphe situla*

○ **gjarpër lumi** *[Zool]* dice snake *Natrix tessellata*

○ **gjarpër me brirë** *[Zool]* sand viper, nose-horned viper *Vipera ammodytes*

○ **gjarpër me çapare** *[Zool]* chicken-snake, four-lined rat snake *Elaphe quatuorlineata*

○ **gjarpër me çikë** *[Zool]* horned viper *Cerastes cerastes*

○ **gjarpër me dy koka** very dangerous enemy

○ **gjarpër me gjyzlykë/syze** *[Zool]* Indian cobra, spectacled cobra *Naja naja*

○ **gjarpër me hajmali** *[Zool]* sand viper, nose-horned viper *Vipera ammodytes*

○ **gjarpër me hundë** *[Zool]* = **nepërkë**

○ **gjarpër me lara** *[Zool]* cat snake *Teleskopus fallax*

○ **gjarpër me nuska** *[Zool]* sand viper, nose-horned viper *Vipera ammodytes*

○ **gjarpër me zile** *[Zool]* rattlesnake *(Crotalus)*

○ **gjarpri me zile** "snake with a bell" *[Zool]* rattlesnake

○ **gjarpër minjsh** *[Zool]* Aesculapian snake *(Elaphe longissima)*

○ **gjarpër qorr** *[Zool]* blindworm, slowworm = **boll'ëverbët**

○ **gjarpër shigjetë** *[Zool]* Montpellier snake *(Malpolon monspessulanus)*

○ **gjarpër shtëpie** *[Zool]* Aesculapian snake *(Elaphe longissima)*

○ **Gjarprit shtypi kokën!** "Stamp on the snake's head!" *(Prov)* Evil must be stamped out!

○ **gjarpër shullani** *[Zool]* sand viper, nose-horned viper *(Vipera ammodytes)*

○ **gjarpër uji** *[Zool]* = **gjarpëru'jës**

○ **gjarpër i vogël** *[Zool]* wall lizard *Lacerta muralis*

○ **gjarpër i zi** *[Zool]* smooth snake *Coronella austriaca*

gjarpër'i'm *nm ger* **1** <**gjarpëro·n** **2** sinuous curve, sinuous movement

gjarpër'i'nj *np* <**gjarpër**

gjarpër'o·n *vi* **1** to take a sinuous course: snake around, wind around; twist, meander; make a sinuous movement **2** *(Fig)* to avoid <> slyly

gjarpër'o'r *adj* = **gjarpëru'es**

gjarpër'u'es *adj* winding, twisting

gjarpër'u'e'se *nf [Tech]* (refrigeration/heating) coil

gjarpëru'jës *nm [Zool]* grass snake, water snake *(Natrix natrix)*

gjarpër'u'sh

I§ *nm* **1** small snake **2** *[Tech]* (refrigeration/heating) coil

II§ *adj (Poet)* sinuous

gjarpër'u'she *nf* **1** female snake **2** *(Fig Pej)* malicious and trouble-making woman: viper **3** *(Old Poet)* long-barreled pistol in use up to the nineteenth century

gjarpër'zi *nm (np ⁓ nj)* **1** *[Zool]* = **gjarpëru'jës** **2** clever and wily person

gja'rpë'zi *adv* sinuously

gjarp'i'nj *np* <**gjarpër**

gjarp'u'jc *nm [Zool]* = **gjarpëru'jës**

gjarp'u'js *nm [Zool]* = **gjarpëru'jës**

gja's· *vi* = **ngja·**n

*gjas = **ngjas**

*gja'sênd OR **gjë'se'nt** *(Reg Gheg)* = **gjëse'nd**

gja·së
I § nf 1 likelihood; probability, chance 2 symptom, sign
II § nf (Old) *anchorage; landing platform
  ◦ gjasët janë të mira the chances are good
  ◦ gjasët i ka· për jo chances are that {} won't
  ◦ gjasët i ka· për po chances are that {} will

gjasë'll nm [Bot] navelwort (Cotyledon umbilicus)

gja·s|ëm adj (i) [Math] probable

***gjas|ëra·me** np (Old) wailings, sounds

gja·s|ës|isht adv probably

gjas|i' nf = ngjashm|ëri

gjas|im nm = ngjasim

gjas|o··n vi = ngjaso··n

gja·s|shëm adj (i) (Book) possible but not certain: likely, probable

***gjas|uer** adj (fem ~ ore) (Old) concrete, real

gjasho're nf [Bot] common vine (Vitis vinifera)

gjashta're nf (Old) 1 six-shooter, revolver 2 old Turkish coin worth 6 grosh

gja·shtë
I § num six; number six
II § adj (i), n (i) sixth
III § nf the number six; the grade six (where ten is the highest possible grade)
IV § nf (e) 1 (fraction) a sixth 2 sixth grade (in elementary school); sixth grade class/classroom
V § np (të) a group of six, six at one time; all six

***gjashtë|çi'p** nm hexagon = gjashtëkëndësh

***gjashtë|çi'p|ët** adj (i) hexagonal = gjashtëkëndor

gjashtë|dhjetë
I § num sixty
II § adj (i), n (i) sixtieth

gjashtë|dhjetë|vjeça'r
I § adj 1 lasting for sixty years 2 sixty years old; sexagenary
II § n sexagenarian

gjashtë|dhjetë|vjeto'r nm sixtieth anniversary

gjashtë|fa'q|ësh
I § adj having six surfaces: hexahedral
II § n hexahedron

gjashtë|fi'sh
I § nm a quantity six times as great as another: sextuple, sixfold amount
II § adv sixfold, six times greater

gjashtë|fish|o··het vpr to increase sixfold

gjashtë|fish|o··n vt to increase [ ] sixfold

gjashtë|gar|ësh nm [Sport] contest consisting of six events

***gjashtë|gi'shte** nf [Bot] common columbine (Aquilegia vulgaris)

gjashtë|kë'mb|ësh
I § nm 1 [Entom] six-legged bug: insect 2 [Lit] pentameter
II § nm hexameter

gjashtë|kë'nd|ësh
I § nm [Geom] hexagon
II § adj hexagonal

gjashtë|kënd|o'r adj [Geom] hexagonal

gjashtë|mbë|dhjetë
I § num sixteen; number sixteen
II § nf the number sixteen
III § adj (i), n (i) sixteenth

gjashtë|mbë|dhjetë|me'tër|sh nm [Sport] penalty area (line) in soccer

gjashtë|mbë|dhjetë|rro'k|ësh
I § adj [Lit] composed of sixteen syllables
II § nm [Lit] sixteen-syllable line of verse

gjashtë|mu'aj|sh adj having completed six months: six-month, six-month old, semi-annual

gjashtë|muj|o'r
I § nm six-month period: half a year
II § adj of six-month duration, lasting six months; six-month

gjashtë|qi'nd
I § num six hundred; number six hundred
II § nf the number six hundred

gjashtë|qi'nd|të adj (i) six-hundredth

gjashtë|rro'k|ësh
I § adj composed of six syllables: hexasyllabic
II § nm [Lit] hexasyllabic line

gja·shtë'sh
I § adj (Colloq) in six parts; measuring six units in value
II § adv in six parts/units

gja·shtë'she nf 1 group of six 2 (Old) = gjashta're

gjashtë|va'rg|ësh
I § adj [Lit] composed of six lines
II § nm stanza composed of six lines: sestet

gjashtë|vjeça'r
I § adj six years old; six years long: lasting six years
II § nm six-year period
III § n six-year old child

gjashto're = gjashta're

gjasht|o'r|ësh
I § adj lasting for six hours
II § nm six-hour period; six-hour workday
III § n person assigned a six-hour workday

gjat|ahu'l adj (Impol) tall and thin: skinny

gjat|ama'n
I § adj (Colloq) conspicuously tall/long: lanky; lengthy, oblong
II § n (Colloq) lanky person

gjat|ani'k adj = gjatama'n

***gjat|a'r** = gjahtar

gjat|aru'sh adj (Pet) tall and thin: slim, lanky, slender

gja·tas adv lengthwise, in length

gja·tazi adv 1 = gja·tas 2 at great length

gja·të
I § adj (i) 1 long 2 tall
II § adv 1 the long way around 2 for a long time 3 at great length
III § prep (abl) 1 along 2 extending for the length of: during, throughout
  ◦ nuk e di· më gjatë not know anything more about it
  ◦ gjatë e gjerë 1 far and wide 2 in full detail
  ◦ nuk do të <> marrë gjatë {it} won't take <> long
  ◦ më gjatë 1 longer 2 any longer, anymore
  ◦ nuk e shpie· më gjatë 1 (of a sick/elderly person) not have long to live 2 not go on; go no further

gjat|ë'si nf 1 length 2 height 3 [Geog] longitude

***gjatë|si'në** (Reg Gheg) = gjat|ësi

gjatë|so'r adj 1 in length; in height 2 in a lengthwise direction/dimension: lengthwise, longitudinal

gja·ti adv (së) 1 along the long side: lengthwise 2 in length

gja·t|im nm ger < gjato··n, gjato'·het

gja·tje adj (of fruit) oblong, elongated

gjatoⁱ·*het vpr* = **zgjat**·*et*

gjato·*n*
   I § *vt* to make [] longer: lengthen; extend
   II § *vi* **1** to get longer: lengthen *2 = **gjahto**·*n*

gjatojë *nf (Colloq)* very tall person: beanpole

gjatok *adj (Colloq)* **1** pretty tall, lanky *2 *(Old)* oblong

gjator
   I § *adj* **1** (of plums) oblong, elongated **2** rather long: longish **3** in a lengthwise direction/dimension: lengthwise
   II § *nm* * = **gjahta**r

gjatosh
   I § *adj* **1** *(Pet)* slim **2** (of fruit) oblong, elongated
   II § *nm* middle (long) finger

gjatovinë *adj (Reg)* tall, of high stature

*gjatu**e**sh**ë**m *adj (i)* extending, extensible

gjatush *adj* = **gjato**sh

*gjä**za**gja**zë *nf (Reg Gheg)* = **gjëegjë**zë

gjazë *nf* thicket in a meadow/plain

*gjë(n) *nm (Reg Gheg)* stall for livestock

gje·*n vt* **1** to find **2** to find [] (in a particular condition); deem, judge, consider **3** to encounter, come upon [], run into [] **4** to discover; find out []; manage to find [] **5** *(Iron)* (used in past definite tense to express irony or displeasure about an action) certainly managed to find
   ∘ <> **gje**·*n* **ajthin** to find the very essence of <>
   ∘ <>a **gje**·*n* **anën** to find a way to get a handle on <>; find a way to manage/convince <>
   ∘ **s'e gje**·*n* **asnjë morr dëm** *(Crude)* to suffer not the slightest damage: not lose a damn thing
   ∘ **gje**·*n* **belanë (me** []) to get into a lot of trouble (with [])
   ∘ <>**i gje**·*n* **burgjitë** "find the screws for <>" **1** to find a way to get a handle on <> **2** to find a way to reach an understanding with <>
   ∘ <>**i gje**·*n* **burmat** "find the screws for <>" **1** to find a way to get a handle on <> **2** to find a way to reach an understanding with <>
   ∘ <> **gje**·*n* **çelën** to find the appropriate opportunity for <>
   ∘ [] **gje**·*n*³ˢᵍ **e mira vetë** "luck *finds* []" [] *is a* very lucky person, [] *is* lucky in everything
   ∘ **gje**·*n* **fjalën me** [] to come to an agreement with [], find a common language with []
   ∘ **gje**·*n* **fole 1** to settle down **2** to appear, take shape
   ∘ <> **gje**·*n* **fundin** to study/investigate <> in depth
   ∘ **gje**·*n* **fushë të lirë** to encounter no impediments, have one's way clear
   ∘ **e gje**·*n* **gojën** "find one's mouth" to choose the food one likes
   ∘ **gje**·*n* **gropën e gurit** to fall into sudden riches, suddenly recover one's economic health
   ∘ **E gje**·*n*³ˢᵍ **guri vendin.** "The rock *finds* its place." A person (eventually) *finds* a job.
   ∘ **e gje**·*n*³ˢᵍ **guri vendin** "the building stone finds its place" everything eventually *finds* its right place
   ∘ **gje**·*n* **gjuhën e përbashkët** to come to a meeting of the minds, find common ground
   ∘ <>a **gje**·*n* **havalenë** to find <>'s weak spot
   ∘ **gje**·*n* **hazinenë** to come into wealth
   ∘ **gje**·*n* **jetë** to come to life, come into force
   ∘ **nuk** <>**i gje**·*n* **(dot/kurrë) këmbët** to have no idea what is going on in <>'s mind; have no idea how to solve <>; not be able to find a trace of <>

   ∘ **gje**·*n* **kishë ku të fal**·*et* "find a church to pray in" *(Iron)* to look for help in the wrong place
   ∘ **e gje**·*n* **kokën e kandilit** [*CrudeImpolite*] to (ask for trouble and) get what one deserves, it *serves* {} right
   ∘ **e gje**·*n* **lëmë të shirë** to find everything ready without having had to do anything oneself
   ∘ **e gje**·*n* **lëmin shtruar** to find everything all ready/prepared
   ∘ **e gje**·*n* **lugën në pilaf** "find the spoon in the rice" to find everything already prepared (so there *is* nothing left for {} to do but enjoy it)
   ∘ [] **gje**·*n* **llome** to find [] already prepared
   ∘ **s'i gje**·*n* **majë vetes** "not find one's own hilltop" not know how to get out of a predicament
   ∘ [] **gje**·*n* **me presh në dorë** to catch [] red-handed
   ∘ [] **gje**·*n* **me hamendje** to arrive at [] by guesswork, guess []
   ∘ [] **gje**·*n* **ndër lakra** to catch [] red-handed
   ∘ **nuk** [] **gje**·*n* **në rrugë** {} won't find [] growing from trees, {} must work to get []
   ∘ **Gjej njëherë bari, pastaj shko e bli dhi!** "Once you find a goatherd, then go and buy goats." *(Prov)* Prepare what you need before you commit yourself to action!
   ∘ **e gje**·*n* **për kollaj** to take the easiest way
   ∘ **gje**·*n* **qimen në *vezë/të bardhën e vezës*** "find the hair in (the white of) an egg" to try to find fault, pick at details
   ∘ <>a **gje**·*n* **rrëfanën 1** to find the way to solve/resolve <> **2** to find the way to get to <*someone*>
   ∘ **e gje**·*n*³ʳᵈ **rrugën për** [] to begin to enter [], start to appear in []
   ∘ **e gje**·*n* **sofrën shtruar** to find everything already prepared, not have to put out any effort oneself
   ∘ **gje**·*n* **shesh e bë**·*n* **përshesh** "find a flat place and make pudding" to make a mess by taking advantage of the circumstances
   ∘ **gje**·*n* **shesh të lirë** to encounter no impediments, have one's way clear
   ∘ **gje**·*n* **talën** to find the solution, solve the problem
   ∘ <>**i gje**·*n* **telat** *(Colloq)* to know how to please <> so that <> will do what one wants: find the right button to press with <>, know how to please <>
   ∘ [] **gje**·*n* **të udhës** to deem [] to be quite proper, consider [] to be all right
   ∘ **e gje**·*n*³ʳᵈ **udhën për** [] to begin to enter [], start to appear in []
   ∘ **gje**·*n* **ustanë** to meet one's master, lose to a better opponent
   ∘ <>a **gje**·*n* **vaun** to find the way to get one's revenge on <>
   ∘ **gje**·*n* **vdekjen** to meet one's death
   ∘ <>a **gje**·*n* **veglën** "find the tool for <>" to find a way to handle <>
   ∘ **s'i gje**·*n* **vend dot vetes** "not find any place for oneself" to be so upset than one doesn't know what to do
   ∘ **gje**·*n* **vend** to take root, find a home
   ∘ **nuk gje**·*n* **vend** to be restless
   ∘ **gje**·*n* **vendin** *(Impol)* to get one's comeuppance, get what's coming to one
   ∘ **gje**·*n* **verigë (për** []) to find an excuse to get involved (with [])
   ∘ <>a **gje**·*n* **verigën 1** to find a way to get a handle on <> **2** to find a way to reach an understanding with <>

○ **gje·**n **vezët e thëllëzës 1** to manage to do something almost impossible **2** *(Iron)* to realize that one's unrealistic pursuit of easy treasure has led one into a tight spot

○ **<>/gje·**n **vidhat** "find the screws for<>" **1** to find a way to get a handle on <> **2** to find a way to reach an understanding with <>

○ **<>a gje·**n **vjegën** to find a way to get a handle on <>

○ **gje·**n **xhami ku të fal·**et "find a mosque to pray in" *(Iron)* to look for help in the wrong place

gjedh *nm* cattle

*****gjedh·** *vt* to yoke [] together, join

gjedhe *nf* model, example; exemplar, sample

gjedh|e'shtër *nf (Old)* interest (on money borrowed from a person)

gjedh|ër *adj (i)* coming from or composed of cattle: of cows, cow, beef

gjedh|i'm *nm* [*Spec*] adjustment or graduation of a measuring device by comparison to a precise standard: calibration

*****gjefshe'k** *adj (i)* infirm

*****gje'fshk|ët** *adj (i)* feeble, ailing

gje'gun *nm* [*Bot*] gum succory (*Chondrilla juncea*)

gjegj·

  I § *vi* to answer = **përgjí'gj·**et

  II § *vt* to listen, consent, heed, listen, obey

gje'gj·et *vpr* **1** to answer = **përgjí'gj·**et **2** to listen, consent, pay heed, obey **3** to be heard

gje'gje *nf* '**1** answer = **përgjí'gj**e **2** listening, consent, paying heed, obedience

gje'gj|ës

  I § *adj* responsible

  II § *n* authorized person; person responsible

gjegj|si'sht *adv* respectively

gje'gj|shëm *adj (i)* **1** obedient, receptive **2** responsible, guilty

gjekët|i·n *vi* to rumble, resound

gjekët|i'më *nf ger* **1** <**gjekëti·**n **2** rumble

*****gje'ku** *adv* = **çoku'**

gjel *nm* **1** [*Ornit*] rooster, cock **2** *(Pej)* pompous or pretentious person: cock-of-the-walk; person looking for an argument: feisty person **3** object or device with a rooster-like shape **4** *(Old)* flintlock firing mechanism **5** popcorn **6** piece of a divided nut kernel; piece of diced fruit **7** [*Ichth*] piper *Trigla lyra* **8** old gold coin

○ **gjel dallëndyshe** [*Ichth*] streaked gurnard *Trigloporus lastoviza*

○ **gjel deti** "sea rooster" [*Ornit*] turkey cock, tom turkey; turkey (*Meleagris gallopava domesticus*)

○ **gjel dushku** [*Ornit*] pheasant (*Phasianus colchicus*)

○ **gjel i egër** "wild rooster" [*Ornit*] capercaillie (*Tetrao urogallus L.*)

○ **gjel gri** [*Ichth*] gray gurnard *Eutrigla gurnardus*

○ **gjel kandil** [*Ichth*] = **gjel-kandi'l**

○ **gjel i kuq** [*Ichth*] red gurnard *Aspitrigla cuculus*

○ **gjel me gropë** [*Ichth*] large-scaled gurnard *Lepidotrigla cavillone*

○ **gjeli i oxhakut** weather vane

○ **gjel pulastreni** young cock

○ **gjel pylli** "forest rooster" [*Ornit*] black cock, black grouse (*Lyrurus tetrix*)

○ **gjel i sheqertë** rooster-shaped candy on the end of a stick: rooster-shaped sucker

○ **gjel ujës** [*Ornit*] = **gjelu'jës**

○ **gjel i vërtetë** [*Ichth*] cardinalfish *Apogon imberbis*

gjela'c *nm* [*Ornit*] **1** water rail (*Rallus aquaticus*) **2** *(Reg)* = **qukapí'k**

○ **gjelaci symadh** [*Ornit*] stone curlew *Burhinus oedicnemus L.*

○ **gjelaci i vogël** [*Ornit*] little stint *Calidris minuta Leisl.*

gjela'ft·et *vp recip (Reg)* = **gjelafy't·**et

gjela'fyt·et *vp recip* to struggle fiercely against one another: fight like roosters

gjela'ma'n *nm* [*Entom*] common European swallowtail butterfly (*Papilio machaon, Iphichides podalirius, Papilio podalirius L.*)

gjela's *adv (Colloq)* **1** (falling) sideways and backwards **2** *(Fig)* constantly brawling, always arguing, on bad terms

gjela'strak *nm* = **gjelastre'n**

gjela'stre'n *nm* young rooster that has not yet begun to crow

gjela'sh *adv*

gjelati'në *nf* gelatine

*****gjelatino·**n *vt* to gelatinize = **xhelatino'·**n

*****gjelatino'r** *adj* gelatinous = **xhelatino'r**

gjela'ze'z *nm* [*Ornit*] cormorant (*Phalacrocorax carbo*)

gjel'azi *adv (Colloq)* = **gje'las**

*****gjelba'b**ë *nf* firefly

gjelbër

  I § *adj (i)* **1** green **2** [*Agr*] (activity) performed when leaves have sprouted

  II § *nf (e)* (the color) green

○ **gjelbër e mbyllur/errët** dark green

gjelbër|ak *adj* = **gjelbëre'm**ë

gjelbër|e'më *adj (i)* greenish in color

gjelbër|i' *nf* = **gjelbërsi'**

gjelbër|i'm *nm ger* **1** <**gjelbëro'·**n, **gjelbëro'·**het **2** greenery, verdure **3** verdancy

gjelbër|i'me *np* <**gjelbëri'm** verdant areas

gjelbër|i'me *nf* **1** green vegetable **2** green leafy plant used as fodder

gjelbër|i'sht *adv* verdantly

gjelbëro'·het *vpr* **1** to become/turn green with new leaves: grow verdant **2** to have a green appearance

gjelbëro'·n

  I § *vi* = **gjelbëro'·**het

  II § *vt* **1** to make [] appear green **2** to plant trees or other greenery

gjelbër|o'r *adj* = **gjelbëre'm**ë

gjelbër|o'sh *adj (Poet)* = **gjelbër**

gjelbër|si' *nf* the quality or condition of being green: greenness

gjelbër|t *adj (i)* = **gjelbër**

gjelbër|u'ar *adj (i)* made green with plant life: verdant

gjelbër|u'e's *adj* bestowing a green appearance

gjelbër|u'sh *adj (Poet)* verdant

gjelbër|u'she *nf* **1** [*Ornit*] cirl bunting (*Emberiza cirlus*) **2** [*Bot*] finger grass (*Chloris chloris L.GJ*)

*****gjelb|so'·**n *vt* to taste [food] for salt

gjelda'sh *nm* popcorn

gjelde't *nm* [*Ornit*] = **gjel deti**

○ **gjeldeti i Adriatikut** [*Ichth*] streaked gurnard *Trigloporus lastoviza*

○ **gjeldeti i vërtetë** [*Ichth*] cardinal fish *Apogon imberbis*

gjel|det|ës *nm* [*Ornit*] tom turkey = **gjel deti**

gjel|e *nf* [*Ornit*] = **gjelëz**

gjel|egër *nm* [*Ornit*] = **gjel i egër**

*__gjelek__ *nm* yearling sheep

gjelëz *nf* [*Ornit*] wild pigeon-sized water fowl with a long yellow beak and black plumage with wings tipped in white

○ **gjelëza gushëkuqe** [*Ornit*] curlew sandpiper *Calidris ferruginea*

○ **gjelëza gushëzezë** [*Ornit*] dunlin *Calidris alpina Fall.*

○ **gjelëza e madhe** [*Ornit*] knot *Calidris canutus L., Tringa canutus L.*

○ **gjelëza pikaloshe** [*Ornit*] red-backed sandpiper, dunlin *Squatarola squatarola L.*

gjel|i|në *nf* (*Reg*) new bride; bride

gjel-kandil *nm* [*Ichth*] yellow gurnard (*Trigla lucerna*)

gjel|koko|sh *nm* (*Colloq*) **1** (as a character in folk literature) rooster, cock **2** (*Pej*) pompous or pretentious person: show-off

gjel|mitër

I § *nf* comb used to disentangle the strands of washed wool

II § *np* < **gjalm**

gjel|ore

I § *np* [*Ornit*] galliform

II § *np* Galliformes

gjel|uc *nm* **1** bantam rooster **2** (*Pej*) small, skinny rooster **3** (*Fig Pej*) terrible braggart who is weak and incompetent

○ **gjeluc deti/furke** [*Ichth*] armed gurnard *Peristedion cataphractum*

gjel|uj|ës *nm* [*Ornit*] water rail (*Rallus aquaticus*)

*__gjel|u|sh__ *nm* = **gjelujës**

gjelza|uj|ore *np* [*Ornit*] Charadriiformes

gjell|ë *nf* **1** prepared food, dish **2** meal

○ **gjellë kazani** (*Impol*) lousy food

○ **gjellë llurbë** bad food: slop

○ **Gjella me kripë e kripa me karar.** "Food with salt and salt in moderation." (*Prov*) Moderation in all things: Not too little and not too much.

○ **gjellë pa kripë 1** tasteless/bland food **2** dull person/thing/event

○ **gjellë qeni** badly prepared food, food fit only for dogs

○ **gjellë e rremë** (*CollogImpolite*) food without any meat in it

gjell|ëbër|ës *n* cook, chef

gjell|ëtar *n* = **gjellëbërës**

gjell|ëtar|i *nf* culinary arts, the art of food preparation and cooking, cooking, cookery

gjell|ëtore *nf* small eatery with food served at a counter: fast food diner, food bar, meal counter

gjell|ëz *nf* table salt

gjem *nm* bridle

gjemb *nm* **1** thorn; barb; sharp spine; prickle; bristle; splinter **2** bramble, bramblebush **3** (*Fig*) person who sticks to you and is a nuisance: pest **4** (*Reg*) table fork = **pirun 5** (*Reg*) pitchfork = **sfurk**

○ **gjemb i bardhë** [*Bot*] field eryngo *Eryngium campestre*

○ **gjemb gomari** [*Bot*] thistle

○ **gjemb lugati** [*Bot*] spiny clotbur, spiny cocklebur (*Xanthium spinosum*)

○ **gjemb në sy** speck in the eye

○ **gjemb peshku** [*Bot*] fishbone

○ **gjemb sybardhë** teasel

○ **gjemb ujku** [*Bot*] holly *Ilex acquifolium* = **ashe**

gjemb|a|ckë *nf* (*Reg*) [*Bot*] thistle, teasel

gjemb|a|c

I § *nm* **1** [*Bot*] thistle (*Silybum*) **2** sharp spine **3** (*Reg*) [*Zool*] hedgehog = **iriq**

II § *adj* = **gjembash**

gjemb|a|k *adj* = **gjembash**

gjemb|a|sh *adj* thorny, spiny, barbed

gjemb|bardhë *nm* [*Bot*] = **gjemb i bardhë**

gjemb|ërisht|e *nf* [*Bot*] hawthorn (*Crataegus*)

gjemb|ëzo·het *vpr* (*Book*) to sprout thorns, have thorns, be covered by thorns

gjemb|isht|e *nf* brier patch, bramble thicket

gjemb|je *adj*

gjemb|o·het *vpr* to get pricked

gjemb|o·n

I § *vt* to prick

II § *vi* to be the locus of a stabbing pain, hurt with a sharp pain

gjemb|or *adj* **1** [*Bot*] thorny, spiny, barbed **2** covered with brambles **3** thorn-shaped

gjemb|të *adj* (*i*) thorny, spiny, barbed

gjemb|th *nm* **1** rooster's foot-spur **2** small thorn, bristle

gjemenxhe *nf* [*Mus*] three-stringed violin

*__gjemë__ *nf* = **gjëmë**

gjemi *nf* (*Old*) large sailing vessel: galley

gjemi|tar *nm* (*Old*) sailor on a galley

gjemi|xhi *nm* (*np* ~ nj) (*Old*) **1** owner/captain of a galley **2** sailor on a galley

gjem|th *nm* = **gjembth**

gjen *nm* [*Biol*] gene

gjend·et *vpr* **1** to be found; be located, be situated, stand **2** to happen to be; be available; be present, be there, exist **3** to find oneself in a position/situation/condition; be accorded/admitted a status

○ <> **gjend·et** {*immediate family member*} to be of help/comfort to <> like one's own {}

○ <> **gjend·et** to be of help/comfort to <>: be there for <>

○ **s'<> gjend·et**³ˢᵍ **ana** there's practically nothing left of <>

○ **nuk <> gjend·et**³ˢᵍ **as nami as nishani** there *is* no trace of <>: <> *disappears* without a trace

○ **s'<> gjend·et**³ˢᵍ **çifti** <> *has* no match/equal, <> *is* incomparable

○ **nuk i gjend·et**³ˢᵍ **filli** it's a real mess

○ <> **gjend·et gjak** to be a real brother to <>

○ <> **gjend·et havale 1** to stand in <>'s way, become an obstacle to <> **2** to be a nuisance to <>

○ **s'i gjend·et**³ˢᵍ **i tilli** such another *cannot* be found, {} *has* no equal

○ **s'<> gjend·et**³ˢᵍ **karari** <> never *knows* what <> wants; something is always wrong with <>

○ <> **gjend·et në ditë të ngushtë** to be helpful to <> in difficult times, be there for <> in times of need

○ **nuk gjend·et**³ˢᵍ **nishani** not a single one *is* to be found

○ **s'<> gjend·et**³ˢᵍ **orta** (*Old*) there *is* not another like <>, <> *has* no match

○ <> **gjend**·*et* **pranë** to be a big supporter of [ ]
○ **gjend**·*et* **qiri në këmbë** to spring to one's feet
○ **nuk** <> **gjend**·*et³ˢᵍ* **shoku/shoqja** <> *has no peer,* <> *is incomparable*

***gjenda'r** = xhanda'r

gjenda'rm = xhanda'r

gjendarm|*ëri* = xhandarmëri'

gje'nd|**je** *nf* **1** situation, circumstances; position; state, condition **2** wealthy circumstances **3** *(Book)* presence
○ **gjendje e jashtëzakonshme** state of emergency
○ **gjendje lufte** martial law
○ **ësh·të në gjendje** to be rich
○ **gjendje shtetrrethimi** state of siege

gje'nd|**ur** *adj (i) (Colloq)* ready to help others in need

gje'ne *adv* yet, still; however

gjenea|**logj**|**i'** *nf* genealogy

gjenea|**logj**|**i'k** *adj* genealogical

gjene'ral *nm* [*Mil*] general

gjeneral|**i'sim** *nm* [*Mil*] highest military rank: generalissimo, commander-in-chief, general of the armies

gjeneral|**kolone'l** *nm* [*Mil*] general in charge of an entire army: lieutenant general

gjeneral|**lejtë**|**na'nt** [*gje-ne-ral-lej-të-na'nt*] *nm* [*Mil*] general in charge of a whole division: major general

gjeneral|**majo'r** *n* [*Mil*] general in charge of a whole brigade, lowest-ranking general: brigadier general

gjenera'të *nf* generation

gjenerato'r *nm* [*Tech*] generator

gjener|**i'k** *adj (Book)* generic

gjenet|**i'k** *adj* genetic

gjenet|**i'kë** *nf* **1** genetics **2** *(Colloq)* textbook on genetics

Gjene'vë *nf* Geneva

gjen|**e'zë** *nf (Book)* genesis

gjengjefi'l *nm* [*Bot*] ginger (*Zingiber officinale*)

gjeni'
I § *nf* high degree of talent or ability: genius
II § *nm* genius

***gje'n**|**i** *obl* <*gje(n)*

gjenia'l *adj* of genius, brilliant

gjenita'l *adj* genital

gjeniti'v *nm* [*Ling*] genitive

gjenoci'd *nm (Book)* genocide

Gjeno'vë *nf* Genoa

gjeo| *formativ* geo-

gjeodet|**i'k** *adj* geodetic

gjeo|**dez**|**i'** *nf* **1** geodesy **2** *(Colloq)* textbook on geodesy

gjeo|**dez**|**i'k** *adj* geodesic

gjeo|**dez**|**i'st** *n* geodesic scientist, geodesist

gjeo|**fiz**|**i'k** *adj* geophysical

gjeo|**fiz**|**i'kë** *nf* **1** geophysics **2** *(Colloq)* textbook on geophysics

gjeo|**gra'f** *nm* geographer

gjeo|**graf**|**i'** *nf* **1** geography **2** *(Colloq)* textbook on geography

gjeo|**graf**|**i'k** *adj* geographic, geographical

gjeo|**lo'g** *n* geologist

gjeo|**logj**|**i'** *nf* **1** geology **2** *(Colloq)* textbook on geology **3** *(Colloq)* exploration for valuable minerals

gjeo|**logj**|**i'k** *adj* geologic, geological

gjeo|**me'tër** *nm* land surveyor

gjeo|**metr**|**i'** *nf* **1** geometry **2** *(Colloq)* textbook on geometry
○ **gjeometri në hapësirë** solid geometry, stereometry
○ **gjeometri plane/rrafshore** plane geometry, planimetry

gjeo|**metr**|**i'k** *adj* geometric, geometrical

gjeo|**polit**|**i'kë** *nf (Book)* geopolitics

gjeo|**qendr**|**o'r** *adj* geocentric

Gjeorgji' *nf* Georgia

gjeorgjia'n *adj, n* of/from Georgia, inhabitant of Georgia: Georgian

gjeorgjia'n|**çe** *adv* Georgia-style; in Georgian (language)

gjep *nm* **1** spool, bobbin (in the shuttle of a loom) **2** nozzle, spout; narrow spout at the end of a millrace **3** pitcher with a narrow neck and a spout = ibri'k

***gjepogje'rra** *np (Old)* odds and ends

gje'pur *nf (Colloq)* **1** meaningless nonsense, drivel **2** obvious untruth: poppycock, crap

gjeq *nm* fine mist

gjer
I § *prep (acc) pcl* up to/till, until
II § *nm* [*Zool*] dormouse, loir (*Glis glis*)
○ **gjer më/në** [ ] up to/till [ ], until [ ]
○ **gjer në cakun e fundit** up to the very last, up to the bitter end
○ **gjer në fund** in full detail
○ **gjer në fyt** up to the ears

gjera'k *nm* [*Ornit*] male sparrow hawk, falcon

***gjera'q** *nm* [*Ornit*] crane (*Grus grus*)

gjeraqi'në *nf* **1** [*Ornit*] goshawk (*Accipter gentilis*) **2** *(Fig)* woman who is fast and agile
○ **gjeraqinë këmbëshkurtër** [*Ornit*] shikra *Acipiter badius*

gje'ras *adv* breadthways, breadthwise, across

gjer|**atë**|**her**|**shëm** *adj (i)* = deriatëhershëm

gjera|**to're** *nf* **1** yarn-winder = qe'rthull **2** whirlpool, eddy

gje'razi *adv* **1** = gje'ras **2** expansively, broadly, at length

gjerb· *vt* to sip

gje'rbë *nf* **1** sip **2** drop of water falling from a roof; part of the roof from which the water drips **3** roof overhang, eaves

gje'rb|**je** *nf ger* **1** <gje'rb· **2** sip

gjerb|**o'·n**
I § *vt* = gje'rb·
II § *vi* to drip, leak water

gjerda'n *nm* **1** necklace **2** cartridge belt **3** lengthwise half of a slaughtered animal carcass: side of meat
○ **gjerdan fishekësh** cartridge belt

gjerda'n|**e** *nf* sheep or goat with a circle of white or black around the neck

gjerde'k *nm* nuptial room prepared for the bride and groom to spend the first night of their wedding: bridal chamber

gjer|**dje**|**shëm** *adj (i)* = deridje'shëm

gjerdh|**a'c** *adj, n (Colloq)* clever and mischievous (child)

***gjerdha'k** *nm* = gjerde'k

***gjerdha'n** *nm* = gjerda'n

gje'rdh|**e** *np* <gardh

***gjerdhi'** *nf* cunning, craft

gjerdhīshtë *nf* **1** [*Bot*] tall bush with fuzzy silvery branches, red flowers and small pleasantly aromatic black berries **2** bramble fence

*****gjeremez** *nm* curdled milk

gjerë
I § *adj (i)* **1** wide; broad **2** vast, spacious, roomy; loose **3** wide apart **4** with broad participation; general, massive **5** broad-minded, liberal, magnanimous, big-spirited **6** [*Ling*] (of vowels) open **7** [*Math*] (of an angle) obtuse
II § *adv* **1** spaciously; loosely **2** *(Fig)* extensively elaborated **3** *(Fig)* broad-mined; lax **4** generally; over a broad range
∘ **gjerë e gjatë 1** far and wide **2** in full detail

gjerësī *nf* width, breadth
∘ **gjerësī gjeografike** latitude

gjerësīsht *adv* **1** broadly, widely; generally **2** extensively, at length **3** with plenty of room, spaciously

*****Gjergj** *nm* George (male name)

gjergjef *nm* **1** embroidery hoop/frame **2** weaving frame

gjerī *adv (së)* across the width: crosswise, breadthwise, across

gjerkëtushëm *adj (i) (Colloq)* = **derikëtushëm**

gjerman *adj, n* German

Gjermani *nf* Germany

gjermanik *adj* Germanic

gjermanisht *adv* in German (language)

gjermanishte *nf* German language

gjermanoperëndimor *adj, n* West German

gjermë *nf* = **gjirmë**

gjeroˑhet *vpr* = **zgjeroˑhet**

gjeroˑn *vt* = **zgjeroˑn**

gjerore *nf* [*Zool*] female dormouse

*****gjerpazi** *adv* in a creeping position, crawling

gjersa *conj* = **derisa**

gjersotëm *adj (i)* = **derisotëm**

gjersotshëm *adj (i)* = **derisotëm**

gjertanishëm *adj (i)* = **deritanishëm**

gjerund *nm* [*Ling*] gerund

gjerush *adj* broad-shouldered

gjerratore *nf (Reg)* skein winder for cotton

*****gjerrë** *OR* **gjerrël** *nf* humming top

gjest *nm* gesture

gjesh• = **ngjesh**•

*****gjeshje** *nf* formation, growth

gjeshk *I §* *nm* OR **gjeshkë** *II §* *nf* fallen leaf, dried-up leaf

*****gjeshse** *nf* ribbon; tape

gjeshtare *nf (Old)* midwife

gjeshtër *nf* [*Bot*] = **gjineshtër**

gjet *2nd & 3rd sg pres* <**gjas**•
∘ **Gjeti i çali të tatëpjetën.** "The lame person found the downhill slope." *(Prov)* {} lucked out.
∘ **Gjeti hajduti thesin.** "The thief found the sack." *(Prov Pej)* The devil has found his mate
∘ **gjeti mendja mendjen** "the mind found another mind just like it" they think just alike, birds of a feather flock together

*****gjetˑet** *vpr (Reg Gheg)* = **gjendˑet**

gjet *stem for pdef, opt, adm, part* <**gjeˑn**
∘ **[ju/të] gjeta/kam gjetur (me dolli)** "I found you with a toast" I challenge [you] to a competition of toasting (in order to honor someone)

∘ **I gjeti mushka drutë.** "The mule found the logs." *(Pej)*: {} is just getting the punishment {} was asking for.

gjete *nf* stepchild (from the husband's previous marriage)

gjetës
I § *n* **1** finder; discoverer **2** challenger to a competition of honoring toasts
II § *adj* * *(Colloq)* inventive

*****gjetësi** *nf* treasure trove, find

gjetiu *adv* elsewhere, somewhere else

gjetje *nf ger* **1** <**gjeˑn**, **gjendˑet 2** find, discovery **3** *(Fig)* felicitous discovery

gjetkë *adv* = **gjetiu**
∘ **gjetkë daullet e gjetkë dasma** "Drums somewhere and the wedding elsewhere." (said of one who says one thing and does another)

gjetkëz *nf* wattled enclosure where livestock are kept for fattening: fattening pen

gjetull *nf* [*Zool*] = **shigjetull**

gjetur
I § *part* <**gjeˑn**
II § *adj (i)* **1** found, discovered **2** arrived at by calculation: total, calculated **3** (child) of a former marriage: step- **4** (child) of unknown parentage: foundling **5** *(Fig)* apt, felicitous
∘ **i ka-**^{pl} **gjetur telat bashkë** to have found some common ground, have established common ties, have buried the hatchet

gjetura *np (Euph)* menstruation, menstrual period: monthlies

gjeturinë *nf* found objects of no value: worthless odds and ends

gjeth
I § *nm* **1** leaf **2** foliage **3** plant foliage used as fodder **4** tree leaf held to the lips and blown through as a musical instrument
II § *adj* whole-leaf (unprocessed, raw)

gjethˑet *vpr* = **gjethoˑhet**

gjethanik *nm* [*Food*] hearty pasty filled with leafy vegetables such as leeks and scallions

gjethatak *adj* having many leaves; with heavy foliage

gjethe *nf* **1** leaf **2** foliage **3** plant foliage used as fodder **4** blade of a woodplane
∘ **gjethe delli** [*Bot*] = **gjethedell**
∘ **gjethe fiku** "fig leaf" vain attempt to mask the truth
∘ **ësh-të gjethe plepi 1** to be very light in weight **2** to feel fit as a fiddle again **3** *(Iron)* not have a penny to one's name
∘ **gjethe thue-pulë** love-in-a-mist *Nigella arvensis*

gjethebardhë *adj* = **fletëbardhë**

gjethebri *nm* [*Bot*] hornwort *(Ceratophyllum)*

gjethedell *nm* [*Bot*] plantain *(Plantago)*

gjethedendur *adj* having dense foliage

gjethegjatë *adj* having long leaves: long-leafed

gjethegjelbër *adj* having green leaves: green-leafed

gjethegjerë *adj* having broad leaves: broad-leafed

gjethehapët *adj* = **fletëhapët**

gjethehollë *adj* having thin leaves: thin-leafed

gjetheimët *adj* having delicate leaves: fine-leafed

gjethemadh *adj* having large leaves: big-leafed

gjethe|mbajt|ës *adj* **1** evergreen **2** [*Bot*] leaf-bearing: *(foliferous)*

gjethe|mís|ër *nm* [*Bot*] common aspidistra (*Aspidistra elatior)*

gjethe|ngrën|ës *adj* [*Zool*] leaf-eating

gjethe|ngushtë *adj* having long narrow leaves: narrow-leafed

gjethe|përdredh|ës|e *nf* = **fletëpërdredhës**e

gjethe|rën|ës *adj* having falling leaves: deciduous

gjethe|shum|ë *adj* having many leaves, with heavy foliage

gjethe|tra|shë *adj* = **fletëtra**shë

gjethe|vogël *adj* having small leaves: small-leafed

gjeth|ëro·n *vi* = **gjetho·**n

gjeth|ës|ím *nm ger* = **gjethím**

gjeth|ës|o·het *vpr* = **gjetho·**het

gjeth|ës|o·n *vi* = **gjetho·**n

gjeth|ëz *nf*[*Bot*] small leaf, leaflet

gjeth|ím *nm ger* < **gjetho·**n, **gjetho·**het

gjeth|ím|e *nf* [*Bot*] = **krífsh**ë

gjeth|ín|ë *nf* **1** patch of ground with leafy shrubs and trees **2** leafy bough

gjeth|ís· *vi* to eat leaves: browse

gjeth|íshtë *nf* **1** fallen leaves lying on the ground **2** patch of ground with leafy shrubs and trees **3** leafy bough

gjeth|najë *nf* **1** tree foliage **2** fallen leaves lying on the ground

gjeth|o·het *vpr* to get covered with new leaves, sprout leaves

gjeth|o·n

I § *vi* to burst into leaf, sprout leaves

II § *vt* to cover [] with verdant new leaves

gjeth|or *adj* [*Bot*] **1** having leaves (rather than needles) **2** of or pertaining to leaves or foliage: leafy, foliar, foliate

gjeth|ore *np fem* broad-leafed/deciduous trees

gjeth|tak *adj* leafy

gjeth|urína *np* leaves fallen from trees, fallen foliage

*gjevalltís *stem for 1st sg pres, pl pres, 2nd & 3rd sg subj, pind* < **gjevalltí**t·

*gjevalltít· *vt* to gossip about [], slander

*gjever *nm (Old)* horse trainer

*gjeverdare *nf (Old)* flintlock gun

gjevrek

I § *nm* ring-shaped cracker: pretzel

II § *adj (Colloq)* brittle; crumbling, falling apart

gjezap

I § *nm (Colloq)* hydrochloric acid used to clean metals preparatory to soldering: acid

II § *adj* caustic, searing, sharp

gjezdís· *vi, vt (Colloq)* = **shëtí**t·

gjezdís|je *nf(Colloq)* = **shëtí**t·

gjezdís|ur *adj (i) (Colloq)* = **shëtí**tur

*gjezme *nf* = **xhe**zve

gjë

I § *nf* **1** thing **2** (in questions and with negatives) anything, a thing **3** livestock, cattle **4** *(Colloq)* belongings, possessions, property **5** *(Colloq)* person (of a sort designated by the following adjective)

II § *pred* **1** something, anything **2** *(Colloq)* related by blood

III § *interrog pcl* by any chance

○ **s'ësh·të gjë** to be nothing; be nothing of value, be of no importance

○ **gjë e gjallë 1** living thing **2** domestic animal, livestock, cattle

○ **s'ka gjë 1** it doesn't matter, never mind **2** (in response to an expression of gratitude) you're welcome, not at all, don't mention it

○ **s'e ka· (për) gjë** to consider it a small matter, not think it to be a big thing

○ **e ka· (për) gjë të madhe 1** to take it very seriously **2** to find it too difficult

○ **s'ka· gjë në kusi** not have a nickel to his name

○ **s'ka· gjë në sofër** "not have anything on the table (to eat)" to live in abject poverty, be very poor

○ **s'ka· gjë në strajcë 1** not have things going right, not have things under control **2** not have any brains, not have much upstairs

○ **s'ka· gjë në të 1** things *are* not going well for {}, it *doesn't* look good for {} **2** there is nothing in what {} is saying

○ **s'ka· gjë në torbë/trastë** "not have anything in the bag" **1** things *are* not going well for {}, it *doesn't* look good for {} **2** {} *doesn't* have anything concrete

○ **s'ka· gjë pas shpirtit** "have nothing behind one's soul" to have nothing to one's name, be poor; have nothing but one's own two hands

○ **s'[] ka· gjë** to have no family relationship with []: not be related to []

○ **s'mba·nn gjë në trup** {} can't keep a secret

○ **nuk ësh·të pa gjë 1** *is* not without guilt/fault **2** to be involved/implicated

○ **s'ësh·të për gjë** (of a person) not be worth a dime; be incapable of doing anything

○ **nuk ësh·të gjë përpara <>** to be nothing in comparison with <>, not to be compared with <>

○ **gjë prej gjëje/gjëri** nothing

○ **s'ësh·të³ˢᵍ gjë ajo/kjo punë** that/this *is* not possible

○ **gjë e rastit** happenstance, accident

○ **gjë tjetër** something/anything else

○ **gjë e trashë 1** cattle **2** *(Pej)* stupid person

gjë(r) *nm* **1** livestock, cattle **2** *(Colloq)* belongings, possessions, property **3** *(Colloq)* person (of a sort designated by the following adjective)

*gjëagjë *nf* **1** small thing; something **2** = **gjëegjëz**ë

*gjëç *pron (Colloq)* = **xhe**ç

gjëegjëzë *nf* riddle, word puzzle

gjëkafshë *pron* something; anything

gjëkund = **gjëku**ndi

gjëkundi *adv* **1** somewhere, anywhere **2** nowhere **3** *(Colloq)* not at all, in no way: no how, no way

○ **s'ësh·të gjëkundi** not be doing/going well

gjëlpërë *nf* = **gjilpër**ë

gjëll|í·n

I § *vi* **1** *(Fig)* to have an empty life, just eating to stay alive **2** to live (in a particular habitat) **3** *(Old)* to stay alive

II § *vt, vi* **1** (of animals) to forage (for [food]); feed **2** to seek and choose []: pick out []

gjëll|ím *nm* life, existence

gjëllíme *np* scattered remnants of hay left after a harvest; sparse fruit left on the tree or vine after a harvest

gjëmb = **gjemb**

gjëmë *nf* **1** loud rumbling sound; boom **2** calamity, catastrophe; death and disaster **3** news of death in the family **4** [*Ethnog*] wailing for the dead: keening **5** (*Colloq Pej*) something so ugly and bad as to be almost unbearable **6** plethora, huge amount

gjëmëmadh
I § *adj* **1** calamitous, catastrophic, disastrous; foreboding a disaster: sinister **2** stricken by woe, struck by disaster; wretched **3** loudly booming/rumbling **4** (*Fig*) very well-known, famous **5** (*Pej*) notorious, infamous
II § *n* **1** wretch **2** notorious person

gjëmëshumë *adj* calamitous, catastrophic, disastrous

gjëmëtar *nm* (*Old*) person who eulogizes the dead in a loud wailing voice: keener

gjëmëzi *adj, n* (*fem sg ~ëz, masc pl ~inj, fem pl ~eza*) (one) afflicted by disaster; long-suffering (one); hapless (person)

gjëmim *nm* **1** boom, thundering sound **2** powerful resounding boom muffled by distance: rumble

gjëmimtar *adj* (*Poet*) = gjëmues

gjëmo·n
I § *vi* **1** to boom, thunder; rumble loudly **2** to roar **3** to groan, moan **4** to rush, run
II § *vt* **1** (*Colloq*) to pursue **2** (*Old*) to eulogize the dead in a loud wailing voice: keen
  ◦ <> gjëmo·n³ᵖˡ veshët <> *feels a booming sensation in the ears*

gjëmshëm *adj* (*i*) calamitous, catastrophic, disastrous

gjëmto·n *vi* = qëmto'·n

gjëmues *adj* powerful and prolonged like thunder: thundering

gjëmushkë *nf* thicket = gajushë

gjënd = gjend

gjëndër *nf* **1** [*Anat Bot*] gland **2** lump under the skin created by swollen lymph nodes; inflamed or swollen lymph node
  ◦ gjëndër mbrojtëse [*Med*] prostate gland
  ◦ gjëndra të pështymës salivary glands
  ◦ gjëndrat e yndyrës [*Anat*] sebaceous glands

gjëndëro·het *vpr* to get lumps under the skin due to swollen lymph nodes, be scrofulous

gjëndëror *adj* [*Anat*] glandular

***gjëngallë** OR **gjënkallë** = gjinkallë

gjëra *np* **1** <gjë **2** circumstances, conditions
  ◦ gjëra të vjetra familiar things

gjëri|i *obl* <gjë(r)

gjëri *nf* = gjini

***gjërpazi** *adv* **1** in serpentine fashion, snake-like, sinuously ***2** crawling, creeping

gjërpinj *np* <gjarpër

gjësend OR **gjësendi**
I § *pron* something, anything
II § *interrog pcl* by any chance

gjëshëm *adj* (*i*) wealthy, rich

***gjëvez** *nm* purple color

gjëzë *nf* **1** = gjëegjëzë **2** puzzle

gji(r) *nm* **1** breast; udder, teat **2** milk from a breast **3** [*Veter*] mastitus **4** bosom **5** [*Geog*] bay, inlet **6** [*Bot Med*] sinus ()

gjibardhë *adj* (*Poet*) white-bosomed

***gjibon** *nm* [*Zool*] gibbon = gibon

Gjibraltar *nm* Gibraltar

gjibutë *adj* having a soft, easy-to-milk udder

gjicilojcë *nf* [*Bot*] annual hair grass (*Aira capillaris*)

gjidele *nf* [*Bot*] curled dock (*Rumex crispus*)

***gjie**
I § *nf* low house
II § *np* <gjë (*Reg Gheg*)

gjifryrë *adj* (*Poet*) firm-breasted, full-chested

gjigant
I § *nm* giant; colossus
II § *adj* gigantic

***gjigjë** *nf* **1** scrap, rag, rubbish **2** spark = xixë

gjihedhur *adj* having a well-developed bosom, full-chested

***gjije** *nf* = gjë

***gjikallë** = gjinkallë

Gjikë *nf with masculine agreement* Gjikë (male name)

gjilpërë *nf* **1** needle **2** pin **3** [*Med*] hypodermic needle; hypodermic injection **4** firing pin **5** (*Colloq*) prickly spine (of a hedgehog) **6** door/window jamb **7** (*Fig Pej*) sly person who secretly does something bad
  ◦ ësh-të gjilpërë to be catty
  ◦ gjilpërë kapëse safety pin; hairpin
  ◦ gjilpërë me kokë pin
  ◦ gjilpërë qyqeje = gjilpërëqyqe

gjilpërëqyqe *nf* [*Bot*] common storksbill (*Erodium cicutarium*)

gjilpërëz *nf* **1** (*Dimin*) <gjilpërë **2** [*Ichth*] broadnosed pipefish (*Syngnathus typhle*) **3** [*Bot*] common storksbill (*Erodium cicutarium*) **4** (*Reg*) darning needle

gjilpëro·n *vt* to inject [] (with a hypodermic needle)

gjilpëror *adj* [*Spec*] needle-shaped, acicular, aciculate

gjilpëryer *nm* **1** thick, heavy duty needle: awl, bodkin **2** (*Reg*) knitting needle **3** peg that attaches the tongue to the bed of a cart/wagon **4** (*Reg Euph*) diphtheria

gjillësë *nf* flavor, savor

gjimadhe *adj* having large breasts: big-breasted

***gjimbishtë** *nf* [*Bot*] = gjipishtë

gjimbushur *adj* (*Book*) having well-developed breasts: full-breasted

***gjimëtar** *n* bully, braggart

***gjimnas** = gjimnaz

gjimnast *nm* [*Sport*] gymnast

gjimnastikë *nf* **1** physical exercise; physical education **2** (*Fig*) exercise **3** [*Sport*] gymnastics

gjimnastikor *adj* gymnastic

gjimnaz *nm* gymnasium (in the European sense): secondary school, high school

gjimnazist *n* student at a secondary school

***gjimo·n** *vi, vt* = gjëmo'·n

***gjimto·n** *vi, vt* = qëmto'·n

***Gjin** *nm* Gjin (male name)

gjinatore *nf* [*Entom*] bumble bee *Bombus*

gjind *np collec* (*Colloq*) people right there, people who are around; household members, members of the family

gjind·et *vpr* = gjend·et

gjind = gjend

***gjindar** *nm* = xhandar

gjindës *n* person ready to help others in need

gjindje *nf collec* (*Colloq*) whole populace

gjindo're *nf* [*Ling*] genitive

gji'ndshëm *adj* (i) helpful in times of need, ready to help = **gje'ndur**

gjineko'lo'g *n* gynecologist

gjineko'logjí *nf* gynecology

gjineko'logjík *adj* gynecological

gjine'shtër *nf* [*Bot*] ginestra, Spanish broom, weaver's broom (*Spartium junceum L.*)

gjine've'rdhë *nf* [*Bot*] type of genista from whose flowers and roots a yellow dye is extracted

*gji'në *nf* = **gli'në**

*gji'nga'llë = **gjinka'llë**

*gji'ngël *nf* = **qi'ngël**

gjingjivit *nm* [*Med*] gingivitis

gjiní *nf* 1 [*Hist*] clan 2 [*Ethnog*] matrilineal family 3 close family relationship; close relative 4 [*Biol*] genus 5 [*Ling*] gender 6 [*Art Lit*] genre 7 sort, type
  ○ **gjinia njerëzore** (*Book*) the human race, mankind

gjiní'sh *nm* 1 router plane 2 the groove of a tongue-and-groove joint

gjinka'llë *nf* 1 [*Entom*] cicada 2 tree cricket (*Oecanthus pellucens*) 3 (*Tibicen plebejus*) 4 (*Fig*) person who talks incessantly 5 (*Reg*) small bell with a piercing sound
  ○ **gjinkalla gungashe** [*Entom*] buffalo cicada *Ceresa bubalus Fabr.*

gjinkallo're *np* [*Invert*] Cicadidae

*Gjinoka'stër = **Gjirokastër**

gjino'ku'q *nm* [*Ornit*] = **gushëku'q**

gjino'r
  I § *adj* 1 [*Hist Ethnog*] of or pertaining to clans: clan, clannish 2 [*Biol*] of the genus 3 genital 4 [*Ling*] pertaining to gender 5 [*Art Lit*] of the genre
  II § *nm* [*Zool*] animal of a particular genus

gjino're *adj*, *nf* [*Ling*] genitive (case)

Gjinu'sh *nm* Gjinush (male name)

gji'nj *np* < **gji**(r)

gji'nj'ës *nm* [*Veter*] mastitis

gji'pës *nm* [*Bot*] privet (*Ligustrum*) = **vo'shtër**

gji'pi'shtë *nf* [*Bot*] wild almond tree (*Amygdalus webii*)

gji'plo'të *adj* (*Poet*) having a bounteous bosom: full-chested, big-breasted

gjips *nm* [*Min*] gypsum

gjir *nm* whirlpool, eddy
  ○ **gjiri i vezëve** [*Anat*] ovary

gjira'fë *nf* giraffe

gjira'k
  I § *adj* [*Bot*] sinuate
  II § *nf* [*Ornit*] hawk

gji're *np* < **gji** [*Geog*] bays, inlets

gjire'shtër *nf* [*Bot*] chaste tree (*Vitex agnus-castus*)

*gji're'm *nf* = **gji'rmë**

gji'r'i *obl* < **gji**(r)

gji'ri *nf* = **gjiní**

gjiri'z *nm* (*Colloq*) 1 waste sewer; septic hole 2 drainage canal covered by stone slabs

gji'rmë *nf* firepit in a fireplace

gjiro'·n *vt* (*Reg*) = **mbrus·**

Gjiroka'stër *nf* city and district in southern Albania: Gjirokastra, Argyrokastron

gjirokastrí't *adj*, *n* of/from Gjirokastra, native of Gjirokastra

gjis *stem for 2nd pl pres, pind* < **gja s·**

---

*gji'sht = **gisht**

gji'sht'ëz *nf* thimble = **gi'shte**

gjit *stem for 2nd pl pres, pind, imper, vp* < **gja s·**
  * = **ngjit**

gjita'r
  I § *nm* [*Zool*] mammal
  II § *adj* mammalian

gjita're *nf* (e) (of a milk animal) having a large udder; high in milk productivity

gjito'n *nm* (*Reg*) neighbor = **fqi'një**

gjith'andej *adv* everywhere

gjith'ane'sí *nf* = **gjithanshm'ëri**

*gjith'a'nsh = **gjitha'nshëm**

gjith'a'nshëm *adj* (i) 1 affecting every aspect: general, complete, thorough; in all regards: all-round, comprehensive, overall 2 from all points of view, in all aspects 3 of broadly ranging interest and ability: many-sided, polymath

gjith'a'nshm'ëri *nf* totality

gjith'a'q *adv* (*Colloq*) 1 to the same degree: just as, that much 2 (in negative contexts) not even that much

gjith'a'rm'ësh *adj* [*Mil*] combined-arms

gjith'a'shtu *adv* 1 likewise, in the same way; also, too 2 as well as

gjith'a'zi *adv* 1 in general, generally 2 altogether, in entirety

gjith'çka *pron* everything

gjith'ç'mo's *pron* (*Colloq*) everything possible, everything imaginable, what not

gjith*ë*
  I § *determiner* 1 all, all of; all the, the whole, the entire; all that 2 (*Reg*) every = **çdo**
  II § *pcl* entirely, completely, fully
  III § *adj* (i) whole, entire
  IV § *nm* 1 the whole 2 all remaining; all there is
  V § *np* (të) all; everything, everyone
  ○ **gjith*ë* i/e** {*intimate kinship term*} exactly/just like
  {} **gjith*ë* e ëma** just like his/her/their mother **gjith*ë* i ati** just like his/her/their father **gjith*ë* e motra** just like his/her/their sister
  ○ **gjith*ë* bota** everybody
  ○ **gjith*ë* buzë** having a disappointed look on one's face
  ○ **ësh·të gjith*ë* caka** to be a thief, have one's hand in the till
  ○ **gjith*ë* ç'** whatever, all that
  ○ **gjith*ë* ditën e bekuar** all day long
  ○ **gjith*ë* ditën e gjatë** all day long
  ○ **gjith*ë* ditën e lume** all the livelong day
  ○ **gjith*ë* ditën e nderme** all day long
  ○ **gjith*ë* ditën** all day long
  ○ **gjith*ë* kohën** the whole time; all the time
  ○ **gjith*ë* natën e gjatë** all night long
  ○ **Qafsha të gjith*ë*!** "May I mourn for the whole family!" (*Colloq*) I swear it by all I hold sacred (that I'm telling the truth)!
  ○ **gjith*ë* sa** whatever, all that
  ○ **gjith*ë* si** just like
  ○ **gjith*ë* sy e veshë** all eyes and ears
  ○ **ësh·të gjith*ë* tule** (of a person) to be very fleshy

gjith*ë*'ci'l *n* (definite case forms only), determiner, *pron* = **gjith*ë*seci'l**

gjith*ë*'di'je *nf* (*Book*) omniscience

gjith*ë*'di'j'ës *adj* (*Book*) all-knowing: omniscient

gjith*ë*'fuqi *nf* (*Book*) overriding power

gjith**ë**fuqi**shëm** adj (i) (Book) omnipotent, all-powerful

gjith**ë**fuqi**shm**|**ëri** nf (Book) 1 overriding power 2 omnipotence

gjith**ë**-gjith**ë** adv (Colloq) all in all

gjith**ë**komb**ë**ta**r** adj of, encompassing, or pertaining to the whole country

gjith**ë**ku**sh** = gjithku**sh**

*gjith**ë**lloj**sh** = gjith**ë**lloj**shëm**

gjith**ë**lloj**shëm** adj (i) (Book) of all kinds; of many kinds, various

gjith**ë**mba**rë** pron absolutely everybody, everyone without exception

gjith**ë**popull**o**r adj involving the whole people

gjith**ë**pushte**t** nm omnipotence

gjith**ë**pushte**tshëm** adj (i) 1 all-powerful: omnipotent 2 plenipotentiary

gjith**ë**sa**he**r**ë** conj whenever, anytime

gjith**ë**se**ci**l n (definite case forms only), determiner, pron each and every one (of them)

gjith**ë**se**ku**sh pron each person (in a group), everybody, everyone

gjith**ë**se**si** adv 1 somehow or another, by some means or another 2 in complete detail, down to the slightest detail 3 in any way, anyhow, however

gjith**ë**si nf (Book) 1 universe 2 (Old) total

gjith**ë**si**shëm** adj (i) (Book) universal

gjith**ë**si**sht** adv in general; completely, totally

gjith**ë**shqiptar adj all-Albanian

gjith**ë**vjet**o**r adj for a whole year

gjithfar**ë** determiner (followed by abl pl case) all sorts/kinds of, various, diverse

gjithfar**ë**lloj determiner (followed by abl pl case) every kind of, the most diverse sorts of

gjithfar**ë**lloj**shëm** adj (i) of all kinds, of every sort

gjithfar**ë**soj
  I § determiner (followed by abl pl case) all sorts/kinds of, various, diverse
  II § adv (Colloq) in all kinds of ways

gjithfar**ë**sh adj of all kinds, of every sort, variegated

gjithfar**shëm** adj (i) = gjithfar**ësh**

gjithhe**r**ë adv all the time, every time, always

gjithhe**r**shëm adj (i) constant, continual, eternal

*gjith**ici**l adj, pron each/every (one)

gjithka**h** adv in/from all directions and on/from all sides: everywhere

gjithkështu adv in this same way: likewise

gjithku**jt** dat <gjithku**sh**
  ○ Gjithkujt i duhet një fre. Everyone needs to be under some limits.
  ○ Gjithkujt murrizi i vet duket i njomë. "To everyone his own blackberry bush seems harmless (tender)." (Prov Iron) If they are your own, you ignore their shortcomings. Your own children are just little angels.

gjithku**nd** adv in every place and on every side: everywhere

*gjithku**nd**i adv from every direction, from everywhere

gjithku**sh** pron everyone

*gjithku**shi** pron (Reg Gheg) = gjithku**sh**

*gjith**ky** determiner this very (one), the very same (one)

*gjithma**r** = gjithmba**r**

gjithmba**rshëm** adj (i) including everything without exception: in everything, universal, general

gjithmo**n**ë adv 1 forever; for the whole time, constantly, always 2 every time, on every occasion

gjithmo**n**shëm adj (i) constant; continual, perpetual

gjithndu**er** determiner (followed by abl pl case) (Old) = gjithfa**r**ë

gjithndu**er**sh
  I § adv in various ways
  II § adj = gjithfa**r**ësh

gjithndu**er**shëm adj (i) = gjithfa**r**ësh

gjithnj**ë** adv 1 always, for the whole time, every time 2 constantly, forever, ever

*gjithq**i**sh adv (Reg Tosk) = gjithqy**sh**

gjithqy**sh**
  I § adv 1 in any way whatever, by any means possible, somehow, anyhow 2 in total
  II § conj by whatever means: however

*gjithsa**do** adv however much/many

gjith**sej**
  I § adv 1 in total, in all 2 wholly, entirely
  II § pcl exclusively, utterly

gjith**sej**ë nf entirety, sum total; final result, upshot

gjith**sej**t adv in entirety: all included, all together

gjith**sej**të adj (i) complete, entire

gjith**sesi** OR gjith**si** adv 1 no matter how, however 2 in every way, in complete detail, thoroughly

*gjith**shënjt** adj (i) (Reg Gheg)
  ○ i gjithshënjti _ (Reg Gheg) the very reverend _

*gjith**shka** = gjith**çka**

*gjith**shka**fe = gjithshka**h**e

gjith**shka**h|e nf entirety, the whole

gjithun**ji** adv (Old) 1 all together, together in unity 2 completely, totally, wholly

gjithun**ji**shëm adj (i) (Old) universal, without exception

gji**vo**gël adj small-breasted

*gjivre**k** nm = gjevre**k**

gjiza**ni**k nm [Food] layered pastry filled with cheese curds

gjiza**r** n [Dairy] maker of cheese curds; dairy assistant

gji**z**ë nf [Dairy] cheese curd; unsalted cottage cheese, pot cheese

gjize**to**re nf [Food] baked dish made with corn meal, cottage cheese and onions

gjoba**r** n (Old) 1 person who imposes and collects fines 2 = bekçi

gjo**b**ë nf fine, penalty

gjob**ë**ta**r** n (Old) 1 person who imposes or collects fines 2 person fined by clan elders

gjob**ï**m nm ger <gjobo·**n**, gjobo**·het**

gjob**i**s stem for 1st sg pres, pl pres, 2nd & 3rd sg subj, pind <gjob**i**t·

gjob**i**t· vt = gjobo**·**n

gjob**i**tje nf ger 1 <gjob**i**t· 2 fine, penalty

gjob**o·**n vt to fine, penalize

gjoc nm 1 small earthenware baking pan 2 [Entom] = gjonth

*gjoc**â**(n) nm (Reg Gheg) deep basin in rock eroded by water

*gjo**dh**| stem for pdef <gje**dh**·

gjo**ja** pcl (Colloq) supposedly, allegedly

○ **gjoja se** under the pretext that, pretending that

***gjo'je** nf = gjah

gjok
　　I § nm gray/white horse
　　II § adj gray-haired

gjo'ke nf gray/white mare or mule

gjoks nm **1** chest, thorax **2** breasts; breast **3** [Food] meat from the chest area: ribs, rib steak **4** (Fig) (as a symbol of human emotions) the heart
　　○ **gjoks këpucari** [Med] funnel breast
　　○ **gjoks për/më gjoks** (in wrestling) body to body; (in fighting) hand-to-hand
　　○ **gjoks pule** [Med] chicken breast

gjoks·gje'rë adj broadchested

gjoks·ja'shtë adj, adv bare-chested

gjoks·ma'dh adj big-chested

gjoks·mba'jt·ese nf brassiere

gjoks·mbro'jt·ese nf [Mil] outer embankment of a defensive fortification: breastwork, earthwork, rampart, bulwark

gjoks·mbro'jtje nf =gjoksmbro'jtëse

gjoks·ngu'shtë adj narrow-chested

gjoks·o're nf **1** [Hist] = parzmo're **2** breast collar of a horse harness **3** vest-like undergarment for women: bodice; brassiere **4** [Mil] bandolier ***5** bib

gjoks·shkë'mb adj (Poet) strong and resolute, powerful and steadfast

gjoks·zbul·u'ar adj bare-chested

gjok·sha'r [gjok-sha'r] nm men's wool flannel shirt

gjol nm (Colloq) **1** lake, pond **2** sea of thick mud: mire

gjol·i'shte nf (Colloq) wet area; pond

gjoll nm separate and slightly elevated plot of land used to grow a particular crop: patch of ground

gjo'lle-gjo'lle adv unevenly (distributed) over an area: in patches

gjo'llë nf slab on which salt for livestock is placed: salt lick; stony ground to which livestock are taken to be given salt

gjoll·i't·et vpr to lose hair/wool in patches, lose hair; have skin peeling in patches

gjon nm [Ornit] Scops owl (Otus scops) = **qok**

Gjon nm John

gjoni nf [Constr] carpenter's square (for checking angles)

gjo'nth nm [Entom] fruit louse

***gjo'një** nf **1** = gjon **2** ox tongue

***gjorda'n** nm = gjerda'n

gjo'rdë nf [Hist] single-edged saber

gjo'rë adj (i) in sorry circumstances: miserable, wretched, poor

***gjo'rës** nm = gjon

gjorqina'k nm (Old) **1** poor villager with neither tools nor land **2** farmer who shares cattle for a certain time with another farmer **3** (Fig) person with no family and no possessions

***gjo'së** nf black nanny goat with white markings on the head

gju(r) nm **1** knee **2** (Colloq) bend, curve
　　○ **gju më/për gju 1** in casual and informal proximity, getting down to an intimate level **2** in close friendship

gju·het vp recip to hit/strike one another

gjua·n vt **1** to hunt **2** (Fig) to lie in wait for [ ] **3** to impel [an aimed projectile]: shoot, throw **4** (Fig) to prick, cut, hurt **5** (Reg) to chase/drive [ ] out
　　○ [ ] **gjua·nn me gur** to heap abuse upon [ ]
　　○ **gjua·nn peshk** to fish

gjua'jt stem for pdef, opt, adm, part <**gjua·n**

gjua'jt·ës nm **1** hunter (of sea animals) **2** [Av] fighter/pursuit plane **3** [Mil Sport] person skillful in hitting a target: sharpshooter **4** [Text] person who catches and ties off broken threads

gjua'jt·ës-bombard·u'es nm [Av] fighter-bomber

gjua'jtje nf ger **1** <**gjua'j·**, **gju·het 2** (Sport) action made to impel a projectile aimed at an object: shot, kick (in soccer), throw (in basketball), stroke (in billiards)
　　○ **gjuajtje e lirë** [Sport] (soccer) free kick; (basketball) free throw
　　○ **gjuajtje personale** [Basketball] free throw
　　○ **gjuajtje peshku** fishery, fishing industry

***gjuble'të** nf = xhuble'të

gju'cë nf [Ichth] = gju'hcë

***gju·e·n** vt (Reg Gheg) = gjua·n

gjueta'r
　　I § nm hunter, huntsman
　　II § adj skilled in hunting
　　○ **gjuetar i peshkut** fisherman

gjue'ti nf hunting
　　○ **gjuetia e peshkut** fishing

***gjuga'ç** nm puddle
　　○ **gjuh·et**pl **me fjalë** to taunt one another

***gjuha'n** nm hunted animals/birds: game

gju'hcë nf [Ichth] **1** bleak (Alburnus albidus alborella De Filip.) **2** (Colloq) anchovy; sprat, pilchard

gju'hë nf **1** tongue **2** bell-clapper **3** language **4** (Colloq) Albanian language as a subject taught in school **5** (Colloq) textbook on language
　　○ **ësh·të i gjuhës** to be good with words
　　○ **Gjuha çan gurin/shkëmbin.** "the tongue can cut through iron" (Prov) Words are more powerful than steel. The pen is mightier than the sword.
　　○ **gjuhë dele** [Bot] ***1** golden-chain laburnum (Laburnum anagyroides) **2** marvel-of-Peru (Mirabilis jalapa)
　　○ **gjuhë dreri** [Bot] hart's tongue fern = tjegullo're
　　○ **Gjuha është prej tuli.** "the tongue is made of soft flesh" (Prov) Words are malleable. Words can be made to say anything.
　　○ **s'ka· gjuhë fare** to be well-behaved and soft-spoken; be quiet and obedient; be sparing in speech
　　○ **s'ka· gjuhë** not be good with words; be taciturn
　　○ **gjuhë kau** [Bot] madwort (Asperugo procumbens)
　　○ **Gjuha s'ka e kocka thyen.** "The tongue has no bone, but it can break bones." (Prov) Words can really hurt.
　　○ **gjuhë lepuri** [Bot] (Nonea alba)
　　○ **gjuha letrare (kombëtare)** the (Albanian national) standard language
　　○ **gjuhë lope** [Bot] = gjuhëlo'pe
　　○ <> **mbërthe·het**3sg **gjuha** "<>'s mouth/tongue is stuck tight" <> is unable to speak
　　○ **ta nxjerr gjuhën nga qafa** "{} pulls the tongue out of your neck" , you are forced to talk, you are made to speak out (and criticize someone who has made a mistake)
　　○ **nuk ësh·të pa gjuhë** (Pej) to talk too much; speak out in opposition inappropriately

○ **Preje gjuhën!** Don't talk so much! You've talked long enough!

○ **Gjuha pret hekurin.** "the tongue can cut through iron" *(Prov)* Words are more powerful than steel. The pen is mightier than the sword.

○ **gjuhë resmi** formal language

○ **<>u thaftë gjuha!** "May <>'s tongue dry up!" *(Curse)* May <> be struck dumb!

○ **gjuhë e ujit** [*Bot*] *=* gjuhujës*e*

○ **gjuhë vjehrre** [*Bot*] tuna, prickly pear *(Opuntia tuna)*

gjuhë́bilbíl *adj (Poet)* eloquent, honey-tongued

gjuhë́brísk *adj* articulate; quick-witted in speech

***gjuˈhë́c** *=* gjuˈhcë́

gjuhëˈçaˈrë́ *nf* [*Mus*] simple musical instrument made of a rye leaf stuck in a crack in a stick and blown

gjuhëˈdeˈle *nf* [*Bot*] "sheep's tongue" **1** goldenchain laburnum *(Laburnum anagyroides)* **2** marvel-of-Peru *(Mirabilis jalapa)*

gjuhëˈdreˈri [*Bot*] hart's tongue *(Scolopendrium officinale)*

gjuhëˈgjaˈrpër *adj* hurtful in tone, venomous (in language), biting, acerb

gjuhëˈgjaˈtë *adj* endlessly talkative, garrulous

gjuhëˈheˈlm *adj* having a poisonous tongue

gjuhëˈkrijˈueˈs *adj* given to creating neologisms: linguistically creative

***gjuhëˈkuˈq** *nm* gypsy

gjuhëˈlaˈshtë *adj* **1** *=* gojëndyˈrë ***2** talkative

gjuhëˈlëshˈuaˈr *adj* unrestrained in speech, talking without thinking

gjuhëˈliˈdhˈur

I § *adj* taciturn, close-mouthed

II § *adv* without speaking, close-mouthed

gjuhëˈloˈpatë *adj (Disparaging)* talkative: garrulous, prattling

gjuhëˈloˈpatˈkë *adj (Disparaging)* gossipy woman

gjuhëˈloˈpë *nf* [*Bot*] true alkanet, bugloss *(Anchusa officinalis)*

gjuhëˈlloˈmˈkë *adj (Disparaging)* *=* gjuhëˈloˈpatë

gjuhëˈmbajˈtur *adj* **1** clumsy in speech: inarticulate, tongue-tied **2** economical in speech: laconic

gjuhëˈmpiˈrë *adj* tongue-tied (from strong emotion)

gjuhëˈmpreˈhtë *adj* skillful in speaking: articulate

gjuhëˈnepërˈkë *adj* (of women) sharp-tongued, spiteful in speech: nasty and catty

gjuhëˈnuˈse *nf* **1** [*Bot*] rocket larkspur *(Delphinium ajacis)* **2** *=* ferrënuˈse

***gjuhëˈpreˈˈmë** *adj (Reg Gheg) =* gjuhëpreˈrë

gjuhëˈpreˈrë *adj* **1** whose tongue has been cut off **2** *(Fig)* unable to speak **3** laconic **4** *(Curse)* be damned! (with tongue cut off)

gjuhëˈqeˈn *nm* [*Bot*] hound's-tongue *(Cynoglossum officinale)*

gjuˈhëˈra *np* <gjuˈhë

gjuhëˈrrëndˈuaˈr *adj* **1** speaking disparagingly of others: backbiting **2** speaking to deceive others: lying, deceitful **3** *(Curse) =* gjuhëthaˈrë

gjuhëˈsiˈ *nf* linguistics

○ **gjuhësi zbatuese** [*Ling*] applied linguistics

gjuhëˈsiˈsht *adv* linguistically

gjuhëˈsoˈr *adj* of or pertaining to language/linguistics: linguistic

gjuhëˈshkuˈrtˈer *adj* laconic

gjuhëˈshkurtˈuaˈr *adj (Curse)* be damned! (with a shortened tongue)

gjuhëˈshpaˈtë *adj* masterful in speaking, articulate; succinct and to the point

gjuhëˈshthuˈrˈur *adj* = gojështhuˈrur

gjuhëˈtaˈr

I § *n* linguist

II § *adj* linguistic

gjuhëˈtraˈshë *adj* **1** barely able to speak **2** speaking with a thick regional accent: provincial in speech; clumsy in speech

gjuhëˈthaˈrë *adj (Curse)* be damned! (with a dried up tongue)

gjuhëˈthiˈkë *adj* articulate; speaking right to the heart of the matter; quick-witted in speech

gjuˈhëz *nf* **1** clapper/tongue of a bell **2** (of land) promontory, tongue **3** [*Mus*] reed of a musical instrument **4** [*Anat*] = njerith **5** [*Bot*] sheath surrounding the leaf and stem of a grass plant: ligule, ligula **6** [*Ichth*] scaldfish *(Arnaglossus laterna laterna)* **7** [*Constr*] tongue (of wood), mortise

○ **gjuhëz e Adriatikut** [*Ichth*] nosed sole *Solea impar*

○ **gjuhëz e bardhë** [*Ichth*] Rueppeli's scaldfish *Arnaglossus ruppelli*

○ **gjuhëz bari** [*Ichth*] *Arnaglossus kessleri*

○ **gjuhëz e bravës** spring bolt, latch bolt

○ **gjuhëz bregu** [*Ichth*] common sole *Solea vulgaris vulgaris*

○ **gjuhëz deti** [*Ichth*] ***1** = gjuhëz bregu *Solea solea L.* **2** snouted sole *Solea nasuta*

○ **gjuhëz dheu** [*Geog*] narrow outlet of land in the water: tongue

○ **gjuhëz e egër** [*Ichth*] Thor's scaldfish *Arnaglossus thori*

○ **gjuhëz kanali** [*Ichth*] common sole *Solea vulgaris vulgaris*

○ **gjuhëz me brezare** [*Ichth*] thickback sole *Microchirus variegatus*

○ **gjuhëz me njolla** [*Ichth*] = gjuhëz syzake

○ **gjuhëz pene** nib of a pen

○ **gjuhëz rëre** [*Ichth*] sand sole, lascar *Solea lascaris*

○ **gjuhëz syzake** [*Ichth*] eyed sole *Microchirus ocellatus*

○ **gjuhëz toke** [*Ichth*] scaldfish *Arnoglossus imperialis*

○ **gjuhëz turke** [*Ichth*] Klein's sole *Solea kleinii*

○ **gjuhëz e verdhë** [*Ichth*] yellow sole, little sole *Buglossidium luteum*

gjuhëzëˈnë *adj* = gjuhëmbajtur

gjuhëzoˈ•n *vt* [*Constr*] to join [] (in tongue-and-groove construction)

gjuhoˈr

I § *adj* **1** [*Ling*] of language: linguistic **2** [*Anat*] lingual **3** [*Bot*] tongue-shaped: linguiform **4** [*Med*] glossal

II § *nf* [*Ling*] language sound

***gjuhˈtiˈ** *nf* = gjueti

gjuhˈujˈëˈse *nf* [*Bot*] broad-leaved pondweed *(Potamogeton natans)*

gjuhˈuˈstˈer *adj (Insult)* spiteful and talkative: catty, tongue-wagging

***gjuhˈushtˈer** = gjuhustˈer

***gjuhˈzˈuˈer** *adj (fem ˜ore) (Old) =* gjuhoˈr

***gjûj** *(Reg Gheg) =* gjuˈnj

*gjuk = gjyk

gjullurdí *nf(Colloq)* loud commotion; big to-do

gjumásh
  I § *adj* 1 fond of sleeping, who sleeps a lot 2 sleepy
  II § *nm* sleepyhead

gjumë *nm* 1 sleep, slumber 2 *(Fig)* torpor, lethargy 3 *(Fig)* suspension of normal activity in winter: hibernation
  ○ gjumi i afjontë narcosis
  ○ gjumë dimëror hibernation
  ○ gjumin e ëmbël! *(Felic)* sweet dreams!
  ○ Gjumi është vëllai i vdekjes. "Sleep is the brother of death" *(Prov)* Sleeping like that, you might as well be dead.
  ○ gjumë gjarpri long sleep
  ○ gjumi i madh *(Euph)* the big sleep: death
  ○ gjumi i parë first stage of (deep) sleep
  ○ gjumi i përjetshëm *(Euph)* the eternal sleep: death
  ○ gjumë qengjash *(Colloq)* pleasant/calm sleep (sleep like a lamb)
  ○ gjumë qeni restless sleep
  ○ gjumë qensh *(Colloq)* disturbed/interrupted sleep
  ○ gjumë i rëndë sound sleep, slumber
  ○ gjumi sjell gjumin nothing is achieved by sloth
  ○ gjumë i shkurtër nap
  ○ gjumi i vdekjes unconscious state preceding death
  ○ [] zëntë gjumi i madh! *(Curse)* Death to []!

gjumëdhënës
  I § *adj* = ndjellës
  II § *nm* sleep-inducing drug: soporific

gjumëlehtë *adj* easily awakened from sleep: light-sleeping

gjumëlepur *adj* very light-sleeping; sleeping in fits and starts

gjumëmadh *adj* 1 = gjumash 2 *(Curse)* be damned! (to the sleep of the dead), I hope you go to sleep and never wake up!

gjumëndjellës *adj* sleep-inducing: soporific

gjumërëndë *adj* 1 difficult to awaken from sleep: heavy-sleeping 2 = gjumash

gjumës *nm* sleep-inducing drug: soporific

gjumësí *nf* 1 sleepiness, drowsiness 2 torpor, lethargy

gjumësjellës *adj* sleep-inducing: soporific

gjumëshumë *adj* = gjumash

gjumëtis·*et* *vpr* to doze off

gjumëz *nf* insect cocoon; silk cocoon

gjumëzí *adj, n (fem sg ˜ ez, masc pl ˜ inj, fem pl ˜ eza)* 1 unfortunate/unlucky (person) 2 *(Curse)* may he sleep the sleep of the dead!

gjumëtës *adj* inducing sleepiness: soporific, stultifying

gjumo·*n* *vi* to sleep

gjumth *nm* short sleep: nap, cat nap

gjumthe *np* = gjumth bunch of hardened cocoons of small dead insects which is hung around a child's neck as a charm to induce sleep

gjunjak *nm* white woolen leggings

gjunjar *nm* = gjunjak

gjunjas *OR* gjunjazi *adv* on one's knees, in kneeling position; on bended knee

gjunjë *np* <gju(r) knees, as symbolizing a person's strength to keep upright and to continue walking: strength in the legs

○ në/më gjunjë kneeling, on one's knees

gjunjëprerë *adj* lacking the strength to keep upright and to continue walking

gjunjëse *nf* 1 knee pad 2 *[Hist]* piece of armor protecting the knee: polayn

gjunjëz *nf[Bot]* joint-fir, ephedra *(Ephedra)*

gjunjëzím *nm ger* 1 <gjunjëzo·*n*, gjunjëzo·*het* 2 *(Fig)* submission

gjunjëzo·*het* *vpr* 1 to kneel, kneel down, fall to one's knees; genuflect 2 *(Fig)* to prostrate oneself, submit, bow down

gjunjëzo·*n* *vt* 1 to bring/force [] to []'s knees 2 *(Fig)* to subdue, defeat

gjunjëzore *np [Bot]* joint-pine family *Ephedraceae*

gjunjëzuar *adj (i)* kneeling, on one's knees

gjuras *stem for 1st sg pres, pl pres, 2nd & 3rd sg subj, pind* <gjurat·

gjurat· *vt* to glean

*gjurgjak *adj (Old)* cantankerous, testy

gjurjí *obl* <gju(r)

gjurmashkë *nf* heavy wool foot sock worn indoors over regular stockings

gjurmë *nf* 1 mark of an earlier presence: track, trail, spoor, scent; (foot)print, (wheel) rut; trace, sign; (archeological) vestige 2 = gjurmashkë 3 *(Old)* foot (as a unit of measurement)
  ○ gjurma-gjurmës in the very footsteps, close on the trail; following closely; following exactly the same path
  ○ gjurmë mushke *[Bot]* = gjurmëmushkë
  ○ gjurmë për gjurmë in the very footsteps, following closely, following the same path
  ○ gjurmë ujku buttercup, crowfoot *Ranunculus*

gjurmëlënës *adj, nm [Mil]* tracer (ammunition) *()*

gjurmëmushkë *nf [Bot]* coltsfoot *(Tussilago farfara)*

gjurmím *nm ger* <gjurmo·*n*

gjurmíme *np* <gjurmím scientific investigations: research

gjurmo·*n*
  I § *vt* 1 to track, track [] down, pursue 2 to spy on [] 3 *(Fig)* to investigate; do research on []
  II § *vi* to wander, walk
  ○ gjurmo·*n* qimen në vezë "look for the hair in an egg" to try to find fault, pick at details

gjurmues
  I § *adj* 1 *[Mil]* scouting, reconnaissance 2 *[Phys]* used for tracing: trace 3 *(Fig)* investigative 4 for research
  II § *n* 1 scout, tracker 2 investigator; researcher
  III § *nm [Phys]* trace element

gjurulldí *nf* hue and cry, clamor, din

*gjurunti *nf* = gjurulldí

*gjutí *nf* = gjuetí

*gjya *adv* = gjoja

gjybekë *np [Food]* small sweet pastry with an indentation or hole in the middle and scalded with sweet syrup

*gjybletë *nf* = xhubletë

gjyç *nm (Colloq)* 1 lump/knot in the throat 2 internal reluctance to do something: inhibition; bashfulness, hesitancy

gjyfqe·*het* *vpr* to get tired, get worn out by exertion

gjyfqe·*n* *vt* = gjyfqe·*het*

*gjyft = gjyfq

*gjyg OR gjygj = gjyk

*gjyk|ata'r n (Old) = gjykatës
  ◦ gjykatar hetues (Old) coroner
  ◦ gjyktar paktues (Old) justice of the peace

gjyk|ata'të nf 1 [Law] law court, tribunal 2 court building 3 (Colloq Old) misfortune, evil
  ◦ gjykatë e diktimit (Old) [Law] appeals court; appeals court office
  ◦ Gjykatë e Lartë [Law] Supreme Court
  ◦ gjykatë penale [Law] criminal court
  ◦ gjykatë popullore "people's court" [Law] trial court

gjyk|at|ës n judge

gjyk|ato're nf court building; court

*gjyk|bje'rr|ës n (Old) = gjyqbje'rrës

*gjyk|fit|o'nj|ës n (Old) = gjyqfito'njës

gjyk|i'm nm ger 1 <gjyko·n, gjyko·het 2 judgment; opinion; criticism 3 reasoning, logic 4 [Law] trial

*gjyk|i'mt|ë adj (i) reasonable, sensible

gjyk|o'·het vpr 1 (Colloq) to become a party in a legal dispute 2 (Old) to engage a clan elder to settle an argument 3 to be judged/evaluated

gjyk|o'·n
  I § vt 1 to judge; adjudge 2 [Law] to try [a case]; render [a judicial decision] 3 [Sport] to referee, serve as umpire for [ ]
  II § vi to deliberate, think, reason
  ◦ gjyko·n me mendje të vet to make up one's own mind, act according to one's own lights
  ◦ gjyko·n shkurt to make a ◇ hasty judgment

*gjyk|su'er OR gjyk|u'er adj (fem ˜ ore) (Old) juridical, judicial

gjyk|u'a'r n (i e) [Law] defendant in a criminal trial: the accused
  ◦ gjykuar në mungesë tried in absentia

gjyk|u'e's
  I § adj judicial
  II § n judge

gjyk|u'e|she'm adj (i) 1 judicious, prudent, rational, reasonable 2 juridical, judicial

gjyl|a'ç nm [Food] meringue

gjyl|a'p nm rose water

gjy'l|e nf 1 cannonball 2 (Colloq) artillery shell 3 [Sport] (shotputting) shot

gjylj|a'k nm attar of roses

*gjylmi'së'n nf twisted thong of wool used to attach moccasins

*gjylpân| nf (Reg Gheg) = gjilpërë

*gjylpân|kë nf dimin (Reg Gheg) little needle

gjym nm tall copper/aluminum ewer with a large curved handle
  ◦ gjym i shpuar useless piece of junk

*gjymbry'k nm (Old) = dogane

gjy'mër nf hoofbeat

*gjy'm|ës nf = gjysmë

*gjy'm|ët adj (i) impaired, damaged, defective

gjym|ë'tar nm (i) clan elder charged with assessing damages in disputes under traditional law

*gjym|i'm nm = gjëmim

gjymle'k nm 1 men's shirt made of cotton print fabric 2 women's blouse

*gjymna's = gjimnaz

*gjyms| = gjysm|

*gjyms|a|ha'në nm (Reg Gheg) = sembër

*gjyms|ata'r nf (Reg Gheg) = gjysmëhënë

*gjyms|a'te'rr nm dimness

gjyms|a|zo'g nm [Ornit] wren

*gjyms|përshku'e's adj semi-transparent

*gjy'mt|as adv defectively

gjy'mt|ë adj (i) 1 handicapped; crippled 2 [Ling] missing an expected part of a paradigm: defective

gjymt|i' nf 1 infirmity, handicap 2 crippling defect: maiming, amputation

gjymt|i'm nm ger 1 <gjymto·n, gjymto·het 2 crippling defect

gjymt|i's· vt (Reg) to annihilate [a clan or family] completely

gjymt|i's·et vpr (Reg) to die out/off

gjymt|o'·het vpr to become crippled/maimed; diminish

gjymt|o'·n vt 1 to mutilate/amputate [a limb]: maim 2 to cut/break off a part; mutilate

gjymt|u'a'r adj (i) 1 having a missing or seriously injured part: lame, crippled, maimed 2 damaged in appearance so as to look abnormal and ugly: mutilated, disfigured

gjymt|y'r|e nf 1 [Anat] human/animal limb 2 component part: component, constituent 3 [Anat] joint

gjymt|yr|o'r adj [Ling] constituent

gjym|y'sh nm embroidery thread made of gold/silver

gjyna'h
  I § nm 1 [Relig] sin 2 (Colloq) error, mistake; wrong; a terrible thing 3 (Colloq) pity, compassion; sorrow
  II § interj what a shame! what a pity! too bad!
  ◦ gjynah të qa·het it is a sin for one to complain (without a reason)

gjynah|qa'r
  I § n 1 [Relig] sinner 2 (Colloq) person to feel sorry for: poor guy, wretch
  II § adj sinful; sinning

*gjyp nm [Ornit] griffon vulture (Gyps fulvus Habl.)

*gjy'paj np [Ornit] (Accipitridae)

gjyq nm 1 trial; judicial process; litigation 2 law court, tribunal 3 (Colloq) meeting whose purpose is to clarify facts or to settle a dispute: parley 4 judgment, good sense, prudence
  ◦ gjyq i diktimit (Old) [Law] appeals court
  ◦ gjyqi i Linçit lynch justice
  ◦ Gjyq i Malit/Kanunit (Old) settlement of disputes according to the traditional law of the mountains
  ◦ gjyq para masave public trial before a mass audience
  ◦ gjyq shoqëror trial by one's peers, neighborhood trial

gjyq|bje'rr|ës n loser in a law case

gjyq|ë'so'r adj [Law] juridical, judicial, legal

gjyq|fit|o'nj|ës n winner in a law case

gjyq|ta'r n 1 [Law] judicial officer: magistrate 2 [Sport] referee, umpire
  ◦ gjyqtar anë'sor [Sport] linesman
  ◦ gjyqtar kryesor [Sport] head referee, chief umpire

gjyq|tar|i' nf collec 1 [Sport] sports referees/umpires as a whole 2 [Law] judicial body

*gjy'r|ë = ngjy'rë

*gjyr|ë|the'll|ë adj dark (in color) = ngjyrëthellë

*gjyr|ë|ze'z|ë nf = karabojë

*gjy'rm|ë nf = gju'rmë

gjyry'k
I § nm bellows (of a forge)
II § adv in a gust, bursting forth

gjyry'k·thi *adv* in a rush, quickly, hurriedly

gjyryllti = **gjurulldi**

*** gjys·a·gje'l** *nm* = **gjysmagje'l**

*** gjys·ata'r** *nm* half-caste

*** gjys·ë** *nf (Colloq)* = **gjys·ëm**

gjysleme' *nf [Food]* sweet pastry like baklava except with less dough

gjysly'kë *nf* = **gjyzly'kë**

gjysly'qe *np* = **gjyzly'kë**

*** gjysma·çe'rr** *nm [Ornit]* wren = **cinxami'**

gjysma·gje'l *nm [Folklore]* a half rooster-like figure in folktales thought to be very clever and capable

gjysma'k
I § adj **1** half missing, incomplete; halfway, partial **2** incompletely educated, half-trained, semiliterate **3** half-witted
II § nm [Hist] sharecropper who paid half his earnings to the owner of the land/livestock

gjysma'k·ësi' *nf* incompleteness

gjysma·me'nd·sh
I § adj half-witted
II § nm half-wit

gjysma·mi' *nm* **1** *[Ornit]* wren = **cinxami'** **2** *[Zool]* bat *(Chiroptera)*

gjysm·analfabe't *adj* **1** semiliterate **2** bungling, inept

gjysm·a·na'sh *adv* leaning to one side

gjysma'r *adj* half as much as expected/usual

gjysma·ra'k *adj (Pej)* half-grown, stunted

gjysma're *nf (Old)* **1** measure of weight for grain usually equal to twenty kilograms; container holding this much grain **2** container holding half a liter

gjysma·ta'r
I § nm [Hist] **1** poor farmer who takes turns with another farmer using a yoke of oxen to which each has contributed one ox (half a yoke) for plowing **2** *[Hist]* sharecropper who paid half his earnings to the owner of the land/livestock: métayer
II § adj on the métayage system, in métayage

gjysm·atari' *nf [Hist]* tenant farm

gjysm·automa't *adj, nm [Tech]* semi-automatic (device/machine/tool)

gjysm·azo'g *nm (np ˜gj)* = **cinxami'** *[Zool]* bat *(Chiroptera)*

gjysm·end·aca'k *adj* spending half the year settled down and the other half wandering from place to place: semi-nomadic

gjysm·err·ë·si'rë *nf* half-darkness; dimly lit place

gjys·më
I § nf **1** half **2** semi- **3** (of shoes) half-sole **4** *(Colloq)* low shoe (as opposed to boot/high-tops): shoe, low-tops **5** *(Old)* = **gjysma're** **6** *(Colloq)* rectangular kerchief worn on the head by women
II § adv **1** into two equal parts: in half **2** partly, partially; halfway, half
∘ **s'tho·të asnjë gjysmë fjale** "not say half a word" not say a single word
∘ **Gjysma e mijës (është) peseqind!** No sense worrying/thinking about it: whatever will be will be, things will happen in their own way
∘ **gjysmë njeriu** thin and feeble; demented/distraught/deranged

∘ **gjysma e së keqes** not all that bad, could be worse

gjys·më *formativ* semi-, hemi-, demi-, half-

*** gjysmë·automati'k** *adj* semiautomatic

gjysmë·bo'sht *nm* **1** *[Spec]* semi-axis *()* **2** *[Tech]* half-axle *()*

gjysmë·bujq·ë·so'r *adj* semi-agricultural

gjysmë·bu'rrë *nm* middle-aged man

gjysmë·di'të *nf* half of a day

gjysmë·dja'tht·as *adv* partly to/on the right, half right

gjysmë·do'r·ë'z *nf* mitten

gjysmë·drejtë'z *nf [Geom]* half-line *(GJ)*

gjysmë·err·ë·si'rë *nf* semidarkness

gjysmë·fabrika't *nm* semifinished product

gjysmë·fina'le *nf, adj [Sport]* semifinal

gjysmë·fje'tur *adv* half asleep

gjysmë·flatra·fo'rtë *np [Entom]* Hemiptera

gjysmë·flatro'rë *np [Entom]* = **gjysmëflatrafo'rtë**

gjysmë·fu'shë *nf [Sport]* half of a playing field; midfield

gjysmë·gja'llë *adj* barely alive

gjysmë·gjat'ë·si *nf* half-length

gjysmë·ha'pur *adv* half-open, ajar

gjysmë·ha'rk *nm* semicircle, half-circle

gjysmë·hë'në *nf* **1** half-moon **2** crescent **3** *[Spec]* tool with a semicircular shape

gjysmë·hi'je *nf* **1** penumbra **2** *[Cine]* half-shadow

gjysmë·ka'fshë *nf [Folklore]* creature with the body of an animal and the head of a man

gjysmë·ka'lë *nm* centaur

gjysmë·ki'l·ësh *adj* half a kilogram in weight or capacity

gjysmë·kodrin·o'r *adj* **1** having low hills **2** somewhat hilly

gjysmë·koloni' *nf* semicolony

gjysmë·lakuri'q *adj* half-naked, semi-nude

gjysmë·larg'ësi *nf [Sport]* half the distance

gjysmë·lart'ësi *nf* half the height

gjysmë·lë'msh *nm [Geog]* hemisphere = **gjysmërru·zull**

gjysmë·li'tër·sh *adj* half a liter in capacity

gjysmë·majt·as *adv* partly to/on the left, half left

gjysmë·mal·o'r *adj* **1** having low mountains **2** somewhat mountainous

gjysmë·mbrojt'ës *nm [Sport]* fullback (in soccer)

gjysmë·mbrojtje *nf [Sport]* secondary defense (in soccer)

gjysmë·me'tër·sh *adj* half a meter in length

gjysmë·mug·ë·ti'rë *nf* semi-twilight

gjysmë·nde'njur *adv* half standing, half lying-down: semierect

gjysmë·ndi'hm·ës *adj [Ling]* semi-auxiliary

gjysmë·njeri' *nm* weak, incompetent, and useless person

gjysmë·perëndi' *nf [Folklore]* demigod

gjysmë·pe'shk *nm [Folklore]* merman

gjysmë·përcje'll·ës *nm [Phys]* = **gjysmëpërçu·es**

gjysmë·përçu·e·s
I § nm [Phys] semiconductor
II § adj semiconductive

gjysm*ë*përku'lje *nf* bending over in less than a full bow: half bow, shallow bow; shallow bending of the knees: slight curtsy

gjysm*ë*përku'lur *adv* in a shallow bow; somewhat bent over

gjysm*ë*prole'ta'r
I § adj **1** working for wages having additional income from one's own small business: semi-proletarian **2** only partially proletarian in character
II § n wage-earner with a small business on the side

gjysm*ë*qa'rk *nm* [*Math*] semicircle ()

*****gjysm*ë*qa'rkull** *OR* **gjysmë'qe'rthull** *nm (Old)* = **gjysmëqa'rk**

gjysm*ë*rra'fsh *nm* [*Math*] half plane

gjysm*ë*rre'th *nm* [*Math*] semicircle

gjysm*ë*rro'g*ë* *nf* half-pay

gjysm*ë*rrotull*i*'m *nm* semirotation

gjysm*ë*rru'zull *nm (np ˜ j)* [*Geog*] hemisphere (of the earth)

gjysm*ë*sfe'r*ë* *nf* hemisphere

gjysm*ë*spaka't*ë* *nf* [*Gymnastics*] half-split position

gjysm*ë*sulmu'e's *nm* [*Sport*] inside forward (in soccer)

gjysm*ë*she'kull *nm (np ˜ j)* half century

gjysm*ë*shekull'o'r *adj* lasting or including a half century

gjysm*ë*shkëmb'o'r *adj* consisting largely of rock

gjysm*ë*shkret*ë*ti'r*ë* *nf* [*Geog*] semidesert

gjysm*ë*shku'rre *nf* [*Bot*] suffruticose plant: subshrub

gjysm*ë*shti'z*ë* *nf*

gjysm*ë*shtri'r*ë* *adv* half lying down

gjysm*ë*tru'p *adj* of the torso

gjysm*ë*thell'*ë*s*i*' *nf* [*Sport*] middle distance

gjysm*ë*vago'n *nm* [*Rr*] (railroad) gondola, open freight car

*****gjysm*ë*va'rr'ur** *adj (i)* at half mast

gjysm*ë*vde'kur *adj* half-dead, barely alive

gjysm*ë*vez'a'k *adj* [*Geom*] semioval ()

gjysm*ë*vi't *nm* half a year

gjysm*ë*zan'o're
I § nf [*Ling*] semivowel
II § adj semivocalic

gjysm*ë*zej'ta'r *adj* partially hand-crafted

gjysm*ë*zgj'u'a'r *adv* half awake

gjysm*ë*zyr'ta'r *adj* semiofficial

gjysm*i*'m *nm ger* = **përgjysmi'm**

gjysm*i*ndustria'l *adj* semi-industrial

gjysm*o*'·*het* *vpr* = **përgjysmo'·*het***

gjysm*o*'·*n* *vt* to halve = **përgjysmo'·*n***

gjysm*o*ka'r *nm* = **gjysmo'kësh**

gjysm*o*ka're *nf* measuring container with a capacity of about 700 grams

gjysm*o*'k'ës *nm* = **gjysmoka're**

gjysm*o*'ka'sh *adj* having a capacity of some 700 grams

gjysm*o*pi'ng*ë* *nf* poor person; person in suffering: wretch

gjysm*u*a'r *adj (i)* = **përgjysmu'ar**

gjysm*u*na'z*ë* *nf* **1** [*Tech*] tool or machine part with the shape of half a ring **2** anything with a semicircular shape

gjysm*u*shtar'a'k *adj* quasi-military; partly of military composition

*****gjys'o're** *nf* half-an-hour

gjysh *nm* **1** grandfather **2** *(Colloq)* honorific term for an elderly man **3** [*Relig*] religious head of an organization of Bektashi congregations
   ○ **gjysh pas gjyshi** generation after generation
   ○ **gjysh stërgjyshi/katragjyshi 1** generation after generation **2** since ancient times

*****gjysh'a'r** *adj* grandfatherly, grandmotherly

gjysha't*ë* *nf* [*Relig*] organization of Bektashi congregations; seat of such an organization

gjy'sh'e *nf* **1** grandmother **2** *(Colloq)* honorific term for an elderly woman

gjy'sh'ër *np* **1** < **gjysh 2** ancestors

gjysh'ër'i' *nf collec* **1** grandfathers taken as a whole; ancestors **2** [*Relig*] = **gjysha't*ë***

gjysh'ër'o'r *adj (Book)* **1** ancestral **2** [*Relig*] of or pertaining to organizations of Bektashi congregations or their heads

gjysh'stërgjy'sh *nm* ancestors of long ago, ancestors of eld, ancestors

*****gjyte't** = **qyte't**

gjytyry'm = **gjytyry'm**

gjytyry'm *adj, n (Colloq)* **1** (person) with paralyzed limbs: invalid **2** *(FigImpolite)* sluggish and clumsy: doltish

gjyve'ç *nm* **1** [*Food*] stew prepared in a deep earthenware pot **2** deep two-handled clay potcopper pan

gjyzly'k*ë* *np* eyeglasses, glasses, spectacles = **sy'ze**

Hh

over 'Their

h [*hë*] *nf* **1** the consonant letter "h" **2** the voiceless aspirate represented by the letter "h"

*ha *interj* = hë

ha. *abbrev* = hekta*r*

ha·

I § vt **1** to eat **2** to eat away [ ], eat away at [ ]: gnaw on [ ], nibble away at [ ]; erode; corrode **3** to bite **4** to mumble, mouth **5** to itch **6** to eat up [ ], spend, cost, waste **7** (in chess) to capture **8** (*Colloq*) to receive [a blow], get hit by [ ], suffer [ ] **9** (*Fig*) to bother [ ] very much **10** to be able to manage [ ]: stand/take, endure, accept; achieve **11** (*Fig*) to belie; take back, go back on **12** (*Fig*) to gobble up [ ] illicitly **13** (*Fig Colloq*) to understand, comprehend **14** (*Fig Colloq*) to be up to taking on [ ], be able to confront [ ] **15** (*Fig Colloq*) to pass/spend [a difficult time]

II § vi **1** to have a meal, take nourishment: eat, feed oneself **2** (*Fig*) to lean

○ **e ha·** to get it in the neck
○ [ ] **ha·**^{3sg} **ana (me** [ ]**)** to be biased (in favor of [ ])
○ [ ] **ha·**^{3sg} **ana** [ ] *leans badly*
○ **nuk ha· arsye** not listen to reason
○ **<> ha· arrat** "eat <>'s walnuts" {} can run rings around <>
○ **s'e ha· atë kokërr ulliri** "know better than to eat that olive pit" not be so easily cheated, not be taken in by that
○ **nuk i ha· ato gorrica/vadhëza/kumbulla** not be so easily fooled/cheated, not be taken in by that: not swallow that
○ **ha· baltë 1** to suffer a great deal **2** (*Impol*) {} bites the dust, {} buys the farm, {} dies
○ **nuk ha· bar** not be easily cheated, not be so stupid
○ **e ha·**^{past} **barin 1** (*Colloq*) to be over the hill; {}'s time is past **2** {} got it in the neck
○ **e ha· barin pa shkop** (*Pej*) to get to do whatever one damn pleases
○ **s'e ha·**^{3sg} **barku për** [ ] (*Scorn*) not give a damn about [ ]
○ **e ha· barutin me grushte** "eat gunpowder by the fistful" to be very courageous
○ **s'ha· bodec 1** {} *does not need goading/reminding* **2** {} *is* not responsive to goading/reminders
○ **<> ha·**^{3pl} **brirët** <> *is asking/looking* for trouble
○ **ha· bukë e mjaltë me** [ ] "eat bread and honey with [ ]" to get along very well with [ ]
○ **ha· bukë 1** to have/eat a meal **2** to earn a living **3** to be of use **4** (*Crude*) to have a job
○ **nuk ha bukë ky zanat** "this profession doesn't provide a living" this profession doesn't do you much good; this profession doesn't put food on the table
○ **ha· bukë me grushte barkut** to gulp down food
○ **ha· bukë veç/veçan të tjerëve** to have no peers
○ **e ha· bukën kot** not deserve what one gets, not get it by the sweat of one's own brow
○ **<>a ha· bukën** to take what rightfully belongs to <>
○ **ha· bukën e përmbys kupën.** "{} *eats* the food and *overturns* the bowl" to *show* one's ingratitude

by doing harm to one's benefactor: bite the hand that feeds you
○ **<> ha bukën gomari** "even the donkey steals (eats) <>'s bread" (*Impol*) to be very slow and lazy
○ **e ha· bukën me lot** to live a miserable life
○ **ha· buzët me dhëmbë** to bite one's tongue, regret what one has said/done
○ **e ha·**^{past} **çairin 1** (*Colloq*) to be over the hill; {}'s time is past **2** {} got it in the neck
○ **ha· çallëza** to gulp
○ **ha· çelikun me dhëmbë 1** to be very brave; be able to do anything **2** to grit one's teeth with anger, be unable to contain one's anger
○ **<> ha· djersën** to live at <>'s expense, live off of <>: live by the sweat of <>'s brow
○ **<> ha·**^{3sg} **dora** "<>'s hand *is itching*" <> *is getting* ready to hit someone
○ **ha· dru** to get a heavy beating; be severely reprimanded; suffer a serious defeat
○ **ha· duart me dhëmbë 1** to give one's all (in order to achieve something) **2** to be angry with oneself
○ **ha· dynjanë** to suffer great hardship
○ **ha· dhé(në)** (*Scorn*) {} bites the dust, {} buys the farm, {} dies
○ **<> ha·**^{3pl} **dhëmbët** <>'s teeth are itching, <> is very eager
○ **ha· egjër** to be reduced to eating sawdust, be very poor
○ **ha· fjalën** "eat one's word" to go back on one's word
○ **ha· fjalët** "eat words" to mince words
○ **e ha· grurin që në arë** "eat grain right in the field" to be unable to wait to spend money, be a spendthrift
○ **ha· grushta** to receive blows, be beaten
○ **ha· gur e dru** to take an oath: swear
○ **s'**[ ] **ha guri i mullirit** [ ] is very hard, [ ] is difficult to penetrate
○ **ha· gurin me dhëmbë 1** to be very brave; be able to do anything **2** to grit one's teeth with anger, be unable to contain one's anger
○ [ ] **ha·**^{3sg} **gjarpri me dy koka** terrible misfortune *befalls* [ ]
○ **<> ha·**^{3sg} **gjetkë** <> *suspects* something else; something else worries <>
○ **<> ha·**^{3sg} **gjuha** "<>'s tongue itches" <> cannot keep from talking, <> *talks* too much
○ **ha· gjuhën 1** to bite one's tongue: keep silent; be sorry for what one has said **2** (*Contempt*) to kick the bucket, die
○ **ha· gjysmën e lekut** (*Scorn*) to eat lead, get shot dead
○ **<>a ha· hakun** not give <> what <> deserves
○ **ha· hekurin me dhëmbë 1** to be very brave; be able to do anything **2** to grit one's teeth with anger, be unable to contain one's anger

○ <>*a* ha· **hijen** "eat <>'s shadow" to wipe <> out, do <> in

○ <> ha·^{3pl} **hundët** "<>'s nostrils *itch*" <> *is asking/looking* for trouble

○ ha· **inat (me []**) to make a challenge (against [])

○ ha· **inat** to put one's foot down, insist

○ **nuk** ha· **kashtë** not be easily cheated, not be so stupid

○ ha· **këmbët e** {*pronominal adjective*} "bite one's feet" to gnash one's teeth (in agony)

○ **nuk e** ha· **kilën për okë** "not buy a kilo at the price of an oke" not be gullible, be no fool

○ <> ha· **kohën** to waste/take <>'s time

○ <> ha·^{3sg} **koka (për brirë)** "<>'s head itches (for horns)" <> *is asking/looking* for trouble

○ <>*a* ha· **kokën** (*Fig*) to bring <> to <>'s death, cause <>'s death, kill <>

○ <>*a* ha· **kokën me të keq/egër** to change <>'s mind by force

○ <>*a* ha· **kokën me të mirë/butë** to change <>'s mind by softening <> up

○ <> ha· **kokërdhokun (e syrit)** to pester <> constantly (until one gets what one wants)

○ ha· **kopaçe** to get a heavy beating; be severely reprimanded; suffer a serious defeat

○ [] ha·^{3sg} **krimbi** something *keeps* eating/gnawing at []

○ <>*a* ha· **kryet** (*Fig*) to bring <> to <>'s death, cause <>'s death, kill <>

○ <> ha·^{3sg} **kurrizi** "<>'s back *itches*" <> *is asking/looking* for trouble

○ **s'ha· kuvend** {} won't listen to reason

○ ha· **lak e lëmsh** to eat in haste

○ **Ha lesh, pi lesh, vish lesh, vdes tu qesh** "Eat wool, drink wool, dress wool, and die laughing." (*Prov*) Eat mutton, drink ewe's milk, wear wool, and you will die happy.

○ <> ha·^{3sg} **lëkura** <> *is asking/looking* for trouble

○ **e** ha·^{past} **livadhin** *1 (Colloq)* to be over the hill; {}'s time is past **2** {} got it in the neck

○ <> ha **macja bukën në dorë** "even the cat steals food out of <>'s hand" (*Impol*) <> is too inept to prevent others from taking the food right out of <>'s mouth: <> always lets others get the better of <>

○ **S'i ha macja cironkat!?** "Does a cat not eat fish!?" (*Iron*) Are you kidding!? Do you expect me to believe that!?

○ ha· **majë me majë** to eat just a little bit of each dish

○ **s'**[] ha·^{3sg} **malli** (*Irony*) [] should worry?! why should [] worry?

○ ha· **me dy gryka** to eat/drink a great deal

○ **e** ha· **me dhëmbë** to be confident of one's ability to handle something difficult

○ [] ha· **me gjithë pupla** "eat [] feathers and all" to defeat [] utterly, overwhelm []

○ ha· **me lugë të florinjtë** "eat with a golden spoon" to be very rich

○ <> ha· **me sy 1** to stare at <> greedily **2** to put the evil eye on <>

○ [] ha· **me të butë/mirë** (*Fig*) to soft-soap [a person], use cajolery on [a person]

○ ha· **me zgrip** to be very thrifty in spending

○ ha· **me gjysmë luge** "eat with half a spoon" (*Iron*) to be nothing but a bag of bones, be practically dead

○ [] ha· **me limë** to use a file on [], file []

○ <>*a* ha· **mendja** to be confidant of one's ability

○ <> ha·^{3sg} **mendja për** [] <> *is* suspicious of/ about [], have doubts about []

○ <>*a* ha·^{3sg} **mendja se** __ <> *believes/thinks* that __, <> *gets* the feeling that __, it *looks* to <> like __

○ [] ha·^{3sg} **meraku** "worry *eats* []" [] *is* really worried/concerned

○ <> ha· **mëlçinë** "eat <>'s liver" to pester <> beyond all endurance, pester <> constantly: drive <> up the wall

○ <>*i* ha· **mushkëritë** to cause <> a lot of suffering, cause <> nothing but grief

○ [] ha· **në besë** to break one's word to []; betray []'s trust

○ [] ha· **në kob** to betray [someone]

○ ha· **në një çanak me** [] "eat at the same trough with []" (*Pej*) to share []'s evil objectives and interests, be in on it together with []; act in collusion with []

○ ha· **në një sofër me** [] to share common interests and goals with []

○ ha· **nga dhjami i** {*pronominal adj*} to live off {*one's*} savings

○ **nuk** [] ha· [a large task] *is* too much for {}

○ ha· **një çapë bukë** to have a bite to eat, eat something

○ ha· **një dru të shëndoshë** to get badly beaten up; get lambasted

○ ha· **një dush** (*Colloq*) to be rebuked, get told off, really get it

○ ha· **një shi të mirë** to get a good soaking from the rain

○ ha· **një tepsi të tërë** "eat a whole trayful" to eat a lot

○ <>*a* ha· **palcën** to work <*a person*> to the bone

○ **nuk** <> ha·^{3sg} **palla** <> *is* callous

○ <> ha· **para** to cost <> money

○ ha· **paratë** (*Colloq*) to spend/waste money

○ ha· **pare** to take bribes

○ **s'**[] ha·^{3sg} **pazari** [] *is not going* to be accepted in the marketplace: [] *is not going* to go over, [] *will not* sell

○ <> ha· **përsheshin macja** <> *is* so sluggish/ slothful ("that the cat eats <>'s porridge")

○ **e** ha· **plumbin** (*Colloq*) to get shot: get a taste of lead, eat lead

○ **e** ha· **preshin nga bishti** to start from the wrong end; put the cart before the horse

○ <> ha·^{3sg} **pula qurrat** "the chicken *eats* <>'s snot" (*Impol*) <> *is* a totally incapable person

○ **s'**<>*i* ha·^{3sg} **pulat dhelpra** "the fox *does not eat* <>'s chicken" <> *is* nobody's fool, no one *puts* anything over on <>

○ **s'ha· pulë të ngordhur** to be no fool, not be gullible

○ [] ha· **pushka** [] *is* within rifle range

○ **nuk** ha· **pykë** not accept advice/criticism

○ <> ha·^{3sg} **qafa për këmborë (dashi)** "<>'s neck itches for a (ram's) bell" <> *is* just itching/ asking for trouble

○ <> ha· **qafa për këmborë** <> *is asking/looking* for trouble

○ **nuk** [] ha·^{3sg} **qederi** [] doesn't give a damn

○ ha· **qen e shpend** "eat dog and fowl" to (be willing to) eat anything

○ **s'ia ha qeni shkopin** "a dog does not bite the stick" {} *is* very shrewd

○ <> ha·^{3sg} rruaza 1 <> *is looking* for trouble
2 <>'s back *itches*

○ ha· sa <> del· *nga hundët/për hundësh* to eat so much it *is coming* out of <>'s ears ("nose")

○ e ha· sapunin për djathë "eat soap as cheese" to foolishly trade something of value for something worthless

○ ha· sedër (me [ ]) to make a challenge (against [ ])

○ ha· si çerr to eat like a bird, eat very little

○ ha· si kaçi to eat like a horse, eat insatiably

○ ha· si kone to eat very little

○ ha· si lugat to eat like a monster, be gluttonous

○ <>a ha·^{3sg} syri <> *thinks* <> can manage/handle/ do it

○ <>[] ha·^{3sg} syri në qime <> *has* a good view of [ ] for shooting, <> *has* a good shot at [ ]

○ e ha· shapin për sheqer "eat/accept alum as sugar" to trade something of value foolishly for something worthless

○ ha·^{3sg} sharra "<>'s saw *is biting*" things *are going* very well for <>

○ ha· shenjtërisht "eat like a saint" *(Iron)* to eat/ drink well

○ <> ha·^{3sg} shpina "<>'s back *itches*" <> *is asking/looking* for trouble

○ <> ha· shpirtin 1 to break <>'s heart, sadden <> deeply; cause <> great suffering 2 to bring <> to the end of <>'s patience

○ <>a ha· shpirtin me të keq/egër to change <>'s mind by force

○ <>a ha· shpirtin me të mirë/butë to change <>'s mind by softening <> up

○ ha· shqip to understand clearly

○ nuk ha· shqip not understand simple Albanian: not listen to reason, not obey

○ ha· shtatin to walk backwards in a bowed position

○ I ha shyta e i nxjerr me brirë. "One eats them without horns and brings them out with horns." One believes lies and even embellishes them in repeating them to others.

○ nuk ha· të gdhendur not accept advice/criticism, be incorrigible

○ e ha· të gjallë to be confident of one's ability to handle something difficult

○ [ ] ha· të gjallë to make [ ] suffer, cause [ ] a lot of trouble

○ ha· të hequr (of a task) to be long and drawn out, take a long time

○ ha· të shara to be scolded

○ ha· tokën me dhëmbë to be about to explode with anger

○ e ha· turpin me bukë "eat shame with one's bread" 1 to eat crow 2 to be shameless

○ nuk e ha· thatë 1 not be easily cheated, not be taken in readily: be no chump, be nobody's fool 2 to be as good as anyone, do as well as anyone

○ ha· thikën to be stabbed by a knife; undergo surgery

○ ha· urov to suffer through a difficult time, undergo great hardship

○ <> ha·^{3sg} vendi <> *can't* sit still, <> *is* restless

○ <> ha· veshët to pester <> for something by incessant talk; chew <>'s ears off, talk <>'s head off

○ ha· veten me dhëmbë 1 to give one's all (in order to achieve something) 2 to be angry with oneself

○ ha· veten nën lëkurë to be eating oneself up inside

○ i ha· vitet "eat the years" to claim to be younger than one is

○ <> ha·^{3sg} zemra <> *has* a gnawing suspicion

○ s'<>a ha·^{3sg} zemra <> *doesn't* want to believe it

○ <>a ha· zemrën 1 to pester <>; wear <> out by pestering 2 to win <>'s heart; win <> over; gain <>'s favor

○ <> ha· zorrët "eat <>'s guts" to drive <> nuts, become unbearable to <>

○ <> ha·^{3pl} zorrët për [ ] <> cannot stand [ ], [ ] *drives* <> nuts

ha·*het vpr* <ha· 1 to be edible/eatable 2 *(Fig)* to be agreeable 3 to become worn/eaten away gradually; get smaller and smaller little by little 4 *(Fig)* to contend/compete with; confront 5 to quarrel; argue

○ <> ha·*het*^{3sg} 1 <> feels like eating, <> is hungry 2 it tastes to <>

○ nuk ha·*het*^{3sg} has no taste

○ s'<> ha·*het*^{3sg} arra në dorë "one wouldn't eat a walnut from <>'s hand" <> is slovenly and unclean

○ nuk ha·*het*^{3sg} as me limon "be inedible even with lemon" to be so annoying as to be unbearable

○ s'ha·*het*^{3sg} as me vaj, as me uthull "not be edible neither with oil, nor with vinegar" to be completely unendurable/unacceptable

○ nuk <> ha·*het*^{3sg} buka me [ ] to be on bad terms with [ ]

○ s'<> ha·*het*^{3sg} goja <> *doesn't* hesitate to talk, <> *doesn't* mind talking

○ ha·*het* hëna the moon wanes

○ <> ha·*het*^{3pl} hundët <> *is itching* for a fight

○ s'<> ha·*het*^{3pl} këmbët <> *doesn't* mind the walk

○ ha·*het* me dhëmbë to quarrel severely

○ ha·*het* me fjalë "eat one another with words" to bandy words, have an argument

○ ha·*het* me veten (e vet) to struggle with *one*self; struggle (mentally)

○ <> ha·*het*^{3pl} mendtë (ndër vete) 1 to beat one's brains out thinking 2 to go back and forth in one's mind

○ <> ha*h*et muhabeti me [ ] <> likes talking with [ ]

○ ha·*het* në pazar to haggle/quarrel about price

○ ha·*het*^{3pl} si merimangat në qyp "argue like the spiders in a storage pot" to keep bickering

haber *nm (Colloq)* information; news, report

○ s'ka· haber nga { } not be well informed about { }

○ s'ka· haber për [ ] not be well informed about [ ]

○ s'merr· haber not get the point

haberd[i]s· *vt (Old)* to inform

haberma[d]h *adj (Colloq Pej)* spreading the news around, blabbermouth

haber[t]a[r]
  I § *nm (Old)* bringer of news: herald
  II § *adj* 1 *(Colloq)* signalling 2 *(Old)* bringing news: heralding

haber[z]i *adj, n (fem sg ˜ez, masc pl ˜inj, fem pl ˜eza)* *(Colloq)* (one) whose death has just been announced

*Habe[sh] *nm (Old)* Abyssinia = Abisin[i]

hab[i] *nf* surprise, wonder, amazement, astonishment

*habi[dër]sh*ë*m *adj (i)* = habi[ts]h*ë*m

*habin[o]·n *vt* to curse

hab|**is** _stem for 1st sg pres, pl pres, 2nd & 3rd sg subj, pind_ <**habit**•

habit• _vt_ **1** to instill wonder in [ ], cause an unexpected or incredulous reaction from [ ]: surprise, amaze **2** to bewilder, dumbfound, stupefy; confuse; astonish, astound

habit•_et vpr_ **1** to be surprised, be amazed; find it odd, wonder about, be dubious **2** to be bewildered/dumbfounded/stupefied; be confused

habit|**ës** _adj_ surprising, distracting

habit|**je** _nf ger_ <**habit**•, **habit**•_et_

habit|**ore**
  _I §_ _adj_ [_Ling_] expressing a fact contrary to expectation: admirative
  _II §_ _nf_ [_Ling_] admirative mood

habit|**shëm**
  _I §_ _adj_ (i) **1** surprising, amazing; astonishing, astounding; marvelous, wonderful; extraordinary **2** strange, abnormal **3** (_Colloq_) easy to confuse/bewilder
  _II §_ _adv_ in a surprised manner: with surprise; in bewilderment

habit|**ur** _adj (i)_ **1** surprised, amazed; bewildered **2** expressive of surprise/bewilderment

***haçidhe** _nf_ kind of disease

hadëm _nm_ eunuch

***hadh** _nm (Old)_ Hades, hell

***hale** _nf_ food

***hales** _adj_ edible

hafëz _nm_ hafiz

hafif _adj (Old)_ **1** (of a face or body) thin and drawn **2** light in weight **3** (of food) easy to digest: light **4** delicate; exquisite **5** (_Fig_) simple-minded, stupid

hafije _nf_ **1** (_Old_) spy = **spiun 2** (_Colloq HistPK_) (secret) agent in the Ministry of Internal Affairs

Hagë _nf_ the Hague

***hagrep** _nm_ (_Reg Gheg_) = **agrep**

ha-ha-ha! _interj_ expresses laughter: ha ha!

***haham** _nm (Reg Old)_ rabbi

haharis• _vi_ = **haharis**•_et_

haharis•_et vpr_ to roar with laughter

***hahas** _stem for 1st sg pres, pl pres, 2nd & 3rd sg subj, pind_ <**hahat**•

***hahat**• _vi_ to chuckle, laugh

hahat•_et vpr_ **1** to stand open-mouthed in astonishment **2** to laugh

***hain** _nm_ = **hajn**

hair _nm_ (_Colloq_) success (in life); gain, benefit, profit; value, utility, use
  ○ **hair qoftë!** I hope it's good news!; I hope so!

hairtë _adj (i)_ (_Colloq_) **1** causing happiness and success **2** of benefit, beneficial

haj _interj_ (_Colloq_) expresses sadness or suffering
  ○ **haj __ haj** either __ or

hajat _nm_ **1** porch; vestibule; entrance hall **2** (_Colloq_) ground-floor stable **3** shed for farm tools/implements **4** (_Old Fig_) = **limer**
  ○ **Të zënçin hajat!** (_Curse_) Damn you!

hajde
  _I §_ _hortative_ (_Colloq_) **1** come! **2** come on! come along! hey! let's go!
  _II §_ _interj_ **1** used to enhance an emotional expression by calling attention to it: hey now! **2** precedes a suggestion in order to dismiss a possible difficulty or objection: how could you even think of __?

○ **hajde** {_noun_}, **hajde!** (expressing great admiration) that's some {}! what a {}!
  ● **Hajde baba të të tregoj arat/vreshtin** "Come along, father, so I will show you the fields/vineyards" (_Iron_) Look who's trying to tell who!
  ○ **hajde de!** (_Crude_) (in exasperation) come on, now! right now!
  ○ **hajde mendje, hajde!** (_Impol Iron_) that's some mind (you have)!

hajde|**ni** _pl_ <**hajde**

***hajdu**|**çe** _adv_ like a thief: furtively, stealthily

***hajduk** _nm_ = **hajdut**

hajdut _n_ (_Colloq_) **1** person who steals: thief, robber, pickpocket, burglar **2** renegade outlaw, mountain brigand = **kaçak**
  ○ **hajdut dyqanesh** shoplifter
  ● **Gjeti hajduti thesin.** "The thief found the sack." (_Prov Pej_) The devil has found his mate.
  ○ **hajdut me damkë/çizme/doreza/dorashka** professional thief
  ● **U poq hajduti me thesin.** "The thief met up with the sack." "The thief met up with the sack." (_Prov Pej_) The devil has found his mate.
  ○ **hajdut xhepash** pickpocket

hajdut|**çe**
  _I §_ _adv_ (_Colloq_) = **hajdutërisht**
  _II §_ _adj_ = **kaçakçe**

hajdut|**ëri** _nf collec_ **1** thieves/outlaws taken as a whole **2** thievery, brigandage

hajdut|**ërisht** _adv_ like a thief: stealthily

hajdut|**kë** _nf_ <**hajdut**

haje _nf_ food provisions; feed, fodder

haje|**keq** _adj_ = **ngrënëkeq**

hajë _nf_ = **haje**

hajger _adj_ = **hamshor**

***hajhuj** _adj, nm (Old)_ vagrant, homeless (person)

***hajin** = **hajn**

***hajlar** _nm_ brawler, bully

hajmali _nf_ (_Old_) talisman, amulet, charm

hajmedet _interj_ expresses deep suffering, sadness, sorrow, or fear: woe is me!

hajmë _adj (i)_ = **hajthëm**

hajn _nm_ (_Reg_) thief, crook, scoundrel

hajni _nm_ (_Reg_) = **hajdutëri**

hajnisht _adv_ (_Reg_) = **hajdutërisht**

hajno•_n vt_ to rob

hajnjeri _nm_ [_Folklore_] man-eating cyclops

***hajr** = **hair**

***hajshëm** _adj (i)_ edible

hajt _interj_ (_Colloq_) = **hajde**

hajth•_et vpr_ to become lean/thin

hajth|**ëm** _adj (i)_ thin, lean, skinny; frail; willowy, lithe, graceful

hajthm|**ëri** _nf_ frailty; skinniness; willowiness

hajujk _nm_ (_Euph_) devil: fiend, evil one

hajvan
  _I §_ _nm_ (_Colloq_) **1** domestic animal; beast of burden **2** amount that can be carried by a beast of burden: oxload, load **3** (_Fig Crude Insult_) dummox, dumb ox, stupid/dumb ass, jackass
  _II §_ _adj_ (_Crude_) stupid, dumb

hajvan|**çe** _adv_ (_Crude_) in the manner of a dumb beast: like a dumb ox

hak *nm (np ˜ qe) (Colloq)* **1** revenge **2** payment for work done: earnings, reward **3** what one has coming, what is deserved: just deserts
  ◦ **hak për hak** credit for work done

****haka′s** *stem for 1st sg pres, pl pres, 2nd & 3rd sg subj, pind* <**haka′t·**

****haka′t·** *vi* = hakat·*et*

haka′t·*et vpr (Colloq)* to try hard, make every effort: strive, toil

hak̇çe *adv (Colloq)* rightfully, by right, just as it should be, truly

ha′kë *nf (Colloq)* = hak

hakërr′e·*het vpr* = hakërro′·het

hakërr′i *nf* **1** sexual excitement (in pigs), lust **2** = hakërrimë *****3** declivity, slope

hakërr′im *nm ger* **1** <hakërro′·het **2** = hakërrimë

hakërr′imë *nf* **1** ferocious and menacing voice/tone: snarl, threat, scowl, menacing glare **2** ferociousness; defiant challenge

hakërr′izë *nf* = hakërri

hakërro′·*het vpr* **1** to make a menacing roar; scold ferociously; become ferocious **2** to show off, strut **3** (of a sow) to be mounted by a boar

hakërro′·*n vt* to provoke [] to anger: rile

hakërru′a⃒r *adj (i)* **1** enraged, ferocious **2** lustful

hakërru′es *adj* menacing, threatening

Haki′ *nm* Haki (male name)

hakika′t *nm (Old)* certainty, certitude

hakma′rr *stem for opt, adm, part* <hakmerr·*et*

hakma′rrë *adj* **1** retaliatory **2** avenging a blood wrong; in vengeance **3** vengeful, vindictive

hakma′rrje *nf* **1** retaliation **2** vengeance for a blood wrong; vengeance **3** vindictiveness, spite

hakme′rr·*et vpr* **1** to retaliate **2** to take vengeance for a blood wrong; take revenge, avenge oneself

hakmi′rr *stem for pind* <hakmerr·*et*

hakmo′r *stem for pdef* <hakmerr·*et*

hakmua′r *pl pdef* <hakmerr·*et*

hako′·*n vt (Old)* to agree on the price for work to be done; pay for work done

hako′ç *nm* boar = harç

hala′ *adv (Colloq)* yet, still

halaru′c *nm* = halës

****halbaro′·***n vt* **1** to invigorate **2** to abound

hale′ *nf (Colloq)* **1** place for urination and defecation, toilet: privy, john **2** despicable/dirty person

ha′lë
  I § *nf* **1** fishbone **2** beard of grain: awn **3** leaf of a conifer: needle **4** [*Bot*] Austrian pine, black pine *(Pinus nigra)* **5** pointed tip
  II § *adj* having a pointed tip: sharp
  ◦ **<>u bëftë halë në grykë!** *(Curse)* May <> get a fishbone stuck in <>'s throat!
  ◦ **hal̇ë breshkëz** mouse barley *Hordeum murinum*
  ◦ **halë në sy** speck in the eye

halë′ba′rdhë *adj* (a variety of wheat) with a white awn: white-bearded

halë′ku′q *adj* (a variety of wheat) with a red awn: red-bearded

ha′lës *nm* fish with many small bones: bony fish

ha′lëz *nf* [*Bot*] **1** Austrian pine, black pine *(Pinus nigra)* **2** herbaceous poisonous weed that grows in moist ground, has green or reddish spikes and a stem that is rough on top *****3** speck, mote

halë′zi′ *adj, n* (variety of wheat/rice) with a white awn: white-bearded (wheat/rice)

halë′zi′m *nm ger* <halëzo′·n

halë′zo′·*n vi* to sprout awns

halë′zu′a⃒r *adj (i)* (of grain) with many awns, profusely bearded; whose beards have formed

hali′ç *nm* pebble, small rock; gravel

hali′çë *np* <hali′ç discards: rubbish, trash

halije′r
  I § *nm (Old)* **1** public land, common ground: commons **2** unowned property
  II § *adj* abandoned

Hali′l *nm* Halil (male name)

****halino′s·***et vpr* **1** to decay, rot **2** to faint, swoon = alivano′s·*et*

****halino′sje** *nf ger* <halino′s·, halino′s·*et*

hali′q *nm* = haliç

hali′qshëm *adj (i)* skinny, scrawny, lean

hali′shtë *nf* pine forest = pishnajë

Hali′t *nm* Halit (male name)

****halivano′s·***et vpr* to be dumbfounded/bewildered

halmu′cë *nf* [*Bot*] German clover *(Dorycnium germanicum)*

halogje′n *nm* [*Chem*] halogen

halo′r
  I § *adj* **1** needle-like, like fishbones **2** [*Bot*] of or pertaining to evergreen conifers: coniferous **3** [*Text*] bristle-like
  II § *nm* evergreen conifer tree

halo′rë *np* [*Bot*] evergreen conifer trees having needlelike leaves *Coniferae*

****halqidho′n** *nm (Old)* chalcedony = kalcedo′n

hal′th *nm* [*Bot*] **1** needle (of an evergreen conifer): aciculum *()* **2** *(Reg)* = halmu′cë

halucinacio′n *nm* hallucination

haluri′në *nf* **1** fishbone, bristle; bunch of bristles **2** *(Impol)* fish with a lot of bones **3** *(Colloq)* needle-bearing tree: evergreen conifer
  ◦ **halurinat e degëve** kindling, firewood

halveti′ *nm* [*Relig*] Moslem hermetic sect; Moslem hermit

hall *nm (Colloq)* **1** predicament, plight: bad trouble, tough situation **2** troublesome thing: problem, trouble, worry **3** solution for a problem, way out of a difficult situation
  ◦ **ësh·të³ˢᵍ halli që/se** __ the point/problem *is* that __, what should really be of concern *is* __
  ◦ **hall __ hall** in trouble whether __ or __
  ◦ **hall me buaj, hall me qe** damned if you do, damned if you don't; it's bad either way

halladi′s *stem for 1st sg pres, 1st & 3rd pl pres, 2nd & 3rd sg subj, pind* <halladi′t·

halladi′t· *vt* to fan, cool, refresh

halladi′tshëm *adj (i)* refreshing

hallagre′p *adv (Reg)* without much thought: off the wall, just to be doing something; at random, haphazardly, disordered

hallajkë *nf (Colloq)* female servant

hallaka′s *stem for 1st sg pres, 1st & 3rd pl pres, 2nd & 3rd sg subj, pind* <hallaka′t·

hallaka′t· *vt* **1** to scatter, disperse; strew, spread, broadcast [seed] **2** to mess [] up **3** to give [] the runaround

○ **<> hallakat· brinjët** to beat <> so badly that <>'s ribs are broken, bust <>'s ribs

hallakat·*et* *vpr* **1** to get scattered, be dispersed; get around, get all over the place **2** to wander around **3** to get messed up **4** to be given the runaround

hallakat·ës *adj* **1** *(Fig)* inattentive, absent-minded, distracted **2** destructive

hallakat·je *nf ger* **1** < **hallaka***t*·, **hallakat·***et* **2** incoherence

hallaka·tur *adj (i)* **1** scattered, dispersed **2** open and exposed, open and discovered **3** *(Fig)* inattentive, absent-minded, distracted

halla·ll
I § *nm (Colloq)* **1** that which is deserved, something that is one's right: just reward, right **2** decent person
II § *adj* decent

hallall·o·*het* *vpr (Colloq)* to beg apology when leaving; take one's final leave

hallall·o·*n* *vt (Colloq)* to forgive

hallall·o·s· *vt* = **hallall·o·***n*

hallall·o·s·*et* *vpr* = **hallall·o·***het*

hallashti·s· *vt (Colloq)* = **hallall·o·***n*

hallashti·s·*et* *vpr (Colloq)* t = **hallall·o·***het*

halla·t *nm (Colloq)* implement, tool, equipment

hall|**avi·s** *stem for 1st sg pres, pl pres, 2nd & 3rd sg subj, pind* < **hallavi·t·**

hallavi·t· *vt* to give [ ] pleasure: entertain

hallavi·t·*et* *vpr* to spend time in casual pleasure

halldu·p *nm* **1** *(Contempt Old)* Turk, dirty Turk; Ottoman lackey **2** *(Insult)* crude or stupid person, barbarian; bad person

halldu·p|**çe**
I § *adv, adj (ColloqImpolite)* in the language/manner of the Ottoman occupiers: Turkish
II § *adv (Fig Pej)* without thinking; like an idiot

halldup|**ëri** *nf collec (Old)* Ottoman occupiers taken as a whole: Ottoman occupation; Ottoman lackey

hall·e·ma·dh *adj* **1** *(Colloq)* beset by many troubles: trouble-laden **2** having suffered much: miserable, wretched

*halle**sti·s·** *vi* to be in pain: suffer

hall|**e·shu·më** *adj (Colloq)* = **hallema·dh**

hall|**exhe·shë** *nf female (Colloq)* < **hallexhi**

hall|**exhi** *nm (np ~ nj) (Colloq)* person with serious troubles: poor guy, hapless wretch

hall|**e·zi** *adj, n (fem sg ~ ez, masc pl ~ inj, fem pl ~ eza) (Colloq)* (person) beset by many troubles, (one) with big problems = **hallema·dh**

hall·ë *nf* **1** father's sister: aunt *(sister of collateral male relative in patriline ascending from father's sister)* **2** auntie (term of respect for addressing an older woman) **3** *(Reg)* wife of mother's brother or of father's brother: aunt

○ **Halla di të bëjë byrek, po i mungon mielli.** "The aunt knows how to make byrek, but lacks the flour." *(Prov)* It's not the knowledge but the means that are lacking.

hall·i *nf* large wool or silk rug decorated with colorful floral patterns to ornament a floor or wall

hall·k *nm collec (Colloq)* mankind, humanity, people

hall·ka *np* < **hall·kë 1** handcuffs, fetters, restraining chain **2** *(Reg)* hoop earrings

hall·ka·n *nm* thick metal dog-collar

hall·ke·q *adj* **1** *(Colloq)* having serious problems, in deep trouble **2** weak and powerless

hall·kë *nf* **1** ring-shaped metal fastener; iron ring; hoop **2** link in a chain **3** collar **4** noose, noose snare

*hall·k·o··*n* *vt* to link [ ] with a ring

hall·ko·më *nf* pothole filled with mud, mud hole

**hall·m·o··*n* *vt (Reg)* to make potholes in [ ]; break [ ] down, wear [ ] down

hallmu·ar *adj (i) (Reg)* worn away, eroded; broken down

hallva·shi·t·ës *n* halvah seller

hallva·xhi *nm (np ~ nj) (Colloq)* **1** = **hallvashi·t·ës 2** *(Old)* halvah maker/merchant

hallv·ë *nf* halvah
○ **hallv·ë e bardhë** plain halvah
○ **<> bëfsha/ngrënsha/ndafsha hallvën!** *(Crude Curse)* May I eat/serve/make the halvah (at <>'s wake)!
○ **hallv·ë e ftohtë** hopeless situation
○ **hallv·ë e pjekur** completed work/thing
○ **hallv·ë e zezë** halvah made with caramelized sugar

*hâm** *nm (Reg Gheg)* **1** tether for horse walking around threshing floor **2** stud horse = **hamsho·r**

hama·ll *nm (np ~ j) (Colloq)* manual laborer who carries things: porter; manual laborer who loads and unloads things: stevedore

hama·ll·çe *adv (Colloq) (Old)* = **hamalli·sht**

hama·ll·e *nf* **1** grain stubble used as pasture for livestock **2** = **hama·llë**

hama·ll·ë *nf* woods used as source of leaves that are kept in stacks for winter fodder

hama·llë·k *nm (np ~ qe)* **1** work of a porter/stevedore: porterage **2** *(Fig)* drudgery, back-breaking job **3** payment for work done by a porter/stevedore **4** *(Fig Pej)* menial labor

hama·ll·i *nf (Colloq)* = **hamallë·k**

hama·ll·i·sht *adv (Old)* crudely, clumsily; strenuously, back-breaking, hard

hama·m *nm* **1** *(Old)* sauna, steam-bath, Turkish bath **2** *(Reg)* toilet, privy

hamam|**xhi·k** *nm* bedroom corner that has been partitioned off for washing and provided with a drain hole leading to the outside

hama·sh·tër *nf (Old)* large trough for tanning hides

hamba·r *nm* **1** grain bin, granary **2** storage bin **3** ship's hold

hambar·tha·të *nf* hot dry crop-damaging wind from the south

hame·j *np* < **hama·ll**

hame·nd·as *adv* presumably; approximately

hame·nd·je *nf* guessing, guesswork, estimate

hame·nd·shëm *adj (i)* guessed at, presumed, supposed

hame·nd·thi *adv* = **hame·nd·as**

hame·nj *np* < **hama·ll**

ha·më *1st pl pres* < **ha·**

ha·m|**ës**
I § *adj* gluttonous
II § *n* glutton

ha·më·to·r *adj* **1** gluttonous **2** greedy

hamgji·s *stem for 1st sg pres, pl pres, 2nd & 3rd sg subj, pind* < **hamgji·t·**

hamgji·t· *vt* to entice, lure, tempt, attract; seduce, deceive

hamgji·t·je *nf ger* < **hamgji·t·**

ham-ham *onomat* sound of a dog barking: woof-woof, arf-arf

ha·mje *nf* **1** way of eating **2** food

hamsho·r *nm* **1** stallion kept for breeding purposes: stud horse **2** *(Fig Iron)* big, strong, and uncontrollable person

hamuli·t *vi* (of a dog) to woof, bark

ha·mull
I § *nm* **1** blazing fire *2** breach, rupture, fracture
II § *nf* **1** = hamullo·re **2** = hama·llë
III § *adj* hot, torrid

hamulli·shtë *nf* = hamullo·re

hamullo· *·het* *vpr* to unleash an angry attack: make an assault, assail

hamullo· *·n* *vi* to blaze/flame up, catch fire

hamullo·r *adj* **1** (of a field) left in stubble **2** (of a field of stubble) sown late for use as fresh pasture

hamullo·re *nf* field of stubble

hamuri·k *nm (np ~q)* [*Zool*] mole = uri·th

hamuri·q *nm* [*Bot*] kind of heath (*Erica manipuliflora* Salisb. (*Erica verticillata*))

Hamza· *nm* Hamza (male name)

han *nm* **1** *(Old)* roadside shelter for travellers and their animals: roadside hostelry, caravanserai, inn **2** *(Pej)* fleabag hotel **3** messy place with no control of who comes and who leaves, regular flophouse

hana·k *nm* thin pastry made of nettles and wheat-flour dough

*****han|a·r** *nm (Old)* = hanxhi·

handako·s· *vt* *(Colloq)* to inflict serious damage: crush

handako·s·et *vpr* *(Colloq)* to be badly damaged, be crushed, be ruined

handako·s·ur *adj (i)* *(Colloq)* badly damaged: crushed, ruined; beaten and suffering badly; exhausted

handa·r *nm (Reg)* = lloz

*****hând·ër** *nf (Reg Gheg)* waste silk

handra·k *nm (np ~ qe) (Reg)* **1** pus = qelb **2** nose mucous = qurra **3** excrement, feces, manure; filthy object **4** remnant, debris **5** *(Fig)* filth; dregs, refuse

ha·ne
I § *adv (Colloq)* **1** since long ago, long ago; for ages **2** in olden days, in early times
II § *pcl* expresses a heightened degree of surprise: wow! my God!
○ **hane __, hane __** introduces contrasted alternatives: the one __, the other __
○ **hane ku** God knows where: in some remote place
○ **hane kur** God knows when: at some indefinite time

*****ha·në** *nf (Reg Gheg)* = hë·në

ha·|në *3rd pl pres* <ha·

hanë·me *nf (Old)* **1** lady, wife **2** term used by a Moslem man to address his wife

*****ha·nërr** = hând·ër

ha·nëz *nf* [*Ichth*] angler, anglerfish (*Lophius piscatorius*)

hanga·r *nm* **1** open shed for drying or storing agricultural products: drying shed, storage hangar **2** airplane hangar

*****hângëlli··n** *(Reg Gheg)* = hingëlli··n

ha·ngër *stem for pdef, adm* <ha·

*****hângër·m**
I § *adj (i) (Reg Gheg)* worn, stripped (of a screw-thread)
II § *nf (e)* food

*****hâng|me** *nf (e) (Reg Gheg)* eating

*****ha·ng|shëm** *adj (i)* edible

*****ha·|ni** *interj pl* = hë

ha·nko *nf (Old)* **1** term used by a Moslem man to address his wife **2** term used by a new wife to address her mother-in-law or sister-in-law

*****hân|** *(Reg Gheg)* = hën|

*****han|o·r** *nm (Reg Gheg)* = hëno·r

hanxha·r *nm* **1** *(Old)* large double-edged cleaver-like sword: broadsword **2** butcher's cleaver

hanxhe·shë *nf female* <hanxhi·

han|xhi· *nm (np ~nj)* innkeeper, hosteler

hap *nm* **1** step **2** = ha·pje
○ **hap më/për hap** **1** keeping even, maintaining the same pace **2** at every step
○ **hap pas hapi** **1** step by step, one step at a time **2** at one's heels; doggedly; without interruption
○ **hap rreshtor** marching step, drill step, goosestep
○ **hapa të gjata** long strides
○ **hap vrulli** [*Track*] bounding step: bound

hap·
I § *vt, vi* **1** to open; open up/out **2** to start in operation: turn on **3** *(Fig)* to expose; disclose
II § *vi* **1** to dawn **2** (of weather) to clear up
○ <> **hap· barkun 1** to touch/move <> deeply, break <>'s heart (with pity) **2** *(Pej)* to give <> the creeps, make <>'s flesh crawl **3** to disclose every personal detail to <>; pour out one's feelings to <>: spill one's guts to <>
○ **hap· defterët (e vjetër)** *(Pej)* to dredge up old wrongs
○ **hap· dyert** "open the doors" to lead the way
○ **e hap· dheun me thonj** to make enormous efforts
○ **hap· dhëmbët** *(Pej)* to snicker
○ **e hap· gojën çorap** "make/open the mouth like a stocking" to be too talkative
○ **hap· gojën e mbyll· sytë** "open the mouth and close the eyes" to speak without thinking, speak without due consideration
○ **hap· gojën e shiko· n qiellin** "look at the sky with mouth agape" to do nothing and expect everything to be done for one
○ <> **hap· gojën** "open <>'s mouth for <>" **1** to open undue cause for <> to speak out, give <> an excuse to open <>'s trap **2** to lead <> into making excessive demands
○ <> **hap· gropën** "dig <>'s grave" **1** to destroy <> utterly; kill **2** to plot <>'s destruction
○ **hap· gjoksin** "bare one's chest" to display bravery, face danger bravely
○ <> **hap· kartat** to put one's cards on the table for <> to see; tell <> what one has been hiding
○ **hap· kat e (më) kat** to open both parts of a double window/door all the way
○ <> **hap· kokën 1** to wound <> badly in the head; kill <> **2** to cause constant problems for <>
○ **hap· konak 1** to build a new house **2** to get married and start one's own family
○ **hap· krahët** to turn one's arms out (in a gesture indicating one's ignorance/helplessness in a matter)
○ **e hap· kuletën** to begin to spend money more freely: stop being so tight-fisted, open one's purse-strings a bit
○ **i hap· letrat** to lay one's cards on the table
○ **hap· listën** to be first on the list
○ **hap· lojën 1** to play first; start the game **2** *(Colloq)* to hand out treats to friends
○ **hap· llogore** to dig trenches

○ **hap e mbyll dollapin** "open and close the wardrobe" to idle away time

○ **hap· mesele të reja** to cause new problems

○ **<> hap· oreksin** to increase <>'s appetite/greed

○ **e hap· qesen** to begin to spend money more freely: stop being so tight-fisted, open one's pursestrings a bit

○ **<> hap· rrugë** to give way to <>, step aside for <>, step out of the way of <>

○ **<> hap· syrin** to overindulge <>, spoil <>

○ **hap· sytë** to pop out one's eye's in amazement

○ **Hapi sytë!** Keep your eyes open! Stay alert!

○ **hap· shtëpi më vete** to set up a separate household

○ **hap· shtëpi të re** to set up one's own place/household

○ **e hap· trastën** to begin to spend money more freely: stop being so tight-fisted, open one's pursestrings a bit

○ **<> hap· trutë 1** to wound <> badly in the head; kill <> **2** to cause constant problems for <>

○ **<> hap·**^{3pl} **trutë** <>'s head is splitting, <> has a splitting headache

○ **hap· vallen** to start the dancing, be the first to start dancing

○ **<> hap· varrin** "dig <>'s grave" **1** to destroy utterly; kill **2** to plot <>'s destruction

○ **hap· vend** to make room

○ **hap· veshët** to keep one's ears open, stay alert

○ **<> hap· zemrën** to pour out one's heart to <>, unburden one's heart to <>

○ **hap· zërin 1** to turn the volume up on a (radio/television) loudspeaker **2** to speak up (about a matter)

○ **hap· zjarr** to start shooting, open fire

○ **<> hap· zorrët 1** to rip open the belly of <> **2** to touch/move <> deeply, break <>'s heart (with pity) **3** (*Pej*) to give <> the creeps, make <>'s flesh crawl

ha·p·et *vpr* **1** to open up, open out **2** to spread, spread out **3** to leave place, make room **4** (of weather/daylight) to become clear/bright

○ **<> hap·et**^{3sg} **barku** <> is sickened (by a horrible sight)

○ **nuk <> hap·et**^{3sg} **barku për** [] (*Scorn*) <> *doesn't* give a damn about [], <> *doesn't* lose any sleep over []

○ **<> hap·et**^{3sg} **dera** <>'s family line now will be continued (said when the first son is born)

○ **<> hap·et**^{3sg} **goja** <> *starts* speaking without timidity/bashfulness

○ **s'<> hap·et**^{3sg} **goja 1** <> *has* no appetite **2** <> *does* not open <>'s mouth (to speak)

○ **<> hap·et**^{3sg} **hunda (për duhan)** <> *is dying* for a smoke

○ **hap·et**^{3sg} **koha** the weather *clears* up

○ **<> hap·et**^{3sg} **oreksi 1** <> *has* an increase of appetite **2** <> *gets* greedy

○ **<> hap·et**^{3sg} **punë** <> *faces* many problems

○ **<> hap·et**^{3pl} **qiejt** "the skies open up for <>" <> *is* in seventh heaven

○ **hap·et si vaji në lakra/ujë** "spread all over like oil on lettuce/water" **1** to spread quickly in all directions **2** to act as if one owns the place

○ **<> hap·et**^{3sg} **syri 1** <> *picks* up courage **2** <> *gets* overindulged/spoiled

○ **<> hap·et**^{3pl} **trutë** <> *has* a splitting headache

○ **<> hap·et**^{3sg} **varri nën këmbë** "the grave *is* opening under <>'s feet" <> *is dying, is dying* out: <> *has* one foot in the grave

○ **<> hap·et**^{3sg} **zemra 1** <> *has* <>'s heart in <>'s mouth **2** <> *is* deeply touched/moved, <>'s heart *breaks* (with pity)

hapa·çe·l *adj* having a broad stride; walking in wide steps

hapa·dollap·a *adv* (*Colloq*)

hapa·gjat·as *adv* (*Colloq*) **1** walking in big steps; lengthening the stride **2** with legs extended

hapa·këmb·as *adv* = **hapashalthi**

hapa·këmb·azi *adv* = **hapashalthi**

hapa·krah *adv* (of doors/windows) open on both sides: wide open

hapa·s *adv* = **hapashalthi**

hapa·shal·as *adv* = **hapashalthi**

hapa·shal·ë = **hapshalë**

hapa·shal·thi *adv* with legs apart, astride

hapdrenu·shë *adj* (*Poet*) walking in quick little steps (like a doe)

ha·pe *nf* pill, capsule, tablet

hape· *nf* (*Colloq*) **1** outer end of an opening into a voluminous space **2** (*Fig*) abundance, opulence, affluence

*****ha·pë** *nf* **1** = **hap 2** pitch (of a screw)

hapër·co·n *vt* to rip/tear [] to pieces, rip/tear [] up

hapër·da··het *vpr* to get scattered, be dispersed; get around, get all over the place

hapër·da·n *vt* to scatter, disperse; strew, spread, broadcast [seed]

ha·pës

I § *adj* serving to open something: opening, starting, turning on (of an electrical switch)

II § *nm* key, opener = **çel·ës**

III § *n* worker who opens holes in the ground: digger

○ **s'ësh·të në hapës** to have a screw loose, not be in one's right mind

ha·pëse *nf* tool used to open something, opener: can opener, bottle opener, letter opener

*****hap·ësi** *nf* openness, frankness

hapësino·r *adj* **1** spatial **2** spacious

hapësirë *nf* **1** space **2** expanse; interior (space) **3** open space; chink, cleft *****4** (*Old*) full bloom

hapësiro·r = **hapësino·r**

ha·pët

I § *adj* (i) **1** without obstruction: open, clear **2** (of colors) light **3** spacious, broad

II § *adv* openly = **ha·pur**

III § *nn* (*të*) (*Old*) *****capacity, volume, space

hap·gja·të *adj* having a long stride: long-striding

ha·pje *nf ger* **1** <**hap·**, **hap·et 2** beginning part: opening **3** [*Skiing*] stemming

○ **hapje e shigjetës** [*Archery*] draw length

hapleh·të *adj* having a light step

hap·madh *adj* walking in big steps; having a long stride

hap·ore *nf* wickerwork used instead of a gate for a fenced enclosure

*****hapr·ro·n** *vt* to rip [] up

○ **haprro·n gojën** to yawn

haps *nm* (*Old*) **1** = **burg 2** jailed person: prisoner

haps·a·në *nf* (*Old*) prison = **burg**

haps·inë *nf* (*Reg Gheg*) = **hapësirë**

*haps¦o's· *vt (Old)* to imprison

*haps¦uer *n (obl ˜o'ri, fem ˜o're) (Old)* prisoner

hap¦sha'lë *[p-sh] nf* distance measured from heel to heel of a step: pace, stride

hap¦shku'rtër *[p-sh] adj* walking in short steps; having a short stride

hap¦shpe'jtë *[p-sh] adj* walking quickly; having a fast stride

hap¦tas OR **hap¦ta'zi** *adv* **1** openly, forthright, candidly, frankly **2** plainly, clearly

ha'pur
  I § part <**hap·**, **ha'p·et**
  II § adj (i) **1** open **2** spread out, spacious **3** overt **4** exposed **5** (of colors) having a low degree of color saturation: light **6** (of sky) clear **7** in operation, activated; turned on **8** *(Fig)* straightforward
  III § nf (e) open space: opening
  IV § adv **1** openly; overtly **2** straightforwardly, frankly
  ○ **e hapur me të dyja kanatet** (of an indoor space) completely exposed, wide open; (of an event) open to the public

ha¦qe *np* <**hak** *(Colloq)*

harabe'l *nm [Ornit]* **1** sparrow **2** house sparrow *(Passer domesticus L.)* = **trumca'k 3** *(FigImpolite)* featherbrained person: birdbrain
  ○ **harabel fushe** *[Ornit]* tree sparrow *(Passer montanus L.)*
  ○ **harabeli i gurëve** *[Ornit]* rock sparrow *Petronia petronia L.*

harabel¦o're *np [Ornit]* passeriformes

hara'ç *nm [Hist]* **1** payment to acknowledge submission or to buy protection: tribute **2** special head tax exacted by Ottoman rulers on non-Moslems in exchange for excusing them from military service

haraç¦pagu'es *adj [Hist]* paying tribute as the price of submission or protection

hara'jk¦ëz *nf (Reg)* = **skërpi'cje**

haraki'ri *indecl masc (Book)* **1** hara-kiri **2** *(Fig)* sacrifice; pointless sacrifice

*harako'p OR **harago'p** *nm* coarse jokester

harakopi' *nf* coarse/off-color joke

harakopi'¦t·et *vpr* to tell coarse/off-color jokes

haraku'q· *vt (Reg)* **1** to rotate [], turn [] **2** to tumble [] down

haraku'q·et *vpr (Reg)* **1** to rotate, turn **2** to tumble down

hara'm
  I § nm (Colloq) **1** something forbidden: taboo **2** something unearned and undeserved **3** bad person; good-for-nothing
  II § adj **1** bad; of no use **2** forbidden

hara'n *nm* = **tenxhe're**

hara'p
  I § nm **1** = **ara'p 2** tadpole
  II § adv in wild disorder, in a complete mess

*haraqi'në *nf [Bot]* valerian *(Valeriana officinalis)*

*haraqi'nëz¦ë *nf [Bot]* lamb's lettuce *(Valerianella)*

hara'r *nm* = **thes**
  ○ **harar i shpuar/grisur 1** person who owns nothing, poor man **2** person who can't hold on to money: spendthrift, compulsive spender **3** person who can't keep a secret: blabbermouth

*harasa'n *nm (Colloq)* cement = **çeme'nt**

*haravâng *adj (Reg Gheg)* = **vë'ngër**

harbi' *nf (Old)* **1** ramrod (for a musket) **2** (weapon) pike
  ○ **ësh·të harbi nga mendja** to have no brains

harb¦i'm *nm ger* **1** <**harbo'·n**, **harbo'·het 2** outburst **3** unbridled lust

*harb¦ke'q *adj* malicious, malevolent

harbo'·het *vpr (Colloq Pej)* **1** to run around from one place to another: ramble **2** to scurry; get away fast **3** to bounce around noisily while playing: make a ruckus **4** = **harli's·et 5** *(Pej)* to act in uncontrolled fashion: run wild, run riot; storm **6** *(Fig Pej)* = **azdi's·et**

harbo'·n
  I § vt **1** to spoil, ruin **2** to stimulate exuberant growth in [a plant] **3** *(Fig Pej)* to drive [] wild, make [] ecstatic, transport **4** to enrage
  II § vi = **harbo'·het**

harbu'a¦r *adj (i) (Colloq)* **1** rampant, rambling; (of plants) growing profusely **2** *(Pej)* unruly, out-of-control: vulgar, rude; ornery; enraged

harbu't
  I § nm **1** *(Old)* member of the rabble: commoner, riffraff **2** *(Impol)* ill-bred/uncouth/coarse person: boor, oaf; brute, barbarian
  II § adj **1** *(Old)* uncouth, common, vulgar **2** *(Contempt)* rude and barbarous: coarse, brutish, vulgar

harbut¦çe *adv (Colloq Pej)* = **harbut¦ëri'sht**

harbut¦ëri' *nf* **1** *(Old)* the lower class: rabble, riffraff **2** *(Contempt)* brutish/uncivilized behavior: churlishness, rudeness; coarseness

harbut¦ëri'sht *adv (Pej)* churlishly

*harb¦zi' *adj, n (fem sg ˜ez, masc pl ˜i'nj, fem pl ˜eza)* = **harbke'q**

harc *nm* **1** rock formation with sharp edges: jagged rock **2** area with such rock formations: rocky terrain

harç *nm* uncastrated male pig used to service sows: boar

harda'll
  I § nm **1** *[Bot]* mustard = **sina'p 2** *[Food]* (condiment) mustard **3** *(Fig)* tall, stupid person: lout
  II § adj stupid
  ○ **hardall i egër** scorpion senna *Coronilla emerus*
  ○ **farë/lëng hardalli** *(Iron)* barely related (by blood)

hardall¦o's· *vt (Colloq)* **1** to stimulate profuse growth **2** *(Fig)* to derange

hardall¦o's·et *vpr (Colloq)* **1** to grow profusely **2** to have one's clothes in disarray **3** *(Fig)* to go crazy **4** *(Fig)* to show off

hardall¦o's¦ur *adj (i)* **1** profuse, growing profusely; overgrown **2** with clothes in disarray **3** *(Fig)* crazy, deranged

*ha'rdh¦ë *nf (Colloq) [Med]* diphtheria

ha'rdh¦ël *nf [Zool]* = **ha'rdhje**

hardhi' *nf [Bot]* grapevine *(Vitia vinifera L.)*
  ○ **hardhi amerikane** *[Bot]* fox grape *Vitis labrusca*
  ○ **hardhi e bardhë** traveler's joy, old man's beard *Clematis vitalba*
  ○ **Hardhia bën rrushin, ferra merr uratën.** *(Prov)* One person does the work and somebody else gets the credit. The wrong person gets the credit.
  ○ **hardhi e egër** *[Bot]* wild vine *(Vitis sylvestris)* = **laru'shk**

hardhi'ç *nm* tonic made from juniper extract and used as a digestive or to relieve pain or thirst

hardh¦i'çk¦ë *nf [Zool]* = **ha'rdhje**

hardhi¦o're *np [Bot]* (grape)vine family *Vitaceae*

hardhi'shte *OR* **hardhi'shtë** *nf* **1** vineyard **2** pruned or broken-off shoot of a grapevine

hardhje *nf* **1** [*Zool*] lizard **2** wall lizard *(Lacerta muralis)* **3** *(Colloq)* [*Med*] diphtheria
  ○ **hardhje e blertë** [*Zool*] emerald lizard, green lizard *Lacerta viridis* = **zhapi**

hardhjeshkë *nf* [*Zool*] = **hardhje**

hardho·*n vt (Reg)* = **hedh**

hardhuca'n *adj* very quick and agile; constantly moving, restless

hardhucë *nf* [*Zool*] lizard
  ○ **hardhucë bari** [*Zool*] Crimean lizard *Lacerta taurica*
  ○ **hardhucë gurësh** [*Zool*] Balkan rock lizard *Lacerta erhardi*
  ○ **hardhucë muresh** [*Zool*] wall lizard *Lacerta muralis*
  ○ **hardhucë paremadhe** [*Ichth*] = **luspëmadhe**
  ○ **hardhucë shkembinjsh** [*Zool*] common lizard *Algyroides nigropunctatus*

hardhuckë *nf* [*Zool*] wall lizard *(Lacerta muralis)* = **hardhje**
  ○ **hardhuckë uji** [*Zool*] smooth newt *Triturus vulgaris*

*__hardhu'shkë__ = **hardhuckë**

hare' *nf* great joy, elation; merriment, gaiety

harem *nm* harem

hare'ngë *nf* [*Ichth*] herring *(Clupea harengus)*

hare'plo'të *adj (Poet)* full of joy: joyful, merry

hare'shëm
  I § *adj (i)* elated; joyful, merry
  II § *adv* merrily

ha'rgull *nm* **1** scaffold **2** hut **3** = **kukuvriqe**

*__hari__ *nm* = **ari**

*__hari·n__ *vi* = **arri·n**

Harilla *nf with masc agreement* Harilla (male name)

*__haristis·__ *vt* to thank

*__harje__ *nf* midge, gnat

hark
  I § *nm (np ~ qe)* **1** [*Geom*] arc **2** [*Archit*] arch **3** curve, curved portion **4** (archery) bow **5** bow (for a stringed instrument); bow fitted with a gut string and twanged to loosen and remove small impurities from wool **6** springe
  II § *adj* arched, curved
  III § *adv* in a circle

harkargje'ndtë *adj (Poet)* having a silver bow

harka'rtë *adj (Poet)* **1** having a golden bow **2** in a shining crescent

harka't *adj* made of silk and cotton

harka'te *nf* veil made of silk and cotton

harkavile *nf* birdsnare made of a noose attached to a bow: springe

harkëta'r *nm* [*Hist*] archer, bowman

harkëto'r = **harkëtar**

harki'm *nm ger* **1** < **harko·n**, **harko·het 2** arch, curve, bend

harkmbajt'ës *nm* [*Hist*] = **harkëta'r**

harkna'jë *nf* arched vault: arcade

harko'·het *vpr* to bend over, bow; wind around

harko·n *vt, vi* **1** to form into a bowed shape: arch, bow, bend **2** to curve/wind/bend around

harko'r *adj* curved, arched

harko're *nf* scythe

harkprarua'r *adj (i) (Poet)* = **harka'rtë**

harktë *adj (i)* = **harko'r**

harkua'r *adj (i)* **1** curved, curvy **2** arched

harlis·
  I § *vt* **1** to stimulate exuberant growth [in a plant] **2** *(Fig)* to stimulate [] to exuberant behavior: make frisky; spoil
  II § *vi* **1** to grow exuberant **2** *(Fig)* to act in an overstimulated way

harlis·et *vpr* **1** to grow profusely, grow rampant **2** *(Fig)* to become uncontrollable; be unable to contain oneself, go wild; become enraged

harli'sje *nf ger* **1** < **harlis·**, **harlis·et 2** exuberant growth

harli'sur *adj (i)* **1** (of plants) profuse, exuberant; lush, luxuriant **2** *(Fig)* uncontrollable; unable to contain oneself, wild; enraged **3** *(Fig)* unlimited, boundless, unbridled

harma'n *nm* blend of tobaccos; tobacco shredded for a cigarette blend

harmani'zim *nm ger* < **harmanizo·n**

harmani'zo·n *vt* to blend [tobaccos]

*__harmëshor__ = **hamshor**

harmi' *nf* **1** [*Veter*] tuberculosis of the bone in animals **2** tooth decay, rotting of teeth **3** *(Fig)* terrible fear, panic, terror

harmo'·het *vpr* **1** to get reduced to tiny pieces: be shredded, be chewed up, crumble **2** to get eaten away little by little **3** to rot, spoil; get infected *__4__ to mourn, grieve

harmo·n *vt* **1** to make [] into tiny pieces: shred, chew up, crumble **2** to rot [], spoil []; infect **3** to eat away at [] little by little; eat [] into shreds

harmo'ç *nm* **1** [*Bot*] stone pine *(Pinus pinea)* **2** mortar mixed with small rock fragments from a wall **3** *(Reg)* hollow in a creek bed; part of a brook where the water pools

harmoni' *nf* harmony

harmoni'k *adj (Book)* **1** harmonic **2** = **harmonishëm**

harmoni'kë *nf* **1** harmonica **2** accordion

harmoni'kisht *adv* harmonically

harmoni'st *n* accordionist

harmoni'shëm *adj (i) (Book)* in harmony

harmonizi'm *nm ger* **1** < **harmonizo·n**, **harmonizo·het 2** harmonization

harmonizo'·het *vpr* to become harmonized

harmonizo'·n *vt* to bring [] into harmony: harmonize

harmonizua'r *adj (i)* harmonized

harmuri' *nf* loose soil that does not hold water

*__haromë__ *nf (Old)* money

haro'në *nf* round baking sheet, round cake pan

ha'rpë *nf* harp

harpi'st *n* harpist

ha'rqe *np* = **hark**

Ha'rta *nf* Harta (female name)

ha'rtë *nf* map, chart
  ○ **hartë memece** [*Geog*] unlabeled/blank/skeleton map: base map

harti'm *nm ger* **1** < **harto·n 2** (student) composition, essay, theme

harti'në *nf* [*Bot*] Scotch pine *(Pinus silvestris L.)*

harti's· *vt (Colloq)* = **harto'·n**

harto'·n *vt* to compile; draft, draw up []

hartograf *nm* cartographer

hartografi *nf* cartography

hartografik *adj* cartographic

hartosë *nf* roof lath, roof sheathing

*****hartuer** *adj (fem ~ore) (Old)* compositional, stylistic

hartues
I § *adj* compiling, drafting
II § *n* compiler, author; drafter

*****harû(n)**
I § *nm (Reg Gheg)* (ungelded) ram
II § *adj* in a stupor/daze; stupid
III § *adv* stupidly

harup *nm [Bot]* = çiçibanoz

*****harushan** *adj* strong as a bear

*****harushë** *nf* = arushë

*****harvallëri** *nf* rascality

harvallinë *nf* 1 dilapidated old house, hovel 2 *(Pej)* scrawny old hag

harxh *nm (Colloq)* 1 material required: supplies, provisions; makings, ingredients; embroidery materials 2 outlay, expense

harxhim *nm ger (Colloq)* 1 <harxho·n, harxho·het 2 expenditure 3 consumption

harxho·het *vpr* <harxho·n

harxho·n *vt (Colloq)* 1 to expend, spend: use up 2 to cause [] to spend money: cost [someone] money
○ harxho·n qimet/leshtë e kokës "spend the hair on one's head" to spend a fortune

harxhuar
I § *adj (i) (Colloq)* 1 used up, eaten up, spent: shot 2 drained by expenditure
II § *nn (të)* expenditure

harzane *nf (Reg)* small votary candle

harr· *vt* 1 to weed, cultivate 2 to thin out [corn or other planted crops]; prune [vines or trees] 3 *(Fig)* to excise weak or superfluous material from []: cull

harraman *adj* = harrestar

harraq *adj (Colloq)* forgetful = harrestar

harresë *nf* 1 loss of memory, forgetfulness; lapse of memory 2 *(Fig)* neglect; oblivion 3 = harrim

harrestar *adj* forgetful

harrë *nf* = bitërr

harrës *n* person who prunes trees/vines or thins out crops

*****harriço** *nf (obl ~ua) with masculine agreement (Colloq Old)* freshman

*****harrijtje** = arrijtje

harrim *nm ger* 1 <harro·n, harro·het 2 = harresë 3 forgetfulness, absent-mindedness; forgetting, amnesia

*****harris·** *vt* = harro·n

harrje
I § *nf ger* <harr·
II § *nf* 1 = bitërr 2 *[Entom]* tiny biting fly: stinging gnat, black fly, sand fly *(Simulium, Culicidae)*

harro·het *vpr* 1 to be so absorbed in something as to lose track of everything else; be preoccupied 2 to doze off 3 to stay away longer than expected 4 *(Colloq)* to go into one's dotage: go dotty 5 to go out of mind, be forgotten/lost

harro·n *vt* to forget
○ <>a harro·n derën "forget <>'s door" to stop coming to visit <>, forget the way to <>'s house, stop being close friends

○ <>u harroftë emri! "May <>'s name be forgotten!" *(Curse)* May <> drop dead and be forgotten!
○ Harro mushkë Valarenë! "Forget the Valarene mule!" *(Iron)* You are living in the past! Those easy times are gone.
○ E harro·n^{3sg} pordha vërën. "the fart forgets the hole" *(Crude)* How the mighty have fallen.

harrok *nm (Reg)* uncastrated male goat used for breeding

harruar
I § *adj (i)* 1 forgotten 2 involved in something to the point of losing track of everything else: totally absorbed, in deep thought, preoccupied, absentminded, bemused 3 *(Colloq)* in one's dotage: senile, dotty
II § *n (i)* preoccupied/absentminded person

harrur
I § *adj (i)* 1 rid of weeds: weeded 2 thinned out, pruned 3 *(Fig)* rid of weak or superfluous material
II § *nf (e)* = bitërr

*****harrutë** *nf* dungeon

*****has** *nm* 1 = hasi 2 = as

has·
I § *vt* 1 to meet [] by accident: come/happen across [], run into [] 2 *(Fig)* to bump into [], find, notice
II § *vi* to have a chance encounter
○ <> has·^{3sg} sharra në gozhdë "<>'s saw *hits a nail*" <>'s plan *hits a snag*; <> *runs* into a dead end

has·et *vpr* 1 to meet by accident, have a chance encounter 2 *(Fig)* to come up suddenly, be found, be noticed 3 *(Reg)* to have a verbal argument: quarrel 4 *(Old)* to be bewitched, be under a spell
○ has·et me to meet with, come upon

Hasan *nm* Hassan (male name)

hase *nf (Reg)* cambric = kambrik

haset *nm (Colloq)* envy

hasetçeshë *nf (Colloq)* envious woman

hasetçi *nm (Colloq)* envious man

hasetmadh *adj (Colloq)* very envious, green with envy

hasetqar *adj (Colloq)* envious

hasëll *nm* grasses (barley, rye, or oats) planted in late summer or fall to serve as fresh pasture for livestock; late-sown pastureland
○ hasëll qeni *[Bot]* bermuda grass *(Cynodon dactylon)*

hasëllore *nf* pastureland sown in barley, rye, or oats

hasër *nf* 1 floor mat made of woven reeds = rrogoz 2 area of about the size of a floor mat

*****hasi** *nf* insurrection: revolt, mutiny

hasje *nf ger* 1 <has·, has·et *(Old)* 2 meeting, appointment 3 quarrel, argument

hasm *nm* 1 enemy in a blood feud 2 *(Colloq)* enemy

hasmeshë *nf* <hasm

hasmëri
I § *nf* 1 blood feud 2 *(Colloq)* enmity
II § *nf collec (Colloq)* enemies considered as a group

hasmëro·het *vpr* 1 to become blood enemies 2 to become hostile, make enemies

hasmëro·n *vt* 1 to stir up trouble in []: create a blood feud among [] 2 *(Colloq)* to create hostilities among [], cause antagonism between [] = armiqëso·n

hasmëruar *adj (i)* 1 engaged in a blood feud 2 *(Colloq)* = armiqësuar

hasrabërës *n* = rrogoztar

hasratar *nm* = **rrogoztar**

***hastrit** = **astrit**

hasude *nf* [*Food*] sweet pudding made of starch, sugar, oil, and butter

***hasull** *adj* **1** stocky, solid; robust **2** = **hasëll**

***hasun** *nn* (*të*) (*Old Regional Gheg*) bewitchment

hasur *adj* (*i*) casually acquainted

hasha *interj* (*Impolite*) **1** expresses doubt or disbelief: like hell! **2** forms idiomatic phrases with verbs to express disagreement or denial

hashari *adj* disobedient, naughty

hashash *nm* **1** [*Bot*] opium poppy (*Papaver somniferum*) **2** opium

***hashef** = **ashef**

***hashëra** *np* sawdust

***hashërim** *nm* wooden fence

hashish *nm* hashish

***hashtull** *nm* winter fodder; field sown for winter fodder

***hashure** *nf* = **ashure**

hata
I § *nf*(*Colloq*) **1** calamity, disaster **2** = **tmerr**
II § *adv* **1** very much: awfully, terribly **2** (*Informal*) very good

hatashëm *adj* (*i*) (*Colloq*) **1** catastrophic, disastrous **2** terrible, awful, ugly; shameful, dirty, filthy **3** extraordinarily large: gigantic, monstrous **4** (*Informal*) wonderful, excellent

hatëk *nm* [*Ornit*] bird's ventricule ()

hatër *OR* **hatër** *nm* **1** mind = **mendje 2** special favor/behalf, sake **3** desire, preference **4** favoritism, partiality

hatërmadh *adj* (*Colloq*) **1** willing to go along, agreeable **2** disagreeable, touchy

hatërmbetur *adj* (*Colloq*) **1** touchy **2** with hurt feelings, indignant

hatëro·n *vt* (*Colloq*) **1** to show bias toward [], unfairly take []'s side: favor **2** to satisfy [], do as a favor to []

hatull *nf* = **hatulla**

hatulla *np* <**hatull 1** space between the roof and the ceiling; roof truss, roof timbers **2** [*Constr*] reinforcing timbers in a masonry wall **3** spiked metal collar worn by dogs to protect them from wolves **4** = **petavër**

haur *nm* = **ahur**

hauz *nm* water reservoir; pond

hava *nf*(*Colloq*) **1** weather; climate **2** open air, sky

Hava *nf* Hava (female name)

havadan *adv* (*Colloq*) **1** in the open air, up in the air **2** aimlessly

havale *OR* **havale** *nf* (*Colloq*) **1** bother, annoyance, nuisance, trouble **2** difficult problem; problem maker **3** (*Euph*) epilepsy **4** vantage point *****5** the symbolic veiling and seclusion of women

havan *nm* **1** mortar (for pounding and grinding) **2** (*Old*) (artillery) mortar = **mortajë 3** tobacco shredder

***havaz** *nm* = **avaz**

havër *nf* **1** woman's dress/skirt **2** sultry heat, mugginess

havi *nf* soldering iron used in the metal crafts

havjar *nm* caviar

havlli *nf*(*Old*) **1** towel = **peshqir 2** kerchief = **shami**

---

havros· *vt* to oppress [] with sultry heat, stifle [] with mugginess

haxhi *nm* (*np* ~*lerë*) [*Relig*] hadji, pilgrim

haxhilejlek *nm* [*Ornit*] stork

haxhillëk *nm* (*np* ~*qe*) [*Relig*] hadj, pilgrimage

hazdis·et *vpr* = **azdis·et**

hazdisur *adj* (*i*) = **azdisur**

hazër *adv* (*Old*) ready = **gati**

hazërllëqe *np* preparations (for a wedding)

hazëro·het *vpr* (*Old*) to get ready, be prepared = **përgatite·t**

hazëro·n *vt* (*Old*) to make ready, prepare = **përgati/·**

hazërta *np* (*të*) ready food

hazërtë *adj* (*i*) prepared, ready = **gatshëm**

hazërxhevap
I § *adj* (*Old*) fast in reply, quick on the comeback
II § *adv* right away, immediately

hazine *nf*(*Old*) = **thesar**

haznë *nf* = **hazine**

HC *abbrev* <**Hidrocentral** Hydroelectric Plant

he *interj* **1** hey you! **2** used before expressions of cursing, bragging, mocking, or pleasure: how about that! boyoboy!

hebraik *adj* of or pertaining to the Hebrews; Jewish

hebraisht *adv* in Hebrew (language)

hebraishte *nf* Hebrew (language)

hebre *nm* Hebrew (person)

***hec** = **ec**

***heckë** *nf* short-sleeved jacket

heder *nm* [*Agr*] header (cutter of a combine harvester)

hedh·
I § *vt* **1** to cast; throw; heave; hurl; toss, fling **2** to broadcast [seeds], sow [grain] **3** to impel, propel, launch; shoot; drop **4** to make [] fall: fell, knock down **5** (*Colloq*) to toss [] off, toss [] down **6** to pour, spray **7** to emit, give off [], issue **8** to put **9** (*Fig*) to lay; lay out [] **10** to set [] up, build **11** to put [] aside for later **12** to note [] down **13** (*Colloq*) to miscarry [] (abort) **14** (*Fig Colloq*) to manage to survive **15** (*Fig Colloq*) to appoint to a new position
II § *vi* **1** (*Colloq*) (of bees) to swarm **2** (of rain or snow) to pour down heavily
∘ <>**a hedh· 1** to lay the blame on <> **2** (*Colloq*) to cheat <>
∘ **hedh· armët** to lay down arms, throw down one's arms: stop fighting, stop resisting, surrender
∘ <> **hedh· baltë** to throw mud on <>'s reputation
∘ **hedh· bazat (e <>)** to lay the foundations (of <>)
∘ **i hedh· benzinë zjarrit** to exacerbate an argument, pour oil on the fire, make matters worse
∘ **hedh· cipën e zezë** to put on mourning clothes
∘ <> **hedh· çakëll** to muddy the waters in a debate
∘ <> **hedh· çeçen** (*Old*) to cast a spell over <>
∘ **hedh· çengelat** to settle down for a long stay, put down roots
∘ **hedh· çengelin** to take the first step (toward achieving something); gain a foothold
∘ [] **hedh· dëm** to ruin []; [] *goes* for nothing, [] *comes* to naught
∘ **ta hedh· dobiçin në prehër** (*Crude*) {} would let you take the blame for something you didn't do
∘ **hedh· dorë mbi** [] to take possession of [], seize []

○ **hedh· dorë** {*in a place*} to steal something while {*in a place*}

○ **<> hedh· dorën** to give a (helping) hand to <>

○ **hedh· dritë mbi** [] to throw light upon [], make [] clear

○ [] **hedh·**^{3sg} **dheu përpjetë** "the earth *throws/lifts* []" []'s life *is* in great turmoil, <> *is* under a lot of stress

○ **<>a hedh· fajin** to shift the blame to <>

○ **hedh· fall** to tell someone's fortune, divine

○ **hedh· farë në ujë/det/lumë/shkëmb** "broadcast seed in the water/sea/river/rock" to do work of no value, do useless work

○ **e hedh· festen** *mbi sy//mënjanë* "throw one's cap over the eyes (and rest)" to have nothing more to worry about, have no more worries, be free of care

○ **<>a hedh· fjalën** *rrotull/vërdallë//larg e larg* to beat around the bush with <>

○ **e hedh· gardhin** to overcome an obstacle

○ **<>a hedh· grepin** to cast bait for <>; try to attract <>

○ **hedh· grepin** to take the first step (toward achieving something); gain a foothold

○ **ia hedh· grykës** to eat/drink it all up (and leave nothing for anybody else)

○ **<> hedh· gunën** to hide <> with a cover-up

○ **hedh· gur në rrota** to throw a monkey wrench into the works

○ **hedh· gurë mbi** [] to reprimand/rebuke [] severely

○ **hedh· gurin e fsheh dorën** "throw the rock and hide one's hand" **1** to do something wrong and pretend to be innocent: play the innocent; evade taking the blame **2** to do things in a sneaky way

○ **hedh· gurin e fundit** to play one's final card

○ **<> hedh· gjobë** to impose a fine against <>

○ **<> hedh· gjylen** [*Sport*] to put the shot

○ **<> hedh· hallkat** to handcuff <>

○ **hedh· një hap** to take a step, step

○ **i hedh· hapat sipas avazit të <>** to do whatever <> wants, agree with everything <> says: march to <>'s beat

○ **<> hedh· hekurat** to handcuff <>, shackle <>: put the cuffs on <>

○ **e hedh· hendekun** to overcome an impediment, get out of trouble

○ **e hedh· hendekun** to put it (one's past problem/difficulty) behind one

○ **<> hedh· hi syve** to throw dust in <> eyes: delude, deceive, cheat

○ **<> hedh· hije** to try to hide <> **2** to make <> look suspicious/doubtful, cast doubt on <>

○ **hedh· hije** to grow up/big

○ **hedh· kanxhat** to settle down for a long stay, put down roots

○ **e hedh· kapelën** *mbi sy//mënjanë* "throw one's cap over the eyes (and rest)" to have nothing more to worry about, have no more worries, be free of care

○ **e hedh· kapërcyellin** to put it (one's past problem/difficulty) behind one

○ **<>a hedh· kapistrën** to make use of <*a person*> to serve one's own interests: exploit/use <*a person*>, take advantage of <*a person*>

○ **hedh· kartën e fundit** to play one's final card

○ **<> hedh· kashtë syve** to throw dust into <>'s eyes, practice deception on <>: fool <>

○ **hedh· këmbën sipas valles** to adapt one's actions to fit the circumstances; change one's opinions to suit the circumstances

○ **i hedh· këmbët sipas daulles** to follow along like a sheep

○ **e hedh· kësulën** *mbi sy//mënjanë* "throw one's cap over the eyes (and rest)" to have nothing more to worry about, have no more worries, be free of care

○ **ta hedh· kopilin në prehër** (*Crude*) {} would let you take the blame for something you didn't do

○ **<> hedh· kthetrat** to get one's claws into <>

○ **hedh· kupëza** to apply cupping glasses (as a medical treatment)

○ **hedh· kurorë** (*Colloq*) to get married

○ **<>a hedh· lakun/litarin në fyt/grykë/qafë** "put a noose around <>'s neck" to lead <> into a trap, ensnare <>

○ **<>i hedh· leckat në erë** (*Scorn*) to exterminate <*someone*>, make mincemeat of <>

○ **<> hedh· ledh** to find some way to fix <> up

○ **hedh· letrën e fundit** to play one's final card

○ **<> hedh· lule** to praise <> undeservedly

○ **e hedh· lumin** to put it (one's past problem/difficulty) behind one

○ **e hedh· lumin pa (u) lagur (këmbët)** to come away without a scratch

○ **u hedh· mballomë këpucëve** to mend/patch shoes

○ [] **hedh· me këmbë përpjetë** (*Impol*) to kill [] dead, knock [] off

○ **<>a hedh· me lezet** to cheat <> with finesse

○ [] **hedh· me një gisht** "flick [] with a finger" to knock [] over with a feather

○ **hedh· ndyrësira mbi** [] to say vile things about []: throw mud on []

○ [] **hedh· në burg** (*Colloq*) to throw [] into prison

○ [] **hedh· në dorë 1** to win [] over, have one's way with [] **2** to force [] to surrender

○ **hedh· në erë 1** (of a structure) to blow up, explode **2** to winnow [grain]

○ [] **hedh· në fund të pusit** "throw [] to the bottom of the well" to ignore [] completely, give [] no consideration

○ [] **hedh· në gjyq** to sue, bring a lawsuit; prosecute

○ [] **hedh· në hava** to blow [] up, explode; destroy

○ [] **hedh· në hendek** to give [] up, discard, abandon

○ [] **hedh· në koshin/shportën e plehrave 1** to throw [] into the trash bin: discard **2** to treat [] with disdain, reject

○ **hedh· në krahët e <>** (*Pej*) to collaborate with <>

○ **hedh· në letër** to commit to paper, write down, put in writing

○ **e hedh· në lotari** to determine the matter by lot, to decide by drawing straws

○ [] **hedh· në mes të katër udhëve** to kick [] out into the street

○ [] **hedh· në mes të** *rrugës//katër rrugëve* to abandon [] completely

○ [] **hedh· në mes të udhës** to kick [] out into the street

○ **hedh· në peshë** to throw into the balance

○ [] **hedh· në pluhur 1** to reduce [] to dust; destroy [] completely **2** to give [] up, abandon; reject []

○ **hedh· në rrugë (të madhe)** to abandon [] completely

○ [] **hedh· në sokak** to toss [] out on the street; toss [] away

○ **hedh· në short** to cast lots

○ **e hedh· në shportën e lugëve** to keep [] secret, not tell [] to anyone

○ [] **hedh· në udhë (të madhe)** to kick [] out into the street

○ **hedh· në yll** to tell fortunes, soothsay

○ [] **hedh· në greminë** to ruin []'s life

○ [] **hedh· nga shkallët** *(Scorn)* to expel [] forcibly, kick [] out

○ <> **hedh· nigjahun** *(Old)* to wed <>

○ <> **hedh· një brez (rakisë)** to eat a little something (to form a protective layer in the stomach) while drinking (raki)

○ **hedh· një fjalë 1** to hint **2** to allude, refer

○ **hedh· një gotë** to have a drink (alcoholic)

○ <> **hedh· një gur në këpucë** to plant a seed of doubt/hatred in <>

○ <> **hedh· një gur në opingë** to plant a seed of doubt/hatred in <>?Move item after dividing

○ <> **hedh· një gur në shollë** to plant a seed of doubt/hatred in <>

○ **hedh· një gur në ujë/lumë/ferrë** "throw a rock into the water/river/brambles" to give it a try, have a go at it

○ <> **hedh· një hije** to cast suspicion/doubt on <>

○ **hedh· një pushkë 1** (with a rifle) to get off only a single shot, fire only once **2** to fight only for a short time

○ **hedh· një sy** to cast an eye, have a look

○ **hedh· një valle 1** to lead a line dance; dance **2** to get into a predicament

○ **hedh· pare poshtë** just throw money away: waste/squander money

○ [] **hedh· pas krahëve/kurrizit/shpinës** to put [] out of one's mind, stop thinking about []

○ <>*i* **hedh· patkonjtë (në erë)** *(Scorn Colloq)* to knock [] off, kill

○ **hedh· pendët** to moult

○ **e hedh· përruan** to put it (one's past problem/difficulty) behind one

○ <> **hedh· pështymë** to spit at <>

○ **nuk i hedh· pluhur faqes** not bring shame upon oneself: not shame oneself

○ <> **hedh· pluhur syve** to throw dust in <> eyes: delude, deceive, cheat

○ **hedh· plumbin** to shoot, fire (a bullet)

○ [] **hedh· poshtë *1** to throw [] down **2** to defeat, bring [] down **3** to denigrate [] **4** to refute [an argument] **5** to reject []

○ <> **hedh· prangat** to put handcuffs on <>

○ [] **hedh· prapa krahëve/kurrizit/shpinës** to put [] out of one's mind, stop thinking about []

○ **hedh· pushkë** to shoot

○ **e hedh· qeleshen** *mbi sy/mënjanë* "throw one's cap over the eyes (and rest)" to have nothing more to worry about, have no more worries, be free of care

○ **hedh· qeveri** to store away winter provisions

○ **hedh· qiqrat** *(Colloq)* to tell fortunes, soothsay

○ **i hedh· rezen derës/shtëpisë** "put the latch on the door/house" to die and bring one's family line to an end

○ **hedh· rrënjë** to take root; settle down, take up permanent residence: become implanted

○ **hedh· skortin të zërë troftën** to give up something of little value in hopes of getting something of greater value

○ **hedh· shikimin larg** to look off in space

○ **hedh· shkelma 1** to let kicks fly: kick **2** to make unreasonable objections: kick

○ <> **hedh· shpirt** to inspire courage in <>

○ **hedh· shtat** to grow tall

○ **e hedh· takijen** *mbi sy/mënjanë* "throw one's cap over the eyes (and rest)" to have nothing more to worry about, have no more worries, be free of care

○ [] **hedh· tej** to reject [] completely; cast [] out

○ <> **hedh· trutë e gomarit** "they have stuck him with the brain of the donkey" they have brain-washed <>, <> doesn't think with an independent mind any more

○ <>*i* **hedh· trutë në erë** to blow <>'s brains out

○ **hedh· tutje** to reject [] completely; cast [] out

○ **hedh· themelet e <>** to establish the foundations of <>: found <>, establish <>

○ **hedh· themelet** to lay the foundations

○ <> **hedh· thonjtë** to get one's claws into <>

○ <> **hedh· thumba** to needle <>

○ **hedh· ujë verës** "add water to the wine" to try to make things look not so bad, try to put a good face on things

○ **hedh· ujë zjarrit** "throw water on the fire" to calm the situation down

○ **u hedh· ujë luleve** to water the flowers

○ **hedh· valle** to dance a folk dance

○ **hedh· vallen e vdekjes** "dance the dance of death" *(Book)* to be in the final moments of life: be at death's door

○ **e hedh· vaun** to put it (one's past problem/difficulty) behind one

○ **hedh· vështrimin larg** to look off in space

○ **hedh· vicka 1** (of an animal) to be a kicker, kick **2** to be cantankerous/crotchety/peevish: kick against the traces

○ **hedh· votën** to cast one's vote

○ **hedh· zaret** to test one's luck

○ **hedh· zarin e fundit** to play one's final card

hedh·a-hedh·a *adv* in large, fleecy flakes; in strands

hedhë OR **hedhe** *nf* **1** fine chaff; fine sawdust **2** dandruff = zbokth **3** (of snow) flake

***hedh|ëm** *adj (i) (Reg Gheg)* thrown, cast

hedh|ës
I § n **1** one who throws: thrower **2** person who joins in with the third voice in polyphonic folk singing **3** = shkopecingël
II § adj used to release something with force

hedh|ëse *nf* device/tool used to throw something: thrower, launcher

hedhje *nf ger* **1** < hedh· *(Reg)* **2** head kerchief
○ **hedhje pa vrull** [Track] standing throw

hedh|ur
I § adj (i) **1** thrown away, discarded **2** transported from somewhere else **3** tall and good-looking **4** high **5** extending forward: thrust forward; extending upward: elevated, raised **6** *(Fig)* adroit, adept; energetic, active, enterprising, lively
II § nf (e) **1** long leap **2** something said obliquely and indirectly: insinuation, innuendo **3** amount of food prepared at one time in a utensil

hedh|ur|a *np (të)* scraps, discards, rubbish

hedh|ur|azi *adv* with innuendo, insinuatingly

hedh|ur|in·e *nf* scrap, junk; rubbish, trash

hegjemo'n *adj* ruling, in the controlling position, hegemonic

hegjemoni *nf* hegemony

hegjemonïst *n* having hegemonic tendencies, aiming for political control

hegjemonïzëm *nm* attempt to exert political control: hegemonism

hegjïrë *nf* hegira

he-he *onomat* sound of laughter: hah-hah

hej
I § *interj* hey!
II § *nm* newly weaned lamb
III § *np* = **hell**

hejbe OR **hejbe** *np* double shoulderbags/saddlebags

hejdë *nf* 1 [*Bot*] buckwheat *(Fagopyrum esculentum)* 2 knotgrass, allseed *(Polygonum aviculare)*

heje *np* <**hell**

hejë *nf* 1 lance, spear 2 blade 3 *(Reg)* = **he'së**

hejzë *nf* mountain/hill ridge that forms a watershed, saddle of a mountain/hill

*****hek·** = **heq·**

hekakeq *adj* long-suffering, wretched, miserable

hekato'mbë *nf (Book) (Old)* hecatomb

he'kë *nf* = **he'që**

he'kës *nm* [*Anat*] collarbone, clavicle = **he'qës**

he'ksjëm *adj (i)* transparent = **tejdukshëm**

heksï *nf* chicken gizzard

hekta'r *nm* hectare

hekto'gram *nm* hectogram

hekto'litër *nm* hectoliter

hekto'metër *nm* hectometer

he'kur
I § *nm* 1 iron (the element) *(Fe)* 2 [*Chem*] iron salt 3 object or device made of iron 4 iron (for pressing clothes) 5 [*Naut*] anchor 6 [*Sport*] horizontal (in gymnastics)
II § *adj* 1 very strong 2 very hard
∘ **hekurat e frerit** bit on a bridle
∘ **hekurat e kalit** hobble on a horse
∘ **hekur i rrahur** wrought iron
∘ **Hekuri rrihet sa është i nxehtë.** "Iron is hammered only when it is hot" *(Prov)* Strike while the iron is hot.

he'kura *np* <**he'kur** irons, shackles

Hekura'n *nm* Hekuran (male name)

hekura'qe *np (Colloq)* iron scraps

hekurbeto'n *nm* [*Constr*] reinforced concrete

hekurïmtë *adj (i)* of iron

hekurïna *np (Colloq)* 1 iron scraps 2 iron object

hekurïshte
I § *nf* ironware
II § *np* pieces of iron; iron things; scraps of iron

hekurkthye's *nm* construction-worker who builds iron framework: ironworker

hekurmbajtës *adj* [*Min*] containing iron: ferrous

he'kur-nike'l *nm* [*Min*] mineral that contains iron and nickel: ferro-nickel

hekuro'r *adj* 1 containing iron: ferrous 2 *(Old)* = **hekurtë**

hekuro're *nf (Old)* railroad = **hekurudhë**

hekuro's· *vt* 1 to iron, press [clothes] 2 *(Fig Crude)* to crush flat, mash
∘ **<> hekuros· trutë** "iron <>'s brains" *(Crude)* to smash <> flat

hekuro's·et *vpr* to be neatly dressed, wear well-ironed clothes

hekuro'sje *nf ger* <**hekuro's·, hekuro's·et**

hekuro'sur *adj (i)* 1 ironed, pressed 2 *(Joke)* (of cigarettes) machine-rolled 3 *(Fig Iron Crude)* stiff and awkward, clumsy

hekurpunue's *nm* ironworker: blacksmith, toolmaker

he'kurt *adj (i)* 1 (made) of iron 2 strong/hard/tough as iron

hekurta'r *nm* = **hekurpunue's**

hekuru'dhë *nf* railroad, railway

hekurudho'r *adj* of or pertaining to railroads

hekza'klora'nt *nm* [*Spec*] insect spray, hexachloride

hekza'metër *nm* hexameter

hela'q *adv (Colloq)* filthy

helbete *parenth (Colloq)* well sure, well of course, sure

helen
I § *nm* Hellene
II § *adj* Hellenic

helenïk *adj* 1 Hellenic 2 Hellenistic

helenïst *n* Hellenist

helenistïk *adj* Hellenistic

helenistïkë *nf* Hellenistics

*****helïk** *nm* = **haliç**

helïkë *nf* (helical) propeller/fan

helikoptër *nm* helicopter

helikoptermbajtëse *nf* [*Mil*] helicopter carrier

helio *formativ* helio-

heliocentrïk *adj* [*Astron*] heliocentric

heliocentrïzëm *nm* heliocentrism

heliogra'f *nm* heliograph

heliografï *nf* heliography

heliografïk *adj* heliographic

helioterapï *nf* [*Med*] heliotherapy

heliu'm *nm* [*Chem*] helium

helm
I § *nm* 1 poison, toxin; venom, bane 2 *(Fig)* sorrow 3 helmet
II § *adj* 1 bitter 2 *(Fig)* sad
∘ **helm e pikë** very depressed/sad

helmarïnë *nf* [*Bot*] belladonna, deadly nightshade *(Atropo belladonna)*

helmatïm *nm ger* = **helmïm**

helmatïs· *vt* = **helmo'·n**

helmatïs·et *vpr* = **helmo'·het**

helmatïsje *nf ger* = **helmïm**

helmatïsur *adj (i)* = **helmu'ar**

helmato'·n *vt* = **helmo'·n**

helmatue's *adj* = **helmue's**

he'lme *nf* 1 [*Bot*] oleander = **he'lmës** ***2 [*Invert*] mite *(Acarina)*

helmetë *nf* steel helmet
∘ **helmetë gungëzake** [*Invert*] prickly helmet *Galeodea echinophora, Cassidaria echinophora*

he'lmës
I § *adj* = **he'lmues**
II § *nm* [*Bot*] oleander, rosebay *(Nerium oleander)*

helmësï *nf* 1 toxicity, virulence 2 *(Fig)* sorrow, great sadness

helmësïrë *nf* 1 bitterness, bitter taste 2 poisonous plant 3 ground whose grass is poisonous

he'lmët *adj (i)* 1 poisonous, toxic, virulent 2 very bitter 3 *(Fig)* deeply sad

he'lmëz *nf* [*Bot*] dodder *(Cuscuta)*

helmím *nm ger* **1** <**helmo´·n, helmo´·het 2** *(Fig)*
bitter sadness: sorrow **3** [*Med*] intoxication

helmllëshu|e|s *adj (Book)* poison-emitting: poi-
sonous, toxic

helmo´·het *vpr* **1** to get poisoned **2** *(Fig)* to become
very sad

helmo´·n *vt* **1** to poison **2** *(Fig)* to embitter, sadden;
afflict
  ○ <> **helmo·n zemrën/shpirtin** to make <> bitterly sad

helmo´s· = **helmo´·n**

helmo´sje *nf ger* = **helmím**

he´lmshëm *adj (i)* virulent, poisonous

he´lmt|ë *adj (i)* = **helmu|e|s**

helmu|a´|r *adj (i)* **1** poisoned; drugged **2** *(Fig)* embit-
tered, saddened, sad **3** *(Reg)* poisonous = **he´lmët**

helmu|e|s *adj* poisonous, venomous, toxic; noxious,
harmful

helm|u|e|shëm *adj (i)* sorrowful

he´lmz|ë *nf* **1** [*Bot*] water hemlock *(Cicuta)* **2** hiccup

*helve´t|as** *adv (Old)* Swiss = **zvicëra´n**

helvetík *adj (Old)* Swiss = **zvicëra´n**

hell *nm (np ˜ je)* **1** skewer, spit **2** something long and
pointed
  ○ **hell akulli** icicle
  ○ **hell guri** stalagmite
  ○ **hell i këmbës** shinbone
  ○ **hell i mullarit** = **strumbulla´r**

hell|í|shte *nf* long, straight piece of wood suitable for
use as a spit/skewer

hem *conj.*
  ○ **Hem __, hem __** *(Colloq)* Both __ and __.
  ○ **Hem qeros, hem qibar/fodull.** "Both bald and
  vainglorious" Rich in desires but poor in means. Big
  appetite and small purse
  ○ **Hem të vë plak, hem të rruan mjekrën.** "One
  treats you like a sage, and then shaves your beard."
  (Prov) They put you in charge and then don't even
  listen to what you say!

hematít *nm* [*Min*] hematite, bloodstone

hemipte´r|ë *np* [*Zool*] hemiptera

hemisfe´r|ë *nf* hemisphere

hemistík *nm* [*Lit*] hemistich

hemo´fili *nf* [*Med*] hemophilia

hemo´globín|ë *nf* hemoglobin

hemo´rragjí *nf* [*Med*] hemorrhage

hemo´rroí´d|e *np* [*Med*] hemorrhoids

hendbo´ll *nm* [*Sport*] game similar to soccer but using
hands rather than feet: European hand-ball

hendbollíst *n* [*Sport*] player of European hand-ball

hende´k *nm (np ˜ qe)* **1** ditch; trench **2** moat **3** *(Fig)*
impediment, barrier

hendeklídhje *nf* [*Mil*] trench that serves to link
together a defensive system: communication trench,
connective trench

hendeko´·n *vt* to trench

hende´qje *np* <**hende´k**

heník *nm (Old)* [*Mil*] mortar; small cannon

hep *nm* **1** fissure, crack **2** shallow hollow place: cavity, hollow **3** cavern; cave **4** pointed tip: tine, thorn

*hep·** *vi (Reg Tosk)* = **ep·**

hepatík *adj* [*Med*] hepatic

*he´pe** *nf* **1** *(Reg Gheg)* waterhole, hole; cave, cavity
2 baking pan

*hep|ësí** *nf* = **epshm|ëri**

*hep|ëz** *nf* grotto

*he´pje** *nf ger (Reg Tosk)* <**e´pje**

*hepo´·n** *vi (Reg Tosk)* = **epo´·n**

*he´pshëm** *adj (i)* = **e´pshëm**

*he´pur** *adj (i)* = **e´pur**

heq·

I § *vt* **1** to pick up and take away [] **2** to exert force
toward the energy source: pull; attract **3** to pull on:
drag, draw, wrench on **4** to pull in: draw on, suck,
drink; smoke [tobacco] **5** to separate [] from the main
part: pull out, extract; cut off, cut out; pull off, pick
[fruit] **6** to remove: take away [] from <>; take
off [a covering]; wipe [] out, extirpate; subtract [a
number]; expurgate [a book] **7** to discontinue; relieve
[one's worry/curiosity/doubt/desire]; lift [a siege]
8 to withdraw: pull out; resign **9** to lead **10** *(Fig
Colloq)* to retract **11** to draw [a geometric figure]
12 *(Colloq)* to hit/shoot <> with [] **13** *(Colloq)* to
give <> a quick [] **14** *(Colloq)* to give <> a quick
going over with [] **15** *(Fig)* to get through/over [some
difficulty]; suffer [a misfortune] **16** *(Fig Colloq)* to
pass [] off as **17** *(Colloq)* to grow, raise **18** *(Colloq)*
to mate/breed [an animal]

II § *vi* **1** (of a chimney) to draw **2** *(Colloq)* to get
going, go **3** *(Colloq)* (of rain or snow) to fall heavily
  ○ **heq· ajkë** to skim the cream off, skim milk
  ○ [] **heq·**[3sg] **ana (me [])** to be biased (in favor of
  [])
  ○ [] **heq·**[3sg] **ana** [] leans badly
  ○ **heq·**[3sg] **bark** [] has diarrhea
  ○ **heq· bishtin e gjarprit 1** to suffer greatly **2** to
  become very tired
  ○ [] **heq·**[3sg] **bizgë** [] has the runs, [] has diarrhea
  ○ <>a **heq· bojën** "remove <>'s paint" to reveal
  <>'s true colors, pull off <>'s mask
  ○ **heq· bojën** to scratch the paint
  ○ <>a **heq· bricën** to give up all hope for <>
  ○ **heq· buront** to take snuff
  ○ <> **heq· cipullin** to drive the evil spirits out of <>
  ○ <>a **heq· dera** to be in <>'s (family) tradition
  ○ <>a **heq·**[3sg] **dera trimërinë** <> gets <>'s coura-
  geousness from <>'s family
  ○ **heq· dorë (nga {})** **1** to withdraw/resign (from
  {}), take no more responsibility (for {}) **2** to change
  one's mind (about {}); lose interest (in {})
  ○ **heq· dorë** to withdraw; give up
  ○ **heq· dorë nga []** **1** to break relations with []
  2 to renounce []
  ○ **ua heq· dushkun fjalëve** to speak frankly, say
  how things are
  ○ **heq· faqen** to remove hair from the face with a
  depilatory
  ○ <> **heq· fasha** "take off <>'s bandages" to give
  <> the full treatment, put <> through the mill, give
  <> a hard time
  ○ <>a **heq· fillin** to lose interest in <>; pay no more
  attention to <>, ignore <>; stop caring for <>
  ○ **heq· gunën** to wash one's dirty linen in public
  ○ <> **heq· gurin e fundit 1** to lambaste <> thoroughly **2** to leave <> without a leg to stand on
  ○ **heq· gjakun me [] []** *puts* {} through Hell
  ○ <>a **heq· hallkën** to lose interest in <>; have no
  more concern for <>
  ○ <> **heq· kapelen 1** to doff one's hat **2** to demonstrate respect for <>

○ **<>a heq· kapistallin** to lose interest in <>; have no more concern for <>

○ **<>a heq· kapistrën** to lose interest in <>; have no more concern for <>

○ **heq· keq** to eke out a living; suffer

○ **i heq· këmbë sipas avazit të <>** to do whatever <> wants, agree with everything <> says: dance to <>'s tune

○ **heq· këmbën zvarrë/rrëshqanë** "drag one's foot" **1** to want others to follow one's lead **2** to bring good luck **3** to attract others by one's example

○ **<> heq·³ˢᵍ kërraba nga vetja** (Pej) <> looks out only for <>self, <> is completely selfish: <> always looks out for number one

○ **<> heq· kryq** to remove <> from a list, remove <> from consideration: cross <> out, cross <> off; have nothing to do with <> any more; give up thinking about <>

○ **heq· lebeti** to be terrified and horrified

○ **heq· lëngun e ullirit** to suffer severe hardship

○ **heq· lotari** to draw straws, cast lots

○ **heq· lotarinë** to try one's fortune

○ **<> heq· mallin** to awaken <>'s longing

○ **e heq· maskën** to take off one's mask, reveal one's true character

○ **e heq· mendjen nga { }** to stop caring about { }

○ **heq· mirë** to live well

○ **<>a heq· mysin** <asaj pune> to give up any hope of fixing <that matter>

○ **[ ] heq· në baltë** to lead [ ] down the wrong path

○ **[ ] heq· në zemër (për [ ]) 1** { }'s heart aches (for [ ]) **2** to steam with anger, be in a huff

○ **[ ] heq· nëpër gojë** to gossip about [ ], slander

○ **[ ] heq· nga defteri** "delete from the list" **1** to stop counting on [ ] **2** to stop caring about [ ]; stop paying attention to [ ]

○ **s'[ ] heq· nga goja** to keep talking nicely about [someone], praise [ ] continually, keep remembering [ ]

○ **[ ] heq· nga mendja** to get [ ] out of one's mind

○ **[ ] heq· nga palltoja** "pull [ ] by the overcoat" to grab [ ] by the sleeve: pull at [ ] insistently

○ **<> heq· një dredhë 1** to beat <> up; beat <> with a whip **2** to rebuke/reprimand <> severely

○ **<> heq· një dru të mirë** to beat <> up; beat <> severely

○ **<> heq· një llabut** to beat <> up, thrash, wallop

○ **<> heq· një rrip** "pull off a strip of <>'s skin" to give <> a good hiding, whip <>

○ **heq· një tel** (Colloq) to send a telegram: send a wire

○ **heq· një valle 1** to lead a line dance; dance **2** to get into a predicament

○ **<> heq· një vishkull** to whip <> with a switch

○ **<> heq· një [ ]** to give <> a quick/casual action with [ ], give <> a quick [ ]ing

○ **heq· paftë** [Tech] to plane a metal plate

○ **ia heq· petën lakrorit** to bring everything out in the open

○ **[ ] heq· për/prej hunde/hundësh** to lead/have [ ] by the nose

○ **[ ] heq· për kapistalli/kapistre** to make [ ] do what one wants; lead by the nose

○ **[ ] heq· për veshi** "pull [ ] by the ear" to lead/have [ ] by the nose

○ **heq· pikën e zezë 1** to knock oneself out trying, break one's back **2** to suffer greatly

○ **[ ] heq· qafe** to get rid of [ ], get [ ] off one's neck

○ **<>a heq·³ˢᵍ rrënja për** [ ] "<>'s root pulls for [ ]" <> itches for [ ]

○ **<> heq· rrugën** to take the lead of <>

○ **<>a heq· saçin** to relieve <> of a big worry: take a load off <>'s chest, get <> out of a tight spot

○ **heq· sisë** to suck at the breast: suckle

○ **i heq· spik jetës** to live a very good life

○ **<>i heq· sytë** to take one's eyes off <>, stop watching <>

○ **<> heq· shapkën 1** to doff one's hat **2** to demonstrate respect for <>

○ **<> heq· shiritat** "remove <>'s stripes" (Colloq) to take away <>'s officer commission: bust <>

○ **<> heq· shkallët** to pull the ladder out from under <>, leave <> without support

○ **e heq· shkopin zvarrë** "drag one's stick" to be a quiet kind of person who doesn't bother anyone

○ **heq· shpirt** to be on { }'s last legs, be fading fast

○ **po heq· shpirt 1** to be in the throes of death, be dying **2** to be falling into ruin; be breaking down

○ **e heq· shpresën** to give up hope

○ **<>a heq· shtëpia** to be in <>'s (family) tradition

○ **heq· tespihet 1** to count off one's prayer beads **2** (Fig) to kill time

○ **heq· të zitë (e ullirit)** to suffer bitter/severe hardship, go through Hell

○ **[ ] heq· tëhu** to tow [ ] along

○ **heq· udhën** to lead the way

○ **heq· vallen** to lead the dance

○ **<> heq· velenxën** "remove <>'s protective covering" to leave <> exposed; expose <>

○ **<> heq· veshin/veshët** to chastise/scold <>

○ **e heq· veten (si) { }** to pretend to be { }, represent oneself as { }

○ **ia heq· vetes** to commit suicide

○ **<> heq· vërejtje** to deliver a disciplinary warning to <>, scold <>

○ **<> heq· vijë/vizë 1** to draw a line through <>, line <> out **2** to wash one's hands of <>, have nothing more to do with <>

○ **heq· zahmet** (Colloq) to wear oneself to a frazzle

○ **<>[ ] heq·³ˢᵍ zemra** <> likes [ ] very much

○ **e heq· zinë** to come to the end of the time of mourning; (of women) take off one's (black) mourning clothes

○ **heq· zor** to be having a difficult time

○ **e heq· zvarrë** to be (just) getting by, be getting along

○ **[ ] heq· zvarrë** to drag [ ]; drag [ ] along; drag [ ] out

○ **s'<>a heq· zhiblën nga zyri** "not take a speck out of <>'s eye" not give <> the slightest help in a time of need

he'q̈ë nf dying breath, death rattle

he'q̈ël nf "pull-on" open-heeled house slipper

he'q̈ës nm **1** [Anat] collarbone, clavicle; wishbone (of a fowl) **2** [Agr] linchpin securing the beam of the plow to the yoke **3** [Agr] tongue of a cart **4** (Colloq) sharpshooter **5** (Colloq) steelyard **6** drawknife, drawshave **7** [Mil] safety catch on a weapon; trigger **8** trawling net **9** (Old) [Fin] person authorized to withdraw money for someone else **10** (Reg) hard layer of ground lying under the soft layer being cultivated **11** worker whose job it is to remove objects (after they have been processed) **12** guide, leader **13** (Old) scout/lookout/accomplice for a thief or assassin **14** leader in a line dance **15** ram or billy goat

that leads the flock **16** person treated badly by life, wretch
○ **ĕsh·tĕ nĕ heqĕs** to breathe one's last, be at death's door

he'qĕse nf **1** slipper **2** hole in the ceiling through which smoke escapes from a fireplace: smoke hole **3** (Reg) desk drawer, table drawer **4** hard layer of ground lying under the soft layer being cultivated **5** [Bot] horsetail = **kĕpu'tj**e

heq'ĕsi nf(Old) **1** service as a scout/lookout/accomplice for a thief or assassin **2** (Fig) = **dredhi' 3** traction; tractility

heqi'm nm (Old) = **mjek**

he'qje
I § nf ger <**heq·, hi'qe·t**
II § nf **1** emendation/expurgation of a text **2** (Fig) terrible suffering, pain **3** (Old) [Phys] gravity = **rĕnde'sĕ 4** = **he'qĕl**
○ **heqje nga gjiri** [Med] ablactation, weaning

heq'keqĕs
I § adj wretched, miserable
II § n miserable person, wretch

***he'qkĕ** nf(Reg Tosk) = **he'qĕl**

***he'qsĕ** nf traction

he'qur
I § part <**heq·, hi'q·et**
II § adj (i) **1** long and thin **2** emaciated, drawn **3** (Colloq) who has suffered much in life, used to suffering: who has been through the mill
III § nf (e) travail, fatigue, suffering
IV § nn (tĕ) **1** traction **2** diarrhea

her'aca'k
I § adj early, early-rising
II § nm early riser, early bird

her'a'her'shĕm adj (i) occasional, sporadic

her'a'k adj **1** early, early-rising **2** early-blooming; early-ripening

herald'i'k adj heraldic

herald'i'kĕ nf heraldry

herald'i'st n heraldist

herb'ariu'm nm (Book) herbarium = **bimĕto're**

herb'ici'd nm [Agr Chem] herbicide

herc nm [Phys] hertz

Hercegovi'nĕ nf Herzegovina

herdh'a'gje'l
I § adj having large kernels/fruit
II § nm olive or grape with large fruit

herdh'a'qe'n nm [Bot] **1** European spindle tree (Euonymus europaeus) = **fshikaku'q 2** variety of early-ripening fig with small light green fruit

he'rdh'e
I § np testicles
II § nf (Reg) nest, hive

***he're'jt** = **he'rĕt**

***heresi'** = **herezi'**

***he're't** = **he'rĕt**

hereti'k
I § nm heretic
II § adj heretical

herezi' nf heresy

he'rĕ
I § nf **1** time, instance; occasion **2** multiplied or repeated instance: time **3** times, multiplied by
II § adv **1** at times **2** (Old) season = **sti'nĕ**
○ **hera·herĕs** once in a while

○ **herĕ mĕ herĕ 1** always, continuously **2** from time to time, occasionally, now and then **3** time after time, time and again, frequently
○ **herĕ pas here 1** from time to time, occasionally, now and then **2** time after time, time and again, frequently

he'rĕ·he'rĕ adv **1** sometimes, from time to time, once in a while **2** occasionally, infrequently

her'ĕ'ke'qe nf [Ornit] owl = **kukuva'jkĕ**

her'ĕ'pas'her'shĕm [her-pas-he'r-shĕm] adj (i) occasional, from time to time; periodical

he'r'ĕs nm [Math] quotient

he'rĕt
I § adv **1** early **2** long ago, at some time in the past, in olden times
II § adj (i) = **he'rshĕm**
○ **herĕt a/ose vonĕ** sooner or later

hergjele'
I § nf **1** group of draft animals allowed to browse freely **2** one of a pack of wild horses **3** (Fig) plump young woman or girl **4** (Fig Pej) unruly and undisciplined young female
II § adj half-wild, semi-domesticated; not yet trained for the saddle or the yoke: unbroken, unbridled
III § adv in disorderly groups

hermafrodi't
I § nm (Book) hermaphrodite
II § adj hermaphroditic

hermeli'nĕ nf [Zool] ermine (Mustela erminea)

hermeti'k adj (Book) **1** hermetically sealed **2** (Fig) obscurantistic

hermet'iki'sht adv (Book) hermetically

hermet'izĕm nm (Book) obscurantism

hermet'izi'm nm [Tech] hermetic sealing

hermet'izu'es adj [Tech] sealing hermetically

he'rmĕth nm [Bot] false carrot (Caucalis)

hermo·'n vt (Reg) = **gĕrmo'·n**

hermo'q nm drainage ditch

he'rnie nf [Med] hernia

hero' nm (pl ˜ nj) hero
○ **hero i heshtur** unsung hero

hero'i'k adj heroic

hero'i'kĕ nf heroic quality/nature/character/substance/aspect of something; that which is heroic

hero'iki'sht adv heroically

hero'i'nĕ nf **1** heroine **2** heroin

hero'izĕm nm **1** heroism, heroic spirit **2** heroic act

hero'nj np <**hero'**

***herq** OR **he'rqje** np <**hark**

***her'si'** nf service period, time served

hershe'm nm (Reg) **1** stormy weather **2** (Fig) = **vrull**

her'shĕm adj (i) **1** early **2** ancient

her'shi'm nm ger <**hersho'·n**

her'shm'ĕri' nf (Book) earliness

hersho'·n
I § vt to do [ ] early
II § vi to give birth prematurely

***her'ue'r** nm (obl ˜ o'ri) (Old) timetable

herr nm [Folklore] gnome, dwarf

herr· vt = **harr·**

he'rr'e np <**ha'rrĕ**

he'rr'ĕs n grapevine pruner

he'rr'je nf ger <**herr·**

herrta'r nm = **ha'rrĕs**

hesa·p *nm (Colloq)* **1** account, count; calculation **2** calculation of charges: bill
  ◦ {*derogatory name*} **hesapi** *(Crude)* indicates scorn and derision for {} **kungull hesapi** stupid fool
  ◦ **bëj/bëni hesap sa __!** just think/imagine how much/many __!
  ◦ **një hesap (ësh·të^{3sg})** it *makes* no difference which
  ◦ **Hesapi i shtëpisë nuk del/nxirret në pazar.** "The household budget is not to be taken out in the market." **1** *(Prov)* Some things should not be aired in public. **2** Things don't always come out the way they're planned.
  ◦ **është tjetër hesap** that is quite a different matter

he's·*ë* *nf (Reg)* food provisions, annual supplies and provisions

hesperi·de *nf [Bot]* rocket *Hesperis*

****he'sull** = e'sëll

****hesh** *nm* curl/lock of hair

hesht· *vi* **1** to stop making any sound; stop talking **2** to keep silent, be quiet

hesht·a·k *adj* lance-shaped: lanceolate

hesht·a·r *nm* soldier armed with a lance/spear: lancer, spearman

he'sht·as *adv* = he'shtazi

he'sht·azi *adv* **1** without speaking: mutely **2** silently, noiselessly **3** *(Fig)* uncomplainingly, unquestioningly

hesht·*ë* *nf* spear, lance

hesht·ë·mbajt·ës *nm [Hist]* spearman, lancer

hesht·ë·si·r·*ë* *nf* silence

hesht·i *nf (Book)* = he'sht·je

hesht·im *nm ger* = he'sht·je

he'sht·je *nf ger* **1** <hesht· **2** stillness; silence **3** *[Ling]* pause
  ◦ **heshtje varri** absolute silence; silence of the grave

hesht·je·rë·nd·*ë* *adj (Poet)* in deep/heavy/gloomy silence; in absolute stillness

hesht·or *adj* lance-shaped: lanceolate

he'sht·shëm *adj (i)* silent

he'sht·ur *adj (i)* **1** silent; taciturn **2** quiet, still **3** tacit

heterogjen *adj (Book)* heterogeneous

het·im *nm ger* **1** <heto'·n **2** inquest, investigation, inquiry

het·im·or *adj [Law]* pertaining to a judicial inquiry, inquest, or examination: investigatory; inquisitional

heto'·n *vt* **1** to investigate **2** *[Law]* to conduct an inquest into [], investigate [a crime] **3** to look into [] carefully, examine **4** to notice, discover

het·ue's
  I § *adj* **1** investigatory **2** *[Law]* pertaining to a judicial inquiry **3** highly attentive
  II § *n* **1** investigator **2** *(Old)* judicial officer conducting an inquest

het·ue·si *nf [Law]* government office responsible for conducting inquests in criminal matters

****he'the** = e'the

he'u *interj* **1** expresses sympathy for suffering: oh my! **2** expresses sudden surprise: say now! hey! **3** expresses great joy or great admiration: boy! hey!

hezit·im *nm* **1** <hezito'·n **2** hesitation

hezit·o'·n *vt* to hesitate

hë
  I § *interj (Colloq)* **1** encourages action: go on! let's go! move it! **2** precedes and reinforces an expression of emotion: well now! hey!
  II § *pcl* **1** asks for an answer or confirmation: hunh? well? **2** asks for confirmation after a negative expression: right?
  ◦ **hë __, hë __ 1** introduces uncertain alternatives: maybe __, or maybe __; at times __, at others __ __ **2** *(Reg)* whether __ or __
  ◦ **hë, hë** (moving) gradually, little by little
  ◦ **hë për hë** = hëpërhë

hëm *interj (Colloq)* **1** expresses displeasure, doubt, or irony: oh sure! **2** expresses reluctance or indecision: wait a minute! whoa!
  ◦ **hëm __, hëm __** first __, but then __
  ◦ **hëm <> vë· plak, hëm <> rrua·nn mjekrën** "make <> the leading elder and then shave <>'s beard" to make <> the leader and then ignore <>

hën·a·bre·nd·a *adv* before the moon comes up
  ◦ **ësh·të^{pl} parë hënabrenda** "have seen one another before the moon comes up" to be on close terms with one another

hën·a·ja·sht·*ë* *adv* when there is a moon, when the moon is up
  ◦ **ësh·të^{pl} parë hënajashtë** to be on bad terms with one another

hën·a·ke·q *adv* = hënapra·pë

hën·a·pra·p·*ë* *adv* at a bad/unlucky time

hën·*ë*
  I § *nf* **1** moon **2** *(Old)* lunar month
  II § *nf (e)* Monday
  ◦ **lëngata/sëmundja e hënës** *(Colloq) [Med]* epilepsy
  ◦ **hën·ë e ngrënë** waning moon; crescent moon
  ◦ **ësh·të^{pl} parë me hënë të keqe** to be on bad terms with one another
  ◦ **hën·ë e prerë** crescent moon
  ◦ **hëna e vjet·ër** waning moon

hën·ë·plo't·*ë*
  I § *nf* full moon
  II § *adj (Poet)* moonlit

hën·ë·z *nf* **1** *(Dimin)* <hën·ë **2** crescent **3** *[Archit]* lunette **4** *[Tech]* steady rest (on a lathe) **5** *[Anat]* lunule, half-moon **6** *[Ichth]* anglerfish *(Lophius piscatorius)* **7** *(FigImpolite)* person who slavishly follows another's bidding: yesman, toady
  ◦ **hën·ë·z buke** small end piece of bread pinched from the loaf
  ◦ **hën·ë·za e derës** arch over a door
  ◦ **hënëz deti** *[Ichth]* anglerfish *Lophius piscatorius*
  ◦ **hën·ë·za e makinës qepëse** bobbin case (in a sewing machine)
  ◦ **hënëz vezake** *[Ichth]* mola *Ranzania laevis*

hë·nger· *stem for pdef, opt, adm* <ha·
  ◦ **e hën·ger·^{pdef} barin/çairin/kullotën/livadhin/tagjinë** *(TeaseImpolite)* **1** to have lived out one's life; have reached the end of one's life **2** to have had it, have bought the farm
  ◦ **hëngri botë** *(Crude)* {} kicked off, {} died
  ◦ **<> hëngri gjuha** <> said something which should not be mentioned, <> let something slip, <>'s tongue slipped
  ◦ **<>i hën·ger·^{pdef} sytë 1** {} made <> suffer **2** {} pestered <> constantly

hë'ni *pl* <hë

hёnо́r

I § *nm* **1** uncastrated male sheep or goat used for breeding **2** person who acts on whim, capricious person; moody person

II § *adj* **1** lunar **2** *(Poet)* moonlit **3** *(Fig)* moon-like in appearance: moon-shaped; pale **4** capricious; moody

hёpёrhё *adv (Colloq)* for the time being

hёpёrhёshёm *adj (i)* *(Colloq)* of the moment; momentary; temporary; of today: contemporary

hi(r) *nm* **1** ash, ashes **2** = **hith** **3** dust of corpses, corpse; memory of the dead

hiát *nm* [*Ling*] hiatus

***hі́be** = **hejbe**

hibrі́d *nm, adj* [*Bot Zool*] hybrid

hibridizі́m *nm ger* **1** < **hibridizо́·n** **2** hybridization

hibridizо́·het *vpr* to become hybridized

hibridizо́·n *vt* to hybridize

hibridizuа́r *adj (i)* hybridized

***hі́ckёl** *nf* = **vі́ckё**

hiç

I § *nm* **1** nothing **2** something of no value or importance

II § *adv (Colloq)* **1** not at all, not any **2** never, not once

III § *adj* empty

○ **hiç fare** nothing at all

○ **hiç me hiç** neither winning nor losing, neither ahead nor behind

○ **Hiç mos ndі́e·n!** "Don't feel anything!" Don't worry!

hiçasgjё *pron (Colloq)* nothing at all, absolutely nothing

hiçgjё *pron (Colloq)* **1** not a thing, absolutely nothing, nothing at all **2** nothing important

hiçgjёkáfshё *pron (Colloq)* nothing, not a thing: zip

hiçgjёkúnd OR **hiçgjёkúndi** *adv (Colloq)* nowhere, not anyplace

hiçgjёsénd OR **hiçgjёséndi** *pron (Colloq)* nothing at all

hiçmosgjё *pron (Colloq)* absolutely nothing

hі́de *nf* [*Bot*] common jujube *(Zizyphus jujuba)*

hі́dёr *nf* hydra

hidrát *nm* [*Chem*] hydrate = **hidroksі́d**

hidratuár *adj (i)* hydrated

hidraulі́k *adj* hydraulic

hidraulі́kё *nf* hydraulics

***hidravіо́n** *nm* = **hidroplán**

hidrі́k *adj (Book)* = **ujо́r**

hidro *formativ* hydro-

hidrocentrál *nm* hydroelectric power station

hidrodinamі́k *adj* [*Tech*] hydrodynamic

hidroelektrі́k *adj* hydroelectric

hidroenergjetі́k *adj* of or pertaining to hydroelectric energy

hidrofі́l *adj* [*Spec*] hydrophilic

hidrofobі́ *nf* hydrophobia

hidrografі́ *nf* hydrography

hidrografі́k *adj* hydrographic

hidrogjén *nm* [*Chem*] hydrogen *((H)H)*

hidrokarbúr *nm* [*Chem*] hydrocarbon

hidroksі́d *nm* [*Chem*] hydroxide

hidrolі́zё *nf* [*Chem*] hydrolysis

hidrolо́g *n* hydrologist

hidrologjі́ *nf* hydrology

hidrologjі́k *adj* hydrological

hidromát *nm* water-soluble powder added to lime to give walls more durable color

hidrometeorolо́g *n* hydrometeorologist

hidrometeorologjі́ *nf* hydrometeorology

hidrometeorologjі́k *adj* hydrometeorological

hidrométёr *nf* hydrometer

hidrometrі́ *nf* hydrometry

hidrometrі́k *adj* hydrometric, hydrometrical

hidromotо́r *nm* [*Tech*] hydraulic motor

hidronyjё *nf* system for the regulation of water flow; node in a network of water-control stations

hidropizі́ *nf* [*Med*] hydropsy, hydrops

hidroplán *nm* [*Av*] airplane designed to land on and take off from water: seaplane, floatplane

hidrosférё *nf* [*Geog*] hydrosphere

hidrosilikát *nm* [*Chem*] hydrosilicate

hidrostát *nm* [*Tech*] bathysphere

hidrostatі́kё *nf* [*Tech*] hydrostatics

hidroteknі́k

I § *nm* hydrotechnologist

II § *adj* hydrotechnical

hidroteknі́kё *nf* hydrotechnology

hidroterapі́ *nf* [*Med*] hydrotherapy

hidroturbі́nё *nf* [*Tech*] hydroturbine

hidrovо́r *nm* [*Hydrol*] water-scooping machine

hidroxhúntё *nf* [*Tech*] hydraulic coupling

hі́dh·et *vpr* **1** to launch oneself: (into the air) jump, leap, spring, bound; hop **2** to surmount an obstacle: get by, pass, overleap **3** *(Colloq)* to drop by **4** *(Fig)* to take immediate action: jump to it **5** *(Fig)* to leap to one's feet (to speak); enter in abruptly **6** *(Fig Colloq)* to ascend higher, rise (on what is conceived as a scale) **7** *(Colloq)* to grow quickly/rampant, take form quickly

○ <> **hidh·et**[3sg] **gjoksi/zemra pёrpjetё** <>'s heart *rejoices,* <> *is* elated

○ **hidh·et kodёr mё kodёr** to talk without making sense

○ **hidh·et nё flakё** "jump into the fire" to plunge right in, act without fear of the dangers

○ <> **hidh·et nё grykё 1** (said of someone who is sensitive to what <> says and reacts strongly) to jump down <>'s throat **2** to go for <>'s throat; assail <>, attack <> **3** to try to shut <> up

○ <> **hidh·et nё qafё** to hug <> energetically

○ **hidh·et nga vendi** to flare up in anger

○ **hidh·et pёrpjetё 1** to be taken aback **2** to react vehemently

○ **hidh·et si gjel** to fly off into a rage at the least thing

hі́dh *stem for 2nd pl pres, pind, imper, vp* = **hedh·**, **hі́dh·et**

○ **hidh farё, nxirr farё** "cast the seed, pick up the seed" unproductive, of no value

○ **hidhu pёrpjetё!** complain all you like, for all the good it will do you

○ **hidhu nё qiell!** complain all you like, for all the good it will do you

hidhёrák *adj* **1** bitter, sour; embittered **2** *(Fig)* = **hidhnák**

hidhërim *nm ger* 1 <hidhëro' •*n*, hidhëro' •*het* 2 bitterness, sour taste 3 *(Fig)* spite, embitterment, anger 4 *(Fig)* sorrow, affliction, sadness

hidhëro' •*het vpr* 1 to become bitter/sour 2 to get a bitter taste (in the mouth) 3 *(Fig)* to be/get bitterly angry 4 *(Fig)* to suffer anguish; be saddened, grieve

hidhëro' •*n vt* 1 to make [] bitter/sour 2 *(Fig)* to make bitterly sad 3 *(Fig)* (of weather) to freeze to the very marrow, make very cold 4 *(Fig)* to vex, make angry

  ∘ [] hidhëro•*n* në zemër to make [] deeply sad

hidhërua'r *adj (i)* 1 (having become) bitter, sour 2 *(Fig)* sad, grieving 3 *(Fig)* vexed, sore

hidhërue's *adj* 1 making sour/bitter; poisonous 2 *(Fig)* causing suffering; making sad/angry

hidhë's *nm (Reg)* [*Bot*] nettle = hithër

hidhësi *nf* 1 = hidhësirë 2 embitterment; poignancy

hidhësirë *nf* 1 bitter taste, bitterness 2 *(Fig)* anguish; sadness, grief

hidhët *adj (i)* = hidhur

hidhëti *nf* = hidhësi

hidhna'k *adj, n* 1 cranky (person); impetuous (person) 2 *(Fig)* capricious, wild 3 *(Fig)* (of weather) bitterly cold

hidhna'kth *nm* [*Bot*] hog's fennel (*Peucedanum officinalis*)

hidhna'q *nm* [*Bot*] black nightshade (*Solanum nigrum*)

hidhta'k *adj* = hidhëra'k

hidhtas *adv (Reg)* bitterly = hidhur

hidhur
  I § *adj (i)* 1 bitter 2 *(Fig)* harsh, acute, grievous, biting 3 *(Fig)* testy; embittered
  II § *nf (e)* 1 something bitter 2 bitter taste 3 bitterness, acridity
  III § *adv* 1 in such a way as to cause distress: bitterly 2 sadly, woefully 3 angrily

*hie = hije

hie'në *nf* 1 [*Zool*] hyena 2 *(Fig)* cruel and vicious person

hierarki *nf* hierarchy

hierarkik *adj* hierarchical

hieroglif *nm* 1 hieroglyph 2 hieroglyphics

hieroglifik *adj* hieroglyphic

hierore *nf* chancel

hieshëm *adj (i)* = hijshëm

higrometër *nf* hygrometer

higjiene *nf* hygiene

higjienik *adj* hygenic

higjienizim *nm ger* <higjieno'•*n*

higjienizo'•*n vt* to make [] hygenic

hi-hi' *onomat* indicates laughter: hee-hee

hijaca'k *adj (Colloq)* superstitious

hije *nf* 1 shadow; shade 2 darkness; semi-darkness, murkiness 3 *(Fig)* cloud (of suspicion or distrust) 4 mere shadow (said of someone emaciated by illness) 5 dark blotch/spot 6 *(Fig)* dignified beauty: grace, charm 7 shadowy figure, apparition 8 *(Fig)* ghostly figure, ghost 9 *(Fig)* faint image; slight trace 10 patronage

  ∘ nuk i bë•*n* hije askujt not be in anybody's way
  ∘ matu me hijen tënde! let your reach not exceed your grasp! take heed of your own limitations

  ∘ <>u shoftë hija e diellit! "May <>'s shadow disappear!" *(Curse)* May <> disappear from the face of the earth! May <> never have a happy day!

hije'ç *adj* = hijeda'shës

hijeda'shës *adj* [*Bot*] shade-loving: umbriphilous

hijedendur *adj* providing dense shade: shady

hijedritë *nf* 1 [*Art*] chiaroscuro 2 partly shaded place; penumbra

hijegjerë *adj* casting a broad shadow, giving a broad shade

hijekeq *adj* 1 casting a dark shadow 2 *(Fig)* downfaced, somber

hijelehtë *adj* 1 casting little shadow, offering little shade 2 *(Fig)* modest, amiable, easy-going

*hijelutës *adj* superstitious = hijaca'k

hijema'dh *adj* 1 providing much shade: shady 2 *(Fig)* = hijerëndë

hijeno'•*n*
  I § *vt* 1 *(Reg)* to cast a shadow on []: shade 2 to make [] pretty, grace
  II § *vi* to stay in the shade to escape the heat

hijerëndë *adj* 1 casting a dark/oppressive shadow 2 *(Fig)* somber; proud and dignified: grand

hijerinë *nf (Reg)* = hijesirë

hijerore *nf (Old)* [*Relig*] chancel of a church, sanctuary; prayer chapel

hijesi *nf* = hijeshi

hijesim *nm ger* <hijeso'•*n*

hijesira *np* underbrush

hijesirë *nf* shaded ground: shade; area without sunshine (which is cool in summer and cold in winter)

*hijesisht *adv* gracefully = hirësisht

hijeso'•*n vt* 1 to cast a shadow over []: shade; put in the shade; make dark 2 *(Fig)* = hijeso'•*n*

hijeshi *nf* elegant beauty: loveliness, grace, charm

hijeshim *nm ger* 1 <hijesho'•*n*, hijesho'•*het* 2 = hijeshi

hijesho'•*het vpr* to gain in loveliness, become beautiful

hijesho'•*n*
  I § *vt* to enhance [] in beauty/loveliness: grace, adorn
  II § *vi* to shine with beauty, be beautiful

hijeshua'r *adj (i)* graced with beauty, adorned

hijeshue's *adj* gracing with beauty, adorning

*hijeta'r *adj* shady

hijetore *nf* sunshade

hijevrenjtur *adj* gloomy in appearance, gloomy; somber

hijezim *nm ger* <hijezo'•*n*

hijezo'•*n*
  I § *vt* 1 = hijeso'•*n* 2 to shade [a drawing], add shading [to a picture] 3 *(Fig)* = errëso'•*n*
  II § *vi* to cast a shadow

hijëz *nf* 1 *(Old)* umbrella 2 *(Reg)* = ëndërr

hijo'•*n vt* to turn [] into ashes: incinerate

hijor *adj (Book)* of ghostly mien; shadowy

*hijo's• *vt* 1 = hijeso'•*n* 2 to turn [] to ash

*hijo'sun *adj (i) (Reg Gheg)* ashy

hijshëm
  I § *adj (i)* 1 possessing grace and beauty: good looking, handsome; lovely, charming 2 becoming, tasteful; proper, fitting
  II § *adv* handsomely; tastefully; becomingly

*hik|=ik|

hi'kërr *nf* 1 whey = hi'rrëcurdled/sour milk 2 [*Bot*] buckwheat (*Fagopyrum esculentum*) 3 [*Bot*] knotgrass, allseed (*Polygonum aviculare*) 4 [*Veter*] = hi'rrëz 5 [*Veter*] = ngalo'së

hikrr|a'q
  I § *nm* [*Veter*] = hi'rrëz
  II § *adj* 1 [*Dairy*] (of milk) turned to whey 2 [*Veter*] (of sheep or goats) afflicted by a disease that thins their milk

hikrr|o·het *vpr* 1 (of milk) to turn into whey, turn sour 2 (*Fig*) to become thin and weak

hikrr|o·n *vt* [*Dairy*] to make milk into whey

hile' *OR* hi'le *nf* (*Colloq*) chicanery

hile|ma'dh *adj* very tricky, deceitful; fraudulent

hile|qa'r
  I § *adj* = hileta'r
  II § *n* cheat, charlatan, trickster, swindler

hileta'r *adj* deceptive, tricky

Himala'jë *nf* Himalaya

himarjo't *adj, n* of/from Himara, native of Himara

hi|mbajt|ëse *nf* 1 ashtray = taketu'ke 2 urn for keeping ashes of the dead: crematory urn

*himbaxhi' *nm* [*Zool*] chimpanzee = shimpanze'

hi'me *nf* 1 bran = kru'nde 2 chaff 3 sawdust

hi'men *nm* [*Med*] hymen

himenopte'rë *np* [*Entomol*] Hymenoptera

*hi'më *adj* (*i*) gray

*him|i'k *adj* (*Old*) chemical = kimi'k

*him|i'st *n* (*Old*) chemical = kimi'st

himn *nm* 1 song/poem of praise: hymn, anthem 2 (*Fig*) glowing praise: eulogy, laudation

himn|izi'm *nm ger* < himnizo·n

himn|izo·n *vt* 1 to compose/perform [a song/poem of praise] 2 (*Fig*) to laud, acclaim, eulogize

himn|izu'a'r *adj* (*i*) acclaimed, highly praised

himn|izu'e's
  I § *adj* laudatory, praising, eulogistic
  II § *n* lauder, eulogist, encomiast

*himoni'k *nm* watermelon

him'të *adj* (*i*) = hi'rtë

hina'rdh *nm* [*Bot*] artichoke = angjina're

*hind
  I § *nm* [*Anat*] tissue = ind
  II § *adj* Indian (of India) = india'n

*hindi'k *adj* indigo = llulla'q

*hi'nj|ë = hi'nkë

hing|ëlli·n *vi* to neigh, whinny

hing|ëlli'm *nm ger* 1 < hing|ëllo·n 2 = hing|ëlli'më

hing|ëlli'më *nf* sound of neighing: whinny

hing|ëllo·n *vi* = hing|ëlli·n

hi'nkë *nf* 1 funnel 2 [*Biol*] infundibulum ()
  o hinka e shumëzimit cone filled with earth and used to root the branch of a fruit tree

hi'nk|ët *adj* (*i*) funnel-shaped

hino're *nf* urn for keeping ashes of the dead: crematory urn, funerary urn

*hi'nj|të *adj* (*i*) = hi'rtë

hi'p·ën *vi, vt* 1 to move/increase ([]) from a lower to a higher level: rise, arise; raise 2 to move ([]) onto or into a means of transportation: climb, mount, board

  o <> hip·ën^{3sg} {} <> *is* overwhelmed by {*a feeling*}

  o <> hip·ën^{3sg} damari <> *loses* <>'s temper, <> *flies* off the handle

  o <> hip·ën^{3sg} gjaku në fytyrë the blood *rushes* to <>'s face

  o <> hip·ën^{3sg} gjaku në kokë/tru <>'s temper *mounts* sharply

  o <> hip·ën^{3pl} kacabunjtë <> *becomes* angry: <>'s blood *begins* to boil

  o i hip·ën kalit lakuriq 1 (*Impol*) to get an undeserved job 2 to become immediately swell-headed

  o i hip·ën kalit mbrapsht/së prapthi to put the cart before the horse

  o i hip·ën kalit qorr to go into it blind

  o <> hip·ën mbi kokë to keep hovering over <*a person*>; keep hanging around <*a person*>

  o <> hip·ën mendja në qiell <> *puts* on airs, <> *is* swellheaded; <> *gets* very conceited

  o <> hip·ën^{3sg} mërzia <>'s annoyance/boredom *mounts*

  o hipi miza në rigon "the fly got on top of the oregano" {} thinks he's a bigshot

  o <> hip·ën^{3pl} mizat në kokë <> becomes greatly worried/troubled

  o <> hip·ën^{3pl} nervat <> *loses* <>'s temper

  o <> hip·ën në shpinë/kurriz 1 to take advantage of <>, exploit <> 2 to put <> under one's thumb

  o nuk hip·ën në degë të hollë not take risks

  o hip·ën në fron to assume the throne

  o hip·ën në fuqi to assume power

  o <> hip·ën^{3sg} në kokë/tru <> *gets* it into <>'s head, <> cannot get it out of <>'s mind

  o <> hip·ën në majë të kokës "mount on top of <>'s head" to become an unbearable annoyance to <>

  o <> hip·ën në qafë to have <> under one's complete control: have <> by the neck

  o [] hip·ën në qiell to praise [] to the skies; brag about []

  o <> hip·ën^{3sg} një avull në kokë <> *loses* <>'s temper, <> *gets* angry

  o <> hip·ën^{3pl} orët <> *is* possessed by fairies (said when someone is acting crazy with rage)

  o <> hip·ën përsipër 1 to force <> to submit, subjugate <>, subdue <> 2 to be a nuisance to <>

  o <> hip·ën^{3pl} qipujt "the goblins *jump* on <>" <> *is* possessed by demons; <> *flies* into a rage

  o i hip·ën qypit to get very angry, fly off the handle

  o <> hip·ën^{3pl} rrebet <> *bursts* into a rage

  o <> hip·ën^{3pl} xhindet "the jinni *jump* on <>" <> *is* possessed by demons; <> *flies* into a rage

  o <> hip·ën^{3sg} zemra në fyt "<>'s heart *leaps* to <>'s throat" <> *gets* very angry, <> *becomes* enraged

  o <> hip·ën^{3sg} zjarri the fire *covers* <> in flame

hiper| *formative prefix* hyper-

hiper|bo'lë *nf* 1 [*Lit*] hyperbole 2 [*Geom*] hyperbola

hiper|boli'k *adj* hyperbolic

hiper|bolizi'm *nm ger* (*Book*) < hiperbolizo·n

hiper|bolizo·n *vt* (*Book*) to hyperbolize

hiper|tensio'n *nm* [*Med*] hypertension, hyperpiesis

hiper|termi' *nf* [*Med*] hyperthermy

hiper|toni'k *adj* [*Med*] hypertensive, hypertonic

hiper|trofi' *nf* hypertrophy

hi'p|ës *nm* 1 (*Reg*) Dutch oven made of terra cotta 2 wooden ladder 3 (*Old*) horseman

hípǁi *1st sg pres* <**híp·ën**

hipí *nf* **1** = **mullar 2** = **stívë 3** hippie

hipík *adj* [*Sport*] **1** equestrian **2** for horses

hipíẑëm *nm* [*Sport*] equestrian sports, horsemanship

hípǁje *nf ger* <**híp·ën**

hipnotík
  I § *adj* **1** hypnotic **2** hypnotized
  II § *nm* **1** sleep-inducing drug **2** person in a hypnotic state

hipnotíẑëm *nm* hypnotism

hipnotizím *nm ger* <**hipnotizó·n**

hipnotizó·n *vt* to hypnotize

hipnotizúar *adj (i)* hypnotized

hipnotizúes
  I § *adj* hypnotic, hypnotizing
  II § *n* hypnotist

hipnozë *nf* hypnosis

hipo *formativ (Book)* **1** hypo- **2** hippo-

hipodróm *nm* hippodrome; race track

hipoidál *adj* [*Tech*] hypoid

hipokondrí *nf* hypochondria

hipokrít
  I § *adj* hypocritical
  II § *n* hypocrite

hipokrizí *nf* hypocrisy

hipopotám *nm* hippopotamus

hipostaẑë *nf* hypostasis

hipotekár *adj* [*Econ*] secured by mortgage

hipotekë *nf* [*Econ*] mortgage; mortgage office

hipotekím *nm ger* <**hipotekó·n**

hipotekó·n *vt* to mortgage []; give a mortgage on []

hipotenuzë *nf* [*Geom*] hypotenuse

hipotetík *adj* **1** hypothetical **2** [*Ling*] conditional

hipotezë *nf* hypothesis
  ∘ **hipotezë pune** working hypothesis

hípur
  I § *part* <**híp·ën**
  II § *adv* mounted, up
  ∘ **ësh-të hipur mbi kalë** to be riding high, be doing well

hiq·et *vpr* <**heq·ë 1** to move from one place to another: move away, move **2** to crawl **3** (of animals) to mate sexually **4** (*Reg*) to go, walk **5** (*Colloq*) to move well (in sales), be popular **6** (*Pej*) to get away, get out, scram **7** (*Colloq*) to distance oneself, avoid <> **8** to become emaciated, get thin/weak **9** to pretend, pretend to be
  ∘ **s'<> hiq·et nga dera** {} doesn't leave <> alone for a minute, {} doesn't give <> a moment's peace
  ∘ **s'<> hiq·et nga rruga/udha** "not get out of <>'s way" to be a constant hindrance to <>
  ∘ **hiq·et zvarrë/rrëshanë/rrëshqanë/rrëshkanjas 1** to go in a ponderous fashion: drag along, shuffle along, creep, crawl **2** to barely get along, have a hard life

hiq *stem for 2nd pl pres, pind, imper, vp* <**heq·**
  ∘ **Hiq e mos këput.** "Pull and don't break." Getting by, but just barely. Making some progress, but very slowly.
  ∘ **Hiqe mys** []! Stop worrying any more about []!
  ∘ **Hiqmu sysh!** Get out of my sight!

hir *nm* **1** kindness, favor; sake **2** will, willingness, good will; desire; love **3** good looks, beauty: grace, charm **4** [*Relig*] heavenly grace

  ∘ **hiri i Hënës** moon dust
  ∘ **hir e pa hir** willingly or unwillingly, willing or not, willy-nilly

híre *np* <**hir** religious relics

hírës *nm* plant disease caused by an oidium: powdery mildew

hirësí *nf* **1** good looks, beauty, grace **2** title or term of very polite address: (to a bishop or archbishop) Eminence, Holiness

hírësísht *adv* gracefully

hirësó·n *vt (Old)* [*Relig*] **1** to absolve [] of sin **2** to exalt

hírët *adj (i)* gray, dun-colored

hírǁi *obl* <**hi(r)**

hirmádh *adj* **1** very beautiful, extremely good looking, exquisite **2** very sympathetic toward others, good-hearted; forgiving **3** (*Old*) [*Relig*] merciful, full of forgiveness

hiró·het *vpr (Old)* **1** to entreat/beg <> **2** to flatter

hiró·n *vt* **1** to caress; flatter **2** to wish [] luck, felicitate, congratulate

*****hiró·n·et** *vpr (Reg Gheg)* = **hiró·het**

hirplótë *adj (Poet)* full of beauty, of beauteous mien, quite handsome

hirshëm *adj (i)* very good looking; very pleasant, amiable

hírtë *adj (i)* light gray

Hirúshe *nf* figure in Albanian folktales who appears as a beautiful, hard-working, and sweet little girl who is maltreated by her stepmother: Cinderella

hirráq *adj* thin and liquid like whey: runny; producing whey

hírrë *nf* **1** whey **2** [*Veter*] = **hírrëz, ndalosë**
  ∘ **hirrë breshke** (*Crude*) too watery (said of liquid foods)

hírrët *adj (i)* **1** of the color of whey: very pale **2** (of liquids) murky, cloudy, milky

hírrëz *nf* [*Veter*] a serious contagious viral disease of sheep and goats that thins their milk

hirrëzó·n *vi* to give off whey

*****hirrnúer** *adj (fem ˜ore) (Old)* serous

hirró·n *vi* to ooze with whey

hise *OR* **híse** *nf* **1** (*Colloq*) person's proper share; allotted portion of an inheritance **2** [*Ethnog*] offspring in the patrilineal line **3** (*Reg Colloq*) times (multiplied by): fold

hisëll *nm* (*Reg*) [*Bot*] = **híthër**

*****Hispaní** *nf (Old)* Spain = **Spanjë**

histerí *nf* hysteria

histerík *adj* hysterical

histeríẑëm *nm* hysterics

histologjí *nf* [*Anat*] histology

historí *nf* **1** history **2** story
  ∘ **historia hesht·**^{3sg} **për** [] history *is* silent about []

historián *n* historian

historík
  I § *adj* **1** historical **2** historic, memorable
  II § *nm* story

historikísht *adv* historically

historiografí *nf* historiography

historishkrúes *nm* historiographer

historízë *nf* short narrative/story

historíẑëm *nm* historicism

hish interj shoo! (to chase away fowl)

hitas stem for 1st sg pres, pl pres, 2nd & 3rd sg subj, pind <hitat·

hita't· vt to urge [] on, hurry, rush

hitatës adj, n (person) in a hurry/rush; hasty (person)

hitat'shëm adv in a hurry/rush; hastily

hiti' nf (Reg) **1** haste, hurry, rush; impetus, impulse **2** great care, heed; zeal

hith nm **1** [Bot] downy mildew **2** = **vrug**

*__hith__ = hidh

hithëbut'ë = hithërbut'ë

hithëbut'ëz nf [Bot] yellow archangel (Lamiastrum)

hithër

I § nf **1** [Bot] nettle (Urtica) **2** (Fig) vexing person, real pest

II § adj nettling, vexing

∘ **hithër deti** [Zool] stinging jellyfish

hithërbut'ë nf [Bot] dead nettle (Lamium)

hithërisht'ë nf place that is full of nettles

hithëror'e np **1** [Bot] nettle family Urticaceae **2** [Invert] Cnidaria

hith'ës nm **1** [Bot] wych elm, Scotch elm (Ulmus glabra) **2** [Med] nettle rash

hith'ëth nm **1** head kerchief made of black chiffon **2** [Bot] nettle tree (Celtis australis) = **carac**

hithkë nf (Reg) **1** [Bot] = **ajdës 2** = **hithër**

*__hiva'dhe__ nf [Zool] scallop

*__hjedh__ = hedh

*__hje'dhët__ adj (i) tall and thin: slender, slim; (of a mountain) high

*__hje'kës__ n person who betrays someone to help a thief or a person taking blood vengeance

*__hjek__ (Reg Gheg) = heq

*__hjeksë__ nf [Bot] marsh horsetail (Equisetum telmataia)

*__hjeksi'__ nf betrayal to help a thief or a person taking blood vengeance

*__hjekso·n__ vi to betray someone in order to help a thief or a person taking blood vengeance

hobe' nf **1** slingshot, sling **2** [Hist] catapult

hobeta'r nm [Hist] catapult artilleryman

*__hobo'rr__ = obo'rr

*__ho'dë__ = o'dë

Ho'do nf with masc agreement Hodo (male name)

ho'dh stem for pdef <he dh·

∘ **hodh**^{pdef} **gurë prapa** {} leave once and for all

*__hof__ = hov

ho-ho-ho' onomat sound of laughter: ho-ho-ho

hoj conj (Colloq)

∘ **hoj** __ **hoj** __ either __ or __

ho'je np <hu'all

*__ho'jë__ nf (Old) **1** escarpment, crag **2** = **hu'all**

hoj'ëz nf **1** honeycomb **2** nostril **3** [Anat] alveolus

hojë'zo'r adj [Anat] of or relating to alveolae: alveolar

hoj'më adj (i) extremely sweet (said of fruit)

ho'ka np jokes, kidding

hoka'ta'r

I § n kidder

II § adj jocular

hoke'ist n [Sport] hockey player

hoke'j nm [Sport] hockey

ho'kë nf **1** joke; prank *__2__ canister, box

hoko'·het vpr to be kidding around, be joking/teasing

∘ **hoko·**het me [] to be kidding/teasing []

hoko'·n

I § vi to be kidding

II § vt to kid, tease

holande'z

I § adj of/from Holland, Dutch

II § n native of Holland, Dutchman

Holandë nf Holland

holandi'sht adv in Dutch (language)

holandi'shte nf Dutch (language)

ho'le nf swinging cradle used outdoors for babies: baby hammock

holl nm hall; lobby

ho'lla np (të) **1** money **2** underwear; light summer underclothing **3** dry tinder for fire **4** (Reg) crops

holla'k adj slim, slender: thin, skinny; sharp

ho'llazi adv **1** thinly **2** (Fig) meagerly

ho'llë

I § adj (i) **1** delicate, fine; thin **2** (of bodies) slim, lean, slender **3** long and narrow **4** coming to a fine point or edge: sharp **5** in fine detail: detailed; delicate, fine, precise **6** composed of fine particles: fine **7** sparse; weak, watery **8** pleasantly light: delicate **9** (of a sound) high in pitch **10** sharply cold **11** (Fig) of delicate sensibilities; perceptive, intelligent, bright **12** (Fig) barely perceptible **13** (Colloq) weak; poor

II § adv **1** in a thin sheet: thinly; thinly clad **2** in small particles: finely **3** (of bowel movement) highly liquid, watery: loosely **4** in fine detail: precisely **5** with mental acuity/sharpness **6** with great care: very carefully **7** (Colloq) meagerly **8** in a high voice **9** (Fig) barely perceptibly

III § nn (të) **1** waist **2** shin, shinbone **3** (Old) moment, second **4** = **fi'kët**

ho'llë-ho'llë adv **1** in great detail **2** in a high-pitched voice; in a fine high voice

hollërina np fine threads

hollësi' nf **1** thinness; fineness, delicacy; highness (of a voice); acuity **2** detail, particularity

hollësi're nf **1** precision part **2** tiny, delicate thing; delicate detail **3** small particular, detail

hollësi'shëm adj (i) in complete detail

hollësi'sht adv finely, in detail, in fine detail, minutely

holli' nf fineness, sharpness; cleverness, subtlety

*__holli'__ obl <hu'all

holli'm nm ger **1** <hollo'·n, hollo'·het **2** (Reg) layer of pastry crust **3** (Fig Old) detail; precision; sharpness of mind *__4__ sharpness, edge

hollo'·het vpr **1** to get thin; get thinner; taper **2** to become diluted **3** (Fig Colloq) to become sharper in mental ability; gain precision **4** (Colloq) to become weaker, get worse, taper off **5** (Fig Colloq) to grow poorer

∘ <> **hollo·**het^{3sg} **gjaku** <>'s blood runs thin: <> gets old; <> gets cold/ill easily

∘ <> **hollo·**het^{3pl} **kikëzat** <> is growing weak; <>'s mind is going; <> is losing <>'s social standing

hollo'·n vt **1** to make [] thin, make [] thinner: tighten; sharpen; flatten, roll [] out; narrow **2** to make [the voice] go high **3** to refine **4** to make [] more watery: dilute **5** (Colloq) to weaken; make [] poorer **6** (Fig

Colloq) to tell [] in (overabundant) detail **7** *(Fig)* to make [] clearer and more comprehensible: clarify; simplify
○ **i hollo·n duart (së fërkuari)** to rub one's hands
○ **hollo·n majën e lapsit** to sharpen the pencil

hollojë́se *nf* **1** woman who rolls out dough; woman who prepares delicate pastry well **2** female bakery worker who prepares dough and brings it to the proper thickness; worker responsible for getting a mixture to the proper thickness

hollokroqe *nf, adj (Reg)* numbskull, dimwit

holluar *adj (i)* **1** made sharp: sharpened, pointed **2** made less thick: (of wood) planed down, (of dough) rolled out **3** thinned out with liquid: diluted **4** (sound) of high timbre

hollues
I § *nm* **1** rolling pin **2** [*Tech*] dilution device/apparatus **3** [*Tech*] diluting substance, diluent; thinner
II § *adj* serving to make thinner

holluese *nf* **1** woman who rolls out dough; woman who prepares delicate pastry well **2** female bakery worker who prepares dough and brings it to the proper thickness; worker responsible for getting a mixture to the proper thickness **3** rolling pin

*****holluet** *adj (i) (Reg Gheg)* pointed

hollush *adj (Pet)* slender

homazh *nm (Elev)* homage

homogjen *adj* homogeneous

homogjenësí *nf (Book)* homogeneity

homogjenitet *nm (Book)* = homogjenësí

homolë *nf* [*Invert*] kind of deepwater crab *Homola barbata*

homolog *nm* person in a corresponding position: opposite number

homonim
I § *nm* [*Ling*] homonym
II § *adj (Book)* having the same name/title

homonimí *nm* [*Ling*] homonymy

homonimík *adj* [*Ling*] homonymous

homor *nm* [*Med*] body fluid

homoseksual *adj, n (Book)* homosexual

homoseksualízëm *nm (Book)* homosexuality

hon
I § *nm* **1** gorge, ravine, gulch; deep crevasse **2** *(Fig)* dark abyss, deep emptiness **3** *(Reg)* = hínkë
II § *adj* empty

honder *nf* thick and knobby thread from the first or last stages of unwinding a silk cocoon = glytër

honeps· *vt (Colloq)* **1** to digest **2** to consider [] edible **3** *(Fig)* to put up with [ ]; bear, stand, abide

honepsje *nf ger* **1** < honeps· **2** digestion

*****honestër** *nf* = hon

honi *nf (Reg)* **1** = vrimë **2** = hínkë
○ **honia e sëpatës** socket in the head of an axe for a handle

*****honi** *obl (Reg Gheg)* < hue

honingím *nm* [*Tech*] honing

honingo·n *vt* [*Tech*] to hone

honinguese *nf* [*Tech*] honing machine: hone

honorar *nm (Book)* honorarium

honxho bonxho *nf with masc agreement (Contempt Insult)* **1** masked mummer at a festival; mock politician **2** vile and unprincipled person/organization: scalawag, rapscallion

hop
I § *nm* **1** very short time: moment **2** time, occasion **3** sudden leap forward **4** small strip (of land)
II § *interj* cry that accompanies or encourages a sudden burst of action: whoop! up we go! there we go!
○ **hop për hop 1** at any moment **2** now and then **3** for the time being
○ **ësh·të hop top** to move around from place to place, not stay in one place

hopa
I § *interj* = hop
II § *adv (Colloq)* held/cradled in one's arms

hopakallas *adv* = brezahypthi

hope-hope *adv* **1** = herë-herë **2** by fits and starts

hopthi *adv* **1** hopping, leaping **2** = hopa

hopthikallas *adv* = brezahypthi

hoq *stem for pdef* < heq·
○ **hoq gazepin e zi** had a really tough time

*****hor** *nm* = horr

*****horar** *nm* timetable

horas *adv* in chorus

horasan *nm (Colloq) (Old)* **1** = llaç **2** = gëlqere

hordop *nm* snowdrift

hordhí *nf* **1** [*Hist*] barbarian horde **2** *(Fig)* horde

*****hordhís·** *vi* to be boorish

*****hore** *nf* = horre

horë
I § *nf (Colloq)* **1** (field) weed to be burned **2** straw scarecrow that is set afire in a field **3** flame, fire **4** *(Reg Arb)* inhabited place: town
II § *adv* in flames, flaming

horiat *nm* stingy person: skinflint, niggard, miser

horizont *nm* **1** horizon **2** [*Hydrol*] water level

horizontal *adj* horizontal

horizontale *nf* **1** [*Geom*] horizontal line **2** [*Geod*] elevation contour line

horizontalisht *adv* horizontally

*****horrllëk** *nm (np ~ qe)* = horrllëk

hormon *nm* [*Physiol*] hormone

hormoq *nm* [*Bot*] Norway spruce *(Picea abies)*

*****horro** = horro

horoskop *nm* horoscope

hortikulturë *nf (Book)* horticulture = kopshtarí

horr *nm (Colloq)* **1** *(Insult)* vile/offensive person: stinker, rat, louse, bastard **2** *(Old)* bum, hobo **3** *(Contempt)* skinflint, miser *****4** deserter, coward
○ **horri i horrave** stinking rat/bastard, rotten louse

horras *adv (Colloq)* shamelessly

horre *nf* slut

horrllëk *nm (np ~ qe) (Colloq)* **1** immorality, baseness **2** *(Old)* extreme poverty, penury

horro·het *vpr* **1** *(Book)* to suffer humiliation **2** to behave/act shamelessly

horro·n *vt (Colloq)* to humiliate, vilify: tell off, bawl out

hosi *nf* aroma

hosten *nm* **1** drover's stick: goad, prod **2** two-pronged spear for fishing in shallow water **3** measure of length of roughly two or three meters: rod

hostenar *n* person who drives draft animals with a prod: drover

hoshaf
I § *nm* dessert made of dried fruit and custard; compote of dried fruit; dried fruit

II § *adj (Colloq)* dried up and wrinkled
○ **hoshaf me pala** [*Food*] dried figs boiled in sugar syrup

hoshafkë *nf* long black plum from which a prune is made

hoshmar *nm* [*Food*] dish made of finely ground corn bread crumbs mixed with butter and fresh cheese

*****hosht**ï**m**ë = **usht**ï**m**ë

hotel *nm* hotel

hotel**ïs**t *n* **1** hotel worker; hotel manager **2** hotel owner

hotel**-pensio**n *nm* residential hotel, rooming/boarding house

hotel**-restora**nt *nm* hotel with a restaurant

hotel**xhi** *nm (np ~nj)* hotel-keeper = **hote**l**ïs**t

hoth = **hodh**

hov *nm* **1** action/movement with sudden force: surge, leap; burst of energy/growth **2** *(Colloq)* time, occasion

hov·
I § *vi* **1** to move forward forcefully: leap, spring, lunge **2** to rush, mount an assault, attack **3** *(Fig)* to grow or develop suddenly: surge
II § *vt* **1** to ascend/climb/mount [] quickly **2** to leap across []
○ <> **hov**· **ndër këmbë** to prostrate oneself before <>, kneel before <>
○ <> **hov**· **në qafë** to hug <> energetically
○ **hov**· **përpjetë 1** to make a sudden upward motion: jump up, start **2** to overreact

hovarda *adj, nm (Colloq)* (person who is) free-spending: generous (person); excessively generous (person)

hovardal**lë**k *nm (np ~qe) (Colloq)* generosity; excessive generosity

*****hovardha** *adj* = **hovarda**

hovardhenj *np* <**hovarda** *(Colloq)*

hov**a**s *adv* with sudden impetus/force, with a sudden surge/push/rush/burst

hovdhën**ë**s *adj (Book)* lending impetus

hove-**hov**e *adv* spasmodically, sporadically; once in a while

*****ho**v**je** *nf ger* <**hov**·

hov**shë**m *adj (i), adv* in a sudden surge/burst

hoxhal**la**rë *np* <**hoxh**ë

hoxhe**s**ë *nf* wife of a Moslem clergyman

hoxh**ë** *nf with masc agreement* Moslem clergyman/muezzin, Moslem religious teacher
○ **Ali Hoxha, Hoxhë Aliu** it's all the same, it makes no difference
○ <> **foltë/këndoftë hoxha!** "May the khoja speak/sing for <>!" *(Curse)* May a priest give last rites to <>!: I hope <> *dies!*

hozheg *nm* long pole used in a bakery to poke the fire or to remove pans from the oven

hrushovian *nm* Khrushchevian

HSINHUA *abbrev (Chinese)* <**Kina e re (Agjencia e Lajmeve e RP të Kinës)** New China = Chinese News Service

hu(n)
I § *nm* **1** *(Old)* measure of grain equal to some 80-150 kg; grain repayment for a debt or for rent **2** *(Old Fig)* large amount
II § *np (Old)* **1** measures of grain; grain repayments **2** *(Old Fig)* large amounts

hu(r)
I § *nm (np ~nj)* **1** wooden post; fencepost, stake, pole **2** *(Fig)* blockhead
II § *adj (Fig)* oafish, stupid

hu·**het** *vpr* <**hu**a·n to take a loan

hua *nf* loan
○ **ta paça hua!** *(Felic)* I hope I can do the same for you some time, I owe you (one)

hua·n *vt* **1** to lend **2** to borrow

huadhë**n**ë**s** *n* lender, creditor

huadhë**n**ï**e** *nf* lending

hua**j**
I § *adj (i)* **1** foreign **2** strange **3** extraneous
II § *n (i)* foreigner, alien; stranger, outsider

hua**j**t *stem for pdef, opt, adm, part* <**hu**a·n

hua**j**t**ë**s *n* = **huadhë**n**ë**s

hua**j**t**je** *nf ger* <**hu**a·n, **hu**·*het*

*****huaj**t**o**·n *vt* to estrange, alienate

hua**j**t**ur** *adj (i)* loaned, lent

*****hu**a**j**thi *adv* in foreign manner

*****huaj**z**o**·n *vt* to give [] lodgings, put [] up: quarter, lodge

hua**ll**
I § *nm* honeycomb
II § *adj* very sweet: sweet as honey

huama**rr**ë**s**
I § *adj* borrowing, in debt
II § *n* borrower, debtor

huama**rr**je *nf* taking a loan: borrowing

hua**s** *n* lender = **huadhë**n**ë**s

hua**z**a *adv* **1** sometimes yes and sometimes no; now and then *****2** = **hu**a**zi**

*****hu**a**zash** *adv* = **hu**a**zi**

hua**zi** *adv* by give and take, with mutual exchange, to one another: reciprocally

huaz**ï**m *nm ger* **1** <**huaz**o·*n*, **huazo**·*het* **2** [*Ling*] borrowing, loan

huaz**ï**sht *adv* = **hu**a**zi**

huazo·n *vt* to take [] on loan, borrow

huaz**u**a**r** *adj (i) (Book)* borrowed

hubi *nf (Reg)* **1** serious damage, bad loss **2** *(Fig)* destructive group/horde

*****hubli**n**ë** = **huli**n**ë**

*****hubu** *adv* madly, wildly

*****hu**d**ë**r = **hu**dh**ë**r

*****hud**l**o** = **huto**

hudh**ë**r
I § *nf* **1** [*Bot*] garlic **2** *(Fig)* bad person
II § *adj* very
○ **hudhër arïnjsh** ramsons, bear's-garlic *Allium ursinum*
○ **hudhër e egër** [*Bot*] field garlic *Allium oleraceum*
○ **nuk hahet as me hudhra** *****1** (of a person) to be unbearable **2** to be unbelievable

*****hudh**ë**r**o·*het* *vpr* to leap in; hop to it

*****hudh**ë**r**o·n *vt* to throw

*****hu**dhje = **he**dhje

*****hudh** *(Reg Gheg)* = **hedh**

*****hu**e *nm (Reg Gheg)* honeycomb = **hu**all

*****huhni** *nf (Old)* espionage

*****huhni**t**ë**s *n (Old)* spy

hu-**hu** *interj* sound made to shoo away poultry

*****huj** *nm* **1** = **huq 2** wrath

hujaks· *vt* to give [ ] the evil eye: put a hex on [ ]

hujaks·et *vpr* to be under a hex, be hexed

hujem *nm* **1** grist **2** commission payment

*****hujme** *nf* vice

hujnajë *nf* structure built on piles

hukamë *nf* **1** warm breath created by huffing; deep breathing; sound of heavy breathing **2** yell, cry

hukas *stem for 1st sg pres, pl pres, 2nd & 3rd sg subj, pind* <**hukat·**

hukat·
    I § *vt* **1** to breathe warm air on [ ] **2** *(Old)* to cast a spell on [ ] (with a breath) **3** to shoo away [poultry] by yelling "hu-hu"
    II § *vi* **1** to exhale with force through the mouth: huff **2** to yell, cry out

hukat·et *vpr* **1** to huff and puff with fatigue **2** to yawn and sigh sleepily

hukatje *nf ger* **1** <**hukat·**, **hukat·et 2** huffing and puffing

*****hukubet** *nm* monster, boogieman

*****hukubetshëm** *adj (i)* monstrous

*****hulajë** *nf (Old)* seesaw

*****hulas** *stem for 1st sg pres, pl pres, 2nd & 3rd sg subj, pind* <**hulat·**

*****hulat·** *vt* to rock [ ] up and down

*****hulat·et** *vpr (Reg)* to rock, seesaw, sway

hulinë *nf* **1** fine chaff, dust **2** *(Fig)* good-for-nothing (person); worthless residue: dregs
    ○ **Duhen ndarë kokrrat nga hulina.**. "The kernels must be separated from the chaff." *(Prov)* One must separate the wheat from the chaff. You have to distinguish what is good from what is bad.

*****hulmëto·n** *vt* = **hulumto·n**

*****hulmëtues** = **hulumtues**

hulumtim *nm ger* **1** <**hulumto·n 2** investigation, inquiry; written report of an investigation **3** research

hulumto·n *vt* **1** to track [ ] down by scent: sniff [ ] out **2** to scan [ ] carefully, search [ ] closely **3** to investigate; do research on [ ]

hulumtuar *adj (i)* thoroughly investigated

hulumtues
    I § *adj* pertaining to research
    II § *n* researcher

*****hull·** *vt* to bring [ ] close

*****hull·et** *vpr (Reg Gheg)* to come close, approach

hulli
    I § *nf* **1** furrow **2** *[Med]* sulcus **3** *(Fig)* groove; wrinkle; proven path **4** ribbon; sash, belt
    II § *adj* empty

hullim *nm ger* **1** <**hullo·n 2** = **hulli 3** puff paste

hullizë *nf [Bot]* small groove in a plant stalk: (*canaliculus*)

*****hullna** *np (Old)* convolutions

hullo·n
    I § *vi, vt* to plow a furrow (in [ ])
    II § *vt* **1** to roll out [dough] *****2** = **hollo·n**

*****hullor** *adj* grooved, ridged, fluted

*****hulluveqkë** *nf [Ornit]* = **kukuvajkë**

humai *nf* fine cambric = **kambrik**

humakush *nm (Reg)* ostrich = **struc**

humanist
    I § *n* **1** humanist **2** humanitarian
    II § *adj* humanistic

humanitar *adj* **1** humanitarian **2** humanistic

humanizëm *nm* **1** humanism **2** humanitarianism

humb·
    I § *vt* **1** to lose **2** *(Colloq)* to cause to disappear: rub [ ] out, kill
    II § *vi* **1** to lose oneself, get totally absorbed **2** to get lost, go astray, stray **3** to disappear
    ○ <> **humb·**^{3sg} **batha** <> *gets confused,* <> *loses* the thread
    ○ <> **humb·**^{3sg} **boja** there *is* not a trace of <>, <> *disappears*
    ○ <>a **humb· derën** not visit <> anymore
    ○ **humb·**^{3sg} **dielli** *(Colloq)* the sun *is going* away; the sun *sets*
    ○ **humb· dritën e syrit/syve 1** to lose one's sight **2** to lose one's only child
    ○ <> **humb·**^{3sg} **fara** "<>'s seed *disappears*" completely *disappears*
    ○ <>a **humb· farën** to get rid of <> completely, make <> disappear completely
    ○ <> **humb· filli i lëmshit** to become completely confused, get all mixed up; lose one's train of thought
    ○ e **humb· fillin** to become confused, lose one's bearings
    ○ e **humb· fiqirin** to go out of one's mind, go crazy
    ○ <> **humb·**^{3sg} **fjala nga goja** <> *loses* <>'s tongue, <> *becomes* speechless
    ○ **humb· flamurin** *(Book)* to lose back the victory one has won
    ○ e **humb· gojën** to lose one's tongue; keep silent
    ○ **humb· klasën** to fail the class
    ○ **Humb kokën e pyet për flokët.** "Lose your head and ask about your hair." *(Prov)* Ignore what is important and worry about trifles.
    ○ <> **humb·**^{3sg} **krakëllima** <> voice *fades* into the distance, <> *is* heard from no more; <> *disappears* without a trace
    ○ e **humb· lojën** to suffer failure after expending effort to succeed
    ○ <> **humbtë mandata** "May <>'s death notices be lost!" *(Curse)* I can't wait for <> to be gone forever!
    ○ e **humb· mendjen** to go out of one's mind, go crazy
    ○ <> **humbtë nami/nishani/vula!** "May <>'s mark disappear!" *(Curse)* May <> disappear and be forgotten!
    ○ **humb· në gjumë** to fall into a deep sleep
    ○ **humb· në peshë** to suffer a loss in weight; get rid of some weight, lose weight
    ○ **humb· në vaj e fito·n në presh.** "lose in oil and gain in leeks" to lose more in a deal than one makes in another
    ○ **humb· në sytë e <>** to lose favor in <>'s eyes
    ○ **humb· pa shenjë** to disappear without a trace
    ○ **Nuk humbi pazari për gjilpëra.** "The market never runs out of needles." *(Prov)* There are plenty more fish in the sea.
    ○ i **humb· pikët para <>** to lose { } points (of favor) with <>
    ○ <> **humb·**^{3sg} **pisha** "<>'s torch *gets lost*" <> *disappears* without a trace
    ○ **humb· provimin** to fail the examination
    ○ e **humb· pusullën** to become confused, lose one's bearings
    ○ **Humb qetë e pyet për brirët.** "Lose the ox and ask about the horns." *(Prov)* Ignore what is is important and worry about trifles.

○ **humb· qetë e pyet· për brirët** *(Prov)* to be concerned about trifles when there is something really important to worry about

○ **humb· si fasulja në vegsh** "disappear like the bean in the cooking pot" to drop out of sight completely

○ **humb· si guri në lum/ujë** to disappear without a trace

○ **humb· si gjilpëra në kashtë** "get lost like the needle in the haystack" to disappear completely

○ **humb· si meli në haliç/rërë** "disappear like millet in gravel/sand" to be nowhere in evidence, seem to have disappeared completely

○ **humb· si pluhur në erë** "get lost like dust in wind" **1** to disappear without a trace **2** to go for naught

○ **humb· si re** to disappear/vanish like a cloud

○ **humb· si sëpata pa bisht** to be a total waste

○ **humb· si shurra e pulës** "get lost like hen's piss" *(Crude)* to disappear without a trace: be down the toilet

○ **e humb· si Xhaferi simiten** to become confused, lose one's bearings

○ **humb· si vesa e mëngjesit//në diell** "disappear like the dew *of morning//in the sun*" to disappear fast, vanish quickly without a trace

○ **humb· sytë** to lose one's eyesight

○ **humb· tokë** *(Book)* to be forced to concede

○ **e humb· toruan** to become totally confused

○ **e humb· udhën në oborr** "lose one's way in one's backyard" to be a person who gets lost easily, be easily confused; be hopelessly incompetent

○ **<> humbtë varri!** *(Curse)* May <>'s grave be lost! Hanging is too good for <>!

○ **humb· vitin** to fall back a year, fail the grade

○ **<> humb·**^{3sg} **vula** "<>'s mark *disappears*" <> *vanishes* without a trace

○ **e humb· vulën** to lose one's way, become totally confused

○ **humb· zemër/ zemrën** to lose heart; become cowardly

○ **<> humb·**^{3sg} **zëri** "<>'s voice gets lost" <> *is* never heard from, <> *disappears*

hu'mb·et *vpr* = përhu'mb·et

○ **humb·et lartësi** to lose altitude; descend

○ **humb·et nën lëkurë** *(Scorn)* to keep quiet and try to hide one's guilt, try to look innocent

○ **humb·et**^{3sg} **nishani** not a single one *is* left

hu'mb|a *adv (Reg)* = hu'mbazi

hu'mb|a-hu'mb|a *adj* pitted with holes (in the ground); with deep crevasses, full of ravines

humb|a'k *nm* quicksand; deep mud

humb|ala'q *adj, n (Pej)* feckless (person)

hu'mb|as *adv* = zhy'tas

humb|a's| *stem for 1st sg pres, 1st & 3rd pl pres, 2nd & 3rd sg subj* <humbet·

*****humb|a'tje** *nf(Old)* shipwreck

hu'mb|azi *adv* without getting anything in return: for nothing

humb|e'll|ë *nf* sinkhole

humb|et· *vt, vi* = humb·

○ **e humbet· udhën në oborr** "lose one's way in one's backyard" to be a person who gets lost easily, be easily confused; be hopelessly incompetent

hu'mb|ë *nf* **1** hole in the ground; gorge, crevasse **2** poor soil, barren land; clay

humb|ë's
I § *adj* losing
II § *n* loser

humb|ë'sir|ë *nf* **1** ravine; abyss, chasm **2** remote place, distant/forgotten land **3** *(FigImpolite)* feckless person

humb|ë't *adj (i)* **1** remote; deep **2** lost, vanished

humb|ë'tir|ë *nf* = humb·ësirë

humb|i'm *nm [Geol]* subsidence, sinking

humb|i's *stem for 2nd pl pres, pind* <humbet·

humb|i'sht|ë *nf* **1** gorge, ravine, gulch; deep crevasse, abyss **2** subterranean bed of a stream or river

humb|i't *stem for pdef, opt, adm, part, pind, 2nd pl pres, imper, vp* <humbet·

hu'mb|je *nfger* **1** <humb·, humb·as· **2** loss **3** waste **4** defeat **5** casualty, loss **6** delirium, daze **7** *(Fig Colloq)* far-off place, nowhere

○ **humbje e shërbimit** *[Volleyball]* loss of service: side out

*****humb|o'·het** *vpr* to yield to pressure: sink, give

humb|o'·n *vi* **1** to sink into the earth, subside into the ground **2** to fall in and be immersed: sink in

humb|o're *nf* **1** uninhabited and forgotten distant land, far-off/remote place, remote wilderness **2** ravine; abyss, chasm

hu'mb|sh|ëm *adj (i)* apt to get lost

humb|ull|o'·n *vi* **1** = humbo'·n **2** *(Fig)* to disappear without a trace

hu'mb|ur
I § *adj (i)* **1** lost **2** wasted **3** *(Fig)* in a daze, bewildered; in a permanent daze, totally out of it; totally incompetent **4** feckless **5** forgotten, remote; of little importance; secluded, wild and uninhabited **6** lost in battle **7** haggard, gaunt; battle-worn **8** extremely weak; barely audible: dying out
II § *adv* unprofitable, in vain, bootless, for nothing

humne're *nf* **1** deep gorge; precipice; abyss, crevasse **2** *(Fig)* abysmal darkness; depths of despair

humo'r *nm* **1** humor **2** mood, temper

humor|i'st *n* humorist

humor|i'st|ik *adj* humoristic

humor|i'z|ëm *nm* humorous character/feature/nature, humor

hu'mus *nm [Agr]* humus

humus|o'r *adj (Book)* consisting of or containing humus: humous

hun *nm [Hist]* Hun

huna'p *nm [Bot]* wild olive, oleaster *(Elaeagnus angustifolia)*

hunap|o're *n [Bot]* oleaster family *Elaeagnaceae*

hunda'c = hunda'ç

hunda'ç *adj* **1** pug-nosed; having a big turned-up nose **2** having a nasal voice: nasal **3** *(Fig)* haughty, arrogant, conceited

hunda'k *adj* **1** = hunda'ç **2** *(Old)* *[Ling]* = hundo'r

hundara'k *adj (Pej)* big-nosed

hund|ç *nm* = hu'ndës

*****hund|çy'ç** *adj* = hundështy'pur

hunde' *nf* **1** muzzle strap on a halter **2** spiked metal ring around an animal's muzzle to prevent suckling, grazing, or biting

hunde'c *adj* = hunda'ç

hu'nd|ë *nf* **1** nose **2** tapered protrusion; prow of a ship; promontory **3** *(Colloq)* spout = lëfy't **4** *(Colloq)* *[Geog]* = kep **5** *(Colloq)* quantity that can be inhaled

in one sniff: noseful, sniff **6** [*Zool*] nose-horn of a sand viper
◦ **hundë dheu** headland, cape
◦ **(tërë) hundë e buzë 1** having a disappointed look on one's face **2** with a cold look
◦ **<>a heq hunda** (*Colloq*) <>'s nose *is* twitching, <> *has* a premonition
◦ **hundë me majë** nose that curves up nicely to a point
◦ **hundë me samar** hooked nose
◦ **hundë më hundë 1** very close to one another; face to face **2** under one's very nose
◦ **Hunda në lis, morri në kurriz.** "The nose in the oak, the louse down the back" (*Prov*) A person who shows off will suffer for it. Pride goeth before a fall.
◦ **<> rri· (tërë) hundë e buzë** to maintain an unfriendly demeanor toward <>
◦ **hundë si qiri** straight nose
◦ **hundë shkabë = hundëshkabë**
◦ **hundë të zëna** stuffed-up nose
◦ **hundë toke** [*Geog*] headland, cape
◦ **ta vjedh·³ʳᵈ hundën** *midis//në mes të syve* "{} can steal your nose from between your eyes" {} *is* an accomplished thief

hundëbri *nm* [*Zool*] **1** rhinoceros = **rinoqeront 2** rhinoceros beetle (*Dynastes*)

hundëçip *adj* **1** having a small and pointed nose **2** (*Pej*) haughty, arrogant, conceited, stuck-up

hundëdash *adj* having a nose bent-in like a ram

hundëderr *adj* (*Insult*) **1** pig-nosed **2** stubborn

hundëdrejtë *adj* having a straight nose

hundëfeçkë *adj* (*Insult*) having a nose like a snout: snout-nosed

hundëgjatë *adj, n* **1** having a long nose or muzzle **2** [*Entom*] snout beetle, weevil (*Curculionidae*)

hundëgjerë *adj* having a wide nose: broad-nosed

hundëhequr *adj* having a long thin nose

hundëkalem *adj* (*Poet*) having a nice-looking long straight nose

hundëkërrabë *adj* having a nose turned down at the tip

hundëkërrutë *adj* having a hooked nose

hundëkuq *adj* having a bulbous nose with a red tip

hundëlesh *adj* **1** having profuse nose hair **2** (*Fig*) daring and foolhardy, audacious

hundëmadh *adj* **1** big-nosed **2** (*Pej*) conceited

hundëmprehtë *adj* **1** having a thin, pointed nose **2** (*Fig*) having a good sense of smell: sharp-nosed

hundëngrënë
I § *adj* having a nose eaten away (by some disease)
II § *nm* (*Colloq*) rotten-nosed syphilitic person; syphilitic

hundëngushtë *np* [*Zool*] catarrhina ()

hundëpatate *adj* (*Insult*) potato-nosed, bulbous-nosed

hundëpatëllxhan *adj* (*Insult*) eggplant-nosed, having a great big nose

hundëpërpjetë *adj* **1** having a turned-up nose **2** (*Pej*) stuck-up, conceited, arrogant

hundëqiri *adj* having a nose as straight as a candle

hundëquirre *adj* runny-nose

hundëro·n *vi* **1** (of horses) to snort softly: snuffle **2** to pronounce vowels nasally, speak through the nose

hundërrjepur *adj* whose nose has peeking skin: with a peeling nose

hundës
I § *n* person with a nasal voice
II § *adj* *nasal = **hundor**

hundëse *nf* **1** halter strap that fits around the nose of a horse **2** = **hundëz**

hundëspec *adj* (*Insult*) **1** red-nosed **2** (*Fig*) quarrelsome, looking for trouble

hundësqep *adj* (*Insult*) beak-nosed

hundëshkabë *adj* = **hundëshqiponjë**

hundëshqiponjë *adj* having an aquiline nose

hundështrembër *adj* having a crooked/lopsided nose

hundështypur *adj* having a flattened nose

hundëtrashë *adj* having a thick nose: big-nosed

hundëvarur *adj* displeased and unhappy: downcast

hundëz *nf* **1** spiked metal ring around an animal's muzzle to prevent suckling, grazing, or biting **2** muzzle strap on a horse halter **3** [*Tech*] nozzle **4** (*Dimin*) little nose

hundëzaj *adv* downcast, with fallen face

hundim *nm ger* **1** <**hundo·n, hundo·het 2** offense, insult, affront; outrage, umbrage

***hundis** *stem for 1st sg pres, pl pres, 2nd & 3rd sg subj, pind* <**hundit·**

***hundit·** = **hundëro·n**

***hundluq** *adj* = **hundështypur**

hundo·het *vpr* **1** to take umbrage/offense, be outraged **2** to turn up one's nose; sneer

hundo·n *vt* to put []'s nose out of joint: affront, offend, insult

hundor *adj* nasal

hundore *nf* [*Ling*] nasal consonant/vowel

hundorësi *nf* [*Ling*] nasalized pronunciation

hundorëzim *nm* [*Ling*] nasalization

hundos·et *vpr* to get in a snit, get angry

***hundpaç** *adj* = **hundështypur**

***hundreç** *nm* curb bit

hundro·n *vi* **1** to speak gruffly ***2** = **hungëro·n**

hunduar *adj* (i) **1** affronted, offended, insulted, outraged ***2** glum

***hundzim** *nm* nasality

hungarez *adj, n* of/from Hungary, native of Hungary

Hungari *nf* Hungary

hungarisht *adv* in Hungarian (language)

hungarishte *nf* Hungarian language

hungëri·n *vi* = **hungëro·n**

hungërim *nm ger* <**hungëro·n** = **hungërimë**

hungërimë *nf* **1** howl, wail **2** growl; snarl **3** whine (of machines)

hungërit· *vi* = **hungëro·n**

hungëritje *nf ger* = **hungërim**

hungëro·n *vi* **1** to howl, wail; keen **2** to growl; snarl **3** (of machines) to whine

hungërues *adj* **1** howling, wailing **2** growling; snarling **3** whining (if machines)

hun¦i *obl* <**hu(n)**

***hunxë** *nf* nib, tip; pen

hunj *np* <**hu(r) 1** poles, stakes, posts, fenceposts **2** (*Fig*) blockheads

hunjas *adv* using posts/stakes, with posts/stakes

hup· *vt* **1** to press hard on [] **2** *(Fig)* to smack, hit hard **3** = humb·

hu'p·et *vpr* **1** (of bread) to get stale and hard *2 to coagulate, thicken

hu'pës
I § *n* **1** person whose killing cannot be avenged because the killer is unknown or because no one in the family is left to take revenge: unavenged person **2** *(Reg)* one who has lost his way
II § *adj (Reg)* = hu'mbur

hu'pët *adj (i)* **1** compressed and hard, solid; coagulated **2** lacking in freshness: stale **3** *(Reg)* = hu'mbur **4** *(Reg)* eaten out inside, hollowed out **5** *(Reg)* loosely packed, uncompacted

*hu'pje *nf ger* = hu'mbj*e*

huq
I § *nm (Colloq)* **1** quirk, eccentricity, peculiarity; foible, vice **2** failed move: miss
II § *adv (Colloq)* **1** in vain, in failure **2** amiss, awry, afield, wrong

huqe'ma'dh *adj, n* having many foibles/peculiarities

huq'lli *adj, n* = huqema'dh

hurb· *vt* to drink [] by sucking in swallows: swig, gulp, sip

hu'rb·a-hu'rb·a *adv* in swigs/gulps/sips

hurba's stem for *1st sg pres, pl pres, 2nd & 3rd sg subj, pind* <hurba'·

hurba't· *vt* = hurb·

hu'rbë
I § *nf* gulp, sip
II § *adj* (of eggs) soft-boiled

*hurdh *nm* tubercle

*hurdh'ata'k *adj (Old)* marshy

*hu'rdhe *nf* ivy = urth

hurdhe'le *nf* small pond

hurdhë *nf* **1** marsh; pond **2** deep pool in a river **3** *(Fig)* neighborhood, neck of the woods
∘ ësh·të³ˢᵍ hurdhë e pagjuajtur "be in virgin ivy/woods" to be well off; (of a place) rich in unexploited resources

hurdhi'q *adj* thoroughly wet: drenched, soaking wet, soused

hurdho're *nf* area with pools of water

hur'li *obl* <hu(r) **1** pole, stake, post, fencepost **2** *(Fig)* blockhead
∘ i hurit e i litarit brutally criminal, evil/vicious

*hurm = hurb

hurma' *nf* = hurmë

hu'rmë *nf [Bot]* **1** date palm; date *(Phoenix dactylifera)* **2** Japanese persimmon, kaki *(Diospyros kaki)* **3** date plum *(Diospyros lotus)* **4** *(Reg)* = vadhëvi'çe
∘ hurmë Stambolli date plum, date-plum persimmon *Diospyros lotus*

*hurp = hurb

*hurpa's stem for *1st sg pres, pl pres, 2nd & 3rd sg subj, pind* <hurpa'·

*hurpa't· *vi* to drink in gulps

*hurth = urth

huruve'jkë *nf (Reg) [Ornit]* = kukuvajkë

*hust *interj* command directed at oxen: giddyup

hushku'lur *adj (Pej)* vagrant, vagabond

hut
I § *nm* **1** *[Ornit]* woodland owl with a mournful cry: hoot owl **2** *(Fig Insult)* numskull, blockhead; senile person, dotard
II § *adv (Reg)* very well, just fine
∘ hut me vesh *[Ornit]* horned owl

huta'q *adj, n (Pej)* scatterbrained/absent-minded (person)

hute'së *nf* bewilderment, puzzlement; absentmindedness, distractedness

hutë *nf* **1** *[Ornit]* buzzard *(Buteo buteo L.)* **2** *[Ornit]* female hoot owl **3** *(Fig)* dimwitted girl or woman; senile/dotty woman **4** ewe with very small ears **5** *(Old)* rear-loading single-shot flintlock gun with four rifling grooves
∘ hutë e bardhë *[Ornit]* Egyptian vulture *Neophron percnopterus* = kali i qyqes
∘ hutë deti *[Ornit]* = pul'ebardhë
∘ hutë grënzangrënëse *[Ornit]* honey buzzard *Pernis apivorus L.*
∘ hutë me kalxa *[Ornit]* rough-legged buzzard *Buteo lagopus Brunn.*

hut'erro·het *vpr* = huto'·het

hut'erro'jë *nf* **1** *[Ornit]* vulture = hu'të **2** *(Reg)* scatterbrained girl or woman

huti'm *nm ger* **1** <huto'·n, huto'·het **2** *(Reg)* error, mistake **3** *[Med]* stupor

huti'm'thi *adv* in bewilderment, in a confused state

huti'n *nm [Ornit]* = hut

hutlo'·het *vpr (Reg)* = huto'·het

hutlo'·n *vt* **1** *(Reg)* = huto'·n **2** to hoodwink, deceive

huto'·het *vpr* **1** to be bewildered, confused **2** to be amazed/dazzled

huto'·n
I § *vt* **1** to cause bewilderment in []: stupefy, bewilder, confuse **2** to surprise [] greatly: daze, stun, shock, dazzle
II § *vi* to make a mistake, err

*hut'rro·het = huto'·het

hutu'ar *adj (i)* bewildered, confused, stunned, taken aback

hutu'es *adj* stupefying, bewildering; amazing; confusing

hutu'e'shëm *adv* in a state of bewilderment, in a confused way; absentmindedly = huti'mthi

*huturi'·n *vi* = uturi'·n

*hy *nm* = hyj

hy'·het *vp impers* there *is* an entrance, it *is* enterable

hy'·n *vi* **1** to enter; enter on the scene **2** to shrink **3** to sag **4** *(Colloq)* = perëndo'·n
∘ <> hy·n to get down to work on <>, get busy with <>; attack <> vigorously
∘ <> hy·n brenda to understand <> thoroughly: get <it>, get a thorough grasp of <it>
∘ Hyn derri e dosa. "The boar comes in and the sow." Anybody (no matter how bad) can get in.
∘ <> hy·n në dorë **1** to take <> in hand: get down to work on <something> **2** to take a hand to <> in order to give <> a beating
∘ Nuk hyn drapri në thes. *(Prov)* It is impossible to hide such an obvious thing. It's too big to sweep under the rug.
∘ hy·n e del· me <> to be on friendly social terms with <>
∘ hy·n e del· e tund· peshqirin *(Impol)* to waste time doing useless things
∘ hy·n e del· si në shtëpinë e vet "come and go as if in one's own home" to do whatever one likes
∘ <> hy·n³ᵖˡ ferrat <> becomes uneasy

○ <> hy·n^{3sg} **frika** <> *gets* frightened; <> *becomes* overcome with fear; <> *lives* in fear
○ <> hy·n^{3sg} **gjembi** <> *is* obsessed
○ s'<> hy·n^{3sg} **gjë në thes** "not go at all into <>'s sack" **1** to be of no concern to <>; not be any of <>'s business **2** <> *gets* nothing out of it
○ **nuk** <> hy·n^{3sg} **gjë në xhep** <> *gains* nothing from it, <> *gets* nothing out of it
○ **Nuk hyn hosteni në thes.** *(Prov)* It is impossible to hide such an obvious thing. It's too big to sweep under the rug.
○ <> hy·n^{3sg} **i paudhi në bark** "the devil *enters* <>'s belly" <> *starts* to have wicked thoughts
○ <> hy·n^{3sg} **krimbi** something *keeps* eating/gnawing at []
○ <> hy·n **lepuri në bark** "the hare *enters* <>'s belly" <> *becomes* terribly afraid, <> *is trembling* with fear
○ <> hy·n^{3sg} **lezeti për** [] "pleasure *enters*<> in respect to []" <> *begins* to like []
○ <> hy·n^{3sg} **madhështia** <> *becomes* conceited
○ <>**a** hy·n **me dru** to start giving <> a beating
○ <> hy·n **me gjithë opinga** "get down to work on <> even with one's clogs" to become totally committed to working on <>, devote all one's energies to <>
○ <> hy·n **me laps** to calculate <> accurately, figure <> all out carefully
○ <>**a** hy·n **me** [] to get down to work on <> with [a tool]
○ <> hy·n **meraku për** [] <> *gets* worried about []
○ **Nuk hyn minarja në thes.** *(Prov)* It is impossible to hide such an obvious thing. It's too big to sweep under the rug.
○ hy·n **mish e del· peshk** "go in meat and come out fish" *(Impol)* not learn a thing
○ <> hy·n^{3pl} **mizat 1** <> *is* very eager: <> has ants in <>'s pants; <> *is* in a rage **2** <> *becomes* unsettled/disquieted
○ <> hy·n **ndër hundë** to get in <>'s way (when <> is trying to accomplish something)
○ <> hy·n **ndër petka** to get to know <>'s problems intimately
○ hy·n **në bri të buallit/kaut** to go into hiding, hole up
○ hy·n **në dhe 1** *(Colloq)* to die **2** to vanish into thin air, not be seen anymore; vanish out of embarrassment
○ <> hy·n **në fjalë** to understand <> finally, get <>'s point
○ <> hy·n **në gjak** to get into <>'s blood, become part of <>'s body
○ <> hy·n **në gji** to get to know <>'s problems intimately
○ <> hy·n **në gjynah** to stick a knife in <>'s back; bear false witness against <>
○ hy·n **në gjynah** to commit a sin; do wrong
○ hy·n **në hak** not deal justly with <>
○ <> hy·n **në hatër** to come into favor with <>, start to appeal to <>
○ <> hy·n **në hesap 1** to interfere/meddle in <>'s affairs **2** to get an undeserved portion of what rightfully belongs entirely to <>
○ **nuk** hy·n **në hesap** not be worth dealing with, not be worth the trouble, be of no account
○ <> hy·n **në hise** to get an undeserved portion of what rightfully belongs entirely to <>

○ hy·n **në histori** to become famous/unforgettable, go down in history
○ hy·n **në punë** to be useful
○ hy·n **në jetë** to enter adult life
○ hy·n^{3rd} **në jetë** to be part of daily life
○ **nuk** hy·n **në kallëp** not be suitable/proper
○ <> hy·n^{3sg} **në kokë/krye 1** to stick in <>'s mind **2** <> *gets* it into <>'s head, <> cannot get it out of <>'s mind
○ <> hy·n^{3pl} **në kokë miza të këqija** "bad flies enter <>'s head" <> *is* not <>self, <> *is* not quite in <>'s right mind
○ **nuk** <> hy·n **në kokë/krye** not penetrate <>'s skull, <> just *can't* understand {}, <> *doesn't* get {}
○ <> hy·n^{3sg} **në kokë/krye për** [] <> *gets* [] into <>'s head, <> cannot get [] out of <>'s mind
○ <> hy·n **në krah** to come to <>'s aid/support
○ hy·n **në livadh të huaj** to encroach on another's territory
○ hy·n **në lojë** to get oneself into a complicated and dangerous game
○ <> hy·n **në llafe** to get what <> is driving at
○ hy·n **në mend e del· pa mend** to have one's breath taken away, be astonished
○ hy·n **në mes** to intercede, intervene
○ hy·n **në modë** to come into fashion
○ **nuk** <> hy·n **në punë/qese/kut/trastë/xhep 1** to be of no use/interest to <> **2** not be <>'s business
○ hy·n **në një pyll të thellë** "enter a deep forest" to take on a complicated task and not know how to get started on it
○ hy·n **në një rabush me** [] *(Pej)* to take up with []
○ hy·n **në një thes me** [] "go into the same sack with []" to be put in the same category as [], be compared/equated with []
○ <> hy·n^{3sg} **në një vesh e** <> **del nga tjetri** *(Impol)* it *goes* in one ear (of <>) and out the other
○ hy·n **në ofshin e** <> to become the object of <>'s curses
○ hy·n **në pazar me** [] to bargain with []
○ **Hy·**n **në pus e del· pa u lagur.** "go into a well and come out without getting wet" to be very tricky/clever
○ hy·n **në pus** to get into deep trouble
○ <> hy·n **në qejf** {} <> *starts* to like {}
○ hy·n **në rrogë** *(Colloq)* to get a (paying) job
○ hy·n **në rrogë te** {} *(Old)* to enter into {}'s employ: start to work for {}
○ hy·n **në rrugë të shtrembër** to take the wrong ("crooked") road/path
○ s'<> hy·n^{3sg} **në sy asgjë/askush** nothing/nobody *can* fill in the emptiness left in <>'s heart
○ s'<> hy·n^{3sg} **në sy** not catch <>'s fancy
○ <> hy·n **në shpirt/zemër** "enter <>'s heart" to enter into <>'s affections, <> *begins* to love {}
○ hy·n **në të** {*number*} **in** to reach the age of {}
○ **nuk** <> hy·n^{3rd} **në tru** <> just *can't get* {} into <>'s head
○ hy·n **në thike** *(Colloq)* to undergo surgery
○ hy·n **në vathë** "enter the fold" to join others who are behaving themselves
○ s'<> hy·n **në vesh (fjala)** "the word *doesn't* enter <>'s ear" **1** <> *doesn't* listen, <> *is unwilling* to listen **2** <> *doesn't understand*
○ <> hy·n **në vesh që/se** __ <> *hears* accidentally that __, <> *happens* to hear that __

○ **hy·**_n_ **në vrimë të miut** "go into the mouse hole" to scamper into hiding, be so afraid that one doesn't know where to hide

○ **hy·**_n_ **në zgjedhë** to submit to the yoke, submit

○ **hy·**_n_ **në** [] **1** to get into [] in a real way: enter [], enter into []; go in []; get included in []; become part of []; start to participate in []; sink down into [], settle [] **2** to get down to work on/at/with [place/tool used for work] **3** = hy/h_et_

○ **hy·**_n_ **nën udhë** to take the wrong path

○ **hy·**_n_ **nëpër lakër** to get unnecessarily mixed up in a complicated matter

○ **hy·**_n_ **për** {_number_} **1** to be {_number minus one_} going on {_number_} (in age) **2** to reach the age of {}

○ <> **hy·**_n_^{3pl} **pleshtat (në trup)** <> _is starting to get nervous:_ <> _get ants in_ <>_'s pants_

○ **i hy·**_n_ **pyllit** to take on a complicated task and not know how to get started on it

○ **hy·**_n_ **si fanti spathi** [] sticks []'s nose in where it doesn't belong

○ **hy·**_n_ **si luga në pilaf** "enter like the spoon in the rice" _(Pej)_ to intrude without invitation; stick one's big nose in

○ **hy·**_n_ **si pykë** to stick one's nose in where it doesn't belong

○ **hy·**_n_ **si xhol** "come in like a joker" to poke one's nose into everything, intrude in matters that are none of one's business

○ **hy·**_n_ **shul e del·/vje·**_n_ **lloz** "come in as a rod and go out as a bar" to gain nothing (from a lesson/experience)

○ **hy·**_n_^{3sg} **të ftohtët** <> _gets cold_

○ <> **hy·**_n_^{3sg} **ujët/uji nën rrogoz/hasër** "the water _is coming_ in under the floor mat" to get into a tight spot all of a sudden

○ <> **hy·**_n_^{3sg} **veremi (për** []) **1** <> _gets sick with worry (about_ []) **2** <> _gets lovesick (for_ [])

○ <> **hy·**_n_^{3sg} **vetja në qejf** <> _becomes_ very conceited

○ <> **hy·**_n_^{3sg} **vrasa** "killing enters <_them/us/you_>" to begin to kill <_each other_> (in a blood feud)

○ <> **hy·**_n_^{3sg} **zjarri (në shtëpi)** discord/dissension _enters_ <>'s into the family, strife rears its ugly head in the family

*__hye'në__ _nf_ [_Zool_] hyena = hie'në
__hyj__ _nm_ god
*__hy'je__ _np_ <__hyll__ stars = __yj__
*__hyj'esi__ _nf_ divinity
*__hyj'esim__ _nm ger_ = __hyjnizim__
*__hyj'eso·__*_n_ _vt_ = __hyjnizo·__*_n_
*__hyj'lindse__ _nf (Old)_ morning star
*__hyj'nderim__ _nm (Old)_ veneration, worship
__hyj'neshë__ _nf (Poet)_ goddess
__hyj'ni__ _nf_ divinity, god
__hyj'nim__ _nm ger_ = __hyjnizim__
__hyj'nizim__ _nm ger_ <__hyjnizo·__*_n_
__hyj'nizo·__*_n_ _vt_ to deify
__hyj'nizua'r__ _adj (i)_ deified; venerated
__hyj'no·__*_n_ _vt_ = __hyjnizo·__*_n_
__hyj'no'r__ _adj_ **1** divine, godly **2** _(Fig)_ miraculous, marvelous; extraordinary **3** _(Old)_ religious

__hyj'no're__ _nf_ [_Bot_] aster _(Aster)_
__hyj'nori__ _nf_ divinity, holiness
__hyj'nua'r__ _adj (i)_ = __hyjnizua'r__
__hyj'nue's__ _adj_ = __hyjnizu'es__
__hyj'nue'shëm__ _adj (i)_ = __hyjno'r__
*__hyj'plime__ _nf (Old)_ Milky Way
*__hyj'sim__ _nm ger_ = __hyjnizim__
*__hyj'so·__*_n_ _vt_ = __hyjnizo·__*_n_
*__hyll__ _nm_ star = __yll__
○ **hylli i karvanit** the planet Venus
*__hyll'ësi__ _nf_ constellation = __yjësi__
*__hy'llëz__ _nf_ anemone
*__hy'me__ _nf (e)_ _(Reg Gheg)_ = __hyrë__
*__hymn__ = __himn__
*__hymno'·__*_n_ _vt_ to praise [] in songs/poems of praise: laud
*__hy'mun__ _part_ <__hy·__*_n (Reg Gheg)_
*__hy'muna__ _np (të)_ _(Reg Gheg Old)_ [_Fin_] income, revenue
*__hyna'da'las__ _adv (Reg Gheg)_ going in and out
*__hy'p__ _(Reg)_ = __hip__
*__hyq__ = __huq__
__hyr__ _stem for pdef, part, imper_ <__hy·__*_n_
○ **hyri në këtë der**ë, (e) **doli në atë der**ë "entered through this door, (and) left through that door" {} learned nothing from it
__hy'ra__ _np (të)_ [_Fin_] revenues, income
○ **të hyra e të dala** friendly social visits
__hy'rë__
I § _part_ <__hy·__*_n_
II § _nf (e)_ **1** opening by which one can enter: entry, ingress; entrance, portal **2** friendly social visit **3** hole, pit
III § _nn (të)_ entering, beginning
__hy'rës__
I § _adj_ **1** entering; introductory **2** _(Old)_ preliminary
II § _nm_ son-in-law who moves in with his wife's family
__hyri__ _nf (Old)_ **1** houri; beautiful maiden (in Moslem paradise) **2** _(Fig)_ extremely beautiful girl/woman
○ **hyria e detit** mermaid
__hy'rje__ _nf ger_ **1** <__hy·__*_n_ **2** opening by which one can enter: entry, ingress; entrance, portal **3** friendly social visit **4** introduction (in a book) **5** [_Fin_] income, revenue **6** [_Mus_] prelude
○ **[e] bë·**_n_ **hyrje** [_Fin_] to receive [a shipment/deposit]
○ **hyrje e dalje** friendly social visit
○ **hyrje në vegël** [_Gymnastics_] mount (on the apparatus)
__hy'rje-da'lje__ _nf_ **1** coming and going, entry and exit **2** friendly social visit **3** [_Fin_] inventory control
*__hyrybe'l__ OR __hyrybe'sh__ _adj_ tall, lanky
*__hysa'r__ _nm_ hussar
__Hy'skë__ _nf with masc agreement_ Hyskë (male name)
*__hysht·__ = __ysht·__
__hy'shtër__ _nf (Reg)_ [_Bot_] forsythia = __bo'shtër__
__hyxhy'm__ _nm (Colloq)_ sudden surge of energy, rush; sudden assault
__hyzmeqa'r__ _n (Colloq)_ servant
__hyzme't__ _nm (Colloq)_ care; service
__hyzmet'çi__ _nm (Old)_ person who serves customers or guests: server

Ii

i [i] *nf* **1** the letter "i" **2** the unrounded high front vowel represented by that letter

i *proclitic attributive article* marks agreement with a masculine nominative referent

i *pronominal clitic preceding a verb, or suffixed to a verb stem in the imper* **1** indicates that the verb has a 3rd sg referent: to/for/of him/her/it **2** indicates that the immediately following transitive verb has an identifiable 3rd pl object: them

i *interj* expresses disgust: ugh, yech

ia *sequence of clitics* (3rd sg referent + 3rd person object)

iberík *adj, n* Iberian

ibërshím *nm* twisted embroidery thread made of lustrous silk

ibërshím|të *adj (i)* of lustrous silk thread

Ibrahím *nm* Ibrahim (male name)

IBRD *abbrev (English)* International Bank for Reconstruction and Development

ibret
  I § *adv (Colloq)* horrible, hideous, ugly
  II § *nm* **1** deterrent **2** misshapen/loathsome person
  *3 horror

ibrík *nm* teakettle

ibri|qe *np* <ibrík

ICC *abbrev (English)* Interstate Commerce Commission

íckël *nf* light kick

iç *nm* [Food] (in pastry) filling, stuffing: forcemeat, nut layer, custard filling

*****idáre** *nf* control, supervision; economic management

ide' *nf* idea

*****íde** = híde

ideál *nm, adj* ideal

ideal|íst *n* idealist

ideal|ízëm *nm* idealism

ideal|izím *nm ger (Book)* **1** <idealizo·n **2** idealization

ideal|izo·n *vt (Book)* to idealize

identifikím *nm ger* **1** *(Book)* <identifiko·n **2** identification

identifik|o·n *vt (Book)* to identify

identík *adj (Book)* identical

identite't *nm (Book)* identity

ideo|artistík *adj* artistic and ideological

ideo|estetík *adj* aesthetic and ideological

ideolo'g *n* ideologue, ideologist

ideologjí *nf* ideology

ideologjík *adj* ideological

ideologjikísht *adv* ideologically

ideo|politík *adj* political and ideological

ideór *adj* conceptual, in terms of ideas: ideational

ide|shëm *adj (i) (Book)* imbued with the correct ideology, ideal

ide|shm|ërí *nf(Book)* ideational content

idërshah *nm [Bot]* = barbaro'zë

idíl *nm* [Lit] idyll

idil|ík *adj* [Lit] idyllic

idiocí = idiot'ësí

idiomatík *adj* idiomatic

idiomat|ízëm *nm* [Ling] idiomaticness

idio'më *nf* idiom

idio't
  I § *adj* idiotic
  II § *n* idiot

idiot|ësí *nf* idiocy

idiot|ízëm *nm* = idiot'ësí

*****idjo't** = idio't

idolatrí *nf* idolatry

idh|cë *nf (Colloq)* gall bladder

*****ídhe** *nf* [Bot] monkshood (Aconitum)

*****idhën|a'r** *n* = hidhna'k

*****ídhër| = hídhër|

*****ídh|ët** *adj (i)* bitter = hídhur

idh|n = hidhër|

idh|na'k = hidhna'k

*****idh|na'kth** *nm [Bot]* = hidhna'kth

*****idh|na'q** *nm* = hidhna'q

idh|na'r *adj* = hidhna'k

*****idh|ni|ta'r** *adj* = hidhna'k

*****idhrovola'nt** *nm (Old)* = hidropla'n

*****idh|sí|në** *nf(Reg Gheg)* = hidhësí|rë

*****ídh|shëm** *adj (i)* bitter, angry

*****ídh|tas** = hídhtas

*****idh|t|ím** *nm* **1** <ídhto·n **2** embitterment; bitterness, sorrow

*****idh|to'·n** *vt* to embitter; sadden

idhujta'r
  I § *adj* idolatrous
  II § *n* idolator

idhujtarí *nf* idolatry

ídhull *nm (np ~ j)* idol

*****idhull|atrí** = idhujtarí

*****idhull|ta'r** = idhujtarí

ifta'r *nm* **1** [Relig] meal eaten after fasting during Ramadan; the time of the day when this meal is eaten *2 festive meal at the beginning of Ramadan

igrasí *nf(Colloq)* small amount of moisture: dampness, slight humidity

igume'n *nm* abbot of an Orthodox monastery

ij|as *OR* **ij|azi** *adv* **1** sidelong, sidewise, along the side, on the side **2** alongside, beside **3** aslant, obliquely; askew, awry, lopsided

íje *nf* **1** pain, spasm **2** trouble

ij|ë *nf* (left or right) side (of the body); flank
  ∘ **íjë më íjë** from one side to the other

ij|o'r *adj* of the flank; costal

ik·ën *vi* **1** to leave, depart, go away, go **2** to flee, run away **3** to vanish, disappear; come to an end, come to one's end, die **4** to elapse, pass, pass by **5** to flow, pour **6** to go alop: become lopsided **7** to be spent too fast: be wasted
  ∘ <> **ik·ën 1** to leave without <>, <> *misses* {} **2** <> *loses the use of* {an organ}; <> *loses* {a dear one}, <>'s {} *dies*

○ <> **ik·ën**^{3sg} **barku** <> *is* sickened (by a horrible sight)

○ <> **ik·ën**^{3sg} **bizgë** <> *has* the runs, <> *has* diarrhea

○ <> **ik·ën**^{3pl} **furkat** <> loses <>'s mind, <> goes crazy

○ <> **ik·ën**^{3sg} **fytyra** <>'s face *falls*, <> suddenly *turns* pale

○ <> **ik·ën**^{3sg} **gjaku (nga fytyra)** the blood *drains* from <>'s face

○ **ësh·të "ikë të ikim"** to be a total panic

○ <> **ik·ën**^{3sg} **koka** <> *gets* killed

○ **ik·ën ku sytë këmbët** to take to one's heels

○ <> **ikën lopa me gjithë viç.** "<>'s cow leaves with the whole calf." <> is too lax (as a supervisor).

○ **ik·ën me bisht në shalë** *(Colloq)* to leave with one's tail between one's legs, leave in shame

○ **ik·ën me bisht nën shalë** to leave in shameful defeat

○ **ik·ën me të katra** to run away fast: take off on all fours; run on all fours

○ <> **ik·ën**^{3sg} **mendja (e kokës) 1** <> *loses* <>'s mind, <> *goes* crazy **2** <> *is* stupefied

○ <> **ik·ën**^{3sg} **nga mendtë/mendsh** to slip <>'s mind

○ <> **ik·ën**^{3sg} **mosha** <> *gets* old; <> *gets* too old, *becomes* overage

○ <> **ik·ën nëpër duar** to slip out of <>'s grasp, slip away from <>

○ <> **ik·ën nga dora/duart 1** to get away from <> (<> *loses* a good opportunity with {}) **2** to get out of <>'s control, <> *loses* control of {}

○ **ik·ën nga faza** *(Colloq)* to go out of one's mind, go crazy

○ **ik·ën nga mendja** to escape <>'s mind

○ **ik·ën nga meseleja** to break one's word/promise, go back on one's word

○ <> **ik·ën nga sytë 1** to leave without <>'s noticing **2** to escape <>'s notice

○ **ik·ën nga sytë këmbët** to take to one's heels

○ **ik·ën nga shiu e bie**$_1$ **në breshër** "escape the rain and fall into hail" out of the frying pan into the fire

○ **ik· nga tymi e bie**$_1$ **në zjarr.** "{} *goes* from the smoke and *falls* into the fire." Out of the frying pan and into the fire

○ **Ik o qar, se kam zarar.** "Leave, oh profit, for I have a loss." *(Prov)* I'd like to do it but it's too dangerous.

○ **Ik, or, tutje! 1** *(Impol)* Hey you, get out of here! Hey you, beat it! **2** You can't mean it! You must be kidding!

○ **i ik·ën pazarit të parë** to change from one's original price

○ **ik·ën rrozga me bjezga** to leave hurriedly and in disorder, flee in haste

○ **ik·ën si djalli/shejtani nga temjani** "distance oneself like the devil from incense" to get the hell out of there, flee in terror

○ **ik·ën si reja me breshër/furtunë** "leave like a hail/storm cloud" to leave in a great rush

○ **ik·ën si vetëtima e beharit** "leave like the lightning of summer" to leave very quickly

○ <> **ik·ën**^{3sg} **shpirti** <>'s heart *stops*, <> *is* frozen in fear

○ <> **ik·ën**^{3pl} **trutë (e kokës)** "<>'s brains (of <>'s head) *leave*" **1** <> *goes* into a state of shock **2** <> *goes* crazy, <> *loses* <>'s mind

○ <> **ik·ën**^{3sg} **turbullira** <>'s head *clears* up

○ <> **ik·ën**^{3sg} **zemra** <>'s heart *stops*, <> *is* frozen in fear

○ <> **ik·ën**^{3sg} **zogu nga dora** "the bird *escapes* from <>'s hand" <> *lets* the opportunity slip away

ik|aca|k
  I § *adj (Disparaging)* cowardly, chickenhearted
  II § *nm* cowardly person who runs away from danger

ik|aca|ke *nf (Pej)* woman who has abandoned her husband

ik|ana|k *nm (Pej)* = **ikacak**

ik|e *nf (Colloq)* girl/woman who spends time running around to see other people rather than staying at home

ik|ë
  I § *nf* **1** departure; escape **2** *(Reg)* death: passing
  II § *interj (Colloq)* go on! (you must be kidding!), oh sure! yeah sure!
  ○ **ikë e ikë** (used in tales to indicate a prolonged period of walking) continuing on and on

ik|ër *nf* **1** egg of a fish/amphibian/crustacean/mollusk **2** caviar; dry salted roe of the mullet

ik|ës *adj, n* fugitive, refugee

ik|i *1st sg pres* <**ik·ën**

ik|je *nf ger* **1** <**ik·ën 2** departure, leaving **3** escape, getaway, flight

ikon|ë
  I § *nf* icon
  II § *adj (Colloq)* having a face that is pale and drawn; lacking spirit, lifeless

ikon|o|graf *nm (Book)* iconographer

ikon|o|grafi *nf (Book)* iconography

ikon|o|grafi|k *adj (Book)* iconographic, iconographical

ikon|o|kla|st *nm (Book)* iconoclast

ikon|om *nm (Old) [Relig]* lowest clerical title in the Orthodox church: deacon, simple priest

ikon|osta|s *nm* iconostasis

ikra *np* fish roe, caviar

iks *nm* **1** the name of the letter "x" in the Roman alphabet used to represent a mathematical variable **2** *(Book)* used to indicate anonymity of a following noun: "a certain __"

*****ik|shëm** *adj (i)* fleeting

*****iktill** *nm (Old)* evil spirit

iktio|log *n* ichthyologist

iktio|logji *nf* ichthyology

ik|ur *adj (i)* **1** escaped, fugitive; refugee **2** *(Colloq)* insane, deranged: crazy, nutty **3** *(Fig Colloq)* past saving, beyond hope: gone

ILA *abbrev* <**Instituti i Lartë i Arteve** Academy of Arts

ila|ç *nm* **1** medicine, drug, medicament; cure, remedy **2** *(Colloq)* chemical used for cleaning or disinfecting; pesticide
  ○ **ilaç i vjetër në shishe të re** *(Pej)* old wine in a new bottle

*****ilaka** *nf* = **afri**

ilaritet *nm (Book)* hilarity

ILB *abbrev* <**Instituti i Lartë Bujqësor** College of Agriculture

ildi *nf* basted stitch

ildis· *vt* (in sewing) to baste

ildisje *nf ger* **1** <ildis· **2** (in sewing) basting work: basting

ilegal
 I § *adj* **1** illegal **2** clandestine
 II § *nm* person working illegally

ilegalisht *adv* **1** illegally **2** surreptitiously

ilegalitet *nm* **1** illegality **2** clandestine activity; the underground taken as a collective whole

****ilektrik = elektrik**

ilet *nm (Colloq)* **1** epilepsy **2** chronic illness **3** *(Fig)* custom, habit; vice

****iliber** *(Old)* = ylber

ilik *nm* **1** buttonhole **2** loop made to hang something from; belt loop **3** one of the loops forming a mesh; hole in a woven textile

iliqe *np* <ilik

ilir
 I § *adj* Illyrian
 II § *n* native of Illyria

Ilir *nm* Ilir (male name)

Iliri *nf* Illyria

Ilirian *nm* Ilirian (male name)

ilirik *adj* Illyrian

ilirishte *nf* Illyrian (the language)

ilis *stem for 1st sg pres, pl pres, 2nd & 3rd sg subj, pind* <ilit·

ilit· *vt* to hem

****iliver** *(Old)* = ylber

ILKF *abbrev* <Instituti i Lartë i Kulturës Fizike Institute of Physical Culture

****ilne** *OR* ilnje = ilqe

ilnjë *nf [Bot]* = ilqe

ILO *abbrev (English)* ILO = International Labor Organization

ILP *abbrev* <Instituti i Lartë Pedagogjik College of Education

ilqe *nf [Bot]* evergreen oak, holm oak *(Quercus ilex)*

ilqishte *nf* forest of evergreen oak

iluminist *adj, n (Book)* illuminist

iluminizëm *nm (Book)* illuminism

ilustrim *nm ger* **1** <ilustro·n **2** illustration, picture **3** illustration, example

ilustro·n *vt* to illustrate

ilustruar *adj (i)* illustrated

ilustrues *adj* illustrative

iluzion *nm (Book)* illusion

iluzionist *n (Book)* illusionist

iluminist *n* = iluminist

iluminizëm *nm* = iluminizëm

im
 I § *pronominal adj masc sg* my, of mine
 II § *nm* **1** mine **2** my male relative/friend

im· *vt* to make thin

imagjinar *adj* imaginary

imagjinatë *nf (Book)* imagination

imagjino·het *vpr (Book)* to imagine to oneself

imagjino·n *vt (Book)* to imagine, dream up

imagjinueshëm *adj (i)* imaginable

imak *nm* round clump of dough to be rolled out to form a leaf of pastry

imam *nm [Relig]* imam

imam bajalldi *nf [Food]* stuffed eggplant

iman *nm [Relig]* faith in Allah

imanent *adj (Book)* immanent

imar *nm* swath of grass

imazh *nm (Book)* image

****imblaq**
 I § *adj* foolish, silly
 II § *n* fool

ime
 I § *pronominal adj fem sg* my, of mine
 II § *nf* **1** mine **2** my female relative/friend

imediat *adj (Book)* immediate

imët
 I § *adj (i)* **1** consisting of very small particles or filaments: fine **2** characterized by fineness of texture: fine **3** of small dimensions; of very little width or thickness: thin, fine **4** skinny, frail **5** *(Fig)* in great detail, down to the last detail; finely detailed **6** of or pertaining to sheep and goats
 II § *adv* in fine detail

imëta *np (të)* **1** tiny particles; small details **2** sheep and goats **3** small change, cash

imëtak *adj* slight of build, somewhat skinny

IMF *abbrev (English)* International Monetary Fund

imigracion *nm* immigration = imigrim

imigrant *nm* immigrant

imigrim *nm ger* **1** <imigro·n **2** immigration

imigro·n *vi* to immigrate

imitacion *nm (Book)* imitation = imitim

imitim *nm ger (Book)* **1** <imito·n **2** imitation

imito·n *vt (Book)* to imitate

imonik *nm (Reg)* = shalqi

imoral *adj* immoral

imoralitet *nm* immorality

impedencë *nf [Electr]* impedance

imperativ *nm [Ling]* imperative

imperator *n* emperor

imperatori *nf* empire

imperfekt *nm [Ling]* imperfect = pakryer

imperialist *n, adj* imperialist

imperializëm *nm* imperialism

impersonal *adj [Ling]* impersonal

impiant *nm [Tech]* physical plant, plant; factory equipment

imponim *nm ger* <impono·n

impono·n
 I § *vt* to exert force on [], importune
 II § *vi* to be impressive, impress <>, make an impression on <>

import *nm* **1** import, importation **2** *(Collec)* imports

importim *nm ger* **1** <importo·n **2** importation **3** imported goods

importo·n *vt* to import

importues *nm* importer

impostim *nm ger* <imposto·n

imposto·n *vt* to send [] by mail: post, mail

impozant *adj* impressive, imposing

impresionist *n, adj* impressionist

impresionizëm *nm* impressionism

improvizim *nm ger* **1** <improvizo·n **2** improvisation

improvizo·n *vt* to improvise

improvizues *nm* improvisator, improviser

impuls *nm (Book)* impulse

impulsiv *adj (Book)* operating by impulse: impulsive

imshta**j**ë *nf* grove of young saplings

imshta**k** *nm* young tree, sapling; seedling, sprig

imshtë *nf* **1** coppice **2** flour hopper in a mill; grain hopper

imshto·*n* *vt* to mill, grind [] up = blu**'**a·*n*

imtas *adv* = imtësi**'**sht

imtë

I § *nf* very short period of time: moment, instant, second

II § *adj* (*i*), *adv* * = i**'**mët

imtësi *nf* **1** smallness, minuteness **2** fine detail

imtësi**'**m *nm ger* <imtëso**'**·*n*

imtësi**'**sht *adv* in detail; minutely

imtës**o**·*n* *vt* **1** to break [] up into small particles: fragmentize, pulverize **2** (*Fig*) to analyze [] carefully and in detail

imti *nf* **1** fine detail **2** acumen, keenness of mind, intelligence

imti *adv* (*së*) = imtësi**'**sht

imti**'**m *nm ger* **1** <imto**'**·*n* **2** fine detail

imto**'**·*n*

I § *vt* **1** = imtës**o**'·*n* **2** to chop [] into thin fibers; make [] thinner

II § *vi impers* it *is* drizzling; it *is* snowing in fine flakes

imun *adj* immune

imunite**'**t *nm* (*Book*) immunity

imunizi**'**m *nm ger* **1** <imunizo**'**·*n* **2** immunization

imunizo**'**·*n* *vt* to immunize

imunizua**'**r *adj* (*i*) immunized

imzo**'**t *nm* **1** [*Relig*] title or term of respect for a bishop or archbishop: Monsignor **2** (*Old*) term by which a servant addressed his master or a wife (in some regions) addressed her husband: my lord, milord, master

inat *nm* (*Colloq*) **1** spite; wrath; ill will, grudge **2** spiteful stubbornness

○ **Kija inatin por hakun mos ia ha!** Give the devil his due!

○ **Kija inatin dhe/por foli hakun!** Give the devil his due!

○ **ësh·të me inat** to be in an angry mood

○ **(si) për inat** as if for spite, ironically; just for spite

inatçe**'**shë *fem adj* (*Colloq*) <inatçi**'**

inatçi**'** *adj* (*Colloq*) **1** short-tempered, bad-tempered, spiteful, choleric **2** filled with rancor: rancorous, vindictive **3** stubborn, pig-headed; strong-minded

inatçi**'**nj *np* <inatçi**'**

inatos·*vt* (*Colloq*) to cause [] to be angry: make [] mad, rile

inatos·*et vpr* (*Colloq*) **1** to lose one's temper/patience: get mad/sore, get all riled/worked up **2** (*Fig*) to lash out, rage

inato**'**sur *adj* (*i*) (*Colloq*) sore, miffed, in a huff; mad, angry; worked up, angered

inauguri**'**m *nm ger* **1** <inaguro**'**·*n* **2** inauguration

inauguro**'**·*n* *vt* to inaugurate

incide**'**nt *nm* (*Book*) incident

*incis = inci**'**z

incizi**'**m *nm ger* **1** <incizo**'**·*n* **2** incision; trace/scar/ sign of an incision: engraved image **3** recording

incizo**'**·*n* *vt* **1** to cut a record of []: record [] **2** to make a skin incision **3** to engrave/carve/cut into wood or other hard medium: incise

ind *nm* **1** yarn used to weave across the warp: weft; spun fiber: yarn **2** (*Fig*) sketched design: sketch **3** [*Anat*] tissue

○ **s'ësh·të as për ind as për majë** to be too little, be insufficient

○ **ind e majë 1** from beginning to end **2** smart; cunning; troublemaking

*indak *nm, adj* indigo = llulla**'**q

indeks *nm* index

independencë *nf* independence

*indës *nm* [*Bot*] wayfaring tree (*Viburnum lanata*)

Indi *nf* India

indian

I § *adj* Indian

II § *n* **1** American Indian **2** native of India

indic *nm* **1** indication, symptom **2** [*Law*] evidence

indiferencë *nf* (*Book*) indifference; resignation

indiferent *adj* indifferent

indiferentiz**ë**m *nm* indifference, detachment, lack of concern

indigjen

I § *n* (*Book*) indigenous native, aborigine

II § *adj* indigenous, aboriginal

indikati**'**v *nm* [*Ling*] indicative

indikato**'**r *nm* indicator

indinjatë *nf* (*Book*) indignation, resentment

indinjo**'**·het *vpr* (*Book*) to become indignant

indinjo**'**·*n* *vt* (*Book*) to arouse indignation/resentment in []

indinjue**'**s *adj* (*Book*) indignant

indirekt

I § *adj* indirect

II § *adv* indirectly

indisiplini**'**m *nm* lack of discipline

indisht *adv* [*Ling*] in (an) Indian (of India) language

indishte *nf* [*Ling*] Indian (of India) language

individ *nm* **1** individual **2** (*Colloq*) person unattached to a larger unit: private person

individual *adj* individual

individuali**'**st

I § *adj* individualistic

II § *n* individualist

individuali**'**sht *adv* individually

individualite**'**t *nm* individuality

individuali**'**zëm *nm* individualism

individualizi**'**m *nm ger* **1** <individualizo**'**·*n* **2** individualization

individualiz**o**·*n* *vt* to individualize

*indjak *adj, n* (*Old*) = india**'**n

indo**'**·*n* *vi, vt* to weave; darn

indoevropia**'**n *adj* (*Book*) Indo-European

Indokine**'**z

I § *adj* Indochinese

II § *n* native of Indochina

Indokinë *nf* Indochina

indoktrini**'**m *nm ger* **1** <indoktrino**'**·*n* **2** indoctrination

indoktrino**'**·*n* *vt* to indoctrinate

indonez

I § *adj* Indonesian

II § *n* native of Indonesia

Indonezi**'** *nf* Indonesia

indonezia**'**n *adv* in Indonesian (language)

*Indo-Qin**ë *nf* (*Old*) Indochina

indo'r *adj* [*Biol*] of or pertaining to tissue: histological

Indrit *nm* Indrit (male name)

indukcio'n = induksio'n

induksio'n *nm* induction

induktim *nm ger* 1 <indukto' ·n 2 induction

induktiv *adj* inductive

induktivite't *nm* [*Phys*] inductance

indukto' ·n
I § *vi* [*Log*] to draw a logical induction
II § *vt* [*Electr*] to induce an electrical current

induktor *nm* [*Tech*] inductor coil, inductor

industri *nf* industry

industrial *adj* industrial

industrialist *n* industrialist

industrializim *nm ger* 1 <industrializo' ·n 2 industrialization

industrializo' ·n *vt* to industrialize

industrializuar *adj* (i) industrialized

inerci *nf* [*Phys*] inertia

infarkt *nm* [*Med*] infarct

infekcio'n = infeksio'n

infeksio'n *nm* infection

infektim *nm ger* 1 <infekto' ·n, infekto' ·het 2 infecting, (process of) infection

infektiv
I § *adj* infectious
II § *nm* department/division of infectious diseases

infekto' ·het *vpr* to become infected

infekto' ·n *vt* to infect

infektuar *adj* (i) infected

inferio'r *adj* inferior

inferiorite't *nm* (*Book*) inferiority

infermeri = infermieri

infermie'r *n* [*Med*] hospital nurse

infermieri *nf* 1 [*Med*] infirmary, sick-ward 2 the nursing profession

infiltrat *nm* [*Med*] infiltration

infiltrim *nm ger* 1 <infiltro' ·n, infiltro' ·het 2 infiltration

infiltro' ·het *vpr* [*Med*] to infiltrate, percolate

infiltro' ·n *vt* [*Med*] to infiltrate, permeate

infinitiv *nm* [*Ling*] infinitive

inflacio'n *nm* [*Econ*] inflation

inflamacio'n *nm* [*Econ*] inflammation

*inflator *adj* inflationary

influenc*ë* *nf* influence = ndikim

influencim *nm ger* <influenco' ·n

influenco' ·n *vt* to influence = ndiko' ·n

informacio'n *nm* 1 information, report 2 agency or location responsible for releasing information

informa't*ë* *nf* 1 information revealed during an inquiry/inquest 2 information, report

informativ *adj* informative; informational

informator *n* informant, informer

informim *nm ger* 1 <informo' ·n 2 = informa't*ë*

informo' ·n
I § *vt* to inform
II § *vi* to give out information

informuar *adj* (i) informed

informue's *nm* = informator

infrakuq *adj* infrared

infuzor*ë* *np* [*Zool*] Ciliophora

*Ingelter*ë* *OR* Ingliter*ë* *nf* (*Old*) England = Angli

*ingla *np* decorations, finery

*inglez = angle'z

*inglisht = anglisht

*ingliz = angle'z

ingrana'zh *nm* 1 [*Tech*] toothed wheel, gear 2 gear mechanism 3 (*Fig Book*) interconnected internal components of a complex structure/operation: machinery 4 (*Fig Book*) actual operation of a complex social structure/organization: workings 5 (*Fig Book*) working component of a complex activity/organization: mechanism

*ingjine'r = inxhinie'r

inhalacio'n *nm* inhalation

inhere'nt *adj* inherent

iniciativ*ë* *nf* initiative, initial step = nism*ë*

iniciator
I § *n* initiator
II § *adj* initiatory, initiating

*inisiat = iniciat

inkandeshe'nt *adj* [*Spec*] incandescent

*inkasatue'r *nm* (obl ~ o'ri) (*Old*) payee

*inkase *np* (*Old*) cash payments

inkasim *nm ger* <inkaso' ·n

inkaso' ·n *vt* 1 to encase 2 to deposit [money] in a bank

inkastrim *nm ger* 1 [*Spec*] <inkastro' ·n 2 insertion

inkastro' ·n *vt* [*Spec*] to insert

inklinacio'n *nm* [*Phys*] inclination

inkludo' ·n *vt* to include

inkluziv *adj* inclusive

inkluzivisht *adv* inclusively

inkuadrim *nm ger* 1 <inkuadro' ·n 2 [*Cine*] framing

inkuadro' ·n *vt* 1 to frame, enclose [] in a frame 2 to incorporate, include 3 to engage [personnel], place [] in position

inkubacio'n *nm* [*Spec*] incubation

inkubator *nm* incubator

inkuizicio'n *nm* [*Hist*] Inquisition

inkuizitor *n* [*Hist*] inquisitor

inkurajim *nm ger* 1 <inkurajo' ·n 2 encouragement

inkurajo' ·n *vt* to encourage

inkurajue's *adj* encouraging

inkursio'n *nm* 1 incursion, raid 2 [*Sport*] sudden attack/rush on the goal

*inonda't*ë* *nf* inundation

inorganik *nm* [*Chem*] inorganic = joorganik

inovacio'n *nm* innovation

inse'kt *nm* insect = kandërr

insekta'r *nm* case for keeping insects

insektembyt*ë*s
I § *adj* insecticidal
II § *nm* insecticide

insektengrën*ë*s *adj* insectivore

insektevra's*ë*s *nm* insecticide

insistim *nm* 1 <insisto' ·n 2 insistence

insisto' ·n *vt* to insist

inspektim *nm ger* 1 <inspekto' ·n 2 inspection

inspekto' ·n *vt* to inspect, make an inspection of

inspekto'r *n* inspector

inspektora't *nm* state agency charged with conducting inspections; office of the inspector

inspektori *nf* **1** inspector's duty/job: inspection **2** = **inspektorat**

inspiracion *nm* inspiration

inspirim *nm ger* <**inspiro'·n**

inspiro'·n *vt* to inspire

instalim *nm ger (Book)* **1** <**instalo'·n, instalo'·het 2** installation

instalo'·het *vpr (Book)* to settle, become established

instalo'·n *vt (Book)* to install

instancë *nf* **1** [*Law*] judicial level at which a legal proceeding is heard **2** [*Offic*] administrative level in a state agency

instinkt *nm* instinct

instinktiv *adj* instinctive

instinktivisht *adv* instinctively

institucion *nm* institution

institut *nm* **1** institute **2** [*Law*] social institution; social mores

instruksion *nm (Book)* instruction

instrukto'·n *vt (Book)* to instruct

instruktor *n* **1** instructor *2* [*Sport*] trainer

instrument *nm (Book)* instrument

instrumental *adj* [*Mus*] instrumental

instrumentist *n* [*Mus*] instrumentalist

insulinë *nf* insulin

integral *nm* [*Math*] integral

integrim *nm ger* **1** <**integro'·n, integro'·het 2** integration

integritet *nm (Book)* integrity

integro'·het *vpr* to be integrated

integro'·n *vt* to integrate

intelekt *nm* intellect

intelektual *adj, n* intellectual

intelektualist *adj (Pej)* affected by intellectualism: intellectualistic

intelektualizëm *nm (Pej)* intellectualism

inteligjencë *nf* intelligence, intellect

inteligjencie *nf* intellectual class of society: intelligentsia

inteligjent *adj* intelligent

intendencë *nf* **1** [*Mil*] supply services; quartermaster section **2** office of the quartermaster

intendent *nm* [*Mil*] quartermaster

intensifikim *nm ger (Book)* **1** <**intensifiko'·n, intensifiko'·het 2** intensification

intensifiko'·het *vpr (Book)* to increase in intensity, become stronger; grow, get more frequent

intensifiko'·n *vt (Book)* to intensify

intensitet *nm* intensity

intensiv *adj* intense, intensive

intensivisht *adv* intensely, intensively

inter *formative prefix in borrowed words* between, among: inter-

interes *nm* interest

interesant *adj* interesting

interesaxhi *nm (np ~ nj)* person pursuing greedy self-interests, avaricious person

interesim *nm ger* **1** <**intereso'·n, intereso'·het 2** concern, attention

intereso'·het *vpr* to be interested, get interested, interest oneself with; busy oneself in, get involved with

intereso'·n *vi* **1** to attract the attention of <>: interest <> **2** to be in the interest of <>

interesuar
I § *adj (i)* **1** interested **2** having a stake in: of interest
II § *n (i)* interested person/party

interferencë *nf* [*Tech*] insertion by force

interferencë *nf* interference

interjeksion *nm* interjection

intermexo *nf* **1** [*Mus*] intermezzo **2** [*Theat*] skit or short presentation between the acts at the theater

internacional *adj* international

internacionale *nf* **1** international socialist organization **2** l'Internationale: name of the hymn of the international communist movement

internacionalist *n* internationalist

internacionalizëm *nm* internationalism

internat *nm (Old)* boarding school; school dormitory = **konvikt**

internatist *n (Old)* student in a boarding school

internim *nm ger* **1** <**interno'·n, interno/he 2** internment

interno'·n *vt* to punish [] by sending to a place of internment: intern

internuar *n (i)* person punished by being sent into internment: internee

interpelancë *nf (Book)* interpellation

interpelo'·n *vt (Book)* to interpellate

INTERPOL *abbrev (English)* Interpol

interpret *nm* (language) interpreter

interpretim *nm ger (Book)* **1** <**interpreto'·n 2** interpretation

interpreto'·n *vt* to give an interpretation of []: interpret

interpretues *nm* interpreter

interval *nm* interval

intervencion *nm* intervention

intervencionist *n* interventionist

intervenim *nm ger* **1** <**interveno'·n 2** intervention

interveno'·n *vt* to intervene

intervistë *nf* interview

intervisto'·n *vt* to interview

interruptor *nm* [*Electr*] switch; circuit breaker; interrupter *( )*

intim *adj (Book)* intimate

intimitet *nm (Book)* intimacy

intolerancë *nf* intolerance

intonacion *nm* intonation

intransigjent *adj* intransigent

intranzitiv *adj* [*Ling*] intransitive

intrigant
I § *n* schemer
II § *adj* involved in intrigue: scheming, plotting

intrigë *nf* **1** intrigue, scheme **2** plot **3** intrigant, intriguer, schemer

intrigo'·n
I § *vi* to plan an intrigue, scheme
II § *vt* to plot

intrigues *adj* = **intrigant**

intuicion *nm* = **intuitë**

intuitë *nf* intuition

intuitivë *nf* intuitive

invadim *nm* [*Mil*] <**invado'·n** invasion

invado'·n *vt* [*Mil*] to invade

invadues *n* [*Mil*] invader

invalid *nm* chronically ill or disabled person: invalid

invaliditet *nm* invalidism

invariant nm [Math] invariant

*****invazor** n = invadues

inventar nm inventory
  ○ **inventar i gjallë** inventory of livestock
  ○ **inventar i imët** [Fin] inventory of items most often consumed
  ○ **inventar i vdekur** [Econ] inventory of tools and work supplies

inventarizim nm ger <**inventarizo**•n

inventarizo•n vt to take inventory of []: inventory

invertebratë np collec [Zool] invertebrates

investim nm ger 1 <**investo**•n 2 investment

investo•n vt to invest

inxh. abbrev <**inxhinier** B.S. in Engineering

inxhi nf pearl

inxhinier n engineer

inxhinieri nf (the field of) engineering

*****inxhinjer** = **inxhinier**

*****iny** interj well, well!

injekcion = **injeksion**

injeksion nm [Med] 1 injection = **injektim** 2 injection, substance injected

injektim nm ger 1 <**injekto**•n 2 injection

injekto•n vt to inject

injektor nm [Tech] injector

injorancë nf ignorance

injorant
  I § adj ignorant
  II § nm 1 ignorant person 2 (Pej) ignoramus, lout

injoro•n vt to ignore, disregard

*****iod** = **jod**

*****ip** stem for 2nd pl pres, pind, imper, vp <**je**•

ipekakuanë nf [Bot] ipecac, ipecacuanha

ipeshkëv nm (np ~ ij) [Relig] Catholic bishop

ipeshkvi [Relig] nf bishopric, diocese

*****ipi** nf = **mullar**

*****ipotekë** = **hipotekë**

ipsilon nm 1 the name of the 20th letter "y" in the Greek alphabet 2 (Book) designates an indefinite anonymous person ("y") as alternative to another designated as "iks" ("x")

ipso nf gypsum, plaster of paris

ipshtak nm young oak

*****ipshtë** nf 1 forest of young oaks 2 = **dishtë**

*****iqindi** nf Moslem evening prayer

ir nm spot in a fertilized egg

ir-et vpr 1 = **irno**•het 2 (Fig) to become depressed/ disheartened

Irak nf Iraq

irakian adj, n Iraqi

Iran nf Iran

iranian
  I § adj Iranian
  II § n Irani, native of Iran

iranishte nf Iranian language

irat nm (Old) assured income; income from real estate
  ○ **ësh-të me irat** to have considerable income

ireal adj (Book) fictional, unreal

irëmadh adj daring, courageous

*****irrët** adj (i) (Reg Gheg) = **hirët**

*****iri** nf (Old) fear, funk

*****iridace** np [Bot] iris plants Iridaceae

iridë nf [Anat] iris

iriq nm 1 [Zool] hedgehog (Erinaceus) 2 [Med] tumor
  ○ **iriq deti** [Zool] sea urchin, echinus
  ○ **iriqi i zi** "black tumor" (Colloq) [Med] cancer

*****iriqëz** nf [Bot] 1 knotted hedgeparsley (Torilis nodosa) 2 saxifrage (Saxifraga)

irith nm [Anat] uvula

irizë nf [Med] cancer

irlandez
  I § adj Irish, of or pertaining to Ireland
  II § nm Irishman

irlandezoverior adj, n Northern Irish

Irlandë nf Ireland

irlandishte nf Irish (language)

Irma nf Irma (female name)

irmë nf = **irnë**

irnë nf permanently dingy color (of clothing)

irnim nm ger <**irno**•n, **irno**•het

irno-het vpr 1 to become dingy 2 to become leadenfaced, turn livid

irno•n vt to make [a piece of clothing] permanently dingy

irnos• vt = **irno**•n

irnos-et vpr = **irno**•het

irnosje nf ger = **irnim**

irnosur adj (i) = **irnuar**

irnuar adj (i) made permanently dingy

ironi nf 1 light sarcasm 2 [Lit] irony

ironik adj 1 lightly sarcastic 2 ironic(al)

ironikisht adv ironically

ironizo•n vt to treat [] with irony, deride

*****irul** OR **irun** nm dun color

irracional adj irrational

irredentist n, adj (Book) irredentist

irredentizëm nm (Book) irredentism

ISIS abbrev <**Instituti Shtetëror i Sigurimeve Shoqërore** State Institute for Social Security

*****iskër** nf spark; touchwood

*****iskro**•n vi to sparkle

islam adj [Relig] Islamic, Moslem

islamizëm nm [Relig] 1 Moslem religion 2 Islam

islamizim nm ger <**islamizo**•n

islamizo•n vt to convert/adapt [] to Islam: Islamize

islandez
  I § adj Icelandic, of or pertaining to Iceland
  II § nm Icelander

Islandë nf Iceland

islandisht adv in Icelandic (language)

islandishte nf Icelandic (language)

iso nf 1 droning voice used in folk singing as accompaniment to the melody: drone 2 monotone

*****israelit** = **izraelit**

istëm nm [Geog] isthmus

*****istër** nm (Reg Gheg Old) star

istikam nm (Old) [Mil] trench = **llogore**

ish interj used to frighten away chickens, shoo!

ish
  I § stem for pind <**ësh-të**
  II § formative prefix former: ex-, past-
  ○ **ishte për t'u bërë** it was just fate, it must have been meant to be.

ishalla interj let's hope, God willing!

*****ishtitutë** nf = **institut**

ishull *nm (np ˜j)* island
*ishull|a'n = ishulla'r
ishulla'r *n* islander
*ishull|naj'ë *nf* archipelago
ishullo'r *adj* insular
Itali' *nf* Italy
italia'n
 I § *adj* Italian
 II § *n* native of Italy
itali'sht *adv* in Italian (language)
itali'sht|e *nf* Italian language
ital|o|shqipta'r *n* Italo-Albanian
itinera'r *nm* itinerary
ith
 I § *nm* **1** back side: back **2** *(Reg)* heat/vapor given
   off by earth **3** warm vapor, warmth
 II § *adv, prep (abl)* behind, after
ith· *vt* to follow behind/after [ ]
*ith|ës *n* person in the know
i'thi *adv (së)* from behind
*ithme *nf* [*Bot*] bitter weed that grows in wheat fields
ith|ta'r *n* follower, supporter
*ith|ti'm *nm* <**ithto'·n, ithto'·het = hidhëri'm**
*ith|ti'në *nf* = **hidhësi'rë**
*ith|to'·het *vpr* = **hidhëro'·het**
*ith|to'·n *vt* = **hidhëro'·n**
iu *sequence of pronominal clitics* **1** (3rd person referent + 3rd pl object) **2** (3rd sg referent + reflexive)
*iv *nm* [*Ornit*] = **pulëba'rdhë**

ivë *nf* an embroidered part of a piece of clothing
*izla'm = isla'm
*izlemi'k *nm* = **çita'r**
Izmi'r *nm* Izmir (formerly Smyrna)
izo|ba'rë *nf* [*Phys*] isobar
izo|bari'k *adj* [*Phys*] isobaric
izoglos'ë *nf* [*Ling*] isogloss
izo|ho'rë *nf* [*Phys*] isochore
izolacio'n *nm* **1** isolation **2** insulation
izolacioni'st *n* isolationist
izolacioni'z|ëm *nm* isolationism
izola'nt *nm* [*Electr Phys*] insulating material, insulation
izolato'r *nm* [*Electr Phys*] insulator
izoli'm *nm ger* **1** *(Book)* <**izolo'·n, izolo'·het 2** insulation
izolo'·het *vpr* to become isolated
izolo'·n *vt* **1** *(Book)* to isolate **2** [*Spec*] to insulate
izolu'a'r *adj (i)* **1** *(Book)* isolated **2** *(Tech Elect)* insu-
   lated
izolu'e's *adj (Book)* non-conductive, insulating
izo|mo'rf *adj* isomorphic
*izo|she'l *adj* [*Geom*] isosceles
izo|te'rmë *nf* [*Phys*] isotherm
izo|termi'k *adj* [*Phys*] isothermal
izoto'p *nm* [*Spec*] isotope
Izrae'l *nm* Israel
izraeli't
 I § *adj, n* Israeli
 II § *nm* [*Hist*] Israelite

Jj

j [*jë*] *nf* **1** the consonant letter "j" **2** the high front unrounded voiced glide represented by the letter "j"

ja

I § *pcl* **1** accompanies a hand gesture indicating that something is close at hand: here! there! take this! **2** begins a story or introduces a new topic: now then! well now! **3** expresses immediacy: right now! in just a second! **4** emphasizes pointing of a deictic word (beginning in a- or kë-): this very, that very, just, exactly **5** calls for listener's attention: so! behold! lo!

II § *sequence of clitics* = **ia**
○ **ja ç'** _ so here's what _
○ **ja çfarë 1** that's what, this is what _ **2** and what _!
○ **ja hop, ja pop!** here goes nothing!
○ **ja_ ja_** either _ or _
○ **ja ke/ku** _ here is _
○ **ja që** what can you do! there's nothing you can do about it
○ **ja se ç'/çfarë** that's what
○ **ja shyt, ja fyt** come Hell or high water

jaban|xhe'shë *nf* <**jabanxhi**

jaban|xhi *nm* (*np* ~ *nj*) foreigner to a community, stranger

*jabixha'k *nm* [*Bot*] common vine (*Vitis vinifera*)

jací *nf* [*Relig*] Moslem evening prayer

jagua'r *nm* [*Zool*] jaguar

jahni

I § *nf* [*Food*] stew made of meat and vegetables: stew

II § *adj* stewed

jaht *nm* yacht

*jahudi *nm* (*Old*) Jew = **çifu't**

*jahudi'je *nf* (*Old*) Jewess

ja'jë *nf* **1** tool made of a stick and a thin wire and used to separate wool fibers to prepare them for felting ***2** father's sister: aunt

jak *nm* [*Zool*] yak

jak|a'ta'r *n* tailor

ja'kë *nf* **1** collar (on a piece of clothing); open collar **2** large hood on a man's cloak **3** (*Reg*) wool remaining on neck of sheared sheep
○ **jakë golf** turtle-neck collar

ja'kë *hortative* (*Colloq*) come! come on! come along!

jak|ë|mbërth|y'er *adj* **1** with collar closed **2** overly meticulous in dress

ja'kë|ni *hortative pl* <**jakë**

ja'kë|z *nf* **1** collar on a short-sleeved wool jacket **2** large hood on a man's cloak **3** = **llaba'ne**

jak|ë|z|bërth|y'er *adj* **1** with collar open **2** careless in dress

jaki *nm* **1** poultice; cast for a broken/sprained limb **2** incision made to allow a wound or sore to flow: lancing ***3** cautery

jak|o're *nf* lightweight folk costume with a high collar

*jakshti's· *vt* to suit

jak|u'ce *nf* man's short-sleeved wool jacket with fringed collar

jaku't *nm* ruby

*jale'k (*Reg Gheg*) = **jele'k**

Ja'ltë *nf* Yalta

jalla'n *adj* deceitful, mendacious

jalla'q *nm* coppersmith's leaching tank

jallí *nf* (*Old*) open field next to a river or sea; salty seaside land; open field

jam *1st sg pres* <**ësh·të** I am

jama'ke *nf* large clay stewing pot

jamb *nm* [*Lit*] iamb, iambic foot

jamba'll *nm* [*Bot*] licorice (*Glycyrrhiza glabra*)

jambi'k *adj* [*Lit*] iambic

jambru'k *nm* [*Bot*] glasswort (*Salicornia*)

jamor|kûje *np* (*Reg Gheg*) wailing, moans

jamulli *nf* wool blanket

jana'r *nm* January

ja'në *3rd pl pres* <**ësh·të** they are

Ja'ni *nm* Jani (male name)

*janiçe'r *nm* = **jeniçe'r**

janki

I § *nm* (*Contempt*) Yankee

II § *adj* American (considered as imperialistic and exploitative)

jap *stem for 1st sg pres, 1st & 3rd pl pres, 2nd & 3rd sg subj* <**je'p·**
○ **japin e marrin me gishta** "they give and take with finger signs" they understand each other immediately

japa'nxhe *nf* (*Old*) broad-collared, sleeveless, long coat worn by Catholic women in Scutari

japí *nf* (*Old*) physical characteristics of a person's face and body, physique and face, physical appearance: build

japí|shëm *adj* (*i*) fine-looking, comely, handsome

japon|e'z *adj, n* Japanese

japon|e'zçe

I § *nf* = **japoní'shte**

II § *adv* in the Japanese manner

Japoní *nf* Japan

japoní|sht *adv* in Japanese

japoní|shte *nf* Japanese language

japra'k *nm* [*Food*] grape/cabbage leaves stuffed with rice: dolma

jara'n *nm* (*Old*) **1** beau, lover **2** close friend

jaraní *nf* (*Old*) **1** love, especially clandestine love: romance **2** close friendship **3** playful joke among close friends

ja'rbë *nf* worthless thing

jard *nm* yard (36 inches)

jarg|ama'n *nm* drooler; slobberer

jarg|a'sh *adj* (*Impol*) slobbering; drooling

jarg|ava'n *nm* [*Bot*] lilac (*Syringa vulgaris*)
○ **jargavan i egër** [*Bot*] Judas tree *Cercis siliquastrum*

jargavec
I § adj (Impol) drooling; slobbering
II § nm [Invert] slug

jargavel *adj (Impol)* **1** drooling; slobbering **2** breaking down emotionally; crying easily, crybaby **3** pest, nuisance

jargavit·*et vpr* **1** to drool; slobber **2** *(Colloq)* to have one's mouth be watering **3** *(Impol)* to become emotional over nothing **4** *(Impol)* to be a disgusting pest

jargavitur *adj* bathed in drool

jargё *nf* **1** dribbling saliva: drool **2** thin sticky excrescence of a terrestrial invertebrate (worm, slug, snail): slime

jargёmadh
I § adj drooling heavily
II § nm drooling old man

jargёs
I § nm **1** *[Invert]* terrestrial invertebrate that excretes a slime; slug **2** drooling child
II § adj drooling

jargёz *nf [Bot]* nostoc *(Nostoc)*

jargёzim *nm ger* **1** <**jargёzo·het 2** spittle drooling from the mouth **3** sogginess **4** *[Med]* salivation

jargёzo·het *vpr* **1 = jargos·et 2** to become soggy

jargёzor *adj* **1** slobbery **2** giving off a slimy excrescence: slimy

jargёzuar *adj (i)* **1** bathed in drool **2** soggy

jargor *adj* **1** *[Biol]* mucous *()* **2** *[Med]* mucoid, blennoid

jargos· *vt* to drool on [], slobber all over []

jargos·*et vpr* **1** to drool; slobber **2** *(Colloq)* to have one's mouth be watering

jargosur *adj (i)* bathed in drool

jargshёm *adj (i)* slimy

jariçkё *nf (Reg)* chick; (of a little girl) chickie

jasemin *nm [Bot]* **1** jasmine *(Jasminum officinale)* **2** false indigo *(Amorpha fruticosa)*

***jase** *(Reg)* **= ose**

***jaspidhё** *nf [Min]* jasper

***jastek = jastёk**

jasteçkё *nf* **1** small pillow: pad **2** pin cushion **3** piece of wool as an ink pad

jastёk *nm* pillow, cushion; bolster
 ○ **jastёk elektrik** electric heating pad
 ○ **jastёku i fjalёs** the gist
 ○ [] **hёng**ё*r^{opt}*/**ngrёn**^{opt} **nё jastёk!** "May {} eat [] on a pillow!" *(Curse)* May {} eat [] in his sick bed! I hope {} never gets to enjoy eating []!

jastёkore *nf [Entom]* scale insect
 ○ **jastёkorja e hardhisё** *[Entom]* wooly currant scale *Pulvinaria betulae (vitis) L.*

jastёqie *np* <**jastёk**

***jastritё** *nf [Invert]* rag worm *(Lumbricus)*

jashmak *nm (Old)* yashmak

***jashta** *adv* **= jasht**ё

jashtё
I § adv **1** out **2** outside **3** outdoors
II § prep (abl) outside, beyond, out of, out
 ○ **ёsh·tё jashtё botёs** *(Pej)* to live in one's own little world
 ○ **ёsh·tё jashtё caranit tё vatrёs** to be outside of the matter at hand
 ○ **jashtё loje 1** *[Soccer]* offside **2** left out, excluded
 ○ **jashtё masёs** beyond measure

 ○ **ёsh·tё jashtё mendjes** to be out of the question, be unthinkable
 ○ **jashtё mendjes** unthinkable, out of the question; out of the realm of possibility, impossible
 ○ **jashtё moshe** excluded by age, not of the right age: outside the age limits
 ○ **jashtё tharkut** outside the family

jashtё *formative prefix* extra-, exo-

jashtё**buxhetor** *adj [Econ Fin]* not provided for by the budget: extra-budgetary

jashtё**fisnor** *adj* from outside the clan/family

jashtё**gjinor** *adj* extra-familial

jashtё**gjuh**ё**sor** *adj* outside the language, exolinguistic, extra-lingual

jashtё**gjyq**ё**sor** *adj* outside the court system: out-of-court, extra-judicial

jashtё**klasor** *adj* unconnected with social class, not based on social class

jashtё**kohor** *adj* timeless

jashtё**ligjor** *adj [Law]* not provided for in law, outside the law, extra-legal

jashtё**ligjshёm** *adj (i)* illegal, unlawful; outlawed

jashtё**m** *adj (i)* external, outside; outer, exterior; outward; foreign; adjunct
 ○ **nxёnёs i jashtёm** student not living in a dormitory

jashtё**martesor** *adj* extra-marital

jashtё**parlamentar** *adj* extra-parliamentary

jashtё**qendror** *adj [Math]* not sharing a common center: eccentric

jashtё**qit·** *vt [Biol]* to evacuate/eliminate waste material

jashtё**qit**ё**s**
I § adj [Biol] excremental
II § nm [Mil] cartridge ejector

jashtё**qitje** *nf ger* **1** *[Biol]* <**jasht**ё**qit· 2** *(Book)* excrement *3 ejection

***jasht**ё**rendshёm** *adj (i)* **= jasht**ё**zakonshёm**

***jasht**ё**rregull**ё**m** *nm* irregularity, exception, deviation

jashtё**s**ё**m** *nm (i) (Euph)* the devil

jashtё**s**ё**me** *np (tё) (Euph) [Myth]* mountain nymphs who inveigle hapless young men and women into dancing to death: oread

jashtё**shkollor** *adj* extra-curricular

jashtё**shkrua·n** *vt [Geom]* to circumscribe

jashtё**shkruar** *adj (i) [Geom]* circumscribed

jashtё**tok**ё**sor** *adj* extraterrestrial

jashtё**zakon**ё**sht** *adv* extraordinarily, unusually, very

jashtё**zakonshёm** *adj (i)* **1** extraordinary, unusual **2** special

jashtme *nf (e)* exterior part

jashtmi *adv (sё)* from outside

***jasht**ё**uar** *adj (i) (Reg Tosk)* exceptional, extraordinary

jatagan *nm* yataghan

jatak *nm* **1** bed; mattress; bedsheet; bed covering **2** *(Reg)* seedbed **3** *(Pej)* lair

***jat**ё**r** *adj, nm nf* other

***jati** *def stem* <**at**ё the father

jau *sequence of clitics (Reg Colloq)* **1** (3rd pl referent + 3rd sg object) **2** (3rd pl referent 3rd pl object)

javash *adv* **= avash**

java'she *nf* wooden clamp used to keep a horse from biting the farrier

java'shëm *adj (i)* = ava'shēm

javashllëk *nm* slowness, sloth

java'to're *nf* woman in an extended household whose weekly turn it is to do the chores

ja'vë *nf* **1** week **2** children's circle game; circle divided into seven parts for playing this game
  ○ **Java e bardhë** *(Old)* [*Rel*] the first seven days of Lent during which Christians may eat eggs and dairy products, but not meat
  ○ **Java e madhe** *(Old)* [*Rel*] Holy Week
  ○ **javë për javë** weekly, week after week, every week
  ○ **java shtatë, ai tetë** there are seven days in a week, but he seems to come (to visit) eight days a week: he comes too often
  ○ **Java e zezë** Passion Week

ja'v ese *nf* [*Ethnog*] woman assigned by the bride's parents to visit her at the beginning of the first week of marriage

*****javit·et** *vpr* = avit·et

javo'r *adj* **1** weekly **2** lasting a week

javo're *nf* *(Old)* notebook in which teachers keep their weekly plans and records

jaz *nm* **1** millrace, sluice **2** stream bed, water channel **3** water reservoir **4** *(Fig)* source, beginning, origin **5** mourning

jaz ëk *interj (Impol)* shame on you!

*****ja'zmë** *np* **1** mumps **2** = aja'zmë

je *2nd sg pres* ‹ësh·të you are

*****jebri'k** = ibri'k

jeh *nm* = jeho'në

jeho·n *vi* **1** to echo, resound *****2** to yell; exult

jeho'në *nf* echo; resounding effect

*****jehue'shëm** *adj (i)* echoing, resounding

je'kën *nf* [*Ichth*] = kora'n

*****jel** *nm* rheumatism

je'lcë *nf* [*Ichth*] nase *(Chondrostoma nasus)*

je'le *nf* horse's mane

jele'a'rtë *adj* (of horses) golden-maned

jele'ba'rdhë *adj* (of horses) having a light-colored mane

jele'gja'të *adj* (of horses) long-maned

jele'k *nm* waistcoat, vest, jerkin
  ○ **jelek shpëtimi** life jacket

jele'ku'q *adj* (of horses) having a reddish mane

jele'zi *adj, n (fem sg ˜ez, masc pl ˜inj, fem pl ˜eza)* (horse) with a dark mane

jem *1st sg subj* ‹ësh·të I may be

Jeme'n *nm* Yemen

Jeme'n *nm* Yemen

jeme'n'as
  I § *adj* Yemenite
  II § *n* native of Yemen

jemen'i *nf* **1** black head kerchief worn by women **2** large piece of cloth used to wrap things in

je'mi *1st pl pres* ‹ësh·të we are

jen *nm* Japanese money, yen

*****jena'r** = jana'r

je'në
  I § *nf* first-born (lamb or kid)
  II § *3rd pl subj* ‹ësh·të they may be

je'ni *2nd pl pres* ‹ësh·të you are

jeniçe'r *nm* [*Hist*] janissary

jep·
  I § *vt* **1** to give **2** to give off [], form **3** to give [] in marriage, marry [] off
  II § *vi* **1** *(Colloq)* to put ‹› into motion; drive **2** to begin suddenly and unexpectedly: burst out
  ○ **s'‹› jep· afat** not give ‹› enough time
  ○ **jep· alarmin 1** to give the alarm **2** to make a big fuss
  ○ **jep· andej, jep· këtej** to try in every way
  ○ **jep· armët** to give up one's arms: stop fighting, stop resisting, surrender
  ○ **‹› jep· arsye** to give grounds for ‹›
  ○ **‹› jep· arratinë** to force ‹› into hasty retreat: rout ‹›
  ○ **s'të jep· as gur për të çarë kokën** {} is very stingy
  ○ **nuk të jep· as një majë cipali** {} wouldn't give you a nickel, {} *is* very stingy
  ○ **s'të jep· as një majë gjilpëre/thoi** "not give you even a tip of a needle/fingernail" to be too stingy even to give you the time of day
  ○ **s'të jep· as sa maja e gjilpërës/thoit** "not give you even as much as the tip of a needle" to be too stingy even to give you the time of day
  ○ **jep· ballë** to loom into view
  ○ **‹› jep· barin e ballkotit 1** to make it impossible for ‹› to think/concentrate **2** to put ‹› under a spell, charm ‹›
  ○ **‹› jep· barut** to kill ‹› by shooting
  ○ **‹› jep· besë 1** to give ‹› one's word not to exercise one's right to take blood revenge **2** to believe in ‹›; trust ‹›
  ○ **‹› jep· besën** to make a pledge to ‹›, guarantee ‹›
  ○ **‹› jep· besim** to put one's faith in ‹›, trust ‹›
  ○ **‹› jep· bojë 1** to apply color to ‹›, color, dye, paint **2** to embellish ‹›
  ○ **s'‹› jep· bukë, kërko·n edhe gjellë** to ask ‹› for more after being turned down by ‹› for even less
  ○ **‹› jep· bukuri** to add to ‹›'s beauty
  ○ **‹› jep· çehre** to greet ‹› with open arms
  ○ **jep· çikë** start to appear
  ○ **‹› jep· datën** to make ‹› afraid
  ○ **i jep· dërrmën armikut** to put the enemy to flight, cause a rout
  ○ **‹› jep· dërrmën 1** to force ‹› to leave, force ‹› out **2** to defeat‹›, crush ‹›
  ○ **‹› jep· dorë** to be of great help to ‹›
  ○ **i jep· dorën e fundit** to give the finishing touch, polish
  ○ **‹› jep· dorën 1** to extend one's hand to ‹› for a handshake **2** to give ‹› a hand: help
  ○ **‹› jep· dorën e fundit** to give ‹› the final touch: give ‹› a final polish
  ○ **jep· dorën** to make a pledge, give a guarantee: swear
  ○ **‹› jep· dritë** to shed light on ‹›; enlighten ‹›
  ○ **‹› jep· drunë** *(Impol)* to force ‹› to leave, force ‹› out; expel ‹› from an organization: give ‹› the old heave-ho
  ○ **‹› jep· duart** *(Colloq)* to give ‹› the old heave-ho, kick ‹› out
  ○ **‹› jep· dum** to figure ‹a problem› out, figure out how to handle ‹a problem›
  ○ **‹› jep· dushkun** to kick ‹› out, give ‹› the boot
  ○ **‹› jep· dhenë** to keep/drive ‹› out by force
  ○ **jep· e bot** to do one's best, try hard

○ **jep· e merr· me** [] **1** to have dealings with [someone] **2** to wrestle with [something]

○ **jep· e jep·** to do one's best, try hard

○ **jep· e merr· 1** to do one's best, try hard, do one's utmost **2** to be on friendly social terms **3** to do business **4** [*Ethnog*] to engage in intermarriage

○ **jep· faliment** to declare bankruptcy

○ **jep· faqe 1** to begin to dry up **2** to begin to ripen **3** (for bread) to start to form a crust **4** (of a wall) to bulge

○ **i jep· fill punës** to put things in order, fix the matter

○ **<> jep· fjalën 1** to call upon <> to speak: give <> the floor **2** to make a promise to <>: give <> one's word

○ **jep· fjalën (e nderit)** to give one's word (of honor)

○ **<> jep· flakë** to inflame <>'s feelings: set <> afire

○ **<> jep· flakën** to cause <> to burn: set <> on fire, set <> afire

○ **<> jep· fletë 1** to give <> great joy: elate <> **2** to give great encouragement to <>

○ **<> jep· flokët në dorë 1** to yank <>'s hair **2** to beat <> severely

○ **u jep· formë flokëve** to style hair

○ **<> jep· frymë** to help <> get out of great difficulty; revive

○ **jep· frymën e fundit** to breathe one's last

○ **<> jep· fund** to bring <> to an end; put an end to <>

○ **i jep· fund jetës** to put an end to one's life, kill oneself

○ **<> jep· fytyrë 1** to treat <*someone*> especially nice; pamper/spoil <> **2** to shape <*something*>

○ **i jep· gojës 1** to treat oneself well with food, like to eat well **2** to be too talkative, talk too much

○ **<>a jep· grumbull** to give <> a piece of one's mind, lambaste <>

○ **<> jep· grushtin e fundit** to deliver <> the final blow: finish <> off

○ **jep· gjakun për** [] "give one's blood for []" to be willing to die for []; make the supreme sacrifice for []

○ **i jep· gjuhës** to talk too much

○ **<> jep· gjumë** to make <> sleepy

○ **jep· gjyq** to explain oneself, answer for one's actions

○ **jep· gjysmën e lekut** (*Scorn*) to fill <> with lead, shoot <> dead

○ **<> jep· hajat** to give support to <*a liar/lie*>

○ **<> jep· hakën** to give <> what <> *deserves*

○ **<> jep· hall** to find a solution for <>; solve <>'s problem

○ **nuk <> jep· hesap askujt** to be accountable to no one

○ **<> jep· jetë** to enliven <>; energize/arouse <>

○ **jep· jetën** to give up one's life, make the supreme sacrifice

○ **<>a jep· karmën** to expel <*someone*> rudely: kick <> out, give <> the boot

○ **ta jep kaun në vorbë dhe shpatën pa dorëz.** "{} gives you the ox in a pot and the sword without a handle." {} is exceedingly brave.

○ **ua jep· këmbëve** to run away as fast as possible, take to one's heels

○ **<> jep· kënd** to figure <*a problem*> out, figure out how to handle <*a problem*>

○ **<>i jep· këpucët në dorë** (*Impol*) to hand <> <>'s hat (indicating forcibly that <> should leave)

○ **jep· kohën** to say hello (in the manner appropriate to the time of day)

○ **jep· kokën për** [] to be willing to die for []

○ **<> jep· krahë 1** to give <> great joy: elate <> **2** to give great encouragement to <>

○ **s'<> jep· kush një gotë ujë** "no one *gives* <> a glass of water" no one gives <> any help

○ **<> jep· lak** to dodge/evade <*an obligation*>

○ **jep· lak** to warp

○ **<> jep· lamtumirën e fundit** (*Elev*) to pay one's final respects to <*someone dead*>, bid a final farewell to <> (at a cemetery)

○ **<> jep· lavër** to till <>, cultivate <>

○ **<>i jep· leckat (në dorë)** "give <> <>'s rags (in hand)" (*ColloqImpolite*) to make <> take <>'s stuff and clear out: kick <> out (with all <>'s damn belongings)

○ **<> jep· leshrat në dorë 1** to yank <>'s hair **2** to beat <> severely

○ **<> jep· ligj** (*Colloq*) to admit/concede that <> is right

○ **<> jep· limë 1** to file <> down; smooth <> with a file **2** (*Fig*) to polish <> up, give <> a final polish

○ **<> jep· liri gjuhës** to give free rein to one's tongue, be uncontrolled in one's speech, let one's tongue wag

○ **<> jep· llasë** to mollycoddle/pamper <>

○ **<>a jep· llokum në gojë** "give <> candy right in <>'s mouth" give <> everything right in <>'s lap, make everything easy for <>

○ **<> jep· majë** to figure <*a problem*> out, figure out how to handle <*a problem*>

○ **<> jep· malin** to force <> to flee (to the mountains)

○ **<> jep· mallkim** to curse <>

○ **jep· me grushte** "give by handfuls" to spend freely

○ **e jep· me dorë dhe e merr· me këmbë** to get it back but only by strenuous effort

○ [] **jep· me buzë e pa zemër** to give [] unwillingly, give [] halfheartedly

○ **<> jep· mend *1** to give <> unwelcome advice **2** to show off how much one knows to <>

○ **<> jep· mendtë në dorë** "give <> <>'s brains in <>'s hand" to take <>'s breath away

○ **<> jep· munxat/ munxët = munxo·s·**

○ **<> jep· namëzat** to make deprecatory gestures toward <> (expressing disgust at <>)

○ **<> jep· nder** to bring honor upon <>

○ **<>a jep· nderin në dorë/grusht** "give <> <>'s honor in <>'s hand/fist" to insult <> (publicly), humiliate <>

○ **<>a jep· në dorë** [] **1** to make [] clear to <> **2** to give [] to <> on a silver platter

○ **<> jep· ngjyrë 1** to apply color to <>, color, dye, paint **2** to embellish <>

○ **<> jep· një dajak/dru/kopaçe 1** to beat <> badly **2** to scold <> severely **3** to defeat <> badly

○ **<> jep· një duman** to work on <> with a burst of energy

○ **<> jep· një dhëmb** to bawl <> out with a stern warning/injunction

○ **<> jep· një faqe 1** to form a crust on <> **2** to give shape to <>

○ **<> jep· një gisht mjaltë** "give one finger of honey" to persuade <> with a very small inducement

○ **<> jep· një hekur** to iron <*clothes*>

○ **<> jep· një kallaj** to give <> a false sheen: misrepresent

○ **jep· një kurë** to prescribe a treatment

○ <> **jep· një përdaf** "give <*a wall*> a float" **1** to plaster <> **2** *(Fig)* to do (some) fix-up work on <> **3** *(Fig)* to give <> a false sheen

○ <> **jep· një sheqerkë** *(Pej)* to give <> a small bribe

○ <> **jep· një të sharë** to cuss at <>

○ <> **jep· një thembër** to give <> a token gift/amount

○ <> **jep· një thes bukë** "give <> a sackful of bread" to be of great help to <>

○ **jep· një valë** to heat <> to a boil; let <> boil

○ <> **jep· një vishkull** to whip <> with a switch

○ <> **jep· një zë** to call out to <>, call <>

○ **jep· një zë** to give a roar/bellow/yell/scream

○ **jep· një** [] to give <> a quick/casual action with [], give <> a quick []ing

○ **jep· oksigjen** "give <> oxygen" **1** to give <> help in an emergency **2** *(Book Pej)* to encourage <> to do something bad: stir <> up, egg <> on

○ <>**i jep· opingat në dorë** *(Impol)* to hand <> <>'s hat (indicating forcibly that <> should leave)

○ <> **jep· partallet** "give <> <>'s rags (in hand)" *(Colloq)* to kick <> out (with all <>'s damn belongings)

○ <> **jep· pazar** to propose a price to <>, enter into bargaining/haggling with <>

○ <>**a jep· përgjigjen më/në këmbë** to answer <> on the spot without thinking

○ [] **jep· përsëri** to give [] back

○ <> **jep· plumbin** *(Colloq)* to shoot <>: give <> a taste of lead

○ <> **jep· porropinë** to send <> off to a remote region

○ [] **jep· prapë** to give [] back

○ <> **jep· qepën** *(Colloq)* to kill <>, knock <> off

○ <> **jep· rëndësi** to consider <> important

○ **nuk** <> **jep· rëndësi** to ignore <>

○ <> **jep· rrugë** to find a solution for <>, find a way out of <>

○ <> **jep· rrugët** to make <> leave, kick <> out on the street

○ <>[] **jep· si lëmoshë** to give [] to <> for nothing/free

○ **jep· shembull** to set an example

○ **jep· shenja për** [] to give indications of an aptitude for []

○ <> **jep· shkas** to give rise to <>

○ <> **jep· shkelmin** to expel <> forcibly: kick <> out

○ <> **jep· shpirt 1** to cheer <> up; enliven <>; give encouragement to <> **2** to keep <> alive

○ **jep· shpirt** *(Euph)* to give up the ghost, breathe one's last: pass away, die

○ **po jep· shpirt 1** to be in the throes of death, be dying **2** to be falling into ruin; be breaking down

○ **e jep· shpirtin** to give up one's life: die

○ **i jep· shtatit** to make a sudden move with one's body

○ <> **jep· shteg** to make way for <>; leave room for <>

○ **i jep· shtrëngim vetes** to give it one's all

○ <> **jep· shuplakën** *(Old)* to cast the evil eye on <>, put <> under the spell of the evil eye

○ <> **jep· shushavën/shushavat 1** to send <> off to various places **2** to throw <> out on the street, abandon <> to their fates

○ <> **jep· të drejtë** to concede that <> is right

○ **Të jep· një thelë e të merr·/rrëmbe·**n **një pelë** "" **1** *(Pej)* {} *gives* you a slice and *takes* a mare **2** {} *gives* you a little but {} *takes* a lot

○ <> **jep· të njohur** to let <> know who one is

○ <> **jep· tonin** *(Book)* to set the tone

○ **i jep· trupit** to make a sudden move with one's body

○ <> **jep· thonjtë** *(Colloq Pej)* to kick <> out, give <> the boot

○ **s'e jep·**^{3sg} **udha** ... *it* is not right to ...

○ <> **jep· udhë** to find a solution for <>, find a way out of <>, find the way to solve/resolve <>; make the decision concerning <>

○ <> **jep· udhët** to make <> leave, kick <> out on the street

○ **i jep· ujë (hekurit)** to temper steel

○ <> **jep· ujë me shoshë** "give <> water with a winnowing screen" to lead <> on

○ **jep· urdhër** to give an order, give orders

○ **jep· vaktin** to say hello (in the manner appropriate to the time of day)

○ **jep· valë** to inspire <> with energy

○ <> **jep· vendim** to make a decision about <>

○ <> **jep· veshët në dorë 1** to yank <>'s ears **2** to beat <> severely

○ **nuk e jep· veten 1** not give oneself away **2** not give up, not surrender

○ **i jep· vetes** to make a sudden move with one's body

○ <>**a jep· vetë bishtin** to be to blame oneself for inflating <>'s ego

○ **jep· {***number***} vjet** to give the impression of being {} years old

○ **jep· votën për** [] to cast one's vote for []

○ <>**a jep· vrapit** to take to one's heels, speed away

○ <> **jep· zemër** to give <> encouragement

○ <> **jep· zë** to call to <>, tell <> in a loud voice

○ <> **jep· zgjidhje** to provide a solution for <>

○ <> **jep· zjarr** to inflame <>'s feelings: set <> afire

○ <> **jep· zjarr barutit** to light the powder (that sets off an explosion)

○ <> **jep· zjarrin** to cause <> to burn: set <> on fire, set <> afire

○ <> **jep·** [] to provide [] for <>

jep·et *vpr*

I § *vpr* <**je**p· **1** *(Fig)* to give in; give up, surrender **2** to bend over/down **3** to appear suddenly

II § *vp impers* <> *has* the necessary skill/competence

○ <> **jep·et**^{3sg} **1** <> *is* gifted, <> *has* a knack **2** <> *gets* it in <>'s head

○ **jep·et pas** <> to be attracted/devoted/dedicated to, be much given to <>, be crazy about <>

○ <> **jep·et**^{3sg} **rasti** <> *is* given the chance/opportunity

jep·i *hortative imper* encourages action: go on! come on!

***jepra·k** = **japra·k**

***jeremi** *nf with masc agreement* **1** eremite **2** eremitic seclusion: hermitage

***jeremi·ni** *nf* solitude, wilderness

jerevi *nf (Old)* **1** room on the ground floor; small, one-storied house **2** ground floor animal shed or storage room = **katu·a**

***Jeri·k** *nm* Jericho

***jeri·t**·et *vpr* = **ir**·et

***je·rkull** *nm* gorge, ravine, precipice

jerm *nm* **1** delirium, raving ***2** madman

jerm·ẽ·sïn|ë nf [Bot]savine, savin (Juniperus sabina)

jerm·ï nf delirium; frenzy, madness

jermïk nm rice flour

jerm·o·n vi to be/become delirious; rave

*****jerm·o·r** adj frenzied, raving, mad

*****jesemïn** nm [Bot] = **jasemïn**

jesïr nm (Old) prisoner of war

jesïr·thi adv

je·sh 2nd sg subj <**ë·sh·të** you may be

jeshïl
  I § adj (Colloq) green (in color) = **gje·lbër**
  II § nm [Ornit]mallard (Anas platyrhynchos)

jeshïl|e
  I § nf the color green
  II § nf collec green plants: verdure, greenery; green vegetables, greens; verdant land

jeshïl|o·het vpr 1 to be/become verdant, turn green 2 to turn pale; change facial color from the cold or from strong emotion

jeshïl|o·n
  I § vt to make [] verdant
  II § vi to become green: bloom

jeshïl|lëk nm (np ~ qe) (Colloq) 1 verdure, greenness 2 green vegetables

Jet|a nf Jeta (female name)

jet·es|ë nf 1 way of life 2 living conditions; living

jet·es·ẽta'r n person especially concerned with improving the material conditions of his life

je·të nf 1 life 2 way of life 3 existence 4 lifetime
  ○ **jeta ime!** my darling!
  ○ **për (në) jetë të jetëve** for all eternity
  ○ **pleqtë/plakat e jetës** very old men/women (around 100 years old)
  ○ **jetë e vockël** (Fig Pej) life full of pettiness

je·të 3rd sg subj <**ë·sh·të** be

jet·ë·ba'rdh|ë adj 1 having a happy life 2 (Felic) I hope you are very happy!

jet·ẽ·dhën|ẽs adj life-giving: nourishing; invigorating

jet·ẽ·gja'të adj 1 long-lived; perennial 2 (Felic) May you have a long life!

jet·ẽ·gjat·ẽsï nf 1 lifetime 2 longevity

jet·ẽ·këpu'tur
  I § adj cut off in the prime of life, dying before one's time
  II § n (Euph) dead person

jet·ẽ·nga'th|ët adj lazy, idle

jet·ẽ·ngry's|ur adj very old, aged

jet·ẽ·nxï'r|ë adj 1 having a miserable life 2 causing misery 3 (Curse) May you live in misery!

jet·ẽ·panï's|ur adj very young and inexperienced

jet·ẽ·pa·so's|ur adj 1 having died before one's time 2 (Curse) May you die early!

jet·ẽ·pru'r|ẽs adj life-giving, vital

jet·ẽr·s|ïm nm ger (Book) = **tjetërsïm**

jet·ẽr·s|o·het vpr = **tjetërso·het**

jet·ẽr·s|o·n vt to alienate = **tjetërso·n**

jet·ẽr·su|e's adj = **tjetërsue's**

jet·ẽr·su|e'sh|ëm adj (i) [Law] = **tjetërsue'shëm**

jet·ẽsï nf 1 vitality *2 nature, disposition

jet·ẽ·sïm nm ger <**jet·ẽso·n**

jet·ẽso·n vt (Book) to give life to, bring to life, realize

jet·ẽso'r adj 1 of or pertaining to life 2 vital, essential, decisive

jet·ẽshkre'të adj 1 having a miserable and lonely life 2 (Curse) May you live in lonely misery!

jet·ẽshkrï'm nm biography

jet·ẽshkrim·o'r adj biographic, biographical

jet·ẽshkru|e's nm biographer

jet·ẽshku'rtër adj 1 short-lived 2 (Fig) ephemeral

jet·ẽ·zbra'z|ët adj having spent a useless life

jet·ẽ·zï adj, n (fem sg ~ez, masc pl ~ïnj, fem pl ~eza) 1 (person) with a miserable life 2 (Curse) may he have a lifetime of misery!

jetïk
  I § adj 1 vital, fundamental 2 (Old) for the rest of one's life: for life, lifetime 3 ancient
  II § nm very old man; decrepit/infirm old man

jetïm
  I § n orphan
  II § adj 1 orphaned 2 abandoned and alone

jetim·o're nf orphanage

Jetmïr nm Jetmir (male name)

*****jet·no'r** (Reg Gheg) = **jet·ẽso'r**

jet·o·het vp impers one can live/survive; one can put up with it, (it) is bearable

jet·o·n vi, vt 1 to live; live through 2 to be alive; stay alive, survive 3 to reside 4 to last
  ○ **jeto·n me iratin e vet** to live on one's own income
  ○ **jeto·n me sot (e) me nesër** to live from day to day
  ○ **jeto·n me të vërtetën** to live an honest life, be incapable of not telling the truth
  ○ **jeto·n me thembrat e botës** to live a wretched life, live in abject poverty
  ○ **jeto·n me zgrip** to live on very little, live very thriftily
  ○ **jeto·n** pl **në një lëkurë** to all have the same living conditions, live pretty much the same
  ○ **jeto·n në shkueri** to live a nomadic life in the mountains
  ○ **jeto·n si gogla mbi ujë** to have no support or help; be in an insecure situation: live in a house of cards
  ○ **jeto·n si kush** (Colloq) to live well
  ○ **jeto·n veresie** to live an aimless life

Jeto'n nm Jeton (male name)

jet·o's adj (of a person) very old; old and infirm

jet·o's·et vpr to get very old, age terribly; become infirm

jet·o's·ur adj (i) aged terribly; old and infirm

jetu|a'r
  I § adj (i) experienced, known, felt, savored
  II § nn (të) living; experiencing, living through; surviving, survival

jetu'll nf (Reg) hair ribbon

Jetu'sh nm Jetush (male name)

jevg nm (np ~ gj) settled gypsy = **evgjït**

je·vg|ë nf 1 = **evgjïte** *2 [Bot] goosegrass, cleavers (Galium aparine)

*****je·vk|ë** = **je·vgë**

jeze'r nm fog

jezï't nm bloodsucker; evil person

jezuït
  I § nm Jesuit

II § adj 1 Jesuitical 2 (Contempt) hypocritical, deceptive, sly: jesuitical

jezuit izëm nm 1 Jesuitical faith/behavior 2 (Contempt) Jesuitry

je zull nm sweltering heat

*jezull i nf = zagushí

jezull o ·n vt to swelter in the heat

ji stem for imper, 2nd pl pres < ësh·të

ji p stem for 2nd pl pres, pind, imper, vp <jep·

jo pcl 1 no 2 not
  ○ jo __, jo __ (indicates speaker's exasperation with another's indecision between opposite alternatives)
  ○ Jo besa-besë e pesë e pesë If you give your word, you are honor bound to keep it.
  ○ jo gjatë 1 not long 2 in brief
  ○ Jo që/se jo.. 1 (accusation of obstinate refusal) Insist(s) on saying no! 2 By no means..
  ○ jo për duké e për pashi not just for show
  ○ jo veç, po __ not just that, but also __
  ○ jo vetëm (që) __, por edhe __ not only __, but even __
  ○ jo vetëm (që) __, porse __ not only __, but also __
  ○ jo vetëm aq, por __ (interpolation) not only that, but __
  ○ jo vetëm kaq not only that
  ○ jo vetëm që __ porse __ not only __ but also __

jo formativ non-

jo alkool ik adj nonalcoholic

jo antagon ist adj not inconsonant, not antagonistic

jo bujq ësor adj nonagricultural

jod nm [Chem] iodine ((I))

jo demokrat ik adj nondemocratic

jo detyrue s adj nonrequired, not required

jo dialekt ik adj nondialectic

jo dio nf = jod

jod izëm nm [Med] iodism

jo dur nm [Chem] iodide

jo ekonom ik adj 1 noneconomic 2 uneconomical

jo feta r adj nonreligious

jo frut or adj non-fruitbearing

jo frym or adj 1 nonbreathing 2 [Ling] inanimate

jo helmue s adj nonpoisonous

jo higjen ik adj nonhygenic

jo histor ik adj nonhistoric, nonhistorical

jo hund or adj [Ling] nonnasal

jo kalim ta r adj [Ling] intransitive

jo kapital ist n noncapitalist, noncapitalistic

jo kërbisht or adj, nm [Zool] invertebrate

jo klas or adj not pertaining to social classes; without class consciousness; classless

jo komb ëta r adj 1 without a country 2 nonnationalistic; unpatriotic

jo larg pam ës adj not farsighted: shortsighted

jo lënd or adj 1 nonmaterial 2 [Phil] immaterial

joli np (Colloq) [Mus] = saze

jo marks ist n non-Marxist

jo metal nm [Chem] nonmetal

jo më conj so consider how much more: even the more so, even more, all the more so

jo mikprit ës adj inhospitable, unfriendly

jo miq ësor adj unfriendly

jon nm [Spec] ion

Jon nm Jon (male name)

*Jon nm

*jo ne np fem <jonë

Jonel la nf Jonela (female name)

jo në nf 1 echo = jehonë 2 aria

jo në
  I § pronominal adj fem sg <ynë our
  II § nf ours

jonga r nm 1 three-stringed, long-necked mandolin 2 double flute

jonian adj of or pertaining to the Ionian Sea, Ionian

jon iz im nm ger 1 <jonizo·n, jonizo·het 2 ionization

jon iz o ·het vpr to be/become ionized

jon iz o ·n vt to ionize []

jon izu e s adj ionizing

jo normal adj abnormal

jon o sfer ë nf ionosphere

jonus ba llëk nm (Old) [Zool] dolphin

Jonu z nm Jonuz (male name)

jo nxh ë nf [Bot] alfalfa, lucerne (Medicago sativa)

jonxh isht e np <jonxhishtë [Bot] a quantity of alfalfa; alfalfa

jonxh isht ë nf [Bot] alfalfa field

jo njer ëz or adj 1 nonhuman 2 inhuman

jo objekti v adj nonobjective

jo oksidue s adj 1 = pandryshkshëm 2 [Chem] non-oxidizing ()

jo organ ik adj 1 nonorganic 2 inorganic

jo paq ësor adj 1 non-peaceloving, opposed to peace 2 not peaceful: belligerent 3 nonpacifist

jo parim or adj 1 unprincipled 2 not based on the right principles, wrong

jo përçue s adj [Spec] nonconductive, nonconducting

jo për parim ta r adj unprogressive

jo pjell or adj infertile

jo prodh im ta r adj unproductive

jo prodh ue s adj infertile, unproductive, nonproducing

jo proleta r adj nonproletarian

jordan ez
  I § adj Jordanian
  II § n native of Jordan

Jordan i nf Jordan

jo real adj 1 unreal; imaginary 2 unrealistic, unrealizable

jo real ist adj unrealistic; non-realistic

jorga n nm bedquilt, quilt

jorgan punue s nm professional quilt maker

jorgan xhi nm (np ~ nj) = jorganpunues

*jorg ta r adj balky (horse)

jo ritm ik adj non-rhythmic

jose conj = ose

*jo se ma conj = jomë

jo se më conj = jomë

*jo si gurt adj (i) = pasigurt

jo simetri nf asymmetry

jo simetr ik adj [Tech] asymmetric

josh· vt to be alluring to []: entice [], lure []
  ○ <> josh· zemrën to capture <>'s heart, capture <>'s admiration, captivate <>, charm <>

jo sh·et vpr to snuggle up, rub up against, cuddle up to

jo'shë nf 1 endearment 2 allure, enticement; lure 3 (Reg) mother's mother: grandmother

jo'sh|ës adj alluring, enticing

jo'shje nf ger 1 <josh•, josh•et 2 allure, enticement; enchantment, spell

jo'shkenc'o'r adj nonscientific

jo'shoq|ër'o'r adj 1 non-social; unsocial 2 unsociable

jo'shqu'e's adj [Ling] indefinite

jo'shter'ue's adj not thorough, not exhaustive: cursory

jo'shtër nf strong crop-damaging hot wind from the sea

*jo'sh|un adj (i) (Reg Gheg) 1 charmed 2 charming

jot adj (used when preceding the feminine noun it modifies) = jo'te

jo'te
    I § pronominal adj fem sg nom <yt thy
    II § nf 1 thine 2 female relative/friend of thine

jo'tok|ës'o'r adj unearthly, not of this world

jo'vend'im'ta'r adj playing no decisive role: inconsequential

jo'vet'o'r adj [Ling] impersonal

*jo'zm = dhio'zmë

jo'zyr'ta'r adj unofficial

ju
    I § pron you (plural or polite)
    II § 2nd pl pronominal proclitic

jua sequence of pronominal clitics = 2nd pl referent + 3rd object

ju'aj
    I § pronominal adj pl nom your
    II § pron 1 yours 2 relative/friend of yours

jua'n nm basic unit of Chinese money, yuan

jubil'a'r adj pertaining to a jubilee: commemorative

jubile' nf jubilee

jud nm [Folklore] boogieman who fights with people, particularly drunks

ju'dë nf (Pej) Judas; base traitor/spy

*ju'dh|ë = ju'dë

ju'fk|e nf 1 egg noodle 2 dessert pancake served with hot sugar syrup

jug nm south

ju'gë nf 1 warm and humid southern wind; wind from the south 2 south
    ○ juga e bardhë breeze from the south that blows in the spring

○ juga e zezë cold winter wind (injurious to plants)

jug'l'ind'je nf southeast

jug'l'ind'o'r adj southeastern

jug'o'r
    I § adj 1 southern, of the south 2 (of wind) blowing from the south
    II § n southerner

jug'o'slla'v
    I § adj Yugoslavian
    II § nm Yugoslav

Jug'o'slla'vi' nf Yugoslavia

jug'perëndim nm southwest

jug'perëndim'o'r adj southwestern

jug'vietname'z adj South Vietnamese

ju'ha onomat derisive hoot aimed at driving the victim away
    ○ juha-juha derisive hooting (accompanied by head and arm gestures)

ju'k|e nf [Bot] yucca (Yucca L.)

Ju'li nm with fem agreement Juli (female name)

julia'n adj Julian

julla'r nm halter, bridle

ju'ntë nf (Pej) junta

Jupiter nm Jupiter

juri' nf jury

juridi'k adj juridical, judicial

juridik'i'sht adv [Law] juridically

juridik'sio'n nm [Offic] jurisdiction

jurisprudenc'ë nf (Book) jurisprudence

jur'i'st n jurist; professor of law

*jur'd'e'r adj (fem ~ ore) (Old) juridical

*jurra' interj = urra'

justifik'i'm nm ger 1 <justifiko'•n, justifiko'•het 2 justification; evidence; excuse, defense

justifik'o'•het vpr to try to justify oneself: make excuses

justifik'o'•n vt 1 to justify 2 to make excuses for []: excuse []

justifik'ue'shëm adj (i) 1 justifiable, excusable 2 justifying, exculpatory

ju'sh abl <ju

ju'të nf [Bot] jute (Conchorus capsularis)

ju've
    I § pron 2nd pl dat/acc <ju you
    II § pron 2nd pl nom/abl (Colloq)

Kk

k [kë] *nf* **1** the consonant letter "k" **2** the voiceless velar stop represented by the letter "k"

k = **kë**

ka·

  I § *vt* to have

  II § *auxiliary forming perfect tenses* to have

  III § *auxiliary forming future tenses followed by infinitive* to feel/experience

  IV § *existential declarative (3rd sg forms only)* there *is*

  ∘ **ka·** {*quantifier + expression of time*} {*somewhere*} to have been (somewhere) for {} **kam dy ditë në Berat** I have been in Berat for two days

  ∘ **ka·** {*quantifier + expression of time*} {} ago, since {}

  ∘ [] **·ka·** {*noun expressing a close personal relationship*} {} *is* one's {} **e kam kushëri** he's my cousin **e kisha mik** he was my friend

  ∘ **ka· amel** to have diarrhea

  ∘ **ka· anë** to enjoy special favor

  ∘ **nuk ka·**^{3sg} **anë e udhë** it *doesn't* make any sense

  ∘ **<> ka·**^{3sg} **ardhur qumështi i nënës në majë të hundës** <> *is* at the end of <>'s endurance, <> *can*not take it any more

  ∘ **<> ka·**^{3sg} **ardhur uji në mulli** "the water has come to <>'s mill" things *have* gone well for <>, <> *has* done well, <> *has* been very lucky

  ∘ **ka· arsye** to have good reason

  ∘ **e ka· arsyen në majë të shpatës** "have the argument on the point of one's sword" to win arguments by force: get one's way by bullying

  ∘ **s'ka·**^{3sg} **as kokë, as këmbë** to be formless, be a shapeless mess; be hard to know where/how to begin

  ∘ **s'ka·**^{3sg} **as këmbë as krye** "have neither foot nor head" to have no internal cohesion, be incoherent

  ∘ **nuk** [] **ka· as në shpatull të pulës** [] doesn't even enter into {}'s account, {} doesn't consider [] to be in the same league

  ∘ **s'**[] **ka· as për mirë as për keq** {} *cannot* count on []

  ∘ **e ka· ballin të hapur** with a clear conscience

  ∘ **ka· bark 1** to have diarrhea **2** to have a big belly

  ∘ **e ka· barkun pa brez** "have a belly without a belt" to have a huge appetite

  ∘ **ka· barkun garroqe** to be very hungry

  ∘ **ka· barkun plloçë** to have a stomach that is absolutely empty

  ∘ **e ka· barkun të ftohtë** to have few expectations, have little hope, be pessimistic

  ∘ **e ka· barutin (të) thatë** to keep one's powder dry, be ready for battle

  ∘ **e ka· barutin të lagur** "have one's gunpowder wet" to be unprepared for conflict, lack the guts to fight

  ∘ **s'i ka· bathët mirë** not have one's affairs in order

  ∘ **ka· besë** to be worthy of trust, be trustworthy

  ∘ **ka· besim** to have faith; be convinced, believe

  ∘ **ka· bezdi** to be bored

  ∘ [] **ka· bezdi** to find [] annoying

  ∘ **s'i ka· bërë ende ditët** (*Impol*) to be still wet behind the ears

  ∘ **<> ka· bërë gurin e gjakut** to have caused <> much torment

  ∘ **e ka· bërë syrin gozhdë** to have a heart of stone

  ∘ **ka· bërë shkollën e shejtanit** "have gone to the devil's school" (*Pej*) to have had lessons from the devil in being bad, be as bad as they come

  ∘ **e ka· bërë vijë/vazhdë** "have made a rut" to have worn a rut (by constant repetition)

  ∘ **s'ka·**^{3sg} **bir nëne të __** "there *is* no mother's son to __" there *is* no one on the face of the earth who can __

  ∘ **sikur ka· bjeshkën në shpinë** to be in a bad way

  ∘ **e ka· bllok me** [] to be inseparable from []

  ∘ [] **ka· bollë** not be able to stand []

  ∘ **ka· borxh të __** to be quite capable of __; {} wouldn't hesitate to __

  ∘ [] **ka· brengë** to have deep and persistent regret about [ ]

  ∘ **nuk ka·**^{3sg} **brirë** one doesn't need a sign, it *is* perfectly obvious

  ∘ [] **ka· bukë e djathë** to find [] very easy, be able to do [] without difficulty: find [] a snap

  ∘ **i ka· burimet të thella 1** to have deep-rooted causes **2** to have sources of power that go deep

  ∘ **i ka· buzët me qumësht** "have lips with milk on them" (*Impol*) <> *is* still wet behind the ears

  ∘ **s'ka·**^{3sg} **ç'<> du·***het*^{3sg} to be none of one's business

  ∘ **s'ka·**^{3sg} **ç'të <> ha·**^{3sg} **miu pas darke** "there *is* nothing left for the mouse to eat after <>'s supper" <> *is* so poor that <> *eats* up every last crumb

  ∘ **ka· çelësat e kashtës** "hold the keys to the straw" (*Iron*) to have no influence/power

  ∘ **e ka· çerepin në zjarr** "have the baking pan in the fire" to have a big problem to worry about; have an urgent matter to take care of

  ∘ **nuk ka· çetë këtu** to have no relatives locally

  ∘ **ka·**^{3sg} **çosa** (*Colloq*) to be a while, some while ago/before; for some while/time

  ∘ **<> ka·**^{3sg} **çukitur pula mendtë** "the chicken *has* pecked/eaten/drunk <>'s brains" <> *is* completely stupid, <> *has* completely lost <>'s senses

  ∘ **<> ka·**^{3sg} **çukitur sorra mendtë** "the crow *has* pecked/eaten/drunk <>'s brains" <> *is* completely stupid, <> *has* completely lost <>'s senses

  ∘ **s'**[] **ka· dadë** not be [] 's baby any more, not have to listen to advice or take orders from []

  ∘ **s'<> ka·**^{3pl} **dalë (ende) pupla** "<>'s feathers *have* not (yet) sprouted" <> *is* still young and immature: <> *is* still wet behind the ears

  ∘ **<> ka·**^{3sg} **dalë bari (në faqe/sy)** "the grass *has* grown (on <>'s face/eye)" <> *has* been dead a long time; it *is* too late for <> now

  ∘ **s'<> ka·**^{3pl} **dalë dhëmbët** "<>'s teeth *have* not come out" (*Impol*) <> *is* wet behind the ears, <> *is* immature

○ **s'ka· dalë ende nga** *veza//lëvozhga e vezës* "not yet have emerged from the egg/eggshell" *(Impol)* to be young and lacking in experience: still be wet behind the ears

○ **<> ka·**^{3sg} **dalë fryma** <> *has* lost <*its*> appeal

○ **<> ka·**^{3pl} **dalë kockat** <>'s bones *are sticking out*, <> *is* very skinny

○ **ka· dalë nga defteri** to have lost the ability; have become too old; have become undependable

○ **ka· dalë nga hullia** to set out on the wrong path: live an improper life

○ **s'<> ka·**^{3sg} **dalë qimja ende** "<>'s beard *has not* yet sprouted" <> *is* still immature, <> is not grown-up yet

○ **<> ka·**^{3sg} **dalë rrënja** "<>'s root *has come* out" <> *is* left without descendents

○ **s'<> ka·**^{3sg} **dirsur qimja ende** "<>'s beard *has not* yet grown out" <> *is* still immature, <> is not grown-up yet

○ **<> ka· ditët të shkurtra** <> *won't* last long: <>'s days *are* numbered

○ **<>a ka·**^{3sg} **djegur qulli/luga buzën** "the mush/spoon *has* burned <>'s lip" <> *has had* a good taste (and wants no more), <> knows from bitter experience

○ **s'<> ka·**^{3sg} **djersitur ende mustaqja** "<>'s moustache *has* not yet grown out" <> *is* still young; <> *is* still wet behind the ears

○ **ka· dorë** *(Pej)* **1** to be given to hitting others **2** to be given to stealing, be of a thieving nature

○ **ka· dorë të lirë** to have a free hand, be able to act without constraints

○ **ka· dorë të rëndë** "have a heavy hand" to be heavy-fisted; be clumsy (in working with one's hands), be all thumbs

○ **e ka· dorën lopatë** to be greedy, never have enough

○ **e ka· dorën grusht** to be tight-fisted, be stingy

○ **e ka· dorën të gjatë** *(Pej)* **1** to like to hit other people **2** to be given to stealing

○ **e ka· dorën të lirë 1** to be loose with money, be (too) free with money **2** to be too easy-going in supervision: lax in discipline

○ **e ka· dorën të thatë** to be unable to hold onto money, money just slips through {}'s fingers

○ **[] ka· dritë në sy** consider [] to be the apple of one's eye

○ **i ka· duart flori** to be extraordinarily skillful with one's hands

○ **i ka· duart me kallo** to have callused hands: have worked hard all one's life; be a hard worker

○ **i ka· duart me vrima** "have hands with holes, have leaky hands" to be a spendthrift: have a hole in one's pocket

○ **i ka· duart të gjata** *(Pej)* **1** to like to hit other people **2** to be given to stealing

○ **i ka· duart të lidhura** "have one's hands tied" to be prevented from acting

○ **i ka· duart të lira** to have a free hand, be able to act without constraints

○ **i ka· duart të mpira** one's arms/legs *are* numb; work as if one's limbs were numb: be maddeningly slow in one's work

○ **i ka· duart të prera** "have one's hands cut off" to have been deprived of power

○ **i ka· duart të shkurtra** not have much pull

○ **i ka· duart të shpenguara** to be one's own boss, have a free hand

○ **i ka· duart të thara 1** to be lazy; be slow in doing things **2** to have butterfingers **3** to be incapable of taking care of oneself

○ **<> ka· duk** to last <> a long time

○ **s'<> ka·**^{3sg} **duk fjala** <>'s words *carry* no weight; what <> *says has* no effect

○ **ka· duk 1** to last long **2** (of foods) to rise/expand

○ **s'<> ka·**^{3sg} **duk puna** <>'s work *is* ineffective

○ **ka· durim prej guri** to be very patient: have the patience of Job

○ **e ka· dyfekun me** to be on hostile terms with

○ **ka· dhëmbë e çaporre** to know what one is doing

○ **i ka· dhëmbët me bukën time** "my bread is still in {}'s teeth" to show one's ingratitude to me

○ **i ka· dhëmbët rruazë** to have small and regular pearly white teeth, have teeth like pearls

○ **ka· dhënë e ka· marrë (me []**) to be linked (to []) through the marriage of one's children

○ **<> ka· dhënë ujë çeliku** to make <> pitiless and cruel

○ **ka· edhe gojë të flet·**^{subj}**/tho·të**^{subj} *(Pej)* to even have the nerve to criticize others

○ **ka· edhe gojë të kërko·n**^{subj} *(Pej)* to have a lot of nerve asking, even have the nerve to ask (for something)

○ **ka· etje për []** to long for []

○ **ka· etje** to be thirsty

○ **<>[] ka·**^{3sg} **ënda** *(Colloq)* <> likes/enjoys []; <> wants [], <> would like []

○ **ka· faj** to be guilty

○ **e ka· faqen të larë 1** to have one's honor intact, have a clear conscience, have clean hands: be completely innocent **2** to look innocent

○ **i ka· faqet gur** to be chubby-cheeked

○ **ka· fat** to be lucky

○ **[] ka· ferrë për qafe** [] *is* a pain in {}'s neck, [] *is* a thorn in {}'s side

○ **[] ka· ferrë në sy** to bear a grudge against [], hate [] terribly

○ **i ka· fijet mbarë** to have things going well, be succeeding

○ **ka· fjalën** {*pronominal adjective*} **1** to have one's say (in the matter) **kam fjalën time 2** I have my say (in the matter)

○ **ka· fjalën** to be talking; have the floor

○ **e ka· fjalën plumb** "have leaden speech" to be capable of saying hurtful things

○ **i ka· fjalët me grosh** [he] talks little, but wisely

○ **i ka· fjalët të shkurtra** to be a person of few words

○ **s'ka·**^{3sg} **flamë që s'[] zë·** "there *is* no flu that *does* not catch []" [] *is* easily influenced

○ **i ka· florinjtë me bisht** to have money to burn

○ **i ka· florinjtë me hejbe** to be extremely rich, have buckets of money

○ **ka· frikë** to be afraid

○ **i ka· futur duart deri në bërryl** *(Pej)* to be in it up to the elbows

○ **e ka· fytin të gjatë/madh** to be a big eater; be a glutton

○ **e ka· fytyrën aba** to have a weather-beaten face

○ **e ka· fytyrën petë-petë** to have a deeply wrinkled face

○ **ka· gisht në** "have a finger in" to be involved in

○ **e ka· gishtin në këmbëz** to have/keep one's finger on the trigger, be ready for battle

○ **ka· gojë 1** *(Pej)* to have a big mouth, say bad things about others **2** to assert something that is self-evident
○ **e ka· gojën arkë** "have a mouth like a safe" to be able to keep secrets, be tight-lipped
○ **e ka· gojën baltë** "have a muddy mouth" to have a bad taste in the mouth
○ **e ka· gojën bilbil** "have a mouth like a nightingale" to be good with words
○ **e ka· gojën brisk** "have mouth like a razor" to have a sharp tongue
○ **e ka· gojën e hapur** "have an open mouth" to have a complete right to say something
○ **e ka· gojën fushë** "have a mouth like a field" to have no teeth left
○ **e ka· gojën kamare** "have a mouth like a niche" to have a big mouth (both literally and figuratively)
○ **e ka· gojën lopatë** "have a shovel of a mouth" to say/make up all sorts of things, true or untrue
○ **e ka· gojën vesh më vesh** "have a mouth ear-to-ear" to have a big mouth (both literally and figuratively)
○ **e ka· gojën ajkë** to have a pleasant disposition, always have a nice word to say
○ **e ka· gojën arkë** to be good at keeping secrets
○ **e ka· gojën brisk 1** to be eloquent; be fast on one's feet **2** to have a sassy tongue
○ **e ka· gojën fushë** to have no teeth in one's mouth
○ **e ka· gojën huall** to be very nice and friendly in speech
○ **e ka· gojën hudhër** to be offensive/nasty in speech; speak gruffly/rudely
○ **e ka· gojën kamare** to have a big mouth
○ **e ka· gojën lopatë** to be a terrible gossip
○ **e ka· gojën llokum** "have a candy mouth" to speak kindly/sweetly
○ **e ka· gojën mish** to have an inflamed mouth full of sores
○ **e ka· gojën si kuti** to have a beautiful little mouth
○ **e ka· gojën sheqer** to be pleasant in speech
○ **e ka· gojën të hapur 1** to have a clear conscience; have every right (to do something) **2** to be courageous
○ **e ka· gojën të keqe** to have a dirty mouth, use bad language
○ **e ka· gojën të mbërthyer/kyçur** to be unable to speak
○ **e ka· gojën të shthurur/prishur/rëndë 1** *(Pej)* to be imprudent in speech; be insolent **2** to use indecent speech: be foul-mouthed
○ **e ka· gojën vetëm për bukë** "have a mouth good for nothing but eating" to be unable/unwilling to speak up when one should
○ **e ka· gozhdë në zemër** to feel constant regret
○ **s'<> ka·³ˢᵍ grat puna** <>'s work *is* ineffective
○ **ka· grurë me** to be on very good terms with
○ **ka· gjak në fytyrë/faqe** to be honorable
○ **[] ka· gjak në sy** to bear a grudge against [], hate [] intensely
○ **ka· gjak prej <> 1** to be a direct descendant of <> **2** to owe blood vengeance against <>
○ **ka·³ˢᵍ gjasë** it *is* likely
○ **[] ka· gjemb në sy** to bear a grudge against [], hate [] terribly
○ **S'[] ka· gjetur në rrugë.** "{} has not found [] on the street" {} *has* not come by [] easily: {} *holds* [] very dear. [] is very precious to {}.
○ **ka· gjetur pelena të buta** "have found soft diapers" to have settled into a life of comfort

○ **Ka·³ˢᵍ gjetur tenxherja kapakun.** "The cooker *finds* its lid." *(Pej)* The devil has found his mate.
○ **[] ka· gjethe** to find [] easy to defeat
○ **ka· gjilpërat majë më majë** to be at loggerheads
○ **e ka· gjoksin e gjerë** to be bighearted/tolerant/generous
○ **(e) ka· gjuhë(n) të gjatë/madhe** to be loose-tongued, be a blabbermouth
○ **ka· gjuhë të shkurtër** to be tongue-tied
○ **ka· gjuhë 1** *(Pej)* to talk too much **2** to backbite
○ **e ka· gjuhën bilbil** to have an eloquent/fluid tongue, speak easily and quickly
○ **e ka· gjuhën brisk 1** to be eloquent; be fast on one's feet **2** to have a sassy tongue
○ **e ka· gjuhën lëpjetë 1** to be insolent in speech **2** to be bitingly cruel in speech: have a sharp and nasty tongue; be a nasty gossip
○ **e ka· gjuhën një pashë** to talk too much
○ **e ka· gjuhën një pëllëmbë** "have a tongue as big as the palm of a hand" to be a talkative gossip, have a wagging tongue
○ **e ka· gjuhën shpatë** to be an eloquent and persuasive speaker
○ **e ka· gjuhën të keqe** to have a dirty mouth, use bad language
○ **nuk <> ka·³ˢᵍ gjumë trimëria** "<>'s bravery *does not sleep* in <>" *(Elev)* <> *is* extremely brave
○ **e ka· gjumin si të lepurit** "sleep like a rabbit" to sleep lightly
○ **e ka· gjumin si të pleshtit** "have sleep like that of the flea" to be a light sleeper
○ **ka· hak** to have every right, have the right
○ **s'<> ka· hak** not be obligated to <>, not be indebted to <>
○ **[] ka· halë në sy** to bear a grudge against [], hate [] terribly
○ **e ka· halën në grykë** "have a fishbone in one's throat" to be great difficulty; have a tough life
○ **ka· hall sa të** {+ *verb*}ˢᵘᵇʲ <>'s problem is just to {*do something*}
○ **[] ka· hallall** to have [] coming, well-deserve []
○ **e ka· hanxhar në zemër** to feel constant regret
○ **ka· hapëset e kashtës** "hold the keys to the straw" *(Iron)* to have no influence/power
○ **e ka· hapur shumë gojën** to talk too much (about things which shouldn't be talked about)
○ **ka· hedhur dashuri për** [] to have come to love []
○ **<> ka·³ˢᵍ hequr shumë lëkura** <> *has* gone through great suffering
○ **ka· hesap** to be worth the trouble, be worth it
○ **<> ka· hije 1** to befit <>, be suitable/proper for <> **2** to fit <> well, look well on <>
○ **nuk ka· hije lisi për** [] "there *is* no oak shade for []" it *is* not comfortable for [], [] does not feel comfortable
○ **<> ka· hije si shala gomarit** "fit <> like a saddle on a donkey" *(Iron)* to fit <> badly: fit like a glove on a foot
○ **i ka· hime trutë/mendtë** to have sawdust for brains
○ **i ka· hipur atij kali** to have already started work necessary; know perfectly well what one *is doing*
○ **i ka· hipur breshkës** *(Iron)* to go/work at a snail's pace
○ **ka· hipur në barkë pa vela** "have jumped into a boat without sails" to be totally without direction

○ <> **ka·** hipur në kurriz/qafë/zverk to have <> under one's thumb

○ <> **ka·**^{3sg} hipur zekthi/miza **1** to be very uneasy **2** to be on the warpath, be up in arms, be in a terrible mood

○ <> **ka·**^{3sg} humbur guri <> lost control of <>self

○ **ka·** humbur pa opt to have disappeared without a trace

○ **ka·** humbur rripin e këmborës "have lost one's bell strap" to speak/behave stupidly

○ <> **ka·** humbur rrumbi "<>'s bellclapper *has* gotten lost" something essential to <>'s well-being *is* gone

○ e **ka·** humbur rrumbi kambanën "the clapper *has* lost the bell" confusion *reigns*

○ e **ka·** humbur rrumbin e këmborës "have lost one's bellclapper" **1** to have lost one's train of thought **2** to lose one's high estate, fall low

○ e **ka·** humbur yzengjinë "have lost one's stirrup" to have gone wild

○ **ka·** hundë e buzë të __ to have the audacity to __

○ **ka·** hundë **1** to have a premonition **2** to be snooty

○ nuk **ka·** hundë për [] *(Impol)* not be good enough to deserve []

○ e **ka·** hundën lart/përpjetë *(Iron)* to have one's nose in the air: be stuck up

○ e **ka·** hundën në lis to have one's nose in the air, be stuck-up

○ e **ka·** hundën të gjatë/madhe to have one's nose in the air, be conceited

○ e **ka·** hundën të hollë to have a good sense of smell

○ [] **ka·** huq {} will fail/miss []

○ <> **ka·**^{3pl} hyrë (punët) në torishtë matters *are* well in hand, things *are* under control

○ <> **ka·**^{3sg} hyrë bukla the person who *is* to ferret out the truth (and ascertain who is to blame) has arrived on the scene

○ <> **ka·**^{3sg} hyrë djalli në bark something has gotten into <> to make <> so bad: the devil has gotten into <>, <> *has* turned into a terrible person

○ <> **ka·**^{3sg} hyrë dreqi në bark something has gotten into <> to make <> so bad: the devil has gotten into <>, <> *has* turned into a terrible person

○ nuk <> **ka·**^{3sg} hyrë ferrë në këmbë "no thorn has entered <>'s foot" **1** <> *has* had too easy a life; <> *has* had an easy time of it **2** <> always *lands* on his feet; <> always *comes* through unscathed

○ <> **ka·**^{3sg} hyrë fitili *(Crude)* <> *has* fallen in love

○ <> **ka·**^{3sg} hyrë lepuri në bark "the hare has entered <>'s belly" <> *is* in constant fear

○ <> **ka·**^{3sg} hyrë macja në bark something has gotten into <> to make <> so bad: the devil has gotten into <>, <> *has* turned into a terrible person

○ <> **ka·**^{3sg} hyrë maçoku në bark something has gotten into <> to make <> so bad: the devil has gotten into <>, <> *has* turned into a terrible person

○ <> **ka·**^{3sg} hyrë shejtani në bark something has gotten into <> to make <> so bad: the devil has gotten into <>, <> *has* turned into a terrible person

○ <> **ka·**^{3sg} hyrë tenja "the tapeworm *has* entered <>" <> *has* become seriously ill

○ <> **ka·**^{3sg} hyrë vemja <> *is* ill/sick; <> *has* become consumptive

○ <> **ka·**^{3sg} hyrë zekthi/miza **1** to be very uneasy **2** to be on the warpath, be up in arms, be in a terrible mood

○ <> **ka·**^{3pl} ikur disa iliqe/iliqet <> *is losing* all sense of morality, <> *is going* downhill morally

○ <>a **ka·** inatin to remember a past wrong done by <>, hold a grudge against <>

○ **ka·** interes to be interesting, be of interest

○ **ka·** kaluar në prehistori to have faded into distant memory

○ **ka·**^{3sg} kaluar shumë ujë "*have drunk* many kinds of water" a lot of time *has* passed

○ [] **ka·**^{3pl} kapur dallgët "the waves have caught []" [] *is* overcome by anger

○ [] **ka·** kapur nga majat e flokëve to have considered [] very superficially; have learned only the least important parts of []

○ sikur **ka·** kapur qiellin me dorë "as if one has grasped the sky by the hand" to act as if one has performed a miracle

○ **ka·** katërqind mendje *(Pej)* **1** to be of constantly changing mind **2** to have opinions that keep changing: be of different minds

○ e **ka·** keq me [] to be on bad terms with []

○ s'e **ka·** keq that's not a bad idea that {} *has*

○ [] **ka·** keq {}'s [] is in a bad way

○ nuk **ka·** këmbë njeriu not a trace of a single living person *is* left

○ **ka·** këmbë të rënda to drag one's feet

○ e **ka·** këmbën të prapë to be a jinx

○ i **ka·** këmbët brisk to have a smooth and very fast gait

○ i **ka·** këmbët kulvarë to have one's legs hanging down (riding horseback)

○ i **ka·** këmbët të lidhura "have one's feet tied" to be tied down, be unable to go/get anywhere

○ i **ka·** këmbët të mpira one's arms/legs *are* numb; work as if one's limbs were numb: be maddeningly slow in one's work

○ i **ka·** këmbët të shpenguara to be one's own boss, have a free hand

○ i **ka·** këmbët të thara to be barely able to walk; walk very slowly

○ <> **ka·**^{3sg} kënduar huti <> *is* blessed with luck, things *are going* well for <>

○ <> **ka·**^{3sg} kënduar kukuvajka "The owl has sung its song for <>." <> *must be* under a bad omen

○ <> **ka·**^{3sg} kënduar qyqja "the cuckoo has sung for <>" <> *has* had <>'s day, <> *is* gone forever

○ <> **ka·**^{3sg} kënduar qyqja në derë "the cuckoo *has* sung for <> at the door" <> *is* the last of <>'s line, <> *is* all alone in the world; <> *has* suffered terrible misfortune

○ <> **ka·** kërcyer në kurriz/qafë/zverk to have <> under one's thumb

○ <> **ka·**^{3sg} kërcyer zekthi/miza **1** to be very uneasy **2** to be on the warpath, be up in arms, be in a terrible mood

○ s'**ka·** kockë to lack the necessary ability, not have what it *takes*, not *be* the right person

○ s'**ka·**^{3sg} kohë as të rrehë qerpikët "there *isn't* even time to blink" there *isn't* enough time left; (one is so busy that) there *is* not enough time in a day

○ [] **ka·** kokë e lart to put [] on a pedestal, revere [] above all others

◦ **ka· kokë më vete** to insist on doing things one's own way, be headstrong

◦ **e ka· kokën bosh** not know a single thing; not have a thought in one's head

◦ **e ka· kokën cangë** to be stubborn, be obstinate

◦ **e ka· kokën daullë** {}'s head feels as if someone has been banging on it all day

◦ **e ka· kokën fushë** to be completely bald

◦ **e ka· kokën gdhe** to be very stubborn

◦ **e ka· kokën gur** to be pig-headed, be stubborn

◦ **e ka· kokën harc** to be hard-headed/obstinate/stubborn

◦ **e ka· kokën lart 1** to hold one's head high, be proud **2** to think too highly of oneself

◦ **e ka· kokën me cepa** to be thickheaded, be hard to get through to

◦ **e ka· kokën në prush** "have one's head on a bed of hot coals" to be in great danger: be playing with fire

◦ **nuk e ka· kokën në vend** not have one's head on straight; not be in one's right mind

◦ **e ka· kokën në vend të lig/keq** "have one's head in a bad place" *(Pej)* to have one's head not tied on straight, not be thinking right

◦ **e ka· kokën plot 1** to know a lot; be wise **2** to be completely convinced

◦ **e ka· kokën plumb** "have a leaden head" to have a splitting headache

◦ **e ka· kokën shkëmb 1** to be hardheaded/obstinate **2** to be thickheaded/dense

◦ **e ka· kokën shtalp** *(Impol)* to be still immature: be wet behind the ears

◦ **e ka· kokën të cekët** to be shallow, frivolous, superficial, flighty

◦ **e ka· kokën të fortë** to be hard-headed/obstinate

◦ **e ka· kokën të lehtë** one's head has cleared up, one's head no longer feels stuffed up

◦ **e ka· kokën vare** to be very stubborn

◦ **e ka· kokën zjarr** {}'s head *is burning* (with fever)

◦ **nuk ka· krah andej** not be going in that direction

◦ **i ka· krahët të prerë** "have one's arms cut off" to have been deprived of power

◦ **i ka· krahët të tharë** to be sluggish/lazy; be unwilling to move a finger

◦ **ka· krimbat** to be unable to sit still for a minute, be constantly squirming

◦ **e ka· kripën të thatë** to have one's affairs in good order, have one's ducks in a row

◦ **s'ka·**^{3sg} **ku <> var·**et^{3sg} **trasta** "there is nowhere for <>'s pouch to hang" <> *is* wretchedly poor

◦ **s'ka·**^{3sg} **ku** [] **kap·**^{3sg}/**zë·**^{3sg} **qeni** "a dog wouldn't know where to grab []" [] *is* poor as a churchmouse

◦ **ka· kujdes** to be careful

◦ [] **ka· kujdes** to be seeing to [], take care of []

◦ **e ka· kuletën të shpuar** "have a leaky pocket/wallet" to have no money because one spends all that one has; have wasted all one's money

◦ **s'ka·**^{3sg} **kuptim** it *makes* no sense; it *is* useless

◦ **e ka· lafshën të madhe** to be cocky

◦ [] **ka· lakra në kopsht** *(Iron)* to have no particularly close relationship with []

◦ **e ka· lakun në fyt/grykë** "have a noose around one's neck" to be in serious trouble

◦ **e ka· lejën** *me pashë*/**plot pashin** to have complete authority

◦ **ka· lepe** to be respectful and receptive to requests

◦ [] **ka· leqendi** to annoy [] greatly

◦ **<> ka· lezet** to be becoming to <>; look good on <>

◦ **ka·**^{3sg} **lezet** to be pleasurable/enjoyable

◦ **nuk <> ka·**^{3sg} **lezet të** {+ *verb*}^{subj} it *is* not nice for <> to {*do something*}

◦ **ka· lëkurë bualli** to be impervious to insult/criticism: be thick-skinned

◦ **e ka· lëkurën si të buallit** to have thick skin; be thick-skinned

◦ **ka· lëkurën e ujkut** "have the skin/hair of a wolf" to be a constant victim of bad luck: be a bad-luck Charley

◦ **ka· lëkurën e ujkut në kurriz/shpinë** "have the skin of a wolf on one's back" **1** to bear a burden of shame (for everyone to see) **2** to be guilty

◦ **e ka· lëkurën shollë 1** <>'s skin *is* tough as leather **2** <> *is* hardened and indifferent: <> *is* thick-skinned

◦ **e ka· lëkurën të trashë** to be thick-skinned

◦ [] **ka· lëmë** to have more than enough []

◦ [] **ka·**^{3pl} **lënë sytë** "the eyes have abandoned []" [] *can* barely see

◦ [] **ka·**^{3rd} **lënë** {*part of the body in nominative definite*} "[]'s {} has abandoned []" [] has lost the use of []'s {}, [] has lost []'s {}

◦ **<>i ka·**^{3sg} **lëpirë lopa trutë/mendtë** "the cow *has* licked up <>'s brain" *(Tease)* <> *is* empty-headed, <> *is* stupid

◦ [] **ka·**^{3sg} **lëpirë lopa** "the cow licked []" **1** *(Joke)* [] *is* all dolled up **2** *(Pej)* [] *has* no sense of shame: [] *is* shameless

◦ [] **ka·**^{3sg} **lëpirë miu** "the mouse licked []" [] *has* become miserably poor

◦ **ka·**^{3sg} **lëshuar merimangë** "{} *is* full of spiders" {} *is* full of cobwebs: {} has been unused/neglected for a long time

◦ **nuk <a ka· lëshuar poganikun** not manage to have gotten to know <> in any depth

◦ [] **ka·**^{3pl} **lëshuar rrathët** [] *has* flipped (his lid)

◦ **i ka· lidhur dengjet** to have matters well in hand

◦ **ka· lidhur mish** to have put on weight, have filled out

◦ **ka· ligj** *(Colloq)* to have good reason; be in the right

◦ **e ka· ligjin në teh të shpatës** "have law on the blade of one's sword" to use one's superior power to get one's way: get one's way by bullying

◦ **ka· limë të fortë** to be very persuasive

◦ **ka· lindur me këmishë/yll** "born with a caul/star" to have been born lucky, be lucky

◦ **ka· lindur për atë punë** to be perfectly suited to that

◦ **ka· lindur përpara shejtanit** "have been born before the devil" *(Pej)* to be more diabolical than the devil

◦ **ka· lindur prej gurit** "be born of stone" **1** to be unemotional; be hard-hearted **2** to be able to resist hardship/pain: be tough/patient

◦ **i ka· litarët nëpër këmbë** "have the ropes between one's legs" to be still embroiled/entangled in one task (and unable to take on another)

◦ **e ka· litarin në fyt/grykë** "have a noose around one's neck" to be in serious trouble

◦ **i ka· lotët në majë të qepallave** "have tears at the edges of one's eyelids" to be on the brink of tears

○ i ka· lotët në majë të syrit to cry easily; be a crybaby

○ <> ka·^{3sg} luajtur çikriku ◇ *has* lost ◇'s marbles, ◇ *is* off in the head, ◇ *has* a screw loose

○ e ka· luajtur gishtin (e pushkës) "*has* wiggled one's gun finger" to have shot a gun; know how to shoot a gun; have fought in a war

○ ka· luajtur nga vidhat/burgjitë "◇ has played around with ◇'s screws" ◇ *has* a screw loose

○ e ka· lubinë në bark *(Pej)* to eat like a horse

○ s'ka·^{3sg} lugë për [] "there *is* no spoon for []" [] *does* not get []'s rightful share

○ i ka· lyer buzët to have gotten involved in some dirty matter: {}'s hands are not clean

○ ka· llafe to be a big talker

○ (e) ka· llapë(n) të gjatë/madhe 1 to be loose-tongued, be a blabbermouth 2 to be a big talker

○ e ka· llapën të keqe to have a dirty mouth, use bad language

○ <>a ka·^{3sg} marrë era çatinë "the wind has taken ◇'s roof" ◇ *doesn't* have a roof over ◇'s head, ◇ *is* very poor

○ <>a ka·^{3sg} marrë era mjellin "the wind has taken ◇'s flour" 1 ◇ *is* confused/depressed by a shock 2 ◇ *is* stupid

○ i ka· marrë erë barutit "have gotten the smell of gunpowder" to have been in battle, be an old hand at war

○ <> ka· marrë erë në qafë "have smelled ◇ on the neck" 1 to know ◇ inside out 2 to have no respect for []

○ <>a ka· marrë erën to know ◇ well enough to be unintimidated

○ ka· marrë fitilin to have caught a cold; have tuberculosis; be seriously ill

○ <> ka· marrë flokët të birit "have taken ◇'s son's hair" [*Ethnog*] (have served as godparent at ◇'s son's first haircutting) to be ◇'s son's godparent

○ ka· marrë krye 1 to turn ornery 2 to act crazy

○ ka· marrë llasë/llastim to have gotten spoiled, get overly pampered?

○ <>i ka·^{3sg} marrë mendtë era "the wind has taken ◇'s mind" ◇ *has* gone crazy: ◇ *has* gone nuts, ◇ *has* flipped ◇'s wig

○ ka· marrë musht "have drunk must" to have become newly energized

○ [] ka· marrë në/për gazep to be disgusted by [], be unable to stand []

○ [] ka·^{3sg} marrë rrëkeja "the torrent has taken []" things are going rapidly downhill for [], [] has had a spate of bad luck

○ [] ka·^{3sg} marrë shëndeti për keq []'s health has taken a turn for the worse

○ s'e ka· marrë shpirtin me qira to be unwilling to risk one's health/life

○ e ka· marrë vdekjen në sy "have stared death in the eye" to have no fear of death, be fearless

○ ka· mbetur akull to be broke

○ ka· mbetur si qeni në qerre "wind up like a dog on a cart" to be weak and emaciated; be in a state of shock

○ <> ka·^{3sg} mbirë bari (në faqe/sy) "the grass *has* grown (on ◇'s face/eye)" ◇ *has* been dead a long time; it *is* too late for ◇ now

○ [] ka·^{3sg} mbuluar bari "the grass has covered [] over" [] *has been* dead for years

○ <>a ka·^{3sg} mbuluar varrin bari "the grass *has* covered ◇'s grave" ◇ *has* been dead for a long time

○ <>a ka· mbyllur derën "have closed the door on ◇" no longer allow ◇ in one's home

○ [] ka· me bereqet [] will last {} a long time

○ ka· me grusht "have by handfuls" to be rich

○ <>a ka· me hile to go behind ◇'s back in order to cheat ◇

○ ka·^{3sg} me kile there *is* plenty, there *are* tons of it

○ [] ka· me pekule 1 to treat [] with special favor 2 to consider [] a very close personal friend

○ nuk <>a ka· me sevda to lose one's passion for ◇

○ ka· me spol to have plenty (of money)

○ [] ka· me sy të mirë to look at [] with a kind eye

○ [] ka· me sy të shtrembër/keq/lig 1 to have a low regard for []; look at/on [] with disfavor 2 to have no interest in []'s welfare

○ [] ka· me shtrëngatë to have only a restricted amount of []

○ e ka· me tallje to be kidding

○ [] ka· me të shkrepur to do [] when one feels like it, do [] at one's whim

○ <>a ka· me të shtrembër to go behind ◇'s back in order to cheat ◇

○ e ka· me të tekur to act on whim

○ [] ka· me vete to have [] on one's side; have [] under one's command/control

○ [] ka· me zgrip to have very little/few []

○ ka· me {*participial verb stem*} *(Reg Gheg)* 1 (expresses future tense of {}): will {}, shall {} 2 (expresses obligation) have to {}

○ [] ka· me kimet to treasure []

○ ka· mendje të keqe/ligë 1 to always think negatively 2 to have bad/malicious intentions

○ e ka· mendjen në kokë to have brains in one's head, have a good head on one's shoulders

○ ka· mendjen to be careful, watch out

○ e ka· mendjen (me) okë to be very capable/wise: have a good head on one's shoulders

○ e ka· mendjen (në) majë (të) kësulës 1 to be silly/foolish, be superficial 2 to keep coming back to the same thing over and over

○ e ka· mendjen akull to have clear judgment

○ e ka· mendjen çarçaf to lack concentration, be unfocused; be undecided

○ e ka· mendjen femër to have a fertile mind

○ e ka· mendjen fije peri "have a mind like a piece of thread" to have a sharp mind, be sharp as a tack; be of sound mind

○ e ka· mendjen kobure 1 to be thick-headed, not understand much 2 to be obstinate, mulish

○ e ka· mendjen në tufë të festes "have one's mind on a tassel of a fez" to have no more brains than a turnip, {}'s brains would fit on the head of a pin

○ nuk e ka· mendjen në vend not have one's head on straight; not be in one's right mind

○ e ka· mendjen *prapa kokës//pas qafe/shpine* not have one's head on straight

○ e ka· mendjen të fjetur to have one's mind easy, not be worried

○ e ka· mendjen të hollë 1 to have a good brain 2 *(Iron)* to be finicky/fussy

○ e ka· mendjen të prishur "have one's mind broken" to be in a very unsettled state of mind

○ e ka· mendjen top to be of sound mind, be sharp as a tack

○ e ka· **mendjen trangull** "have the mind of a cucumber" to have the brain of a turnip, be a fool, be stupid

○ e ka· **mendjen veri/si veriu** "have a mind like the north wind" to be flighty

○ nuk i ka· **mendtë e** {*pronominal adj*} not be expressing {*one's*} own ideas

○ i ka· **mendtë majë thanës** to have no more brains than a turnip, {}'s brains would fit on the head of a pin

○ i ka· **mendtë në kokë** to have a brain in one's head, have some intelligence

○ i ka· **mendtë në tra/nga trarët/qofkat** (*Impol*) to have one's mind off in the clouds

○ i ka· **mendtë në tufë të festes** "have one's brains in the tassel of one's fez" to be foolish, not have a brain in one's head

○ i ka· **mendtë prapa kokës/pas qafe/shpine** not have one's head on straight

○ ia ka· **mendtë vetes** to be very cautious

○ e ka· **merakun për** []/**pas** <> to love []/<>, be devoted to []/<>

○ [] ka· **më vijë** "have [] in line" to have [] well in order/hand, have [] all arranged

○ [] ka· **më zgrip** to be undecided about []

○ e ka· **mëndjen brisk** to have a razor-sharp mind

○ [] ka· **mëri** to dislike []

○ ka· **mik** {} to have a friend with pull {*somewhere*}

○ e ka· **mirë me** [] to be in []'s special favor

○ nuk e ka· **mirë** it is not good for {} to do that; not do what one should, not behave properly

○ nuk i ka· **mish brinja** to be very thin (said of animals): have no meat on its bones

○ ka·[3rd] **miza në kokë** "have flies in the head" to seem to be wrestling with too many problems

○ e ka· **mizën nën kësulë/shapkë/feste** "have the fly under one's cap" to have a guilty conscience

○ ka· **mizën pas veshi** "have the fly behind the ear" to have a guilty conscience

○ e ka· **mjaltë e sheqer/gjalpë/qumësht me** [] to be on very good terms with []

○ nuk ka· **mjekër për Qabe** "not have the beard for Qabe" (*Impol*) not have the ability required

○ nuk ka· **mort** to be very durable

○ [] ka· **mort** {} can't stand/bear []

○ [] ka· **mortje (të dytë)** to really hate [], be unable to stand []

○ e ka· **moshën** to have reached the right age

○ i ka· **mprehur brirët** to have sharpened one's horns, be ready to fight

○ ka· **muhabet me** [] to be on friendly terms with []

○ ka· **ndër mend** to have in mind: be thinking, intend

○ [] ka· **ndër mend** to have [] in mind: be thinking of [], consider []

○ e ka· **ndërgjegjen të qetë** to have a clear conscience

○ [] ka· **në begeni** to treat [] with polite consideration/condescension

○ [] ka· **në besë** to have [] under one's protection

○ [] ka· **në bërryl** to hold [] in low esteem

○ [] ka· **në dorë** to have [someone] in one's hip pocket; have [] in the bag

○ [] ka· **në gojë *1** to keep talking nicely about [someone], praise [] continually, keep remembering [] **2** to talk often about [] **3** to have [it] on the tip of one's tongue

○ [] ka· **në grusht** "have [] in the fist" to have [] under one's complete control

○ [] ka· **në gjak 1** to have [] as a deeply embedded habit **2** to have [] as part of one's personality; have [] in one's blood

○ [] ka· **në hundë** (*Contempt*) not be able to bear/endure [], *cannot* stand []

○ [] ka· **në inventar** to be responsible for [an object]

○ [] ka· **në krah** [] *is* next to {}

○ e ka· **në majë të gjuhës 1** to have it on the tip of one's tongue **2** to be quick with the answer/retort **3** to answer back audaciously

○ [] ka· **në majë të hundës** (*Pej*) to be fed up with []; be about to blow up

○ ka· **në mend** to intend, have in mind, be thinking

○ [] ka· **në mend** to have [] in mind, be thinking of []

○ [] ka· **në ngarkim** to have [] in one's charge

○ [] ka· **në pekule 1** to treat [] with special favor **2** to consider [] a very close personal friend

○ [] ka· **në pëllëmbë të dorës** to know [] like the back of one's hand; have plenty of experience with [], know one's way around []

○ [] ka· **në pjatë** to have [] in the bag

○ s'[] ka· **në sy** not like []

○ [] ka· **në shenjë** to target [] for criticism; keep [] under constant attack

○ [] ka· **në tavë** to have [] safely in hand

○ [] ka· **në thembër** to have [] nearby; have [] ready to help

○ [] ka· **në thes** to have [someone] in one's pocket

○ e ka· **në thua** to have it an inbred characteristic, it *is* just part and parcel of {}

○ [] ka· **në vijë** "have [] in line" to have [] well in order/hand, have [] all arranged

○ [] ka· **në xhep** to have [someone] in one's hip pocket; have [] in the bag

○ [] ka· **në zgrip** to be undecided about []

○ [] ka· **nëpër duart** to be in the process of doing [], be working on []

○ [] ka· **nëpër këmbë 1** to (still) have [a small child] to be concerned about **2** to (still) have [unfinished work] to do

○ s'ka· **nga ia mba·**nn to have nowhere to turn

○ e ka· **nga zori** to be due to one's bashfulness

○ ka· **ngecur si gomari në akull** "stuck like the donkey in ice" to be extremely stubborn

○ <>a ka· **ngenë** to feel ready for <>; have the time for <>; have the wherewithal for <>

○ nuk ka· **ngenë** {*possessive adjective*} not have time to deal with {}'s problem, not have to worry about {}'s problem

○ e ka· **ngrënë barin/çairin/kullotën/livadhin/tagjinë** (*TeaseImpolite*) **1** to have lived out one's life; have reached the end of one's life **2** to have had it, have bought the farm

○ e ka· **ngrënë çorbën përpara** <> to have more experience than <>, have been around more than <>, know more than <>

○ <> ka·[3sg] **ngrënë gomari veshët** "the donkey *has* eaten <>'s ears" (*Iron*) (said of someone whose silence is interpreted a failure to understand what others are saying)

○ ka· **ngrënë lule thane** "must have eaten cornel flowers" **1** to be in good health **2** to have learned to be cautious from bitter experience

○ ka· **ngrënë me një lugë me** [] "have eaten with a spoon with []" to be a close friend of []; know [] very well

◦ **ka· ngrënë më shumë mjaltë se bukë** "have eaten more honey than bread" **1** to have become healthy and good-looking, look pleasingly plump **2** to have become pleasant in speech

◦ **ka·**$^{-pl}$ **ngrënë një** *furrë bukë/thes/barrë kripë/hambar mjell* **bashkë** "have eaten *an ovenful of bread//a sack/load of salt/hopperful of flour* together" to have known each other for a long time, be friends/colleagues of long-standing

◦ **ka· ngrënë plëndës pule** "have eaten chicken gizzard" *(Joke)* to be unusually gabby, be full of chatter

◦ **nuk <>a ka· ngrënë poganikun** "not have eaten <>'s birth celebration wafer" not know when <> was born, not know how old <> is; not know <> very well

◦ **<> ka·**^{3sg} **ngrënë pula/sorra mendtë** "the chicken *has* pecked/eaten/drunk <>'s brains" <> *is* completely stupid, <> *has* completely lost <>'s senses

◦ **ka· ngjeshur dy breza** *(Pej)* to claim to be mature enough to ignore parental authority: be too big for one's britches

◦ [] **ka· ngjitur për thembre** to have [] nearby; have [] ready to help

◦ **e ka· ngjyer gishtin** to have taken part in a robbery; have profited from a misdeed

◦ **ka·**^{3sg} **nisur t'<> dalë gjuha** "<>'s tongue has begun to come out" <> *has* begun to answer back audaciously

◦ **ka· nishan** to be a good shot, have a good eye

◦ **ka· nuhatje të hollë** to have a great deal of foresight

◦ **ka· nxehtë** to feel the heat

◦ **s'ka·**^{3sg} **njeri të gjall**ë there *is* no one to be seen, there *is* no one around

◦ **e ka· një ashkë nga** [] to get the characteristic from [a blood relative]: inherit it from []

◦ **ka· një burgji mangët** "have one screw missing" *(Impol)* to be missing a screw, have a screw loose

◦ **e ka· një damar marrëzie** to have a tendency towards foolhardiness, have a streak of foolhardiness

◦ **ka· një fytyrë** to be a completely honest person

◦ **ka· një gur në zemër** to be very disappointed/disheartened

◦ **ka· një letër të mirë në dorë** to be holding a strong hand, be in a strong position

◦ **ka· një mend okë në kokë** to be very capable/wise: have a good head on one's shoulders

◦ **ka· një mendje më tepër** to have a better brain than the others, be smarter than the others

◦ **ka· një mjegull në sy** to have blurred vision

◦ **ka· një vidhë mangët** "have one screw missing" *(Impol)* to be missing a screw, have a screw loose

◦ **ka· njërën dorë në baklava e tjetrën në re-vani/kabuni/mjaltë** *(Pej)* to be living high from having a hand in two pots, live well by double dipping

◦ **nuk ka· ogur me** [] things *don't* go well when one *is* with []

◦ **e ka· orën gjallë** *(Old)* to be always lucky, always have good luck

◦ **ka· orientim të mirë 1** to accommodate easily to new surroundings: adjust quickly **2** to have a good sense of direction

◦ **nuk ka· paha** to be beyond price: be priceless

◦ **ka· para me thes/thasë** "have money by the sackload" to have a barrel of money, be rolling in dough

◦ **i ka· paratë me bisht** to have money to burn

◦ **e ka· parë diellin para <>** "have seen the sun before <>" to have been born before <>; have more experience than <>

◦ **ka· parë botë/dynja me sy** "have seen the world with one's own eyes" to have traveled (abroad) extensively

◦ **ka· parë jetë** "have seen life" to have had a life of comfort

◦ **nuk <>a ka· parë derën** "not have seen <>'s door" never have visited <>, not have stepped foot in <>'s house

◦ **s'<>a ka· parë pragun** never have been in <>'s home

◦ **e ka· parë ujkun që** *i vogël//në vogëli/fos-hnjë* "have seen the wolf since childhood" to have grown up with menacing danger, be used to danger

◦ **e ka· peng** to regret it, be sorry

◦ **e ka· peng në zemër** to still bear the scars in one's heart

◦ **nuk ka· perde** to have no ear for music

◦ [] **ka· perëndi** to consider/treat [] as if [] were a god

◦ **e ka· për fis 1** to have it as a family trait, inherit the habit **2** to behave in a typical (for oneself) way

◦ **s'e ka· për gajle 1** to be unashamed/thick-skinned about it **2** [] considers it very easy

◦ **s'e ka· për gjë (të __)** {} wouldn't be afraid/ashamed: think nothing of (doing __)

◦ **nuk [] ka· për gjë** to be able to do [] with no trouble at all; have no qualms about doing []; [] *is* nothing to <>

◦ [] **ka· për hiçmosgjë** to think nothing of []

◦ **e ka· për keq** to think it causes bad luck, think it unlucky

◦ [] **ka· për mall** [] *is* dear to one's heart

◦ **e ka· për mburrje** to consider it something to be proud of

◦ **e ka· për mirë** to mean well

◦ [] **ka· për nder** to consider [] an honor

◦ **s'<>a ka· për pesë** to not be afraid of <> for five seconds: <> *doesn't scare* {} for a minute

◦ [e] **ka· për piri** to have the habit of []

◦ **s'[] ka· për sy** not like []

◦ **e ka· për të mirën të <>** to do it for <>'s own good

◦ **ka· për të** {*participle*} (expresses obligation with intention) have to, ought to {}, should {}

◦ **e ka· për thua** to have it an inbred characteristic, it *is* just part and parcel of {}

◦ [] **ka· për xhins** to have [] in one's blood/genes, get [] from one's family

◦ **nuk e ka· përgjakur dyfekun** not have made one's first kill (with a gun); never have fired one's gun; {} *has* never been tested in battle

◦ **e ka· përgjigjen në majë të gjuhës** to be quick with one's answer; retort immediately; talk back

◦ **e ka· përgjigjen te buza** to have the answer on the tip of one's tongue

◦ **e ka· pikë në zemër** to still bear the scars in one's heart

◦ **<> ka· pirë djersën** to exploit <> unmercifully: make <> sweat blood

◦ **e ka· pirë këtë ujë** "have drunk this water" *(Impol)* to have been down that path before, not be so gullible as before

◦ **ka· pirë** "have drunk" to be drunk

◦ **ka· pirë kupën e hidhur** *(Book)* to have suffered greatly in life

○ <> **ka·**^{3sg} **pirë pula mendtë** "the chicken *has* pecked/eaten/drunk <>'s brains" <> *is* completely stupid, <> *has* completely lost <>'s senses

○ <> **ka·**^{3sg} **pirë sorra mendtë** "the crow *has* pecked/eaten/drunk <>'s brains" <> *is* completely stupid, <> *has* completely lost <>'s senses

○ **ka·** **pirë shumë ujëra** "*have drunk* many kinds of water" to have seen much in one's life; have a lot of experience

○ **ka·**^{pl} **pirë ujë në një krua·**n**n** "*have drunk water from the same source*" to have known one another for a long time

○ **ka·** **pirë ujë në shumë burime/kroje** "*have drunk* water in many springs" to have suffered a lot in life, have gone through a lot in one's life

○ <> **ka·**^{3sg} **pjellë lopa** "<>'s cow *has* given birth" <> *is* very comfortably fixed

○ **i ka·** **plaçkat nëpër këmbë** to have one's things spread all over helter-skelter

○ **e ka·** **plafin të madh** to have many influential friends

○ **e ka·** **plagë në zemër** to still bear the scars in one's heart

○ <> **ka·**^{3sg} **plasur cipa/peta e ballit** <> *has lost* all sense of shame/honor

○ <> **ka·**^{3sg} **plasur damari i ballit** <> *has* become utterly shameless, <> *has* lost all sense of shame

○ <> **ka·**^{3sg} **plasur delli i marres** "<>'s blood vessel supplying <>'s shame *has* burst" <> *has* become totally shameless

○ <> **ka·**^{3sg} **plasur turpi** *(Pej)* <> *has lost* all sense of shame

○ [] **ka·** **pranë** to be very close to []; be a big supporter of []

○ [] **ka·** **prej vetiu** to have [] as a natural characteristic: [] is in {}'s nature, [] *is* inherent in {}

○ **s'** <> **ka·** **prerë kërthizën** not owe <> any great favor

○ <> **ka·** **prerë kokën** "cut off one's head" to look exactly like <>: be the spitting image of <>

○ [] **ka·** **prerë një sharrë** "one saw cut []" [] are cut from the same cloth

○ [] **ka·** **presh në kopsht** *(Iron)* to have no particularly close relationship with []

○ **nuk** <> **ka·**^{3sg} **prirë** things *have* not gone well for <>

○ [] **ka·** **prush në gji** "have [] as a hot ember at one's breast" *(Iron)* to hate [] with a passion, dislike [] intensely

○ **s'ka·** **pulë në tra** "not have a chicken on the roof beam" to be poor as a churchmouse

○ **ka·** **punë me** [] to have business to do with []

○ **ka·** **punë** to have work to do: be busy; have something to attend to

○ **e ka·** **punën në dorë** to have the matter resting in one's hands, the matter *is* in {}'s hands

○ **e ka·** **punën me teka** to work only when one is in the mood, work only when one feels like it

○ **e ka·** **punën në çark** to have everything in order, have the matter well in hand

○ **e ka·** **punën si në lak** to have the matter practically finished

○ **i ka·** **punët *në vijë*/*për fije*** to have matters in good order, be in good shape, be getting along quite well

○ **i ka·** **punët në hulli** to have one's affairs in good shape

○ **i ka·** **punët pilë** "have one's things in an unstable heap" {}'s affairs *are* in an uncertain state

○ **i ka·** **punët pus** "{}'s affairs *are* a well" to be in deep trouble

○ **s'ka·** **qafë për atë këmborë** "<> *doesn't* have the right neck for that bell" <> is incompetent for that job

○ <> **ka·**^{3sg} **qafën të shkurtër** "<> has a short neck" **1** <> *can't keep* a secret long **2** <> *talks* off the top of <>'s head, <> *talks* without thinking

○ **e ka·** **qafën me një dell** to be very feeble; be emaciated; hanging on by a thread, on the point of dying

○ **nuk ka·** **qederin** <*e vet*> not care about <> **nuk kam qede**·**rin e tij** I don't lose any sleep about him **nuk kishte qede**·**rin tim** he didn't give a damn about me

○ **ka·** **qejf** __ to feel like __, {} would like __

○ **e ka·** **qemerin kordhë** to be a doughty warrior, be dauntless, be a seasoned veteran; be brave and daring

○ **ka·** **qenë buka e fukarasë** to have always helped the poor

○ **e ka·** **qerre me** [] to be on friendly terms with []

○ **e ka·** **qesen të nxehtë/ngrohtë** to have plenty of money

○ **ka·** **qimen e ujkut** "have the skin/hair of a wolf" to be a constant victim of bad luck: be a bad-luck Charley

○ **i ka·** **qiqrat të ftohta me** [] to be on bad terms with []

○ **i ka·** **qiqrat të mbara** "have one's chickpeas doing well" to be prospering, be doing well; have one's ducks in a row

○ **s'ka·**^{3sg} **qoshe** to be beyond repair

○ **ka·**^{3sg} **raste** there *are* circumstances/times

○ [] **ka·** **rëndë** [] is a burden on one; [] is burdensome for one

○ **s'ka·**^{3sg} **rëndësi** not be important; not matter

○ <> **ka·**^{3sg} **rënë bora (në krye)** "snow *has* fallen on <>('s head)" <> has become gray-haired

○ **s'** <> **ka·** **rënë brisk fytyrës** "a razor has. not touched <>'s face" <> *is* still a child; <> *is* still wet behind the ears

○ <> **ka·**^{3sg} **rënë flaka** <> *is* all gone, <> *is* nowhere to be found: <> *has* gone up in smoke

○ <> **ka·**^{3sg} **rënë flama** <> *is* all gone, <> *is* nowhere to be found: <> *has* gone up in smoke

○ <> **ka·**^{3pl} **rënë leshtë/qimet e kokës** "<>'s hair has fallen out" <> has spent a good part of <>'s life (in a place)

○ <> **ka·**^{3pl} **rënë leshtë/qimet e kokës me** [] "<>'s hair has fallen out with []" <> has spent a good part of <>'s life and is very experienced with []

○ **ka·** **rënë në** [] "{} *has* fallen into []" {} has come into an abundance of [], {} is swimming in []

○ **ka·** **rënë nga dega** to have lost authority/position

○ **ka·** **rënë nga dynjallëku** to have become impoverished

○ **ka·** **rënë nga hëna** *(Iron Pej)* to think one is something special

○ **ka·** **rënë nga shtatë degët** to have been through some tough times, have a lot of experience in life

○ **ka·** **rënë për tokë** "{} fell to the ground" to be feeling very low, be terribly depressed

○ <> **ka·**^{3sg} **rënë pjergulla në fik** luck *has* come <>'s way

○ **s'<> ka·**^{3sg} **rënë zgjedha në vesh** "the yoke *has* not fallen on <>'s ears" <> *hasn't* seen enough of life's hardships

○ **i ka·**^{pl} **rregulluar telat bashkë** to have found some common ground, have established common ties, have buried the hatchet

○ **ka· rreze** to radiate beauty, be radiantly beautiful

○ **i ka· rrënjët mbi ujë** "have roots on water" to have a foundation built on sand, have no solid basis

○ **i ka· rrënjët të shkulura** "have one's roots pulled out" to be left with no family

○ **ka·**^{3sg} **rrjedhur shumë ujë** "*have drunk* many kinds of water" a lot of time *has* passed

○ **i ka· rrobat në finjë** "have clothes soaking in lye" to be very busy, have no time to turn around

○ **sikur ka· rrokur qiellin me dorë** "as if one has grasped the sky by the hand" to act as if one has performed a miracle

○ **i ka· sahanët pa kapak** to be straightforward and frank

○ **nuk ka· sarkë** not have a good physique

○ **<>a ka· sevdanë** to be jealous/envious of <>

○ **[] ka· si bukë e djathë** to find [] very easy, be able to do [] without difficulty: find [] a snap

○ **[] ka· si dy sytë** "consider [] like one's two eyes" to hold [] very precious: treasure []

○ **[] ka· si gjuhën në gojë** to find [] indispensable, have an absolute need for []

○ **e ka· sininë gjithnjë plot** "always have the serving tray full" to be ready for guests at any time: be very hospitable

○ **[] ka·**^{3sg} **sjellë laraska** *(Iron)* (said of an anonymous source) a little birdie must have brought/said []

○ **e ka· sofrën gjithnjë plot** "always have the serving tray full" to be ready for guests at any time: be very hospitable

○ **ka· sprijën në bark** *(Iron)* to have an endless appetite; stay thin even though one eats a lot: {} must have swallowed a tapeworm

○ **e ka· sqepin të gjatë** *(Pej)* to be garrulous

○ **ka· stof** *(Colloq)* to have a lot of brain matter: be brainy

○ **e ka· stomakun të rëndë** to have eaten too much, feel bloated, feel too full; have eaten something that disagrees with one, have eaten something that one cannot digest

○ **[] ka· sy në ballë** "consider [] like the eye in one's face" to hold [] very precious: treasure []

○ **ka· sy të keq/lig** *(Old)* to have the power to cast spells: have the evil eye

○ **e ka· syrin atje/aty** that's what {} has in mind, that's what {} wants

○ **e ka· syrin bakër** to have a sharp/keen eye

○ **e ka· syrin boçe** not care about the cost

○ **e ka· syrin për** [] to be thinking of []; be thinking of going to [place noun]; have the look of someone ready to {participle}

○ **e ka· syrin pishë/kokërr 1** to have sharp eyes; have eyes in the back of one's head, see everything that is going on **2** to be fearless/courageous; have a confident look

○ **e ka· syrin plot** to have seen everything: {} *cannot* be impressed

○ **e ka· syrin plumb/plumbç** "have a lead eye" **1** to be very lively; have flashing eyes **2** to be very perceptive; be very sharp (of a person)

○ **e ka· syrin pushkë/shigjetë** "have an eye like a gun/arrow" to have sharp eyesight

○ **e ka· syrin te** {} **1** to have one's eye on {} **2** to hang one's hopes on {}

○ **e ka· syrin të hapur 1** to have a clear conscience **2** to be erudite/knowledgeable

○ **e ka· syrin të madh për** [] **1** to have [something grand] in mind, want [something grand] **2** to be overly ambitious in respect to []

○ **e ka· syrin xixë 1** to have a sharp eye, have good eyesight **2** to have eyes that glisten with courage, have unblinking courage, be undaunted

○ **i ka· sytë dollap** to be unable to fall asleep

○ **i ka· sytë me jakëz** *(Impol)* to be blind to what is going on, be easily duped/confused

○ **i ka· sytë me majë** to have sharp eyes

○ **i ka· sytë në ballë 1** to be perfectly able to see: have eyes in one's head **2** to take care, keep one's eyes open

○ **nuk i ka· sytë në vend** "not have one's eyes in the right place" not keep one's mind on one's work

○ **ka· sytë si të urithit** to have the eyes of a mole: barely be able to see, have very poor eyesight

○ **i ka· sytë te** {} to hang one's hopes on {}

○ **[] ka· shemër (e) jo zemër** [] *is* {}'s enemy and not {}'s friend

○ **ka· shenjë** to have good aim, be a good shot

○ **ka· shiritin në bark** *(Iron)* to have an endless appetite; stay thin even though one eats a lot: {} must have swallowed a tapeworm

○ **ia ka· shitur shpirtin shejtanit** "sell one's soul to the devil" **1** *(Pej)* to be the epitome of evil **2** to live a joyless life with nothing but suffering

○ **<> ka·**^{3sg} **shkarë syri** "<>'s eye *has* slipped" <>'s mind has become fixed on it, <> has become fixated, have made up one's mind

○ **<> ka· shkelur hijen** to have given <> offense: have stepped on <>'s toes

○ **[] ka·**^{3sg} **shkelur koha** time *has* left [] behind: [] *is* behind the times, [] *is* out of step and old-fashioned; [] has failed to keep up with the others

○ **nuk <>a ka· shkelur njeri hijen prapa** "no one has stepped on <>'s shadow from behind" <> is so fast that no one can catch <>

○ **s'<>a ka· shkelur pragun** never have been in <>'s home

○ **ka·**^{3sg} **shkuar dielli një hosten** "the sun has already gone the length of an ox-goad" it *is getting* late (in the morning)

○ **ka· shkuar në fije** to become all skin and bones; become exhausted

○ **ka· shkuar të bëjë ponica** "have gone to make flower pots" *(Impol)* to be pushing daisies, be dead

○ **<> ka· shkuar thika në kockë/asht/palcë** "the knife *has* gone into <>'s bone" <> *gets* to the point of desperation, <> *can't* take it any more

○ **<>i ka·**^{3sg} **shkundur era trutë** "the wind has shaken <>'s brains" <> *has* gone crazy: <> *has* gone dotty, <> *has* flipped <>'s wig

○ **i ka· shokët të rrallë** to be one in a million

○ **i ka· shpatullat të ngrohta** "*has* warm shoulders" **1** to have powerful protectors **2** to have influential friends

○ **nuk ka· shpirt** to be cruel/merciless/heartless: be hardhearted/unfeeling: have no heart

○ **e ka· shpirtin helm/zeher** to be deeply grieved

○ **e ka· shpirtin në fyt** "have one's soul in one's throat" to be very angry

○ e ka· shpirtin të thellë to hold on to life (tenaciously), cling tenaciously to life, refuse to die

○ ka· shprehje (Book) to have a gift for speaking well: be eloquent

○ ka· shpretkën (Colloq) to have an enlarged spleen

○ <> ka· shterur mendja "<>'s mind *has dried* up" (Disparaging) <> has become senile: *has* gone dotty

○ ka· shtënë dashuri për [] to have come to love []

○ e ka· shtëpinë në prevë to live right beside the road

○ nuk [] ka·³ˢᵍ shtrënguar këpuca "the shoe never *pinches* []" [] [] *has* never felt what it is to be very poor; *has* never had to suffer hard times

○ ia ka· shtrënguar vegjës/avlëmendit to get down to proper work

○ ka· shumë çoqe mbi kokë to have big problems, have a lot of worries

○ [] ka· shushull në sy to bear a grudge against [], hate [] terribly

○ [] ka· tabako (Impol) to find [] easy, be able to do [] without difficulty: find [] a snap, [] is a piece of cake for {}

○ s'<>a ka· takatin not have the strength/ability/time (necessary) for <>

○ ka· taraf të madh to have a lot of helpful friends and relatives

○ ka· tenjën në bark (Iron) to have an endless appetite; stay thin even though one eats a lot: {} must have swallowed a tapeworm

○ s'ka·³ˢᵍ terezi there *is* not much chance

○ e ka· të ardhmen përpara to have a long future ahead of one

○ e ka· të shpejtë to have it coming up very soon

○ ka· të drejtë to be in the right

○ ka· të nxehtë to have a fever; feel hot/feverish

○ ka· të gjitha të mirat to have everything one needs, have all one's needs satisfied

○ nuk e ka· të gjatë not last much longer, be almost gone; not have long to live

○ ka· të njohur me [] to know [] (as one who can be called on for help/favors)

○ s'ka·³ˢᵍ të paguar to be very valuable: be priceless

○ i ka· të pakta bukët "have few meals ahead" not have long to live

○ i ka· të pakta fjalët to be a person of few words

○ ka· të paudhin në bark "have the devil in one's belly" to be wicked, to have evil intentions; be deceitful and treacherous

○ s'ka·³ʳᵈ të sosur to be inexhaustible/boundless/endless

○ s'ka·³ʳᵈ të sharë there *is* nothing there to find fault with, {} *is* really special

○ e ka· të shkruar në ballë to have it written all over one's face

○ i ka· të shpejta to be soon to die

○ e ka· të vështirë to find it difficult

○ [] ka· të qartë to have [] clear in one's mind

○ Nuk [] ka·³ˢᵍ tokal "The earth does not have [] !" There's no one on earth who can match []! [] *is* the best there is!

○ nuk ka· tragë të __ not intend to __; not have the least intention of __

○ nuk e ka· trastën në kurriz/shpinë "not have the burden on one's back" not be the one who suffering/hurting, not be the one in need

○ s'ia ka· treguar njeriu të gjallë to have told absolutely no one about it

○ ka· trup (of a person) to have a nice body; (of wine) to have body

○ e ka· trupin si selvi "have a body like a cypress" to be tall, well built, and good looking

○ i ka· trutë në bark to be irrational, be mindless

○ i ka· trutë në fund të këmbëve "have one's brains at the bottom of one's legs" to be a brainless fool, be stupid

○ ka· tujet to be full of joy, be in high spirits

○ s'<> ka· tundur djepin "{} has not rocked <>'s cradle" to have no idea how old <> is

○ ka· turinj 1 to have a premonition 2 to be snooty

○ nuk ka· turinj për [] (Impol) not be good enough to deserve []

○ i ka· turinjtë si të maces "have a snout like a cat" (Impol) to have a face like a rat

○ s'ia ka· thënë njeriu të gjallë to have told absolutely no one about it

○ [] ka· thikë në zemër to feel [] like a knife in one's heart, have [] in one's heart as a constant painful memory

○ e ka· thikën në fyt/grykë "have a noose around one's neck" to be in serious trouble

○ [] ka· thithur bashkë me qumështin e nënës "*have sucked* [] together with the milk of one's mother" to have learned [] at one's mother's bosom, have grown up with [] since early age

○ i ka· thonjtë pa hequr to be a thief

○ i ka· thonjtë të prerë 1 (Impol) to be harmless 2 to no longer be a thief

○ e ka· thuan të keq (Pej) to be given to stealing, be a thief

○ e ka· thuan të mirë to be no thief

○ nuk <>a ka· thyer poganikun not manage to have gotten to know <> in any depth

○ <> ka·³ˢᵍ ujdisur gjaku <>'s differences *have* been ironed out

○ ka· ujin në arë to have something urgent to do; be extremely busy

○ i ka· ulur flamurët "lower the flags" to have come down off <>'s high horse

○ Ka· ulur pak hundën, por ka· ngritur sqepin. "{} *has* lowered {}'s nose a little, but *has* raised {}'s beak." (Iron) {} *continues* preening despite {}'s previous come-down.

○ [] ka· unazë në gisht to keep [] always in mind

○ ka· urdhër to be under orders

○ ka· uri to be hungry

○ e ka· vajin në buzë "have a lament on the lip" to make constant complaints, be always ready to complain

○ ka· vajtur të bëjë ponica "have gone to make flower pots" (Impol) to be pushing daisies, be dead

○ <> ka· vajtur thika në kockë/asht/palcë "the knife *has* gone into <>'s bone" <> *gets* to the point of desperation, <> *can't* take it any more

○ <>a ka· vaktin (Colloq) to feel ready for <>; have the time for <>; have the wherewithal for <>

○ [] ka· vath në vesh "have [] as an earring in one's ear" to try never to forget []; make a reminder of [] for future revenge

○ [] ka· vdekje to detest []

○ <> ka·³ˢᵍ vdekur mendja "<>'s mind *has* died" <> *has* lost <>'s mind, <> *has* become senile

○ <> ka·^{3sg} **vdekur ora** "<>'s fairy *has* died" **1** *is* on <>'s last legs, <> *is* not long for this world **2** <> *is* all set, <> *cannot* be changed any longer

○ ka·^{3sg} **vend për** [] there's room for []

○ ka·^{3sg} **veshë dheu** "the ground has ears" the walls have ears

○ ka· **veshë e rëndë** to have poor hearing

○ i ka· **veshët pipëz** to have very good hearing; be all ears

○ i ka· **veshët të hollë** to have a fine sense of hearing: have good ears

○ ka· **veshur lëkurën e qengjit** "have donned the fleece of a lamb" to be a wolf in sheep's clothing

○ <> ka· **veshur sytë** "have veiled <>'s eyes" to have clouded <>'s vision

○ [] ka· **vëlla e shkuar vëllait** "consider [] a brother and more than a brother" to be closer to [a friend] than to a brother

○ <> ka·^{3pl} **vënë cergë sytë** "<>'s eyes have grown cobwebs" <> *is* blind to the truth; <> *is* unaware of what is going on

○ ka· **vënë gojë 1** to have started using foul language **2** to have started gossiping

○ s'ka· **vënë kurorë me** [] not have a particularly close relationship with []

○ <> ka·^{3pl} **vënë sytë perde 1** "<>'s eyes *have put* on a filmy membrane, a filmy membrane has formed over the eyes **2** *(Fig)* <> *has become* blind to a danger

○ <> ka·^{3pl} **vënë sytë tis** "<>'s eyes have put on a veil" <> *has* put blinders on, <> *won't* listen to reason

○ ka· **vlagë** to be still hanging on, be able to hold out with what one has

○ s'[] ka·^{3sg} **vrarë samari/këpuca** "the saddle/shoe has not hurt []" [] has never known real suffering

○ [] ka· **xhan** *(Child)* to just love []

○ e ka· **xhepin plot** to have plenty of money; have no unsatisfied needs

○ e ka· **xhepin të ngrohtë** "<>'s pocket *is* warm" to have a lot of money

○ e ka· **xhepin të shpuar** "have a leaky pocket/wallet" to have no money because one spends all that one has; have wasted all one's money

○ nuk e ka· **zbrazur asnjëherë** "not once have fired (one's gun)" never have been in a gunfight

○ ka· **zemër luani** to have the heart of a lion: be very brave

○ ka· **zemër të fortë** "have a strong heart" to be thick-skinned

○ ka· **zemër me kockë** to have a heart of steel

○ ka· **zemër murgeshe** to open one's heart to all without distinction: have the heart of a saint

○ e ka· **zemrën hambar** to be very tolerant/patient/generous

○ e ka· **zemrën hazinenë** to be bighearted/generous

○ e ka· **zemrën pasqyrë** to be completely honest

○ e ka· **zemrën plagë** to have a deep hurt, be in terrible grief

○ e ka· **zemrën pleh** to feel depressed, feèl very sad

○ e ka· **zemrën prej lime 1** to be very patient; be able to stand great suffering **2** to be hard-hearted/pitiless

○ e ka· **zemrën të ftohtë** to have little hope, have few expectations, be pessimistic

○ e ka· **zemrën të ngrohtë** "<>'s heart *is* warm" to feel secure/relieved about the future

○ [] ka· **zënë (atje) ku s'rrëfe·***het*^{3sg} "have grabbed [] (there) where it doesn't show" **1** to get [] by the short hairs, grab [] where the sun don't shine **2** to put [] into a difficult situation: get [] into a tight spot

○ ka·^{3sg} **zënë dëbora roga-roga** the snow *has* settled in uneven patches

○ s'<> ka·^{3sg} **zënë goja lesh** "<>'s mouth *does* not grow wool" <> would like some (food) also, do you think <> *doesn't* eat?

○ <>a ka·^{3sg} **zënë këmbët fërtoma** "the rope has grabbed <>'s legs" <> *has* a problem that creates an impossible obstacle

○ [] ka·^{3sg} **zënë magjja** "the washtub has gotten []" all the family problems *have* fallen to [], all the family woes *have* fallen on <>

○ ka·^{3sg} **zënë merimangë** "{} *is* full of spiders" {} is full of cobwebs: {} has been unused/neglected for a long time

○ sikur ka· **zënë qiellin me dorë** "as if one has grasped the sky by the hand" to act as if one has performed a miracle

○ <> ka·^{3pl} **zënë sytë lesh** "<>'s eyes *have taken* on wool" <> *is* blind to what's wrong, <> *is* easily duped/confused

○ <> ka·^{3pl} **zënë sytë perde 1** <>'s eyes *have taken* on a filmy membrane, a filmy membrane has formed over the eyes **2** *(Fig)* <> *has become* blind to a danger

○ <> ka·^{3sg} **zënë shosha/hambari merimanga** "the spiders have taken over <>'s sieve/granary" <> *is* very poor: <>'s cupboard is bare

○ nuk <>a ka· **zënë trari kurrizin** "the wooden beam *has* not gotten on <>'s back" <> *is* not ready for responsibility because <> *has* not known what it is to suffer

○ e ka· **zërin pushkë** to have a strong and resonant voice

○ [] ka· **zët** to detest []

○ e ka· **zgjatur gjuhën/gojën** "have lengthened one's tongue/mouth" *(Pej)* to have become a loudmouth; have become a gossip

○ ka· **zhurin e detit** to have an abundance, have plenty

ka *3rd sg pres* <ka·

○ s'ka **as gëk as mëk** there's no choice, just do it; don't give me any lip

○ **S'ka berra e shet lesh.** "He doesn't have sheep and he sells wool." Something fishy is going on.

○ <> ka **bërë kokën** she has given <> birth

○ **S'ka ç'i bën gomarit (e) i bie samarit.** "There's nothing to do about the donkey so one hits the packsaddle." *(Prov)* When you can't get at the real cause of your anger, you take it out on something/somebody else.

○ **S'ka ç'i bën shkëndija eshkës së njomë/lagur.** "There's nothing a spark can do with wet punk." *(Prov)* You can't make a silk purse out of a sow's ear.

○ s'ka **çare** there's no way out: certainly, of necessity, necessarily, inevitably, like it or not

○ s'ka **çelës që** <> **bie** it's like trying to pull teeth to get money from him: <> is stingy

○ **S'ka dele me pesë këmbë.** "There is no such thing as a sheep with five legs." *(Prov)* No one is perfect. Nothing is perfect.

○ **S'ka fushë pa breshkë.** "There is no field without a tortoise." *(Prov)* Nothing's perfect.

○ **s'ka gajle** never mind, it doesn't matter

○ **Ka gjetur eshi eshin** They are alike as two peas in a pod

○ **Ka gjetur shkopi doçen** *(Pej)* The devil has found his mate.

○ **s'ka gjëkafshë 1** it doesn't matter, never mind **2** (in response to an expression of gratitude) you're welcome, not at all

○ [] **ka lëshuar kripa** "the salt has gone out of []" [] says tasteless things

○ [] **ka lëshuar ora** "the fairy has abandoned []" [] has not been blessed by luck

○ **ka lëshuar toka merimangë** "the soil is full of spiders" the land is past due for planting; the time is right for the land to be planted

○ **S'ka mbetur laraskë pa bisht** "There's not a magpie left without a tail." Everyone has to settle down sometime.

○ **ka me duzinë** *(Impol)* there are too many, they aren't worth much

○ **ësh-të ka me një bri** to be a broken-spirited person, be like a beaten dog

○ **s'ka më qofte te daja** "there are no more meatballs at one's uncle's house" the time is past when things came on a silver platter, you have to work for your supper now

○ **Ka ngordhur ajo pulë, që bënte ato vezë.** "The chicken that was making those eggs has died." Those times are long gone. That was a long time ago.

○ **S'ka oriz pa gur.** Nothing's perfect.

○ **ka pak *= nga pak**

○ **S'ka perde me mua!** "There is no veil with me!" Don't try to hide things from me! Tell me frankly!

○ **s'ka përse** (in response to thanks) don't mention it! you're welcome!

○ **ka plak ahuri** hey! this place already has one boss, you know!

○ **i ka prerë një gërshërë** they are very much alike

○ **ka sa të hanë qentë/lopët** "enough for (even) the dogs/cows to eat" *(Crude)* more than enough, plenty

○ **s'ka si bëhet** it can't be done, there's no way

○ **ka të gjarë** it's likely, it's possible, it could be

○ **Ka thelb buka.** *(Prov)* (said of someone who shows a lack of gratitude for hospitality received) Don't bite the hand that feeds you.

○ **e ka zemrën prush/zjarr** "have a heart of fire" to be energetic and daring

○ **ka zënë toka merimangë** "the soil is full of spiders" the land is past due for planting; the time is right for the land to be planted

○ **ka zot ahuri** hey! this place already has one boss, you know!

ka
I § nm ox; steer
II § 3rd sg pres <**ka· 1** has **2** there is
○ **kau i hullisë** (stronger) member (of a team of oxen) that walks in the furrow
○ **kau i kularit** yoke ox
ka (Reg Gheg) **= nga**

kaba
I § adj (Colloq) **1** bulky, unwieldy **2** (of a voice) bass **3** lacking in the expected content: empty, sparse

4 made in poor taste and without great care **5** *(Fig)* stupid and speaking nonsense
II § nf [Mus] **1** droning bass voice accompanying a singing duet in folk music **2** *[Mus]* folk music played on clarinet/violin
III § adv carelessly, superficially

***kabardís·et = kapardís·et**

kabardhë *nf* goat with whitish hair

kabare *nf* cabaret

kabash *nm (Reg)* water jug, can

kabashëm *adj (i) (Colloq)* bulky

kabël *nm* **= kabllo**

kabëz *nf* flat part of the metal plate at the end of a plowman's goad that is used to scrape earth from the plowshare

kabinet *nm* **1** small room used as a study, office, or laboratory: chamber **2** (government) cabinet

kabinë *nf* small enclosed room: (telephone) booth; cabin; cab of a piece of machinery; dressing room

kabisht *nm [Entom]* earwig **= gërshërëz**

kablesh *nm* **1 = shark 2** seed cone of a conifer

kablosh *nm* **1** wool left on sheep's heads after shearing **2 = balluke**

kabllo *nf* cable

kabllogram *nm* cablegram

kabllombështjellëse *nf [Tech]* cable drum, cable reel

kaboqe *nf* hilltop; low hill

kabot *nm [Text]* tightly woven twilled fabric: twill

kabotazh *nm [Naut]* coastal sea commerce: coasting trade **2** fleet of ships engaged in coastal sea commerce
○ **kabotazh i madh** *[Naut]* international coastal sea commerce
○ **kabotazh i vogël** *[Naut]* coastal sea commerce within national boundaries

kabull *nm (Colloq)*

***kabune** *nf* tuft (on a plant)

kabuni *nf* rice dessert: caramelized rice pudding with raisins/almonds or slivers of mutton

kacabu(n) *nm [Entom]* **= furrtare**

kacabun|i *obl* <**kacabu(n)**

kacabu·nj *np* <**kacabu(n)**

○ <> **kërce·n³ᵖˡ kacabunjtë** <> *seethes* with anger

kacadre(r) *nm (np ~ nj) [Entom]* stag beetle *(Lucanus cervus)*

kacadre|nj *np* <**kacadre(r)**

kacadrer|i *obl* <**kacadre(r)**

kacafik *nm* **1** stack of hay or straw having three or four support poles **2** (straw) hut used by a guard of a field or vineyard **3** hut, hovel

***kacafit· = kacafyt·**

kacafyt· *vt* **1** to grab [] by the throat **2** *(Fig)* (of an emotion) to seize

kacafyt·et *vpr* **1** to wrestle, fight hand-to-hand, scuffle **2** *(Fig)* to come to grips with; be at each other's throats

kacafytas *adv* grappling

kacafytje *nf ger* <**kacafyt·et**

kacagjel
I § nm **1** *[Entom]* carpenter ant, sugar ant *(Camponotus)* **2** *(FigImpolite)* cocky show-off, empty braggart

II § *adv* = **kacagjelthi**

*****kacagjelë** *nf* repercussion

kacagjelo·het *vpr* to show off pretentiously: strut, swagger

kacagjelthi *adv (Impol)* pretentiously showing off, in a swaggering manner

*****kacalec** *nm (Reg Gheg)* = **karkalec**

kacalytë *nf [Ornit]* crested lark *(Galerida cristata)*

*****kacambit·et** = **kacafyt·et**

*****kacambitj·et** = **kacafytje**

kacambyt·et *vpr* = **kacafyt·et**

*****kacamic** *nm* roebuck

*****kacamill** *nm* **1** = **kaçamill** **2** = **kërmill**

*****kacamillçë** *nf (Reg Gheg)* oyster

*****kacamit** *nm* stag

*****kacamitë** *nf* doe, hind

kacan *adj (Pej Insult)* stingy, miserly

*****kacandre** = **kacadre**

*****kacanuk·** *vt* = **kaçanduk·**

kacarra(n) *nm (np ~nj)* long stick ending in an angled hook

kacarran *nm* = **kacarra**

kacarrik *nm* = **furkaçe**

kacarro·het *vpr* **1** to climb by hugging on with hands and feet **2** *(Fig)* to show off

kacarro·n *vt* to hug

kacarrum *nm* corncob

kacaturrë *nf (Old)* **1** long, sharp, curved and double-edged dagger carried in a scabbard at the belt **2** double-edged bayonet

kacavar·et *vpr* **1** to cling and climb: clamber up **2** to twine around in an upward direction **3** *(Fig)* to persevere, stick to

kacavarës *adj* twining upward

kacavarje *nf ger* < **kacavar·et**

*****kacavidhe** *nf* = **kaçavidë**

kacavirr·et *vpr* = **kacavar·et**

kacavjerrë *part* < **kacavirre·t**

kacavjerrës *adj* = **kacavarës**

kacavjerrie *nf* = **kacavarje**

kacavor *stem for pdef* < **kacavirre·t**

*****kace·n** = **kërce·n**

kacek *nm* **1** bag made of sheepskin/goatskin **2** blacksmith's bellows **3** *(Colloq)* bagpipe **4** *[Med]* utricle

kacer *adj* = **kacerr**

kacerr *adj, n* **1** (man) with a turned up handle-bar mustache; (goat/ram) with horns pointing straight up **2** very naughty/mischievous (child)

*****kacetan** *adj* frisky, bouncy

kacë *nf* cask

kaci *nf* **1** small scoop used to shovel cinders and ashes **2** *(Fig Pej)* servile person: toady

kacibardh·et *nf[Bot]* dog rose *(Rosa canina)*

kacidhe *nf* **1** *(Old)* (former coin of low value) half-piaster coin, twenty-para coin **2** *(Impol)* very short person: shorty

  ○ **s'bë·n një kacidhe** not be worth a farthing/nickel

*****kacik** = **kacek**

kacilore *nf* one-liter measure and container for liquids

*****kacimare** *nf [Bot]* = **kacirom**

kaciq *nm* **1** baby goat: kid **2** = **kacek**

*****kacirom** *nm [Bot]* water chestnut *(Trapa natans)*

  ○ **kacirom toke** *[Bot]* common storksbill *Erodium cicutarium*

kacis *stem for 1st sg pres, pl pres, 2nd & 3rd sg subj, pind* < **kacit·**

kacit· *vi* to stick (in <>'s throat)

*****kacoji** *nm (obl)* < **kacua**

*****kacû** *adv (Reg Gheg)* = **kacuk**

kacua *nm (obl ~oi)* servant

*****kacubane** *nf [Ornit]* skylark *(Alauda arvensis)*

*****kacubri** *nm [Invert]* beetle *(Coleoptera)*

kacuk *adv* in squatting position

kacule *nf* **1** small sheaf of grain **2** muzzle used to prevent baby animal from suckling at the udder

kacull *OR* **kacull** *nm [Bot]* bagpod *(Vesicaria utriculata Lam.)*

*****kacup** = **kaçup**

*****kacybet** = **kaçubet**

*****kacye** *stem for sg pdef, part* < **kace·n**

kaç *nm (Reg)* weaver

kaçabek = **kaçubet**

kaçaberr *nm* corncob with only a few kernels

*****kaçabet** = **kaçubet**

*****kaçabro·n** *vt* to block, trip

*****kaçadel** *nm (Reg Gheg)* shoot growing out of a bulb

kaçadredhë *nf* curled object: curl; curl of hair

kaçak

  I § *nm (Old)* renegade outlaw, mountain brigand *II §* *adj (Old)* contraband, illegal

kaçakçe *adv, adj (Colloq)* **1** in the manner of a mountain brigand: secretly, sneakingly **2** as contraband

kaçalyt *nm* pigeon with a tuft of feathers on top of the head

kaçamak *nm [Food]* porridge made of corn and butter: corn mush, polenta

*****kaçamik·** *vt* to pinch, nip

kaçamill *nm (np ~j) [Invert]* snail; sea snail

kaçamol *nm* corn with small ears; corn with few kernels

kaçanduk· *vt* **1** to pluck **2** to pinch, tweak

*****kaçarrel** = **kaçurrel**

*****kaçarrênë** *nf(Reg Gheg)* whopping lie

kaçarret *nm* men's jacket with short sleeves and wool-fringed collar

kaçarrum = **kacarrum**

kaçavidë *nf* screwdriver

*****kaçavidhe** *nf* = **kaçavidë**

*****kaçavilë** = **kaçavidë**

kaçe

  I § *nf [Bot]* **1** dog rose *(Rosa canina)* **2** common crocus *(Crocus vernis)* **3** meadow saffron, autumn crocus *(Colchicum autumnale)* **4** herbal used for tea *II §* *adj* off-white, cream colored

kaçel *adj* lame

kaçerr *nm* icicle hanging from a tree branch

kaçezë *nf* = **kaçe**

kaçe *nf* **1** empty walnut **2** corncob

kaçi

  I § *nf* upper part of the human thigh *II §* *adv* astride the shoulders

kaçibardhë *nm [Bot]* dog rose *(Rosa canina)*

*****kaçik** *nm* year-old chicken

kaçikërr *nf[Entom]* **1** small grasshopper **2** cicada

kaçile *nf* round basket with a narrow neck; basket, hamper

kaçirubë *nf* 1 tuft of feathers on the head: crest 2 rooster's comb 3 forelock; mane

kaçkarit·et *vpr* 1 to make false promises; prevaricate, tell lies; talk nonsense 2 (*Impol*) to brag, boast 3 to avoid hard work

kaçkaritje *nf* false promise; lie; nonsense

kaçkavall *nm* [*Dairy*] salty cheese made of ewe's milk: caciocavallo cheese

kaçkë *nf(Colloq)* 1 walnut 2 empty walnut 3 *(Contempt)* empty-headed person
  ◦ **kaçka e fytit** [*Anat*] Adam's apple
  ◦ **kaçka e gjurit** [*Anat*] kneecap

kaçkët *adj (i)* 1 made of walnut (wood) 2 stained with an infusion made from the outer husk of the walnut fruit; of the color of the walnut husk

kaçkin *nm* = kaçak

kaçkinj· *vt* to remove the soft outer hull of [walnuts]

kaçole *nf* cork of a bottle

kaçorr *nm* 1 baby rabbit, leveret 2 small ear of corn, corn with few kernels

kaçorre *nf* 1 small thatched hut 2 improvized shelter made of branches 3 chicken coop

kaçuban
  I § *adj* 1 having coarse hair sticking up 2 having a tuft of feathers
  II § *nm* [*Ornit*] = çafkëlore

kaçubet *nm* [*Ornit*] kite (*Milvus*)

kaçubë *nf* bush, shrub

kaçubishtë *nf* 1 bushy area, thicket: brushwood 2 bush

kaçubor *adj* 1 [*Bot*] bushy 2 covered with bushes

kaçul *nm* 1 tuft (of feathers), crest 2 rooster's comb 3 [*Ornit*] horned lark (*Eremophila alpestris L., Alauda alpestris*) 4 (*Fig*) child dressed in raggedy clothes; very poor child

kaçular *n* (*Impol*) braggart

kaçule *nf* 1 hood of a cloak or raincoat 2 pointed wool cap typically worn by children

*kaçulerë *nm* [*Ornit*] woodcock

kaçulitë *nf* 1 tuft of feathers 2 [*Zool*] nose-horn of a sand viper

kaçulore *nf* chicken with a tuft of feathers on the head

*kaçull *adv* = kacuk

kaçullar *n* = kaçular

kaçullatë *nf* 1 tuft of feathers 2 crested fowl

kaçulle *nf* = kaçule

*kaçume *nf* wooden bowl

*kaçunar *nm* leg of mutton

kaçup *nm* 1 small leather bottle 2 blacksmith's bellows 3 tuft of feathers 4 corn tassel 5 small sheaf of corn

kaçurela *np* = kaçurrela

kaçurrec *nm* hood (on clothing)

kaçurrel *adj* curly; curly-headed

kaçurrelë *nf* ringlet, curl

*kaçybet = kaçubet

kad *nm* (*Old*) incense

kadaif *nm* 1 dessert made by pouring boiled sugar syrup over thin noodles baked with walnuts and almonds 2 thin extruded noodle used for this dessert

kadaifbërës *n* person who makes thin dessert noodles

kadaifçi *nm* = kadaifbërës

*kadall = ngadal

*kadalli = ngadalësi

kadastër *nf*[*Offic*] registry of land for tax purposes: cadaster
  ◦ **kadastra e ujërave** register of river information

kadastral *adj* = kadastror

kadastrim *nm* ger[*Offic*] <kadastro·n

kadastro·n *vt* [*Offic*] to register in a cadaster

kadastror *adj*[*Offic*] cadastral

kade *nf* 1 wooden tub; vat, wine vat, tun 2 storage cask 3 funnel-shaped millrace

kadebërës *nm* cask/vat/tub maker: barrel maker

kadencë *nf* cadence; cadenza

kadet *nm* cadet in a military high school

kadexhi *nm* (*np ~nj*) = kadebërës

kadi *nm* [*Hist*] Ottoman official with power to judge on both civil and religious matters: cadi

kadife *OR* **kadife**
  I § *nf* velvet, plush
  II § *adj* velvety

kadifenjtë *adj (i)* 1 made of velvet 2 velvety

kadilerë *np* = kadil

*kadim *nm* = kufi

*kadis *stem for 1st sg pres, pl pres, 2nd & 3rd sg subj, pind <kadit·

kadishtë *nf* small cask

*kadishtëri *nf* barrel making, cooperage

*kadit *adv* of yore, long since

*kadit· *vt* to perfume

kaditshëm *adj (i)* 1 long past 2 of long ago: bygone, of yore

kadmium *nm* [*Chem*] cadmium

kadoriqe *nf* = përpajnë

Kadri *nm* Kadri (male name)

kadril *nm* quadrille

*kadro *nf* cadre, staff personnel, staff = kuader

*kadyfe = kadife

kadhë *nf* billhook with a long handle = kmesë

kadhëm *nm* = kadhë

kaf *nm* 1 tinder, fire-starter, punk = eshkë *2 headland, cape

*kafalet *nm* haycock

*kafanoz *nm* bowl, basin

*kafariç *OR* kafariq *nm* spiked metal ring around an animal's muzzle to prevent suckling, grazing, or biting = hundëz

*kafas = kafaz

kafaz *nm* 1 cage, coop 2 storage bin 3 shutter (outside a window) 4 structure containing a stairway: staircase 5 radioman in an embassy (who works in the barred security room) 6 bodyguard of a high functionary
  ◦ **kafaz i kraharorit** [*Anat*] rib cage

kafazli *nf* grillwork outside a window

kafe *OR* **kafe**
  I § *nf* 1 coffee; coffee plant; coffee bean 2 café; coffee house
  II § *adj* dark brown, coffee-colored
  ◦ **kafe e egër** [*Bot*] sharp-leaved asparagus *Asparagus acutifolius*
  ◦ **kafe ekspres** espresso
  ◦ **kafe e gjelbër** alluring but dangerous enterprise
  ◦ **kafe e hidhët** black coffee without sugar

○ **kafe e madhe** the final betrothal ceremony
○ **kafe sade** coffee without sugar
○ **kafe shpuzë** strong coffee boiled slowly over hot embers to bring out the flavor
○ **kafe e vogël** the preliminary betrothal ceremony

kafe|**ha'ne** *nf* **1** = **kafe**, **kafene** **2** *(Pej)* dirty, run-down coffee house

kafei'në *nf* caffeine

kafe|**ne** *nf(Colloq)* café; coffee house, pub that sells coffee

kafe|**njt**ë *adj (i)* coffee-colored, brown

kafe-restora'nt *nm* cafe-restaurant

***kafe**|**ta'r** *nm* café proprietor = **kafexhi'**

***kafe**|**to're** *nf* coffee house = **kafene'**

kafe|**xhi** *nm (np ˜ nj) (Colloq)* **1** person who makes the coffee in a café **2** owner of a café

***kafillo'ne** *nf* pin

kafja'll *nm (Old)* morning snack, breakfast

***kafjo'll**ë *nf(Old)* = **kafja'll**

kafka'llë *nf(Reg)* = **ka'fkull**

***Kafka'z** *(Old)* = **Kauka'z**

ka'fkë *nf* **1** skull, cranium **2** = **ka'fkull**

kafko'r *adj (Book)* cranial

ka'fkull *nm (np ˜ j)* carapace: turtle/snail shell

***kafo're** *nf* coffeepot

***kafsh**|**a'k** *adj (Old)* zoological = **zoologji'k**

kafsh|**a'r** *n* herdsman in charge of draft animals; drayman in charge of haulage with animals

kafsh|**ara'k** *adj* = **shtazara'k**

kafsha'të *nf* **1** bite, mouthful, morsel **2** *(Fig)* tiny amount yet to be overcome or finished
○ **Kafshata e madhe të zë fytin.** "Big bites stick in your throat" *(Prov)* If you are too greedy you will suffer for it.

ka'fshë *nf* **1** animal; beast, brute **2** *(Fig Crude Insult)* stupid and ill-behaved person: dumb brute **3** thing
○ **kafsh**ë **barrabajtëse** beast of burden, pack animal
○ **kafshë barre** beast of burden, pack animal
○ **kafshë prodhimi** livestock animal
○ **kafshë samari** pack animal

kafshë|**mba'th**|**ës** *nm* farrier

kafshë|**ri** *nf* **1** *(Collec)* animals; a group of animals; livestock **2** the life of an animal: brutish life **3** *(Fig)* brutish behavior: bestiality, brutality

kafshë|**ri'm** *nm ger* **1** <**kafsho'·n**, **kafsho'·het 2** brutalization

kafshë|**ri'sht** *adv (Book)* in a bestial way, like an animal; brutally

kafshë|**ro'·het** *vpr* to turn into a beast

kafshë|**ro'·n** *vt* **1** to treat [ ] like an animal: brutalize **2** to turn [ ] into an animal

kafshë|**ro'r** *adj (Book)* **1** of or pertaining to animals; characteristic of animals **2** bestial, brutish

kafshë|**ru'a'r** *adj (i)* = **shtazëru'ar**

kafshë|**rri't**|**ës** *n* person who tends livestock; person involved in raising livestock

kafshë|**si** *nf* brutishness, bestiality

kafshë|**so'r** *adj (Old)* = **kafsh**ë**ro'r**

ka'fshë**z** *nf* riddle

kafsh|**i'm** *nm ger* **1** <**kafsho'·n**, **kafsho'·het 2** bite mark

kafsh|**i't**ë *nf* = **kafsha't**ë

kafsh|**o'·het** *vpr* to fight tooth and nail

kafsh|**o'·n** *vt, vi* **1** to bite; bite/snap at (with teeth/fangs); bite on; bite into **2** to sting, prick **3** to strike, hit
○ **kafshoi botë** *(Crude)* { } kicked off, { } died
○ **kafsho·n buzët me dhëmbë** to bite one's tongue, regret what one has said/done
○ **kafsho·n gjuhën 1** to bite one's tongue: keep silent; be sorry for what one has said **2** *(Contempt)* to kick the bucket, die

kafsh|**o'r** *adj* **1** of or pertaining to animals; characteristic of animals **2** *(Colloq)* beastly, bestial

kafsho're *nf* = **kafsha't**ë

kafsh|**u'ar**
I § *adj (i)* bitten
II § *nf (e)* **1** bitten place: bite **2** amount that can be taken in one bite: biteful, bite

kafsh|**u'e's** *adj* biting

kafta'n *nm (Old)* **1** caftan **2** fancy embroidered silk kerchief carried by a bride

***kâgj** *nm (Reg Gheg)* = **kënde's**

***kagjarrâ(n)** *nm (Reg Gheg)* hook for hanging up weapons/meat

kah *I §* *nm OR* **ka'he** *II §* *nf* direction (of motion) *III §* *prep (nom)* = **nga**

***ka'ha'ne** = **kahe'rë**

ka'he'rë *adv* some time ago; formerly

ka'he'rshëm *adj (i)* of long ago, long past; former, previous

***ka'h**ë *adv* just now

kahmo's *adv* in every direction

***kah'mo't** *adv (Colloq)* ages ago; formerly

kahni's *stem for 1st sg pres, pl pres, 2nd & 3rd sg subj, pind* <**kahni't·**

***kahni't·** *vt* = **vogëlo'·n**

kahti's *stem for 1st sg pres, pl pres, 2nd & 3rd sg subj, pind* <**kahti't·**

kahti't· *vt* to remove the soft outer hull of [ ]

kahti't|ur *adj (i)* with the soft outer hull removed

ka'ike
I § *nf(Colloq)* caïque
II § *adj* (of kitchenware) oval in shape and shallow

kai'l *adv (Old)* ready to obey/act/accept

ka'ish *nm (Colloq)* **1** narrow sash around the waist: belt **2** leather strop **3** *(Fig Insult)* blockhead

ka'ishtë *nf* white clay, kaolin

***kaja'k** *nm [Sport]* kayak

***kajga'sh** *nm [Ornit]* nightingale

***kaj'he're** *adv (Colloq)* = **ngandonjëhe're**

***kaji's** *stem for 1st sg pres, pl pres, 2nd & 3rd sg subj, pind* <**kaji't·**

***kaji't·** *vt* to yelp, bark

***ka'jk**ë *nf* **1** forest **2** keel of a ship

***kâjk**ë *(Reg Gheg)* = **kë'ng**ë

kajku'shkë *nf* **1** variety of pear with small round autumn-ripening fruit that become softer and sweeter in storage **2** = **gorri'c**ë

kajlë *nf* catkin

kajma'k *nm* fat-rich top layer that forms on a boiled or fermented liquid: cream = **ajk**ë

kajmakli'e *nf [Food]* meringue

***kaj'm**e *np* <**kalla'm** reeds, rushes

kajmeka'm *nm [Hist]* provincial vicegerent during the Ottoman occupation

kajna'cë *nf* latch

***ka'jo** *np*

Ka'jro *nf* Cairo

kajsi *nf* apricot

kajs i'shtë *nf* apricot orchard

***kâj shëm** *adj (i) (Reg Gheg)* = **këndshëm**

kajti's· *vt* **1** to flush [game] out of hiding ***2** to rouse; irritate

kaju'ke *nf* **1** short-sleeved and buttonless man's wool jacket with a drooping collar in back **2** the collar of such a jacket

ka-ka-ka *onomat* cluck-cluck

kaka'o *nf* cocoa

kakara'ç *nm* boiled corn

kakare'ç *adj, nm* unripe (fruit)

kaka ri'më *nf* = **kakari'sje**

kaka ri's· *vi* to cackle, cluck
   ○ **kakaris· si pula në veri∥pa grurë** "cackle like a hen *in the north wind∥without grain*" to talk and talk on and on to no purpose

kaka ri'sje *nf ger* **1** <**kakaris· 2** cackling sound

kaka rit = **kakaris·**

***kakatu'a** *nm (obl ~ oi, np ~ o'nj)* [*Ornit*] cockatoo

kakaviç *nm* **1** small sweet melon with greenish-yellow skin **2** *(FigImpolite)* immature person

ka'kë *nf (Child)* feces, doodoo

***kakërdha'c·** *vi* to open one's eyes wide: goggle

kakërdha'çe *nf* [*Zool*] blindworm, slowworm = **bollëve'rbët**

kakër'dhi *nf* **1** (of sheep or goats) excrement, droppings **2** *(FigImpolite)* small, ugly person

***kakërdhiçkë** *nf* [*Zool*] = **zhapi**

kakërdho'c *nm* frog

***kakër'dhok** = **kokërdho'k**

***kakëri·n** *vi* to cackle

***kakëri'më** *nf ger* <**kakëri·n**

***kakër'llo'cë** *nf* saffron

***kakëru'kë** *nf* walnut

ka'kë'za *np* **1** residual dried snot in the nose **2** pieces of dried up earwax

kakë zo'gëz *nf* **1** [*Zool*] blindworm, slowworm = **bollëve'rbët 2** *(Reg)* = **bretko'së**

kaki
   I § *nf* [*Bot*] Japanese persimmon (*Diospyros kaki*)
   II § *adj* khaki colored

***kaki(n)** *nm (Reg Gheg)* iron pan, waffle iron = **kaki'n**

kaki'n *nm* = **saç**

kakofoni *nf* cacophony

kakofonik *adj* cacophonic

kako'le *nf* = **kërdho'kull**

kakri *nm* [*Bot*] cachrys (*Cachrys*)

***kakrri'qe** *nf* wart

kakrru'k
   I § *nm* **1** walnut still wet from having its outer soft husk removed **2** hard-shelled walnut **3** walnut shell **4** fruit with a large hard pit
   II § *adv* **1** all hunched up, in a lump **2** empty inside

kakto're *np* [*Bot*] cactus family *Cactaceae*

ka'ktus *nm* [*Bot*] **1** cactus **2** cactus flower

***kakule'të** *nf* hood

kaku'shë *nf* **1** blister, vesicle **2** pimple

kaku'të *nf* **1** [*Bot*] black henbane (*Hyosciomus niger*) **2** corn stubble left in a field

kala *nf* **1** castle, citadel **2** fortress **3** [*Chess*] castle, rook
   ○ **kala prej karte/letre** house of cards

kalabre'z *n, adj* Calabrian

Kalabri *nf* Calabria

kala dibra'nçe *adv*

***kal a'do'ras** *adv* feeling one's way, gropingly

kala dredh'has *adv* **1** twisting and turning **2** *(Fig)* shiftily, deceptively

kala dre'dhë *nf (Intens)* sharp curve, curl

kala gju'nj'azi *adv* **1** in squatting position **2** on one's knees

kala ki'ç *adv* **1** astride the shoulders: piggyback **2** astride, astraddle

kala kry'q *adv* in a string of crosses

kalama(n)
   I § *nm (Colloq)* **1** young child: little kid **2** *(Pej)* person who behaves childishly, immature person
   II § *adj* childish

kalama'j *np* <**kalama(n)**

kalama'k *OR* **kalama'q** *(Colloq)* = **kalama(n)**

kalama'llëk *nm (np ~ qe) (Colloq)* childish behavior

kalama'llëqe *np* <**kalama'llëk**

kalama'n ‖ *obl* <**kalama(n)**

***kalama'r** *nm (Reg Kos)* = **kallama'r**

kalambu'r *nm* [*Lit*] pun; play on words

kala me'nd· *vt* **1** to rock/swing/whirl [ ] to the point of dizziness **2** to make dizzy, bewilder

kala me'nd·et *vpr* **1** to lose consciousness, faint **2** to get dizzy, become bewildered

kala me'nd'ës *adj* dizzying, bewildering

***kalami'të** *nf* calamity

***kalami'tun** *adj (i) (Reg Gheg)* tired out, exhausted

***kalamu'q** *adv* in a disorderly heap

kalande'r *nm* **1** [*Relig*] itinerant dervish **2** poor man, beggar

kalandë'r *nf* **1** [*Ornit*] calandra lark (*Melanocorypha calandra*) **2** [*Entom*] = **farëngrënës 3** [*Tech*] calender *()*

kalandri'm *nm* [*Tech*] calendering *()*

kala'ngërç
   I § *adj* afflicted with cramps/epilepsy; in bad health, sickly
   II § *nm* *cramp

***kala'ngërç·et** *vpr* to writhe with pain, be bent over with a cramp

***kalangi'ç** = **kallangi'ç**

kal a'pe'le *nf* [*Bot*] corn poppy (*Papaver rhoeas*)

kalapi'ç *adv* = **kalaki'ç**

kala qa'fë *adv* piggyback = **kaliqa'fë**

kalari'm *nm ger* <**kalaro'·het**

kalaro'·het *vpr* **1** to wrap hands and feet around and hold on **2** to clamber = **kacava're·t**

***kalaro'·n** *vt* **1** to clamber up [ ]: climb **2** = **kalëro'·n**

***kalaru'es** *adj* clambering, climbing; sprawling

ka'las *adv* on all fours = **këmbado'ras**

***kala'stër** *nm* [*Ornit*] cockerel

kala va'r·et *vpr* **1** to clamber down **2** to hang down from one's hands

***kalave're** *nf* drinking cup

kala ve'sh *nm* **1** cluster of grapes/cherries **2** forked stick = **biga'çe**

kala ve'sh as *adv* with great difficulty

kala ve·sh|azi *adv* = **kalaveshas**

kala vigj|as *adv* by the hands and feet

*****ka llaza** *adv* on all fours

kalb· *vt* **1** to rot [], cause decay in []; putrefy **2** *(Fig)* to ruin, spoil, do [] in
  ○ **na kalbi dimri/shiu** the long winter/rain has done us in

ka lb·et *vpr* to become rotten: rot, decay, spoil, fester
  ○ **kalb·et në burg/shtrat/spital** to languish for a long time in prison/bed/hospital
  ○ <> **kalb·***et*[3pl] **trutë** *(Impol)* <> *becomes* senile, <> *goes* dotty

kalb|aro q *n* sick person, invalid

kalb|ç *adj* rotten, putrid

ka lb|ës *adj* rotting, putrescent

kalb|ëse·het *vpr* = **kalb·***et*

kalb|ësi *nf* rot, putrescence

kalb|ësi m *nm ger* < **kalb·***et*

kalb|ësiqe *nf* **1** rotted thing: rot **2** *(Fig)* worthless thing/person

kalb|ësirë *nf* **1** decayed material: rot, rotted part, putrefaction, decay **2** *(Fig)* worthless old thing/person; thin and weak person **3** rottenness, putrefaction

kalb|ësit·et *vpr* = **ka lb·***et*

kalb|ësor *adj* putrid, festered, spoiled

ka lb|ët *adj (i)* rotten, putrid, spoiled

kalb|ëze·het *vpr* = **kalb**ëzo·*het*

kalb|ëze·n *vt* = **kalbëzo·***n*

kalb|ëzim *nm ger* **1** < **kalbëzo·***n*, **kalb**ëzo·*het* **2** rotten part, rotten thing **3** *[Bot]* rot
  ○ **kalbëzim i butë** *[Bot]* gradual browning of plant parts, slow rotting
  ○ **kalbëzim unazor** *[Bot]* disease that causes rot in the shape of rings around potato tubers

kalb|ëzo·het *vpr* **1** to begin to rot/spoil **2** to become putrefied: putrefy **3** *(Fig)* to undergo moral decay

kalb|ëzo·n *vt* **1** to cause [] to rot/spoil **2** to cause putrefaction **3** *(Fig)* to cause moral decay

kalb|ëzu ar *adj (i)* in the process of rotting, putrifying

kalb|ëzu es *adj [Med]* putrescent

kalb|ëzy er *adj (i)* = **kalb**ëzu ar

kalb|ishte *nf* decaying/rotten thing, rotting material

ka lb|je *nf ger* < **kalb·**, **kalb·***et*

*****kalb n|o·n** *vt (Reg Gheg)* = **kalb·**

*****kalb o·het** *vpr* = **kalb**ëzo·*het*

*****kalb s|e·n** OR **kalb s|o·n** *vt* = **kalbëzo·***n*

ka lb|ur *adj (i)* **1** rotten **2** *(Fig)* emaciated; worn out **3** *(Fig)* morally corrupt
  ○ **ësh-të i kalbur në para** *(Colloq)* to be rolling in dough, be very rich

kalcedo n *nm [Min]* chalcedony

ka lc|ë *nf* = **ka llc**ë

ka lcium *nm [Chem]* calcium

kalda j|ë *nf [Tech]* boiler

kaldaj|ist *n* heating-plant worker

kale c *nm (Colloq Pej)* (popular derogative term for Albanian State Security agents: secret police, spy) government fink

kale c|ë *adv* = **kale ht**ë

ka le ht|as *adv* = **kale ht**ë

ka le ht|ë *adv* very softly/quietly

ka leht or *adj* very soft/quiet

kaleidosko p *nm* kaleidoscope

kale m *nm* **1** pencil **2** *(Fig Colloq)* reading and writing **3** rod-shaped tool **4** tip of a tooth of a saw **5** *[Agr]* cutting/scion used for grafting

kalem xhi *nm (np ~ nj) (Pej)* petty writer: pencil pusher, scribbler, hack

kalenda r *nm* calendar

kalendar ik *adj* calendrical

kale s|ë *nf* **1** *(Old)* = **kali m** **2** passageway **3** *[Tech]* removal of a piece by a one movement of a tool: *(pass, bite, cut)*

kale stër *nf* *[Ethnog]* = **dark**ëçi k**ë**

kalesto r *n* guest at a party given to honor a new son-in-law's first visit

kale sh
I § *adj*, *nm* **1** wooly (animal) **2** (small livestock) with dark markings on the head and around the eyes **3** (person) with bushy, dark eyebrows and dark eyes; pretty
II § *adj* (of hair) dark

ka lesha n *adj* wooly

ka le sh|e *nf* **1** sheep with black circles around the eyes **2** term of endearment for a girl: sweetie

ka lesh o·het *vpr* **1** (of land) to be left overgrown and unworked **2** (of a person) to be left abandoned and with nothing

*****kaleto re** *adj fem* deft

ka lë *nm* **1** horse; stallion, male horse **2** *(Colloq)* amount that a horse can bear: horseload **3** *[Chess]* knight **4** *[Mus]* bridge (of a stringed instrument)
  ○ **kalë barre** pack horse
  ○ **kali i belarave** person who bears the burden of others' troubles; person who bears the burden of work
  ○ **Kali i botës të lë në mes të udhës.** "The stranger's horse will leave you in the middle of the road." *(Prov)* It is better to rely on yourself than on others.
  ○ **kali i detit 1** *[Ichth]* sea horse *(Hippocampus hippocampus)* **2** walrus
  ○ **kali i dreqës** *[Entom]* dragonfly ***=** **pilive s**ë
  ○ **kalë drush** each of the two stones that support the fire logs in a hearth; firedog, andiron
  ○ **kalë gërxhall** *(Pej)* **1** scrawny nag **2** *(Fig)* scrawny person
  ○ **kalë gjakpastër** thoroughbred
  ○ **Kali ha tagjinë, gomari mbart bucelat.** "The horse eats fodder, the donkey carries the water jugs." *(Prov)* Some people sit around and have a good time while others break their backs working.
  ○ **Kali i huaj të lë në mes të udhës.** "The stranger's horse will leave you in the middle of the road." *(Prov)* It is better to rely on yourself than on others.
  ○ **Kali humbi, gomari s'duket.** "The horse is lost and the donkey cannot be seen." *(Prov)* (describes a mob of people)
  ○ **(Edhe) kali i mirë/kuq e ka një huq.** "(Even) the good/brown horse has a defect" *(Prov)* Even the best of us has some defect. No one is perfect.
  ○ **kalë karroce 1** dray horse **2** person who lacks initiative/vision
  ○ **kali i kuq** sorrel horse
  ○ **Kali i mirë e shton (vetë) tagjinë** "A good horse adds his own fodder (himself)." *(Prov)* If you work hard and behave yourself, good things come your way.

○ **Kali i mirë njihet nën mutaf.** "A good horse is recognized only under the horse blanket." *(Prov)* A person's worth can only be determined on the job.
○ **kal**ë **ngarkese** pack horse
○ **kal**ë **i ngordhur** *(Pej)* scrawny nag
○ **Kali nuk ka prask.** "The horse has no veil." Horses have a seventh sense of things. Horses can smell what's going to happen.
○ **kalë për së gjëri** [*Gymnastics*] side horse
○ **kalë për xhambaz** horse that is hard to handle, unruly horse
○ **kali i qyqes 1** [*Ornit*] Egyptian vulture *(Neophron percnopterus)* **2** [*Entom*] devil's coach-horse, Tasmanian devil, cock-tail beetle *(Ocypus (Staphylinus) olens)*
○ **kal**ë **samari** pack horse
○ **kal**ë **shale** saddlehorse
○ **kal**ë **shtrigash/shtrige** [*Entom*] praying mantis *(Mantis religiosa)*
○ **Kalë të preshtë nuk ka.** "There are no green horses" *(Prov)* There is no such thing.
○ **U rrëzua kali, t'i presim këmbët!** "The horse fell down, let's cut off his legs!" *(Iron)* Are we to punish severely a good and faithful worker for one little mistake!

kalë**-fuqi** *nm* [*Phys Tech*] horsepower
*__**kal**ë**píç** *adv* = **kalaki̧ç**
kalë**rím** *nm ger* <**kal**ë**ro·***n
kalë**ro·***n
  I § *vi* to ride/go on horseback
  II § *vt* to straddle/bestraddle [ ]
kalë**shal**ë *adv* astraddle
ka'lfët *adj (i)* murky
*__**kali** *nf* alkali = **alka'l**
*__**kaliba'ç** *adv* = **kalibo'ç**
kali'be *nf* = **kolíbe**
kali'bër *nm* **1** caliber **2** [*Tech*] micrometer **3** [*Tech*] passage of metal between rolls in a mill: pass
kalibo'bë *nf* [*Bot*] nettle tree *(Celtis australis)*
kalibo'ç *adv* astride the shoulders: piggyback
kalibrím *nm ger* [*Tech*] **1** <**kalibro·***n **2** calibration
kalibro·*n vt* **1** [*Tech*] to refine [a machine] to bring into conformity with final specifications; calibrate; measure [ ] with a calibrated tool **2** [*Spec*] to assort [ ] into categories
kalibru'a'r *adj (i)* **1** [*Tech*] refined [a detail] to conform with specifications; calibrated; measured with a calibrated tool **2** [*Spec*] assorted into categories
kalibru'e's
  I § *adj* serving to calibrate: calibrating
  II § *nm* tool calibrated to make exact measurements
kalíf *nm* [*Hist*] caliph
kalifa't *nm* [*Hist*] caliphate
kalife'r *nm* [*Bot*] garden sage *(Salvia officinalis)*
Kaliforní *nf* California
*__**kaliga'q** *adv (Reg Gheg)* = **kalaki̧ç**
kaligrafí *nf* calligraphy, penmanship
*__**kalika'ç** *adv* = **kalaki̧ç**
kalikí̧ç *adv* = **kalaki̧ç**
*__**kaliko'ç** OR **kaliku'sh** *adv* = **kalaki̧ç**
kaliko't *nm* calico
kalím *nm ger* **1** <**kalo·***n **2** passage **3** place that allows passage: passageway, pass, crossing
  ○ **kalim lumi** ford, river-crossing
  ○ **kalim pengesash** [*Mil*] obstacle course

kalimta'r
  I § *adj* **1** transitory, ephemeral, momentary **2** transitional **3** [*Ling*] transitive (of verbs)
  II § *n* **1** passer-by **2** pedestrian
kalimtarí *nf* [*Math*] transitivity
kalímthi *adv* in passing, incidentally; superficially; hastily
kalipí̧ç *adv* = **kaliqa'fë**
*__**kalí̧q** *nm* biscuit, small loaf
kaliqa'fë *adv* piggyback
kaliqe *nf* wooden sandal/clog = **nalla'n**e
*__**kaliqy'ës** *nf* [*Ornit*] = **mjellba'rdh**ë
*__**kaliro·***n = **kal**ë**ro·***n
kalí̧s·et *vpr* to sit astride the neck
kalí̧s *stem for 1st sg pres, pl pres, 2nd & 3rd sg subj, pind* **1** <**kalí̧t·** *__**2** = **skalí̧s**
kalisher *nm* a rope of onions or garlic
kalí̧t· *vt* **1** to harden [ ] by tempering: temper, steel **2** to dress/shape [a scythe] by hammering; dress [a millstone] *__**3** = **skalí̧t·**
kalí̧t·et *vpr* **1** to become tempered/hardened/steeled deeply **2** = **skalí̧t·***et
kalí̧të**s** *adj* **1** serving to make stronger and harder: tempering **2** = **skalí̧tës**
kalí̧tje *nf ger* **1** <**kalí̧t·**, **kalí̧t·et 2** = **skalí̧tje**
kalí̧tur *adj (i)* **1** tempered **2** dressed/sharpened/shaped by hammering *__**3** = **skalí̧tur**
kaliu'm *nm* [*Chem*] potassium *((K)K)*
kaliva'ç *nm* fruit hung in clusters on a branch for drying
kaliva're
  I § *nf* **1** rod from which strings of agricultural products are hung for drying **2** string of agricultural products hung up for drying **3** something hanging or flowing down **4** trace left by a liquid flowing down
  II § *adv* in a spate, torrentially
  ○ **kalivare uji** waterfall
*__**kalí̧ve** *nf* = **kolíbe**
kalk *I §* *nm* OR **ka'lk**ë *II §* *nf* **1** transparent tissue used to copy drawings **2** [*Ling*] calque
kalka're *np* **1** weeds and brambles **2** driftwood in a stream of water
kalkopirí̧t *nm* [*Min*] chalcopyrite
kalkula'triçe *nf* calculating machine
kalkulím *nm ger* **1** <**kalkulo·***n **2** calculation
kalkulo·*n vt* to calculate
Kalku'të *nf* Calcutta
kalma'r *nm* [*Invert*] cuttlefish = **kallama'r**
kalmu'q
  I § *nm* compost heap; garbage pile
  II § *adj* *covered by mud/dust
kalmu'th *nm* [*Bot*] restharrow *(Ononis)* = **ferrënu'se**
kalo·*n
  I § *vi* **1** to pass, pass/go by; get past/through/down **2** to proceed
  II § *vt* **1** to ride **2** to pass over [ ]: traverse, cross; surpass, exceed **3** to pass [ ] on; send [ ] forward, transmit **4** to swallow [ ] down **5** to pass/spend [time] **6** to excel
  ○ <> **kalo·***n*^{3sg} it *gets away from* <>, it *gets by* <>
  ○ <> **kalo·***n* **anash** to try to avoid/ignore <>
  ○ **i kalo·***n* **gur më gur** to get it done at low cost
  ○ **e kalo·***n* **gjumë e brumë** to live a life of leisure with plenty to eat: live the life of Riley

◦ **e kalo**·*n* **hendekun/kapërcyellin/lumin/përrruan/vaun** to get around/through a problem

◦ <> **kalo**·*n*^{3sg} **koha** <>'s time *has passed*

◦ **e kalo**·*n* **lumin në va 1** to cross (a river) at a ford: ford **2** to take the best and easiest path to a solution

◦ **e kalo**·*n* **lumin pa (u) lagur (këmbët)** to escape without a scratch

◦ **kalo**·*n* **me urë/pishë në dorë** "pass with torch in hand" to spread devastation in one's path

◦ <> **kalo**·*n*^{3sg} **mendja** <> *goes out of* <>'s mind, <> *goes crazy*

◦ <> **kalo**·*n*^{3sg} **mosha 1** <> *gets old* **2** <> *becomes* overage

◦ [ ] **kalo**·*n* **në sitë 1** to pass [ ] through a sieve: sift [ ] **2** to screen [ ] carefully

◦ **të kalo**·*n* **në vrimë të gjilpërës** "put you through the eye of a needle" to be extraordinarily adept

◦ [ ] **kalo**·*n* **në vrimë të gjilpërës 1** to reprimand [ ] severely **2** to make [ ] do something, force **3** to examine [ ] carefully and in detail

◦ <> **kalo**·*n* **nën hundë** to pass under <>'s very nose

◦ **kalo**·*n* **nga faza** *(Colloq)* to go out of one's mind, go crazy

◦ [ ] **kalo**·*n* **për anash** to mention [ ] only in passing, hardly mention [ ], barely touch on [ ]

◦ <> **kalo**·*n* **radha** <> *has* <>'s turn

◦ **kalo**·*n* **si erë/fortunë** to pass quickly

◦ **kalo**·*n* **si reja me breshër/furtunë** "pass like a hail/storm cloud" to pass quickly

◦ **e kalo**·*n* **të shtatën** "survive the seventh day (after birth)" to get past the danger, survive safely

◦ **e kalo**·*n* **trashë** to have plenty to eat and drink, have a good time

◦ **ta kalo**·*n*^{3sg} **ujët/ujin nën rrogoz/hasër/vete** "put water under your floor mat" to always be doing things behind your back

◦ **kalo**·*n* **vapë** to take a break during the hot time of the day: take a siesta

*__**kalo'çe**__ = **gallo'sh**e*

*__**kalofe'r**__ *nm* flavoring herb

kalo'jë *nf* passageway (bridge) across a stream

*__**kalo'r**__ *n* = **kalo'rës**

kalo'ras *adv* = **kaladibra'nçe**

kalo'razi *adv* = **kaladibra'nçe**

kalo're
I § *nf* **1** switch used to urge on horse or mule: riding stick **2** shoulder of a packsaddle **3** rumpstrap joining the packsaddle to the cinch or to the crupper **4** part of the halter that passes over the animal's nose **5** hard septum dividing the nutmeat of a walnut **6** rooftile covering two others which have been turned hollow side up
II § *adj (Fig)* (of a girl or woman) slender and lithe; (walking) with her nose in the air
III § *adj, adv* (sewing) with a basting stitch

kalo'rës *nm* **1** rider, horseman **2** [*Mil*] cavalryman **3** knight (as a title) **4** [*Ornit*] black-winged stilt *(Himantopus himantopus L.)*

kalo'rësi *nf* **1** *(Collec)* horseback riders **2** [*Sport*] horseback riding, equitation **3** [*Mil*] cavalry **4** chivalry *__**5** knighthood

kalo'rësia'k *adj* chivalric; chivalrous

kalori *nf* [*Phys*] calorie

kalo'ri *nf* **1** *(Collec)* horseback riders **2** [*Mil*] cavalry **3** [*Sport*] horseback riding, equitation

kalorife'r *nm* radiator (in a building)

kalorifi'k *adj* calorific

kalori'k *adj* caloric

kalo'rim *nm* ride

kalori'metër *nm* calorimeter

kalo'rthi *adv* = **kalu'ar**

kalo'shin *nm* small two-wheeled horse cart

kalpëto·*n* *vt* to plug [a leaky wooden container] up

kalpëty'rë *nf* plug used to stop leakage

*__**kalqit** *nm* limestone

kal'qy'qe *nf* [*Ornit*] = **mjellbardh**ë

kalt'ër *adj* (i), *nf (e)* sky blue, clear blue

kaltëri'm *nm ger* **1** < **kaltëro**·*n*, **kaltëro**·*het* **2** azure color/coloring

kaltëri'më *nf* = **kaltërsi**

kaltëri'në *nf* patina on copper, verdigris

kaltëro·*het* *vpr* to turn blue (in color); take on a bluish tinge

kaltëro·*n*
I § *vi* to be/appear blue (in color)
II § *vt* to color [ ] blue, make/paint/dye blue

kaltëro'r *adj (Poet)* shiny blue

kaltëro'sh *adj (Poet)* shiny blue, azure

kaltërsi *nf* blueness; the color blue, azure

*__**kalt'ër** = **ka'lt**ër

*__**kaltër'ti** *nf* azure, blue

*__**kaltër'to**·*het* = **kaltëro**·*het*

kaltëru'ar
I § *adj* (i), *nm* **1** (something) which has turned blue/bluish **2** blue
II § *n* (i) **1** *(Fig)* person who has suffered a terrible blow, wretch **2** *(Euph)* corpse

kaltë'rremë *adj (i)* of a bluish cast, bluish; light blue

kalthe'dër [*kal-the-dër*]
I § *nf* brushwood
II § *adj (Fig)* frail, skinny

*__**kalth'ër** = **ka'lt**ër

kal'thi *adv* **1** on all fours like a horse **2** mounted astride, astraddle **3** = **kaliqa'fë**

kalu'ar
I § *adj* (i) **1** past; over and done **2** outdated, old-fashioned **3** aged, old **4** (in expressions of time) last, previous **5** [*Ling*] past
II § *nm* (i) aging person
III § *nf* (e) the past; time gone by
IV § *adv* **1** on horseback **2** astride the shoulders **3** *(Fig)* without a problem; in comfortable circumstances, well-off; handily, effortlessly **4** (sewing) with a basting stitch **5** fitting together closely one atop the other

◦ **të kaluara** *(Colloq)* said to someone with current or recent personal problems: May all this be quickly behind you!

◦ **i kaluar nga mosha** of advanced age: old, aged

kalu'arthi *adv* **1** = **brezahy'pthi 2** = **kalí'mthi 3** = **kalu'ar**

kalu'ç *nm* [*Gymnastics*] vaulting horse: buck, long horse, side horse

kalu'es
I § *adj* **1** passing, transitory **2** passing, successful in class **3** passable, satisfactory
II § *n* student who has passed into a higher grade

kal`ue`shëm
I § adj (i) traversable, passable
II § adv passably

kal`ue`shm`ëri` *nf (Book)* **1** traversability, passability **2** competence to pass; percentage of students passing

kal`ush` *nm* **1** pony; small horse **2** colt **3** [*Sport*] = **kaluç**

kalva'r *nm* **1** hanging/falling object **2** calvary, ordeal
○ **kalvar rrushi** bunch of grapes
○ **kalvar uji** waterfall

kalvin`ist` *n* Calvinist

kalvin`izëm` *nm* Calvinism

***kalvo'z** *adj* filthy

***kaly'be** = **kolibe**

kall· *vt* **1** to put [] inside: insert, stick in, intrude, bury **2** to incite, stir up **3** to instill [something bad], provoke **4** *(Fig)* to deceive, trick **5** *(Reg)* to light, ignite
○ <> **kall· barut** to kill <> by shooting
○ <> **kall· bretkun** *(Crude)* to let <> go to pot/seed
○ <> **kall· datën** to make <> shudder, strike terror into <>, scare <> stiff, scare <> to death
○ <> **kall· djallin/dreqin** *(Crude)* not give a damn about <>, let <> go to hell
○ <> **kall· flamën/murtajën/ujkun 1** *(Crude)* not give a damn about <>, let <> go to hell **2** to scare <> to death, terrify <>
○ **kall· krupën** to cause nausea; horrify
○ <>**a kall· në vesh** to put a bug in <>'s ear, put it into <>'s head
○ <>**a kall· qimen** *(Crude)* to neglect []: let [] go to pot
○ <> **kall· spicat** to provoke <> to do something (wrong); cause <> to quarrel

ka'll·et *vpr* **1** to get inside: enter **2** to catch fire = **ndiz·et**

kall *stem for pdef, opt, adm, part, pind, vp, 2nd pl pres, imper* <**këllet·**

ka'lla *np* provocations, calumny

kall`aba`llëk *nm (np ~qe) (Colloq)* big crowd, throng
○ **mblidhe/mblidheni kallaballëkun!** *(Crude)* use your brain!

kalla`fa`s *stem for 1st sg pres, pl pres, 2nd & 3rd sg subj, pind* <**kallafat·**

kalla`fa't· *vt* **1** to do [] with no particular care, do [] in slapdash fashion, bungle **2** *(Fig)* to deceive, fool

kalla`fat`im *nm ger* <**kallafato'·n**

kalla`fato'·n *vt* **1** to caulk holes and cracks in [] with tar **2** *(Fig)* to fix defects in []

kalla`fato'r *n* ship caulker

kalla`fy's *stem for 1st sg pres, pl pres, 2nd & 3rd sg subj, pind* <**kallafyt·**

kalla`fy't· *vt* to compress

kallaj *nm* [*Chem*] **1** tin **2** tin solder **3** *(Fig)* superficial shine

kalla`je
I § nf cup made of tinplated copper
II § np tinplated utensils: tinplate

kallaj`is· *vt* **1** to coat [] with tin: tin, tinplate **2** to repair [] with solder **3** *(Pej)* to make [] all dirty **4** *(Fig)* to give [] a false appearance, disguise

kallaj`is·et *vpr* to get all dirty

kallaj`isje *nf ger* <**kallajis·**

kallaj`is`ur *adj (i)* **1** tinned, tinplated; soldered **2** *(Pej)* soiled, all dirty **3** *(Fig)* having a superficial veneer (that hides the truth)

kallaj`të *adj (i)* made of tin

kallaj`xhi` *nm (np ~nj)* tinsmith

kallam
I § nm **1** tall grass of the wetlands with a hollow, jointed stalk: reed, cane, rush **2** [*Bot*] giant reed *(Arundo donax)* **3** long hollow plant stalk; any object that is long, thin, and straight **4** spindle (for thread) **5** reed pipe (folk musical instrument) **6** shotgun cartridge **7** shank (of a leg or of a stocking)
II § pred (Fig Colloq) hollow inside, empty; with empty pockets: flat broke
○ **kallam i dorës** radius bone (of the arm)
○ **kallam i këne.tës** [*Bot*] great reed mace *(Typha latifolia)*
○ **kallam peshkimi** fishing pole/rod
○ **kallam sheqeri** [*Bot*] sugar cane

kallama'r *nm* **1** inkstand; ink bottle, inkwell **2** [*Invert*] cuttlefish *(Sepia)*

kallam`ate` *nf* brandy flavored with mastic: ouzo

kallam`boq` *nm (Reg)* corn, maize
○ **kallamboq i hollë** [*Bot*] millet

kallam`boq`të *adj (i) (Reg)* = **misërt**

kalla`me *nf* **1** grain stubble; straw **2** field of stubble

kallam`idhe` *nf (Reg)* **1** cartridge case **2** grain stubble **3** corncob

kallam`ishte` *nf* **1** grain stubble; straw **2** area with reedy plants: reed marsh, cane brake; clump of reeds **3** [*Bot*] reed grass, common reed *(Phragmites communis)*

***kallam`ite`** *nf (Old)* magnet

kallam`oq`ishte *nf* field of corn/maize

kallamper *nm* [*Bot*] tansy *(Tanacetum vulgare)*

kallam`sheqer` *nm* [*Bot*] sugar cane *(Sacharum officinarum)*

***kallam`urdhë`** *nf* wool yarn

***kallangiç** *nm* little boy

kallap`is` *stem for 1st sg pres, pl pres, 2nd & 3rd sg subj, pind* <**kallapit·**

kallap`it· *vt* = **kollofit·**

***kallatu'mb`a** *adv* head over heels

kallau'z *nm (Old)* **1** local guide **2** *(Pej)* paid spy **3** belled sheep or goat that leads the flock: bellwether **4** go-between; go-between for arranged marriages **5** pass key **6** hole punch

ka'llc`ë *nf* **1** thick woolen foot warmer: gaiter; legging **2** chain mail greave (worn by Illyrian soldiers) **3** = **tirq** ***4** *(Reg Gheg)* stocking, hose

***kallç** *nm* shoe last, boot-tree

kallçij *np* <**ka'llcë**

kallç`in`ë *nf* **1** = **ka'llcë 2** upper part of boots

kalldrë'm *nm* cobblestone pavement

kalldrëm`im` *nm ger* <**kalldrëmo'·n**

kalldrëm`o'·n *vt, vi* to pave with cobblestone

kalldrëm`o'r *adj* = **kalldrë'mtë**

kalldrëm`shtru`e's *nm* person who lays cobblestones: cobblestone layer

kalldrë'm`të *adj (i)* of cobblestone

kalldrëm`xhi` *nm (np ~nj)* = **kalldrëmshtrues**

***ka'llë**
I § part <**kall**
II § nf slander

kallëkeq *adj* inciting others to argue/dispute, provoking a quarrel: troublemaking

kallëp
I § *nm* 1 object whose form determines derived objects: mold, form, die, template, model 2 *(Pej)* blindly followed model 3 *(Pej)* rigid person incapable of independent judgment 4 *(Pej Fig)* ilk 5 exemplar of a type: bar (of soap), ear (of corn)
II § *adv* 1 just as it should be, to the exact fit 2 *(Pej)* on the basis of surface judgements, in a shallow way
∘ **i fut· (gjërat) në kallëpe** *(Pej)* to put (things) into pigeonholes; think dogmatically
∘ **kallëp këpucësh** shoe last, shoe tree
∘ **të një kallëpi** *(Pej)* of a feather, alike

****kallës** *nm* 1 slanderer 2 plunger

kallëz *nf* husk of grain

kallëza *np* 1 <**kallëz** 2 scattered grain left by reapers: gleanings

kallëzambledhës *n* gleaner (of grain)

kallëzim *nm ger* 1 <**kallëzo·n** 2 narration 3 denunciation, denouncement

kallëzimtar
I § *adj* 1 tattling, talebearing 2 *(Old)* [*Lit*] narrative
II § *n* tattler, tattletale

kallëzo·n
I § *vt* 1 to narrate, tell 2 to tell/tattle on []
II § *vi* 1 to report, show 2 (of grain) to form a spike

kallëzor *adj* [*Ling*] accusative

kallëzore *nf* [*Ling*] accusative case

kallëzues *nm* 1 tattler; denouncer 2 [*Ling*] predicate

kallëzuesor
I § *nm* [*Ling*] predicate complement
II § *adj* of the predicate; functioning as a predicate

kallfë *nf* apprentice

kalli(r) *nm (np ~ nj)* 1 head of grain: ear, spike 2 [*Bot*] elongated inflorescence: spike 3 shank (of a leg or of a stocking) 4 forearm
∘ **ësh·të kalli** to have nothing left, be flat broke
∘ **kalli e killë** well-filled out spike/cob of grain; plentiful grain harvest
∘ **kalli pa bukë** "spike of grain without a kernel" *(Pej)* person who is nothing but show, all fluff and no substance

kalliartë *adj (Poet)* golden-spiked

kalligjatë *adj* having a long spike

kalligjerë *adj* having spikes spread wide

kallihollë *adj* having thin spikes

kallimadh *adj* having large spikes

kallimbledhës *n* = **kallambledhës**

kallinj *np* <**kalli**

kalliplotë *adj* heavy with grain, loaded with grain

kallirëndë *adj* heavy with grain, loaded with grain

kallir *i obl* <**kalli(r)**

****kallis·** = **kall·**

kallishtë *nf* stunted ear of corn

kallje *nf ger* <**kall·**, **kall·et**

kallkan *nm* 1 *(Colloq)* ice, icicle 2 loft of a building 3 room partition 4 *(Reg)* shield 5 *(Reg)* gate bolt

kallkanos· *vt (Colloq)* 1 to turn [] to ice 2 *(Fig)* to cause [] to freeze to death

kallkanos·et *vpr (Colloq)* 1 to turn to ice, become ice 2 *(Fig)* to freeze to death

kallkanosur *adj (i) (Colloq)* = **akulluar**

kallkantë *adj (i) (Colloq)* = **akullt**

kallm *nm* 1 *(Reg)* [*Bot*] cattail, reed mace *(Typha)* 2 tall grass of the wetlands with a hollow, jointed stalk: reed, cane, rush 3 thin hollow stalk, straw 4 rolling pin 5 leg-warmer; shank of a stocking 6 strip of land planted in vegetables
∘ **kallm i egër** [*Bot*] false carrot *(Calamagrotis pseudophragmites)*

****kallminj** *np* <**kallm** reeds, rushes

kallmishtë *nf* 1 = **kallamishte** 2 = **kallminj**

****kallmo·n** *vt* to sweep away []

****kallmore** *np fem* [*Bot*] cattail family *Typhaceae*

kallni *nf* thick stew of meat

kallnor *nm (Old)* January

kallo *nf* callus, corn, bunion

kallogre *nf* 1 Orthodox nun 2 *(Colloq)* pitiful woman left without family

kallogrinjë *nf* = **kallogre**

kallogjer *nm* 1 Orthodox monk 2 *(Pej)* man leading a withdrawn life

****kalloshtë** *nf* corncob

kallp
I § *adj (Colloq)* 1 counterfeit, false 2 fraudulent 3 without foundation, lacking basis; of no value, worthless
II § *nm* slab, block, bar

****kallpabâs** *nm (Reg Gheg)* = **kallpazan**

kallpak *nm (Old)* tall cap made of lamb fleece

kallpazan *n (Pej)* counterfeiter, forger

****kallpuer** *adj (fem ~ ore) (Old)* stereotyped

kallume *nf (Reg)* 1 big pile, tall heap 2 cesspool

kallumë *nf* [*Naut*] keel

kallumshor *adj* shaped in a tall heap

kam *1st sg pres* <**ka·** I have
∘ **aty/këtu e kam** that's precisely it! that's the point!

****kamahi** *nf* frozen snow on plants

****kamalec** *nm* 1 [*Entom*] = **karkalec** 2 = **kambalec**

kamalle *nf* burrow, foxhole

kamare *nf* 1 wall niche, alcove 2 small opening over an arch of a bridge 3 *(Reg)* brood nest for poultry: hen roost = **furrik** 4 ship cabin

kamarier *n* = **kamerier**

kamaroshë *nf* [*Bot*] geranium *(Geranium)*

kamastër *nf* fireplace chain for holding pothook

kamatar *n* lender of money at interest: usurer

kamatari *nf* lending of money at interest: usury

kamatë *nf* 1 interest on borrowed money 2 banking charge 3 penalty fee for lateness

kamatëmarrës *n* one who receives interest from loans: moneylender

kamatëmarrje *nf* receiving interest from loans: moneylending

kamatëpagues *nm* payer of money borrowed at interest

kamatëvonesë *nf* interest charged for overdue payments

****kamati** *nf* frame

****kambadoras** *adv* on all fours, on hands and knees

****kâmbajkë** *nf (Reg Gheg)* treadle

kambalec *nm* 1 stand (on a bicycle/motorcycle) 2 scaffolding

kambanar *n* bell ringer

****kambanarë** = **kambanore**

****kambanec** *nm* 1 pedestrian 2 person who limps

kamba·në
I § nf 1 loud bell; church bell; warning/alarm bell 2 [Sport] gong 3 [Spec] bell jar
II § adj having a very loud resonating sound: booming
○ **duhen dëgjuar të dyja kambanat** both sides of the story should be heard
○ **të gjithë i bien një kambane** everyone tells the same story
○ **kambana e vdekjes** the death knell

kamba·nëz nf 1 (Pet Dimin) little bell 2 small bell jar 3 [Bot] bellflower (Campanula)

kamban·or adj 1 bell-shaped 2 [Bot] campanulate

kamban·ore
I § nf belltower, belfry
II § np [Bot] bellflower family Campanulaceae

*__kâmba·shína__ np (Reg Gheg) woolen socks worn as slippers

*__kâmba·tí__ nf (Reg Gheg) structure erected on supports

*__kamba·tís·__ vt [Constr] to prop [] up, support

*__kamba·tísje__ nf 1 [Constr] < kambatís· 2 supporting structure

*__kâmbc__ nm (Reg Gheg) support, stand, rest

*__kâmbcar__ nm (Reg Gheg) legging worn by women

*__kâmbe__ nf (Reg Gheg) andiron

*__kamberícë__ nf place of ambush: covert

kambe·se nf (Reg Gheg) 1 treadle on a loom 2 foot stuck out to trip someone 3 protective felt pad protecting a pipemaker lap

*__kâmbgjith·kurí__ adv (Reg Gheg)

kambia·l nm [Fin] secured note: bill of exchange

ka·mbio OR **ka·mbjo** nf 1 [Tech] gearbox 2 rate of exchange (for money)

*__kâmbís·__ (Reg Gheg) = këmbatís·

*__kâmbít·et__ vpr (Reg Gheg) 1 to lean, loll 2 to shuffle (one's feet)

kambi·zëm nm money exchange

*__kâmbj__ (Reg Gheg) = këmb

Kamboxhia nf Cambodia

kamboxhia·n adj, n Cambodian

kambri·k nm cambric

*__kamçík__ = kamxhík

*__kame__ nf coulter

kameleo·n nm 1 chameleon 2 (Contempt) person whose convictions and behavior change to suit his advantage

kamelí·në nf [Bot] false flax, gold of pleasure Camelina sativa

kamerdar·e nf inner tube; rubber bladder inside a ball

kamer·e nf 1 camera oscura 2 camera
○ **kamera me mulli** [Cine] turret motion camera

kamerí·e nf 1 upper story outdoor flowerbox 2 seat of a student desk; stool with back support

kamerie·r nm waiter (in a restaurant)

kamerie·re nf waitress

*__kamestër__ nf (Reg Gheg) = këmbestër

ka·më nf double-edged dagger carried in a scabbard as a sidearm

kam·ës
I § n wealthy person
II § adj financially well off: wealthy

*__kamësí__ = kamje

*__kâmëz__ (Reg Gheg) = këmbëz

*__kamfo·rë__ OR **kamfu·rë** nf = kamfur

ka·mfur nm [Pharm] camphor

*__kamfura__ nf = kamfur

*__kamíle__ nf camel = gamíle

kamilla·f nm cylindrical miter worn by Orthodox priests and monks

*__kamillopardha·llë__ nf (Old) giraffe = gjirafë

*__kamine__ nf lime pit

kamin·etë nf small portable stove

kamí·në nf 1 kiln 2 blacksmith's hearth 3 pile, heap

kamio·n nm truck, lorry
○ **kamion vetëshkarkues** dump truck

kamí·sh nm long-stemmed pipe (for smoking tobacco)

kamja·llë nf grain stubble

*__kamje__ nf three-legged trivet in a fireplace

ka·mje nf wealth; assets; property

ka·mnë nf [Bot] small-flowered fumitory (Fumaria parviflora)

kamomi·l nm [Bot] wild camomile, German camomile (Matricaria chamomilla)

kamo·sh nm chamois leather, chamois skin

kamo·shë nf [Zool] chamois
○ **kamoshë fushe** *= antilopë [Zool] antelope

kamo·shtë adj (i) made of chamois leather

kamo·tshëm adj (i) (Colloq) age-old, ancient, of long ago

kamp nm 1 camp 2 (Colloq Euph) prison camp
○ **kamp shfarosje** extermination camp

kampanulace np fem bellflower family Campanulaceae

*__kampeqí__ nm [Bot] logwood, campeachy (Haematoxylon campechianum) = bakëm

kampio·n nm 1 champion 2 [Spec] sample

kampiona·t nm championship

kampi·st n camper

kampu·lëz nm (Reg) = mjedër

*__kamso·r__ (Reg Gheg) = këmbësorrë

*__kamshík__ nm = kamxhík

kamufli·m nm ger 1 < kamuflo·n, kamuflo·het 2 camouflage

kamuflo·het vpr to conceal one's intentions

kamuflo··n vt to camouflage, disguise, conceal

kamuflua·r adj (i) 1 camouflaged, concealed 2 (Fig) with concealed intentions

ka·mur adj (i) wealthy, rich

kamxhík nm 1 whip 2 [Biol] flagellum ()

kamxhiko··n vt 1 to whip 2 (Fig) to lash out against [faults and failings]

kamxhiko·rë np [Zool] flagellatae lucius

kamzhík nm = kamxhík

Kanada nf Canada

kanade·z
I § adj Canadian
II § n native of Canada

kanade·z adj, n Canadian

kanaka·r adj, n pet, favorite

kana·l nm 1 canal 2 channel 3 [Med] duct
○ **kanal i ujrave të zeza** sewer, sewage canal

kanal·gërm·ues
I § adj used for digging canals
II § nm canal-digging machine

kanal·ha·pës nm canal-digging machine

kanaliq *nm* extender into which a knitting needle can be inserted to give extra length

kanalizim *nm ger* 1 <**kanalizo·n** 2 canalization; drainage
　∘ **kanalizimi i ujrave të zeza** sewerage

kanalizo·n *vt* to channelize

kanalith *nm* [*Med*] tubule

kaname *nf* small circular pot, usually made of copper

****kanap** *nm* hemp = **kërp**

kanape *nf* 1 long low wooden bench with a back: couch 2 [*Food*] canapé

****kanar** = **kanarinë**

kanarinë *nf* [*Ornit*] canary

****kanarqis·** *vt* (*Old*) to plot, contrive

kanat
　I § *nm* 1 shutter 2 leaf of a door 3 side leaf of a cart/ wagon 4 panel of a blouse
　II § *adv* totally, completely
　∘ **kanat dyfletësh** double-leafed shutter

kanatiere *nf* = **kanotiere**

kanavacë *nf* 1 canvas; canvas stiffening use as interlining for clothes 2 (*Reg*) thin towel

kanavetë *nf* 1 small box for keeping valuables 2 (*Reg*) suitcase *3 drawer = **sirtar**

****kanavur** *nm* hempseed

kancelar *nm* chancellor

kancelari *nf* 1 chancellery, office of the chancellor 2 embassy 3 stationery

kancer *nm* [*Med Veter*] cancer

kancerogjen *adj* [*Med*] carcinogenic

kancerollog *nm* [*Med*] cancer specialist

kanceroz *adj* [*Med*] cancerous

KANÇ *abbrev* <**Këshilli Antifashist Nacional-çlirimtar** [*Hist*] Anti-fascist National Liberation Council

****kançë** = **kanxhë**

****kandak** *nm* gun butt = **kondak**

kandar *nm* 1 spring balance, steelyard 2 (*Fig Colloq*) precise measurement, precise and careful calculation
　∘ **s'[]ço·n**[3sg]/**he q·**[3sg]/**mba·n**[3sg]**ngre·**[3sg] **kandari** 1 [] *is* too heavy/big; [] *is* excessive 2 [] *is* totally unacceptable

kandelë *nf* [*Tech*] spark plug

****kândle** (*Reg Gheg*) = **ëndle**

kandër *nf* narrow-necked painted container with a capacity of about a quart of oil

kandërr *nf* insect

kandërrngrënës *adj, nm* insectivore

kandidat *nm* candidate
　∘ **kandidat i shkencave** academic degree (awarded after 5-7 years of postgraduate research or study) requiring extensive examinations and publication of at least two articles: doctor of science, doctor of philosophy

kandidaturë *nf* candidacy, candidature

kandil *nm* 1 oil lamp 2 [*Invert*] jellyfish, sea nettle
　∘ **kandil deti** [*Invert*] jellyfish, sea nettle

kandilenaft *nm* verger, sacristan, sexton

kandiler *nm* candelabra, chandelier, candle holder

kandillonaft *nm* person who lights the candles in church, candle-lighter

kandis·
　I § *vt* to persuade, convince
　II § *vi* to make up one's mind about [], decide

kandis·et *vpr* to make up one's mind

****kândje** (*Reg Gheg*) = **ëndje**

****kând** (*Reg Gheg*) = **kënd**

kandos· *vt* to find [] by searching; manage to put in order

kanelë *nf* [*Tech*] welding torch

kanellë *nf* [*Bot*] cinnamon

****kanep** *nm* hemp = **kërp**

kanepngrënës *nm* [*Ornit*] linnet (*Carduelis cannabina*)

kanë *nf* water jug/can

kanë
　I § *3rd pl pres* <**ka·** they have
　II § *sg acc def* <**ka** the ox

****kâng** (*Reg Gheg*) = **këng**

kangur *nm* [*Zool*] kangaroo

****kanguro** *nf* [*Zool*] = **kangur**

kangjele *nf(Reg Arb)* [*Lit*] canto in a long poem

kangjella *np* balustrade

****kangjellar** (*Old*) = **kancelar**

****kângj** (*Reg Gheg*) = **këndes**

kanibal *nm* 1 [*Hist*] cannibal 2 (*Pej*) bestial, barbarous

kanibalizëm *nm* 1 [*Hist*] cannibalism 2 (*Pej*) bestiality, barbarism

kanicë *nf* sheath for a knife or dagger

kanike *nf* small temporary thatched hut built by a shepherd or by a vineyard guard

kanion *nm* canyon

kanisk *nm (np ˜ qe)* 1 [*Ethnog*] gift of bread sent by the groom to the bride during the wedding-week 2 gift

kanistër *nf* 1 round and shallow two-handled wicker basket 2 disk-shaped device made of wicker or goat-hair macramé used to press olives 3 straw weaving made by children as wall decoration

kanoçe *nf* 1 small hut 2 metal canister

****kanoe** *nf* [*Sport*] canoe

kanon *nm* cannon, gun

****kanonar** *n* gunner

kanonierë *nf* [*Mil*] gunboat

kanonik *adj* [*Relig*] canonic

kanonizo·n *vt* to canonize

kanos· *vt* to menace, threaten; pose a menace/threat to, endanger

kanos·et *vpr* to make menacing gestures, be threatening, make a threat; pose a menace/threat

kanosës *adj* menacing, threatening

kanosi *nf* threatening/menacing situation: threat, menace

kanosjar *nm* [*Hist*] 1 person appointed secretly by village elders to keep watch over farmland 2 member of the council of elders who imposed fines for damages

kanosje *nf ger* = **kërcënim**

****kanosqar** *nm (Old)* 1 outpost, patrol 2 = **kanosjar**

kanotazh *nm* [*Sport*] rowing

kanotierë *nf* undershirt (sleeveless)

****kanoz** *nm* walnut smoothed for playing with

****kanp** *nm* = **kërp**

****kanpashë** *nf* [*Zool*] = **kanushë**

****kanqellar** = **kancelar**

*kantalio·n *nm* [*Bot*] centaury, drug centaurium *Centaurium umbellatum* = **trikë**

*kanta·r *nm* [*Entom*] soldier beetle (*Cantharidae*)

kanta·të *nf* **1** [*Mus*] cantata **2** [*Lit*] solemn lyric poem inspired by a important historical event

*ka·ntër *nf (Old)* wharf

kantie·r *nm* work place, workshop
  ○ **kantier detar** shipyard
  ○ **kantier ndërtimi** construction site

*kantikaçík *adv* on one foot

kantí·në *nf* **1** cool storage cellar for beverages, wine cellar ***2** basket

kanto·n *nm* canton

*kanu·l *nm* shuttle (on a loom)

kanu·n *nm* **1** [*Hist*] the body of unwritten laws and traditional customs that governed former Albanian life: Canon **2** *(Old)* law = **ligj**

kanuna·r *adj* = **kanuno·r**

*kanu·nët *adj (i)* according to the Canon; canonic

*kanuní·k *nm (Old)* prebendary, canon

*kanuní·sht *adv (Old)* according to the Canon

kanunizí·m *nm ger* **1** <**kanunizo·**·*n* **2** canonization

kanunizo··*n* *vt (Book)* **1** to incorporate [] into the canon: canonize **2** to treat [] dogmatically; treat as if cast in stone

kanuno·r *adj* canonic; according to the traditional Canon

kanuno·re *nf (Old)* body of laws and customs that govern a society or institution; regulatory code

kanu·shë *nf* [*Ornit*] stork = **lejle·k**

ka·nxhë *nf* **1** hook **2** fireplace poker with a hook at the end **3** (*Colloq*) [*Naut*] anchor **4** anchors driven into telephone poles or lamp posts to aid in climbing

kanxhí·m *nm* [*Naut*] anchorage, anchoring

kanje·lë *nf* barrel tap; bung

kanju·shë *nf* [*Ornit*] = **kanu·shë**

kaolí·n *nm* kaolin, clay for porceline

kao·s *nm* chaos, confusion

kaotí·k *adj* chaotic

ka·p-
  I § *vt* **1** to catch, grasp, grab, seize, clutch **2** to capture **3** to comprise; include **4** to catch up with [], overtake **5** to get to []: reach **6** *(Fig)* to perceive, get
  II § *vt, vi* **1** to touch **2** to start
  ○ **ia kap· anën** to get a hold on <*a matter*>, find the best way to approach <>
  ○ **s'**[] **kap· as sharra, as lima** "neither a saw nor a file could bite into []" (there's not enough there to saw, let alone file) [] *has* nothing to []'s name, [] *is* dirt poor
  ○ <> **kap·**.*3sg* **dora** <> *has* a tendency to take things that don't belong to <>: <> *has* sticky fingers
  ○ **ia kap· fillin** to get a hold on <*a matter*>, find the best way to approach <>
  ○ [] **kap·**.*3sg* **gjumi** [] *falls* asleep
  ○ **kap· ik**ë**n** to run away, flee
  ○ [] **kap·**.*3sg* **kalemi për ters** to have it in for []
  ○ [] **kap·**.*3sg* **kalemi** [] *is* selected/chosen arbitrarily; good/bad luck *falls* to [] completely by chance
  ○ **Kape laro, prite balo** "Catch it, Spot; grab it, Fido." *(Tease)* It looks like a circus in there with all that noise and confusion.

  ○ **e kap· lepurin/dhelprën me qerre** "catches the hare/fox with a cart" to be able to accomplish difficult tasks without wasteful haste: have a quiet but steady competence
  ○ [] **kap· me presh në dorë** to catch [] red-handed
  ○ [] **kap· me** {*plural noun*} to land blows on [] with {}
  ○ [] **kap· më** {*plural noun*} to land blows on [] with {}
  ○ [] **kap· ndër lakra** to catch [] red-handed
  ○ [] **kap· në zarar** to catch [] red-handed, catch [] in the act
  ○ [] **kap· në** {*plural noun*} to land blows on [] with {}
  ○ [e] **kap· nga bishti** to go about [] in the wrong way, start [] off wrong
  ○ [] **kap· nga veshi** "grab [] by the ear" to give [] a severe scolding, chastise [] strongly
  ○ [] **kap· ngushtë** to catch [] unprepared
  ○ **s'**[] **kap· njeri me dorë/për bishti** "no one takes [] by the hand/tail" no one *is* interested in []
  ○ **nuk ia kap· perin lëmshit** "not grab the end of the ball of thread" not find a starting point for unraveling a complicated matter: not know where to start in solving the mess, not be able to get a handle on it
  ○ **nuk** <>**a kap·**.*3sg* **pëllëmba** "<>'s palm does not span it" **1** <> *has* no standard by which to measure it **2** there *is* no way for <> to do it
  ○ [] **kap· për degësh** to treat [] by looking at unimportant components
  ○ [] **kap· për rrënjësh e jo për degësh** "grab [] by the roots and not by the branches" to go right to the heart of [the problem]
  ○ [] **kap· për fyti/gryke** to put heavy pressure on []
  ○ <> **kap· për mëngë** "grab <>'s sleeve" to remind <> persistently (of one's request), keep pulling at <>
  ○ [] **kap· për palltoje** "grab [] by the overcoat" to remind [] persistently of one's request, keep pulling at []
  ○ [] **kap· për veshi** "grab [] by the ear" to give [] a severe scolding, chastise [] strongly
  ○ [] **kap· prej jake** to compel/coerce []
  ○ [] **kap·**.*3pl* **qipujt** "the goblins *grab* []" [] *is* possessed by demons; [] *flies* into a rage?
  ○ [e] **kap· së prapi** to go about [] in the wrong way, start [] off wrong
  ○ <>[] **kap·**.*3sg* **veshi** "<>'s ear *catches* []" <> *hears* [] in passing, <> *happens* to hear [], <> accidentally *hears* []
  ○ [] **kap·**.*3pl* **xhindet** "the jinni *grab* []" [] *is* possessed by demons; [] *flies* into a rage?

ka·p·*et* *vpr* **1** to extend the hand in a grasping motion **2** to come to blows/grips: grapple, fight **3** to climb up **4** to latch/hang/hold on **5** to begin to regain one's economic well-being: get back on one's feet
  ○ **kap·***et* **me** [] to pick on [] unfairly
  ○ **kap·***et* **pas** <> to hang/hold/latch on to <>; stick to <>
  ○ **kap·***et* **pas fijes së perit/flokut/kashtës** to rest on an unsound basis, be built on sand; be grasping at straws, have vain hopes
  ○ **kap·***et* **pas fjalësh/fjalësh** to give undue emphasis to words grabbed out of context
  ○ **kap·***et* **për fyti/gryke me** [] to quarrel/fight bitterly with []

○ **S'kapet qielli me dorë.** "The sky cannot be grasped by the hand." *(Prov)* That is an impossible proposal. No way!

○ **kap·***et pas shkumëve/për shkume* to be wasting one's effort

kapacitet *nm* capacity

kapadai *nm (Colloq)* conceited braggart

kapadaillëk *nm (np ~ qe) (Colloq)* bragging, blustering

kapadaillëqe *np (Colloq)* <**kapadaillëk**

kapak *nm* **1** lid, cover **2** wrapper, cover

○ **kapak floriri** "lid of gold" the best possible outcome

○ **kapaku i fytit** [*Anat*] uvula

○ **kapaku i gjurit** kneecap

○ **kapak i kafkës** [*Med*] calvarium

○ **kapaku i kokës** braincap

○ **kapak syri** eyelid

kapakllie *nf (Old)* old-fashioned gun loaded through a lidded opening in the breech

*****kapallis·** *vt* = kaplo·n

kapama *nf* [*Food*] **1** dish made by browning meat in a sauce and then boiling it in water and wine **2** rice dish made with lamb and spices

kapan *nm* steelyard

kapanxhë *nf* trap door

kapar *nm* [*Fin*] down payment, earnest money

kapardis·*et vpr* **1** to sit insolently with limbs in improperly casual position **2** to brag, boast

○ **kapardis·***et si maçoku në thekër* "prance around like a tomcat in the rye" to strut around showing off

○ **kapardis·***et si gjeli/këndesi/kaposhi majë plehut* to strut like a rooster on a pile of manure, make a fool of oneself trying to show off

○ **kapardis·***et si qeni në qerre* "stretch out like a dog on a cart" to act like a big shot

kapardisje *nf ger* <**kapardis·***et*

kapardisur *adj (i)* **1** all dressed up as if going to a party **2** swaggering

kaparo·n *vt* = kaparos

kaparos· *vt* to make a down payment on [ ]

kaparosje *nf ger* <**kaparos·**

kaparosur *adj (i)* assured by the giving of a down payment

kaparthi *adv*

kaparuar *adj (i)* = kaparosur

kapasë *nf* **1** large clay vat for oil or flour **2** = vorbë

kapastër *nf* [*Bot*] sugar maple *(Acer dasycarpum)*

*****kapatruc** *adj* contracted, crumpled up

kapcel· *vt* to patch/caulk [a leaky wooden water jug]

kapcele *nf* patch of leather or ground pine bark used to plug leaks in a wooden water jug

*****kapeçul** *nm* [*Astron*] Big Dipper

kapedan

I § *n* **1** *(Old)* commander of a military unit; brave commandant **2** *(Fig)* brave person **3** *(Colloq)* ship captain **4** [*Hist*] = bajraktar

II § *adj* brave, courageous

kapelabërës *n* hat maker: hatter

kapelapunues *nm* = kapelabërës

kapelashitës *n* hat seller

kapelexhi *nm* = kapelabërës

kapelë *nf* **1** hat; cap with a brim **2** cap shape

○ **kapelë kineze** [*Invert*] Chinese hat (mollusc) *Calyptraea chinensis*

○ **kapelë republike** felt hat with a high crown and a brim: Stetson; top hat, derby, bowler

*****kapellxhi** *nm (np ~ nj)* [*Bot*] puffball fungus

kapë *nf* **1** = kapelë **2** sheaf of grain **3** rubber nipple, pacifier

kapëllo·n *vt* to overcome

kapërce·het *vpr* **1** to swallow **2** (of animals) to mate sexually

kapërce·n

I § *vt* **1** to get [ ] over/across a barrier, cross; overcome, surmount **2** to surpass **3** to manage to get [ ] down, swallow [food]

II § *vt, vi* to manage to pass [a period of time]

III § *vi (Impol)* to overstep the limits (of propriety): go too far

○ **e kapërce·n bregun** to go too far, overstep the limits

○ **e kapërce·n fjalën 1** to deliberately sidestep an issue **2** to change the subject on purpose

○ **e kapërce·n gardhin/hendekun/kapërcyellin/lumin/përruan/vaun** to overcome a difficulty

○ **e kapërce·n kufirin** to go too far, overstep the limits

○ **e kapërce·n lumin pa lagur këmbët** to escape without a scratch

○ **e kapërce·n masën** to go too far, overstep the limits

○ **<> kapërce·n^{3sg} mendja (e kokës)** <> loses <>'s mind, <> goes crazy

○ **kapërce·n piramidën** to cross the border

○ **e kapërce·n pragun** to go too far, overstep the limits

kapërcej *np* <**kapërcell**, kapërcyell

kapërcell *nm (np ~ j)* **1** passageway through a fence; turnstile over a fence; narrow passageway; mountain pass **2** *(Fig)* transitional period/phase **3** [*Anat*] gullet = gurmaz

kapërcim *nm ger* **1** <**kapërce·n**, kapërce·het [*Lit*] **2** enjambment

kapërcimthi *adv* by surmounting obstacles; by leaps and bounds; by a series of leaps = kalimthi

kapërcyell *nm* = kapërcell

kapërcyer *adj (i)* **1** (of an obstacle) overcome **2** *(Impol Colloq)* loony; out of one's mind

kapërcyes *nm* passageway through a fence

kapërcyeshëm *adj (i)* surmountable, passable, traversable

*****kapërdak** *nm (Old)* cylinder

kapërderdhës *nm* overflow discharge in a dam or dike: spillway

kapërdi·het *vpr* **1** to tumble **2** to swallow

kapërdi·n *vt* to swallow; gulp [ ] down without chewing

kapërdimje *nf* [*Gymnastics*] headlong fall, tumble, somersault

kapërdimthi *adv* down headfirst

kapërto·n *vt* = kapto·n

*****kapërton** *nm* = koperton

kapërthe·het *vpr* **1** to grapple **2** to become all entangled/interwoven **3** to be overloaded with work

kapërthe·n *vt* **1** to clutch; entangle, bind **2** (of an emotion) to overwhelm and hold [ ], take [ ] over

○ **kapërthe·n duart** to intertwine one's fingers

kapërthim *nm ger* <**kapërthe·n**, kapërthe·het

kapërx|e·n *vt* = **kapërce·n**

ka'p|ës
I § *nm* **1** pump **2** clothespin; hairclip, hairpin
II § *n* catcher
III § *adj* *seizing, grasping, holding; prehensile

kap'ëse *nf* device for holding something in place: clasp, clamp, clip
  ○ **kapëse flokësh** hairpin
  ○ **kapëse rrobash** clothespin

ka'p|ëz *nf* **1** handle (of a bladed instrument); hilt **2** armful of grain, sheaf **3** rubber nipple **4** [*Tech*] clamping device, clamp **5** [*Electr*] clamp used to make electrical contact: alligator clip

kapíce
I § *nf* **1** pile (of wood), heap **2** (*Old*) crocheted and embroidered cap worn by brides ***3** knitted white cap; cap worn by Montenegrins **4** armful of grain, sheaf
II § *adv* in a heap

kapida'n = **kapeda'n**

kapi'n|ë *nf* [*Bot*] = **manafe'rrë**

kapin|ok *nm* [*Bot*] horehound, white horehound (*Marrubium vulgare*)

kap'is| *stem for 1st sg pres, pl pres, 2nd & 3rd sg subj, pind* < **kapi't·**

kapista'll *nm* = **kapi'stër**

kapista'll·et *vpr* **1** to show off, get decked out **2** to wander around

kapi'stër *nf* halter (for controlling animals)

kapi't· *vt* **1** to wear [] out: overtire, overstrain **2** to cause/allow to droop

kapi't·et *vpr* **1** to be overtired, be worn out **2** to droop

kapita'l
I § *nm* **1** [*Econ*] capital **2** (*Colloq*) lots of money **3** capitalistic class; capitalism
II § *adj* **1** (*Book*) capital **2** [*Tech*] complete, full, general
  ○ **kapital i vdekur 1** [*Econ*] idle capital **2** (*Book*) idle thoughts **3** (*Book*) impractical idea

kapital|i'st
I § *n* **1** capitalist **2** (*Colloq*) very rich person
II § *adj* capitalistic

kapital|i'zëm *nm* [*Econ*] capitalism

***kapita'n** = **kapeda'n**

kapitaneri' *nf* captain's office (of a ship or a harbor)

kapite'l *nm* [*Archit*] capital (of a column)

kapite'n *nm* captain
  ○ **kapiten i parë** [*Mil*] highest level captain, senior captain

kapi't|ës *adj* extremely tiring, exhausting

kapi'tje *nf ger* **1** < **kapi't·**, **kapi't·et** **2** weariness, lassitude

kapi'tu|ll *nm* (*np* ~ *j*) chapter

kapitull|i'm *nm ger* **1** < **kapitullo'·n** **2** capitulation

kapitull|o'·n *vi* to capitulate

kapitull|u'e|s *adj, n* (cowardly person) who capitulates easily, who is quick to surrender

kapi'tur *adj* (*i*) **1** extremely tired, worn out, exhausted **2** drooping

ka'p|je *nf ger* **1** < **ka'p·**, **ka'p·et** [*Sport*] **2** pin (scoring a point in wrestling)
  ○ **kapje çengel** [*Weightlifting*] hooking grip

kapl|i'm *nm ger* < **kaplo'·n**, **kaplo'·het**

kapl|i's· = **kaplo'·n**

kapl|o'·het *vpr* **1** to become covered all over **2** to appear suddenly and spread everywhere

kapl|o'·n
I § *vt* **1** to cover [] with the wings and nestle down; weigh down on [] while covering; cover [] completely; enshroud **2** to overpower; overwhelm
II § *vi* to appear suddenly and spread all over, surge forth

kaplo'q *nm* top part of the distaff on which the skein to be spun is placed; skein of wool or flax

kaplo'qe *nf* (*Impol*) **1** noggin, head, noodle **2** stupid person, pumpkin head

***kapl|u'em** *adj* (*i*) (*Reg Gheg*) overwhelmed, beset

kaplladi's| *stem for 1st sg pres, pl pres, 2nd & 3rd sg subj, pind* < **kaplladi't·**

kaplladi't· *vt* **1** to cover a quilt (for a bed) with a sheet **2** to cover [upholstery] with a piece of cloth; decorate [upholstery] with gold thread **3** to overwhelm, overpower **4** to clasp/sew [torn clothing] together **5** to plate

kaplla|i's| = **kaplladi's|**

***kaplla|i't·** = **kaplladi't·**

kaplla'n *nm* (*Old*) tiger (in folk tales)

***kapllat'** = **kapllad**

kapllu|çi'n *nf* felt pad protecting the neck of draft animals from chafing by the yoke

kapo'le *nf* **1** hood of wool felt **2** cover protecting a haystack from rain

kapora'ne *nf* men's plain short-sleeved jacket with a hood; plain jacket without tassels

kapo'sh *nm* **1** rooster, cock = **këndes** **2** (*Fig*) braggart, show-off **3** [*Entom*] large reddish ant = **kacagje'l** **4** popcorn **5** cross-stitch (in embroidery)
  ○ **kaposh deti** [*Zool*] = **gjel deti**
  ○ **kaposh i egër** [*Zool*] = **gjel i egër**
  ○ **kaposh shege** pomegranate section containing a cluster of seeds

kapo't|ë *nf* long heavy overcoat; military overcoat

kap|qie'll *nm* (*np* ~ *j*) skyscraper

kapria't|ë *nf* [*Constr*] = **qepra't|ë**

kapri'ç *nm* **1** caprice, whim, fancy ***2** busy woman

kapri'ço *OR* **kapri'ço'z** *adj* capricious, whimsical; headstrong, willful

kapro'll *nm* (*np* ~ *j*) [*Zool*] roebuck (*Capreolus capreolus*)

kapro'lle *nf* **1** [*Zool*] roe doe (*Capreolus capreolus*) **2** reddish-brown cow/goat with bent horns

***kapru'a|ll** *nm* (*obl* ~ *o'i*, *np* ~ *o'j*) = **kapro'll**

kaprro'ç
I § *nm* **1** = **kapro'll** **2** (*Fig*) strong and spry man
II § *adj* strong and spry

kaps *pred* with difficulty in defecation: constipated

kapsalli's| *stem for 1st sg pres, pl pres, 2nd & 3rd sg subj, pind* < **kapsalli't·**

kapsalli't· *vt* **1** to blink/flutter [the eyelids] **2** to narrow/half-close [the eyes] ***3** to wink

kapsalli'tje *nf ger* < **kapsalli't·**

***kapsi'** *nf* grape stem

kapsi's| *stem for 1st sg pres, pl pres, 2nd & 3rd sg subj, pind* < **kapsi't·**

kapsi't· *vt* **1** to winnow **2** = **kapsalli't·** ***3** to congest ***4** to dazzle [the eyes]

kapsi'tje *nf ger* < **kapsi't·**

kapsllëk *nm* constipation

*kapsoll nm = **kapsulë**

kapsollaqe nf [Hist] musket

kapsollë nf 1 [Mil] (cartridge) primer 2 metal eyelets for shoelaces 3 (FigImpolite) empty-headed person, idiot
○ **kapsollë detonuese** [Mil] blasting cap
○ **kapsollë ndezëse** [Mil] percussion cap

kapsulaçe = **kapsollaqe**

kapsulë nf 1 capsule 2 laboratory crucible
○ **kapsulë fishekësh** cartridge case

*kapshall = **kapsall**

*kapshatë = **kafshatë**

kapshëm adj (i) 1 graspable 2 (Fig) easily comprehensible

kapshitë nf [Bot] frog-bit (Hydrocharis morsus-ranae)

*kapsho·n = **kafsho·n**

kapshto·n vt to encompass

kapt nm 1 ditch in a field 2 field studded with ditches and embankments

*kaptej nm skinny person

kaptell nm 1 pommel of a packsaddle, saddle-bow 2 high front part of a cradle

kapter nm [Mil] sergeant

kaptë nf narrow path; defile

kaptim nm ger 1 <**kapto·n**, **kapto·het** 2 = **kapërderdhës**

kaptinë nf 1 head; knob, bulb 2 top part 3 (Old) chapter (of a book)

kaptinëz nf [Bot] capitulum ()

kaptirë nf wood screw

kapto·het vpr to get food down: swallow

kapto·n
I § vt 1 to cross over [], go/cross over [] 2 to surpass = **kapërce·n**
II § vi (of the sun or moon) to set

*kaptyell = **kaptell**

kapth nm narrow mountain trail

kapua nm (obl ˜ oi, np ˜ onj) [Zool] = **kaposh**

*kapuc = **kapuçe**

kapucar n (Old Pej) 1 private detective, gumshoe 2 person who informs on another: stool pigeon, spy

kapucari nf (Old Pej) 1 private detective work 2 spying

kapuç nm 1 hood of a cloak/coat/jacket 2 brimless cap that tapers to a point on top; object shaped like such a cap 3 popcorn 4 cigarette filter *5 cigarette butt
○ **kapuçi i cigares** ash on a lit cigarette
○ **kapuçi i gjurit** [Anat] kneecap
○ **kapuçi kundragazit** gas mask

kapuçambrojtas adv

kapuças adv

kapuçashkelmas adv

kapul I § nm OR **kapule** II § nf 1 sheaf (of grain) 2 pile, heap

kapulan nm (Old) 1 leader of a quasi-military group 2 leader of the common people

kapule nf 1 sheaves of grain standing together in a stack 2 heap, pile

*kapuletë nf monk's robe

kapulis stem for 1st sg pres, pl pres, 2nd & 3rd sg subj, pind <**kapulit·**

kapulit· vt = **pulit·**

kapulit·et vpr = **pulit·et**

*kapullo·n vt = **kaplo·n**

*kapun adj (i) (Reg Gheg) (of plants) blighted, under attack

*kapuxhak nm drawer (in furniture)

kaq adv, quant 1 this much/many, so much/many, so 2 only this much/many; only so much/many; so few/little
○ **kaq dua!** that's exactly what I need, I don't need anything more
○ **kaq gjë** so little/few (as this)
○ **kaq mend ka·!** that's how much sense {} has!
○ **kaq e pati!** well that's the end of that
○ **kaq _, sa _** so/such _ that _
○ **kaq tepër** so much

kaqol nm 1 large walnut thrown in a children's game 2 (Fig Pet) little idiot

kar nm (Colloq Crude) (penis) prick, cock

kara nm (Old) very dark horse 2 pigeon with very dark plumage

karabina nf framework, framing (of a house)

karabinë nf carbine

karabinier nm 1 Italian policeman during the occupation of Albania 2 carbineer; sharpshooter, marksman

karabinieri nf 1 infantry 2 police force during Italian occupation of Albania: carabinieri

*karabishte nf [Entom] earwig

karabobe nf [Bot] = **kalibobë**

karabojë nf 1 dark dye for leather 2 green fungicidal solid soluble in water, used to spray the trees

karabot nm [Bot] caraway (Carum carvi)

karabullak nm 1 [Ornit] cormorant (Phalacrocorax carbo L.) 2 [Ornit] pygmy cormorant (Phalacrocorax pygmaeus Pall.) 3 (Fig) big lout/oaf
○ **karabullak deti** [Ornit] cormorant Phalacrocorax carbo L.
○ **karabullak me çafkë** [Ornit] shag Phalacrocorax aristotelis L., Pelicanus Graculus L.

Karaburun nm name of a mountainous peninsula in southwestern Albania

karabush nm 1 [Bot] panicle 2 empty corncob 3 (Fig) blockhead, dolt

karadake nf (Old) six-shooter, large revolver

karadrinë nf [Entom] small mottled willow moth (Laphygma exigua Hb.)

karadyzen nm (Old) [Mus] small mandolin-like instrument with two or four strings

*karaf = **karav**

karafil nm 1 [Bot] carnation; pink 2 clove (spice) 3 (Pej) flighty person

karafilore np fem [Bot] family of pinks Caryophyllaceae

karafkopë nf perforated iron slab used by coppersmiths to make nails

karagjoz nm clown; buffoon

karagjozllëk nm (np ˜ qe) buffoonery

Karaibe np Caribbean Islands, Caribbees

Karaibik adj, nm Caribbean (Sea)

karajfile nf (Old) long flintstone musket

karajpel nm [Bot] tansy (Tanacetum vulgare)

*karakaçe nf [Ornit] = **laraskë**

karakafte nf [Bot] snake's head iris, widow iris (Hermadactylis tuberosus) *karaka'skë nf [Ornit] magpie (Pica pica L.) = lara'skë

karakati'në nf hovel; jalopy

karake'skë nf [Ornit] common jay (Garrulus glandarius)

karako'll nm (Old) 1 [Mil] sentry box 2 sentry, sentinel 3 guard troops, guard

karakte'r nm character

karakteristi'k adj characteristic

karakteristi'kë nf 1 characteristic, distinctive character 2 official document assessing an individual's moral, social, political and work reputation

karakterizi'm nm ger 1 <karakterizo' ·n, karakterizo' ·het 2 characterization

karakterizo' ·het vpr to have a distinguishing characteristic; be/become distinctive

karakterizo' ·n vt to characterize

karaku'sh nm [Veter] laming disease of horses and mules manifested as swelling of the leg joints: greaseheels (bursitis)

karamanjo'llë nf (Old) guillotine-like mechanism used by the Ottoman Empire for capital punishment

karambo'l nm 1 carom (in billiards) 2 (Colloq) collision

karame'le nf caramel

*karanfi'l = karafi'l

karanti'në nf quarantine

karantino'r adj pertaining to a quarantine

*kara'nxhë nf [Entom] ant

kara'r nm (Colloq) 1 resolution, solution 2 settled condition: calm, respite 3 proper amount

kara's nm [Ichth] crucian carp (Carassius carassius)
  ∘ karasi i artë [Ichth] goldfish Carassius auratus gibelo

karaska'q adj shameless

karashti's· vt (Colloq) 1 to mix, stir 2 to turn [a sheaf of grain]

karashti's·et vpr = përzí·het

karashti'sje nf ger <karashti's·, karashti's·et

kara't nm carat (measurement of weight)

*karata'ne nf [Bot] nettle tree (Celtis australis) = cara'c

*kara'v nm boat

*karava't·et vpr to nod off

karave'le
  I § nf (Old) caravel
  II § adj round loaf of bread = çyre'k

kara'vë nf ship

karavi'dhe nf 1 crab-like crustacean: lobster; crab; shrimp 2 (Fig Pej) restless person who can't stay still and won't let others sit still
  ∘ karavidhe kanali [Invert] Norway lobster (Nephrops norvegicus)
  ∘ karavidhe lumi [Invert] freshwater crayfish (Astacus astacus)
  ∘ karavidhe xhuxhë [Invert] slipper lobster Scyllarus pygmaeus

karbi'd nm [Chem] carbide

karbi't nm [Chem] calcium carbide

karbohidra't nm [Biol Chem] carbohydrate

karbo'n nm 1 [Chem] carbon ((C)) 2 charcoal pencil 3 [Tech] carbon-arc electrode 4 (Colloq) carbon paper

karbona't nm 1 [Chem] carbonate ((COdu)) 2

∘ karbonat plumbi lead carbonate, white lead

karboni'k adj [Chem] carbonic

karbonizi'm nm ger (Book) 1 <karbonizo' ·n, karbonizo' ·het 2 carbonization

karbonizo' ·het vpr (Book) to become carbonized

karbonizo' ·n vt (Book) to carbonize

karbonizu'ar adj (i) (Book) carbonized

*karbu'n nm rabies, hydrophobia

karbu'r nm [Chem] carbide compound

karbura'nt nm motor fuel

karburato'r nm carburetor

karburizu'es adj, nm [Tech] carbonaceous (material)

*karci'(n) nm (pl ˜ j) (Reg Gheg) = karçi'n

*karcu'ell nm (obl ˜ olli) flowerpot

*karcye'll nm (obl ˜ elli, np ˜ ej) [Entom] locust

karçi'n nm weanling kid, yearling goat

*kardami'në nf [Bot] bitter cress (Cardamine)

karda'n nm [Tech] Cardan shaft

kardia'k
  I § adj [Med] cardiac
  II § n person with heart trouble

kardina'l
  I § nm cardinal in the Catholic church
  II § adj cardinal, main, fundamental

kardiokiru'rg n heart surgeon

kardiolo'g n cardiologist

kardiologji' nf cardiology

*kardhi'(n) nm (Reg Gheg) = ka'rthje

kare' adv (of hair) styled short all around but slightly longer in front

*kare'kllë nf (Reg) = karri'ge

kare'l nm [Spec] sliding carriage on a machine: carriage, saddle

*kare'm = karre'm

*kare'në nf [Naut] bilge

karfi'cë nf hairpin; safety pin; brooch

*karfjo'll nm (Reg Kos) cauliflower

karfo's· vt 1 to attach [a pin] 2 to sew loosely: baste 3 to attach [] tightly; grab by the throat 4 (Fig) to suppress 5 (Fig) (of an emotion/illness) to overwhelm

karfo's·et vpr 1 to stick close 2 to grapple 3 to be overwhelmed by an emotion/illness

karfo'sje nf ger <karfo's·, karfo's·et

kargati's· vt 1 to stretch 2 to make [] worse, aggravate *3 to stuff, cram *4 to numb, paralyze

*kargati's·et vpr to get stiff/numb/paralyzed

*karhân nm (Reg Gheg) = gërha'në

karie'rë nf rock quarry

ka'ries nm [Med] caries

*kari'ge = karri'ge

karikato'r nm [Mil] cartridge clip

karikatu'rë nf [Art] caricature; cartoon

karikaturi'st n [Art] caricaturist; cartoonist

karikaturizo' ·n vt to characterize

kari'q nm rectangular fishing net with corners tied to two crossed rods: lift net

*kari'qe nf follicle; seed capsule

*karje're nf career

karjo'llë nf 1 plank bed 2 (Reg) bed frame, bedstead

karkacu'l adj (Colloq Pej) 1 tall and skinny 2 dressed poorly, in rags; naked *3 goblin

karkalec *nm* **1** [*Entom*] grasshopper, locust **2** [*Invert*] prawn **3** (*Colloq Tech*) small excavator **4** (*Fig*) tall and skinny person; thin person who moves and jumps around

  ◦ **karkalec deti** [*Invert*] peneid shrimp (*Penaeus kerathurus*)

  ◦ **karkalec i egër** [*Invert*] squilla (*Squilla mantis*)

  ◦ **karkaleci i errët** "dark grasshopper" [*Entom*] *Chorthippus apricarius L.*

  ◦ **karkaleci flatrazi** "winged grasshopper" [*Entom*] *Stauroderus scalaris*

  ◦ **karkaleci këmbëgjatë** [*Entom*] kind of grasshopper *Acrotylus longipes*

  ◦ **karkalec i kuq** [*Invert*] deepwater prawn *Aristaeomorpha foliacea*

  ◦ **karkalec me mustaqe** [*Invert*] striped shrimp *Lysmata seticaudata*

  ◦ **karkaleci i ndryshueshëm** [*Entom*] *Chorthippus biguttulus*

  ◦ **karkaleci i ranishteve** [*Entom*] blue-winged locust *Sphingonotus coerulans*

  ◦ **karkalec rëre** [*Invert*] brown shrimp *Crangon crangon*

  ◦ **karkalec uji** [*Invert*] prawn

  ◦ **karkaleci i zakonshëm** [*Entom*] green grasshopper *Aiolopus thalassinus*

  ◦ **karkalec i zi** [*Entom*] band-winged grasshopper *Psophus stridulus L.*

*karkall** *nm* **1** tuft/crest on a bird's head **2** helmet

karkanaqe *nf* **1** [*Food*] cookie topped with butter and eggs before baking **2** [*Bot*] cyclamen

*karkanoqe** *nf* clump, clot

karkanxholl *nm* [*Folklore*] elf endowed with magic powers and clad in a shirt of mail

*karkanjoze** *nf* shallot

*karkapiq** *nm* deadly nightshade

*karkari** *nf* (*Old*) shark = **peshkaqen**

karkas *stem for 1st sg pres, pl pres, 2nd & 3rd sg subj, pind* <**karkat**·

karkasë *nf* [*Constr*] carcass, framework, skeleton frame

karkashinë *nf* **1** thin lamb or kid; runt *2 bushranger, highwayman

karkat· *vi* **1** to croak (like a frog) **2** (*ColloqImpolite*) to talk nonsense in a loud harsh voice

karkë *nf* overbaked tile

karkërimë *nf* dry and barren land full of stones = **bokërrimë**

*karkopje** *nf* apricot = **kajsi**

*karkore** *nf* (*Reg Tosk Old*) shark = **peshkaqen**

*karm** *nm* (*Old*) song, ode

karmë *nf* **1** rocky hill overlooking a body of water; barren cliffs **2** large heap of things

karmo·**het** *vpr* **1** to fall off a cliff **2** to descend a steep precipice

karmo·**n** *vt* **1** to expel [] rudely: kick [] out, give [] the boot **2** to knock [] down, demolish

*karmshis** *stem for 1st sg pres, pl pres, 2nd & 3rd sg subj, pind* <**karmshit**·

*karmshit**· *vt* to smash, shatter

karnaval *nm* **1** carnival celebration **2** (*Fig*) person dressed like a clown **3** (*Fig*) frivolity

*karnavale** *np* <**karnaval** carnival days before Lent: Shrovetide

karo *nf* diamond (playing cards)

*karoc** = **karroc**

*karos** *adv* bareheaded

karotë *nf* [*Bot*] carrot (*Daucus carota L.*)

*karov** = **karav**

*karp** *nm* (*Reg Gk*) wrist

Karpate *np fem* Carpathian Mountains, Carpathians

karpentier *nm* carpenter

karpë *nf* rocky hill with sharp peak

karpushkë *nf* [*Ichth*] carp (*Cyprinus carpio L.*) = **krap**

karpuz *nm* watermelon

  ◦ **karpuz llambe** (*Old*) lampshade

*karsellë** *nf* = **sënduk**

karst *nm* [*Geog*] karst

karstik *adj* [*Geog*] karstic

karsh *nm* region strewn with rocks and boulders, rocky slope

karshi

  I § *adv* (*Colloq*) opposite, facing across, in front

  II § *prep* (*abl*) **1** facing, across from, opposite, in front of **2** in respect to: toward **3** in comparison with

kartagjenas *adj, n* [*Hist*] Carthaginian

Kartagjenë *nf* [*Hist*] Carthage

kartel *nm* [*Econ*] cartel

kartelë *nf* file/index card, card

kartelist *n* person who maintains file cards

karter *nm* crankcase

kartë *nf* **1** paper **2** = **kartelë** **3** political charter

kartëmonedhë *nf* paper money: bill, banknote

*kartëpirës** *nm* blotting paper

*kartëpostale** OR **kartëpostare** *nf* postcard

*kartëshitës** *nm* (*Old*) stationer

*kartët** *adj* (*i*) (*Old*) of paper

kartëvizitë *nf* visiting/calling card

*kartëzo**·**het** *vpr* to carry on a correspondence by mail

*kartograf** *nm* cartographer = **hartograf**

*kartografi** *nf* cartography = **hartografi**

kartografik *adj* **1** of or pertaining to cardboard products *2 cartographic = **hartografik**

kartografike *nf* printing plant for cardboard products (such as postcards, invitations, documents)

kartoleri *nf* (*Old*) stationery store, stationer's

kartolinë *nf* postcard

  ◦ **kartolina e zjarrit** [*Mil*] battle plan that indicates gun positions and lines of fire

kartollë *nf* (*Reg Gheg*) potato

karton *nm* cardboard, pasteboard

  ◦ **karton katramat** = **katrama**

kartotekë *nf* record file; place where record files are kept

*kartroz** *adj, n* (*Old*) Carthusian

kartuç *nm* **1** cardboard = **karton** *2 book cover

*karturina** *np* (*Old*) stationery

*kartushkë** *nf* card, ticket

*karth** *nm* [*Agr*] linchpin securing the beam of the plow to the yoke

karthë *nf* [*Bot*] = **ajdës**

  ◦ **karthë e egër** **1** terebinth (*Pistacia terebinthus*) **2** bean trefoil (*Anagyris foetida*)

karthi *nf* = **karthje**

karthje *nf* **1** kindling, brushwood; dry twigs **2** oak boughs used as fodder

karthpulë nf [Bot] bladder senna (Colutea arborescens)

*karubë OR karumbë nf [Bot] carob = çiçibanoz

karukullë nf [Tech] pulley

karvan
I § nm 1 caravan 2 line of people/animals/vehicles
II § adv in a long line

karvanar n leader of a caravan

karvariq nm small long-handled basket-shaped net used to remove fish from a large net

*karvele = karavele

*karx = kërc

karra bisht nm [Entom] earwig = gërshërëz

karrace nf yearling mule

karranì·n OR karranìs· = karranìt·

karranìt· vt to stretch [ ] out flat, stretch [a dead body] out on the ground

karrapìt·et vpr to get tired/exhausted, get weak

karrapuc
I § nm 1 dense lump 2 (Fig) strong, skillful, resolute
II § adv in a lump; in a squat, crouching

*karratyq nm beehive in a hollow = korube

*karravagj adj paralytic

karravesh nm long stick with a hook used to pick fruit

*karrazuem adj (i) (Reg Gheg) = karravagj

karrcin nm yearling male goat, male kid

karrekëll nf (Reg) = karrige

karrel nm [Spec] 1 sliding carriage on a machine: carriage, saddle 2 mine car

karrelë nf [Cine] dolly, truck

karrelim nm [Cine] travelling shot
∘ karrelim optik [Cine] zooming

karrem nm 1 [Zool Reg] earthworm 2 fishing worm 3 (Fig) bait, lure

karrierë nf career

karrierist adj, n (Pej) careerist

karrierizëm nm (Pej) careerism

karrige nf 1 chair 2 (Colloq Fig Pej) privileged and easy position

karrigepunues nm chairmaker

*karrike OR karrikël = karrige

*karril nm [Ornit] crane (Grus grus)

karriq nm (Reg) 1 = shinik 2 = brokë

karro nf 1 cart 2 pushcart; wheelbarrow 3 [Tech] truck

karrocabërës nm cartwright

karrocapunues nm cartwright

*karrocar OR karrocatar nm = karrocier

karrocaxhi nm (pl ˜ nj) = karrocier

*karrocer = karrocier

karroceri nf coachwork, bodywork on a vehicle

karrocë nf 1 carriage, coach; wagon 2 pushcart; wheelbarrow 3 baby carriage, pram

karrocier nm coachman; carter; cab driver

karrok nm blockhead

karrooficinë nf mobile workshop, van equipped with machine tools

karropunues nm cartwright

karroqe nf 1 wooden bucket used as a measure of approximately 10 kilograms: peck 2 (Reg) = vedër 3 (FigImpolite) blockhead, dolt *= korriqe

*karrsh adj (Old) arid, barren

---

karrt·et vpr (Reg) 1 to ripen 2 to dry up and wilt

*karrube nf beehive in a hollow = korube

*karruce = karrocë

karruke nf = karrup

karrule nf (Old) tall fez worn by dervishes

karrup nm dip net for catching fish

kas adv 1 (of animals) rearing up on the back feet *2 cassia

kasaba nf (Old) city, casbah = qytet

kasaforte nf safe, strongbox

*kasan = kazan

kasap nm butcher

kasaphane nf slaughterhouse

*kasarolle nf saucepan

kasatë nf [Dairy] ice-cream confection: cassata

kasaturrë nf broadsword

kasavet nm (Colloq) worry, care

*kasdej adv the day after the day after tomorrow, three days from now

*kasellë nf = arkë

Kasem nm Kasem (male name)

kasetë nf case, small box

kasë nf 1 safe, cashbox 2 gunstock 3 door/window frame forming part of a wall

kaskadë nf cascade

*kaskandër nf cascade, waterfall

kasketë nf cap with brim in front

kaskë nf helmet
∘ kaskat blu blue helmets: soldiers of the United Nations Organization

kasmot adv two years from now = prapmot

kasnak nm 1 handle of a cradle *2 embroidery frame *3 embroidery

kasnec nm 1 (Old) herald 2 (Disparaging) = tellall

kasnecim nm ger < kasneco·n announcement, promulgation

kasneco·n vt (Old) 1 to proclaim, announce 2 (Pej) to boast [ ] loudly

kasolle nf shed; shack, hut
∘ kasolle e qenit doghouse

kasollë nf = kasolle

Kaspik adj, nm Caspian

kast nm (Colloq) intention, forethought

*kastan adv (Reg Gheg) = kastile

kasten adv (Reg Gheg) = kastile

kastë nf caste

kastërmbesë nf daughter of one's niece/grand-daughter

kastërnip nm son of one's nephew/grandson

kastile adv (Colloq) 1 on purpose, deliberately, intentionally 2 for a particular purpose: especially, expressly

kastor nm [Zool] beaver

kastravec
I § nm 1 [Bot] cucumber (Cucumis sativus L.) 2 [Bot] type of fig with big, long fruit
II § adj (Fig Pej) immature, stupid, and inexperienced: wet behind the ears

Kastriot nm Kastriot (male name)

kastriq nm [Zool] chicken-snake, four-lined rat snake (Elaphe quatuorlineata)

kashaï nf currycomb

kashaïs· vt to curry [ ] (with a currycomb)

kashaïsje *nf ger* <**kashais·**

kashaït· = **kashais·**

kashaloʹt *nm* [*Zool*] sperm whale *(Physeter macrocephalus)*

kashelaʹshë *nf* riddle

kasheʹr *nm* [*Dairy*] type of soft cheese

*****kashë** *nf* 1 = **kasë** 2 traditional story/verse 3 = **kashelaʹshë**

kaʹshër *nf (Reg)* [*Bot*] = **xunkth**

*****kashkavaʹll** = **kaçkavaʹll**

kashmiʹr *nm* cashmere

kashnjeʹt *nm* chestnut grove

*****kashtaʹllë** *nf* radius bone (of the arm) = **gëzhdaʹllë**

kashtaʹr *nm* bonfire; burning straw

kashtaʹrë *nf* 1 heap of hay/straw 2 = **hamulloʹre** 3 rattan chair 4 blacksmith's small wire-handled broom used to sprinkle water on hot coals 5 bonfire, big fire

kaʹshtë *nf* 1 straw 2 thatch 3 [*Bot*] pycreus *(Pycreus)* 4 [*Bot*] great reed mace *(Typha latifolia)* 5 *(Fig Colloq)* outer appearance; height, stature 6 *(Fig)* worthless thing
∘ **kashtë frytje** [*Bot*] great reed mace *(Typha latifolia)*
∘ **kashtë kënete** [*Bot*] pycreus *(Pycreus)*
∘ **Kashta e Kumtrit** [*Astron*] The Milky Way

kashtëbaʹrdhë *nf* [*Bot*] broadleafed bulrush, great reed mace *(Typha latifolia)*

kashtëbuʹtë *adj* having soft hay/straw

kashtëkuʹqe *nf* [*Bot*] marsh plant with a tripartite red stalk

kashtëmbleʹdhëse *nf* part of a combine in which the straw collects after threshing

kashtënxjeʹrrëse *nf* part of the combine serving to remove the straw after threshing

kashtërmeʹnë *nf* 1 thin straw; thin and weak stem of a grain plant 2 *(Fig)* weak and sickly person or living thing

kashtërraʹbë *nf* stilt (for walking)

kashtërroʹjë *nf* 1 straw remaining on ground after harvesting; straw stubble 2 [*Bot*] Venus-cup teasel *(Dipsacus sylvester)*

kaʹshtët *adj (i)* of straw

kashtoʹ·n *vt* 1 to cover [] with straw; thatch 2 to feed [] with hay/straw 3 to beat [] up badly

kashtoʹr *adj* made of straw; thatched

kashtoʹre *nf* 1 thatched cottage 2 hayshed; hay barn 3 stack of hay/straw 4 demijohn covered with wickerwork 5 straw hat 6 rattan chair 7 corn stubble 8 blacksmith's small wire-handled broom for sprinkling water on hot coals

kashtoʹs· *vt (Crude)* to beat up badly

kashtroʹje *nf* corn straw

*****kashtuʹ(n)** *nm (Reg Gheg)* = **kashuʹn**

kaʹshtull *nf* [*Astron*] The Milky Way

kashtuʹp *nm* cornhusk

kashturiʹna *np* straw residue left after threshing

kashuʹn *nm* 1 wickerwork basket 2 large wooden storage chest 3 beehive in an apiary = **kosheʹre**

kat *nm* 1 level of a building: storey, floor 2 shelf of a closet 3 [*Bot*] zonal flora; set of plants that grow at the same altitude

kataʹc
I § *nm* small bird trap

II § *adj* = **ngaʹthët**

kataklizëm *nm* cataclysm

katakoʹmb *nm* catacomb

katalepsiʹ *nf* catalepsy

*****kataliʹ** *nf* tiredness, fatigue

katalizaʹtor *nm* [*Chem*] catalyst 2 catalyzer

kataliʹzë *nf* catalysis

kataloʹg *nm* catalog

katalogizoʹ·n *vt* to catalog

katallaʹn
I § *nm* [*Folklore*] cyclops-like character in folk tales
II § *adj* gigantic

katanaʹ
I § *nf* paper kite
II § *adj* tall but not very solid in build

katandiʹ *nf (Colloq)* 1 belongings, worldly goods 2 plight

katandiʹs·
I § *vt* to reduce [] to misery/poverty; seriously reduce [] in value
II § *vi* = **katandiʹs·et**

katandiʹs·et *vpr* 1 to reach a miserable state 2 to be reduced to poverty; be brought low
∘ **U katandisi kokoshi/kaposhi një thelë** "The rooster was reduced to a single slice" Out of what seemed a lot there's almost nothing left.

kataniʹke *nf* small caique

kataʹnkë *nf* [*Tech*] wire rod

katapiʹ *nf (Reg)* door bolt, door bar = **mandaʹll**

*****kataplaʹzmë** *nf* cataplasm

katapuʹltë *nf* catapult

kataraʹf *nm* 1 attic door; trap door 2 grilled door opening onto a stairway

kataraʹk *nm (Reg)* door bolt, door bar = **mandaʹll**

kataraʹkt *nm* cataract

kataʹrë *nf* curse, imprecation

katariʹm *nm* [*Ethnog*] crying of a bride when she leaves home

kataroʹsh
I § *nm* snaggletooth
II § *adj* 1 having dense and irregularly arranged grain 2 (of ram or billy goat) having two pairs of horns; having forked horns 3 naughty, causing mischief

kataʹrr *nm* catarrh

katastrofaʹl *adj* catastrophic

katastroʹfë *nf* catastrophe, disaster

kateʹdër *nf* 1 podium 2 department (at a university)

katedraʹle *nf* cathedral

kategoriʹ *nf* 1 category 2 classification rank according to professional training

kategoriʹk *adj* categorical

kategoriʹkisht *adv* categorically

kategoriziʹm *nm ger* 1 <**kategorizoʹ·n**, **kategorizoʹ·het** 2 categorization

kategorizoʹ·het *vpr* to qualify

kategorizoʹ·n *vt* to categorize

katekiʹzëm *nm* [*Relig*] catechism

*****katenaʹr** *nm* padlock = **dry**

kateʹt *nm* [*Geom*] (of a right triangle) leg, side

kateteʹr *nm* [*Med*] catheter

kateʹk *nm* = **rrëcoʹk**

katëʹr
I § *num* four; number four

II § *nf* the number four

III § *np (të)* a group of four, the four of them, all four

○ [ ] **çofshin me katër veta** "May they take [ ] with four people!" *(Curse)* May the pallbearers come for [ ]!

○ **katër hapa (larg)** "four steps (away)" quite near

*katëra·n·sh *adj* four-sided, quadrilateral

katëra·n·shëm *adj (i)* four-sided; rectangular

katërbrinj·ësh *adj [Geom]* quadrilateral

katërce·p·sh *adj (Old) [Geom]* quadrangular

katërçip

I § *nm* quadrangle

II § *adv* = **katërçipërisht**

katërçipërisht *adv (Book)* **1** completely, on all sides **2** clearly and definitively

*katërçipje *nf* quadrangle; rectangle = **katërkëndësh**

katërçiptazi *adv* = **katërçipërisht**

katërçiptë *adj (i)* **1** quadrangular **2** complete, full; completely clear

katërditor *adj* of four days, four-day

katërdoras *adv* on all fours

*katërdhetë *(Reg)* = **dyzet**

*katërdhetkâmbës *nm (Reg Gheg)* millipede

katërdhjetë *(Reg)* = **dyzet**

katërfaqësh

I § *adj* tetrahedral, four-sided; four-page, having four pages

II § *nm* tetrahedron

katërfarësh *adj* of four kinds

katërfijësh *adj* consisting of four strands

katërfish

I §· *nm* a quantity four times as great as another: quadruple

II § *adv* four times as great

III § *adj* = **katërfishtë**

katërfishim *nm ger* < **katërfisho·n, katërfisho·het**

katërfisho·het *vpr* to increase fourfold, quadruple

katërfisho·n *vt* to cause a fourfold increase, quadruple

katërfishtë *adj (i)* **1** quadripartite **2** four times greater than the basis of comparison: quadruple, fourfold

katërfishuar *adj (i)* quadrupled

katërfletësh *adj* in four panels: four-paneled; four-page

katërgrykësh

I § *adj [Mil]* four-barreled

II § *nm* four-barreled antiaircraft machine-gun

katërkatësh *adj* four-storey

katërkëmbësh *adj* **1** four-legged, four-footed **2** *[Zool]* quadruped **3** *[Lit]* tetrameter

katërkëndës *adj* = **katërkëndësh**

katërkëndësh

I § *adj [Geom]* quadrangular

II § *nm* quadrangle

○ **katërkëndësh këndrejtë** rectangle

katërkohësh *adj* four-stroke

katërkrerësh *nm [Anat]* quadriceps

katërlëmsh *adv* rolling like a ball

katërliq *adj [Text]* woven in a loom with four harnesses: four-harness (weave)

katërmbëdhjetë

I § *num* fourteen; number fourteen

II § *nf* the number fourteen

III § *adj (i), n (i)* fourteenth

*katërmëzo·n *vt* to multiply [ ] by four

katërmotorësh *adj* four-motor (of airplanes)

katërnak *nm (np katërneq)* quadruplet

katërorësh *nm* **1** four-hour block of time **2** four-hour workday

katërpalësh *adj* on the part of four parties: quadripartite

katërqind

I § *num* four hundred; number four hundred

II § *nf* the number four hundred

○ **ësh-të katërqind qyqesh** "be four hundred generations of cuckoos" to be ancient

katërqindtë *adj (i)* four hundredth

*katërqoshës *adj (Old) [Geom]* = **katërcepsh**

katërrokësh *[kat-ër-rrok-ësh]*

I § *adj* composed of four syllables

II § *nm [Lit]* four-syllable line of verse, normally accented on the third syllable

*katërskâjç *adj (Reg Gheg Old)* *[Geom]* = **katërcepsh**

katërsor *nm* Quaternary (geological era)

katërsh

I § *adj* **1** consisting of four parts; quadripartite **2** with a measure or value of four

II § *nm* **1** group of four, tetrad **2** a grade of four

III § *adv* in four parts, in fours, four by four

○ **ësh-të ta ça·n**^{subj} **katërsh** to be too fat; be really big

*katërshëm *adj (i)* quarterly

katërshor *adj* four-cornered, tetragonal; having a four-sided surface or shape

katërshore *nf (Old)* **1** school notebook ***2** set square

katërt

I § *adj (i), n (i)* fourth, quarter

II § *nf (e)* fourth grade (in elementary school); fourth grade class/classroom

*katërtar *adj (Old)* = **katërsor**

*katërtuem *adj (i) (Reg Gheg)* fourfold

katërvargësh *adj [Lit]* having four lines

katërvargëshe *nf* quatrain

katërvendësh *adj* with room for four, four-place, four-seated

katërvjeçar *adj* **1** quadrennial **2** four-year-old

*katërvjetshëm *adj (i)* four-year-old

*katërzim *nm ger* **1** < **katërzo·n 2** quarter (phase of the moon)

*katërzo·n *vt (Old)* to square [a number]

katikule *np (Colloq)* flattering words: overdone praise

katil

I § *adj* criminal, murderous; inhuman, bestial

II § *n* criminal, murderer

katil-ferman *nm* death edict

katinar *nm* padlock = **dry**

kation *nm [Phys]* cation, positive ion

katis *stem for 1st sg pres, pl pres, 2nd & 3rd sg subj, pind* < **katit·**

katit· *vt* **1** to tire [ ] out, exhaust; defeat **2** to tenderize and cook vegetables or meat by boiling in a small amount of water

katit·*et vpr* **1** to become soft from boiling in a small amount of water **2** to get dim gradually

katitur *adj (i)* exhausted, completely tired out

katmel *nm* [*Bot*] poppy

katmerr
I § *adj* delicate, fragile; feeble
II § *nm* **1** defect **2** disquieting concern: worry, uneasiness

katmerr-katmerr
I § *adj* having many leaves/petals
II § *adv* in sheet form

katmore *nf* dessert made of filo dough twisted into snail shape

katode *nf* cathode

kato ∙ i *obl* <**katu**a

katolicizëm *nm* Catholicism

katolik *adj, n* Catholic

katonj *np* <**katu**a

katoq *nm dimin* <**katu**a

katrabrez *nm* **1** fourth generation (of people descended from a common ancestor) **2** distant relationship

katragyshër *np* <**katragy**sh ancestors

katragjysh *n* great-great-grandparent

katrahurë *nf(Colloq)* disorderly mess

katrakushëri(r) *nm (np ~ nj)* fourth cousin; very distant cousin

katralig *nm* very bad person: scoundrel, rat

katralojë *nf* amusement/fun with much talk and music

katrama *nf* tar paper

katramat *adj* coated/impregnated with tar

katramëz *nf* buckle (for belt or shoes)

katran
I § *nm* **1** tar, pitch **2** *(Reg)* = **zift 3** miserable person **4** rotten person
II § *adj (Colloq)* **1** pitch black **2** very dirty **3** *(Fig Colloq)* black-hearted
III § *adv*
∘ **katran me bojë** very bad; in very bad condition
∘ **katran i zi** pitch black

katrano ∙ n *vt* to coat [] with tar/pitch

katrano s· *vt* **1** to coat [] with tar/pitch **2** *(Crude)* to make [] dirty, soil **3** *(Fig Crude)* to louse [] up, botch **4** *(Fig Crude)* to manage [] somehow, manage [] by hook or crook

katrano s·*et vpr (Crude)* **1** to get very dirty **2** to get screwed up

katrano sur *adj (i)* **1** tarred, covered with pitch **2** totally incompetent, ne'er-do-well

katranuar *adj (i)* = **katrano**sur

katrapilas *adv* **1** disorderly, messy **2** up to the very top, up to the brim

katrapilëzo ∙ n *vt* to create disorder, ruin

katrasyll *adj* cock-eyed in both eyes

katrash *adv (së)* in great haste

katravesh *nm* **1** [*Entom*] flying black insect with four antennae that lives in rotting tree trunks **2** [*Folklore*] man-eating monster

katro ∙ n
I § *vt* **1** to tell <*someone*> [something] straightforwardly **2** to lament loudly for [a dead person] in a wailing eulogy
II § *vi* **1** to pronounce a curse **2** *(Colloq)* to talk blather

katroqe *nf* leather bag carried by shepherds

katror *adj, nm* square

katrore-katrore *adj* square-shaped

katrosh
I § *adj* square-shaped
II § *nm* ram with forked horns

*katrov = **katruv**

*katrumë *nf* bunch of flowers

katruvar *n* maker of earthenware vessels: potter

katruve *nf* **1** earthenware pitcher **2** squat-bellied wooden bowl for water

katua *nm (obl ~ oi, np ~ onj)* **1** utility/storage shed; cellar **2** animal shed = **ahu**r **3** coop for fowl

katulesh *nm* **1** shaggy dog **2** *(Pej)* shaggy-haired person

katulesh·*et vpr* = **leshëro** ·*het*

katund *nm* **1** village **2** [*Hist*] community of herdsmen; widely spread-out village

*katundak *adj* rustic

katundar
I § *n* **1** villager, rustic; peasant **2** [*Hist*] village chief
II § *adj* of or pertaining to a village, rustic, rural

katundarçe *adv (Colloq)* = **fshata**rçe

katundari *nf* **1** peasantry **2** *(Pej)* peasant rabble
*3 rural countryside, country

katundarisht *adv* = **katund**isht

katundës *n* = **fshata**r

katundësi *nf* **1** = **fshatarësi 2** [*Hist*] = **bashki**

katundisht *adv* as a whole village, all together

kath *nm* [*Med*] sty on eyelid

*kathedër *nf* = **kate**dër

*kathë = **ngathtë**si

kathic *nm* [*Anat*] clitoris

kathistër *nf* chicken coop

*kathuer *nf (obl ~ ori) (Reg Gheg)* = **kathi**stër

kalu *sg def form* <**ka**

kauboj *nm* cowboy

kauçuk
I § *nm* rubber, caoutchouc
II § *adj* rubber-like

kauk *nm (Old)* fez around which a turban is wrapped; fez worn by dervishes

Kaukaz *nf* Caucasus

kaukazian *adj, n* Caucasian, native of/to the Caucasus

kaull *nm (Colloq)* **1** guarantee, warranty **2** bet

kaun *nm (Reg Kos)* melon (casaba, honeydew, cantaloupe)

kaur *nm (Old)* **1** contemptuous term used by the Turks for non-Moslems: infidel **2** [*Relig*] Christian

kaurdis· *vt* **1** to roast [meat, coffee] **2** *(Fig Colloq)* to manage to accomplish []

kaurdis·*et vpr (Colloq)* to manage, get by, get along
∘ **kaurdis**·*et me dhjamin e <>* to manage entirely on <*one's*> own

kaurdisje *nf ger* <**kaurdis**·, **kaurdis**·*et*

kaurdisur *adj (i)* roasted

kaurma *nf* [*Food*] liver and intestines cooked with spices in a flour gravy

kaurr *nm (Pej Scorn)* = **kau**r

*kaurreshë *nf (Pej Scorn)* female infidel

*kaurri *nf (Pej Scorn)* non-Moslems: the infidel world

kaustik *adj* caustic

kaush *nm* **1** paper bag; paper cone (used to hold a small purchase) **2** *(Old)* dormitory room in a barracks; prison cell

kauzal *adj (Book)* causal

kauzalitet *nm (Book)* causality

kauzë *nf* noble cause

KAV *abbrev* <**Kooperativa e Artikujve të Veshmbathjes** *(Old)* Clothing Cooperative

kavajas
I § *adj* Kavajan
II § *n* native of Kavaja

Kavajë *nf* Kavajë

kavak *nm* [Bot] Lombardy poplar (Populus italica)

kavaleri *nf* cavalry

kavalet *nm* **1** easel **2** trestle

kavaletë *nf* large covered haystack with a flat top; tightly bound sheaf (of grain)

kavalier *nm* cavalier; open-hearted and generous person

kavaljet *nm* epoch, era

kavall *nm* fife, shepherd's pipe
  ○ **kavall deti** [Ichth] sea lamprey (Petromyzon marinus)
  ○ **kavall lumi** [Ichth] river lamprey (Lampetra fluviatilis)

kavanoz *nm* glass jar

*__kavardis__ OR **kaverdis** = **kaurdis**

kavariqe *nf* = **karvariq**

kavernë *nf* [Med] cavity caused by disease *cavern*

kavërdis = **kaurdis**

*__kaviti__ *nf(Old)* motive

kavitshëm *adj* (i) = **kamotshëm**

kavo *nf* metal cable

kaza *nf (Old)* administrative unit governed by a provincial vicegerent in the Ottoman empire; administrative center of such a unit

kazak *adj, n* Kazakh

Kazakistan *nm* Kazakhstan

*__kazami__ = **kalendar**

kazan *nm* **1** cauldron **2** [Tech] boiler **3** still (for distillation of liquids) **4** *(Pej)* boiling pot, center of unrest

kazanpunues *adj* boilermaker

kazanxhi *nm (np ~ nj)* **1** = **kazanpunues 2** raki distiller

kazeinë *nf* [Chem] casein

kazermë *nf* **1** [Mil] barracks **2** *(Pej)* large house or apartment house with miserable living conditions

kazermim *nm ger* <**kazermo**•n, **kazermo**•het

kazermo•het *vpr* [Mil] to take quarters in barracks

kazermo•n *vt* [Mil] to quarter [soldiers] in barracks

kazezë *nf* black cow

kazil *nm* black bull/ox/steer

*__kazinë__ = **kazino**

kazino *nf* casino

kazmë *nf* two-headed pick; pickax
  ○ **bjeri kazmës!** get to work, kid!
  ○ **kazmë me veshë** pickax

*__kazmir__ = **kashmir**

*__kazhup__ = **gozhup**

ke
I § 2nd sg pres <**ka**• you have
II § prep (nom) conj = **te**
  ○ **ke parë ti** "have you yourself seen!" *(Scorn)* have you ever heard of such a thing!

Kebek *nm* Quebec

kec *n (masc np ~ ër)* kid, goat less than a year old

kecan *nm (Old)* **1** domestic servant used for heavy work **2** *(Pej)* lackey

kecelushe *nf (Euph)* = **dosëz**

kecer *nf* **1** hand reel for winding thread **2** small skein of thread

kecër *np* <**kec**

*__keç__
I § *n* = **kec**
II § *np* <**kaç**

kece *nf (Reg)* young girl

keçër *np* <**kaç**

*__kêdo__ (Reg Gheg) = **këdo**

kedh *n (Reg)* = **kec**

Kejptaun *nm* Capetown

kek *nm* cake

kekllish• *vi* (of crickets) to chirp

Kelmend *nm* mountainous ethnographic region in northwestern Albania: Kelmend

kelmendas
I § *adj* Kelmendite
II § *n* native of Kelmend

*__kelshejt__ *nm* [Relig] chalice

kelt
I § *adj* Celtic
II § *n* Celt

keltisht *adv* in Celtic

keltishte *nf* Celtic language or languages

kem *nm* incense = **temjan**

kem *1st sg subj* <**ka**• I may have

kemi *1st pl pres* <**ka**• we have

kemo•n *vt* to cense = **temjanis**•

*__kêmos__• *vt(Reg Gheg)* to cense = **kemo**•n

KEMP *abbrev* <**Komisioni i Ekspertimit Mjekësor të Punës** board of medical examiners of work fitness

*__kêmtar__ I § *nm* OR **kêmtore** II § *nf(Reg Gheg)* censer, thurible = **temjanicë**

kenë *3rd pl subj* <**ka**• they may have

*__kênë__ (Reg Gheg) = **qenë**

keni *2nd pl pres* <**ka**• you have

*__kên__ (Reg Gheg) = **qen**

*__kênsi__ (Reg Gheg Old) = **qensi**

kentaur *nm* centaur

kep
I § *nm* **1** crag **2** [Geog] cape, promontory, point **3** hoe **4** spalling mallet, spallpeen hammer *5 edge
II § *adj* clever, sharp, witty

kep• *vt* **1** to sharpen [ ] by spalling, dress [a stone] by flaking **2** to hoe **3** to peck at; peck away at

kepcë *nf (Reg)* **1** [Bot] basket willow, osier willow, osier (Salix viminalis) **2** willow withe

kepës *nm* **1** stone dresser, tool sharpener: spaller **2** hoer, cultivator **3** person who nibbles at food **4** pickpocket

kepët *adj* (i) craggy

kepje *nf ger* <**kep**•

keplor *nm* [Ornit] woodpecker = **qukapik**

kepore *nf* hatchet

keptar *nm* = **kepës**

keq
I § *adj* (i) **1** bad **2** wrong **3** of a high order, of high quality
II § *adv* **1** badly **2** wrongly, amiss **3** ill **4** very much, badly, like mad

○ **keq e mos më keq** very very bad, terrible

○ **ësh·të keq nga** [] to have trouble with []

○ **e pa**^{pdef} **keq** {} found {}self in deep trouble

○ **s'ësh·të keq për** [] not be badly off in terms of []: not lack/need []

○ **s'është keq për** [] there is plenty of []

keq·et *vpr* **1** to get worse **2** to speak/answer harshly; threaten **3** to have a falling out, be on bad terms

keqadministrim *nm* poor/bad administration

keqan *adj (Pej)* **1** wicked **2** ugly **3** sickly; in bad health

keqardhje *nf* regret

keqas *adv* badly, gravely, seriously

keqbesim *nm* mistrust, distrust

keqbërës
I § adj harmful, injurious
II § n evildoer, criminal; malefactor

keqbërje *nf* harmfulness, harm

keqdashës *adj, n* malevolent/hostile/malicious (person)

keqdashje *nf* malevolence, hostility, malice

keqe *nf (e)* **1** bad situation **2** bad thing, trouble, problem; cause of the trouble **3** bad action/deed **4** bad feature/aspect/part **5** bad illness; epilepsy
○ **e keqja e të këqijave** the very worst

keqel *adj, n* thin and weak (person)

keqësim *nm ger* <**keqëso**·*n*, **keqëso**·*het*

keqëso·*het* *vpr* **1** to get/grow worse, worsen; become exacerbated/aggravated **2** to fall into discord

keqëso·*n* *vt* to make [] worse, exacerbate, aggravate

keqësues *adj* **1** causing to get worse, exacerbating **2** degrading; derogatory

keqfolje *nf* defamation; discredit

keqinterpretim *nm ger* **1** <**keqinterpreto**·*n* **2** *(Book)* misinterpretation

keqinterpreto·*n* *vt (Book)* to misinterpret

keqkuptim *nm* misunderstanding

keqkupto·*het* *vpr* to have a misunderstanding

keqkupto·*n* *vt* to misunderstand

keqmëso·*het* *vpr* to be brought up badly; be badly behaved

keqmëso·*n* *vt* to bring up [] badly

keqo·*n* *vt* to commiserate with [], feel sorry for []

keqotë *adj (i)* unwell, sickly

keqpërdor *vt* = keqpërdoro·*n*

keqpërdorim *nm ger* <**keqpërdoro**·*n* **2** abuse

keqpërdorje *nf ger* <**keqpërdor**·, keqpërdor·*et*

keqpërdoro·*n* *vt* **1** to abuse; maltreat, mistreat **2** to misuse

keqpësim *nm* mishap, accident; calamity

keqprurës *adj* harmful, injurious; calamitous

keqsjellje *nf* bad manners/conduct

keqtingëllim *nm* dissonance

keqtrajtim *nm ger* **1** <**keqtrajto**·*n* **2** maltreatment, mistreatment

keqtrajto·*n* *vt* to maltreat, mistreat

kequdhëzo·*n* *vt* to give [] poor guidance

keqveprim *nm* wrongdoing

kercul = kërcul

kerdi = kërdi

kerdhokullë *nf* = kërdhokull

kerë *nf* dog that runs along with a cart/wagon

kersh *np* <karsh

kerubin *nm* cherubim

kerr *nm* [*Ichth*] stone bass, wreckfish *(Polyprion americanus)*
○ **kerr bari** [*Ichth*] = kerr thellësie
○ **kerr bilbil** [*Ichth*] painted comber *Serranus scriba*
○ **kerr guri** [*Ichth*] painted comber *Serranus hepatus*
○ **kerr thellësie** [*Ichth*] comber *Serranus cabrilla*

kerrkë *nf* she-colt

kerrmë *nf* = ferrishtë

kerrmëz *nf* purring

kerrn *nm* [*Ichth*] **1** dusky grouper *(Epinephelus guaza)* = sqoh **2** = kerr
○ **kerrn i artë** [*Ichth*] golden grouper *Epinephelus alexandrinus*
○ **kerrn i bardhë** [*Ichth*] dogtooth grouper *Epinephelus caninus*
○ **kerrn i hirtë** [*Ichth*] = kerrn i bardhë
○ **kerrn i verdhë** [*Ichth*] white grouper *Epinephelus aeneus*

kerrnjo·*n* *vi* (of a cat) to purr

kesë = kezë

kesh *2nd sg subj* <ka· you may have

ketë *3rd sg subj* <ka· he may have

ketër *nm* [*Zool*] squirrel

kezë *nf (Reg Arb)* bride's ceremonial gold-embroidered red/green silk/velvet headdress

kë *sg acc* <kush whom, which

kë *formativ* proximal deixis, near: this, here

këc· *vt (Child)* = kafsho·*n*

këc = kërc

këdo *acc* <kushdo whomever

këha *adv* here, right here

këhë *adv (Old)* in this vicinity: around here

këkli OR *këklish* *nf* chirping (of crickets)

këlbaz· *vt* **1** to cause liver rot in [livestock] **2** to cause [an animal]'s nose to run; cause [an animal] to form phlegm

këlbaz·et *vpr* **1** to come down with liver rot **2** to develop phlegm in the lungs and throat **3** *(Fig)* to get sick and tired of staying too long in one place

këlbazë *nf* **1** phlegm, sputum **2** [*Veter*] liver rot

këlbazur *adj (i)* [*Veter*] afflicted with liver rot

këlboqe *nf* phlegm

këlc = kërc

këlcatës *nm (Colloq)* squirt gun, popgun

këlfas stem for *1st sg pres, 1st & 3rd pl pres, 2nd & 3rd sg subj* <këlfet·

këlfet· *vt* to peck at [], peck

këlfis stem for *2nd pl pres, pind* <këlfet·

këlfit stem for *pdef, opt, adm, part, pind, 2nd pl pres, imper, vp* <këlfet·

këlfitur *adj (i)* pockmarked, pitted

këlkajë *nf*
○ **këlkajë uji** [*Bot*] water-plantain *Alisma plantago-aquatica*

këlkas stem for *1st sg pres, pl pres, 2nd & 3rd sg subj, pind* <këlka·*t*·

këlka·t· *vt* to stop up []: plug, bung

këlkatës *nm* shutter; valve

këlkazë *nf* [*Bot*] Italian arum *Arum italicum*

këlkëzë = këlkazë

këlkëzore *np fem* [*Bot*] arum family Araceae

këlkim *nm ger* <këlko·*n*

këlko·n *vt* to tickle, excite; irritate

këlkos· = këlko·n

këlkues *nm* irritator

Këln *nm* Cologne

këlpishtë *nf* [*Bot*] = gjipishtë

*këlpudhë = kërpudhë

*këlqer = gëlqer

*këlsaç = kësaç

*këlsaça *np* <këlsaç 1 fangs 2 pincers, tongs

këlshedër *nf* grapevine shoot

këlshejt *nm* (*Old*) chalice used in a Catholic mass

këlthas *stem for 1st sg pres, 1st & 3rd pl pres, 2nd & 3rd sg subj* <këlthet·

këlthet· *vi, vt* to yell, shout, scream; call loudly, scream; cry loudly

këlthi *OR* këlthimë *nf* loud yell/call/cry

këlthimë *nf* = klithmë

këlthis *stem for 2nd pl pres, pind* <këlthet·

këlthit *stem for pdef, opt, adm, part, pind, 2nd pl pres, imper, vp* <këlthet·

këlthitës *adj* 1 yelling, loud 2 [*Ling*] exclamatory

këlthitje *nf ger* <këlthet·

këlthitur
I § *part* <këlthet·
II § *adj* (*i*) loudly publicized, noised abroad

këlysh *nm* 1 young offspring of a quadruped mammal, baby animal: pup, cub, kitten, colt 2 (*Fig Pej*) child of despicable parents 3 (*Fig Insult*) young sprout, offshoot 4 small pustule that forms around an abscess 5 branch of a waterway or canal

   ◦ këlysh dheu [*Zool*] = dosëza

   ◦ këlysh sokaku (*Impol*) young hooligan/bum, street tough

këlyshëz *nf* 1 hangnail 2 [*Bot*] = ndajgjethëz

këllas *stem for 1st sg pres, 1st & 3rd pl pres, 2nd & 3rd sg subj* <këllet·

këllcacë *nf* blowpipe

këlle·het *vpr* 1 to become turbid 2 (of female animals) to mate sexually

   ◦ këlle·het³ˢᵍ gjaku ◇ gets angry, ◇ gets all stirred up

   ◦ <> këlle·het³ˢᵍ mendja ◇ gets dizzy

këlleqkë *adj* rotten egg = kllënjkë?

këllet· *vt* to put [] in; insert, intrude = kall·

   ◦ këllet· krupën to make ◇ sick to the stomach, disgust ◇

këlleç *nm* two-edged saber

këllëf *nm* 1 close-fitting encasement: sheath; holster, scabbard; instrument case 2 cap on a broken tooth 3 [*Bot*] leaf sheath: vagina (*) 4 [*Anat*] vagina

   ◦ këllëf dysheku mattress case/ticking

   ◦ këllëf dysheku fabric case enclosing a mattress: mattress ticking, tick

   ◦ këllëf enëzor [*Anat*] external connective-tissue coat of a blood vessel: vascular sheath *tunica adventitia*

   ◦ këllëf jastëku pillowcase

këllfishte *nf* (*Reg*) casing of a cartridge

këlli *nf* 1 bran mash for livestock 2 = këllirë

këlliç *adv* 1 lengthwise 2 alongside; sideways

këllirë
I § *nf* 1 filth remaining from washing wool 2 dirty sediment, grime 3 dirty/polluted water; waste material 4 (*Fig Pej*) dregs of society, filthy good-for-nothing; filthy thing
II § *adj* unclean, dirty; murky

këllis *stem for 2nd pl pres, pind* <këllet·

këllit *stem for pdef, opt, adm, part, pind, 2nd pl pres, imper, vp* <këllet·

këllk *nm* (*np ~qe*) 1 hip, haunch 2 (*Fig*) mental/physical strength

*këllkaç *nm* = gëlçomë

këllqe *np* <këllk

këllqegjerë *adj* broad-hipped

këllyer *part* <këllehe

këmashën *nf* [*Bot*] mouse ear (*Hieracium pilosella*)

   ◦ këmbe·n fjalë to exchange words; exchange bitter words

këmbac *adj* 1 lame *2 one-legged

këmbadoras *adv* on hands and knees, on all fours

këmbajkë *nf* wooden trestle for crossing streams

këmbakëmbas *adv* = këmbas

këmba-këmbës *adv* 1 at one's heels; doggedly 2 simultaneously

këmbal *nm* 1 treadle 2 stilt

këmbale *nf* leather strap on a soldier's boottop

këmbalec *nm* 1 anchor bar driven into telephone poles or lamp posts to aid in climbing 2 horizontal crossbrace 3 easel 4 = shalok 5 = kambalec 6 trestle *7 gangway; slipway

këmbalkë *nf* 1 stilt 2 easel

këmbaloshe *nf* (*Pet*) little foot: footie

këmbanë = kambanë

këmbanik *nm* = këmbësor

*këmbanim *nm ger* <këmbano·n

*këmbano·n *vi* (of bells) to peal, chime

këmbanore *nf* = kambanore

*këmbar *nm* prop, trestle

këmbargjend *adj* (*Colloq*) 1 (of a woman) having beautiful fair-skinned legs 2 = këmbëmbarë

këmbas *adv* on foot

këmbatis· *vt* to prop [] up, support

këmbe·het *vpr* 1 to change directions after meeting 2 to change, become different 3 (*Fig*) to go crazy

këmbe·n *vt* 1 to exchange 2 to barter 3 to change

këmbes *nm* (*Old*) money changer

këmbese *nf* 1 alteration, change 2 = shkëmbesë

këmbestër *nf* foot stuck out to trip someone; impediment

këmbë *nf* 1 leg 2 foot 3 footstep 4 footrest 5 stairstep 6 branch (of a stream of water) 7 skein of yarn 8 cutting/scion for planting

   ◦ s'lua·*nn* asnjë këmbë "not move a single leg" 1 not bestir oneself: not even get up (when someone enters), move a finger (to help) 2 to make no progress

   ◦ i bie \ së mirës \ bukës me këmbë "kick away *something good//food*" to throw it all away, throw away a good opportunity

   ◦ Këmbët e lehta e faqja e bardhë! Honor unscathed by dint of his fast legs! (said admiringly of someone who has just escaped danger by running fast)

   ◦ i ndeu/mblodhi këmbët (*Impol*) to kick the bucket, die

   ◦ s'ka· këmbë to be unable to walk

○ **këmbë e krye 1** head over heals **2** every one, the whole lot; from beginning to end

○ [] **lanë këmbët e duart** []'s old bones just won't carry [] any more; [] is too old and feeble to work

○ **ju lumshin këmbët** "good for you that you came!" *(Felic)* welcome!

○ **këmbë mbi këmbë** with legs crossed

○ **<>u mblodhën këmbët** *(Impol)* <> died: <> kicked the bucket

○ **ësh·të më/në këmbë** to be in good health

○ **Këmbë për baltë, gojë për mjaltë.** "Foot in mud, mouth in honey." *(Prov)* He who works gets to eat.

○ **këmbët si drapër** bowed legs

○ **këmbë stërgu/stërku** [*Bot*] wild geranium

○ **këmbë të rreme** [*Zool*] pseudopod

○ **nuk i trego·n këmbët** to be tricky; act in secret

○ **Nuk i tregon gjarpri/bolla këmbët.** *(Prov)* An evil person hides his intentions.

○ **ua hipi këmbëve** *(Joke)* to start walking somewhere

○ **këmbë e urës** pier of a bridge

këmbëbardhë *nf* **1** (of sheep and goats) having white feet **2** = **këmbëmbarë**

këmbëcingthi *adv* standing on one foot

këmbëcipal *adj* having very thin legs

këmbëcorr *nm* pedestal

këmbëcalë
  I § *adj* lame
  II § *adv* walking on one foot, jumping on one foot

këmbëdac *nm* [*Bot*] cat's foot *(Antennaria dioica)*

këmbëdele *nf* [*Bot*] = **radhiqe**

këmbëdrapër *adj* bowlegged

këmbëgjarpër *adj* acting slyly and in secrecy

këmbëgjatë
  I § *nf* long-legged
  II § *np* [*Entom*] crane flies *(Tipulidae)*

këmbëhollë *nf* having thin legs

këmbë-këmbë *adv* **1** leaving foot tracks **2** step by step; in small bits, little by little

këmbëkithi *adv* on one leg

këmbëkizë
  I § *adj* bowlegged
  II § *adv* = **hopthi**

këmbëkryq *adv* **1** sitting on crossed legs **2** *(Fig)* calmly and coolly; in a relaxed manner, comfortably; feeling completely at home

këmbëkular *adv* = **këmbëkryq**

këmbëkuq *adj* (of animals) having brownish or reddish legs

këmbëkuqe *nf* **1** [*Ornit*] = **thëllëzë 2** *(Euph)* = **dhelpër 3** [*Food*] sweet cornmush; fried cornbread crumbs served with sugar, jam, or honey **4** [*Bot*] Russian thistle *(Salsola kali)* = **cimlë**

këmbëlehtë *adj* light-footed

këmbëlesh *adj* "hairy-legged" **1** having a furry stalk **2** having feathered legs

këmbëlëpirës *n* bootlicker, toady

këmbëlikaçik *adv* on one leg/foot

*****këmbëlopë** *nf* [*Ornit*] eagle

këmbëmaçok *nm* [*Bot*] Mediterranean salt grass *(Aeluropus littoralis)*

këmbëmbarë *adj* luck-bearing, lucky

këmbëmbrapshtë *nm* *(Euph)* the devil

këmbëmes· *nm* = **stërkëmbës**

këmbëngul· *vi* to put one's foot down: insist

këmbëngulës *adj* insistent, persistent; obstinate

këmbëngulje *nf ger* **1** <**këmbëngul· 2** insistence, persistence; stubbornness

këmbëngultas *adv* obstinately

këmbënyjëtuar *np* [*Invert*] arthropods *(Arthropoda)*

këmbëpambuk *adj* light-footed

këmbëpandier *adj* walking noiselessly

këmbëpatë
  I § *adj* **1** goose-footed; having a large and wide foot **2** having large palmate leaves
  II § *nf* [*Bot*] goosefoot *(Chenopodium album)*

*****këmbëpatore** *np fem* [*Bot*] goosefoot family *Chenopodiaceae*

këmbëpërpjetë *adj* **1** with legs up **2** *(FigImpolite)* dead

këmbëplloçak *adj* flat-footed

këmbëprapë *adj* bringing bad luck, unlucky

këmbëprerë *adj* having one or both legs cut off, missing one or both legs

këmbëpulë *nf* [*Bot*] bermuda grass *(Cynodon dactylon)*

këmbëpupël *adj* = **këmbëpambuk**

këmbëpupthi *adv* = **tingthi**

këmbëqiri OR **këmbëqirith** *nm* [*Ornit*] sandpiper, shank *(Tringa)*

këmbës *nm* **1** person on foot, pedestrian **2** [*Mil*] infantryman, foot-soldier **3** small two-legged wooden ladder = **shelqeror 4** *(Fig)* assistant, aide

këmbëse *nf* small two-legged wooden ladder

*****këmbësi** *nf (Old)* infantry

këmbësor
  I § *n* **1** pedestrian **2** [*Mil*] foot-soldier, infantryman
  II § *adj* **1** for pedestrians **2** of/for the infantry

këmbësore *nf* sidewalk

këmbësori *nf* [*Mil*] infantry

këmbësorrë *nf* [*Bot*] bulb buttercup *(Ranunculus bulbosus)*

këmbësutë *adj (Poet)* doe-footed, light-footed

këmbëshakull *adj* heavy-footed, barely able to move

këmbëshesh OR **këmbësheshtë** *adj* having flat feet: flat-footed

këmbëshkurtër
  I § *adj* short-legged
  II § *np* [*Invert*] terebratula, lamp shells *(Terebratulidae)*

këmbëshpejtë *adj* fleet-footed

*****këmbështo·n** *vi.* to go on foot, walk

këmbështrëmbër *adj* having crooked legs

këmbëshumëz *nf* [*Zool*] = **dyzetkëmbëz**

këmbëters *adj* = **këmbëprapë**

këmbëtrung *adj* crippled in the legs, unable to walk

këmbëtul *adj* having plump/fat legs

këmbëthadër *adj* having thin weak legs

këmbëtharë *adj* **1** slow and awkward in gait **2** *(Curse)* may his legs wither!

këmbëthirë *nf*

këmbëthyer *adj* broken-legged; limping

këmbëthyerazi *adv* **1** standing on one foot **2**

këmbëujk *nm* [*Bot*] gipsy-wort *(Lycopus europaeus)*

këmbë**vo'gël** *adj* having small feet
këmbë**z**
  I § *nf* **1** stairstep; ladder rung **2** upright supporting post in a house: wall stud, jamb, post **3** foot stuck out to trip someone **4** cuff on trousers or long bloomers **5** *(Mil)* trigger
  II § *nf dimin* **1** small leg/foot/footstep/footrest **2** small skein of yarn **3** [*Biol*] peduncle **4** gaiter, legging **5** [*Tech*] treadle, pedal
  ○ **ësh-të këmbëza e urës** "be the supporting pier of a bridge" (of a person) to be a constant source of trouble
  ○ **këmb**ë**z e urës** supporting pier of a bridge
këmbë**zba'th ur** *adj* **1** barefooted **2** poverty-stricken
këmbë**ze'z**ë *nf* [*Veter*] blackleg (*emphysema gangrenosum*)
këmbë**zë'n**ë *adj* **1** paralyzed in the legs **2** = **këmb**ë**tharë**
këmbë**zi** *adj (fem sg ˜ëz, masc pl ˜inj, fem pl ˜eza)* = **këmb**ë**prap**ë
këmbë**zo·n** *vi* to begin to sprout
këmbë**zva'rr**ë *adv* shuffling along
këmb'im *nm ger* **1** <**këmbe·n, këmbe·het 2** exchange; deal **3** change, conversion (of money)
këmb'je *nf* **1** trivet **2** cuff on trousers or long bloomers **3** upright supporting post in a house: wall stud, jamb, post
këmbo're *nf* **1** bell worn by pastoral animals: cowbell, sheep-bell **2** (*Fig Pej*) subservient person exploited by others; spineless toady
këmb'una'zë *adj* having a white ring of feathers/wool around the legs
këmb'y'er *adj (i)* **1** exchanged **2** alternate, in alternation **3** (*Fig*) crazy
këmb'y'erazi *adv* one after the other, in order
këmb'y'es *nm* **1** substitute **2** [*Tech*] = **fto'h**ë**s 3** money changer
këmb'y'e'shëm *adj (i)* exchangeable, convertible
kë**me'nd**ë *nf* fleece of a goat
kë**me's**ë *nf* [*Agr*] = **kme's**ë
**këmi = kumi
\>*këmi'n**ë** = kami'n**ë
kë**mish'a'r** *nm* = **k**ë**mishëqe'pës**
kë**mish'a'ri** *nf* workshop for making shirts; shop for selling shirts
kë**mi'sh**ë *nf* **1** shirt **2** [*Anat*] outer membrane covering a new-born baby or larva, caul; membranous covering of an organ or animal **3** (*Colloq*) layer that forms on spoiled vinegar **4** [*Tech*] protective cover: jacket
  ○ **nuk i beso·n as këmishës së trupit** "not even believe the shirt on one's back" not even trust one's own mother: not trust anyone
  ○ **këmisha e gjarprit** snakeskin that has been molted
  ○ **këmish**ë **hekuri** [*Hist*] shirt of mail
  ○ **këmish**ë **me avull** [*Tech*] steam jacket
  ○ **këmish**ë **me tiranda** woman's slip with straps
kë**mish**ë**'bër'**ë**s** *n* = **k**ë**mishëqe'pës**
kë**mish**ë**'gri's'ur** *adj* **1** having a torn shirt **2** (*Fig*) poverty-stricken
kë**mish**ë**'ku'q** *nm* [*Hist*] Redshirt (Garibaldi follower)
kë**mish**ë**'la'r'**ë**se** *nf* laundrywoman
kë**mish**ë**'qe'p'**ë**s** *n* shirtmaker

kë**mish**ë**'ste'rr**ë *nf, adj (Colloq Contempt)* = **k**ë**mishëzi**
kë**mish**ë**'zi** *adj, nm (Contempt)* Blackshirted (Italian) fascist
këna *nf* henna
këna'ce = këna'çe
këna'çe *nf* **1** one-handled water jug/pitcher; ladle **2** cup/mug with a handle **3** metal canister
**këna'll = kana'l
këna'lle *nf* [*Entom*] cicada
këna'q· *vt* **1** to please, delight **2** to satisfy, gratify; indulge
  ○ **kënaq· kureshtjen** to indulge one's curiosity
këna'q·et *vpr* **1** to experience pleasure: feel pleased; enjoy oneself **2** to feel satisfied
  ○ <> **kënaq·et**[3sg] **syri** <> *is* pleased at the sight, <> *enjoys* looking
  ○ <> **kënaq·et**[3sg] **shpirti/zemra** "<>'s soul has delight" (*Colloq*) <> *is* delighted, it *gives* <> a big kick, it *is* a real pleasure for <>
  ○ <> **kënaq·et**[3sg] **veshi** <> *is* pleased by the sound, <> *enjoys* listening; <> *is* pleased to hear it; <> *is* happy to listen
këna'q|ë = kënaq|ë'si
kënaq|ë'si *nf* **1** pleasure **2** satisfaction
këna'q|je *nf ger* **1** <**kënaq·, kënaq·et 2** = **kënaqë'si**
këna'q|shëm *adj (i)* **1** pleasant, pleasing **2** satisfactory
këna'q|ur *adj (i)* **1** pleased, happy **2** satisfied, contented
këna'të *nf* = **këna'çe
kënd *nm* **1** [*Geom*] angle **2** corner area **3** cozy nook **4** special area for an activity **5** remote area **6** (*Fig*) point of view
  ○ **kënd i drejtë** [*Geom*] right angle
  ○ **kënd i gjallë** special area near a secondary school in which live animals are kept for demonstration purposes
  ○ **kënd i gjerë** [*Geom*] obtuse angle
  ○ **kënd jo i drejtë** [*Geom*] oblique angle
  ○ **këndi i kuq** board/stand (with a red background, usually located in a corner) for displaying announcements, honors, and photographs connected with an enterprise/institution
  ○ **këndi i lojnave** playground
  ○ **këndi i marrjes** [*Cine*] shooting angle
  ○ **kënd më kënd** from one end to another, on every side, everywhere; exactly, in every detail
  ○ **kënd i ngushtë** [*Geom*] acute angle
  ○ **kënd përgjegjës** [*Geom*] corresponding angle
  ○ **kënd i plotësues** [*Geom*] complementary angle
  ○ **kënd sportiv** sports area
  ○ **këndi i shëndetit** stand displaying information about health and hygiene: health corner
  ○ **këndi i shënimit** [*Mil*] sighting angle
  ○ **kënd i shtrirë** [*Geom*] straight (180-degree) angle
  ○ **kënd i vdekur** [*Mil*] area that lies out of the line of fire: dead angle
kënd·et *vp impers* <> would like [], <> feels like having []
kënd'ajtë *nf* pleasure
kënda'lle *nf* whirlpool
**kënda'q = këna'q·
kënd'dre'jtë
  I § *adj* rectangular, orthogonal, right-angled
  II § *nm* rectangle

kë|ndej *adv, prep (abl)* = **këte'j**
  ○ **këndej pari** over this way, around over here
  ○ **këndej e tutje** from now on
këndej|më *adj (i)* = **këte'jmë**
këndej|shë**m** *adj (i)* = **këte'jsh**ë**m**
këndell· *vt* **1** to revive, vitalize; refresh **2** *(Fig)* to enliven; cheer [] up **3** = **skuq**
këndell·et *vpr* **1** to become enlivened; revive, be refreshed **2** to blush, become flushed **3** *(Fig)* to become happy; be full of life
këndellë**t** *adj (i)* fresh, thriving
këndell|je *nf ger* **1** < **këndell·**, **këndell·et 2** freshness; briskness
këndell|ur *adj (i)* **1** enlivened; revived, refreshed **2** *(Fig)* happy, satisfied; full of life
*****kë|nde'naj** *(Reg)* = **këtej**
kënde's *nm* **1** rooster, cock **2** *(Iron)* braggart, showoff **3** *(Colloq)* rooster's early morning crow
kënde'z *nm* = **kënde's**
këndë *nf* = **ë'ndje**
kënd'gjerë *adj* containing an obtuse angle, obtuse (said of a triangle)
*****kënd'ik** *nf(Old)* harmony, tune
kënd'im *nm ger* **1** < **këndo'·n**, **këndo'·het 2** reading ability; reading lesson **3** elementary reader (book) containing an assortment of readings: short stories, poems, essays **4** *(Old)* education, book knowledge: learning
këndirr· *vt* **1** to suffocate [] **2** *(Fig)* to bear [misfortune] with great patience and endurance
këndirr·et *vpr* **1** to be out of breath **2** *(Fig)* to become very depressed
kënd'is *stem for 1st sg pres, pl pres, 2nd & 3rd sg subj, pind* < **kënd'it·**
kënd'it· *vt* to attract, win [] over
kënd'it·et *vpr* to become satiated
*****këndje'll·** = **kënde'll·**
kënd'mat'es *nm* tool for measuring angles: protractor
kënd'ngu'shtë *adj* (of triangles) acute
këndo'·het *vp impers* it *is* easy to see, it *is* obvious
këndo'·n
  I § *vt, vi* **1** to sing **2** *(Colloq)* to read **3** to sing praises
  II § *vt* = **ysht·**
  III § *vi* to say (in writing)
  ○ **<> këndo·n aliilluja** *(Pej)* **1** to praise <> excessively, praise <> to the skies; flatter <> **2** to agree with whatever <> says: say amen to anything <> says
  ○ **nuk <> këndo·n**^{3sg} **buza** <> *does* not smile
  ○ **<> këndo·n fermanin** *(Old)* **1** to sentence <> to death **2** to treat <> very badly
  ○ **<> këndon gishti** "<>'s finger sings" <> is very skillful with a gun
  ○ **<> këndo·n**^{3p1} **dyzet gjela përmbi kokë** <> *has* too many things to worry about
  ○ **<> këndo·n**^{3sg} **gjeli në samar** "the rooster is crowing on the saddle" everything *is going* well for <>
  ○ **<> këndo·n kollofruthin** *(Colloq)* to have nothing more to do with <>, desert: dump, break up with <>; give <> up, pull out of <>; give up on <>
  ○ **nuk këndo·n me perde** to sing off-key
  ○ **s'këndon më ajo qyqe** "that cuckoo sings no more" those days are gone forever
  ○ **nuk <> këndo·n**^{3sg} **më gjeli në shtëpi** none of <>'s family *is* alive
  ○ **<> këndo·n në tru** *(Tease)* <> goes crazy
  ○ **<> këndo·n në vesh** "blow/whisper/sing in <>'s ear" to egg <> on
  ○ **këndo·n**^{3p1} **njësh** to sing a drone
  ○ **këndo·n**^{3sg} **qyqja për** [] "the cuckoo *sings (mourns)* for []" **1** [] *has* a premonition of disaster **2** no one cares about [] anymore
  ○ **<> këndoftë qyqja!** "May the cuckoo sing for <>!" *(Curse)* May <> die!
  ○ **këndo·n sipas avazit të <>** to do whatever will please <>, agree with anything <> says
  ○ **<> këndo·n**^{3sg} **veshi (i djathtë)** "<>'s (right) ear *is singing*" <> *has* a presentiment of something bad
  ○ **<> këndo·n**^{3sg} **zemra** <> *is* very happy
  ○ **<> këndoftë zemra** "May <>'s heart sing!" *(Felic)* I wish <> happiness!
  ○ **<> këndo·n**^{3p1} **zorrët** <>'s stomach is growling/rumbling (from hunger)
  ○ **S'këndon zhaba në të thatë.** "The frog does not croak on dry land." **1** *(Prov)* The action must be suited to the situation. **2** *(Pej)* (said of someone who has to be bribed to do something)
këndo'r *adj* angular
këndo're *nf* **1** cornerstone *****2** *(Old)* lectern, reading-desk
kënd'shëm *adj (i)* **1** pleasant, nice, agreeable, congenial **2** happy, pleasurable
këndu'ar *adj (i)* **1** *(Colloq)* well-read, schooled, educated **2** (of dancing) accompanied by singing
*****këndu'es** *nm* *(Colloq)* reader = **lexu'es**
këndu'eshëm *adj (i)* **1** easy to sing and to learn: singable *****2** *(Colloq)* educated, learned
kënd'vështr'im *nm* point of view
*****kënell·** = **kënde'll·**
kënellë *nf* bunghole
kënetë *nf* marsh, bog, wetlands
kënetëz'im *nm ger* **1** < **kënetëzo'·het 2** marshland
kënetëzo'·het *vpr* to turn into a marsh
kënetëzu'ar *adj (i)* turned into a marsh
kënet'ishtë *nf* marshy area: marsh, swamp
kënet'or *adj* **1** growing in a marsh; pertaining to marshes; marshlike **2** having marshes
*****kë'në** *nf* [*Bot*] henna (*Lawsonia inermis*)
këngë *nf* **1** song **2** canto
  ○ **këngë ahengu** song suitable for weddings
  ○ **këngë majëkrahut** unaccompanied epic song of the northern mountainous region of Albania sung on a high pitch by one or two singers placing one hand behind the ear
  ○ **këngë mbi krah** = **këngë majëkra'hut**
  ○ **këngë e Mukës** the same old story
këngë**ta'r**
  I § *n* singer
  II § *adj* skilled in singing
  ○ **këngëtar shëtitës** wandering minstrel
këngë**to'r** *adj* = **këng**ë**ta'r**
*****kënko'l** *nm* [*Bot*] = **kuko'l**
*****këno'çe** = **këna'çe**
kënu't *adj* (of animals) light gray
këpuca'r *n* shoemaker, cobbler

këpucarí *nf* **1** shoemaking (as a profession), shoecraft **2** shoemaker's workshop, shoe factory *3 footwear

këpucë *nf* **1** shoe **2** agent's fee
○ **këpucë me qafë** low boot, hiking boot
○ **këpucë të larta** high-heeled shoes

këpucëbërës *nm* = **këpucar**

këpucëbërësí *nf* = **këpucëtore**

këpucëgrísur
I § adj **1** having worn-out shoes **2** poverty-stricken
II § nm **1** poor man; person with worn-out shoes **2** *(Old Pej)* spy

këpucëpastrónjës *nm* bootblack

këpucëtar *nm* = **këpucar**

këpucëtarí *nf* = **këpucari**

këpucëtore *nf* **1** = **këpucari 2** *(Old)* shoestore

*këpucínë *nf* half-shoe

këpuckë *nf dimin* little shoe

*këpuje *nf(Old)* arc, sector, segment

këpujë *nf* **1** round fruit; berry **2** drop of liquid, blob **3** *(Colloq)* button **4** *(Ling)* copula

këpujór *adj* [*Ling*] copular

këpurdhë = **kërpudhë**

këpus *stem for 1st sg pres, pl pres, 2nd & 3rd sg subj, pind* <**këput**·

këpushë *nf* **1** [*Entom*] tick **2** person who is a social parasite
○ **këpusha e hardhisë** [*Entom*] grape leaf blister mite *(Eriophyes vitis P.)*

këput·
I § vt **1** to sever; break; break [] off **2** to wean **3** to cause [] despair **4** *(Colloq)* to kill **5** *(Fig Colloq)* to smack; damage [] badly **6** to redirect, divert **7** *(Fig)* to take a shortcut in [] **8** to plow [] a second time, plow [] again
II § vi *(Colloq)* to talk in an offensive manner; blather away
○ *<>***a këput**· *(Colloq)* to hit <> (hard), get <> **na e këputi me sa fuqi kishte** he struck us as hard as he could **Afrohu dhe këputja mu në ballë!** Get close and shoot him right through the forehead!
○ **këput· arrëzën/qafën!** "Break your neck!" *(Pej)* Get the hell out of here! To Hell with you!
○ **këput· arrëzën 1** to fall and get badly hurt, break one's neck **2** to leave at last
○ **këput· edhe qimen** to be a sharpshooter
○ *<>***a këput· frymën** to touch <> to the quick, affect <> deeply
○ **ia këput· gjumit 1** to fall into a deep sleep **2** *(Crude)* to fall asleep on the job, sleep at the switch
○ *<>* **këput· ijët 1** to make <> split <>'s sides laughing, break <> up **2** to tell <> a pack of lies
○ *<>***a këput· kokën** to take care of <> for good; kill <>
○ *<>* **këput· lakun** to get <> out of trouble, get <> out of a jam
○ **këput· mish** to get a sprain, sprain oneself
○ [] **këput· në mes 1** to break [] off before the end, interrupt/stop [] in the middle **2** to hurt [someone] very badly, do [] a lot of damage
○ **e këput· pazarin** "cut/break the haggling" to stop haggling, settle on a price
○ *<>* **këput· plumbin** *(Colloq)* to shoot <>: make <> eat lead
○ **këput· prangat/vargonjtë** to gain one's freedom

○ **e këput· punën** to be very straightforward
○ **këput· qafën 1** to fall and get badly hurt, break one's neck **2** to leave at last
○ *<>***a këput· shpirtin** to touch <> to the quick, affect <> deeply
○ **këput· prangat/vargonjtë** to gain one's freedom
○ **këput· zverkun 1** to fall and get badly hurt, break one's neck **2** to leave at last

këput·*et vpr* **1** to break, fall apart **2** to get very tired, become exhausted **3** to become faint **4** to break off and fall down **5** *(Fig)* to stop suddenly, break off **6** *(Fig)* to feel deep sadness
○ **këput**·*et^{3sg}* **beli 1** <> gets very tired from hard work **2** <>'s back hurts (at the waist), <> *has* lumbago
○ *<>* **këput**·*et^{3pl}* **brinjët** <>'s ribs are caving in; <> *gets* tired to the bone, <> *becomes* utterly exhausted
○ *<>* **këput**·*et* **gërbet** to get bone tired; break one's bones with effort
○ *<>* **këput**·*et* **këllqet** to get bone tired; break one's bones with effort
○ *<>* **këput**·*et* **kërbishtet** to get bone tired; break one's bones with effort
○ *<>* **këput**·*et^{3pl}* **krahët** <> *breaks* <>'s bones working, <> *works* <>'s tail off
○ *<>* **këput**·*et^{3pl}* **kryqet** <> *becomes* physically exhausted: <> *gets* bone tired **2** <> *breaks* <>'s bones with effort
○ *<>* **këput**·*et^{3sg}* **kurrizi** <>'s back *is breaking* from overwork
○ *<>* **këput**·*et^{3sg}* **mesi** <>'s back *is breaking*, <> *is* worn out from backbreaking work
○ **këput**·*et* **ndër vete** *(Euph)* to get a hernia
○ **këput**·*et* **për gjumë** *(Colloq)* to be badly in need of sleep
○ *<>* **këput**·*et^{3sg}* **rripi i pallës** "the belt holding <>'s sword breaks" <> *is* knocked off <>'s high horse
○ *<>* **këput**·*et^{3sg}* **shpina** <>'s back *is breaking* from overwork
○ **këput**·*et^{3sg}* **ylli** "the star *falls*" there *is* a falling star

këputaqafas *adv* running away very fast

këputë
I § nf **1** sole of the foot **2** = **gjurmashkë**
II § adv *(Reg Gheg)* *quite

*këputëm *adj* finished, cut-and-dried

këputës *adj* **1** tiring, exhausting **2** used for cutting apart

këputje *nf ger* **1** <**këput**·, **këput**·*et* **2** break; break point; breaking point **3** [*Bot*] marsh horsetail *(Equisetum telmataia)*

këputur
I § adj (i) **1** broken apart by pulling or twisting: severed **2** very tired, exhausted, worn out **3** *(Fig)* very poor **4** separated from the mother for weaning **5** snapped, broken off suddenly
II § n (i) very poor person

*këputhër *nf* = **kërpudhë**

*këpuzë *nf* [*Bot*] corolla of a flower

këqíj *pl (të)* <**keq**

këqíja *pl (të) fem* sorrows, misfortunes; evils, bad deeds

*këqís *nm* evildoer, criminal

këqy·r

I § *vt* **1** *(Reg Gheg)* to examine [ ] with care, study [ ] carefully: inspect, scrutinize **2** to treat with care. *II §* *vi* to watch/observe carefully, conduct a careful inspection

këqy·r·et *vpr (Reg Gheg)* to look at one's reflection

këqy·r·ës *n (Reg Gheg)* inspector; observer

këqy·rje *nf ger (Reg Gheg)* <**këqy·r·**, **këqy·r·et**

kërba·ç *nm* **1** instrument used to beat people: cudgel, club; whip **2** blow of a club/cudgel/whip

kërbë *nf* barrel, cask

kërbi·l *nm* steep/precipitous slope

kërbi·sht *nm* [*Anat*] sacrum

kërbi·shtje *np* haunches; loins

kërbishto·r *adj, nm* [*Zool*] **1** vertebrate **2** [*Med*] sacral

kërbo·ç *nm* <**kërbo·t**

kërbo·t *nm* pulverized red rock that is added to hot iron to anneal it

kërbo·tull *nf* red clay

*** kërbu·l** = **gërbu·l**

*** kërbu·lzo··n** *vt* to infect with leprosy

*** kërbu·llë** *nf* = **ko·rbull**

kërbu·nj· *vt* to bend [a part of the body used in posture]

kërbu·nj·et *vpr* to become bent over (in posture)

kërbu·njas *adv* in bent-over posture

kërby·thje *nf* **1** tail portion of a bird **2** corn stubble

kërca·cë *nf* = **stërfy·tës**

kërca·ç *nm* pod of the bladder senna

kërca·s stem for *1st sg pres, 1st & 3rd pl pres, 2nd & 3rd sg subj* <**kërce·t·**

kërce

I § *nf* **1** [*Anat*] cartilage **2** crust **3** [*Biol*] chondrin *()* *II §* *adj* brand new, crisp and clean

kërce·n

I § *vi* **1** to leap; leap up/forward/out **2** to gambol, frisk *II §* *vt, vi* to dance *III §* *vt (Colloq)* to put [ ] in quickly

○ <> **kërce·n³ˢᵍ damari** <> *bursts* into a rage, <> *loses* 's temper, <> *flies* off the handle

○ <> **kërce·n delli i ballit 1** <> *flies* off the handle, <> suddenly gets angry **2** <> *has* a capricious idea, *has* a whim

○ **e kërce·n gardhin** to overcome an obstacle

○ <> **kërce·n³ˢᵍ gjaku në kokë/tru** <>'s temper *mounts* sharply

○ <> **kërce·n³ˢᵍ gjoksi përpjetë** <>'s breast *rejoices*: <> *is* elated

○ <> **kërce·n³ˢᵍ gjuha në fyt** <>'s heart is in <>'s mouth (with fear)

○ <> **kërce·n³ˢᵍ inati** <> *explodes* with anger

○ <> **kërce·n³ᵖˡ kacabunjtë** <> *becomes* angry: <>'s blood *begins* to boil

○ <> **kërce·n³ˢᵍ kandari** <> suddenly *takes* affront, <> suddenly *gets* angry

○ <> **kërce·n në shpinë** to keep bothering <>

○ <> **kërce·n³ˢᵍ në kokë/tru** <> *gets* it into <>'s head, <> cannot get it out of <>'s mind; <> *has* a sudden whim

○ **kërce·n njëkëmbthi** to hop

○ **kërce·n përpjetë 1** to be taken aback **2** to react vehemently

○ **Kërcen prifti nga belaja.** "The priest dances because of the trouble (it would cause otherwise)" *(Tease)* Like it or not, there's no real choice.

○ **kërce·n pupthi** to hop with both feet together

○ <> **kërce·n³ᵖˡ qipujt** "the goblins *jump* on <>" <> is possessed by demons; <> *flies* into a rage?

○ <> **kërce·n³ᵖˡ rrebet** <> *bursts* into a rage

○ **kërce·n si gjel** to fly off into a rage at the least thing

○ <> **kërce·n³ˢᵍ trilli** <>'s temper *flares*, <> *flies* off the handle

○ <> **kërce·n³ᵖˡ trutë në kokë** *(Pej)* <>'s blood *boils*, <> *flies* into a rage

○ <> **kërce·n³ᵖˡ xhindet** "the jinni *jump* on <>" <> *is* possessed by demons; <> *flies* into a rage?

○ <> **kërce·n³ˢᵍ zemra përpjetë** <>'s heart *rejoices*: <> *is* elated

kërce·ll *nm (np ˜ j)* **1** stalk, stem **2** = **kërci·**

○ **kërcell kacavarës** clinging vine

kërcello·r *adj* **1** having one or more stalks: cauline *()* **2** stalk-like

kërcell‖pështje·llës *adj* (*Bot*) (of a leaf) wrapping around the stem: *(amplexicaul)*

kërce·t *vi* **1** to make a sharp percussive noise: crack, crackle, crash, crunch, creak, clatter, click **2** to set off suddenly, leave quickly **3** to start suddenly and violently: break out; (of objects used to hit people) to start to fly **4** to smack <>, bang <>

○ **kërcet·³ˢᵍ** {*object*} people *are hitting* each other with {}, {*objects*} *are flying/flailing*

○ <> **a kërcet· derën në fytyrë** to slam the door in <>'s face

○ <> **kërcet· dhëmbët** to bare one's teeth at <>, threaten <>

○ **kërcet· dhëmbët** to grate one's teeth

○ **kërcet· gishtërinjtë 1** to snap one's fingers; crack one's knuckles (fingers) **2** *(Fig)* to spend time idly

○ <> **kërcet·³ᵖˡ zorrët** <>'s stomach is growling/rumbling (from hunger)

kërcë *nf* **1** = **kërce** *2 (Fig)* unhappy woman

kërcëlli··n *vt, vi* = **kërcëllo··n**

kërcëlli·m *nm ger* **1** <**kërcëllo··n 2** = **kërcëllimë 3** bitter cold

kërcëllimë *nf* rattling sound: rattle

kërcëllitje *nf ger* = **kërcëllim**

kërcëllo··n *vt, vi* to clack, clink; crackle; rattle

○ **kërcëllo··n dhëmbët 1** to clack one's teeth **2** *(Fig)* to make a show of hostility

*** kërcënge·l** *nf* candy; dried fruit

kërcëni·m *nm ger* **1** <**kërcëno··n**, **kërcëno··het 2** threat

kërcëno··het *vpr* **1** to threaten **2** to impend

kërcëno··n *vt* **1** to threaten **2** to endanger, menace

kërcënue·s *adj* **1** threatening **2** endangering, menacing

kërcënue·shëm *adv* in a threatening manner

kërci· *nf* **1** shin, shank; lower leg; shinbone **2** part of the stocking that covers the lower leg **3** *(Reg)* stalk, stem

*** kërcie·ll** = **kërce·ll**

kërcigja·të *adj* having lower legs that are long

kërciho·llë *adj* having thin lower legs

kërc|ím *nm ger* **1** <kërc*e*·*n* **2** dance **3** [*Sport*] jumping, vaulting
  ○ **kërcim barkush** [*Track*] straddle jump
  ○ **kërcim gërshërë** [*Track*] scissors jump
  ○ **kërcim me shkop** [*Track*] pole vault
  ○ **kërcim nga vendi** [*Track*] jump from a standing position: standing jump
  ○ **kërcim së gjati** [*Track*] broad jump, long jump
  ○ **kërcim trihapësh** [*Track*] hop-and-step jump
kërc|im|ta'r *n* **1** dancer **2** [*Sport*] jumper, vaulter **3** acrobat
kërc|ím|thi *adv* in leaps and bounds
kërcí|nj *np* <kërcí
kërcí|ri *sg def, sg abl indef* <kërcí
kërcí|s *stem for 2nd pl pres, pind* <kërc*e*t·
kërcí|t *stem for pdef, opt, adm, part, pind, 2nd pl pres, imper, vp* <kërc*e*t·
kërc|ít|je *nf ger* **1** <kërc*e*t· **2** sharply percussive noise: rattling, clicking, cracking, crackling, creaking, snapping, chattering, clacking, popping
kërc|o·n *vt* to take a small bite of [something hard]: nip
kërc|o|distrofí *nf* [*Med*] achondroplasia
kërco'r *adj* cartilaginous, gristly
kërcu(r)
  I § *nm* **1** tree stump **2** log **3** block of wood
  II § *adj* **1** (*Fig Pej*) block-headed, stupid; standing in a stupor; just sitting there **2** forsaken and alone, forlorn
  ○ **kërcu përmbi samar/shkarpa** yet one more burden on top of all the others
kërcu|l *nm* clay pot
kërcun|a'r *n* wretch; idler
kërcu|nj *np fem* <kërcu(r)
kërcu|q *nm* **1** small stump; small stump of wood **2** (*Fig*) wretched person left all alone
kërcu're *nf* woman left all alone, woe-befallen woman
kërcu'ri *sg def, sg abl indef* <kërcu(r)
*****kërc|y|ell** = kërc*e*ll
kërc|yer *adj (i)* **1** protruding, bulging, jutting out **2** soured, spoiled **3** (*Fig*) impatient, impulsive **4** (*Pej*) crazy
kërc|ye's *nm* **1** (*Sport*) jumper **2** dancer
kërç = kërríç
kërça'b|ë *nf* triangular collar for a pig to prevent it from getting through a fence/hedge
kërçanja'r *nm* unripe melon
kërçe'p
  I § *nm* **1** root of the stump; stump **2** knotty log **3** hook formed in the trunk by the angle of a chopped-off branch **4** pole left with branch stumps to form the core of a haystack; haystack with such a core
  II § *adj (Fig Pej)* thickheaded, stupid
kërç|ík *nm* **1** = kërcí **2** (*Fig*) strength, skill
kërdí *nf* mass killing, massacre, slaughter
kërdí|s· *vt* **1** to massacre **2** to exhaust; beat, abuse **3** (*Fig*) to abuse [] severely with words
kërdí|s·et *vpr* **1** to suffer heavy loss or damage **2** to be exhausted **3** to do to an excess
kërdho'kull *nf* [*Anat*] **1** hipbone **2** haunch **3** bone joint
kë're *nf* [*Ornit*] teal duck (*Anas crecca L.*)
*****kë'rer** *(Reg Tosk)* = gërhan*ë*
kërëndí *nf* ruins of a wall

*****kërë'p** = kërp
kërha'n *nm* [*Ichth*] great scallop (*Pecten jacobaeus*)
kërk|a'ç *nm* **1** beggar **2** (*Pej*) person who frequently borrows things
*****kërka'h** OR **kërkahít** *adv (Reg Gheg)* from any direction, from anywhere
kërk|e's|ë *nf* **1** request **2** requirement **3** [*Econ*] demand
kërk|es|ë|padí *nf* [*Law*] writ for petition of legal rights
kërk|ím *nm ger* **1** <kërko'·*n*, kërko'·*het* **2** search; inquiry **3** research
kërk|im|o'r *adj* pertaining to research
kërk|im|ta'r
  I § *n* researcher, explorer
  II § *adj* = kërkimo'r
kërk|o·het *vp impers* it *is* required
kërk|o·n
  I § *vt* **1** to seek; search for [] **2** to do research on [] **3** to ask for [] **4** to try, attempt **5** to require **6** to claim, demand [recognition of a right] **7** to deserve; need **8** (*Colloq*) to wander around
  II § *vi* **1** to be demanding **2** (of animals) to rut, try to find a sexual mate
  ○ <>**a kërko·n** **1** to ask <> for [] **2** (*Crude*) to ask <> to have sex: ask <> for [it]
  ○ **kërko·n dardha nga boriga** to ask for the impossible
  ○ **kërko·n derë e ferrë** to search everywhere
  ○ **kërko·n dynjanë** to look everywhere: beat the bushes looking
  ○ **kërko·n dheun** to look everywhere: beat the bushes looking
  ○ **kërko·n fjalë** to be looking for an argument, be asking for a fight
  ○ **kërko·n fjalën** to try to get a word in, try to get the floor
  ○ **kërko·n gjilpërën në kashtë/mullar/bar** to look for a needle in a haystack
  ○ **kërko·n halën në përpeq** "look for the hair in the cheese pastry" to try to find fault with everything
  ○ <> **kërko·n hesap** to call <> to account, demand an explanation from <>
  ○ **kërko·n hënën** to make an impossible demand
  ○ **kërko·n kallëza në borë** to ask for the impossible
  ○ **kërko·n kaun në gji** to look for [] in the wrong place
  ○ **kërko·n këmbë për gjemb** to look for a fight, ask for trouble
  ○ **kërko·n litar prej rëre/kumi** "want a rope made of sand/" to want something impossible, ask for something impossible
  ○ <> **kërko·n llogari** to call <> to account, demand an explanation from <>
  ○ [] **kërko·n me gjak e me lak** to seek out [] in a rage
  ○ [] **kërko·n me qiri** to look for [] everywhere
  ○ **kërko·n me mend** to think out
  ○ **Kërko·n**[opt] **murin me dorë!** "May {} look for the wall with {}'s hands" (*Curse*) May {} go blind!
  ○ [] **kërko·n në gur të shpuar** to search very hard for []
  ○ [] **kërko·n në qiell dhe** [] **gje·n në tokë** "look for [] in the sky and find [] on the ground" to search everywhere for [] before finding [] in a place that should have been obvious

○ **kërko**·*n* **petulla me gjalpë** "want pancakes with butter (rather than with the usual oil)" to want too much; have a desire for things that are too expensive

○ **kërko**·*n* **për mokra** *(Pej)* to chatter away

○ **kërko**·*n* **pleshta në kashtë** "look for fleas in straw" **1** to look for a needle in a haystack **2** to fritter away the time

○ **kërko**·*n* **qimen në vezë** "look for the hair in an egg" to try to find fault, pick at details

○ **kërko**·*n* **qimen në kashtë/mullar/bar** to look for a needle in a haystack

○ **kërko**·*n* **qimen në përpeq** "look for the hair in the cheese pastry" to try to find fault with everything

○ **kërko**·*n* **qimet e kokës** "ask for the hairs of the head" to demand an exorbitant price

○ **kërko**·*n* **qiqra në hell** to ask the impossible

○ **e kërko**·*n* **si breshka te nallbani** to be looking for trouble

○ **e kërko**·*n* **sherrin me qiri 1** to be looking for any excuse to fight **2** to be asking for trouble

○ **kërko**·*n* **shtjerrat e deshve** "look for ram's lambs" to ask for the impossible

○ **kërko**·*n* **ta ndalë ujin me këmbë** "try to block the water with the feet" to try to do something hopeless, try to do the impossible

○ **kërko**·*n* **të arri**·*n*^{subj} **erën** to try to achieve the impossible

○ **kërko**·*n* **të ha**·^{subj} **me dy lugë** "try to eat with two spoons" *(Pej)* opportunistically play both sides to one's advantage

○ **kërko**·*n* **të ha**·^{subj} **me lugë të madhe** "try to eat with a big spoon" *(Pej)* to try to get more than one's share: be greedy

○ **kërko**·*n* **të ngec**·^{subj} **me** [] to pick a fight with [], look for an excuse to fight []

○ **kërko**·*n* **të zërë peshk në prevë** "try to catch fish at the river ford" to go to a lot of trouble for nothing; do useless work

○ [] **kërko**·*n* **vend më vend e mal më mal** to search high and low for []

○ **kërko**·*n* **vendin** to look everywhere: beat the bushes looking

kërku'ar *adj (i)* **1** requested, asked for **2** recherché, esoteric

kërku'es

I § *adj* **1** demanding, exacting **2** = **kërkimo'r**

II § *n* **1** *(Offic)* applicant; petitioner **2** researcher **3** searcher; prospector

kërku'eshëm *adj (i)* in great demand

kër'ku'q *nm* children's disease manifested by red blotches on the skin

*****kërku't**ë *nf* [*Bot*] khella *(Ammi visgana)*

kërle'sh·*et vpr* **1** to have one's hair stand on end **2** to fight **3** to get interwoven; get entangled/complicated

kërle'shje *nf ger* **1** < **kërlesh**·*et* **2** fighting with fists and kicking: tussle

kërle'shur *adj (i)* touseled, frizzy

kërlu'k *nm* shepherd's crook

*****kërma's**ëm *nf* millrace

kër'më *nf* **1** carrion **2** *(Colloq)* carcass **3** *(Fig Insult)* walking corpse

kërmë'z

I § *nm* dark red dye

II § *adj* scarlet

kërmi'll

I § *nm (np ˜j)* **1** [*Invert*] snail **2** [*Anat*] cochlea

II § *adj* spiral

○ **kërmill deti/uji** [*Invert*] sea slug

○ **kërmill lakuriq** slug

○ **kërmill me samar** snail

○ **kërmill i veshit** [*Med*] cochlea

○ **kërmill i zhveshur** "unclothed snail" [*Zool*] slug

kërmillo'r *adj* **1** snail-shaped **2** [*Med*] cochlear

kërmi'në *nf* stomach of a ruminant: rumen

kërna'c

I § *adj* stingy, miserly

II § *nm* skinflint, miser

kërna'ckë *nf (Reg)* rolled meat patty

*****kërna'l** *adj* bald

*****kërna'l**·*et vpr* to grow bald

kërna'lle

I § *nf* barren land

II § *adj* empty

kër'ndez·*et vpr* to get all worked up (into a rage), get angry

kërne'të *nf (Colloq)* clarinet

*****kërnja'll**ët *adj (i)* brisk

kërp *nm* hemp *(Cannabis sativa)*

○ **kërp dheu** [*Zool*] = **uri'th**

kërpa'ç *nm (Colloq)* **1** = **arnu'es 2** *(Pej)* person incompetent in his profession

kërpaç'ë'ri *nf (Pej)* professional incompetence

kërpana'k *nm* dapple-gray horse

kërpe'sh *nm* = **kapi'st**ër

kër'p'ët *adj (i)* = **kë'rpt**ë

kër'p'ëz *nf* [*Ornit*] goldfinch *(Carduelis carduelis)*

kërpi'·*n* *vi* to eat a snack with one's (alcoholic) drink

kërpi'cë

I § *nf* disorderly heap

II § *adv* **1** completely full **2** in a disorderly heap

kërpi'shtë *nf* = **kërpo're**

kër'pi't· *vt* **1** to eat [] all up **2** to do well; fix up

kërpi't·*et vpr* **1** to eat a lot **2** to get fat **3** to get well, recover **4** to get dressed and adorned (for a wedding): get all fixed up

kërp'najë *nf* = **kërpo're**

kërpo're

I § *nf* field planted in hemp

II § *np* [*Bot*] hemp family *Cannabaceae*

kër'ptë *adj (i)* **1** hempen, made of hemp **2** light gray

*****kërpu'c** *nm* pinch of snuff

kërpu'dhë *nf* **1** [*Bot*] large fungus: mushroom, toadstool **2** [*Bot*] pileus *()* **3** [*Biol*] fungus infection **4** *(Fig)* person who is a social parasite

○ **kërpudhë dashe** [*Bot*] edible pink mushroom

○ **kërpudhë derri** [*Bot*] poisonous mushroom: Satan's mushroom, blood-red boletus *Boletus satanus, Dictyopus tuberosus*

○ **kërpudhë gjarpri** [*Bot*] inedible toadstool with white cap and black underside

○ **kërpudhë e helmët** toadstool

○ **kërpudhë jevgu** [*Bot*] granulated boletus *Boletus granulatus*

○ **kërpudhë pipiriqe** [*Bot*] kind of fungus

○ **kërpudhë plehu** "manure fungus" completely worthless person, low-life

○ **kërpudhë qeni** [*Bot*] kind of mushroom usually found growing on wood *Hypholoma fascicularis*

○ **kërpudhë trashje** [*Bot*] edible mushroom with abundant white flesh

kërpudho'r *adj* fungal

kërpu'sh· *vt* to remove the plush from [ ]

kërpu'sh·*et vpr* to lose its plush

kërpu'shje *nf ger* 1 <kërpu'sh·, kërpu'sh·*et* 2 removal/loss of plush

*__kërqabë__ = kërçabë

kërqel'o·*n vt* = gëlqero's·

kërqel'lë *nf* 1 doorhinge 2 = kërqel'ë

*__kërqil'lik__ *OR* **kërqil'lik** *nm* trigger guard

*__kërs__ = kërc|

*__kërsne'qe__ *nf* = kërci|

*__kërshë__ *nf* = karsh

kërshënde'lla *nf(Old)* Christmas

kërshëri *nf* curiosity, inquisitiveness, lively interest

*__kërshle'ma__ = kërshënde'lla

kërshnje't *nm* [*Bot*] tree phillyrea *(Phillyrea media)*

*__kërte'së__ *OR* **kërte'zë** = kërrabëz

kërtil·*et vpr* = kano's·*et*

kërto'le *nf* thighbone; long bone

kërto'llë *nf* (*Reg*) potato

*__kërtyl__ *adj* fat, fattened

kërtyl· *vt* 1 to feed [ ] till full: gorge 2 to sate

kërtyl·*et vpr* to be sated; get fat

kërtyl'ë *adv* more full, full

kërth'azi
 I § *adv* 1 along/on the side; sidelong, obliquely 2 by a shortcut
 II § *prep (abl)* by the side of

*__kërthe'la__ *np* = karthje

kërth'ët *adj (i)* 1 oblique 2 cross-eyed

kërthi *(r)*
 I § *nm (np ~nj)* 1 suckling lamb or kid; runt lamb or kid; lamb or kid born out of season 2 newborn child, infant; small and weak child; premature baby 3 *(Pet)* baby of old parents, parent's pet child: little darling 4 young and tender plant; plant stunted in growth, dwarf plant
 II § *adj* 1 newborn, young, immature 2 *(Fig)* immature, unripe

*__kërthi'·n__ *vt* to soften; crumble

kërthi'çël *nf* short, skinny, sickly woman

*__kërthija'k__ *adj* bristly

kërthi'ngël *nf* [*Ornit*] lapwing = piskë

kërthi'nj *np* <kërthi

kërthi'nja *np* late harvested crops

kërthi'njak *adj* new-born baby; premature baby; sickly baby

kërthi'një *nf* = kërthi

kërthinji *nf* early childhood, infancy

kërthi'njtë *adj (i)* 1 newly born; premature 2 not yet ripe

kërthi'ri *sg def, sg abl indef* <kërthi

kërthiza'k *nm* very small cucumber

kërthi'zë *nf* 1 [*Anat*] umbilical cord 2 belly button, navel 3 carved rose 4 *(Fig)* center, middle

kërthi'zëku'q *adj* having a red spot in the middle; having a red center (of some fruits and vegetables)
 ○ **fasule/groshë kërthizëkuqe** type of large bean with a large dark spot in the middle, black-eyed pea

kërthizo'r *adj* 1 umbilical; shaped like an umbilical cord 2 *(Fig)* central

kërth'nde'z·*et vpr* 1 to grow into healthy adulthood 2 to become refreshed 3 to flourish 4 *(Fig)* to get angry

kërth'nde'zët *adj (i)* = kërthnde'zur

kërth'nde'zur *adj (i)* 1 grown into healthy adulthood 2 refreshed 3 well-developed, exuberant 4 *(Fig)* angry

*__kërth'ne'z__ = kërthnde'z

*__kërva'll·***et vpr* to bray = gërva'll·*et*

kërve'sh· *vt* to contort [parts of the face]

kërve'sh·*et vpr* 1 to grimace, make faces 2 (of parts of the face) to become contorted

kërve'shje *nf ger* 1 <kërve'sh·, kërve'sh·*et* 2 grimace

*__kërve'sh'ur__ *adj (i)* grimacing, wry-faced

*__kërx__ = kërc|

kërr
 I § *nm* 1 = kërri'ç 2 light gray horse, dappled gray horse
 II § *onomat* sound of crunching
 III § *adj* 1 grayish 2 (of land) barren

kërra'bë *nf* 1 shepherd's crook 2 forked prop 3 hook from which something is hung 4 mattock
 ○ **kërrabë deti** [*Bot*] kind of small red alga *Hypnea musciformis*

kërra'bës *nf* = kërrabëz

kërra'bëz *nf* 1 crochet hook, crochet needle 2 small hook

*__kërrcu'kës__ *nm* somersault

kërrç = kërri'ç

*__kërre__ = kerrkë

kërre's *stem for 1st sg pres, pl pres, 2nd & 3rd sg subj* <kërret·

kërret· *vi* (of pigs) to grunt; (of cats) purr; (of crows) caw

kërri'ç *n* 1 [*Zool*] donkey colt 2 *(Fig Insult)* immature and foolish young child: silly kid

kërri'gë *nf* 1 thin knitting needle; embroidery hook; crochet needle 2 = gjilpëry'er

*__kërri'kull__ *nm (np ~j)* 1 = shelqëro'r 2 forked prop in a vineyard

kërri's *stem for 1st sg pres, pl pres, pind* <kërret·

kërri't *stem for pind, imper, pdef, 2nd pl pres, part* <kërret·

kërri'tje *nf* repetitive sound made by certain animals: cawing (of crows); grunting (of pigs); purring (of cats)

*__kërr'kund__ = kurrku'nd

*__kërr'kush__ = kurrku'sh

kërr'lë *nf* thin mud, muck

kërrmi *nf* [*Entom*] wood worm, larva of the furniture/deathwatch beetle *(Anobium punctatum (domesticum))*

*__kërrna'm__ *nm* impertinence, audacity

kërrna'me *np* = naze

kërrnjo't·*et vpr* 1 to get infected with distemper 2 = përqu'rre·t 3 to doze off and snore 4 *(Fig Pej)* to spend time in idleness

kërrnjo'të *nf* [*Med Veter*] farcy

kërro'çe *nf* 1 new-born mule, mule foal 2 one or two year old mule

kërru's· *vt* 1 to bow [part of the body], bend [ ] down, hunch over 2 to make [ ] shrunken and stooped-over 3 *(Fig)* to bring to one's knees: subjugate

kërru's·et *vpr* **1** to become hunched over; hunch over **2** *(Fig)* to bow down, submit

kërru'slëm OR **kërru'slët** *adj (i)* = kërru'sur

kërru'sur *adj (i)* **1** hunched over; stooped **2** hunchbacked **3** *(Fig)* brought to one's knees: submissive **4** *(Old)* [*Publ*] = kursi'v

kërru'të *nf, adj* (animal) with backward-curling horns; (ewe) with small horns

kësa'ç *nm* pliers

kësaj
  I § *dat/abl* <kjo
  II § *gen (i)* of this, of this one, of her <kjo
  ○ **kësaj shultinë** one of these days

***kësaj't** *adv* this way

këse·n *vi impers* ◇ feels a twinge/pang

kësi *masc abl (Old)* this kind of, like this <ky, këta'

kësilloj *determiner* = kësiso'j

*kësimjeti** *adv* hereby, herewith, thus

kësisoj
  I § *determiner* of this sort, such, this sort of
  II § *adv* in this manner, in such a way; just like this, in the same way, thus, so

kësish *dat/abl* <këta'

kësmet *nm (Colloq)* kismet: good luck; fate

këso' *fem dat/abl* this kind of, like this <kjo, këto'
  ○ **këso dore 1** of this kind **2** in this way

kësodo're
  I § *determiner* such, of this sort
  II § *adv* in this manner/way

këso'llë *nf (Reg Gheg)* = kaso'lle

këso'sh *dat/abl* <këto'

këst *nm* installment payment

kësule'r *nm [Ornit]* = çafkëlo're

kësu'lë *nf* **1** brimless cap, skullcap **2** game in which children in a circle try to capture a cap placed in their center **3** [*Spec*] object shaped like a skullcap: dome **4** [*Anat*] second chamber of the stomach of a ruminant: reticulum

kësulë ba'rdhë *adj* white-capped

kësulë ku'qe *nf* **1** [*Folklore*] girl in a folktale who wears a red cap, Little Red Riding Hood **2** [*Bot*] small mushroom with a reddish cap

kësulta'r *nm* cap-maker

*kësu're** *nf(Old)* carrot

*kësy'eme** *nf (e)* sharp/stabbing pain

*këshet** *nm* = gërshe't

*këshete** *np fem* = gërdhu'shta

kështill *nm* **1** council **2** high government body: board
  ○ **kështilli gjyqësor** council of judges acting as an appeals court

kështi'llë *nf* advice, counsel

kështillë mba're *adj* good at taking advice: amenable, responsive; compliant

kështillë mi're *adj* giving good advice; of good counsel

kështill im *nm ger* **1** <kështillo·n, kështillo·het **2** consultation **3** = kështi'llë **4** warning admonition
  ○ **kështillim i gjyqtarit** [*Soccer*] warning by the referee: caution

kështill imo'r *adj* advisory; consultative

kështill imo're *nf* = konsulto're

kështillo·het *vpr* to consult/confer

kështillo·n *vt* to advise

kështillta'r *n* **1** counselor, advisor; counsel **2** consultant **3** council member

kështillue's *adj* offered as advice; advisory

kështillue'shëm *adj (i)* advisable

*kështne'lla** = kërshënde'lla

*kështqe'l** *nm* = kështje'llë

kështa'llë *nf* splint = gëzhda'llë

kështallo·n *vt* to immobilize [ ] with a splint, put [ ] into splints = gëzhda'llë

*kështa'rpë** *nf* [*Bot*] setaria, foxtail millet *(Setaria)*

*kështellja'n** *(Old)* = kështjella'r

*kështe'një** = gështe'një

kështjella'r *n* [*Hist*] **1** castle owner/commander *(Old)* *2 castle guard *3 (Old)* steward

kështje'llë *nf* **1** [*Hist*] castle, fortress, citadel **2** [*Mil*] metal shield protecting a gun emplacement **3** *(Fig)* symbol of success won by overcoming difficulties
  ○ **kështjellë në rërë** "castle on sand" something built on an unstable foundation: house of cards; footprint in the sand
  ○ **kështjellë prej karte/letre** house of cards

*kështjello·n** *vt* to garrison

kështjello'r *adj* of or pertaining to castles/fortresses

*kështo·n** = kushto'·n

*kësht** *(Old)* = këst

kështu *adv* **1** I like this, thus, in this way **2** so **3** okay
  ○ **Kështu i do mushka drutë.** "This is how the mule wants the logs." *(Pej)* That's what { } deserves. { } is just getting the punishment { } deserves.
  ○ **e kështu me radhë** and so on (and so forth)
  ○ **kështu ë? 1** is that clear!?; right!? **2** is that so!?
  ○ **kështu e ka·** { } it's in { }'s nature/character to act that/this way
  ○ **kështu e ka·** this *is* how { } *does* things; that's just the way { } *is/behaves*, that's { }'s manner
  ○ **kështu e ka·**[pl] **kuvendin** this is what { } agree on
  ○ **kështu e kështu** and so on and so on
  ○ **kështu nuk shkohet** this just won't do, one can't go on like this
  ○ **kështu ose ashtu** in any case, however it may be
  ○ **kështu që** this being the case: so that; therefore, so
  ○ **kështu qoftë** I hope so!
  ○ **kështu e tutje** from now on, from here on out
  ○ **kështu ësh·të**[3sg] **(e) thënë** "so it *is* said (written)" that's how the cookie crumbles, that's the way it goes

kështu tu'tje *adv* from now on

kështy're *nf* mountain trail

kët

këta *proximal 3rd pers pl masc determiner* **1** they, these **2** recent (with units of time)

*këtan shëm** *adj (i)* near here, over this way

këtej
  I § *adv* **1** over here, this way; in this direction, hither **2** around here **3** from here; from this point (in time) **4** in consequence of this
  II § *prep (abl)* on this side of
  ○ **këtej <> hy·n**[3sg] **(e) këtej <> del·**[3sg] *(Impol)* it *goes* in one ear (of ◇) and out the other
  ○ **Këtej të pi· verën, andej të shan derën** "here one drinks your wine, there he curses your whole family" (said of someone who is a hypocritical ingrate
  ○ **këtej e tutje** from now on, from this point on

këtejas *OR* **këtejazi** *adv* = këtej

këtejbregas *adj, n* (person) dwelling/situated in territory on this side (of a river/lake)

këtejdetas
I § adj pertaining to territory on this side of the sea
II § adj, n (person) inhabiting or coming from territory on this side of the sea

këtejlumas *adj, n* (person) dwelling/situated in territory on this side of the river

këtejmë *adj (i)* = këtejshëm

këtejmi *adv (së)* from here

*këtejna *adv* = këtej

këtejsë *adj (i)* = këtejshëm

këtejshëm *adj (i)* from here, from around here: local

këtejza *adv* = këtej

këtë
I § acc <ky this; him
II § acc <kjo this; her
○ **këtë çast** right now
○ **këtë udhë** this time, this time around

*këti

këtij *dat/abl* <ky

këtillë *adj (i)* **1** such as this, like this **2** such

*këtje *proximal adv* **1** = këtu **2** from here to there

këto *proximal 3rd pers pl fem determiner* **1** these, they **2** recent (with units of time)

këtu *proximal adv* here, over here
○ **këtu-këtje** here and there
○ **këtu drejt** in this direction
○ **këtu e/ta ka·** (fjalën) that's what {} *is driving* at, here is what {} *is trying* to say
○ **këtu e kam** that's precisely it! that's the point!
○ **këtu e këti** this way and that
○ **këtu rrotull** around here somewhere, somewhere around here
○ **këtu <>a sjell·** (said while touching the tip of one's nose) to bring <> to the end of <>'s patience: <> *has* had it up to here with {}
○ **këtu e tutje** from now on: henceforth

këtupari *adv* somewhere around here, somewhere close by

këtushëm *adj (i)* located here, of this place, from around here, from here: local

këtyre *dat/abl* <këto, këta

këth = kth

*këthmill = kërmill

k.f. *abbrev* hp. (horsepower)

KGB *abbrev (Russian)* <**Komitet Gosudarstvennoj Bezopasnosti** KGB = (Soviet) State Security Committee

Khs *abbrev* <**krahaso** c.f. = compare

khu-khu *onomat* coughing sound of someone choking

ki *imper* <ka·

ki·het *vpr*
○ **s'<> kihet me** [] <> doesn't get along with []

ki·n *vt* to trim [] by lopping off extra branches, prune [a grapevine]

kiamet
I § nm (Colloq) **1** [Relig] end of the world, apocalypse **2** disaster, calamity, catastrophe **3** terrible storm; flood; heavy rain
II § adv very much, completely

kiavetë *nf* [Tech] **1** machine key **2** dowel

kibernetikë *nf* cybernetics

kic· *vt* **1** to bite down on [] lightly **2** *(Child)* to bite on [] with the teeth

kica *np* child's first teeth, milk teeth

kicilo·n *vt (Colloq)* to tickle = gudulís·

*kicimic *nm (Old)* goblin, demon

kiciribë *nf* * [Ornit] lapwing *(Vanellus vanellus)*

kiç *nm* stern (of a boat/ship); poop deck

kiçe *nf* **1** small container for liquids **2** crag

Kiço *nf with masc agreement* Kiço (male name)

*kiemas *adv* obliquely

kijas *stem for 1st sg pres, pl pres, 2nd & 3rd sg subj, pind* <kijat·

kijat· *vi* **1** to whine **2** to sob

*kijtas *adv (Reg Gheg)* tilted, sloping, awry

*kikatim *nm* crowing: cockadoodledoo

kikë *nf* **1** sharp tip, point **2** highest point: peak, crest, top **3** mane of a horse **4** head of grain; corn tassel

kikël *nf* fine tip, sharp point

kikëz *nf* **1** tendon **2** spout of a water kettle/pitcher **3** Adam's apple

*kikiku *onomat* cockadoodledoo

kikirik *nm* [Bot] peanut *(Arachis hypogaea)*

kikiriki *onomat* sound of a rooster: cockadoodledoo

*kilas *stem for 1st sg pres, pl pres, 2nd & 3rd sg subj, pind* <kilat·

*kilat· *vt* to incite, provoke, rouse, excite

kile *nf* **1** *(Colloq)* kilogram **2** cartridge case **3** = kilzë

*kilë *nf* **1** joint (of meat) **2* roll, bread

kilësh *adj* of a kilogram in weight, weighing a kilogram

Kili *nm* Chile

Kili *nm* Chile

kilian *adj, n* Chilean

kiliko·het *vpr (Colloq)* = kilikos·et

kiliko·n *vt (Colloq)* = kilikos·

kilikos· *vt (Colloq)* to tickle = gudulís·

kilikos·et *vpr (Colloq)* = gudulís·et

kilikosje *nf ger (Colloq)* = gudulísje

*kilivishe
I § nf, adj (Old) spiral = spirale
II § adv (Old) in a spiral

*kilivishuer *adj (fem ~ore) (Old)* spiral

*kilizo·n *vt* = gudulís·

*kilkazë *nf* = këlkazë

kilo *formativ* thousand, kilo-

kilogram *nm* kilogram

kiloliter *nm* kiloliter

kilometër *nm* kilometer

kilometrazh *nm* speed/distance/area expressed in kilometers

kilota *np* **1** breeches that fit tightly below the knee **2** shorts; sports trunks

kilovat *nm* [Electr] kilowatt

kilovat-orë *nf* [Electr] kilowatt-hour

kilus *nm* [Med] chyle

kilzë *nf* cloth button used to secure the ends of cloth spacers in a padded mattress: mattress button

*kilzi *nf* = gudulí

*kilzim *nm ger* = gudulísje

kilzo·n *vt* **1** to sew on [mattress buttons] **2** to tickle = gudulís·

ki'llë nf(Old) **1** measure of grain of about 50-60 kilograms: bushel **2** measure of land of approximately 3 square kilometers

*__kima__ nf = ki'më

ki'mce nf [Bot] jujube = hi'de

*__ki'mçë__ nf [Entom] bedbug

kimere nf **1** chimera **2** [Ichth] rabbitfish (Chimaera monstrosa)

kimeri'k adj chimerical

kime't nm (Colloq) worth, value

ki'më nf [Food] dish prepared with minced meat and fried onions; minced meat

kimi' nf chemistry

kimi'k adj chemical

*__kimika'l__ nm = kimika't

kim ika't nm chemical

kim iki'sht adv chemically

kim i'st n **1** chemist **2** chemical worker

kim izi'm nm ger <kimizo'·n

kim izo'·n vt **1** to apply chemical means to improve [a field of endeavor] **2** to develop chemical industry in [a place]

kinaki'n nm [Bot] = ki'në

kind nm **1** pleat **2** (triangular) cloth patch **3** angle; corner; edge, border **4** small piece of land
  ◦ **kind dëbore** snowdrift

kind a gje're adj having broad pleats

kine a'st nm [Cine] film maker

kinema' nf **1** cinema, movie theater **2** (Colloq) the movies
  ◦ **kinema e hapur** open-air cinema
  ◦ **kinema e mbyllur** (indoor) movie theater
  ◦ **kinema verore** open air theater used in summer to show films

kinemati'kë nf kinematics

kinematogra'f nm cinematographer

kinemato grafi' nf cinematography

kinemato grafi'k adj cinematographic, of motion pictures

kineti'k adj kinetic

kineti'kë nf kinetics

kin e'z adj, n Chinese

kin e'zçe
  I § nf = kinezi'shte
  II § adv in the Chinese manner

kinez e'ri' nf (Pej) something cleverly complicated, but odd or apparently pointless

kin ezi'sht adv in Chinese (language)

kin ezi'shte nf Chinese language

ki'në nf [Bot] cinchona (Chinchoma officinalis)
  ◦ **kinë fushe** [Bot] centaury, drug centaurium Centaurium umbellatum

Ki'në nf China

ki'ng ël nf **1** (for a saddle) bellyband, girth, cinch *__2__ [Bot] danewort (Sambucus ebulus)

kini'në nf [Pharm] quinine

kini'no nf = kini'në

kinkaleri'
  I § nf shop that sells household and personal sundries
  II § np **1** sundries *__2__ glassware

ki'no formativ film, movie, cinemato-

kino apara't nm [Cine] movie camera

kino dita'r nm **1** [Cine] short film portraying daily life **2** newsreel

kino dokumenta'r nm documentary film

kino fi'lm nm [Cine] motion picture film

kino klu'b nm club equipped to show movies

kino komedi' nf film comedy

kino kroni'kë nf film chronicle, news film

kino operato'r n movie cameraman

kino regjizo'r n film director

kino stu'dio nf film studio

kino tea'tër nm movie theater

ki'nse
  I § pcl supposedly
  II § conj as if, supposedly as if

*__kin u'z__ nm lamb = qengj

kio'sk nm kiosk, stall, stand, booth

kipc nm person bearing a striking resemblance to someone else: double

Kirgi'z
  I § adj of the Kirghiz people
  II § nm member of the Kirghiz people

kiroptere np [Zool] Chiroptera

kiru'rg nm surgeon

kirurgji' nf surgery (as a branch of medicine)

kirurgji'k adj surgical

*__kirrç__ = rrëshi'q

kisme't nm = kësme't

kist = këst

kisto'r adj paid in installments

*__kish__ conj if only

kish stem for pind <ka· used to have, had

kisha'r n sexton, church warden

*__kish ata'r__ nm, adj (Old) = kishta'r

ki'shë nf church

ki'shë z nf [Archit] chapel

kishk nm (Reg) **1** donkey colt **2** domestic buffalo calf

ki'shkë nf = kishk

kishta'r
  I § nm clergyman, churchman; sexton
  II § adj pertaining to the church or to churchmen: churchly, ecclesiastic

ki'sh te 3rd sg pind **1** (3rd sg subject) used to have, had **2** there was, used to be <ka·

kita're nf guitar

kitari'st n guitarist

ki't as adv = kithi

ki'të nf(Reg) **1** icicle **2** spike of grain

*__ki'tër__ = ke'tër

kito'n nm chiton

kith nm seasonal mist

kith·
  I § vi = këlthe't·
  II § nm *icicle

ki'th ët adj (i) askew, awry; on a slant

ki'th i adv **1** by an indirect route: indirectly **2** along the side(s); on the side **3** on a diagonal, obliquely

kithmi'll = kërmi'll

ki'ze nf **1** billhook, bushhook, pruning knife **2** [Ornit] hobby (Falco subbuteo)

*__kj__ (Reg) (orthographic variant) = q

*__kjasi'në__ nf ground from which water oozes

*__kjas o'·n__ vi to ooze, leak liquid

kjo proximal 3rd sg fem determiner this, this one, she, it
  ◦ **Kjo është nusja, ky është dhëndri.** "This is the bride and this is the bridegroom." (having explained

the situation thoroughly) That's how things are, take it or leave it. That's the long and the short of it.
∘ **kjo është punë për** [ ] it's a matter for [ ] to decide, it's up to [ ]
∘ **Kjo është ç'është!** That tops everything!
∘ **Kjo kockë e di.** If there's anyone that knows, it's me (because of personal experience).

kjo'çolë nf [Tech] screw nut, female screw

kjo'më nf plum/cherry juice

KK abbrev <**Kooperativa e Konsumit** (Old) Consumer's Cooperative

KKK abbrev (American) Ku Klux Klan

*****kla'jk**ë nf doorlatch, doorhandle

klan nm clan

klandestin adj clandestine

klarinet'e nf clarinet

kla'së nf 1 class; classroom 2 level, grade 3 social class
∘ **klasa e dytë** 1 second grade 2 (in writing a long number) the numbers in the second group from the right (before the decimal point)
∘ **klasa e mijësheve = kla'sa e dytë**
∘ **klasa e parë** first grade

klasic'ist adj classicist

klasic'izëm nm classicism

klas'ifik'i'm nm ger 1 <**klasifiko'·n, klasifiko'·het** 2 classification; system of classification

klas'ifik'o'·het vpr to take one's proper place

klas'ifik'o'·n vt to classify

klasik
I § nm 1 author of a classic 2 [Lit] classicist 3 [Lit] Classical author
II § adj classical, classic, Classical

*****klas'ist** (Old) = **klaso'r**

klas'o'r adj of or pertaining to social class

klauzol'e nf [Law] clause (in a legal document); stipulation

klavi'kul nf [Anat] clavicle

*****kleba'c**ë nf [Bot] cleavers, catchweed, goosegrass (Galium aparine)

*****kle'b**ë = **gle'p**ë

kle'çkë nf 1 sliver of wood 2 wooden peg 3 small defect/flaw 4 (Fig) hidden secret: skeleton in the closet 5 (Fig) unconvincing, spur-of-the-moment argument 6 (Fig) stumbling block
∘ **kleçkë dhëmbësh** toothpick
∘ **kleçka këpucësh** wooden pins used to fasten shoe soles to their uppers

kle'kë nf [Bot] mountain pine, mugho pine (Pinus mughus)

klen nm [Ichth] white chub = **mlysh**

kle'një nf [Ornit] European kingfisher (Alcedo atthis)

kleptoman adj, n kleptomaniac

kleptoman'i nf kleptomania

kler nm collec 1 clergy *2 (Reg Gheg) wild drake

*****kler** = **krel**

kler'ik nm clergyman

kler'ik'a'l adj 1 of or pertaining to the clergy: clerical 2 clericalistic

kler'ikal'izëm nm clericalism

kle'shte nf coppersmith's tongs

klie'nt n customer, regular customer; client, patron

kliente'l'e nf clientele

*****klija**| = **kija**|

kli'kë nf [Polit] clique

klimat'eri'k adj having a healthful climate, noted for its good climate

klimat'i'k adj 1 climatic 2 = **klimateri'k**

klimatiz'i'm nm 1 <**klimatizo'·n** 2 acclimatization, acclimation

klimatiz'o'·n vt to acclimatize, acclimate

kli'më nf climate

*****klind** = **kind**

*****klind'o's·** vt to pleat, fold

klinic'ist nm clinician

klini'k
I § adj clinical
II § nm clinician

klini'kë nf clinic

kli'pë nf [Geol] klippe ()

kliri'ng nm [Fin] settling accounts: clearing

*****kli'rt**ë nf lowland

klisy'rë nf narrow pass, mountain defile

klishe' nf 1 [Publ] stereotype plate used in printing: cliché; image reproduced from such a plate 2 (Fig Pej) cliché

*****kli'sh**ë nf handle, crank

kli'të nf (Reg) 1 thin film/membrane/curtain 2 snow clinging to the boughs of trees

klitor nm [Anat] clitoris

klith
I § stem for pdef, opt, adm, part, vp, imper <**këlthet·**
II § alternate stem for pres, subj, pind to shout, yell <**këlthet·**

kli'th'je nf ger 1 <**këlthet·** 2 = **kli'thm**ë

kli'th'më nf sudden loud yell/cry, shout; exclamation

klizmë nf 1 enema 2 apparatus for giving an enema

klo'këz nf [Bot] campion, catchfly (Silene)
∘ **klok**ëz **gale** [Bot] French silene, English catchfly Silene gallica
∘ **klok**ëz **italiane** [Bot] Italian catchfly /silene Silene italica
∘ **klok**ëz **e natës** [Bot] night-flowering campion/silene Silene noctiflora
∘ **klok**ëz **pluskuese** [Bot] Nottingham catchfly, nodding silene Silene nutans

klor nm [Chem] chlorine ((Cl))

klor'a't nm [Chem] chlorate

klor'hidri'k adj [Chem] hydrochloric

klor'i'k adj [Chem] chloric

klorofi'l nm chlorophyll

klorofo'rm nm chloroform

kloru'r nm [Chem] chloride

klo'un nm 1 clown 2 (Impol Insult) person who acts like a clown

klub nm 1 social club 2 (Colloq) meeting hall for social gatherings and entertainment at which refreshments are available

*****klyty'r**ë nf (Old) cover, lid; shutter, flap, valve

*****klla'b**ë nf pick, pickaxe

klla'çë nf 1 small muddy pothole 2 pond of stagnant water, mudhole

*****kllaf** = **këllëf**

klla'gër nf 1 clod of earth (turned up by plowing) 2 slab of ice

klla'jkë nf 1 cotter pin, linchpin 2 door bolt, door bar

kllani'k nm = **gllani'k**

klla'pa-klla'pa adj bracketed

klla'pë nf 1 clamp; clasp 2 hooked end 3 reed of a wind instrument 4 gravestone 5 (Colloq) handcuff

6 wooden hobble **7** mortise **8** each arm of a supporting bracket/brace **9** parenthesis, bracket, brace **10** *(Fig Colloq)* trap, snare ***11** catchment
◦ **kllapa gjarpë́ruese** curly brackets: braces { }

kllapí *nf* delirium, raving, nightmare

kllapí·s *stem for 1st sg pres, pl pres, 2nd & 3rd sg subj, pind* <**kllapít·**

kllapít· *vt* to gulp [ ] down

*kllapíẗës *adj* voracious, greedy

kllapodá̈n *nm (Old)* gold brocade

kllapó·s *vt* **1** to shut; lock shut **2** to trap **3** *(Colloq)* to lock [ ] up; put the cuffs on [ ], handcuff, cuff **4** (of a feeling) to seize *<a person>*

kllapó·s·et *vpr* **1** to remain inside; close oneself in **2** to get mired down

kllapurí·s *stem for 1st sg pres, pl pres, 2nd & 3rd sg subj, pind* <**kllapurít·**

kllapurít· *vi* to talk deliriously; rant

*kllá̈që = **kllaçë́**

*kllás· = **kall·**

*kllásë *nf* = **klasë**

*kllasík *adj* classical

kllásḧë *nf* heavy cloak made of wool and goathair

*kllef *OR* **kllëf** = **këllëf**

*kllenjkë *nf* = **kllënjkë**

*kllesë *nf(Old)* particle

kllëk *nm* click

kllë́njkë *nf* rotten egg

kllëp *nm* splashing of waves

*kllikár *adj* shameless

*kllímcë = **kllínzë**

kllínzë *nf* [*Ornit*] bee-eater *(Merops apiaster)*

*kllírtë *nf* mound, ridge

*kllít = **kall**

*klloçí *nf* brood, clutch

klloçí·s *stem for 1st sg pres, pl pres, 2nd & 3rd sg subj, pind* <**klloçít·**

klloçít·
I § *vt* to brood over [eggs]
II § *vi* **1** to brood **2** to cluck while brooding; make clucking sounds

klloçíẗës *nm* **1** *(Colloq)* incubator **2** chatterbox

klloçítje *nf ger* **1** <**klloçít·** **2** brooding period, incubation **3** soft clucking by a brooding hen

kllóçkë *nf* **1** brood hen **2** *(Colloq)* [*Astron*] Pleiades

*kllogjën = **kllogjër**

*kllogjënár *n* charcoal-burner

kllogjër *nf* **1** [*Bot*] ergot *(Claviceps purpurea)* ***2** charcoal

*kllogjëreshë *nf* = **kallogre**

*kllopáshkë *nf* throttle

*klloq = **klloç**

*klloqímë *nf* chatter

*kllub = **klub**

*klluf = **këllëf**

*klluk· *vt* = **klloçít·**

*kllukás *stem for 1st sg pres, 1st & 3rd pl pres, 2nd & 3rd sg subj* <**klluket·**

*klluket· *vt* = **klloçít·**

kllúkë *nf* **1** brood hen **2** brood egg **3** infertile brood egg; rotten egg

kllukímë *nm* = **klloçítje**

*kllukí·s *stem for 2nd pl pres, pind* <**klluket·**

*kllukít *stem for pdef, opt, adm, part, pind, 2nd pl pres, imper, vp* <**klluket·**

kllup· *vt* to wolf/gobble down [ ]

kllup̈ít· = **kllup·**

km *abbrev* kilometer

kme̋së *nf* billhook, bushhook, pruning hook

kmesë́tár *nm* **1** worker using a billhook **2** [*Hist*] soldier armed with a billhook

KNER *abbrev* <**Këshilli i Ndihmës Ekonomike Reciproke** Council of Reciprocal Economic Aid (for Warsaw Pact nations)

ko·n *vt* **1** to feed **2** to bait [a hook] **3** to replace [a crop plant] with a healthy seed/sprout **4** *(Fig)* to bribe

ko *stem for pdef, opt, adm* <**ku·het**

koalició̈n *nm* coalition

kob *nm* **1** calamity, disaster; death **2** betrayal, deceit

*kobáj *nm* [*Zool*] rat

kobált *nm* cobalt *((Co))*

kobár
I § *nm* petty thief, pilferer; pickpocket
II § *adj* prone to stealing: thieving, pilfering

kobásh *adj* thieving, pilfering

kobashí·s *stem for 1st sg pres, pl pres, 2nd & 3rd sg subj, pind* <**kobashít·**

kobashít· *vt, vi* = **kobít·**

*kobéc *adj (Old)* crafty

kobë *nf* **1** pilferage; petty theft **2** shameful act; wicked thing **3** bad/naughty word

kobër *nf* [*Zool*] cobra

kobím *nm* **1** <**kobo·n** **2** deception, fraud

kobimtár *n* swindler, faker, cheater

kobí·s *stem for 1st sg pres, pl pres, 2nd & 3rd sg subj, pind* <**kobít·**

kobísht *nm* [*Entom*] = **gërshë́rëz**

kobít *nm* [*Ichth*] river loach *(Cobitis taenia)*

kobít· *vt* **1** to pilfer **2** to deceive [ ] with fine words and false promises **3** to betray, break one's word to [ ]

kobíẗës *n* = **kobimtár**

kobítje *nf ger* <**kobít·**

kobndjé̈llës *adj* calamitous, disastrous

kobó·n *vt* to fool, deceive, take [ ] in, dupe

kobshëm *adj (i)* **1** calamitous, disastrous; fatal **2** wicked, shameful, bad **3** ominous

kobtár *adj* **1** causing great damage: pernicious **2** treacherous, traitorous **3** baleful, ominous, sinister

kobúre *nf* **1** *(Old)* muzzle-loading flintlock pistol **2** *(Colloq)* pistol, revolver **3** *(Fig)* servile servant, catspaw **4** *(Fig Colloq)* foolhardy person; numskull **5** *(Fig Crude)* drunkard: boozer, lush
◦ **Koburja bosh tremb dy veta.** *(Prov)* An empty pistol frightens two people (the one who knows it is empty and the one who does not know it is empty).
◦ **kobure teke** single-shot pistol

kobzí *adj (fem sg ˜ëz, masc pl ˜ínj, fem pl ˜eza)* darkly portentous: sinister, ominous, baleful

koc *nm (Reg)* = **kockë**

kocák *nm* saddle horn; cinchpost

kocá̈n *nm* black billy goat

kóce *nf* **1** long, reedy grassplant used to make partition walls and ceilings; woven grassplant ***2** prepubescent girl (8-10 years old)

kóce *OR* **kócë** *nf* [*Ichth*] gilthead *(Sparus auratus)*

○ **koce deti** [*Ichth*] sea bream *(Pagrus pagrus)*
○ **koce e egër** [*Ichth*] black roach *Pachychilon pictum Heck et Kner.* = **mëru'në**
○ **koce pendëgjatë** [*Ichth*] crowned dentex *Dentex gibbosus*

ko'cë *nf* **1** black nanny goat **2** = **koca'k 3** wattled fence

kock|ama'n *adj* scrawny, rawboned, bony

kock|anja'r *adj* down to skin and bones, very weak

ko'ckë *nf* **1** bone **2** die used by children playing a dice game **3** *(Fig)* something of no great value given as a kind of bribe: trinket **4** *(Fig)* core of a person's character; essential nature; strong character
○ **ësh·të kockë e fortë 1** to be no pushover; be strong-willed **2** to live long and be strong throughout
○ **kockë e këmbës** shinbone, shank
○ **kockë e kofshës** thigh bone
○ **kockë e lëkurë** skin and bones, skinny, scrawny
○ **kockë e nofullës** jawbone
○ **kockë e supit** shoulderbone, clavicle
○ **Kocka e thatë nuk lëpihet.** "One can't lick a dry bone." *(Prov)* You can't get blood out of a turnip.

kock|bu'të *adj* soft-boned

kock|ë|da'lë *adj* rawboned, bony; very thin

kock|ë|fo'rtë *adj* **1** having strong bones **2** able even at an advanced age to take on hard work: wiry **3** *(Fig)* able to withstand great difficulties; of strong and stable character

kock|ë|gje'rë *adj* wide-boned, big-boned

kock|ë|ho'llë *adj* thin-boned

kock|ë|ma'dh *adj* big-boned

kock|ë|ri'na *np* = **kockuri'na**

kock|ë|tra'shë *adj* thick-boned

kock|ë|vo'gël *adj* small-boned; having bones that don't show

kock|ë|zu'es *adj* [*Med*] ossifying

kock|o'r *adj (Book)* osseous; of bone; bony

kock|uri'na *np fem* pieces of bone; pieces of meat that are mostly bone

* **koco'k** *adj* vile, base

koco|mi *nm* **1** *(Colloq)* little mouse **2** [*Folklore*] clever little man/child who appears as a character in folktales

koco|na'r *nm* bone knob

koç *nm* **1** domestic buffalo calf = **koto'rr 2** ram or billy goat with only one horn **3** *(Colloq Fig)* strong, muscular person

koç|a'k *nm* livestock enclosure: coop, cote, sty, pen

koç|alla'k *nm* thigh bone

koça'n
I § *nm* **1** bare corncob **2** hard stalk/core of a cabbage/lettuce/artichoke/cauliflower
II § *adj* **1** (of limbs) frozen from the cold **2** knobbed, stumpy

ko'çe *np* decorations, finery

koçe'k *nm* **1** granary, corncrib **2** = **çarrani'k**

koçe'le *nf* **1** basket, hamper **2** wooden trough through which grain falls from the grain hamper to the millstone **3** spoon rack

* **koçema're** *nf* [*Bot*] = **mare**

koçe're *nf* metal jug/can, tankard

koçi *nf (Old)* **1** horse-drawn coach **2** contest prize

koçima're *nf* [*Bot*] = **mare**

koçira'më = **koçirë'në**

koçirë'në *adj* partially paralyzed

* **koçi'tun** *adj (i) (Reg Gheg)* pampered, spoiled; affected, foppish

ko'çkull *nf* [*Bot*] chickling vetch, grass pea *(Lathyrus sativus)*

koçoba'sh *nm* [*Hist*] chief elder of a village (during the Ottoman occupation)

koçomi'l|a *np* **1** bones and bone remnants **2** nonsense, empty talk

* **koçomi'll**
I § *adj* farcical
II § *nm* simpleton

koçopa'n
I § *adj (Reg)* stunted
II § *nm* **1** stunted person **2** thicket

koçu'me *nf* **1** small pitcher **2** small ink bottle

kod *nm* code

* **koda'c** *adj* (of animals) ruptured

ko'dër
I § *nf* **1** hill; low mountain; mound **2** raised irregularity on an otherwise flat surface
II § *adj* *potbellied
○ **kodër pas bregut** nonsense

kodër|lis|na|jë *nf* hill covered with oak trees

kodër|shko'zë *nf* hill covered with hornbeam trees

* **kodërta'r** *adj* hilly

kodër|va'rr *nm* [*Archeol*] grave mound: tumulus, barrow *(K)*

kod|ifik|i'm *nm ger* **1** < **kodifiko'·n 2** codification **3** [*Postal*] coding

kod|ifik|o'·n *vt* to codify

kod|ifik|u'es *adj* codifying

kodi'k *nm* codex

kodi'm *nm* [*Postal*] < **kodo'·n**

kod|o'·n *vt* to encode

kodo'sh *nm (Pej)* pimp; scoundrel, rascal

kodre'c *nm* hillock

kodri'cë *nf* = **kodri'në**

kodri'në *nf* **1** low hill, knoll **2** hilly land

kodrin|o'r *adj* **1** hilly **2** suitable for work in hilly country

kodri'she *nf* knoll, small hill covered with grass or brush

kodri'shtë *nf* = **kodri'në**

* **kodru'e|m**
I § *adj (i) (Reg Gheg Old)*
II § *nm* dotted with hills, hilly

* **kodhe'c** *nm (Reg Tosk)* plait

koeficie'nt *nm* **1** coefficient **2** relative intensity/amount: extent, degree
○ **koeficienti i punës së dobishme** degree of efficiency
○ **koeficienti i tretshmërisë së ushqimit** nutritional value/efficacy

ko'fano *nf* [*Tech*] hinged metal cover over an engine: hood

* **kofçe'k** = **koçe'k**

kofi'n *nm* large basket

kofsha're *np* **1** ankle-length winter underwear **2** white-flannel pants with narrow legs

ko'fshë *nf* **1** thigh **2** drumstick (of a fowl)
○ **kofshë topi** [*Mil*] trail (of a gun carriage)

kofshë|tra'shë *nf* part of the fowl just above the drumstick: thigh

kofshi'në *nf* pad protecting the neck of oxen from chafing by the yoke *kofta'rë *np* = korta'rë

ko'ftër *nm* long two-handed saw

koftor *nm* potbellied heating stove

kohani'k *nm* contemporary = bashkëko'hës

koherenc'ë *nf* coherence

koherent *adj* coherent

kohezion *nm* cohesion

ko'hë *nf* 1 time; period of time 2 weather 3 [*Ling*] grammatical tense
  ○ koha e ardhme [*Ling*] future tense
  ○ kohë e artë 1 beautiful ("golden") weather 2 halcyon days
  ○ kohët e fundit 1 recentlylately 2 in the last period: toward/at the end
  ○ kohët e para in the early period: in the beginning, in the early days
  ○ s'ka· kohë as të ha·^*subj* bukë to be busy all the time, {} doesn't even have time to eat
  ○ kohë e kryer [*Ling*] perfect tense
  ○ koha ligjore daylight saving time, summer time
  ○ kohë me erë windy weather
  ○ Koha e Mesme [*Hist*] the Middle Ages
  ○ s'ësh·të më i kohës to be out of date
  ○ kohë më kohë 1 from time to time 2 at just any time
  ○ koha e ngeshme free time, leisure time
  ○ kohë e pa kohë 1 no matter what the weather 2 with no regard for the proper time
  ○ kohë pas kohe from time to time
  ○ Koha s'lidhet me litar. (*Prov*) Time doesn't stand still.
  ○ koha e tanishme [*Ling*] present tense
  ○ kohë e tashme present tense
  ○ kohë e vdekur [*Basketball*] time with the game clock stopped
  ○ koha e vjetër ancient times
  ○ kohë e vrenjtur overcast weather

*kohë'di *nf(Old)* chance

*kohë'di'tun *adj (i) (Reg Gheg) (Old)* chance, accidental

kohë'mat'ës *nm* device for measuring time

kohë'mba'jt'ës *n* timekeeper

kohë'ni'k *adj, n* contemporary

kohë'pas'koh'shëm *adj (i)* occasional

ko'hë'ra *np* <ko'hë

kohë'rrëf'yes *nm* 1 weathervane 2 timepiece

*kohë'si *nf* = kohë'vazhdi'm

kohë'shën'ues *nm* timekeeper

kohë'shku'rtër *adj* of short duration; short-time

*kohë'tar
  I § *adj* = kohani'k
  II § *n* chronicler

kohë'vazhdi'm *nm* duration period, duration

kohë'vra'sës
  I § *adj* time-killing
  II § *n* time waster

koho'r *adj* 1 of time, chronological, temporal 2 [*Ling*] of or pertaining to grammatical tense: temporal

koho'rtë *nf* [*Hist*] cohort (military unit in Roman times)

*koh'shëm *adj (i)* = koho'r

koili'k *nm* curlew (*Numenius*)
  ○ koiliku i madh [*Ornit*] curlew *Numenius arquata* L.

○ koiliku mesatar [*Ornit*] whimbrel *Numenius phaeopus* L.
  ○ koiliku i zi [*Ornit*] glossy ibis *Plegadis falcinellus* L.

koincidenc'ë *nf* coincidence

koincidi'm *nm* 1 <koincido·*n* 2 = koincidenc'ë

koincido·*n* *vt* to coincide

koje *nf* 1 rat of hair added to women's braids 2 breadcrust

kojë *nf* 1 bait *2 crust; skin

koje's *nf* bait

*kojga'sh = kajga'sh

kojkë *nf* barren hilltop

kojli'k = koili'k

*kojo·*n* *vt* to wheedle

kojri'lë *OR* kojrri'llë *nf* [*Ornit*] crane = kurri'llë

*kojshi = komshi'

kok *nm* 1 = koks 2 [*Med*] round bacterium: coccus () *3 (Reg Gheg) coconut

kokai'në *nf* cocaine

koka'llë
  I § *nf* bone
  II § *np* [*Anat*] hip-bone, ilium

koka're *nf* [*Bot*] = qepujk'ë

kokaru'shë *adj* = kokëma'dh

*koka'zë = kokëz

*kokcine'll *nm* [*Entom*] cochineal insect

*kok'dha'n *nm* [*Ichth*] = kryegja't'ë

ko'ke *nf* = bonbo'ne

ko'kë *nf* 1 head 2 heading 3 spherical object: knob, bulb 4 top/front/main part 5 (*Fig*) the essence of something 6 (*Colloq*) (in tossing a coin) heads
  ○ kokën (le) të hanë! (*Impol*) let them kill each other for all I care!
  ○ Nuk ka kokë dëbora në maj. "The snow in May doesn't last." (*Prov*) It won't last long. It will never last
  ○ s'ka· kokë (of a period of bad weather) to have lost its main force, be unable to continue its intensity
  ○ kokë e këmbë 1 including the whole body, from head to foot 2 head-over-heels; completely
  ○ Kokën këtu, këmbët atje. one (is) here but one's mind (is) elsewhere: Out to lunch.
  ○ kokë e madhe great mind, genius
  ○ kokën mbi shpatulla e ke "you have your head on your shoulders" use your head!
  ○ kokë më kokë (with their upper parts) right next to one another; head to head; face to face; tête a tête, personal
  ○ kokë për kokë individually, one by one, separately
  ○ {*noun*} për kokën e {*same noun in the genitive case*} really wonderful {}, {} of the best kind, {} above all others djalë për kokën e djalit boy above all others, a boy to beat all boys
  ○ kokë pojellë lunkhead, stupid
  ○ Qafsh kokën tënde! "May you cry your head off!" (*Curse*) I hope you die!
  ○ kokë stërgu/stërku [*Bot*] wild geranium
  ○ koka e turkut scapegoat

kokë'ba'rdhë *adj* white-haired; gray-haired

kokë'bo'sh *adj (Pej)* empty-headed, incompetent

kokë'bu'all *adj (Insult)* 1 having a large head 2 (*Fig*) thickheaded, stupid; stubborn

kokë'buce'l *adj (Insult)* having a large head

kokë'cja'p *adj (Insult)* having a head like a billy goat

kok**ë**ça'rje *nf* "head-splitting" **1** problem, dilemma, difficulty: headache **2** worry

kok**ë**da'c *adj* having a completely shaved head

kok**ë**da'rdh**ë** *adj* having a small pear-shaped head

kok**ë**de'le *adj (Colloq)* **1** having white hair since birth **2** gray-haired (usually said of women)

kok**ë**de'rr *adj, n (Disparaging)* pigheaded (person)

kok**ë**dru' *adj (Disparaging)* thick between the ears, dense, stupid

*kok**ë**dhë'mbje *nf* headache

kok**ë**dhë'n**ë** *nm* [*Ichth*] = kryegja'të

kok**ë**dhi' *adj (Disparaging)* (of women or girls) having a head like a nanny goat, goatface

kok**ë**fo'rt**ë** *adj* **1** hard-headed, obstinate **2** *(Fig)* undeniable

kok**ë**fort**ë**si' *nf* hard-headedness, obstinacy

kok**ë**fy'ell *adj* rattlebrained

kok**ë**garu'zhd**ë** *nf* [*Zool*] tadpole

kok**ë**gdhe' *adj (Disparaging)* **1** thick between the ears, dense, stupid **2** stubborn, willful, disobedient

kok**ë**goma'r *adj (Insult)* **1** having a large head like a donkey **2** extremely thickheaded

kok**ë**ja'sht**ë** *adj* bareheaded

kok**ë**kë'rcu *adj* **1** thickheaded, slow-witted **2** stubborn

kok**ë**kri'sur *adj* foolhardy; cracked in the head

kok**ë**ku'ngull *adj (Disparaging Pej)* **1** having a large wide head, pumpkin-headed **2** shorn of all hair **3** thickheaded, softheaded

kok**ë**ku'q *adj* having a reddish-brown head

ko'k**ë**l *nf* **1** lump, clump **2** knot; tangled knot **3** pit of a fruit **4** knob-like object **5** *(Fig)* complication, impediment: kink **6** bonbon *7 (Colloq)* testicle

kok**ë**la'rt *adv* with head held high: proudly

kok**ë**la'rt**ë** *adj* proud

kok**ë**lart**ë**si' *nf* pride

kok**ë**le'sh *adj (Pej)* = qafële'sh

kok**ë**li'dh**ur** *nm (OldImpolite)* term of disrespect for a Moslem priest

kok**ë**lo'p**ë** *adj (Disparaging)* **1** having a large head like a cow **2** *(Fig)* thickheaded, softheaded

kok**ë**lu'nd**ë**r *adj* [*Anat*] scaphocephalus

kok**ë**lla'n *nm* thin-lipped gray mullet (*Mugilidae ramada*)

kok**ë**ma'dh *adj* having a disproportionately large head

kok**ë**ma'dh**e** *nf* [*Bot*] reed canary grass (*Phalaris arundinacea*)

kok**ë**mbro'jt**ë**se *nf* [*Hist*] headguard: battle helmet

kok**ë**mënja'n**ë** *adv* silently offended, put off, in a dudgeon

kok**ë**mi'sh *adj (Disparaging)* thickheaded, softheaded: meathead

kok**ë**moll**ë**çi'nk**ë** *adj (Disparaging)* **1** having a very small head **2** *(Fig)* featherbrained

kok**ë**mu'shk**ë** *adj (Insult Pej)* stubborn as a mule

kok**ë**nde'zur *adj* hotheaded, rash

kok**ë**ndry'shk**ur** *adj* rusty in the brain, incapable of understanding

kok**ë**ngu'lthi *adv* head down, headfirst; upside down

*kok**ë**ngu'lur *adj* obstinate

kok**ë**ngu'sht**ë** *adj* [*Anat*] leptocephal

*kok**ë**ngje'shje *nf* obstinacy

kok**ë**ngje'sh**ur** *adj* = kok**ë**fo'rt**ë**

kok**ë**ngjy'lmas OR kok**ë**ngjy'lm**azi** *adv* = kryengu'lthi

kok**ë**një's**ore** *nf* [*Ichth*] rabbitfish (*Chimaera monstruosa*) = bishtmi'

kok**ë**përpje't**ë**

I § *adj* arrogant, stuck-up

II § *adv* in an arrogant way, nose in the air

kok**ë**po'sht**ë** *adv* **1** head down, headfirst; upside down **2** *(Fig)* completely crooked, backward, wrongwise

kok**ë**pre'r**ë** *adj* **1** beheaded **2** *(Fig)* in dire straits, in deep trouble; in despair

kok**ë**qe'th**ur** *adj* with head completely shorn

*kok**ë**rând**ë** *adj (Reg Gheg)* thickheaded

kokërdha'k

I § *nm* round, spherical

II § *adv* face to face; publicly, openly; frankly

*kokërdhi' *nf* = kakërdhi'

kokërdhi'c**ë** *nf* small object

kokërdho'k

I § *nm* eyeball

II § *adv* popeyed

ko'kërr *nf* **1** somewhat round and small detachable unit of a concrete solid: head (of fruit or vegetable); piece (of fruit), berry, nut, kernel (of grain); chunk (of coal), granule, bead, ball, nugget **2** small roundish object seen as an exemplar of a class: piece, head **3** countable individual of a class **4** *(Colloq)* nub of the matter, issue, problem

  ○ kokërr-breshri hailstone

  ○ kokrra e keqe/zezë [*Med*] sunstroke

  ○ kokrra e motit (*Colloq*) lightning

  ○ kokërr për kokërr one piece at a time, one by one

  ○ kokrra e syrit eyeball

kokërrdu'çe *nf* gallnut, oak gall, oak apple

kokërrdhe'se *nf* [*Bot*] Jerusalem artichoke (*Helianthus tuberosus*) = mollë dheu

kokërrfo'rt**ë** *adj* having hard fruit

kokërrgja't**ë** *adj* having elongated fruit

kokërri'mët *adj* having fine granules, finely beaded

kokërrma'dh *adj* bearing large fruit, characterized by large chunks

kokërrro't**ë** *adj (Disparaging)* **1** having a large round head **2** *(Fig)* thickheaded, softheaded

kokërrru'ar *adj* having a shaven head

kokërrru'j**ë** *nf* [*Bot*] common gromwell (*Lithospermum officinale*)

kokërrvo'g**ë**l *adj* bearing small fruit, characterized by small chunks

kokërrze'z**ë** *nf* [*Bot*] elder (*Sambucus nigra*)

kokërrzi'm *nm ger* < kokërrzo'•n

kokërrzo'•n

I § *vt, vi* to consolidate [] into granules; turn into granules: granulate

II § *vi* to form fruit; form a head (of grain)

kokërrzo'r *adj* granular

ko'k**ë**s

I § *nm* **1** (Old) headman **2** ram that leads a flock **3** front part of a cradle = ballu'k

II § *adv* [*np*] local dignitaries, elders

kok**ë**sepe'te *adj (Disparaging)* **1** having a big, rectangular head **2** *(Fig)* hard-headed, obstinate

*kok**ë**stë'rg *nm* [*Bot*] cranesbill (*Geranium*)

kokë·shinik adj (Disparaging) **1** bushel-headed, having a large head **2** (Fig) thickheaded, stupid

kokë·shkëmb adj hard-headed; obstinate

kokë·shkrepur adj = kokëkrisur

kokë·shkretë adj **1** obstinate **2** = kokëkrisur

kokë·shtrëmbër adj head awry

kokë·shtypur adj having a squat head, flat-headed

kok·ët adj (i) smart, intelligent

kokë·tatëpjetë adv **1** = kokëposhtë **2** (Fig) topsy-turvy, backwards, all wrong

kokë·trashë adj (Pej) thickheaded, stupid

kokë·trashlësi nf thickheadedness, stupidity

*__kokë·trokë__ adj heady, intoxicating

kokë·trung adj = kokëgdhe

kokë·tul adj (Insult) soft in the head, feebleminded

kokë·turr adj = kokëdac

kokë·thatë
I § adj foolish, stupid
II § n idiot

kokë·thinjur adj gray-headed, grizzled

kokë·varur adj **1** head alop **2** (Fig) ashamed, embarrassed; sad

kokë·viç adj (Insult) **1** having a head as big as a calf's **2** (Fig) stupid

kokë·vogël adj having a disproportionately small head

kokëz nf dimin little head

kokë·zbrazët adv (Pej) empty-headed

kokë·zbuluar adj bareheaded

kokë·zezë nf [Veter] blackhead (a poultry disease), infectious enterohepatitis (Enterohepatitis infectiosa Melagridum)

kokë·zo·n vt = koksifiko·n

kokë·zog nm [Bot] globe amaranth (Gomphrena)

kokë·zhabë adj (Disparaging) **1** toad-face **2** (Fig) slow-witted; empty-headed

kokë·zhangël adj stupid

kokilë nf [Tech] chill mold (for shaping a liquid/plastic substance)

kokje nf protective head covering: hat, hood

*__koklan__ = kokllan

koklav·is stem for 1st sg pres, pl pres, 2nd & 3rd sg subj, pind < koklavit·

koklavit· vt **1** to entangle, tangle **2** (Fig) to complicate

koklavit·et vpr **1** to get entangled **2** (Fig) to get badly mixed up in something

koklavitje nf ger **1** < koklavit·, koklavit·et (Fig) **2** complication; complicated mess

koklavitur adj (i) **1** entangled, tangled up **2** (Fig) complicated

koklëz nf grain, seed

kokliçe nf mountain top, summit, peak

*__koklutë__ nf gallnut, oak apple

kokllan nm [Ichth] = kryegjatë

kokme nf **1** ladle, dipper, mug **2** small container holding freshly ground coffee **3** coffeepot **4** (Reg) = kumbara

koko nf (Child) candy, chocolate

koko·çel nm [Bot] **1** knapweed (Centaurea) **2** light blue

koko·çule nf wax with which bees seal the cracks of a hive

koko·dash nm **1** little ball of cloth soaked in a greasy sop of bread and cheese and given to a baby to hold and eat **2** = pupagjel

*__kokoleps·__ = koklavit·

koko·lëmsh nm **1** entangled wad of wool yarn **2** (Fig) very complicated matter

*__kokolit·__ = koklavit·

*__kokomish__ nm hood

*__koko·nesh__ = kokorosh

koko·ne nf **1** = kukull **2** (Fig Pet) pretty girl/woman

*__koko·ni__ sg def, abl indef < kokua

*__koko·nosh__ = kokorosh

kokoraq nm [Bot] spurge (Euphorbia)

kokore nf winter hat with ear flaps

*__kokoresh__ = kokorosh

*__kokoris·__ vi to crow, cackle

kokorosh
I § adj **1** having a stout, sturdy body **2** (Impol) dressed like a dandy; strutting and showing off like an old rooster
II § nm popinjay, fop, dandy

kokorr nm **1** wooden draining shelf for cheese or other wet products **2** platform used by the warden guarding a field of crops; field hut (usually elevated above the ground) used by the crop warden **3** elevated haystack supported on wooden posts

kokorreth
I § nm **1** round bundle of rags or straw placed on the head to help balance a pot **2** [Food] wheat cracker spread with butter or oil
II § adv in the shape of a disk, in the form of a circle

kokos nm (Reg Kos) coconut

kokosh nm **1** rooster, cock **2** (Pej Fig) popinjay **3** [Entom] large dark red ant = kacagjel **4** popcorn ○ **kokosh i egër** [Ornit] hoopoe (Upupa epops)

*__kokoshar__ n poultry raiser

kokoshare nf spicy/hot pepper with a round pod

*__kokoshep__ nm poultry louse

kokoshke nf popcorn

*__kokoshurdh__ nm [Ornit] waterfowl

*__kokot__ nm (Reg Gheg) **1** large rooster **2** fool

kokrra-kokrra adv in little bits

kokrrizë
I § nf **1** granule; grain **2** [Med] skin rash **3** (Reg) hailstone = breshër
II § adj = kokrrizor

kokrrizim nm ger **1** < kokrrizo·n **2** granulation

kokrrizo·n vt to form into granules: granulate

kokrrizor adj composed of granules; granular

kokrrizueshëm adj (i) readily formed into granules

kokrro·het vpr to flow out in a stream (of grain); disperse into small bits; divide up into groups

kokrro·n vt **1** to pick/pluck at [] one at a time **2** to examine [] one at a time; pick through []

*__kokrrone__ nm [Bot] wheat (Triticum vulgare)

*__kokrruk__ nm (Reg Tosk) seed, grain

koks nm coke (from coal)

*__koksë__ nf wheel hub = bucelë

koksifikim nm ger [Tech] < koksifiko·n, koksifiko·het

koksifiko·het vpr [Tech] to turn into coke

koksifiko·n vt [Tech] to convert [] to coke: coke, carbonize

koktej nm 1 cocktail composed of layers of differently colored alcoholic beverages 2 cocktail 3 cocktail party

*koku'a nm (obl ~o'ni, np ~o'nj) = kukule

*ku'dh nm (Reg Tosk) = kukudh

koku'lët adj, adv = kokulur

kokulur
I § adj 1 head-bowed; humble 2 oppressed, humbled 3 (Fig) ashamed and embarrassed 4 modest; well-behaved; obedient 5 (Fig) industrious, diligent
II § adv minding one's own business

koku'll adj curved outward, convex

*koku'lle nf cowl

*kok'unjë nf (Old) brothel

*kok'unjur adj (i) = kokulur

kokurllëk nm wall protecting the outlet of a water spring

kolaboracionist
I § adj collaborationist
II § nm 1 [Hist] collaborator with Fascists/Nazis 2 (Pej) collaborator, traitor

kolaboracionizëm nm 1 [Hist] collaboration with Fascists/Nazis 2 (Pej) collaborationism, treason

kolandinë nf children's swing; seesaw

kolandis· vi to swing, sway

*kolandris stem for 1st sg pres, pl pres, 2nd & 3rd sg subj, pind <kolandrit·

*kolandrit· vt to collect

*kolanë nf = kollan

kolaps nm [Med] collapse

kolar nm 1 person paid to haul loads with horses: drayman *2 sausage 3 collar = kollare

*kolas'ur adj (i) hesitant

kolash nm cornmush, polenta

*kolatun adj (i) (Reg Gheg) shiny

kolaudim nm ger 1 <kolaudo·n 2 preliminary test, check-out

kolaudo·n vt to check/try out [apparatus] before using; check [] out before selling

kolce nf 1 = kolës *2 [Bot] = kolëz

kole nf 1 [Food] liver sausage 2 clothing starch 3 [Tech] distance between wheels on an axle: wheel track, gauge

koleg
I § n (Book) colleague
II § nm * (Book Old) college

kolegj nm 1 college 2 [Law] council associated with the Supreme Court

kolegjial adj collegial

kolegjialisht adv in a collegial manner, collegially

kolegjialitet nm (Book) collegiality

kolegjium nm executive committee/council

koleksion nm collection

koleksionist n collector, fancier of collectibles

koleksiono·n vt to collect

kolektiv
I § adj collective
II § nm socialist collective

kolektivë nf (Old) labor union

kolektivisht adv collectively

kolektivitet nm (Book) collectivity

kolektivizëm nm collectivism

kolektivizim nm ger 1 <kolektivizo·n, kolektivizo·het 2 collectivization

kolektivizo·het vpr 1 to form a collective 2 to become collectivized

kolektivizo·n vt to collectivize

kolektivizuar adj (i) collectivized

kolektor n 1 [Spec] collector 2 [Tech] manifold (of an automobile motor)

kolendare np (Old) 1 child who goes door to door on Christmas eve to ask for kulaç 2 Christmas caroler

kolendër nf (Old) [Ethnog] kulaç prepared for children on Christmas

koleopter nm [Entom] beetle (K)

koleoptere np [Entom] Coleoptera

kolerë nf 1 [Med Veter] cholera 2 (Fig Insult) bad/dirty person/thing

kolerik adj [Psych] choleric

kolesterinë nf cholesterol

koleshkë nf barrow; wheelbarrow

*kolet nm collar = kollare

Kolë nf with masc agreement male name

kolës nm solder

kolëz nf [Bot] colza (Brassica napus var. oleifera DC)

koli nf parcel

kolibe nf 1 hut, shack, hovel 2 doghouse

kolibër nm [Ornit] hummingbird (Trochilidae)

kolik nm 1 mountain slope *2 hillock, mound

kolikë nf [Med] colic

kolimator nm [Phys] collimator

koliposte nf postal parcel

*kolir nm 1 rip/tear (in clothes), split 2 [Med] eye drops, eyewash, eye lotion

*kolirë nf bib

kolis stem for 1st sg pres, pl pres, 2nd & 3rd sg subj, pind <kolit·

kolit nm [Med] colitis

kolit· vt, vi to attach, stick

kolit·et vpr to become attached, get stuck

kolkoz nm Russian commune, kolkhoz

kolkozian
I § adj communal (pertaining to the kolkhoz)
II § nm member of a kolkhoz

kolmë adj (i) having a good figure; pleasingly plump

kolmuth nm [Bot] = ferrënuse

kolo nf [Ichth] chub mackerel (Scomber japonicus)

kolofon nm 1 [Chem] colophon 2 colophony, rosin = çamçakëz

kolokium nm test (over lectures and assigned reading material)

*kolomend| (Reg) = kalamend|

*kolomurdhë = kollomurde

kolon nm 1 [Hist] freed slave or tenant farmer in Roman times 2 colonist

*kolonatë = kollonatë

*kolondris stem for 1st sg pres, pl pres, 2nd & 3rd sg subj, pind <kolondrit·

*kolondrit· vt to gather, glean

*kolonec nm (Old) cramp; spasm

kolonel nm [Mil] colonel

kolonë nf 1 column 2 [Tech] opening for feeding liquid into a mold: sprue
○ kolona vertebrale spinal column

○ **kolon**ë **zanore** [*Cine*] sound track

koloni *nf* colony

kolonial *adj* colonial

*kolonia**le** *np* groceries

kolonialist *adj, n* colonialist

kolonializëm *nm* colonialism

kolonist *n* colonist

kolonizator *n* colonializer; colonizer

kolonizim *nm ger* 1 <**kolonizo**·n 2 colonization

kolonizo·n *vt* to colonize

kolonizuar *adj (i)* colonized

kolonizues

I § *adj* colonizing, colonializing

II § *n* colonizer, colonializer

kolonjar

I § *adj* of or pertaining to Kolonja

II § *n* 1 native of Kolonja *2 *(Old)* colonist

*kolonja**r**ë *(Old)* = **kolo**një

kolonjë *nf* cologne

Kolonjë *nf* southeastern ethnographic region of southeastern Albania bordering Greece: Kolonja

kolopuc

I § *nm (Colloq Pet)* chubby little kid (child)

II § *adj (Colloq)* chubby

kolorit *nm* 1 harmonic blend of colors 2 coloring, hue

kolos *nm* colossus, giant

○ **kolos me këmbë argjile** *(Impol)* big and strong in appearance, but in reality quite weak, paper tiger

kolosal *adj (Book)* colossal

kolovajzë *nf* 1 children's swing 2 seesaw 3 *(Reg)* steep snow-covered hill used by children as a slide

kolovat·*et vpr* to nod off from weakness and exhaustion, get extremely tired

kolovat*ë*s *nm* [*Ornit*] penduline tit *(Remis pendulimnus L.)*

kolovatje *nf ger* <**kolova**·et

kolovatur *adj (i)* weak and exhausted

kolovis *stem for 1st sg pres, pl pres, 2nd & 3rd sg subj, pind* <**kolovi**t·

kolovit· *vt* to cause to swing: swing

kolovit·*et vp* 1 to swing through the air 2 to sway

kolovitje *nf ger* <**kolovi**t·, **kolovi**t·*et*

*kolt <**kuajt** *(Colloq)* horses

*koltri**në** *nf* curtain

*koltu**k** = **koltu**k

Kolumbi *nf* Columbia

kolumbian *adj, n* Columbian

*kolumr**i** *nf* [*Bot*] = **kullumbri**

kolupuç *n* chubby-faced little child

*kolu**shë** *nf (Colloq)* coarse woman; fat hussy

koll *nm* 1 starch (used to stiffen cloth) 2 plowbeam 3 cough

koll·*et vpr* to cough

kolljace *nf* coughed-up phlegm

*kollaçkë *nf* elbow (of a sleeve)

kolljaj *adv (Colloq)* easily, easy

kollajllëk *nm* ease, easiness, facility

kollajshëm *adj (i) (Colloq)* easy

kollajtë *adj (i)* easy

kollan *nm* 1 cartridge belt 2 belt; bellyband, girth for a saddle

*kollandë *nf with masc agreement* idler, loafer

kollap *nm* [*Anat*] upper-arm bone *(humerus)*

*kollar *nm* collar = **kolla**re

kollare *nf* 1 cravat, tie 2 starched collar

kollaris· *vt* to stiffen [] with starch

kollarisje *nf ger* <**kollaris**·, **kollaris**·*et*

kollarisur *adj (i)* stiffened with starch: starched

*kollaro *nf* collar = **kolla**re

kollçakë *np* forearm part of a tunic sleeve strengthened by decorative braided piping

kollçik *nm* = **kallc**ë

kollçinë *nf* card game for two or four players each dealt four cards, whose object is to win the most cards or the most spades

kollë *nf* 1 cough 2 coughed-up phlegm

○ **kollë e bardhë/ëmbël/mirë** *(Euph)* [*Med*] whooping cough

○ **kollë duhani** [*Med*] smoker's cough

○ **kollë e keqe** [*Med*] tuberculosis

○ **kollë e njomë** cough with phlegm

○ **kollë e zezë** [*Med*] tuberculosis

kollit· *vt* to affect [] with a cough, cause [] to cough

○ [] **kollit**·[3sg] **kolla** [] *has* a cough

kollit·*et vpr* to come down with a cough; cough

kollitje *nf ger* 1 <**kollit**·, **kollit**·*et* 2 = **ko**llë

*kollobëllëk *nm (Reg Gheg)* = **kallaballë**k

kollodok *nm* crankshaft

kolloface *nf* sausage

kollofis *stem for 1st sg pres, pl pres, 2nd & 3rd sg subj, pind* <**kollofi**t·

kollofisk *nm* = **kulufi**sk*e*

kollofit· *vt* to gobble/gulp [] down, swallow quickly; swallow [] up, engulf

*kollofi**të** *nf* chasm

kollofruth *nm* [*Med*] = **fruth** 2 *(Old)* blessing said by a priest to ward off measles

*kollogje**r** *nm* [*Zool*] reptile

*kollogji**n** *nm* [*Bot*] whitebeam *(Sorbus aria)*

kollogjonë *nf* [*Bot*] = **murr**iz

*kollomo**q** *nm (Reg Gheg)* corncrib

*kollomu**rde** OR **kollomu**rdhë *nf* 1 silk waste; waste 2 slums; rabble

kollonate *nf (Old)* 1 piaster: silver or gold coin used during the Ottoman occupation before introduction of the <**mexhi**te 2 [*Ethnog*] coin or silver disk used to adorn a bride *3 colonnade = **shtyllinaj**ë

kollonë *nf* column; pillar

*kolloni = **koloni**

kollotumbë *nf* somersault

kollovar *nm* 1 man who lives with his wife's family 2 lackey

kollovizhë *nf* [*Invert*] oriental cockroach *(Blatta orientalis)*

kollozhek *nm (Old)* January

*kollta**k** *nm* = **koca**k

kolltuk *nm* 1 fully upholstered comfortable armchair/settee 2 *(Pej)* comfortable position of authority; throne

kolltukofag *nm* person with a cushy desk job

kollum *nm* blunged clay

kollume *nf* 1 blunging trough 2 boat bottom

kom *nm* 1 horsehair; goathair 2 horse's mane 3 fabric made of goathair: mohair

komandant *nm* [*Mil*] commander, commandant

komandë nf command, authority

komandím nm ger <**komando**·n

komando·n vt to command, head, lead

komandúes adj 1 of headquarters, command 2 commanding, imperious 3 [Tech] controlling

komb nm 1 nation; nationality, ethnic group 2 knot 3 [Anat] Adam's apple 4 drop of liquid; swig

kombajnér nm [Agr] combine operator

kombajnë nf [Agr] farm machine that combines the tasks of mowing threshing: combine

kombe nf hollow tree trunk

kombësí nf 1 nationality, nationhood 2 ethnic character: nationality 3 (Colloq) nation, ethnic group

kombëtar adj 1 national, ethnic 2 nationalist

kombëtare nf national characteristic, ethnic quality

kombëtarísht adv nationally, ethnically

kombëtarizím nm ger <**kombëtarizo**·n, **kombëtarizo**·het

kombëtarizo·het vpr to take on ethnic characteristics

kombëtarizo·n vt to endow [] with ethnic characteristics

*__kombiar__ adj (Old) national, ethnic

kombinacion nm (Book) 1 combination 2 accidental or ad hoc alliance/relationship

kombinat nm 1 industrial complex consisting of related production or processing units: industrial combine 2 combination food mixer and processor

kombinezon nm woman's slip, chemise

kombiním nm ger (Book) 1 <**kombino**·n 2 combination 3 [Sport] prepared play strategy: play

kombino·n vt (Book) 1 to combine 2 to coordinate

kombísht nm 1 melon that never ripens 2 young, immature, and inexperienced boy

komblík nm [Anat] pelvis

*__komçar__ nm hook (for an eye/eyelet)

komçë nf button = **kopsë**

kome nf two-eared earthenware pitcher

komedí nm [Lit] comedy

komediograf nm writer of comedies

koment nm 1 commentary; explication 2 annotation

komentar nm commentary

komentím nm ger <**komento**·n

komento·n vt 1 to deliver a commentary on [] 2 to annotate; explicate

komentúes n 1 commentator 2 annotater

kometë nf [Astron] comet

komë nf [Med] coma

*__komëz__ nf [Invert] botfly (Gasterophilus)

komfort nm comfort, luxury

komík
  I § adj 1 pertaining to comedy: comic 2 comical, funny
  II § n comedian, comic

komíke nf [Lit Art] comedic element: the comic

kominë nf dregs

kominoshe np overalls; work clothes

KOMINTERN [kominte'rn] nm abbrev (Russian) [Hist] Cominterm

komisar n 1 commissar 2 commissioner

komisariat nm 1 commissariat 2 office of the commissioner of police

*__komiser__ nm = **komisar**

komision nm agent's fee: commission

komisionar n person paid by commission: agent, broker

komisioner nm = **komisionar**

komít nm [Hist] guerilla fighter, mountain outlaw; patriotic rebel

komitaxhi nm (np ⁓ nj) [Hist] = **komít**

komitet nm committee

komízëm nm comicality, humorousness, humor

*__komlík__ = **komblík**

komo nf low chest of drawers for keeping bed linen and underwear: commode

komod adj comfortable

komodínë nf table by the side of a bed: night table, nightstand

komodítet nm comfort

*__komotít__·et vpr to grow numb, stiffen

komp nm lump (in one's throat)

kompakt adj 1 compact 2 (Fig) (of a group) internally cohesive and well-coordinated

kompaktësí nf 1 compactness 2 (Fig) cohesiveness

kompaní nf 1 company 2 (Pej) henchman

komparatív nm [Ling] comparative

kompas nm 1 drawing compass 2 (Old) compass (for indicating direction) = **busull**

kompensatë nf plywood

kompensato nf = **kompensatë**

kompensím nm ger 1 <**kompenso**·n 2 compensation

kompenso·n vt to compensate

kompetencë nf competence

kompetent adj competent

kompilacion nm compilation

kompilím nm ger (Book) 1 <**kompilo**·n 2 compilation

kompilo·n vt (Book) to compile

kompjuter nm computer

kompleks
  I § nm, adj complex
  II § nm [Mus] small group of performing musicians: band, chorus, combo

kompleksív adj complex; in toto, total

kompletím nm ger 1 <**kompleto**·n, **kompleto**·het 2 completion

kompleto·n vt to complete

komplicitet nm (Law) complicity

kompliko·n vt to complicate

komplikuar adj (i) complicated

kompliment nm (Book) compliment

komplot nm plot, conspiracy

komplotíst n participant in a plot, plotter, conspirator

komploto·n vi to plot against someone or something: conspire

komplotúes adj involved in a plot, conspiratory

komponent nm component

kompomím nm [Chem] compound

komposté nf = **komposto**

kompostím nm ger <**komposto**·n

komposto nf stewed fruit: compote

komposto·n vt [Agr] to compost

kompozicion nm [Lit Art] composition

kompozim *nm ger* **1** <kompozo·n **2** [*Lit Art*] composition

kompozitë *nf* **1** [*Ling*] composite/compound word **2** [*Bot*] composite flower

kompozitor *n* composer (of music)

kompozo·n *vt* [*Lit Art*] to compose

kompresë *nf* [*Med*] compress

kompresor *nm* [*Tech*] compressor

komprimo·n *vt* [*Spec*] to compress

komprimuar *adj (i)* [*Spec*] compressed

komprometim *nm ger* <komprometo·n, komprometo·het

komprometo·het *vpr* to become compromised, lose one's reputation

komprometo·n *vt* to put [] in a compromising situation: compromise []; involve [] in a dishonorable matter

komprometuar *adj (i)* compromised, discredited

komprometues *adj* threatening one's reputation: compromising

kompromis *nm (Book)* compromise

kompromisaxhi *nm (np ˜ nj) (Pej)* compromiser

KOMSOMOL [*komsomol*] *nm abbrev (Russian)* Comsomol

komsomollas *n* komsomol member

komshi
  I § *nm (np ˜ nj)* neighbor = **fqinj**
  II § *nf (Colloq Collec)* the people in the neighborhood, neighbors, neighborhood

komtë *adj (i)* made of horsehair

komunal *adj* **1** communal **2** of or pertaining to a commune

komunale *nf (Colloq)* communal enterprise

komunë *nf* commune

komunikacion *nm* communication, communication system

komunikatë *nf* communiqué

komunikim *nm ger* **1** <komuniko·n **2** communication **3** short communication: notice, announcement

komuniko·n
  I § *vt* to report, announce
  II § *vi* to communicate

komunikues *adj* communicative, communicating

komunist *adj, n* communist

komunitet *nm* community

komunizëm *nm* communism

komutator *nm* [*Electr*] commutator

kon *nm* cone

KON *abbrev* <Komiteti Olimpik Ndërkombëtar International Olympic Committee

konak *nm (Reg)* **1** hostel **2** upstairs parlor for receiving guests: guest parlor **3** residence, home; family
  ○ **fjalë/vërejtje me konak** wisely spoken remark

konakar *adj* domestic-minded, good at housekeeping

konaqe *np* <konak

KONARE *abbrev* <Komiteti Nacional Revolucionar [*Hist*] National Revolutionary Committee (1925-1927)

*konc *nm* keel

koncentrat *nm (Book)* **1** dehydrated food: food concentrate **2** [*Agr*] bran concentrate **3** [*Min*] mineral concentration

koncentrik *adj* [*Geom*] concentric

koncentrim
  I § *nm*
  II § *nm ger* **1** <konsentro·n **2** concentration

koncentro·het *vpr* to think hard and with a focus: concentrate

koncentro·n *vt* to concentrate [a substance]

koncentruar *adj (i)* concentrated

koncept *nm* **1** concept **2** preliminary draft

koncepto·n *vt* **1** to form/have a conception of []: conceive of **2** to gain insight into, manage to understand **3** to outline in concept, draft out, sketch

koncern *nm* syndicate made up of companies

koncert *nm* **1** concert **2** concerto

koncesion *nm* concession

koncesiv *adj* [*Ling*] concessive

koncil *nm* council

konciz *adj* concise

*konco·n *vt* to careen [a boat], heel

kondak *nm* **1** butt (of a gun) **2** swaddling clothes; swaddling band

kondensator *nm* [*Spec*] condenser
  ○ **kondensator elektrik** [*Phys*] capacitor

kondensim *nm ger* **1** <kondenso·n **2** condensation

kondenso·n *vt* to condense

*kondicë *nf* passage (in a book)

*kondicional OR **kondicionel** *adj (Law)* conditional

kondicionalisht *adv (Book)* conditionally

*kondicioner *nm* [*Tech*] air conditioner

kondicionim *nm ger* **1** *(Book)* <kondiciono·n **2** stipulation, condition

kondiciono·n *vt* **1** *(Book)* to set limits/conditions on []: condition **2** to air-condition

kondicionuar *adj (i) (Book)* conditional, provisional

kondis·
  I § *vi* to roost
  II § *vt* **to put [] up: lodge, quarter

konditë *nf* condition = **kusht**

kondor *nm* [*Ornit*] condor

kondosh *nm* heavy cloak; fur cloak

*kondruf *adj* branchy

konduktor *n* conductor (on a train or bus); (heat/electrical) conductor
  ○ **konduktor asnjanës** [*Electr*] neutral conductor = **neutër**

*kondur *nm (Reg Tosk)* tree stump; log

kone *nf* **1** puppy, pup **2** small pet dog: lapdog

konfederatë *nf* confederation

konferencë *nf* **1** conference **2** lecture

konferencier *n* master of ceremonies

*konfetari *nf (Old)* confectionery

konfirmim *nm ger* **1** <konfirmo·n **2** confirmation

konfirmo·n *vt* to confirm

konfiskim *nm ger* **1** <konfisko·n **2** confiscation

konfisko·n *vt* to confiscate

konflikt *nm* conflict

konfondo·n *vt (Book)* to mix [] up, confound

konform *adj* in conformity: conform

konformist *adj, n (Book Pej)* conformist

konformitet *nm (Book)* conformity

konformizëm *nm (Book Pej)* conformism

konfuz *adj* in confusion: confused, muddled

konfuzion *nm* confusion, disorder; loss of self-possession: abashment

*__kongare__ OR __kongerë__ *nf* = mbledhlj*e*

konglomerat *nm* 1 [*Geol*] conglomerate 2 (*Book*) conglomeration

Kongo *nf* Congo

kongolez *adj, n* Congolese

kongres *nm* congress

kongresist *n* 1 participant in or delegate to a congress 2 congressman

kongjestion *nm* congestion (of blood)

kongjill *nm (np ~ j)* live coal, burning ember

konicitet *nm* (*Book*) [*Tech*] conicity

konifere *np* conifers *Coniferae* = halorë

konik *adj* conic; conical

*__konil__ = kunel

*__konis·__ = kondis·

koniuktivë *nf* [*Med*] conjunctiva

koniunksion *nm* [*Ling*] conjunction

koniunktiv *nm* [*Ling*] subjunctive (mood)

koniunkturë *nf* (*Book*) complex of circumstances: conjuncture

konizmë *nf* = ikonë

konkav *adj* concave

konkë *nf* [*Anat*] concha
  ○ **konkë e hundës** [*Med*] nasal concha
  ○ **konkë e veshit** [*Med*] concha auriculae

konkludo·n *vi* to arrive at conclusion

konklusion *nm* conclusion

*__konkol__ *nm* [*Bot*] corn cockle (*Agrostemma githago*)

konkordat *nm* concordat

konkret *adj* concrete, real

konkrete *nf* that which is concrete, substance; something concrete

konkretësi *nf* concreteness

konkretisht *adv* concretely

konkretizim *nm ger* 1 <konkretizo·n 2 concretization

konkretizo·n *vt* (*Book*) to concretize

konkurs *nm* competitive contest

konkurrencë *nf* competition

konkurrent *n* competitor

konkurrim *nm ger* 1 <konkurro·n 2 competition

konkurro·n
  I § *vt* to compete
  II § *vt* [*Econ*] to drive [] out of the market by competition

konkurrues
  I § *adj* contesting, competing
  II § *n* contestant

konop *nm* rope, cord

konopicë *nf* [*Bot*] = marenë

konopishtë *nf* [*Bot*] = marenë

konseguencë *nf* = konsekuencë

konsekuencë *nf* (*Book*) 1 consistency 2 persistence 3 consequence, result

konsekuent *adj* 1 consistent 2 persistent

konsentrik *adj* = koncentrik

konsentrim *nm ger* = koncentrim

konsentro·n *vt* = koncentro·n

konservator
  I § *adj* conservative

  II § *n* political conservative; member of the conservative party
  III § *nm* conservatory, conservatorium

konservatorium *nm* conservatorium, conservatory

konservatorizëm *nm* conservatism

konservë *nf* 1 canned food, preserves 2 container of preserved food: can, tin, jar

konservim *nm ger* 1 <konservo·n, konservo·het

konservo·het *vpr* to become/stay fresh; be preserved

konservo·n *vt* to preserve [food] (in an air-tight container)

konservuar *adj* (*i*) preserved

konsideratë *nf* (*Book*) 1 consideration 2 esteem

konsiderim *nm ger* 1 <konsidero·n 2 consideration

konsidero·n *vt* to consider

konsiderueshëm *adj* (*i*) (*Book*) considerable

konsisto·n *vi* to consist

konsol *nm* 1 cantilever 2 [*Archit*] console; corbel; cornice

konsolidim *nm ger* 1 <konsolodo·n 2 consolidation

konsolido·n *vt* to consolidate

konsonant *nm* [*Ling*] consonant

konsorcium *nm* (*Book*) consortium

konspekt *nm* overview, digest

konspekto·n *vt* to give an overview/digest of [ ]

konspiracion *nm* conspiracy

konspirativ *adj* conspiratorial

konspirator *n* conspirator

konspirim *nm ger* <konspiro·n

konspiro·n *vt* to conspire

Konstandin *nm* Konstantine (male name)

konstant *adj* constant

konstante *nf* (mathematical) constant

konstatim *nm ger* (*Book*) <konstato·n

konstato·n *vt* (*Book*) 1 to notice 2 to ascertain, observe

konstelacion *nm* constellation

konstitucion *nm* constitution

konstitucional *adj* constitutional

konstruksion *nm* [*Tech*] construction

konstrukt *nm* (*Book*) structure; body structure, build

konstruktim *nm* (*Book*) construction

konstruktiv *adj* (*Book*) 1 structural, constructional 2 constructive

konstruktor *n* designer

konsultacion *nm* (*Book*) consultation

konsultativ *adj* (*Book*) consultative = këshillimor

konsultë *nf* (*Book*) consultation

konsultim *nm ger* 1 <konsulto·n, konsulto·het 2 consultation

konsulto·het *vpr* to take counsel: consult (with), confer (with)

konsulto·n *vt* to consult

konsultore *nf* consultation clinic for maternity health care and child rearing

konsull *nm (np ~ j)* consul

konsullatë *nf* consulate

konsullor *adj* consular

konsum *nm* consumption

konsumator *n* consumer

konsumim *nm ger* <**konsumo**' •*n*

konsumo' •*n vt* to consume

konsumues *adj* consumer = **konsumator**

kont *nm [Hist]* count (aristocratic title)

kontabël *adj [Econ Fin]* of or pertaining to book-keeping; engaged in bookkeeping

kontabilitet *nm (Book)* bookkeeping

kontakt *nm (Book)* contact

kontaktor *nm [Electr]* contactor

kontator *nm* meter (for gas/electricity/water)

kontekst *nm (Book)* context

*__kontenjer__ *nm* 1 container *2 (Reg Kos)* waste container, waste can

kontest *nm (Elev)* contest

kontestim *nm ger (Elev)* <**kontesto'** •*n*

kontesto' •*n vt (Elev)* to contest, dispute

kontestues *adj (Elev)* = **kontestueshëm**

kontestueshëm *adj (i) (Elev)* contestable, disputable

konteshë *nf* countess

kontinent *nm [Geog]* continent

kontinental *adj* continental

kontingjent *nm* contingent

kontrabandë
 I § *nf* 1 contraband, smuggling 2 black marketeering
 II § *adj* smuggled, black-market
 III § *adv* secretly and illegally

kontrabandist *n* smuggler, black marketeer

kontrabas *nm [Mus]* contrabass

kontradiksion *nm* = **kontradiktë**

kontradiktë *nf* contradiction; opposition
 ◦ **kontradiktë antagoniste** unreconcilable opposition
 ◦ **kontradiktë joantagoniste** reconcilable opposition

kontradiktor *adj* contradictory

kontraksion *nm [Anat Ling]* contraction

kontraktim *nm ger* <**kontrakto'** •*n*

kontrakto' •*n vt* to contract for [ ]

kontraktues
 I § *adj* contractual; contracting
 II § *n* party to a contract, contractor

kontrapunkt *nm [Mus]* counterpoint

kontrast *nm (Book)* contrast

*__kontratar__ *n (Old)* 1 contractor = **sipërmarrës** 2 notary

kontratë *nf* 1 [Law] contract *2 bond, deed

kontribuo' •*n vi* to make a contribution, contribute

kontribut *nm* contribution

kontroll *nm* 1 check, verification 2 examination; inspection 3 regulation 4 control; oversight, command 5 police
 ◦ **kontrolli punëtor** inspection by a visiting team of workers
 ◦ **kontroll rrugor** highway patrol

kontrollim *nm ger* <**kontrollo'** •*n*, **kontrollo'** •*het*

kontrollo' •*het vpr* to get a (medical) check-up

kontrollo' •*n vt* 1 to check, verify; examine; inspect 2 to check up on; give [ ] a check-up

kontrollor *n* 1 inspector 2 [Tech] regulatory device/ person: controller
 ◦ **kontrollor biletash** ticket collector

 ◦ **kontrollor biletash treni** train conductor
 ◦ **kontrollor rrugor** highway patrolman

kontrollues *nm* 1 controller, inspector 2 control device

kontrollueshëm *adj (i)* subject to inspection and control

kontur *nm* contour, outline

*__konup__ *nm* gnat, mosquito

*__konushmen__ *nm (Old)* bill of lading

konvaleshencë *nf [Med]* convalescence

konvejer
 I § *nm* 1 conveyor, conveyor belt 2 *(Fig)* assembly line
 II § *adv* using an assembly line system
 ◦ **konvejer i gjelbër** green foodstuffs held in reserve for winter consumption by animals and humans

konveks *adj* convex

konvencion *nm* agreement, convention

konvencional *adj* conventional

konventë *nf* 1 convention, covenant 2 formal meeting: convention

konvergjencë *nf (Book)* convergence

konvergjent *adj* convergent

konvertibël *adj [Fin]* convertible

konvertim *nm ger* <**konverto'** •*n*

konvertitor *nm* converter

konverto' •*n vt* to convert [funds]

konvikt *nm* school dormitory

konviktor *n* dormitory student, student living in a dormitory

konvulsion *nm* convulsion

*__konxhe__ *nf* bud = **gonxhe**

Konxhe *nf* Konxhe (female name)

konjak *nm* reddish-brown Albanian brandy, cognac

*__konjar__ *nm* rogue, rascal

*__konjare__ *nf [Entom]* firefly

kooperativ *adj* cooperative

kooperativë *nf* cooperative, co-op
 ◦ **kooperativë e shitblerjes** *(HistPK)* cooperative whose function was to arrange the commercial transactions between agricultural and industrial cooperatives

kooperativist
 I § *adj* of or pertaining to a cooperative
 II § *n* member of a cooperative

kooperativizëm *nm* economic system based on cooperatives

kooperim *nm ger* 1 <**koopero'** •*n*, **koopero'** •*het* 2 cooperation 3 cooperative arrangement; cooperative system

koopero' •*het vpr* to join a cooperative

koopero' •*n vi* to enter into a cooperative arrangement with an institution

kooperuar *adj (i)* joined into a cooperative arrangement; belonging as a member of a cooperative

kooptim *nm ger [Law]* <**koopto'** •*n*

koopto' •*n vt [Law]* to appoint [ ] to a vacant position without a new election

koordinatë *nf [Spec]* coordinate (on a graph)

koordinim *nm ger* 1 <**koordino'** •*n* 2 coordination

koordino' •*n vt* to coordinate

kopaç *nm* 1 block of wood, tree stump 2 hipbone 3 hammer

kopa çe *nf* **1** fire log; cudgel, bludgeon **2** beating using a cudgel; severe reprimand

kopa l *nm* copal

kopa lla *np* valueless talk, nonsense

kopa n
I § *nm* **1** wooden paddle for beating clothes during washing: wash paddle, clothes beater **2** flail **3** wooden mallet for pounding meat **4** grape cluster **5** spoke of a wheel
II § *adv* **1** in swaddling clothes **2** [*Entom*] beetle

kopan e c
I § *nm* swaddled baby
II § *adv* in swaddling clothes

kopan e c ë *np* swaddling clothes

kopan is· *vt* **1** to pound [clothes] with a wooden bat during washing **2** (*Colloq*) to beat [ ] severely: thrash, drub

kopa nj *nm* **1** shallow basin used for separating cream from milk **2** bath basin **3** hod for mortar

*kopc i t· = **kopsi t·**

*ko pçë = **kopsë**

kope *nf* flock/herd of livestock

kopeda n *nm* [*Bot*] European wild ginger (*Asarum europaeum*)

kope k *nm* kopek, unit of Russian money

Kopenha gë *nf* Copenhagen

kope ri *nf collec* livestock flocks taken as a whole

koperti në *nf* cover, wrapper; book cover

koperto n *nm* outer casing of a tire or ball with an inner tube

ko për *nf* [*Bot*] common dill (*Anethum graveolens*)
  ○ **kop ër e egër** [*Bot*] = **mara skë**
  ○ **kopër qeni** "dog dill" [*Bot*] bitter fennel = **mara skë**

kopi cë *nf* [*Entom*] **1** moth (*Microlepidoptera*) **2** moth larva

*kopij = **kopj**

kopi l
I § *nm* **1** illegitimate male child: bastard son **2** (*Old*) male houseman, drudge **3** (*Crude*) clever/sly person **4** (*Crude*) brat **5** barren new shoot that impedes productive plant growth
II § *adj* **1** (*Old*) born out of wedlock: illegitimate **2** (*Colloq*) sly, clever, devilish **3** appearing as an nonproductive offshoot that interferes with the proper growth of a plant

kopila n *nm* young rascal

kopi le *nf* **1** (*Old*) illegitimate female child: bastard daughter **2** (*Old*) female servant **3** (*Colloq*) clever/sly woman **4** [*Tech*] cotter pin

kopil eri *nf* bastardy

kopili *nf* cleverness, slyness, devilishness; guile, fraud

kopil isht *adv* using guile, deceptively

kopil kë *nf* lascivious girl

kopilo·n *vi* **1** (*Colloq*) to practice fraud, use deception; escape by guile **2** (*Old*) to work as a household drudge

kopi st *n* copyist; low-level clerk

kopist eri *nf* copy office

*kopi t· *vt* to make [ ] ill

kopi të *nf* [*Veter*] soft part of a horse's hoof

kopj ativ *adj* used for making copies: copying

ko pje *nf* copy

kopj i m *nm ger* <**kopjo·n**

kopjo·n *vt* to copy

kopju es *adj* for copying, duplicating

*kopo n = **kupo n**

kopra c *adj, n* = **koprrac**

koprac i *nf* = **koprrac i**

kopra n *adj* (*Reg*) metal tip of a goad

kopre sh *nm* (*Reg*) animal halter = **kapi stër**

*ko pr ëz *nf* = **ko për**

kopri k *nm* rocky heath

koprra c
I § *nm* stingy person: miser, skinflint
II § *adj* stingy, miserly

koprrac i *nf* stinginess, miserliness

ko psë *nf* button

kops i t· *vt* to button [clothes]

kops i t·et *vpr* to button up, get buttoned

kops i tje *nf ger* <**kopsi t·**, **kopsi t·**et

kopsi tur *adj* (i) buttoned, buttoned up

*ko psh ë = **kopi cë**

kopsht *nm* **1** garden; orchard **2** kindergarten **3** piece of land (approx. a tenth of an acre) granted by a cooperative farm to a family for its own use
  ○ **kopsht me lule** "flower garden" wonderful place, heavenly paradise
  ○ **kopsht zoologjik** zoological garden: zoo

kopsht a qe *np* (*Colloq*) garden vegetables

kopsht ar *n* gardener, horticulturist

kopsht ari *nf* **1** gardening **2** horticulture

kopsht ore *nf* (*Old*) **1** small garden **2** kindergarten

*kopti rë *nf* flask, bottle

*kopti s· *vi* to go off (somewhere)

kopu k *nm* (*Colloq Insult*) scoundrel

kopu lë OR **ko pul** *nf* [*Ling*] copula

kopura n *nm* coarse wide cloth of felt or flannel

ko qe *nf* **1** kernel, grain **2** (*Crude*) ball (testicle)
  ○ **koqe lepuri** [*Bot*] European gooseberry (*Ribes reclinatum*, *Ribes grossularia*)
  ○ **koqja e ligë/zezë** [*Veter Med*] anthrax = **pla sje**
  ○ **koqe e mirë** (*Euph*) [*Med*] abscess in the skin: boil, furuncle

*koqe mi llë *nf* [*Entom*] cochineal insect (*Dactylopius coccus*)

koqe zë = **ko qëz**

koq ërina *np* small skin blisters caused by heat: heat rash

ko q ëz *nf* **1** (*Dimin*) small kernel, grain; granule; pimple **2** [*Bot*] herbaceous annual with ramate stem, long lanceolate leaves, small white flowers, and fruit filled with black seeds **3** small, very sweet August-ripening white fig

*koqi n a *np* cereal grains

*koqini l = **kokcine ll**

koqi s *stem for 1st sg pres, pl pres, 2nd & 3rd sg subj, pind* <**koqi t·**

koqi skë *nf* small kernel/bean, grain; berry

koqi t· *vt* **1** to pick/gather [fruit] piece by piece **2** to eat [a fruit cluster] by breaking off one piece at a time

ko qkë = **ko qëz**

kor *nm* **1** chorus; choir **2** [*Mus*] choral piece

Kora b *nm* **1** Mount Korab **2** Korab (male name)

koraca të *nf* [*Mil*] armored warship, battleship

kora cë *nf* [*Mil*] **1** (*Old*) cuirass **2** carapace, shell

koracu ar *adj* (i) armored, steel-clad

*kora'k nm [Ornit] raven (Corvus corax)

kora'l nm 1 coral 2 choral

kora'n adj [Ichth] speckled trout (Salmo letnica Karaman, Trutta dentex Heck.)

korani'k nm [Food] dish prepared by frying pig's blood

kora'q nm farrier's hammer

ko'ras adv in chorus, in turns; one by one, little by little

korb
I § nm 1 [Ornit] raven (Corvus corax) 2 [Ichth] corb (Umbrina cirrosa L.) 3 black-haired domestic animal
II § adj 1 dark black 2 black-haired
∘ korbi i bardhë [Ornit] hooded crow = gallo'f
∘ Korbi korbit s'ia nxjerr sytë. "A raven doesn't peck out the eyes of another raven" (Prov) A bad person is safe from harm from other bad people.
∘ korbi sqepbardhë [Ornit] rook Corvus frugilegus
∘ korb uji [Ornit] cormorant (?)
∘ korbi i verdhë [Ichth] corb Umbrina cirrosa
∘ korb i zi 1 pitch black 2 [Ichth] brown meagre Sciaena umbra, corvina nigra

korba'sh nm black billy goat

ko'rbe nf gunwale; side of a boat

korbe'c nm black-haired domestic animal

ko'rbë
I § nf 1 [Ornit] raven (Corvus corax) 2 (Fig) hapless/wretched woman
II § adj wretched
∘ korba unë (woman's lament on learning of a personal tragedy to herself) woe is me! oh my poor soul! oh no!

ko'rbull nf wooden dairy tub; cask, keg

korcu'lle'shë nf [Ichth] female striped mullet after spawning (Mugil cephalus)

korça'r
I § adj of or pertaining to Korça
II § n native of Korça

Ko'rçë nf southeastern district of Albania bordering Greece and its capital city: Korça, Koritza

korde'le nf silk ribbon
∘ kordele deti [Zool] Vidalia volubilis

ko'rdë nf 1 [Geom] chord 2 [Anat] body sinew: tendon, ligament, cord 3 [Mus] guitar/mandolin string
∘ kordat e zërit the vocal cords

kordo'n nm 1 cordon 2 electric cord 3 watch chain
∘ kordon sanitar cordon sanitaire: quarantine, embargo

kordhe'le nf winding road

kordhe'lë nf = korde'le

ko'rdhë nf 1 [Hist] single-edged saber 2 sword *3 = ko'rdë

kordhë'ta'r nm 1 person armed with a saber: swordsman 2 (Elev) great warrior

ko'rdhë'z nf 1 [Food] sheep or goat intestines twisted together and fried or broiled 2 bowstring

*kordho'kull nf = kërdho'kull

ko're
I § nf 1 crust 2 tree bark 3 scab on a wound 4 (Reg) = turp 5 [Entom] bedbug 6 old age 7 [Bot] = radhi'qe
II § np harmful spirits who are burned in night bonfires during Easter
∘ korja e trurit [Anat] membrane covering the brain

Kore' nf Korea

korea'n adj, n Korean

korea'no'jugo'r adj, n South Korean

*kore'kt = korre'kt

*kore'lë nf girl

*kore'në nf [Ichth] = kora'n

kore'nt = korre'nt

koreogra'f nm choreographer

koreografi' nf choreography

koreografi'k adj choreographic

*korespond = korrespond

kore'shtë nf land covered by a coppice

kore't nm black and red pleated wool skirt for women

ko're nf(Old) 1 appointed time = afa't 2 generation = brez 3 icon 4 crust; tree bark

korë'zi'm nm [Geol] incrustation

Korfu'z nm Corfu

*korfuza'n
I § adj of/from Corfu
II § nm native of Corfu

kori' nf(Reg) shame = turp

kori'çkë nf 1 grove, thicket 2 piece of bread crust 3 scab on a wound

*korido'r nm corridor = korrido'r

korie'r = korrie'r

korife' nm 1 [Theat] leader of the chorus in ancient Greek tragedy: coryphaeus 2 (Elev) distinguished person in any sphere of science or art

korife'ne nf [Ichth] common dolphin-fish Coryphaena hippurus

*korigj = korrigj

korije' nf grove of oaks or other low-lying trees: coppice

kori'lë nf [Ornit] crane = kurri'llë

korinti'k adj [Archit] Corinthian

kori'nth nm [Ornit] little crake (Porzana parva)

kori's stem for 1st sg pres, pl pres, 2nd & 3rd sg subj, pind <kori't·

kori'st n member of a chorus: chorister

korishto'·n vt to humiliate

kori't· vt to shame, dishonor, disgrace
∘ <> korit· mustaqet to shame <> publicly in his old age; cause <> to lose his honor as a man

kori't·et vpr to fall into disgrace

kori'të nf trough; mill trough; feed/water trough

kori'tje nf ger 1 <korit·, korit·et 2 disgrace, dishonor

kori'tur adj (i) very hungry/thirsty

kori'th nm large thick-skinned grape with a long, tapering shape

*korkodri'l = krokodi'l

korkole'ps· vt to tangle up, make a mess of

korkoli't·et vpr to swing, sway, rock; totter, waver

*korkorri'm nm stomach rumbling

*korkosha'në nf [Bot] fruit of the Judas tree

*korkoshi'në nf = karkashi'në

korkozhe'l nm a swing

kormi'në nf = plë'ndës

*kormora'n nm [Ornit] cormorant

korne' nf 1 cornea 2 [Soccer] corner; corner kick

*korni'çe = korni'zë

korni'zë nf 1 frame; picture frame 2 (Fig) action frame 3 (Fig) limiting boundaries 4 [Constr] cornice 5 crossbar from which things are hung to dry: drying bar

○ **korniz**ë **për perde** curtain valance

korno I § *nf* OR **kornu**a II § *nm (obl ˜o̤i, np ˜o̤nj)* horn, French horn

*__koro__o *-n vt* = **korit·**

korobace *nf [Ichth]* = **gjuhc**ë

*__koro__bisht *nm (Colloq) [Anat]* coccyx

korolar *nm [Math]* corollary

korolë *nf [Bot]* corolla

koromane *nf* **1** *(Old)* stale bread issued to soldiers, commissary bread; piece of bread **2** bread of poor quality **3** *(Fig)* daily bread, livelihood; bare minimum wages

*__koron__ec
I § *nm (Reg Tosk)* silo
II § *adj* stingy

korronë *nf* crown

*__korove__c *nm [Bot]* melon, cantaloupe *(Cucumis melo cantalupensis)*

*__korove__sh *nm* water pitcher

korozion *nm* corrosion

korp *nm* corps

korparma**t**ë *nf* **1** *[Mil]* armored corps, largest unit of Albanian army **2** = **truparmat**ë

korporatë *nf* **1** corporation **2** professional union

kor**pus** *nm* **1** *(Book)* main building **2** *[Mil]* army corps **3** *[Tech]* main part of a mechanism or machine **4** *(Book)* body of published work: corpus

korse *nf* corset

korsel *nm* alum

*__korse__t *nm* = **korse**

*__kors__ëm *pcl* supposedly

korsi *nf* lane (in sports or traffic)

korsiv *nm* = **kursi**v

kortarë *np* **1** limbs severed from the body **2** strips of meat prepared for smoking

kortarë-**korta**rë *adv* in strips, into separate pieces

korte *nm (Book)* = **korte**zh

*__korte__l *nm (Reg Gheg)* sword

kortesh *nm* **1** *[Med]* eczema; pruritus **2** *(Fig)* lust

kortezh *nm (Book)* cortege, procession

*__kort__ës *nm* surface, texture

kortinë *nf* curtain

*__korth__ë *nf* shell, hard crust

korthinë = **korthit**ë

korthitë *nf [Bot]* tree sprout growing from a stump

*__korth__pul*ë = **karthpul**ë

*__korth__ta**r**
I § *nm [Invert]* crustacean
II § *adj* carapacial

korube *nf* **1** hollow in a tree trunk or in a rock cliff; beehive in such a hollow **2** small box used as a beehive **3** small trunk for clothes borne by a beast of burden **4** *(Disparaging)* hut

*__korz__ë *nf [Entom]* bedbug

korr· *vt* to mow; mow down; reap, harvest, garner
○ **korr· bar** to mow hay
○ **korr· duartrokitje** to garner applause
○ **korr· e gri·**n to be able to do anything one *wants*, be unstoppable
○ **korr· e nuk/mos lidh·** to do [ ] in a flawed and incomplete way, leave [ ] incomplete and unfinished
○ **korr· para** to reap (huge) profits
○ **korr· përmbi kallinj** to do something fruitless

korra *np (të)* **1** harvest **2** harvest time

*__korraca__të *nf* battleship = **koracat**ë

korracë *nf* = **korac**ë

*__korrac__o *-n vt* to plate with armor, armor

korrekt *adj* proper, correct

korrektes**ë *nf* = **korrektës**i

korrektës**i *nf* **1** correctness **2** propriety

korrektim *nm ger (Book)* **1** <**korrekto·**n, **korrekto·het 2** correction

korrekto *-het vpr (Book)* to mend one's ways

korrekto *·n vt [Publ]* to correct
○ **korrekto·**n **boca** to read proof, correct proof-sheets

korrekto**r** *n* proofreader

korrektu**es** *adj* corrective

korrektu**r**ë *nf [Publ]* **1** proof copy **2** correction

korrelacion *nm* correlation

korrent *nm* current

korrespondenc**ë *nf* correspondence

korrespondent *n* correspondent

korrespondo *·n vi* to correspond, match up

*__korr__ë *nf* **1** *(Reg Tosk)* icon, image = **kor**ë **2** = **korra**

kor**r**ës
I § *nm* mower, harvester, reaper
II § *adj* used for harvesting

kor**r**ese *nf* mowing/reaping machine, harvester

korridor *nm* **1** corridor, lobby **2** *[Alpinism]* chasm
○ **korridor kërcimi** *[Riding]* jumping lane

korrier *n* courier, messenger

korrigjim *nm ger* **1** <**korrigjo·**n, **korrigjo·het 2** correction

korrigjo *·het vpr* to mend one's ways = **ndreq·**et

korrigjo *·n vt* to correct

korrik *nm* July

korrikje *nf* July-ripening

*__korri__kull *nm (np ˜j)* = **kërri**kull

*__korri__l I § *nm* OR **korri**lle II § *nf [Ornit]* crane = **kurri**lle

korriqe *nf (Old)* measure of grain equal to about one and a half kilograms

kor**rje** *nf ger* **1** <**korr· 2** harvest

*__korrni__cë = **korni**zë

korrobac *adj* slim, lean, thin

korrobace *nf [Ichth]* **1** bleak *(Alburnus albidus alborella)* **2** small fish, young fish

korrocak *nm* gizzard

*__korroi__l· = **kolovi**t·

*__korroi__lë *nf* = **kolandin**ë

korronec *nm* = **koshta**r

korropesh *adj (Reg)* = **korrozi**

korropit·*et vpr* to get tired, give out: tire, flag

*__korrotiq__ *nm* beehive in a hollow = **koru**be

korrovesh
I § *nm* **1** jug/pitcher with one handle **2** person or animal missing an ear **3** *(Reg)* cluster of grapes
II § *adj* missing an ear or earlobe

korrozi *adj (fem sg ˜ez, masc pl ˜inj, fem pl ˜eza)* swarthy, dark-haired

*__korr__ta**r** *n* mower, reaper, harvester

korrupcion = **korrupsio**n

korrupsion *nm* corruption

korruptim *nm ger* <**korrupto·**n <**corruption**

korrupto *·n vt* to corrupt

korruptua**r** *adj (i)* corrupt; corrupted

korruptˈuˈes *adj* corruptive, corrupting

korruptˈuˈeˈshëm *adj (i)* corruptible

kos *nm* yogurt
○ **kos i kulluar** solid yogurt (from which the liquid has been filtered off)

kosˈaˈr *n* = **kosˈitës**

kosˈaˈxhiˈ *nm (np ⁓ nj)* person who makes and sells yogurt

kosˈaˈxhiˈk *nm* packsaddle post to which a rope is tied to secure the load

koˈsˈeˈ *nf* 1 scythe 2 cutting, harvest (first, second, last, etc.) 3 braid of hair

*ˈkoˈsˈër** *nf* scythe

kosˈëˈraˈk *adj* bent like a scythe

kosˈëˈtaˈr *n* = **kosˈitës**

kosinuˈs *nm* [*Geom*] cosine

kosˈiˈs *stem for 1st sg pres, pl pres, 2nd & 3rd sg subj, pind* <**kosiˈt·**

kosˈiˈt· *vt* to mow/reap with a scythe
○ **ësh·të pre e mos kosit** "be 'cut and don't reap!'" to mindlessly/pointlessly

kosˈiˈtˈës
I § *n* reaper, scythe wielder
II § *adj* used for harvesting

kosˈiˈtˈese *nf* mowing/reaping machine, harvester

kosˈiˈtje *nf ger* 1 <**kosi·n, kosit·et** 2 reaping period, harvest time 3 harvest

kosˈiˈtur *adj (i)* reaped by scythe, mowed

*ˈkoˈskë** *nf* bone = **koˈckë**

KOSMET *abbrev* <**Kosovë e Metohi** *(Old)* Kosova and Metohia (Albanian-speaking areas of Yugoslavia)

kosˈoˈre *nf* bush hook/scythe

kosovaˈr
I § *adj* of or pertaining to Kosovo
II § *n* native of Kosovo

Kosoˈvë *nf* southern region of Serbia with a large Albanian speaking population: Kosova, Kosovo

Kostandiˈn *nm* = **Konstandiˈn**

*ˈkosˈtaˈr** *n* 1 = **korrtaˈr** 2 [*Invert*] long-legged ground-spider

*ˈkosteriˈcë** *nf* [*Zool*] small lizard

*ˈkoˈsˈtëˈr** *nf* scythe

koˈstoˈ *nf* [*Econ*] cost

kostreˈvë *nf* 1 [*Bot*] foxtail millet, bristle grass, pigeon grass *(Setaria)* 2 hooked bristle grass *(Setaria verticillata)*

kostuˈm *nm* 1 suit (of clothes) 2 ethnic/regional costume
○ **kostum banje** bathing suit
○ **kostum me porosi** made-to-order clothes

kosh *nm* 1 large basket that widens at the opening 2 funnel-shaped fish pot; wicker creel 3 container for kitchen spoons, forks, and salt: spoonbox 4 trash basket 5 hamper 6 sidecar 7 [*Basketball*] basket
○ **kosh filmi** [*Cine*] film bin
○ **kosh letre** wastepaper basket
○ **kosh motoçiklete** motorcycle sidecar
○ **kosh teli** [*Constr*] gabion
○ **kosh zhvillimi** [*Cine*] developing basket

koshaˈdhe *nf* 1 patrol 2 [*Hist*] Ottoman soldier in pursuit squads sent out to capture outlaws and revolutionaries

*ˈkoshaˈk** *nm* wooden bar/doorbolt

*ˈkoshaˈll** *nm* pocket

koshaˈr *nm* grain silo

koshaˈre *nf* 1 corn hamper; grain silo 2 fence around a fruit-tree serving as protection 3 = **farashë**

koshariˈqe *nf* 1 small basket for fruit, pannier; weight of fruit held by such a basket 2 hen roost made of wicker

*ˈkoˈshˈas** *np* = **koˈshëz**

*ˈkoshelˈ** *nm* hammock, swing

koshˈeˈre *nf* 1 box/hamper containing a hive of bees in an apiary: beehive 2 hive of bees *3* = **koshaˈre** *4* kiln

koˈshˈëz *nf* [*Invert*] 1 warble fly maggot; warble fly *(Hypoderma)* *2* edible thistle, artichoke

koshieˈncë *nf (Book)* conscience

koshieˈnt *adj* 1 conscious 2 conscientious

koshiˈq *nm (Old)* measure of grain of about 35 kilograms

koshiˈqe *nf* 1 small basket 2 food cooler made of wire 3 bushel measure of grain of 10-50 kilograms

koshtaˈr *nm* 1 large hamper for corn: corn crib 2 basket/hamper maker

*ˈkoshteˈk** *nm* reserve supply, store

*ˈkoshtutˈ** = **kushtetuˈt**

kot· *vt* to cause to nod off

koˈt·et *vpr* 1 to nod off while sitting: doze, nap 2 to rave, speak deliriously

kot *adv* 1 in vain, without effect, for nothing, of no avail 2 for no reason, without purpose
○ **kot më kot** 1 in vain 2 aimless(ly), to no purpose

kot *nm* = **kotoˈr**

koˈtangjeˈnte *nf* [*Geom*] cotangent

kotaˈr
I § *nm* 1 animal enclosure: pigsty, sheepcote, chicken coop 2 food pantry, larder
II § *adj* * = **koˈtë**

koˈtas *adv* 1 for nothing, for no reason 2 just to pass time

koteˈc *nm* 1 shelter for poultry: chicken coop, hen house 2 [*Agr*] corn crib 3 *(FigImpolite)* shanty

kotele *nf* kitten, puss

koteˈsha *np*

koˈtë *adj (i)* 1 futile, vain, useless, fruitless 2 without any particular purpose, random; for no particular reason 3 silly, worthless, superfluous 4 meaningless, vain, empty

koˈtëleˈtë *nf* cutlet = **bërxoˈllë**

*ˈkoˈtëll** = **koˈtull**

koˈtëm = **koˈtë**

*ˈkoˈtës** *adj* soporific

kotˈësiˈ *nf (Book)* 1 futility, inefficacy, ineffectiveness; uselessness, worthlessness 2 worthless effort; folly

*ˈkotˈësiˈna** *np (Colloq)* nonsense, rubbish

koˈtiˈ *adv (së)* in vain

kotiledoˈn *nm* [*Bot*] cotyledon

koˈtkë *nf* knot, hitch

*ˈkoˈtla** *np* copper coins

*ˈkotˈniˈ** *nf (Reg Gheg)* = **kotësiˈ**

koˈtoˈ·het *vpr* 1 to rave, speak deliriously 2 to be silly/foolish to put in effort, work/try in vain

kotoleˈtë *nf* cutlet = **koˈtëleˈtë**

*ˈkotomeˈn** *adj* chubby, plump; broad-backed

kotoˈrr *n* calf of the domestic (water-) buffalo

kotova'l· *vt* to create wavelike movement in [ ], cause ripples in [ ]

kotova'l·et *vpr* to move in waves, ripple

*__kotrova'r__ *n* = katruva'r

*__kotro've__ *nf* = katruv'e

kotru'p *nm* ancestral origins, clan ancestors, trunk of a clan's genealogical tree

kotru've *nf* = katruv'e

*__kotsi'm__ *nm* 1 <kotso·*n* 2 frustration

*__kotso·__*n* *vt* to thwart, frustrate

ko'tull *nf* 1 cambric underskirt with lace 2 skirt, dress

*__kotulla'ç__ *adj, adv* in spiral coils

kotulli'm *nm ger* 1 <kotullo'·het 2 drowsy state

kotull'o·het *vpr* to get drowsy, doze

*__kotull'o·__*n* *vt* 1 to make [ ] drowsy; befuddle *2 to foil, frustrate

*__kotull'ue'm__ *adj (i) (Reg Gheg)* drowsy

*__ko'tun__ *adj (i) (Reg Gheg)* sluggish

*__kothe'c__ = kote'c

kother'a'k [ko-the-ra'k] *nm* person raised in total poverty

kothe're [ko-the'-re] *nf* 1 dry crust of bread, piece of dry bread 2 *(Fig)* stingy person

koth'ër *nf* ring of a sieve; rim of a pie

koth'ishtë [ko-thi'sht] *nf* tree stunted in growth by frequent pruning

kov *stem for 1st & 2nd sg pdef forms* <ko·*n*, ku·*het*

kova'ç *nm* 1 blacksmith = farkëta'r 2 [Ichth] John Dory *(Zeus faber)* = peshk-kova'ç

kovaça'në *nf* smithy, forge = farkëtari'

kova's *stem for 1st sg pres, pl pres, 2nd & 3rd sg subj, pind* <kova't·

kova't·
  I § *vt* to set a brood hen on [a clutch]
  II § *vi* to brood

ko've *nf* 1 pail, bucket 2 socket in the head of a metal tool into which the handle is inserted

Koz *nm* Koz (male name, nickname for Kozma)

koza'k *nm* Cossack

*__ko'z__ë *nf* trump

Kozma *nm* Kozma (male name)

kozmeti'k *adj* cosmetic

kozmeti'kë *nf* cosmetics

kozmeti'st *n* cosmetician, beautician

kozmi'k *adj* 1 cosmic 2 involved with interplanetary space or space travel

kozmodro'm *nm* spaceship station

kozmografi' *nf* cosmography

kozmografi'k *adj* cosmographic

kozmonau't *nm* cosmonaut, astronaut

kozmopoli't *adj* cosmopolitan, supporting cosmopolitanism

kozmopoliti'zëm *nm* cosmopolitanism

ko'zmos *nm* cosmos

kozhe'l *nm* = kolova'jz'ë

*__kozhu'f__ = gozhu'f

*__kozhu'p__ = gozhu'p

KP *abbrev* <Këshilli Popullor People's Council

KPP *abbrev* <Konfederata e Përgjithshme e Punës General Confederation of Labor

KQ *abbrev* <Komiteti Qendror Central Committee

*__kra'b__ë *nf* = kërra'be

*__kra'b__ë'z *nf* = kërra'bëz

*__kra'c__ë *nf* tinsel

krah *nm* 1 arm 2 shoulder and back area (used for carrying) 3 left/right side (of something) 4 armload, armful 5 armrest 6 side, direction 7 wing 8 *[Mil]* flank 9 branch 10 laborer, farm hand 11 strength for manual labor 12 *(Fig)* support, help, protection
  ○ **krah për krah** arm in arm; together, alongside; at the same time/level
  ○ **<>u prenë krahët** "<>'s arms went numb" 1 <> *is* numb from shock 2 <> is left with no one to be of help
  ○ **krah vinçi** boom/jib of a crane

krah'abisht'shku'lë *adj* with feathers missing from wings and tail

krah'a'në *nf* group of supporters: side, camp, party

krah'aqa'fë *adv* 1 in place over one shoulder and under the other arm: slung cross-shouldered 2 suspended from the shoulders

krah'aro'r *nm* 1 chest area, thorax 2 *(Colloq)* woman's bosom, breast 3 *(Fig)* bosom, heart, soul

krah'a'rtë *adj (Poet)* golden-winged

krah'as
  I § *adv* 1 arm in arm; side by side 2 alongside; close by, right beside 3 together, simultaneously 4 equally, the same
  II § *prep (abl)* 1 alongside, next to 2 besides, along with, in addition to 3 just like, the same as

krah'asi'm *nm ger* 1 <krahaso'·*n*, krahaso'·het 2 comparison 3 *[Lit]* simile

krah'asim'ta'r *adj* = krahasu'es

krah'as'o'·het *vpr* to consider oneself the equal of others

krah'as'o·n *vt* to compare

krah'as'o'r *adj* [Ling] comparative

krah'as'o're *nf* [Ling] comparative (degree)

krah'as'ua'r *adj (i)* compared, comparative

krah'as'u'es *adj* comparative

krah'as'ue'shëm *adj (i)* comparable

krah'as'ue'shmëri *nf* comparability

krah'ash'o·het *vpr* 1 to make a fair division; make an even split 2 to give back something borrowed

krah'ash'o·n *vt* to divide into equal parts; split evenly/fairly

krah'ata'r *n* 1 *(Old)* day laborer 2 manual laborer

krah'atha'dër *nf* [Ornit] peregrine falcon *(Falco peregrinus)*

krah'atha'të *nf* [Ornit] = krahatha'dër

krah'azi'm *nm ger* <krahazo'·*n*

*__krah'azim'ta'r__ *(Old)* = krahasu'es

*__krah'az'o·__n *vt* to be in partnership with; cooperate on a project with

krah'bardhë *nf* livestock animal that is white on one side

*__krah'ce__ *nf* bangle

*__krah'c__ë *nf* shirt

krah'cu'ng *adj* missing all or part of an arm

*__krah'ejt__ *adv* amiss, wrong

krah'ëdre'jtë *np* [Entom] grasshoppers *(Orthoptera)*

krah'ë'flu'tur *adj* [Poet] with butterfly wings, flitting silently

krah'ëfo'rtë *np* [Entom] beetles *(Coleoptera)*

krah'ëgja'të
  I § *adj* long-armed; large-winged
  II § *nm* [Ornit] skylark *(Alauda arvensis)*

krahë ha'pët *adj (i)* open-armed

krahë ha'pur *adj* with open arms

krahë leht ë *adj* having wings so light that they make no noise in flight

krahë luspo'r ë *np* [*Entom*] butterflies and moths *Lepidoptera*

*kra'hëm *adj (i)* grayish

krahë ma'rr *stem for 1st sg pres, pl pres, 2nd & 3rd sg subj, opt, adm, part* <krahëmerr·

krahë ma'rr ës *adj* [*Mil*] serving for a flank attack: flanking

krahë ma'rrje *nf ger* [*Mil*] 1 <krahëme rr· 2 flank attack

krahë me'rr *vt* [*Mil*] to attack [] on the flank

krahë mírr *stem for 2nd pl pres, pind, imper* <krahëme rr· [*Mil*]

krahë mo'r *stem for pdef* <krahëme rr· [*Mil*]

krahë mua'r *stem for pl pdef* <krahëme rr· [*Mil*]

*kra'h ën *nm (Reg Gheg)* = kre'hër

krahë ngro'ht ë *adj* feeling well protected and secure

krahë njo'm ë *adj* foolish, inexperienced

krahë pra'rua'r *adj* gilt-winged

krahë pre're *adj* having cropped wings

krahë ro'r *nm* = kraharo'r

*krahë rua'r *adj* = kraharo'r

kra'h ës *nm* = kra'hëse

krahë se *nf* shirt/blouse with sleeves

krahë shkru'a r *adj (Poet)* dapple-winged

krahë shku'rt ër *adj* short-armed, short-winged

krahë shpër vje'l ë *adj, adv* with sleeves rolled up; ready for work

krahë tha'të

    I § adj, n 1 lazy (person) 2 unhandy/clumsy/inept (person); helpless/hapless (person) *3 penniless

    II § nf [*Ornit*] = petri't

kra'h ëz *nf* 1 braces (to hold up trousers), suspenders 2 [*Ethnog*] gold-embroidered armlet worn over the sleeves of women's blouses 3 (*Old*) rope woven of linden bark and used for tying faggots together and carrying them on one's back *4 armrest

*krahë za *np* withers, shoulders

krahë zi *nm* [*Ichth*] flying fish (*Hirundichthys rondeletii*)

krahina'r

    I § n regional officer, provincial administrator

    II § adj * (*Old*) = krahino'r

krahin ar i *nf* regional administrative unit: province

krahín ë *nf* 1 region 2 province 3 country (in contrast with urban areas)

    ○ Krahinat e Ulta the Netherlands

krahin o'r *adj* regional; provincial

krahin or iz ëm *nm* 1 regionalism 2 provincialism

krah ís *stem for 1st sg pres, pl pres, 2nd & 3rd sg subj, pind* <krahí·

krah ísht *adv* in orderly arrangement; one next to the other

krah isht im *nm ger* <krahisht o'·n

krah isht o'·n *vt* to put [] in order, arrange [] properly

krah í t· *vt* 1 to prune [a tree] 2 to weed [a field] 3 to winnow [grain]

krah í tje *nf ger* <krahí t·

krah í tur *adj (i)* 1 pruned 2 weeded 3 winnowed

krah je't ë *nf* [*Bot*] = mështe'kën

*krah mba'jtje *nf* force, might

krah ne'z *nf* 1 snow frozen on tree branches; groundfrost 2 icy cold weather

krah ní c *nf* = fa'lm ë

krah no'c *nm* herdsman's food pouch

*krah no'r ce *nf (Reg Gheg)* belt

krah no'r ëse *nf* 1 backpack *2 basket

krah nje'r *nm* [*Bot*] spring heather (*Erica carnea*)

*krah nje'z *nf* light snowfall

krah o'l *nm* vest (for men)

krah o'sh

    I § adj broad-chested

    II § nm backpack, knapsack

krah o'she *np fem* braces, suspenders; garters

*krah o'she *nf* 1 bodice; doublet 2 thorax 3 backpack, knapsack

*krah urí n ë *nf* = bokëri'm ë

*kraja't ë *nf (Reg Gheg)* hardship, misery, toil

krajl *nm* king (in an Albanian folk epic)

krajl í *nf* kingdom (in an Albanian folk epic)

krajl í ce *nf* queen (in an Albanian folk epic)

*krajl o'·n *vt* to suffer

krakëll í·n *vi* to caw

krakëll í m ë *nf ger* <krakëll í·n

kra-kra' *onomat* caw-caw

kral *nm (Old)* = krajl

kramshí n ë *nf* damp area where wood rots

*krand *nm* = krënd

*kra'nd·et *vpr* = krë'nd·et

*krând ç *nm (Reg Gheg)* shrub, plant

kra'nde *nf* = krë'nde

krand o'·het *vpr* = krë'nd·et

*krand ull i *nf (Reg Gheg)* = krëndi'sht ë

*kran th *nm* = krëndth

krap *nm* 1 carp (*Cyprinus carpio*) 2 (*Fig*) stupid and clumsy person: oaf

krap an í k *n* [*Ichth*] = kora'n

kra'pe *nf* 1 [*Anat*] ovary *2 shoulder blade; collarbone

*kra'p ëz *nf* anchor

kra'pje *nf* 1 soft and sweet black cherry 2 [*Anat*] collarbone, clavicle = he'qës 3 (*Colloq*) = amane't

krap ul íq *nm* [*Ichth*] 1 fry of the carp 2 gudgeon (*Gobio gobio*)

kras ís *stem for 1st sg pres, pl pres, 2nd & 3rd sg subj, pind* <krasí·

kras í t· *vt* 1 to cut off [unnecessary parts, excess]: prune; lop [] off, trim, crop 2 (*Fig*) to kill [] in large numbers, decimate

kras í t ës *n* tree-pruner

kras í tje *nf ger* <krasí t·

    ○ krasitje e gjelbër [*Agr*] pruning done when the plant has sprouted leaves

*krastave'c = kastrave'c

kra'st ë *nf* hill quarried for its stone; arid and barren ground; rocky land

*krast í t· = krasí t·

*krashn ík = kreshní k

*krasht í t· = krasí t·

krate'r *nm* [*Geog*] crater

*krat í m ë *nf* bottle

krava't ë *nf* necktie, cravat

*krave'le *nf* = karave'le

kre·n *vt* to pull/take [] out/off

*kre *I §* *nf* OR *II §* *nm* = **kry**e
  ○ **kreu i grupit** [*Track*] leading bunch (in a race)

kre2 *stem for pdef, opt* <**kry**e·n

kreator
  I § *adj* creative
  II § *n* creator

krecë *nf* 1 needle of an evergreen tree 2 thorn; thorn tip 3 fishbone 4 fishbone-like object

kreçe *nf* head of cabbage

kredencial *adj* credential

kredi *nf* 1 credit 2 [*Fin*] loan

kredibilite̱t *nm (Book)* credibility

kredit *nm* [*Fin*] = **kred**i

kredito·n *vt* to extend credit to []

kreditor *adj, n* creditor

kredo *nf (Book)* credo

kredh· *vt* to plunge [] into a liquid; immerse, submerge

kredhara̱k *nm* 1 [*Ornit*] great crested grebe (*Podiceps cristatus*) 2 (*Old*) submarine
  ○ **kredharaku gushëzi** [*Ornit*] black-necked grebe *Podiceps caspicus, Colymbus caspicus H.*
  ○ **kredharaku i madh** [*Ornit*] = **kredhara**k
  ○ **kredharaku me veshë** [*Ornit*] horned grebe, Slavonian grebe *Columbus auritus L., Podiceps auritus*
  ○ **kredharaku i vogël** [*Ornit*] little grebe, dabchick *Tachybaptus ruficollis, Colymbus ruficollis Pall.*

kredhara̱kë *np* [*Ornit*] grebes (*Colymbiformes*)

kredẖës *n* diver

kredhje *nf ger* <**kre**dh·, **kri**dh·*et*

**kre*f̱ës *n (Old)* hairdresser

kref̱ëz *nf* trap, snare

**kre*f̱këz *nf* fancy cake, tart

krefsẖë *nf* 1 currycomb = **kasha**i **2* = **kre**shtë

kreh· *vt* 1 to comb 2 (*Fig*) to edit [a text] to remove errors and superfluous matters: comb through []
  ○ **<> kreh· bishtin** to curry favor with <>, butter <> up

kreẖër *nf* 1 haircomb 2 reed (on a loom) 3 carding comb 4 rake 5 cartridge clip 6 [*Ichth*] young carp 7 [*Bot*] dandelion (*Taracacum officinale*)
  ○ **krehër fishekësh** cartridge clip
  ○ **krehër zvarranik** "drag comb" comb used to raise the nap on wool flannel

krehëṟorë *np* [*Zool*] ctenophora, comb jellies

kreẖës *n* operator of a wool-combing machine

kreẖëse *nf* 1 currycomb; comb for wool 2 female operator of a wool-combing machine

krehje *nf ger* < **kreh·, krih·**et 2 coiffure 3 (*Colloq*) wool-combing mill or section

kreẖur *adj (i)* combed, carded

kreishtë *nf* mountain peak

kre*iṯ OR **krejt *sg gen/abl def (Reg Gheg)* <**kry**e

kre*jn = **kren

**kre*jni̱ *nf (Reg Gheg)* pride, confidence, vanity

krejt
  I § *adv* completely, entirely, totally, fully
  II § *determiner* 1 the entire, absolutely all, the whole 2 all, every
  III § *pcl* exactly like, just like, the very image of

**kre*jṯë *adj (i) (Reg Gheg)* complete, entire; utter

krejtës̱isht *adv* utterly = **krejt**

**kre*jṯshëm *adj (i) (Reg Gheg)* utter

krekacor *n (Disparaging)* braggart; conceited person

krekco·n
  I § *vi* to clash
  II § *vt* to batter

krekë *nf* [*Bot*] hedge maple, common maple (used to make musical instruments) (*Acer campestre*)

krekëz *nf* 1 [*Bot*] cain of the willow tree 2 [*Bot*] = **kre**kë 3 [*Bot*] Montpellier maple (*Acer monspessulanum*)

krekëzo·n *vt* to trim [tree branches]

kreko *adv (Colloq)* 1 dressed in clean and pressed clothes: all decked out in fresh clean clothes; dapper 2 with erect posture

kreko·het *vpr* = **kreko**s·et

krekos· *vt (Colloq)* to tense [one's body or body part]; raise [one's head and body] erect; prick up [one's ears]
  ○ **i krekos· veshët** to start to put on airs, begin to act high and mighty

kreko̱s·et *vpr (Colloq)* 1 to strut; act stuck-up, act snooty 2 (*Fig*) to show off
  ○ **krekos·et si maçoku në thekër** "prance around like a tomcat in the rye" to strut around showing off
  ○ **krekos·et si gjeli/këndesi/kaposhi majë plehut** to strut like a rooster on a pile of manure, make a fool of oneself trying to show off

kreko̱sje *nf ger* <**kreko**s·, **kreko**s·*et*

kreko̱sur *adj (i) (Colloq)* 1 stuck-up, snooty 2 showy, ostentatious

krela-kre̱la *adj* curly

krelë *nf* hair curl

krelo·n *vt* to curl (hair), make curls

krem
  I § *nm* 1 custard made with honey 2 cosmetic cream 3 [*Dairy*] creamy derivative from milk
  II § *adj* creamy in color

kremalie̱r *nm* [*Tech*] toothed rack (for meshing with a gear)

kremasta̱r *nm* 1 clothes hanger 2 = **vargo**r

kremato̱r *nm* crematorium

kremë *nf* paste, cream

kremte *nf (e)* religious holiday, holy day

kremti̱m *nm ger* <**kremto**·n

kremto·n *vt* to celebrate [a holiday]; commemorate

**kre*n *nm* horseradish

krena̱jë *nf* 1 peak of a hill or mountain; top 2 top/front part 3 top and choice part of a food dish

krena̱r *adj* 1 proud 2 (*Pej*) arrogant

krena̱ri̱ *nf* 1 pride 2 (*Pej*) arrogance

krena̱ri̱sht *adv* 1 proudly 2 (*Pej*) arrogantly

krend *nm*
  ○ **krend lepuri** [*Bot*] mistletoe *Viscum album*

kre*nde *nf* = **krende

**kre*ni̱ *nf (Reg Gheg)* pride

**kre*ni̱k *adj (Reg Gheg)* proud

**kre*ni̱sht *adv (Reg Gheg)* proudly

kreno·het *vpr* 1 to take/feel pride, feel proud 2 (*Pej*) to act arrogant/haughty; brag, boast

krep
  I § *nm* 1 silk or wool crepe 2 rocky crag; icy crag **3* clay pot used for baking
  II § *np* <**krap**
  ○ **krep rreze** rayon crepe

krep|ato· ·_het vpr_ **1** to become alarmed; get roused to action *__2__ to become strong/vigorous

krepato·*o· ·n vt* **1** to cry [] for help **2** to alarm

***kre·pçë** _nf_ = **gjep**

***kre·pël** _nf_ [_Bot_] whorled clary _(Salvia verticillata)_

krep|i·s· _vt_ to blink [one's eyes]

krepo··*n vi* to cry hard; cry out loud

kre|rë _np_ <**kry·e 1** head (of livestock) **2** leading citizens, prominent persons, dignitaries **3** loan funds **4** capital assets

kres _nm_ currycomb

kre·s _nf_ **1** pillow = **jastëk 2** top/front part **3** beginning part **4** scraper **5** = **kres**

***kres|ëm**| _nf_ = **krezm**|

kresni·cë _nf_ [_Ichth_] = **je·kën**

krest _nm_ = **kres**

krestomaci _nm (Book)_ chrestomathy, educational anthology

***kresh** = **kre·shtë**

kreshk _nm_ fish soup

kre·shkë _nf_ **1** foliage; leaf **2** peeling bark (on a tree) **3** scale (on a fish) **4** mountain range

kre·shk|ëm _adj (i)_ = **kre·shkët**

kre·shk|ët _adj (i)_ (of stone) layered and fissile, brittle: foliated

kre·shmë _nf_ [_Relig_] period of fasting for Christians
  ○ **kreshmët e gushtit** [_Relig_] in Eastern Orthodox religion the Lenten period dedicated to the Virgin Mary in the first half of August
  ○ **kreshmët e vogla** [_Relig_] six-day Lenten period preceding Christmas
  ○ **kreshmët e mëdha** [_Relig_] the seven weeks preceding Easter: Lent
  ○ **Kreshma e Këshnellavet** [_Relig_] Advent
  ○ **ësh·të me kreshmë** (for Christians) to observe a period of fasting, observe Lent

kreshm|i _nf_ fasting

kreshm|o··*n vi* **1** [_Relig_] to observe Lent **2** to fast

kreshm|or _adj_ **1** [_Relig_] Lenten **2** lacking in flavor

kreshm|or|e _nf_ Lenten food; food with little substance

***Kreshne|lla** _np fem_ Christmas

kreshn|ik
  _I §_ *n* valiant hero
  _II §_ _adj_ valiant; valorous

Kreshn|ik _nm_ Kreshnik (male name)

kreshnik|ëri _nf_ **1** _(Elev)_ chivalry; knightly order **2** = **kreshniki**

kreshnik|i _nf_ **1** _(Elev)_ valor **2** _(Collec)_ valiant people

kreshnik|isht _adv (Elev)_ chivalrously; valiantly

kre·shpe _nf_ sheep with coarse long wool

kreshp|ër|im _nm ger_ <**kreshpëro·**·*n*, **kreshpëro·**·_het_

kreshp|ëro··_het vpr_ **1** (of hair) to stand on end: bristle **2** _(Fig)_ to become aroused to anger; become very menacing **3** (of wool) become coarse

kreshp|ëro··*n vt* **1** to cause [hair] to stand on end **2** to rouse to anger **3** to make [wool] more coarse

kreshp|ër|u·ar _adj (i)_ **1** with hair standing on end: bristling; very angry **2** (of wool) coarse **3** wild, turbulent

kre·shpët _adj (i)_ = **ngra·thët**

kresht _nm_ [_Bot_] Austrian pine, black pine _(Pinus nigra)_

kresht|ak _adj_ tufted, fringed, bristling

kresht|an _nm_ large-combed (rooster)

---

kresht|ar _adj_ bristly

kresht|ashpër _adj_ (of a mountain) having a steep crest; sharply ridged

kre·shtë
  _I §_ _nf_ **1** tufted crest on the head or neck of a bird or animal: crest, mane; cock's comb **2** mountain crest; crest of a wave **3** tufted root **4** rough surface on a leaf **5** chair back **6** ridge between furrows
  _II §_ _adj (i)_ bristly, prickly; rough, coarse

kresht|ëba·rdhë _adj_ **1** (of mountains) white-crested, snow-ridged **2** (of waves) foam-crested

kresht|ëku·q _adj_ **1** (of mountains) having a reddish-brown crest **2** (of birds) red-crested

kresht|ëmu·rrmë _adj_ dark-crested

***kreshtëri|m** _nm_ Christianity = **krishteri·m**

kreshto··_het vpr_ = **kreshpëro·**·_het_

kreshtu·ar _adj (i)_ = **kreshpër|u·ar**

kretak _adj, nm_ cretaceous (era)

kre·të _nf_ [_Geol_] chalk

Kre·të _nf_ Crete

kretin _nm_ cretin

***kreth·** _vt_ = **kre·dh·**

kre|lu _oblique_ <**kry·e**

kreva·t _nm_ bed (for sleeping)

kre·vë _nf (Reg)_ = **fu·rkëz**

krezm _nm_ [_Relig_] holy oil, unction: chrism

krezm|im _nm ger_ [_Relig_] **1** <**krezmo·**·*n* **2** confirmation

krezm|o··*n vt* [_Relig_] **1** to confirm (in the Catholic faith) **2** to anoint with oil

***kre·h|ër** = **kre·hër**

krënd
  _I §_ _nm_ <**krënd**e
  _II §_ _nf_ **1** dry thin branches and twigs used as tinder **2** fodder composed of tender thin twigs cut up with leaves

krënd··*et vpr* to bud, sprout; go into leaf; become all leafy

krënd|ishtë _nf_ area thick with dry bush; grove of saplings used for tinder

krëndo··_het vpr_ = **krënd·**·*et*

krënd|th _nm_ sprout/bud on a tree

krëndulli _nf_ = **krëndi·shtë**

kri _nf_ [_Invert_] **1** woodworm **2** furniture beetle _(Anobium punctatum)_

***kri·ç** = **kërri·ç**

kri·dh··*et vpr* <**kre·dh·** to submerge, dive

kri·dh| _stem for 2nd pl pres, pind, imper, vp_ <**kre·dh·**

kri·dhë _nf_ mudhole

krif _nf_ **1** mane; crest **2** pile/sheaf of corn stalks left in a field during a harvest

krif|ëba·rdhë _adj_ white-maned

krif|ëgja·të _adj_ long-maned

kri·fshë _nf_ [_Bot_] evergreen shrub used for firewood/charcoal: phillyrea _(Phillyrea)_

kri·h··*et vt* to comb one's hair

kri·h| _stem for 2nd pl pres, pind, imper, vp_ <**kreh·**

krije·së _nf_ **1** creature **2** creation

krij|im _nm ger_ **1** <**krijo·**·*n*, **krijo·**·_het_ **2** creation **3** establishment, foundation, formation

krijim|tari _nf_ creation

krijo··_het vpr_ to come into existence, be created

krijo··*n vt* to create

kriju·ar _adj (i)_ imagined, dreamed-up

krijues
I § adj creative
II § n creator, innovator, author
krik nm [Tech] jack (for lifting heavy objects)
krikëll nf large beer mug made of thick glass
krikëllin·n vi = krikëllo·n
krikëllo·n vi to creak, squeak
kriko nf [Tech] jack
krikull nf forked prop
krillë nf [Ornit] crane = kurrillë
*krillo·het vpr = krih·et
krim nm crime; felony
krimb nm 1 worm 2 grub, larva
  ○ **krimbi i bardhë** [Entom] June beetle = zhuzhaku i majit
  ○ **krimbi i bizeles** [Entom] larva of the pea midge Contarinia pisi Winn.
  ○ **krimbi i boçeve** [Entom] bollworm larva Chloridea obsoleta F.
  ○ **krimbi i drurit** [Invert] = kërrmí
  ○ **krimbi i dheut** [Invert] earthworm
  ○ **krimbi i grurit** [Invert] grain/granary weevil, corn weevil Calandra granaria
  ○ **krimb jargavec** [Invert] slug
  ○ **krimbi i kashtës (së grurit)** [Entom] larva of the wheat stem sawfly, wheat sawfly borer Cephus pygmaeus
  ○ **krimbi i mëndafshit** [Invert] silkworm Bombyx mori L.
  ○ **krimbi i misrit** [Entom] European corn/maize borer Ostrinia (Pyrausta) nubilalis Hb.
  ○ **krimbi i murrmë** [Entom] turnip dart Agrotis segetum Schiff.
  ○ **krimbi i shiut** [Invert] rainworm, earthworm
  ○ **krimbi i shtypur** [Invert] pork tapeworm
  ○ **krimbi i teltë** [Invert] wireworm Agriotes lineatus
  ○ **krimbi i tokës** [Invert] earthworm, rainworm
krimb· vt 1 to make [] very dirty by wearing too long: make [] grubby 2 (Fig Pej) (said of stingy people) to accumulate [] so long that it spoils 3 (Colloq) to supply [] with a surfeit, dish out too much to []
krimb·et vpr 1 to get wormy/grubby 2 to go bad, spoil 3 to become filthy 4 (Colloq) to be infested: abound, teem, be up to one's ears (in something) 5 (Fig) to suffer a wasting disease
krimbalesh nm 1 wooly caterpillar 2 insect larva: grub
krimbçe adj wormy
krimbëri nf collec 1 larval swarm, grubs as a whole 2 crowd, throng, multitude
krimbje nf ger < krimb·, krimb·et
*krimbore nf annelida
krimbos· vt to make [] wormy
krimbur adj (i) 1 wormy; worm-eaten 2 [Med] rotten, decayed 3 (Fig Pej) rotten 4 filthy 5 (Contempt) lousy, worthless
  ○ **i krimbur (në para/flori)** filthy rich, rolling in dough
Krime nf Crimea
kriminal adj criminal
kriminalíst n criminologist
kriminalistíkë nf criminology
kriminalitet nm collec 1 crime 2 criminality
kriminel n criminal
krinë nf 1 bee swarm 2 horse's mane; horsehair 3 mattress filling

krip nm (Old) head of hair
krip· vt 1 to salt 2 to sprinkle [] with a powdery or granular substance 3 to give salt to [livestock] 4 to add flavor/zest/life to []
  ○ <> **krip· kokën** to kill <>: knock <> off
  ○ <>a **krip· lëkurën** 1 to kill <>: knock <> off 2 to skin you alive, take you for everything you've got
  ○ **të kripsha mendjen/trutë** (Impol Iron) I think you've gone bananas, are you crazy?
krip·et vpr 1 to eat something salty; taste salt 2 to get salty; get pickled (in brine)
kripaník
I § nm 1 saltshaker, saltcellar 2 [Food] pasty made with cornmeal and salty cheeses 3 very poor person with nothing to his name
II § adj salty
*kripç nm [Bot] = krifshë
kripë
I § nf 1 salt, table salt 2 salt, chemical compound formed by from an acid and a metal 3 laxative salt, magnesium sulfate 4 (Colloq Fig) appetizing flavor; tasty bit 5 pungent wit
II § pred broke, with no money
  ○ **ësh·të kripë** to have nothing left, be flat broke
  ○ **kripë e bardhë** clean salt, crystallized salt
  ○ **ësh·të kripë derri** to be completely broke, be miserably poor
  ○ **kripë guri** mineral salt, rock salt
kripëra np salts < kripë
kripërishtë nf salty infertile coastal land
kripës
I § nm saltceller
II § adj salted (for preservation), pickled
kripësí nf 1 saltiness 2 salinity
kripësim nm ger < kripëso·n
kripësirë nf 1 brine 2 salty taste, salty flavor 3 saltiness, salinity
kripësník nm wooden box on the wall that holds tableware and salt
kripëso·n vt to salt thoroughly; pickle with salt
kripëzím nm ger (Book) < kripëzo·n, kripëzo·het
kripëzo·het vpr to become salty
kripëzo·n vt (Book) to add salt to []; make [] salty
kripje nf ger 1 < krip·, krip·et 2 salt trough for livestock
kripor adj salty, saline
kripore nf 1 salt works, salt mine 2 saltcellar
  ○ **kripore e zeza** salt works for black salt
kripshëm adj (i) salty, salted
kripshmëri nf salinity
kriptogame np [Bot] Cryptogamae
kriptogram nm cryptogram
kripth nm 1 saline soil 2 [Bot] mistletoe (Viscum; Loranthus europaeus) 3 [Zool] cilium
kripur adj (i) 1 salty 2 pickled in brine 3 (Fig Colloq) too expensive 4 (Fig) (of speech) pungent, piquant
krir nm nacre = sedef
kris nm couch grass, quack grass (Agropyron repens)
kris·
I § vi 1 to crack 2 to make a sharp explosive noise: crack, clap, crash 3 (of an action) to begin suddenly, break out 4 to set off suddenly, leave quickly
II § vt to cause [] to crack: crack, snap
  ○ <>a **kris**· to suddenly begin <>: break out in <>

○ **kris·**[3pl] **grushtet** fists *begin* to fly

○ **<> kris·**[3sg] **koka/mendja** <> *becomes* cracked in the head, <> *goes* nuts

○ **kris· pushka** the battle *starts*

kris·*et vpr* to develop a crack: crack, get cracked

kris| *stem for pdef, opt, adm, part, vp, imper* <**kërcet·**

kris|**ë** *nf* crack, fissure

kris|**je** *nf ger* 1 <**kris·**, **kris·***et* 2 = **kris**|**ë** 3 [*Bot*] = **gram**

***kris**|**kë** *nf* poker (for a fire)

kris|**kull** *nm* [*Anat*] sternum, breastbone

kris|**më** *nf* sharp explosive noise: crack, clap, crash, snap

krista|**l**
  I § *nm* crystal
  II § *adj* crystal clear; crystal clean/pure

kristal|**in** *adj* crystalline; of crystal

kristal|**iz**|**im** *nm ger* 1 <**kristalizo**·*n*, **kristalizo**·*het* 2 crystallization

kristal|**izo**·*het vpr* to become crystalized, crystalize

kristal|**izo**·*n vt* to crystalize

kristal|**izu**|**ar** *adj (i)* in crystalized form, crystalized

kristal|**o**|**grafi** *nf* crystallography

kristal|**or** *adj* 1 in crystal form, crystal 2 (*Book*) crystal clear; crystal pure

kristal|**të** *adj (i)* 1 in crystal form, crystal 2 crystalline, crystal clear 3 crystal clean/pure; genuine; sincere

kristal|**th** *nm* [*Med*] crystalline lens

kristia|**n** *adj* Christian

kristian|**izëm** *nm* Christianity = **krishterim**

Kristofor *nm* Christopher

kris|**ur** *adj (i)* 1 cracked, fissured 2 (*Fig*) cracked (in the head), loony

Krisht *nm* Christ

krisht|**er**|**ë** *adj (i), n (i)* [*Relig*] Christian

krisht|**er**|**im** *nm* 1 [*Relig*] Christianity 2 Christendom

krisht|**lind**|**je** *nf* [*Relig*] Christmas

Krisht|**ngja**|**ll**|**je** *nf* (*Relig*) Resurrection

krite|**r** *nm* 1 criterion 2 regulation, specification

kriti|**k**
  I § *adj* 1 at a critical point 2 critical
  II § *nm* critic

kritik|**a**|**n** *nm* (*Pej*) 1 grumbler, complainer 2 = **kritize**|**r**

kritik|**ë** *nf* criticism, critique

kritik|**o**·*n vt, vi* to criticize

kritik|**ues**
  I § *adj* criticizing, critical
  II § *n* critic

kritik|**ue**|**sh**|**ëm** *adj (i)* criticizable

kritize|**r** *nm* (*Pej*) carping critic

***kritha**|**më** *nf* [*Bot*] = **krith**|*ëm*

kritha|**ra**|**q** *nm* grain-shaped pasta, semolina

krith|**ëm** *nm* [*Bot*] rock samphire (*Crithmum maritimum*)

krizante|**më** *nf* [*Bot*] chrysanthemum

kriz|**ë** *nf* crisis

Kroaci|**ï** *nf* Croatia

kroa|**t** *adj, n* Croatian

kro|**cë** *nf* [*Bot*] dog rose (*Rosa canina*)

***kro**|**çë** = **kerrkë**

kro|**dh**| *stem for pdef* <**kredh·**

kro|**dhë** *nf* 1 crust 2 scab (of a wound)

kro|**i**
  I § *obl* <**krua**
  II § *stem for 3rd sg pdef, opt* <**krua**·*n*

○ **Kroi i mirë njihet në kohë të thatë.** "The good wellspring becomes known in dry times." (*Prov*) A friend in need is a friend indeed.

kro|**j**|**çe** *nf* little wellspring/fountain

kro|**je** *np* <**krua**

kro|**jt**| *stem for 3rd sg pdef, opt, part* <**krua**·*n*

***kroka**|**r** *nm* small bulb/onion

kroka·**t** *vi* = **karka**t

kroka|**tje** *nf ger* = **karka**t

krokodil *nm* [*Zool*] 1 crocodile 2 (*Fig Pej*) deceptive scoundrel

krol *nm* [*Sport*] crawl (stroke)

***krol**|**ist** *n* [*Sport*] crawl swimmer

krom *nm* 1 [*Chem*] chromium ((*Cr*)) 2 chrome

krom|**ash**
  I § *adj, n* (*Pej*) scabious
  II § *nm* (*Insult*) person afflicted with scabies

kro|**më** *nf* 1 [*Med*] scabies = **zgjebe** 2 [*Agr*] fungal infection of plants: scab () 3 [*Bot*] = **krocëK**

krom|**im** *nm ger* <**kromo**·*n*

krom|**mbajt**|**ës** *adj* containing chromium

krom|**o**·*n vt* to plate with chrome

krom|**or** *adj* containing chromium, of chrome: chrome

krom|**os**· *vt* to afflict with scabies

krom|**os**·*et vpr* 1 to become afflicted with scabies 2 (*Fig*) to get stinking dirty, become putrid

krom|**os**|**ur** *adj (i)* 1 scabious 2 (*Fig*) stinking dirty, putrid

kromozom *nm* [*Biol*] chromosome

***krona**|**k** = **kronikë**

krongji|**ll** *nm* (*np ˜ j*) icicle

kronik *adj* chronic

kronika|**n** *nm* = **kronist**

kroni|**kë** *nf* chronicle, record

kron|**ist** *n* chronicler

krono|**logji** *nf* chronology

krono|**me**|**tër** *nm* 1 chronometer; stop-watch 2 (*ColloqJocular*) punctual person

krono|**metr**|**im** *nm ger* <**kronometro**·*n*

***krono**|**metr**|**ist** *n* [*Sport*] timekeeper, timer

krono|**metro**·*n vt* 1 to measure [] with a chronometer 2 (*Colloq*) to time [] accurately

krono|**logji**|**k** *adj* chronological

krono|**logji**|**k**|**isht** *adv* chronologically

kronshtejn *nm* [*Tech*] arbor support

***kro**|**nj** *np* <**krua**

kropa|**llë** *nf* hooked metallic dirt-scraper at the tip of a plowman's goad

***kro**|**pje** = **kra**|**pje**

kro|**qe** *nf* 1 = **krip**|**ësnik** *2 bucket *3 skull *4 drying rack for cheese

***kroqi** *nf* sketch, outline

kros *nm* 1 [*Sport*] cross-country racing 2 = **qeros**

kros·*et vpr* = **qeros**e

kros|**ë** *nf* = **qeros**ë

***kros**|**ist** *n* [*Sport*] cross-country runner

***krosh** *nm* (*Reg Kos*) box for cutlery

*krota n = kruta n

krov *stem for 1st & 2nd sg pdef* <kru a·n

kru·het *vpr* <kru a·n 1 to scratch an itch, scratch oneself 2 to itch
  ○ <> kru·het³ᵖˡ hundët <> *is itching* for a fight
  ○ <> kru·het³ˢᵍ kurrizi/shpina "<>'s back *itches*" <> *is looking* for trouble

kru a nm (obl ˜o i, np ˜o je) freshwater spring, fountain spring

kru a·n *vt* 1 to scratch [an itch] 2 to scrape 3 to search everywhere for []
  ○ krua·nn fytin/gurmazin/zërin to clear [one's throat]
  ○ krua·nn thonjtë (*Tease*) to twiddle one's fingers, sit around not doing anything; do something useless
  ○ krua·nn veshin "scratch one's ear" to make a nervous gesture (tug at one's ear, wriggle one's finger in the ear, nervously scratch the ear) as a way to stall answering a question

*krua çkë *nf (Reg Tosk)* = krojçe

kru ajt ese *nf* = kru ese

kru ajt je *nf ger* <kru a·n, kru·het

kru ajt ur *part* <kru a·n

*krua r
  I § *part* <kru a·n
  II § *nm (i)* madman

kru a ra *np* 1 itching 2 food scraped out of a cooking vessel

kru arje *nf ger* 1 = kru ajtje 2 [*Med*] pruritus

kru ashkë *nf* potter's wooden tool for smoothing/scribing

krucife re *nf* [*Bot*] crucifer

kru es *nm* = kru ese

kru ese *nf* 1 scraper for cleaning off metal 2 toothpick 3 food scraper

*krueta n = kruta n

*kruja n = kruta n

Kruj ë *nf* city north of Tirana: Kruja

*kru ll·et *vpr* to double (oneself) up, get bent

kru nde *np* 1 bran, wheat husks 2 (*Fig*) worthless person
  ○ ësh·të krunde (*Colloq*) to be broke/penniless

krup *nm* [*Med*] croup
  ○ krup i remë [*Med*] subglottic laryngitis

kru p ë *nf* 1 urge to vomit, nausea 2 disgust, loathing

kru p shëm *adj (i)* 1 nauseated 2 disgusted 3 disgusting, loathsome

*krupullo s un *adj (i) (Reg Gheg)* raggedy

*kruq = kryq

*kru s·et *vpr* = kërru s·et

*kru s je *nf* gesture of respect: bow, reverence

krusma r *nm* (torture) rack

kru s më *nf* 1 terrible suffering 2 exhaustion, destruction

kru spull *adv* compacted/contracted into a small space, drawn up in a heap: curled/hunched/huddled/shriveled/wadded/pinched up

kruspull im *nm ger* <kruspullo ·n, kruspullo ·het

kruspullo ·het *vpr* to contract into a ball: hunch/huddle/curl up; crouch

kruspullo ·n *vt* to contract [] into a ball, compress [] into a small space, compact [] into a heap

kruspull or *adj* contracted into a ball, curled up

kruspullo s· *vt* = kruspullo ·n

kruspullo s·et *vpr* = kruspullo ·het

kruspullo s je *nf ger* <kruspullo s·, kruspullo s·et

kruspullo s ur *adj (i)* = kruspullu ar

kruspullu ar *adj (i)* 1 in a pile/heap 2 hunched up into a ball, curled up

kruspullu k *nm* [*Bot*] = madërgo në

krustace *np* [*Zool*] crustaceans *Crustacea*

krushk *nm (np ˜ q)* 1 [*Ethnom*] member of the escort group from the groom's family that come to fetch the bride 2 relative by marriage
  ○ krushku i madh = krushkapa rë
  ○ krushku i parë = krushkapa rë

krushk a ma dh *nm* [*Ethnom*] = krushkapa rë

krushk a pa r ë *nf* [*Ethnog*] leader of the escort group from the groom's family that come to fetch the bride

kru shk ë *nf* 1 [*Ethnom*] female member of the escort group from the groom's family that come to fetch the bride 2 female relative by marriage

krushk o ·het *vpr* to become related by marriage

krushk o ·n *vi* to make a marriage (with another family), marry up (with another family)

krushq *np* <krushk

krushq a r *n* [*Ethnom*] marriage broker

krushq ë si *nf* escort group from the groom's family that come to fetch the bride

krushq i *nf* 1 alliance by marriage 2 (*Collec*) escort group from the groom's family that come to fetch the bride; relatives by marriage

kruta n
  I § *adj* of/from Kruja
  II § *n* native of Kruja

kry·het *vpr* to be accomplished/completed, come to an end: terminate

kry be *nf* coarse fiber removed by combing flax or hemp: tow, oakum

krydh· *vt* (*Colloq*) to take/pick [] from <>'s pocket: steal, filch, lift

krye
  I § *nm* 1 head 2 head, chief 3 heading 4 river source 5 beginning 6 (*Fig*) best and most-honored position, head
  II § *nn* 1 head 2 mind 3 self 4 head portion 5 river source 6 beginning 7 (*Fig*) best and most-honored position, head 8 chapter (of a book)
  ○ kryet e punës the person in charge
  ○ krye jave/muaji/viti (on a) weekly/monthly/yearly (basis)
  ○ krye më krye (with their upper parts) right next to one another; head to head; face to face; tête à tête, personal

krye·n *vt* 1 to bring [] to a successful conclusion: accomplish, complete 2 to fulfill [a duty/charge/expectation]: satisfy 3 to do, perform, execute; commit/perpetrate [a crime] 4 to expend, finish off [] 5 to live out [a period of time], last []
  ○ krye·n detyrën to do one's duty, fulfil one's obligation

krye *formativ* chief, head

krye agrono m *nm* chief agronomist

krye ark ë ta r *n* chief treasurer, comptroller

krye armi k *nm* archenemy

krye a r të *adj* 1 (of a bird) golden-headed 2 [*Poet*] golden-haired

krye a r t ëz *nf* [*Ornit*] goldfinch (*Carduelis carduelis*)

krye artiku ll *nm (np ˜ j)* lead article

krye|aru'shë adj having a large ugly head
krye|bandi't nm bandit chieftain; brutal criminal
krye|ba'rdhë adj **1** white-headed *2 lucky
krye|bari' nm head shepherd
*krye|bi'sht** adv from front to back
krye|bo'sh adj = kokëbo'shë
krye|bra'zdë nf [Agr] deep furrow plowed first before plowing the rest of the field
krye|buri'm nm principal source
krye|cull'a'k adj having no more hair: bald
krye|cu'ng adj = kokëfo'rtë
krye|dasm'o'r n person who organizes a wedding
krye|da'sh nm battering ram
krye|de'll nm (Fig) mainspring
krye|dru' adj = kokëfo'rtë
krye|du'kë nm [Hist] archduke = arkidu'kë
krye|dhje't'ës nm (Old) [Mil] leader of a ten-man squad: corporal
krye|e'ngj'ëll nm (pl ~ j) archangel
krye|familj'a'r n head of the family, pater familias
krye|feta'r n head of the faith, church leader
krye|fi'll nm starting point, very beginning
*krye|fit'u'es** nm (Old) champion
krye|fja'l'ë nf **1** [Ling] grammatical subject *2 motto; slogan, watchword
krye|fjal'o'r adj [Ling] serving as grammatical subject
krye|fo'rtë adj willful, stubborn
*krye|fsha't** nm (Old) main village (in a village cluster)
krye|fu'nd adv from head to toe
krye|gjah'ta'r nm experienced hunter heading a hunting party
krye|gja't'ë nm **1** [Ichth] thin-lipped gray mullet (Liza ramada, Mugil ramada) **2** long-headed, dolichocephalic
krye|gjeo'lo'g n chief geologist
krye|gjet'ës nm [Ethnog] person who offers the first toast at a wedding
krye|gjë nf(Old) capital asset, capital
krye|gjyk'a't'ës nm [Law Old] presiding judge
krye|gjymty'r'ë nf [Ling] major sentence constituent: whole subject/predicate
*krye|gjy'q** nm (Old) = kryegjyqta'r
krye|gjyq'ta'r n **1** [Law Old] chief justice **2** [Sport] head referee, chief umpire
krye|gjy'sh nm **1** [Relig] head of the Bektashi faith **2** (Old) = stërgjy'sh
krye|gjysh'a't'ë nf[Relig] **1** central directorate of the Bektashi faith, seat of the Bektashi faith *2 (Old) presbytery
krye|ha'rk'ës nm [Ornit] siskin (Spinus spinus)
krye|her'sh'ëm adj (i) earliest, oldest, most ancient
krye|ho'll'ë nm [Ichth] = kryegja't'ë
krye|infermie'r n chief/head nurse
krye|inspekto'r n chief inspector
krye|inxhinie'r n chief engineer
*krye|ipe'shk** = kryepeshko'p
krye|ja'sht'ë adj bareheaded = kokëja'sht'ë
krye|ja'v'ë nf **1** first part of the week **2** the day a week after the point of reference: a week from today
krye|kallogre' nf [Relig] mother-superior, abbess

krye|kallogje'r nm [Relig] abbot, prior
krye|kamerie'r n headwaiter
*krye|katund'a'r** n (Old) mayor; headman
krye|këcy'er adj impetuous, hotheaded, impulsive
krye|këpu't adv utterly, downright, absolutely
*krye|kërru's'ë** = kryekërru'sur
krye|kërru's'ur adj **1** bent by illness or old age **2** modest and withdrawn **3** deeply suffering; deeply troubled
krye|këshill'ta'r n chief counselor
krye|kështje'll'ë nf **1** command fortress **2** (Fig) national leader, commander-in-chief
krye|kiru'rg nm chief surgeon
krye|ki'shë nf main church, cathedral
krye|komanda'nt nm [Mil] commander-in-chief
krye|komi't nm [Hist] guerilla chieftain
krye|ko'nsull nm (np ~ j) consul-general, chief consul
krye|konsull'a't'ë nf consulate-general
*krye|kqy'r-** vt (Reg Gheg Old) to supervise
krye|kre'je
  I § adv above all; first of all
  II § adj *1 main, principal, chief *2 (Reg Gheg) absolute
krye|kre'jet adv above all; first of all
krye|kru'shk nm [Ethnog] = krushkapa'r'ë
*krye|kumand'a'r** n (Colloq Reg) commander-in-chief
krye|ku'ngull adj (Pej Scorn) pumpkin-head = kokëku'ngull
krye|ku'q nm [Ornit] **1** = kryea'rt'ëz **2** [Bot] club rush, great bulrush (Scirpus lacuster)
krye|ky'ç nm master key
krye|labora'nt nm chief technician (in a laboratory)
krye|la'kër nf [Bot] Savoy cabbage (Brassica oleracea var. capitata)
krye|la'n'ë nf **1** [Food] mixture of crumbled corn bread and cheese topped with melted butter; pasty made of corn and cheese **2** confection made of boiled bread crumbs and honey
*krye|la'r** nm kind of pancake/fritter
krye|la'rtë adj **1** proud **2** haughty
krye|la'rt'ës'i nf **1** pride **2** haughtiness
krye|lo'p'ë adj (Disparaging) = kokëlo'p'ë
krye|lundër'ta'r n captain (of a ship), pilot
krye|llogari'ta'r n chief accountant
krye|ma'dh
  I § adj big-headed
  II § nm [Ichth] stargazer (Uranoscopus scaber L.)
krye|mami' nf head midwife
*krye|mbro'jt'ës** nm (Old) champion, protector
*krye|me** nf (e) (Reg Gheg) **1** accomplishment **2** [Ling] = e kry'er
krye|mekani'k nm chief mechanic
krye|mëdhe'nj adj (të) masc pl nm < kryema'dh
*krye|më'ngë** nf with masc agreement chief
*krye|mësa'll'ë** nf with masc agreement (Old) man who presides at the table
krye|mës'u'es nm (Old) head teacher, headmaster
krye|mës'u'es'e nf (Old) head teacher, headmistress
krye|mës'ues'i' nf (Old) headmaster's office
krye|minato'r n chief miner
krye|mini'stër nm prime minister

krye ministrï *nf* **1** council of chief ministers **2** prime ministry

krye mje k *nm* chief/head doctor

krye mje shtër *nm* **1** foreman **2** [*Art*] old master

krye mo t *nm* **1** New Year's Eve; New Year's Day **2** [*Ethnog*] March 1 celebration of the arrival of spring

krye mpre h të *nm* [*Ichth*] = **kryegja**të

krye mu shk *adj* pig-headed

krye myftï *nm* [*Relig*] grand mufti

*****krye na lt** *(Reg Gheg)* = **kryela rt**

krye ne ç *adj* obstinate, stubborn; headstrong

krye neç ë sï *nf* obstinacy, stubbornness

*****krye ne q**·*et vpr* to be obstinate

*****krye neq ë sï** = **kryeneç ë sï**

krye ngri t ë s *adj, n* insurgent

krye ngri t je *nf* insurgency

*****krye ngu c ë s** *adj* fomenting, instigating

*****krye ngu lm**ë *nf (Old)* somersault

krye ngu l tas *adv* head-down

krye ngu l thi *adv* upside-down; headfirst, headlong

*****krye ngje sh** *adj* tenacious, persistent; stubborn

*****krye ngje shje** *nf* tenacity, persistence; stubbornness

krye ngje sh ur *adj (i)* persistent, obstinate

*****krye ngjy sh** = **kryegjysh**

krye ni sje *nf* starting point

krye pa rë *adv* first and foremost, in the first place

*****krye parï** *nf* primacy

krye peshko p *nm* [*Relig*] archbishop

krye peshkopa të *nf* [*Relig*] diocese headed by an archbishop: archbishopric, archdiocese

*****krye peshkopï** = **kryepeshkopa t**ë

krye përpje të

   I § *adv* **1** with head held high **2** *(Pej)* in a arrogant manner, insolently

   II § *adj* insolent

krye përpjet ë sï *nf* insolence

krye pici ngu l *adv* = **kryengu lthi**

krye pla k *nm (Old)* official headman of a rural community

   ○ **kryeplak në fshat të huaj** person who tries to act the boss outside his own territory

krye ple q *np* < **kryepla k**

krye pleq ë sï *nf (Old)* council of elders

krye po shtë

   I § *adv* = **kok ë po sht**ë

   II § *nf* * [*Bot*] snowdrop (*Galanthus nivalis*) = **boçëbo r**ë

*****krye pri ft** *nm* [*Relig*] high priest, chief priest; provost (of a cathedral chapter)

krye pri j ë s *n* leader, guide

*****krye profe t** *nm* [*Ichth*] = **kryegja t**ë

krye prokuro r *n (Old)* [*Law*] attorney-general, chief prosecutor

krye pun ë to r *nm (Old)* foreman

krye qe nd ë r *nf* **1** administrative center; district capital **2** *(Fig)* headquarters

krye qind l ë s *nm* centurion

*****krye qi tas**

   I § *n (Old)* rebel

   II § *adj* rebellious

*****krye qi t je** *nf (Old)* rebellion, revolt

krye qyte t *nm* capital city; metropolis

*****krye qytet a r** *(Old)* = **kryeqyte tas**

krye qyte tas

   I § *adj* of or pertaining to the capital city; metropolitan

   II § *n* inhabitant of the capital city

krye r

   I § *adj (i)* accomplished, performed, achieved, executed, done

   II § *nf (e)* [*Ling*] present perfect tense, perfect tense

   ○ **e kryera e tejshkuar** [*Ling*] pluperfect

   ○ **e kryera e plo t**ë [*Ling*] past perfect tense

   ○ **e kryera e thjeshtë** [*Ling*] simple past tense, past definite tense

krye ra dhë *nf* indented first line of a paragraph; headline

krye redakto r *n* editor-in-chief

krye regjiso r *n* head director, chief director

krye r je *nf ger* **1** < **kry e**·*n*, **kry**·*het* **2** accomplishment, fulfilment, performance, execution, achievement, completion

krye rre sht *nm* = **kryera dh**ë

krye sekreta r *n* chief secretary, office head

krye sï *nf* **1** directorate **2** leadership, management **3** presidency; chairmanship

krye sï m *nm* **1** directorate **2** leadership, management

krye si sht *adv* chiefly, mainly

krye so·*n*

   I § *vt* to head, head up [], lead; preside over/at []

   II § *vi* to take the leadership role

krye so r *adj* main, chief, leading

krye so re *nf* most important thing/matter, main thing

krye specia lï st *n* chief specialist

krye su es *adj* person in charge at an event: leader, director, manager

krye shëndo shë *nf* condolence visit

krye shërbe to r *n* **1** chief of servants: household head, major-domo **2** *(Pej)* lackey

krye shka llë *nf* top of the stairs; landing between flights of stairs

*****krye shkro nj**ë *nf* capital letter

krye shte rë OR **krye shte rr**ë

   I § *adj* empty-headed

   II § *n* fathead

krye shtro·*het vpr* to take one's hat off, bare one's head

krye shty llë *nf* capital (of a column/pillar)

krye ta r *n* chief, head; chairman, leader, boss

krye tarï *nf* leadership, chairmanship, presidency, captaincy

krye tekni k *nm* chief technician

krye ti ngull *nm (np ˜ j)* initial sound

krye ti tull *nm (np ˜ j)* main title

krye to llë

   I § *adj* bald-headed, bald

   II § *nf* bald head

krye tra (r) *nm (np ˜ rë)* [*Constr*] architrave; lintel

krye tra shë *adj* thickheaded, slow, stupid

krye tre g *nm* central market

krye tri m *nm* hero of heroes, principal hero

krye tu l *nm (Insult Tease)* = **kok ë tu l**

krye tu llë *adj (Tease)* bald-pated

kry'e·th _nm dimin_ **1** small head/knob **2** short chapter; subchapter; subchapter heading

krye·tha'tё _adj (Pej)_ thickheaded, dense, stupid

krye·thi'nj·ur _adj_ = kok*ё*thi'nj·ur

krye·u·l'ët _adj_ = koku'lur

krye·ul·t'ë·si _nf_ humility, modesty

krye·ul·t'ë·sï·sht _adv_ humbly, modestly

krye·u·l'ur _adj_ = koku'lur

krye·u·r'ë _nf_ bridgehead

krye·ve·nd _nm_ **1** = kryeqe·nd*ё*r **2** place of honor **3** _(Old)_ capital city

krye·ve'p·ër _nf_ masterpiece; magnum opus

krye·veqil·harxhi' _nm_ chief deputy attorney, chief prosecutor

krye·veterine'r _nm_ chief veterinarian

krye·vi't _nm_ New Year's day/eve; New Year

*****krye·vje't·it** _adv_ at the beginning of the year

krye·zbul·u·a'r _adj_ = kok*ё*zbulu·ar

krye·ze'z·e _nf_ **1** [_Ornit_] black-headed bunting _(Emberiza melanocephala)_ **2** black-headed goat

krye·zi'
  _I §_ _adj masc sg_ (of birds and animals) having a solidly black head
  _II §_ _nm_ [_Bot_] reed grass, common reed _(Phragmites communis)_
  ∘ **kryezi qepës** [_Ornit_] penduline tit _Remis pendulinus_

krye·zo'njё _adj fem sg_ < kryezo't

krye·zo't
  _I §_ _nm (np ˜ ëri'nj)_ feudal overlord; chief, head
  _II §_ _adj (Old)_ leading, chief

*****krye·zot·i'm** _nm_ dominance

*****krye·zyrta'r** _n (Old)_ chief official

*****kry'·gj**ё _nf(Old)_ cross

*****kry'k·ës** _nm (Old)_ capstan, windlass

*****krymb** _(Reg Gheg)_ = krimb

*****kryp** = krip

  kryp·ane'c _nm_ pastry with nettle filling

*****kry'p·c**ё _nf_ saltcellar = kri'p·ёs

*****kry'p·ësht** _nm_ [_Bot_] sweet alison _(Lobularia maritima, Alyssum maritimum)_

kryq
  _I §_ _nm_ **1** cross; crucifix **2** _(Fig)_ heavy burden to bear; great misfortune **3** [_Gymnastics_] crucifix position
  _II §_ _adj, adv_ crosswise, crossways
  ∘ **kryqi i thyer** swastika

kryq·a'k _adj_ [_Med_] cruciform

kryq·ali'
  _I §_ _n (Colloq)_ Christian
  _II §_ _pred_ *in the shape of a cross

*****kryq·a'r** _nm (Old)_ rafter

kry'q·as _adv_ crosswise, crossways, transversely

kryq·a's· _vt_ to crucify = kryq*ё*zo·n

krye·qe _nf_ **1** cross-tied head kerchief **2** quarter portion of a loaf of bread **3** rope cross-tie that secures a pack saddle to the animal **4** _(Fig)_ crossroads **5** cross brace

kry'qe _np_ **1** _(Anat)_ small of the back; sacrum **2** rear horns of a cross-tied pack saddle frame

*****kryq·eli'** = kryqali'

*****kry'q·ës** _nm_ axletree

*****kry'q·ës** = kryq*ё*z

kryq·ë's·o'r _adj_ crossing, intersecting

kryq·ë's·ore _nf_ **1** crossbeam; bracing post, brace **2** ladder rung

kry'q·ëz _nf_ small metallic cross placed under the top millstone

kry'q·ëza _np_ **1** rear horns of a cross-tied pack saddle frame **2** [_Anat_] sacral bones: sacrum **3** loins
  ∘ **kryqëzat e kurrizit** lumbar regions, lower back

kryq·ëza't·e _nf_ crusade

kryq·ëza't·ës _nm_ crusader

kryq·ëz·i'm _nm ger_ **1** < kryqёzo·n, kryqёzo'·het **2** crossing of roads: crossroad, grade crossing (for railroad tracks) **3** crucifixion ***4** crossbreed

kryq·ëzo'·het
  _I §_ _vpr_ **1** to intersect, meet in a cross **2** to cross paths **3** to be enmeshed (with one another)
  _II §_ _vp reflex_ to cross oneself (as a religious gesture)

kryq·ëzo·n _vt_ **1** to form a cross with []: cross [objects/limbs], crossbreed [animals], cross-fertilize/cross-pollinate [plants] **2** to crucify **3** to exchange [glances]; cross [paths]
  ∘ **kryqёzo·n duart 1** to fold one's arms together **2** to stand by with arms folded: make no attempt to be helpful

kryq·ëz·o'r _nm_ [_Mil_] cruiser

kryq·ëz·u·a'r _adj (i)_ **1** in crossed position, crossed **2** [_Hist_] crucified **3** [_Bot_] cross-fertilized, cross-pollinated **4** [_Bot_] cruciate

kryq·o're _np_ [_Bot_] cabbage family _Cruciferae, Brassicaceae_

*****kryq·o's·** _vt_ = kryqёzo·n

*****kryq·o's·et** _vpr_ = kryqёzo'·het

*****kryq·o'sje** _nf_ = kryqёzim

kryq·ta'r _nm_ crusader

*****kryq·tari'** OR **kryq·tari'm** _(Old)_ = kryqёza't*ё*

kry'q·thi _adv_ crosswise

*****krysanthe'm** _nm_ [_Bot_] chrysanthemum = krizante'mё

*****kry'th·** _vt_ = krydh·

*****krr** = kёrr, gёrh

*****krra·jk** _nf_ [_Ornit_] roller _(Coracias garrulus)_

krra-krra _onomat_ sound made by a raven: caw-caw

*****krre** _nf_ she-ass

krrёk _adv_ **1** up to the limit: cram full, completely **2** close-fitting, fitting tightly; skintight

*****krri'ç·et** _vpr_ to form a hook, bend, curve

*****krri'çe** = ke'rrk*ё*

*****krrik** _nm_ breeze

krri'lё _nf_ [_Ornit_] crane = kurri'll*ё*

*****krri'm**ё _nf_ death rattle

*****krri's** _stem for 1st sg pres, pl pres, 2nd & 3rd sg subj, pind_ < krrit·

*****krri't·** _vi_ to make a rattling noise in the throat; grunt = gёrhi'·n

*****krri't·et** _vpr_ to talk twaddle, prate

*****krri'tje** _nf ger_ < krri't·, krrit·et

*****krro** = kro

krro·k· _vi_ = krroka·t·

krroka't· _vi_ to caw

krrok·ёrri't· _vi_ to caw

krrok·ёrri'tje _nf ger_ **1** < krrokёrrit· **2** cawing sound, caw

krro·kull _nf_ **1** hipbone **2** saffron

*****krrom** = kro'm

*****krrom·o'z** _adj_ having scabs from itching; leprous

*****krro'qe** = kro'qe

*****krru·**_het_ = kru·_het_

*krru'a·*n* = kru'a·*n*

krru's· = kërru's·

*krru'sje = kru'sje

*krru't *nm* forefinger; ring finger

krru'të = kërru'të

*krrut'z'o·*het vpr* to become bent

KS *abbrev* <**Klubi Sportiv** Sports Club

KSAK *abbrev* <**Krahina Socialiste Autonome e Kosovës** Autonomous Socialist Region of Kosova

ksant *nm* [*Bot*] cocklebur *Xanthium*

ksenofo'b

    I § *nm (Book)* xenophobe

    II § *adj* xenophobic

ksenofobi'ï *nf (Book)* xenophobia

kse'ste'r *nf* clay pot for keeping oil or fatty substances

ksilofo'n *nm* [*Mus*] xylophone

ksilografi' *nf* xylography

ksi'ste'r *nf* metal spatula used to scrape dough from the bread board

kso'mbël *nf (Old)* exemplar or fragment of a printed text; rare copy

*ksy'me *nf (e)* pang, pain

*ksha'nzë *nf* roof-timbering

*kshe'të *nf* [*Folklore*] = gërshe'tëz

kshe'tëz *nf* [*Folklore*] = gërshe'tëz

*kshta'rpë *nf* wild millet

*ktapo'dh = oktapo'd

KTL *abbrev* <**Kooperativë e tipit të lartë** "cooperative of the higher level" merger of cooperatives

*ktha'p *nm* 1 = gërtha'p 2 fork prong

kthe·*het vpr* 1 to return 2 to turn 3 to drop in, pay a short visit, stop by 4 (*Colloq*) to regain health: recover 5 (*Colloq*) to address <> in a menacing tone

    ○ kthe·*het* me trofe to return from a successful endeavor

    ○ kthe·*het* nga të fryjë era to swing whichever way the wind is blowing

kthe·*n*

    I § *vt* 1 to turn []; turn [] over/up 2 to bend [] 3 to drink up/down 4 (*Colloq*) to alter, change 5 to convert 6 (*Colloq*) to translate 7 to return 8 to fail [] (in an examination), give [] a failing grade 9 (*Colloq*) to regain health: recover 10 (in folk music) to sing an accompaniment to a melody line already in progress

    II § *vi* 1 to return 2 (*Colloq*) to regain health: recover 3 to change one's mind

    ○ <>a kthe·*n* to retort to <>; answer <> right back; respond to <> in kind

    ○ <> kthe·*n* armët 1 to turn one's weapons on <> 2 to make an armed response to <>

    ○ e kthe·*n* barkun nga del dielli "turn one's belly toward where the sun appears" (*Scorn*) to change one's convictions with every change in the weather; change one's principles to fit one's self interest

    ○ <> kthe·*n* bërrylin "show <> one's elbow" to turn <> down, turn one's back on <>

    ○ kthe·*n* bukë to lay out food

    ○ <>a kthe·*n* dalë to retort immediately to <>, answer <> right back; answer <>'s fire with fire

    ○ kthe·*n* dorë to hit back (when it is wrong to do so)

    ○ <>a kthe·*n* dorën 1 to turn down what <> hands to one 2 (*Fig*) to reject <>'s hand in marriage, turn down <>'s marriage proposal, turn <> down

    ○ <> kthe·*n* dyfekun "turn the gun on <>" to fight against <>

    ○ e kthe·*n* festen mbi sy/mënjanë "turn one's cap over the eyes (and rest)" to have nothing more to worry about, have no more worries, be free of care

    ○ <> kthe·*n* fjalë to answer <> right back; retort to <>

    ○ kthe·*n* fjalë to talk back, answer back

    ○ (e) kthe·*n* fjalën (mbrapsht) to go back on one's word, break one's promise, renege on an oath

    ○ e kthe·*n* fletën (*Pej*) 1 change the subject (in order to avoid embarrassment) 2 change sides/allegiance, be a turncoat

    ○ kthe·*n* fytyrën nga {} to address one's attention to {}

    ○ kthe·*n* gëzofin nga fryn/të fryjë era "turn one's fur toward where the wind blows" (*Scorn*) to change one's convictions with every change in the weather; change one's principles to fit one's self interest: sway with the wind

    ○ si të jetë moti, kthe·*n* gëzofin "as the weather is, turn one's fur" (*Scorn*) to change one's convictions with every change in the weather, sway with the wind; change one's principles to fit one's self interest

    ○ kthe·*n* gunën nga fryn/të fryjë era "turn one's cloak toward where the wind blows" (*Scorn*) to change one's convictions with every change in the weather; change one's principles to fit one's self interest: sway with the wind

    ○ e kthe·*n* gjuhën to change what one has said

    ○ <>a kthe·*n* huan me babune to avenge a harm done by <> by doing much greater harm to <>: pay <> back in spades

    ○ e kthe·*n* kapelën mbi sy/mënjanë "turn one's cap over the eyes (and rest)" to have nothing more to worry about, have no more worries, be free of care

    ○ e kthe·*n* kësulën mbi sy/mënjanë "turn one's cap over the eyes (and rest)" to have nothing more to worry about, have no more worries, be free of care

    ○ <> kthe·*n* krahët to turn one's back on <>; leave <> in the lurch

    ○ kthe·*n* krahët nga fryn/të fryjë era "turn one's arms toward where the wind blows" (*Scorn*) to change one's convictions with every change in the weather; change one's principles to fit one's self interest: sway with the wind, be an unprincipled opportunist

    ○ <> kthe·*n*kurrizin to turn one's back on <>; leave <> in the lurch

    ○ kthe·*n* kurrizin nga fryn/të fryjë era "turn one's back toward where the wind blows" (*Scorn*) to change one's convictions with every change in the weather; change one's principles to fit one's self interest: sway with the wind

    ○ [] kthe·*n* mbrapsht to turn [] upside down, make a mess of []

    ○ <>a kthe·*n* me grykë to start singing a drone accompaniment (in music from Labëria) to <>

    ○ [] kthe·*n* me këmbë përpjetë (*Impol*) to kill [] dead, knock [] off

    ○ [] kthe·*n* me kokë poshtë to turn [] upside down

    ○ <>a kthe·*n* me të njëjtën monedhë (*Book*) to pay <> back in kind, respond to <> in kind; pay <> back in <>'s own coin

    ○ <>[] kthe·*n* me të tepërt to repay <> for [] with interest

    ○ <>a kthe·*n* mendjen to change <>'s mind

    ○ [] kthe·*n* në jetë to bring [] back to life

    ○ <>a kthe·*n* nga myka to turn away from <>, become totally indifferent towards <>, ignore <>

○ **kthe·n nishanin** [*Ethnog*] return the betrothal token: break off the engagement

○ **e kthe·n pllakën** *(Pej)* **1** change the subject (in order to avoid embarrassment) **2** change sides/allegiance, be a turncoat

○ **i kthe·n** ^{pdef} **potkonjtë nga dielli** "turned one's horseshoes toward the sun" *(Crude)* {} kicked the bucket, died

○ **<> kthe·n pushkën** "turn the gun on <>" to fight against <>

○ **e kthe·n qeleshen** *mbi syl/mënjanë* "turn one's cap over the eyes (and rest)" to have nothing more to worry about, have no more worries, be free of care

○ **kthe·n rrugën** to change path, take a different road

○ **kthe·n sytë nga qielli** "turn one's eyes toward the sky" to kick the bucket, die

○ **kthe·n sytë nga** {} **1** to turn one's attention to {} **2** to turn for help to {}

○ **kthe·n shenjën** to break off an engagement of marriage

○ **<> kthe·n shpatullat** to turn one's back on <>; leave <> in the lurch

○ **<> kthe·n shpinën** to turn one's back on <>; leave <> in the lurch

○ **kthe·n shpinën nga** *fryn//të fryjë* **era** "turn one's back toward where the wind blows" *(Scorn)* to change one's convictions with every change in the weather; change one's principles to fit one's self interest: sway with the wind

○ **e kthe·n takijen** *mbi syl/mënjanë* "turn one's cap over the eyes (and rest)" to have nothing more to worry about, have no more worries, be free of care

○ **e kthe·n thesin me grykë poshtë** "empty the sack" to spend all one has

***kthell** = thell

***kthell**|**oj**ë = thello|më

***kthell**|**tin**ë = thelli|në

***kthe**|**pë** nf = ktha|p

***kthe**|**pët** adj (i) hooked

kthes|ë nf **1** bend in the road, curve; turn (in direction) **2** change, turnaround **3** [*Mus*] refrain ***4** return

○ **kthes**|**ë e fortë** sharp curve/turn/bend

kthet|ër nf claw, talon

kthetra|**zi** adj (fem sg ~ ez, masc pl ~ inj, fem pl ~ eza) black-taloned

***kthill**· vt = kthjello'·n

***kthi**|**ll**·et = kthjello'·het

***kthill**|**ët** adj (i) = kthje'llët

kthi|**m** nm ger **1** <kthe·n, kthe·het **2** return

kthi|**në** nf **1** partitioned off space in a house: room; alcove ***2** = kthis

kthis nm partition wall, inner wall

kthis·

I § vi to whimper, whine

II § vt (Old) *to construct, build

***kthis**|**ër**i nf (Old) building

kthis|**ës** nm = kthista'r

***kthis**|**je** nf ger (Old) <kthis·

***kthista**|**r** nm (Old) mason, bricklayer = murato'r

***kthista**|**ri** nf (Old) masonry, bricklaying = muratori

***kthiz**|ë nf (Old) wall

kthjell· vt = kthjello'·n

kthje|**ll**·et vpr = kthjello'·het

***kthjell**|**es**ë nf (Old) revelation, disclosure

kthjell|**ësi** nf clarity

kthje|**llët**

I § adj (i) **1** clear; pure **2** (*Fig*) bright-eyed, happy

II § adv clearly; purely

kthjell|**i** = kthjell|tësi

kthjell|**im** nm ger <kthjello'·n, kthjello'·het

kthjell|**o**·het vpr **1** to become clear, clear up **2** to brighten up

kthjell|**o**·n vt **1** to cause [] to become clear: make clear, clear up; clarify **2** [*Cine*] to brighten [the colors]

kthjell|**tazi** adv with clarity, clearly

kthjell|**tës**i nf **1** clarity, clearness; lucidity **2** (*Fig*) brightness

kthjell|**t**|**es**im nm ger **1** = kthjelli|m **2** = kthjell|ësi

kthjell|**t**|**es**o·het vpr = kthjello|he

kthjell|**t**|**es**o·n vt = kthjello'·n

kthjell|**ti** nf = kthjell|tësi

kthjell|**u**|**a**|**r** adj (i) clear, limpid, transparent, lucid

kthjell|**u**|**e**|**s**

I § adj explanatory

II § n explainer

kthy|**e** stem for 1st & 2nd sg pdef, part <kth·et

kthy|**er**

I § part <kth·et, kthe·het

II § adj (i) **1** curved, bent **2** (of soil) tilled, turned **3** (of worn clothes) turned inside out and resewn: reversed **4** (of clothes) turned up **5** (of a woman) divorced and returned to her family **6** (*Colloq*) recovered (from an illness)

III § nf (e) **1** curve, bend **2** (of clothes) hem, cuff

kthy|**e**|**sh**|**ëm** adj (i) reversible; turnable; pliable

ku adv conj **1** where **2** in rhetorical questions indicates the absurdity of the proposition that follows

○ **Ku i bie çekanit?** What are you driving at?

○ **Ku i bie daulles unë e ku e hedh vallen ti!** "I beat the drum in one place and you dance somewhere else." *(Prov)* I say one thing and you do another!

○ **ku bun, s'bun** one who never stays long in one place

○ **Ku di derri këmborë.** "Where does a pig know a cowbell!" *(Impol)* How could you expect appreciation (of the value/significance) from someone like that!

○ **Ku di dhia ç'është tagjia.** "How does the goat know what fodder is." *(Impol)* It's like casting pearls before swine.

○ **s'di· ku ka· kokën/kryet** to have no idea what to do, not know where to begin; be scatterbrained; have so many things to worry about that one cannot think straight

○ **s'di· ku të fut· kokën** (to be beset by so many problems that) one does not know which way to turn, be at a loss at what to do first

○ **ku di·**het ^{3sg}? who knows?: perhaps, maybe

○ **Ku dhemb dhëmbi vete gjuha.** "Ehe tongue goes where the tooth hurts." *(Prov)* You think and talk about what bothers you the most.

○ **ku <> dhemb e ku <> djeg** where it hurts <> most

○ **Ku është fushë bëhet breg.** "Even when there is a plain a hill may arise." *(Prov)* Difficulties may arise at any any time.

○ **Ku futet gjilpëra, do të futet edhe peri.** "Where the needle is inserted, the thread will go." *(Prov)* Where you find one, you'll find the other.

○ **ku ha pula gur** (place) that is bare; poor (land)

∘ **ku ha pula strall** (place) that is bare; poor (land)
∘ **e ku di unë** "and where should I know" *(Disparaging)* and God knows what else
∘ **Ku ishe? Asgjëkundi** (rhetorical question expressing disappointment with the result of efforts made) What's the use!
∘ **ku janë (e) ku s'janë** all without exception
∘ **Ku ka zë, s'është pa gjë.** "Where there's talk, it is not for nothing." *(Prov)* Where there's smoke, there's fire.
∘ **ku e ka· hallin?** what is {} driving at?
∘ **s'ka· ku të gjejë/nxjerrë qime** "have nowhere to find/yank a hair" to be unable to find fault anywhere
∘ **s'ka· ku të përpjekë/përplasë kokën** to have no one to turn to
∘ **s'ka· ku të vij rrotull/rreth/vërdallë** to have no room to turn around in, be very cramped for space
∘ **Ku i ke sytë?** What are you thinking about? Keep your mind on your work!
∘ **(për) ku kështu** {*someone*}**?** where is {} off to?
∘ **(për) ku kështu?** where are you off to?
∘ **ku e ku më** __ much much more __, by far the most
__
∘ **Ku lë laroja të hajë baloja.** "Why would the big dog leave anything for the little dog to eat." You can't expect the big guy to let the little guy have anything.
∘ **Ku mbill·***et* **s'korr·***et.* "{} is not reaped where {} is sown." {} keeps moving from one place to another. {} never settles down.
∘ **ku mbjell· nuk korr·** "where one sows one doesn't reap" to keep moving from one place to another, never settle down
∘ **ku ngrys·***et,* **s'gdhi·***het* "one does not pass the dawn where one passes to the evening" to keep moving from one place to another; keep changing residences/jobs
∘ **Ku nis·***et* **e ku degdis·***et.* "One *starts* up somewhere and *ends* up somewhere else." Things *end* up different from the way they *start.*
∘ **Ku ⟨⟩ qëndro·***n³ˢᵍ* **shpirti!** "Where does ⟨⟩'s soul stay?" How can ⟨⟩ stay alive (since ⟨⟩ is nothing but skin and bones)!
∘ **ku rafsha mos u vrafsha.** "where I may fall may I not get killed" devil-may-care, completely irresponsible
∘ **ku shkrep·***³ˢᵍ* **kjo fjalë** "where is this word striking" what is that supposed to mean!, what's the point?
∘ **Ku ⟨⟩ shp***ie·³ˢᵍ***/ço·***n³ˢᵍ* **mushka!?** "where *is* the mule taking ⟨⟩?" Can't ⟨⟩ see that ⟨⟩ *is* headed for trouble? What on earth *does* ⟨⟩ think ⟨⟩ *is doing?*
∘ **Ku ta dish?** Who knows? Maybe.
∘ **ku ta mbaj unë e ku ma mban ti** "where I'm headed and where you're headed" you and I are on different wavelengths
∘ **ku ta nxjerrë trapi** "wherever the furrow takes you" however it comes out, whatever happens
∘ **Ku ta shkruajmë?** "Where shall we write it down?" *(Iron)* Go get the record book! (in order to write down a rare accomplishment by a usually lazy or incompetent person)
∘ **Ku të tregojnë copën e madhe, merr lugën e vogël.** "Where they display the big piece to you, take your small spoon (because it will not be as good as they say)." **1** *(Prov)* When they make it sound too good to be true, don't expect much from it. **2** A lot of

smoke, but no fire. Don't get fooled by a lot of razzle-dazzle.
∘ **Ku** [] **zë·***³ˢᵍ* **dreka, s'**[] **zë·***³ˢᵍ* **darka.** "Where lunchtime *finds* [], dinnertime *does* not find []." [] *keeps* on the move. [] never *stays* in one place long enough to hang []'s hat.

ku·*het* *vpr* to get a skin rash from sunburn, windburn or other irritation that causes redness and peeling
ku'a·*n* *vt* to feed = **ko·***n*
kua|
  I § *stem for pl pdef, opt, adm, part* ⟨**ko·***n,* **ku'·***het*
  II § *stem for 3rd sg pdef* ⟨**ku'·***het*
kua'cë *nf* sheep with a reddish brown muzzle
kuaçi's| *stem for 1st sg pres, pl pres, 2nd & 3rd sg subj, pind* ⟨**kuaçi't·**
kuaçi't· *vi* to cluck
kuaçi'tje *nf ger* **1** ⟨**kuaçi't·** **2** clucking sound, cluck
*∗**kua'çke** *nf* brood hen
kua'dër
  I § *nm* **1** picture, painting **2** [*Cine*] film clip, film sequence **3** [*Electr*] control panel, control board; switch panel, switchboard **4** (*Book Fig*) framework, context **5** (*Offic Collec*) cadre, staff personnel, staff **6** (*Offic*) member of the managerial staff **7** (*Offic*) personnel office
  II § *nf* [*Tech*] hand-held shield used in welding
  ∘ **kuadër i mesëm** personnel with high school education
kuadra't *nm* square
kuadrati'k *adj* quadratic
kuadratu're *nf* quadrature
kua'drio *np* = **kua'dër**
ku'aj *np* ⟨**ka'lë**
kuaj-fuqi *np* [*Phys Tech*] ⟨**kalë-fuqi**
kua'k· *vi* to make the sound of a frog: croak
__**kua'kje** *nf ger* **1** ⟨**kuak·** **2** sound of croaking, croak
kuak-kua'k *onomat* sound made by a duck: quack-quack
kualifiki'm *nm ger* **1** ⟨**kualifiko'·***n,* **kualifiko'·***het* **2** qualification, level of qualification
kualifiko'·*het* *vpr* to qualify, become qualified, achieve qualification
kualifiko'·*n* *vt* to train [] for a higher step of qualification
kualifiku'a|**r** *adj* (*i*) **1** qualified; highly qualified **2** requiring a high degree of qualification
kualifiku'es *adj* for the purpose of determining qualification: qualifying
kualitati'v *adj* qualitative
kualite't *nm* (*Book*) quality
*∗**kua'll** *nm* bassoon = **fago't**
kua'nt *nm* quantum
kuantitati'v *adj* quantitative
kuantite't *nm* (*Book*) quantity
kua'rc *nm* [*Min*] quartz
kua'rt *nm* **1** [*Mus*] interval of a fourth; chord of the tonic and the fourth **2** quarter of a liter
kuarte't *nm* [*Mus*] quartet
kua's| *stem for 1st sg pres, pl pres, 2nd & 3rd sg subj, pind* ⟨**kua't·**
*∗**kua'skë** *nf* incrustation, glaze, enamel, scum (on a liquid)
*∗**kua't** *nm* goblet; double-handled pitcher
kua't· *vt* to croak

kub
I § *nm* cube
II § *adj* cubic

kuba'n *adj, n* of/from Cuba, native of Cuba

kubatu'rë *nf* volume in cubic measurement: cubature, cubage

kube *nf* 1 [*Archit*] arched/vaulted enclosure: cupola, dome; vaulted cellar 2 crown of a tree

Ku'bë *nf* Cuba

ku'bël *nf* [*Ichth*] (marine) Twaite shad *(Alosa falax nilotica)*
   ◦ **kub**ël **liqenore** [*Ichth*] (freshwater) Twaite shad *Alosa falax lacustris*

kub'ik
I § *adj* cubic
II § *nm* small mound of fertilized earth in which a seed or seedling is planted

kub'ist *n* [*Art*] cubist

kub'izëm *nm* [*Art*] cubism

*****kub'o'**·n *vt* to cheat; betray

*****kubra't**ë *nf* bird trap made from a hollowed-out marrow bone

*****kubu're** *nf* = kobure

*****kuc** *adj* lame

*****kucale'c** *nm* fig that has burst on its tree

*****ku'c**ë *nf* whelp, pup

ku'ckë
I § *nf* 1 stump and root of a cut plant *2 pot with a handle
II § *adj* fitting tight, tight

kuç *nm* 1 earthenware cauldron for cooking or boiling water 2 *(Colloq Child)* doggie, bowwow

kuçe'dër *nf* 1 [*Folklore*] multi-headed dragon, hydra 2 *(Colloq Pej)* harpy, termagant, shrew

ku'çkë *nf* 1 female dog, bitch 2 *(Crude)* slut, whore, bitch

ku'dër *nf* female dog, bitch

ku'do' *adv* anywhere, everywhere
   ◦ **kudo ku i thonë bukës bukë e ujit ujë** wherever Albanian is spoken, wherever there are Albanians
   ◦ **kudo oka katërqind dërhemë është** the cost is the same everywhere
   ◦ **kudo që** wherever
   ◦ **kudo qoftë** wherever, anywhere

kudh *nm* 1 large anvil 2 single-handled clay pot used for storing dairy products; small clay jar 3 = ku'dh'ër

ku'dhë *nf* = ku'dh'ër

ku'dhër *nf* 1 anvil 2 [*Anat*] anvil bone in the middle ear: incus

*****kuejt**ë *nf* = ko'jës

kuestiona'r *nm* questionnaire = pyet'ëso'r

kuesto'r *nm* 1 [*Hist*] Roman quaestor 2 Italian chief of police

kuestu'rë *nf* Italian police headquarters

*****kufeta'r** *n* confectioner

*****kufet'ari** *nf* confectionery

*****kufe't**ë *nf* confection, candy

*****ku'f**ër *nf* box, chest

kufi'(r) *nm* 1 border, borderline 2 limit 3 frontier

*****kufia'r** = kufita'r

kufi'j *np* < kufi'(r)

kufi'lme = kufi'rm'ë

kufi'nda'rës *adj* border-dividing

*****kufi're'm**ë = kufi'rm'ë

kufi'r'li *obl* < kufi'(r)

kufi'rmë *nf* [*Bot*] comfrey *(Symphytum officinale)*

kufita'r
I § *n* 1 border resident; neighbor 2 [*Mil*] border guard
II § *adj* 1 of or pertaining to a frontier/border 2 bordering, neighboring 3 border-marking

kufi'të *nf* sugared almond

kufi'treg'ues *adj* border-marking

kufi'zë *nf* [*Math*] element representing a sum or product in a mathematical expression: term

kufi'zi'm *nm ger* 1 < kufizo'·n, kufizo'·het 2 limitation, limit

kufi'zo'·het
I § *vpr* to share a border
II § *vp reflex* to limit oneself, keep within bounds

kufi'zo'·n
I § *vt* 1 to delimit; mark the borderline of [] 2 to limit, restrict
II § *vi* to share a border

kufi'zo'r *adj* 1 = kufizues 2 *(Old)* = kufitar

kufi'zu'a'r *adj (i)* limited, restricted

kufi'zu'es *adj* limiting, restrictive

ku'fje *nf* earphone

ku'fkë
I § *nf* snail shell
II § *adj* hollow, empty inside

kufo'më *nf* 1 dead body: corpse; cadaver 2 *(Reg)* animal carcass 3 *(Fig)* very thin and weak person: walking corpse
   ◦ **kufomë e gjallë** living corpse

kufom'o're *nf (Book)* mortuary, morgue = morg

kuh-kuh *onomat* coughing sound of someone choking

kuinta'l *nm* a hundred kilograms: quintal

kuintese'ncë *nf (Book)* quintessence

kuinte't *nm* quintet

kuis· *vi* to whine; squeal

kui'sje *nf ger* 1 < kuis· 2 whining/squealing sound

kuisli'ng *nm, adj* quisling, traitor

kuita'ncë *nf* [*Offic*] document authorizing delivery of money or other item of value: voucher

*****ku'jb**ë *nf* [*Ichth*] = ku'b'ël

kujde's *nm* 1 care, attention 2 responsibility, charge 3 caution 4 diligence

kujde's·et *vpr* 1 to take care; be cautious 2 to be concerned, be worried
   ◦ **kujdes**·et **për** [] 1 to take care of [] 2 to worry too much about []

kujde'si *nf* 1 carefulness; caring, concern; sense of responsibility 2 caution

kujde'si'm *nm ger* 1 < kujdeso'·het 2 concern, caring

kujde'sje *nf ger* 1 < kujde's·et 2 concern, care, attention

kujde'so'·het *vpr* = kujde's·et

kujde'sshëm *adj (i)* 1 careful 2 caring 3 diligent, responsible

kujdesta'r
I § *n* 1 person in charge: supervisor, custodian 2 (in an educational setting) person in charge of enforcing regulations or maintaining discipline: monitor 3 [*Law*] legal guardian
II § *adj* responsible, in charge

kujdes·ta·re nf 1 <kujdesta·r 2 (Old) kindergarten teacher

kujdes·tar·i nf 1 custodianship, custodial service; custody; responsibility, charge; tutelage; aegis 2 [Law] guardianship; trusteeship

kuj·ë nf wailing, loud lament; keening

*kûj·ët adj (i) (Reg Gheg) wedge-shaped

kuj·is\ stem for 1st sg pres, pl pres, 2nd & 3rd sg subj, pind <kujít·

kuj·ít· vt to howl, whine

*kûj (Reg Gheg) = kunj

kujo·re np incisor teeth (of a horse)

kujri nf, adj [Hist] (land) shared by a whole village: village common land

*kujrril·ë nf [Ornit] crane = kurríllë

kujt

I § dat/abl whom <kush

II § adj (i) whose <kush

○ Kujt i djeg· le të kruhet. "Let the one who itches scratch." If the shoe fits, wear it.

○ Kujt i flet·, murit? "Talk to whom, to the wall?" It's like talking to a wall!

○ Kujt i ha miza nën kësulë, le të kruhet!. "Whoever is itching from the fly under his cap, let him scratch!" Let the guilty person pay!

kujt·do

I § dat/abl <kushdo

II § gen (i) of whomsoever, of anyone, of everybody <kushdo

kujt·es·ë nf 1 memory 2 (Old) = kujtim

kujt·im nm ger 1 <kujto·n, kujto·het 2 remembering, recollection, memory 3 remembrance, souvenir, memento, keepsake

Kujt·im nm Kujtim (male name)

kujt·o·het vpr 1 to have it occur to one: remember, recall; be reminded 2 to get the point quickly, understand right away

kujt·o·n

I § vt 1 to recall [] from memory: remember 2 to call [] to mind 3 to remind, bring [] to mind

II § vi to think, form an opinion, get an impression

○ Kujto qenin, rrëmbe/bëj gati shkopin. "Mention the dog, grab the stick." (Prov Pej) Speak of the devil (and here he is).

kujt·ue·sh·ëm adj (i) 1 quick-witted, sharp 2 cognizant of friends and past favors: appreciative, grateful 3 (Old) oft-remembered

kujun·xhi nm (np ~ nj) (Old) artisan who works with precious metals and jewels = argjendar

*kuj·xhi = kujunxhi

*kujz·a np <kunjëz

kuk adv all alone

kuka·fsheh·thi adv

kuka·fshet·as adv hide-and-seek

kuka·më nf loud wail

kuka·n nm humpbacked person, hunchback

kuka·s\ stem for 1st sg pres, pl pres, 2nd & 3rd sg subj, pind <kuka·t·

kuka·t· vi 1 to wail, lament loudly; keen 2 to make the sound of the cuckoo 3 to plug

kuka·të nf patch of leather or ground pine bark used to plug leaks in a wooden water jug = kapce·le

kuka·tje nf ger 1 <kuka·t· 2 loud lament, wail, shriek 3 sound of the cuckoo

*kukavíc·ë nf cuckoo

kuke·s·ë nf crutch

*ku·kë nf 1 (Reg Tosk) = ko·kë *2 (Old) [Med] water on the brain (hydrocephalus)

*ku·këll nf = ku·kull

Ku·kës nm city in northeastern Albania: Kukës

ku·këz nf crutch

kukëzo·het vpr 1 to bend over, hunch over 2 (of animals) to get one's back up, hunch up 3 to appear as the top of an arch: arch up

kukëzo·n vt to curve [] into the shape of an arch

ku·kluks-kla·n nm Ku Klux Klan

kukma·n adj slow-witted, slow, retarded; stupid

kuko·het vpr to become humpbacked

kuko·n vt 1 to curve [] into the shape of an arch 2 to plug/patch/caulk [a leaky wooden container]

kuko·l nm [Bot] corn cuckle (Lychnis githago)

*kukrru·kë nf pomegranate seed = kokrru·k

kuks·ia·n

I § adj of or pertaining to Kukës

II § n native of Kukës

ku·k·thi adv

kuku·

I § interj expresses sudden pain/sorrow or unexpected surprise

II § onomat 1 sound made by a cuckoo: cuckoo 2 [Ornit] cuckoo

*kukuba·n nm [Entom] firefly

kuku·dh

I § nm 1 [Folklore] goblin 2 (Pej) evil person 3 (Fig) imaginary fear, phobia

II § adj wretched and alone

ku-ku-ku· onomat 1 coughing sound of someone choking 2 sound of girls laughing

*kuku·l nm peak

kuku·le nf silk cocoon

kukuli·qe nf (Disparaging) = kaplo·qe

ku·kull nf 1 doll 2 puppet

kukuma·l· vt to throw upward with force

kukuma·le nf mound/heap with an apex

kukuma·l·thi adv 1 up high, high in the air 2 in a tall pile

kuku·mja·çkë nf [Ornit] = kukuva·jkë

○ kukumjaçkë e detit [Ichth] = kryema·dh

*kuku·n nm cocoon

*kukuna·r nm cone

kuku·nj np hives, skin rash

kuku·nj·az np heat rash; rash

*kukura·k nm [Bot] = kukura·q

kukura·q I § nm OR **kukura·qe** II § nf [Bot] hellebore = ta·çe

kukurbita·ce np fem = kungullo·re

kukure·c nm [Food] pieces of sheep liver held together by lamb/kid gut and roasted

kuku·r·ë nf quiver (for arrows)

kukuri·s· vi to giggle

kukuri·s·et vpr to giggle

kukuri·s·je nf ger 1 <kukuri·s·, kukuri·s·et 2 giggling sound, giggle

*kukurja·k nm [Bot] goat's rue, French lilac (Galega officinalis)

*kuku·të nm [Bot] 1 meadow rue (Thalictrum) 2 poison hemlock (Conium maculatum)

kuku|vaj|kë *nf* **1** owl **2** [*Ornit*] little owl (*Athene noctua*) **3** [*Ichth*] eagle ray (*Myliobbatis aquila*)
○ **kukuvajkë deti** [*Ichth*] bull ray *Pteromylaeus bovinus*
○ **kukuvajka mjekëroshe** [*Ornit*] barn owl *Tyto alba Scop., Strix alba Scop.*
○ **kukuvajka e pyjeve** [*Ornit*] tawny owl *Strix aluco L.*

kuku|vriq
I § *nm* **1** newly hatched chick **2** male owl **3** [*Folk-lore*] ghost
II § *adv* in a shrivelling manner

kuku|vriq|e *nf* female owl

****kukz|o·** -*het vpr* to crouch over, crouch low

****kukz|o·n** *vt* to bend/arch [ ] over

kul·et *vpr* (of a wall) to bow out

kulaç
I § *nm* **1** unleavened dough (made of flour, eggs, and water) that is rolled into strips, twisted into ring or spiral form, and cooked on a stove top or in an oven: kulaç **2** circlet of cloth worn on the head to assist in carrying a jug or vase **3** flower disk **4** cotter for attaching a yoke
II § *adv* curled up in a ball, hunched up

kula|çe
I § *nf* **1** round clump of dough to be rolled out to form a leaf of a pasty **2** unleavened dough (made of flour, eggs, and water) that is rolled into strips, twisted into ring or spiral form, and cooked on a stove top or in an oven: kulaç **3** circlet of cloth worn on the head to assist in carrying a jug or vase **4** flower disk
II § *adj* having round, slightly squat fruit

kula|jkë *nf* **1** linchpin securing the beam of a plow to the yoke = **qajkë 2** locking bolt on a door or cabinet

kula|k *nm* kulak

kulak|ëri *nf collec* kulaks as as collective group

kula|r
I § *nm* **1** bow of a yoke, collar, oxbow **2** wooden training harness for teaching a child to walk: go-cart **3** felly = **gavy|ell 4** [*Text*] wooden bow that serves as a tensioning device on a loom **5** bow for a bowed lute **6** (*Colloq*) arch (of a bridge) **7** (*Fig*) yoke of oppression
II § *adj* arched, bowed, bent
III § *adv* curled up, hunched up into a ball

kula|r|shëm = kulartë

kula|r|të *adj* (i) bent in the shape of an oxbow, arched

kula|r|th *nm* **1** horseshoe magnet **2** [*Anat*] clavicle

ku|lbë [*Ichth*] = **ku|bël**

ku|le *nf* **1** disordered heap **2** thick mass of thorns: thicket

kule|ç *np* < **kulaç**

kule|ks *nm* [*Entom*] mosquito *Culex*

kule|të *nf* **1** wallet, purse (for carrying money) **2** (*Colloq Fig*) money at one's disposal, spending money **3** (*Colloq*) cartridge belt

****kule|zë** *nf* ball, marble

kulihu|m *adv* headlong, headfirst; head down, upside down

****kuli|k** OR **kuli|q** *nm* = **franxholl|ë**

kuli|m
I § *nm* **1** shameless bum, scoundrel **2** clever/sly person
II § *adj* **1** base, villainous; mischievous **2** clever, sly

kuli|se *np* [*Theat*] backstage, wings, behind-the-scenes

kuli|s|ë *nf* [*Tech*] slotted guide plate, slotted link

kuli|sh = kely|sh

****kuli|vi|thër = kulluvi|thër**

kulm
I § *nm* (*Colloq*) **1** peak, apex **2** highest point: height, top; acme **3** culminating point: climax, culmination **4** [*Geom*] vertex
II § *adv* up to the top, fully

kulma|k *nm* [*Bot*] marsh plant used for withes: rush (*Juncus*)

kulm|ar *nm* [*Constr*] ridgeboard (of a roof), ridgepole

kulm|a|re *nf* [*Constr*] **1** peak/apex of a roof **2** = **kulm|ar**

kulm|i|m *nm ger* < **kulmo·n**

kulm|o·n
I § *vt* **1** to top off [a building with a peaked roof]; erect [a peaked roof] **2** to arrange [long objects] vertically with their tops coming together: stack
II § *vi* to reach the peak

kulm|o|r *adj* **1** of or pertaining to the rooftop **2** [*Geom*] perpendicular **3** standing on end **4** pointed, tipped

kulm|o|re *nf* **1** [*Geom*] perpendicular line **2** = **kulm|a|re**

kulm|o|s· *vt* [*Mil*] to stack [arms] in a pyramidal pile

kulm|o|s|je *nf ger* [*Mil*] < **kulm|o|s·**

kulo|mb *nm* [*Electr*] coulomb

kulo|t|ës *n* one who takes animals to pasture: herds-man, shepherd

****kulp** *nm* [*Bot*] traveller's joy, old man's beard (*Clematis vitalba*)

ku|lp|ër *nf* **1** [*Bot*] clematis (*Clematis*) **2** [*Ethnog*] head garland of clematis worn by children to cele-brate the coming of spring *****3** [*Bot*] bryony
○ **kulp|ër e bardhë/egër** [*Bot*] traveller's joy, old man's beard *Clematis vitalba*
○ **kulp|ër e butë** [*Bot*] **1** fragrant clematis *Clematis flammula* **2** traveller's joy, old man's beard *Clematis vitalba*
○ **kulp|ër deti** [*Zool*] *Caulerpa prolifera*

****kulp|i|cë** *nf* (*Reg*) **1** tip, peak **2** (*Fig*) height

****kulshe|d|ër = kuçe|d|ër**

kult *nm* cult

kulte|re *np* water-eroded grooves in stone

ku|l|tër *nf* cushion, pad, pillow

kultivato|r *nm* [*Tech*] implement for cultivating soil: cultivator

kultivi|m *nm ger* **1** < **kultivo·n 2** cultivation

kultiv|o·n *vt* to cultivate

kultiv|u|es *nm* one who cultivates: cultivator, grower

kultura|l *adj* cultural

kultu|r|ë *nf* **1** culture **2** [*Agr*] cultivation; that which is cultivated: crops

kultur|ë|dashës *adj* desiring culture: culture-loving

kulturi|m *nm ger* < **kulturo·n, kulturo·het**

kultur|o·het *vpr* to become cultured

kultur|o·n *vt* to make [ ] cultured, provide culture for [ ]

kultur|o|r *adj* **1** cultural **2** [*Agr*] of or pertaining to cultivation

kultur|u|ar *adj* (i) cultured

****kulty|r|ë** *nf* **1** splinter, chip **2** ice floe

kulth *nm* [*Bot*] hop (*Humulus lupulus*)

kulufiska|n *n, adj* (person) afflicted with consump-tion, tuberculosis: consumptive, tubercular

kulufíske *nf* consumption, tuberculosis

kulumbrí = **kullumbrí**

kuluvér *nm* rainbow

kulvárë *adv*

kull *nm* horse with hair of a yellowish tan: palomino

***ku'll**·*et vpr* = **ko'll**·*et*

kullák = **kull**

kullandrís· *vt (Colloq)* **1** to manage [] well; use [] appropriately **2** to put [] in order, arrange; fix up ***3** to use

kullandrís·*et vpr (Colloq)* to be able to manage; manage to get by; manage

kullandrísje *nf ger (Colloq)* <**kullandrís**·, **kullan-dris**·*et*

***kullár** = **kulár**

***ku'lle** *nf* pan (for milk)

***kulle'ndër** = **kole'ndër**

kulle'së *nf* **1** lees **2** colander, strainer; filter

kulle'stër *nf* colander, strainer; filter

ku'llë *nf* **1** tower; turret **2** [*Chess*] rook, castle **3** small anvil used for sharpening scythes **4** children's playground slide **5** multi-storied dwelling designed to house and defend an extended family and its livestock; upper room in such a house

∘ **kulla e gjyqtarit** [*Volleyball*] referee's platform

∘ **kulla me gjizë** castles in the air

∘ **kullë sane** hay barn

∘ **kullë zjarri** gun turret

ku'llëz *nf* turret

kull·ím *nm ger* **1** <**kullo'·n**, **kullo'·het** **2** filtration **3** [*Agr*] drainage, draining

kull·ínë *nf* very weak coffee

kull·íshte *nf* [*Dairy*] cloth filter used in making cheese: cheesecloth; filter

kull·ímë *adj (i)* yellowish tan, honey-colored

***ku'llmë** *nf (Reg Gheg)* = **ku'dhër**

kullo'·het *vpr* **1** (of a liquid) to settle out, become clarified **2** *(Fig)* to get cleared up, get clarified, become clear

kullo'·n

I § *vt* **1** to cleanse [liquid] of unwanted matter: filter, strain; clarify, distill; decant **2** *(Colloq)* to clarify, clear up, solve **3** to drain [] **4** *(Colloq)* to drink up

II § *vi* **1** (of a liquid) to settle, become clarified **2** to drip **3** *(Colloq)* to pour

∘ <> **kulo·n**^{3sg} **goja mjaltë** "<>'s mouth *flows* with honey" <> *speaks* pleasantly; <> *speaks* beautifully

∘ <> **kullo·n**^{3pl} **hundët** <>'s nose *runs*

∘ **kullo·n në lotë** to dissolve in tears

∘ <> **kullo·n**^{3pl} **sytë për** [] [] *makes* <> want to weep

∘ <> **kullo·n**^{3sg} **shpirti/zemra për** [] <>'s heart *bleeds* for []

∘ <> **kullo·n**^{3sg} **zemra gjak** "<>'s heart *drips/flows* blood" <>'s heart *bleeds*

kullo'jcë *nf* = **kullo're**

kullo'jë *nf* = **kullo're**

kullo'më *nf* sediment, lees

kullo're *nf* sieve, colander, strainer; filter

kullo's *stem for 1st sg pres, pl pres, 2nd & 3rd sg subj, pind* <**kullo't**·

kullo'së *nf* = **kullo'të**

kullos·o'r *adj (Book)* serving as pasturage

kullo'shtër

I § *nf* foremilk, beestings, colostrum

II § *adj* thick and fatty

kullo'shto'r *nm* thin-leafed pasty made with colostrum

kullo't·

I § *vt* **1** to pasture [livestock] **2** *(Fig Colloq Iron)* to feed, provide food for

II § *vi* **1** to graze, browse **2** *(Fig ColloqImpolite)* to move about in leisure fashion: run around, hang around, ramble

∘ <> **kullo't**·^{3sg} **hunda lart** *(Iron)* <> *is* snooty

∘ [] **kullo't· me shkop** "pasture [] with a stick" to keep [animals] grazing in controlled strips

∘ <> **kullo't· mendja (gjetkë)** <>'s mind *is* off somewhere, <>*has* <>'s mind elsewhere: <> *is* wool-gathering somewhere

∘ **ku të kullo't**·^{3sg} **mendja?!** what are you dreaming about!?

∘ [] **kullo't· pa shkop** "pasture [] without a stick" to allow [animals] to graze freely

∘ **kullo't· retë** to wool-gather

∘ **kullo't· sytë** to look around idly, just look around; let one's eyes take in the scene

kullo'të *nf* pasture

kullo't|es|o'r *adj* = **kulloso'r**

kullo'tje *nf ger* **1** <**kullo't**· **2** pasturage, pasture

***kulltu'k** = **kolltu'k**

kullu'ar *adj (i)* **1** cleansed of objectionable or foreign elements: filtered; clarified; clear, transparent; pure **2** free of excessive water: drained **3** *(Fig)* faultless; innocent, pure; frank, open; clean

kullu'arje *nf* filtration, straining

kullu'es *adj* used for drainage

kullu'ese *nf* filter

kullufi's *stem for 1st sg pres, pl pres, 2nd & 3rd sg subj, pind* <**kullufi't**·

kullufi't· *vt* = **kollofi't**·

kullumbri *nf* [*Bot*] blackthorn, sloe (*Prunus spinosa*)

kullu're *nf* sweet biscuit made from twisted dough

kullu'smë *nf* thicket

***kullutu'mbë** = **kollotu'mbë**

***kulluve'qkë** *nf* [*Ornit*] = **kukumja'çkë**

***kulluvi'thër** *nf* baptismal font

***kulluvri'qe** *nf* shanty, hovel

kum

I § *nm* **1** sand = **rë're** ***2** sad news, news of a death = **manda'të** ***3** = **kumba'r**

II § *adj* sandy

kum·

I § *vt* to fill [] up, fill [] to capacity

II § *vi* to suffice

ku'm·*et vpr* <**kum**· to fill out, get plump, become completely full

kuma'c *nm* enclosure for small domestic animals: coop, cote; dog kennel; pig pen, sty

kumaha'rk *nm (np ~ qe)* [*Entom*] dragonfly = **kumiha'rk**

kuma'k *nm* [*Bot*] field marigold (*Calendula arvensis*)

***kuma'nd** *nm (Old)* = **koma'ndë**

kumanda'r *nm (Old)* = **komanda'nt**

***kumanjo're** *nf (Old)* = **kambano're**

kuma'r *nm* gambling

***kuma're** *nf* **1** flue **2** [*Bot*] = **mare'**

kumar·xhi *nm (np ˜ nj)* gambler

kuma·sh *nm* thin and shiny silk fabric: damask

*****kuma'sh·ët** *adj (i) (Old)* of damask

kumb *nm* resonant sound; sound of a musical instrument

kumba·r *I § nm OR* **kumba·rë** *II § nf* **1** [*Ethnog*] person who holds the baby at baptism or gives the baby its first haircut: godparent **2** [*Ethnog*] ceremonial witness at a religious wedding who becomes the special friend of the new couple ***3** [*Relig*] confessor

kumbara *nf* **1** children's coin bank, piggy bank **2** *(Old)* bomb

kumbari *nf* **1** [*Ethnog*] friendly relationship between families created by marriage; the relationship between godparent and godchild **2** *(Collec)* special friendship created by acting as a ceremonial witness at a religious wedding

kumbaris·et *vpr* [*Ethnog*] = **kumbaro·het**

kumbaro·het *vpr* **1** [*Ethnog*] to become a godparent **2** to become a special family friend by acting as a ceremonial witness at a religious wedding

kumbim *nm ger* **1** <**kumbo·n 2** distant rumble, echoing sound **3** [*Phys*] resonance

kumbis· *vt* **1** to put [one's head/body] down to rest/ sleep **2** to lean against [], rest on [] **3** to support

kumbis·et *vpr* to lie down for a rest

kumbo·n *vi* to resound; resonate

*****kumbona·re** = **kambano·re**

kumbo·nçë *nf (Reg Gheg)* = **kamba·nëz**

*****kumbo·në** *OR* **kumbo·rë** = **kamba·në**

kumb·ues *adj* resounding, resonating

kumb·ue·shëm *adj (i)* resonant

ku·mbull *nf* **1** [*Bot*] plum; plum tree *(Prunus domestica L.)* **2** *(Fig Colloq)* healthy and beautiful girl or young woman
  ○ **kumbull bardalike** [*Bot*] variety of plum with long, dark fruit
  ○ **kumbull e bardha** green plum
  ○ **kumbull e egër** [*Bot*] blackthorn, sloe = **kullumbri**
  ○ **kumbull gjatore/valldarje** [*Bot*] long red plum *(Prunus domestica L.)*
  ○ **kumbull myshku/shinine** [*Bot*] cherry plum *Prunus cerasifera*
  ○ **kumbull surgjatë** plum with oblong fruit
  ○ **kumbull sheqeri** sugar plum
  ○ **kumbull e thatë** prune
  ○ **kumbull e zezë** purple plum

kumbullishtë *nf* plum orchard

kumbullor *adj* (of fruit) full-bodied and sweet

kumbullore *nf* **1** sweet green plum with large, slightly oblong fruit: Victoria plum **2** small thin-skinned tomato ***3** grafted plum tree

ku·me *nf* **1** godchild **2** godparent

*****kume·rë** *nf* apprehension, fear

ku·më *nf* **1** godmother ***2** pleasant sound ***3** small bubble caused by dripping rain ***4** fox

*****ku·mëll** *nf (Reg)* = **ku·mbull**

kumi *nf* kiln (for baking tiles)

kumiha·rk *nm (np ˜ qe)* [*Entom*] dragonfly = **pilives·ë**

*****kumina·r** *nm* chimney sweep

*****kumi·në** *nf* **1** = **kumi 2** chimney

kum-kum *onomat* coughing sound of someone choking

kumri *nf* **1** [*Ornit*] collared turtle dove, ringdove *(Streptopelia decaocto)* **2** [*Bot*] = **kullumbri**.

kumt *nm* (bad) tidings, news

kumta·r *n* bearer of bad tidings, messenger

kumt·es·ë *nf* **1** communication of information: report **2** scientific paper, report **3** *(Old)* (bad) tidings **4** *(Old)* official public notice

ku·mtër *nm* [*Ethnog*] = **kumba·r**

kumtëri *nf collec* [*Ethnog*] **1** = **kumbari 2** gift of clothing from the groom to the bride before the wedding; sweets served when the gift is delivered

*****kumti** *nf (Old)* announcement, notification; communiqué

kumtim *nm ger* **1** <**kumto·n**, **kumto·het 2** announcement, notification; notice

kumto·het *vpr* to be reported, become known, become public information

kumto·n
  I § *vt* to notify
  II § *vi* to deliver a report, read a paper at a conference, speak; speak (with someone), converse

*****kumt·uer** *adj (fem ˜ ore) (Old)* communicative

kumt·ues *nm* notifier, announcer; person who delivers a report: reporter

kum·utri *nf* clothes sent by the bridegroom to the bride as his wedding gift

kuna·dhe *nf* [*Zool*] = **shqarth**

kuna·t *nm* brother-in-law

kuna·të *nf* sister-in-law

*****kuna·tës** *nm* animal's stomach: craw

kunati *nf collec* the set of one's siblings-in-law

kunato·ll *nm* = **kunat**

kunato·lle *nf* = **kunatë**

*****kuna·ve** *OR* **kuna·vje** = **kuna·dhe**

kund
  I § *adv* **1** somewhere, anywhere **2** nowhere
  II § *determiner* about, some, approximately

kundali *nf* swing, seesaw

*****kundalis·** = **lëku·nd·**

ku·nde *nf* [*Bot*] = **kalim**

ku·ndër *adv, prep (abl)* **1** against **2** opposite, facing, across **3** opposing, in opposition

kundër *formative prefix* opposite, anti-, counter-, contra-

kundëradmira·l *nm* [*Mil*] rear admiral

kundërajro·r
  I § *adj* anti-aircraft
  II § nm **1** anti-aircraft weapon **2** soldier manning an anti-aircraft weapon

kundëratomi·k *adj* anti-atomic

kundërbërtham·o·r *adj* anti-nuclear

kundërda·do *nf* [*Tech*] locknut

kundëre·rë *nf* wind blowing in the opposite direction and with the same force as another: answering wind

kundërfaqe *nf* opposite/facing page

kundërfeta·r *adj* anti-religious

*****kundërfja·lë** *nf* contradiction

kundërforc·ë *nf* **1** counterforce **2** buttressing wall

kundërgaz *nm* gas mask

kundërgoda·s *stem for 1st sg pres, 1st & 3rd pl pres, 2nd & 3rd sg subj* <**kundërgodit·**

kundërgodi·s *stem for 2nd pl pres, pind* <**kundërgodit·**

kundër·god·ít· *vt* **1** to counterstrike **2** to deliver a counterblow

kundër·god·ít·ës *adj* striking back, in retaliation

kundër·god·í·tje *nf* **1** counterblow, retaliation **2** [*Mil*] counter strike

kundër·grímc·ë *nf* [*Phys*] antiparticle

kundër·gru·sht *nm* counterpunch, counterblow; counterstrike
∘ **kundërgrusht shteti** counter-coup

kundër·gje·gje *nf* response, reply

*****kundër·gjy·q·ës** *n* (*Old*) [*Law*] opposing side, opponent

kundër·he·lm *nm* antidote; antitoxin

kundër·kërk·es·ë *nf* counterdemand, counter-request

kundër·kim·ík *adj* protective against chemicals

kundër·kritík·ë *nf* rebuttal, counter-criticism

kundër·lënd·ë *nf* antimatter

kundër·ligj·ór *adj* [*Law*] against the law, counter-legal, illegal

kundër·lígj·sh·ëm *adj* (*i*) [*Law*] illegal

kundër·malar·ík *adj* antimalarial

kundër·mano·vër *nf* counter-maneuver

kundër·mas·ë *nf* countermeasure

kundër·mësy·m·ës *adj* counteroffensive

kundër·mësy·m·je *nf* counteroffense, counteroffensive

kundër·m·ím *nm ger* **1** <kundërmo·*n* **2** strong smell: aroma, fragrance; stink

kundër·m·o··n *vi* **1** to give off a strong odor, have a strong smell **2** to smell putrid: stink

kundër·m·ues *adj* giving off a strong odor: fetid, smelly; fragrant

kundër·njer·ëz·ór *adj* inhumane; mean; cruel

kundër·o··n *vt* **1** to contradict **2** to oppose

kundër·ofensív·e *nf* = kundërmësymje

kundër·pad·í *nf* [*Law*] countercharge; countersuit

kundër·pag·es·ë *nf* payment collected on delivery, C.O.D. payment

kundër·paru·ll·ë *nf* password, countersign

kundër·pe·sh·ë *nf* counterweight, counterpoise, counterbalance

kundër·pesh·ím *nm ger* <kundërpesho··*n*

kundër·pesh·o··n *vt* to counterpoise, counterbalance

kundër·përgjígj·et *vpr* **1** to give a sharp counter reply/retort **2** to act in response: respond, react, counter

kundër·përgjígje *nf* countering reply/response

kundër·propoz·ím *nm* counterproposal

kundër·qëndr·ím *nm ger* **1** <kundërqëndro··*n* **2** resistance

kundër·qëndr·o··n *vt* to resist

kundër·rake·t·ë *nf* anti-missile missile

kundër·revolucio·n *nm* counterrevolution

kundër·revolucion·ar *adj, n* counterrevolutionary

kundër·sje·ll·je *nf* (of a weapon) recoil, kick

kundër·spiun·ázh *nm* **1** counterespionage **2** counterespionage agency

kundër·su·lm *nm* **1** counterattack, counteroffense **2** instant retaliation

kundër·sulm·ím *nm ger* <kundërsulmo··*n*

kundër·sulm·o··n *vt* **1** to counterattack **2** to retaliate immediately

kundër·shën·ím *nm ger* **1** <kundërshëno··*n* **2** countersignature

kundër·shën·o··n *vt* to countersign

*****kundër·shit** *nm* (*Old*)

kundër·sht·ar
I § *n* opponent, antagonist, rival, adversary
II § *adj* opposing

kundër·shtet·ëror *adj* against the state

kundër·sht·í *nf* opposition, objection; contradiction

kundër·sht·ím *nm ger* **1** <kundërshto··*n* **2** = kundërshtí

kundër·sht·o··n
I § *vt* to oppose; defy, refuse; contradict, reject, deny
II § *vi* to stand opposed: object

kundër·sht·or *adj* [*Ling*] contrastive

kundër·sht·u·e·shëm *adj* (*i*) opposable, disputable, contestable

kundër·shty·pje *nf* [*Tech*] back pressure

kundër·t
I § *adj* (*i*) **1** contrary; contradictory **2** opposite; facing
II § *nf* (*e*) the contrary, the reverse; polar opposite

kundër·ta·nk
I § *nm* antitank gun
II § *adj* antitank

kundër·terror *nm* anti-terrorist warfare

kundër·te·z·ë *nf* antithesis

kundër·t·í *nf* **1** [*Phil*] polar opposite, contradictory **2** contrast, opposition

*****kundër·tíngull** *nm* (*Old*) counterpoint, harmony

kundër·tru·p *nm* [*Med*] antibody

kundër·thë·n·ës *adj* contradictory

kundër·thë·n·ie *nf* contradiction

kundër·thi *adv* (*së*) to the contrary

kundër·urdh·ër *nm* counter-order, countermand

kundër·vajt·ës
I § *n* person committing a violation: violator, transgressor
II § *adj* contravening, in violation, transgressing

kundër·vajt·je *nf* contravention, violation, infraction, transgression
∘ **kundërvajtje penale** [*Law*] misdemeanor

kundër·ve·n *stem for opt, adm, part* <kundërvë·

kundër·vepr·ím *nm ger* **1** <kundërvepro··*n* **2** reaction, counteraction, antagonism

kundër·vepr·o··n *vi* to react, counteract, counter

kundër·vepr·ues *adj* reactive, counteracting, countering, antagonistic, reactionary

kundër·ve·r *stem for imper* <kundërvë·

kundër·vë· *vt* to put into opposition: contrast; oppose, confront

kundër·vë·n *stem for opt, adm, part* <kundërvë·

kundër·vë·n·ie *nf ger* **1** <kundërvë·, kundërvi·*het* **2** opposition; contrast **3** [*Ling*] antonymy

kundër·vë·r *stem for imper* <kundërvë·

kundër·vi··het *vpr* <kundërvë· to be in opposition: contrast, clash

kundër·vi· *stem for 2nd pl pres, pind, imper, vp* <kundërvë·

kundër·vle·ft·ë = kundërvlerë

kundër·vle·r·ë *nf* [*Fin*] equivalent value, equivalent

kundër·vu· *stem for pl pdef, 3rd sg pdef vp* <kundërvë·

kundër·vu·r *stem for sg pdef, sg imper* <kundërvë·

kundërzbulim *nm* **1** counterespionage **2** counterespionage agency

*__kundërzim__ *nm* contrast

kundërzjarr *nm* [*Mil*] counterfire

kundërrymë *nf* countercurrent

kundje *nf* [*Bot*] thin reed stalk commonly used as lathing material: giant reed (*Arundo donax*)

kundra = **kundër**

kundraje *nf (Old)* opposite side

*__kundrajruer__ *adj (fem ˜ore) (Old)* = **kundërajror**

kundrarrymë *nf* [*Electr*] reverse current, back current

*__kundrashoqnor__ *adj (Old)* antisocial

kundravajtës *n* [*Law*] lawbreaker, violator

kundraxhi *nm (np ˜nj) (Old)* = **këpucar**

kundrejt
  I § *adv* across, opposite, facing
  II § *prep (abl)* **1** across, opposite, facing **2** with respect to, in relation to; toward, towards **3** in exchange for, for **4** in comparison with

*__kundresht__ *nm (Old)* contrast, distinction, set-off

kundri *nf* **1** contrast, opposition *__2__ antithesis

kundrim *nm ger* <**kundro·n**

kundrinë *nf* [*Ling*] grammatical object
  ∘ **kundrinë e drejtë** direct object
  ∘ **kundrinë e zhdrejtë** indirect object

kundrinor
  I § *nm* [*Ling*] (direct or indirect) object
  II § *adj* [*Ling*] serving as (direct or indirect) object: objective

kundro·n *vt* **1** to watch [] carefully, observe **2** to look [] over carefully, consider [] carefully

*__kundror__ *nm* = **kundri**

kundruall
  I § *adv* opposite, facing
  II § *prep (abl)* opposite, across from, facing

kundruelltë *adj (i)* opposite; alternate, corresponding

kundrueshëm *adj (i)* observable

*__kundulli·__ *(Reg Gheg)* = **lëkund·**

kuneiform *adj* in cuneiform

kunel *nm* [*Zool*] **1** rabbit, cony (*Oryctolagus cuniculus*) **2** leveret, young rabbit; bunny

kunetër *np* <**kunat**

kunetëri *nf collec* siblings-in-law, the set consisting of brothers-in law and sisters-in law

*__kuneti__ = **kunetëri**

kunë *nf* seesaw, swing

*__kunës__ *nm* [*Zool*] = **shqarth**

kungallë [*Entom*] = **gjinkallë**

kungar *nm* **1** thick wooden corner post in the construction of a hut **2** roof rafter connecting a corner post to the ridge beam: hip rafter, principal rafter

*__kungardë__ *nf* cockade

*__kungas·__ = **kunjas·**

kungatë *nf* [*Relig*] communion bread and wine: Eucharist

kungatës *n* **1** [*Relig*] communicant **2** caulker

kungë *nf* [*Archit Relig*] chancel of a church, sanctuary

kungim *nm ger* [*Relig*] **1** <**kungo·n, kungo·het** **2** communion

kungo·het *vpr* [*Relig*] to receive communion

kungo·n
  I § *vt* [*Relig*] to give/offer communion
  II § *vi* to receive communion

kungore *nf* = **kungë**

kungull
  I § *nm (np ˜ j)* **1** [*Bot*] gourd; squash; pumpkin (*Cucurbita* L.) **2** water gourd, gourd bottle **3** wide-bellied bottle **4** *(Fig CrudeImpolite)* head; mind **5** *(Fig Crude Insult)* idiot
  II § *adj (Fig)* idiotic
  ∘ **kungull i egër** [*Bot*] white bryony *Bryonia alba*
  ∘ **kungull ferracak** [*Bot*] redberry bryony *Bryonia dioica* = **stërkungull**
  ∘ **u bë/rrit kungulli e mori/zuri gardhin** "the squash grew and took over the fence" **1** *(Iron)* (said about someone still wet behind the ears who acts like a big shot) **2** *(Pej)* (said about someone who harms a former close friend after the friendship breaks up)
  ∘ **kungull lakrorës** fleshy squash/pumpkin used as a pie filling
  ∘ **kungull pa fara** *(ColloqImpolite)* completely brainless, really stupid
  ∘ **U dogj nga kungulli, e i fryn edhe kosit.** "He was burned by the squash, and he blows even on the yogurt." *(Prov)* Once bitten, twice shy.
  ∘ **kungull ujës** [*Bot*] = **kungullujës**

kungullac *nm (Disparaging)* **1** *(Impol)* skull **2** *(Fig Insult)* idiot

kungullaç
  I § *nm* **1** unripe melon **2** *(FigImpolite)* immature person
  II § *adj* **1** unripe **2** *(Fig)* immature, foolish

kungullak
  I § *nm* dried gourd used as a water jug: water gourd
  II § *adj* gourd-shaped

kungullas *adv*

kungulleshë *nf* saltceller

kungulleshkë *nf* **1** [*Bot*] zucchini, vegetable marrow **2** small wide-bellied flask

kungullhaes *nm* [*Bot*] winter squash; pumpkin (*Cucurbita maxima*)

kungullishtë *nf* **1** = **kungullujës 2** field of plants of the gourd family: pumpkin patch, field of squash

kungullnik *nm* [*Food*] pumpkin pie

kungullor *adj* [*Bot*] having elongated oval fruit; belonging to the gourd family

kungullore *np fem* gourd family *Cucurbitaceae*

kungullujës *nm* [*Bot*] wild gourd that is dried and used to make utensils: bottle gourd, calabash (*Lagenaria vulgaris*) = **susak**

kungullush *nm* [*Bot*] squirting cucumber (*Ecballium elaterium*)

*__kungurec__ *nm* [*Invert*] intestinal worm: roundworm = **rre**

kungjero·n *vi (Old)* to curse, swear

*__kunik__ *adj* conical

*__kunilë__ *nf* = **kunel**

*__kunorë__ *(Reg Gheg)* = **kurorë**

*__kuntrat__ = **kontrat**

kunup *nm* [*Entom*] = **mushkonjë**

kunupice *nf* [*Bot*] = **marenë**

kunupidhe *nf* [*Bot*] = **lulelakër**

kunupierë *nf* mosquito netting over a bed, canopy

kunj

I § *nm* **1** peg **2** *(Colloq)* matchstick **3** *(Fig)* horse's molar (tooth) **4** *(Fig)* barbed word

II § *adv* *(Fig Crude)* standing (in a daze) like a stick of wood

kunj **a·s·** *vt* to plug up [a leaky wooden container] with rags

kunj **ëz** *nf* **1** small peg; sliver of wood **2** hangnail **3** blisters on an animal's gums

kunj **ëzim** *nm ger* **1** <kunjëzo·*n* **2** [*Mil*] picket posted as a guard

kunj **ëzo·*n*** *vt* **1** = kunjo·*n* **2** [*Mil*] to stake out a guard for [], picket

kunj **im** *nm ger* <kunjo·*n*

kunj **o·*n*** *vt* to drive a peg into []; close up [] with a peg

kunj **or** *nm* incisor (tooth) of a horse

kuocient *nm* quotient

kuotë *nf* **1** elevation of land; height of that elevation; height (above sea level) **2** quota
○ **kuotë (anëtarësie)** *(Colloq)* membership dues

kuotizacion *nm* membership dues

kup *nm* heap

kupa *np* <kupë hearts (card game)

kupac *nm* **1** wooden bowl with a tight-fitting lid used by shepherds to carry moist or liquid food provisions; bowlful **2** wooden bowl for crushing nuts or seasonings; garlic press

kupalicë *nf* = kup

kupanicë *nf* goblet, cup

***kupatë** *nf* heart (in card games)

kupe *nf* **1** train compartment **2** *(Old)* four-wheeled enclosed carriage for two people

kupë *nf* **1** bowl **2** = kupac **3** large round and concave space **4** cupping glass (formerly used in cupping as a medical treatment) **5** [*Bot*] calyx **6** *(Fig Colloq Pej)* booze, cups **7** one of the two red suits in playing cards: heart
○ **kupa e gjurit** [*Anat*] the kneecap
○ **kupa e kokës** [*Anat*] skull
○ **kupa e liqenit** lake bed
○ **kupa e murit** [*Bot*] navelwort *Cotyledon umbilicus*
○ **kupa e qiellit** dome of the sky
○ **kupë e rrotës** hubcap

***kupël** = kubël

kupëz *nf dimin* **1** small cup-shaped/concave space or object: little cup/bowl, cupping glass, calyx **2** [*Bot*] cupule, cyathys ( )
○ **kupëz e bërrylit** [*Anat*] knob of the elbow
○ **kupëza e gjurit** [*Anat*] kneecap

kupëzak *adj* shaped like a little cup

kupëzor *adj* dome-shaped

kupicë *nf* heap (of corn), pile

kupkë *nf dimin* *(Reg)* little cup
○ **kupkë në faqe** dimple

kuplet *nm* [*Lit Mus*] couplet

kupolë *nf* cupola, dome

kupoliferе *np* [*Bot*] cupuliferae

kupon *nm* coupon

kupor *adj* bowl-shaped

kupore *nf* food bowl; deep soup bowl

***kuprec** = koprrac

***kupresh** *nm* halter

***kupri** *nf* box for butter

kupshelle *adj* (of dishes) bowl-shaped

kupshore *nf* = kupore

kuptim *nm ger* **1** <kupto·*n*, kupto·het **2** meaning **3** [*Ling*] signification, sense **4** *(Colloq)* ability to understand: comprehension
○ **kuptimi i drejtpërdrejtë** [*Ling*] denotation
○ **kuptim i kundërt** opposite sense

kuptimisht *adv* semantically, in terms of meaning

kuptimor *adj* [*Ling*] semantic

kuptimplotë *adj* full of meaning, highly significant

kuptimshëm *adj (i)* meaningful, significant

kupto·het *vpr* **1** to arrive at an understanding, come to realize; have an understanding **2** to be understandable
○ **kupto·het**[3sg] **vetvetiu/vetiu** to be self-evident, be obvious

kupto·*n* *vt, vi* to understand, comprehend; realize

***kuptos·** *vt (Old)* to conquer, defeat

kuptuar *adj (i)* understood, understanding

kuptueshëm

I § *adj (i)* understandable, comprehensible, intelligible

II § *adv* **1** understandably **2** significantly, with significance

kuptueshmëri *nf* intelligibility, comprehensibility

kuq

I § *adj (i)* red

II § *nm (të)* **1** redness, the color red; flushed color **2** lipstick, lip rouge **3** egg yolk
○ **i kuq si thana** rosy-cheeked: very healthy
○ **të kuqtë e madh** erysipelas (a disease characterized by deep-red inflammation)

kuq· *vt* **1** to cause [] to be red, make [] red; color [] red, give a red color to [] **2** to fry **3** to heat [] red-hot
○ <>**a kuq·** **1** *(Fig)* to cheat <> **2** to give <> a severe scolding

kuq·et *vpr* **1** to get red, redden **2** to get red in the face: become flushed; blush
○ **as kuq·et as verdh·et** to be shameless

kuqal

I § *n* **1** person with red hair and ruddy complexion: redhead **2** livestock animal with a reddish-brown coat: sorrel

II § *adj* having red/reddish/sorrel hair

kuqalak *adj* = kuqërremë

kuqalan *nm* person with red hair and ruddy complexion: redhead

kuqalash

I § *adj* **1** reddish, ruddy **2** having a ruddy complexion

II § *nm*
○ **kuqalashi çafkëzi** [*Ornit*] bullfinch *Pyrrhula pyrrhula* L.

kuqalosh *adj* = kuqalash

kuqar *nm* land with red soil

kuqash *adj* (animal) with reddish-brown hair

kuqe

I § *nf (e)* **1** redness, the color red **2** egg yolk

II § *np (të)* red clothes

kuqele *nf* reddish-brown (nanny) goat

kuqeshë *nf* cow with reddish-brown hair

kuqeverdhë *adj (i)* orange; reddish-brown

kuqezi *adj* red and black (colors of the Albanian national flag)

ku'qël nf **1** reddish-brown liquid pressed from olives; reddish-brown sediment in olive oil **2** [Ornit] female of the mallard Anas platyrhynchos **3** livestock animal with reddish-brown hair **4** [Bot] = kuqëla're **5** dead-nettle straw used to pad the bottom of a cradle **6** [Bot] dogtooth violet, canary clover Erythroniumdens-canina **7** [Bot] dogtooth violet, Ravenna-grass Erianthus ravennae

kuqëla're nf [Bot] dead nettle (Lamium)

kuqëli'm nm reddish light/glow

kuqëli'në nf **1** (sandy and infertile) reddish soil **2** reddish color

kuqëli'shtë nf (sandy and infertile) reddish soil

kuqëlo' •n vi to become reddish; glow/shine red

kuqëlo're nf [Bot] edible golden mushroom: orange-milk agaric, royal agaric, Caesar's amanita (Amanita caesarea)

kuqëlo'sh = kuqala'sh

ku'qër adj (i) (Reg Tosk) = kuqërre'më

*****kuqëri's** = kuqërri's

kuqërre'më adj (i) reddish, ruddy, rubicund; reddish-brown, rust-colored

kuqërre'mtë adj (i) = kuqërre'më

kuqërre'shëm adj (i) = kuqërre'më

kuqërre'shkët adj (i) = kuqeve'rdhë

kuqërri'm nm bright red/reddish light

kuqërri's • vt to brown [ ] (in the oven), sear

kuqërri's •et vpr **1** to become brown (in the oven) **2** (of fruit) to start to turn red, begin to look ripe **3** to blush

kuqërro' •n vi to shine with a bright red color, glow with a scarlet light

kuqësi' nf redness

*****kuqësi'r** = kuqësi'

kuqëso' •n vt to imbue with a red color: redden

kuqile'stër nf = kuqëli'në

kuqi'shtë nf = kuqëli'në

ku'qje nf ger <kuq•, kuq•et

kuqle'mtë adj (i) = kuqërre'më

ku'qo nf with masc agreement **1** domestic animal with reddish hair **2** red pigeon **3** (Colloq) person with reddish hair and florid complexion **4** large earthenware pot without handles

kuqo' •n vi to have a red color; shine with a red light, shine red

kuqo'r adj reddish

*****kuqrra'k** nm [Ichth] cardinalfish (Apogon imberbis L.)

*****kuquna're** nf poppy

ku'qur adj (i) **1** colored red **2** glowing red with heat: red-hot **3** browned, fried

kuqurri'k adj bay (horse)

*****kuqve'rdhë** = kuqeve'rdhë

kur adv conj when

  ○ **Kur dëgjon se ka shumë pema, merr shportën e vogël.** "When you hear that there is a lot of fruit, take your small basket." (Prov) If there is talk of great abundance, don't expect to get much.

  ○ **Kur fle koka, lëviz gjuha.** "While the head rests/sleeps, the tongue moves." (Prov) That's just talking without thinking.

  ○ **kur këndo•** n[3sg] gjeli/këndesi i parë when the first cock crows, at daybreak

  ○ **kur këndo•** n[3sg] gjeli/këndesi i tretë when the third cock crows, in full daylight

  ○ **Kur kërce•** n[3sg] fukarai, ça•het[3sg] daullja. "When the poor man is dancing, the drum breaks." A poor man never gets a break.

  ○ **kur e kur 1** time after time; many times **2** a long time ago

  ○ **kur __ kur __** at times __ at other times __, sometimes __ other times __

  ○ **Kur m'u dogjën mullarët, njoha miqtë e kumbarët.** "When my haystacks burned down, I came to know my (family) friends." (Prov) You find out who your friends are when you are in trouble. A friend in need is a friend indeed.

  ○ **Kur rri koka, lëviz gjuha.** "While the head rests/sleeps, the tongue moves." (Prov) That's just talking without thinking.

  ○ **Kur s'është maca, minjtë hedhin valle.** (Prov) When the cat's away the mice will play.

  ○ **Kur s'ha kumbulla, s'të mpihen dhëmbët/dhëmballët.** "If you don't eat plums, your teeth don't get numb." (Prov) (said to someone pretending not to be guilty) If you didn't do anything wrong, you have no reason to worry.

  ○ **Kur s'ke grurë, e mirë është edhe thekra.** "When you don't have wheat, even rye is good." (Prov) You make do with what you have.

  ○ **Kur s'ke pula, mos bëj ish!** "If you don't have chickens, don't say 'shoo'!" When it's none of your business, keep your nose out of it!

  ○ **Kur s'ke pula, mos u merr me dhelprat!** "When you don't have chickens, don't get involved with foxes!" (Prov) Since it's none of your business, keep your big nose out of it.

  ○ **Kur s'ke pula, pse hahesh me dhelprat?** "If you don't have chickens, why are you quarrelling with the foxes?" (Prov) Since it's none of your business, keep your big nose out of it.

  ○ **Kur s'ke pulën, ha (edhe) sorrën.** "If you don't have chicken, you (even) eat crow." **1** (Prov) You do what you have to do **2** You can get used to anything. You learn to get by with what you have.

  ○ **Kur s'ke punë, luaj derën!** "When you have no work to do, move the door back and forth." Always find something to do to keep busy! Don't just hang around.

  ○ **Kur s'ke rrush, ha edhe larushk.** "When you don't have grapes, you even eat wild grapes" (Prov) You take what you can get. You make do with what you have.

  ○ **Kur s'ke shkallën, merr litarin//është mirë edhe litari.** "When you don't have a ladder, take a rope//even a rope will do." (Prov) In a pinch, you use whatever is available.

  ○ **Kur shkoi lata, të shkojë edhe sëpata.** When you lose the axe-head, you don't need the axe-handle. Once the main part is gone, the rest is of little use.

  ○ **Kur i shtie drutë, hap sytë!** (Prov) When you are doing something important, be particularly careful!

  ○ **Kur t'i hipësh kalit, shihi potkonjtë!** "When you mount the horse, look at the horseshoes!" (Prov) Look before you leap! Make sure of what you are doing before you begin!

  ○ **kur e tek** very seldom, rarely

  ○ **Kur të bëhen dy ditë bashkë.** "When two days merge into one." (Iron) when Hell freezes over: never

  ○ **kur të bashkohet qielli me tokën//e toka** (Iron) when the sky joins the earth: never, no way

○ **kur të bë·**het^{3sg} **deti kos** "when the sea turns to yogurt" *(Iron)* when hell freezes over

○ **kur të bëjë larushku rrush** "when the wild grapevine yields grapes" *(Iron)* when Hell freezes over: never

○ **kur të bëjë qarri arra** "when the Adriatic oak bears walnuts" when Hell freezes over: never

○ **kur të bjerë shi i kuq** "when red rain falls" when Hell freezes over: never

○ **kur të qethen dhentë e kuqe** "when red ewes get sheared" never: when Hell freezes over

○ **kur të hipë gomari në fik/majë të fikut** "when the donkey climbs (the top of) the fig tree" *(Colloq)* when Hell freezes over, never

○ **kur të flasin lopët** "when cows talk" when Hell freezes over, never

○ **kur të këndojë qyqja e kuqe (nga bishti)** "when the red cuckoo sings (from his tail)" *(Iron)* never

○ **kur të pjellë mushka** when your mule gives birth, when Hell freezes over, never

○ **kur të puqet qielli me tokën/e toka** *(Iron)* when the sky touches the earth: never, no way

○ **kur të qethen viçat** "when calves get haircuts" *(Iron)* when pigs can fly: never

○ **kur të sheh gropën e zverkut** "when one can see the back of one's neck" **1** when Hell freezes over, • gropën e zverkut "when onecan see the back of one's neck" **2** when Hell freezes over, never

○ **kur të shoh**^{subj} **shpatullat/kurrizin/veshët/zverkun/qafën** "when {} sees {}'s shoulders/back/ears/nape/neck" never, when Hell freezes over

○ **kur të takohet qielli me tokën/e toka** *(Iron)* when the sky meets the earth: never, no way

○ **Kur të varësh zilen, duhet t'i biesh.** "If you hang the bell, you should strike it." *(Prov)* If you take on a responsibility, you should perform it well.

○ **kur të bëhet gjethja sa këmba e patës** "when the leaf becomes as big as a goose's foot" when the weather turns fair, when spring comes

○ **kur (të) zbardh·**et^{3sg} **penda e korbit** "when-(ever) the raven's plumage turns white" when hell freezes over: never

○ **Kur zgjatet muhabeti, pakësohet bereqeti.** "When the talking grows longer, the harvest grows shorter." *(Prov)* When there is too much talking, too little work gets done.

kura *nf (Old)* **1** *(Collec)* age cohort drafted into military service, group of conscripts **2** military service

kurajë *nf* courage, heart = **guxím**

○ **kuraj**ë **gjarpri** [*Bot*] = **hidhnaq**

kurajo = **kuraj**ë

kurajo·z *adj* **1** courageous **2** encouraging

kuralë *nf*

○ **kural**ë **gjarpri** [*Bot*] = **hidhnaq**

kuran *nm* [*Relig*] **1** Koran **2** [*Ichth*] = **koran**

****kuras** *adv* in turn

kuratív *adj* [*Med*] curative, remedial

kurbalinjë *nf* [*Tech*] French curve

kurban *nm* **1** [*Relig*] sacrificial animal **2** *(Fig Colloq)* sacrifice, martyr

○ **<>u bë**^{opt} **kurban** "May {} become <>'s sacrifice!" *(Curse)* <> hopes that {} *drops* dead!

○ **T'u bëfsha kurban!** "May I become a sacrifice for you" *(Pet)* my sweet little thing! my little dear!

○ **T'u bëftë kurban nëna!** "may your mother become a sacrifice for you" *(Pet)* mother's little dear!

○ **kurban nëna/motra!** "mother/sister would sacrifice her life" *(Pet)* you are the sweetest little thing (to your mother/sister)! you little dear!

kurban bajram *nm* lesser Bairam = **bajram i vogël**

kurbat *nm* **1** = **arixhí 2** bohemian

kurbate *nf* = **arixheshk**ë

kurbatk*ë *nf* = **arixheshk**ë

kurbatu·rë *nf* [*Math*] curvature

kurbet *nm (Colloq)* **1** foreign land to which one emigrates **2** emigration **3** journey to a foreign land

kurbetçi *nm (np ~ nj) (Colloq)* emigrant

kurbetli *nm* = **kurbetçi**

kurbë *nf* [*Geom*] curve

****kurbu·ll**ë *nf* mill-hopper

****kurc** = **kurs**

kurdís· *vt* **1** to prepare [] for operation by a series of rotary motions, wind up: wind [a clock/toy]; tune [a stringed instrument] **2** *(Fig Colloq Pej)* to get [someone] all wound up: incite **3** *(Fig Pej)* to contrive [a scheme], cook up [a plot] **4** *(Pej)* to contrive, prearrange **5** *(Colloq)* to fix up

kurdís·et *vpr* to start talking in a rush without a pause

kurdís·je *nf ger* **1** <**kurdís·, kurdís·et 2** contrivance

Kurdistan *nm* Kurdistan

kurdís·ur *adj (i)* **1** wound up **2** *(Fig Colloq Pej)* all wound up: excited **3** *(Pej)* contrived, prearranged **4** *(Colloq)* [*Mus*] tuned

kurdo *adv* anytime; all the time, always

○ **kurdo që** whenever

kurdoherë *adv* at all times, every time; always, all the time; at any time, ever

○ **kurdoherë që** whenever

kurdohershëm *adj (i)* constant; perpetual, continual; permanent

****kurdhís·** = **kurdís·**

****Kurdhistan** *nm* = **Kurdistan**

****kurent** *nm (Colloq)* [*Electr*] current = **korrent**

kureshtar

I § *adj* **1** inquisitive, curious **2** *(Pej)* overinquisitive, nosy, snoopy

II § *n* **1** inquisitive person **2** *(Pej)* nosy person: snoop

****kureshte** = **kureshtí**

****kureshtëm** *adj (i)* inquisitive, curious

kureshtí *nf* **1** inquisitiveness, curiousness **2** curiosity

kureshtje *nf* **1** inquisitiveness, curiosity **2** *(Pej)* overinquisitiveness

kurë *nf* curative treatment, cure

○ **kur**ë **për t'u dobësuar** treatment for losing weight

****kurí** *nf* shame

****kurier** *nm* courier, messenger = **korrier**

kurím *nm ger* **1** <**kuro·n, kuro·het 2** treatment, therapy, tonic

kurioz *adj* curious

kuriozitet *nm (Book)* curiosity, notable sight, special object of interest

kurishto·n *vt* to bring discredit upon []

kurje *nf* end of a field at which one starts an activity; entrance to a field

****kurkull·o·n** *vt (Old)* to wait for [], expect

****kurkurís·** *vi* to gobble (like a turkey) = **glluguro·n**

*__kurku__|__vajkë__ = kukuvajkë

*__kurkuvikë__ nf hut, shack

*__kurkuviq__ adv, adj (Reg) in a crouch

__kurm__ nm 1 torso, trunk; tree trunk, bole 2 dorsal portion of the body (of a fish/fowl) 3 slice (of meat/fish/pastry)

__kurm__|__agjak__ nm blood pudding, black pudding: blood sausage

__kurm__|__a__-__kurm__|__a__ adv in slices; in pieces

__kurm__|__ërisht__ adv with the body, bodily, physically

__kurm__|__ëzo__ ·__het__ vpr 1 to fold (one's body), double/buckle up 2 (of cats/snakes) to arch the back, hump up

__kurm__|__ëzo__ ·__n__ vt 1 to fold [one's body], double up [one's body] 2 to arch [the back], bend [one's back]

__kurm__|__ëzuar__ adj (i) bent, arched; twisted

__kurm__|__o__ ·__n__ vt to cut into pieces/slices

__kurm__|__ore__ nf(Old) mortuary

__kur__|__mos__ adv at any time, always

__kurm__|__uar__ adj (i) sliced up, cut into pieces

__kurnac__ adj stingy, miserly

__kurnac__|__ëri__ nf stinginess, miserliness

*__kurni__ nf alley

*__kurnos__ adj shrewd, clever

__kur__|__o__ ·__het__ vpr to undergo treatment (for a health problem); be under medical supervision

__kur__|__o__ ·__n__ vt to cure; give [] medical treatment

*__kuronë__ = kurorë

__kurorë__ nf 1 crown 2 wreath, garland 3 circlet of cloth worn on the head to assist in carrying a jug or vase 4 (Old) ornamented crown worn by a bride 5 marriage; wedlock 6 legal household; married couple 7 [Bot] corolla 8 [Astron] corona, halo
  ◦ __kurorë dafine__ laurel wreath
  ◦ __kurorë me gjemba__ (Book) crown of thorns
  ◦ __kurorë varrimi__ funeral wreath

__kurorë__|__z__ nf 1 small wreath 2 [Bot] coronule ()

__kurorë__|__zim__ nm ger 1 <kuroro ·n, kuroro ·het 2 coronation 3 (Old) religious wedding, marriage ceremony

__kurorë__|__zo__ ·__het__ vpr 1 to get married (in a traditional crowning ceremony) 2 (Fig) to come to a successful conclusion

__kurorë__|__zo__ ·__n__ vt 1 to crown 2 to crown [a wedding couple] in marriage: wed 3 to surround 4 to bring [] to a successful conclusion

*__kurpël__ = kulpër

__kurpër__ = kulpër

*__kurpnishtë__ nf (Reg Gheg) field of hops; place overgrown with bryony

*__kurpth__ = kulpër

*__kurqel__ nm = kërqelë

*__kurqë__ conj whereas, as, since

__kurs__ nm 1 course 2 annual course of studies; body of students following a course of studies in a given year 3 rate of exchange (of money)
  ◦ __kursi i valutës__ exchange rate for foreign currency

__kursant__ n person engaged in a course of studies

__kurse__ OR __kurse__ conj whereas, while, on the other hand, in contrast

__kurs__|__e__-__het__ vpr to be sparing with one's energy; hold back in giving help

__kurs__|__e__·__n__
  I § vt 1 to expend [] in a thrifty manner: spare [], spend/use [] thriftily; be sparing with [] 2 to save (not waste) []
  II § vi to be thrifty/frugal, economize

__kurse__|__nac__ adj (Pej) = kurnac

__kurs__|__im__ nm ger 1 <kurse·n, kurse·het 2 economy, thrift

__kurs__|__ime__ np money saved: savings

__kurs__|__imtar__ adj, n thrifty (person)

__kurs__|__ist__ n = kursant

__kursiv__
  I § nm [Publ] cursive script; italic script, italics
  II § adj cursive; italic

__kurs__|__ye__ stem for pl pdef, adm, part <kurse·n

__kurs__|__yer__ adj (i) 1 thrifty; parsimonious; stingy 2 few and well-considered, sparing and careful

__kurs__|__yes__ nm = kursimtar

*__kurt__ nm (royal) court

*__kurtar__ n courtier = oborrtar

__kurta__|__zh__ nm [Comm] (sales) commission

__kurt__|__esh__ nm [Med] nettle rash; tickling itch

*__kurt__|__inë__ nf 1 courtyard 2 curtain

__kurtizane__ nf courtesan

__kurtuk__ nm 1 unharvested corn left in the field *2 iron trap *3 hunting spear

__kurth__ nm 1 trap, snare 2 ambush

__kurth__|__e__ np 1 tangle of creeping vines of gourd-like or melon-like plants 2 seed holes for such plants

__kurth__|__im__ nm ger <kurtho·n, kurtho·het

__kurth__|__o__·__het__ vpr to be tongue-tied

__kurth__|__o__·__n__
  I § vt to trap, ensnare; set a trap for []
  II § vi to produce a new branch, branch out

__kurth__|__tar__ nm trapper

__kur__|__ueshëm__ adj [Med] remediable

__kuruk__|__uc__ adj (Pej) lame, limping, gimpy

*__kuruna__|__c__ = kurnac

*__kurunt__|__inë__ nf quarantine = karantinë

*__kuru__|__sh__- vt to hurl/bring down, prostrate, crush

*__kuruve__|__jkë__ nf [Ornit] = kukuvajkë

__kurv__|__anik__ adj adulterous

__kurv__|__ar__ n whoremaster, whoremonger

__kurv__|__ash__ nm pimp, procurer

*__kurv__|__atë__ nf(Old) brothel = bordel

__Kurvelesh__ nm a district in southwestern Albania: Kurvelesh

__kurvelesh__|__as__
  I § adj of/from Kurvelesh
  II § n native of Kurvelesh

__kurvë__ nf sexually promiscuous woman, prostitute: whore

__kurv__|__ëri__ nf 1 sexually promiscuity (for a woman); whoring, prostitution 2 (Collec) the whores (of a place) as a collective whole

__kurv__|__ërim__ nm whoring, prostitution

__kurv__|__ëro__·__n__
  I § vi 1 to whore 2 to become a whore
  II § vt to turn [] into a whore

*__kurv__|__tore__ (Old) = kurvatë = bordel

*__kurre__|__shtëm__ = kureshtëm

__kurrë__
  I § adv 1 never 2 (in negative or interrogative contexts) ever

kurrfa·rë

II § nf eternity
  ○ **kurrën e kurrës** absolutely never: never ever, no way, not in a million years!

kurrfa·rë *neg quant* not even a little, not a single; none of, no; no _ of any kind, no kind of _

kurr·gjë *neg pron* **1** nothing, not a thing, nothing at all, nothing of any kind; none **2** nothing of value, nothing important

kurri·lë = **kurrí·lë**

kurrí·lë *nf* [*Ornit*] crane (*Grus grus*)

****kurrís** = **kurríz**

****kurrís·qit·ëm** *adj (i)* = **kurrizda·lë**

kurrí·z *nm* **1** back **2** (*Colloq*) spinal column, spine **3** hunched back **4** back part of a chair/building/dress **5** dorsal part **6** mountain ridge **7** [*Agr*] crest of a plowed furrow
  ○ **kurrizi i anijes** keel (of the ship)
  ○ **kurrizi i hundës** bridge (of the foot)
  ○ **kurrizi i këmbës** instep (of the foot)
  ○ **kurriz më kurriz** back to back

kurrí·z·et *vpr* to become hunchbacked

kurriza·ç (*Pej*) = **kurrizda·lë**

kurriz·bre·shkë *adj (Disparaging)* having a back that looks like a turtle shell: turtle-backed

kurriz·da·lë *adj* **1** with one's back hunched forward, slumping forward **2** hunchbacked, humpbacked

kurrí·ze *nf* cut of meat from the animal's back

kurriz·gja·të *adj* long in the back

kurriz·gje·rë *adj* broad-backed and muscular

kurrí·zo
  I § adj **1** with one's back hunched forward, slumping forward **2** hunchbacked, humpbacked
  II § nf with masc agreement **1** person hunched forward **2** person with a hump on his back: hunchback

kurrizo·r *adj* **1** pertaining to or located on the back: dorsal **2** pertaining to or located on the spine: spinal **3** having a spine: vertebrate **4** humped, humpbacked

kurrizo·rë *np fem* [*Zool*] vertebrates

****kurrja·lle** *np* animal entrails

kurr·ka·h *neg adv* nowhere, no place

kurr·kë·nd *acc* = **kurrku·sh**

kurr·ku·jt *dat/abl* = **kurrku·sh**

kurr·ku·nd *neg adv* nowhere, not anywhere, no place
  ○ **s'ësh-të kurrkund 1** to have gotten nowhere **2** not be oneself at all (today), not be thinking

kurr·ku·sh *neg pron* no one, nobody; not a single person, not even one person

****kurrne** *OR* **kurrní** = **gurrní**

****kurr·nja** (*Reg Gheg*) = **asnjë**

****kurr·nji·se·nd** (*Reg Gheg*) = **asgjë·se·nd**

kurr·qy·sh *neg adv* in no way, in no manner; not at all; (in negative or interrogative contexts) in any way

kurr·sesí *neg adv* in no way, in no manner; under no circumstances, in no case; (in negative or interrogative contexts) in any case, in any way

****kurru·s** = **kërru·s**

kusa·r
  I § n brigand, bandit; robber, thief
  II § adj thieving; piratical
  ○ **kusar deti** pirate

kusara·k *adj* piratical, rapacious

kusarí *nf* banditry, brigandage; piracy

kusarísht *adv* rapaciously, piratically

kusaro··het *vpr* to take up the brigand's life, turn to banditry/piracy

kusaro··n *vi* to live the brigand's life: rob, plunder

****kusër** = **kusar**

kusí *nf* flat-bottomed kettle/pot
  ○ **Kusia mbi prush, thëllëza në fushë.** "The pot is already on the fire, but the partridge is still in the field." (*Prov*) There's many a slip 'twixt cup and lip.

kusku·të *nf* [*Bot*] dodder (*Cuscuta*) = **he·lmëz**

****ku·spull**
  I § adj = **kru·spull**
  II § nm ***ball

kusu·r *nm* **1** money received back for amount paid in excess of price: change **2** money remaining from a larger amount: balance **3** (*Colloq*) part left over: tag end, the rest of it, remaining part, remnant **4** (*Colloq*) defect, failing, vice; fault **5** (*Colloq*) trouble, worry
  ○ **Ç'kusur (e) kam unë!** Why should I pay for that?!.
  ○ **s'lë· kusur** to spare no pains, do one's utmost

kusure·ma·dh *adj* (*Colloq*) afflicted by woes: with lots of worries, unlucky

kusure·shu·më *adj* afflicted by woes: long-suffering

kush
  I § interrog pron who; exactly who
  II § pron anyone
  III § conj anyone who
  ○ **Kush fle me qenin/qentë, ngrihet me pleshta** (*Prov*) Lie down with dogs and you get up with fleas.
  ○ **Kush ha bukë, bën edhe thërrime.** "He who eats bread, also makes crumbs." (*Prov*) You can't eat bread without leaving a few crumbs: You can't expect to make no mistakes.
  ○ **Kush ha djathë nga të hoxhës, pëlcet për ujë.** "Whoever eats cheese from that of the khoja bursts with thirst." (*Prov*) Don't expect anything good from the clergy!
  ○ **Kush ka ditën të mos presë mesditën.** "Whoever has the day should not wait for midday." (*Prov*) Don't put off for tomorrow what you can do today.
  ○ **Kush ka shteg, s'ka mot të lig.** "He who has a journey to make does have bad weather." (*Prov Reg*) The determined traveler is not put off by bad weather. He who knows where he is going is not deterred by the difficulties in the path.
  ○ **kush e kush 1** everyone **2** every man for himself
  ○ **kush _ e kush** _ some _ and others _
  ○ **Kush luan këmbët, luan (edhe) dhëmbët.** "He who moves his feet also moves his teeth." (*Prov*) Only he who works, eats.
  ○ **Kush mbjell erën, do të korrë furtunën/ stuhinë.** "He who sows the wind will reap the storm." (*Prov Book*) Sow the wind and reap the whirlwind.
  ○ **Kush mbjell duhi, korr breshër e shi.** "He who sows storms reaps hail and rain." (*Prov*) They have sown the wind and they shall reap the whirlwind.
  ○ **Kush ndot këmbët luan dhëmbët.** "He who gets his feet dirty moves his teeth." (*Prov*) (He who works eats.) If you don't work, you don't eat.
  ○ **Kush ngutet, përmutet.** "He who hurries too fast shits in his pants." (*Prov Crude*) Haste makes waste.
  ○ **Kush nuk lëviz këmbët nuk luan as dhëmbët.** "He who does not move his feet does not moves his teeth either." (*Prov*) If you don't work, you don't eat.
  ○ **kush pak kush shumë** some more, some less

○ **Kush shkon pas brumbullit, te plehu do ta shpjerë** follow the dung beetle and you'll wind up on the dung heap

○ **E kush thotë pa!** Look who's talking!

○ **Kush vete në mulli doemos do të përmiellet.** "Whoever goes into a mill will inevitably get coated with flour." *(Prov Colloq)* If you lie down with dogs you get up with fleas.

kushane *nf* fireplace kettle used to boil water or food

****kushar** = koshar

****kushdi** *parenth adv* = kushedi

kushdo *pron* **1** anyone, anybody; everyone, everybody **2** someone, somebody

○ **kushdo që** whoever

kushdoqoftë *pron* anyone at all = kushdo

kushedi

I § *parenth* (rhetorical question) who knows; perhaps

II § *pcl* of indeterminate quantity: who-knows

○ **kushedi (se) çfarë/ç'_ 1** *(Iron)* so what makes _ such a big deal!? **2** who-knows-what-all _!?

○ **kushedi (se) ku** who-knows-where

○ **kushedi (se) kur** who-knows-when

○ **kushedi për të satën herë** "who knows for how many times" for the umpteenth time

○ **kushedi (se) pse** who-knows-why

○ **kushedi (se) sa** who-knows-how-much, a lot, very much/many, very

○ **kushedi (se) si** who-knows-how

kushedisatë *adj (i)* umpteenth

kushëri(r) *nm (np ⁓ni)* (male) cousin

kushërini *nf collec* **1** people related as cousins **2** cousinly relationship

kushërirë *nf* female cousin

kushinetë *nf* [Tech] bearing; bushing

○ **kushinetë me bila** *(Old)* ball bearings

○ **kushinetë me rula** [Tech] roller bearing

○ **kushinetë me sfera** [Tech] ball bearing

kusht *nm* **1** condition; requirement **2** stipulation, term **3** bet/wager between two people **4** *(Old)* [Relig] vow made to a god in repayment for an answered prayer

○ **kusht paraprak** premise, condition, conditional requirement

kushtesë *nf* dedication

kushtetim *nm ger* <kushtetoⁿn

kushtetoⁿn *vt* to decide [] on the basis of a constitution

kushtetor *adj (i)* = kushtetues

kushtetues *adj* constitutional

kushtetutë *nf* constitution

kushtëzim *nm ger* <kushtëzoⁿn, kushtëzoⁿhet

kushtëzoⁿhet *vpr* to be conditional, depend

kushtëzoⁿn *vt* to serve as a condition for [], be prerequisite for []

kushtëzuar *adj (i)* conditioned; conditional

kushtim *nm ger* **1** <kushtoⁿn, kushtoⁿhet **2** dedicatory preface, dedication ****3** cost, value

kushtoⁿhet *vpr* **1** to devote oneself, be devoted **2** to be dedicated; be consecrated

kushtoⁿn

I § *vt* **1** to dedicate; consecrate **2** to devote [] to <>

II § *vi, vt* to cost

kushtor *adj* [Ling] conditional

kushtore *nf* [Ling] conditional mood

****kushtri** *nf (Old)* campaign

kushtrim *nm* clarion call, alarm; call to arms

Kushtrim *nm* Kushtrim (male name)

kushtrimdhënës *adj* serving to give the alarm; rallying

kushtrimoⁿn *vi* to sound the alarm

kushtrimtar *adj* rousing, exhortative

kushtueshëm *adj (i)* **1** costly; expensive **2** valuable, highly esteemed

****kushtutë** *nf* **1** constitution = kushtetutë ****2** charter, patent

kushtutor *adj (Book)* = kushtetues

****kushull** *(Old)* = konsull

kut *nm* **1** *(Old)* measure of length equal to 6 or 80 centimeters: ell **2** forearm; cubit **3** stick used as the bat in tipcat

○ **nuk e nxjerr· në kut** not work/come out well

kutalak *nm* stick used in playing tipcat

****kutaresë** *nf* = kuturesë

kutë *nf* young dog, pup

kuti *nf* **1** box, case **2** tin can

○ **kuti e lugëve** spoon rack

○ **kutia postës** mailbox

○ **kuti e shpejtësisë** [Tech] gearbox.

○ **kuti votimesh/e votimit** ballot box

kutiçeⁿles *nm* can opener

kutiçkë OR **kutizë** *(Dimin) nf* <kuti

kuti-kuti *adj* patterned with small squares: having a grid design, with little boxes; (of fabric) check

kutizë *nf dimin* little box/case

****kutlas** *nm* scullion

****kutrul** *I §* *nm* OR **kutrule** *II §* *nf* = kutruli

kutruli *nf* beardless wheat with round light-colored grains; easy-to-work flour made from this wheat

kutulishte *nf* mortar for mashing ingredients such as walnuts and garlic; pestle for this mortar

kutull *nf (Old)* measure of grain (weighing 6-9 kilograms)

kutullaç *adv* in (the shape of) a circle

****kuturesë** *nf* decision, resolution, determination

kuturi *nf* **1** rough estimate; guess, wild guess **2** reckless impulse

kuturiar *adj* brash, impetuous, daredevil

kuturimthi *adv* off the top of one's head; on an impulse; recklessly

kuturis· *vi* **1** to make a risky decision: venture, take a risk, dare ****2** to make a decision, resolve, determine

kuturisje *nf ger* **1** <kuturis· **2** venture, uncertain undertaking

kuturisur *adj (i)* **1** reckless **2** resolute, determined

kuturu *adv* **1** unselectively, at random **2** without direction or plan: haphazardly, aimlessly **3** by estimate

kuturum *adv* = kuturu

kuturumthi *adv* = kuturu

Kuvajt *nm* Kuwait

kuvajtjan *adj, n* Kuwaiti

kuvar *nm* **1** ball of twine **2** [Text] thread loosely wound into a ball

kuvare *np* [Food] stuffed pickled cabbage leaves

kuvaristër *nf* **1** bobbin of embroidery thread; cardboard tube wrapped with embroidery thread **2** spool of wool/cotton yarn

kuvend *nm* **1** conversation, discussion **2** public assembly (for purposes of general discussion) **3** *(Old)*

assembly of elders: district council **4** convention, meeting; conclave **5** [*Relig*] monastery, convent
◦ **s'rri· në kuvend** not keep to what one has said: not keep one's word; change what one has said

kuve·nd· *vt, vi (Colloq)* = kuvendo· ·n

kuvenda·r
I § *adj* skillful in public speaking: eloquent, articulate, well-spoken
II § *n* **1** orator **2** assemblyman **3** participant in a convention

kuvend·ëmb·ël *adj* gentle and kind in speech: soft-spoken

kuvend·ím *nm ger* **1** <kuvendo· ·n **2** discussion

kuvendo· ·n
I § *vi* to have a quiet and unhurried discussion
II § *vt* to discuss []

kuvend·shtru·a·r *adj* capable of discussing things in a sensible way

kuvend·ue·s *nm* **1** participant in a discussion **2** articulate orator, skillful speaker

kuvend·vo·g·ël *adj* laconic, of few words, untalkative

kuve·rtë *nf* **1** bedcover **2** deck of a ship

****kuvi·s·et** *vpr (Old)* to converse, chat

****kuvi·s·e** *np (Old)* conversation, chat

kuvli· *nf* **1** cage **2** (*Pej*) poorly lit small room

****kux·** = gux

ku·ze *nf* large shallow pan, baking pan

****kuzi·në** = kuzhi·në

kuzhi·në *nf* **1** kitchen **2** cuisine **3** (*Pej*) organization that cooks up intrigues or propaganda
◦ **kuzhi·në ekonomike** efficient kitchen stove used for both heating and cooking

kuzhin·ie·r *n* cook, chef

kw. *abbrev* kilowatt

ky
I § *proximal 3rd pers sg masc determiner* this
II § *proximal pron 3rd sg masc* this one, he, it

kyç
I § *nm* **1** key **2** padlock **3** [*Anat*] joint
II § *adj* crucial, most important: key
◦ **kyç i dorës** wrist joint
◦ **kyç i këmbës** ankle

kyç· *vt* to lock [] with a key; lock [] up
◦ **kyçe gojën** shut up! button your lip!

ky·ç·et *vpr* to lock oneself in

kyça·r *n* locksmith

kyçeni·cë *nf* lock = bra·vë

kyç·is *stem for 1st sg pres, pl pres, 2nd & 3rd sg subj, pind* <kyçi·t·

kyçi·t· *vt* = kyç·

ky·çje *nf* [*Electr*] connection

kyço·s· *vt* = kyç·

kyçta·r = kyça·r

ky·çur *adj (i), pred* **1** locked by key, locked up **2** (*Fig*) locked up inside, very private

kyçyly·të *nf* [*Zool*] nose-horn of a sand viper

****ky·e·m** *adj (i)* wasted, ruined

kyl· *vt* (*Reg*) to fill to the brim, fill full

****kylbo·qe** = këlbo·qe

****kyly·sh** = këly·sh

****ky·ne** OR **ky·në** *emphatic acc form* <ky this here

****ky·q** = kyç

****kyta·re** *np (Old)* honeycomb

l [*lë*] *nf* **1** the consonant letter "l" **2** the palatal lateral liquid represented by the letter "l"

la *nf* [*Mus*] the note "la" on a musical scale

la *3rd sg pdef* <**lë**·

la·*het vpr* **1** to get washed, bathe **2** (of the sky) to clear up, become clear **3** *(Fig)* to clear one's debts **4** *(Fig)* to be exonerated, clear oneself **5** to have diarrhea **6** (of fish) to spawn

○ **la**·*het* **me lëngun e** {*pronominal adj*} (of livestock) to be of some value, not be too bad

la·

I § *vt* **1** to wash; bathe **2** to wash away [] **3** *(Colloq)* to cleanse; clear; lick [] clean **4** *(Fig)* to exonerate; expiate, atone **5** *(Fig Colloq)* to liquidate [a debt], pay off []; avenge **6** *(Fig)* to seize in a violent flow: suck away **7** *(Colloq)* to make smooth and even: trim (branches from a log), plane

II § *vi* to flee quickly; suddenly disappear

○ **la**·*n* **ballin** to clear one's honor

○ **la**·*n* **ballin para** <> to expunge one's guilt in the eyes of <>

○ [] **la**·*n*[^3sg] **barku** []'s bowels *are running*

○ **e la**·*n* **çetë** to overdo, take excessive revenge

○ **la**·*n* **çetëzën** to end one's turn in this game

○ **i la**·*n* **duart nga** {} to wash one's hands of {}

○ [] **la**·*n* **dhe** [] **lëpi**·*n* to flatter and kiss up to []

○ **la**·*n* **e qa**·*n* to suffer terribly

○ **la**·*n* **enët** to wash the dishes

○ **e la**·*n* **fajin** to make amends, atone for one's guilt: make up for what one has done

○ **Laje gojën mirë (me uthull)!** "Wash your mouth well (with vinegar)" *(Iron)* How dare you criticize!

○ **Laj gojën! (Impol)** First wash your own dirty mouth!

○ **e la**·*n* **gjakun** to pay one's blood debt

○ **la**·*n* **hesap** to settle an account

○ **t'<> lash këmbët e t'<> pish ujin** "you should wash <>'s feet and then drink the water" <> *deserves* some greater respect from you

○ **la**·*n* **këpucët** *(Colloq)* to be betrothed by payment of money

○ **i la**·*n* **kokën/kryet gomarit** to do worthless/useless work

○ **<>a la**·*n* **kokën 1** to give <> a serious scolding/punishment **2** to bleed <> dry, pluck <> clean

○ **la**·*n* **lesh me** [] **1** to mop the floor with [], beat [] to a pulp **2** to get back at [] many times over

○ [] **la**·*n* **me lot** to shed tears for [], mourn [] deeply; feel very sorry for []

○ **e la**·*n* **me majë të gishtit** "wash it with the fingertips" to do a hasty and superficial job

○ [] **la**·*n* **me majë të gishtit** "wash [] with a fingertip" to do a superficial and hasty job on []

○ **la**·*n* **me sy** to cast one's eyes about, glance all around

○ [] **la**·*n* **me të puthura** to bathe [] in kisses

○ **e la**·*n* **mendjen** to get [] out of one's mind

○ [] **la**·*n* **në lot** to shed many tears for [], mourn [] deeply; feel very sorry for []

○ [] **lau dhe** [] **ngau** [] had an epileptic fit

○ **i la**·*n* **rrugët me lot** to fill the streets with tears: cry a lot; live a miserable life

○ **<>i la**·*n* **sytë 1** to give <> a hasty and superficial going over **2** to cover up <*something wrong*>, hide <*defects*>

○ **la**·*n* **sytë** to feast one's eyes, enjoy looking around; relax and look around

○ **e la**·*n* **zemrën ndaj** <> to rid oneself of doubts about <>

○ **<>i la**·*n* **zorrët** to give <> the runs (diarrhea)

○ **e la**·*n* [] **me gjak** to spill one's blood on [a place] (in a terrible battle)

*lä· *(Reg Gheg)* = **lë·**

la *stem for pdef* <**lë·**

lab

I § *adj* of or pertaining to Labëria

II § *n* native of Labëria

laba'th *nm* [*Ornit*] whooper swan (*Cygnus cygnus*)

la'b·çe *adv* *(Colloq)* = **labëri'sht**

labea't

I § *nm* [*Hist*] member of one of the Illyrian tribes that formerly inhabited territory between Lake Scutari and Northern Malësia

II § *adj* of or pertaining to these people

la'bër *nf* [*Ichth*] green wrasse (*Labrus viridis*)

la'bër *np* * = **lab**

labëre'shë *nf* = **la'be**

labërgi'm *nm ger* <**labërgo'·n, labërgo'·het**

labërgo'·het vp *vr* **1** to get loose, become loose **2** to become emaciated

labërgo'·n *vt* **1** to loosen **2** to unloose **3** to make [] weak and flabby

labërgua'r *adj* (*i*) [*Ling*] lax

Labëri' *nf* ethnographic region of southwestern Albania

labëri'sht

I § *adv* in the manner or language of the Lab people

II § *adj* made/done/created by Labs

labëri'shte *nf* language spoken by Labs

*labërko'·n *vt* **1** = **labërgo'·n 2** = **shkallmo'·n**

*labërko's· = **labërko'·n**

labërqa'r *adj, n (Pej)* (person) wanting something for nothing, parasitic on others

labia'l *adj* [*Ling*] labial

labia'te *np* [*Bot*] mint family *Labiatae*

labiri'nt *nm* labyrinth

labora'nt *n* laboratory technician/assistant

laborato'r *nm* laboratory

laboratori'k *adj* of or pertaining to the laboratory

labo't *nm* [*Bot*] orach, garden orach, mountain orach (*Atriplex hortensis*)

○ **labot i egër** [*Bot*] lamb's quarters (*Chenopodium album*)

labri'k *nm* [*Ichth*] rainbow wrasse (*Coris julis, Symphodus mediterraneus*) = **peshk bari, buzoç bari**

labro'ç *nm* <**levre'k** [*Ichth*] young sea bass (*Dicentranchus labrax*)

[^3sg]: 3sg

lac *nm (np ˉaj)* **1** highwayman, robber **2** parti-colored billy goat

lacan *nm* spotted white ram or billy goat

la'cë *nf* **1** speckle or small spot on an animal **2** small piece, scrap **3** small plot of unworked land **4** spotted white ewe or nanny goat

la'cër
 I § nf **1** gristle **2** open space in filigree or lace work
 II § adj (Fig) very thin (person)

***lacmac = gjizë**

laç *nm* floodplain; wetland

la'çkë *nf*

ladicë *nf* white felt gaiter/spat

ladri *nf* [*Veter*] tapeworm disease in pigs (*Cestodosis, Tenia suis*)

ladut
 I § adj (Colloq) **1** gluttonous, ravenous **2** mean, wicked **3** crazy, mad
 II § nm greedy person

ladut'ëri *nf (Colloq)* **1** gluttony **2** predation **3** *(Collec)* gluttons taken as a whole; predators taken as a whole

lafarak *adj* **1** in rags, raggedy **2** *(Fig Scorn)* ragtag

***lafatë = lofatë**

lafsha gjele *nf* **1** comb of a rooster: cockscomb **2** [*Bot*] cockscomb mushroom (*Cantharellus cibarius Fr.*)

lafsh ak *adj, n* (fowl) with a large comb

la'fshë *nf* **1** crest, comb (on fowl) **2** loose flap of skin: dewlap, wattle, flab; foreskin
 ∘ **lafshë gjeli** [*Bot*] cockscomb (*Celosia christata*)
 ∘ <> **ësh-të rritur lafsha** <> *has* gotten cocky

lafshë kuq *adj* having a red comb

la'fsh ët *adj (i)* resembling a cockscomb

lafshinë *nf* [*Bot*] periwinkle (*Vinca*)

***laft** *nm = lëvdatë*

lag- *vt* **1** to make [] wet **2** *(Colloq)* to water **3** (of a body of water) to wash [a body of land]
 ∘ <>*a* **lag· bishtin** to bring shame/dishonor upon <>
 ∘ <>*a* **lag· dorën** "moisten <>'s hand" **1** to give <> a tip or small bribe: grease <>'s palm **2** *(Old)* to give alms to <>
 ∘ **lag· drutë me benzinë** "wet the logs with gasoline" to add fuel to the fire
 ∘ **lag· fytin** to wet one's whistle
 ∘ **lag· gojën 1** to wet one's mouth: drink a small amount **2** to give a small amount of charity
 ∘ **s'e lag· këmbën** to make not the slightest effort
 ∘ **s'i lag· këmbët 1** to escape without a scratch, get away clean **2** to have insufficient experience with hardship, not be used to suffering
 ∘ [] **lag· me djersë** to sweat hard over []
 ∘ **e lagu, s'e lagu (bishtin) (dhelpra)** "did he (the fox) get it (his tail) wet or not" it's a dispute over a trivial and dead issue
 ∘ **i lag· sytë** to make one's eyes wet with tears: weep tearfully
 ∘ **e lag·** [] **me gjak** to spill one's blood on [a place] (in a terrible battle)

la'g·et *vpr* to get wet
 ∘ <> **lag·***et³ˢᵍ* **baruti** "<>'s powder *gets* wet" <> *loses* <>'s nerve, <> *gets* cold feet
 ∘ **s'**<> **lag·***et³ᵖˡ* **drutë** "<>'s wood *is* not getting wet" <> doesn't need to care; <> doesn't really care

∘ <> **lag·***et³ˢᵍ* **edhe gjuha** to get drenched to the bone
 ∘ **Lagu sot e rruhu mot.** "Wet (your beard) today and shave it next year." It's taking entirely too long.

lagaterë
 I § nf **1** changeable weather: sometimes wet, sometimes dry **2** land that is wet in places **3** children's game played by guessing whether a flipped flat piece of rock will land on its wet or dry side
 II § adj **1** (of weather) changeable **2** *(Colloq)* two-faced

lagatershëm *adj (i)* (of weather) changeable

lagavi *nf* scribble, scribbling

lagavis *stem for 1st sg pres, pl pres, 2nd & 3rd sg subj, pind* <**lagavit·**

lagavit· *vt* to scribble

la'gcë *nf* watering can

la'gë *nf* **1** drop of liquid; dampness, moisture **2** watery portion of the planet **3** wet side of the rock (in the game of lagaterë)

la'gës
 I § nm = **lagëse = stërlagës**
 II § adj used for watering

la'gëse *nf* **1** watering can **2** moistening sponge, moistener **3** worker in a bakery who adds water to make the dough

lagësi *nf =* **lagështirë**

lagësirë *nf* **1** = lagështirë **2** damp area; wetland

lagëso·het *vpr* to become damp/moist

lagëso·n
 I § vi **1** to bleed/drip with moisture **2** to swell with sap
 II § vt to moisten, dampen

la'gësht ëm *adj (i)* wet

la'gësht *adj (i)* **1** moist, damp **2** (of weather) rainy

lagështi *nf* **1** moisture, dampness, wetness **2** rainy weather **3** humidity

lagështidashës *adj (Book)* moisture-loving

lagështim *nm ger* **1** <**lagështo·n**, **lagështo·het** *(Reg)* **2** = **lagështirë 3** fine rain, mist

lagështimatës *nm* [*Spec*] hygrometer, psychrometer

lagështirë *nf* **1** moisture **2** humidity **3** rainy weather **4** *(Reg)* fine rain, mist

lagështis *stem for 1st sg pres, pl pres, 2nd & 3rd sg subj, pind* <**lagështit·**

lagështit· *vt =* **lagështo·n**

lagështo·het *vpr* to get damp, become liquid/diluted

lagështo·n
 I § vt **1** to make [] damp/wet/moist **2** to make [] into a liquid; dilute
 II § vi (Reg) to form dew

la'gët
 I § adj (i) **1** wet, moist, damp, humid **2** rainy
 II § nn (të) = **lagështirë**

lagëtyrë *nf* moist and twisted straw used to bind sheaves of grain

la'gje [*la'g-je*] *nf ger* <**lag·**, **lag·et**

lagraç *nm* pronged stick used to handle the hot top of a dutch oven

la'gshtë *nf* **1** dew; drizzle **2** early dawn **3** fungus disease that afflicts crops

la'gur

  I § *part* <**lag·**, **la'g·et**

  II § *adj (i)* **1** wet, moist, damp, humid **2** soaked **3** irrigated, watered

  ○ **Të fut·**^{3rd} **në ujë/lumë/pus/det e të nxjerr pa (u) lagur** "Puts you in the water/river/well/sea and pulls you out without getting wet" So slick that he could steal the watch off your wrist and you wouldn't even know it.

lagu'sh *nm collec* rotting wet leaves

la'gje *nf* **1** district in a town: neighborhood, quarter, ward **2** big crowd of people **3** *(Colloq)* camp

  ○ **lagje e jashtme** outlying area, suburb, outskirts

lagji'n

  I § *nm* **1** clay container for liquid **2** clay pot used for making dough **3** = **legen**

  II § *adj* of bright red color

lahu'r *nm* **1** thin fabric used to make women's clothes **2** large fringed head kerchief worn by women **3** towel with fringes on both ends

lahuri' *nf* **1** = **lahur 2** *(Reg)* = **lahu'të**

lahuta'r *n* player of a bowed lute

lahu't'ë *nf [Mus]* in northern Albania, a bowed single-string musical instrument with an egg-shaped body and a long neck; in southern Albania, a lute with four double courses of strings

  ○ **lahuta bridashe 1** lute (in Albanian epic songs) **2** epic folk poetry

  ○ **lahutë e butë** *[Mus]* lyrical song

lai'k *adj* laic, lay

la'jka *np* <**lajkë** *(Pej)* words spoken in a mincing/baby voice

lajka'ma'dh *adj (Pej)* terrible flatterer: lickspittle

lajka'ta'r

  I § *adj (Pej)* **1** flattering **2** kittenish, coquettish

  II § *n (Pej)* flatterer, wheedler

lajkatari' *nf* flattery

lajka'ti'm *nm ger* **1** <**lajkato'·n**, **lajkato'·het 2** = **la'jkë**

lajka'ti's· *vt* = **lajkato'·n**

lajka'to'·het *vpr* to snuggle up affectionately and playfully

lajka'to'·n *vt* **1** to win [] over by niceness: wheedle, cajole **2** to caress **3** *(Pej)* to flatter

lajka'tu'a'r *adj (i)* pampered, treated affectionately

lajka'tu'es *adj, n* **1** (person) who wins one over by niceness **2** *(Pej)* (person) who flatters insincerely

la'jkaxhi *nm (np ˜ nj) (Colloq Pej)* insincere flatterer

la'jkë *nf* **1** caress; compliment **2** *(Pej)* flattering word or act: flattery

lajkë'ro'·n *vt* to flatter

la'jk'ës

  I § *adj (Pej)* insincerely flattering

  II § *n* insincere flatterer

lajk'ësi' *nf* = **lajkatari'**

lajk'ëso'·n = **lajkato'·n**

lajki'm *nm* **1** <**lajko'·n 2** flattery; eulogy

*****lajk'meni** *nf* flattery

lajko'·n *OR* **lajko's·** *vt* = **lajkato'·n**

lajkti's· = **lajkto'·n** = **lajkato'·n**

lajkto'·n *vt* = **lajkato'·n**

la'jle *nf* ornamental tracery/scrollwork; floral decoration

la'jlelu'le *nf* flowery ornamentation, flourish

lajlo'·n *vt* to ornament [] with tracery or floral decoration

lajm *nm* **1** report; message **2** news, information

  ○ **i lajmi** his/her/their courier/envoy/emissary

lajm'dhën'ës *n* **1** reporter; correspondent **2** news announcer

lajme'se *nf (Old)* **1** = **lajmërim 2** written notification: notice

lajm'ërim *nm ger* **1** <**lajmëro'·n 2** announcement, notification

lajm'ërimthirrje *nf* notice sent by mail that a telephone call is to be made to the originating party by the addressee at a designated time

lajm'ëro'·n *vt* to let [] know: inform, notify

lajm'ëru'es

  I § *adj* informing, notifying, announcing

  II § *n* announcer of news, messenger; envoy

lajm'ës *n* **1** *[Ethnog]* marriage broker, go-between, matchmaker **2** messenger sent to announce a death or wedding **3** military scout

lajm'ësi' *nf [Ethnog]* marriage engagement arranged by a go-between = **mblesëri'**

lajm'ëso'·n

  I § *vi [Ethnog]* to act as go-between for a marriage

  II § *vt* = **lajmëro'·n**

lajm'ëta'r

  I § *n* **1** messenger; notifier **2** *(Fig)* herald of something to come, augury, harbinger

  II § *adj* **1** announcing, news-bearing **2** harbingering, signalling

lajm'im *nm ger (Colloq)* <**lajmo'·n**

lajmo'·n *vt (Colloq)* = **lajmëro'·n**

lajm'pru'r'ës *n* = **lajmëtar**

lajm'thirrje *nf* **1** written notification that the addressee is to appear somewhere at a designated time **2** = **lajmërimthirrje**

Lajpci'g *nm* Leipzig

*****lajta'r** *n (Old)* washer; washbasin

lajtmoti'v *nm (Book) [Mus]* leitmotif

lajto're *nf* **1** washbasin, sink **2** shower room **3** washing machine/device **4** washerwoman

lajtha'të *nf [Bot]* = **lofa'të**

lajthi' *nf [Bot]* hazelnut; hazel tree/bush *(Coryllus avellana L.)*

lajthi'm *nm* mistake, error

lajthi'njtë *adj (i)* made of hazelnut wood

lajthi's *stem for 1st sg pres, pl pres, 2nd & 3rd sg subj, pind* <**lajthit·**

lajthi'shtë *nf* grove of hazelnut trees

lajthi't·

  I § *vi* **1** to make a mistake, commit an error **2** to err, fall into error **3** to go out of one's mind, go crazy

  II § *vt* to drive [] crazy

  ○ **lajthit· nga mendtë** to go out of one's mind, go crazy

lajthi't·et *vpr* **1** to make a mistake, commit an error **2** to go out of one's mind

lajthi'tje *nf ger* **1** <**lajthi't·**, **lajthit·et 2** accidental error, slight mistake, slip

lajthi'tshëm *adj (i)* **1** *(Colloq)* capable of being very silly; capable of going off the deep end *****2** erroneous

lajthi'tur *adj (i)* wrong by chance, accidentally mistaken

lajthí·zë *nf* [*Bot*] **1** herbaceous tassel-shaped annual that grows in hilly country and has slightly aromatic flowers **2** = **lajthí**

laju·sh *nm* black sheep

lak *nm* **1** curve **2** bight, loop **3** snare, noose **4** twisted leather thong used for tying up moccasins **5** halter/saddle rope; stirrup loop **6** horsehair bow for a bowed lute **7** tendon at the rear hollow of the knee: hamstring **8** knuckle **9** bowed declivity/pass in a range of hills/mountains; area with many steep declivities
  ◦ **nuk i bë·n lak fjalës** to keep one's word
  ◦ **lak bore** snowdrift, mound of snow
  ◦ **laku i qafës** (*Contempt*) rope wound around a woman's neck and used to carry loads; symbol of a woman's subjugation and hard work

laka·dredh· *vt* to wind [] this way and that
  ◦ **lakadredh· fjalën** to take back one's words

laka·dredh·as *adv* bending and winding, sinuously, tortuously

laka·dredhë *nf* **1** sinuous/curvy/winding line **2** [*Text*] bow fitted with a gut string and twangied to loosen and remove small impurities from raw wool/cotton **3** (*Reg*) double stick used to shuck corn **4** (*Fig*) = **dredhi**

laka·dredhje
  I § *nf ger* <**lakadredh·**, **lakadridh·et**
  II § *nf* zigzag

laka·dridh·et *vpr* **1** to meander, wind this way and that **2** (*Fig*) to equivocate

laka·dridh *stem for 2nd pl pres, pind, imper, vp* <**lakadredh·**

laka·drodh *stem for pdef* <**lakadredh·**

lakander *adj, n* (person) of poor/shaky character, slatternly (person)

lakandraq *nm* = **lakander**

lakanís· *vt* = **lakëro·n**

lakanís·et *vpr* = **lakëro·het**

lakas *adv* with loops, in looping fashion

lakat· *vt* **1** to teasel **2** (*Colloq*) to crumple

lakat·et *vpr* to become crumpled

lakatur *adj (i)* **1** teaseled **2** incompletely twisted **3** (*Colloq*) crumpled

lakazi *adv* = **lakas**

lake *nm* (*Book Pej*) lackey

lakeç *nm* [*Ichth*] young carp

lakenj *np* (*Book Pej*) <**lake**

lakesë *nf* curve

***lakë** *nf* lacquer = **llak**

***lakën** (*Reg Gheg*) = **lakër**

lakër *nf* **1** [*Bot*] cabbage (*Brassica oleracea capitata*) **2** green leafy vegetable
  ◦ **lakër e bardhë** [*Bot*] Savoy cabbage (*Brassica oleracea var. capitata*)
  ◦ **lakër deti** [*Bot*] sea kale, sea cole (*Crambe marittima*)
  ◦ **lakër pate** [*Bot*] prostrate knotweed, knotgrass (*Polygonum aviculare L.*)
  ◦ **lakër qeni** [*Bot*] (*Theligonum cynocrambe*)
  ◦ **lakër e verdhë** [*Bot*] black mustard *Brassica nigra, Sinapis nigra*
  ◦ **lakër e zezë** [*Bot*] black mustard *Brassica nigra*
  ◦ **lakër zogu** [*Bot*] = **kërkutë**

lakër·arme *nf* pickled cabbage; sauerkraut

***lakërço·n** *vt* to cloud, muddy

lakëríshtë
  I § *nf* **1** cabbage patch **2** [*Bot*] white butterbur (*Petasites albus*)
  II § *np* leafy plants, green vegetables

***lakërlule** *nf* cauliflower = **lulelakër**

lakëro·het *vpr* to become all tattered; get cut to shreds

lakëro·n *vt* to cut/tear [] into small pieces: shred, tatter, cut [] up; cut to shreds

lakës *n* unreliable/shifty person

lakím *nm ger* **1** <**lako·n**, **lako·het** **2** road curve **3** [*Ling*] grammatical declension

lakínë *nf* **1** saddle of a mountain/hill; precipitous mountain pass **2** winding road up a mountain

***lakmec** OR **lakmes** *adj, n* (*Pej*) greedy (person): pig

lakmesë *nf* = **lakmí**

lakmí *nf* **1** (*Pej*) voracious desire: avarice, greed **2** inordinate fondness/passion **3** envy

lakmím *nm ger* **1** <**lakmo·n**, **lakmo·het** **2** = **lakmí**

lakmitar *adj, n* avaricious, greedy/envious (person); (person) having an inordinate fondness/passion

lakmo·het *vpr* to get a sudden craving for []

lakmo·n *vt, vi* **1** to have a voracious desire/appetite (for []); be avaricious/greedy **2** to have an inordinate fondness/passion (for []) **3** to be envious (of []); envy
  ◦ **lakmo·n në** [] **// pas <>** to be greedy for []/<>

lakmonjës = **lakmues**

lakmuar *adj (i)* inordinately desirable, much coveted

lakmues
  I § *adj* covetous; greedy
  II § *n* covetous/greedy person
  III § *nm* (*Colloq*) skirt-chaser, womanizer

lakmueshëm *adj (i)* inordinately desirable, much coveted

lakníshtë = **lakërishtë**

***lakno·n** = **lakëro·n**

***lako** *indecl* = **loc**

lako·het *vpr* **1** to bend; curve **2** (*Fig*) to be shifty **3** (of a noun, adjective, pronoun, number, article) to be declined

lako·n
  I § *vt* **1** to bend; curve **2** [*Ling*] to decline
  II § *vi* (*Fig*) to be shifty
  ◦ **e lako·n gjuhën** to bend one's own words so as to go back on a promise

lakoç *adj, nm* **1** castrated (animal) **2** (*Impol*) sexually impotent (man)

***lakom** *nm* glutton

***lakomí** *nf* avarice, greed

***lakomic** *adj* avaricious, greedy

***lakomicë** *nf* (*Reg Gheg*) funnel, tundish

lakoník *adj* (*Book*) laconic

lakor *adj* [*Spec*] bent in a curve

lakore *nf* **1** [*Geom*] curve, curved line **2** curve in a road/river **3** winding road **4** waist-length short-sleeved black woolen jacket worn by men

lakra *np* <**lakër 1** green leafy vegetables **2** (*Colloq Fig*) silly ideas
  ◦ **ësh·të lakra në kopsht me** [] (*Iron*) to have no particularly close relationship with []

lakror *nm* [*Food*] large round pie filled with some combination of vegetables, eggs, cheese, and meat: vegetable pie

lakrurína *np* green leafy vegetables

lakrushkë *nf* [*Bot*] brussels sprout *(Brassica oleracea gemmifera)*

lakshte *nf* dew; drizzle

laktë *adj (i)* **1** curved, bent **2** sewn with leather thongs

laktozë *nf* [*Med*] lactose

lakth *nm dimin* < **lak** interstice

lakuar *adj (i)* **1** bent, curved **2** curvy, sinuous

lakues *nm* = **lakës**

lakueshëm *adj (i)* **1** flexible, pliable **2** [*Ling*] declinable

lakueshmëri *nf (Book)* flexibility

lakuqe *adj, n* red (clay/earth)

***lakur** *adj* naked

lakurekës = **lakuríqës**

***lakurí** *nf* nakedness

lakuriq
  I § adj **1** naked, bare **2** nude
  II § nm **1** [*Zool*] bat **2** [*Food*] pasty without the upper layer of dough **3** [*Food*] = **laropítë**
  III § adv **1** nakedly **2** barefooted
  ○ **lakuriq trependësh** [*Ichth*] blue whiting *Micromesistius poutassou*

lakuriq·*et vpr* **1** to become naked **2** *(Fig)* to become impoverished **3** *(Fig)* to be nakedly exposed

lakuriqës *nm* [*Zool*] bat

lakuriqësi *nf (Book)* nakedness; nudity

lakuriqëzím *nm ger* < **lakuriqëzo**·*n*

lakuriqëzo·*n vt* to lay [] bare, strip

lakuriqos· *vt (Colloq)* to strip; denude

lakut *adj, n* greedy/gluttonous (person or animal)

lakutëri *nf* greed, gluttony

***lalabe** *nm* rainbow

lale *nf* **1** red poppy; corn poppy **2** floral ornament ***3** larva, grub ***4** infatuation, love

laleshë *nf (Old)* ancient inhabitant of Myzeqé (female)

laletatë *adj* intimate

lalë
  I § nf with masc agreement **1** *(Old)* name of ancient inhabitants of Myzeqé **2** derisive term of address for poor Myzeqé villagers **3** term used by Moslems of Myzeqé for Christians of the area **4** *(Colloq)* young father: daddy **5** elder brother; (paternal) uncle **6** term expressing respect and intimacy for someone
  II § nf speckled rock

***lalík** *adj* frivolous

lalush *nm* darling, sweetheart

lalush· *vt* to be affectionate toward []: pet, fondle, caress

lamash *adj (Colloq)* **1** poor, beggarly **2** *(Insult)* hooligan **3** *(Pej)* social parasite

lamashëri
  I § nf (Pej) behavior of a social parasite: sponging
  II § nf collèc social parasites as a whole

***lambadhë** *nf* torch

lambík *nm* **1** apparatus used for distilling liquids: alembic, still **2** water heater used in washing clothes **3** wash basin

***lambrík** *nm* [*Ichth*] shark

***lamburík** *nf* [*Entom*] firefly

lamelibranke *np* [*Invert*] Lamellibranchia

***lame** *(Reg Gheg)* = **lamjë**

lamë *nf* **1** [*Zool*] llama **2** saw blade

***lâmë** *(Reg Gheg)* = **lëmë**

laminat *nm* [*Tech*] laminated metal

laminím *nm* [*Tech*] lamination

***lamje** *(Reg Gheg)* = **larje**

***lamjë** *nf* harpy, dragon-woman, spook

***lâmnues** *(Reg Gheg Old)* = **lëmar**

***lampër** *nf* [*Éntom*] firefly

***lâmshkë** *nf (Reg Gheg)* globule

***lâmsh** *(Reg Gheg)* = **lëmsh**

***lâmshuer** *adj (fem ~ore) (Reg Gheg Old)* = **lëmshor**

lamtumír·*et vpr* to say goodbye

lamtumírë
  I § nf long-time or final goodbye: farewell
  II § interj Goodbye!

***lamuth** *nm* [*Bot*] spiny restharrow *(Ononis spinosa)*

***lamzë** *adv* full, up to the brim

landar *nm* large amount/bunch

***lândar** *n (Reg Gheg Old)* woodworker

landare *nf* **1** sparse cluster of grapes **2** tendril of squash

***lândë** *(Reg Gheg)* = **lëndë**

lander *nf* [*Bot*] **1** oleander *(Nerium oleander L.)* **2** tendril (of a gourd/squash)

lando *nf* landau

***lândore** *nf (Reg Gheg)* forest

landro *nf* [*Bot*] oleander *(Nerium oleander L.)*

lanet *n (Colloq)* demon, devil
  ○ **lanet qofsh!** damn you!

lanetís· *vt* to make [] possessed with demons: curse

***lânë** *(Reg Gheg)* = **lënë**
  ○ **lâng e plâng** *(Reg Gheg)* bag and baggage

langaros· *vt* to soil [] by spattering

langarosur *adj (i)* soiled; spotted

***lângcínë** *(Reg Gheg)* = **lângurínë**

***lângël** *nf (Reg Gheg)* jug, pitcher

langoli *obl* < **langua**

***lâng** *(Reg Gheg)* = **lëng**

langonj *np* < **langua**

***langor** = **langua**

langore *nf* < **langua** **1** female hunting dog **2** *(Fig)* very capable woman

***lângsínë** *(Reg Gheg)* = **lângurínë**

langua *nm (obl ~oi, np ~onj)* **1** hunting dog **2** *(Fig)* very perceptive person

***lângurínë** *nf (Reg Gheg)* hogwash

***lângzo**·*n (Reg Gheg)* = **lëngëso**·*n*

***lângje** *(Reg Gheg)* = **lëngje**

lanís· *vt* to chop [meat] up: mince

***lânje** *nf ger (Reg Gheg)* = **lënie**

***lânme** *nf (e) (Reg Gheg)* abandonment, desertion

lanok *nm* thief

lansím *nm* **1** < **lanso**·*n* **2** rocket launch

lanso·*n vt* to launch [a rocket]

***lânje** *np (Reg Gheg)* = **lëngje**

***lanjse** *nf* washerwoman

***lanjtore** = **lajtore**

Laos *nm* Laos

laosian *adj, n* Laotian

***lap** *nm* native of Labëria = **lab**

lap· *vi* to slobber

lapagreth *nm* [*Bot*] **1** frogbit *(Hydrocharis morsus-ranae)* **2** naiad *(Naias)*

lapagreth o re *np* [*Bot*] naias family *Naiadaceae*

***lapa n** *nm* (*Old*) chalk

lapanda r *adj* tattered, raggedy

lapangjo z
I § *adj* (*Colloq*) filthy; filthy in behavior
II § *nm* filthy bastard, shameless louse

lapardh o s ur *adj* (*i*) = **laturi sur**

laparo s· *vt* (*Colloq*) = **laturi s**

laparo s·et *vpr* (*Colloq*) = **laturi s·et**

laparo s ur *adj* (*i*) (*Colloq*) = **laturi sur**

lapata n *nm* [*Ornit*] wood pigeon (*Columba palumbus*)

***lap de le** *nf* [*Bot*] purple loosestrife (*Lythrum salicaria*)

lape *nf* dewlap on a goat

laper *adj, n* (*Colloq Pej*) **1** (person) in rags **2** (*Insult*) foulmouthed (person)

lape t *nf* **1** fleshy/membranous layer over flank meat; flank meat **2** covering flap; decorative flap sewn on an outer garment

***lapeti** *nf* shimmer of color, sheen

***lapeti t un** *adj* (*i*) (*Reg Gheg*) shimmery

la pe *nf* **1** thin piece of tough flesh/skin/hide; inedible gristle **2** earflap, earlap, pinna; earlobe **3** loose piece of skin: dewlap, wattle, paunch; deep wrinkle **4** flap, cover **5** broad flat piece: blade; leafblade, leaf **6** pad placed under the yoke to protect the neck of the ox
  ○ **lap e e syrit** eyelid
  ○ **lap e e veshit** (outer) ear, flap of the ear

la për *nf* **1** thin piece of tough flesh/skin/hide; inedible gristle **2** loose piece of skin: dewlap, wattle, paunch; deep wrinkle **3** small piece of loose/peeling skin; hangnail **4** flat blade **5** (*Colloq*) slap/box in the ear **6** [*Med*] aponeurosis

lapërdh a r *adj, n* foul-mouthed (person); (person) behaving rottenly

lapërdhi *nf* dirty words, foul language; obscenity; obscene behavior

***lapërko ·n** *vt* to release, remove, undo

***lapërki thi n a** *np* = **lapërdhi**

lapëru she *nf* [*Bot*] fairyring marasmius, fairyring mushroom (*Marasmius oreades, Scorteus oreades*)

lapëru sh kë *nf* [*Bot*] = **lapëru she**

la përz *nf* dewlap

***lapërzo ·n** *vt* to defile

lapida r
I § *nm* memorial monument
II § *adj* (*Fig Book*) laconic

***la pke** *nf* (*Reg Tosk*) earlobe

la p ker *nf* **1** dewlap **2** box on the ear, slap in the face

***laplu ng ë** *nf* = **lëplu ng ë**

lapo n *nm* Lapp

Laponi *nf* Lapland

laponi shte *nf* Lappish (language)

lapo t ë *nf* [*Bot*] = **lëpje t ë**

laps *nm* **1** pencil **2** pencil-shaped object
  ○ **laps kopjativ** indelible pencil

laps·
I § *vi* (*Reg*) **1** to become exhausted, get completely tired out **2** to have a craving
II § *vt* to exhaust [], tire [] out

***la psh ë** = **la fsh ë**

lapura k
I § *nm* [*Zool*] **1** bat **2** [*Invert*] slug

II § *adj, n* **1** featherless (bird); (bird) lacking neck feathers **2** (*Fig*) (poor person) without clothes to wear

***lapu sh** *adj* = **llapu sh**

lar *nm* [*Bot*] laurel, bay (*Laurus nobilis L.*)
  ○ **lari i egër/zi** [*Bot*] = **a she**

la ra *np* (*të*) **1** dirty wash water **2** (*Fig*) thin and tasteless food **3** fodder consisting of chaff and water **4** (*Reg*) menses **5** (*Reg*) underwear

laraca k = **laraga n**

laraco ·het *vpr* to become speckled/mottled; start to turn ripe

laraco ·n *vt* to speckle, mottle

lara da sh *nm* **1** [*Ornit*] pelican **2** popcorn **3** somersault

laraga n *adj* **1** variegated, motley: multi-colored, pied, piebald, parti-colored **2** (*Fig*) insincerely flattering, deceitful

lara k *adj, n* mottled (animal)

laraka shë *nf* (*Colloq*) magpie

laraku q *adj* (animal) having patches of red/brown

laraku qe *nf* [*Zool*] weasel (*Mustela nivalis*)

lara-lara *adj* **1** having patches of different color **2** insincerely flattering

larama n *adj, n* **1** (animal/plant) having variegated color: motley, particolored **2** [*Ichth*] cuckoo wrasse (*Labrus bimaculatus*) **3** (*Fig*) insincerely flattering (person)

larama ne *nf* **1** [*Ornit*] red-breasted goose (*Rufibranta ruficollis*) **2** [*Zool*] spotted salamander = **pikë lo re**

lara n *adj* parti-colored, variegated, motley

laraqu k *adj* **1** spotted, speckled **2** with kernels of variegated color **3** having spots on the face from chicken pox

lara skë *nf* **1** [*Ornit*] magpie (*Pica pica L.*) **2** (*Insult*) ugly and contentious woman
  ○ **laraska e detit** [*Ornit*] oyster catcher (*Haematopus ostralegus L.*)

lara sh
I § *adj, n* (animal) of variegated color
II § *nm* **1** [*Ornit*] golden eagle (*Aquila chrysaetos*) **2** [*Ornit*] sheldrake (*Tadorna tadorna*) **3** pasty made with cabbage, leeks, or onions

laravi *nf* insincerity, two-facedness

laravi dhe *nf* [*Invert*] centipede

lara ze ze *adj, nf* ewe or nanny goat with dark patches

lara zo ·n = **laraco ·n**

lardh *nm* fat bacon, bacon

lare *nf* nanny goat with variegated coat

***lare skë** *nf* [*Ornit*] magpie = **lara skë**

la rë
I § *nf* **1** blotch, patch **2** domestic animal of motley color **3** multi-colored decoration on clothes **4** multi-colored wool cloak **5** clearing in a mountain forest; patch of open ground **6** [*Ichth*] = **lo jb ë** ***7** beam of light between clouds
II § *adj* = **la rmë**

la rë
I § *part* < **la ·n**
II § *adj* (*i*) **1** washed; cleansed, clean; clear (of something undesirable) **2** plated (with a precious metal) **3** (*Colloq*) smoothed; polished to a shine
III § *adj* multi-colored, motley, pied
IV § *nf* (*e*), *nn* (*të*) **1** scrubbing, washing **2** payment of a debt ***3** underwear/linen to be washed: laundry

○ **ësh·të larë e shkuar** "be washed and gone" {} *is* as good as dead, {} *is* as much dead as alive

la'rëc *adj* spotted, speckled, mottled

larë'ku'q|e *nf* brown-speckled ewe

larë'mu'shkë *nf* gray nanny goat with dark patches on her body or muzzle

la'rë's
I § *n* **1** person who does washing: launderer **2** wooden clothes beater **3** sharp plane **4** *(Old)* witness who exonerates a defendant **5** [*Ethnog*] bracelet or necklace of silk or wool yarn worn by children on the first day of spring
II § *adj* **1** (of a plane) sharp **2** used for washing

la'rë's|e *nf* **1** washerwoman **2** washing machine **3** soap flakes

larë've'rdhë *adj, nf* (cow or goat) with light brown patches on the hide

la'rëz *nf* **1** [*Bot*] **= laru'shk 2** [*Bot*] vetch-like plant with multicolored fruit **3** [*Ornit*] multi-colored sparrow-like bird **4** [*Ichth*] gambusia **= barkule'c 5** [*Med*] disease that causes blotches on the skin
○ **larëza tripikaloshe** [*Ichth*] guppy *Lebistes reticulatus*
○ **larëza vizake** [*Ichth*] fartet *Aphanius iberus*

larë'ze'zë *nf* **=larazezë**

larë'zo'·het *vpr* to contract a disease that causes blotches on the skin

larg
I § *adv* **1** far (in terms of space or time): far away/ apart; long ago; far in the future **2** distantly related **3** very different **4** indirectly
II § *prep (abl)* **1** far from **2** (in expressions of time) long before
○ **larg duart** hands off!
○ **larg e larg = la'rgas**
○ **ësh·të larg mendsh 1** to be impossible to believe; be out of the question **2** to be beyond question/ doubt
○ **Larg nesh!** "Far from us!" I hope it doesn't get this far!
○ **Larg qoftë!** I hope it (a calamity) stays away!
○ **Larg sysh/syve, larg zemrës.** *(Prov)* Out of sight, out of mind.

larga'la'rgas *adv* **= la'rgas**

la'rg|as *OR* **la'rg|azi** *adv* **1** from far away; far apart **2** indirectly and by implication, the long way around; beating around the bush

large'së *nf* **1** distance between points **2** *(Old)* **= largi'm 3** length of separation

la'rg|ë *adj (i)* far, far-off

la'rg|ëm *adj (i)* **= la'rgët**

larg|ësi'
I § *nf* **1** distance **2** remoteness **3** length of time/ space: interval, space
II § *np* remote places
○ **largësi e vrullit** [*Track*] approach distance (for a jump)

larg|ësi'ma't|ës *nm* [*Tech*] telemeter

larg|ësi'r|ë *nf* remote place, distant region

la'rg|ët
I § *adj (i)* **1** distant, far-off, remote **2** distant (relative/friend) **3** very different
II § *nm (i)* distant relative/friend
III § *nf (e)* **1** distant time or space **2** the unfamiliar

larg|he'dh|ës *adj* [*Mil*] long-range

larg|he'dh|je *nf* **1** long-range firing/shelling/bombing **2** range (of a weapon)

larg|i'm *nm ger* **1** <**largo'·n, largo'·het 2** removal; departure **3** **= largësi'**

larg|i'n|ë *nf* remote place

larg|kë'tej *nm (Euph)* the devil

larg|ne'sh *nm (Euph)* the devil

largo'·het *vpr* **1** to get away; leave; move apart **2** to be/become distant; be absent **3** *(Fig)* to be evasive, dodge **4** (of a time or event) to become more distant **5** to differ

largo'·n
I § *vt* **1** to move [] from a position: remove, take/ send/move [] away; banish **2** *(Fig)* to alienate, keep at a distance **3** to postpone; evade **4** to differentiate
II § *vi* **1** (of a time or event) to become more distant **2** to differ
○ **e largo·n mendjen nga** {} to stop caring about {}
○ **largo·n si djalli/shejtani nga temjani** "distance oneself like the devil from incense" to get the hell out of there, flee in terror
○ **e largo·n vëmendjen nga** [] to stop thinking about []; begin to neglect []

larg|pam'|ës *adj, n* farseeing (person), (person) with foresight

larg|pa'm|ësi *nf (Book)* farsightedness, foresight

larg|pa'm|je *nf (Book)* **= largpamësi'**

larg|qo'ftë *nm (Euph)* the devil

larg|shiku'es *adj* **1** powerful in range of vision: telescopic **2** farseeing (person), (person) with foresight

la'rgu *adv (së)* afar, from afar, from far away, at a distance

largu'ar *adj (i)* far away; distant, remote

largu'es
I § *adj* **1** *(Book)* differentiating; distancing **2** [*Med*] abducent, abducting
II § *n* transporter

larg|va'jt|ës *n* achiever

lari' *nf* **1** variegation **2** [*Biol*] variety

lari'c|ë *nf* **1** multi-colored cloth **2** multi-colored ewe or nanny goat **3** *(Fig)* insincere flatterer, hypocrite

lari'k *adj* **= larmë'**

lari'm *nm ger* **1** <**laro'·n, laro'·het 2** variegated decoration

larі'ng *nm* [*Anat*] larynx

laring|i't *OR* **laringji't** *nm* [*Med*] laryngitis

lari's *nm* horse of mixed color; grey horse

lari's· *vi* to make a croaking sound: croak, quack, caw

lari'sk *adj, n* multi-colored (livestock)

lari'shtë *nf* laurel grove, bay forest

lari't· *vi* to change one's opinion/attitude

lari't·et *vpr* **1** to get patchy **2** *(Fig)* to flatter insincerely

la'rje *nf ger* <**la·n, la·het**

*   *lark = larg

la'rm|ë *adj (i)* **1** parti-colored, variegated, motley **2** *(Colloq)* (of weather) changeable **3** *(Fig)* flattering insincerely **4** **= larmi'shëm**

larm|i' *nf* **1** variegation **2** assortment; large assortment

larmi'shëm *adj (i)* highly variegated

larmo'·n *vt* **1** to decorate [] with a variegated design **2** to create variety in

larmu'shkë *nf* spotted nanny goat

laro *nf with masc agreement* **1** dog with a coat of different colors **2** *(Fig Pej)* rascal

laro · *het vpr* to develop patches of different color in the process of ripening

laro · *n vt* **1** to make [] variegated in color **2** *(Fig)* to flatter [] insincerely

Laro *nf with masc agreement* Spot (name for a spotted dog)

laro‖**i** *obl* <**laru**a

larok *adj (Pet)* = la·ra-la·ra

laronj *np* <**laru**a

laropitë *nf [Food]* pasty make of corn flour, green vegetables, and cheese

laros· *vt* = laro·n

laros·et *vpr* = laro·het

larosh
  I § *adj, n (Pet)* spotted (thing/animal)
  II § *nm [Ornit]* golden eagle = lara'sh

larosh·et *vpr* to develop spots as a sign of ripening

larosh|e *nf* **1** multi-colored wool cloak **2** *[Ornit]* shelduck *(Tadorna tadorna L.)*

larosh|ë *nf* particolored sheep/goat

****la**rsh**ë**m *adj (i) (Reg Tosk)* washable

lart
  I § *adv* **1** up, higher; above **2** at a high level, up high
  II § *prep (with abl)* above; atop
  ∘ **lart e poshtë 1** high and low, everywhere **2** up and down

lartas
  I § *n* mountaineer, highlander
  II § *adv* = la'rtazi

la'rt**azi** *adv* **1** upwards **2** at a high level

lartesë *nf* height

lartë
  I § *adj (i)* **1** high; high-pitched; high-level **2** tall **3** raised; elevated **4** loud **5** upper **6** *(Fig)* highly valued
  II § *nn (të) (Colloq)* = lartëësi

lartëm *adj* = la'rtë

****la**rtë**r *adj* = la'rtë

lartësi *nf* **1** height; altitude **2** high place; high part; high pitch; high level **3** Highness

lartësi'm *nm ger* **1** <lartëso'·n, lartëso'·het *[Mil]* **2** elevation (of a gun)

lartësi'mat|ës *nm* altimeter

lartësi'rë *nf* **1** plateau **2** *[Geog]* zonal area more than 200 meters above sea level

lartëso'·het *vpr* to rise, ascend

lartëso'·n *vt* **1** to elevate; raise, lift **2** to value highly; exalt, glorify

la'rti *adv (së)* **1** = lart **2** from above **3** *(Fig)* haughtily

lartmadh|ëri *nf* Highness

lartmadh|ëri *nf* majesty (as a title)

larto'·het *vpr (Colloq)* = lartëso'·het

larto'·n *vt (Colloq)* = lartëso'·n

****larto**re *nf(Old)* laundry; washerwoman

lartpërme'nd|ur *adj (i)* above-mentioned

la'rtshëm *adj (i)* upper

lartshën|ua'r *adj (i) (Book)* noted above

larttreg|ua'r *adj (i) (Book)* = lartpërme'ndur

larth *nm [Bot]* **1** = a'she **2** = urth

larua *nm (obl ~ o'i, np ~ o'nj)* multi-colored ox/bull

laruk *adj, n* **1** multi-colored (animal) **2** *(Fig)* insincere flatterer

****la**'run *adj (i) (Reg Gheg)* multi-colored

larush
  I § *adj, n (Pet)* multi-colored/piebald (animal)
  II § *adj (Pej)* of mixed composition: motley, heterogeneous
  ∘ **larushi kokëkuq** *[Ornit]* woodchat shrike *Lanius senator L.*
  ∘ **larushi kurrizkuq** *[Ornit]* brown shrike *Lanius cristatus L.*

larushan
  I § *adj* = la'ra-la'ra
  II § *nm* multi-colored animal

****larush**ë *nf [Ornit]* = lara'skë

****larush**ësi *nf* = lari

larushi *nf* = larmi

larushit·
  I § *vt* **1** to variegate with patches of color; speckle, spot **2** to soil with spots
  II § *vi* to have a multi-colored appearance

larushit·et *vpr* **1** to get dirty in spots **2** to develop spots in the process of ripening

larushk *nm* **1** *[Bot]* wild grapevine *(Vitis sylvestri)* **2** dark grape used to make raki or vinegar **3** *(Reg)* green branches of a grapevine used as fodder

larushkë *nf* **1** multi-colored cow **2** *[Bot]* = laru'shk

****larush**ko'·n = laro'·n

larushtë *adj (i)* = la'rmë

larvë *nf* larva

larvo'r *adj [Spec]* larval

larysht|ë *adj (i)* = laru'sh

larzim *nm* **1** <larzo'·n **2** decorative pattern, design, tracery

larzo'·n *vt* to cover with designs

****larzue**m *adj (i) (Reg Gheg)* mottled, checkered

****la**'rrë *nf* cloak, cape

****las** *nm* **1** witness who testifies to one's innocence **2** = lac

la'së *nf* **1** wooden clothes beater **2** *(Old)* old Moslem woman who washes corpses **3** leafless branch used to thresh grain **4** *(Reg)* stiff bristles of grass used for scouring kitchen utensils

****lasi**në *nf* arquebus = arkebu'z

laskande'r *nm* good-for-nothing

laskar *nm* **1** long thick wooden crowbar/lever **2** litter/stretcher made with sticks slung between two poles and used to carry dirt or other heavy loads **3** paddle **4** = landa're **5** *(Fig Insult)* big lout

laskare *nf* **1** = le'skë **2** land fallen in a landslide; scree

laskaro'·het *vpr* **1** = lecko'se·t **2** to fall in a landslide

laskaro'·n *vt* **1** = lecko's· **2** to cause a landslide, create scree

laskar|ua'r *adj (i)* **1** = lecko'sur **2** fallen in a landslide

****la**'skë = lara'skë

****la**'skër *nf* tumor, growth

****lasku**'ndër *nm [Zool]* bat = lakuri'q

laskuraç *nm [Invert]* slug

laskuri'q *nm [Zool]* bat = lakuri'q
  ∘ **laskuriq i natës** bat

****la**'so're *nf(Old)* wash-house, laundry

****lasp**ëro'·het *vpr* to be slatternly

lastar *nm* **1** shoot, sprout; offshoot, scion **2** *(Fig)* tall well-built person **3** tendril, runner

la·stër nf **1** thin flat piece of material: plate, sheet **2** [Publ] printing plate

*lastik·ë nf **1** elastic **2** rubber tire

*lastik·ët adj (i) elastic; springy, rubbery

lastik·shëm = lastikët

*last·o ·n vt = llast·o ·n

lastro·k adj **1** filthy **2** (Fig) dissolute, vile

*lastu·k nm tuft, crest

lastu·një nf = përpa·jnë

la·shë 1st sg pdef < lë·

*lashkava·r adj sloppy, slovenly

la·shkë nf **1** = ashkë **2** small wooden cup/bowl **3** [Ornit] magpie (Pica pica) **4** [Ichth] roach (Rutilus rutilus)

lasht I § nm OR la·shtë II § nf (Reg) time; past, former times, ancient time, a long time ago

la·shtë·a np (të) grain crops sown in late autumn and harvested in early summer: early grain harvest

lasht·ak nm lamb/kid that is born dead

lasht·as OR la·sht·azi adv long ago; in the distant past, in olden times

la·shtë
I § adj (i) **1** ancient, antique; very old **2** early-ripening **3** (meat) of old animals **4** (Colloq) made of flour from grain harvested in early summer
II § nf = la·gshtë
III § adv **1** early **2** long ago

lasht·ëri nf = lashtësi

lasht·ëri·sht adv (Colloq) **1** in olden times **2** in the fashion of the past

lasht·ërishte
I § fem adj ancient; old-fashioned
II § nf past event; old song about ancient times

lasht·ësi nf antiquity

la·shti I § adv OR II § adv (së) in ancient times, in olden times, long ago; formerly, at one time
∘ asi/aty lashti at that time long ago, in those days of yore

lasht·o ·het vpr **1** to grow old, age **2** to grow up, mature **3** (of plants) to grow, ripen

lasht·o ·n
I § vi **1** to get old **2** to ripen faster than usual **3** to give birth prematurely, abort **4** to hurry
II § vt to finish early

lasht·ore nf field sown in grain

lasht·ua·r adj (i) aged, old

lata·r n woodcarver

late·nt adj latent

late·së nf carved wood, carved wooden object

la·të nf **1** blade used in a chopping tool **2** hatchet **3** meat cleaver **4** dressed timber; carved wooden object **5** wooden hook **6** ration coupon **7** record of a driver's traffic offenses kept with his driver's license

la·tër nf stretcher, litter

lati·cë nf = latore

latifo·nd nm **1** [Hist] latifundium **2** large landed estate

latifond·ist n **1** [Hist] latifundista **2** feudalistic large landowner

lati·m nm ger < lat·o ·n

lati·n adj Roman, Latin

latin·i·sht adv in Latin

latin·i·shte nf Latin (language)

lat·o ·n vt **1** to smooth [] by chipping/trimming: dress [wood/stone] **2** (Fig) to smooth out [a person]'s rough spots, gradually fix [a child]'s behavioral problems **3** to carve [] with an adze; carve

lato·jsë nf wood chip

lato·r adj **1** = latu·es **2** (Old) = mbla·tës

lato·re nf hatchet

lato·she nf = latore

latrape·c nm [Bot] celandine (Chelidonium majus)
∘ latrapec i madh greater celandine Chelidonium majus

la·tre·dh nm ram or billy goat that cannot be castrated because of the strangled position of the testicles

latu·a·r adj (i) (of wood or stone) dressed to provide a flat surface; carved

latu·es nm woodcarver; stonecarver

*latu·k nm tassel

*latu·r·ës n boor

latu·ri nf bungled/dirty mess

latu·ri·s· vt (Colloq) **1** to make [] all messy/dirty **2** to apply too much makeup

latu·ri·s·et vpr (Colloq) **1** to get all messy/dirty **2** to wear too much makeup

latu·ri·s·ur adj (i) (Colloq) **1** messy, dirty **2** wearing too much makeup

latu·she nf = latore

Latvi nf Latvia

laty·rë nf **1** dishwater **2** mire

*lathi nf error, mistake = lajthi·tje

*lathu·re nf [Bot] everlasting pea Lathyrus

laurea·t nm honored person, laureate

Lauresh·a nf Lauresha (female name)

laure·shë nf [Ornit] **1** crested lark = çafkëlo·re **2** skylark (Alauda arvensis)
∘ laureshë me kaçirubë/brirë [Ornit] horned lark Eremophila alpestris L., Alauda alpestris L. = kaçu·l

la·u·r nf **1** [Folklore] witch who dwells in hillside streams and ponds and can turn into a small shrieking animal **2** arbor, bower

lauro ·het vpr to win with the highest honor

lauro ·n vt **1** to award [] the highest honor **2** = lëro ·n

*lau·z nm (Old Colloq Regional Gk) = llau·z

lava·ç
I § nm (Reg) = lava·re
II § adv in a bent shape, round

lavama·n nm washbasin, sink

lavanderi nf place for doing laundry: laundry

*lava·ndë nf [Bot] common lavender (Lavandula spica)

lava·pja·të nf dishwashing sink

lava·r nm **1** = lava·re **2** (Old) lintel, arch

lava·re
I § nf **1** rope with a noose; noose; halter **2** loop used to attach or tighten **3** collar for an animal **4** rope of dried fruit **5** ornamental chain worn by girls **6** bail by which a kettle, pail or similar container is held **7** skin or feathers hanging down: dewlaps, wattles **8** link in a chain **9** [Bot] tendril **10** [Bot] catkin, ament
II § adv = lava·ç

*lavarr·ës = lavje·rrës

*lava·rr·ëz nf **1** goat's beard; dewlap **2** pot handle

lava·tri·çe nf washing machine

lava·zh nm [Med] lavage

lavd *nm* = **lëvdatë**

lavdëresë *nf (Old)* = **lëvdatë**

lavdëri *nf (Old)* **1** = **lavdi 2** = **lëvdatë**

lavdërím *nm ger* **1** <**lavdëro**·*n*, **lavdëro**·*het* **2** praise

lavdëro·*het vpr* to brag

lavdëro·*n vt* to praise, laud, extol

lavdëruar *adj (i), nm* (person) who is praised

lavdërues *adj* laudatory, praising

lavdërueshëm *adj (i)* laudable, praiseworthy

lavdí *nf* glory

lavdidashës *adj (Book)* hungry for glory

lavdidashje *nf* hunger for glory

Lavdím *nm* Lavdim (male name)

lavdimadh *adj (Poet)* full of glory: glorious

lavdiplotë *adj (Poet)* = **lavdimadh**

lavdishëm *adj (i)* glorious

****lavdo**·*n* = **lëvdo**·*n*

****lavdra** OR **lavdurí** *np* = **lëvdatë**

****lavdueshëm** *adj (i)* = **lavdërueshëm**

****lavduro**·*het* = **lëvdo**·*het*

****laver** *nm (Old)* [*Mil*] aide-de-camp

laverdhëz *nf* [*Bot*] honeysuckle (*Lonicera*)

　　∘ **laverdhëz erëkëndshme** [*Bot*] = **dorëzonjë**

lavë *nf* **1** lava ****2** *(Reg Gheg)* crowd, gang, pack

lavër *nf* **1** tillage, plowing **2** tillable land **3** piece of land that can be plowed with a yoke of oxen in a day **4** measure of age of oxen reckoned from the time they are first used for plowing

****lavërda**(*n*) *nm* = **lavërdan**

lavërdan *nm* large open space, open field

lavërtar *nm* **1** farmer using oxen for plowing: plowman **2** *(Fig)* hard worker

lavërtarí *nf* land cultivation, tillage

****lavinë** *nf* avalanche = **ortek**

lavir·*et vpr* to hang down, droop

****lavír** *stem for 2nd pl pres, pind, imper, vp* <**lavjerr**·

lavire *nf* **1** hanging tatter, rag; dirty rag **2** *(Contempt)* dirty whore **3** torrent

lavjerr· *vt* to suspend, hang, dangle

　　∘ **lavjerr**· **buzët** to pout

lavjerrë

　　I § part <**lavjerr**·

　　II § nf * (Old) waterfall

lavjerrës *nm* **1** [*Phys*] pendulum **2** hanging wickerwork feeder with fodder for livestock **3** girls' necklace

lavomë *nf (Reg)* = **plagë**

lavor *adj* of or pertaining to lava

lavor *stem for pdef* <**lavjerr**·

lavos· *vt (Reg)* = **plagos**·

lavos·*et vpr (Reg)* = **plagose**·*t*

****lavr** = **lëvr**

lavrak

　　I § adj skinny

　　II § nm * [*Ichth*] = **levrek**

****lavreshë** OR **lavroshë** *nf* = **laureshë**

lavrosë *adj (i)* ravenously hungry

****laxon** *nm* ornamental linen rug (in the countryside around Scutari)

****laxue** *nm (obl ˜ oni, pl ˜ oj) (Reg Gheg)* = **laxon**

****laxhë** *nf* goblin, gnome

laxhyhelr *nm* spangle, paillette

****laz** = **lac**

lazanjë *nf* lasagna

lazdrak *adj, n* = **ledhatar**

lazdrím *nm ger* <**lazdro**·*n*, **lazdro**·*het*

lazdro·*het vpr* = **llasto**·*het*

lazdro·*n vt* to fondle, caress; pamper

lazdruar *adj (i)* = **llastuar**

Laze *nf with masc agreement* Laze (male name)

****lazínë** *nf* paddock, corral

lazmít·*et vpr* = **lazmo**·*het*

lazmo·*het vpr* to wheedle

lazmo·*n vt* = **llasto**·*n*

****lb-** = **lëb-**

le

　　I § invar jussive pcl let

　　II § 2nd sg pdef <**lë**

　　∘ **le gomari që na ngordhi, po s'na lënë rehat as mizat** "not only did the donkey die on us, but the bugs don't leave us alone" on top of disaster, we have this nuisance

　　∘ **le që 1** let alone that, not only, not to mention, although **2** conceding that

　　∘ **le që __ por edhe __.** let alone __ but even __

　　∘ **le që __ por __.** let alone (not to mention) __ but __

　　∘ **le që __ por as (që) __.** let alone __ but not even (that) __

　　∘ **nuk** [] **le të ngrejë/çojë kokë** not let [] come into []'s own

　　∘ **le të** {*verb + subj*} (marks jussive mood of the following verb) let's __, let __ **le të shkojmë** let's go!

le·*n vi* **1** to be born = **lind**· **2** (of a heavenly body) to rise

　　∘ **le**·*n* **e mbi**·*n* **aty** "be born and grow up right there" to stay in one place, not move (away)

　　∘ <> **le**·*n* **në zemër për** [] to give rise to a desire for [] in <>

lebetí *nf (Colloq)* **1** terror, horror = **tmerr 2** cry of horror

lebetí·*n vi* = **lebetít**·

lebetís *stem for 1st sg pres, pl pres, 2nd & 3rd sg subj, pind* <**lebetít**·

lebetít·

　　I § vt (Colloq) = **tmerro**·*n*

　　II § vi (Colloq) to cry out in terror/woe

lebetít·*et vpr (Colloq)* **1** = **tmerro**·*het* **2** to cry out in terror/woe

lebetítje *nf ger* **1** *(Colloq)* <**lebetít**·, **lebetít**·*et* **2** *(Colloq)* cry of terror/woe

lebetítshëm *adj (i)* terrifying; woeful

lebetítur *adj (i)* = **tmerruar**

lebër

　　I § nf [*Med Veter*] **1** leprosy **2** mastitis, garget **3** [*Med Veter*] scabies

　　II § np <**lab** people of Labëria

lebros·*et vpr* to become leprous; (of animals) be afflicted with mastitis/garget/scabies

lebrosur *adj (i)* leprous; mastitic, gargety; scabious

lebrosh *adj* leprous

****lec** *nm (Reg Gheg)*

****lecë** *nf* maypole

lecka *np* raggedy old clothes

lecka-lecka *adj, adv* in rags, raggedy

leckamán *adj, n* **1** (person) dressed in rags **2** poverty-stricken/poor (person)

leck a nŏr *adj* clad in rags, poor

leck a pan *OR* **leck a tar** = **leckaman**

le·ckë *nf* **1** rag, tatter **2** *(Fig Pej)* person or thing of no importance

le·ckët *adj (i)* **1** raggedy *2** overburdened

leck o·s· *vt* to tear/tatter []

leck o·s·et *vpr* to become torn/tattered; get <>'s clothing torn/tattered

leck o·s je *nf ger* <**lecko·s·**, **lecko·s·**et

leck o·s ur
   I § adj (i) ragged, tattered; shabby
   II § n (i) shabbily dressed person

leck ur inë *nf* **1** rag; tattered clothes **2** *(Colloq)* swaddling clothes

*****leco·**·n *vt* **1** = **lehtë·so·**·n **2** *(Reg Gheg)* = **lexo·**·n

*****leçi** *nf (Reg Gheg)* proclamation, bann; ban

leçi s *stem for 1st sg pres, pl pres, 2nd & 3rd sg subj, pind* <**leçi t·**

leçi t· *vt* **1** to proclaim; preach **2** to read

*****leçi ta r** *n* lecturer, reader

leçi t ës *n* announcer; reader

*****leçi t je** *nf* **1** <**leçi t·** **2** proclamation

*****leçi t shëm** *adj (i)* legible

*****led i në** = **lëndi në**

ledh *nm* **1** embankment; river levee, dike **2** narrow strip of land planted with a crop, narrow patch (of a crop) **3** *(Fig)* obstacle **4** *(Colloq)* alluvial land/soil; mud

le dh as *adv* affectionately

ledh a ta r
   I § adj **1** caressing **2** pampered
   II § n **1** caresser; flatterer; cajoler **2** pampered person: pet

ledh at im *nm ger* **1** <**ledhato·**·n, **ledhato·**·het **2** = **ledh**ë

ledh ato·het *vpr* to be pampered/coddled

ledh at o··n *vt* to caress, fondle; flatter; cajole, coax

ledh at o·s· = **ledhato·**·n

ledh at u a r *adj (i)* pampered, coddled

ledh at u es *adj* caressing; pampering; cajoling

ledh at u e shëm *adj (i)* = **ledhat u es**

le dhë *nf* **1** show of affection: caress; flattery; cajolery **2** wheedling

ledh i shtë *nf* **1** area with embankments **2** = **ledhnaj**ë **3** alluvial soil; area covered by alluvial soil **4** muddy area, mudbed; mudbank

ledh naj ë *nf* fortification wall

ledh o··n *vt* to erect an embankment; surround with a fortification wall

ledh o re *nf* page margin

le dht ë *adj (i)* made of banked earth: earthen

*****lef a ta r**
   I § adj barking
   II § n dog

*****lef ten a r** *n (Old)* lieutenant = **toge r**

*****le fun** *nn (të) (Reg Gheg)* barking = **le hur**

legal *adj* legal, lawful; open and aboveboard

legal i sht *adv* legally, lawfully

legal i te t *nm (Book)* legality

Legal i te t *nm (Hist)* monarchist political party during World War II

legal iz im *nm* **1** <**legalizo·**·n **2** legalization

legal iz o··n *vt* to legalize

lega të *nf* legate, legation

lege n *nm* **1** basin, washbasin **2** *(Fig ColloqImpolite)* contemptible good-for-nothing **3** moldboard of a plow **4** *[Anat]* pelvis
   ∘ **legen i shpuar** "leaky washbasin" *(Impol)* intolerable prattler/blabbermouth

legen mbajt ëse *nf* washstand

le gë *nf* **1** measure of distance: league **2** whirlwind

*****le gë tyr ë** *nf* **1** ligament **2** cord used as a belt

leg ues *adj* *[Tech]* forming an alloy, alloying

*****legje** = **leqe**

legjend a r *adj* legendary

legjend ë *nf* legend

legjio n *nm* legion

legjion a r *n* legionnaire

legjislacio n *nm* legislation, body of laws and statues

legjislat i v *adj* legislative = **ligjvë nës**

legjislato r *n* legislator

legjislatu r ë *nf* legislature

legjit im *adj* legitimate

legjit im i te t *nm (Book)* legitimacy

leh- *vi* **1** to bark, bay, yap **2** *(Fig Scorn)* to prattle on; tell vicious gossip using dirty language
   ∘ **leh-**³ᵖˡ **si qentë në hënëz/hënë** "bark like dogs at the moon" *(Pej)* (of a group of people) to be as loud as a bunch of howling dogs

leh a qe n *nm (Disparaging)* dirty gossipmonger

*****lehco·**·n *vt* = **lehtë·so·**·n

le he *nf* **1** strip of cultivated land: bed **2** furrow; irrigation/drainage furrow

le he-le he *adv* in strips; strip by strip

leh ëro··n *vt* to divide a piece of land into cultivatable strips; cultivate a field strip by strip

le hje *nf ger* **1** <**leh·** **2** sound of barking/baying

leho n ë *nf* woman in confinement following childbirth

lehon ëri = **lehoni**

lehon i *nf* confinement period for a woman after giving birth, postpartum period: lying-in

lehon o r *adj [Med]* puerperal

le ht as *OR* **le ht azi** *adv* = **le htë**

le htë
   I § adj (i) **1** light **2** soft; gentle **3** easy **4** agile **5** dilute **6** slight **7** *(Fig)* simple-minded; frivolous
   II § nn (të) **1** being light: lightness **2** = **lehtë si** **3** = **fi kët**
   III § nm (i) (Colloq) epilepsy
   IV § adv **1** lightly; slightly **2** softly; gently **3** easily
   ∘ **lehtë e lehtë** = **le htë-le htë**
   ∘ **i lehtë nga mendja** foolish, simple-minded

le htë-le htë *adv* **1** very lightly; very slightly **2** very softly; very gently **3** very easily

leht ë si *nf* **1** easiness; facility **2** amenity; relief

lehtë s im *nm ger* **1** <**lehtë·so·**·n, **lehtë·so·**·het **2** reduction; attenuation; mitigation **3** relief; solace **4** amenity

lehtë si r ë *nf* amenity, facility

lehtë s i sht *adv* = **le htë**

lehtë s o·het *vpr* **1** to lighten one's load **2** to become lighter (in weight) **3** to get relieved; be alleviated; gain in ease **4** to be reduced/eased **5** to lose one's mind gradually, become senile
   ∘ <> **lehtë·so·**het³ᵖˡ **krahët** <> *is given a free hand*

lehtë s o·n vt 1 to reduce, lighten; mitigate, attenuate 2 to make easier: facilitate 3 to alleviate: assuage, relieve; give solace to
 ○ <>a lehtëso·n dorën to give <> a free hand
 ○ <>a lehtëso·n zemrën to relieve <>'s anxiety
lehtë s onjës = lehtësues
lehtë s or adj (fem ¯ore) = lehtësues
lehtë s ues adj 1 facilitative, easing 2 [Law] mitigating
lehtoshe nf toy balloon
leh ur
 I § nf (e) 1 = lehje 2 (Fig) yapping insult
 II § nn (të) = lehje
lei nm unit of Rumanian money: leu
leje nf 1 permission; written permit, license; authority 2 time off granted by special permission: leave
leje da lje nf = fletëdalje
leje hy rje nf = fletëhyrje
leje kal ím nm written pass: passage permit, safe-conduct pass
leje qark ull ím nm motor vehicle registration document
leje s ë nf [Tech] tolerance
lej ë = leje
lej ím nm ger 1 <lejo·n, lejo·het 2 permission; permit
*lejlla k nm [Bot] lilac
lejle k nm 1 [Ornit] stork Ciconia ciconia L. 2 [Ichth] garfish Belone belone gracilis 3 [Agr] long scythe used to mow corn 4 [Tech] monkey wrench, shifting spanner 5 (Colloq) [Tech] hoisting crane 6 (FigImpoliteJocular) thin person with long legs and neck
 ○ lejleku i zi [Ornit] black stork Ciconia nigra L.
lej o·het
 I § vp (Book) to permit oneself a right
 II § vp impers it is permissible
lej o·n vt to permit, allow
lej o r adj [Ling] concessive
*lej o s· = lejo·n
lejtmotí v nm (Book) [Mus] leitmotif = lajtmotív
*lej to re nf (Old) permit, pass
*lejthí = lajthí
lejthí z nf = lajthíshtë
leju a r adj (i) permitted
leju e shëm adj (i) permissible
leju e shm ërí nf permissibility
lek nm 1 lek, basic monetary unit of Albania equal to 100 qindarka 2 money
 ○ s'bë·n asnjë/një lek not be worth a plugged nickel, be absolutely worthless
 ○ lekë të vogla "small money" small change, small bills
*leka n nm basin, bowl; tank, reservoir
le k e adj (for sheep) having brown patches under the eyes
le k ë
 I § nf top of the head
 II § np mountaineers of Mbishkodra
Le k ë nf with masc agreement Lekë (male name)
le k ën nf [Ichth] female speckled trout
 ○ lekna e verës [Ichth] salmon trout Salmo trutta
lek íst n (Pej) person whose pursuit of money occupies all his time: money-hungry person
Leks nm Alex (male name)

leksí k nm [Ling] lexicon, vocabulary
leksiko graf nm lexicographer
leksiko grafí nf [Ling] lexicography
leksiko grafí k adj [Ling] lexicographical
leksiko gramatik o r adj [Ling] lexicogrammatical
leksik o lo g n lexicologist
leksik o logjí nf [Ling] lexicology
leksik o logjí k adj [Ling] lexicological
leksik o r adj [Ling] lexical
leksio n nm (Book) lecture
lekti·n vi = lektis·
lektí s·
 I § vi
 II § vpr to yearn/long, have a longing
lektí s·et vpr to feel a yearning/longing
 ○ <> lektís·et^{3sg} zemra për [] <> has a heartfelt longing for [], <> longs for []
lektí s je nf ger 1 <lektís·, lektís·et 2 deep longing
lektor n lecturer
*le le nf horse's mane = jele
*lele k = lejlek
le l ë adj, nf slovenly (woman)
*le m nn (të) (Reg Gheg) birth
 ○ të lemit e diellit (Reg Gheg) sunrise
lemaca k OR lemara k
 I § adj 1 greedy, gluttonous 2 miserly
 II § nm 1 glutton 2 miser
*le mc ë nf 1 uterus (of animals) 2 = lemzë
lemerí nf 1 great terror 2 multitude
*lemerím nm catastrophe, terror
lemerí s· vt to terrify
lemerí s·et vpr 1 to be terrified; cry with terror 2 (Fig Colloq) to try a hard as possible: beat one's brains out
lemerí s je nf ger 1 <lemerís·, lemerís·et (Fig Colloq) 2 utmost effort
lemerí s ur adj (i) (Colloq) 1 terrified 2 (Fig) exhausted
lemerí shëm adj (i) terrifying, dreadful
lemero·het vpr <to be overcome with terror
le m ë nf [Math Ling] lemma
*le m n ë nf [Bot] duckweed (Lemna minor)
*lemn o re np [Bot] duckweed family Lemnaceae
le mzë nf hiccough, hiccup
lemzo·n vi to have hiccoughs/hiccups
*len nm = legen
Len a nf Lena (female name)
lend nm = lende
le nde nf 1 acorn 2 pine cone
lendí nf (Reg) = mëri
*lendí n ë = lëndínë
leng nm = lëng
leni nf (Reg) 1 generation (of people); populace; nation, ethnic group 2 place, area
lenic ë nf [Ichth] = jekën
leniní st adj, n Leninist
lenini zëm nm Leninism
Len k a nf Lenka (female name)
len o·het vpr = lehtëso·het
len o·n vt (Colloq) 1 = lehtëso·n 2 = pakëso·n
lentí m nm ger <lento·n
lent o·n vt = krijo·n

leopard *nm* [*Zool*] leopard

lepe *interj (Colloq)* **1** indicates respectful attention to another person's needs or requests: yes? **2** requests repetition of something just said, but not heard well: excuse me? **3** indicates a polite request: please!

lepec *nm (Reg)* **1** ox/bull too old to work **2** *(Fig)* old and sickly person

lepericë *nf* [*Ichth*] = **gjuhëz**

*****lepër** *nf* [*Med*] leprosy

*****Lepër** *np* <**Lap**

lepidopterë *np* [*Entom*] butterflies and moths *Lepidoptera*

lepitkë *nf* **1** *(Reg)* open-heeled house slipper **2** *(Colloq)* cutting blade

lepizë *nf* blaze (on the muzzle of large livestock)

*****lepizmë** *nf* [*Entom*] silverfish *Lepisma saccharina*

leprolog *nm* [*Med*] leprologist

lepros·et
　I § *vpr*
　II § *nf* [*Med*] to contract leprosy

leprozar *nm* [*Med*] leprosarium

leprushkë *(Reg Tosk)* = **lepurushë**

leptyrë *np* <**lepur** muddy place, slippery ground

lepuj *np* <**lepur**

lepur *nm* **1** [*Zool*] hare, rabbit **2** *(FigImpolite Insult)* coward **3** *(Fig)* person who walks fast
　○ **lepur i butë** rabbit *(Oryctolagus cuniculus)*
　○ **lepur deti** [*Zool*] sea hare *Tethys*
　○ **lepur i egër** hare *(Lepus europaeus)*
　○ **Lepuri në mal e vala/kusia në zjarr** "You have the pot already on the fire, but the hare is still in the field." *(Iron)* There's many a slip 'tween cup and lip.
　○ **Kapi/zuri qeni një lepur.** "The dog caught a hare." *(Impol Iron)* Such luck strikes only once in a blue moon.

lepuras *adv*

lepurit·et *vpr* to begin to dawn; get white/light

lepurore *nf* rabbit hutch

lepurush *nm* **1** leveret, young rabbit **2** *(Pet)* bunny, bunny rabbit

lepurushë *nf* doe of the hare, female rabbit

lepurushkë *nf* **1** baby hare/rabbit **2** nanny goat with long ears **3** [*Bot*] edible mushroom with a large head

*****leq** *nm* = **lak**

leqe *nf (Colloq)* = **njollë**

leqe *np* <**lak** **1** leather thongs used to make moccasins **2** hamstrings **3** road curves; winding road

leqe-leqe
　I § *adj* very curvy; in loops
　II § *adv* with a lot of curves

leqendi *nf (Colloq)* **1** great feebleness **2** sorrow, sadness, woe, affliction

leqendis· *vt (Colloq)* **1** to make feeble: weaken **2** to sadden; afflict

leqendis·et *vpr (Colloq)* **1** to become enfeebled **2** to be afflicted, suffer woe

leqendisje *nf ger (Colloq)* **1** <**leqendis·**, **leqendis·et** **2** sadness, woe, affliction

leqendisur *adj (i) (Colloq)* physically or emotionally weakened: enfeebled, afflicted

leqenik *nm* thin corn bread made with cold water

leqetis· *vt* to make [] dirty: soil, spot

leqikë *nf* [*Bot*] **1** = **marule** **2** = **radhiqe**

leqo·n
　I § *vt* **1** to weave [moccasins] (out of leather thongs) **2** to tie on [moccasins]
　II § *vi* **1** to travel in a winding path, snake along **2** *(Fig)* to be evasive

ler *stem for 3rd sg subj, imper* <**lë·**

leranë *nf* **1** scree; stretch of sand with an accumulation of rocks; creek bed full of rocks from the mountains; river debris **2** rock heap **3** piece of wood supporting the mill axle

lerash *adj, n* **1** (person who is) muddy/dirty/filthy **2** *(Fig)* lewd (person)

*****lerdh** = **lerth**

lerë
　I § *nf* **1** thin mud; mudhole **2** grime, dirt **3** *(Fig)* opprobrium, blame **4** dirty language **5** quicksand **6** scree; stretch of sand with a accumulation of rocks; creek bed full of rocks from the mountains
　II § *adv* completely filthy

lerë
　I § *part* <**le·n** born
　II § *nn (të)* birth
　○ **të lerët e diellit** sunrise

*****lerg** *adv (Reg Gheg)* = **larg**
　○ **së lergut** from far off; in the distance

*****lergas** *adv* at a distance, distantly

*****lerje** *nf ger (Reg Tosk)* le•**n 2** birth

leros· *vt* **1** to make [] filthy: soil, dirty **2** *(Fig)* to disgrace **3** *(Fig Colloq)* to ruin

leros·et *vpr* **1** to get dirty **2** *(Fig)* to be disgraced **3** (of ground) to collapse

lerosur *adj (i)* **1** muddied, soiled; filthy **2** *(Fig Colloq)* badly ruined **3** *(Colloq)* disgraced, sullied **4** (of ground) collapsed, sunken

lerth *nm* [*Bot*] **1** = **urth** **2** field garlic *(Allium oleraceum)*

lesë *nf* **1** wattled grate, wickerwork; wicker rack/panel; small wattled gate; sledge with a wicker back; barrow **2** harrow (originally made with a wickerwork frame) **3** tassel
　○ **lesë në ujë** raft
　○ **për çdo derë/shteg ka· një lesë** there's a cure for everything, there's some way out of every problem

*****lesëm** *nf* showy adornment = **sqimë**

lesim *nm ger* <**leso·n**

leskër *nf* **1** surface fragment: flake, peeling, scale, shred **2** *(Colloq)* rag **3** *(Colloq)* spark **4** slate; layer (of bee's wax)
　○ **leskër peshku** scale of a fish, fish scale

leskëro·het *vpr* **1** to peel off, flake, scale **2** to become tattered

leskëro·n *vt* **1** to peel [] off in shreds **2** to cause [] to tatter, shred

leskëruar *adj (i)* **1** flaking, peeling **2** tattered

leskërzë *nf* thin layer: film

*****leskic** *nm* [*Zool*] squirrel = **ketër**

Leskovik *nf* town in the most southeastern part of Albania: Leskovik

leskoviqar
　I § *adj* of or pertaining to Leskovik
　II § *n* native of Leskovik

leskra-leskra *adj* **1** coming off in flakes, flaking off, peeling **2** *(Fig)* all in tatters

lesnik *nm* haystack built around a tree

lesnishtë *nf* dry wood

leso·n *vt* **1** to harrow **2** *(Fig)* to smooth [] out

lesh *nm, nn* **1** wool; hair (of an animal); (human) body hair **2** fleece **3** fuzz on plants or fruit; fuzz on insects or caterpillars **4** wooly fiber used as packing material or insulation **5** *(Fig Colloq)* tangled-up mess
  ○ **lesh arapi** tangled-up mess
  ○ **lesh barxhe** wool of little value
  ○ **lesh i kokës** hair of the head
  ○ **lesh e li** in/into disarray, in/into a hodgepodge: topsy-turvy
  ○ **të leshit e të lirit** "woolens and linens" both the good and the bad; all the dirt
  ○ **lesh xhami** glass wool

le·sh·*et vpr* **1** to start to grow hair on the face **2** *(Fig Colloq)* to start to become a man **3** (of plants) to develop a wooly surface **4** *(Pej Fig)* to try to cover up

*__**Lesh**__ *nm* = Le·zh*ë*

lesh|**a'n** *adj* = qafële·sh

lesh|**a·shp***ër adj* **1** having coarse wool **2** bushy-haired

lesh|**ata'k** *adj* **1** = leshto·r **2** shaggy

lesh|**ato·**-het *vpr* **1** to grow wool; grow shaggy **2** to fray

lesh|**ato'r** *adj* **1** wooly; shaggy **2** hairy; hirsute **3** covered with plush; downy **4** having feathered legs

lesh|**a·ve·sh** *adj, adv* helter-skelter

lesh|**ba'rdh***ë adj* having a white fleece; white-haired, gray-haired

lesh|**bozhu're** *adj* having soft and shiny reddish blond hair

lesh|**bu't***ë adj* having soft wool

lesh|**de'nd**|**ur** *adj* having thick hair

lesh|**dre'dh**|**ur** *adj* having curly wool; curly-haired

lesh|**e·g***ër adj* **1** having coarse wool **2** with disheveled hair

lesh|**e·li** *adv* in disarray

lesh|**e·mi·sh** *adv* in confusion, topsy-turvy

lesh|**ër·o·**-het *vpr* to have unkempt long hair covering the neck

lesh|**gu'r** *nm* [*Bot*] greenish-gray lichen used in folk medicine and in perfume manufacture

lesh|**ho'll***ë adj* having thin wool

*__**leshja'n**__
  I § *adj (Old)* of/from Alessio
  II § *nm* native of Alessio

le·sh|**je** *nf* **1** wool scrub brush **2** small woolen mop used to collect flour **3** pincushion **4** [*Med*] = u'rdhj*e*

le·sh|**ko** *adj, nf (with masculine agreement)* gullible/simple-minded (person): dupe

lesh|**ko'rr***ë nf (Old)* widow who affirms her vow not to remarry by shaving off her hair

lesh|**ku'q** *adj* having reddish-brown wool; red-headed, having auburn hair

lesh|**lësh**|**ua'r** *adj* = flokëlëshu·ar

lesh|**mënda'sht***ë adj (Poet)* silken-haired

lesh|**m'rru·dh'ët** *adj* = leshdre'dhur

*__**le·sh**|**na**__ *np (Reg)* **1** types of wool **2** area of a market where wool is sold

lesh|**ni·c***ë nf* [*Bot*] sharp-pointed fluellin (*Kickxia elatine*)

lesh|**ni'k** *nm* **1** wool or goathair cloak with false sleeves **2** [*Food*] dessert made of sheep's milk and flour

*__**lesh**|**nja'n**__ = lezhja'n

le·sh|**nje** *nf* [*Bot*] moss

lesh|**pala'r***ë adj* = flokëlëpala·r*ë*

*__**lesh**|**pre'**|**me**__ *nf* amazon

*__**lesh**|**pre'**|**me***__ *adj* **1** (of girls) with bobbed hair, with hair cut short **2** frivolous

lesh|**pre'r**
  I § *adj* = flokëpre·r*ë*
  II § *nf (Old)* = leshko'rr*ë*

lesh|**pun**|**u'es**
  I § *adj* wool-working
  II § *n* wool worker

le·sh|**ra** *np* <lesh **1** fleeces; wools **2** (human) hair (on the head)

lesh|**ra·ba'rdh***ë adj* gray-haired

lesh|**ra·de'nd**|**ur** *adj* = flokëde'ndur

lesh|**ra·dre'dh**|**ur** *adj* = flokëdre'dhur

lesh|**ra·gja't***ë adj* = flokëgja't*ë*

lesh|**ra·ku'q** *adj* = flokëkuq

lesh|**ra·lësh**|**ua'r** *adj* = flokëlëshu·ar

lesh|**ra·pre'r***ë adj, nf* = leshpre·r*ë*

lesh|**ra·shku'rt***ër adj* = flokëshku·rtër

lesh|**ra·thi'nj**|**ur** *adj* = flokëthi·njur

lesh|**ra·ve'rdh***ë adj* = flokëve'rdhur

lesh|**ra·zi** *adj (fem sg ˜ e'z, masc pl ˜ i'nj, fem pl ˜ eza)* = flokëzi

lesh|**rë'n***ë adj* **1** = flokërë·n*ë* **2** having wool that has fallen out

lesh|**shit**|**ë's** *n* wool merchant

lesh|**shku'rt***ër adj* **1** = flokëshku·rtër **2** having short wool

lesh|**ta'k** *adj* [*Bot*] **1** hairy, hirsute **2** having long thin fibers

lesh|**tak**|**ë'si** *nf* [*Med*] excessive hairiness: pilosity

lesh|**teri'k** *nm* [*Bot*] **1** seaweed, alga **2** eel-grass, grass-wrack (*Zostera marina*) **3** [*Invert*] (*Posidonia oceanica*)
  ○ **leshterik deti** [*Bot*] eel-grass, grass-wrack (*Zostera marina*)
  ○ **leshterik kënete** [*Bot*] kind of eel-grass (*Zostera noltii*)

le·sh|**të**
  I § *adj (i)* **1** woolen; wooly **2** of sheep, ovine **3** *(Colloq)* rich, wealthy **4** *(Fig)* warm, honest, and generous **5** thickheaded, stupid
  II § *nf(e)* **1** woolen cloth: woolen **2** *(Euph)* epilepsy
  III § *nn (të)* = lesh
  ○ **leshtë e barkut** "belly hair" **1** *(Crude)* absolutely nothing, nothing at all **2** *(Iron)* that's a laugh! big chance! oh sure!
  ○ **të leshtat dhe të dhirtat** sheep and goats
  ○ **të leshtat e të linjtat** "woolens and linens" both the good and the bad; all the dirt
  ○ **Leshtë e ujkut, thonjtë e bufit** "Hair of a wolf, claws of an owl" *(Prov)* Sometimes it is necessary to use raw force.

le·sht|**ërr** *nf* [*Bot*] Alpine epimedium (*Epimedium alpinum*)

lesh|**to'k** *adj, n* = leshta'k

lesh|**to'r** *adj* **1** = leshato·r **2** = le·sht*ë*

lesh|**to'rm***ë adj (i)* having long thick wool/hair

le·sh|**ur** *adj (i)* **1** having thick wool/hair **2** *(Fig)* thick-headed

lesh|**ve'rdh***ë adj* **1** = flokëve·rdh*ë* **2** having yellowish-tinged wool

lesh|**zi** *adj (fem sg ˜ e'z, masc pl ˜ i'nj, fem pl ˜ eza)* **1** = flokëzi **2** having dark wool

*letanore *nf* lining of the stomach

letargji *nf* **1** lethargy **2** [*Biol*] hibernation

letargjik *adj* **1** [*Biol*] hibernating **2** lethargic

*letas *OR* **letazi** *adv* (*Old*) = **lehtas**

*letë *adj* (*i*) (*Old*) = **lehtë**

letër *nf* **1** paper **2** sheet of paper; page **3** written message: letter **4** official letter, credentials; document **5** playing card
  ○ **letër ankimi** [*Law*] written complaint
  ○ **letër bakalli** (*Pej*) sloppy writing on grimy paper
  ○ **letër dashurie** love letter
  ○ **letër detyrimi** [*Law*] written order
  ○ **letër dylli** mimeograph stencil
  ○ **letër gjykimi** [*Law*] written judgment
  ○ **letër e hapur 1** = **letër qarkore 2** open letter
  ○ **letër higjenike** toilet paper
  ○ **letër karboni** carbon paper
  ○ **letër katramaje** tar paper
  ○ **letër katramat** = **katrama**
  ○ **letër kopjative** carbon paper
  ○ **letra kredenciale** (diplomatic) credentials = **letërkredenciale**
  ○ **letër me vlerë** [*Fin*] negotiable instrument; certificate
  ○ **letër milimetrike** graph paper
  ○ **letër e mirë** winning card
  ○ **letër njoftimi** = **letërnjoftim**
  ○ **letër parafine** wax paper
  ○ **letër përfaqsimi** (*Old*) [*Law*] written authorization; warrant
  ○ **letër e porositur** registered letter
  ○ **letër qamatar** (*Old*) letter of complaint
  ○ **letër qarkore** *= **qarkore**
  ○ **letër e vdekur** (*Book*) dead issue, dead matter
  ○ **letër zotimi** (*Old*) [*Law*] promissory note, bond

*letërftesë (*Old*) [*Law*] subpoena, summons

letërgaranci *nf* (*Offic Old*) = **fletëgaranci**

letërkëmbim *nm* correspondence

letërkredenciale *np* (diplomatic) credentials

letërmarrës *n* addressee

*letërndarës *n* (*Old*) postman

letërnjoftim *nm* identification document: identity card

letërpërcjellëse *nf* = **fletëshoqërim**

letërprerëse *nf* letter-opener

letërprurës *n* letter carrier

letërsi *nf* literature

letërshkëmbim = **letërkëmbim**

letërshkrues *nm* letter writer

letërshpërndarës *n* mailman, postman, letter carrier

letërthirrje *nf* = **fletëthirrje**

letërthithëse *nf* blotting paper: blotter

leto·*het vpr* to go dotty

leton *adj, n* Latvian

Letoni *nf* Latvia

letonisht *adv* in Lettish (language)

letonishte *nf* Latvian, Lettish (language)

letra *np* **1** = **letër 2** (*Old*) letters = literature

*letrandamës = **letërndarës**

letrar
  I § *adj* literary
  II § *n* literary person: man of letters

*letrari *nf* (*Old*) = **literaturë**

*letrator *adj, n* = **letrar**

*letratyrë *nf* (*Old*) = **literaturë**

leucemi *nf* [*Med*] leukemia

leukocit *nm* [*Physiol*] leucocyte

leukoplast *nm* [*Med*] adhesive bandage, sticking plaster, Band-Aid

*levand *nm* lavender = **livandë**

levarash *adj* **1** very energetic, constantly moving **2** unstable, changeable, shifting **3** (*Fig*) having loose morals

levend *adj* (*Colloq*) frisky, spry

levenxë *nf* wool blanket

leverdi *nf* (*Colloq*) profit, gain, advantage, interest, benefit

leverdi·s· *vi* (*Colloq*) to be profitable, be advantageous/fruitful

leverdishëm *adj* (*i*) profitable, advantageous, fruitful

leverdishmëri *nf* profitability, fruitfulness

levë *nf* **1** [*Phys*] lever **2** [*Tech*] steering lever **3** (*Fig*) initiating mechanism **4** monetary unit of Bulgaria: lev
  ○ **levë stakimi** [*Tech*] trip rod

*levis *OR* **leviz** = **lëviz**

*levore = **lëvore**

levrek *nm* **1** [*Ichth*] sea bass (*Dicentranchus labrax L.*) **2** (*Fig*) spry/agile person
  ○ **levrek pikalosh** [*Ichth*] common guppy *Licentrarchus punctatus*

lexim *nm ger* **1** < **lexo**·*n*, **lexo**·*het* [*Tech*] **2** instructions for operation of a device
  ○ **lexim jashtë klase** reading for homework: outside reading
  ○ **lexim letrar** literary anthology (with helpful questions and explanatory notes) used in grammar schools

lexo·*het vpr* to be legible

lexo·*n vt* to read
  ○ **lexo**·*n në mes të radhëve/rreshtave* (*Book*) to read between the lines

lexues *nm* person who reads, person who is reading: reader

lexueshëm *adj* (*i*) legible

lez *nm* **1** facial mole **2** (*Med*) wart

leza *nm* **1** crossbar on which grapevines are hung **2** thin wooden stick on which meat and sausages are hung for drying

lezbike *adj, nf* lesbian

lezbizëm *nm* [*Med*] lesbianism

leze *nf* = **lez**

lezeçëm = **lezetshëm**

lezet *nm* (*Colloq*) **1** flavor **2** pleasure **3** (*Fig*) nice; nice-looking
  ○ **{girl} me lezet** nice-looking girl

lezetar *adj, n* (*Colloq*) (person) having grace and beauty

lezeto·*het vpr* (*Colloq*) **1** to gain good flavor **2** to become good-looking
  ○ **<> lezeto**·*het* to begin to be pleasant for <>, <> starts to enjoy {}

lezeto·*n vt* (*Colloq*) **1** to flavor **2** to make [] pleasurable **3** to make [] good-looking, give [] a fine appearance

lezetshëm *adj* (*i*) (*Colloq*) **1** delicious, tasty, savory, good-tasting **2** good-looking **3** pleasant

*lezëm *adv* quietly, in a whisper

lezio·n *nm* [*Med*] lesion

lez·u·a·r *adj (i)* pleased, content

Le·zhë *nf* town and district in northwestern Albania: Alessio, Lezha, Lesh

lezhja·n

I § *adj* of or pertaining to Lezha (Alessio); made/done/created by people in Lezha

II § *n* native of Lezha

lezhja·n·e *nf* **1** female from Lezha **2** southern wind blowing through the Lezha mountain pass toward Shkodra (Scutari) and bringing bad weather with much rain

lë· *vt* **1** to leave **2** to leave [] behind: lose; forget; leave [] as inheritance **3** to leave [] out: omit, miss **4** to leave/let [] alone, allow [] to stay **5** to let **6** to let go: release **7** to give up []; stop using/doing [], cease; stop producing [] **8** to put, set

○ [] **lë·** {*adverbial*} to ruin [] {*in some way/place, by some means*}

○ **lë·** **amanet** to make one's final wishes (before dying)

○ [] **lë·** **amanet** to leave [] as (part of) one's final wishes

○ **lë·** **arallëk** to leave room, give free entry

○ **lë·** **armët** to lay down one's arms: stop fighting, stop resisting, surrender

○ **nuk <> lë·** **baltë nën thua** not omit even the most sordid details about <>: spill all of <>'s dirty little secrets

○ **nuk e lë·** **barutin të laget** to keep one's powder dry, stay prepared to fight

○ **<>[] lë·** **barrë** to give over [a responsibility] to <>, leave [] in <>'s charge

○ [] **lë·** **biçak** to leave [] without a shirt on his back, leave [] with nothing

○ **lë·** **bishtin** to take to one's heels suddenly, escape suddenly

○ **<> lë·** **çetën 1** to put the blame on <> **2** to cheat/deceive <>

○ **i lë·** **çetëzën** to make and hit in such a game and yield one's turn to an opponent

○ **s'<>a lë·** **dalë** "not let <> get ahead" to be inferior in no way to <>, be just as good as <>

○ **lë·** **dasmën e shko·n për shkarpë** "leave the wedding and go looking for kindling" to abandon an urgent task for something of no urgency

○ [] **lë·** **daulle** to leave [] with nothing, not leave [] a thing

○ **e lë·** **derëbabën** to get married (of women only)

○ **s'<> lë·** **din e iman** (*Colloq*) to leave nothing out in one's vigorous criticism of <>, blast <> with both barrels

○ **<>a lë·** **dobiçin në derë/prehër** (*Crude*) to lay one's own blame at <>'s door; leave <> holding the bag

○ **<>a lë·** **doçin në derë/prehër** (*Crude*) to lay one's own blame at <>'s door; leave <> holding the bag

○ [] **lë·**^{3sg} **drita (e syve)** "the light *goes out* (of []'s) eyes" [] *loses* []'s sight, [] *goes* blind

○ **nuk lë·** **dy gurë bashkë** to be mischievous

○ [] **lë·** **dyshek** "leave [] like flat as a mattress" to kill [] dead

○ **e lë·** **dyshekun** to leave one's sickbed

○ **lë·** **dhomën me pleh e fshi·n oborrin** "leave the living room filthy and sweep out the garden" to neglect what is important and do what is unimportant

○ [] **lë·**^{3sg} **fiqiri** [] *loses* his senses/mind

○ **s'e lë·** **fjalën të bjerë në tokë/përdhe/përtokë** "not let a word fall on the ground" to be very bright and alert

○ **<> lë·** **fushë të lirë** to allow <> complete freedom; open the gates wide for <>

○ [] **lë·** **gisht** to leave with [] nothing, abandon [] with no means of support

○ **<> lë·** **glasën** "leave <> birdshit" (*CrudeImpolite*) to leave <> unexpectedly; leave <> high and dry

○ **<>a lë·** **gozhdë** to give <> a gnawing feeling in <>'s innards

○ **nuk lë·** **gur në këmbë 1** to leave no stone unturned **2** to get into everything

○ **nuk lë·** **gur mbi gur** to get into everything; be mischievous

○ **nuk lë·** **gur pa lëvizur/luajtur/trazuar/kthyer** to leave no stone unturned

○ **nuk lë·** **gjemb këmbë** to leave nothing standing, destroy everything

○ **s'<> lë·** **gjë mangët/metë** "be missing nothing that <> has" to be inferior in no way to <>, be just as good as <>

○ **nuk lë·** **gjë në sofër** "not leave anything on the table (to eat)" to eat everything in sight, be a glutton

○ **s'<> lë·** **gjë pa thënë** to lambaste <> in the strongest possible language

○ **nuk lë·** **gjë për sofër** "not leave anything for the table" ready to do any work, quick to do work, unhesitant to work

○ [] **lë·**^{3sg} **gjiri** []'s breast *stops* giving milk

○ **e lë·** **gjirin** "leave the breast" (of a baby) to stop nursing, be weaned

○ [] **lë·** **havadan** to leave [] in the lurch; leave [] hanging

○ **<> lë·** **hije të zezë** to leave a black cloud over <>: dishonor <>, shame <>

○ **<> lë·** **hijen** "leave <> one's shadow" (*Iron*) to leave <> unexpectedly and rudely: leave <> flat, leave without so much as a by your leave

○ **nuk lë·**^{3sg} **hunda të hajë/kullotë bar** (*Tease*) []'s nose is so high up in the air that [] can't see the ground: [] is stuck up

○ [] **lë·** **jashtë valles** "leave [] out of the dance" leave [] out, not include []

○ [] **lë·** **jashtë vëmendjes** to leave [] out of consideration, take no interest in []

○ **e lë·** **jatakun** to leave one's sickbed

○ [] **lë·** **kalli** to leave [] with nothing, not leave [] a thing

○ **<>a lë·** **kapelën mbi ujë** "leave <>'s hat on the water" (*Impol*) to drown <>

○ **lë·** **kockat 1** to lose one's life: leave one's bones to dry **2** to put in a lot of hard work and suffering

○ **i lë·** **kockat rrugëve/udhëve** to die far from home and family, die in the streets

○ **lë·** **kokën/kryet** to die as a result of one's actions: lose one's life

○ **lë·** **kokën/kryet për** [] to be willing to die for []; be totally devoted to []

○ **<>a lë·** **kokën poshtë** "leave <> head down" to cause shame to fall on <>

○ [] **lë·** **kopan** "leave [] dead as a log" to kill [] dead

○ **<>a lë·** **kopilin në derë/prehër** (*Crude*) to lay one's own blame at <>'s door; leave <> holding the bag

○ **<>a lë·** **koren te dera** "leave one's shame at <>'s door" to leave <> to face the disgrace (caused by <>)

○ **e lë·** **krevatin** to leave one's sickbed

○ **nuk <> lë· kusur** to let loose an endless stream of verbal abuse on <>

○ [ ] **lë· lakror** to leave [the matter] unclear

○ [ ] **lë· lakuriq** to leave [ ] destitute

○ **lë· lamtumirën** to say goodbye, bid farewell

○ <> **lë· lamtumirën** to say goodbye to <> forever

○ [ ] **lë· lehe** to give [ ] up, abandon [ ]

○ <> **lë· leqe** to leave <> a stain on <>'s honor

○ [ ] **lë·^{3pl} leqet e këmbëve** "the sinews of the legs release [ ]" [ ]'s legs *won't* hold [ ] up (because [ ] is so old/sick/scared)

○ **lë· lesh kudo** to keep on the move, never settle anywhere; never sit still

○ **lë· leshin në vrimë** "leave one's fleece in the hole" to come out a big loser, lose one's shirt

○ **lë· leshtë e kokës për** [ ] "leave the hair of one's head for [ ]" to devote a lot of effort to [ ]; be willing to die for [ ]

○ **lë· leshtë 1** to lose one's life: leave one's bones to dry **2** to put in a lot of hard work and suffering

○ [ ] **lë· në letër** (*Book*) to leave [ ] undone

○ **lë· lëkurën 1** to die as a result of one's actions: lose one's life, leave one's bones to dry **2** to put in a lot of hard work and suffering; knock oneself out trying, break one's back

○ [ ] **lë· lëmsh** "leave [ ] collapsed in a lump" to kill [ ] dead

○ [ ] **lë· lëmuq (përdhe)** to hit [ ] and leave [ ] for dead

○ <>**i lë· lëpendrat në dorë** "leave one's feathers in <>'s hand" to escape cleverly from <>'s clutches, slip out of <>'s hands

○ **i lë· litarët zvarrë** "let the ropes drag" to be slack in one's work

○ **nuk ta lë· mangët për nesër** "not put off responding to you until tomorrow" to be quick in repartee, be fast on one's feet in an argument

○ <> **lë· mbarre** to bring shame upon <>, disgrace <>

○ [ ] **lë· me duar në gji** to leave [a woman] alone and forsaken

○ [ ] **lë· me duar në ije** to cause [ ] to hold [ ]'s sides with laughter

○ **e lë· me fjalë** to agree on it in advance

○ [ ] **lë· me fjalë në gojë** "leave [ ] with words in [ ]'s mouth" to leave [ ] frustrated because [ ] hasn't finished talking: leave [ ] with a mouth full of words

○ [ ] **lë· me gisht në gojë** to leave [ ] with nothing, not leave [ ] a thing

○ [ ] **lë· me këmbë të lira** to allow complete [ ] freedom of action

○ **e lë· me thonj në trokë** to leave [ ] with nothing, not leave [ ] a thing

○ [ ] **lë·^{3sg} mendja** [ ] *loses* his senses/mind

○ **lë· mendjen pas <> 1** to be spellbound by <>; be astonished by <> **2** to lose one's head over <>, be crazy about <>

○ [ ] **lë·^{3pl} mendtë** "[ ]'s brains leave [ ]" [ ]'s brains go out of [ ]'s head, [ ] *loses* [ ]'s mind

○ **nuk ta lë· metë për nesër** "not put off responding to you until tomorrow" to be quick in repartee, be fast on one's feet in an argument

○ **lë· nam** to achieve notoriety; get a (bad) reputation

○ <> **lë· nder** to bring honor upon <>

○ <>[ ] **lë· në kurriz/shpinë** to lay [ ] on <>; blame [ ] on <>

○ [ ] **lë· në ahe** to leave [ ] in misery

○ **lë· në ahur** treat badly

○ [ ] **lë· në arkiv** (*Book*) to relegate [ ] to oblivion, file [ ] away forever

○ [ ] **lë· në baltë** to leave [ ] in the lurch

○ <>[ ] **lë· në besë** to entrust [something valuable] to <>

○ <>a **lë· në daltë** to outwit <>

○ <>[ ] **lë· në dorë** to leave [ ] in <>'s hands

○ <>a **lë· në dorë** to lay the blame on <>

○ [ ] **lë· në gjumë** to leave [ ] on the shelf, leave [ ] undone/undisturbed

○ [ ] **lë· në hava** to leave [ ] in the lurch; leave [ ] hanging

○ [ ] **lë· në heshtje 1** not mention [ ] **2** not deal with [ ], put [ ] aside

○ [ ] **lë· në hije** to keep [ ] secret/hidden: keep [ ] under wraps

○ [ ] **lë· në mes të katër rrugëve** to abandon [ ] completely

○ [ ] **lë· në mes të katër udhëve** to kick [ ] out into the street

○ [ ] **lë· në mes të rrugës** "leave in the middle of the road/highway" **1** to quit [ ] half way through, leave [ ] half done **2** to abandon [ ] completely

○ [ ] **lë· në mes të udhës 1** to kick [ ] out into the street **2** to leave [ ] undone/unfinished: leave [ ] in the middle

○ [ ] **lë· në mes** to leave [ ] half done, leave [ ] unfinished

○ [ ] **lë· në mëshirë të fatit** "leave [ ] to the mercy of fate" to abandon [ ] to the elements, abandon [ ] completely

○ [ ] **lë· në një cep** to put [ ] aside, abandon [ ]

○ <>[ ] **lë· në qafë** "hang [ ] onto <>'s neck" to place [a burden] on <>

○ [ ] **lë· në qull** to leave [ ] in hot water, leave [ ] in the lurch

○ [ ] **lë· në rrugë të madhe** to abandon [ ] completely

○ [ ] **lë· në rrugë** "leave in the middle of the road/highway" **1** to quit [ ] half way through, leave [ ] half done **2** to abandon [ ] completely

○ **e lë· në shportën e lugëve** to keep [ ] secret, not tell [ ] to anyone

○ <>a **lë· në tallagan** to deceive/cheat <>

○ [ ] **lë· në të vetën/tijën/sajën/tyrën** to let [ ] go on, give [ ] his/her/their head **e lashë Agimin në të tijën** I let Agim go on **i lë në të tyrën** she gives them their head

○ <>a **lë· në trastë** to cheat <> by browbeating, deceptively push <> into a bad bargain

○ [ ] **lë· në udhë (të madhe)** to kick [ ] out into the street

○ [ ] **lë· në udhë** to leave [ ] undone/unfinished: leave [ ] in the middle

○ [ ] **lë· në vend** to kill [ ] with a single blow; knock [ ] down; drop [ ] with a single shot

○ [ ] **lë· në zall** to leave [ ] in the lurch

○ [ ] **lë· në rrenë/gënjeshtër** to double-cross [ ]

○ [ ] **lë· në rrenë** to break one's promise and leave [ ] in the lurch

○ **s'[ ] lë· nga goja** never cease to speak (well) of [ ], praise [ ] constantly

○ <> **lë një qime ujku te dera** "leave a wolf hair at <>'s door" to leave <> with a mess to clean up, leave <> with a messy problem to solve

○ [ ] **lë· pa fuqi** (*Book*) to leave [a law] without force, nullify = **shfuqizo'·n**

○ <> **lë· pa mend/gojë** to take <>'s breath away

○ [ ] **lë· pa sy** "leave [ ] without eyes" to blind [ ]

○ [] **lë· pa veshë** "leave [] without ears" to deafen []

○ **nuk e lë· pa** {*intransitive verb participle*} not fail to {*verb*}

○ **nuk** [] **lë· pa** {*transitive verb participle*} leave no [] un-{*verb past participle*}: not fail to {} []

○ [] **lë· pas dore** to neglect []: let [] go to pot

○ **<>***i* **lë· pendët** "leave one's feathers to <>" (*Iron*) to leave <> unexpectedly: leave <> high and dry, leave <> flat

○ **<> lë· pendët** "take one's final leave of <>" (*Impol*) to die on <>

○ [] **lë· (si) peng 1** to give [] as hostage **2** to pawn/ mortgage []

○ **<>***a* **lë· peng** to give <> a gnawing feeling in <>'s innards

○ [] **lë· pikë gjallë** to kill [] on the spot

○ [] **lë· pirg** "leave [] collapsed in a heap" (*Colloq*) to kill [] dead

○ **<>***a* **lë· plumbin në lëkurë/mish** "leave the bullet in <>'s skin/flesh" to say something disquieting to <>: plant a seed of worry in <>

○ *i* **lë· potkonjtë** "leave one's horseshoes" (*Scorn*) to kick the bucket: die

○ **e lë· punën bllacë** to leave the job unfinished

○ **e lë· punën në gjysmë** to leave things in the middle

○ *i* **lë· punët gjetur** "leave matters as found" to leave matters as they are

○ **<>***i* **lë· puplat** "leave one's feathers to <>" (*Iron*) to leave <> unexpectedly: leave <> high and dry, leave <> flat

○ [] **lë· pykë** to leave/knock [] flat on the ground; leave [] dead on the spot

○ [] **lë· qull** to let [] go to pot; leave [] unfinished/ undone

○ **<> lë· radhë** to give way to <>, let <> go first; let [] have []'s way

○ [] **lë· rehat** to leave [] in peace: leave [] alone

○ **e lë· rrashtën** {*somewhere*} "leave one's skull" to leave one's bones to dry {*somewhere*}

○ **<> lë· rrikën** to blame the whole thing on <>

○ **lë· rruazën (duke punuar)** to break one's back (working)

○ **<> lë· rrugë 1** to deliberately try to forget <>: put <> behind one **2** to let <> go/leave <> **3** to let <> have the right of way: give way to <>

○ **<>***a* **lë· samarin nën bark** "leave <>'s packsaddle under the belly" to leave <> in a terrible predicament

○ [] **lë·***³ᵖˡ* **sendet** "the things all left []" [] *is* left with nothing

○ [] **lë· si carani i vatrës** to abandon [], leave [] alone in the world

○ **s'<> lë· sy e faqe** to make <> ashamed to look anyone in the face

○ **lë· sytë pas <>** to be captivated by <>'s beauty

○ [] **lë· shajak** to leave [work] in a bad state

○ [] **lë· shakull** "leave [] collapsed like a leather pouch" to kill [] dead

○ **<> lë· shesh të lirë** to allow <> complete freedom; open the gates wide for <>

○ **lë· shëndenë 1** to take leave, bid farewell **2** (*Euph*) to pass away, die

○ **<> lë· shëndetin** to bid farewell to <> "take one's final leave of <>: die on <>"

○ [] **lë· shirk** (*Impol*) to leave [] collapsed and lifeless on the ground: kill []

○ [] **lë· shkretë e lugëthatë** to leave [] with absolutely nothing, leave [] high and dry

○ **lë· shteg (për** []**) 1** to leave/raise doubts (about []) **2** to open a path (for [])

○ **<> lë· shteg 1** to leave/raise doubts (about <>) **2** to make way for <>; open a path for <>; leave room for <>

○ **e lë· shtratin** to leave one's sickbed

○ **lë· shtratin** to get out of bed; get well

○ **<>**[] **lë· shtupë** to leave [] to <> in a mess

○ [] **lë· shul** to leave [] without finishing

○ [] **lë· shurdh** to leave an empty space in []'s life, leave [] the worse

○ **<>**[] **lë· takë** to give <> a gnawing feeling in <>'s innards []

○ **<>***a* **lë· tangë 1** to give <> a gnawing feeling in <>'s innards **2** to leave <> in debt

○ **nuk** [] **lë· të bë· çap** not let [] make a single move

○ **s'**[] **lë· të bjerë përdhe** not let [an opportunity] slip through one's fingertips

○ **nuk** [] **lë· të gjallë** not allow [] to remain alive

○ **s'<> lë· të krua·***nn^{pres, imperf}* **dhëmbin** "not let <> even pick <>'s teeth" to be constantly on <>'s back, never allow <> to do anything

○ [] **lë· të shurdhër** to leave an empty space in []'s life, leave [] the worse

○ **lë· të vdekurin e shko·***n* **në dasmë** "leave the funeral and go to a wedding" (*Pej*) to leave urgent work for the sake of something less urgent

○ [] **lë· të qetë** to leave [] in peace, let [] be

○ **e lë· tokën bar** to leave land fallow

○ [] **lë· top** "leave [] collapsed in a clump" to kill [with a single blow/shot, kill [] dead

○ **S'të lënë topat të dëgjosh dyfekët.** "The cannon don't allow you to hear the rifles." (*Prov*) When something really bad happens to you, you forget about your less serious problems.

○ [] **lë· trashë** to leave [] whole (not cut [] up)

○ **<>***a* **lë· turpin te dera** "leave one's shame at <>'s door" to leave <> to face the disgrace (caused by <>)

○ **s'e lë· thatë 1** to be no chump, be nobody's fool **2** to be as good as anyone, do as well as anyone

○ [] **lë· thes në vend** to leave [] dead on the spot/ ground

○ [] **lë· thes** "leave [] collapsed like a sack" to kill [] dead

○ **lë· uniformën** to quit the (military) service

○ **<> lë· uratën 1** to die (and leave one's blessing on <>) **2** (*Iron*) to leave <> forever, wave goodbye to <> for good

○ [] **lë· vakëf** to devastate [], leave [] in ruin

○ **lë· vend për dyshime** to leave room for doubt

○ *i* **lë· vend vetes** "leave a place for oneself" to leave in good repute

○ **<> lë· veshët në lesh** to turn a deaf ear to <>; not give a thought to <>, not think about <>

○ **e lë· vrapin** to take a rest after great exertion, hold up

○ **nuk lë· vrimë pa u futur** "not leave a hole unentered" to stick one's big nose into everything

○ **Lë zanat e zë zurnanë.** "Leave a profession and take up an aulos (musical instrument)." Quit one's job to join the circus.

○ **S'më lënë zilet e mia të dëgjoj këmboret e tua.** "My bells don't let me to listen to your chimes." I can't take on your troubles because I have too many of my own. That's all I need: somebody else's problems!

◦ **Nuk më lënë zilet e mia të dëgjoj çokanet e tua.** "My bells don't let me hear your hammer." *(Prov)* I've got trouble enough of my own without worrying about yours.

lëbardh·
I § *vt* to give [ ] a white appearance
II § *vi* = lëbardh·*et*

lëbardh·et *vpr* **1** to have a white appearance, shine white **2** to dawn

lëbardhë
I § *nf* early dawn
II § *adj* **1** whitish; white **2** fair-haired, blond

lëbarke *nf (Colloq) [Med]* dysentery

lëbyr *nm [Anat]* filmy membrane over the eye

lëbyr· *vt* **1** to veil [the eyes] with a hazy film **2** to veil **3** *(Fig)* to dazzle/blind **4** *(Fig)* to spend [one's time] in depressing darkness
◦ **<>a lëbyr· mendjen** to confound/bewilder <>

lëbyr·et *vpr* **1** to have a hazy film veiling one's eyes **2** *(Fig)* to become dazzled/blinded

lëbyrës *adj* blinding

lëbyrje *nf ger* **1** <lëbyr·, lëbyr·et **2** blinding light, glare

lëbyrtë *adj (i)* faint, faded

lëçis *stem for 1st sg pres, pl pres, 2nd & 3rd sg subj, pind* <lëçit·

lëçit· *vt (Old)* = lexo·*n*

lëçitës *n (Old)* = lexues

lëçitje *nf ger (Old)* = lexim

*lëdinë = lëndinë

lëfar· *vt (Reg)* to destroy totally

lëfar·et *vpr (Reg)* to disappear without a trace

*lëfetë = lëpjetë

lëfore *nf* = lëvore

lëfos *nm* glutton

lëfostër *nf* seed husk

*lëftim *nm* heartbeat

*lëfto·n *vt* = lufto·*n*

lëfyt
I § *nm* **1** throat **2** spout
II § *adv* spouting out in a thin stream, spurting

lëkitër *nf [Zool]* = ketër

lëkojë *nf* **1** fruit rind *2 stagnant pond

lëkoq *nm* = latredh

lëkore *nf* **1** *[Bot]* phloem; bast **2** filmy layer/skin that forms on a surface: scab, scum, film **3** *[Bot]* chicory = radhiqe

lëkostër *nf* **1** *[Bot]* phloem; bast *()* **2** *[Bot]* skin/rind of fruit; seed husk **3** crust/film that forms on a surface

lëkua *nm (obl ˜o i, np ˜onj) [Bot]* European white water lily *(Nymphaea alba)*

*lëkujmë *adj (i)* reddish

lëkund· *vt* to cause back and forth motion: shake [ ], vibrate [ ], rock [ ]
◦ **<>a lëkund· zemrën** to touch <>'s heart: touch <> deeply, move <> (emotionally); disturb/upset <>

lëkund·et *vpr* **1** to move back and forth: shake, vibrate, quake; rock **2** to waver; hesitate, be reluctant

lëkundës *nm* **1** children's swing, seesaw **2** *[Spec]* pump/jack that works by a rocking motion **3** indecisiveness, vacillation, fickleness

lëkundje *nf ger* **1** <lëkund·, lëkund·et **2** movement with back and forth motion: shaking, vibrating, rocking, quaking, oscillation **3** wavering, hesitation

lëkundshëm *adj (i)* **1** shaky, wobbly **2** wavering, hesitant **3** weak and unstable

lëkundur *adj (i)* **1** wavering, hesitant **2** weak and unstable

lëkuq
I § *n* livestock animal with reddish-brown hair
II § *adj (i)* having a reddish tinge

lëkuq·
I § *vt* to give [ ] a reddish tinge
II § *vi* to have a reddish tinge

lëkuq·et *vpr* to get a red tinge; blush

lëkuqe *nf* infertile reddish soil

lëkur· *vt* to turn [ ] into skin and bones: emaciate

lëkur·et *vpr* to turn into skin and bones: become emaciated

lëkurashpër *adj* having rough skin

lëkuraxhi *nm (np ˜ nj)* leather tanner: currier

lëkurçë *nf* **1** short sheepskin cloak **2** sheepskin rug **3** small leather pouch **4** lambskin sheath used over a broomhead to apply whitewash to walls; whitewash applier **5** fruit rind; seed husk

lëkurë *nf* **1** outer covering layer: skin, hide (of animal); rind/husk/pod (of fruit/seed/vegetable); bark (of a tree) **2** leather; pelt **3** *(Colloq)* leather bag for food **4** outer cover; outer appearance **5** gristle, cartilage
◦ **<>a bëfshin lëkurën def!** *(Prov Crude)* May they make <>'s skin into a tambourine-head!
◦ **<>a bëri lëkura** "<>'s skin did it" <> has only <>self to blame
◦ **ta krip· lëkurën** { } would skin you alive, { } would take you for everything you've got
◦ **lëkurë e njomë** fresh pelt, unprocessed hide
◦ **ësh-të³ˢᵍ lëkurë për të hequr** to be something that simply *has* to be done, be unavoidable
◦ **lëkurë e regjur** leather
◦ **<>u thaftë lëkura e barkut!** "May the skin of <>'s belly go dry!" *(Curse)* May <> never bear a child!

lëkurëbardhë
I § *adj* having light-colored skin
II § *nm* **1** person of Caucasian race **2** fair-skinned person **3** fruit with light-colored skin

lëkurëbutë *adj* soft-skinned, tender-skinned

lëkurëfishkur *adj* having wrinkled skin

lëkurëgjemborë *np [Spec]* echinoderms

lëkurëhollë *adj* thin-skinned

lëkurëkuq
I § *adj* red-skinned
II § *nm* redskin, American Indian

lëkurëlëmuar *adj* smooth-skinned

lëkurënxirë *adj* tanned (by the sun)

lëkurëplasur *adj* **1** (of fruit) burst open from ripeness **2** (of people) having erupted skin

lëkurëpunues
I § *adj* leather working
II § *n* **1** leather worker; currier **2** tannery worker

lëkurëregjës *nm* leather tanner: currier

lëkurërrjepës *nm* flayer of hides: skinner

lëkurërrjepur *adj* flayed, skinned

lëkurërrudhur *adj* having wrinkled skin

lëkurës
I § *nm* = lëkurërrjepës
II § *adj* easy to peel

lëkurëshitës *nm* leather merchant

lëkurëta·r *n* 1 currier 2 leather merchant

lëkurëtarí *nf* 1 leather industry 2 leather mill

lëkurëtra'shë *adj* thick-skinned

lëkurëverdhë
 I §ldj 1 having yellowish skin 2 jaundiced
 II § n 1 person of Mongoloid race 2 person with jaundiced skin

lëkurë·z *nf* 1 membrane covering an internal body organ 2 [*Anat*] cuticle

lëkurëzi *adj, n (fem sg ˜ez, masc pl ˜inj, fem pl ˜eza)* dark-skinned (person/fruit); Negro, Black

lëkuro·r *adj (Spec)* of or pertaining to skin: cutaneous, dermal; leathery, coriaceous

lëkurtë *adj (i)* 1 made of leather 2 [*Bot*] leathery, coriaceous

lëkurur *adj (i)* skin and bones: emaciated

lëmajë *nf* 1 archer's bow 2 bow-shaped object 3 [*Archit*] arch

lëmak
 I § nm ball of thread or yarn: clew
 II § adj, n well-fed (one) with skin made smooth by plumpness

lëmaqe *nf* scree, stoneslide

lëma·r *n* thresher

lëmashk *nm* 1 [*Bot*] = lëmyshk 2 scum indicating spoilage/disease: slime, mold, film (on the eyes)

lëmashkët *adj (i)* 1 mossy *2 slimy, moldy

lëmata·r *n* person who threshes grain on the threshing floor

lëmazë *nf* 1 thin and transparent membrane between layers 2 thin layer

lë mba·r·et *vpr* to be in suitable condition; be amply prepared

lë mbu·rr·et *vpr* to boast, brag; show off

lëme·-het *vpr* to put on makeup; get cleaned up

lëmek· *vt* 1 to moisten; drench 2 to touch lightly, graze 3 (*Fig*) to tire [ ] out, exhaust

lëmek·et *vpr* 1 to become moist; get drenched 2 to become completely drained of strength: go limp, faint, die 3 (of a voice) to lose all strength, fade out

lëmekët *adj (i)* = lëmekur

lëmekur *adj (i)* 1 moist, damp; drenched, soaked 2 completely drained of strength 3 (of a voice) faded out

lëmenj *np* <lëmë

lëmes· *vt (Reg)* to caress, show affection to

lëmes·et *vpr (Reg)* to invite a show of affection

lëmesë *nf* 1 wet, slippery ground 2 membrane; septum 3 [*Dairy*] film/scum that forms on top of a boiled liquid

lëmë
 I § nm 1 threshing floor, threshing yard 2 threshing 3 harvest time 4 quantity of grain threshed at one threshing 5 production run 6 (*Colloq*) passel 7 (*Colloq*) hive (of bees) 8 (*Colloq*) flat, open space 9 production yard; workyard 10 (*Fig*) field of endeavor, domain 11 aureole around a heavenly body 12 big wheel of an olive press 13 bag under the eyes
 II § adv (Colloq) in large numbers
 ∘ **lëmë i hedhur** 1 wheat from which the husks have been removed 2 honest man
 ∘ **ësh·të lëmë nga koka** to be empty-headed, have empty space between one's ears
 ∘ **lëmë pa drithë/bereqet** (somebody/something) of no help at all

lëmim *nm ger* <lëmo·n, lëmo·het

lëmishte
 I § nf 1 chaff left by threshing; piece of straw; small stick/twig, brushwood; kindling 2 small grove of young beech
 II § np trash

***lëmizhda** *OR* **lëmizhde** *np* = lëmishte

lëmo·het *vpr* 1 to rub up against 2 to invite a show of affection 3 (*Fig*) to provoke an argument 4 to smooth down one's hair by combing 5 to clear up (of weather)

lëmo·n *vt* 1 to file down [a surface] 2 to smooth [a surface] (down) 3 to stroke; caress

lëmojzë *nf* smoothing/polishing tool

***lëmonçe** *nf (Reg Gheg)* = limonadë

***lëmoqe** = lëmaqe

lëmoshë *nf* 1 alms; charity 2 (*Old*) boiled grain served to poor people in commemoration of a dead person

lëmoshëta·r *n* 1 almsgiver 2 person who lives from alms: beggar

lëmoshtër *nf* breadcrumb

lëmpitë *nf* [*Bot*] lesser dodder, devil's gut (*Cuscuta epithymum*)

lëmpjejtë = lëpjetë

lëmsh
 I § nm 1 ball of thread/yarn: clew 2 sphere 3 (*Fig*) disorderly mess 4 (*Fig*) (emotional) knot
 II § adv 1 in the shape of a ball 2 in(to) a lifeless/dead heap
 ∘ **lëmshi i dheut** world globe
 ∘ **lëmshet e njeriut** (*Old*) human testicles
 ∘ **lëmsh gjaku** (*Old*) leucocyte; erythrocyte
 ∘ **lëmshi i syrit** (*Old*) eyeball
 ∘ **lëmshi i topit** (*Old*) cannonball

lëmsho·r *adj (Book)* spherical

lëmshuk
 I § nm [*Bot*] spherical cluster of flowers/fruit
 II § adj, n = shkurtabíq

lëmth *nm* [*Med*] areola

lëmua·r
 I § adj (i) polished, smooth; (of a fabric) worn (out)
 II § adv smoothly

lëmues
 I § adj serving to smooth: smoothing
 II § n polisher

lëmueshëm *adj (i)* polishable

lëmuq
 I § nm snowball; small heap
 II § adv 1 in the shape of a ball 2 in a heap 3 in an inanimate/insensient heap, lifelessly, in a dead heap

lëmyshk *nm* 1 [*Bot*] moss 2 (*Fig*) shrouding layer of dust over something in the past

lën *stem for opt, adm, part* <lë·

lëna *np (të)* 1 leavings; leftovers, food scraps, garbage 2 debris left by ebbing water

lëndak *adj* = lëndo·r

lënda·r = lëndo·r

***lëndarísht** *adv* materially; concretely

***lëndë** *nf* 1 substance, material, matter; subject matter 2 timber, lumber 3 acorn
 ∘ **lëndë djegëse** fuel
 ∘ **lëndë druri** wood material: timber, lumber
 ∘ **lëndë mësimore** 1 school subject 2 educational material
 ∘ **lëndë e parë** raw material

lëndët *adj (i)* = **lëndor**

lëndëtar *n* **1** sawmill worker **2** *(Old)* wood merchant

lëndëzo *·het vpr* = **materializo** *·het*

lëndëzo *·n vt* = **materializo** *·n*

lëndi *nf* point of irritation, sore point; peeve = **mëri**

lëndim *nm ger* **1** <**lëndo** *·n*, **lëndo** *·het* **2** injury, wound **3** pain

lëndim thi *adv* slowly and carefully: painstakingly

lëndinë *nf* **1** untilled field; grassy field/meadow **2** *(Reg)* = **lëndishtë**

*****lëndishëm** *adj (i) (Old)* irritable

lëndishtë *nf* timber forest

lëndo *·het vpr* **1** to get hurt (at a sore point) **2** *(Fig)* to feel hurt

lëndo *·n vt* to touch [ ] at a sore point; hurt

lëndor *adj* **1** concrete; substantive; material; substantial **2** pertaining to a school subject **3** *(Book)* pertaining to timber

lënduar *adj (i)* hurt (at a sore point)

lëndues *adj* damaging/painful (at a sore point)

lëndueshëm *adj (i)* irritable, touchy

lëndyrë *nf (Reg)* = **yndyrë**

lëneshë *nf (Pej)* woman that no one will consider for marriage: leftover old maid

lënë
  I § *part* <**lë**·
  II § *adj (i)* **1** leftover, left **2** inherited **3** debris from ebbing water **4** *(Pej)* woman who has been divorced by her husband **5** abandoned; orphaned **6** disheveled, personally neglectful **7** weak (from illness or old age) **8** insane, crazy

lënësi *nf* **1** insanity **2** weakness (from illness or old age)

lëng *nm (np ~ gje)* **1** liquid **2** juice **3** *(Colloq)* soil moisture **4** *(Colloq Fig)* wealth **5** *(Colloq Fig)* good flavor **6** *(Reg)* whey
  ○ **ësh·të zier në lëng çeliku** to have experienced the hardships of life, be tempered by experience, have been through the mill
  ○ **lëng i djegur** gravy
  ○ **lëng i drurit** tree sap
  ○ **lëng gështenjash** weak coffee; bland food
  ○ **lëng groshe** *(Impol)* unimportant person, worthless person
  ○ **lëng gjaku** *(Old)* lymph
  ○ **lëng kamomili** chamomile tea
  ○ **lëng mishi** gravy
  ○ **lëng ndër lakra** worthless trash
  ○ **lëng pas lëngu** *(Impol)* hardly related (by blood) at all
  ○ **lëng qumështor** *[Med]* chyle
  ○ **lëng stërlëngu** *(Impol)* hardly related (by blood) at all
  ○ **U derdh lëngu e ra në lakra** "The liquid spilled and fell back into the vegetables" No harm done: it wound up in the right place eventually.
  ○ **lëng xhami** *[Tech]* water glass, sodium silicate

lëng *·et vpr* = **lëngëzo** *·het*

lëngarak *adj, n* **1** *(Impol)* (person) who eats in a sloppy/messy manner **2** *(Contempt)* (person) who eats slop **3** *(Fig)* (person) who gets nothing to eat but slop

lëngaraq *adj* = **lëngarak**

lëngatë *nf* **1** ailment requiring lengthy bed rest: lingering illness **2** *(Fig)* deep suffering, great sorrow; languishment **3** epidemic disease in plants/animals

○ **lëngata e hënës** *(Colloq)* epilepsy
○ **lëngata e thatë** *(Colloq)* *[Med]* tuberculosis
○ **lëngata e verdhë** *(Colloq)* *[Med]* jaundice

lëngatëmadh *adj (Colloq)* languishing with a serious illness

lëngato *·het vpr* **1** to languish with a serious illness **2** *[Veter]* to suffer from liver rot **3** *(Fig)* to suffer great sorrow; languish

lëngese *nf* deep suffering; languishment

lëngë *nf* small terraced field; vegetable patch

lëngës
  I § *adj* juicy
  II § *n (Pej)* person who freeloads on others' food or drink

lëngësi *nf* juiciness

lëngësim *nm ger* <**lëngëso** *·n*, **lëngëso** *·het*

lëngësirë *nf* **1** fruit juice **2** tree sap **3** *(Colloq)* beverage

lëngëso *·het vpr* **1** to become liquefied **2** to water at the mouth **3** to become full of juice/sap

lëngëso *·n*
  I § *vt* **1** to liquefy **2** to moisten
  II § *vi* to become full of juice/sap

lëngësht *adj (i)* = **lëngët**

lëngështim *nm ger* <**lëngështo** *·n*, **lëngështo** *·het*

lëngështirë *nf* juice; sap

lëngështo *·het vpr* **1** to become liquefied **2** to become full of juice/sap

lëngështo *·n*
  I § *vt* **1** to liquefy **2** to make [ ] wet, humidify
  II § *vi* **1** to become full of juice/sap **2** to ooze with moisture

lëngështuar *adj (i)* **1** liquefied **2** full of juice/sap

lëngështueshëm *adj (i)* liquefiable

lëngët *adj (i)* liquid

lëngëtor *adj (Old)* *[Ling]* liquid (consonant)

lëngëtore *nf (Old)* *[Ling]* liquid (consonant)

lëngëtyrë *nf (Pej)* watery food: slop

lëngëzim *nm ger* **1** <**lëngëzo** *·n*, **lëngëzo** *·het* **2** liquefaction

lëngëzo *·het vpr* **1** to become liquified **2** to become full of juice/sap **3** (of soil) to absorb water, become damp **4** to bleed/drip moisture **5** to water at the mouth

lëngëzo *·n*
  I § *vt* **1** to liquefy **2** to cause [ ] to water at the mouth
  II § *vi* **1** to become full of juice/sap **2** to ooze with moisture **3** to water at the mouth

lëngëzor *adj* *[Ling]* (of consonants) liquid

lëngëzuar *adj (i)* **1** liquefied **2** full of juice/sap

lëngëzues *adj* *[Med]* liquefacient

lëngie *adj, nf* very juicy (fruit)

lëngim *nm ger* **1** <**lëngo** *·n (Fig)* **2** deep suffering, great sorrow; languishment **3** epidemic disease of plants/animals

lëngo *·n*
  I § *vi* **1** to have a long debilitating illness **2** *(Fig)* to suffer greatly, languish; pine away **3** to become full of juice/sap
  II § *vt* to moisten
  ○ <> **lëngo** *·n³ˢᵍ* **zemra** <>'s heart languishes, <> suffers deeply; <> pines away

lëngosh = **lëngshëm**

lëngshëm *adj (i)* **1** liquid **2** juicy, succulent

lëngshtrydhe *nf* *[Bot]* = **luleshtrydhe**

lëng·urînë *nf* **1** liquid food **2** *(Pej)* = **lëngëty·rë**

lëng·uth *nm* sap of a young tree

lëngj·e *np* <**lëng**

lëngj·ere *nf* large pot

lëngj·e·rë *nf* **1** juice from pressed olives; juice from residue of olive pressing **2** oily lees **3** mud puddle **4** *(Fig Insult)* dirty stinker

lëngj·y·rë *nf* **1** lingering illness **2** *(Fig)* deep suffering **3** *(Fig)* terrible fear, terror **4** *(Reg)* = **butër**

lëni·e *nf ger* **1** <**lë·**, **li·het 2** *(Old)* resignation

lënur· *vt* **1** to comb/card/hackle [fibers] **2** *(Fig)* to damage [] by tearing/scratching: lacerate, tear off parts of [] **3** *(Fig)* to cause terrible suffering
  ◦ [] **lënur· nga mendtë 1** to confuse [] totally **2** to drive [] crazy, rile

lënur·et *vpr* **1** to have parts of one's outer surface torn (off): suffer laceration **2** *(Fig)* to suffer terribly, be torn up
  ◦ **lënur·et nga mendtë 1** to be totally confused **2** to go crazy, go insane

lënur·ëse *nf* woman who combs fibers

lënur·je *nf ger* <**lënur·**, **lënur·et**

lënur·ur *adj (i)* **1** combed **2** badly damaged by tearing/scratching, lacerated **3** *(Fig)* in terrible suffering **4** *(Fig)* crazy, insane

*****lëny·er·** = **lënur·**

lëpe *nf* **1** mist, haze **2** hazy film over the eyes

lë·pendër *nf* **1** feather **2** rag **3** bottom end of the cornhusk that is wrapped around the stem

lëpi·het *vpr* **1** to lick one's lips **2** *(Fig Pej)* to get all slicked up **3** to reach the borders in a fleeting way **4** *(Fig Pej)* to kiss up to, act in a servile manner
  ◦ **lëpi·het pas** <> (of an amorphous entity) to lick up against <>

lëpi· *n vt* **1** to lick [] (with the tongue), lick up [], lap up [] **2** to take a taste of [], taste [] with the tongue **3** to smooth []down **4** *(Fig Pej)* to admit having said [something bad]
  ◦ **lëpi·n atë që pështy·n** "lick up what one spit" to take back in embarrassment what one has said publicly: eat crow
  ◦ **lëpi·n aty ku pështy·n** "lick up where one spit" to take back in embarrassment what one has said publicly: eat crow
  ◦ **lëpi·n çanakët e** <> *(Pej)* to lick <>'s boots
  ◦ **lëpi·n**^{3pl} **çibanët e njëri-tjetrit** "{} lick each other's sores" *(Pej)* to cover up each other's mistakes
  ◦ <> **lëpi·n çizmet** *(Pej)* to lick <>'s boots
  ◦ <> **lëpi·n këmbët** *(Pej)* to lick <>'s feet
  ◦ **lëpi·n kockat e hedhura** "lick discarded bones" to be willing to debase oneself for even the smallest gain, crawl on one's belly for a penny
  ◦ **Lëpi mjaltin, po mos e ha gishtin!** "Lick the honey, but don't bite your finger!" *(Prov)* Have a good time, but don't overdo it! Don't let your greed get the best of you!
  ◦ **lëpi·n**^{3pl} **plagët e njëri-tjetrit** "{} lick each other's wounds" *(Pej)* to cover up each other's mistakes
  ◦ **lëpi·n sahanët e** <> *(Pej)* to lick <>'s boots

lëpi·rë
  I § *part* <**lëpi·n**
  II § *adj (i)* **1** licked **2** slicked down **3** soft and smooth

lëpir·ës *nm* **1** bootlicker, lickspittle **2** *(Colloq)* index finger

lëpír·je *nf ger* <**lëpi·n**, **lëpi·het**

lëpís *nm (Colloq)* index finger

*****lëpîs**
  I § *adj (Reg Gheg)* licking; lambent
  II § *n* licker

lëpískë *nf* scale of a fish = **lu·sp**ë

lëpítkë *nf (Reg)* = **lepítk**ë

lëpízë *nf* **1** wall shelf for kitchenware *****2** = **lepíz**ë

lëpjetë *nf [Bot]* **1** dock, sorrel *(Rumex)* **2** garden sorrel *(Rumex acetosa)*
  ◦ **lëpjetë e alpeve** *[Bot]* alpine dock, monk's rhubarb *Rumex alpinus*
  ◦ **lëpjetë bjeshke** *[Bot]* garden sorrel *Rumex acetosa*
  ◦ **lëpjetë e bukur** *[Bot]* fiddle-leaved dock *Rumex pulcher*
  ◦ **lëpjetë deti** *[Bot]* golden dock *Rumex maritimus*
  ◦ **lëpjetë kaçurrele** *[Bot]* = **uthulla·ke**
  ◦ **lëpjetë kokëkau** *[Bot]* small dock-like plant *Rumex bucephalopheous*
  ◦ **lëpjetë lepuri** *[Bot]* = **uthullísht**ë
  ◦ **lëpjetë livadhi** *[Bot]* garden sorrel *Rumex acetosa*
  ◦ **lëpjetë e madhe** *[Bot]* water dock *Rumex hydrolapathum*
  ◦ **lëpjetë majhoshe** *[Bot]* = **uthullí·sht**ë
  ◦ **lëpjetë mali** *[Bot]* mountain sorrel *Rumex paucifolius*
  ◦ **lëpjetë e rëndomtë** *[Bot]* bitter dock *Rumex obtusifolius*
  ◦ **lëpjetë e thartë** *[Bot]* garden sorrel *Rumex acetosa*
  ◦ **lëpjetë thartushë** *[Bot]* French sorrel *Rumex scutatus*
  ◦ **lëpjetë uji** *[Bot]* water dock *Rumex hydrolapathum*

lëplu·ngë *nf* **1** cheesecloth strainer *****2** *(Old)* webbing used to tie a cradle to a mother's back

lëpozë *nf* **1** ceiling *****2** soot

lë·pushë *nf* **1** *[Bot]* purple butterbur *(Petasites officinalis)* **2** *[Bot]* clasping mullein *(Verbascum phlomoides)* **3** *[Bot]* large tongue-shaped leaf: spathe *()* **4** cornhusk **5** *(ColloqImpolite)* paper money **6** *(Reg Arb)* letter (for mailing)

lëpushkë *nf* **1** *[Bot]* purple butterbur *(Petasites officinalis)* **2** *[Bot]* large tongue-shaped leaf: spathe **3** *(ColloqImpolite)* paper money **4** *(Pej)* a worthless newspaper
  ◦ **lëpushkë dejsh** *[Bot]* plantain *Plantago*

lëpushk·ët *adj (i)* having a husk

lëpushtër *nf [Bot]* marsh marigold *(Caltha palustris)*

lëputë *nf* earlobe

lëqe·shtë *nf [Bot]* = **ílqe**

lër *stem for 3rd sg subj, imper* <**lë·**
  ◦ **Lëre lëngun e hyrë në thela!** "Leave the gravy and get to the chops!" *(Iron)* Get to the point! Stop beating around the bush!
  ◦ **Lëre mos (e) nga!** "Leave it don't touch it!" Don't even talk about it! Too terrible to even talk about!
  ◦ **Lëre (që) mos pyet!** "Leave it don't ask!" Don't even talk about it! Too terrible to even talk about!

lër·e *interj* builds up expectation: just wait! don't think that's all there is to it

lër·e·n *vi* to let up, cease

lërím *nm ger* **1** <**lëro··n 2** cultivation, tillage, plowing

lëro·*n*

  I § *vt, vi* to cultivate, till, plow

  II § *vt* to make a deep and thorough study of []

  ○ **lëro**·*n* **në ujë** to do something pointless, waste one's effort

***lëro'sё** *nf* mire

lëru'ar *adj (i)* **1** tilled, plowed **2** *(Fig)* cultivated, educated

lëru'arshëm *adj (i)* arable

lëru'es

  I § *nm* **1** tiller (of the soil), cultivator, plowman **2** person who makes a deep and thorough study

  II § *adj* tilling, cultivating

lëru'eshëm *adj (i)* suitable for plowing: arable

lës *nm* [*Geol*] loess

lëshe' *nf* burst of energy: rush

***lëshendёrr** *nf* resin

lëshe'sё *nf* **1** *(Old)* divorce ***2** *(Old)* negligence **3** [*Tech*] tolerance

***lëshё'c** *nm* [*Bot*] velvet grass, Yorkshire fog (*Holcus lanatus*)

lëshi'm *nm ger* **1** <**lësho**·*n*, **lësho**·*het* **2** lenience; looseness, overindulgence **3** *(Old)* divorce **4** *(Reg)* swarm of bees looking for a new hive **5** [*Tech*] tolerance = **tolera'nc**ё **6** [*Sport*] release **7** launch **8** [*Tech*] start (of a machine)

lësho'·*het vpr* **1** to cease efforts suddenly: lie down, give up, let go **2** to dash

  ○ **lësho**·*het* **në shpinë** to stay right at <>'s back, follow <> closely behind

  ○ **lësho**·*het* **në të** {*participle*} to be busy {}ing, be given over to {}, be deep into {}ing

  ○ **lësho**·*het* **pas** <> to be much given to <>, be crazy about <>

  ○ **lësho**·*het* **rrezga-bjezga** to run pell-mell

lësho'·*n*

  I § *vt* **1** to release, let go of [], let/set [] loose, set [] free, launch [a ship] **2** to let up on []: stop affecting/hurting [] **3** to let [] fall, drop **4** to give [] up, quit **5** to drop [] off, deliver, give **6** *(Colloq)* to divorce **7** to unleash the power of []; turn []; on; launch [a projectile]; start [a machine] **8** to give (forth/out) []: emit, issue, generate, create, sprout **9** to make room for [], give way to []

  II § *vi* **1** *(Colloq)* to swarm **2** to be overindulgent, be too tolerant

  ○ <> **lësho**·*n* {*an illness or bad emotional state*} *(Colloq)* <> get over {}

  ○ [] **lësho**·*n* **(me qira)** to rent [] out

  ○ [] **lësho**·*n*^{3rd} {*part(s) of one's body*} []'s {} *get too weak:* []'s {} *fail*

  ○ **lësho**·*n* **afsh** to exhale air (with a whoosh)

  ○ **lësho**·*n* **armёt** to lay down one's arms: stop fighting, stop resisting, surrender

  ○ **e lësho**·*n* **bajgёn** *(Crude)* to do a sloppy job; be careless in speech

  ○ **lësho**·*n* **bark 1** to bulge, bulge out; warp **2** to get a fat belly

  ○ <> **lësho**·*n* **be** to beseech <>

  ○ **lësho**·*n* **be** *(Intens)* = **beto'**·*het*

  ○ **lësho**·*n* **brezin** "take off one's belt (for use as a weapon)" **1** to get ready to fight; get the fight started "drop one's belt" **2** to back out of a fight

  ○ <> **lësho**·*n* **buzёt një pёllёmbё** "let one's lips/nose/snout hang down about six inches" to get a sullen expression on one's face; take on a gloomy look; look offended

  ○ [] **lësho**·*n* **dore** to leave/abandon []; let [] out of one's hands

  ○ **lësho**·*n* **dorë kundër** <> to raise one's hand against <>

  ○ **e lësho**·*n* **dorën 1** to be too generous **2** to be injudicious, act without thinking

  ○ <>**a lësho**·*n* **fillin** to let [] act freely, no longer maintain control over []

  ○ **nuk e lësho**·*n* **fjalёn nga goja** "not let up on the word from one's mouth" to always have something more to say: be too talkative

  ○ **i lësho**·*n* **fjalёt si lopa bajgёn** *(Crude)* to talk irresponsible nonsense: talk crap

  ○ **i lësho**·*n* **fjalёt veresie** to talk nonsense

  ○ <>**a lësho**·*n* **frerin** *(Pej)* to let go of the reins: maintain no discipline over <>, let <> go out of control

  ○ **ia lësho**·*n* **frerin gojёs** to speak without much thought, talk without stop

  ○ **lësho**·*n* **fronin 1** to leave the throne: abdicate; fall from power **2** to give up one's position

  ○ <> **lësho**·*n*^{3sg} **goja lëng** <>'s mouth is watering: <> *has* a craving

  ○ <> **lësho**·*n* **gojë** to abuse <> verbally: insult

  ○ **e lësho**·*n* **gojёn** to talk too much; have a loose mouth

  ○ **lësho**·*n* **gushё** to get a double chin

  ○ **e lësho**·*n* **gjuhёn** to talk too much; have a loose mouth

  ○ [] **lësho**·*n*^{3sg} **gjumi** "sleep *releases* []" *(Poet)* [] *wakes* up

  ○ **lësho**·*n* **hije pa dalё dielli** *(Impol)* to do something before the proper time: act too hastily, put the cart before the horse

  ○ <> **lësho**·*n* **hundёt një pёllёmbё** "let one's lips/nose/snout hang down about six inches" to get a sullen expression on one's face; take on a gloomy look; look offended

  ○ <>**a lësho**·*n* **kapistallin** *(Pej)* to let go of the reins: maintain no discipline over <>, let <> go out of control

  ○ <>**a lësho**·*n* **kapistrёn** *(Pej)* to let go of the reins: maintain no discipline over <>, let <> go out of control

  ○ <> **lësho**·*n*^{3sg} **koka tym** <>'s head is absolutely spinning with all the things <> has to worry about

  ○ [] **lësho**·*n*^{3pl} **leqet e kёmbёve** "the sinews of the legs release []" []'s legs *won't* hold [] up (because [] is so old/sick/scared)

  ○ [] **lësho**·*n* **lёmuq** to drop [] into a heap, knock [] over into a heap, knock [] out

  ○ <> **lësho**·*n* **litar** to give <> too much rope, let <> have too much freedom

  ○ **lësho**·*n* **loze 1** (of a person) to take a long time with it, draw it out too long **2** (of a thing) to expand greatly and show a lot of progress

  ○ **e lësho**·*n* **/llapёn** to talk too much; have a loose mouth

  ○ [] **lësho**·*n*^{3pl} **mendtё** "the brains *abandon* []" [] *is losing* []'s mind

  ○ **lësho**·*n* **mjaltё nga goja** "release honey/sugar from one's mouth" to speak pleasantly/beautifully

  ○ **lëshofsh mjekёr** "may your beard sprout!" *(Felic)* may you reach an old age!

  ○ **s'**[] **lësho**·*n* **nga goja** never cease to speak (well) of []

  ○ **nuk** [] **lësho**·*n* **nga sytё** not let [] out of one's sight; never take one's eyes off of []

○ <> **lësho**·*n* **një gjëmë** to put a heavy curse on <>
○ <> **lësho**·*n* **pe** to give <> too much rope, let <> have too much freedom
○ [] **lësho**·*n* **pikë gjallë** to kill [] on the spot
○ **lësho**·*n* **rrënjë** to take root; settle down, take up permanent residence: become implanted
○ <>*a* **lësho**·*n* **rripin** *(Pej)* to let go of the reins: maintain no discipline over <>, let <> go out of control
○ <> **lësho**·*n* **rrugë** to give way to <>, step aside for <>, step out of the way of <>
○ <> **lësho**·*n* **samarin nën bark**∥**nëpër këmbë** "loosen <>'s packsaddle to fall *under the belly*∥ *around the legs*" to put <> in a terrible predicament
○ [] **lësho**·*n*^{3pl} **sendet** "the things all left []" [] *is* left with nothing
○ **lësho**·*n*^{3pl} **si miza në mjaltë** "swarm like ants to honey" to gather in swarms
○ [] **lësho**·*n* **si pula glasën** *(Crude)* to say/do [] impetuously/irresponsibly
○ **lësho**·*n* **sogje** to change the guard
○ <> **lësho**·*n* **spangon** to put the measuring tape on <>, measure <>
○ <> **lësho**·*n*^{3pl} **sytë shkëndija/çika/xixa** "<>'s eyes make sparks of light" (when <> is hit in the head <>'s vision goes dark) <> *sees* stars
○ **lësho**·*n* **sheqer nga goja** "release honey/sugar from one's mouth" to speak pleasantly/beautifully
○ **lësho**·*n* **shtat** to grow tall
○ **i lësho**·*n* **shumë ujë mullirit.** "release a lot of water to the mill" *(Impol)* to talk a lot without thinking
○ **lësho**·*n* **trup** to grow bigger
○ <> **lësho**·*n*^{3sg} **truri** <> *can't* keep anything in <>'s head
○ <> **lësho**·*n* **turinjtë një pëllëmbë** "let one's lips/nose/snout hang down about six inches" to get a sullen expression on one's face; take on a gloomy look; look offended
○ **s'i lësho**·*n* **udhë as më të mirit** not take second place to anyone, be the best
○ **ta lësho**·*n*^{3sg} **ujët/ujin nën rrogoz/hasër/ vete** "put water under your floor mat" to always be doing things behind your back
○ <> **lësho**·*n* **vend** to give <> too much rope, let <> have too much freedom
○ <> **lësho**·*n* **vendin** to take off one's hat to <>, have to give <> credit
○ **lësho**·*n* **vendin** to give up one's position
○ **e lësho**·*n* **veten** to give up, not resist any further
○ <> **lësho**·*n* **vetullat** *1 to frown 2 to get angry
○ **lësho**·*n* **vigmën** to let out a shriek/yell; bellow with pain
○ **Lëshoje vrapin sa ke hapin!** "Make your speed match your stride!" *(Prov)* Adjust your wants in accordance with your abilities!
○ **lësho**·*n* **(helm e) vrer** "unleash (poison and) bile" to pour out one's hatred, speak with unmitigated spite: pour out one's bile
○ [] **lësho**·*n*^{3sg} **zemra** []'s heart *is* not in it anymore
○ <> **lësho**·*n* **zë 1** to cry out to <>, call to <>, yell at <> **2** to tell <> in a loud voice, tell <>, let <> know
lëshojë *nf* mill sluice
***lëshojë**s *adj* resilient, supple
***lështarpë** *nf* [*Bot*] setaria, foxtail millet *(Setaria)*

lëshuar *adj (i)* **1** hanging loose, unbound **2** *(Old)* (of a woman) divorced **3** weak and in poor health **4** *(Fig)* completely demoralized, enervated **5** of loose morals
lëshues
I § *nm* **1** person who issues a document **2** [*Tech*] device for starting a mechanism going: starter; launcher **3** sluice
II § *adj* **1** issuing **2** overindulgent, permissive
__lëti__ (n) *nm* **1** *(Reg Gheg)* West European **2** Frenchman **3** Roman Catholic
*__lëtinë__ *nf* *(Reg Gheg)* smooth-bore gun
lëtyrë *nf* **1** dirty water **2** fodder consisting of chaff and warm water **3** *(Fig)* = **lëngëtyrë** **4** body/clothes dirt **5** *(Fig Pej)* trash
lëthur· *vt* to knit tightly
lëthur·*et* *vpr* to become tightly interlaced
lëvar *nm* [*Bot*] drooping inflorescence: *ament, catkin*
lëvar· *vt* to hang [] down, let [] sag
○ <> **lëvar**· **buzët/hundët/turinjtë një pëllëmbë** "let one's lips/nose/snout hang down about six inches" to get a sullen expression on one's face: take on a gloomy look; look offended
○ <> **lëvar**· **vetullat 1** to frown **2** to get angry
lëvar·*et* *vpr* **1** to hang down loosely: dangle **2** *(Fig)* to be all tired out **3** *(Fig Pej)* to be servile, hang on
lëvare *nf* **1** waterfall **2** cliff **3** steep mountain road **4** trace, track
lëvarës *nm* **1** leather loop used for hanging things **2** [*Bot*] amentiferous plants *(Amentaceae)* **3** overripe fig **4** *(Colloq)* = **lavjerrës**
*__lëvarëse__ *nf* [*Bot*] silk vine *(Periploca graeca)*
lëvarur *adj (i)* **1** hanging, dangling **2** *(Fig)* all tired out
lëvarr· *vt* **1** to scratch, gash **2** to hang [] up
lëvarr·*et* *vpr* to get wounded; get scratched
lëvdatar
I § *adj* boasting, boastful
II § *n* boaster
lëvdatë *nf* **1** praise **2** boasting
lëvdat*ë*madh *adj (Pej)* bragging, boastful
lëvdat*ë*s
I § *adj* boasting, boastful
II § *n* boaster
*__lëvdator__ *adj (Old)* laudatory
*__lëvdi__ = lavdi
lëvdim *nm* <**lëvdo**·*n*, **lëvdo**·*het*
lëvdo·*het* *vpr* to boast, brag
○ **lëvdo**·*het* **në të thatë**∥**për së thati** to boast unjustifiably, brag without justification
lëvdo·*n* *vt* to laud, praise, extol
lëvduar *adj (i), n (i)* (person) praised
lëvdues *adj* = **lavdërues**
lëvdueshëm *adj (i)* = **lavdërueshëm**
lëverdh·
I § *vt* to imbue [] with a tinge of yellow
II § *vi* to appear yellowish
lëverdh·*et* *vpr* to get a tinge of yellow
lëverdhë *adj (i)* having a tinge of yellow
lëvere
I § *nf* **1** rag **2** *(Colloq)* kerchief **3** *(Fig Pej)* worthless person/thing: trash **4** *(Fig Scorn)* worthless newspaper
II § *np* **1** underwear **2** *(Reg)* clothes **3** laundry

*lëve'xhgë *OR* lëve'zhgë = lëvo'zhgë

lëvir·*et vpr* **1** to beseech humbly: implore, plead **2** to humble oneself

lëvir'ë *nf* **1** waterfall **2** trace, track **3** *(Pej)* servile begging, plea

*lëvi's = lëvi'z

*lëvi'smë *nf (Colloq)* movement

lëviz·
  I § vt to change the position of []: move []
  II § vi **1** to change position: move, change **2** *(Pej Colloq)* to move suggestively **3** *(Colloq)* to go crazy
  ∘ Nuk <> lëviz·³*sg* as bebja e syrit. "Not even the pupil of <>'s eye *wavers*." <> *is* fearless/intrepid.
  ∘ nuk <> lëviz·³*sg* bebja e syrit. "<>'s eye never *blinks*" <> *is* fearless/intrepid
  ∘ lëviz· bishtin "waggle one's tail" **1** *(Pej)* to have loose sexual morals: be a slut **2** to waver in loyalty, be untrustworthy; be unreliable
  ∘ lëviz· gurët "move rocks" to make great efforts, try every possible means; go to any lengths, try by hook or by crook
  ∘ <> lëviz·³*sg* kapaku/tabani i kokës/kafka/ tepja e kokës **1** <>'s head *is splitting*, <> *has* a terrible headache **2** <> *is* overwhelmed by problems to worry about **3** <> *is* shocked/astonished
  ∘ nuk lëviz· nga vendi not worry about anything
  ∘ lëviz· si murrjelë to keep moving around: flit around from place to place, never stand still
  ∘ <> lëviz· tepeleku i kokës **1** <>'s head *is splitting*, <> *has* a terrible headache **2** <> *is* overwhelmed by problems to worry about **3** <> *is* shocked/astonished
  ∘ <> lëviz·³*sg* thepi (in shooting) <> loses aim, <> is unsteady in <>'s aim
  ∘ <> lëviz·³*sg* zemra <> *feels* very worried, <> *is* uneasy; <> *is* deeply afraid

lëviz'ak *adj* mobile, active

lëviz'ës *adj* **1** in movement: moving **2** movable: mobile **3** motive: propelling, driving

*lëviz'ësi *nf* mobility

lëvi'zje *nf ger* **1** <lëviz· **2** movement; motion **3** traffic, circulation

*lëvizje'tar *adj* seditious

lëviz'or *adj (Book)* **1** pertaining to movement: moving **2** causing movement, motor **3** movable

lëviz'shëm *adj (i)* **1** movable, mobile **2** in constant motion, in flux **3** *(Fig)* variable **4** *(Pej Colloq)* moving suggestively

lëviz'shm|ëri *nf* **1** *(Book)* mobility **2** variability, mutability

*lëviz'tar *nm* agile, mobile

lëviz'ur *adj (i)* **1** moved (from one place to another) **2** in constant motion **3** *(Pej Colloq)* moving suggestively

*lëvo'çkë *(Reg Tosk) = lëvo'zhgë

lëvo're *nf* **1** protective outer cover of a plant: husk, rind, skin, bark, shuck **2** fish scale **3** *(Old)* earth's crust **4** *[Bot]* quassia *(Quassia)*
  ∘ lëvore e hidhët Surinam quassia *Quassia amara*

lëvore'brejt|ës
  I § adj (Book) bark-boring
  II § nm [Entom] bark beetle

lëvore'holl|ë *adj* thin-skinned

lëvore'ku|q *adj* having a russet skin

lëvore'ngrën|ës *adj = lëvorebrejtës

lëvore'plas|ur *adj* having a burst skin

lëvore'trash|ë *adj* thick-skinned

lëvore'zi *adj, n (fem sg ˜ez, masc pl ˜inj, fem pl ˜eza)* dark-skinned

lëvore'zo·*het vpr = lëvoro·het

lëvore'zo·*n vt = lëvoro··n

lëvore'zua|r *adj (i) = lëvoru'ar

lëvoro'·het *vpr* **1** to get peeled **2** *(Fig)* to be worn/ tired out

lëvoro·*n vt* **1** to peel off the skin of [] **2** *(Fig)* to tire [] out, wear [] down, exhaust

lëvoru'a|r *adj (i)* **1** peeled **2** *(Fig)* tired out, exhausted

*lëvorxo'·*het vpr* to be worn/tired out

*lëvo'zhg· *vt* to remove the protective covering of [a plant or plant part]: peel, husk, shell

lëvo'zhgo·*het vpr* to get peeled/husked/shelled

lëvo'zhgë *nf* **1** tough covering of a plant part: rind, peel, husk, shell, pod, shuck **2** *(Fig)* outer mask

lëvozhgë'bu|të *adj* soft-skinned

lëvozhgë'for|të *adj* hard-skinned

lëvozhgë'hol|lë *adj* thin-skinned

lëvozhgë'tra|sh|ë *adj* thick-skinned

lëvri·*n vi* **1** to wriggle; wiggle **2** *(Fig)* to be in constant motion **3** to roll in mire ***4 = lëvro··n
  ∘ <> lëvri·*n*³*sg* gjaku <>'s blood is heating up: <> *is* very lively and energetic
  ∘ lëvri·*n* gjuhën *(Impol)* to keep one's tongue wagging, prattle on

*lëvri'cë = lëvri'zë

lëvri'm *nm ger* **1** <lëvro··n **2** cultivation, tillage, plowing

lëvri'zë *nf [Invert]* tapeworm *(Cestoda)*

lëvro·*n*
  I § vt to cultivate, till, plow
  II § vt **1** to make a deep and thorough study of [] **2** to comb (wool)

lëvro'r *adj* ox used to pull a plow

lëvru'a|r *adj (i)* **1** plowed **2** combed (of wool) **3** thoroughly studied (of a subject)

lëvru'es *nm* **1** plowman; small farmer, yeoman **2** *(Fig)* person who does yeoman service in an artistic or scientific field: industrious contributor

lëvru'e'shëm *adj (i)* arable, plowable

*lëvy'r·*et = lënur·et

li·*het vp impers* <li· it is allowed

li *nf* **1** smallpox, pox **2** *[Bot]* disease of fruits that leaves irregular blemishes over which a dark powder forms
  ∘ lia e bardhë/mirë/dushkut/dhenve/pyllit chicken pox
  ∘ lia e madhe *[Med]* smallpox
  ∘ lia e ullirit *[Agr] = sypallu'a

li(r) *nm* flax *(Linum)*
  ∘ të lirit e të mullirit both the good and the bad; all the dirt

li *stem for 2nd pl pres, pind, vp* <lë·

Liba'n *nm* Lebanon

liban'e|z *adj, n* Lebanese

libera'l *adj, n* liberal

libera'l|iz|ëm *nm* liberalism

Liberi *nf* Liberia

*libe'r *nf* platter, plate

li'bër *nm* **1** book **2** omasum (in the stomach of a ruminant) **= paraplë'ndës

∘ lib**ë**r i art**ë** golden book in which the names of distinguished people are kept

∘ lib**ë**r i bardh**ë** official report on a major issue: white paper

∘ lib**ë**r i bordit logbook; ship's register

∘ lib**ë**r famullie parish register

∘ lib**ë**r gatimi cookbook

∘ lib**ë**r i lidhur bound book

∘ lib**ë**r me kujtime memoirs

∘ lib**ë**r i zooteknikut zootechnician's logbook

libër**lidh**ës = librali**dh**ës

libër**lidh**je *nf* bookbinding

libër**mbajt**ës *n* bookkeeper

libër**shit**ës = librashi**t**ës

libër**shit**je *nf* bookselling

*libërta**r** *n (Old)* = librashi**t**ës

*libërtar**i** *nf (Book Old)* the world of books, reading world

*libërto **·n** *vt* 1 to loosen 2 to unloose

*libërto**re** *nf(Old)* bookshop; bookcase; library; bibliography

lib**ë**rz *nm dimin* booklet

Libi *nf* Libya

libia**n** *adj, n* Libyan

*libo **·n** *vt* to unload/discharge cargo from [a ship/ boat] (to a barge)

libra *np* <li**b**ër

librali**dh**ës *n* bookbinder

librapre**r**ese *nf* page-cutter, paperknife, letter-opener

libra**r**

I § *n* 1 bookseller 2 bookstore owner

II § *adj* *of or pertaining to books; bookish

librar**i** *nf* bookstore

librashit**ës** *nf* bookseller, book salesman

*librathith**ës** *nf* bookworm

Librazhd *nf* city and district in eastern Albania bordering Yugoslavia: Librazh

librazhdas

I § *adj* of or pertaining to Librazhd

II § *n* native of Librazhd

libre**t** *nm* [*Mus*] libretto

libre**z**ë *nf* small booklet (like a passport) containing personal data: personal record book

∘ libre**z**ë anëtarësie record of membership dues paid

∘ libre**z**ë kursimi savings book

∘ libre**z**ë e notave personal record of courses taken and grades received

*li**b**rëz *nf* = libre**z**ë

libro**r** *adj* [*Ling*] bookish

libru**shk**ë *nf dimin* <li**b**ër 1 small book, booklet 2 *(Pej)* cheap little book

lice **·** *nf* lycée, high school offering liberal education; middle school

lice**ist** *n* student in a lycée

li**c**ë *nf* 1 bat for beating flax 2 [*Ichth*] = lo**j**bë

*licitacio**n** *nm* auction

lider *nm (Book)* political leader (often with pejorative implications)

lidh**·**

I § *vt* 1 to tie; tie [ ] up; tie [ ] on; bind [ ] together 2 to keep [ ] busy: tie up 3 to put on a leash 4 *(Fig Colloq)* to tie [ ] up in knots 5 to connect; couple

6 to establish [a relationship]; pledge [a mutual agreement] 7 *(Fig Colloq)* to secure [a regular payment] for <*someone*> 8 to spellbind 9 *(Fig Colloq)* to swear off [ ]

II § *vt, vi* to bear [fruit]; form [a head] (of grain); (in grafting) take

∘ lidh**·** besën to give one's word of honor

∘ lidh**·** cigare to roll a cigarette

∘ nuk lidh**·** dot dy fjalë (bashkë) "be totally unable to join two words (together)" to be incapable of expressing oneself clearly

∘ <>i lidh**·** duart to tie <>'s hands, make it impossible for <> to act

∘ lidh**·** duart 1 to fold one's arms together 2 to stand by with arms folded: make no attempt to be helpful

∘ lidh**·** e zgjidh**·** to do whatever one wants/likes

∘ lidh**·** fejesë to make an engagement agreement; get engaged

∘ lidh**·** fjalë me [ ] "join words with [ ]" to make a deal with [ ]

∘ lidh**·** fjalën 1 to give one's word; pledge oneself 2 to mutually agree, concur

∘ lidh**·** fjalët to put words together

∘ lidh**·** foshnjën to swaddle the baby

∘ s'e lidh**·** gishtin me [ ] not trust [ ]

∘ <>a lidh**·** gojën me fashë "tie <>'s mouth with bandage" to gag; not let <> speak

∘ <>a lidh**·** gjuhën to force <> to keep silent, compel <> to hold <>'s tongue

∘ lidh**·** inat to form a grudge

∘ [ ] lidh**·** këmbë e duar 1 to tie [ ] up hand and foot, tie [ ]'s hands; keep [ ] busy 2 to take away [ ]'s rights; enslave [ ]

∘ <>i lidh**·** këmbët "fasten <>'s legs" to hobble <>; tie <> down; make it difficult for <> to move, make it hard for <> to do anything; keep <> from going/ getting anywhere

∘ lidh**·** këmbët me gjalmat e vet to get involved unnecessarily; tie one's own hands, make it impossible to act further

∘ lidh**·** kontratën to conclude/make a contract

∘ <>i lidh**·** krahët to tie <>'s hands, make it impossible for <> to act

∘ lidh**·** kreshmët [*Relig*] to fast (for a holiday), observe a religious fast

∘ i lidh**·** krye me krye to get/bring them into order

∘ lidh**·** kuvendin to give one's word; pledge oneself

∘ e lidh**·** lekun me ushkur "tie up a lek with a waistband" *(Impol)* to be very stingy with money, be a penny-pincher

∘ e lidh**·** lekun nyjë to be tight with money, count one's pennies

∘ lidh**·** martesë to get married

∘ [ ] lidh**·** me ballamar to moor [ ]

∘ lidh**·** mendimet to pull one's thoughts together

∘ lidh**·** mendjen to make up one's mind

∘ lidhe në gisht "tie it on your finger" don't forget it

∘ lidh**·** një plagë to bandage/bind up a wound

∘ e lidh**·** paranë nyjë to be tight with money, count one's pennies

∘ <> lidh**·** qafolin to give <> a very tough job to do

∘ e lidh**·** qesen "tie his purse strings" to keep careful control of one's purse: be stingy; be careful with one's money

∘ <>i lidh**·** sytë to blindfold <>

li**dh**·et *vpr* 1 to form a knot; be joined 2 to be attached 3 to be attached to, be very fond of 4 to hold together,

bind **5** to form a connection; bind together **6** [*Chem*] to combine (in a compound) **7** [*Sport*] to tie, draw
○ <> **lidh·***et* **buka (në grykë/fut)** the food *sticks* in <>'s throat (out of fear or from loss of appetite)
○ **nuk lidh·***et* **dot** to be impossible to persuade
○ <> **lidh·***et*^{3pl} **duart** <>'s hands *are* tied
○ <> **lidh·***et*^{3sg} **fjala komb** <>'s tongue *freezes* in <>'s mouth; <> *gets* utterly tongue-tied; *is left* speechless
○ <> **lidh·***et*^{3sg} **goja** "<>'s mouth/tongue *is* tied/cut" = *is* unable to utter a word; <> /is/ at a loss for words; <> *gets* utterly tongue-tied
○ <> **lidh·***et*^{3sg} **gjuha** "<>'s mouth/tongue *is* tied/cut" = *is* unable to utter a word; <> /is/ at a loss for words; <> *gets* utterly tongue-tied
○ **lidh·***et* **keq** to be perplexed (by one's complicated situation)
○ **lidh·***et* **këmbë e duar** to be all tied up
○ <> **lidh·***et*^{3pl} **këmbët** <> /is/ tied down, <> /is/ unable to go/get anywhere
○ <> **lidh·***et*^{3pl} **krahët** <>'s hands *are* tied
○ **nuk lidh·***et* **lehtë** to be difficult to persuade
○ **lidh·***et* **me kusht** to engage in a wager
○ **nuk lidh·***et* **në një hu** to be inconstant, fickle
○ <> **lidh·***et*^{3sg} **nyjë jeta** "<>'s life *is* tied up in a knot" <>'s life *becomes* unbearable, <>'s life *is* a living Hell
○ <> **lidh·***et* **një nyjë në grykë/fyt** <> *gets* an emotional lump in <>'s throat
○ **lidh·***et* **pas bishtit të** <> (*Pej*) to be at <>'s beck and call
○ **lidh·***et* **pas qerres së** <> to jump on <>'s bandwagon, join <>'s camp, follow <>'s lead
○ **lidh·***et*^{3sg} **sherbeti** the sugar syrup thickens

lidha'k
I § *nm* **1** person who binds grain into sheaves **2** stone wall held together by supports
II § *adj* (of a person) well-built

*****lidh|a'n** *nm* tablecloth, napkin, towel

*****li'dh|ëm** *nf* knot, tie

li'dh|ës
I § *n* **1** tie; bond **2** garter **3** [*Constr*] binding material, binder **4** [*Tech*] connector **5** [*Rr*] railroad switch; switchman **6** paddle-like diverter that switches flow of water to and from a waterwheel
II § *adj* **1** connective **2** binding

li'dh|ëse *nf* **1** thong **2** (clinging) tendril **3** machine or device for binding sheaves: binder **4** hairband **5** stapler **6** [*Anat*] ligament **7** [*Ling*] conjunction
○ **lidh|ëse këpucësh** shoelace

li'dh|ëz *nf* **1** thong **2** (clinging) tendril **3** [*Ling*] conjunction *****4** = **li'dhës**

lidh|ëzo'r *adj* [*Ling*] conjunctional

li'dhje *nf ger* < **li'dh·**, **li'dh·***et* **2** connection, link; relationship **3** bond; (binding) tie **4** knot **5** agreement **6** (clinging) tendril **7** support beam in a roof **8** hairband **9** [*Electr*] coupling **10** binding force **11** membership document **12** association **13** [*Publ*] binding (of a book) **14** [*Chem*] alloy **15** [*Lit*] crux (of the plot)
○ **lidhje gjaku** blood relationship, blood ties, kinship
○ **Lidhja e Kombeve** League of Nations
○ **lidhje metalike** alloy
○ **lidhje shah** [*Tech*] staggered joint
○ **lidhje të gjalla** close and continuous relationship

li'dhk|ë *nf* (*Reg Tosk*) measure of distance: league

*****lidh|ni** *nf* (*Reg Gheg*) union, association; connection, bond

lidh|o'r *adj* **1** [*Anat*] connective **2** [*Ling*] relative **3** [*Ling*] subjunctive, conjunctive

lidh|o're *nf* [*Ling*] subjunctive mood

li'dh|ur
I § *part* < **lidh·**, **li'dh·***et*
II § *adj* (i) **1** tied, linked, connected, related; bound **2** strongly tied, tight **3** well-constructed, well-built; coherent **4** bandaged; swaddled **5** [*Spec*] coupled; alloyed
III § *nf* (e) *****1** alloy *****2** bond, security
IV § *adv* **1** in a bound/bandaged condition **2** on tenterhooks
○ **i lidhur bisht me bisht** (*Colloq*) closely allied
○ **lidhur me** [ ] in regard to [ ], regarding [ ], concerning [ ], in reference to [ ]
○ **ësh·të**^{3sg} **lidhur me pe merimange** "be held together by spider silk" (*Colloq*) to be held together in very insecure fashion: held together by spit and by golly
○ **lidhur pas** <> devoted to <>
○ **i ka·**^{pl} **lidhur telat bashkë** to have found some common ground, have established common ties, have buried the hatchet

li'dh|ura *np* (të) **1** [*Anat*] joints **2** [*Relig*] Shrove Tuesday; Shrovetide

lidh|ure'c *nm* swaddled child

*****lidh|zi'm** *nm* ligature, ligament, joint

*****lie'zë** *nf* [*Entom*] firefly

lifqe'r *nm* waterfall = **ujëva're**

lig
I § *adj* (i) **1** evil, wicked **2** whorish **3** bad **4** nasty **5** (*Colloq*) in poor health, sick **6** (*Reg*) pregnant, with child **7** weak and cowardly **8** *nm* (i) **9** the devil, evil one
II § *nn* (të) **1** wickedness, evil **2** illness **3** terror **4** = **fi'kët**
III § *adv* (*Colloq*) = **ligsht**
○ **i lig për vdekje** very seriously ill

lig· *vt* **1** to cause [ ] to be ill, make [ ] ill; aggravate **2** to emaciate

lig·*et* *vpr* **1** to grow thin and weak, become emaciated, waste away **2** to grow sick with sorrow; fall ill; faint **3** to lose strength; dwindle **4** (of soil) to lose fertility
○ <> **lig·***et*^{3sg} **ora** "<>'s fairy *is* pining" <> *is* in low spirits, all the heart *goes* out of <>
○ <> **lig·***et*^{3sg} **zemra** to be deeply wounded/hurt

liga'ç
I § *nm* **1** (*Impol*) weak, frail; ailing **2** (*Contempt*) mean, rotten **3** (*Impol*) cowardly
II § *nm* drivelling coward, driveller

*****lig|ama'n** *nm* slobberer

*****lig|ara'sh** *adj* frail; ailing

liga't· *vt* to make sick with liver rot

liga't·*et* *vpr* to become sick with liver rot

liga'të *nf* **1** liver rot = **këlba'zë 2** = **ligatî'në**

ligati'në *nf* wet grassy area: marsh

liga'tî'shtë *nf* = **ligatî'në**

liga'tur *adj* (i) sick with liver rot

ligave'c
I § *nm* **1** [*Invert*] slug; snail **2** (*FigImpolite*) sniveling coward
II § *adj* (*Impol*) = **jargave'c**

○ **ligavec lakuriq** slug

*__lig·da·sh|ës__ adj malevolent

li'g|ë

I § *nf* **1** *(Book)* league, association **2** *(Colloq)* = **jarg**ë *II* § *nf (e)* **1** bad situation **2** immoral behavior/attitude: vice **3** serious/fatal disease; epilepsy **4** *(Reg)* = **pëgë**rë **5** *(Reg)* = **nevojto**re
○ **e liga e të ligave** worst of all

__lig|ë·ba·rdh__ nm [Ornit] hobby (Falco subbuteo)

lig|ë·sí *nf* **1** maliciousness, wickedness, meanness **2** mean behavior, malice **3** cowardice

lig|ë·sí·në *nf* evil, vice

lig|ë·sí·sht *adv* maliciously

lig|ë·so·het *vpr* **1** to become thin and weak **2** to get worse **3** to faint

lig|ë·so·n *vt* **1** to enfeeble [ ], make [ ] weak **2** to make [ ] worse

lig|ë·su·ar *adj (i)* **1** thin and feeble **2** afflicted with a wasting illness

lig|ë·shtí *nf* **1** infirmity; weakness, feebleness **2** fainting spells **3** cowardice **4** sorrow

lig|ë·shti·m *nm ger* **1** <**ligeshto·n**, **ligeshto·het** **2** long, serious illness

lig|ë·shto·het *vpr* **1** to become weak and frail; get ill **2** to faint **3** *(Fig)* to be deeply wounded/hurt; feel great sorrow **4** (of soil) to lose fertility
○ <> **ligështo·het**[3sg] **ora** "<>'s fairy *is pining*" <> is in low spirits, all the heart *goes* out of <>

lig|ë·shto·n *vt* **1** to make [ ] weak, debilitate, enfeeble **2** to make ill **3** to reduce the fertility of [soil]
○ <>**a ligështo·n zemrën 1** to make <> heartsick; touch <>'s heart deeply **2** to discourage <> greatly

lig|ë·shtu·ar *adj (i)* **1** enfeebled, weakened, infirm **2** made ill **3** reduced in fertility **4** disheartened, depressed

li'g|ët *adj (i)* *(Colloq)* weak; thin and emaciated; weakened, worn out

lig|o·sh *adj (Pej)* (sexually) loose, of bad morals

__lig|ro·het__ vpr to swoon, faint; languish

li'g|sht *adv* **1** in poor health, frail; ill **2** feeling poorly **3** maliciously **4** unfavorably, badly, poorly

li'g|shtë *adj (i)* **1** frail, weak **2** ill **3** of poor quality

ligta'r *adj, n* ill

lí'g|ur *adj (i)* emaciated

ligu·stër *nf* [Bot] = **vo·sht**ër

ligj *nm* law
○ **ligj i jashtëzakonshëm** martial law
○ **ligji i Linçit** lynch law
○ **ligj lufte** martial law
○ **ligji marcial** martial law

ligj|bër|ës *adj, n* lawmaker = **ligjvë·nës**

ligj|dhën|ës *adj, n* lawgiver = **ligjvë·nës**

lí'gje *np (Old)* rhythmic eulogy for the dead spoken in a wailing voice

ligj|ë·ra·të *nf* **1** formal discourse: lecture, speech **2** conversation **3** [Ling] speech style **4** *(Old)* ritualized lamentation
○ **ligjëratë e drejtë** direct discourse
○ **pjesët e ligjëratës** [Ling] parts of speech
○ **ligjëratë e zhdrejtë** indirect discourse

ligj|ë·re·së *nf* declamation

ligj|ë·rí *nf(Old)* **1** word = **fja**lë **2** elegy **3** legislation **4** = **drejtë**sí

ligj|ë·rí·m *nm ger* **1** <**ligjëro·n**, **ligjëro·het** **2** discourse; speech **3** ritualized lamentation **4** [Law] legalization

ligj|ë·rim|or *adj* [Ling] pertaining to discourse

ligj|ë·rim|ta'r *n* speaker

ligj|ë·rí·sht *adv (Book)* legally, lawfully

ligj|ë·ro·het *vpr (Colloq)* **1** to converse **2** to complain

ligj|ë·ro·n

I § *vi* **1** to speak; give a speech, lecture **2** to examine a matter thoughtfully and carefully **3** to legislate **4** to wail out a rhythmic eulogy for a dead person **5** (of a bird) to warble
II § *vt* **1** to recite **2** to enact [ ] into law; legalize **3** to confirm
○ **ligjëro·n**[3sg] **zemra** <>'s heart is glad

ligj|ë·ru·ar *adj (i)* = **ligjësu**ar

ligj|ë·ru|es

I § *adj* **1** twittering **2** [Ling] pertaining to discourse
II § *n* **1** speaker, lecturer **2** *(Old)* = **lexue**s **3** = **ligjvë**nës

ligj|ë·sí *nf* = **ligjshm**ërí

ligj|ë·sí·m *nm ger* **1** <**ligjëso·n** **2** legalization

ligj|ë·so·n *vt* **1** to make [ ] a law; legalize; make [ ] legitimate **2** to corroborate, confirm

ligj|ë·so·r *adj (Book)* lawful

ligj|ë·sorí *nf* lawfulness

ligj|ë·su·ar *adj (i)* legalized

ligj|ë·shm|ërí *nf* legality, legitimacy, lawfulness

*__ligj|ë·shtyrë__ (Old) = legjislatur*ë

ligj|í·m *nm ger* **1** <**ligjo·n**, **ligjo·het** **2** legitimation; verification **3** proof of innocence, exculpation, exoneration

ligj|o·het *vpr* to be given last rites (by a priest)

ligj|o·n

I § *vi (Old)* to talk
II § *vt* **1** to prove [ ] innocent **2** to console **3** = **pagëzo·n** **4** *(Old)* to corroborate, confirm

ligj|o·r *adj* **1** legal **2** forensic

*__ligj|or|í·m__ nm legalization = ligj*ërim

ligj|or|í·sht *adv* lawfully, legally, legitimately

*__ligj|or|o·n__ vi to legislate = ligj*ërim

li'gj|shëm *adj (i)* legal, lawful, legitimate

ligj|shm|ërí *nf* **1** legitimacy **2** legitimization **3** legality, lawfulness

ligjta'r *adj, n* = **ligjvë·nës**

__ligj|ue|s__ adj legislative = ligjvë·nës

ligj|vë·n|ës

I § *n* **1** legislature **2** legislator, lawmaker
II § *adj* legislative

ligj|vë·n|ie *nf* legislation

__lih__ stem for pind <leh·

__liha·nzë__ nf caraway seed

__lihudhí__ nf gastronomy; gluttony

__li'jë__ nf = li(r)

lij|ë·vra·rë *adj* = **liju**ar

lij|í·m *nm ger* <**lijo·n**, **lijo·het**

lij|o·het *vpr* to be infected with smallpox

lij|o·n *vt* to infect with smallpox

lij|o·s· *vt* = **lijo·n**

lij|o·s·et *vpr* = **lijo·het**

lij|o·sje *nf ger* = **lijí·m**

lij|o·sur *adj (i)* = **liju**ar

lijo·sh *adj* **1** scarred by smallpox, pock-marked **2** knotty (of trees)

liju·ar *adj (i)* afflicted with smallpox; scarred by smallpox, pock-marked

lik
  I § *nm* **1** level surface; level *2 braid, lace
  II § *adv* **1** level with the surface, to the brim **2** precisely, directly
  III § *prep (abl)* right next to
  ○ **lik i detit** *(Colloq)* sea level

***lik·** *vt* = **lig·**

li·ka·rdh·ë *nf* [*Med*] chicken pox

lika·të *nf* ball of embroidery thread

Li·ke *nf* Like (female name, nickname for Liri)

like·n *nm* [*Bot*] lichen

like·r *nm* liqueur; glass of liqueur

like·r·na *np* <**like·r**

likiri·c·e *nf* locoweed, milk vetch *(Astralagus)*

liko· *nf* [*Food*] candied fruit (served to guests) = **gliko·**

likogjo·ne *nf (Reg)* = **kry·qe**

***lik·sh** = **ligsh**

likty·r·ë *nf* twisted straw/withes used to bind a sheaf of grain; withe used to bind a bunch of faggots

likuidato·r *n (Book)* liquidator

likuid·im *nm ger* **1** <**likuido··n 2** liquidation

likuido··n *vt* to liquidate

***liku·nd·** = **lëku·nd·**

likuri·sht·ë *nf* [*Invert*] octopus = **tetëkë·mbësh**

***lil** *nm* **1** lily **2** shout

li·la *np* fetters, chains

lila·k *nm* [*Bot*] lilac

li·l·ë *nf* **1** ring, link *2 mesh

liliace· *np* [*Bot*] lily family *Liliaceae*

Lilia·n·a *nf* Liliana (female name)

***lili·çk·e** *nf* pendant, trinket

lili·ng·ë *nf* child's rattle

lilingo·sh *nm* **1** = **lili·ng·ë 2** toy

lilth *nm* [*Anat*] uvula

***lima·c** *nm* gray horse

lima·n *nm* **1** harbor **2** *(Fig)* haven **3** large pool of water

***liman·o··n** *vt* = **limano··n**

liman·o·r *adj (Book)* pertaining to harbors

lim·atri·ç·e *nf* [*Tech*] shaping machine, shaper

li·mb·ë *nf* **1** covered deep glass dish for serving sweets **2** plate, dish

lime·r *nm* **1** lair **2** *(Old)* hideout for outlaws **3** *(Fig)* action arena **4** *(Fig Pej)* cozy little den **5** *(Old)* = **lima·n**

lime·t·ë *nf* [*Bot*] sweet lemon *(Citrus limetta)*

li·m·ë *nf* **1** (abrasive) file, rasp **2** *(Reg)* cornhusking tool = **li·mëz 3** [*Invert*] file shell *(Lima lima)*
  ○ **Lima e butë të ha trutë.** "The smooth file eats away your brain." *(Prov)* It is the person who works in small ways against you who is most dangerous.
  ○ **lim·ë e hollë** smooth file

li·m·ët *adj (i)* filed smooth, smooth

li·m·ëz *nf dimin* <**li·m·ë** charred corncob used to remove cornhusks

limfati·k *adj* [*Anat*] lymphatic

li·mf·e *nf* **1** lymph **2** [*Bot*] sap

limiji·r *nm* metal block inserted into the work for hammering by a coppersmith

lim·im *nm ger* <**limo··n, limo··het**

lim·it
  I § *nm* limit
  II § *adj* within a limit, limiting

limo··het *vpr* = **lëmo··het**

limo··n *vt* to file, file [] down; file [] smooth

limo·n
  I § *nm* [*Bot*] lemon *(Citrus limonia Osbeck)*
  II § *adj* **1** greenish yellow **2** very sour
  ○ **limon i ëmbël** [*Bot*] = **lime·t·ë**
  ○ **limon i shtrydhur** "squeezed lemon" person who has been exploited and then abandoned

limon·a·dë *nf* lemonade

***limon·a·dh·e** = **limona·dë**

limon·ashtry·dh·ës *nf* lemon-squeezer

limon·i·sht·ë *nf* lemon grove

limo·n·të *adj (i)* lemon-colored

limonti· *nf* **1** idleness, lethargy **2** apathy

limon·to·z *nm* citric acid in powdered form

limo·s· *vt* = **limo··n**

limo·sje *nf ger* <**limo·s·**

limo·s·ur *adj (i)* = **limu·ar**

limo·zhdra· *np* filings

limu·ar *adj (i)* filed down, filed; polished

limuri·në *nf* filings, filedust

linace· *np* [*Bot*] flax family *Linaceae*

Linç *nm* (Judge) Lynch

linç·im *nm ger* <**linço··n**

linço··n *vt* to lynch

lind *nm (Reg)* **1** [*Bot*] pollen **2** scab covering the pus of a wound

lind·
  I § *vi* **1** to be born; begin life **2** to appear on the horizon, rise (said of a heavenly body) **3** to arise
  II § *vt* **1** to give birth to [] **2** to give rise to
  ○ **S'lind burri me mustaqe.** "No man is born with a mustache." *(Prov)* Rome wasn't built in a day.
  ○ **lind· e mbi·n aty** "be born and grow up right there" to stay in one place, not move (away)
  ○ **lind· me lëmesë** to be born with a caul
  ○ <> **lind· në zemër për** [] to give rise to a desire for [] in <>

li·nd·et *vpr* to be born; begin life

***li·nd·a** *np (të)* = **li·njta**

Li·nd·a *nf* Linda (female name)

***li·nd·ër** *nf* flash, twinkling of an eye

li·nd·ës
  I § *nm (Old)* = **prind**
  II § *adj* birth-giving

li·nd·ëse *nf* birth mother

***lind·ja·k**
  I § *adj* eastern, oriental
  II § *nm* son, offspring

li·nd·je *nf ger* **1** <**lind·, lind·et 2** birth **3** *(Colloq)* offspring, child; descendants as a collective whole **4** east **5** *(Colloq)* dry wind from the east
  ○ **lindja e djellit** sunrise

lind·o·r
  I § *adj* **1** eastern, oriental **2** pertaining to the place of birth: native **3** genital
  II § *n* oriental

li·ndsh·ëm *adj (i)* innate, inborn

lindshm·ëri *nf* **1** capability of giving birth: fertility **2** birthrate, natality

lindur

I § *part* <**lind·**, **lind·et**

II § *adj (i)* **1** aboriginal **2** inborn, innate **3** gifted from birth: born

III § *n (i)* newborn baby

∘ **ka·**^{pl} **lindur për njeri-tjetrin** to have been born for each other, be perfectly suited to one another

∘ **si/siç** [] **ka lindur nëna** "as []'s mother gave [] birth" naked as the day [] was born, naked as a newborn babe

lineár *adj (Book)* linear

linjë *nf* [*Ichth*] tench *(Tinca tinca)*

linërt *adj (i)* (of hair) flaxen

ling

I § *nm* **1** quick gait: pace, trot **2** hurry, haste

II § *adv* quickly, in a hurry/rush; at a fast pace

****lingárdhë = likardhë

lingë *nf* **1** small bell that jingles; bell worn by livestock **2** clapper on a bell

lingëri *nf* skirmish

****lingëro·n *vi* to skirmish

lingëz *nf dimin* <**lingë**

****lingo·n *vi (Reg Gheg)* = **lëngo·n**

lingotë *nf* [*Tech*] ingot

lingrënë *adj, n* (person) scarred by smallpox, pockmarked

lingthi *adv* **1** at a fast pace **2** in a rush/hurry, quickly

linguíst *nm* linguist = **gjuhëtar**

linguistík *adj* linguistic

linguistíkë *nf* linguistics = **gjuhësi**

lingjerë *nf* marshy/swampy spot

linkthi *adv* briskly, quickly; at a trot

lino *nf* cloth made from flax: linen

linoleum *nm* linoleum

linore *np* [*Bot*] flax family *Linaceae*

linotíp *nm* [*Publ*] linotype

linotipíst *n* [*Publ*] linotypist

linsh *nm* **1** sack made of linen cloth **2** cloth potholder

****línt = línjt

****linzë *nf* [*Zool*] lynx

línjë *nf* **1** line **2** [*Tech*] assembly line **3** [*Bot*] lineage

línjë *nf* **1** white shirt **2** linen sheet

linjít *nm* lignite

línjta *np (të) fem* underpants, shorts, drawers; underwear

línjtë *adj (i)* made of linen: linen

****linjyrë *nf* laceration, scratch, wound

****lios· *vt* to pockmark, pit

****liosur *adj (i)* pockmarked, pitted

lipacák *OR* **liparák** *adj, n* = **lypsar**

lipë *nf* [*Bot*] large-leaved lime tree *(Tilia platyphyllos Scop.)*

****lípës = lypës

****lipësi = lypsí

****lipjejtë = lëpjetë

****lip *(Reg)* = lyp

lips·

I § *vi (Colloq Pej)* (of someone disliked) to scram

II § *vt* to kick [] out

∘ **Lipsur qoftë!** To hell with it! Forget it! Who needs it!

lips·et *vpr (Colloq Pej)* **1** (of someone disliked) to scram **2** = **lyps·et**

lipsán *I §* *nm OR* **lipsánë** *II §* *nf (Old)* corpse *III §* *np* remains

****lipsár *OR* **lipcár = lypsar**

****lípsë *nf* dearth

****lípsëm = lypsëm

liq *np* **1** [*Text*] harness (of a loom) ****2** weft ****3** *(Old)* rent payment, rent

∘ **liq dhënës** *(Old)* person who rents out something: renter, leaser, letter

líqe *nf* **1** [*Bot*] = **xínë 2** *(Old)* repayment; rent

liqen *nm* lake

liqenór *adj* **1** of or pertaining to lakes: lacustrine **2** rich in lakes

liqenzë *nf* wind blowing from the lake

****liqer *nm* = liker

liqos· *vt (Old)* **1** to rent **2** to rent out []

****liqth *nm (Reg Gheg)* mountain lake: tarn

lirák *nm* [*Bot*] (of leaves) deeply lobed

lirár *n* lyre player

liratë *nf (Old)* **1** permission, right **2** liberty, freedom

liretë *nf* Italian lira

lirë

I § *adj (i)* **1** free **2** loose; unattached **3** inexpensive

II § *adv* **1** freely **2** loosely **3** cheaply

∘ **Jeni/Je i lirë!** You may go now! You are dismissed!

∘ **I lirë në miell, i shtrenjtë në krunde.** "Careless with the flour, careful with the bran." *(Prov)* Penny-wise and pound-foolish.

∘ **lirë stërlinë** pound sterling

lírë *nf* **1** lyre **2** *(Fig)* poetic inspiration **3** Turkish lira

lirësí *nf* **1** inexpensiveness **2** offering at especially low prices: sale

lirësím *nm ger* <**lirëso·n**, **lirëso·het**

lirëso·het *vpr* to become cheaper

lirëso·n *vt* to reduce in price

lirët *adj (i)* loose

lirëtínë = lirísht

liri *sg def, sg abl indef* <**li(r)** flax

liri *nf* **1** liberty, freedom **2** horse's mane

∘ **liri e fjalës** freedom of speech

∘ **liri e shtypit** freedom of the press

Liri *nf* Liri (popular female name)

líri *obl* <**li(r)**

∘ **liri i breshkës/egër** [*Bot*] bitter lowland weed with dense thin leaves and yellow flowers *Linum*

Líri *nm* Liri (male name)

liridálje *nf* permission to leave: military pass, pass

liridáshës *adj* freedom-loving

liridáshje *nf* love of liberty

****liridashurí *(Old)* = lirídashje

lirík

I § *adj* lyrical

II § *nm* **1** [*Lit*] writer of lyrical literature, lyric poet **2** [*Mus*] singer of lyrical music

Liríka *nf* Lirika (female name)

liríkë *nf* [*Lit*] lyric

lirím *nm ger* **1** <**liro·n**, **liro·het** *(Old)* **2** liberation = **çlirim**

Lirím *nm* Lirim (male name)

****lirimtár *(Old)* = çlirimtar

liriplotë *adj* **1** *(Poet)* free as the air **2** *(Old Offic)* unconstrained

liri|prurës
I § *adj (Book)* freedom-bringing
II § *n* = çlirimtar

liri|shke|lës
I § *adj (Book)* freedom-crushing
II § *n* destroyer of freedom: liberticide

liri|sht *adv* 1 freely, without impediment 2 easily, fluently 3 without reticence or artifice

liri|shtë *nf* 1 forest glade/clearing 2 field sown in flax

liri|shtyp|ës *adj, n (Book)* = lirishkelës

liri|zëm *nm* lyricism

liro·*het vpr* 1 to gain freedom 2 to be discharged from military service or prison 3 to get loose; become loosened 4 to get disencumbered 5 to get relief 6 *(Euph Colloq)* to give birth to a baby 7 *(Euph)* to relieve oneself (evacuate body wastes) 8 to become lower in price

liro·*n vt* 1 to set [] free: free, liberate 2 to release, let go; let up 3 *[Chem Phys]* to radiate 4 *[Mil]* to discharge (from service) 5 to clear (a place) 6 to loosen (something tight-fitting) 7 *(Old)* = shfajëso'·*n* 8 to allow 9 to lower [the price]
  ○ e liro·*n* dorën 1 to spend money freely; overspend 2 to lower one's demands
  ○ e liro·*n* dorën 1 to become less tight-fisted, loosen one's spending habits 2 to relax discipline, become more lenient
  ○ <>a liro·*n* frerin/kapistallin/kapistrën/rripin *(Pej)* to let go of the reins: maintain no discipline over <>, let <> go out of control
  ○ <>a liro·*n* rripin to loosen the reins on <>: relax the constraints on <>
  ○ <>i liro·*n* vidhat/burgjitë to become less strict with <>, loosen up on <>'s discipline

lir|shëm
I § *adj (i)* 1 loose, relaxed, unconstrained, unhampered 2 loose-fitting 3 not occupied, not busy: free
II § *adv* 1 in a loose/easygoing manner 2 freely; without reticence, readily 3 not busy, unoccupied: free
III § *pred* loosely

lir|shm|ëri *nf* freedom of motion

lir|të = linjtë

liru|ar
I § *part* <liro·*n*, liro·*het*
II § *adj (i)* 1 freed 2 released from service; released from prison 3 loose; run away, escaped 4 fitting loosely: loose 5 unloosed 6 (of a field) harvested 7 lowered in price
  ○ <> janë liruar burmat/burgjitë/vidhat "<>'s screws have come loose" <> has a screw loose

lir|ues *nm* 1 liberator, emancipator 2 *(Old) [Relig]* Deliverer 3 *[Tech]* screwdriver 4 *[Anat]* depressor (muscle)

lis
I § *nm* 1 *[Bot]* oak *(Quercus)* 2 tall tree 3 *[Ethnog]* lineage
II § *adj* tall and powerful
  ○ lis i bardhë *[Bot]* Turkey oak = qarr
  ○ lis bujk *[Bot]* Macedonian oak *(Quercus trojana)*
  ○ lis i butë *[Bot]* pubescent oak = bungëbutë
  ○ lis i egër *[Bot]* holly = ashe
  ○ lisi i gjaku patrilineal descendents
  ○ lisi i gjinisë matrilineal descendents
  ○ ësh·të lis me rremba to be a valuable person with many virtues

  ○ ësh·të lis me shumë degë to be strong and have many allies
  ○ lis me shumë degë "oak with many branches" person with many relatives

lis *np* = liq

lis|are *nf* oak grove

Lisbone *nf* Lisbon

*li` s|ë *nf (Reg) [Text]* 1 heddle 2 woof, weft

lis|ëm *nf* 1 stony field 2 clay

lis|ën *nf [Bot]* thyme *(Thymus)*

lisgav|is *stem for 1st sg pres, pl pres, 2nd & 3rd sg subj, pind* <lisgavit·

lisgav|it· *vt* to flood

lisk *nm* clapper (of a bell)

lis|më *nf* = grill

lis|najë *nf* oak grove/forest

lis|ni *nf* = lisnajë

lis|nik *nm* 1 stack of oak or beech branches left out as winter fodder 2 thin branch of oak 3 = lisnajë

lisn|ishtë *nf* = lisnajë

lis|nore = lisnajë

liste|le *nf [Constr]* lath, batten

lister|ik = leshterik

li` stë *nf* list; register, roll
  ○ listë emërore list of names, roll (of names)
  ○ listë e gjellëve menu
  ○ lista e zezë blacklist

lis|të *adj (i)* oaken, of oak

listë|page|së *nf* payroll

lis|tër *nf [Bot]* thyme *(Thymus)*

*lis|tin*ë = lisnajë

listopa|dh *nm* 1 rotted oak leaves used as compost 2 October

*listrik*e *nf* = leshterik

lisha|kë *nf* seesaw

*lish|es*ë *nf* = lëshesë

lish|ëz *nf [Bot]* Canadian pondweed *(Helodea canadensis)*

litani *nf [Relig]* litany

litantra|ks *nm* low-grade anthracite

litar
I § *nm* 1 rope; line (on a boat) 2 *(Fig)* long line (of something) 3 measure of length of 10-12 meters
II § *adv* very much, heavily
  ○ i hurit e i litarit brutally criminal, evil/vicious

litarë-litarë *adv* in large quantities, heavily

litar|pun|ues *adj* rope maker

litar|të *adj (i)* made of rope

litar|th *nm dimin*
  ○ litarth i kërthizës *[Med]* umbilical cord

litar|thi *adv*

literatu|rë *nf* body of written work in a field: literature

*lit*ë *nf* sheet

li` tër
I § *nm* liter
II § *nf [Text]* skein

li` tër|sh *adj* of one-liter capacity

litograf *nm* lithographer

litografi *nf* lithography

litorinë *nf [Invert]* periwinkle *Littorina*

litro|re *np [Bot]* loosestrife family *Lythraceae*

litro|sh
I § *adj (Colloq)* = litërsh

II § *nm* one-liter bottle

litua'n *adj, n* Lithuanian

Lituani *nf* Lithuania

lituani'sht *adv* in Lithuanian (language)

lituani'sht|e *nf* Lithuanian language

liturgji *nf* liturgy

liturgji'k *adj* [*Relig*] liturgical

*****li'thk|ë** *nf* (*Reg Tosk*) ribbon, lace

li'thm|e *np* [*Relig*] Shrove Tuesday, Mardi gras

liva'dh *nm* **1** grassy meadow, meadowland **2** (*Fig*) bed of roses, easy life
  ○ **S'korret livadhi me gërshërë.** "The meadow is not reaped with scissors." (*Prov*) You need the right tools to do a job.

livadhi's· *vi* **1** to graze in meadows **2** (*Fig Pej*) to wander aimlessly **3** (*Fig Pej*) to act improperly and go one's own way

livadhi's|je *nf ger* <**livadhi's·**

livadhi'sht|ë *nf* **1** area with many (small) meadows **2** small meadow

livadh|o'r *adj* (*Book*) used as meadow, characteristic of meadows

liva'nd|ë *OR* **liva'nd|o** *nf* **1** [*Bot*] lavender (*Lavandula*) **2** lavender water; cologne, perfume

*****li'va'r** = **lëva'r**

*****li'va'rt|ë** *nf* appendage

liva'rz *nf* [*Bot*] catkin, ament

live'l *nm* [*Constr*] spirit level; bubble in a spirit level

*****live're** (*Reg Gheg*) = **lëve're**

*****live'zhg|ë** = **lëvo'zhg|ë**

*****livo'shk|ë** *OR* **livo'zhg|ë** = **lëvo'zhg|ë**

livri'm *nm ger* [*Commerc*] **1** <**livro'·n 2** delivery

livri'z|e *nf* tapeworm

livro'·n
  I § *vt* [*Commerc*] to deliver
  II § *vi, vt* (*Reg Gheg*) to move

Li'z||a *nf* Liza (female name)

*****li'zm|e** *nf* clay

*****lje'rsh|ëm** *adj* (i) = **ly'rsh|ëm**

*****Inje**| stem for *pdef, opt* <**Injy'e·n**

*****Injy'e·n** *vt* to flay

*****Injy'e|r** *part* <**Injy'e·n**

*****lo** = **lu'a|**

lob *nm* [*Anat*] lobe

lo'bul *nm* [*Med*] lobule = **vrigth**

loc *nm* **1** youngest brother **2** (*Fig Pet*) buddy, close friend

lo'c|e *nf* **1** youngest sister **2** (*Fig Pet*) close girlfriend, best friend

lo'çk|ë *nf* **1** inedible hard-shelled fruit of certain plants: acorn, pine cone, cotton boll **2** small round object: ball **3** (*Fig*) kernel, core, heart **4** (*Fig Pet*) darling

*****lo'çmi** *nf* flock of chickens

lo'ço *nf* (*Colloq*) ninny, simpleton

*****lo'de** *nf* = **lot**

lo'dër *nf* **1** toy, plaything **2** (*Fig*) game **3** big drum, bass drum **4** eardrum **5** (*Euph*) epilepsy
  ○ **Lodra bie₁.³ˢᵍ për tjetër valle.** "The drum beats for a different dance." The real point *is* something quite different.

lodërta'r
  I § *n* **1** drummer **2** playful person
  II § *adj* playful

lodër'ti
  I § *nf* **1** large drum *****2** (*Old*) play, comedy
  II § *np* instruments used for folk music

lo'dër|z *nf* **1** small drum **2** (*Euph*) epilepsy

*****lodra'r** = **lojta'r**

*****lo'drëz** *nf dimin* riddle

lodri'm *nm ger* **1** <**lodro'·n 2** amusement, game **3** play on words

lodro'·n
  I § *vi* **1** to play, frisk **2** to play around
  II § *vt* to play around with [ ]

lodro'r *adj* [*Med*] tympanal, tympanic

lodru'|es *adj* playful

lodh· *vt* **1** to make [ ] tired: tire, tire [ ] out **2** to be tiresome to [ ]: irk, bother
  ○ **shumë e lodh· gojën** "make one's mouth very tired" to wear out one's mouth talking
  ○ **nuk i lodh· këmbët** "not tire one's legs" not take the trouble to go/come: be too lazy to go/come, not care enough to go/come
  ○ **Lodhi këmbët!** Walk faster! Get a move on!

lo'dh·et *vpr* **1** to get tired **2** to try very hard
  ○ **lodh·et e bë·het përshesh** "get tired and become sop" to get completely tired out

lo'dh|ës *adj* tiring

lo'dh|ët
  I § *adj* (i) **1** = **lo'dhur 2** miserable
  II § *nm* wretch

lo'dh|je *nf ger* **1** <**lo'dh·, lo'dh·et 2** fatigue, tiredness

*****lodhni'm** *nm* (*Old*) period following childbirth

lo'dh|shëm *adj* (i) tiring

lo'dhur *adj* (i) **1** tired, fatigued, weary **2** bored, fed up
  ○ **i lodhur nga** { } tired of { }

lofa'sht|ë *adj* (i) made of the wood of the Judas tree

lofa't|ë *nf* [*Bot*] Judas tree, redbud (*Cercis siliquastrum*)

lofato're *np* [*Bot*] trees of the redbud family *Cercis*

log *nm* (*np ~ gje*) **1** small forest clearing in the mountains; level patch of ground **2** (*Old*) combat ground: list

logari't|ëm *nm* [*Math*] logarithm

logaritmi'k *adj* [*Math*] logarithmic

logaritmi'm *nm ger* [*Math*] <**logaritmo'·n**

logaritmo'·n *vt* [*Math*] to take the logarithm of [ ]

lo'ge *nf* runtish sheep/goat

logetro'g *adv* in great disorder, in a big mess

loglo'·n *vt* to level out ground containing potholes

*****logo're** *nf* burrow; tunnel; passage

logori *nf* (*Colloq*) loud wailing and mourning: keening

logori's· *vt* (*Colloq*) to wail for [ ]

*****logori'sh|ëm** *adj* (i) mournful

lo'gje *np* <**log**

logji'k *adj* **1** logical **2** reasonable

logji'k|ë *nf* **1** logic **2** reasonability

logji'ki'sht *adv* logically

logji'k|shëm *adj* (i) **1** logical, reasonable **2** consistent, coherent

*****lo'j** *2nd sg imper* <**lu'a·n**

lo'jbë *nf* [*Ichth*] pompano (*Lichia amia*)
  ○ **lojbë dhembake** [*Ichth*] Guelly jack *Pseudocaranx dentex*

○ **lojb**ë **me shirita** [*Ichth*] pompano, derbio *Trachinotus ovatus* = **bishtdallëndy'she**

○ **lojb**ë **pikaloshe** [*Ichth*] vadigo *Campogramma glaycos*

lojc *adj* = lojca'k

lojca'k *adj* **1** playful, funloving; frisky **2** in constant motion, overactive **3** (*Fig*) inconstant and unreliable **4** (*Fig*) loose in morals

lojë *nf* **1** play **2** game **3** plaything, toy **4** (*Fig*) practical joke, trick **5** (*Old*) military training **6** beautiful fairskinned woman

○ **loj**ë **fëmijësh** child's play

○ **loj**ë **fjalësh** play on words; playing with words

○ **loj**ë **e hapur** [*Sport*] game played with players spread out

○ **loj**ë **me letra** card game

○ **loj**ë **me topa të lartë** [*Soccer*] play that keeps the ball in the air

lojës *adj* **1** playful, funloving **2** mocking

****lo'jkë** *nf* tadpole

lojna *np* <loj*ë*

lojna'k *adj* playful

****lojn**ë *nf* plaything, toy

****lo'jt** *stem for pdef, part* <lua•n

lojta'k *adj* (*Colloq*) movable

lojta'r

    I § *n* **1** player **2** (*Old*) actor
    II § *adj, n* (person) who likes to joke with others; (person) who likes to mock others

lojtës

    I § *adj* (*Colloq*) **1** playing **2** acting
    II § *n* **1** (*Colloq*) player; contestant, entrant; sportsman **2** (*Old*) actor

lojtje *nf ger* = lua'jtje **1** <lua•n (*Colloq*) **2** play, sport **3** (*Old*) acting

lojtur *adj* (*i*) = lua'jtur

****lojz**ë *nf* (*Reg Gheg*) tendril

lokaçi's = londi's

lokaçi't• = londi't•

lokal .

    I § *nm* **1** locale for public functions **2** pub, café, cafeteria, bar, restaurant
    II § *adj* local

lokali'st *adj, n* **1** clannish **2** local booster

lokali'tet *nm* **1** administrative unit consisting of a few villages: township **2** small inhabited area: locality

lokali'zëm *nm* (*Book*) clannishness

lokali'zim *nm ger* **1** <lokalizo'•n, lokalizo'•het **2** localization

lokalizo'•het *vpr* to be localized

lokalizo'•n *vt* to localize

****lokana'r** *n* intriguer

****loka'ndë** *nf* (*Reg Gheg*) inn

****loka'ndës** *nm* (*Reg Gheg*) innkeeper

lokati'v *adj* locative

****lokavi's** = londi's

lokavi't• = londi't•

lo'ke *nf* (*Reg Gheg Pet*) **1** mom **2** father's mother: grandmother, gran'ma **3** term of respectful address for an old woman

****lo'këm** *nf* tine, cog, spike

lokie *np* [*Med*] lochia

****lokoçi's** = lokaçi's

****lokoçi't•** = lokaçi't•

****loko'dre'dh** = lakadre'dh

****loko'dri'dh** = lakadri'dh•

****loko'dro'dh** *stem for pdef* <lakadre'dh•

lokome'nd•et *vpr* to be dizzy/giddy

****lokomi'ç** *nm* = hi'nkë

lokomobi'lë *nf* locomobile

lokomoti'vë *nf* locomotive

lokomotivi'st *nm* locomotive driver, railroad engineer

****lokovi's** = lokoçi's

****lokovi't•** = lokoçi't•

lokucio'n *nm* [*Ling*] locution

lo'le *nf* naive, gullible woman

loli' *nf* **1** bad/dirty word; dishonorable action; stupidity **2** person who is the object of ridicule

loli's *stem for 1st sg pres, pl pres, 2nd & 3rd sg subj, pind* <loli't•

loli't• *vt* **1** to cuss at [] **2** to curse **3** to make [] the object of ridicule

loli't•et *vpr* to be humiliated/ridiculed

lo'lo *nf* (*Colloq*) **1** laughingstock **2** (*Old*) court jester

lo'mçkë *nf* (*Reg*) acorn; pine cone

Lo'ndër *nf* London

****lo'ndërz** = lu'ndërz

londi's *stem for 1st sg pres, pl pres, 2nd & 3rd sg subj, pind* <londi't•

londi't• *vt* to shake/move/wag/rattle []

londi't•et *vpr* to shake, sway, move, wag, rattle

****loni'shtë** *nf* splinter, chip

lo'nxho *nf* (*Contempt*) **1** person with no sense of shame **2** laughingstock

****lonja'k** *adj* = lëvi'zshëm

lonjara'k *adj* = lozonja'r

lopa'r *n* cowherd

lopata'r *n* oarsman

lopa'të *nf* **1** shovel **2** boat paddle, oar **3** fin **4** (*Colloq*) sole of the foot [*Zool*] = lopa'tëz

○ **lopat**ë **brezi** [*Mil*] trench shovel

○ **lopat**ë **ekskavatori** excavator bucket

lopa'tëz *nf* **1** [*Zool*] tadpole **2** flat metal scraper at the end of a plowman's goad **3** trowel

lopa'tkë *nf dimin* (*Reg Tosk*) **1** little shovel, dustpan **2** [*Zool*] tadpole

lopça'r *n* = lopa'r

lo'pë *nf* cow

○ **lop**ë **deti 1** [*Zool*] walrus **2** [*Ichth*] common eagle ray *Myliobatis aquila* = **shqiponjë deti 3** [*Ichth*] devil ray *(Mobula mobular)*

○ **Të merr lopën me gjithë viç.** "{} takes your cow together with the whole calf." {} will take everything you have and leave you nothing.

○ **Lopa në mal, përsheshi në vatër/xham** "You have the warm sop already soaking (in milk) in the hearth/glass, but the cow is still in the field." (*Iron*) There's many a slip 'twixt cup and lip.

○ **lop**ë **e ngurtë** cow with stiff teats

○ **lop**ë **qumështi** milk cow

lopëla'rë *nf* **1** multi-colored cow **2** (*Fig*) glutton **3** [*Folklore*] girl cowherd

lopë**ri'na** *np* cattle

lo'pë'rt *adj* (*i*) of cowhide

lo'pë'z *nf* [*Entom*] roach

****lo'pkë** *nf* (*Old*) coin worth quarter of a lek

lopo'r *adj* fat

*lop|qa'r *n* = **lopar**

lo'p|thi *adv* humped up against each other like mating cows: cow-fashion, dog-fashion

*lop|u'er *adj (fem ~ore) (Old)* of cows, bovine

lo'qe
  I § *nf (Crude Colloq)* male organ: prick
  II § *np* genitals: crotch

lord *nm* lord (title in English aristocracy)

Lore'në *nf* Lorraine

lo'rëz *nf* [*Ornit*] Scops owl *(Otus scops)*

lorëzo'·n *vi* **1** to wail (like a Scops owl) **2** *(Fig)* to speak with a hoarse voice

*los· = **loz·**, **lua·n**
  ○ **los· damadam** to play checkers

lo'së *nf* [*Ichth*] grayling *(Thymallus thymallus)*

losh *adj, n (Colloq)* (person) who cries easily

lot
  I § *nm* **1** liquid shed by the eyes: tear, teardrop **2** drop of liquid **3** small spot
  II § *adj* very clear
  ○ **lot e shpirt** (of a resemblance) in every detail: the very image
  ○ **◇ vajtën/shkuan lotët pas kokës** "◇'s tears have all been shed" ◇ is no longer grieving about a past loss
  ○ **lot qyqje** "cuckoo's tear" beech nut

*lof· *vt* = **los·**
  ○ **nuk ◇ lot·**^{3sg} **mendja** ◇ *does* not waver in ◇'s opinions

lot|a'k *adj* tearful

lotari *nf* **1** lottery **2** lottery ticket

*lo'të *nf (Old)* draft lottery (for military service) in Turkish times

lot|i'm *nm ger* **1** <**loto'·n 2** [*Med*] lacrimation

*lot|it· = **loto'·n**

lot|ma'dh *adj, n* (person) who has suffered much

loto'·n
  I § *vi* **1** to shed tears, weep, cry **2** to drip moisture
  II § *vt* to mourn [] with tears, shed tears for [], cry over []

*lot|o'r *adj* lacrimal

lot|o're *nf (Book)* flask for collecting tears: tear bottle, lachrymatory

lot|sje'll|ës *adj* tear-provoking

lot|u'a'r *adj (i)* = **përlo'tur**

lot|u'es *adj* tear-producing

lot|ue'shëm *adj (i)* plaintive, sad; tearful

lot|zo'nj|e *nf* [*Bot*] lily-of-the-valley *(Convallaria majalis)*

*love'zhgë = **lëvo'zhgë**

lovi'dhe *nf* string bean

*loxhi'kë *nf* lettuce

loz· *vi, vt* = **lua·n**

loz|a'k *adj* **1** playful **2** having vines

lo'ze *nf* **1** vine; tendril **2** = **gu'zhmë 3** *(Fig Colloq)* sort, kind

lo'zë *nf* [*Ichth*] Albanian lake trout *(Salmo trutta macrostigma)*

loz|o'nja'r *adj, n* **1** playful (child) **2** kittenish (girl) **3** *(Fig Pej)* coquettish (woman)

lo'zhë *nf* **1** [*Theat*] loge **2** [*Constr*] loggia

*lo'zhëra *np fem* sweepings

*lpe *nf* fog, mist

*lpo'zë *nf* ceiling

*lter *nf* = **alta'r**

lu· *het vpr vp* <**lua·n**

lua·n
  I § *vi* **1** to play; play around **2** to move freely/loosely: be loose, wiggle **3** *(Colloq)* to go crazy
  II § *vt* **1** *(Fig Colloq)* to move [] energetically: really make [] move, make [] sizzle **2** *(Colloq)* to play around with []; tease
  ○ **lua·n bajrakas** to play a game in which players hit with sticks another stick set in the ground like a flag
  ○ **lua·n bakthi** to play a jumping game
  ○ **lua·n batbat** to play a game whose object is for one player to try to tell which of those men seated in a circle around him has the knotted kerchief that is being passed around behind them
  ○ **lua·n batinas** to play a children's game that uses three flat rocks
  ○ **nuk ◇ lua·n**^{3sg} **bebja e syrit.** "◇'s eye never blinks" ◇ *is* fearless/intrepid
  ○ **lua·n bidakthi** to play a children's game in which a stick is hit and sent flying through the air as far as possible
  ○ **◇ lua·n bishtin** *(Pej)* to lead ◇ on; flirt
  ○ **lua·n bishtin** "waggle one's tail" **1** *(Pej)* to have loose sexual morals: be a slut **2** to waver in loyalty, be untrustworthy; be unreliable
  ○ **lua·n bixhas** to play a children's gambling game with flat pebbles
  ○ **lua·n biz** to play a game in which a player is secretly tapped on the palm of a hand held behind his back
  ○ **lua·n (me) bizë** to play a mumblety-peg game with homemade awl-like darts
  ○ **lua·n bletas** to play a children's game involving exchanges of light jabs between one player and a circle of other players
  ○ **lua·n breshkazi** to play a children's pushing game
  ○ **lua·n brezahypthi** to play a boy's game in which members of one team try to build a tower by jumping onto the huddled backs of members of their team, without being struck by the sash of a member of the other team
  ○ **lua·n bufthi** to play a game in which one child plays the owl and the others the chickens
  ○ **lua·n bukagjellë** play a game in which children pretend to be bakers
  ○ **lua·n bukas** to play a game in which cards are turned over to see who wins
  ○ **lua·n bukthi** to play a game in which two children in a circle of players race to get the seat vacated by the child into whose lap the "it" player has just dropped a kerchief
  ○ **lua·n buzët** to talk; move one's lips without being heard distinctly: mumble
  ○ **lua·n cakthi** to play a hockey-like game in which one player tries to throw a corncob (or piece of wood) into a hole in the ground protected by the sticks of the other players
  ○ **◇ lua·n caranin në vatër** to insult ◇ terribly
  ○ **lua·n cekash** to play tag
  ○ **lua·n cicmic me** [] **1** to give [] the runaround **2** to fiddle around with []
  ○ **lua·n cingël me** [] to give [] the runaround
  ○ **lua·n cingëlthi** to play tipcat
  ○ **lua·n cingëlthi me** [] to give [] the runaround

○ <> lua·n^{3sg} **çafka e kokës** <> *is losing* <>'s mind, <> *goes crazy*

○ **lua·*n* çakaçukthi** to play the children's game of throwing awls and trying to make them stick in soft ground

○ **lua·*n* çelembyll 1** to play hide-and-seek **2 = ci-cmíc**

○ **lua·*n* çetash** to play a game of tag between two opposing teams

○ **lua·*n* dans** to dance

○ **lua·*n* doçash** to play a hockey-like game using a corncob (or piece of wood) as a puck

○ **lua·*n* fiçor** to play a game like marbles

○ **lua·*n* filxhanash** to play the shell game with inverted teacups hiding small objects

○ **lua·*n* flamuras** to play a game of capture-the-flag

○ **lua·*n* fshehalogas** to play blindman's buff

○ **lua·*n* fugimthi** to play tag

○ **lua·*n* gishtazi** to play a game involving counting off with the fingers

○ **e lua·*n* gishtin (e pushkës)** "wiggle one's gun finger" **1** to be quite a capable person **2** to be very brave

○ **e lua·*n* gishtin e pushkës 1** to be very brave **2** to be very skillful

○ **e lua·*n* gishtin e shëllirës/lëngut** "move the index finger (the finger used to soak up the brine/juice)" **1** to be brave **2** to be clever enough not to come out of any situation empty-handed: be very skillful

○ **lua·*n* gropas** to play a game whose object is to throw small stones into holes made in the ground

○ **lua·*n* gropthi** to play a children's game whose object is to get a small ball into an opponent's hole

○ **lua·*n* guraçokthi** to play a game of jacks with pebbles

○ **lua·*n* gurashenjash = lua·*n* rrasash**

○ **lua·*n* gurët** "move rocks" to make great efforts, try every possible means; go to any lengths, try by hook or by crook

○ **lua·*n* gurin e fundit** to play one's final card

○ **lua·*n* gurthi** to juggle two small rocks with one hand

○ **lua·*n* gurthimurthi** to play a game in which children look for something hidden in fists placed one on top of another

○ **lua·*n* gjelash** to play a game in which each player standing on one leg tries to shoulder another player into putting his other leg down

○ **lua·*n* gjyrykthi** to play a game in which one player throws his stick high into the air and another player tries to hit it

○ **lua·*n* hapadollapa** to play blindman's buff

○ **lua·*n* jesirthi** children's game played in which each team tries to capture prisoners from the other team

○ **lua·*n* kajot** to play a game with small round stones

○ **lua·*n* kaladibrançe** to play a game in which members of one team try to build a tower by jumping onto the huddled backs of members of their team, without being tagged by a member of the other team

○ **lua·*n* kalorthi** to play a game in which boys battle each other while riding piggyback

○ **lua·*n* kâmbgjithkuri** *(Reg Gheg)* to play hop-scotch

○ <> lua·n^{3sg} **kapaku i kokës/kafka/tepja e kokës 1** <>'s head *is splitting*, <> *has* a terrible headache **2** <> *is* overwhelmed by problems to worry about **3** <> *is* shocked/astonished

○ **lua·*n* kaparthi** to play a game of drop the handkerchief

○ **lua·*n* kapuçambrojtas** to play a game in which one person tries to keep the others from taking away the cap he is wearing

○ **lua·*n* kapuças** to play a game in which the hidden object is placed under one of several cap-shaped covers

○ **lua·*n* kapuçashkelmas** to play a game in which one person tries to kick one of the people circled around him, and the person kicked must take off his cap for the others to kick around

○ **lua·*n* kartën e fundit** to play one's final card

○ **lua·*n* këmbadoras** to play a game in which players on all fours try to catch the legs of the players standing up who in turn are trying to grab the caps of the players on all fours

○ **lua·*n* këmbë e duar** "move feet and hands" to move heaven and earth, make every effort, do everything necessary

○ **lua·*n* këmbëcingthi** to play a game in which players stand on one foot and push one another in the shoulder until one of them puts down his other foot or falls over

○ **lua·*n* këmbëçalë** to play a sort of hopscotch game whose object is to hop and kick a flat stone around a marked course

○ **lua·*n* këmbëthirë = këmbëçalë**

○ **lua·*n* kukafshehthi = lua·*n* kukafshetas**

○ **lua·*n* kukafshetas** to play hide-and-seek

○ **lua·*n* kukthi** to play hide-and-seek

○ **lua·*n* kumar** to gamble

○ **lua·*n* kungullas** to play a game in which children chase after a hollowed-out rolling gourd

○ **lua·*n* laradash** to do a forward somersault

○ **lua·*n* lepuras** to play a game of hounds and hares, in which one child is the hare and is chased by the other children

○ **lua·*n* letrën e fundit** to play one's final card

○ **lua·*n* litarthi** to play a game of jump-rope

○ **lua·*n* lodrën/lojën e <>** "play <>'s game" be <>'s pawn, be at <>'s beck and call

○ **lua·*n* luftash** to play a game of dodgeball

○ **lua·*n* lulebukthi** to play the game of kick-the-cap

○ **lua·*n* mbyllasyzash 1** to play blindman's buff **2** *(Fig)* to have no way of knowing what one is doing: be operating in the dark **3** *(Fig)* to play a trick on someone, be pulling someone's leg

○ **lua·*n* me fjalë** to be playing with words

○ **lua·*n* me kokën** to stake one's life

○ **lua·*n* me kungulleshka** to play a game in which each player is assigned a number and must respond quickly when a phrase containing his number is said

○ **lua·*n* me pllaka = lua·*n* petas**

○ **lua·*n* me zjarrin** to be playing with fire

○ <> lua·n^{3sg} **mendja (e kokës)** <> *loses* <>'s mind, <> *goes crazy*

○ po <> lua·n^{3sg} **mendja (e kokës) 1** <> *has* a splitting headache **2** <> *has* some really tough problems: <> *has* a real headache on <>'s hands

○ **lua·*n* mendsh** to go crazy

○ **lua·*n* mendsh për** [ ] to be crazy about [ ]

○ [ ] **lua·*n* mendsh** to drive [ ] out of [ ]'s mind

○ **lua·*n* mjaltas** to play a children's game in which one child tries to keep others from touching a cap placed on the ground and called the "pot of honey"

○ [ ] **lua·*n* në litar** to poke fun at [ ]; ridicule [ ]; deride [ ]

∘ [] **lua·***n* **në majë të gishtit** to have [] wrapped around one's little finger

∘ [] **lua·***n* **në tel** to be able to do as one likes with [], have [] in one's pocket

∘ [] **lua·***n* **nëpër gishta** "play [] upon one's fingers" to know [] like the back of one's hand; understand/ master [] quickly

∘ **lua·***n* **nga fiqiri/mendtë** to go out of one's mind

∘ **lua·***n* **nga kondaku** to go out of one's mind, lose one's marbles

∘ **lua·***n* **nga mendja** to go crazy

∘ **<> lua·***n* **një rreng** to play a dirty trick on <>

∘ **lua·***n* **pesagurthi** to play the children's game of jacks with five pebbles

∘ **lua·***n* **petash** to play a form of hopscotch requiring competing players to move a flat stone around a sectioned course marked on the ground

∘ **lua·***n* **pështymas** to play blindman's buff

∘ **lua·***n* **picimajthi** to play a mumblety-peg game with homemade awl-like darts

∘ **e lua·***n* **pjesën** to put on a clever act

∘ **lua·***n* **pulaqorrthi** to play blindman's buff

∘ **lua·***n* **qiteprit** to play a game whose object is for a player to hit with his stick the stick that another player has thrown as high as possible into the air

∘ **lua·***n* **qokthi** to play a game with several players in which the object is to throw tokens into two holes

∘ **lua·***n* **qorras** to play hide-and-seek

∘ **e lua·***n* **rolin e <>** to make a deceptive pretense of being <>: play the <>

∘ **lua·***n* **rrasash** to play a children's game in which the object is to knock down the opponents' three rock slabs standing on their ends before your own are knocked down

∘ **lua·***n* **rrasbuq** to play a children's game in which the object is to knock over a corncob or flat rock perched at the edge of a hole

∘ **lua·***n* **rripas** to play a children's game in which a strip of cloth is passed in secret from hand to hand

∘ **lua·***n* **rruvijash** to play hopscotch

∘ **lua·***n* **si gjethja e plepit** to waver on a promise

∘ **lua·***n* **si qeni me leckë me** [] "play with [] like a dog with a rag" to jack [] around

∘ **lua·***n* **spathinjsh** to play a card game in which clubs are counted as special

∘ **lua·***n* **stricë në kurriz të <>** "play tic-tac-toe on <>'s back" to pull a swindle on <>

∘ **lua·***n* **syllambyllthi** to play blindman's buff

∘ **lua·***n* **symbyllas** to play blindman's buff

∘ **lua·***n* **symbyllthi** to play blindman's buff

∘ **<> lua·***n* **syrin** to give <> the eye, wink at <>

∘ **lua·***n* **shalahipas = lua·***n* **topahípas**

∘ **lua·***n* **shatorrthi = rra·**sash

∘ **lua·***n* **shelikademën** to play leapfrog

∘ **lua·***n* **shenjas *= lua·***n* **rrasash**

∘ **lua·***n* **shilarthi** to play on a swing/seesaw

∘ **lua·***n* **shkopacingthi/shkopaxingël/shkopax-inglash** to play tipcat

∘ **<> lua·***n* **shpatullash** to play a team game in which players use sword-shaped paddles to keep an acorn from touching the ground

∘ **lua·***n* **shpendthi** to play a game testing one's skill in making various birdcalls

∘ **lua·***n* **shregullash** to play on swings

∘ **lua·***n* **shtëpiash** to play house

∘ **<> lua·***n*^{3sg} **tabani i kokës/kafka/tepja e kokës *1** <>'s head *is splitting*, <> *has* a terrible headache **2** <> *is* overwhelmed by problems to worry about **3** <> *is* shocked/astonished

∘ **lua·***n* **teatër me** [] to try to be amusing at []'s expense; put/have [] on

∘ **i lua·***n* **telat** to know how to pull strings

∘ **lua·***n* **topahípas** to play a game in which members of one team throw a ball back and forth while mounted on the backs of crouching members of the other team

∘ **lua·***n* **topgropthi** to play a children's game in which the players try to roll a ball into one of the small holes lined up in the ground

∘ **s'**[] **lua·***n*^{3sg} **(as) topi** "not (even) a cannon can shake []" **1** [] *is* absolutely definite **2** [] *can't* be budged

∘ **lua·***n* **topkalorthazi** to play a ball game in which opposing players are riding piggyback

∘ **lua·***n* **topthi** to play ball

∘ **Luaji të tharat** "Move those numb things (arms/ legs)" Get a move on!

∘ **lua·***n* **thikas** to play at throwing a knife accurately

∘ **lua·***n* **unazash** to shoot marbles between thumb and finger formed in a ring

∘ **lua·***n* **uras** to play a game in which one boy is stretched in the air between two others to form a bridge under which other boys pass

∘ **lua·***n* **urët** "poke the andirons" **1** to try to heat/ hurry things up **2** *(Pej)* to incite a fight, stir the pot

∘ **Luaj vendit!** "Move your position!" (expresses shock at something just said) Say it isn't so! You can't mean it!

∘ **lua·***n* **xhamthi** to play a game in which children from one team standing in a circle try to catch children running from the other circle

∘ **lua·***n* **zarin e fundit** to play one's final card

∘ **<> lua·***n*^{3sg} **zemra** <> *feels* very worried, <> *is* uneasy; <> *is* deeply afraid

∘ **lua·***n* **zhizh-bubazi** to play blindman's buff

∘ **lua·***nn* **arazi** to play a game in which one player tries to prevent another from entering a space pretended to be freshly sown land

∘ **lua·***nn* **arushë me** [] to toy with []

∘ **Nuk <> lua·***nn*^{3sg} **as bebja e syrit.** "Not even the pupil of <>'s eye *wavers*." <> *is* fearless/intrepid.

∘ **nuk lua·***nn* **as gishtin e dorës/këmbës** "not even move the fingers/toes" *1 not lift a finger, not do a thing; not move at all **2** not worry a bit, be totally indifferent

∘ **lua·***nn* **badbadbad** *(Reg)* to play a game of hunt-the-slipper

lua·dh *nm* = liva·dh

lua·jt *stem for pdef, opt, adm, part* <lua·*n*

lua·jtje *nf ger* <lua·*n*

lua·jt·shëm *adj (i)* **1** movable **2** unstable **3** *[Law]* (of property) movable (not real estate)

lua·jt·ur

  I § part <lua·*n*, lu·*het*

  II § adj (i) (Colloq) **1** rambling **2** crazy, insane

  III § nm (i) **1** *(Colloq)* rambler **2** lunatic

  ∘ **<> kanë luajtur vidhat/burmat/burgjitë** "<>'s screws have come loose" <> *has* a screw loose

lua·n *nm [Zool]* lion

  ∘ **luan deti** *[Zool]* sea lion

Lua·n *nm* Luan (male name)

luane·shë *nf* lioness

lua·n·kë *nf dimin (Reg Tosk)* lion cub

luan·or *adj [Spec]* leonine

luarí *nf* herd of cows

lubardhë *nf* [*Zool*] fast lynx-like animal: wildcat
lubenicë *nf* watermelon
lubertinë *nf* mud, slush
lubi *nf* **1** [*Folklore*] ogre **2** *(Fig Pej)* terrible glutton **3** *(Reg)* storm
lubitur *adj (i)* **1** monstrous **2** stormy, raging
lubrifikant
  I § *adj* [*Tech*] = **lubrifikues**
  II § *nm* lubricant
lubrifikator *nm* lubricator
lubrifikim *nm ger* [*Tech*] **1** <**lubrifiko**·*n* **2** lubrication
lubrifiko·*n* *vt* [*Tech*] to lubricate
lubrifikues
  I § *adj* [*Tech*] lubricating
  II § *nm* lubricant
luc *nm* [*Ichth*] zander *(Stizostedion lucioperca)*
*****lucaviq** *nm* boor
*****luc**ë *nf* = **lluc**ë
*****luc**ët *adj (i)* muddy, dirty
*****luck** *nm* = **lugaç**
*****luco**·*n* OR **lucos**· = **llucëro**·*n*
luçidim *nm ger* [*Spec*] <**luçido**·*n*
luçido·*n* *vt* [*Spec*] to polish
luçidues
  I § *adj* [*Spec*] used in polishing
  II § *n* polisher
luçie *nf* [*Ichth*] pike *Esox lucius*
luçis *stem for 1st sg pres, pl pres, 2nd & 3rd sg subj, pind* <**luçit**·
luçit· *vt* to boil/bubble up
*****ludi** *nf* body odor
*****lue** = **lua**
*****luejtsh**ëm = **luajtsh**ëm
luftanije *nf* warship
luftar = **luftëtar**
Luftar *nm* Luftar (male name)
luftarak *nm* **1** of war **2** military; martial **3** militant
luftash *adv*
luftë *nf* **1** war **2** battle, combat
  ○ **luftë qytetare** civil war
luftëdashës
  I § *adj* war-loving, warlike, bellicose
  II § *n* warmonger
luftëndezës
  I § *adj* provoking to war
  II § *n* warmonger
luftënxitës
  I § *adj* warmongering
  II § *n* warmonger
luftëtar
  I § *n* **1** warrior, fighter; combatant **2** [*Ornit*] ruff (male), reeve (female) *(Philomachus pugnax L.)*
  II § *adj* **1** in combat; fighting **2** *(Old)* = **luftarak**
luftim *nm ger* **1** <**lufto**·*n* **2** combat, fight; battle
  ○ **luftim me dema** bullfight
Luftim *nm* Luftim (male name)
luftime *np* hard and fast beating of the heart; deep pulsating pain
lufto·*n*
  I § *vt* to fight, combat, battle, wage war against []
  II § *vi* **1** to fight, struggle **2** to throb; pulsate with pain

○ <> **lufto**·n^{3sg} **gjaku/zemra** <>'s blood *starts to* rise, <>'s heart *is* surging (with eagerness/excitement)
luftues
  I § *adj* **1** in combat; combative **2** militant
  II § *n* = **luftëtar**
lug *nm (np* ¨ *je)* **1** trough **2** duct; channel; gully **3** groove; hollow **4** dale
  ○ **lugu i mullirit** millrace
  ○ **lugu i zemrës** pit of the stomach
lugaç *nm* adze with a curved blade: spout adze
lugaj *nf* deep, wide and long valley
lugare *nf* **1** mason's hod **2** deep and steep valley **3** spoon rack
lugat *nm* **1** dark and evil ghost who rises from the grave to frighten and harm people at night **2** *(Pej)* ugly and evil person
lugatë *nf* oar
lugetër *np* <**lugat**
lugë *nf* **1** spoon **2** trowel; scoop, shovel
  ○ **lug**ë **gacash/thëngjish** cinder scoop
  ○ **ësh·të lug**ë **e lar**ë not have a nickel: be poor as a churchmouse
  ○ **lug**ë **lulesh** garden trowel
  ○ **Luga e madhe të shqyen gojën.** "The big spoon will rip your throat." *(Prov)* You can choke on greed.
  ○ **Luga e madhe të zë fytin/gojën.** "The big spoon will stop up your throat/mouth." *(Prov)* You can choke on greed.
  ○ **ësh·të lug**ë **për vegsh** "be a spoon for a stew pot" to be the right person for the job
*****lugëlang**ës = **lugëlëng**ës
lugëlëngës *nm (Contemp)* bootlicking parasite
lugë-**lug**ë
  I § *adv* one spoon after another
  II § *adj* in spoon-formed heaps
lugës
  I § *nm* **1** adze with a concave blade: spout adze; gouge **2** concave grater **3** small concave metal scraper **4** spoon rack **5** shoe spoon **6** ladle **7** *(Contemp)* bootlicking parasite **8** [*Ornit*] = **sqeplug**ë
  II § *adj* = **lug**ët
lugësim *nm ger* <**lugëso**·*n*, **lugëso**·*het*
lugësnik *nm* spoon rack
lugëso·*het* *vpr* to become concave
lugëso·*n* *vt* to make concave
lugësore woodworking adze with concave blade
lugështirë *nf* depressed place: depression, hollow, basin
lugët *adj (i)* **1** concave **2** curved
lugëtar *n* **1** carver of wooden spoons **2** knife with a curved blade for carving spoons **3** spokeshave used to peel the bark from trees **4** concave grater
lugëti *nf* concavity
lugëthatë *adj* very poor, without a bite to eat
lugë**vesh**ëz *nf* [*Entom*] earwig *(Dermaptera)* = **gërshë**rëz
lugëz *nf* **1** container used for bailing water from a boat **2** abdominal cavity **3** groove **4** teaspoon
lugim *nm ger* **1** <**lugo**·*n*, **lugo**·*het* **2** groove, slot *****3** fluting, molding
luginë *nf* valley, gorge
luginor *adj (Book)* **1** pertaining to a valley **2** having valleys **3** valley-shaped

lug·my'stë *adj (i)* concavo-convex

lug·na'jë *nf* = **lugajë**

lugo'·het *vpr* to become hollow/concave; become drawn haggard

lugo'·n *vt* to make [] concave: hollow [] out, gouge out []

lug'or *adj* concave, hollow

lugo're *nf* 1 wooden basin 2 wooden mold with a handle for making tiles 3 small valley
  ○ **lugorja e duarve/këmbëve** wooden basin for washing hands/feet
  ○ **lugorja e hudhrave** wooden mortar for pressing garlic

*****lugo's·** = **lugo'·n**

lugo's·et = **lugo'·het**

*****lu'gshtë** *nf* mountain gorge

lugth *nm* 1 small water trough/spout through which water flows from a spring 2 [*Anat*] abdominal cavity; belly

lugthe'llë *nf* deep depression in the mountains

*****lugth'uer** *adj (fem ˜ore) (Old)* gastric

luguminoze *np* [*Bot*] legumes

*****lu'gun** *adj (i) (Reg Gheg)* hollow

lugu'r *nm* curved knife used to peel squash

lugu'ru'zhdë *nf* 1 large wooden spoon 2 *(Old)* thick wood or clay crucible for metals

lugu'tkë *nf* = **luleshtry'dhe**

lu'gje *np* <**lug**

luha'çe *OR* **luha'çe** *nf* swing, seesaw

luha're *nf* large wooden ladle

luha's *stem for 1st sg pres, pl pres, 2nd & 3rd sg subj, pind* <**luha't·**

luha't· *vt* to cause [] to move freely through an arc from a base point: rock, swing; make [] sway; wag; dangle

luha't·et *vpr* 1 to rock; sway, swing 2 *(Fig)* to waver, vacillate; fluctuate

luha't· *vt* to rock; sway, swing 2 *(Fig)* to waver, vacillate; fluctuate

luha't·ëse *nf* swing

luha'tje *nf ger* 1 <**luha't·**, **luha't·et** 2 *(Fig)* vacillation; fluctuation

luha'tshëm *adj (i)* 1 subject to swaying, rockable 2 *(Fig)* unstable

*****lu'jtshëm** *adj (i)* = **lu'ajtshëm**

lu'kër *nf* 1 sheep; lamb; small flock of sheep 2 *(Fig Pet)* small child: little lamb

luks
  I § *nm* luxury; finery
  II § *adv (Colloq)* in a deluxe manner, in finery
  III § *adj (Colloq)* deluxe

Luksembu'rg *nm* Luxembourg

luks'oz *adj* luxurious

luk'th *nm* = **lugth**
  ○ **lukthi i barkut** pit of the stomach

lukuni' *nf* 1 pack of (hungry) wolves 2 *(Fig)* horde

lukura'më *nf* = **rrokulli'më**

lu'l·et *vpr* = **lulo'·n**

lula'r *nm* [*Bot*] lesser celandine, pilewort *(Ranunculus ficaria, Ficaria verna)*

Lu'lash *nm* Lulash (male name)

lul'bu'kur *nf* [*Bot*] sweet William *(Dianthus barbatus)*

lu'le
  I § *nf* 1 flower 2 patch of color on an animal's body 3 clump of gray hair 4 fleshy part of the fingertip

5 middle of the forehead 6 the very middle, right in the center 7 pupil of the eye 8 *(Fig)* the best of, the best part of
  II § *np* 1 *(Euph)* menstrual period, menstruation 2 *(Euph)* male genitalia
  ○ **ësh·të lule** to be in relatively good health, have nothing to complain about: be in good condition
  ○ **lule agrepi** [*Bot*] yellow vetch
  ○ **lule akshami** [*Bot*] = **luleakshami**
  ○ **lule akulli** "flower of ice" [*Bot*] perpetual begonia *(Begonia semperflorens)*
  ○ **lule alle** [*Bot*] balsamine, garden balsam *(Impatiens balsamina)*
  ○ **lule argjendi** "flower of silver" [*Bot*] crown daisy, garland chrysanthemum *(Chrysanthemum Coronarium)*
  ○ **lule arushe** "bear flower" [*Bot*] honeysuckle
  ○ **lule baku** [*Bot*] daisy *(Bellis perennis)*
  ○ **lule balsami** [*Bot*] common St.-John's-wort, klamath weed *(Hypericum perforatum)*
  ○ **lule e ballit** 1 middle of the forehead; right between the eyes 2 [*Med*] glabella *()*
  ○ **lule bare** [*Bot*] ground ivy, bugle
  ○ **lule behari** [*Bot*] gentian *(Gentiana)*
  ○ **lule bezele** [*Bot*] sweet pea *(Lathyrus odoratus)*
  ○ **lule blete** [*Bot*] sweet honeysuckle *(Lonicera caprifolum)*
  ○ **lule bollë** [*Bot*] bellbine, greater bindweed *(Calystegia sepium)*
  ○ **lule bore** [*Bot*] *=* **lulebo'rë**
  ○ **lule breshke** [*Bot*] = **lulebre'shkë**
  ○ **lule bretku** [*Bot*] buttercup, crowfoot *(Ranunculus)* = **zhabinë**
  ○ **lule brezi** [*Bot*] white currant *(Ribes sativum)*
  ○ **lule bualli** [*Bot*] = **ta'tull**
  ○ **lule çallme** [*Bot*] = **çallma're**
  ○ **lule daci** [*Bot*] sun spurge *(Euphorbia helioscopia)*
  ○ **lule dashurie** [*Bot*] = **lule mosmëharro**
  ○ **lule deleje** [*Bot*] = **lulede'le**
  ○ **lule dielli** [*Bot*] common sunflower *(Helianthus annuus L.)*
  ○ **lule dimri** [*Bot*] = **luledi'mër**
  ○ **lule djathi** "cheese flower" [*Bot*] globe artichoke *(Cynara scolymus)* = **bar djathi**
  ○ **lule dredhje** [*Bot*] bellbine, greater bindweed *(Calystegia sepium)*
  ○ **lule dredhkël** [*Bot*] traveller's joy, old man's beard *(Clematis vitalba)*
  ○ **lule dushku** "oak flower" [*Bot*] mother chrysanthemum *(Chrysanthemum indicum)*
  ○ **lule dylli** 1 [*Bot*] common waxplant *(Hoya carnosa)* 2 = **lulequmështo're**
  ○ **lule dhensh** [*Bot*] = **lulede'le**
  ○ **lule dhije** [*Bot*] = **luledhi'**
  ○ **lule ethesh** [*Bot*] centaury, drug centaurium *(Centaurium umbellatum)* = **trikë**
  ○ **lule filxhani** [*Bot*] foxglove = **lulefilxha'n**
  ○ **lule floriri** "gold flower" [*Bot*] strawflower *(Helichrysum)* = **a'kës**
  ○ **lulet e frudhit** [*Med*] rash from measles
  ○ **lule fshese** [*Bot*] summer cypress *(Kochia trichophylla)* = **micu'kth**
  ○ **lule fushe** wildflower
  ○ **lule gishti** [*Bot*] foxglove = **lulefilxha'n**
  ○ **lule gomari** [*Bot*] = **lulequmështo're**

○ **lulet e gomës** [Tech] tread design of the tire; tire tread

○ **lule gramafoni** [Bot] jimsonweed, thorn apple *(Datura stramonium)* = **ta'tull**

○ **lule gruri** [Bot] = **lulegru'r**

○ **lule gypëz** [Bot] flosculous (VD)

○ **lule gjaku** "blood flower" [Bot] common St.-John's-wort *(Hypericum perforatum)*

○ **lule gjarpri** "snake flower" [Bot] dragon arum *(Drancunculus vulgaris)* = **stërgji'**

○ **lule gjeli** "cock flower" [Bot] = **lulëku'qe**

○ **lule gjembi** "thorn flower" [Bot] = **gjemba'ç**

○ **lule gjize** [Bot] yarrow *(Achilea millefolium)*

○ **lule gjuhëz** [Bot] floret (of a composite flower)

○ **lule gjyle** [Bot] kind of valerian *(Valeriana tuberosa)*

○ **lule hashashi** [Bot] = **hasha'sh**

○ **lule helmi** [Bot] = **lulehe'lm**

○ **Lulet i ka të bukura, po t'i shohim pemlat.** "It has beautiful flowers/leaves, but let's see the berries." It looks all right now, but we have to see how it turns out.

○ **lule kacidhe** [Bot] daisy *(Bellis perennis)*

○ **lule kadifeje** [Bot] marigold *(Tagetes)*

○ **lule kambane** [Bot] = **lulekëmbo're**

○ **lule kashte** "straw flower" [Bot] strawflower *(Helichrysum)*

○ **lule këmbore** [Bot] = **lulekëmbo're**

○ **lule kishe** [Bot] oleander, rosebay *(Nerium oleander)*

○ **lule koreje** [Bot] chicory, succory *(Cichorium intybus L.)* = **radhi'qe**

○ **lule krehri** "comb flower" [Bot] venuscup teasel *(Dipsacus silvestris)*

○ **lule krishti** [Bot] passionflower *(Passiflora)*

○ **lule kryeshtrëmbër** [Bot] snowdrop *(Galanthus nivalis)*

○ **lule kulish** [Bot] purple orchid

○ **lule kumbonë** [Bot] = **lulekamba'në**

○ **lule kunde** [Bot] = **luleku'nde**

○ **lule kungulli** "squash flower" [Bot] nasturtium *(Tropaeolum majus)*

○ **lule lakre** [Bot] cauliflower *(Brassica oleracea L.)* = **lulela'kër**

○ **lule lepuri** "rabbit flower" [Bot] lungwort *(Pulmonaria officinalis)*

○ **lule letre** "paper flower" [Bot] zinnia *(Zinnia elegans)*

○ **lule lini** [Bot] Mediterranean needlegrass, feathergrass *(Stipa mediterranea)*

○ **lule maji** [Bot] = **lulema'j**

○ **lule mbrëmjeje** [Bot] = **lule akshami**

○ **lule merimange** [Bot] love-in-a-mist *(Nigella damascena)*

○ **lule mëllage** [Bot] = **lulemëlla'gë**

○ **lule mëngjesi** "morning flower" [Bot] morning glory *(Ipomoea purpurea)*

○ **lule Milani** [Bot] hybrid dahlia *(Dahlia variabilis)*

○ **lulja e mirë** *(Euph)* [Med Veter] anthrax

○ **lule misiri** [Bot] common wallflower *(Cheiranthus cheiri)*

○ **lule mize** [Bot] = **lulemi'zë**

○ **lule mosmëharro** [Bot] forget-me-not *(Myosotis)*

○ **lule mosmëprek** [Bot] touch-me-not *(Impatiens noli-tangere)*

○ **lule mosprek** [Bot] touch-me-not = **lule mosmëprek**

○ **lule murgeshe** [Bot] common columbine *(Aquilegia vulgaris)*

○ **lule mustaku** [Bot] honeysuckle *(Lonicera)*

○ **lule nate 1** [Bot] = **lule akshami 2** [Bot] columbine *(Aquilegia)*

○ **lule ngjitëse** [Bot] = **lulengji'tëse**

○ **lule pashke** "Easter flower" **1** [Bot] wallflower, gillyflower *(Cheiranthus cheiri)* **2** common toadflax *(Linaria vulgaris)*

○ **lule patate** [Bot] earthnut *(Conopodium denudatum)*

○ **lule pavodë** [Bot] silk tree *(Albizzia julibrissin)*

○ **lule peshku** [Bot] kind of mullein *(Verbascum longifolium)*

○ **lule pini** *(Reg Gheg)* [Bot] yellow bedstraw *(Galium verum)*

○ **lule pleshti** [Bot] Dalmatian pyrethrum *(Chrysanthemum cinerariaefolium)*

○ **lule pranvere** [Bot] primrose *(Primula vulgaris)* = **aguli'çe**

○ **lule preshi** [Bot] common iris *(Iris germanica)*

○ **lule qengji** [Bot] = **luledə'le**

○ **lule qeni 1** [Bot] wild chamomile *(Chamomilla recutita)* **2** corn chamomile *(Anthemis arvendsis)*

○ **lule qumështore** [Bot] = **lulequmə'shtore**

○ **lule qyqeje** [Bot] = **luleqy'qe**

○ **lule rrenëse** flower that blooms but never develops fruit

○ **lule rruaze** [Bot] = **lulerrua'zë**

○ **lule sabahu** [Bot] = **lule mëngjesi**

○ **lule sahati** [Bot] blue-crown passionflower *(Passiflora caerulea)*

○ **lule saksie** potted plant

○ **lule sapuni** [Bot] bitter cress *(Cardamine)*

○ **lule sefa** [Bot] hollyhock *(Althaea rosea)*

○ **lule semini** [Bot] jasmine *= **jasemi'n**

○ **lule squfuri** [Agr] flowers of sulfur

○ **lule syri** [Bot] wild pansy, heartsease *(Viola tricolor)*

○ **lule sharre** [Bot] leaf cactus *(Epiphyllum)*

○ **lule sheboje** [Bot] = **luleshebo'jë**

○ **lule shëmitri** [Bot] crown daisy, garland chrysanthemum *(Chrysanthemum coronarium)*

○ **lule shëngjergji 1** [Bot] crosswort *(Galium cruciata)* **2** common gladiolus *(Gladiolus communis)*

○ **lule shëngjini** [Bot] = **luleshëngji'n**

○ **lule shigjete** [Bot] = **luleshigje'të**

○ **lule shkrepse** [Bot] field cow-wheat *(Melampyrum arvense)*

○ **lule shpate/shpatëz** [Bot] = **luleshpa'të**

○ **lule shqerre** [Bot] = **luleshqe'rrë**

○ **lule shqiponje** [Bot] = **luleshqipo'një**

○ **lule shtërgu** [Bot] flowering rush *(Butomus umbellatus)*

○ **lule tambli** [Bot] common dandelion *(Taraxacum officinale)* = **tambëlto're**

○ **lule thoi** [Bot] stonecrop *(Sedum acre)*

○ **lule vathi** [Bot] fuchsia *(Fuchsia)* = **luleva'th**

○ **lule vedre** [Bot] = **luleve'dër**

○ **lule veje/veze** [Bot] = **luleve've**

○ **lule verdhë** [Bot] buttercup

○ **lule vëllamë** [Bot] burning bush *(Dictamnus albus)*

○ **lule vile** [Bot] = **lulevi'le**

○ **lule vizhe** "beetle flower" [Bot] = **lulevizhë**

○ **lule vjeshte** [*Bot*] = **lulevje'sht**ë

○ **lule vreshti** [*Bot*] = **dorëzo'një**

○ **lule ylli** [*Bot*] = **luley'll**

○ **lule zabzun** [*Bot*] anemone *(Anemone)*

○ **lule zjarri** [*Bot*] = **lulezja'rr**

○ **lule zogu** [*Bot*] rocket larkspur *(Delphinium ajacis)* = **gjuhënu'**s*e*

○ **lule zonje** [*Bot*] = **lulezo'nj**ë

○ **lule zyre** [*Bot*] common portulaca *(Portulaca grandiflora)*

Lu'le *nf* Lule (popular female name)

lule aksha'm *nm* [*Bot*] four o'clock, marvel of Peru *(Mirabilis jalapa)*

lule a'lle *nf* [*Bot*] balsamine, garden balsam *(Impatiens balsamina)*

lule a'r *nm* [*Bot*] figroot buttercup *(Ficaria verna)*

****lule ba'rdh**ë *nf* [*Bot*] marguerite, moon-daisy, ox-eye daisy *(Leucanthemum vulgare)*

lule ba'rtë*s* *adj* [*Bot*] floriferous ()

lule basa'n *nm* [*Bot*] common St.-John's-wort, klamath weed *(Hypericum perforatum)*

lule ble'te *nf* [*Bot*] sweet/perfoliate honeysuckle *(Lonicera caprifolium)*

lule bli'ri *nm* [*Bot*] linden flower

lule bo'reë *nf* [*Bot*] "snow flower" big-leafed hydrangea *(Hydrangea macrophylla)*

lule bre'shkë [*Bot*] rockrose used as a source of labdanum balsam *(Cistus villosus)*

lule bri'gje *nf* [*Bot*] salsify, goatsbeard *(Trapapogon)*

lule bu'fkë *nf* [*Bot*] pompon flower

lule bu'kje *nf* [*Bot*] strawflower *(Helichrysum)*

lule bu'k'thi *adv*

lule buri' *nf* [*Bot*] ornamental bushy plant up to ten meters high, pendulous leaves, tubular rust-colored flowers ()

lule cinga're *nf* [*Bot*] = **lulekamba'n**ë

lule de'le *nf* [*Bot*] "sheep flower" garden daisy, English daisy *(Bellis perennis)*

lule di'ell i *nm* [*Bot*] sunflower *(Helianthus annuus L.)*

lule di'mër *nm* [*Bot*] globe candytuft *(Iberis umbellata)*

lule dre'dhë *nf* [*Bot*] wild strawberry *(Fragaria vesca L.)*

lule dhi' *nf* [*Bot*] perfoliate honeysuckle *(Lonicera caprifolium)*

lule dhri' *nf* [*Bot*] water dropwort *(Oenanthe)*

****lule e'n**ë *nf* [*Bot*] fritillary *(Fritillaria)*

lule e'thesh *nm* [*Bot*] centaury, drug centaurium *(Centaurium umbellatum)* = **tri'k**ë

lule fasu'le *nf* [*Bot*] ivy arum *(Scindapsus aureus)*

lule filxha'n *nf* [*Bot*] foxglove *(Digitalis)*

lule fi'n *nm* [*Bot*] mercury () *(Mercurialis)*

lule fro'së *nf* [*Bot*] white water-lily *(Nymphaea alba)*

lule fy'le *nf* [*Bot*] tubular water dropwort *(Oenanthe fistulosa)*

lule go'jë *nf* [*Bot*] common snapdragon *(Antirrhinum majus)*

lule gre'reë*z* *nf* [*Bot*] = **qum**ë**shtor**e

lule gru'r *nm* [*Bot*] knapweed *(Centaurea)*

lule he'lm *nm* [*Bot*] poisonous plant of the genus Berberidaceae *(Gymnosperium Spach)*

lule kabuni' *nf* [*Bot*] crocus-like flower *(Romulea bulbucodium)*

lule ka'cidh jare *nf* [*Bot*] garden daisy *(Bellis perennis)*

lule ka'çe *nf* [*Bot*] cowslip *(Primula officinalis)*

lule kadi'fe *nf* [*Bot*] marigold *(Tagetes)*

lule kamba'në *nf* [*Bot*] bellflower *(Campanula)*

○ **lulekambanë fitemë** [*Bot*] rampion *Campanula rapunculus*

○ **lulekambanë gjethepjeshke** [*Bot*] peach-leaved bellflower *Campanula persicifolia*

○ **lulekambanë gjetherrumbullake** [*Bot*] harebell *Campanula rotundifolia*

○ **lulekambanë e hapur** [*Bot*] rambling/spreading bellflower *Campanula patula*

○ **lulekambanë lëmshore** [*Bot*] Dane's-blood bellflower, clustered bellflower *Campanula glomerata*

○ **lulekambanë e ndërmjeme** [*Bot*] Canterbury bell *Campanula medium*

○ **lulekambanë piramidale** [*Bot*] chimney bellflower *Campanula pyramidalis*

○ **lulekambanë e Siberisë** [*Bot*] Siberian bellflower *Campanula sibirica*

○ **lulekambanë e trakelit** [*Bot*] Coventry bells, throatwort *Campanula trachelium*

lule ka'shtë *nf* [*Bot*] strawflower *(Helichrysum)*

lule këmbë'**pu'l**e *nf* [*Bot*] sowbread *(Cyclamen neapolitanum)*

lule këmbo're *nf* [*Bot*] bellflower *(Campanula)*

lule kërdho'kull *nf* [*Bot*] sowbread *(Cyclamen neapolitanum)*

****lule ki'she** *nf* [*Bot*] oleander *(Nerium oleander)*

lule kokërdho'kull *nf* [*Bot*] spring snowflake *(Leucojum vernum)*

lule komi'sht *nm* [*Bot*] burnet *(Sanguisorba)*

lule kopsu'të *nf* [*Bot*] auricula *(Primula auricula)*

lule ko'rcull *nf* [*Bot*] common St. John's wort *(Hypericum perforatum)*

lule kre'hër *nm* [*Bot*] venuscup teasel *(Dipsacus silvestris)*

****lule krye po'sht**ë OR **lule krye shtre'mb ët** *nf* [*Bot*] snowdrop *(Galanthus nivalis)*

lulekumbo'ne *nf* [*Bot*] = **lulekamba'n**ë

lule ku'nde *nf* [*Bot*] wood anemone *(Anemone nemorosa)*

lule ku'ngull *nm* [*Bot*] nasturtium *(Tropaeolum majus)*

lule ku'pë *nf* [*Bot*] nodding navelwort *(Umbilicus, pendulinus, Cotyledon umbilicus)*

lule ku'qe *nf* [*Bot*] = **lul**ë**ku'q**e

lule la'kër *nf* [*Bot*] cauliflower *(Brassica oleracea)*

lule le'she *nf* [*Bot*] woundwort, kidney vetch anthyllis *(Anthyllis vulneraria)*

lule le'tër *nf* [*Bot*] zinnia *(Zinnia elegans)*

lule liva'ndë *nf* [*Bot*] lavender *(Lavandula)*

lu'le-lu'le *adj* flowery, flowered, all in flowers, floral

lule ma'j *nm* [*Bot*] May lily *(Majantheum bifolium)*

lule mba'jtë*se* *nf* flower holder

lule merima'ngë *nf* [*Bot*] love-in-a-mist *(Nigella damascena)*

lule mëlla'gë *nf* [*Bot*] pelargonium, stork's-bill *(Pelargonium)*

lule mi'ne *nf* [*Bot*] verbena, vervain *(Verbena hybrida)*

lulemisïr *nm* [*Bot*] wallflower, gillyflower (*Cheiranthus cheiri*)

lulemizë *nf* [*Bot*] **1** forget-me-not (*Myosotis*) **2** speedwell (*Veronica*)

○ **lulemizë alpine** [*Bot*] alpine forget-me-not *Myosotis alpestris*

○ **lulemizë e arës** [*Bot*] field forget-me-not *Myosotis arvensis*

○ **lulemizë bishtakrep** [*Bot*] true forget-me-not, mouse ear *Myosotis scorpioides*

○ **lulemizë pyjore** [*Bot*] woodland forget-me-not *Myosotis sylvatica*

lulemos-më-harro *nf* [*Bot*] = **lule**mizë

lulemustak *nm* [*Bot*] sweet honeysuckle (*Lonicera caprifolum*)

lulengrënësi *nm* [*Entom*] **1** pollen beetle, blossom beetle (*Meligethes aeneus*) "blossom eater" **2** (*Oxythyrea funesta*)

lulengjïtëse *nf* [*Bot*] red German catchfly, clammy campion (*Lychnis viscaria*)

○ **lulengjitëse luleqyqe** [*Bot*] ragged robin *Lychnis flos-cuculi*

○ **lulengjitëse me kurorë** [*Bot*] rose campion *Lychnis coronaria*

lulenïshte *nf* [*Bot*] **1** balsamine, garden balsam (*Impatiens balsamina*) **2** oleander, rosebay (*Nerium oleander*)

lulenure *nf* [*Bot*] leopard's bane, panther strangler (*Doronicum pardalianches*)

lulenuse *nf* [*Bot*] = **lule**kunde

lulepashkë *nf* [*Bot*] plant (of various species) with large flowers (*Primula grandiflora*)

lulepatate *nf* [*Bot*] hybrid dahlia, garden dahlia (*Dahlia variabilis*)

lulepëllumb *nm* [*Bot*] fumitory (*Fumaria*)

luleplesht *nm* [*Bot*] pyrethrum (*Tanacetum cinerariifolium*)

lulepllatkë *nf* [*Bot*] gillyflower, wallflower = shebojë

lulepresh *nm* [*Bot*] common iris (*Iris germanica*)

luleprues *nm* flowering

luleqershi *nf* [*Bot*] common globe amaranth (*Gomphrena globosa*)

lulequmështore *nf* [*Bot*] **1** common dandelion (*Taraxacum officinale*) **2** euphorbia (*Euphorphia*)

luleqyqe *nf* [*Bot*] **1** buttercup (*Ranunculus*) **2** soapwort (*Saponaria officinalis*)

luleradhïqe *nf* [*Bot*] dandelion (*Taraxacum officinale*)

lulerrïtës *n* florist, flower grower

lulesapun *nm* [*Bot*] soapwort (*Saponaria officinalis*)

lulesë *nf* [*Bot*] **1** inflorescence **2** decorated figure in textiles; tread design on tires

lulesy(r) *nm* [*Bot*] wild pansy, heartsease (*Viola tricolor*)

luleshebojë *nf* [*Bot*] common wallflower (*Cheiranthus cheiri*)

luleshëngjïn *nm* [*Bot*] clary, clary sage (*Salvia sclarea*)

luleshïgjetë *nf* [*Bot*] gladiolus (*Gladiolus*)

luleshïtës *n* flower seller

luleshpatë *OR* **lule**shpatëz *nf* [*Bot*] common iris (*Iris germanica*)

luleshqerrë *nf* [*Bot*] garden daisy, English daisy (*Bellis perennis*)

○ **luleshqerrë amerikane** [*Bot*] pineapple weed *Matricaria matricaroides*

○ **luleshqerrë e Kaukazit** [*Bot*] Caucasian pyrethrum, florist's pyrethrum *Chrysanthemum roseum*

luleshqiponjë *nf* [*Bot*] monstera (*Monstera*)

luleshtrydhe *nf* [*Bot*] wild strawberry (*Fragaria vesca L.L*)

luleshumë *adj* (*Poet*) rich in flowers

luleshurdhë *nf* [*Bot*] dandelion (*Taraxacum officinale*)

○ **luleshurdhë mjekësore** [*Bot*] "medicinal dandelion" common dandelion *Taraxacum officinale*

luletaçe *nf* [*Bot*] hellebore = taçe

luletogëz *nf* [*Bot*] foxglove (*Digitalis*)

○ **luletogëz e purpurt** [*Bot*] purple/common foxglove *Digitalis purpurea*

○ **luletogëz e verdhë** [*Bot*] straw foxglove *Digitalis lutea*

○ **luletogëz leshatake** [*Bot*] Grecian foxglove *Digitalis lanata*

○ **luletogëz lulemadhe** [*Bot*] large yellow foxglove *Digitalis grandiflora*

lulevath *nm* [*Bot*] fuchsia (*Fuchsia*)

○ **lulevath i egër** [*Bot*] comfrey *Symphytum officinale*

luleve *nf* [*Bot*] aubergine, eggplant (*Solanum melongena*)

luleverdhë *nf* [*Bot*] = zhabinë

lulevezë *nf* [*Bot*] = luleve

lulevïle *nf* [*Bot*] Chinese wisteria (*Wistaria sinensis*)

lulevizhë *nf* [*Bot*] campion, catchfly (*Silene*)

lulevjeshtë *nf* [*Bot*] **1** common autumn crocus, meadow saffron (*Colchium autumnale*) **2** crown daisy, crown daisy chrysanthemum (*Chrisanthemum coronarium*)

lulevreshtë *nf* [*Bot*] = dorëzonjë

lulexixëllonjë *nf* [*Bot*] forget-me-not (*Myosotis*)

luleyll *nm* [*Bot*] common waxplant (*Hoya carnosa*)

lulezemër *nf* [*Bot*] **1** common bleedingheart (*Dicentra spectabilis*) **2** Tripoli aster, sea aster (*Aster tripolium*)

lulezjarr *nm* [*Bot*] scarlet sage (*Salvia splendens*)

lulezonjë *nf* [*Bot*] felty germander (*Teucrium polium*)

lulezhabinë *nf* [*Bot*] buttercup, crowfoot (*Ranunculus*)

lulëbardhë

I § *nf* **1** [*Bot*] marguerite, moon-daisy, ox-eye daisy (*Leucanthemum vulgare*) **2** [*Bot*] good-tasting vegetable with white flowers **3** [*Med*] pemphigus

II § *nm* [*Bot*] common bladder senna (*Colutea arborescens*) = fshikartë

lulëbukur *nm* [*Bot*] sweet William (*Dianthus barbatus*)

lulëgjake *nf* [*Bot*] common St. John's wort (*Hypericum perforatum*)

lulëkuqe

I § *nf* [*Bot*] red poppy, corn poppy, field poppy (*Papaver rhoeas L.*)

II § *np* (*Euph*) menstruation, menstrual period

○ **lulëkuqe e dyshimtë** [*Bot*] long-pod poppy *Papaver dubium*

○ **lulëkuqe lindore** [*Bot*] Oriental poppy *Papaver orientale*

lulë·kuqo're *np* [*Bot*] poppy family *Papaveraceae*

lulë'se *nf* ornate broach/necklace worn by women

lulë'si *nf* inflorescence

lulë'ta'r *n* florist

lulë'tari' *nf* floriculture

lulë'z *nf* **1** [*Med*] red-eye: conjunctivitis, ophthamalia **2** [*Med*] sty **3** [*Zool*] = lubardhë

lulë'zi'm *nm ger* <lulëzo·*n*, lulëzo·*het*

lulë'zo'·het *vpr* to blossom

lulë'zo'·n
 I § *vi* **1** to flower, bloom **2** (*Fig*) to flourish, thrive; prosper
 II § *vt* (*Fig*) to adorn

lulë'zua'r *adj* (i) blossomed, flowering, in flower

lulë'zueshëm *adj* (i) flowering, blooming; flourishing

Luli
 I § *nm* Luli (male name, nickname for Lulzim)
 II § *nm with fem agreement* Luli (female name, nickname for Lulzime)

luli'm *nm ger* <lulo'·*n*

luli'shta'r *n* flower gardener; groundskeeper at a public park

luli'shtari' *nf* flower gardening

luli'shte *nf* **1** flower garden **2** (*Colloq*) public park

lulnajë *nf* flowery meadow

lulo'·n
 I § *vi* to flower, blossom, bloom; sprout; bud
 II § *vt* (*Fig*) to adorn
 ○ <> lulo·*n*^{3sg} bahçia (edhe) në dimër. "<>'s garden even *blooms* in winter." Things always go well for <>. Good luck follows <> around.

lulo'r *adj* floral

*****lulshkro'·n** OR **lulshkru'e·n** *vt* (*Old*) to tattoo

luluku'q *adj* red as a poppy

lulusha'n
 I § *adj*
 II § *adj* (of fabric) with a floral design: flowered
 III § *adj, n* (*Impol*) foppish (person)

Lulzi'm *nm* Lulzim (male name)

Lulzi'me *nf* Lulzime (female name)

lum
 I § *pcl* expresses warm approval/blessing
 II § *adj* (i) **1** = lumtur **2** (*Fig*) lucky, blessed
 III § *nf* (e) (*Euph*) chicken pox
 ○ **Lum** {} që të ka! "Lucky {} that has you!" {} must be very proud of you!
 ○ **Lum ti!** Lucky you!

lu'm *opt only*
 ○ <> **lumshin** {} "may <>'s {*instruments or body part used in an achievement*} be blessed by good fortune! bless <>'s {}!" well done! nice going! bravo!
 ○ <> **lumtë** {} "may <>'s {*instrument or body part used in an achievement*} be blessed by good fortune! bless <>'s {}!" well done! nice going! bravo! **të lumtë goja!** "may thy mouth be blessed" well said!, bless you for saying it

luma'k *nm* **1** sprout, leafbud **2** tender branch, sprig **3** (*Fig*) tall and thin person

luma'qe *np* <lumak

lumara'k *nm* river dweller

luma're
 I § *nf* area along the sides of a river: riverbanks
 II § *np* river driftwood

lum·ba'rdhë *nf* **1** (*Reg*) female pigeon **2** bomb

*****lu'mb|u'r = lumtur

lu'me *np* (*Euph*) powerful and beautiful mountain fairies

Lu'me *nf* Lume (female name)

lume'nj *np* <lumë

lumë
 I § *nm* river
 II § *adv* pouring out in a veritable flood/river
 ○ (për) lumë e (për) det in miserable condition; in misery
 ○ ësh·të për lumë to be badly off
 ○ lumë e përrua in miserable condition

Lu'më *nf* northeastern ethnographic region of Albania bordering Yugoslavia

lumë·ba'rdhë *adj* fortunate, lucky

lumë·ma'dh *adj, n* unfortunate/unlucky (person)

*****lumë'ri' = lumturi

lumë'ro'·n
 I § *vt* = lumturo'·*n*
 II § *vi* to live happily

lu'më'th = lumth

lumë'zi *adj, n* (*fem sg* ~ëz, *masc pl* ~inj, *fem pl* ~eza) unfortunate/unlucky (person)

*****lumi'** *nf* sandy beach

lumineshe'ncë *nf* luminescence

lumineshe'nt *adj* luminescent

*****lumi'në** *nf* wick

lumi'shtë *nf* **1** area along the sides of a river: riverbanks **2** field by the river

lumja'n
 I § *adj* of or pertaining to Luma
 II § *n* native of Luma

lumnajë *nf* river of moving people/objects

*****lumni'm** *nm* (*Reg Gheg*) welfare, happiness

*****lumnja'n = lumjan**

lumo'r *adj* of or pertaining to a river: fluvial

lumo's· *vt* (*Colloq*) to destroy

lumo's·et *vpr* (*Colloq*) to suffer disaster

lumo'sur *adj* (i), *nm* (i) (*Colloq*) (person) who has suffered disaster

*****lumpa'r** *nm* [*Invert*] oyster = borboçinezë

lumpenproletaria't *nm* lumpenproletariat

*****lu'mshëm** *adj* (i) (*Old*) blessed

*****lumtër** = lumtur

lumti'në *nf* turmoil; disquiet

Lu'mto *nf* (female name)

lu'mtur *adj* (i), *n* (i) (person) blessed with good fortune: happy/fortunate (person)

lumturi' *nf* **1** good fortune, happiness **2** [*Relig*] beatitude

Lumturi'i *nm with fem agreement* Lumturi (female name)

lumturi'sht *adv* fortunately, luckily, happily

lumturo'·het *vpr* to become happy

lumturo'·n
 I § *vt* **1** to make [ ] happy **2** to give [ ] congratulations
 II § *vi* to lead a happy life

lumth *nm* river tributary

lu'mthi *pcl* (*Colloq*) = lum

*****lu'm|ur** *adj* (i) = lumtur

*****luna're** *nf* [*Bot*] honesty *Lunaria*

lundër
  I § nf 1 boat; punt 2 [Tech] river raft 3 [Zool] fresh-water otter
  II § adj (Reg Tosk) *bulky, burly

*lundërt adj (i) fat, flabby

lundërta'r nm boatman; navigator; steersman

lundërtari' nf the art of controlling the course of a ship: navigation

*lundërthyemje (Old) = anijethyerje

lu'ndërz nf [Zool] Old World otter, river otter, otter (Lutra lutra)
  ○ lundërz gjatoshe [Zool] common otter shell, large conch Lutraria lutraria (magna)
  ○ lundërz e ngushtë [Zool] kind of bivalve mollusc Lutraria angustior
  ○ lundërz e rreme [Zool] "false otter" wavy Venus Mysia undata

lundërza'k nm (Colloq) small ball of thread

lundra'r n = lundërta'r

lundrari' nf = lundërtari'

*lundrata'r = lundërta'r

lundri'cë nf covered river boat; skiff

lundri'm nm ger 1 < lundro' ·n 2 travel by boat or ship 3 voyage
  ○ lundrim detar maritime navigation
  ○ lundrim lumor inland navigation
  ○ lundrim me varkë rowing
  ○ lundrim me vela sailing

lundro' ·n vi 1 to travel by boat or ship 2 to float 3 to be insecure
  ○ lundro· ·n në një/dy gisht ujë "swim/sail in one/two finger(s) of water" to be very skillful

lundru'es
  I § adj 1 used for travel by boat or ship 2 navigable
  II § n traveller by boat or ship

lundrue'shëm adj (i) navigable, floatable

lundrue'shmëri' nf navigability, floatability

lune'të n f [Tech] support for steadying work or cutting tool: rest

lu'ngë nf 1 boil, carbuncle; abscess 2 tumor
  ○ lungë e keqe/zezë malignant tumor

*lu'ntër nf = lu'ndërz

Lunxhëri' nf ethnographic region of southern Albania between Gjirokastra and Tepelena

lunxhi'ot
  I § adj of or pertaining to Lunxhëria
  II § n native of Lunxhëria

lu'pë nf loupe

lupi'n nm [Bot] lupine Lupinus

luqe'bull nm (np ~ j) [Zool] lynx = rrëqe'bull

*luqsi' nf folly

*lu'rbë = llu'rbë

*lurblo· ·n vi = luro' ·n

lure'k nm swaddled child

luri' nf 1 (Colloq) = ngjyrë 2 herd, flock

*luri'm nm ger < luro' ·n

lu'rkë nf 1 = jaku'ce 2 sheep with long, coarse wool

*luro' ·n vi to howl, wail = ulëri· ·n

lurti'm nm ger 1 < lurto' ·n 2 = lurti'më

lurti'më nf 1 caress; flattery, cajolery 2 (Pej) = mashtri'm

lurto' ·n vt 1 to caress; flatter, cajole 2 (Pej) = mashtro' ·n

lus| stem for 1st sg pres, pl pres, 2nd & 3rd sg subj, pind < lut·

*lu'sje = lu'tje

lu'skë nf sharp piece of shale

luspa'k nm 1 = luspor 2 [Med] squamous

luspargje'ndtë adj (Book) silver-scaled

luspa'rtë adj (Book) golden-scaled

lu'spë nf 1 covering layer of cold-blooded animals: scale (of fish), scaly skin (of reptiles or amphibians), exoskeleton (of insects) 2 removable covering layer of a fruit or vegetable 3 sliver that has come loose from a hard surface 4 (Fig) mask

luspëma'dhe nf [Ichth] true lizardfish (Saurida undosquamis)

*luspi'm nm [Med] exfoliation, desquamation, scaling off

luspo'r adj 1 scaly; scalelike 2 [Med] desquamative

lu'stër nf 1 luster, gloss, shine 2 = lustri'm 3 (Fig Pej) false sheen

lustrafi'n nm patent leather

*lustra'r n (Old) polisher

lustra'xhi nm (np ~ nj) 1 bootblack, shoeshine boy 2 (Fig) person who can present things in a deceptively good light 3 (Fig) flatterer

lustri'm nm ger < lustro' ·n

lustri'në nf 1 patent leather 2 glossy polish

lustro'· ·n vt 1 to apply a lustrous finish to [ ]: lacquer, polish/shine [ ] 2 (Fig Pej) to give [ ] a deceptive sheen

lustro's· vt = lustro' ·n

lustro'sje nf ger < lustro's·

lustru'a'r adj (i) 1 polished, shiny 2 (Fig Pej) with a deceptive sheen

lustru'es
  I § adj used for polishing
  II § n 1 polisher 2 (Fig Pej) person who gives a deceptive sheen

lush nm 1 male dog 2 (Fig Pej) man who is out of control: wild man, mad dog, savage

lu'sh|ë nf 1 female dog, bitch 2 (Fig Pej) woman who is out of control: wild woman, mad bitch, savage

lushnja'r
  I § adj of or pertaining to Lushnja
  II § n native of Lushnja

Lu'shnjë nf district and its capital city in the Myzeqe region of central western Albania: Lushnja

lut·
  I § vt 1 to ask for [ ], request 2 to beg for [ ], beseech, solicit 3 [Relig] to celebrate [a rite/ritual/holiday]
  II § vi to hope

lu't·et vpr 1 to beg, implore 2 [Relig] to pray
  ○ ju/të lutem! "I beg you!" please!

lutera'n adj, n Lutheran

lu'te nf 1 bitch, female dog *2 (Fig) glutton 3 plea, prayer, request

lu'tles
  I § n 1 petitioner, applicant 2 [Relig] person praying
  II § adj beseeching, suppliant

lu'tesore nf [Relig] chancel

lu'tje nf ger 1 < lu'r·, lu't·et 2 polite verbal request; petition, request, plea 3 [Relig] prayer

lutjeso're nf [Relig] prayer book

lutjeshkru'es nm 1 applicant in writing 2 scrivener of prayers

lutra'n nm huge swarthy man

lu·tur
 I § *adj (i) (Book)* **1** invitee **2** person to whom a request is made
 II § *nf (e)* = **lutje**
*****luturís·** *vt* to bespatter; beslobber
*****luturís·et** *vpr* to wallow
 luvari *nf [Bot]* bay, laurel *(Laurus nobilis L.)*
*****luveq** *nm* = **kukuvajkë**
 lu'vër *nf [Bot]* hop *(Humulus lupulus)*
*****luvgat** *nm (np luvgjetër)* = **lugat**
 lu'zmë
 I § *nf* swarm (of bees)
 II § *adv* in a swarm
 luzmló·n *vi* to swarm
 ly·het *vpr* <**lye·n** **1** to apply lotion on one's face or body; put on makeup **2** to become bedaubed, get dirty **3** *(Pej)* to become morally stained **4** *(Reg)* to become a sticky nuisance
 ∘ **Nuk lyhet dielli me baltë.** "The sun cannot be painted over with mud." *(Prov)* Truth will out. You can't hide the truth.
 ∘ **Nuk ly·het**[3sg] **dielli me baltë** "the sun cannot be smeared with mud" the truth cannot be hidden by lies
 ∘ **ly·het e ngjy·het** to put on too much makeup
*****lyce** *nf (Old)* secondary school (modeled on the French lycée) = **lice**
 lyç *adv* in a muddle/mess
 lye·n *vt* **1** to apply an adhering liquid to []: daub, smear, coat; paint, whitewash; grease, oil, butter; paste, glue **2** to soil, bedaub **3** *(Fig Pej)* to dishonor **4** *(Fig Pej)* to disguise/misrepresent []
 ∘ **<a lye·n dorën/duart** *(Pej)* to grease <>'s palm: give <> a bribe
 ∘ **i lye·n duart me gjak** to stain one's hands with blood: participate in murder
 ∘ **i lye·n duart në** [] to dirty one's hands in [the matter]
 ∘ **lye·n me gjak** to stain with blood
 ∘ [] **lye·n me sheqer** "coat [] with sugar" to sugarcoat []
 ∘ **<> lye·n rroten** "grease <>'s wheels" to give <> a bribe
 lye'r
 I § *part* <**lye·n**
 II § *adj (i)* **1** painted **2** bedaubed, dirty **3** *(Pej)* morally stained
 lye'rës
 I § *n* person who applies a sticky liquid coating: painter
 II § *adj* used for applying a sticky liquid coating
 lye'rje *nf ger* <**lye·n, ly·het**
 lyes
 I § *nm* marriage broker, go-between
 II § *adj, nm* lubricant
 lye'shëm *adv* with a few clouds, slightly cloudy/overcast
*****lyktyrë** *nf* band (of cloth); bandage
 ly'lë *nf* bubble
 lyle'zo·n *vi* to bubble
*****lyly'kës** *nm* [*Ornit*] redshank *(Tringa totanus)*
*****lylyve'r** *nm* rainbow
 lym
 I § *nm* alluvial/silty soil: alluvium
 II § *adj* created by sedimentation: alluvial
 lyma'k *adj* = **lymor**

*****lymb** *nm (Old)* limbo, dark regions
 lym|erí'shtë *nf* = **lymíshtë** = **ly'shtër**
 lymíshtë *nf* alluvial area, alluvial land; mudbed, mudpit
 lym|o'r *adj* alluvial, silty; muddy
 lym|o're *nf* = **lymíshtë**
 ly'm|të *adj (i)* = **lymor**
 lyp· *vt* **1** to beg for [] **2** to ask for [], request **3** to need; want **4** *(Colloq)* to look for []
 ∘ **lyp· dru kurrizit** to ask for a beating ("on the back"): be asking for it
 ∘ **lyp· gavër** "ask for a hole" to ask for a little place to use as a hideout
 ∘ **Lyp për derë e ndan për shpirt.** "{} begs at the door and divides it out of goodness" {} shares what little {} has, {} would give you the shirt off {}'s back
 ∘ **lyp· qimen në vezë** "look for the hair in an egg" to try to find fault, pick at details
 ∘ **lyp· shumë për** [] to ask a high price for []
 ∘ **lyp· të falur** to ask to be forgiven, beg for forgiveness
 ∘ **<> lyp· vajzën për djalin** to ask for <>'s daughter to marry one's son
 lyp·et *vpr* **1** to be in demand **2** to be necessary, be needed
 lyp|aca'k *OR* **lyp|ara'k** *adj* begging
 lyp|aní'k *nm* = **lypës**
 lyp|anja'r *adj, n* = **lypsar**
 lyp|ara'k *adj, n* = **lypës**
*****lyp|c** *adj, n* = **lypës**
 lyp|ë *nf* **1** *(Old)* alms **2** begging for alms
 ∘ **Lypa e ka faqen e zezë, por s'të lë pa gjë.** "Begging has a dark face, but it doesn't leave you begging (does not leave you without anything)." Begging is shameful, but it's better than nothing. Better beg than starve.
 ly'p|ës *n* beggar, mendicant
 lyp|ësí *nf* **1** beggary; begging **2** *(Collec)* beggars
 lyp|ëso'·n *vt* to beg [for alms]
 ly'pje *nf ger* <**lyp·, lyp·et**
*****lypje'të** = **lëpjetë**
*****ly'p|me** *nf (e) (Reg)* beggary, begging, panhandling
 ly'ps·et *vpr* **1** to need, be in need of **2** to be necessary/needed; be lacking
 lyp|sa'gjet *nm* person who asks for trouble
 lyp|sa'r *adj, n (Scorn)* (person) who goes begging door-to-door = **lypës**
*****ly'ps|ëm** *adj (i)* needful, necessary, requisite
 ly'p|ur
 I § *adj (i)* **1** sought as alms **2** *(Colloq)* necessary, requisite
 II § *nf (e)* = **ly'pje**
 ly'p|ur|a *np (të)* alms = **lypë**
 lyr· *vt* **1** to grease, make [] oily **2** to stain, make [] dirty
 lyr·et *vpr* **1** to become oily/greasy **2** to become stained/dirty
 lyr|dhëz *nf [Med]* wart
 lyr|ë *nf* **1** grease; cooking fat, shortening **2** dirty grease, grime **3** *(Fig Colloq)* flavor, appeal
 lyr|ës
 I § *nm [Tech]* lubricant
 II § *adj* greasy
 lyr|ësí *nf* greasiness
 lyr|ësím *nm ger* <**lyrëso·n, lyrëso·het**

lyr̈ëso·het *vpr* to get greasy

lyr̈ëso·n *vt* **1** to make [] greasy **2** [*Tech*] to lubricate: grease

lyr̈ësues *adj* [*Tech*] **1** greasy **2** lubricant

lyr̈ët *adj (i)* **1** = lyrshëm **2** dirty **3** *(Fig Pej)* shameless, disgusting

lyrikur *adj (Disparaging)* **1** lacking all dignity, shameless, base, disgusting **2** unappealing, dull, lacking flavor

lyrim *nm ger* < lyro·n, lyro·het

lyro·het *vpr* = lyro se·t

lyro·n *vt* = lyros·

lyros· *vt* to dirty [] with something greasy

lyros·et *vpr* to get dirty with something greasy

lyrosur *adj (i)* dirty with something greasy

lyrshëm *adj (i)* **1** greasy **2** made dirty by something greasy

lyrth *nm* **1** [*Agr*] black rot **2** [*Med*] = urdhje

lyrthan *adj, n* **1** (plant) infested with black rot **2** [*Med*] (person) suffering from impetigo

lyruar *adj (i)* = lyrosur

*****lyspë** = luspë

lystër *nf* [*Bot*] savory *(Satureia)*

lyshtër *nf* **1** alluvium **2** steep part of a mountain subject to landslide **3** *(Fig Pej)* mob of people

lyshtëror *adj* alluvial

lyth *nm* **1** wart **2** callus; corn (on the foot) **3** red or black mole on the skin **4** [*Bot*] small bump in the bark of a tree: verruca *()* **5** *(Fig)* vice, defect

lyth·et *vpr* to get red or black moles on the skin

lythët *adj (i)* [*Bot*] having small bumps/warts in the bark: *(verrucose)*

LLII

ll [*llë*] *nf* **1** the consonant digraph letter "ll" **2** the velar lateral liquid represented by the digraph letter "ll"

lla·n *vt (Colloq)* to nurse [a baby] from the breast until satiated; gorge

llaba·ne *nf* large shepherd's hood made of waterproof goat hair

llabata·n *nm (Reg)* [*Ornit*] = **guhak**

llabi·ç
  I § *nm (Reg)* **1** = **lugat** **2** *(Fig)* glutton
  II § *adj* * *(Reg)* ghostly

llabu·t *nm* strong young sprout

llabu·zhdë *nf* [*Bot*] great burdock (*Arctium lappa*)

*****llabu·zhdër** *nf* = **lëpjetë**

llac *nm* bricklayer's assistant, apprentice brick mason

llacama·n *adj, n (Colloq)* **1** (animal) late in being weaned from its mother **2** (person) used to good (especially sweet) food

llacë *nf* **1** knitted loop in fabric or mesh **2** loose-fitting garment, cloak

*****llaci·s** = **llucis**

*****llaci·t·** = **llucit·**

*****llacka** *np* balustrade

*****llackë** *nf (Colloq)* = **njollë**

llacko·s· *vt (Colloq)* **1** to make dirty, soil; spatter **2** *(Pej)* to put on too much make-up

llacko·s·et *vpr* **1** to get dirty **2** *(Pej)* to wear too much make-up

llacko·sur *adj (i)* **1** dirty; spattered with dirt **2** *(Pej)* with too much make-up on

llaç *nm* **1** mortar **2** slushy substance (such as cement/asphalt) used in construction: slush **3** dirty slush; thin mud

llaça·vër *nf (Colloq)* nasty woman who chatters too much

llaçka·r *adj, n (Colloq)* foolish/stupid (person)

*****llaçka·t·et** *vpr* to turn flat, become insipid

llaçkë *nf (Colloq)* **1** hair bun; knot tied to keep the corners of a kerchief together on top of the head **2** *(Pej)* foolish/stupid woman **3** *(FigImpolite)* brain, head

llaçpërzie·rëse *nf* [*Tech*] concrete mixer, cement mixer

*****lladicë** *nf* deposit charge

lladigë *nf* **1** grape skin **2** = **llastar**

lladi·k
  I § *nm* **1** variety of melon that is juicy but poor-tasting **2** overripe melon
  II § *adj* juicy but poor-tasting

lladromë *nf* cleansing of silver with wine marc

lladro·n *nm* wine marc used to polish silver; acid made from grape sediment

llaf *nm (Colloq)* **1** word **2** talk, chat, conversation
  ○ **Pikë llaf!** Stop talking! Shut up, now!

llafato·r *adj* = **llafaza·n**

llafaza·n
  I § *adj, n* talkative, garrulous, long-winded
  II § *nm* windbag; chatterer

llafazanëri *nf* talkativeness, garrulousness, long-windedness

llafe *np* <**llaf** gossip; slander

llafema·dh *adj, n (Colloq)* **1** verbose, talkative, garrulous, long-winded **2** windbag; big talker, braggart

llafepa·kë *adj (Colloq)* of few words; not given to making long speeches

llafeshu·më *adj* verbose, very talkative, very long-winded

llafo·s·
  I § *vi* to chat, talk
  II § *vt* to discuss, talk about

llafo·s·et *vpr* to speak together, chat

llaftari·s· = **llahtari·s·**

llaga·p *nm (Colloq)* **1** nickname, moniker **2** surname

llaga·r
  I § *adj* pure
  II § *nm* * *(Old)* emaciation, phthisis

llagari·s· *vt* **1** to clarify **2** to purify ***3** *(Old)* to refine [metal] ***4** to clean

llaga·rtë *adj (i)* clear, limpid

llagavi·t· *vt (Colloq)* to make dirty, soil

llagavi·t·et *vpr (Colloq)* to get dirty, become soiled

*****llagavi·tje** *nf ger* **1** <**llagavit·**, **llagavit·et** **2** inkblot

llagëm *nm (Colloq)* **1** public sewer **2** tunnel

*****llagërese** *nf* time due, term

*****llagëro·n** *vi* to fall due

lla·h·et *vpr* **1** to eat until stuffed, stuff/gorge oneself **2** (of a baby) to nurse (at the breast) until satiated

*****llahêg** *nm (Reg Gheg)* shepherd's wool cloak

llahtar *I §* *nm OR* **llahtarë** *II §* *nf (Colloq)* = **llahtari**

llahtari *nf (Colloq)* **1** terror; terrible anxiety **2** *(Fig)* horrible thing, nightmare

llahtari·s·
  I § *vt (Colloq)* to terrify
  II § *vi* = **llahtari·s·et**

llahtari·s·et *vpr (Colloq)* to become terrified

llahtari·sur *adj (i) (Colloq)* terrified, full of dread

llahta·rshëm *adj (i) (Colloq)* terrifying, dreadful

llahta·rtë *adj (i), adj (i) (Colloq)* = **llahtarshëm**

*****llahurdë** *nf* = **ferexhe**

llahu·së *nf (Colloq)* = **lehonë**

llahusi *nf (Colloq)* = **lehoni**

*****llahu·të** = **lahutë**

*****llaïk**
  I § *adj* laic, lay = **laik**
  II § *nm* layman

llajë
  I § *nf* **1** black cow or ewe **2** *(Reg)* = **hinkë**
  II § *adj* (of cows and sheep) having black hair

*****llajës** *nm (Old)* wire

llajkë *nf* **1** wickerwork gate in a sheep pen; wattled fence surrounding a sheep fold **2** wooden bar used to close something shut

llaju·sh
  I § *nm* black ram/ox/bull

II § adj (of a ram/ox/bull) having black hair
llak nm lacquer
*****llakabe're** = llogobe're
*****llakaq'ís** = llokoçís
*****llakaqít** = llokoçít
lla'kë nf **1** watering hole for animals, mountain pool serving as a waterhole; standing pool of water *****2** = **llak**
llakím nm ger <**llako'**·n
llako'·n vt to coat [] with lacquer
*****llaku'c** adj parasitic
*****llaku'cë** nf parasite
*****llakucí** nf parasitism
*****llakuco'**·n vt to infect, blight
llallë nf **1** [Entom] large moth that lays eggs in bee-hives, driving bees from the hive: honeycomb moth, wax moth, greater wax moth (Galleria melonella) **2** (Fig) something causing quarrels: trouble maker **3** (Colloq) wetnurse = **mëndeshë**
llamarínë nf sheet metal, galvanized iron
llamaríntë adj (i) made of sheet metal, made of galvanized iron
*****llama'shkë** nf [Invert] snail
llambada'r nm lamp fixture
llamba'dhe nf **1** votary candle, thick candle **2** lamp
llamba'ris· vi = **llamburít**·
*****llambaritës** = **llamburítës**
llambë nf **1** lamp **2** electrical tube/bulb; light bulb
llambík nm washtub
*****llambiko'**·n vt to distill
*****llambro'** nf [Entom] firefly
*****llambu'rd** nm scion of a fruit tree
llamburís stem for 1st sg pres, pl pres, 2nd & 3rd sg subj, pind <**llamburít**· (Reg Calab)
llamburít· vi **1** to shine, shine brightly **2** to sparkle with beauty/cleanliness
llamburítës adj brilliant, resplendent, shining
llamburítje nf ger **1** <**llamburít**· **2** radiance, illumination
llambu'shkë nf small lamp; small light bulb
lla'mje nf [Folklore] man-eating dragon who lives in springs or wells
llampada'r nm = **llambada'r**
llampa'dis stem for 1st sg pres, pl pres, 2nd & 3rd sg subj, pind <**llampadít**·
llampadít· vt to glare; dazzle
*****llampanda'r** nm = **llambada'r**
lla'mpë nf = **lla'mbë**
llana'r nm **1** comb **2** weaver's reed
*****lla'në** nf (Reg Gheg) = **llé'rë**
llango's nm **1** dog that barks but does not bite **2** stray dog **3** (FigImpolite) person with nothing to do but wander around: bum; idle chatterer
llango's· vt to bedaub [] with mud, make [] filthy
llango's·et vpr to get bedaubed with mud, made [] filthy
llango'sje nf ger **1** <**llango's**·, **llango's**·et (Fig) **2** something dirty and disgusting: muck, filthy business
llango'sur adj (i) filthy
llangja'sh adj, n (person) with a hoarse voice
*****lla'os**· vt to check, baffle, halt
*****lla'os**·et vpr to be baffled, stop dead

*****lla'o'sur** adj (i) baffled, checked
llap·
I § vt **1** to lap/lick [] up; slurp **2** to lick **3** to gulp [] down, swallow [] up
II § vi **1** (Fig) to prattle on, chatter; talk irresponsibly: tattle, blab **2** to slobber, slurp
llapa
I § nf **1** mush, porridge, pap **2** poultice made out of boiled herbs
II § adj mushy
llapada'n
I § adj bearing large elongated fruit
II § nm large elongated fig without much sweetness
llapa'n
I § adj **1** having large broad leaves **2** (Fig Pej) very talkative
II § nm very talkative person
llapa'qen adj, n (Disparaging) (person) who talks without let-up; who gossips
llapa'r nm [Agr] wooden shoe-like block reinforcing the sole and functioning as a moldboard for the iron plowtip on a wooden plow
*****llapa's** stem for 1st sg pres, pl pres, 2nd & 3rd sg subj, pind <**llapa't**·
llapa'shít· vt to splash [feet/hands] in something wet
llapa'shít·et vpr to slosh along
llapa'shítje nf ger **1** <**llapashít**·, **llapashít**·et **2** sloshing sound
*****llapa't**· vt to prate, chatter, twaddle
*****llapa'të** nf clod, lump
llapaza'n
I § adj talkative
II § n chatterbox
*****llapazo'r** adj, n = **llapaza'n**
llapa'zha'r adj (Colloq) **1** sloppily dressed, sloppy in dress **2** voracious and undiscriminating in eating: gluttonous, swinish
lla'pë nf **1** (Colloq) tongue **2** earflap, earlap, pinna; earlobe **3** flap **4** blade of a plant leaf; plant leaf **5** goat or sheep with long hanging ears **6** anything tongue-shaped *****7** = **llapa'**
  ◦ **llapa e parmendës** = **llapa'r**
llapë'gje'rë adj = **gjethegje'rë**
llapë'ho'llë adj = **fletëho'llë**
*****llapë'ka'ple's** adj, n = **llapaza'n**
llapë'ma'dh adj **1** = **gjethema'dh 2** very talkative
*****lla'për** adj muddy, dirty
llapërçínë nf **1** muddy patch worn in much-traveled paths; mud puddle, mud slick **2** sleet **3** (Fig) thin mush without much taste
llapërçít· vt = **llapashít**·
llapërçít·et vpr = **llapashít**·et
*****llapërçítun** adj (i) (Reg Gheg) restless
llapërka'jë nf slush; sleet
llapë'ro'·n vi to prattle, chatter on and on
lla'pës adj, n = **llafaza'n**
llapëtí'-n
I § vi to shine; sparkle
II § vt to make [] shiny, cause to gleam
llapë'tímë nf shine, sparkle, gleam
llapë'to'r adj = **llafaza'n**
llapë'tyrë
I § nf tasteless gruel
II § np (Fig) dirty language, cussing

llapís *stem for 1st sg pres, pl pres, 2nd & 3rd sg subj, pind* <**llapít**

llapít *vt* = **llapo**·*n*

llapo·*n*

I § *vt* to lap [ ] up, slurp; guzzle, wolf [ ] down, gobble [ ] up

II § *vi (Pej)* to chatter away

llapore *nf* front-buttoning sleeveless wool vest for men

llaps·

I § *vi* to gleam, shine

II § *vt* to make [ ] gleam: polish, shine

*****llaptar** *n* 1 glutton 2 chatterbox

*****llaptarí** *nf* gluttony

*****llaptí**·*n vt* to gulp down [ ]

*****llaptim** *nm* chatter

*****llaptís** *stem for 1st sg pres, pl pres, 2nd & 3rd sg subj, pind* <**llaptít**

*****llaptít**· *vt* to shine

*****llaptojkë** *OR* **llaptore** *nf* gossip, chatterbox

llaptyra *np* <**llaptyrë** invective, vituperation

llaptyrë *nf* feed (for animals): slop

llapua *nm (obl ~ oi, np ~ onj)* [*Bot*] purple butterbur *(Petasites officinalis)*

llapush *adj* 1 having big floppy ears: lap-eared, long-eared 2 having the shape or dimensions of a tongue, tonguelike, linguiform

llapushë *nf* [*Bot*] 1 great mullein *(Verbascum thapsus)* 2 white water-lily *(Nymphaea alba)* = **lëkua** 3 purple butterbur *(Petasites officinalis)* 4 cornhusk

*****llas** *nm* wash paddle

llasë *nf* 1 excessive caressing, pampering: spoiling, mollycoddling 2 excessive impetuousness and daring: recklessness

*****llaskë** *nf (Reg Gheg)* barrier, dam

llaskonjë *nf* new twig; young shoot, seedling

llaskore *nf* = **llaskonjë**

llaskuç *nm (Pej)* 1 freeloader = **qelepirxhi** 2 person who sticks his nose into other people's business

llastar = **lastar**

*****llastarshëm** *adj (i)* bearing sprouts, sprouting

llastër = **lastër**

llasticë *nf* spoiled little girl, pampered brat

llastík *nm* 1 rubber 2 elastic band, rubber band, garter 3 slingshot 4 elastic fabric: elastic *****5 rubber tire

llastíka *np* <**llastíkë** *(Colloq)* rubber boots: rubbers

llastíkë *nf* 1 = **llastík** 2 *(Colloq)* rubber nipple for babies

*****llastikor** *adj* [*Spec*] = **llastíktë**

llastikshëm *adj (i)* = **llastíktë**

llastíktë *adj (i)* 1 made of rubber 2 *(Colloq)* elastic, flexible, pliant; adaptable

llastim *nm ger* 1 <**llasto**·*n*, **llasto**·*het* 2 fussy behavior of a spoiled child

llastiqe *np* <**llastík**

llasto·*het vpr* to behave like a pampered child: be fussy, fawn, demand affection

llasto·*n vt* to pamper/mollycoddle [a child]: indulge, spoil

llastor *adj, n* (person) who likes to be pampered; spoiled (brat)

llastrak *nm* = **krëndth**

*****llastrues** *adj* 1 *(Old)* foppish 2 = **llastuar**

llastuar *adj (i)* pampered, coddled, spoiled

llashkë

I § *nf, adj* = **llashkore**

II § *nf* = **përpajnë**

llashkore *nf, adj* (animal) which has given birth before reaching maturity

llashtër *nf* 1 [*Bot*] = **ullastër** 2 wheat straw 3 herbaceous weed with small thin leaves and clusters of white flowers whose dried stems are used as toothpicks

*****llatínkë** *nf* Italian/Catholic/Latin woman

*****llatoz**

I § *adj* limp, slack

II § *nm (Reg Gheg)* lazybones

*****llatuk** *nm* = **lastuk**

*****llaturímë** *nf* stain

*****llaturíq**·*et vpr* to twaddle, chatter

llaturís *stem for 1st sg pres, pl pres, 2nd & 3rd sg subj, pind* <**llaturít**

llaturít· *vt* to stain, soil; dishonor

llautë *nf* 1 eight-stringed lute plucked with a quill 2 wooden mold with a handle used to shape bricks before baking

llauz *nm (Old Colloq Regional Gk)* whole populace

llavesh *adj* having big floppy ears: lap-eared, long-eared

llavë *nf* 1 wolf pack 2 lava

Llazar *nm* Llazar (male name)

*****llazdro**·*n* = **llasto**·*n*

llazínë *nf* grass pasture for draft animals in or near a village

*****llazuer** *nm (obl ~ ori) (Old)* street singer

llazurë *nf* din; tumult

*****llazyrë** *(Old)* = **llazurë**

*****llendër** *nf* 1 carol 2 = **kolendër**

Llesh *nm* Llesh (male name)

*****lleshk** = **dhesk**

*****lleshko**·*n vt* to hold [ ] at bay; trap, corner; constrain

*****llevë** *nf (Reg Gheg)* = **llavë**

*****llëk** *nf (Old)* toy

*****llëkue** *nm (obl ~ oi, np ~ onj) (Reg Gheg)* white water lily

llëngë *nf* 1 mudhole 2 small valley with soft grass

llënor *adj* [*Med*] ulnar

llënjëz *nf* mud, slush

llërë *nf* 1 upper arm 2 arm; forearm 3 [*Med*] ulna

llërëbardhë *adj (Poet)* having white arms: fair-armed

llërëçelíktë *adj (Poet)* having strong and powerful arms

llërëdjegur *adj (Poet)* 1 having sun-tanned arms 2 *(Fig)* hard-working

llërëjashtë *adj* bare-armed; having rolled-up sleeves

llërëpërveshur

I § *adj* having rolled-up sleeves

II § *adv (Fig)* unsparingly and with great energy

llërëplotë *adj (Poet)* having well-filled-out arms: plump-armed

llërëshpërvjelur *adj* = **llërëpërveshur**

llërëzbuluar *adj* bare-armed; having rolled-up sleeves

llërëzhveshur *adj, adv* with arms bare; with sleeves rolled-up

llixhë *nf* thermal spa

llockë *nf* olive mash

lloç
I § *nm* 1 muddy slush 2 mortar
II § *adj* (of fruit) over-ripe, mushy
○ **lloç gëlqere** whitewash

*****lloçar** *nm* (Old) curse, oath

*****lloçergë** *nf* = lloqe

lloçë *nf* [Ichth] 1 (Anguilla latirostris) 2 young shad between four months and a year old

*****llockë** *nf* (Old) eyeball

llof *nm* (Colloq) gluttony

lloftar *n* (Colloq) glutton

*****llog** *adj* limp, flabby

llogaçe *nf* stagnant pool, pond; mud puddle

*****llogar** *nm* 1 accountant 2 account

llogari *nf* 1 account 2 accounting 3 economic calculation 4 (Fig Colloq) preparatory reckoning *5 bill, reckoning
○ **llogari rrjedhëse** [Fin] running account

llogaridhënës *adj* (Book) pertaining to the rendering of accounts

llogaridhënie *nf* (Book) account rendering

*****llogarim** *nm* rhythmic time: rhythm, beat

llogaris stem for 1st sg pres, pl pres, 2nd & 3rd sg subj, pind <**llogarit**·

llogarit· *vt* 1 to calculate, compute, reckon 2 to take [] into account
○ [] **llogarit**· to think [] through

llogaritar *n* accountant

llogaritëm *nm* logarithm

llogaritës
I § *nm* 1 calculating device 2 [Mil] firing control specialist: firing calculator 3 (Old) accountant
II § *adj* used for calculating

llogaritje *nf ger* 1 <**llogarit**· 2 calculation, computation, accounting

llogaritshëm *adj* (i) calculable, computable; accountable

llogaritur *adj* (i) taken into account; accounted for

*****llogarithëm** *nm* = **llogaritëm**

*****llogë** *nf* 1 doorlatch 2 splint

llogobere *nf* 1 full-blown flower past its prime and no longer beautiful 2 (Fig) blabbermouthed girl or woman 3 [Ornit] wild duck left behind during summer migration

llogore *nf* [Mil] trench, entrenchment
○ **llogore e rreme** [Mil] decoy entrenchment

*****llogjikë** = logjikë

llohë *nf* 1 sleet 2 cold, wet, and windy weather
○ **llohë akullore** (Old) sleet and hail

llohëtershëm *adj* (i) gloomy, pitch dark

*****llois**· *vi* to think
○ **llois**· **për** [] to think of []

*****llois**·*et vpr* to reflect, think

lloj *nm* 1 sort, kind, type 2 [Biol] variety 3 characteristic nature (of something)

*****llojc** *adj* moody

lloj-lloj
I § *determiner* (followed by abl pl case) various kinds of, all sorts of
II § *adj* of various kinds, of all sorts

llojllojshëm *adj* (i) varied, of various kinds

llojllojtë *adj* (i) = **llojllojshëm**

llojor *adj* (Book) according to type/kind/species: by type

llojshmëri *nf* diversity, variety

llok· *vt* = **llokoçit**·

*****llokaçkë** *nf* (Reg Tosk) vine shoot

llokaje *nf* 1 muddy/dirty water 2 watery mud

*****llokan** OR **lokantë** = **lokandë**

*****llokëm** *nf* (Old) flounce, furbelow

llokme *nf* 1 morsel of food; slice 2 (Fig Pej) undeserved profit/gain, unearned benefit

llokmëmadh *adj* (Pej) voracious profiteer

llokoçis stem for 1st sg pres, pl pres, 2nd & 3rd sg subj, pind <**llokoçit**·

llokoçit·
I § *vt* to agitate [a liquid] forcefully: churn, churn up []
II § *vi* to make a churning/splashing sound: churn, slosh

llokoçit·*et vpr* 1 to make a churning sound: churn 2 to slosh, splash

llokoçitje *nf ger* 1 <**llokoçit**·, **llokoçit**·*et* 2 sloshing sound

*****llokoçitun** *adj* (i) (Reg Gheg) turbulent, restless

*****llokoqis** = **llokoçis**

*****llokoqit**· = **llokoçit**·

*****llokotis** stem for 1st sg pres, pl pres, 2nd & 3rd sg subj, pind <**llokotit**·

*****llokotit**· *vi* to gurgle

llokum I § *nm* OR **llokume** II § *nf* 1 gelatinous candy: Turkish delight, Turkish paste 2 [Spec] small piece of a soft explosive material III § *adj* very soft/tender
○ **nuk hahen çdo ditë llokume** "candies are not eaten every day" not every day can be celebrated as a holiday
○ **Llokumja e hasmit/armikut të mbetet në fyt.** "The candy of the enemy sticks in your throat." (Prov) Beware of Greeks bearing gifts.

llom *nm* = **llum**

*****llomat** = **llomot**

llome *nf* 1 alluvial soil left by a overflowing river or stream 2 residue, sediment 3 (Fig) profit derived from someone else's work

llomështi *nf* 1 dirty mud, sludge; filth 2 (Fig) rubbish

*****llomicë** *nf* = **lymishtë**

llomis stem for 1st sg pres, pl pres, 2nd & 3rd sg subj, pind <**llomit**·

llomishtë *nf* = **lymishtë**

llomit· *vt* 1 to make [] dirty with mud 2 to smash [] to a pulp

llomit·*et vpr* 1 to get muddy 2 to get smashed to a pulp

*****llomitun** *adj* (i) (Reg Gheg) muddy

*****llomkë** *nf* 1 lump, chunk 2 (Reg Kos) abusive language

llomotar *adj, n* 1 talkative and foolish (person); gossiping (person) 2 blustering/brawling/noisy (person)

llomoti *nf* 1 prattle; gossip 2 bluster, brawling, noisy chatter

llomotis stem for 1st sg pres, pl pres, 2nd & 3rd sg subj, pind <**llomotit**·

llomotít· *vi* **1** to prattle, blabber; gossip **2** to bluster, brawl, chatter noisily

llomotítje *nf ger* **1** <llomotít· **2** mumbling **3** prattle, gossip

llom·shtí *nf* filth, mire, mud; grounds, dregs

Llondёr *nf* = Londёr

*llondóne *nf* landau = lando

*llónxё = llónxhё

llónxhё
I § *nf* **1** vegetable or flower garden strip near a house **2** large rain puddle; pond **3** hole used as an animal lair: burrow, den, foxhole **4** *(Old)* village gathering; council of village elders; village elders; meeting place of village elders/council **5** *(Fig Colloq)* long leisurely conversation **6** *(Fig Colloq)* noise made by many people talking at the same time without understanding each other; din; tumult
II § *adj (Fig)* full of good things
III § *adv (Fig)* **1** with a lot of food and drink **2** in loud and disorderly tumult

llóp·es *adj, nm* [*Bot*] light-colored September-ripening (fig) with very large sweet fruit

llópje *nf* large white bean

lloq = lluq

*llóqe *nf* slut

*llóqesh *nf* linchpin

lloskár = llozkár

lloskё *nf* [*Ichth*] red-eye, rudd *(Scardinius erythrophthalmus scardafa, Leuciscus scardafa)* = drangё

*llost *nm* heavy metal bar (used to make an opening in a wall)

llosh
I § *nm* **1** [*Bot*] widely found long grass with thin pointed leaves eaten by livestock **2** area covered by tangles of long grass: marsh, bog **3** *(Fig)* disorderly tangle **4** hair grime *5 = llozh *6 lair
II § *adj, n (Pej)* **1** disheveled (person) **2** stupid/crazy (person)

lloshíra *np* garbage; house trash

llotarí *nf* lottery = lotarí

llóto *nf* lotto

llovrák *nm (Reg)* straw chaff

lloxhё *nf* loggia

lloz *nm* **1** doorbolt **2** crowbar **3** [*Phys*] lever **4** *(Colloq)* [*Mil*] gun bolt **5** *(Colloq Fig)* tall dolt

llozkár *nm* **1** door bolt **2** long wooden lever used to increase the pressure on an olive press

*llozh *nm* rubbish

llozhё *nf* box in the theater: loge = lozhё

llubátё *nf* sediment that has settled to the bottom of a liquid, dregs

lluburdínё *nf* = llurbёtírё

llucё *nf* thin mud; muddy place

llucёro ·het *vpr* to get all muddy

llucёro ·n *vt* **1** to make [] muddy; bespatter, soil **2** *(Fig)* to foul up [], make a mess of []

*llucís *stem for 1st sg pres, pl pres, 2nd & 3rd sg subj, pind* <llucít·

*llucít·
I § *vi* to paddle/splash around in the mud
II § *vt* to make [] muddy; bespatter, soil

*lluém *adj (i) (Reg Gheg)* maimed

llufaník *nm* type of dry spicy sausage

llufás = llufís

llufís *stem for 1st sg pres, pl pres, 2nd & 3rd sg subj, pind* <llufít·

llufít· *vt (Colloq)* to gobble up

llufít·es *n (Colloq)* person who gobbles up food; glutton, gobbler

llufítje *nf ger* <llufít·

llugáçe *nf (Colloq)* puddle

llukaník *nm* = llufaník

llukё *nf* **1** spoiled and infertile egg **2** *(Reg)* brood hen **3** *(Fig)* dunce **4** *(Reg)* [*Bot*] = bli

lluks = luks

*lluksóze *np* luxuries

llulláq
I § *nm* indigo
II § *adj* dark blue

llullё *nf* **1** pipe (for smoking tobacco); long-stemmed pipe; pipe bowl **2** condenser pipe in a raki still **3** metal bushing in the hub of a cart/wagon wheel

llum *nm* **1** sludge, crud **2** sediment, dregs **3** grime on unwashed hair, body, or clothes **4** crud left in a (smoking) pipe **5** *(Fig)* rubbish

*llumb = llum

*llumér *nm* landmark; boundary stone

llumё *nf* stagnant and filthy puddle; large waterhole in which sheep are dipped before shearing

llumíshtё OR **llumíshte** *nf* = lymíshtё

*llump = llum

*llumtár *adj* sedimentary

llumtё *adj (i)* **1** covered with alluvial soil **2** *(Fig)* cloudy

llup· *vt (Colloq)* **1** to gobble down; eat gluttonously **2** *(Fig)* to seize greedily, pillage

llupásh *adj, n (Pej)* gluttonous/greedy (person)

llupё *nf (Colloq)* gluttony

llup·es
I § *adj* gluttonous
II § *n* glutton

llupёsí *nf* gluttony

lluq
I § *adj* **1** wet and mushy **2** *(Fig Pej)* sluggish; slow-witted
II § *nm (Pej)* sluggish/slow-witted person

lluqe *nf* thick piece of wood

llurbё *nf* **1** muddy place; mud sediment; slush **2** sludge, dregs **3** mash fed to animals **4** mushy, overcooked food **5** *(FigImpolite)* flabby fat woman

llurb·es *adj* somewhat soft and mushy

llurbёt *adj (i)* **1** soft and muddy **2** mushy **3** *(FigImpolite)* flabby *4 unsteady

llurbёtírё *nf* **1** thin mud; slush; slushy/muddy area **2** sediment, lees, dregs **3** murky liquid without a good taste **4** mash fed to animals **5** mushy, overcooked food **6** *(Fig Pej)* rubbish

*llusё *nf* luxury

*lluskё *nf* meat; pork

llustёr *nf* luster, gloss, shine = lustёr

*llustrár *nm* = llustraxhí

llustraxhí *nm* bootblack, shoeshine boy = lustraxhí

llustrínё *nf* patent leather = lustrínё

llustró·n OR **llustrós·** *vt* = lustró·n

llustruár *adj (i)* polished = lustruár

*lluxё = llucё

m [*më*] *nf* **1** the consonant letter "m" **2** the bilabial nasal consonant represented by the letter "m"

m'i *sequence of pronominal proclitics preceding a transitive verb; represents the complex of 1st sg referent + 3rd pl object clitics: më + i* (generally indicates that the verb has a 1st sg referent and an identifiable 3rd pl direct object) them to/for me

m'u *pronominal clitic preceding a nontransitive verb form; represents the complex of the object clitic më + the reflexive particle u* generally indicates that 1st sg has an underlying interest in a nontransitive action

m *largely fossilized prefix preceding verbal roots beginning with a bilabial stop em-*

ma *sequence of pronominal clitics* (1st sg referent + 3rd sg object)

*****mä** *adv, pcl* (*Reg Gheg*) more; some more, any more = **më**

ma·het *vpr* to become fat

*****macallu'g**ë *nf* round-headed club

ma'ce
   I § *nf* **1** cat **2** (*Insult Pej*) quarrelsome and shrewish female
   II § *adj* (of females) sickly and haggard
   ○ **mace deti** [*Ichth*] small-spotted dogfish (*Scyliorhinus caniculа L.*)
   ○ **mace e egër** [*Zool*] wild cat (*Felis sylvestris sylvestris*)
   ○ **Macja lëmon/lëpin gjithnjë bishtin e vet.** "The cat licks its own tail." (*Prov*) People praise their own. There's comfort in thinking your own is the best.
   ○ **mace zjarri** "fire cat" (*Colloq*) iron firedog

ma'ce *nf* **1** cat **2** (suit in card games) spade

ma'ckë *nf* (*Reg*) **1** cat **2** tip of a peak: very top, tip top point

maco'lle *nf* wooden mallet

macu'kë *nf* shepherd's staff

macu'rr *nm* (*Colloq*) ear of corn

maç *nm* **1** (suit in card games) spade **2** (*Reg*) = **ma'ce** *****3** = **maço'k 4** [*Sport*] sports event: match

*****maçaru'ng**ë = **macallu'g**ë

ma'çë *nf* = **ma'ck**ë

ma'çkë *nf* hard ground, densely packed soil

maço'k *nm* **1** male cat, tomcat **2** (*Fig*) person who is constantly caterwauling and squabbling; person who is sly and untrustworthy
   ○ **maçok me brirë** "tomcat with horns" **1** very difficult to get along with, rowdy, unruly **2** very ugly

maço'rr *nm* = **maço'k**

made'm *nm* **1** mineral; ore **2** (*Old*) mine = **minie'r**ë
   ○ **madem guri** stone quarry = **guro're**

madërgo'në *nf* **1** [*Bot*] henbane, hogbean (*Hyoscyamus niger*) **2** mandrake (*Mandragora officinarum*) **3** (*Fig*) hindrance

madje *pcl* what's more, in fact, furthermore, moreover, indeed

madravi'dë *OR* **madrevi'd**ë *nf* [*Tech*] thread-cutting die

madriga'l *nm* (*Old*) [*Lit Mus*] madrigal

madh
   I § *adj* (i) **1** big; large; tall **2** great; grand **3** long (in time) **4** adult, mature, grown-up; elder **5** major, important; prominent **6** (of something bad) serious, severe **7** big-hearted, tolerant **8** (*Pej*) exaggerated
   II § *nm*(i) **1** adult **2** (*Colloq*) big shot
   III § *nn* (*të*) (*Old*) **1** importance, majesty; pride **2** magnitude; bulk
   ○ **i madh e i vogël** every single person

ma'dh·et *vpr* **1** = **madho' ·het 2** (*Pej*) to get big-headed; act pompous

ma'dh|e *nf* grandmother = **gjy'sh|e**

madh|ëri' *nf* **1** majesty, grandeur **2** (*Offic*) Majesty

madh|ëri'|shëm *adj* (i) (*Elev*) **1** grand, majestic **2** historically important, of monumental importance

madh|ëri'|shm|e *nf* (e) [*Phil*] that which is great

madh|ëri'|sht *adv* (*Book*) majestically

madh|ëro'·het *vpr* **1** (*Book*) = **madho' ·het 2** (*Pej*) to get big-headed; act pompous

madh|ëro'·n *vt* **1** (*Book*) to elevate [] to a higher position, promote **2** to exalt

madh|ësi' *nf* **1** size **2** [*Spec*] magnitude

madh|ësht'i *nf* **1** grandeur **2** (*Pej*) conceit, conceitedness; pomposity

madh|ësht|o' ·het *vpr* **1** to be celebrated with great pomp **2** (*Pej*) to be conceited, be pompous

madh|ësht|o' ·n *vt* to exalt

madh|ësht|o'r
   I § *adj* **1** majestic **2** (*Old pej*) conceited, pompous
   II § *n* (*Old Pej*) conceited/pompous person

madh|ësht|o're *nf* **1** majesty, grandeur **2** that which is majestic

*****ma'dh|ëz** *adj* cocky

madh|o' ·het *vpr* **1** to get bigger; grow larger/taller/longer; grow up **2** = **zmadh|o' ·het 3** to grow in esteem

madh|o' ·n *vt* **1** to grow [] **2** = **zmadh|o' ·n 3** (*Pej*) to overrate, overestimate

madh|o'r *adj* **1** [*Law*] of age, adult **2** [*Mil*] of senior rank (major or colonel) **3** of major value or importance: major

madh|o'sh *adj* hefty, bulky, massive, stocky

ma'dh|t|e *nn* (*të*) magnitude, size; value; strength

mafe's *nm* head kerchief of cotton or silk

ma'fër *nf* (*Colloq*) **1** black head kerchief for women **2** handkerchief

mafi'she *nf* meringue

maga'r *nm* (*Reg*) ass, donkey

*****maga'ze** *OR* **magazi'** *nf* = **magazi'n**ë

magazi'në *nf* **1** department store **2** storage room/building: warehouse

magazinie'r *n* storeroom manager

magazini'm *ng ger* **1** < **magazino' ·n 2** storage

magazino' ·n *vt* to put into storage: warehouse

magdano's *OR* **magdano'z** *nm* = **majdano'z**

*****ma'g**ë *nf* (*Old*) caul

ma'gmë *nf* [*Geol*] magma

magnat *nm* magnate

***magnes** *nm* [*Chem*] = **magnez**

magnet *nm* magnet

magnetik *adj* magnetic

magnetizëm *nm* magnetism

magnetizim *nm ger* [*Tech*] **1** <**magnetizo·**n, **magnetizo·**het **2** magnetization

magnetizo·het *vpr* [*Tech*] to gain magnetic properties: become magnetized

magnetizo·n *vt* to magnetize

magnetofon *nm* tape recorder

***magnetshëm** *adj* (i) = **magnetik**

magnez *nm* [*Chem*] magnesium ((*Mg*))

magnezium = **magnez**

magrip *nm* large clay storage pot for oil

***magunë** *nf* hemlock

magjar *nm* (*Reg*) **1** = **gomar 2** = **ur**ës **3** bridge of a stringed instrument

magje *nf* **1** wooden tub: kneading trough, washtub, mill hopper **2** (*Old*) boat

magjeplotë *adj* well supplied with living provisions: well-off

magjeps· *vt* to enchant, bewitch

magjeps·et *vpr* to be enchanted, become bewitched

magjepsës *adj* enchanting, bewitching

magjepsje *nf ger* **1** <**magjeps·**, **magjeps·et 2** enchantment, bewitchment

magjepsur *adj* (i) enchanted

magjetore *nf* **1** woman who prepares the family bread on a kneading trough **2** woman/girl who is a good cook

magjethatë *adj* poorly supplied with living provisions: poorly off

magjëreshë *nf* = **magjetore**

magjëtore *nf* **1** (female) cook/baker *2 kitchen

magji *nf* **1** magic, witchcraft **2** (*Fig*) enchantment

magjibërës
I § adj magic-working, magical
II § n magician

magjik *adj* **1** having magical powers, magical **2** secretive **3** (*Fig*) enchanting, bewitching

***magjikë** *nf* = **magjistricë**

magjiplotë *adj* (*Poet*) enchanting, bewitching, charming

magjistar
I § nm **1** sorcerer **2** magician
II § adj *magical

magjistari *nf* sorcery, witchcraft

magjistral *nm* [*Tech*] main pipe: main

magjistrat *nm* [*Hist*] magistrate

magjistricë *nf* sorceress, witch

magjishëm *adj* (i) (*Poet*) magically enchanting, captivating, magical

magjyp *n* settled gypsy

magjypthi *adv* **1** gypsy-fashion **2** lewdly

mah· *vt* to fatten, feed

***mahagon** *nm* (*Old*) mahogany

***mahallë** *nf* = **mëhallë**

mahi *nf* [*Constr*] **1** principal rafter of a roof **2** joking, teasing; mockery; trick, joke **3** (of a wound) festering, inflammation, infection

mahis·
I § vt to aggravate [a wound], inflame, irritate

II § vi to fester

mahis·et *vpr* **1** to fester, become inflamed **2** (*Fig*) to get worse: become exacerbated

mahisës *adj* inflammatory

mahisje *nf ger* **1** <**mahis·**, **mahis·et 2** inflammation

mahisur *adj* (i) inflamed, festering, sore

mahit· *vt, vi* to make fun of []; mock

mahit·et *vpr* to joke around, jest

mahitar *n* mocker; jester

***mahitqar**
I § n sneerer, mocker
II § adj sneering, mocking

mahmur *adv* (*Colloq*) tipsy; dopey from drinking: hung-over; sleepy

Mahmut *nm* Mahmut (male name)

mahnis *stem for 1st sg pres, pl pres, 2nd & 3rd sg subj, pind* <**mahnit·**

mahnit· *vt* to astound, amaze

mahnit·et *vpr* to be astounded/amazed

mahnitës *adj* astounding, amazing

mahnitje *nf ger* **1** <**mahnit·**, **mahnit·et 2** astonishment

mahnitshëm *adj* (i) astounding, amazing

mahnitur *adj* (i) astounded, amazed

***mahrama** *nf* cloak, wrap

***maistrall** *nm* mistral

maj *nm* **1** (the month) May **2** large hammer used by blacksmiths **3** heavy wooden device used as a soil compactor: soil rammer **4** heavy wooden mallet; maul

***maj·** = **majm·**

***maj·et** = **majm·et**

maja *nf* **1** yeast = **tharm 2** (*Fig Colloq*) choice part, the cream **3** (*Fig Colloq*) essential element/factor: heart of the matter

majacuk *adj* having sharp peaks

maja-maja *adj* having many peaks

Majami *nm* Miami

majarak *adj* pointed, sharp

***majas·** *vt* to soak

majasëll *nm* (*Colloq*) [*Med*] hemorrhoids, piles

***majasill** = **majasëll**

majçe *OR* **majçe** *nf* [*Bot*] upper leaf of a herbaceous annual (especially tobacco)

majdanoz *nm* [*Bot*] parsley (*Petroselinum*)

***majde** *conj* = **madje**

majere *nf* **1** steep slope; steeply terraced land **2** [*Naut*] plank of a boat's hull: (*carvel plank, strake*)

majë
I § nf **1** tip; point **2** top; peak **3** [*Text*] warp yarn/thread **4** (*Fig Colloq*) choice part, the cream
II § prep (*abl*) atop, upon, on top of
○ (**shko·**n) **majë më majë/e brisk** (to be) at loggerheads
○ **maja e çorapit** toe of the stocking
○ (**një**) **majë gishti/gjilpëre** just a tiny bit; (in negative sentences) even a little bit
○ **majë gishti** fingertip
○ **majë gjilpëre** minutely, in extreme detail
○ **s'ke ku të hedhësh majën e gjilpërës** "you don't have anywhere to throw in the tip of a needle" they're packed in like sardines

○ **s'kishe ku të hidhje majën e gjilpërës** "you didn't have anywhere to throw in the tip of a needle" they were packed in like sardines

○ **Nuk ka majë pa rrëzë.** "There can be no top with a solid bottom." *(Prov)* Every building needs a strong foundation.

○ **majë e kokës** [*Med*] bregma

○ [] **nxjerr· në majë** "take [] to the very top" **1** to finish [] successfully: pull [] off **2** to solve []

○ **majë për majë** completely full, up to the brim

majëkrahut *adj*

majëmal *nm* mountaintop

majëmprehtë
   I § *adj* sharp tipped; pointed
   II § *nf* [*Ichth*] thinlip gray mullet *(Liza ramada)*

majëz *nf* tip

majhosh *adj* slightly sour, bittersweet

majiskë *nf* leaf at the tip of a plant

majkë *nf (Reg)* stinger (of a bee)

Majlinda *nf* Majlinda (female name)

majm· *vt* **1** to make [] beefy/fat: fatten, fatten up [] **2** to fertilize **3** *(Fig Colloq Pej)* to fatten the bellies of []: make [] filthy rich

majm·et *vpr* **1** to become beefy/fat; put on weight **2** *(Fig Colloq Pej)* to become filthy rich **3** *(Fig Colloq)* to boast

*****majmal** *nm (Reg Tosk)* mountain summit

majmë
   I § *adj (i)* **1** hefty, beefy; fat **2** fertile, productive, rich **3** *(Fig Colloq)* filthy rich
   II § *nn (të)* **1** being fat/beefy, corpulence **2** *(Fig Colloq)* being filthy rich: affluence

majmëri *nf* **1** weight increase created by good feeding: beefiness **2** heftiness; corpulence, obesity **3** (of soil) fertility, productiveness

majmje *nf ger* <**majm·**, **majm·et**

majmok *adj* chubby

majmun *nm* monkey, ape **2** *(Fig Pej)* ugly person: ape-face; hairy person

majmunëri *nf(Pej)* **1** monkeyshines; making monkey faces **2** blind imitation: aping

*****majmun·is·** *vt* to ape, mock

majmur *adj (i)* = **majmë**

*****majnishtë** *nf* private pasture

*****majno·het** *vpr* (of a milk animal) to give no milk

majo·n *vt* **1** to top off [a haystack] **2** *(Fig)* to bring [] to a close; complete []

majoke *nf* treetop

majole *nf* low peak

majolikë *nf* majolica

majonezë *nf* [*Food*] mayonnaise

major *nm* [*Mil*] (military rank) major

major *adj (Book)* apical

majos· *vt* **1** to fill [] up to the top *****2** to fatten

*****majosh** = **majhosh**

*****majsë** *nf* **1** outer skin of an onion/egg **2** fontanella

majtas *OR* **majtazi** *adv* **1** leftward, on the left **2** to the left

majtasrrotulluës
   I § *adj* **1** wheeling to the left **2** counterclockwise
   II § *adv* [*Mil*] (command) wheel left!

majtë
   I § *adj (i)* left
   II § *nf (e)* **1** left side **2** political left

majtist *adj, n* [*Politics*] leftist

majtizëm *nm* [*Politics*] leftism

majth *nm* **1** small hammer *****2** [*Anat*] malleus bone in the ear

majuc *nm* tip; pointed tip

majuckë *nf dimin* very tip; topmost point, highest level, pinnacle

majuk *nm* blunt end of the wooden paddle used to beat cloth in the fulling process

majung *nm* **1** sledge hammer, forge hammer **2** wooden club used to break up clods of earth

makalush
   I § *adj, n (Impol)* **1** easily fooled: simple, gullible **2** stupid
   II § *nm* simpleton

makar *pcl (followed by a subjunctive verb phrase) (Colloq)* **1** expresses unwilling approval: okay (said in a resigned and bitter voice) **2** expresses a scaled-down desire: at least __

○ **makar __, makar __** (introduces balanced alternatives) either __, or __

makara *nf* [*Tech*] **1** pulley; windlass, reel **2** spool (of thread)

makarona *np* macaroni

○ **makarona deti** [*Bot*] wormlike red seaweed *Nemalion helminthoides*

*****makarune** = **makarona**

maket *nm* **1** maquette, model, mock-up **2** prepublication draft of a book circulated for comment: bound galleys, reading copy; dummy

makë *nf* **1** film that forms on a liquid; scum, skin **2** = **makrosë** **3** spiderweb, cobweb **4** paste made of flour and cornstarch, glue

makër *nf* animal's fluid discharge before giving birth

makiavelizëm *nm* Machiavellianism

makijazh *nm* **1** theatrical makeup; maquillage **2** profession of the makeup artist: maquillage

makijazhist *n* makeup artist

makinacione *np* machinations

MAKINAIMPORT *abbrev* agency for the importation of machinery

makinandërtues *adj* producing various machines

makineri *nf* machinery

makinë *nf* **1** machine **2** vehicle; automobile

○ **makinë fotografike** *(Old)* camera

○ **makinë korrëse** reaping machine, reaper

○ **makinë kositëse** mowing machine: mower

○ **makinë larëse** washing machine

○ **makinë lidhëse** binding machine: binder

○ **makinë mbjellëse** sowing machine, seed drill

○ **makinë mbledhëse** [*Agr*] machine for gathering straw: hay rake

○ **makinë me avull** steam engine

○ **makinë ngrohëse** **1** heating plant **2** *(Colloq)* hot-water heater

○ **makinë qepëse** sewing machine

○ **makinë rroje** safety razor

○ **makinë shkrimi** typewriter

○ **makinë shkruese** *(Old)* typewriter

○ **makinë shpimi** drilling machine, driller

○ **makinë shtypi** printing press

makinist *n* machinist

*****maklen** *nm* [*Bot*] Montpellier maple *(Acer monspessulanum)*

makllada *np (Colloq)* nonsense, rubbish

maknore *nf* [*Zool*] = **shumëkëmbësh**

◦ **sill·***et* (gjithë ditën) si maknore *(Crude)* to spend all one's time walking around doing nothing

makro'·*het vpr* to form a scum, form a scab; grow moldy; spoil

makro' *formativ (Book)* macro-

makro'bo'të *nf (Book)* macroworld

makro'organi'zëm *nm* macroorganism

makro'se' *nf* **1** greenish scum; green mold; film that forms on liquid **2** [*Anat*] placenta; afterbirth **3** earwax

maksima'l
I § *adj* maximal
II § *nf* maximum limit

maksimu'm
I § *nm* maximum
II § *adv* at most, at the maximum

makth *nm* **1** [*Bot*] sweet clover, melilot *Melilotus* **2** common St.-John's wort *Hypericum perforatum* **3** baby rabbit, leveret; rabbit **4** [*Anat*] placenta; afterbirth **5** *(Colloq)* nightmare **6** [*Folklore*] bogeyman who comes at night to steal away your spirit, but if caught may grant anything you wish

◦ **makth i bardhë** [*Bot*] white sweet clover *Melilotus albus*

◦ **makth i dhëmbëzuar** [*Bot*] dentated melilot *Melilotus dentata*

◦ **makth indian** [*Bot*] annual yellow clover *Melilotus indica*

◦ **makth i lartë** [*Bot*] tall melilot *Melilotus altissimus*

◦ **makth i verdhë** [*Bot*] white sweet clover *Melilotus officinalis*

****maku'sh** *nm* [*Ornit*] ostrich = **struc**

maku't *adj, n (Pej)* greedy/insatiable/gluttonous (person)

makut'ëri' *nf (Pej)* **1** gluttony **2** greed

makut'kë *nf* greedy/insatiable woman

mal
I § *nm* **1** mountain **2** *(Colloq)* mountainous region **3** *(Old)* small mountain district comprising a distinct ethnic unit **4** *(Old)* = **pyll 5** *(Fig Colloq)* huge stack/pile/heap
II § *adv* enormously

◦ **male të shkreta** barren and arid mountains

◦ **male thinjoshe** *(Poet)* mountains covered with a light layer of snow: grizzled mountains

◦ **U mbars mali e polli një mi.** *(Prov)* The mountain rumbled and gave forth a mouse.

mal'aca'k *adj, n* (person) living in the mountains, mountaineer

Malajzi' *nf* Malaysia

mal'a'ma'l *adv* reaching from one bank (of a body of water) to the other

mala'rie *nf* [*Med*] malaria

malari'k
I § *adj* **1** ill with malaria **2** malarial
II § *n* person afflicted with malaria, malarial

mal'ata'k
I § *adj (Impol)* crude and uncultured: uncouth
II § *n* hillbilly, boor

****mal'a'ze'stë** *adj (i)* Montenegrin = **malaze'z**

mala'ze'z *adj, nm* Montenegrin

mala'ze'ze *adj, nf* Montenegrin

mala'zi'as *adj, n* Montenegrin

Malbo'r *nm* Malbor (male name)

malc'im *nm ger* **1** <**malco'·***n*, **malco'**·*het* **2** infection

malc'o'·*het vpr* to fester

malc'o'·*n vt* to infect [a wound], inflame; make sore, irritate

malc'ua'r *adj (i)* infected, festering

****maldano's** = **majdano'z**

malea'bël *adj* [*Spec*] malleable

malena'ke *adj*

mal'ësi' *nf* **1** mountainous region; mountain range **2** *(Collec)* mountaineers

mal'ëso'r
I § *adj* from the mountains, of or pertaining to mountaineers or the mountains
II § *n* mountaineer

mal'ëso'rçe *adv* mountain-style

Mali i Zi *nm (definite cases only)* Montenegro

Mal'li *nm* Mali (male name)

maliher *nm* old five-shot rifle

malije *nf* cold wind from the mountains; north wind

malinj *adj* [*Med*] malignant

malinj'itet *nm* [*Med*] malignancy

Maliq *nm* town in southeastern Albania

mal'ishtë *nf* small district in the mountains

Malo *nf with masc agreement* Malo (male name)

malo'k *nm (Impol)* **1** = **malëso'r 2** crude and uncultured person: hillbilly

malo'kçe *adv (Impol)* **1** = **malësorçe 2** boorishly, like a hillbilly

malo'r *adj* **1** mountainous; located in the mountains **2** living or growing in mountainous areas **3** appropriate for mountains

malo're *nf* uphill slope

mal'she'she *nf* mountain plateau

malt *nm* malt

mal'ta'r *nm* mountain lumberman

malto'r *n* = **malta'r**

malto'zë *nf* [*Chem*] maltose

maluka't *nm (Colloq Insult)* monster

maluk'e'tër *np* <**maluka't**

malvace' *np* [*Bot*] mallow family *Malvaceae*

mall *nm* **1** feeling or longing for someone or something that one deeply misses; fond yearning **2** property, possessions **3** goods, merchandise; article of merchandise; cargo

◦ **mall pa zot** property that belongs to no one: loose property, abandoned property

◦ **mall azat** abandoned property

◦ **mall belik** "state property" property not owned by anyone; public property

◦ **mall bërllok** junk, worthless stuff

◦ **do t'<> ka-***subj* **mallin** to miss <> when <> is gone

◦ **ësh·të për mall** to be permanently pleasurable: be a constant joy

****mallaga'n** *adj, n* (one that) furtively sneaks things away

Mallaka'stër *nf* ethnographic region of southwestern Albania: Mallakastra

mallakastrio't
I § *adj* of or pertaining to Mallakastra
II § *n* native of of Mallakastra

****mallau'rë** *nf* [*Ornit*] owl

****malle'së** *nf* pasture

mallëngj'e·*het vpr* **1** to feel deeply touched, feel emotional **2** to have a deep longing, yearn

mallˈëngje·*n vt* to move [] emotionally, move [] to a deep emotion: touch [] deeply, stir

mallˈëngjiˈm *nm* deep feelings/sentiment; nostalgia

mallˈëngjyˈer *adj (i)* **1** emotionally touched, deeply moved, emotional **2** nostalgic, full of longing; feeling sentimental

mallˈëngjyˈes *adj* **1** sentimental, emotional; deeply touching/moving ***2** pathetic; wistful

mallˈëngjyeˈshëm *adj (i)* emotionally touching, deeply moving, piquant; sentimental

*mallˈim *nm* **1** yearning, longing **2** = **malleˈs**ë

*mallkˈes *nm (Old)* priest

mallkˈesë *nf(Old)* malediction, anathema, curse

mallkiˈm *nm ger* **1** <**mallkoˈ·***n* **2** malediction, curse; denunciation

mallkoˈ·*n vt, vi* **1** *[Relig]* to pronounce a malediction/anathema (upon []) **2** to curse ([]) **3** *(Elev)* to denounce, damn

mallkuaˈr
  I § *adj (i)* cursed, damned
  II § *nm (i)* devil, satan

malloˈ·*het vpr* to be moved by tender emotions; be nostalgic; feel a longing

malloˈ·*n vt (Reg)* to drive [] to pasture

malloˈs·*et vpr* to yearn, long

malloˈsur *adj (i)* **1** homesick **2** wistful

malloˈtë *nf(Reg)* heavy wool overcoat for men

maˈllshëm *adj (i)* wistful, sentimental, yearning, desirous

mallˈtar *adj, n* (person) having many possessions of value, rich (man)

mallth *nm* pad of an animal's paw

malluaˈr *adj (i)* affected by nostalgia, made nostalgic; homesick

mama *nf(Pet)* baby's term for his mother: mama

*mamaliˈgjë *OR* **mamaling**ë *nf* porridge made of corn

*mamˈar *adj* suckling, mammalian

*mamˈçoˈre *adj* = **mamshoˈre**

*mameˈshë *nf (Old)* = **mamí**
  ○ **mâm**ë **e ftoft**ë *(Reg Gheg)* foster mother

*mâmë *(Reg Gheg)* = **mëm**ë

mamí *vocative (Child)* term of affectionate address for one's mother: mommy

mamí *nf* **1** midwife ***2** wetnurse

mamícë *nf* = **mamí**

mamifeˈrë *np [Zool]* mammalia

*maˈmkë *nf* oat-bag for horses

*mamˈosh *adj* mother's

*mamˈshoˈre *adj* yielding milk

mamuˈz *nm* rider's spur with spiked rowel

man *nm [Bot]* mulberry *(Morus L.)*
  ○ **man i bardhë** *[Bot]* white mulberry *(Morus alba)*
  ○ **man i kuq** *[Bot]* red mulberry *(Morus rubra)*
  ○ **man toke** *[Bot]* wild strawberry *(Fragaria vesca L.)*
  ○ **man i zi** *[Bot]* common mulberry *(Morus nigra)*

mana *pcl (Reg)* indeed, in fact, in truth, to tell the truth

*manaç *adj* peculiar, odd, curious

manˈaferrë *nf [Bot]* blackberry bush, bramble; blackberry *(Rubus)*
  ○ **manaferr**ë **e but**ë raspberry *(Rubus idaeus)*

manˈaferrës *nm [Ornit]* wren *(Troglodytes troglodytes)*

manaˈk *nm [Ethnog]* bracelet or necklace twisted with a few strands of red and white wool or silk and worn by children on the first day of spring

*manapo *adv* well and good, finally

manaˈr *n* **1** pet lamb that tags along after its master **2** *(Fig Pet)* pampered and well behaved little child that stays close to its parents

manaˈrkë *nf dimin* <**manaˈr**

manastíˈr *nm* monastery
  ○ **manastir pa hair** *(Old)* close-fisted person, miser; an inhospitable household

*manaˈt = **mana**

manˈatoke *nf [Bot]* wild strawberry *(Fragaria vesca L.)*

Mançuˈri *nf* Manchuria

mançuriˈan *adj, n* Manchurian

mandaˈll *OR* **mandaˈll**ë *nm, nf* pivoting bar used to keep a door/window closed

mandaˈpostë *nf* postal money order

mandaríˈnë *nf [Bot]* mandarin orange; tangerine *(Citrus reticulata)*

mandaˈt *nm* **1** mandate **2** *[Law]* authority; authorization, warrant
  ○ **mandat reshtimi** arrest warrant

mandatarkëˈtiˈm *nm [Fin]* payment order to a cashier

mandaˈtë *nf(Colloq)* **1** notice of death in the family; bad news, sad news ***2** = **mandaˈt**

mandatpageˈsë *nf[Fin]* payment order to a bank or cashier

mandeˈj *adv* = **pastaj**

*mândˈeshë *nf (Reg Gheg)* = **mëndˈesh**ë

manˈdër *nf* enclosure for livestock: pen, stable, corral; mountain corral, fold

*mandërgoˈre = **madërgoˈn**ë

*mândˈëz *(Reg Gheg)* = **menˈdër**

*mandíˈle *nf* kerchief

mandolinˈatë *nf[Mus]* mandolin concert

mandolíˈnë *nf[Mus]* mandolin

mandoliníˈst *nm* mandolin player

mandrí *nf* herd, flock

mandríˈnë *OR* **mandríˈno** *nf[Tech]* lathe chuck

mandríˈno *nf [Tech]* mandrel, chuck

manekíˈn *nm* **1** mannequin; clothes model **2** *(Impol)* puppet under control of other people

maneˈvˈër *nf* = **manoˈvˈër**

*manˈevˈr *nm* = **manoˈvˈr**

manˈeroˈsë *nf[Bot]* duckweed *(Lemna minor)*

mangaˈj *np* <**mangaˈll**

mangaˈll *nm (np ~j)* brazier for holding burning coals or charcoal

mangaˈn *nm [Chem]* manganese *((Mn)M)*

mangaˈnˈez *nm* = **mangaˈn**

*manganíˈs· *vt* to card [wool]

*mangerˈush *adj* left-handed

maˈngë *nf(Insult)* **1** hobo, bum **2** sly person

*mângˈë *nf(Reg Gheg)* = **mëˈng**ë
  ○ **mâng**ë **lini** *(Reg Gheg)* flax breaker

mangˈësi *nf* deficiency, lack; insufficiency, weakness

maˈngët *adj (i)* **1** deficient, wanting, missing, lacking **2** insufficient; incomplete **3** *(Colloq)* defective

○ **ësh·të mangët për** [] to lack []; need [one's comeuppance]

*mângo'o·*n* *vt (Reg Gheg)* to press [] between rollers: mangle, calender

*mângo're *(Reg Gheg)* = mëngo're

*mangth *nm* [*Folklore*] bogeyman = makth

mangut *adv* = mangët

mani *nf* 1 [*Med*] mania, obsession; addiction 2 eccentricity

mania k

I § *adj* [*Med*] suffering from a mania/obsession: obsessive

II § *nm* obsessive person, maniac

manifaktu're *nf* 1 cottage industry 2 *(Old)* yard goods, textile fabric

manifest *nm* 1 manifesto 2 *(Old)* proclamation

manifestim *nm ger* 1 <manifesto·*n*, manifesto·*het* 2 demonstration 3 manifestation

manifesto·*het vpr (Book)* to become evident, be evinced: become manifest

manifesto·*n*

I § *vi* to take part in a march/rally, participate in a group demonstration/protest: demonstrate

II § *vt* to manifest, display

manifestues *nm* participant in a group demonstration/protest: demonstrator

manikyr *nm* 1 manicure 2 nail polish

manipulim *nm ger (Book)* 1 <manipulo·*n* 2 manipulation

manipulo·*n vt (Book)* to manipulate

*maniqe'te *nf* cuff (on clothing) = manshe'te

*maniqyr *nf* manicure = manikyr

*manis = mahnis

*manit = mahnit

manivelë *nf* [*Tech*] crank handle, crank

maniviq *nm (Old)* 1 [*Ethnog*] = poganik 2 gift for the birth of a child

manliher *nm* = maliher

*mano·*n (Reg Gheg)* = mëno·*n*

manometër *nm* [*Phys*] manometer, pressure-gauge

*manore *np* [*Bot*] mulberry family *Moraceae*

*manorels *nm* [*Tech*] monorail

*mano'v *nm (Old)* dark-complexioned Turkish soldier of Oriental ancestry

manovakum metër *nm* [*Tech*] vacuum gauge

*manovelë = manivele

mano'vër *nf* 1 maneuver 2 *(Fig Book)* trick

manovrim *nm ger* 1 <manovro·*n* 2 trickery

manovro·*n*

I § *vt* to maneuver

II § *vi* 1 [*Mil*] to go on maneuvers 2 *(Fig Book)* to finagle

manovrueshëm *adj* (i) maneuverable

manshe'te *nf* cuff (on sleeves), wrist band

mantel *nm* 1 long overcoat 2 exterior covering used to hide the truth: secret mantle, guise *3 mantle, cloak

mantiqe *nf* [*Naut*] hoisting/trimming line for a sail: sheet, tack ( )

manto *nf* light topcoat worn by women

manual *nm* manual, handbook; textbook

manure *nf* 1 [*Dairy*] round cheese made of ewe's milk; wheel of such cheese 2 fig bread made in a round shape

manushaqe *nf* [*Bot*] violet = vjollcë

○ **manushaqe e verdhë** [*Bot*] yellow vetch *Viola lutea*

Manushaqe *nf* Manushaqe (female name)

manushaqore *np* [*Bot*] violet family *Violeceae*

manxura'në *nf* [*Bot*] sweet marjoram *(Origanum majorana)* = rigon

manzhe'të *nf* = manshe'te

manj *nf* ewe or nanny goat with one defective teat

*manjolie *nf* magnolia

mapo *nf* <magazinë popullore department store

maqedonas *adj*, *n* Macedonian

Maqedoni *nf* Macedonia

maqedonisht *adv* in Macedonian (language)

maqedonishte *nf* Macedonian language

*maqellar *nm* butcher

*maqelli *nf* slaughterhouse; butcher shop

*maqellos· *vt* to butcher, slaughter

*maqineri *nf* machinery, machine equipment

*maqinë *nf* = makinë

○ **maqinë shtrydhëse** mangle

*maqinist *n* machinist

Maqo *nf with masc agreement* Maqo (male name)

maraj I § *nm OR* maraje II § *nf* [*Bot*] fennel *(Foeniculum vulgare)*

*mara'më *nf* = mahrama

marangoz *nm* 1 woodworker, carpenter 2 [*Ornit*] woodpecker = qukapik

*maranxhë *nf* [*Bot*] grapefruit *(Citrus paradisi)*

maraq *nm* [*Bot*] mayweed chamomile *(Anthemis cotula)*

○ **maraq i ëmbël** [*Bot*] fennel *Foeniculum vulgare*

maraskë *nf* [*Bot*] bitter fennel *(Foeniculum piperitum)*

maratonë *nf* marathon

maratonist *nm* [*Sport*] marathon runner

*marauzhgë *nf* [*Entom*] horsefly, gadfly

maraz *nm (Colloq)* 1 envy, jealousy 2 deep sadness

marcanik *nm* [*Ichth*] = ferracak

marcapane *nf* marzipan

marcel *nm (Old)* gold-color disk worn by women as ornaments on clothes or ears

marcial *adj*

*mardanoz = majdanoz

mardh· *vi* to feel ice cold, suffer from the icy cold

mardha *nf* 1 hidden defect 2 hidden locus of a disease/illness 3 = hile

mardhë *nf* freezing cold; frost

mardhur

I § *part* <mërdhi·*n*

II § *adj* (i) numb with cold, frozen, very cold

mare *nf* [*Bot*] 1 strawberry madrone, strawberry tree *(Arbutus unedo L.)* 2 fruit of this tree

mare *nf* fecund stage/state (of an animal), readiness for mating

*marendo·*n* = merendo·*n*

marenë *nf* [*Bot*] 1 lilac chaste tree, monk's pepper tree *(Vitex agnuscastus)* 2 [*Ichth*] = mërenë

marenëkuqe *nf* [*Bot*] = marenë

mareshal *nm* [*Mil*] (military rank) marshal

mare·shtë *nf* **1** grove of strawberry trees **2** area with dense bushes that afford good hiding **3** strawberry tree = **mare**

margaç *nm* = **magar**

margarinë *nf* margarine

Margarit·a *nf* Margarita (female name)

margarita·r *nm* pearl

margjëno·r *nm* shelter provided by a cliff overhang

marhama *nf* large towel

***Mari** *nf (Reg)* Mary, Marie

***mariana·k** *nm (Old)* cabinetmaker

maridh·ë *nf* [*Ichth*] (*Spicara flexuosa*)
  ∘ **maridhë boshtake** [*Ichth*] *Spicara smaris*
  ∘ **maridhë e rreme** [*Ichth*] *Centracanthus cirrus*
  ∘ **maridhë e zezë** [*Ichth*] *Spicara maena*

marifet *nm (Colloq)* **1** skill needed to handle a (delicate) matter successfully: special knack, special know-how, expertise **2** craftiness, finagling

marifetçi *nm (np ~ nj) (Colloq)* finagler

maril·lë *nf*
  ∘ **marillë thellësie** [*Ichth*] small-toothed argentine *Glossanodon leioglossus*

***marima·ngë** *nf* = **merima·ngë**

marina·r *nm* sailor (by profession)

marin·ë *nf* **1** naval forces: navy, merchant marine **2** [*Bot*] tamarisk (*Tamarix*)

Maringle·n *nm* Maringlen (male name) acronym

marin·kuqe *nf* = **marenë**

marin·ore *nf* [*Bot*] plants of the tamarisk family *Tamaricaceae*

marione·të *nf (Book)* marionette

Marjan·a *nf* Marjana (female name)

Mark *nm* Mark (male name)

marketim *nm* labelling with the brand name; brand label

marke·z *nm* [*Hist*] marquis

marke·ze *nf* [*Hist*] marchioness

mark·ë *nf* **1** (German or Finnish monetary unit) mark **2** factory label, trademark; brand name **3** *(Fig Colloq Pej)* type, sort (of person)

***Marko** *nf with masc agreement* Mark

markofili *nf* [*Postal*] postmark collecting

marksist *adj, n* Marxist

marksist-leninist *adj, n* Marxist-Leninist

marksizëm *nm* Marxism

marksizëm-leninizëm *nm* Marxism-Leninism

markuç *nm* rubber hose

marmalatë = **marmelatë**

marmelatë *nf* fruit preserves: jam, marmalade

marmitë *nf* [*Tech*] muffler (for a motor), silencer

marmotë *nf* [*Zool*] marmot

***marmur** = **mermer**

***marne·shë** *nf* [*Bot*] = **manushaqe**

***maro** *nf* [*Invert*] firefly

***maroc·ë** *nf* [*Invert*] snail

Marok *nm* Morocco

maroke·n *adj, n* Moroccan

***marozhe** *nf* = **kërmill**

mars *nm* **1** March (the month) **2** Mars (the planet)

marsake *nf* [*Ornit*] = **marsatore**

marsatore *nf* [*Ornit*] garganey (*Anas querquedula*)

marse *np* <**mars** [*Ethnog*] bracelet or necklace of silk or wool yarn worn by children on the first day of spring

Marsejë *nf* Marseille

marsiliore *nf* [*Bot*] plants of the marsilia family *Marsiliaceae*

marsh
  I § *nm* **1** [*Mus*] march **2** [*Tech*] transmission setting for a motor: gear
  II § *interj* military command to move: march!

marshall *nm* [*Mil*] = **mareshal**

***marshalla** = **mashalla**

marshallojë *nf* [*Bot*] oleander, rosebay (*Nerium oleander*)

marshim *nm ger* **1** <**marsho·n** **2** march

marsho·n *vi* to march

***marshto·n** OR **marshtro·n** *vi* = **mataro·n**

***marshtrue·s**
  I § *adj* administrative
  II § *n* administrator, steward, bailiff

Mart·a *nf* Marta (female name)

martalloz *nm* [*Hist*] **1** armed marshal during the Ottoman occupation of Albania **2** *(Old)* = **bekçi**

Martane·sh *nm* mountainous region east northeast of Tirana

martanesh·as *adj, n* of/from Martanesh, native of Martanesh

martes·ë *nf* **1** marriage, matrimony **2** wedding

martesor *adj (Offic)* matrimonial

mart·ë *nf (e)* Tuesday

martin *nm*
  ∘ **martin peshkatari** [*Ornit*] European kingfisher (*Alcedo atthis*)

martin·ë *nf* Martini rifle

martir *n (Elev)* martyr

martirizim *nm ger* **1** <**martirizo·n, martirizo·het 2** martyrization; martyrdom

martirizo·het *vpr* to make a self sacrifice; become a martyr

martirizo·n *vt* to martyrize

marto·het *vpr* to get married
  ∘ **marto·het dhe selit·et** to get married and start a family

marto·n *vt* **1** to marry off [] **2** to graft [figs] **3** *(Fig Colloq)* to get rid of []; lose []

marto·së *nf* (on a roof) overtile, ridge tile; wood lap used to cover joints in a roof

martuar *adj (i), nm (i)* married person
  ∘ **Mukajeti të lë pa martuar.** "Your (excessive) solicitude will leave you unmarried." **1** *(Joke)* Your oversolicitude (with what you are doing) will keep you from ever getting married. **2** Your fussiness will be the cause of your remaining unmarried.

marule *nf* [*Bot*] lettuce (*Lactuca sativa*)

marxh·ë *nf* **1** skinned carcass of livestock **2** *(Colloq)* very thin and weak livestock animal

***marzipan** *nm* marzipan = **marcapane**

marr *stem for 1st sg pres, pl pres, 2nd & 3rd sg subj, opt, adm, part* <**merr**
  ∘ <> **marr**^*opt* **hijen!** *(Curse)* May {} disappear from <>'s sight forever!: I hope {} *dies*!
  ∘ <> **marr**^*opt* **të keqen/ligat** "May {} get <>'s bad stuff!" *(Curse)* (in response to an insult/threat) May {}'s curse on <> be turned back on {} instead! Same to {}!

∘ <> marrtë e mira/mbara! "May good fortune take <>!" *(Felic)* May things continue to go well for <>! Good luck to <>!

marra'k *adj* deranged, crazy

marra'ko't· *vt* to make dizzy, befuddle

marra'ko't·et *vpr* to be dizzy/befuddled; walk dizzily

marrame'ndje *nf* = marrame'nth

marrame'nth *nm* **1** dizziness; befuddlement, stupor **2** [*Med*] vertigo

marrame'nthi *adv* dizzily; in a stupor

marra'sh *nm* person who is out of his mind: madman, lunatic

*****marra'z** = mara'z

ma'rre *nf(Colloq)* shame, disgrace = turp

ma'rrë
  I § *part* <merr·
  II § *adj (i)* **1** deranged, out of one's mind; crazy, mad **2** foolhardy; silly, idiotic, senseless **3** turbulent **4** *(Reg Gheg)* shameful
  III § *n (i)* **1** lunatic **2** idiot

marrë'dhë'nie *nf* relationship

ma'rrës
  I § *n* **1** receiver; recipient **2** [*Postal*] addressee **3** [*Mus*] person who starts the singing of a polyphonic folksong, songleader; person who leads a folkdance **4** [*Ethnog*] father of the bridegroom
  II § *adj* receiving

*****ma'rrët** *adj (i) (Reg Gheg)* **1** pallid **2** crazy, mad

marrë've'shje *nf* understanding, agreement, accord

marrë'zi *nf* **1** insanity, madness **2** preposterousness, absurdity

marrë'zi'shëm *adj (i)* preposterous, absurd, senseless

marrë'zi'sht *adv* insanely; foolishly

*****marrfundo'·n** *vt (Old)* to terminate, conclude

*****marrha'kje** *nf* revenge = hakma'rrje

marri *nf* = marrë'zi

*****marri'në** *nf (Reg)* = marrë'zi

*****marri'shëm** *adj (i)* foolhardy

marri'sht *adv* = marrë'zi'sht

ma'rrje *nf ger* **1** <merr·, me'rr·et **2** capture, seizure **3** reception **4** [*Volleyball*] change of service

marro'·het *vpr* **1** = marro'se·t **2** to feel shame, be ashamed of oneself, feel dishonored **3** to be shamed, be dishonored

marro'·n *vt* **1** = marro's· **2** to shame, dishonor

marro'q *adj (Insult)* **1** idiotic, imbecilic, foolish **2** slightly crazy

marro's· *vt* to make crazy; addle; befuddle, delude

marro's·et *vpr* **1** to go crazy **2** *(Fig)* to act crazy
  ∘ **marros·et pas <>** to be crazy about <>

marro'sje *nf ger* <marro's·, marro's·et

marro'su'r *adj (i)* crazy; foolish

ma'rrshëm *adj (i) (Colloq)* bashful

ma'rrtas *adv* dimly, faintly

ma'rrtë *adj (i)* **1** dim; non-glossy, matted **2** murky, clouded; opaque

marr'th *nm* [*Bot*] weed that resembles wheat

marru'k *adj (Insult)* = marro'k

mas *stem for 1st sg pres, pl pres, 2nd & 3rd sg subj, pind* <ma'·

masa'kër *nf* massacre

masakri'm *nm ger* **1** <masakro'·n, masakro'·het **2** massacre

masakro'·n *vt* **1** to massacre **2** *(Fig)* to butcher [an artistic work]

masa't *nm* piece of steel used to strike sparks from a flintstone = uro'r

masa'zh *nm* massage

masazh'ato'r *n* = masazhi'st

masazh'ist *n* masseur

ma'së *nf* **1** measure **2** measurement; size; scope **3** mass *(Fig)* (proper) limits, limitation
  ∘ **masë e njomë** "wet mass" fodder consisting mainly of fresh hay
  ∘ **masë vëllimtare** cubic capacity

masi'v
  I § *adj* **1** massive **2** of the masses
  II § *nm* **1** [*Geog*] massif **2** *(Book)* large mass

masivite't *nm (Book)* mass participation

masivizi'm *nm ger* <masivizo'·n, masivizo'·het

masivizo'·het *vpr* to attract mass participation; take on a mass character, come to belong to the masses

masivizo'·n *vt* to engage mass participation in [ ]

maskara' *nm (np ˜ e'nj) (Insult)* dishonorable and unprincipled person: scoundrel

maskara'de *nf* masquerade

maskara'llë'k *nm (np ˜ qe) (Colloq)* **1** activity or behavior of scoundrels: dirty work, dirty business **2** dirty word/language

maskare'nj *np* <maskara'

maskari' *nf* dirty trick

maskaro'·n *vi* to play a dirty trick

ma'skë *nf* mask

*****mas'këndaj** = mbasanda'j

maski'm *nm ger* **1** <masko'·n, masko'·het **2** camouflage

masko'·het *vpr* **1** to put on a mask/disguise **2** to hide by means of camouflage/disguise

masko'·n *vt* to mask; camouflage

masku'a'r *adj (i)* **1** masked, disguised **2** camouflaged

masku'es *nm* [*Mil*] camoufleur

maso'n *nm* mason

masoneri' *nf* Freemasonry

masovi'k
  I § *adj* large-scale: mass
  II § *n* person who is good at organizing popular activities

masta'p *nm (Colloq)* **1** long stick, staff **2** *(Fig)* tall and thin

masta'r *nm* **1** board used for applying and levelling plaster: float **2** board used as a mason's level

*****maste'lë** *nf* barrel, tub, vat

masti'kë *nf (Reg)* **1** ouzo = u'zo **2** chewing gum

*****masto'·n** *vi* = mbasto'·n

mastra'pa *nf* = mashtra'pë

masu'r *nm* **1** spool, bobbin (in the shuttle of a loom) **2** corncob

mashalla'
  I § *interj (Colloq)* said before a compliment in order to ward off the evil eye: bless God! knock on wood!
  II § *nf* **1** *(Old)* silver or gold coin placed on a baby's forehead to ward off the evil eye: talisman **2** tin can filled with oil and ashes and used as a lamp **3** burning torch
  III § *adv* very well; very much

mashan *nm* fireplace tongs

mashbigë *nf* tongs with two curved prongs

mashë *nf* **1** tongs **2** *(Fig)* person used as a tool by another: tool
○ **duhet kapur me mashë e duhet flakur** "it must be grabbed by tongs and thrown away" {*something*} should be thrown away without even touching it; {} must be dismissed out of hand

mashën *nf* **1** place in the mountains in which sheep or goats are kept: mountain sheepfold, mountain corral for goats **2** shed for keeping winter fodder, hayshed **3** herder's hut in winter pasture

****mashinë** *OR* **mashinkë** *nf* **1** submachine gun ****2** = **makinë**

mashkë *nf* hairpin

mashkull
I § *nm* **1** male **2** *(Reg)* deep wooden bowl for food **3** [*Bot*] large seed-bearing stalk **4** [*Tech*] tap (for cutting internal screw threads)
II § *adj* masculine
○ **mashkulli i misrit** cornstalk
○ **mashkulli i qerres/karrocës** tongue of the cart/wagon

mashkulli *nf* **1** masculinity **2** males taken as a collective whole: male population

mashkullim *nm* males taken as a collective whole: male population

mashkullo·n *vi* (of animals) to give birth to male offspring

mashkullor
I § *adj* **1** male **2** masculine, manly **3** (of soil or female animals) infertile, sterile
II § *nm* **1** drone bee **2** grapevine cutting that produces no grapes

mashkullore *nf* **1** [*Ling*] masculine gender **2** woman with masculine characteristics and behavior; woman who produces no children

mashkulloresi *nf* [*Med*] virilism

mashkullorezim *nm* [*Med*] virilization

****mashkulluer** *nm (obl ˜ori) (Old)* grapevine shoot that bears no fruit

mashnor *n* animal herder who accompanies the herd or flock to summer pasture in the mountains

mashterk *nm (np ˜q)* = **mashtër**

****mashtë** = **majtë**

mashtër *nf (Old)* deep wooden bowl/dish; wooden platter

mashtrapë *nf* tankard

mashtresë *nf* = **mashtrim**

mashtrim *nm ger* **1** <**mashtro·n, mashtro·het** **2** deceit; swindle, fraud

mashtro·n *vt* to deceive; cheat, swindle

mashtrues
I § *adj* deceptive; fraudulent
II § *n* deceiver; swindler, cheat

mashurka *np fem* [*Bot*] **1** snap bean, string bean (*Phaseolus vulgaris*) ****2** [*Bot*] pod: *(silique)*

mat *nm* **1** seacoast; river bank **2** = **ranishtë** **3** [*Chess*] mate, checkmate
○ ([]) **mat· e çmat·** **1** to measure and remeasure ([]) to make sure **2** to wander aimlessly up and down [] **3** to turn [] over well in the mind; think [] through carefully, scrutinize [] with care

mat· *vt* to measure
○ **mat· armët** to match arms, pit forces, enter into battle

○ **e mat· detin me filxhan** "measure out the sea with a coffee cup" to be able to endure slow and arduous work
○ **mat· forcat me** [] "measure forces with []" to match forces with [], engage [] in a fight
○ **Mat tri/shtatë/dhjetë herë e pre një herë!** "Measure three/seven/ten times and cut one time." *(Prov)* Look before you leap.
○ [] **mat· me kutin e vet** to measure [] by one's own standards
○ **mat· me pëllëmbë** to wander over every inch of the ground
○ [] **mat· me sy** to measure [somebody] with one's eyes
○ <> **mat·pulsin 1** to take <>'s pulse **2** to try <*a candidate*> out
○ **mat· rrugët** to wander aimlessly
○ **Mate vrapin sa ke hapin!** "Make your speed match your stride!" *(Prov)* Adjust your wants in accordance with your abilities!

mat·et *vpr* **1** to take one's own measurements **2** *(Fig)* to measure up (well) **3** to take measures toward action: get ready to, prepare to; be about to; have a mind to, intend; threaten
○ **S'matet deti me pëllëmbë.** "The sea is not to be measured with the hand." *(Prov)* You need the right tool to do a big job.
○ **mat·et e çmat·et** to think carefully
○ **mat·et me hijen e** {*pronominal adj*} to overrate {*oneself*}, think too much of {*oneself*}
○ **mat·et me hijen e mëngjesit//diellin e mbrëmjes** "measure oneself by the *shadow of morning//sun of evening*" *(Pej)* to think too highly of oneself, be conceited

Mat *nm* river and district in north-central Albania: Mati

Mat *nm* mountainous region north of Tirana

matanë
I § *adv* <**më-atë-anë** on the other side, on that side; over there
II § *prep (abl)* on the other side of: beyond, across

matanëdetas *adj, n* overseas

matanëlumas *adj, n* resident on the other side of the river

matanëmalas *adj, n* resident on the other side of the mountain

matanshëm *adj (i)* on the other side

matanujas *adj, n* resident on the other side of the shore/bank

matara *nf* [*Dairy*] large metal container for milk or other liquids: milk can

****matare** *nf* flask, bottle

matarim *nm ger* <**mataro·n**

mataro·n *vt* **1** to get [] into good order; tidy [things] up; make proper arrangements for [] **2** to finish [] up

****mâtejshëm** *adj (i) (Reg Gheg)* = **mëtejshëm**

matem *nm* [*Relig*] ten-day fast observed by people of the Bektashi faith

matematik *adj* mathematical

matematikan *nm* mathematician

matematikë *nf* mathematics

matematikisht *adv* mathematically

matematikor *adj* = **matematik**

material *nm, adj* material
○ **materiale të imëta elektrike** electrical accessories: fuses, resistors, etc.

◦ **materiale të im**ë**ta ndërtimi** building hardware (such as locks, nails, door handles)

materiali**st** *adj, n* materialist

materiali̇**sht** *adv* from a materialist point of view

materiali̇**zëm** *nm* materialism

materiali̇**zim** *nm ger* <**materializo**̇**·n, materi-alizo**̇·*het*

materiali̇**zo**̇·*het vpr* to become concrete and substantive: materialize

materiali̇**zo**̇·*n vt* to give [] concrete substantive form, make [] concrete: materialize

materialo**-teknik** *adj* material and technical

mate**rie** *nf* [*Phil*] material substance: matter

materik *nm* [*Geol*] parent rock

maternitė**t** *nm* maternity hospital

matë**s**
I § *n* **1** measurer, surveyor **2** measuring device/vessel/indicator/instrument: meter
II § *adj* for measuring

matinë *nf* = **shta**gë

matjȧ**n** *adj, n* of/from the Mat district, native of the Mat district

mȧ**tje** *nf ger* **1** <**ma**̇*t·*, **mat·**et **2** measurement; measure, dimension

matkȧ**p** *nm* auger, gimlet; Archimedes drill

matkë *nf* **1** queen bee **2** brood turkey whose chicks have hatched **3** largest goose at the head of a flock ***4** goose leading her goslings

mȧ**tkëz** *nf (Dimin)* <**matk**ë

matorik *nm* **1** hole dug in the ground to hold water; waterhole **2** irrigation/drainage ditch

matrahul *adj (Old Colloq)* **1** dunderheaded, dull-witted, simple-minded **2** stolid

matrapȧ**z** *nm (Colloq Pej)* **1** black-marketer **2** *(Fig)* person who engages in any sort of dirty business to gain his ends; huckster **3** (business) speculator

matrapazl**lëk** *nm (np ˜ qe) (Colloq Pej)* dirty business

*matravidë *nf* [*Tech*] = **madravid**ë

matriarkȧ**t** *nm* [*Hist*] matriarchate

matricë *nf* [*Spec*] **1** mold/die for casting metal objects: matrix, drawing die, type mat **2** [*Math*] matrix

*matriç̇ë *nf* type matrix

matrikull *nm (np ˜ j)* **1** *(Old)* registered list of members; livestock register; register of armaments in a detachment; registry office **2** registration number; identification tag

*matrisë *nf* = **matri**çë

mȧ**tsh**ëm *adj (i)* **1** measurable **2** commensurate

matuf *nm* person grown senile in the mind: dotard; feeble-minded person

matufė**ps·** *vt* = **matufo**̇**s·**

matufė**ps·**et *vpr* = **matufo**̇**s·**et

matufl**lëk** *nm* childish behavior: dotage, senility

matufȯ**s·** *vt* to make [] dotty, dull the mind of []; confuse

matufȯ**s·**et *vpr* to become dotty, go into one's dotage

matufȯ**sje** *nf ger* <**matufo**̇**s·**, **matufo**̇**s·**et

matufȯ**sur** *adj (i)* in one's dotage, senile, feeble-minded

*matullë *nf* bunch (of vegetables)

maṫ**ur**
I § *adj (i)* **1** of a measured/limited amount/size **2** well-calculated **3** judicious, prudent: mature, sober
II § *nf (e)* [*Food*] cake made by boiling together flour, sugar, butter or oil, and water and then baking it in a pan

maturȧ**nt** *nm* **1** student in the final year of middle school: secondary-school senior **2** secondary-school graduate

maturë *nf* **1** final examinations for graduating from secondary school ("middle school"); final term of secondary school; senior year **2** senior class in secondary school

maturi̇ *nf* prudence; wisdom

matushȯ·*n vt (Reg)* to break [] into tiny pieces, crumble

math = **madh** * = **mbath**

mau̇**n**ë *nf* **1** barge **2** semitrailer, semi, long-haul truck

mȧ**ur** *nm* Moor

mauthi *nf* [*Folklore*] beautiful girl dressed in gold and wearing a jeweled cap

mauzė**r** *nm* **1** five-shot repeating rifle **2** Mauser pistol

mauzole *nm* [*Archit*] mausoleum

mavi̇ *adj (Colloq)* blue; (of a bruise) black and blue

mavijȯ·*n* = **mavijo**̇**s·**

mavijȯ**s·** *vt (Colloq)* to color [] blue, cause [] to turn blue

mavijȯ**s·**et *vpr (Colloq)* **1** to turn blue; turn blue with cold; turn black and blue **2** to get dark, get dark with anger

mavijȯ**sje** *nf* black-and-blue mark, bruise

*mȧ**vonsh**ëm *(Reg Gheg)* = **mëvonësh**ëm

mavriak *nm* [*Ichth*] thicklip gray mullet *(Chelon labrosus)* = **qefull dimri**

*mavzė**r** *nm* repeating rifle: Mauser

maxhallë**k** *nm (np ˜ qe) (Old)* = **paja**ndër

maxhar *adj, n* Magjar, Hungarian = **hungare**z

*Maxhari̇ *nf* Hungary = **Hungari**̇

mȧ**xh**ë *nf (Reg)* flour bin

mazȧ**tar** *adj* [*Dairy*] (of unseparated and unchurned milk) containing all its butterfat

mazȧ**tor** *nm* bull calf, steer

mazȧ**tore** *nf* heifer

mȧ**z**ë *nf* **1** [*Dairy*] butterfat-rich part of milk: cream **2** [*Dairy*] cream cheese **3** [*Dairy*] creamy scum of heated milk **4** thin covering layer; membrane **5** [*Food*] corn-meal cake

mazgȧ**ll**ë *nf* **1** crack, slit; leak **2** embrasure, loophole = **frëngji** **3** fireplace alcove where coffee-making and drinking vessels are kept **4** hollow in a cliff or tree trunk

mazi *nf* **1** plowed earth ready for sowing **2** oak gall from which a dark hair dye is extracted; dark hair dye from oak gall

mazĭ**s** *stem for 1st sg pres, pl pres, 2nd & 3rd sg subj, pind* <**mazi**̇*t·*

mazi̇**t·** *vt* [*Dairy*] to skim [milk]

mazi̇**tje** *nf ger* <**mazit·**, **mazit·**et

mazi̇**tur** *adj (i)* [*Dairy*] (of milk) skimmed; made of skimmed milk

mazo're adj **1** [Dairy] (of milk animals at the beginning of the lactation period) having thick milk, giving foremilk ***2** filly

mazu'rkë nf mazurka

mazu't nm dark viscous industrial fuel oil: mazut

ma'zhë adj, nf (sheep) with a dark brown head

mba·het vpr **1** to hold on **2** to hold up, last; hold firm; survive **3** to support oneself; take care of oneself **4** (Fig) to consider oneself to be __; carry on like __, act like __ **5** (Book) to hold true to $\diamond$, be faithful to $\diamond$ **6** (Fig Colloq) to take sides **7** to be stopped up, not flow easily **8** (of meetings) to be held

○ **Nuk mbahen dy kunguj/shalqinj nën (një) sqetull/në një dorë.** (Prov) You can only do so many things at once.

○ $\diamond$ **mba·het** ^{3sg} **goja** $\diamond$ stutters

○ **nuk** $\diamond$ **mba·het** ^{3sg} **gjaku** $\diamond$ cannot hold $\diamond$'s temper: $\diamond$ loses $\diamond$'s temper

○ **mba·het gjallë** just to keep oneself alive; be still alive

○ **mba·het gjallë** to be holding one's own

○ **mba·het me qesen e tjetrit** "be supported by someone else's sack" to live off of someone else's money

○ **nuk mba·het** ^{3sg} **mend qysh kur** it is beyond recall how long ago

○ **mba·het më të madh** to have one's nose in the air, act arrogant/haughty; boast; show off, strut

○ **mba·het në jetë** to stay alive, hang on to life, be still alive

○ **mba·het në këmbë** to be holding one's own

○ **mba·het pas flokëve të** {pronominal adj} "be supported by {one's} hair" (Iron) to rely on a weak kind of support: be standing on thin ice

○ $\diamond$ **mba·het** ^{3sg} **ujët** (Euph) $\diamond$ is unable to urinate

mba·n

I § vt **1** to bear, carry; wear **2** to hold; contain **3** to hold on to []; keep; maintain; support **4** to keep going in [a direction]: keep to [] **5** to hold [] off **6** [Mus] to sing the supporting voice or drone in polyphonic folk singing; join in [the dance] **7** to deliver [] by speaking, give [a lecture/speech/lesson] **8** to consider [] as, take [] for **9** (Colloq) to aim at [] (with a gun) **10** to last [a length of time]; (of a trip) take [a length of time]

II § vi to last; continue

○ $\diamond$a **mba·n 1** (Colloq Crude) $\diamond$ dares: $\diamond$ has the guts **2** (Colloq) to hit $\diamond$ (hard), get $\diamond$ **Afrohu dhe mbaja mu në ballë!** Get close and shoot him right through the forehead!

○ **ia mba·n** to head (in a direction), set out

○ **nuk** $\diamond$a **mba·n** (Colloq) $\diamond$ does not dare: does not have the guts

○ [] **mba·n** {} (Colloq) to sell [] {for a price}

○ $\diamond$ **mba·n anën** to show bias toward $\diamond$, be partial to $\diamond$

○ **s'**[] **mba·n** ^{3sg} **as qielli, as dheu/toka** "neither the sky nor the earth can bear [the affront]" [it] is too much to put up with, [it] is too much to take: that is just too much!

○ $\diamond$[] **mba·n avaz** to keep reminding $\diamond$ of [], keep throwing [] in $\diamond$'s face

○ $\diamond$ **mba·n avazin** to do anything to please/satisfy $\diamond$

○ **e mba·n ballin lart** to hold one's head high, stand proud

○ **s'**$\diamond$ **mba·n** ^{3sg} **barku gjë** $\diamond$ can't keep a single secret

○ **mba·n barkun me dorë** "hold one's belly with one's hands" **1** to go without food, do without eating **2** to break up with laughter

○ **e mba·n barutin (të) thatë** to keep one's powder dry, be ready for battle

○ $\diamond$ **mba·n bishtin** to follow $\diamond$ slavishly as a lackey

○ **e mba·n bishtin cakërr** (said of women) to be snooty: keeps her nose in the air

○ **mba·n bishtin përpjetë** "hold one's tail up in air" to be swell-headed, be conceited

○ **mba·n brinjët me duar** to break up with laughter

○ **e mba·n çapin** to halt, hold up

○ **mba·n çelësat e kashtës** "hold the keys to the straw" (Iron) to have no influence/power

○ **e mba·n derën hapur/çelur 1** to keep one's door open: welcome visitors at any time **2** (Old) to continue the family line

○ **mba·n dizgjinët** to hold the reins: be in control

○ **e mba·n dorën** to be sparing with, be careful about spending

○ $\diamond$a **mba·n dorën** to show special concern to $\diamond$, treat $\diamond$ special

○ **mba·n dorën 1** to refrain from hitting (someone) **2** to control one's spending, spend sparingly

○ **e mba·n dorën në çark të pushkës** to keep one's hand on the trigger: be ever ready

○ **mba·n drejtimin** to hold course

○ **i mba·n dyert hapur/çelur 1** to keep one's door open: welcome visitors at any time **2** (Old) to continue the family line

○ **s'**$\diamond$ **mba·n** ^{3sg} **dheu** $\diamond$ can't sit still

○ $\diamond$ **mba·n erë** to give $\diamond$ a sniff: smell $\diamond$

○ **mba·n** ^{3sg} **erë barut** "there is the smell of gunpowder" there is a smell of war/battle in the air

○ **mba·n erë myk 1** to smell musty **2** to have old-fashioned ideas

○ **mba·n erë** {} to have the smell of {}, reek of {}, smell of {}

○ **mba·n ferra lakuriq** "carry thorns naked" to be involved in something very difficult

○ **mba·n fjalën 1** to keep one's word **2** to give a speech

○ **mba·n flamurin** "hold the flag" **1** to have the leading position **2** to be famous/notorious

○ **mba·n frerin** to hold the whip hand, be in the driver's seat; be at the controls, be in control

○ **e mba·n frerin ngrehur** to be strict; maintain tight control

○ **e mba·n frymën** {} "hold one's breath until reaching {}" to make a quick getaway {to somewhere}

○ **mba·n frymën gjallë me** [] to live on []

○ **mba·n frymën** to hold one's breath

○ **e mba·n gishtin në këmbëz** to have/keep one's finger on the trigger, be ready for battle

○ **s'**$\diamond$ **mba·n** ^{3sg} **goja arra** "$\diamond$'s mouth can't hold walnuts" $\diamond$ never stops talking, $\diamond$ is a big windbag

○ **s'**$\diamond$ **mban goja arra** "$\diamond$'s mouth can't hold walnuts" $\diamond$ is a chatterbox

○ $\diamond$ **mba·n** ^{3sg} **goja erë qumësht** "$\diamond$'s mouth still has a milk smell" to still be a child; still be wet behind the ears

○ $\diamond$ **mban goja erë qumësht** "$\diamond$'s mouth smells of milk" to be very young

○ **e mba·n gojën** to hold one's tongue

◦ **mba·**_n_$^{2ndimperativ/subj}$ **gojën** hold your tongue! stop saying such things!

◦ **mba·**_n_ **gjarprin në gji** to harbor a viper in ◇'s bosom

◦ **mba·**_n_ **gjilpërat majë më majë** to be at loggerheads

◦ **mbaje gjuhën pas/prapa dhëmbëve!** "keep your tongue behind your teeth" don't speak!

◦ **mbaje gjuhën!** you should watch your tongue!; hold your tongue!

◦ **mba·**_n_ **hapëset e kashtës** "hold the keys to the straw" _(Iron)_ to have no influence/power

◦ **mba·**_n_ **hapin/hapat 1** to keep in step **2** to stop walking (and hold still)

◦ **<> mba·**_n_ **hapin** to keep ◇ back, stop ◇

◦ **nuk mba·**_n_^{3rd} **hekur** not keep _its_ crease, _wrinkles_ easily

◦ **e mba·**_n_ **hundën lart/përpjetë** _(Iron)_ to have one's nose in the air: be stuck up

◦ **e mba·**_n_ **hundën në qiell** "hold one's nose in the sky" to become stuck up, become conceited

◦ **<> mba·**_n_ **inatin** to hold a grudge against ◇

◦ **<> mba·**_n_ **ison 1** to sing the drone accompanying _<the lead singer>_ **2** _(Pej)_ to be ◇'s yes-man

◦ **mba·**_n_ **ison** to sing the accompanying drone

◦ **mba·**_n_ **jaz** _(Old)_ to remain in mourning

◦ **<> mba·**_n_ **kandilin** to be present and helpful during ◇'s wrongful act

◦ **mba·**_n_ **këmbët** to stop walking (and hold still)

◦ [ ] **mba·**_n_ **kokë e lart** to put [ ] on a pedestal, revere [ ] above all others

◦ **<>a mba·**_n_ **kokën mënjanë** to avoid ◇ out of resentment

◦ **e mba·**_n_ **kokën lart 1** to hold one's head high, be proud **2** to think too highly of oneself

◦ **<> mba·**_n_ **konferencë** _(Iron)_ to lecture ◇ at long length, give ◇ a long lecture

◦ **mba·**_n_ **krahun e <>** to take ◇'s side, support ◇

◦ **mba·**_n_ **krahun** to stay in one's own traffic lane

◦ **<> mba·**_n_^{3sg} **kuleta** ◇ _has_ money

◦ **nuk <>a mba·**_n_^{3sg} **kurrizi** it would take more than ◇ _can_ bear, ◇ is not up to it

◦ **nuk <>a mba·**_n_^{3sg} **lëkura** ◇ _can't_ take/stand it anymore

◦ [ ] **mba·**_n_ **mbi trup** to be burdened by [ ], [ ] _is_ a burden to {}, [ ] _is_ a weight on {}'s back

◦ [ ] **mba·**_n_ **me erë të mollës** to placate [ ] by dangling false promises before [ ]'s nose; lead [ ] on by dangling a carrot before [ ]'s nose

◦ [ ] **mba·**_n_ **me bukë e me gjellë** to keep [ ] in food, provide [ ] with food

◦ [ ] **mba·**_n_ **me llafe/fjalë** to keep [ ]'s hopes up with words

◦ **Mbaje me shëndet!** "Wear it in good health!" _(Iron)_ It's your own fault.

◦ [ ] **mba·**_n_ **me ujë të ngrohtë/vakët** "keep [ ] in warm water" to treat [ ] with nice words but no action, forestall [ ] with nice words

◦ [ ] **mba·**_n_ **me kimet** to treasure [ ]

◦ **mba·**_n_ **mend** "hold in mind" to remember

◦ **mba·**_n_$^{2ndimperativ/subj}$ **mendjen!** (you should) use your brains! keep calm!

◦ [ ] **mba·**_n_ **më këmbë** to keep [ ] alive; prop [ ] up, hold [ ] together: maintain [ ]

◦ **nuk mba·**_n_^{3sg} **më kupa!** "the cup _doesn't_ hold any more" that _is_ the limit!

◦ **nuk mba·**_n_^{3sg} **më ujë orizi/pilafi/kosi/vera** "the rice/yogurt/wine won't hold/take more water" matters _have_ come to a head, things _have_ gone too far

◦ [ ] **mba·**_n_ **në fre** to keep [ ] under control

◦ [ ] **mba·**_n_ **në gojë** to hold [ ] dear in thought and word, keep talking (kindly) about [ ]; constantly mention [ ], be always talking about [ ]

◦ **mba·**_n_ **në gjirin e** {_pronominal adj_} to contain in {_one's_} midst: harbor in {_one's_} bosom

◦ [ ] **mba·**_n_ **në pëllëmbë/shuplakë të dorës** to provide well for [ ], assure [ ] a comfortable life

◦ [ ] **mba·**_n_ **në shenjë** to keep a careful watch on [ ]

◦ [ ] **mba·**_n_ **në të hostenit** to take good care of [ ], put under one's aegis

◦ **e mba·**_n_ **në torbë bukën e barutin** "keep food and gunpowder in one's pouch" to be prepared to meet any danger

◦ [ ] **mba·**_n_ **në vend** to hold [ ] in place, keep [ ] from moving; not allow [ ] to get ahead, hold [ ] back

◦ [ ] **mba·**_n_ **nën hije të hostenit** to take good care of [ ], put under one's aegis

◦ [ ] **mba·**_n_ **nën hijen e** {_pronominal adj_} to have [ ] under {_one's_} own care/protection

◦ [ ] **mba·**_n_ **nën jastëk** to bear [ ] in mind

◦ **<> mba·**_n_ **nën kërbaç** to keep ◇ under the constant threat of force: hold a sword over ◇'s head

◦ [ ] **mba·**_n_ **nëpër gojë** _(Pej)_ to gossip about [ ]

◦ **mba·**_n_ **një drugë** to keep saying the same thing every time: sing the same tune over and over

◦ **mba·**_n_ **një fjalim** to deliver a speech, make a speech

◦ **(<>) mba·**_n_ **pajë** to show unjustified bias (in favor of ◇)

◦ ([ ]) **mba·**_n_ **parasysh** to keep clearly [ ] in mind, keep [ ] always before [ ], pay attention

◦ **mba·**_n_ **pehriz në** [ ] to refrain from [ ]

◦ **e mba·**_n_ **penën të mprehtë** "keep the pen sharp" not lose one's ability to write

◦ [ ] **mba·**_n_ **për asgjë** "consider [ ] as nothing" to look down one's nose on [ ], despise [ ]

◦ [ ] **mba·**_n_ **për** to consider [ ] as, take [ ] to be

◦ **<> mba·**_n_ **pishën** to be present and helpful during ◇'s wrongful act

◦ **nuk mba·**_n_ **pluhur mbi vete** "not keep dust in one's ear" not take an affront lightly

◦ **nuk mba·**_n_ **pluhur në vesh** "not keep dust in one's ear" to be easily offended, be prickly/touchy

◦ [ ] **mba·**_n_ **pranë** to be of constant support to [ ]

◦ **e mba·**_n_ **qefinin me vete** "carry one's shroud by oneself" **1** to have no fear of death **2** to sense the approach of death

◦ **<> mba·**_n_^{3sg} **qesja** ◇'s money will hold out, ◇ _can afford_ it, ◇ _has_ enough money

◦ **mba·**_n_ **radhimin** [_Mil_] to stay in formation/rank

◦ **rakia mba·**_n_^{3sg} **zinxhir** "the raki forms chains (of bubbles when shaken)" the raki is very strong

◦ **mba·**_n_ **sehir** _(Pej)_ to look on without helping or taking part, sit comfortably on the sidelines

◦ **mba·**_n_ **sëpatën nën gunë** to be capable of stabbing one in back, not to be trusted

◦ [ ] **mba·**_n_ **si breshka dheun** to guard [ ] carefully

◦ **<> mba·**_n_ **si penez në pëllëmbë të dorës** "hold ◇ like a coin in the palm of one's hand" to give ◇ the best of treatment; keep/treat ◇ as something precious

◦ [ ] **mba·**_n_ **si ujët e paktë** "treat [ ] like water in short supply" to treat [ ] as precious

∘ [] **mba·**n **si zogun majë gjembit** to treat [] with special favor

∘ **mba·**n **syrin në shtjekëz** to keep one's eyes peeled, stay vigilant

∘ **i mba·**n **sytë dollap** to keep one's eyes open, be vigilant

∘ **i mba·**n **sytë hapur** to keep one's eyes open, be ever vigilant

∘ **mba·**n **sytë nga** {} to keep an eye on {}

∘ **i mba·**n **sytë te** {} to hang one's hopes on {}

∘ **e mba·**n **shatin në ujë** "hold one's hoe in water" to work in vain, waste one's effort

∘ **mba·**n **shënim për** [] to take note of [], bear [] in mind

∘ <> **mba·**n^{3pl} **shpatullat** <> *has* the ability/backbone required for []: <> *has* what it takes

∘ **nuk** <>a **mba·**n^{3sg} **shpina** it would take more than <> *can* bear, <> *is* not up to it

∘ **mba·**n **shpirtin gjallë me** [] to live on []

∘ [] **mba·**n **të mprehtë** to keep [] ready to use at a moment's notice

∘ **nuk** [] **mba·**n^{3sg} **toka** "even the earth *does* not tolerate []" **1** [such things] *cannot* be tolerated, [something] *is* utterly contemptible, [] is unspeakable **2** []'s feet *don't touch* the ground (because [] *is* so happy); [] *flies* off the handle (with anger)

∘ **e mba·**n **trupin beng** to hold one's body erect

∘ **mba·**n$^{2ndimperativ/subj}$ **udhën** "keep to your path" *(Colloq)* mind your own business

∘ **mba·**n **ujë me shoshë/shportë** "hold water with a screen/basket" to do useless work

∘ **ia mba·**n **va pa va** to leave without knowing where one is going

∘ [] **mba·**n **vath në vesh** "keep [] as an earring in one's ear" to try never to forget []; make a reminder of [] for future revenge

∘ **mba·**n$^{2ndimperativ/subj}$ **vendin** "keep your place" *(Colloq Pej)* stick to your own business, keep your big nose out of other people's business

∘ **mba·**n **verë e pi· ujë** "keep wine and drink water" **1** to be miserly **2** to get no advantage from a position from which one might be expected to gain

∘ <> **mba·**n **vesh** to listen to <> obediently: listen to <>, obey <>

∘ **mba·**n **vesh** to listen, listen attentively

∘ **i mba·**n **veshët kapëz** to keep one's ears open

∘ **i mba·**n **veshët përpjetë/ngritur** to stay alert: keep one's ears pricked/open

∘ **i mba·**n **veshët pipëz/bigë/curr/çift/gërshërë/katër** to listen (in) attentively: listen with all ears, be all ears

∘ **mba·**n **veten për të madh** to think oneself to be so high and mighty, act self-important

∘ **e mba·**n **veten 1** to keep oneself in good condition, take good care of oneself **2** to dress neatly **3** to keep oneself under control **4** to maintain one's pride

∘ **mba·**n **veten gjallë me** [] to live on []

∘ **mba·**n **vezë në tundës** "keep an egg in the churn" to hold on to everything; be very careful and thrifty

∘ **e mba·**n **vrapin** to take a rest after great exertion, hold up

∘ **nuk** <>a **mba·**n^{3sg} **xhepi** <> *cannot* afford to pay

∘ **nuk** <>a **mba·**n **zava** "the hook won't support <>" it would take more than <> *can* bear, <> *is* not up to it

∘ <> **mba·**n **zërin** to do as <> wants; agree with whatever <> says

∘ **mba·**n **zi** "wear mourning clothes" to be in mourning

∘ **Mbaje zogun sa e ke në dorë!** "Hold on to however many birds you have in hand!" *(Prov)* Use whatever opportunities you have! Don't miss your chances!

*****mba**jc*ë* = mba**js*ë*

mbajs*ë* *nf* support, prop; holder; banister

mbajt *stem for pdef, opt, adm, part* <**mba·**n

∘ <>[] **mbajti dhëmbi** <> stopped just short of saying [], <> bit <>'s tongue to keep from saying []

*****mba**jt*ë* *nf* standard of living

mbajt*ës*

I § *adj* bearing, supporting, reinforcing

II § *n* **1** bearer, carrier; wearer **2** supporter, support **3** keeper, maintainer **4** [*Mus*] singer of the supporting (second) voice or drone **5** prop, support

mbajt*ëse* *nf* **1** holder; container **2** forked stick supporting a grapevine

mbajtje *nf ger* **1** <**mba·**n, mba·het **2** containment; maintenance; holding

mbajt*ur*

I § *part* <**mba·**n

II § *adj* (i) **1** well-kept, well-maintained, well-preserved; well-grown, well-raised; healthy and young-looking **2** previously worn/used: used **3** *(Colloq)* restrained, conservative, cautious, prudent

III § *n* (i) paralyzed person, paralytic

*****mball**afa*qe* *adv* = ballafa**qe

mballes*ë* *nf (Reg)* = kullo**t*ë*

mballi*m* *nm (Reg)* path trodden down by livestock on their way to pasture

mballo·*n* *vt* **1** *(Reg)* to drive [livestock] to pasture **2** = mballo**s·**

mballom*ata*r *nm (Colloq)* shoe repairman

mballom*axhi* *nm (np ~ nj) (Colloq)* = mballo**mata**r

mballo*më* *nf (Colloq)* **1** patch (for old shoes/clothes) **2** *(Fig Pej)* quick and dirty patch, temporary fix

mballos· *vt (Colloq)* **1** to patch **2** *(Fig Pej)* to patch over [a deficiency] by a cover-up

∘ <>a **mballos·** *(Fig Pej)* to lay [the blame] on <>

*****mball**os*ës* *nm (Old)* cobbler

mballos*ur* *adj* (i) *(Colloq)* patched

mban*ë*

I § *adv* **1** alongside; nearby **2** on the other side, beyond

II § *prep (abl)* **1** beside, by, next to **2** on the other side of, beyond

∘ **mbanë tjetër** *(Colloq Regional Tosk)* on the other hand

*****mba**n*shëm* *adj* (i) lateral

*****mba**nj*ës* = mba**jt*ës*

mbar· *vt* = mbar**t·**

mbar·et *vpr* = mbart·et

*****mbar**as = bar**as

*****mbar**az = bar**az

mbarazi *adv* right side up

*****mbarc**o ·*n* = mbarso·*n*

*****mbarc**u̇es *adj* fertilizing, inseminating

mbar|e's∙ë *nf* **1** [*Ling*] inflectional ending **2** termination, ending

mba'rë
I § *adj (i)* **1** with the good side showing: right side up, front side facing forward/out **2** decent, proper; well-behaved **3** developing nicely, growing well; bountiful **4** favorable, proper; going well, successful; prosperous
II § *nf (e)* **1** the good/right/front side (of a material object) **2** benefit, advantage
III § *adv* **1** with the good side showing: right side up, front side facing forward/out **2** successfully; well, prosperously **3** just as it is, in its entirety; just as it comes, in due order
IV § *determiner* the entire __; all __ without exception
V § *nf* = **ba'rrë**
  ○ **mbarë e mirë** extremely well, couldn't be better
  ○ **mbarë e prapë/mbrapsht** from one end to another, thoroughly
  ○ **Të vaftë pushka mbarë** "May your gun have success!" *(Felic)* Good luck in battle!
  ○ [] **sjell∙ në rrugë/udhë të mbarë** "bring [] to the right path" to put [] on the right path; get [] in order

mbar|ë|kthi'm *nm* [*Postal*] facing (up)

mbar|ë|si *nf* good luck/fortune; success

mbar|ë|si'sht *adv* in a good way, nicely, well

mbar|ë|s|o'∙het *vpr* to get on the proper track; head for success

mbar|ë|s|o'∙n *vt* **1** to put [] on the proper track; make [] successful **2** = mbarështo'∙n

mbar|ë|sht|i'm *nm ger* < mbarështo'∙n

mbar|ë|sht|o'∙n *vt* **1** to put [] right, straighten [] up, put [] in proper order: manage [] properly **2** to breed

mbar|ë|shtr| = matar|

mbar|ë|sht|u'es *nm* **1** caretaker **2** breeder

mbar|ë|vajtje *nf* successful progress; progress (toward success)

mbar|i *adv (së)* **1** properly, well **2** enjoying good luck: successfully

mbar|i'm *nm ger* **1** < mbaro'∙n, mbaro'∙het **2** termination, end; finish, conclusion

mbar|o'∙het *vpr* **1** to come to an end; (of a period of time) pass **2** to be finished up; run out **3** to waste away (because of some affliction or illness)

mbar|o'∙n
I § *vt* **1** to bring [] to completion: complete, finish **2** to bring to a finish: stop **3** to finish [] up/off, use up **4** to comply with [a request/order]
II § *vi* **1** to come to an end; expire **2** *(Colloq)* to die; be unable to continue **3** to end up
  ○ **mbaro∙n me liq e me shpatë** to lose one's health; fall upon hard times
  ○ **mbaro∙n me të gjitha 1** to lose everything; have nothing left **2** to have come down to the end
  ○ **mbaro∙n**^{past} **me të tëra** to have nothing at all left, be down to nothing
  ○ **mbaro∙n pas <>** *(Fig Colloq)* (hyperbole) be crazy about <>, be infatuated with
  ○ **mbaro∙n për gjumë** *(Colloq)* to be badly in need of sleep
  ○ **mbaro∙n për** [] *(Fig Colloq)* (hyperbole) be dying for [], crave []
  ○ **<> mbaro∙n punë** to help <> out

mbar|o's|ë *nf (Old)* [*Ethnog*] = **bu'llë**

mbars∙
I § *vt* to make [] pregnant, impregnate; inseminate

II § *stem for 1st sg pres, pl pres, 2nd & 3rd sg subj, pind* * < mbart∙

mba'rs∙et *vpr* (of animals) to get pregnant, conceive
  ○ **Nuk mbarset mushka të pjellë mëz.** "A mule does not get pregnant to give birth to a foal." *(Prov)* There are some things that are just impossible.

mba'rs|ë *adj* **1** (of animals) pregnant: with calf, in foal **2** to become loaded/heavy/full; swell up, fill up

*mbars|i *nf* mating season, rut, heat

*mbarsi'sht *adv* favorably, happily

mba'rs|je *nf ger* **1** < mbars∙, mbars∙et **2** pregnancy

mbars|m|ëri *nf (Book)* **1** (in animals) ability to get pregnant: fertileness **2** (in animals) pregnancy

*mbars|o'∙n *vt(Old)* **1** = mbars∙ **2** *(Fig)* to infect **3** to forward, dispatch

*mba'rs|un *adj (i)* *(Reg Gheg)* fertilized, fertile

mbars|ur|i *nn (të)* impregnation, fecundation

mbart∙ *vt* **1** to bear, carry, transport, convey **2** [*Fin*] to carry over [] **3** *(Fig)* to possess, hold
  ○ **mbart∙ plaçkat** to change residences: move
  ○ **mbart∙ verë e pi∙ ujë** "keep wine and drink water" **1** to be miserly **2** to get no advantage from a position from which one might be expected to gain

mba'rt∙et *vpr* to take one's belongings and change residence: move

mba'rt|ës
I § *adj* carrying
II § *n* carrier

mba'rt|je *nf ger* < mbart∙, mbart∙et

*mba'rth = mardhë

mbar|u'ar *adj (i)* **1** complete **2** completed, finished **3** fulfilled **4** over and done with; dead; out of stock, all gone

*mba'rre *nf(Reg)* shame, dishonor, disgrace

*mba'rrë = barrë

*mbarr|o'∙het *vpr* **1** to be ashamed; be bashful/shy **2** to fall into disgrace

*mbarr|o'∙n *vt(Reg)* to bring shame upon [], disgrace []

*mba'rr|shëm *adj (i)* bashful

mbas *adv, prep (abl)* = pas
  ○ **mbas gjase** probably, likely

*mbas *stem for 1st sg pres, pl pres, 2nd & 3rd sg subj, pind* < mbat∙

mbas|anda'j *adv* = pastaj

mbas|bje'shkë *nf* region lying beyond the high mountain pastures

mbas|da'rkë *nf* = pasda'rkë

mbas|di'te *adv* = pasdi'te

mba'se *pcl* perhaps, maybe

mbas|gru'shtë *nf* = pasgru'shtë

mbas|i *conj* = pasi

*mbas|kë'nda|j = paskëtaj

mbas|kre *nf* = paskry'e

mbas|kry'e *nn* = paskry'e

mbas|ne'sër *adv* = pasne'sër

mbas|qa'fe *nf* = pasqa'fe

*mbashk|o'∙n = bashko'∙n

*mbashtr|o'∙n *vt* **1** to feed [] from the hand **2** *(Fig)* to tip; bribe *3* = mashtro'∙n

*mbat∙ *vt* to try [] out

mbath∙ *vt* **1** to clothe all or part of the lower body (below the waist): put on [legwear/footwear] **2** to provide <> with [legwear/footwear] **3** to shoe [a horse/mule] **4** *(Colloq)* to put tires on [a vehicle] **5** to repair

[] by applying a metal patch **6** to fill up and cover over [an empty space or hole] **7** [*Agr*] to bank loose soil around [a plant]: earth up [] **8** [*Agr*] to mulch **9** (*Colloq*) to stuff/gorge [] with food **10** (*Fig Colloq*) to lay [blame/fault] on <>, pin [blame] on <> **11** (*Fig Colloq*) to chastise []: really lay it on []
○ **ia mbath·** (*Colloq*) to get away quick: scram
○ **ua mbath· këmbëve** to run away as fast as possible, take to one's heels
○ **<>i mbath· këpucët** (*Impol*) to give <> a good lesson (in proper behavior)
○ **ia mbath· me të katra** to run away fast: take off on all fours
○ **mbath· pleshtat me potkonj** "put horseshoes on fleas" to waste time trying to do the impossible, just be spinning one's wheels
○ **<>i mbath· potkonjtë** "shoe <> with horseshoes" (*Impol*) to teach <> a good lesson
○ **<>a mbath· vrapit** to take to one's heels, speed away

mbath·et *vpr* **1** to wear/put on clothes on the lower body (below the waist) **2** to provide oneself with legwear/footwear **3** to be shod; be wearing legwear/footwear **4** to get covered on the bottom with a layer of something **5** (*Colloq*) to get stuffed (with food); gorge oneself

mbathë *nf* **1** repair patch made of wood or metal **2** horseshoe **3** footwear

mbathës
I § *adj* used for heaping loose soil around a plant; for mulching
II § *nm* **1** shoehorn *2 farrier

mbathje *nf ger* **1** <mbath·, mbath·et **2** [*Agr*] mulch covering around a plant **3** footwear **4** [*Geol*] aggradation *()* **5** underwear

mbathtar *nm* farrier

mbathtore *nf* place for shoeing draft animals: farriery

mbathur *adj (i)* **1** wearing legwear/footwear: clad in shoes and stockings **2** shod **3** (*Fig*) provided with the bare necessities of life **4** (of tools) patched up with a new part **5** overlaid with a covering of earth/rock

mbathura *np (të)* = brekë
mbeç *stem for opt* <mbet·
*mbes· *vt* to dazzle
mbes *stem for 1st sg pres, pl pres, 2nd & 3rd sg subj, pind* <mbet·
mbesë *nf* **1** daughter of one's son or daughter: granddaughter **2** daughter of one's brother or sister: niece
*mbesim = besim
*mbeso·n = beso·n
mbesollë *nf* = mbesë
mbet· *vi* **1** to stay **2** to remain; be left (over); come out of it, come away **3** to stick without moving: stay concentrated; get stuck **4** to end one's life: die **5** (*Colloq*) to come to an agreement **6** (*Colloq*) to start, begin
○ **nuk mbet·**^{3sg} **as një për qyqe** "not even one *remains* to serve as cuckoo (mourner)" not a single one *is* left
○ **s'<> mbet·**^{3sg} **asnjë pikë lëndyrë** "not a bit of (protective) fat *remains* on <>" <>'s shameful character *is* revealed
○ **mbet· bërllok** to still be a mess
○ **mbet· bic** to remain empty-handed, be left with nothing

○ **mbet· bilbil** to have nothing left, be flat broke
○ **mbet· birë në zemër** to stick in <>'s heart (as a deep regret)
○ **mbet· në bisht të urës//te bishti i urës** "remain at the end of a bridge" (of a person) to lag behind
○ **mbet· bitërr** to be stunted in growth, remain thin and weak
○ **<> mbet· brengë** to remain a constant source of regret for <>
○ **mbet· brisk 1** to have nothing left, be flat broke **2** to get stuck with nothing
○ **<> mbet· cingare** to be a burden on <>; weigh heavily on <>, hang over <>'s head
○ **mbet· dërrasë** to have nothing left, be flat broke
○ **mbet· fishek** (*Colloq*) **1** to have nothing left: be flat broke **2** to be abandoned and left all alone
○ **mbet· gisht 1** to remain all alone **2** to have nothing left, be flat broke
○ **<> mbet·**^{3sg} **goja** <> *cannot* speak any more, suddenly *falls* silent
○ **<> mbet·**^{3sg} **goja çark** (*Pej*) <>'s mouth never *stops*, <> *talks* without a stop: <> *runs* off at the mouth
○ **<> mbet·**^{3sg} **goja për** []*//tek* {} <> *keeps* talking about []/{}
○ **mbet· gojëthatë** to be left with nothing; be left out in the cold
○ **<> mbet· gozhdë** to be a constant cause of regret to <>
○ **s'<> mbet· gjë në shpatull** <> *has* nothing left, <> *has* nothing left in the house
○ **mbet· havadan//në hava 1** to hover **2** to be wavering, be undecided **3** to be in uncertain circumstances: be hanging in air
○ **mbet· jashtë çanakut** (*Pej*) to be left out of a shady deal, get no share of the haul/loot
○ **mbet· jashtë** (*Colloq*) to be left out, be excluded
○ **mbet· kalli 1** to be left all alone; be left very poor/wretched **2** to be left naked **3** to have nothing left, be flat broke
○ **Mbet·**^{3sg} **kaposhi/kokoshi një thelë** "The rooster *is* reduced to one slice" Out of what seemed a lot there's almost nothing left.
○ **nuk mbet· këmbë njeriu** not a trace of a single living person *is* left
○ **<> mbet·**^{3sg} **kocka në fyt** <> *suffers* the consequences of <>'s own failure
○ **<> mbet· kunj** to be a constant cause of regret to <>, still sticks in <>'s heart
○ **<> mbet·**^{3sg} **lëkura në bishtin e sëpatës** "<>'s skin *remains* on the handle of <>'s axe" <>'s whole life *is* dedicated to logging
○ **<> mbet·**^{3sg} **luga në pilaf** "<>'s spoon *is* stuck in the cooked rice" (*Iron*) to be embarrassed by one's obvious guilt
○ **<> mbet·**^{3sg} **luga në qull** "<>'s spoon *stays* in the mush" (*Iron*) <> *is* not even listened to, <>'s opinion doesn't count
○ **mbet· mbrapa** to survive
○ **mbet· me dhëmbë jashtë** (*Pej*) to keep baring one's teeth and laughing: keep up a cackle
○ **mbet· me gojë hapur** to be very surprised/amazed
○ **mbet· me gojë thatë** "remain with a dry mouth" to get nothing to eat

○ **mbet· me lugë** *të zbrazët/bosh* "stay with empty spoon" to be left with nothing; have nothing to eat

○ **mbet· me një grusht miza** "be left with a handful of flies" to be left with nothing, get no share

○ **mbet· me vaj në buzë** "stay with a lament on the lip" **1** to be in constant mourning **2** to be a constant complainer, never stop complaining

○ **mbet· me veshë përpjetë** "stand still with ears pricked up" to listen for something, scan one's ears

○ **mbet· në mes të rrugës** "be left in the middle of the road" **1** to be left high and dry **2** to hang around in the streets

○ <> **mbet· mëllë** to be a constant cause of regret to <>

○ <> **mbet·**^{3sg} **murriz në zemër** "remain a thorn in <>'s heart" to weigh heavily on <>'s heart

○ **mbet· në bisht** to lag behind

○ <> **mbet· në derë** "be left at <>'s door" **1** to annoy <> with frequent visits **2** to be a constant burden on <>

○ **mbet· në derë të prindërve** "be left at one's parents' door" to remain an old maid

○ **mbet· në diell** to be left destitute

○ <> **mbet· në dorë 1** to fall apart right in front of <>, fall apart in <>'s hands **2** to faint/die right in front of <>, faint/die in <>'s hands

○ <> **mbet·**^{3rd} **në dorë** to collapse while in <>'s hands, break/faint while under <>'s responsibility

○ <> **mbet· në kokë** "remain in <>'s mind" <> *can't get {something} out of* <>'s head

○ **mbet· në mish** to be left naked

○ <> **mbet· në qafë** "get stuck on <>'s neck" to pick on <> unfairly

○ **mbet· në** *rrugë/mes të rrugës* to be left undone, remain unfinished, still be only partly done

○ **mbet· në udhë** to still be on the road, not finish the trip

○ **mbet· në** *udhë/mes të udhës* to be left in the middle of the road, be left in midstream

○ **mbet· në vend 1** to stay put **2** to get stuck in place **3** to drop dead on the spot

○ **mbet· në vend-numëro** to make no progress: spin one's wheels

○ **mbet· në zall** to be left in the lurch

○ **mbet· në** [ ] to flunk [ ]

○ <> **mbet·**^{3sg} **njolla me bojë** "be left with dyed spots" <> *is* stained with shame forever

○ **mbet· pa çati** not have a roof over one's head, have no place to call home, be homeless

○ **mbet· pa gojë** to be speechless (out of surprise, happiness, etc.), be amazed, stand speechless

○ **mbet· pa mend (në kokë)** to be shocked/awestricken/amazed

○ **mbet· pa mend/gojë** "be stuck without mind/speech" to be speechless with amazement: be dumbfounded

○ **mbet· pa para e pa pullë** "be left without money and without a button" to left without a penny

○ <> **mbet· peng** to remain a constant cause of regret to <>

○ <> **mbet· peronë** to be a constant cause of regret to <>

○ **mbet· pezul** to be stuck in one place; not make a move, just lie/sit there for a long time

○ s'<> **mbet·**^{3sg} **pikë gjaku në fytyrë** "not a drop of blood *remains* in <>'s face" <>'s face *goes* ashen, <> *goes* completely pale

○ **mbet· pip** to have nothing left, be flat broke

○ <> **mbet· plëng** to become the object of <>'s longing and immediate concern: <> *misses* and really *worries* about { } now

○ **mbet· plloçë** to sit dead in one place

○ <> **mbet·**^{3sg} **pushka mbi gozhdë** *(Old)* "<>'s gun *remains* on the nail" to have no males left in <>'s family (who could shoot a gun)

○ **mbet· pykë** to be in trouble, be in a tight spot

○ <> **mbet·**^{3sg} **qejfi** <> still *feels* indignant from an affront

○ **mbet· qiri** to be in a tight spot, be in difficulty

○ **mbet· qiri në këmbë 1** to stand up straight without moving for a long time, stand at attention for a long time **2** to wait a long time

○ **mbet· rrasë në diell** "remain like a rock slab in the sun" to be left flat broke, be left with nothing to one's name

○ **mbet· rrip daulleje** to be flat broke

○ **mbet· në rrugë të madhe** "be left in the highway" **1** to be left high and dry **2** to hang around idly, loaf around in the streets

○ **mbet· rrugëve 1** to hang around idly, loaf around in the streets **2** to leave forever; drop out of sight; die **3** to be left high and dry

○ **mbet·**^{3sg} **sahati** the watch/clock *stops*

○ <> **mbet·**^{3sg} **samari nën bark** "<>'s packsaddle to *hangs* under the belly" <> *is* in serious trouble

○ **mbet· si bariu pa bagëti** to be abandoned by one's followers

○ **mbet· si caran i vatrës** to be left alone in the world

○ **mbet· si dyfeku pa lloz** "remain like a rifle without a bolt" to be left unable to do anything, be left helpless

○ **mbet· si gisht i lëpirë** "remain like a licked finger" to be left with nothing

○ **mbet· si guri në mes të pellgut** "remain like a rock in the middle of a pond" to be left all alone in the world

○ **mbet· si guri në mes të pellgut** to be left all alone in the world and miserable: be forlorn

○ **mbet· si guri në ujë/zall/lumë** to be left all alone, be forlorn

○ **mbet· si hu (gardhi) 1** to be dumbfounded **2** not know what to say/do

○ **mbet· si lis pa degë** to be left all alone in the world

○ **mbet· si peshku në gjanë/zall** "be left like a fish in mud/gravel" be left high and dry

○ **mbet· si peshku pa ujë** "be left like a fish without water" be left high and dry

○ **mbet· si pika në lis** to be left all alone in the world

○ **mbet· si qyqe në degë** "remain like a cuckoo on a branch" to be in a miserable situation

○ **mbet· si rosa në mjegull 1** not know which way to go **2** not know which way to turn, be in a tight spot

○ **mbet· si ujku/zagari në thekër** "remain like a wolf/hound in rye" to be stuck in a hopeless situation

○ **mbet· si zogjtë e korbit** to be left homeless and helpless

○ **mbet· si zogjtë pa klloçkë** to be left helpless

○ s'<> **mbet·**^{3sg} **sy e faqe** "for <> no eye and face sticks" <> is too ashamed to face anyone; <> is covered with shame

○ <> mbet·^{3sg} **syri te/tek** {} <> *keeps* looking at {}

○ <> mbet·^{3pl} **sytë te/tek** {} <> *keeps* looking at {}

○ mbet· **shtang** to go rigid, be paralyzed with shock/fear

○ mbet· **shul** to be left with nothing

○ <> mbet· **takë** to remain a constant cause of regret to <>

○ <> mbet· **tangë** to remain a constant cause of regret to <>

○ mbet· **teneqe** to have nothing left, be flat broke

○ mbet· **top në vend** to be dead on the spot

○ mbet· **trëndelinë** *(Colloq)* to have not a penny in one's pocket, have nothing to one's name

○ mbet· **thes në vend** to drop dead on the spot

○ s'<> mbet· **thërrime** not a particle of <> remains, there *is* not even a little bit of <> left

○ <> mbet· **thikë në zemër** to cause <> deep emotional anguish: strike <> to the heart

○ mbet· **udhëve 1** to leave forever; drop out of sight; die **2** to be on the road all the time **3** to hang around idly, loaf around in the streets

○ <> mbet·^{3sg} **vetëm hija** <> *is* a mere shadow of one's former self

○ mbet· **zhyt** to remain totally in the dark

○ <> mbet· [] to still owe <> [an amount of something]

mbet·*et* vpr to remain; be left (over); come out of it, come away

○ <> mbet·*et*^{3sg} **goja** <> *goes* on and on talking about the same thing

○ <> mbet·*et*^{3sg} **gjalmi nëpër këmbë** a big problem remains for <>

○ mbet·*et* **jashtë në shi si kocomi** "remain outside in the rain like a little mouse" to be left out, be given the cold shoulder

○ mbet·*et* **me barrë** to get pregnant

○ mbet·*et* **me duar në gji** (of a woman) to be left alone and forsaken

○ mbet·*et* **me gisht në gojë** "stand with finger in mouth" **1** to end up with nothing **2** to be dumbstruck with surprise **3** to stand in shame

○ mbet·*et* **midis katër rrugëve** "be left between four roads" to be left in the lurch

○ mbet·*et* **në ajër** to be left hanging in air; be up in the air, be not yet decided

○ mbet·*et* **në hije** to keep [] secret/hidden: keep [] under wraps

○ mbet·*et* **në rrugë / gjysmë të rrugës** to be stuck on the road

○ mbet·*et* **për ibret** to be in a miserable state

○ mbet·*et* **si çobani pa bagëti** "remain like a shepherd without a flock" to be a leader who has lost his followers

mbet·*ës*
  I § *adj* remaining; vestigial, residual
  II § *n* student who must repeat an examination/subject/class

mbet·*ëz* nf remains, vestige, relic

*mbet·**i·na** *np fem* = mbeturi·na

mbet·je** *nf ger* **1** <mbet·i·, mbet·*et* **2** remainder; remnant

mbet·shëm** *adj (i)* remaining to be done, left to do

mbet·ur** *adj (i)* **1** remaining, leftover **2** left behind: (of girls) still unmarried; (of children) orphaned; (of old people) without close kin **3** *(Fig)* retarded, slow

mbetur·a *np (të) fem* **1** remnants, leftovers; remainder **2** waste products **3** bird or animal wastes: droppings **4** [*Fin*] surplus

mbetur·ë *nf (e)* = mbetura

mbeturi·na *np* <mbeturi·në leftover waste: wastes, refuse; debris, residue, sediment, dregs

mbeturi·në *nf* **1** leftover; scrap, remnant; vestige **2** *(Pej)* outmoded idea

mbeturin·o·r *adj (Book)* **1** residual; waste **2** vestigeal

*mbë*ë* = më

*mbë*dy·sh*ë** = mëdy·shje

mbëdha = mëdha

mbëdhe·nj = mëdhe·nj

*mbëfa·s** = mbufa·s

*mbëfa·t·** = mbufa·t·

mbëhi *nf* **1** *(Colloq)* = nevojë *2** urgency, exigency

*mbëhi·s** stem for 1st sg pres, pl pres, 2nd & 3rd sg subj, pind <mbëhi·t·

*mbëhi·shëm** *adj (i)* *(Reg Calab)* urgent, pressing

*mbëhi·t·** *vt* to urge, press

*mbëhi·t·et** *vpr* to be obliged, be forced

mbëhita·r *n (Colloq)* needy person = nevojta·r

*mbëhi·tur** *adj (i)* obliged, forced

*mbë*je·dh·** = mble·dh·

*mbë*kâmb** *(Reg Gheg)* = mëkëmb

*mbë*kâmb·si·m** *(Reg Gheg) nm* authorization, authority = manda·t

*mbë*krejc·ë** *nf* **1** patch (on clothes) **2** unploughed patch (in a field)

mbëlti·m *nm ger* <mbëlto··n

mbëlto··n *vt* **1** to plant [seedlings/bulbs/cuttings/rootstocks] **2** *(Reg)* to bury

*mbëltue·s** *nm* planter; dibble stick

*mbërdha·s·et** = mërdhe·z·et

mbërdhe *adv* on/to the ground; down

*mbërdhe·c·ë** *nf* young vineyard

*mbërdhe·shëm** *adj (i)* ground-level, ground-floor

mbërdhe·z·et *vpr (Colloq)* = mërdhe·z·et

mbërdhi··n *vi* = mërdhi··n

*mbërdhi·h·** *vi* = mërdhi··n

*mbërdhi·h·et** *vpr ()* = mërdhi··n

*mbërdhi·je** *nf* chilliness

mbërdho·k *nm (Reg)* (round) pebble

mbërthe·het *vpr* **1** to button up **2** to grab tight: cling; stand still, stick **3** to grapple; quarrel

mbërthe··n *vt* **1** to fasten together securely; button [] up, secure [] with a clasp **2** to secure by nailing: nail **3** to attach **4** to grip tight: clamp, clutch **5** to hitch up: yoke [oxen], harness [horses]

○ <> mbërthe·*n*^{3sg} **goja** "<>'s mouth *gets* fastened shut" <> *buttons* up <>'s mouth

○ e mbërthe·*n* **gojën** to keep one's mouth shut

○ [] mbërthe·*n* **me shpatulla në mur / pas murit** "nail [] to the wall" to put the squeeze on [] until [] *is* forced to admit <>'s guilt.

○ [] mbërthe·*n* **me shpatulla pas murit / në mur** "nail [] with []'s back to the wall" to defeat [] with incontrovertible arguments/evidence

○ [] mbërthe·*n* **në shtyllën e turpit** "nail [] to a pillar of shame" *(Book)* to mark/brand [] with shame

○ [] mbërthe·*n* **në vend** "attach/fix [] in place" to hold [] in place, keep [] from moving; not allow [] to get ahead, hold [] back

○ [] **mbërthe·***n* **për fyti/gryke** to put heavy pressure on []

○ [] **mbërthe·***n*^{3sg} **rakia** the raki *makes* [] drunk, the raki *takes* [] over

○ **i mbërthe·***n* **sytë** to finally die

mbërthe'ce = **mbërthe'ckë**

mbërthe'ckë *nf* **1** fastener (on clothes): button, snap, clasp **2** metal fastener: catch, buckle, latch **3** clamp **4** part of the foot of a lamb or kid used to close up the belly of the carcass for roasting on a spit

mbërthe'së *nf* **1** buttonhole ****2** parenthesis

mbërthe'zë *nf* fastener on clothes: buckle, snap; belt, suspenders

mbërth'im *nm ger* <**mbërthe·***n*, **mbërthe·***het*

mbërth'yer *adj (i)* **1** buttoned up **2** attached; fixed in place **3** *(Fig)* transfixed **4** nailed on tight **5** *(Fig)* dead drunk: nailed

○ **mbërthyer krah për krah** locked arm in arm

mbërth'yer·a *np (të)* [*Anat*] joints

mbërth'yes·e *nf* **1** fastener **2** fibula

mbërri·*n* *vi, vt* = **arri·***n*

mbërri't *stem for pdef, opt, adm, part* <**mbërri·***n*

mbërri'tje *nf ger* = **arri'tje**

mbërri'tsh·ëm *adj (i)* = **arri'tsh·ëm**

mbërru't·*et* *vpr* **1** to wither, wither away **2** *(Fig)* to fall into moral decay: go bad

***mbësha'k·** *vt* **1** to blunt, dull **2** *(Fig)* to stupefy

***mbësha'k·ët** *adj (i)* **1** blunt, dull **2** *(Fig)* stupefied, puzzled

***mbëshe'l·** *vt* to close [] up/in; close, shut

mbë'shenj·o·*het* *vpr* to stand out, be distinguished

***mbëshi'l** *stem for 2nd pl pres, pind, imper, vp* <**mbëshel·**

***mbëshi'l·e** *nm* = **mbëshi'le**

***mbë'shi'l·e** *nf* lid, cover, shutter

mbë'shte's *stem for 1st sg pres, pl pres, 2nd & 3rd sg subj, pind* <**mbështe't·**

mbështe't· *vt* **1** to provide a basis/base: set/lay [] firmly **2** *(Fig)* to support []; rest []

○ **e mbështet· brinjën** *(Impol)* to finally die

mbështe't·*et* *vpr* **1** to have a basis/base: rest; lie, sit, lean **2** to lie down **3** to rely, depend

○ **mbështet·***et* **(vetëm) me/më një këmbë** to have a weak basis, rest on a shaky foundation

○ **mbështet·***et* **në të dyja këmbët** to rest on a firm basis, rest on a strong foundation

***mbë'shte't·ëm** *adj (i)* supported

mbë'shte't·ës

   I § *adj* supporting

   II § *n* supporter

   III § *nm* support, prop, rest, stand

mbështe't·ëse *nf* **1** support, prop **2** armrest; backrest; head support

mbështe'tje *nf ger* **1** <**mbështe't·**, **mbështet·***et* **2** support, supporting bracket; prop **3** *(Book)* foundation, basis

mbështe'tsh·ëm *adj (i)* worthy of support

mbë'shte'tur

   I § *adj (i)* well supported, well grounded

   II § *adv* while being supported: leaning on something

mbë'shti'll·*et* *vpr* **1** to get wound onto a spool; coil/ furl up into ball shape; coil/wind/wrap around into convoluted form **2** to wrap oneself up **3** to hunch/

double up into a ball-shaped mass **4** to huddle together, form a crowd **5** *(Fig)* to attack <> in one fell swoop

○ <> **mbështill·***et* **gardh** to be completely surrounded

○ **po** <> **mbështill·***et*^{3sg} **kapistalli** <> *is getting near the end of life*

○ <> **mbështill·***et*^{3sg} **lëmshi** "<>'s ball of yarn *is winding up*" <> *is nearing the end of (of life)*, <> *is dying*

mbë'shti'll *stem for 2nd pl pres, pind, imper, vp* <**mbështje'll·**

mbë'shtje'll· *vt* **1** to wind [] onto a spool; coil, furl, wrap **2** to wrap [] up, envelope, assemble **3** to wad/ double [] up **4** *(Fig)* to gather [] into one place, heap [] together **5** *(Fig)* to clutch [] closely **6** *(Reg)* to cause [mill] to curdle

○ **mbështjell·** **mendtë/trutë** to come to one's senses

mbë'shtje'll·e

   I § *part* <**mbështje'll·**

   II § *adj (i)* **1** spooled, wound on, coiled up **2** wrapped up

   III § *nf* **1** material used for wrapping: wrapping material **2** *(Colloq)* complicated mystery

mbë'shtje'll·ës

   I § *adj* used for spooling/winding/coiling

   II § *nm* spool winder

mbë'shtje'll·ëse *nf* **1** material used for wrapping: wrapping material **2** outer covering of fruit/grain: hull, husk **3** spooling device: spooler

mbë'shtje'll·je *nf ger* **1** <**mbështje'll·**, **mbështi'll·***et* **2** material used for wrapping: wrapping material **3** enveloping layer: envelope **4** *(Crude)* meeting, gathering: parley

mbë'shto'll *stem for pdef* <**mbështje'll·**, **mbështi'll·***et*

mbë'tra'zë *nf* attic, garret

mbi *prep (acc)* **1** on, upon; over; above **2** engaged/ busy with **3** *(Book)* about, concerning = **për 4** *(Book)* on the basis of

○ {*noun*} **mbi** {*same noun*} one {} on top of another, one {} after another

○ **mbi gjithçka** above all

○ **mbi themele prej balte** "on foundations of mud" built on sand

mbi·*n* *vi* **1** to take root, sprout, germinate; sprout up **2** to teethe; develop claws/nails

○ <> **mbi·***n*^{3sg} **bari në faqe** "grass *sprouts* in <>'s face" <> *waits* a long time

○ <> **mbiftë ferra në derë** "May the thorn bush grow at <>'s door!" *(Curse)* May no one in <>'s family remain!

○ <> **mbi·***n* **në bark** "take root in <>'s stomach" <> *gets tired of eating the same thing all the time*

○ <> **mbi·***n* **në derë** "take root at <>'s door" *(Pej)* to annoy <> with frequent visits

○ <> **mbi·***n* **në kokë/mendje** "take root in <>'s mind" *(Pej)* <> *can't get* {*something*} out of <>'s mind

○ <> **mbi·***n* **në sy** *(Impol)* to keep showing up in <>'s face

○ <> **mbi·***n* **në tru** to stick in <>'s mind

○ <> **mbi·***n*^{3sg} **sherri midis hairit** "Discord *sprouts* at <> in the midst of prosperity." A terrible thing *happens* to <> when <> least *expects* it.

mbi *formativ* over-, sur-, super-, hyper-

mbibi'sht *nm* rump, croup

mbi|bi'sht|ëz *nf* harness strap that fits over the tail of a beast of burden: crupper

mbi|çm|im *nm ger* 1 <mbiçmo'•n 2 overestimation, overestimate

mbi|çmo'•n *vt* to overvalue, overestimate

mbi|de'rmë *nf* [*Med*] = mbilëku'rë

mbi|det|a'r *adj* above sea level

mbi|dialekt|o'r *adj* supradialectal

mbi|dhe'sh|ëm *adj (i)* above-ground

*mbiell = mbjell

mbi|em|ër *nm* 1 [*Ling*] adjective 2 family name: surname

mbi|em|ër|im *nm ger* <mbiemëro'•n, mbiemëro'•het

mbi|em|ëro'•het *vpr* = mbiqu'•het

mbi|em|ëro'•n *vt* = mbiqua•n

mbi|em|ër|o'r *adj* [*Ling*] adjectival

mbi|em|ër|u'ar *adj (i)* nicknamed

mbi|em|ër|zim *nm ger* [*Ling*] 1 <mbiemërzo'•n 2 adjectivization

mbi|em|ër|zo'•n *vpr* [*Ling*] to make into or use as an adjective: adjectivize

mbi|em|ër|zu'ar *adj (i)* [*Ling*] made into or used as an adjective: adjectivized

mbi|fa'qe *nf* surface

mbi|fit|im *nm* [*Econ*] excess profit

*mbi|fo'lje *nf (Old)* = ndajfo'lje

mbi|fu'nd *nm* [*Agr*] upper leaf of tobacco

mbi|fuqi'sh|ëm *adj (i)* extraordinarily powerful

mbi|fu'shë *nf* area just above a plain, foothill area

mbi|harxh|im *nm* overexpenditure

mbi|he'rdhe *nf* [*Anat*] epididymis

mbi|hi'pje *nf* [*Geol*] tectonic slippage of one plate over another: *overthrust, thrust, thrusting*

mbi|jet|e'së *nf (Book)* <mbijeto'•n

mbi|jeto'•n *vi (Book)* to survive

mbi|jet|o'jë *nf* surviving relic

*mbi|jtje *nf ger* = mbi'rje

mbi|kal|e'së *nf* overpass

mbi|kal|im *nm* = mbikale'së

mbi|këqy'r• *vt* to supervise, oversee; inspect

mbi|këqy'r|ës

I § *adj* supervising; supervisory
II § *n* 1 supervisor; inspector 2 *(Old)* school inspector

mbi|këqy'rje *nf ger* 1 <mbikëqy'r• 2 supervision; charge; surveillance

mbi|klas|o'r *adj* transcending class

mbi|ko'hë *nf* [*Econ*] overtime (work)

mbi|kra'h *nm* 1 upper wing 2 upper arm

mbi|lëku'rë *nf* [*Anat Bot*] outer skin layer: epidermis

mbi|lo'dhje *nf* overtiredness: overfatigue

mbi|lu'kth *nm* [*Anat*] epigastrium

mbill•-*et* *vpr* <mbje'll•

mbi|ll *stem for 2nd pl pres, pind, imper, vp* <mbje'll•
◦ **mbill farë, korr farë** "sow the seed, reap the seed" unproductive, of no value
◦ **mbill e mos korr** "sow-and-don't-reap" total mess

*mbi|më = bi'më

*mbi|mje *nf ger (Reg Gheg)* = mbi'rje

mbi|natyr|o'r *adj* = mbinaty'rshëm

mbi|naty'r|shëm *adj (i)* supernatural

mbi|nde'mje *nf* excess voltage/tension

mbi|ndërt|im *nm* superstructure

mbi|ndjesh|mëri *nf (Book)* supersensitivity; hypersensitivity

mbi|ngacm|im *nm (Med)* overexcitement

mbi|ngark|e'së

I § *nf* overload; overburden
II § *nf ger* <mbingarko'•n, mbingarko'•het

mbi|ngark|im *nm ger* 1 <mbingarko'•n, mbingarko'•het 2 overload; overburden

mbi|ngark|o'•het *vpr* to be overburdened

mbi|ngark|o'•n *vt* to overload; overburden

mbi|ngark|u'ar *adj (i)* overloaded; overburdened

mbi|ngo'p• *vt* [*Spec*] to oversaturate

mbi|ngo'pje *nf* [*Spec*] oversaturation

mbi|ngo'pur *adj (i)* [*Spec*] oversaturated

mbi|ngro'•het *vpr* to be overwarm

mbi|ngro'h• *vt* to overwarm

mbi|ngro'hje *nf ger* <mbingro'h•, mbingro'•het

mbi|normativ|ë *nf* [*Econ*] 1 record of an excess (over a planned amount) 2 overproduction (amount that exceeds norms)

mbi|nxe'h• *vt* 1 to overheat 2 [*Tech*] to superheat

mbi|nxe'h•-*et* *vpr* 1 to get too hot: overheat 2 [*Tech*] to become superheated

mbi|nxe'h|ës *nm* [*Tech*] superheater

mbi|nxe'hje *nf ger* <mbinxe'h•, mbinxe'h•-*et*

mbi|ny'ell *nm* [*Med*] epicondyle

mbi|njer|ëz|o'r *adj* superhuman

mbi|njeri *nm* superman

mbi|pas|ne'sër *adv* day after the day after tomorrow, three days from today = tje'tërpasne'sër

mbi|pe'shë *nf* overweight

mbi|pe'tk *nm* overgarment, outer garment

mbi|popull|im *nm* [*Geog*] overpopulation

mbi|popull|u'ar *adj (i)* overpopulated

mbi|presio'n *nm* [*Tech*] overpressure

mbi|produ'kt *nm* [*Econ*] surplus product

mbi|prodh|im *nm ger* [*Econ*] 1 overproduction 2 = mbiprodu'kt

mbi|pu'në *nf* [*Econ*] surplus labor

mbi|qe'ndër *nf* epicenter

mbi|qu'•het *vpr* to be nicknamed

mbi|qua•n *vt* to nickname

mbi|qu'ajt *stem for pdef, opt, adm, part* <mbiqua•n

mbi|qu'ajtje *nf* nickname

mbi|qu'ajt|ur *adj (i)* nicknamed

*mbi|qy'r = mbikëqy'r

mbi|rë

I § *part* <mbi-n
II § *adj (i)* germinated, sprouted

mbi'r|ës *adj* for germinating

mbi'rje *nf ger* 1 <mbi-n 2 germination; rooting; plant growth

mbi|rro'jt|ës *adj (Book)* surviving

mbi|ry'më *nf* [*Electr*] excess current: overcurrent

*mbi|si *nf (Reg Gheg)* germination

mbi|sund|im *nm ger* 1 <mbisundo'•n 2 domination, superiority

mbi|sund|o'•n *vi* to predominate

mbi|sund|u'es *adj* predominating, predominant

mbi|su'p *nm* strip of cloth on the shoulder of a military uniform for displaying military insignia: epaulet

mbi·shartes̈ë *nf* [*Agr*] upper portion of a plant graft: scion

*****mbi·shikím** *nm ger* = **mbikëqy'rje**

mbi·shiko̱·*n vt* (*Book*) = **mbikëqy'r·**

mbi·shiku'es *adj, n* (*Book*) = **mbikëqy'rës**

mbishkrím *nm* 1 <**mbishkrua·n** 2 inscription

mbi·shkru̱a·*n vt* (*Book*) to inscribe

mbi·shkru̱ar *adj* (*i*) inscribed

mbishpenzím *nm* overexpenditure = **mbiharxhím**

mbi·shte̱gth *nm* [*Anat*] epiglottis

mbishtes̈ë *nf* additional increase/increment

mbi·shteẗëro̱r *adj* [*Law*] transcending the state

mbishtres̈ë *nf* overlay; superstratum

mbishtres̈ím *nm ger* <**mbishtreso̱·n**, **mbishtres-o̱·het** upper/later stratum; superstratum

mbishtreso̱·het *vpr* to gain an additional layer

mbishtreso̱·*n vt* to add another layer: overlay

mbitakse̱ *nf* surtax

mbitaksím *nm ger* 1 <**mbitakso̱·n** 2 overtaxation

mbitakso̱·*n* 1 to surtax 2 to overtax

mbitarife̱ *nf* surcharge; extra tariff

mbitensio̱n *nm* [*Electr*] excess voltage: *overvoltage*

mbito̱ke̱ *nf* land surface; surface of the ground

mbitok̈ëso̱r *adj* 1 above-ground 2 extraterrestrial 3 supernatural

mbitrusni̱ *nf* [*Tech*] overpressure

*****mbi̱·tur** *part* (*Reg*) <**mbi·n**

mbithartí *nf* [*Med*] hyperacidity

mbiuj̈ë *nf* ground located well above the water: high ground

mbi̱uj̈ës *adj* resting/operating on the surface of the water

mbi̱uj̈ëse *nf* device that operates on the surface of the water: surface vessel

mbi̱ujo̱r *adj* [*Spec*] = **mbiujshëm**

mbi̱ujshëm *adj* (*i*) located/happening on the surface of the water

mbi̱varrshëm *adj* (*i*) = **përmbivarrshëm**

mbi̱ve̱tull *nf* area above the eyebrows: brow

mbi̱vështrím *nm ger* (*Book*) = **mbikëqy'rje**

mbi̱vështro̱·*n vt* (*Book*) = **mbikëqy'r·**

*****mbi̱vle̱·***n vi* to prevail

mbi̱vle̱fte̱s = **mbivlerës**

mbi̱vlere̱ *nf* surplus value

mbi̱vlere̱sím *nm ger* 1 <**mbivlereso̱·n** 2 overestimation

mbi̱vlere̱so̱·*n vt* to overestimate

*****mbi̱vo̱ll** *nf* snare, ambush

mbizoẗërím *nm ger* 1 <**mbizotëro̱·n** 2 superiority, domination

mbizoẗëro̱·*n vi* 1 to predominate 2 to be superior, dominate

mbizoẗëru̱es *adj* 1 superior, dominant 2 dominating

mbje̱ll· *vt* 1 to sow; plant 2 (*Fig*) to disseminate, propagate 3 (*FigJocular*) to strew, scatter around; lose here and there

∘ **mbje̱ll· bostan e <> de·l·**[3pl] **kastraveca** "sow melons and have cucumbers come up for <*one*>" (*Iron*) things turn out differently/worse than what one expects

∘ **mbje̱ll· ferra nëpër këmbë** to create difficulties/complications along the path

∘ **mbje̱ll· misër e korr tallë** "sow corn and reap bare corncobs" to work hard with high hopes and have it come to naught

∘ **mbje̱ll· në dushk** to do careless/superficial work

∘ **mbje̱ll· thekër e <> de·l·**[3sg] **grurë** "sow rye and have wheat come up for <*one*>" to be prospering, be doing well

mbje̱lla *np* (*të*) 1 sown/planted fields 2 grain crops

mbje̱lle̱
I § *part* <**mbje̱ll·**
II § *adj* (*i*) sown, planted

mbje̱ll·ës
I § *adj* for sowing/planting
II § *n* sower, planter

mbje̱llje *nf ger* <**mbje̱ll·**, **mbíll·et**

mbje̱ll·shëm *adj* (*i*) suitable for planting/sowing

mbje̱lltar *n* sower

*****mblaçís** = **mbllaçís**

*****mblaçít·** = **mbllaçít·**

*****mblade̱** *nf* (*Reg Gheg*) reward, recompense, recognition

*****m·bla̱k·** *vt* = **plak·**

*****m·bla̱kur** *adj* (*i*) (of a person) aged, old

mbla̱t· *vt* [*Relig*] to consecrate [communion wafers]

mbla̱ẗë *nf* [*Relig*] communion wafer, eucharistic bread: host

mbla̱ẗës *nm* [*Relig*] wooden seal used to stamp communion wafers with a holy symbol

*****mblatím** *nm* imprinted mark

mbledh·
I § *vt* 1 to gather, gather in [ ], gather up 2 to gather/fasten [ ] together; pull [ ] in, fold [ ] up, tuck [ ] in/under 3 to collect; accumulate 4 to call together [a gathering]: assemble 5 [*Math*] to add 6 to wrap
II § *vt, vi* to collect [pus]; fester

∘ **<>a mbledh· (keq/mirë)** (*Colloq*) to pull in the reins on <>, teach <> a (good) lesson, discipline <>, set <> straight

∘ **mbledh· ballin** to frown sadly, look glum

∘ **mbledh· bishtin** 1 (*Contempt*) to put one's tail between one's legs (from shame) 2 to turn tail, run away

∘ **mbledh· buze̱t** to make a wry face to express disappointment/disapproval

∘ **mbledh· buze̱t** to purse one's lips

∘ **mbledh· çaklat** to leave lock stock and barrel, leave with all one's junk

∘ **i mbledh· çoparkat** (*Iron*) to pack up and leave; leave in a hurry

∘ **e mbledh· dore̱n** to become careful with expenses

∘ **e mbledh· fillin** to recover; come back to one's senses

∘ **<> mbledh· frerin** to tighten the reins on <>

∘ **<>i mbledh· gjalmat** to tighten the reins on <>

∘ **e mbledh· gjuhën** "gather one's tongue back in the mouth" stop talking so much/freely

∘ **mbledh· kallinj** to glean (wheat from the fields)

∘ **mbledh· këmbët për të fshehur gjurmët** to disguise one's true character by a false show of regret

∘ **i mbledh· këmbët** to reduce one's demands

∘ **mbledh· kockat** to pull oneself together (after being exhausted): rest up

∘ **mbledh· kup** to pile up

∘ **<>i mbledh· leckat** (*ColloqImpolite*) to make <> pick up <>'s lousy belongings and clear out: kick <> out (with all <>'s damn belongings)

○ **mbledh· leckat** *(ColloqImpolite)* to pick up one's goddam belongings and clear out

○ **i mbledh· lotët** to stop one's tears, cease crying

○ [] **mbledh· me bar blete** to attract [] by using inducements

○ **mbledh· me** [] to wrap in []

○ **e mbledh· mendjen 1** to finally make up one's mind **2** to come to one's senses; gather one's wits together

○ **mbledh· mendtë** to come to one's senses

○ **i mbledh· plaçkat** "gather/pick/load up all one's stuff" *(Iron)* to finally pack up one's stuff and leave; pick up and leave

○ **mbledh· retrat 1** to tie up one's moccasin laces **2** to tighten one's belt, practice greater thrift

○ **<> i mbledh· rraqet** *(ColloqImpolite)* to make <> pick up <>'s lousy belongings and clear out: kick <> out (with all <>'s damn belongings)

○ **mbledh· rraqet/rreckat** *(ColloqImpolite)* to pick up one's's goddam belongings and clear out

○ **<> mbledh· rripat** to tighten the reins on <>

○ **mbledh· rripat 1** to tie up one's moccasin laces **2** to tighten one's belt, practice greater thrift

○ [] **mbledh· si plaga qelbin** "collect [] like a wound collects pus" to collect [] by dint of great effort

○ **mbledh· supet 1** to shrug one's shoulders **2** to answer with a shrug of the shoulders: how should I know!?

○ **e mbledh· të** {+ *verb*}^{subj} *(Fig Colloq Crude)* to finally make up one's mind to {}

○ **mbledh· trutë** to come to one's senses

○ **e mbledh· veten 1** to pull oneself together **2** to rest up

○ **mbledh· vetullat** to frown sadly, look glum

mbledha˙k *adj* having a strong and robust body

mble˙dh|ës
I § *adj* **1** for gathering/collecting; for adding **2** [*Phys*] for focussing: concentrating
II § *n* collector, gatherer; harvester
III § *nm* **1** [*Math*] addend **2** water collector

mble˙dh|ëse *nf* **1** adding machine, calculator **2** collecting device: collector

mbledh|ëta˙r *n (Old)* **1** participant in an assembly **2** adding machine

mble˙dhje *nf ger* **1** <mble˙dh·, mbli˙dh·*et* **2** (of a group) assembly, meeting, gathering **3** [*Math*] addition; sum, total

○ **mbledhje e fundit** grand total

○ **mbledhje e këmbëve** [*Sport*] tuck position

mble˙dh|shëm *nm (i)* addend

mble˙dh|ur
I § *adj (i)* **1** concentrated in or near one place: compact; pursed; folded/curled up **2** calm and collected, well-behaved ***3** festered
II § *adv* with limbs folded, contracting the body together

*mbleks· = **pleks·**

*mbler| = **bler|**

mbles *nm* [*Ethnog*] marriage broker, go-between

mble˙se *nf* [*Ethnog*] marriage engagement arranged by a go-between

mblese˙ri *nf* [*Ethnog*] *(Old)* matchmaking, marriage brokerage

mblese˙ri˙m *nm ger* [*Ethnog*] **1** <mblese˙ro·*n* **2** = **mblese˙ri**

mblese˙ri˙në *nf* marriage brokerage, matchmaking

mblese˙ro˙·n *vt* [*Ethnog*] to arrange a marriage engagement as a go-between

*mblese˙r|ue˙r *nm (obl ˜ori) (Old)* of or pertaining to matchmaking

mblese˙ta˙r *n* [*Ethnog*] = **mbles**

mble˙s|kë *nf* woman matchmaker

*mblet|ani˙k *nm (Old)* apiary

*mbleta˙r *n (Old)* beekeeper = **bleta˙r**

*mble˙të *nf (Old)* = **ble˙të**

mbli˙dh·*et vpr* **1** to get together in one place: assemble; have a meeting **2** *(Colloq)* to join one's family at home: come home **3** to crouch, crouch down, hunch up, curl up, cringe, cower **4** to shrink; shrink up **5** *(Fig)* to become calm and collected; become well-behaved, gain poise

○ **<> mblidh·***et*^{3sg} to become more constrained

○ **mblidh·***et* **grusht** to become hunched up into a ball

○ **mblidh·***et* **kulaç** to squat

○ **<> mblidh·***et*^{3sg} **laku** "<>'s noose *is getting* tighter" <> *is coming* to the end of <>'s rope; <> *is nearing* the end (of life), <> *is dying*

○ **mblidh·***et* **lëmsh** to curl up

○ **<> mblidh·***et*^{3sg} **lëmshi** "<>'s ball of yarn *is winding* up" <> *is nearing* the end (of life), <> *is dying*

○ **<> mblidh·***et*^{3sg} **litari** "<>'s rope *is getting* tighter" <> *is coming* to the end of <>'s rope; <> *is nearing* the end (of life), <> *is dying*

○ **mblidh·***et* **me** [] to wrap oneself in []

○ **<> mblidh·***et* **një nyjë në grykë/fyt** <> *gets* an emotional lump in <>'s throat

○ **S'mblidhen pleshtat në grusht.** "Fleas won't be gathered in a fist." *(Prov)* It's like catching fish with your hands. It can't be done. There's no way.

○ **mblidh·***et* **shukthi** to huddle up

○ **<> mblidh·***et*^{3sg} **zemra lëmsh/shuk** <>'s heart *is* full (of emotion); <> *becomes* very sad

○ **<> mblidh·***et*^{3pl} **zorrët në grykë/fyt/te goja** "<>'s guts *rise* to <>'s throat/mouth" <> *feels like* throwing up

mbli˙dh| *stem for 2nd pl pres, pind, imper, vp* <mbli˙dh·

○ **mblidhe çafkën (e kokës)!** come to your senses!

○ **Mblidh dhitë!** "Gather your goats!" Come to your senses!

○ **mblidhe gjuhën!** you should watch your tongue!; hold your tongue!

*mbli˙të *nf* castle keep

*mblo·*n vt* **1** = **mbush·** **2** to affiance, betroth

*mblo˙cë *nf* covering; cover, lid; breastplate

mblo˙dh| *stem for pdef* <mble˙dh·

*mblo˙k·*et vpr* to heal up (leaving a scar): scar over

*mblo˙më *nf* roof

*mbl|ue˙m *adj (i) (Reg Gheg n (i))* = **feju˙ar**

*mbl|ue˙t *adj (i) (Reg Gheg)* covered up, hidden

mblla˙çë *nf* puddle

mbllaçi˙s| *stem for 1st sg pres, pl pres, 2nd & 3rd sg subj, pind* <mbllaçi˙t·

mbllaçi˙t· *vt* **1** to chew on [] noisily: munch on [] **2** *(Fig)* to mutter

mbllaçi˙t·*et vpr* **1** to chew and chew noisily; munch and munch **2** to chew one's cud, ruminate **3** to mumble one's words

mbllaçít|ës *adj* ruminating, cud-chewing: ruminant

mbllaçí|tje *nf ger* **1** < **mbllaçí**•, **mbllaçít**•*et* **2** noise made by chewing, munching noise

***mbllá**|**stër** *nf* poultice

***mbode**|**c** = **bode**|**c**

mbodhi|*nf (Reg)* delay; hindrance = **vones**|ë

mbodh|**ís**• *vt (Reg)* to delay; hinder = **vono**|•*n*

mbodh|**ís**•*et vpr (Reg)* **1** = **vono**|•*het* ***2** to stumble, trip

***mboh**|ës *adj* negative = **mohu**|es

***mboh**| *(Old)* = **moh**|

***mbo**|**le** *nf (Old)* testicle

mboll| *stem for pdef* < **mbje**|**ll**•

mboll|**ís**• *(Reg)* = **mbodhí**|s•

***mbraçi**|**s** *stem for 1st sg pres, pl pres, 2nd & 3rd sg subj, pind* < **mbraçí**|t•

***mbraçí**|t• *vt* to soak

mbra|**më** *adj (i)* = **pra**|**pm**ë

***mbrâ**|**më**|t *adj (i) (Reg Gheg)* rear, back; last

***mbrâm**| *(Reg Gheg)* = **mbrëm**|

mbra|**pa** *adv, prep (abl)* = **pra**|**pa**

mbrapa|**mbe**|**tur** *adj (i)* = **prapambe**|**tur**

mbrapa|**aník** *nm* cotton apron worn in back by women to protect clothes from getting dirty while sitting

mbrapa|**ro**|jë = **praparo**|jë

mbrapa|**skë**|në = **prapaskë**|në

mbrapa|**sht**|**es**|ë = **prapashtes**|ë

mbrapa|**ví**|jë = **prapaví**|jë

mbra|**p**|**ëm** *adj (i)* = **pra**|**pm**ë

mbra|**p**|**mi** *adv (së)* at last, finally

mbra|**ps**• *vt* = **zmbraps**•

mbra|**p**|**s**•*et vpr* = **zmbraps**•*et*

mbra|**p**|**sje** *nf ger* = **zmbrapsje**

mbra|**psht** *adv* **1** inside out, reversed **2** backwards, in reverse **3** wrong; perversely; naughtily **4** wickedly

mbra|**pshtas** *adv* from behind

mbra|**pshtë** *adj (i)* **1** perverse; naughty, mischievous **2** nasty; wrong, improper

mbrapshtí|*nf* = **prapësí**

mbrapshtë|**ím** *nm ger* **1** < **mbrapshto**|•*n*, **mbrapshto**•*het* **2** = **prapësí**

mbrapshto|•*het vpr* **1** to draw back, retreat, withdraw **2** to suffer a drawback; suffer a foul-up **3** to go wrong; go bad

mbrapshto|•*n vt* **1** = **zmbraps**• **2** to pervert, deprave; foul [ ] up, mess [ ] up

***mbrapt**|**ue**|**s** *adj* retroactive

mbra|**pthi** *adv (së)* = **pra**|**pthi**

***mbra**|**të** *adj (of animals)* pregnant: with calf, in foal

mbr|**e**•*n vt* = **mbreh**•

***mbref**• *vt (Reg Gheg)* = **mpreh**•

mbreh• *vt* to yoke up [draught animals]
  ○ **i mbreh**• **qetë (me** [ ]**)** to start to quarrel acrimoniously (with [ ]): go at [ ] hot and heavy

mbre|**h**•*et vpr* **1** to be yoked up for draught work **2** *(Fig)* to grapple; quarrel

***mbre**|**jt** *stem for pdef, opt, adm, part, vp* < **mbre**•*n*

***mbre**|**lë** *nf* umbrella

***mbre**|**nd**|**a** = **bre**|**nd**|**a**

***mbrend**|**i** = **brend**|**i**

***mbre**|**nd**|**shëm** = **bre**|**nd**|**shëm**

mbres| *stem for 1st sg pres, pl pres, 2nd & 3rd sg subj, pind* < **mbre**|*t*•

mbre|**s**|ë *nf* **1** scar **2** trace left on a surface: impression

mbret *nm (np ~ ër)* **1** king **2** *[Bot]* silver fir *(Abies alba)*
  ○ **mbreti i kafshëve** the lion
  ○ **mbreti i luleve** the rose
  ○ **mbreti i pemëve** the grape
  ○ **mbreti i shkurtës** *[Ornit]* corncrake *Crex crex L.*
  ○ **mbreti i shpendëve** the eagle

mbret• *vt* to bruise badly

mbre|**t**•*et vpr* **1** to get a badly bruised **2** to become infected (from a wound) **3** (of fruit) to rot from bruising; get soft and spoil

mbret|**ër** *np* < **mbret**

mbret|**ër**|**esh**ë *nf* queen

***mbret**|**ër**|**eshkë** *nf [Bot]* common columbine *(Aquilegia vulgaris)*

mbret|**ër**|**í** *nf* kingdom

mbret|**ër**|**ím** *nm ger* **1** < **mbretëro**|•*n* **2** reign

mbret|**ër**|**o**•*n vt* to reign

mbret|**ër**|**o**|**r** *adj* **1** royal **2** *(Fig)* regal, kingly

mbret|**th** *nm [Ornit]* = **mbreth**

mbret|**vra**|**s**|ës *n (Book)* regicide

***mbreth** *nm [Ornit]* goldcrest *(Regulus regulus)*
  ○ **mbrethi vetullbardhë** *[Ornit]* firecrest *Regulus ignicapillus Temm.*

mbre|**zhd**ë *nf* temporary pen for sheep used to collect sheep manure

mbrëm|**a** *adv* in the evening

mbrëm|**anet** *adv* toward evening time, towards dusk; during the evening, at evening time

mbrëm|ë *adv* yesterday evening; last night

mbrëm|ë|**sore** *nf* = **mbrëmjesor**

mbrëm|**je** *nf* **1** evening **2** evening party/entertainment: soiree
  ○ **mbrëmje akademike** evening commemorative ceremony

mbrëm|**je**|**sor** *adj (Book)* of the evening: vesperal

mbrëm|**je**|**sore** *nf* evening prayer: vespers

mbrëm|**shëm** *adj (i)* of yesterday evening, last night's

***mbrija**|**za** *adv* = **tërtho**|**razi**

mbrijo|•*het vpr* to have a fight

m|**brinj**•*et vpr* **1** to lean over, lean to one side, tilt **2** to be lopsided, bulge out

m|**brinjo**|•*het vpr* = **mbrínj**•*et*

mbro|•*het vpr* **1** to take defense measures, protect oneself **2** to arm oneself

mbro|•*n vt* **1** to shield, protect **2** to defend **3** to uphold, support

mbro|**çkull** *nf (Colloq)* nonsense

***mbrodh**• *vt* to be good for [ ], be of benefit to [ ]

mbrojt| *stem for pdef, opt, adm, part* < **mbro**•*n*

mbro|**jt**|ës
  I § *nm* **1** protector, defender; member of the defense **2** *[Soccer]* fullback
  II § *adj* for defense: defensive, protective

mbro|**jt**|**ese** *nf* protective device/object: protection

mbro|**jt**|**je** *nf ger* **1** < **mbro**|•*n*, **mbro**|•*het* **2** protection **3** defense
  ○ **mbrojtje beton** *[Soccer]* solid defense: rock-solid defense
  ○ **Mbrojtja e Popullit** state security agency in Albania during 1944-46
  ○ **mbrojtje rrethore** *[Mil]* perimeter defense

mbrojto·re *nf* protected area, game preserve (no hunting permitted)

mbro·jt·shëm *adj (i)* defendable

mbro·jtur
I § *part* <mbro·n
II § *adj (i)* protected; defended

*****mbro·lje** *nf* 1 intrigue 2 *(Reg Calab)* rope attached to the leech of a sail, clew-line, brail

*****mbro·qër** *nf* brussels sprout

mbroth *adv (Colloq)* without a hitch, successfully

mbroth·
I § *vi (Colloq)* to go without a hitch, succeed
II § *vt* to help [] get through a difficulty

mbroth·ësi *nf (Colloq)* flourishing success

mbru··het *vpr* 1 to get fattened up 2 to become formed by absorbing knowledge or a set of principles

mbru··n *vt* 1 to prepare [dough] by kneading/leavening 2 to prepare [mortar/cement] by mixing 3 to fatten [livestock] 4 *(Fig)* to form [someone] by instilling knowledge/principles *5 *(Old)* to ferment

mbru·jt *stem for pdef, opt, adm, part* <mbru··n

mbru·jtje *nf ger* <mbru·jt·, mbru·jt·et

mbru·jtur *adj (i)* 1 kneaded and leavened 2 *(Fig)* inspired and ennobled 3 (of livestock) fattened

*****mbrum** *nm (Old)* leaven

mbru·më
I § *adj (i)* leavened, fermented
II § *nf* leavened bread

*****mbrum·im** *nm ger (Old)* <mbrumo··n

*****mbrumo··n** *vt (Old)* to leaven, ferment

mbrus· *vt* 1 to fill [] to capacity 2 to load [] heavily, load [] to capacity
∘ **e mbrus· shtëpinë** to fill one's home with many good things

mbrus·et *vpr* to be filled to capacity

*****mbru·shëm** *adj (i)* tart, harsh

mbry·dh· *vt* to make [] soft: soften [fruit]

mbry·dh·et *vpr* (of ripening fruit) to become soft

mbry·dhët *adj (i)* (of fruit) very soft and ripe; overripe

*****mbry·shëm** = mbru·shëm

*****mbry·ta·r** *n* brewer

*****mbry·tari** *nf* brewery

*****mbrri·më** *adj (i) (Reg Gheg)* = arri·rë

*****mbrri·shëm** *adj (i)* = arri·rë

*****mbrro··n** = mbro··n

*****mbrrol·** *vt* = vrenjt·
∘ **mbrrol· sytë** to scowl, glare

*****mbrro·l·et** *vpr* to scowl, glare

*****mbrrola·r** *n* intriguer

*****mb·rrudh·** = mrrudh·

*****mbrru·t·et** *vpr* to dry up, wither

*****mbshe·lë** *nf* gag (in the mouth)

*****mbshe·re** *nf* mold for cheese

*****mbshikze·zë** *nf* furuncle; tumor

*****mbshi·së** = fshi·së

*****mbsho··n** = mësho··n

mbudh· *vt* 1 to meet [] along the way: run into [] 2 to show [] the way 3 *(Old)* to waylay

mbu·dh·et *vpr* 1 to meet along the way 2 to start on the way, start out

mbufa·s *stem for 1st sg pres, pl pres, 2nd & 3rd sg subj, pind* <mbufa·t·

mbufa·t· *vt (Colloq)* 1 to puff [] up 2 to fill [] full, stuff 3 to soak 4 *(Fig)* to exaggerate

mbufa·t·et *vpr (Colloq)* 1 to swell up 2 (of dough) to rise 3 *(Fig)* to get stuffed full 4 *(Fig)* to be exaggerated

*****mbufa·të** *adj (i)* = mbufa·tur

mbufa·tje *nf ger* <mbufa·t·, mbufa·t·et

mbufa·tur *adj (i)* 1 swollen 2 soaked 3 (of dough) risen

mbuja·k *adj* (of ground) soaking in water, under water: boggy

mbule·së *nf* 1 protective covering: wrapping, cover 2 envelope 3 lid 4 *[Fin]* precious metal reserves that guarantee the value of money in circulation 5 *[Text]* tensioner on a loom
∘ **mbulesë e gërmacit** epiglottis
∘ **mbulesa e lules** *[Bot]* perianth

mbuli·cë *nf* veil (for the face)

mbul·im *nm ger* <mbulo··n, mbulo··het

mbulo··het *vpr* 1 to put on a covering 2 to hide by covering up 3 to get covered over
∘ **Nuk mbulohet dielli me shoshë.** "The sun cannot be covered by a sieve." *(Prov)* Truth will out. You can't hide the truth.

mbulo··n *vt* 1 to cover; close 2 to cover [] up 3 to bury 4 (on a loom) to wrap [cloth] around a roller
∘ **Mbulo balta baltën.** "Dirt covers dirt." (said when a bad person dies) Good riddance to bad rubbish.
∘ **e mbulo··n dobiçin** "cover up the bastard" to conceal one's guilt
∘ **i mbulo··n këmbët** "cover one's legs" to hide one's true intentions: be sneaky
∘ **[] mbulo··n me plaf** to hide [something wrong], sweep [] under the rug
∘ **e mbulo··n në hi** to keep it (a feeling/secret) pent up inside

mbuloj *nf* 1 cover, covering; bed covering, blanket 2 roof 3 note/notebook cover

mbulo·më *nf* = mbule·së

mbulu·ar
I § *adj (i)* 1 covered; clothed, wrapped 2 roofed over 3 covered/clouded over: overcast 4 latent 5 *(Fig)* masked, hidden
II § *adv* under a protective/concealing covering; veiled

mbulu·es *adj* serving as a covering

mbure·së *nf* railing, banister

*****mbur·im** *nm* = burim

mburo··n *vt* 1 = mbro··n *2 = buro··n

mburoja·k *nm [Anat]* thyroid

mburo·jë *nf* 1 shield 2 earthwork, bulwark 3 carapace

*****mburu·es** = mbrojtës

mburr· *vt* to vaunt, boost, praise, extol

mbu·rr·et *vpr* 1 to brag, boast 2 to feel proud
∘ **mburr·et në të thatë/për së thati** to boast unjustifiably, brag without justification

mburraca·k
I § *nm* braggart; show-off
II § *adj* boastful; swaggering; ostentatious

mburrama·n *adj* boastful; swaggering; ostentatious

mburrani·k = mburrama·n

mburrave·c *adj, nm* = mburraca·k

mburr·ësi *nf (Book)* excessive boasting; ostentation

mburrit·et *vpr* to fight by butting horns: butt horns

mbu'rrje *nf ger* **1** <mbu'rr·, mburr·*et* **2** feeling of pride

mburru's'ët *adj (i)* oppressive

mbush· *vt* **1** to fill **2** to fill [] in/up **3** to load [a gun] **4** to complete [a period of time] **5** to backfill [a plant] to protect the roots **6** *(Fig Colloq)* to fulfill, comply with [], satisfy
   ◦ **ia mbush·** *(Colloq)* to run away, skedaddle
   ◦ **e mbush· barkun** *(Impol)* to stuff one's belly
   ◦ **<>i mbush· faqet** to make <> plump-cheeked (and healthy)
   ◦ **ua mbush· (këmbëve)** *(Colloq)* to run away, skedaddle
   ◦ **<>a mbush· kokën** to convince/persuade <>
   ◦ **e mbush· kokën** to get it all into one's head, learn it all
   ◦ **<>a mbush· kokën me ashkla** to bother <> with trivial details
   ◦ **e mbush· kuletën** to fill one's pockets with gold, make a lot of money
   ◦ **e mbush· kupën** to do too many bad things, exceed the limits: go too far
   ◦ **[] mbush· majë me majë** to fill [] to the very top/brim
   ◦ **<> mbush· mendjen** to convince/persuade <>
   ◦ **<>a mbush· mendjen** to convince/persuade <>
   ◦ **e mbush· plëndësin** *(Impol)* to stuff one's belly
   ◦ **e mbush· qesen** "fill one's sack" to make a lot of money, make whole sackful of money
   ◦ **e mbush· qindin** to do too many bad things, exceed the limits: go too far
   ◦ **mbush· qindin** to become a hundred years old, reach the age of a hundred
   ◦ **[] mbush· rraxhë** to fill [] to the brim
   ◦ **i mbush· sytë (me lot)** "fill one's eyes with tears" to get ready to cry
   ◦ **e mbush· shtëpinë 1** to fill one's home with many good things **2** to fill the whole house with one's presence
   ◦ **e mbush· të shtatën** "survive the seventh day (after birth)" to get past the danger, survive safely
   ◦ **i mbush· trutë** to get it all into one's head, learn it all
   ◦ **e mbush· thesin** to do too many bad things, exceed the limits: go too far
   ◦ **mbush· ujë me shoshë/shportë** "fill water with a screen/basket" to do useless work
   ◦ **[] mbush· vrer** to fill [] with bitter grief; make [] bitter/sore, vex []
   ◦ **i mbush· xhepat** "fill one's pockets" to earn/make a lot of money, become rich
   ◦ **e mbush· zorrën** "fill one's gut" *(Crude)* to eat one's fill: stuff one's belly

mbush·*et* *vpr* **1** to become full: fill up/out **2** (of a period of time) to be completed; (of a deadline) to be met **3** *(Fig Colloq)* to be fulfilled, be complied with, be satisfied **4** *(Colloq)* to scram, skedaddle
   ◦ **s'<> mbush·***et*^{3sg} **barku** "<>'s belly *does* not get full" *(Impol)* <> *has* a bottomless belly; <> *is* never satisfied
   ◦ **mbush·***et* **deri/gjer në fyt/grykë** to have had more than enough, not be able to take it any more; be fed up (to the gills)
   ◦ **nuk <> mbush·***et*^{3sg} **koka** "<>'s head *is* not to be filled" <> *is* impossible to convince/persuade; <> *is* incapable of learning
   ◦ **mbush·***et*^{3sg} **kupa** "the bowl *fills*" they *are* going too far, it (the situation) *is* unbearable

   ◦ **mbush·***et* **me majë** to get filled to the top/brim
   ◦ **<> mbush·***et*^{3sg} **mendja** "the mind *is* filled" <> *makes up* <>'s mind; <> becomes convinced
   ◦ **<> mbush·***et*^{3sg} **mendja qyp** <> *is* absolutely convinced
   ◦ **s'<> mbush·***et*^{3sg} **plëndësi** "<>'s belly *does* not get full" *(Impol)* <> *has* a bottomless belly; <> *is* never satisfied
   ◦ **S'mbushet pusi me pështymë/gjilpëra.** "The well cannot be filled with spit/needles." *(Prov)* You need the right equipment to do a job
   ◦ **<> mbush·***et*^{3sg} **syri (plot)** "<>'s eyes *get* filled (with pleasant things)" <> *is* made happy just by looking
   ◦ **mbush·***et*^{3sg} **tala** the limit *is* reached, that *is* the limit!
   ◦ **<> mbush·***et*^{3sg} **zemra (plot)** "<>'s heart *gets* filled (full)" <>'s heart *wells* up with joy

mbu'shël *nf* small fragment that lands in a liquid/container

mbu'shës
   I § *adj* used for filling something
   II § *nm* **1** filler **2** filling device or machine **3** loader (of guns) **4** [*Mus*] third voice in polyphonic folk music

mbu'shëse *nf* filling device or machine

mbush|ëtirë *nf* something stuffed/padded; stuffing, padding

mbu'shje *nf ger* **1** <mbu'sh·, mbu'sh·*et* **2** filler material (for holes or cracks): caulk **3** sedimentary sludge **4** [*Food*] = **iç 5** [*Agr*] cultivation of crops by filling the soil around the stem: earthing up = **mba'thje**

mbush|ta'r *n* [*Agr*] person who cultivates crops by filling the soil around the stem

mbush'ulli *nf* large amount, mass

mbushull|im *nm ger* **1** <mbushullo·*n* **2** large amount, mass

mbushullo·*n* *vt* to fill to overflowing; provide/give/bring a very large amount

mbu'shur
   I § *adj (i)* **1** full **2** filled; filled in/up/out; stuffed **3** fattened; plump; swollen **4** (of weapons) loaded **5** filled with important events
   II § *nf (e)* filling (of a tooth)

mbuto·*n* *vt* to stop up []: cap, cork, seal, bung

mbu'z·*et* *vpr* to come very near: approach the very edge

mbu'zë
   I § *adv* at very edge, on the brink/verge
   II § *nf* * *(Reg Gheg)* very edge: brink, verge

mbyl|ëse *nf* **1** closing device **2** closing machine: sealer

mbyll·
   I § *vt* **1** to shut []; close []; seal [] **2** to put a stopper/lid on []; close off []; stop up [] **3** to conclude []; put an end to []; turn off, hang up (a telephone) **4** to shut [] in; enclose [] **5** *(Colloq)* to put [] away for safekeeping
   II § *vi* (of an institution) to close, close down
   ◦ **mbyll· arkën** "close the cashbox" [*Fin*] to tally up the cash receipts
   ◦ **mbylle atë hale!** shut your dirty mouth!
   ◦ **mbylle buçen** shut up! shut your trap!
   ◦ **e mbyll· defterin** to close the book on the matter, bring the matter to an end

○ **T'u mbylltë dera/oxhaku** "May your door/ hearth be closed!" *(Curse)* May you die and leave no survivors!

○ **<>a mbyll· derën** to wipe out all the members of <>'s family; bring <>'s family line to a close

○ **e mbyll· derën** to bring one's family line to a close: die and leave no survivors

○ **<>a mbyll· derën me ferra** "close <>'s door with thorn bushes" to put an end to <> and <>'s whole family

○ **<>a mbyll· derën përpara hundës** to slam the door in <>'s face; forcibly show [ ] the door

○ **mbyll· dymbëdhjetë dyer me një shul** "close twelve doors with one bar" to be totally capable

○ **<>a mbyll· gojën 1** to get <> to keep <>'s mouth shut; make it impossible for <> to say anything more, make <> shut up **2** to beat <> down with words and arguments

○ **e mbyll· gojën** to shut one's mouth, shut up; keep one's mouth shut

○ **<>a mbyll· gojën me shtupë** "close <>'s mouth with oakum" to forcibly prevent <> from speaking: shut <> up good

○ **mbylle këtë muhabet** let's not talk about it! drop it!

○ **mbyll· me kyç** to lock up

○ **[ ] mbyll· me shtatë kyçe/palë çelësa** "lock [ ] with seven (sets of) keys" to lock/hide [ ] away safe and secure

○ **[ ] mbyll· në burg** to put in prison/jail: lock [ ] up

○ **mbyll· një sy 1** to wink **2** to pretend not to notice **3** to be lenient

○ **mbyll· një vesh e një sy** "close one ear and one eye" to turn a blind eye, let it go, ignore it; not let it upset one very much

○ **mbyll· një sy e një vesh para <>** to act as if one does not see or hear <>, pretend not to notice <>

○ **<>a mbyll· oxhakun** to wipe out all the members of <>'s family; bring <>'s family line to a close

○ **i mbyll· plagët** "close up the wounds" to repair the damage, come back to normal

○ **<> mbyll· rrugën** "close the path/road for <>" to bar <>'s way, block <>'s path

○ **<> mbyll· sytë** to close <>'s eyes (for the last time); be with <> at the moment of <>'s death

○ **<>i mbyll· sytë** to pull the wool over <>'s eyes

○ **mbyll· sytë 1** to pretend not to notice; ignore the danger **2** *(Euph)* to close one's eyes forever, die

○ **<> mbyll· shtegun** "close the path/road for <>" to bar <>'s way, block <>'s path

○ **e mbyll· shtëpinë** to bring one's family line to a close: die and leave no survivors

○ **mbyll· veshët (para <>)** "close one's ears (to <>)" to turn a deaf ear (on <>); refuse to listen (to <>)

mbyll·et *vpr* **1** to close **2** to close together; fold up; close up **3** (of an institution) to close, close down **4** to come to the end: conclude **5** to shut/seal oneself in; close oneself off from others **6** to get dark; be covered/clouded over: become overcast

○ **<> mbyll·et**[3sg] **dera/shtëpia** <> *dies* and *leaves* no survivors, <> *brings* <>'s family line to a close

○ **nuk <> mbyll·et**[3sg] **goja** <>'s mouth never *stops* talking: <> never shuts up

○ **mbyll·et në lëvozhgën/guaskën e vet** to enclose oneself in one's own private world

○ **<> mbyll·et**[3sg] **plaga** the wound is beginning to heal

○ **<> mbyll·et**[3pl] **sytë** <> is very sleepy, <>'s eyes keep closing on <>

mbyll|as *adv* = mbyllur

mbyll|a|sy|za *np* blindman's buff

mbyll|a|sy|zash *adv* **1** while blindfolded **2** *(Fig)* blindly

mbyll|azi *adv* = mbyllur

mbyll|ëm *adj (i)* = mbyllur

mbyll|ës

I § *adj (i)* used for closing/sealing/concluding

II § *nm* closer; closing device

mbyll|ët *adj (i)* **1** having a cover or roof: covered **2** closed-off; private **3** (of colors) deep and dark

mbyll|je *nf ger* **1** <mbyll·, mbyll·et **2** conclusion, closing

mbyll|të|si *nf (Book)* enclosedness; isolation; darkness (of colors)

mbyll|tin|ë *nf* enclosure

mbyll|to|re *nf* **1** [*Ling*] stop/plosive consonant **2** conclusion

mbyll|ur

I § *adj (i)* **1** closed **2** closed-off; private; (of a person) introverted **3** having a cover/roof: covered **4** (of colors) deep and dark **5** (of weather) overcast

II § *adv* in a closed condition: closed

○ **i mbyllur në kuti** *(Pej)* shut off from the world

mbys *stem for 1st sg pres, pl pres, 2nd & 3rd sg subj, pind* <mbyt·

mbyt· *vt* **1** to kill [ ] by depriving of breath: choke, strangle; suffocate **2** to stifle **3** to drown **4** *(Fig)* to overwhelm/drown [ ] (with an excess) **5** to sink/scuttle [a boat] **6** to kill [animal/insect pests] by spraying **7** *(Reg)* to kill [ ] by striking **8** *(Colloq)* to beat [ ] up; beat [ ] to death **9** *(Colloq)* to plant [a cutting/root/sprout] in the ground **10** to saturate

○ **mbyt· kafe** *(Reg Tir)* to make coffee

○ **s'e mbyt·**[past] **macen** "did not strangle the cat" *(Iron)* not have taken control from the beginning (by symbolically strangling a cat); be henpecked

○ **[ ] mbyt· që në bark/vezë** "stifle [ ] in the womb/ egg" to nip [ ] in the bud

mbyt·et *vpr* **1** to suffocate; drown **2** to choke (on an impediment in the throat) **3** (of a boat) to sink **4** to drown in an excess, be overwhelmed **5** *(Fig)* to be immersed in an activity **6** to be extinguished: go out, die out

○ **(s'ka) ku të mbyt·et**[subj] "(not have) where one may drown" (not have) anywhere to turn, be in a hopeless situation

○ **mbyt·et në lumë pa ujë** "drown in a dry river" **1** to have one's whole plan ruined by a trivial mistake **2** to be easily led off track; get hung up on a trivial problem

○ **mbyt·et në një pikë/lugë/gotë/filxhan/gisht ujë** "drown in a tiny amount of water" *(Impol)* to be easily led off track; get hung up on a trivial problem

mbyt|as *adv* = mbyturazi

mbyt|azi *adv* = mbyturazi

mbyt|ës

I § *adj (i)* **1** stifling, suffocating **2** used for exterminating insects: pesticidal **3** (of fruit) astringent **4** stifling

II § *nm* **1** animal exterminator **2** stifler; strangler

mbyt|je

I § *nf ger* **1** <mbyt·, mbyt·et **2** astringent fruit **3** [*Med*] asphyxia

II § adj **1** astringent **2** covert

mbyt'shë**m** *adj (i)* choking, stifling

mbyt'ur

I § *adj (i)* **1** drowned **2** (of a boat) sunken **3** soaking, soaked **4** barely audible: muffled, faint **5** barely visible: vague, faint

II § n (i) drowned person

III § *adv* **1** deeply, completely: up to the neck **2** = **mby'turazi**

mbyt'ur·azi *adv* **1** with only a faint/muffled sound; in a mumble **2** softly and quietly, unnoticed

m byth·im

I § *adv* in a sitting position (but not in a seat), sitting on the ground

*II § nm * = byth*ë

*m byth· *vt* to kick [ ] in the rear

*m byth'ar *nm* sodomite = by'thar

*mçef *OR* *mçeh* = fsheh

**m çel'sh*ë*m* *adj (i)* concludable

**mçes*ë *nf* = ndodhj*e

*mço·n *vi* = ndodh·

**mdhe'sh*kë *nf* = mëdhes*ë

me *prep (acc)* **1** with **2** having **3** by (instrumental) **4** according to, in terms of: by **5** added to: plus

 ○ me {*expression of duration*} within a period of {} me dy javë within a two-week period

 ○ {*noun in nom def form designating a time period*} me {*same time-period noun in acc indef form*} {} after/by {}: every {} dita me ditë every day: day by day dreka me drekë every lunchtime java me javë every week: week after week mëngjesi me mëngjes every morning muaji me muaj every month: month after/by month viti me vit every year: year after/by year

 ○ me afërsi approximately

 ○ me afsh passionately

 ○ me agjërim në gojë without eating anything

 ○ me ah e me bah with deep groans, constantly complaining

 ○ me akull të mendjes *(Book)* by cold logic

 ○ me alete në brez ready for anything

 ○ me anë të <> by means of <>; with <>'s help

 ○ me anën {*e* <>} by means of <>; with <>'s help

 ○ me armë në dorë ready for battle; with sword in hand, not surrendering

 ○ me avancë *(Book)* before the deadline, before the designated time: in advance

 ○ me bakra e me çakra with the whole kit and kaboodle, with bag and baggage

 ○ me ballë/ballin lart head held high

 ○ me ballë hapur = ballë ha'pur

 ○ me ballë të hapët/çelur **1** courageously **2** proudly

 ○ me ballë të larë **1** possessed of a clean conscience **2** having pride, proud

 ○ me ballë të hapur/çelur courageous; proud

 ○ me ballë të larë unstained by guilt, completely innocent

 ○ me bar e me gjethe with everything but the kitchen sink

 ○ me bark zbuluar not hiding anything: openly, frankly

 ○ me bark të gjerë tolerant; generous

 ○ me bark zbuluar "with belly uncovered" hiding nothing, openly

 ○ me barkun te buza in the final month of pregnancy

 ○ me barkun te buza/goja ready to give birth

 ○ me barrë pregnant

 ○ me batakçi fraudulently

 ○ me bel të këputur narrow-waisted, with a very thin waist

 ○ me besë good to one's word, trustworthy

 ○ me bisht *(Pej)* too much, too many

 ○ me bisht ndër shalë with one's tail between one's legs

 ○ me bot with great intensity

 ○ me brekë nëpër këmbë "with one's shorts down around the ankles" *(Tease Crude)* in total shame, humiliated

 ○ me brirë përpara in a mean manner, savagely

 ○ me bukë e kripë (e zemër të bardhë) with generous hospitality

 ○ me buzë të fryra bloated in appearance

 ○ me buzë të ciflosur embittered, depressed, unhappy, downcast

 ○ me buzë të plasur dispirited, down in the mouth

 ○ me buzë të varura/varur frowning

 ○ me bythë përpjetë upside down

 ○ me cektësi superficially

 ○ me çdo çmim at all costs, at whatever cost, no matter what it costs

 ○ me çdo kusht at any cost, in any case

 ○ me çika distinguished above all the others

 ○ me dashje e pa dashje willy-nilly

 ○ me dashje intentionally, on purpose

 ○ me dashje e me mosdashje willing or not

 ○ me derë pas dragging the whole family behind

 ○ me dëshirën e {*pronominal adj*} of {*one's*} own accord, of {*one's*} own free will

 ○ me din e me iman **1** by might and main, by gosh and by golly **2** everything, everyone

 ○ me dollap underhandedly

 ○ me dorë në zemër **1** fairly, justly **2** warmly; with pity **3** worried; anxious **4** respectfully

 ○ me dorë të lëshuar **1** free-spending, (too) free with money **2** too easy-going in supervision: lax in discipline

 ○ me dorë në qafë in a friendly way

 ○ me dorën në kobure ready/threatening to use a firearm: with one's hand on the gun

 ○ me dorën të thatë empty-handed

 ○ me duar kryq **1** with arms folded **2** sitting on one's hands, doing nothing

 ○ me duar lidhur "with hands tied" **1** sitting on one's hands, doing nothing **2** handcuffed, with hands tied

 ○ me duar ne xhepa **1** empty-handed **2** unprepared

 ○ me duar të lira with a free hand, without any constraint

 ○ ësh·të me dy fije brinjë to be weak and sick, be all skin and bones

 ○ me dy fytyra/faqe two-faced, hypocritical

 ○ ësh·të me dy krënde në vatër to be miserably poor, not have two sticks to rub together

 ○ me dy kuptime equivocal, ambiguous

 ○ me dyer te hapur open to the public

 ○ me dyer të mbyllura behind closed doors, in private session

 ○ me dhëmbë jashtë *(Pej)* grinning like a stuck mule

 ○ me faqe në dhe shamefacedly

 ○ me faqe të bardhë successfully

 ○ me faqe të zezë "with a dark face" shamed

 ○ me fat lucky, fortunate

 ○ me ferman *(Pej)* with a bad reputation

◦ **me fëmijë e me rropulli** with all one's family and belongings: with the whole kit and kaboodle

◦ **me fjalë të tjera** in other words, that is; otherwise

◦ **me fjalë të prera** in words of one syllable, flat out

◦ **me fjalën e parë** no sooner said than done, at the first word, immediately on hearing it

◦ **me fjalët e mia** "in my own words" in plain language; without going into detail, in a word

◦ **me forcë 1** by force **2** with insistence, insistently

◦ **me forcën** <*e vet*> relying entirely on one's own resources

◦ **me forcën e bajonetës** at the point of a bayonet, by force of arms, by violence

◦ **me frymën pezull** with bated breath

◦ **me frymën e shenjtë** (*Iron*) by supernatural power, as if by magic

◦ **me frymën pezull** "with breath/heart in suspension" in a state of great anxiety

◦ **me furi** frantically

◦ **me fytyra të prera** looking upset

◦ **me fytyrë** with a frown on one's face; looking angry/upset

◦ **me gëzim** joyfully

◦ **me gojë hapur/hapët 1** spellbound **2** watering at the mouth, eagerly

◦ **me gojë të qepur** not saying anything, without saying a word

◦ **me gojën plot** sincerely, openly; with confidence; courageously; impudently

◦ **me grurë në gojë** very ill, about to die

◦ **me grykën pushkës** "with the muzzle of a gun" by force: at the muzzle of a gun

◦ **me gur në kokë** at the cost of great personal hardship

◦ **me gjak të butë 1** mild mannered **2** calmly, unexcitedly, without making a fuss

◦ **me gjak të ftohtë** with a cool head, cool-tempered

◦ **me gjak të ndezur** with blood boiling, in rage

◦ **me gjak të ngrirë** "with frozen blood" with blood run cold: frozen with fear, in great fear

◦ **me gjak të nxehtë** with blood boiling, blazing with rage

◦ **me gjak të zemrës** "with one's heart blood" with all one's heart

◦ **me gjasë 1** apparently, it seems **2** perhaps, chances are

◦ **me gjashtë gishta** having a tendency to take things that don't belong to one: sticky-fingered

◦ **me gjithë dëshirë** with pleasure; willingly

◦ **me gjithë lecka** including/with everything

◦ **me gjithë mend** in earnest, seriously

◦ **me gjithë opinga** (*Colloq*) with everything, in entirety

◦ **me gjithë qejf** (expresses warm approval of an offer or request) with pleasure, delighted; pleased to do it; yes, certainly

◦ **me gjithë zemër** sincerely, honestly, gladly

◦ **me gjithë** [ ] together with [ ], including [ ], and all [ ]

◦ **me gjoks hapur** courageously; without hesitation

◦ **me gjoks 1** with all one's might, unsparingly **2** resolutely, with determination

◦ **me gjoks të hapur** courageous

◦ **me gjysëm goje** hesitating, undecided, gingerly

◦ **me gjysmë zëri** speaking without conviction; speaking timidly; expressing reluctance

◦ **me gjysmë fryme** barely breathing; looking ghastly and pale

◦ **me gjysmë goje** speaking without conviction; speaking timidly; expressing reluctance

◦ **me gjysmë hapi** moving hesitantly/slowly

◦ **me gjysmë mendjeje** reluctantly

◦ **me gjysmë shpirti** thin and barely able to stand, emaciated and feeble

◦ **me gjysmë zemre** reluctantly

◦ **me gjysmë fjale** "with half words" hesitatingly, without conviction; with quivering voice, with fear and trembling

◦ **ësh·të me gjysmë opinge** "be with half a clog" to be very poor, live in abject poverty

◦ **me hapin e breshkës** too slowly, at a snail's pace

◦ **me hata** by force; unwillingly, against one's will, reluctantly

◦ **me hesap** while careful with one's expenses: thriftily

◦ **me hënë përpjetë** during the waxing of the moon

◦ **me hënë poshtë** during the waning of the moon

◦ **me hënë të mirë** in a good mood

◦ **me hënë** moody

◦ **me hënëz** moody

◦ **me hënëz të mirë** in a good mood

◦ **me hir** willingly, voluntarily

◦ **me hir e me pahir** willingly or unwillingly, willy-nilly

◦ **me hollësi** in detail

◦ **me hope** (*Fig*) with irregular bursts of activity

◦ **me hosten prapa** unwillingly, against one's will

◦ **me humbje** yielding a loss, at a loss

◦ **me humor** humorous

◦ **me humor të mirë/keq** in a good/bad humor

◦ **me hundë plloçak** pug-nosed, snub-nosed

◦ **me hundë** *të varura* ∥ *varur* frowning

◦ **me hundën çip** having a pointed nose turned up at the tip

◦ **me hundën përpjetë** arrogantly: nose in the air

◦ **s'ësh·të me inat** it *can*not be done by force

◦ **me interes** of interest, of importance

◦ **me intervale** now and then, from time to time; by fits and starts

◦ **me jakë të ngrirë** with a well-ironed collar

◦ **me kalem në dorë** (pencil poised and) ready to work

◦ **me katër duar** light-fingered/skillful/professional/real (thief)

◦ **me këmbë e me duar** by might and main, with all one's might

◦ **me këmbë në kapërcell** unable to get out of a predicament, in a predicament, at one's wit's end

◦ **ësh·të me këmbë në yzengji** "be with one's foot in the stirrup" **1** to be about to leave **2** to have an easy work environment

◦ **me këmbë nga dielli** "with legs pointed to the sky" (*Impol*) dead as a doornail

◦ **me këmbë prej balte** with feet of clay

◦ **me këmbë si kleçka** having skinny legs

◦ **me kët** (*Colloq*) in small amounts: sparingly

◦ **me këte sebep** on this occasion

◦ **me kobure në brez 1** by force and threat of force: belligerent(ly) **2** boastful(ly)

◦ **me kohë 1** long ago **2** after a length of time: in time **3** soon enough: in time, in plenty of time, with time to spare

◦ **me kokë në qiell 1** very tall **2** (*Pej*) conceited

◦ **me kokë në torbë/trastë/thes** in great danger

◦ **me kokë poshtë** with head bowed (in shame/submission)

○ **(ve·te/vje·n/shko·n/rri·) me kokë të prerë** "come/go/stay with head cut off" (to go/come/sit) with head bent low, looking downcast

○ **me kokë ulur** with head bowed = **koku'lur**

○ **me kokën në gërshërë** in great danger

○ **me kordhë (në dorë)** by force or threat of force

○ **me krahë të zbuluar** [Mil] having exposed flanks

○ **me krye në hi** in a depressed/miserable mood, downcast

○ **me krye në qiell 1** very tall **2** (Pej) conceited

○ **me kryet në torbë/trastë/thes** in great danger

○ **me kuadrat** checkered

○ **me kuç e me maç** with the whole kit and kaboodle, with everything but the kitchen sink

○ **me kujdes** carefully, attentively; cautiously, gingerly

○ **me kujë e me bujë** with noisy confusion, in a loud hubbub

○ **me kulaç e me kërbaç** by threats and blandishments, sometimes the carrot and sometimes the stick

○ **me kurriz** with one's back hunched forward, slumping forward

○ **me kurriz ulur** with bended back: submissive; humble

○ **me kuturi** off the top of one's head

○ **me laçkë e me plaçkë** with all one's family and possessions

○ **me lak e me gjak** (by means of) great pain and suffering

○ **me lak në qafë** "with a noose around one's neck" in serious trouble; pregnant

○ **me laps në dorë** (pencil poised and) ready to work

○ **me lecka e me pecka** with all one's belongings

○ **me lecka në krah** unsettled and always on the road; just waiting to move with all one's family and baggage

○ **me lecka në zemër** in a state of fearful anxiety

○ **me lepe e me peqe** (Pej) kowtowing, servile

○ **me lesh** hairy

○ **me lëng e me piëng** with bag and baggage

○ **me lot përfaqe** with tear's in one's eyes

○ **me lugë në brez** "with spoon in the belt" **1** (Pej) interested only in eating **2** always freeloading

○ **me masë 1** in just the right/proper amount **2** economically, in sparing amounts

○ **me mbarësi** nicely, well

○ **me mendje të fjetur** unworried: with one's mind at ease

○ **me mendje të lehtë** foolishly

○ **me mendje të ngritur** having one's mind elsewhere, mentally distracted

○ **me mendje të shtruar 1** in a calm manner, coolly **2** with differences put to rest

○ **me mijë për qind** with absolute certainty: a hundred ("thousand") per cent sure

○ **me mish e me gjak/kocka** alike in every detail: exactly alike

○ **me mish e me shpirt** body and soul, with all one's might

○ **me natë** at night

○ **me nder jush** (used before saying/doing something very impolite) excuse me, begging your pardon

○ **me nder qofsh** "may you be with honor" (in answer to a thank you) you're welcome

○ **me ndezje automatike** with automatic ignition: self-starting

○ **me ndërgjegje (të plotë) 1** fully conscious **2** conscientiously

○ **me nerva** with nerves on edge; nervous; hot-tempered

○ **me ngalëz** with a haunting fear caused by guilt

○ **me nge** in no hurry

○ **me ngjyra të trëndafilta** "with rosy colors" (Book) (painted over) in rosy colors, made to look rosy

○ **me nishan** marked with distinction

○ **me numër 1** each already assigned, all reserved **2** very few; sparingly

○ **me një fjalë** briefly, in short, in other words

○ **me një frymë** with a single breath, in one go, at one stretch; quickly

○ **me një gojë** "with one mouth" in unison, in chorus; unanimously

○ **me një grusht miza** "with a handful of flies" **1** buzzing/raging with anger **2** in a sullen/unfriendly manner

○ **me një të rënë të penës/lapsit** with a stroke of the pen/pencil

○ **me një të rënë të shkopit** with a wave of the magic wand: without apparent effort, as if by magic; miraculously

○ **me një zë** (Fig) with a single voice: unanimously

○ **me okë** (Impol) in large amount: by the ton, up the kazoo

○ **me orar e pa orar** (Book) without regard to time limits: at any hour of the day; with or without an appointment; around the clock

○ **ësh·të me orë të këqija/liga** "be with the bad fairies" to be in a bad mood

○ **me orë të tëra** for hours at a time, for hours on end

○ **me pa të keq** without malice, innocently

○ **me padashje** unwillingly, involuntarily

○ **me pahir** against one's will: unwillingly, reluctantly; by force

○ **me pakicë** at retail

○ **me pallë të zhveshur** "with sword/knife unsheathed" with the open threat of force

○ **me pa-të-keq** without malice, innocently

○ **me pe e me gjilpërë** in complete detail

○ **ësh·të**³⁸ᵍ **me pehriz** to be scarce, be hard to find

○ **me periudha** with interruptions, in stops and starts

○ **me pesë para në xhep** "with five cents in the pocket" having very little money/property

○ **me peshoren e farmacistit** "with apothecary scales" measured out with precision; measured out to the last bit; with detailed precision

○ **me përpikëri matematike *1** with absolute certainty **2** with mathematical precision

○ **me plaçka në shkop** "with all one's belongings at the end of a stick" **1** homeless and poor **2** acting like a vagabond, moving around from place to place

○ **me plaçkë e me laçkë** with the whole kit and kaboodle, with bag and baggage

○ **me plotësi zërash** (Book) as one, unanimously

○ **me pohe e me bujë** (Pej) with much pomp and circumstance, making a big to-do about it

○ **me potencë** (Colloq) very influential; powerful

○ **me pula e me zogj** with the whole family

○ **ësh·të me pushkë në faqe** "be with a gun at one's cheek" to be ready to shoot/fight

○ **me qefin nën sqetull//në kokë** "with one's shroud under the armpit//on one's head" in great danger

○ **me qen e me mace** with the whole kit and kaboodle, with everything but the kitchen sink

○ **me që ra fjala** now that it (the subject) has come up, since it has been mentioned, by the way, incidentally

○ **me që __** since __, given that __

○ **me qëllim** on purpose

○ **me qëllim që** in order that, so that, with the aim that

○ **me qind për qind** with absolute certainty, without any doubt

○ **me qira** for rent/hire

○ **me radhë** in a row; in order; by turn, in turn

○ **me rast e pa rast** without any particular occasion, at any time at all

○ **me rastin e __** on the occasion of __

○ **me rendë** at a run

○ **me rob e robi** including everyone in the household, old and young

○ **me rrezik koke** dangerous to life and limb

○ **me rrënjë** down to the last detail

○ **me rrjeta të paprekura** "with the nets untouched" [*Sport*] in/to a scoreless tie

○ **me rroc e me koc** with the whole kit and kaboodle; with the whole family; with everything but the kitchen sink

○ **me rrugë të tërthortë** in a roundabout way, indirectly; by devious means

○ **me sa dëgjohet qyqja në dimër** "as much as the cuckoo is heard in winter" keeping completely silent, saying nothing

○ **me sa ka· në kokë** at the top of one's voice

○ **me sa palë mend?** "with how many piles of brains?" what kind of brains were used (to do something foolish)?

○ **me se** with what, the wherewithal, the means

○ **me siguri matematike** with absolute certainty

○ **me siguri** certainly, most assuredly

○ **me sistem rrethi** [*Sport*] round robin

○ **me sjellje të lehtë** frivolous, irresponsible

○ **me sot me nesër** one of these days; pretty soon, in the near future

○ **me strajcë në krah** with one's hand out: begging, begging for alms

○ **me sustë** with total ease, without any problem

○ **(çmo·n/mat·/përcakto·n) me sy** (to estimate/measure/determine) by eye, (make) a rough estimate, eyeball it

○ **me sy hapur/hapët** courageously; without hesitation

○ **me sy të lirë** with the naked eye

○ **me sy të perënduar** barely able to keep one's open

○ **me sy të vlagët** with eyes wet with tears

○ **me syrin/sytë xixë** keeping a sharp lookout, vigilant

○ **me sytë duman** with eyes fogged over

○ **me sytë e zemrës** "with the heart's eye" out of pure love, relying only on one's heart

○ **me shajak e me dajak** by threats and blandishments, sometimes the carrot and sometimes the stick

○ **me shkëmbim të <>** in trade, by exchange

○ **me shkop** by force/compulsion

○ **me shkopin magjik** with a wave of the magic wand: without apparent effort, as if by magic; miraculously

○ **me shkumë në gojë** foaming at the mouth; in a foaming rage

○ **me shpatë në brez** *(Pej)* out for blood, up to no good, ready to strike

○ **me shpatë të zhveshur** "with sword/knife unsheathed" with the open threat of force

○ **me shpinë në tokë** "with back on the ground" **1** down on one's knees: subjugated **2** defeated, vanquished

○ **me shpinë ulur** with bended back: submissive; humble

○ **ësh·të me shpirt ndër dhëmbë** to be in a terrible state of health; be in a terribly difficult situation

○ **me shpirt ndër dhëmbë 1** with great pain and effort **2** at death's door

○ **me shtatë zemra** "with seven hearts" incredibly courageous, absolutely fearless, dauntless

○ **me shtëpi e bagëti** with all one's family and possessions

○ **me tahmin 1** *(Colloq)* as a guess **2** by groping; by trial and error

○ **me terezi** very carefully; cautiously

○ **me tesha e kotesha** with everything but the kitchen sink; bag and baggage

○ **me të parë e me të bërë** see how things go before deciding anything, let's first see how it goes

○ **me të dy duart** unstintingly

○ **me të keq** by pure force, forcibly

○ **me të butë** with good will, without bitterness, softly

○ **me të fortë** by force, under pressure, unwillingly

○ **me të shpejtë** in a hurry, quickly

○ **me të urtë 1** quietly and calmly, gently **2** by gentle persuasion

○ **me të vërtetë** in fact, indeed, really; truly

○ **me të gjitha të mirat** having everything one needs, with all one's needs satisfied

○ **me të mirë** by gentle persuasion

○ **me të qeshur e me të ngjeshur** pretending to be in fun, but in fact intended with malice

○ **me të qeshur** in fun, not seriously, as a joke

○ **me të gjallë e me të vdekur** "with the living and with the dead" including everyone living or dead

○ **me të** {*adjective*} {*adjective*}ly

○ **me të** {*participle*} when it {}-ed

○ **me tërë forcën** "with all one's strength" **1** with all one's might **2** with vigorous insistence, vigorously insisting

○ **me tërë mend** seriously

○ **me trastë e me torbë** in huge amounts: in abundance; by the carload

○ **me tre pash diell** (Turkish time) at three o'clock

○ **me tru e me zemër** devoted body and soul

○ **me trup e me zemër** completely, entirely: body and soul

○ **me trup si ngjalë** slim and lithe; slim

○ **me urinj *të varura//varur*** frowning

○ **me themel** on a solid basis

○ **me thes** by the sackful: in large quantities

○ **me pallë të zhveshur** "with sword/knife unsheathed" with the open threat of force

○ **me thikë ndër dhëmbë** *(Pej)* with teeth bared, in a threatening way

○ **me thonj e me dhëmbë** *(Pej)* with might and with main

○ **me thonjtë e duarve** by one's own efforts/sweat

○ **me urdhër të peshkut** "by command of the (magic) fish" *(Iron)* without putting oneself out, not requiring much effort

○ **me urë e pa urë** "with or without a bridge" by all manner and means, at all costs

○ **me veshë të mprehur** with keen ears

○ **me veshë të ngritur** ears cocked, listening alertly

○ **me veshët ngrehur** with ears cocked

○ **me veshët pip** with ears pricked attentively; sharp-eared

○ **me vrap** hastily; speedily

○ **(njeri) me vulë** (person) with a bad reputation,

○ **me xhepin e huaj** at someone's else expense

○ **me yll në ballë *1** distinguished from the crowd, heads and shoulders above the others **2** outstanding in valor, courageous

○ **me zarar** risky

○ **me zemër në fyt** choking with anger

○ **me zemër të bardhë** generous and amiable

○ **me zemër të copëtuar** deeply touched/moved, with a broken heart

○ **me zemër të çjerrë** heartbroken

○ **me zemër të gjerë** tolerant; generous

○ **me zemër të hapur/çelur** honestly

○ **me zemër të ngrirë** "with frozen heart" in terrible dread: with one's heart in one's throat, frozen with fear, in great fear

○ **me zemër të plasur 1** dispirited, down in the mouth **2** brokenhearted; pining

○ **me zemër të plotë** without any reservation; wholeheartedly

○ **me zemër të prishur 1** heartbroken **2** in a bad mood

○ **me zemër të thyer 1** with great reluctance, reluctantly **2** hurting from a serious emotional blow, grieving deeply

○ **me zemrën pezull** "with breath/heart in suspension" in a state of great anxiety

○ **me zë 1** aloud **2** in oral form, orally

○ **me zile të madhe** "with a big bell" with a lot of influence, influential

○ **me** [ ] [ ](al)ly **me gëzim** joyfully

me·n

I § vt **1** to reduce [ ] gradually in amount: drain away **2** to reduce [ ] gradually in intensity: diminish [ ] , gradually stop [ ], alleviate [ ]

II § vi **1** to let up, stop gradually **2** to be still/quiet, stop (talking)

meazallah *adv (Colloq)* God forbid

mec *nm (Reg)* lad

mecen *nm (Book)* generous patron: Maecenas

mecenatë *nf (Book)* patronage: maecenatism

meçe *nf* small clay jug

***meçitun** *adj (i) (Reg Gheg)* exhausted by hunger

meçkadin *nm [Bot]* = **bujgër**

***meçkar** *nm [Bot]* = **bujgër**

meçke *nf* female dog: bitch

***medajë** = **medalje**

medalje *nf* medal

○ **ana tjetër e medaljes** *(Fig)* the other side of the coin/matter

medaljon *nm* medallion

medet

I § interj (Colloq) woe is me! oh god!; (commonly expressed in English by groaning)

II § nm **1** terrible disaster, catastrophe **2** help, remedy, salvation

mediane *nf [Math]* median

mediçinë *nf (Book)* medicine (as a field)

mediokër *adj (BookImpolite)* mediocre

mediokritet *nm (Book)* mediocrity

***mediqinë** *nf (Old)* medicine = **mjekësi**

***meditje** *nf* = **meditje**

medium *nm (Book)* person who acts as a go-between to communicate with dead spirits: medium

medoemos *adv* unquestionably, certainly, definitely, absolutely

medrese *nf [Relig]* school for advanced training of Moslem priests and teachers of Moslem law: Moslem seminary

meduzë *nf* **1** Medusa **2** [Invert] medusa = **kandil deti**

mefshtë *adj (i)* sluggish, lethargic; slothful, indolent

mefshtësi *nf* sluggishness, lethargy; slothfulness, indolence

mega *format* mega-

megafon *nm* megaphone

megaloman *nm* megalomaniac = **mendjemadh**

megalomani *nf* megalomania = **mendjemadhësi**

***megashtër** = **mëgashtër**

mego·n *vi 3rd*

○ **mego·**n^{3sg} **dita** *(Reg)* day breaks, it dawns

***megj·**et *vpr* (of fruit) to burst open

***megje** *nf* **1** border; boundary **2** railing

***megjetar** *n* inhabitant of a border area; neighbor

megjithatë *conj* even so, despite that, in spite of that; nevertheless, all the same

megjithëkëtë *conj* even so, in spite of this, despite this; nevertheless, all the same

megjithëqë *conj* although, even though

megjithëse *conj* although, even though

○ **megjithëse ... përsëri ...** although ... still ...

meh·et *vpr* to dwindle, diminish; dwindle away, fade away

meh *stem for pdef, opt, adm, part* <**me·**n

***mehane** = **mejhane**

mehir *adv* willingly, voluntarily = **me hir**

***mehit·**et = **mahit·**et

mehje *nf ger* **1** <**meh·**et ***2** stagnation

○ **mehje pune** work slow-up

Mehmet *nm* Mehmet (male name)

mehur *adj (i) (Reg Tosk)* inert, idle, static, stagnant

meit *nm (Colloq)* human corpse, cadaver: stiff

mejdan *nm (Old)* open ground: plain **2** battlefield; place for settling disputes by fighting **3** *(Fig)* open battle/contest

***mejdis** *(Old)* = **midis**

meje *pron 1st sg abl* <**unë**

mejhane *nf* **1** = **pijetore 2** *(Pej)* noisy smoke-filled saloon

mejhanexhi *nm (np ~ nj)* saloon-keeper

***mejt** *stem for pdef, opt, adm, part* <**me·**n *(Reg Gheg Old)*

***mejt** = **mend**

mejtep *nm (Old)* primary parochial school for Moslem children

***mejtës** *adj, nm (Old Regional Gheg)* palliative

mek· *vt* **1** to tire [ ] out completely: exhaust, wear out **2** to weaken, make faint **3** to make limp [ ] by moistening; soak

mek·et *vpr* **1** to grow limp with fatigue; get worn out from laughing or crying; grow faint **2** to go completely slack: be petrified, be dumbfounded **3** to get stuck **4** to get limp from moisture; get a little wet **5** to slacken, die down gradually, fade away

○ <> **mek·**et^{3sg} **goja** <> *stutters*

○ <> **mek·**et^{3sg} **jeta** <>'s life *dwindles* away, <> *is* gradually dying

meka'm *nm (Old)* **1** tomb of a Moslem saint, holy sepulcher **2** [*Mus*] melody

mekanik
  I § *adj* mechanical
  II § *nm* mechanic

mekani'kë *nf* **1** mechanics **2** machinery

mekaniki'sht *adv* mechanically

mekanizato'r *n* repair mechanic

mekanizëm *nm* **1** mechanism **2** mechanics, procedural details

mekanizi'm *nm ger* **1** <mekanizo'·n **2** mechanization

mekanizo'·n *vt* to mechanize

mekanizu'ar *adj (i)* mechanized

****meka't** = mëkat

mekëri·n *vi* (of a goat) to bleat = vërret·

mekërimë *nf* <mekëri'·n

mekëris *stem for 1st sg pres, pl pres, 2nd & 3rd sg subj, pind* <mekëri't·

mekërit· *vt* = mekëri·n

me'k'ës *nm* soft part of the sole = me'ngës

me'kët *adj (i)* **1** damp **2** weak, faint, dim

mekëto'·n *vt* to dampen

me'kje *nf ger* <mek·, mek·et

****meko·n** = mëko'·n

meksika'n *adj, n* Mexican

Meksi'kë *nf* Mexico

meksh *nm* = mushko'r

me'kshëm *adj (i)* gasping, faint

mekto'·n *vt* to make [] wet, moisten

mekth *nm* **1** brief loss of consciousness: faint, swoon **2** baby rabbit, leveret

****mekth·** *vi* to blink, wink

me'kur *adj (i)* **1** tired and limp, exhausted; ready/about to faint **2** worn out from laughing or crying; feeling faint **3** dampened: faint, dim **4** damp and limp; withered and limp; limp

mel
  I § *nm* [*Bot*] millet, broom corn millet, hog millet, proso millet (*Panicum miliaceum*)
  II § *adv* *quiet, mum
  ○ **meli egër** [*Bot*] = kostre'vë

melankoli' *nf* melancholy

melankoli'k *adj (Book)* melancholic

melanu're *nf* [*Ichth*] saddled bream *Oblada melanura*

mela'qe *nf* [*Folklore*] mountain nymph

mela'së *nf* molasses
  ○ **melasë e helmuar** poisoned molasses used as a spray insecticide on fruit trees

me'lcë *nf* [*Ichth*] young shad

meleku'qe *nf* [*Bot*] broomcorn, sorghum (*Sorghum vulgare*)

****mele'm** = melhe'm

mele'në *nf* [*Med*] bloody stool

mele'z
  I § *adj* of mixed race/breed: crossbred
  II § *nm* crossbreed, halfbreed

mele'ze *nf* **1** fine silk thread **2** thin textile made of silk and cotton

mel'ës *nm* variety of white grape with small fruit

mel'ëse *nf* livestock animal that is small

melhe'm *nm (Colloq)* **1** [*Med*] ointment, salve **2** balm for the spirit

meli'cë *nf* wooden hackle (for pounding flax)

****meli'ngër** *nf* **1** [*Entom*] plant louse, aphid **2** Aphidodea

****melingo'në** = milingo'në

melisdra'v *nm* = mëzhdra'vë

****melixha'ne** OR **melixha'në** *nf* = patëllxha'n

****melki'm** *nm ger* <melko'·n

****melko'·n** *vt* to care for [], foster, feed

****melme·n** *vt* **1** = mëlme·n **2** to prepare [food]

melodi' *nf* melody

melodi'k *adj* of or pertaining to melody: melodic

melodio'z *adj* melodious, musical, melodic, dulcet

melodi'shëm *adj (i)* = melodio'z

melodrama'tik *adj* melodramatic

melodra'më *nf* melodrama

melo're *nf* field of millet

me'ltë *adj (i)* made of millet

melth *nm* [*Bot*] compound raceme: (*panicle*)

****melxha'ne** *nf* = patëllxha'n

****mell** *nm* [*Bot*] kind of mistletoe (*Loranthus europaeus*)

mella'n *nm (Old)* ink (for writing)

me'llë *nf (Reg)* **1** kind of white clay used for pottery, marl **2** alluvial mud

mellu'rë *nf* [*Bot*] vine blight (*Peronospora*)

membra'në *nf* membrane

meme'c *adj, n* **1** mute; dumb; deaf-mute **2** (*Fig*) desolate

memeci' *nf* [*Med*] mutism

****meme'li'ke** = mëmëli'gë

Me'mo *nf with masc agreement* Memo (male name)

memorandu'm *nm* [*Dipl*] memorandum

memu'll *nm* [*Ichth*] = menu'll

memu'r *nm (Old)* functionary

me'mzi' *adv (Colloq)* with difficulty, barely

MENA *abbrev (English)* Middle East News Agency

****me'na'tet** *adv* **1** in the morning; next morning **2** = mena'të

me'na'të *adv* early in the morning: not yet light, still dark, before daybreak

****me'na'ti** *adv* = mena'të

me'nçëm *adj (i)* = me'nçur

me'nçur
  I § *adj (i)* **1** smart; intelligent **2** knowledgeable **3** wise; sage
  II § *n (i)* brainy/wise/knowledgeable person

mençuri' *nf* intelligence, wisdom, sagacity

mend
  I § *np* brains, mind, intellect
  II § *pcl* nearly, almost
  ○ **nuk ka· (as) pesë/dy para mend** not have (even) a nickel's worth of brains
  ○ **ësh-të ndër mend** (only in questions or negative sentences) to be in one's right mind
  ○ **mend për tjetër herë** next time we'll know better; keep it in mind for next time

menda'k *adj* = mendalo'k

mendalo'k *adj* smart, intelligent

menda'r *adj* **1** smart, intelligent **2** thinking, deep in thought **3** (*Old*) = mendo'r

****menda'ri'** *nf (Old)* intelligence; mentality

****mendata'r** (*Old*) = mendimta'r

me'nde *nf* mind, will

****mende'hû** *adj* pigheaded, obstinate

me'nd_ër *nf* [Bot]mint *(Mentha L.M)*

  ◦ **mend_ër e 'butë** [Bot] peppermint *Mentha piperita L.* = **nenexhik**

  ◦ **mend_ër e egër** pennyroyal *Mentha pulegium L.*

mend_ë'risht *adv* mentally

me'nd_ër'z *nf* [Bot] peppermint *(Mentha piperita L.)*

mend_ësi *nf* (Book) conceptual manner: mentality

*****mendil** *nm* handkerchief

mendim *nm* 1 thinking 2 thought 3 opinion, judgment

Mendim *nm* Mendim (male name)

mendimtar *n* thinker

me'ndje *nf* 1 thinking ability, mental capacity, intelligence: intellect, mind 2 opinion, judgment; advice 3 attention 4 thinking, mental activity 5 memory, mind 6 (Colloq) intention

  ◦ **<> është bërë mendja** {sport/muzikë} <> thinks of nothing but {sports/music}

  ◦ **Mendja e madhe e zeza e të zot.** "A big head, suffering for its owner" (Prov) Pride goeth before a fall.

  ◦ **Mendja e madhe ta thyen qafën/zverkun.** "A big head will break your neck" (Prov) Pride goeth before a fall.

  ◦ **mbaj/mbani mendjen!** "keep your mind!" (said to someone in a rage) keep cool! calm down! take it easy!

  ◦ **ta merr/pret mendja** "your mind gets it" (Colloq) it is obvious/self-evident, of course; there's no doubt, undoubtedly; obviously! of course!

mendje akre'p *adj* malevolent

mendje ba'rdhë *adj* prepossessing, confidence-inspiring

mendje ça'lë *adj* weak-minded

mendje fe'mër *adj* having a fertile mind: creative

mendje fje'tur *adj* 1 mentally calm and assured 2 (Pej) mentally sluggish

mendje flu'tur *adj* frivolous, flighty

mendje fry'rë *adj* swell-headed

mendje fshe'h ur *adj* secretive

mendje fy'çkë *adj* featherbrained, empty-headed

mendje fy'ell *adj* rattlebrained

mendje gje'rë *adj* broadminded; knowledgeable

mendje gjer_ë'si *nf* broadmindedness; broad knowledge

mendje ho'llë *adj* quick-witted, sharp, smart, clever

mendje holl_ë'si *nf* quick-wittedness, sharpness, cleverness

mendje hu' *adj* hard-headed, obstinate, stubborn

mendje hu'mb ur *adj (i)* not in one's right mind, not right in the mind

mendje ke'q *adj* malevolent, evil-minded

mendje ko'të *adj* frivolous

mendje kthje'll ët *adj* clear-minded

mendje lara'skë *adj, nf* foolish/silly (woman)

mendje la'rtë *adj* (Poet) high-minded

mendje le'ht *adj (i)* lacking good sense: foolish; shallow, silly

  ◦ **mendjelehtë si miza** flighty, featherbrained, foolish

mendje leht_ë'si *nf* lack of good sense: foolishness; shallowness, silliness

mendje li'g *adj* evil-minded, malevolent

*****mendje li'rë**

  I § *adj* freethinking; liberal; frank

  II § *n* freethinker, liberal

*****mendje li'r'i** *nf* freedom of thought

mendje ma'dh *adj* arrogant, conceited

mendje madh_ë'si *nf* arrogance, conceit

mendje mble'dh ur *adj* mentally composed; decided in the mind

me'ndje-me'ndje *adv* 1 irresolute 2 of different minds, having different opinions

mendje mëdhe'nj *adj masc pl* <**mendjema'dh**

mendje mi'rë *adj* well-intentioned

mendje mpre'htë *adj* mentally sharp, smart, clever

mendje mpreht_ë'si *nf* mental sharpness, cleverness

mendje my'kur *adj* old-fashioned (in mentality)

mendje ndri'tur *adj* enlightened

mendje ndry'shk ur *adj* 1 mentally retarded 2 outmoded in one's thinking

mendje ngri'tur

  I § *adj* nervous; highstrung; preoccupied

  II § *adv* nervously

mendje ngu'shtë *adj* narrow-minded; ignorant

mendje ngusht_ë'si *nf* narrow-mindedness; ignorance

mendje pa'k = **mendjepakët**

mendje pa'kët *adj, n* (person) without much upstairs, dim-witted/foolish (person)

mendje plo'gë = **mendjeplo'gët**

mendje plo'gët *adj* slow-witted, sluggish in thinking, stupid

mendje pri'sh_ës *adj* puzzling, persuasive

mendje pri'sh ur *adj* out of one's wits

mendje pu'lë *adj* featherbrained

*****mendje si** *nf* astuteness, ingenuity

mendje shka'th ët *adj* quick-witted, bright, clever

mendje shkre'të *adj* = **kokëshkre'të**

*****mendje shku'rtë** = **mendjeshku'rtër**

mendje shku'rtër *adj* thinking only of the short term: short-sighted

mendje tra'shë *adj* thickheaded, stupid

mendje trash_ë'si *nf* thickheadedness, stupidity

*****mendje u'lët** *adj* humble

mendje ve'ri *nf* scatterbrained

mendje zi

  I § *adj, n (fem sg ~ e'z, masc pl ~ i'nj, fem pl ~ e'za)* 1 (person) always having something bad to say; predicting, and therefore inviting, bad fortune 2 = **xhelo'z**

  II § *n (fem sg ~ e'z, masc np ~ i'nj, fem np ~ e'za)* pessimist

mendo'·het *vpr* 1 to ponder; think; worry 2 to be conceivable/thinkable

  ◦ **mendo'**·het e çmendo'·het to go crazy thinking about, really think hard about

  ◦ **mendo'**·het për [] to think [] over, reflect upon []

  ◦ **mendo'**·het të {verb} to think of {}ing, consider {}ing

mendo'·n *vi, vt* 1 to think; think of [], imagine 2 to consider, think about [] 3 to think over; contemplate 4 to remember, think about

  ◦ **mendo'**·n e çmendo'·n to turn over in the mind to find a solution, wrestle with (in the mind)

  ◦ **mendo'**·n e shmendo'·n to beat one's brains out thinking scenario's

  ◦ **mendo'**·n keq për [] to think ill of []

○ **mendo·n për** [] **1** to think of [], have an opinion of [] **2** to think about []; be concerned about []

○ **mendo·n shkurt** to make a <> hasty judgment

○ **mendo·n të** {*verb*} to intend to {}, think of {}ing

○ **mendo·n zi** to have a premonition of something bad

mendo'r *adj* **1** mental **2** intellectual **3** (*Colloq*) = **mendar**

me'nd shëm *adj (i)* = **mençur**

***mênd sh** *(Reg Gheg)* = **mënç**

***mend tari sht** *adv (Old)* mentally

***mend tret un** *adj (i) (Reg Gheg)* foolish

***mend tu'er** *adj (fem ¨ ore) (Old)* = **mendo'r**

mendu'ar

I § *adj (i)* **1** deep in thought, thoughtful **2** well-considered, given a lot of thought

II § *adv* deep in thought, in the process of thinking

III § *nn ger (të)* **1** < **mendo·n**, **mendo·het** **2** [*Psych*] the thinking process

***mendu'em** *adj (i) (Reg Gheg)* sensible

mendu'eshëm

I § *adj (i)* deep in thought, thoughtful

II § *adv* thoughtfully, deep in thought

menekshe *nf* [*Bot*] **1** = **shebo'jë 2** (*Reg*) violet

○ **menekshe gomari** periwinkle (*Vinca*)

***me'në** *nf* queen bee = **më'më**

mengene *nf* vise

***mêngë** *(Reg Gheg)* = **mëngë**

me'ng ës *nm* arch of the foot

***mêng ët** *(Reg Gheg)* = **mangët**

***mengjene** = **mengene**

meni'ngje *np* [*Anat*] meninges

meningji't *nm* [*Med*] meningitis

meni'sk *nm* [*Phys*] meniscus

menopa'uzë *nf* [*Med*] menopause

me'nsë *nf* institutional cafeteria

menso'lë *nf* [*Archit*] = **konso'l**

menstruacio'ne *np* (*Book*) menstruation

menshevi'k *adj* Menshevik

menshev i'zëm *nm* Menshevism

menta'k

I § *adj* brainy

II § *n* *thinker

mentalite't *nm* (*Book*) mentality = **mendësi**

***menta'r**

I § *adj* intelligent

II § *n* thinker

***menta'r ë** *np (Old)* intelligentsia

mente'shë *nf* hinge

***mento·n** = **mendo·n**

mento'r *nm* mentor

Mento'r *nm* Mentor (male name)

***me'nt shëm** = **mendshëm**

menue't *nm* [*Mus*] minuet

menu'll *nf* [*Ichth*] brown wrasse (*Labrus merula*)

***me'njan ësi** = **mënjanësi**

me'një *nf* **1** (*Colloq*) nectar from leaves = **mënjë 2** dairy animal that continues to give milk after an aborted birth

me'një he'rë *adv* **1** at once, immediately; all at once, suddenly **2** at the same time, simultaneously

me'një he'r shëm *adj (i)* **1** immediate; sudden **2** simultaneous

***me'njı zâ** *nf* = **me një zë** (*Reg Gheg*) unison

me qe'në që *conj* = **meqe'nëse**

me qe'në se *conj* it being the case that, given that, inasmuch as: since

me që *conj* = **meqe'nëse**

mera' *nf (Old)* pasture = **kullo'të**

mera'k *nm* (*Colloq*) **1** disquieting concern: worry, uneasiness, trouble **2** emotional distress: worry **3** eagerness to know something: nosiness **4** craving, yen **5** great care: devotion; love; conscientiousness **6** deepseated suspicion **7** (*Fig*) regret

merak le shë *nf* < **merakli**

merakli'

I § *adj* (*Colloq*) **1** conscientious **2** overly zealous **3** quick to fall in love **4** solicitous, concerned, worried **5** uneasy

II § *nm* zealot

merako's· *vt* (*Colloq*) to cause [] to worry, cause [] to feel uneasy: trouble, sadden

merako's·et *vpr* (*Colloq*) **1** to feel worried; feel uneasy **2** to feel conscientious: care

merako'sur *adj (i)* (*Colloq*) worried; uneasy; anxious

merak shëm *adj (i)* given to worrying, constantly anxious

mercena'r

I § *adj* mercenary; venal

II § *nm* **1** mercenary soldier **2** (*Colloq*) venal person

mercenari' *nf (Book)* **1** mercenary forces **2** mercenary soldiering

merceo'log *n* merchandise technologist

merceo logji' *nf* merchandise technology

merdo'stë *adj* (*Colloq*) **1** having a rough surface **2** (*Fig*) frowning, gloomy; cruel, bestial

Me'reme *nf* Mereme (female name)

meremeti'm *nm ger* **1** < **meremeto·n 2** repair work, repair

meremeto·n *vt* **1** to repair, mend **2** (*Fig*) to fix [] up temporarily, patch [] temporarily

meremetu'ar *adj (i)* repaired

meremetu'es *nm* repairman

me rendo·n *vt* (*Colloq*) to arrange in order, sort

mereqe'p *nm* (*Reg*) writing ink

***mere'sh ni'k** *nm* perfume

***mere'shtë** *nf* (*Reg Tosk*) strawberry tree = **mare**

me'rë *nf* **1** pleasant smell: aroma, fragrance **2** fear

me'r ëm *adj (i)* aromatic, fragrant

me'rgë *nf* [*Text*] thin patch

mergju'r *nm (Old)* [*Ethnog*] money given by bridegroom to bride's family to provide bride's trousseau

merhu'm *nm (Old)* the deceased

meridia'n *nm* [*Geog*] meridian

***merima'gë** = **merimangë**

merima'ngë *nf* **1** [*Invert*] spider; mite **2** (*Colloq*) spider-web, cobweb **3** (*Fig Colloq*) cleverly laid trap **4** (*Fig*) annoying person who sticks to like a burr **5** [*Invert*] (*Tetranychus telarius L.M*)

○ **merimanga e agrumeve** [*Invert*] red spider, red spider mite *Tetranychus telarius L.*

○ **merimanga e argjendtë** [*Entom*] citrus rust mite *Phyllocoptruta oleivora*

○ **merimangë deti** [*Invert*] spider crab *Maja squinado*

○ **merimanga e kopshteve** [*Invert*] garden spider *Aranea diademata*

○ **merimanga me kryq** [*Invert*] garden spider *Aranea diademata*

○ **merimanga e kuqe** [*Invert*] European red mite, red spider, red spider mite *Panonychus Ulmi Koch*

○ **merimanga e pambukut** [*Entom*] two-spotted spider mite *Tetranychus urticae Koch.*

merimango're *np* [*Invert*] arachnids *Arachnida*

*meringo'në = milingo'në

merino's *adj, n* merino (sheep)

meri'të *nf* merit

merito·n *vt* to merit; deserve

meritu'ar *adj (i)* **1** merited; deserved **2** (as a title conferred by an official body) meritorious, worthy

merit'ue'shëm *adj (i)* meritorious, commendable

merka'të *nf* retail market that sells food and household goods: grocery store, market

merku'r *nm* [*Chem*] mercury *(Hg)*

***Merku'r** *nm* = Mërkurr

merlu'c *nm* [*Ichth*] hake *(Merluccius merluccius)*

○ **merluc trependësh** [*Ichth*] blue whiting *Micromesistius poutassou*

merme'r

I § *nm* marble

II § *adj (Fig)* hard as marble

mermeri'zim *nm ger* <**mermerizo'·n**

mermeri'zo·n *vt* to marble

mermer'pun'ue's *nm* craftsman with marble, marble cutter

merme'r'të *nf* **1** of marble **2** *(Fig)* cold, frozen

merme' *adj (i)* fragrant, sweet-smelling

mero'·het *vpr* to suffer greatly; get very tired, be falling apart

***mersi'në = mërsi'në**

***merti's· = mërti's·**

merudhi'

I § *nf (Reg)* [*Bot*] = majdano's

II § *np* spices

Meru'she *nf* Merushe (female name)

merxha'n *nm* **1** = kora'l **2** ox with hair of a mixed brownish color **3** red wattle on fowl

merr·

I § *vt* **1** to take **2** to take [] away from <> **3** *(Colloq)* to take [] away; arrest []; capture **4** to take up []; start **5** to take on []: acquire; hire, engage **6** *(Colloq)* to take in []: include, contain **7** to get **8** to receive; accept **9** to gain/achieve; reach to [] **10** to be struck by [] **11** to contract/catch [a disease]; catch [something thrown] **12** to shorten, cut off [] **13** to head for []

II § *vi* to take a particular direction/path

○ **e merr·** {*verbal noun*} to commence {}, begin {}

○ **ia merr·** to head (in a direction), set out

○ [] **merr·** {*a quantity of money*} to pay {} for [], get [] for {}

○ **merr· ajër = ajros·***et*

○ [] **merr· ana 1** [] leans badly to one side **2** [] *is deteriorating*

○ **merr· anë 1** to lean **2** to take a breather, rest up a bit **3** *(Old)* to take part, participate

○ **<>a merr· anën** to come to understand <>; get the hang of <>

○ **merr· anën e <>** to side with <>

○ **<> merr· anët 1** to trim the sides of <>'s hair **2** to flank/outflank <>

○ **merr· anët** to get the sides of one's hair trimmed

○ **<> merr· arrat** "eat <>'s walnuts" {} can run rings around <>

○ [] **merr·**.³*ˢᵍ* **arratia** things *are getting* worse and worse for []

○ **merr· arratinë** to flee; make a getaway

○ **<a merr· avull** to get used to <>, get to know <> well

○ **merr· avull** to become heated, get angry

○ **<>a merr· avullin** to defeat <> badly, break the spirit of <>, take all the steam out of <>,

○ **merr· ballin e ballin** to take the best part

○ **<> merr· bashkën** to fleece <>, take <> to the cleaners

○ **merr· bishtin nën shalë** to leave in shameful defeat

○ **s'merr· bojë** that's not the way it should be (done)

○ **merr· botën** to spread to the entire world, become known everywhere

○ **merr· botën ndër sy** to go very far away from home; emigrate; flee to a far-off place

○ **merr· brijën** to run away somewhere, take to the hills

○ **<> merr· bukën të harro·n***ˢᵘᵇʲ* **djathin** "take <>'s bread in order that <> will forget about the cheese" to deprive <> of something of greater importance in order to forestall requests for an associated thing of less importance: block off a road to prevent complaints about the potholes

○ **merr· burrë** to get a husband

○ **merr· cen** to get scarred for life, get an infirmity; develop a paranoia

○ **merr· cifël** to begin to splinter

○ **i merr· çoparkat** *(Iron)* to pack up and leave; leave in a hurry

○ **<> merr· çupërinë** to deprive <> of her virginity: deflower <>

○ **merr· dallgë** to act with a sudden burst of energy/rage

○ **merr· detin me sy** "take the sea in the eye" to think too big

○ **merr· dërrmën** to scatter in confusion

○ **merr· dita** "daylight *increases*" the days *are getting* longer

○ **<> merr· dorën 1** to ask <>'s permission **2** to kiss <>'s hand as a form of very respectful greeting

○ **<>a merr· dorën** to come to understand <>; get the hang of <>

○ **merr· drejtqëndrimin 1** [*Mil*] to come to attention **2** to do as one is told, be compliant/deferential

○ **merr· dritë filmi** film *becomes* lightstruck

○ **merr· dynjanë** to spread to the entire world, become known everywhere

○ **merr·**.³*ˢᵍ* **dhenë dielli** "the sun *is reaching* to the earth" it *is getting* late

○ **merr· dhenë** to run away

○ **merr·**.³*ˢᵍ* **dheun** news *spreads*, the word *gets* around

○ **merr· dheun ndër sy** to go very far away from home; emigrate; flee to a far-off place

○ [] **merr·**.³*ˢᵍ* **era** "the wind *takes* []" **1** [] *goes* up in smoke: [] *comes* to naught; [] *disappears* **2** [] is*skinny*

○ **merr·**.³*ˢᵍ* **erë** to become known, come out in public

○ **s'merr· erë nga** {} to be completely ignorant about {}; not suspect a thing about {}

○ **<> merr· erë** to sniff <>; smell <>

◦ **merr· erë** to begin to smell bad = **qe lb·***et*

◦ **<> merr· erzin** "take away <>'s honor!" to insult <> terribly; humiliate <>; make <> suffer

◦ **merr· faqe** form a crust

◦ **i merr· faqen nuses** to remove facial hair from a bride

◦ **merr· fije** to develop cracks: crack

◦ **merr·**[3sg] **fjala dheun/dynjanë** news *spreads*, the word *gets* around

◦ **<> merr· fjalën** to make <> give <>'s word/promise

◦ **merr· fjalën** to take the floor (in order to speak at a meeting)

◦ **ta merr· fjalën nga goja** "take the word out of your mouth" to be quick-witted, get what you mean quickly (even before the word is out of your mouth)

◦ **i merr· fjalët nga këmbët** "take the words from the feet (from the wrong end)" to misinterpret what is said

◦ **i merr· fjalët e i vë· në rabush** "take the words and put them in the onion stalk" to let it go in one ear and out the other, ignore what is said

◦ **<> merr· fjalët nga këmbët** to misunderstand what <> *says*

◦ **merr· flakë 1** to get angry quickly: see red **2** to develop quickly: take fire

◦ **<> merr· flakë shpirti** "<>'s spirit *catches* fire" <> becomes inflamed (by a passionate feeling), <> *is* overcome by emotion

◦ **merr· fletë** to become enthusiastic/inspired; pluck up courage

◦ **e merr· frerin nëpër këmbë** to behave arrogantly as if no one can tell one what to do

◦ **merr· frikë** to become afraid

◦ **merr· frymë** to breathe, take a breath, inhale; be alive

◦ **<> merr· frymën 1** to tire <> out, exhaust <> **2** to make <> suffer, torture <>

◦ **merr· fund** to come to an end, finish

◦ **merr· fushat** to run away somewhere, take to the hills

◦ **<> merr·**[3sg] **fytyra zjarr** <>'s face becomes flaming red

◦ **merr· fytyrë** to take shape/form; become concrete/definite

◦ **merr· gardhin** to exceed the normal limit

◦ **merr· grua** to get a wife

◦ **merr· guximin** to have the audacity = **guxo·** ·*n*

◦ **merr· guximin të** _ to make bold to _

◦ **<>a merr· gjakun** to take blood revenge in behalf of <>

◦ [] **merr·**[3sg] **gjumi** [] *falls* asleep

◦ **<> merr· gjurmën** to follow <>'s tracks, trace/pursue <>

◦ **e merr· gjurmën mbrapsht** to start out the wrong way, take the wrong path

◦ **merr· gjysmën e lekut** (*Scorn)* to eat lead, get shot dead

◦ **merr· hakun** to take revenge

◦ **merr· hamull** to catch fire

◦ **merr· hekurat zvarrë** to act quickly/hastily

◦ **<> merr· horë shpirti** "<>'s spirit *catches* fire" <> becomes inflamed (by a passionate feeling)

◦ **merr· hundë për** [] to pluck up courage for [an action]

◦ **merr· huq** to take affront, get angry

◦ **merr· hyxhym** to act with a sudden surge of energy

◦ **<> merr· ijët** to occupy <>'s flank

◦ **merr· ikën** to run away, flee

◦ **merr· inat** to become indignant/huffy; take affront

◦ [] **merr· inat** to come to hate/dislike []

◦ **merr· jetë** to become lively; come to life

◦ **<> merr· kafshatën nga goja 1** to take the bread from <>'s mouth, take away <>'s last means of support; leave <> in helpless misery **2** <> is too inept to prevent others from taking the food right out of <>'s mouth: <> always lets others get the better of <>

◦ **e merr· kalanë nga brenda** "capture the castle from within" to succeed through one's connections to insiders

◦ [] **merr·**[3sg] **kalemi** [] *is* selected/chosen arbitrarily; good/bad luck *falls* to [] completely by chance

◦ **merr· karar** (*Colloq)* to get (back) on track

◦ **merr· këmbë 1** (of a small child) to begin walking **2** (of a thing/matter) to start to go well

◦ **merr·**[3sg] **këmbë (fjala)** it (the word) *gets* around, *gets* all over town

◦ **<> merr· këmbën** "take <>'s leg" take <>'s place, substitute for <>

◦ **merr· këmbët në krahë 1** to leave right away, take off like a bird **2** to be too tired to walk any more

◦ **merr· këmbët** to take to one's heels, get out of there fast

◦ **i merr· këmbët** *mbi supe**/**në krahë* "take one's legs over one's shoulders" to run away fast, take to one's heels

◦ **t'i merr· këpucët nga këmba/këmbët 1** to be a real thief: {} would steal the shirt off your back **2** to be entirely capable of doing something terrible to you

◦ **merr· kërrabën** "take up the shepherd's crook" to become a shepherd

◦ **<> merr·**[3rd] **kokaerë** <> *has* a screw loose, <> *has* flipped

◦ **<> merr· kokën** "take <>'s head" to kill <>

◦ **merr· kot 1** to get uptight/excited over nothing **2** to become conceited: get swell-headed

◦ **merr· krahë** to become enthusiastic/inspired; pluck up courage

◦ **<> merr· krahët** "take <>'s arms" **1** [*Mil*] to take <>'s flanks **2** to defeat <> by trickery

◦ **<>a merr· krahun** to come to understand <>; get the hang of <>

◦ **merr· krahun e <>** to take <>'s side, support <>

◦ **merr· krezmim** to be confirmed (in the faith)

◦ **merr· krisë** to develop a crack: crack

◦ **i merr· krundet për miell** "take bran to be flour" to be easy to deceive, be very gullible

◦ **<> merr·**[3rd] **kryet erë** <> *has* a screw loose, <> *has* flipped

◦ **merr· lak** to warp

◦ **merr· lartësi** to gain altitude; climb/rise high

◦ **merr· lebetinë** to become terrified

◦ **merr· lëng nën bisht** "get wet under the tail" to behave in an unrestrained manner: run wild

◦ **s'<> merr·**[3sg] **luga gjë** "<>'s spoon *gets* nothing" (*Tease)* <> *comes* out of it empty-handed

◦ **<>a merr· lumi të keqen** <> *is* rescued from a bad predicament; <> *escapes* from trouble

◦ [] **merr· lumi** "the river *takes* []" [] *suffers* a terrible blow, [] *gets* wiped out

◦ **merr· llasë** to get too much mollycoddling, get overly pampered

○ **merr· majë me majë** to eat just a little bit of each dish

○ **merr· malet** "take the mountains" **1** *(Colloq)* to take refuge in the mountains; take to the hills **2** to go out of one's mind: go crazy

○ **merr· malin me sy** to take to the hills and disappear

○ **<> merr·**^{3sg} **malli për** [] <> *has* a nostalgic longing for []; <> *misses* []

○ [] **merr· mbi shpatull/kurrizin/vete** to take [] upon oneself

○ [] **merr· me bu** to do [] hastily

○ [] **merr· me cep** to take [] amiss; take umbrage at [], resent []

○ [] **merr· me gur e me dhé** to take [] on willingly; take [] as gospel

○ **merr· me grushte** "get by handfuls" to make a lot of money

○ **<> merr· me ledha** to cajole, coax

○ **merr· me lopatë** "take by the shovelful" *(Colloq)* to do really well for oneself, earn a lot: *be making* a pile

○ [] **merr· me sy të keq** to consider [] in a bad light

○ [] **merr· me tallje** to treat [] as a joke, not take [] seriously

○ [] **merr· me teneqe** to humiliate [] publicly

○ [] **merr· me të keq** to treat [] roughly

○ [] **merr· me të mirë** to treat [] nice; talk nice(ly) to []; soothe []

○ [] **merr· me valë** to attack [a project] with great fervor, make a massive assault on []

○ **merr·** to treat []ly

○ [] **merr· me mend** to picture [] in one's mind: imagine []

○ **merr· mend** to listen to reason, understand

○ **<> merr·**^{3rd} **mendja erë** <> *has* a screw loose, <> *has* flipped

○ **<>a merr·**^{3sg} **mendja se** __ <> *believes/thinks* that __, <> *gets* the feeling that __, it *looks* to <> like __

○ **merr· mendjen e botës/të tjerëve** to be excessively influenced by the opinion of others

○ **<>a merr· mendjen 1** to make it impossible for <> to think/concentrate **2** to put <> under a spell, charm <>

○ [] **merr· mendsh** to make it impossible for [] to think/concentrate: take away []'s concentration, spoil []'s concentration

○ **<> merr· mendtë** to dazzle <>; bamboozle <>

○ **<>a merr· mendtë 1** to make it impossible for <> to think/concentrate **2** to put <> under a spell, charm <>

○ **merr· mendtë e botës/të tjerëve** to be excessively influenced by the opinion of others

○ **nuk merr· më frymë** to stop breathing; be dead

○ [] **merr·**^{3sg} **më qafë gryka** "[]'s throat gets [] into trouble" **1** [] *is* ruined by expenses for eating and drinking **2** [] *is* ruined by strong drink

○ [] **merr· më qafë 1** to embrace [] **2** to do [] a lot of harm, hurt [] badly; get [] into a lot of trouble, get [] into a jam/mess

○ [] **merr· më sysh** to put [] under a spell: give [] the evil eye

○ **merr· mëri** to bear a grudge

○ [] **merr· mësysh** to put [] under a spell, give [] the evil eye

○ **merr·**^{pl} **miell hua** to be close friends, be on especially friendly terms

○ **<> merr· nder** to rob <> of <>'s honor

○ **<> merr· nderin** "take away <>'s honor!" to insult <> terribly; humiliate <>

○ [] **merr· ndër krah** to embrace/hug []

○ **e merr· në bisht** to get it in the neck, take it on the chin

○ **merr· në film** to shoot a movie; film

○ [] **merr· në fill** to give consideration to [], consider []

○ [] **merr· në qafë 1** to embrace [] **2** to do [] a lot of harm, hurt [] badly; get [] into a lot of trouble, get [] into a jam/mess

○ [] **merr· në rrogë** to hire []

○ [] **merr· në sy** to face up to [a danger] courageously

○ [] **merr· në shenjë** to pick on []

○ **merr· në thua 1** to stumble **2** to blunder

○ [] **merr· nëpër gojë** to say bad things about [] behind []'s back

○ [] **merr· nëpër këmbë 1** to trample on []'s rights **2** to mistreat [], abuse []; bully

○ **merr· nga torba e hedh· në thes** to take from the poor and give to the rich

○ [] **merr· ngrykë** to hug [] (around the neck)

○ **merr· nishan** to take aim, aim at a target

○ **merr· nuse** (of a boy) to get married, take a bride

○ **e merr· nusen lakuriq** to marry a woman with no dowry

○ **merr· një bark zjarr** to get warmed up

○ **merr· një notë** to sing/play a note

○ **merr· një sy gjumë** to take a short nap

○ **merr· një zjarr** to get a bit of warmth, get warm

○ **merr·**^{3sg} **njësoj** (of an object being colored/painted/dyed) to become colored evenly

○ **t'i merr· opingat nga këmba/këmbët 1** to be a real thief: {} would steal the shirt off your back **2** to be entirely capable of doing something terrible to you

○ [] **merr·**^{3sg} **ora e ligë** "the bad fairy *gets* []" [] *is* completely ruined, *is* visited by disaster; [] *suffers* an untimely death

○ **merr· pafajësinë** [*Law*] to win on appeal, be exonerated

○ **e merr· pajë me vete** to bear the mark of one's shame forever

○ **<> merr· palcën** "suck the marrow from <>" *(Colloq)* to make <> suffer mercilessly; exploit <> mercilessly

○ **merr· palcën** to start going downhill

○ **merr· parasysh** to consider

○ [] **merr· parasysh** to take [] into account/consideration; consider []

○ **merr· pe e gjilpërë** "take thread and needle" *(Colloq)* to take everything but the kitchen sink

○ **merr· pezëm** to become inflamed, become sore

○ **(<>)[] merr· për (të) keq** to think <> is bad-intentioned: take (what <> does/did) [] wrong, get <> wrong

○ **merr· për (të) keq** to take a turn for the worse

○ [] **merr· për cep** to come to hate/dislike []

○ [] **merr· për flokësh** to grab [] by the hair, take [] by force

○ [] **merr· për kapital** to take [] as if it were serious

○ **nuk <> merr·**^{3sg} **{} për mbarë** <>'s {} *is* not going well

∘ [] **merr· për veshi** "take [] by the ear" to drag [] kicking and screaming, pull [] by the ear

∘ [] **merr· përpara 1** to push forward victoriously against [] **2** to put forth the argument that defeats [] **3** to squelch []

∘ **merr· përpjetë** to hit the ceiling, fly into a rage

∘ [] **merr· përsipër** to assume responsibility for []

∘ **merr· pisha nga të dy anët/krerët** "the pine log *is burning* from both sides" to get worse and worse

∘ **merr· pjesë** to take part, participate

∘ **merr· plasaritje** to develop a crack, develop cracks; (of skin) get chapped

∘ **e merr· plumbin** (*Colloq*) to get shot: get a taste of lead, eat lead

∘ **merr· porropinë** to be headed for destruction, be on the way to ruin

∘ **merr· postërojën** [*Mil*] to assume sentry duties

∘ **merr· poshtë** to take a downward direction: descend, go down

∘ [] **merr· prapa 1** to take [] on to follow in one's footsteps **2** to take [] back

∘ **nuk merr· pykë** not accept advice/criticism

∘ **merr· radhimin** [*Mil*] to get in rank, line up

∘ **merr· revan** to be on the road to ruin, go to Hell in a handbasket

∘ **merr· rrahën** to rush

∘ **merr· rrethin e daulles** "get the hoop of the drum" (*Iron*) to get off with nothing, come away with nothing

∘ [] **merr· rrezga-bjezga** to drag [] along behind

∘ [] **merr· rrëshqanë** to drag []

∘ **merr· rripat** to take to the hills, flee

∘ **merr· rripën** to go downhill

∘ [] **merr·**^{3sg} **rrjedha** [] *is* on a downhill course, [] *is* in rapid decline, [] *is getting* worse and worse

∘ **merr· rrokullimën** to tumble downhill; take a tumble

∘ **merr·**^{3sg} **rrugë** to get well under way

∘ **merr· rrugën** *1** to take to the road, leave home **2** to set off (on a trip/journey)

∘ **merr· rrugën për në** [] to set out for []

∘ **merr· rrugët 1** to leave home to seek one's fortune **2** to disappear without trace **3** to take to one's heels

∘ [] **merr· rryma** "the current takes []" [] *is carried* along by the current; [] *has* no choice but to go along with the crowd

∘ **merr· skërkat** to take to the hills, flee

∘ **merr· sokakët 1** to bum around after being expelled from one's home/country **2** to start travelling around, take to the road

∘ **merr· sokakun përpjetë** to climb (straight up)

∘ <>[] **merr· sot për nesër** to take [] from <> for a supposedly short time

∘ <>a **merr·**^{3sg} **syri** <> *thinks* <> can manage/handle/do it

∘ s'[] **merr·**^{3sg} **syri** [] *is* too vast for the eye to encompass

∘ **merr· sytë (e iku)** to get out fast, leave quickly, take to one's heels

∘ <> **merr· sytë 1** to dazzle <>, take <>'s breath away **2** to bamboozle

∘ **e merr· shapin për sheqer** "eat/accept alum as sugar" to trade something of value foolishly for something worthless

∘ **merr· shatë toka** "the soil *takes* a hoe" the ground *is* easy to hoe/cultivate

∘ **merr· shenjë** to take aim

∘ [] **merr· shenjë** to pick on []

∘ **merr· sheshin/sheshit** to become publicly known, be exposed; come out in the open

∘ **merr· shënim për** [] to take note of [], make special note of []

∘ **merr· shpirt 1** to become lively, become enlivened **2** to take heart

∘ <> **merr· shpirtin** to make <> suffer, put <> through Hell

∘ **merr· shuplakën** (*Old*) to get bewitched, be put under a spell

∘ **merr· shushavat** to flee in all directions; run far away

∘ **merre ta marrim** "take it so that we take it" catch-as-catch-can

∘ **merr· (të) tatëpjetën** to go downhill; take a turn for the worse, get worse and worse

∘ **merr· teposhtënn** to go downhill; take a turn for the worse, get worse and worse

∘ [] **merr· ters** to take [] amiss

∘ **merr· tesqere** (*Impol*) to cash in one's chips: die

∘ **nuk merr· të gdhendur** not accept advice/criticism, be incorrigible

∘ **merr· të keqen/ligën në sy** to face up to danger courageously

∘ **merr· të zezën** to reach the lowest point of misfortune/unhappiness: hit/touch bottom

∘ **merr· tingtingën** to go downhill; take a turn for the worse, get worse and worse

∘ **merr· torbën/trastën** to become a beggar

∘ **merr· trup** to grow bigger

∘ **merr· udhët/udhën e madhe 1** to leave home to seek one's fortune **2** to disappear without trace **3** to take to one's heels

∘ **merr·**^{3sg} **udhë** to get well under way

∘ **merr· udhë/udhën 1** to take to the road, leave home **2** to set off (on a trip/journey)

∘ **merr· udhën për në** [] to start out for [], leave/depart for []

∘ **merr· udhën e ujqve** to take the wrong path in life

∘ **nuk** <> **merr·**^{3sg} **ujë lopata/shati** "<>'s shovel can't lift much water" **1** <> *has* no influence, <> does not pull much weight **2** <> *does* not succeed

∘ **merr· ujë me shoshë/shportë** "take water with a screen/basket" to do useless work

∘ **merr· urdhër** to get one's orders

∘ <> **merr·**^{3sg} **uria** <> gets hungry

∘ **merr· valë 1** to reach a boil, start boiling **2** (*Fig*) to heat up, take a surge; get a big push, become animated

∘ **ia merr· valles** to begin to dance; dance

∘ **merr· vendim** to make a decision: decide

∘ **merr· vesh/vesht 1** to understand **2** to (come to) understand/know; become aware, find out, hear

∘ **nuk e merr·**^{3sg} **vesh i pari të dytin** "the first *does* not understand the second" there *is* utter confusion

∘ **nuk** <> **merr·**^{3sg} **vesh koka** "<>'s head *does* not hear" **1** <> *does* not listen/obey, <> *is* headstrong **2** <> simply *will* not get it into <>'s head, <> *is* pigheaded

∘ **e merr· vesh ku rreh·**^{3sg} **çekani** to understand the heart of the matter, get the real point, understand what's really going on

∘ **merr· vesh nga** [] to have some understanding of [], have some knowledge of []

∘ **(e) merr· veten** to get back to normal: recover

∘ <> **merr· ymrin** to make <>'s life a living Hell

○ <>*a merr· zejen* to get the hang of <>, master <>
○ **merr· zemër** to pluck up courage
○ <> **merr· zemrën** to win <>'s heart
○ [ ] **merr· zët** to take a dislike to [ ]
○ **merr· zjarr 1** to start burning, catch on fire, catch fire **2** take fire: (of work) gain impetus, come to life; (of something in the sky) become red **3** to become enraged
○ **merr· zjarr pushka** <>'s gun *goes off*
○ [ ] **merr· zvarrë 1** to drag [ ] **2** to keep [ ] from coming into [ ]'s own
○ [ ] **merr· zhagas** "take [ ] by dragging [ ]" to drag [ ]

me·rr·et *vpr* **1** <*merr·* **2** to be taken up (with), be involved/engaged (in) **3** *(Colloq)* to be engaged/married
○ **S'merret bota në krahë.** "The world can't be taken in one's arms." *(Prov)* Rome wasn't built in a day.
○ <> **merr·***et³ˢᵍ* **goja** <> *stutters*
○ <> **merr·***et³ᵖˡ* **këmbët** <> *walks* unsteadily: <> totters/staggers/toddles
○ **merr·***et* **me hekura** to be an ironworker
○ **merr·***et* **me mend 1** to be imaginable **2** to be self-evident/obvious
○ <> **merr·***et³ᵖˡ* **mendtë** <> *is* dizzy
○ **merr·***et* **në grykë** to embrace (one another)
○ **merr·***et* **vesh (me [ ])** to come to a mutual understanding (with [ ])
○ **merr·***et* **vesh 1** to be understandable **2** to reach an understanding, come to an agreement

merrkot *nm* = **mëshere**

mes
I § *nm* **1** middle; middle part **2** waist **3** ambiance, environment
II § *prep (abl)* **1** in/through the middle of **2** between
○ **në atë/këtë mes 1** in that/this regard, concerning that/this **2** just at that/this moment, at that/this very moment
○ **mes për mes** right across/through the middle

*mesak *adj* mediocre, middling, fair

mesap *adj, n* [*Hist*] Messapian

mesapishte *nf* [*Hist*] Messapian (language)

mesarak *nm* narrow strip of land between two other pieces of land

mesarë *nf* field strip between two other fields

mesatar *adj* **1** of medium size; of medium build **2** of medium temperature; mild (of weather) **3** of medium quality/strength **4** average

mesatare *nf* mean, average

mesatarisht *adv* on the average

*mesavis *stem for 1st sg pres, pl pres, 2nd & 3rd sg subj, pind* <*mesavit·*

mesavit·
I § *vt* to slander
II § *vi* to gossip

mesazh *nm* formal message sent by a head of state

*mesbrinjë *nf* small of the back, waist, loins

*mesditar *adj* = mesditës

mesditë *nf* **1** midday, noon; lunchtime **2** midday meal, lunch

mesditës *nm* [*Geog*] = meridian

mesdredhur *adj (Poet)* (of a girl/woman) having a thin and flexible waist: supple-waisted

Mesdhe *nm* Mediterranean Sea/Area

mesdhetar *adj* **1** Mediterranean **2** [*Geog*] (of a sea) surrounded by land

mesehe *nf* wherewithal, means

mesele *nf* **1** *(Colloq)* story one tells about one's experience: (personal) story **2** matter, issue, problem **3** chat

mesë *nf* **1** covering membrane; peritoneum **2** thin skin; film

mesëm *adj (i)* **1** middle **2** medium; middling; average; intermediate **3** (of a specialist) with a secondary school education
○ **e mesmja e artë** the golden mean

mesës *nm* **1** intermediary **2** [*Ethnog*] marriage broker

mesfushë *nf* [*Soccer*] midfield

mesfushor *n* [*Soccer*] halfback

mesgjuhor *adj* [*Ling*] palatal

mesgjuhore *nf* [*Ling*] palatal consonant

meshollë [*mes-hollë*] *nf* narrow-waisted, thin-waisted, slender

mesit *nm (Old)* = mestar

mesjetar *adj* medieval

mesjetë *nf* medieval period, Middle Ages

meskall *nm (np ~ j)* small file-like tool used by jewelers to make gold or silver filigree sparkle

*meskâmbje *nf (Reg Gheg)* buttress, pier

meskëputur *adj, nf (Poet)* (of a girl/woman) having a thin waist, having a beautiful figure: slender in waist

meskin *adj (Book)* stingy; small-minded; narrow, limited

meskohë *nf* interlude = ndërkohë

meslakore *nf* narrow-waisted, thin-waisted

mesnatë *nf* midnight

mesnik *adj* meat pasty

*mesno·n *vt* to betroth

mesoburrë *nm* middle-aged man

mesogra *np* <meso-grua

mesogrua *nf* middle-aged woman

mesor *adj* [*Ling*] having passive form but intransitive meaning: of middle voice, middle

mesore *nf* **1** small room in the middle of other rooms: vestibule; passageway, corridor **2** partition wall **3** strip of land between two fields **4** [*Geom*] bisector **5** [*Ling*] palatal

mespërdredhur *adj* = mesdredhur

mespurtekë *adj (Poet)* very thin-waisted: svelte

mestar *n (Old)* go-between, intermediary, middle-man

meste *nf* slippers

mestingull *nm (Old)* [*Ling*] medial sound

*mestis *stem for 1st sg pres, pl pres, 2nd & 3rd sg subj, pind* <*mestit·*

*mestit· *vt* to announce, proclaim

*mestitës *n* announcer

*mestori *nf* hall, passage, lobby

mesun *nm* = mesarak

mesunazë *adj* very thin-waisted

meshar *nm* [*Relig*] missal

meshë *nf* **1** [*Relig*] mass (the ceremony) **2** communion wafer

meshinë I § *nf OR* **meshin II** § *nm* thin leather
○ **meshinë llustrinë** patent leather

meshìntë *adj (i)* **1** made of thin leather **2** covered in thin leather

meshk *nm (np ˜q)* **1** bull; bull used as an ox **2** young bull

*meshkë *nf (Old)* bitch; whore

meshkuj *np* <**mashkull**

*meshkur *nm* = **ushkur**

*meshmë *nf* trimming, fringe

meshno·het *vpr* to become senile, go dotty

*meshnuer *adj (fem ˜ore) (Old)* dotty, childish

mesho·n *vi [Relig]* to conduct mass; hold a commemorative mass

meshq *np* <**meshk**

meshtar *nm [Relig]* person who conducts the mass: celebrant

meshtari *nf [Relig]* **1** the duties of the celebrant of a mass **2** *(Collec)* those who conduct mass

*meshtni *nf (Old)* skin bag

*meshto·n *vi* **1** = **mesho·n** **2* to moderate; modify

Met *nm* Met (male name)

meta *formative prefix* meta-

metabolizëm *nm [Biol]* metabolism

metafizik *adj* metaphysical

metafizikë *nf [Phil]* metaphysics

metaforë *nf [Lit Ling]* metaphor

metaforik *adj* **1** metaphorical **2** rich in metaphors

metakarp *nm [Anat]* metacarpus

metal *nm [Chem]* metal
- **metali i bardhë** babbitt metal; white metal
- **metal me ngjyra** nonferrous metal
- **metale të çmuara** precious metals
- **metal i zi** ferrous metal

metale *nf* snowdrift; pile, heap

metalik *adj* metallic

METALIMPORT *abbrev* agency for the importation of metals

metalizim *nm ger [Tech]* <**metalizo·n**

metalizo·n *vt* **1** *[Tech]* to plate with metal **2** to patch [a crack/leak] with metal **3** to give [ ] a metallic sheen or semblance

metalmbajtës *adj (Spec)* metal-bearing, metalliferous

metaloid *nm [Chem]* metalloid

metaloqeramik *adj [Chem]* sintered alloy

metalor *adj* containing metal

metalprerës *adj [Tech]* metal-cutting

metalpunues
I § *adj* metal-working
II § *n* metal worker

metalshkrirës
I § *adj* **1** for melting metal **2** working as a melter of metal
II § *n* metal melter: foundryman, furnaceman

metaltë *adj (i)* made of metal

metalurg *nm* metallurgist

metalurgji *nf* metallurgy
- **metalurgji me ngjyra** metallurgy of non-ferrous metals
- **metalurgji e zezë** metallurgy of ferrous metals

metalurgjik
I § *adj* metallurgical
II § *nm (Colloq)* metallurgical complex: mill

metamorfozë *nf* metamorphosis

metan *nm [Chem]* methane

metani *nf [Relig]* penance on one's knees before a holy figure: prostration

metastazë *nf* metastasis

metatezë *nf [Ling]* metathesis

*metef *nm* **1** border area **2** high ground, elevation, rise (in an otherwise flat area)

metelik *adj (Old)* coin worth 5 thousandths of a Turkish lira

metempsikozë *nf* metempsychosis

meteor *nm* **1** *[Astron]* meteor **2** *(Fig)* person or thing famous for only a short period of time

meteorit *nm [Astron]* meteorite

meteorolog *n* meteorologist

meteorologji *nf* meteorology

meteorologjik *adj* meteorological

meteriq *nm (Reg)* womb

meteriz *nm [Mil]* trench

metë
I § *adj (i)* **1** deficient; defective **2** *(Fig)* mentally defective, crazy
II § *nf (e)* **1** deficiency; defect **2** weakness, flaw; failing, fault
III § *nf* swig
IV § *adv* short of the expected or required amount: missing, short, lacking, hanging, incomplete

metër
I § *nm* **1** meter **2** (meter-long) measuring rod/tape/stick **3** *(Fig)* means of measurement
II § *nf* small clay pot with handles

*metil *nf [Invert]* larva of the leech

metilik *adj* methyl

*meting *nm* = **miting**

*metis *stem for 1st sg pres, pl pres, 2nd & 3rd sg subj, pind* <**metit·**

*metit· *vt* to crossbreed

metodë *nf* **1** method **2** book containing the rudiments of a subject: primer

metodik *adj* methodical

metodikë *nf* **1** set of methods employed in a given field **2** set of principles governing a given subject **3** *(Colloq)* textbook for learning the methods and principles of a subject

metodikisht *adv* methodically

metodist *n* educational specialist: subject matter specialist, methodologist

metodologji *nf* methodology

metodologjik *adj* methodological

metonimi *nf [Ling Lit]* metonymy

metonimik *adj [Ling Lit]* metonymical

metoq *nm (Reg)* single-storey structure for keeping grain or animals

metrazh *nm* **1** *[Spec]* area or length in meters; (film) footage **2** cloth sold by the meter **3** store that sells such cloth: fabric shop

metrik *adj* metric

metrikë *nf [Lit]* metrics

metro *nf* underground urban train: subway, metro

metropol *nm* **1** imperialistic nation **2* metropolis **3** motherland

*metzë *nf* leftover; scrap, remnant

*mevetsi = **mëvetësi**

mevlud *nm* commemoration of Mohammed's birth

mexhite *nf (Old)* silver coin worth a fifth of a Turkish lira

mezat *nm (Colloq)* auction = **ankand**

*****mezatar** *nm* = **mesatar**

*****mezatarisht** = **mesatarisht**

meze OR **meze** *nf* **1** [*Food*] appetizer; tidbit **2** choice part; best of a group **3** bait ***4** setting, milieu

mezellëqe *np* appetizers

mezeri *nf* food shop that serves charcoal-broiled sausages and other snacks

mezi *adv* **1** with difficulty; by great effort **2** barely, hardly **3** impatiently

  ○ **mezi** [ ] **ka·** to hold [ ] very dear, [ ] *is* very dear to one

  ○ **mezi mba·n frymën** to be miserably poor: be barely able to stay alive

  ○ **mezi merr· frymë 1** to barely have time to breathe **2** to be in a tight spot

*****meznatë** = **mesnatë**

mezolit *nm* Mesolithic Age

mezhdë *nf (Colloq)* embankment, low ridge

*****mezhdnik** *nm* rock marking the border between fields

më *1st sg object pronominal clitic preceding a transitive verb, or suffixed to a transitive verb stem in the imper* **1** indicates that the verb has an identifiable 1st sg referent or object: me **2** *(Colloq)* indicates a feeling of intimacy or affection on the part of the speaker

  ○ **më qafsh!** "may you mourn for me!" *(Colloq)* I beg you! please! for my sake!

më *adv, pcl* more; some more, any more

  ○ **ësh·të³ˢᵍ më afër mendsh/mendjes** it *is* more likely

  ○ **më andej** later, afterward

  ○ **më cazë** in a little while, in a little while **2** towards dusk, in the evening

  ○ {*adverb*} **e më** {*adverb*} ever more {}, more and more {}

  ○ **më i madh zarari, se qari** "greater the loss than the gain" more to lose than to gain

  ○ **më pas <> dëgjo·het³ˢᵍ muzika** "later on <>'s music is heard" the consequences of <>'s actions *become* apparent only later

  ○ **më i tejmë** the furthest/farthest, at the extreme edge

më *prep (acc)* **1** indicates position in time or space: at, on, in **2** indicates manner/means: by

  ○ {*countable noun*} **më** {*same noun*} every single {}

  ○ {*noun*} **më** {} at/in/to every single {}: {} by {}

  ○ **më atë anë** = **matanë**

më *short form* = **mëmë**

  ○ **im më** my mother, mom

*****mëbarkazi** *adv* on the belly

*****mëditë** = **mëditje**

mëditës *nm* person hired by the day: day laborer

mëditje *nf* daily wages

mëdorës *nm* **1** drayman leading the animal at the head of a caravan **2** animal caretaker

mëdysh = **mëdyshas**

mëdysh·et *vpr* to be of two minds: be undecided/ uncertain

mëdyshas *adv* of two minds: in doubt, undecided, uncertain

mëdyshje *nf* **1** doubt, uncertainty **2** suspicion

mëdyzaj *adv* = **mëdyshas**

mëdha *fem pl* <**madh**

*****mëdhajs** *nf (Old)* capital letter

mëdhenj *masc pl* <**madh**

mëdhesë *nf (Colloq)* single-storey dwelling

mëgashtër *nf* [*Bot*] sage = **sherbelë**

mëgojëz *nf* bridle bit = **ngojëz**

*****mëgojsë** *nf* = **ngojëz**

mëgje *nm (np ¯ nj) (Reg)* shed for livestock

*****mëgjile** OR **mëgjilë** *nf* **1** something shaped like a sickle: crescent **2** iron band securing a scythe to its handle

mëgjunjazi *adv* = **gjunjas**

*****mëgjunjë** = **gjunjas**

mëhallë *nf* **1** [*Hist*] district in which everyone is of the same religion **2** *(Colloq)* residential section/ward = **lagje 3** large number: bunch, pile

mëhas *stem for 1st sg pres, pl pres, 2nd & 3rd sg subj, pind* <**mëhat·**

mëhat· *vt* to bleat = **mekëri·n**

mëhorr *nm* [*Bot*] = **muhar**

mëk *onomat (Colloq)*

  ○ **(s'bë·n) as gëk as mëk** not make a sound; not say boo

*****mëkâmb·** *(Reg Gheg)* = **mëkëmb·**

mëkat *nm* sin

mëkatar *n* sinner

mëkatim *nm ger* <**mëkato·n**

mëkato·n *vi* to sin

mëkatshëm *adj (i)* sinful

mëkeq· *vt* to make [ ] worse

mëkeq·et *vpr* **1** to get worse **2** to grow infuriated, be incensed: get roaring mad

mëkequr *adj (i)* **1** grown worse **2** infuriated, roaring mad

mëkëmb· *vt* **1** to stand [a child] on [his] feet, start [a child] walking; put [a sick person] back on [his] feet **2** *(Fig)* to cause to recover

mëkëmb·et *vpr* **1** to stand up on one's own feet, begin to walk; get back on one's feet **2** *(Fig)* to recover

mëkëmbës *n* **1** deputy; viceroy, regent **2** *(Old)* [*Dipl*] diplomatic representative: envoy

mëkëmbësi *nf* operational organization of a viceregental government; seat of a vice-regental government

mëkëmbje *nf ger* **1** <**mëkëmb·**, **mëkëmb·et 2** recovery

mëkëmbur *adj (i)* **1** standing/walking on one's own feet; on one's own two feet, adult; back on one's feet **2** *(Fig)* recovered

mëkim *nm ger* <**mëko·n**, **mëko·het**

mëko·het *vpr* to take nourishment, be nourished

mëko·n *vt* **1** to feed [a helpless person/bird] **2** to breast-feed [a baby] **3** *(Fig)* to nourish

mëkrahëzaj *adv* on one side

mëkrejcë = **mëkrejsë**

mëkrejsë *nf* **1** unplowed strip of land in a field: balk **2** top end of a field **3** top part of clothing **4** *(Fig)* deceptive trick

mëkresë *nf* gravestone

mëkuarit *nn (të)* breast-feeding

mëlakë *nf* [*Bot*] herb bennet, wood avens *(Geum urbanum)*

mëlco·n
I § vt 1 (Colloq) to make [] sweet: sweeten 2 (Fig) to reduce the amount of pain in [something painful]: relieve 3 (Fig) to strop [a razor]
II § vi <> experience a twinge, <> feel a dull/slight pain

mëlçi nf 1 [Anat] liver; innards 2 (Colloq) lungs
∘ **mëlçia e bardhë** the lungs
∘ **mëlçi derri** worthless thing
∘ **mëlçia e zezë** the liver

mëlko·het vpr to get along with what one has: get by; be happy with what there is: make do

mëlko·n
I § vt to use sufficient fat in preparing [food]; add shortening
II § vi to suffice, be enough

mëlme·n vt to add flavoring to [food]

mëlme·së nf fat added to food, shortening; food eaten on or with bread

mëlmye·r adj (i) [Dairy] enriched with fat: buttered, creamed, triple-cream

mëlmye·shëm adj (i) fatty; greasy

mëlqinjë nf [Bot] barberry (Berberis vulgaris)

mëlqinjo·re np [Bot] barberry family Berberi-daceae

mëlto·n vt [Bot] to graft

mëlla·gë nf [Bot] mallow (Malva)
∘ **mëllag**ë **e butë** [Bot] hollyhock (Althaea rosea)
∘ **mëllag**ë **Stambolli** [Bot] hollyhock
∘ **mëllag**ë **uji** [Bot] = mëllanja·dhe

mëllago·re np [Bot] mallow family Malvaceae

mëlla·gjër nm [Bot] eastern strawberry tree (Arbutus andrachne)

mëllanja·dhe nf [Bot] marshmallow (Althea officinalis)

mëllenja·n nm [Ornit] male blackbird

mëllenjë nf [Ornit] 1 blackbird (Turdus merula) 2 black goat
∘ **mëllenj**ë **e bardhë** = mullibardhë
∘ **mëllenj**ë **sqepgjatë** [Ornit] water ouzel, dipper Cinclus cinclus L. = **mulliujëse**
∘ **mëllenj**ë **thumbverdhë** [Ornit] blackbird Turdus merula
∘ **mëllenj**ë **uji** [Ornit] water ouzel, dipper Cinclus cinclus L. = **mulliujëse**

mëlle·zë nf 1 [Bot] hop hornbeam (Ostrya carpinifolia) 2 [Ornit] blackbird (Turdus merula)

mëllë(r) nm (np ˜ nj) 1 = bullu·ngë 2 [Med] = breshkëz 3 hard piece of bread or bread crust

mëllënksh·et vpr [Dairy] (of milk) to start to curdle and go bad

mëllënkshur adj (i) (of milk) curdled, sour

mëllënjë = mëllenjë

mëllija·n nm = mëllenja·n

***mëlli·nj**ë = mëllenjë

mëllu·gë nf [Bot] scale: (squama)

mëmë nf 1 mother 2 queen bee 3 (Colloq) used as a term of affection and respect for mother-in-law or another elderly woman 4 [Anat] womb 5 [Bot] plant that supplies the ovules for cross breeding 6 source (of a stream) 7 (Fig) source, cause, origin

mëmë**dhe** nm (Elev) motherland = atdhe

mëmë**dheta·r** n (Elev) = atdheta·r

***mëm**ë**la·l**ë nf paternal grandmother

mëmë**li·g**ë nf [Food] corn mush, polenta

***mëm**ë**ra·k** adj maternal

mëmë**si·** nf 1 [Law] maternity; maternal rights 2 motherhood

mëmë**z** nf 1 [Entom] queen bee 2 (Pet) mom, mommy, mummy

mëmë**zi·m** nm ger (Book) 1 <mëmëo·n 2 feeding of milk to a newborn animal

mëmë**zo·**n vt 1 (Book) to provide a steady supply of milk to a newborn animal 2 to suckle [a newborn animal]

mëmë**zo·nj**ë nf grandmother = gjy·she

***mëmo·r** adj [Zool] mammalian

mëna·të adv in the early morning; early this morning

*mëna·tje nf eve

*mënç pl abl <mend

mënçëm adj (i) = mençëm

*mënd
I § nm = mend
II § adv almost
∘ (për) një mënd almost

mënd· vt to suckle; breast-feed, nurse

*mënd = mend

mënda·fsh
I § nm silk
II § adj silky

mëndafsh·punues nm worker in the silk industry

mëndafshtë adj (i) made of silk; silken

mënda·ra·k nm 1 lamb or kid that nurses at the breast of a mother other than its own 2 baby raised by a wet nurse

mënde·shë nf wet nurse

më·ndër = mendërz

*mëndërgo·re = madërgonë

*mëndi·n**ë nf suckling animal

*mëndja·k adj pithy, witty

*mëndja·ke nf sage remark, pithy saying

mëndje nf ger 1 <mënd· *2 = mendje

*mëndjeçka·th**ët = mendjeshka·thët

*mëndjemu·gur adj stupid

*mëndjengjesh**ur adj obstinate

*mëndjeshi·t**ës
I § adj pedantic; showing off
II § n pedant

mëndjethe·llë adj profound

mëndo·re nf [Ethnog] = ndo·re

mëne·së nf (Colloq) = vone·së

*mën**ë nf 1 (Reg) fate 2 = man

mënga·sh adj = mëngjara·sh

mëngë nf 1 sleeve 2 extended part of a geographical entity: branch, prong 3 sleeved vest 4 armful *5 crowd, pack; corps
∘ **mëng**ë **deti** arm of the sea
∘ **mëng**ë **në mes të kurrizit** "sleeve in the middle of the back" superfluous thing; extra burden; something completely out of place

mëngë**gja·t**ë
I § adj long-sleeved
II § nm (Tease) priest

mëngë**përve·sh**ur
I § adj having rolled-up sleeves
II § adv with sleeves rolled up

mëngë**r** nf 1 wooden trough 2 = melicë

mëngë**shku·rtër** adj short-sleeved

mëngo·*n*
 I § *vi* to get up in the very early morning: get up very early, get to work early; hurry
 II § *vt* to put [livestock] to pasture in early morning

mëngojë *nf (Old)* living provisions given to a childless widow

mëngore *nf* **1** double-breasted waistcoat decorated with gold braid and long sleeves slung behind the arms rather than worn **2** shirt with long loose sleeves *3 embroidered waistcoat with sleeves

**mënguar *adj (i)* early in the morning

*mëngut = **mangët**

mëngjarak = **mëngjarash**

mëngjarash
 I § *adj* **1** left-handed; left-footed **2** awkward, clumsy **3** *(Iron)* (politically) supposedly leftist, leftish
 II § *n* left-hander

mëngjes *nm* **1** morning **2** breakfast

*mëngjes·*et vpr* to have breakfast

mëngjesor *adj* of, pertaining to, appropriate for, or occurring in the morning

mëngjesore *nf* breakfast café; snack bar

mëngjez = **mëngjes**

mëngjezor *adj* [*Spec*] matutinal

mëngjër *adj (i)* **1** left (as opposed to right) **2** cross-eyed, cockeyed

mëngjërash *adj* = **mëngjarash**

mëngjërosh *adj* = **mëngjarash**

mëngji *nf* **1** folk medication, folk healing **2** = **magji**

*mëngjim *nm* remedy, cure

*mëngjirë *nf* ewe or nanny goat only one teat

mëngjis· *vt* to treat [] by folk remedies

mëngjis·*et vpr* to medicate oneself with folk remedies

*mëngjistar *n* **1** folk healer **2** = **magjistar**

mëngjosh = **mëngjarash**

*mëni *nf* hatred, loathing

mëni·*het vpr* to get angry

mëni·*n vt* to hate, loathe

mënik *adj* puppy dog

*mënim *nm ger* **1** <**mëno**·*n* **2** delay **3** handicap

*mënimtar = **mëngjitar**

mënishëm *adj (i)* hateful, loathsome

mënishte *nf* [*Bot*] rockrose (*Cistus*) = **bedunicëM**

mënishtore *np* [*Bot*] rockrose family *Cistaceae*

*mënko·*n* = **mëko**·*n*

mëno *interj* used to call back a hive of bees

mëno·*n*
 I § *vi (Colloq)* to be late/tardy
 II § *vt* **1** *(Colloq)* to delay, make [] late **2** to put off [] until later

mënoje *nf* = **mëru**

*mënt *pcl* nearly, almost = **mend**

*mënt = **mend**

mënuar *adv* tardy, late, delayed

mënuarje *nf* tardiness, delay

*mënuje OR **mënye** *nf* haft

mënyrë *nf* **1** manner, way; process **2** [*Ling*] mode

*mënyrësi *nf (Old)* mannerism, affectation

*mënyrëshëm *adj (i)* mannered, affected

mënyror *adj* [*Ling*] **1** modal **2** of manner

mënjan·*et vpr* to step aside, sidestep; be evasive

mënjanë
 I § *adv* **1** aside, separately **2** on one side, to one side
 II § *prep (abl)* **1** alongside, beside **2** besides, in addition to

mënjanëri *nf* "standing on the sidelines" detachment, lack of concern, indifference

mënjanës *adj* aloof

mënjanëse *adj* with just one teat (on the udder)

mënjanësi *nf* = **mënjanëri**

mënjanim *nm ger* <**mënjano**·*n*, **mënjano**·*het*

mënjano·*het vpr* **1** to keep oneself apart from others **2** to step aside

mënjano·*n vt* **1** to turn [] to one side; move [] to one side **2** to push [aside], parry; avert, prevent, avoid **3** to exclude; shun

mënjanisht *adv* indifferently

mënjanshëm *adj (i)* indifferent

mënjanuar *adj (i)* **1** apart; segregated **2** withdrawn; isolated

*mënjanuar *adj (i)* = **mënjanuar**

mënjë *nf* **1** drizzle **2** nectar from leaves *3 manna

mënjësh *adv* in/into one piece, together

mënjëzaj *adv* in a single strand

mënjill *nm* evening feast before a Catholic religious holiday

mënjille *nf* [*Relig*] fasting (for Roman Catholics); fasting period

mënjollë *nf* **1** thin sapling that sprouts near a tree trunk **2** thin branch; withe **3** *(Fig)* young child (as representing hope for the future)

mëparshëm *adj (i)* former; of earlier days

mëpasshëm *adj (i)* following, subsequent

mëpastajshëm *adj (i)* later, future, coming

mëposhtëm *adj (i)* further below, lower

mëqak·*et vpr (Colloq)* to try hard

mëqik *adj* [*Text*] shuttle (on a loom); spool, bobbin

mërajë *nf* fennel

*mërca·*n vt* to crush, squash

*mërcajt *stem for pdef, opt, adm, part* <**mërca**·*n*

*mërcel *nm* medallion, pendant; sequin

mërç *nm* = **kallo**

mërdhac *adj, n* (person) oversensitive to cold, (person) who gets cold too easily

mërdhacan *adj* = **mërdhac**

mërdhas *stem for 1st sg pres, pl pres, 2nd & 3rd sg subj, pind* <**mërdhet**·

mërdhet· *vi* to feel ice cold, suffer from the icy cold

mërdhez·*et vpr* **1** *(Colloq)* to become flushed with emotion, get red with anger **2** to get hot; light up, glow; burn

mërdhi·*n vi* to feel ice cold, suffer from the icy cold

mërdhis *stem for 2nd pl pres, pind* <**mërdhet**·

mërdhit *stem for pdef, opt, adm, part, pind, 2nd pl pres, imper, vp* <**mërdhet**·

*mërdhuz·*et vpr* to get too fat, become obese

mëre·*het vpr* **1** to get the evil eye, fall under a spell **2** to be surprised/amazed

mëre·*n vt* to give [] the evil eye, cast a spell over []

mërenë OR **mërengë** *nf* [*Ichth*] southern barbel = **mustak**

*mëret *nm* [*Bot*] myrtle (*Myrtus communis*)

mërgatë *nf collec* exiles/emigrants taken as a whole

mërgím *nm ger* 1 < **mërgo**· *n*, **mërgo**·*het* [*Law*]
2 exile; emigration 3 land of exile/emigration
4 (*Old*) moving away, departure

mërgim|ta'r *n* person in exile: exile

mërgo'·*het vpr* 1 to go into exile; emigrate 2 to
depart

mërgo·*n*
I § *vt* to exile; banish
II § *vi* 1 to go into exile; emigrate 2 (of birds) to
migrate

mërgu|a'r
I § *adj (i)* exiled; in exile
II § *adv* in exile; away from the homeland

mërg|u'e|s *adj* migratory

mërgji'l *nm* [*Bot*] field marigold (*Calendula arvensis*)

****mërgji'zë** *OR* **mërgjy'zë** *nf* [*Bot*] = mërgji'l

mëri *nf* grudge; malice; rancor, hatred

****mëri**· *vi (Reg Gheg)* = arri·*n*

mëri··*het vpr* to harbor/develop a grudge; be full of
rancor, feel bitter

mëri·*n vt* 1 to dislike []; hate [] 2 to cause rancor in
[]: turn [] against

mëri'në *nf* moray eel
∘ **mërinë e zezë** [*Ichth*] brown moray *Gymnotho-
rax unicolor*

mëri|shëm
I § *adj (i)* 1 with rancor: rancorous 2 deserving of
hate: hateful, detestable
II § *adv* with rancor: rancorously

mërit·*et vpr* = mëri·*het*

mërit *stem for pdef, opt, adm, part* < mëri·*n*

****mëri'tje** = arri'tje

mëri'tur *adj (i)* carrying a grudge

****mërkata'r** *nm (Old)* = tregta'r

****mërka'të** *nf* = merka'të

****mërkato're** *nf (Old)* = dyqa'n

****mërk|e**·*het vpr* to fly into a passion

mërkëmb· *vt* to trip []; hamper, hinder

mërkëmb·*et vpr* to stumble, trip = pengo'·*het*

mërko'sh *nm (Hist)* [*Ethnog*] man who lies in bed to
receive visitors after his wife has given birth: husband
in couvade

mërku'rë *nf (e)* Wednesday

****Mërku'rr** *nm* Mercury

****mërku'rrë** *nf (e)* = mërku'rë

mërla'q·*et vpr (Colloq)* to eat gluttonously

****mërlu'a** *nm (obl ˜o'i, np ˜o'nj)* [*Entom*] hornet

mërmëri'më *nf* = murmuri'më

mërmëri's *stem for 1st sg pres, pl pres, 2nd & 3rd
sg subj, pind* < mërmëri*t*·

mërmëri't· *vi* = murmuri't·

mërmëri't|ës *adj* = murmuri'tës

mërmëri'tje *nf ger* = murmuri'tje

****mërmi'ng** *nm* [*Entom*] = milingo'në

****mërqe'jtë** *nf (Old)* heartburn = urth

mërqi = mërqi'një

mërqi'një *nf* [*Bot*] 1 Christ's thorn (*Paliurus spina-
christi Mill.*) = dri'zë 2 (*Reg*) common jujube (*Ziziphus jujuba*) = hi'de

****mërqi'r** *nm (Old)* [*Ethnog*] bride price

mërs|e·*n vt (Colloq)* to bring to completion: finish
up, complete

mërsi'në *nf* [*Bot*] myrtle (*Myrtus communis*)

mërsino're *np* [*Bot*] myrtle family *Myrtaceae*

mërshë *nf* 1 rotting corpse; carrion; bad meat
2 flabby flesh, flab

****mërshë'rísht** *adv* carnally

mërshët *adj (i)* (of meat) rotting

mërshi'në *nf* 1 leather sack *2 = mërsi'në

mërte'k *nm* thin wooden beam: rafter

mërti'k *nm* [*Bot*] = rici'n

mërti's· *vt* to veil

mërti's·*et vpr* to veil the face; have one's face veiled

****mërthe'cë** = mbërthe'ckë

mëru'(r) *nm* handle for a blade

mëru'në *nf* [*Ichth*] Albanian minnow (*Pachychilon
pictum*)

mëru'|i *obl* < mëru

****mëry'er|shëm** *adj (i)* = mrekullu'eshëm

mërze·*n*
I § *vi* 1 (of livestock) to rest in the shade during hot
weather 2 (*FigImpolite*) to lie around doing nothing:
loiter *3 (*Old*) to lie at anchor
II § *vt* to herd livestock into a shady place to escape
the heat

****mërze|jtë** *nf (Old)* anchorage

mërzi *nf* 1 boredom; worry, annoyance, nuisance
2 apathy, torpor

mërzi'm *nm ger* 1 < mërze·*n* 2 shady place for livestock

mërzi's *stem for 1st sg pres, pl pres, 2nd & 3rd sg
subj, pind* < mërzi*t*·

mërzi't· *vt* 1 to bore 2 to annoy 3 to worry
∘ **mërzit· gur e dru** to be a terrible pest/nuisance

mërzi't·*et vpr* to feel bored; be annoyed; be worried

mërzi'tje *nf ger* 1 < mërzit·, mërzit·*et* 2 = mërzi

mërzit|shëm
I § *adj (i)* boring; bothersome, annoying, worrisome
II § *adv* with boredom: boringly

mërzi'tur *adj (i)* 1 bothered, annoyed, worried; saddened 2 = mërzit'shëm

mërzy'e *stem for 1st & 2nd sg pdef* < mërze·*n*

mërzy'er *part* < mërze·*n*

****mërri|** = arri

****mërro'kul** *nf* idle chatter, prattle

mërrol· *vt (Reg)* to have a somber face: frown

mërrol·*et vpr (Reg)* to become somber

mërrol|a'n *adj, n (Reg)* (person) with a somber face

mërrol|shëm *adv (Reg)* with a somber face

mërru'dh· *vt* to wrinkle/crease []

mërru'dh·*et vpr* 1 to wrinkle/crease one's face:
frown 2 to get crumpled 3 to crouch; cringe

****mërry'e|shëm** *adj (i)* wild and blustery

mësa *conj* 1 (*Colloq*) to the same (impossible) de-
gree/extent that, no more than 2 (*Reg*) so long as,
while, as
∘ **mësa ___ aq ___** as (much) ___ as ___

mësa'llë *nf* 1 napkin, serviette 2 [*Ethnog*] large napkin (serviette) for guests 3 tablecloth 4 dining table
5 (*Fig Colloq*) dinner; banquet
∘ **mësallë djathi** cheesecloth
∘ **mësallë me dy faqe** two-faced hypocrite

****mësdra'ke** *nf (Old)* = mëzdra'k

mësi'm *nm ger* 1 < mëso'·*n*, mëso'·*het* 2 lesson
3 instruction, education
∘ **mësim i qytetarisë** (*Old*) civics

mësimdhënës
I § adj [Spec] **1** instructional, educative **2** instructive
II § n [Spec] instructor

mësimdhënie *nf [Spec]* teaching, instruction

mësimor *adj* instructional, educational, academic

*__mësimtar__ *adj, n (Old)* = mësimdhënës

mësipërm *adj (i)* **1** upper **2** above-mentioned

mëso· *het vpr* to become accustomed, get used to
∘ **mëso·het me vezë në tigan** "be accustomed to eggs on a frying pan" to be too accustomed to an easy life
∘ **mëso·het me** [] to get used to []
∘ **mëso·het pa** [] to get used to doing without [], get along without []

mëso·n
I § vt **1** to teach, instruct; train **2** to let [] know; advise, counsel **3** to find out [], find out about [], hear/learn about [] **4** to accustom, habituate
II § vi to study
∘ **S'mëso·n**[3sg] **kali revan në pleqëri.** "A horse does not learn a racing gait in old age." *(Prov)* You can't teach an old dog new tricks.
∘ **mëso·n me gojë** to learn by heart

mësonjës *(Old)* = mësues

mësonjëtore *nf (Old)* (elementary) school

*__mëstrejc__ *nm* long-tailed sheep

*__mëstruk·__ *et vpr* = struk·et

mësuar
I § part <mëso·n, mëso·het
II § adj (i) **1** educated; trained **2** knowledgeable, learned **3** gained through experience: acquired **4** accustomed
∘ **ësh·të mësuar në pupla** to have been used to a life of ease and comfort, have been raised in a life of ease and comfort, {}'s life has been a bed of roses

mësues *n* teacher; educator; instructor

mësuesi *nf* teaching profession

mësukë *nf* wooden mallet used to beat out the twist in fibers during the combing process

mësy·n *vt* **1** [Mil] to launch a series of fierce assaults on [] **2** (Fig) to attack []
∘ <>a mësy·n to appear suddenly at <>'s doorstep

*__mësyjë__ *nf [Mil]* = mësymje

*__mësymë__ = mësymje

mësymës *adj [Mil]* in a sudden all-out offensive, assailing, assaulting

mësymje *nfger* **1** <mësy·n [Mil] **2** sudden all-out offensive, assault

*__mësyrje__ = mësymje

mësysh *adv* under a spell

*__mështal__ *nm* two-three year old colt

*__mështale__ *nf* filly

*__mështef·__ OR **mështeh·** *vt (Reg Gheg)* = fsheh·

*__mështehësinë__ *nf (Reg Gheg)* = fshehësirë

*__mështehtas__ *adv (Reg Gheg)* = fsheh·

*__mështel·__ *vt (Reg)* = mbështel·

mështenjo·n *vt* to make [] stand out, make [] distinctive; pick [] out, select

mështere [më-she-re] *nf [Dairy]* wheel of cheese, whole cheese

*__mështesë__ *nf (Reg)* = fshesë

*__mështi·n__ *vt* = fshi·n

*__mështik·__ *vt* = fshik·

∘ [] **mështik·**[3sg] **pika** [] *suffers* a stroke

*__mështik·__ *et* = fshik·et

mështikëz *nf* bladder = fshikëz

*__mështil·__ *vt (Reg)* to close [] tight, seal

*__mështils__ *(Reg)* = mbështilc

mështim [më-shim] *nm ger* <mësho·n

mështirë [më-shir] *nf* **1** compassion, pity **2** mercy

mështirëmadh *adj (Elev)* merciful; compassionate

mështirëplotë *adj (Elev)* = mështirëmadh

mështirëshumë *adj (Elev)* = mështirëmadh

mështirim *nm ger* <mështiro·n = mështirë

mështiro·n *vt* **1** to take pity on [] **2** to forgive [someone]; absolve

mështirshëm *adj (i)* **1** merciful; tender-hearted, compassionate **2** soft-hearted, indulgent

mështirues *adj* compassionate

mështirueshëm *adj (i)* pitiable

*__mështkajë__ *nf [Entom]* mosquito

*__mështkall__ *nm* corner cupboard

mështkenjë *nf* carrion, carcass

mësho·n *vi (Colloq)* **1** to put pressure on <>: bear down on <>; step on <> **2** to press on <> with one's full weight, push down hard **3** to move <an object> quickly and with force: shove/swing/slam <> **4** (Fig) to emphasize <> strongly **5** (Colloq) to eat/drink gluttonously: guzzle <food/drink> down **6** to lean, tilt
∘ **i mësho·n dorës mbi** [] to give [] a hard smack with the hand
∘ **mështoji/mështojini vendit!** *(Pej)* stay where you are! stay out of it!

mështqerrë *nf* = mështjerrë

*__mështriak__ *nm* highland shepherd

mështekën *nf [Bot]* white birch (*Betula verrucosa*)

mështekër *nf [Bot]* = mështekën

mështeknore *np [Bot]* birch family *Betulaceae*

mështeko· *het vpr* to get furious, become angry; have one's hackles rise

mështjerrë *nf* heifer

mëteh *nm* ridge that marks a field borderline; border, limit

mëtejmë *adj (i)* **1** = mëtejshëm **2** located further away

mëtejshëm *adj (i)* **1** later, subsequent; ultimate **2** to a greater extent: further

*__mëtëhap·__ *et vpr* to boast

*__mëtëkeq·__ *et vpr* to get worse: worsen

mëti *nf* wooden churn

mëtim *nm ger* <mëto·n

mëto·n *vt* **1** to claim **2** (Colloq) to find [] out **3** (Colloq) to fix [] up, put [] in order

mëtrik *adj [Bot]* periwinkle (*Vinca major*)

mëtues *nm* claimant

mëtutjeshëm *adj (i)* = mëtejshëm

mëveshët *adj (i)* apathetic, indifferent

mëveshti *nf* apathy, indifference

mëvetësi *nf* autonomy, independence

mëvetësishëm *adj (i)* autonomous, independent

*__mëvitje__ *nf (Old)* anniversary

*__mëvitshëm__ *adj (i) (Old)* annual

mëvonë *adj (i)* = mëvonëshëm

mëvonëshëm *adj (i)* later, subsequent; ultimate

mëz *nm* foal; two-three year old colt

mëzak nm bull calf from six months to a year old

mëzat nm bull calf from one to three years old; young bull

mëzator nm = mëzat

mëzatore nf 1 heifer calf; heifer 2 cow nursing her calf for more than a year and thus not getting pregnant

mëzdrak nm (Old) 1 spear, lance, javelin; pointed post 2 = topuz

mëze nf filly

*mëze·n vt to suckle = mënd·

*mëzenj np <mëz

mëzetër np <mëzat bull calves

mëzëmër nf = zëmërherë

*mëzër np <mëz

mëzirë nf symptom

mëzo·n vt to put [a cow/calf] to nurse

mëzor nm = mëzat

mëzore

I § nf 1 unimpregnated cow still (after a year) able to nurse her calf 2 heifer calf; heifer

II § adj [Dairy] (of a cow) not pregnant and still giving milk: still fresh

mëzhdravë nf [Bot] mahaleb cherry (Prunus mahaleb)

mëzhdredhë nf [Bot] = mëzhdravë

*mfry = fry

*mfshikë = fshikë

*mfytyrim = fytyrim

*mgoj = ngoj

*mgje nm livestock shed/barn

mi pronominal adj (të) masc pl <im my, mine
  ○ të mitë my close relatives, those near and dear to me

mi nm 1 mouse (pl ˜nj) 2 (Fig Insult) good-for-nothing person; coward; sneaky person
  ○ mi fushe/kanalesh [Zool] rat
  ○ Miu ha grepin, macja ha miun. "The mouse eats the beetle, the cat eats the mouse." There's always a bigger fish to eat the fish that eats the little fish.
  ○ mi shtëpie [Zool] house mouse (Mus musculus)

mi nf [Mus] the note "mi" on a musical scale

mia pronominal adj (të) fem pl <ime my, mine
  ○ të miat my (woman speaking) close friends and relatives

*miagullo·n = mjaulli·n

miau onomat sound made by a cat: meow

*miaulli·n = mjaulli·n

miazmë nf miasma

mic
  I § nm (Reg Pet) little baby
  II § adj having a small body

micak nm [Ornit] = cinxami

*micamin nf blindman's buff

mice nf (Reg Gheg) cat = mace

micëro·n
  I § vt to nibble at [food]
  II § vi (Fig) to occupy oneself with trivial matters

mickël nf trivial matter = vogëlsirë

micukth nf 1 [Bot] summer cypress (Kochia trichophylla) 2 (Alopecurus utriculatus)

miçe nf = lëneshë

miçman nm [Naut] = bocman

mide nf (Colloq) 1 = stomak 2 hunger, appetite 3 (Fig) = qejf

midër nf (Reg) = mjedër

*midërr nf = mitër

midis
  I § prep (abl) 1 between; among; amidst 2 in the middle of
  II § nm 1 middle 2 ornamental binding strip

*midh nm = midhje

*midhe nf = midhje

*midhër nf = mitër

midhje nf [Invert] 1 mussel 2 Mediterranean mussel (Mytilus galloprovincialis)
  ○ midhje mjekroshe [Invert] bearded mussel Modiolus barbatus

miell nm 1 flour 2 finely ground product or by-product: powder, dust
  ○ miell nga thesi i botës/huaj "flour from a stranger's sack" (Iron) someone else's work/ideas
  ○ nuk ësh-të miell i thesit të {pronominal adj} "not be flour from {one's own} sack" not be the product of {one's own} mind
  ○ miell zero flour of the highest quality

miellazë nf powdery snow blowing in the wind

miellës adj (of fruit) mealy

miellishtë nf food made with flour

miello·n vt to cover [] with flour: flour

miellor adj (Elev) containing flour; like flour: floury

miellt adj (i) 1 powdered 2 made of flour: farinaceous = miellës

miellzim nm ger <miellzo·n

miellzo·n vt to mill [flour]; make [something hard and dry] into powder/dust

miellzuar adj (i) milled, powdered

*miêmën = mbiemër

*miemno·n = mbiemëro·n

*mif· = mih·

*miftar n (Reg Gheg) (Reg Gheg) tiller of the soil

migrenë nf [Med] migraine

mih· vt 1 to break/dig into [soil]: till [land], dig up [the ground] 2 to hoe, cultivate 3 (Fig) to give [] a severe beating
  ○ mih· në ujë to do something pointless, do useless things, waste one's effort/time
  ○ mih· para vetes "dig in front of oneself" to look after one's own personal affairs

Mihal nm Mihal (male name)

mihës
  I § n 1 tiller of the soil 2 digger
  II § adj digging

*mihis· vt (Reg Gk) to fornicate

mihje nf ger <mih·

mijë nf (np ˜a or ˜ra) thousand

mijëfisho·het vpr to increase a thousand times

mijëfisho·n vt to increase [] a thousandfold

mijëkëmbësh nm [Invert] millipede (Myriapoda)

mijëravjeçar adj thousands of years old; of thousands of years ago, ancient

mijëshe nf 1 [Math] set/unit of a thousand; number/numeral in the thousands column 2 (Old) paper money worth a thousand leks 3 (Colloq) 100-lek bill

mijëvjeçar
  I § adj of a thousand years; a thousand years old
  II § nm period of a thousand years: millennium

mijëvjetor nm millennial anniversary/commemoration

*mijëvjetore nf millennium

mijtë adj (i), nf (e) thousandth

mik nm (np ~q) **1** friend on whom one relies: reliable friend, real friend, friend **2** visitor, guest **3** [Ethnog] male member of the bride's family (affinal relative, in-law) **4** supporter, devotee: aficionado **5** (Colloq) guy **6** (Colloq) lover, sweetheart
  ○ **mik i familjes/shtëpisë** family friend
  ○ **mik me/për kokë** best friend
  ○ **mik i paftuar** uninvited guest: intruder
  ○ **mik për fiq** "friend (who comes) for your figs" (Colloq) friend purely after his self interest: fair-weather friend, false friend
  ○ **mik i rëndë** guest who expects special treatment: difficult guest
  ○ **mik i rëndë** guest who expects to treated as some-one important
  ○ **mik vatre** close/family friend

mik'e OR **mik'e'shë** nf **1** female friend **2** female visitor/guest **3** female supporter/devotee **4** (Colloq) gal **5** (Colloq) female lover, sweetheart

mi'kë nf [Min] mica

mikl'i'm nm ger **1** <**miklo'** •n **2** flattery

miklo •n vt **1** to pet, caress **2** to cajole, flatter
  ○ [] **miklo**•n to appeal to [], captivate []

mikl'u'es adj **1** caressing, affectionate **2** flattering

mik'pre'rë nm [Ethnog] person who has not avenged a wrong done to his guest

mik'pre'rje nf [Ethnog] failure to avenge a guest

mik'prit'ës adj hospitable

mik'prit'je nf hospitality; hospitableness

mik'prit'shm'ëri nf hospitableness

mikro formative prefix (Book) micro-

mikro'b nm **1** [Med Biol] microbe **2** (Fig) insidious seed/germ **3** (Fig) social parasite

mikrobe'mby't'ës adj germicidal

mikro'biolo'g n microbiologist

mikro'biolo'gji nf microbiology

mikro'biolo'gjik adj microbiological

mikro'borgjez adj, n petty bourgeois

mikro'borgjez'i nf petty bourgeoisie

mikro'bo'të nf (Book) microworld

mikro'bu's nm microbus, minivan

mikrob'vra's'ës adj [Med] bactericidal

mikro'eleme'nt nm trace element

mikro'fi'lm nm microfilm

mikro'film'i'm nm ger <**mikrofilmo'** •n

mikro'filmo' •n vt to microfilm

mikro'flo'rë nf [Biol] microflora

mikro'fo'n nm microphone

mikro'kli'm'ë nf microclimate

mikro'me'tër nm micrometer

mikro'n nm micron

mikro'organi'z'ëm nm [Biol] microorganism

mikro'sko'p nm microscope

mikro'skop'ik adj microscopic

miks'i'ne nf [Ichth] hagfish Myxine glutinosa

*****mik'so'** •n vt to befriend

*****mik'th** nm dimin <**mik**

mil stem for 2nd pl pres, pind, imper, vp <**mjel**•

*****mila'çe** nf nymph-like folktale character

mila'k nm **1** = **lepuru'sh 2** (Pet) baby

mi'lcë nf [Bot] lemon balm, common garden balm, sweet balm (Melissa officinalis)

mile't nm **1** [Hist] under the Ottoman Empire an autonomous community of people of the same religion under the direction of their religious leader **2** (Colloq) = **po'pull**

*****mile'z** nm [Bot] yellow vetchling (Lathyrus aphaca)

*****mi'lë** nf **1** = **mi'lje** ***2** = **mi'jë**

*****milënde'rë** nf = **pullande'r**

mi'lëz nf [Bot] scorpion senna (Coronilla emerus)

milia'rd nm billion

miliard'e'r nm billionaire

mili'c nm militiaman

milic'i nf (Old) army group with police functions, militia

mili'gra'm nm milligram

mili'li'tër nm milliliter

mili'me'tër nm millimeter

milingo'ne nf [Entom] ant (Formicidae)

milio'n nm million

*****milion'a'r** = **milione'r**

milion'e'r nm millionaire

milio'n'ësh adj of millions

milio'n'të adj (i) **1** millionth **2** = **milio'n'ësh**

milita'nt adj (Book) militant

militant'i'z'ëm nm (Book) militancy

militari'st
  I § n militarist
  II § adj militaristic

militari'z'ëm nm militarism

militari'z'i'm nm ger **1** <**militarizo'** •n, **militarizo'** •het **2** militarization

militari'zo' •het vpr to become militarized

militari'zo' •n vt to militarize

milito' •n vi (Book) to become militant; take on a militant role; play a militant role

milit'u'es adj (Book) militant

*****milja'rdë** nf milliard, billion

mi'lje nf mile

*****miljo'n** nm = **milio'n**

Mi'lo nf with masc agreement Milo (male name)

milo'nje nf (Old) kind of long rifle

milo'r nm young ram

Milo'sh nm Milosh (male name)

*****mi'lzë** = **mi'lcë**

mill nm scabbard, sheath

*****mi'llë** nf alms

*****mill'ë'to'** •n vt to intend

millocfa'ke nf [Bot] three-lobed sage (Salvia triloba)

mimi'kë nf **1** facial expression **2** miming

*****mi'mk'ët** adj (i) lumpy

Mimo'z'a nf Mimoza (female name)

mimo'z'ë nf [Bot] mimosa (Mimosa)

mina'he'dh'ës nm [Mil] **1** trench mortar, mortar **2** soldier armed with a mortar: mortarman

mina'heq'ës
  I § adj [Mil] for minesweeping
  II § nm person specialized in minesweeping

mina'heq'ese nf [Mil] minesweeper (ship)

mina'kërk'u'es
  I § adj [Mil] mine-detecting
  II § nm [Mil] mine detector

mina'lësh'u'es adj [Mil] **1** minelaying device on a ship **2** mortar

mina'mble'dh'ës adj [Mil] for gathering in mines

mina|mble'dh|ëse *nf*[*Mil*] = minahe'qëse

mina|nde'z|ës *n* [*Min*] person who sets off explosives

mina|pastru|es *adj* [*Mil*] for clearing mines: blaster, shooter, chargeman

mina|pastru|es|e *nf*[*Mil*] = minahe'qëse

mina're *nf* minaret

mina|spastru|es = minapastru'es

mina|shpërnda'r|ës *adj*[*Mil*] for minelaying

mina|shpërnda'r|ëse *nf*[*Mil*] minelaying machine

mina|to'r *n* miner

mina|vën|ës
  I § *adj*[*Mil*] for setting mines
  II § *nm* mine setter

mina|vën|ëse *nf*[*Mil*] minelayer

mina|zbul|u|es
  I § *adj*[*Mil*] mine-detecting
  II § *nm* mine detector

minde'r *nm* wooden bench built into the walls of a room, divan; straw-padded mattress covering such a bench

minera'l *nm, adj* mineral

MINERALEKSPORT *abbrev* <**Ndërmarrja e eksportit të mineraleve** agency for the exportation of minerals

mineral|iz|i'm *nm ger* 1 <**mineralizo'**·*n*, mineralizo'·*het* 2 mineralization; mineral enrichment; mineral content

mineral|izo'·*het vpr* to become mineralized

mineral|izo'·*n vt* to mineralize

mineral|mba'jt|ës *adj* mineral-bearing

minera|log *n* mineralogist

minera|logji' *nf* mineralogy

minera|logji'k *adj* mineralogical

minera'r *adj* mining, mineral

min'ë *nf* 1 mine (explosive) 2 mine (for extracting minerals)
  ∘ **min'ë fluturuese** mine dropped by parachute
  ∘ **min'ë me sahat** mine with a time fuse

***mi'n'ëz** *nf* pupil (of the eye)

miniatu'r|ë *nf* miniature

miniatur|i'st *n* miniaturist

minie'r|ë *nf* mine, quarry

mini|fu'nd *nm* miniskirt

min|i'm *nm ger* <**mino'**·*n*

minima'l
  I § *adj* (*Book*) minimal
  II § *nm* (*Book*) lower limit

minim|iz|i'm *nm ger* (*Book*) 1 <**minimizo'**·*n* 2 minimization

minim|izo'·*n vt* (*Book*) to minimize

minimu'm *nm* minimum

mini'stër *n* minister (of state)

ministri' *nf* government ministry

ministro'r *adj* (*Offic*) ministerial

min'o'·*n vt* 1 to lay explosive mines in []: mine 2 (*Fig*) to sabotage/undermine []

***mino'lla** *nm* (*np* ~ë*nj*) miller = mulli's

minori'ta'r
  I § *n* member of a minority
  II § *adj* of or pertaining to a minority

minorite't *nm* 1 minority 2 (*Fig*) small-sized group

minta'n *nm* padded jacket

minto'n *nm* (*Reg Gheg*) tight-fitting vest with big puffed sleeves (worn by a new bride)

min|u'a'r *adj* (*i*) mined (set to explode); boobytrapped

minue'r *nm* [*Bot*] goosefoot (*Chenopodium L.*)

minue't *nm* minuet

mi|nu'k *nm* 1 little mouse 2 (*Fig Colloq*) small child 3 (*Fig ColloqImpolite*) short person: shorty

*****minu'r** *nm* [*Bot*] = minue'r

minu'rth [*Bot*] Jerusalem oak, Jerusalem oak goosefoot (*Chenopodium botrys*)

minu's *nm, prep* (*nom*) minus

minu'sh|ë *nf* female mouse

minu'të *nf* minute; moment

mi|nj *np* <**mi** mice

*****minje'r** *nm* mine, pit = xe'he

mioka'rd *nm* [*Anat*] myocardium

mio'p *adj* myopic

miopi' *nf* myopia

miq *np* <**mik**

*****miq|ëri'** = miq*ë*si'

miq|ë'si *nf* 1 friendship 2 (*Collec*) friends and relatives
  ∘ **miq*ë*si e sëmurë** friendship based on doing favors

miq|ë'si'm *nm ger* <**miqëso'**·*n*, miqëso'·*het*

miq|ë'si'sht *adv* in friendly fashion, in a friendly way; as/like a friend

miq|ë'so'·*het vpr* to become friends; become reconciled

miq|ë'so'·*n vt* 1 to make [] friends; establish friendship with []; make peace between [] 2 to befriend

miq|ë'so'r *adj* friendly

*****miqi'k** *nm* shuttle

mi'ra *np* (*të*) 1 necessities of life 2 [*Folklore*] the Fates

Mir|a *nf* Mira (female name)

mira|di'as *adj* = mirënjo'hës

mira|di'je *nf* = mirënjo'hje

mira|di'j|shëm *adj* (*i*) = mirënjo'hës

mira|ka'nde *nf* fun, pleasure; whim; tidbit

miralla'j *nm* colonel

mira'n *adj, n* benevolent (person)

Mira'nd|a *nf* Miranda (female name)

*****mir|a'rdh|je** = mir*ë*sea'rdhje

mi'ra's *adv* in a friendly relationship: on friendly terms

Mira'sh *nm* Mirash (male name)

mirat|i'm *nm ger* 1 <**mirato'**·*n* 2 approval

mirato'·*n vt* 1 to give [] official approval: approve, ratify, sanction 2 to approve of []; indicate approbation of []
  ∘ **mirato'**·*n një ligj* to pass a law

mirat|u'es *adj* expressing approval, indicating approbation: approving, ratifying, sanctioning

mira'zh *nm* mirage

Mirba'rdh *nm* Mirbardh (male name)

mirdi't|as
  I § *n* native of Mirdita: Mirditan
  II § *adj* = mirdito'r

Mirdi't|ë *nf* mountainous district of northern Albania: Mirdita

mirdito'r
  I § *adj* of or pertaining to Mirdita, characteristic of Mirdita or of Mirditans; made by Mirditans

II § *n* = **mirdjtas**
*mire'ngë *nf* [Ichth] southern barbel = **mustak**
mirë
 I § *adv* 1 well 2 pleasantly 3 very much 4 *(Iron)* oh
 fine!
 II § *interj* okay, fine
 III § *adj (i)* good
 IV § *nf* good (as a grade assessment)
 V § *nf (e)* 1 well-being 2 favor, service, kindness
 3 benefit, virtue, value; good purpose, good 4 *[Folk-
 lore]* each of the three Fates; fate 5 *(Euph)* epilepsy
 6 *(Euph)* *[Zool]* weasel = **nuselalë**
 ◦ **mirë a keq** for better or worse, like it or not
 ◦ **mirë <>a bë·**n to give <> what <> *has* coming,
 teach <> a lesson
 ◦ **mirë e bukur 1** in ample/generous amount:
 enough to satisfy, plenty 2 thoroughly, very well
 ◦ **e mira e të mirave** best of all
 ◦ **E mira e ka të mirën.** *(Prov)* Good deeds are
 repaid a hundredfold. Do good and you will do well.
 ◦ **i miri i dheut** (of a person, also said ironically)
 best in the world, wonderful
 ◦ **mirë ju gjetsha!** (I hope to see you well!) so long
 for now, stay well!
 ◦ **e ka· (punën) mirë** "have one's affairs in good
 order" to have nothing to worry about, be all right
 ◦ **mirë mbeç** keep well! goodbye!
 ◦ **ësh·të me të mirat** to be in a good mood
 ◦ **mirë e mirë** thoroughly, very well
 ◦ **për (të) mirë 1** on a good occasion 2 with good
 intentions
 ◦ **mirë <>a puno·**n to give <> what <> *has* coming,
 teach <> a lesson
 ◦ **mirë se ju gjejmë!** (greeting) Good to see you!
 ◦ **mirë se vje·**n$^{2ndpdef/pres}$! nice of you to
 come!: welcome!
 ◦ **mirë e tumirë** better and better, ever better
 ◦ **Mirë vafsh!** "May you go well!" *(Felic)* Have a
 good trip!
mire'besim *nm* good faith: trust
mirëbë'rës
 I § *adj* 1 beneficent; benevolent 2 charitable, philanthropic
 II § *n* benevolent person: do-gooder, benefactor,
 philanthropist
mirëbë'rësi *nf* 1 benevolence 2 charity, philanthropy
*mirëbë'rje = mirëbërësi
*mirëda'lje *nf* success = **mbarësi**
*mirëda'sh|ës *adj, n* benevolent/generous/kind (per-
 son)
mirëda'shje *nf* benevolence, generosity, kindness
mirëdi'ta *interj* good day! hello!
*mirëdi'tun *adj (i)* *(Reg Gheg)* wellknown
mirëfilli *adv* 1 quite well, perfectly well 2 quite
 clearly
mirëfilltë *adj (i)* genuine, real, proper; true; direct
mirëkuptim *nm* solid mutual understanding: agreement; good will
mirëkupto·het *vpr* to come to a mutual understanding
mirëkupto·n *vt* to understand [ ] perfectly well
mirëmba·n *vt* to maintain [ ] well, take good care of
 [ ]
mirëmba'jt *stem for pdef, opt, adm, part*
 <**mirëmba·**n

mirëmba'jtje *nf ger* 1 <**mirëmba·**n 2 (proper)
 maintenance
mirëmbrë'ma *interj* good evening!
mirëmëngje's = **mirëmëngjesi**
mirëmëngje'si *interj* good morning!
mirëni *nf* prosperity; wealth
*mirënjo'f *(Reg Gheg)* = **mirënjoh**
mirënjoh|ës *adj* grateful, appreciative
mirënjoh|ësi *nf* = **mirënjohje**
mirënjo'hje *nf* gratitude, appreciation; acknowledgement
mirënjo'hur *adj (i)* well-known; famous
*mirënjo'jt OR mirënjo'ft *(Reg Gheg)* = **mirënjoh**
mirëpo *conj* 1 even so 2 even though 3 however
mirëpre's *stem for 1st sg pres, 1st & 3rd pl pres, 2nd
 & 3rd sg subj* <**mirëpret·**
mirëpret· *vt* to welcome
mirëpris *stem for pind, 2nd pl pres, imper*
 <**mirëpret·**
mirëprit *stem for part, pdef, pind, 2nd pl pres, imper,
 vp* <**mirëpret·**
mirëprit|ës *adj, n* hospitable/friendly (person)
mirëpri'tje *nf ger* 1 *(Book)* <**mirëpret·** 2 welcome
mirëpri'tur *adj (i)* welcome
*mirëpru'rës *adj* beneficial
mirëqenë *adj (i)* appropriate, fitting
mirëqe'nie *nf* well-being: prosperousness; good
 health
mirëru'ajtje *nf* good maintenance: preservation
mirërri's *stem for 1st sg pres, pl pres, 2nd & 3rd sg
 subj, pind* <**mirërrit·**
mirërri't· *vt* to rear [ ] well: give [ ] a good upbringing;
 grow [crops] well; raise [animals] well
mirërri'tje *nf ger* 1 <**mirërrit·** 2 proper raising/
 rearing; good upbringing
*mirërri'tur *adj (i)* well brought up
*mirërro'jtje *nf* high living, luxury
mirëse'ardh = **mirëserdh**
mirëse'ardhje *nf* welcome
mirëse'ardhur *adj (i)* welcomed, welcomed back,
 welcome
mirëse'rdh· *vt (pdef only)* bade welcome, welcomed
 back
 ◦ **:mirëserdhët** Welcome (to several guests)!
 ◦ **mirëserdhe** Welcome (to a single guest)!
mirësi *nf* 1 goodness 2 kindness 3 benefit; sake
 4 virtue 5 well-being 6 *(Colloq)* a drink to honor
 someone: toast
*mirësje'll|ës *adj* polite
mirësje'llje *nf* proper behavior; good manners, politeness, etiquette
mirëso·het *vpr* to improve, get better
mirëso·n *vt* 1 to improve [ ], make [ ] better 2 to
 benefit [ ]
mirëva'jtje *nf* smooth running, successful perfor-
 mance/progress
mirëz *nf* 1 pleasant aroma, fragrance *2 fairy
 *3 darling
Mir'i *nm* Miri (male name)
Miria'n *nm* Mirian (male name)
miriapo'dë *nf* *[Entom]* millipede, centipede
mirjollogi's· OR mirjollojis· *vt* to wail/mourn
 over a dead person

mir|kë adv (Reg Southeast) fairly/pretty well

Mirlind|a nf Mirlinda (female name)

mir|meni nf gracious act: favor

mir|ni nf prosperity

mir|o nf [Relig] holy oil/ointment

mir|os· vt 1 [Relig] to anoint [] with holy ointment, administer unction 2 (Colloq) to improve, enrich

mir|os·et vpr to recuperate

mir|o|sje nf ger 1 <miros· 2 [Relig] anointment ceremony, unction; confirmation 3 (Colloq) improvement

mir|si|shëm adj (i) kindly, well-disposed

mirta|cë np fem [Bot] myrtaceae ()

mir|upa|fsh|im interj goodbye! so long!

mir|up|je|k|sh|im interj = mirupafshim

Miru|sh nm Mirush (male name)

mirr stem for 2nd pl pres, pind, imper, vp <merr·

mirrë nf myrrh

mis

I § nm (np ~e) 1 body member, limb 2 facial feature
II § nm (np ~ a) (Old) member of the government/family

mis|ardh|je = mirësea|rdhje

mis|dit|ë = mesditë

Misejugje|ta! interj (Colloq) Glad to be here! Thanks for your welcome!

mis|e|ma|dh adj having notably large body or facial features

mis|serdh = mirëserdh

mis|ë nf
  ○ mis|ë e arës [Bot] *= helmarinë

mis|ër nm [Bot] corn, maize (Zea mays)
  ○ misër deti corn (plant) that yields small kernels
  ○ misër hamullor corn sown in a field of stubble
  ○ misër mashkull corn plant that does not produce any ears
  ○ misër qyqeje [Bot] = këlkazë

misër|i nf collec (Colloq) corn crop

misër|isht|ë OR **misër|isht|e** nf 1 field of corn; field of corn stubble 2 empty cornstalk; empty cornhusk 3 bare corncob

misër|nik|e nf cornbread

misër|o|k n [Ornit] turkey (Meleagris gallopava domesticus) = gjel deti, pulë deti

misër|o|re nf corn field; field of corn stubble

mis|ër|t adj (i) made with corn meal

mis|io|n nm mission

mis|iona|r nm missionary

Misi|r nm (Old) Egypt = Egjipt

misir|ës adj, n (Old) = egjiptian

misk
  I § nm musk (scent)
  II § interj command to a mule: giddyap!

miska|t nm muscatel wine

mi|skë nf 1 turkey hen = pulë deti 2 white ewe with black spots on her face

mis|këll nf personal grooming: toilet

miskëll|o·het vpr to perform one's toilet; put on makeup

miskëll|o·n vt to bamboozle

miskër nf [Ichth] young of the bleak

miskërro|nj|ë nf anthill

miskojë OR **miskojzë** nf mosquito, gnat = mushkonjë

---

mis|ma|dh adj large-bodied, big

miste|r nm mystery

misterio|z adj (Book) mysterious

misterioz|isht adv (Book) mysteriously

miste|rshëm adj (i) (Book) = misterioz

misticizëm nm mysticism

mistifik|im nm ger (Book) 1 <mistifiko·•n 2 mystification

mistifik|o·n vt (Book) to mystify

mistik adj mystical

mistre|c
  I § n 1 short and skinny person; runt 2 (Pej) troublemaking rascal
  II § adj runtish

mistr|i nf 1 trowel 2 [Tech] shaped trowel

mistro|s· vt to plaster [] (with a trowel)

misu|r nm large bowl

mish nm, nn (pl ~ra) 1 flesh 2 meat 3 naked skin 4 (Colloq) shop that sells meat
  ○ mish dashi mutton
  ○ mish derri/thiu pork
  ○ mish i dobët meat that is too lean
  ○ mish i dhëmbëve "flesh of the teeth" [Anat] gums
  ○ mishi i dhëmbëve gums (holding the teeth)
  ○ mish i egër [Med] exuberant granulation tissue
  ○ ësh-të^{pl} mish e gjak to be inseparable (companions)
  ○ mish i hollë goat meat, mutton, lamb
  ○ mish i huaj 1 tumor 2 (Fig) foreign body, alien presence
  ○ ka· (shumë) mish to be beefy and clumsy
  ○ mish kau beef
  ○ mish me presh e presh me mish "meat with leeks and leeks with meat" (Impol) there's not a dime's worth of difference between them, one's just as bad as the other
  ○ mishi i mishit children of one's own children
  ○ mish në mashë without a stitch to wear, body naked (and poor)
  ○ mish i ngordhur meat that is too lean
  ○ mish i njomë meat from a young animal: lamb, kid, veal
  ○ mish pas lajmësi request/message transmitted indirectly from mouth to mouth; unreliable/uncertain result of dependence on an intermediary
  ○ mish për top (Pej) cannon fodder
  ○ mish rrufak very tough meat
  ○ mish sade meat without any side dishes
  ○ (Edhe) mishi të piqet, edhe/e helli të mos digjet. "The meat may (even) roast and still not burn the spit." (Prov) The potentially dangerous situation can be handled without harm to what is important.
  ○ mish i trashë beef
  ○ mish i thatë dried and smoked meat: jerky
  ○ mish i therur meat carcass
  ○ mish i varfër (Colloq) diaphragm
  ○ mish viçi veal

mish|ata|k adj = mishtak

mish|dre|dhe nf strawberry = luleshtrydhe

mish|e|le|sh nm fouled-up mess

mish|ër nf 1 vocal cords/bands 2 [Anat] sinew, tendon 3 [Bot] meaty mushroom with a light brown underside

mish|ër|im nm ger 1 <mishëro·•n, mishëro·•het 2 embodiment

mish ëro·het *vpr* to take concrete form, find expression

mish ëro·n *vt* to make [] concrete/substantive, give substance/life to []: embody, incarnate; flesh out

mishëronjës *nm* embodiment

mishëz *nf* 1 [*Med Veter*] anthrax 2 [*Med*] caruncle

*****mishfortë** *nf* gizzard

mishje *adj* (said of fruit difficult to detach from the pit or of nuts whose meat is difficult to detach from the shell) flesh-clinging: clingstone (as opposed to freestone)

*****mishkonjë** *nf* gnat, mosquito = **mushkonjë**

*****mishkr** = mbishkr

mishkuq *adj* (of certain fruit) red-fleshed

mishlesh = mishelesh

mishmash
  I § *nm* (*Colloq*) general disorder and confusion; mishmash
  II § *adv* in general disorder and confusion, in disarray

mishmë *adj* (i) = mishtë

mishngrënës
  I § *adj* 1 carnivorous 2 (*Colloq*) (one) that eats a lot of meat
  II § *n* carnivore

*****mishno·het** (*Reg Gheg*) = mishëro·het

mishnjë *nf* 1 [*Bot*] soft moss on tree bark 2 = leshterik

*****mishqerë** = mështjerrë

*****mishro·n** = mështiro·n, mishëro·n

mishshitës *n* meat seller

mishtak *adj* = mishtë

mishtar *nm* (*Old*) butcher = kasap

mishtë *adj* (i) 1 fleshy, meaty; pulpy 2 [*Med*] pulpous

*****mishtjerrë** = mështjerrë

*****mishto·n** = mishëro·n

mishtor *adj* fleshy, meaty; plump

mishtore *nf* slaughterhouse

mishtormë *adj* (i) 1 plump, stout 2 fleshy, meaty

*****mishtrishte** = misërishtë

*****mishzo·het** *vpr* to put on flesh, get fleshy

*****mishzo·n** *vt* to make [] beefy: fatten, fatten up []

mit *nm* myth

mitake *adj* [*Bot*] adventitious

mitan *nm* 1 long-sleeved vest 2 plain white shirt 3 cotton-padded jacket

mitar *adj* 1 immature 2 tame 3 attractively innocent and unsophisticated: ingenuous

*****mitare** *nf* (*Old*) whore; brothel

*****mitavan** *nm* attic = nënçati

mitelë *nf* [*Med*] arm sling

mitë *nf* 1 tree sprout growing from a stump 2 stunted sprout of a plant 3 (*Pej*) bribe 4 [*Ethnog*] bride price paid by bridegroom's family to bride's family; payment to a marriage broker

mitëdhënës *n* bribe giver

*****mitëm** *adj* (i) corrupt, soft, effete

mitëmarrës *n* bribe taker

mitër *nf* 1 [*Anat*] uterus, womb 2 [*Bot*] stunted sprout of a plant 3 miter worn by bishop or other high cleric

mitëri *nf* gift brought by a guest

Miti *nm* Miti (male name)

mitik *adj* mythical

*****mitil** *adj* stunted

*****mitilës** *nm* [*Entom*] poultry louse

miting *nm* (*np* ~ *je*) large public gathering; political rally

mitingash *nm* (*Iron*) person who loves to attend rallies

mito·n = mitos·

mitologji *nf* mythology

mitologjik *adj* mythological

mitos· *vt* to corrupt, bribe

mitralim *nm ger* < mitralo·n

mitraljer *nm* [*Mil*] machine gunner

mitralo·n *vt* [*Mil*] to machine-gun

mitraloz *nm* [*Mil*] machine gun

mitropoli *nf* [*Relig*] see of an Orthodox metropolitan

mitropolit *nm* Orthodox archbishop: metropolitan

mitur
  I § *adj* (i) 1 immature, juvenile; childlike; inexperienced 2 [*Law*] underage, minor
  II § *n* (i) youth, juvenile, child

miturak
  I § *adj* 1 young, immature; youthful 2 (*Fig*) pertaining or belonging to childhood/youth
  II § *n* young person: youth

mituri *nf* 1 youth; immaturity, childishness; inexperience, innocence 2 childish act 3 childhood 4 (*Collec*) young people, children

miturine *nf* little girl, young girl

miturisht *adv* ingenuously, artlessly; childishly

miturishte *adj* of, for, or pertaining to children; juvenile; childish

mithër *nf* (*Reg*) = mjedër

miu *onomat*

miush *nm* little mouse

*****mivjetore** = mijëvjetore

mixan *nm* type of small-fruited black olive that is rich in oil

*****mixllo·n** *vi* to regain health, convalesce, improve; (of plants) turn green (again)

mixhë *nf with masc agreement* (*Reg*) uncle = xhaxha

mizakapës *nm* [*Ornit*] flycatcher (*Muscicapidae*)
  ○ **mizakapës i përhimë** [*Ornit*] spotted flycatcher *Muscicapa striata Pall.*
  ○ **mizakapës i zi** [*Ornit*] pied flycatcher *Ficedula hypoleuca, Muscicapa hypoleuca*

*****mizake** *nf* [*Entom*] beetle

mizambytës
  I § *adj* for killing bugs
  II § *nm* bug poison, bug killer

miza-miza *adv* with a prickly feeling
  ○ <> **bëhet miza-miza koka** <> is on pins and needles

mizangrënës *adj* insectivorous

mizanskenë *nf* [*Cine*] mise-en-scene, staging, stage setting

mizantrop *nm* (*Book*) misanthrope

mizantropi *nf* (*Book*) misanthropy

mizerje *nf* misery

mizë
  I § *nf* 1 fly; winged bug 2 noxious parasitic insect 3 (*Fig ColloqImpolite*) person/animal with a very small body: runt 4 (*Fig Colloq Impol*) weak or insignificant person who can be easily squashed: worm

II § adv (Colloq) in large numbers/amount: crawling, loaded, rife
○ **mizë e bardhë** something impossible; something very rare
○ **mizë e bukur** honey bee
○ **mizë dhensh** [*Entom*] sheep parasite *Melophagus ovinus* = **bite'm**
○ **mizë dheu** ant
○ **miza e farave** [*Entom*] bean seed fly/maggot, corn maggot *Phorbia platura*
○ **miza hesen** [*Entom*] Hessian fly *Mayetiola destructor Say.*
○ **mizë kali 1** horsefly, botfly, gadfly **2** *(Fig Pej)* annoying pest
○ **mizë e kërcu** lots and lots, a multitude
○ **miza e lakrës** [*Entom*] cabbage root fly, cabbage maggot *Phorbia (Hylemyia) brassicae*
○ **mizë lisi** *(Colloq)* lots, in hordes
○ **miza e mesdheut** [*Entom*] Mediterranean fruit fly *Ceratitis capitata Wied.*
○ **miza nëpër trup** [*Med*] formication
○ **ësh·të mizë pa kokë/krye** to be utterly brainless: be a flybrain/featherbrain/pinhead
○ **miza e panxharit** [*Entom*] sugar-beet fly *Pegomyia betae Curt.*
○ **mizë pashke** ladybug, ladybird = **mollëku'qe**
○ **mizë përdhese** [*Entom*] ant
○ **miza e qepës** [*Entom*] onion fly *Hylemyia antiqua Mg.*
○ **miza e qershisë** [*Entom*] fruit fly *Rhagoletis cerasi L.*
○ **miza suedeze** [*Entom*] frit fly *Oscinella frit L.*
○ **mizë toke** [*Entom*] ant = **milingo'në**
○ **miza e ullirit** [*Entom*] olive fruit fly *Dacus oleae Rossi*
○ **mizë xanxare** pesky insect
mizëpla'kë *nf* queen bee
miz|ëri *nf collec* swarm, horde, multitude, throng
miz|ëro'·n *vi* **1** (of body parts) to feel all tingly, cause ◇ to feel pins and needles **2** to be crawling/teeming (with people) ***3** to shatter
○ **<> mizëro·n**^{3sg} **koka** ◇ *has* tons of problems, ◇'s head *is* buzzing with problems
miz|o'·n *vi* **1** to snow in fine flakes ***2** *(Reg Gheg)* to rant and rage
mizo'r *adj, n* vicious/cruel/heartless (person)
mizori *nf* **1** viciousness, cruelty **2** vicious/cruel act; massacre
mizori'sht *adv* cruelly, viciously
***mizhdra'k** *(Old)* = **mëzdra'k**
mjaft
I § adv **1** in sufficient degree/amount: enough **2** in moderate degree/amount: in fair amount, rather, pretty **3** *(Colloq)* a lot, quite a bit; quite
II § pron quite a few, quite a number
○ **mjaft më!** that's enough already!, stop it!
mjaftë *adj (i)* sufficient, enough
mjaftëm *adj (i)* = **mjaftë**
mjafti *OR* **mjaftësi** *nf (Book)* sufficiency, adequacy
mjafto'·het *vpr* to get by, make do, do all right
mjafto'·n *vi* **1** to be enough; suffice **2** to be adequate
mjaftue'shëm
I § adj (i) adequate, satisfactory
II § adv adequately, satisfactorily
mjak·et *vpr* to feel dry in one's mouth, feel parched

mjak'ë *nf* furring of the tongue from fever or thirst
mjal'cë *nf* **1** = **ble'të 2** plant nectar
mjaltas *adv*
mjaltë
I § nm **1** honey **2** liquid exuded by an overripe fig
II § adj very sweet
III § adv (Fig) without a problem: very well, smooth as silk
○ **mjaltë i ëmbël** sweet as honey
○ **ësh·të mjaltë e qumësht** to be very pleasant/nice
○ **mjaltë e qumësht** ointment used in folk medicine to treat the bite of a weasel
○ **Mjalti i tërheq mizat.** "Honey draws ants." *(Prov)* (said of someone buttering up a powerful/wealthy person in order to get something)
mjaltëdhën|ës *adj* yielding plant nectar, rich in nectar
mjaltës *adj* nectar-producing; honey-producing
mjaltëz *nf* honeybee
mjalto'r *adj* **1** = **mjaltës 2** very sweet
mjaltshëm *adj (i)* very sweet, honey-sweet
mjallo'·n *vi* = **mjaulli'·n**
***mjaru'sh** *nm* = **milingo'në**
***mjaru'shkë** *nf (Reg Tosk)* = **milingo'në**
mjaulli'·n *vi* **1** to meow **2** *(Disparaging)* to complain in a whining voice; prattle on; gossip
mjaulli'me *nf ger* **1** < **mjaulli'·n 2** cat's sound: meow
mjaulli's *stem for 3rd pl pres, 3rd sg subj, 3rd pind* < **mjaulli't·**
mjaulli't· *vi* = **mjaulli'·n**
mjaulli'tje *nf ger* **1** < **mjaulli't· 2** = **mjaulli'më**
***mje** *prep (acc) (Reg)* = **gjer**
mje'dër *nf* [*Bot*] raspberry *(Rubus idaeus L.)*
mjedi's *nm* **1** environment, surroundings **2** circumstances, ambiance
○ **mjedis ushqyes** [*Biol*] culture medium (for growing microorganisms)
mjediso'r *nm* = **mes**
mjediso're *nf* center rod/beam
mjedhër = **mje'dër**
***mjeft** = **mjaft**
mje'gull *nf* **1** fog; haze that obstructs vision **2** [*Bot*] downy mildew = **hith**
mjegulli *nf* fogginess, haze; semi-darkness; twilight
mjegulli'm *nm ger* **1** < **mjegullo'·n, mjegullo'·het 2** haziness; vagueness
mjegulli'më = **mjegulli'në**
mjegulli'në *nf* **1** haze; mist **2** [*Med*] nebula (on the cornea)
mjegullna'jë *nf* **1** thick fog over a large area **2** [*Astron*] nebula **3** *(Fig)* murky darkness
mjegullo'·het *vpr* to get foggy; get covered in fog; get hazy
mjegullo'·n *vt* **1** to befog, cloud; cover [ ] with fog/haze **2** *(Fig)* to obscure
mjegullo'r *adj (Book)* clothed in fog, deep in fog
mjegullt *adj (i)* **1** foggy **2** *(Fig)* hazy, obscure, vague
mjegullua'r *adj (i)* **1** covered by fog, foggy **2** hazy, misty **3** *(Fig)* obscure, murky, vague
mjek *n* medical doctor, physician
○ **mjeku i dhëmbëve** *(Colloq)* tooth doctor
○ **mjek grash** *(Colloq)* women's doctor
○ **mjeku për fëmijë** *(Colloq)* children's doctor

○ **mjeku i syve** *(Colloq)* eye doctor
○ **mjeku i zemrës** *(Colloq)* heart doctor

*__mjeke'shë__ *nf* <mje• lady doctor

mjeke'r *nf* 1 chin 2 beard

mjekër bardhë *adj* 1 white-bearded; grizzled 2 *(Fig)* sage, prudent, mature

mjekërbore *adj* have a snowy white beard

mjekërbu'all *adj* *(Tease)* having a chin like a buffalo: double-chinned

mjekërbutë *adj* (of a woman) having a gently rounded chin; (of a man) having a soft beard

mjekërcja'p *adj, nm* (person) with a long pointed beard like a goat

mjekërde'nd ur *adj* having a thick beard

mjekërdhi'zë *nf* [*Bot*] St. Bernard's lily *(Anthericum liliago)*

mjekërfshe'së *adj* "broom-bearded" having a wide and rather sparse beard

mjekërgja'të
I § *adj, nm* person (with a long beard)
II § *nm* *(Impol)* priest

mjekërku'q *adj* red-bearded

mjekëro'r *nm* [*Ichth*] *(Ophidium rochei)*

mjekëro'sh *nm* 1 [*Ichth*] snake blenny *(Ophidium barbatum)* 2 man with a long beard

mjekërshtëllu'ngë *adj* having a soft thick woollike beard

mjekërthinj ur *adj, nm* 1 (man) with a grizzled beard 2 *(Fig)* sage (person)

mjekërzi' *adj, nm* (man) with a dark beard

mje'k ës *n* *(Old)* person who treats others with folk remedies: folk healer

mjek ësi' *nf* medical science: medicine

*__mjek ësi'm__ *nm* = mjeki'm

*__mjek ësi'në__ *nf* = mjeki'm

mjek ëso'r *adj* of or pertaining to medicine: medical

mjeki' *nf* *(Colloq)* medical treatment: physic, cure

mjeki'm *nm ger* 1 <mjeko• n, mjeko•het 2 medical treatment: medication, remedy

mjek je *np* folk remedies

mjeko•het *vpr* to be under medical treatment; be taking/using medicine

mjeko•n *vt* to treat [] with medicine: medicate

mjeko ligjo'r *adj* pertaining to forensic medicine: medicolegal

mjekra *np* <mjekër beard (of a man or animal)

*__mjekre'zë__ *nf* *(Reg Gheg)* barbel

mjekro'sh *nm, adj* (person) wearing a beard; (person) with a long beard

*__mjekrra'r__ *nm* *(Reg Gheg)* barber

mjekta'r *n* 1 *(Old)* medical practitioner: doctor, healer 2 = magjistar

*__mjeku er__ *adj (fem ~ore) (Old)* = mjekëso'r

mjeku'es
I § *adj* used for medical treatment: medical
II § *n* person who gives medical treatment, person giving health care: medic

mjeku eshëm *adj (i)* [*Med*] curable, remediable; treatable

mjel• *vt* to milk
○ **mjel• dy qyqe dele/dhi** "milk only two miserable old ewes/goats; be a poor peasant with only two miserable old ewes/goats left" to be a miserably poor peasant

mjelc ë *nf* [*Dairy*] milk bucket, milk pail

*__mjelc or__ *n* = mjelës

mjel ë *part* <mjel•

mjel ës *adj* [*Dairy*] 1 milk-giving, lactific 2 used for milking

mjel ëse *nf* [*Dairy*] 1 female dairyworker; milkmaid 2 milking machine 3 = mjelcë

mjel je *nf ger* <mjel•

mjel m *nm* teat of an udder; nipple; breast

mjell *nm* = mi'ell

mjell azë *nf* 1 = miellazë *2 snowdrift

mjell bardhë *nf* [*Ornit*] Egyptian vulture *(Neophron percnopterus)*

mjellmë *nf* 1 [*Ornit*] mute swan *(Cygnus olor)* 2 *(Fig Pet)* wise and beautiful young woman or girl
○ **mjellma qafëdrejtë** [*Ornit*] whooper swan *Cygnus cygnus L.*

*__mjeqe__ *np* folk medicine

mjera'n *n* wretch

mjerë
I § *adj* wretched, miserable, poor
II § *n (i)* wretch

*__mjerësi'__ *nf* = mjeri

*__mjergullë__ *nf* = mjegull

*__mjergull ore__ *nf* nebula of stars

mjeri' *nf* miserable existence: woe, misery; woeful poverty

mjeri'm *nm ger* 1 <mjero•n, mjero•het 2 misery; extreme poverty 3 great misfortune, calamity

mjeri'sht *adv* unfortunately

mjero•het *vpr* 1 to fall into a wretched state, become miserable 2 to feel very sorry (for someone)

mjero•n
I § *vt* 1 to desert 2 to make [] miserable/wretched 3 to pity; mourn
II § *vi* to suffer miserably

mjeru'ar *adj (i)* 1 visited by misfortune; wretched, miserable 2 deserted, abandoned and helpless

mjeru eshëm *adj (i)* woeful, pitiable

mjeru'sh *adj* sad

*__mjes__ *nm (Colloq)* 1 = mëngjes 2 *(Reg)* = mes

*__mjesa__ *adv* *(Reg Gheg)* = ndërsa

*__mjesta'r__ *nm* = mestar

mjeshta'k *nm* husband of one's wife's sister, brother-in-law

mjeshtër *nm* 1 master (of a skill), professional; master craftsman 2 mason, bricklayer
○ **mjeshtër vegle** master/professional instrumentalist

mjeshtëri' *nf* 1 mastery; skill; craftsmanship 2 craft, profession 3 *(Colloq)* craftiness

mjeshtëri'sht *adv* masterfully, skillfully, professionally

mjeshtëro•n *vt, vi* 1 to do/make/perform [] masterfully 2 to practice [a craft/skill]

mjeshtëro'k *nm* 1 *(Old)* poor (indigent) mason/ bricklayer 2 *(Impol)* poor (unskillful) craftsman 3 *(Impol)* uncultivated person

mjeshtëro'r *adj* 1 masterful, masterly, professional 2 pertaining to a master's craft/skill/profession 3 *(Fig)* belonging to or appropriate for a master: of a master

*__mjeshtra'k__ *adj* 1 = mjeshtëro'r 2 artificial

mjet *nm* **1** means **2** means of transportation: vehicle **3** device **4** partition wall

mjetë *nf* [*Text*] left-over yarn on a loom after the cloth is removed: thrums

mjetër *nf* (*Reg*) [*Bot*] = mjed*ër*

***mjet**ërr *nf* (*Reg*) [*Bot*] = mjed*ër*

***mjet**rra *np* <mjet*ër*r nonsense

***mjez** *nm* (*Colloq*) = mëngjes

***mjez**dit*ë* *nf* (*Colloq*) = mesdit*ë*

***mj**o •*n* *vi* to kick up a row, raise cain, cause a fracas

MK *abbrev* <Ministria e Komunikacioneve Ministry of Communication

***m**kâmb| (*Reg Gheg*) = mëkëmb|

***m**kejmë *adj* (*i*) wasted, ruined

***m**kryec|im *nm* rabidity, rage

***m**kry|em *adj* (*i*) peculiar, abnormal

MKZ *abbrev* <Mbrojtja kundër zjarrit protection against fire

***mlat**ë = mblat*ë*

mlepish *nm* [*Bot*] = gjipisht*ë*

mles (*Reg*) = mbles

***mleto**n-*et* *vpr* to become worn through long use

***mle**z*ë* = mbul*ës*e

mlysh *nm* (*Leuciscus cephalus albus*) (*Fig*) [*Ichth*] stupid person, pinhead

mllef *nm* built-up rage, pent-up fury

mllefqar *adj, n* (person) ready to burst with rage

***mlluzg**ë *nf* marl

***mndo**re *nf* (*Old*) = mjet

***mne**f-*et*-*vpr* to be abusive, be annoying

***mne**lë *nf* diaper

***mne**rë I § *nf* OR **mner** II § *nm* terror, horror, dread

***mne**rshëm *adj* (*i*) dreadful, horrible, terrible

***mnimo**re *nf* monument, memorial = përmendo*re*

***mnji**lle = mënji*lle*

***mo** = mos

mobilie *nf* furniture, room furnishings

mobilier *n* furniture maker, cabinetmaker, joiner

mobilieri *nf* **1** (*Collec*) furnishings **2** furniture making

mobilim *nm ger* <mobilo•*n*

mobiliz|im *nm ger* **1** <mobilizo•*n* **2** mobilization

mobiliz|o•*het* *vpr* to get mobilized, prepare all one's forces for concentrated action

mobiliz|o•*n* *vt* to mobilize

mobiliz|u|a|r
  I § *adj* (*i*) mobilized
  II § *nm* [*Mil*] person called up by mobilization

mobiliz|u|es *adj* mobilizing

***mobil**je *nf* = mobi*lie*

***mobil**jeri = mobi*lieri*

mobilo•*n* *vt* to furnish [] (with furniture/furnishings)

mobilu|a|r *adj* (*i*) furnished (with furniture/furnishings)

***moc**
  I § *adj* one-year-old
  II § *n* age-mate, contemporary; schoolmate

***mo**cë *adv* (*Reg Gheg*) of the same age
  ○ **i rritun mocë** (*Reg Gheg*) brought up together

moco *nf* [*Tech*] wheel hub, boss

moç *nm* year-old wether

moçal *nm* swamp, mire

moçalik *adj* = moça*lor*

moçalishte OR **moça**lisht*ë*
  I § *nf* swampy soil; swampland, bog
  II § *adj* swampy, boggy

moçaliz|im *nm ger* <moçalizo•*n*, moçalizo•*het*

moçaliz|o•*het* *vpr* to become a swamp

moçaliz|o•*n* *vt* to make [] into a swamp

moçalor *adj* **1** swampy, boggy **2** growing in swamps/bogs

moçallëke *nf* damp wood that fails to burn and turn into charcoal

moç|ëm
  I § *adj* (*i*) **1** advanced in years: aged **2** ancient
  II § *n* (*i*) old one; ancient; ancestor

moçim *nm ger* **1** <moço•*n* **2** terrible insult

***moç**kë *nf* rough barren ground

***moç**no•*het* *vpr* (*Reg Gheg*) = mosho•*het*

moço•*n* *vt* to insult terribly

***moço**licë *nf* = meli*cë*

model *nm, adj* model; style
  ○ **model flokësh** hair style, hairdo

modelim *nm ger* **1** <modelo•*n* **2** exemplary standard: model

modelist *n* person who builds models: model maker

modelo•*n* *vt* to make an exemplary [], produce a sample [] to serve as a model: make a model [], model []

moderator *nm* [*Phys*] moderator

modern *adj* modern

modernist *adj, n* (*Book*) modernist

moderniz|ëm *nm* [*Art Lit*] **1** modernism **2** modernistic appearance

moderniz|im *nm ger* **1** <modernizo•*n*, modernizo•*het* **2** modernization

moderniz|o•*het* *vpr* **1** to become modernized **2** (*Iron*) to put on modernistic airs

moderniz|o•*n* *vt* to modernize

modest *adj* (*Book*) modest

modesti *nf* (*Book*) modesty

***mode**shë *nf* milliner

modë *nf* fashion, mode

modifikim *nm ger* **1** <modifiko•*n* **2** modification

modifiko•*n* *vt* to modify

modiste *nf* (*Book*) modiste

modulacio*n* *nm* [*Mus*] modulation

***modh** *nm* **1** = mo*de* **2** fancy, notion

***mo**dhë *nf* [*Bot*] rye-grass (*Lolium*)

***modh**istër *nf* = mode*shë*

modhull *nf* [*Bot*] yellow vetchling (*Lathyrus aphaca*)

***moga**n I § *nm* OR **moga**në II § *nf* mahogany

***mogi**lë *nf* = gomi*lë*

moh *nm* = mohim

mohameda|n *n* Mohammedan = muhamedan

mohaq *nm* [*Bot*] = moha*r*

***moha**r *nm* [*Bot*] bristlegrass (*Setaria germanica*)

moh|ës *adj* **1** = mohu*es* **2** worthless, bad

mohim *nm ger* **1** <moho•*n* **2** denial; negation; contradiction **3** refusal **4** [*Phil*] antithesis

***moh**imtar *adj, n* (*Old*) renegade

moho•*n* *vt* **1** to deny; negate; contradict, refute, belie **2** to refuse

mohor *adj* [*Ling*] negative

moh|u|es *adj, nm* negative

mohueshëm *adj (i)* deniable

Moisi *nm* Moses

moj *interj pcl* appellative addressed to a woman or girl: hey, hey you; appellative title preceding a feminine noun to indicate intimacy: my dear

*moje *np* <**muaj** *(Reg Gheg)*

moker *nf* **1** millstone **2** hand mill, grinder; grindstone **3** big heavy rock

mokërr *nf* [*Invert*] = **shumëkëmbësh**

moknore *nf* [*Geol*] lime-rich sandy soil: *(pozzolana)*

*mokrar *nm* miller

*mokth *nm* *(Reg)* [*Bot*] poet's narcissus, pheasant's eye *(Narcissus poeticus, Narcissus radiflorus Salisb.M)*

mol *nm* mole, breakwater; quay, pier

mol *stem for pdef* <**mjel**•

molar
  I § *adj* **1** *(Colloq)* sticky-fingered; thieving, swiping **2** filthy, slovenly **3** slatternly
  II § *n* **1** filcher, poacher, thief **2** filthy person

molare *nf* slut, slattern

mole *nf* [*Chem*] mole (measure of quantity)

molekular *adj* [*Chem*] molecular

molekulë *nf* **1** [*Chem*] molecule **2** *(Fig)* smallest part of something

moleps• *vt* to contaminate, pollute, infect

moleps•et *vpr* to become contaminated/polluted/infected

molepsje *nf* **1** <**moleps•**, **moleps•et 2** contamination, pollution, infection

molepsur *adj (i)* contaminated, polluted, infected

molë *nf* **1** [*Entom*] moth, clothes moth **2** [*Med*] mole (in the uterus containing fetal tissue) **3** *(Fig)* person who is a constant irritation: pest
  ○ **mola e drithërave** [*Entom*] Angoumois grain moth *Sitotroga cerealella Oliv.*
  ○ **mola e grurit** [*Entom*] European grain moth, mottled corn clothes moth *Nemapogon granellus*
  ○ **mola e lindjes** [*Entom*] Oriental fruit moth *Cydia molesta*
  ○ **mola e qepës** [*Entom*] leek smudge *Acrolepsis assectella*

molëz *nm* [*Invert*] = **molë**

molibden *nm* [*Chem*] molybdenum *(Mo)*

molikë *nf* [*Bot*] Balkan pine *(Pinus peuce)*

molimolybdenums• *vt* **1** to tire/wear [ ] out, make [ ] weary; enfeeble ***2** (of moths) to eat away at [ ]

molis•et *vpr* **1** to get all tired out; become enfeebled **2** *(Fig)* to become emotionally drained ***3** to get moth-eaten; get infected

*molisës *adj* infectious

molisje *nf ger* **1** <**molis•**, **molis•et 2** exhaustion, fatigue

molisur *adj (i)* **1** all tired out, exhausted; enfeebled **2** *(Fig)* to become emotionally drained

molit• *vt* (of moths) to eat a hole in [clothing]

*molitë *nf* [*Entom*] moth

molitur *adj (i)* moth-eaten

*molivë *nf* *(Reg Gk)* pencil, crayon

molo *nf* mole, jetty, pier

molusk *nm* *(np ~qe)* [*Invert*] mollusk = **butak**

*molushë
  I § *nf* **1** toad **2** *(Fig)* fat and disgusting woman
  II § *adj* fat and disgusting

*mollafaqe *nf* bluntly

mollaftua *nm (obl ~oi, np ~onj)* [*Bot*] large-fruited quince grafted to a apple tree

mollak *nm* rusty-colored ox

mollakuqe *nf* [*Entom*] ladybug, ladybird = **mollëkuqe**

*mollamuç *nm* = **mushmollë**

mollapjeshkë
  I § *nf* chubby young woman with rosy cheeks
  II § *adj* chubby and rosy-cheeked

mollaqe *np* buttocks, rump

mollash *adj* chubby; having chubby rosy cheeks

mollatartë *nf (Reg)* [*Bot*] tomato

mollatoke *nf (Reg Gheg)* potato

*mollavis *stem for 1st sg pres, pl pres, 2nd & 3rd sg subj, pind* <**mollavit**•

*mollavit• *vt* to sadden, touch

mollçinë *nf* [*Bot*] crab apple, wild apple *(Malus silvestris)*

mollçinkë *nf* **1** [*Bot*] = **mollçinë 2** *(Pej)* small misshapen apple that is not good to eat

molldragë *nf* **1** [*Med*] whitlow; felon **2** [*Bot*] = **bordullak**

mollë *nf* **1** apple, apple tree *(malus domestica)* **2** cheek
  ○ **molla e Adamit** [*Anat*] Adam's apple
  ○ **mollë e artë** tomato
  ○ **molla e bejlegut** [*Ethnog*] apple thrown to challenge one's opponent to a duel
  ○ **molla e dasmës** [*Ethnog*] the apple of good luck thrown by one of the bride-fetching group to the guests waiting in the yard of the bride's house: whoever catches it will be happy
  ○ **molla e derës** doorknob
  ○ **mollë dheu** [*Bot*] ***1** Jerusalem artichoke *Helianthus tuberosus* **2** *(Reg)* potato
  ○ **mollë egër** [*Bot*] crab apple, wild apple *Malus silvestris*
  ○ **molla e fytit** [*Anat*] Adam's apple
  ○ **molla e gishtit** pad of the finger; ball of the toe
  ○ **mollë e pandarë** bosom buddies, inseparable friends
  ○ **Mollët i qëro, dardhët i numëro!** *(Prov)* Eat as many apples as you like (since they won't hurt you), but count out the pears carefully (since they are hard on the stomach).
  ○ **s'ke ku të hedhësh/hidhje mollën** "there is/was no room for you to add an apple" they are/were packed in like sardines
  ○ **molla e shalës** pommel of the saddle
  ○ **mollë sherri** cause of a quarrel: the apple of discord
  ○ **molla të dala** prominent cheekbones
  ○ **mollë verige** small reddish apple
  ○ **molla e veshit** earlobe

mollëkuqe *nf* "red-apple beetle" **1** [*Entom*] *(Phytodecta fornicata Brugg.)* **2** ladybird beetle, ladybug *(Coccinella septempuncata)*

mollëmuçe *nf* [*Bot*] = **mushmollë**

*mollëmushe *nf* [*Bot*] = **mushmollë**

mollët
  I § *adj (i)* **1** pale orange ***2** pale green; chlorotic
  II § *nn (të)* ***chlorosis**

mollëviçe *OR* **mollëviçëz** *nf* [*Bot*] wild service tree *(Sorbus torminalis)*

mollëz nf 1 cheek 2 finger/toe pad 3 [Bot] = modhull
○ mollëza e fytit [Anat] Adam's apple
○ mollëza të dala prominent cheekbones
*mollis·et vpr to dally, tarry, be late
mollishtë nf apple orchard
mollmuçe nf [Bot] = mushmollë
*mollo nf = mol
*mollofrenxë nf venereal disease, syphilis
*mollojis· vt to tell, confess, declare
mollok
I § nm 1 massive object; massive piece/portion 2 massive rock: boulder
II § adj massive; (of a boy/girl) strapping
○ mollok akulli ice floe
*mollovit·et vpr to swell up
mollure nf [Agr] fungal parasite that dries up the leaves of crops such as tobacco, grapes, and onions
mollusk nm [Invert] mollusk
moment nm moment
*momë nf (Reg Gheg) = mëmë
*momullë nf = mobilie
monark nm monarch
monarki nf monarchy
monarkik adj monarchic, monarchial
monarkist n monarchist, royalist
monarkizëm nm monarchism
monarko-fashist adj, n monarcho-fascist
*monarqi = monarki
*monastir = manastir
Monastir nm city in Macedonia which was the site of the 1908 congress of Albanians (before their independence from Turkey) at which the Latin alphabet was permanently adopted for Albanian: Monastir, Bitola
mondan adj (Npc) worldly
*mone nf walled enclosure
*monedhar = monetar
monedhë nf coin; currency, money
○ ç'monedhë ësh·të^{sg} (Impol) what kind of louse {} is
○ monedhë qarkulluese currency
*monedhuer adj (fem ˜ ore) (Old) = monedhar
monetar adj monetary
mongol adj, n Mongolian, Mongol
mongolishte nf Mongolian language
mongolizëm nf [Med] mongolism
mongoloid adj Mongoloid
monist nm 1 adherent of a single political party line 2 monist
monizëm nm [Philos] monism
mono formativ mono-
monogami nf monogamy
monografi nf monograph
monografik nf monographic
monokël nm monocle
monokotiledon nm [Bot] monocotyledon
monokulturë nf [Agr] monoculture
monolishtë nf [Bot] oregano, pot marjoram (Origanum vulgare)
monolit
I § nm monolith
II § adj monolithic
monolog nm [Lit] monologue

monom nm [Math] monomial
monopat nm narrow path, goat trail
monopol nm monopoly
monopolist n monopolist
monopolizim nm ger 1 <monopolizo·n 2 monopolization
monopolizo·n vt to monopolize
monosilabik adj monosyllabic
monoteist n monotheist
monoteizëm nm monotheism
monotip nm [Publ] typesetting machine that casts individual letters and assembles them in a single line: Monotype
monotipist n Monotype operator
monoton adj monotonous
monotoni nf monotony
*monozig OR monozik nm trapeze
monstruoz adj monstrous
montator n assembler, fitter
montazh nm montage
montim nm ger 1 <monto·n 2 assembly, assembly work 3 montage, assemblage
monto·n vt to assemble, fit [] together; edit [film]
montues n 1 assembler, fitter 2 (film) editor
montueshëm adj (i) capable of being assembled and disassembled, mountable and dismountable: collapsible
monument nm monument
monumental adj monumental
*mor = more
mor stem for pdef <merr·
○ e mori ferra fjalën everyone knows about it, it's all over town
○ e mori ferra uratën it's all over, there's nothing that can be done about it now
moraçë nf [Bot] = maraskë
morajë nf [Bot] fennel = maraj
○ moraj qeni *= maraskë
moral nm 1 morality 2 sense of morality/honor: morals 3 moral (of a story) 4 morale
moralist n moralist
moralisht adv 1 morally 2 in terms of morale
moralizim nm ger (Pej) 1 <moralizo·n 2 moralization; tedious moralizing
moralizo·n vt (Pej) to moralize
moralizues adj, n (Pej) (tediously) moralizing (person)
moralo-politik adj moral and political
moralshëm adj (i) 1 moral 2 of high morale
*moraskë nf [Bot] wild fennel = maraskë
moratorium nm moratorium
Moravë nf mountain in southeastern Albania
*morç nm corpse, carcass
*mord = mort
more interj pcl appellative addressed to a man or boy: hey, hey you; appellative preceding a masculine noun to indicate intimacy: my dear
More nf Morea
*morekuje nf curse, scourge
morenë nf 1 [Ichth] moray eel Muraena helena 2 [Alpinism] moraine
morenxë nf [Bot] smilax, greenbrier (Smilax aspera)

*mo'rë *nf* alpine pasture

morfe'm'ë *nf* [*Ling*] morpheme

morfi'n'ë *nf* [*Pharm*] morphine

morfo logji'i *nf* morphology

morfo logji'k *adj* morphological

morg *nm* morgue

mori *nf* large number: multitude, swarm, flock

mori'n'ë *nf* [*Bot*] goat willow *(Salix caprea)*

morni'c a *np* 1 shivers, shudders 2 goosebumps 3 [*Med*] shivering caused by a chill: rigor

*Moro'ko *nf* = Maro'k

*morollo'k *adv* = zhyt

morovi'n'ë *nf* muggy weather: sultriness, stifling heat

moro'ze *nf* (*Pej*) paramour of a married man: mistress

mors *nm* [*Spec*] Morse code

morse'te *nf* [*Tech*] small vise

mo'rsë *nf* 1 [*Tech*] vise 2 [*Zool*] = elefant deti
  ◦ mors*ë* ballore [*Tech*] end screw
  ◦ mors*ë* e bangos [*Tech*] bench vise

mort *nm* (*Colloq*) death
  ◦ ësh·të (fare) mort to be very ugly, be ugly as sin
  ◦ [] hëngërt morti! (*Curse*) May death take ("eat") []! I hope [] dies!
  ◦ Goja/fjala s'bën mort. (*Prov*) Words don't kill. Just mentioning it can't do any harm.

morta'j'ë *nf* [*Mil*] mortar (weapon)

morta'j ist *n* [*Mil*] mortarman

mortali'te't *nm* (*Book*) mortality; death rate

morta'r *adj* of or pertaining to death

*mo'rt e *nf* = mo'rtj e
  ◦ ësh·të^{3sg} mortjae <> ⬦ hates {}
  ◦ Të harroftë mortja! "May death forget you!" (*Iron*) (said in jest to someone who has just done something very impressive)

*mort'ë'ni *nf* = mori'

mo'rtj e *nf* Death

morto'r *adj* 1 pertaining to death: mortal, death 2 pertaining to a funeral 3 resulting in death: fatal 4 causing terrible suffering

mort sh'ë'm *adj* (i) 1 mortal = vde ksh'ë'm 2 = morto'r

morth *nm* chilblain

morr *nm* [*Entom*] 1 louse 2 plant louse: aphid *(Aphidodea)*
  ◦ morri i bahçeve [*Entom*] cotton aphid *Aphis gossypii Glov.*
  ◦ morrat e bimëve [*Entom*] aphids *Aphidodea*
  ◦ morri i drithërave [*Entom*] greenbug, spring grain aphid, wheat louse, corn leaf aphid, corn root aphis *Schizaphis (Toxoptera) graminum*
  ◦ morri i lakrës [*Entom*] kind of cabbage aphid *Brevicoryne ornata L.*
  ◦ morri i misrit [*Entom*] elm leaf aphid, corn root aphis *Tetraneura ulmi*
  ◦ morri i panxharit [*Entom*] black bean aphid *Aphis fabae Scop.*
  ◦ morri i përgjakshëm [*Entom*] wooly apple aphid *Eriosoma lanigerum Hausm.*
  ◦ morri i pjeshkës [*Entom*] green peach aphid *Myzus persicae Sulz.*
  ◦ morri i qershisë [*Entom*] black cherry aphid *Myzus cerasi*
  ◦ morri i rrënjës [*Entom*] elm leaf aphid, corn root aphis *Tetraneura ulmi*

morra'c *adj* (*Pej*) = morraca'k

morra'ca'k
  I § *adj* (*Pej*) 1 infested with lice, lousy 2 filthy; rotten
  II § *nm* (*Pej*) 1 louse-infected person 2 filthy/rotten person

morr ama'n = morraca'k

morra's *stem for 1st sg pres, pl pres, 2nd & 3rd sg subj, pind* < morra't·

morra'sh *adj* (*Pej*) = morraca'k

morra't· *vt* = morrit·

morra't·et = morrit·et

morrc *nm* chicken/animal/plant louse

mo'rr ës *n* (*Pej*) = morraca'k

morri's *stem for 1st sg pres, pl pres, 2nd & 3rd sg subj, pind* < morri't·

morri't· *vt* to inspect [] for lice; delouse []

*morri'z = murri'z

mos *negative pcl* 1 don't 2 lest, that __ not 3 I wonder whether it isn't the case: wouldn't that be right? might it not? 4 (in exclamations) expresses surprise or dissatisfaction: come on now!
  ◦ Mos a mos! You don't mean it! You must be kidding! No!
  ◦ Mos arrifsh "May you not arrive!" (*Curse*) I hope you die young!
  ◦ Mos bëj hop pa kapërcyer/hedhur gardhin. "Don't say whee! until you are over the fence." (*Prov*) Don't count your chickens before they're hatched.
  ◦ Mos u bëj plak në shtëpinë e botës! "Don't act like an elder in someone else's house!" (*Prov*) Don't be bossy when you're not the boss!
  ◦ Mos <> bëj/bëni vapë! "Don't make <> hot." (*Crude*) Stop bugging <>! Get off <>'s back!
  ◦ Mos e ço·n^{opt3rd} kokën shëndoshë! (*Curse*) May {} never have a healthy day!, I hope {} dies!
  ◦ Mos i çoftë kryet shëndoshë! (*Curse*) May {} never have a healthy day!, I hope {} dies!
  ◦ Mos e dëgjo·n^{opt} qyqen! "May {} not hear the cuckoo!" (*Curse*) May {} die before spring comes!
  ◦ Mos <>i fryj/fryni shkotat! Don't make <> mad! Don't mess with <>!
  ◦ Mos e fut në hambar pa e shoshitur "Don't put it in the granary without sifting it." Don't consider someone a friend without knowing him well. Don't trust anyone you don't know well.
  ◦ Mos gjetsh vend e trevël (*Curse*) May you never have a moment's peace!
  ◦ Mos e hap/hapni vallen shumë! "Don't open up the dance too much!" Don't go overboard and include too many people!
  ◦ Mos e hap· postatin! 1 Don't spend more than you have! 2 Don't carry things too far! 3 Don't open a hornet's nest! Don't open Pandora's box!
  ◦ Mos hyr në pus me litarin e botës! "Do not go into a well using someone else's rope!" (*Prov*) You can't always rely on somebody else! You need to be more self-reliant.
  ◦ mos <> jep faqe don't give <> support, encourage <>; don't pamper <>
  ◦ Mos mburr degët pa parë rrënjët! "Don't praise the branches without seeing the roots!" (*Prov*) Don't judge a book by its cover!
  ◦ Mos <> nxeh kryet! (*Crude*) Stop bugging []!
  ◦ Mos <>i pafsha sytë/surratin "May I not see <>'s eyes/face!" (*Scorn*) I never want to see <> again!

○ **Mos <>i pafsha sytë!** "May I never see <>'s eyes!" I don't even want to hear about <>!

○ **Mos <> paftë syri keq** "May <>'s eye not see bad things!" *(Felic)* May <> never suffer! I wish <> happiness!

○ **Mos pjektë dy bukë në një hi!** *(Curse)* may he see no more tomorrows

○ **Mos e prek në bisht, se të ha në gisht!** *(Prov)* Play with fire and you get burned!

○ **Mos e prish jahninë për një qepë.** "Don't spoil the stew for one onion" Don't ruin the whole thing by stinginess over a minor detail.

○ **Mos e prish kazanin/jahninë për një qepë!** "Don't spoil the cauldron/stew for the sake of an onion!" *(Prov)* Don't take a chance of ruining something important for the sake of something minor!

○ **mos fol prishur** don't use offensive language

○ **mos [] qit pas mendsh!** "don't push [] behind your brains" don't put [] aside, don't forget []

○ **Mos <> rëntë shpina për tokë!** "May <>'s back not touch the ground!" May <> never die! Long live <>!

○ **Mos i shiko shkallët, por shikoji oborrin!** "Don't look at the stairway, but look at the garden!" *(Prov)* Don't judge a person by what he has inherited from others, but by what he does himself.

○ **Mos i shiko shpatullat, por shikoji zemrën!** "Don't look at shoulders, but look at one's heart!" *(Prov)* What counts is not someone's physical strength, but his character.

○ **mos e shtier në pus!** "don't stick it in the well" be sure not to forget it!

○ **Mos i shtjer hidhërim vetes!** Try not to be so sad!

○ **Mos e trazo/prek gjarprin në bisht!** "Don't touch the snake by the tail!" *(Prov)* Let sleeping dogs lie!

○ **Mos [] zëntë ora!** *(Curse)* May [] not last through the hour!

○ **Mos <>a zgjat·!** Don't drag it out with <>! Don't go into any details with <>!

mos *formativ* (forms negatives of pronominals or deverbal nouns) mis-, dis-, non-, un-

mos a rdh je *nf* failure to come

mos arri t je *nf* failure to arrive/achieve

mos baraz i *nf* inequality

mos baraz im *nm* [*Math*] inequality

mos bes im *nm* **1** mistrust, distrust; lack of confidence **2** disbelief; lack of faith

mos bes u e s
  I § *adj* sceptical
  II § *n* sceptic, non-believer

*mos bër je** *nf* non-performance

mos bind ës *adj* disobedient

mos bind je *nf* disobedience

mos blu a rje *nf* indigestion

mos cën im *nm* nonviolation

*mos cil ës i** *nf* disqualification

*mos cil ës u e s** *adj* disqualifying

*mos çm im** *nm* disregard; underestimation

mos da shje *nf* unwillingness; reluctance

*mos dash uri** *nf* dislike

mos dëgj im *nm* **1** failure to hear **2** failure to listen; failure to pay attention

mos di je *nf* ignorance

mos duk je *nf* non-appearance, absence

*mos dur im** *nm* impatience, intolerance

*mos dhi mbje** *nf* anesthesia

mos fit im *nm* defeat, loss

mos fjet je *nf* sleeplessness; alertness, vigilance

mos godi t je *nf* failure to hit: miss

mos gjë *pron (Colloq)* nothing = **asgjë**

mos ha pje *nf* non-openness

mos hy rje *nf* non-entry

mos interes im *nm (Book)* lack of interest

*mos je** *nf* negation, negative

*mosk** *nm* musk

mos kal im *nm* **1** blocked passage **2** (in examinations) failure

*mos ka mje** *nf* poverty

mosketier *nm* daredevil, musketeer

Mo skë *nf* Moscow

mos kënaq ës i *nf* dissatisfaction, displeasure

mos kok ë ça rës *adj* lacking conscientiousness: negligent, careless

mos kok ë ça rje *nf* lack of concern, indifference; neglect

mos ko ndër *nf* [*Bot*] burning bush, dittany *(Dictamnus albus)*

mos konsekue nc ë *nf* inconsequentiality

moskovit *adj, n* Muscovite

mos kry erje *nf* failure to achieve/accomplish/complete

mos kth im *nm* failure to return

mos kufi z im *nm* boundlessness, unrestrictedness

*mos kujde s je** *nf* negligence, carelessness; indifference; neglect

*mos kujde s ur** *adj (i)* negligent, careless; indifferent

mos ku nd *adv* not anywhere, nowhere else

mos kundër sht im *nm* lack of opposition/contrariness: obedience

mos kupt im *nm* **1** failure to understand **2** misunderstanding

mos ku rrë *adv* not ever, no other time

mos ku sh *pron* not anyone, no one else

mos lej im *nm* refusal (of permission)

mos luft u e s *adj* noncombatant

mos marr ë ve shje *nf* **1** disagreement, discord **2** misunderstanding

mos mbar ë va jtje *nf (Book)* lack of progress/success; failure

mos me rë *nf (Reg)* = **përbi ndësh**

mos merit im *nm (Book)* undeservedness

mos më harro *adj*

mos më prek *adj*

*mos më sy rje** *nf* nonaggression

mos mirat im *nm* disapproval

mos mir ë mba jtje *nf (Book)* lack of maintenance, failure to maintain well

mos mir ë njo h ës *adj* **1** ungrateful *2* thankless

mos mir ë njo hje *nf* ingratitude, ungratefulness

*mos mjaft im** *nm* insufficiency, inadequacy

*mos mu ndje** *nf* inability

mos një rhy rje *nf (Book)* non-intervention, non-interference

*mos ndo dhje** *nf* absence

mos nën sht rim *nm* lack/refusal of support; failure to support *mos|ngjajtje nf inequality

mos|ni pcl pl <mos don't do that!

mos|njeri pron (Reg Arb) = asnjeri

mos|një herë adv (Reg Arb) = asnjëherë

*mos|nji herë adv = asnjëherë

mos|njohje nf(Reg Gheg) 1 lack of knowledge/information: ignorance 2 nonrecognition, nonacceptance

mos|njohuri nf unawareness, ignorance

*mos|pagesë nf = mospagim

mos|pagim nm nonpayment

mos|pajtim nm 1 lack of agreement; failure to agree; discrepancy; disagreement 2 incompatibility, incongruity

mos|paraqitje nf failure to appear; failure to report in

mos|pasje nf 1 deficiency, insufficiency, lack 2 (Old) poverty

mos|pëlqim nm disapproval

*mos|përdorim nm nonuse, disuse; desuetude

mos|përfillës adj disdainful, disrespectful; scornful

mos|përfillje nf 1 disrespect; disregard 2 disdain; disparagement

mos|përgatitje nf unpreparedness

mos|përgjegjje nf failure to reply

mos|përkim nm = mospërputhje

mos|përkujdesje nf (Book) negligence, neglect

mos|përmbushje nf nonfulfilment

*mos|përparim nm lack of progress

mos|përputhje nf 1 lack of fit, mismatch; disparity, discrepancy 2 incompatibility

mos|përshtatje nf inappropriateness; incompatibility

mos|përzierje nf nonintervention

*mos|pika sje nf failure to detect/spot/notice

mos|plotësim nm failure to complete, failure to carry through: non-fulfilment

mos|pranim nm 1 failure to accept: nonacceptance, rejection 2 disapproval, refusal

mos|prek adj

mos|prishje nf (Book) preservation
  ◦ mosprishje e gjakut avoidance of excitement

mos|provim nm lack of proof, failure to prove

mos|punim nm inactivity; idleness; leisure

mos|puthitje nf misfit, non-contact, slack

mos|qenie nf 1 nonexistence 2 absence

mos|qëndresë nf 1 lack of resistance *2 instability

mos|realizim nm (Book) nonperformance, nonfulfilment

mos|respektim nm (Book) disrespect: disregard, non-observance; disdain

mos|sigurim nm (Book) 1 failure to secure necessities 2 lack of safety measures

mos|suksesе nm failure, flop, fiasco

mos|sulmim nm nonaggression

*mos|shpëtuarshëm adj (i) inevitable

mo|stër nf 1 sample, specimen, exemplar 2 model, prototype

mos|tjetër adv at least

mostopite nf [Food] sweet dish made with grape juice or wine and a small amount of flour

mos|tretje nf 1 non-solubility 2 indigestion

mos|tror adj illustrative, sample, specimen

*mos|ujdisje nf (Colloq) failure to agree, disagreement; incongruity

mos|veprim nm 1 inactivity; inaction 2 (of a law) failure to function, non-functioning

mos|veprues adj inactive, inert; ineffective

*mos|vërejtje nf oversight, disregard

mos|violencë nf nonviolence

mos|zbatim nm failure to carry out/through, failure to execute/perform/operate: nonperformance; failure to enforce

mos|zgjidhje nf (Book) failure to solve (a problem)

mos|zhvillim nm lack of development, stuntedness

*mosh|ar adj 1 of age, adult, mature 2 aged

*mosh|ari nf coming of age, maturity; seniority; adulthood

mosh|atar
  I § adj of the same age, contemporary
  II § n age-mate, contemporary

mo|shë nf 1 age 2 (Collec) those of the same age: generation
  ◦ mosha e artë (Book) years of one's prime
  ◦ moshë e gjirit infancy
  ◦ të një moshe of the same age
  ◦ moshë e njomë tender age, childhood
  ◦ moshë e regjur ripe old age
  ◦ mosha shkollore school age (ages 6-19)
  ◦ moshë e shkuar/vjetër old age
  ◦ moshë e thyer one's declining years

*mo|shëm adj (i) = moshar

moshë|thyer adj past the halfway mark in one's life, more than fifty years old

mosh|o·het vpr 1 to come of age 2 to reach old age

*mosh|tar adj, n adult

*mosh|tuar adj (i) (Reg Tosk) = moshuar

mosh|uar adj (i) overaged; over sixty years old, aged

mot
  I § nm 1 weather 2 year
  II § adv next year
  ◦ mot i brishtë leap year
  ◦ mot e zaman over a long period of time; since time immemorial
  ◦ mot e jetë always, forever
  ◦ moti me motin (Colloq) every year; year by/after year
  ◦ Moti i mirë duket që në mëngjes. "Nice weather is evident by morning." (Prov) You can tell right from the start if something will go well. You can tell right from the start if someone will do well.

motaçillë nf [Ornit] white/pied wagtail (Motacilla alba)

motak
  I § adj one-year-old
  II § n yearling

motar adj, n = motak

*mota vi = motovile

motele nf
  ◦ motele me mustaqe [Ichth] shore rockling Gaidropsarus mediterraneus
  ◦ motele e zezë [Ichth] black rockling Gaidropsarus megalokynodon

*mote|një nf [Bot] goosegrass, cleavers (Galium aparine)

motër nf 1 sister 2 [Ethnog] = motërmë 3 term of address for a nun: sister
  ◦ motër gishti = motërmë
  ◦ motër e gjetur step-sister

○ **s'ka· (as) motër as shoqe** "have neither sister nor friend" to be unlike anyone/anything else: be unique

○ **motër prej babe/nëne** sister from the same father/mother: step-sister, half-sister

○ **motër qumështi** "milk sister" sister only in the sense of having shared the same wet nurse

○ **ësh·të**[pl] **motër e vëlla** to be as if {} were sister and brother

motëri nf **1** sisterhood **2** (Collec) sisters

motërmë nf [Ethnog] female friend pledged to another (by drinking a drop of each other's blood): sworn sister, sister in blood

motërmëmë nf (Colloq) mother's sister, maternal aunt = **teze**

motërsi = **motëri**

motërsor adj sisterly

motërtatë nf (Colloq) father's sister, paternal aunt = **hallë**

motërz nf **1** (Pet) sis **2** = **motërmë 3** each of a pair of threads that pass through the comb of a loom together

motërzezë nf (Colloq) unfortunate sister left with no brother who can support her

motërzim nm ger **1** [Ethnog] <**motërzo**·het **2** [Folklore] variant

motërzo·het vp recip [Ethnog] to pledge sisterhood to each other (by drinking a drop of each other's blood)

mot·ës adj **1** (fruit) that keeps for a year **2** = **moshatar**

motëse nf pear that keeps for a year

***motësi** nf **1** (weather) temperature **2** date **3** anniversary

motësim nm ger **1** <**moteso**·n **2** (weather) temperature **3** climate

***motësinë** nf **1** (weather) temperature **2** date **3** anniversary

motëso·n vi to ripen, age, cure

motit OR **moti** adv (Colloq) a long time ago, long ago, in the old days, formerly

motiv nm **1** motive; rationale **2** motif

motivacion nm motivation

motivim nm ger **1** <**motivo**·n **2** motivation

motivo·n vt to provide a rationale for []: explain, motivate

motivueshëm adj (i) explicable, possibly motivated

motje nf **1** = **motëse** *2 honeysuckle

motkeqe nf wind from the south (that brings unwelcome rainy weather)

motmoçar adj = **motak**

motmot nm a full year, one whole year

○ **Motmoti i Ri** (Old) New Year = **Viti i Ri**

motmotak adj (Colloq) one-year-old

motmotar adj **1** (Colloq) one-year-old **2** yearly, annual

***motno**·het vpr (Reg Gheg) = **mosho**·het

moto nf (Book) motto

moto·het vpr **1** = **mosho**·het **2** to become dated, go out of date **3** to get stale

○ **moto**·het[3sg] **koha** (Old) time passes

moto·n vi to spend a year (somewhere)

motobarkë nf motorboat

motoçikletë nf motor-bike; motorcycle

motoçiklist n motorcyclist

motoçiklizëm nm motorcycling; motorcycle racing

motolundër nf motorboat

motopeshkatore nf motorized fishing trawler

motopompë nf [Tech] motorized pump, motor pump

motor nm **1** motor, engine **2** (Colloq) motorcycle; moped **3** (Fig) driving force

○ **motor asinkron** [Phys] induction motor

○ **motor katërkohësh** four-stroke engine

○ **motor reduktor** [Tech] gear motor

motoranije nf (Reg) motorboat

motorik adj **1** [Tech] of or pertaining to motors: motoric **2** [Physiol] motor

motorist n person who repairs, runs, or tends a motor/engine/machine: motor/engine mechanic, engineer

motorizim nm ger **1** <**motorizo**·n, **motorizo**·het **2** motorization

motorizo·het vpr to become motorized

motorizo·n vt to motorize

motorizuar adj (i) motorized

motoskaf nm speedboat, powerboat

motosharrë nf [Tech] power saw

***mototrap** nm pontoon raft powered by a motor and used as a ferry

motovelier nm powered sailboat

***motovi** = **motovile**

motovile nf powered reel for winding yarn or thread: winding frame

motrani vocative pl <**motër** (Reg) oh sisters!

motras adv **1** in a sisterly way **2** (of threads) passing through the comb of the loom joined together

motshëm = **moçëm**

motuar adj (i) **1** overdue **2** overaged **3** stale; past its prime

mozaik nm **1** mosaic **2** [Agr] mosaic disease

mpak· vt **1** to lessen, reduce, make [] smaller **2** to make [] breathless, exhaust; cause [] to faint

mpak·et vpr **1** to be out of breath; feel woozy/dizzy; faint **2** to grow weaker: dwindle, weaken

○ **s'<> mpak**·et[3sg] **zemra** <>'s heart does not break (over it), <> doesn't lose any sleep (about it)

mpakur adj (i) **1** out of breath; feeling faint/woozy/dizzy **2** very weak

mpi·het vpr **1** to grow/go numb **2** (Fig) to get sluggish/clumsy **3** (like a blade) to become dull **4** to become stunted in growth

○ **<> mpi**·het[3sg] **gjuha** the words freeze in <>'s mouth: <> becomes speechless

mpi·n vt **1** to make [] numb: numb, benumb **2** (Fig) to make [] sluggish/clumsy **3** to dull [a blade] **4** to stunt the growth of []

mpiks· vt to cause [] to become viscid/rigid, cause [] to thicken and set: congeal, gel, clot, coagulate, curdle, freeze, stiffen

mpiks·et vpr to become viscid/rigid, thicken and set: congeal, gel, clot, coagulate, curdle, freeze

mpiksës adj causing to thicken and set: coagulant, clotting, curdling

mpiksje nf ger <**mpiks**·, **mpiks**·et

mpiksur adj (i) thickened and set: gelled, coagulated, clotted, curdled, frozen hard

mpi'rë *adj (i)* **1** numb, benumbed **2** *(Fig)* sluggish, awkward, clumsy **3** (of a blade) dulled, dull **4** stunted

mpi'rje *nf ger* **1** <mpi·*n*, mpi'·*het* **2** numbness; pins and needles sensation

*__mpi'si__ *nf* = mpitsí

mpi'të *adj (i)* numb; sluggish

*__mpi'tësí__ *nf* numbness

*__mpi'tje__ *nf* cramp

m'plak· *vt* = plak·

m'pla'k·*et vpr* = plak·*et*

*__m'pla'kje__ *nf ger* = pla'kje

m'pleks· *vt* = pleks·

m'ple'ks·*et vpr* = pleks·*et*

m'posht· *vt* **1** to suppress, subdue; quash, put down []; defeat, bring down; top **2** to overpower; weaken [] badly, break [] down

m'po'sht·*et vpr* **1** to yield, give up **2** to weaken, get very weak **3** to feel defeated, despair

m'po'sht·ës *adj* overpowering, crushing; degrading; humbling

m'po'shtje *nf ger* **1** <mpo'sht·, mpo'sht·*et* **2** suppression

*__m'pra'p·***et vpr* to retrogress; lag behind

*__m'prapa'shtes·ë__ = prapashte's·ë

*__m'pra'ps·** *vt* = zmbraps·

*__m'pra'ps·***et vpr* = zmbraps·*et*

*__m'prapsím__ *nm ger* = zmbrapsje

*__m'pra'psje__ *nf ger* = zmbrapsje

*__m'prapso'·***het vpr* = zmbraps·*et*

*__m'pref__ = mpreh

m'preh· *vt* **1** to sharpen **2** to exacerbate; aggravate
  ∘ **e mpreh· (mirë) penën/lapsin** *(Book)* to sharpen one's attack (in writing)
  ∘ **mpreh· armët** to sharpen one's spears: prepare for war/battle
  ∘ **mpreh· dhëmbët** "sharpen one's teeth" **1** to get ready to attack, sharpen one's claws; bare one's teeth **2** *(Iron)* to lick one's chops in anticipation
  ∘ **i mpreh· fjalët (me [])** to exchange sharp words (with [])
  ∘ **mpreh· kunja kot** to waste one's efforts, do a lot of work for nothing
  ∘ **mpreh· sytë** to try to see better, look close
  ∘ **mpreh· shpatën** "sharpen the sword" to get ready to deliver the decisive blow
  ∘ **mpreh· veshët** "sharpen the ears" to listen keenly: sharpen one's ears

*__m'pre'h·ëm__ *adj (i)* keen, sharp

m'pre'h·ës
  I § *adj* serving for sharpening/honing
  II § *n* person who sharpens blades

m'pre'h·ëse *nf* **1** pencil sharpener **2** blade sharpener: hone, sharpening file

m'pre'h·je *nf ger* <mpre'h·, mpre'h·*et*

m'pre'h·të *adj (i)* **1** sharp **2** requiring delicacy to solve: delicate **3** piercing; shrill **4** *(Fig)* right to the point, expressively precise
  ∘ **i mprehtë nga gjuha** skillful in speaking: highly articulate

m'pre'h·tësí *nf* **1** sharpness **2** shrillness **3** sharpness of thought/expression

m'pre'h·ur *adj (i)* **1** sharpened **2** ready to fight; exacerbated, inflamed

m'pri·het *vpr* **1** to become exacerbated **2** *(Iron)* to build up false hopes

*__mpri'm__ *nm ger* = mbro'jtje

*__mpro'·***n** *vt* = mbro·*n*

*__mpro'jt__ = mbrojt

*__mpru'a'r__ *adj (i)* = mbrojtur

*__m'psalte'ro'·***n** *vi* to sing psalms

*__mpsherëtí'më__ *nf* sigh = psherëtí'më

*__mpsherëtí's__ *stem for 1st sg pres, pl pres, 2nd & 3rd sg subj, pind* <mpsherëti·*t·*

*__mpsherëtí't·** *vt* = psherëti·*n*

*__mpshi'kë'z__ = fshi'këz

*__mpsht__ = mbësht

*__mqer__ *nm* *(Old)* due time: term

*__mr-__ = mbr-

mraz *nm* bad weather: rainstorm, bad frost

*__mre__ *interj* = bre

mre'çë *nf* [*Bot*] tree heath, brierroot *(Erica arborea)*

*__mref__ = mpreh

mrekullí
  I § *nf* **1** miracle **2** marvel, wonder
  II § *adv (Colloq)* wonderfully, marvelously

mrekullibërës *adj* = çudibë'rës

mrekullíshëm *adj (i)* = mrekullu'eshëm

mrekullísht *adv* wonderfully, marvelously, miraculously

mrekullo'·*het vpr* to marvel, be astonished/amazed

mrekullo'·*n** *vt* to astonish, amaze

mrekullu'ar *adj (i)* astonished, amazed

mrekullu'eshëm *adj (i)* marvelous, wonderful

*__mre'q__ = mre'çë

*__mreqna'r__ *adj, n* mercenary

mre'shtë *nf* grove of tree heath

mret *nm* [*Bot*] phillyrea *(Phillyrea)* = krí'fshë
  ∘ **mret i egër** butcher's-broom *Ruscus aculeatus*

mre'te *nf* [*Bot*] = mret

mre'zhë *nf* catch net

mrijo'·*n** *vt* to raise [the lid of a pot/pan] slightly to let out steam and prevent food from bubbling over

Mrík·a *nf* Mrika (female name)

mriz *nm* **1** cool and shady place for livestock to stay out of the summer heat **2** hottest period of a hot summer day

mrizím *nm* = mriz

mrizo'·*n** *vt, vi* = mërze·*n*

*__mrok__ *nm* suckling pig

*__mrol·** *vt (Reg)* = mrrol·
  ∘ **mrol· sytë** *(Reg)* to glower

*__mroth__ = mbroth

*__mru'l·***et vpr* *(Reg)* = mrrol·*et*

*__mry'të__ *adj (i)* crushed together, cramped

mrra'gël *nf* [*Entom*] **1** ant = milingo'në **2** seed-harvesting ant *(Messor structor)*

mrre'çë *nf* [*Bot*] = mre'çë

mrrol· *vt (Reg)* to darken, cloud = vrenjt·

mrrol·*et vpr (Reg)* = vrenjt·*et*

mrrola'n *adj, n (Reg)* gloomy looking (person)

mrrol'shëm *adv (Reg)* with a dark visage, looking gloomy, glowering

mrro'lur *adj (i) (Reg)* dour, frowning = vrenjtur

m'rrudh· *vt* to screw up [], wrinkle, pucker
  ∘ **<>a mrrudh· gojën** to shut <> up, not let <> say anything

○ **e mrrudh· gojën** to keep one's mouth shut, not say a word

mᵢrru·dh·_et vpr_ **1** (of the face) to become wrinkled **2** to fold up one's body: curl/hunch up, cringe

mᵢrru·dh·ur _adj (i)_ **1** (of the face) wrinkled **2** curled/hunched up, cringing

*__mrru·l·__*_et_ = **mrro·l·**_et_

*__mrrut__*ë _nf_ old and wrinkled

*__mrry·t__*ë _nf_ (of animals) dark-colored, dun

__mshef__ OR **msheh** = **fsheh**

__msheftᵢa·r__ OR **msheh·tᵢa·r**

_I §_ _adj_ secretive

_II §_ _nm_ secretive person

__mshe·l·__ = **mᵢshil·**

__mshertᵢi·s__ _stem for 1st sg pres, pl pres, 2nd & 3rd sg subj, pind_ <**mshertᵢi·t·**

__mshertᵢi·t·__ _vt (Reg Tosk)_ = **psherëti·**_n_

__mshikᵢë__ = **fshikᵢë**

__mshikᵢëz__ = **fshikᵢëz**

__mti__ _nm (pl ˜ni)_ milk churn

MTI _abbrev. (Hungarian)_ <**Magyar Tarivati Iroda** Hungarian news agency

*__mtᵢo·__*_n_ = **mbuto·**_n_

*__mtᵢro·__*_n_

_I §_ _vt_ **1** to delude **2** to decoy

_II §_ _vi (Fig)_ to be pretentious; be hypocritical

mu

_I §_ _onomat_ sound made by a cow: moo

_II §_ _pcl_ right there, right, exactly

○ **mu te hunda** right there (under <>'s nose)

muᵢa

_I §_ _pron 1st sg acc/dat_ <**uᵢnë** me

_II §_ _pron 1st sg nom (Colloq)_ (used after prepositions that take the nominative case)

muᵢaj _nm_ month

○ **muaj i gjatë** 31-day month

○ **muaji i mjaltit** honeymoon (period)

__muajᵢo·r__ = **mujo·r**

__muallᵢi·s__ _stem for 1st sg pres, pl pres, 2nd & 3rd sg subj, pind_ <**muallᵢi·t·**

__muallᵢi·t·__ _vt_ to moo

__muallᵢi·tje__ _nf ger_ **1** <**muallᵢi·t·** **2** cow's sound: moo

muaᵢr _pl pdef_ <**merr·**

__muc__ _nm_ muzzle, snout, mouth

__mu·ckᵢë__ _nf dimin_ = **muc**

muçᵢi·t· _vi_ to moo, bellow

muçᵢi·t·_et vpr_ **1** (Reg) to swell up **2** to collect in one place and not move or flow: stagnate

○ <> **muçᵢi·t·**³ˢᵍ **zemra** "<>'s heart _swells_ with sadness" <> grieves deeply

mueᵢt· _vi_ to moo, low

muf

_I §_ _adj_ **1** (of figs) unripe **2** (Fig Pej) mentally immature

_II §_ _adv_ * = **muft**

mufaᵢs _stem for 1st sg pres, pl pres, 2nd & 3rd sg subj, pind_ <**mufaᵢt·**

mufaᵢt· _vt_ = **buhavi·**

mufaᵢt·_et_ = **buhavit·**_et_

mufaᵢtje _nf [Med]_ imbibition

mufaᵢtur = **buhavitur**

muᵢfkᵢë

_I §_ _adj_ **1** unripe, immature **2** round and well filled out: plump **3** (Fig) mentally immature **4** (Fig) unfruitful

_II §_ _nf (Pej)_ poorly thought out words or actions

mufkᵢo·_het vpr_ (of figs) to be just beginning to ripen

muft _adv_ (Old) without paying, for nothing: by freeloading

mufti _nm_ chief jurist

mug _nm (np ˜ gje)_ twilight = **muzg**

muᵢg·_et vp impers_ = **mugëllo·**_n_

muga·shtᵢër _nf [Bot]_ aromatic inula (Dittrichia viscosa)

muᵢgë _nf_ **1** twilight = **muzg 2** half-light; half-shadow, penumbra

muᵢgëll _adv_ obscurely, unclearly

mugᵢëllo·_n vi impers_ it grows twilight, it _begins_ to get dark

mugᵢësi _nf_ = **mugᵢësirᵢë**

mugᵢësirᵢë _nf_ = **mugᵢësirᵢë**

*__mugᵢëso·__*_n vi_ = **mugëllo·**_n_

muᵢgët

_I §_ _adj (i)_ **1** semidark; murky; overcast **2** (Fig) gloomy **3** (Fig) obscure, vague

_II §_ _nn (të)_ = **mugëtirᵢë**

mugᵢëtirᵢë _nf_ **1** twilight, dusk **2** semidarkness, half-light **3** (Fig) murkiness, haze, haziness

mugᵢëto·_het vp impers_ it grows dark; it _becomes_ twilight

__mugollaᵢr__ _nm [Invert]_ shellfish

muᵢgull _nm (np ˜j) [Bot]_ sprout, bud

mugullᵢi·m _nm ger_ <**mugullo·**_n_, **mugullo·**_het_

mugullᵢo·_n vi_ **1** to sprout, bud; begin to grow **2** to get covered in fresh greenery

mugjᵢet _nm [Bot]_ lily of the valley (Convallaria majalis)

muhabet _nm (Colloq)_ chat, conversation, talk

○ **ësh·të i muhabetit** to be good in conversation, be a lively speaker

○ **muhabet pa kokë** talk/discussion that fails to come to a point

○ **muhabet/muhabete pazari** common gossip

○ **muhabet i vjetër** old story (with nothing new in it)

muhabetᵢqar

_I §_ _adj (Colloq)_ chatty, talkative

_II §_ _nm (Colloq)_ chatty conversationalist

muhabetᵢshëm _adj (i) (Colloq)_ charming in conversation

muhalebi _nf [Food]_ light pudding made of sugar and milk together with cornstarch or rice flour

muhamedᵢan _adj, n_ Muhammedan

muhamedᵢanizëm _nm [Relig]_ Muhammedanism, Islam

Muhamᵢet _nm_ Muhamet (male name)

__muhaᵢq__ _nm [Bot]_ = **mohar**

muhaᵢr _nm [Bot]_ barnyard grass, barnyard millet, barn grass (Echinochloa crusgalli)

*__muhavi·t·__*_et_ = **buhavit·**_et_

muhaxhiᵢr _nm (Colloq)_ refugee

*__muhᵢo·__*_n vt (Reg Gheg)_ = **moho·**_n_

__mu·htᵢë__ _adv_ **1** gratis, free, for nothing **2** cheap

__muj__ _nm (Reg Gheg)_ = **muaj**

__mujᵢa·k__ = **mbujaᵢk**

mujᵢo·_n vt_ to refute

mujᵢo·r _adj_ **1** monthly **2** month-long

mujshᵢa·r _adj_ bullying

mujshᵢi _nf_ bullyragging

mujsho·n *vt* to use power to abuse [ ]: bully

***mujtësi** = mundësi

mujzë *nf* tool used to beat felt into caps: felt beater

***muk** = muk

mukaje·t *nm (Colloq)* involved concern: solicitude, personal involvement
  ○ **(ësh·të) (njeri) i mukajetit** (to be) someone who shows initiative: (be) a go-getter, (be) a doer

mukava *nf (Old)* = karton

muko·n *vi* to bellow for [a calf], moo

mukozë *nf* mucus

mulat *adj, n* mulatto

***mulë** *nf [Zool]* mule

***muli** *nf (Old)* mold, mildew

muliçkë *nf* pockmark

***mulidhë** = molivë

muline *nf [Text]* embroidery floss; small skein of floss

mulko·n = mëlko·n

***mulmesë** = mëlmesë

mull *nm* = mull

mulla *nm (Old)* mullah

mullac *adj* **1** *(Pej)* potbellied, paunchy; fat **2** having a swollen face

mullacak *adj* = mullac

mullaçkë *nf* bump/bulge on a tree

mullafarë *nf* rod used by jeweler for making rings wider or narrower

mullagë *nf [Bot]* = mëllagë

***mullagëmadhe** *nf [Bot]* = mullanjadhe

***mullanjadhe** *nf [Bot]* hollyhock *(Althaea rosea)*

mullar *nm* **1** haystack, strawstack **2** heap

mullarthi *adv* turning round and around

mullenjë *nf [Ornit]* = mëllenjë

mullë *nf* **1** *(Colloq)* belly; paunch **2** = mullëz

mullëmadh *adj, n* = barkmadh

***mullënjë** *nf* = mëllenjë

***mullëtërçuk** *adj* potbellied

mullëz *nm* **1** fourth chamber of the stomach of a ruminant: abomasum **2** [Dairy] cheese starter extracted from the inner lining of the stomach of a suckling ruminant: rennet, rennin **3** *(Colloq)* stomach (of a human being)
  ○ **kështu e ka· zënë mullëzën** "have gotten one's stomach this way" this is how one *was* brought up

mullëzak *nm* retarded child

mulli(r) *nm (np ~ nj)* **1** mill: grist mill, flour mill, coffee mill; hammermill, pounding mill; oil press **2** cylinder of a revolver
  ○ **Mulliri bluan me aq ujë sa ka.** "The mill grinds with the water that it has." *(Prov)* You can only do what you can do.
  ○ **mulli ere** windmill
  ○ **ësh·të gur mulliri** to be very heavy/durable/strong
  ○ **mulli me erë** windmill
  ○ **sikur ësh·të zënë në mulli** "as if one *has been* conceived in a mill" *(Impol)* { } just can't stop talking: { } *is* a born chatterbox

mullibardhë *nf [Ornit]* **1** thrush **2** mistle thrush *(Turdus viscivorus)*

mullinar *nm* = mullis

mullinj *np* <mulli

mullirri *obl* <mulli

mullis *nm* miller

mullithi *adv* = mullarthi

mulliujcë = mulliujëse

mulliujëse *nf [Ornit]* **1** water ouzel, dipper *(Cinclus cinclus)* **2** European kingfisher *(Alcedo atthis)*

mullixhi *nm (np ~ nj)* = mullis

mullizezë *nf [Ornit]* blackbird *(Turdus merula)*
  ○ **mullizezë uji** [Ornit] = mulliujëse

***mullojë** *nf* roan cow

mullos *vt (Colloq)* to swell up <>'s belly

mullos·et *vpr (Colloq)* **1** to swell up in the belly from overeating or drinking **2** to become swollen/bloated

mullosur *adj (i) (Colloq)* swollen/bloated

mullosh *adj (ColloqImpolite)* having a swollen belly, big-bellied

mumie *nf* **1** mummy **2** *(Fig)* inert and listless person

***muncë** *nf* wooden bar/bolt

mund *nm* **1** effort **2** reward for one's efforts

mund·
  I § semi-auxiliary modal **1** be able; be capable **2** be possible: can, could; may, might
  II § *vt* to overcome, defeat; resist, stand up to [ ]
  ○ **S'mund të jetë diell për të gjithë.** You can't please everyone.

mund·et *vpr* **1** to be able, can; be capable **2** to be possible **3** to be allowed, be permitted **4** to wrestle; struggle
  ○ **s'mund·et** to be unable to continue: *can't* stand/ take it, *can't* go on
  ○ **mund·et me atë të** {timen/tënden/tonën/tuajën/ tijën/sajën/tyren/vetën} to try with all {my/your/ our/your/his/her/their, one's} might

mundac *nm* hard worker, toiler; one who strives in vain

mundaq *adj* = mundqar

mundbjerrë *adj* = mundimhumbur

mundbjerrët *adj* = mundimhumbur

***mundçar** = mundqar

***mundebare** *adv* at least

***mundëm** *adj (i)* possible

***mundërshëm** *adj (i)* filthy

mundërr *nf* sediment in a viscous substance (such as oil, honey, butter)

mundës
  I § *n* **1** winner, victor **2** [Sport] wrestler
  II § *adj* winning, victorious

mundësi *nf* **1** possibility **2** resource, facility; potentiality, potential ***3** *(Old)* authority, right

mundësisht *adv* as much as possible, if possible, possibly

mundëso·het *vpr* to be/become possible

mundëso·n *vt* to make [ ] possible, enable

***mundështir** = manastir

mundim *nm ger* **1** <mundo·n, mundo·het **2** effort, pains, trouble, difficulty

mundimhumbur *adj* having cost a lot of effort for nothing, difficult and to no avail

mundimmadh *adj* **1** having suffered miserably **2** demanding great effort: arduous, toilsome, tedious

mundimplotë *adj* strenuous; full of difficulties

mundimshëm *adj (i)* **1** arduous, laborious, tiring, strenuous **2** causing suffering: difficult, burdensome

mundimtar *adj* worrisome, onerous, burdensome

mundimtë *adj (i)* = mundimshëm

mundje nf ger **1** <mund·, mund·et **2** defeat **3** [Sport] wrestling
○ **mundje e lirë** free-style wrestling

mundo·het vpr **1** to try hard, strive; go to great pains **2** to experience great suffering

mundo·n vt **1** to demand great effort of []; tire [] out **2** to torment
○ **mundo·het për bishtin e gjarprit 1** to suffer greatly **2** to become very tired

mundqar
I § adj hard-working; toiling, laboring
II § n hard worker, toiler, laborer

mundshëm adj (i) **1** possible **2** requiring great effort: demanding

mundshme nf (e) that which is possible: everything possible

mundshto·n vt to reprove [] sharply: lambaste, scold, bawl [] out

*__mundtar__ adj, n **1** = mundqar **2** (Old) victor, winner; champion

munduar adj (i) **1** tired out, exhausted **2** beaten-down, long-suffering, tormented

mundur
I § adj (i) **1** defeated, vanquished **2** possible = mundshëm
II § n (i) defeated one: loser

mundzi adj (fem sg ˘ ez, masc pl ˘ inj, fem pl ˘ eza) = mundimhumbur

*__mungade__ nf = manastir

*__mungar__ nm = murg

mungesë nf **1** absence **2** lack **3** weakness, failing

mungesor adj [Ling] (of a paradigm) defective; incomplete

mungestar nm = mungues

*__mungeshë__ = murgeshë

mungicë nf **1** absence **2** lack, dearth, need

mungim nm = mungesë

*__mungll__ = mugull

mungo·n
I § vi **1** to be missing; be absent **2** to be lacking/deficient/inadequate
II § vt to allow [] to remain lacking/deficient/inadequate; leave [] undone; neglect
○ **nuk <> mungo·n asnjë qime** "not lack a single hair" <> lacks for nothing, <> has everything <> could want
○ **<> mungo·n³pl dhitë** "<>'s goats are missing" <> has something missing upstairs
○ **<> mungo·n³sg shprehja** (Book) <> lacks the gift of eloquence, <> does not speak well

mungonjës adj missing, lacking

mungues nm missing one, absentee

*__mungull__ = mugull

*__mungullë__ nf [Bot] Jerusalem sage (Phlomis fruticosa) = bezgë

municion nm [Mil] munitions

Munih nm Munich

*__munikël__ nf [Bot] star-of-Bethlehem (Ornithogalum)

munk nm
○ **munku i grurit** [Bot] = kllogjër

munxë nf (Colloq) gesture of disrespect made by pointing the open palm of the hand at a person and moving it from the wrist (= thumbing the nose)

○ **<> mbeçin munxët nga prapa!** "May insulting gestures stick to <> from behind!" (Curse) May <> suffer a life of disrespect!

munxos· vt (Colloq) **1** to make a disrespectful hand gesture of rejection toward [] **2** to treat [] with disdain; turn one's back on []; reject with scorn **3** to curse []; cuss at []

*__muq__ adv higgledy-piggledy

mur
I § nm wall
II § adj * = murrmë
○ **Muri luan, burri s'luan.** "A wall may waver, a man may not." (Prov) A real man keeps his word.
○ **mur mbushës** non-bearing wall: panel wall, partition wall
○ **mur i thatë** stone wall made without any mortar

*__murajzë__ nf [Bot] hawk nut (Bunium)

*__murak__ nm [Ornit] house sparrow = murrash

muranë nf **1** cairn marking where someone was killed or hanged **2** pile of stones; stone ruins

*__murash__ = murrash

Murat nm Murat (male name)

murator n builder of walls: mason, bricklayer

muratori nf masonry (as a profession); wall construction

muraturë nf wall structure, masonry

murçak nm [Ornit] red-crested pochard (Netta rufina Pall.)

murdar adj filthy; vulgar

*__murdhiz·et__ vp impers it grows twilight = mugëllo·n

murenë nf [Ichth] Lake Ohrid gudgeon (Gobio gobio ohridanus)

muresë nf = muraturë

*__murë__ = murrmë

*__murët__ = murrët

murëzim nm [Min] brickwork lining of a mine tunnel

murg
I § nm (np ˘ gj) monk
II § adj gloomy, grumpy
○ **murgu i natës** [Myth] malevolent old man who roams at night hurting people: boogieman

murgar nm = murg

murgash
I § adj dark gray, dun-colored
II § n nickname for a dark grey animal

murgator
I § adj (Colloq) miserable, wretched
II § n poor wretch

murgeshë nf **1** nun **2** [Entom] pine butterfly (Neophasia menapia) **3** [Entom] praying mantis (Mantis religiosa)

murgë nf **1** = murgeshë **2** (Colloq) unmarried woman, spinster; girl or woman with a miserable life **3** dregs of cooking oil; marc from olives

murgëri nf **1** monastic life, monkery **2** monkhood

*__murgësi__ = murgëri

*__murgëtore__ nf convent, nunnery

murgëz nf sparrow-like bird that winters in Albania

*__murgullo·n__ vi to get dark

murgjan OR **murgjar** nm saddle horse

murgjëri nf collec monkdom

murgjïn
I § nm **1** dun-colored ox *__2__ (Old) retired person
II § adj * (Old) morose, grumpy

murgjinˈë *nf* chestnut-colored cow; dun cow

*****murgjinˈ**ërˈ *nf (Old)* retirement

*****murgjinˈ**ˈ *nf (Old)* boarding house

murˈim *nm ger* <muroˈ•*n*

murˈinˈë *nf* [*Ichth*] bicolored false moray *(Chlopsis bicolor)*

murˈishtë *nf* ruins of walls

*****murjeˈl**ë = murrjeˈlë

murkullˈo•*n vt (Colloq)* to put an end to [the matter], put a lid on [], bring [] to a close

*****murlaˈn** = murrlaˈn

muˈrlë *nf* = murrlaˈn

*****muˈrm**ë = muˈrrmë

*****murmˈo**ˈ•*n vi* to take on a dun color: turn brown/grey = murrëte•*het*

*****murmuraˈk** *nm* [*Ornit*] lark

murmurˈi•*n vi* = murmurˈit•

murmurˈim *nm ger* 1 <murmuroˈ•*n* 2 = murmurˈitje

murmurˈimë *nf* muttering sound; murmuring/rustling sound

murmurˈis stem *for 1st sg pres, pl pres, 2nd & 3rd sg subj, pind* <murmurˈit•

murmurˈisje *nf* = murmurˈimë

murmurˈit• *vi* 1 to mutter; murmur 2 to make a rustling sound

murmurˈitje *nf ger* 1 <murmurˈit• 2 = murmurˈimë

murmurˈo•*n vi* = murmurˈit•

*****murˈna** *np* <mur *(Reg Gheg)*

*****murnˈim** *nm (Reg Tosk)* fortification

muroˈ•*n vt* = muroˈs•

*****murojˈe** *nf* = mburojˈë

murˈoˈr *adj* 1 of or pertaining to walls: mural 2 [*Anat*] parietal

murˈoˈs• *vt* 1 to enclose [] by a wall; wall [] in 2 to immure 3 *(Fig)* to preserve [] in memory; preserve [] unchanged

muroˈs•*et vpr* 1 to live closed off from the outside 2 to remain immured in memory

murˈoˈsje *nf ger* 1 <muroˈs•, muroˈs•*et* 2 immurement

murˈoˈsˈur *adj (i)* 1 enclosed by a wall; walled in 2 immured

*****murtaˈd** *nm* deserter, traitor

murtajˈak *adj* plaguey

murtajˈe *nf* 1 plague, pestilence 2 cholera 3 *(Fig)* pest

   ◦ **murtaja e bardhë** *(Euph)* tuberculosis

*****murtaˈr** = muratoˈr

*****murtaˈt** = murtaˈd

*****murteˈ•*het* OR **murtoˈ**•*het* = murrëte•*het*

*****murteˈ•*n* OR **murtoˈ**•*n* = murrëte•*n*

*****murtuaˈr** *adj (i)* livid

murr

   I § *nm* murrain (that reduces grape yield)

   II § *adj (i)* * = muˈrrmë

murraˈk *adj* = murraˈsh

murraˈn *nm* = murrlaˈn

murraˈsh

   I § *adj* (of things) chestnut-colored; (of animals) dun

   II § *nm* 1 [*Ornit*] = trumcaˈk 2 [*Ichth*] blackfish *(Centrolophus niger)*

murrçimˈë *adj (i)* very dark grayish green

murreˈlë *nf* [*Entom*] horsefly *(Tabanus bovinus)*

muˈrrë *nf* dark gray cow

   ◦ **murrë e egër** [*Ichth*] bronze bream *Pagellus acarne*

murrˈët *adj (i)* 1 dark gray 2 = vreˈnjtur 3 *(Fig)* gloomy, grumpy

murrˈëte•*het vpr* 1 to take on a dark gray color 2 (of the sky) to grow dark; become overcast 3 (of the skin/countenance) to become dark with cold or strong emotion 4 *(Fig)* to become gloomy

murrˈëte•*n vt* 1 to give [] a dark gray color 2 to darken [the sky], make [] overcast 3 to darken [the skin/countenance] with cold or strong emotion 4 *(Fig)* to make gloomy

murrˈëto•*het vpr* = murrëte•*het*

murrˈëto•*n vt* = murrëto•*n*

murrˈëtuaˈr *adj (i)* = murrëtyˈer

murrˈëtyˈer *adj (i)* 1 grown dark; overcast 2 (of the skin/countenance) dark with cold or strong emotion 3 *(Fig)* gloomy

*****murrˈik** *nf* dark brown, dun-colored

murrˈikë *nf* = muˈrrë

murrˈiz *nm* [*Bot*] hawthorn *(Crataegus)*

   ◦ **murriz i butë** [*Bot*] silver hawthorn *(Crataegus orientalis)*

   ◦ **murriz dybërthamës** [*Bot*] English hawthorn, European hawthorn *Crataegus oxyacantha*

   ◦ **Fshiji buzët për murrizi** *(Iron)* to get all ready for nothing

   ◦ **murriz i kuq** [*Bot*] = ushiˈnth

   ◦ **murriz njëbërthamës** [*Bot*] single-seed hawthorn *Crataegus monogyna*

   ◦ **murriz i zi** [*Bot*] European black hawthorn *(Crataegus nigra)*

murrˈizˈt**ë** *adj (i)* 1 of hawthorn 2 *(Fig)* prickly, thorny

murrjeˈlë *nf* 1 [*Entom*] horsefly *(Tabanidae)* 2 *(Fig)* person who is constantly irksome: pest

murrlaˈn *nm* strong and bitterly cold wind from the north

murrmaˈsh *adj* (of animals) light gray-brown

muˈrrmë *adj (i)* 1 dark gray 2 dusky, murky, (of sky/weather) overcast

muˈrrˈo *nf with masc agreement* dark gray ox/dog

Muˈrrˈo *nf with masc agreement* Murro (dog's name)

murroˈk *nm* [*Ichth*] = murraˈsh

murruneˈc *nm* [*Ichth*] = mëruˈnë

*****mus** *adj* foolish

Musaˈ *nm* Musa (male name)

*****musaˈf** *nm* the Koran

musakaˈ *nf, adj* [*Food*] (dish) made of ground meat, potatoes/zucchini/eggplant, onions, eggs, and spices and baked in the oven: moussaka

musaˈndër *nf* = museˈndër

*****museliˈn**ë *nf* = musuˈll

museˈndër *nf* wall cupboard; linen cabinet

*****muˈsg**ë = muzgë

*****musk** *nm* [*Bot*] moss = myshk

muˈskul *nm (np ˙j)* muscle

   ◦ **muskul afrues** [*Anat*] adductor

   ◦ **muskul brendakthyes** [*Anat*] pronator muscle

   ◦ **muskul i herdhes** [*Anat*] cremaster muscle

   ◦ **muskul jashtëkthyes** [*Anat*] supinator

   ◦ **muskul mbyllës** [*Anat*] constrictor

   ◦ **muskul nderës** [*Anat*] tensor

   ◦ **muskul ngritës** [*Anat*] erector, levator

   ◦ **muskul rrudhës** [*Anat*] corrugator muscle

   ◦ **muskul shtrëngues** [*Anat*] constrictor

○ **muskul shtrirës** [*Anat*] tensor muscle

muskulatu·rë *nf* musculature

muskulo·r *adj* muscular

muskulo·z *adj* having well-developed muscles: muscular

*mu**skull** *nm (np ⁓ j)* = mu**skul**

*musli**man** = mysli**man**

*musli**në** = musu**ll**

musllu**k** *nm (np ⁓ qe)* cannister with a spigot; spigot

musokra**t** *nm* [*Ichth*] = buza**k**

musta**k** *nm* **1** = musta**qe 2** [*Ichth*] southern barbel (*Barbus meridionalis petenyi Heck.*)

○ **mustak lumi** [*Ichth*] butterfly blenny (*Blennius ocellaris L.*) = barbur**iq**

mustako**ç** *adj, nm* (*Colloq*) (man) with a bushy mustache

mustako**re** *nf* [*Ichth*] shore rockling *Gaidropsarus mediterraneus*

musta**qe** *nf, np* **1** mustache **2** (on animals) whiskers, feelers; (on fish) barbels **3** filament clusters growing out of seed spikes: (corn) tassel, silk

○ **mustaqe thurur pisk** tightly twisted mustache

○ **mustaqe kacadre** mustache with turned-up ends

mustaqe**ba·rdhë** *adj* having a gray/white mustache

mustaqe**bi·gë** *adj* having a handlebar mustache

mustaqe**di·rsur** *adj* having a newly-sprouted mustache: newly adolescent

mustaqe**fshe·së** *adj* having a broom-like long thick mustache with bristly hairs

mustaqe**gja·të** *adj, nm* (person) with a long-haired mustache

mustaqe**gje·mb** *adj* having a mustache with tapered tips

mustaqe**ho·llë** *adj* having a thin mustache

mustaqe**ku·q** *adj, nm* (person) with a red mustache

mustaqe**li** *adj, nm* (*Colloq*) (man) with a bushy mustache

mustaqe**ma·dh** *adj* having a bushy mustache

mustaqe**mi** *adj* having a mouse-like mustache with few hairs

mustaqe**pa·di·rsur** *adj* having a mustache that has barely sprouted, not yet mature

mustaqe**përdre·dhur** *adj, nm* (person) with a twisted mustache

mustaqe**përpje·të** *adj* having an upturned mustache

mustaqe**po·shtë** *adj* having a mustache hanging down at the ends

mustaqe**r** *nm* [*Ichth*] = buza**k**

mustaqe**rru·ar** *adj* **1** with mustache shaved off, without a mustache, clean-shaven **2** (*FigImpolite*) put down; left with nothing to brag about

mustaqe**spi·cë** *adj* having a thin pointed mustache

mustaqe**shtëllu·ngë** *adj* having a soft fluffy mustache

mustaqe**shti·zë** *adj* having a wide mustache with spear-like tips

mustaqe**thi·njur** *adj, nm* (person) with a grizzled/white mustache

mustaqe**va·rur** *adj* having a drooping mustache

mustaqe**ve·rdhë** *adj, nm* (person) with a blond mustache

mustaqe**zi** *adj, nm* (man) with a mustache

musta**rdë** *nf* prepared mustard, mustard sauce

*musta**rdhë** = musta**rdë**

***musteqe** = musta**qe**

mu**stë** *nf* [*Bot*] = musht

***musu·ll** *nm* muslin

musha**·** *nf* **1** (*Old*) land allowed to lie fallow for a specific time and to be used as commonland pasture **2** pastureland shared by a village

***musha·h** *nm* = musha

musha**ma** *nf* waterproof cloth: raincoat, tarpaulin, oilcloth, oilskin

***mushamali·zim** *nm ger* < mushamalizo·+n

***mushamali·zo·** +n *vt* to cloak, disguise

***musha·rkë** *nf* shell (of pulse), seed pod = mashu·rkë

mush**i·cë** *nf* **1** [*Entom*] fruit fly (*Drosophila*) **2** = harr**je**

mush**i·qe** *nf* = mushko·nj**ë**

mush**k** *nm (np ⁓ q)* **1** [*Zool*] he-mule; male hinny

***2** = musk

mushk**a·r** *nm* mule driver

mushk**a·sh** *adj* having hair the color of a mule: dark gray

mushk**a·zëm** *adj (i)* honey-colored

mushket**a·r** *nf* [*Hist*] musketeer

mushke**të** *nf* [*Hist*] musket

mushketo**·n** [*Hist*] to shoot (with a musket)

mu**shko·** *n* [*Zool*] mule, she-mule; female hinny

○ **Mushkës xanxare ia vënë drutë më të trasha/barrën më të rëndë.** "The heaviest load is put on the ornery mule" (*Prov*) The person who kicks and complains the most is given the heaviest workload.

mushk**ëlle·**·*het vpr* (of fruit at early stage of ripening) to take on a reddish tan color

mushk**ëlli·tur** *adj (i)* in an early stage of turning gray: graying

mushk**ëlly·er** *adj (i)* dull reddish brown

mu**shkër** *adj (i)* = mushka·sh

mushkër**i** *nf* lung

○ **mushkëri çeliku** [*Med*] Drinker respirator: iron lung

○ **me (të) gjithë/tërë mushkëritë** with all the power of one's lungs: in a loud voice; with a deep breath

mushkëro**·r** *nm* pulmonary

mushkëro**re** *np* [*Invert*] *Pulmonata*

mu**shkët** *adj (i)* = mushka·sh

mushko**një** *nf* [*Entom*] mosquito

○ **mushkonja këmbëgjatë** [*Entom*] common crane fly *Tipula oleracea L.*

○ **mushkonja e ullirit** "olive-tree gall midge" [*Entom*] *Dasyneura oleae*

mushko**r** *n* calf of the domestic buffalo = koto·rr

mushko**re** *nf* heifer of the domestic buffalo

mushlli·**nzë** *nf* [*Bot*] lesser/field bindweed (*Convolvulus arvensis*)

mushlli·**zë** = mushlli·nz**ë**

mush**ma·tse** *nf* (*Old Reg*) thermometer

mush**mo·llë** *nf* [*Bot*] medlar (*Mespilus*)

○ **mushmollë dimri** [*Bot*] medlar (*Mespilus germanica*)

○ **mushmollë vere** [*Bot*] loquat (*Eriobotrya japonica*)

***mush·mu·llë** = mushmo·ll**ë**

mush**q** *np* < mush**k**

mushqe·**re** OR mushqe·**rrë** *nf* = mështje·rr**ë**

***mushqet** (*Old Hist*) = mushket

musht *nm* must (from fruit)

mushta'k *nm* sweet and juicy grape used to make a jam

mushtëk'o·-*het vpr* to become accustomed/familiarized

***mushtje'r** *nm* = mështje'rrë

mushto·-*het vpr* **1** (of fruit juice) to turn into must **2** *(Fig)* to be ripened by experience

mushtua'r *adj (i)* ripened by experience; mature, experienced

mushtullu'k *nm* **1** (*Old*) good news, happy tidings **2** [*Ethnog*] small gift to acknowledge a happy event: gift to the messenger of good news; gift to acknowledge a new birth or wedding engagement; bride's gift to members of the groom's family

mut *nm (Crude)* human excrement: shit

muta'f *nm* heavy coverlet made of goat hair; horse blanket made of goat hair; saddle blanket

mut'ësi *nf (Crude)* dirty job, filthy work: shitwork

***muza'ik** *nm* mosaic

***muza't** *nm* = mëza't

muze *nf* museum

muze'or *adj* of or pertaining to museums

muze'tër *np* <muza't

muze'um *nm* = muze

mu'zë *nf* muse

muzg *nm (np ~ gje)* twilight, gloom; gloomy weather

mu'zg·-*et*

  I § *vpr* to become overcast, get dark

  II § *vp impers* (it) *grows* twilight

mu'zg·ë *nf* dark swamp mud: black mire

mu'zg'ët *adj (i)* **1** turning/growing dark, dark **2** overcast, gloomy

muzgëti'në *nf* = muzg

muzgëti'rë *nf* = muzg

***muzgo'·n** = munxos·

***muzgro'më** *nf* [*Bot*] broom grass = gjine'shtër

muzika'l *adj* musical

muzikalite't *nm* (*Book*) musicality

***muzika'n** OR **muzika'nd** = muzika'nt

muzika'nt *n* musician

muzi'kë *nf* **1** music **2** instrumental (as distinct from vocal) portion of a song **3** harmonica **4** orchestra, band

  ○ **muzikë dhome** chamber music

  ○ **muzikë goje** harmonica

muziko'·n *vt* [*Mus*] to set [] to music: score

muziko'log *n* musicologist

muzikologji' *nf* musicology

muziko'r *adj* musical

muzikta'r *n* (*Colloq*) = muzika'nt

***muz'mu'llë** = mushmo'llë

muzha'ngë *nf* dewlap

muzhga'dra *np* **1** uprooted weeds and other plant debris ***2** rubbish, debris, junk

muzhi'k *nm* Russian muzhik

***m'va'r** = var·

***m'va'r'ës** OR **va'rtës** = va'rtës

***m'va'r'ësi'** OR **m'vart'ësi'** *nf* = var'ësi'

***m'va'r'shëm** *adj (i)* dependent, attached = va'rtës

m'veht'ësi' *nf* independence, individuality

m'veht'ësi'shëm *adj (i)* independent, individual

***m've'rdh·** *vt* = verdh·

m've'rdh·et vpr* = verdh·*et*

***m've'sh·** *vt* = vesh·

***m've'shje** *nf* = ve'shje

m'vi'sh·et vpr* <mvesh· = vish·*et*

m've·-*het vpr* = vrenjt·*et*

***m've·n** *vt* = vrenjt·

***m're'hje** *nf* clouding over; frown, scowl

***m've'jtur** OR **m'vro'jtur** *adj (i)* = vre'njtur

***my** OR **my'e** *nf* = myj'ë

my'cë *nf* **1** rotten and crumbling dry wood ***2** half-burned piece of dry wood

myderri'z *nm* teacher of theology and religious law in a Moslem seminary

myezi'n *nm* [*Relig*] muezzin

***myfli'z**

  I § *nm* bankruptcy

  II § *adj* bankrupt

myfta'r *nm* chief elder of a village or district

myfti' *nm* (*np ~ le'rë*) [*Relig*] judge of Moslem law: mufti

***my'gëz** = my'këz

myhi'b *nm* [*Relig*] novice in a Moslem religious community

myhy'r *nm* **1** ring (for the finger) **2** signet ring/seal

myj'ë *nf* **1** [*Bot*] heartwood, duramen **2** *(Fig)* the middle/central part: heart

myj'shë *nf* **1** ash that forms over a burning ember **2** greenish slime/mold that forms on wood or stone

myj'të *adj (i)* (made) of heartwood

myk *nm* (*np ~ qe*) **1** mold-causing fungus: mold; mildew **2** *(Fig)* outdated thinking, cobwebs of the mind; antiquated impediment to social progress

myk· *vt* **1** to make [] moldy; allow [] to get moldy **2** *(Fig)* to make [] lethargic/rusty; retard

my'k·*et vpr* **1** to get moldy, become mildewed **2** *(Fig)* to become lethargic/rusty; become retarded

  ○ **myk·***et* **nga trutë 1** to start losing one's mind **2** to be out of date in one's thinking; think in an old-fashioned way

  ○ <> **myk·***et*[3pl] **paratë** <>'s money *gets* moldy (from little use)

my'kë *nf* blunt side of a bladed tool

  ○ **Myka e di sa e fortë është gozhda.** "The hammer head knows how hard the nail is." *(Prov)* The person who does the work knows what the difficulties are.

***my'k'ët** *adj (i)* mildewed; musty, dry as dust

my'këz *nf* [*Bot*] downy mildew

my'kje *nf ger* <my'k·, my'k·*et*

myk'llo'·*het vpr* to become covered with mildew; get moldy

myk'o'r *adj* mold-like, mildewy

mykth *nm* [*Med*] thrush (*stomatamycosis*)

my'kur

  I § *part* <myk·, my'k·*et*

  II § *adj (i)* **1** moldy, musty **2** *(Fig)* grown lethargic **3** *(Fig)* outdated, antiquated

  ○ <> **ësh·të**[3sg] **mykur buka** "<>'s bread *has* become moldy" <> *has* a black mark on <>'s record, <> *is* on the blacklist

  ○ <> **ësh·të**[3pl] **mykur trutë** "<>'s brains *have* rusted" <>'s thinking *has* become old-fashioned, <> *is* behind the times

my'kzë *nf* [*Agre*] = lyrth

mylk *nm* (*np ~ qe*) [*Hist*] large landed estate consisting of heritable or transferrable real property

***myll** *nm* = mill

***mynafik** *nm* troublemaker, schemer; tattletale.

mynxyrë *nf* **1** calamity, disaster **2** terrible disgrace

mynxyrë**madh** *adj (Colloq)* **1** cursed by calamity **2** causing a calamity: calamitous

mynxyro**s·** *vt (Colloq)* to cause a calamity in [ ], turn [ ] into a calamity

mynxyro**s·**et *vpr (Colloq)* to experience a calamity, have a disaster; have one's life turn into a disaster

mynxyro**s**ur *adj (i)* visited by disaster: miserable, wretched

mynxyrsh**ë**m *adj (i)* *(Colloq)* (of things) causing calamity: disastrous, calamitous

***mynxyr**ta**r** *adj* (of people) causing calamity: pernicious, baneful

***my**qe *nf* = mykë

***my**rtë *nf* [*Bot*] myrtle *(Myrtus communis)*

***myrtis·**et *vpr* to cover the face

mys

  I § *nm* **1** convex elevation, protuberance: hump; hillock, knoll **2** dome-like shape: arch

  II § *adj* = mysët

   ∘ **mysi i bukës** top of a loaf of risen bread

   ∘ **mysi i dheut** top of the furrow

mysafir *n* guest

  ∘ **mysafir i rënd**ë guest who expects special treatment: difficult guest

mysët *adj (i)* humped, arched; convex

mysëti *nf* convexity, protuberance

mysliman *adj, n* [*Relig*] Moslem

myslimanizëm *nm* **1** Moslem religion **2** *(Collec)* Islam

***myster** = mister

myshk

  I § *nm (np ~ qe)* [*Bot*] moss

  II § *nm* **1** musk; fragrance **2** scented face soap

  III § *adj* fragrant

   ∘ **Myshk e sheqer!** "Perfume and sugar!" *(Felic)* (said to a sneezing child) Gesundheit! Bless you!

***myshk**er**o·**n *vi* to be fragrant

myshkët *adj (i)* **1** fragrant; musky, scented with musk **2** mossy

***my**shkëz *nf* [*Entom*] sheep louse

myshkor *adj* mossy

myshkore *np* = myshqe

myshnjë *nf* [*Bot*] moss

myshqe *np* <myshk [*Bot*] mosses

myshteri *nm (Colloq)* client, regular customer

myteber *nm (Colloq Iron)* smart guy, big shot

mytesarif *nm* [*Hist*] chief administrator of a sanjak

***my**të *adj (i)* = myjtë

***mytil** *nm* [*Invert*] mussel

myxyrë = mynxyrë

myzavë *nf* powdery track left in wood by termites or other insects

myzeqar

  I § *adj* of or pertaining to Myzeqe

  II § *n* native of Myzeqe

myzeqarçe *adv (Colloq)* in the manner of people from Myzeqe

Myzeqe *nf* flat coastal ethnographic region of central Albania: Myzeqe

***mzith** *nm* [*Anat*] ankle joint

  ∘ **mzith i dorës** wrist

  ∘ **mzith i këmbës** ankle

Nn

n [*në*] *nf* **1** the consonant letter "n" **2** the apical nasal consonant represented by the letter "n"

na *1st pl pron dat/acc clitic preceding a verb, or suffixed to a verb stem in the imper* < **ne** us; to/for us; our
- **na lë·** (**për gjithmonë**) "leave us forever" *(Euph)* to pass away, die
- **na (e) merr· të keqen/ligën** "take away {}'s evil from us" *(Impol)* to get the bad end {} *deserves*
- **Na rrofsh për dimër, se për verë jemi vetë.** "May you live for us in winter, for in summer we are self-sufficient." *(Colloq Iron)* We have no need of fair-weather friends.
- **Na theve brinjët** "you broke our ribs" *(Iron)* You're cracking us up! You make me laugh!

na *interj* vocal gesture indicating that something is being handed to the listener: here! take this!

NA *abbrev* < **Ndërmarrja e asfaltimit** agency for putting asphalt on roads

nacional *adj* national

nacionalçlirimtar *adj* of or pertaining to national liberation

nacionalist *adj, n* nationalist

nacionalitet *nm* *(Book)* nationality

nacionalizëm *nm* nationalism

nacionalizim *nm ger* **1** < **nacionalizo·n 2** nationalization

nacionalizo·n *vt* to nationalize

nacionalizuar *adj (i)* nationalized

nacionalo-socialist *adj* national socialist .

nacional-socializëm *nm* national socialism

****nacist** *n, adj* Nazi = **nazist**

nade *nf (Reg Gheg)* morning

nadir *nm* [*Astron*] nadir

nafaka *nf* luck

nafakë *nf(Colloq)* luck

nafakëbardhë *adj (Colloq)* lucky

nafakëkëputur *OR* **nafakëprerë** *adj (Colloq)* unlucky; (of a woman) unwed

nafakëzi *adj (fem sg ˜ez, masc pl ˜inj, fem pl ˜eza) (Colloq)* ill-fated, unlucky

****nafe** *OR* **nafë** *nf* **1** goatee **2** catkin, tassel

****nafele** *nf* white patch in the fur of a stone/beech marten

naforë *nf[Relig]* sacramental bread (in the Orthodox church): host

****naft** *nm* seaman, mariner

naftalinë *nf* naphthalene

naft-e-gazmbajtës = **naftëgazmbajtës**

naftë *nf* **1** petroleum **2** diesel oil
- **naftë e papastruar** crude oil

naftëgazmbajtës *adj* containing oil and natural gas

naftëmbajtës *adj [Geol]* containing petroleum: oil-bearing, petroliferous

****naftër** *np* < **naft** crew

****naftësi** *nf* seamanship

naftësjellës *nm* oil pipeline

naftëtar *nm* petroleum worker, oilman

nagaçe *nf* = **naxhake**

nagant *nm* six-shooter, revolver

****nagas·** *vt* to prevail upon [], coerce

****nagër** *adj* very dark: dark brown, black

****nagjasëm** *nf* [*Bot*] peppermint (*Mentha piperita*)

nahije *nf* **1** *(Colloq Reg)* region, district **2** [*Hist*] smallest administrative subdivision of a sanjuk during the Ottoman occupation: commune

nailon *nm* = **najlon**

Naim *nm* Naim (male name)

naiv *adj* naive

naivitet *nm* *(Book)* naiveté

najadë *nf* [*Bot*] naiad

najë *nf* anvil used by coppersmith

najlon *nm* nylon

****najo·n** *vt* to warm [a liquid] up a little

nakar *nm (Colloq)* envy, jealousy

nakarmadh *adj (Colloq)* envious, jealous

****nakati** *nf* confusion

nakatos· *vt (Colloq)* **1** to mingle, mix [] together; get [] mixed up **2** *(Pej)* to get [] mixed up in something

nakatos·et *vpr (Colloq)* **1** to become intermingled, get mixed together **2** *(Pej)* to get tangled up, become enmeshed

nakël *nf * (Old)* tale
- <> **bëhet nakël** <> can't get it out of <>'s mind; <> can't stop worrying

naks *adj, n (Colloq)* touchy/hotheaded (person)

****nalt** = **lart** *(Reg Gheg)*

****naltë** *adj (i)* high, high up; elevated; prominent, superior

nallane *nf* wooden sandal held on by a single strap: clog, sabot

nallban *nm* **1** farrier **2** *(Fig Pej)* person incompetent at his trade

nallçë *nf* **1** metal plate with a hole in the middle used as horseshoe **2** protective metal plate on the bottom of a shoe

nallë *nf* = **nallban**

nallëne = **nallane**

nam *nm (Colloq)* **1** reputation, repute, fame **2** *(Fig)* terrible damage, great destruction
- **ësh-të me nam** to have a reputation, be famous
- **S'u bë nami!** *(Colloq)* It's not such a big deal! It's nothing to get excited about!

****namatar** *n* charmer, exorcist, conjurer

****namati** *nf* salutary spell: charm

namatis·
- *I* § *vi (Old)* **1** to whisper a salutary charm **2** to mutter incomprehensibly
- *II* § *vt (Old)* **1** to exorcise [an afflicted person] *****2** to enchant, fascinate

namatisje *nf ger* **1** < **namatis· 2** incantation

namaz *nm* [*Relig*] Moslem prayer that is repeated several times a day *na'meta = nam*ë*ta'

*nam*ë*na' *adv*

*nâm*ë*t *adj (i) (Reg Gheg)* damned, accursed, wretched

nam*ë*ta'
  I § *adv (Reg)* just then, right then: all of a sudden; at that moment, meanwhile
  II § *pcl* here you are!

na'm*ë*z *nf* = mu'nx*ë*

namibia'n
  I § *adj* of/from Namibia
  II § *n* native of Namibia

namlli' *nf* 1 = navlli' *2 plant stem: stalk, blade

*namus'li' *nf* = namusqa'r

namus'qa'r *adj (Colloq)* having a sense of dignity/honor/decency

nana'ç
  I § *nm* obstinate/headstrong person
  II § *adj* *boorish

*nana'm*ê*nd *adj (Reg Gheg)* imbecilic

*nând*ë *nf (Reg Gheg)* = n*ë*nt*ë

na'n*ë *nf (Reg Gheg)* = n*ë*n*ë

*nan*ë*ma'dhe *nf (Reg Gheg)* = n*ë*n*ë*gjy'she

*nani' *adv* = tani'

nani'c*ë *nf* [*Bot*] common fennel (*Foeniculum vulgare*)

nan'iz*ë*m *nm* [*Med*] nanism, dwarfism

nan'sho'rje *nf (Reg Colloq)* wet nurse

nanu'q *nm* [*Anat*] second chamber of the stomach of a ruminant: reticulum

nanuri's· *vt* 1 to lull/sing [] gently to sleep 2 *(Fig)* to caress [] gently: soothe

nanuri'sje *nf ger* 1 <nanuri's· 2 lullaby

nanuri't· *OR* nanuro'·*n* *vt* = nanuri's·

*nap *(Colloq Reg)* = jap|

napa'lm *nm* napalm

na'p*ë *nf* 1 cheesecloth 2 cambric cover; piece of cambric worn as a head kerchief by women 3 *(Fig)* veil 4 diaper *5 tablecloth; sheet

nap*ë*lu'ng*ë *nf* = l*ë*plu'ng*ë

Na'pol'i *nm* Naples

napolita'n *adj* Neapolitan

napolo'n *nm* [*Hist*] napoleon (gold coin)

*napra'n *adj, n* = nopra'n

*nara'nc*ë *nf* orange = portoka'll

narci's *nm* [*Bot*] narcissus *Narcissus*

narde'n *nm* [*Food*] extract of a sour fruit (plum/cherry extract) used in cooking

nargji'le *nf* water-pipe for smoking tobacco: narghile

*nari' *nf* small hammer used by a coppersmith

*nari'c *nm* fool

narkoma'n *nm* drug addict

narkomani' *nm* drug addiction

*narko's· = narkotizo'·*n

narkoti'k *adj, nm* narcotic

narkotiz'i'm *nm ger* 1 <narkotizo'·*n*, narkotizo'·*het* 2 narcotization

narkotizo'·*het* *vpr* to become addicted (to a narcotic)

narkotizo'·*n* *vt* 1 to put []into a narcotic sleep: anesthetize 2 *(Fig)* to becloud the mind

narko'z*ë *nf* [*Med*] narcosis

*narqi'z = narci's

na'rt*ë *adj (i)* (of water) limpid, pellucid; sparkling clean

Na'rt*ë *nf* Narta: town in southwest Albania known for its wines: Narta

nartjo't
  I § *adj* of/from Narta
  II § *nm* native of Narta

*narva'le *nf* [*Zool*] narwhal

narrati'v *adj* narrative

narrati'v*ë *nf* [*Lit*] narrative, narration

nasqiri' *nf* cleaning/tidying up, housework

nasqiri's· *vt* to clean/tidy up [a house]

*na'shl'a *np fem* entrails

*nashti' *(Reg Tosk)* = tashti'

*nashti'sh*ë*m *(Reg Tosk)* = tani'sh*ë*m

na'ta-na't*ë*s *adv* every night, night after night

*nata'r *adj* clever, quick-witted

na't*ë *nf* night
  ○ nata e buzmit Christmas night
  ○ Nat*ë*n e mir*ë*! *(Felic)* Goodnight!
  ○ Nata *ë*sht*ë* me barr*ë*. *(Prov)* The night is full of unexpected dangers.
  ○ nata e gjerdekut the wedding night

na't*ë*n *adv* at night

*na't*ë*l'sh*ë*m *adj (i)* nocturnal, nightly

nato'·*n* *vi (Colloq)* to spend the night

NATO
  I § *abbrev*
  II § *nf (English)* <Organizata e Traktatit t*ë* Atlantikut Verior NATO: North Atlantic Treaty Organization

natriu'm *nm* [*Chem*] sodium, soda *(Na)* = sodiu'm

*natur' = natyr'

natyra'l *adj* natural

natyrali'st
  I § *adj* naturalistic
  II § *n* naturalist

natyrali'z*ë*m *nm* naturalism

natyrlaliz'i'm *nm ger* 1 <naturalizo'·*n* 2 naturalization

natyr'alizo'·*n* *vt* to naturalize

natyr'alizu'ar *adj (i)* naturalized

naty'r*ë *nf* nature
  ○ natyra e gjall*ë* living things/beings
  ○ natyr*ë* e qet*ë* [*Art*] still life
  ○ natyra e vdekur inert nature

natyr'ësi' *nf* = natyrshm*ë*ri'

natyr'i'sht *adv* naturally, of course

natyro'r *adj* of or pertaining to nature; not artificial, real: natural

natyr'sh*ë*m
  I § *adj (i)* in accord with nature; not artificial, real; relaxed: natural
  II § *adv* naturally

natyr'shm*ë*ri' *nf* naturalness

*nava's· *vt* to harness

*nava's *stem for 1st sg pres, pl pres, 2nd & 3rd sg subj, pind* <nava't·

*nava't· *vt* 1 to manage, run, control 2 to get; procure; extract

nava't*ë *nf* [*Archit*] nave = ani'jat*ë

*nava't*ë*s *n* manager, administrator

navi'g *nm (np ~ gje)* door bolt = lloz

navlli' *nf* barrel of a gun

na'vllo *nf (Old)* transportation charge on a vessel: fare for passage; shipping charge, freight cost

*****navll'o·n** *vt (Old)* to charter [a vessel]

naxha'ke *nf* small hatchet, cleaver

naza'l *adj* [*Ling*] nasal

na'ze *np* **1** affected manners, affectation **2** pretense of dislike: finicky/fussy behavior; squeamishness **3** cute/coquettish/impish behavior intended to draw attention: coyness, impishness

naze'li *adj* = nazeqa'r

naze'ma'dh *adj* very fussy in eating; very finicky

naze'qa'r *adj* finicky, picky; fussy, fastidious; affected; squeamish

naze'ta'r *adj* = nazeqa'r

naze'to'r *adj* **1** mannered, affected; coy; fussy **2** dressing so that others will notice: showy in dress **3** = nazeqa'r

nazi'ball'ist *adj, n* [*Hist npc*] (person) involved with Albanian Balli Kombëtar forces said to be allied with the German Nazis

nazi'fashi'st *adj, n (Npc)* [*Hist*] Nazi-Fascist

nazi'k *adj (Colloq)* **1** good-looking, comely **2** fastidious; with refined tastes

nazi'st *n, adj* Nazi

nazi'zëm *nm* Nazism

Nazmi *nm* Nazmi (male name)

NB *abbrev (Italian)* < Nota bene N.B.

NB *abbrev* < Ndërmarrja blegtorale **1** agency for stock-farming < Ndërmarrja e bonifikimit **2** agency for land reclamation < Ndërmarrja bujqësore **3** agency for agriculture

NBK *abbrev* < Ndërmarrja bujqësore e kullotave agency for agriculture and grazing

NBSh [*në-bë-shë*] *abbrev* < Ndërmarrja bujqësore shtetërore *(Old)* state agricultural agency

NBShL *abbrev* < Ndërmarrja bujqësore shtetërore lokale local state agricultural agency

nc = cq

NÇ *abbrev* < Nacionalçlirimtare National Liberation

nda·het *vpr* **1** to become separated; separate; go in separate ways, split up **2** to get divorced **3** *(Fig)* to come/make out, end up **4** to be of a different opinion: part ways, disagree ***5** to be a descendant/offshoot
  ○ **nuk/mos/s'<> nda·het** *(Fig)* to stick to <>; not leave <> alone; never leave <>
  ○ **nda·het mirë** to come out well
  ○ **nda·het**^{3sg} **moti** the weather *clears* up
  ○ **nda·het në shenjë** to be easily distinguishable
  ○ **nda·het nga gjiri ynë** to be taken from our midst (die)
  ○ **nda·het nga jeta** to depart this life (die)
  ○ **nda·het nga lëngu e nga përsheshi** (said of a poor person who dies or leaves his people forever) to go away forever
  ○ **nda·het nga vatha** to leave the flock
  ○ **nda·het**^{pl} **për së gjalli (me [])** not have social contact (with []) for a long time, not see [] for ages
  ○ **nda·het prej nesh** to be taken from us (die)
  ○ **nuk u nda·het shokëve** to keep up with the others, not lag behind
  ○ **s'<> nda·het**^{3sg} **shpirti** <> *are* inseparable companions
  ○ **<> nda·het**^{3sg} **zemra dysh** "<>'s heart *divides* in half" <>'s heart *is breaking*?

nda·n

I § *vt* **1** to separate; divide; keep [] apart **2** to separate from []; divorce **3** to apportion [] into shares, distribute **4** to put [a portion] aside **5** *(Fig)* to share **6** *(Fig)* to make a joint [decision]; bring [a matter] to a final conclusion: decide **7** *(Fig)* to discern, make [] out

II § *vi (Colloq)* to be distinctive from others: stick out
  ○ **nuk <>[] nda·n** to never allow <> to go without [], never deprive <> of [], never neglect <> in terms of []; take [] away/off/from <>
  ○ **i nda·n bathët** to bring it all out in the open, expose it all to public view
  ○ **nda·n bejlegun** to fight a duel
  ○ **e nda·n bukën me** [] to break off one's friendship with [], stop seeing []
  ○ **e nda·n bukën në zjarr** to be very hospitable
  ○ **nda·n bykun nga gruri** to separate the wheat from the chaff
  ○ **nda·n bykun nga kokrrat** to separate the wheat from the chaff
  ○ **nuk <>a nda·n hapin** follow <> wherever <> goes
  ○ **i nda·n hesapet me** [] to settle accounts definitively with; break up with [] once and for all
  ○ **nda·n kafshatën e gojës/fundit me** [] to share one's last morsel with [], give [] the shirt off one's back
  ○ **nda·n kalli** (of plants) to sprout spikes/ears
  ○ **i nda·n lakrat me** [] to settle accounts definitively with; break up with [] once and for all
  ○ **<>i nda·n leshtë** to get <> untangled; straighten <> out, put <> all in order
  ○ **nda·n letrat** to deal the cards
  ○ **i nda·n llogaritë me** [] to settle accounts definitively with; break up with [] once and for all
  ○ **[] nda·n me shpatë** "decide [] by the sword" to decide [] definitively by use of force
  ○ **[] nda·n me thikë** to divide/separate [] sharply; distinguish [] clearly
  ○ **e nda·n mejdanin (me []) 1** *(Old)* to select a date for a duel (with []) **2** to straighten matters out (between [each other])
  ○ **e nda·n mendjen** to make up one's mind
  ○ **s'[] nda·n nga goja** never cease to speak (well) of [], praise [] continually, always mention []
  ○ {*period of time*} **<> nda·n**^{3rd} [] **nga** {} <> *is* {*period of time*} away from {} **dy javë na ndajnë nga zgjedhjet** we are two weeks away from the elections
  ○ **e nda·n punën dysh** to solve the problem neatly
  ○ **e nda·n punën** to be very straightforward
  ○ **nda·n qimen (më) katërsh/dysh** "divide the hair in four/two" **1** to be extremely skillful/clever **2** *(Pej)* to be very stingy/miserly **3** to disagree about trivial details: quibble
  ○ **[] nda·n rrethas** to divide [] evenly among all around
  ○ **nda·n shapin nga sheqeri** "separate the alum from the sugar" to separate what is valuable from what is worthless: separate the grain from the chaff; straighten out a complicated matter
  ○ **nda·n sherrin** to settle a dispute; reconcile the quarreling parties
  ○ **e nda·n xhevapin** "divide the answer" to answer yes or no
  ○ **nda·n []** *prej gjirit* to wean [a suckling]

○ **S'ndahet mishi prej thoit.** "The flesh does not separate from the nails." *(Prov)* (said of people who cannot do without one another) They are inseparable.

ndaj
I § *prep (abl)* **1** toward **2** in respect/regard to
II § *conj (Colloq)* therefore: so

***ndajafërsí** *nf* [*Ling*] genetic relationship: affinity

***ndajafërt** *adj* [*Ling*] genetically related

ndajfolje *nf* [*Ling*] adverb

ndajfoljezím *nm ger* [*Ling*] < **ndajfoljezo·het**

ndajfoljezo·het *vpr* [*Ling*] to become adverbialized

ndajfoljor *adj* [*Ling*] adverbial

ndajgjend·et *vpr (Book)* to be there (for someone in times of difficulty), stand by, be supportive

ndajgjethëz *nf* [*Bot*] stipule

ndajnate *adv* towards evening, at twilight, just before dark

ndajnatë
I § *nf* evening dusk, twilight
II § *adv* towards evening, at twilight, just before dark

ndajnatëherë
I § *adv* towards evening, just before dark
II § *nf* * = **ndajnatë**

ndajshtesë *nf* [*Ling*] affix

ndajshtesím *nm* [*Ling*] affixation

ndajshtesor *adj* [*Ling*] affixal

ndajshtím *nm* [*Ling*] apposition

ndajshtimor *adj* [*Ling*] appositional

ndajshtresë *nf* [*Ling*] adstratum

ndajt·es *adj* divisive; severing

ndajthith· *vt* [*Chem*] to adsorb

ndajthithje *nf* [*Chem*] adsorption

ndal·
I § *vi* **1** to halt; stop **2** *(Colloq)* to stop by/in, drop in
II § *vt* **1** = **ndalo·n 2** *(Fig)* to keep [] in one place: fix, retain, rivet, keep **3** *(Colloq)* to put out [], extinguish, quench
○ **ndal· diellin me fjalë** "halt the sun with words" to be too talkative
○ **<> ndal· dorën** to bring <>'s (bad) actions to an end, make <> stop (doing harmful things)
○ **e ndal· vrapin** to take a rest after great exertion, hold up

ndal·et *vpr* **1** to come to a stop/rest: halt **2** *(Colloq)* to stop over, stay over **3** *(Fig)* to keep one's attention focused: concentrate **4** to maintain restraint, hold back
○ **Ndalu beg se ka hendek.** "Stop, bey, because there is a ditch." Wait a minute, we've hit a little snag.

ndalesë *nf* **1** temporary stopping point: pause, rest period, rest **2** stopping place: station, stop, halt; stopover, stay **3** obstacle **4** withheld money, withholding **5** detention, arrest; prohibition, ban

ndalë *nf* stopping place: station, stop, halt

ndalím *nm ger* **1** < **ndalo·n, ndalo·het 2** halt, stoppage **3** *(Colloq)* prohibition: don't
○ **ndalim kalimi** no entrance
○ **ndalim kazerme** *(Old)* [*Mil*] confinement to quarters (as a punishment)

ndalimqarkullím *nm* curfew

ndalje *nf* **1** rest stop during travel **2** pause; stoppage **3** withheld salary, garnisheed wages

ndalk *nm (np ˜q)* [*Ichth*] suckerfish, remora *(Remora remora)*

ndalo·het *vpr* **1** to come to a stop; halt; stop flowing **2** *(Colloq)* to stop over, stay over **3** to be forbidden, be prohibited
○ **Ndalohet Duhani** No Smoking
○ **Ndalohet Hyrja!** No Entrance, Entrance Forbidden

ndalo·n
I § *vt* **1** to stop; stop [] temporarily, detain **2** to prohibit, forbid; prevent **3** to garnishee, withhold **4** [*Law*] to arrest
II § *vi* to halt, stop, discontinue

ndaluar *adj (i)* prohibited, forbidden

ndalues *adj* prohibitive

***ndam** *(Reg Gheg)* = **ndar**

ndanë
I § *adv* alongside, nearby
II § *prep (abl)* along/to the edge of: beside, along

ndaras OR **ndarazi** *adv* in a separated manner, separately; spaced apart

ndarë
I § *part* < **nda·n** divided
II § *adj (i)* **1** separate **2** not living with one's spouse: separated
III § *nf (e)* partitioned-off section: room (of a building); compartment (of a train); shelf (of a closet); square (of a chess board)
○ **ndarë për** [] divided by []

ndarës
I § *adj* separating, dividing, partitioning
II § *nm* **1** divider, separator *2 divisor

ndarje *nf ger* **1** < **nda·n, nda·het 2** separation; divorce **3** part **4** parting **5** departure, leave-taking **6** division, allocation, distribution **7** deal (in card game) **8** compartment, shelf

***ndas** *nm (Old)* dividend

***ndase** *nf* partition

ndasí *nf* rift, split, schism

ndasor *adj (Old)* [*Ling*] disjunctive

ndashëm *adj (i)* dividable, partible; divisible

ndashmëri *nf* **1** dividability, separability; divisibility **2** [*Min*] fissility

***ndashtí** = **tashtí**

nde·het *vpr* **1** to stretch out **2** *(Fig)* to spread out and form a covering **3** = **tendos·et** *4 (Old)* = **deh·et**
○ **<> nde·het** to stick tight to <>, dog/shadow <>

nde·n *vt* **1** to stretch/spread [] (out) **2** to strain; tense
○ **<> nde·n dorën** to have one's hand out to <>: beg <>

ndeh· *vt* = **nd·et**

ndejas *adv* in sitting position, while sitting

ndejë *nf* **1** = **ndenjje 2** residence; sojourn **3** informal gathering of friends

***ndejës** *adj* sedentary

ndejëtar *n* long-time resident: native, indigene

ndejme *nf* dwelling place, residence, place of sojourn

ndejshëm
I § *adj (i)* **1** calm, stable, judicious *2 inhabitable
II § *adv* deliberately, unhurriedly

ndejt *stem for pdef, part, adm* < **rri·**

ndejtësor *adj* [*Anat*] = **ndenjësor**

***ndek** = **tek**

ndemje *nf* = **nderje**

ndenj *stem for pdef, opt, adm, part* < **rri·**

nde·nj|as *adv* in/to a sitting/stationary position

nde·nj|ës *n (Old)* occupant, resident

nde·nj|ëse *nf* sitting place: seat

nde·nj|ës|o·r *adj [Anat]* gluteal

nde·nj|je *nf* staying in one place/position; stationary posture

nde·nj|ur
I § *part* <rri·
II § *adj (i)* 1 stationary 2 stagnant; stale
III § *adv* in a sitting position
IV § *nn (të)* stationary posture

nde·nj|ur|a *np (të) (Colloq)* buttocks: hind end, backside

nder *nm* 1 honor; sense of honor 2 honesty, fidelity 3 good name, esteem 4 favor, good turn 5 most honored person of __ , pride of __

nder· *vt* 1 = ndero·n 2 = nde·n

nde·razi *adv* face to face, opposite

*****nder|ba|më** *adj (Reg Gheg)* = nderbërës

nder|bë·r|ës *adj, n* (person) willing to do favors, helpful (person)

nde·re *OR* **nde·rë** *nf (Reg)* = nder

nde·rë *adj (i)* 1 stretched out 2 shallow, flat 3 *(Fig)* tense; taut, tight 4 *[Ling]* (of vowels) tense

nder|im *nm ger* 1 <ndero·n, ndero·het 2 respect; homage

Nder|im *nm* Nderim (male name)

Nder|ime *nf* Nderime (female name)

*****nder|im|ta·r** *adj* respectful; reverent

nde·r|je *nf ger* 1 <nde·n, nde·het 2 strain 3 *[Ling]* tensing

nder|më *adj (i)* 1 = nde·rë 2 *(Colloq)* = nde·rshëm

nder|mir|ë *adj* very generous and helpful in times of need

ndero·het *vpr* to emerge with honor, be honored

ndero·n *vt* 1 to honor; respect; esteem; show [] appreciation and respect 2 to do/bring honor to [] 3 to salute

nder|shëm
I § *adj (i)* 1 honest; honorable; respectable 2 decent, fair 3 chaste
II § *adv* honorably
○ **i ndershëm gjer në thember** honest to the core; totally honorable; completely respectable

nder|shm|eri *nf* honesty, integrity

nder|shm|ër|isht *adv* honorably, honestly

nde·rt|ë *adj (i)* 1 = nderu·ar 2 flat, level; smooth; open

nder|ua·r *adj (i)* 1 honored, esteemed, respected 2 with honor and success: successful

*****nder|ue·shëm** = nderrshëm

*****ndes|** = ndezl

ndesh *adv*

ndesh· *vt* 1 to encounter [] accidentally: run/bump into [], come upon [] 2 to happen to find []: come across [], hit upon []
○ **ndesh· në** [] = ndesh·
○ **ndesh· sytë/veshtrimin e** <> to catch <> looking at one
○ **<> ndesh·**[3sg] **sharra në gozhdë** "<>'s saw hits a nail" <> 's plan *hits* a snag; <> *runs* into a dead end

nde·sh·et *vpr* 1 to appear by chance: come up 2 to meet by chance 3 to come up against: collide 4 to enter into a contest/game/battle: fight; be opponents

nde·shë *nf (Reg)* (chance) encounter

○ **Ndesha e mirë!** *(Reg)* (greeting upon meeting someone in the street) How nice to bump into you!

*****ndë·sh|ëm** *adj (i) (Reg Gheg)* extended, protracted; drawling

nde·sh|ës
I § *adj* competitive
II § *n* contestant, player

nde·sh|je *nf ger* 1 <nde·sh·, nde·sh·et 2 competitive struggle: contest; battle, fight; (in sports) match, game
○ **ndeshje e kthimit** *[Sport]* return match

*****ndeshk|im** = ndëshkim

ndesh|tra·shë *nf* 1 phenomenon 2 *(Colloq)* omen

ndez·
I § *vt* 1 to cause [] to burn: ignite [], kindle [a fire], light [a lamp/cigarette] 2 to start [] in energetic operation: turn on [a mechanical/electrical device], start [a motor] 3 to excite vigorous activity/emotion: inflame, stimulate; incite/excite <> to []; provoke [a battle/argument] 4 to cause [] to feel hot 5 *(Fig)* to strike []
II § *vi* 1 to catch fire 2 (of a gun) to fire 3 *(Fig Colloq)* to get into trouble; get on bad terms (with someone)
○ **e ndez·** to smoke (tobacco)
○ **nuk <> ndez·**·*(Colloq)* not work out for <>
○ **nuk <> ndez·**[3sg] **fisheku** "<>'s cartridge *doesn't* fire" <>'s plan misfires
○ **<> ndez·**[3sg] **groshi me** [] [] *puts* <> into a terrible predicament
○ **<> ndez· gjakrat** to cause <>'s tempers to flare
○ **<>i ndez· mizat** 1 to enrage <>, set <>'s blood boiling 2 to disquiet <>, upset <>; get <> riled, stir <> up
○ **<> ndez·**[3sg] **pushka në ujë** "<>'s rifle *fires* even in water" 1 <>'s voice is heard everywhere, <>'s influence is felt everywhere 2 <> is very brave
○ **<> ndez· qiririn** to expect <> to die at any moment
○ **ndez· shkëndijën** to spark, ignite the flame
○ **<> ndez· trutë** to blow out <>'s brains
○ **<> ndez· zemrat** to ignite <>'s spirits
○ **i ndez· zemrat horë** to be inspiring, set hearts aflame
○ **<>a ndez· zemrën flakë/zjarr** to fire <> up, inspire <> with passion
○ **e ndez· zjarrin në ujë** "<> lights fire even in water" <> *is* very capable, <> *can* work miracles

nde·z|ç *adj* = nde·zës

nde·z|çë *nf (Reg)* = çakma·k

nde·z|ë *nf* 1 burning envy *2 zeal

*****nde·z|ëm** *adj (i)* inflamed, lit up, kindled, burning

nde·z|ës
I § *adj* 1 serving to start fires: incendiary, inflammatory 2 inflammable 3 *(Fig)* exhilarating, rousing
II § *nm* 1 firing mechanism on an explosive device, fuse 2 *(Old)* lamplighter

*****nde·z|ët** *adj (i)* = nde·zëm

nde·z|je *nf ger* 1 <ndez·, ndiz·et *(Colloq)* 2 high fever = zjarrmi 3 ignition 4 inflammation
○ **Ndezja e zjarrit nuk fillon nga trungu.** "Lighting the fire does not start from the log" *(Prov)* First things first!

nde·z|shëm *adj (i)* inflammable

*****ndez|ta·r** *nm* lamplighter

nde·z|të *adj (i)* 1 = nde·zur 2 *(Fig)* = zja·rrtë

ndezulli *nf* **1** high temperature, fever **2** *(Colloq)* zeal/enthusiasm for work

ndëzur
 I § *part* <**ndez·**, **ndiz·***et*
 II § *adj (i)* **1** on fire, burning; lit, lighted **2** in energetic operation: (of a mechanical/electrical device) turned on, on; (of engines) running **3** *(Fig)* hot-tempered; red with anger **4** *(Fig)* emotionally heated: fiery, animated; charged, tense **5** (of colors) vivid, bright **6** [*Med*] (of eyes) bloodshot
 III § *adv* on fire, afire; lit, alit; (of a mechanical/electrical device) turned on: on, running

*ndë *prep (acc)* = në

*ndëgj = dëgj

 ndëjt *stem for part, pdef, adm* <**rri·**

*ndële·*n vt* = ndj·*et

*ndëles**e** *nf* = ndje's**e**

*ndën *OR* **ndë·në** *prep (acc)* = nën

 ndënj *stem for pdef, opt, adm, part* <**rri·** = ndenj

*ndënjtje *nf* = nden*je

 ndër *prep (acc)* between; among, amidst, in; throughout, through
 ∘ **ndër domna** *(Reg)* in a quandary, perplexed; up in the air, unresolved
 ∘ **ndër sy** to one's face

*ndër· *vt* = nde·*n

*ndër·*et vpr* to stretch out, extend = shtri·*het

 ndër *formative prefix* inter-, intra-

 ndëra'kt *nm* [*Theat*] entr'acte, intermission

 ndëralea't *adj* interallied

*ndërbe·*n vi* (of rivers) to rise

 ndërçel'ës *nm* [*Electr*] commutator = komutato'r

 ndërçe'lje *nf* [*Electr*] reversal of electric current: commutation

 ndërdialekto'r *adj* [*Ling*] interdialectal

 **ndërdy·*het vpr* to waver between alternatives: be ambivalent

 **ndërdy·*n vi* to be of two minds: be doubtful/hesitant

 ndërdy'më *adj (i)* of two minds: ambivalent

 ndërdy'sh *adv* = ndërdy'shas

 ndërdy'shas *adv* of two minds: ambivalently

 ndërdy'zash *adv* = ndërdy'shas

 ndërdhëmbë'zi'm *nm* interlocking, intermeshing

 ndërdhëmbo're *nf* [*Ling*] interdental

*ndërë *adj (i)* = nder'ë

 ndërfu's *stem for 1st sg pres, pl pres, 2nd & 3rd sg subj, pind* <**ndërfu'·**

 ndërfu't· *vt (Book)* to put [] in between: interpose

 ndërfu't·*et vpr (Book)* to enter in between; intrude

 ndërfu'tje
 I § *nf (Book)* <**ndërfu'·**, **ndërfu't·***et
 II § *nf* intrusion

 ndërfu'tur *adj (i)* **1** inserted *(Book)* **2** intrusive **3** [*Ling*] parenthetical

 ndërgishtle *nf* [*Bot*] creeping cinquefoil, fivefinger, five-leaf grass *(Potentilla reptans)*

 ndërgi'shtëz *nf* whitlow

 ndërgo'·*n vt* **1 to suck the teat of [a livestock animal] *2 (Old)* to water [livestock]

 ndërgje'gje *nf* **1** conscious mind **2** consciousness **3** conscience; sense of responsibility
 ∘ **të rrahurit e ndërgjegjes** "the pounding of one's conscience" compunction, qualm

*ndërgjegje'si *nf (Book)* conscientiousness

*ndërgjegje'si'sht *adv (Book)* conscientiously

*ndërgjegjë'si'm *nm ger* <**ndërgjegjëso'·**n

*ndërgjegjë'so·*n vt (Book)* to make [] conscientious

 ndërgje'gjshëm *adj (i)* **1** conscious **2** conscientious; feeling responsible

 ndërgjegjshm'ëri *nf (Book)* **1** consciousness **2** conscientiousness; responsibleness

*ndërgjo·*n (Old)* = dërgo'·*n

 ndërgjuh'ëso'r *adj* [*Ling*] between languages: cross-linguistic; interlingual

 ndërgjyq'ës *adj, n* [*Law*] litigant

*ndërgjyq'shëm *adj (i)* litigating, litigant

 **ndërhundë'zo·*n vi* to speak in a nasal voice

 ndërhu'ndsh *nm* person who speaks in a nasal voice

 ndërhy·*n vi* **1 to intrude, interfere **2** to intervene **3** to intercede

 ndërhy'r *stem for pdef, part* <**ndërhy'·**n

 ndërhy'rës
 I § *adj* invading; intrusive
 II § *n* **1** intruder **2** go-between; matchmaker **3** [*Law*] intervenor, interpleader

 ndërhy'rje *nf ger* **1** <**ndërhy'·**n **2** intrusion; incursion **3** intervention; intercession

 ndërishullo'r *adj* among the islands: interisland

*ndërkal·*vt (Book)* to intercalate

 ndërka'q *adv* during this time: meanwhile, in the meantime; at this moment

 ndërka't *nm* [*Constr*] = sole'tё

*ndërkejm *adj (i)* wasted, ruined

 ndërkë'mb· *vt* = nëpërkë'mb·

 ndërkë'mbas *adv* trying to knock one's opponent down by tripping

 ndërkë'mbës *n* sly person who strikes out of the blue

 ndërkëmbi'm *nm (Book)* interchange, reciprocal exchange

 ndërkë'mbje *nf* **1** hobble (on a horse's feet) **2** treadle on a loom

 ndërkë'mbye'shëm *adj (i) (Book)* interchangeable

 ndërkëshilli'm *nm* [*Law*] group deliberation

 ndërkocko'r *adj* [*Anat*] interosseal

 ndërko'hё
 I § *nf* period of time between events, between time: interim, interlude
 II § *adv* meanwhile, in the meantime

 ndërko'hshëm *adj (i)* **1** concurrent **2** intermittent

 ndërkombëta'r *adj* international

 ndërkombë'ta're *nf* = internaciona'le

 ndërkombё'tarë'si *nf (Book)* internationality

 ndërkombё'tariz'ëm *nm* [*Ling*] internationalism

 ndërkombё'tarizi'm *nm ger* **1** <**ndërkombёtarizo·**n **2** internationalization

 **ndërkombё'tarizo·*n vt* to internationalize

*ndërkombia'r = ndërkombёta'r

 ndërkontinenta'l *adj* intercontinental

 ndërkrahino'r *adj* interregional

 **ndërkre·*het vpr* to fly into a rage; (of animals) go wild

 ndërkre·*n vt* **1 to drive [] into a rage, madden; stupefy, befuddle *2 (of goats) to butt

 ndërkry'e *stem for 1st & 2nd sg pdef* <**ndërkre·**n

 ndërkry'er *adj (i)* furious, in a rage

*ndërkry'erje *nf* **1** fury, rage **2** insurrection

*ndërky'·*het vpr* = ndërkre'he

ndërla'k·*et vpr* = ngo'p·*et*

ndërlidh· *vt* 1 to make liaison with []; bring [] into
contact: interconnect, communicate 2 *(Fig)* to intertwine, interweave

ndërlidh·*et vpr* 1 to establish connections, enter
into communication 2 *(Fig)* to be interconnected/in-
terwoven

ndërlidh|ës
  I § n 1 agent for communication: liaison 2 operator
  of communications equipment, communicator
  II § adj serving for communication/liaison, connective, interconnecting, communicative

ndërlidhje
  I § nf ger <ndërlidh·, ndërlidh·*et*
  II § nf 1 liaison; communication; communications
  2 interrelationships, interconnections; reciprocal relations

ndërlidh|ur *adj (i)* 1 in communication, communi-
cating 2 *(Fig)* interconnected, intertwined, interwoven

ndërlidh|uri *nf* interconnectivity, interconnected-
ness

ndërlik· *vt* 1 to interweave, interlace 2 to twist/
sprain/dislocate [a part of the body] 3 *(Fig)* to complicate; confuse, bewilder

ndërlik·*et vpr* to get tangled up; get confused

ndërlik|ë *nf* 1 wickerwork; wattle, fence wattle
2 latticework, window lattice *3 (Fig)* flattery

ndërlikim *nm ger* 1 <ndërliko·*n*, ndërliko'·*het*
2 complication, intricacy 3 tangle; involvement, implication

ndërliko'·*het vpr* 1 to get tangled up; become confused 2 to become entangled/involved 3 *[Med]* to
encounter complications

ndërliko'·*n vt* 1 to complicate 2 to entangle/involve
[someone] in a matter

ndërliks· *vt* = ndërlik·

ndërliks·*et vpr* to get tangled up; get confused

ndërliks|je *nf ger* 1 <ndërliks·, ndërliks·*et* 2 com-
plication 3 entanglement

ndërliks|ur *adj (i)* complicated; tangled up, entan-
gled

ndërlik|uar *adj (i)* complex, intricate

*ndërlikue|shëm *adj (i)* 1 = ndërlikur 2 correlat-
able, correlated

*ndërliq· = ndërlik·

*ndërliq·*et vpr* = ndërlik·*et*

*ndërliqe *nf* = ndërlikim

*ndërluft|ar *adj, n* = ndërluftues

ndërluft|ues
  I § adj at war, engaged in fighting, belligerent
  II § n belligerent

*ndërlum *nm* tributary

ndërlu'mna *np fem* area between two rivers

ndërmarte's|ë *I § nf OR* ndërmartim *II § nm*
intermarriage

ndërmarto'·*het vpr* to intermarry

ndërma'rr *stem for 1st sg pres, pl pres, 2nd & 3rd sg
subj, opt, adm, part* <ndërmerr·

ndërma'rrje *nf ger* 1 <ndërmerr· 2 enterprise
3 undertaking, project

ndërme'nd *nm (Reg)* memory held of someone

*ndërme'nd·*et vpr* to bring [] to mind: recall

ndërme'nd·*et vpr* to regain consciousness: come to

ndërme'rr· *vt* to undertake

*ndërmesta'r *n* intermediary

*ndërmestim *nm ger* = ndërmjetesim

*ndërmesto'·*n vt* = ndërmjeteso·*n*

ndërmirr *stem for 2nd pl pres, pind, imper, vp*
  <ndërme'rr·

ndërmje|më *adj (i)* = ndërmjetem

ndërmjet
  I § prep (abl) between; among; amongst, amidst
  II § adv in between, in the middle
  III § nm [Anat] waist

ndërmjet|ëm *adj (i)* 1 in-between; intermedi-
ate, intermediary; linking 2 *[Ling]* parenthetic 3 of
medium quality, middling

ndërmjet|ës
  I § adj 1 = ndërmjetëm 2 *[Agr]* of a crop grown to
  replenish soil fertility: intercalary
  II § n 1 mediator, intermediary, negotiator 2 marriage broker, go-between 3 intermediate link

ndërmjet|ësi *nf* 1 negotiation by an intermediary:
mediation, intermediation *2 interval

ndërmjet|ësim *nm ger* 1 <ndërmjeteso·*n* 2 in-
tercession; mediation

ndërmjet|ëso·*n vi* to act as intermediary: inter-
cede, mediate

*ndërmjet|ëso'r *adj* intermediate

ndërmje'tëz *nf* 1 narrow valley; meadow between
two fields 2 intervening time, interlude 3 *[Constr]*
partition wall *4 interstice

ndërmjetim *nm (Book)* 1 indirect way of expressing something 2 intermediate link 3 = ndërmjetesi

ndërmjetshëm *adj (i)* = ndërmjetem

ndërmjetu|ar *adj (i) (Book)* by intermediary means:
indirect

*ndërmlis *stem for 1st sg pres, pl pres, 2nd & 3rd sg
subj, pind* <ndërmlit·

*ndërmlit· *vt* = përdre'dh·

ndërmo'r *stem for pdef* <ndërme'rr·

ndërmuar *stem for pl pdef* <ndërme'rr·

*ndërmvar|ësi *nf* interdependence, mutual depen-
dence

ndërnyjë *nf [Bot]* internodal part of a stem

ndërloqean|ik *adj* 1 linking two oceans 2 involved
in travel across the ocean: oceanic, transoceanic

*ndërpa'm|ës *adj (i)* = ndërpare'shëm

*ndërpa're'shëm *adj (i)* transparent = tejduk'shëm

ndërplaneta'r *adj* interplanetary

ndërpre' *stem for pdef, part, imper sg, adm, opt*
  <ndërpret·

ndërpre're *adj (i)* interrupted; cut short; broken off/
up

ndërpre'rje *nf ger* 1 <ndërpret·, ndërprit·*et* 2 interruption; disruption 3 *[Geom]* intersection

ndërpres *stem for 1st sg pres, pl pres, 2nd & 3rd sg
subj* <ndërpret·

ndërpret· *vt* 1 to intersect, cross; intercept 2 to cut
[] short: leave [] unfinished, interrupt 3 to interfere
with []: interrupt, disrupt 4 *[Mil]* to locate [] by
triangulation

ndërpris *stem for pind, 2nd pl pres* <ndërpret·

ndërprit·*et*
  I § vp recip 1 to intersect (one another) 2 *(Reg)* to
  kill one another
  II § vpr to break off, cease, quit

ndërprit *stem for pind, imper, vp* <ndërpret·

ndërqelizo'r *adj [Biol]* intercellular

ndërqytetar = ndërqyteti̇̈s

ndërqyteti̇̈s adj interurban

ndërqyteto̊r adj = ndërqyteti̇̈s

ndërradhë nf [Postal] interline spacing

ndërsa conj 1 while, when, as 2 whereas, while

ndërse·het vpr to assail ◇

ndërse·n vt 1 to incite [a dog] to attack, set [dogs] on 2 (Fig) to incite *3 = ndërze·n

ndërsektoriål adj intersectional

ndërsi̇m nm ger 1 <ndërse·n, ndërse·het *2 = ndërzi̇m

*__ndërsimo̊r__ adj provocative

ndërsje̊llë adj (i) reciprocal; mutual

ndërsje̊lltas adv vice versa; reciprocally

ndërsje̊lltë = ndërsje̊llë

*__ndërsulje__ nf [Mil] breakthrough

ndërsundim nm (Book) interregnum

ndërsye stem for sg pdef <ndërse·n

ndërsye̊r adj (i) 1 stirred up, whipped up (like dogs prepared for the hunt) 2 (Reg) raging; out of control

ndërsye̊s adj inciting, agitating, provocative

ndërsyno̊·het vp recip to confront one another eyeball to eyeball

ndërsyno̊·n vt to confront

ndërshej adv 1 riding astride a loaded packsaddle *2 (Old) in the middle

*__ndërshit__ adv between the two sides of a load on a horse's back

ndërshkollo̊r adj interscholastic

ndërshteti̇̈ro̊r adj interstate

ndërshtënë adj (i) 1 interposed 2 [Ling] parenthetical

ndërshtre̊së nf 1 interlayer [Geol] 2 interstratum: (interbed)

*__ndërshtre̊zuår__ adj (i ˜) [Geol] interstratified, interbedded

ndërshtreso̊r adj [Geol] interstratal

ndërte̊së nf (large) building

ndërti̇ nf 1 woman's makeup, cosmetics *2 compound; combination

ndërti̇m nm ger 1 <ndërto̊·n, ndërto̊·het 2 construction; structure

ndërtimo̊r adj (Book) constructional; structural

ndërtimtår
I§ adj (Elev) used for construction, constructional; constructive
II§ nm (Elev) constructor, builder

ndërtimtåri nf (Elev) building construction

ndërto̊·het vpr to be built/structured

ndërto̊·n vt 1 to construct 2 (Colloq) to fix up []; decorate, adorn 3 (Colloq) to prepare [food]; add flavorful ingredients to [food] *4 to compose; compound

ndërtuår adj (i) finished in construction, built, erected

ndërtue̊s
I§ adj constructive
II§ n builder, constructor

ndërthu̇r· vt to intertwine, interlace, interweave

ndërthu̇r·et vpr to become intertwined/interlaced/ interwoven

ndërthu̇rje nf ger 1 <ndërthu̇r·, ndërthu̇r·et 2 woven object: weaving

*__ndëru̇l·__ vt (Old) [Ling] to inflect, decline = lako̊·n

*__ndëru̇lje__ nf (Old) [Ling] inflection, declension = lakim

*__ndëru̇lshëm__ adj (i) (Old) [Ling] inflectable, declinable = laku̇eshëm

ndërvår·et vpr (Book) to be interdependent

ndërvarë̇si nf (Book) interdependence

ndërvårje nf (Book) = ndërvarë̇si

ndërvårur adj (i) (Book) mutually dependent

ndërveprim nm (Book) interaction

ndëryjo̊r adj (Book) interstellar

ndërzano̊r adj [Ling] intervocalic

ndërze·het vpr (of livestock animals) to mate, have coitus

ndërze·n vt 1 to mate [livestock animals] 2 to mount, inseminate/impregnate

ndërzi̇m nm ger <ndërzo̊·n, ndërzo̊·het

ndërzye stem for sg pdef, part <ndërze·n

ndërzye̊s adj used for insemination: at stud

ndërre̊sa np fem 1 underwear, underclothes 2 dirty linen, laundry 3 (Euph) menstruation

ndërre̊së nf 1 duty period for alternating groups: (for workers) workshift, shift; (for military or naval personnel) watch 2 change, changing, replacement, turn

ndërri̇m nm ger 1 <ndërro̊·n, ndërro̊·het 2 change
∘ **ndërri̇m fushe** [Soccer] change of ends

ndërro̊·het vpr 1 to change clothes 2 to undergo replacement/exchange: change 3 (of animals) to molt 4 to change places: move

ndërro̊·n
I§ vt 1 to replace 2 to exchange; change [money], get change for [] 3 to change, alter 4 [Agr] to transplant 5 to change [residence]: move 6 (of animals) to molt [skin/hair/feathers] 7 = përpajno̊·n
II§ vi to become different: turn, change
∘ **ndërro̊·n bajrak** (Pej) to turn traitor, switch allegiance
∘ **ndërro̊·n biseden** to change the subject (in conversation)
∘ <> **ndërro̊·n**[past] **din e iman** {} really work ◇ over
∘ **ndërro̊·n fjalë me** [] to exchange bitter words with [], have words with []
∘ **ndërro̊·n flamur** to turn traitor
∘ **e ndërro̊·n fleten** (Pej) 1 change the subject (in order to avoid embarrassment) 2 change sides/allegiance, be a turncoat
∘ **ndërro̊·n fytyrën** to go pale, lose one's smile, {}'s face drops
∘ **ndërro̊·n jetë** (Elev) to pass on to a better life, pass away, pass on: die
∘ **ndërro̊·n kë̇mbë** to change step/gait
∘ **ndërro̊·n lëku̇rën** to change one's outer appearance: change the way one looks
∘ **ndërro̊·n plagën** to change the dressing on a wound
∘ **e ndërro̊·n pllakën** (Pej) 1 change the subject (in order to avoid embarrassment) 2 change sides/ allegiance, be a turncoat
∘ **ndërro̊·n**[3sg] **puna** that changes matters; that's an entirely different matter
∘ **i ndërro̊·n si mbreti gratë** (Pej) to change [] as often the king changes his wives: constantly replace one's things with new ones
∘ **i ndërro̊·n telat** to be too changeable to trust: be untrustworthy/unreliable,

ndërrojë *nf* **1** transplantation **2** = përpajnë

ndërruar
- *I §* *part* <**ndërro·n**, **ndërro·het**
- *II §* *adj (i)* wearing clean underwear and new clothes
- **∘ i ndërruar orësh** "changed by fairies, fairy changed" off one's rocker, crazy, loony

ndërrues
- *I §* *nm* **1** person who replaces old things with new **2** [*Rr*] switchman
- *II §* *adj (Book)* used as replacement: fresh

ndërrueshëm *adj (i)* replaceable; exchangeable; convertible

ndërrueshmëri *nf* replaceability; exchangeability; convertibility

ndëshkim *nm ger* **1** <**ndëshko·n** **2** punishment; penalty

ndëshkimor *adj* [*Law*] serving as punishment: punitive; retaliatory

ndëshko·n *vt* **1** to punish; penalize; chastise **2** to retaliate

ndëshkues *nm* **1** intended as punishment: punitive **2** penal; disciplinary

ndëshkueshëm *adj (i)* punishable

*****ndi** *sg imper* <**ndi·e·n**

ndi·het *vpr* <**ndi e·n** **1** to be heard; be felt; be detected **2** to make one's presence felt **3** to experience a feeling, be conscious of one's condition: feel, feel oneself **4** to be evident/perceptible
- **∘ nuk ndi·het³ˢᵍ as miza** not even a fly *can* be heard: you *can* hear a pin drop, there *is* complete silence
- **∘ nuk ndi·het i gjallë** not move a muscle: remain completely still, not make a sound; not lift a finger

*****ndiç** *adv* = në ditsh (*Colloq*) so to say

ndiç·et *vpr* to get stale/rancid

ndiçëm *adj (i)* stale, rancid

ndi·e·n *vt* **1** to experience [ ] with the senses: sense **2** to experience a feeling of [ ]: feel **3** to hear
- **∘ <>a ndie·n lezetin** "feel pleasure for <>" to taste the pleasure offered by <>, learn how nice <> can be
- **∘ ndie·n një limë në zemër** to feel just terrible (in one's heart)
- **∘ <>a ndie·n shije** to start to like <>; begin to get used to <>
- **∘ e ndie·n shpinën të ngrohtë** "<>'s back *is* warm" **1** to have powerful protectors **2** to have influential friends
- **∘ e ndie·n shpirtin të lehtë** to feel relieved (of worry)
- **∘ e ndie·n veten në pekule** to feel that one has everything one could want
- **∘ <>a ndie·n zemra** <> *has* a feeling in <>'s heart, <> *has* a premonition
- **∘ e ndie·n zemrën të lehtë** to feel relieved (of worry)
- **∘ s'e ndie·n** [ ] not feel the passage of time during [ ]

*****ndie** = ndje

*****ndiejtshëm** *adj (i)* perceptible, sensible

ndier *adj (i)* **1** well-known, famous **2** created with deep sensitivity: sensitive

*****ndierkaq** = ndërkaq

*****ndierse** = ndërsa

*****ndies** *adj* sensitive; sensory

*****ndiesor** = ndjesor

*****ndiestar** *adj* tolerant, indulgent

*****ndieshëm** *adj (i)* = ndjeshëm

*****ndigj** = dëgj

ndih· *vt, vi* to help

ndihmesë *nf* contribution, assistance

ndihmë *nf* **1** help; aid; assistance **2** (*Colloq*) helper: help
- **∘ ndihmë e parë** [*Med*] first aid
- **∘ ndihmë e shpejtë** [*Med*] emergency care

*****ndihmëqar** *n* helper

ndihmës
- *I §* *adj* auxiliary
- *II §* *n* assistant, aide; helper, supporter

ndihmës *formativ* assistant-, vice-, deputy-

ndihmësdrejtor *n* (*Old*) assistant director

ndihmësgjyqtar *n* assistant judge (elected by popular vote)

ndihmësministër *nm (Old)* deputy minister

ndihmësmjek *n* medical aide: paramedic

ndihmësmurator *n* assistant mason, mason's assistant

ndihmëtar
- *I §* *n* (*Old*) **1** charitable contributor **2** assistant; helper
- *II §* *adj* **1** charitable **2** auxiliary

ndihmo·n *vt* **1** to help **2** to give charitable assistance to [ ]: help [ ] out

ndihmues *adj* = ndihmës

ndijë *nf(Old)* = ndijim = shqisë

ndijim *nm* [*Psych*] **1** sensation **2** (mental) impression

ndijo·n *vt* [*Psych*] to sense

ndijor *adj* [*Spec*] sensory

ndikesë *nf* = ndikim

ndikim *nm ger* **1** <**ndiko·n** **2** influence

ndiko·n *vi, vt* to be influential, have influence (on): influence
- **∘ ndiko·n për mbarë** to be a good influence

ndikues *adj* influential

ndill *stem for 2nd pl pres, pind, imper, vp* <**ndje ll·**

*****ndim** *nm* stool by the hearth: fireside stool

ndiq·et *vpr* (of carnivorous animals) to mate

ndiq *stem for 2nd pl pres, pind, imper, vp* <**ndjek·**

*****ndirëz** *nf* (*Old*) linen, laundry = ndërresa

*****ndishëm** (*Reg Gheg*) = ndiçëm

ndishk *nm* **1** (*Colloq*) [*Med*] consumption, tuberculosis = tuberkuloz ***2** = ndyshk

*****ndishkun** *adj (i) (Reg Gheg)* consumptive

ndit shëm *adj (i)* = ndiçëm

*****ndivnesë** *nf* divination, oracle, prophesy

*****ndivnim** *nm* = ndivnesë

ndiz·et *vpr* **1** to catch fire; begin to burn **2** to begin to give off light/heat: (of a motor) start; (of a light) turn on; (of eyes) sparkle; (of the face) blush, get flushed **3** to heat up, get hot **4** (of grain/flour) to begin to spoil from excessive moisture **5** (*Fig*) to become angry/furious
- **∘ <> ndiz·et³ˢᵍ damari** <> loses <>'s temper, <> flies off the handle
- **∘ ndiz·et³ᵖˡ gjakrat** tempers start to flare
- **∘ <> ndiz·et³ˢᵍ gjaku** <> loses <>'s temper
- **∘ <> ndiz·et³ᵖˡ shkotat** (*Crude*) <> gets furious: <>'s bowels *get* into an uproar

ndiz *stem for 2nd pl pres, pind, imper, vp* <**ndez·**

° **ësh·të ndiz e shuaj** (of people) to be of no use (because {} waste {}'s effort)

ndje·*het vpr* to end a quarrel by mutual forgiveness

ndje·*n vt* 1 to forgive, pardon 2 = **ndi**/**e**·*n*

° [] **ndjeu Perëndia/Zoti** "God forgave []" (said of a recently dead person) thank God that []'s suffering has ended

ndje/ *stem for pdef, opt* <**ndi**/**e**·*n*

***ndjef**· OR **ndjeh**· *vi (Old)* to be conscious of one's condition: feel = **ndi**·*het*

***n**/**djegulluem** *adj (i) (Reg Gheg)* inflamed, sore

***ndje**/**shëm** *adj (i)* pardonable, excusable

ndjek·

I § *vt* 1 to chase; pursue; follow 2 to pursue [a course of studies]: attend [school/courses] 3 *(Colloq)* to chase/drive [] out, force [] to leave: get rid of 4 to persecute

II § *vi* to come next: follow

° **e ndjek**· **gjurmën mbrapsht** to start out the wrong way

° **ndjek**· **gjurmët** to follow in the footsteps

° **ndjek**· **gjurmët e** <> 1 to follow <>'s track 2 *(Fig)* to follow in <>'s footsteps

° [] **ndjek**· **në gur e në galinë** to pursue [] every step of the way, dog []'s trail

° **ndjek**· **(pas) qerren e** <> to jump on <>'s bandwagon, join <>'s camp, follow <>'s lead

ndjek/**ës**

I § *n* 1 pursuer 2 follower, adherent, disciple 3 *[Mil]* pursuit airplane

II § *adj* 1 following, succeeding, next 2 *[Mil]* for pursuit

ndjek/**je** *nf ger* 1 <**ndjek**·, **ndji**/**q**·*et* 2 pursuit 3 persecution

° **ndjekje gjyqësore/penale** *[Law]* criminal prosecution

ndjek/**ur**

I § *part* <**ndjek**·, **ndji**/**q**·*et*

II § *adj (i), n* persecuted (person)

ndjell· *vt* 1 to use food to entice [a domestic animal] to come near 2 *(Fig)* to lure; attract 3 *(Fig)* to invite/attract [something bad] by mentioning it 4 *(Fig)* to have a premonition of [] 5 *(Fig)* to awaken [thoughts/emotions], arouse a feeling of [] in <> 6 to suck in, inhale

° **ndjell**· **keq** to bring bad luck

° **<>a ndjell**· **zemra** <> *has* a feeling in <>'s heart, <> *has* a premonition

ndjell/**ake**/**q**

I § *adj* 1 of ill omen, ominous; inauspicious 2 pessimistic

II § *nm* bad omen

ndjell/**amir**/**ë**

I § *adj* 1 of good omen; auspicious 2 optimistic

II § *nm* good omen

ndjell/**azi** *adj (fem sg ˜ez, masc pl ˜inj, fem pl ˜eza)* = **ndjellake**/**q**

ndjell/**ë** *part* <**ndjell**·

ndjell/**ës**

I § *adj* enticing, alluring

II § *nm [Bot]* bee balm used to attract bees

ndjell/**ëse** *nf* lure used to attract livestock

ndjell/**je** *nf ger* 1 <**ndjell**· 2 enticement

ndjenj/**ak** *adj* sentimental

ndje/**nj**/**ë** *nf* 1 subjective feeling, sensation 2 consciousness; sense 3 emotion, feeling

ndje/**rë**

I § *adj (i)* (in speaking of the dead) beloved, the late

II § *n (i)* the loved one (a dead person)

***ndje**/**rs**·*et vpr* to sweat = **djersit**·*et*

ndje/**s**/**ë** *nf* <**ndje**·*n* 1 forgiveness, pardon 2 *[Relig]* remission of sins: indulgence

° **ndjesë pastë** (tag of respect added to the name of someone dead) may he rest in peace

ndjes/**ë**/**madh** *adj (Old)* (of a respected dead person) rest-in-peace, blessed

ndje/**s**/**ë**/**pastë**

I § *parenthetical* (said to honor a dead person) may-he/she-be-blessed!

II § *n (Euph)* he/she of blessed memory

ndje/**si** *nf* 1 sensory impression: sensation, feeling 2 emotion

ndjesi/**holl**/**ë** *nf* highly sensitive; of refined sensibility

ndje/**sor** *adj* sensitive

ndje/**shëm** *adj (i)* 1 sensitive; easily affected 2 *(Fig)* evident, obvious

ndje/**shm**/**ëri** *nf* 1 sensitivity; sensitiveness 2 sentience

ndo *conj (Colloq)*

° **ndo__ ndo__** either__ or __, whether__ or__

ndoba/**re** *adv* at least

ndo/**ca**

I § *adv (Colloq)* a little, in some amount, to some degree

II § *pron, quant* some, several

ndodh· *vi* 1 to take place, occur 2 to happen (by chance) 3 = **ndo**/**dh**·*et*

° **ndodh**· **pa punë** to happen for no reason

ndo/**dh**·*et vpr* 1 to be situated/located 2 to be (somewhere) at the moment; happen to be (somewhere); be present 3 to be in <>'s possession at the moment; <> happens to have 4 *(Fig Colloq)* to be there (to help) for <>

° **ndodh**·*et* **bosh** to be caught unprepared, be caught short

° **<> ndodh**·*et* **në ditë të ngushtë** to be helpful to <> in difficult times, be there for <> in times of need

° **ndodh**·*et* **në mes dy zjarresh** "be situated between two fires" to be between the devil and the deep blue sea

° **<> ndodh**·*et* **pranë** to be a big supporter of []

ndodh/**i** *nf* 1 empirical event: incident, case 2 true story: story

ndo/**dh**/**ije** *nf ger* 1 <**ndo**/**dh**·, **ndo**/**dh**·*et* 2 event, incident; occurrence; situation

ndo/**fta** *adv* = **ndo**/**shta**

***ndo**/**full** = **no**/**full**

***ndoh**· *vt* = **ndy**·*n*

***ndo**/**h**·*et vpr* = **ndy**·*het*

***ndoh**/**t**· *vt* = **ndy**·*n*

***ndo**/**h**/**t**·*et vpr* = **ndy**·*het*

***ndo**/**h**/**të** *adj (i)* = **ndy**/**rë**

***ndo**/**h**/**t**/**ësi** OR **ndoh**/**t**/**ësi**/**rë** *nf* = **ndy**/**rësi**

***ndo**/**h**/**ti** OR **ndoh**/**t**/**je** *nf* disgust, loathing, repugnance = **neveri**

***ndo**/**h**/**t**/**ur** *adj (i)* = **ndy**/**rë**

***ndo**/**h**/**t**/**ura** *np (të) fem* = **ndo**/**tura**

***ndo**/**jkë** *nf* elevated plain, plateau

ndo/**kë**/**nd** *acc* <**ndoku**/**sh**

ndo/**ku**/**jt** *dat* <**ndoku**/**sh**

ndo·ku̇nd *adv* somewhere, anywhere

ndo·ku̇sh *pron* some person, somebody; anybody

ndo·ll *stem for pdef* <**ndje**ll·

ndo·ne̊se *conj* even though, although

*__ndo·nja__ *pcl* approximately, about

ndo·nje̊
  I § *determiner* some (unidentified): any, a certain
  II § *pcl* (followed by a unit of measurement) some (a positive, but unspecified amount), approximately, about
  ○ **ndonjë gjë** something

ndo·nje̊he·re̊ *adv* at some time, sometimes; at any time: ever

ndo·nje̊r *nm, nf (definite case forms only)* some person, someone

ndo·pak *adv* a few, a little; a little while

ndo·q *stem for pdef* <**ndjek**·

ndor·et *vpr* to descend from the mountains

ndo·re
  I § *nf (Old)* protection accorded by the Law of the Mountains to a person in life-threatening peril; person under such protection; safekeeping, trust
  II § *adv* in safekeeping/trust

ndo·resh *adv* manageable, easy

*__n·do·re̊__ *adv* <**në dorë**

*__ndo·re̊si̇__ *nf (Old)* nonage, minority, juniority

*__ndo·re̊she̊m__ *adj (i) (Old)* handy, convenient

*__ndo·re̊tar__ *n* patron, protector

*__n·do·re̊zo·n = doreʹzo·n

ndo·rme̊ *adj (i)* unleavened

ndo·rm̊te̊ *adj (i)* ordinary, commonplace; banal, corny

*__n·do·ro·n__ *vt* to control, manage

*__n·do·rue̊m__
  I § *adj (i) (Reg Gheg)* under tutelage
  II § *n (i)* ward, minor

*__ndo·rushe̊__ *nf [Ornit]* pelican

*__ndo·sa = ndoca

*__ndo·se = ndone̊se

ndo·shta *pcl* maybe, perhaps

ndot *nm* nausea, disgust, loathing

ndot·
  I § *vt* 1 to make [] filthy 2 to pollute, befoul
  II § *vi (Euph)* to urinate/defecate: make dirty

ndot·et *vpr* 1 to get filthy 2 (*Euph*) to urinate/defecate: make dirty, dirty one's pants

ndo·te̊
  I § *adj (i)* filthy; foul, polluted; sordid
  II § *np (të)* = ndot

ndot·e̊si̇ *nf* 1 filthiness, filth 2 pollution 3 (*Fig*) piece of filth; dirty business 4 = ndot

ndo·tje *nf ger* 1 <**ndot**·, **ndot**·et 2 pollution

ndo·tshe̊m *adj (i)* = ndo·te̊

ndo·tur *adj (i)* polluted, foul; filthy

ndo·tura *np (të) fem* 1 soiled/wet diapers 2 feces, excrement

ndrag· *vt* to soil, make filthy

ndra·g·et *vpr* to get soiled/filthy

*__ndra·ge̊s__
  I § *adj* defiling
  II § *n* defiler

ndra·ge̊t *adj (i)* soiled, filthy

ndra·gie *nf ger* <**ndrag**·, **ndra·g**·et

ndra·gur *adj (i)* soiled

*__ndrash· = trash·

*__ndre**
  I § *nm* = dre
  II § *interj pcl* = **more**

*__ndrejt = drejt

*__ndrejti̇m__ *nm* correction

ndreq· *vt* 1 to bring [] back into proper condition: fix, repair, restore, mend; adjust; correct, rectify 2 (*Fig Colloq*) to resolve [an argument]; make peace between [] 3 (*Colloq*) to perform expected services/chores in respect to [guests/children/animals]: take care of [ ]; prepare [food]; add flavorful ingredients to [food] 4 (*Colloq*) to straighten up [the body] 5 (*Old*) to pay off [debts/debtors]: make things right with [ ]
  ○ <>a **ndreq·** bërroren/kurrizin/samarin/shpinën to punish <> severely for doing something wrong: give <> the beating that <> deserves
  ○ **ndreq·** gojën to mind/watch one's language
  ○ i **ndreq·** hesapet me [] to square accounts with []: get one's revenge on []
  ○ <>i **ndreq·** kryqet to beat sense into <>
  ○ <>a **ndreq·** orët me [] "fix <>'s clock together with []" (*Pej*) to cook up a plot with [] against <>
  ○ <>a **ndreq·** qejfin to teach <> a lesson, correct <>'s wrongful behavior; give <> the beating that <> deserves
  ○ **ndreq·** tryezën to set the table (and lay out the food)

ndre·q·et *vpr* 1 to put on new clothes; get all dressed up 2 (*Fig*) to mend one's ways 3 to make up (after an argument) 4 (of weather) to get better, improve

ndre·qe *nf [Ethnog]* day when the bride is brought to the groom, wedding day

ndre·qe̊s *n* 1 repairman 2 (*Colloq*) peacemaker

ndre·qje *nf ger* 1 <**ndre·q**·, **ndre·q**·et 2 repair; correction, correction mark

*__ndre·qshe̊m__ *adj (i)* corrigible, rectifiable, reparable

ndre·qur *adj (i)* repaired, fixed; corrected

ndri·n *vi* 1 to radiate light: shine 2 to gleam 3 (*Fig*) to go very well for <>

ndriçi̇m *nm ger* 1 <**ndriço·n** 2 illumination; brightness 3 sheen 4 (*Book*) [*Hist*] illuminism = iluminize̊m
  ○ **ndriçim avarie** emergency lighting

Ndriçi̇m *nm* Ndriçim (male name)

ndriçimtar *n (Book)* person who lights the way, guide to enlightenment

ndriço·n
  I § *vt* 1 to infuse [] with light: illuminate, light up [] 2 (*Fig*) to shed light on; enlighten
  II § *vi* 1 to become infused with light: light up 2 (*Fig*) to emerge in clear light, become clear

ndriçue̊s
  I § *adj* 1 luminous 2 serving for illumination: illuminating 3 (*Fig*) enlightening; guiding
  II § *nm* illuminating device, lamp
  III § *n* 1 person responsible for lighting: lighting technician/director 2 (*Fig*) = ndriçimtar

*__ndridh· = dre·dh·

ndri·kull *nf* 1 (*Old*) wife of one's godfather: godmother 2 mother of the baby getting its first haircut from its godfather 3 bridesmaid 4 (*Impol*) woman who talks too much: old biddy

ndrikulli̇ *nf* 1 (*Collec*) godmothers 2 the status of being a godmother: godmotherhood

ndris stem for 1st sg pres, pl pres, 2nd & 3rd sg subj, pind <ndrit·

ndrit·

I § vi 1 to shine brightly 2 (Fig) to go very well for ◇

II § vt 1 to illuminate, light; enlighten 2 (Iron) to spoil/ruin []: sure fixed that!

○ <> ndrit· nuri ◇'s face lights up

○ s'<> ndrit· nuri ◇ never smiles

○ <> ndrit· rrugën to show ◇ the (correct) path

○ <> ndrit· sytë/dhëmbët "show ◇ one's teeth, glare with hostility at ◇" to menace ◇, speak roughly to ◇, threaten ◇

○ <> ndritrtë shpirti "may ◇'s soul find light" (parenthetical formula accompanying the mention of someone dead, as a sign of respect and gratitude) bless his/her soul!

*ndrite nf (Old) brightness, splendor

*ndritëllis stem for 1st sg pres, pl pres, 2nd & 3rd sg subj, pind <ndritëllı·

*ndritëllit· vt to brighten

*ndritës adj illuminating, shining

*ndritësi nf glory

*ndritim nm brightness, shininess

ndritshëm adj (i) 1 shining brightly: brilliant, glistening 2 (Fig) illustrious

*ndritullimë nf brightness, splendor

ndritur adj (i) 1 bright 2 (FigElevated) illustrious 3 (Fig Elev) made lucid: illuminated

ndrizë nf wool strap to hold a baby in a cradle

ndrojt·et vpr to be afraid = dru·het

ndrojtje nf = druajtje

*ndrojtso·het vpr = dru·het

ndrojtur adj (i) = druajtur

ndru·het vpr = dru·het

ndrua·n vi = drua·n

ndruajt stem for pdef, opt, adm, part <ndrua·n

*ndruarshëm adj (i) mutable, variable

ndry·het vpr to stay in one place, not move: stay

ndry·n vt 1 to lock [] up; keep [] locked up 2 (Fig) to keep [] hidden inside oneself

ndrydh· vt 1 to apply heavy pressure on []: bear down on, knead, squeeze 2 to sprain/dislocate [one's limb] 3 (Fig) to repress

ndrydh·et vpr 1 to become sprained/dislocated 2 (Fig) to keep everything locked up inside 3 to frown; have a gloomy look

○ <> ndrydh·et³ˢᵍ zëmra (për []) "◇'s heart is squeezed" 1 ◇'s heart bleeds (for []), ◇'s heart is anguished (with sympathy) 2 ◇ feels very bad (about [])

*ndrydhë nf 1 bridle bit 2 torture rack

ndrydhës

I § adj 1 repressive 2 weighing heavily on one: oppressive

II § nm device for applying heavy pressure: wringer, mangle, press, roller, stamp, clamp

ndrydhët adj (i) overripe

ndrydhje nf ger 1 <ndrydh·, ndrydh·et [Med] 2 sprain; dislocation

○ ndrydhje në zemër wrenching of the heart: emotional suffering

ndrydhur adj (i) 1 compressed 2 sprained 3 shy; introverted

ndrymje nf [Geol] inclusion

ndryp· vt 1 to squeeze [] by hand 2 (Fig) to fell

ndryq·et vpr to stretch one's limbs (as when yawning)

ndrys· vt 1 to massage 2 to caress 3 to plunge

ndryshe

I § adv differently, in another way; in a different (improper/abnormal) way; something else again

II § conj otherwise, or else

○ ësh·të më ndryshe to have changed quite a bit; be quite another thing

○ ndryshe nga {} in contrast to {}

ndryshesë nf 1 change, alteration 2 [Spec] variation

ndryshëm adj (i) 1 different; other 2 diverse, varied; miscellaneous, sundry

ndryshim nm ger 1 <ndrysho·n, ndrysho·het 2 difference; dissimilarity 3 alteration, change 4 [Spec] variation

ndryshk nm rust

ndryshk· vt to make rusty: rust

ndryshk·et vpr to become rusty

ndryshkët adj (i) rusty

ndryshkje nf ger <ndryshk·, ndryshk·et

ndryshkull nf festering sore/abscess on the foot/toe

ndryshkull nm (np ˜ j) [Bot] 1 cypress euphorbia (Euphorbia cyparissias) 2 burning bush, dittany (Dictamnus albus)

ndryshkur adj (i) rusted, rusty

ndrysho·het vpr to undergo change, become transformed

ndrysho·n vt, vi to change

○ e ndrysho·n moshën "lower/raise/change the age" to put down a lower/higher/different age (on a document)

○ ndryshon puna that changes matters; that's an entirely different matter

○ ndrysho·nᵖˡ si nata me ditën to be as different as day and night

ndryshore nf [Math] variable

ndryshuar adj (i) transformed, changed

ndryshueshëm adj (i) 1 changeable; variable 2 unsteady, unsettled

ndryshueshmëri nf (Book) changeableness; variability

*ndug·et vpr = ndulk·et

*ndugjët adj (i) = ndulkët

nduk· vt 1 to pinch, nip 2 to pluck; pull at [], tug lightly on [] 3 to nibble on [] 4 to wrinkle up [] in one's hand

nduk·et vpr 1 to scratch one's face and tear out one's hair with grief 2 to pinch one another

ndukë nf shorn fleece

*ndukës adj, n (Old) depilatory

ndukje nf ger <nduk·, nduk·et

ndulk·et vpr (of fruit) to ripen and get soft after being picked

ndulkët adj (i) (of fruit that ripens after picking) very soft and ripe; overripe

ndulkje nf ger <ndulk·et

*ndull·et vpr to be faint (with hunger)

ndy·het vpr 1 to get dirty 2 to make ◇ sick, nauseate ◇ 3 (Euph) to make dirty: defecate

ndy'·n

I § *vt* **1** to make [] dirty/filthy: smear [] with dirt,
soil **2** *(Fig)* to defile, besmirch; foul **3** to make <>
lose <>'s appetite for []

II § *vi* *(Euph)* to make dirty: defecate

○ **ndy·n gojën 1** to talk dirty, use obscene language
2 to argue using foul language

***ndye'r**

I § *adj (i)* *(Reg Tosk)* recently deceased: the late

II § *n (i)* person who has recently died: the deceased

***ndye'si** *nf (Reg Gheg)* = ndyrësí

***ndye't** *adj (i)* *(Reg Gheg)* = ndo'të

***ndy'k·et** OR **ndy'lk·**et *vpr* = ndu'lk·et

***ndy'k'ë** *adj (i)* = ndu'lkët

***ndy'kur** OR **ndy'lk'ur** *adj (i)* = ndu'lkët

ndy'llt'ë *adj (i)* soft and mushy

ndyn'ara'q *nm* **1** one who wallows in filth, filthy
person, pig; obscene talker **2** dirty person; slattern,
slut

***ndyr·** *vt* = ndy'·n

ndyraca'k

I § *adj* habitually dirty; having base morals, slatternly; foul-mouthed, obscene

II § *n* dirty person; slattern, slut

ndyrama'n OR **ndyr'ana'k** *adj* = ndyraca'k

ndyr'a'q OR **ndyr'avi'q** *adj* = ndyraca'k

ndyra'zi OR **ndy'ra's** *adv* **1** using dirty language
2 in a foul manner, in a dirty way **3** outrageously;
very badly

ndyr'ë

I § *adj (i)* **1** dirty, filthy **2** *(Fig)* vile, despicable; sordid; disgraceful

II § *adv* = ndyra'zi

ndyr'ësi' *nf* **1** dirtiness, filthiness; filth **2** *(Fig)* shameful behavior

ndyr'ësi'r'ë *nf* **1** = ndyrësí **2** *(Fig)* disgusting person
3 human filth

ndyr'ës'i'sht *adv* in a filthy manner

ndyri'sht *adv* = ndy'ras

ndyr'je *nf ger* <ndy'·n, ndy'·het

ndy'së'ke'q *adj* touchy, easily offended

ndy'si'n'ë *nf* = ndyrësí'r'ë

***ndys'ke'q** *nm* *(Old)* mischief-maker, disrupter

***ndy'sh'ëm** *adj (i)* sickening, abominable

***ndyshk** *nm* chip/splinter still attached to wood/bone

***ndysh'ke'q** *(Old)* = ndyske'q

ndy't'ë

I § *adj (i)* **1** unclean **2** filthy, polluted **3** = ndy'r'ë

II § *nn (të)* nausea, disgust

ne

I § *pron nom* we

II § *pron acc* us

III § *prep (nom)* * = tek

neandertal *nm* Neanderthal man

nebulo'z'ë *nf* *[Astron]* nebula = mjegullnaj'ë

ne'çe *nf* woolen apron worn in some regions of Albania

ne'd'ër *nf* anise, aniseed

Nedi'n *nm* Nedin (male name)

nef *nm* *[Archit]* church nave = anija't'ë

nefe's *nm* *[Med]* **1** *(Old)* breath **2** asthma

nefri't *nm* *[Med]* **1** nephritis **2** *[Min]* nephrite

***neft** *nm* = na'ft'ë

negacio'n *nm* negation

negati'v *adj, nm* negative

negativi'sht *adv* negatively

ne'g'ër *nm* Negro = zeza'k

***negligj* = neglizh

neglizhe'nc'ë *nf* negligence

neglizhe'nt *nf* negligent

neglizh'o· *vt* to neglect

negocia't'ë *nf* negotiation

ne'jc'ë *nf* *[Bot]* = ne'jç'ë

ne'jç *adj* **1** *[Bot]* knotty, gnarly **2** *[Med]* nodose

ne'jç'ë *nf* *[Bot]* knotweed *(Polygonum L.N)*

ne'jç'o're *np* *[Bot]* dock family *Polygonaceae*

ne'je *np* <ny'e

ne'j'ës *nm* wart

ne'jse *pcl* *(Colloq)* no matter, nevertheless; be that as
it may, anyhow

***ne'jv'ëm** *nf* = ndi'hm'ë

***nek** *prep (nom)* = tek

nekrologji *nf* death notice, obituary

nekropo'l *nm* *[Archeol]* ancient cemetery: necropo-
lis

nekta'r *nm* **1** nectar **2** *(Fig)* best/choice part

nektar'mba'jt'ës *adj* *[Bot]* nectariferous *( )*

nektar'o'r *adj* **1** *[Bot]* of or pertaining to nectar: nec-
tarous **2** = nektarmbajtës

***nema'k** *adj* with a stammer

***nêm'e** *nf (e)* *(Reg Gheg)* = në'm'ë

***neme'c** *nm* = meme'c

***neme't·et** = nemít·et

nemit·et *vpr* **1** to be rendered speechless: be struck
dumb; be stupefied **2** to become silent **3** to become
deaf and dumb

nemi't'je *nf ger* <nemít·et

nemi'tur *adj (i)* dumbfounded; rendered speechless,
struck dumb, mute

***nemose** *adv* at least

nemru't *nm* bad man, villain, rogue

ne'mte *nf* woman's long jerkin decorated with braid

nen *nm* **1** numbered subdivision of a law: paragraph/
article/section (of a statute); clause (of a contract/
statute) **2** *(Reg)* ankle

ne'ne *nf* wife of mother's brother: aunt

nenexh'i'k *nm* *[Bot]* peppermint *(Mentha piperita
L.)*

ne'n'ë *nf* *[Bot]* amaranth *(Amaranthus)*

○ **nen'ë e bardh'ë** *[Bot]* tumbleweed *Amaranthus albus*

ne'n'ëz *nf* *[Bot]* = ne'n'ë

***nën** *(Reg Gheg)* = nën

nen'o're *np* *[Bot]* cockscomb family *Amaranthaceae*

neo *formativ* neo-

neo'fashi'st *adj, n* neofascist

neo'fashi'z'ëm *nm* neofascism

neofi't *nm* *(Book)* neophyte

neo'klasi'k *adj* neoclassical

neo'klasi'z'ëm *nm* neoclassicism

neo'kolonia'l *adj* = neokolonial'i'st

neo'kolonial'i'st *adj* neocolonialist

neo'kolonial'i'z'ëm *nm* neocolonialism

neo'lati'n *adj* neo-Latin; Romance

neoli't

I § *adj* *[Archeol]* Neolithic

II § *nm* Neolithic Age

neolitïk *adj* [*Archeol*] Neolithic

neologjïzëm *nm* [*Ling*] neologism

neo'n *nm* **1** neon (*Ne*) **2** neon lamp/light

NEP *abbrev* (*Russian*) <**Novaja Ekonomiçeskaja Politika** [*Hist*] New Economic Policy

nepale'z *adj, n* Nepalese, Nepali

nepërkë *nf* **1** viper, adder **2** [*Zool*] sand viper, nose-horned viper (*Vipera ammodytes*) **3** (*Fig*) crafty and dishonorable person: snake-in-the-grass; person with a venomous tongue
  ○ **nepërkë e shkruar** beautiful and coquettish woman
  ○ **nepërkë shullëri 1** poisonous snake basking in the sun **2** very clever woman/girl with a sharp and biting tongue
  ○ **nepërkë uji** [*Zool*] dice snake (*Natrix tessellata*)
  ○ **nepërkë e zakonshme** [*Zool*] sand viper (*Vipera ammodytes L.*)

nepërkëro'·n *vi* to make sinuous curves

*****nepërtkë = nepërkë**

nepkër *nf* [*Zool*] sand viper, nose-horned viper (*Vipera ammodytes*)

nepotïzëm *nm* nepotism

neps *nm* **1** strong appetite, greed **2** lust, lechery

nepsqar *adj* (*Colloq*) **1** ravenously hungry, greedy **2** lustful, lecherous

neqe'z
  I § *adj* (*Colloq*) stingy
  II § *nm* stingy person: miser

nerde'n *nm* plum syrup

nerënxë *nf* [*Bot*] bitter orange, Seville orange, sour orange (*Citrus aurantium, Citrus amara, Citrus vulgaris*)

ne'rgut *adv* on purpose, intentionally, deliberately

Nerita'n *nm* Neritan (male name)

*****nerqïze** *nf* narcissus = **narcïs**

nerv *nm* **1** nerve **2** (*Fig*) nub
  ○ **nerv endacak** [*Anat*] vagus nerve
  ○ **nervi ndenjësor** sciatic nerve

*****nervësi** *nf* [*Anat*] nervation

nervëzïm *nm* **1** [*Anat*] nervation **2** [*Bot*] venation

*****nervlïs** *stem for 1st sg pres, pl pres, 2nd & 3rd sg subj, pind* <**nervlït**·

*****nervlït**· *vt* to use, adopt; concern, involve

nervo'r *adj* [*Anat*] neural

nervo'z *adj* edgy, irritable: nervous

nervozïte't *nm* nervousness

nervozïzëm *nm* nervousness

nervozo'·het *vpr* to get nervous

nervozo'·n *vt* to make [] nervous

ne'sër *adv* tomorrow
  ○ **nesër mbrëma** tomorrow night
  ○ **nesër një javë** a week from tomorrow
  ○ **nesër, pasnesër** some day; someday

*****nesërejt** *adv* on the next day, the day after

ne'sërm *adj* (*i*) of tomorrow, tomorrow's

ne'sërme *nf* (*e*) **1** the next day, the day after, the morrow **2** the future, tomorrow

nesh *pron abl* <**ne** us

*****neshk**
  I § *nm* (*Reg*)
  II § *nm* donkey colt = **kërrïç**

*****neshkë** *nf* (*Reg*) = **neshk**

neshte'r *nm* [*Med*] bistoury

neshtra'she *nf* **1** bad omen, sign; adversity; bad luck
*****2** (*Reg Gheg*) mishap, accident

net *np* <**natë**

netër *OR* **ne'tërz** *nf* [*Bot*] = **ko'për**
  ○ **netër qeni** [*Bot*] = **maraskë**

ne'to *adj* remaining after subtraction from the gross amount: net (weight/amount)

neto'·n *vt* (*Reg*) to blind = **verbo'·n**

ne'tull *nf* **1** [*Bot*] Aaron's rod, great mullein (*Verbascum thapsus*) **2** [*Bot*] heath (whose fibers are used to make brooms): heather (*Erica*) = **shqo'pë 3** (*Reg*) broom = **fshe'së 4** selvage

neth *nm* birthmark; mole

neurït *nm* [*Med*] neuritis

neurokiru'rg *nm* neurosurgeon

neurokirurgjï *nf* [*Med*] neurosurgery

neurolïzë *nf* [*Med*] neurolysis

neurolo'g *n* [*Med*] neurologist

neurologjï *nf* [*Med*] neurology

neuropsikiatër *nm* neuropsychiatrist

neuropsikiatrïk *adj* [*Med*] neuropsychiatric

neuro'zë *nf* [*Med*] neurosis

ne'utër *nm* **1** [*Ling*] neuter **2** [*Electr*] neutral conductor

neutra'l *adj* (*Book*) neutral = **asnja'nës**

neutralïte't *nm* (*Book*) neutrality

neutralïzïm *nm ger* (*Book*) **1** <**neutralizo'·n**, neutralizo'·het **2** neutralization

neutralizo'·het *vpr* (*Book*) to become neutral

neutralizo'·n *vt* (*Book*) to neutralize

neutro'n *nm* [*Phys*] neutron

ne've
  I § *pron 1st pl dat/acc* <**ne** us; to/for us
  II § *pron 1st pl nom* (*Colloq*) we

neverï *nf* **1** urge to vomit: nausea **2** (*Fig*) disgust, loathing, revulsion

neverïs *stem for 1st sg pres, pl pres, 2nd & 3rd sg subj, pind* <**neverït**·

neverït· *vt* **1** to make [] nauseating; fill <> with disgust for [] **2** (*Fig*) to make [] too difficult/incomprehensible; make [] loathsome **3** to abandon, neglect, desert **4** (*Fig*) to speak ill of [someone/something] previously dear to one: repudiate

neverït·et *vpr* **1** to feel nausea **2** to feel disgust/loathing, be disgusted

neverïtës *adj* nauseating, disgusting

neverïtje *nf ger* **1** <**neverït**·, **neverït·et 2** = **neverï**

neverïtshëm *adj* (*i*) **1** nauseating, disgusting **2** (*Fig*) despicable, contemptible

neverïtur *adj* (*i*) **1** = **neverïtshëm** *****2** despised

neve'rt *nm* fine overcast stitching on a hem

*****neve'rthi** *adv* using overcast stitching, oversewn

neve'stër *nf* [*Bot*] = **ferrënu'se**

nevoja'r *adj, n* = **nevojta'r**

nevojë *nf* **1** necessity; need **2** (*Euph*) excrement
  ○ **nevoja e madhe** (*Euph*) need to defecate, defecation
  ○ **nevoja e vogël** (*Euph*) need to urinate, urination

nevojïsht *adv* **1** in terrible need, in poverty **2** by necessity

nevojït·et *vpr* to be necessary, be required; be needed; be of use

nevojshëm *adj* (*i*) necessary, requisite; useful

nevojtar _adj, n_ needy/poor (person)

nevojtore _nf_ place for defecation/urination: toilet, bathroom, outhouse, privy
  ○ **nevojtore publike** public toilets

nevralgji _nf_ [_Med_] neuralgia

nevralgjik _adj_ 1 [_Med_] neuralgic 2 (_Fig_) most sensitive, most important: critical

nevrasteni _nf_ [_Med_] neurasthenia

nevrastenik _adj_ 1 neurasthenic 2 easily upset, touchy; short-tempered

nevrik _adj_ quick-tempered, touchy

nevrikos· _vt_ 1 to get on [ ]'s nerves, exasperate 2 to enrage

nevrikos·et _vpr_ to have one's nerves set on edge: get exasperated

nevrikosje _nf ger_ <**nevrik·**, **nevrik·et**

nevrikosur _adj_ (i) with one's nerves set on edge: exasperated

nevruz _nm_ [_Relig_] March holiday celebrated by the Bektashi to mark the arrival of spring

në
  I § _prep (acc)_ 1 in; on, upon; into; to 2 at (followed by an expression of time or event) 3 approaching; at the point of
  II § _conj_ if; whether
  ○ **në adresë të <>** 1 addressed to <> 2 concerning <>
  ○ **në ah të vdekjes** in the throes of death
  ○ **në akord** in tune
  ○ **në anë të anës** very far away
  ○ **në anën tjetër të barrikadës** on the side of the opponent
  ○ **në aq e (në) kaq** on so few, in the few
  ○ **në asnjë mënyrë** no way, not on your life
  ○ **në asnjë rast** "on no occasion" under no circumstances, in no case
  ○ **Në atë anë fli!** (_Iron_) Don't take that attitude!
  ○ **Në atë krahë/anë/brinjë fli!** (_Iron_) You're dreaming if you think that!
  ○ **Në atë shtëpi nuk qesh as vera.** "In that house even summer _doesn't laugh_" It _is_ an joyless and inhospitable family.
  ○ **në ato e sipër** meanwhile, at that time
  ○ **ësh·të në ato ujëra** 1 to be working on it 2 to be involved/implicated somehow
  ○ **në ballë** in the forefront, at the head, in the lead; at the beginning, at first
  ○ **në bankat e shkollës** "on the school benches" in/during one's schooldays
  ○ **në bankën e të pandehurve** in court as a defendant, in the prisoner's dock
  ○ **në barazim me** [ ] in comparison with [ ]
  ○ **në barkun e** {} in the middle of the {_time word in the genitive case_}
  ○ **në bazë fshati** on a local village basis
  ○ **në befasi** unawares, offguard
  ○ **ësh·të në bend të mirë** to be in good humor
  ○ **në brez i ka· të shtatat** to be at death's door
  ○ **në bukë të <>** in the employ of <>, hired by <>
  ○ **në bukë të qeverisë** employed by the government
  ○ **ësh·të në buzë të varrit** "be on the edge of one's grave" 1 to have one foot in the grave 2 to be facing grave danger
  ○ **në cep të krahut** on the shoulder
  ○ **në cirë** naked, undressed
  ○ **në çast** right away, without delay

  ○ **në çastin e prapmë/fundit** at the hour of death, at the last
  ○ **në çastin kur __** at the moment that __
  ○ **Në çati ngjiten me shkallë.** "To climb a roof they use a ladder." (_Prov_) In a case like this, one needs a different tool.
  ○ **në çdo gjellë majdanoz** "parsley in every dish" (_Iron_) (said of someone who gets involved in everything, whether invited or not) just has to get into everything! can't stay out of it!; (said of something repeated unnecessarily) we really needed that again!
  ○ **në çdo gjë** in all directions
  ○ **në çdo mënyrë** no matter what, in any event
  ○ **në çdo rast** "on every occasion" at any time
  ○ **në derë të huaj** from/with strangers
  ○ **ësh·të në det të zi** "be on a dark sea" to be in a difficult predicament, be in deep trouble
  ○ **në din** on the right (moral) path
  ○ **në diskutim** under discussion
  ○ **në ditë të errët** 1 in trouble 2 in an unenlightened way: improperly
  ○ **ësh·të në ditë të hallit** to be in the depth of despair/misery/poverty
  ○ **në ditë të pikës** in desperate straits
  ○ **ësh·të në ditët e veta** to be about to give birth
  ○ **Në djall të vejë!** "May he go to the devil!" (_Curse_) Devil take him!
  ○ **në dobi të <>** to <>'s benefit, for the good of <>
  ○ **në dorë** [_Math_] (in division) left over, remainder; (in multiplication/addition) carried over
  ○ **në dorë të fundit** almost at the end, in the final phase
  ○ **në drejtim të <>** in the direction of <>, toward <>; with regard to <>, concerning
  ○ **në emër të <>** on behalf of <>, representing <>
  ○ **në është se __** if it is the case that __, if __
  ○ **në favor të <>** to the advantage of <>: favoring <>
  ○ **në fill të këmishës** wearing nothing but a shirt, standing in his/her shirttails
  ○ **ësh·të në fill të vdekjes** "be at the start of one's death" 1 to be on the verge of death: have one foot in the grave 2 to be in mortal danger
  ○ **në fjalë** under discussion, in question, concerned, mentioned
  ○ **në fjalë qoftë** so to speak
  ○ **në flakë të agzotit** very quickly: in a flash, in the twinkling of an eye
  ○ **në flakë të pushkës** "in the flash of a gun" very quickly, instantly: in a flash
  ○ **në flurë** in flight, fleeing
  ○ **në front të gjerë** over a broad front, ranging widely over an area
  ○ **në frymë të <>** very near <>
  ○ **në frymën e <>** in the spirit of <>, following the principles of <>
  ○ **në fund e në bisht** and finally, when it comes right down to it
  ○ **në fund e në krye/majë** from top to bottom: completely
  ○ **në fund të herës** during/at/on the last (of a sequence): the last time
  ○ **në fund të fundit** and finally, in the final analysis, in any case
  ○ **në glazurë** glazed
  ○ **në gojë të qenit** "in the dog's mouth" in the lion's den

○ **në gojë të ujkut** "in the wolf's mouth" surrounded by enemies, in a dangerous position: in the lion's den

○ **në gropët** *(Reg)* (old locative form) in the grave/hole

○ **ësh·të në grykë të varrit** "be on the edge of one's grave" **1** to have one foot in the grave **2** to be facing grave danger

○ **në gjak (me** [ ]**)** in a blood feud (against [ ])

○ **ësh·të në gjendje të** __ to have the ability to __; be able to __; be capable of __

○ **në gjysmështizë** at half-mast

○ **ësh·të në hall për** [ ] to be in great need of [ ]

○ **ësh·të në hënë të fëmijës** to be in the final month of pregnancy

○ **në hënëz 1** *(Crude)* in vain **2** (speaking) mindlessly

○ **ësh·të në hije të** {*a person*} to be the very image of { }

○ **në hijen e** <> *(Pej)* under <>'s protection/rule

○ **në instancë/pikë të fundit** *(Book)* in the final analysis, in the end

○ **në kalim e sipër** in passing, incidentally; hastily

○ **në katror** squared

○ **në këmbë e në dorë/duar** quickly, on the run

○ **në këmbë** on foot

○ **në këmbë të** <> in the stead of <>

○ **në këmishë 1** in shirtsleeves **2** having nothing but the clothes on one's back, very poor; having no dowry

○ **në këto e sipër** meanwhile, at this time

○ **në kohën e baba Qemos** in ancient times, in an era long ago

○ **në kohën e duhur** just in time

○ **në kohët e para** in early days/times

○ **(edhe/tani) në kokën tëndе!** *(Felic)* Next time we will celebrate for you (or for your wedding)!

○ **në kokërr të shpinë** flat on one's back

○ **në krah të** <> at <>'s side; alongside <>

○ **në krye** at the head, in the lead

○ **në krye të** <*a definite period of time*> after <>

○ **në krye të detyrës** at work; while working

○ **në krye të vatrës** in the place of honor next to the hearth

○ **në krye të vendit** in the place of honor

○ **në krye** {*të vet*} acting on { }'s own without consulting anyone else

○ **(edhe/tani) në kryet tënde!** *(Felic)* Next time we will celebrate for you (or for your wedding)!

○ **në kthetrat e vdekjes** in the final moments of life: at death's door; in the clutches of death

○ **në kundërshit** *(Old)* at cross purposes

○ **në kundërshtim me** [ ] contrary to [ ]

○ **në kurriz të** <> at the expense of <>; to the disadvantage <>

○ **në lëmë të qytetit** *(Colloq)* in the main square in a town/village/city: downtown

○ **në lidhje me** [ ] in connection with, concerning [ ]

○ **ësh·të në majë të kalit** "be on top of the horse" to be sitting pretty

○ **në majë e në puç** at loggerheads

○ **në majë të gjilpërës** minutely, in extreme detail

○ **në malt** *(Reg)* (old locative form) in mountain country

○ **ësh·të në marrëdhënie pune** to have a regular job: be employed

○ **ësh·të në merak (për** [ ]**)** to be worried (about [ ])

○ **në mes të** <> among, between; in the middle of <>, in the midst of <>

○ **në mes të tjerave/tjerash** *1** among other things **2** in addition, additionally

○ **në mes** {*noun*^{abl}} among { }, amongst { }, between { }

○ **në mënyrë që** __ in order that __, so that __

○ **Në mos del, tepron.** "If it is not enough, it is more than enough." It will be more than enough.

○ **Në mos rrjedhtë, pikon.** "If it doesn't flow, it leaks" Even if it (a profession) doesn't offer much directly, it offers a chance to make something on the side.

○ **në mos sot, nesër** if not today then tomorrow; maybe not now but then later

○ **në moshë** of age, adult; of proper age

○ **në natyrë** *[Econ]* in goods or commodities (rather than in money): in kind

○ **në ndihmë të** <> in order to help <>

○ **në nevojë** in need

○ **në një afat rekord** (meeting a deadline) in record time

○ **në një fjalë me** [ ] in agreement with [ ], of one mind with [ ]

○ **në një kohë rekord** in record time

○ **në një mëngjes të bukur** (unexpectedly) one fine morning

○ **Në një tel i bie₁·jongarit.** "{ } *play* the mandolin on the same string" { } *keeps* harping on the same theme.

○ **në orët e vona** late at night (after 10 P.M.)

○ **në pe e në gjilpërë** in complete detail

○ **në përgjithësi** in general; in general terms; universally, without exception

○ **në pikë të gazepit** at the worst possible point

○ **ësh·të në pikë të hallit** to be in the depth of despair/misery/poverty

○ **në pikë të hallit** in dire straits

○ **në pikë të mëngjesit** at the crack of laylight

○ **në pikë të moshës** {*së vet*} in {*one's*}'s prime (of life)

○ **në pikë të vapës** at the hottest part of the day

○ **në pikë të vrapit** running at top speed, at top speed

○ **në pisk të diellit** in the heat of the sun

○ **në piskun e mëngjesit** at the break of day

○ **në pishë të** <> *(Fig Colloq)* at the most intense moment of <>: smack in the middle of <>, right at the height of <>, in the prime of <>

○ **në pishë të diellit** *(Colloq)* in the heat of the sun, in the hottest part of the day

○ **Në plumb!** (cry of a mob calling for execution) Death by shooting!

○ **në pragun e jetës** in the bloom of youth

○ **në prehër** *(Fig)* at/in/into the very heart, right in/into the arms, in the very bosom

○ **në profesion të lirë** (working) as a free-lance artist/writer

○ **në punë të qeverisë** employed by the government

○ **në qiell të hapur** *(Book)* in open air; out of doors

○ **në qoftë se** __ if it be the case that __, in case __, if __, provided that __

○ **në qoshe të vatrës** in the place of honor next to the hearth

○ **në radhë të parë** first of all

○ **në radhët e para** at the forefront; in the front ranks

○ **në raport me** [ ] in comparison with [ ]

○ **në rast se** __ in case __, in the event that __, if __

○ **në rast të kundërt** otherwise, if not
○ **ësh·të**[3rd] **në rendin e ditës** to be the order of the day, be the main concern
○ **në rogë të ballit** smack in the middle of the forehead
○ **në rojë të <>** guarding/protecting <>
○ **në rreshtat e parë** at the forefront; in the front ranks
○ **në rrezë të veshit** very close by: if it were any nearer it would bite (you)
○ **në rrjedhë të <>** *(Book)* in the course of <>
○ **ësh·të në rrugë e sipër** to be on the way
○ **në rrugë e sipër** in passing, along the way
○ **në saje/sajë të <>** with the aid of <>, thanks to <>
○ **në saje të <>** with the help of <>, thanks to <>; owing to <>, because of <>
○ **në skaj të botës** at the edge of the earth, in a far off place
○ **në stil të gjerë** on a broad scale: widely, broadly
○ **Në sulm!** *[Mil]* Attack!
○ **në sy të botës** out in public
○ **në sy të ditës** in broad daylight
○ **në syrin e diellit** in broad daylight
○ **në sytë e <> 1** in <>'s view, as <> sees it; in <>'s estimation **2** to <>'s face, in <>'s presence
○ **në shenjë** taking aim
○ **në shesh** out in the open
○ **në shesh të burrave** out in the open
○ **në shkëmbim të <>** in exchange for <>, as a replacement for
○ **në shtëpi** at home
○ **Në shtëpinë e të varurit nuk e zënë në gojë litarin.** "In the house of a hanged man they don't mention the word rope." *(Prov)* Watch what you say (because there are some hurt and delicate sensitivities here).
○ **ësh·të në shtratin e vdekjes** "be in death's bed" to be on one's death bed
○ **ësh·të në terezi tjetër** "be in another state of mind" *(Euph)* to have epilepsy
○ **në të mirë të <>** to <>'s benefit
○ **në të kundërt** on the contrary
○ **në të pamë** *(Reg Gheg)* at sight
○ **në të prishur të pazarit** when the market breaks up, at the end of the market day
○ **në të zezë 1** darkish, blackish **2** right on target, dead center
○ **në të** {*color adjective*} with a {}-ish tinge, {}-ish
○ **në të** {*participle*} (indicates an approximation of {}) getting/approaching {}
○ **në të katër anët 1** in all parts, everywhere, all over **2** in all directions: to the four winds
○ **në tërësi** broadly speaking, in general
○ **ësh·të në trup të** <*vet*> to be of the proper body size
○ **në thekun e zemrës** in the depths of one's heart
○ **në thellësi të shekujve** *(Book)* in olden times
○ **në thellësi të shpirtit** to the depths of one's soul, deep in one's heart: down deep (in one's heart)
○ **ësh·të**[pl] **në thikë e në pikë** to be at dagger points, stand toenail to toenail
○ **ësh·të**[pl] **në thikë** to be ready to kill one another, be implacable enemies
○ **ësh·të në udhë e sipër** to be on the way
○ **në udhë e sipër** in passing, along the way
○ **në valë të gjakut** "with blood aboil (in boil of the blood)" in the fullness of youth

○ **në varësi nga** {} *(Book)* depending on
○ **në varg indian** *(Book)* in Indian file, one after another in succession
○ **në veçanti** especially
○ **Në vend - num**ë**ro·n!** *[Mil]* Mark time - march!
○ **në vend i ati/e ëma** just like his/her father/mother
○ **në vend** right there, immediately; right on the spot
○ **Në vend që t'<> vë· vetulla, <> nxjerr· sytë.** "Instead of putting eyebrows on <>, {} *takes* out <>'s eyes." Instead of making <> better, {} *ruins* <> completely.
○ **në vend që të** {*verb*} instead of {}ing
○ **në vend të <>** in place of <>, instead of <>
○ **në vend të lig/keq** "in a bad place" *(Euph)* in the groin (of a man), in his privates
○ **në vetvete 1** in/into oneself **2** natively; intrinsically
○ **në vija të përgjithshme/kryesore/të trasha** in broad outline, in general terms, broadly speaking
○ **në vijë të parë** at the forefront, on the front line
○ **në vijën e parë të luftës/zjarrit** in the front line of battle
○ **ësh·të në zgrip të varrit** "be on the edge of one's grave" **1** to have one foot in the grave **2** to be facing grave danger
○ **në zjarr** (of livestock) in heat, rutting
○ **në zjarrin e <>** in the heat of <>, at the critical moment of <>

***në·kë·mb**i**ës** *n* deputy, agent, lieutenant; regent
***nëk·i·m** = rënki·m
***nëk·o·n** *vi* = rënko·n
nëm· *vt, vi* to curse ([]) angrily
○ **nëm· gur më gur** to cuss up and down
nëm| *imper* <je·p· give!
nëmë *nf* **1** heavy curse, imprecation, blasphemy **2** *[Bot]* kind of mistletoe (*Loranthus europaeus*)
***nëm**ë**r** = num**ë**r
nëm|ës *n* one who curses: curser
***nëm·o·n** *vt, vi* = nëm·
***nëm·o·s·** *vt, vi* = nëm·
nëm|ur *adj (i)* **1** accursed, damned **2** wretched, pitiful
nën *prep (acc)* under
○ **nën armë** in/into military service
○ **nën bajonetën e armikut** in the midst of danger
○ **nën banak** "from under the counter (where things are covertly kept)" *(Pejor)* under-the-table
○ **nën dorë** clandestine, under the table (sale),
○ **nën dhé** sneakily, underhandedly
○ **nën grykën e pushkës/topit** at the barrel of a gun, under threat of arms
○ **nën gunë** secretly
○ **nën hundën e mjekrën e <>** under <>'s very nose
○ **nën një kulm** under the same roof
○ **nën rrogoz** surreptitiously, covertly
○ **nën sqetull** under the wing, under protection
○ **nën thua** underhanded; in an underhanded manner
○ **ësh·të nën urdhërat e <>** to be at <>'s command
○ **nën vartësinë/varësinë e <>** *(Book)* subordinate to <>
○ **nën vërejtje** "under observation" under surveillance
nën| *formative prefix* sub-, under-, hypo-
***nën|admira·l** *nm* rear admiral
nën|bana·k *nm* space under a service counter
***nën|ba·rk** *nm* lower abdomen

nën|bark|ёs *nm, adj* sycophant(ic), toady

nën|bark|ёz *nf* under-belly girth used to secure a saddle: cinch

nën|bark|je *nf* = nënbarkёz

nën|bark|o·*het vpr* to grovel obsequiously, toady

nën|bishte *nf* crupper

nën|buzё *nf* curb strap (around the lower jaw of the horse) on a bridle

nën|central *nm* = nënstacion

*** nën|cipё** *nf* underlayer; substratum, subsoil; hypodermis

nën|çati *nf* attic space, attic

nën|çm|im *nm ger* 1 <nënçmo·*n* 2 underestimation

nën|çm|o·*n vt* to underestimate, underrate; undervalue

*** nёnd** = nёnt

*** nën|da|si** *nf* subdivision

nën|detar *adj* underwater

nën|det|ёse *nf* submarine (boat)

nën|det|shёm *adj* (i) underwater, submarine

nën|dialekt *nm* [Ling] subdialect

nën|dialektor *adj* [Ling] subdialectal

*** nёndor** = nёntor

nën|dorё
   I § adj underhanded, in secret
   II § nf bribe

nën|dorёs *adj* under-the-table; in secret, on the sly

nën|drejtor *n* deputy director, assistant director

*** nën|dhe** *adj* = nёndheshёm

nën|dhe|cё *nf* basement, cellar

nën|dhe|s *adj* = nёndheshёm

nën|dhe|shёm *adj* (i) underground; subterranean

*** nën|dhe|të** *adj* (i) = nёndheshёm

nёnё
   I § nf 1 mother 2 (Colloq) term of respect for addressing an older woman
   II § prep (acc) = nën
   ○ **Nёnё Heroinё** title given to a woman who has raised and educated eight or more children

nënё|daj|ё *nf* (Colloq) mother's mother: grandmother

nënё|gjysh|e *nf* 1 grandmother 2 grandmother's mother: great-grandmother

nënё|lok|e *nf* (Pet) mommy

nënё|madh|e *nf* 1 = nёnёgjyshe 2 granny

nënё|ri *nf* 1 motherhood 2 (Collec) mothers taken as a whole

nënё|ris stem for 1st sg pres, pl pres, 2nd & 3rd sg subj, pind <nënёrit·

nënё|rit· *vt* to mutter

nënё|z *nf* (Pet) mom

nënё|zez|ё *nf* mother who has lost her children through misfortune

*** nën|fis** *nm* subspecies

nën|fish *nm* 1 subdivision of a larger unit 2 [Math] submultiple, factor

nën|fletё *nf* 1 article printed at the bottom of the page of a periodical publication 2 serialized novel printed part by part at the bottom of the page of a periodical 3 newspaper supplement 4 [Postal] printed insert/enclosure

nën|fush|ёz *nf* [Sport] subdivision of a playing field

nën|grup *nm* subgroup

nën|gry|kёz *nf* piece of cloth put under the neck of a sack to catch spilled grain

*** nën|gush|ё** *nf* chinstrap

nën|gjuh|ё *nf* [Bot] adder's tongue (Ophioglossum vulgatum)

*** nën|kam|cё** *nf* pedal

*** nën|kam|ёz** *nf* = nёnkёmbёz

nën|kapitull *nm* (np ~j) subchapter

nën|kёmb· *vt* to defeat [an opponent]

nën|kёmb|ёz *nf* 1 obstacle intended to trip someone 2 (Fig) stumbling block 3 treadle of a loom 4 footstool 5 bottom sole of a stocking

nën|klas|ё *nf* [Biol] subclass (in taxonomy)

nën|kolonel *nm* [Mil] lieutenant colonel

nën|komandant *nm* (Old) vice commander

nën|komite|t *nm* subcommittee

nën|konsull *nm* (np ~j) viceconsul

nën|kre|jcё OR **nën|kre|jё** = nёnkresё

nën|kre|sё *nf* pillow = jastёk

nën|kry|e *nf* [Veter] disease of cattle, sheep, and goats caused by a brain parasite

nën|krye|si *nf* deputy chairmanship, vice-presidency

nën|krye|tar *n* vice chairman

nën|kuptim *nm* implication, suggestion, innuendo; inference

nën|kupt|o·*het vp impers* it is implied/self-evident, it goes without saying

nën|kupt|o·*n vt* 1 to imply, suggest; infer 2 to presume

*** nën|leftenar** *nm* (Old) = nёntoger

nën|lёkurё *nf* [Anat] subcutis

nën|lёkuror *adj* [Anat] subcutaneous

nën|ligjor *adj* [Law] falling under the law: legal

nën|lloj *nm* [Biol] subspecies

*** nën|mbret** *nm* (Old) viceroy

*** nën|ministёr** *nm* (Old) undersecretary

nën|nda·*n vt* to subdivide

nën|ndarje *nf* subdivision

nënó *nf* (Colloq) 1 (Pet) mom 2 granma

*** nën|ock|ё** = nёnoke

nën|oficer *nm* [Mil] non-commissioned officer, warrant officer, subaltern

nën|ok|e *nf* (Colloq Pet) endearing term of address for one's mother: mommy, mummy

nën|ol|e *nf* (Colloq Pet) 1 = nёnoke 2 (Reg) = lёneshё

*** nën|or** *adj* maternal

nën|petёl *nf* [Bot] sepal

nën|pik|ё *nf* subtopic

nën|prefekt *nm* subprefect

nën|prefekturё *nf* subprefecture

nën|president *n* vice president

nën|produkt *nm* = nёnprodhim

nën|prodhim *nm* by-product

*** nën|pun|ёs** = nёpunёs

*** nën|pun|o**·*n vi* to understudy; act as second

nën|qaf|ёz *nf* neck strap on a beast of burden

nën|qesh· *vi* to smile

nën|qesh|ёs *adj, n* smiling/smirking (person)

nën|qesh|je *nf* 1 <nёnqesh· 2 smile

*** nën|qind|ёs** *nm* = nёntoger

nën|qingje *nf* [Bot] peppermint (Mentha piperita)

nën·rendís | stem for 1st sg pres, pl pres, 2nd & 3rd sg subj, pind < **nënrendí**t·

nën·rendít· vt = **nënrendo**·n

nën·rendít es adj [Ling] subordinating

nën·rendít je nf[Ling] subordination

nën·rendít ur adj (i) [Ling] subordinate

nën·rendó·n vt to subordinate

nën·repárt nm smallest military subunit: squad

*nën·rrogo·sët adj (i) underhanded, shady

nën·sistém nm [Ling] subsystem

nën·sqe'tull nf 1 armpit 2 underarm piece (of clothing) 3 [Agr] sprout that appears at the bottom of a leaf near the end of a graft: subaxillary sprout

nën·stación nm substation (with telephone or electrical transmission lines)

nën·sharte·së nf [Agr] lower portion of a plant graft: stock, rootstock

*nën·shestím nm (Old) protractor, sextant

nën·shkrím nm ger 1 < **nënshkrua**·n 2 signature

nën·shkrua·n vt 1 to affix a signature: sign [] 2 to undersign, pledge to uphold []
∘ nënshkrua·n në të bardhë to sign a blank check

nën·shkruar n (i) (Offic) the undersigned

nën·shkrues nm party to a formal agreement

nën·shtetas n 1 citizen (in a monarchial state): subject 2 citizen = shte'tas

nën·shtete·sí nf 1 citizenship (in a monarchial state) 2 = shtetësí

nën·shtre·së nf underlying level: substratum

nën·shtrím nm ger 1 < **nënshtro**·n, **nënshtro**·het 2 subjugation 3 submission 4 subordination

nën·shtro·het vpr 1 to submit 2 to be submissive 3 to undergo suppression/oppression

nën·shtro·n vt 1 to force [] to submit: subjugate 2 to subdue 3 to submit [] to < the judgment of others> 4 to subordinate

nën·shtruar adj (i) 1 subjugating, oppressed, exploited 2 submissive

nën·shtrues adj subjugating; oppressive, repressive

*nën·shty'pje nf oppression, suppression

nëntat np (të) (Old) [Relig] the commemorated ninth day after a death; the meal served at such a commemoration

nën·tekst nm covert meaning: subtext

nën·teshëm adj (i) lower, under

nëntë
I § num nine, number nine
II § adj (i) ninth
III § nf 1 the number nine 2 the grade nine (where ten is the highest possible grade)
IV § nf (e) (fraction) a ninth
V § np (të) a group of nine, nine at one time; all nine

nëntë adv in/at/to the lowest part: down below

nëntë·dhjete·nen'ta np (të) (Colloq) every conceivable bad thing

nëntë·dhje'të
I § num ninety; number ninety
II § nf the number ninety
III § adj (i), n (i) (ordinal number) ninetieth
IV § nf (e) (fraction) a ninetieth

nëntë·mb'ë·dhje'të
I § num nineteen; number nineteen
II § nf the number nineteen

III § adj (i), n (i) (ordinal number) nineteenth
IV § nf (e) (fraction) a nineteenth

nëntë·mua'jsh adj nine-month-old

nëntë·mujo'r
I § adj lasting nine months: nine-month-long
II § nm nine-month period of time, three-fourths of a year

nëntë·qínd
I § num nine hundred; number nine hundred
II § adj (i) (ordinal number) nine hundredth
III § nf (e) (fraction) a nine hundredth

nëntë·qínd·të adj (i), nf (e) = **nënt**ë·qínd

nëntë·rro'kësh
I § adj consisting of nine syllables: nonasyllabic
II § nm [Lit] nonasyllabic line of verse

nëntë·sh nm game played by two players with nine stones on three squares with lines drawn through them

nëntë·she nf group of nine

nën·të·shëm adj (i) [Spec] in a position underneath: nether, inferior

nën·típ nm [Spec] subtype

nën·títull nm (np ⁻j) subtitle

nën·toger nm [Mil] second lieutenant

nën·tokë nf ground below the surface: subsurface, earth underground, subterranean level/stratum, subsoil

nën·tokë·so'r adj subterranean, underground

nën·tokë·shëm adj (i) = **nëntokë**so'r

nën·tor nm November

nën·tra nm (np ⁻ rë) [Archit] support beam placed under another beam

nën·tropika'l adj [Geog] subtropical

nën·truall nm [Geol] subsoil

nën·thartí nf [Med] hypochlorhydria

*nën·the·k'ës adj (Old) [Ling] accented, stressed

nën·tho·nj'ëz nf [Med] whitlow, felon

*nën·uj'cë nf (Old) submarine

nën·uj'e np fem underground water

nën·uj'ës
I § adj living/operating underwater
II § nm [Mil] submarine

nën·ujo'r adj located underwater

nën·uj·shëm adj (i) underwater

*nën·urdh'as n (Old) subject (of a monarch)

*nën·urdhëra't ës OR nën·urdhëronj'ës adj, n (Old) = **nënu**rdhës

*nën·urdh'ës adj, n (Old) subordinate

*nën·urí·s· = **nanur**í·s·

nën·ve·shje nf undergarment, underclothing

nën·ve'te nf 1 (Euph) [Anat] inguinal area: groin 2 [Anat] perineum

nën·vetë·dí'je nf [Psych] subconsciousness, the subconscious

nën·vetë·dí'jshëm adj (i) [Psych] subconscious

nën·veto'r adj [Med] perineal

nën·ve'tull nf underbrow

nën·vizím nm ger 1 < **nënvizo**·n 2 underline

nën·vizó·n vt to underline, underscore

nën·vizua'r adj (i) underlined, underscored

nën·vleft = **nënvle**r

nën·vlerës'ím nm ger 1 < **nënvlerëso**·n 2 undervaluation; underestimation

nën·vlerëso'·n vt to undervalue, underrate, underestimate

nën|vler|ës|u|es *adj* underrating, underestimating, slighting

nëpër *prep (acc)* in and among; among; through, throughout
- **nëpër dhëmbë** in a mutter, unclearly
- **nëpër ëndërr** in one's dreams; while dreaming
- **nëpër tym** dimly, unclearly, obscurely
- **Nëpër vende! 1** To your places! Take your places! **2** [*Track*] On your marks!

nëpër|duk·et *vpr* **1** to appear through something transparent: become apparent **2** to appear intermittently

nëpër|duk|shëm *adj (i)* transparent, transpicuous

nëpër|këmb· *vt* to trample on []; abuse, mistreat, oppress

nëpër|këmb|je *nf ger* **1** <nëpërkëmb· **2** abuse, maltreatment, oppression

nëpër|këmb|ur *adj (i)* trampled down; maltreated

nëpërk|o·n *vt* to take a sinuous course around []: snake/twist around []

nëpër|me|s
I § *adv* from one side to the other: across
II § *prep (abl)* **1** by way of: through, across **2** = **nëpërmjet**.

nëpër|mje·t *prep (abl)* by means of: through

nëpër|nde|shje *nf* [*Optics*] interference

*****nëpër|se** *nf (Old)* [*Ling*] interjection

*****nëpër|shk|o·**n *vt* to penetrate

*****nëpër|shndri't|sh**ëm = nëpërdu|kshëm

në|pun|ës *n* white collar employee; office worker

në|pun|ësi *nf* white collar work; office work

në qoftë|se *conj* in case that, if it should be that, if = në qoftë se

*****nër** = ndër

*****nër|he|qje** *nf (Old)* [*Phys*] gravity = gravite't

*****nër|hy·**n = ndërhy·n

*****nër|hy|rje** = ndërhy'rje

*****nër|mje·t** = ndërmje't

*****nërv|** *nf* = nerv|

*****nërv||** *nf* = nervl|

në|se *conj* if; whether

*****në|shty'p|je** *nf* impression

NFB *abbrev* <Ndërmarrja e furnizimit të bujqësisë agency for agricultural equipment

NFN *abbrev* <Ndërmarrja e furnizimit të ndërtimit agency for construction equipment

NFP *abbrev* <Ndërmarrja fruta-perime **1** agency for fruits and vegetables <Ndërmarrja e furnizimit të punëtorëve **2** agency for provision of labor

NFPM *abbrev* <Ndërmarrja e furnizimit të punëtorëve të minierave agency for mining equipment

NG *abbrev* <Ndërmarrja e grumbullimit agency for stockpiling of goods

nga
I § *prep (nom)* **1** from; out of; of **2** by means/way/agency/reason of: by, through **3** toward; at **4** starting/originating from **5** in terms of **6** (followed by a noun or pronoun) than **7** (followed by a number) in equal number: each, every
II § *interrog adv* **1** from where, whence; towards where **2** from what, how
III § *relative conj* from/toward which; from/toward where; in whatever direction that
- **nga** {*number*} {} each, {} apiece; {} at a time, {} at the same time
- **nga** {*time word in nom def form*} **në** [{*same time noun in acc indef form*}] {} by [] **nga** {*dita/dreka/java/mëngjesi/muaji/viti/...*} **në** {*ditë/drekë/javë/mëngjes/muaj/vit/...*} day by day, every lunchtime, week by week, every morning, month by month, year by year, ... **nga muaji në muaj** every month, month by month
- **nga** {} **te** {} through the whole range from {} to {}
- {*number*} **nga** {*same number*} {} at a time
- **nga ana e** <> on <>'s part, if it were up to <>
- **nga ana e anës** from the end of the world, from a very long distance
- **nga buka në bukë** from one year to the next
- **Nga del fjala, del shpirti.** "Where the word comes from, the heart comes from." **1** *(Prov)* You can't go back on your word. **2** What a person has in his heart comes out in what he says.
- **nga dita në ditë** daily, day in day out, from day to day, day by day
- **Nga ferra e vogël del lepuri i madh.** "From the little thorn bush the big hare emerges." *(Prov)* Great oaks from little acorns grow. Big problems start out as little problems.
- **nga frika se __** for fear that __
- **nga fry·**n³ˢᵍ **era kthe·**n **gunën/gëzofin/shpinën** (said of an opportunist) {} *turns* whichever way the wind *is* blowing
- **nga fundi/thelbi i zemrës/shpirtit** from the bottom of one's heart, in all sincerity
- **nga fundi në krye/majë** from top to bottom: completely
- **nga gjiri i tokës** from the bowels of the earth
- **nga halli** out of necessity, by necessity
- **nga janë (e) nga s'janë** all without exception
- **nga e keqja** by necessity, out of necessity
- **Nga këmbët borroviq, nga mendja eksiq** mature in body, but not in mind
- **nga koka deri te thembrat** from head to toe, entirely, up to the neck
- **nga larg** from afar, from a distance
- **Nga një anë të puth, nga tjetra të pret** "*Kisses* you on one side, *cuts* you on the other" {} *smiles* in your face while {} *stabs* you in the back.
- **nga një vesh** <> **hy·**n³ˢᵍ**, nga tjetri** <> **del** (*Impol*) it *goes* in one ear (of <>) and out the other
- **nga njëra anë __ nga ana tjetër __** on the one hand __ on the other hand __
- **nga njëri çast në tjetrin** at any moment, shortly; very soon
- **nga pak** just a little, a little bit
- **Nga peri mund të kapet edhe lëmshi.** "From the strand, the whole clew can be captured." *(Prov)* One little detail may be enough to solve a whole problem.
- **ësh-të nga rrëza** "be from the outskirts" *(Old Pej)* to be from the poor section of town, be from the other side of the tracks
- **nga shkaku** <> because of <>
- **nga shkaku që/se __** for the reason that __: because __
- **Nga ta di·** {}?! How *is* {} supposed to know?!
- **nga të katër anët** from all over
- **nga vë· ballin, vë· thembrën.** "where {} *puts* {}'s forehead, {} *puts* {}'s heel" *(Tease)* to turn tail and leave

nga' *stem for pdef, opt, adm, part, imper* <nge't·

*****nga'c|ë** *nf* snag, catch, impediment

*****nga'c|ës** *adj* impeding, preventing

*ngackë = **ngacë**

ngacmim *nm ger* **1** <**ngacmo**·*n*, **ngacmo**·*het* **2** excitation **3** *(Fig)* irritation

∘ **ngacmim në seri** [*Electr*] series excitation

∘ **ngacmim i pavarur** [*Electr*] separate excitation

ngacmimtar

I § *adj* provocational, exacerbating

II § *nm* provoker, inciter; provocateur, mischief-maker

ngacmo·*het vpr* to arouse one another; get stirred up, become excited; exchange taunts

ngacmo·*n vt* **1** to poke, poke at [] **2** to taunt; provoke **3** to irritate **4** to excite **5** *(Fig)* to incite

∘ [] **ngacmo**·*n*³*ˢᵍ* {*a disease*} [] *suffers an attack of* {}

∘ **ngacmo**·*n* **urët** "poke/disturb the burning embers" to exacerbate bad feelings: stir the pot

*ngacmor *adj* irritating

ngacmues

I § *adj* **1** exciting, stimulating **2** irritating

II § *n* instigator, inciter; provocateur

III § *nm* **1** [*Physiol*] excitant () **2** [*Electr*] exciter ()

ngacmueshëm *adj (i)* easily provoked; excitable; high-strung

ngacmueshmëri *nf* **1** oversensitivity; irritability **2** [*Physiol*] excitability

*ngacrr *(Colloq)* = **ngatërr**

*ngacun *adj (i) (Reg Gheg)* **1** halted, caught **2** lame, paralytic

ngadalë

I § *adv* **1** slowly **2** without making much sound **3** gradually

II § *interj* calm down!

ngadalësi *nf* slowness

ngadalësim *nm ger* **1** <**ngadalëso**·*n*, **ngadalëso**·*het* **2** slowdown

ngadalëso·*het vpr* to slow down, get slower

ngadalëso·*n vt* to slow [] down

ngadalësuar *adj (i)* slowed down, slow

ngadalësues

I § *adj* serving to slow down: slowing

II § *nm* [*Tech*] speed reducer

ngadalshëm *adj (i)* **1** slow **2** delayed

ngadalshmëri *nf* = **ngadalësi**

ngadaltë *adj (i)* = **ngadalshëm**

ngadita OR **ngaditë** *adv* every day, daily

*ngaditëshëm *adj (i)* daily

ngado *adv* in or from every/any direction; whichever way, wherever

ngadhënje·*n*

I § *vi (Elev)* to triumph

II § *vt* to triumph over [], vanquish; conquer

ngadhënjim *nm ger (Elev)* **1** <**ngadhënje**·*n* **2** great victory, triumph

ngadhënjimísht *adv (Elev)* victoriously; triumphantly

ngadhënjimtar

I § *adj (Elev)* victorious; triumphant

II § *nm* victor; conqueror

ngadhënjyes *adj, n (Elev)* = **ngadhënjimtar**

ngaha *adv* from where, whence

ngahera OR **ngaherë** *adv* every time, all the time, continually

ngahershëm *adj (i)* constant, continual, perpetual

ngajë *nf* motive, cause

*ngajk *nm* = **ngajë**

*ngajko·*n vt* to mount/ride [a horse]

*ngajo·*n vt (Reg Tosk)* to occasion, cause

*ngakto·*n vt* to acquire

ngal·*et vpr* **1** to shuffle along slowly; barely move **2** *(Fig)* to be behind in one's work

ngalakaq *adj (Pej)* shuffling, sluggish, slothful

*ngalëc *nm (Old)* = **ngalës**

ngalës *nm* **1** *(Old)* gun trigger ***2** person who shuffles along slowly: shuffler

ngalët *adj (i)* with feet of lead, moving sluggishly, at a shuffling gait, ungainly

ngalëz *nf (Colloq)* obstacle: stumbling block

*ngaliro·*het vpr* <to clamber up

ngalo·*het vpr* = **ngal**·*et*

ngalo·*n vi* = **ngal**·*et*

ngalos·*et vpr* **1** = **ngal**·*et* **2** to limp from foot rot

ngalosë *nf* [*Veter*] = **hírrëz**

ngallë *nf* **1** young plant sprout **2** tasseled stalk of an onion **3** corn tassel

ngallicë *nf* **1** = **ngallë 2** woman who makes trouble, woman who stirs the pot

*ngallínë *nf* excrescence, growth

ngallís *stem for 1st sg pres, pl pres, 2nd & 3rd sg subj, pind* <**ngallít**·

ngallít·

I § *vt* **1** to prick **2** *(Fig)* to provoke, annoy

II § *vi (Fig)* (of plants like onions and corn) to display tassels

ngallít·*et vpr* to devote oneself entirely to <>

ngallítje *nf ger* <**ngallít**·, **ngallít**·*et*

ngallmim *nm ger* <**ngallmo**·*n*

ngallmo·*n vt* **1** to nail [] together **2** *(Fig)* to incite **3** *(Fig)* to bring about, cause

ngallo·*n vi* to sprout

ngalluar *adj (i)* sprouted; (of vegetables) not fresh

ngandonjëherë *adv* occasionally, sometimes

nganjëherë *adv* from time to time, now and then, once in a while

ngapak *adv* little by little, gradually

ngaqë *conj* inasmuch as: since

ngaraz *adv* using a covering plow (to plant seed in already plowed land)

ngarduliqe *nf* [*Ornit*] goldfinch (*Carduelis carduelis*)

*ngardh· *vt* to blemish, stain; stigmatize, brand

ngardhe *nf (Old)* **1** snag **2** disfiguring mark: stigma, blot, blemish ***3** fastener, clasp ***4** cheating trick

ngarend· *vi* to run fast; hurry

ngarendas *adv* in a hurry, quickly

ngarendje *nf ger* <**ngarend**·

ngarë *part* <**nget**·

ngarkaçe *nf* forked prop used to load packsaddles

ngarkesë *nf* **1** load, burden; freight, cargo **2** task, charge **3** [*Phys Electr*] charge, load **4** explosive charge

∘ **ngarkesë goditëse** [*Spec*] blast load

∘ **ngarkesë e lëvizjes** traffic load

∘ **ngarkesë ndezëse** [*Spec*] firing charge

∘ **ngarkesë plasëse** [*Spec*] explosive charge

ngarkicë *nf* small load (that can be carried by one person)

ngarkim *nm ger* **1** <**ngarko**·*n*, **ngarko**·*het* **2** charge, responsibility

ngarkim-shkarkim *nm* loading-and-unloading; stevedoring

ngarko·*het vpr* **1** to take on a load **2** to become loaded **3** to get pregnant

ngarko·*n vt* **1** to place a burden on/in []: load **2** to charge **3** *(Fig)* to overload [], load [] down
 ○ **i ngarko·n plaçkat** "gather/pick/load up all one's stuff" *(Iron)* to finally pack up one's stuff and leave; pick up and leave
 ○ **ngarko·n vezë në lak** "load eggs in the loop of a rope" to try to do something really stupid

ngarkojsë *nf* thick woolen packstrap used to carry loads on one's back

ngarkuar
 I § *adj (i)* **1** loaded **2** *(Fig)* loaded with work to do **3** *(Colloq)* pregnant
 II § *n (i)* person charged with a responsibility
 ○ **i ngarkuari me punë** [*Dipl*] chargé d'affaires

ngarkues
 I § *adj* serving to carry freight; draft (animal)
 II § *nm* loader; stevedore

ngarmo·*n vt* **1** to drive [] away, expel **2** to drive/ goad [] on, prod; compel

ngarris *stem for 1st sg pres, pl pres, 2nd & 3rd sg subj, pind* <**ngarrit**·

ngarrit· *vi* to spend time idly, waste time, loiter

*****ngarrit**-*et vpr (Reg Gheg)* = **ngarrit**·

ngarro·*n vt* to gather/crowd around [], surround

ngas *stem for 1st sg pres, pl pres, 2nd & 3rd sg subj* <**nget**·

ngase
 I § *conj* given that, inasmuch as: since
 II § *nf (Colloq)* reason why, what-for, reason

ngasëkeqe *nf (Colloq)* trigger of a gun

ngasës
 I § *n* **1** pesterer **2** tempter, seducer **3** *(Book)* drover; driver **4** instigator, inciter; provocateur
 II § *adj* **1** serving to arouse an urge **2** inciting, provocative

ngasje *nf* **1** urge **2** [*Relig*] sinful urge **3** [*Bot*] = **prrall**

*****ngaskeq** *nm* **1** trigger **2** frog of a (violin) bow **3** nuisance

ngastër *nf* **1** strip of land; farm plot **2** piece of meat, cheese or vegetable pasty **3** *(Reg)* vegetable quiche made with corn meal ***4** *(Old)* district

ngastëro·*n vt* to divide land into plots for sowing

ngashenjyes *adj* alluring, seductive

ngashënje·*het vpr* to be lured by sweet talk or gentle action

ngashënje·*n vt* to lure by sweet talk or gentle action: seduce; enchant

ngashënjim *nm ger* **1** <**ngashënje**·*n*, **ngashënje**·*het* **2** alluring trait

ngashëre·*het vpr* **1** to feel emotionally moved/ touched, feel deep sentiments **2** to break out in sobs

ngashëre·*n vt* to move emotionally, touch []'s sentiments

ngashëri *nf* deep sentiment

ngashërim *nm* **1** feeling of great sentiment, deep emotion **2** sobbing

ngashëro·*het vpr* = **ngashëre**·*het*

ngashëro·*n vt* = **ngashëre**·*n*

ngashëryer *adj (i)* deeply touched, emotionally moved

*****ngashnim** *nm ger* **1** <**ngashno**·*n* **2** apprehension, concern

*****ngashno**·*n vt* to cause [] concern, worry

*****ngashnje**·*n vt* to allure, entice, tempt

ngatërr *nf* ribbon to keep woman's hair in order: hair ribbon

ngatërrac *adj, n* = **ngatërrestar**

ngatërresë *nf* confused and disordered situation or thing: mess, tangle, muddle; disturbance

ngatërrestar
 I § *adj* troublemaking, agitating, disturbing
 II § *n* troublemaker, agitator, disturber

ngatërri *nf* disorderly confusion

ngatërrim *nm ger* **1** <**ngatërro**·*n*, **ngatërro**·*het* **2** complication
 ○ **ngatërrim zorrësh** [*Med*] volvulus

ngatërro·*het vpr* **1** to be tangled up; be all mixed up **2** to become embroiled/entangled **3** to get confused **4** to get more complicated
 ○ **ngatërro**·*het³ᵖˡ* **fijet** "the strands *get* tangled" things *get* all fouled up, matters *get* all complicated
 ○ **ngatërro**·*het³ᵖˡ* **fijet** matters *get* more complicated/confused
 ○ **ngatërro**·*het³ˢᵍ* **lëmshi** the matter *gets* more complicated/confused
 ○ <> **ngatërro**·*het* **nëpër këmbë 1** to get tangled up in <>'s feet **2** *(Fig)* to get in <>'s way, be a hindrance to <>.

ngatërro·*n vt* **1** to tangle, mix [] up **2** to embroil, entangle **3** to create confusion/complication in []; confuse []; upset [], complicate []
 ○ **ngatërro**·*n* **hapin** to get out of step
 ○ <>**i ngatërro**·*n* **letrat** "mix up <>'s cards" to upset <>'s plans
 ○ **ngatërro**·*n* **lëmshin/fijet/penjtë** to make matters more complicated
 ○ [] **ngatërro**·*n* **nëpër dhëmbë** to say [] unclearly, mumble []
 ○ **ngatërro**·*n* **ujërat/ujin** to muddy the waters, confuse matters

ngatërruar *adj (i)* tangled, entangled; complicated; embroiled

ngatërrueshëm *adv* confusingly, in disordered manner

ngath· *vt* **1** to make [] numb: numb, benumb; stun **2** to make [] sluggish; cause [] to be clumsy

ngath-*et*
 I § *vpr* **1** to get numb from the cold **2** to lose spryness, become sluggish/stiff, get clumsy
 II § *adv* sluggishly, stiffly; clumsily

ngathët *adj (i)* **1** clumsy, awkward; sluggish **2** numb, stiff, wooden

ngathtësi *nf* **1** clumsiness, awkwardness; sluggishness **2** numbness

ngathtësisht *adv* clumsily

ngazëlle·*het vpr* = **ngazëllo**·*het*

ngazëlle·*n vt* = **ngazëllo**·*n*

ngazëllim *nm* feeling of great joy: exultation, merriment

ngazëllimtar *adj* = **ngazëllues**

ngazëllo·*het vpr* to express elation: rejoice

ngazëllo·*n*
 I § *vt* to arouse great joy in []: elate, delight
 II § *vi* to rejoice; light up with joy, beam

ngazëllu·ar *adj (i)* elated

ngazëllu·es *adj* **1** expressing a feeling of great joy: joyous, merry, exultant **2** arousing great joy: joyful

***ngazít·**et *vpr* = gazít·*et*

***ngdhi·**n = gdhi·n

nge *nf* free time, leisure
  ○ **më nge** in one's free time, at one's leisure

nge·het *vpr* to take a break from work; have/find (free) time

nge·n *vi* to have free time, have time free

ngec·
  I § vi **1** to get stuck: stick, jam, catch
  II § vt **1** to attach [] in a hanging position: stick [] up **2** (*Fig Colloq*) to stick <*someone*> with [an unwanted task]; stick <*someone*> with [the blame] **3** [*Sport*] to dink [a volleyball]
  ○ **Ngeci karkaleci.** "The earth mover got stuck." (*Tease*) Okay, big shot, now you're stuck.
  ○ **ngec· në vend** to be stuck; stay in one place; not move, not change; lag behind
  ○ <> **ngec·**^{3sg} **plori në rrënjë** "<>'s plow *gets stuck* on a root" <>'s schemes *hit* a snag
  ○ <> **ngec·**^{3sg} **sharra në gozhdë** "<>'s saw *gets stuck* on a nail" <>'s plans *hit* a snag
  ○ <> **ngec·**^{3sgpast} **veza kryq** "<>'s egg got stuck crosswise" <>'s plan *hit* a snag; <> *ran* into a dead end

ngec·et *vpr* to find an excuse to quarrel/fight

ngec|ë *nf* **1** quagmire **2** (*Fig*) obstacle = **pengesë 3** (*Fig*) bone of contention

ngec|je *nf ger* <ngec·
  ○ **ngecje e topit** [*Sport*] dropping the ball just over the net: drop shot (in racket games); dink (in volleyball)

ngec|ull *nf* obstacle

ngec|ur *adj (i)* stuck, jammed

***ngehshëm** = ngeshëm

ngehur *adj (i)* = ngeshëm

***ngejtun** *adj (i)* (*Reg Gheg*) = ngeshëm

ngel *nm* = ngërç

ngel·
  I § vi **1** to remain stuck in one place, be unable to move: get jammed, get stuck **2** still not manage to do something; still not find the time to do something **3** still to remain in an undesirable situation **4** (of items of value) to remain still unused/unspent **5** to remain still uncompleted **6** to remain intact ***7** (of dogs/bulls) to mate **8** (*Colloq*) to fail to pass [a student] to the next grade in school, flunk [a student]
  II § vi (*Colloq*) to fail to pass to the next grade in school, flunk
  ○ <> **ngel· goja** "<>'s mouth *gets* stuck" <> *goes* on and on talking about the same thing
  ○ **ngel· kërcu** to be left in pitiful misery without any family
  ○ <> **ngel·**^{3sg} **kërrabëza** an obstacle *arises* for <>
  ○ **ngel· me gisht në gojë** "stand with finger in mouth" **1** to end up with nothing **2** to be dumbstruck with surprise **3** to stand in shame
  ○ **ngel· në derë** "be left at <>'s door" **1** to annoy <> with frequent visits **2** to be a constant burden on <>
  ○ <> **ngel·**^{3rd} **në dorë** to collapse while in <>'s hands, break/faint while under <>'s responsibility
  ○ <> **ngel· në qafë** "get stuck on <>'s neck" to pick on <> unfairly

  ○ **ngel· në vend** to be stuck; stay in one place; not move, not change; lag behind
  ○ **ngel· pa frymë** "be stuck without breath" to be unable to breathe
  ○ **ngel· pa mend/gojë** "be stuck without mind/ speech" to be speechless with amazement: be dumbfounded
  ○ **ngel· për vjeshtë** to flunk spring examinations and have to retake them in autumn
  ○ <> **ngel·**^{3sg} **qejfi** <> still *feels* indignant from an affront
  ○ **ngel· qyqe** (of a woman) to be left in pitiful misery without any family
  ○ **s'<> ngel·**^{3sg} **sy e faqe** "for <> no eye and face sticks" <> is too ashamed to face anyone; <> is covered with shame
  ○ <> **ngel·**^{3sg} **syri te/tek** {} <> *keeps* looking at {}
  ○ <> **ngel·**^{3pl} **sytë te/tek** {} <> *keeps* looking at {}
  ○ <> **ngel·**^{3sg} **sharra në gozhdë** "<>'s saw *gets stuck* on a nail" <>'s plans *hit* a snag

ngel·et *vpr* to get stuck

ngela|c *adj* = ngela|q

ngela|q *adj* clumsy; inept

ngel|ës *n, adj* (*Colloq*) (student) failing to pass to the next grade in school

ngel|je *nf ger* <ngel·

ngel|ur *adj (i)* intact; not used up, remaining

***ngeq·** *vt* to make [] worse, impair

***ngerç** = ngërç

***ngerm|ë** *nf* taunt

***ngermo·**n = ngërmo·n

ngeshëm
  I § adj (i) **1** having free time; at/for/of leisure **2** convenient, opportune
  II § adv leisurely

nget· *vt* **1** to touch; handle **2** to prod [a draught animal] with a prick; urge/drive [] on **3** (*Fig*) to provoke, incite **4** (*Fig*) to prick; annoy **5** (*Colloq*) to afflict **6** to drive [a vehicle/caravan] **7** (*Reg*) to plow **8** (*Colloq*) to pursue [a subject of interest] **9** (*Reg*) to sharpen = **mpreh**
  ○ **e nget· reja** "the cloud is provoking it" it hasn't stopped raining
  ○ **e nget· fjalën** to seize on something said in order to pick a fight fjalën ng*et*· ::ng*et*· fjalën to stir up conversation; keep the conversation going
  ○ **e nget· gotën** "touch one's glass" to be a (habitual) drinker
  ○ **nget· këmbët** to walk faster
  ○ [] **nget·**^{3sg} **shkuma** []'s blood freezes in []'s veins

***ngeth|ët** = ngathët

***ngëc·** = ngec·

***ngëlleq·**et *vpr* = ngërdhaq·et

***ngëlli·** *vt* (*Reg Gheg*) to vent, let out []

***ngërc|ëll** = kërc|ell

ngërç *nm* muscle cramp/spasm

***ngërdhaq·**et *vpr* to tipple, carouse

ngërdhesh· *vt* to sneer, snicker
  ○ **ngërdhesh· fytyrën** to contort one's face: make a face, grimace

ngërdhesh·et *vpr* **1** to contort one's face: make a face, grimace **2** to make a mocking face

ngër|dhe·shje *nf ger* 1 <**ngërdhe·sh·et** 2 painful/ scornful grimace

ngër|dhe·sh|ur *adj (i)* grimacing

ngër|dhu·c·et *vpr* 1 to snarl; threaten <> ferociously 2 to turn up one's nose at food, be finicky in eating

ngër|dhu·za *np fem* pickiness in eating

ngërfo·s·et *vpr* = ngrefo·s·et

*****ngërhi|s|** = gërha·s, gërhi·s|

*****ngërhi·t·** = gërhe·t

ngër|le·sh·et *vpr* = kërle·sh·et

ngërmo··n *vt* 1 to goad; goad [] into; rouse [] into anger 2 to affect [] with an urge

  ∘ <> **ngërmo··n**[3sg] **për bukë** <> *feels* really hungry

ngër|th = ngërç

ngërthe·het *vt* 1 to become intimately joined: be intermeshed, mesh 2 to squeeze up

ngërthe··n *vt* 1 to join [] tightly together; grab [] tight 2 *(Fig)* to pull [] together, comprise *3 to mesh/ engage [gears]

  ∘ **ngërthe··n vetullat** to knit one's brow

ngërthe·s|ë *nf* 1 gear mechanism, gear train 2 *(Fig)* intermeshed network

ngërth|im *nm ger* <**ngërthe··n**, **ngërthe·het**

ngër|thy|er *adj (i)* 1 bent sharply 2 (of brows) wrinkled

ngër|zi·s| stem for 1st sg pres, pl pres, 2nd & 3rd sg subj, pind <**ngërzi·t·**

ngër|zi·t· *vt* to get [] stirred up; stir up trouble among []

*****ngërri·t·et** *vpr* to mutter

*****ngërr|nja·r** *adj* irritable, testy

*****ngëth·et** = nga·th·et

*****ngëth|ës|i** = ngathtë·si

*****ngëth|ur** *adj (i)* = nga·thët

ngi··het *vpr* 1 to become satiated 2 to get saturated

ngi··n *vt* 1 to satiate 2 to saturate

ngi|m|je *nf ger* 1 <**ngi··n**, **ngi··het** 2 satiation; saturation

ngi|nj·et *vpr* = ngi··het

ngi|nj|ur *adj (i)* 1 gorged, sated, satiated 2 saturated

ngi|s| stem for 2nd pl pres, pind <**nget·**

ngi|shëm *adv* in a satiated/saturated condition

*****ngi|sht|e** = gi·shte

ngi|t·et *vpr* to become provoked

ngi|t| stem for pind, 2nd pl pres, imper, vp <**nget·**

n|goj|cë *nf* 1 bit (on a bridle) 2 muzzle (for a dog)

n|goj|e *OR* adv in the mouth

n|goj|e| *nf* = ngojcë

n|goj|ëz *nf* = ngojcë

n|goj|im *nm ger* <**ngojo·|n**

n|goj|o··n *vt* to speak ill of [], bad-mouth, slander

ngol|o··n *vt* to taste, sample [food/drink]

ngop· *vt* 1 to sate/satiate [] (with food/drink), gorge; stuff 2 *(Fig Colloq)* to unload something undesirable onto [someone], stick [] with something bad 3 to saturate

  ∘ [] **ngop· me dru** to give [] a good walloping

ngo·p·et *vpr* 1 to gorge oneself, become satiated; feel full 2 to get saturated

  ∘ **s'ngopet ariu me miza** it's never enough, there's no satisfying him!

  ∘ **ngop·et deri në grykë** to eat till one bursts

  ∘ **ngop·et me bathë** to get sick and tired of the same old thing

  ∘ **ngop·et me erë** to be satisfied by false promises/ words

  ∘ **ngop·et me lugë të zbrazët** "gorge oneself with an empty spoon" to be very gullible

  ∘ **ngop·et me shkumë** "get satisfied with mere foam" to be too easily satisfied

ngo|p|je *nf ger* 1 <**ngop·**, **ngop·et** 2 saturation

ngo|p|ur *adj (i)* sated, satiated, gorged; saturated

ngordh· *vi* 1 (said of animals) to die 2 *(Colloq)* to die like an animal: croak, kick off 3 *(Fig Colloq)* to die trying, wear oneself out doing, become exhausted in the process; suffer

  ∘ [] **ngordh· në dru** *(Colloq)* to beat the living daylights out of []

ngordh|aca|k *adj (Pej)* = ngordhala·q

ngordh|ala·q

  I § *adj* 1 *(Pej)* emaciated and barely able to stand, tottering on the brink of the grave 2 lacking in vitality and spirit: lethargic

  II § *nm* bag of bones, walking cadaver

ngordh|a·q *adj (Pej)* = ngordhala·q

ngordh|e|si·r|ë *nf* 1 animal carcass, carrion 2 *(FigImpolite)* bag of bones, walking cadaver 3 *(Fig Insult)* totally inept person

ngo|rdh|ët *adj (i)* = ngo·rdhur

ngo|rdh|je *nf* 1 <**ngo·rdh·** 2 animal's death

  ∘ **ësh·të**[3sg] **ngordhje me thes në kokë** to be freezing cold out

ngo|rdh|ur *adj (i)* 1 dead, fallen over dead (said of animals) 2 lacking in vitality and spirit: lethargic

*****ngore·n** = gore·n

*****ngos|** = ngop

NGP *abbrev* <**Ndërmarrja e grumbullim-përpunimit** agency for stockpiling and processing material

*****ngrafi·s·** *vt* to bewitch, hypnotize

*****ngrah·** *vt* to whip, lash

ngra|t|ë *adj (i)* pitiful, wretched

ngra|thët *adj (i)* (of hair) bristly

ngre· *vt* 1 to move [] to a higher physical or social position: lift, raise; elevate 2 to put [] into the air, make [] fly 3 to erect; construct 4 to stimulate [] into activity: awaken, arouse; flush [prey] from a hiding place 5 to increase [] in magnitude 6 to recruit 7 *(Fig)* to bring up, put [] on the table

  ∘ **ngre· bishtin** 1 to be about to take action 2 *(Colloq)* to take a downward moral path 3 to think too highly of oneself

  ∘ **ngre· çengelat** 1 to weigh anchor 2 *(Fig)* to leave finally

  ∘ **i ngre· çoparkat** *(Iron)* to pack up and leave; leave in a hurry

  ∘ **ngre· dollinë** to raise a glass in proposing a toast: propose a toast

  ∘ **ngre· dorë/dorën kundër** <> to raise one's hand against; take up battle against <>

  ∘ **ngre· duart lart/përpjetë** to raise one's hands (in surrender), give up; give up (on a difficult task)

  ∘ [] **ngre·**[3sg] **dheu përpjetë** "the earth *throws/ lifts* []" []'s life *is* in great turmoil, <> *is* under a lot of stress

  ∘ **ngre· flamurin e bardhë** to raise the white flag, surrender

  ∘ **ngre· flamurin** to raise the flag, take the lead in speaking up

  ∘ **ngre· fole** 1 to settle down 2 to appear, take shape

○ **ngre· gotën** to raise a glass in proposing a toast: propose a toast

○ **ngre· grushtin** "raise the fist" to protest; be ready to fight

○ **ngre· hundën (përpjetë)** to get conceited

○ **ngre· hundën me** [] *(Pej)* to get unreasonably miffed at []

○ **nuk ngre· kandar** to be of no value/importance, not matter, not count; have no effect on the outcome

○ **ngre· këmbën e i bie₁· kokës** to punish oneself for one's own failure

○ **ngre· këmbën e vë· gozhdën** to act without due caution and get hurt

○ **i ngre· këmbët bigë** *(Crude)* to keel over and die, kick the bucket

○ **ngre· kokë/krye 1** to rise up; revolt, rebel **2** to raise one's head: make an appearance

○ **s'e ngre· kokën nga** {} to work on [] without stopping

○ **ngre· krye** to rebel, revolt

○ **ngre· kupën** to raise a glass in proposing a toast: propose a toast

○ **e ngre· lafshën përpjetë** to strut around like a bantam rooster

○ **<> ngre· lart emrin** to bring glory to <>'s name

○ **<> ngre· lart zemrën** "raise <>'s heart high" to inspire courage/self-confidence in <>, give <> heart

○ **[] ngre· lart** to praise [] highly

○ **<>i ngre· leckat** *(ColloqImpolite)* to make <> pick up <>'s lousy belongings and clear out: kick <> out (with all <>'s damn belongings)

○ **ngre· leckat** *(Impol)* to pick up <>'s goddam belongings and clear out

○ **[] ngre· me rrënjë e me degë** "lift [] up by root and by branch" to expel [] together with []'s entire family

○ **[] ngre· me këmbë përpjetë** *(Impol)* to kill [] dead, knock [] off

○ **[] ngre· me frymë** to threaten [] with a loud voice

○ **[] ngre· më/në këmbë 1** to raise [a child] until [] can stand on []'s own two feet; help [someone ill] to recover, put [someone ill] back on []'s feet; put [] (back) into working order; get [a building] up **2** to get [] to stand up (in rebellion); get [] to become active **3** to get [] organized, arrange []

○ **<> ngre· monument 1** *(Book)* to erect a monument to <> **2** *(Fig)* to extol <>, praise <> to the skies

○ **<> ngre· nervat** to get on <>'s nerves

○ **[] ngre· në art** to raise [] to the level of art, make [] into an art form

○ **[] ngre· në gjyq** to take [] to court

○ **[] ngre· në qiell** to praise [] to the skies; brag about []

○ **ngre· orën kundër <>** "sic the fairies on <>" to initiate action directed against <>

○ **ngre· peshë (mendjen/zemrën)** to lift (people's) spirits, be uplifting

○ **nuk ngre· peshë** to be of no value/importance, not matter, not count; have no effect on the outcome

○ **[] ngre· peshë** to lift [] up

○ **[] ngre· pezull** to lift [] into the air

○ **i ngre· plaçkat** "gather/pick/load up all one's stuff" *(Iron)* to finally pack up one's stuff and leave; pick up and leave

○ **ngre· pluhur në llaç** "raise dust in mortar" to be/get involved in useless work, busy oneself in an impossible task

○ **<> ngre· rehatinë** to disturb <>'s peace and quiet

○ **<>i ngre· rraqet** *(ColloqImpolite)* to make <> pick up <>'s lousy belongings and clear out: kick <> out (with all <>'s damn belongings)

○ **ngre· rraqet** *(Impol)* to pick up <>'s goddam belongings and clear out

○ **ngre· rreckat** *(Impol)* to pick up <>'s goddam belongings and clear out

○ **ngre· spirancë 1** to weigh anchor **2** *(Fig)* to leave finally

○ **ngre· supet 1** to shrug one's shoulders **2** to answer with a shrug of the shoulders: how should I know!?

○ **ngre· shëndetin** to raise a glass in proposing a toast: propose a toast

○ **ngre· tavolinën/tryezën/trapezën** to clear the table

○ **ngre· tryezën** to clear off the table after eating

○ **ngre· ugar** to bring a fallow field back into cultivation

○ **nuk <> ngre·³ˢᵍ ujë lopata/shati** "<>'s shovel can't lift much water" **1** <> *has* no influence, <> does not pull much weight **2** <> *does* not succeed

○ **ngre· ujin përpjetë** "make the water flow upward" to be very capable, be able to work miracles

○ **<> ngre·³ˢᵍ vendi** <> *is* troubled and uneasy; be in an agitated state

○ **i ngre· veshët bigë** *(Impol)* to prick up one's ears, pay close attention

○ **ngre· veshët curr = curro·n veshët**

○ **ngre· veshët çark** to prick up one's ears, listen attentively

○ **i ngre· veshët çip** to prick up one's ears, listen closely

○ **i ngre· veshët** to start to put on airs, begin to act high and mighty

○ **ngre· veshët** to prick up one's ears, pay close attention

○ **i ngre· veshët pipëz** to listen in closely; be all ears

○ **ngre· veten** to have a high opinion of oneself, think highly of oneself

○ **ngre· zërin (në qiell)** to raise one's voice (to the high heavens); make one's voice heard (all the way to the top)

*ngref = ngreh|

ngrefo·s·et *vpr* **1** to fan one's feathers (like a turkey cock) **2** to strut, act cocky **3** *(Fig)* to take on a menacing posture

ngrefo·sur *adj (i)* with one's feathers fanned out (like a turkey cock); strutting, cocky

ngreh· *vt* **1** to prepare [] for use by putting under tension: stretch [a hide], wind [a watch], cock [a gun] **2** to set up [], erect; pitch [a tent] **3** *(Fig Colloq)* to get ready for [a complex event]: prepare (for battle, for a wedding) **4** *(Fig Colloq)* to pull [] along

○ **ngreh· e shkreh·** to waste effort by constantly undoing what one has just done

○ **ngreh· e mos këput· 1** to act prudently/cautiously **2** to be too tolerant

○ **ngreh· gjyq kundër <>** to bring a legal action against <>, prosecute <>

ngreh·et *vpr* to strut

ngreh|alu'c *nm (Pej)* braggart, show-off

ngreh|alu'c·et *vpr (Pej)* to strut around; brag, show off

ngreh|ë *nf* **1** structural frame (of a house) **2** skeleton

ngreh·hës *adj* **1** wooden apparatus for raising and lowering the upper millstone to regulate the fineness of the grind **2** [*Text*] lever for turning the warp beam of a loom ***3** jack **4** roof strut **5** pendulum

ngrehi̱në *nf* **1** industrial building **2** (*Fig*) mental structure

ngre̱hje *nf ger* **1** = ngri̱tje ***2** fabric

ngre̱hur
I § *adj (i)* **1** ready for use under tension: stretched, wound, cocked, at the ready **2** (*Fig*) strutting, cocky
II § *adv* **1** at the ready **2** in a cocky manner

ngre̱jt *stem for pdef, opt, adm, part* <ngre·

ngre̱shtë *adj (i)* = ngra̱thët

ngrën *stem for part, opt, adm* <ha·

ngrën̲ç *stem for opt* <ha·
○ **Të ngrënçim dasmën!** "May we eat at your wedding!" (*Felic*) May we next celebrate your wedding!
○ **<> ngrënça drekën!** "May I eat <>'s dinner (at <>'s wake)!" (*Curse*) I hope to see <> dead!

ngrënë
I § *part* <ha·
II § *adj (i)* **1** that has eaten: fed **2** eaten away: corroded, eroded, eaten
III § *nf (e)* **1** the act of eating food; food **2** amount eaten at a meal
IV § *nn (të)* eating (of food)

ngrën̲ëkeq *adj* **1** with no appetite: not hungry **2** picky in eating

ngrën̲ës *adj, n* = hame̱s
○ **ngrën̲ësja e drurit** [*Entom*] leopard moth *Zeuzera pyrina L.*

ngrën̲ie *nf ger* **1** <ha·, ha·het **2** (*Colloq*) food; fodder

ngrën̲shëm *adj (i)* edible

ngri·het *vpr* **1** to rise **2** to arise **3** to get up; stand up; (of a baby) to begin to walk **4** to rise into the air; (of something that can fly) take off **5** to rise up (in rebellion) **6** (*Colloq*) to move away from one's home base: leave home **7** to increase in magnitude **8** to freeze; grow numb with cold **9** to grow numb, become paralyzed; get stiff; (of a penis) become erect
○ **<> ngri·het**[3sg] **damari** <> *loses* <>'s temper, <> *flies* off the handle
○ **Ngri·het**[3pl] **këmbët e i bie**₁·[3pl] **kokës.** "The legs rise up and hit the head" The servant thinks he can get away with beating the master.
○ **ngri·het me gjelat** to get up very early in the morning ("at cockcrow") get up with the chickens ("roosters")
○ **ngri·het me yje** "get up with the stars" to get up very early in the morning
○ **<> ngri·het**[3sg] **mendja** <> *cannot* stop thinking about it
○ **ngri·het më/në këmbë 1** (of a small child) to begin walking **2** (of someone ill) to get back on one's feet after a long illness: recover **3** to gather all one's forces, get everyone together (in order to work on an important task) **4** to rise up in protest
○ **<> ngri·het**[3pl] **nervat** <> *loses* <>'s temper
○ **ngri·het nga shtrati/krevati/dysheku/jataku** "get out of bed" to get up from one's bed
○ **nuk ngri·het nga shtrati** "not get out of bed" to be unable to get out of bed: be really very ill
○ **ngri·het peshë** to spring to one's feet, get up quickly; spring into action
○ **<> ngri·het**[3sg] **pluhuri nga prapa** "<> *raises* dust in back" <> *is* talked about everywhere, <> *creates* a stir wherever <> *goes*

○ **ngri·het me vesë** "get up with the morning dew" to get up early in the morning
○ **<> ngri·het**[3sg] **zemra** "<>'s heart *freezes*" <> *gets* scared to death
○ **<> ngri·het**[3pl] **zorrët në grykë/fyt/te goja** "<>'s guts *rise* to <>'s throat/mouth" <> *feels* like throwing up

ngri·n
I § *vi* **1** to freeze **2** to become stiff/numb (with cold); feel extremely cold; become paralyzed
II § *vt* **1** to freeze; freeze-dry **2** to frost/coat/embroider with gold/silver
○ **ngri·n çark** to be struck with amazement
○ **<> ngri·n gjakun** to make <>'s blood run cold, terrify <>
○ **ësh·të ngrij shkrij** to be on pins and needles, be anxious and worried

ngri̱ *stem for 2nd pl pres, pind, imper, vp* <ngri·et
○ **Ngrije qafën!** "Lift your neck!" **1** Don't let yourself be exploited! **2** Keep your chin up!

ngri̱cë *nf* freezing weather, frost

ngri̱dh·et *vpr* **1** (of leavened dough) to rise **2** (*Fig*) to come into heat: rut **3** (*Fig*) (of animals) to get all worked up; fuss and pester (to be fed)

ngri̱dh·ur *adj (i)* (of leavened dough) risen
○ **<> ngrih·et**[3pl] **flokët përpjetë 1** <>'s hairs *stand* on end (with fear) **2** <>'s body *shakes* with rage
○ **Ngrihu prift të ulet/rrijë hoxha!** "Get up, (Catholic) priest, so that the (Moslem) priest can sit down!" Why should one person give up what he has just so some equal person can have it!?

ngri̱jë *nf* something frozen; frost, ice

*ngri̱më = ngri̱rë

ngri̱rë *adj (i)* **1** frozen; frozen stiff/solid; stiff **2** starched; well-ironed **3** frosted/embroidered in gold/silver

ngri̱rje *nf ger* <ngri·n

ngri̱shëm *adj (i)* capable of freezing, freezable

ngri̱t *stem for pdef, opt, adm, part* <ngre·, ngri·het

ngri̱të
I § *adj (i)* **1** frozen; icy; cold **2** (referring to a death) unfortunate
II § *n (i)* poor soul, loved one (dead person)

ngri̱tës
I § *adj* used for lifting
II § *nm* **1** wooden beam that raises and lowers the upper millstone to regulate the fineness of the grind = ngre̱hës **2** [*Tech*] apparatus for raising something heavy: lift rig **3** [*Sport*] weight lifter

*ngri̱tësi *nf* severe frost

ngri̱tje *nf ger* **1** <ngre·, ngri·het **2** rise: elevation, increase, improvement **3** elevation of land: rise ***4** (*Old*) inflation

ngri̱tur
I § *part* <ngre·et
II § *adj (i)* **1** raised, elevated **2** standing straight up; stiff and erect **3** (*Fig*) at an advanced/higher level ***4** frozen; frosted
III § *nf (e)* swelling, bump, protuberance
IV § *adv* **1** in a vertical position: up **2** no longer in bed: up

*ngri̱thët *adj (i)* distorted, wry

*ngrof = ngroh

ngroh·

I § *vt* **1** to make [] warm: warm; heat **2** *(Fig)* to excite

II § *vi* to give off heat

○ **s'**[] **ngroh·** [] *cannot get much satisfaction from* {}

○ **ngroh· dajren** to warm up the skin on the tambourine (in order to improve the sound of the instrument)

○ **e ngroh· në hi** to keep it (a feeling/secret) pent up inside

○ **ngroh· vezët 1** to brood/incubate eggs **2** to sit around doing nothing; take all day (at a task)

○ **<>a ngroh· xhepin** to fill <>'s pockets with money; give <> a lot of money

○ **s'<>a ngroh· zemrën** <> *cannot get much satisfaction from* {}

ngro'h·et *vpr* to get warm; warm up

○ **ngroh·et në diell** "bask in the sun" *(Colloq)* to do nothing, be idle; have no work to do

○ **ngroh·et në leshin e** {*pronominal adj*} "keep warm inside {*one's*} own fleece" to keep entirely to oneself

○ **ngroh·et në shullë** to sit around idly

○ **<> ngroh·et**³ᵍᵍ **zemra/shpirti** <> *feels* very much relieved; <> *feels* encouraged

***ngroha'dor'cë** *nf* muff

ngro'h¦ës

I § *nm* **1** heater, stove **2** [*Tech*] boiler of a steam engine **3** person who tends a furnace or oven

II § *adj* serving to heat

ngroh¦ësi¦ma't¦ës

I § *nm* [*Tech*] calorimeter = **nxehtësima't¦ës**

II § *adj* [*Tech*] calorimetric

ngroh¦ësi¦veç¦ue's *adj* heat-insulative

ngro'h¦je *nf ger* **1** <**ngroh·**, **ngro'h·et** **2** heating

ngroh¦ta'r *n* worker in a heating plant

ngro'h¦të

I § *adj (i)* warm

II § *nn (të)* warmth; means of generating/maintaining warmth

III § *adv* warm; warmly

ngroh¦t¦ë'si *nf* warmth

ngroh¦t¦ë'si¦ma't¦ës *nm* = **nxehtësima't¦ës**

ngroh¦t¦ë'si¦sht *adv* warmly

ngroh¦t¦o're *nf* heating system; heating plant

ngro'h¦ur

I § *part* <**ngroh·**

II § *adj (i)* **1** warmed, heated **2** *(Fig)* enheartened

○ **ësh·të ngrohur nën një diell** *(Iron)* to have no relationship (except to have been warmed by the same sun); be completely unrelated

***ngro'p¦ët** *OR* **ngro'p¦ur** *adj (i)* crippled

n¦grushto'·n *vt* to squeeze [] to extract its liquid: wring, squash

ngry'dh·et *vpr* to crowd together; get squashed

ngry'dh¦ët *adj (i)* compressed, dense, firm

n¦gry'k· *vt* = **ngryko'·n**

n¦gry'k¦as *adv* = **ngry'kë**

n¦gry'kë *adv* **1** (embrace) around the neck, hug **2** cradled in one's arms

n¦gry'k¦o'·n *vt* to embrace = **përqafo'·n**

ngrys· *vt* **1** to stay over for [a period of time] until darkness sets in **2** to spend [a period of time] unpleasantly; spend [the final period of life] **3** to give [a facial feature, one's face] a dark look, make [one's

face] look gloomy **4** *(Colloq)* to cause [] to be late: delay []

○ **ngrys· vetullat/ballin** to frown sadly, look glum

ngry's·et

I § *vp impers* it *grows* dark, it *becomes* evening

II § *vpr* **1** (of a day) to pass **2** to remain until darkness falls: spend a day (somewhere); stay late **3** *(Fig)* to put on a dark countenance: look gloomy, scowl

○ **ngrys·et e nuk gdhi·het** "one passes the evening and does not pass the dawn" to die before daybreak, die in one's sleep

ngrys¦ala'q *adj* always frowning: gloomy-faced, dour

ngry's¦ët *adj (i)* = **ngry'sur**

ngry's¦je *nf ger* **1** <**ngry's·**, **ngry's·et 2** period of time just after sunset: dusk of evening

ngry's¦ur

I § *adj (i)* gloomy

II § *nn (të)* evening time, dusk

III § *adv* **1** late in the day, toward dusk **2** *(Fig)* gloomily

***ngry'th¦ët** *adj (i)* inept, lazy, careless, slow, timorous

nguc· *nm (Pej)* = **ngu'cës**

nguc· *vt* **1** to poke **2** *(Fig)* to heckle/goad **3** *(Fig)* to incite, egg [] on **4** to cram, squeeze

ngu'c·et *vpr* **1** to cram/squeeze in **2** *(Fig)* to heckle/goad one another

ngu'c¦ës *n* person who tries to stir up trouble among others: provocateur, agitator, rabble-rouser

***nguc¦ë'ti'r¦e** *nf* velocity, speed

ngu'c¦je *nf ger* **1** <**ngu'c·**, **ngu'c·et 2** nuisance

ngu'c¦ta'r = **ngu'cës**

ngu'c¦ur *adv* squeezed/crammed together

ngufa's *stem for 1st sg pres, pl pres, 2nd & 3rd sg subj, pind* <**ngufa't·**

ngufa't· *vt* **1** to puff [] up **2** to open [one's eyes] wide

ngufa't·et *vpr* (of eyes) to bulge

nguji'm *nm ger* **1** <**ngujo'·n**, **ngujo'·het 2** siege, blockade **3** *(Old)* self-confinement to keep from being killed (in a blood feud)

ngujo'·het *vpr* **1** to stay indoors **2** to take protection inside a fortification; remain confined **3** to stake oneself in a good position; station oneself well

ngujo'·n *vt* **1** to shut and secure [a door] in a closed position, shut [] tight **2** to besiege; keep [] confined (indoors), shut [] in **3** to keep [] from moving

ngujo're *nf* heavy wooden door bar

nguju'ar *adj (i)* **1** blocked shut **2** besieged, under siege **3** confined

ngul

I § *nm* inherent characteristic, character trait

II § *adv* directly, straight

ngul·

I § *vt* **1** to thrust/drive [] in; insert, implant **2** to plant; plant/set [] securely, embed

II § *vi* to stay in one place, settle down; take up residence

○ **e ngul· bririn** "plant one's horn" *(Contempt)* to bite the dust: die

○ **ngul· cak** *(Colloq)* to put down one's roots: settle down

○ **ngul· çadrat** to stake one's tents, make camp

○ **ngul· hunj e shkul· hunj** "drive in posts and pull out posts" **1** to do useless work **2** to make provocative/sarcastic remarks

○ **ngul· këmbë** to insist

◦ **ngul· këmbë si mushkë** to be stubborn as a mule
◦ **ngul· këmbët në akull** "plant one's feet on ice" to have nowhere to turn for help
◦ **e ngul· me pullë (fjalën)** "seal it with a stamp" to drive the point home
◦ **ngul qepë e shkul hudhra** "plant onions and dig up garlic" to do useless work
◦ **ngul· rrënjë** to take root; settle down, take up permanent residence: become implanted
◦ **<> ngul· sytë** to stare at <>
◦ **ngul· thembrat** to dig in one's heels, refuse to budge
◦ **<> ngul· thikën prapa kurrizit/shpinës** to stick a knife in <>'s back, betray <>

ngu'l·*et vpr* **1** to be implanted **2** to become ensconced **3** *(Fig)* to take up residence: settle down to live
◦ **<> ngul·***et* **thikë në zemër** to cause <> deep emotional anguish: strike <> to the heart

ngu'las OR **ngu'lazi** *adv* persistently; insistently

*****ngulç**i**m = gulçim**

ngulç**i**š**i** *nf* persistence, zeal

ngu'lë**t** *adj (i)* **1** fixed in position: stationary, fast, firm **2** *(Fig)* persistent, steadfast; permanent

nguli**m** *nm ger* **1** <**ngul·***et* **2** settlement

nguli**s** *stem for 1st sg pres, pl pres, 2nd & 3rd sg subj, pind* <**ngul**i**t·**

nguli**t·** *vt* **1** to implant [] in mind: fixate **2** to institute

nguli**t·***et vpr* **1** to hold on tight **2** to become fixated **3** *(Fig)* to make an indelible impression **4** *(Fig)* to become well established
◦ **ngulit·***et* **pas <>** to be hold on tight to <>

nguli**t**ë**s** *nm, adj* [*Chem*] fixative

nguli**tje** *nf ger* **1** <**ngul**i**t·**, **ngul**i**t·***et* **2** establishment

ngu'lje *nf ger* <**ngul·**, **ngul·***et*

ngu'lm *nm* persistence, perseverance

ngulmë**r**o**·***n* **= ngulmo·***n*

ngulmë**s**i *nf* [*Phys*] tenacity, ductility

ngu'lmë**t** *adj (i)* persistent

ng**ulm**i**m** *nm ger* **1** <**ngulmo·***n* **2** persistence; insistence

ngulmo**·***n vi* to insist, persist

ngulmu**es** *adj* relentless; persistent

ngulo**·***n vi* to take up residence: settle down to live
◦ **<>***i* **ngulo·***n* **këmbët** "fasten <>'s legs" to hobble <>; make it difficult for <> to move, make it hard for <> to do anything; be a terrible burden on <>

ngu'lshë**m** *adj (i)* persistent, steadfast

ngu'ltas *adv* steadily, persistently

ngu'lthi *adv* **= kryengulthi**

ngu'lur *adj (i)* **1** fixed in place, immobile **3** permanently settled **4** persistent

*****n**g**uq·**
  I § *vt* to make [] red/brown
  II § *vi* to look red/brown, have a red/brown appearance

*****n**g**uq·***et vpr* to become red: redden, turn brownish

*****n**g**ur·** **= nguro's·**

ng**ur·***et* **= nguro's·***et*

ng**ura**ç**a'k** *adj* very firm and hard

ng**ura**ç**a**ç**ke** *nf* type of pear with firm and hard fruit

nguraf**ë**t *adv* hesitantly

ng**ur**ë**s**i *nf* hardness

ng**ur**i**m** *nm ger* <**nguro·***n*

ngurmazo**·***n vi* to talk until hoarse

ng**ur**o**·***het vpr* **= guro'·***het*

ng**ur**o**·***n vt* **1** to make [] hard as rock **2 = nguros·** **3** (of a dog) to howl

ng**ur**o**s·** *vt* to turn [] to stone: petrify, fossilize

ng**ur**o**s·***et vpr* to become petrified/fossilized

ng**ur**o**sje** *nf ger* **1** <**nguros·**, **nguros·***et* **2** fossil

ng**ur**o**sur** *adj (i)* petrified; fossilized

*****n**g**ur**s**i**na** *np* *(Reg Gheg)* solids

ng**ur**t**ë**
  I § *adj (i)* **1** [*Phys*] solid **2** rigid, inflexible
  II § *adv* inflexibly

ng**urt**ë**s**i *nf* **1** hardness; solidity **2** *(Fig)* rigidity, inflexibility

ng**urt**ë**s**i**m** *nm ger* **1** <**ngurtëso·***n*, **ngurtëso·***het* **2** rigid object

ng**urt**ë**s**o**·***het vpr* to become hard and rigid

ng**urt**ë**s**o**·***n vt* **1** to make [] hard and rigid, turn into a solid: harden **2** *(Fig)* to cause [] to lose feeling: numb

ng**urt**ë**s**u**ar** *adj (i)* **1** solidified; hardened, made rigid **2** rigid, inflexible

ngurr·
  I § *vt* **1** to make [] rigid **2** *(Fig)* to check [an onrush/impulse]
  II § *vi* to be fixed in one spot, stand transfixed

ngu'rrët *adj (i)* hesitant, halting; halted

ngurri**m** *nm ger* **1** <**ngurro'·***n* **2** hesitation, hesitance, hesitancy

ngurro**·***n vi* to hesitate

*****n**g**urr**o**s·** **= nguros·**

*****n**g**urr**o**sje** *nf* stubbornness

*****n**g**urr**o**t**o**·***n* **= nguro'·***n*

*****n**g**urr**u**ç**·***et vpr* to huddle up, cower

ngurru**es** *adj* hesitant, reluctant

*****ngurr**u**e**s**h**ë**m** *adj (i)* hesitantly, reluctantly

ngus *stem for 1st sg pres, pl pres, 2nd & 3rd sg subj, pind* <**ngut·**

ngush· *vt* to hug

ngu'sh·*et vpr* to hug one another: embrace

ngushë**ll**i *nf* comforted/cheered-up feeling: cheer

ngushë**ll**i**m** *nm ger* **1** <**ngushëllo·***n*, **ngushëllo'·***het* **2** condolence **3** consolation

ngushë**ll**i**mta'r** *adj, n (Elev)* **= ngushëllu'es**

ngushë**ll**o**·***het vpr* to find consolation, be comforted; be cheered up

ngushë**ll**o**·***n vt* **1** to try to cheer up []: console **2** to offer condolences to [], express one's sympathy to []

ngushë**ll**u**ar** *adj (i)* consoled, comforted, cheered-up

ngushë**ll**u**es** *adj* affording solace/consolation, serving to cheer one up

ngu'shtë
  I § *adj (i)* **1** narrow **2** small in area **3** confining a small space: tight; tight-fitting; close together **4** *(Fig)* causing difficulty
  II § *adv* **1** tightly, closely **2** with little space, squeezed in **3** *(Fig)* in a difficult situation, in trouble **4** *(Fig)* narrowly
  ◦ **ësh·të ngushtë me** [] to be having trouble with []

ngushtë**s**i *nf* **1** narrowness **2** tight space **3** *(Fig)* tight situation (economically)

ngushtë**s**i**r**ë *nf* **= ngushtësi**

ngushtë**s**i**sht** *adv* narrowly

ngushtícë *nf* **1** strait **2** difficult situation; tight economic situation, economic straits **3** [*Anat*] isthmus

ngushtím *nm ger* **1** <ngushto·*n*, ngushto·*het* **2** [*Med*] stenosis **3** constriction **4** (*Old*) difficult situation, tight straits

ngushtínë *nf* **1** strait **2** tightness

ngushto·het *vpr* **1** to become narrower; narrow down **2** to squeeze closer together **3** to become reduced in size/scope/perceptibility **4** (*Fig*) to be tightly constrained, be forced; be in a tight spot
  ∘ <> **ngushto·**het[3sg] **zemra** <>'s heart bleeds

ngushto·n *vt* **1** to make [] narrower; make [] smaller; reduce [] in scope, restrict **2** to tighten **3** (*Fig*) to constrain tightly, force [] to do something; put in a tight spot

ngushtúar *adj* (*i*) **1** made narrower: narrower **2** (*Fig*) in a tight spot, in difficulty

ngushull = ngushëll

ngut *nm* haste, rush; urgency

ngut· *vt* to pressure [] into haste: rush []

ngut·et *vpr* to act in haste, act hastily

ngutas *adv* hastily

ngutësí *nf* **1** urgent need, urgency **2** haste, forcefulness; impetus

ngutësísht *adv* hastily; urgently

ngutje *nf ger* **1** <ngut·, ngut·et **2** haste; urgency

ngutshëm *adj* (*i*) **1** urgent **2** without delay: immediate, instant **3** hasty

ngutshmërí *nf* **1** urgency **2** haste

ngutthi *adv* hastily

ngutur
  I § *part* <ngut·, ngut·et
  II § *adj* (*i*) hasty

NGV *abbrev* <Ndërmarrja e grumbullimit të vjetërsirave agency for wholesaling of used clothes

NGj *abbrev* <Ndërmarrja gjeologjike geological agency

ngja·n *vi* **1** to resemble <>, be similar **2** to suit **3** to seem, appear **4** to occur, happen
  ∘ <>a **ngja·**n (*Colloq*) to imitate <>
  ∘ **ngja·**n[pl] **si dy pika uji** "be alike as two drops of water" to be alike as two peas in a pod

ngjaçë *nf* [*Ichth*] fish testicles

ngjak *nm* **1** blood clot **2** (*Fig*) obsessive guilt feeling

ngjalan *nm* eel pond

ngjalë *nf* **1** [*Ichth*] eel (*Anguilla anguilla*) **2** (*Fig Pej*) wily person able to get out of a bad situation
  ∘ **ngjalë balçe/balte** [*Ichth*] (*Anguilla latirostris*) = goçe
  ∘ **ngjalë deti** [*Ichth*] = ngjalë e egër
  ∘ **ngjalë dyngjyrëshe** [*Ichth*] bicolored false moray *Chlopsis bicolor*
  ∘ **ngjalë e egër** [*Ichth*] conger eel *Conger conger*
  ∘ **ngjalë fërgëlluese** [*Ichth*] electric eel

ngjalístër *nf* small and very thin eel

***ngjalshëm** *adj* (*i*) eel-like

ngjall· *vt* **1** to bring [] back to life: revive; reawaken: rouse, enliven **2** (*Colloq*) to heal, cure **3** to feed [] in order to make fat: fatten [livestock]
  ∘ **ngjall· të vdekurin nga varri** "bring the dead back from the grave" **1** to be capable of performing miracles **2** to be extraordinarily delicious

ngjall·et *vpr* **1** to come back to life: revive **2** (*Colloq*) to recover from an illness: get well **3** to gain a lot of

weight: get fat **4** (*Fig*) (of a mental state) to arise, be generated

ngjallëm = ngjallur

***ngjallis** *stem for 1st sg pres, pl pres, 2nd & 3rd sg subj, pind* <ngjallít·

***ngjallít·** *vt* = ngjall·

***ngjallítës** *adj* reviving, refreshing

ngjallje *nf ger* **1** <ngjall·, ngjall·et **2** revival, resurrection

***ngjallmë** *adj* (*i*) fat

ngjallo·n *vi* (*Reg*) to rush, run

ngjallur *adj* (*i*) stocky, beefy, fat

ngjamë
  I § *part* <nga·n
  II § *nf* (*e*) resemblance

***ngjamës** *adj* = ngjashëm

ngjarë
  I § *part* <ngja·n <ngjas·
  II § *nf* (*e*) (*Colloq*) incident, happening, event
  ∘ **ka (pak/shumë) të ngjarë** there's a (slight/good) possibility, it could be

ngjarje *nf* happening, event, incident

ngjas *stem for 1st sg pres, 1st & 3rd pl pres, 2nd & 3rd sg subj* <ngjet·

ngjasí *nf* = ngjashmërí

ngjasím *nm* = ngjashmërí

ngjaso·n *vi* to bear a similarity

***ngjasshëm** *adj* (*i*) **1** = gjasshëm **2** = ngjashëm

ngjashëm *adj* (*i*) similar, alike

***ngjâshëm** *adj* (*i*) (*Reg Gheg*) = gjëshëm

ngjashmërí *nf* similarity; resemblance

ngjat
  I § *adv* (*Colloq*) alongside
  II § *prep* (*abl*) **1** alongside, next to **2** in comparison with, next to

ngjat· *vt, vi* to lengthen = zgjat·

ngjat·et *vpr* = zgjat·et

ngjatangjatas *adv* very close/near

ngjatesë *nf* prolongation, extension, projection

ngjatë *adj* (*i*) (*Reg*) proximate in time or social relationship, near

***ngjatím** = zgjatím

ngjatje = zgjatje

ngjatjeta *interj* (*Colloq*) = tungjatjeta

ngjatjetím *nm* (*Colloq*) salutation, greeting

ngjatjeto·het *vpr* to exchange friendly and polite greetings

ngjatjeto·n *vt* (*Colloq*) **1** to greet politely in a friendly fashion **2** to congratulate ***3** to acknowledge, thank

***ngjatjetúar** *nn* (*të*) acknowledgement, thanks

ngjato·n *vt* **1** = zgjato· *n* **2** to tether [an animal]

ngje *stem for pdef, opt* <ngjy·et

***ngjedh·** = ngjesh·

ngjelkë *nf* (*Colloq Pej*) gossipy woman

***ngjelmësí** *nf* saltiness

***ngjelmëso·n** *vt* to add salt: salt

***ngjelmët** *adj* (*i*) salty

ngjelthi *adv* without advantage to either: even, equal

***ngjell·** *vt* = ngjall·

***ngjeq·** *vt* to stifle

ngjesh· *vt* **1** to apply pressure on []: compress; squeeze; squeeze/tamp [] down **2** (*Fig*) to stuff, cram **3** to knead **4** (*Colloq*) to strike hard; bludgeon, beat

5 to attach [] tightly to the body: gird [] on **6** to encircle [] tightly with a hoop
○ **<>a ngjesh·** **1** *(Colloq)* to lay the blame/responsibility wrongly on <> **2** *(Colloq)* to hit [] in <>, hit [] suddenly: lay one on [], paste [] one
○ **e ngjesh· barkun** to stuff one's belly full
○ **ngjesh· radhët** to join ranks, unite forces

n|gjeshár *nm* roof beam, tie beam, girder

n|gjeshátar|e *nf* masseuse; midwife

n|gjesh|ës *nm* (gas) compressor = **kompresór**

n|gjeshët *adj (i)* **1** dense **2** = **ngje'shur**

n|gjesh|je *nf ger* **1** <**ngje'sh·**, **ngji'sh·**et **2** compression

n|gjeshmërí *nf* compressibility

n|gje'shur
I §ˌ part <**ngjesh·**
II § adj (i) compressed; compact, dense; tightly packed, sturdy; felted
III § nn (të) = **ngje'shje**
IV § adv close together

n|gjeshurí *nf* denseness

ngje't· *vi* **1** to happen, occur **2** = **ngja·n**

*****ngje'tshëm** *adj (i)* adjoining, close-by

n|gjeth· *vt* to cause to shudder/shiver
○ **<> ngjeth· mishtë/zemrën** to make <>'s flesh crawl

n|gje'th·et *vpr* **1** to shudder, shiver **2** to break out in gooseflesh **3** to break out in leaves, be clothed in leaves **4** *(Fig)* to be revitalized
○ **<> ngjeth·**et^{3sg} **mishtë** "<>'s flesh *crawls/shivers*" **1** <>'s flesh *crawls*; <> *shakes* with fright **2** <> *is deeply touched/moved*

n|gje'th|ës *adj* causing one to shudder/shiver: chilling, eerie

*****ngje'thlí** *nf* foliage

n|gje'th|je *nf ger* **1** <**ngje'th·**, **ngje'th·**et **2** shudder, shiver

n|gje'tho·n *vt* to cover/intertwine with leafy branches

n|gje'thshëm *adj (i)* = **ngje'thës**

n|gje'thur|a *np (të)* convulsive tremors: shudders, the shivers, the shakes

ngjërátë *nf* dip to be eaten with bread

ngjëro·n
I § vt to sample [food] for flavor: taste
II § vi **1** to walk gingerly/carefully to avoid getting dirty **2** *(Fig)* to kill time

ngjícë *nf* fishing net with cork floats and lead or stone weights to make it lie vertical in the water

*****n|gjidhur**
I § adj (i) complicated, intricate
II § nn (të) critical point: crux, crisis, node

*****ngjilít** *nm* javelin, spear, dart

*****ngjín·**et *vpr* = **ngí·het**

*****ngjínd·**et = **gje'nd·**et

ngjine'së *nf* = **agjëre'së**

ngjir *nm* = **gjir**

ngjir· *vt* to make [] hoarse

ngjir·et *vpr* **1** to get hoarse **2** *(Fig)* to yell oneself hoarse

*****ngjirr** = **ngjirr**

ngjirís· *vt* to make [milk] curdle: sour

ngjírje *nf ger* **1** <**ngjir·**, **ngjir·**et **2** hoarseness; raucousness

ngjirur *adj (i)* hoarse; raucous

ngjís
I § stem for 1st sg pres, pl pres, 2nd & 3rd sg subj, pind <**ngjít·**
II § stem for 2nd pl pres, pind <**ngjet·**

ngjís·et *vpr* **1** to become more compact, get denser **2** to get very close **3** to bind arms to one's waist: gird on arms **4** *(Fig)* to eat till stuffed

ngjísh *stem for 2nd pl pres, pind, imper, vp* <**ngjesh·**

ngjít·
I § vt **1** to attach; affix; stick with [] **2** to attach [] together: bond, weld **3** to stick close to [] **4** to climb [] **5** to move [] to a higher position, take [] up **6** to infect <> with [one's disease/emotion] **7** *(Colloq)* to smack []
II § vi **1** to be sticky **2** to stay in place: stick **3** (of food) to agree with <> and taste good
○ **<> ngjít· dorën/krahun** to help <> out of trouble: lend <> a helping hand
○ **<> ngjít· dhëmbin** to fasten one's teeth in <>, bite <>
○ **<> ngjít·**$.^{3sg}$ **fjala** what <> says has an effect, <> *is* effective as a speaker
○ **[] ngjít· me barrë** to make [] pregnant, stick [] with a big belly
○ **<> ngjít· në zemër** to become very dear to <>, <> *gets* deeply attached to {}
○ **<> ngjít· si pullë poste** "stick to <> like a postage stamp" to follow <> closely: stick to <> like glue, not let <> out of one's sight
○ **<>i ngjít· sytë** to fasten one's eyes on <>
○ **i ngjít· shkallët një nga një** "ascend the stairs one at a time" to act/speak carefully and prudently

ngjít·et *vpr* **1** to become/remain attached: stick, stick together **2** (of bones) to knit **3** to infect <> **4** *(Old)* to become apprenticed **5** to climb; rise **6** *(Fig)* to reach a high level
○ **<> ngjít·**et^{3sg} **barku pas shpine/ me kurrizin** "<>'s stomach *sticks* to <>'s back" <> *is starving*
○ **ngjít·et edhe pa shkallë** "climb even without a ladder" to be extremely resourceful, be ingenious
○ **nuk <> ngjít·**et^{3sg} **ferra gjëkundi** "brambles *don't* stick to <> anywhere" <> can't hold on to money, <> *doesn't* have a nickel to <>'s name
○ **<> ngjít·**et^{3sg} **gjuha pas qiellze** the words *stick* to the roof of <>'s mouth: <> *becomes* speechless
○ **ngjít·et lart 1** to go uphill **2** to get higher, grow
○ **ngjít·et me barrë** to be pregnant: be stuck with a big belly
○ **ngjít·et pas <> 1** to stick to <> **2** *(Colloq)* to be obsessed with <>
○ **s'<> ngjít·**et^{3sg} **qimja në trup** "<>'s hair *doesn't* stick to <>'s body" <> *is* always clean and well-groomed
○ **ngjít·et si pallaska pas brezit** to stick like a leech
○ **<> ngjít·et si rriqër** "stick to <> like a tick" to keep pestering <>
○ **ngjít·**et^{pl} **shpinë për shpinë** to stand back to back (defending each other), stand shoulder to shoulder (helping each item
○ **ngjít·**et^{pl} **shpinë për shpinë** to stand back to back (defending each other), stand shoulder to shoulder (helping each other)

ngjít *stem for pind, 2nd pl pres, imper, vp* <**ngjet·**

ngjítas *adv* **1** immediately adjacent, very next, next-door **2** sticking close

ngjitë *adv* = **ngji**tas

ngjitë
  I § *adj* **1** adhesive; sticky **2** infectious, contagious **3** rising, ascending **4** [*Bot*] creeping, clinging, climbing **5** [*Bot*] glutenous
  II § *n* climber; mountain climber
  III § *nm* **1** adhesive **2** [*Bot*] ivy, English ivy *Hedera helix* **3** [*Bot*] catchweed, bedstraw *Galium*

ngjitëse *nf* **1** welding torch; soldering iron **2** adhesive

ngjitje *nf ger* **1** < **ngji**t·, **ngjit**·et **2** juncture between two joined pieces **3** ascent **4** [*Bot*] zinnia *(Zinnia)*

ngjitshëm *adj (i)* **1** adhesive; sticky **2** viscous

ngjitshmëri *nf* **1** adhesiveness; stickiness **2** [*Chem*] viscosity

ngjitur
  I § *adj (i)* **1** adjacent, adjoining, contiguous, abutting **2** *(Fig)* affectionate, loving **3** *(Fig Pej)* annoyingly clinging
  II § *adv* **1** contiguously **2** clingingly
  ∘ **i ngjitur me pështymë** "held together by spit" not securely fastened, held together by chewing gum

ngjiz· *vt* **1** [*Dairy*] to create a clotted product: make [a curdled dairy product (cheese, yogurt)], clot [blood] **2** to form [a hard object] out of an initially soft substance: pot

ngjiz·et *vpr* **1** [*Dairy*] to curdle into cheese/yogurt; coagulate, clot **2** (of an embryo) to take shape in the mother's womb **3** *(Fig)* to start to take shape

ngjizës *nm* coagulant

ngjizje *nf ger* **1** < **ngji**z·, **ngji**z·et **2** something made up, imaginary object: fabrication

ngjizshëm *adj (i)* coagulable

ngjizur *adj (i)* **1** curdled; coagulated **2** *(Fig)* fabricated, imagined

*ngjo·n = dëgjo·n

ngjok· *vt* **1** to sting, prick **2** *(Fig)* to pester

ngjok·et *vpr* to wrestle

ngjollë = njo**ll**ë

*ngjo·më = njo·më

*ngjomështí = njomështí

ngjy·het *vpr* **1** to apply too much make-up **2** to dye one's hair **3** to be receptive to dye: dye well

ngjye·n
  I § *vt* **1** to dip [] in liquid **2** to dye **3** to change the color of []: color, paint
  II § *vi (Fig Colloq)* to grease palms; fix things up, arrange matters
  ∘ **e ngjye·n (bukën) në dhallë** "soak (bread) in buttermilk" to be very poor: be down to eating nothing but beans
  ∘ **e ngjye·n turpin me bukë** "dip one's bread in shame" **1** to eat crow **2** to sell one's soul to the devil

ngjyer *adj (i)* colored by immersion in a liquid: dyed

ngjyerje *nf ger* < **ngj**ye·n, **ngjy**·het

ngjyes *OR* **ngjy**ës *nm* dyer

ngjyesë *nf* dye, tincture

ngjyranë *nf* inkpot

ngjyra-ngjyra *adj* colorful, multicolored; motley, parti-colored

ngjyrartë *adj (Poet)* golden

ngjyresë *nf* overall distinguishing character of a time or place

ngjyrë *nf* **1** color **2** coloring liquid: dye, paint, ink, stain **3** complexion **4** = **ngjy**resë

∘ **ngjyr**ë *{noun in the indefinite ablative case}* names or attributes the color of ◇ **ngjyr**ë **molle** apple-colored
∘ **ngjyrë açike** amber colored
∘ **ngjyrë arre** dark brown
∘ **ngjyrë bube** yellowish brown
∘ **ngjyrë gjaku** blood red, scarlet
∘ **ngjyrë hashashi** light violet color
∘ **ngjyrë limoni** greenish yellow
∘ **ngjyrë qumështi** cream-colored
∘ **ngjyr**ë **e rëndë** ugly color
∘ **ngjyra sapuni** pastel color
∘ **ngjyrë tulle** brick red

ngjyrëçelët *adj* light-colored

ngjyrëgështenjë *adj* chestnut-colored, brown

ngjyrëkafe *adj* coffee-colored, brown

ngjyrëkaki *adj* khaki

ngjyrëkashtë *adj* straw-colored, light tan

ngjyrëlimon *adj* lemon-colored

ngjyrëmanushaqe *adj* violet

ngjyrëmjaltë *adj* honey-colored

ngjyrëndezur *adj* bright-colored

ngjyrëportokall *adj* orange

*ngjyrët *adj (i)* colored, dyed, tinted

ngjyrëtrëndafil *adj* rose

ngjyrëtullë *adj* brick-colored

ngjyrëthellë *adj* dark-colored

ngjyrëvishnje *adj* dark cherry-colored

ngjyrëvjollcë *adj* violet

ngjyrëzezë *adj (i)* = karabojë

ngjyrim *nm ger* **1** < **ngjyr**o·n, **ngjyr**o·het **2** shade of color, tint

ngjyro·het *vpr* to take on a color

ngjyro·n *vt* to color; lend color to []

ngjyro**s**· *vt* **1** to apply color to []: color, dye, paint, stain **2** to dirty [] with a liquid: stain

ngjyro**s**·et *vpr* to take on color

ngjyrosje *nf ger* < **ngjyr**os·, **ngjyr**os·et

ngjyrosur *adj (i)* colored; multicolored

ngjyrshëm *adj (i)* colorful, variegated in color

ngjyruar *adj (i)* of a particular color; altered in color; adorned with color: rouged

ngjyrues
  I § *nm* **1** coloring substance/matter: dye **2** dye technician
  II § *adj* serving to alter color: coloring

*Niderland *nm* Netherlands

*nieri *nm* = njeri

*nierz = njerëz

*nigël *nf (Old)* water nymph, mermaid

nigjah *nm (Old)* concluding part of a Moslem religious wedding in which the bride gives money to her husband as a bond to be returned if he divorces her; the money bond

nihilist *n* nihilist

nihilizëm *nm* nihilism

nijet *nm (Colloq)* intention

nikel *nm* nickel *(Ni)*

nikelim *nm ger* **1** < **nikel**o·n **2** nickelplating; coating of nickelplate

nikelo·n *vt* to plate with nickel

nikeluar *adj (i)* nickelplated

Niko *nf with masc agreement* Niko (male name)

Nikodïm *nm* Nicodemus

nikoqïr *nm* **1** good family provider and manager, provident and thrifty head of the family, householder; man of the house **2** economically responsible person

nikoqïr|e *nf* woman who is a good house manager; lady of the house

nikoqïr'llë k *nm (np ~ qe)* thrift; thriftiness; economicalness

nikoqïrth *nm* [*Ornit*] eagle owl (*Bubo bubo*)

nikotïn|e *nf* nicotine

NIL *abbrev* <**Ndërmarrja industriale lokale e... (Old)** local agency for industrial ...

NILRG [*nil-rë-gë*] *abbrev* <**Ndërmarrja industriale lokale e rrobave të gatshme** agency that makes ready-made garments

nim *nm* low sofa-bed along the wall of a room = **minde'r**

nimfe' *nm* [*Archeol*] nymphaeum

nimfë *nf* nymph

ninana'në *nf* lullaby

nin ëz *nf* **1** pupil of the eye **2** (*Fig*) lasting visual impression

***ninu'l·** OR **ninuli's** *vt* to rock [] in a cradle = **nanu'ri's·**

***ninu'llë** *nf* (*Reg Arb*) cradle

ninu'llë *nf* lullaby

nip *nm (np ~ ër)* **1** grandson **2** nephew

nipa'sh *nm* son of one's sister or daughter: nephew

ni'p|çe *nf* (*Pet*) young grandson/nephew

ni'p|ër *np* **1** <**nip 2** grandchildren, descendants

nip|ëri *nf collec* grandchildren; posterity

nip|ësi *nf* nepotism

ni'ples *nm* [*Tech*] pipe coupling threaded on both ends: nipple

nip'o'll *nm* (*Reg*) = **nip**

***niq-** *vt* (*Old*) to rent, hire

NIQ *abbrev* <**Ndërmarrja e industrializimit të qumështit** agency for industrial milk processing

***niqa's·** *vt* (*Old*) to rent [] out, let

***niqa'sje** *nf ger* (*Old*) <**niqa's·**

Nïqi *nm with fem agreement* Niqi (female name)

nis·
I § *vt* **1** to start, begin; begin to eat [] **2** to start [] off: send [] off, dispatch **3** to bedeck [] for a wedding **4** (*Colloq*) to start and drive (a vehicle)

II § *vi* **1** to commence, set in, begin **2** to open, start
o **nis· rrugën 1** to take to the road, leave home **2** to set off (on a trip/journey)
o **nis· udhë/udhën 1** to take to the road, leave home **2** to set off (on a trip/journey)
o **nis· ulërimën** to start howling; begin the wailing (for the dead)
o **Nisën vallet kur pushuan daullet.** "They began the dances when the drums stopped." (said when an action is taken tardily) They locked the stable door after the horse was stolen.

ni's·et *vpr* **1** to start off/out; set out, depart **2** to get bedecked for a wedding
o **nis·et me yje** "get started with the stars" to get up very early in the morning
o **nis·et nuse** to get dressed and adorned as a bride on her wedding day
o **nis·et va pa va** to leave without knowing where one is going

***nisa'k** *nm* = **nisja'k**

niseso's *adv* = **gjithnjë**

niseshte' *nf* starch

***ni's|ë** *nf* (*Old*) finery

ni's|ës
I § *adj* beginning, initial
II § *n* beginner

***nisi** *nf* (*Reg Gk*) island

***nisiatïv|ë** *nf* initiative

***nisiato'r** *n* **1** initiator; entrepreneur *2 enterprising

nisja'k *nm* novice, beginner

ni'sje *nf ger* **1** <**ni's·**, **ni's·et 2** start, beginning; departure, outset **3** origin, source **4** [*Sport*] starting place: start

ni'smë *nf* **1** initiative **2** point of departure

ni'smë's *nm* = **nismëta'r**

nismëta'r *n* person who takes the initiative: initiator

nista'r *adj* initiatory, starting

nisto'r *adj* [*Ling*] initial

nisto're *nf* [*Ling*] initial sound

ni'sur *adj* (*i*) **1** begun, started **2** bedecked for a wedding
o **e nisur dhe e stolisur 1** dressed and adorned as a bride **2** all dressed up, dressed to kill **3** dressed ostentatiously, putting on the dog

NISh *abbrev* <**Ndërmarrja industriale shtetërore** (*Old*) state agency for industry

nisha'dër *nm* **1** sal ammoniac (*ammonium chloride*) **2** (*Colloq*) saltpeter

nisha'n
I § *nm* **1** birthmark mole; scar **2** distinguishing mark **3** [*Ethnog*] token exchanged as a symbol of betrothal: engagement ring **4** (*Colloq*) target *5 gunsight **6** omen **7** (*Old*) decoration awarded to mark distinction: medal
II § *adj* distinguished
o **nishanet e mishit** choice cuts of meat served to the most honored guests

nisha'n|xhi *nm (np ~ nj)* (*Colloq*) sharpshooter, marksman

***nisha'ste** OR **nishe'ste** *nf* = **niseshte'**

nishk *nm* (*Colloq*) **1** chip/splinter of wood **2** twinge in the chest that interferes with breathing; pleurisy **3** lung fever

***ni'shk|ë** *nf* (*Reg Kos*) waist

NIShPF *abbrev* <**Ndërmarrja industriale shtetërore e prodhimeve farmaceutike** (*Old*) state agency for industrial pharmaceutical products

***nishte'r** *nm* chisel

nitra't *adj* [*Chem*] nitrate

nitrïk *nm* [*Chem*] nitric

nitroglicerïn|ë *nf* [*Chem*] nitroglycerine

nitrogje'n *nm* nitrogen

nitrolla'k *nm* nitrocellulose

nitro'r *adj* [*Chem*] nitrous

nive'l *nm* level

nivelïm *nm ger* <**nivelo'·n**, **nivelo'·het**

nivelo'·het *vpr* to reach the same level; even out

nivelo'·n *vt* **1** to make [] level, level [] out; bring to the same level **2** to adjust the level of [] **3** (*Fig*) to consider [] to be at the same level **4** (*Fig Pej*) to equate [] (falsely)

nivelu'a'r *adj* (*i*) evened/leveled out

nivelu'es
I § *nm* **1** earth leveler **2** [*Tech*] altimeter
II § *adj* serving to level/flatten out

niza'm *nm* [*Hist*] recruit/soldier in the Turkish army during the Ottoman Empire

*n|ka'h|e *OR* **n|ka'h|je** *nf* (*Reg Gheg*) = **shkak**

NKB *abbrev* < **Ndërmarrja komunale e banesave** public utility company for residential dwellings

NKEL *abbrev* < **Ndërmarrja komunale elektrike** agency for providing local electrical utilities

NKEM *abbrev* < **Ndërmarrja komunale elektromekanike** communal electromechanical utility

n|keq· *vt* to make [] worse; spoil, ruin

n|ke'q·et *vpr* to go bad: spoil, be ruined; get worse

*n|kra'h|ë *adv* **1** (resting) in the arms **2** on the shoulders

NKU *abbrev* < **Ndërmarrja komunale e ujësjellësit** communal water utility

*n|kuq. *vt* = **kuq·**

*n|ku'q·et *vpr* = **ku'q·**et

*n|kuraji'm *nm ger* **1** < **nkurajo'·**n **2** encouragement

*n|kurajo'·n *vt* to encourage

NMD *abbrev* < **Ndërmarrja e metal-drurit** agency that provides services for metal- and woodwork

NMN *abbrev* < **Ndërmarrja e materialeve të ndërtimit** agency for construction materials

NN *abbrev* < **Ndërmarrja e ndërtimit** agency for construction

NNI *abbrev* < **Ndërmarrja e ndërtimeve industriale** agency for industrial buildings

NNU *abbrev* < **Ndërmarrja e ndërtimit të urave** agency for bridge construction

*nobare' *adv* at least

nobo't *nm* hayfork for pitching grain sheaves

*noc *nm* dwarf

no'ca *np fem* necklace of metal disks or coins

*no'ca = **ndoca**

nocio'n *nm* **1** [*Phil*] concept **2** notion

*no'ç|ë *nf* = **no'çkë**

no'ç|kë *nf* **1** protruding part of a bone or bone joint; ankle, knuckle, fetlock **2** nodule; knot (in wood) **3** snout, trunk
- **no'çkë e do'rës** wrist
- **no'çkë e gishtit** knuckle
- **no'çkë e kë'mbës** ankle

no'fk|ë *nf* nickname

no'full *nf* **1** [*Anat*] jaw, jawbone **2** [*Tech*] clamping device, clamp

nofull|da'l|ë *adj* having a protruding jaw

nofull|gje'r|ë *adj* wide-jawed

nofull|o'r *adj* [*Anat*] maxillary, mandibular

nofull|o'r|ë *np* [*Invert*] mandibulata

nofull|shtrë'mb|ër *adj* having a twisted jaw

no'jm|ë *nf* (*Colloq*) communicative gesture: nod, wink

noka'ut *nm* **1** [*Sport*] knockout **2** (*Fig*) bad defeat

nokda'un *nm* [*Boxing*] knockdown

noksa'n
  I § *nm* (*Colloq*) **1** defect, infirmity **2** wacky and cantankerous person: crank
  II § *adj* **1** (*Colloq*) broken-down, crippled, defective **2** cranky

nom *nm* (*Old*) law, legal code
- **Nom i dytë** Deuteronomy

noma'd
  I § *nm* nomad
  II § *adj* nomádic

*nomati's· *vt* **1** to invoke; conjure up [], incant ***2** to cite

*nom|bër|ë's *nm* lawmaker

*nom|dhën|ë's *nm* lawgiver

nome' *nf* corral

nomenklatu'r|ë *nf* = **emërte's|ë**

*nom|ë'rísht *adv* lawfully, legally

*no'më|shëm *adj* (i) legitimate, legal

nomina'l *adj* nominal

nominati'v *nm* [*Ling*] nominative

*nom|ta'r *nm* man of law, doctor of law

*no'm|të *adj* (i) lawful, legal

no'nius *nm* [*Tech*] vernier scale

*nonto'·n *vt* to suit, fit; match

nopra'n *adj* (*Colloq*) perverse, intractable: ornery

nor *nm* [*Ornit*] diver (bird) (*Gavia*)
- **nori gushëku'q** [*Ornit*] red-throated diver *Gavia stellata*
- **nori gushë'zi** [*Ornit*] black-throated diver *Gavia arctica L., Columbus arcticus L.*
- **nori pola'r** [*Ornit*] great northern diver *Gavia immer*

norma'l *adj* normal

norma'le *nf* **1** that which is normal **2** [*Math*] normal line **3** (*Old*) normal school, school of pedagogy

norma'l|íst *n* (*Old*) student at a normal school

norma'l|ísht *adv* in a normal way: normally

norma|lizi'm *nm ger* **1** < **normalizo'·**n, **normalizo'·**het **2** normalization

norma|lizo'·het *vpr* **1** to return to normal **2** [*Ling*] to become normalized, become established as standard

norma|lizo'·n *vt* to normalize

norma|lizu'e's *adj* **1** normalizing **2** setting norms: standardizing

norma'n *nm, adj* [*Hist*] Norman

normati'v *adj* normative

normati'v|ë *nf* economic norm/standard

no'rm|ë *nf* norm, standard

norm|ëzi'm *nm ger* **1** < **normëzo'·**n, **normëzo'·**het **2** standardization

norm|ëzo'·het *vpr* [*Ling*] to become standardized

norm|ëzo'·n *vt* [*Ling*] to standardize

norm|ëzu'a'r *adj* (i) [*Ling*] standardized

norm|i'm *nm ger* **1** < **normo'·**n **2** [*Ling*] = **norm|ëzi'm**

norm|íst *n* person who calculates and establishes work standards

normo'·n *vt* to calculate and establish work standards for []; determine material and energy requirements for []

norm|u'a'r *adj* (i) **1** in accordance with the work standard: determined by norm **2** [*Ling*] standardized

norm|u'e's *n* = **norm|íst**

norvegj|e'z *adj, n* Norwegian

Norvegj|i' *nf* Norway

norvegj|i'sht *adv* in Norwegian (language)

norvegj|í'sht|e *nf* Norwegian language, Norse

nosi't *OR* **nosí'tës** *nm* (*Reg*) [*Ornit*] pelican

nostalgj|i' *nf* (*Book*) nostalgia

nostro'm *nm* [*Naut*] boatswain

no'sht|ër *nf* [*Bot*] sprout, shoot

not *nm* swimming
- **not bretko'së** breaststroke
- **not flutur/baterfla'i** butterfly stroke
- **not gërshë'rë** sidestroke
- **not pa'sh** [*Swimming*] crawl stroke
- **not qe'ni** dog paddle
- **not shpi'në** backstroke

◦ **not urdhësjellës** *(Old)* crawl stroke

no'ta *np fem* <**no'të** written music; musical score

nota'r *n* **1** swimmer *2 = **note'r**

notara'k *adj (Old)* swimming; water-dwelling

note'r *nm* notary, notary public

noteri' *nf* [*Law*] notary office

noteria'l *adj* [*Law*] pertaining to the duties of the notary: notarial

no'të *nf* **1** musical note **2** *(Fig)* tone, mood **3** evaluation on a scale: grade **4** [*Dipl*] diplomatic note
◦ **notë pozitive** passing grade/mark (in school)

noti' *nf (Reg)* **1** moisture, humidity **2** rainy weather; humid wind

noti'm *nm ger* <**noto'**·*n*
◦ **notim bretkosë** [*Swimming*] breaststroke
◦ **notim flutur** [*Swimming*] butterfly stroke
◦ **notim qeni** [*Swimming*] dog paddle

****noti'shëm** *adj (i)* damp, dank

noti'shte *nf* headwaters (of a river)

****no'tkë** *nf* mark, sign

noto'·*n vi* to swim; float
◦ **noto·***n* **në një/dy gisht ujë** "swim/sail in one/two finger(s) of water" to be very skillful
◦ **noto·***n* **në të njëjtat/po ato ujëra (me** []**)** "swim in the same water (with []**)**" **1** to be involved/implicated somehow in the same mess (as []) **2** to have the same problem (as []): be in the same boat (as [])

not'ues *adj* **1** floating **2** used in swimming

nova'cio'n *nm* innovative thing: innovation

nova'to'r
I § *n* innovator
II § *adj* innovative; innovational

nova'to'r'e *nf* innovative thinking: innovation

nova'tori'st *adj* innovative

nova'tori'zëm *nm* **1** inventiveness, originality **2** innovative movement; innovative activity **3** innovation

nove'lë *nf* long short story, short novel, novelette: novella

noveli'st *n* writer of novellas

****novi'cë** *nf (Old)* long Montenegran rifle

no'zull *nm (Colloq)* food put aside and saved for winter; food taken along for a long trip: stock of food

nozull'i'm *nm ger (Colloq)* **1** <**nozullo'**·*n*, **nozullo'**·*het* **2** foodstuff, provisions

nozullo'·*het vpr (Colloq)* to lay up provisions

nozull'o'·*n vt* to supply [] with food

NP *abbrev* <**Ndërmarrja pyjore** forestry agency

NPA *abbrev* <**Ndërmarrja e prodhimeve të artizanatit** agency for artisan products

NPB *abbrev* <**Ndërmarrja e parafabrikateve bujqësore** agency for agricultural prefabricated units

NPD *abbrev* <**Ndërmarrja e përpunimit të drurit** lumber company

NPM *abbrev* <**Ndërmarrja e prodhimeve metalike** agency for metal products

NPN *abbrev* <**Ndërmarrja e prodhimeve të ndryshme** workshop that produces miscellaneous small articles

NPV *abbrev* <**Ndërmarrja e prodhimit të veshjeve** agency for clothing production

nr. *abbrev* <**numër** no. = number

NRNMP *abbrev* <**Ndërmarrja e riparim-ndërtimit të mjeteve të peshkimit** agency for repair and construction of fishing equipment

NRSh *abbrev* <**Ndërmarrja e riparim-shërbimeve** agency for repair services

NSh *abbrev* <**Ndërmarrja shtetërore** *(Old)* state agency

NShAFES *abbrev* <**Ndërmarrja shtetërore e artikujve farmaceutikë e sanitarë** *(Old)* state agency for pharmaceutical and sanitary articles

NShFDT *abbrev* <**Ndërmarrja shtetërore e flotës detare tregtare** *(Old)* state agency for the merchant marine fleet

NShFM *abbrev* <**Ndërmarrja tregtare shtetërore e furnizimit të mensave** *(Old)* commercial state agency for provisioning of institutional cafeterias

NShFMN *abbrev* <**Ndërmarrja shtetërore e furnizimit të materialeve të ndërtimit** *(Old)* state agency for provision of construction materials

NShG *abbrev* <**Ndërmarrja shtetërore e grumbullimit** *(Old)* state agency for wholesaling

NShGID *abbrev* <**Ndërmarrja shtetërore e grumbullimit e të industrializimit të duhanit** *(Old)* state agency for the accumulation and industrialization of tobacco

NShMN *abbrev* <**Ndërmarrja e shfrytëzimit të makinerive të ndërtimit** state agency for the utilization of construction machinery

NShN *abbrev* <**Ndërmarrja shtetërore e ndërtimeve** *(Old)* state agency for buildings

NShOA *abbrev* <**Ndërmarrja shtetërore e oficinave automobilistike** *(Old)* state agency for automobile repair shops

NShRAK *abbrev* <**Ndërmarrja shtetërore e riparimit të autoveturave e të kamionëve** *(Old)* state agency for repair of automotive vehicles and trucks

NShTJ *abbrev* <**Ndërmarrja shtetërore e tregtisë së jashtme** *(Old)* state agency for foreign commerce

NTAN *abbrev* <**Ndërmarrja tregtare e artikujve të ndryshëm** agency for dealing in miscellaneous articles

NTASh *abbrev* <**Ndërmarrja e transportit automobilistik shtetëror** *(Old)* state agency for automotive transportation

NTFM *abbrev* <**Ndërmarrja tregtare e furnizimit të mensave** commercial agency for provisioning of institutional cafeterias

NTFP *abbrev* <**Ndërmarrja tregtare e fruta-perimeve** commercial agency for fruit and vegetables

NTI *abbrev* <**Ndërmarrja e transportit e industrisë 1** industrial transportation agency <**Ndërmarrja tregtare industriale 2** industrial trade agency

NTLAI *abbrev* <**Ndërmarrja tregtare lokale e artikujve industrialë** *(Old)* commercial local agency for industrial articles

NTLAP *abbrev* <**Ndërmarrja tregtare lokale e artikujve të përzjerë** *(Old)* commercial local agency for miscellaneous articles

NTLAU *abbrev* <**Ndërmarrja tregtare lokale e artikujve ushqimorë** *(Old)* commercial local agency for food articles

NTLUS *abbrev* <**Ndërmarrja tregtare lokale e ushqimit social** local agency for providing and provisioning public eating places

****n'trash·** = **trash·**

NTSh *abbrev* <**Ndërmarrja tregtare shtetërore e <> 1** *(Old)* commercial state agency for <> <**Ndërmarrja tregtare e shitblerjes 2** agency for commercial business

NTShAI *abbrev* <**Ndërmarrja tregtëre shtetërore e artikujve industrialë** *(Old)* commercial state agency for industrial articles

NTShAP [*në-të-shap*] *m abbrev* <**Ndërmarrja tregtare shtetërore e artikujve të përzier** *(Old)* commercial state agency for miscellaneous articles

NTShAU [*në-të-sha´u*] *m abbrev* <**Ndërmarrja tregtare shtetërore e artikujve ushqimorë** *(Old)* commercial state agency for food articles

NTShShK *abbrev* <**Ndërmarrja tregtare shtetërore e shpërndarjes së karburanteve** *(Old)* commercial state agency for distribution of motor fuels

NTShUS [*në-të-shu´s*] *m abbrev* <**Ndërmarrja tregtare shtetërore e ushqimit social** *(Old)* agency for providing and provisioning state-owned eating places

NTT *abbrev* <**Ndërmarrja e transportit të tregtisë** agency for commercial transport

NTU *abbrev* <**Ndërmarrja tregtare ushqimore** agency in charge of distributing food to stores

NTUS *abbrev* <**Ndërmarrja tregtare e ushqimit social** agency for providing and provisioning state-owned eating places

nua´ncë *nf* nuance

nuga *nf* nougat

nuha´r
I § *nm* deer's hiding place
II § *adj* *greedy, gluttonous

nuha´s| *stem for 1st sg pres, pl pres, 2nd & 3rd sg subj, pind* <**nuha´t·**

nuha´t· *vt* **1** to sniff [ ] with the nose: smell **2** to sense [ ]; gain insight about [ ]

nuha´t·et *vpr* to smell/sniff/sense one another

nuha´t|ës
I § *adj* olfactory
II § *n* person with a sensitive sense of smell

nuha´tje *nf ger* **1** <**nuha´t·**, **nuha´t·et 2** ability to smell, olfactory sense: olfaction **3** *(Fig)* insight

nuha´to´r *adj* olfactory

nuha´tur *nn (të)* sense of smell

***nuh|ëri´t·** = **nuhuri´t·**

***nuh|ëri´tje** *nf* scent, odor

nuh|uri´t· *vt* to sniff out [ ]; catch the scent of [ ]

nuk *pcl* negative particle before verbs: not
  ○ **a nuk 1** isn't that so **2** *(Colloq Reg)* = **nu´ku**

nuklea´r *adj* nuclear

***nu´ku** *tag question (Colloq Reg)* don't you think so? right?

nul *nm* [*Electr*] neutral

nu´l|ë *nf (Colloq)* grandma, granny

nulipa´re *nf* [*Med*] nullipara

nu´ll|ë *nf* [*Anat*] gum (tissue in which the teeth are embedded) *(gingiva)*

nu´ll|ëz *nf* [*Anat*] = **nu´llë**

***null|i´m** *nm ger* **1** <**nullo´·n 2** nullification, annulment

***null|o´·n** OR **null|o´s·** *vt* to nullify, annul, cancel, repeal

numeri´k *adj* numeric

numeri´kisht *adv (Book)* numerically

nu´mër *nm* **1** number **2** size (of clothing)
  ○ **numër cub** *(Old)* [*Math*] odd number
  ○ **numër çift** [*Math*] even numbers
  ○ **numri i futazhit** [*Cine*] edge-numbering
  ○ **numër i thjeshtë** [*Math*] prime number

numëra´to´r *nm* **1** calculator = **njehso´r 2** telephone switchboard **3** telephone book

numëra´to´re *nf* [*Math*] abacus

numëri´m *nm ger* **1** <**numëro´·n**, **numëro´·het 2** enumeration

numëro´·het *vpr* to reach a certain size
  ○ <> **numëro·het**^{3pl} **brinjët** you can count <>'s ribs
  ○ **numëro·het**^{3pl} **me gishtat e dorës** to be countable on the fingers of one hand

numëro´·n
I § *vt* **1** to number **2** to count **3** to enumerate
II § *vi* to count sequentially
  ○ **a numëro·n 1** to fire off shots at <> one by one **2** to enumerate <>'s mistakes
  ○ <>**i numëro·n brinjët** "count <>'s ribs" to give <> a severe beating
  ○ **nuk** [ ] **numëro·n fare** not (even) count [ ], not consider [ ]
  ○ **numëro·n gishtat** "be counting fingers" to have flipped one's wig, have gone crazy
  ○ **numëro·n miza (gjithë ditën)** "count/kill/catch flies (all day long)" *(Impol)* to waste time idly: sit around (the whole day) twiddling one's thumbs
  ○ **numëro·n në vend** to mark time (in one place); stay in place, not change; lag behind
  ○ **numëro·n qimet/fijet e postiqes** "count the hairs of the goatskin pad" to waste time on trivia; in waste time on trivial pursuits
  ○ **numëro·n rrënjët** to do useless work: twiddle one's thumbs
  ○ **numëro·n tespihet 1** to count off one's prayer beads **2** *(Fig)* to kill time
  ○ <>**a numëro·n të gjashta** to count off six shots at <>, shoot <> (with a six-shooter) six times; kill <> dead
  ○ <>**a numëro·n të shtata** "count out seven to <>" **1** to pump <> full of lead, shoot <> dead **2** to cuss <> out with every word in the dictionary, really let <> have it
  ○ **numëro·n yjet** "count the stars" to be unable to fall asleep

numëro´r
I § *adj* numeric, numerical
II § *nm* **1** [*Ling*] number (as a part of speech), number word **2** [*Mil*] member of a gun crew
  ○ **numëror shtesor** number or numerical phrase consisting of more than one component: composite number
  ○ **numëror shumëzor** compound number
  ○ **numërorët e thjeshtë** [*Ling*] the number words from one to ten

***numër|tar**
I § *adj* numerical
II § *n* counter

nu´mërtë *adj (i)* numerous

numërti´m *nm ger* <**numërto´·n**

numërto´·n *vt* to apply numbers in sequential order: number

numërua´r *adj (i)* counted; numbered

numërue´s *nm* **1** [*Math*] numerator **2** person charged with keeping track of numbers: counter, scorekeeper

numërue´shëm *adj (i)* countable; denumerable

numizmati´k *adj* numismatic

numizmati´kë *nf* numismatics

***nu´mur** = **nu´mër**

nun *nm* [*Ethnog*] = **kumba´rë**

nu´n|e *nf (Old)* = **ndri´kull**

nu´nël *nf (Reg)* mother's mother: grandmother

nu·nër *nf* place for storing and drying wood in back of a fireplace

nun|ëri *nf* = kumbarí

nun|ëro's·et *vpr* 1 [*Relig*] = nunos·et 2 to get someone to act as godfather

nuno's· *vt* [*Relig*] (of a priest) to hear the confession of []: confess

nuno's·et *vpr* [*Relig*] to confess (as a Christian rite)

*nun|o's|ës

I § *adj* (*Old*) confessional

II § *nm* (*Old*) confessor (priest)

nun|o's|je *nf ger* 1 <nuno's·et 2 confession

nunur|is| *stem for 1st sg pres, pl pres, 2nd & 3rd sg subj, pind* <nunurit·

nunurit· *vi* 1 to mumble softly 2 to mourn in a soft voice

*nuq *nm* refusal

nur *nm* (*Colloq*) 1 facial expression 2 attractive appearance 3 outward appearance; radiance

nur|bardhë *adj* (*Colloq*) happy-faced, smiling, radiant

Nuredín *nm* Nuredin (male name)

nur|madh *adj* (*Colloq*) extraordinarily charming, lovely

nur|sëz *adj* (*Colloq*) having an unhappy face, dour

nur|shëm *adj* (*i*) beautiful, radiant

nur|zi *adj* (*fem sg ˜ ez, masc pl ˜ inj, fem pl ˜ eza*) (*Colloq*) dour-faced, always frowning

nu|se *nf* 1 bride; young wife 2 daughter-in-law 3 granddaughter

○ nuse e arës [*Bot*] yellow bedstraw, yellow cleavers (*Galium verum*)

○ nuse e bukur [*Zool*] = nusela'lë

○ nuse deti [*Myth*] siren

○ nuse e djemvet [*Zool*] = nusela'lë

○ nuset e malit [*Myth*] mountain nymph: oread = jashtësme

○ nuse kopshti scarecrow

○ Nuse, ku kalle këmbët? "Bride, where did you put your feet?" (*Colloq*) (said to a new bride who has apparently made a bad marriage) Hey girl, what have you gotten yourself into?

○ nuse lale [*Zool*] = nusela'lë

○ nusja e lalës = nusela'lë

○ nusja macë queen of spades

○ nuse me tela "bride with wires" 1 bride in her wedding adornment 2 very beautiful girl

○ nuse e mirë [*Zool*] = nusela'lë

○ nuse misri scarecrow

○ nuse për mur/muri young wife (of earlier times) who remains standing to serve guests

○ nuse pashke [*Entom*] ladybug = mollëku'qe

○ ësh·të nuse e re "be the new wife" to be new on the job

○ nusja e syrit pupil of the eye

○ nusja e ujërave [*Myth*] water nymph: naiad = gërshe'tëz

nuse|bu'kur *nf* [*Zool*] = nusela'lë

nuse|la'lë *nf* 1 [*Zool*] weasel (*Mustela nivalis*) 2 ermine (*Mustela ermina*)

nuse|ze'zë *nf* wretched bride

nus|ël *nf* [*Zool*] = nusela'lë

nus|ëri *nf* 1 period of a woman's life from marriage until the birth of her first child: bridehood 2 (*Collec*) newly married women

nus|ërím *nm ger* <nusëro·n

nus|ërísht *adv* in bridal fashion

nus|ëro·n *vi* to act as a proper bride: sit mutely on a chair with head bowed on one's wedding day; stand up for members of the husband's family and serve them during one's first days of marriage

nus|ëror *adj* (*Book*) bridal

nus|ërore *nf* (*Old*) = gjerde'k

nu's|ëz *nf* [*Zool*] = nusela'lë

nus|ísht *adv* = nusërísht

nu'skë *nf* 1 doll 2 sheaf of corn = kapu'le 3 triangular-shaped talisman 4 (*Colloq*) triangular or rhomboid piece of sweet pastry *5 scarecrow

nu'sk|ëz *nf* sheaf of corn = kapu'le

nuve'g *nm* [*Ornit*] eagle owl (*Bubo bubo*)

*nu'zull|ë *nf* = no'zull

*n|vesh| = mvesh|

nxeh·

I § *vt* 1 to make [] hot/hotter: heat 2 to add fuel to [a heat source] 3 (*Fig*) to inflame, make [] irate, rile

II § *vi* to generate heat

○ <> nxeh· gjakrat to cause <>'s tempers to flare

nxe'h·et *vpr* 1 to get hot/hotter; heat up 2 (*Fig*) to lose one's composure: become angry

○ nxeh·et³ᵖˡ gjakrat tempers start to flare

○ <> nxeh·et³ˢᵍ gjaku <> loses <>'s temper

nxe'h|ës

I § *adj* making hot

II § *nm* [*Tech*] heater

nxe'h|je *nf ger* 1 <nxe'h· 2 heat 3 [*Sport*] warm-up

nxe'h|shëm *adj* (*i*) 1 heatable 2 irritable

nxe'h|të

I § *adj* (*i*) 1 hot 2 (of friendly behavior) warm 3 (*Fig*) hot-tempered

II § *nm* (*të*) 1 heat 2 high temperature, feverish heat

III § *adv* in/with high temperature

nxeht|ësí *nf* 1 heat; hotness 2 feeling of being hot 3 [*Phys*] heat energy 4 (*Colloq*) emotional tension

nxeht|ësi|ma't|ës *nm* thermometer

nxeht|ësí|sht *adv* warmheartedly, warmly; fervently

nxe'h|ur *adj* (*i*) 1 heated 2 angry; excited

*nxe'|mje *nf* [*Sport*] warm-up

nxen| *stem for opt, adm, part* <nxë·

nxer| *stem for imper, 3rd sg subj* <nxë·

nxë· *vt* 1 to have a capacity of [measure of capacity]: be able to hold/accommodate/take 2 to be large enough for [] to fit through/in 3 to learn

○ nuk <>[] nxë·³ˢᵍ koka/mendja <> cannot imagine []

○ nuk [] nxë·³ˢᵍ lëkura "the skin *does* not contain/hold []" (*Joke*) [] *is* bursting out of <>'s skin, [] *is* too fat

○ nxë· mend to learn a (good) lesson

○ s'<> nxë·³ˢᵍ vendi <> *is* troubled and uneasy; be in an agitated state

nxën| *stem for opt, adm, part* <nxë·

nxën|ës *n* 1 pupil 2 apprentice; disciple

nxën|ësí *nf* capacity = kapacite't

nxën|ie *nf* learning, studying

nxër| *stem for imper* <nxë·

nxi·het *vpr* 1 to get dark/darker; darken 2 (*Fig*) to darken in the face with emotion 3 to take on a gloomy appearance: become dour

○ <> nxi·het³ˢᵍ balli <> *gets* covered with shame

○ <> **nxi·**het³ˢᵍ **buza** <>'s lips *turn* blue (with cold); <>'s lip *gets* black and blue

○ **s'<> nxi·**het³ˢᵍ **faqja/fytyra** <> *has* absolutely no sense of shame

○ <> **nxi·**het³ˢᵍ **faqja** "<>'s face *gets* blackened" <>'s honor *gets* sullied, <> *becomes* disgraced

○ <> **nxi·**het³ˢᵍ **jeta** life *becomes* a living Hell for <>

○ **nxi·**het³ˢᵍ **koha** (of the weather) to get dark and cloudy, become overcast

○ **nxi·het me bojë** to be overtaken by misfortune

○ <> **nxi·**het³ˢᵍ **mishi** <>'s skin *turns* black and blue

○ <> **nxi·**het³ᵖˡ **vetullat** "<>'s eyebrows darken" <> *becomes* terribly ashamed

nxi·*n*
   I § *vt* **1** to make [] dark/black: blacken; darken **2** *(Fig)* to denigrate
   II § *vi* **1** to have a black/dark appearance: look black/dark **2** *(Fig)* to take on a dark countenance, become/look gloomy
   ○ **<>a nxi·**n **faqen/fytyrën** to cause <> public shame; humiliate <> publicly
   ○ **<>a nxi·**n **jetën** to make <>'s life a living Hell
   ○ **nxi·**n³ˢᵍ **misri** the corn *gets* a healthy dark green (promising a good yield)
   ○ **<>a nxi·**n **mishin** to give <> a severe beating: tan <>'s hide, beat <> black and blue
   ○ **<>i nxi·**n **mishrat** to give <> a severe beating: tan <>'s hide, beat <> black and blue

nxi| *stem for 2nd pl pres, pind, imper, vp* <**nxë·**
   ○ **s'<> nxih·**et³ˢᵍ **lara** <> *has* no sense of shame, <> *has* no concern for what people might think

nxi|**rak** *adj* **1** incompetent in one's own profession: inept = **kërpaç 2** unfortunate, wretched

nxi|**rë** *adj* **1** blackened, darkened **2** *(Fig)* visited by misfortune: unfortunate, wretched

nxi|**rim** *nm ger* = **nxirje**

nxi|**rje** *nf ger* <**nxi·**n, **nxi·**het

nxi|**ro·**n
   I § *vt* **1** = **nxi·**n **2** *(Fig)* to kill
   II § *vi* *(Fig Colloq)* to die

nxi|**ros·** *vt* **1** to dye [] black; blacken **2** *(Fig Colloq)* to foul [] up
   ○ **<>a nxiros· jetën** to make <>'s life a living Hell
   ○ **<>a nxiros· zemrën/shpirtin** to make <>'s life joyless and empty; cause <> great suffering

nxi|**ruar** *adj (i)* = **nxirë**

nxirr| *stem for 2nd pl pres, pind, imper, vp* <**nxjerr·**

nxis| *stem for 1st sg pres, pl pres, 2nd & 3rd sg subj, pind* <**nxit·**

nxit· *vt* **1** to stimulate; instigate; give [] an incentive **2** to spur [] into going faster

nxit·*et vpr* to have/get an incentive

nxit|**ës**
   I § *adj* stimulating
   II § *n* instigator; inciter
   III § *nm* stimulant

nxit|**im** *nm ger* **1** <**nxito·**n, **nxito·**het **2** high speed; hurry **3** hurried action: haste, rush **4** [*Phys*] acceleration

nxit|**im**|**thi** *adv* quickly, rapidly

nxi|**tje** *nf ger* **1** <**nxit·** **2** stimulation

nxito·*het vpr* **1** to be in a hurry; hasten, hurry **2** to act hastily

nxito·*n*
   I § *vt* to press/urge to go faster, urge on; speed [] up
   II § *vi* **1** to go faster, speed up; make haste, hurry, rush **2** to act in haste

nxit|**uar** *adj (i)* **1** in too much of a rush: hasty, hurried **2** in a hurry; quickly, fast **3** accelerated

nxjerr· *vt* **1** to cause [] to move from in to out: get [] out, push/pull [] out; extract; select **2** to generate from within: issue, produce, emit, release, present **3** to move [] (to a different place/position); wrench/dislocate [one's limb] **4** to remove [covering material] **5** *(Crude)* to take off [a piece of clothing] **6** to expose; reveal; display; offer **7** to manage to get []; earn, gain **8** to make [a copy/photograph] **9** to manage to get through [a period of time] alive: survive [] **10** to allay [an emotional need/desire] **11** *(Colloq)* to make up, fabricate, create
   ○ [] **nxjerr· birërie** to consider [] no longer one's child
   ○ **<>a nxjerr· bishtin** "take off <>'s tail" to engage in <*the activity*> for too long, be overdoing <>
   ○ **<>a nxjerr· bojën** "remove <>'s paint" to reveal <>'s true colors, pull off <>'s mask
   ○ **nxjerr· brirët** *(Pej)* to show one's true colors
   ○ **<>a nxjerr· cifundin** to ruin <> completely, damage <> beyond repair
   ○ [] **nxjerr· çirak** (sometimes said ironically) to put [] on []'s feet
   ○ **e nxjerr· çupën** to marry off one's daughter
   ○ **<> nxjerr· djersë** to really make <> sweat, tire <> out completely
   ○ **nxjerr· dufin** to vent one's anger
   ○ **<> nxjerr· dhëmb e dhëmballë** to exhaust <>, put <> through a lot of pain and suffering
   ○ [] **nxjerr· faqe** to clear [] of a charge
   ○ [] **nxjerr· fare** to get rid of [] completely; annihilate []
   ○ **nxjerr· filiz** to sprout, form a bud
   ○ **nxjerr· fjalë për** [] to spread a story about []
   ○ **nxjerr· fjalën në pazar** to spread the news all around town
   ○ **nxjerr· frymë** to breathe out, expel one's breath: exhale
   ○ **<>a nxjerr· fundin *1** to ruin <> completely, damage <> beyond repair **2** to study/investigate <> in depth
   ○ **i nxjerr· gështenjat nga zjarri me duart e të tjerëve//botës** "take chestnuts out of the fire with someone else's hands" to get someone else to do something that one wants not to do oneself
   ○ **<> nxjerr·**³ˢᵍ **goja mjaltë** "<>'s mouth *flows* with honey" <> *speaks* pleasantly; <> *speaks* beautifully
   ○ **nuk nxjerr· gjë në breg** to be incapable of accomplishing anything
   ○ **nuk nxjerr· gjë në dritë** {} *is* incapable of finishing anything, {} *is* unproductive
   ○ **nuk nxjerr· gjë në shesh/treg** "not get anything out in public" not manage to bring anything to a successful conclusion, not manage to achieve anything
   ○ **nuk nxjerr· gjë në vijë** "not get a thing in line" not unable to accomplish anything
   ○ **<> nxjerr· gjoksin** to stand up to <>, meet <> head on, confront <> courageously
   ○ **<> nxjerr· gjuhën** to stick one's tongue out at <> (make a derisive gesture)

∘ <>*a* nxjerr· gjuhën një pëllëmbë/pash to make <>'s tongue hang out a mile, tire<> out completely

∘ po e nxjerr· gjuhën to become audacious and answer back

∘ <> nxjerr· gjumin to make <> no longer sleepy: wake <> up

∘ <> nxjerr· hanxharin to threaten <> strongly

∘ <>[] nxjerr· *nga hundët/për hundësh* 1 *(Pej)* to take [] away from <> by force, draw [] out of <> by force 2 to spoil <>'s enjoyment of [] 3 to make <> pay for [] through the nose

∘ e nxjerr· hundën jashtë *(Iron)* to go into action, take the initial step

∘ ia nxjerr· için lakrorit to reveal the ugly truth

∘ <>*a* nxjerr· inatin to take it out on <>

∘ [] nxjerr· jashtë ligji to outlaw []

∘ [] nxjerr· jashtë ligjit to outlaw []

∘ nxjerr jashtë *(Colloq)* to export

∘ [] nxjerr· jashtë përdorimit to make [] useless

∘ nxjerr· kafshatën e gojës to eke out a living

∘ t'i nxjerr· këpucët nga këmba/këmbët 1 to be a real thief: {} would steal the shirt off your back 2 to be entirely capable of doing something terrible to you

∘ <> nxjerr·^{3sg} koka tym <>'s head is absolutely spinning with all the things <> has to worry about

∘ nxjerr· krye/kokë to make an appearance

∘ <>*i* nxjerr· lakrat në shesh to reveal one's mistakes, disclose one's guilt

∘ Nuk nxjerr· lepur nga strofulla. "{} can't even get a hare out of its hole" {} *can't* do anything right

∘ [] nxjerr· lyç to make a mess of [], muddle [] up

∘ <> nxjerr· mallin to awaken <>'s longing

∘ nxjerr· mallin e <> to satisfy one's longing for <>

∘ <>*a* nxjerr· me çengel to try hard to get <> to speak, struggle to get some words out of someone; it's like pulling teeth to get <> to talk

∘ <>*a* nxjerr· me grep përgjegjen/fjalën to drag the words out of <>

∘ <>[] nxjerr· me kllapë to get [] out of <> by special efforts

∘ nxjerr· mend 1 to learn from bitter experience 2 to be obedient, listen

∘ [] nxjerr· mendsh to drive [] out of []'s mind

∘ <>*i* nxjerr· mendtë to drive <> out of <>'s mind

∘ [] nxjerr· më krye to get [] done

∘ nxjerr· mjaltë nga goja "emit honey/sugar from one's mouth" to speak pleasantly/beautifully

∘ nxjerr· mjaltë nga guri "extract oil/honey/water from rock" to have the ability to make something good out of anything, be able to do well in any circumstances, be a wonderworker

∘ <>[] nxjerr· në lëndinë to bring <>'s [secret] out into the open

∘ [] nxjerr· në ankand 1 to auction off [], put [] up for auction 2 *(Fig)* to treat [something sacred and precious] as if it something cheap

∘ [] nxjerr· në breg to rescue [] from a difficult or dangerous position: pull [] out of the fire

∘ [] nxjerr· në dritë 1 to expose [] to the light of day 2 to put [] on []'s feet

∘ e nxjerr· në faqe to succeed

∘ [] nxjerr· në fotografi to take a photograph of []

∘ [] nxjerr· në furkë to bring [] out into the open, make [] completely public

∘ [] nxjerr· në jetë 1 to save []'s life; show [] how to live 2 to bring [] to light

∘ [] nxjerr· në krye to get [] done

∘ [] nxjerr· në mes të *rrugës/katër rrugëve* to abandon [] completely

∘ [] nxjerr· në mezat to bring [] out into the open, make [] public

∘ [] nxjerr· në pah 1 to make [] public, bring [] out into the open 2 to give [] special emphasis

∘ [] nxjerr· në portë pazari "expose [] at the market gate" to reveal all []'s private information in public

∘ e nxjerr· në rrasë të gjallë to be capable of performing miracles, be extremely able

∘ [] nxjerr· në rrugë (të madhe) to abandon [] completely

∘ [] nxjerr· në selamet to rescue [] from a bad situation

∘ [] nxjerr· në shesh to bring out in the open, reveal; expose []

∘ [] nxjerr· në shteg to help [] find a way out (of a problem)

∘ [] nxjerr· në *udhë/mes të udhës/udhë të madhe/mes të katër udhëve* to kick [] out into the street

∘ [] nxjerr· në va to get [] out of trouble; get [] back on the right path

∘ [] nxjerr· në anë to get [] out of a tough spot

∘ [] nxjerr· nga buka to deprive [] of a living

∘ [] nxjerr· nga dera "get [] out of the family" to manage to marry [a girl] off

∘ [] nxjerr· nga dera, (e) hy-*n* nga deriçka "one *kicks* [] out of the front door, [] *enters* through the back door" [] *keeps* showing up like a bad penny

∘ [] nxjerr· nga dheu to leave no stone unturned in looking for []

∘ e nxjerr· nga guri to do the impossible

∘ nxjerr· një ligj to issue a law

∘ t'i nxjerr· opingat nga këmba/këmbët 1 to be a real thief: {} would steal the shirt off your back 2 to be entirely capable of doing something terrible to you

∘ [] nxjerr· pa kapuç *(Pej)* to exploit [] to the utmost limit: leave [] without a shirt on []'s back, take [] to the cleaner's

∘ (<>)[] nxjerr· për brirësh to use great force to get [] out of <>

∘ nxjerr· për faqe *(Old)* to publish

∘ [] nxjerr· për qafë "take [] out through one's neck" to pay through the nose for []

∘ <> nxjerr· pijen to sober <> up

∘ të nxjerr· po në atë/një qafë to come to the same conclusion

∘ nxjerr· prej goje to utter

∘ s'e nxjerr· (dot) qimen nga qulli "not be able to get the hair out of the mush" to be totally clumsy and inept

∘ [] nxjerr·^{3sg} rruga "the road *brings* [] {*somewhere*}" chance *takes* [] {*somewhere*}, [] *happens* to be {*somewhere*}

∘ [] nxjerr· si simite nga furra "produce [] like buns from the oven" to turn out [] one after another in haste and without due care, grind [] out like sausages

∘ nxjerr· sy/syrin to begin to peek out; just be beginning to appear

∘ <> nxjerr· sytë to do terrible harm to <>

∘ le të nxjerr·^{3rdsubj} sytë let one dig one's own grave

∘ nxjerr· sytë to strain/overstrain one's eyes

○ <> **nxjerr·**^{3pl} **sytë shkëndija/çika/xixa** "<>'s eyes make sparks of light" (when <> is hit in the head <>'s vision goes dark) <> *sees* stars

○ **nxjerr· sheqer nga goja** "emit honey/sugar from one's mouth" to speak pleasantly/beautifully

○ <> **nxjerr· shkumë nga goja** "make <> foam at the mouth" **1** to beat the living daylights out of <> **2** to cause <> great suffering

○ <> **nxjerr· shpirtin** to make <> suffer, put <> through Hell

○ <> **nxjerr· tabanin** to investigate <> to the very core, delve into <> deeply

○ **nxjerr· të vdekurin nga varri** "take the dead from the grave" **1** to be very naughty; be evil and vicious **2** to be able to perform miracles

○ <>*i* **nxjerr· trutë** to drive <> out of <>'s mind

○ <>*a* **nxjerr· turpin** to help <> get over <>'s shyness

○ <> **nxjerr· thinjat** to give <> gray hairs

○ [] **nxjerr·**^{3sg} **udha** "the road *brings* [] {*somewhere*}" chance *takes* [] {*somewhere*}, [] *happens* to be {*somewhere*}

○ <> **nxjerr· ujë të zi** "take out <>'s dirty water" **1** to demolish <> completely **2** to make <> suffer terribly, put <> through Hell **3** to give <> a severe dressing down

○ **nxjerr· ujë në vatër** "get water out of the hearth" **1** to be very mischievous **2** to be very capable, be a miracleworker

○ **nxjerr· ujë nga guri** "extract oil/honey/water from rock" to be a wonderworker

○ <> **nxjerr· ujët** to squeeze <*someone*> dry; exploit <> mercilessly

○ <> **nxjerr· vaj** to work <> to exhaustion

○ **nxjerr· vaj nga guri** "get oil from a rock" to have the ability to make something good out of anything, be able to do well in any circumstances: be a wonderworker

○ **e nxjerr· vajzen** to marry off one's daughter

○ <> **nxjerr· veshët** "deafen/remove <>'s ears" to bore <*a listener*> to death; hammer constantly at <>

○ **nxjerr· veshët** "stick one's ears out" *(Pej)* to show one's true colors

○ **nxjerr· (helm e) vrer** "emit (poison and) bile" to pour out one's hatred, speak with unmitigated spite: pour out one's bile

○ <> **nxjerr· xhigerin** to pull/cut out <>'s guts <>; kill <> cruelly

○ **nxjerr· xhunga** raise lumps

○ **nxjerr· zogj** "hatch chicks" **1** *(Iron)* to lie in bed with a long debilitating illness **2** to remain idly in one place, hang around not doing anything

○ **nxjerr· zorrët (e barkut)** to vomit up everything (in one's stomach)

nxje·rrë
I § *part* <**nxjerr·**

II § *nn (të)* *

nxje·rrës
I § *adj* extracting, mining
II § *nm* [*Tech*] remover; extractor

nxje·rrje *nf ger* **1** <**nxje·rr· 2** extraction; removal **3**

*****nxon**i**s** *stem for 1st sg pres, pl pres, 2nd & 3rd sg subj, pind* <**nxoni**t·

*****nxoni**t· *vt* to constrain, restrain

*****nxoni**tje *nf* constraint, restraint

nxo·r *stem for pdef* <**nxjerr·**

*****nxo·rr** *stem for pdef* <**nxë·**

nxu *stem for pl pdef, 3rd sg pdef vp* <**nxë·**

nxuar *stem for pl pdef* <**nxjerr·**

*****nxu**c·*et vpr* = **nxus·**et

nxu·r *stem for sg pdef, sg imper* <**nxë·**

*****nxu**s·*et vpr* (of a plant) to coil around and up a tree; (of an animate subject) clamber up a tree

nyç *adj* **1** = **nejç 2** *(Fig)* headstrong **3** *(FigJocular)* old but still fit as a fiddle

nye *nf* = **nyj**e

nye**ll** *nm (np ˜ j)* **1** gnarl **2** [*Anat*] anklebone

nyje *OR* **nyj**ë *nf* **1** knot; gnarl **2** *(Fig)* connecting link: bond, tie, joint **3** junction; junction point **4** node **5** *(Fig)* nub, crux **6** central production plant **7** [*Ling*] article

○ **nyja e dimrit** thick of winter

○ **nyja e fytit** Adam's apple

○ **nyjë gordiane** Gordian knot

nyjë**s** *nm* joint

nyjë**t** *adj (i)* jointed

nyjë**ti·m** *nm* [*Ling*] articulation

nyjë**to·**n *vt* **1** [*Ling*] to articulate ***2** to say further: add

nyjë**tu·a·r** *adj (i)* [*Ling*] articulated

nyjë**z** *nf* nodule

nyjë**zi·m** *nm ger* **1** <**nyjëzo·**het **2** [*Anat*] articulation

nyjë**zo·**het *vpr* **1** to come together at a node; form a joint **2** [*Ling*] to take an article

nyjo**r**
I § *adj* **1** [*Spec*] nodal **2** jointed, articulated **3** [*Biol*] arthropodal
II § *nm* [*Zool*] arthropod

nyjsh**ëm** *adj (i)* [*Ling*] taking a preposed article

nyjti·m *nm* hinge, joint

*****ny**lk**ët** *adj (i)* overripe = **ndu**lkët

*****nymënta·r** *n* informer; messenger

*****nymënto·**n *vt* to inform

*****nysht**ë**ri** *nf* contrition; tenderness

*****nytë**ri**m** *nm (Old)* whisper, murmur

*****nz** = **nx**

nj [një] *nf* **1** the consonant letter "nj" **2** the palatal nasal consonant represented by the letter "nj"

nja *pcl followed by a number (Colloq)* approximately, or so

*njac OR njaç *nm* roe = nja'ça

nja'ç|a *np* spawn, roe

nja'çë *nf* [*Ichth*] fish testicle

*nja'do *pron* some, a few, a little

*nj|a'i *distal pron 3rd pers sg masc (Reg Gheg)* that very one, he, it

nja'j = njaj

nja'jo *distal pron 3rd pers sg fem (Reg Gheg)* that very one, she, it

*nja'jshëm = një'shëm

*nja'jtë = njëjtë

*njajzo'·n *vt* to make [] uniform

*njak *nm* suckling pig

*njall· *vt (Reg Gheg)* = ngjall·

nja'nj *nf (Reg)* half-baked bread, bread that is still doughy

*nja|për'nja *adv* = njëpër'një

njaq *adv (Reg)* to that very same degree: just so

*njariç *adj (Old)* eccentric, moody

*nja'saj

   I § *dat/abl* <njajo'

   II § *gen* (i) <njajo'

nja'shtu *adv (Reg Gheg)* in that very same manner: just like that

   ◦ njashtu si njashtu likewise

*njat *adv, prep (abl)* = ngjat

*nj|a'ta *distal 3rd pers pl masc determiner (Reg Gheg)* those very ones, they

*nj|a'të *acc* <njai', njajo'

*nj|a'tij *dat/abl* <njai'

*nj|a'tje *adv* at that very place; right over there, over there yonder

*nj|a'to' *distal 3rd pers pl fem determiner (Reg Gheg)* those very ones, they

nj|a'ty *adv (Reg)* in that very same place: right there

*nja'ty|ne *dat/abl* <njato', njata

*nj|a'y = njai

*nje'fkë *nf* [*Bot*] sepal

*nje'fme *nf (e)* gesture, nod

*nje'fsi'm *nm* counting, arithmetic

*nje'fshë *nf (Old)* gesture

njeh-

   I § *vt* **1** to come to know []: experience **2** to know the meaning of [] **3** to become acquainted/familiar with []: meet, learn; know [] (whom one can call on for help/favors) **4** to be acquainted/familiar with []: know, recognize **5** to acknowledge **6** to acquaint

   II § *vt* = numëro'·n

   ◦ <>a njeh· beben e syrit to know/appreciate <>'s valor; know <>'s quality

   ◦ <> njeh· dhëmb e dhëmballë to know <> intimately, know all <>'s weaknesses

   ◦ [] njeh· e çnjeh· **1** to count up [] carefully, count [] out several times **2** to think hard about [], consider and reconsider []

   ◦ nuk [] njeh·^{3sg} historia [] *is* unheard of; [] *is* unprecedented

   ◦ [] njeh· me rrënjë e me degë "know [] by root (and by branch)" to be deeply familiar with [] in every detail: know [] backwards and forwards, know [] inside out

   ◦ [] njeh· me pëllëmbë to know every inch of [the place]

   ◦ [] njeh· me rrënjë "know [] by root" to be very familiar with []

   ◦ [] njeh· me {} to make [] acquainted with {}: introduce [] to {}

   ◦ [] njeh· në majë të gishtrinjve "know [] to the fingertips" to know [] down to the last detail, know [] backwards and forwards

   ◦ [] njeh· në pëllëmbë të dorës to know [] like the back of one's hand; have plenty of experience with [], know one's way around []

   ◦ [] njeh· në thumb e në potkua to know [] in detail, know [] backwards and forwards

   ◦ [] njeh· pëllëmbë për pëllëmbë to know every inch of [the place]

   ◦ s'e njeh·^{3sg} qeni të zotin "the dog *doesn't* know his master" there *is* utter chaos

   ◦ njeh· shumë to know a lot of people (whom one can call on for help/favors)

   ◦ <>a njeh· të tëra (of a keener who enumerates the good deeds of the deceased) to mention every single thing about <>

   ◦ njeh· zhurin e detit "know the sand of the sea" to know all kinds of things, be very knowledgeable

*njeha'në *nf* container, ball holder

njeha'to're *nf (Old)* woman who is good at enumerating the good deeds of the deceased: mourner

nje'hje *nf* = nume'rim

njehs|i'm *nm ger* **1** <njehso'·n **2** calculation *3 counting; arithmetic

njehs|o'·n *vt* to calculate

njehs|o'r *nm* metering device: flow/rate meter

njehs|ue'shëm *adj (i)* calculable

nje'kë *nf (Reg)* = shkak

*nje'lb|ët = nje'lmët

nje'lmë *adj (i)* salty

njelm|ë'si *nf* saltiness; salinity

njelm|ë'si'm *nm ger* <njelmëso'·n, njelmëso'·het

njelm|ë'si're *nf* food that is too salty; salty taste

njelm|ë'so'·het *vpr* to become salty

njelm|ë'so'·n *vt* to add salt to []: make [] more salty, salt; add flavor to []: flavor

nje'lm|ët *adj (i)* **1** salty **2** saline

njelm|i'shtë OR njelm|i'shte *nf* salty soil/land

njelm|o'·het *vpr* = njelmëso'·n

njelm|o'·n *vt* = njelmëso'·n

nje'll|ët *adj (i)* light blue

*njellíme *nf* swan = mje'llm*ë*

njer'ëz *np* <njeri **1** people **2** relatives, family, kin members

njer'ëzí *nf collec* **1** people, inhabitants, populace **2** cordiality; politeness, courteousness **3** *(Collec)* relatives, family, kin members

njer'ëzillëk *nm (Colloq)* politeness, courtesy, decency

njer'ëzi'm *nm* mankind, humankind, humanity

njer'ëzi'shëm
I § *adj (i)* cordial; courteous, polite
II § *adv* cordially; courteously, politely

njer'ëzi'sht *adv* cordially; courteously, politely

njer'ëzo'r *adj* **1** human **2** humane

njerí
I § *nm* **1** human being; person **2** person on one's side: supporter; relative, family/kin member
II § *pron* someone; anyone
○ **njeri i besës** trustworthy/honorable person, man of his word
○ **njeri i brendshëm** person with close family or social ties
○ **njeri i detit** person whose life revolves around the sea
○ **njeri i djersës** hard-working person
○ **njeri enciklopedik** person with encyclopedic knowledge
○ **njeri i fushës** lowlander
○ **njeri i hekurave** person who is good with metal-working tools: mechanic
○ **njeri i hiçit** worthless person
○ **njeri i hilesë** cheat, charlatan, swindler
○ **njeri i humbur** feckless person
○ **njeri i hurit dhe i litarit** stinking rat/bastard, rotten louse: gallows bird
○ **njeri i jashtëm** person without blood relationship to a family; outsider
○ **njeri i kazmës** manual laborer
○ **njeri i librit** person devoted to books
○ **njeri i luftës** war veteran
○ **njeri i Luftës** *(HistPK)* Albanian veteran of the War of National Liberation
○ **njeri me dyzet/njëqind flamur** "person with 20/200 flags" person without principles
○ **njeri me hënë/hënëz** moody person
○ **njeri me kokë** person with a head on his shoulders
○ **njeri me orë** person who acts on whim, capricious person
○ **ësh·të njeri me pikë** to be a person with a spotted/stained past
○ **njeri me rrebe** person with a temper
○ **njeri me taban** person of stalwart character
○ **njeri me taraf** well-connected person
○ **njeri me teka** person given to indulging his whims: capricious person
○ **njeri me tru** person with a great mind
○ **njeri me thopërç** hot-tempered person
○ **njeri me yll** lucky man
○ **njeri me gramë** literate/learned person
○ **njeri i minderit** *(Pej)* big shot who would rather sit in his comfortable sofa than do real work
○ **njeri që nuk ndi·***het³ˢᵍ* a person who is quiet and well-behaved; person who never speaks up
○ **njeri në shenjë** distinguished person, person of distinction
○ **njeri pa cipë** shameless person
○ **njeri pa kripë** dull/boring person, bland personality

○ **njeri pa leqe** "person without twists or turns" a thoroughly honest person, completely sincere person
○ **njeri pa lyrë** dull person
○ **njeri pa njeri** person left with no family
○ **njeri pa shpirt 1** cruel/merciless person: heartless person **2** person without any warm feelings: cold fish
○ **njeri pa shtrak** person who speaks straightforwardly
○ **njeri pa taban** person of weak and shifting character
○ **njeri pa yndyrë** bland/dull person
○ **njeri i penës** person who is good at writing: skillful/effective writer; (professional) writer
○ **Njeriu për njeriun është.** People should help one another.
○ **Njeriu për njeriun është ujk.** "Man is a wolf for man." *(Prov)* It's a jungle out there.
○ **njeri i punës** hard worker
○ **njeri i pushkës** person willing and able to fight with a gun: fighter
○ **njeri i rrogozit** common man; man of the people
○ **njeri i shpellave** caveman
○ **njeri i shtëpisë** friend who has become one of the family
○ **njeri i shtresës** *(Colloq)* person at the bottom level of society
○ **njeri i vickave** cantankerous/crotchety/peevish person
○ **njeri i zbortë** snowman

njeri'da'sh'ës
I § *adj (Book)* having good will towards other people
II § *n* person kind to others: philanthropist

njeri'da'shje *nf (Book)* kindness towards others: philanthropy

njeri'ngrën'ës
I § *adj* man-eating
II § *adj* man-eater

*njeri'njt*ë* *adj (i) (Old)* = njerëzo'r

njeri'th *nm* **1** [*Anat*] uvula **2** *(Impol)* short person: little stump of a man

njeri'vra's'ës *n (Book)* person who kills a human being: homicide

njeri'vra'sje *nf (Book)* killing of a human being: homicide

njeri'zi'm *nm ger* **1** <njerizo'·*n*, njerizo'·*het* **2** humanity, humankind; human society

njeri'zo'·het *vpr* to become humanized/civilized

njeri'zo'·*n* *vt* to humanize, civilize

njerk *nm* stepfather

njerk'*ë* *nf* **1** stepmother **2** *(Fig)* cruel stepmother
○ **zemër/shpirt njerke** vicious, mean (to children)

njerk'*ëri* *nf* status of a stepparent; time during which one is a stepparent

njerk'o'r *adj* like/as/of a stepparent

*njer'o'·*n* *vi* to spend time idly, putter around

*nje'sh = njësh

*nje'sh'ëm *adj (i)* uniform, even = njësi'sh*ë*m

*njesht'o'·*n* *vt* = lëvdo'·*n*

nje'tër *nf (Reg)* = mje'd*ë*r

*nje'ti *adv* = gjet'u

*njeth·
I § *vt* to fertilize; impregnate
II § *vi* to be fertile; grow

njeth·et *vpr* **1** to bud; (of trees) break into leaf **2** to come to life, become enlivened

*nje'th|ët *adj (i)* green and tender, growing

*nje'thje *nf ger* <njeth·

një

　I § num one; number one

　II § determiner **1** a, an **2** one and the same, the same, single **3** one in particular

　III § adj **1** single, unitary **2** one of a kind

　IV § nf the number one

　V § nf, nm (np ˜ra) a single one: one, unit

　VI § pron **1** one (as opposed to another) **2** someone; something

　VII § pred (Colloq) together as one

　◦ **Një fytyrë** <> **vje·**-*n³ˢᵍ*, **një fytyrë** <> **shko·**-*n³ˢᵍ*. "One face of <> comes, one face of <> goes." <>'s face goes from flush to pale.

　◦ **ësh·të një që s'bëhet dy** to be one of a kind

　◦ **ësh·të**ᵖˡ **një rraxhë** to be exactly the same size

　◦ **një vatër** {*plural noun*} a lot of {}, a whole bunch of {}

një|aks|ial *adj* [*Spec*] uniaxial, monaxial

një|akt|ësh *adj* [*Theat*] (of a play) having a single act

një|akt|ëshe *nf* [*Theat*] one-act play: one-acter

një|an|ësi *nf* = njëanshm|ëri

një|an|ësisht *adv* = njëanshm|ëri

një|an|ësor *adj* **1** positioned on one side **2** [*Ling*] lateral **3** one-sided, biased

një|an|ësh *adj* having a single side; involving only one side

një|an|shëm *adj (i)* **1** one-sided, single-sided; biased **2** having a single focus/direction/interest; narrowly focussed **3** unilateral

një|an|shm|ëri *nf* one-sidedness

një|an|shm|ërisht *adv (Book)* one-sidedly

një|atom|ësh *adj* [*Chem*] monoatomic

një|bazík *adj* [*Chem*] monobasic

një|boshtor *adj (Spec)* uniaxial

një|brir|ësh

　I § adj single-horned

　II § nm unicorn

një|buzor *adj* [*Bot*] having a single-lipped flower: unilabiate

një|ckë *num (Colloq Reg)* just a single one

një|de'g|ësh *adj* having a single branch

një|dialekt|or *adj* based on a single dialect

një|direk|ësh *adj* single-masted

një|dit|ësh *adj* of one day; one day old

një|dit|ëz *adv* = njëditëzaj

një|dit|ëzaj *adv* on the day before yesterday; a few days ago, the other day

një|ditor *adj* one day long

një|dit|shëm *adj (i)* **1** = njëditor **2** *(Old)* of the day before yesterday; of a few days ago

një|drejt|im|ësh *adj (i)* (of a road) permitting traffic in only one direction: one-way

një|dynym|ësh *adj* of one dynym in size

një|dhom|ësh *adj* consisting of a single room: single-room, one-room

një|emër|ak *nm* = njëemërsh

një|emër|sh *nm* namesake

një|enj|ëze *nf* riddle

një|fare *determiner (followed by abl pl case)* **1** a certain; a so-called, supposedly a **2** *(Pej)* the worst kind of

një|far|ë|lloj *adv* = njëfarësoj

një|far|ë|s *adj* [*Bot*] having a single seed: monospermous

një|far|ë|si *nf* equality of type/status

një|far|ë|soj *adv* **1** in some way: somehow **2** neither too badly nor too well: so-so

një|far|ë|sh *adj* **1** = njëfarës **2** of the same type; homogeneous

një|fa'z|ësh *adj* **1** (of a rocket) one-phase, single-phase **2** = njëfazor

një|faz|or *adj* [*Electr*] single-phase, one-phase

një|fe'tar *adj (Old)* of the same faith: co-religionist

një|fi'll|ësh *adj* consisting of a single strand: simple

një|fish

　I § adj single; single-stranded; single-ply

　II § adv just as it is, just the one

　III § nm base (value/price/cost)

një|fish|të *adj (i)* single, simple; single-ply; onefold

një|fjal|ësh *adj* type of rebus puzzle whose solution is a single word

një|fjal|ëz|im *nm ger* <njëfjalëzo'·n, njëfjalëzo'·het

një|fjal|ëzo'·het *vpr* [*Ling*] to become compounded into a single word

një|fjal|ëzo'·n *vt* [*Ling*] to compound [a word sequence] into a single word

një|fle't|ësh *adj* (of textiles) in a single panel: single-paneled; single-leafed

një|form|ësh *adj* having a single form

një|gjak|ës *n (Book)* person of the same lineage: blood relative, kinsman; compatriot, countryman

*një|gjak|ësi *nf* consanguinity

një|gji're *nf* [*Bot*] woodruff (*Asperula*)

një|gjymtyr|ësh *adj* **1** [*Math*] monomial **2** [*Ling*] having only one constituent

një|her|azi *adv* **1** at the same time: simultaneously **2** to the same extent

një|herë

　I § adv **1** at some time in the past: at one time, once, one day **2** at sometime in the future: sometime, some day, one day **3** before anything else: first **4** for right now, for the moment, for the time being

　II § pcl **1** in particular **2** (after a verb) just this once **3** (softens the force of an imperative verb) once

　◦ **na ishte njëherë** once upon a time

　◦ **njëherë e një kohë** a long time ago, at one time

　◦ **njëherë për njëherë** for right now, for the moment, for the time being

　◦ **njëherë si sot** on a similar occasion in the past

një|her|ësh *adv* all at one time, all together; together; at the same time, simultaneously

një|her|shëm *adj (i)* **1** erstwhile, bygone, old-time **2** one-time, one only **3** at the same time: simultaneous

një|hop|shëm *adj (i)* instantaneous, instant, immediate

një|jar *adj* **1** (of a recorder-like musical instrument) single-barreled **2** (of fruit) having a single seed/pit

një|jare *nf* **1** recorder-like musical instrument with a single-barrel **2** fruit with a single seed/pit

*një|jatër|m *adj (i)* reciprocal

një|ja'v|ësh *adj* **1** one-year-old **2** = njëjavor

një|ja'v|ëshëm *adj (i)* one-week-old

një|javor *adj* one year long

një|j|ës *adj, nm* [*Ling*] singular

një|j|ësi *nf* **1** equality **2** unity, oneness

njëjë̈si̇́m nm ger 1 <njëjësoˑ•n *2 parity, equality

*njëjëˈsi̇́sht adv solely

njëjëˈso•het vpr (Book Old) = barazoˑ•het

njëjëso•n vt (Book) 1 = njëjtësoˑ•n 2 (Old) = barazoˑ•n *3 to unify

*njëjshëm adj (i) equal, like; alike

njëjtë adj (i) 1 same; identical 2 equal

njëjtë̈si̇́ nf 1 sameness; identicality 2 equality

njëjtë̈si̇́m nm ger <njëjtësoˑ•n, njëjtësoˑ•het

njëjtëso•het vpr (Book) to become identical/equal

njëjtëso•n vt (Book) 1 = identifiko•n 2 to equalize

*njëkaq adv then and there, on the spot

njëkaˈtë̈sh adj having only one storey: single-storey, one-level

*njëkëmbˈas adv on equal footing

njëkëmbë̈sh
  I § adj monopodal
  II § n monopode

njëkëmbthi adv on one leg

njëkilë̈sh adj weighing one kilogram

njëkoˈhë̈s adj (Old) = bashkëkohës

njëkohësi̇́ nf 1 simultaneity, contemporaneity 2 [Ling] synchrony

njëkohë̈si̇́sht adv at the same time: simultaneously

njëkoˈhshëm adj (i) at the same time: simultaneous

njëkoˈmbˈas adv = njëkombës

njëkoˈmbë̈s n (Book) compatriot, fellow countryman

njëkryeˈgjymtyˈrë̈sh adj [Ling]

njëkthi̇́në̈sh adj having only one room: one-room

njëkuintalˈë̈sh adj weighing one quintal

njëkuptimë̈si̇́ nf [Ling] monosemy

njëkuptimoˈr adj (Book) unambiguous

njëkuptiˈmshëm adj (i) monosemous

njëkuroˈrë̈she adj

njëleˈkë̈sh (Offic) worth/costing one lekadj, nm (Colloq)(coin) worth ten cents

njëleˈkë̈she nf (Offic) money worth one lek

njëli̇́të̈rsh adj having a capacity of one liter

njëˈlloj adv = njësoj

njëˈllojˈshëm adj (i) = njëllojtë

njëˈllojshmˈëri̇́ nf (Book) alikeness; identicalness; selfsameness

njëˈllojtë adj (i) same

njëˈllojtë̈si̇́ nf (Book) = njëllojshmˈëri̇́

njëmbë̈dhjetˈë
  I § num eleven; number eleven
  II § nf the number eleven
  III § adj (i), n (i) eleventh

njëmbë̈dhjetë̈meˈtë̈rsh nm [Soccer] penalty kick zone; penalty kick; penalty spot

njëmbë̈dhjetë̈rrokˈë̈sh
  I § nm, adj [Lit] (a verse line) having eleven syllables: hendecasyllabic
  II § nm hendecasyllabic line

njëmbë̈dhjetë̈sh nm [Sport] team of eleven players

njëmbë̈dhjetë̈vjeçaˈr adj 1 eleven years long 2 eleven years old

njëmeˈnd adv (Colloq) 1 right now; right away, immediately 2 really meaning it, in earnest: genuinely; seriously

njëmeˈnd• vt (Book) = njëjtësoˑ•n

njëmendë̈si̇́ nf (Book) reality = realitë̱t

njëmendë̈so•n vt (Book) to make real: realize

njëmeˈndi = njëmend

njëmendi̇́m nm ger (Book Old) <njëmendoˑ•n, njëmendoˑ•het

njëmeˈndje nf agreement

njëmendo•het vpr 1 (Book Old) to become of one mind 2 to melt into one's surroundings: conform

njëmendo•n vt (Book) to ascertain the truth of [ ]

njëmeˈndshëm adj (i) = njëmeˈndtë

njëmeˈndtë adj (i) actual, real

njëmenjë adv without doubt, right away: one-two-three
  ◦ është njëmenjë kjo punë it will happen for sure, you can count on it, it's all settled

njëmë̈sht adj (i) = njëfi̇́llësh

njëmë̈zaj adv = njëfi̇́sh

njëmi̇́jë = një mijë

njëmijë̈leˈkë̈sh
  I § adj (Offic) worth/costing a thousand leks
  II § adj, nm (Colloq) (bill) worth a hundred leks

njëmijë̈leˈkë̈she nf 1 (Offic) bill worth a thousand leks 2 (Colloq) bill worth a hundred leks

njëmijë̈she nf (Old) = njëmijëleˈkë̈she

njëmi̇́jtë adj (i) thousandth

njëmilioˈnë̈sh adj with a value/population of a million

njëmilioˈntë adj (i) millionth

njëmoˈshˈas n = moshataˈr

njëmoˈshë̈s n = moshataˈr

njëmoshoˈr adj [Geol] of the same age: coeval

njëmotoˈrë̈sh adj [Spec] single-motor

njëmujoˈr adj 1 of one-month duration 2 monthly

njënaˈtë̈zaj adv (Colloq) night before last; a few nights ago/earlier

njëngjyˈrë̈sh adj 1 single-colored, monochromatic 2 (Fig) humdrum, monotonous 3 (Book) (of certain political parties) indistinguishable

*njëni̇́ nf unity

njënjë adv (Colloq) alike

njënjë̈shëm adj (i) just the same: identical, equal, uniform

*njënji̇́sht adv uniformly

njëoˈrë̈sh adj hour-long

njëpasˈnjëshëm adj (i) one-after-another: continual; consecutive

njëpë̈llëmbˈë̈sh adj as big as a thumb: thumb-sized

njëpë̈rnjë adv exactly the same

njëpjeˈllˈë̈shˈe
  I § adj fem
  II § nf [Biol] bearing only one offspring in a litter; having borne only one litter

njëpjesˈë̈sh adj consisting of a single piece: one-piece

njëpoloˈr adj [Electr] unipolar

njëqelizoˈr adj consisting of a single cell: one-celled, unicellular

njëqendroˈr adj [Spec] having a single center

njëqi̇́nd nm the number one hundred; one hundred

njëqindfi̇́sh
  I § nm a hundred times the amount: hundredfold
  II § adv by a hundredfold, multiplied by a hundred; very much

një|qind|gra·dë·sh *adj* (of a measuring instrument) scaled into a hundred units

një|qind|këmbë·sh *nm* [*Invert*] centipede (*Chilopoda*)

një|qind|le·k·ësh
I § *adj* (*Offic*) worth/costing a hundred leks
II § *adj, nm* (*Colloq*) (bill) worth ten leks

një|qind|le·k·ëshe *nf* 1 (*Offic*) bill worth a hundred leks 2 (*Colloq*) bill worth ten leks

një|qind|me·tër·sh *nm* [*Sport*] track 100 meters long; 100-meter run

një|qind|ta *np (të)* one's hundredth year of age

një|qind|të
I § *adj (i)* (ordinal number) hundredth
II § *nf (e)* (fraction) a hundredth

një|qind|vjeç·ar
I § *adj* hundred-year-long; a hundred years old
II § *nm* century

një|qind|vjet·o·r *nm* hundredth-year anniversary: centenary

njër *nm, nf (definite case forms only)* < një 1 one (of them): either one, any one 2 (the) one (in contrast with the other) 3 (*Colloq*) someone; (in negative or interrogative contexts) anyone
◦ **njëri i bie gozhdës, tjetri potkoit** everyone is working at cross purposes
◦ **Njëri i bie trokes, tjetri i bie këmborës.** "One hits the small bell, the other hits the large bell." They are not even trying to understand each other.
◦ **njëri (i bie₁·³ˢᵍ) kudhrës, tjetri çokut/çekiçit** (to work) at cross purposes
◦ **Njëri ia thotë e tjetri ia pret.** "One person tells it to him and the other catches it for him." Whatever one says, the other will back up.

njër|a-tjetr|a *nf recip nom* one another

njër|a-tje·tr·ën *nf recip acc* one another

njër|a-tje·tr·ës *nf recip dat* one another
◦ **njëri përpjetë e tjetri tatëpjetë** some (people) do well, some/others don't

njër|i-tje·tr|i *nm recip nom* one another

njër|i-tje·tr|in *nm recip acc* one another

njër|i-tje·tr|it *nm recip dat* one another

njër|ro·k·ës = njërro·kësh

njër|ro·k·ësh
I § *adj* [*Ling*] monosyllabic
II § *nm* [*Ling*] monosyllable

një|rro·k·shëm *adj (i)* = njërro·kësh

një|seks·o·r *adj* [*Bot*] unisexual

një|si *nf* unit; unity
◦ **njësi hamullore** [*Agr*] basic unit to measure agricultural work, officially equal to one hectare plowed 17-20cm deep
◦ **njësi e rendit të dytë** [*Math*] unit of the second order: number/numeral in the ten's column
◦ **njësi e rendit të tretë** [*Math*] unit of the third order: number/numeral in the hundred's column
◦ **njësi ushqimore** [*Agr*] nutritional unit of forage (defined as the nutritional value equivalent to a kilogram of oats or barley)

një|si *nm ger* 1 < njëso·n, njëso·het 2 unification; consolidation; standardization *3 unity

një|sipër|fa·q·shëm *adj (i)* [*Geom*] equilateral

një|si·shëm *adj (i)* unitary; unified

një|si·sht *adv* 1 (*Book*) uniformly, evenly, equally 2 jointly

një|si·t *nm* [*Mil*] 1 [*Hist*] guerilla unit during the struggle for national independence 2 squad

një|so·het *vpr* to become unified

një|so·n *vt* 1 to unify; consolidate 2 to make [] uniform, standardize

një|soj *adv* 1 alike; in the same way 2 equally, to the same extent/degree

një|soj|shëm *adj (i)* = njëllojtë

një|so·j·të *adj (i)* = njëllojtë

një|s·o·r *adj* 1 (*Book*) = njësi·shëm 2 [*Spec*] per unit *3 individual *4 singular

një|s·u·ar *adj (i)* unified

një|s·u·es *adj* 1 unifying 2 standardizing

një|sh
I § *nm* 1 number one 2 lowest grade: one (where ten is the highest grade); highest grade: one (where four is the lowest grade) 3 ace (in card games)
II § *adv* 1 together 2 uniform, even; alike; equal; level 3 (*Colloq*) at the same time: simultaneously 4 in one piece, undivided
◦ **më njësh** in a single piece: unfolded completely; (of filament) in a single strand

një|sh|e
I § *adj* suitable for just one
II § *nf* something suitable for just one: single room, one-cup coffeepot, monophonic song
III § *np* primary numbers

një|shekull|o·r *adj* century-long

një|shëm *adj (i)* (*Old*) 1 = njëjtë 2 = njësi·shëm 3 = baraba·rtë

një|sh|kolon·ë
I § *nf* single-file column
II § *adv* in single file

një|shkro·nj·ësh *adj* [*Ling*] with each letter representing a single sound

*****një|sh|të** *adj (i)* single, sole, unique

një|shtres·o·r *adj* [*Spec*] monolayer

*****një|ta·sh** *adv* (*Reg Gheg*) right now, at once

një|te·h|ësh *adj* single-bladed

një|te·l|ësh *adj* single-stringed

një|ti·ngull·t *adj* sounding the same

një|ton|ësh *adj* 1 weighing one ton 2 with a capacity of one-ton

një|trajt|ës·i *nf* = njëtrajtshm|ëri

një|trajt|ës·i·m *nm ger* < njëtrajtëso·n, njëtrajtëso·het

një|trajt|ës·i·sht *adv* (*Book*) uniformly

një|trajt|ës·o·het *vpr* 1 (*Book*) to become uniform 2 to conform

një|trajt|ës·o·n *vt* 1 (*Book*) to make [] uniform 2 to bring [] into conformity: conform

një|trajt|ësh *adj* having a single form, invariable in form

një|trajt|shëm *adj (i)* uniform

një|trajt|shm|ëri *nf* uniformity

një|tru·ng|ësh|e *adj* (boat) constructed from a single log: dugout

një|thelb·o·r
I § *nm* [*Bot*] monocotyledon
II § *adj* [*Bot*] monocotyledonous

një|thundr·a·k
I § *adj* [*Zool*] odd-toed ()
II § *nm* [*Zool*] family of odd-toed ungulates (*Equus*)

një|vale·nt *adj* [*Chem*] univalent, monovalent

një|ve·gj·ësh *adj* (of vessels) one-handled

njëve·nd[ë**sh** *adj* having space for one person to sit

njëve·to·r *adj* [*Ling*] (of verbs) used only in the third person

njëvëllim[ë**sh** *adj* published as an individual volume; in a single volume

njëvëllim·shëm *adj (i)* [*Geom*] of equal volume

njëvi·ti *adv* a year ago; a couple of years ago

njëvi·tmë *adj (i)* (*Colloq*) = njëvi·tshëm

njëvi·tshëm *adj (i)* **1** = parvje·tshëm **2** of a couple of years ago

njëvjeça·r
  I § *adj* **1** lasting for one year; year-long **2** [*Bot*] having a one-year life cycle: annual **3** one-year-old
  II § *nm* **1** yearling **2** [*Bot*] annual (plant)

njëvjeto·r
  I § *nm* first anniversary
  II § *adj* *one-year-old

njëvle·fshëm *adj (i)* = njëvlershëm

njëvle·r[ë**s** *nm* [*Spec Ling*] equivalent

njëvle·r[ë**s**[**i** *nf* [*Spec Ling*] equivalence

njëvle·rshëm *adj (i)* equivalent

njëvlershm[**ëri** *nf* (*Book*) = njëvlerësi

një·zaj
  I § *adv* together; at the same time: simultaneously
  II § *adv (së)* once again; from the beginning

njëze·t
  I § *num* twenty; number twenty
  II § *nf* the number twenty
  ○ **njëzet e katër karatësh** (*Book*) (person) of sterling quality, (person) of the very best quality

njëze·ta *np (të)* twenty years of age

njëzetdito·r
  I § *adj* of twenty days
  II § *nm* period consisting of the first twenty days of a month

njëzete·dy[**të** *adj (i)* twenty-second

njëzete·katëror[ë**sh** *adj* lasting twenty-four hours

njëzete·katër[**t** *adj (i)* twenty-fourth

njëzete·një[**të** *adj (i)* twenty-first

njëzete·pes[**të** *adj (i)* twenty-fifth

njëze·t[ë *adj (i)* twentieth

njëze·t[ë**sh** *nm* number twenty; group of twenty of the same kind, a score

njëzetfisho··n *vt* to increase [] twentyfold

njëzetkënd[ë**sh** *adj* [*Geom*] icosahedron

njëzetqinda·rk[ë**sh** *adj* worth twenty cents; priced at twenty cents

njëzetqinda·rk[ë**sh**[**e** *nf* coin worth twenty cents; priced at twenty cents

njëzetvje·ç *adj* twenty-year-old

njëzetvjeça·r *adj* **1** twenty years in duration: twenty-year-long **2** twenty-year-old

njëzetvjeto·r *nm* twentieth anniversary

një·z[ë *num* (*Pet Dimin*) teeny one
  ○ **njëzë e njëzë** riddle = njëenjë·zë

njëzë·ri *adv* **1** with a single voice, all together **2** (*Fig*) unanimously

njëzë·shëm *adj (i)* unanimous

njëzëshm[**ëri** *nf* unanimity

njëzi·m *nm ger* = njësim

njëzo··het *vt* = njëso··het

njëzo··n *vt* = njëso··n

njëzua·r *adj (i)* = njësua·r

○ **nji·**-*het* **me gisht** "be known by (pointing) finger" to have a bad reputation

○ **nji·**-*het* **si paraja e kuqe** "be recognized like red money" (*Impol*) to be immediately recognizable; be notorious, be in the public eye

*nji (*Reg Gheg*) = një

nji·c[ë *nf* = ngjic[ë

*njif·-*et* = njih·*et*

njih·-*et* *vpr* <nje·h· **1** to become acquainted; get to know one another, meet **2** to be met with, occur **3** to be revealed/known, reveal oneself/itself, come to be known
  ○ **S'njihet burri nga mustaqet.** "A man is not known by his mustache." (*Prov*) You can't tell a book by its cover.
  ○ **njih·**-*et* **nga afër me** [] to become thoroughly familiar with []
  ○ **njih·**-*et* **si kau balash** "be recognizable as the dappled bull" **1** to stand out like a sore thumb **2** to be notorious

njih stem for 2nd pl pres, pind, imper, vp <nje·h·

*njik[ë**saj**
  I § *dat/abl* <njikjo
  II § *gen (i)* <njikjo

*njik[ë**shtu** *adv* (*Reg Gheg*) in just this way, just like this

*njik[ë**ta** *proximal 3rd pers pl masc determiner* (*Reg Gheg*) these very ones, they

*njik[ë**të** *acc* (*Reg Gheg*) <njiky, njikjo

*njik[ë**tij** *dat/abl* <njiky

*njik[ë**to** *proximal 3rd pers pl fem determiner* (*Reg Gheg*) these very ones, they

*njik[ë**ty·ne** *dat/abl* <njik[ë**to**, njik[ë**ta** (*Reg Gheg*)

*njikjo *proximal pron 3rd pers sg fem* (*Reg Gheg*) this very one, she, it

*njiky *proximal pron 3rd pers sg masc* (*Reg Gheg*) this very one, he, it

njil[ë *nf* [*Ichth*] Lake Ohrid nase (*Chondrostoma nasus ohridanus*) = skobu·z

njimta·r *n* (*Old*) fraud, swindler

njimt[ë *adv* (*Old*) fraudulently

njimti *nf* (*Old*) fraud, deceit; equivocation

*njimto··n *vt* to swindle, cheat

*njin·es[ë *nf* fasting

*njino··n *vi* to fast

*njirënd[**uer** *adj* (*fem ~ore*) (*Old Regional Gheg*) first-class

*nji·si = njësi

*nji·si·sht = njësi·sht

*nji·so··n = njëso··n

njish[ë *nf* long and low shed with straw bedding for sheep or goats

*nji·shtu *adv* (*Reg Gheg*) in the same way, likewise

*nji·tas = ngji·tur

*nji·tash *adv* = njëta·sh

*njiz = ngjiz

*nji·za·ni *adv* = njëzë·ri

*nji·zâ·shëm (*Reg Gheg*) = njëzë·shëm

*njof (*Reg Gheg*) = njoh

njoftim *nm ger* **1** <njofto·**·n **2** announcement, communique; news **3** information; knowledge

njofto··n *vt* to announce, notify, inform, communicate, report

njoftu·es *nm* announcer; notifier

njoh· _stem for 1st sg pres, 1st & 3rd pl pres, 2nd &_
3rd sg subj, pdef, part, opt, adm <**njeh·**

njoh|ës
_I §_ _n_ expert, savant
_II §_ _adj_ informative, informational

njoh|je _nf ger_ **1** <**njeh·**, **njih·**_et_ **2** cognition; knowl-
edge **3** acquaintance; familiarity **4** recognition; acknowledgement

njoh|shëm _adj (i)_ knowable; recognizable

*njoh|tím = njoftím

njo'h|ur
_I §_ _adj (i)_ **1** familiar, known **2** well-known, famous
_II §_ _nf (e)_ something known; what is known; (math-
ematics) known quantity
III § _n (i)_ person who is known: acquaintance; per-
son who can be called on for help/favors
_IV §_ _nn (të)_ = **njo'hje**

njoh|urí _nf_ knowledge, information

*njo'jt|ës _n (Old)_ connoisseur, expert

*njo'jtje _nf_ **1** acquaintance **2** consciousness

*njo'jt|ur _adj (i)_ known; well known = **njo'hur**

njo'lla-njo'lla
_I §_ _adj_ covered with patches, blotchy
_II §_ _adv_ in variegated color

njo'llë _nf_ **1** patch of color; blotch, blemish **2** _(Fig)_
mark of dishonor; fault, failing **3** bud on a plant
○ **njollë e bardhë** unstudied area, clear field, un-
charted territory
○ **njollat e barrës** spots appearing on a woman's
face when she is pregnant
○ **njollat e Hënës** dark spots on the moon
○ **njollat e vdekjes** spots on a dying person's body
indicating the approach of death
○ **njollë e verdhë** [_Anat_] yellow spot (in the retina)
macula lutea

njoll|o·_het vpr_ = **njollo's·**_et_

njoll|o·_n vt_ = **njollo's·**

njoll|o's· _vt_ **1** to get spots/dirt on [ ]: spot, soil, stain
2 _(Fig)_ to stain [ ]'s reputation; dishonor [ ]

njoll|o's·_et vpr (Fig)_ to bring dishonor upon oneself

njoll|o'sje _nf ger_ **1** <**njollo's·**, **njollo's·**_et_ [_Agr_] **2** =
pikalo're

njoll|o's|ur _adj (i)_ spotted; stained

njom· _vt_ **1** to make [ ] wet: moisten, dampen **2** _(Colloq)_ to water lightly: sprinkle **3** to dip/soak [ ] in liquid
○ **e njom· buzën/gojën** to drink a small amount;
eat a small amount of juicy fruit
○ <>**a njom· dorën** "moisten <>'s hand" **1** to give
<> a tip or small bribe: grease <>'s palm **2** _(Old)_ to
give alms to <>
○ **e njom· fytin/gurmazin/grykën** to drink something: wet one's whistle
○ <> **njom· gojën** to make <>'s mouth water, give
<> an appetite
○ <>**a njom· udhën** "moisten <>'s path" to make
<>'s life easier
○ **e njom· zorrën** "make one's intestines wet"
*1 (of a poor person who has had nothing to eat for a

long time) to slake one's hunger, get something into
one's belly **2** _(Fig)_ to at least have something to eat
now (after having been financially strapped)

njom·_et vpr_ **1** to become soft with moisture **2** to get
wet
○ <> **njom·**_et_ **luga** "<>'s spoon is getting moist"
<>'s financial situation _is improving_, <> _is getting_
back on <>'s feet

njo'me _nf (Pet)_ baby born to old parents, parent's pet
child: little darling

njo'më _adj (i)_ **1** damp, moist **2** juicy; tender; young
and tender **3** _(Fig)_ young and immature **4** (of food)
fresh **5** employing liquid means: wet

njo'm|ës
_I §_ _adj_ [_Spec_] serving to dampen or make moist
_II §_ _nm_ moisturizer

njom|ësí _nf_ **1** moisture; dampness; humidity **2** _(Fig)_
tenderness; freshness

njom|ësíra _np_ green vegetables

njom|ësírë _nf_ **1** = **njomësí** **2** wet place, wet spot

njom|ëso·_het vpr_ to be revived/revitalized; be re-
freshed

njom|ëso·_n vt_ to revive, revitalize; refresh

njo'm|ësht _adj (i)_ = **njomë**

njom|ështí _nf_ **1** = **njomësí** **2** wetness **3** green leafy
plants used as animal fodder: hay **4** green leafy vegetables **5** _(Poet)_ tender age

njom|ështírë _nf_ **1** = **lagështí** **2** green leafy plants
used as animal fodder: hay **3** green leafy vegetables
4 = **njomësírë**

njom|ështo·_het vpr_ **1** to become juicy **2** _(Fig Book)_
to become soft and tender

njom|ështo·_n vt_ **1** to make [ ] juicy and tender
2 _(Fig Book)_ to soften [ ] and make tender

njo'm|ëz _nf_ sapling; tender new foliage

njom|ëza'k
_I §_ _adj (Pet)_ soft and tender, babyfaced
_II §_ _nm_ cute little baby
III § _adj, n_ inexperienced/green (person): (person)
still wet behind the ears

njom|íshte _nf_ **1** green leafy plants used as animal
fodder: hay **2** green leafy vegetables **3** verdant land
4 place that is constantly wet

njo'mje _nf ger_ <**njo'm·**, **njo'm·**_et_

*njom|sís| _stem for 1st sg pres, pl pres, 2nd & 3rd sg
subj, pind_ <**njomsít·**

*njom|sít· _vt_ to moisturize, sprinkle

njom|sh _nm_ green grass; fresh hay

njo'm|ur _adj (i)_ moistened, made damp; wet

njom|urína _np fem_ green vegetables

*nju'fkë _nf_ small feather; down; vein of a leaf

njuha's = **nuha's**

njuha't· = **nuha't·**

Nju-Jo'rk _nm_ New York

njuto'n _nm_ [_Phys_] newton

*njyro·_n vt_ = **ngjyro's·**

Oo

o *nf* **1** the letter "o" in the alphabet **2** the rounded back mid vowel represented by that letter

o
  I § *conj* or; either
  II § *vocative pcl* O, hey
  III § *interj* expresses suffering or regret, surprise, pleasure or admiration: oh!

OA *abbrev* <**Oficina e automjeteve** Workshop for Auto Repair

OAS *abbrev (French)* <**Organisation Armee Secrete** OAS = secret military organization in France after World War II

OAT *abbrev* <**Oficina e automjeteve të tregtisë** Workshop for Repair of Commercial Vehicles

oa'zë *nf* oasis

*oba'd *nm* [*Invert*] horsefly (*Tabanus bovinus*)

obeli'sk *nm* obelisk

obje'kt *nm* object

objekti'v *nm* **1** objective **2** objective lens

objektivi'st *adj, n* [*Phil*] objectivist

objektivi'sht *adv* objectively

objektivite't *nm* objectivity

objektivi'zëm *nm* [*Phil*] objectivism

obligacio'n *nm* **1** [*Fin*] bond of indebtedness: bond **2** (*Book*) obligation

obli'k *adj* [*Tech*] oblique

obobo' *interj* expresses great sorrow, suffering, or surprise: oh no!

obo'rr *nm* **1** enclosed area belonging to and adjacent to a building: courtyard, garden, yard **2** royal court ◦ **oborr kooperativist** (*HistPK*) garden and animals assigned to a family in an agricultural cooperative for its personal use

oborr|ë'si *nf* **1** membership in a royal court **2** courtliness

oborrta'r
  I § *adj* **1** pertaining to a royal court **2** courtly
  II § *n* courtier

oborrta'ri *nf collec* **1** members of a royal court **2** courtliness

obro'kth *nm* (*Reg*) = **pu'çërr**

observato'r *nm* observatory

obskuranti'st *adj, n* (*Book*) obscurantist

obskuranti'zëm *nm* (*Book*) obscurantism

obstruksio'n *nm* (*Book*) (political) obstruction

obstruksioni'st *adj, n* (*Book*) obstructionist (in political matters)

obstruksioni'zëm *nm* **1** (*Book*) obstructionism **2** filibuster **3** delaying tactics

obturacio'n *nm* [*Spec*] interruption of light in a camera

obturato'r *nm* [*Spec*] camera shutter

o'bu'rra *interj* expresses encouragement and exhortation: way to go! attaboy! keep at it!

oburra'ni *pl* <**obu'rra**

obu's *nm* [*Mil*] howitzer

odata'r *n* (*Old*) person who cleans up rooms in an inn or hotel

o'de *nf* [*Lit*] ode

oderra *exhortative interj* onward! keep at it!

oderra'ni *pl* <**oderra**

odë *nf* **1** (*Colloq*) = **dho'më** **2** room used for receiving guests: guest parlor **3** = **o'de**
  ◦ **odë e mirë** room for receiving guests, guest parlor
  ◦ **oda e revoles** (*Old*) percussion chamber of a revolver
  ◦ **oda e zjarrit** living room with a fireplace

*odë'tare *nf* (*Old*) chambermaid

odontome'tër *nm* [*Postal*] perforation gauge

OECD *abbrev (English)* Organization for Economic Cooperation and Development

oenotero're *nf* [*Bot*] evening primrose *Oenothera*

*of *interj* = **ofsh**

ofendi'm *nm ger* **1** (*Book*) <**ofendo'·n, ofendo'·het** **2** offense, affront

ofendo'·het *vpr* (*Book*) to feel offended, take affront

ofendo'·n *vt* (*Book*) to offend

ofendu'es *adj* offensive, insulting

ofensi'vë *nf* **1** military offensive **2** (*Fig*) forceful attack

ofe'rtë *nf* [*Econ*] offering, offer

*ofertu'es *nm* (*Old*) supplier, contractor

ofice'r *n* **1** officer **2** [*Chess*] bishop

ofiçi'në *nf* workshop, repair shop

ofi'q *nm* **1** (*Old*) position of authority: office; official title **2** disparaging nickname

ofiqa'r *n* (*Old*) official

ofro'·n *vt* to offer

ofsa'it *nm* [*Soccer*] offside

ofse't *nm* [*Publ*] offset printing

ofsh
  I § *interj* expresses suffering or sorrow: ow! oh!
  II § *nm* = **ofsha'më**

ofsha'·n *vi* to moan and sigh with pain or suffering: groan

ofsha'më *nf* **1** moaning and sighing; terrible suffering **2** imprecation of terrible suffering: curse

o'fshë *nf* = **ofsha'më**

ofsh|ë'ti·n *vi* **1** = **ofsha'·n** **2** = **ushto'·n**

*oft *nm* meal
  ◦ **oft darke** supper

ofti'kë *nf* (*Old*) consumption, tuberculosis: phthisis

*oftikja'su'r *adj (i)* (*Reg*) = **oftiko'sur**

*oftiko's·et *vpr* to become phthisic/consumptive, contract tuberculosis

*oftiko'su'r *adj (i)* consumptive, tubercular: phthisic

*ofti'm *nm* sigh

ogi' *nf* (*Reg*) defect, deficiency, failing

ogi'ç *n* **1** large sheep wearing a bell to lead the other sheep **2** pet lamb **3** (*Fig*) (of a person) good little lamb

*ogradi's· *vt* to annoy, bother

ogra'jë *nf* grazing meadow in/near a grove of trees: forest meadow

*ogri'shte *nf* [*Bot*] prickly lettuce (*Lactuca scariola*)

ogu·r *nm* augury, omen

ogur·ba·rdhë
   I § *adj* **1** boding well **2** = **fatba·rdh**ë
   II § *nf* good omen

ogur·ke·q
   I § *adj* **1** boding ill **2** = **fatke·q**
   II § *nf* bad omen

ogur·mi·rë *adj, n* = **ogurba·rdh**ë

ogur·sëz *nm (Colloq)* **1** grouch, grumbler; cusser, curser **2** unlucky fellow: poor guy

ogur·zi *adj (fem sg ˜·ez, masc pl ˜·inj, fem pl ˜·eza)* = **ogurke·q**

oh *interj, nm* expression of fatigue, shock, admiration, fear, desire, or pleasure: oh!

****o·h·ët** *adj (i)* sultry

oho· *interj* **1** expresses newly discovered admiration or pleasure: aha! **2** teasingly expresses pretended admiration: oho!

ohoho· *interj* = **oho·**

****ohti·k**ë = **ofti·k**ë

ohu· *interj* **1** expresses sarcastic indifference and lack of respect: who cares! **2** expresses reluctance to go further into a matter: well Hell! **3** expresses a feeling of being overwhelmed by the magnitude of what follows: oh boy! (said with a sigh) **4** emphasizes that some event is far in the past

oi·
   I § *nf onomat* sound of a person crying: boo-hoo
   II § *interj* used by women and girls **1** expresses suffering: oh! ow! ouch! **2** teasingly makes fun of the person addressed **3** expresses annoyance with the person addressed: oh you!

oj·
   I § *onomat* sound of wailing
   II § *interj* **1** expresses fright (used by women and girls) **2** expresses discovered surprise: well! **3** expresses teasing disagreement: come on now!
   III § *vocative pcl* = **moj**

oja·rë *nf* = **oj**ë

ojë *nf* decorative trimming on cloth edges: trimming

****oj·bâ·s**ë *nf (Reg Gheg)* needlewoman

ojme *nf* = **oj**ë

oj·na *np fem* < **oj**ë **1** = **na·ze** **2* needlework **3 (Fig)* high spirits, horseplay

ojn·a·k *adj* = **ojnata·r**

ojnata·r *adj* **1** attempting to be cute **2** playful; playing games

ojn·e· *nf* **1** finickiness; coyness **2** attempt to act cute: cutesiness **3** = **oj**ë **4** *(Fig)* ornamentation, decoration

ojn·i·k *nm* light sea breeze

ojtni· *nf (Old)* custom, tradition

okapi· *nm [Zool]* okapi

oka·r
   I § *adj* **1** using the okë as the unit of weight **2** = **okata·r**
   II § *nm* = **o·kj**e

oka·re *nf* = **okata·r**e

oka·ta·r
   I § *adj* **1** having a capacity of one oke **2** *(Fig Pej)* drinking alcohol to excess: hard-drinking
   II § *n (Fig Pej)* hard-drinking person: drunkard

okata·re *nf* liquid measure of one oke

OKB [*o-kë-bé*] *abbrev nf* < **Organizata e Kombeve të Bashkuara** U.N. = the United Nations

o·kë *nf* old measure of weight: oke

◦ **e bë·**n **(mendjen) okë (për** [ ]) to make up one's mind (about [ ])

◦ **ok**ë **e madhe** full measure: a weight of 1408 grams

◦ **nuk ësh·të në okë** not right in the head, off one's rocker

◦ **Okën pije, pikën mos e derdh!** "Drink the whole container, don't spill a drop!" *(Prov)* When it comes to matters of health, don't try to save, but don't waste anything either!

◦ **ok**ë **e vogël** light measure: a weight of 1250 grams

o·kër *nf [Bot]* einkorn *(Triticum monococcum)*

ok·ëri·shtë *nf* field planted in einkorn

o·k·ës *nm* = **okata·r**e

oki·të *nf* snow frozen on boughs and branches

ok·je *nf* **1** dry measure of one okë **2** weighing scale that measures in okë-based units

okli·m *nm [Bot]* tree with elliptic downy leaves, whose thin, pith-filled branches are particularly suited to be made into cigarette holders

oklo·nje *nf [Invert]* sea snail

okllai· *nf* rolling pin = **pe·tës**

oko·ll
   I § *nm* circle, circuit; circuitous excursion
   II § *adv* around, all around

okre· *nf [Bot]* ocrea, ochrea

oksalido·re *nf [Bot]* sorrel family *Oxalidaceae*

oksi·d *nm [Chem]* oxide

oksidi·m *nm ger* **1** *[Chem]* < **oksido·**n, **oksido··het 2** oxidation

oksido··het *vpr [Chem]* to become oxidized; get rusted

oksido··n *vt [Chem]* to oxidize; rust

oksidue·shëm *adj (i)* **1** subject to rust, not rustproof **2** *[Chem]* oxidizable *()*

oksigje·n *nm [Chem]* oxygen *((O))*

oksigjeni·m *nm ger* **1** < **oksigjeno··n 2** oxygenation

oksigjeno··n *vt [Chem]* to oxygenate

oksigjenua·r *adj (i) [Chem]* oxygenated

oksito·n *adj [Ling]* oxytonic

oktae·dër *nf [Geom]* octahedron

oktapo·d *nm* **1** *[Invert]* octopus **2** *(Fig)* evil person whose harmful activities spread quietly all around

****oktapo·dh** = **oktapo·d**

okta·vë *nf [Mus Lit]* octave

okte·t *nm [Mus]* octet

oktro·v *nm* customshouse

okula·r *nm* eyepiece of an optical device: ocular

okuli·st *n* ophthalmologist

okulisti·kë *nf* ophthalmology

****okulli·m** *nm* multitude, crowd

okupacio·n *nm (Book)* occupation (by military action) = **pushti·m**

okupato·r *n (Book)* occupier (by military action) = **pushtue·s**

okupo··n *vt* to occupy [ ] (by military action)

****Ola·nd**ë *nf* Holland = **Hola·nd**ë

oleace· *nf [Bot]* olive family *Oleaceae*

olea·nd·ër *nf [Bot]* oleander *Nerium oleander* = **he·lmës**

ole·r *nm (Reg)* = **shta·lp**ë

olifë *nf [Tech]* drying oil, linseed oil

oligarkí *nf* oligarchy

oligarkík *adj* oligarchic

olimpiadë *nf* olympiad

olimpík *adj* Olympic

olivikulturë *nf* [*Agr*] cultivation of olives = ullishtari

om *nm* [*Phys*] ohm

oma·n *nm* [*Bot*] elecampane *(Inula helenium)*

ombeliferë *nf* [*Bot*] = ombrellóre

ombrellë *nf* 1 umbrella 2 [*Bot*] foliage, leafage 3 [*Bot*] umbel, umbella *()*

*ombrellëz** *nf* [*Bot*] umbellule *()*

ombrellóre *nf* [*Bot*] carrot family *Umbelliferae*

omega *indecl* the Greek letter omega

*omer** *nm* measure equal to about eight pounds: omer

omëletë *nf* omelet

ommetër *nf* [*Phys*] ohmmeter

OMT *abbrev* < **Oficina mekanike e tregtisë** workshop for repairing equipment used by NTU

*ona·gër** *nm* [*Zool*] wild ass, onager

onanizëm *nm* (*Book*) onanism

*oncë** *nf* ounce

ondulacio·n *nm* undulation

onkolo·g *nm* [*Med*] oncologist

onkologjí *nf* [*Med*] oncology

onomastíkë *nf* [*Ling*] onomastics

onomatope· *nf* [*Ling*] onomatopoeia

onomatopeík *adj* [*Ling*] onomatopoeic

opa·ç *nm* [*Ichth*] female striped mullet

*opa·ngë** = opíngë

Opa·r *nm* largely pastoral ethnographic region in southeastern Albania

opara·k
    I § *adj* of or pertaining to Opar
    II § *n* native of Opar

opcio·n *nm* (*Book*) option

OPÇ *abbrev* < **Organizata për Çlirimin e Palestinës** PLO = Palestine Liberation Organization

OPEC *abbrev* (*English*) OPEC

operacio·n *nm* operation
    ◦ **operacion cezarian** [*Med*] cesarean section
    ◦ **operacion i gjelbër** [*Agr*] pruning a plant to increase its productivity

*operatë** *nf* (surgical) operation

operatív
    I § *adj* operative; operational
    II § *nm* (*Colloq*) person in charge

operato·r *n* 1 operator (of complex equipment) 2 operating surgeon 3 cameraman; projectionist

operetë *nf* [*Mus*] operetta

operë *nf* [*Mus*] opera
    ◦ **operë gazmore** light opera

operím *nm ger* 1 < opero·∙n 2 operation

opero·∙n
    I § *vt* [*Med*] to operate on [a body part]
    II § *vi* [*Mil*] to engage in military operations

*opet** *adv* again

opingabërës *nm* = opinga·r

opinga·r *n* 1 maker of clogs/moccasins 2 (*Old*) merchant who sells clogs/moccasins

opingaxhi *nm* (*np* ˜ *nj*) = opinga·r

opíngë *nf* 1 moccasin tied on with thongs; clogs with hard rubber soles and rubber or leather uppers 2 (*Pej Old*) lower class, riffraff
    ◦ **opinga gogishte** pointed cowhide moccasins with thongs tied around the shin
    ◦ **Të <> marr**^{subj} **opingat!** (*Crude*) "Let {} take <>'s very clogs (if {} catch <>)." ({} *would be* welcome to everything <> had if {} could catch/find <>) let {} just try to catch/find <>!

opinio·n *nm* general opinion/judgment

opium *nm* 1 opium 2 (*Fig*) opiate

opone·nt *n* 1 official critic: challenger at a thesis defense 2 prepublication manuscript reader

opopo· *interj* expresses astonishment

oportuníst
    I § *n* opportunist
    II § *adj* opportunistic

oportunízëm *nm* opportunism

opozíta·r *adj* in opposition: opposed

opozítë *nf* opposition

opt *nm* (*Reg*) face; countenance

optatív *nm* [*Ling*] optative

optík *adj* optic; optical

optíkë *nf* 1 optics 2 optical equipment

optimal *adj* (*Book*) optimal

optimetër *nf* [*Tech*] optimeter

optimíst
    I § *n* optimist
    II § *adj* optimistic

optimízëm *nm* optimism

oputa *np* lace for moccasins

oqea·n *nm* ocean
    ◦ **oqeani ajror** (*Book*) the (earth's) atmosphere
    ◦ **oqean botëror/i përbotshëm** (*Book*) [*Geog*] the (earth's) hydrosphere
    ◦ **Oqeani Paqësor** Pacific Ocean

oqeaník
    I § *adj* oceanic
    II § *nm* large ocean-going vessel: ocean liner

or *interj pcl* (*Colloq*) = more

ora·kull *nm* (*np* ˜ *j*) (*Old*) oracle

oral *adj* oral

oranguta·ng *nm* [*Zool*] orangutan

ora·r *nm* time schedule; timetable
    ◦ **orar unik** work schedule without a break for lunch

orato·r *n* (*Book*) orator = gojëta·r

oratorí *nf* (*Book*) oratory = gojëtarí

oratorík *adj* (*Book*) oratorical = gojëta·r

orbítë *nf* orbit

*orcallaba·nda** *interj* [*Naut*] heave to!

*ordí** = ordhí

ordina·ncë *nf* (*Old*) [*Mil*] orderly, batman

ordinatë *nf* [*Math*] ordinate

ordinato·r *nm* (mainframe) computer = kompju·ter

ordine·r *adj* 1 ordinary 2 (*Pej*) common, vulgar

*ordhí** = hordhí

ore· *interj pcl* (*Colloq*) = more

ore·ks *nm* appetite

orendí *np fem* 1 furnishings; furniture 2 equipment

orendís- *vt* 1 to supply furniture for []: furnish 2 (*Reg*) to tidy up [a house]

ore·shkë *nf* (*Reg*) [*Bot*] Jerusalem artichoke *(Helianthus tuberosus)*

o'rë *nf* 1 hour 2 time 3 timekeeping mechanism: clock, watch 4 [*Folklore*] helpful magical sprite that takes form as a woman, girl, child, or snake: nymph, fairy 5 (*Fig*) luck
○ **orë (akademike)** academic hour (about 50 minutes): class hour; hour of academic credit
○ **orë e çast** at every moment: constantly, continually
○ **orë dore** wristwatch
○ **orët e maleve** mountain spirits, oreads
○ **<>a hëngri orën** "eat away <>'s destined hour of death" (*Fig*) to shorten <>'s life, cause <>'s death, kill <>
○ **orë e kohë** at every moment: constantly, continually
○ **ora me dorë** 1 quickly and thoroughly 2 without any doubt, of course, absolutely
○ **ora me një** 1 quickly and thoroughly 2 without any doubt, of course, absolutely
○ **orë mësimore** class period
○ **orë e minutë** at every moment: constantly, continually
○ **orë muri** wall clock
○ **orë e pa kohë** 1 with no regard for the proper time 2 quite often, frequently
○ **sa ora** at that moment, immediately
○ **i orës së fundit** most recent, latest
○ **i orës së parë** 1 among the earliest (members), there at the very start: one of the first 2 enthusiastic, fervent
○ **ora e shtëpisë** (*Euph*) Aesculapian snake = bo'llë
○ **i orëve të para** 1 among the earliest (members), there at the very start: one of the first 2 enthusiastic, fervent
○ **orë tryeze** table clock
○ **orë xhepi** pocket watch

orë'ba'rdhë *adj* = fatba'rdhë
orë'çu'et *adj* (*Reg*) ever-lucky, blessed by fate
orë'fje'tur *adj* trying hard but without success: hapless, unlucky
orë'ke'q *adj* (*Colloq*) = fatke'q
orë'li'gë *adj* (*Colloq*) = fatke'q
orë'ma'tës *nm* [*Spec*] timer
orë'mi'rë *adj* (*Colloq*) = fatmi'rë
orë'ndre'qës *n* clock/watch repairman: watchmaker
o'rë-no'rmë *nf* [*Econ*] amount of work to be done in one hour
o'rë-nje'ri *nm* [*Econ*] man-hour
o'rë-o'rë *adv* (*Colloq*) from time to time = he'rë-he'rë
orë'pra'pë *adj* (*Colloq*) luckless, unhappy
orë'pre'rë *adj* (also used as a curse) hapless, unlucky, unhappy
orë'sha'rë *adj* luckless, unlucky, unhappy
orë'shi'tës *n* clock/watch seller
orë'shu'ar *adj, n* (also used as a curse) (*Colloq*) (person) cursed with bad luck
*orë'tu'ndë *nf* large stewpot
orë'zi *adj, n* (*fem sg ~ ez, masc pl ~ i nj, fem pl ~ eza*) (*Colloq*) (one) cursed by fate: unfortunate
orga'n *nm* 1 organ (of the body) 2 institutional organ 3 organ, periodical
organe't *nm* [*Mus*] barrel organ
organi'k *adj* organic
organi'kë *nf* table of organization; set of positions under a superior administrative unit

organiki'sht *adv* organically
organi'st *n* organ-player: organist
organiza'të *nf* organization
○ **organizatë-ba'zë** party cell
organizati'v *adj* organizational
organizati'vi'sht *adv* (*Book*) organizationally
organizato'r *n* organizer = organizu'es
organi'zëm *nm* organism
organizi'm *nm ger* 1 < organizo'•n, organizo'•het 2 organization
organizo'•het *vpr* 1 to become organized 2 to join an organization
organizo'•n *vt* to organize
organizu'ar
  I § *adj (i)* 1 organized 2 belonging to an organization
  II § *n (i)* member of the Party; member of the Communist Youth Organization during World War II
organizu'es
  I § *n* organizer
  II § *adj* 1 involved in organizing 2 organizational, organizing
o'rgano *nf* [*Mus*] organ
orgji *nf* orgy
*orgjy'n *nm* (*Old*) [*Zool*] small cetacean: grampus, porpoise, narwhal
*orhe'stër = orke'stër
ori *interj pcl* appellative addressed to a woman or girl: hey, hey you; appellative preceding a feminine noun to indicate intimacy: my dear
orie'nt *nm* Orient
orienta'l *adj* Oriental
orienta'li'st *n* Orientalist
orienti'm *nm ger* 1 (*Book*) < oriento'•n, oriento'•het 2 orientation
oriento'•het *vpr* to be well-oriented: get oriented
oriento'•n *vt* to orient; provide orientation to [ ]
orientu'es
  I § *adj* serving to give orientation: orienting, orientational
  II § *nm* [*Mil*] guiding landmark, orientation point
origjina'l *adj, nm* 1 original 2 (*Colloq*) unusual
origjinali'tet *nm* originality
origji'në *nf* origin
ori'z *nm* [*Bot*] rice (*Oryza sativa*)
○ **oriz i rrahur** polished rice
○ **oriz i veshur** brown rice
oriznaj'ë *nf* = orizo're
*orizo'nt = horizo'nt
orizo're *nf* rice field
orke'stër *nf* [*Mus*] orchestra; band (of musicians)
orkestra'l *adj* [*Mus*] orchestral
o'rkë *nf* [*Zool*] killer whale (*Orca*)
orkidace' *nf* [*Bot*] orchid family *Orchidaceae*
orkide' *nf* [*Bot*] orchid *Orchis*
*orki'dhë *nf* [*Bot*] nettle tree (*Celtis australis*)
*orl *nm* eagle = shqipo'një
ormi' *nf* 1 (*Reg*) special preparation 2 gift for a special occasion
ormi's• *vt* (*Reg*) to get [ ] ready; dress [ ] up
ormi's•et *vpr* (*Reg*) to make elaborate preparations, get all ready; get dressed up
ormi'sje *nf ger* (*Reg*) < ormi's•, ormi's•et

ORMN *abbrev* <**Oficina e remontit të makinerive të ndërtimit** Workshop for Repair and Restoration of Construction Machinery

ornamen't *nm* ornament

oro'k *nm* appointed time

oro'qe *nf (Old)* wish, desire

orospi' *nf* whore

*****orqe'stër = orke'stër**

orta'k *n* **1** partner, associate **2** *(Reg)* spouse **3** *(Fig Pej)* conspirator

ortak'e *nf (Old)* = **she'mër**

ortak'ëri *nf* partnership

*****ortak'i = ortakëri**

orte'k *nm* avalanche of snow; avalanche

o'rtë *nf (Old)* cohort of people at the same level: social category/class, social level

*****ortiqe** *np* <**orte'k**

ortodo'ks
  I § *adj* **1** Orthodox **2** *(Fig Pej)* dogmatic
  II § *n* person of the Orthodox religion

ortodoks'i *nf* Eastern Orthodox religion: Orthodoxy

ortoepi' *nf* [*Ling*] orthoepy = **drejtshqiptím**

ortoep'ik *adj* [*Ling*] orthoepic = **drejtshqiptimo'r**

ortografi' *nf* [*Ling*] orthography = **drejtshkrím**

ortograf'ik *adj* [*Ling*] orthographic = **drejtshkrimo'r**

ortope'd *nm* [*Med*] orthopedist

ortoped'i *nf* [*Med*] orthopedics

ortoped'ik *adj* [*Med*] orthopedic

*****ortopte'rë** *np* *Orthoptera*

ortu'ndë *nf* large clay pot used for cooking

*****orthodho'ks = ortodo'ks**

*****oru'm** *nm* **1** gold coin *****2** *(Old)* Greek = **grek**

orva't·et *vpr* to exert oneself: strive

orva'tje *nf* striving with all one's might

*****orve'të** *nf* [*Invert*] slowworm, blindworm = **bollëverbët**

*****orrl** *nm* [*Ornit*] buzzard *(Buteo buteo)*

osa'kë *nf* [*Bot*] Jerusalem sage *(Phlomis fruticosa)*

o'se *conj* or; either
  ○ **ose hu ose thupër** *(Prov)* whether robust or weak

osma'k *nm (Old)* grain measure of about 40 or 50 kilograms

osma'n *adj, n* Ottoman

osmani'shte *nf* [*Ling*] Ottomanic Turkish

osmo'zë *nf* [*Phys*] osmosis

o'ste *nf* [*Relig*] consecrated wafer: host = **nafo'rë**

*****oste'n** *nm* ox goad = **hoste'n**

ostri' *nf* warm rain-bearing wind from the southwest that is damaging to olive trees

*****ostri'k** *nm* [*Ornit*] ostrich

osh
  I § *nm (Colloq)* pleasant satisfaction, relaxed pleasure
  II § *adv* in a dragging manner: draggingly

III § *nm* *harrow

osh· *vt, vi* **1** *(Colloq)* to cause [ ] to stop, halt; quiet [ ] down **2** to pet; treat nice: make nice

osha'f *nm* **1** compote made from dried fruit **2** *(Reg Kos)* prune

oshëna'r *n* religious recluse: hermit, anchorite, eremite

oshënar'i *nf* [*Relig*] **1** *(Collec)* eremites **2** eremitic way of life

oshëti·n = ushto'·n

*****oshëti'më** *nf* = **ushti'më**

oshilacio'n *nm* [*Spec*] oscillation

oshilogra'f *nm* oscillograph

oshma'k *nm* part of the chimney that rises above the roof: smoke stack

oshni'k *nm* light breeze

o'shtë *nf* [*Agr*] tongue of a cart, plow, or other pulled farm implement

oshti·n = ushto'·n

oshti'më *nf* = **ushti'më**

ota'vë *nf* second cutting of hay, second hay harvest

otoma'n *adj, n* = **osma'n**

otra' *nf* strong and heavy twine

otre'sh *nm* linchpin securing the beam of a plow to the ox yoke; iron peg or ring that keeps the hub from slipping off the axle of a cart/wagon

otura'k *nm* chamber pot: potty

o'u *interj* **1** *(Colloq)* expresses a surprised or mocking tone: well now! ah so! **2** expresses physical pain: ouch! ow!

OUA *abbrev* <**Organizata e Unitetit Afrikan** Organization for African Unity

ovacio'n *nm* ovation

ova'l *adj* oval

ovalite't *nm* *(Book)* [*Tech*] ovality

ovi'skë *nf* cradle strap

OVRA *abbrev (Italian)* <**Opera Vigilanza Repressione Antifascismo** [*Hist*] Fascist secret police organization in Italy

*****ovra't** *nm* dike, ditch

ovu'l *nm* [*Bot*] ovule

o'vull *nf (Old)* copper coin of the lowest value in Turkish money, worth one para

oxha'k *nm* **1** chimney **2** fireplace, hearth, fireside **3** *(Fig Colloq Old)* family **4** [*Hist*] old family of high repute; rich family **5** long tube connecting the inside to the outside: shaft **6** seed furrow **7** *(Old)* kiln
  ○ **oxhak pa tym** family that has come to an end

oxhak'ëri *OR* **oxhak'ësi** *nf collec* [*Hist*] upper classes, rich stratum of society; feudal lords

oxhakfshi'r'ës *nm* = **oxhakpastru'es**

oxhakpastru'es *nm* chimney sweep

oxhaqe *np* <**oxha'k**

OZNA *abbrev (Serbian)* [*Hist*] Serbian secret police

ozo'n *nm* [*Chem*] ozone

Pp

p [pë] *nf* **1** the consonant letter "p" **2** the voiceless bilabial stop represented by the letter "p"

P.S *abbrev* < **passhkrim** P.S. = postscript

pa
I § *prep (acc)* **1** without; minus **2** not counting [], even without counting []
II § *adv (Colloq)* (only) after that: then
III § *pcl* **1** (before an imperative) attenuates a command or suggestion: so let's just, so how about **2** indicates items forming a sequence: and then **3** (forms the negative of a following participle) without **4** (at the end of a clause) after all!
IV § *conj (Colloq)* therefore **2** else, otherwise
V § *interj* expresses pleased surprise at an outcome: whew! boy! well now! well-well!
○ {*noun/adverb/adjective*} **pa** {*same noun/adverb/adjective*} it doesn't matter whether {} or not: {} or not, {} or no {}, whether {} is right or not
○ **pa u lagur 1** without getting wet **2** without a scratch, totally unharmed
○ **pa u ngutur** without haste: carefully and prudently
○ **ësh·të pa opinga në këmbë** "be without clogs on one's feet" to be very poor, live in abject poverty
○ **pa <>u pjekur ashti** at a tender age
○ **pa pyetur** without regard to, disregarding; unheeding
○ **pa u trashur filli** before the problem gets bigger and more complicated
○ **pa u tharë (mirë) gjaku** before the blood was yet dry
○ **pa u tharë boja** before the paint even dries: quickly, soon
○ **pa u vënë re** without being noticed

pa *formativ* **1** forms antonyms of nouns and adjectives: un-, in- **2** forms privative compound adjectives indicating absence or lack of the second element of the compound: -less

pa *stem for 3rd sg pdef, pl pdef, opt, adm, part* < **sheh·, shi·***het*
○ **<> u pa**^*pdef* {*adjective*} *(Colloq)* {} looked {*adjective*} to < **Agimi iu pa i lodhur nënës** Agim looked tired to his mother
○ **pa**^*pdef* **ç'pa**^*pdef* having sized the situation up, having taken a good look
○ **e pa**^*pdef* **keq** {} found {}self in deep trouble
○ **nuk pa**^*pdef* **(udhën) nga shko·**^*npdef* **/vete**^*pdef* "{} didn't even see where {} was headed" {} took off as fast as {} could, took to {}'s heels
○ **u pa** "it was seen" (written notation indicating that a piece of writing has been looked at and that appropriate action was taken) seen and noted
○ **pa**^*pdef* **vdekjen me sy** "saw death with one's eyes" {} came close to dying

pa *formativ prefix* **1** forms antonyms of nouns and adjectives: un-, in- **2** forms privative

pa|afirm|u|a|r *adj (i)* unacknowledged; unrecognized, not famous; unconfirmed

pa|afru|a|r *adj (i)* = **paafru·eshëm**

pa|afru·e|shëm *adj (i)* **1** unfriendly, stiff, unsociable: unapproachable **2** *(Book)* inaccessible

pa|aft|ë *adj (i)* **1** unable, incapable: unfit **2** lacking in aptitude: inept, incompetent

pa|aft|ë|sí *nf* unfitness, incapability; lack of aptitude, incompetence

pa|a|jër *adj (i)* lacking in air; not airy

pa|ajr|u|a|r *adj (i)* **1** not aerated **2** unventilated; having stale air

pa|akord|u|a|r *adj (i)* [*Mus*] untuned; out of tune

pa|a|mëz *adj (i)* lacking flavor: flavorless, tasteless

pa|a|n|a *np (të) fem* undershorts, drawers

pa|a|n|ë *adj (i)* **1** boundless, endless **2** = **paanshëm**

pa|a|n|e|sí *nf* **1** impartiality; neutrality **2** boundlessness

*pa|a|n|ë|sím *nm ger* **1** < **paanëso·** ·*n* **2** neutralization

pa|a|n|ë|sí|sht *adv (Book)* without bias: impartially

*pa|a|n|ë|so· ·*n vt* to neutralize

pa|a|n|ët *adj (i)* = **paanshëm**

pa|angazh|u|a|r *adj (i) (Book)* disengaged, neutral

pa|a|n|shëm *adj (i)* impartial, unbiased; unprejudiced; neutral

pa|a|n|shm|ërí *nf* = **paanësí**

pa|anull|u|e|shëm *adj (i)* irrevocable

pa|apel|u|e|shëm *adj (i)* [*Law*] without possibility of appeal: non-appealable

pa|aprov|u|a|r *adj (i)* unapproved

*pa|a|që|shëm *OR* **pa|a|q|të** *adj (i)* = **pabarabartë**

*pa|a|që|tí *nf* = **pabarazí**

pa|ardh|ur
I § *adj (i)* (of dough) not yet risen: unrisen; (of bread) unleavened; (of soil) not ready for cultivation
II § *nm (Colloq Curse)* person who should never have been born

*pa|arga|s|ur *adj (i)* (of hides) untanned, raw

pa|argument|u|a|r *adj (i)* unargued

pa|armat|o|s|ur *adj (i)* without a weapon: unarmed

pa|arsim|u|a|r *adj (i)* having no formal education

pa|arsy|e|shëm *adj (i)* unreasonable, irrational, unjustified, unwarrantable

pa|artikul|u|a|r *adj (i)* = **panyjëtuar**

pa|arri|r|ë *adj (i)* **1** unripe **2** *(Fig)* not worked out completely, not perfected

*pa|arri|t|ësi = **paarritje**

pa|arri|t|je *nf* unripeness, immaturity

pa|arri|t|shëm *adj (i)* **1** unattainable, unachievable, infeasible **2** beyond the abilities of other to equal: matchless, peerless

pa|arri|t|ur *adj (i)* unsuccessful, ineffective, bootless

pa|asfalt|u|a|r *adj (i)* not covered with asphalt: unpaved

pa|asgjë|s|u|e|shëm *adj (i)* not subject to obliteration: non-destructible, indestructible

pa·atdhe *adj (i)* **1** without a homeland/country **2** *(Pej)* expatriate

pa·autorizu·a·r *adj (i)* not authorized, unauthorized

pa·ba·bë *adj (i)* fatherless

pa·ba·ft *adj (i) (Old Colloq)* = **pafa·t**

***pa·bâ·më** *(Reg Gheg)* = **pabë·rë**

pa·ban·ua·r *adj (i)* uninhabited

pa·ban·ue·shëm *adj (i)* uninhabitable

pa·bara·ba·rtë *adj (i)* **1** unequal; uneven **2** dissimilar

***pa·bara·bi·t·shëm** *adj (i)* = **pabarazu·e·shëm**

***pa·bara·s** = **pabaraz**

pa·bara·zi *nf* inequality

pa·bara·zi·m *nm* [Math] inequality

pa·bara·zu·e·shëm *adj (i)* noncomparable, incomparable

pa·bari *adj (i)* **1** unattended by a herdsman: without a shepherd **2** (of a child) lacking parental supervision

pa·bashkë·ma·t·shëm *adj (i)* [Math] incommensurable

pa·bazu·a·r *adj (i)* unfounded, groundless

pa·be·ft *adv* unexpectedly, suddenly, all of a sudden

pa·be·së

I § *adj (i)* **1** disloyal, unfaithful; dishonest, deceitful; untrustworthy **2** *(Old)* = **pafe**

II § *nn (të)* = **pabesi**

pa·bes·ë·ri = **pabesi**

pa·besi *nf* dishonesty, deceptiveness; disloyalty, faithlessness, perfidy

pa·besi·m

I § *nm* **1** = **mosbesim 2** = **pabesi 3** absence of religious belief, impiety; lack of (religious) faith

II § *adj (i) (Old)* lacking (religious) faith

pa·besi·sht *adv* disloyally, treacherously, perfidiously; in bad faith

pa·besu·e·shëm *adj (i)* **1** unbelievable **2** untrustworthy

pa·bë·rë

I § *adj (i)* **1** unripe, not yet ready **2** not done, undone

II § *nf(e)* something not done; something not acceptable in polite society

pa·bina·rë *adj (i)* = **panjeri**

***pa·bi·nd·shëm** *adj (i)* unconvincible, not to be persuaded

pa·bi·nd·ur *adj (i)* **1** unconvinced, unpersuaded **2** disobedient, unruly

pa·bisedu·e·shëm *adj (i)* = **padiskutuesh**ëm

pa·bi·sht *adj (i)* having no tail/stem: tailless, stemless

pa·bo·jë *adj (i) (Colloq)* shameless

pa·botu·a·r *adj (i)* unpublished

pa·botu·e·shëm *adj (i)* unpublishable

pa·bre·dh·ur *adj (i)* untraveled, provincial

pa·bre·ng·ë *adj (i)* untroubled, without problems

pa·bru·më *adj (i)* **1** unleavened **2** *(Fig)* lacking in mental ability or training

pa·bru·m·o·sur *adj (i)* lacking in proper training/education

pa·bu·jë *adj (i)* = **pabujsh**ëm

pa·bu·j·shëm *adj (i)* unpretentious, modest

***pa·bu·j·t·shëm** *adj (i)* inhospitable

pa·bu·kë *adj (i)* **1** poverty-stricken; starving **2** (of a plant) lacking well-developed fruit/grain **3** *(Fig Colloq)* fruitless **4** *(Fig)* lacking in mental ability or training

pa·bu·k·shëm *adj (i)* **1** unproductive; infertile, barren **2** poverty-stricken; starving **3** *(Fig Colloq)* fruitless

pa·bu·kur *adj (i)* not as one would like: not right; unattractive

pa·bulme·t *adj (i)* = **pabulme·t·sh**ëm

pa·bulme·t·shëm *adj (i)* "not giving much milk" unproductive

pa·bu·rrë *adj (e)* (of women) left without a husband

pa·bu·rr·ë·ri

I § *nf* unmanliness, weakness of character; cowardice, faint-heartedness

II § *adj (i)* unmanly, weak in character; cowardly

pac *nm* [Zool] pelican

pa·ca·k *adj (i)* **1** boundless, unlimited **2** *(Pej)* unsettled, vagrant, homeless

***pa·ca·k·ti** *nf* inaccuracy

***pa·ca·k·ti·m** *nm* indefiniteness; indeterminacy

pa·ca·k·tu·a·r *adj (i)* **1** unspecified; undetermined, undecided; undefined, unknown **2** [Ling] indefinite

pa·ca·k·tu·e·shëm *adj (i)* = **papërcaktu·e·shëm**

***pacani·k** *nm* apron worn by mountaineers

***pacave·l** *nm* dishcloth

pa·ce·k·shëm *adj (i)* untouchable, immune

pa·ce·n *adj (i)* without defect: faultless

pa·cen·u·a·r *adj (i)* unblemished, intact, untouched

pa·cen·u·e·shëm *adj (i)* **1** inviolable **2** [Law] irrevocable

pa·cen·u·e·shm·ë·ri *nf* inviolability

pacifi·st *adj, n* pacifist

pacifi·zëm *nm* pacifism

pa·ci·k·shëm *adj (i)* = **pacenu·a·r**

pa·cil·ë·su·a·r *adj (i) (Book)* **1** not clearly distinguishable: indeterminate **2** lacking proper qualifications: unqualified

pa·cil·ë·su·e·shëm *adj (i)* *(Book)* unqualified

pa·ci·p·ë *adj (i)* barefaced, shameless; impudent

pa·cop·ë·zu·a·r *adj (i)* unfragmented

paç *stem for opt* < **ka·**

○ [] **paçim/paça sa malet** "May we/I have [] as much as the mountains!" *(Felic)* May [] live as long as the mountains!

○ **I paç ymër!** "May you have life for them!" *(Felic)* May your children live long!

paça *nf* **1** stomach of an animal **2** [Food] spicy stew made with tripe or headcheese

paçamu·r *nm* = **papa·re**

paçari·z *nm* *(Colloq)* confusion, chaos: mess

***pa·ça·r·t·shëm** *adj (i)* unbreakable, inviolable

***pa·ça·r·tur** *adj (i)* unbroken, intact

pa·ça·shëm *adj (i)* unsplittable

***paça·ve·r** *nf (Reg Gheg)* = **paçavu·re**

paçavu·re *nf* **1** scrap of cloth: rag; cleaning rag; pot-holder **2** *(Pej Scorn)* scrap of worthless writing **3** *(Fig)* base and worthless person: good-for-nothing louse

○ **paçavure letrash** scraps of paper

paçe *np* = **mu·nx**ë

paçe *nf* [Food] spicy stew made with tripe or headcheese

paçebërë**s** *nm* person who prepares and sells spicy stew made with tripe or headcheese

****paçe'l**ë**m** *adj (i)* **1** unopened **2** *(Fig)* undeveloped

****paçfaqsh**ë**m** *adj (i)* inexpressible, ineffable

****paçfaqur** *adj (i)* unexpressed, implicit

****paçikur** *adj (i)* untouched, unaffected

paçim *1st pl opt* <**ka**·

paçka *conj (Colloq)* even though, even so

****paçkëputur** *adj (i)* (of an obligation/debt) unsettled, unpaid = **pashlyer**

paçmuar *adj (i)* = **paçmueshëm**

paçmueshë**m** *adj (i)* extremely valuable: priceless

****paçqitur** *adj (i)* unseparated

****paçquajtje** *nf* = **pashquarsi**

****paçquar** *adj (i)* = **pashquar**

****paçrrënjossh**ë**m** *adj (i)* ineradicable

****paçuem** *adj (i) (Reg Gheg)* inexperienced, green

****pada** *adv (Reg Gheg)* incessantly

padalë *adj (i)* **1** not widely traveled, provincial **2** *(Colloq)* without a way out, with no exit: (of a street) blind

padalluar *adj (i)* undistinguished; indistinct

padallues**h**ë**m** *adj (i)* indistinguishable, imperceptible

****padâm**ë *adj (i) (Reg Gheg)* = **padëmtuar**

****padâmsh**ë**m** *adj (i) (Reg Gheg)* = **padëmshëm**

****padasisht** *adv* = **pandashmërisht**

padash *adv* unintentionally; involuntarily

****padashje** *nf* unwillingness

padashka *adv (Colloq)* = **padashur**

padashur
I § *adv* unintentionally; involuntarily
II § *adj (i)* ***unintentional, accidental

padashuri *nf* lack of cordiality: unfriendliness, coolness

padatuar *adj (i)* undated

padegë**zuar** *adj (i)* not divided into branches: nonramate

padeklaruar *adj (i)* undeclared

padenjë *adj (i)* unentitled, unworthy; shameful

padenjë**sisht** *adv* in an unworthy manner: shamefully

padepërtues**h**ë**m** *adj (i)* impenetrable, impermeable

paderrë *adj (i)* homeless

padert *adj (i) (Colloq)* without a worry in the world: unworried; unconcerned

padeshifrues**h**ë**m** *adj (i)* indecipherable

****padesh'tas** *adv* involuntarily, accidentally = **padashur**

padetyrues**h**ë**m** *adj (i)* not obligatory: noncompulsory

padëgjuar *adj (i)* **1** not well-known **2** unheard of **3** disobedient *****4** unheeded

padëgjues**h**ë**m** *adj (i)* **1** disobedient **2** impossible to hear: inaudible

padëmë**m** *adj (i)* = **padëmshëm**

padëmshë**m** *adj (i)* harmless, innocuous

padëmtuar *adj (i)* undamaged, unharmed

padënuar *adj (i)* **1** never convicted of a crime **2** unpunished

padënues**h**ë**m** *adj (i)* **1** guiltless **2** unpunishable

****padëpërtuarsh**ë**m** *OR* **padërptue**s**h**ë**m** = **padepërtueshëm**

padëshiruar *adj (i)* undesired

padëshirues**h**ë**m** *adj (i)* undesirable

padëshmuar *adj (i)* unattestable

padi *nf* [*Law*] charge, accusation; legal action, suit

padije
I § *nf* lack of knowledge: ignorance
II § *adj (i)* = **paditur**

padijeni *nf* lack of information: ignorance, unawareness

padijshë**m** *adj (i)* = **paditur**

padiktimues**h**ë**m** *adj (i) (Old)* [*Law*] not subject to appeal: non-appealable

padiktuar *adj (i)* undiscovered

padiktues**h**ë**m** *adj (i)* **1** undetectable, indiscernible **2** *(Old)* [*Law*] = **padiktimueshëm**

padis *stem for 1st sg pres, pl pres, 2nd & 3rd sg subj, pind* <**padit**·

padisiplinë *nf* lack of discipline: indiscipline

padisiplinuar *adj (i)* undisciplined

padiskutues**h**ë**m** *adj (i)* **1** not subject to further discussion: non-debatable **2** indisputable

padishah *nm* [*Hist*] title of the absolute sovereign under Islamic rule: padishah

padit· *vt* [*Law*] to accuse [] of legal wrongdoing, file/press charges against [], bring suit against [], sue
○ [] **padit**· **te** {} to tell on [] to {}

paditë**s**
I § *n* **1** [*Law*] plaintiff; complainant **2** *(Colloq)* accuser
II § *adj* [*Law*] complaining

paditje *nf ger* <**padit**·

paditur *nm (i)* [*Law*] defendant

paditur
I § *adj (i)* **1** unknowledgeable, uneducated, uninformed **2** *(Colloq)* ignorant **3** unknown
II § *n (i)* unknowledgeable person, ignoramus
III § *adv* unknowingly

padituri *nf* ignorance

padjallë**zi** *nf* ingenuousness, innocence, forthrightness

padjallë**zuar** *adj (i)* guileless, artless, ingenuous, innocent, forthright

padjegshë**m** *adj (i)* noncombustible, incombustible

padjersë *adj (i)* not earned by the sweat of one's brow: unearned

****padjerrsh**ë**m** *adj (i)* indestructible

padlirë *adj (i)* **1** sacrilegious, profane **2** impure, unchaste

****padlir**ë**si** *nf* **1** sacrilege *****2** impurity, unchasteness; dirt

padobi
I § *adj (i)* = **padobishëm**
II § *nf* ***fruitlessness

padobishë**m** *adj (i)* fruitless, useless

padorë *adj (i)* **1** missing a hand **2** anonymous **3** *(Fig)* not given to stealing: honest

padorë**s** *adj (i)* without signature, unsigned by the writer: anonymous

****pador**ë**zuem** *adj (i) (Reg Gheg)* undelivered

padredhur adj (i) 1 unspun *2 unbending, inflexible

padrejtë

I § adj (i) unjust; wrong, unfair

II § nf (e) something unjust: injustice

padrejtësi nf lack of justice: injustice, unfairness

padrejtësisht adv unjustly, wrongly, unfairly

padrejtueshëm adj (i) incapable of being straightened out: unstraightenable

padrojtur adj (i) = padruajtur

padron n boss; proprietor

padruajtur adj (i) 1 unflinching, unwavering: staunch 2 not bashful, not timid

padry adj (i) 1 not secured by a lock: unlocked 2 (Fig Pej) open to just anybody

paduhur adj (i) undue, unnecessary

paduk adj (i) 1 not long-lasting 2 (of foods) not rising well 3 without much effect

****padukëm** = padukshëm

padukshëm adj (i) invisible

padukshmëri nf invisibility

padukur

I § nm (i) (Euph) the Devil

II § nf (e) (Euph) anthrax

III § adj (i) = padukshëm

paduresë nf = padurim

padurim nm impatience

paduruar adj (i) impatient

padurueshëm adj (i) 1 impatient 2 intolerable

****padyshim** adv = pa dyshim without doubt, no doubt

padyshimtë adj (i) 1 indubitable, doubtless, certain *2 unsuspected, unsuspicious

padyshueshëm adj (i) not subject to doubt: indubitable, unquestionable

padhembë adj (i) toothless

padhembshëm adj (i) 1 heartless, pitiless, unfeeling 2 [Med] causing little pain: indolent

****padhëmbje** adj = pa dhëmbje without pain, painless

****padhëmçur** OR **padhëmshur** = padhembshëm

padhimbshëm = padhembshëm

****padhimsur** OR **padhimshëm** = padhembshëm

padhjamë adj (i) lacking fat, (of meat) lean

****padhjatë** adj (i) intestate

padhunueshëm adj (i) [Law] inviolate

padhunueshmëri nf [Law] inviolability

paedukata adj (i) ill-behaved, impolite

paedukuar adj (i) 1 not properly brought up: ill-bred 2 ill-behaved, impolite

paefektshëm adj (i) ineffective

paekuilibruar adj (i) (Book) intemperate, immoderate

paelektrifikuar adj (i) not powered by electricity; not supplied with electricity, not electrified

paemër

I § adj (i) 1 having no name: nameless 2 anonymous; unsigned 3 (Fig) not famous, unknown, unheard of 4 (Fig) beyond naming: unspeakable 5 (Curse) unmentionable

II § nm (i) 1 the unmentionable 2 (Euph) the Devil 3 [Med] muscle spasm: tic

III § nf (e) 1 (Euph) [Med] shingles, tetter 2 (Euph) [Med] splenitis; splenomegaly 3 (Euph) [Med] anthrax

IV § np (të) 1 (Euph) [Med] varicose veins 2 [Bot] herbaceous perennial marsh plant with long stem and broad leaves that is used in folk treatment of shingles/tetter 3 [Bot] type of moss appearing as whitish blotches on rock surfaces

****paemërshëm** nm (i) "the unnamable" (Euph) the Devil

paemërtuar adj (i) unnamed, nameless

paepshëm adj (i) unbendable; inflexible, rigid

paepur adj (i) 1 unyielding, unflinching, unwavering 2 (Fig) stalwart

paerë adj (i) 1 windless, calm 2 flavorless

paerrësueshëm adj (i) forever bright, never-fading, stainless, everlasting

****paesëll** adj unsober, tipsy

****paesëlli** nf insobriety

paevitueshëm adj (i) inevitable, unavoidable

pafaj adj (i) = pafajshëm

pafajësi nf [Law] exoneration

pafajëso·n vt to exonerate

pafajshëm adj (i) guiltless; not guilty; innocent

pafalshëm adj (i) unpardonable, unforgivable

pafamilje adj (i) having no family

pafarë adj (i) 1 seedless 2 (Fig) without number, innumerable

pafat adj (i) unlucky; ill-fated

pafatshëm adj (i) = pafat

pafe adj (i) 1 of no religious faith 2 [Hist] heretical 3 (Fig Colloq Old) = pabesë

pafejuar adj (i) not engaged to be married: not affianced

pafeshëm adj (i) irreligious; infidel

****pafëlliqur** adj (i) unsoiled, immaculate

pafikshëm adj (i) unquenchable, inextinguishable

****pafill** nm (Old) wireless (radio)

pafillë nf 1 (Colloq) tin; container made of tin 2 shell of a cartridge 3 narrow strip 4 thin rug; saddle blanket

pafilltë adj (i) (Reg) made of tin

pafilluar adj (i) = panisur

pafisëm adj (i) low-born, lowly, mongrel

****pafisnik** adj (Old) base (metal); ignoble

pafisshëm adj (i) impolite, rude

****pafitimshëm** OR **pafitimtë** adj (i) unprofitable

pafjalë adj (i) 1 sparing in speech: taciturn 2 compliant, agreeable; modest 3 well-behaved and soft-spoken 4 (Book) unspeaking, mute; unspoken *5 doubtless

pafjetur adj (i) 1 not having slept, not having slept sufficiently 2 (Fig) unsleeping, ever alert; indefatigable

pafkë nf = paftë

****pafolë** adj (i) unspoken

pafolur adj (i) speechless; taciturn

paformuar adj (i) 1 not fully formed 2 not well-developed, not well brought-up, not well-trained

pafre adj (i) unbridled, acting by whim; unrestrained, acknowledging no bounds

pafrenueshëm adj (i) unbridled, uncontrollable

pafrikë adj (i) = pafrikshëm

****pafrikësi** nf fearlessness, intrepidity

pa|fri̇k|shëm *adj (i)* unafraid, afraid of nothing

pa|fru̇t *adj (i)* without fruit, not bearing fruit

***pa|frymb|u̇|e̊r** *adj (fem ˜ore) (Old)* inanimate; inorganic

pa|fry|më *adj (i)* not breathing: lifeless, dead

***pa|frym|ësi̇** *nf* lifelessness

***pa|frẏt** *adj (i)* = pafrẏtshëm

pa|frẏt|shëm *adj (i)* fruitless, vain

***pa|fsheh|u̇r** *adj (i)* undisguised, patent

***pa|fshi̇|më** *adj (i)* = pafshi̇rshëm

pa|fshi̇|r|shëm *adj (i)* ineffaceable, indelible

pȧft|a *np* < pȧftë metal hinges

***pȧfte** *nf* [*Bot*] Balkan maple *(Acer obtusatum)*

pȧftë
I § *nf* **1** small flat piece of metal: metal plate/disk **2** small flat object **3** button = ko̍psë ***4** metal sheet; armor ***5** *(Old)* stratum
II § *adj* disk-shaped
 ○ **pȧftë dysheku** *(Reg)* = ki̇lze
 ○ **pafta e misrit** endosperm in a kernel of corn

paft|ë|zi̇m *nm ger* [*Tech*] < paftëzo̍·n

paft|ë|zo̍·n *vt* [*Tech*] to make [metal] into thin plate

pa|ftill|u̇e|shëm *adj (i)* unable to be disentangled; unresolvable; inexplicable

pa|ftu̇|ȧr *adj (i)* not invited, uninvited

pa|fu̇nd *adj (i)* endless; boundless; infinite; bottomless

pa|fu̇nd|ëm *adj (i)* = pafu̇nd

pa|fund|ësi̇ *nf* **1** *(Book)* boundlessness **2** infinity

pa|fund|ës|i̇sht *adv* without end, endlessly, infinitely

pa|fundi̇ *nf (Book)* infinitude

***pa|fundi̇m** *nm* infinity

***pa|fu̇|ndje** *nf* bottomless depth, abyss; eternity; infinity

pa|fu̇nd|më *adj (i)* **1** = pafu̇nd **2** [*Math*] infinite

pa|fu̇nd|shëm *adj (i)* = pafu̇nd

pa|fuqi̇
I § *nf* **1** condition without physical strength: feebleness, weakness **2** inability, powerlessness, impotence
II § *adj (i)* **1** feeble; unable, powerless, impotent **2** *(Old)* [*Law*] having no legal force, inoperative **3** [*Med*] adynamia

pa|fuqi̇|si̇ *nf (Book)* debility, weakness

pa|fuqi̇|shëm *adj (i)* without adequate force/energy/ability: powerless, impotent

pa|fyėr *adj (i)* not offended

pa|fytẏ|rë *adj (i)* barefaced, shameless, unabashed

pa|fytyr|ësi̇ *nf* shamelessness, unabashedness

***pa|gabi̇m** *adv* = pa gabi̇m without fail, unfailingly

pa|gabi̇m|të *adj (i)* unfailing, unerring

pa|gab|u̇ȧr *adj (i)* unmistaken; correct

pa|gabu̇e|shëm *adj (i)* unerring, infallible; unfailing; unmistakable

pa|gabue|shm|ëri̇ *nf* infallibility; inerrancy

***pagȧ|çe** *nf* bread roll, bun

pa|gȧ|jle *adj (i)* carefree, unworried; indifferent, unconcerned

pagȧn *adj (i), n* pagan

pagan|i̇z|ëm *nm* paganism

pa|garant|u̇ȧr *adj (i)* without guarantee, not guaranteed

***pa|gati̇m|shëm** *adj (i)* unprepared, poorly prepared

pa|gati̇|tur *adj (i)* = papërgati̇tur

pagȧto̍r *n* [*Spec*] wage distributor; paymaster

pa|gat|u̇ȧr *adj (i)* unprocessed for eating, uncooked

pa|gdhe̍nd|ur *adj (i)* **1** unpolished, coarse, rough **2** *(Fig)* uncouth, ill-bred, crude

***page̍l** *nm* [*Ichth*] sea bream, porgy *(Pagellus mormyrus L.)*

page̍s|ë *nf* **1** payment **2** = pa̍gë **3** = pagi̇m
 ○ **pagesë me kohë** payment according to time spent working: hourly wages

pa̍gë *nf* pay, wage, wages
 ○ **pagë me cope** payment by the piece: piecework wage
 ○ **pagë me kohë** hourly wage

pagë|dhën|ës *n* payer, paymaster

pagë|ma̍rr|ës *n* payee

pagë|tẏrë *nf* = pa̍gë

pagë|zi̇m *nm ger* **1** < pagëzo̍·n, pagëzo̍·het [*Relig*] **2** baptism
 ○ **pagëzim i zjarrte** baptism by fire (in battle)

pagë|zi̇m|o̍re *nf* [*Relig*] = pagëzo̍re

pagë|zi̇m|ta̍r *n* [*Relig*] = pagëzo̍r

pagë|zo̍·het *vpr* **1** [*Relig*] to get baptized **2** to participate (in an activity) for the first time

pagë|zo̍·n *vt* **1** [*Relig*] to baptize **2** *(Fig)* to christen **3** *(FigJocular)* to thin out [ ] with water

pagë|zo̍r *n* [*Relig*] baptizer

pagë|zo̍re *nf* [*Relig*] baptismal font; baptistry

pagë|zu̇ȧr *adj (i)* [*Relig*] baptized

pa|gëz|u̇ȧr *adj (i)* dying before enjoying the happiness that comes with being married or seeing one's children married

pagë|zu̇es *nm* baptist; baptizer

pagi̇m *nm ger* **1** < pagu̇a·n, pagu̇·het **2** payment

pagi̇m|ta̍r *n (Old)* payer

pago̍·n *= pagu̇a·n

pago̍| *stem for 3rd sg pdef, opt, adm* < pagu̇a·n

pago̍dë *nf* pagoda

pa|go̍j|ë
I § *adj (i)* dumb, mute
II § *nm (i) (Euph)* **1** the Devil **2** wolf

***pa|goj|ësi̇** *nf* dumbness, muteness

pa|goj|ët *adj (i)* dumb, mute

***pagrȧç** *nm* copper ewer

pa|grȧt *adj (i)* **1** = padu̇k **2** *(Fig)* unsuccessful, futile, fruitless

pa|grȧt|shëm *adj (i)* **1** (of rice/flour) not rising when cooked **2** not productive, infertile **3** *(Fig)* unsuccessful, futile, fruitless

***pa|gri̇s|ë** *adj (i)* untorn

pa|gri̇s|shëm *adj (i)* wear-resistant, very durable

pa|gru̇a *adj (i)* without a wife, wifeless

pagu̇·het *vpr* **1** to clear one's debt **2** *(Old)* to discharge an obligation in a blood feud

pagu̇a *nm (obl ˜o̍i, np ˜o̍nj)* = pallu̇a

pagu̇a·n
I § *vt* **1** to pay for [ ] **2** to pay off; repay, pay b ack
II § *vi* to pay
 ○ **është të paguash e të ikësh** "it is for you to pay and leave" it is a very unpleasant/uncomfortable place
 ○ **pago·n leshtë/qimet e kokës** "pay the hair on one's head" to spend a fortune

○ **Paguan një grosh e hyn në valle, paguan njëqind e s'del dot.** "You pay a farthing to get into a dance, pay a hundred and not be able to get out." *(Prov)* You can easily get yourself into a situation, but not so easily get out of it.

○ **për pak e pagua·**n^{past} "almost paid for it" escaped by a hair, barely escaped

○ [] **pagua·**n **sa frëngu pulën** "pay as much for [] as a foreigner pays for a chicken" to pay too much for []; pay an arm and a leg for []

○ [] **pagua·**n **si prifti sorrën** "pay for [] like the priest for the crow" to pay too much for []; pay an arm and a leg for []

○ **e pagua·**n **si ujku me lëkurë** "pay for it like the wolf with his hide" to pay dearly for what one has done

○ **e pagua·**n **ujin për raki** "buy water for the price of raki" to pay too much for something usually costing less

pagu'a'r
I § *adj (i)* paid-off, repaid; paid for
II § *nn (të)* = **pagi'm**

pagu'e's *nm* = **pagato'r**

pagu'e'shëm *adj (i)* payable

pagu'në *adj (i) (Old)* very poor, broke

pagu'r I § *nm* OR **pagu're** II § *nf* 1 canteen for carrying water 2 small flask for raki

***pagu'rkë** *nf dimin (Reg Tosk)* hip flask

pagux'i'm *adj (i)* = **paguxi'mshëm**

pagux'i'mshëm *adj (i)* lacking in boldness/courage

***pagjâ** *nf(Reg Gheg)* void, vacuum, space

***pagja'jshëm** *adj (i)* = **pagja'shëm**

pagja'k *adj (i)* 1 anemic; pallid 2 *(Fig)* lacking vigor: lethargic, weak 3 *[Med]* exsanguine

pagja'kësi *nf* lack of vigor: lethargy, lifelessness

***pagja'kshëm** *adj (i)* bloodless

pagja'lpë *adj (i)* 1 *[Dairy]* (of milk) without cream: skimmed 2 *(Fig)* (of a person) bland, insipid, dull

pagja'llë *adj (i)* 1 inanimate; dull, lifeless 2 *(Old)* inorganic

***pagja're** *nf* unlikely, improbable

pagja'së *adj (i)* unlikely, implausible, improbable

pagja'shëm *adj (i) (Colloq)* unseemly, improper, undue

***pagje'gjur** *adj (i)* unheeded

pagje'shëm *adj (i) (Colloq)* without property, having nothing but the shirt on one's back: broke, poor

pagje'the *adj (i)* leafless

pagji'nd *adj(i)* left alone in this world, without family or friend

pagji'ni *adj (i)* having no kinfolk

pagju'ajtur *adj (i)* (of rich wilderness) unexploited by hunting and fishing: virgin

pagju'hë *adj (i)* without language: dumb

pagju'më *adj (i)* 1 (of a period of time) spent without sleep: sleepless 2 sleepy

pagju'mësi *nf* 1 sleeplessness, insomnia 2 sleepiness

pagju'njëzu'ar *adj (i)* never brought to one's knees: indomitable

pagju'rmu'e'shëm *adj (i)* untraceable

pagjyki'm *adj (i)* = **pagjyku'e'shëm**

pagjyki'm'të *adj (i)* = **pagjyku'e'shëm**

pagjyku'e'shëm *adj (i)* 1 injudicious, imprudent; unreasonable 2 *[Law]* not subject to the judicial process

***pagjy'm'ët** *adj (i)* unimpaired, undamaged

***pagjyq'ësi** *nf* lack of judgment; tactlessness

pah *nm* 1 finely milled flour 2 fine chaff and dust from harvested grain 3 sawdust 4 pollen 5 fine snow flakes; thin layer of snow 6 dandruff; body grime 7 outward appearance

pah *interj* expresses pleased surprise at an outcome: whew! boy! well now! well-well!

paha' *nf(Colloq Old)* 1 worth, price 2 *(Fig)* importance, value

pa'ha'ir *adj (Colloq)* without utility, of no use: no good

pa'ha'lë *adj (i)* (of certain wheat) beardless

pa'harru'a'r *adj (i)* 1 unforgotten 2 = **paharru'e'shëm**

pa'harru'e'shëm *adj (i)* unforgettable

pa'heku'ro's'ur *adj (i)* not ironed, unironed

***pa'he'p** = **pae'p**

***pa'hep'ësi** *nf* inflexibility, rigidity

*pah'ërinë *nf* pollen

pahi' *nf(Colloq)* 1 wooden fence/balustrade 2 wattled hurdle (used as a gate for a fence) 3 harrow 4 tobacco leaves in pairs preparatory to being hung in chains

pa'hije *adj (i)* without shade, offering no shade = **pahi'jshëm**

*pa'hije'si *nf* unseemliness, impropriety

pa'hij'shëm *adj (i)* 1 unpleasing to the sight: unattractive, not good-looking, ugly 2 indecorous, unseemly; improper, indecent, shameful

pa'hi'r *indecl masc* unwillingness

*pa'hir'ësi *nf* 1 reluctance, unwillingness, repugnance 2 ruthlessness

*pa'hir'ës'i'sht *adv* = **pahi'ri**

pa'hir'ët *adj (i)* 1 unwilling; reluctant; ungracious 2 ruthless *3 indecorous, unseemly

pa'hi'ri *adv (Reg)* unwillingly; reluctantly

*pa'hir'so·n *vt* to force

pahi's *stem for 1st sg pres, pl pres, 2nd & 3rd sg subj, pind* < **pahi'r·**

pahi't· *vt* 1 to winnow [grain] 2 to air out [tobacco leaves] (by moving them apart to prevent mold from forming) 3 to fan [] (in order to cool off)

pahi't·et *vpr* 1 (of a powdery substance) to billow up and around 2 to become covered with a powdery substance; become covered with mold 3 to cool off

pahi'tur *adj (i)* 1 covered with mold 2 tinged with gray; grizzled

*pa'hone'psje *nf* indigestion

*pa'hone'ps'shëm *adj (i)* indigestible

*pah'u'er *adj (fem ˜ore) (Old)* powdery, dusty, floury; farinaceous

pa'hu'mb'shëm *adj (i)* never-to-be-lost, imperishable

pa'i'de *adj (i)* lacking in ideas

pa'imagjinu'e'shëm *adj (i)* unimaginable = **papërfytyru'e'shëm**

pa'imitu'e'shëm *adj (i)* inimitable

pa'intere's *adj (i)* 1 of no particular interest: unimportant 2 free of selfish motives: disinterested, sincere

pa'interesu'a'r *adj (i)* uninterested

***paj** *interj (Reg Gheg)* damn it!

paja'gë *nf* **1** fungal plant disease: peronospora; rust disease **2** warm wind that dessicates plants and fruit

paja'mba· *n* *vt* to be partial to [ ], exhibit bias towards [ ], take [ ]'s side

paja'mba'jt *stem for pdef, opt, adm, part* <**pajamba·***n*

paja'mba'jtas *adv* in a biased way, showing partiality

paja'mba'jtës
I § *n* biased person
II § *adj* showing bias

paja'ndër *nf* [*Constr*] timber that supports a wall: shoring post, strutting piece

pajazhi'në *nf* spiderweb

*__pajce'__ = pa'lcë

*__pajci'm__ *nm ger* **1** <pajco·*n* **2** pacification

*__pajco·__*n* *vt* to appease, placate, reconcile; pacify

paje'të *adj (i)* lifeless, inert

pajetërsue'shëm *adj (i)* [*Law*] = **patjetërsue'shëm**

*__paje'tme__ *nf (e) (Old)* nitrogen

paje' *nf* **1** [*Ethnog*] bride's trousseau; dowry **2** *(Colloq)* load carried by each side of a packsaddle **3** *(Fig)* unjustified partiality, bias **4** *(Colloq)* burden
  ○ **Bëhu pajë!** *(Pej)* Get out of here!

paji'm *nm* **1** equipment; supply, provision *__2 endowment *__3 dowry

paji'me *np* <**pajim** set of belts worn by soldiers to hold arms and provisions; set of harness for horses

*__pajimênd__ *nm (Reg Gheg)* outrage

paji's· *vt* to equip, outfit; furnish, supply, provide; endow

pajis·et *vpr* to be outfitted with supplies; get one's supplies ready
  ○ **pajis·et me** [ ] to provide oneself with [ ]

paji'sje *nf ger* **1** <**pajis·**, **pajis·et 2** materials needed for a particular activity or enterprise: equipment, supplies, furnishings

paji'sur *adj (i)* outfitted, supplied

*__pajla'të__ *nf* [*Bot*] Judas tree *(Cercis siliquastrum)*

pajma'k *adj* = **bajma'k**

*__pajni__ *nf* endowment; talent, gift

*__pajno·__*n* *vt* = **pajis·**

pajo·*het *vpr* **1** to prepare a trousseau **2** = **pajis·***et*

pajo·n* *vt* **1** to prepare a trousseau for [a girl] **2** = **pajis**

pajo'llë *nf* **1** removable wooden grating on the bottom of a boat **2** *(Reg)* snare, trap *__3 *(Fig)* intrigue, ruse

pajo's· *vt* = **pajis·**

*__pajo'sje__ *nf* = **pajis'je**

*__pajta'r__ *n* **1** veterinarian *__2 authority

pajte'së *nf (Old)* **1** reconciliation **2** monthly or annual salary

*__pajti__ *nf (Old)* contract, pact

pajti'm *nm ger* **1** <**pajto·***n*, **pajto·***het* **2** accord, accordance; placation, conciliation **3** subscription

Pajti'm *nm* Pajtim (male name)

pajtimbë're's
I § *adj* peacemaking
II § *n* peacemaker

pajtimta'r *n* **1** conciliator **2** subscriber

pajto·*het* *vpr* **1 to become reconciled: make up **2** to come to an agreement: agree, concur **3** to reconcile oneself: acquiesce **4** to be in accord **5** to agree

to terms of employment: hire oneself out, take employment **6** to subscribe

**pajto·*n*
I § *vt* **1** to bring [ ] into accord: reconcile; conciliate **2** *(Colloq)* to placate, assuage; still the crying of [ ], soothe **3** to hire, employ; engage, rent **4** to enroll [ ] as a subscriber
II § *vi* **1** to go together without clashing: comport, harmonize **2** *(Colloq)* to reach an agreement: concur
  ○ **pajto·*n* gjaqet** [*Ethnog*] to conciliate between the feuding parties; reach settlement of a blood feud

pajtua'r *adj (i)* hired

*__pajtu'ar__ *nm (obl ˜ o'ri)* patron saint, patron

pajtue's
I § *adj* **1** conciliatory **2** placating, soothing
II § *n* **1** person who tries to reconcile differences: conciliator **2** hirer: employer (of people), renter (of things)

pajtue'shëm *adj (i)* **1** compatible; reconcilable *__2 for hire

pajtue'shmëri *nf* reconcilement, rapprochement; reconcilability

*__pajua'r__ *adj (i)* endowed; provided

*__paju'er__ *nm (obl ˜ o'ri) (Old)* mast (of a sailing ship)

pajustifikua'r *adj (i)* unjustified

pajustifikue'shëm *adj (i)* unjustifiable, inexcusable

pajva'n *nm* pastern

pak
I § *quant* **1** not much: little; not many: few **2** a little; a few
II § *adv* **1** a little, somewhat, slightly **2** a little while
III § *pcl* (mitigates a command or request) please; just
  ○ **më pak** less, fewer

pak·*et* *vpr* **1 to shrink up (from old age or illness) **2** = **mpak·***et*

pa'ka *nf (e)* the smaller/smallest part

paka'lb'shëm *adj (i)* imperishable

paka'lb'ur *adj (i)* not rotten, unspoiled

paka'li'tur *adj (i)* **1** (of metal) untempered; (of tools) not sharpened by hammering; (of a millstone) not dressed **2** *(Fig)* (of a person) not toughened enough (by life experience)

pakalue's *adj (i)* **1** (of a pupil/grade) not passing (into a higher class) **2** *(Old)* [*Ling*] intransitive

pakalue'shëm *adj (i)* **1** impassable, impenetrable, insuperable, insurmountable **2** *(Fig)* unsurpassable; highest (mark in school)

pakallaji'sur *adj (i)* (of a copper utensil) uncoated with tin

paka'llur *adj (i) (Impol)* left unburied

*__pakând'shëm__ *(Reg Gheg)* = **pakë'nd'shëm**

*__pakanu'n__ *adj* = **pakanu'nët**

*__pakanu'nët__ *adj (i)* illicit, illegal

*__pakanu'nshëm__ *OR* **pakanu'ntë** *adj (i)* = **pakanu'n**

pakapërcye'shëm *adj (i)* **1** insurmountable, impassable, untraversable **2** *(Fig)* unsurpassable

paka'pshëm *adj (i)* **1** uncatchable **2** ungraspable; incomprehensible **3** ephemeral

*__pakaptua'rshëm__ *OR* **pakaptue'shëm** *adj (i)* unsurpassable; unattainable

paka'pur *adj (i)* = **paka'pshëm**

pakarakter *adj (i)* lacking strength of character, lacking moral firmness

pakare *np fem* small number of goats or sheep not pastured with the others but kept near home for milking

paketë *nf* small cardboard case/box: pack, package, packet
  ○ **paketë e aksioneve** block of shares
  ○ **paketë individuale** [*Mil*] first aid kit
  ○ **paketë ligjesh** set of laws
  ○ **paketë tymuese** [*Mil*] smoke pot

paketim *nm ger* < **paketo·n**

paketo·n *vt* to pack, package

paketues
  I § *adj* used for packing/packaging
  II § *n* person who work as a packer

pakë
  I § *nf* pork belly, side of pork
  II § *adj (i)* (*Colloq*) = **paktë**

pakëmbë *nf* without legs, legless; lame, crippled.

pakëmbyeshëm *adj (i)* nonconvertible

pakënaqësi *nf* 1 displeasure; discontent, dissatisfaction 2 complaint expressing dissatisfaction

pakënaqshëm *adj (i)* unsatisfactory

pakënaqur
  I § *adj (i)* dissatisfied; discontented; displeased
  II § *n (i)* malcontent

pakënd *adj (i)* without anyone: all alone

pakëndshëm *adj (i)* 1 unattractive, unappealing 2 displeasing, unpleasant

*****pakënduéshëm** *adj (i)* (*Colloq*) illegible; unreadable

pakëputshëm *adj (i)* 1 unbreakable 2 (*Fig*) indissoluble

pakëputur *adj (i)* 1 unbroken 2 unweaned 3 (*Fig*) uninterrupted, continuous

pakërcell *adj (i)* [*Bot*] (of certain plants) stemless: (*acaulescent, acauline*)

pakërro·het *vpr* to be timid about speaking; stay in the background

pakërrusur *adj (i)* 1 not bent over: unbowed, straight-backed 2 (*Fig*) indomitable, undaunted

*****pakësi** *nf* paucity

pakësim *nm ger* 1 < **pakëso·n**, **pakëso·het** 2 decrease, reduction, diminution

pakëso·het *vpr* to get smaller, become reduced, decrease; abate

pakëso·n *vt* to decrease, reduce, lessen, diminish; subtract

pakësues *adj* lessening, reducing

pakësueshëm *adj (i)* reducible

pakëshilluéshëm *adj (i)* inadvisable

pakët *nn (të)* = **fikët**

*****pakëthjellt** *adj (i)* unclear

pakëz *adv* a little bit; a little while

pakicë *nf* 1 small amount/number 2 the smaller/smallest part; minority

pakiderm *nf* [*Zool*] pachyderm

pakkush *pron* hardly anybody, few people

pakmos *adv* 1 (followed by a number) more or less, of the order of, about 2 at least

pako *nf* package

pako·het *vpr* = **pakëso·het**

pako·n *vt* = **pakëso·n**

pakohë *adj (i)* = **pakohshëm**

pakohshëm *adj (i)* not appropriate (in terms of time): untimely, inopportune, unseasonable; premature

pakomendje *nf with masc agreement* simpleton, imbecile

*****pakontestar** *adj (i)* uncontested; incontestable

pakontrolluar *adj (i)* 1 not checked carefully: unexamined, uninspected 2 not given proper thought: careless, rash

pakontrolluéshëm *adj (i)* 1 uncontrollable 2 not subject to inspection/examination

pakorë
  I § *adj (i)* immoderate in eating/drinking: overindulgent, intemperate
  II § *nf* immoderation in eating/drinking: overindulgence, intemperance

pakorrigjuéshëm *adj (i)* = **pandreqshëm**

pakositur *adj (i)* unmown

pakrahasuéshëm *adj (i)* 1 noncomparable 2 (*Fig*) incomparable

pakrasitur *adj (i)* unpruned; untrimmed

pakrehur *adj (i)* unkempt, disheveled; uncombed

pakrijuéshëm *adj (i)* (*Book*) incapable of being created

pakrijueshmëri *nf* (*Book*) incapability of being created

pakrimbur *adj (i)* not wormy

pakripë *adj (i)* 1 lacking salt 2 (*Fig*) flavorless, tasteless: bland

pakripur *adj (i)* unsalted, fresh

pakristalizuar *adj (i)* uncrystallized

pakritikuéshëm *adj (i)* not subject to criticism, uncriticizable

pakrye *adj (i)* 1 dead-end 2 (*Fig*) leading nowhere 3 (*Fig*) mindless

pakryer
  I § *adj (i)* 1 unfinished, uncompleted 2 [*Ling*] imperfect
  II § *nf (e)* [*Ling*] imperfect tense

*****pakryesi** *nf* lack of leadership: anarchy

*****pakrypë** OR **pakrypët** *adj (i)* = **pakripë**

paksa *adv* just a little/few, a little bit

paksel *vt* to plug [a crack/hole]: caulk, stop up

paksel·et *vpr* to squeeze in

paksëpaku *adv* no less than, at least

pakt *nm* pact

paktë
  I § *adj (i)* 1 small in quantity/number: few, little 2 insufficient, inadequate; in short supply, scarce 3 puny; frail
  II § *n (i)* few
  III § *nf (e)* smaller/smallest part: minority
  IV § *adv* (*Colloq*) no less than, at least
  V § *adv (të)* at the very least, at minimum
  ○ **nuk ësh-të e paktë** (of an event) not be a trivial matter, be no slight matter
  ○ **nuk ësh-të i paktë** 1 (of a person) not be without value, be of considerable value 2 (of a person) not be without fault
  ○ **të paktën** at least
  ○ **(në) të paktën e herëve** rarely

*****paktues** *adj (Old)*

*****pakthelluéshëm** *adj (i)* inexplicable

pakthyer adj (i) not turned: unbent, straight; (of soil) untilled; (of worn clothes that have not been turned inside out and resewn) unreversed

paku adv (së) no less than, at least

pakualifikuar adj (i) **1** unqualified; not having special qualifications **2** not requiring special qualifications

pakufi adj (i) **1** boundless, immense **2** (Fig) infinite

pakufishëm adj (i) **1** boundless, limitless: infinite **2** [Ling] indefinite

pakufizuar adj (i) unbounded, unlimited

pakufizueshëm adj (i) illimitable

pakujdes adj (i) = pakujdesshëm

pakujdesi nf **1** carelessness **2** negligence

pakujdesshëm adj (i) **1** careless **2** uncaring; negligent

pakujdesur adj (i) = pakujdesshëm

*__pakujti__ nf inadvertence, heedlessness

pakujtimas adv inadvertently

pakujtuar adv = pakujtimas

pakujtueshëm adj (i) **1** impossible to remember: unmemorable **2** not quick-witted, unintelligent **3** thoughtless; unappreciative, ungrateful

pakulturë adj (i) lacking in culture, not broadly knowledgeable

pakulturuar adj (i) not well brought up: uncultivated, uncultured; not broadly cultured

*__pakun__ nn (të) (Reg Gheg) faint, swoon

pakundërshtuar adj (i) undisputed, unchallenged, unopposed

pakundërshtueshëm adj (i) indisputable

pakundshoq adj (i) = pashoq

pakuptim
   I § nm **1** inability to understand **2** something not understood correctly: misunderstanding
   II § adj (i) meaningless; undefined, vague

pakuptimshëm adj (i) unintelligible, incomprehensible; meaningless

pakuptuar adj (i) **1** unintelligible, misunderstandable; muddled, confused **2** slow-witted, dense

pakuptueshëm adj (i) **1** unintelligible, unclear **2** incomprehensible, mysterious

pakurdisur adj (i) (of a mechanism driven by a spring) not wound up

pakureshtje adj (i) (Book) incuriosity

*__pakurmë__ = pakorë

pakurorë adj (i) **1** (Old) living together without being officially married **2** (Colloq) unmarried **3** born out of wedlock: illegitimate

pakursyer adj (i) unstinting; unstintingly helpful

pakursyeshëm adj (i) = pakursyer

pakusht adj (i) unconditional

pakushtëzuar adj (i) not contingent: independent

pakushtueshëm adj (i) inexpensive

*__pakuximshëm__ adj (i) = paguximshëm

pakyçur adj (i) unlocked

*__Pal__ nm Paul

*__palaçi__ nf = palaçollëk

palaço nf with masc agreement **1** (Old) jester **2** clown

palaçollëk nm (np ~ qe) (Colloq) tomfoolery

palafike nf pair of dried fig halves

palagështi adj (i) lacking moisture: arid, dry

palagshëm adj (i) impervious to water, waterproof

*__palajthim__ adv = pa lajthim without error, infallibly

*__palajthitshëm__ OR **palajthitur** adj (i) unerring, infallible

palakuar adj (i) unbent, straight

palakueshëm adj (i) **1** inflexible **2** [Ling] indeclinable

*__palamid__ nm [Ichth] Atlantic bonito (Sarda sarda)

*__palamit__ = palamid

*__palamute__ nf [Bot] common restharrow, common ononis (Ononis vulgaris)

palandy·het vpr (Colloq) to get all dirty

palandy·n vt (Colloq) to make [] all dirty

palandytë adj (i) (Colloq) all dirty

palanik nm pasty made by adding successively baked and buttered layers

pala-pala adv = palë-palë

palapalë adv in pairs

palapetë
   I § nf **1** kick pleat **2** disk-shaped object
   II § adj flat

palara np (të) fem improper activities kept hidden from others: dirty linen, dirty business

palare nf **1** round, smooth board used for rolling out dough: pastry board **2** large, shallow ceramic platter **3** (Old) [Relig] dish of boiled wheat taken to an Orthodox church and shared with others to commemorate a death

palarë
   I § adj (i) **1** unwashed; unclean **2** (Fig) not cleared from the account: unsettled, unpaid
   II § nf (e) debt

*__palargueshëm__ adj (i) **1** inevitable, unavoidable **2** inalienable

pallas adv folded up

palatal nm palatal

*__palatuem__ adj (i) (Reg Gheg) unpolished; unrefined, coarse

palavdi adj (i) = palavdishëm

palavdishëm adj (i) (Book) unpraiseworthy; inglorious

palavi nf **1** uncleanliness, filth; pus **2** infestation of lice/fleas in a human body **3** (Collec) infestation of weeds **4** (Fig) filthy language

palavig nm (np ~ gje) narrow wooden bridge over a creek; thick log laid across a ditch or muddy area

palavo·het vpr **1** to become unclean **2** to form pus

palavo·n
   I § vt to make [] unclean: soil
   II § vi to use foul language, talk dirty

palavos
   I § adj **1** (of a person who does not keep himself clean) filthy, slovenly, unclean **2** foul-mouthed
   II § nm dirty bum, pig

palavos· = palavo·n

palavose nf slattern, slut

*__palavosur__ adj (i) **1** unhurt, unwounded **2** soiled

*__palavrak__ nm flatterer

palavruem adj (i) (Reg Gheg) = palëvruar

palcak nm **1** back of the neck: nape **2** = palcar

palcar nm ear of fresh corn: green/unripe corn

palcë
   I § nf **1** marrow **2** [Bot] pith **3** (Fig) very center, very core; central part, heart; best part: cream
   II § adj **1** very soft and tender **2** immature, unripe
   ○ palca e arrës meat of a walnut, nutmeat

○ **palcë gjëri** the best part
○ **palca e kurrizit** spinal cord
○ **palca e·lumit** main current in a river; part of a river where the current is strongest
○ **palca e shtyllës kurrizore** spinal cord

pa'lcët adj (i) (of certain trees) having a pith: pithy

palco'r adj 1 [Spec] of or pertaining to marrow/pith 2 [Med] medullary

palco're nf 1 fresh corn = **palca'r** 2 (Old) small metal box worn at the waist and used for carrying one's supply of grease for a gun

*** pa'lçë = palcë**

pale' pcl (Colloq) 1 expresses speaker's uncertainty: whether maybe, maybe 2 (at the beginning or end of a sentence) expresses speaker's distaste or mockery: oh sure! 3 expresses speaker's softening of a suggestion or request: let's just

palej'ua'r adj (i) prohibited, forbidden; illicit

palej'ue'shëm adj (i) inadmissible, impermissible

pale'më adj (i) (Reg Gheg) unborn

paleogra'f nm paleographer

paleografi' nf paleography

paleografi'k adj paleographic

paleoli't nm [Archeol] Paleolithic Age

*** paleoliti'k** adj [Archeol] Paleolithic

paleonto'lo'g n paleontologist

paleonto'logji' nf paleontology

paleonto'logji'k nf paleontological

*** pale'qe** adj without mistakes

*** palere'** = **palare'**

pale'stër nf gymnasium

palestine'z adj, n Palestinian

Palesti'në nf Palestine

palestri'në nf [Soccer] shin guard, shin pad

pales'ua'r adj (i) (of soil) not broken up by a harrow: unharrowed

pale'sh adj (i) hairless; bald

pale'sh'ur adj (i) not yet covered by hair: beardless, hairless

*** paletër'si** nf ignorance, illiteracy

*** pale'tra** adj unlettered, illiterate

paleverdi'shëm adj (i) of no advantage, disadvantageous, unprofitable

paleverdi'shmëri nf unprofitability, disadvantage

palexue'shëm adj (i) unreadable, illegible

paleze't adj (i) = **paleze'tshëm**

paleze'tshëm adj (i) 1 (Colloq) tasteless, flavorless 2 unattractive 3 distasteful

pale'
I § nf 1 pair; couple 2 set, collection, group 3 fold; crease; pleat; convolution 4 dried fig (flattened or cut before drying) 5 pile of cured tobacco leaves ready for shredding
II § adv in piles, pile upon pile
III § adv folded (in two)
○ **palat e trurit** [Anat] convolutions of the brain gyri
○ **palë e palë** = **pa'lë-pa'lë**

pa'lëçi'tshëm adj (i) (Old) = **palexue'shëm**

pa'lëku'nd'shëm adj (i) unwavering, steadfast

pa'lëku'nd'ur adj (i) unwavering, steady, constant

pa'lëm'ua'r adj (i) unpolished

pa'lënd'ët adj (i) [Phil] immaterial, incorporeal, abstract

pa'lëng'shëm adj (i) lacking in liquid: not juicy

pa'lë-pa'lë adv 1 with multiple folds, in folds: pleated; wrinkled 2 pile upon pile; in piles

palër'ua'r adj (i) unplowed; uncultivated

palë'tim nm ger < **palëto'·n**, **palëto'·het**

palë'to'·het vpr to bend over

palë'to'·n vt to fold [ ] (up)

*** palëvi'z'ëm** adj (i) unmoving, still

palëvi'z'shëm adj (i) 1 motionless; immobile; immovable, unmovable 2 stable, constant; invariable; unchangeable; fixed, established

palëvi'z'shmëri nf motionlessness; immobility, constancy, stability, invariability

palëvi'z'ur adj (i) motionless

palëvr'ua'r adj (i) in its primitive state, not yet worked on: uncultivated, undeveloped

palë'z nf 1 earlobe 2 fold, pleat, tuck 3 spool of silk thread 4 amount of wool taken at a time from a carding comb 5 dried fig (flattened or cut before drying)
○ **palëz akulli** ice pack
○ **palëz llape/pape** poultice
○ **palëza e veshit** the earlobe

palë'zim nm ger < **palëzo'·n**, **palëzo'·het**

palë'zo'·het vpr to get folded/pleated/creased/wrinkled

palë'zo'·n vt to fold, pleat; crease; wrinkle

*** pa'li'dhje**
I § nf incoherence
II § adj disconnected, incoherent

pali'dh'ur adj (i) 1 unbound, untied; unconnected; separate 2 [Ling] unbound, independent 3 (Fig) lacking coherence: incoherent 4 of poor build 5 not coagulated and set: ungelled

palig'ësht'ua'r adj (i) 1 in reasonably good health, not ill 2 not depressed, not in low spirits

pali'gjë
I § nf cow, sheep, or goat that gives birth at an unusually early age = **lla'shkë**
II § adj < **pa ligjë** *illegal

pali'gj'ësi = **paligjshm'ëri**

pali'gj'shëm adj (i) illegal, unlawful; illegitimate

pali'gj'shmëri nf (Book) illegality, unlawfulness; illegitimacy

*** pali'm** nm ger < **palo'·n**

*** pali'nd'ur** adj (i) yet unborn, unborn

*** pali's·** vt = **palëzo'·n**

*** palk** nm [Theat] loge, box

palme'të nf [Naut] (on a ship) berth; cabin

pa'lme nf [Bot] palm tree
○ **palma feniks** [Bot] date palm Phoenix dactylifera
○ **palmë sagutare** [Bot] sago palm Coelococcus, Metroxylon

palmo're np [Bot] plants of the palm family Palmaceae

palmu'ç adv all in a heap; stooped, bent

*** palmu'ç** = **palmu'ç**

pa'lnjë nf [Bot] maple tree

*** palo'·n** vt = **palëzo'·n**

palo- pejorative formative prefix crummy old __, a devil of a __; big old __

*** palo'dh'ësi** nf tirelessness, indefatigability

*** palo'dhje** nf = **palodhësi**

palo'dh'shëm adj (i) 1 tireless, indefatigable 2 not tiring: effortless, easy

palo·dhur *adj (i)* unremitting, inexhaustible, assid-uous

palogjíkë *adj (i)* = **palogjíkshëm**

palogjíkshëm *adj (i)* illogical; unreasonable

***palojtshëm** *adj (i)* motionless, still

palok *nm* string of split figs hung up to dry

***palomb** *nm* [*Ichth*] smooth hound (*Mustelus mustelus* L)

palombár *nm* **1** underwater diver *2 hawser = **pal-lamar**

palóre *nf* small, flat flask for raki

***palo-rróba** *np* crummy old clothes

palós· *vt* **1** to fold; fold up; crease; pleat **2** to bend [ ] down **3** (*Colloq*) to beat [ ] down, smash [ ] down, smash

○ **palós· buzët** to make a pouting gesture, make a face (expressing one's displeasure); get ready to cry

palós·et *vpr* to bend down, bend over

palós·ës
  I § *adj* [*Spec*] used for folding
  II § *n* person whose work is to fold something

palósje *nf ger* **1** <**palós·**, **palós·et 2** [*Sport*] pike (in diving/gymnastics)

palósshëm *adj (i)* foldable, collapsible

palósur *adj (i)* folded; pleated

palpím *nm* [*Med*] palpation

***palpurís** *stem for 1st sg pres, pl pres, 2nd & 3rd sg subj, pind* <**palpurít·**

***palpurít·** *vt* to bounce

***palsë** *nf* **1** shock of hair, topknot; tuft **2** earlobe

***paltar** *nm* = **palues**

paltim *nm ger* = **palósje**

palto·n *vt* = **palós**

paluajtshëm *adj (i)* **1** unmovable, rigid; immobile **2** [*Law*] immovable **3** (*Fig*) steadfast

***paluejtshëm** = **paluajtshëm**

***paluftueshëm** *adj (i)* unassailable, invulnerable

paluhatshëm *adj (i)* unwavering, steadfast = **palëkundshëm**

***palumtëri** *nf* unhappiness

***palumtsísht** *adv* unfortunately

palumtur *adj (i)* unhappy; unfortunate

palumur *adj (i)* ill-fated, hapless

palundrueshëm *adj (i)* unnavigable

paluze OR **paluze** *nf* [*Food*] sweet pap (for ba-bies) made of starch or rice flour, sugar and hot water

palyer *adj (i)* **1** unpainted; not whitewashed **2** (*Fig*) not mixed up in something bad: untainted, unstained

***palyeshëm** *adj (i)* indelible

palyrë *adj (i)* **1** [*Food*] (of food) lacking in fat, hav-ing too little fat; flavorless, tasteless, dry **2** (*Fig*) dull, vapid

***palzë** = **palcë**

pall *nm* **1** finely milled flour **2** fine chaff and dust from harvested grain **3** dandruff

pall· *vi* = **pëllet·**

***palláckë** *nf* = **pallaskë**

pallagajë *nf* (*Old*) = **poganík**

pallak *adj* [*Bot*] spatulate

pallamar *nm* **1** cinch strap **2** [*Naut*] hawser; anchor hawser **3** [*Bot*] tall, thick weed **4** person with thick legs **5** oar

pallamáre *nf* protective wooden handguard worn on the left arm while reaping with a sickle

***pallamut** *nm* [*Ichth*] codfish

pallangë *nf* **1** (*Old*) large village with houses, a few stores, and an open market place **2** (*Colloq*) sliding door bolt **3** wind vane in a windmill

pallanxë *nf* weight (on a scale)

pallasártë *nf* [*Naut*] main stay

pallaskë *nf* **1** carved piece of wood; plaque **2** [*Ethnog*] medallion worn on the chest or waist **3** (*Impol*) military medal; epaulet on a uniform **4** (*Old*) belt pouch or case for cartridges or gunpow-der; cartridge belt; cartridge case **5** (*Colloq*) shank of the foot

○ **pallaska e belit** footrest on a spade handle (used to apply foot pressure for digging)

○ **pallaskë buke** (*Joke*) thick slice of bread

○ **pallaska e derës/dritares** pivoting bar used to keep a door/window closed

○ **pallaskat e kalit** leather blinders for a horse, blinkers

pallat *nm* **1** large multi-storied building; block of flats, apartment building **2** palace

pallavesh
  I § *n* (*Impol*) **1** person with big ears **2** person who is slow on the uptake, slow-witted person
  II § *adj* big-eared; slow-witted

pallavra *np* (*Colloq*) palaver, idle talk

pallavro·n *vi* to chatter

pallavrues *nm* chatterer, chatterbox

palldëm *nm* girth used to secure pack saddle on a draft animal: cinch strap

pallë *nf* **1** (*Old*) battle sword **2** paddle used to beat clothes while washing **3** flail **4** [*Agr*] colter; plow-share **5** (*Colloq*) spoke of a cart wheel **6** (*Colloq*) door bolt **7** rollicking good time

○ **ësh·të bishti i pallës** to be lowest in importance, be totally disregarded: be low man on the totem pole

pallëlárë *adj* **1** (*Poet*) with sword bathed in gilt, with glistening sword **2** (*Fig*) glorious in battle

pallëngjeshur *adj* (*Poet*) sword girt to the waist: ever ready for battle

pallëvetëtímë *adj* (*Poet*) with sword flashing like lightning; masterful in swordsmanship; valiant

pallëzhveshur *adj* (*Poet*) sword unsheathed and ready to do battle

***pallï(n)** *nm* (*Reg Gheg*) marble, taw

pallje *nf ger* = **pëllitje**

pallmë *nf* **1** = **pëllitje 2** (*Pej*) loud bellow

pallmëmadh *adj* (*Impol Colloq*) with screaming voice

pallo·het *vpr* (*Crude*) to burst at the seams with eating, eat gluttonously

pallo·n *vt* **1** to beat [clothes] with a paddle while washing **2** (*Crude*) to bash, wallop **3** (*Crude*) to stuff [food] down gluttonously, pig out on [ ]; stuff [some-one] with food

pallogaritshëm *adj (i)* **1** incalculable **2** (*Fig*) enor-mously important; extraordinary

pallogaritur *adj (i)* uncounted; uncalculated

palloi *obl* <**pallua**

○ **palloi i ditës** [*Entom*] peacock butterfly *Vanessa io*

pallonj *np* <**pallua**

pallo·sh *adj* **1** *(Colloq)* tall and stout **2** *(Fig)* good-hearted; somewhat unsophisticated, ingenuous **3** *(Impol)* simpleminded

*pallta·ke *nf* bomb

pa·llto *nf* **1** heavy overcoat **2** [*Tech*] galvanized coating of a metal container/vessel

pall·u̇a *nm (obl ~ o·i, np ~ o·nj)* [*Ornit*] peacock

pa·maj̇ë *adj (i)* rounded-off, without sharp points

pa·majṁë *adj (i)* lacking in fat: lean

pamanovru̇e·shëm *adj (i)* difficult to maneuver: unmaneuverable

*pamaqëri *nf* predicament, bad trouble

pa·marte·së *nf (Book)* celibacy

pa·martu̇a·r *adj (i)* unmarried, single

*pama·rre *nf (Reg Gheg)* shameless impudence, insolence: cheek

pa·marrë *adj (i)* *(Reg Gheg)* shamelessly impudent, insolent: cheeky

pa·marrë·ve·sh *adj (i)* deaf to advice, headstrong; disobedient

*pa·marr·shëm *adj (i)* *(Reg Gheg)* = pama·rrë

pa·ma·së *adj (i)* beyond measure: immeasurable; innumerable, incalculable

pa·ma·shkull *adj (i)* **1** unmanly **2** (of a family) without a man; without a male child

pa·mashtru̇e·shëm *adj (i)* **1** undeceivable **2** not deceptive

pa·maṫësi *nf (Book)* measurelessness

pa·ma·t·shëm *adj (i)* immeasurable

pa·ma·tur *adj (i)* **1** immoderate; impetuous, hasty **2** of unknown size: unmeasured **3** immense

pa·matu̇ri *nf* immatureness

pa·mazi̇·tur *adj (i)* [*Dairy*] (of milk) unskimmed; made of whole milk

pa·mba·rë *adj (i)* not going well; unsuccessful

pa·mbari̇·m *adj (i)* interminable; endless

pa·mbari̇·m·isht *adv* **1** *(Book)* interminably; constantly **2** [*Math*] without limit

pa·mbaru̇a·r *adj (i)* **1** unfinished; uncompleted **2** interminable; endless **3** inexhaustible

pa·mbaru̇e·shëm *adj (i)* **1** inexhaustible **2** interminable; endless

*pa·mba·rrë *adj (i)* = pama·rrë

*pa·mba·tun *adj (i)* *(Reg Gheg)* badly maintained, ill-kept, neglected; unpreserved

pa·mbërri̇·t·shëm *adj (i)* = paarrit·shëm

pa·mbështe·tje *adj (i)* **1** unsupported; without family support **2** = pambro·jtje

pa·mbikqẏr·shëm *adj (i)* *(Reg Gheg)* unsupervisable

pa·mbi̇·rë *adj (i)* non-germinating

pa·mbje·llë *adj (i)* [*Agr*] (of plowed land) not yet planted: unsown

pa·mbra·p·shëm *adj (i)* irreversible = paprapsu̇e·shëm

*pa·mbret·ëri *nf* anarchy

pa·mbro·jë *adj (i)* = pambro·jt·shëm

pa·mbro·jt·shëm *adj (i)* indefensible; defenseless, vulnerable

pa·mbro·jt·ur *adj (i)* **1** unprotected; undefended **2** = pambro·jtje

*pa·mbro·tḣë·shëm *adj (i)* unfavorable

*pa·mbru̇·më *adj (i)* = pabru̇·më

pambu̇·k

I § *nm* **1** cotton *(Gossypium L.)* **2** cotton fiber

II § *adj* very soft; soft and gentle

∘ **pambu̇k i egër** [*Bot*] bristly-fruited silkweed *Gomphocarpus fruticosus*

∘ **pambu̇k guri** [*Min*] asbestos

∘ **pambu̇k mjek̇ësor** [*Med*] absorbent cotton

∘ **pambu̇k xhami/qelqi** [*Tech*] glass wool = **lesh xhami**

pambu̇·k·ët *adj (i)* of cotton

pambu̇·kje *adj*

pambuk·o·r *adj* **1** puffy and white, cottony **2** very soft

pambuk·o·re *nf* **1** field sown in cotton, cotton field **2** heavy twill jacket with cotton padding **3** [*Entom*] citrus mealy bug *(Pseudococcus citri Risso)*

∘ **pambukorja e agrumeve** [*Entom*] cottony-cushion scale, which causes a disease of citrus trees manifested by a white foam near branch nodes *Icerya purchasi Mack*

∘ **pambukorja e ullirit** [*Entom*] olive psyllid *Euphyllura olivina Costa*

pambu̇·kṫë

I § *adj (i)* made of cotton cloth

II § *nf (e)* cotton cloth; clothes made of cotton

pa·mbu·lu̇a·r *adj (i)* **1** not closed, not covered over, uncovered **2** unburied **3** [*Fin*] unpaid **4** [*Sport*] unguarded, uncovered

*pa·mby·ll *adj (i)* not closed, unlocked, open

pa·mby·ll·ur *adj (i)* unfastened; unclosed/unhealed (wound); unlocked

*pa·mejtu̇a·r *adj (i)* = pamendu̇a·r

pa·me·nd *adj (i)* **1** mindless; thoughtless **2** inadequately considered: impetuous

*pa·me·ndje *nf* absurdity, nonsense

pa·mendu̇a·r *adj (i)* not thought out, with inadequate deliberation: ill-considered, imprudent, foolish

*pameni *nf (Reg Gheg)* = pa·mje

pa·meritu̇a·r *adj (i)* unmerited, undeserved

pa·meritu̇e·shëm *adj (i)* = pameritu̇a·r

*pame·ta = pa·mëta

*pa·me·t·shëm *adj (i)* unimpaired

pa·më *nf* protective covering of leaves over a stack of hay or grain

pa·më

I § *1st pl pdef <*she h·

II § *part (Reg Gheg) <*she h·

pa·mëka·të *adj (i)* **1** [*Relig*] without sin; chaste **2** *(Colloq)* innocent; not adulterous, faithful in marriage

pa·mëkaṫësi *nf (Book)* sinlessness

pa·mëka·t·shëm *adj (i)* = pamëka·të

pa·mënḋ·ëri *nf* mindlessness, foolishness, folly

pa·mënjanu̇e·shëm *adj (i)* = pashma·ngshëm

pa·mërzi̇·t·shëm *adj (i)* not bothersome, not troublesome

*pa·m·ës *n* onlooker, spectator

pa·mësu̇a·r *adj (i)* uneducated; untrained

pa·mësye·shëm *adj (i)* unassailable

pa·mëshi̇·rë *adj (i)* = pamëshi̇r·shëm

pa·mëshi̇r·shëm *adj (i)* merciless, ruthless

*pa·mëta *adv* again

pamfle·t *nm* [*Lit*] pamphlet

pamflet·i·st *n* pamphleteer

pa·mi̇·q *adj (i)* friendless

pa·miq̇·ësi *nf (Book)* friendlessness

pa|mira|di|je
I § _nf_ = **mosmir**_ënjo_**hje**
II § _adj (i)_ = **mosmir**_ënjo_**hës**
pa|mira|díj|shëm _adj (i)_ = **mosmirënjohës**
pa|mir_ë_ _adj (i)_ not right/good: improper; unpleasant
*pa|mir**ë**|**pri**|**t|un** _adj (i) (Reg Gheg)_ unwelcome
pa|mir_ësí_ _nf (Book)_ unfriendliness; uncharitableness
*pa|mir**ë**|**s**|**u|e|shëm** _adj (i)_ incorrigible
pa|mí|sh _adj (i)_ not meaty: skinny; (of fruit) without much flesh
pa|mjaft_ë_ _adj (i)_ = **pamjaftu|esh**_ëm_
pa|mjaft_ë|_**sí** _nf_ = **pamjaftueshm**_ërí_
pa|mjaft|u|a|r _adj (i)_ = **pamjaftu|esh**_ëm_
pa|mjaft|u|e|shëm _adj (i)_ insufficient, inadequate
pa|mjaft|u|e|shm|_ërí_ _nf (Book)_ inadequacy; insufficiency
pa|m|je _nf_ **1** outer appearance, countenance, look; aspect, facet **2** view, sight; scene, panorama **3** visual image **4** ability to see: vision; range of vision
pam|je|çe|l|ur _adj (Poet)_ having a happy countenance: ever-smiling
pa|mje|kër _adj (i)_ beardless
pa|mje|ku|e|shëm _adj (i)_ not medicable: untreatable, incurable
pa|mje|lë _adj (i) [Dairy]_ unmilked
pam|je|rën|dë _adj_ of stern countenance, stern-faced
pa|moh|u|a|r _adj (i)_ indisputable, incontrovertible; undisputed
pa|moh|u|e|shëm _adj (i)_ undeniable
*pa|mol|í|sje _nf (Old)_ immunity (from infection)
pam|o|r _adj_ visual; optical
pa|mora|l _adj (i)_ = **pamora|sh**_ëm_
pa|mora|l|shëm _adj (i)_ amoral; immoral
pa|mo|rt _adj (i) (Colloq)_ capable of lasting a long time: durable **2** _(Fig)_ immortal
pa|mo|shë
I § _adj_ not of age: minor, juvenile
II § _n (i)_ minor, juvenile
*pa|mosh**ë**|**sí** _nf_ minority, juvenility
pa|motiv|u|e|shëm _adj (i)_ unmotivated
*pam|po|r _nm (Old Colloq)_ = **vapo**_r_
pam|po|sht|shëm _adj (i)_ **1** unsuppressible, irrepressible **2** undefeatable, invincible
pam|po|sht|ur _adj (i)_ undefeated = **pam|po**_sht_**shëm**
*pa|m|pro|jt|shëm _adj (i)_ = **pambrojtshëm**
*pam|pu|a|r = **vapo**_r_
*pa|msh|u|a|r = **pashu**_a_**r**
*pa|mu|je _nf (Reg Gheg)_ impotence
*pa|mu|jt|un _adj (i) (Reg Gheg)_ **1** powerless, impotent **2** unconquered
*pa|mu|k| _(Colloq)_ = **pambu**_k_|
pa|mund_ësí_ _nf_ impossibility, infeasibility
pa|mund|ím|shëm _adj (i)_ not requiring great effort: effortless, easy
*pa|mu|nd|je _nf_ illness, indisposition
pa|mu|nd|shëm _adj (i)_ **1** impossible **2** undefeatable, invincible
pa|mu|nd|shm|e _adj (i)_ = that which is impossible
pa|mund|u|a|r _adj (i)_ not having experienced suffering; untormented
pa|mu|nd|ur _adj (i)_ **1** impossible **2** insufferable **3** _(Colloq)_ unwell, slightly ill

pa|mung|u|e|shëm _adj (i)_ never absent; ever available
*pa|mvar| = **pavar**|
pan _nm [Hist]_ land baron in Poland, Slavic lord
pan| _formative prefix (Book)_ **pan–**
pa|nafak_ë_ _adj (i)_ **1** = **pafa**_t_ **2** naughty
*panagji**r** _OR_ **panagjy|r** _(Old)_ = **panaí**_r_
panaí|r _nm_ **1** market fair; fair; annual fair; exposition, exhibition **2** _(Fig Colloq)_ noisy and bustling place
*pa|nají|r = **panaí**_r_
panama _nf_ panama hat
Panama _nf_ Panama
pana|me|z _adj, n_ Panamanian
*pana|ve|t**ë** _nf_ side table, sideboard
pancí|r _nm [Hist]_ = **parzmo**_re_
*pa|ndaj _conj_ = **prandaj**
*pa|nda|l|ëm _adj (i)_ unhalted, uninterrupted
*pa|nda|l|je _nf_ permission, leave
pa|nda|l|shëm _adj (i)_ unhaltable, unstoppable; unrestrainable, uncontrollable
pa|nda|l|u|e|shëm = **panda|lsh**_ëm_
pa|nda|r_ë_ _adj (i)_ **1** undivided, whole, unitary; integral **2** inseparable; indivisible
*pa|nda|r**ë**|**shëm** = **panda**_'sh_**ëm**
pa|nda|shëm _adj (i)_ **1** indivisible; inseparable, impartible; undivided **2** _[Econ]_ not designated for division among members of the cooperative: reserved **3** = **pandar**_ë_
pa|nda|shm|_ërí_ _nf_ indivisibility; inseparability
pa|nda|shm|ër|í|sht _adv_ indivisibly; inseparably; integrally
*pa|nde·|_n_ = **pandeh·**
pande|h·
I § _vi_ to have the impression, suspect; suppose, think, presume, assume
II § _vt_ **1** to deem, adjudge **2** to expect [a certain behavior]
  ○ [] **pandeh· për** to consider [] to be, take [] for, think of [] as
*pande|h|**ë**|**m** _nf_ supposition, presumption; illusion
pandeh|_ësí_ _nf (Old)_ = **pande|hj**_e_
*pande|h|je _nf_ supposition, assumption; suspicion
pande|h|ur _adj (i) [Law]_ suspect; defendant
*pa|nde|nj|ur _adj (i)_ uninhabited
pa|nde|r _adj (i)_ = **pande|rsh**_ëm_
*pa|nde|r**ë** _nf_ embroidery
pa|nde|r|shëm _adj (i)_ dishonorable, disgraceful; dishonest
pa|nder|shm|_ërí_ _nf_ dishonor, disgrace; dishonesty
pa|nder|shm|ër|í|sht _adv_ dishonorably, disgracefully
*pa|ndeshkí _nf (Old)_ impunity
*pa|ndeshk|u|e|m _adj (i) (Reg Gheg)_ unpunished
pa|nde|z|shëm _adj (i)_ incombustible, nonflammable
pa|nde_r_ _nf_ frame and roof of a house
pa|ndëgje|s_ë_ _nf_ disobedience, insubordination
pa|ndëgj|u|e|shëm _adj (i)_ disobedient, insubordinate
*pa|nd**ë**l _nf_ scrap, bit
pa|ndërgje|gje _nf_ lack of conscientiousness, irresponsibility
*pa|ndër|gjegj|ësí _nf (Book)_ = **pandërgjegj**_e_

pa·ndër·gje·gj·shëm *adj (i)* **1** not conscientious, lacking conscientiousness; irresponsible **2** unconscious

pa·ndër·gjegj·shm·ërï *nf* **1** *(Book)* lack of conscientiousness; irresponsibility **2** unconsciousness

pa·ndër·mje·më *adj (i)* = **pandërmjetëm**

pa·ndër·mje·tëm *adj (i)* **1** without intermediation, unmediated, direct **2** immediate

pa·ndër·pre·rë
I § *adj (i)* uninterrupted, continuous
II § *adv* without interruption, uninterruptedly, continuously; constantly

pa·ndër·va·rur *adj (i)* not interdependent

pa·ndër·ru·ar *adj (i)* not replaced (by something fresh), unfreshened: (of air) stale, (of water) stagnant, (of dirty clothes) not changed

pa·ndër·ru·e·shëm *adj (i)* **1** non-interchangeable **2** [*Ling*] = **pandryshu·e·shëm**

***pa·ndëshkï** *nf* impunity

pa·ndëshk·u·a·r *adj (i)* unpunished

pa·ndëshk·u·e·shëm *adj (i)* unpunishable

pa·ndie·r *adj (i)* **1** unheard, quiet **2** lacking deep feeling, cold

pa·ndïh·më *adj (i)* helpless

***pa·ndï·shëm** OR **pa·ndje·j·shëm** *adj (i)* = **pandje·shëm**

pa·ndje·një *adj (i)* without·feeling: emotionless, unfeeling; insensitive

***pa·ndje·rë** *adj (i)* inexcusable, unpardonable

pa·ndje·sï *nf* inability to react to one's environment: insensibility

pa·ndje·shëm *adj (i)* **1** imperceptible; insignificant, inconsequential; impalpable **2 = pandje·një**

pa·ndje·shm·ërï *nf* insensitivity; insensitiveness

***pa·ndo·dh·un** *adj (i) (Reg Gheg)* absent

***pa·ndo·flë** *nf* = **panto·fël**

***pa·ndo·më** *nf* hope

pa·ndonjë·të·me·të *adj (i)* without any defect: flawless, immaculate

pa·ndo·tur *adj (i)* unsoiled, unsullied

pa·ndreq·shëm
I § *adj (i)* unrepairable, irreparable; irremediable; incorrigible, irredeemable
II § *n (i)* irredeemable reprobate

pa·ndre·q·ur *adj (i)* unrepaired; unemended

***pa·ndro** *nf* [*Bot*] oleander, rosebay *(Nerium oleander)*

pa·ndro·jt·je *nf* fearlessness; unbashfulness

***pa·ndrysh·ï** *nf* changelessness; monotony

pa·ndry·shk·shëm *adj (i)* rustproof, stainless (steel)

pa·ndry·shk·ur *adj (i)* unrusted

pa·ndrysh·u·a·r *adj (i)* unchanged, unchanging

pa·ndrysh·u·e·shëm *adj (i)* **1** unchangeable, unalterable; changeless, immutable **2** [*Ling*] invariable

pa·ndrysh·u·e·shm·ërï *nf (Book)* immutability

***pa·ndy·rë** *adj* undefiled; unsullied

pa·ne *nf* parsnip *(Pastinaca sativa)*

pane·fte *nf* mold used for casting precious metal jewelry

panegjer·ïk *nm, adj* **1** panegyric **2** *(Iron)* inflated praise

panegjer·ïst *n* **1** composer of panegyrics **2** *(Iron)* insincere flatterer

pane·l *nm* **1** panel, panelling, wainscot *2 [Bot]* = **pane**
  ◦ **panel montimi** wiring panel
  ◦ **panel muri** wall slab
  ◦ **panel ndërkati** roof slab

***pane·rkë** *nf (Reg Tosk)* small basket

pa·nevo·j·shëm *adj (i)* unnecessary

pa·në *3rd pl pdef* < **she·h·**

pa·në *nf* **1** thin covering on a surface: filmy layer on milk, filmy substance on the eyes; eggshell, onion husk *2* poodle

pa·nën·ë *adj (i)* motherless

pa·nën·shkr·u·a·r *adj (i)* without signature: unsigned

pa·nën·shtr·u·a·r *adj (i)* **1** unsubjugated, unconquered; free, independent; not subservient/submissive **2** = **panënshtru·e·shëm**

pa·nën·shtr·u·e·shëm *adj (i)* indomitable

pa·nën·viz·u·a·r *adj (i)* not underlined

***pa·ngadhnj·ye·shëm** *adj (i)* unconquerable, invincible

pa·nga·rë *adj (i)* untouched; uncultivated

pa·nga·shëm *adj (i)* = **papre·kshëm**

pa·nge·h·ur *adj (i)* = **pangeshëm**

pa·nge·shëm *adj (i)* having no free time: busy

***pa·ngi·më** *adj (i) (Reg Gheg)* not having eaten one's full; unsatiated; hungry

***pa·nginj·ësï** *nf* = **pangopësï**

***pa·nginj·e·shëm** *adj (i)* = **pango·pshëm**

pa·ngï·nj·ur *adj (i)* = **pango·pur**

pa·ngï·shëm *adj (i)* = **pango·pshëm**

pa·ngop·ësï *nf* **1** insatiability **2** [*Med*] bulimia

pa·ngop·ësï·sht *adv* insatiably

***pa·ngo·pje** *nf* = **pangopësï**

pa·ngo·pshëm *adj (i)* insatiable; gluttonous

pa·ngo·pur *adj (i)* **1** not having eaten one's full; unsatiated; still hungry **2** *(Fig Pej)* = **pango·pshëm** **3** [*Spec*] unsaturated

***pa·ngo·sur** = **pango·pur**

pa·ngrë·në
I § *adj (i)* not having eaten: unfed, ill-fed; famished
II § *nn (të)* chronic lack of sufficient food: hunger, starvation

pa·ngrën·ie *nf* chronic lack of sufficient food: hunger, starvation

pa·ngrë·n·shëm *adj (i)* inedible

***pa·ngu·l·un** *adj (i) (Reg Gheg)* not set firmly: unsettled, unfixed

pa·ngush·ëllu·e·shëm *adj (i)* **1** inconsolable **2** unassuageable

pa·ngut·shëm *adj (i)* unhurried, leisurely

***pa·ngja·j** = **pangja·**

***pa·ngja·më** *adj (i) (Reg)* **1** weak, frail; ailing **2** not good-looking

pa·ngja·rë
I § *adj (i)* non-occurrent; exceptional, extraordinary, unheard of
II § *nf (e)* something extraordinary

***pa·ngjâse** *nf (e) (Reg Gheg)* = **pangjashm·ërï**

pa·ngja·shëm *adj (i)* **1** dissimilar **2** improper, unfit, unseemly

pa·ngja·shm·ërï *nf (Book)* dissimilarity

pa·ngje·shje *nf* looseness, flabbiness

pa'ngje'shur *adj (i)* uncompressed: loose, flabby, slack

*pa'ngji'tun *adj (i) (Reg Gheg)* not touching: disjoined, separate

pa'ngjyrë *adj (i)* colorless; uncolored

pa'ngjyrësi *nf (Book)* colorlessness

pa'ngjyrët *adj (i)* = pangjyrë

*pani'cë *nf* = palare

panik *nm* panic

panine *nf* small loaf of white bread; roll

pani'sur *adj (i)* 1 unbegun, unstarted; untouched, intact (not bitten into) 2 unadorned; not dressed

pankartë *nf* slogan-bearing placard attached to a stick

*pa'nkë *nf (Reg Tosk)* = palare

pankrea's *nm [Anat]* pancreas

panku'she *nf [Bot]* edible mushroom with a thick brownish stem and a round cap that is dark-gray on top and white underneath

*pano'm *adj* = pa nom *(Old)* lawless; illegal; iniquitous

*pa'nom'ëri *nf(Old)* illegality

*pa'nom'ëri'sht *adv(Old)* illegally

*pa'nom'të *adj (i)(Old)* illegal

panoramë *nf* 1 panorama 2 *[Cine]* pan-shot

panoramik *adj (Book)* panoramic

panoramim *nm ger [Cine]* <panoramo'•n

panoramo'•n

I § *vt [Cine]* to pan (a camera) over []

II § *vi* to pan

pan'sllavizëm *nm* pan-Slavism

pantallo'na *np (fem)* trousers, pants

pante'ist

I § *n* pantheist

II § *adj* pantheistic

pante'izëm *nm [Phil]* pantheism

panteo'n *nm* pantheon

pante'rë *nf [Zool]* panther

panto'fël *nf* open-heeled house slipper

*panto'lla *np fem (Colloq)* = pantallo'na

pantomi'më

I § *nf* pantomime

II § *adj* pantomimic

*panthe'r *nm [Zool]* = pante'rë

*panu'ç *adj (Reg)* bespattered by mud

pa'numërt *adj (i)* countless, innumerable; vast

pa'numëru'ar *adj (i)* = panu'mërt

pa'numërue'shëm *adj (i)* = panu'mërt

pa'nxë'në *adj* 1 uneducated 2 uncomprehended, unlearned 3 intangible; incomprehensible

panxhar *nm* 1 root of the beet, beetroot 2 *[Bot]* beet plant *(Beta vulgaris)* = pazi 3 *(Colloq) [Bot]* = panxharsheqer

  ○ panxhar sheqeri = panxharsheqer

panxhar'sheqe'r *nm [Bot]* sugar beet *(Beta vulgaris L. var saccharifera)*

pa'nxhë *nf* 1 paw 2 short rod; door bolt

*pa'nye'shëm *adj (i)* = panyjshëm

pa'nyjë *adj (i) [Ling]* = panyjshëm

pa'nyjë'tu'ar *adj (i ˘)* unarticulated

pa'nyjshëm *adj (i) [Ling]* having no attributive article

*panzëhe'r *nm* talisman made of a hardened wart taken from the skin of a horse/donkey

*pa'nje = pa'një

pa'njeh'sue'shëm *adj (i)* non-calculable; incalculable

*pa'nje'jtë *adj (i)* unequal

pa'njerëzi

  I § *adj (i)* = panjerëzi'shëm

  II § *nf* 1 incivility, impoliteness, discourtesy *2(Old)* inhumanity

pa'njerëzi'shëm *adj (i)* 1 uncivil, impolite, discourteous 2 *(Old)* inhumane

pa'njerëzi'sht *adv* 1 impolitely, discourteously 2 *(Old)* inhumanely

panjeri *adj (i)* without family: forlorn and alone

pa'një *nf [Bot]* maple *(Acer L.P)*

*pa'njëj'ësi *nf* 1 nonuniformity, unevenness 2 inequality

pa'një'su'ar *adj (i)* not unified

*pa'njisi *nf (Reg Gheg)* = panjëjësi

*pa'njo'fshëm *adj (i) (Reg Gheg)* = panjo'hshëm

*pa'njo'ftun *adj (i) (Reg Gheg)* = panjo'hur

pa'njo'hshëm *adj (i) [Phil]* unknowable

pa'njo'hur *adj (i)* 1 unfamiliar, unknown 2 not well-known, not famous 3 *[Math]* unknown

pa'njo'llë *adj (i)* 1 without spots: unspotted; spotless, unstained 2 *(Fig)* = panjollo'sur

pa'njollësi *nf* spotlessness

pa'njollo'sur *adj (i)* 1 unblemished, unstained; spotless, clean 2 *(Fig)* unbesmirched

panjo're *np [Bot]* maple family *Aceraceae*

pa'njtë *adj (i)* of maple, made of maplewood

pa'oksidue'shëm *adj (i)* 1 = pandry'shkshëm 2 *[Chem]* non-oxidizable *()*

pa'ore'ks *adj (i)* without appetite, not hungry

pa'organizu'ar *adj (i)* 1 lacking organization; disorganized 2 not belonging to a political organization: unorganized, unaffiliated

pa'oxha'k *adj (i)* homeless; having no family

PAP *abbrev (Polish)* <Po'lska Age'ncja Preso'wa Polish Press Agency

*papafing *nm* terrace = tarra'cë

papafingo *nf with masc agreement [Archit]* attic

papaga'll *nm [Ornit]* parrot

pa'pagu'ar *adj (i)* unpaid

*pa'pajcu'ar'shëm = papajtue'shëm

pa'paji'sur *adj (i)* unprovided

*pa'pajtim *nm* = papajtueshmëri

pa'pajtu'ar *adj (i)* unreconciled

pa'pajtue'shëm *adj (i)* irreconcilable, implacable; incompatible, inconsistent

pa'pajtue'shm'ëri *nf* irreconcilability, implacability; incompatibility, inconsistency

*papali'në *nf [Ichth]* sprat *(Sprattus sprattus)*

pa'pande'hur

  I § *adv* unexpectedly

  II § *adj (i)* *unexpected

*pa'pande'hur'azi *adv* = papande'hur

*pa'pand'ye'r *adj (i)* unanticipated, unexpected = papande'hur

*pa'pand'ye'rthi *adv* unexpectedly

*pa'pa'qëm *adj (i)* unclean

*pa**paqtu**e**shëm** *adj (i)* **1** bellicose, war-like **2** restless

pa**para**men**du**ar *adj (i)* unpremeditated

*pa**para**pa**më** *adj (i) (Reg Gheg)* = **paparaparë**

pa**para**pa**rë** *adj (i)* = **paparashikuar**

pa**para**shik**u**ar *adj (i)* unforeseen

pa**para**shik**ue**shëm *adj (i)* **1** unforeseeable **2** [*Law*] indefeasible

pa**pa**re *nf* [*Food*] (breakfast) food made of pieces of wheat bread boiled in water with spices and butter or olive oil

pa**pa**rë *adj (i)* **1** not seen before: unfamiliar, unknown; unprecedented **2** inexperienced, unworldly **3** *(Colloq)* insatiable, gluttonous

*pa**parë**mejt**u**ar *adj (i)* unpremeditated, not on purpose

*pa**parë**shëk**u**ar *adj (i)* = **paparashikuar**

pa**par**im *adj (i)* unprincipled

pa**par**im**shëm** *adj (i)* = **paparim**

pa**parti** *adj (i)* without party membership

pa**parti**shëm *adj (i)* nonpartisan

*pa**paru**në *nf* poppy
 ◦ paparunë uji [*Zool*] anemone

pa**pa**sje *nf* poverty

*pa**pa**sme *nf (e)* = **papasje**

pa**pa**stër
 I § *adj (i)* impure; unclean
 II § *nf (e)* first draft with emendations still on it, rough draft

pa**pastër**ti *nf* impurity; uncleanliness

pa**pastri** *nf* = **papastërti**

pa**pa**sur *adj (i)* impoverished, poor

pa**pas**uri *nf* impoverishment, poverty

pa**pa**shëm *adj (i)* **1** invisible = **padukshëm 2** not good-looking

pap**a**t *nm* papacy

*pa**peça**tun *adj (i) (Reg Gheg)* = **panjollë**

pa**pe**më *adj (i)* non fruit-bearing; fruitless

pa**pem**ësi *nf* fruitlessness

*pa**pe**mët *adj (i)* fruitless

*pa**pe**mshëm *adj (i)* = **papemë**

*pa**pend**im *nm* impenitence

pa**pengu**ar *adj (i)* unhindered

pa**percept**ue**shëm** *adj (i)* **1** imperceptible **2** incomprehensible

pa**peshë** *adj (i)* **1** of little weight, weightless **2** *(Fig)* not weighing one's thoughts and actions judiciously **3** *(Fig)* not given much weight by society: uninfluential

pa**pesh**uar *adj (i)* **1** unweighed **2** *(Fig)* not thought through carefully: ill-considered

pa**pë**
 I § *nf with masc agreement* [*Relig*] pope
 II § *nf (Child)* food

pa**pëlq**y**er** *adj (i)* = **papëlqyeshëm**

pa**pëlq**y**e**shëm *adj (i)* **1** unsatisfactory **2** unpleasant, disagreeable **3** undesirable, inappropriate

pa**për**ball**ue**shëm *adj (i)* impossible to withstand: irresistible

pa**për**cakt**u**ar *adj (i)* unspecified, undetermined; undecided, uncertain; vague, murky

pa**për**cakt**ue**shëm *adj (i)* indeterminable, indeterminate; uncertain, vague

pa**për**cakt**ue**shm**ëri** *nf* indeterminability, indeterminacy; uncertainty, vagueness

*pa**për**ça**më** *adj (i) (Reg Gheg)* = **papërçarë**

pa**për**ça**rë** *adj (i)* undivided

pa**për**dor**shëm** *adj (i)* unusable

pa**për**dor**ur** *adj (i)* unused, brand-new

pa**për**dhok *nm* **1** *(Colloq)* pebble **2** eyeball

pa**për**fill**shëm** *adj (i)* insignificant

pa**për**fill**ur** *adj (i)* **1** disrespected, slighted; disregarded, neglected **2** = **papërfillshëm**

*pa**për**fund**shëm** *adj (i)* inconclusive; not final

pa**për**fund**u**ar *adj (i)* unfinished, uncompleted

pa**për**fytyr**ue**shëm *adj (i)* unimaginable, inconceivable

pa**për**gati**tje** *nf (Book)* unpreparedness

pa**për**gati**t**ur *adj (i)* unprepared, not ready

pa**për**gënjeshtr**u**ar *adj (i)* unrefuted, uncontroverted

*pa**për**gja**jt**ur *adj (i)* incomparable

*pa**për**gja**shëm** *adj (i)* dissimilar

pa**për**gjegj**ësi** *nf* negligence, irresponsibility

pa**për**gjegj**shëm** *adj (i)* **1** [*Law*] not responsible for one's actions **2** negligent, irresponsible; careless and irresponsible

pa**për**ka**tshëm** *adj (i)* irrelevant

pa**për**këmb**ur** *adj (i)* (of a baby) not yet able to walk; not yet able to fend for oneself; not yet back on one's feet (after an illness)

*pa**për**kor**ë** *adj (i)* immoderate, intemperate, greedy

*pa**për**kor**i** *nf* immoderation, intemperance, greed

pa**për**kra**hje** *adj (i)* without anyone to lend a helping hand: unsupported

pa**për**kthy**er** *adj (i)* untranslated

pa**për**kthy**e**shëm *adj (i)* untranslatable

pa**për**kujde**s**shëm *adj (i)* careless; incautious; inattentive

pa**për**ku**l**ët = **papërkulshëm**

pa**për**ku**l**shëm *adj (i)* **1** unbendable, inflexible **2** *(Fig)* indomitable, resolute

pa**për**kul**shm**ëri *nf* **1** *(Book)* inflexibility **2** *(Fig)* indomitability

pa**për**ku**l**ur *adj (i)* **1** unbent: straight, erect **2** *(Fig)* unyielding, resolute

pa**për**lig**j**shëm *adj (i)* unjustifiable

pa**për**lig**j**ur *adj (i)* unjustified

pa**për**lyer *adj (i)* **1** not grimy/greasy: unsoiled **2** immaculate; chaste, virginal

*pa**për**lyer**shëm** *adj (i)* non-tarnishable, immaculate

pa**për**mbajt**shëm** *adj (i)* uncontainable; uncontrollable

pa**për**mbajt**ur** *adj (i)* **1** out of control, hot-tempered, hot-headed; impulsive, impetuous, rash **2** = **papërmbajtshëm**

pa**për**mble**dh**shëm *adj (i)* incomprehensible

pa**për**men**d**shëm *adj (i)* unmentionable, unspeakable

*pa**për**men**d**shun *adj (i) (Reg Gheg)* unmentioned

pa**për**mirës**u**ar *adj (i)* unimproved

pa**për**mirës**ue**shëm *adj (i)* not improvable: hopeless

pa**për**pikt**ë** *adj (i)* **1** imprecise, inexact **2** careless; unpunctual

papërpjesëtueshëm *adj (i)* **1** not in proportion; disproportionate **2** [*Math*] irrational

papërpunuar *adj (i)* unprocessed: raw, rough, crude

papërqendruar *adj (i)* not concentrated on a particular object; unconsolidated, dispersed; unfocused

papërsëritshëm *adj (i)* unrepeatable; unique

papërsosur *adj (i)* imperfect

papërsosuri *nf* imperfection

papërshkruar *adj (i)* = **papërshkrueshëm**

papërshkrueshëm *adj (i)* indescribable

papërshkueshëm *adj (i)* impenetrable, impermeable; impassable

papërshkueshmëri *nf* impenetrability, impermeability; impassability

papërshpirtshëm *adj (i)* not devout

papërshtatshëm *adj (i)* unsuitable; inappropriate

papërshtatshmëri *nf (Book)* unsuitability; inappropriateness

papërshtatur *adj (i)* unsuited

papërtuar *adj (i)* = **papërtueshëm**

papërtueshëm *adj (i)* ready to do any work, quick to do work, unhesitant to work

papërtypshëm *adj (i)* unchewable

papërthyer = **papërthyeshëm**

papërthyeshëm *adj (i)* inflexible

papërullur *adj (i)* unvanquished, untamed

papërvetësuar *adj (i)* **1** unassimilated, unabsorbed **2** [*Biol*] undigested

papërvetësueshëm *adj (i)* **1** unassimilable, unabsorbable **2** [*Biol*] undigestible

papërvojë *adj (i)* inexperienced

papërzier *adj (i)* **1** not consisting of a mixture/blend; not mixed **2** unadulterated **3** unscrambled **4** *(Fig)* uninvolved in other's affairs

papësuar *adj (i)* unaffected, untouched; inexperienced

papijshëm *adj (i)* undrinkable; unpotable

papilionace *np fem* [*Bot*] *Papilionaceae*

papirus *nm* papyrus

papishëm *adj (i)* undrinkable

papizëm *nm (Pej)* [*Relig*] papism

papjekur
  I § adj (i) **1** uncooked, raw; (of meat) rare **2** unripe **3** *(Fig)* immature (in body or mind); injudicious, imprudent
  II § nf (e) injudicious word

papjekuri *nf* immaturity

papjellë *adj (e)* (of a female) barren, sterile

papjellësi (of a female) barrenness, sterility

papjellori *nf* = **papjellësi**

papjesë *adj (i)* not having a share; non-participant

papjesëtueshëm *adj (i)* **1** indivisible; nondivisible; impartible **2** [*Math*] irrational

papjesëtueshmëri *nf (Book)* indivisibility; nondivisibility

papjesi *nm (i) (Colloq euph)* the Devil

paplakshëm *adj (i)* never aging, unaging

paplakur *adj (i)* (of a person) not yet old; not senile

paplangë *adj (i)* without worldly goods: destitute

paplanifikuar *adj (i)* not according to plan: unplanned

paplasshëm *adj (i)* non-exploding

paplasur *adj (i)* **1** without any cracks: uncracked *2** unexploded

paplotë *adj (i)* **1** incomplete; imperfect **2** [*Math*] having a decimal fraction

paplotësi *nf (Book)* incompleteness

paplotësuar *adj (i)* not completed: not filled out, uncompleted, incomplete; unsatisfied, unfulfilled

paplotësueshëm *adj (i)* impossible to satisfy/fulfill

papluguar *adj (i)* unplowed

papllomë *nf* feather quilt, eiderdown

papni *nf (Reg Gheg)* **1** [*Relig*] papacy **2** popery

papnor *adj (i)* [*Relig*] papal

papopulluar *adj (i)* unpopulated

papor = *vapor*

paprâ *adv (Reg Gheg)* incessantly

paprâjshëm *adj (i) (Reg Gheg)* incessant

paprâjtë *adj (i) (Reg Gheg)* = **paprâshëm**

papranishëm
  I § adj (i) not present: absent
  II § n (i) absent person

papranuar *adj (i)* unaccepted, unadopted

papranueshëm *adj (i)* unacceptable, inadmissible

paprapsueshëm *adj (i)* irreversible

paprapshëm *adj (i)* = **paprapsueshëm**

paprâshëm *adj (i) (Reg Gheg)* = **paprâjshëm**

papregatitur *adj (i)* unprepared

paprehje = **pa prehje** without pause, incessantly

paprekëm *adj (i)* untouched, intact

paprekshëm *adj (i)* **1** not to be touched: untouchable **2** inviolable, sacrosanct

paprekshmëri *nf* **1** untouchability **2** [*Law*] inviolability **3** [*Law*] immunity

paprekur *adj (i)* untouched, intact (not yet bitten into); untainted, chaste, virginal

papremë *adj (i)* (*Reg Gheg*) = **paprerë**

papreras *adv* without interruption, continually, incessantly

paprerë
  I § adj (i) **1** uncut **2** uninterrupted, incessant, continual
  II § adv = **papreras**

paprehje *nf* unrest, disturbance

paprimë *adj (i) (Reg Gk)* = **papritur**

paprind *adj (i)* (left) without parents

paprishur *adj (i)* undamaged; unspoiled; unscathed; unpolluted

papritë *adv* unexpectedly, suddenly = **papritur**

papritje *nf* surprise

papritmas OR **papritmazi** *adv* = **papritur**

papritme *nf (e)* surprise

papritueshëm *adj (i)* = **papërtueshëm**

papritur
  I § adj (i) unexpected, sudden
  II § adv unexpectedly, suddenly
  III § nf (e) something unexpected; unexpected event

paprivilegjuar *adj (i)* unprivileged

paprodhimshëm *adj (i)* unproductive

paprogramuar *adj (i)* unprogrammed

paprokop *nm* destitute person

paprokopsur *adj (i)* unfortunate; destitute

paprovuar *adj (i)* **1** never yet experienced: unexperienced **2** unproven

paprovu|e|shëm *adj (i)* unprovable, undemonstrable

****paptu|ng**
 I § *nm* **1** peeled chestnut **2** *(Fig)* darling
 II § *adj* plump, chubby

papu|çe *nf* light woolen slipper worn in the house

papu|në
 I § *adj (i)*, *n (i)* **1** not busy working; unemployed **2** of no use, doing no good: useless
 II § *n (i)* person not busy working; unemployed person

papun|ë|si *nf* **1** not keeping busy: sloth, idleness **2** unemployment

papun|u|ar *adj (i)* **1** uncultivated, unplowed: standing idle, fallow **2** = **papërpunuar**

****pa|pu|q|un** *adj (i) (Reg Gheg)* detached, disjoined

papusht|u|e|shëm *adj (i)* impregnable

papushu|ar
 I § *adj (i)* ceaseless, unceasing
 II § *adv* ceaselessly

****pa|puth|i|s|ur** *adj (i)* fitting badly together; unstuck, unjoined

papyll|ë|zu|ar *adj (i)* unforested

paq *adv (Colloq)* **1** clean, pure **2** in A-one condition; just right: swell **3** up to the limit, to the full **4** *(Joke)* as deserved, (as served someone) right
 ○ **ësh·të**^pl **paq me njeri tjetrin // bashkë** *(Colloq)* to be all square in accounts with one another: be all even, be even Steven

****paq** *OR* **paq|ë** = **paqe**

****pa|qa|m|un** *adj (i) (Reg Gheg)* unwept, unmourned

pa|qa|r|ë *adj (i)* unmourned

pa|qar|t|ë *adj (i)* unclear

pa|qart|ë|si *nf* unclarity

****pa|qa|s|shëm** *adj (i)* inaccessible

paqe *nf* peace

paqe|bë|r|ës
 I § *adj* peacemaking
 II § *n* peacemaker

paqe|da|sh|ës *adj* **1** peace-loving **2** pacifist; peaceful

paqe|da|sh|je *nf* pacifism

****pa|qef|ë|si** *nf* **1** indisposition **2** dislike

paqe|jf *adj (i)* *(Colloq)* not feeling well, unwell, slightly ill

paqe|në
 I § *adj (i)* unreal, non-existent
 II § *nf (e)* imaginary thing
 III § *nm (i) (Colloq Euph)* the Devil

paqe|ne|si|shëm *adj (i)*, *nf(e) (Book)* non-essential

****paqe|n|shëm** *adj (i) (Book)* unreal, non-existent

****paqe|pri|sh|ës** *n* person who disturbs/disrupts the peace: disrupter, rioter

paqe|prur|ës *adj* contributing to peace: peace-bringing

paqe|sh|ur *adj (i)* serious

paqe|të *adj (i)* **1** never quiet, noisy **2** troubled, disquieted **3** never quiet: always moving around

****paqe|të** *nf* = **paketë**

paqet|ë|si *nf* disquiet

paqet|ë|su|e|shëm *adj (i)* **1** unrelievable, unassuageable **2** restless, uneasy

paqe|th|ur *adj (i)* needing a haircut: (of hair) uncut, untonsured; (of sheep) unsheared

pa|qëll|i|m *adj (i)* **1** aimless; pointless; fruitless **2** unintended

****pa|qëll|i|m|ët** *adj (i)* = **paqëllim**

pa|qëll|i|m|shëm *adj (i)* unintentional

****pa|q|ëm** *adj (i)* clean, pure

****pa|qëndr|e|s|ë** *nf* = **paqëndrueshm|ëri**

pa|qëndr|u|ar *adj (i)* = **paqëndru|eshëm**

pa|qëndr|u|e|shëm *adj (i)* unstable; unsteady; inconstant; constantly moving, unsettled

pa|qëndr|ue|shm|ëri *nf* instability; unsteadiness; inconstancy

****pa|që|në** = **paqe|në**

****pa|qërt|u|ar|shëm** *OR* **pa|qërt|u|e|shëm** *adj (i)* = **paqortu|e|shëm**

pa|qër|u|ar *adj (i)* not rid of an unwanted outer layer: (of fruit) unpeeled, (of chickens) unplucked, (of fish) unscaled, unshelled; (of language/culture) unpurged, unpurified

****paq|ë|si** *nf* **1** peacefulness **2** cleanliness

paq|ë|s|im *nm ger* **1** *(Colloq)* < **paq**ës|o·n, **paq**ës|o·het **2** conciliation; reconciliation **3** alleviation, relief

paq|ë|s|i|sht *adv* peacefully

paqës|o·**het** *vpr* **1** to become reconciled **2** to subside, abate, slacken **3** *(Colloq)* to get all clean and in good order

paqës|o·**n** *vt* **1** to reconcile **2** to pacify; conciliate **3** to alleviate, relieve **4** to set [ ] right/straight

paqës|o**r** *adj* **1** peace-loving; peaceable **2** pacific; peaceful **3** during peacetime **4** concerning peace

****paq|i|m** *nm* purification

****paqlo|re** *nf* [*Bot*] grapevine (*Vitis vinifera*)

****paq|llë|k** *nm* purity, cleanliness

pa|q|m|ë *adj (i)* *(Colloq)* = **pa|st|ër**

paqo·het *vpr* **1** to subside, abate, slacken **2** *(Colloq)* to get all clean and in good order

paqo·n
 I § *vt* **1** to reconcile **2** to alleviate, relieve **3** *(Colloq)* to clean [ ] and put in good order: clean [ ] up, cleanse
 II § *vi* to subside, abate, slacken

pa|qort|u|e|shëm *adj (i)* **1** irreprehensible, beyond reproach **2** irreparable

****paq|t** = **paq**ës

****paq|t|i|m|bë|r|ës** *adj*, *n* = **paqe|bë|r|ës**

****paq|to|r** *OR* **paq|tu|e|s** = **paqës|or**

pa|qum|ësht *adj (e)* [*Dairy*] not lactating, giving no milk

pa|q|y|ll *nm (Colloq Insult)* nitwit, ninny, imbecile

pa|qytet|ër|u|ar *adj (i)* **1** uncivilized **2** ill-bred

****par** *nm* **1** pair; couple **2** [*Math*] even number
 ○ **par a cub/tek** even or odd (number)
 ○ **par e cub** *(Old)* odd and even

pa|r·et *vpr (Colloq)* to progress, proceed, advance

para *nf* **1** money **2** *(Old)* coin worth one-twentieth of a grosh or five ten-thousandths of a Turkish lira during the Ottoman empire: para
 ○ **para bakër** "copper money" something of little or no value: a tuppence, a farthing
 ○ **paraja e bardhë për ditë të zezë** "white money for a black day" money put aside for a rainy day
 ○ **s'lidh· para** not bring much money when sold, not sell for much money; not be very profitable
 ○ **para saklame** hard currency
 ○ **para të holla** small change (money)
 ○ **para të hup|ëta** money thought to be lost; unexpected money

○ **para të ime̱ta** small bills, small change, change
○ **para të thata** hard cash
○ **para të vëna** cash savings
○ **para të vogla** "small money" small change, small bills

pa'ra
I § *adv* **1** = **përpa'ra 2** forward: in front
II § *prep (abl/dat)* **1** before; ahead of **2** in front of, facing; in comparison with
○ **para** {*quantity of time in the ablative indefinite case*} {} ago **para gjashtë vjetësh** six years ago **para një jave** one week ago
○ **para kohe** before the expected time: too early, premature(ly)

pa'ra *nf(e)* **1** (feminine) the first **2** the beginning; first course (of a meal)
○ **e para e punës** first of all; the main thing

para *pcl (appears only after a negative pcl)* hardly, barely, not very much **nuk para dalim në kinema** we hardly ever go out to the movies **s'para ishte i ri** he wasn't all that young **mos para i flisni** better not talk to him
○ **mos para** {*imperative verb*}! don't {} so much! better not {}
○ **nuk para** {*verb*} not likely to {}; hardly {}
○ **nuk/s' para** {*verb*} hardly/barely {}; not {} very much

para *formative prefix* pre-, fore-, para-
para a'rdh|**ës**
I § *nm* **1** forerunner; predecessor **2** forefather, ancestor
II § *adj* **1** preceding, previous **2** [*Agr*] planted or harvested earlier

para bi'më *nf* [*Agr*] crop planted or harvested earlier
parabo'lë *nf* **1** [*Math*] parabola **2** [*Lit*] parable
para burgi'm *nm* [*Law*] time between the arrest and the sentencing of a suspect: detention
para burgo's· *vt* [*Law*] to jail [] before trial
para cakti'm *nm ger* < **paracakto'**·*n*
para cakto'·*n vt* to specify [] in advance: pre-set, preestablish; predetermine, predestine
para caktu'ar *adj (i)* predetermined; inevitable
para cu'kë *nm (Colloq)* shortened form of a person's name: name for short; nickname
para çliri'm *nm* pre-liberation
para'dë *nf* **1** parade **2** (*Fig*) succinct report of a sequence of matters or events without evaluative comment: bare report
paradi'gmë *nf* [*Ling*] paradigm
para di'te *adv* in the forenoon
para di'te *nf* period of the day between breakfast and lunch: forenoon
*****para do'**·*n vi* to parade
parado'ks *nm (Book)* paradox
paradoks a'l *adj (Book)* paradoxical
para dre'ke *adv* in the forenoon
para dre'ke *nf* period of the day before lunch
para dhëmba'llë *nf* [*Anat*] premolar
para dhën|**ës** *n* payer of a down/advance payment
para dhënie *nf* down payment; advance payment, prepayment
*****paradhi's** *nm (Reg Tosk)* paradise
pa|radhi'tur *adj (i)* **1** not in order, unordered **2** [*Publ*] (of type) not yet set up
para dho'më *nf* anteroom, antechamber; vestibule
para elektora'l *adj* pre-electoral

para fabrik a't *nm* [*Constr*] prefabricated unit
para fabrik i'm *nm ger* **1** [*Constr*] < **parafabriko'**·*n* **2** prefabrication
para fabriko'·*n vt* [*Constr*] to prefabricate
para fabriku'ar *adj (i)* [*Constr*] prefabricated
para fa'ngo *nf* [*Tech*] mudguard, fender
parafi'në *nf* **1** paraffin **2** [*Chem*] hydrocarbon
parafin i'm *nm ger* [*Tech*] < **parafino'**·*n*
parafino'·*n vt* [*Tech*] to coat with paraffin
para fja'l|**ë** *nf* [*Ling*] preposition
para fjalo'r *adj* [*Ling*] prepositional
para fla's *stem for 1st sg pres, pl pres, 2nd & 3rd sg subj, pind* < **paraflet**·
para flet· **1** to speak first; make an introductory speech **2** to speak out of turn *****3** to foretell
para fli's *stem for 2nd pl pres, 3rd sg pind* < **paraflet**·
para fli't *stem for 2nd pl pres, pind, vp* < **paraflet**·
para fo'l *stem for imper, pdef, opt, adm, part* < **paraflet**·
para fol|**ës**
I § *adj* **1** speaking previously *****2** prophetic
II § *n* previous speaker
*****para fol je** *nf* introductory speech
para fra'zë *nf (Book)* [*Lit*] paraphrase
para frazi'm *nm ger (Book)* [*Lit*] < **parafrazo'**·*n*
para frazo'·*n vt (Book)* [*Lit*] to paraphrase
*****pa'ra fshë** *adj (i)* = **parra'fshët**
para fu'nd it *adj (i)* next to last; prefinal
para fundo'r *adj* [*Ling*] penultimate; prefinal
*****para fyty'rë** *nf* model, example, exemplar
para fytyri'm *nm* = **përfytyri'm**
para fytyro'·*het vpr* = **përfytyro'**·*het*
para fytyro'·*n vt* = **përfytyro'**·*n*
para fytyru'ar *adj (i)* = **përfytyru'ar**
para gati'tje *nf* advance preparation
para gati'tor *adj* preparing in advance, preparatory
para gra'f *nm* paragraph
Paragua'i *nm* Paraguay
para gjuho'r *adj* [*Ling*] (speech sound) made with the tip of the tongue: apical
para gjuho're *nf* [*Ling*] apical speech sound
para gjyki'm *nm* prejudice
para gjyko'·*n vt (Book)* to prejudge
para gjyq|**ës o'r** *adj* [*Law*] pretrial
*****para rahati'** *nf* disquiet, uneasiness
para histori' *nf* prehistory
para histori'k *adj* prehistoric
para imperiali'st *adj* antedating imperialism: pre-imperialistic
*****para i's** OR **para js** *nm* = **para jsë**
para js|**ë** *nf* paradise
para'k *adj* = **primiti'v**
para kali'm *nm ger* **1** < **parakalo'**·*n* **2** procession, parade
para kalo'·*n*
I § *vi* to pass in procession: parade
II § *vt* to overtake, pass, pass by []
para kalu'es
I § *adj* **1** passing by in parade; parading *****2** passing by
II § *n* *****passerby

parakapitalíst *adj* antedating capitalism: precapitalistic

*__paraklís__ *I §* *nm* OR **paraklíshë** *II §* *nf* private chapel: oratory

parakohës *adj* prior, anterior

parakohshëm *adj (i)* premature, too early

*__parakolp__ *nm* bumper

parakombëtar *adj* antedating the formation of the nation

parakrah *nm* [*Anat*] lower arm, forearm

parakthim *nm* [*Med*] anteversion

parakthinë *nf* **1** = **paradhomë** **2** [*Med*] vestibule

*__parakujdesun__ *adj (i) (Reg Gheg)* taking precautions: cautious, precautious

parakuptó ·*het* *vpr (Book)* to be evident, be understood

parakuptó ·*n* *vt (Book)* to consider [] as self-evident, assume

parakúsht *nm (Book)* necessary condition: precondition, prerequisite

paralajmërím *nm ger* **1** <**paralajmëró** ·*n* **2** warning; warning notice

paralajmëró ·*n* *vt* **1** to notify [] in advance **2** to forewarn; warn **3** to foreshadow, portend

paralajmërúes
I § *adj* forewarning, heralding, presaging
II § *n* harbinger, herald

*__paralajmëtar__ OR **paralajmúes** = **paralajmërúes**

paralel
I § *adj, nm* parallel
II § *adv* in parallel

paralele
I § *nf* **1** [*Geom*] parallel line **2** class at the same level as another
II § *np* parallel bars (in gymnastics)

paralelepiped *nm* [*Geom*] parallelepiped

paralelísht *adv* in a parallel way; in parallel

paralelízëm *nm* parallelism

paralelogram *nm* [*Geom*] parallelogram

paraletrar *adj* **1** [*Ling*] preliterate **2** before standardization of the language

paralíndës
I § *n* **1** *(Book)* person of an older generation, senior **2** first born, primogenitor
II § *adj* first-born, primogenital, eldest

paralíndje *nf* **1** period of pregnancy a few months before giving birth; prenatal period **2** preparation room in a maternity hospital **3** primogeniture

paralíndur *adj (i)* of an earlier generation: senior

paralitík *adj* **1** paralytic; paralyzed **2** *(Fig)* stagnant

paralizë *nf* [*Med*] paralysis

paralizí = **paralizë**

paralizím *nm ger* **1** <**paralizó** ·*n*, **paralizó** ·*het* **2** paralysis

paralizó ·*het* *vpr* to become paralyzed, suffer paralysis

paralizó ·*n* *vt* to paralyze

paralizúar *adj (i)* paralyzed

paralizúes *adj* causing paralysis, paralyzing

*__paralojë__ *nf* prelude

paralúftë *nf* prewar period

paralúftës *adj (i)* prewar

parallogarít· *vi* to precalculate; make a preliminary accounting

parallogarítur *adj (i)* precalculated

paramanë *nf* safety pin

paramarksíst *adj* antedating Marxism: pre-Marxist

parambró ·*het* *vpr* to take precautionary measures

parambró ·*n* *vt* to protect [] by preventive measures

parambrójtës *adj* preventive, protective, precautionary

parambrójtje *nf ger* <**parambró** ·*n*, **parambró** ·*het*

*__paramejtím__ *(Reg)* = **paramendím**

*__paramejto__ ·*n* *(Reg)* = **paramendo** ·*n*

paramendím *nm* **1** forethought **2** [*Law*] premeditation

paramendó ·*n* *vt* **1** to consider [] in advance: premeditate **2** = **përfytyró** ·*n*

paramendúar *adj (i)* **1** given forethought, preconsidered **2** [*Law*] premeditated

*__paramesditë__ *nf* forenoon

parametër *nm* parameter

paramjekím *nm* [*Med*] premedication

paramonopolíst *adj* antedating monopoly capitalism: pre-monopolistic

paramúr *nm* outer wall, bulwark

parandalím *nm ger* **1** <**parandaló** ·*n* **2** prevention [*Med*] **3** prophylaxis

parandaló ·*n* *vt* to prevent

parandalúes *adj* preventive

parandej *adv* before that, earlier

parandérë *adj (i)* [*Tech*] prestressed

parandérje *nf* [*Tech*] prestressing (of steel rods use in reinforced concrete)

parandíe·*n* *vt* to sense [] beforehand, foresee

parandjenjë *nf* presentiment, premonition

parango *nf* [*Tech*] pulley block hoist

*__parangjyllëz__ *nf* *(Old)* antimacassar

paraník *nm* **1** black woolen apron worn as part of a woman's costume **2** firstborn, eldest

paraník *ë np* <**paraník** forefathers, ancestors

parantezë *nf* parenthesis

paranjoftím *nm* preliminary report/notice

paraodë *nf* front parlor

parapa *stem for 3rd sg pdef, pl pdef, opt, adm, part* <**parasheh**·

parapagesë *nf* prepayment

parapagím *nm ger* **1** <**parapagúa**·*n* **2** = **parapagesë**

parapagúa·*n* *vt* to prepay

parapagúar *adj (i)* prepaid

*__parapame__ *np* = **parapara**

*__parapamës__ *adj* foresighted

parapamje *nf* [*Fin*] preliminary estimate, cost estimate

parapandeh· *vt* to have a premonition

parapandehje *nf* **1** presupposition **2** premonition

parapara *np* [*Fin*] expenditures provided for in a budget

paraparë
I § *part* <**parasheh**·
II § *adj (i)* foreseen, anticipated, expected; estimated, presumed

*__paraparës__
I § *adj* anticipating
II § *n* anticipator

para|pa'shë *1st pdef* <**parashe**h·

para|pe' *2nd sg pdef* <**parashe**h·

parape't *nm* parapet

para|pëlqe·n *vt* to like [] better: prefer

para|pëlqi'm *nm* **1** preference **2** preliminary approval

para|përcakti'm *nm ger* <**parapërcakto'·n**

para|përcakto'·n *vt* to specify [] in advance: preset, preestablish; predetermine; foreshadow

para|përgati's *stem for 1st sg pres, pl pres, 2nd & 3rd sg subj, pind* <**parapërgati**t·

para|përgati't· *vt* to make [] ready beforehand, prepare [] ahead of time, prearrange

para|përgati't·et *vpr* to get ready beforehand; make early preparations, make prearrangements

para|përgati'tje *nf ger* **1** <**parapërgati**t·, **parapërgati**t·et **2** preliminary preparations

para|përgati'to'r *adj* preparatory, preliminary

para|përgati'tur *adj (i)* prearranged

para|përku'lje *nf* [Med] anteflexion

*****para|përme'ndun** *adj (i) (Reg Gheg)* aforementioned

*****para|pika's** *stem for 1st sg pres, pl pres, 2nd & 3rd sg subj, pind* <**parapika**t·

*****para|pika't·** *vt* = **parandi'e·n**

para|pjek'ës *adj* early-ripening

para|pleq'ëri *nf* old age prior to senility: pre-senile age

para|plënd'ës *nm* [Anat] third section of a ruminant's stomach: omasum

para|pra'k *adj* **1** preliminary **2** preventive

para|praki'sht *adv (Book)* in advance

*****para|pregati't·** *vt* to get [] ready in advance, prepare [] beforehand

para|pre's *stem for 1st sg pres, 1st & 3rd pl pres, 2nd & 3rd sg subj* <**parapre**t·

para|pret· *vt* **1** to forestall **2** [Mil] to aim a weapon in front of [a moving target]: lead [a target]

para|pri·n *vi, vt* **1** to lead **2** to precede

para|prij'ës *adj* preceding

*****para|pri's** *nm* leader, pioneer

para|pri's *stem for pind, 2nd pl pres, imper* <**parapre**t·

para|pri't *stem for part, pdef, pind, 2nd pl pres, imper, vp* <**parapre**t·

para|pri'të *nf* barrier

para|pri't'ës *adj* [Mil] interdictive, interdictory

para|pri'tje *nf ger* [Mil] <**parapre**t·

para|provi'm *nm* qualifying examination graded on a pass/no pass basis and given to advance a student to a higher level of training

para|prur'ës *adj, nm* [Tech] serving to return a machine part to its operating position: recuperative (device)

para|qe's *stem for 1st sg pres, 1st & 3rd pl pres, 2nd & 3rd sg subj* <**paraqe**t·

para|qet· *vt* = **paraqi't·**

para|qi's *stem for pind, 2nd pl pres, imper* <**paraqi**t·

para|qi't· *vt* **1** to present, exhibit; present [] for examination; exhibit [] as evidence **2** to introduce [a person] **3** *(Book)* to express [a feeling or opinion]

∘ [] **paraqit· me ngjyra të zeza** "present [] in dark colors" to make [] seem worse than [] is, depict [] as being worse that [] is: paint [] in dark colors, present [] in the worst light

∘ **paraqit· për** []**//si** {} to depict/represent as [ ]/{}, make sound/seem like [ ]/{}

∘ **e paraqit· të bardhën të zezë** "make white black" to make a misrepresentation, distort the truth

∘ **e paraqit· veten për** []**//si** {} to pretend to be [ ]/{}

para|qi't·et *vpr* **1** to appear **2** to introduce oneself **3** to report in; report for duty **4** to present oneself, make a showing; represent oneself, pass oneself off, misrepresent oneself

para|qi't'ës
I § *adj* introductory
II § *n* presenter; introducer

para|qi'tje *nf ger* **1** <**paraqi**t·, **paraqi**t·et **2** outward appearance, look; attractive appearance **3** presentation

para|qi'tsh'ëm *adj (i)* **1** suitable for presentation **2** good-looking, attractive

para|re'nd· *vi* to be the forerunner

para|re'nd'ës
I § *adj* preceding; antecedent
II § *n* forerunner, precursor; predecessor

para|revoluci'o'n *nm* pre-revolutionary era

para|ro'jë *nf, adj* vanguard

para|si'll *stem for 2nd pl pres, pind, imper, vp* <**parasje**ll·

*****parasiti'** *nf (Book)* parasitism

*****parasi't** *(Colloq)* = **parazi't**

para|sje'll· *vt* **1** to present, deliver **2** to allege

para|sje'll'ë *part* <**parasje**ll·

para|sje'llje *nf ger* **1** <**parasje**ll· **2** presentation, delivery

para|ske'në *nf* forestage (of a theater): apron

*****para|so'·n** *vt* = **barazo'·n**

para|sociali'st *adj* antedating socialism: presocialist; not fully socialistic

para|so'll *stem for pdef* <**parasje**ll·

*****paraspo'r** *nm* farmer with insufficient fertile land

*****para|ste·n** *vt* to be present at []: attend

para|stërvi'tje *nf* preparatory exercise

para|stoma'k *nm* [Anat] = **paraplë'ndës**

para|studi'm *nm ger* <**parastudio'·n**

para|studio'·n *vt* to make a preliminary study of []

para|sy'sh *adv* at the focus of one's attention: in mind

*****para|she'f·** *vt* = **parashe**h·

para|she'h· *vt* <**parashiko'·n**

para|she's *stem for 1st sg pres, 1st & 3rd pl pres, 2nd & 3rd sg subj* <**parashe**t·

para|she't· *vt* to sell in advance

*****para|shëk** = **parashik**

*****para|shi'f** = **parashi'h**

para|shi'h *stem for 2nd pl pres, pind, imper, vp* <**parashe**h·

para|shiki'm *nm ger* **1** <**parashiko'·n** **2** forecast, prediction, prognosis; anticipation, expectation

para|shiko'·n *vt* to foresee, envision; forecast, predict; anticipate, expect

para|shikua'r *adj (i)* foreseen, predicted, anticipated, expected

para|shiku'e's
I § *adj* **1** prophetic; foresighted **2** provided for, anticipated
II § *n* predictor; forecaster

para·shiku·eshëm adj (i) **1** predictable **2** = parashiku·ar

para·shis stem for pind, 2nd pl pres, imper < parashet·

para·shit stem for part, pdef, pind, 2nd pl pres, imper, vp < parashet·

*para·shke·në nf (Reg GK) [Theat] = paraske·në

para·shkollor
I § adj preschool
II § n child (3-6 years old) in nursery school: preschool child

para·shkrim nm ger **1** [Law] < parashkrua·n, parashkru·het **2** statute of limitations **3** prescription

*para·shkronjë nf initial (letter)

para·shkru·het vpr [Law] to be subject to a time limitation

para·shkrua·n vt **1** [Law] to subject [] to a time limitation *2 to prescribe

para·shkru·eshëm adj (i) [Law] subject to a time limitation

*para·shof = parashoh

para·shoh stem for 1st sg pres, 1st & 3rd pl pres, 2nd & 3rd sg subj = parashe·h·

para·shtesë nf [Ling] prefix

para·shtes·im nm [Ling] prefixation

para·shtesor adj [Ling] prefixal; formed with a prefix

para·shtresë nf **1** [Offic] short presentation; memorandum **2** summary report

para·shtrim nm ger **1** < parashtro·n **2** = parashtresë

para·shtro·n vt **1** [Offic] to put forward []: propose, suggest, submit **2** to lay out [] in summary fashion

*para·shty·n vt to push/thrust [] forward: propel

*para·shtynjë nf = parashtytje

*para·shtytës
I § adj propelling, propulsive
II § nm propellant

para·shtytje nf propulsion

para·shtytsë nf buffer

parashutë nf parachute

parashutist
I § n **1** parachutist **2** [Mil] paratrooper
II § adj [Mil] consisting of paratroops

parashutizëm nm parachute jumping (as a skill); sky-diving (as a sport)

para·tifo nf [Med Veter] paratyphoid

*parator n = përçor

para·trajto·n vt to predispose of [], prearrange

para·tren nm [Agr] forecarriage

para·trinë nf [Anat] carpus; tarsus (P)
  ◦ **paratrinë e dorës** [Anat] carpus
  ◦ **paratrinë e këmbës** [Anat] tarsus

para·tha stem for pdef < paratho·të

para·tha·shë 1st sg pdef < paratho·të

para·the 2nd sg pdef < paratho·të

para·theksor adj [Ling] before the stressed syllable: pretonic

para·them 1st sg pres < paratho·të

para·themi 1st pl pres < paratho·të

para·thetë 3rd sg subj = paratho·të

para·thën stem for part, opt, adm < paratho·të

para·thënë
I § adj (i) **1** mentioned before, already mentioned, aforesaid **2** foreordained, predestined
II § part < paratho·të

para·thënës nm **1** (Old) seer, prophet **2** previous speaker

para·thënie nf **1** foreword, preface **2** (Old) prophecy

paratho·të vt **1** to predict **2** (Old) to prophesy

*para·thom 1st sg pres = parathem

*para·thomi 1st pl pres = parathemi

para·thonë 3rd pl pres < paratho·të

para·thoni 2nd pl pres < paratho·të

para·thosh stem for pind < paratho·të

para·thu stem for vp < paratho·të

para·thua
I § 2nd sg pres < paratho·të
II § 2nd sg pres & imper = parathuaj

para·thuaj 2nd sg imper < paratho·të

para·thuash 2nd sg subj < paratho·të

*para·udhës nm precursor

para·ushtarak
I § adj **1** pertaining to military training prior to induction into the army **2** paramilitary
II § n **1** person in military training prior to induction into the army **2** paramilitary soldier

para·vajtës
I § adj (Book) progressing; increasing
II § n *predecessor

*para·vajtje nf progress, advancement; welfare, well-being

*para·vë· = paravë·

*para·ven stem for opt, adm, part < paravë·

para·vendos· vt to decide [] beforehand, predetermine

para·vendosje nf ger **1** < paravendos· [Ling] **2** preposing

para·vendosur adj (i) **1** predetermined **2** [Ling] preposed

*para·ver stem for imper < paravë·

para·verë nf (Old) = pranverë

para·vesh nm (Colloq) slap (in the face)

*para·vë· vt [Offic] to put [] forward: propose

*para·vështro·n vt = parashiko·n

*para·vi stem for 2nd pl pres, pind, imper, vp < paravë·

para·vithe nf **1** hindquarters (of a horse) **2** blanket covering the hindquarters of a horse

*para·vjet = parvjet

*para·vu stem for pl pdef < paravë·

*para·vume nf [Ling] sentence

*para·vumë part (Reg Gheg) < paravë·

*para·vur stem for imper < paravë·

parazit
I § nm parasite
II § adj parasitic

parazitar adj parasitic

parazitizëm nm parasitism

parazitologji nf parasitology

parcelë nf [Agr] strip of farm land, parcel of land, plot of ground

parcelo·n vt [Agr] to divide a field into plots (that are to be planted with various crops)

*par|ci|vje|ti *adv* the year before last, two years ago

pardesy *nf* lightweight overcoat: topcoat

par|dje *adv* day before yesterday

par|dje|shëm *adj (i)* of the day before yesterday

*pardh *nm* [*Zool*] leopard

pa|re *nf* 1 (*Colloq*) money = **para** 2 scale (of a fish)
  ∘ **s'bë-**n **asnjë pare** not be worth a nickel
  ∘ **pare të namista** tons of money

pa|realiz|u|a|r *adj (i)* unrealized

pa|realiz|u|e|shëm *adj (i)* unrealizable

pa|reg|jur *adj (i)* 1 untanned, uncured 2 (*Fig*) (of a person) not toughened enough (by life experience)

pa|rehat|í *nf* (*Colloq*) uncomfortableness; uneasiness; restlessness

pa|reha't|shëm *adj (i)* (*Colloq*) not providing comfort: uncomfortable, unrelaxing

pare|ma'dhe *nf* [*Ichth*] = **luspëma'dhe**

*parema'ne *nf* brooch; pin

*pa|rênd *adj* = **pa rend** (*Reg Gheg*) disorderly, in disorder

*parente'zë *nf* parenthesis

pa|respektu|e|shëm *adj (i)* disrespectful

pa|resh *adv* shortly before, a little earlier

pa|re|sht|ur
  I § *adj (i)* incessant, ceaseless, uninterrupted
  II § *adv* incessantly, constantly

pare't *nm* partition (wall)

pare'tkë *nf* 1 fence lath: paling *2 (Reg Tosk)* = **pare't**

pa're
  I § *adj (i)* 1 first 2 most important, highest, principal; best; earliest; oldest
  II § *n (i)* 1 highest ranking person: chief, number one 2 (*Old*) = **parësí**
  III § *np (të)* ancestors, forefathers
  IV § *nn (të)* 1 [*Ethnog*] formal first visit of a bride back to her natal family home 2 pair, couple
  V § *nf (e)* first grade (in elementary school); first grade class/classroom
  VI § *adv* (*Colloq*) a little earlier, a little while ago
  VII § *adj (Reg)* even (as opposed to odd) = **çift**
  ∘ **më pa'rë e më da'lë** first and foremost
  ∘ **më pa'rë** 1 earlier 2 in the first place: first
  ∘ **e para nga të parat** the very best of all
  ∘ **nuk e njeh-**³ˢᵍ **i pari të dytin** "the first *does* not know the second" there *is* utter confusion

pa|rë
  I § *part* < **she h·**
  II § *nn (të)* 1 ability to see: sight, vision 2 scrutiny, observance 3 outer appearance, seeming
  ∘ **nuk ësh-të parë e as dëgjuar** "not be seen and not heard" to be totally unheard of

*pa|rë = **para**

*pa|rë|di|je *nf* foreknowledge

*pa|rë|fja'lë *nf* prologue

*pa|rë|fjal|ím *nm* foreword, preface = **parathë'n**ie

pa|rë|lind|ur *adj (i)* firstborn

*pa|rë|mbrë'më *adv* on the evening/night before last

pa|rë|mbrë'm|shëm *adj (i)* of the evening/night before last

pa|rënd|ësí *adj (i)* = **parënd**ësí**shëm**

pa|rënd|ësí|shëm *adj (i)* unimportant

pa|rë|para'tor *n* = **kryedasmo'r**

pa|rë|se *nf* front portion: face

pa|rë|sí *nf* 1 primacy 2 (*Old Collec*) = **parí**

pa|rë|so'r *adj* (*Book*) primary; of highest priority

par|ë|so're *nf* matter of highest priority

pa|re'ti *nf* [*Ethnog*] 1 bride's first visit back to her old home 2 first party given by the father-in-law after the wedding in honor of the new son-in-law

*pa|rë|vënd|o's· = **paravendo's·**

*pa|rë|vështr|ím *nm* prevision

pa|rëz *nf* queen bee

pa|rë|zím *nm ger* < **parëzo·**n, **parëzo·**het

pa|rë|zo·het *vpr* to pair up; become coupled

pa|rë|zo·n *vt* to couple [a pair]; pair up []; make [] even

parfu'm *nm* perfume
  ∘ **parfum i rëndë** strong and obnoxious perfume

parfum|erí *nf* perfumery

parfum|ím *nm ger* < **parfumo·**n, **parfumo·**het

parfumo·het *vpr* to put on perfume

parfumo·n *vt* to perfume

pa|rí *adv (së)* from the beginning: first; at first, to begin with; for the first time

parí *nf collec* leading citizenry, local dignitaries

pa|ríce *nf* = **pa|rëz**

*parigorí *nf* consolation, comfort

*parigorís· *vt* to console, comfort

par|ím *nm* principle

par|im|ësí *nf* (*Book*) principled basis, standing on principle: consistency

par|im|isht *adv* on a principled basis; in principle

par|im|o'r *adj* 1 in terms of principle, fundamental; in principle 2 of strong principle, highly principled

*par|im|ta'r *n* chief, boss

parite't *nm* (*Book*) parity

*pa|rje *nf* (*Old*) [*Ling*] = **parafja'l**ë

park *nm* (*np* ⁓*qe*) 1 park 2 parking lot 3 [*Tech*] place where motor pool vehicles are kept and repaired: garage

*parkali'dhë *nf* [*Bot*] chicory (*Cichorium intybus*)

parke't *nm* parquetry; floor made of parquetry

parketo·n *vt* to parquet

parlame'nt *nm* parliament

parlamenta'r
  I § *adj* parliamentary
  II § *n* member of parliament

parlament|ar|íz|ëm *nm* parliamentary government

parlo'të *nf* [*Bot*] lily-of-the-valley (*Convallaria majalis*)

parma'k *nm* 1 balustrade 2 window sill/ledge 3 window shutter 4 row of wooden hooks for hanging agricultural tools under the eaves

par|mbrë'më *adv* in the evening of the day before yesterday, two evenings ago; two nights ago

par|mbrë'm|shëm *adj (i)* of the evening before yesterday; remaining from two evenings ago

parme'ndë *nf* 1 [*Agr*] wooden plow 2 one of a series of plowings: plowing

pa'rmë
  I § *adj (i)* 1 in the front: fore-, anterior 2 [*Ling*] consisting of a single root: simple, prime
  II § *nf* 1 forefinger, index finger 2 = **pa'rmëz**
  ∘ **parmat e fytit** [*Anat*] neck arteries (carotid)

pa'rmëz *nf* breastbone of a fowl

parodí *nf* [*Lit*] parody

parodizo·n *vt* to parody; satirize

*pa|roj|t|ur *adj (i)* unguarded

paroksito:n *nm* [*Ling*] paroxytone

paro:m *nm* ferry-boat; raft

paroni:m *nm* word similar in form to another

***paroqi:** *nf* parish

paro:r *nm* sweet dough for making buns

paro:s *nm* chaffinch (*Fringilla coelebs*) = **bo:rës**

paro:she *nf* [*Ichth*] spotted flounder (*Citharus lin-guatula*)
  ○ **paroshe e bardhë** [*Ichth*] spotted flounder *Eu-citherus linguatula* Gill.

***par:par:dje** *adv* the day before the day before yester-day, three days ago

parpuli:s *stem for 1st sg pres, pl pres, 2nd & 3rd sg subj, pind* <**parpuli:t**

par:puli:t *vt* to give [ ] a beating: beat, thrash

par:puli:t·*et vpr* to struggle, strive

***parqe:t** *nm* = **parke:t**

***parsi:m** *nm* = **pari**

pa:r:shëm *adj (i)* 1 previous, preceding 2 foremost, front; first

parta:lle *nf* 1 (*Colloq*) old and worthless odds and ends: old junk 2 (*FigImpolite*) dead bones

partalli:s· *vt* (*Colloq*) = **shpartallo:**·*n*

***parta:s**· *nm* partition, division

parti: *nf* 1 political party 2 (*Old*) group/team of people working toward a common goal; team 3 (*Book*) batch for shipment: lot *4 sentry duty, patrol party *5 = **darkëçi:kë**
  ○ **Parti** (*HistPK*) communist party in Albania: before 1948 = Partia Komuniste e Shqipërisë; after 1948 = Party of Labor of Albania: Partia e Punës e Shqipërisë
  ○ **parti dyfishe** [*Fin*] double-entry bookkeeping

partici:p *nm* [*Ling*] participle

partikulari:zëm *nm* (*Book*) particularism

parti:n *nm* [*Hist*] member of one of the Illyrian tribes that dwelt on the shores of the Mati River

parti:në *nf* (*Reg*) 1 enclosing structure, frame: picture frame 2 slap, clout, smack (on the face/ears)

parti:shëm *adj (i)* of or pertaining to a political party

partishm:ëri: *nf* partisanship; party spirit

partitu:rë *nf* [*Mus*] orchestration, scoring; score

partiza:n *adj, n* partisan

partiza:nçe *adj* 1 (*Colloq*) like a partisan 2 (*Pej*) hastily organized

partne:r *nm* partner; social escort

***pa:rthi** *adv* a short time ago

***paru:ejtun** *adj (i)* (*Reg Gheg*) = **paro:jtur**

paru:kë *nf* wig, peruke

paru:llë *nf* 1 password 2 slogan; watchword

paru:r *nm* = **paro:r**

parva:z *nm* 1 door frame; window frame 2 window ledge; window sill 3 long and narrow shelf along a wall

***par:ve:rë** *nf* = **pranve:rë**

***par:vje:më** *adj (i)* = **parvje:tshëm**

par:vje:t *adv* year-before-last, two years ago

par:vje:tmë *adj (i)* = **parvje:tshëm**

par:vje:tshëm *adj (i)* of the year before last; held over from two years ago

pa:r:zëm *nf* chest, breast, bosom

***par:zi:m** *nm ger* <**parzo:**·*n*

parzma:k *adj* = **parzmo:r**

parzmo:r *adj* covering the chest

parzmo:re *nf* 1 [*Hist*] breastplate armor, coat of mail 2 [*Anat*] sternum 3 carapace

***parzo:**·*n vt* to pair off

***parradi:** *nf* (*Old*) fracas, squabble; uprising, revolt

pa:rra:fshë *adj (i)* = **parra:fshët**

parra:fshët *adj (i)* having an uneven surface: rugged, rough

parra:fshu:ar *adj (i)* = **parra:fshët**

parra:hur *adj (i)* 1 unchurned 2 untrodden 3 (*Fig*) inexperienced

***parrai:s** *OR* **parra:js** *nm* = **parajs:ë**

parregulli: = **parregullsi:**

***parregulli:m** *nm* breach of rules: violation, infringe-ment

parregullsi: *nf* irregularity

parregulli:t *adj (i)* irregular

parre:shtur *adj, adv* = **pare:shtur**

parreth:pre:rë *adj (i)* uncircumcised

parreth:u:ar *adj (i)* not surrounded by a wall or fence: unenclosed

parrezi:k *adj (i)* = **parrezi:kshëm**

parrezi:kshëm *adj (i)* 1 innocuous, harmless 2 not hazardous/dangerous, unrisky

parrezikshm:ëri: *nf* innocuousness; absence of dan-ger

parrëfye:shëm *adj (i)* inexpressible, indescribable; unspeakable

parrënue:shëm = **parrëzue:shëm**

parrë:një *adj* = **pa rrë:një** rootless

parrënjë:zu:ar *adj (i)* [*Agr*] not yet rooted: un-rooted

parrëzue:shëm *adj (i)* indestructible

parri:tur *adj (i)* 1 not yet grown into adulthood: not yet grown, ungrown 2 not advanced in growth, un-developed; stunted

***parri:z** *nm* = **parajs:ë**

***parro:jtur** *adj (i)* unshaven

***parro:tulltë** *adj (i)* invertebrate

parru:ar *adj (i)* 1 unshaven 2 (of an adolescent boy) not yet shaving

parru:dhë *adj (i)* unwrinkled

parru:dhët = **parru:dhëshëm**

parru:dh:shëm *adj (i)* wrinkle-proof; unshrinkable

parru:gë
  I § *adj (i)* 1 without a road, lacking roads; (of roads) rough, impassable *2 illicit, wrong
  II § *adv* *wrongly

pas
  I § *adv* behind
  II § *prep (abl)* 1 behind; along behind, following 2 after 3 according to; in respect to = **sipas** 4 (*Col-loq*) by means of, via, through
  ○ **pas perdes** surreptitiously, sneakily

pas *nm* [*Sport*] pass

pa:s *stem for part, adm* <**ka**·

pasagje:r *n* passenger

pasa:ktë *adj (i)* 1 inaccurate 2 unreliable; imprecise

pasa:kt:ësi: *nf* inaccuracy; imprecision; imperfection

pasa:kt:ës:isht *adv* inaccurately, imprecisely, inex-actly

pasa:kt:ësu:ar *adj (i)* not determined precisely, un-determined, indefinite

pasaldue:shëm *adj (i)* unweldable

pasanda:j *adv* (*Colloq*) = **pasta:j**

pasanïk n 1 member of the wealthy upper class: rich person 2 (Old) subservient follower, lackey *3 adherent, devotee, enthusiast

pasapor̈te nf 1 (Colloq) identity card = letërnjoftïm 2 passport 3 user's manual for a vehicle with vehicle identification information

pasaportizïm nm ger 1 < pasaportizo'·n, pasaportizo'·het 2 official permission to live in a particular city or town

pasaportizo'·het vpr 1 to get a passport 2 to get officially registered as having the right to live in a particular city or town

pasaportizo'·n vt 1 to issue a passport to [] 2 to register [someone] officially as having the right to live in a particular city or town 3 to provide a user's manual

*pasa̋r nm [Ornit] sparrow

pasa̋rdhës
I § n 1 member of a later generation of a lineage: descendant 2 successor 3 (Colloq) child; heir
II § adj succeeding, next, following

pasa̋rdhje nf 1 result, consequence 2 succession

pasçlirïm nm 1 post-liberation 2 (Npc) in Albania, the period following November 29, 1944

pasda̋lje nf [Anat] anus

pasda̋rke
I § nf period of time after dinner and before bedtime, evening time
II § adv during the period of time after dinner and before bedtime, in the evening

pasdïte adv in the afternoon

pasdïte nf afternoon

pasdre̋ke adv after lunch, in the afternoon

pasdre̋ke nf afternoon

pasdre̋këshëm adj of/in the afternoon

pasë alternative short form of participle used in speech and occasionally also in writing to form doubly-compounded remote perfect tenses < ka· used to

pasgodïtje nf (Book) aftershock (of an earthquake)

pasgrűshtë nf 1 back of the hand 2 shirt cuff

pasï
I § conj 1 after 2 since, because
II § nf [Ethnog] = parëtï

pasigurï nf 1 insecurity 2 uncertainty

pasïgur̈t adj (i) 1 insecure 2 uncertain

pasigurűar adj (i) 1 uninsured 2 insecure

pasïm nm [Sport] pass

pasinqer̈të adj (i) insincere

pasion nm passion

pasiono'·het vpr (Book) to be imbued with passion: be passionate

pasiono'·n vt (Book) to imbue with passion: impassion

pasionűar adj (i) (Book) impassioned, passionate

pasïtur adj (i) unsifted

pasïv
I § adj 1 passive; inactive 2 [Fin] pertaining to liabilities; having liabilities greater than assets: showing a loss
II § nm [Fin] liability

pasivïsht adv (Book) passively

pasivite̋t nm (Book) passivity

*pasja̋tër̈t adj (i) (Old) alternate, successive

pa̋sje nf ger 1 < ka· 2 possessions, property, wealth; possession

pasje̋llë adj (i) = pasje̋llshëm

pasje̋llshëm adj (i) ill-behaved; without good manners: ill-mannered

paska̋jë nf finely milled flour

paskajőre
I § nf [Ling] infinitive
II § adj (Old) infinitival

paskajshëm adj (i) interminable, infinite

paska̋jtë adj (i) = paskajshëm

*paskajue̋m adj (i) (Reg Gheg) [Ling] = pashqűar

Paska̋l nm Pascal (male name)

paska̋q
I § nm flour dust, fine flour
II § adj *coated with dust, dusty

*paskënda̋j OR paskësa̋j = paskëta̋j

paskër̈ stem for adm < ka·

paskësḧ stem for pind admirative forms < ka·

paskëta̋j adv from now on, after this

*paskëta̋jm adj (i) = paskëta̋jshëm

paskëta̋jshëm adj (i) subsequent, future

*paskëta̋jthi adv from right now on, after this

paskra̋h nm [Anat] upper arm

paskreműar adj (i) [Dairy] unskimmed/whole (milk)

paskrűpull adj (i) (Book) unscrupulous; unconscionable

paskry̋e nn back of the head

*paskűsh pron each one, everyone

paslïndje nf 1 period (of a few weeks) after giving birth: postpartum period 2 room in a maternity hospital in which a woman stays for a few days following delivery

paslïndur adj (i) of a later generation: junior

paslűftë nf postwar period

*paslűgjë nf [Ornit] = sqeplűgë

pasmbe̋së nf great-granddaughter; great-niece

*pasmejtïm nm (Reg) afterthought

pasmesdïtë nf time period just after noon: early afternoon

pasmesna̋të nf time period just after midnight

pa̋smë adj (i) 1 in back: rear, posterior 2 later in time 3 behind in education and culture: backward

*pa̋smi adv (së) in the end, at last, lastly

pasndje̋kës
I § adj following, succeeding, next
II § n successor

pasne̋sër adv day after tomorrow

pasne̋sër adj (i) of the day after tomorrow

*pasnesër̈tje̋tër adv the day after the day after tomorrow, three days from now

paso'·n
I § vt, vi 1 to follow 2 to pass
II § vi [Ethnog] to visit one's parents for the first time after the wedding

pasőjë nf consequence, upshot

pasőr n [Ethnog] member of the groom's family who accompanies the bride to the house of her parents for the first time following the wedding

*pasősősëm adj (i) = pasősur

pasősur adj (i) boundless, endless; innumerable, enormous

*paspa̋jë nf finely ground flour

paspalístë *nf* [*Bot*] common goosefoot *(Chenopodium)*

*paspallós· *vt* **1** to sweeten **2** *(Fig)* to elaborate, heighten

*pa|spjegue|shëm = pashpjegueshëm

*pas|pjes·ë *nf* analogy, counterpart

pas|provua|r *adj (i)* untested by experience, unproven

pas|qafe *nf* **1** back of the neck: nape **2** *(Euph)* death (of someone disliked)

pas|qaru|a·r *adj (i)* unclear, unsettled

pasqyr·ë
  I § *nf* **1** mirror **2** summarized representation of information in a concise and orderly visual form: table **3** *(Fig)* panorama
  II § *adj* sparkling with cleanliness
  ∘ **pasqyra e lëndës** table of contents

pasqyr|ë·z *nf* chart, table

pasqyr|im *nm ger* **1** <pasqyro·n, pasqyro·het **2** reflection; image **3** [*Phil*] mental representation

pasqyro·het *vpr* to cast a reflection, be reflected

pasqyro·n *vt* **1** to mirror, reflect **2** *(Fig)* to present [] in a concise and orderly visual form **3** [*Phil*] to form a mental representation of []

pasqyr|or
  I § *nm* reflector
  II § *adj* [*Tech*] reflecting; reverberatory

pasqyru|e·s *adj* **1** reflecting; reflective **2** representational

pas|rregull *nf* dizziness, vertigo, fainting

*pas|si *conj* = pasi

*pas|shën|im *nm ger* **1** <passhëno·n **2** addendum, postscript

*pas|shën|o·n *vt* to add [] on (as an addendum/ postscript)

pas|shkrim *nm* postscript

*pastafa·t *adv* on purpose, expressly = apostafa·t

pastaj *adv* **1** afterwards, later, then **2** further on, beyond that **3** furthermore, in addition **4** (introducing the second part of a threat) or else, otherwise

pastajm·ë *adj (i)* **1** later, subsequent **2** last, final

*pastaj|na *adv* = pastaj

pastel *nm* [*Art*] pastel

paste·n *nm* *(Reg)* wool blanket worn over the head to keep off the rain: shepherd's cloak, rain cloak

*pastena·g *nm* [*Ichth*] electric ray

*pasterellós *nm* [*Veter*] pasteurellosis

pasteriz|im *nm ger* **1** <pasterizo·n **2** pasteurization

pasteriz|o·n *vt* [*Spec*] to pasteurize

pa|st·e *nf* **1** cream pastry, French pastry **2** paste **3** [*Ichth*] flounder *(Platichthys flesus luscus)*
  ∘ **past**ë **druri** wood pulp
  ∘ **past**ë **dhëmbësh** toothpaste
  ∘ **past**ë **xhamash** window putty

pa|st·ë *3rd sg opt* <ka·
  ∘ **Past**ë **Drit**ë "May {} Have Light" (inscription on tombstones) Rest In Peace

pa|stër
  I § *adj (i)* **1** clean **2** clear (of unwanted elements): pure; cloudless **3** cleanly, fastidious **4** *(Fig)* free of deceit: honest, sincere
  II § *nf (e)* clean sheet on which final copy is written without errors and corrections: clean copy

  III § *adv* in clean condition; without mistakes; clearly; using pure language

*pastër *nm* [*Ornit*] = harabe·l
  ∘ **past**ë**r deti** [*Invert*] starfish, sea star *Asteroidea*

pastërma· *nf* dried and smoked meat: jerky

pastërm|o·n *vt* to cure strips of [meat] by salting and then smoking: make [] into jerky; smoke []

pastërti *nf* **1** cleanliness **2** purity **3** drycleaner's, laundry

pastërto·r
  I § *adj* habitually clean: cleanly
  II § *n* cleanly person

pa|stërvít|ur *adj (i)* untrained; inexperienced

*pastíç *nm* pasty, tart

pastíçe *nf* [*Food*] noodles baked with cheese, eggs, and milk: cheese pastry

pastiçe·r *nm* confectioner

pastiçeri *nf* confectionery = ëmbëltore

pastíço *nf* [*Food*] = pastíçe

*pastíl·ë *nf* pastille

pastinak·ë *nf* [*Bot*] = pane·l

pa|stok·ë *nf* [*Geog*] = prapatok·ë

pa|stoli *adj (i)* unadorned: (of a woman) dressed simply, not dressed up; (of a room) furnished simply, not furnished well

pa|strehe
  I § *adj (i)* **1** unsheltered; roofless, open **2** *(Fig)* homeless
  II § *n (i)* homeless person

pa|strehua·r *adj (i)* **1** left out in the open, unsheltered **2** unprovided with a place to live

pastri *nf* = pastërti

pastrim *nm ger* <pastro·n, pastro·het.

pastro·het *vpr* **1** to clean up, get clean **2** to clear up, become clear; become purified

pastro·n *vt* **1** to clean; cleanse **2** to clear [] up, clarify **3** to rid [] of unwelcome elements; purify, clean [] off/out, clear [] away/off; purge
  ∘ **pastro·n ahuret e Augjiasit** *(Book)* to cleanse the Augean stables
  ∘ **pastro·n fytin/gurmazin/zërin** to clear [one's throat]
  ∘ **Pastro gojën!** *(Impol)* First wash your own dirty mouth!

pastru|e·s
  I § *nm* person or substance that cleans: cleaner
  II § *adj* used for cleaning

pastru|ese *nf* **1** cleaning woman **2** eraser **3** machine used for cleaning: cleaner

pa|studju|a·r *adj (i)* unstudied, unexplored; not yet learned

pas|theks|or *adj* [*Ling*] posttonic

pas|thën|ie *nf* short commentary added to the end of a book: afterword

pas|thirrm·ë *nf* [*Ling*] interjection

pas|thirrm|or *adj* [*Ling*] interjectional

pas|ue·s
  I § *nm* follower, adherent
  II § *adj* following, succeeding

pa|sukse·s|shëm *adj (i)* unsuccessful

pas|una·r
  I § *adj* = pa|sur
  II § *n* = pasaník

pas|universita·r *adj* postgraduate

pa sur
 I § *part* <**ka·** had
 II § *adj (i)* propertied; wealthy; rich
 III § *nm (i)* rich person

pas uri *nf* property, wealth
 ◦ **pasuri e patundshme/paluajtshme** [*Law*] real estate, real property
 ◦ **pasuri e tundshme/luajtshme** [*Law*] movable property, effects

pas urim *nm ger* **1** <**pasuro·n**, **pasuro·het** **2** enrichment

pas uro·het *vpr* to get rich; become enriched

pas uro·n *vt* to enrich

pas uror *adj* **1** [*Law*] pertaining to property *2 of or pertaining to the rich

pas uruar *adj (i)* enriched

*****pasva n** *nm* night guard, nocturnal watch

pas vdekje *nf* period of time following a death

*****pas vere** *nf* autumn = **vjeshtë**

*****pa sy** *adj (i)* blind = **verbët**

pash *nm* length of two outstretched arms: fathom

pasha *nm* [*Hist*] high government official during the Ottoman occupation, military and civil governor of a region: pasha

*****pa sha** *prep (acc)* (swear) by

pashai *nf (Reg)* neckerchief or shawl worn by women

pashallarë *np* <**pasha**

pashallëk *nm (np ~ qe)* [*Hist*] **1** the position or title of a pasha **2** region governed by a pasha; in Albania, a group of districts ruled by a pasha striving for autonomy from the sultan

pashaport = **pasaport**

*****pa shêjtë** *adj (i) (Reg Gheg)* unholy, profane

*****pa shêjun** *adj (i) (Reg Gheg)* unmarked, unblemished

pa shembshëm *adj (i)* not subject to collapse, sturdy

pa shembullt *adj (i)* unprecedented, unparalleled

*****pasheqe** *nf* origin, source = **burim**

pa sherr *adj (i)* **1** (*Colloq*) staying out of trouble, quiet **2** not malicious: kindly, agreeable

*****pashesë** *nf* wife of a pasha

*****pa sheshuar** *adj (i)* not level/flat: uneven

pa shë *1st sg pdef* <**she·h·** I saw

pashë *nf* with masc agreement [*Hist*] **1** = **pasha 2** title of respect placed after the name of a pasha
 ◦ **pashë mbi pashë** pompously

*****pa shëllirëshëm** *adj (i)* insipid

pa shëm *adj (i)* good-looking, pretty, handsome

pa shëmbull *adj* <**pa shëmbull** = **pashembullt**

pa shëndet *adj (i)* not healthy: sickly

*****pa shëndetësi** *nf* illness, infirmity

pa shëndetshëm *adj (i)* = **pashëndet**

pa shëndosh = **pashëndet**

*****pa shënuar** *adj (i)* insignificant; unmarked

*****pa shënjtë** *adj (i)* unholy, profane, impious

pa shëruar *adj (i)* = **pashërueshëm**

pa shërueshëm *adj (i)* incurable

pa shëtitur *adj (i)* untraveled, unworldly

pa shfaqshëm *adj (i)* inexpressible, indescribable

*****pa shfryem** *adj (i)* unexpressed

pa shfrytëzuar *adj (i)* unexploited, unutilized

pashi *nf* physical beauty

*****pa shigur** = **pasigur**

pa shije *adj (i)* **1** having no flavor; flavorless **2** (*Fig*) bland, insipid; unpleasant

pa shijësi *nf (Book)* flavorlessness, tastelessness, blandness

pa shijshëm *adj (i)* (of food) tasteless

pa shitshëm *adj (i)* unsalable

pa shitur *adj (i)* unsold; not for sale

pa shkak *adj (i)* without apparent cause

pa shkelshëm *adj (i)* untraversable; unconquerable; inviolable

pa shkelur *adj (i)* untrodden; untrampled

pa shkë *nf, np* **1** [*Relig*] major Christian holy day **2** [*Entom*] ladybug, ladybird = **mollëku qe**
 ◦ **Pashkët e vogla** Christmas
 ◦ **Pashkët e mëdha** Easter

*****pa shkëlqyeshëm** *adj (i)* not bright: dull

pa shkëputshëm *adj (i)* unbreakable; indissoluble

pa shkëputur *adj (i)* **1** unbroken, uninterrupted **2** integral, inseparable, indivisible **3** unweaned

pa shkollë *adj (i)* uneducated; illiterate, ignorant

pa shkolluar *adj (i)* without formal education: unschooled

pa shkoqitur *adj (i)* unexplained, unresolved; complicated and unclear

pa shkoqur *adj (i)* **1** not separated from a containing outer layer: unshucked, unshelled **2** (*Colloq*) (of money) not converted into change

pashkor *adj* of or pertaining to Easter: paschal

pa shkrehshëm *adj (i)* inexplosive

pa shkrirë *adj (i)* unmelted

pa shkruar *adj (i)* **1** unwritten; unrecorded **2** unwritten on: blank

pa shkueshëm *adj (i)* **1** uncongenial, unsociable **2** impassable

pa shkulshëm *adj (i)* impossible to uproot; impossible to get rid of

*****pa shkurtuem** *adj (i) (Reg Gheg)* unabridged

pa shlyer *adj (i)* **1** (of an obligation/debt) unrepaid, unsatisfied, undischarged **2** (*Fig*) unexpunged, unforgotten *3 = **pashlyeshëm**

pa shlyeshëm *adj (i)* **1** inexpungible, indelible; unforgettable, unforgivable; unatonable **2** (of an obligation or debt) unrepayable, undischargeable

pashmagje *np fem* **1** women's slippers; embroidered sandal/shoe **2** (*Old*) short heavy woolen socks worn as house slippers

*****pashmângë** *nf (Reg Gheg)* = **pashmagje**

pa shmangësi *nf (Book)* inevitability

pa shmangshëm *adj (i)* unavoidable, inevitable

pa shmangshmëri *nf (Book)* = **pashmangësi**

pa shmangshmërisht *adv (Book)* inevitably

*****pa shmëri** *nf* visibility = **dukshmëri**

pash nik *nm (Old)* **1** piece of thin cloth; thin kerchief worn over the head by old women **2** shroud *3 handkerchief; towel

pa shoq *adj (i)* peerless, matchless, incomparable, unequaled; unique

pa shoqëruar *adj (i)* **1** unaccompanied, unescorted **2** = **pashoqërueshëm**

pa shoqërueshëm *adj (i)* unsociable

pa shoshitur *adj (i)* **1** = **pashoshur 2** (*Fig*) unexplained, unresolved

pa shoshur *adj (i)* unsifted

pashpall ur adj (i) undeclared, unproclaimed; unannounced

pashpërblyer adj (i) 1 unrecompensed, uncompensated 2 (Fig) gratuitous; unappreciated

pashpërblyeshëm adj (i) 1 giving no recompensation, not for pay: unpaying, unpaid 2 (Fig) beyond possibility of ever being repaid: unrepayable, invaluable

***pashpërdhi** nf (Reg) clumsiness, awkwardness

***pashpërdhitë** adj (i) (Reg) nimble, agile

pashprëthyer adj (i) unexploded

pashpirt adj (i) 1 lifeless, dead 2 (Fig) lacking in spirit: spiritless 3 (Fig) heartless, ruthless

pashpirtësi nf heartlessness, callousness

***pashpirtshëm** adj (i) inanimate

pashpjegueshëm adj (i) inexplicable

pashporrshëm adj (i) 1 impossible to get rid of, impossible to drive away 2 irrefutable

pashprehshëm adj (i) inexpressible, ineffable

pashprehur adj (i) 1 unexpressed 2 = pashprehshëm

pashpresë adj (i) without hope; hopeless

pashpresuar adj (i) unhoped for, unexpected

pashpronësuar adj (i) expropriated

pashpyllëzuar adj (i) (of land) not cleared of forests: not deforested, uncleared

***pashqiptuar** adj (i) inarticulate, incoherent, indistinct

pashqiptueshëm adj (i) unpronounceable

***pashqizë**
I § adj (i) inquisitive, nosy
II § nf inquisitiveness

pashquar adj (i) [Ling] (of nouns) indefinite

pashquarsi nf [Ling] (grammatical category of nouns) indefiniteness

***pashtatshëm** adj (i) bodiless, formless

pashteg adj (i) 1 impassable 2 (Fig) with no way out: hopeless, insoluble

pashtershëm adj (i) never running dry: inexhaustible, unfailing

pashteruar adj (i) = pashtershëm

pashterueshëm adj (i) = pashtershëm

pashterur adj (i) = pashtershëm

pashtëpi adj (i) 1 homeless 2 (Pej) (of a person) who doesn't properly stay at home: running around in the streets

pashtër nf untrodden meadowland: virgin pasture

pashtjelluar adj (i) 1 unelaborated; not spelled out in detail 2 [Ling] (of verbs) unconjugated for person and number

pashtrak nm (np ~ qe) [Hist] 1 pastureland within the borders of a clan district 2 fee imposed for grazing animals on a pasture

pashtref nm [Hist] = pashtrak

pashtruar adj (i) 1 not covered properly: (of a room) without floor or wall coverings, bare, uncarpeted, without drapes; (of a table without food) unladen; (of a road) unpaved 2 unruly, disobedient 3 = panënshtruar

pashtrueshëm adj (i) untamable, indomitable, intractable

pashtypur adj (i) not crushed into small particles: uncrushed

pashuar adj (i) 1 still burning: unquelled, unextinguished, unslaked 2 not wiped out: unerased 3 not

mixed with water: undiluted, undissolved 4 at full strength: undamped

pashueshëm adj (i) inextinguishable; indelible

***pashujtun** (Reg Gheg) = pashuar

pat
I § nm 1 = kat 2 room on the ground floor 3 [Chess] stalemate
II § adv 1 [Chess] in a draw 2 equal for both: even

pat
I § stem for pdef, opt, part <ka·
II § 3rd sg pdef <ka·

patakt adj (i) without tact: tactless

patalentuar adj (i) untalented

patalok nm (np ~ qe) (Reg) flat piece of ground; fight arena

patan nm = patok

patar n gooseherd

***patare** nf = potere

patate nf [Bot] potato (Solanum tuberosum L.)
∘ **patate e ëmbël** sweet potato
∘ **patate e kuqe** red potato
∘ **patate e verdhë** Irish potato

patatore nf [Entom] potato weevil

***patavër** = petavër

patejdukshëm adj (i). not transparent: opaque

patejdukshmëri nf (Book) non-transparency: opacity

patejkalueshëm adj (i) (Book) insuperable

patekë nf narrow street, alley

pateklif adv without inhibitions, with no embarrassment

patellë nf [Invert] limpet Patella

patentë nf 1 patent 2 certificate of training; license 3 (Old) commercial tax on craftsmen
∘ **patentë benzine** driver's license (for a gasoline-powered vehicle)
∘ **patentë nafte** driver's license (for a diesel-powered truck/lorry)

patenzonë adj (i) 1 merciless, pitiless 2 atheistic

patenj np <patan

patericë nf 1 crutch 2 (Fig) hasty repair/patch *3 crosier *4 (Reg Gk) barrel stave

patetik adj (Book) 1 enthusiastic, passionate *2 pathetic

patetikë nf (Book) 1 enthusiasm, passion 2 pathetic tone

patë nf [Ornit] goose (Anser anser domestica)
∘ **patë amë** brood hen/goose
∘ **pata e arave** [Ornit] bean goose Anser fabalis Latham = belbe
∘ **pata e bardhë** [Ornit] snow goose Anser caerulescens L.
∘ **pata belbë** [Ornit] = pata e arave
∘ **pata e detit** [Ornit] cormorant
∘ **pata e egër** [Ornit] graylag goose (Anser anser L.)
∘ **pata e vogël** [Ornit] red-breasted goose Rufibranta ruficollis

patë 2nd pl pdef <sheh·

patëholluar adj (i) (of pastry dough) not rolled thin

patëkeq adj (i) unmalicious: guileless, ingenuous

patël nf [Zool] limpet Patellidae

patëllxhan nm 1 eggplant, aubergine (Solanum melongena L.) 2 = patëllxhanës

patëllxha·n·ës *nm* sweet purple fig whose long fruit ripens in the autumn

pa·tëme·të *adj (i)* without defect: impeccable, flawless, faultless

*patërdí *nf* = batërdí

pa·tërma·l *adj (i) (Colloq)* abject, long-oppressed, long-suffering

patërsha·n·ë *nf (Old)* [*Hist*] spear, pike

*patërxha·ne *nf* = patëllxha·n

*patërza·n·ë *nf (Old)* [*Hist*] = patërsha·n·ë

patështí·n·ë *nf (Reg)* = bërsí

*pa·të·zo·n·ë

I § *adj (i) (Old)* godless, atheistic

II § *n (i)* atheist

patí·ck·ë *nf* type of short-barreled rifle

patí·m *nm* flooring, planking

patin·ato·r *n* ice-skater, roller-skater: skater

patina·zh *nm* ice-skating, roller-skating: skating

patí·n·ë *nf* ice skate, roller-skate: skate

∘ **patina akulli** ice skates

∘ **patina me rrotëza** roller skates

patiní·m *nm ger* [*Spec*] <patino·n

patino·n *vt* [*Spec*] to coat [a surface] with gypsum

pa·tje·tër *adv* without fail, no matter what, in any case, no buts about it; unquestionably, undoubtedly, absolutely

pa·tjetër·su·e·shëm *adj (i)* [*Law*] inalienable; not subject to sale

patku·a *nm (obl ~o·i, np ~o·nj)* horseshoe = potku·a

*patlixha·n *nm* = patëllxha·n

patlla·ke *nf (Old)* six-shooter, revolver

patllixha·n *nm* = patëllxha·n

pato·n *vt (Colloq)* to cover [] with boards: lay a floor on []; board [] up, board over []

patogje·n

I § *adj* [*Med*] pathogenic

II § *nm* [*Med*] pathogen

pato·k *nm* 1 [*Ornit*] male goose: gander 2 = darda·ll·ë

pato·k·ë *adj (i)* landless

pa·toleru·e·shëm *adj (i)* intolerable

pato·lo·g *n* [*Med*] pathologist

pato·logjí·í *nf* [*Med*] pathology

pato·logjí·k *adj* [*Med*] pathological

pato·m·ë *nf* 1 (*Reg*) sole of the foot; sole of a stocking 2 innersole of a shoe: insole 3 *(Old)* storey, floor = dysheme

patorí·k *nm* lamb's wool, short-stapled wool

pa·tos *nm* 1 intellectually or aesthetically inspired feeling: passion 2 pathos

pato·z *nm* 1 earth packed down by trampling; dirt floor 2 ground floor stable, livestock shed with a dirt floor

pa·tra·jt·ë *adj (i)* [*Chem Lit*] amorphous

pa·trazu·a·r *adj (i)* 1 unmixed, pure 2 undisturbed: unperturbed, intact

pa·tre·dh·ur *adj (i)* uncastrated

pa·tregu·a·r *adj (i)* = patregu·e·shëm

pa·tregu·e·shëm *adj (i)* indescribable, inexpressible, ineffable

pa·tre·mb·ur *adj (i)* undaunted, fearless

pa·tre·t·shëm *adj (i)* 1 insoluble 2 indigestible

pa·tre·t·shm·ërí *nf* insolubility

pa·tre·t·ur

I § *adj (i)* undissolved, unmelted; undigested, indigested

II § *nm (i)* *indigestion

patria·rk *nm* patriarch

patriarka·l *adj* patriarchal

patriarka·lí·zëm *nm* 1 *(Hist)* patriarchalism 2 set of characteristics typical of a patriarch

patriarka·t *nm* patriarchate

*patriarqí·í *nf* = patriarka·t

patrí·c *nm* [*Hist*] patrician

*patrí·dh·ë *nf* fatherland = vata·n

patrí·k *nm* [*Relig*] patriarch (of the Orthodox church)

patrika·n·ë *nf* [*Relig*] patriarchate

*patrimërí *nf* cowardice

patrio·t

I § *n* 1 patriot 2 *(Colloq)* compatriot = bashkëatdheta·r

II § *adj* patriotic

patrioti·k *adj* patriotic

patrioti·zëm *nm* patriotism

*patrixha·n·ë *nf* = patëllxha·n

patrona·zh *nm* patronage

pa·trondi·t·shëm *adj (i)* 1 not shocking 2 unflappable

pa·trondi·t·ur *adj (i)* unshaken; not shocked

patru·ll·ë *nf* patrol

patrullí·m *nm ger* <patrullo·n

patrullo·n *vi* to be on patrol: patrol

*pa·tru·p *adj (i)* pa trup bodiless

*pa·tu·nd·ësí *nf* unshakableness; firmness

pa·tu·nd·shëm *adj (i)* 1 unshakeable 2 unwavering, secure, stable, steady

pa·tu·nd·ur *adj (i)* 1 unshaken, steadfast, firm 2 unshakeable

*pa·tu·r

I § *part* <ka·

II § *adj (i)* wealthy, rich = pa·sur

*patu·r *adj* stupid, silly

patu·rp *adj (i)* shameless

pa·turp·ësí *nf* 1 shamelessness, indecency 2 shameless behavior

pa·turp·ësí·sht *adv* shamelessly

pa·tu·rp·shëm *adj (i)* shameless

patu·sh *nm* gosling

patushtí·n·ë *nf (Reg)* = bërsí

*pa·tu·t·ur *adj (i)* = patre·mbur

*patva·lle *nf (Old)* supporting crossbeam, transom

pa·theksu·a·r *adj (i)* [*Ling*] stressless, unstressed

*pa·the·llë *adj (i)* not deep, shallow

pa·thellu·e·shëm *adj (i)* 1 not carefully considered, not well thought through/out: hasty 2 given to hasty action/thought

*pa·theme·l *adj (i)* = pathemel·të

pa·themel·ësí *nf (Book)* baselessness

pa·theme·l·të *adj (i) (Book)* without basis: baseless, unfounded

*pa·thë·n·ë·shëm *adj (i)* unspeakable

pa·thí·nj·ur *adj (i)* not yet gray-haired

pa·thje·sht·ë *adj (i)* not simple, composed of more than one part

*patho·logjí·k *adj* pathological

patho·s = pato·s

*pa·thu·r·ur *adj (i)* (of hair) unbraided, loose

pathyer *adj (i)* **1** unbroken **2** (of money) not converted into small change **3** not folded, unfolded **4** *(Fig)* undefeated **5** = **pathyeshëm**

pathyeshëm *adj (i)* **1** unbreakable **2** inflexible, unbendable **3** *(Fig)* indomitable; adamant

pathyeshmëri *nf* **1** unbreakability: toughness **2** indomitability

paudha *np (Colloq)* = **paudhësi**

paudhë
I § *adj (i)* **1** troublesome; mischievous, naughty **2** evil; illegal; wrong; unjust
II § *nm (i) (Colloq Euph)* the devil

*paudhëni *nf* = **paudhësi**

paudhësi *nf* **1** troublesomeness; mischievousness, naughtiness **2** wrong, bad deed

paudhi *nm def* the Devil

*paugurshëm *adj (i)* of ill omen, ill-omened: not boding well

*paujdisëm *adj (i)* disorderly; unsuitable

paujë *adj (i)* **1** having no water: arid **2** undiluted

*paunjur *adj (i)* undaunted

*paurkë = **pagurkë**

paurtësi = **paurti**

paurti *nf* imprudence, injudiciousness, folly

paushqim *nm* undernourishment

paushqyer *adj (i)* undernourished; unfed

pauzë *nf* **1** pause **2** [*Mus*] rest

pavaditur *adj (i)* **1** unwatered, unirrigated *2 unaccustomed; inexperienced; untrained

pavajtuar *adj (i)* unwept, unmourned

*pavalle *(Old)* = **patvalle**

*pavarëm *adj (i)* independent

pavarësi *nf* independence

pavarësisht *adv* independently

pavarur *adj (i)* independent

pavatër *adj* homeless

*pavazhdim *nm* intermittence

pavazhdimësi *nf* discontinuity, break

*pavazhduar *adj (i)* intermittent

pavdekësi *nf* immortality, deathlessness

pavdekëso·het *vpr* to become immortal

pavdekëso·n *vt* to immortalize

pavdekshëm *adj (i)* deathless; immortal; immemorial, never-to-be-forgotten

pavdekshmëri *nf* **1** immortality **2** deathlessness, permanence

*pavdekur *adj (i)* immortal

pavdirë *adj (i)* undying, unfading

*pavdirshëm *adj (i)* indestructible

*pavegluar *adj (i) (Old)* inorganic

pavend *adj (i)* inappropriate; improper

*pavendësi *nf* inappropriateness; impropriety

pavendosmëri *nf* indecisiveness, irresolution

pavendosur *adj (i)* **1** undecided, unresolved **2** indecisive, irresolute

*pavendshëm *adj (i)* inappropriate; improper

pavenitshëm *adj (i)* unwithering, unfading

pavenitur *adj (i)* **1** unfaded; (of health) unfailing **2** undiminished

pavepri *I §* *nf OR* **paveprim** *II §* *nm (Book)* inactivity, inaction

pavetëdije *nf* unconsciousness

pavetëdijshëm *adj (i)* unconscious, unaware

*pavetësor *adj* [*Ling*] = **pavetor**

pavetor *adj* [*Ling*] impersonal

pavëlla *adj (i)* having no brother, brotherless

pavëmendje *nf* inattention

pavëmendshëm *adj (i)* **1** inattentive **2** careless, negligent

pavënë *adj (i)* not previously used/worn: brand new

pavënëre *adj (i)* unnoticed; neglected, ignored

*pavënur *adj (i)* not guilty: innocent

*pavërejshëm *adj (i)* inattentive, heedless; unnoticeable

pavërejtje *nf* = **pavëmëndje**

pavërtetë *adj (i)* untrue

pavërtetësi *nf* lack of truth: falsity, falseness

pavërtetuar *adj (i)* unverified, unconfirmed

pavërtetueshëm *adj (i)* unverifiable

pavëzhgueshëm *adj (i)* unobservable; inscrutable

pavijon *nm* **1** hospital ward **2** (in an exposition or fair) pavilion

pavijueshëm *adj (i) (Book)* discontinuous

pavijueshmëri *nf (Book)* discontinuousness, discontinuity

pavirtytshëm *adj (i)* without virtue, lacking virtue: unvirtuous

*pavishmë *adj (i)* = **pavënur**

pavlefshëm *adj (i)* **1** worthless **2** [*Law*] invalid; null **3** ineffective

pavlefshmëri *nf* **1** *(Book)* worthlessness **2** [*Law*] invalidity; nullity

pavlerë *adj (i)* without value: valueless, worthless = **pavlefshëm**

*pavlerësi *nf* worthlessness; uselessness

pavlershëm *adj (i)* worthless, valueless; useless = **pavlefshëm**

pavodë *nf* [*Ornit*] peahen

pavolitëm *adj (i)* inconvenient

*pavolitje *nf* inconvenience

pavolitshëm *adj (i)* **1** unsuitable, inadequate **2** inconvenient

pavolitur *adj (i)* inappropriate, undue

*pavon *nm* [*Ornit*] peacock *Pavo cristata*

*pavorruem *adj (i) (Reg Gheg)* unburied

pavrarë *adj (i)* **1** unbruised; undamaged **2** *(Fig)* unscathed by suffering **3** *(Colloq)* untrodden

pavullnet *adj (i) (Colloq)* [*Dairy(of milk)* unskimmed; (of cheese) made of whole milk] = **pavullnetshëm**

pavullnetshëm *adj (i)* **1** involuntary **2** lacking drive/zeal

*pavyer *adj (i)* unworthy, undeserving

payndyrë *adj (i)* **1** low in fat content; (of meat) lean **2** *(Fig)* dull, vapid, flavorless

payndyrshëm *adj (i)* [*Dairy*] low in fat content; unfattened, lean; (of milk) skimmed

pazakonshëm *adj (i)* unusual; extraordinary; special

pazakontë *adj (i)* = **pazakonshëm**

pazanat *adj (i)* having no special skill or trade

pazar *nm (Colloq)* **1** bazaar, market; marketplace **2** bargaining, haggling **3** *(Fig)* large and disorderly place or group of people

pazarak *nm (Old)* person selling wares at a market: marketer

pazarllëk *nm (np ~ qe)* **1** bargaining conversation: haggling **2** *(Pej)* dirty business

pazarllëqe *np* <**pazarllëk**

pazbardhur *adj (i)* unbleached

pazbatueshëm *adj (i)* impracticable

pazbërthyer *adj (i)* unresolved

pazbërthyeshëm *adj (i)* unanalyzable

pazbuluar *adj (i)* undiscovered

pazbutshëm *adj (i)* untamable, tameless

pazbutur *adj (i)* untamed, undomesticated, wild

pazemër *adj (i)* **1** heartless **2** easily unnerved: faint-hearted **3 lifeless, dull

pazë *adj (i)* **1** = **pazëshëm 2** quiet, silent; still

pazënë *adj (i)* **1** not taken, unoccupied, vacant **2** uncovered, open **3** not busy, free **4** *(Colloq)* not engaged to be married; not spoken for **5** not yet sprouted

pazënëfill *adj (i)* unused, unbegun, untouched: brand new

pazëshëm *adj (i)* **1** unvoiced, not using the voice **2** *[Ling]* voiceless

pazëvendësuar *adj (i)* unreplaced

pazëvendësueshëm *adj (i)* irreplaceable

pazgjedhur *adj (i)* unselected; non-elected

pazgjidhshëm *adj (i)* **1** indissoluble; inseparable **2** unsolvable, insoluble; unresolvable

pazgjidhshmëri *nf* **1** indissolubility; inseparability **2** unsolvability, insolubility; unresolvability

pazgjidhshmërisht *adv* inextricably, inseparably

pazgjidhur *adj (i)* unsolved; unresolved

pazi *nf [Bot]* Swiss chard, chard *(Beta vulgaris cicla)*

pazier *adj (i)* not boiled; uncooked

pazmbrapshëm *adj (i)* non-repulsable

pazonja *adj (e) fem nf (e)* <**pazoti**

pazot *adj (i)* unowned

pazotësi *nf* incompetence, incapability

pazoti *adj (i), nm (i)* incompetent/inept (person); clumsy (person)

pazvan *nm* **1** *(Old)* night watchman paid to guard a marketplace **2** *(Pej Contempt)* person whose loyalty is bought with money: lackey

pazvjerdhur *adj (i)* unweaned

pazvogëluar *adj (i)* undiminished

pazvogëlueshëm *adj (i)* incapable of being made smaller

****pazhdërvjellti** *nf* crudeness

****pazhik** *nm (Reg)* barren land near a house

pazhurmë *adj (i)* **1** noiseless, soundless **2** quiet, silent

pazhveshur *adj (i)* **1** not undressed, fully clothed **2** unpeeled; still in the husk

pazhvilluar *adj (i)* **1** undeveloped; not fully formed **2** unsolved, unresolved

PD *abbrev* = **Partia Demokratike** the Democratic Party

pe *2nd sg pdef* <**she h·** you saw

pe(r) *nm (np ~ nj)* thread, yarn

****pebrinë** *nf [Entom]* disease that affects silkworms

pec *adj, n* **1** (person) with very poor eyesight: near-sighted/blind (person) **2** *(Reg South)* long rolling pin (for rolling out dough) = **petës**

pece *nf* **1** (cleaning) rag **2** foot wrapping used by soldiers instead of stockings **3** gauze bandage

pecëtë *nf* **1** tablecloth **2** *(Colloq)* = **peshqir**

pecë *nf* **1** = **pece 2** cloth patch

peckë *nf dimin* <**pece**

****peco·n** *vt* to patch [clothing]

****peças** *stem for 1st sg pres, pl pres, 2nd & 3rd sg subj, pind* <**peçat·**

****peçat·** *vt* to touch; harm

****peçatshëm** *adj (i)* touchable; easily hurt/harmed, vulnerable

****peçatur** *adj (i)* touched; harmed, spoiled

peçe *nf* face veil (for Moslem women)

****peçell** *nm [Bot]* chickpea = **qiqër**

****peçinë** *nf* cave = **shpellë**

pedagog *nm* **1** instructor in a university **2** educational specialist: pedagogue **3** educator

  ○ **pedagog i jashtëm** adjunct instructor/professor

pedagogji *nf* pedagogy

pedagogjik *adj* pedagogical

pedal *nm* pedal; treadle

****pedanë** *nf [Sport]* (diving/gymnastics) springboard; (in throwing events) circle; (in weight-lifting) platform

pedant *nm* pedant

pedanteri *nf* pedantry

pedantizëm *nm* pedantry

pederast *nm* pederast

pederasti *nf* pederasty

pediatër *nm* pediatrician

pediatre *nf* female pediatrician

pediatri *nf [Med]* pediatrics

****pedinë** *nf (Old) [Chess]* pawn

pedolog

  I § *n* pedologist

  II § *adj* pedological

pedologji *nf* science of soils: pedology

pef *nm* **1** *(Colloq)* flimsy rug **2** bedsheet

****pegâ·** *vt (Reg Gheg)* to soil, defile

pegamber *nm* (Moslem) prophet

pegelë *nf* large pin used on clothing

pegull *nf* tar

pegullo·n *vt* to coat with tar: tar

pegun *nm* baby rabbit, bunny; leveret

****pegurkë** *nf* mushroom; fungus

****peh** *nm* = **pe(r)**

pehar *nm (Old)* **1** large spoon: ladle **2** drinking glass; chalice

pehlivan *nm (Colloq)* acrobat, tightrope-walker

pehlivanllëk *nm (np ~ qe) (Pej)* ruse, stratagem

pehriz *nm (Colloq)* **1** regimen for eating and drinking: diet **2** *(Fig)* thrifty use of something

peizazh *nm* depiction or view of the countryside: landscape

peizazhist *nm* landscape photographer

pej *prep (abl) (Old Reg)* = **prej**

pejan

  I § *adj* of/from Peja

  II § *n* native of Peja

****pejcë** *nf* lint

****pejë** *nf (Reg)* = **pe(r)**

Pejë *nf* city in Kosovo near the northern border of Albania: Peja

pejo'r *adj* = fijezo'r

pe'jzë *nf* **1** = te'jzë **2** [*Bot*] black borony *(Tamus communis)*

pejzo'r *adj* sinewy

*__**pek**__ *nm (np ~ qe)* regret

*__**peka'n**__ë *nf* sheet = çarça'f

pekme'z *nm* concentrated fruit jam treated with lime or lye: fruit paste

peksima'dhe *nf* bread baked twice to make it dry and long lasting: zwieback, hardtack, hard biscuit

peksi'met = peksima'dhe

peku'l *nm* **1** *(Old)* property leased for high rent or for a large share of the profits **2** personal property accumulated over time; personal property to which an individual (not other family members) has exclusive rights **3** family friend **4** *(Fig)* personal care/attention **5** *(Colloq)* = pekuli
  ∘ **pekuli i nuses** *(Dimin)* bridal dowry

pekula'të *nf* = pekuli

pekul'i *nf* **1** *(Colloq)* small present given to a child: treat **2** *(Fig)* pampering, indulgence

*__**pekulo'**__•*n vt* to give [ ] a gift/tip, reward

*__**pekulo're**__ *nf (Old)* treasury

*__**pekul'uer**__ *adj (fem ~ore) (Old)* of or pertaining to a treasury

pe'la *np fem* huge waves; breakers

pela'r *n* herdsman who looks after mares: horse wrangler

pe'llas *adv* = kaladibra'nçe

*__**pe'le**__ *nf* sharp-tongued woman, shrew

pelegri'n *nm* pilgrim, haji

pelegrina'zh *nm* pilgrimage, haj

*__**peleka'n**__ = pelika'n

pele'në *nf* diaper; swaddling cloth; baby blanket
  ∘ **ësh-të në pelena** "still be in diapers" *(Scorn)* to be still wet behind the ears; still in its early beginnings, not yet really developed

peleqis• *vt* to reduce [ ] to small pieces: mince

peleri'në *nf* **1** cape, cloak **2** [*Med*] pallium (of the brain)

*__**pelesga'r**__ *nm* [*Ornit*] stork

pe'lë *nf* mare

peli'çe *nf* fur coat; fur

peligo'rgë *nf* [*Ornit*] bee-eater = bre'gçë

peligo'rk *nm* [*Ornit*] = bre'gçë

pelika'n *nm* [*Ornit*] pelican
  ∘ **pelikan kaçurel** [*Ornit*] Dalmatian pelican *Pelecanus crispus B.*
  ∘ **pelikan rozë** [*Ornit*] white pelican *Pelecanus onocrotalus L.*

peliko'r *nm* fainting, swoon

peli'kulë *nm* [*Anat*] pellicle

peli'n *I* § *nm OR* **peli'n**ë *II* § *nf* **1** wormwood, absinthe *(Artemisia absinthium)* **2** *(Fig)* great sorrow *III* § *adj* **1** bitter **2** *(Fig)* sorrowful
  ∘ **pelin i hidhur** very bitter; very sad

*__**pelivra'm**__ *nm (Old)* = sifi'llz

pelq• *vt* to make [liquid] turbid

pe'lte *nf* **1** sweet pap (for babies) made of starch or rice flour, sugar and hot water **2** concentrated liquid mush made by boiling fruit/vegetables for a long time; thick mush **3** *(Fig Colloq)* person who is fat and flabby

pelu'sh *nm* soft and plushy fabric: plush

pella'zg *adj, n* [*Hist*] Pelasgian

pellazgji'shte *nf* Pelasgian language

pe'llë *nf* **1** weaver's reed (on a loom) *(Reg)* **2** panel of a carpet **3** fool, idiot **4** = pe'tull **5** [*Text*] bombazine

*__**pelle'ng**__ *nm* = pëlle'ng

pellg *nm (np ~ gje)* **1** standing body of water: puddle, pool, pond **2** large quantity of a liquid: pool **3** deep part of a body of water **4** [*Geog*] basin comprised of a body of water and the land surrounding it; bight in a body of water; basin of land containing mineral resources **5** *(Fig Pej)* sinkhole

pellga'çe *nf* small pool of water: puddle, pond

pellgi'shte *nf* ground with many puddles

pellgo're *nf* large pool of watersea basin; open sea

pellgovi'në *nf* marshland, swamp

pe'llgje *nm* <pellg

*__**pellta'r**__ *nm* rump (of cattle)

pema'xhi *nm (np ~ nj)* = pemëshi'tës

*__**pe'mb**__ë *adj* rose-colored

pe'më *nf* **1** tree cultivated for its fruit: fruit tree **2** fruit **3** shade tree; tree
  ∘ **pem**ë **gjenealogjike** family tree
  ∘ **Pema e kalbur kalb/kalbëzon edhe shoqet.** "The rotten fruit also spoils its neighbors." *(Prov)* One rotten apple spoils the whole barrel.
  ∘ **Pemën, kur s'pjell, e presin se i bën hije dardhës.** "When a fruit tree stops bearing, they cut it down because it is shading the pear tree." *(Prov)* An unproductive person should be removed before he influences others.
  ∘ **ësh-të pemë me rremba** to be a valuable person with many virtues
  ∘ **pem**ë **mushkërore** [*Anat*] pulmonary system
  ∘ **pem**ë **pa kokrra 1** person who can do nothing to help you; person who spends time without accomplishing anything **2** fruitless activity; something that offers no gain
  ∘ **Pema pa u pjekur s'hahet.** "Fruit is not eaten before it is ripe." *(Prov)* One must wait for the proper time.
  ∘ **pem**ë **uratë** [*Bot*] Persian lilac, Indian bead tree *Melia azedarach*
  ∘ **pema e Vitit të Ri** "New Year's tree" Christmas tree

pe'më**l** *nf* berry
  ∘ **Fletët/Lulet i ka të bukura, po t'i shohim pemlat.** "It has beautiful flowers/leaves, but let's see the berries." It looks all right now, but we have to see how it turns out.

pemë**pru'r**ë**s** *adj* fruit-bearing, fructiferous, fruiting

pemë**ri'n**ë *nf collec* **1** fruit **2** orchard

pemë**si'm** *nm* = frytë**zi'm**

pemë**so'**•*n vt* = frytë**zo'**•n

pemë**so'r** *adj* = frytdhe'nës

pemë**shi't**ë**s** *n* fruit seller, fruiterer

pemë**ta'r** *n* fruit grower, fruit farmer

pemë**tar'i** *nf* **1** fruit growing, fruit farming **2** *(Collec)* fruit crop

pemë**to're** *nf* **1** orchard **2** fruit shop/store
  ∘ **pemëtore mëmë** tree nursery

pemi'shtë *OR* **pemi'shte** *nf* land planted in fruit trees: fruit plantation, orchard

*__**pemni'sht**__ë = pemi'shtë

*__**pemno'**__•*n vt* to plant [ ] with trees

pemuri'na *np fem (Colloq)* various fruits, a variety of fruits

pemzë *nf* [*Med*] herpes, tetter, shingles

penal *adj* [*Law*] penal; criminal

penalist *n* [*Law*] criminal lawyer

penalisht *adv* [*Law*] according to criminal law: penally

penalitet *nm* [*Law*] criminal law; criminal penalty

penallti *nf* [*Soccer*] penalty kick zone; penalty kick = **njëmbëdhjetëmetërsh**

*Pendakos *nm* Pentecost

pendar *nm* 1 plowman who drives a yoke of oxen 2 rural watchman who guards crops 3 [*Hist*] sharecropper on a baronial estate, tenant farmer = **çifçi**
○ **Pendari i ruan vreshtat.** "The watchman guards the vineyard." (*Prov*) It is fear of being caught that keeps people honest.

pendaricë *nf* = **pendarishtë**

pendarishtë *nf* 1 high ground on which watchman's bower is built 2 watchman's bower

pendaro·het *vpr* to take a mate

pendartë *adj (i)* (*Old*) [*Relig*] high mass celebrated to commemorate the dead: requiem mass

pendesë *nf* 1 penitence, repentance 2 [*Relig*] (in Roman Catholicism) confession

pendespanjë *nf* [*Food*] = **bukësheqere**

pendestar
I § *n* penitent, repenter
II § *adj* penitent, penitential

*pëndestore *nf* (*Reg Gheg Old*) penitentiary

pendë
I § *nf* 1 feather, quill 2 = **penë** 3 fin (of a fish) 4 vane; vane of a waterwheel; waterwheel 5 dike, levee, dam 6 pair of draft animals yoked together: yoke of oxen, team 7 measure of land equal to what a yoke of oxen can plow in a single day: juger
II § *adj* light as a feather
○ **pendë bersalierësh** tuft of rooster plumes worn in the helmets of Italian infantrymen in World War II
○ **pendë deti** [*Zool*] sea pen *Pennatula*
○ *Kjo është//Kësaj i thonë* **tre qe e dy pendë.** "This is (called) three oxen and two yokes." This disparity (between resources to needs) is impossible to bridge.
○ **pendë fijëzore** [*Ichth*] = **pendëfijëzore**
○ **pendë mulliri** clapper on a mill hopper

pendëbardhë *adj* white-feathered

pendëdendur *adj* with thick plumage

pendëfijëzore *nf* [*Ichth*] Mediterranean flagfin (*Aulopus filamentosus*)

pendëgjatë
I § *adj* long-feathered
II § *nf* [*Ichth*] = **pendëfijëzore**

pendëhirtë *adj* gray-feathered

pendëkaposh *nm* [*Bot*] 1 feather grass (*Stipa pennata*) 2 herbaceous perennial found on rocky slopes with a dense cluster of leaves near the root

pendëkuq *nm* 1 [*Ichth*] red-finned carp 2 red-feathered

pendël *nf* small feather

pendërënë *adj* whose plumage has fallen out, featherless

pendëshkruar *adj* having variegated plumage

pendëshkurtër *adj* short-feathered

pendëz *nf* [*Mus*] plectrum, pick

*pendikosti *nf* [*Relig*] Pentecost

pendim *nm ger* 1 <**pendo·het** 2 = **pendesë** 3 regret

*pendimas *adv* = **pendueshëm**

pendo·het *vpr* 1 to be sorry for what one has done: have regrets; be penitent, repent; have second thoughts 2 [*Relig*] to confess one's sins (to a priest)

pendor *adj* [*Bot*] pinnate

pendore *nf* plot of land that can be plowed with a yoke of oxen in one day

pendos·et *vpr* to fledge

pendrec *nm* knife colter, colter

penduar *adj (i)* penitent, repentant; sorry

pendues *adj, n* penitent

pendueshëm *adv* grudgingly, reluctantly; regretfully, with regret

pendulin *nm* [*Ornit*] penduline tit (*Remis pendulimnus L.*) = **kolovatës**

pendull *nf* feather

penel *nm* small paintbrush

*penell *nm* = **penel**

penetrim *nm ger* 1 <**penetro·n** 2 penetration

penetro·n *vt* to penetrate

penez *nm* 1 (*Old*) very thin silver coin worn as an ornament 2 something very thin; thin fabric

penezore *nf* medium-sized ceramic water urn with a long narrow neck and one or two handles

penë *nf* 1 writing pen; pen point, nib 2 (*Fig*) writer

*penëro·het *vpr* (of a horse) to rear up

peng *nm* (*np ˉ gje*) 1 collateral (left as security for a loan) 2 hostage (left to assure compliance) 3 feeling of regret (for one's failure) 4 (*Fig*) token of assurance

pengac *adj* crumpled/doubled up, contracted

pengashkë *nf* (*Reg*) brake rod on the roller of a loom

pengatë *nf* rope used to hobble an animal's forelegs: hobble

pengcë *nf* object left as security/collateral on a loan: pawn

pengdhënës *n* (*Book*) person who leaves collateral for a loan: pawner, mortgagor

pengesë *nf* 1 obstacle, obstruction; hindrance, encumbrance; impediment, handicap; restriction 2 [*Sport*] hurdle 3 = **pengatë**
○ **pengesë guri** rock barrier
○ **pengesë natyrale** natural barrier, terrain obstacle
○ **pengesë rrugore** road blockage, road block

pengë *nf* 1 leg stuck out to trip someone 2 hobble used on an animal

pengëz *nf* 1 hobble used on an animal 2 leg stuck out to trip someone

pengicë *nf* tether

pengim *nm ger* 1 <**pengo·n**, **pengo·het** 2 = **pengesë**

pengimtar
I § *n* (*Book*) obstructionist
II § *adj* **obstructive

penglënës *nm* (*Book*) = **pengdhënës**

pengmarrës *nm* (*Book*) person who accepts collateral for a loan: pawnbroker; mortgagee

pengo·het *vpr* 1 to stumble 2 to get hung up by some difficulty, be stuck

pengo·n *vt* 1 to impede, hamper, hinder; obstruct 2 to hobble 3 to mortgage; pawn

pengojcë *nf* hobble on an animal

pengoʹjë nf **1** barrier to keep livestock inside a corral **2** latch, catch

pengoʹre nf **1** hobble on an animal's forelegs **2** sturdy pole stuck in between the vanes of a water wheel to stop it from turning **3** chock

pengruʹajtёs nm depositary

*__pengsʹim__ nm surety, hostage

*__penguʹemʹe__ nf (e) (Reg Gheg) hindrance

penguʹes adj obstructive; impeding

*__penguʹeshёm__ adj (i) = **penguʹes**

penicilʹinё nf [Pharm] penicillin

peniʹk nm [Bot] variety of millet with small brown or tan seeds; bread made of the flour of this millet (Panicum miliaceum)

penʹoʹ ·n vt to mark a straight line on [ ] with a stretched wet string

penoʹbetoʹn nm foam concrete

pensiʹoʹn nm **1** pension **2** pensioned status **3** boarding house = **hotel-pensioʹn**
∘ **pension familiar** pension paid to a non-working member of the family of the deceased

pensioʹniʹst
I § n pensioner
II § adj living on a pension

pentaʹedёr nf [Geom] pentahedron

pentaʹgram nm [Mus] five-line musical staff

pentatʹloʹn nm [Sport] pentathlon

Pentekoʹstё nf [Relig] Pentecost

penxheʹre nf (Colloq) window = **dritaʹre**

penxheʹrʹkё nf dimin (Reg) little window

peʹnj np <pe threads, strings

*__peʹnjё__ nf [Bot] broadleafed bulrush, great reed mace (Typha latifolia)

peʹnjёz nf **1** filament, thin fiber **2** [Anat] = **eʹshtё**

penjёʹzoʹ ·n vt to spin into thread; make [ ] into the form of thread

penjёʹzoʹr adj composed of fibers, having fibers: fibrous **2** [Med] fibrillar

peʹnjtё adj (i) made of fiber

pepeʹq nm [Food] kind of cheesecake scalded with syrup

peperuʹnё nf [Ethnog] boy clothed only in fern and hellebore leaves and sprinkled with water in a ceremony to attract rain

*__peperuʹqe__ nf [Bot] red pepper (Capsicum)

pepsiʹnё nf pepsin

*__pepûʹ(n)__ nm (Reg Gheg) wine made from berries

peʹqe pcl (Colloq) expression of compliance: at your service

*__peqeʹr__ OR **peqiʹ** = **pёqiʹ**

Peqiʹn nm town in central Albania: Peqin

peqiʹnʹas
I § adj of or pertaining to Peqin
II § n native of Peqin

*__peraʹjkё__ nf (Reg Tosk) wash paddle

perandoʹr nm emperor

perandoʹraʹk adj imperial

perandoʹreʹshё nf empress

perandoʹriʹ nf empire

*__perandoʹriʹk__ adj = **perandoʹraʹk**

perceptiʹm nm [Psych] perception

perceptoʹ ·n vt **1** [Psych] to perceive **2** (Book) to comprehend

*__perç__ nm **1** = **pёrç** **2** bell-wether

perçarʹtё adj (i) incoherent, delirious

perʹçe nf **1** (Colloq) shock of hair, tress; forelock; mane **2** corn silk **3** thin black veil worn over the face by Moslem women
∘ **perçe e pemёs** crown of a tree

perçeʹbardhё adj **1** white-maned **2** (Poet) (of waves) white-crested

perçeʹgjaʹtё adj (of man or beast) having long forelocks; long-maned

perçeʹngriʹtur adj having a bristling mane

perçeʹshkuʹmё adj (Poet) (of waves) foam-crested; abounding in waves; foamy

perçiʹnё nf rivet

perçiʹnʹoʹ ·n vt to rivet

perçiʹnʹuʹesʹe nf [Tech] riveting device

perçollaʹk nm = **pёrçollaʹk**

perdaʹh nm = **pёrdaʹf**

peʹrde nf **1** curtain; drapery; drapery material **2** screen **3** partition **4** [Anat] = **lёbyʹr** **5** [Mus] (on a stringed instrument) fret **6** (Fig Colloq) sense of shame/honor **7** (Colloq) woman's face veil *__8__ parapet of a bridge
∘ **perde tymi** [Mil] smoke screen
∘ **perde zjarri** [Mil] simultaneous discharge of a battery of guns for defense: curtain of fire

*__pereniʹk__ n trusty guide; reliable person

perёndeʹshё nf **1** [Relig] goddess **2** (Fig) paragon of beauty among women

perёndiʹ nf god

perёndiʹm nm ger **1** <perёndoʹ ·n **2** sunset **3** west **4** (Fig) demise

perёndiʹmoʹr adj western

perёndiʹshёm adj (i) godly, divine

perёndiʹt· vt = **pёrandiʹt·**

perёndoʹ ·n
I § vi **1** (of a heavenly body) to set, go down **2** to come to an end, have its demise **3** (Reg) to go high into the air and disappear
II § vt (Colloq) to throw high into the air and cause to disappear
∘ **perёndoʹ·n mbas** <> to set one's lights by <>, live according to <>'s lights
∘ **perёndoʹ·n nga kjo botё** to take leave of this world, depart this life
∘ **i perёndoʹ·n sytё** **1** to be unable to keep one's eyes open **2** to close one's eyes for the last time, die
∘ <> **perёndoi ylli** "<>'s star set" <> is past its prime; <> is coming to the end of <>'s life

perёnduʹaʹr
I § part <perёndoʹ ·n
II § adj (i) defunct, at an end, no more, gone

*__perёnduʹsh__ nm Cupid

perfeksiʹoʹn nm perfection

perfeksiʹoniʹm nm ger <pёrfeksionoʹ ·n

perfeksiʹonoʹ ·n vt to perfect, improve

perfeksiʹonuʹaʹr adj (i) perfected; perfect

perfeksiʹonuʹes adj perfectible; improvable

perfeʹkt
I § nm [Ling] perfect (tense)
II § adj perfect

perfoleʹntё nf [Tech] punched tape

*__perfosfaʹt__ nm [Agr] superphosphate

pergamenë
  I § *nf (Old)* parchment
  II § *adj* parchment-like
***pergjím** *nm* consolation visit
pergjel *nm (Old)* 1 = **shalok** 2 compass (for drawing arcs) = **kompas**
perri *obl* <**pe**(r)
  ○ **t'i shkojë peri gëzofit** "that the thread match the fur" so that everything matches; that everything be done with great care
periferi *nf* 1 outskirts 2 periphery
periferik *adj* 1 in the outskirts 2 peripheral
perifrazë *nf* 1 paraphrase 2 [*Lit*] periphrastic expression
perifrazim *nm ger* 1 <**perifrazo**•*n* 2 annoying circumlocution
perifrazo•*n*
  I § *vi* to speak in circumlocutions
  II § *vt* to paraphrase
perigje *nm* [*Astron*] perigee
perikot *nm* brick, tile
perime *np* vegetables
  ○ **perime gjethore** green leafy vegetables
perimekulturë *nf* = **perimtari**
perimerritës *n* vegetable grower
perimeshitës *n* vegetable seller
perimetër *nm* 1 perimeter 2 line of circumference
perimor
  I § *adj* of or pertaining to vegetables
  II § *nm collec* vegetables, the vegetable
perimore *nf* field of vegetables, vegetable garden
perimtari *nf* horticulture
perinjak *nm* [*Bot*] Mediterranean mezereon (*Daphne gnidium*)
perioda *np* 1 <**periodë** 2 menstrual period(s)
periodë *nf* 1 = **periudhë** 2 [*Chem*] periodic table 3 [*Phys*] period (of a wave)
periodicitet *nm* (*Book*) periodicity
periodik
  I § *adj* periodic; periodical
  II § *nm* periodical
periodikisht *adv* (*Book*) periodically
periodizim *nm ger* (*Book*) <**periodizo**•*n*
periodizo•*n* *vt* (*Book*) to divide [a process] into time periods
peripeci *nf* problem in one's life, vicissitude
***peripeti** = **peripeci**
***perís** = **pehríz**
periskop *nm* periscope
perishane *np fem* [*Ethnog*] chaplet of coins or sequins laced together with thin wire and worn around a bride's forehead: bridal crown
perishtup *adj* leap-year
peritonit *nm* [*Med*] peritonitis
periudha *np* menstrual period(s) = **perioda**
periudhë *nf* 1 time period: epoch, era 2 developmental period: stage 3 [*Math*] period (of an iterative function) 4 division of a school according to yearly progress: grade 5 [*Ling*] complex/compound sentence
  ○ **periudha e qumështit** period during which a baby drinks milk from the breast: suckling/nursing period
perivol *nm* garden, orchard

***periz** = **pehriz**
***perkë** *nf* [*Ichth*] perch (*Perca fluviatilis*)
perkuizim *nm* authorized search of a house/body for evidence in a criminal investigation: perquisition
Perlat *nm* Perlat (male name)
perlë *nf* pearl = **margaritar**
permanent
  I § *adj* permanent, continuous
  II § *nm* 1 (for hair) permanent wave 2 hairdressing salon, beauty shop
permanganat *nm* [*Chem*] permanganate
permanganik *adj* [*Chem*] permanganic
***permë** *nf* 1 heartbreak, regret, disappointment *2 timorousness, reluctance
permutacion *nm* [*Math*] permutation
peronas *nm* nail maker
peronë
  I § *nf(Colloq)* nail, spike; rivet
  II § *adj* (of water) very cold
***peronígë** *nf* [*Bot*] spring flower with a strong odor
***perpelugë** *nf* [*Entom*] butterfly
  ○ **perpelugë uji** [*Entom*] dragonfly
pers *adj, n* [*Hist*] = **persian**
***persan** *adj, n* = **persian**
***persejatje** = **përsiatje**
***persekutim** *nm ger* 1 <**persekuto**•*n* 2 persecution
persekuto•*n* *vt* to persecute
Persi *nf* Persia
persian *adj, n* Persian
persisht *adv* in Persian (language)
persishte *nf* Persian language
person *nm* 1 (*Book*) person, individual 2 [*Theat*] character, persona 3 [*Law*] entity with rights and duties under the law: legal person
personal *adj* personal
personale *nf* [*Basketball*] free throw
personalisht *adv* personally
personalitet *nm* 1 personality; dignitary, authority 2 social standing
personazh *nm* [*Lit*] personage
personel *nm collec* personnel
***personë** *nf* person = **vetë**
personifikim *nm ger* (*Book*) 1 <**personifiko**•*n* 2 personification 3 [*Lit*] anthropomorphic character
personifiko•*n* *vt* to personify
perspektiv *adj* (*Book*) 1 perspective 2 prospective
perspektivë *nf* 1 (*Book*) perspective projection/representation; perspective 2 outlook on the future, prospect
peruan *adj, n* Peruvian
***perukë** *nf* peruke, wig = **parukë**
perusti *nf* trivet, tripod
***perushane** *nf* = **perishane**
***pervazë** *nf* = **arkitra**
pervers *adj* perverse; wicked, depraved
perri *nf* 1 [*Folklore*] houri 2 = **xhind**
perrik *nf* (*Colloq*) very small amount
***perrupi** *nf* = **porropi**
p. e. s. *abbrev* <**para erës së re** "before the new era" B.C.
pesagurthi *adv*
pesar *nm* [*Med*] pessary

pesa're nf (Old) = pese're

pese're nf (Old) small Ottoman coin equal to five para

pe'së
I § num five; number five
II § nf 1 the number five 2 lowest passing grade in a scale of one to ten; highest grade in a scale of one to five
III § np (të) a group of five, five at one time; all five
◦ **pesë dhi gjashtë zile** a lot of noise but not much getting done
◦ **pesë me hiç** (Crude) without any worthwhile result; worthless
◦ **pesë më shumë, pesë më pak** "five more, five less." a little bit more or a little bit less (doesn't make much difference)
◦ **ësh·të pesë para burrë/njeri** "be a nickel's worth of man" to be small and scrawny, not be much of a man; be a person of no importance
◦ **pesë para burrë** man with a small and weak body, weakling
◦ **pesë para gjë** "thing worth five para" a trifling amount; a trifle
◦ **pesë para oka** (Impol) dirt cheap
◦ **Pesë pordhë, dhjetë grosh.** (Crude) Costs an arm and a leg.

pesëce'p|ësh adj five-cornered, five-pointed

pesëdit|ësh
I § adj lasting five days, five days long
II § nm five-day period

pesëdhje'të
I § num fifty
II § adj (i), n (i) fiftieth
◦ **të pesëdhjetat** fifty years of age

pesëdhjetëlek|ësh
I § adj UIOffic worth/costing fifty leks
II § adj, nm (Colloq) (bill) worth five leks

pesëdhjetëlek|ëshe 1 (Offic) bill worth fifty leks 2 (Colloq) bill worth five leks

pesëdhjetëqinda'rk|ësh adj (Offic) worth/costing fifty cents

pesëdhjetëqinda'rk|ëshe nf (Offic) fifty-cent coin

pesëdhjetëvjeça'r
I § adj 1 lasting/taking fifty years 2 fifty years old
II § n fifty year old person

pesëdhjetëvje't|ësh nm fifty-year period; half a century

pesëdhjetëvjeto'r nm fiftieth anniversary; fifty-year celebration

pesëfi'sh
I § nm a quantity five times as great as another: quintuple, fivefold amount
II § adv fivefold, five times greater
III § adj (i) fivefold; five-ply

pesëfish|i'm nm ger <pesëfisho'·n, pesëfisho'·het

pesëfisho'·het vpr to increase fivefold, get five times greater; increase greatly

pesëfisho'·n vt to increase [] fivefold: quintuple; increase [] greatly

pesëfi'sh|të adj (i) 1 five-ply 2 five times greater, quintuple 3 five-part, five-faceted

pesëfish|ua'r adj (i) increased fivefold, quintupled; greatly increased

pesëga'r|ësh nm [Sport] pentathlon

pesëgar|i'st n [Sport] pentathlon athlete

pesëgi'shte nf [Bot] 1 creeping cinquefoil, fivefinger, five-leaf grass (Potentila reptans) 2 = halmu'cë 3 Turkish micromeria (Micromeria)

pesëka't|ësh
I § adj five-storey
II § nm five-storey building

* **pesëkë'mb|ës** adj five-legged

pesëkë'mb|ësh
I § adj [Lit] pentameter
II § nm pentameter line

pesëkënd|ësh
I § adj [Geom] pentagonal
II § nm [Geom] pentagon

pesëlek|ësh
I § adj (Offic) worth five leks; costing five leks
II § adj, nm (Colloq) (coin) worth fifty cents

pesëlek|ëshe nf five-lek bill

* **pesëluft|i'm** nm [Sport] = pesëga'r|ësh

pesëmbëdhje'të
I § num fifteen; number fifteen
II § nf the number fifteen
III § adj (i), n (i) fifteenth

pesëmbëdhjetëdito'r adj lasting fifteen days, fifteen days long

pesëmbëdhjetëdit|ësh
I § adj lasting fifteen days, fifteen days long; fifteen-day old
II § nm fifteen-day period

pesëmbëdhjet|ësh adj 1 size fifteen 2 on the fifteenth day of its period: (of the moon) full

* **pesëmëzo'·n** = pesëfisho'·n

pesëminut|ësh nm (Colloq) five-minute period of time

pesëqi'nd
I § num five hundred; number five hundred
II § nf the number five hundred

pesëqi'nd|të adj (i) five-hundredth

pesëqind|vjeto'r nm five-hundredth year anniversary; five-hundredth year anniversary celebration

pesërro'k|ësh
I § adj composed of five syllables: pentasyllabic
II § nm [Lit] pentasyllabic line

pe'së|sh adj 1 five-part; five-line 2 worth five 3 (Old) old Turkish coin worth five para

pe'së|she nf 1 group of five 2 (Colloq) five-lek bill

pesëshekull|o'r adj five centuries old; five centuries long; lasting five centuries

pesëto'n|ësh adj five-ton

pesëva'rg|ësh
I § adj five-line
II § nm five-line stanza

pesëvë'nd|ësh adj having room for five to sit: seating five

pesëvjeça'r
I § adj five-year-old; five years long; lasting five years
II § nm 1 five-year-old (child) 2 five-year period; five-year plan

pesim|i'st
I § n pessimist
II § adj pessimistic

pesim|i'zëm nm pessimism

pesme'rç nm son born after the death of his father

peso'r|ësh
I § adj lasting five hours: five-hour

II § *nm* five-hour workday

pe'stë
I § *adj (i), n (i)* fifth
II § *nf (e)* fifth grade (in elementary school); fifth grade class/classroom

pestíl
I § *nm* pulp of cooked plums that has been mashed and dried: plum paste
II § *adj (Fig)* flattened out; skinny
III § *adv* drenched to a pulp

pestílkë *nf* = **hosha'fkë**

pestro've *nf* [*Ichth*] trout

*****pesh** *nm* farthing, penny

peshë
I § *nf* 1 weight 2 load 3 *(Fig)* influence; importance 4 heavy stone (used for throwing)
II § *adv* (lifted) bodily
○ **peshë bruto** gross weight
○ **ësh·të pesha e dheut** to be the most important person: be the big shot/man, be the boss
○ **pesha flutur** *(Old)* [*Boxing*] flyweight
○ **peshë e gjallë** live weight (of an animal before slaughtering)
○ **pesha gjel** [*Weightlifting*] bantamweight
○ **pesha e këndesit** [*Sport*] bantamweight
○ **ësh·të peshë e madhe** to be a very influential person, have a lot of influence
○ **peshë neto** net weight
○ **peshë e rëndë** [*Sport*] heavyweight
○ **pesha specifike 1** [*Phys*] specific weight 2 *(Fig)* special importance/significance
○ **peshë e therur** slaughtered weight, weight of the carcass
○ **peshë e vdekur 1** dead weight 2 useless/worthless material

peshë'matje *nf* 1 checking and calibration of weight measures 2 *(Book)* measurement of weight

peshë'mbajtje *nf* load capacity, weight-carrying capacity

peshë'ngritje *nf* 1 *(Book)* weight capacity 2 [*Sport*] weight-lifting

peshi'm *nm ger* 1 < **pesho'·n** 2 *(Fig Colloq)* = **vëme'ndje**

peshi'mthi *adv* 1 (lifted) into the air, bodily 2 according to weight, by weight

peshi'n *adv (Old)* with money in hand: in cash

peshk *nm (np ~ q)* 1 [*Ichth*] fish 2 *(Colloq)* spinal column: spine, backbone
○ **peshk i artë** [*Ichth*] goldfish *Carassius auratus gibelio*
○ **peshk bari 1** [*Ichth*] axillary wrasse *Symphodus (Crenilabrus) mediterraneus* 2 rainbow wrasse = **buzoç bari**
○ **peshk bilbil** [*Ichth*] = **peshk-bilbi'l**
○ **peshk bishtvel** [*Ichth*] = **peshk-bishtve'l**
○ **peshk dac** [*Ichth*] black bullhead *Ictahurus melas*
○ **peshk dallëndyshe** [*Ichth*] flying gurnard, flying robin
○ **peshk elektrik** [*Ichth*] marbled electric ray *(Torpedo marmorata)*
○ **peshk flutur** "butterfly fish" [*Ichth*] *(Callionymus risso)*
○ **peshk fluturak** [*Ichth*] flying fish *Cheilopogon heterurus*
○ **peshk furtunali** [*Ichth*] butterfish *Stromateus fiatola*
○ **peshk gomari** [*Ichth*] southern barbel = **musta'k**

○ **peshk guri** [*Ichth*] 1 painted comber *Serranus scriba* = **deli'l** 2 blue-spotted sea bream *Pagrus coeruleostictus*
○ **peshk gjel** [*Ichth*] piper *Trigla lyra* = **gjel-dallëndy'she**
○ **peshk gjilpërë** [*Ichth*] syngnathoid fish, pipefish *Solenichthyes*
○ **peshk hënë** [*Ichth*] = **peshk-hë'në**
○ **peshk jevg** [*Ichth*] Albanian minnow = **mëru'në**
○ **peshk kavall** [*Ichth*] river lamprey *Lampetra fluviatilis*
○ **peshk krehër** [*Ichth*] = **peshk-kre'hër**
○ **peshk i kuq** [*Ichth*] goldfish *(Carassius auratus)*
○ **peshku i kurrizit** [*Anat*] spinal column
○ **peshk lakuriq** [*Ichth*] poor-cod *Trisopterus minutus capelanus*
○ **peshk lejlek** [*Ichth*] garfish *Belone belone gracilis*
○ **peshk lepur** [*Ichth*] mola *Ranzania laevis* = **hënëz vezake**
○ **Peshku i madh e ha të voglin.** "The big fish eats the little ones." *(Prov)* The big guy always wins against the little guy.
○ **peshk me ventuza** [*Ichth*] sharksucker *Echeneis naucrates*
○ **peshk i mermertë** [*Ichth*] = **peshk elektrik**
○ **Peshku në det, tigani në zjarr.** "The fish is in the sea, the frying pan on the fire." *(Prov)* There's many a slip 'twixt cup and lip.
○ **peshk pëllumb** [*Ichth*] smooth hound *Mustelus mustelus L*
○ **peshk përroi** [*Ichth*] *Paraphoxinus minutus Kar.* = **grunc**
○ **peshk pikalosh** [*Ichth*] spotted dragonet *Callionymus maculatus*
○ **peshk pilot** [*Ichth*] = **peshk-pilo't**
○ **ta pjek peshkun në buzë.** "{} cooks the fish in your mouth." {} will get your job done but you will suffer for it by having to keep after {}
○ **peshku qen** [*Ichth*] = **peshkaqe'n**
○ **peshk rrotullak** [*Ichth*] Atlantic bluefin tuna, tunny *Thunnus thynnus*
○ **peshk sqepalugë** [*Ichth*] Atlantic saury *Scomberesox saurus*
○ **peshk sqyt** [*Ichth*] perch
○ **peshk sqyt** [*Ichth*] perch *Perca fluviatilis*
○ **peshk shirit** [*Ichth*] ribbon fish *Trachipterus trachipterus*
○ **peshk shushunjë** [*Ichth*] sharksucker, suckfish *Remora brachyptera, Echeneis brachyptera*
○ **peshk trumpetë** [*Ichth*] boarfish *Capros aper*
○ **peshk turigjilpërë** [*Ichth*] white marlin *Tetrapturus albidus*
○ **peshk i thatë** dried and salted fish
○ **peshk therës** [*Ichth*] common weever, greater weever *Trachinus draco* = **dreqi i detit**
○ **peshk uji** [*Zool*] smooth newt *Triturus vulgaris*
○ **peshk i vnerit** [*Ichth*] lesser weever *Echiichthys vipera, Trachinus vipera*

peshka'gjel *nm* [*Ichth*] flying gurnard, flying robin *(Dactylopterus volitans)*

*****peshka'qej** *np* = **peshkaqe'n**

peshkaqe'n *nm* [*Ichth*] 1 great blue shark *(Prionace glauca)* 2 spiny dogfish *(Squalus acanthias)* 3 gray shark *(Galeorhinus galeus)* 4 [*Zool*] tadpole
○ **peshkaqen blu** [*Ichth*] blacktip reef shark *Carcharhinus melanopterus*

◦ **peshkaqen dhëmbëgjarpër** [*Ichth*] **1** small-tooth sand tiger shark *Odontaspis ferox* **2** sharpnose seven-gill shark *Heptranchias perlo*

◦ **peshkaqen i egër** [*Ichth*] sharpnose seven-gill shark *Heptranchias perlo*

◦ **peshkaqen gjembak** [*Ichth*] kitefin shark *Dalatias licha*

◦ **peshkaqen i hirtë** [*Ichth*] sandbar shark *Carcharhinus plumbeus*

◦ **peshkaqen kokështypur** [*Ichth*] bluntnose six-gill shark *Hexanchus griseus*

◦ **peshkaqen lëkurashpër** [*Ichth*] porbeagle *Lamna nasus*

◦ **peshkaqen i madh** [*Ichth*] basking shark *Cetorhinus maximus*

◦ **peshkaqen njeringrënës** "man-eating shark" [*Ichth*] great white shark *Carcharodon carcharies*

◦ **peshkaqen rrashpë** [*Ichth*] = **peshkaqen gjembak**

◦ **peshkaqen turihollë** [*Ichth*] shortfin mako shark *Isurus oxyrinchus*

◦ **peshkaqen xhuxh** [*Ichth*] = **peshkaqen lëkurashpër**

◦ **peshkaqen i zi** [*Ichth*] velvet belly shark *Etmopterus spinax*

◦ **peshkaqen zumpara** [*Ichth*] gulper shark = **peshkaqen-zumpa·re**

peshka·qen-bisht·dhe·lpër *nf (np ˜ q)* [*Ichth*] = **peshk-dhe·lp**ër

peshka·qen-bu·a·ll *nm* [*Ichth*] sand tiger shark *Eugomphodus taurus*

peshka·qen-de·rr *nm* [*Ichth*] angular rough shark *Oxynotus centrina*

peshka·qen-zumpa·re *nf* [*Ichth*] gulper shark *Centrophorus granulosus*

peshka·r *nm* **1** [*Ornit*] crane **2** gull

peshka·ta·r *n* fisherman

peshka·ta·ri· *nf* fishing (as a profession, sport, industry, or technology)

peshka·to·re *nf* **1** fishing vessel, fishing boat **2** [*Tech*] long metal pole hooked at the end to retrieve broken pieces of oil-drilling pipe **3** fish hatchery; fishing area

peshk-bishtve·l *nm (np ˜ q)* [*Ichth*] scalloped ribbon fish *(Zu cristatus)*

peshk-çeka·n *nm (np ˜ q)* [*Ichth*] smooth hammerhead shark *(Sphyrna zygaena)*

peshk-çeki·ç *nm (np ˜ q)* [*Ichth*] hammerhead, hammerhead shark *(Sphyrna fudes)*

peshk-çibu·k *nm (np ˜ q)* [*Ichth*] stargazer *(Uranoscopus scaber)*

peshk-de·rr *nm (np ˜ q)* [*Ichth*] gray triggerfish *(Balistes carolinensis)*

peshk-dre·q *nm (np ˜ q)* [*Ichth*] velvet belly shark *(Etmopterus spinax)*

peshk-dhe·lpër *nf (np ˜ q)* [*Ichth*] thresher shark *(Alopias vulpinus)*

****peshk·e·q** *adj* frivolous

peshk·|**e·ta·r** *nm* [*Ornit*] kingfisher *(Alcedo atthis)*

peshk-fi·k *nm (np ˜ q)*

◦ **peshk-fik i bardhë** [*Ichth*] greater fork-beard *Phycis blennoides*

◦ **peshk-fik i zi** [*Ichth*] *Phycis phycis*

peshk-flu·tur *nf (np ˜ q)* [*Ichth*] sea butterfly *Callionymus risso*

peshk-flutur|**u·es** *nm (np ˜ q)* [*Ichth*] flying fish *Cheilopogon heterurus*

peshk-gështe·një *nf (np ˜ q)* [*Ichth*] damsel fish *Chromis chromis*

peshk-gjinka·llë *nf (np ˜ q)* [*Ichth*] dragonet *Callionymus lyra*

peshk-hardhu·cë *nf (np ˜ q)* [*Ichth*] Atlantic lizard-fish *Synodus saurus*

peshk-hënë *nf (np ˜ q)* [*Ichth*] moonfish *Mola mola*

peshk|**i·m** *nm ger* < **peshko·** • *n*

peshk-jataga·n *nm (np ˜ q)* [*Ichth*] silver scabbard fish *(Lepidopus caudatus)*

peshk-karabinie·r *nm (np ˜ q)* [*Ichth*] = **peshk-çeka·n**

peshk-kava·ll *nm (np ˜ q)* [*Ichth*] sea lamprey *(Petromyzon marinus L.P)*

peshk-kita·rë *nf (np ˜ q)* [*Ichth*] common guitarfish *Rhinobatos rhinobatos*

peshk-kova·ç *nm (np ˜ q)* [*Ichth*] John Dory *(Zeus faber)*

peshk-kre·hër *nm (np ˜ q)* [*Ichth*] cleaver wrasse *Xyrichthys novacula*

peshk-lara·skë *nf (np ˜ q)* [*Ichth*] spiny butterfly ray *Gymnura altavela*

peshk-lejle·k *nm (np ˜ q)* [*Ichth*] garfish *Belone belone*

peshk·ngrën|**ës** *adj* fish-eating

peshko· • *n vt* to fish

◦ **peshko·** • *n* **në ujë të turbullt / ujëra të turbullta** *(Pej)* to be fishing in troubled waters

peshko·p *nm* **1** [*Relig*] bishop **2** *(ColloqJocular)* person who studies all the time at the expense of normal social activities: bookworm

peshkop|**a·t**ë *nf* [*Relig*] bishopric; bishop's residence

peshk·o·r *adj* *(Book)* pertaining to fish or fishing

peshk·o·re *nf* **1** fishing area **2** fish nursery

peshk-pallu·a *nm (np ˜ q)* [*Ichth*] ornate wrasse *Thalassoma pavo*

peshk-papaga·ll *nm (np ˜ q)* [*Ichth*] parrot sea perch *Callanthias ruber*

peshk-pëllu·mb *nm (np ˜ q)* [*Ichth*] smooth hound *Mustelus mustelus*

peshk-pilo·t *nm (np ˜ q)* [*Ichth*] pilot fish *Naucrates ductor*

****peshk·qe·n** = **peshkaqe·n**

peshk·rri·t|**ës** *n* fish nurseryman

peshk·rrotull|**a·k** *nm* [*Ichth*] Atlantic bluefin tuna, tunny *Thunnus thynnus*

pe·shk-sha·rrë *nm (np ˜ q)* [*Ichth*] **1** sawfish *(Pristis pristis)* **2** smooth hammerhead shark *(Sphyrna zygaena)*

pe·shk-shigje·të *nm (np ˜ q)* [*Ichth*] **1** garfish *(Belone belone)* **2** smooth hammerhead shark *(Sphyrna zygaena)*

pe·shk-shiri·t *nm (np ˜ q)* [*Ichth*] **1** red bandfish *Cepola rubescens, Cepola macrophthalma* **2** ribbon fish, deal fish *Trachipterus trachypterus*

peshk·shi·t|**ës** *n* fishmonger

pe·shk-shpa·t *nm (np ˜ q)* [*Ichth*] **1** swordfish *(Xiphias gladius)* **2** silver scabbard fish *(Lepidopus caudatus)* **3** barracuda *(Sphyraena sphyraena)*

peshk-trumpe·të *nf (np ˜ q)* [*Ichth*] boarfish *Capros aper*

peshk-tullë *nf (np ~q)* [*Ichth*] four-spotted megrim *Lepidorhombus boscii*

peshkth *nm* **1** (*Dimin*) [*Ichth*] small fish **2** clothes moth

peshkues|e *nf* fishing vessel, fishing boat

peshkuj|ë *nf* fishing hole, fishing area; fishpond

peshkulliz|ë *nf* [*Bot*] European glorybind (*Convolvulus arvensis*)

peshkve *nf* pitch, tar; bitumen
∘ **peshkve minerale** crude oil

peshkvo·*n vt* to cover [] with tar

peshli *nf* **1** man's waistcoat worn with detached hanging sleeves **2** woman's waist-length tunic with long, wide sleeves **3** baby's long-sleeved flannel sweater

*peshme*ngë *nf* stoup/basin for holy water

pesho·*n*
I § *vt* **1** to ascertain the weight of []: weigh **2** (*Fig*) to weigh [a matter] carefully: consider [] with care **3** (*Fig*) to value, appreciate
II § *vi* **1** to be of a certain weight: weigh **2** to be heavy [] (*Fig*) to be of some importance, have some influence
∘ **i pesho**·*n* **arrat pa i shkundur** "weigh the walnuts without shelling them" to talk without thinking; be hasty, make a hasty decision
∘ **pesho**·*n*[3rd] **mbi** [] (of a burden) to fall upon []
∘ **Peshoje shtypkën mirë!** Check that angle (between two walls using a plumb line) well!

peshoj|ë *nf* = **pesho**re

peshor *adj* (*Book*) pertaining to weight, in terms of weight

peshore *nf* **1** device for determining weight: balance, scale **2** the constellation or zodiac sign Libra

peshpr = pëshpër

peshq *np* < **peshk**

peshqesh *nm* (*Colloq*) gift, present

peshqir *nm* **1** towel **2** [*Anat*] suet **3** (*Reg*) square apron worn by women **4** (*Reg*) tablecloth; napkin

peshta|f *nm* small decorated box for jewelry or cosmetics

peshtamall *nm* **1** large tablecloth **2** large shawl worn by women **3** long woven decorated apron **4** white cloth placed around the neck of a person getting a shave or haircut

peshu|ar *adj* (*i*) **1** weighed **2** (*Fig*) arrived at after due thought: well-considered, proper **3** (*Fig*) thoughtful, sober, deliberate

peshu|es *nm* person engaged to weigh objects or people: weigher, weighman

pet *nm* stairstep

peta|k *adj* having a thin slab-like shape, plate-like

peta|l *nm* [*Bot*] petal

petani|k *nm* **1** [*Food*] pasty made with flat layers of dough alternating with fillers such as meat, rice, or beans; multi-layered pastry **2** pasty made by adding successively baked and buttered layers

petano|r *nm* **1** steep mountain slope descending in a series of small plateaus **2** stratified seacoast cliff

petari|shte *np fem* leaves of pastry dried for winter storage

petas *OR* **pet**ash *adv*

petashu|q *adj* = **pet**ak

petato|r *adj* wrinkled, wrinkled in the face

petav|ër *nf* [*Constr*] roof sheathing; roof lath; roof shingle

petaxhi *nm (pl ~nj)* puff pastry maker

petë
I § *nf* **1** rolled-out dough, flat/thin layer of dough; layer of pastry crust **2** (*Colloq*) dish prepared with thin layers of dough: pasty **3** pasta **4** thin layer: sheet, stratum **5** thin object (in vertical dimension): slab, flat stone, piece of tile/slate **6** (*Colloq*) [*Dairy*] layer of cream on milk
II § *adj* small in vertical dimension: flat

petë|l *nf* **1** [*Bot*] petal **2** flat stone

petë-**pe**të
I § *adv* in thin layers
II § *adj* layered

petë|s *nm* **1** long rolling pin (for rolling out dough) **2** [*Anat*] = **fle**tës

petë|shore *nf* decorated flat unleavened biscuit baked on the stove

petë|z *nf dimin* = **pe**të **1** very thin surface layer or piece of that layer: flake, scale, film, squama **2** [*Bot*] petal **3** thin piece of cherry bark used as a plectrum for the buzuk

petë|zak *adj* thin and flat

petë|zim *nm ger* **1** [*Tech*] < **petëzo**·*n*, **petëzo**·*het* **2** lamination

petë|zo·*het vpr* [*Tech*] to become laminated/rolled out

petë|zo·*n vt* to press/roll [] into flat sheets: laminate, roll [] out

petë|zu|es *nm* laminator

petë|zue|shëm *adj* (*i*) [*Tech*] capable of being pressed/rolled into sheets

*petic*ë *nf* five-shot repeating rifle

peticio|n *nm* (*Book*) petition

petiskë *nf* thin layer

petk *nm* **1** outer garment **2** set of outer garments: suit **3** (*Fig*) cloak; guise **4** (*Reg Arb*) property

petka *np* < **petk** underclothes; linens; clothes

petkala|rëse *nf* washing machine (for clothes)

petkash *adv* = **petash**

petki|cë *nf dimin* < **petk** (*Reg*) small-sized garment

peto·*het vpr* to become thin and drawn

peto·*n vt* to roll out [dough] into a sheet, make [] into a flat leaf

peto|r *nm* pasty filled with dried and crumbled pastry leaves

petra = petarishte

petrahi|l *nm* [*Relig*] knee-length gilt-embroidered stole worn by orthodox priests on important occasions: pallium

*petrel *nm* [*Ornit*] storm petrel (*Hydrobates pelagicus*)

petrifikim *nm ger* **1** < **petrifiko**·*het* **2** petrification

petrifiko·*het vpr* to become stone: petrify

petrik *nm* [*Bot*] birthwort (*Aristolochia*)

petrikore *np* [*Bot*] birthwort family *Aristolochiaceae*

petrit
I § *nm* [*Ornit*] peregrine falcon (*Falco peregrinus*)
II § *adj, nm* (*Fig*) brave, strong, agile, and daring (man)

Petrit *nm* Petrit (male name)

petrografi *nf* [*Geol*] petrography

petrokimi *nf* [*Chem*] petrochemistry

petro|kim|ik *adj* [*Chem*] petrochemical

petroleum *nm* petroleum
○ **petroleum i njomë** crude oil

__petrosel__ *nf* [*Bot*] parsley (*Petroselinum*) = **maj-danoz**

Petrush *nm* Petrush (male name)

pe'tull *nf* pancake, crepe
● **Nuk hahen ato petulla që t'i jep/sjell shig-jetulla.** "Those pancakes that the poisonous snake gives/brings to you are not to be eaten." (*Prov*) Beware of Greeks bearing gifts.

petull|ak *adj* like a pancake: round and flat

petull|icë
I § *nf* **1** pancake pan **2** flat cornbread
II § *adj* = **petullak**

petull|o·het *vpr* = **përdridhe·t**

petull|o·n *vt* to make [] into pancake form

petull|or *adj* round and flat; round and puffed up

peth *nm* **1** [*Anat*] membranous fold that attaches the underside of the tongue to the jaw: frenum **2** tendon, sinew

pezaul *nm* small hand-held fishing net

Pezë *nf* town southwest of Tirana

pe'zëm *nm* **1** inflammation (of a wound) **2** (*Fig*) soreness, irritation; outrage, grudge

__pezmatar__ *adj* harsh, rude

pezmat|i *nf* inflammation; irritation; affliction, sorrow

pezmat|im *nm ger* **1** <**pezmato·n, pezmato·het** **2** inflammation; irritation; affliction, sorrow

pezmat|o·het *vpr* **1** to become inflamed; become irritated/sore **2** (*Fig*) to be deeply annoyed by a wrong, be bitterly angry: be incensed; take offense **3** to become deeply disappointed

pezmat|o·n *vt* **1** to inflame [a wound]; irritate, make [] sore **2** to drive [] to anger: irk, outrage, offend **3** to afflict [] with disappointment

pezmat|uar *adj* (*i*) **1** inflamed; irritated, sore **2** (*Fig*) deeply annoyed by a wrong: outraged; bitterly angry: incensed

__pezmatues__ *adj* inflammatory

pezmat|ue|shëm *adj* (*i*) **1** touchy, sensitive **2** ready to take offense: irritable *__3__* irritating, annoying

pezmat|ue|shm|ëri *nf* irritability, irascibility, thin skin

pezul *nm* **1** (*Colloq*) windowsill **2** bench outside the door to a house **3** upper side of a wall **4** fireplace mantle **5** embankment to prevent overflow of water: levee **6** (*Old*) mound of earth serving to mark land boundaries **7** pile, heap

pe'zull *adv* **1** suspended in the air **2** (*Fig*) up in the air, in abeyance, hanging in air, undecided **3** (*Fig*) dangling

pezull|im *nm ger* **1** <**pezullo·n, pezullo·het** **2** suspense; suspension

pezull|o·het *vpr* to be held in abeyance: be suspended temporarily

pezull|o·n *vt* to suspend [] temporarily; hold [] in abeyance

pezull|uar *adj* (*i*) held in abeyance; temporarily suspended

__pezh__ = **peshë**

pe'zhgve *nf* [*Min*] pitch = **pisë**

pezhishkë *nf* (*Reg*) **1** spiderweb; cobweb **2** (*Fig*) net; snare **3** hazy screen

__pë(r)__ *nm* (*np* ~ *nj*) = **pe'(r)**

__pëdhe'te__ *nf* apron

__pëgâm__ *adj* (*i*) (*Reg Gheg*) = **pëgërë**

pëgë·het *vpr* to soil oneself, get filthy/dirty

pëgë·n *vt* to make [] filthy/dirty: soil

pëgërë
I § *adj* (*i*) soiled, filthy
II § *nf* (*e*), *nn* (*të*) (*Euph*) (baby's) excrement
III § *nf* = **pëgërësi**

__pëgërës__ *adj* stinking, foul

pëgërësi *nf* stinking filth

pëgërje *nf ger* <**pëgë·n, pëgë·het**

pëgërtë *adj* (*i*) soiled, filthy; sordid; indecent, obscene

__pëhar__ = **pehar**

__pëlandër__ *nf lye* = **pullandër**

pëlca's *stem for 1st sg pres, 1st & 3rd pl pres, 2nd & 3rd sg subj* <**pëlcet·**

pëlce't·
I § *vi, vt* **1** to explode; burst; burst out **2** to crack
II § *vt* (*Colloq*) to throw [] with force: slam, bang
○ **nuk <> pëlcet·**^{3sg} **barku për** [] (*Scorn*) <> doesn't give a damn about [], <> doesn't lose any sleep over []
○ **pëlcet· edhe gurin** to be exasperatingly lazy/disobedient
○ **<> pëlcet·**^{3pl} **faqet** "<>'s cheeks *are bursting*" <> *is fat*

pëlcis *stem for 2nd pl pres, pind* <**pëlcet·**

pëlcit *stem for pdef, opt, adm, part, pind, 2nd pl pres, imper, vp* <**pëlcet·**

pëlcit|ës *adj* explosive, bursting

pëlcit|je *nf ger* **1** <**pëlcet·** **2** explosion

__pëlcisë__ *nf* [*Ichth*] anchovy, pilchard

pëlhur|end|ës *n* textile worker

pëlhur|end|ese *nf* weaving machine; weaver

pëlhu're *nf* **1** woven cloth, textile, fabric **2** sail of a ship **3** spiderweb **4** (*Fig*) screen **5** [*Folklore*] ghostly white figure that appears to night travelers blocking their path
○ **pëlhura e bardhë** (movie/cinema) screen
○ **pëlhura e merimangës** spiderweb; cobweb
○ **pëlhura e Penelopës** (*Book*) work that seems never to end: the web of Penelope

__pëlhu'rëra__ *np* <**pëlhu're** *__textiles__*

__pëlhur|ëtar__ *n* textile worker; weaver

pëlhur|ëz *nf* afterbirth

__pëlhur|të__ *adj* (*i*) of cloth, textile

pëlqe·het *vp recip* to like one another

pëlqe·n *vt* **1** to like [] **2** to please <>; be pleasing to <>, be enjoyable for <>; be approved by <> **3** to inspire love in <>
○ **<> pëlqe·n**^{3sg} **mendja (e** {*pronominal adj*}**)** **1** = *is too pleased with* <>*self* **2** = *does just as* <> *likes* (without proper concern for other's views)

__pëlqe'r__ *nm* **1** thumb **2** quantity that can be held between the thumb and an opposed finger: pinch

pëlqim *nm ger* **1** <**pëlqe·n, pëlqe·het** **2** approval

Pëlqim *nm* Pëlqim (male name)

pëlqyer *nm* = **pëlqer**

pëlqyer *adj* (*i*) **1** approved **2** pleasant

pëlqye|shëm *adj* (*i*) pleasing, pleasant; proper, satisfactory

__pëls__ = **pëlc**

*pëltu'c· *vt* to exert pressure on [ ]: press, squeeze

pë'lyr· *vt* **1** to make [ ] grimy by handling, soil [ ] slightly **2** to bloody *3 to veil

pë'lyr·et *vpr* **1** to get grimy from use, get slightly dirty **2** to get bloodied

pë'lyr·ur *adj (i)* **1** somewhat grimy from use **2** bloody, bloodied

pë'lla's *stem for 1st sg pres, 1st & 3rd pl pres, 2nd & 3rd sg subj* <pëllet·

*pë'llc = pëlc

pë'lle' *nf [Dairy]* ewe or nanny goat with milk in her udders (having recently given birth): fresh ewe/nanny

pë'lle'shëm *adj (i)* fertile; productive

pë'llet· *vt* **1** to moo; bray, bellow **2** *(Fig Crude Mocking Pej)* to bellow (in an offensively loud voice)

pë'llëmbë *nf* **1** palm (part of the hand) **2** slap **3** measure equalling the size of a palm: span, six inches **4** *(Fig)* small amount/number: handful **5** *(Fig)* small plot of land; small/crowded space; small amount of time
∘ pëllëmbë e flori very fertile soil; land rich in mineral wealth
∘ një/dy pëllëmbë njeri little guy

pë'llë'mbëz *nf [Ichth] (Brama brama)*
∘ pëllëmbëz buzoçe *[Ichth]* black sea bream *Spondyliosoma cantharus*
∘ pëllëmbëz deti *[Ichth]* = pëllë'mbëz
∘ pëllëmbëz me yllëza *[Ichth]* starry smoothhound *Mustellus asterias*

pë'llëmbgje'rë *adj* having big hands

pë'llëmbo'r *adj* **1** *[Bot]* palm-shaped: palmate **2** *[Med]* palmar

pë'llëng
I § nm **1** stagnant pond **2** wash pit, washtub
II § adj thoroughly wet: soaked

pë'lli'm *nm ger* = pëlli'tje

pë'lli's *stem for 2nd pl pres, pind* <pëllet·

pë'lli't *stem for pdef, opt, adm, part, pind, 2nd pl pres, imper, vp* <pëllet·

pë'lli'tje *nf ger* **1** <pëllet· *(Fig Colloq)* **2** offensive bellowing

*pë'llo'r *adj* fertile

*pë'llo're *nf* = pë'lle

pë'lltu'm *onomat* sound of something suddenly hitting the water: plop

pë'llu'a *adv (Colloq)* **1** without a scratch, unharmed **2** *(Fig)* lucky

pë'llu'mb *nm* **1** *[Ornit]* pigeon, dove *(Columbidae)* **2** *(Fig Pet)* term of endearment for a child
∘ pëllumbi borizan *[Ornit]* collared dove *Streptopelia decaocto*
∘ pëllumbi i egër i shkëmbit *[Ornit]* rock dove, feral pigeon *Columba livia*
∘ pëllumb i egër *[Ornit]* stock dove *(Columba oenas L.)*
∘ pëllumb guaku/gugashi *[Ornit]* woodpigeon *(Columba palumbus L.)* = guak
∘ pëllumb me yllëza *[Ichth]* starry smoothhound shark *Mustelus asteria*
∘ pëllumb poste carrier pigeon
∘ pëllumb pylli stock dove *(Columba oenas)*
∘ pëllumb shkëmbi *[Ornit]* wild pigeon, rock pigeon, rock dove *Columba livia Gm* = goge'sh

Pë'llumbe'sh|a *nf* Pëllumbesha (female name)

pë'llumbe'shë *nf* <pë'llumb hen pigeon

*pë'nda'r
I § nm = penda'r
II § adj *of the pen, written

*pë'ndë = pe'ndë

*pë'ndë'plu'mp *nm* lead pencil

pe'ni'k *nm [Bot]* = peni'k

*pë'nj *(Reg Tosk)* = pe'nj

pë'qi'(r) *nm (np ~ nj)* **1** hem of a garment **2** lap (formed by sitting down) **3** *(Fig)* protected nook, bosom
∘ Në bark mba-*n*^opt e në pëqi mos ka-^opt! "May {} carry in {}'s belly and not have in {}'s lap!" *(Curse)* May {}'s children die stillborn!

*pë'qi'rë *nf (Old)* breastplate

pë'qi'së *nf (Reg)* kiln-dried brick

pë'r
I § prep (acc) **1** for **2** in regard to, about; as for; as **3** per **4** pro (vs. con), in favor **5** through; throughout; (swear) by
II § prep (abl) by means/way of: by, through
III § formative prefix trans-, thorough-
IV § pcl (semantically empty element preceding an adverbial expression that begins with së) për së gjati lengthwise
∘ {*countable noun*} për {*same noun*} {} by {}, every single {}, every {}
∘ ësh·të për t'<> pirë dollinë <> is worthy of a toast
∘ ësh·të për t'i hedhur telat "be ready for adorning <> with the bridal wires" to be pretty as a new bride
∘ ësh·të për t'ia gërryer trutë me kazmë "be fit for scooping out one's brains with a pickaxe" to be brainless, be very stupid
∘ ësh·të për t'u lidhur në grazhd "is fit to be kept in a stable" to be thickheaded/stupid
∘ ësh·të për t'u përplasur në mur//pas murit "be fit to smash against the wall" to be absolutely worthless
∘ ësh·të për t'ua hedhur qenve (of food) to be only good for dog food
∘ ësh·të për ta humbur/zhdukur me gur në ujë "{} should disappear like a rock in water" {} is unspeakable and should never be mentioned again
∘ ësh·të për ta ngjitur pas muri "be fit for pasting to the wall" to be sickly and scrawny, be all skin and bones
∘ ësh·të për të rrahur murin me [ ] "be fit for beating the wall with [ ]" *(Impol)* [ ] *is* completely worthless/useless
∘ ësh·të për të {} to be ready to be {*past participle*}, be fit/suitable for {*present participle*} jam për të ngrënë I'm ready to eat, I am about to eat ishte për t'u ngrënë it was fit for eating, it was ready to be eaten
∘ ësh·të për [ ] to be suitable for [ ]
∘ ësh·të^3rd për të lëpirë me gjuhë to be clean enough to eat off of
∘ ësh·të^3sg për t'i rrëmbyer/prerë kokën "<>'s head*is* fit for snatching" *is* very beautiful, *couldn't be* more beautiful
∘ (gjysmë) për gjysmë **1** in halves **2** in two equal parts; fifty-fifty
∘ Për nder - armë! *[Mil]* (command given to hold guns upright and to one side as an expression of honor) Present - arms!

për *formative prefix* trans-, thorough-

*pë'ra'fëri'sht = përa'fërsi'sht

pë'ra'fë'rm *adj (i)* = përa'fërt

përafë**rsi** *nf,* approximation

përafë**rsi'sht** *adv* approximately, more or less; roughly speaking

përafë**rt** *adj (i)* **1** approximate **2** similar

përafri' *nf* = përafërsi'

përafri'm *nm ger* **1** <përafro'•n [*Math Optics*] **2** approximation

përafro'•n *vt* to move/bring [] closer

*****përaft**o'•n** *vi* to last, continue

përa'llë *nf* = përra'llë

*****përa'n-***et* *vpr* to deviate, swerve

përandi't- *vt* **1** to scatter [], disperse []; shoo [] away **2** to transplant; thin out [plants] **3** *(Fig)* to estrange **4** *(Fig)* to distract [] from work **5** *(Fig)* to cause [] to waver/hesitate; cause [] to give way

përandi't-*et* *vpr* **1** to scatter in fear, disperse **2** to become estranged, drift apart **3** to have inhibitions, be unsure of oneself, hold back, hesitate; give way

  ○ **s'<> përandi't-***et*^{3sg} **syri** <> *has no fear:* <> *doesn't bat an eye*

*****përa'n**ës

  I § *adj (Old)* supporting, partisan

  II § *n* supporter, partisan

përa'nshëm *adj (i)* **1** by the side: alongside **2** indirect; devious, evasive

*****përarëndi'm** *nm* [*Agr*] crop rotation

përarëndi's *stem for 1st sg pres, pl pres, 2nd & 3rd sg subj, pind* <përarëndi't•

përarëndi't- *vt* = përandi't•

përavull-*et* *vpr* to get warm (from a nearby heat source)

përavullo'•het *vpr* to turn to steam; evaporate

*****përba'lc** *nm* **1** = pehliva'n **2** fop, dandy

përba'lcë *nf* wrestling (match)

përba'lt- *vt* to soil with mud; make muddy

përba'lt-*et* *vpr* to get muddy

përba'ltës *n (Old)* winner, victor

përba'ltësh *nm* person who is always soiled with mud

përba'll- *vt* = përballo'•n

përba'llë

  I § *adv* face-to-face, directly opposite

  II § *prep (abl)* facing, across from; in confrontation with, confronting

*****përba'll**ës

  I § *adj* opposing

  II § *n* opponent

përballi'm *nm ger* **1** <përballo'•n, përballo'•het **2** direct comparison; confrontation

*****përba'llje** *nf ger* = përballi'm

përballo'•het *vpr* to face up

  ○ **përballo'•het me** [] to be confronted with []

përballo'•n *vt* **1** to confront, face [] squarely; stand up to [], defy; oppose; face down [], withstand **2** to face successfully, deal with [] successfully; overcome

përballu'eshëm *adj (i)* capable of being faced successfully, that can be dealt with

*****përbâm**ë *adj (i) (Reg Gheg)* = përbërë

përba'rkje *np* innards of small livestock

*****përba'rs** *stem for 1st sg pres, pl pres, 2nd & 3rd sg subj, pind* <përba'rt•

*****përba'rt-** *vt* to transport, transfer, conduct

*****përba'rt**ës *n* conductor (of electricity)

*****përba'rtje** *nf ger* **1** <përba'rt• **2** transportation, transfer

*****përbâs** *(Reg Gheg)* = përbë'rës

përba'shkët *adj (i)* **1** communal, common; in common **2** mutual; shared **3** done together: joint

përbashku'a'r *adj (i)* united

*****përbe'** *nf* **1** oath **2** incantation, spell

përbe'•het *vpr* **1** to make a vow to <>; swear an oath, swear **2** to threaten <>

përbe'•n *vt* **1** to beseech [] with an invocation of something sacred **2** to make [] swear an oath, put [] under oath

përbeti'm *nm ger* **1** <përbeto'•n, përbeto'•het **2** vow, oath **3** secret conspiracy bound by vows

përbeto'•het *vpr* **1** to take an oath, make a pledge, swear; swear allegiance **2** to threaten <>

përbeto'•n *vt* **1** to beseech [] with an invocation of something sacred **2** *(Old)* to mutter an oath to drive off [an evil spirit]

përbetu'a'r

  I § *adj (i)* committed; unrelenting, inexorable

  II § *nm (i)* conspirator

përbë'•het *vpr* to be constituted: consist

përbë'•n *vt* to constitute, make up [], form

përbë'rë *adj (i)* composed of more than one part: compound; composite

përbë'rës *adj, nm* constituent, component

përbë'rje *nf* composition, make-up

*****përbi'nd**ës *adj (Old)* surprising

përbi'ndësh *nm* imaginary monster

përbi'ndshëm *adj (i)* monstrous

përbinjo're *nf* ewe or nanny goat giving birth for the second time

përbi'r- *vt* = përbiro'•n

përbiro'•het *vpr* to get through a difficult place: thread one's way through

përbiro'•n

  I § *vt* to put [] through a hole

  II § *vi* **1** to open a path through difficult terrain **2** *(Fig)* to break new ground, make a breakthrough

përbi'sht- *vt* to cause [] to turn tail, put [] to flight, rout; disperse [a crowd]

përbi'sht-*et* *vpr* to turn tail and scatter away, scatter away

*****përble's**ë *nf* small amount of grain; just enough flour to make one loaf

përblu'a-n *vt* **1** to turn [] over in one's mind; consider [] carefully; plan out [] **2** to digest **3** *(Fig)* to plot, scheme

përbo'ç *nm (Colloq)* **1** large clod of mud/earth; large rock used as a hunting weapon **2** big firelog

përbo'r- *vt* to heap snow on [], throw snow at []

përbo'rme *adj (i)* snow-covered, snow-filled: snowy

*****përbot**ë'si *nf* universality

përbo'tshëm *adj (i)* **1** throughout the entire world: worldwide, universal **2** *(Old)* public

përbre'nda

  I § *adv* inside; internally

  II § *prep (abl)* within; inside

përbre'ndë'sa *np fem* innards of a freshly killed animal/human: pluck, guts

përbre'ndë'se *np fem* = përbre'ndshme

përbre'ndë'so'r *adj* [*Med*] visceral

pёr|bre'nd|shёm *adj (i)* internal, interior

pёr|bre'nd|shm|e *np* internal organs: innards

pёr|bri'
  I § *adv* alongside, adjacent
  II § *prep (abl)* beside

pёr|bri'j|ёse *nf* sidebeam of the rackwagon bed to which the railings are fixed

*pёr|bri'j|ёt *adj (i)* = pёrbri'jshёm

pёr|bri'j|shёm *adj (i)* adjacent; adjoining

*pёr|bri'nj|ёt *adj (i)* = pёrbri'jshёm

*pёr|bri's|a *np fem* the two side beams at the bottom of a cart

*pёr|bry'll·et *vpr* to rest on one's elbows, lean on an elbow

pёr|bu'·n
  I § *vt* **1** to provide overnight lodgings to [ ]: lodge [ ] overnight **2** to stay up with [ ] all night
  II § *vi* to spend the night, stay overnight

pёr|bu'j|tё *adj (i)* left standing overnight: stale

pёr|bu'j|t|ёs *n* **1** host who provides overnight lodgings **2** [*Biol*] host (of a parasite)

pёr|bu'j|tje *nf ger* < pёrbu'·n

pёr|bu'j|tur *adj (i)* **1** provided with overnight lodgings: quartered, having living quarters **2** left standing for a period of time, allowed to settle; stagnant; stale

*pёr|bule·n *vt* to transmit [a contagious disease]

pёr|bu'z· *vt* **1** to sneer/scoff at [ ], laugh off [ ], ignore **2** to find [ ] contemptible: despise **3** to treat [ ] with contempt, reject [ ] contemptuously: scorn **4** to look down on [ ]

*pёr|bu'z|ё *adv* to the very brim, to the brink

pёr|bu'z|ёs
  I § *adj* **1** contemptuous, scornful, derisive **2** [*Ling*] derogatory
  II § *n* *scoffer, scorner

pёr|bu'z|je *nf ger* **1** < pёrbu'z· **2** scorn, contempt

pёr|bu'z|shёm *adj (i)* despicable, contemptible

*pёr|bu'z|ta'r *n* mocker, jeerer

pёr|bu'z|ur *adj (i)* **1** despised **2** hated, despised; hateful

pёr|by'k· *vt* **1** to winnow [grain] **2** *(Fig Pej)* to remove [someone] from his environment

pёr|by'th· *vt (Colloq)* to maltreat, abuse

pёr|by'th·et *vpr (Colloq)* to squeeze up close, sit very close

*pёr|cakt|i' *nf* precision, accuracy, exactitude

pёr|cakt|i'm *nm ger* **1** < pёrcakto'·n, pёrcakto'·het **2** specification, determination **3** definition

pёr|cakt|o'·n *vt* **1** to specify; determine, fix, decide, set **2** [*Ling*] to modify, determine

pёr|cakt|o'r
  I § *adj* [*Ling*] modifying, determinative
  II § *nm* **1** [*Ling*] attribute **2** [*Math*] determinant

pёr|cakt|u'a'r *adj (i)* **1** determined, fixed; delimited, defined **2** predetermined, specified **3** [*Ling*] determined

pёr|cakt|u'e's *adj* **1** determining **2** [*Ling*] modifying, determining

pёr|cakt|u'e|shёm *adj (i)* determinable

pёr|cakt|u'e|shm|ёri *nf* determinability

pёr|ce' *nf* [*Bot*] butcher's broom (whose small myrtlelike leaves crackle when burned) *(Ruscus aculeatus)*

*pёr|ce'l = bёrce'l

*pёr|ce'n|ёs
  I § *adj* irritable, testy

  II § *nm* irritant

*pёr|ce'p|ёt *adj (i) (Old)* diagonal

pёr|cё'll|a'k
  I § *nm* **1** short-lasting burst of flame **2** cracker toasted over hot ashes **3** *(Fig)* person who is and thin and pale as ashes **4** [*Bot*] butcher's broom *(Ruscus aculeatus)*
  II § *adj* **1** ashen-faced **2** smarting, stinging

pёr|cё'll|i'·n *vt, vi* = pёrcё'llo'·n

pёr|cё'll|i'm *nm ger* < pёrcё'llo'·n, pёrcё'llo'·het

pёr|cё'll|i'm|ё *nf* **1** forest fire; fire with intense flames: blazing fire **2** forest showing scars of fire; burned-off meadow **3** heat given off by flames: scorching heat

pёr|cё'll|i'n|ё *nf* parched land

pёr|cё'll|i's *stem for 1st sg pres, pl pres, 2nd & 3rd sg subj, pind* < pёrcё'lli't·

pёr|cё'll|i't· *vt* = pёrcё'llo'·n

pёr|cё'llo'·het *vpr* **1** to get slightly burned: get singed; get lightly charred **2** to be consumed by fire, burn to a crisp

pёr|cё'llo'·n
  I § *vt, vi* **1** to scorch, singe; roast, toast; scald; parch **2** to cause [ ] to smart
  II § *vt* **1** to consume [ ] by flame: burn [ ] up **2** *(Fig)* to burn; inflame
  III § *vi* **1** to become parched **2** *(Fig)* to be consumed by flame **3** to smart, sting

pёr|cё'll|u'a'r *adj (i)* toasted, broiled; singed; scalded; parched

pёr|ci'll·et *vpr* < pёrcje'll· to make swallowing motions: swallow

pёr|ci'll *stem for 2nd pl pres, pind, imper, vp* < pёrcje'll·

*pёr|ci'p|e *adv* = pёrci'ptas

*pёr|ci'p|je *nf (Old)* surface

pёr|ci'p|tas *OR* pёr|ci'p|t|azi *adv* superficially

pёr|ci'p|tё *adj (i)* superficial

pёr|cje'll· *vt* **1** to swallow [ ] **2** to accompany, go along with [ ] **3** to see [a traveler] off **4** to conduct [ ] (somewhere); conduct [energy] **5** *(Colloq)* to put [ ] off (using some pretext)
  ∘ [ ] **pёrcje'll· me fjalё tё mira** to put [ ] off with fine words (and empty promises)
  ∘ [ ] **pёrcje'll· me njё grusht miza/pleshta** "put [ ] off with a handful of flies/fleas" to put [ ] off with empty promises

pёr|cje'll|ё *nf collec* entourage, attendants

pёr|cje'll|ёs
  I § *n* **1** conductor (of energy); carrier (of an idea/ document) **2** person who sees another off; escort, guide **3** [*Ethnog*] member of the party conducting the bride to the groom's house
  II § *adj* **1** accompanying; escorting **2** conductive

pёr|cje'll|ёsi *nf* [*Electr*] conductivity

pёr|cje'll|je *nf ger* **1** < pёrcje'll·, pёrcje'll·et **2** sendoff **3** = pёrcje'llё

pёr|cje'll|o're *nf* [*Ling*] construction consisting of duke + participle and indicating an attendant action or state

pёr|cje'll|shm|ёri *nf* [*Phys Electr*] conductivity

pёr|co'll *stem for pdef* < pёrcje'll·

*pёr|cuk|a'r *n (Old)* wigmaker

*pёr|cu'k|ё *nf (Old)* wig = paru'kё

përç
I § nm **1** uncastrated billy goat **2** odor given off by an uncastrated billy goat
II § adj pigheaded

përça·*het vpr* to be split by dissension; split apart, split up

përça·*n vt* **1** to cut [] apart; split, divide [] in two **2** to split [] apart, cause dissension in [] **3** to cut across [], cross

përçak *nm* uncastrated male goat used as stud

përçap· *vt* to chew on [], chew
∘ **i përçap· fjalët 1** to consider one's words carefully, think before speaking **2** to deny having said what one has said **3** to mumble: swallow one's words

përçap·*et vpr* **1** to make chewing motions: chew **2** *(Fig Pej)* to indicate displeasure by making slow circular motions of the jaw **3** *(Fig)* to exert effort

përçapje *nf ger* **1** <**përçap**·, **përçap**·*et* **2** endeavor

përçarë *adj (i)* split by dissension

përçarë**s**
I § adj causing dissension
II § nm cause of dissension

përçarje *nf ger* **1** <**përça**·*n*, **përça**·*het* **2** rift, dissension

përçart
I § adv in a delirious state: deliriously, raving
II § nm = **kllapí**

përçartje *nf* **1** delirium **2** raving

*****përças** *stem for 1st sg pres, 1st & 3rd pl pres, 2nd & 3rd sg subj* <**përçet**·

përçes *nm* = **përçor**

*****përçet**· *vt* = **përçít**·

*****përçík** *nm* **1** = **bërçík** *****2** speck

përçím *nm ger* **1** <**përço**·*n* **2** conduction

përçín = **perçín**

përçís *stem for 1st sg pres, pl pres, 2nd & 3rd sg subj, pind* <**përçít**·

përçit· *vt* (of a billy goat) mount and impregnate [a goat]

përçit·*et vpr* **1** (of a nanny goat) to get pregnant; rut *****2** *(Fig Colloq)* to screw up

përçitë**s** *nm* uncastrated male goat permitted to breed

përçitje *nf ger* <**përçit**·, **përçit**·*et*

*****përçkëmbes**ë *nf (Old)* alternation

përçllan *nm [Bot]* = **urth**

përçmím *nm ger* **1** <**përçmo**·*n* **2** contempt

përçmo·*n vt* **1** to have a low opinion of [], have contempt for []: disdain, despise, scorn **2** to show disrespect for []: scoff at [] *(Colloq)* to make [] ugly, disfigure

përçmuar *adj (i)* **1** disdained, despised; despicable **2** *(Colloq)* made ugly

përçmues *adj* contemptuous, scornful, disdainful

përçmueshëm *adj (i)* contemptible, despicable

përço·*n vt* **1** to guide, lead, pilot **2** to conduct [energy] **3** to carry [an idea/document], be the messenger/bearer of []

përçollak *nm [Invert]* scorpion

përçor *nm* male sheep/goat that leads a flock: bellwether

*****përçud**ë**s** *n* conjurer

*****përçudní** *nf* horror

përçudním *nm ger* **1** <**përçudno**·*n*, **përçudno**·*het* **2** disfigurement; ugliness

përçudno·*het vpr* **1** to become ugly/disfigured **2** *(Fig)* to become perverted

përçudno·*n vt* **1** to make [] ugly, disfigure **2** *(Fig)* to pervert

përçudshëm *adj (i)* monstrous, deformed; cruel, savage

përçues
I § adj **1** conductive **2** *[Anat]* afferent
II § n **1** leader, guide; driver (of a vehicle), pilot **2** bearer (of an idea/document)
III § nm [Phys Electr] conductor (of energy)

përçuesí = **përçueshm**ërí

përçueshmërí *nf [Phys Electr]* conductivity

*****përçuk** *nm* forelock

përda·*n* = **përnda**·*n*

përdaf *nm* **1** plasterer's float **2** marble form used by a felt cap maker to mold wool into the proper shape **3** *(Fig Pej)* false sheen

përdalë *adj (e) fem (Pej)* wanton

*****përdalme** *adj (e) fem (Pej)* = **përdal**ë

përdalur *adj (e) fem (Pej)* = **përdal**ë

*****përdarje** = **përndarje**

përdas
I § adj distributive
II § nm mailman

përdat· *vt* to terrify, scare

përdat·*et vpr* to get thoroughly scared, be terrified

përdeg·*et vpr* **1** to divide into many branches: branch out **2** *(Fig)* to spread out in many directions: spread oneself thin

përdegje *nf ger* <**përdeg**·*et*

përder·*et vpr* to beg door to door, go around begging

*****përderdh**· *vt* to spread [] in various directions, pour out [] in a flood; disseminate, propagate

përderdhje *nf ger* <**përderdh**·

përderë**s** *n* person who goes begging door-to-door: itinerant beggar, mendicant

përderisa *conj* insofar as, since

përdëlle·*het vpr* to feel/be consoled

përdëlle·*n vt* **1** to have sympathy for []: pity **2** to offer solace: console

përdëllesë *nf* = **përdëllím**

përdëllestar
I § adj (Elev) **1** compassionate, sympathetic **2** consoling, comforting
II § n compassionate/sympathetic person

përdëllím *nm* **1** compassion, sympathy **2** solace, consolation; consolation visit

përdëllimtar *adj, n* = **përdëllestar**

përdëllyer *adj (i)* **1** deeply touched, emotionally moved **2** emotionally moving: poignant, touching

përdëllyeshëm *adj (i)* compassionate, sympathetic

*****përdí**·*n vt* = **përpí**·*n*

*****përdierr**· *(Old)* = **përdje**rr·

përdígj·*et vpr* to get scorched

përdígj *stem for 2nd pl pres, pind, imper, vp* <**përdje**g·

*****përdír** *stem for 2nd pl pres, pind, imper, vp* <**përdje**rr· *(Old)*

*****përdírr**·*et vpr (Old)* to go astray, stray

*****përdite** *nf (Old)* daily work

përdítë *adv* daily, every day; constantly

përdítësím *nm ger* (*Book*) <**përdítëso·***n*, **përdítëso·***het*

përdítëso·*het* *vpr* (*Book*) to bring oneself up to date

përdítëso·*n* *vt* (*Book*) **1** to bring [] up to date: update **2** to postpone

përdítshëm *adj (i)* **1** daily **2** everyday, usual: quotidian

përdítshme *nf (e)* daily newspaper: daily

*****përdjal·** *vt* to adopt [a child]

përdje·g· *vt* to scorch

përdjersur *adj (i)* soaked/bathed in sweat

*****përdjerr·** *vt* **1** (*Old*) to mislead, misguide; seduce **2** to destroy

*****përdjerrje** *nf* destruction

përdogj *stem for pdef* <**përdje·g·**

përdor· *vt* **1** to use; utilize **2** to wear [an article of clothing]
  ◦ **përdor· letrën/kartën/gurin/zarin e fundit** to play one's final card
  ◦ [] **përdor· si joshë** to use [] as lure/bait

përdorak *adj* **1** convenient to use: handy, useful *****2** manageable, docile

përdoresh *adv* at hand, handy

përdorëse *nf* hand tool

përdorím *nm ger* **1** <**përdoro·***n*, **përdor·** **2** use, utilization; usage

përdorje *nf* <**përdor·** = **përdorím**

përdoro·*n* *vt* = **përdor·**

përdorse *nf* tool, instrument

përdorshëm *adj (i)* usable; useful; handy

përdorues *nm* user; consumer

përdorur *adj (i)* used

përdredh· *vt* **1** to twist; twirl **2** to curl, coil **3** to shake/trill [one's voice] **4** (*Fig*) to cause the death of []: kill []
  ◦ **përdredh· bishtin** "waggle one's tail" **1** (*Pej*) to have loose sexual morals: be a slut **2** to waver in loyalty, be untrustworthy; be unreliable
  ◦ **i përdredh· buzët** to screw up one's lips in an expression of disbelief/contempt/disappointment/disapproval: make a wry face
  ◦ **i përdredh· fjalët** to go back on ones' word
  ◦ <**a përdredh· kokën** "twist <>'s head" (*Impol*) to knock <> off, do <> in, kill <>

përdredhas *adv* evasively, deviously

përdredhë *nf* [*Med*] helix (of the external ear)

përdredhët *adj (i)* winding, tortuous; devious, roundabout; wily, tricky; fascinating

përdredhës
  I § *adj* [*Bot*] having a vine-like stem that twists around another plant: twining
  II § *nm* **1** [*Tech*] tool for twisting hard: torsioning tool **2** [*Mus*] tuning peg on a stringed instrument
  III § *n* twister; hypocrite

përdredhëse *nf* [*Bot*] tendril

përdredhëz *nf* coil

përdredhím *nm* **1** twisting, wrenching **2** sharp curve/bend **3** [*Mus*] trilling **4** (*Fig*) evasive action/trick, wile **5** curling, waving

përdredhje *nf ger* **1** <**përdredh·**, **përdridh·***et* **2** coil, twist **3** [*Tech*] torsion

përdredhore *nf* [*Hist*] catapult propelled by a coil put under tension

përdredhshëm *adj (i)* curly

përdredhur *adj (i)* tortuous, winding, spiral

*****përdrejt** *prep (abl)* toward

*****përdrejto·***het* *vpr* to head straight, make a beeline, make one's way

përdreqno·*n* *vt* (*Crude*) to bungle

përdridh·*et* *vpr* **1** to twist from the waist; walk with a swiveling gait; walk in a weaving line **2** to twist and turn; twirl/curl around **3** (*Fig*) to falter, waffle, hesitate; be evasive, equivocate, pussyfoot

*****përdris** *stem for 1st sg pres, pl pres, 2nd & 3rd sg subj, pind* <**përdrit·**

*****përdrit·** *vt* to illuminate

*****përdritësí** *nf* transparency

*****përdritët** *adj (i)* = **përdukshëm**

*****përdritso·***n* *vt* to shine upon []

përdrodh *stem for pdef, adm, opt* <**përdredh·**

përduarsh *adv* by the hand

*****përdukje** *nf* showing off

*****përdukshëm** *adj (i)* transparent

përdyjavshëm *adj (i)* biweekly, fortnightly

përdylko·*n* *vi* to be pliant: bend

përdymuajshëm *adj (i)* bimonthly

përdyt· *vt* to do [] for the second time: repeat

*****përdha** *stem for pdef* <**përja·p·**

*****përdhashë** *1st sg pdef* <**përja·p·**

përdhe
  I § *adv* on the ground; toward the ground, down
  II § *nm* (*Colloq*) = **përdhes**

*****përdhe** *2nd sg pdef* <**përja·p·**

përdhe·*n* *vt* to cover the roots of [] with earth

përdhec *nm* [*Agr*] sole of a wooden plow

përdheck *adj* = **përdhes**

përdhel· *vt* to deceive [] by flattery, inveigle

*****përdhelmë** *nf* deception by flattery, inveiglement

përdhes
  I § *adj* on the ground; ground-level
  II § *nm* **1** (*Euph*) snake **2** [*Med*] arthritis, rheumatism

përdhese *nf* room on the ground floor; one-storey house

përdheshëm *adj (i)* on the ground

përdhëmb· *vt* to gnaw on []

*****përdhën** *stem for opt, adm, part forms* <**përja·p·**

*****përdhënie** *nf* (*Reg Tosk*) delivery

*****përdhies** *nm* large ant

*****përdhíkul** *nn* (*Reg*) variety of fig

*****përdhimbëtím** *nm* (*Old*) expression of condolences, condolences

përdhos· *vt* **1** to make [] grimy/dirty: soil; besmirch **2** (*Fig*) to corrupt, pervert

përdhos·*et* *vpr* to become corrupt/perverted

përdhosje *nf ger* <**përdhos·**, **përdhos·***et*

përdhosur *adj (i)* **1** begrimed, soiled, dirty **2** polluted, perverted, corrupted; vile

përdhunë *nf* raw/brute force; violence

*****përdhunëshëm** *adj (i)* violent

përdhunët *adj (i)* by violent force

përdhuni *adv* by force, under coercion

përdhuní *nf* use of violent force, coercive act; rape

përdhuním *nm ger* **1** <**përdhuno·***n* **2** forcible rape

përdhunisht *adv* under coercion, by force; by rape

përdhun|o· ·n *vt* **1** to coerce [] by violent force; rape [a woman/girl], violate **2** to suppress [] with violent force: squash, trample on []

përdhun|shëm *adj (i)* violent, forcible

përdhunu|e|s
I § *adj* using violent coercion, violating, violent
II § *n* rapist; violator

përemër *nm* [*Ling*] pronoun

përemëror *adj* [*Ling*] pronominal

përend·et *vpr* to wander up and down, wander around

****përerëso· ·n** *vt* to scent, perfume

përfal·et *vpr* to exchange greetings/salutations (upon meeting or departing)

përfalje *nf ger* **1** <përfal·et **2** exchange of salutations (upon meeting or departing) **3** *(Relig)* prayer, blessing

****përfalur** *adj (i)* devout; humble, meek

përfaq· *vt (Colloq)* = shfaq·

përfaq·et *vpr (Colloq)* = shfaq·et

përfaqe
I § *adv (Colloq)* **1** openly, publicly **2** face-to-face, directly opposite **3** *(Fig)* for the sake of appearances, just for show **4** on the face
II § *prep (abl)* facing, across from

përfaqez *adv (Colloq)* face to face, right to someone's face

****përfaq|ës** *n* representative

përfaq|ësi *nf (Collec)* representatives, representative body; representation, agency

përfaq|ës|im *nm ger* **1** <përfaqëso· ·n, përfaqëso· ·het **2** representation

përfaq|ës|im|tar *adj* representational

përfaq|ës|o· ·het *vpr* to participate through representatives: be represented

përfaq|ës|o· ·n *vt* to represent

përfaq|ës|uar *adj (i)* represented

përfaq|ës|ue|s *adj, n* representative

përfaq|ës|ue|se *nf* [*Sport*] all-star team; representative team

përfaqëz *adv* openly, publicly

përfaqtë *adj (i)* **1** outwardly; just for show, for the sake of appearances; perfunctory **2** ostensible; apparent

përfarim *nm ger* = shfarosje

përfaro· ·het *vpr* = shfaros·et

përfaro· ·n *vt* = shfaros·

****përfati** *nf* treatment with honor

****përfatit·** *vt* **1** to do [] an honor **2** = gostit·

****përfato· ·n** *vt* = përfatit·

****përfeto· ·n** *vt* to tell; show

****përfëlit·** *vt* = përcëllo· ·n

****përfërkas|** *stem for 1st sg pres, pl pres, 2nd & 3rd sg subj, pind* <përfërka·t·

****përfërka|t·** *vi* to come to a stop: halt; stay

përfik· *vt* **1** to reduce the moisture in []: dry **2** to increase the moisture in []: moisten

përfik·et *vpr* to get dry

****përfikos·et** *vpr* to shudder with horror = përqeth·et

përfikto· ·het *vpr* = përfik·et

përfikto· ·n *vt* = përfik·

përfill· *vt* **1** to regard [] highly, have a lot of respect for [] **2** to show [] polite consideration **3** to take [] into account, give consideration to []: consider

****përfill|ës** *adj* considerate, respectful

përfill|je *nf ger* **1** <përfill· **2** esteem; consideration, regard

****përfisk·** *vt* = përfit·

përfit|im *nm ger* **1** <përfito· ·n, përfito· ·het **2** gain, profit, value

përfito· ·het *vpr* to gain value

përfito· ·n *vt, vi* to gain [something of value]: profit, benefit

përfitu|e|s
I § *nm* person who gains/profits: gainer, winner
II § *adj* profitable, beneficial

****përfjalo· ·n** *vt* to dispute

përflak· *vt* **1** to engulf [] in flame, burn [] with a flame; broil; scorch **2** *(Fig)* to tinge [] with red **3** to hurl []

përflak·et *vpr* **1** to catch on fire; burn in flames **2** *(Fig)* to become tinged with red

përflak|ës *n* incendiary, agitator

përflak|je *nf ger* <përflak·, përflak·et

përflak|o· ·n *vt* = përflak·

përflak|shëm *adj (i)* **1** inflammable **2** flaming, flame-like

përflaktë *adj (i)* flaming, fervent, ardent

përflas| *stem for 1st sg pres, pl pres, 2nd & 3rd sg subj, pind* <përflet·

përfles| *stem for 1st sg pres, pl pres, 2nd & 3rd sg subj, pind* <përfle·t·

përflet· *vt* to leaf through [] page by page, peruse

përflet· *vt* **1** to speak ill of [] **2** to blame **3** to remind [] of a favor done **4** to tell [something] heard from someone else: repeat
  ∘ <>[] **përflet·** to remind <> impolitely of [] (involved as a favor to <>)

****përfleto· ·n** *vt* = përfle·t·

përflis| *stem for 2nd pl pres, pind* <përflet·

përflit·et *vpr* to have a verbal argument: bicker; debate
  ∘ **përflit·et**[3sg] **se** _ there *is* a lot of talk going around that _, there *are* rumors that _

përflit| *stem for pind, 2nd pl pres, vp* <përflet·

përfoll| *stem for imper, pdef, opt, adm, part* <përflet·

****përfolje** *nf* conversation; quarrel

****përfo·** *vt* to dry out [soil], parch

****përfora|s|** *stem for 1st sg pres, pl pres, 2nd & 3rd sg subj, pind* <përfora·t·

****përfora|t·** *vt* to seek, look for []

përforc|im *nm ger* **1** <përforco· ·n, përforco· ·het **2** reinforcement

përforco· ·het *vpr* **1** to get reinforced **2** [*Phys Electr*] to gain in amplification

përforco· ·n *vt* **1** to reinforce **2** [*Phys Electr*] to amplify

përforcu|ar *adj (i)* **1** reinforced **2** [*Phys Electr*] amplified

përforcu|e|s
I § *adj* **1** reinforcing **2** [*Phys Electr*] amplifying
II § *nm* [*Spec*] amplifier

****përfrigue|shëm** *adj (i)* terribly frightening, terrifying

****përfry|rë** *adj (i)* swollen up

përfshi·*het vpr* to be included; take part, participate

përfshi·*n vt* **1** to sweep [ ] into one's arms: embrace, gather [ ] up **2** to seize **3** to include; comprise, contain; encompass **4** *(Fig)* to take it all in (visually or mentally): comprehend instantly

****përfshij**ës *adj* sweeping, drastic, comprehensive

përfshirje *nf ger* **1** <**përfshi**·*n*, **përfshi**·*het* **2** inclusion

përftesë *nf* created/generated/procreated entity: creation, product

****përftik**· *vt* to dry [ ] up completely

përftim *nm ger* **1** <**përfto**·*n*, **përfto**·*het* **2** creation; procreation

përfto·*het vpr* to come into being

përfto·*n vt* **1** to create, generate, yield **2** *(Book)* to procreate

përftore *nf* [*Geom*] generatrix

përftues

I § *adj* creative, generative, productive; procreative
II § *nm* [*Phys*] generator

përftuese *nf* [*Math*] generatrix

përfund

I § *adv* **1** at the bottom **2** down; below
II § *prep (abl)* **1** at/along the bottom of **2** underneath, below

****përfundes**ë *nf* final result

****përfund**ëm *adj (i)* = përfundimtar

****përfund**ërisht = përfundimisht

****përfund**ese *nf* women's long bloomers that fasten at the ankle

përfundët *adj (i)* bottom, lowest

përfundi *adv* **1** at the bottom, underneath **2** down; below

përfundim *nm ger* **1** <**përfundo**·*n* **2** conclusion **3** result; outcome **4** *(Colloq)* final grade (in school)

përfundimisht *adv* **1** conclusively; once and for all **2** in the end: finally **3** in conclusion

përfundimtar *adj* final, ultimate; definitive, conclusive, decisive

****përfundisht = përfundimisht

****përfundit = përfundi

****përfundje** *nf* termination, ending

përfundo·*n*

I § *vt* to bring [ ] to an end: conclude; successfully conclude [ ]: finish
II § *vi* **1** to come to an end, be over: terminate **2** to end up; result **3** to arrive at a conclusion

përfundos· *vt* to submerge, sink

përfundshëm *adj (i)* **1** lower, under **2** *(Old)* = përfundimtar

përfunduar *adj (i)* finished

përfundues

I § *n* person who brings a task to completion; finisher
II § *adj* ultimate, final

****përfuntëm** *adj (i)* = përfundimtar

****përfuqisim** *nm ger* <**përfuqiso**·*n*

****përfuqiso**·*n vt* = përforco·*n*

përfush· *vt* to bring [ ] out into the open: expose, reveal

përfush·*et vp reflex* to expose/reveal oneself

përfushtë *adj (i)* **1** completely flat/level **2** *(Fig)* out in the open: open ***3** on the ground floor, groundfloor

përfyt·*et vpr* **1** to engage in hand to hand fighting; grapple; wrestle **2** *(Fig)* to engage in mortal combat; struggle boldly

përfytës *nm (Colloq)* necktie = **krava**të

përfytje *nf ger* **1** <**përfyt**·*et* **2** hand-to-hand combat

përfytyrim *nm ger* **1** <**përfytro**·*n*, **përfytro**·*het* **2** creation of the mind: mental image; imagination **3** image

përfytyro·*het vpr* to come to mind

përfytyro·*n vt* **1** to call [ ] to mind, conceive **2** to imagine

përfytyrueshëm *adj (i)* imaginable

****përgaç** *nm* bib

përgaçe *nf* apron, pinafore

****përgaçk**ë *nf* little apron; bib (for a child)

përgatesë *nf* [*Spec*] = **prepara**t

përgatis *stem for 1st sg pres, pl pres, 2nd & 3rd sg subj, pind* <**përgatit**·

përgatit· *vt* to prepare

përgatit·*et vpr* to make preparations

përgatitës

I § *adj* preparatory; preliminary
II § *n* preparer

përgatitje *nf ger* **1** <**përgatit**·, **përgatit**·*et* **2** preparation **3** [*Mil*] training

përgatitor *adj* preparatory, preparative

përgatitore *nf* preparatory school

përgatitur *adj (i)* trained

përgënjeshtrim *nm ger* **1** <**përgënjeshtro**·*n*, **përgënjeshtro**·*het* **2** refutation, denial

përgënjeshtro·*het vpr* to turn out to be false: prove false

përgënjeshtro·*n vt* to assert/show [ ] to be false: deny; refute

përgënjeshtruar *adj (i)* asserted to be false; proved false

përgëzim *nm ger* **1** <**përgëzo**·*n*, **përgëzo**·*het* **2** pleasure, joy, satisfaction

përgëzime *np* congratulations

përgëzo·*n vt* **1** to exchange congratulations; pat each other on the back **2** (of a dog) to engage in ingratiatory behavior

përgëzo·*n vt* **1** to congratulate **2** to fondle; pet and play with [ ]

përgëzues *adj* cheering, approving; congratulatory

****përgishte** *nf (Old)* duel

****përgledh**· = përkëdhel·

****përgo**·*n vt* = përgojo·*n*

përgojim *nm ger (Pej)* **1** <**përgojo**·*n* **2** gossip

përgojo·*n vt, vi* **1** *(Pej)* to spread gossip (about [ ]); backbite, slander ***2** to enunciate, pronounce

****përgrîm** *adj (i) (Reg Gheg)* contrite

****përgrimos**·*ur adj (i)* weak, feeble

****përgush**ë *nf* ruff, frill

****përgja**·*n* = përngja·*n*

****përgja** = përngja

përgjak· *vt* **1** to cause [ ] to bleed: bloody **2** to drench/stain [ ] with blood **3** *(Fig)* to circumcise

përgjak·*et vpr* **1** to become all bloody; bleed **2** *(Fig)* to fight fiercely **3** *(Fig)* to turn red; take on a red tinge

përgjakëm *adj (i)* bloody, bloodstained

përgja'kje *nf ger* **1** <përgja'k·, përgja'k·*et* **2** bloody combat, battle

përgjako'·n *vi* to bleed

*__përgjako's·__ *vt* to stain [] with blood

përgjakshë**m** *adj (i)* **1** bloody; bloodstained **2** cruel, savage

përgja'ktë *adj (i)* = përgja'ksh**ë**m

përgja'kur
  I § *part* <përgja'k·
  II § *adj (i)* bloodied, wounded; bloody
  III § *nn (të) (Old)* ritual circumcision = **synet**

përgjall'o·n *vt* to enliven, invigorate

*__përgjanj'tor__ *adj (Old)* comparative

përgja'të *prep (abl)* alongside

*__përgja'tshëm__ *adj (i)* lengthwise, longitudinal

përgje'gj *stem for pdef, opt, adm, part, vp* <përgji'gj·*et*

*__përgje'gje__ = përgji'gj*e*

përgje'gjë**s**
  I § *adj* **1** bearing responsibility: accountable, responsibility **2** parallel in function: corresponding
  II § *n* person in charge: manager

përgje'gjë**sí** *nf* responsibility; sense of responsibility

përgje'gjshëm *adj (i)* answerable for one's actions: responsible

*__përgje'gjun__ *nn (të) (Reg Gheg)* answer

*__përgje'jm__ *adj (i)* horrible

*__përgje'll·__ *vi, vt* to turn

përgje'seë *nf* = përgji'm

përgje't· *2nd & 3rd sg pres* <përgja's·

*__përgjëni'shëm__ *adj (i)* affectionate, intimate

përgjëra'të *nf* **1** ugly monster, boogieman **2** = përgjëri'm

përgjëri'm *nm ger* **1** <përgjëro'·n, përgjëro'·*het* **2** devotion *__3__ vow

përgjëro'·het *vpr* **1** to pledge one's love/devotion; make a personal commitment **2** to have a deep yearning, have a longing; have a strong desire **3** *(Fig)* to plead by invoking something precious

përgjëro'·n
  I § *vt* to beseech [] with an invocation of something precious
  II § *vi* to take a vow, swear

përgjëru'ar *adj (i)* **1** touched with affection: affectionate **2** filled with longing; filled with a strong desire

përgjëru'es
  I § *adj* deeply touching; heartwarming
  II § *n* *__blasphemer

përgji'gj·et *vpr* **1** to reply; respond; answer **2** to be answerable, be responsible **3** to explain oneself, answer for one's actions **4** to be responsive to <> **5** to correspond to/with <>, be the same as <>
  ◦ përgji'gj·*et* maj**ë** për maj**ë** to answer back, retort
  ◦ <> përgji'gj·*et* me të njëjt**ë**n monedh**ë** *(Book)* to pay <> back in kind, respond to <> in kind; pay <> back in <>'s own coin

përgji'gje *nf* **1** reply; response; answer **2** backtalk

*__përgji'gj__ë**s** = përgje'gjës

*__përgji'gj__ë**sí** = përgje'gjësí

përgji'm *nm ger* **1** <përgjo'·n **2** concentrated observation: monitoring, surveillance **3** *[Mil]* reconnaissance

përgji'mta'r
  I § *n* eavesdropper, spy
  II § *adj* eavesdropping, spying

*__përgji's__ *stem for 2nd pl pres, pind* <përgja's·

*__përgji'it__ *stem for pdef, opt, adm, part, pind, 2nd pl pres, imper, vp* <përgja's·

*__përgjith__ë**ri'sht** = përgjithësi'sht

përgjithë**si** *indecl*

përgjithë**si'm** *nm ger* **1** <përgjithëso'·n, përgjithëso'·*het* **2** generalization

përgjithë**si'sht** *adv (Book)* generally; generally speaking

përgjithë**so'·het** *vpr* **1** to become general, spread more broadly: generalize **2** *[Med]* to spread

përgjithë**so'·n** *vt* **1** to generalize **2** to make [] universal

përgjithë**su'ar** *adj (i)* generalized, general

përgjithë**su'es** *adj* that expresses or makes a generalization: generalizing

përgjithmo'në *adv* for all time, forever

përgjithnjë *adv* **1** forever, for all time **2** *(Reg)* every time, many times

përgji'thshëm *adj (i)* general
  ◦ komandant i përgji'thshëm commander in chief

përgji'thshme *nf (e)* that which is general: the general, generality

*__përgji'tht__ë *adj (i)* = përgji'thshëm

përgjo'·n
  I § *vt* **1** to observe [] surreptitiously: peep in on [], spy/eavesdrop on []; watch [] indirectly **2** to ambush **3** to watch (all night) over [someone sick/dying]
  II § *vi* to stand watch (at night); stand around waiting: wait in ambush: lurk

*__përgjo's·__ *vt* to weaken, enfeeble

përgjo'es
  I § *nm* surreptitious observer: eavesdropper, peeping Tom, spy; person on watch: sentinel; guardian; person waiting in ambush
  II § *adj* listening-in, eavesdropping

përgju'm· *vt* **1** to put [] to sleep; make [] sleepy/ drowsy **2** *(Fig)* to take []'s mind off the main issue; dull []'s mind

përgju'm·et *vpr* to fall asleep, doze off

*__përgju'm__ë *nf* slumber

përgju'më**sí** *nf* **1** = përgju'mje **2** *[Med]* somnolence

përgju'më**sh** *adv* in a sleepy state: drowsy, sleepy, somnolent

përgju'mje *nf ger* **1** <përgju'm·, përgju'm·*et* **2** drowsiness, sleepiness

*__përgju'mo'·n__ *vt* = përgju'm·

përgju'mshëm
  I § *adv* = përgju'mësh
  II § *adj (i)* = përgju'mur

përgju'mur *adj (i)* **1** still sleepy, sleepy, drowsy **2** *(Fig)* lethargic; indolent

përgju'nj· *vt* **1** to force [] to []'s knees **2** *(Fig)* to subjugate, vanquish, defeat

përgju'nj·et *vpr* **1** to kneel; fall to one's knees **2** *(Fig)* to bow down, submit; be submissive, humble oneself

përgju'njur *adj (i)* brought to one's knees; on one's knees, kneeling

*__përgjy's__ë**s** *nm (Old)* equator

përgjy'sët *adj (i)* half, halved

përgjy'smë *adv* 1 in two halves/parts 2 half way; partially; not completely

***për'gjysm**|ës *nm (Old)* participle = pjeso're

përgjysm|im *nm ger* 1 <përgjysmo'·n, përgjysm-o'·het 2 division in halves 3 [*Geom*] bisection

për'gjysmo·*het vpr* to divide in half; split in two 2 to become smaller by half

përgjysm|o·*n vt* 1 to divide [] in half; bisect 2 to reduce by half, halve

përgjysm|ore *nf* [*Geom*] bisector of an angle

përgjysm|ua'r *adj (i)* 1 half gone, half used up, not whole; reduced by half 2 (of speech) having many mistakes, poorly pronounced: broken

përgjysm|ue|s *adj* [*Geom*] bisected

***për'ha'n|un** *adj (i) (Reg Gheg)* epileptic

për'ha'p· *vt* 1 to spread []; spread [] out 2 to disperse [], scatter [], propagate

për'ha'p·*et vpr* 1 to spread 2 to disperse, scatter; become spread thin, become diffuse

  ◦ **përhap·***et³ˢᵍ* **fjala vesh më vesh** "the word *spreads* ear to ear" the word/rumor/news *spreads* mouth to mouth

për'ha'p|ëm *adj (i)* = përha'pur

për'ha'p|ës

  I § *n* disseminator, broadcaster; publicizer; carrier (of a disease), spreader, propagator

  II § *adj* of or pertaining to dissemination/publicity, broadcasting

për'ha'p|je *nf ger* 1 <përha'p·, përha'p·et 2 dispersion area

për'ha'p|ur *adj (i)* spread out; widespread

për'hedh· *vt* 1 to throw [] away, heave [] out; reject 2 to shake [] hard

për'hedh|ë *nf* 1 thin layer of snow *2 jump

***për'hedh|ët** *adj (i)* nimble, spry; vigorous, sprightly

për'hedh|je *nf ger* <përhe'dh·, përhi'dh·et

për'hedh|ur *adj (i)* 1 bulging out 2 grown high and fast: bursting up 3 *(Fig)* sprightly, spry

për'he'q·

  I § *vi* to be in the throes of death, be dying

  II § *vt* to speak ill of [], malign; gossip about []

për'he'q|ës *nm* slipknot

për'he'q|ur *part* <përhe'q·, përhi'q·et

për'he're *adv* all the time, always; constantly

për'her|ëble'r|të *adj (i)* [*Bot*] evergreen

për'her|ët *adj (i)* = përhe'rshëm

për'her|shëm *adj (i)* permanent; perpetual, constant; perennial; fixed

për'hën|ur *adj (i)* vacillating, capricious

***për'hë'sh|ëm** *adj (i)* temporary = hëpërhë'shëm

për'hi·*het vpr* 1 to become covered with ashes 2 to become gray-haired: get gray 3 to appear to <> in a phantasmagoric vision

  ◦ **<> përhi**·*het³ˢᵍ* it *comes to* <> in a vision

për'hi·*n vt* 1 to scatter/sprinkle ashes on [] 2 [*Relig*] to bedaub []'s head with ashes (on Ash Wednesday) 3 to turn []'s hair gray

për'hidh·*et vpr* 1 to leap, bound; bound up and down 2 to bounce up and down 3 to wave; sway 4 to burst up; grow exuberantly 5 to show off, swagger, swank

për'hidh| *stem for 2nd pl pres, pind, imper, vp* <përhe'dh·

***për'hier|im** *nm ger* <përhiero'·n

***për'hiero**·*n vt* to consecrate, dedicate

për'hijo·*n vi* to look like a shadow

për'hi'më *adj (i)* light gray

për'himë't *adj* = përhi'më

për'himn|o·*n vt (Elev)* to sing the praises of []: extol

për'hi'q·et vpr* to be in the throes of death, be dying

për'hiq| *stem for 2nd pl pres, pind, imper, vp* <përhe'q·, përhje'k·

***për'hi're** *adj (i)* gracious

për'hir|im *nm ger (Elev Old)* 1 <përhiro'·n 2 congratulation *3 acknowledgement of gratitude: thanks

***për'hir|im|ta'r** *adj* congratulatory

për'hiro·*n vt (Elev Old)* to congratulate

***për'hir|shëm** *adj (i)* = përhi're

për'hir|të *adj (i)* having become gray: turned gray, gray

për'hi't·*et vpr* 1 to be soiled/covered/bedecked with ashes 2 to get gray (hair)

për'hi't|je *nf* apparition

për'hi't|ur

  I § *adj (i)* 1 covered with ashes 2 greying, grizzled

  II § *nf (e)* [*Folklore*] Cinderella

***për'hje'k·** = përhe'q·

***për'hje'k|ë** *nf* death struggle, throes of death

për'hodh| *stem for pdef* <përhe'dh·

për'holl|ësh *nm* very skinny person

për'ho'q| *stem for pdef* <përhe'q·, përhje'k·

për'ho'sh· *vt (Colloq)* to fondle, caress; cajole

***për'ho'sh|ës**

  I § *adj* caressing; cajoling

  II § *n* fondler; cajoler

për'hu'dh·et vpr* = përhi'dh·e

***për'huka's|** *stem for 1st sg pres, pl pres, 2nd & 3rd sg subj, pind* <përhuka't·

***për'huka't·** *vt* to perfume

për'hu'mb·*et vpr* 1 to go astray; get lost 2 *(Fig)* to become obsessed/infatuated 3 *(Fig)* to lose awareness, go into a daze

për'hu'mb|je *nf ger* <përhu'mb·et

për'hu'mb|ur *adj (i)* 1 obsessed, infatuated 2 bewildered 3 in a daze 4 forsaken

***për'hu'nd|shëm** *adj (i) (Reg Gheg)* nasal

***për'hy'r|je** *nf* (book) introduction

***për'hysht** = ysht|

***për|** || *obl* <pë(r)

për'ikje *nf* escape, getaway, flight

***për'imênd** *adv (Reg Gheg)* = përnjëme'nd

për'imtim *nm ger (Book)* <përimto'·n

për'imto·*n vt (Book)* to examine [] minutely

***për'itë** *adj (i) (Reg Gheg)* of brass, brazen

***për'ja'p·** *vt* to hand [] over, deliver

për'ja'rg· *vt* to make [] wet with spittle; slobber all over []

për'ja'rg·*et vpr* 1 to slobber []; excrete slime 2 to get all wet and slimy 3 *(Pej Iron)* to slobber all over one another in kissing

për'ja'rg|ur *adj (i)* covered with slobber; slimy

për'ja'sht|a

  I § *adv* outside; outdoors; out of the country; out

  II § *prep (abl)* outside of; outside

***për'ja'sht|azi** *adv* outwardly, externally

për'ja'sht|ëm *adj (i) (Intens)* 1 outer, exterior; outward 2 external, superficial

përjasht im _nm ger_ **1** <përjashto· ·n, përjashto· ·het **2** exception

përja'shtme _nf (e)_ exterior

përjashto·het _vpr_ **1** to be excluded from consideration: be out of the question **2** to be an exception

përjashto·n _vt_ **1** to expel **2** to exempt; except **3** to put [] out of consideration: exclude

përjasht uar _adj (i)_ expelled; exempted

përja'va _adv_ every week, weekly

përja'vshëm _adj (i)_ weekly

përja'vshme _nf (e)_ periodical that appears once a week: weekly

*__përje k·__ = prek·

*__përje'p__ _2nd & 3rd sg pres_ <përja'p·

*__përje'r·__ = prier·

përje të _adv_ **1** for a lifetime, for life: lifelong **2** forever

përjetë si _nf_ permanence, timelessness; perpetuity, eternity

përjetë sim _nm ger_ **1** <përjetëso· ·n, përjetëso· ·het **2** perpetuation, perpetuance

përjetë sisht _adv_ continually, perpetually, eternally

përjetëso·het _vpr_ to become permanently implanted in memory

përjetëso·n _vt_ **1** to perpetuate **2** to impress [] in memory forever: memorialize

përjet im _nm ger_ **1** <përjeto· ·n **2** deep imprint left by significant experience(s); mental scar

përjeto·n _vt_ to experience [], go through the experience of []; bear the imprint of [an experience]

përje'tshëm _adj (i)_ eternal; perpetual; permanent; timeless

*__përjul__ _nm_ flat stone for skimming over water

përka'll ës _n_ pretender, hypocrite, poser

*__përkâmb__ = përkëmb

përkarshi _adv (Reg Gheg) (Colloq)_ right in front, directly facing

përka's _stem for 1st sg pres, 1st & 3rd pl pres, 2nd & 3rd sg subj_ <përket·

*__përka'sje__ _nf_ encounter, meeting

përkat ës _adj_ **1** appropriate, proper; requisite; suitable; corresponding **2** pertinent, relevant

përkat ësi _nf_ **1** one's social class **2** jurisdiction, purview, responsibility *__3__ relevancy, suitability; relationship

përkat ësisht _adv (Book)_ respectively

përka'tshëm _adj (i)_ = përkatës

përka'va _ë nf_ **1** = velenxa ̈ **2** saddle cloth, saddle blanket

përke q· _vt_ **1** to make [] ugly: disfigure **2** to make [] sad

përke q·et _vpr_ to grow ugly

përkeq ëso·n _vt_ to make [] much worse, seriously aggravate

përket·
  _I § vt_ to touch [] lightly (with the hand)
  _II § vi_ **1** to belong to <> **2** to be proper/appropriate for <>: be up to <>

përkë dhel· _vt_ **1** to stroke [] softly and repeatedly: pet **2** to caress, fondle **3** _(Fig)_ to speak to [] in affectionate terms: baby **4** _(Fig Pej)_ to treat [] with undeserved softness: coddle, baby, pamper, spoil

përkë dhel·et _vpr_ to rub up against someone affectionately: cuddle up; behave in a fawning manner

*__përkë dhel e__ _np fem_ caresses: fondling

përkë dhel ës _adj_ **1** soothing, caressing; doting; fawning **2** [Ling] affectionate

përkë dheli _nf_ **1** fondling, caress **2** _(Fig Pej)_ coddling: babying, pampering

përkë dhel im _nm ger_ = përkëdhelje

përkë dhel je _nf ger_ **1** <përkëdhel·, përkëdhel·et **2** = përkëdheli **3** flattery, cajolery

*__përkë dhel or__ _OR_ **përkë dhel osh** _adj_ caressing, affectionate; flattering

përkë dhel ur _adj (i)_ **1** treated as the favorite child **2** _(Pej)_ badly brought up: spoiled, pampered

përkë mb· _vt_ **1** to help [a baby] walk (on its own two feet); rear [a child] **2** _(Fig)_ to help [] get back on []'s feet

përkë mb·et _vpr_ **1** to grow up (and learn to walk on one's own two feet) **2** _(Fig)_ to get back on one's feet: recover, recuperate

përkëmb im _nm_ [Math] permutation

përkëmb je _nf ger_ **1** <përkëmb·, përkëmb·et **2** recuperation, recovery

përkëmb ur _adj (i)_ **1** able to walk **2** back on one's feet; (of grain in a field) recovered after a heavy wind or rain

*__përkënaq shëm__ _adj (i)_ thoroughly pleasant

përkëtej
  I § adv over here, in this direction
  II § prep (abl) on this side of <>

*__përkëthe·n__ = përkthe·n

përkim _nm ger_ **1** <përko· ·n **2** coincidence, conformity **3** [Ling] agreement

përkis _stem for 2nd pl pres, pind_ <përket·

përkit _stem for pdef, opt, adm, part, pind, 2nd pl pres, imper, vp_ <përket·

përkit azi _adv_ **1** relevant, apropos **2** respectively
  ◦ përkitazi me [] in accordance with []

përkit je _nf ger_ <përket·

*__përkjell·__ = përkëdhel·

përko·n _vi_ **1** to fit/conform; coincide; agree **2** [Ling] to agree grammatically *__3__ = përket·

përkohë si _nf (Book)_ temporariness; impermanence, transitoriness

përkohë sisht _adv_ for a short time, for the time being: temporarily

përko'h shëm _adj (i)_ temporary; provisional; momentary, transitory

përko'h shme _nf (e)_ periodical (publication), magazine

përko'h shm eri _nf (Book)_ = përkohësi

përko q· _vt_ to pick out [] one by one, select [] individually

përko re _nf_ **1** moderation in drinking/eating **2** abstinence, temperance; self-restraint

përko'r ë _adj (i)_ **1** moderate in drinking/eating: abstemious **2** _(Fig)_ temperate, self-controlled

*__përkori__ _nf_ = përkore

përko'rm ë _adj (i)_ = përkore

*__përkorsi__ _nf_ = përkore

*__përkovaç e__ _nf_ winding sheet (for a corpse)

*__përkqyr ës__ _n_ overseer, bailiff

përkrah
  I § adv side-by-side, adjacent, alongside; at hand, nearby

II § *prep (abl)* **1** beside, next to **2** in support of: backing, supporting, helping

për|kra·h· *vt* **1** to support; back; assist; advocate, endorse *2 to uphold

për|kra·h·et *vpr* **1** to be adjacent, be nearby **2** to be supportive of <>; be helpful to <>

për|kra·h|as *adv* arm in arm

për|kra·h|ës *n* supporter, backer; follower, advocate

për|kra·h|je *nf ger* **1** <përkra·h·, përkra·h·et **2** support, backing, help

për|kra·h|shëm *adj (i)* supportable, maintainable

për|kra·hu *adv* by the arm

*përkre·n *n* *(Reg Gheg)* = përkry'e·*n*

*për|krejc*ë *nf (Old)* index

*për|krejt|ëm *adj (i)* *(Old)* extreme

për|krena·re *nf* [*Hist*] sallet

për|kreno·n *vt* [*Text*] to join [warp threads on a loom] end to end: tie on [the warp]

për|kre'së *nf* **1** pillow for the head = **jastë·k 2** cap

për|kry·het *vpr* to become perfect/perfected, increase in perfection

për|kry'e·n *vt* **1** to perfect []; do/make [] perfectly; finish [] up **2** *(Intens)* to bring [] to utter completion: accomplish, achieve, fulfil, consummate

*për|kry'e|me *nf (e)* perfection

për|kry'er *adj (i)* done/made perfectly: perfect

për|kry'erje *nf ger* <përkry'e·*n*, përkry·het

*për|kry'p· *vt* to sprinkle [] with salt; heavily salt []

për|kry'qët *adj (i)* **1** shaped in a cross: crossed, cross-shaped **2** transversal

për|kth'e·n *vt* **1** to translate **2** to turn [] around: rotate

*për|kth|enjë·s = përkthy'es

për|kth'e·së *nf* **1** [*Mus Lit*] refrain = refre·n **2** [*Ling*] accidence: declension, conjugation *3 translation

për|kth'im *nm ger* **1** <përkthe·*n*, përkthe·het **2** translation **3** *(Old)* [*Ling*] grammatical declension

për|kthjello·n *vt* to clear [] up, clarify; reveal, expose

për|kth'y'er *adj (i)* **1** translated **2** bent, curved

për|kthy'e·s *n* translator

*për|kthy'e|t *adj (i)* = përkthy'er

*për|ku'e|shëm *adj (i)* = përka·tës

për|kufiz'im *nm ger* **1** <përkufizo·*n*, përkufizo·het **2** definition

për|kufizo·n *vt* to define

për|kujde's·et *vp (Intens)*

° **përkujdes·et për** [] **1** to look after [], (provide) care for [] **2** to be show concern for []; take pains with []

për|kujde's|je *nf* custodial care, nursing care

për|kujde's|shëm *adj (i)* cautious; vigilant; attentive

për|kujde's|ta·r

I § *n* supporter, patron; custodian

II § *adj* showing great care, careful

për|kuj'ë *nf (Intens)* great wailing, loud mourning; prolonged keening

për|kujte's|e *nf* [*Offic*] memorandum

për|kujt'im *nm ger* **1** <përkujto·*n* **2** memorial celebration: commemoration **3** remembrance

për|kujt|imo'r *adj* commemorative, memorial

për|kujt|imo're *nf* publicly posted notice of the anniversary of a death, inviting friends of the dead person to come to pay their respects: memorial notice

për|kujto·n *vt* to commemorate

për|kujt|ore *np* memoirs

*për|kujt|ue|shëm *adj (i)* **1** of solemn remembrance; reminiscent *2 solemn

për|ku'l· *vt* **1** to bend [] down/over **2** to cause [] to submit, vanquish

° **përkul·²ⁿᵈ mesin** "bend your back (to the task)" get down to work

për|ku'l·et *vpr* **1** to bend/lean down; stoop **2** to bend over **3** *(Fig)* to bow; bow down **4** *(Fig)* to bow down to <>: submit, yield

për|ku'l|ëm *adj (i)* = përku'lur

për|ku'l|ës *adj* causing to bend down

për|ku'l|ët *adj (i)* **1** = përku'lur **2** = përku'lshëm

për|ku'l|je *nf ger* <përku'l·, përku'l·et

për|ku'l|shëm *adj (i)* bendable, pliable, flexible; supple, pliant

për|ku'l|shm|ëri *nf (Book)* flexibility, pliability; suppleness, pliancy

për|ku'l|ur *adj (i)* **1** bent, curved; crooked **2** bent/stooped over, crouched, bowed

për|ku'nd· *vt* **1** to cause to rock/sway [] gently: lull **2** to shake, rattle

për|ku'nd·et *vpr* **1** to rock, sway gently **2** *(Fig)* to be lulled into false dreams

për|ku'ndër

I § *pcl* = përku'ndrazi

II § *prep (abl)* opposed to, against

për|ku'ndë·rt *adj (i)* directly opposite; contrary

për|ku'nd|je *nf ger* <përku'nd·, përku'nd·et

për|ku'ndra *adv* = përku'ndrazi

për|ku'ndrazi *pcl* on the contrary, quite the opposite

për|ku'ndrejt

I § *adv* in front, directly opposite, facing

II § *prep (abl)* directly facing, facing toward

për|kupto·n *vt* to perceive, apperceive

për|ku'qët *adj (i)* bright red

për|ku'qur *adj (i)* = përsku'qur

për|kushti *nf (religious)* devotion, dedication

për|kusht'im *nm ger* <përkushto·*n*, përkushto·het

për|kushto··het *vpr* **1** to devote oneself; become dedicated, make a commitment **2** [*Relig*] to take vows (in a religious order)

për|kushto·n *vt* to dedicate

për|la··het *vpr* to grapple; have a fight

për|la·n *vt (Colloq)* **1** to grab [someone] quickly; engage in hand to hand combat: wrestle **2** to sweep [] away with force: wipe [] out **3** to steal [] away: snatch **4** to gobble up []

° **përla·n edhe** [] "even gobble up [the person in sight]" *(Crude Iron)* to gobble up [anything in sight]

për|la'g· *vt* to soak

*për|la'k *nm* **1** uncastrated donkey *2 donkey colt

*për|la'|mje *nf* **1** = përla'rje **2** flood

për|la'|rje *nf ger* <përla·*n*

*për|la|sí|na *np* = shpërlasína

*për|le'htë *adj (i)* very light, dainty

për|le'sh· *vt* to tousle, rumple, tangle; pull [] to pieces

për|le'sh·et *vpr* to engage in heavy struggle

për|le'shë *nf* tangle

përle´shje *nf ger* **1** <përle´sh· **2** heavy struggle

përle´shur *adj (i)* in complete disorder, all messed up

përlëfy´t·et *vpr* to be at each other's throat, go for the throat: scuffle, fight

përlëku´r·et *vpr* to grovel

përlëmi´m *nm ger* **1** <përlëmo´·n **2** polish

përlëmo´·n *vt* to polish

përlëng·et *vpr* = përlot·et

përlëpi´·n *vt* **1** to smooth down [] ***2** to hack

përlëvdo´·het *vpr* to boast

përlëvdo´·n *vt* to praise [] extravagantly, extol, glorify

përli´ast *adj (i)* infected with smallpox; scarred by smallpox

përli´dh· *vt* to plait, weave

përligso´·het *vpr* to get worse, deteriorate

përligj· *vt* **1** to legitimize, justify, excuse; vindicate **2** *(Old)* to pay off [], repay

përligj·et *vpr* **1** to consider oneself justified/vindicated: rationalize **2** to be justifiable/justified

përligj´ë *nf* **1** = përligjje **2** = detyrë **3** = shpagim

përligj´ës *adj* justifying; vindicating; legitimizing

përligjje *nf ger* **1** <përligj·, përligj·et **2** exculpatory evidence; vindication **3** [*Lit*] consistency (for a character), motivation

përligjshëm *adj (i)* justifiable, rational

përligjur *adj (i)* **1** justified; vindicated; validated **2** = përligjshëm

përlim *nm* duty

përlind· *vi, vt* (*Book Old*) = rilind·

*përlind·et *vpr* (*Book Old*) = rilind·et

përlindje *nf* (*Book Old*) = rilindje

përlinë *nf* badly eroded land, wasteland; area prone to landslides: unstable ground

përlo´dhshëm *adj (i)* tiring

*përlo´q·et *vpr* to whisper

përlo´sh·et *vpr* to sob without shedding tears; pretend to cry; cry about nothing

përlosha´n *adj* always ready to cry, always on the point of tears; always crying

përlo´t· *vt* to make [the eyes] of <> tearful

përlo´t·et *vpr* (of eyes) to well up with tears, become tearful

përlo´tëm *adj (i)* = përlotur

përlotim *nm ger* <përloto´·n

përloto´o·n *vt* to shed tears for [], bathe [] in tears, pity

përlotue´shëm *adj (i)* tearful; pitiable

përlo´tur *adj (i)* tearful

*përlufta´r *n* (*Old*) champion, crusader

përlugëto´·het *vpr* (*Pej*) to get bloated with food and drink; gorge/stuff oneself

përlu´më *adv* down the drain: for nothing, in vain

përlundri´m *nm* passage (by ship)

përlu´s *stem for 1st sg pres, pl pres, 2nd & 3rd sg subj, pind* <përlu´t·

përlu´t· *vt* to intercede with []: implore, supplicate

përlu´tje *nf ger* **1** <përlu´t· **2** intercession, supplication

përly´·het *vpr* **1** to get all greasy; be coated with grease **2** to become spattered with spots, get dirty

all over **3** to get infected; catch a contagious disease **4** *(Fig)* to be involved up in dirty business

përly´e·n *vt* **1** to get [] all greasy **2** to make [something that was clean] dirty: get spots on []; pollute **3** *(Fig)* to sully, defile

përly´er *adj (i)* **1** soiled, greasy, dirty **2** *(Fig)* mixed up in dirty business

përly´erje *nf ger* <përly´e·n, përly·het

përly´eshëm *adj (i)* soiling; defiling

*përly´et *adj (i)* = përlyer

përllo´ç· *vt* to make [] dirty with mud: make [] muddy

përllo´ç·et *vpr* to become dirty from mud: get all muddy

përllogari´s *stem for 1st sg pres, pl pres, 2nd & 3rd sg subj, pind* <përllogari´t·

përllogari´t· *vt* to figure out [] well, calculate [] exactly

përllogari´tje *nf ger* **1** <përllogari´t· **2** extensive calculation: computation; accounting

*përma´jësh *adv* up to the top, to the very brim

përma´l *adv* uphill, up

përma´ll *nm* **1** person for whom another yearns ***2** wistfulness; regret

përma´ll· *vt* = përmallo´·n

përmalli´m *nm ger* **1** <përmallo´·n, përmallo´·het **2** sentimental longing; emotional tenderness

përmallo´·het *vpr* **1** to feel deeply touched (emotionally) = mallëngje·het **2** to feel nostalgia/longing, yearn

përmallo´·n *vt* **1** to infect [] with longing, instill a sense of nostalgia in [] **2** = mallëngjo´·n

përmallshëm

I § *adj (i)* touching tender emotions: sentimental, touching, moving; nostalgic

II § *adv* sentimentally

përmallue´s *adj* deeply touching, heartbreaking, sentimental

përmarrshëm *adj (i)* **1** bashful **2** shamefaced

përma´së *nf* dimension; extent

○ **përmasa gabarite** overall dimension

përmata´në

I § *adv* over yonder, yonder

II § *prep (abl)* beyond, on the other side of

përmba´·het *vpr* to be self-restrained; contain oneself, keep oneself in check

përmba´·n *vt* **1** to keep [] in check: hold in, restrain **2** to keep [] within limits: constrain, confine **3** to contain **4** *(Old)* to maintain

përmba´jt *stem for pdef, opt, adm, part* <përmba·n

përmba´jtës *nm* container, receptacle; keeper

përmba´jtje *nf ger* **1** <përmba·n, përmba·het **2** content; contents **3** table of contents ***4** maintenance, support

*përmba´jtse *nf* vessel, container

përmba´jtshëm *adj (i)* **1** = përmbajtur ***2** supportable ***3** containable

përmba´jtur *adj (i)* capable of self-restraint: self-possessed, composed; sober, moderate

*përmba´mës *adj* **1** preservative **2** containing

përmbari´m *nm ger* **1** <përmbaro´·n **2** [*Law*] enforcement (of a civil matter) **3** [*Law*] bureau responsible for enforcing decisions (of the civil court) **4** [*Spec*] final preparation of a product: finishing touch, final treatment, finishing

përmbaro·*n vt* 1 to carry out [], implement, perform; accomplish 2 to give [] the finishing touches 3 *(Old)* [*Law*] to execute/enforce [a civil matter]

përmbarua*r adj (i)* finished, accomplished; perfect

përmbarue*s*
I § *adj* 1 [*Law*] implementing civil court judgments 2 *(Old)* having executive power 3 [*Spec*] in final preparation of a product: as a finishing touch, as a final treatment
II § *n* [*Law*] deputy charged with implementing civil judgments of a court

***përmba**rrsh*ëm adj (i)* bashful; blushing easily, easily shamed

përmbas *prep (abl)* immediately after; right behind

***përmba**s*i conj* since, as

***përmbes**o·*n vt* to accredit

***përmbet**un *adj (i) (Reg Gheg)* permanent

përmbë shti*ll stem for 2nd pl pres, pind, imper, vp* <përmbë dh·

përmbë shtje*ll· vt* 1 to wrap around []; seize by encircling 2 to gather [] together and then scatter
○ **përmb**ë shtje*ll·* **veten/shpirtin/frymën** to pull oneself together

përmbë shtje*ll ë part* <përmbë shtje ll·

përmbë shto*ll stem for pdef* <përmbë shtje ll·

përmbi *prep (acc)* on top of []: over; more than [an amount]; on [a surface]; concerning/about [a topic]; in addition to []
○ **përmbi këto** furthermore, moreover

***përmb**ie*mër nm* 1 *(Old)* surname = mbiemër 2 alias

***përmb**i fja*lë nf (Old)* epilogue

***përmb**i kqyr*ës adj, n (Old Regional Gheg)* = mbikëqyrës

***përmb**i kqy*rje nf ger (Old Regional Gheg)* = mbikëqyrje

përmbi par dje *adv* on the day before the day before yesterday

përmbi pas ne sër *adv* on the day after the day after tomorrow

***përmb**i qyr*ës (Old)* = mbikqyrës

***përmb**i sh*ëm adj (i)* upper, superior, on top

***përmb**i shkre s*ë nf (Old)* inscription

përmbi va rrsh*ëm adj (i)* graveside, funerary

përmbledh· *vt* 1 to gather [] together: compile, collect 2 to summarize, consolidate 3 to sum, sum [] up 4 to encompass, comprise 5 to restrain, constrain
○ <>**a përmbledh·** *(Colloq)* to strike/hit <>

përmble dhë*s*
I § *adj* 1 summary, summarizing 2 [*Ling*] collective
II § *nm* 1 book composed of items by the same author or on the same theme: anthology, collection, compilation 2 summarizer; compiler; anthologist
○ **përmbledhësja e llogarisë** *(Old)* [*Econ*] balance statement

përmble dhje *nf ger* 1 <përmble dh·, përmbli dh·et 2 summary; compendium

përmble dht*as* OR **përmble dh**t*azi adv* in summary manner/form

përmble dhur *adj (i)* 1 in summary form: succinct 2 closely aggregated 3 *(Fig)* composed/temperate in thought and action: collected; frugal

***përmble**s *stem for 1st sg pres, 1st & 3rd pl pres, 2nd & 3rd sg subj* <përmble t·

***përmble**t· *vt* to add shortening/fat to []

përmbli dh·et *vpr* 1 to huddle/hunch up, cringe 2 to pull oneself together 3 to gather up one's forces 4 to be included

përmbli dh *stem for 2nd pl pres, pind, imper, vp* <përmble dh·

***përmbli**s *stem for pind, 2nd pl pres, imper* <përmble t·

***përmbli**t *stem for part, pdef, pind, 2nd pl pres, imper, vp* <përmble t·

përmblo dh *stem for pdef* <përmble dh·

përmbrapa *adv* immediately after, right in back, just behind

***përmbra**pcë *nf* (of an animal) buttock

***përmbra**p sh*ëm adj (i)* rear, back

***përmbre**nd = përbrend

përmbre nd shme
I § *nf (e)* interior
II § *np (të)* entrails

***përmbrë**nd = përbrend

përmbush· *vt* 1 to fulfill [a responsibility/duty]; accomplish [a task] 2 to satisfy [a requirement/desire/condition] *3 to supplement

përmbush je *nf ger* <përmbu sh·

përmbyll·
I § *vt* 1 to bring [] to an end: conclude 2 to comprise
II § *vi* to come to the end: conclude

përmby llë*s adj* [*Ling*] consequent, consequential; resultative

përmby llje *nf ger* 1 <përmby ll·, përmby ll·et 2 conclusion

***përmby ll**t*as adv* = përmby s

***përmby ll**to*r adj* conclusive

përmbys *adv* upside down; face down; inverted; stooped over

përmbys·
I § *vt* 1 to turn [] upside down, upset; turn [] over; overturn 2 to lay [] face down; knock down 3 [*Agr*] to turn [the soil]; work manure into [the ground] 4 *(Fig)* to defeat badly: overwhelm, overcome 5 *(Fig)* to change [] around completely: invert, reverse 6 *(Fig)* to subvert
II § *stem for 1st sg pres, pl pres, 2nd & 3rd sg subj, pind* <përmbyt·
○ **e përmbys·** *(Crude)* to put on a real celebration; have a wild time, have rip-roaring fun

përmbys·et *vpr* 1 to fall face down, fall over; lie face down 2 (of a vehicle) to turn/roll over with great force 3 (of a situation) to change radically

përmbys*ëm adj (i)* = përmbys ët

përmbys ës
I § *n* 1 person who causes radical changes: subverter 2 [*Tech*] device for emptying a loaded vehicle by turning it over: dumping/tilting mechanism
II § *adj* subversive

përmbys ët *adj (i)* upside-down; topsy-turvy

përmbys je *nf ger* 1 <përmbys·, përmbys·et 2 overturn, upset

përmbys sh*ëm adj (i)* reversible

përmbys ta*r adj* rebellious

***përmby**s ur *adj (i)* in reverse, reversed, inverted

përmbyt· *vt* 1 to flood [] 2 *(Fig)* to stifle; drown
○ [] **përmbyt· nga rrënjët/me rrënjë** "stifle at the root(s)" to eradicate []

përmbyt·et *vpr* to become flooded

përmbytje *nf ger* 1 <**përmby**t·, **përmbyt**·*et* 2 deluge

***përmbyz**·*et vpr* to prostrate oneself, kneel down

përmend· *vt* 1 to mention; cite 2 to call [] to mind; call [] to <>'s attention, remind <> about [] 3 to revive, reawaken: rouse
  ◦ **përmend· mbi** [] *(Old)* to make mention of []

përmend·*et vpr* 1 to wake up from a deep sleep; regain consciousness 2 to gain distinction; earn mention

përmendje *nf ger* 1 <**përmend**·, **përmend**·*et* 2 mention; citation

përmendore *nf* 1 memorial, monument 2 *(Old)* [*Dipl*] = **përkujtes**ë

***përmends**ë *nf* record, document

përmendsh *adv* from memory, by heart; perfectly; mechanically, by rote

***përmendshëm** *adj (i)* memorable; worthy of mention, noteworthy

përmendur *adj (i)* oft-mentioned, noteworthy, famous

përmes
  I § adv 1 from one side to the other; throughout 2 right in the middle
  II § prep (abl) 1 through; throughout 2 among, between
  III § nm * *(Old)* diameter

***përmesëm** *adj (i)* average

Përmet *nf* city and its surrounding area in southeastern Albania

përmetar
  I § adj of or pertaining to Përmet
  II § n native of Përmet

***përmeto**·*n vt* to permit, allow

***përmë**ë *nf* desire, wish

përmëkat·*et vpr* to sin

***përmëkatnueshëm** *adj (i)* sinful

përmëles *stem for 1st sg pres, 1st & 3rd pl pres, 2nd & 3rd sg subj* <**përmële**t·

përmëlet· *vi* to cause <> to stop fasting

përmëlis *stem for pind, 2nd pl pres, imper* <**përmële**t·

përmëlit·*et vpr* to stop fasting

përmëlit *stem for part, pdef, pind, 2nd pl pres, imper, vp* <**përmële**t·

***përmëndëshëm** *adj (i)* worthy of note, worth remembering: notable, memorable

përmënim *nm ger* <**përmëno**·*n*

përmëno·*n vi* to be somewhat late: be tardy

përmidis *nm* center

përmiell· *vt* 1 to get/put flour on []: coat/cover/sprinkle [] with flour 2 *(Fig)* to grizzle

përmiell·*et vpr* 1 to get coated/covered/sprinkled with flour 2 *(Fig)* to become grizzled

***përmier** = **përmj**err·

përmih· *vt* 1 to break up [soil] into smaller pieces prior to planting *2 to cultivate

***përmillzo**·*n vt* to cover with flour/powder

përmiqëso·*het vpr* to become/make friends, be chummy

***përmiq**ëso·*n vt* to reconcile

***përmiqyr**· *vt* to observe, inspect = **mbik**ëqyr·

***përmirr**·*et* = **përmi**rr·*et*

përmirësim *nm ger* 1 <**përmirëso**·*n*, **përmirëso**·*het* 2 improvement

përmirëso·*het vpr* to improve, get better

përmirëso·*n vt* to improve []; perfect

përmirësuar *adj (i)* improved

përmirësues *adj* serving to improve: beneficial

përmirr·*et vpr* to pass urine; urinate involuntarily: wet one's pants

përmirr *stem for 2nd pl pres, pind, imper, vp* <**përmj**err·

përmishëro·*n vt* to make [] concrete, incarnate, embody

përmjalt· *vt* 1 to sweeten/smear [] with honey 2 *(Fig)* to give pleasure to []

përmjaltshëm *adj (i)* honeyed

përmjaltur *adj (i)* 1 made with honey; sweetened with honey 2 *(Fig)* pleased

***përmjer** = **përmj**err·

përmjerr·
  I § vi to urinate
  II § vt 1 to wet [] (with urine) 2 *(Crude)* to piss [a liquid]

përmjerrë
  I § part <**përmj**err·
  II § adj (i) wet/dripping with urine; full of piss

përmjet *prep (abl)* = **nëpërmjet**

përmjeto·*n vt* to fill [] half full

***përmnershëm** *adj (i)* really horrible

përmor *stem for pdef* <**përmj**err·

përmortshëm
  I § adj (i) 1 of or pertaining to a funeral; in mourning 2 funereal
  II § adv as a sign of mourning, in mourning; in a funereal manner

përmortur *adj (i)* in mourning

përmorr *stem for pdef* <**përmj**err·

përmorrtë *adj (i)* infested with lice: lousy

përmot *adv* every year

përmotje *nf (Old)* anniversary

përmotshëm *adj (i) (Colloq)* yearly

***përmqyr** = **mbik**ëqyr·

përmuaj shëm *adj (i)* monthly = **mujo**r

përmuaj shme
  I § nf (e) monthly periodical: monthly
  II § np (të) fem [*Physiol*] menses: monthlies

përmuar *stem for pl pdef* <**përmj**err·

përmullëz *nf* [*Anat*] fourth chamber of the stomach of a ruminant that contains the abomasum: rennet sac

përmut·*et vpr* to soil oneself (with feces): shit in one's pants

***përmys**· *(Colloq)* = **përmbys**·

përnar *nm* [*Bot*] kermes oak = **prrall**
  ◦ **përnar i eg**ër [*Bot*] = **a**she

përnatë *adv* nightly, every night, at night

përnatshëm *adj (i)* happening every night: nightly, nocturnal

përnda·*het vpr* to go off in different directions: disperse, scatter; become diffused, thin out

përnda·*n vt* to distribute; disperse, scatter

***përndamje** = **përndarj**e

përndarë *adj (i)* separated and apart: dispersed

përndarës *nm* = **shpërndar**ës

përnda`rje *nf ger* **1** <përnda·*n*, përnda·*het* **2** distribution; dispersal

*****përndejshëm** *adj (i)* stationary, still; sedentary; stable

përnderim *nm (Book)* reverence; low bow as a sign of respect

*****përnde`rje** *nf* courteous bow, curtsey

përndero·*n* *vt (Book)* to revere; bow low to show respect

*****përnde`rshëm** *adj (i)* = përnderua`r

përndeiua`r *adj (i)* **1** *(Book)* revered **2** *[Relig]* title of respect for a Christian clergyman: Reverend

*****përndën** *prep (acc)* <për nën under

*****përndiq** *stem for 2nd pl pres, pind, imper, vp* <përndje`k·

përndjek· *vt* to persecute

*****përndjek`ës** *n* persecutor

përndjekje *nf ger* **1** <përndje`k· **2** persecution

**përndjeku`r** *part* <përndje`k·

**përndo`q** *stem for pdef* <përndje`k·

*****përndo`r·** = përdo`r·

*****përndris** *stem for 1st sg pres, pl pres, 2nd & 3rd sg subj, pind* <përndri`t·

përndri`t· *vt* to light up [], illuminate

përndritshëm *adj (i)* **1** *(Old)* *[Relig]* title of respect for a high-ranking Christian clergyman: Eminence **2** brilliant, glorious

përndritu`r *adj (i)* illuminated

përndry`dh· *vt* to sprain [] badly

përndry`she *adv* otherwise, or else

*****përndrrim** *nm* thorough alteration, complete change

*****përne** *prep (acc)* <për në heading for, bound for, off to

*****përnën`ë** *prep (abl)* under, underneath

përnga`herë *adv* forever; all the time, always; any time

*****përngroh·** *vt* to warm [] up

përngu`l· *vt* **1** to transplant, replant; plant **2** to push in [], force **3** to establish residence in []: settle

përngu`l·*et* *vpr* to become established: settle

përngu`lje *nf* establishment of a population: settlement

përngu`lur *adj (i)* **1** fixed in place: lodged **2** permanently settled (in residence) *****3** transplanted *****4** stubborn

përngu`t *adv* in a hurry/rush, in haste

përngu`tshëm *adj (i)* urgent, pressing

përngja·*n* *vi* to be very much like <>, resemble <> strongly
  ○ **përngja·*n* si** {} to be very much like {}, resemble {} strongly

përngja`ll· *vt* to enliven, animate; revive, rouse

përngja`ll`ës *adj* animating, rousing, reviving

*****përngja`m`ë** = përngja`rë

përngja`rë *part* <përngja·*n*

**përngja`rje** *nf* = përngjasi`m

**përngja`s** *stem for 1st sg pres, pl pres, 2nd & 3rd sg subj, pind* <përngje`t·

përngjasi`m *nm* similarity, resemblance

përngja`shëm *adj (i)* similar

përngja`shm`ëri *nf* = përngjasi`m

përngja`shmi`m *nm [Ling]* assimilation

përngje`sh· *vt* **1** to compress [] strongly, squeeze [] hard **2** *(Fig)* to smack

përngjet· *vi* = përngja·*n*

përngjetshëm *adj (i)* similar

përngjis *stem for 2nd pl pres, pind* <përngje`t·

përngji`t· *vt* **1** to stick [things] together **2** *[Ling]* to agglutinate []

përngji`t·*et* *vpr* **1** to be in close fit, fit well (together); match up well **2** to press up close **3** *[Ling]* to become agglutinated

përngjit *stem for pind, 2nd pl pres, imper, vp* <përngje`t·

përngji`tje *nf [Ling]* agglutination; agglutinate

përngji`tur *adj (i) [Ling]* agglutinated

*****përnzi`·*n*** *vt* = nxi·*n*

përnjë`çastm`ë *adj (i)* momentary; instantaneous

përnjë`herë** OR **përnjë`herë`sh *adv* **1** at once, right away, immediately; at that very moment, right then **2** at the same time, simultaneously **3** all at once, suddenly

*****përnjë`herë`t** *adj (i)* = përnjëhershëm

përnjë`hershëm *adj (i)* instantaneous, immediate; spontaneous, sudden

përnjë`herthi *adv* = përnjëherë

përnjë`mend *adv* really meaning it, in earnest: genuinely; seriously

përnjë`mendt`ë *adj (i)* genuine, true, real; serious

*****përnjiher** *(Reg Gheg)* = përnjëher

*****përnjimënd`ët** *adj (i) (Reg Gheg)* = përnjëmendt`ë

*****përnjiso·*n*** = njëso·*n*

*****përnji`shëm** *adj (i)* uniform, unified

përnjo`hje *nf [Mil]* reconnaissance

përnjom· *vt* to get [] wet

*****përon`ë** = peron`ë

*****përor`ë** *adv* continuously, always

*****përpa** *stem for 3rd sg pdef, pl pdef, opt, adm, part* <përsho`f·

përpajn`ë *nf [Agr]* grapevine stock from which cuttings are taken for layering: *(layer)*

përpajni`m *nm ger* **1** *[Agr]* <përpajno·*n* **2** propagation by grafting: *(layerage)*

përpajno·*n* *vt [Agr]* to propagate [grapevines] by layering: layer *(P)*

përpa`k *adv* nearly

përpa`l`ë *nf* = përpare`se

**përpa`ll·** *vt* **1** *(Old)* to bring [] out into the open, make [] public: divulge **2** *(Pej)* = tellalli`s·

përpa`llet·*et* *vpr* to become known publicly, get bruised around

përpa`ra
I *§* *adv* **1** ahead; forward **2** earlier, before
II *§* *prep (abl)* ahead of, in front of, before; in comparison with
  ○ **nuk <> dil·*et*³ʳᵈ përpara 1** there *is* none better than <> **2** there *is* no use trying with <> {}, there *is* no point in talking to <>
  ○ **përpara hundës** right there (under <>'s nose)
  ○ **më përpara 1** earlier **2** first of all, in the first place
  ○ **Përpara rripë e prapa thik`ë.** "precipice behind and knife ahead" Damned if you do and damned if you don't. Bad either way.
  ○ **përpara se __** before __
  ○ **përpara syve të <>** before <>'s very eyes; in <>'s presence; before the whole <>

*për|par|ande'j *adv* in the past, previously, beforehand

*për|par|ande'j|shëm *adj (i)* former, previous

*për|pa'razi *OR* për|pa'razit *adv* in front, towards the front; first of all

për|pa'rcë *nf* = përpa'rëse

*për|pa'rë *part* <përsho'f•

për|pa'rëse *nf* 1 apron 2 smock (worn to protect clothes at work or school) 3 front panel of an upper garment

*për|pa'rës|ëm *adj (i)* = përparm'ë.

për|par|esi' *nf* primacy, priority

për|pa'rim *nm ger* 1 <përparo'•n 2 advance; progress, headway

Përpa'rim *nm* Përparim (male name)

për|par|im|da'sh'ës *adj, n (Book)* progressive

për|par|im|da'shje *nf (Book)* favoring progress, progressiveness

për|par|im|ta'r *adj* favoring/contributing to progress: progressive

për|par|im|ta're *nf* progressive element

për|par|im|tari' *nf* progressiveness

për|pa'rje *nf* 1 = përpa'rëse 2 = përpa'jnë

për|pa'rmë *adj (i)* 1 in front: forward, front 2 [*Ling*] anterior; preposed; front

për|paro'•n *vi* to move forward: advance; make progress, progress

për|par|she'm *adj (i)* 1 previous, earlier 2 = përparm'ë

për|par|shm|eri' *nf* precedence, priority

për|par|thi *adv* in front

për|pa|ru'ar *adj (i)* 1 advanced 2 up-to-date, modern 3 progressive

për|pa|ru'es *adj (Book)* increasing in graduated steps: gradual, progressive

*për|pa's *adv* behind

për|pa's|ëm *adj (i)* rear, hind, hindmost

*për|pa'shë *1st sg pdef* <përsho'f•

*për|pe' *2nd sg pdef* <përsho'f•

për|pe'q *nm* [*Food*] kind of cheese custard with a crust; kind of cheese pastry

për|pel|is *stem for 1st sg pres, pl pres, 2nd & 3rd sg subj, pind* <përpëli't•

për|pël|i't• *vt* to make a small quick movement with [part of the body]: blink [eye], jerk [body], wiggle [finger], flap [wing]

për|pël|i't•*et vpr* 1 to make small energetic movements repeatedly: thrash around, writhe, squirm; quiver, twitch, wiggle 2 (*Fig*) to suffer terribly; struggle to escape, wriggle

  ○ përpëlit•*et* në shtratin e vdekjes "struggle in death's bed" to be struggling with death, be in one's death throes

  ○ përpëlit•*et* si petulla në tigan "wriggle like a pancake on the frying pan" to have an insatiable burning desire; have an agonizing problem: be like a cat on a hot tin roof

*për|pël|i't|ës *adj* making a quick movement of part of the body: spasmodic, convulsive, twitching; quivering

për|pël|i'tje *nf ger* 1 <përpëli't•, përpëli't•*et* 2 repeated quick movement of the body or a body part; tossing and turning 3 [*Med*] jactitation 4 strenuous effort to escape

*për|përi'•*n OR* për|përo'•*n vi* 1 to make a purring sound: purr; murmur 2 to make a rustling sound: rustle, whisper

*për|përi'm *I§ nm OR* për|përi'm'ë *II§ nf* 1 <përpëri'•n 2 purr

për|pi'•*het vpr* to disappear without a trace

për|pi'•*n vt* to swallow [] greedily; swallow [] up: devour, gulp down [], gobble up []

  ○ [] përpi•*n* me sy to devour [] with one's eyes; stare at <> greedily

  ○ përpi•*n* retë "devour the clouds" to be a miracle-working hero

  ○ e përpi•*n* rrugën "gobble up the road" to cover a distance in a short time: eat up the road

  ○ [] përpi•*n* të gjallë "devour [] alive" to devour [] in entirety (leaving nothing), gobble [] all up; make [] disappear in an instant

për|pik|eri' *nf* precision, exactitude; special care

për|pik|meri' = përpik'eri

për|pi'k|she'm *adj (i)* = përpi'ktë

për|pi'ktë *adj (i)* 1 exact; precise; on target; prompt, punctual 2 with particular care, especially careful

*për|pi'k|un *adj (i) (Reg Gheg)* 1 shrewd; witty 2 = përpi'ktë

për|pil|i'm *nm ger* 1 <përpilo'•n 2 compilation

për|pilo'•*n vt* to compile; draft, draw up []

për|pil|u'es *nm* compiler; formulator, drafter

*për|pi'll = përpil

për|pi'q•*et vpr* 1 to struggle; strive, endeavor 2 to writhe, thrash around

  ○ përpiq•*et* si gjarpër to try hard, do one's utmost

  ○ përpiq•*et* si zorra/veza në prush "struggle like an intestine/egg on a bed of hot coals" to be very uneasy, have ants in one's pants, be very antsy

për|pi'q| *stem for 2nd pl pres, pind, imper, vp* <përpje'k•

për|pi'r|ës *I§ n* 1 one who grabs and gobbles up everything in sight 2 (*Reg*) hidden hole in the ground into which rain water disappears *II§ adj* overwhelming

për|pi'r|je *nf ger* <përpi•n, përpi•het

për|pje'k•
  I§ vt 1 to cause [] to impact with force (and noise): bang [], bang against [], clap [hands], click [heels], slam [door], smack [lips] 2 to run into: encounter *II§ vi* 1 to meet 2 (*Fig*) to get along together: click

  ○ i përpjek• fjalët me [] to exchange angry words with [], quarrel with []

  ○ përpjek• këmbët to stamp one's feet (with insistence); pound the table, keep insisting

  ○ përpjek• pallat/ushtat me [] to cross swords with [], get into a fight with []

  ○ i përpjek•*pl* pipat bashkë to act in cahoots

për|pje'kë *nf* big effort, great pains, much difficulty

*për|pje'k|ës *n* struggler; fighter, wrestler

për|pje'kje *nf ger* 1 <përpje'k•, përpi'q•*et* 2 great effort; struggle 3 short battle, skirmish: clash, affray

për|pje'k|ur
  I§ part <përpje'k•, përpi'q•*et* *II§ adj (i)* 1 making great efforts: striving, eager, hard-working 2 struck together, collided

për|pje'së *nf* = përpjes'ëtim

për|pje's|ëm *adj (i)* = përpjes'she'm

përpjesëtim nm 1 proportion 2 ratio 3 scale, dimension *4 allocation; distribution

përpjesëtimëri nf (Book) = përpjesëtueshmëri

përpjesëtimi nf (Book) = përpjesëtimëri

përpjesëtimisht adv (Book) in proportion, proportionately

përpjesëtimor adj (Book) proportional

përpjesëto·n vt 1 to put [] into proportion 2 to apportion/divide/distribute [] according to a plan: allot, allocate

përpjesëtuar adj (i) having the right dimensions; proportioned as required; in the right proportion

përpjesëtueshëm adj (i) proportionable, proportionate

përpjesëtueshmëri nf (Book) proportionality

*përpjesisht = përpjesëtimisht

*përpjesor = përpjesëtimor

përpjesshëm adj (i) 1 [Math] proportional *2 partial

*përpjestisht = përpjesëtimisht

përpjetë
I § adv 1 uphill; upward 2 up; upright, erect
II § prep (abl) up
III § nf 1 uphill slope 2 men's circle dance with high kicks and leaps
IV § adj (i) 1 uphill; sloping upward 2 (Fig) on the rise, rising
V § nf (e) uphill slope
○ {after an expression of amount} e përpjetë {} and up/more
○ s'bë·n përpjetë (of someone/something in poor health/economic condition) {} will not get any better
○ nuk i hy·n asaj së/të përpjete to be unwilling to do anything that is not easy: not want to take on a hard task

përpjetëm adj (i) 1 sloping up, uphill 2 [Bot] (of a plant stalk) that lies low to the ground and then rises sharply upward

përpjeto·n vt to praise [] to the heavens: extol

përpjetshëm adj (i) = përpjetëm

përplas· vt 1 to smack, slam, bang; bounce [a ball] 2 to hurl [] to the ground, slam down [], dash 3 (Fig) to unload [a burdensome responsibility] onto ○ 4 (Fig) to plop [] down (in an inappropriate place), clap [] (into an undesirable place)
○ <>[] përplas· to hit ○ with [the plain facts/truth]
○ <>a përplas· derën në fytyrë to slam the door in ○'s face
○ përplas· duart to clap hands
○ përplas· këmbët to stamp one's feet (with insistence); pound the table, keep insisting
○ <>a përplas· në fytyrë to say it right to ○'s face
○ <>a përplas·³ˢᵍ në sy to say it right to ○'s face

përplas·et vpr 1 to collide; crash: (of waves) dash, (of a ball) bounce, (of glasses) clink 2 to plop; plop down 3 (Fig Colloq) to look for help/support

përplasje nf ger 1 <përplas·, përplas·et 2 crash

*përplis· vt 1 to entangle, entwine; complicate 2 to puzzle, perplex

*përplisje nf complexity

përplot adv completely full

përplotës
I § adj supplementary
II § nm supplement

përplotësim nm ger 1 (Book) <përplotëso·n, përplotëso·het 2 augmentation, supplement

përplotëso·het vpr (Book) to become augmented

përplotëso·n vt (Book) to augment, supplement

përplotësor adj (Old) = përplotësues

përplotësues adj (Book) augmenting, supplementing; supplementary

përpoq stem for pdef <përpjek·

*përporit·et vpr to be in doubt, be perplexed

përpos prep (abl) aside from; besides, in addition to

përposh
I § adv below; down
II § prep (abl) beneath; down, below

përposhtazi adv downwards, toward the bottom

përpraps·et = praps·et

përprish· vt (Intens) 1 to ruin [] utterly, mess [] up; totally destroy [], nullify; break [] down 2 to break off [a relationship] completely

përprish·et vpr 1 to break off a social relationship completely 2 to have a mental breakdown: go crazy, lose one's mind

përprishje nf ger <përprish·, përprish·et

përprishur adj (i) out of one's mind, crazy

*përpshtjellë nf extract (from a book)

përpunim nm ger 1 <përpuno·n, përpuno·het 2 treatment, refinement

përpuno·n vt 1 to work on [] to yield a desired result: process [], refine [oil], revise [a manuscript], process [fruit], treat [milk], perfect [a plan] 2 (Pej) to work on [someone] to do something in one's own interest: attempt to influence []

përpunuar adj (i) refined, improved, revised; processed, treated

përpunues
I § adj serving to process/refine/improve
II § n 1 processor, refiner, reviser/editor, finisher, detailer 2 [Postal] sorting clerk, sorter

përpuq· vt to fit/join/connect [] together tightly

përpuq·et vpr to fit together tight/well

përpuqje nf ger <përpuq·, përpuq·et

*përpuris stem for 1st sg pres, pl pres, 2nd & 3rd sg subj, pind <përpurit·

*përpurit· vt to stir [] up, rouse

përpurth nm = përpurthë

përpurth· vt to soil [] with diarrhea

përpurth·et vpr to have diarrhea; dirty oneself in defecating

përpurthë nf (Colloq) diarrhea: the runs

përpush· vt 1 to poke [a fire], stir up [live coals/embers] 2 (of chickens) to scratch [the ground] 3 to rumple/tousle []

përpush·et vpr 1 (of chickens) to scratch the ground while foraging; rummage around 2 to twitch

përpushje nf ger 1 <përpush·, përpush·et 2 twitch

*përpushto·n vt to comprise

përputh· vt to fit/join/connect [] together tightly, interlock, clasp

përputh·et vpr 1 to fit together, dovetail, interlock 2 to stick to the body; fit tight 3 (Fig) to agree completely; fit well, match exactly

përputhje nf ger 1 <përputh·, përputh·et 2 agreement; conformity

* **për·pu'th·un** ,*adj (i) (Reg Gheg)* dovetailed, interlocked, clasped

përqa'f· *et vpr* to engage in friendly hugging

përqa'fe *adv* < **për qa**fe around the neck

për qafi'm *nm ger* 1 < **përqafo**´·*n*, **përqafo**´·*het* 2 embrace

për qafo´·*het vp recip* to hug each other around the neck; embrace

për qafo´·*n vt* to hug [] around the neck; embrace

për qa'll· *et vpr* to court favor by servile behavior/ affection: fawn

për qa'rk *adv prep (dat)* all around

për qa'rk *nm (np ~ qe)* 1 ornamental border 2 border, periphery *3 compass, scope

për qa'rkje *nf* moccasin thong that ties around the leg

* **për·qa'rq e** *np* < **përqa**rk environs, outskirts, surroundings

përqa's· *vt* to bring [] close for comparison: compare, collate

për qa's·*et vpr* to be comparable

për qa's je *nf ger* 1 < **përqa**s·, **përqa**s·*et* 2 close comparison; collation

* **për qe'll** = **përqe**sh

për qendri'm *nm ger* 1 < **përqendro**´·*n*, **përqendro**´·*het* 2 concentration

për qendro´·*het vpr* 1 to assemble in one place: concentrate 2 to focus one's attention: concentrate

për qendro´·*n vt* to concentrate, centralize

për qendru a'r *adj (i)* 1 concentrated 2 mentally focussed: concentrating, attentive

për qendru e's *nm* [*Tech*] concentrator

për qendru esh ëm *adj (i)* 1 able to concentrate; capable of being concentrated *2 persistent

për qendru eshm ëri´ *nf (Book)* ability to concentrate

për qe'sh· *vt* to mimic, mock; scoff at [], deride

për qe'sh ës

I § *adj* mocking; scoffing

II § *n* mocker; scoffer

○ **përqeshësi i gjelbër** [*Ornit*] icterine warbler *Hippolais icterina*

○ **përqeshësi i ullinjve** [*Ornit*] olivaceous warbler *Hippolais pallida*

për qe'sh je *nf ger* 1 < **përqe**sh· 2 derisive word/ gesture/attitude; derision

* **për qesh ta'r** *adj, n* = **përqe**shës

për qe'sh ur *n (i)* person mocked

për qe'th· *vt* to cause to shudder/shiver

për qe'th·*et vpr* to shudder, shiver

për qe'th *ë nn (të)* shudder, shiver

për qe'th ës *adj* causing one to shudder/shiver: horrifying, dreadful; shocking

për qe'th je *nf ger* 1 < **përqe**th·, **përqe**th·*et* 2 shudder, shiver

për qe'th ur a *np fem (të)* shivers, shudders, shakes

për qëndr = **përqendr**

* **për qëndr o'r** *adj (Old)* [*Geom*] concentric = **bashkë**-**qendro**r

për qi' *nf* = **paj**ë

* **për qind es ë** *nf (Old)* = **përqi**ndje

* **për qi'nd** ës *adj* percentile

* **për qi'nd** ëshe *nf* percentile, percent

për qi'ndje *nf* 1 percentage 2 percentage payment: interest (on money); (salary) commission

○ **përqindje e lindjeve** "percentage of births" birthrate

* **për qi'nd sh e** *nf* percentage

* **për qi'nd t** é *adj (i)* = **përqi**ndës

* **për qi's·** *vt* to knock, knock [] down

për qo'k· *vt* to pick [fruit] up/out (selectively); (of fowl) pick up with the beak: get [] by pecking

për qok o´·*n* = **përqo**k·

* **për qu'k·** = **përqo**k·

për qu'll·*et vpr* to slobber

për qu'rr·*et vpr* to issue mucous from the nose: have a runny nose, snivel, snuffle

për qy'rr· *vt (Crude)* to bedaub with snot

për qy'rr·*et* = **përqu**rr·*et*

* **për·ra'hje** [*për-rra´h-je*] *nf* repercussion, reverberation

për re'th [*për-rre´th*] *adv, prep (abl)* around

* **për·rëpi'n** ë [*për-rrë-pi´n*] *nf* steep/precipitous slope; ravine = **rrëpi**rë

* **për·rëpi't** ë [*për-rrë-pi´t*] *adj* steep/precipitous = **rrëpi**rët

për s afri´ *adv* very soon

për se'

I § *adv conj* for what (reason): why

II § *nf* reason, cause

* **për se' he** *nf* reason, ground

për sekut o´·*n vt* = **përndje**´k·

për së ba'shku *adv* all together

për së drejti *adv* straightforwardly; honestly

* **për së dy's** *stem for 1st sg pres, pl pres, 2nd & 3rd sg subj, pind* < **përsëdy**t·

për së dy't· *vt* to do [] for the second time, do [] again: repeat

për së dy't·*et vpr* to happen for the second time, happen again: repeat

* **për së dy'ti** *adv (së)* for the second time, again; secondly, in the second place

për së dy'tje *nf ger* 1 < **përsëdy**t·, **përsëdy**t·*et* 2 repetition

* **për së fu'nd i** *adv (së)* recently

për së gje'ri *adv* crosswise

për së ja'sht m i *adv* from the outside

për së kthje'llti *adv* in/under a clear sky

* **për së la'rg ëm** *adj (i)* far-away, distant, remote

për së la'rg u *adv* from far away, from afar

* **për së la'rk·***et vpr* = **përsëlargë**m

* **për s ëll** = **përc**ëll

për së pra'pi OR **për së pra'p thi** *adv* wrongly; perversely

për së ri´ *adv* for another time: again

për së ri's *stem for 1st sg pres, pl pres, 2nd & 3rd sg subj, pind* < **përsëri**t·

për së ri't· *vt* 1 to say/do [] again: repeat 2 *(Old)* to rejuvenate, renew = **ripërtëri**·*n*

për së ri't·*et vpr* to occur again, be recurrent: recur

për së ri't ës

I § *n* repeater

II § *adj* 1 repeating 2 [*Ling*] iterative

për së ri'tje *nf ger* 1 < **përsëri**t·, **përsëri**t·*et* 2 repetition; exercise, drill 3 [*Lit*] reiteration

për së ri'tsh ëm *adj (i) (Book)* repeatable; replicable

për·së·ri·tur adj (i) **1** repeated, repeating **2** (Old) rejuvenated, renewed = **ripërtëritur**

për·së·shpejt·i adv very soon

për·së·te·pri adv excessively, too much, in excess

*****përsi** = **përsëri**

përsi·as stem for 1st sg pres, pl pres, 2nd & 3rd sg subj, pind <**përsia**t·

përsia·t· vt to think [] out/over/through, consider [] carefully: deliberate about []

përsia·t·et vpr to think carefully: deliberate, ponder

përsia·tje nf ger **1** <**përsia**t·, **përsia**t·et **2** deep thought, cogitation; musing

përsia·tur adj (i) well thought out, well-considered.

*****përsikë** nf [Ichth] = **perke**

*****përsill** = **përcill**

*****përs·imt·i** adv in great detail; minutely

përsipër
I § adv **1** on the upper surface: on top; in the upper part; above **2** up
II § prep (abl) on top of, on; above, over

përsipshëm adj (i) upper, top

*****përsje·ll·** vt = **përcje·ll·**

*****përsjell·ës** adj, n = **përcjell·ës**

*****përsjellje** nf ger = **përcjellje**

përskaj
I § adv superficially
II § prep (dat) along the edge of <>

për·ske·q·et vpr to get very angry

për·sku·q· vt to cause to redden

për·sku·q·et vpr to take on a red color: become rosy, blush, redden

për·sku·q·ur adj (i) reddened, rosy; flushed, blushing

*****përso·ll·** = **përco·ll·**

për·so·s· vt to perfect, refine, polish; complete

për·so·s·et vpr to become perfected/refined/polished

*****përso·së·m·i** = **përsosuri**

përso·s·je nf ger **1** <**përso·s**·, **përso·s**·et **2** = përsosuri

përso·s·më·ni = **përsosuri**

përso·s·më·ri = **përsosuri**

përso·s·ur adj (i) perfected; refined, polished; perfect, complete

përsosuri nf perfection; refinement

*****përspër** = **pëshpër**

*****përspjek** adv on the contrary

përspjet· vi (Colloq) to appear unexpectedly to <>: pop up

përsykt·e adj (i) **1** (of horses) red-roan ***2** flea-bitten gray

për·sy·sh· vt **1** to cast the evil eye on []: bewitch **2** to ogle

për·sy·sh·et vpr to be afflicted by the evil eye: be bewitched, have a jinx

përsha··het vpr to exchange terrible insults

për·sha··n vt to revile [] badly, abuse

*****përshef** stem for 2nd & 3rd sg pres <**përsho·f**·

për·she·nj· vt to cause [] to show signs of ripening

për·she·nj·et vpr **1** to start to show signs of ripening **2** (Fig) to show signs (of maturity)

përshesh nm **1** sop made with pieces of bread; bread dressing/stuffing; bread pudding **2** (Fig) big mess, hodgepodge

○ **di· vetëm të ha·**ˢᵘᵇʲ **/rras·**ˢᵘᵇʲ **përshesh** to be good for nothing but eating and drinking

për·she·sh· vt **1** to crumble [bread] into a sop **2** (Fig) to crumble/pulverize []; raze
○ **<>i përshesh· trutë** (Impol) to split <>'s head open

për·she·sh·et vpr **1** to fall to pieces: crumble **2** (Fig Colloq) to get badly hurt, bruise oneself **3** (Fig) to scuffle hard

përshesh·të adj (i) flat and shallow

përshënde·s stem for 1st sg pres, pl pres, 2nd & 3rd sg subj, pind <**përshënde**t·

përshënde·t· vt to give salutations to []: greet; salute; say one's goodbyes to []; congratulate

përshënde·t·et vpr to exchange salutations

përshënde·t·ës adj in salutation; congratulatory

përshënde·tje nf ger **1** <**përshënde**t·, përshënde·t·et **2** greeting, salutation; congratulations
○ **përshëndetja e fundit** final homage (to the dead), final farewell

përshëndo·sh· vt = **përshënde**t·

përshëndo·sh·et vpr = **përshënde**t·et

përshëndo·shje nf ger <**përshëndo·sh**·, përshëndo·sh·et = përshënde·tje

përsh·ndri·t·shëm adj (i) **1** = **shndritshëm** ***2** transparent ***3** illustrious

*****përshën·im** nm ger **1** <**përshëno**·n **2** insinuation

*****përshëno··n** vt to insinuate

përshënjt·ëro··n vt to consecrate

për·shi··n vt to crumble [bread]

*****përshif** stem for 2nd pl pres, pind, imper, vp <**përsho·f**·

përshit·et vpr to sell off everything

*****përshit·as** adv (Reg Gheg) inclusively

përshit·ës n (Pej) profiteer; black-marketer

për·shka·rdh· vt to enslave; treat [] like a slave

për·sh·këlli··n vt (Colloq) to soil with a blot, get ink on []

*****përshkënde··n** vt to scatter [light], refract

përshkënd·is stem for 1st sg pres, pl pres, 2nd & 3rd sg subj, pind <**përshkendi**t·

përshkëndi·t·
I § vt **1** to scatter [] broadly **2** to poke [embers/fire] into giving off sparks; cause to sparkle
II § vi to sparkle

përshkëndi·t·et vpr **1** to scatter far and wide **2** to give off sparks: sparkle

përshkëndi·tje nf ger **1** <**përshkëndi**t·, përshkëndi·t·et **2** sparkle

*****përshkëti** nf **1** herpes = **shpërgëti** ***2** = **gërshet**

përshk·im nm ger **1** <**përshko**·n, përshko·het **2** basting stitch

përshko··het vpr to be permeated/imbued

përshko··n vt **1** to pass [] through; thread [a needle] **2** to cross over/through []; traverse [a route] **3** to permeate **4** to sew [] temporarily with a basting stitch: baste []; string [] together
○ [] **përshko·n me ngjyra të zeza** "describe [] with dark colors" to make [] seem worse than [] is, depict [] as being worse that [] is: paint [] in dark colors, present [] in the worst light

përshko·q· vt **1** to divide [] into small pieces: crumble **2** to scatter [] **3** to snatch

përshko·q·et vp to become widely dispersed: scatter

përshko qje *nf ger* <përshkoq·, përshko qe·t

përshkrím *nm ger* 1 <përshkrua·n 2 description 3 [*Lit*] (descriptive) sketch

përshkrim ta r *adj (Book)* descriptive

përshkrua·n *vt* to describe

përshkrue s *adj* descriptive

përshku a r *adj (i)* permeated, imbued

përshku e s *adj* conductive

përshku e shëm *adj (i)* permeable; penetrable

përshku e shmëri *nf* permeability; penetrability

përshku l· *vt* to yank out []; keep pulling out []

përshku l·*et vpr* to move away/out; emigrate

*përshkye·n *vt* to grab [] away from <>

*përshof· *vt* to perceive

*përshoq ërо·n *vt* to be associated with [], accompany

*përshoq no·n = përshoqërо·n

përsho sh· *vt* 1 to sift [] thoroughly; sift [] again 2 (*Fig*) to scrutinize carefully

*përshpa ll· *vt* to proclaim = shpall·

përshpatë *adv* at/from the side

përshpejtim *nm ger* 1 <përshpejtо·n, përshpejt-о·het 2 acceleration

përshpejtо·het *vpr* to get/go/grow faster: accelerate

përshpejtо·n *vt* to increase the speed/development of []: accelerate

përshpejtua r *adj (i)* accelerated

përshpejtue s *adj* 1 accelerative, accelerating 2 [*Phys*] accelerator

*përshpëritje = pëshpëritje

*për shpirt *nm* memorial service: requiem

përshpirt·*et vpr* to beg/plead to <> on bended knee: beseech <>

*përshpirt ës *adj* edifying, uplifting

përshpirtje *nf [Relig]* 1 (Christian) requiem 2 food and gifts passed out to honor the dead person *3 piety

përshpirt shëm *adj (i)* 1 devout, reverent, pious 2 respectful of the dead; compassionate

përshqa s *stem for 1st sg pres, pl pres, 1st & 3rd pl pres, 2nd & 3rd sg subj* <përshqet·

përshqet· *vt* to slide/glide over

përshqi s *stem for 2nd pl pres, pind* <përshqet·

përshqi t *stem for pdef, opt, adm, part, pind, 2nd pl pres, imper, vp* <përshqet·

përshqua·n *vt* to distinguish, discern

*përshqua r ët *nn (të)* distinction

*përshqye·n *vt* to rip/tear [] up

përshta s *stem for 1st sg pres, pl pres, 2nd & 3rd sg subj, pind* <përshtat·

përshta t· *vt* 1 to alter [] to suit a purpose: adapt 2 to change [] to meet new conditions: adjust; get used to [] 3 to translate and adapt [a literary work]

përshta t·*et vpr* 1 to accommodate to new conditions: adjust 2 to be suitable: suit <>, befit <> 3 [*Ling*] to agree grammatically

përshta tas *adv* in an appropriate way, suitably

përshta t ës *n* adapter

përshta t ësi *nf (Book)* adaptability

përshta tje *nf ger* 1 <përshta t·, përshtat·et 2 (literary) adaptation 3 [*Ling*] grammatical agreement

përshta t shëm *adj (i)* suitable

përshtat shm ëri *nf* suitability

*përshta tur *adj (i)* made suitable, adapted

*përshti je *nf* nausea = pështirо sje

*përshti ll· = mbështill

*përshtim *nm* propagation

*përshtimë *adj* adjacent, adjoining

*përshti t shëm *adj (i)* = pështirë

*përshtje ll· = mbështje ll

*përshto ll· = mbështoll

*përshtro·n *vi* to comply

*përshtye·n *vt* to push [] out; repel

përshty pje *nf* impression

përshu mët *adj (i)* excessive

përshurr· *vi, vt (Crude)* = përmjerr·

*përshutë *nf* prosciutto, ham = proshutë

përta c
    I § *adj,* 1 slothful/lazy (person)
    II § *nm* [*Zool*] sloth

përta ci *nf* sloth, laziness

përtani shëm *adj (i)* = përta shëm

*përta rdhme *nf (e)* future

përta sh ëm *adj (i)* (*Fig*) made suitable/good for the moment, for now

përtej
    I § *adv* 1 over there, on the other side: yonder, further 2 more
    II § *prep (abl)* 1 on the other side of: beyond 2 exceeding, more than: over and beyond, over

përtejar *n* = përtejas

përtejarak *nm* = përtejas

përtejas *n* inhabitant of the other side (of a river/lake)

përtej bre gas *adj, n* (person) dwelling/situated in territory beyond the shore (of a river/lake)

përtej de t *nm* territory beyond/across the sea: overseas territory

përtej detas
    I § *adj* pertaining to territory beyond/across the sea: transmarine
    II § *adj, n* (person) inhabiting or coming from territory beyond the sea

përtej lumas *adj, n* (person) dwelling/situated in territory beyond the river

përtejmë *adj (i)* located beyond/across: on the other side; far distant

përtej oqean *nm* territory beyond/across the ocean

përtej shëm *adj (i)* = përtejmë

përtej varr *nm* life beyond the grave: afterlife

*përtek *prep (nom)* <për tek headed for, directed to: to, towards

*përtengun *adj (i) (Reg Gheg)* prejudiced

përte po shtë = përtëpo shtë

përter· *vt* to dry [] out somewhat

përter·*et vpr* to dry out somewhat

përte s *n* = përtо najs

përtese *nf* laziness; sluggishness

*përtes ës *n* idler, dawdler

*përtesi *nf* idleness, laziness

përtë gjallë *adv* during one's lifetime

përtëke q·*et vpr* 1 to fester *2 to fly into a rage

përtëmi rë *adv* meaning well, with good intentions

përtë po shtë *adv* 1 sloping downward 2 falling, waning, declining

përtëri·_het_ _vpr_ **1** to become like new, come back like new: revive, recover; be renewed/rejuvenated/refreshed/restored/reinvigorated **2** to reappear; get repeated (again and again)

përtëri·_n_ _vt_ to make [] like new: rejuvenate; refresh, restore, renew; reinvigorate; revive; renovate

*përtërimë _nf_ repetition; renewal

përtëri·s _stem for 1st sg pres, pl pres, 2nd & 3rd sg subj, pind_ <**përtërit·**

përtëri·t· _vt_ = **përtëri·**_n_

përtëri·t·_et_ _vpr_ = **përtëri·t·**_et_

përtëri·t·_ës_ _adj_ rejuvenating, refreshing, restorative, reinvigorating

përtëri·t·je _nf ger_ **1** <**përtëri**_t·_, **përtëri·t·**_et_ **2** rejuvenation, reinvigoration, renewal, restoration

*përtëri·t·shëm _adj (i)_ = **përtëri·t·ës**

përtim

_I §_ _nm ger_ <**përto·**_n_

_II §_ _nm_ = **përtes**_ë_

përto·_n_ _vi_ to dawdle, loiter; hesitate; idle, laze
∘ **s'<>a përto·**_n_ not hesitate a minute

përtoka _adv_ on the ground, down

përtokas _adv_ dragging along the ground

përtokë _adv_ **1** on the ground; to the ground, downward **2** _(Fig)_ very low/weak; touching bottom

përtokëz _nf_ **1** [_Agr_] brush harrow **2** tree stump

përtonjës _n_ lazy person: lazybones, sluggard, dawdler

përtop· _vt_ **1** to hit [] with a ball **2** _(Fig)_ to chew [] out roughly, scold [] harshly

përtret· _vt_ **1** to dissolve/melt [] completely **2** to digest/absorb [] completely; wear [] away completely; rot [] away completely **3** to banish [] to a forsaken place

përtret·_et_ _vpr_ to go into exile far from home

përtrojcë

_I §_ _nf_ vineyard with short bare grapevines

_II §_ _adj_ low-lying

përtrojëse _nf (Reg)_ ant

përtroll· _vt_ to fell [] to the ground, lay out [] on the ground

përtrollës

_I §_ _adj_ on the ground; ground-level

_II §_ _nm (Euph)_ snake

përtrollëse _nf_ house all on one floor, one-storey house

përtrollëz _nf_ = **përtrollës**_e_

përtrollis _stem for 1st sg pres, pl pres, 2nd & 3rd sg subj, pind_ <**përtrolli**_t·_

përtrollit· _vt_ to hurl [] to the ground, throw/slam [] down

përtuar _adj (i)_ **1** exhibiting laziness: barely moving, lethargic, dawdling **2** _(Fig)_ slow in development: slow-growing; sluggish

përtueshëm _adj (i)_ = **përtuar**

përtumbledhur _adj (i)_ = **mbledhshëm**

përtupjesëtuar _adj (i)_ = **pjesëtueshëm**

përtupshëm _adj (i)_ = **turpshëm**

përtushumëzuar _adj (i)_ = **shumëzueshëm**

përtuzbritur _nm (i)_ [_Math_] = **zbritshëm**

përtym· _vt_ **1** to preserve [] by smoking **2** to make [] smoky

përtym·_et_ _vpr_ to become smoky

përtymo·_n_ = **përtym·**

përtymur _adj (i)_ smoke-covered, smoke-filled, smoky; smoked

përtyp· _vt_ **1** to chew [] up **2** (of ruminants) to rechew **3** _(Fig)_ to take in [], absorb [] **4** _(Fig)_ to be able to endure/stand [something unpleasant]
∘ **i përtyp· fjalët** _vt_ **1** to consider one's words carefully, think before speaking **2** to deny having said what one has said **3** to mumble: swallow one's words
∘ **e përtyp· mendimin** to think carefully before speaking

përtyp·_et_ _vpr_ **1** to make chewing motions: chew, masticate **2** (of ruminants) to re-chew: ruminate **3** _(Fig)_ to move the jaw and perhaps mumble something unintelligible: struggle with words

përtypës

_I §_ _adj_ **1** [_Anat_] serving for mastication: masticatory **2** [_Zool_] ruminant

_II §_ _nm_ ruminant = **ripërtypës**

përtypëse _nf_ chewing gum

përtyppje _nf ger_ **1** <**përtyp·**, **përtyp·**_et_ **2** mastication

përtha·_het_ _vpr_ **1** to dry up completely; become dehydrated; wither **2** (of a wound) to close up and form a scab

përtha·_n_ _vt_ **1** to dry [] out, dry [] thoroughly **2** to cause [a wound] to close up and form a scab **3** to numb [] with cold **4** to wither []

*përtha _stem for pdef_ <**përtho·të**

përtharë _adj (i)_ **1** dried up, parched, completely dry; withered **2** (of a wound) closed up and forming a scab

përtharje _nf ger_ <**përtha·**_n_, **përtha·**_het_

*përthashë _1st sg pdef_ <**përtho·të**

*përthe _2nd sg pdef_ <**përtho·të**

përtheko·_n_ _vt_ **1** _(Reg)_ to button [] **2* to stitch a buttonhole

përthello·_het_ _vpr_ to delve deeply into a matter

përthello·_n_ _vt_ to investigate [] deeply

*përthem _1st sg pres & subj_ <**përtho·të**

*përthemi _1st pl pres_ <**përtho·të**

*përthen _stem for part, opt, adm_ <**përtho·të**

përthenë

_I §_ _part_ <**përtho·të**

_II §_ _adj (i)_ **repeatedly said/told, retold

*përthërres _stem for 1st sg pres, 1st & 3rd pl pres, 2nd & 3rd_ <**përthërret·**

*përthërret· _vt_ to invoke

përthi·_het_ _vpr_ = **përthinj·**_et_

*përthikës _nm_ bully, brawler

përthimë _adj (i)_ = **përthinjur**

përthinj·_et_ _vpr_ to begin to get gray hairs

përthinjur _adj (i)_ (completely) gray, gray-haired

përthirrës _adj_ exclamatory = **thirrmor**

përthith· _vt_ to suck [] all up; absorb; suck

përthithës _adj_ absorbent

përthithje _nf ger_ **1** <**përthith·** **2** absorption

*përthjermë _adj (i)_ grayish

*përtho·të _vi_ to recite

*përtho _stem for pind_ <**përtho·të**

*përthom _1st sg subj_ = **përthem**

*përthomi _1st pl pres_ = **përthemi**

*përthoni _2nd pl pres_ <**përtho·të**

*përthosh _stem for pind_ <**përtho·të**

*përthu _stem for vp_ <**përtho·të**

*përthua _2nd sg pres_ <**përtho·të**

*për'thu'aj 2nd sg imper <përtho'·të

*për'thu'a'sh 2nd sg subj <përtho'·të

për'thu'r· vt 1 to make [] well by interlacing of components: braid; interweave 2 to surround [] thoroughly by a fence

për'thu'rë nf texture

përthu'rje nf ger <përthu'r·

për'thy·het vpr 1 to bend (sharply), turn up/down 2 [Phys] to refract 3 to be pliable

për'thye·n vt 1 to fold [] at the edges 2 to bend double [] (at a joint) 3 [Phys] to refract 4 (Fig) to bend [] to one's will, force [] to submit: humble

për'thye'r adj (i) 1 folded, pleated; bent at the joint 2 (of terrain) rugged, hilly, mountainous

përthye'rje nf ger 1 <përthy'e·n, përthy·het [Phys] 2 refraction

për'thye's
    I § adj [Phys] refractive, refracting
    II § nm [Phys] refractor

për'thye'she'm adj (i) 1 bendable 2 [Optics] refractive

për'thye'shm'ëri nf (Book) [Optics] refractability

për'u'dh· vt to put [] on the right path, show [] the way; guide, lead; brief

për'u'dhë adv on the way, en route

për'u'l· vt 1 to force [] to submit: subdue, humble, vanquish 2 (Fig) to abase, belittle, deprecate

për'u'l·et vpr 1 to bow down 2 belittle oneself; debase oneself 3 to bow down, acknowledge defeat, submit 4 to bow (as a mark of respect)

për'u'lës adj 1 degrading, humbling, denigrating; humiliating 2 repressive

*për'u'lësi nf (Book) abasement, submissiveness; humility; obsequiousness

për'u'lësisht adv (Book) submissively, humbly; obsequiously, subserviently

për'u'lje nf ger 1 <për'u'l·, për'u'l·et 2 abasement; servility, submissiveness; humility *3 [Ling] declension

për'u'lshëm adj (i) humble

për'u'ltas adv with servility, submissively; humbly

për'u'lur adj (i) servile, subservient; humble

*për'u'ngj OR për'u'nj (Reg) = për'u'l

*për'u'nj· = për'u'l·

*për'u'njësi nf humility

për'u'njësisht adv with humility, humbly = për'u'ltas

*për'u'njët adj (i) humble

për'u'rim nm ger <për'u'ro'·n, për'u'ro'·het = inaugurim

për'u'ro'·n vt to inaugurate = inauguro'·n

për'va'jshëm
    I § adj (i) 1 mournful, plaintive, dolorous 2 (Fig) pathetic, pitiful
    II § adv 1 mournfully 2 wailing and crying

për'vaj'tim nm ger 1 <për'vajto'·n 2 plaintive mourning

për'vaj'to'·n vt to mourn [] with a plaintive wail

për'vaj'tu'ar adj (i) afflicted by sorrow: sorrowful

për'vaj'tu'eshëm adj (i) pathetic, pitiful; deplorable, dolorous

për'va'k· vt to make [a liquid] tepid

*për'va'l = për'vël

për'va'r· vt 1 to dangle [] from the hands 2 (Fig) to evade [a requirement] by looking for loopholes

për'va'r·et vpr 1 to dangle from a handhold 2 (Fig) to bow down to <>, be servile

për'va'shë nf [Bot] = për'va'shëz

për'va'shëz nf [Bot] vervain (used to make garlands) (Verbena officinalis)

*për'vda'rëje nf deterioration

për'vdir·et vpr 1 to squint 2 to fade away; vanish

për'vdje'rr stem for opt, adm, part <për'vdir·et

për'vdje'rr·et part <për'vdir·et

për'vdo'r stem for pdef <për'vdir·et

*për've'·het vpr = për'vsh·et

për've'ç prep (abl) apart from, except; in addition to, besides

për've'çëm adj (i) special, distinctive

për've'ço'·n vt to separate, isolate

për've'çqë conj not only __

për've'çse conj 1 except, unless 2 = për've'çqë

*për'vehtës = për'vetës

për've's·et vpr to become wet with dew

*për've'së nf trial, test

për've'so'·het vpr = për'ves·et

për've'sh· vt to roll/tuck up [one's sleeves/pant-legs]; turn up/over [a hem], reverse [a hem]
    ○ <>a përvesh· (Colloq) to smack
    ○ përvesh· buzët "roll one's lips up" to extend one's lower lip out in an expression of contempt
    ○ <> përvesh· krahët/llërët/mëngët to get down to work on <>

*për've'sh·et vpr = për'vish·et

për've'shje nf ger <për'vesh·, për'vish·et

*për've'shtr = për'vështr

për've'shur adj (i) (of sleeves/pants) rolled/tucked up; (of forearms) bare

*për've't·et vpr to be fulfilled; come true

*për've'të adj (i) = për've'çëm

për've'tësim nm ger 1 <për'vetëso'·n 2 mastery 3 (Pej) misappropriation; embezzlement

për've'tësime np fem stolen property

për've'tëso'·n vt 1 to make [] one's own: acquire, appropriate 2 to assimilate/absorb [a subject/skill]: master 3 to put [] to good use: exploit [a natural resource] 4 to misappropriate, embezzle 5 [Biol] to assimilate, digest

për've'tësu'ar adj (i) 1 appropriated, acquired 2 assimilated, learned, acquired 3 misappropriated, embezzled

për've'tësu'es
    I § adj 1 [Biol] assimilative 2 mentally able to assimilate material well
    II § n misappropriator, embezzler

për've'tim nm ger 1 <për'veto'·n 2 assimilation; digestion 3 = për'vetësim

për've'to'·n vt 1 [Biol] to assimilate; digest *2 = për'vetëso'·n

*për've'tshëm adj (i) 1 personal 2 = për've'çëm

për've'tu'es adj 1 [Biol] assimilative, digestive 2 = për'vetësu'es

për'vëla'k nm 1 thin corn bread prepared in boiling water 2 corn mush = mëmëli'gë

përvëlim nm ger 1 <përvëlo ·n, përvëlo ·het 2 injury caused by scalding: scald

përvëlo ·het vpr 1 to get scalded; get seared badly 2 to be burning with fever 3 (Fig) to experience great suffering: suffer terribly; be devastated

 ∘ <> **përvëlo** ·het³ˢᵍ zemra/shpirti (për []) "<>'s heart burns (for [])" 1 <> is yearning (for []), <> has <>'s heart set on []) 2 <>'s heart is suffering

përvëlo ·n vt 1 to scald; sear; burn [] (by liquid or chemical means) 2 to prepare [food] by browning; prepare [a dessert] by scalding it with a hot syrup 3 to cause [] to feel extremely hot; cause <> to feel a burning sensation (in []) 4 to devastate; cause [] terrible damage/pain 5 (Fig) to rouse [] to anger; consume [] (with emotion)

përvëlorë nf small pieces of bread boiled in water, mixed with oil or butter and usually cheese, and then fried in lard

përvëluar adj (i) 1 badly burned/parched 2 (Fig) filled with a burning desire 3 (Fig) seared by misfortune

përvëlues adj 1 searing, burning 2 (Fig) (of emotion) consuming

****përvështrim** nm ger 1 <përvështro ·n 2 close observation

****përvështro** ·n vt to observe closely

përvidh ·et vpr to sneak in/out without being noticed

përvier part <përvir·et

****përvijësim** = përvijim

përvijim nm ger 1 <përvijo ·n, përvijo ·het 2 outline

përvijo ·het vpr to appear in general outline

përvijo ·n vt to outline, sketch [] out

përvijos· = përvijo ·n

përvil stem for 2nd pl pres, pind, imper, vp <përvjel·

****përvir**·et vpr = prir·et

****përvir** stem for 2nd pl pres, pind, imper, vp <përvjerr·

përvish·et vpr to roll up one's sleeves/pant-legs to get ready for work

 ∘ <> **përvish**·et (Colloq) to get right down to work on <>; go at <> with might and main, tear into <>; get ready to attack <>

****përvitje** nf (Old) = përvjetor

përvitshëm adj (i) yearly, annual

përvizim nm ger 1 <përvizo ·n *2 outline; description

përvizo ·n vt 1 to outline 2 to fill [] with lines

përvjedh stem for opt, adm, part <përvidh·et

përvjel· vt 1 to roll/tuck up [] 2 to shear [sheep] only on the underside and around the neck and tail

përvjelë

 I § nf (e) relatively weak and short-staple wool shorn from the underside and from around the neck and tail of sheep

 II § nf *hem, tuck

përvjelje nf ger <përvjel·

****përvjerr**· vt = prier·

****përvjetim** = përvjetor

përvjetor nm 1 anniversary *2 annual

përvjetore nf (Old) yearbook

****përvjetshëm** adj (i) = përvitshëm

****përvner**· vt 1 to embitter 2 to nauseate, sicken

****përvnershëm** adj (i) nauseating, sickening

përvodh stem for pdef <përvidh·et

përvoje nf experience; previous experience

përvol stem for pdef <përvjel·

****përvor** stem for pdef <përvjerr·

****përvra**·n vt to cloud, darken

përvuajtje nf humbleness, humility

përvuajtshëm adj (i) = përvuajtur

përvuajtur adj (i) 1 humbled/hardened by experience, long-suffering, wretched 2 reflecting long suffering: abject, miserable 3 humble

****përvuejtnisht** adv (Reg Gheg) = përvujtësisht

përvujtëri nf 1 long suffering 2 humility

****përvujtësisht** adv 1 in constant suffering 2 humbly

përvujtni nf (Reg Gheg) = përvujtëri

****përvujtshëm** adj (i) = përvuajtur

****përvujtë** adj (i) 1 long suffering 2 humble

përzalishëm adj (i) causing dizziness, sickening

përzemërsi nf cordiality

përzemërsisht adv cordially

përzemërt adj (i) cordial

****përzet** interj oh my god!

përze· vt 1 to force to leave: force [] out 2 to dismiss, fire; expel

 ∘ [] **përzë· me daulle** to heckle and harass [] loudly and publicly

****përzemërisht** adv = përzemërsisht

****përzemërsi** nf = përzemërsi

****përzemërt** adj (i) = përzemërt

përzën stem for opt, adm, part <përzë·

përzënie nf ger <përzë·, përzi·het

përzër stem for imper <përzë·

****përzgjatshëm** adj (i) widespread

përzgjatur adj (i) somewhat elongated: oblong

përzgjedh· vt to make a selection of []: pick out [], select

përzgjedhës

 I § adj selective

 II § n selector

përzgjedhje nf ger 1 <përzgjedh· 2 selection; eugenic selection

përzgjidh stem for 2nd pl pres, pind, imper, vp <përzgjedh·

përzgjodh stem for pdef <përzgjedh·

përzi·het

 I § vpr 1 to become mixed together, get mingled 2 to meddle 3 to mingle (with other people)

 II § vp impers <> is nauseous, <> feels like vomiting

 ∘ **përzi**·het³ˢᵍ moti the weather turns bad

 ∘ **përzi**·het³ᵖˡ retë the clouds are getting dark: it looks like bad weather ahead

përzi stem for 2nd pl pres, pind, imper, vp <përzë·, përzie·n

përzie·n vt 1 to mix [] together: mix up [], stir; stir [] up; mix [] up, confuse 2 (Fig Pej) to get [] mixed up in something 3 to till [] a second time: rework [the soil]

 ∘ **përzie**·n bukë [Ethnog] to go to one's relatives by marriage for a meal for the first time

 ∘ **përzie**·n lëmshin/fijet/penjtë to make matters more complicated

përzier

 I § part <përzie·n

 II § adj (i) mixed, heterogeneous; complex; assorted

III § *nf (e)* nausea

përzíerës *I* § *nm OR* **përzíerëse** *II* § *nf [Spec]* mixing machine: mixer

përzíerje *nf ger* **1** <përzí·et, përzí·het **2** mixture **3** nausea ***4** digestion
  ◦ **përzierja e bukës** *[Ethnog]* meal for the bride at her paternal home a week after the wedding

përzíeshëm *adj (i)* **1** feeling nauseous ***2** confused
  ◦ **përzih·et si bolla me ngjalën** to be in a total mess, be terribly confused

***përzím** *nm* **1** hodgepodge, mess **2** disparagement, slander

***përzímas** *adv* in disorder, untidily

***përzímje** *nf* mixture, mess

***përzímtar** *n* meddler, mischief-maker

***përzís** *adj* mixing; mixing up, confusing; mixing in, meddling

përzíshëm
  I § *adj (i)* **1** wearing black as a sign of mourning; in mourning **2** macabre, lugubrious, mournful; gloomy, sad ***3** mixed together, mingled ***4** meddlesome ***5** slanderous
  II § *adv* in mourning

përzítës *nm (Old)* participant in a temporary merger of livestock belonging to different owners for purposes of common herding and pasturing

përzítur *adj (i)* (dressed) in black as a sign of mourning

***përzivúe** *nm (obl* ˜*oi, np* ˜*onj) (Reg Gheg)* = **pezaúl**

përzjarrshëm *adj (i)* **1** on fire, burning **2** *(Fig)* fiery, fervent, ardent

përzje = **përzíe**

përzjeríese *nf [Constr]* mixing machine: mixer

përzu *stem for pl pdef, 3rd sg pdef vp* <**përzë·**

përzur *stem for sg pdef, sg imper* <**përzë·**

***përzhël** = **përzh**

përzhis *stem for 1st sg pres, pl pres, 2nd & 3rd sg subj, pind* <**përzhít·**

përzhít· *vt* **1** to scorch, char, singe, sear **2** *(Reg)* to fry

përzhít·et *vpr* to get scorched/charred

përzhítje *nf ger* <**përzhít·**, **përzhít·et**

përzhítur *adj (i)* **1** scorched, singed; charred; toasted; suntanned; sunburned **2** *(Fig)* badly charred, left in ashes, destroyed

***përzhollë** *nf* = **bërzollë**

përzhúrg· *vt* to make [ ] dirty: besmear, stain

***përzhyt·et** *vpr* to get smothered/covered with a powdery substance

përrall·et *vpr* **1** to chat and joke around **2** to spend time idly, waste time

***përrallar** = **përrallëtar**

përrallë *nf* **1** folktale; fable **2** tale, story; fictional account **3** *(Colloq)* made-up story: fanciful tale, fantasy, lie
  ◦ **përralla me mbret** "stories with a king" *(Impol)* mere fairy tales, a pack of lies; false promises
  ◦ **përrallë mizash** hogwash, nonsense

përrallëtar *n* story teller

përrallëz *nf* short prose fable

përrallím *nm ger* <**përrallo·n**, **përrallo·het**

përrallís· *vi, vt* **1** to make up [stories]: tell tales, spread tales **2** to spin out [a story]; recount

përrallís·et *vpr* to chat/talk idly

përrallísje *nf ger* **1** <përrallís·, përrallís·et **2** idle talk

***përrallítje** = **përrallísje**

përrallo·het *vpr* to chat for a long time; chat to pass the time

përrallo·n *vi, vt* to tell [tales]; tell [a story], recount [a parable]

përrallor *adj* **1** of or pertaining to folktales/fables **2** fictitious; fabulous, legendary

përrallos· *vi* = **përrallís·**

përrallos·et *vpr* = **përrallís·et**

përrallshëm *adj (i) [Poet]* fabled, legendary

përrallueshëm = **përrallshëm**

përrallzatór *nm* tale/story teller

***përrallzím** *nm* tale/story telling = **përrallím**

***përrallzor** = **përrallor**

përrenj *np* <**përrua**

përrënd· *[për-rrënd] vt [Dairy]* to add rennet to [milk]

përrlë *nf* **1** *(Colloq)* chip of rock **2** *(Fig)* squabble, argument

përroi *obl* <**përrua**

përroiske *nf* small stream of water; spring freshet, rill; mountain pool formed by a freshet; hill/mountain gully

përrua *nm (obl* ˜*oi, np* ˜*onj)* **1** torrent, rapid stream; bed of a rapid stream **2** *(Fig)* large quantity of something (moving in a rush): torrent, gush

pësím *nm ger* **1** <pëso·n **2** cause of suffering

pësimor *(Old)* = **pësor**

pëso·n *vt, vi* to undergo, experience; suffer

pësor *adj [Ling]* passive

pësore *nf [Ling]* passive voice

pësúar
  I § *adj (i)* experienced in suffering, deeply experienced
  II § *nm (i)* person who has experienced much suffering; person with deep experience

***pështkardh·** *vt* to violate; rape

pështko·n *vt* to wash [clothes], rinse out [ ], rinse

pështpërímë *nf* whisper; whispered rumor; whispered complaint

pështpërís *stem for 1st sg pres, pl pres, 2nd & 3rd sg subj, pind* <**pështpërít·**

pështpërít· *vt, vi* to whisper; sigh

pështpërít·et *vpr* **1** to be rumored ***2** to sigh; whisper

pështpërítës
  I § *adj* in a whisper
  II § *n* **1** rumormonger, gossiper **2** *[Theat]* prompter

pështpërítje *nf ger* **1** <pështpërít·, pështpërít·et **2** = **pështpërímë**

***pësh-pësh** *adv* in whispers

***pështpëshje** *nf* whispering

pësht *onomat* indicates a swift and sudden movement: whoosh, zing

pështes *stem for 1st sg pres, pl pres, 2nd & 3rd sg subj, pind* <**pështet·**

pështet· *vt* = **mbështet·**

pështëllí·n *vi (Reg)* = **pështpërít·**

pështëllímë *nf (Reg)* = **pështpërítje**

pështíll·et
  I § *vpr* = **mbështíll·et**

II § *vp impers* <> *feels* like vomiting

pështill *stem for 2nd pl pres, pind, imper, vp* <**pështje**ll·

*****pështim** *nm* = shpëtim

pështirë
I § *adj* (i) nauseating, disgusting, loathsome
II § *nn* (të) nausea, disgust, loathing

pështiros· *vt* to tell something about [] that makes <> sick

pështiros·et *vpr* to be disgusting to <>

pështirosje *nf ger* 1 <**pështiros·**, **pështiros·et** 2 disgust, loathing; nausea

pështjell· *vi* = mbështjell·

pështjellak *nm* 1 white wool flannel apron worn by some women in northern Albania; pleated and embroidered skirt worn as part of a woman's ethnic costume 2 kerchief wrapped around the head of women in some mountainous areas of northern Albania

pështjellas *adv* in disorderly confusion

pështjellë *nn* (të) 1 vomiting, vomit 2 (*Fig*) nausea

pështjellëse *nf* = mbështjellëse

pështjellim *nm ger* 1 <**pështjello**·n, **pështjello**·het 2 disorder, chaos, confusion 3 [*Electr*] winding, magnetic coil = pështjellje

pështjellizë *nf* [*Bot*] European glorybind (*Convolvulus arvensis*)

pështjellje *nf ger* 1 = mbështjellje [*Electr*] 2 magnetic coil

pështjello·het *vpr* to get entangled; get all mixed up

pështjello·n *vt* 1 to lump [diverse things] together without rhyme or reason 2 to make a confused mess of []; create disorder in []

pështoll *stem for pdef* = mbështoll

pështrik *nm* [*Bot*] grape-hyacinth (*Muscari*)
  ○ **pështrik me baluke** [*Bot*] tassel hyacinth *Muscari comosum*

pështy·n *vt* [] 1 to spit out [] 2 to spit 3 (*Fig*) to make a spitting gesture as a sign of contempt and hatred 4 (of flies) to contaminate [] by laying eggs: flyblow
  ○ **pështy·n lart** "spit high" to be conceited, think one is so great
  ○ **pështy·n në çorbë/gjellë** "spit in the soup/food" to foul things up deliberately, deliberately spoil everything

pështym· *vt* to dry out [wood]

pështym·et *vpr* (of wood) to dry out

pështymas *adv* (while) spraying spit

pështymë *nf* 1 spit, spittle, saliva 2 (*Colloq*) soot

pështymor *adj* salivary

pështymore *nf* cuspidor, spittoon

pështyrje *nf* spittle, spit = pështymë

*****pëtrore** *OR* **pitrore** *nf* camera

*****pëves·** = pyes·

*****pëvet·** = pyet·

pi·
  I § *vt* 1 to drink [liquid]; drink down [medicine] 2 to smoke [tobacco] 3 to soak up [a liquid], absorb 4 (*Fig Colloq*) to suffer [a blow], get struck badly
  II § *vi* to be a regular drinker of alcohol: drink, drink too much
  ○ <> **pi·**^{3pl} {bugs} (*Colloq*) {bugs} *are eating* <> up alive, <> *is* plagued by {bugs}
  ○ **e pi·** to get it in the neck

○ [] **pi·**^{3sg} **e zeza** "grievous misfortune *befalls* []" a terrible thing *happens* to []
○ **pi· gjak me** [] [*Ethnog*] to pledge blood fellowship with [] (by drinking a drop of each other's blood)
○ <> **pi· gjakun** "drink/suck <>'s blood" 1 to exploit <> mercilessly: make <> sweat blood 2 to inflict terrible pain on <>, torture <> to death
○ **e pi·**^{past} **(gjithë) kupën (e hidhërimit/mjerimit)** (*Book*) to have drunk from the bitter cup of life: have experienced terrible misfortunes
○ **pi· lëngun e gjarprit (prej <>)** "drink snake poison from <>" to taste bitterness in life, has suffered a lot (from <>), go through hell (because of <>)
○ <>a **pi· lëngun** "taste <>'s juice" (*Impol*) to learn from experience that <> *is* not to be feared, learn from experience that <> *is a* paper tiger
○ **pi· llullë** to have a lot of fun
○ **Nuk pi macja uthull** "The cat doesn't drink vinegar." (*Iron*) That can't just happen.
○ **Pi macja uthull.** "The cat drinks vinegar." (*Iron*) (said to a child who smokes or drinks something too strong for him)
○ **pi· me dy gryka** to eat/drink a great deal
○ [] **pi· me hundë** to drink/smoke [] a lot
○ **e pi· me opingë** "drink it with a moccasin" to be a hard drinker
○ **pi· (raki) me opingë** "drink (raki) out of one's clogs" to be a heavy/drinker (of raki)
○ **pi· mendjen** "drink one's mind" to get so drunk that one does not know what one is doing: get stoned out of one's head
○ **pi·**^{3pl} **në një kungull** "{} drink from the same cup" 1 {} *are* like peas in a pod, *are* alike 2 {} *know* each other very well
○ **pi· retë** "drink the clouds" to be very fast and capable
○ **pi· shenjtërisht** "drink like a saint" (*Iron*) to eat/drink well
○ **e pi· sherbetin** "soak up the syrup" (*Impol*) to kick off: die
○ **nuk pi· ujë** "not drink water" (*Pej*) to make no sense: not hold water
○ **pi· ujë te** {} "drink water at {}'s place" (*Pej*) to be {}'s stooge/minion/tool
○ **pi· ujë nga një shishe** "drink water from one and the same bottle" to be a man of his word

pi·het *vpr* 1 to get drunk 2 to be potable/drinkable
  ○ <> **pi·het**^{3sg} <> *feels* like drinking, <> *is* thirsty

*****piacë** = pjacë

*****pianak** *OR* **pianik** = pianec

*****pianec** *nm* heavy drinker, drunkard

*****pianik** = pianec

*****pianik**ësi *nf* heavy drinking, drunkenness

pianist *n* pianist

piano *nf* [*Mus*] piano

pianoforte *nf* [*Mus*] pianoforte

piastër *nf* piaster

*****piatelë** *nf* [*Sport*] clay pigeon

piavicë *nf* leech = shushunjë

*****pic** *nm* tip, top, end

picak *adv* completely unclothed: naked

picarak *nm* little fellow, dwarf

picas *stem for 1st sg pres, pl pres, 2nd & 3rd sg subj, pind* <**picat·**

picat· *vt* to filch, pilfer

*****picetë** *nf* (table) napkin, serviette

*pic̈ë nf little girl

pic̈ël nf (sewing) stitch

pic̈lim nm ger 1 <pic̈lo'·n, pic̈lo'·het 2 fine stitching

pic̈lo'·het vpr to get dressed up

pic̈lo'·n vt to dress [] up

pic̈ërr
   I § nf burning particle: spark
   II § adj little, tiny

pic̈ërrak
   I § adj small-bodied: tiny
   II § nm 1 undersized child 2 [Zool] European spotted salamander (Salamandra salamandra salamandra)

pic̈ërrimë nf faint/weak voice

pic̈ërrina np fem worthless trivia of no importance

pic̈ërro'·het vpr 1 to shrink *2 to lose heart

pic̈ërro'·n
   I § vt to make [] very small; screw up [the eyes]: squint
   II § vi to pilfer

pic̈ërruk adj tiny

picigonë nf = pilipizgë

picigjatë adj oblong

picimaj adv headlong, headfirst

picimajthi adv headfirst

*picinakë nf [Zool] = pic̈ërrak

picingul
   I § adv upside-down, headfirst
   II § nm (Impol) person who is short and weak
   III § adj vertical, perpendicular; steep, sheer

picingul̈ët adj (i) vertical, perpendicular; steep, sheer

picingul̈thi adv 1 (Colloq) vertically 2 headfirst, headlong

picir adj covered with small spots: dotted; freckled, spotted

picirruk
   I § adj, nm (Colloq) small-bodied: tiny
   II § nm undersized person, runt

*pick = pisk

pickatë nf 1 [Entom] stinging gnat, mosquito = mushicë 2 sting

*pickatore nf tweezers

*pic̈kë nf (Crude) = pic̈kë

pickim nm ger 1 <picko'·n, picko'·het 2 sting, prick, pinch

picko'·n vt 1 to pinch, nip; sting, prick 2 [Mus] to pinch down [a string] (so as to create a vibrato)

pickuar
   I § adj (i) stung, pricked, pinched
   II § nf (e) prick, sting; nip, bite

pickues adj stinging, pricking, pinching

picnok nm [Zool] European fire salamander, spotted salamander (Salamandra salamandra)

picorr
   I § nm undersized child
   II § adj undersized, tiny

picrrak nm 1 [Zool] = pik̈ëlore 2 = picorr

picunare nf slowly trickling spring issuing from a rock

pic̈ nm (Crude) = pic̈kë

pic̈kë nf (Crude) woman's pudenda: pussy

*piçmagë OR piçmakë (Old) = merimangë

*piçul nm dimin (Crude Old) girl's pudenda: pussy

pidh nm (Crude) woman's pudenda: cunt, pussy

pidhar nm (Crude) cunt-fucker

piedestal nm pedestal

*piell = pjell

*pier· OR pierr· = pjerr·

*pierrme nf (e) tendency, leaning

pigal nm spout (of a container)

pigamer nm = pegamber

*pigan nm [Bot] rue (Ruta)

*pigël nf stone jar for oil

pigme nm (np ˜ nj) 1 pygmy 2 (Fig) insignificant person; selfish person

pigment nm pigment

*pigun nm 1 [Zool] = pegun *2 [Ornit] pigeon (Columba)

*pihar pred

piha't·et vpr to become completely tired/exhausted

pijanec
   I § nm drunkard
   II § adj constantly drunk

pijanik nm = pijanec

*pijar n (Old) guest at a spa

pije nf 1 beverage; alcoholic beverage: drink 2 drinking (as a vice) 3 (Colloq) tipsiness
   ∘ pije ëmbël (Colloq) liqueur

*pijell nf lane, passage

*pijesinë nf beverage, drink

pijeshiẗës n seller of alcoholic beverages: bartender

pijetore nf pub, bar, saloon, tavern

pijor adj of or pertaining to drinking

pijshëm adj (i) potable, drinkable

pik nm = pikth

pik·
   I § vi 1 to drip, leak 2 to fall straight down to the ground 3 to begin
   II § vt 1 to stop [] from leaking 2 to solder 3 to spray, sprinkle; paint 4 to sadden [] deeply 5 [Dairy] to curdle [milk]
   ∘ <> pik·³ˢᵍ në zemër (për []) "sadden <> in the heart for []" 1 <> feels very bad/sad (about []) 2 <> has <>'s heart set on []
   ∘ <> pik· në zemër "sadden <> in the heart" 1 to make <> feel very bad/sad 2 <> has <>'s heart set on {}

pik·et vpr 1 to fall straight down to the ground 2 to be frozen to the spot (because of a strong and sudden emotion)

pikabardh adj covered with white spots

pikakuq adj (of animals) covered with reddish brown spots

pikalar adj = pikalarme

pikalarmë adj speckled, freckled; dappled, mottled

*pikalas· vt = pikalos·

pikalash OR pikali adj = pikalosh

pikalec = pikalosh

pikaleckë nf 1 small spot/mark 2 [Zool] spotted snake

pikalor adj = pik̈ëlor

pikalore nf [Bot] plant disease that appears as leaf blotches: (anthracnose, bird's-eye rot; scab)

*pikalos· vt to cover [] with small spots: speckle/freckle; spatter

pikalo's·*et vpr* to become speckled/freckled; get spattered

pikalo's|ur *adj (i)* dotted, spotted, freckled

pikalo'sh *adj* freckled; speckled

pikalo'sh|e *nf* **1** [*Ichth*] luvar (*Luvarus imperialis*) **2** [*Ichth*] = **pendëfijëzo're**
  ○ **pikaloshe bostani** [*Entom*] melon ladybird beetle *Epilachna chrysomelina*
  ○ **pikaloshe deti** [*Ichth*] spotted dragonet *Callionymus maculatus*

pi'ka-pi'ka
  I § *adv* one drop after another: in drops, dripping
  II § *adj* covered with small spots: dotted; freckled, spotted
  ○ **Pika-pika bëhet lumi.** "The river grows drop by drop." *(Prov)* Little strokes fell great oaks. Constant dripping wears away the stone. Little by little and bit by bit.

pikarri'tje *nf* **1** point of arrival, terminal point **2** *(Fig)* goal

pika's·
  I § *vt* to spot, notice; detect; find out
  II § *vi* to be particularly evident: be noticeable/distinctive, stick out

*****pika's·***et vpr* to guess, find out

pika's| *stem for 1st sg pres, pl pres, 2nd & 3rd sg subj, pind* <**pika'·**

pika'sje *nf ger* <**pika's·**

pika't· *vt* **1** = **stërpi'k·** **2** to grab

pikato're *nf* medicine dropper, eyedropper

pika'tshëm *adj (i)* notable, prominent, distinctive

*****pika'tur** *adj (i)* **1** = **pikatshëm** **2** likable, attractive

pi'ke *OR* **pi'k|ese** *nf* fruit that falls to the ground when ripe

pike'të *nf* **1** wooden stake used as a marker: picket (stake) **2** picket line **3** *(Fig)* objective, goal

piketi'm *nm ger* <**piketo'·n**

piketo'·n *vt* **1** to set [picket stakes] in the ground **2** to picket **3** *(Fig)* to set [objectives/goals]

piketu'e|s *nm* picket setter

pi'kë
  I § *nf* **1** drop (of liquid) **2** small amount: a little bit **3** small spot, speck; freckle **4** dot **5** period (punctuation mark) **6** point **7** leak (in a roof) **8** [*Med*] stroke, apoplexy **9** *(Reg)* stroke of lightning **10** *(Fig Colloq)* quintessential point: peak, very middle, stroke (of noon/midnight), dead (of night); the best (of a type)
  II § *nm* [*Ornit*] woodpecker
  III § *adv* **1** *(Colloq)* looking perfect **2** (indicating finality) period!
  ○ **pikë çuditjeje/çuditëse** = **pikëcudi'tje**
  ○ **pika e diellit** sunstroke
  ○ **pikë e gjak** very expensive: costing an arm and a leg
  ○ **pika e hapjes** [*Mil*] supply point
  ○ **pika heshtjeje** ellipsis (punctuation mark)
  ○ **pika e komandimit** [*Mil*] command post
  ○ **ësh·të pikë në vetull** to be the very best of all
  ○ **pikë nga shërbimi** [*Volleyball*] service point
  ○ **pika e ngrirjes** freezing point
  ○ **pikë parapritëse** predicted collision point, futurepoint
  ○ **pika e parë** first and strongest raki from the still
  ○ **pikë pas pike** in every detail, point by point
  ○ **pikë e pesë** widely scattered: scattered like flies/straw

  ○ **pika pezullimi** ellipsis (punctuation mark)
  ○ **pikë për pikë** in every detail/respect; point by point, precisely
  ○ **pikë së pari/dyti** in the first/second place, first/second of all
  ○ **Pika shpon gurin.** "The drop pierces the stone." *(Prov)* Little strokes fell great oaks. Constant dripping wears away the stone. Little by little and bit by bit.
  ○ **pika të zeza** blackheads
  ○ **pikë e valë** very depressed/sad
  ○ **pikë e vdekur** *1 dead end **2** [*Tech Phys*] dead center/point
  ○ **pikë e vrer** very depressed/sad
  ○ **Pikë e zezë!** Scandalous!

pikë bashki'm *nm* point of juncture

pikë cudi't|ëse *nf* = **pikëcudi'tje**

pikë cudi'tje *nf* exclamation point (punctuation mark)

pikë de'rdh|je *nf* dumping point

pikë grumbulli'm *nm* collection/assembly point

pikë gja'llë *adv* dead on the spot

pikë kali'm *nm* crossing point/place

pikë l *nf* **1** little drop **2** small spot, dot **3** spoiled fruit that drops to the ground **4** *(Reg)* = **cingël**

pikë l|a'n *adj* freckle-faced, freckled

pikë lo'·het *vpr* **1** to be speckled; get spattered **2** to get freckled

pikë lo'·n
  I § *vt* to sprinkle; spatter
  II § *vi* to drip; drizzle

pikë lo'r *adj* speckled

pikë lo're *nf* [*Zool*] European spotted salamander (*Salamandra salamandra salamandra*)

pikë lli'm *nm ger* **1** <**pikëllo'·n**, **pikëllo'·het** **2** bereavement, sorrow (at the death of a loved one)

pikë llo'·het *vpr* to be saddened, be bereaved

pikë llo'·n *vt* to sadden; bereave

pikë llu'ar *adj (i)* saddened, sad; bereaved

*****pikë llue'shëm** *adj (i)* saddening, dolorous, grievous

pikë ma'dh
  I § *adj* **1** falling in big drops **2** having suffered apoplexy **3** *(Curse)* may-he-have-a-stroke!
  II § *nm* person with apoplexy

pikë mbërri'tje *nf* = **pikarri'tje**

pikë mbështe'tje *nf* **1** point of support **2** [*Mil*] fortified support point **3** *(Fig)* supporting material
  ○ **pikëmbështetje e levës** fulcrum

pikë ni'sje *nf* starting point

pikë pa'mje *nf* viewpoint, point of view

pikë pe's|ë *adv* widely scattered: scattered like flies/straw

pi'kë-pi'kë *adv* = **pika-pika**
  ○ **Pikë-pikë zgavrohet guri.** "The rock is eroded drop by drop." *(Prov)* Little strokes fell great oaks. Constant dripping wears away the stone. Little by little and bit by bit.

pikë pje'kje *nf* meeting time: appointment, date; meeting place

pikë pre's|ë = **pikëpre'sje**

pikë pre'sje *nf* semicolon

pikë py'etje *nf* question mark

*****pikë qa'rk|ës** *n* drawing compass = **kompa's**

pikë rënë *adj* **1** very sad, depressed; bewildered **2** (as a cursing epithet) may-he-drop-dead!; (as an expression of affection) blessed; (as an expression of regret) poor me! poor guy! poor thing!

pikë·rīsht *pcl* **1** precisely, exactly **2** especially

pikërrīm *nm ger* **1** <**pikërro·n** **2** slow rain with heavy drops

pikërro·n
I § *vi impers* it *rains* lightly in big drops
II § *vt* to sadden, depress

pīkës *adj* **1** used for soldering utensils *2 serving to congeal: congealing

pikësëparī *adv* first of all, in the first place, above all

pikësī *nf* precision; punctuality

pikësīm *nm* [*Ling*] punctuation

pikëso·het *vpr* to stand out

pikëso·n *vt* **1** [*Ling*] to punctuate **2** to stipple, dot

pikësynīm *nm* goal, objective

pikësyno·n *vt* to set [a goal]

pikëshkrīrje *nf* [*Spec*] melting point

pīkët *adj (i)* **1** (of cheese) turned bitter and sour: rancid **2** *(Fig)* full of bitterness; full of grief

pikëtakīm *nm* point of juncture, junction; meeting place

pikëto·n
I § *vt* to picket
II § *vi* **1** to eat frequently but a little at a time: be constantly nibbling at []; pick at [food] **2** to caper, cavort **3** to cause <> to feel very sad: eat at <>, sadden <>, embitter <>

pikëthīrrëse *nf* = pikëcudītje

pikëvështrīm = pikëvrojtīm

pikëvrojtīm *nm* [*Mil*] observation point

pikëz *nf* **1** droplet **2** dot; fleck

pikëzīm *nm ger* **1** <**pikëzo·n** [*Min Geol*] **2** mineral fleck **3** [*Sport*] scoring, score-keeping

pikëzo·n *vt* to put dots all over []: dot []

pikiadë *nf* downward plunge, nosedive

pikīm *nm ger* <**piko·n**, **piko·het**

pīkje *nf ger* <**pīk·**, **pīk·et**

pikllōre *nf* [*Ornit*] woodpecker = qukapīk

piknīk *nm* picnic

piko·het *vpr* **1** to become covered with spots: get spattered/flecked/freckled **2** to have a stroke/apoplexy

piko·n
I § *vi* **1** to drip; leak **2** to fall to the ground when ripe or rotten
II § *vt* **1** to spatter, sprinkle **2** to stop [] from leaking **3** to solder
∘ <> **piko·n**^{3sg} <> *feels* a stabbing pain
∘ <> **piko·n**^{3sg} **gjak shpata** "<>'s sword *drips* blood" to have the blood of innocent people on one's hands
∘ <> **piko·n**^{3sg} **në zemër (për [])** "sadden <> in the heart for []" **1** <> *feels* very bad/sad (about []) **2** <> has <>'s heart set on []
∘ <> **piko·n** **në zemër** "sadden <> in the heart" **1** to make <> feel very bad/sad **2** <> has <>'s heart set on {}
∘ <> **piko·n**^{3sg} **syri gjak** "<>'s eye *drips* blood" <> *sweats* blood
∘ <> **piko·n**^{3sg} **zemra gjak** "<>'s heart *drips/flows* blood" <>'s heart *bleeds*

∘ <> **piko·n**^{3sg} **zemra vrer** "<>'s heart *drips* bile" <> *feels* a terrible bitterness/sadness

piko·sh *adj* spotted, dotted

pikpīkë *nf* [*Ornit*] woodpecker *()*

pikrânë *adj (i) (Reg Gheg)* apoplectic

piks *nm* [*Bot*] boxwood = bush

piks· *vt* = mpiks·

pīks·et *vpr* = mpīks·*et*

piksīsht *adv* exactly; punctually

piksje *nf ger* = mpiksje

pīksur *adj (i)* = mpīksur

piktīm *nm* drawing = vizatīm

piktor *n* maker of pictures: artist
∘ **piktor filmi** [*Cine*] art director
∘ **piktor kostumesh** [*Cine*] costume designer
∘ **piktor multi** [*Cine*] animator, cartoonist
∘ **Piktor i Popullit** "People's Painter" *(HistPK)* highest title accorded a painter

piktorēsk *adj* picturesque

piktorī *nf* picture-making: painting, drawing, art

piktūrë *nf* **1** picture-making: painting, drawing, art **2** picture, work of art

pikturīm *nm ger* **1** <**pikturo·n** **2** depiction, picture

pikturo·n *vt, vi* to paint, draw; picture, depict
∘ [] **pikturo·n me ngjyra të zeza** "picture [] with dark colors" to make [] seem worse than [] is, depict [] as being worse that [] is: paint [] in dark colors, present [] in the worst light

pikturshëm *adj (i) (Old)* picturesque

pikth *nm* **1** [*Ornit*] great spotted woodpecker *(Dendrocopus major)* = qukapīk **2** wick holder

pikūar *adj (i)* **1** having suffered a stroke **2** paralyzed **3** selected, choice, outstanding **4** flecked
∘ **i pikuar nga qielli** "chosen by heaven" person of special excellence: one in a million

pikūes *nm* steel punch used to make holes in metal: metal punch

pikūeshëm *adj (i)* dripping; leaky

pikūeshë *nf (Reg)* = vajtōre

pikūr *adj (i)* **1** having suffered a stroke **2** paralyzed **3** patched with solder **4** *(Fig)* out of it, not knowing what is going on **5** *(Fig)* poor, broke **6** *(Fig)* wanting something badly **7** embittered
∘ **i pikur nga qielli** "chosen by heaven" person of special excellence: one in a million

pilaf *nm* rice boiled with salt and butter and allowed to stand at warm temperature until all the water is evaporated
∘ **pilaf me gozhdë** hard-to-chew food; anything hard to accept

pilangelthi *adv* (in pursuit) sticking to the trail, doggedly

pīlcë *nf* lever (for raising heavy objects)

pīlco·n *vt* to raise [] with a lever

pīle *nf (Reg Tosk Child)* = bīle

pīlë
I § *nf* **1** pile of three walnuts or round stones forming a target in a children's game **2** pile used in foundation or support of a bridge **3** [*Constr*] timber used in masonry structures to fasten or strengthen adjoining parts **4** [*Electr*] battery **5** [*Phys*] energy source: pile **6** stone or wood block used as a fulcrum for a lever **7** hillock, knoll **8** *(Colloq)* (in tossing a coin) tails
II § *adv* in a pile, one on top of the other
∘ **pīlë më pīlë** in a disorderly heap

○ **pil**ë **e thatë** [*Electr*] dry cell, battery
○ **pila e Voltës** [*Electr*] voltaic pile

pilihe'rdhe *adj fem (Colloq)* (of a female) behaving coquettishly; flirtatious

***piliko'r** *nm* = **peliko'r**

***piliku'ri** *pred* naked

pili've'së *nf* **1** [*Entom*] dragonfly *(Odonata)* **2** slender and sprightly girl

pilivro'm *nm* syphilis

pil|**o'**·*het vpr* **1** to dash **2** to chase after <>, pursue <> doggedly

pill|**o'**·*n vt* to heap [] up; put [] in a pile

Pi'lo *nf with masc agreement* Pilo (male name)

***piloca'k** *adj* low-lying, squat

pilo'g *nm* pile, heap

pilo'r *nm* [*Anat*] pylorus

pilo't *nm* pilot

pilot|**a'zh** *nm* the profession or craft of being a pilot: pilotage

pilo'të *nf* pile (of a bridge)

pilot'im *nm ger* **1** <**piloto'**·*n* **2** = **pilota'zh**

piloto'·*n vt* to pilot

pilotu'ar *adj (i)* piloted

***pil'th** *nm* trigger

pilu'lë *nf* pill

pilu'rë *nf* [*Bot*] kind of spiny shrub *(Genista acanthoclada)*

***pi'll**·*et vpr* (of an animal) to be born

pi'll
I § stem for 2p pl pres, pind, imper, vp <**pje'll**·
II § stem for 2p pl pres, pind, imper, vp <**pëll**e·t·

pill|**a't** *nm* water vat at a spring

pi'lle *nf* rectangular stone vat for storing oil; earthenware vat for storing cold and wet comestibles

***pille's**ë *nf* standing censer

pi'llë *nf* **1** board set with hackles for combing flax by hand: hackle board, hackle **2** small pebble used in games **3** = **pi'lle**

***pi'll**ës *n* hackler

***pill'im** *nm ger* **1** <**pillo'**·*n* **2** search

pill|**o'**·*het vpr* = **pispillo's**·*et*

pill|**o'**·*n vt* **1** to hackle [flax], dress [flax] **2** to groom and adorn [] = **pispillo's**·

***pi'm**e *nn ger (të)* = **pi'mje**

***pi'm**ës *nm* drinker; drunkard

***pi'mje** *nf ger* <**pi**· = **pi'rje**

***pim**|**o's**·*et vpr* to be distressed, feel hurt

***pim**|**o's**|**ur** *adj (i)* distress, hurt, sad

***pin** *nm* pine = **pi'sh**ë

***pina'k**ë *nf (Reg Gk)* blackboard

pinakote'ke *nf* picture gallery

pina'r *nm* [*Fish*] fyke net

pince'të *nf* [*Tech*] collet

pi'ncë *nf* **1** pliers; tweezers **2** [*Med*] forceps
○ **pinca prerëse** metal-cutting shears: wire snips, tin shears

pine'skë *nf* thumbtack, drawing pin

pi'në *nf* **1** bubble on the surface of water **2** [*Invert*] pen shell *(Pinna nobilis)*
○ **pinë e ashpër** [*Invert*] fan shell *Pinna rudis*

pi'ngë
I § *nf* extreme end: very tip

II § *adv* **1** full to the brim ***2** in elegant fashion: elegantly, smartly
III § *adj* *elegant, smart

ping'ël *nf (Reg)* = **cing'ël**

pingër'im *nm ger* <**pingëro'**·*n*

pingëro'·*n vi* **1** to twitter, chirp = **cicëro'**·*n* **2** [*Folklore*] (of mountain fairies) to pipe (presaging a significant event)
○ <> **pingëron veshi** <>'s ears *are ringing*

pingpo'ng *nm* ping pong, table tennis

pingpong'ist *n* ping pong player

pingui'n *nm* [*Ornit*] penguin

pingu'l
I § *adj* perpendicular; vertical
II § *adv* **1** straight down; upside-down **2** vertically straight: plumb

pingu'le *nf* [*Geom*] perpendicular

pingu'ltë *adj (i)* vertical

pingu'lthi *adv* vertically; straight down, upside-down

***pingja'll** = **pinja'll**

pino'çe *nf* [*Bot*] lupine *(Lupinus)*

pino'k *nm* small offshoot just issuing from a tree trunk

***pinu'e** *nm* (obl ˜ o'i, np ˜ o'nj) *(Old Regional Gheg)* sailyard

***pi'nz**ë *nf* watchmaker's tweezers

pinja'll *nm* [*Hist*] double-edged dagger, stiletto

pinjo'll *nm* **1** offshoot growing out of or next to a tree trunk **2** *(Fig)* family scion

pinjo'n *nm* [*Tech*] pinion

pioce'lë *nf* [*Med*] pyocele

piome'tër *nm* [*Med*] pyometra

pionie'r *n* **1** pioneer **2** [*Hist*] member of the youth organization sponsored by the Communist party: Young Pioneer

piorre *nf* [*Med*] pyorrhea
○ **piorre hojëzore** [*Med*] periodontosis

pip *nm* **1** offshoot (of a plant), scion, shoot **2** scion used in grafting; cutting planted in the ground **3** cigarette holder **4** [*Mus*] mouthpiece of a wind instrument **5** [*Ornit*] woodpecker
○ **ësh-të pip** to have nothing left, be flat broke
○ **i ka**·*pl* **pipat bashkë** to be in cahoots

pip· *vi* to cheep, chirp

***pi'p**|**a** *np (Reg Gheg)* asparagus

pipano'llë *nf* [*Bot*] meadow rue *(Thalictrum)*

pipapunu'es *nm* maker of pipes (for smoking)

pipa'xhi *nm (pl* ˜ *nj)* = **pipapunu'es**

***pipe'q** *nm* = **pepe'q**

pipe'r *nm* **1** [*Bot*] pepper *(Piper nigrum)* **2** black pepper **3** red pepper (the spice), paprika **4** *(Fig)* hot-temperered and irascible person

***pipe'rc**ë *nf* pepper mill

pipe're *nf* = **piperk**ë

pipe'rkë *nf* **1** [*Bot*] sweet pepper (the plant) *(Capsicum frutescens grossum)* **2** bell pepper (the fruit of that plant) **3** [*Bot*] chile (pepper), red pepper *(Capsicum annuum)* **4** *(Fig)* spiteful and irascible woman

***pipero'**·*n vt* = **pipero's**·

pipe'rore *nf* small container of pepper for the table: pepper shaker, pepper caster

***pipe'r**|**o's**· *vt* to spice [] with pepper, add pepper to []

pipe'të *nf* [*Chem*] pipette

pi'pë *nf* pipe (for smoking); cigarette holder

pip ëlli·*n* = pip·

pip ër *nf* = gjevrek

*pip ët = pipët

pip ëti·*n* *vi*

  ∘ **s'pipëti** not make the slightest sound, not make a peep

pip ëtimë *nf ger* **1** <pipëti·*n* **2** soft, high-pitched sound: peep, squeak, whisper

pip ëz *nf* **1** [*Mus*] pipe with a slit cut near one end of a dry plant stalk to create a vibrating reed, and with four or five finger holes and a thumbhole along the body of the stalk **2** narrow mouthpiece of a wind instrument **3** [*Chem*] pipette

  ∘ pip ëz dyshe [*Mus*] double flute

*pip i·*n* *vi* to sing to oneself, hum

*pipi gjatë *nf* (*Reg Gheg*) variety of plum

*pip il = pipët

pipiri q·*et vpr* to get all dolled up, put on the dog, show off

pipiru q

  I § *adj* (*Tease*) all dolled up, looking spiffy; showing off

  II § *n* dandified and frivolous person: dandy, fop; show off

pipi za ne *nf* "fairies' pipe" [*Mus*] double whistle made of tree bark

pip ke *nf* **1** chanter (on a bagpipe) *2 (*Old*) steam whistle, steam valve *3 (*Old*) [*Anat*] epiglottis **4** [*Vet*] disease of the trachea that causes labored breathing in young fowl: gapes

*pip l = pipët

*pipnu shë *nf* [*Bot*] iris-like plant (*Romulea bulbucodium*)

piprro ·*het vpr* to climb up

pipto ·*n vi* (of a plant) to issue offshoots, give off shoots

pip th *nm* **1** scion (in plant grafting) **2** tube through which the wick goes in an oil lamp; short gas pipe, gas jet; valve stem **3** [*Ornit*] robin (*Erithacus rubecula*) **4** mouthpiece

pipzo ·*n vi* to sprout

*piq *nm* small fragment, bit

pi q·*et vpr* **1** to bake; roast, broil **2** to ripen; mature **3** to come to a head **4** to meet together **5** (*Colloq*) to meet up

  ∘ **Nuk piqet buka me shkarpa** "Bread is not baked with kindling." It takes the right tools to do a job right.

  ∘ <> piq·*et*³ˢᵍ gjaku me [] <> is in perfect agreement/harmony with []

  ∘ piq·*et* në prush për [] to willing to die for []

  ∘ piq·*et*³ˢᵍ qielli me detin "the sky *meets* the sea" there *is* a terrible rainstorm

  ∘ <> piq·*et*³ˢᵍ ylli "<>'s star met" <> *are* meant for each other

pi q *stem for 2nd pl pres, pind, imper, vp* <pjek·

  ∘ **Piqe (një herë) këtu!** "Touch it (once) here!" (simultaneously offering a handshake or a toast as congratulations; simultaneously offering a handshake to a passing friend) Put 'er there!

pir *nm* (*Reg*) = leze t

pir· *vt* (*Reg*) to cram [] full, stuff

*pir r· *vt* = pirr·*et*

pi ra *np* (*të*) *fem* drink provisions: party beverages, drinks

*pira c *nm* bramble, briar

pirajkë *nf* small wooden paddle for beating clothes being washed: clothes-paddle

piramidë *nf* **1** pyramid **2** low concrete or stone pillar marking an international border

*pi ra ne c = pijane c

pira sh *nm* = pijane c

pira t

  I § *nm* pirate

  II § *adj* piratical

*pira t· *vt* to beat [] with a club

*pira t·*et vpr* to overeat

pirat eri *nf* **1** piracy **2** (*Collec*) pirates

pi rdh *stem for 2p pl pres, pind, imper, vp* <pjer dh·

piretik *adj* [*Med*] pyretic

*pi rë *nf* **1** skin pore, pore **2** prick, thorn *3 tall rushlike plant

pi rë

  I § *part* <pi·

  II § *adj* (i) **1** drunk **2** suckling

  III § *nm* (i) person who is drunk

pi rës

  I § *adj* suckling

  II § *n* drinker, drunkard

pi rëse *nf* container out of which animals drink water

pirg *nm* (*np* ˜ *gje*) **1** watchtower, castle tower **2** small haystack **3** tall stack/heap/pile

*pirgo s· *vt* to stack, pile up []

piri

  I § *nf* (*Colloq*) **1** funnel = hinkë **2** = qajkë

  II § *np* nares, nostrils

*piripu t *nm* (*Old*) quixotic adventurer

piri t *nm* [*Min*] pyrite

*pirive sh *nm* scorpion = sfurkth

*pirja n *nm* = piane c

pi rje *nf ger* **1** <pi·, pi·*het* **2** = pije *3 = mpirje

*pirk = pirg

piro grafi *nf* pyrography

piroksili në *nf* [*Mil*] military guncotton, pyroxylin

*piro ll *interj* (*Reg Gheg*) cry of congratulations: bravo!

  ∘ **pirolla të qoftë** Hurray for you!

*pirosti = perusti

piro tekni kë *nf* pyrotechnics

*pirpi r *nm* berry wine

*pirpiri *nf* women's overgarment

*pirpi shkë *nf* (*Reg Tosk*) wheat-straw flute

piru a *nm* (*obl* ˜ *oi*, *np* ˜ *onj*) = piru n

*piru lë *nf* pearl, bead

piru n *nm* **1** table fork **2** fork on a bicycle/motorcycle frame

piru st *nm* [*Hist*] member of one of the major Illyrian tribes that formerly inhabited mountainous territories of northern Albania and that are known to have smelted both copper and iron

pirr·*et vpr* <pjerr· to lean, lean over; lean toward <>, tend

  ∘ pirr·*et* nga {} (*Fig*) **1** to be attracted by {}, be interested in {} **2** to be biassed in favor of {}: favor {}

pirr *stem for 2nd pl pres, pind, imper, vp* <pjerr·

*pirra c

  I § *nm* stingy miser

  II § *adj* stingy, miserly

pi'rrë *nf* [*Bot*] **1** cricket rhaphis (*Chrysopogon gryllus*) **2** moor grass (*Sesleria*)

pirrë gjak ëse *nf* [*Bot*] moor grass (*Sesleria*)

Pirro *nf with masc agreement* Pirro (male name)

pis
I § *adj, adv* (*Colloq*) dirty = pistë
II § *n* (*Insult*) filthy pig!
III § *interj* scat!
○ pis pis here kitty kitty! (call to a cat)

pis anik *adj, n* = pis

*Pisdre'n (*Old*) = Prizre'n

pi'së
I § *nf* **1** pitch, tar **2** (*Fig*) Hell
II § *adj* **1** pitch black **2** [*Ichth*] red-eye, rudd (*Scardinius erythrophthalmus scardafa, Leuciscus scardafa*) = llo'skë **3** [*Famil*] kitty, pussy, tabby
○ pisë i zi pitch black

pisë rëngë *nf* [*Zool*] = pikë lo're

*pisëro·*het vpr* to get exasperated

*pisëro·*n vt* to exasperate

*pisi'r *nm* exasperation

pisk
I § *nm* **1** fastening knot **2** quantity that can be held between the thumb and an opposed finger: pinch **3** (*Fig*) most intense/characteristic part of a process/activity/period: thick, height, middle, heart
II § *adv* **1** in a tight spot, in deep trouble **2** pinching with thumb and finger
○ ësh·të[pl] parë me hënë pisk o be on bad terms with one another
○ pisk e lakuriq stark naked

piska më *nf* loud and penetrating cry: scream, shriek
○ piskamë e hollë shrill cry: shriek, screech
○ piskamë e trashë coarse growl

piska s *stem for 1st sg pres, pl pres, 2nd & 3rd sg subj, pind* < piska t·

piska t· *vi* to utter a loud piercing cry of pain/fear: scream, shriek, squeal, howl, squeak, bray

piska te *nf* **1** pinch, prick **2** wound made by biting: bite
○ piskatë pleshkash fleabites

piskato re *nf* tweezers

*piskavi cë *nf* = piavi cë

piskë *nf* **1** [*Ornit*] Old World plover: lapwing (*Vanellus vanellus*) **2** = piskë
○ piskë batullash [*Ichth*] electric ray *Torpedo nobiliana*
○ piskë korenti [*Ichth*] common torpedo *Torpedo torpedo*

piskë rr *nf* **1** = piskato re *2 small splinter

piskë z *nf* = piskato re

*piski'm *nm* = picki'm

*pisko·*het vpr* to have lumbago

*pisko·*n vt* **1** to pinch, nip; prick, sting, bite = picko'·*n* **2** to fasten [] with a knot **3** (in sewing) to tack, baste

*piskthi *adv* tightly

pis llëk *nm* (*np ~ qe*) (*Colloq*) filth, uncleanliness; something dirty

*pis o's· *vt* to tar, cover [] with tar

*pispila'c *adj* purring

pispili *nf* [*Food*] cornmeal pasty (particularly if made with a green vegetable)

pispili ngë *nf* frivolous and talkative woman who stirs up trouble: busybody

pispilla qe *nf* woman or girl who gets all dolled up

pispilli'm *nm ger* (*Pej*) = pispillo'sje

pispillo·*het vpr* (*Pej*) = pispillo's·*et*

pispillo's· *vt* (*Pej*) to dress [] ostentatiously, doll [] up

pispillo's·*et vpr* (*Pej*) **1** to dress in an extravagant and ostentatious manner: overdress, put on the dog **2** to be overly meticulous in dress

pispillo'sje *nf ger* **1** (*Pej*) < pispillo's·, pispillo's·*et* **2** ostentatious adornment; excessive meticulousness in dress

pispillo's ur *adj (i)* (*Pej*) ostentatiously overdressed, putting on the dog; overly meticulous in dress

pispill u q *nm* (*Pej*) frivolous person unduly attentive to his dress and adornment: dandy

*pispir = pëshpër

*pispir i *nf* whispering, rustling

*pispll = pispill

pispu'th *nm* (*Crude*) shitface, bastard, louse

pisqo'llë *nf* **1** (*Hist*) muzzle-loading flintlock pistol **2** (*Fig ColloqImpolite*) numskull, dolt

pisqoll i s· *vt* to shoot at [] with a pistol

pisre'ngë *nf* [*Zool*] European fire salamander, spotted salamander (*Salamandra salamandra*)

pista ll·*et vpr* = kapista ll·*et*

pi'stë
I § *nf* **1** track (for racing events); sound track **2** large paved area: drying stage; dance floor; train platform; airstrip, runway
II § *adj (i)* (*Colloq*) dirty

pisti'l *nm* [*Bot*] pistil

*pisto'le *nf* = pisqo'llë

pistole të *nf* **1** automatic or semi-automatic pistol **2** [*Tech*] air hammer, pneumatic hammer
○ pistoletë gjashtëshe six-shooter (revolver)

*pistollo·*n vt* to fire at [] with a pistol

pisto'n *nm* [*Tech*] piston

pistra'k *nm* unripe fig

pish a'k *nm* **1** thick pine tree; pine stump **2** pine grove **3** pine torch **4** (*Fig*) intense heat

pi'shë *nf* **1** [*Bot*] pine tree; pine wood; pine chip; pine cone **2** pine kindling; pine torch
○ pishë e bardhë [*Bot*] Scotch pine *Pinus silvestris L.* = harti'në
○ pishë e butë [*Bot*] Italian stone pine *Pinus pinea*
○ pishë deti *1 [*Bot*] cluster pine *Pinus pinaster* **2** [*Bot*] kind of red alga *Halopitys incurvus*
○ pishë e egër [*Bot*] aleppo pine *Pinus halepensis*
○ pishë e kuqe [*Bot*] Heldreich pine *Pinus heldreichi*
○ pishë mali [*Bot*] Heldreich pine *Pinus heldreichi*
○ pishë e zezë [*Bot*] Austrian pine, black pine *Pinus nigra Arn.* = ha lëz

pi'shëm *adj (i)* = pi'jshëm

pi'shët *adj (i)* of pine

pishë vë'në *adj* agitator, troublemaker

*pishi'm *nm* = pëshpëri'tje

pishi'në *nf* **1** pine grove **2** alburnum/sapwood of the pine tree

pishi'në *nf* swimming pool

pishk *nm* line of soil missed by the plow in a cultivated field

Pishka'sh *nm* town in east central Albania

pishkull'o·n vi to whisper into the ear of <>, speak softly

pishll'o·n vt to whisper

pishma'n adv (Colloq) regretful: sorry, repentant

pish'najë nf pine forest

***pish'o·**n vi = pëshpëri't·

pish'ore nf [Bot] pine family Pinaceae

***pishq** np < pesh*k*

pish'ta'r nm 1 pine torch; torch 2 torch-holder; torchbearer

pi'shtë adj (i) made of pinewood

***pisht'ëll** = pëshpër'

pi'sht'ër nf forest meadow = ograjë

***pita'k**ë nf (Old) [Mus] whole note, breve

pita'r nm 1 honeycomb (without the honey) 2 (Old) [Relig] requiem mass

pi'tas adv 1 awkwardly and stiffly 2 with a dull sound

pi'te nf 1 pita bread 2 (Reg) [Food] pasty made of dough baked with a topping 3 honeycomb 4 wreath of dried rose petals

pitekantro'p nm [Paleo] pithecanthropus

pite'ri nf café serving pita sandwiches

pi'të nf dried rose petals (used for clothes closets as an air freshener and insect repellent)

***pitë'gja'rp'ën** nm (Reg Gheg) 1 fruit roll 2 cake made of peas

pi'tër
   I § adj (i) frequent
   II § adv frequently

pitigo'n'e nf silly, carping and talkative female

pito'k nm strong workhorse

pito'n nm [Zool] python

***pitur-bâs**ë nf (Reg Gheg) picture

pit'u'sh nm small loaf of bread; round biscuit of unleavened dough

piuri' nf [Med] pyuria

***piv'is** stem for 1st sg pres, pl pres, 2nd & 3rd sg subj, pind < pivit·

***pivi't·** vt to observe [] surreptitiously: peep in on [], spy/eavesdrop on []

***pivi't'**ës n eavesdropper, peeping Tom, spy

***pi'x**ë nf cap, hood

***pixha'me** nf = pizha'me

***pixhe're** nf = penxhere

***piza't·et** vpr to try hard, strive

pizeve'ng nm (Colloq Insult) dishonorable and base person: rat; deceitful swindler: crook

piz'ël nf 1 tiny speck *2 tiny splinter *3 (Old) atom

***piz'ëri'** nf

pi'zgë
   I § nf 1 musical pipe made of reed or straw; small whistle made of willow bark 2 spurt of liquid, squirt
   3 = pi'zgër
   II § adj having a high piercing sound
   III § adv in a spurt, spurting out

***pi'zg'ër** nf metal shaving; splinter, chip

pi'zg'ëz nf dimin 1 small musical pipe made of reed or straw; small whistle made of willow bark 2 tiny splinter/chip

pi'zgull nf small piece/fragment, splinter/chip

***Pizire'n** OR **Pizre'n** (Old) = Prizre'n

***pizha'ma** OR **pizha'mara** np = pizha'me

pizha'me np fem pajamas

pja'cë nf (Colloq) 1 plaza, piazza; city street used as the main locus for casual walking 2 business street in the main part of the town: downtown 3 (Old) marketplace 4 market value/price; value
   ◦ **s'del· në pjacë** "not go out into the market" not get out of the house much any more

pjalm nm 1 finely ground flour; flour dust; dust 2 fine snow 3 [Bot] pollen *4 blizzard

pjalm'i'm nm ger [Bot] 1 < pjalmo'·n 2 pollination
   ◦ **pjalmim i drejtë** self-pollination
   ◦ **pjalmim i kryqëzuar/tërthortë/zhdrejtë** cross-pollination

pjalm'o'·n vt [Bot] to pollinate

pjalm'o'r adj [Bot] pertaining to pollination: pollinic

pjalm'o're nf [Bot] anther

pjalm'u'e's
   I § adj [Bot] serving to pollinate: pollinizing
   II § nm [Bot] pollinator

***pja'no** = pia'no

***pjarim'ta'r** n = ly'pës

pja'st'ër nf metal plate

pjata'la'r'ës n person who washes dishes: dishwasher

pjata'la'r'ese nf sink used for dishwashing

pjata'mba'jt'ës nm plate holder

pjata'ncë nf large plate

***pjate'll**ë nf (Reg Gheg) plate

pja'të nf 1 plate, dish 2 [Mus] cymbal
   ◦ **pjatë duhani** ashtray
   ◦ **pjatë filxhani** saucer
   ◦ **pjatë zinxhiri** [Cycling] chainwheel

pja't'ëz nf small dish, saucer

***pjavi'c**ë nf leech = piavi'cë

***pje'gull** nf = pe'gull

***pjegull'o** nf = pe'gullo'

pjek nm stick used to knock over the pegs in playing tipcat

pjek· vt 1 to bake []; roast/broil [] 2 to cause [] to feel/get hot 3 [Tech] to anneal 4 to cause [] to ripen/mature 5 to bring [] to a head 6 (Colloq) to run into [], meet 7 (Colloq) to touch, tap 8 (Colloq) = përpu'th·
   ◦ **<>a pjek· buzën** to bring <> to the end of <>'s patience
   ◦ **i pjek·**ᵖˡ **hutat** to join forces against the enemy

pjek'alla'r'thi adv by chance, accidentally

pje'kë
   I § nf 1 (Old) meeting place 2 sheep or goat roasted on a spit 3 hobble on an animal's legs to restrict its movement
   II § np eyelashes

***pje'k'ëm** adj (i) = pje'kur

pje'k'ës
   I § adj used for baking/roasting/broiling
   II § n baker; roaster

pjek'ës'i' nf (Book) maturity, ripeness

pjek'je nf ger 1 < pje'k·, pi'q·et 2 meeting at a pre-arranged time: appointment, date 3 [Tech] annealing
   ◦ **pjekje botanike** natural ripening of botanical seeds

pjek'o'·n vt to hobble [a horse]

***pje'k'shëm** adj (i) 1 suitable for baking 2 becoming mature, maturing

pjek'ta'r n baker, cook

pjek'tari' nf (Book) cookery

pjekto're *nf* café serving roasted/broiled meats

pje'kull *nf* = **tu'll**ë

pje'kur
I § *part* <**pjek•, píq•et**
II § *adj (i)* **1** baked, roasted, broiled **2** ripe; mature; prudent
III § *nn (të)* meeting, encounter

pjekur'i *nf* **1** maturity **2** senior status in secondary school; age of a secondary-school senior
○ **pjekuri teknike** maturity of a plant in terms of its suitability as raw material for industry

****pjelm** *nm* = **pjalm**

pje'll• *vi, vt* **1** to bring forth young, give birth to [] (for non-human births); lay [an egg] **2** *(Colloq)* to bear [fruit]; bear [a child]
○ <> **pjell·**³ˢᵍ **belaja me** [] [] *puts* <> into a terrible predicament
○ <> **pjell·**³ˢᵍ **edhe kau/kёndezi/mushka** "even <>'s bull/rooster/mule *gives birth*" everything *comes* up roses for <>, everything *is going* well for <>
○ <> **pjell·**³ˢᵍ **edhe kёndesi/kokoshi** "even <>'s rooster gives birth" <> *enjoys* constant good luck
○ <> **pjell·**³ˢᵍ **groshi me** [] [] *puts* <> into a terrible predicament
○ <> **pjell·**³ˢᵍ **mendja** <> *has* a creative mind; <> *has* a lively imagination
○ <> **pjell·**³ˢᵍ **sherri me** [] *(Colloq)* <> start a big hassle (by doing something) with []
○ <> **pjell (edhe) viçi** "even <>'s calf bears young" <> is blessed with constant good luck

pjella'k
I § *nm* yearling ram; ram or billy goat that has just begun to mate with females
II § *adj* = **pjello'r**

pjella'k|e *nf, adj* **1** (ewe or nanny goat) able to bear young **2** (ewe or nanny goat) that has borne her first offspring

pje'll|e
I § *part* <**pje'll•**
II § *nf* offspring

pjell|ë's *adj* = **pjello'r**

pje'll|je *nf ger* **1** <**pje'll• 2** animal birth **3** animal offspring

****pje'll|m|e** *nf (e)* animal offspring of a birth: litter, brood, hatch

pjello'r *adj* **1** (of female livestock) able to bear offspring; fertile, prolific **2** fruitful, productive

pjello'r|i *nf* fertility

pjell|shë'm *adj (i)* = **pjello'r**

pjell|shm|ër'i *nf (Book)* fecundity; fertility

pjello'r *adj* producing many eggs ***2** *(Old)* [*Ling*] genitive

****pjello're** *nf (Old)* [*Ling*] genitive case

****pje'll|z|ïm** *nm* fertilization

pje'pёr *nm* **1** [*Bot*] muskmelon *(Cucumis melo)* **2** *(Reg)* cucumber
○ **pjepër i egёr** [*Bot*] squirting cucumber *(Ecballium elaterium)*
○ **s'ka· pjerdhur në ujë** "never have farted in water" *(Crude Scorn)* to have never experienced real danger

pjerdh• *vi* **1** to break wind: fart **2** *(Crude Scorn)* to brag, boast: blow a lot of hot air

pje'r|ëz *nf* [*Bot*] = **arrç**

pje'rgull
I § *nf* grapevine fixed in a frame supported on upright posts; climbing grapevine; grape pergola, grape arbor
II § *adj (Fig)* slender and pretty
III § *adv (Fig)* fully loaded

pjergull|o're *nf* grape trellis

****pjerk** *adj* = **pjerrk**

pjerr• *vt, vi* to tilt, lean

pjerra'k
I § *adj* = **pjerrёt**
II § *nm* post that supports a haystack

pjerra'ke'q *adj, n* evil-minded (person)

pje'rr|ë *part* <**pjerr•**

pjerr|ës'i *nf* **1** downward tilt **2** downhill slope **3** steepness **4** [*Geom*] inclination

pjerr|ës'ïm *nm* = **pjerrësi're**

****pjerr|ës'i|në** *nf* = **pjerrësi're**

pjerr|ës'i're *nf* downward slope: sloping ground, slope, drop

pje'rr|ët *adj (i)* **1** sloping/slanting down, on a downward tilt; steep **2** [*Geom*] inclined

pjerr|i'në *nf* = **pjerrësi're**

pje'rr|je *nf ger* **1** <**pjerr•, pirr•et 2** tilt **3** = **pjerrësi 4** *(Old)* = **pri'rje**

pjerrk *adj* hanging down, hanging

pjerr|o'•het *vpr* to bend over, bend down

pje'rr|tas *adv* **1** on a downward slant **2** aslant; crooked, lopsided

pjerr|t|ës'i *nf* = **pjerrësi**

****pjes|ara'k|e** *nf (Old)* [*Ling*] participle

pje'së *nf* **1** piece; part **2** [*Sport*] period (of a game): half, quarter
○ **pjesë e ndё̈rrueshme/ndryshueshme (e ligjёratёs)** [*Ling*] inflectable part of speech
○ **pjesёt e fjalisë** [*Ling*] sentence/clausal constituents
○ **pjesë kёmbimi/ndёrrimi** spare part
○ **pjesa e luanit** *(Book Iron)* lion's share

pje's|ëm *adj (i)* partial

pjes|ëma'rr|ës
I § *adj* participating
II § *n* participant

pjes|ëma'rr|je *nf* participation

pje'së-pje'së *adv* in pieces, in parts; one part at a time: piecemeal

pjes|ёri'sht *adv* partially, partly; only in part

pjes|ёta'r *n* participant; member

****pjes|ёti** *nf* fraction

pjes|ёtïm *nm ger* **1** <**pjesёto'•n, pjesёto'•het 2** division

pjes|ёto'•het *vpr* [*Math*] to be divisible (into equal parts)

pjes|ёto'•n *vt* **1** to divide [] (into pieces/parts), divide [] up; allot, distribute **2** *(Fig)* to share

pjes|ёto'r *adj* [*Ling*] partitive

****pjes|ёto're** *nf* = **pjeso're**

pjes|ёtua'r *part* <**pjesёto'•n** [*Math*]
○ **pjesёtuar me** [] divided by []

pjes|ёtue's *nm* **1** [*Math*] divisor **2** [*Spec*] potentiometer

pjes|ёtue'shё'm *adj (i)* divisible; partible

pjes|ёtue'shm|ër'i *nf (Book)* divisibility

pje'së|z *nf* particle

****pje's|më** *adj (i)* partial

pjesór adj **1** partial **2** of someone's portion: apportioned, fractional **3** [Ling] = **prejpjesór**

pjesóre nf [Ling] participle

pjesshëm

I § adj (i) **1** partial **2** particular, special

II § nf (e) [Phil] that which is particular rather than universal: particular

*__pjestóre__ = pjesóre

pjeshkë nf [Bot] peach (Prunus persica L.P)
  ○ **pjeshkë çahje/shklese** freestone peach
  ○ **pjeshkë mishje** clingstone peach
  ○ **pjeshkë pa push** nectarine

pjet·et vpr to develop a hernia = **rrënxó**·het

pjet·póshtë adv downwards

pjetís· vt to knit

*__pjetje__ nf inguinal hernia/rupture

PKSh abbrev <**Partia Komuniste e Shqipërisë** Communist Party of Albania (1941-1948)

pkt. abbrev <**përkatësisht** respectively

plaç
  I § stem for opt <**pëlcet·, plas·**
  II § interj (Crude) drop dead!
  ○ **më plaçin sytë!** "may my eyes burst (if I'm not telling the truth)!" I swear! on my honor!
  ○ **Të plaçin sytë!** "May your eyes explode!" (Insult Curse) Dammit, use your eyes! Look what you've gone and done!
  ○ <> **plaçin tëmthat!** (Curse) May <>'s (skull) temples burst! I hope <> drops dead!
  ○ **nuk** <> **tha një herë goja plaç!** <> has never said an unkind word

plaçka np fem **1** <**plaçkë 2** entrails, guts
  ○ **një gjel/këndes/kaposh/kokosh plaçka** small amount of baggage

plaçkatár n **1** (Pej) person overly concerned with material goods **2** = **plaçkítës**

plaçkë nf **1** property taken by force: loot, plunder, booty **2** material goods, personal effects **3** (Colloq) piece of cloth used to make clothing; piece of clothing **4** fabric, cloth **5** (Colloq) land/field overgrown with weeds/brambles **6** speck **7** (ColloqImpolite) (refers to a person or thing to be left nameless) some guy, some thing
  ○ **plaçkë e larme** [Bot] dog's tooth violet Erythronium dens-canina
  ○ **plaçka e maçka/rraçka** the whole kit and kaboodle, bag and baggage
  ○ **plaçkë tregu** (Pej) mere merchandise to be bought and sold

plaçkëró·n vt = **plaçkít**·

plaçkís stem for 1st sg pres, pl pres, 2nd & 3rd sg subj, pind <**plaçkít**·

plaçkít· vt to loot [] by force: rob, plunder

plaçkítës
  I § n looter, pillager, plunderer, robber
  II § adj for looting/pillaging/plundering/robbing

plaçkítje nf ger <**plaçkít**·

plaçkítur adj (i) taken as plunder/spoils

plaçkueshëm adj (i) lootable, plunderable

plaçkurína np fem **1** various old stuff: used clothing **2** belongings; odds and ends **3** (Pej) old junk

plaf nm thick blanket with a tufted fringe; thick covering/rug; horse blanket

plaf· vt (Reg) to cover = **mbuló**·n

plagë
  I § nf **1** traumatic injury: wound; bruise; open wound; running/infected sore **2** (Fig) mental anguish caused by a traumatic injury: hurt
  II § adj wounded, hurt, sore
  ○ **plagë e gjallë** unhealed wound
  ○ **plagë e hapur** open wound
  ○ **plaga e ligë** [Veter Med] anthrax

plagëpambyllur adj **1** open wound **2** (Curse) may his wounds never heal!

plagësjellë nm [Med] ulcerating

*__plagëso__·het vpr to get worn out, become fatigued

*__plagëso__·n vt to weaken, wear [] out, exhaust

*__plagím__ nm ger <**plago**·n, **plago**·het

plagó·het vpr = **plagos**·et

plagó·n vt = **plagos**·

plagómë nf **1** internal injury **2** (Fig) deep hurt/sorrow

plagos· vt to wound, injure

plagos·et vpr **1** to get wounded/injured, suffer an injury **2** to feel wounded/hurt

plagosje nf ger <**plagos**·, **plagos**·et

plagósur
  I § adj (i) wounded, injured; hurt
  II § nm (i) wounded person

plagjiat nm (Book) = **plagjiatór**

plagjiatór n plagiarizer

plagjiatúrë nf (Book) plagiarism

plah· vt to cover [] up, cover

plajë nf (woodworker's) plane

plak
  I § adj masc (pl pleq) **1** old, aged **2** (Fig) veteran, experienced
  II § nm (pl pleq) **1** old man **2** (Colloq) father, paterfamilias **3** [Ethnog] elder acting as an adjudicator of disputes **4** (Colloq) scarecrow **5** [Bot] = **madërgonë 6** [Lit] king; priest
  ○ **plaku i katundit = kryeplak**
  ○ **plak i mykës/në mykë** old person with one foot in the grave
  ○ **U bëftë plak** (Felic) (congratulatory wish on the birth of a son) May he live to a ripe old age!
  ○ **Plaku i Vitit të Ri** white-bearded old man in folklore who delivers presents to children on New Year's Eve: Santa Claus, Father Christmas
  ○ **plak zakoni** (old) man who keeps to the old customs

plak· vt **1** to make [a person] old: age [] **2** (FigColloq) to annoy [] by taking too much time **3** (Colloq) to kill [the remaining time]

plak·et vpr **1** to get/grow old: age **2** (of time periods) to elapse; get dark **3** (Fig) to spend a long period of time together
  ○ **plak**·et **me një palë mend** "get old with the same pile of brains" **1** (Impol) to stick with the same tired old ideas **2** to get older but no wiser

plakaman
  I § adj (Impol) doddering
  II § nm doddering old man

plakarec
  I § adj **1** (Impol) old in appearance: old-looking **2** past its prime: stale
  II § nm withered and ugly old man

plakarúq adj, nm (Impol) = **plakarec**

plakarúsh
  I § adj, nm pleasant and lively (old man)

II § *nm* little old man, old coot

pla'kë
I § *adj fem* old, aged
II § *nf* old woman
○ **pla'kë e jetës** very old woman: old crone

pla'k je *nf ger* <pla'k·, pla'k·*et*

*pla'kne'shë *nf (Reg Gheg)* old woman

*pla'kos· *vt, vi* = pllako's·

plak o'sh = plaku'sh

plak ru'q *nm (Pej)* rotten old man

pla'k ur *adj (i)* (of a person) grown old: aged, old

plak u'sh *nm (Pet)* sweet old guy

plan *nm* 1 plan; (work) schedule 2 plane *3 bait, lure
○ **ka· (vënë) në plan** to have in mind, have the intention, be planning: intend

plan-dety'rë *nf* production/work schedule

pla'ndë *nf (Reg)* = vresht

pla'nd ër
I § *nf* heavy weight
II § *adj* heavy

*pla'ndës *(Reg Gheg)* = plë'ndës

pland o's·
I § *vt (Colloq)* to plop/plump/plunk [] down; drop [] heavily, hurl [] down
II § *vi (Fig)* (of atmospheric/temporal conditions) to arrive suddenly: fall, precipitate

pland o's·et *vpr* 1 *(Colloq)* to fall heavily, plunge to the ground, hurtle down; fall with a crash, plop/tumble down 2 *(Fig)* (of atmospheric/temporal conditions) to arrive suddenly: fall

*pla'ne'ps· *vt (Reg Gk)* to beguile, deceive

pla'ne't *nm* [Astron] planet

planet a'r *adj* 1 [Astron] planetary 2 [Tech] planetary gear

pla'në
I § *nf (Colloq)* low ground, dip in the land; level ground
II § *pred* 1 level 2 concave 3 without moving: stagnant

pla'n ët *adj (i)* 1 *(Old)* flat, level 2 [Geom] plane

plan ë zi'm *nm ger* = planifiki'm

plan ë zo'·n *vt* 1 = planifiko'·n 2 [Mil] to plan out [tactics] in detail

*pla'ng *nm (np gje)* = plë'ng

*pla'ng ço'r *adj* = ve'ndës·

plang pri'sh ës = plëngpri'shës

*plang pri'shje *nf* extravagance, wastefulness

plan ifiki'm *nm ger* <planifiko'·n

plan ifik o'·n *vt* to plan, make plans for []

plan ifik u'ar *adj (i)* planned, planned for

plan ifik u'es *adj* involved in planning: planning

planime'tër *nf* planimeter

planimetri' *nf* 1 [Geom] plane geometry 2 [Constr] plan, blueprint

plan kalenda'r *nm* time plan/schedule

plan kërke'së *nf* request list for a proposed project

plan o'·n *vt* to level [] out, make [] flat

plan o's *nm* decoy bird; stuffed golden oriole

*plan o's· *vt* to entice, lure

plantacio'n *nm* plantation

pla'ntë *adj (i)* 1 flat, level, plane 2 *(Fig)* slow, sluggish; quiet

*pla'pur = përpël

plapur i't·et *vpr (Reg)* = përpëli't·et

Plare'nt *nm* Plarent (male name)

plas·
I § *vi, vt* 1 to explode; burst; burst out 2 to crack
II § *vt (Colloq)* to throw [] with force: slam, bang
○ **<> plas·**^{3sg} **barku** <>'s stomach *becomes bloated*, <> *eats* to the bursting point
○ **plas· barkun** to touch <> deeply
○ **<> plas·**^{3sg} **bomba në duar** "the bomb *goes* off in <>'s hands" 1 <>'s shenanigans *are* suddenly revealed 2 the sky *falls* in on <>'s plans
○ **<> plas·**^{3sg} **buza** <> *comes* to the end of <>'s strength/patience
○ **plasi dreqi** "the devil burst" the bad days are gone, the storm is past
○ **plas· edhe gurin** "afflict even a rock" to exhaust the patience of a saint
○ **<> plasi në kokë** "it burst on <>'s head" 1 <> suddenly got the idea of {} into <>'s mind, <> got it into <>'s mind (to ...), <> had a whim 2 {a terrible calamity} hit <>
○ **<> plas· kokën/kryet** *(Colloq)* to annoy <> badly by a displeasing repeated action: give <> a splitting headache, drive <> crazy with that stuff
■ **Plasi Muçoja për dyfek** "Muço burst for a gun." *(Tease)* (said of someone who is gunning for a high position)
○ **<>[] plas· ndër sy** *(Fig)* to confront <> with [] right to <>'s face
○ **<> plas· në dorë/duar** to blow up in <>'s face
○ **<> plas·**^{3sg} **në kokë për** [] "it *explodes* in <>'s head for []" <> *has* a sudden hankering for []
○ **plas· së ngrëni/duke ngrënë** "burst with eating" to overeat, eat to the bursting point
○ **<> plas· shpirtin** 1 to break <>'s heart, sadden <> deeply; cause <> great suffering 2 to bring <> to the end of <>'s patience
○ **<> plas· tëmblin** "burst <>'s gall bladder" 1 to break <>'s heart, sadden <> deeply; cause <> great suffering 2 to bring <> to the end of <>'s patience
○ **<> plas·**^{3pl} **tëmthat** "<>'s (skull) temples *are bursting*" <>'s head *is splitting*, <> *has* as splitting headache
○ **<> plas· trutë** to annoy <> past endurance
○ **<> plas·**^{3pl} **trutë** <> *gets* exhausted from thinking so much, <>'s brains *are exploding* from so much thinking/work; <> *is going* out of <>'s head in exasperation, <> *gets* completely exasperated
○ **plas· vape** to be dying of the heat
○ **<> plas·**^{3sg} **zemra** "<>'s heart *bursts*" <> *dies* of heartbreak
○ **<> plas· zemrën** "burst <>'s heart" 1 to break <>'s heart, sadden <> deeply; cause <> great suffering 2 to bring <> to the end of <>'s patience
○ **<>a plas· zemrën** "burst <>'s heart" to annoy <> past the breaking point, make <> lose patience

plas ari'në *nf* crack, fissure, chink

plas ari't· *vt* to cause [] to crack; (of skin) crack

plas ari't·et *vpr* to crack; (of skin) get chapped

*plas ari't ëm *adj (i)* liable to cracking, easily cracked

plas ari'tje *nf ger* 1 <plasari't·, plasari't·*et* 2 cracked place: crack, small crack

plas ari't ur *adj (i)* full of cracks, cracked all over

plas da'rm *nm* 1 [Mil] assault base: bridgehead 2 *(Fig Book)* launching point

*pla'se *nf* wool comb, teasel

pla's**ë** nf **1** crack, fissure **2** (Fig) small, reparable defect

pla's**ës** adj explosive; bursting

pla's**je** nf ger **1** <plas· **2** explosion **3** fracture, hairline fracture **4** [Veter Med] anthrax
 ∘ **plasje e lëkurës** [Veter Med] pellagra

plasko**m** nm ravine, gorge; chasm

*plaskue nm (obl ¯ o**i**, np ¯ o**nj**) (Reg Gheg) gorge, ravine

plasteli**në** nf plastic clay used in children's handicrafts: plasteline

pla'st**ër** nf = fash**ë**

plastic**ite't** nm plasticity

plasti**k** adj **1** plastic **2** (Fig) graceful; lithe, adroit

plasti**kë** nf **1** plastics, plastic **2** [Art] plastic arts: sculpture **3** [Choreog] achievement of grace, gracefulness

plast**ma's**ë nf synthetic material, plastic; plastic sheet

pla's**ur**
 I § part <plas·, përcet·
 II § adj (i) **1** cracked **2** (of a sore) burst, open **3** (Fig) heartbreaking
 III § nm heartbroken person

*plasuri**dhë** nf watercress

plashi**cë** nf [Ichth] bleak (Alburnus albidus alborella De Filip) = ciro**nk**ë

*plashka're nf fodder, mash

plate nf parterre (of a theater)

platelmin**të** np [Zool] Platyhelminth

plate's**ë** nf [Ichth] plaice Pleuronectes platessa

platfor**më** nf **1** platform **2** preliminary outline

plati**cë** nf fish that has just emerged from the egg: fingerling

plati**n** nm [Chem] platinum (Pt)

plati**s** stem for 1st sg pres, pl pres, 2nd & 3rd sg subj, pind <plati**t**·

plati**t**·
 I § vt **1** to knock [] flat, beat [] down; flatten; cause [] to crouch down **2** to reduce [] in force/intensity: diminish, lower, dull, quench *3 to invade
 II § vi to abate, die down gradually

plati**t**·et vpr **1** to abate, gradually die down **2** to come to rest and remain without moving **3** to crouch down; flop down

*platit**ës** n (O) (Old) invader

*plati**tje** nf invasion

*plati**tur** adj (i) flattened, levelled

*plati**o's**·et vpr to hurtle down

*plaz = pllaz

pla'z**më** nf plasma

plazh nm bathing beach

plazhi**st** n bather (on a bathing beach)

plazhi**t**· vt **1** to let [] drop with a thud: drop **2** to roll [] down a slope

*pleba**t** nm avalanche

plebe' nm plebeian

plebeja**n** adj plebeian

plebeja**s** = plebeja**n**

*plebesqi**t** = plebishi**t**

plebishi**t** nm plebiscite

pleçgja**je** nf [Bot] Grecian foxglove (Digitalis lanata)

---

pleh
 I § nm **1** manure, dung; fertilizer **2** trash; filth
 II § adj dead tired
 III § adv (as an intensifier with certain adjectives) filthy, very
 ∘ **pleh i gjelbër** green manure
 ∘ **pleh i lëngshëm** liquid manure
 ∘ **pleh pylli** forest litter
 ∘ **pleh shpendësh** bird guano

*ple'h**ën** nm (Reg Gheg) = pleh

*ple'h**ën** (Reg Gheg) = pleh**ër**

pleh·**ëri'm** nm ger **1** <pleh**ër**o·n, pleh**ër**o·het **2** fertilization (with manure)
 ∘ **plehërim i njëanshëm** [Agr] fertilizing with a single fertilizer

pleh·**ëri'sht**ë nf **1** garbage dump; compost heap; manure pile; manure/dung pit **2** pen for livestock: corral, pen, sty **3** junkyard, junk pile
 ∘ **plehërishtë ekonomike** manure pit

pleh·**ëro'**·n vt to spread manure on []: fertilize

pleh·**ërue's** adj serving to fertilize: fertilizing

*pleh**i'm** nm = pleh**ëri'm**

pleh**i'sht**ë = pleh**ëri'sht**ë

*pleh**no's**· vt (Reg Gheg) = pleh**ër**o·n

*pleh**o'**·n = pleh**ër**o·n

ple'h**ra** np <pleh **1** trash, garbage **2** despicable person

pleh**raxhi'** nm (np ¯ nj) (Colloq) garbageman

*pleh**ri'zë** nf grain of dust, mote, speck

pleh**uri'na** np sweepings, rubbish

pleia**d** nm small group of illustrious persons

pleibe**k** nm [Cine] playback

pleibo**j** nm pornographic movie/magazine

pleja**dë** nf **1** [Astron] the Pleiades **2** (Fig Book) pleiad

pleks· vt **1** to form [] by interlacing: interlace, interweave, knit, plait **2** (Pej) to devise [something bad]

pleks·et vpr **1** to get tangled up, get entangled **2** to get intertwined

pleksigla's nm [Tech] plexiglass

pleksi're nf hair ribbon

pleks**je** nf ger <pleks·, pleks·et

pleks**ur** adj (i) **1** entangled; implicated **2** twisted together: braided, intertwined

*plema't nm fishing net

ple'me nf (Reg) = plevi**cë**

plemeni' nf = rrebe'sh

plena'r adj plenary

*ple'nd**ës** = plë'nd**ës**

ple'n**ër** nf [Bot] elecampane (Inula helenium)

pleng
 I § nm (np ¯ gje) **1** (Reg) heavy object **2** (Reg) disgrace, dishonor **3** (Reg) peg (for hanging up something), hook **4** (Reg) bandage of thin cloth *5 = plë'ng
 II § adv like a dead weight: heavily

ple'ng**ë** nf (Reg) = hobe'

pleniu'm = plenu'm

plenu'm nm plenary meeting: plenum

pleonasti**k** adj (Book) pleonastic

pleona'z**ëm** nm (Book) pleonasm

plep
 I § nm [Bot] poplar (Populus)
 II § adj of tall and erect stature
 ∘ **plep i bardhë** [Bot] abele, white poplar Populus alba

○ **plep i butë** [*Bot*] = **kava·k**

○ **plep i egër** [*Bot*] aspen *Populus tremula*

○ **plep kavak** [*Bot*] = **kava·k**

○ **plep i zi** [*Bot*] black poplar *Populus nigra*

ple·p·ët *adj (i)* of poplar

plep·íshtë *OR* **plep·íshte** *nf* poplar grove

pleq *np, adj* <**plak**

○ **pleqtë e besë** [*Ethnog*] council of elders conducting a trial

○ **pleqtë e fshatit** village elders

○ **pleq e të rinj** young and old, everyone

*****pleq|ën| = **pleq**ër

pleq|ëri *nf* **1** old age, senility **2** *(Collec)* old/elderly people **3** [*Hist*] council of elders

○ **pleqëri e shkuar** very old age, senility

pleq|ëri·m *nm ger* <**pleqëro·**·n

pleq|ëri·sht

I § *adv* in elderly fashion, like elders

II § *adj* of or for old people, characteristic of the elderly

pleq|ëro··n

I § *vt* **1** to care for [someone elderly] at home, tend to [one's elders] at home **2** to deliberate [] carefully about [], examine [a matter] and weigh it carefully

II § *vi* **1** to reach a pleasant old age **2** to spend one's old age {*adverbial/adjectival complement*}; spend one's old age as a {*nominal complement*} **pleqëroja i lumtur** I was spending my old age being happy, I was happy in my old age **pleqëroi kryetar i bashkisë** he grew old as mayor of the town *(Old)* to arrive at a peaceful settlement

pleq|ësí *nf* **1** *(Hist)* council of aldermen; advisory council of a district **2** council of elders **3** deliberation by a council of elders **4** leadership responsibility

pleq|ësí·m *nm ger* **1** <**pleqëso·**·n, **pleqëso·**·het *(Old)* **2** decision made by a council of elders in settling a dispute

*****pleq|ësí·në *nf* = **pleqësí**

pleq|ëso··het *vpr* to go over a matter very carefully (with someone), take counsel

pleq|ëso··n

I § *vt* **1** to go over [] very carefully (with someone), examine [a matter] and weigh it carefully **2** to settle [a dispute] peacefully

II § *vi (Old)* to settle a dispute (by a council of elders)

pleq|na·r *nm (Old)* elder elected to settle disputes

*****ple·ra** = **ple·hra**

plesht *nm* **1** [*Entom*] flea **2** *(Fig)* unpleasant pest

○ **pleshti i drith**ë**rave** [*Entom*] barley flea beetle *Phyllotreta vittula*

○ **pleshti i gjelbër** [*Entom*] **1** lucerne flea *Sminthurus viridis L.* **2** alfalfa plant bug *Adelphocoris lineolatus*

○ **pleshti i lakrës** [*Entom*] yellow-striped flea beetle *Phyllotreta nemorum L.*

○ **pleshti me breza** [*Entom*] barley flea beetle *Phyllotreta vittula*

○ **pleshti i panxharit** [*Entom*] beet leaf beetle *Chaetocnema concianna Man.*

○ **pleshti i patates** [*Entom*] potato flea beetle *Psylloides affinis*

○ **do· të di·**^{subj} **ku e ka pleshti syrin** "want to know where the flea has its eye" to want to know something trivial/silly

○ [] **sht**/**e· te pleshtat** "stick [] with the fleas" *(Colloq)* to create difficulties for []: put [] into hot water

○ **pleshti i tokës** [*Entom*] flea beetle *Altica, Phyllotreta, Longitarsus*

○ **plesht uji** [*Entom*] water flea = **dafní**e

plesht|a·ma·dh *adj* covered with fleas, flea-bitten

plesht·ít·et *vpr* = **plesht**ó··**het**

plesht|o··het *vpr* to pick off fleas

plesht|o··n *vt* to pick off fleas from []

*****pleten|íc**ë *nf* brooch worn by highland women

ple·urë *nf* [*Anat*] pleura

pleur·ít *nm* [*Med*] pleurisy

*****plev|a·s| *stem for 1st sg pres, pl pres, 2nd & 3rd sg subj, pind* <**pleva·t·**

*****plev·a·t· *vt* to float; swim = **noto·**·n

*****plev·a·t·**et *vpr* = **pleva·t·**

*****plev|a·t|ës|

I § *adj* natatorial

II § *n* swimmer

*****plev·a·t|je *nf ger* <**pleva·t·**, **pleva·t·**et

plevícë *nf* **1** hay shed, hayloft **2** livestock shed

plevít *nm* **1** [*Med*] pleurisy **2** *(Colloq)* lung fever

plevít|o·s· *vt* **1** to cause [] to get pleurisy; give [] a cold **2** *(Fig)* to make [] feel cold, be the source of []'s feeling cold

plevít|o·s·et *vpr* **1** to get pleurisy; catch a cold **2** *(Fig)* to get very cold

*****plevmo·n** *nm (Old)* [*Med*] pneumonia

ple·vra *np* [*Anat*] pleura

*****plëf|e·nj** *np* <**plaf**

plënc *nm* = **plë·nd**ës

plë·nd|ës *nm* **1** [*Anat*] stomach of a ruminant; rumen **2** tripe **3** paunch, belly **4** *(ColloqImpolite)* fat person: fatty

plëng *nm (np ˉ gje)* **1** *(Colloq)* everything one has: house and home; family; worldly goods, property **2** bosom of one's family **3** *(Colloq)* yearning, longing

plëng|ço·r *adj (Reg)* owner; heir

plëng|prí·sh|ës *adj, n* profligate; wastefully extravagant, prodigal

*****plík**ë *nf* = **plí·ko**

plí·ko *nf* postal package: parcel

*****plí·ks| *stem for 2nd pl pres, pind, imper, vp* <**pleks·**

plim

I § *nm (Reg)* group arranged in loose order, bunch: flock, string

II § *adv* in loose groups: in bunches

plí·ma-plí·ma

I § *adv (Reg)* arranged in loose order, bunch: flock, string

II § *adv* in loose groups: in bunches

*****plím|ëra** *np* sheep/goat entrails

plint *nm* [*Archit*] plinth

pliq *nm (Reg)* cord made of twisted wool

plis

I § *nm* **1** large clod of earth **2** wool felt; felt skullcap **3** pad placed under a yoke or pack saddle to protect the necks of draft animals **4** tree moss **5** *(Reg Kos)* = **qele·sh**e

II § *adv* **1** heavily, with a thud **2** teeming, full; extremely

plis·a·r *nm* = **qeleshepunu·es**

plis|a·thy·es *nm* disk harrow

plí·s|ët *adj (i)* made of felt

*****plis|ím** *nm ger* <**pliso·**·n

*****plis|o·**·n *vt* to cover [] with sod: turf

plista·r *n* maker of felt

plish *nm* [*Bot*] reed grass, common reed *(Phragmites communis)*

plitë *nf* = plitha·r

plitha·r *n* *(Colloq)* sun-dried mud brick: adobe = qerpi·ç

*pliv| = plev|

*plo·çkë *nf* (Reg Gheg) woolen covering for the knees/ legs

plog *nm* (np ˜ gje) haystack, hayrick = mulla·r

*plog|ëri = plogështi

plog|ësi = plogështi

plog|ës'o·-het* *vpr* = plogështo·*-het*

plog|ësht *adj* (i) = plogët

*plog|ësht·as *adv* = plogëtas

plog|ësht·i *nf* 1 sluggishness; sloth; lethargy 2 [*Phys*] inertia

plog|ësht·im *nm ger* <plogështo·*-n*, plogështo·*-het*

plog|ësht·o·*-het* *vpr* 1 to become sluggish/lethargic 2 to loaf, dawdle

plog|ësht·o·*-n* *vt* 1 to make [] sluggish/lethargic 2 to dull, dampen, diminish

plog|ët
I § *adj* (i) sluggish; slow-acting; slothful; lethargic
II § *adv* = plogëtas

plog|ët·as *adv* sluggishly; slothfully; lethargically

plog|ët·i *nf* 1 [*Phys*] inertia 2 sluggishness; sloth; lethargy

plog|shëm *adj* (i) = plogët

plog|sht·as *adv* = plogëtas

plog|shtë *adj* (i) = plogësht

ploje *nf* carnage, bloodbath, slaughter

*plojtë
I § *adj* (i) chubby, round-cheeked
II § *nn* (të) *(Old)* inertia

*plo·kë *nf* *scar

plo·mbë *nf* lead-mercury amalgam (used as tooth fill- ing)

plor *nm* 1 [*Agr*] plowshare; plowtip of a wooden plow 2 prow of a boat 3 [*Zool*] vomer *()*
○ plori e shelqërori *(Colloq)* farming and herding

plor|ishtë *nf* [*Agr*] place at which the plowshare is attached to the sole of the plow

*plo·shtjët *adj* (i) = plogët

plot
I § *adv* 1 full 2 plenty; a lot 3 fully, completely 4 exactly, precisely 5 *(Colloq)* successfully
II § *quant* full of; plenty of, quite a lot of
○ plot e përplot full to the brim, absolutely full
○ plot pashën straight out, blurting out

plo·të *adj* (i) 1 full 2 complete, entire 3 plump; thick

*plot|ërisht = plotësisht

plot|ës *nm* [*Ling*] complement = rrethano·r
○ plotës i çfarësisë [*Ling*] *(Old)* complement of quality: qualifier, modifier
○ plotësi i vepruesit "agentive complement" [*Ling*] agent (of a passive verb)

plot|ësi *nf* *(Book)* fullness, completeness
○ plotësi e pronës [*Ling*] possessive complement

plot|ës·im *nm ger* <plotëso·*-n*, plotëso·*-het* 2 part added for the sake of completeness: supplement, addendum

plot|ësi·sht *adv* fully; entirely, completely

plot|ës·o·*-het* *vpr* to become full: fill up

plot|ës·o·*-n* *vt* 1 to fill, fill up/in/out [] 2 to supple- ment 3 to fulfill; satisfy; grant

plot|ës'o·r *nm, adj* 1 = plotësu·es 2 [*Ling*] = rrethano·r

plot|ësu·es
I § *adj* 1 complementary, supplementary 2 [*Law*] alternate (to replace someone missing)
II § *nm* supplement added for the sake of improve- ment or completeness

plot|fuqi *nf* *(Book)* = plotfuqishm|ëri

plot|fuqi|shëm
I § *adj* (i) 1 fully empowered to act: plenipotentiary 2 almighty, omnipotent
II § *nm* (i) neighborhood policeman

plot|fuqi|shm|ëri *nf* *(Book)* full power to act in a matter: plenipotent

plot|goj·ë *nf* *(Euph)* the devil, Satan

*plot|meni *nf* *(Old)* 1 i *(Old)* 2 intensity, density

*plot|ni *nf* fullness; abundance

plot|o·r *adj* *(Old)* complementary, supplementary

plot|o·re *nf* *(Old)* elementary school (offering grade levels one through six)

plot|për|plot *adv* completely filled, absolutely full

plot|pjes·ët·im *nm ger* 1 [*Math*] <plotpjesëto·*-n*, plotpjesëto·*-het* 2 even division

plot|pjes·ët·o·*-het* *vpr* 1 [*Math*] to be fully divisible 2 *(Book)* to become completely separated/divided

plot|pjes·ët·o·*-n* *vt* 1 [*Math*] to divide [a number] without leaving a remainder: divide [] evenly 2 *(Book)* to divide [] up completely

plot|pjes·ët·u·es *nm* [*Math*] divisor that divides an- other number without leaving a remainder: factor

plot|pjes·ët·u·e·shëm
I § *adj* (i) [*Math*] evenly divisible
II § *nm* (i) [*Math*] evenly divisible dividend

plot|pushtet·shëm *adj* (i) *(Book)* omnipotent, all- powerful

plot|shëm *adj* (i) = plotë

*plot|të *adj* (i) = plotë

*plozhë *nf* splinter, sliver, chip

*plozh|ët *adj* (i) sleepy

*plu·ar *OR* plu·er = plor

plug *nm* (np ˜ gje) [*Agr*] 1 steel plow; gang plow 2 *(Colloq)* one of a series of plowings: plowing 3 amount of earth turned over in a furrow
○ plug mbathës [*Agr*] earthing-up plow
○ plug urith [*Agr*] trench plow

plug|im *nm ger* <plugo·*-n*

plug·o·*-n* *vt* [*Agr*] to plow [] (with a steel/gang plow)

plug·u·ar *adj* (i) plowed

*pluhn|izë *nf* (Reg Gheg) = pluhuri·ë

pluhr|iz·o·*-n* *vt* = pluhurzo·*-n*

pluhr|iz·o·r *nm* pulverizer

plu·hur
I § *nm* 1 powdery substance: dust, powder, flour 2 *(Fig)* something able to impede one's actions and sap one's vitality
II § *adj* powdery, powdered
○ pluhur i kashtës chaff
○ pluhur lulesh pollen
○ mos ngri(ni)/ço(ni) pluhur "don't *raise* dust" keep quiet about it, don't create a stir
○ pluhur sharre/druri sawdust

pluhura·k *adj* = pluhuro·r

pluhurizë *nf* powdery dust suspended in the air; thin layer of dust

pluhuriz·im *nm ger (Book)* = **pluhurzim**

pluhurizo·het *vpr (Book)* = **pluhurzo·het**

pluhurizo·n *vt (Book)* = **pluhurzo·n**

pluhuro·het *vpr* = **pluhuros·et**

pluhuro·n
   I § *vt* = **pluhuros·**
   II § *vi* to stir up dust, raise dust

pluhuror *adj* powdery

pluhuros· *vt* **1** to make [] dusty, get dust on [] **2** to coat [] with a powdery substance: dust (with a chemical); powder **3** to make [] into dust: pulverize

pluhuros·et *vpr* **1** to get dusty **2** to crumble into dust/powder

pluhurosës *adj* serving for powdering/dusting, serving in the making of powder/dust

pluhurosje *nf ger* < **pluhuros·**, **pluhuros·et**

pluhurosur *adj (i)* **1** covered/coated with dust **2** turned to dust

*****pluhurs** = **pluhurz**

pluhurthithës *adj* serving to suck up dust

pluhurthithëse *nf (Book)* vacuum cleaner

pluhurueshëm *adj (i)* pulverizable

pluhurzim *nm ger* **1** *(Book)* < **pluhurzo·n**, **pluhurzo·het** **2** pulverization

pluhurzo·het *vpr (Book)* to become pulverized

pluhurzo·n *vt (Book)* to pulverize

plumb
   I § *nm* **1** *[Chem]* lead *((Pb))* **2** bullet **3** = **plumbçe** **4** pencil lead (graphite) **5** lead-mercury amalgam (used as tooth filling) **6** *(Fig)* killing blow
   II § *adj* **1** very heavy, heavy as lead **2** lead gray
   III § *adv* **1** heavily **2** fast as a bullet, quickly
      ○ **plumb me sheqer** "bullet with sugar" *(Iron)* sugar-coated poison
      ○ **plumb për plumb 1** in a fierce exchange **2** tooth and nail

plumbç *nm* **1** *(Colloq)* pencil lead (graphite); lead pencil **2** lead sinker (on a fishing net) **3** = **plumbçe 4** = **plumbçë**

plumbçe *nf* plumb line; plumb bob

plumbçë *nf* fishing net circled with lead sinkers and thrown by hand: cast net

plumbçore *nf* woman conjurer who tells fortunes by casting pieces of lead

plumbizëm *nm [Med]* lead poisoning: saturnism

*****plumbno·n** *vt (Reg Gheg)* = **plumbos·**

plumbos· *vt* to patch/seal/join/fill [] with lead: solder

plumbosje *nf* lead-work; leading

plumbtë *adj (i)* **1** made of lead: leaden **2** heavy as lead: leaden **3** gray as lead: lead gray

*****plumç** *nm* lead pencil

*****plumçe** *nf* **1** = plumpth **2** = **plumbçë**

*****plump** = plumb

*****plumpth** *nm* = **plumç**

*****plumxhore** *nf* sorceress, witch

plunxher *nm [Tech]* plunger

*****pluq** *interj* plop! splash! = **plluq**

plural *nm [Ling]* plural

pluralist *adj* pluralist, pluralistic

pluralizëm *nm* pluralism

plus *nm* plus

plusk *nm* **1** powdery substance floating in the air; thin layer of a powdery substance; pollen **2** scum that forms on the surface of a liquid ***3** *(Reg Gheg)* fine sleet

pluskim *nm ger* < **plusko·n**

plusko·n *vi* **1** to float ***2** *(Reg Gheg)* to snow in a fine sleet
   ○ **plusko·n në mes të <>** to be swimming in <>, have oodles of <>

pluskues
   I § *adj* floating
   II § *nm* floating object: float

plush *nm* plush

plutokraci *nf (Book)* plutocracy

plutokrat *nm (Book)* plutocrat

plutonium *nm [Chem]* plutonium *((Pu))*

*****plym** = plim

pllajë *nf [Geog]* plateau

pllaka *np*

pllakaqe *nf* floor tile, paving tile, flagstone

pllakas *OR* **pllakash** *adv* = **petas**

pllakashtrues *nm* person who lays a tile pavement: tile layer

pllakat
   I § *nm* placard, poster
   II § *adj* eye-catching and easy to understand

pllakatore *nf* ewer with one or both sides flat

pllakë
   I § *nf* **1** slab of hard material: flagstone, tile **2** *(Old)* school slate **3** plaque **4** photographic plate **5** recording disk: record
   II § *adj* thin and flat
      ○ **ësh·të pllakë gramafoni 1** to talk incessantly **2** to be a mere mouthpiece for someone else
      ○ **pllakë zdrukthi** particleboard

pllakos·
   I § *vt* **1** to come down hard on [], slam [] down, whack; attack [] suddenly **2** to cover [] suddenly with something heavy **3** *(Colloq)* to conceal
   II § *vi* to happen/appear suddenly and with intensity: fall; descend suddenly (on someone, on the scene) and in force: make a sudden attack

pllakthi *adv* **1** making both sides flat **2** = **petash**

*****pllan** *nm* plan = **plan**

*****pllaneps·** *vt* = **planeps·**

pllanga-pllanga *adj, adv* in blotches, blotchy = **njolla-njolla**

pllangë *nf* **1** supporting post, support, pillar **2** lever used to raise heavy rocks; lever for raising and lowering the lower millstone **3** = **njollë**

*****pllaq** *adj* foolish

pllaq-plluq *onomat (Colloq)* sound of water splashed by hands or feet

pllaqurit·et *vpr* to splash water with the hands or feet

*****pllasicë** = **pllashicë**

*****pllaskë** *nf* **1** flake ***2** = **hartos·e**

pllashicë *nf (Reg) [Ichth]* = **gjuhcë**

pllatkë *nf [Bot]* stock *(Matthiola)*

pllaz *nm* **1** sole of the foot; stocking sole **2** *[Agr]* sole of a wooden plow: slade *(P)*

*****plle** *adj (Old)* (of female livestock) fertile = **pjellor**

pllenim *nm ger* **1** *[Biol]* < **plleno·n 2** *(Collec)* livestock that are fertile

plleno·n *vt* to fertilize, impregnate, pollinate

*plle¦she̊m *adj (i)* fruitful, fertile (soil)

pllëmba're *nf* wooden tool held by one hand to gather stalks of grain into sheaves in order to cut them with a sickle held in the other hand

pllock¦ar *n* padlock

pllo̱ç¦ak *adj (Reg)* having a flat surface: flat, slab-like

pllo'çë
I § *nf(Reg)* **1** flagstone, garden stepping stone **2** tile
II § *adj* trampled flat, flat

*pllo'ç¦kë = **pllo'skë**

pllo'ç¦këz *nf* small flagstone; small stone dish

*pllo'kë *nf* scar

pllo'skë *nf(Reg)* flat wooden flask

pllum *onomat* sound of an object falling into a liquid: plop

*pllum¦ = **pëllumb¦**

plluq *interj* plop! splash!

plluqur i s· *stem for 1st sg pres, pl pres, 2nd & 3rd sg subj, pind* <**plluqur¦t·**

plluqur i t· *vi* to splash

plluqur i tje *nf ger* <**plluqur¦t·**

*pllu'skë *nf* bubble = **fllu'skë**

pllu'shë *nf(Reg)* = **gjurma'shkë**

plly'mëz *nf* light flaxen net used to catch fish in shallow waters

pneumoni'a *nf [Med]* pneumonia

po
I § *pcl* **1** affirmative particle: yes; indeed **2** *(Colloq)* (in questions) confirmative tag: is that right? **3** confirmative identifier: exactly, precisely, the very **4** indicates momentaneous action: be {*verb*}ing
II § *interj* oh say! say! but say!
III § *conj* **1** but **2** (in conditional clauses) if; if only
IV § *nf* the word "po": affirmation, confirmation, agreement
  ◦ **e po** (expresses resignation to a disagreeable reality) what can one do? that's how it is
  ◦ **po (gjithë)** {*definite noun or pronoun*} the (very) same {} **po gjithë ai** that very same {*one*}
  ◦ **po <> desh qejfi** if <> would like
  ◦ **Po <> dhe gishtin, të merr/rrëmben dorën.** "If you gave <> your finger, <> would take your hand" Give him an inch and <> will take a mile.
  ◦ **Po <> dhe krahun, të merr/rrëmben kokën** "If you gave <> your arm, <> would take your head." Give <> an inch and <> will take a mile
  ◦ **Po <> hape derën, të rrëmben shtëpinë.** "If you open the door to <>, <> will grab your house" Give <> an inch and he'll take a mile.
  ◦ **po <> vjen/vinte rrotull larashi** "the golden eagle of death is hovering over <>" <>'s final hour is/was near, <> does/did not have long to live
  ◦ **Po <> zgjate gishtin, të merr/rrëmben dorën.** "If you extended <> your finger, <> would take your hand" Give him an inch and <> will take a mile.
  ◦ **Po <> zgjate krahun, të merr/rrëmben kokën** Give <> an inch and <> will take a mile.

*pobratinë *nf (Reg Gheg)* fraternization, fraternity

pocaq i *nf(Colloq)* **1** suffering, distress, trouble; exhaustion **2** filth, uncleanliness; filthy thing

pocaq i s· *vt* **1** to make dirty/filthy **2** to make [ ] suffer: distress, trouble

pocaq i s·et *vpr(Colloq)* to suffer greatly; be done in by hardship

pocaq i s'ur *adj (i) (Colloq)* **1** completely filthy **2** worn-out by hardship and suffering: haggard

*po'cë *nf (Reg)* apron

poç
I § *nm* **1** single-handled pot-bellied vessel for drinking or storing liquids: flagon **2** = **po'çe** **3** bottle gourd **4** *(Colloq)* light bulb; lamp chimney **5** potbellied object **6** *[Tech]* crucible
II § *adj* potbellied
  ◦ **ësh·të poç nga koka/mendja** "be empty in the head" to be empty-headed, be slow-witted

poç a'r *n* potter

poç ar¦i *nf* the art of the potter: pottery

po'çe *nf* earthenware cooking pot with a handle

poçe'k *nm* pigpen, sty

*poçe'm *nm* valley; lowland

poçe'ri *nf collec* earthenware: pottery

poçeri'na *np* objects produced by a potter: pottery

*poçkë *nf* small pot; small tankard, mug

*pod *nm (Reg Gheg)* **1** bottom **2** slope, upland

poda'gër *nf [Med]* gout, podagra

*pod i s· *stem for 1st sg pres, pl pres, 2nd & 3rd sg subj, pind* <**pod¦t·**

*pod i t· *vt* to scare off [birds]

podiu'm *nm* podium

*podru'm *nm* = **bodru'm**

podhe' *nf* **1** apron ***2** waterproof cloth, oilcloth

podh i qe *nf* woolen apron

poe'm¦ë *nf* poem

po e'nde *pcl* furthermore

poe't *nm* poet

poete'sh¦ë *nf* poetess

poet i k *adj* poetic

poet i kë *nf [Lit]* poetics

poet i zo'·n *vt* to poeticize

poet u c *nm* poetaster

poezi *nf* poetry

po'fkë *nf* **1** popcorn ***2** swelling; tumor ***3** clenched fist

po'fte *nf* = **mo'stër**

poga'çe *nf[Food]* **1** wheat wafer; unleavened bread **2** pastry eaten with butter for breakfast **3** wafer-shaped

poga'nik *nm* **1** *[Ethnog]* naming celebration of a boy on the third night after his birth **2** wafer broken on a boy's head and eaten at his naming celebration; meal served on that celebration

Pogo'n *nm* highland ethnographic region east of Gjirokastra in the southern part of Albania: Pogoni

pogo'n¦as
I § *adj* of or pertaining to Pogoni
II § *n* native of Pogoni

pogon i shte
I § *nf* dance characteristic of Pogoni
II § *adj* danced by natives of Pogoni

Pograde'c *nm* district and its capital city in eastern Albania near Lake Ohrid: Pogradeci

pogradec a'r
I § *adj* of or pertaining to Pogradeci
II § *n* native of Pogradeci

pogro'm *nm (Book)* persecution and mass murder of a political or ethnic minority: pogrom

po'he *np* **1** pageantry, pomp ***2** fishing net

po'h¦ës *adj* = **pohu'es**

pohim *nm ger* **1** <**poho·** *·n* **2** affirmation

pohimisht *adv* affirmatively

poho· *·n* *vt* **1** to assert, affirm **2** to admit, acknowledge **3** *(Fig)* to agree with []: support

pohor *adj* **1** affirmative **2** *[Phys Ling]* positive

pohore *nf* *[Ling]* (in comparison) positive degree

pohues *adj* positive (in attitude), affirmative

pojak *nm (Old)* **1** village watchman appointed to guard crops **2** village courier

pojatë *nf* **1** hut covered with a roof of foliage **2** front porch

*****pojellë** *nf* stove

*****pojs** *stem for 1st sg pres, pl pres, 2nd & 3rd sg subj, pind* <**poj·**

*****pojt·** *vt (Reg)* to encounter, meet

poker *nm* poker (card game)

*****pokmol** *nm* untidy mess: litter

pokrovë *nf* sheet; winding sheet, shroud

pol *nm* **1** extremity of an axis/opposition: pole **2** *(Reg)* pleat = **kind 3** *(Reg)* panel (of a textile) **4** hinge *****5** lapel; coattail **6** weaver's reed

polak

  I § *adj* Polish

  II § *n* Pole

*****pola-pola** *adv (Reg Gheg)* in pleats/folds, heavily creased

polar *adj* polar

polarizim *nm ger* **1** <**polarizo·** *·n*, **polarizo·** *·het* **2** polarization *[Phys Electr]* **3** polarity

polarizo· *·het* *vpr* to be polarized

polarizo· *·n* *vt* to polarize

polem *nm (Colloq)* populace, the people; common folk

polemik *adj* polemic

polemikë *nf* polemics; debate

polemizo· *·n* *vi* to enter into polemics; enter a debate

polen *nm* *[Bot]* pollen

polenizim *nm ger* *[Bot]* **1** <**polenizo·** *·n*, **polenizo·** *·het* **2** pollination

polenizo· *·het* *vpr* *[Bot]* to become pollinated

polenizo· *·n* *vt* *[Bot]* to pollinate

poleskë *nf* *[Bot]* = **aguliçe**

poliambulancë *nf* = **poliklinikë**

poliandri *nf* polyandry

polic *nm* policeman

policentrist *n (Book)* adherent of polycentrism

policentrizëm *nm (Book)* doctrine that insists on political autonomy of geographically divided centers: polycentrism

policez *adj* detective (story/film)

policë *nf* **1** *[Commerc]* bill of lading **2** (insurance) policy **3** kitchen shelf, shelf

polici *nf* police; police department

policor *adj* **1** of or pertaining to police **2** detective (story/film)

*****poliç** *nm* donkey colt = **kërriç**

poliedër *nf* polyhedron

poliedrik *adj* **1** *[Geom]* polyhedral **2** *(Fig)* multifaceted

poliestër *nf* **1** *[Chem]* polyester **2** light polyester fabric

polietilen *nm* *[Chem]* polyethylene

polifoni *nf* *[Mus]* polyphony

polifonik *adj* *[Mus]* polyphonic

polifonist *n* polyphonist

poligam *nm* *[Ethnog]* polygamist

poligami *nf* *[Ethnog]* polygamy

poliglot *nm (Book)* polyglot

poligon *nm* polygon

poligonace *np* *[Bot]* *Polygonaceae*

poligonal *adj* polygonal

poligraf *nm* *[Publ]* **1** printing press **2** printer

poligrafi *nf* *[Publ]* printing (technology)

poligrafik

  I § *adj* *[Publ]* pertaining to or involved in printing (on a press)

  II § *nm* *[Publ]* institution that prints books: press, printer

poligrafo· *·n* *vt* *[Publ]* to print [] (on a press)

poligjenezë *nf* polygenesis

polik *nm (Reg)* **1** *[Bot]* water gourd = **susak** *****2** funnel *****3** irrigation furrow

poliklinikë *nf* polyclinic

*****polikromi** *nf* polychrome process

polimerizim *nm* polymerization

polimerizo· *·n* *vt* to polymerize

Polinezi *nf* Polynesia

polinezjan *adj*, *n* Polynesian

poliomielit *nm* *[Med]* poliomyelitis

polip *nm* *[Zool]* polyp

poliprim *nm ger* *[Tech]* <**poliro·** *·n*

poliro· *·n* *vt* *[Tech]* to polish

polisemantik *adj* polysemantic

polisemik *adj* *[Ling]* having multiple meanings: polysemic

polispast *nm* *[Tech]* block and tackle

polistirol *nm* *[Chem]* polystyrene

*****polisht** *nm* donkey foal = **kërriç**

politeist *n* polytheist

politeizëm *nm* polytheism

politeknik *adj* **1** polytechnic **2** (of a person) knowledgeable in many fields; (of a book) containing terms in several fields

politeknikum *nm* polytechnic secondary school

politeknizim *nm ger* **1** *(Book)* <**politeknizo·** *·n*, **politeknizo·** *·het* **2** system of education in a polytechnic school/institute

politeknizo· *·het* *vpr* to take on a polytechnic quality

politeknizo· *·n* *vt* to give a polytechnic quality on []

politik *adj* political

politikan *nm* politician

politikanizëm *nm (Book Pej)* set of typical characteristics of a politician

politikë *nf* **1** politics; political thinking, political principle **2** policy

  ○ **politika në komandë!** *(HistPK)* let political considerations rule!

  ○ **politika e kulaçit dhe e kërbaçit** "policy of candy and cudgel" policy of using enticement alternating with threat: policy of the carrot and the stick

  ○ **politika e tokës së djegur** scorched-earth policy

*****politikërisht** = **politikisht**

politikisht *adv* politically

politi·ko *formativ* politico-
politi·ko-ekonomik *adj* politico-economic
politi·ko-ideologik *adj* politico-ideological
politi·ko-shoqëror *adj* politico-social
politi·ko-ushtarak *adj* politico-social
***politik·uer** *adj (fem ˉore) (Old)* = **politik**
politizim *nm ger (Book)* <**politizo·n**
politizo·n *vt* to politicize
politolog *nm* political scientist
***politrikë** *nf* new shoot, sprout
***polje** *nf* highland, upland
polkë *nf [Mus]* polka
polmonit *nm [Med]* pulmonary inflammation, pneumonia
polo *nf* polo
polonez
   I § *adj* Polish
   II § *n* Pole
poloneze *nf [Mus]* marchlike Polish dance: polonaise
Poloni *nf* Poland
polonisht *adv* in Polish (language)
polonishte *nf* Polish language
***poltis·** *vt* to accept, approve
***poltisshëm** *adj (i)* acceptable
poltronë *nf* settee; easy chair
polucion *nm [Med]* pollution
***pol·uer** *adj (fem ˉore) (Old)* = **polar**
pol·l *stem for pdef* <**pjell·**
   ∘ <> **polli djalli/dreqi** <> *has run* into terrible unexpected trouble; <> *gets* into a terrible predicament
***pollagaç** *nm* youngster
***pollë** *nf* apron
***polloge** *nf* glove worn by reapers
***Pollonjë** *(Old)* = **Poloni**
pomadë *nf* salve; pomade
***pomatë** = **pomadë**
***pombok** *adj* chubby, pudgy
***pombol** *nm* field patch that gets no water
***pomendore** *nf* monument, memorial
***pomendshëm** *adj (i)* memorable
***pomodis** *stem for 1st sg pres, pl pres, 2nd & 3rd sg subj, pind* <**pomodit·**
***pomodit·** *vi* to freeze = **ngri·n**
pompë *nf* pump
pompim *nm ger* <**pompo·n**
pompist *n* workman with a pump, pump attendant
pompo·n *vt* **1** to pump; spray [ ] from a pump **2** to pump out [ ] in large quantities **3** *(Fig Colloq)* to get [ ] all worked up about someone
pompoz *adj (Book Pej)* pompous
pompozitet *nm (Book)* pomposity; pompous activity
***pon** *adv* (expresses uncertainty about a following explanation) might it be the case that: maybe, perhaps
ponç *nm* punch made with alcohol
***pond**
   I § *nm* point, center
   II § *adv* = **pon**
***poni** = **pon**
***poni** *nf (Reg Gheg)* chivalry
ponicë *nf (Reg)* **1** clay vase, flower pot ***2** baking pan made of clay ***3** flagstone; tombstone

***ponori** *nf* abyss, chasm
pont *nm (Colloq)* centimeter
pop *nm* Orthodox priest
***popare** *nf* **1** = **papare** ***2** tall story, humbug
pope *nf* **1** gunwale of a boat; driver's seat on a cart/wagon/carriage **2** bartizan ***3** poop, stern
popël *nf* round piece of earth/rock; stone, boulder
poplin *nm* poplin
popull *nm (np ˉj)* people; populace
   ∘ **populli i thjeshtë** "the simple people" ordinary people; the common man; common folk
popullaritet *nm (Book)* popularity
popullarizim *nm ger* **1** <**popullarizo·n**, **popullarizo·het** **2** popularization
popullarizo·het *vpr* to become popular
popullarizo·n *vt* to popularize
popullarizues *adj* serving to popularize: popularizing, popular
popullatë *nf* population; populace
popullim *nm ger* **1** <**popullo·n**, **popullo·het** [Biol] **2** plant or animal life in an area, biological population: *(biota)*
popullo·het *vpr* to be populated
popullo·n *vt* to populate; settle people in [ ]
popullor *adj* of/by/for the people: popular
popullorce *adv (Colloq)* the way people do, in the manner of the common folk; in the language of the common people
popullorësi *nf (Book)* popularity
popullsi *nf* populace, population, people
   ∘ **popullsia aktiv** people able to work, working population
populluar *adj (i)* populated
popullzim *nm ger* = **popullim**
popullzo·het *vpr* = **popullo·het**
popullzo·n *vt* **1** = **popullo·n** **2** to popularize
popullzuar *adj (i)* populated
poq *stem for pdef* <**pjek·**
poqe *conj (Colloq)* as soon as, just as: right when
poqë *conj* **1** *(Colloq)* as soon as, just as: right when **2** in the event that
por *conj* but
por *nm* **1** *(Book)* pore **2** *(Fig Book)* small part of something: bit, cell **3** axle-ring **4** stove **5** cotter ring holding a wheel on an axle: axle ring ***6** door
por *stem for sg pdef* <**pjerr·**
porcek *nm* **1** *(Reg)* gourd bottle **2** skull; back of the head
porcelan *nm* porcelain
   ∘ **porcelan poroz** porcelain (electrical) insulation
porcion *nm* portion
pordh *stem for pdef* <**pjerdh·**
pordhac
   I § *adj (Insult)* **1** person who farts a lot **2** *(Fig)* full of hot air; talking big, but doing little
   II § *nm (Insult)* **1** big farter **2** big braggart; coward
pordhaman *adj (Insult)* = **pordhac**
pordhash *adj (Insult)* = **pordhac**
pordhashakull *nm (np ˉj)* = **shakullinë**
pordhë *nf* **1** loud fart **2** *(Fig Crude)* nonsense: hot air; crap
pordhëmadh *adj* **1** *(Insult)* making noisy farts **2** = **pordhac**

pordho·sh *nm (Insult)* good-for-nothing loafer

po·re *nf* pore

pore·nd *nm (Reg)* field boundary consisting of bushes and brambles

***pore·ps·** *vt (Reg Gk)* to heal

***pore·ps·et** *vpr (Reg Gk)* to recuperate

***pore·z** *nm* tax

porfi·r *nm* [Geol Min] porphyry

***porfy·rë** *nf* purple

po·rno *nf* = **pornografí**

pornografí *nf* pornography

pornografík *adj* pornographic

***porolí** *nf* grimace

***poro·ník** *(Old)* = **porotník**

porosí *nf* **1** order/request (for merchandise or service to be paid for) **2** merchandise or service delivered by request: order; special order **3** advice, guidance; instruction **4** instructions given as part of one's last wishes **5** [Postal] registration

porosís *stem for 1st sg pres, pl pres, 2nd & 3rd sg subj, pind* < **porosí·t·**

porosí·t· *vt* **1** to place an order for [goods/service], order delivery of []: request, order **2** to entrust [] with a charge/responsibility: engage **3** to give advice/instruction to []: advise, instruct

porosí·t·ës *n* initiator of an order: orderer, requester; customer, buyer

porosí·tje *nf ger* < **porosí·t·**

porosí·tur *adj (i)* **1** encharged **2** made-to-order, requested **3** [Postal] sent by registered mail: certified, registered = **rekomandé**

poro·të *nf (Old)* group of 6-24 witnesses who swear to the innocence of a defendant

***porotník** *nm (Old)* juryman

poro·z *adj* porous

poro·zhdë *nf* tether

***porpollo·k** *nm* [Ornit] skylark *(Alaudo arvensis)*

po·rsa
  I § *adv* just then, just now; hardly, barely
  II § *conj* just as, as soon as

po·rsa *formativ* newly-, just-, recent-

porsa·rdhur
  I § *adj (i)* newly arrived, just arrived, recent
  II § *nm* new arrival

porsa·ce·lur *adj (i)* newly opened (out); newly hatched

porsa·da·lë *adj (i)* **1** newly emerged **2** (of a bride) newly married (and made her appearance with the groom's family)

porsa·emë·ru·a·r *adj (i)* newly appointed, just-named

porsa·fejua·r
  I § *adj (i)* newly engaged (to be married)
  II § *nm (i), nf (e)* new fiancé/fiancée

porsa·fill·u·a·r *adj (i)* recently begun

porsa·form·u·a·r *adj (i)* newly formed

porsa·ha·p·ur *adj (i)* just-opened

porsa·këp·u·t·ur *adj (i)* (of fruit) just-picked

porsa·ko·rr·ur *adj (i)* newly reaped

porsa·kriju·a·r *adj (i)* newly created

porsa·la·rë *adj (i)* newly washed, just-cleaned

porsa·lëru·a·r *adj (i)* newly plowed

porsa·lí·nd·ur
  I § *adj (i)* newly born; newborn

II § *nm* newborn infant

porsa·liru·a·r *adj (i)* **1** newly liberated **2** recently released from military service **3** recently emptied; (of a field) recently cleared (of its crops)

porsa·lye·r *adj (i)* newly whitewashed/painted

porsa·martu·a·r
  I § *adj (i)* newly wedded
  II § *nm (i)* newlywed

porsa·mbaru·a·r *adj (i)* just finished/ended; newly completed

porsa·mbje·llë *adj (i)* newly sown, newly planted

porsa·ndë·rtu·a·r *adj (i)* newly erected, just-built

porsa·përfundu·a·r *adj (i)* newly finished

porsa·pje·k·ur *adj (i)* freshly baked, just-cooked

porsa·rr·u·a·r *adj (i)* freshly shaved

porsa·vje·lë *adj (i)* recently harvested

porsa·zbul·u·a·r *adj (i)* newly discovered; recently uncovered

porsa·zë·në *adj (i)* **1** newly caught **2** newly sprouted **3** newly fermented

porsa·zgje·dh·ur *adj (i), nm ()* newly elected/selected (person)

po·rse *conj* even though, however, whereas

po·rsi *conj* like, just like

port *nm* port, seaport

***portafo·l** = **portofo·l**

***porta·r** *nm* gatekeeper; porter; concierge

porta·re *nf* **1** garden gate (of wicker) **2** animal enclosure: pen

***portare·shë** *nf* concierge; porter' wife

portatív *adj* portable

po·rtë *nf* **1** portal: entrance door/gate; main entrance; double door **2** control gate **3** [Soccer Hockey] goal, net **4** entrance point **5** in a children's game of jacks, the space between stretched thumb and forefinger through which picked up pebbles must go
  ○ **Porta e Lartë** [Hist] The Sublime Porte
  ○ **ësh·të portë pazari** "be the market gate" to be a terrible gossip, have a big mouth

portie·r *nm* **1** gatekeeper; doorman, porter **2** [Sport] goalkeeper, goalie

portík *nm* portico

portofo·l *nm* **1** portfolio; wallet **2** ministerial position: portfolio

***portogale·z** *OR* **portoge·z** *adj, n* = **portuge·z**

***Portogalë** *nf (Old)* = **Portugalí**

portoka·ll
  I § *nm (np ~j)* **1** orange (tree) *(Citrus sinensis Osbeck)* **2** orange (fruit)
  II § *adj* orange (in color)
  ○ **portokall i kuq** blood orange
  ○ **portokall sheg** blood orange

portoka·llíshtë *OR* **portokallíshte** *nf* orange grove

portoka·lltë *adj (i)* orange (in color)

portre·t *nm* portrait

portretíst *n* portraitist; portrait photographer

portretizím *nm ger (Book)* **1** < **portretizo·**·n **2** portrayal

portretizo··n *vt* [Lit] to portray

***Portuga·l** *nm (Old)* = **Portugalí**

Portugalí *nf* Portugal

portugalísht *adv* in Portuguese (language)

portugalíshte *nf* Portuguese language

portuge'z *adj, n* Portuguese

*__porr__ *nm (Reg)* stove = **por**

po'rr *stem for pdef* <**pjerr·**

porrç *nm (Reg)* [*Anat*] = **aliver**

po'rre *nf (Reg)* [*Anat*] = **gurma'z**

porris *stem for 1st sg pres, pl pres, 2nd & 3rd sg subj, pind* <**porrit·**

porrit· *vt* **1** *(Reg)* to put [] out, extinguish **2** *(Fig)* to mollify, quell, allay

porrit·et *vpr* **1** *(Reg)* to die down; die out **2** *(Fig)* to become mollified, quiet down

porropi *nf* **1** *(Colloq)* evil; devastation, utter destruction **2** remote region

pos

I § *prep (dat) (Reg)* apart from, except; in addition to, besides = **përveç**

II § *adv (Reg)* separately, apart

po'sa

I § *adv* just then, just now, hardly

II § *conj* **1** just as, as soon as **2** *(Colloq)* inasmuch as, since

○ **posa që** inasmuch as, considering that

po'sa *formativ* = **porsa**

*__posaç__ *adj* special

*__posaçe__ *adv* apart, separate

po'saçem *adj (i)* special, particular

po'saçërisht *adv* especially; specially

*__posaçi__ *nf* necessity, supply

*__posaçisht__ *adv* = **posaçërisht**

po'sa që *conj* **1** just as, as soon as **2** inasmuch as, considering that, since

*__posaqi__ = **pocaqi**

*__posaqis·__ = **pocaqis·**

posedim *nm* possession

posedo·n *vt* to possess

posedues *nm* possessor

*__po'së__

I § *adv* apart

II § *prep (abl)* apart from, except for

po'si

I § *pcl* **1** of course **2** (with irony) oh sure!

II § *conj* like, as, as if

○ **posi jo** of course! definitely! certainly!

po'si kundër *conj* just as

po'si kundërqë *conj* just as

po'si kur *conj (Colloq)* just as if

post *nm* **1** *(Book)* post **2** = **postiqe**

posta'f *nm* large water trough (used for watering animals or washing clothes)

*__postafa't__ *adv* on purpose, expressly = **apostafa't**

*__postahe__ *nf* = **postiqe**

posta'r

I § *adj* postal

II § *n* *(Old)* postman, mailman

*__postas__ *stem for 1st sg pres, pl pres, 2nd & 3rd sg subj, pind (Reg)* <**postai·**

posta't *nm* **1** strip/plot of land; ground plowed with one burst of energy by ox and man *__2__ catalogue

posta't· *vt (Reg)* to tire [] out completely, exhaust

posta't·et *vpr (Reg)* to get very tired, become exhausted

post'bllo'k *nm (np ˜ qe)* **1** sentry post, checkpoint **2** raisable road barrier **3** *(Fig Book)* preventive barrier

po'ste *nf* **1** sheepskin/goatskin rug **2** rug made of goat hair

*__poste'k__ *nm* = **postiqe**

poste'rk *nm* stepson

*__posterke__ *nf* = **posterkinjë**

posterkinjë *nf* stepdaughter

po'stë *nf* **1** mail, post **2** postoffice **3** [*Mil*] sentry post

postëkomanda'nt *nm* [*Hist*] commandant of the local gendarmerie

postëkoma'ndë *nf* [*Hist*] local gendarmerie under a commandant; building that houses the local gendarmerie unit

postëro'jë *nf* [*Mil*] sentry post; sentry unit; sentry

postë-telegraf *nm* post-and-telegraph office

postie'r *n* postman, mailman

postim *nm ger* <**posto·n**

postiqe *nf* **1** cushion made of fleece, fleece pad; pad stuffed with a soft material **2** pad of hide and hair placed under a yoke to protect the necks of the oxen

*__postje'r__ = **postier**

post'koma'ndë *nf* [*Mil*] local command post

posto·n *vt* to send [] by post: post, mail

postre' *nf (Old)* covered entrance in front of the main door: porch

*__post-telegrafa'në__ *nf (Old)* = **postë-telegraf**

postula't *nm* [*Spec*] postulate

posht'anik *nm* = **poshtarak**

posht'ara'k *nm* lowlander

po'sht'as OR **po'sht'azi** *adv* **1** from below **2** at a low level

po'shtë

I § *adv* **1** low **2** below; lower; less; worse **3** down; downward **4** *(Colloq)* downstairs; on the bottom floor

II § *prep (abl)* **1** below; down **2** *(Pej)* down with __!

○ **s'bie₁· poshtë** **1** to stay in good shape **2** not submit, not give in **3** not be badly off

○ **poshtë e lart** **1** high and low, everywhere **2** up and down

○ **poshtë e më poshtë** lower and lower; worse and worse

○ **poshtë e përpjetë** "up and down" **1** high and low, everywhere **2** without any particular aim or direction: all over the place

po'shtë-lart *pcl* **1** up and down **2** more or less, approximately

po'shtëm *adj (i)* **1** lower, inferior **2** downstream **3** *(Reg)* = **po'shtër**

poshtëpërmendur *adj (i)* *(Book)* below-mentioned

po'shtër *adj (i)* **1** vile; base, low, indecent **2** *(Reg)* lower, inferior

poshtëra'k *adj (i)* villainous

poshtëri *nf* = **poshtërsi**

poshtërim *nm ger* **1** <**poshtëro·n**, **poshtëro·het** **2** degradation, abasement, dishonor **3** = **poshtërsi**

poshtërisht *adv* = **poshtërsisht**

*__po'shtërm__ *adj (i)* = **po'shtëm**

poshtëro·het *vpr* **1** to lose one's reputation; degrade oneself **2** *(Colloq)* to lose value/status/reputation: become debased

poshtër'o·n *vt* **1** to abase, degrade, dishonor **2** to lower [] in value/status/reputation: debase, downgrade **3** *(Colloq)* to defeat

poshtër'si *nf* **1** baseness, indecency, immorality **2** indecent/immoral action

poshtër'si'sht *adv* in a debased manner: indecently

poshtër'u'es *adj* debasing, degrading

poshtë'shën'im *nm (Book)* footnote; postscript

poshtë'shën'u'ar *adj (i)* noted below; footnoted; in the postscript

poshtë'shkr'im *nm* **1** explanatory legend (under a chart/picture) **2** postscript

poshtë'treg'u'ar *adj (i) (Book)* mentioned below

*****poshti'në** *nf* basement

po'shtm'e *nf (e)* lower part

*****poshtni'** *(Reg Gheg)* = **poshtër'si**

*****poshtn'** *(Old)* = **poshtër**

poshto·n *vi, vt (Colloq)* **1** to give birth too early: drop prematurely *****2** to bring [] down, cause [] to collapse

*****poshtra'k** *adj* villainous

pot *nm (Colloq)* **1** baby (animal or human); litter, brood; generation **2** baby (animal or human); litter, brood; generation **3** male animal put out to stud **4** clay crucible used by silversmiths for melting metals **5** hopper that feeds grain/olives into a mill/press

pota's *nm [Chem]* potassium *((K))*

pota'se *nf [Chem]* potash *(potassium carbonate)*

potas'ik *adj [Chem]* of or containing potassium: potassic

poten'ce *nf* power

potencia'l *adj, nm* potential

potenc'im *nm [Math]* <**potenco'·n**

potenc'o·n *vt [Math]* to find the antilogarithm of []

pote're *nf* **1** *(Colloq)* clamor, uproar; din, racket; crashing roar **2** *(Reg)* cry of alarm

potere'ma'dh *adj (Colloq)* very noisy: rackety

potere'xhi' *nm (np ˜ nj)* noisy person; brawler

poter'shëm *adj (i) (Colloq)* noisy = **zhu'rmshëm**

poti'na *np (Reg)* high shoes, boots

poti'r *nm* wine goblet

poti's· *vt* to water [livestock, plants, soil]

poti'ske *nf* square net used for river fishing

po'tk'a *np* **1** <**po'tkë** **2** children's game played with small round stones

*****po'tk'e** *nf* **1** *[Bot]* maple tree **2** scarecrow **3** gravestone **4** willow bough placed in a meadow to indicate that the meadow is to be mowed and therefore not to be grazed by livestock

*****potki's·** *vt* to give birth to []

potku'a *nm (obl ˜ o'i, np ˜ o'nj)* horseshoe
  ◦ **I ranë potkonjtë kalit.** "The horse's horseshoes fell off" **1** The horse has grown old and too weak to work. **2** *(Impol)* The old lion has lost his teeth.

*****potmo'l** *nm* = **moça'l**

*****poto'k** *nm* hiding place, lair, den

*****potpollo'shk'e** *nf [Ornit]* quail *(Coturnix coturnix)*

potpuri' *nf [Mus]* potpourri, musical medley

*****potre'se** *nf* terrible suffering: torture, torment; hardship, suffering

*****potres'i'** = **potre'se**

*****potres'it·** *vt* to subject [] to terrible suffering: torture, torment

*****potres'i'tur** *adj (i) (Fig)* having suffered terrible suffering

potu'ra'k *nm* person who wears poture

potu're *np* traditional white woolen pants worn by men in some Tosk regions, with a loose waist and narrow legs ending at the calf

potu're'çje'rrë *adj* = **poture'gri'sur**

poture'gri'sur *adj* poor, worn-out

poture'va'rur *adj* **1** wearing britches that hang down: slovenly in dress **2** *(FigImpolite)* incapable of pulling up his own britches: incompetent

potur'ezi' *nm (np ˜ nj)* person wearing dark britches

po'thu'aj *adv, pcl* = **pothu'ajse**

po'thu'ajse
  I § *adv* all but, not quite, almost
  II § *pcl* nearly, almost: practically

*****po'thu'e** *(Reg Gheg)* = **pothu'aj**

po'vl'ë *nf* cascading water; brook

*****povo'dë** *nf* runner of a vine; plant shoot

*****povo'jë** *nf* swaddling band

po'ze *nf* pose

pozicio'n *nm* **1** body position: posture **2** relative position: placement **3** military/game position **4** *(Fig)* = **pozi'të**
  ◦ **pozicion jashtë loje** *[Soccer]* offside

pozi'të *nf* **1** location, situation: position **2** station in life: position **3** point of view, attitude: position

poziti'v *adj* positive

poziti'v'ist *adj, n [Philos]* positivist

poziti'v'isht *adv* positively

poziti'v'izëm *nm [Philos]* positivism

pozo'·n *vi (Book)* to pose

pozhe'ge *nf [Bot]* variety of plum with long black fruit

PPSh *[pë-pë-shë]* *abbrev nf* <**Partia e Punës e Shqipërisë** Labor Party of Albania

pra
  I § *adv* **1** so then, consequently; accordingly **2** *(Colloq)* then, afterward
  II § *conj* so, therefore
  III § *pcl (Colloq)* (spoken parenthetically without stress) so; (spoken parenthetically with stress) in fact

pra'·het *vpr (Colloq)* to become infected/diseased

pra·n
  I § *vi, vt (Reg Colloq)* to stop
  II § *vt (Colloq)* to infect <> with [a communicable disease], transmit [an infectious disease] to <>

praf *onomat* (expresses suddenness) suddenly, immediately

prafull'i'më *nf (Colloq)* live spark from a fire

prafull'o·n
  I § *vi (Colloq)* to give off sparks; sparkle
  II § *vt* to sear, toast

prag *nm (np ˜ gje)* **1** threshold; doorsill, windowsill, sill **2** *(Fig)* home; family **3** step-like formation; shelf in a stream bed **4** bridge (of a stringed musical instrument) **5** large stone slab **6** *(Fig)* impediment

Pra'gë *nf* Prague

pragmat'ik *adj* pragmatic

pragmat'ist
  I § *adj* pragmatic
  II § *nm* pragmatist

pragmat'izëm *nm* pragmatism

prag'shu'ar *adj* left completely alone in the world, without close family = **derëshu'ar**

prajë nf 1 microbial disease: infection 2 (Colloq) cessation, lull, stop

*****prajkë** nf drumstick (for drums)

prajshëm adj (i) (Reg) 1 taking a break, at rest; resting 2 calm *3 stagnant, foul; infectious; blasphemous

prak nm (np ~ qe) = prag

*****prakov** = prokof

*****praksim** nm ger < praksö·het

*****praksö**·het vpr to go wrong, fall into error

*****praksuar** adj (i) fallen into error, immoral, errant

prakticizëm nm 1 (Book) practicality; practicability; practicalness 2 naive pragmatism

praktik adj practical; in practice

praktikant n person undergoing supervised practical training: intern

praktikë nf practice
  ○ **praktikë pedagogjike** practice teaching

praktikisht
  I § adv in practice; from a practical point of view
  II § pcl 1 actually, in reality *2 practically

praktiko·het vpr 1 (Book) to undergo exercise, gain practice; become practiced 2 to happen as usual

praktiko·n vt 1 to exercise []; give practice to [] 2 to participate regularly in [a sport] (Old) to practice [a profession]

praktikum nm (Book) practicum

*****prall** nm [Bot] kermes, holly oak (Quercus coccifera)
  ○ **prall i butë** [Bot] = ashe

pramatar n (Old) peddler, itinerant merchant

pramati nf (Old) peddling (as a trade)

*****pramë** adj (i) infected; contaminated

pranadriatik adj located near the Adriatic Sea

prandaj
  I § conj therefore, so
  II § adv for this reason; that's why! that explains it!

*****prandej** = prandaj

*****prandi**·n vt = përandit·

*****prandverë** = pranverë

pranë
  I § adv 1 close; close-by, nearby, near 2 similar
  II § prep (abl) 1 close to; next to; near 2 in regard to 3 (Book) appurtenant to (< an institution/ organization>)
  ○ **pranë e pranë** very close to each other, adjacent

*****pranës** n assistant, helper

pranga np 1 handcuffs 2 (Old) shackles; fetters

prangim nm ger < prango'·n

prango·n vt to handcuff; shackle

prani nf presence

pranim nm ger 1 < prano'·n 2 admission, acceptance 3 person accepted/admitted

pranishëm
  I § adj (i) present
  II § nm (i) person in attendance, participant

*****pranisht** adv nowadays, at present

prano·n vt to accept; admit [] (as a member/participant); tolerate, take

pranuar nm (i) person admitted as a member/participant

pranueshëm adj (i) acceptable; admissible; welcome

Pranvera nf Pranvera (female name)

pranverë nf 1 (the season) spring 2 (Fig Poet) beginning of something good: dawning; happy time of life

pranverör adj of or pertaining to spring: vernal

*****prap**· vt to force/push [] back, repulse

prapa
  I § adv 1 backwards 2 in back, behind 3 late, tardy; slow, backward, retarded 4 afterward, later 5 following behind; left behind 6 long ago
  II § adj = prapmë
  III § prep (abl) 1 in back of; behind 2 after
  ○ **ësh·të prapa botës** to be behind the times
  ○ **prapa gardhit** secretly, secretively
  ○ **s'kthe·het prapa** to be committed/resolute/determined, not turn back
  ○ **prapa malit** far far away, in a far off land
  ○ **prapa perdes** surreptitiously, sneakily
  ○ **prapa skene/skenës** behind the scenes, in secrecy

prapa formativ 1 post- 2 retro-

prapagojë nf [Anat] pharynx

prapagjuhör adj [Ling] dorsal

prapagjuhöre nf [Ling] dorsal consonant

prapakokë nf [Anat] occiput

prapakthehu
  I § interj about face!
  II § nm (Fig) sharp reversal of direction; change of heart

prapakthim nm 1 turnabout, turnaround; about face; reversal; return 2 retreat 3 (Fig) revert

prapalaq adj, n unruly (animal)

prapamal nm, adj (area) on the other side of the mountain

prapamalas n person living on the other side of the mountain

prapambetës
  I § adj, n (person) who is held back (from advancement), passed over, or left behind
  II § n *debtor who is behind in repayment: defaulter, delinquent, deadbeat

prapambetje nf 1 backwardness; retardation 2 keeping from advancement/promotion, keeping back 3 [Fin] arrears

prapambetur
  I § adj (i) 1 left behind 2 still to be done, left 3 behind, slow; backward, retarded 4 old-fashioned, reactionary
  II § nf (e) something left to be done
  III § nn (të) [Fin] arrears

*****prapamejtim** = prapamendim

prapamendim nm ulterior motive, hidden intention

prapanicë nf (Colloq Pej) 1 rear end (of a person) 2 part of a garment that fits over the buttocks: seat

prapanik
  I § adj, n old-fashioned (person); backward (person); (person) who inhibits progress
  II § nm [Ethnog] apron worn in back

prapanike nf 1 old-fashioned/backward thing/ idea, inhibitor of progress 2 (Colloq) = prapanicë

*****prapanikësi** nf backwardness; delinquency

prapaqiellzor adj [Ling] postpalatal, velar

praparoje nf, adj [Mil] rear guard

prapaskene adv behind the scenes, in secrecy

prapaskenë nf 1 [Theat] backstage 2 (Fig) behind-the-scenes plot

prapa·shpinë nf 1 [Mil] rear flank 2 (Fig) secrecy; secret plot

prapa·shtesa np (Fig Pej) 1 superfluous appendages 2 false excuses used to get out of work

prapa·shtesë nf [Ling] suffix
 ○ **prapashtesë zvogëlimi** diminutive suffix

prapa·shtesim nm [Ling] suffixation

prapa·shtesor adj [Ling] formed by a suffix; suffixal

*****prapa·shtim** nm [Ling] suffix = **prapashtesë**

prapa·tokë nf [Geog] hinterland, hinterlands

prapa·vajtës adj 1 (Book) behind in development 2 inhibiting progress: regressive, reactionary

prapa·vajtje nf (Book) retrogression, regress

prapa·vendosje nf 1 positioning in the rear 2 [Ling] postposing, postposition

prapa·vendosur adj (i) [Ling] postposed

prapa·veprues adj (Book) retroactive

prapa·vesh nm [Anat] part of the head behind the ear

prapa·vështrues adj (Book) retrospective

prapa·vijë nf 1 [Mil] rear-line area: rear lines; rear-line units 2 (Fig) supporting force

prap·azi adv in back, behind; from behind

prapë
 I § adj (i) 1 in/on the back side, in back: reverse, obverse 2 (Colloq) rear, hind, hindmost 3 behaving badly: naughty; nasty; unruly, perverse 4 (of weather/terrain) rough 5 (of a person in a function that requires skill) consummate, superb
 II § nf(e) 1 reverse/obverse side, side in back: back, rear 2 bad behavior: wrong; naughtiness 3 misfortune
 III § adv 1 backwards; back; in reverse; inside out 2 (Colloq) again, yet again 3 (Fig Colloq) improperly, perversely

prapë·se nf 1 scissor-shaped rear part of the frame of a packsaddle to which the securing rope is attached 2 wicker endgate on a cart/wagon

prapë·se prapë adv yet again

prapësi nf 1 naughtiness, impropriety, perverseness, mischievousness; wrongdoing 2 bad luck, misfortune; adversity 3 nasty word/talk, bad language *4 retrogression

prapësim nm ger 1 < **prapëso·n**, **prapëso·het** 2 [Law] objection 3 [Med] regression *4 retrogression

prapësinë nf 1 shaded area (in mountains or valleys) behind a high rise 2 heel of a shoe

prapësisht adv (Book) adversely

*****prapësmë** adj (i) = **prapmë**

prapëso·het vpr 1 to step back; withdraw; retreat 2 to stop (doing something) in the middle: break off 3 to take back something said; change one's mind 4 to go bad

prapëso·n
 I § vt 1 to force/turn [] back: repel, repulse 2 to deprave, debauch; foul [] up, get [] fouled up 3 to make [] repeat *4 to reject, refuse
 II § vi, vt 1 to withdraw, withdraw from []; take [something said] back, retract; rescind [a law/command] 2 (Fig) to retreat

prapësor adj reverse

prapësues adj [Med] regressive

prapësueshëm adj [Med] reversible

prapësht adj (i) perverse; naughty; bad, wicked

prapështi nf = **prapësi**

prapësht o·het vt = **prapëso·het**

prapësht o·n vt = **prapëso·n**

prapët
 I § adj (i) 1 wicked, perverse 2 in the back; hidden, secret 3 on the back, supine
 II § adv on the back, with one's back down

prapët OR **prapëta** adv with one's back on the ground, on one's back

*****prapëto·n** vt = **prapëso·n**

prapi adv (së) wrong way first/out/up: in reverse, backwards, upside-down, inside-out

prapmë adj (i) 1 in/on the back side, in back: reverse, obverse 2 rear, hind, hindmost

prapmot adv two years from now

prapo·het vpr (Colloq) 1 to fall backwards; overturn 2 to reverse directions: turn around; withdraw, retreat

prapo·n vt (Colloq) 1 to turn [] upside down 2 to turn [] around 3 to take back [], rescind, cancel

praps· vt to force [] backwards: back; push back: repel

praps·et vpr to move backwards: step back, withdraw, retreat

prapsëm adj (i) = **prapmë**

prapsje nf [Mil] march to the rear: retreat

prapshëm adj (i) in back, back

prapshtas = **praptas**

prapshtë = **praptë**

prapshti = **prapësi**

praptas OR **praptazi** adv backwards, in reverse

praptë adj (i) = **prapë**

prapto·het vpr to overturn, topple over

prapto·n vt to turn [] upside down

prapthi
 I § adv backwards; in reverse, back
 II § adv (së) 1 wrong way first/out/up: in reverse, backwards, upside-down, inside-out 2 in the wrong way 3 unsuccessfully, badly

praqe
 I § nf [Ethnog] sash worn around the waist as part of a woman's costume
 II § np fem 1 crupper and cinch straps on horse harness 2 stirrups

prarán nm (Reg) ditch; trench

prarim nm ger 1 < **praro·n**, **praro·het** 2 golden light, glow

praro·het vpr to glisten with a golden color; glow with pleasure

praro·n
 I § vt 1 to coat [] with gold: gild 2 (Fig) to cause [] to glow with a golden light, imbue [] with a golden color 3 (FigElevated) to elevate, glorify, exalt
 II § vi to glow with a golden light

praruar adj (i) gilded 2 (Fig) glistening with a golden color; glowing with pleasure

prarues n person who gilds: gilder

pras nm = **presh**

*****prase** conj (dismisses what precedes as unimportant and introduces a following clause) So OK! __ anyway. No big deal! so __

prasëm adj (i) at the rear, hindmost, last

prask nm 1 (Reg Gheg) thin covering: membrane, film, veil *2 cataract in the eye

prashajkë nf weeding hoe

prashis| *stem for 1st sg pres, pl pres, 2nd & 3rd sg subj, pind* <**prashi**t·

prashit·

I § vt to break up the soil around [crops] with a cultivator: cultivate; hoe

II § vi (FigImpolite) to blather on and on without effect

∘ **prashit· në erë** to blather away

∘ **prashit· në të thatë** "hoe in dry ground" **1** to do useless work **2** to prattle on, talk to the wind

∘ **prashit· në ujë** to do something pointless, waste one's effort

∘ **prashit· para vetes** "hoe in front of oneself" to look after one's own personal affairs

prashites

I § adj **1** used for cultivating (breaking up the soil around) crops **2** (of crops) requiring cultivation/hoeing to grow properly

II § n cultivator, hoer

prashitëse *nf* **1** cultivating machine: field cultivator, cultivator **2** crop that requires cultivation/hoeing to grow properly

prashitje *nf ger* <**prashi**t·

∘ **prashitje qorre** "blind cultivation" light hoeing done before a plant has sprouted

*__prashtë__ *nf* = **prazhdë**

pratish *nm* [*Bot*] snowbells *(Soldanella)*

pravullim *nm ger* **1** <**pravullo**·*n*, **pravullo**·*het* **2** [*Med*] inhalant

pravullo·*het vpr* to get a vapor treatment; take a steam bath

pravullo·*n vt* **1** to steam **2** to bathe [] in steaming-hot water

∘ **pravullo**·*n* **hundët** "steam the nostrils" to inhale steam (as a treatment)

∘ **pravullo**·*n* **odën** to overheat the room

*__prazhdë__ *nf* sling

∘ **prazhdë shale** stirrup

*__pre__·*n vt* to please

pre *nf* **1** prey **2** *(Fig)* easy prey **3** something stolen or taken by force: plunder, loot, booty **4** person captured and killed: victim; person captured: prisoner of war

pre| *stem for pdef, part, imper, adm, opt* <**pre**t₁·, **prit**·*et* cut

∘ **e pre**^(*past*) **gojën** "cut off the mouth" **1** spoke one's last words: be dying **2** stopped talking/asking

∘ **Pre mish e ha!** "Cut your meat and eat it!" Tend to your own business!

∘ **nuk** [] **preu për** {*pronoun*} [] has no concern for {}, [] is not going to break [] 's back in {} 's behalf

∘ **Preje për vete e vishma mua!** "Cut it for yourself and let me wear it" Don't be selfish!

precedence *nf (Book)* precedence, priority

precedent *nm (Book)* precedent

precipitim *nm ger* [*Chem*] <**precipito**·*n* = **fundërrim**

precipito·*n vi, vt* [*Chem*] to precipitate = **fundërro**·*n*

precizion *nm* precision

*__preçart__

I § adj, adv speaking in a raving manner, in a delirium, not making any sense

II § nm delirium, raving

predestinuar *adj (i)* predestined

predikat *nm* **1** [*Ling*] predicate = **kallëzuues** **2** [*Phil*] logical predicate

predikatar *n* [*Relig*] preacher, pastor

*__predikator__ *n* [*Relig Old*] = **predikues**

predikim *nm ger* **1** <**prediko**·*n* [*Relig*] **2** sermon

prediko·*n vi* [*Relig*] to preach

predikues *nm* [*Relig*] preacher

predispono·*n vt* to predispose

*__predk__ *nm* [*Relig*] preaching, sermon

predomino·*n vt* to predominate

predominonjës *adj* predominant

predhë *nf* **1** [*Mil*] explosive projectile: bomb, cannonball; shell, bullet; missile **2** *(Fig)* something used to deliver a devastating blow

∘ **predhë e drejtuar** guided missile

pref = **mpreh**

prefekt *nm* prefect

prefekturë *nf* prefecture

preferim

I § nm <**prefero**·*n*

II § nm preference

prefero·*n vt (Book)* to prefer = **parapëlqe**·*n*

preferuar *adj (i)* preferred, favorite

preferueshëm *adj (i)* preferable

prefëse *nf* pencil sharpener

*__prefët__ *adj (i) (Reg Gheg)* sharp = **mprehtë**

prefiks *nm* [*Ling*] prefix

prefull *nm* wafer toasted over embers

*__preg__ = **prag**

*__pregaç__ *nm* = **përgaçe**

*__pregat__ = **përgat**

*__pregjim__ *nm* [*Ethnog*] naming celebration of a boy on the third night after his birth

preh··*et vpr* **1** to take a rest; pause; relax **2** to languish **3** *(Iron)* to lie there without anyone paying attention **4** *(FigElevated)* to be in repose (= buried)

∘ **preh·**·*et* **mbi dafina** to rest on one's laurels

*__preh__ = **mpreh**

prehalo·*het vpr (Colloq)* to become emaciated: waste away

prehaluq *adj* emaciated

prehër *nm* **1** lap (formed by sitting down) **2** front part of the body or of clothing between the waist to the knees **3** long apron used to carry loose objects **4** front apron of a fireplace **5** *(Fig)* place in which one feels at home: bosom, home

prehërthatë *adj* unable to conceive a child: barren, sterile

*__prehëshëm__ *adj (i)* restful, relaxing, comfortable; serene, peaceful

prehistori *nf* [*Hist*] prehistory = **parahistori**

prehistorik *adj* [*Hist*] prehistorical = **parahistorik**

prehje *nf ger* **1** <**preh**·*et* **2** rest, relaxation **3** serenity, tranquillity **4** place for stopping to relax: rest stop

*__prehtë__ *adj (i)* = **mprehtë**

prej *prep (abl)* **1** from; starting/originating from; made of; characteristic of; of **2** by means/way/agency/reason of: by

∘ **ësh·të prej xhami** "be made of glass" to be very fragile

prejardhje *nf* **1** origin, source **2** [*Ling*] derivation

prejardhur *adj (i)* derived

prejemëror *adj* [*Ling*] derived from a noun stem: denominal

prejfoljor *adj* [*Ling*] derived from a verb stem: deverbal

prej pjes or adj [Ling] derived from a participle stem: participial

prej se conj (Colloq) inasmuch as, since

*****prej t** stem for pdef, part, imper, adm, opt <**pre**•n

prek• vt 1 to touch 2 (Fig) to touch on [ ] 3 to affect 4 to infect

  ○ **s'**[ ] **prek**•^{3sg} **as me pupël/pendë** "you can't touch [ ] with even with a feather" [ ] is too sensitive/touchy/irritable, [ ] can't stand the slightest criticism

  ○ <> **prek**•^{3sg} **buza në gaz** <>'s lips form into a slight smile, <> smiles slightly

  ○ [ ] **prek**• **në kallo/lyth** to touch [ ]'s most sensitive spot

  ○ [ ] **prek**• **në plagë** to touch [ ]'s sore point

  ○ [ ] **prek**• **në tela** to find [ ]'s soft spot

  ○ <> **prek**• **në zemër/shpirt** to touch <>'s heart, move <> deeply

  ○ <>**i prek**• **telat** (Colloq) to know how to please <> so that <> will do what one wants: find the right button to press with <>, know how to please <>

  ○ **s'e prek**• **tokën** to think one is so high and mighty, be stuck up, have one's nose in the air

  ○ <> **prek**• **xhepin** "touch <>'s pocket" to find out how much money <> has

prek•et vpr 1 to be affected deeply, be touched (emotionally) 2 to take offense 3 to get a disease, get infected

  ○ **nuk prek**•et **(as) me krënde 1** to be so touchy that anything sets one off 2 to be too high and mighty for ordinary people to talk to

prek a tar

  I § adj 1 sensitive to the feelings of others, tactful 2 musically expressive/sensitive

  II § n sensitive person

prek ë nf 1 freckle 2 facial pockmark 3 (Fig Old) blemish, scar 4 (Colloq) hurt feelings 5 [Agr] blight

prek ël nf 1 [Zool] feeler, antenna 2 [Mus] instrument part pressed by a finger to produce a note: fret, key = **tast**

prek ës

  I § adj 1 tactile 2 (Fig) touching (to the sentiments), moving, poignant 3 having a tendency to take things that don't belong to one: sticky-fingered (Old) *****4** [Geom] tangent

  II § n person who obsessively touches/steals

prek je nf ger 1 <**prek**•, **prek**•et 2 tactile sense: touch 3 contact 4 [Wrestling] fall

prek shëm adj (i) 1 touchable; tangible; concrete; readily grasped 2 sensitive; vulnerable, susceptible; impressionable 3 (Fig) touching (to the sentiments), moving, poignant

prek shm ëri nf 1 (Book) vulnerability, susceptibility 2 sensitivity

*****prekula ç** nm [Zool] scorpion = **akrep**

prek ur

  I § part <**prek**•

  II § adj (i) 1 affected with a disease: infected, diseased 2 (Colloq) infected with tuberculosis 3 (Fig) marked for political sanction; under a political cloud: politically tainted 4 (Fig) deeply impressed; sympathetic, touched; disquieted, disturbed; with hurt feelings

  III § nm 1 (Colloq) person affected with tuberculosis 2 (Fig) person under legal/political punishment

  IV § nn (të) sense of touch

prekursor nm precursor

*****prel**•et vpr to hang, dangle

prelat nm prelate

prelud nm prelude

prell nm sunny place out of the wind = **shullë**

prell isht ë nf wide open sunny place

*****pre më** (Reg Gheg) = **prerë**

*****premi** nf (Old) conciseness, terseness

premierë nf premiere

premis e nf (Book) premise

premte nf (e) Friday

  ○ **e Premte e Zezë** Good Friday

premt im nm ger <**premto**•n

Premtime nf Premtime (female name)

premto•n

  I § vt to promise

  II § vi to show promise, be promising

  ○ **nuk** <> **premto**•n^{3sg} **koha** (Colloq Solecism) time does not permit <>

premtu ar adj (i) promised

premt u es adj showing promise: promising

*****prend ver** = **pranver**

*****prenk** = **princ**

prenk ë nf freckle

preokupacion nm concern

preokup im nm <**preokupo**•n

preokupo•het vpr to be concerned

preokupo•n vt to be of concern; cause concern

preokup u es adj of concern, causing concern

preparat nm [Spec] chemical/pharmaceutical/experimental preparation

prepotencë nf (Book Pej) power dominance: prepotency

prepotent adj (Book Pej) dominant in power: dominating, prepotent

*****preps** pcl

  ○ **preps të** {+ verb}^{subj} (Old) ought to {}

*****prepsje** nf dignity, decorum

*****preqe** np <**prak**, **prag**

pre ras OR **pre razi** adv 1 tersely; decisively; frankly *****2** precisely

pre rë

  I § part <**pret**₁• cut

  II § adj (i) 1 cut 2 cut into pieces: cut up 3 cut short: shortened, shortened; cut down: mown 4 flat/flattened on top 5 having an abrupt precipice 6 [Geom] cut off: truncated 7 not thick: thin 8 not subject to discussion: set, decided, definitive 9 terse and stern: curt, brusque, laconic 10 [Sport] (of a play/move) sharply angled: cut 11 adulterated, cut; (of wine) diluted; (of milk) spoiled; curdled 12 completely exhausted; weak, tired

  III § adv 1 = **pre ras** 2 right in the middle; right up to the brim 3 of course

  IV § nf (e) 1 cut place, cut 2 sharp pain

  V § nn (të) passage right through the middle: shortcut

  ○ **i prerë me gërshërë** tailor-made

  ○ **të prerë (barku)** colic

  ○ **ësh·të**^{3sg} **e prerë me thikë** "be cut through with a knife" to be settled once and for all, be absolutely decided

*****pre rë risht** = **prer ësisht**

pre rës

  I § adj 1 cutting; sharp 2 [Geom] intercepting, intersecting

II § *n* **1** person who cuts: cutter **2** = **prestar 3** [*Tech*]
= **prerëse**

III § *nm* incisor

IV § *n* minter of money

prerëse *nf* [*Tech*] cutting device/machine: cutter,
clipper; cutting blade

*****prerësisht** *adv* definitively, decisively

prerje *nf ger* **1** <**pret₁·**, **prit·et 2** cut; cutting
3 slice; section **4** interruption, break **5** sharp pain
6 [*Med*] amputation; section

   ○ **prerja e artë** division that follows the golden mean

pres *n* person who breaks his word

pres *stem for 1st sg pres, 1st & 3rd pl pres, 2nd &
3rd sg subj* <**pret₁·**, **pret₂·**

   ○ **E pres kokën!** "I cut off my head" I swear! I'm
absolutely certain!

presë *nf* **1** cutting edge; blade **2** (*Fig*) crucial part; (in
a fight) crucial blow **3** [*Agr*] water cut-off point into
an irrigation canal; irrigation furrow: corrugation
4 [*Tech*] apparatus that exerts pressure: press **5** =
prerëse *****6** bow (of a ship) *****7** vessel, pot

   ○ **ësh-të presë me dy tehe 1** to cut both ways,
have advantages and disadvantages **2** to require very
careful handling

presës *nm* variety of grass with sharp-blades

presformë *nf* [*Tech*] compression mold

president *n* president

presidium *nm* executive council: presidium, directorate

presim *nm ger* (*Book*) <**preso·n**

presing *nm* [*Basketball*] pressure

presion *nf* **1** pressure **2** physical pressure

presje *nf* **1** [*Ling*] comma **2** [*Bot*] sedge (*Carex*)

   ○ **presje dhjetore** (comma marking the) decimal
point

preso·n *vt* (*Book*) to shape/squeeze [] in a press

presor *nm* (*Colloq*) abbreviated form of address used
by a pupil toward a male teacher = **profesor**

prestar *n* **1** [*Text*] (journeyman) cutter **2** (*Old*) tailor

prestari *nf* **1** the profession of a cutter **2** cutting department (in a workshop) **3** (*Old*) tailor/dressmaker
shop

prestidigjitator *n* **1** circus magician: prestidigitator
2 (*Fig*) charlatan

prestigj *nm* prestige

prestixhiator *n* = **prestidigjitator**

prestore *nf* (*Old*) = **prestari**

presupozo·n *vt* to presuppose

presh *nm* [*Bot*] leek (*Allium porrum L.P*)

   ○ **presh i egër** [*Bot*] wild leek *Allium ampeloprasum*

   ○ **presh gomari** [*Bot*] summer snowflake *Leucolum
aestivum*

   ○ **presh gjarpri** [*Bot*] tassel hyacinth *Muscari comosum*

   ○ **ësh-të presh në kopsht me** [] (*Iron*) to have no
particularly close relationship with []

preshajkë *nf* short-handled cultivating tool with two
claws on one side and a hoe blade on the other:
cultivator = **capë**

*****preshëm** = **prekshëm**

preshkë *nf* spring onion/leek

preshtë *adj* (*i*) light green

preshto·n *vi* to grow verdant

pret₁·

I § *vt* **1** to cut; cut [] up/off/down; cut back [],
prune **2** to slaughter **3** to intercept [] on a road, block
[]'s path; force [] back **4** to take a shortcut through
[] **5** (*Fig*) to interrupt [] **6** (*Fig Colloq*) to set, fix,
establish **7** (*Fig*) to cut out [], give up [], discontinue,
stop **8** (*Fig*) to cut down the strength of []: weaken,
decrease, check; tire [] out **9** to add something to
congeal [a liquid]: curdle **10** to mint [money] **11** to
get [a receipt] for payment; buy a [ticket]

II § *vi* **1** to afflict <> with biting pain/cold **2** (*Colloq*)
to take a shortcut **3** (*Colloq*) (of a mechanism) to
engage/handle (well/badly); steer (to the left/right)

   ○ <> **pret₁·**³ˢᵍ {*the cutting weapon*} **djathtas e
majtas/nga të dyja anët** "<>'s {} cuts both
ways" <> *does* as <> likes because of special privileges

   ○ <>**a pret₁·** (*Colloq*) to cut <> short, not give <>
the time of day

   ○ **u pret₁· ballin** to turn <*animals*> in a different
direction

   ○ [] **pret₁·**³ˢᵍ **barku për** [] "longing cuts []'s
belly" (*Iron*) [] is really dying to see []

   ○ <>**a pret₁·** **bishtin** to take away things from <>
that <> does not deserve

   ○ **e pret₁· bletën** to cut apart the beehive (in order
to take out the combs of honey)

   ○ <>**a pret₁· derën** "cut <>'s door" to close one's
door to <>

   ○ <>**a pret₁· ditën** "cut off <>'s hour/day/life" to
bring <>'s life to an end: kill <>

   ○ **i pret₁· drutë shkurt me** [] to put matters bluntly
to []

   ○ <> **pret₁· duart** to deprive <> of <>'s main source
of strength: cut off <>'s right arm

   ○ **pret₁· e qep·** "cut and sew" to be able to do
whatever one wants, have total control

   ○ <> **pret₁·**³ˢᵍ **edhe myka** "even <>'s blunt side
cuts" <> enjoys everyone's respect, no one *says* no
to <>

   ○ [] **pret₁·**³ˢᵍ **etja** [] *is* very thirsty

   ○ **pret₁· fjalën** to settle the matter decisively

   ○ <> **pret₁· fjalën** to interrupt <>, break in on <>

   ○ **i pret₁· fjalët me sëpatë** "cut through the words
with an axe" to speak in a decisive manner and lay
down the law

   ○ **e pret₁· gojën** "stop one's mouth" **1** to be dying
and no longer able to speak **2** to stop speaking, say
no more

   ○ **pret₁· gozhdë** "cut nails/tacks" to grow numb
with cold

   ○ <> **pret₁·**³ˢᵍ **goja/gjuha brisk/gozhdë/hekur**
"<>'s tongue *cuts* hard" <> *has* a quick tongue, <>
speaks with fluency and precision; <> *is* quick with
<>'s retort; <> gives one a lot of backtalk; <> *has* a
sharp tongue

   ○ <> **pret₁· havalenë** (*Old*) to block <>'s view

   ○ <> **pret·**³ˢᵍ **hollë mendja** <> *has* a good brain

   ○ **pret₁· hollë** "cut fine" **1** to be very shrewd, be
very smart/clever, be quick-minded **2** to speak in
clever and suggestive/allusive language

   ○ <>**a pret₁·** "cut off <>'s hour/day/life" to
bring <>'s life to an end: kill <>

   ○ **pret₁· kokën për** [] "cut off one's head for []"
to be willing to cut off one's arm for []

   ○ [] **pret₁· kryq** to cut [] on the diagonal

   ○ <> **pret₁· lakun** to get <> out of trouble, get <>
out of a jam

○ **pret₁· larg** to have a distant/long-term goal; aim at something further

○ **<>a pret₁· litar** to get [ ] out of a bad predicament

○ [ ] **pret₁·**^{3sg} **malli për** [ ] "longing cuts [ ]'s heart" *(Iron)* *is* really dying to see [ ]

○ [ ] **pret₁·**^{3sg} **malli** [ ] *suffers* from longing

○ **<>[ ] pret· me brisk** to end [the matter] with <> without further discussion

○ **<>a pret₁· me cakorre** "cut it with a hatchet for <>" to tell <> frankly/plainly

○ **<> pret₁· me dy tehe** <> *does* as <> likes because of special privileges

○ **<>[ ] pret· me hanxhar** to say [ ] outright to <>

○ **<>[ ] pret· me sëpatë** to end [the matter] with <> without further discussion

○ [ ] **pret₁· me sëpatë të madhe/sëpatën e dardharit** "cut [ ] with a big axe" to lay down the law on [ ]

○ [ ] **pret₁· me thikë** to divide/separate [ ] sharply; distinguish [ ] clearly

○ **<>a pret₁·**^{3sg} **mendja se** __ <> *believes/thinks* that __, <> *gets* the feeling that __, it *looks* to <> like __

○ **<>a pret₁· (mendja)** "<>'s mind *cuts* <>" **1** *(Colloq)* it *occurs* to <> **2** it *strikes* <>; <> understands/ gets it

○ **e pret₁· misrin** to harvest corn

○ [ ] **pret₁· në besë** to break one's word to [ ]; betray [ ]'s trust

○ [ ] **pret₁· në fjalë** to go back on one's word to [ ]

○ **s'<>a pret₁·**^{3sg} **njeri qimen/perin** "no one *cuts* <>'s hair/thread" no one can put anything over on <>, no one is shrewder than <>

○ **<>a pret₁· orën** "cut off <>'s hour/day/life" to bring <>'s life to an end: kill <>

○ **pret₁· para të madhe** "cut big money" to make a lot of money

○ **e pret₁· pazarin** "cut the haggling" to stop haggling, settle on a price

○ **pret₁· perin** "cut the thread" to be very shrewd

○ **e pret₁· punën** to be very straightforward

○ **pret₁· qafën për** [ ] "cut off one's neck for [ ]" to be willing to cut off one's arm for [ ]

○ **<>a pret₁· qumështin** to wean <>

○ [ ] **pret₁· nga rrënjët/me rrënjë** "cut at the root(s)" to eradicate [ ]

○ **<>i pret₁· rrënjët** "cut out <>'s roots" to get rid of <> forever

○ **<> pret₁· rrugën** "intercept <>'s path" to block/ stop <>, prevent <>

○ **nuk <> pret₁·**^{3sg} **sëpata në një vend** "<>'s axe does not cut at the same place" **1** to change <>'s mind often **2** to say the wrong thing at the wrong time; talk nonsense

○ **<> pret₁·**^{3sg} **shpata nga të dy anët** <> *does* as <> likes because of special privileges

○ **<> pret₁· shtegun** "intercept <>'s path" to block/stop <>, prevent <>

○ **e pret₁· timonin** to turn the steering wheel suddenly and with force: cut the wheel hard

○ **pret₁· trashë** "cut coarse" **1** to be dense/brainless, be thick in the head **2** to say stupid things, talk nonsense

○ **ia pret₁· thekun gruas** *(Old)* to divorce one's wife and shame her publicly by cutting off the tassels of her waist sash

○ **<>i pret₁· thonjtë** "cut <>'s claws" **1** to do away with <>'s ability to do harm: pull <>'s claws, render <> harmless **2** to punish *<the thief>* (in order to discourage further stealing)

○ **pret₁· thumba** "cut nails/tacks" **1** to grow numb with cold **2** to become exhausted from working on something difficult: poop out doing hard work

○ **<> pret₁·udhën** "intercept <>'s path" to block/ stop <>, prevent <>

○ [ ] **pret₁·**^{3sg} **ujët e hollë** "[ ] *suffers* from urine" [ ] badly *needs* to urinate

○ [ ] **pret₁·**^{3sg} **uria** [ ] *is* very hungry

○ **pret₁· verën** to cut/dilute the wine

○ **<>i pret₁· veshët** "cut <>'s ears" to bring <> down from <>'s high horse, bring <> down a peg or two

pret₂·

I § *vt* **1** to wait for [ ]; await; wait expectantly; expect **2** to catch [an approaching object]; (of a goalkeeper) save **3** to receive [visitors/guests], welcome; give [ ] a reception

II § *vi* to wait; wait patiently

○ **ia pret₂· (këngës)** *(Colloq)* (in folk music) to sing the drone accompaniment to a melody line begun by another singer

○ **<> pret₂· ditën** to be just waiting for the day to get back at <>

○ **pret₂· e përcjell·** to be very hospitable; have a lot of visitors/company

○ **pret₂· fëmijë** "expect a child" to be pregnant, be expecting

○ **nuk <> pret₂·**^{3sg} **koha** "time *does not wait* for <>" <> *has* little time, <> *is* in a hurry

○ **s'<>a pret₂·**^{3sg} **luga lugën** "<>'s spoon *doesn't* wait for the spoon" <> *eats* one spoonful quickly after another; <> *eats* in a hurry, <> *is* too hungry to eat slowly

○ **pret· me gojë hapur** to wait with bated breath

○ [ ] **pret₂· me këmbët e para** to give [ ] a cold reception

○ [ ] **pret₂· me lot në sy** to welcome [ ] with nostalgic warmth, welcome [ ] emotionally

○ [ ] **pret₂· me lule** "receive [ ] with flowers" to roll out the red carpet for [ ]

○ [ ] **pret· me muhabet deri në gju** to receive [a visitor/guest] warmly (with friendly conversation and much to eat and drink)

○ [ ] **pret₂· me plumb/pushkë** *(Colloq)* to welcome [ ] with bullets

○ [ ] **pret₂· me pushkë në faqe** to greet [ ] with open arms

○ [ ] **pret₂· me të parat** to give [ ] a cold reception

○ **nuk <> pret₂·**^{3sg} **puna** <> *has* little time, <> *is* in a hurry

○ [ ] **pret· si dhia thikën** "await [ ] like the goat awaits the knife" to be very anxious/fearful/nervous about [ ]

preta'r *n* *(Old)* thief who steals live prey: rustler

prete'kst *nm* pretext

prete'ncë *nf* [*Law*] prosecutor's speech to the court: prosecution argument

pretend/**im** *nm ger* **1** <**pretendo**·*n* **2** illegitimate claim

pretendo·*n*

I § *vt* **1** to claim [ ] (illegitimately); pretend **2** to aspire to [ ]

II § *vi* to make a pretense

pretendu|e's
I § *n* pretender, aspirant
II § *adj* **1** making an illegitimate claim; pretending **2** aspiring

pre'tim *nm ger (Old)* <preto'

pre'to·n *vi (Old)* **1** to steal [livestock]: rustle, raid **2** to plunder, loot

pre'thi *adv* = jesi'rthi

preva'z *nm* casement/wing of a window

prevede' *nf [Food]* fruit jelly

preventi'v *nm [Fin]* amount budgeted for a particular purpose: budget allocation, budget

preve'ë *nf* **1** [Folklore] = vito're **2** (Reg) much-traveled road: beaten path; highway **3** small and shallow river: creek; river ford

prezant|i'm *nm ger* **1** <prezanto'·n **2** presentation, introduction

prezant|o'·n *vt* to present, introduce

prezbi't *adj* myopic

preze'nt
I § *nm [Ling]* present (tense)
II § *adj* present

prezervati'v *nm* condom

***prë·**n *vt* = pre·n

***prëh| = preh|**

***prë'm| = mbrë'm|**

prëmu'llzë *nf [Zool]* abomasum *()*

***prënd\ve're**ë = pranve're

***prënd\ver\o'r = pranver\o'r**

***prë'nga = pra'nga**

prë'njkë *nf* freckle

pri
I § *stem for imper* <pret₁·
II § *nf* *small row, row, line

pri·het *vpr* <pri·n
  o **pri·***het* **nga** __ to follow the guidance of __, base oneself on __

pri·n *vi* **1** to lead; be at the head **2** to be good for <>; go well for <>.
  o **<> prifte e mbara!** May <> achieve success! Good luck to <>!
  o **<> pri·n rrugën** to take the lead of <>

pria'ls *nm* pulse, pulse beat

***pri'ç** *nm* = prinxh

***prie'ç**ë *nf* moccasin/sandal (of poor quality)

pri'er· *vt* to tilt, lean

pri'erje *nf* = pri'rje

prift *nm (np ~ ër|i'nj)* **1** priest **2** [Lit] elder; king **3** [Constr] kingpost = babal'lëk
  o **foltë/këndoftë prifti!** "May the priest speak/sing for <>!" (Curse) May the priest say a (final) prayer over <>!: I hope <> dies!

prift|ere'shë *nf* **1** wife of an orthodox priest **2** [Hist] priestess

prift|ëri' *nf* **1** priesthood **2** (Collec) clergy

prift|ëri'nj *np* <prift

prift|ëro'·n *vi* to officiate as priest

prift|ëro'r *adj* priestly

***prigj| = përgj|**

prija'ta'r
I § *n* leader; leader in group dancing/singing
II § *adj* in the role of leader, at the lead: leading

pri'jë *nf* **1** (Colloq) irrigation/drainage ditch in a field **2** strip of land between two ditches **3** row of fruit trees or vines at the far end of a field **4** leadership, primacy

pri'j|ë's *n* guide; leader; military/clan leader,

***pri'j|ë's|e** *adj* (of cows) fertile

pri'jë'z *nf (Dimin)* irrigation/drainage furrow: corrugation

pri'k *nm* = pje'rrje

pri'kë *nf* dowry

***prik|o's·** *vt* to endow

prill *nm* April
  o **Prilli bën lulen e maji ka nderin.** "April makes the flower and May gets the credit." (Prov) One person does the work and another gets the credit.

***pri'lle** *nf* household furnishing

prima'r *adj (Book)* having highest priority: primary = parës'or

pri'me *np fem* treatment with folk remedies: folk medicine

primigravi'de *nf [Med]* primigravida

primipa're *nf [Med]* primipara

primiti'v *adj* primitive

primitiv|i'zëm *nm* primitivism

primulace' *np fem [Bot]* primrose family *Primulaceae*

princ *nm* prince

***prince's**ë = prince'shë

prince'shë *nf* princess

pri'nc|ër *np* <princ princes

princ|ër|o'r *adj* = princo'r

princi'p *nm* principle = pari'm

princ|ipa'të *nf [Hist]* principality

principia'l *adj (Book)* principled

principia'l|itet *nm (Book)* principled basis

***princ|ni'** *nf* **1** (Collec) the condition or period of being a prince **2** = principa'të

princ|o'r *adj* princely

pri'nç *nm [Bot]* tunicflower (*Tunica* (*Petrorhagia*))

prind *nm (np ~ ër)* parent

***prind|a'r** *adj* = prindëro'r

pri'nd|ër *np* <prind **1** parents **2** earliest ancestors

prind|ër|o'r *adj (Book)* parental

***prind|ësi'** *nf* parentage; affinal kinship

***prind|ës|o'r** *adj (i)* = prindëro'r

***prind|ës|ue's** *adj* consanguinally related

***prind|o'r** *adj* = prindëro'r

pri'nq *nm (obl ~ gji)* = princ

prinxh *nm* brass = tunxh

***prinj|ësi'** *nf* leadership

prior|ite't *nm (Book)* priority, primacy = përparësi'

pripa'lë *nf (Reg)* = përpa'rje

pri'qe *np fem* = cerm'ë

prir·et *vpr* **1** to lean, lean over; incline **2** (Fig) to have a tendency: tend
  o **prir·***et* **nga** {} (Fig) **1** to be attracted by {}, be interested in {} **2** to be biased in favor of {}: favor {}

pri'rë
I § *part* <pri·n, prier·
II § *nf* instep (of the foot)

pri'rët *adj (i)* **1** slanting = pje'rrët **2** bent = përku'lur

pri'rje *nf ger* **1** <prier·, prir·et **2** inclination, tendency; predilection; penchant **3** natural bent, aptitude **4** (Old) = pjerrësi'

*pris *n* = pri·jës

pris *stem for pind, 2nd pl pres* <pret₁·, pret₂·

*prisi *nf* guidance, leadership

prisko *·n vt* to spray

prish· *vt* **1** to break/ruin/spoil []; break [a mechanism/agreement] **2** to break [a larger piece of money into smaller amounts], change; spend [an amount of money] **3** *(Colloq)* to break [] apart/down; unravel, untangle, loosen up [] **4** to demolish, destroy; do [] in, kill; despoil **5** to erase, delete, strike [] out **6** *(Fig)* to mess/foul [] up **7** *(Colloq)* to deflower [a virgin]; rape **8** to bring [] to an orgasm **9** *(Fig Colloq)* to refuse <>'s [request]

∘ **prish· bletën** to take the beehive apart to get at the honey

∘ **prish· bucela e bë·*n* kënaçe** to break something of great value in order to make something of little value

∘ **prish· bucela e bën kënaçe** to ruin something of great value in order to fix something of little value

∘ **prish· buzët** to make a grimace

∘ **i prish· curlet me** [] "break shawms with []" to stop being friends with []

∘ **prish· çehren** to express sudden unhappiness in one's countenance: put on a sad face, {}'s face *falls*

∘ **<> prish· çupërinë** to deprive <> of her virginity: deflower <>

∘ **<>a prish· fiqirin 1** to change <>'s mind **2** to make <> confused, confuse <>

∘ **i prish·*pl* fjalët** to exchange bitter words, have a terrible argument, quarrel

∘ **prish· fytyrën** to express sudden unhappiness in one's countenance: put on a sad face, {}'s face *falls*

∘ **e prish· gojën** to use foul/offensive language

∘ **<>a prish· gjakun** to upset <> greatly, cause <> distress; terrify <>

∘ **nuk e prish· gjakun 1** not get upset/frightened, be unflappable/unexcited; not show any concern, be unworried **2** to show no concern, be uncaring

∘ **e prish· hajatin me** [] to break off relations with []

∘ **prish· martesën** to dissolve the marriage: get divorced

∘ **prish· me zgrip** to be very thrifty in spending

∘ **<>a prish· mendjen 1** to change <>'s mind **2** to make <> confused, confuse <>

∘ **[] prish· mendsh** to drive [] out of []'s mind

∘ **prish· ndoren** *(Old)* to betray one's trust

∘ **<> prish· nervat** to get on <>'s nerves

∘ **i prish· nervat me** [] to lose one's patience with [], become exasperated with []

∘ **i prish· pipëzat** "break the flutes" *(Colloq)* to break off a friendship

∘ **s'prish· punë** it doesn't matter

∘ **<>*i* prish· punët** to cause difficulties for <>, ruin <>'s plans

∘ **s'prish· qejf (me njeri)** *(Colloq)* not want to create any bad feelings (with anyone)

∘ **prish· qejf me** [] to get on bad terms with []

∘ **<>a prish· qejfin** *(Colloq)* to put <> in a bad mood; disappoint <>

∘ **nuk <>a prish· qejfin** to do as <> wants

∘ **prish· radhimin** [*Mil*] to break ranks

∘ **s'po <>a prish·** not going to turn <> down

∘ **prish· syrin (e keq)** to break the (evil) spell

∘ **prish· shtëpi e bë·*n* kasolle** "knock down a house and build a shack" *(Prov)* to ruin something important for the sake of something trivial

∘ **<>a prish· toruan** to change <>'s mind, get <> off on a different track

∘ **nuk ta prish· tymin e duhanit** "not disturb your tobacco smoke" to be very quiet and well-behaved, be no bother

∘ **prish· uri** to appease/slake one's hunger

∘ **<>a prish· zemrën** to break <>'s heart

∘ **e prish· zemrën** to fill one's heart with unkind thoughts

prish·*et vpr* **1** to break; break down; collapse **2** to break off a relationship: break up **3** to get worse **4** to get fouled/tangled/mixed up: get all confused **5** to go bad: spoil, rot; wither away; grow ugly **6** to vanish, disappear **7** *(Colloq)* (of a female animal) to miscarry, abort **8** to have an orgasm: come

∘ **nuk prish·*et3sg* bota/dynaja** *(Impol)* not be a big calamity, not be such a tragedy

∘ **<> prish·*et3sg* çarku** <> *suffers* total breakdown

∘ **<> prish·*et3sg* gjaku** *(Impol)* to get terribly frightened/upset

∘ **<> prish·*et3sg* gjiza** "<>'s cheese *is* not spoiling" *(Crude Iron)* it is of no concern to <>

∘ **<> prish·*et3sg* mendja** <>'s mind *is beginning* to change, <> *is wavering*; <> *is getting* confused

∘ **prish·*et* në fytyrë/çehre** *(Colloq)* to express sudden unhappiness in one's countenance: put on a sad face, {}'s face *falls*

∘ **prish·*et* nga mendja/fiqiri** to go out of one's mind, go crazy

∘ **prish·*et* për një lugë çorbë** "break up over a spoonful of thick soup" to break off a friendship over a trivial matter, break off a social relationship over nothing

prish·a·le·sh *nm* person who combs wool or cotton fibers: comber

prish·ani·k *adj, n* **1** = prisharak **2** crazy, cracked, screwy

prish·a·plëng·as *n* = plëngpri·shës

prish·a·qe·jf

I § adj (of a person) causing frustration by refusal

II § adv = prishaqe·jfas

prish·a·qe·jf·as *adv* **1** with hurt feelings; with annoyance/anger *2 downhearted

prish·ara·k *adj, n* (person) who is wasteful of money: spendthrift

pri·shë *nf* dilapidation, decrepitude

*pri·sh·ëm *adj (i)* = pri·shur

pri·sh·ës

I § n **1** demolisher, wrecker **2** person who despoils/breaks/disrupts {}: despoiler, {}-breaker, disrupter **3** waster, spendthrift **4** person who breaks an agreement

II § adj **1** overspending, extravagant **2** destructive, detrimental, ruinous

*pri·sh·ë·sh·ëm *adj (i)* subject to spoilage/breakage/destruction: ruinable

pri·sh·je *nf ger* **1** <prish·, prish·et **2** breakdown; collapse **3** broken place: break; breakage; interruption; damage **4** [*Geol*] fault **5** *(Colloq)* expense; consumption

∘ **prishje tektonike** [*Geol*] tectonic accident

pri·shur

I § part <prish·, prish·et

II § adj (i) **1** in ruin; ruined **2** broken down, unusable, inoperable **3** fouled/tangled/mixed up: confused **4** gone bad: spoiled, rotten; withered away;

grown ugly **5** grown worse **6** (of a face) in a grimace **7** stunned, dazed; out of one's mind

III § *nm* (i) person in a daze; person out of his mind

prish|ur|a *np (të) (Colloq)* **1** expenses; charges **2** money, change, small change

*prish|urina** *np fem* fragments, rubble

prit *interj* wait a second! hold on a minute!

prit·et* *vpr* **1** (of the body) to get gashed/lacerated **2** *(Fig Colloq)* (of something that has been continuous) to come to a stop: end, halt **3** *[Dairy]* (of milk) to spoil, turn sour **4** to intersect **5** to be expected; be awaited; be received

  ○ <> **1prit·**et*³ˢᵍ* **fytyra** <>'s face *falls*, <> *suddenly turns pale*

  ○ <> **prit·**et*³ˢᵍ* **goja/gjuha/zëri** "<>'s mouth/tongue/voice *is cut*" <> is unable to utter a word, <>'s voice *freezes* in <>'s throat; <> /is/ at a loss for words, <> is struck dumb with amazement; <> *gets* utterly tongue-tied

  ○ <> **prit·**et*³ᵖˡ* **gjunjët 1** <>'s knees *buckle*, <> *can* barely stand **2** *(Fig)* to be numb and unable to act

  ○ <> **prit·**et*³ᵖˡ* **këmbët ∥ leqet e këmbëve 1** <>'s legs *give way*, <> *can* barely stand **2** *(Fig)* to be numb and unable to act

  ○ <> **1prit·**et*³ᵖˡ* **krahët 1** <> *goes* numb, <> *is* unable to continue **2** <> *loses* <>'s base of support

  ○ **S'pritet lisi/druri me një sëpatë∥të rënë të sëpatës.** "The oak/tree is not cut down by a single axe ∥ blow of the axe." *(Prov)* It takes persistent effort to do a difficult task.

  ○ **prit·**et* **në fytyrë** to grow pale from shock, {}'s face *falls* from shock

prit|

  I § *stem for 2nd pl pres, pind, imper, vp* <**pret₁·**, **pret₂·**

  II § *stem for part, pdef, opt, adm, vp* <**pret₂·**

  ○ **Prit të presim!** What can we do: we just have to wait!

  ○ **Prite Zot!** God forbid!

prit|a'r *nm* **1** person who lies in wait: ambusher *2** person who decides whether an informer is telling the truth

prit|e|s|ë *nf* laziness, sluggishness, sloth

prit|ë *nf* **1** place of ambush; group waiting in ambush; ambush **2** embankment/levee erected to prevent flooding or erosion **3** water cut-off point into an irrigation canal **4** *[Spec]* cut-off device **5** *(Fig)* difficulty (to overcome); obstacle

  ○ **pritë druri** wattled dam

  ○ **pritë dheu** earthen dike

*prit|ëm**

  I § *adj* (i) expected, anticipated; future, upcoming, coming

  II § *nm* *the future

  III § *nf (e)* the future

prit|ës *adj* **1** hospitable **2** *[Offic]* involved with receiving delivered commodities **3** *[Agr]* catchwater

prit|ës|i = prit·e|s|ë

prit|ës|o·-n *vt* to intercept

prit|je *nf ger* **1** <**pret₂·**, **prit·**et* **2** welcoming reception **3** reception banquet **4** hearing given to petitions by the public

  ○ **ësh·të në pritje** *(Book)* to be in expectation

prit|je-përcjellje *nf* receiving and seeing off a constant stream of visitors

prit|me *nf (Old) [Ling]* future tense

*prit|meni** *nf* leave of absence

prit|më *adj (i)* expected, awaited

prit|mëri *nf = pritshmëri*

prito·-n *vi = përto·-n*

prit|sh|ëm *adj (i)* **1** expectable; expected, future **2** hospitable *3** acceptable

prit|shm|ëri *nf (Book)* **1** waiting around passively **2** on reserve status

prit|ue|sh|ëm *adj (i)* dawdling, hesitating

prit|ur

  I § *part* <**pret₂·**

  II § *adj* (i) hospitable = **mikpritës**

privat

  I § *adj* private; personal

  II § *n* owner of a private shop

privat|isht *adv* privately

privatiz|o·-n *vt* to privatize

privilegj *nm* special privilege

privilegj|o·-n *vt (Book)* to grant special privilege to []

privilegj|u|a'r

  I § *adj* (i) specially privileged

  II § *nm* (i) member of the privileged class

priv|im *nm* deprivation

  ○ **privim lirie** *[Law]* deprivation of liberty: imprisonment

  ○ **privim i të drejtave** *[Law]* deprivation of (civil) rights

priv|o·-n *vt* to deprive, dispossess

prixhionie'r *nm [Tech]* stud bolt

prizë *nf* **1** *[Electr]* socket **2** *[Hydrol]* sluice *3** stream bed, water channel

  ○ **prizë me fole** *[Electr]* recessed socket

  ○ **prizë uji** water hydrant

priz|ëm *nm* **1** prism **2** *(Fig Book)* point of view, special perspective

prizm|atik *adj* shaped like a prism: prismatic

Prizre'n *nm* old city in Kosovo with a large Albanian population: Prizren

prjer| = prier, pjerr|

pro

  I § *adv (Book)* in favor, pro, for

  II § *prep (abl)* in favor of, on the side of, pro

pro| *formativ pref* pro-

pro|amerika'n *adj, n* pro-American

pro|angle'z *adj, n* pro-English

probabilite't *nm (Book)* probability

probat|e|sh|ë *nf [Ethnog] = motërmë*

probat|i'n *nm [Ethnog] = vëlla'm*

probat|ino·-het *vpr* to become bound/pledged in a blood fellowship

*pro'be** *nf with masc agreement = vëlla'ço*

proble'm *nm* **1** problem **2** *[Math] = problemë*

problem|atik *adj* problematical

problem|atikë *nf* set of problems to be dealt with

proble'm|cë *nf* mathematical problem (in schoolwork)

problem|o'r *adj* setting forth a problem, presented as a problem; problematic

*pro|botim** *nm* **1** adopted brother **2** *(Fig)* boon companion

proced|im *nm* <**procedo·-n**

proced|o·-n

  I § *vi (Book)* to follow a procedure: proceed

II § vt [Law] to proceed against []: prosecute, charge

procedurë *nf* **1** *(Book)* procedure **2** *[Law]* juridical procedure

proces *nm* **1** *(Book)* process **2** *[Law]* proceedings at law, action at law: case

procesion *nm* procession

proces\verbal *nm* official record: proceedings, minutes of a meeting

**proçes = proces

proçka\ma\dh *adj (Pej)* given to making stupid blunders: bungling, blundering; always saying the wrong thing without thinking: boorish

pro\çkë *nf (Pej)* clumsy error made without thinking: faux pas, stupid blunder; silly thing

produkt *nm* product

produktiv *adj* productive

produktivitet *nm* productivity = **prodhimtari**

prodh I § nm OR **pro\dhë II § nf (Old) = **prodhim**

prodhim *nm ger* **1** <**prodho**•*n* **2** production; product, output **3** *[Math]* product

   ◦ **prodhim për shoqërinë** *[Econ]* (in Marxist economics) society's share of a worker's productivity

   ◦ **prodhim për vete** *[Econ]* production for the producer's own needs

   ◦ **prodhimi i vogël i mallrave** *[Econ]* small-scale production of commodities

**prodhim\ësi = prodhueshm\ëri

**prodhim\or = prodhimtar

prodhim\tar *adj* productive

prodhim\tari *nf* productivity

prodho•*n vt* to produce

*prodho\s• *vt* to inform on [], give [] away, betray

**prodhot *nm* informer, police spy

prodhues

   I § adj productive

   II § n producer

   ◦ **prodhuesit e vegjël të mallrave** *[Econ]* small-scale producers of commodities

prodhue\shëm *adj (i)* able to be produced: producible

prodhue\shm\ëri *nf* productiveness; productivity

prof. *abbrev* <**profesor** Prof. = Professor

profan

   I § adj **1** *(Book)* lacking requisite knowledge: ignorant **2** non-religious, secular, profane

   II § nm not having expert knowledge: uninitiated

profan\o•*n vt* to profane

PROFARMA *abbrev* agency for pharmaceutical products

pro\fashist *adj, n* pro-Fascist

profeci *nf* prophesy

profesion *nm* profession

profesion\al *adj* pertaining/leading to a profession: professional

profesion\al\iz\ëm *nm* **1** professionalism **2** *[Ling]* professional jargon

profesion\ist *adj, n* (person) trained for or practicing a profession: professional

profesor *nm* professor, teacher

profesore\shë *nf* (female) professor/teacher

profet *nm* prophet

**profet\ar = profetik

profete\shë *nf* prophetess

**profeti *nf* prophecy

profetik *adj* prophetic

profet\iz\im *nm* prophecy

profet\iz\o•*n vt(Book)* to prophesy

**profik *adj* prophetic

profil *nm* **1** profile **2** *(Fig Book)* major direction of activity: specialization; set of major characteristics

profilaksi *nf* **1** *[Med]* prophylaxis **2** *[Tech]* preventive maintenance

profilaktik *adj* prophylactic; preventive

profil\im *nm* *[Tech]* shaping of metal

profil\iz\im *nm ger* <**profilizo**•*n*, **profilizo**•*het*

profil\iz\o•*het vpr* to gain specialized training: become a specialist in a particular field

profil\iz\o•*n vt* **1** to prepare [] for a specialty, train [] in a particular discipline **2** to develop a specialization program at [a training institution]

profil\iz\uar *adj (i)* specialized; offering specialization

**profis• *vi* to go astray

profit *nm* **1 = **profet** **2 = profeti

**profite\ps *nm* soothsayer, fortune-teller

**profite\ps• = profetizo•*n*

profka\tar *n* person who lies and talks nonsense

pro\fkë *nf* **1** toy squirt gun **2** nonsensical lie: claptrap, twaddle

prog *nm (np ˜ gje)* hobnail

prognozë *nf* **1** *[Med Veter]* prognosis **2** forecast

program *nm* program

programatik *adj* programmatic

program\im *nm ger* <**programo**•*n*

program\o•*n vt* to program

program\or = programatik

progres *nm* progress

progresion *nm* *[Math]* progression

progres\ist *adj (Book)* in favor of progress, for progress; contributing to progress = **përparimtar**

progresiv *adj (Book)* progressive

pro\gje *np* <**prog**

**proh *interj (Reg Gheg)* oh my!

projeksion *nm* **1** *[Geom]* projection **2** projection (on a film screen)

projekt *nm* **1** construction plan, design; construction drawings, blueprint **2** draft of a document under consideration **3** *(Book)* plan for future work: project

projekt\buxhe *nm* *[Fin]* budget projection

projekt\deklara\të *nf* draft declaration

projekt\dety\rë *nf* proposed assignment of duties

projekt\diplo\më *nf* research project presented and defended by a degree candidate (in engineering)

projekt\direkti\vë *nf (Offic)* proposed/draft directive ()

projekt\ide *nf* idea for a project

projekt\im *nm ger* <**projekto**•*n*

projekt\kushtetu\të *nf* proposed/draft constitution

projekt\ligj *nm* proposed/draft law

projekt\marrë\veshje *nf* proposed/draft agreement

projekt\o•*n vt* **1** to draw up a construction plan/design for [] **2** to project [] on a screen

projekt\or *nm* **1** searchlight **2** projector

projekt\plan *nm* proposed/draft plan

projekt\rezolu\të *nf* proposed/draft resolution

projekttraktat *nm* proposed/draft treaty

projektues
I § *adj* **1** engaged in construction designing/planning **2** serving to project images on a screen
II § *nm* **1** construction designer/planner ***2** draftsman

projektvendim *nm* proposed/draft decision

proje *nf* loot, booty

*projt *nm (Old)* harbor

*projt = mbrojt

*prok *nm* = prog

prokat *nm [Tech]* rolled metal

proke *nf* = prog

proklamatë *nf* proclamation

proklamo·n *vt* to proclaim

proklitik *nm [Ling]* proclitic

*prokof *nm* shroud, pall

prokomunist *adj* pro-Communist

prokopi *nf(Colloq)* **1** property, wealth **2** profit, benefit

*prokops· *vi* to prosper

*prokopsur *adj (i)* having profited, benefitted

prokopshëm *adj (i)* prosperous

prokovacë *nf* bed sheet, blanket

*prokudis *stem for 1st sg pres, pl pres, 2nd & 3rd sg subj, pind* <prokudit·

*prokudit· *vt* to pilfer

prokurë *nf [Law]* power of attorney: procuration

prokuror *n [Law]* public prosecutor, state's attorney
○ **Prokuror i Përgjithshëm** Attorney General
○ **prokuror popullor** district attorney

prokurori *nf [Law]* office of the state's attorney

proletar *adj, n* proletarian

proletariat *nm* proletariat

proletarizim *nm ger* <proletarizo·n, proletarizo·het

proletarizo·het *vpr* to become proletarianized

proletarizo·n *vt* to proletarianize

proletarizuar *adj (i)* proletarianized

prolog *n* prologue

promemorie *nf (Book)* memorandum = përkujtesë

Promete *nm* Prometheus

promotor *n (Book)* initiator

pronar *n* proprietor (of a profit-making establishment); owner

*pronarësi *nf* ownership

*pronaro·n *vt* to own

pronarth *nm dimin* proprietor (of a small profit-making establishment), smallholder

*prondim *nm* product, output

*prondis *stem for 1st sg pres, pl pres, 2nd & 3rd sg subj, pind* <prondit·

*prondit· *vt* to produce, yield

*pronditës *adj* productive

*pronditje *nf ger* **1** <prondit· **2** production

pronë *nf* property
○ **pronë vetjake** personal property

pronësi *nf* ownership

pronëso·n *vt* to gain possession of [ ]

pronësor *adj* **1** pertaining to property/ownership: proprietary **2** [Ling] (of a compound element) possessing the attribute embodied in the second component: attributive

pronor
I § *adj [Ling]* possessive
II § *nm* possessive pronoun

*pronjak *adj* proprietary

*pronjëz *nf dimin* small piece of property

propagandë *nf* propaganda; publicity

propagandim *nm ger* <propagando·n

propagandist *n* propagandist; publicist

propagandistik *adj* propagandistic

propagando·n *vt* to propagandize

propagandues *adj* propagandizing

*propë *nf* prow

proporcion *nm* proportion = përpjesëtim

proporcional *adj* proportional = përpjesëtimor

proporcionalisht *adv (Book)* proportionally = përpjesëtimisht

propozim *nm ger* **1** <propozo·n **2** proposal; suggestion; proposition

propozo·n *vt* **1** to propose; suggest **2** to nominate

propozuar
I § *adj (i)* nominated
II § *nm (i)* nominee

propozues *nm* **1** proposer; suggestion maker **2** nominator

pror *stem for pdef* <prier·

prore *adv (Reg)* all the time: constantly, continually

prorevizionist *adj, n* pro-Revisionist

prosek *nm* corral/pen for livestock; sheepfold

*proseqe *np* clippings from a pruned tree

*proskonis· *vt* to pick [ ] up, collect

prosovjetik *adj, n* pro-Soviet

prosperitet *nm (Book)* prosperity

prostat *nm* prostatitis

*prostatë *nf [Anat]* prostate gland

prostitucion *nm* prostitution

prostitutë *nf* prostitute

proshkët *adj (i)* fresh; freshly cooked

proshtimë *nf* freshly flayed skin: raw hide; rawhide

*proshtokuth *nm* rogue, rascal

proshutë *nf* prosciutto, ham

protagonist *n* protagonist

proteinë *nf [Biol]* protein

proteksionist *n (Book)* protectionist

proteksionizëm *nm (Book)* protectionism

protektorat *nm* protectorate

protestant *adj* Protestant

protestantizëm *nm [Relig]* Protestantism

protestë *nf* protest

protestim *nm ger* **1** <protesto·n **2** = protestë

protesto·n *vi* to make a protest: protest

protestues
I § *adj* protesting, in protest
II § *n* protester

protezë *nf [Med]* **1** prosthesis **2** dentures

protokoll *nm* **1** *(Offic)* = procesverbal **2** registry of incoming and outgoing documents in an office; registry/records office **3** [Dipl] protocol **4** understanding between parties to an exchange agreement

protokollar *adj (Offic)* pertaining to a protocol; in accordance with protocol

protokollim *nm ger (Offic)* <protokollo·n

protokollïst *n (Offic)* office worker who maintains the registry of incoming and outgoing documents

protokollo·n *vt (Offic)* to enter [a document] into the office registry

protokolluar *adj (i) (Offic)* (of a document) registered in an official registry

proto'n *nm* [*Phys*] proton

protoplazmë *nf* [*Biol*] protoplasm

prototïp *nm* prototype

protozoar *adj, nm* protozoan

proverb *nm* proverb

proverbial *adj* proverbial

proverbor *adj* = **proverbial**

prove *nf* 1 proof; evidence, argument 2 test; try-out 3 sample taken for testing: test sample 4 empirical test; experiment

  ○ **provë lëndore/materiale** [*Law*] material evidence

  ○ **prova e zjarrit** proof by fire

provëz *nf* [*Chem*] test tube

provïm *nm ger* 1 <**provo·n, provo·het** 2 examination; test, quiz

  ○ **provim me gojë** oral examination

provimdhën'ës *n* examiner

provimtar *adj* experimental

provincë *nf* province

provincial

  I § *adj* provincial

  II § *nm (Impol)* unsophisticated, provincial person

provincializëm *nm* [*Ling*] provincialism

provizor *adj* provisional, temporary, stopgap

provo·het *vpr* to try out, put oneself to the test; measure one's relative strength

provo·n

  I § *vt* 1 to prove 2 to test 3 to put [] to the test 4 to try [] out, try [] on, try; taste 5 to experience [something bad]

  II § *vi* to try hard; strive

  ○ [] **provo·n mbi supe/shpatulla/kurriz** to learn [] from bitter experience

provokacion *nm* provocation

provokator *n* instigator, provoker; agent provocateur

provokïm *nm ger* 1 <**provoko·n** 2 deliberate provocation

provoko·n *vt* to provoke [] deliberately

provokues *adj* deliberately provoking, provocative

provuar *adj (i)* proven; tried and true

provues

  I § *adj* 1 as a test, testing 2 engaged in giving examinations 3 evidentiary

  II § *n* examiner

provueshëm *adj (i)* [*Law*] provable

provueshmëri *nf* [*Law*] capability of proof, verifiability

prozaïk *adj* prosaic

prozaizëm *nm* prosaism

prozator *n* prose writer

prozë *nf* prose

prozodi *nf* [*Lit*] prosody

prozodïk *adj* prosodic

prozval· *vt* 1 to abase, degrade, dishonor 2 to lower [] in value/status/reputation: debase, downgrade

prozh *nm (Reg)* goat manure; enclosure for goats, goat pen

prozhektor *nm* searchlight = **projektor**

prozhëm *nm* grove, copse

prozhmïm *nm ger* 1 *(Reg)* <**prozhmo·n** 2 bad-mouthing, defame

prozhmo·n *vt (Reg)* to speak ill of [] behind []'s back: bad-mouth, defame

prozhmues *adj (Reg)* defamatory, slanderous

pru *stem for 3rd sg pdef vp, pl pdef, opt, adm* <**bie₂·**

prua·n

  I § *vt (Reg)* 1 to plunder 2 to guard

  II § *vi (Reg)* to nurse <> constantly through <>'s treatment with a folk remedy

pruajt *stem for pdef, part* <**prua·n** guarded

prur *stem for sg pdef, part* <**bie₂·** brought

prurë *part* <**bie₂·** brought

prurës

  I § *nm* 1 bringer, bearer; carrier 2 [*Mil*] (in a gun) follower () 3 radio beacon

  II § *adj* [*Physiol*] afferent

  ○ **prurësi i fishekëve** [*Mil*] cartridge follower ()

  ○ **prurësi i topit** [*Mil*] member of the artillery team who brings the shell from the ammunition supply to the loader

prurje *nf ger* 1 <**bie₂·, bír·et** 2 carrying, bearing, bringing 3 material/amount carried by a flow: load, charge, discharge

Prusí *nf* Prussia

prusian

  I § *adj* of/from Prussia

  II § *n* native of Prussia

prush

  I § *nm* 1 bed of hot coals; bed of live charcoal; live ember 2 heat rash 3 *(Colloq)* fever (from an illness) 4 *(Fig)* powerful urge; burning desire 5 *(Collec)* fringe of tassels on a floor/wall covering 6 profuse number

  II § *adj (Fig)* sparkling; audacious and lively

  III § *adv* 1 (intensifying an expression of heat or of red glow): hotly 2 in uncountably high number: profusely

  ○ **prush në hi/dhé/tokë** young and completely helpless

  ○ **do·të nxjerr·**^{subj} **prush me këmbët e maces** "want to take out hot coals with cats' paws" *(Pej)* to try to do something on the sly for one's personal gain

prushanë *nf* brazier for holding burning coals or charcoal = **mangall**

prushaník *nm* wafer baked in hot coals

prushërimë *nf* skin rash

prushís *stem for 1st sg pres, pl pres, 2nd & 3rd sg subj, pind* <**prushít·**

prushít· *vt* 1 to stir up [a fire] 2 to reduce [] to small bits

prushít·et *vpr* to get red in the face

prushka *np* tinsel

prushkurrïze *np fem* heat rash

prushtë *adj (i) (Poet)* burning; burning red, glowing; sparkling; fiery

pruzh *nf* horsehair brush used to sweep crumbs from the table

prrall *nm* [*Bot*] kermes oak *(Quercus coccifera L.P)*

  ○ **prrall i butë** European holly *Ilex aquifolium* = **beronjë**

*prrar *nm* [*Bot*] = prrall

*prra·shtë *nf* sling = prashtë
   ∘ prrashtë shale stirrup

prri·dh· *vt* 1 *(Colloq)* to strangle [] 2 *(Fig)* to suppress [ ]'s freedom of thought/action: suffocate [ ]

prri·dh·et *vpr* 1 *(Colloq)* to strangle 2 *(Fig)* to have no freedom of thought/action: suffocate

prri·dhje *nf ger* 1 < prri·dh·, prri·dh·et 2 suffocation

*prro·skë *nf* 1 small creek, brook 2 gully on a steep mountain slope

PS *abbrev* = **Partia Socialiste** the Socialist Party

psal· *vi* 1 [*Relig*] to chant psalms 2 *(FigImpolite)* to go on and on in a monotonous voice; talk nonsense without letup; talk endlessly about trivia

psalm *nm* [*Relig*] psalm

psalt·ës *nm* [*Relig*] = psalt

psaltir *nm* 1 [*Relig*] Psalter, Bookish of Psalms 2 special part of a church for chanting psalms

psallmo·n *vi* [*Relig*] to chant

psallmtar *n* [*Relig*] psalmist

*psalltar *n* [*Relig*] psalmist

psallter = psaltir

pse
   I § *interrog adv* why; for what reason
   II § *pcl* (precedes a question to indicate a challenging stance) what do you think?
   III § *nf* the why-and-wherefore, reason, cause
   IV § *nm* (*obl* ˜ *hi*) *the why-and-wherefore, reason, cause

pseudo *formativ (Book)* pseudo-, false-

pseudoasnjanës *adj* pretending to be neutral: pseudo-neutral

pseudoasnjanësi *nf* pseudo-neutrality

pseudoatdhetar *n* pseudo-patriot

pseudodemokraci *nf* pseudo-democracy

pseudofilozof *nm* pseudo-philosopher

pseudomarksist *adj* pseudo-Marxist

pseudomarksizëm *nm* pseudo-Marxism

pseudonim *nm* pseudonym

pseudopatriot *nm* pseudo-patriot = pseudoatdhetar

pseudopatriotizëm *nm* false patriotism

pseudoreformë *nf* pseudo-reform

pseudorevolucionar *n* pseudo-revolutionary

pseudosocialist
   I § *n* pseudo-socialist
   II § *adj*, *n* pseudosocialistic

pseudosocializëm *nm* pseudo-socialism

pseudoshkencë *nf* pseudo-science

pseudoshkencëtar *n* pseudo-scientist

pseudoshkencor *adj* pseudoscientific

pseudoshkrimtar *n* pseudo-writer

psikanalizë *nf* [*Psych Phil*] psychoanalysis

psikë *nf* psyche

psikiatër *nm* psychiatrist

psikiatri *nf* [*Med*] 1 psychiatry 2 *(Colloq)* mental hospital; mental ward (in a hospital)

psikiatrik *adj* [*Med*] psychiatric

psikik *adj* psychic; psychological, mental

psikikë *nf* psyche

psiko *nf with masc agreement (Book)* psychopath: psycho

psiko *formativ* psycho-

psikofiziologji *nf* [*Med*] psychophysiology

psikolog *n* psychologist

psikologji *nf* psychology

psikologjik *adj* psychological

psikologjis· *vt (Colloq)* to have psychological insights into [ ]

psikologjizëm *nm* [*Philos*] psychologism

psikometri *nf* [*Psych*] psychometry

psikopat *nm* 1 [*Med*] psychopath 2 *(Colloq)* psycho

psikopati *nf* [*Med*] psychopathy

psikoterapi *nf* [*Med*] psychotherapy

psikozë *nf* psychosis; mental disease

psilozë *nf, adj* [*Med*] sprue

psitacidë *np* [*Ornit*] Psittacidae

*pso·n = mëso·n

psonis· *vt, vi* 1 *(Colloq)* to buy [ ] in the market; go shopping 2 to find [something] and take it

psonisje *nf ger (Colloq)* < psonis·

pst *interj* (attention-getting whisper) pst

*psunis· = psonis·

p.sh. *abbrev* < për shembull e. g., for example

*psha = ofsha *(Reg Tosk)*

*pshe *OR* pshef < psheh = fsheh

pshelinok *nm* [*Bot*] common balm, lemon balm *(Melissa officinalis)*

*psher ëti *nf* = psherëtimë

psherëti·n *vi* to breathe a sigh

psherëtimë *nf* sigh; moan

*psherëtit·ës *adj* sighing; moaning

*psherëto·n *vi* to sigh; moan

*pshesh *nm* = përshesh

*pshi = fshi

*pshik = fshik

*pshikëll = fshikull

*pshikshurrë *nf* [*Anat*] urine bladder

*pshira *np (të)* = fshira

*pshkardh· *vt* to reduce [ ] to slavery; mistreat, abuse

*psho·n *vi* = psherëti·n

*pshtec·ë *nf* = mbështetës
   ∘ pshtecë shkallash bannister

*pshtet = mbështet

*pshtiell *OR* pshtjell = mbështjell

*pshtill *OR* pshtill = mbështill

*pshtim = shpëtim

*pshtjellcë *nf (Colloq)* cyclone = ciklon

*pshtjellueshëm *adj (i) (Colloq)* convoluted, intricate

pshtjerrë *nf* = mështjerrë

*pshtoll = mbështoll

pshtymore *nf* spittoon

pshurr·
   I § *vi* to urinate
   II § *vt* 1 to wet [one's clothes] (with urine) 2 *(Fig Crude)* to pay no mind to [ ], ignore [ ]: piss on [ ]

pshurr·et *vpr* to urinate in one's clothes: piss in one's pants

pshurriqe *nf* piece of waterproof material placed under a baby to keep urine from soaking through

PT *abbrev* < Postë-telekomunikacion postal and telecommunication

*pter = ter

PTT *abbrev* < Postë-telegraf-telefon *(Old)* postal telegraph and telephone

ptu *interj* stylized spitting to represent spite/contempt for someone

*ptyh = ptu

pu·all *stem for pl pdef* <**pjell·**

puanso·n *nm* [*Tech*] upper die, punch

pu·ar *OR* **pu·arr** *stem for pl pdef* <**pjerr·**

puberte·t *nm* (*Book*) puberty

pubi·s *nm* [*Anat*] pubic hair

publici·st *n* person who writes on current (public) affairs

publici·sti·k *adj* dealing with current (public) affairs

publici·sti·k*ë* *nf* writing on current (public) affairs

publici·te·t *nm* **1** public announcement/report **2** publicity

publi·k *adj, nm* public

publiki·sht *adv* publicly

puc *adj, nm* **1** (fig) that is overripe and withered on the branch **2** (*Fig Pet*) spirited and brave (person)

puc·ara·k *adj, n* (*Colloq*) spirited and brave (person)

*pucit·un *adj (i) (Reg Gheg)* tight-fitting, clinging

puç *nm* **1** top of the head: crown, pate **2** top of an egg **3** military takeover: putsch

*puç·e = puçerr

pu·çerr *nf* **1** skin eruption: pimple, pustule, blister **2** (*Colloq*) little bump on a surface
　º **puçrra e zezë/keqe** [*Veter Med*] anthrax

puçerr·ak *adj* pimply

puçerro·het *vpr* to break out in pimples/blisters, get a skin rash

puçerro·s·et *vpr* **= puçerro·het**

puçiba·bë *nf* [*Entom*] type of wingless grasshopper (*Saga italica*)

puçi·k *nm* **1** dimple ***2** catchment, rain pond

puçi·s *stem for 1st sg pres, pl pres, 2nd & 3rd sg subj, pind* <**puçit·**

puçi·st *n* conspirator in a putsch: putschist

puçi·t· *vt*
　º **puçit· buzët** to pout

puçi·zëm *nm* (*Book*) method of gaining political power by a putsch: putschism

*puçkerr = puçerr

puçrr·ak *adj* (*Insult*) **= puçrranjo·s**

puçrr·ama·dh *adj* all broken out in pimples; with a skin rash

puçrr·anjo·s *adj* (*Insult*) always covered with pustules: pimply-faced

puçrri·z·et *vpr* **= puçerro·het**

puçrri·zë *nf dimin* **1** small pustule, vesicle **2** tiny bubble

*puda·r *nm* hostler, stable-boy

pu·dër *nf* powder

pudi·ng *nm* pudding

pudro·het *vpr* **= pudro·s·et**

pudro·n *vt* **= pudro·s·**

pudro·s· *vt* **1** to apply powder to []: powder **2** (*Fig*) to present [] in a false light (by powdering over any defects)

pudro·s·et *vpr* to become covered with powder

pudro·sje *nf ger* <**pudro·s·, pudro·s·et**

pudro·sur *adj (i)* coated with a powdery substance

puf· *vi* **1** (*Colloq*) to blow smoke in puffs: puff away **2** (*Reg*) to explode with a muffled sound: pop

pu·fe *nf* **1** powder puff **2** large cushion used to sit on: puff **3** (*Colloq*) cigarette

---

pu·fk*ë*
　I § *nf (Colloq)* **1** skin blister; leaf blister **2** drop, droplet **3** popcorn **= pupagjel** **4** sudden puff (of smoke/dust) **5** meringue **= mafishe** **6** lung **= mushkëri** **7** large cushion used to sit on: puff
　II § *adj* **1** bulging **2** hollow inside

pu·fte *adj n* empty-headed (person); cowardly and inept (person)

*puga··n = pëgë··n

*puga·n|ës *n* defiler, soiler (in a moral sense)

*pugan|ësi *nf* filth, impurity

*pugë··n = pëgë··n

puha·cë *nf* bellows (for a forge) **= gjyry·k**

puha·s *stem for 1st sg pres, pl pres, 2nd & 3rd sg subj, pind* <**puha·t·**

puha·t· *vt* to fan [] with a bellows

puhi· *nf* breeze

puhi·zë *nf* light breeze

puk *adv* ***foolish**

Pu·kë *nf* city and district in northern Albania: Puka

pukja·n
　I § *adj* of/from Puka
　II § *n* native of Puka

pulagje·l *nm* [*Bot*] sowbread (*Cyclamen hederifolium Aiton, Cyclamen neapolitanum*)

*pulaqi·dhe *np* fowl, poultry

pulaqo·rrthi *adv*

pula·r *nm* (*Old*) Turkish coin worth 25 thousandths of a Turkish lira

pula·ri *nf* **1** poultry husbandry **2** poultry department; poultry area

pularu·ajt|ës *n* **= pularri·tës**

pularri·t|ës *n* person who tends poultry: poultry grower

pu·las *adv* **= gje·las**

pula·stër *nf* **1** corn tassel **2** [*Ornit*] moorhen (*Gallinula chloropus*)

pula·stre·n *nm* young chicken (older than a chick)

*pulazeqi·n *nm* [*Bot*] wild olive

pul·çi·në *nf* [*Ornit*] moorhen (*Gallinula chloropus*)

pule·gër *nf* [*Ornit*] **= pul·ë e egër**

pule·ndër *nf* polenta

pule·xhë *OR* **pule·xhio** *nf* [*Tech*] pulley, pulley wheel

pu·lë *nf* **1** hen **2** chicken **3** popcorn that has not popped **4** (*Fig*) easily intimidated person: chicken
　º **pul·ë amë** brood hen/duck
　º **Pula e botës (të) duket më e majme.** "The chicken of someone else always looks more plump (to you)." (*Prov*) The grass is always greener on the other side.
　º **Pula e botës të duket patë.** "the *neighbor's // other guy's* chicken looks like a goose to you." (*Prov*) The grass always looks greener on the other side.
　º **pul·ë deti** [*Ornit*] turkey hen (*Meleagris gallopava domesticus*)
　º **pul·ë dushke** [*Ornit*] woodcock **= shapto·re**
　º **pul·ë e egër** [*Ornit*] hazel grouse, hazelhen (*Tetrastes bonasia*)
　º **Pula e fqinjit të duket patë.** "the *neighbor's // other guy's* chicken looks like a goose to you." (*Prov*) The grass always looks greener on the other side.
　º **pul·ë fushe** (domestic) hen
　º **pul·ë hindi** [*Zool*] turkey

○ **pulë hini** [*Ornit*] *= **pulëhi**n*e*
○ **pulë me mjekër** [*Ornit*] great bustard *Otis tarda L.* = **ta**rd*e*
○ **<>a merr pula bukën nga dora** "The hen takes the bread from <>'s hand." (*Impol*) (said of someone who is inept and slow)
○ **pulë Misiri** [*Zool*] = **pulë**hi*ne*
○ **nuk e nxjerr· dot pulën nga kopshti** "not able even to chase a chicken out of the garden" to be clumsy and incompetent
○ **s'ka· një pulë përpara derës** "not have a single chicken at the door" to be poor as a churchmouse
○ **pulë e Shën Marisë** [*Entom*] ladybug, ladybird = **mollëku**q*e*
○ **pulë shqerake** (domestic) hen
○ **pulë shqir** [*Ornit*] = **pulçi**n*ë*
○ **Pula e tjetrit të duket patë.** "the *neighbor's// other guy's* chicken looks like a goose to you." (*Prov*) The grass always looks greener on the other side.
○ **pulë uji** [*Ornit*] = **pulçi**n*ë*
○ **pula e vogël e livadheve** [*Ornit*] little bustard *Otis tetrax L.*
pulë·ba·rdhë *nf* **1** [*Ornit*] black-headed gull (*Larus ridibundus L.*) **2** [*Ornit*] little egret (*Egretta garzetta*) **3** (*Colloq*) chestnut that has been roasted and shelled P
○ **pulëbardha e argjendtë** [*Ornit*] herring gull *Larus argentatus L.*
○ **pulëbardha kokëzezë** [*Ornit*] Mediterranean gull *Larus melanocephalus L.*
○ **pulëbardha ngjyrëhiri** [*Ornit*] common gull, mew *Larus canus L.*
○ **pulëbardhë e përhime** [*Ornit*] = **pulëbardhë ngjyrëhiri**
○ **pulëbardha rozë** [*Ornit*] slender-billed gull *Larus genei*
○ **pulëbardha e zakonshme** [*Ornit*] black-headed gull *Larus ridibundus L.*
pulë·da·sh *nm* popcorn
pulë·du·shke *nf* [*Ornit*] woodcock = **shapto**r*e*
pulë·hi·ne *nf* [*Ornit*] Guinea fowl; Guinea hen (*Numida meleagris*)
pulë·pi·te *nf* chicken with short legs covered with feathers
pulë·z *adj* having small fruit
pulë·za *np fem* [*Astron*] Pleiades
pulë·ze·zë *nf* [*Ornit*] coot (*Fulica atra L.*) = **ba**jz*ë*
pulika·re *nf* leech
puli·s *nm* [*Entom*] chicken body louse; nit of the chicken body louse
puli·s stem for 1st sg pres, pl pres, 2nd & 3rd sg subj, pind <**puli·t**·
puli·sht *nm* donkey colt = **kë**rri*ç*
puli·t· *vt* **1** to flutter [the eyelids]; narrow [the eyelids] down to slits, almost close [the eyes] **2** to prick up [the ears]
puli·t-*et vpr* **1** (of eyelids) to flutter; narrow down to slits, almost close **2** to crouch/cringe in hiding **3** (of fire/light) die down, start to go out; get dim
puli·tje *nf ger* <**puli·t**·, **puli·t**·*et*
puli·tur *adj (i)* **1** (of eyes) half-closed, almost closed *2 lurking
puli·th *nm* **1** [*Bot*] groundsel, ragwort (*Senecio*) **2** [*Zool*] chicken louse; nit of the chicken louse **3** late-ripening white fig with small long-stemmed

fruit = **ci·ngull 4** (*Fig Pej*) devious person; trouble-maker *5 short old man
pulive·shë·z *nf* earwig
***puli·zë** *nf* = **puli·s**
pu·lkë *nf* (*Colloq Dimin*) **1** little chicken **2** turkey hen
pulo·re *np masc* [*Ornit*] galliformes
pulo·vër *nm* pullover sweater
***pulpa·zë** *nf dimin* <**pu·lpë** = **pu·lpë·z**
pu·lpë *nf* **1** calf of the leg **2** pulpy part of a fingertip: fingertip **3** udder sac, udder **4** [*Anat*] pulp of a tooth **5** meaty part of a fruit or vegetable: pulp
pu·lpë·z *nf dimin* <**pu·lpë**
○ **pulpë·z gishti** fingertip
pulpo·r *adj* [*Med*] pulpal
pulqe·r *nm* thumb
***pulqye·r** = **pulqe·r**
puls *nm* pulse
pulsacio·n *nm* [*Med*] throbbing
pulsi·m *nm* [*Med*] pulsation
pulso··*n vi* (*Book*) to pulsate
pult *nm* **1** lectern **2** [*Tech*] console, control station, control platform *3 pulpit
***pulti(r)** *nm* [*Entom*] poultry louse, shaft louse (*Meniponidae*)
pulve·sh *nm* small cluster of grapes
pullagje·l *nm* [*Bot*] sowbread (*Cyclamen neapolitanum*) = **burth**
pulla·ke
  I § *nf* young mule not yet broken to the saddle
  II § *adj* not yet broken to the saddle
pulla·li *adj, n* (horse) that is white with black spots or black with white spots: dapple
pulla·ndër *nf* **1** clear solution of lye (used in washing clothes) **2** hot solution of salts used as a soak for aching/tired feet
***pulla·ndri·s** stem for 1st sg pres, pl pres, 2nd & 3rd sg subj, pind <**pullandri·t**·
***pulla·ndri·t**· *vt* to doll [ ] up, bedeck
***pulla·ndri·tun** *adj (i)* (*Reg Gheg*) dolled up, bedecked
pulla·shi·të·s *n* stamp seller
pulla·z *nm* (*Colloq*) roof = **çati**
pullazi·në *nf* **1** = **harto·s**e **2** crawl space under a roof
pu·llë *nf* **1** small spot **2** button **3** patch in clothing **4** head of a tack/nail **5** postage stamp; paper stamp (marking official approval)
pullo·s· *vt* to stamp/frank [a letter]
***pullu·mb** = **pëllu·mb**
***pull·undr** = **pullandr**
***pumba·k** = **pambu·k**
pumbo·s· *vt* **1** to smother [a fire] **2** to darken [a room], make [ ] dark
pumbo·s-*et vpr* (of a fire) to fail to light
pumbo·sje *nf ger* <**pumbo·s**·, **pumbo·s**·*et*
pu·më *nf* [*Zool*] puma
pune·së *nf* **1** piece of work, task, activity **2** work product **3** arable land
pu·në *nf* **1** work **2** (*Colloq*) workplace; job **3** (*Collec*) co-workers of a workplace: collective **4** product of work **5** situation; relationship **6** (*Colloq*) chance, occasion **7** (*Colloq*) matter, affair, business; thing; problem
○ **punë <>** kind/type/sort of a <>

○ **punë e gjallë** [*Econ*] human labor (as opposed to work done by machine)

○ **Puna hap punën.** "work brings more work" Once you get into it you see how much more work there is to do.

○ **puna e herës** *(Euph)* epilepsy

○ **s'ësh·të**³ˢᵍ **punë inati** it *can*not be done by force

○ **ka·** {*period of time*} **punë** to have work to do that will take {}

○ **ësh·të**³ᵖˡ **punët kokë e këmbë/këmbë e krye** things *are* in a big mess

○ **punë korrektuese** [*Law*] court-mandated work sentence

○ **punë krahu** manual labor

○ **Punë e madhe (fort)!** *(Impol)* Big deal! No big deal! It doesn't matter. So what!

○ **punë me spec 1** stressful work **2** something with dangerous risks

○ **punë me shkelma** work done unwillingly, work done under protest

○ **punë e ndyrë** dirty thing; dirty job, dirty work; dirty trick

○ **punë pa punë** just making a lot of work for oneself

○ **punë e pa punë** whether there is a reason or not

○ **punë plëndës** (in sewing) pleating

○ **<>u prish puna!** *(Impol Iron)* <> really cares a lot! (it's nothing to <>, <> doesn't care)

○ **nuk ësh·të**³ˢᵍ **punë që bë·**het³ˢᵍ not be possible

○ **Puna s'ka turp.** "Work has no shame." *(Prov)* All work is honorable.

○ **Puna sjell punën.** "work brings more work" Once you get into it you see how much more work there is to do.

○ **puna e turallit** *(Euph)* epilepsy

○ **punë e verdhë** dirty business; dirty work

punë·ba'rdhë *adj (Colloq)* fortunate

punë·bu'kur *adj, n (Poet)* (person) who does exquisite work

punë·da'sh·ës "work-loving" *adj* hard-working, industrious

punë·do're *nf* handwork: (by women) needlework; (by elementary-school children) découpage

punë·dhë'n·ës

I § *n* employer

II § *adj* employing

punë·he're *nf (Colloq Euph)* epilepsy

punë·he'sht·ur *adj* who works without talking/bragging

punë·hu'mb·ur *adj* whose work was done in vain; whose work is without recognition

punë·ke'q

I § *adj* evil

II § *nm* **1** *(Euph)* the Devil, the Evil One **2** evil person

punë·lu'm·ë *adj, n* (person) whose action is slipshod/sloppy

punë·ma'dh *adj, n* **1** (person) whose work is important; hard-working (person) **2** *(Tease)* (person) who acts like a big shot; (person) who brags

punë·mba're *adj, n* **1** industrious and productive (person) **2** successful (person)

punë·mba'r·uar *adj, n* (person) who gets things done

punë·pa'bit'·is·ur *adj* (person) who leaves things half-done

punë·pa'du'k·ur *adj, n* (person) with nothing to show for his effort

punë·pa'st·ër *adj, n* = **punë·bu'kur**

****punë·qy'r·ës** *n* foreman

punë·rry'e·shëm *adj (i)* acting slowly and with evident difficulty: plodding

punë·si *nf* employment

punë·si'm *nm ger* **1** <**punë·so'·n, punë·so·het 2** employment

punë·so·het *vpr* to become employed: get a job

punë·so·n *vt* to give [] a job: employ

punë·su'ar

I § *adj (i)* employed

II § *n (i)* employee

punë·shpe'jtë *adj* working quickly: fast-working

punë·shtru'a'r *adj* acting carefully and without haste

punë·to'r

I § *n* **1** worker; laborer **2** employee

II § *adj* **1** of or pertaining to work **2** working, employed **3** of or pertaining to working people: labor **4** hardworking, diligent, industrious

○ **punë·tor krahu** manual laborer

punë·to're *nf* <**punë·to'r 1** worker bee **2** *(Old)* workshop

punë·tor·ë'si *nf* workmanship

punë·tor·i *nf collec* labor force; contingent of workers, shop, work group

punë·to'rke *nf* worker bee

punë·tha'të *adj, n* (person) without much to show for his/her work

****punë·z** *nf dimin*

punë·zi *adj (fem sg ˜ ez, masc pl ˜ inj, fem pl ˜ eza)* **1** unfortunate, hapless **2** slow/incompetent in work

punga'ce *nf* [*Bot*] **1** = **bishtdhe'lpër 2** velvet grass, Yorkshire fog *(Holcus lanatus)*

pu'ngë *nf (Reg)* **1** small bag: purse, pouch, wallet **2** pincushion

****puni'l** *nm* young shoot (of tobacco)

puni'm *nm ger* **1** <**puno'·n 2** operation, function **3** work activity: work, manufacture **4** piece of work: work

○ **punim i forcuar** [*Agr*] intensive cultivation

○ **punim i tokës** cultivating the soil, tilling

puni'st *n (Scorn HistPK)* member of the (Communist) Party of Labor

puni'shte *nf* workshop

○ **punishte lëkurësh** tannery

puno·n

I § *vi* **1** to work; be at work **2** to be in operation; be open/functioning/working **3** to be working well; be going well; be working out all right: be successful **4** (of a wound) to be festering **5** *(Colloq)* to work well together, have a good relationship

II § *vt* **1** to work/till [soil] **2** to process [raw material]; make [a product] **3** *(Colloq)* to operate/work [a tool] **4** *(Fig)* to work out the substance of [a text] **5** to work up [a skill]: perfect **6** *(Colloq)* to work at [a trade/occupation]: practice **7** *(Colloq)* to use [a route] regularly (for one's business); ply the road to [] **8** *(Fig Colloq)* to do [something bad] to <>; cheat <> double-cross <>

○ **<> puno·n**³ˢᵍ **bafti** <> gets lucky

○ **s'<> puno·n**³ˢᵍ **dora** "<>'s hand *doesn't* work" <> *is* unable to work anymore

○ **puno·n e rrogo·n** *(Old)* to work long and hard (in order to make a living)

○ **puno·n e rëndo·n** to do hard work

• **Punon kali, ha gomari.** *(Prov)* One does the work, another gets the credit.

○ **s'<> puno·n³ᵖˡ këmbët** "<>'s legs *don't* work" <> *is* unable to walk anymore

• **puno·n me grabujë** to rake

○ **puno·n me pleqësi** to work cooperatively with good will

○ **puno·n me shkelma** to work against one's will, work under protest

○ **puno·n me udhë/rrugë** to act/speak/work in accordance with accepted procedure, act/speak/work with propriety

○ **puno·n në tym** to work without a clear plan

○ **puno·n pa udhë/rrugë** to act/speak/work in disregard of accepted procedure

○ **puno·n për bukën e gojës** to work for one's living

○ **puno·n për hesap të <>** to work for <someone>

○ **puno·n për rriskën e fëmijëve** "work for one's children's slice (of bread)" to make a living for one's family

○ **puno·n për shpirt të gomarit** "work for the donkey's soul" to waste one's efforts

○ **<> puno·n qindin** to give <> Hell; make <>'s life a living Hell

○ **puno·n rraset** to work industriously

○ **puno·n (si) sahat** to work like clockwork, work perfectly

○ **puno·n si nën plaf** to work under cover, act in secret

• **Puno·n sot ha· sot.** "{} works today, eats today." **1** {} *lives* from hand to mouth. **2** {} *spends* everything {} *earns*.

○ **puno·n veresie** to work to no purpose

puno·njës
I § *n* worker
II § *adj* working

puno've *nf (Reg)* arable land; cultivated land

pu'nto *nf [Tech]* drill bit

***pun·tor·si** *nf* diligence

pun·u·ar
I § *part* <**puno·n**
II § *adj* (i) **1** in a form created by work: (of land) tilled (and ready for sowing); (of raw material) processed, treated, refined; (of a project) worked out, refined **2** *(Colloq)* (of a tool/road) much-used, well-worn

pun·u·e·s *adj* **1** for use at work **2** = **puno·njës**

pun·u·e·shëm *adj* (i) capable of being worked: arable, workable

punjashe *nf (Reg)* small bag: pouch

pup *onomat* sound of a fast and sudden action: pop! just like that! (with a snap of the fingers)

pu·pa *adv (Colloq)* **1** = **prapa 2** *(Fig)* very well/successfully

pupa·gjel *nm* **1** popcorn **2** *[Ornit]* hoopoe (*Upupa epops*)

pupa·le·sh *adj (Colloq)* wooly, hairy, downy; plushy

pupa·s *adv* **1** = **pu·pthi 2** in a squatting position = **gali·ç 3** in a kneeling position = **gju·njas**

pup·ce *nf* = **pu·pëz**

pup·co··n *vi* to hop along (on two feet), hop

pupçi·k *adv (Colloq)* in a squatting position = **gali·ç**

pu·pë *nf* **1** *(Colloq)* small cluster, tuft; grape cluster **2** *[Biol]* pupa **3** *(Colloq)* jump with both legs together, hop, bound **4** stride, pace; (for horses) canter, gallop **5** infant's shoe, bootie **6** stern (of a boat or ship); poop deck; raised part of a vehicle on which one may sit; high level of performance/achievement ***7** breast, teat **8** *[Ornit]* hoopoe *Upupa epops*

○ **ësh·të çuar në pupë** to have become swell-headed

pu·pël
I § *nf* **1** pinfeather; down **2** dart (for a dart gun)
II § *adj, adv* downy light, very light

○ **pupël përmbi ujë** "a feather on water" feather-brained

pu·pël·bu·të *adj* having soft downy feathers

pup·ëlo··het *vpr* to develop pinfeathers; become covered with down/feathers

pup·ëlo·r *adj* **1** soft and puffy: downy **2** *[Bot]* pinnate

pu·përr *nf(Colloq)* **1** goosebump **2** = **thek**

○ **puprri i sisës** *[Anat]* nipple

pu·pëz *nf* **1** *[Ornit]* Eurasian hoopoe *(Upupa erops)* **2** *[Ornit]* = **çafkëlo·re 3** tuft of feathers on the head: crest **4** tuft, tassel **5** plant bud

pu·pëzo··n *vi* to make a woofing sound (characteristic of the Eurasian hoopoe)

***pupi·t·** *vi* to re-echo, resound

***pu·pke** *nf* tuft, crest

pup·laj·ë *nf* **1** plumage **2** feather used as adornment, feathery tuft, crest ***3** feathered poultry wing used as a small broom

pup·la·k *adj* downy, feathery

pup·la·ndri·tur *adj (Poet)* brightly feathered

pup·la·ngre·hur *adj* puffed-up, arrogant

pup·la·ngrën·ë·s *np* *[Entom]* biting lice *(Mallophaga)*

pup·la·rë·n·ë *adj* **1** missing some or all of its feathers: featherbare **2** brought low, humbled

pup·la·sh *adj* = **puplak**

pup·le·she *nf* soft and light house slipper with a downy lining

pu·plëz *nf dimin* down

pupli·n *nm* poplin

pupli·t· *vt* to pluck (feathers from) [fowl]

puplo··n *vt* to adorn [] with feathers

pup·rra-pu·prra *adv* **1** *(Colloq)* covered with pinfeathers **2** having many tufts/tassels

puprri· *np fem* **1** papillae **2** *[Med]* caruncle ()

puprri·qe *np fem* *(Colloq)* goosebumps = **mornica**

puprro··het *vpr* to get goosebumps

pu·pthi *adv* with both legs at the same time; with a bound

pupu' *interj* expresses indignation = **bubu'**

pupula·k
I § *adj* plump
II § *n* plump person

pupulo··het *vpr* (of eyes) to fill up with drowsiness and close

pupulo··n *vt (Colloq)* to fill [] to the brim

pupurri·t· *vt* (of birds) to scratch at [the ground]

pupurri·q·et *vpr* **1** = **puprro··het 2** to shrivel up

puq *adv* touching/butting together, into contact; adjacent

○ **puq me** [] right next to [], adjoining []

puq· *vt* **1** to fit [] together, join, combine **2** *(Fig)* to bring [] into agreement
  ○ **puq· shpatat** to cross swords; have a fight
pu'q·et *vpr* **1** to fit together: fit **2** to come to an accord; be in accord, get along well; fit in
  ○ <> **puq·**et³ᵖˡ **fitilat (me** [] **)** <> *fits* in well (with [])
  ○ **nuk** <> **puq·**et³ˢᵍ **lëngu me thelë** "not have just the right amount of gravy with the meat" not get along well (with someone else)
  ○ **s'**<>**puq·**et³ᵖˡ **pipëzat** "the pipes are not in tune" <> are not able to get along
  ○ **puq·**et³ˢᵍ **qielli me detin** "the sky *meets* the sea" there *is* a terrible rainstorm
pu'qas *adv pred* flush
*****pu'qël** *nf* [Bot] turpentine tree, terebinth *(Pistacia terebinthus)*
*****pu'qëm** *adj (i)* fitting tight, flush
pu'qje *nf ger* **1** <**puq·, pu'q·et 2** juncture, contact
pu'qur *adv* joined together
pure *nf* purée
*****pu'rë** *nf* = **pu'ro**
purgativ *nm* [Med] purgative
purgator *nm* [Relig] purgatory
puri'st *n* [Ling] purist
purita'n *nm* puritan
purita'nizëm *nm* puritanism
puri'zëm *nm* [Ling] purism
pu'ro *nf* cigar
puro'·n *vt* to calm [] down, restrain
*****purpër** = **purpur**
pu'rpur *nm* **1** purple/scarlet (dye) **2** purple/scarlet cloth; purple cloth indicating wealth or nobility in ancient times
*****purpuri'në** *nf* = **pu'rpur**
purpu'rtë *adj (i)* **1** purple, scarlet; made of purple cloth **2** [Med] purpuric
purqa'rk *nm* [Bot] water cress *(Nasturtium officinale)*
purte'k·et *vpr* to shiver
purte'kë *nf* **1** slender stick: withe, switch **2** long stick; rod, bar **3** *(Reg)* knitting needle **4** *(Colloq)* beating with a switch
purte'këz *nf* **1** *(Dimin)* small withe/switch **2** small stick/rod/bar **3** [Med] rod-shaped microbe: bacillus
*****purte'së** = **përte'së**
purth· *vt* to soil [] with feces
pu'rth·et *vpr* to have diarrhea
pu'rthë *nf* diarrhea
purthi'derrth *nm* [Bot] treacle mustard *(Erysimum)*
pu'rrë *nf (Reg)* ember = **shpu'zë**
*****purri'(n)** *nm (pl ˜ j) (Reg Gheg)* [Bot] leek = **presh**
purrigja'rpër *nm* [Bot] wild leek *(Allium ampeloprasum)*
pus
  I § *nm* **1** well (for water); well for extracting minerals/gas **2** *(Colloq)* cistern **3** *(Colloq)* deep pot-hole; deep pool
  II § *adj, adv* deep/dark as a well
  ○ **ësh·të pus** to be close-mouthed
  ○ **Pusi i mirë njihet në kohë të thatë.** "The good wellspring becomes known in dry times." *(Prov)* A friend in need is a friend indeed.

○ **pus nafte** oil well
○ **ësh·të pus pa ujë** "be a well without water" **1** to be poor as a rat **2** to be totally incompetent/inept
○ **pus qorr** dry well
○ **Pusi** [] **marrtë!** "May the well take []!" *(Curse)* May [] have nothing but bad luck!
pusi *nf* **1** place to hide in wait, covert; ambush, ambuscade **2** *(Fig)* deception, dishonesty
pusingri'tës *n* person lying in ambush: ambusher, snake in the grass
*****pusita'r** *n* ambusher
pusizë'nës *n* person who sets an ambush: ambusher
pustu'lë *nf* [Med] pustule
*****pustu'llë** = **pusu'llë**
pusu'llë *nf* written message dashed off quickly to someone: note
  ○ **pusullë bakalli** *(Pej)* sloppy writing on grimy paper
push *nm* covering of short fine fiber/hair/pinfeathers: furry covering, fluff, fuzz, plush, down; moss, mold
pu'sh·et *vpr* **1** to grow downy hair **2** to get covered with fine fiber, get lint all over one
pusha'lesh *adj* thickly furred: furry; downy
*****pusha'le'sh|ur** *adj (i)* huddled
pusha'lli *adj* furry, fuzzy
pusha'tak *adj* covered by a furry layer: downy; plushy
pusha'to'·het *vpr* **1** to grow a layer of pinfeathers, get covered with down **2** (of clothing) to get all fuzzy
pushbu'të *adj* **1** covered with soft fine hairs **2** [Bot] (pubescent) (P)
pushëzi'm *nm ger* <**pushëzo'·n, pushëzo'·het**
pushëzo'·het *vpr* to come apart in loose fibers
pushëzo'·n *vt* to make [] fluffy, fluff up []; give [textile] a furry surface texture: nap
pushim *nm ger* **1** <**pusho'·n 2** work-break, break; repose **3** vacation period, vacation **4** [Mus] intermission **5** *(Colloq)* quietness; silence **6** [Sport] time-out
  ○ **pushimi i javës** worker's day off
pushkala'gës *nm (Reg)* = **stërla'gës**
pushka'liqe *nf* = **stërfy'tës**
pushka'tar
  I § *nm* **1** sharpshooter, marksman **2** fighter armed with a rifle: rifleman
  II § *adj* armed with rifles; composed of riflemen; used by riflemen
pushka'tim *nm ger* **1** <**pushkato'·n 2** execution by firing squad
pushka'to'·n *vt* to execute [] by firing squad
pushka'tu'ar *adj (i), n* (person) executed by firing squad
pushkerr|i'zë *nf* = **pu'çrrizë**
pu'shkë *nf* **1** rifle **2** *(Colloq)* fighter armed with a rifle: rifleman **3** rifle fire; armed warfare **4** maximum range of a rifle: rifle range **5** *(Fig Colloq)* argument, squabble
  ○ **ësh·të i pushkës** "be of the gun" **1** to know how to handle a gun **2** to be a real fighter
  ○ **T'u bëftë pushka top!** "May your rifle become a cannon!" *(Felic)* (said to a soldier going off to battle) Kill 'em good!
  ○ **pushka habertare/lajmëtare** *(Old)* signalling gun
  ○ **pushkë e lagët** *(Impol)* good-for-nothing

○ **ta lë· pushkën në faqe** "it leaves the gun at your cheek" **1** {} is a person who leaves your work half done **2** {} is so fast/clever that it gets away from you (before you can shoot)

○ **ësh·të pushkë e mbushur/ngrehur** "be a loaded/raised gun" to be always ready for a fight; have a quick temper

○ **pushkë me çark** person with outdated/antiquated ideas

○ **ësh·të pushkë e plasur** to be too old to work; be broken down, be unsafe

○ **Të puthsha grykën e pushkës!** "May I touch the muzzle of your gun!" *(Felic)* Congratulations on your victory (in battle)!

****pushkërro** ·*het vpr* = puçërro ·*het*

pushkëz *nf* = puçrrízë

****pushkím** *nm* gunshot, volley of rifle fire

****pushkimta**r *n (Old)* = pushkata**r**

****pushkrrítës** *adj* blistering

****pushkrrítun** *adj (i) (Reg Gheg)* blistered

****pushkrrízët** *adj (i)* pimply, blotchy

****pushkzo**·*n vi (Old)* to shoot, fire

pushlo**r** *adj* **1** = pushata**k 2** [*Bot*] tomentose

pusho·n

I § *vi* **1** to pause; halt, stop; let up, ease off **2** to take a break in work, stop working: rest **3** to take a vacation **4** to stop speaking, be silent; shut up **5** *(Book)* to be at repose (= buried), lie in eternal rest

II § *vt* **1** to discharge [] (from a job/assignment), fire **2** to stop, halt, interrupt; silence []

○ **i pusho·n muhabetit** to speak slowly and thoughtfully, weigh one's words carefully

○ **pusho·n nga detyra** to discharge [] from a job

pusht *nm (Contempt Insult)* **1** crook, bastard **2** womanizer

****pushterkë** *nf (Reg)* apron

pushtet *nm* **1** authority; political power; governance **2** *(Colloq)* government = qeverí

****pushtetar** *nm* ruler, master

****pushtetje** *nf* dominion, rule

pushtetplotë *adj* having complete authority: fully empowered, plenipotentiary

pushtetshëm *adj (i)* **1** in authority/power **2** accustomed to giving commands: authoritarian **3** authoritative; not-to-be-questioned

pushtë *adj (i)* furry; plushy; downy

****pushtërí** *nf* adultery; wickedness

pushtërísht *adv (Pej)* like a womanizing scoundrel, wickedly

pushtím *nm ger* **1** <pushto·*n*, pushto·*het* **2** conquest; occupation

pushtimtar *adj, n (Book)* = pushtue**s**

pushto·*het vpr* **1** to hug (one another) **2** *(Fig)* to be overcome (with emotion)

pushto·*n vt* **1** to conquer; overcome; overwhelm; occupy [another's territory] **2** to hug **3** *(Fig)* to encompass/grasp [] (at one glance)

pushtuar *adj (i)* conquered

pushtues

I § *nm* conqueror; occupier

II § *adj* conquering; occupying

****pushueshëm** *adj (i)* **1** easygoing, relaxed, leisurely **2** not subject to dismissal/firing

put *nm (Colloq)* idol = idhull

****putan** *adj* (of a livestock animal) without horns: hornless

putané *nf (Colloq Insult)* whore

putargë *nf* salted and smoked roe of the mullet

puter *nm (Reg Kos)* [*Dairy*] butter made from cream

putë *nf* **1** *(Colloq)* sole of the foot **2** = gjurmashkë

putër *nf* **1** paw; sole of the foot **2** stocking sole

putërgjerë *adj* having broad paws

putërmadh *adj* having big paws

****putír** *nm* = potí**r**

puth· *vt* **1** to kiss **2** *(Fig)* (of a light source) to touch [] gently; just begin to illuminate []

○ **nuk puth·** {} *(Colloq)* not be allowed to be {somewhere}

○ **<> puth· çizmet** *(Pej)* to lick ("kiss") <>'s boots

○ **<> puth· dorën/gjunjët** *(Pej)* to be servile: lick <>'s boots

○ **për çdo punë puth· dorën e <>.** "for every matter kiss <>'s hand" to insist on getting <>'s permission for even the slightest thing

○ **puth· dorën e <> 1** to kiss <>'s hand as a form of very respectful greeting **2** to ask <>'s permission

○ **[] puth· dhe [] vë· në ballë** "kiss [] and put [] to one's forehead" **1** {} would love to have [], {} would be happy to have [] **2** to be thankful for getting at least []

○ **Të puth halla në të dy faqet.** *(Crude Iron)* (expresses the strong belief by one with an obligation that the obligation has been fulfilled); (expresses the strong belief that an obligation owed one was not satisfied and that nothing further will be forthcoming) That was it! No more!

○ **<> puth· këmbë e dorë** "kiss <>'s foot and hand" *(Pej)* to be servile: lick <>'s boots

○ **<> puth· këmbët** "kiss <>'s feet" *(Pej)* to be servile: lick <>'s boots

○ **puth· kryqin** "kiss the cross" to die: meet one's maker

○ **<> puth· pëqirin** "kiss <>'s hem" *(Crude Pej)* to be servile: grovel at <>'s feet, kiss <>'s ass

○ **Puthe pragun (po dole që këtej)!** "Kiss the doorstep goodbye (if you went out of here)!" Just shut the door on your way out!

○ **puth· pushkën** "kiss the gun" to swear to fight to the death

○ **Të puth· dorën.** "{} kisses your hand." {} *sends* you regards.

○ **puth· truallin** "kiss the ground" to be badly bent (by old age)

puth·*et vpr* **1** to kiss (each other) **2** to join, come together **3** *(Fig Colloq)* to come to an understanding: agree

○ **Puthu me Milon!** "Kiss and make up with Milo" *(Crude Iron)* Give it up! It's over now!

puthadór

I § *nm* **1** *(Old)* messenger boy, office boy, office lackey **2** *(Contempt)* servile person: lackey

II § *adj* servile

puthadóras *adv* getting along together very nicely

****puthje** *nf* (said of bread loaves) place where two pieces/parts are joined: juncture

puthís *stem for 1st sg pres, pl pres, 2nd & 3rd sg subj, pind* <puthít·

puthít· *vt* **1** to place [] together in close contact, make [] touch: join, touch **2** *(Fig Colloq)* to fit [] together, tailor, suit

puthit·_et vpr_ **1** to be in close contact, fit together: abut, join, touch **2** _(Fig)_ to be in complete agreement

puthitje _nf ger_ **1** <**puthit·**, **puthit·**_et_ **2** complete agreement: congruity

puthitshëm _adj (i)_ **1** fitting together tightly; closely matching **2** [_Math_] congruent

puthitur _adj (i)_ **1** abutting; conjoined **2** sealed tight; air-tight

puthje _nf ger_ **1** <**puth·**, **puth·**_et_ **2** kiss

puthos· = **puthit·**

*puth**to**·_n vt_ = **puthit·**

puthur
  _I §_ _nf (e)_ kissing, kiss
  _II §_ _adj (i)_

PVC _abbrev (English)_ PVC = polyvinyl chloride

*pves = pyes

*pvet· = pyet·

pyes _stem for 1st sg pres, pl pres, 2nd & 3rd sg subj, pind_ <**4pyet·**

pyet· _vt, vi_ to ask, inquire
  ○ **nuk** [] **pyet· as për osh, as për balosh** _(Colloq)_ to totally disregard []: act as if [] weren't there
  ○ **nuk pyet·** pay no heed
  ○ **nuk pyet· nga ajo anë** not be afraid of that, not worry about that
  ○ **nuk pyet· për njeri** "not ask about anyone" not heed anyone
  ○ **nuk pyet· për të tjerët** "not ask about others" not care what others think, not care whether others like it or not
  ○ [] **pyet· rrip për këpucë** to inquire into [] in every detail
  ○ **Pyet** _njëqind//shtatë a tetë_ **vetë, e bëj si di vetë!** "Ask _a hundred//seven or eight_ people, and then do what you know yourself is right!" _(Prov)_ Get a lot of other opinions, but follow your own judgment!

pyet·_et vpr_ to be the person who must be consulted for the final decision: be the person whose opinion counts

pyetës
  _I §_ _adj_ **1** inquiring, questioning **2** [_Ling_] interrogative
  _II §_ _nm_ **1** _(Old)_ [_Law_] judicial officer conducting an inquest *2 coroner *3 question mark

pyetësi _nf_ [_Law_] _(Old)_ inquest, investigation, inquiry = **hetuesi**

pyetësor _nm_ questionnaire

pyetje _nf ger_ **1** <**pyet·**, **pyet·**_et_ **2** question

pyetje-përgjigje _np fem_ quiz show

pyetur
  _I §_ _part_ <**pyet·**, **pyet·**_et_
  _II §_ _adj (i)_ _(Colloq)_ already considered

*pyh _interj_ pooh!

pyje _np_ <**pyll**

*pyjeshëm _adj (i)_ wooded

pyjor _adj_ **1** of or pertaining to woodlands: forestal, sylvan, woodland **2** of or pertaining to forestry

pykë _nf_ **1** wedge **2** [_Mil_] wedge-like penetration (into an enemy position) **3** _(Impol)_ blockhead
  ○ **Pyka do pykë.** "A wedge is to be driven in/out with a wedge." _(Prov)_ It takes a tough person to handle someone tough.
  ○ **Pykën e shtyn/nxjerr pyka** "You drive a wedge in/out with a wedge." _(Prov)_ It takes a tough person to handle someone tough.
  ○ **ësh-të pykë në diell** to be flat broke, be very poor
  ○ **ësh-të pykë nga veshët** to be stone deaf
  ○ **Pyka nxirret/shtyhet me pykë.** "A wedge is to be driven out with a wedge." _(Prov)_ It takes a tough person to handle someone tough.

pykël _nf_ **1** splinter/chip of wood **2** _(Dimin)_ small wedge

pykëz _nf_ _(Dimin)_ small wedge, peg

pykëzim _nm ger_ **1** <**pykëzo·**_het_ [_Mil_] **2** forward wedge **3** [_Min_] wedge/pinch/feather out

pykëzo·_het vpr_ **1** [_Mil_] to break through enemy lines in a wedge **2** [_Min_] (of a mineral seam) to wedge out

pykëzuar _adj (i)_ **1** [_Mil_] in the shape of a wedge, wedge-shaped **2** [_Min_] (of a mineral seam) tapering out gradually

*pylkë _nf_ = pykë

pyll
  _I §_ _nm_ forest
  _II §_ _adj_ copious
  III § _adv_ in large quantity, copiously
  ○ **Nuk ka pyll pa derra.** "There is no forest without pigs." _(Prov)_ Nothing's perfect.
  ○ **pyll në prag të derës** "forest at the threshold of the door" complicated impediment encountered in starting a task
  ○ **ësh-të**[3sg] **pyll i pagjuajtur** "be in non-hunted-over forest" to be well off; (of a place) rich in unexploited resources

*pyllar _n_ = pylltar

pyllëzim _nm ger_ **1** <**pyllëzo·**_n_ **2** forestation

pyllëzo·_n vt_ to plant a forest in/on []: afforest

pyllëzuar _adj (i)_ reforested

pyllinë _nf_ small stand of trees: grove, copse

pyllishtë _nf_ **1** woodland **2** small forest, wood grove, woods

pyllnajë _nf_ woodland

pyllnor _adj_ = pyjor

pyllosh _adj_ abounding in trees: wooded, woody

pyllrojës OR **pyllrojtës** _n_ forest ranger

pylltar _n_ forester; forest ranger

pylltari _nf_ forestry, wood farming

*pyper _nm_ (fungus disease in grain) rust

*pyramidë = piramidë

*pyrg = pirg

*pyrk = pirg

Qq

q [që] *nf* **1** the consonant letter "q" **2** the voiceless palatal stop represented by the letter "q"

qa·het *vpr (Colloq)* to groan; complain
  ○ <> qa·*het*^{3sg} <> feels like crying

qa·n
  I § *vi* **1** to shed tears: cry, weep **2** to bead with moisture; steam/fog up **3** = **gërvi·**·*n* **4** *(Fig)* to complain *II §* *vt* **1** to mourn/grieve for [] **2** *(Fig Colloq)* to lament (the irretrievable loss of) [something] **3** *(Crude)* to guzzle [] down completely
  ○ **Të qafsha!** "May I wail for you!" **1** *(Colloq)* I beg you! Please! **2** (to a child) You are the cutest little thing!
  ○ [] **qa·n** *(Colloq)* to do/make/perform [] to exquisite perfection
  ○ **qa·n**^{3sg} **dyfeku për zot** "the handgun *cries* for a master" **1** (sentiment expressed when the last man in a family dies and no one is left to use a gun) **2** *(Iron)* (said of a coward carrying a gun)
  ○ **qa·n e bot** *(Colloq)* to keep crying, cry without let-up: flood the place with tears
  ○ <> **qa·n hallin 1** to tell one's troubles to <> **2** to feel sorry for <>; sympathize with <> **3** to worry about <>'s problems
  ○ **I qan hallin kalorësit se i varen këmbët** "You cry over the horseman because his legs are hanging down" You are worrying about a person who is doing just fine.
  ○ **qa·n me lot grabofçi** to cry crocodile tears
  ○ [] **qa·n me lot 1** to do [] to perfection; learn [] perfectly **2** to consider [] lost for good
  ○ **qa·n me shtatë palë lot** "cry with seven sets of tears" to mourn with terrible sadness: mourn deeply/bitterly
  ○ <> **qa·n**^{3sg} **mendja për** [] <> *is* worried about []
  ○ **qa·n nga të majmët/se majmi** to enjoy a good life and still complain: complain without cause, whine
  ○ **qa·n pa rrahur** "cry without being beaten" to complain for no reason, complain before there is anything to complain about
  ○ **qa·n për** [] to be clearly in need of []: cry out for [], beg for []
  ○ <>a **qa·n piten** *(Crude)* to do particularly well with <>
  ○ <> **qa·n**^{3sg} **puna në dorë** "the matter *weeps* in <>'s hand" the work goes slow in <>'s inept hands
  ○ **Qan puna për të zotin.** "The matter weeps for its master." Every task requires the proper person to do it.
  ○ **Qan pylli për sepatë.** "The forest cries for an axe." It's time for some serious cutting back.
  ○ **ta qa·n qoshen** to do things to perfection for you, do excellent work for you
  ○ <> **qa·n**^{3sg} **syri për** [] "<>'s eye *cries* for []" <> really *wants* []
  ○ <> **qa·n**^{3pl} **sytë për** [] "<>'s eyes *cry* for []" <> really *wants* []
  ○ <> **qa·n**^{3sg} **shpirti për** [] "<>'s soul *cries* for []" **1** <> *feels* great compassion for [] **2** <> really *wants* []
  ○ <> **qa·n**^{3sg} **zemra për** [] "<>'s heart *cries* for []" **1** <> *feels* great compassion for [] **2** <> really *wants* []
  ○ <> **qa·n**^{3sg} **zemra te** {} "<>'s heart *cries* at {}" <> *suspects* {}

qaf· *vt (Colloq)* to hug [] around the neck = **përqafo·**·*n*

qa·f·et *vpr* to hug one another around the neck = **përqafo·**·*het*

qafardhëmbër *(Insult)* = **qafështrembër** = **qafërrjepur**

qafalik *OR* **qafalok** *nm* mountain pass of small size

qafarak *adj* having a featherbare neck; scrawny-necked

qafas *OR* **qafazi** *adv* neck-to-neck, head-to-head

***qafcë** *nf* collar

qafe *nf* **1** woolen neck scarf **2** collar (on clothing); horsecollar **3** stocking top

qafere *nf* mountain pass, gorge

qafetë *nf* shirtcollar

qafë *nf* **1** neck **2** back part of the neck: nape **3** collar (on clothing); collar of a yoke **4** narrow part of the forearm or leg: ankle; wrist **5** narrow part connecting the roots of a plant to the main stem **6** stocking top **7** mountain pass, gorge **8** *[Tech]* part of a shaft supported by the bearing: journal
  ○ **m'u hiq/hiqmu qafe!** leave me alone! get off my back!.
  ○ **këput qafën!** scram! get out of here!
  ○ <>u **kheftë qafa prapa!** "May <>'s neck be twisted backward!" *(Curse)* I hope <> *breaks* <>'s neck!
  ○ <>a **lë· (gurin) në qafë** "leave the rock on <>'s neck" to leave the burden on <>'s shoulders
  ○ **Nga lëviz·**^{3sg} **qafa, kthe·het**^{3sg} **koka.** "Where the neck *moves*, the head *turns*." *(Prov)* Something/someone of no apparent importance *has* a big effect.
  ○ **nuk e ngre· kurrë qafën** "not raise one's neck ever" never stand up for oneself, be totally submissive
  ○ **Të paça më qafë/në qafën time!** "May I have it on my neck!" I guarantee it!
  ○ **qafe më/për qafë** in an embrace, embracing
  ○ **Të merr/mirrte më/në qafë!** **1** {} takes/took your breath away with {}'s beauty! **2** {} will/would charm the pants off you! {} is/was utterly charming!
  ○ **thyej qafën!** scram! get out of here!
  ○ **nuk e vë· qafën në litar** "not put one's neck in the rope" not submit to anyone, not bear anyone's yoke

qafëbardhë *adj* white-necked

qafëcullak *adj* = **qafëlakuriq**

qafëcungal *adj* stubby-necked

qafëderr *adj, n (Insult)* (person) with a neck like a pig: fat-necked (person)

qafëdrapër *adj* whose neck is scrawny and crooked

qafëdredhës *nm* [*Ornit*] wryneck *(Jynx torquilla L.)*

qafëgastare *adj* (of a girl or woman) with a slender fair-skinned neck

qafëgjatë
I § *adj* long-necked
II § *nf* **1** long-necked person/thing **2** [*Ornit*] common egret *(Casmerodius albus)*

qafëgjatës *adj, nm* [*Bot*] long-necked (fig)

qafëhark *nm* [*Ornit*] = **qafëdredhës**

qafëhollë *adj* thin-necked, scrawny-necked

qafëkëputur
I § *adj* slender-necked; scrawny-necked
II § *n (Curse Colloq)* person with a broken neck

qafëkuq
I § *nm (Old Mocking Colloq)* gendarme with red insignia on the collar
II § *adj, nm (Colloq)* (pigeon) with a rufous neck

qafëlakuriq *adj* (bird) with a featherbare neck

qafëlarmë *adj* with a speckled neck

qafëlejlek *adj* (of a person) with a stork-like neck

qafëlesh
I § *adj* (of a person) hairy-necked; long-haired
II § *nm (Pej)* term of opprobrium for a man or boy who wears his hair long over the neck

qafëmal *nm* mountain pass

qafëpatë *adj (Impol)* having a long neck; having a plump white neck: goosenecked

qafërrafshët *adj* = **qafëshkurtër**

qafërrashtë *adj* = **qafëshkurtër**

qafërrjepur *adj* having a neck bare of feathers/fur/hair

qafërruar *adj* (of a person) clean-shaven

qafësorkadhe *adj (Poet)* (of a girl or woman) with a beautiful willowy neck

qafëshkurtër *adj, nm* short-necked (person/animal)

qafëshoke *nf* tasseled red sash worn as a belt by young women in parts of northern Albania

qafështrembër *adj, n* (person) whose neck tilts to one side

qafëtrashë *adj, n* thick-necked (person/animal)

qafëthyer
I § *adj* having a neck that looks broken
II § *n (Curse)* may-he-break-his-neck

qafëz *nf* **1** narrow part of the forearm or leg: ankle; wrist **2** stocking top **3** collar on clothing; collar of an ox-yoke; neck-pad under the yoke **4** upper part of the bellstrap around an animal's neck **5** [*Bot*] narrow part of a root at a juncture with the stem: collet **6** (*Reg Arb*) armpit = **sqetull**

qafëzi
I § *adj, n (fem sg ˜ez, masc pl ˜inj, fem pl ˜eza)* dark-necked (animal/fowl)
II § *n* **1** (*Curse*) may-he-break-his-neck-and-die! **2** deadly boring person

qafim *nm* = **përqafim**

qafir *nm* **1** non-Moslem: unbeliever, heathen **2** (*Pej*) troublemaking rascal

*****qafit·et** *vpr* = **përqafo·het**

*****qafkëlore** OR **qafkore** *nf* [*Ornit*] crested lark = **çafkëlore**

qafo·n *vt* = **përqafo·n**

qafok *adj, n* **1** (*Impol Insult*) (person) whose neck tilts to one side **2** (bird) having a neck bare of feathers **3** long-necked (thing) **4** short-necked

qafoke *nf* = **qafalik**

qafol *nm* **1** horsecollar **2** part of a packsaddle that rests on the neck of the animal

qafor
I § *nm* stepfather
II § *adj* [*Med*] cervical

qafore *nf* **1** necklace **2** collar; white collarband attached to the inside of a collar; neck scarf; ornamented collarpiece **3** close-necked shirt without a collar **4** baby bib **5** [*Tech*] bushing; journal (of a shaft) **6** leather neckstrap on a horse halter **7** pad placed under the yoke to protect the neck of the ox **8** stocking top **9** axehead with a narrow neck connecting its sharp and blunt sides: long-necked axe **10** hill pass **11** crab = **gaforre**

qafos· *vt* **1** to embrace = **përqafo·** *n* **2** to shear the neck fleece of [ ]

qafos·et *vpr* = **përqafo·het**

qafosje *nf ger* < **qafos·**, **qafos·et**

qafosur *adj (i)* (of sheep) sheared around the neck

qafsh *stem for opt* < **qa·n**

qafuk
I § *adj, n* **1** (*Impol Insult*) (person) with a crooked neck **2** short-necked (person)
II § *nm* small pass in the mountains

*****qafur** *nm* camphor = **kamfur**

qahi *nf* [*Food*] **1** bun made with wheat and chickpea flour and brushed with eggyolk before baking; small round bun **2** small piece of Albanian pasty

qai *distal 3rd sg masc pron (Colloq)* that one, that very one; he's the one

*****qajgëz** *nf* = **qajkëz**

qajkë OR **qajkëz** *nf* linchpin securing a yoke to the tongue of a cart or the beam of a plow

qajo *distal pron 3rd sg fem (Colloq)* that one, that very one; she's the one

*****qall** *np masc* eyeglasses, spectacles

*****qallkane** *nf* [*Ornit*] crane *(Grus grus)*

*****qamatar** *adj* complaining, protesting

*****qamet** *nm* = **kiamet**

*****qamë** *(Reg Gheg)* = **qarë**

Qamil *nm* Qamil (male name)

*****qandër** *nf (Reg Gheg)* **1** = **qendër 2** resistance

*****qangje** *nf* bud

Qano *nf with masc agreement* Qano (male name)

*****qapell** *nm* string of dried figs

qapë *nf* **1** hobble, fetter **2** window/door latch

qapo·n *vt* **1** to catch and hold [ ]: capture, catch **2** to take [ ] secretly: snatch

qar *nm (Colloq)* profit, gain
∘ **qar e ka· edhe atë/këtë** (*Colloq*) to be lucky to get even that/this

qaramán
I § *adj* **1** (*Pej*) plaintive **2** complaining excessively: cranky, crabby
II § *n* crybaby

qaramash *adj, n (Pej)* = **qaramán**

qarash *adj, n (Pej)* = **qaramán**

qarë
I § *part* < **qa·n**
II § *nf (e)* **1** sobbing voice: crying, sob **2** complaint **3** [*Mus*] sad song, plaintive music: dirge

III § *np (të)* = qa'rje
○ **të merr të qarët** it's enough to break your heart
○ **të qarët e syrit** *(Old)* white of the eye
○ **të qarët e vezës** *(Old)* white of the egg, eggwhite

qa'rës *adj* **1** mournful, plaintive **2** complaining

*qari *nf* = qartësi

*qarim = sqarim

*qarisht = qartësisht

qa'rje *nf ger* **1** <qa·*n*, qa·*het* **2** sobbing voice: crying, sobbing, sob **3** *(Colloq)* complaint

qark
I § *nm (np ˜qe)* **1** circle; circular line **2** *[Geom]* area enclosed by a circle **3** *[Electr]* circuit **4** *(Old)* *[Offic]* (administrative) district: circuit
II § *adv (Colloq)* in a circular path, around
III § *prep* around, about

qa'rk|as *OR* **qa'rk|azi** *adv* around, all around

qa'rk|at|o'·n *vt* to encircle

qa'rke *nf* large intestine, colon

qa'rk|ëz *nf* small bundle of hay left in a field to get dry

qark|im *nm ger* **1** *(Colloq)* <qarko'·*n* **2** encirclement; circular tour

qa'rk|je *np fem* sheep/goat intestines

qark|komanda'nt *nm* *[Hist]* commandant of the district gendarmerie

qark|komandë *nf* *[Hist]* headquarters of the district gendarmerie

qark|o'·n *vt (Colloq)* **1** to encircle, surround **2** to go all around [], make a circuit around []

qark|or
I § *adj* **1** forming a circle: circular **2** *(Old)* pertaining to an administrative/regional district
II § *nm* *[Hist Colloq]* district committee of the Communist party in Albania (during World War II and in the early postwar years)

qark|ore *nf (Offic)* circular (issued by a central administration to satellite offices and departments) containing commands, reports, or guidelines

qark|to're = qarko're

qark|ue's
I § *adj* encircling, surrounding
II § *n* encircler

qa'rk|ull *nm (np ˜j)* circle

qark|ull|im *nm ger* **1** <qarkullo'·*n* **2** circulation; rotation; traffic; flow of materials **3** *[Fin]* currency
○ **qarkullim bujqësor** crop rotation

qark|ull|o'·n
I § *vi* **1** to go out and return: make a (complete) tour; make a circuit, go in a circuit; orbit **2** to rotate (in job position)
II § *vt, vi* **1** to circulate; (of goods and materials) flow **2** to reassign [] to different duty **3* to rotate [crops]

qark|ull|ua'r *adj (i), n (i)* (person/group) reassigned to different duty

qark|ull|ue's
I § *adj* *[Spec]* circulating
II § *nm* circulator

qark|ull|ue'sh|ëm *adj (i)* able to circulate

*qar|o'·n = qartëso'·*n*

qa'rq|e *np* <qark influential/powerful groups of people: circles

qart|as *OR* **qa'rt|azi** *adv* = qartë

qartë
I § *adv* clearly; distinctly
II § *adj (i)* clear; distinct

qart|ësi *nf* **1** clarity; distinctness **2** degree of clarity in a screen image: definition

*qart|ësi|në *nf(Reg)* = qartësi*

qart|ësisht *adv* *(Book)* with great clarity: clearly; distinctly

qart|ëso'·het *vpr* **1** (of weather) to clear up **2** to become clear; get clarified

qart|ëso'·n *vt* to make [] clear, clarify

qart|i = qartësi

*qart|o'·n *vt* = qartëso'·*n*

qarr *nm* * *[Bot]* Adriatic oak, European Turkey oak *(Quercus cerris)*
○ **qarr i kuq** Macedonian oak = bujgër
○ **qarr i leshtë** *[Bot]* = bungëbutë

qarr|a|ba'rdhë *nm* *[Bot]* = bungëbutë

qarr|a|bu'të *nm* *[Bot]* = bungëbutë

qarr|a'zi *nm (np ˜ëz)* *[Bot]* Macedonian oak = bujgër
○ **qarrazi magjyp** *[Bot]* = bujgër
○ **qarrazi i zi/egër/kuq** *[Bot]* = bujgër

qa'rr|ës *adj, nm* (melon) with a rough-textured/densely fissured rind: muskmelon, cantaloupe

qarr|ish|ta'r *n* person who makes things out of Adriatic oak

qarr|i'shtë *nf* **1** forest of Adriatic oak **2** Adriatic oak log **3** *(Fig Colloq)* beating with a club

qa'rr|të *adj (i)* made of Adriatic oak

qarr|u'c|e *nf* kermes oak = prrall

qarr|zi *nm* *[Bot]* = bujgër

qas· *vt (Colloq)* **1** to bring [] closer **2** to allow [] to enter: admit [] inside **3** to be able to take []: tolerate **4** *(Reg)* to oust; push [] away, reject

qa's·et *vpr (Colloq)* **1** to go up close; move nearer **2** to approach (in time), come soon **3** *(Reg)* to get away; get out of the way

qasa'j *abl/dat* <qajo'

qa'se *nf (Old)* **1** grain measure of about 40 kilograms **2** deep basin; large bowl for food

qa'së *nf* place where livestock gather to escape the heat; place where livestock bunch up

qa'sët *adj (i)* *(Reg)* in a far-off corner, hidden away, deep down

*qa'sje *nf ger* **1** <qas·, qas·*et* **2** approach, contact

qa|so'sh *pl fem abl* <qajo'

*qa'sshëm *adj (i)* = qasur*

qa'sur *adj (i) (Colloq)* approachable, sociable

qa'she *nf* **1** thick homespun white wool flannel **2** pleated wool-felt jerkin with decorative black or green braid worn by women in mid-northern Albania

*qashtëri *nf* chastity, virtue*

*qa'shtrë *adj (i)* chaste*

qa|shtu' *adv (Colloq)* exactly that way, just like that

qa|ta' *pl nom/acc* <qai

qatë
I § *acc* <qai
II § *acc* <qajo'

qa'tër
I § *nf* **1** forked pole used to prop up a drooping grapevine or branch of a fruit tree **2** *(Fig)* family mainstay **3** *(Fig Colloq)* sarcastic remark **4* ice slab
II § *determiner* * *(Colloq)* = tje'tër

qatij *abl dat* <**qai**

qatip *nm (Old)* **1** scribe **2** *(Pej)* incompetent pencil-pusher

qatje *adv (Colloq)* exactly at that place: right there

qato *pl nom/acc* <**qajo**

qatrar *n (Colloq)* quipster, joker

qaty *adv (Colloq)* exactly at that place (nearby): right over there, right there

qatyre OR **qatyreve** *pl abl/dat* <**qai**, **qajo**

qaz *nm (Reg)* = **saç**

Qazim *nm* Qazim (male name)

qazhnë *nf* coarse homespun white flannel

qe
I § *2nd & 3rd sg pdef* <**ësh•të** was, were
II § *pcl (Colloq)* look! there you are! there!
III § *stem for pdef, part* <**ësh•të**
IV § *np* <**ka** bullocks, oxen, bulls
○ **Qe si qe e u bë si ka.** "It was as it was and it became like an ox. (qe is both the plural form of ka and the past definite form of ësh•të)" *(Joke)* Let bygones be bygones.

qebap *nm [Food]* **1** kabob: chunks of meat roasted on a spit; baked spicy meat balls; rolled and grilled meat balls **2** coffee roaster

qebaptor *nm* person who makes and sells kabobs

qebaptore *nf* shop that makes and sells grilled meats

*_**qeber** *nm* = **fuçi**

qeçkë OR **qeçkëz** *nf* **1** curved wooden peg that secures the collar to the beam of the ox yoke **2** wooden skewer used to close the belly of a small animal roasted on a spit

qeder *nm (Colloq)* **1** harm = **dëm 2** loss = **humbje 3** *(Fig)* worry, trouble, concern; grief
○ **Mos ki/kini qeder!** *(Colloq)* Don't worry!

qederos *vt (Colloq)* **1** to harm, do harm to [ ]; afflict **2** *(Fig)* to make [ ] sad, worry

qederos·et *vpr (Colloq)* **1** to experience harm **2** *(Fig)* to feel anxious/troubled/sad: worry; grieve

*_**qedër** *nf* = **cedër**

*_**qef** = **qejf**

*_**qefall** *nm* = **qefull**

qefil *nm (Old)* **1** guarantor = **dorëzanë 2** guarantee, bail = **dorëzani 3** *[Bot]* duckweed *(Lemna minor)*

qefin *nm* winding sheet for burial of Moslem dead: shroud
○ **Të prefshin qefinin!** *(Curse)* May they cut (prepare) your shroud!

qefinos· *vt* to wrap [ ] in a shroud

qefleshë *nf, adj* = **qejfleshë**

qefli *nm, adj* = **qejfli**

qeft *nm* long-handled wooden cup; drinking glass, cup

qefull
I § *nm (np ~ j)* gray mullet *(Mugilidae)*
II § *adj (Fig Colloq)* long and thin
III § *adv (Fig Colloq)* hale and hearty
○ **qefull buzëtak** *[Ichth]* boxlip mullet *Oedalechilus labeo* = **buzëmadh**
○ **qefull dimri** *[Ichth]* thick-lipped gray mullet *Liza labrosus Chelon labrosus*
○ **qefull vere** *[Ichth]* common gray mullet *Mugil cephalus* = **cumër**
○ **qefull vjeshte** *[Ichth]* = **kryegjatë**

*_**qegëllë** *nf (Reg Colloq)* = **tjegull**

qehaja *nm (Old)* steward (for a landlord); agent (for a guild)

qehallarë *np* <**qehaja**

qehën *nm* **1** long-handled oval paddle used to put bread into an oven: baker's peel *_**2** pastry board

*_**qehlibar** = **qelibar**

*_**qehlibartë** = **qelibartë**

qej *np* <**qye**

*_**qejë** *nf* evil spirit

qejf *nm (Colloq)* **1** pleasurable time: fun; pleasure, enjoyment **2** active desire, yen; enthusiasm **3** good mood, feeling good; good health, feeling well **4** *(Pej)* whim
○ <>**a do qejfi që __** <> would like __
○ **s'**<>**a paska qejfi** <> *is* not in the mood
○ **Qejf të kesh!** "If you just have the desire!" All you need is the desire/will!

qejfleshë *nf, adj (Colloq)* <**qejfli**

qejfli *nm, adj (np ~ nj) (Colloq)* fun-loving/jovial (man)
○ **ësh•të qejfli për** [ ] to like [ ] a lot

qejfmbetur *adj* resentful

qejfpaprishur *adj* obliging, compliant, congenial, easy-going

qejfprishur *adj, n* (person) having hurt feelings

qejfshëm *adj (i)* pleasant

*_**qejzë** *nf* **1** splinter in the finger **2** cuticle
○ **qejzë bari** *[Agr]* haulm

*_**qek·** *vt* to mention, cite

qekth *nm* **1** rain mixed with dust **2** dust that forms on the dew on leaves **3** plant nectar

*_**qekur** *adv* **1** = **qëkur** *_**2** from time to time, at times

qel *nm (Reg)* person afflicted with ringworm = **qeros**

qelan *adj (Reg)* afflicted with ringworm = **qeros**

qelb *nm* pus
○ **qelb nën thua** "pus under one's nail" **1** *(Fig)* insidious force, cancer **2** sneaky person

qelb·
I § *vt* **1** to foul/pollute [the air] **2** to make [ ] filthy: foul **3** *(Crude)* to foul/mess [ ] up, botch
II § *vi* to smell bad: stink
○ **e qelb· gojën** to use foul language

qelb·et **1** to putrefy **2** to smell bad: be putrid, stink **3** to become filthy **4** *(Fig Crude)* to get fouled/screwed up *_**5** = **kalb·et**

qelbac *adj, n (Insult)* **1** disgustingly filthy (person) **2** *(Fig)* (person) with filthy vices

qelbanik *adj, n (Insult)* **1** (person) who is always filthy **2** *(Fig)* (person) of filthy moral character

qelbash *adj, n (Pej)* (person) who is always filthy

qelbës
I § *adj* putrid, stinking
II § *n* stinker
III § *nm* **1** *[Zool]* polecat *(Mustela putorius)* **2** *[Zool]* skunk **3** *[Bot]* terebinth *(Pistacia terebinthus)* **4** *[Bot]* bean trefoil *(Anagyris foetida)*

*_**qelbësinë** *nf [Bot]* kind of buckthorn *(Rhamnus fallax)*

qelbësirë *nf* **1** putrid/rotten thing **2** filthy person; stinker **3** *(Fig)* disgusting action

qelbëso·het *vpr* to become filthy/putrid

qelbëso·n *vi* to cause [ ] to smell bad: spoil; make [ ] putrid: putrefy [ ]

qelbësuar *adj (i)* = **qelbët**

qe'**lbët** *adj (i)* **1** rotten and bad-smelling: putrid, spoiled **2** *(Fig)* filthy, rotten

qelb|**ëz**'**i**m *nm ger* **1** <**qelbëzo**'·**n**, **qelbëzo**'·**het** **2** suppuration

qelb'**ëz**'**o**'·**het** *vpr* to develop/gather pus: suppurate

qelb'**ëz**'**o**'·**n** *vi* (of a wound) to suppurate

qelb'**ëz**'**u**'**a**'**r** *adj (i)* swollen with pus: putrefied, suppurating

qelbi'**në** *nf* [*Bot*] alpine buckthorn *(Rhamnus alpina)* = **arrç**

qe'**lb**'**ur** *adj (i)* **1** putrid, foul **2** filled with pus, putrefied **3** filthy

qelepi'**r**
  I § *nm (Colloq)* something gotten for nothing (given for some ulterior purpose); food/drink gotten by freeloading
  II § *adv* without paying, for nothing: by freeloading

qelepir|**xhi**' *nm (np ˜ nj) (Colloq Pej)* freeloader

qelepo'**çe** *nf* narrow-peaked summer cap made of stitched white cloth

qele'**r** *nm* **1** cool-storage cellar **2** anteroom

qele'**she** *nf* brimless cap made of white felt: Albanian fez

qeleshe|**pun**'**u**'**e**'**s** *nm* maker/seller of white-felt caps

qeleshe|**xhi**' *nm (np ˜ nj)* = **qeleshepunu**'**es**

qe'**l**'**ë** *nf* **1** *(Old)* residence of a parish clergyman: parsonage **2** cell **3* roof of the mouth, palate

*****qel**'**ëndry**'**she** *nf* [*Ornit*] nightingale

qe'**l**'**ëz** *nf* cell of a honeycomb or of a wasp nest

qeli' *nf* **1** *(Old)* monastic cell **2** jail cell **3** small storeroom in a cellar
  ○ **ësh·të qeli e *mbyllur/pa dritare*** to be completely tight-lipped; be utterly secretive

qeliba'**r**
  I § *nm* amber
  II § *adj* **1** clear, limpid **2** *(Fig)* without guile, honest

qeliba'**rt**'**ë** *adj (i)* **1** made of amber **2** amber (color) **3** *(Fig)* without guile, honest

*****qeliqe**'**r** *nm* [*Entom*] (of insects) poison gland

qeli'|**z**'**ë** *nf* **1** [*Biol*] cell **2** *(Fig)* compartment **3** = **qe**'**lëz**

qeli'**z**'**o**'**r** *adj* [*Biol*] pertaining to cells; cellular

*****qelp-** = **qelb-**

qelq *nm* **1** glass **2** drinking glass **3** pane of glass **4** *(Colloq)* light bulb; lamp chimney

qe'**lq**|**e** *nf (Colloq)* drinking glass

*****qelqëne**'**z** *nm* [*Ornit*] kestrel *(Falco tinnunculus)*

*****qelq**|**ëri**'**na** = **qelquri**'**na**

qelq|**ëz**'**i**'**m** *nm* [*Spec*] becoming vitreous; vitrification

qelq'**o**'**r** *adj (Book)* vitreous

qelq|**pun**'**u**'**e**'**s** *nm* glassworker

qelq|**ta**'**r** *n* = **qelqpunu**'**es**

qe'**lq**|**t**'**ë** *adj (i)* **1** made of glass; vitreous **2** *(Fig)* crystal clear, like glass; sparkling

qelq|**uri**'**na** *np fem* glassware

qell· *vt (Colloq)* = **vono**'·**n**

qe'**ll·**'**et** *vpr (Colloq)* = **vono**'·**het**

*****qe**'**ll**'**ë** *nf* mansion, residence

*****qe**'**ll**'**ëz** *nf* = **qie**'**llz**'**ë**

qem *nm* incense = **temja**'**n**

Qema'**l** *nm* Qemal (male name)

*****qema**'**le** = **qema**'**ne**

qema'**ne** *nf (Colloq)* violin = **violi**'**në**

*****qemba**'**ne** *nf (Old)* = **cimba**'**l**

qeme'**r** *nm* **1** archway; arch **2** waistband; ornamental binding/hem on clothing **3** *(Old)* strong ornamental moneybelt; gilt/silver belt worn on the bridal dress
  ○ **qemer i këmbës** arch of the foot
  ○ **qemer kryq** crossvault
  ○ **qemer kupole** dome vault

qe'**m**'**ë** *1st pl pdef* <**ësh·të** we were, we used to be

qe'**m**'**ër** *nf* sinuous movement made by a snake

qem|**ëz**'**o**'·**n** *vt* = **qemo**'**s**

qemo'**s·** *vt* to cense

*****qe**|**mo**'**ti** *adv* once upon a time; years ago, formerly = **qëmo**'**ti**

*****qe**|**mo**'**t**'**shëm** *adj (i)* ancient, olden = **qëmo**'**tshëm**

*****qemt**' OR **qemt**|**i**'**m** = **qëmt**'

*****qemt**'**o**'·**n** *vt* to garner = **qëmt**'**o**'·**n**

qen *nm* **1** dog **2** *(Fig Insult)* cur
  ○ **qen i arratisur** stray dog
  ○ **qen bahçevani** dog in the manger
  ○ **qen besnik** "loyal dog" *(Pej)* bodyguard
  ○ **qen bir qeni** "dog son of a dog" *(Insult)* bad son from bad parents: son of a bitch
  ○ **qen deti** "sea dog" [*Ichth*] shark = **peshkaqe**'**n**
  ○ **qen gjahu** hunting dog, hound
  ○ **qen kopeje** = **qen stani**
  ○ **qen kopshtari/kopshti** *(Pej)* dog in the manger
  ○ **Qentë le të lehin, karvani shkon përpara.** "Let the dogs bark, the caravan keeps going forward" *(Prov)* Let your opponents rattle on: you go forward.
  ○ **Qeni leh atje ku ha.** "A dog barks where he eats." *(Prov Pej)* He knows which side his bread is buttered on.
  ○ **qen me kreshta/gjemba** *(Pej)* abusive and stern person; merciless person
  ○ **ësh·të qen i punës** to be an assiduous worker: be a dog for work
  ○ **Qeni që leh nuk të ha/kafshon.** *(Prov)* Barking dogs don't bite.
  ○ **qen roje 1** watchdog **2** bodyguard
  ○ **qen i rrahur** "beaten dog" broken-spirited person, like a beaten dog
  ○ **qen rrugësh 1** stray dog **2** good-for-nothing bum
  ○ **qen sallhaneje/sokaku 1** stray dog **2** good-for-nothing bum
  ○ **zihen/hahen si qentë në garroqe** they fight like cats and dogs
  ○ **qen stani** sheep dog
  ○ **qen zinxhiri** vicious dog that is kept on a chain leash
  ○ **qen zorrësh 1** stray dog **2** good-for-nothing bum

qe'**n**' *stem for adm* <**ësh·të**

qena'**r** *nm* **1** strip along the side: border; edge; hem **2** *(Fig)* personal resting place: niche
  ○ **qenar i cohës** selvage

qe'**n**|**çe** *adv (Crude)* like a dog, very badly

qe'**nd**'**ër** *nf* **1** center **2** headquarters
  ○ **qend**'**ër banimi** population center
  ○ **qendër klimaterike** health resort (in a good climate)
  ○ **qendra e rëndimit** *(Old)* the center of gravity
  ○ **qend**'**ër zëri** control room for broadcasting messages on loudspeakers
  ○ **qend**'**ër zjarri** [*Mil*] gun emplacement

qendër|**i**'**k**|**ës** *adj* [*Spec*] centrifugal

qendër|**mbro**'**jtës** *nm* [*Sport*] center back (in soccer)

qendër·sulm|u|e|s *nm* [*Sport*] center forward (in soccer)

qendër·syn|im *nm* **1** (*Book*) centralizing tendency **2** central aim

qendër·syn|u|e|s *adj* [*Spec*] centripetal

qendër·z|im *nm ger* [*Tech*] < **qendërzo** ·*n*

qendër·zo ·*n vt* **1** [*Tech*] to center [a tool] **2** to centralize

qendër·z|ua|r *adj* (*i*) [*Tech*] (of a tool) centered

*qend|i = qëndismë

*qend|im|ë *nf* = qëndistari

*qend|is· *vt* = qëndis·

*qend|is|ta|r = qëndistar

*qendr|ak *nm* (*Old*) diameter

qendr|o|r
  I § *adj* central
  II § *nm* **1** [*Hist Colloq*] Central Committee of the Communist Party (during and immediately after World War II) **2** (*Old*) executive committee ***3** persistent

*qend|dhe *nf* [*Entom*] mole cricket

qe|ne *nf* (*Insult*) bitch

*qe|ne|hu *adv* ostensibly, seemingly, professedly

qen|e|raca|k *nm* dog with a good nose for game

qe|në
  I § *part* < ësh·të been
  II § *3rd pl pdef* < ësh·të they were, they used to be
  III § *nn* (*të*) being, existence; reality

qen|ëri *nf collec* **1** dogs, canine world **2** (*Insult*) despicable people; rabble **3** (*Fig*) despicable thing/act

qen|ërisht *adv* like dogs: in inhumane conditions; ferociously and tenaciously, doggedly; cruelly and without mercy

*qen|ë|s *nm* (*Old*) **1** element **2** essence

qen|ës|ishëm *adj* (*i*) (*Book*) essential

qen|ës|ishme *nf* (*e*) (*Book*) essential part, essence

qen|ës|isht *adv* (*Book*) in essence: essentially, basically

qen|ës|o|r *adj* (*Book*) essential, basic, fundamental

qen|ëz *nf* **1** hangnail **2** splinter (stuck in skin)

*qe|ngj = qingël

qengj *nm* lamb
  ∘ **qëngj qumështi** suckling lamb

qe|ngjë *nf* beehive

*qên|i *nf* (*Reg Gheg*) stubbornness

qe|nie *nf* **1** being, existence **2** [*Phil*] being, reality **3** being, living creature

*qen|ik *OR* **qenik|al** *adj* cynical

qen|isht *adv* = qenërisht

qen|mbyt|ëse *nf* [*Bot*] swallowwort, white swallowwort (poisonous) (*Cynanchum vincetoxicum*)

qen|o|r *adj* canine, dog-like

qen|o|r|ë *np* [*Zool*] canine family *Canidae*

*qe|nse = qenehu

*qe|nshëm *adj* (*i*) essential

*qen|të *adj* (*i*) canine

*qen|th *nm* = qenëz

qen-ujk *nm* German shepherd (dog)

qep *nm* (*Colloq*) **1** beak = sqep **2** (*Fig Iron*) person's mouth: trap **3** spout (of a container) **4** pointed tip of a tool **5** spallpeen hammer ***6** (*Old*) gas-jet, gas-burner ***7** bobbin, reel = gjep ***8** (*Old*) wedge; peg

qep· *vt* **1** to sew; sew [] up **2** to put [] on a string: string [] up **3** [*Med*] to suture **4** (*Fig*) to close [body

orifices] tight **5** (*Fig Colloq*) to catch **6** (*Fig Crude*) to compose, write ***7** (*Fig Crude*) to fuck
  ∘ < >a qep· arnën "sew a patch on <>" to put a black mark on <>'s record
  ∘ i qep· buzët **1** to seal one's lips, keep tight-lipped **2** to close one's eyes for the last time: die
  ∘ qep· e shqep· to proceed slowly without ever coming to an end
  ∘ i qep· gojën to seal one's lips, not speak again
  ∘ qepe gojën shut up! button your lip!
  ∘ i qepur me pe të bardhë "sewn together with white thread" crudely repaired (so that the seams all show)
  ∘ qep· një pëllëmbë e shqep· një pash "sew an inch and unsew a yard" to ruin something of great value in order to fix something of little value
  ∘ < > qep· si pullë poste "stick to < > like a postage stamp" to follow < > closely: stick to < > like glue, not let < > out of one's sight
  ∘ < >i qep· sytë to never take one's eyes off < >, stare at < >
  ∘ i qep· sytë **1** to shut one's eyes tight **2** to close one's eyes for the last time: die
  ∘ qep· [] thuapulë to sew [] with a triangular overcast stitch

qep·et *vpr* **1** to be sewn up, be patched up **2** (of body orifices) to be closed tight **3** (*Fig*) to clutch tight, hang on tightly: adhere **4** (*Fig*) to engage in fierce combat **5** (*Fig*) to climb up with great effort; scramble to get to < > **6** (*Fig Colloq*) to stick tight to < >, keep doggedly to < >; nag at < > to finish; trail < > doggedly, tail < > **7** to be afflicted by lingering or incessant disease/misfortune ***8** (*Reg Kos Fig Crude*) to engage in sexual intercourse: fuck
  ∘ < > qep·et me bukë në trastë to keep after < > persistently
  ∘ < > qep·et³ˢᵍ mulla për shpinë "< >'s stomach sticks to < >'s back" < > *has* an empty stomach
  ∘ qep·et pas < > **1** to stick tight to < >, keep doggedly to < >; nag at < > to finish; trail < > doggedly, tail < > **2** to adhere to < >; be an adherent of < >, be a follower of < >
  ∘ < > qep·et pas to tail < >
  ∘ < > qep·et si rriqër "stick to < > like a tick" to keep pestering < >

qepall|ë *nf* **1** eyelid ***2** eyelash = qerpik

qepall|ëpërve'sh|ur *adj* with eyelids rolled up

qepall|ërënd|ë *adj* with heavy eyelids

qepall|ëtra'sh|ë *adj* = qepallërëndë

qepall|o|r *adj* [*Anat*] palpebral

qepa'r *nm* **1** device for determining a horizontal line: level, bubble level ***2** = qepër

qe|pa|rthi *adv* = qëpa'rë

qepa'ze *adj, n* (*Colloq*) shameful/disgraceful (person)

*qep|ç *adj* thorny

qepe'n *nm* **1** protective metal shutter over shop windows or doors **2** trapdoor

qepe'ng *OR* **qepe'nk** *nm* = qepe'n

qe'p|ë *nf* **1** [*Bot*] onion (*Allium cepa L.*) **2** plant bulb, tuber
  ∘ qepë deti [*Bot*] sea-onion = bo'çkë
  ∘ qepë gjarpri [*Bot*] = xhërro'kull

qe'p|ër *nf* **1** [*Constr*] roof strut **2** bar pushed round and round by a horse to drive a mill

qepëro ·het *vpr* to grapple

qepëro·n *vt* to sheath [a roof], roof in [a house]

qepëros· *vt* = qepëro·n

qepëros·et *vpr* = qepëro·het

qepës
  I § *adj* used for sewing
  II § *n* person engaged in sewing: tailor; sewer, seamstress

qepëz *nf* [*Bot*] bulb

qepgjir *nm* **1** perforated ladle **2** colander, strainer

qepje *nf ger* **1** <qep·, qep·et **2** stitched place: stitch **3** [*Med*] raphe, suture

qepkë *nf* (*Reg Kos*) scallion

qeplo·het *vpr* (*Colloq*) to get pierced/pricked

qeplo·n *vt* **1** (*Colloq*) to pierce/prick *2 to strike, hit

qeplor *adj* [*Bot*] (of plants) bearing bulbs: bulbous

qeplore *nf* **1** [*Bot*] plant which bears bulbs: bulbous plant **2** [*Bot*] bulb **3** tooth enamel *4 swelling, knob

qepratë *nf* **1** [*Constr*] rigid framework composed of wooden members: truss, roof truss **2** (*Colloq*) roof beam, tie beam

qepriatë = qepratë

qepshe *nf* **1** ladle; ladleful **2** wooden ox-bow *3 colander for pasta

*qepsh/qep'ës *n* mischief-maker

qepujkë *nf* [*Bot*] **1** small plant bulb grown from seed **2** tubercle of a herbaceous plant

qepule *nf* = qepujkë

qepur
  I § *adj* (i) **1** ready-to-wear, tailored **2** (*Fig*) closed tight
  II § *nf* (e) **1** seam **2** [*Med*] suture

qepushkë *nf* seedling onion

qer *nm* large round rolling board: pastry board = palare

qeramidhe *nf* roof tile = tjegullë

qeramikë *nf* **1** ceramic clay **2** (*Collec*) ceramics, pottery; earthenware
  ○ **qeramikë e hollë** porcelain
  ○ **qeramikë zakonshme** brick; tile

qeras· *vt* **1** to treat/regale [guests] with food and drink **2** to pay for [ ]'s food/drinks (in a pub), treat [ ] to a round

qeras·et *vpr* to be treated to food/drinks from one's host

qerasje *nf ger* <qeras·, qeras·et

qerasmë *nf* **1** (*Colloq*) = qerasje *2 gratuity, tip

*qerast *nm* [*Bot*] chickweed = cerast

qerbash *nm* [*Bot*] goat's rue, French lilac (*Galega officinalis*)

qerbë *nf* black nanny goat with a brown muzzle

qere *nf* **1** [*Med*] ringworm of the scalp (*Tinea capitis*) **2** (*Tease*) bald pate
  ○ **qerja e këmbëve** [*Med*] athlete's foot *Tinea pedis*
  ○ **qerja e thonjve** [*Med*] ringworm of the nails, onychomycosis *Tinea unguium*

qereç *nm* **1** mortar mixed with lime **2** stone wall secured with lime mortar **3** (*Reg*) lime = gëlqere

qereste *nf* lumber, timber

qerestexhi *nm* (*np ˜ nj*) lumber dealer

*qerevis *nm* celery = sherp

qerëse *nf* uncultivated land; fallow land

qerf *nm* [*Ichth*] = kryegjatë

*qeri *nm* = qiri

*qerish *nm* = qiriç

*qerkë *nf* (*Reg Tosk*) handcart, barrow

qerm *nm* **1** slight ridge marking the boundary between two fields; uncultivated strip of land surrounding an agricultural field **2** ridge along the inside of a fireplace chimney upon which the hearth logs rest **3** ridge surrounding the mouth of a well

qeros *adj, n* **1** (person) afflicted with ringworm of the scalp; (person) made bald by ringworm infection **2** (*Insult*) baldy **3** [*Folklore*] clever bald man/boy in folktales **4** ear of corn with sparse kernels

qeros·et *vpr* **1** to lose hair from a ringworm infection of the scalp **2** to go bald

qerosë *nf* (*Colloq*) [*Med*] = qere

qeroskë *nf* bald-headed girl; girl with ringworm infection of the scalp

qerpí *nf* mason's plumb bob

qerpiç *nm* sun-dried brick: adobe

qerpík *nm* eyelash

qerpikor *adj* [*Anat*] ciliary

qerpikorë *np* [*Zool*] infusoria

qersë *nf* fallow land

qershi *nf* [*Bot*] cherry (*Prunus avium*)
  ○ **qershi e butë** [*Bot*] sweet cherry, mazzard cherry *Cerasus avium*
  ○ **qershi e egër** [*Bot*] **1** = qershigël **2** (*Reg*) wild cherry *Cerasus avium var. sylvestris* **3** (*Reg*) Mahaleb cherry *Cerasus mahaleb* **4** (*Reg*) daphne *Daphne oleoides*
  ○ **qershi krisje** [*Bot*] cherry whose skin bursts slightly when it ripens
  ○ **qershi rrëshqanëse** [*Bot*] creeping cherry *Cerasus prostrata*
  ○ **qershi toke** [*Bot*] = qershigël

qershiçkë *nf* snowberry (*Symphoricarpus albus*)

qershigël *nf* [*Bot*] blueberry, bilberry, whortleberry (*Vaccinium myrtillus*)

*qershior *adj* = qershitë

*qershitë *adj* (i) of cherry

qershizë *nf* [*Bot*] = qershigël

qershor *nm* June

qershore *nf* variety of green apple that ripens in June with fruit of medium size

*qertas *= qartas

qerth *nm* **1** small round bread board made of a single piece of wood *2 hoop, circle, ring

*qerthëll *= qerthull

*qerthënj *np* = qerth

qerthull *nm* (*np ˜ j*) **1** [*Text*] barrel-like reel for winding yarn or thread into skeins **2** small basket, open at the bottom and mounted on an axle and wheels, into which a toddler is placed to assist learning to stand and walk: walker, go-cart **3** circumscribing line or space **4** (*Old*) group, circle **5** (*Fig*) series of phenomena; series of stories on the same theme **6** (*Fig*) whirl of events **7** [*Bot*] shoots that grow around the main stem of a plant **8** (*Fig*) whirl of events **9** [*Bot*] verticil *10 whirlwind *11 picture frame

qerthullak *adj* [*Bot*] = qerthullor

qerthullim *nm ger* **1** <qerthullo·n, qerthullo·het (*Old*) **2** circulation = qarkullim *3 enclosure

qerthullo·het *vpr* to spin around, gyrate, rotate

qerthullo·n *vt* **1** to take a position around [ ]: encircle; surround **2** (*Fig*) to rotate, roll [one's eyes]

qerthullor *adj* [*Bot*] whorled, verticillate

qerthunjë *nf* large spool

qerr *nm* **1** [*Veter*] contagious inflammation of a horse's hoof (*panaritium*) **2** = qe'rre

*****qerrabâs** *nm (Reg Gheg)* = qerrepunu'es

qerra'r = qerrta'r

qerrata' *nm (np ˜ e'nj)* **1** (*Colloq*) crafty person **2** (*Pet*) clever, but slightly naughty child: little imp

qerratallëk *nm (np ˜ qe) (Colloq)* crafty act; crafty attitude; craftiness

qerrate'nj *np* < qerrata'

qe'rre *nf* **1** wooden cart **2** (*Old*) chariot
  ◦ **Qerrja e Madhe** [*Astron*] The Big Dipper *(Ursa Major)*
  ◦ **<>u thye qerrja në derë//te dera** "the cart breaks down right at <>'s front door" <> got a lucky break
  ◦ **Qerrja e Vogël** [*Astron*] The Little Dipper *(Ursa Minor)*

qerre'punu'es *nm* cartwright, wainwright

*****qerreto'r** *adj* suitable for carts

qerre'xhi *nm (np ˜ nj)* = qerrta'r

qerrta'r *n* **1** carter, drayman **2** = qerrepunu'es

qe's *stem for 1st sg pres, 1st & 3rd pl pres, 2nd & 3rd sg subj* < qe't•

qesa'r *nm* **1** (*Old*) = gjyna'h **2** curse

qesa's *stem for 1st sg pres, pl pres, 2nd & 3rd sg subj, pind* < qesa't•

qesa't *nm* economic depression, hard times

qesa't• *vt (Old)* to prune, trim

qesatllëk *nm (np ˜ qe)* = qesa't

qe'se *nf* **1** sack, bag, pouch **2** purse **3** (*Fig Colloq*) amount of money at the disposal of a person/family: means, money, budget, family income **4** [*Anat*] sac for storing body fluids; scrotum **5** (*Colloq*) balls (testicles) **6** wash-mitt made of wool **7** (*Old*) sum of money worth about three Turkish lira
  ◦ **qese e lotëve** [*Anat*] tear sac
  ◦ **qese e tëmthit** [*Anat*] gall bladder
  ◦ **qese e ujit** [*Anat*] urinary bladder

qeseli'dh'ur *adj* close with money, very thrifty; tightfisted, stingy

qesema'dh *adj, n* (person) with a big income, wealthy (person): moneybags

qeseme'r *nm* small pliers used by jewelers

qese'r *nm (Colloq)* **1** adze = sqepa'r **2** weeding hoe = çapë

qeseshpu'ar *adj* loose with money, free-spending, thriftless

qesëndi' *nf* **1** derision **2** derisive language

qesëndi's• *vi, vt* to deride, be derisive, mock

qesëndi's•et *vpr* = qesëndi's•

qesëndi'sës *adj* derisive

qesëndi'sje *nf ger* < qesëndi's•, qesëndi's•et = qesëndi'

qesi'm
  I § *nm (Old)* firm contract at a fixed price
  II § *adv* **1** (*Old*) (buying/selling) without measuring, at one price for all of it **2** (*Fig*) hastily, without giving the matter much thought

qe'skë *nf* **1** small pouch/bag **2** [*Anat*] sac, bursa ()
  ◦ **qeskë e lotëve** [*Anat*] tear sac
  ◦ **qeskë e mjaltit** [*Biol*] honey sac
  ◦ **qeskë e polenit** [*Bot*] pollen sac
  ◦ **qeskë e tëmthit** [*Anat*] gall bladder
  ◦ **qeskë e ujit** [*Anat*] urinary bladder

*****qesqi'** *nf* = qysqi'

qesqi'n *adj* **1** (*Old Colloq*) nimble **2** nattily dressed; careful in dress

*****qe'ste** *nf* zither

*****qeste'ta'r** *n* zither player

*****qesti'** *nf* = qesëndi'

*****qesti's•** *vi, vt* = qesëndi's•

qesh•
  I § *vi* **1** to laugh **2** (*Fig*) to express happiness **3** to be kidding, not be serious **4** to be derisive **5** (*Fig*) to look kindly on <>, smile on <>
  II § *vt* to laugh at []; deride, ridicule
  ◦ **s'<> qesh.**^{3sg} **buza** "<>'s lip *does* not laugh" <> has an unhappy face, <> looks dour/gloomy
  ◦ **qesh.**^{3sg} **drita** to start to get light, begin to dawn
  ◦ **qesh• e bot** (*Colloq*) to keep laughing, laugh without end
  ◦ **qesh• edhe me ujin e kulluar** "be derisive even with filtered water" to be pleased/satisfied by nothing, have something bad to say about everything
  ◦ **<> qesh.**^{3sg} **fytyra** "<>'s face *laughs*" <> lights up with happiness
  ◦ **s'<> qesh.**^{3sg} **fytyra** "<>'s lip/face *does* not laugh" <> has an unhappy face, <> looks dour/gloomy
  ◦ **qesh• me zemër e jo me buzë** "laugh with the heart and not with the lips" to be truly happy
  ◦ **qesh• me sy e qa•n me zemër.** "{} *laughs* with the eyes and *cries* with the heart" {} *laughs* on the outside but *cries* on the inside
  ◦ **[] qesh.**^{3sg} **mendja** [] *is* deluded
  ◦ **qesh• nën hundë/mustaqe** to snicker
  ◦ **qesh e ngjesh** pretending to be in fun, but in fact intended with malice
  ◦ **Qesh, se s'qan dot.** You laugh because it hurts too much to cry.
  ◦ **<> qesh.**^{3sg} **shtegu i ballit** <>'s face *lights* up with joy
  ◦ **në atë shtëpi qesh.**^{3pl} **edhe trarët** "in that house even the wooden beams *laugh*" it *is* a happy family
  ◦ **qesh• vesh më vesh** to laugh heartily
  ◦ **<> qesh.**^{3sg} **zemra** "<>'s heart *laughs*" <> *is* very happy

qe'sh•et
  I § *vpr* **1** to laugh **2** to smile **3** to be joking/kidding **4** (*Fig*) to smile on <>
  II § *vp impers* <> *feels* like laughing/smiling

qesh'ara'k *adj* **1** inducing laughter: funny, risible; laughable, ridiculous **2** absurdly inadequate

qesh'ara'ke *nf (Book)* ridiculous thing: absurdity; humor

qe'shë *1st sg pdef* < ësh•të I was, used to be

qe'sh'ëm *adj (i)* laughing, jovial, merry

qe'sh'ur *nf* roof sheathing, roof lath

qe'shje *nf ger (Book)* **1** < qe'sh•, qe'sh•et **2** laughter, laugh

qeshqe'k *nm* [*Food*] wheat mush boiled with small pieces of meat and scalded with hot butter

*****qe'sh'sh'ëm** *adj (i)* = qeshara'k

qe'sh'ur
  I § *part* < qesh•
  II § *adj (i)* **1** smiling and happy; cheerful; amiable **2** (*Fig*) lit up with joy **3** (of colors) light
  III § *nf (e)* **1** laughing; laughter **2** mocking

IV §   *nn ger (të)* = **qe·shje**

qesh·uri *nf* something laughable: absurdity

qet· *vt* = **qit·**
  ∘ **qet· e bërtet·** to try in every way possible to prove/disprove something

qe·tar *nm* plowman who drives oxen

qe·tas *adv* **1** quietly, noiselessly **2** secretly

qe·tash *adv* right away, immediately

qe·tazi *adv* = **qetas**

qe·të
  I §   *adj (i)* quiet, calm; serene, tranquil
  II §   *adv* quietly, calmly, in a relaxed manner
  ∘ **ësh·të i qetë për** [] not worry about []

qe·të *nf* crag; face of a crag; strip of land along the face of a crag

qe·të *2nd pl pdef* <**ësh·të** you were, used to be

qe·të-qe·të *adv* **1** unhurriedly; calmly and quietly **2** stealthily

qe·tër *nm* large rat

qe·tës *adj, n* *(Pej)* sneaky (person)

qe·tësi *nf* quietness, quiet; calmness, calm; tranquillity
  ∘ **qetësi varri** absolute silence; silence of the grave

qe·tësim *nm ger* **1** <**qetëso·n**, **qetëso·het** **2** [*Med*] sedation

qe·tësisht *adv* **1** quietly; calmly **2** stealthily

qe·tëso·het *vpr* **1** to quiet/calm down **2** to feel comforted **3** to relax, stretch out

qe·tëso·n *vt* **1** to quiet [] (down); calm [] (down) **2** to ease [suffering]: soothe, comfort; sedate

qe·tëso·hu *interj* at ease!

qe·tësuar *adj (i)* **1** calm **2** feeling comforted, with a sense of relief

qe·tësues
  I §   *adj* **1** serving to calm/comfort, soothing **2** [*Physiol*] relieving discomfort: sedative; analgesic
  II §   *nm* [*Pharm*] sedative, palliative; pain-reliever, analgesic

qe·tësueshëm *adj (i)* = **qetshëm**

qe·ti *nf* state of calm, stillness

qe·ti *adv (së)* quietly

qe·tim *nm ger* = **qetësim**

qe·to·het *vpr* = **qetëso·het**

qe·to·n *vt* = **qetëso·n**

****qe·tshëm** *adj (i)* peaceful, tranquil, still

qe·tthi
  I §   *adv* = **qetas**
  II §   *adv (së)* = **qetas**

qe·tuar *adj (i)* = **qetësuar**

qeth· *vt* **1** to trim [something fibrous], clip: cut []'s hair; clip the wool of [], shear; clip the loose ends of [a fabric]; clip the tops of [plants], mow [] **2** *(Fig)* to shorten [something written] by clipping off parts; curtail [expenses] **3** *(Fig Colloq)* to mow down [an enemy] **4** *(Fig Colloq)* to steal from [] by subterfuge: rip off, clip
  ∘ [] **qeth· kokën zero** "cut []'s hair on the lowest clipper setting" *(Colloq)* to give [] a very short hair cut
  ∘ **e qeth· roga-roga** to shear/cut patchily
  ∘ [] **qeth· shkallë-shkallë** to cut []'s hair/wool in uneven patches

qeth·et *vpr* to get a haircut

qeth·ar *n* sheep shearer

qeth·ë *nf ger* = **qethje**

qeth·ëm
  I §   *adj (i), n (Reg)* unfortunate/wretched/poor (person)
  II §   *n (i)* (of a dead person) poor soul

qeth·ës
  I §   *adj* serving to clip/shear
  II §   *n* sheepshearer

qeth·je *nf ger* <**qeth·**, **qeth·et**

qeth·muar *adj (i)* unfortunate, wretched, poor = **qethëm**

qeth·tar *nm* **1** sheepshearer = **qethës** ***2** *(Old)* barber, hairdresser

qeth·tore *nf* **1** sheep-shearing yard **2** *(Old)* barber/ hairdresser shop

qeth·ur
  I §   *part* <**qeth·**
  II §   *adj (i)* **1** shorn; with hair cut; with hair cut short **2** clipped; mown

qeth·urina *np fem* hair or wool residue left after clipping hair or fleece

qeveri *nf* **1** government **2** *(Colloq)* home management **3** *(Old)* food specially prepared to be stored or given away

qeveri·m *nm* governing, manner of governing

qeveri·s· *vt* **1** to govern, rule **2** to manage [household tasks] properly; put [household areas] in order **3** *(Colloq)* to take care of [someone ill]

qeveri·sje *nf ger* **1** <**qeveri·s·** **2** government, management

qeveri·tar
  I §   *adj* of or pertaining to government
  II §   *n* **1** high government official, government executive **2** *(Old)* governor

*****qezap** = **gjezap**

qe·zë *nf* = **qe·hën**

qe·zër *nm* eyetooth, canine (tooth)

që
  I §   *conj* followed by verb in the indicative **1** that **2** which, who
  II §   *conj* followed by verb in the subjunctive **1** in order that, so that **2** whoever, whichever; whatever
  III §   *prep (acc)* **1** since **2** from [] and beyond, from [] on, even from
  IV §   *pcl* from
  ∘ {*verb*} **që** {*same verb in same form*} since {*verb*} anyway
  ∘ **që atëherë** since then
  ∘ **që ç'ke me të** *(Colloq)* **1** willy nilly, whether or no **2** all right, pretty good, okay
  ∘ **që këtej** from now on, from this point on
  ∘ **që kur bota është botë** since the beginning of the world
  ∘ **që kur** from the time when/that, ever since
  ∘ **që lashtë** a long time ago
  ∘ **që me** [] since [], from the time of []
  ∘ **që më natë** before daybreak
  ∘ **Që në gusht nga një grusht.** "Beginning in August one fistful at at time." *(Prov)* Get an early start and do a little at a time.
  ∘ **që në kohën e baba Qemos** "since the time of Father Qemo" *(Colloq)* for as long as anyone can remember: since Hector was a pup
  ∘ **që në lindje** since birth
  ∘ **që në skutina** "since in diapers" *(Colloq)* since infancy
  ∘ **që në vezë** "since in the egg" from the very beginning, ab ovo

○ **që në** [] from [particular date/place] on

○ **që nga koka deri te thonjtë/thembrat** from head to toe

○ **që nga thellësia e zemrës/shpirtit** from deep in one's heart, from the bottom of one's heart

○ **që nga themeli *1** right from the start, from the very beginning **2** with complete thoroughness: to the very foundation, to the very roots

○ **që nga** {} (extending) from {*particular date/place*}

○ **që parthi** just a little while ago

○ **që përpara** in advance

○ **që prej çastit kur** _ since the time when _

○ **që prej çastit që** _ from the time that _

○ **që ta kam fjalën** *(Colloq)* (parenthetically) so to say/speak

○ **që ta ngas fjalën/llafin** "in order to drive the conversation forward" **1** (starts a topic related to something known to both parties in a conversation) incidentally, by the way **2** (used to start or take one's turn in a conversation) well, you know

○ **që tutje e tëhu** from then on: thenceforth

○ **që the/thua ti** *(Colloq)* (parenthetically) they say, you know

qëherthi *adv (Colloq)* quite some time ago, quite a while ago, long ago

qëku'r OR **qëku'ri** *adv* since long ago; a long time ago

qëku'rse *conj* since the time that _

qëku'rshëm *adj (i)* of long ago, bygone

qëku'rthi *adv (Reg)* = **qëku'r**

qëla'shti *adv* in ancient times; long ago

qëlla'të *nf (Old)* particular care/attention, sedulousness

qëll'i'm *nm ger* **1** <**qëllo'·n, qëllo'·het 2** aim, purpose, objective **3** intention

○ **qëllim në vetvete** objective in its own right, independent objective

qëll'i'm'isht *adv* intentionally, deliberately

qëll'im'ke'q *adj (Book)* of evil intention: malevolent

qëll'im'mi'rë *adj (Book)* well-intentioned

qëll'im'o'r *adj* **1** *(Book)* purposeful **2** [*Ling*] of purpose

qëll'i'm'shëm *adj (i)* intentional, deliberate

qëll'im'ta'r *adj* purposeful; intentional

qëll'i'm'thi *adv* on purpose, deliberately

qëll'o'·het *vp recip* to strike/hit one another

○ **qëllo·het me grusht** to box

qëll'o'·n

I § *vt* **1** to strike [an intended target] **2** *(Fig)* to make [] come out just right, hit [] just right

II § *vi, vt* **1** to aim (at); shoot (at) **2** *(Fig)* to criticize [] sharply, be critically biting

III § *vi* to happen to be, be/happen by chance; happen to occur

○ [] **qëllo·n gjumi** sleep strikes []: [] falls asleep

○ [] **qëllo·n me bastun** to beat [] with a cane: cane []

○ **qëllo·n në hi** to be a coward

○ **qëllo·n në shenjë** "hit the target" to be right on target

○ **qëllo·n në xixëllonjë** to be a good shot, shoot very well, be a sharpshooter

qëll'ua'r

I § *adj (i)* hitting the target: successful; apt

II § *nf (e)* combat, fight

III § *nn ger (të)* **1** <**qëllo'·n, qëllo'·het 2** accidental possibility: chance

qëll'ue's *n (Old)* sharpshooter, marksman = **qi'tës**

që'me'na'të *adv* while still night, before dawn

që'mo'çëm *adj (i)* **1** age-old, of long ago, ancient **2** very old, aged **3** former, one-time

që'mo'ti

I § *adv* **1** in olden times, in the old days, once upon a time **2** long ago

II § *nm* olden times, the old days

që'mo't'shëm *adj (i)* = **qëmoçëm**

qëmte'së *nf* = **qëmti'm**

qëmt'i'm *nm ger* **1** <**qëmto'·n 2** garnerment

qëmt'o'·n *vt* **1** to search out []; gather up [bits of material, crops] piece by piece: glean, garner **2** to snow or rain slowly in fine particles

○ **po** [] **qëmto·n**n^{3sg} **gjumi** sleep *is* slowly creeping up on [], [] *is* slowly falling asleep

qëmt'ue's *nm* gleaner (of information)

***qëndër** = **qendër**

***qëndër'si'm** *nm ger* **1** <**qëndërso'·n 2** concentration **3** = **qendërzi'm**

***qëndër'so'·n** *vt* **1** to concentrate **2** = **qendërzo'·n**

qëndi'më *nf* = **qëndi'smë**

qëndi's·

I § *vi* to make embroidery, do needlework

II § *vt* **1** to embroider **2** *(Fig)* to decorate **3** *(Fig Colloq)* to write [] beautifully

○ <>**a qëndis· në lule të ballit** "decorate <> in the center of the forehead" to shoot <> dead, shoot <> right between the eyeballs

○ <>**i qëndis· të gjitha** to count out all <>'s failings/mistakes

qëndi's'je *nf ger* **1** <**qëndi's· 2** embroidery, needlework

qëndi's'më *nf* embroidered figure/cloth; embroidery

qëndis'ta'r *n* embroiderer

qëndis'ta'rí *nf* embroidery

qëndi's'ur *adj (i)* ornamented by embroidery: embroidered

qëndi'zmë *nf* = **qëndi'smë**

qëndra'k

I § *adj* resolute, steadfast

II § *-nm* *diameter

***qëndra'l** *adj* central

qëndre'së *nf* **1** stopping place; passenger station/stop **2** sojourn, stay **3** resistance; firm stance, stand **4** perseverance, steadfastness

qëndres'ta'r *adj* = **qëndrimta'r**

qëndri'm *nm ger* **1** <**qëndro'·n 2** standing position; stance **3** *(Fig)* position; attitude **4** *(Fig)* resistance, stand **5** passenger stop/station

○ **qëndrim i mbledhur** squat (position)

***qëndrim'ta'r** *adj* resolute, firm, steadfast; steady; resistant = **qëndrue'shëm**

qëndri'në *nf* **1** *(Fig)* tough old woman who has withstood hardships ***2** temporary position/station, temporary stopping place; hangout

qëndro'·n

I § *vi* **1** to stand; stand up **2** to maintain the same position/condition/place/behavior for a length of time: remain, stay; keep; stay over, live; stand; persist; resist; hold up well, have enduring value

II § *vt, vi* to bring/come to a halt: halt

○ **S'qëndron breshri mbi breshkë.** "Hailstones won't stay on a turtle's back." *(Prov)* No one can succeed under these circumstances.

○ <> **qëndro·***n* **brisk me brisk** to go head to head with <>, argue with <> right to <>'s face

○ <> **qëndro·***n* **gatitu** to be obedient to <>

○ **qëndro·***n* **havadan***/***në hava 1** to hover **2** to be wavering, be undecided **3** to be in uncertain circumstances: be hanging in air

○ **qëndro·***n* **këmbë mbi/përmbi këmbë** to be/act too casual, be complacent

○ **nuk** <> **qëndro·***n*^{3pl} **këmbët në yzengji** "<>'s feet *don't stay* in the stirrups" not stay in a good job for long, be constantly moving from

○ <> **qëndro·***n* **kokërr** to face <> boldly, stand firm against <>, stand eyeball to eyeball with <>

○ **qëndro·***n* **larg** to be far different, be incomparable

○ **qëndro·***n* **lis** to stand proud and unbending

○ **qëndro·***n* **mbi dy karrige** *(Pej)* to profit from two sides by catering opportunistically to both; lack commitment

○ <> **qëndro·***n* **me fyt** to choke with anger toward <>

○ **qëndro·***n* **me këmbët e veta** to stand on one's own two legs; stand firm

○ **qëndro·***n* **me armë të mprehura** to stand with arms (weapons) at the ready

○ **qëndro·***n* **më/në këmbë 1** to stand on one's feet, stand up **2** (of an object) to stand upright, stand straight; (of an idea/argument) hold up

○ **qëndro·***n* **në ajër** to be left hanging in air; be up in the air, be not yet decided

○ **qëndro·***n* **në bisht** to lag behind

○ **qëndro·***n* **në teh/presë të thikës/briskut/shpatës** to be at the crucial point, be right on the edge; hang in the balance

○ **qëndro·***n* **në vend** to stay in one place; not move, not change; lag behind

○ <> **qëndro·***n* **pranë** to look after [] with great care

○ **qëndro·***n* **prapa shpinës së** <> to use <> as a front; hide behind <>'s skirts

○ **qëndro·***n* **(si) qiri** to stand up straight without moving, stand at attention

○ **qëndro·***n* **si kërcu** just stand/sit there like a bump on a log

○ **qëndro·***n* **si shkëmb (graniti)** "stand like a rock (of granite)" to stand steadfast

*__qëndro__|**jse** *nf* supporting base: stand, rest, support

*__qëndro__|**r** *adj, n* = qendror

__qëndro__|**es** *adj* = qëndrueshëm

__qëndro__|**eshëm** *adj (i)* **1** stationary, fixed; invariable, stable; durable; permanent; enduring; resistant **2** persistent **3** [*Bot*] evergreen

__qëndro__|**eshm**|**ëri** *nf* **1** [*Phys Tech*] stability **2** durability; permanence **3** resistance; persistence

*__qëndro__|**et** *adj (i)* stable, firm

*__që__|**në** = qenë

*__që__|**nër** *np* <qen

*__qëngjë__|**lë** *nf* [*Bot*] danewort (*Sambucus ebulus*)

*__qëpall__|**ë** = qepallë

__që__|**pa**|**rë** *adv* a little while ago, a short time ago

__që__|**pari** *adv* = qëparë

__që__|**parsh**|**ëm** *adj (i)* of just now

__që__|**parthi** *adv* = qëparë

__qër__|**im** *nm ger* <qëro·*n*, qëro·*het*

*__qër__|**imtar** *n* = qortues

__qëro__·*het* *vpr* **1** to become clear: clear up **2** *(Scorn)* to clear out, leave (a place where one is not wanted) **3** to peel

__qëro__·*n vt* **1** to get rid of unwanted elements: 1) to separate an undesired exterior from a desired interior part: peel [an orange], shell [peas, nuts], scale [a fish], clean [a chicken]; 2) to clear away unwanted parts: clear [underbrush], clear [one's throat], clear up [pimples from a face], purge [one's enemies], expel [undesirable students] **2** *(CrudeImpolite)* to eat up [everything] (without leaving anything for others), clean [the plate] **3** *(Crude Pej)* to swipe

○ **i qëro·***n* **hesapet me** [ ] to settle accounts with [ ] definitively; break up with [ ] once and for all

○ **i qëro·***n* **lakrat/llogaritë me** [ ] to settle accounts with [ ] definitively; break up with [ ] once and for all

○ **e qëro·***n* **punën** to be very straightforward

○ [ ] **qëro·***n* **si hudhër** to exploit [ ] terribly, squeeze [ ] dry

*__qëro__|**jcë** *nf* cleaner, brush, wire brush

*__Qërsho__|**r** = qershor

*__qërt__| = qort

__qër__|**ua**|**r** *adj (i)* **1** with outer covering layer removed: peeled, shelled, scaled, shucked, plucked **2** free of undesired elements; unblemished: clear; (of sky) cloudless **3** (of an account) clear of debt, closed

__qër__|**ues** *adj* serving to pare fruit

__qër__|**uese** *nf* paring knife; corn shucker

*__qërr__| *(Reg)* = qër

*__qësëndi__| = qesëndi

qi *conj (Reg Gheg)* = që

qi·*n vt (Crude)* to fuck

qibar

   I § *adj (Colloq)* **1** fastidious about food and dress: persnickety, finicky **2** snobbish

   II § *n* snob

__qi__|**bër** *nf* **1** *(Colloq)* finickiness about food or dress: fastidiousness = sqimë **2** haughtiness

__qibër__|**tar** *adj, n* fastidious/haughty (person)

__qi__|**ej** *np* <qiell

__qi__|**ell** *nm (np ~j)* **1** sky **2** [*Relig*] heaven

○ **s'ësh·të as në qiell, as në tokë/dhé** "not be in the sky nor on earth" to be undecided: be up in the air

○ **asgjë nuk vjen/bie nga qielli** nothing just comes down from the sky, it takes effort and hard work to get anything of value

○ **qiell i mbuluar** cloudy/overcast sky

○ **Qielli me tokën të bashkohen!** "The sky may join with the earth!" It will never happen! Not in my lifetime!

○ **qiell xixa-xixa** sky full of twinkling stars

__qiell__|**gërvisht**|**ës** *nm (Book)* skyscraper

__qiell__|**ha**|**pur** *adj (Book)* (of weather) with a clear, cloudless sky

__qiell__|**or** *adj* celestial, heavenly

*__qiell__|**treg**|**on**|**ë** *nf* astronomy = astronomí

*__qiell__|**uq** *adj* azure, bluish

__qiell__|**zë** *nf* **1** [*Anat*] roof of the mouth: palate **2** vaulted top of an oven/doorway

__qiell__|**z**|**or** *adj* [*Anat Ling*] palatal

__qiell__|**z**|**ore** *nf* [*Ling*] palatal consonant

*__qi__|**ës** *n* **1** *(Crude)* fucker **2** *(Old)* fornicator

qift *nm* [*Ornit*] **1** kite *(Milvus)* **2** red kite *(Milvus milvus)* **3** *(Reg)* falcon = skifter *qi'full nm goblin

qik nm = qiqërim

*qi'kël OR qi'këll = ki'kël

qikë'lo'sh adj tapering to a point, pointed

qikllo'p nm Cyclops = ciklo'p

qiku'të nf poison hemlock (Conium maculatum)

qila'r nm 1 cool-storage cellar 2 (Reg) bridal chamber in a highland house
  ○ **Është më afër dera se qilari.** "The door is nearer than the cellar" People look after their own.

qilar'xhe'shë nf female (Old) < qilarxhi

qilar'xhi' nm (np ~ nj) (Old) person at a wedding who is in charge of distributing the food and drink from the cool-storage cellar

*qile'r nm = qila'r

qili'm nm ornamental rug; carpet
  ○ qilimi i gjelbër "the green carpet" (Book) the soccer field

qilim'e'nd'ëse nf = qilimpunue'se

qilim'pun'u'e's adj involved in rug weaving

qilim'pun'u'e'se nf woman who weaves rugs: rug weaver

*qili'zë = qeli'zë

qili'zmë nf [Agr] deep plowing of land newly under cultivation; land newly under cultivation

*qi'lo OR qi'llo nf (Colloq) = kilogra'm

*qill = qëll

*qi'llë nf container of grain measuring 60 okes

qillo'ta np = kilo'ta

qi'me nf 1 filament of hair: hair, bristle 2 (Collec) animal's coat of hair 3 (Collec Colloq) whiskers (of a beard/mustache) 4 wool filament 5 [Bot] hair, trichome 6 [Anat] villus 7 [Tech] hairspring 8 [Zool] filiform nemertean parasite that infests livestock 9 [Veter] disease of livestock caused by these parasites
  ○ **ësh·të qime e gjallë 1** to be very energetic: be a ball of fire 2 (Pej) (of a person) to be insidiously harmful
  ○ **qime e gjallë** [Invert] filiform nemertean parasite that infests livestock
  ○ **Qimja e tjetrit të duket tra.** "Someone else's hair seems like a wooden beam to you." Someone else's faults are easy for you to see.

qi'm'e nf (e) (Crude Regional Gheg) fucking

qime'a'rtë adj (Poet) (of animals) with a coat of shiny golden hair: golden-coated

qime'a'shpër adj 1 (of animals) with a coat/fleece of coarse hair/wool 2 (of a man) with a coarse beard

qime'ba'rdhë adj 1 (of animals) with a coat of white or light-colored hair 2 white-haired; gray-haired

qime'bri'shtë adj having bristly hair

qime'bu'të adj (of animals) with a coat/fleece of soft hair/wool

qime'de'nd'ur adj having dense/thick hair/wool/bristles

qime'dre'dh'ur adj curly-haired

qime'gështe'një adj (i) chestnut-haired

qime'gja'llë nf 1 [Zool] filiform nemertean parasite that infests livestock *2 [Med] fistula

qime'gja'të adj long haired, long-fibered

qime'hi'rtë adj gray-haired

qime'ho'llë adj having fine/thin hair/fibers

qime'ku'q adj, n (animal) having a reddish-brown coat of hair; redheaded (person)

qime'la'rmë adj having hair of different colors: piebald

qime'mu'rrmë adj having dun-colored hair

qime'ndri't'ur adj (of animals) with shiny hair

qime'rë'në adj whose hair has fallen out

qime'rra'llë adj having sparse hair/bristles

qime'rru'a'r adj 1 whose hair and mustache has been shaved off: clean-shaven 2 (of animals) whose dense short hair lies flat

qime'shku'rtër adj having short hair/filaments

qime'tra'shë adj having thick hair filaments: coarse-haired

qime'thi'nj'ur adj gray-haired

qime've'rdhë adj 1 (of animals) with a light brown/tan coat of hair 2 (of a person) blond, fair-haired

qime'zba'rdh'ur adj gray-haired

qime'zi' adj (fem ~ ez) (of animals) with a dark/black coat

*qi'm'ër nf [Invert] bedbug = çi'mkë

*qi'm'ës nm (Colloq) man who is too involved in sexual intercourse

qim'ëz nf 1 [Veter] disease of domestic animals and fowl caused by filiform parasites (Dictycaulosis) 2 [Med] gangrene

qim'ëzo'·het vpr (Book) to fray

*qimi' (Old) = kimi'

*qimio'n = qimno'n

*qimi'st n chemist; chemistry teacher

qim'ishte np pile of hair

*qimite'r OR qimiti'r nm (Old) cemetery

*qimja'r adj long-haired

*qimjo'n = qimno'n

qimno'n nm [Bot] cumin Cuminum cyminum

qimo'r adj (Book) hairy; fibrous

qimo's·et vpr (of domestic animals and fowl) to contract a disease caused by filiform parasites

qimo'sh adj hairy, hirsute

*qimpanzi' nm [Zool] chimpanzee = shimpanze'

qimto'·n
  I § vi (of snow) to fall in thin flakes = qëmto'·n
  II § vt to glean

qimu'sh nm = gu'në

qind nm (np ~ ra) hundred; a hundred
  ○ qind për qind a hundred percent; complete(ly), total(ly)

qinda're nf (Old) liquid measure of a quarter of an oke

qinda'rkë nf hundredth of a lek: cent, centime

*qind'ëri' nf century

qind'ës nm [Hist] centurion

qind'ësh nm (Colloq) hundred-meter run

qind'ëshe nf 1 [Math] set/unit of a hundred; number/numeral in the hundreds column 2 hundred-lek bill 3 hundred-gram container 4 [Hist] military unit containing a hundred men: century

qindfi'sh nm hundredfold

qindfish'i'm nm ger < qindfisho'·n, qindfisho'·het

qindfisho'·het vpr to increase [] a hundredfold; grow enormously

qindfisho'·n vt to multiply [] hundredfold; increase [] greatly

qindfi'sh'të adj (i) a hundred times greater/more

qindfishu'a'r adj (i) increased a hundredfold; grown enormously *qindïs· = qëndïs·

qindle·k·ësh·e *nf* 1 *(Offic)* hundred-lek bill 2 *(Colloq)* ten-lek bill

*qïndmë·stë *adv* *(Old)* = qindmëzaj

*qïndmë·zaj *adv* *(Old)* a hundredfold

qindor *adj* [*Math*] centesimal

*qindr = qëndr

qindra *np* hundreds

qindravjeça·r *adj* lasting hundreds of years, for many centuries; hundreds of years old

qïndtë *adj (i), n (i)* hundredth

qindvjeça·r

I § *adj* hundred-year-long; a hundred years old

II § *nm* century

qindvjetor *nm* 1 century 2 centennial

*qinema = kinema

*qinez = kinez

qingël *nf* 1 cinch belt of a saddle: girth, saddle belt 2 [*Bot*] Mediterranean herb elder, danewort *(Sambucus ebulus)*

qingj *nm* = qëngj

qingje *nf* cinch belt of a saddle: girth

qingjo·n *vt* to cinch up [], put a girth around []

*qinïk *adj* = qenïk

*qinikïzëm *nm* cynicism

*qininë *nf* quinine = kininë

*qinos· *vt* to merge [livestock] temporarily for common herding and pasturing

*qinosï *nf (Old)* temporary merging of herds belonging to different owners for purposes of common herding and pasturing

*qinosiar *nm* = përzitës

*qip *nm* 1 = qep 2 bow (of a ship)

qiparis *nm* [*Bot*] cypress, funeral cypress *(Cupressus sempervirens)* = selvi

qiparïstë *adj (i)* made of cypress wood

*qïpër·t *adj* *(Old)* copper, bronze

qipi *nf* = mullar

qipriot *adj, n* Cypriot

qiprïqe *nf* edible mushroom with a reddish cap that appears in autumn

Qïpro *nf* Cyprus

*qïpshte *np fem* <kopsht

qïpull *nm (np ~j)* [*Folklore*] evil spirit: ghost, goblin, gremlin

qiqër

I § *nf* [*Bot*] chickpea *(Cicer arietinum)*

II § *adj (Fig)* agile, sprightly

III § *adv (Fig)* in very good heath and condition, feeling fit: chipper

qiqerïm I § *nm* OR qiqerïmë II § *nf* summer mist that stretches to the ground: summer haze

qiqëro··het *vpr* to get all cleaned up and in shape: get spruced up

qiqërvïqër *nf* [*Bot*] = qiqirïq

*qiqireq [*Bot*] spike of wheat

*qiqirïq [*Bot*] peanut = kikirïk

qira *nf* money paid for temporary use or occupancy: rent

qiradhën·ës *n* person who offers something for rent: lessor; landlord

qiradhën·ie *nf* renting out, leasing: lease

qiramarr·ës

I § *n* person who agrees to pay rent: lessee, renter; tenant

II § *adj* paying rent, renting

qiramarr·je *nf* taking a lease, renting

*qiramïdhe *nf* roof tile = qeramïdhe

*qiras· *vt* = qeras·

qiraxhe·shë *nf female* <qiraxhi

qiraxhi *nm (np ~ nj)* 1 tenant, renter 2 *(Old)* person paid to haul loads with horses: drayman; person who rents out horses: hostler, ostler

*qïr·ës *n* 1 *(Crude)* fucker 2 *(Old)* fornicator

*qirgorïnë *nm* [*Ornit*] finch

qiri(r)

I § *nm (np ~ nj)* 1 candle 2 [*Phys*] candlepower 3 [*Tech*] sparkplug 4 candle-shaped object

II § *pred* erect

o qiri akulli icicle

qiribër·ës *n* candlemaker

qirïç *nm* paste; size, sizing; glue

qirimbajt·ëse *nf* candlestick

*qirïnthë *nf* [*Bot*] honeywort *(Cerinthe)*

qirïnj *np* <qiri

qirïnjtë *adj (i)* 1 made of candle wax, waxen; candlelike 2 *(Fig)* very pale

qirïr·i *obl* <qiri(r)

qirïth [*Bot*] = gju·njëz

qirïthi *adv* 1 standing on the hind legs, rearing up 2 standing erect, upright, straight up

qirïu *obl* <qiri(r)

*qirurg *nm* *(Old)* surgeon = kirurg

*qirurgjï *nf* *(Old)* surgery = kirurgjí

qis *stem for 1st sg pres, pl pres, 2nd & 3rd sg subj, pind, imper* <qit·

qisar *nm* [*Bot*] ivy *(Hedera helix)*

*qishdo *determiner* any, any at all, any whatever

*qïshë *nf* church = kïshë

qit·

I § *vt* 1 to move [] out by forcible action: take [] out; expel; dislocate 2 to take off [outer covering]; expose [] to public view, bring [] out to the public, present [] publicly 3 to give off/out [], emit; issue; produce, yield, create 4 to earn [] by effort 5 to treat <> to [] 6 to toss [] away 7 *(Colloq)* to spend/pass [a period of time] (somewhere) 8 to put [] into <> 9 *(Reg)* to start

II § *vt, vi* 1 to shoot (using a firearm), shoot off [] 2 to take a photograph of []

o <> qit· be to beseech <>

o [] qit· birërie to disown [one's son/daughter], banish [one's son/daughter] from the family

o <>a qit· bojën "remove <>'s paint" to reveal <>'s true colors, pull off <>'s mask

o [] qit· borxh (tek {}) to put [] in ({}'s) debt

o e qit· bosh fjalën to treat what was said with arrant disregard

o qit· cekën to decide to do something, intend to do something

o [] qit· çirak (sometimes said ironically) to put [] on []'s feet

o <>a qit· fishekët to damage <> beyond repair, shoot <> full of holes

o qit· fjalë për [] to spread a story about []

o <> qit· fundin to study/investigate <> in depth

○ **nuk qit· gjë në shesh/treg** "not get anything out in public" not manage to bring anything to a successful conclusion, not manage to achieve anything

○ <>[] **qit· nga hundët/për hundësh 1** *(Pej)* to take [] away from <> by force, draw [] out of <> by force **2** to spoil <>'s enjoyment of [] **3** to make <> pay for [] through the nose

○ **ia qit· için lakrorit** to reveal the ugly truth

○ <> **qit·**^{3sg} **koka tym** <>'s head is absolutely spinning with all the things <> has to worry about

○ **e qit· kokën** to show one's true colors

○ **qit· krye/kokë** to make an appearance

○ **qit· kushtrimin** to raise a hue and cry

○ <>*i* **qit· lakrat në shesh** to reveal one's mistakes, disclose one's guilt

○ **Nuk qit· lepur nga strofulla.** "{} can't even get a hare out of its hole" {} *can't* do anything right

○ [] **qit· lyç** to make a mess of [], muddle [] up

○ [] **qit· lyç** to mess/muddle [] up

○ **qit· mallin = çma·ll·**^{*et*}

○ [] **qit· mbanë** to conclude [] successfully

○ [] **qit· mendsh 1** to forget about []: get/wipe [] out of one's mind **2** to drive [] out of []'s mind, drive [] crazy

○ <>*i* **qit· mendtë/trutë** to drive <> out of <>'s mind

○ [] **qit· më/në krye** to get [] done

○ <>*a* **qit· mishin copë** "pull off <>'s flesh in pieces" to beat <> to a pulp

○ **qit· mjaltë nga guri** "extract honey from rock" to be a wonderworker

○ <>[] **qit· në lëndinë** to bring <>'s [secret] out into the open

○ [] **qit· në be** *[Ethnog]* to put [] under oath

○ [] **qit· në doçe** to leave [] with nothing

○ <> **qit· në dorë** to give money/bribe/gift to <>

○ [] **qit· në dritë 1** to expose [] to the light of day **2** to put [] on []'s feet

○ **qit· në fotografi** to take/shoot a picture

○ [] **qit· në harresë** to expunge [] from one's memory, stop thinking about [], deliberately forget []

○ [] **qit· në jetë 1** to save []'s life; show [] how to live **2** to bring [] to light

○ [] **qit· në shteg** to help [] find a way out of (a problem)

○ **i qit· në ujë (paratë)** "toss it (money) in the water" to waste money, just throw money away

○ [] **qit· nga defteri** to cross [] off the list

○ [] **qit· pa kapuç** *(Pej)* to exploit [] to the utmost limit: leave [] without a shirt on []'s back, take [] to the cleaner's

○ [] **qit· pas shpine** to put [] behind one, give [] no more thought or consideration, disregard []

○ <> *q*it· **përgishte** *(Old)* to challenge <> to a duel

○ [] **qit· prej zemre** "dismiss from one's heart" to cast [] out of one's affection: disown []; stop caring about []

○ **i qit· puplat** "shed one's pinfeathers" *1 to grow up **2** *(Fig)* to come to life **3** to show one's true colors

○ <> **qit· rrethin 1** to encircle; surround **2** to hit on the way to put the screws to ruin <>

○ <> **qit· stërdhëmbët** to bare one's teeth at <>

○ <> **qit· sytë** to do terrible harm to <>

○ **qit· shestë** to make a decision

○ **qit· shkelma 1** to let kicks fly: kick **2** to make unreasonable objections: kick

○ <> **qit· shkumë nga goja** "make <> foam at the mouth" to work <> to exhaustion

○ **qit· short** to cast lots, draw straws

○ <> **qit· shpirtin** to make <> suffer, put <> through Hell

○ <>*i* **qit· mendtë/trutë** to drive <> out of <>'s mind

○ **qit· ujë/vaj nga guri** "extract water/oil from rock" to be a wonderworker

○ <> **qit· veshët** "deafen/remove <>'s ears" to bore *<a listener>* to death; hammer constantly at <>

○ **qit· veshët** "stick one's ears out" *(Pej)* to show one's true colors

qit·*et vp impers* it *comes* easy to <>, <> *has* a knack

○ **nuk qit·***et*^{3sg} it cannot go on, it cannot continue

○ <> **qit·***et*^{3sg} **këmba** <>'s foot is sprained

*****qitall·***et vpr* to clear up, get sunny

○ **koha qitall·***et*^{3sg} the weather *clears* up

qita'p *nm* **1** *(Old)* *[Relig]* holy book, the Koran **2** *(Colloq)* book

*****qi'ta'sh** = **qeta'sh**

qite'pri't *invar*

qi'tër *nf* **1** = **qi'tro** ***2** *(Old)* citrus fruit

qit'ës *n* **1** marksman, sharpshooter; target shooter **2** *[Sport]* shooter **3** *[Mil]* gunner

*****qiti'në** *nf* chitin

qi'tje *nf ger* **1** <**qi**t· **2** gunfire **3** target shooting

qi'tro *nf*[*Bot*] **1** citron *(Citrus medica)* **2** lime *(Citrus aurantifolia)*

qi'tur

I § *part* <**qi**t·

II § *adj (i)* **1** sticking/bulging out; dislocated **2** prominent, renowned ***3** fired; launched

qitha'ra'zë *nm* [*Ornit*] turtledove

*****qitha'rë** *nf* guitar = **kita'rë**

*****qitha'ri's·** *vt* to play [a plucked string instrument]: strum, pick

*****qiveri's·** = **qeveri's·**

*****qive'te** *nf* [*Zool*] civet cat

qivu'r *nm* gravestone; pile of stones marking a grave; low wall surrounding a grave; tomb; coffin, bier

qivur'ta'r *nm* coffin-maker; tomb-builder

qivur'thi *adv* = **pe'tash**

*****qi'zgë** *nf* ringworm of the scalp = **qe're**

qo'·het *vpr* = **zgjo'·het**

qo'·n *vt* = **zgjo'·n**

qo *stem for opt* <**ësh·të**

qo'fkë *nf* [*Ornit*] = **mëlle'një**

qo'fsh *stem for opt* <**ësh·të**

○ **Qofsh e bardhë!** May you be happy!

○ <> **qofsha falë!** *(Felic)* May I express my thanks to <>!

○ **Qofsh me jetë!** "May you be alive!" Be well! Stay well!

qo'fte *nf* **1** [*Food*] (spicy) meat patty **2** *(Crude Pej)* clumsy, sluggish and inept person: meatball

qofte're *nf* [*Food*] large spicy meat patty

qofte'shit'ës *nm* person who makes and sells spicy meat patties

qo'ftë *3rd sg opt* <**ësh·të** may it be; whether it be

○ **Të qoftë!** *(Iron)* It's yours! Enjoy it!

○ **qoftë edhe një thua** even a tiny (bit)

○ **qoftë edhe** at least, even

○ **qoftë edhe** {*gradable adjective*} no matter how {}, however {}

○ **Qoftë largl** I hope it (a calamity) stays away!
○ **qoftë _ qoftë_** whether/either _ or _, be it _ or
be it _
qoftëlarg nm "May-he-stay-away!" (Euph) Satan,
the devil
qok nm [Ornit] = **gjon**
qok• vt 1 to strike [] lightly: tap, peck at [] 2 to make a
shallow cut in []: notch 3 to shake [hands] in friendly
fashion
qokaç nm 1 [Ornit] woodpecker = **qukapik**
2 wooden mallet used to castrate livestock
***qokas** stem for 1st sg pres, pl pres, 2nd & 3rd sg
subj, pind < **qokat•**
***qokat•** vt to peck
qokatar
I § adj, n 1 (person) who takes his time and acts
in a deliberate and circumspect way 2 (person) who
observes social proprieties by attending traditional
celebrations
II § n distinguished person
qokë nf 1 nick/notch (made in wood or stone as
a sign); boundary marker 2 marker; game token
3 place set with traps or snares; trap 4 (Fig) constraint
5 (Fig) moderation 6 egg placed in a brood nest
*7 brood hen 8 (Fig) celebration of an important life
event
qokël nf 1 large walnut thrown at target walnuts in a
children's game 2 small spherical object
○ **qokla e syrit** iris of the eye
qokth nm [Ornit] eagle owl (Bubo bubo)
qokthi adv
qole
I § nf with masc agreement (Colloq) 1 serf, slave;
servant; servile person 2 (Pej) person of weak intelligence who is easily taken advantage of by others:
sap, chump, sucker
II § nf [Ornit] woodlark (Lullula arborea)
qollit• vi 1 to turn out well, succeed 2 to take place,
happen, occur
***qollo•n** vi = **qëllo**
***qollopitë** nf kind of cake
qopal nm large stone/clod
qore nf sunless hollow in the mountains
***qorfishek** = **qorrfishek**
***qorim** nm = **qorrim**
***qorollis•** = **qorrollis•**
***qoros•** vt = **qorro•n**
qortim nm ger 1 < **qorto•n**, **qorto•het** 2 reproach,
rebuke, reprimand, censure
qortimemadh adj, n (person) who constantly
scolds
qortimtar adj = **qortues**
qorto•het vpr to get into an argument, have an argument
qorto•n vt 1 to scold, castigate; admonish, reproach,
reprimand; censure 2 to correct [errors]
***qortor** adj = **qortues**
qortues adj admonishing, censorious, critical, cas-
tigating, reproachful
qortueshëm adj (i) 1 deserving reproach: repre-
hensible, blameworthy 2 correctable, corrigible
***qorullis•** = **qorrollis•**
qorr
I § adj 1 (Colloq) blind as a bat 2 having little light:
dim; admitting little light 3 closed off; without an
exit 4 without particular aim: wild

II § n (Colloq) 1 blind one 2 (Pej) scatterbrained person 3 (Child) sleep
○ **fasule/groshë qorre** [Bot] black-eyed peas
(Dolichos unguiculatus L.)
○ **qorr me një sy** one-eyed person/animal
qorras OR **qorrazi** adv blindly
qorrfishek nm 1 blank (bullet) 2 (Old) fireworks
qorrim nm ger 1 < **qorro•n**, **qorro•het** 2 blindness
qorro•het vpr (Colloq) 1 to go blind 2 (Fig) (of a
mirror) to lose its reflectivity: go bad, darken, veil
over 3 (Fig) (of a blade) to become dull
qorro•n vt (Colloq) to blind []
○ **qorro•n njërin sy** to pretend not to see/notice,
turn a blind eye
qorrollis• vt 1 to make [] giddy 2 to humiliate [] in
front of others
qorrollis•et vpr (Colloq) to stumble and fall on an
unfamiliar path
qorrsokak nm (np ~ qe) (Colloq) dead end, blind
alley, cul-de-sac, impasse
qorrthi adv = **qorras**
qos• vt (Colloq) to get [something] accomplished/
arranged
qos•et
I § vpr to lose one's facial hair: be left beardless/
barefaced
II § vp impers it works out all right for <>, <> comes
out okay
***qosarak** adj beardless, hairless
qosarake nf goat with no goatee
qose adj, nf with masc agreement 1 (man) without facial hair: beardless (man) 2 (Fig) in folk tales,
prankster who takes the form of a smooth-cheeked
boy usually in the company of a bald man
***qosëm** adj (i) rich
qostek nm 1 chain on a pocket watch: watch chain
2 hobbling chain: hobble
qostër nf pedal-operated grindstone for sharpening
tools
qoshe nf 1 (Colloq) corner, angle; far corner; hidden
corner, cranny 2 cosy nook by the hearth; best place
to be
○ **qoshe e ngrohtë** (Pej) cushy job
○ **qoshe e rehatshme** soft job
qosheli adj (Colloq) with sharp corners/angles
qoshk nm (np ~ qe) 1 corner, edge, angle 2 oriel,
covered balcony 3 storage shed in the corner of a
yard; kiosk, newspaper stand
qoshtere nf rabbet plane
***qoshtër** nf whetstone
qoti adj (Colloq) timid and somewhat moronic; be-
fuddled
***qoth** nm [Ornit] scops owl (Otus scops)
qu•het vpr to have the name _, be called _
○ **quhet se** _ it is said that _
qua•n vt 1 to call [] (by a name); give [] a name:
name [] 2 (Fig) to consider/declare [] to be _
○ [] **qua•n të udhës** to deem [] to be quite proper,
consider [] to be all right
○ **e qua•n veten (si)** {} to pretend to be {}, represent oneself as {}
quajt stem for pdef, opt, adm, part < **qua•n**
***quanjetore** nf (Old) [Ling] nominative case
quar nm 1 livestock shed; storage cellar; prison
2 (Fig) lair, den

*qu'et adj (i) = zgju'ar

*quk nm beak = qep, sqep

quk· vt 1 to peck at [ ], peck 2 to pierce; prick; (of an insect) sting, bite 3 (Fig) to sting/prick [ ] with words

qu'k·et vpr 1 to get pricked, prick oneself 2 to peck/scratch at one another

qu'ka np freckles

quka'çik̈ë nf freckle = qu'k̈ë

quka'li adj (Colloq) = qukalo'sh

quka'lo's adj = qukalo'sh

quka'lo's· vt 1 to freckle 2 to peck

qukalo'sh adj, n (person) whose face is pock-marked/freckled

quka'n nm [Ornit] turkey, turkey cock, tom turkey

quka'pi'k

I § adj having spots on the face or body: freckled, dappled, mottled

II § nm 1 [Ornit] woodpecker *2 pockmark

∘ qukapiku i gjelbër [Ornit] green woodpecker Picus viridis L.

∘ qukapiku i zi [Ornit] black woodpecker Dryocopus martius L., Picus martius L.

qu'ka-qu'ka adj freckled

quka's stem for 1st sg pres, 1st & 3rd pl pres, 2nd & 3rd sg subj <quka't·

quka't· vt to peck = quk·

qu'k̈ë nf 1 freckle; pock-mark 2 dot 3 dimple 4 [Ornit] turkey hen 5 (Reg) = kukuva'jk̈ë

∘ qu'k̈ë dhjami blob of grease

qu'k̈ëç adj concave

qu'k̈ël nf 1 (Dimin) <qu'k̈ë 2 [Ornit] blackbird

qu'k̈ëli'n̈ë nf (Dimin) small freckle/pockmark/dimple

qu'k̈ës adj having a freckled/pock-marked face

quki'm nm ger 1 <quko'·n 2 peck

qu'km̈ë nf (Colloq) stinger (of an insect)

quko'·n OR quko's· vt, vi to peck at [ ], peck

qukti's· vt to hit, strike

*quku'l̈ë nf (Ornit) large crow

qull

I § nm mush, mash, pap

II § adj soggy

III § adj, n (Colloq) (person) who is slow and clumsy

∘ Mos u fut/hyr në atë qull! "Don't go into that mush!" ⋄ Don't get involved in that dirty business!

∘ Të vraftë qulli! "May the mush kill you!" (Tease) (said to someone who can't do something very easy) If you can't do something this easy you might as well be dead: Maybe it's just too much for you!

∘ U dogj nga qulli, e i fryn edhe kosit. "He was burned by the mush, and he blows even on the yogurt." (Prov) Once bitten, twice shy.

qull· vt 1 to make [ ] completely wet: drench, soak 2 (Fig Colloq) to botch [ ] up completely = qullo's·

qu'll·et vpr to get soaked; become soggy

qulla'c adj, n (Pej) = qullama'c

qullama'c adj, n (Impol) (person) who is slow and clumsy

qullama'n adj (Impol) slow and clumsy

qullama'ne nf [Ichth] bluntsnout snake eel (Echelus myrus)

qullani'k nm [Food] 1 corn pone 2 cheese pie made with corn meal and oil

qulla'sh

I § adj, n (Colloq Pej) (person) who is slow and clumsy

II § nm [Food] large pie made with leeks or cabbage and with eggs and rice between thick layers of dough

qullave'c nm = qullama'c

qu'll̈ëm adj (i) = qu'll̈ët

qu'll̈ës adj = qu'll̈ët

qu'll̈ët adj (i) 1 soggy; mushy; slushy 2 flabby 3 (Fig) slow and clumsy

*qull'ni nf jellied meat, aspic

qull'ni'k nm cheese pie

qullo'·n vt (Colloq) to make [ ] wet through and through: drench, soak

qull'opiẗë nf [Food] 1 large round pie with a thick underlayer of dough; thick layer of dough covered with hot butter 2 thin corn pone fermented in cold water

qullo's· vt 1 (Colloq) to make [ ] sopping wet: drench, soak = qull· 2 (Fig) to botch [ ] up completely, make a botch of [ ]: make a sopping mess of [ ]

qullo's·et vpr 1 (Colloq) = qu'll·et 2 to become over-ripe and soft 3 (Fig) to get completely botched up

qullo'sje nf ger <qullo's·, qullo's·et

qullo'sur adj (i) (Colloq) = qu'llur

qullto'·het vpr to become mushy/soggy

qullto'·n vt to make [ ] into mush: make [ ] soggy, mash

qu'llur adj (i) drenched, soggy

qum̈ësht nm 1 milk 2 white liquid resembling milk 3 (Reg) = hírr̈ë

∘ qum̈ësht i bardhë milk-white

∘ qum̈ështi i bleẗëve bee nectar

∘ qum̈ësht dal̈ëndysheje choice food, delicacy; very rare and precious thing

∘ qum̈ësht i dhirẗë goat milk

∘ qum̈ësht i leshẗë ewe's milk

∘ qum̈ësht nga delja shterp̈ë "milk from a sterile ewe" blood from a turnip, wasted effort

∘ qum̈ësht i parrahur whole milk (before the butter is extracted)

∘ qum̈ësht i ploẗë whole milk

∘ qum̈ësht i rrahur "churned milk" (milk with some of the butterfat removed) skimmed milk

∘ qum̈ësht i shkartisur milk mixed with water, watered-down milk

*qum̈ësht'ar

I § n [Dairy] dairyman

II § adj * (Old) = gjita'r

qum̈ësht'i'm nm [Biol] lactation

qum̈ësht'o'r

I § adj 1 [Dairy] giving a high yield of milk: lactific 2 [Dairy] milk-inducing: lactogenic 3 unweaned, suckling; still young and immature 4 soft and milky white; milky white

II § nm 1 custard; large custard pie with a thick underlayer of dough 2 (Old) [Dairy] dairyman who sells the milk of sheep or goats pastured in the mountains

qum̈ësht'o're nf 1 [Bot] common dandelion (Taraxacum officinale) 2 [Bot] euphorbia (Euphorphia) 3 [Astron] Milky Way 4 [Dairy] farm animal that gives a high yield of milk: milk cow, milking goat/ewe

qum̈ësht'o'riz nm [Food] rice pudding

qum̈ësht'shi'ẗës n [Dairy] seller of milk

qupla'k nm pebble = gurale'c

quplo·het vpr (of a cutting tool) to become dull

*****qur** nm (Old) turkey cock, tom turkey

*****qu're** nf (Old) turkey hen

*****qurk** nm = çurg

qurr'a np nasal mucus: snot

qurr'ac adj (Pej) = qurra'sh

qurr'ak adj (Pej) = qurra'sh

qurr'an nm, adj (Pej) (person) who gets on one's nerves by constant sniffling: sniffler, sniveler

qurr'ash adj, nm 1 (Pej) (person) having a runny nose, (person) who fails to wipe a runny nose: snot-nose 2 (Fig) (person) of weak/cowardly character; (person) who is constantly complaining: sniveler

qurr'ave'c adj (Pej) = qurra'sh

qurr'o·het vpr (Colloq) to get (one's face) all covered with nasal mucus

qurr'o·n vt 1 (Colloq) to soil/soak [] with nasal mucus 2 (Fig Pej) to botch [] up completely

qurr'os· vt (Colloq) = qurro'·n

qurr'os·et vpr (Colloq) = qurro'·het

*****qut** interj shoo! scram!

*****qy** (Reg Tosk) = ky

*****qyç** nm = kyç

qyçeni'c̈ nf bolt (as for a door or a gun)

qy'e nf (Colloq) bottom of a mountain slope: foot of the mountain

qyfte'r nm fruit jam; dried fruit jam

qyfy'r nm (Colloq) wisecrack; something done in fun

qyfyre'ma'dh adj (Colloq) wise-cracker; joker, clown

qyfyre'xhi nm (np ˜ nj) (Colloq) 1 = qyfyrema'dh 2 (Pej) lazy clown, wisecracking loafer

*****qy'kën** nf [Ornit] swan (Cygnus)

qyl
  I § nm 1 mud 2 (Colloq) free hand-out, something for nothing: freebie 3 (Colloq Pej) lazy person who expects something for nothing; inept and lazy person
  II § adv 1 (Colloq) without paying anything, for nothing 2 in vain, for nothing

qyla'f nm 1 white fez with a small tassel 2 [Bot] calyx

qyla'h nm 1 (Old) tall fez worn by dervishes = karru'le *2 = qyla'f

qyla'xhi nm (np ˜ nj) (Colloq Pej) person who habitually avoids paying his share for food and drink: freeloader, sponger

qyl'içe adj 1 (of metals) unalloyed, pure 2 (Fig) unsophisticated, naive; honest

qyl'xhi' = qylaxhi'

qyly'k nm large pickaxe with a broad blade

qyly'ke nf 1 large axe with a broad blade 2 = qyly'k

*****qyly'm** = qili'm

*****qy'me** = qi'me

qyme'z nm chicken coop, dovecote

*****qy'me'z** nm worm that infests sores

qymsy're np fem 1 olives that have been knocked to the ground; stalks of grain left in the field after reaping 2 (Fig) odds and ends of no value

qymy'r
  I § nm 1 charcoal 2 stifling gas produced by incomplete combustion of hot coals: coal gas 3 (Colloq) coal
  II § adj dark as coal: black
  ∘ **qymyr i bardhë** water (as a source of hydroelectric power)
  ∘ **qymyr guri** coal

∘ **qymyri i kaltër** energy generated by the ebb and flow of tide: tidal power

∘ **qymyr shtazor** animal black

qymyr'bër'ës n maker of charcoal (from wood)

*****qymyr'dru(r)** nm charcoal

qymyr'gur nm coal

qymyr'gur'or adj 1 containing coal 2 made of coal; derived from coal 3 of or pertaining to coal mining

qymyr'mbajt'ës adj coal-bearing

qymyr'or adj = qymyrmbajtës

qymyr'shit'ës n charcoal seller

qymyr'ta'r n 1 person who makes charcoal from wood: charcoal maker 2 (Old) person who makes and sells charcoal

qymyr'xhi nm (np ˜ nj) = qymyrta'r

qyng nm (np ˜ gje) tube, duct, pipe, conduit

qy'ngje nf 1 = qyng 2 sugar cube

qyp nm 1 tall, round potbellied clay vessel for keeping wet or liquid foodstuffs 2 (CrudeImpolite) person's head/mind: bean, thick skull 3 (Crude Insult) numskull, blockhead, dimwit

qy'pe nf 1 small jug 2 (Pet) little girl with a plump little body

qypërl'o·het vpr (Colloq) to become inebriated: get potted, get drunk, get stewed

qy'p'ës nm two-handled clay jug

qy'pje nf variety of pear with large yellowish-tan fruit that ripens in September

qyp'or adj pear-shaped

qyp'ore nf small single-handled clay pot used to culture yogurt

*****qyp'thi** adv with the open end upside down

qyq nm (np ˜ ër) 1 person without family or friends, person left all alone in the world 2 unfortunate person: wretch
  ∘ **ësh·të qyq në degë** (of a boy) to know how to get along by himself

qyq'a'n adj = qyqar

qyq'a'r adj, n 1 (person) left without family or friends; (person) all alone in the world 2 (person) who has suffered much misfortune and unhappiness: hapless wretch 3 totally inept (person)

qy'qe nf 1 cuckoo (Cuculus canorus) 2 (Fig) woman left all alone in the world (with no husband and no children); miserable female
  ∘ [] **bë·n (fare) qyqe** to leave [] feeling wretched (by one's merciless criticism)
  ∘ **qyqe bregu** woman with a poisonous tongue and an evil eye
  ∘ **qyqja me çafkë** [Ornit] great spotted cuckoo Clamator glandarius, Cuculus grandurius
  ∘ **ësh·të³ˢᵍ qyqe në degë** "be cuckoo on the branch" (of a girl) to know how to get along by herself
  ∘ **qyqe nga mendja** "cuckoo in the mind" featherbrained, stupid

qy'q'ër np < qyq

qy'qja interj woman's address to another woman, expressing sadness or surprise: my goodness! dear me!; you poor thing!

qyq'o·het vpr to be left all alone in the world

qyq'o·n vt to leave [] all alone in the world

qyr· vt = këqyr·

qyre'k nm 1 garden spade 2 shovel *3 dustpan

○ **qyreku i bukëve** baker's paddle (for pushing bread into the oven)

○ **qyreku i zjarrit** cinder scoop = **kaci**

***qyreta r** *n* inspector; observer = **këqy rës**

qy rë *nf* blunt side of a bladed tool

qyrk *nm (np ˜ qe)* **1** heavy winter cloak made of or lined with fur **2** *(Fig)* covering, cloak

qyrk pun u e s *n* = **qyrkta r**

qyrk ta r *n (Old)* person who makes fur cloaks: furrier

qyrle k *n* [*Ornit*] = **kll nz ë**

qyryly k *nm* [*Ornit*] redshank *(Tringa totanus L.)*

○ **qyrylyku këmbëbojëhiri** [*Ornit*] green sandpiper *Tringa ochropus L.*

○ **qyrylyku i madh** [*Ornit*] greenshank *Tringa nebularia Gunn.*

○ **qyrylyku i murmë** [*Ornit*] spotted redshank *Tringa erythropus*

○ **qyrylyku sqephollë** [*Ornit*] marsh sandpiper *Tringa stagnatilis L.*

○ **qyrylyku i vogël** [*Ornit*] common sandpiper *Tringa hypoleucos L.*

qyrr = **qurr**

***qyski** = **qysqi**

qysqi *nf* **1** crowbar, pry **2** pestle

○ **qysqi mine** [*Min*] drill rod

qysh

I § *adv conj* **1** *(Reg)* how **2** how is it possible!

II § *prep (acc) pcl (Reg)* beginning from the time of/ that: since

○ **qysh at ë herë** since then

○ **qysh kur** since the time when __

qy sh e *nf* way something is done: the how

***qysh k** *nm* condition

qysh ku r *adv* some time ago; for some time

qysh ta sh *OR* **qysh tashti** *adv* right now, immediately

qyte t *nm* **1** city, town **2** urban life **3** *(Collec)* urban community

qytet a r

I § *adj* **1** *(Book)* urban **2** [*Law*] pertaining to civil law: civil **3** *(Book)* characteristic of civilized life/ behavior/society: civilized

II § *n* **1** city dweller, urbanite **2** citizen

qytet ar ësi *nf* official right to live in a particular city; city citizenship

qytet ar i *nf* **1** citizenship = **shtetësi** **2** urban life **3** *(Old)* urban upbringing

qyte t as

I § *adj* urban

II § *n* city dweller, urbanite

qytet ër i *nf* civilization

qytet ër i m *nm ger* **1** < **qytetëro ·n, qytetëro ·het** **2** civilization

qytet ër o ·het *vpr* to become civilized

qytet ër o ·n *vt* to civilize

qytet ër u a r *adj (i)* civilized

qytet ër u e s *adj* civilizing

qyte t ës *adj* operating within city limits: urban

qyte t ëse *nf (Old)* secondary school offering general education in towns

qytet ësi *nf (Old)* = **qytetari**

qyte t-hero *nm (HistPK)* city awarded special status for its special contributions to the country: heroic city

qyte t-muze *nm* city with many historic buildings and monuments: museum city

qytet o r *adj* operating within city limits: urban = **urba n**

qyte t-shte t *nm* [*Hist*] city-state

qyte t th *nm dimin* small town

qyte z ë *nf* **1** inhabited center of an old castle; citadel **2** organized community; small town

qy të *nf* **1** butt of a gun; gun stock **2** blunt side of a bladed tool

qyty k *nm (Colloq)* **1** tree trunk; wooden post; thick wooden beam **2** *(Fig)* person carrying the main burden **3** *(FigImpolite)* backward oaf **4** *(Old)* thick register used for keeping official accounts

Rr

r [rë] *nf* **1** the consonant letter "r" **2** the apical flap represented by the letter "r"

*ra *np* (të) *fem* <**re** (e) **1** young women; brides, daughters-in-law **2** news

ra *stem for pdef, opt* <**bie**₁ fell; hit
  ○ **Ra fyti e na mbyti** "The throat fell and suffocated us" It was greed that caused such a shameful end.
  ○ <> **ra lota** it is <>'s turn
  ○ <> **ra një nur** (of a woman) <> has taken on a new and more beautiful appearance, <> got prettier
  ○ <> **ranë progjet** (*Impol*) <>'s power/strength has faded
  ○ **Nuk ra sheqeri në ujë!** "the sugar did not fall in water" (*Iron*) it's not so terrible! it's no big deal! don't worry about it!

RAB *abbrev* <**Republika Arabe e Bashkuar** [*Hist*] UAR = United Arab Republic

rabat *nm* [*Commerc*] retail markup

*rabec *nm* (*Reg*) [*Ornit*] = **trumcak**

rabeckë *OR* **rabekë** *nf* (*Reg*) [*Ornit*] = **trumcak**
  ○ **rabeckë gamile** [*Ornit*] ostrich

*rabë *nf* cart for rubbish, garbage wagon

rabin *nm* [*Relig*] rabbi

rabush *nm* **1** inedible thick stalk of an onion; tasseled onion stalk **2** tally rod = **çetelë 3** (*Fig Crude*) numbskull, dumb dodo ***4** (*Old*) = **rrabush**

*rabushim *nm ger* (*Old*) <**rabusho**•*n*

*rabusho•*n vt* (*Old*) = **rrabusho**•*n*

racator *adj, n* purebred, thoroughbred

racë *nf* **1** race **2** [*Zool*] breed

*racërisht *adv* racially

racial *adj* **1** racial **2** (*Pej*) racist

racion *nm* ration

racional *adj* rational

racionalist *n* [*Phil*] rationalist

racionalisht *adv* rationally

racionalizator *n* person who makes innovative improvements in the workplace: innovator

racionalizëm *nm* (*Book*) **1** [*Phil*] rationalism **2** rationality

racionalizim *nm ger* **1** <**racionalizo**•*n*, **racionalizo**•*het* **2** application of principles of scientific management: rationalization

racionalizo•*n vt* to apply principles of scientific management to []: rationalize

racionalizuar *adj* (*i*) rationalized

racionalizues *adj* applying principles of scientific management: rationalizing

racionim *nm ger* <**racionizo**•*n*

raciono•*n vt* to ration; apportion

racionuar *adj* (*i*) rationed

racist *adj, n* racist

racizëm *nm* racism

racor *adj* **1** racial **2** purebred, thoroughbred **3** eugenic **4** racist

*raçinë *nf* cap, beret

radar *nm* [*Spec*] radar

---

radiator *nm* radiator

radikal *nm* (*Book*) (political) radical

radikalisht *adv* (*Book*) radically

radikalizëm *nm* (*Book*) radicalism

radio *nf* radio

radio *formativ* (*Book*) radio-

radioaktiv *adj* [*Phys*] radioactive

radioaktivitet *nm* [*Phys*] radioactivity

radioamator *n* ham radio operator

radioamatorizëm *nm* ham radio operation

radioantenë *nf* radio antenna

*radioaparat *nm* radio receiving set, wireless: radio

radiodhënës *nm* radio transmitter

radiofikim *nm ger* **1** [*Spec*] <**radiofiko**•*n* **2** radio installation

radiofiko•*n vt* [*Spec*] to bring radio to [], install radio apparatus in [], provide [] with a radio installation

radiofonik *adj* involving transmission by radio

radiografi *nf* **1** radiography **2** (*Colloq*) radiograph, X ray

radiografik *adj* radiographic

radiogram *nm* radiogram

radiogramafon *nm* combined radio set and phonograph: radio-phonograph console

radioizotop *nm* radioisotope

radiolog *n* radiologist

radiologji *nf* radiology

radiologjik *adj* radiological

radioloje *nf* counter-espionage use of enemy's secret radio to send misleading messages

radiolokacion *nm* [*Spec*] radiolocation

radiolokator *nm* radiolocator

radiomarrës *adj* radio receiving

radionderlidhje *nf* radio connection, radio communication

radiopërhapje *nf* radio diffusion

radioskopi *nf* [*Med*] radioscopy

radioskopik *adj* [*Med*] radioscopic

radiostacion *nm* radio station

radioshkrehës *nm* [*Min*] radio detonator/fuse

radioteknik
  I § *n* radio technician, radio engineer
  II § *adj* pertaining to or engaged in radio technology

radioteknikë *nf* radio engineering

radiotelegrafi *nf* radiotelegraphy

radiotelegrafik *adj* radiotelegraphic

radiotelegram *nm* radio telegram

radiotelevizion *nm* radio and television broadcast station

radioteleviziv *adj* pertaining to radio and television broadcasting

radioterapi *nf* radiotherapy

radiovalë *nf* [*Phys*] radio wave

radis *stem for 1st sg pres, pl pres, 2nd & 3rd sg subj, pind* <**radit**•

radist n person who sends and receives radio signals: radioman, wireless operator

radit· vt to prepare [food]
  ∘ **radit· për** [] to look after [], take care of [], see to []

radites n food preparer, cook

raditje nf preparation (of food)

radium nm [Chem] radium (Ra)

radrizator nm [Tech] rectifier

***radhla** adv = radhas

radhanik nm [Food] pastry snail = dredhanik, rrethanik

radhas OR **radhazi** adv 1 each in turn, taking turns 2 in succession, in a row

radhe
  I § nf 1 series in linear order: row; tier; rank; queue 2 serial order 3 position in a serial order: turn = red 4 instance, time; occasion
  II § adv (Colloq) = radhazi
  ∘ **e kështu me radhë** and so on (and so forth)
  ∘ **Eja në radhë!** "Come into rows!" [Mil] Line up!
  ∘ **radhë e pa radhë** in no particular order

radhë-radhë adv row after row, in rows

radhim nm ger 1 = radhitje 2 objects or people in a straight line: straight row, column 3 [Mil] line-up; rank, formation
  ∘ **Radhimi djathtas/majtas!** [Mil] Dress right/left!

radhiqe nf [Bot] chicory, succory (Cichorium intybus L)

radhis stem for 1st sg pres, pl pres, 2nd & 3rd sg subj, pind <radhit·

radhit· vt 1 to arrange [] in order; list [] in order 2 [Publ] to set [] in type 3 (Fig) to rank [] in comparison

radhit·et vpr 1 to take one's proper place in an ordered group; line up 2 (Fig) to enter the ranks, join the team 3 (Fig) to get ranked in a comparison, be comparable: rank

radhites n compositor, typesetter

radhitje nf ger 1 <radhit·, radhit·et 2 arrangement, order 3 [Publ] bed of type composed in rows for printing: galley

radho·n vt = radhit·

radholi obl <radhua

radhor nm 1 chain of rocks sticking out of the ground; boulder 2 ornamental chain worn as a necklace 3 (Old) notebook, ledger

***radhore** nf(Old) list

***radhos·** vt = radhit·

***radhtor** adj(Old) ordinal

radhua nm (obl ˜ oi, np ˜ onj) (Old) 1 notebook, ledger 2 ornamental chain worn as a necklace

radhues nm [Publ] = radhites

rafineri nf refinery (for refining raw materials)

rafinim nm ger 1 <rafino·n 2 refinement

rafino·n vt to refine [raw material]

rafinuar adj (i) 1 refined 2 (Fig Colloq) cunningly sly

***rafsh** = rrafsh

***rafshatak** adj flat, level

***rafshazi** adv rrafshazi

***rafshnalt** nm plateau, upland = rrafshnaltë

***rafshore** nf 1 plain 2 [Geom] plane

raft nm 1 cupboard, cabinet 2 shelf

***rag** nm = ragnicë

ragabardhë adj, nm (variety of grape) with large white fruit

ragade np [Med] rhagades

***ragazi** nm variety of grape with large black fruit

***ragnicë** nf canvas cloth, canvas

ragu nf [Food] ragout

***ragushë** nf ewe with horns

Raguzë nf Ragusa (Dubrovnik)

Raguzhë nf (Old) = Raguzë

***ragjë** nf jacket made of coarse material

rahani nf grape juice, grape must

***rahat** = rehat

raja nf 1 [Hist] non-Moslem subject of the Ottoman Empire: raya 2 (Old Colloq) poor downtrodden peasant; poor oppressed peasantry, the little people 3 (Pej) servile/obsequious person

raje nf = raja

rajë nf [Ichth] = raxhë

rajon nm 1 large area with distinctive characteristics: region, zone 2 municipal district: ward

rajonal adj 1 regional 2 of or pertaining to a municipal district/ward

rajonizim nm ger [Spec] <rajonizo·n

rajonizo·n vt [Spec] to divide an area into districts

Rajshtag nm Reichstag

raketahedhes
  I § adj [Mil] used for launching rockets; having rocket-launching capability
  II § nf rocket launcher

raketambajtes adj, nm [Mil] (plane/ship) armed with rockets: missile carrier

raketë nf 1 rocket; rocket ship 2 [Mil] missile; rocket flare 3 [Sport] racket
  ∘ **raketë ajër-ajër** [Mil] air-to-air missile

raki nf raki
  ∘ **raki dëllinje** gin (liquor)

Rakip nm Rakip (male name)

rakishites nm raki merchant; liquor dealer

rakit nm [Med] = rakitizëm

***rakitë** nf [Bot] white willow (Salix alba)

rakitik
  I § adj, n (person) afflicted by rickets; rachitic
  II § adj weak and spindly

rakitizëm nm [Med] rachitis, rickets

rakord nm [Tech] (pipe) coupling

rakorderi np [Tech] (pipe) fittings, accessories

rakurs nm foreshortening

***ram** nm = rem

***ramas** adv prostrate

ramazan nm [Relig] Ramazan, Ramadan

rameçë nf [Bot] herbaceous swamp plant used to make brooms: goldmoss sedum (Sedum acre)

ramë nf [Tech] frame

***ramë**
  I § 1st pl pdef <bie₁·
  II § part (Reg Gheg) <bie₁· = rënë

***ramët** adj (i) (Old) of copper/brass; copper-colored

Ramiz nm Ramiz (male name)

***ramtar** n (Old) coppersmith = remtar

***rancë** nf hammock

***randis·** vt (Reg Tosk) = ujit·

***rând** (Reg Gheg) = rënd

ra·në
I § *3rd pl pdef* <bie$_1$· they fell/hit
II § *part* <bie$_1$· (*Reg Gheg*)

rânë
I § *nf(Reg Gheg)* = rërë
II § *part* <bie$_1$· (*Reg Gheg*)

rang *nm (np ~ gje)* rank; level

rangall *adj (Old)* jaded

rangatare *nf. adj* (woman) who does the household chores

range *nf* 1 household chore, housework 2 (*Reg*) duty, charge, responsibility

rangull = rrangull

rangje *np* goods and chattels; personal effects = rraqe

ranishtë OR **ranishte** *nf* 1 sandy shore/beach; sand-covered area 2 sandpit

rânme *nf (e) (Reg Gheg)* playing (of an instrument)

ranor
I § *adj* sandy
II § *nm* sandstone

ranxhë *nf* [Ichth] spotted weever (*Trachinus araneus*)
  ○ **ranxhë helmuese** [Ichth] lesser weever *Echiichthys vipera*
  ○ **ranxhë rrezake** [Ichth] streaked weever *Trachinus radiatus*

rapa-qapa *adv* in a jumble/muddle, topsy-turvy

rapatë *nf* stripping tool; rasp

rapatupa *adv* beating around the bush

rapeshë *nf* = arapeshë

raport *nm* 1 report 2 relation, relationship; ratio, proportion
  ○ **raport i anasjellë** inverse relation
  ○ **ësh-të me raport** (*Colloq*) to be on sick leave

raportim *nm ger* <raporto·n

raporto·n *vt, vi* 1 to report; deliver a report; give a formal presentation at a meeting 2 (*Colloq*) to inform on [someone], give information secretly about [someone]

raportor *nm* [Geom] instrument with a graduated arc for measuring angles: protractor

raportues *nm* person who delivers a report: reporter

rapsall *nm (Reg Tosk)* [Agr] variety of wheat with long awns

rapsinë *nf* = rapsall

rapsod *nm* singer of folk epics; rhapsodist

rapsodi *nf* folk epic; rhapsody

raptimë *nf* rattling noise, clatter

rapto·n *vi* to make a rattling noise, clatter

ra·rë *part* <bie$_1$· = rënë

ras *nm* [Mus] bow for the bowed lute

rasat *nm* 1 seedling (in a plant nursery); seedbed (in a plant nursery) 2 fish eggs used to stock a pool or lake 3 (*Old*) breed/stock (of domestic animals) 4 (*Fig Colloq*) (of people) stock, family, lineage

ra·së *nf* 1 [Ling] (grammatical) case 2 (*Colloq*) = rast 3 [Relig] long black robe worn by Orthodox priest

raskal *nm (np ~ j)* grape leaf

raskapi *nf* utter fatigue, exhaustion

raskapi·t *vt* to tire [] out to the point of exhaustion; overstrain, overexert

raskapit·et *vpr* to become exhausted; overexert oneself

raskapitje *nf ger* <raskapi·t·, raskapíte

raskapitur *adj (i)* tired out, exhausted; overstrained, overexerted

rasketë *nf* [Tech] scraper

rasketim *nm ger* [Tech] <rasketo·n

rasketo·n *vt* [Tech] to scrape

raskutë *nf* cave in the rocks, rock cave

rasor *adj* [Ling] of or pertaining to case, by means of a distinction in case

rast *nm* 1 case; occasion; circumstance 2 accidental circumstance: accident, chance 3 opportunity, chance 4 [Law Ling] case 5 cause, reason
  ○ **rast i pastër** [Sport] wide open shot

rastëm *adj (i)* apposite; convenient

rastërisht (*Reg Tosk*) = rastësisht

rastësi *nf* 1 chance event: accident 2 [Phil] chance

rastësishëm *adj (i)* of accidental character: accidental, chance, fortuitous, casual

rastësisht *adv* 1 accidentally, unintentionally; upon occasion, occasionally 2 by (mere) chance, accidentally, fortuitously

rastësor *adj* = rastësishëm

rastis·
I § *vi* 1 to happen to be (somewhere), be (somewhere) by chance 2 to happen by chance, happen accidentally
II § *vt (Colloq)* to happen to meet []: run into []
  ○ <> **rastis·** _ (*Colloq*) <> has the occasion/opportunity to _; <> chances/happens to {}

rastisje *nf ger* 1 <rastis· 2 = rastësí

rastit *adj (i)* 1 by accident: fortuitous, accidental, chance; adventitious 2 occasional; irregular

rastnisht (*Reg Gheg*) = rastësisht

rastor *adj* = rastësishëm

rastshëm *adj (i)* = rastësishëm

rashë *nf* 1 skirt worn under a sleeveless smock; velvet skirt 2 silk chemise (as a wedding garment)

ra·shë *1st sg pdef* <bie$_1$· I fell/hit
  ○ **O rashë o vdiqa.** "Either I fell or I died." It's that or else. There's really no choice.

rashëm *adj (i)* falling; deciduous

rashqel *nm (Reg)* rake = grabujë

ratas *adv* horizontally

ratë
I § *part (Reg)* <bie$_1$·
II § *pred (Reg)* in horizontal position: fallen, lying down

ratifikim *nm ger* 1 [Dipl] <ratifiko·n 2 ratification 3 ratified document

ratifiko·n *vt* [Dipl] to ratify

ratifikues *adj* ratifying

Rauf *nm* Rauf (male name)

raund *nm* 1 [Sport] round (in boxing) 2 (*Fig*) one of a series of encounters between two parties: round

raven *nm* [Bot] rhubarb (*Rheum*)

ravë *nf* 1 mountain trail/path; path opened up through snow 2 trail, track, trace 3 (*Fig*) well-worn path; proven path

ravg = rravg

ravijëzim *nm ger* 1 <ravijëzo·n, ravijëzo·het 2 outline, schematic

ravijëzo·het *vpr* to begin to appear in outline: take shape

ravijëzo·n *vt* 1 to draw an outline around [] 2 (*Fig*) to outline, delineate

ravis·ë *nf (Reg Gheg)* sketch, drawing

ravitë *nf* alluvial/silty soil: alluvium

raviz = ravijëz

raxhë *nf* [*Ichth*] = rraxhë

 ○ **raxhë e bardhë** [*Ichth*] white skate *Raja (Rostroraja) alba*

 ○ **raxhë bishtshkurtër** [*Ichth*] blond ray *Raja (Raja) brachyura*

 ○ **raxhë e butë** [*Ichth*] Spotted ray *Raja (Raja) montagui*

 ○ **raxhë ferracake** [*Ichth*] shagreen ray *Raja (Leucoraja) fullonica*

 ○ **raxhë gurësh** [*Ichth*] Thornback ray *Raja (Raja) clavata*

 ○ **raxhë laroshe** [*Ichth*] Undulate ray *Raja undulata*

 ○ **raxhë pendëzezë** [*Ichth*] gray skate *Raja batis*

 ○ **raxhë pikaloshe** [*Ichth*] speckled ray *Raja (Raja) polystigma*

 ○ **raxhë e rrumbullakët** [*Ichth*] sandy ray *Raja (Leucoraja) circularis*

 ○ **raxhë syzake** [*Ichth*] brown ray *Raja (Raja) miraletus*

 ○ **raxhë turigjatë** [*Ichth*] longnosed skate *Raja (Dipturus) oxyrinchus*

 ○ **raxhë turishkurtër** [*Ichth*] rough ray *Raja (Raja) radula*

 ○ **raxhë thumbore** [*Ichth*] = raxhë gurësh

 ○ **raxhë yllzake** [*Ichth*] starry ray *Raja (Raja) asterias* = ferrzë

razaki *nf* variety of grape with thick-skinned long red fruit = korith

*__razi__ *adj* disposed, minded, ready

*__razi__ *nf* devoutness, devotion

RDGj *abbrev* < **Republika Demokratike Gjermane** GDR or DDR = German Democratic Republic

re

 I § *invar* attention

 II § *2nd sg pdef* < bie₁ · you (sg) fell/hit

re *nf* 1 cloud 2 (*Reg*) = rrufe 3 (*Reg*) facial expression, countenance 4 (*Old*) permission: leave 5 [*Mus*] second note of a solfeggio scale: re

 ○ **re me breshër** "cloud with hail" 1 irascible person 2 intrepid person who lets nothing stand in his way

re

 I § *adj (e) fem* < ri 1 young 2 new 3 modern

 II § *nf (e)* 1 young girl; member of a youth organization; daughter-in-law 2 report of something new: news; new discovery 3 new arrival; something new, novelty

reagim *nm ger* 1 (*Book*) < reago · *n* 2 reaction

reago · *n vi* to react

reaksion *nm* reaction

reaksionar *adj, n* reactionary

reaktiv

 I § *adj* propelled by reactive force: jet, rocket

 II § *nm* 1 [*Chem*] reagent 2 (*Colloq*) jet (airplane)

reaktor *nm* 1 reactor 2 [*Tech*] apparatus using a chemical reaction as the means of production: reactor

real *adj* 1 real 2 realizable

realist *adj* 1 realistic 2 [*Art Lit*] realist

realisht *adv* 1 in reality, really 2 realistically

realitet *nm* reality

realizëm *nm* realism

realizim *nm ger* 1 < realizo · *n*, realizo · het 2 realization

realizo · het *vpr* to come into existence: be realized

realizo · *n vt* to effectuate, make [] real: realize

realizuar *adj (i)* realized, come true

realizueshëm *adj (i)* realizable

*__rebe__ = rrebe

rebel

 I § *nm* rebel

 II § *adj* rebellious

rebelim *nm ger* 1 < rebelo · *het* 2 rebellion

rebelizëm *nm* rebelliousness

rebelo · *het vpr* to rebel

rebs *nm* [*Med*] pellagra

*__rebull__ *nm* [*Bot*] maple = panjë

rebus *nm* 1 (*Book*) rebus 2 (*Fig*) puzzle

recensent *n* = recensues

recensim *nm ger* 1 < recenso · *n* 2 = recension

recension *nm* critical evaluation: review

recenso · *n vt* (*Book*) to review

recensor *n* (*Book*) = recensues

recensues *n* reviewer

recenzent *n* = recensues

receptor *nm* 1 (telephone) receiver 2 [*Physiol*] receptor

reces *nm* [*Med*] recess

recesiv *adj* [*Med*] recessive

recetë *nf* 1 medical prescription 2 recipe

recidiv

 I § *nm* 1 [*Med*] relapse 2 [*Law*] recidivistic act 3 (*Book*) recidivism

 II § *adj* recidivistic, back-sliding

recidivist *nm* [*Law*] recidivist

recin *nm* 1 [*Bot*] castor bean, castor-oil plant (*Ricinus*) 2 (*Old*) retsina

recinë *nf* [*Bot*] = ricin

reciprocitet *nm* (*Book*) reciprocality

reciprok *adj* reciprocal

reciprokisht *adv* (*Book*) reciprocally

recital *nm* [*Mus*] recital

recitim *nm ger* 1 < recito · *n* 2 recital 3 elocutionary art: elocution

recito · *n vt* to recite [] (expressively and by heart)

recitues *n* eloquent public speaker; person who recites a literary work expressively and by heart

*__reck__ = rreck

reçel *nm* [*Food*] jam

 ○ **reçel shalqiri** watermelon preserves

*__red__ *nm* position in a serial order

redaksi *nf* editorial staff; editorial office/offices

redaksional *adj* engaged in or pertaining to editorial duties: editorial

redaktim *nm ger* 1 < redakto · *n* 2 edition

redakto · *n vt* 1 to edit 2 (*Old*) to be the editor-in-chief

redaktor *n* editor

redaktuar *adj (i)* edited

redaktues *adj, n* (person) who serves/served as editor

redinë *nf* clearing in a forest: glade

redingotë *nf* frock coat, tails

reduktim *nm ger* 1 < redukto · *n* 2 reduction

redukto · *n vt* to reduce

reduktor *nm* [*Tech*] speed reducer

*__redh__ *nm* = rreth

refene' *nf* **1** *(Old)* party with food and drink whose costs are shared by the participants **2** dutch-treat picnic

***refer**' *nm* [*Sport*] referee, umpire = **arbit**ẽr

referạt *nm* lead-off paper at a public forum: discussion paper, conference paper/report, theme paper

referendum *nm* referendum

referent *n* (*Offic Book*) staff member responsible for tracking an area of official interest and reporting it to his chief: watcher

referịm *nm ger* **1** (*Book*) <**refero**'·*n*, **refero**'·*het* **2** short report, paper **3** reference; footnote reference, citation; crossreference

refero'·*het vpr* (*Book*) to have reference to <>; relate to <>

refero'·*n*

I § *vi* (*Book*) to deliver a lecture/report

II § *vt* **1** (*Offic*) to refer [a matter/document] to <>; refer [someone] (to a source) **2** to refer; crossrefer

referụẹs *n* person who delivers a lecture: lecturer, speaker

refkẽtị *nf* heartbeat

refkẽtị·*n vi* to beat rhythmically: pulsate, beat; throb

refkẽtị́m*ẽ* *nf* pulse beat, pulse; beating, beat; throbbing, throb

refleks *nm* reflex

∘ **reflekse të fituara** [*Psych*] acquired reflexes

refleksịon *nm* [*Phys*] reflection

refleksịv *adj* [*Ling*] reflexive

reflektịm *nm ger* **1** <**reflekto**'·*n* **2** (*Book*) reflection

reflekto'·*n vt* to reflect

reflektor *nm* **1** [*Spec*] reflector **2** room heater with an electric reflector

reflektụẹs *adj* reflective, reflecting

reformạtor *n* reformer

reformẽ *nf* reform

reformịm *nm ger* **1** <**reformo**'·*n*, **reformo**'·*het* **2** reform

reformịst *adj, nm* reformist

reformịzẽm *nm* reformism

reformo'·*het vpr* to undergo reform

reformo'·*n vt* to reform

refraktar *adj* (*Book*) refractory

refren *nm* [*Lit Mus*] refrain

refugjat *nm* refugee

refuzịm *nm ger* **1** <**refuzo**'·*n* **2** refusal

refuzo'·*n vt, vi* to refuse

regatẽ *nf* regatta

regẽtị·*n vi* **1** to beat rhythmically: pulsate, beat; throb; (of eyelids) flutter **2** to flicker **3** to sob softly; sputter weakly **4** to gasp for breath; gasp for one's last few breaths, be in the throes of death

regẽtị́m*ẽ* *nf* **1** throbbing of the heart, palpitation **2** dying breath **3** flickering light, flicker **4** flutter; pulsation

regẽtịs· *vi* = **reg**ẽtị·*n*

***reg**ẽtị́z *nf* slight gasp; weak sob

regẽto'·*n vi* = **reg**ẽtị·*n*

regres *nm* (*Book*) regression, regress

regresịv *adj* (*Book*) regressive

***regj** *nm* (*Old*) king

regj· *vt, vi* **1** to tan [hides]; cure; pickle []; preserve; marinate **2** (*Fig*) to toughen [] (by experience or exercise): inure

re'gj·*et vpr* **1** to get tanned/pickled/preserved/marinated: cure **2** (*Fig*) to get toughened up, become hardened/inured; be bedridden for a long time by serious illness

∘ <> **re**'gj·*et*³*ˢᵍ* **lëkura** "<>'s skin is hardened" <> *is* inured

re'gjẹ *nf* **1** tanning **2** (*Fig*) inurement

regjencẽ *nf* regency

regjent *n* regent

***regj**ẽnị *nf* (*Old*) kingdom = **mbret**ẽrị

re'gjẹs

I § *adj* used or involved in the tanning of leather

II § *n* tanner

regjị *nf* **1** [*Theat Cine*] direction (of a film/play); directing (as a profession) **2** (*Collec*) production staff

regjịm *nm* regime

∘ **regjim shtrati** [*Med*] (prescription of) bed rest

regjịment *nm* [*Mil*] regiment

***regjị**ne'shẽ *nf* (*Old*) queen

regjịsor *n* director (of a film/play)

regjịsorịal *adj* directorial

regjịstẽr *nm* register

regjịstrar *n* (*Book*) registrar

regjịstrịm *nm ger* **1** <**regjịstro**'·*n*, **regjịstro**'·*het* **2** recording

regjịstro'·*het vpr* to enroll, sign up, register

regjịstro'·*n vt, vi* **1** to register [] **2** to make a recording of []: record

regjịstrụar *adj* (*i*) registered, enrolled

regjịstrụẹs

I § *nm* registrar

II § *adj* recording

regjịstrụẹshẽm *adj* (*i*) [*Tech*] adjustable

re'gjjẹ *nf ger* <**re**'gj·, **re**'gj·*et*

re'gjjọs· *vt* = **re**'gj·

regjịtar *n* tanner

re'gjjur

I § *adj* (*i*) **1** tanned (of hides); cured; pickled; marinated, steeped; preserved; marinated **2** (*Fig*) toughened; hardened

II § *nn* (*të*) = **re**'gjjẹ

∘ **i regjur me vaj e me uthull** "cured with oil and vinegar" well seasoned by experience

re'gjjura *np* (*të*) pickles

rehabilịto'·*het vpr* (*Book*) to regain one's civil rights

rehabilịto'·*n vt* (*Book*) to restore []'s civil rights; restore []'s good name: rehabilitate

rehanị *nf* grape juice (drunk as a beverage)

rehat

I § *nm* (*Colloq*) = **rehat**ị

II § *adv* (*Colloq*) **1** quietly and without anxiety, in a relaxed manner, at ease **2** without moving: still **3** in comfortable/easy circumstances

∘ **fli/flini rehat!** rest easy! (it's being taken care of)

∘ **Rri/rrini rehat! 1** Keep still! Stop moving around! **2** Don't bother! Don't worry about it!

rehatị *nf* (*Colloq*) peace and quiet, relaxation, calm **2** (*Pej*) laxity **3** comfort

rehato'·*het vpr* (*Colloq*) to become comfortable; find peace and comfort

rehato'·*n vt* (*Colloq*) **1** to calm, soothe **2** to put [] in order, get [] fixed up; take care of [], serve the needs of []; make [] comfortable

rehatshëm *adj (i) (Colloq)* **1** comfortable, restful; quiet and relaxed, peaceful; cosy **2** (of a child) well-behaved

rehen *nm (Old)* = **peng**

rejë *nf* **1** withe **2** curved wooden linchpin securing the plow beam to the ox-yoke **3** piece of wood attached to a log/beam to serve as a drag hook

rejsmus *nm [Tech]* surface gauge

***reketi·n** *vi* = **refketi·n**

***reketim** *nm* pulsation of blood: pulse

***reketimë** *nf* = **refketimë**

***reketit·** *vi* = **refketi·n**

***reketo·n** *vi* = **refketi·n**

reklamë *nf* publicity; advertising; advertisement

reklamim *nm ger* < **reklamo·n**

reklamist *n (Pej)* self-promoter, boaster

reklamo·n *vt* **1** to advertise, publicize **2** *(Pej)* to hawk [ ], huckster

reklamues
  I § *adj* of or pertaining to advertising: promotional
  II § *n* **1** advertiser, publicist **2** *(Pej)* self-promoter, boaster
  III § *nm [Commerc]* advertisement

rekomande *adj* sent by registered mail: certified, registered

rekomandim *nm ger* **1** < **rekomando·n 2** recommendation **3** proposal of a course of action: advice

rekomando·n *vt* to recommend

rekomandues *nm* person making a recommendation/proposal: recommender, proposer

rekomandueshëm *adj (i)* able to be recommended; advisable

rekord
  I § *nm* record (of achievement/production)
  II § *adj* (establishing a) record

rekordist
  I § *n* record setter/breaker
  II § *adj* record-setting

rekordmbajtës *n [Sport]* record-holder

rekordmen *n* person who has achieved a record performance: record holder/setter/breaker

rekrut *nm* (military) recruit

rekrutim *nm ger* **1** < **rekruto·n 2** recruitment

rekruto·n *vt* to recruit

***rekti·n** *vi* = **regeti·n**

***rektifikim** *nm ger* **1** < **rektifiko·n 2** rectification

***rektifiko·n** *vt* **1** to rectify **2** *[Tech]* to grind, reface

***rektimë** *nf* = **regetimë**

***rekto·n** *vi* **1** = **regetis· 2** to sob quietly

rektor *n* rector (of a college)

rektorat *nm* administration (building) of a college: rectorate

rektues *adj [Med]* pulsatile

rekuiem *nm (Book)* requiem

rekuizim *nm ger* **1** < **rekuizo·n 2** confiscation; requisition

rekuizitë *nf* **1** *[Theat]* stage props/properties **2** prop room

rekuizo·n *vt* to confiscate; requisition

relacion *nm* descriptive account given to a superior: report, account, accounting

relativ *adj (Book)* **1** in comparison to a standard: relative **2** *[Ling]* (of an adjective) of substance (derived from a noun designating a substance)

relativisht *adv* relatively

relativitet *nm (Book)* relativity

relativizëm *nm [Phil]* relativism

rele *nf [Electr]* relay

reliev *nm* **1** *[Geog]* topographical surface: relief; relief map **2** sculptured/graphic relief: relief

***religjion** *nm* religion = **fe**

relikt *nm (Book)* relic

rem *nm* **1** copper = **bakër 2** poisonous salt formed in untinned copper vessels

***remar** *n* oarsman, rower = **rremtar**

***remb** *nm* **1** = **rremb 2** = **rrymë**

***rembo·het** = **rrembo·het**

***rembsi** OR **rembsim** *nm* branching out, ramification

***rembso·het** = **rrembo·het**

remde *nf [Ichth]* Twaite shad (*Alosa fallax lacustris*)

***reme** *nf* **1** copper vessel **2** copper

***remë** *nf* **1** = **rremë 2** = **rrymë *3** = **rrem**

remi
  I § *nf [Chess]* draw
  II § *adv* in a draw

reminishencë *nf (Book)* reminiscence

remont *nm* repair, restoration, reconditioning
  ∘ **remont kapital** major overhaul

remtar *nm* coppersmith = **bakërpunues**

remtë *adj (i)* of copper = **bakërtë**

rend *nm* **1** row, series **2** position in a sequence: order **3** orderliness, system: order **4** pathway, course **5** *[Biol]* order (in scientific nomenclature) **6** class **7** fast pace, haste, hurry = **vrap**
  ∘ **rend i ditës** meeting agenda; daily agenda

rend· *vi* **1** to go quickly: run **2** *(Fig)* to pass quickly; flow by
  ∘ **rend· me të katra** to run fast; run on all fours
  ∘ **rend· pas <>** to be obsessed by <>: chase/run after <>
  ∘ **rend· si mëqiku në avlëmënd** to run back and forth

rendar *n (Old)* = **rendëtar**

rende *nf* **1** food grater **2** *[Biol]* radula *()* ***3** towel, dish towel

rendë *nf* **1** running speed; rapidity, speed ***2** food grater

rendëtar *nm (Old)* = **rendëtar**

rendës *n* person who runs: runner

***rendët** *adj (i) (Old)* = **rëndomtë**

rendëtar *n (Old)* person whose turn it is, person next in line; person at the head of a procession, head of the line ***2** part-owner of property

***rendëz** *nf* food grater

rendim *nm ger* **1** *[Mil]* < **rendo·n**, **rendo·het 2** *[Mil]* alignment, position **3** *[Mil]* order of battle, combat formation ***4** classification ***5** *[Biol]* order
  ∘ **rendim luftarak** *[Mil]* order of battle, combat formation, battle array

rendiment *nm* (crop) yield; productivity

rendis stem for 1st sg pres, pl pres, 2nd & 3rd sg subj, pind < **rendit·**

rendit· *vt* **1** to put [ ] in a row, arrange [ ] in order, align **2** to list **3** *(Fig)* to treat [ ] as equal: rank [ ] together, compare

rendit·et *vpr* to line up
  ∘ **rendit·et me** [ ] to consider oneself the equal of [ ]; be the equal of [ ]

renditje *nf ger* **1** <**rendit**•, **rendit**•*et* **2** sequence, order

rendje *nf ger* <**rend**•

rendo•*n vt* **1** to grate [food] **2** = **rendit**•

****rendom** = **rëndom**

****rendomtë** *adj (i)* = **rëndomtë**

rendor *adj* ordinal

****rendore** *nf* systematic list: index, register

****rendshëm** *adj (i) (Old)* = **rëndomtë**

rendur

 I § *adj (i)* willing and able

 II § *nf (e)* = **rendje**

renegat *nm, adj (Contempt)* renegade

rene *nf* [Zool] reindeer *(Rangifer tarandus)*

****reng** = **rreng**

****rengjo**•*n vt* to cheer [] on, encourage

rentabël *adj* [Econ] profitable

rentabilitet *nm* [Econ] profitability

rentë *nf* [Econ] income derived from capital ownership: revenue, rent, income

rentier *n, adj* (person) whose income comes from investments

****renzo**•*n vt* = **rendo**•*n*

reostat *nm* [Electr] rheostat

*****rep**- = **rrjep**•

****repan** *I §* *nm OR* **repane** *II §* *nf* [Bot] radish = **rrepan**

reparacion *nm* reparation; repair

****reparim** = **riparim**

****reparo**•*n vt* = **riparo**•*n*

repart *nm* division charged with particular duties: department, section; (military) detachment; (hospital) ward; action group

 ○ **repart goditës** [Mil] shock troops, strike force

reperkusion *nm (Book)* repercussion

repertor *nm* **1** *(Book)* repertoire **2** catalog

****repë** *nf* **1** barren land **2** [Bot] radish = **rrepan**

****repicë** *nf* [Bot] = **rrepicë**

replikë *nf* **1** *(Book)* answering reply: response; retort; repartee, colloquy **2** [Law] rejoinder = **kundërpërgjigje**

reportazh *nm* reportage, news report

reporter *nm* reporter, correspondent

represalje *nf* reprisal

reptil *nm* reptile

republikan *adj, n* republican

republikë *nf* **1** republic **2** *(Colloq)* the republic of Albania **3** *(Colloq)* derby hat, bowler

repuq *adj* dressed in tattered clothes, shabby

****reqën** *OR* **reqin** *nm* [Entom] wood louse, sow bug *(Oniscus asellus)*

resatak *adj, n* envious (person)

****resedace** *np* [Bot] *Resedaceae*

resë *nf* **1** spiteful envy = **smírë** **2** drooping inflorescence: catkin, ament **3** [Bot] long-fibered swamp grass used for weaving: rush *(Pycreus)* **4** weaving of rushes; funnel-shaped basket made of woven rushes and used to catch fish **5** wickerwork frame under the straw thatch of a roof **6** place in a river where a fish trap is set

resëkeq *adj* = **smírëzí**

resëtar *adj, n* = **smírëzí**

resëzi *adj, n (fem sg ˜ezë, masc pl ˜inj, fem pl ˜eza)* = **smírëzí**

resís *stem for 1st sg pres, pl pres, 2nd & 3rd sg subj, pind* <**resít**•

resít• *vi* to wipe [] clean, wipe [] out: erase

resk *nm* **1** long and coarse fleece **2** (of fleece) long and coarse

****resm** *nm* picture; design

reso•*n vt* **1** to be envious of [], envy [] **2** to put [] under the spell of the evil eye: give [] the evil eye

****resore** *nf (Old)* mooring cable

respekt *nm* respect, high regard

respektim *nm ger* <**respekto**•*n*

respekto•*n vt* to respect

respektueshëm *adj (i)* **1** respectful **2** respected

****restar** *adj* = **resëtar**

restaurim *nm ger* **1** <**restauro**•*n*, **restauro**•*het* **2** restoration; reinstatement; reinstitution

restauro•*het vpr* to become restored, regain power

restauro•*n vt* to restore; reinstate; reinstitute

restauruar *adj (i)* restored (to its previous condition)

restaurues *nm* **1** restorer (of antiquities) **2** advocate of a restoration of previous regime: restorationist

restorant *nm* restaurant

resurse *np (Book)* resources

resh-

 I § *vi* (of rain or snow) to pour down, fall in a downpour

 II § *vt (Fig)* to supply [] with a plethora of good things

resh•*et vpr* **1** (of rain or snow) to pour down, precipitate **2** to become full of good things

reshedi *nf* [Food] = **hasude**

reshje *np fem* precipitation (of water), downpour

reshme

 I § *nf (Old)* vest ornamented with yellowish metal disks and formerly worn by brides

 II § *np* **1** clinking metal disks or coins connected by a chain and worn as a bridal necklace or ornamenting a bridal vest **2** = **rreshme**

reshpe *nf* = **rreshpe**

reshper *nm (Old)* big businessman/merchant; rich person

reshperi

 I § *nf (Old)* big business; commerce

 II § *np fem* merchandise, wares

reshpero•*n vi* **1** to conduct commerce, trade **2** *(Fig)* to bustle; bustle around

reshpje *nf* = **rreshpe**

resht-

 I § *vt* **1** to drive [] away, chase/hold [] off **2** to drive [] ahead; direct/steer [] **3** to gird [] protectively; guard **4** to mollify, control, restrain, abate; stop, stanch

 II § *vi* to die down, come to a halt: cease, stop, afford respite

resht•*et*

 I § *vpr* to get away/out, dodge

 II § *vi* to die down; gradually cease

reshte *np* odds and ends of personal property

reshter *nm* = **rreshter**

reshtje *nf ger* **1** <**resht**•, **resht**•*et* **2** abatement **3** respite, rest

reshtur *spelling variant*

re'sh|ur *adj (i)* full of household objects, filled with odds and ends of personal property

***retere'** *nf* [*Ornit*] = mbreth

re'tër *nf* **1** twisted leather thong; thong for lacing up moccasins **2** woven cradle strap

retifika'to'r *nm* [*Tech*] operator of a grinding machine tool

retifi'kë *nf* [*Tech*] machine tool for grinding, (universal) grinding machine *( )*

retifiko' *-n vt* to grind

reti'në *nf* [*Anat*] retina

reti'nëz *nf* [*Biol*] retinula

retor'ik *adj (Book)* rhetorical

retor'ikë *nf(Book)* rhetoric

retor'izëm *nm (Book)* empty rhetoric

reto'roman'ishte *nf* Rhaeto-Romanic

retrospektiv *adj (Book)* retrospective

retrospektivë *nf (Book)* retrospective view/review/ show/presentation: retrospective

retu'sh *nm* [*Spec*] retouch, retouching; touch-up

retush'im [*Spec*] *nm ger* **1** <retusho' *-n* **2** touched-up area

retusho' *-n vt* [*Spec*] to touch up [], retouch

reumat'ik *adj* [*Med*] rheumatic

reumat'izëm *nm* [*Med*] rheumatism

reumato'log *nm* [*Med*] rheumatologist

reva'n
  I § *nm* **1** fast pacing gait for a horse: pace **2** *(Fig)* fast pace, hurry, haste
  II § *adv* at a fast pace; in a hurry, hurriedly

revani' *nm* [*Food*] kind of pound cake served with sugar syrup

revani'çkë *nf dimin* = revani'

reva'nsh *nm* **1** *(Book)* struggle to regain previously lost territory: revanche; revenge **2** [*Sport*] victory that gets even for a previous loss

revansh'ist *adj, n (Pej)* revanchist

revansh'izëm *nm (Pej)* policy aiming to regain previously lost territory: revanchism

***rev'is** *stem for 1st sg pres, pl pres, 2nd & 3rd sg subj, pind* <revi't•

revi'stë *nf* magazine, journal, periodical (publication)

***revi't•** *vi* to rave wildly

***revi'tje** *nf* wandering mind state: reverie, delirium, ecstasy

revizio'n *nm (Book)* **1** (financial) audit **2** review, revision

revizion'im *nm ger (Book)* **1** <reviziono' *-n* **2** review, revision; audit

revizion'ist *adj, nm* revisionist

revizion'izëm *nm* revisionism

reviziono' *-n vt* **1** to review; revise **2** to audit [financial/economic operations] **3** [*Tech*] to check over and make any necessary repairs of [a machine]; tune up [a motor]

revizo'r *n* (financial) auditor

revok'im *nm ger* **1** [*Law*] <revoko' *-n* **2** revocation, recision, repeal; recall

revoko' *-n vt* [*Law*] to revoke/rescind/repeal [a decision/order]; recall [a representative]

revoku'e'shëm *adj (i)* [*Law*] revocable, rescindable; recallable

revo'le *nf* revolver (handgun)

revo'ltë *nf* **1** revolt **2** revulsion

revolt'im *nm ger* **1** <revolto' *-n*, revolto' *-het* **2** revolt

revolto' *-het vpr* **1** to be filled with revulsion/anger: feel revulsion, feel revolted **2** to rise up in rebellion: revolt

revolto' *-n vt* to cause [] great displeasure, revolt []

revolt'ua'r
  I § *adj (i)* **1** filled with revulsion/anger: revolted **2** in rebellion/revolt: rebelling
  II § *nm (i)* person in rebellion/revolt

revolt'ue's *adj (i)* causing revulsion/anger: revolting

revolucio'n *nm* revolution

revolucio'na'r *adj, n* revolutionary

revolucion'arizi'm *nm ger* <revolucionarizo' *-n*, revolucionarizo' *-het*

revolucion'arizo' *-het vpr* to take on a revolutionary spirit

revolucion'arizo' *-n vt* to revolutionize; fill [] with revolutionary spirit

revolucion'arizu'e's *adj* revolutionizing

revolucion'im *nm ger* = revolucionarizi'm

revolucio'no' *-n vt* = revolucionarizo' *-n*

revolve'r *nm* = revo'le

revy' *nf* [*Theat*] revue

Re'xha *nm* Rexha (male name)

Rexhe'p *nm* Rexhep (male name)

re'ze *nf* **1** small metal ring or hook to which something is temporarily attached **2** hooking lock: latch

reze' *nf* = re'ze

rezerva't *nm* tract of land set aside by a government for special purposes: reservation; nature reserve

reze'rvë
  I § *nf* **1** reserve **2** [*Sport*] substitute
  II § *adj* spare

rezerv'im *nm ger* <rezervo' *-n*, rezervo' *-het*

rezerv'ist *adj, nm* [*Mil*] reservist

rezervo' *-het vpr (Book)* **1** to behave in reserved fashion **2** to be stinting in one's efforts; be a slacker at work

rezervo' *-n vt (Book)* to reserve

rezerv'ua'r
  I § *nm* reservoir
  II § *adj (i)* **1** kept in reserve: reserved **2** reticent, reserved

***re'zë** *nf* **1** wicker fish trap, weir **2** millrace

reziden'cë *nf (Book)* official residence; residence of a high official

rezi'l *adj, nm (Colloq Insult)* shameless/vile (person)

rezisten'cë *nf* **1** resistance **2** [*Electr*] fuse
  ○ **rezistenca e materialeve** [*Tech*] ultimate strength

reziste'nt *adj* resistant

rezisto' *-n vt* **1** to resist **2** to hold up against []: endure, survive

rezisto'r *nm* [*Phys*] resistor

***rezm** *nm* [*Law*] estate portion reserved to the legal heirs and not subject to disposition by the testator: legitim

rezmi'shta *np fem* stakes forming the sides of a cart

rezolucio'n *nm (Book)* = rezolu'të

rezolu'të *nf* (official) resolution

rezona'ncë *nf* **1** [*Phys*] resonance **2** *(Fig Book)* echo, resonance = jeho'në

rezonato'r *nm* [*Spec*] resonator

rezulta'nte *nf* **1** [*Spec*] resultant **2** *(Fig)* joint effect/ result

rezulta't *nm* **1** result **2** [*Sport*] score

rezult'o •*n vi* to result

***rezull'im** *nm ger* **1** <**rezullo'** •*n* **2** mental reflection, meditation

***rezull'o** •*n vi* to reflect, meditate

re'zhd'a *np* <**re'zhdë** empty pods/husks; left-over rubbish, chaff and straw

rezhd'ak *adj* having dewlaps

re'zhd'ë *nf* **1** drooping inflorescence: catkin **2** unripe mulberry **3** dewlap (on a goat); goat with dewlaps **4** ragged threads; rag; tasseled fringe (on cloth)

  ⚬ **rezhda zdrukthi** shavings from a plane, wood curls/shavings

re'zhg'ë *nf* cell in a honeycomb

rëbo'ke *nf* pine bark

rëfyr'ë *nf* knot in wood

***rëgall'inë** = **rrëgalli'në**

***rëk** = **rënk**

rëko're *nf* [*Bot*] chicory = **radhiqe**

rëko'sh *nm* [*Dairy*] cheese made from whole milk

***rële** = **rele**

***rëm'ar'ëm** *adj* (*i*) rumbling, noisy

***rëm'a-rëm'a** *adv* in a rumble, rumblingly

***rëmb** *nm* = **rremb**

***rëmb** = **rrëmb**

***rëmb'ak** *adj* (*Old*) arterial

***rë'mih•** *vt* = **rrëmih•**

***rëm'im'e** *np* archeological diggings; scientific investigations = **gërmime, gjurmime**

***rëm'o** •*n vt* = **rrëmo'** •*n*

***rëm'oj'cë** *nf* toothpick = **rrëmoj'ëse**

***rëmuj'e** = **rrëmuj'e**

***rëmull'ë** = **rrëmull'ë**

rën *stem for part, opt, adm* <**bie₁** • fall, hit, strike

rën'ç *stem for opt* <**bie₁** • = **rënsh**

rënd- *vt, vi* = **rëndo'** •*n*

rënd-et *vpr* to become a burden/difficulty/nuisance to <>

rënd'es'ë *nf* **1** [*Phys*] gravity **2** (*Old*) tax imposition = **taksë**

rënd'ë

  I § *adj* (*i*) **1** heavy **2** ponderous; corpulent and ponderous in movement **3** (*Colloq*) pregnant **4** imposing **5** (*Fig Colloq*) important **6** (*Fig Colloq*) wise **7** difficult; difficult to bear, hard to take; difficult to dissolve/digest **8** (*Colloq*) (of beverages) high in alcoholic content **9** arduous, laborious **10** (*Fig*) severe, grave, serious; harsh **11** [*Sport*] rough

  II § *adv* **1** heavily **2** seriously, badly **3** like a big shot **4** coarsely

  III § *nf* (*e*) (*Euph*) epilepsy

  IV § *nn* (*të*) **1** weight **2** (*Colloq*) fainting spell = **fikët**

  V § *nf* *sperm, seed, semen

  ⚬ **ësh-të i rëndë bishti se sqepari/sëpata** (said when someone tries to act more important than he is) look at the big shot!

  ⚬ **ësh-të i rëndë nga veshët** to be hard of hearing

  ⚬ **të rëndët e dheut** (*Euph*) anxiety

rënd'ë-rënd'ë *adv* with great bearing, without wavering: proudly

rënd'es'i *nf* **1** weight, heaviness **2** (*Fig*) importance; authority; influence **3** heavy feeling in the stomach

rënd'es'im *nm ger* = **rënd'im**

rënd'es'ir'ë *nf* **1** heavy thing: weight **2** heavy feeling in the stomach **3** (*Fig*) load, burden **4** tax imposition

rënd'es'i'shëm *adj* (*i*) important; influential

rënd'es'o' •*het vpr* = **rëndo'** •*het*

rënd'es'o' •*n vt* = **rëndo'** •*n*

rënd'im *nm ger* **1** <**rëndo'** •*n*, **rëndo'** •*het* **2** exacerbation, aggravation (*Old*) ***3** weight

rëndo' •*het vpr* **1** to get heavier; get loaded down **2** to get worse; get more difficult to bear; be burdened **3** (*Fig*) (of a responsibility) to rest, lie, fall **3** to hurt <>'s pride, hurt <>'s feelings **5** to begin to lose one's hearing: gradually go deaf

  ⚬ <> **rëndo'** •*het³ˢᵍ* **shpirti** life *weighs* heavily upon <>, <>'s heart is heavy

rëndo' •*n*

  I § *vt* **1** to make [] heavy; load [] heavily; weigh down [] **2** (*Fig*) to add to []'s burdens/difficulties; increase the severity of [] **3** (*Fig*) to weigh heavily on []; make [] difficult; fatigue **4** (*Fig*) to hurt []'s pride, hurt []'s feelings **5** to exert pressure on <>; give weight to <>

  II § *vi* **1** to weigh; weigh down; weigh heavily **2** (*Fig*) (of a responsibility) to rest, lie, fall **3** (*Fig*) to make <> feel sorry/sad/bad **4** (*Fig*) to exert influence; (of words) to have an effect on <> **5** (*Fig*) to give emphasis to <> **6** (*Fig*) to put one's weight on one side: lean **7** (*Colloq*) to do heavy/difficult work **8** (*Colloq*) (of weather) to increase in severity: get worse

  ⚬ **aq/kaq** <> **rëndo'** •*n³ᵖˡ* that just *shows* how much brains <> has!

  ⚬ **e rëndo'** •*n* **dorën mbi** [] "use a heavy hand on []" to give [] a heavy (undeserved) beating

  ⚬ **i rëndo'** •*n* **dheut** (*Impol*) (of a bad/useless person) to just be taking up valuable space, be a burden on the world, the world would be better off without {}

  ⚬ **e rëndo'** •*n* **gojën 1** to use foul language **2** to argue using foul language

  ⚬ **po rëndo'** •*n³ˢᵍ* **moti** "the weather *gets* getting worse" things *are* taking a turn for the worse, the situation *is getting* serious

  ⚬ <> **rëndo'** •*n³ˢᵍ* **në shpirt** to weigh heavily on <>'s conscience

  ⚬ <> **rëndo'** •*n* **në zemër** to weigh heavily on <>'s mind

rëndo'm *adv* usually, ordinarily

rëndo'm'shëm *adj* (*i*) = **rëndo'mtë**

rëndo'mt'ë *adj* (*i*) usual, customary; ordinary, common

***rëndo'm'thi** *adv* = **rëndo'm**

rëndo'sh *adj, n* heavy/lumbering (person)

rënd'ue's *adj* **1** exacerbating, aggravating **2** contributing heavy weight, weighing down

rë'në

  I § *part* <**bie₁** • fallen; hit, struck

  II § *adj* (*i*) **1** fallen to the ground; fallen **2** hanging down **3** lying down, decumbent **4** past one's prime; frail

  III § *nf* (*e*) blow, sound of a blow: smack

  IV § *adv* lying down, decumbent

  ⚬ **kanë rënë trutë në qafë** "<>'s brains have fallen on <>'s neck" (*Impol*) <>'s brain *has* become senile, <>'s brain *is* fried

  ⚬ **(si) i rënë nga qielli** "(as if) fallen from the sky" **1** wonderful, extraordinary, just perfect **2** (*Iron*) very ordinary

rë'nës *adj* **1** [*Bot*] deciduous () **2** [*Phys Geom*] incident

rëngë nf 1 ringing/reverberating sound 2 deep groan: moan 3 [Ichth] herring

rëngëmadh adj having suffered much: afflicted, harrowed, woeful

rënie nf ger 1 <bie₁· 2 falling, fall 3 decline 4 [Phys Geom] incidence
  ○ rënie e diellit në kokë [Med] sunstroke

rënkesë nf moan, groan; sigh

rënkim nm ger 1 <rënko·n, rënko·het 2 moan, groan; sigh 3 (Colloq) visit to pay one's condolences, consolation visit

*__rënkimtar__ adj moaning, groaning; sighing

rënko·het vpr (Colloq) to complain (about one's troubles)

rënko·n
  I § vi 1 to moan, groan; sigh 2 (Fig) emit a prolonged and muffled sound: rumble
  II § vt (Colloq) to console [a mourner]

rëntë 3sg opt <bie₁·
  ○ <> rëntë flama (Curse) A pox on <>!
  ○ i rëntë gurit e drurit "may it fall on the rock and tree" I hope you come out of it (a calamity) all right
  ○ <> rëntë pas veshit/qafës! "May it fall on <>'s ears/neck!" (Curse) May misfortune/death fall suddenly on <>!

rëntgen nm, adj [Phys] roentgen; x-ray

rëntgenografi nf [Med] roentgenography

rëntgenolog nm [Med] roentgenologist

rëntgenologji nf [Med] roentgenology

*__rënx__ = rrënx

*__rëpjetë__
  I § prep (abl) adv up
  II § nf (e) (Reg Tosk) slope, steep incline

*__rëpjetëm__ adj (i) steep, precipitous

*__rëposh__ adv down

*__rëpuq__ adj bald

*__rëqis·__ = shqis·

*__rëqit·__ = shqit·

rërë nf 1 sand 2 sandy area/surface
  ○ rërë xhami fine sand used for making glass

rërët adj (i) sandy

*__rëshegullë__ nf = shregull

*__rëvit·__ vt to hurl = vërvit·

RFGj abbrev <Republika Federale Gjermane Federal Republic of Germany

ri
  I § adj (i) 1 young 2 new 3 modern
  II § nm (i) 1 young boy/person, youth; member of a youth organization 2 (after a surname) junior
  III § nn (të) period when young: youth

ri·het vpr 1 to become renewed, be reinvigorated 2 to get coated with moisture: become moist/damp
  ○ ri·het³ˢᵍ hëna there is a new moon

ri·n
  I § vt 1 to renew, revive 2 to please 3 to moisten; coat [] with moisture, fog [] up 4 to bait [a hook] for fishing
  II § vi to appear anew, sprout up; newly to appear, be reinvigorated; (of a wound) close up, scab over; (of an area of land) become verdant with new growth

ri formativ re-

riabilitim nm ger 1 <riabilito·n, riabilito·het 2 rehabilitation

riabilito·het vpr to become rehabilitated

riabilito·n vt to rehabilitate

riafrim nm ger 1 <riafro·n, riafro·het 2 reconciliation, resumption of friendship

riafro·het vpr to become reconciled, make up, resume friendship

riafro·n vt to reconcile [estranged people]

*__riaft__ = riaftës

riaftësim nm ger <riaftëso·n, riaftëso·het

riaftëso·het vpr to become rehabilitated; regain skills; gain new skills

riaftëso·n vt 1 to rehabilitate; put [] back into working condition 2 to train [] in new skills, retrain

riaktivizim nm ger 1 <riaktivizo·n, riaktivizo·het 2 reactivation

riaktivizo·het vpr to become active again; go back into action

riaktivizo·n vt to put [] back into action; reactivate

riarmatim nm rearmament

riarmato·s· vt to rearm []

riarmato·s·et vpr to become rearmed: rearm

riarmato·sje nf ger <riarmato·s·, riarmato·s·et

riatdhesim nm ger 1 <riatdheso·n, riatdheso·het 2 repatriation

riatdheso·het vpr to return to one's homeland: become repatriated

riatdheso·n vt to repatriate

riatdhesuar adj (i), n (i) repatriated (person)

ribashkim nm ger <ribashko·n, ribashko·het

ribashko·het vpr to become reunited

ribashko·n vt to reunite []

ribatinë nf [Tech] rivet

ribatinim nm ger <ribatino·n

ribatino·n vt to rivet

ribatinuese nf [Tech] riveting machine

*__ribell__
  I § nm (Old) disorder, confusion
  II § adj (Old) in disorder/confusion

*__ribez__ nm [Bot] currant, gooseberry (Ribes)

ribë·n vt 1 to redo; do [] again, do [] over 2 to remake: rework, revise, repair, rebuild

ribërë adj (i) 1 redone, done over 2 remade: reworked, revised, repaired, rebuild

rible·n vt to buy [] again

ribotim nm ger <riboto·n

riboto·n vt to republish, reprint

ricin nm [Bot] castor-oil plant, castor bean (Ricinus communis)
  ○ ricin i egër [Bot] = çapëz

ridërgim nm ger <ridërgo·n

ridërgo·n vt 1 to send [] back 2 to send [] again: resend

riedukim nm ger <rieduko·n, rieduko·het 2 reeducation

rieduko·het vpr to become a new person, make oneself over

rieduko·n vt to make [] over (into a new person): reeducate

*__riell__ nm [Bot] sun spurge (Euphorbia helioscopia)

riemërtim nm ger <riemërto·n

riemërto·n vt to rename

rifillim nm ger <rifillo·n 2 resumption

rifillo·n vt to resume; begin again/anew

*__rifito·n__ vt to regain, recover

rifreskim nm ger 1 <rifresko·n 2 refreshment

rifreskó·n *vt* to refresh

rifúxhio *nf* refuge, shelter

rig *nm* king (in a deck of cards); high-ranking joker (one of four) in a children's card game

rigásh *nm* *(Reg)* [*Ornit*] = **gjel deti**

rigátë *nf* *(Old)* kingdom, realm = **mbretëri**

rígë *nf* **1** trickle (of liquid) **2** drizzle **3** ruler (measuring stick) = **vizóre** **4** king

*****rígët** *adj* (i) drizzly

rigó·n *vi* **1** to trickle **2** to drizzle

rigón *nm* **1** [*Bot*] oregano *(Origanum heracleoticum)* **2** [*Bot*] origanum *(Origanum)*
○ **rigon i zakonshëm** [*Bot*] wild marjoram *Origanum vulgare*

rigoróz *adj* rigorous

rigorozísht *adv* rigorously

rigorozítet *nm* rigorousness, rigor

*****rigós·** *vt* to draw [lines] with a ruler

rigrupím *nm ger* **1** <**rigrupó·n, rigrupó·het 2** regroupment

rigrupó·het *vpr* to regroup

rigrupó·n *vt* to regroup [forces]

*****rigtó·n** = **rigó·n**

rigjallërím *nm* [*Med*] revivification

rigjetje *nf* rediscovery

riháp· *vt* to reopen

rihápje *nf ger* <**rihap·**

*****ríhës** *n* *(Old)* complainer

rijetó·n *vt* to relive, reexperience

rikán *nm* [*Ornit*] male duck: drake

rikáp· *vt* **1** to seize [] back **2** to overtake

ríkë *nf* **1** [*Ornit*] duckling; duck **2** hen turkey

*****rikëqyr·** *vt* *(Reg Gheg)* to re-examine, revise

*****rikëqyrje** *nf ger* **1** <**rikëqyr· 2** *(Reg Gheg)* re-examination, revision

rikonicíon *nm* [*Mil*] reconnaissance

rikonstruksión *nm* **1** *(Book)* = **rindërtim 2** radical overhaul, reconstruction

rikopjím *nm ger* <**rikopjó·n**

rikopjó·n *vt* to recopy

rikoshétë *nf* ricochet

rikoshetím *nm ger* <**rikoshetó·n**

rikoshetó·n *vi* to ricochet

rikrijím *nm ger* **1** <**rikrijó·n, rikrijó·het 2** re-creation

rikrijó·n *vt* **1** to re-form **2** to give [] artistic embodiment: re-create

rikthe·het *vpr* **1** to return **2** to pick up from where one was before; take up the matter again, turn again (to a a subject)

rikthe·n *vt* to return []

rikthim *nm ger* **1** <**rikthe·n, rikthe·het 2** return

rikujtésë *nf* **1** reminiscence, recollection **2** [*Lit Mus*] recurring motif

rikujtím *nm ger* **1** <**rikujtó·n, rikujtó·het 2** recollection; recall; remembrance

rikujtó·het *vpr* to come back to mind

rikujtó·n *vt* to remember [] again, recall

rikumbím *nm ger* **1** <**rikumbó·n 2** resonance = **rezonáncë**

rikumbó·n *vi* **1** to resound **2** to resonate

rikumbúes
  I § *adj* resounding

  II § *nm* [*Spec*] resonator = **rezonatór**

rikúpero *nf* [*Tech*] factory reject

rilevím *nm ger* [*Spec*] <**rilevó·n**

rilevó·n *vt* [*Spec*] to survey [an area] to establish its topographical relief

rilevúes
  I § *nm* topographical surveyor
  II § *adj* topographical surveying

rilexó·n *vt* to read [] again: reread

rilínd·
  I § *vi* to be reborn, be revitalized
  II § *vt* *(Elev)* to give rise to a rebirth in [], revitalize

rilínd·et *vpr* to begin a new life: be born again

rilíndas *n* = **rilíndës**

rilíndës *n* [*Hist*] renaissance personage/figure

rilíndje *nf ger* **1** <**rilínd·, rilínd·et 2** rebirth **3** [*Hist*] renaissance; national reawakening

rilíndur *adj* (i) reborn, revitalized

rílë *nf* **1** lentil **2** pea = **bizéle**

rim *nm* **1** trail made by flowing rain water: rill **2** narrow path: trail

rimartúar *adj* (i) remarried

rimárr *stem for 1st sg pres, pl pres, subj, opt, adm, part* <**rimerr·**

rimárrje *nf ger* **1** <**rimerr· 2** [*Mus*] repeat

rimbíll *stem for 2nd pl pres, pind, imper, vp* <**rimbjell·**

rimbjéll· *vt* to resow, replant

rimbjéllë
  I § *part* <**rimbjell·**
  II § *adj* (i)

rimbóll *stem for pdef* <**rimbjell·**

rimbúsh· *vt* to refill, replenish

rimbúshje *nf ger* **1** <**rimbush· 2** replenishment; refill

rimerr· *vt* **1** to retake; regain; recapture; get [] again **2** to take up [] again, get back to []; repeat

riméso *nf* veneer

rímë *nf* [*Lit*] rhyme
  ○ **rimë e mbyllur** [*Lit*] rhyme sequence that is conterminous with the stanza: enclosing rhyme
  ○ **rimë e puthur** rhymed couplet

*****rímë** *adj* (i) renewed

rimëkëmb· *vt* **1** to put [] back on [his/its] feet **2** *(Fig)* to cause [] to recover; rehabilitate

rimëkëmb·et *vpr* **1** to get back on [one's] feet **2** *(Fig)* to regain health: recover; become rehabilitated

rimëkëmbje *nf ger* **1** <**rimëkëmb·, rimëkëmb·et 2** recovery; rehabilitation

rimëkëmbur *adj* (i) recovered; repaired, rebuilt; rehabilitated

rimilitarizím *nm ger* <**rimilitarizó·n, rimilitarizó·het**

rimilitarizó·het *vpr* to become remilitarized: remilitarize, rearm for war

rimilitarizó·n *vt* to remilitarize []

rimírr *stem for 2nd pl pres, pind, imper, vp* <**rimerr·**

rimó·n *vi* [*Lit*] to rhyme

rimór *adj* [*Lit*] of or pertaining to rhyme: rhyming

rimór *stem for pdef* <**rimerr·**

rimórk *nm* = **rimórkio**

rimorkiatór *nm* [*Naut*] tugboat; tow boat

rimo'rkio *nf* motorless vehicle pulled by another vehicle: trailer

rimo'rkio · *vt* (of a vehicle) to pull/tow another vehicle

rim|të *adj (i)* azure, blue = **bru'ztë**

***rimto's·** *het* = **rimto'se·t**

***rimto'·n** = **rimto's·**

***rimto's·** *vt* to turn [] blue

***rimto's·et** *vpr* to turn blue

rimth *nm* [*Anat*] clitoris = **kathi'c**

rim|ua'r *adj (i)* rhymed; in rhyme; rhyming

ri|mua'r *stem for pl pdef* < **rime'rr·**

***ri'm|un**

   I § *part* < **ri·n**

   II § *adj (i)* renewed

Ri'n|a *nf* Rina (female name)

ri|nda·het *vpr* to get separated (from a spouse): separate

ri|nda'·n *vt* to divide [] up again: reapportion

ri|nda'rje *nf* re-division

ri|ndërti'm *nm ger* 1 < **rindërto'·n** 2 reconstruction

ri|ndërto'·n *vt* to reconstruct; rebuild

ri|ndërtu'a'r *adj (i)* reconstructed

ri|ndre'q· *vt* to repair, overhaul; restore

***ri|ndre'qje** *nf ger* 1 < **rindre'q·** 2 repair, overhaul; restoration

ring *nm (np ˜ gje)* [*Sport*] boxing ring

***ringegji'nge** *nf* twaddle, nonsense

ri|ngja'll· *vt* to bring [] back to life: revive

ri|ngja'll·et *vpr* to come back to life: revive

ri|ngja'llje *nf ger* 1 < **ringja'll·**, **ringja'll·et** 2 revival, refreshment, reinvigoration

ri|ngja'll|ur *adj (i)* revived, revitalized, reinvigorated

***ringji'nge** = **ringegji'nge**

ri|ni' *nf* 1 youth 2 youthfulness 3 the young 4 *(Crude)* term of familiar address for a young person whose name is not known: squirt 5 *(Fig)* early days/period

ri|ni'm *nm ger* 1 < **rino'·n**, **rino'·het** 2 rejuvenation

***ri|ni'sje** *nf* recommencement, new start

ri|no'·het *vpr* to be/feel rejuvenated

ri|no'·n *vt* to rejuvenate

rinocero'nt *nm* [*Zool*] rhinoceros

***rinoqe'r** = **rinocero'nt**

rinoqero'nt *nm* [*Zool*] rhinoceros = **rinocero'nt**

ri|no'r *adj* of or characteristic of the young: youthful

Rinu'sh *nm* Rinush (male name)

ri|nxe'h· *vt* to reheat

ri'|nj *adj (të) masc pl* < **ri'**

ri|nje'h *2nd & 3rd sg pres* < **rinjo'h·**

ri|nji'h·et *vpr* < **rinjo'h·** to become reacquainted

ri|nji'h *stem for 2nd pl pres, pind, imper, vp* < **rinjo'h·**

ri|njo'h· *vt* to become reacquainted with []

ri|njo'hje *nf ger* 1 < **rinjo'h·**, **rinji'h·et** 2 reacquaintance

ri|organizi'm *nm ger* 1 < **riorganizo'·n**, **riorganizo'·het** 2 reorganization

ri|organizo'·het *vpr* to get reorganized: reorganize

ri|organizo'·n *vt* to reorganize []

ri|organizu'a'r *adj (i)* reorganized

ri|o'sh *adj, n (Book)* youthful/youthful-looking (person)

***rip** = **rrip**

***ri'p·et** *vpr* = **rri'p·et**

***rip|** = **rrip|**

ri|pari'm *nm ger* 1 < **riparo'·n** 2 repair

ri|paro'·n *vt* to repair

ri|paru'a'r *adj (i)* repaired

ri|paru'es *nm* repairman

ri|paru'e'shëm *adj (i)* reparable

***ri|pastri'm** *nm ger* < **ripastro'·n**

***ri|pastro'·n** *vt* to clear/clean [] again

***ri'pë** = **rri'pë**

ri|përtëri'·het *vpr* 1 [*Biol*] to regenerate 2 *(Fig)* to become rejuvenated

ri|përtëri'·n *vt* 1 [*Tech*] to bring [] back into working condition: repair 2 [*Biol*] to regenerate [] 3 *(Fig)* to rejuvenate

ri|përtëri'tje *nf ger* 1 < **ripërtëri'·n**, **ripërtëri'·het** 2 regeneration, restoration, rejuvenation

ri|përty'p· *vt* 1 to rechew, ruminate 2 *(Fig)* to restudy

ri|përty'pës *adj, nm* [*Zool*] ruminant

ri|përty'pje *nf* rumination

***ri'pkë** *nf* shoelace, thong = **rri'pkë**

ri|pohi'm *nm ger* 1 < **ripoho'·n** 2 reassertion; reaffirmation

ri|poho'·n *vt* to reassert; reaffirm

ri|populli'm *nm ger* 1 < **ripopullo'·n** 2 repopulation

ri|popullo'·het *vpr* to get/become repopulated

ri|popullo'·n *vt* to repopulate

ri|prodhi'm *nm ger* 1 < **riprodho'·n**, **riprodho'·het** 2 reproduction

ri|prodhi'mta'r *adj* reproductive

ri|prodho'·het *vpr* to reproduce, propagate

ri|prodho'·n *vt* 1 to reproduce [] 2 to recite

ri|prodhu'a'r *adj (i)* reproduced

ri|prodhu'es *adj* of or pertaining to reproduction

***ri|prondi's** *stem for 1st sg pres, pl pres, 2nd & 3rd sg subj, pind* < **riprondi't·**

***ri|prondi't·** *vt (Reg Gheg)* = **riprodho'·n**

***ri|prondi't·ës** *adj (Reg Gheg)* = **riprodhimta'r**

***ri|prondi'tje** *nf (Reg Gheg)* = **riprodhi'm**

ri|provi'm *nm* retest

ri|puni'm *nm ger* < **ripuno'·n**

ri|puno'·n *vt* to rework

ri|punu'a'r *adj (i)* reworked

ri|pushto'·n *vt* to reconquer, reoccupy

ri|pyll|ëzi'm *nm ger* 1 < **ripyllëzo'·n** 2 reforestation

ri|pyll|ëzo'·n *vt* to reforest

ri|qe *nf* [*Bot*] heath *(Erica)*

ri|rë *adj (i)* = **ri'të**

***ris** *nm (np ˜ ër)* [*Zool*] lynx = **rrëqe'bull**

ri|si' *nf* 1 youth; youthfulness; newness 2 innovation

***ri|si'll** *stem for 2nd pl pres, pind, imper, vp* < **risje'll·**

ri|si'm *nm* new formation, innovation

***ri|sje'll·** *vt* to take/bring [] back, return

***ri|sje'll|ë** *part* < **risje'll·**

risk *nm (Colloq)* destiny, fate, lot; luck

***ri|so'll** *stem for pdef* < **risje'll·**

***ri|stora's·** *vt* to restore, re-establish

ri|she's *stem for 1st sg pres, 1st & 3rd pl pres, 2nd & 3rd sg subj* < **rishe't·**

ri|she't· *vt* to resell; sell [] at retail

***ri'|shëm** *adj (i)* recent, new

ri|shfa'q· *vt* to redisplay, reveal; show [] again

ri|shfa'q·et *vpr* to reappear

rishfa'qje *nf ger* 1 <rishfa'q•, rishfa'q•*et* 2 reappearance

rishikím *nm ger* 1 <rishiko'•*n* 2 review, reexamination

rishiko'•*n vt* to review, reexamine

rishís *stem for pind, 2nd pl pres, imper* <rishet•

rishít *stem for part, pdef, pind, 2nd pl pres, imper, vp* <rishet•

rishítës *n (Old)* retailer

rishítje *nf ger* 1 <rishet• 2 resale; retail sale

rishkrua•*n vt* to rewrite

*rishku'll *nm [Ornit]* nightingale

ri'shmë *adv* recently, newly, just now

*rí'shmi *adv (së)* 1 = rishmë *2 anew, afresh, again = sërish

rishpërnda•*n vt* to redistribute

rishpërnda'rje *nf ger* 1 <rishpërnda•*n* 2 redistribution

rishqyrtím *nm ger* 1 <rishqyrto'•*n* 2 reexamination, reinvestigation

rishqyrto'•*n vt* to reexamine, reinvestigate

rishta'r *n* novice

rishtarí *nf [Relig]* novitiate

rí'shtas *OR* rí'shtazi *adv* 1 recently 2 anew, again

rí'shte *np fem* 1 *[Food]* = petarishte 2 *[Anat]* cartilage, gristle

*rishte *nf* variety of long-stemmed pear

*rishtno'r *adj (Old)* cartilaginous, gristly

*rishtno're *nf* probationary year

rishto'•*n vt* to renew, rejuvenate = përtëri'•*n*

rishty'p• *vt* to reprint

rishty'pje *nf ger* 1 <rishty'p• 2 reprint

rit *nm* rite

rítë *adj (i)* moist; wet with tears

rítëm *nm* rhythm

ritmík *adj* rhythmic

ritmíkë *nf* 1 *[Mus Lit]* rhythmics, metrics; metric/rhythmic form 2 manner of movement/development: rhythm, pace

ritmiki'sht *adv* rhythmically; steadily, without let-up

rito'•*het vpr* (of hard surfaces) to become wet with moisture: fog up, sweat

rito'•*n vt* to make [ ] moist; make [ ] wet (with sweat)

ritransmetím *nm ger [Brdcast]* 1 <ritransmeto'•*n* 2 relay transmission; retransmission

ritransmeto'•*n vt [Brdcast]* 1 to transmit [a radio/television signal] by relay 2 to rebroadcast [a radio/television program]

ritransmetue's *adj, nm [Brdcast]* (apparatus) used for relay transmission

ritregím *nm ger* <ritrego'•*n*

ritrego'•*n vt* to retell, recount (in one's own words)

ritua'l *nm, adj (Book)* ritual

rith = rridh

ritheksím *nm ger* 1 <ritrekso'•*n* 2 reemphasis

ritrekso'•*n vt* to reemphasize

riva'l *n, adj* rival

rivalitet *nm* rivalry

rivalizo'•*n vi* to compete as a rival

rive'n *stem for opt, adm, part* <rivë•

rivendikím *nm ger* 1 *[Law]* <rivendiko'•*n* 2 claim for restoration

rivendiko'•*n vt [Law]* to make a claim for restoration of [ ]: reclaim

rivendo's• *vt* to reestablish, restore; reinstate

rivendo's•*et vpr* to return to a previous place/position

rivendo'sje *nf ger* 1 <rivendo's•, rivendo's•*et* 2 reestablishment, restoration; reinstatement; replacement

rive'r *stem for imper* <rivë•

rivë• *vt* to put [ ] again

rivën *stem for opt, adm, part* <rivë•

rivë'nie *nf ger* <rivë•
    ◦ rivënie anësore *[Soccer]* throw-in

rivë'r *stem for imper* <rivë•

rivështro'•*n vt* to look [ ] over again

rivi *stem for 2nd pl pres, pind, imper, vp* <rivë•

riviérë *nf* scenic coast, riviera

*rivle'ftës = rivlerës

rivlerësím *nm ger* 1 <rivlerëo'•*n* 2 revaluation; reevaluation

rivlerëso'•*n vt* 1 to revaluate; revalue 2 to reevaluate

rivu *stem for pl pdef, 3rd sg pdef, vp* <rivë•

rivu'r *stem for sg pdef, sg imper* <rivë•

rixha *nf (Colloq)* entreaty, request

rizë *nf* 1 face towel 2 shawl 3 *[Anat]* fatty membrane covering internal organs: omentum *4 ladybug

*rizëz *nf dimin* small napkin

rizgjedh• *vt* to reelect [ ] for office

rizgjedhje *nf ger* 1 <rizgje'dh•, rizgjídh•*et* 2 reelection

rizgje'dhur *adj (i)* reelected

rizgjídh *stem for 2nd pl pres, pind, imper, vp* <rizgje'dh•

rizgjodh *stem for pdef* <rizgje'dh•

*rizik = rrëzik

rizo'më *nf [Bot]* rhizome

rizo'r *adj [Anat]* omental

*rje'p• *vt* = rrjep

*rje'paca'k *nm, adj* = rrjepaca'k

*rje'pa-rje'pa *adv* = rrjepa-rrje'pa

*rje'pë *nf* = rrjepë

*rje't = rrjet

*ro'•*n* = rro'•*n*

rob *nm* 1 *[Hist]* landless peasant; serf 2 captive 3 *(Contempt)* thrall 4 *(Colloq)* person; family member

*robala'rse *nf* = rrobala'rëse

*robdisha'm *nm (Colloq)* = robëdësha'mbër

robëdësha'mbër *nm* bathrobe, dressing gown

rob'ër *np* <rob

robëreshë *nf fem* <rob

robërí *nf* 1 slavery 2 *[Hist]* serfdom 3 *(Colloq Collec)* members of a household

robërím *nm ger* 1 <robëro'•*n* 2 enslavement

*robëri'na *np (fem)* clothes, things = roburi'na

robëri'sht *adv* in slave fashion

robëro'•*n*
    I § *vt* 1 to enslave 2 *(Fig)* to enthrall
    II § *vi (Colloq)* to work like a slave, slave away

robëru'ar *adj (i)* enslaved

robëru'es *adj* aimed at or having the effect of enslavement: enslaving

robí *nf (Colloq Collec)* members of a household

robinjë *nf* **1** = **robëreshë 2** [*Bot*] locust (tree) = **akacie**

rob|**is** *stem for 1st sg pres, pl pres, 2nd & 3rd sg subj, pind* <**robit·**

robit· *vt (Old)* **1** to rob, loot **2** to enslave

robit· *et vpr* **1** = **robto**·*het* **2** to get worn out; become haggard; get jaded

* **robitur** *adj (i) (Old)* **1** enslaved, captured **2** jaded, haggard

* **robizgë** *nf* cone (of a conifer tree)

robineshë *nf (Book)* female slave

robot *nm* robot

robotikë *nf* [*Tech*] robotics

robotizim *nm ger* <**robotizo·n**

robotizo·n *vt* to robotize

robti *nf* **1** laborious work * **2** slavery; captivity

robtis· *vt* = **robto**·*n*

robtis·et *vpr* = **robto**·*het*

robtis|**ur** *adj (i)* = **robtuar**

robto·*het vpr* **1** to slave away, work like a slave; work to the point of exhaustion **2** to get worn out; become haggard; get jaded

robto·*n*

I § *vi* = **robto**·*het*

II § *vt* to work [] like a slave

robtuar *adj (i)* exhausted by hard work, toil-worn

* **robull** *nm (np ˜j)* [*Bot*] = **rrobull**

* **roçomil** *nm* simpleton

rod *nm* **1** *(Reg)* patrilineal clan, kin **2** kind, type

rodhan *nm* **1** winding reel (for yarn); spinning wheel **2** bobbin, spool

rodhe = **rrodhe**

* **rodhje** *nf* [*Med*] tuberculosis of the bone

* **rofe** *nf* [*Ichth*] turbot (*Psetta maxima*)

rogaç *nm* **1** castrated animal; steer **2** *(Old)* person dressed in masquerade costume and mask for pre-Lenten carnival; pre-Lenten carnival

roga-roga *adv* characterized by bare patches; in patches

rogeçe *np (Old)* people dressed in masquerade costumes and masks for pre-Lenten carnival

roge *nf* **1** grassy meadow in the midst of a forest: forest glade/clearing **2** bare patch

* **roginë** *nf* = **roge**

rogo·*het vpr* **1** (of snow) to melt in patches **2** to lose hair in patches

rogovece *nf* [*Bot*] **1** carob (*Ceratonia siliqua*) **2** *(Reg)* = **rogovecke**

rogoveckë *nf (Reg)* [*Bot*] = **akacie**

rogja(n) *nm (np ˜nj)* one of the river branchlets in a delta

rogje *nf* small clay jug with a narrow neck; small round-bellied bottle; cruet, carafe

rogjeze *nf* glass vial, ampule

roit· *vi* **1** *(Colloq)* (of bees) to swarm **2** to buzz, drone **3** to leak **4** *(Fig)* to go nuts, become dotty **5** (of land) to slide

roitje *nf ger* <**roit·**

roitur *adj (i)* rickety

roj *nm (Colloq)* bee-swarm; swarming = **luzmë**

* **roje** *nf* product, fruit

rojë *nf* **1** watch/guard duty: watch, guard; duty watch **2** *(Collec)* guard/patrol unit in a military group; garrison **3** watchman, guard; guardsman, sentry; person on duty **4** saving, economy

* **rojjes** *n* **1** = **ruajtes 2** (on a gun) safety catch, safety

* **rojit·** = **roit·**

rojkë *nf* **1** *(Colloq)* beeswarm away from the hive **2** stray livestock **3** *(Fig)* talkative woman, chatterbox * **4** queen bee **5** flock of sheep in the care of a hired shepherd

rojmë *nf (Colloq)* = **rojkë**

rojsi *nf* heavy rain

rojtar *n* person on guard duty: watchman, sentry, guard

rok *nm* **1** variety of wheat with short stalks and beardless heads * **2** period of time, term

rokade *nf* [*Chess*] castling

rokan *nm* **1** plane (for planing wood) **2** *(Fig)* person who gets on one's nerves: nuisance

rokoko *nf* [*Archit*] rococo (style)

rol *nm* role, function

rolete *nf* venetian blind

rolgang *nm* [*Tech*] roller conveyer

* **rom** *nm* (card game) rummy

romak *adj, n* Roman

roman

I § *adj* [*Ling*] Romance (language)

II § *nm* **1** [*Lit*] novel * **2** gate/door bar, door bolt

romancë *nf* [*Lit Mus*] short lyric set to music: romance

romancier *n* novelist

* **romanctar** *(Old)* = **romancier**

romantik

I § *adj* romantic

II § *nm* romanticist

romantikë *nf* something that elicits noble/romantic sentiments: romance, romantic legend

romantizëm *nm* romanticism

romb *nm* [*Geom*] **1** rhombus **2** [*Ichth*] brill (*Scophthalmus rhombus*)

romboedër *nf* rhombohedron

romboid *nm* rhomboid

romuz *nm (Colloq)* snide remark: insinuation, innuendo

rondele *nf* [*Tech*] washer (for a bolt/axle)

◦ **rondele e prerë** [*Tech*] slotted washer

rone *nf (Colloq)* scarecrow = **dordolec**

ron|**is** *stem for 1st sg pres, pl pres 2nd & 3rd sg subj, pind* <**ronit·**

ronit· *vt* **1** to break [] apart into small pieces: break up [clods of soil]; shred [tobacco]; shell [corn]; erode [rock]; fray [cloth] **2** *(Fig)* to render [] helpless, break [] down

ronit·et *vpr* **1** to fall apart: crumble, fall to shreds, fray, erode **2** *(Fig)* to lose all strength, become helpless **3** *(Fig Colloq)* to become senile, go dotty

ronitje *nf ger* <**ronit·**, **ronit·**et

ronitur *adj (i)* **1** fallen apart: crumbled, dilapidated, in rags, eroded **2** *(Fig)* deprived of strength, feeble **3** *(Fig Colloq)* senile, dotty

ronke *np* [*Med*] rales

* **rop** *stem for pdef* <**rjep·**· = **rrop**|

* **ropkë** *nf* slave girl

* **roq**

◦ **roq me roq** from bad to worse

○ **roq me roq** from bad to worse

rosak *nm* [*Ornit*] drake

rosë *nf* **1** [*Ornit*] duck **2** long-handled bedpan
○ **rosa bishtgjelë** [*Ornit*] pintail *Anas acuta L.*
○ **rosa gridhe** [*Ornit*] teal *Anas crecca L.* = **kë**re
○ **rosa kokëbardhë** [*Ornit*] white-headed duck *Oxyura leucocephala Scopoli.*
○ **rosa pikaloshe** [*Ornit*] marbled teal *Anas angustirostris Men.*
○ **rosa e vendit** [*Ornit*] mallard *Anas platyrhynchos* = **ku**qël
○ **rosa e zezë** [*Ornit*] **1** gadwall *Anas strepera L* **2** common scoter *Melanita nigra L.*

*****roskë** *nf dimin* duckling

rosmari = **rozmarin**ë

rosticeri *nf* small café serving roasted meat: rotisserie

rosto *nf* [*Food*] sliced roast (meat)

roshan
  I § *adj, n* (person) scarred by smallpox: pockmarked
  II § *nm* ram (male sheep) with four horns

*****roshan**ë *nf* pock, freckle, spot

roshnica *np fem* [*Food*] rice-shaped pasta: orzo

rotacizëm *nm* [*Ling*] rhotacism

*****rotkë** = **rrotkë**

rotor *nm* [*Spec*] rotor

rozace *np* [*Bot*] rose family *Rosaceae*

rozë
  I § *nf* (*Reg*) knot (in timber), gnarl = **gdhe**
  II § *adj* pink (in color)

rozmarinë *nf* [*Bot*] rosemary (*Rosmarinus officinalis*)
○ **rozmarinë e egër** [*Bot*] tansy *Tanacetum vulgare*

RPSSh *abbrev* < **Republika Popullore Socialiste e Shqipërisë** People's Socialist Republic of Albania

RPSh *abbrev* < **Republika Popullore e Shqipërisë** [*Hist*] People's Republic of Albania

RSFJ *abbrev* < **Republika Socialiste Federative e Jugosllavisë** Federated Socialist Republic of Yugoslavia

RTSh *abbrev* < **Radiotelevizioni shqiptar** Albanian radio and television broadcasting network

RTV *abbrev* < **Radiotelevizioni** radio-television broadcasting network

ru·*het vpr* < **rua**·*n* **1** to avoid harm, be careful **2** to stay away from < *a danger*> **3** to be preserved, last; remain undamaged, remain
○ <> **ru**·*het* **si vdekjes** to fear <> like death itself, be scared to death of []

rua·*n vt* **1** to guard; stand watch/guard over []; watch over [], observe [] carefully; look after [], care for [], have custody of []; preserve; keep, maintain, retain; keep [] separate, save **2** to wait for [a time/opportunity]
○ **rua**·*n* **erërat** "wait for the winds" to wait to see which way the wind *is blowing*, be an opportunist
○ **e rua**·*n* **faqen** to save face
○ **rua**·*n* **fjalën** to keep one's word
○ **rua**·*n* **lëkurën 1** to save one's own skin **2** to look out for one's own interests
○ **Ruan me trastë e prish me thasë.** "Saves by the bag and wastes by the sack." (*Prov*) Penny-wise and pound-foolish.
○ **rua**·*n* **në gjirin e** {*pronominal adj*} to contain in {*one's*} midst: harbor in {*one's*} bosom

○ [] **rua**·*n* **në xhep 1** to keep [] in mind **2** to try never to forget []; make a reminder of [] for future revenge
○ [] **rua**·*n* **si breshka dheun** to guard [] carefully
○ [] **rua**·*n* **si dritën e syve** "guard [] like one's eyesight" to consider [] to be as precious as eyesight, hold [] as precious: treasure []; treat [] carefully
○ [] **rua**·*n* **si i varfri kaun** to treat [] as a precious object
○ [] **rua**·*n* **si qeni mishin/mëlçitë** "watch [] like the dog watches meat/liver" (*Iron*) (said of thieves preparing to steal something) to look over [the place] for a long time: case [the joint]
○ [] **rua**·*n* **si qorri syrin e vetëm** "guard [] like the one-eyed man his only eye" to guard [] as something very precious
○ [] **rua**·*n* **si syrin e vetëm** "guard [] like one's only eye" to regard [] as very precious: treasure []
○ [] **rua**·*n* **si sytë e ballit** "guard [] like the eyes in one's face" to hold [] very precious: treasure []
○ **rua**·*n* **të vdekurin** to watch over the deceased until the funeral
○ **Ruaje zogun sa e ke në dorë!** "Hold on to however many birds you have in hand!" (*Prov*) Use whatever opportunities you have! Don't miss your chances!

ruajt *stem for pdef, opt, adm, part* < **rua**·*n*, **ru**·*het*

ruajtës
  I § *n* **1** guard, watchman, sentry **2** keeper; custodian **3** herdsman
  II § *adj* serving to keep/guard/maintain/preserve: protective, preservative
○ **ruajtësit e rendit** forces/guardians of law and order

ruajtje *nf ger* < **rua**·*n*, **ru**·*het* preservation, protection

ruajtur
  I § *part* < **rua**·*n*, **ru**·*het*
  II § *adj* (i) **1** guarded **2** preserved **3** saved, reserved

*****ruazë** = **rruazë**

*****ruazore** *nf* rosary

rubai *nf* [*Lit*] lyrical Oriental quatrain whose first, second, and fourth lines rhyme: rubai

rubak *nm* sheep or goat whose coat/fleece is patchy

rubë *nf* **1** (black) kerchief, head kerchief *****2** handkerchief

rubël *nf* ruble

rubin *nm* ruby

*****rubinet**ë *nf* faucet

rubintë *adj* (i) made of ruby; ruby-colored

rubo·*n vt* to plug [] up with rags

rubrikë *nf* subject rubric: section, category

ruc *nm* (*Colloq*) petty thief, pilferer

ruc· *vt* (*Crude*) to penetrate <>'s mind: get through to <>

*****ruckë** *nf* flawless walnut

ruco·*n vt* (*Colloq*) to swipe, pilfer

*****rud** = **rudak**

rudak *nm* ram/lamb with a thick high-quality fleece of short, soft, and curly wool

rudë
  I § *adj* (of fleece/hair) short, soft, and curly; having short, soft, and curly fleece/hair
  II § *nf* **1** ewe with a thick high-quality fleece of short, soft, and curly wool **2** [*Bot*] = **ryz**ë

rudëzim *nm ger* (*Book*) < **rudëzo**·*n*, **rudëzo**·*het* rudëzo·het vpr (Book) to gain better quality of wool through crossbreeding

rudëzo·n vt (Book) to crossbreed [sheep] to improve the quality of wool

Rudin||a nf Rudina (female name)

rudinë nf grassy upland meadow, mountain lea/pasture

rudith nm [Bot] false bromegrass Brachypodium

rudo nf with masc agreement (obl ˜ ua) wooly ram

*ru'e| = rua|

rufai nm [Relig] member of a sect of Moslem dervishes

rufet nm guild

*ru'fë = rrufë

*rufis = rrufis·

*rufit· = rrufit·

*rufja'n nm = rrufja'n

*ru'fkë adj = rru'fkë

*ru'full = rru'full

ruk· vt (Colloq) = ruko'·n

ru'kë adj without its outer husk; bare

ruko·het vpr (Colloq) to get rid of unwanted hair: have a shave and a haircut

ruk|o·n vt to remove the outer covering of [ ]

rul nm [Tech] 1 roller 2 tube made of a rolled up sheet

rum nm rum

Ruman|i nf Rumania

ruman|isht adv in Rumanian (language)

ruman|isht|e nf Rumanian language

*rumeg|im nm ger <rumego'·n

*rumego·n vt to bellow

Rumeli nf Rumelia

rumu'n adj, n Rumanian

*rumu'z nm (Colloq) = romu'z

ru'në nf chimney flue

*runga' OR runga'jë OR runga'llë nf = rrunga'jë

rup nm 1 (Old) coin worth ten para: rupee 2 ornamental coin worn in chains by women
  ○ Nuk shkohet me tre rupe në dasmë. "One doesn't go to a wedding with only three rupees." (Prov) You have to be better prepared to consider such a big undertaking.

*rupc nm 1 scree 2 precipice, cliff

*ru'pë nf smell of something burning

ru'pi indecl masc rupee

rupi'zgë nf pine cone

*ruqe'rbull nm (np ˜ j) [Zool] lynx = rrëqe'bull

*ruqe'të nf rocket, signal rocket

ru're nf constant suspicion/worry

ru'r|ëz = ru're

rus
  I § adj, n Russian
  II § adj red-haired

ru's·et vpr to hang down, descend

*ru's|ër np <rus

rusgje'r nm (Old) pouring rain

Rusi nf Russia

rusi'ca np fem 1 (Reg Old) [Relig] holiday celebrated by Orthodox women and children twenty-five days after Easter: Pentecost 2 small biscuit baked for Pentecost

rusi'sht adv in Russian (language)

rusi'sht|e nf Russian (language)

ru'skë adj, n fem (Dimin) <rus

rus|o'ma'dh adj (Pej) pertaining to Russian expansionism

ru'spë nf 1 [Tech] bulldozer blade 2 (Old) small golden coin 3 (Fig Colloq) beautiful girl

ruspie nf (Pej) whore

Ruste'm nm Rustem (male name)

rusha't nm (Old) [Ethnog] = mergju'r

*rushfe't = ryshfe't

rushk nm (np ˜ qe) [Bot] butcher's broom (Ruscus aculeatus)

*ru'shk|ull = rru'shkull

ruti'në nf routine

*ru'xë = ry'zë

*ru'zë nf 1 = rrua'zë 2 [Bot] = lulerrua'zë

*ru'zull = rru'zull

*ry·n vt = hy'·n

*ry'be nf rank, title

*ry'p|kë nf shoelace, thong = rri'pkë

*ry'rë part <ry'

rys· vt 1 to train, exercise, toughen 2 to convince

ry's·et vpr 1 to gain experience/training; get toughened 2 to be convinced

rys|ni nf experience = përvo'jë

ry's|ur adj (i) experienced, trained; toughened

ryshfe't nm bribe, bribery

ryshfet|çi nm (np ˜ nj) (Pej) bribe taker

rytbe nf (Old) rank, title

*ry'thë nf cashbox, till

ry'zë nf [Bot] rue (Ruta)

ryzo·n vt to wear out [clothes], wear [clothes] to a fray

RRrr

rr [rrë] *nf* **1** the digraph "rr" considered to be a single letter in the Albanian alphabet **2** the apical trill represented by the letter "rr"

rra *nf* [*Invert*] threadworm = **rre**

rra·be *nf* unproductive and rocky scrub-land

rrabe·rr *nm* emaciated livestock about to die

rrabo·shtë *nf* [*Bot*] spindle-tree = **fshikaku·q**

***rra·bush** *nm* (*Old*) score, marker; record book, ledger, inventory

***rrabush·im** *nm ger* (*Old*) < **rrabusho·n**

***rrabusho·n** *vt* (*Old*) **1** to enter [] into the record: tally, score, log, record **2** to ration

***rrac·at·u·er** *adj* (*fem ⁓ ore*) (*Old*) racial; of known pedigree, thoroughbred

***rra·çe** *nf* clothes = **rra·qe**

rra·çka *np* = **rra·qe**

rrada·ke *nf* **1** (*Colloq*) skull **2** (*FigImpolite*) thick skull

***rradunga·l** *nm* dwarf with a big head

***rradh**| = **radh**|

***rraf**| = **rrah**|

***rra·fc** *nm* wash paddle, clothes beater

***rra·fse** *nf* = **rrah·ëse**

rrafsh
  I § *nm* **1** flat/level surface **2** plain **3** plane
  II § *adv* **1** level; flat **2** (not erect) low, down, down flat **3** completely full: to the brim, up to the rim
  III § *pcl* neither more nor less: precisely, exactly
    ○ **rrafsh me tokën** flat to the ground, at ground level
    ○ **rrafsh e plot** brimming; full of good things

rrafsh·azi *adv* at ground level

rrafsh·ëri *nf* large amount, mass

rrafsh·ësi *nf* (*Book*) levelness; flatness

rrafsh·ët *adj* (*i*) **1** level; flat **2** shallow **3** (*Fig*) even, uniform **4** (*Fig*) calm and relaxed

rrafsh·im *nm ger* < **rrafsho·n**, **rrafsho·het**

rrafsh·inë *nf* level ground/land: plain

rrafsh·inor *adj* characteristic of a plain; having a flat/level surface: planar

rrafsh·ja·n *n* inhabitant of a lowland/plain

rrafsh·kodër *nf* level ground in the hills: hill plain

rrafsh·naltë *nf* [*Geog*] plateau, upland

rrafsho·het *vpr* to become level/flat/smooth

rrafsho·n *vt* **1** to make [] flat with the ground: level, flatten **2** to cause [] to be level: level [] to the ground; make [] level; fill [] to the brim **3** (*Fig*) to conciliate, pacify, smooth down []
    ○ **rrafsho·n thepin me shtjekëzën** to line up the sighting pin, the gunsight notch, and the target

rrafsh·or *adj* **1** level, flat **2** [*Geom*] planar, plane

rrafsh·u·ar *adj* (*i*) **1** leveled out, flat **2** flattened to the ground, utterly destroyed

rrafsh·u·es *adj* **1** used for levelling; having levelling effects: levelling **2** (*Pej*) ignoring essential differences

rrafsh·u·es·e *nf* [*Tech*] trowel

rrafsh·u·l·ët *nf* [*Geog*] lowland plain

rraga·m *nm* large rocky crag

rraga·në *nf* scuffle

rraga·nic·ë = **rragnic·ë**

rragat·et *vpr* (*Colloq*) to have a spat, bicker, squabble

rragat·ar *adj, n* contentious, bickering

rragat·ë *nf* (*Colloq*) strife; verbal spat, squabble, bickering

rragat·ës *adj, n* quarrelsome (person)

rra·gë *nf* **1** linen sackcloth **2** protective apron (worn by women) made of linen sackcloth: linen duster **3** = **rragatë**

rragnic·ë *nf* thick dustcloth used for cleaning the floor

rrah
  I § *nm* arable clearing in a forest
  II § *adv* prostrate, laid flat

rrah *stem for 1st sg pres, 1st & 3rd pl pres, 2nd & 3rd sg subj* < **rre·h·**

rrah·a·der·ë *adj, n* (person) begging from door to door, beggar

***rra·h·c·ë** *nf* ramrod

rrah·ça·k *nm* tree stump with roots

rrah·çë *nf* conical fishing net used to catch spawning fish

rrah·e *nf* **1** narrow path: trail **2** part in the hair (created by combing)

rra·h·ëm *nf* (*i*) (*Reg Gheg*) = **rra·hur**

rrah·ës *nm* **1** beater; bat, paddle; knocker; clapper; gun hammer; pestle **2** [*Med*] pulsatile

rrah·ës·e *nf* **1** ramrod **2** beating tool: beater **3** churn
    ○ **rrahëse vezësh** eggbeater

***rra·h·ëz** *nf dimin* = **rra**

rrah·inë *nf* forest clearing left uncultivated

rrah·ishtë *nf* = **rrah**

rrah·it·et *vpr* (of woodland) to become cleared for cultivation, be cleared of trees

rra·hje *nf ger* **1** < **rre·h·**, **rrih·et** ***2** fighting: fight, scuffle, brawl ***3** ridge of land, hill

***rra·h·me** *nf* (*e*) beating

rraho·n *vt* **1** to clear [land] (for cultivation or for pasture) **2** to knock [] flat/down, lay [] out flat

rrah·stul·ë *nf* = **dërstil·ë**

rra·hur
  I § *part* < **rre·h·**, **rrih·et**
  II § *adj* (*i*) **1** processed by pounding/beating: hammered; beaten, whipped; churned **2** (*Euph*) castrated **3** (*Fig*) much-traveled (route): beaten (path), familiar (road/problem); well-explored (method/issue) **4** (*Fig*) having endured endless hardship
    ○ **i rrahur me vaj e me uthull** "beaten with oil and vinegar" well seasoned by experience

***rrâj·ça·k** *adj* (*Reg Gheg*) stump with roots attached

rra·jë *nf* [*Ichth*] thornback ray (*Raja (Raja) clavata*)

***rrâj·ë**| (*Reg Gheg*) = **rrënj·ë**|

***rraj·ë·shkul·ët** *adj* = **rrënj·ëshku·lur**

rra·jzë *nf* **1** (*Reg*) [*Invert*] earthworm, rainworm ***2** threadworm ***3** rootlet, root

rrakat adj (Colloq) mindless, unthinking: dotty, dizzy

rrakat· vt to make a noise by shaking []: tinkle/ring [a bell], rattle

rrakatake nf = rrake

rrake nf rattle, noisemaker; toy rattle

rrakel nm = rodhan

rraketake nf 1 toy rattle 2 sound of the beater against the millstone

rrakoq nm laxative medicine

rrallaçik adj = ralluk

rrallas adv sporadically; sparsely

rrallazi = rrallas

rrallesë nf 1 something taken out for thinning-out purposes 2 = rrallësi

rrallesh nm ear of corn with few kernels

rrallë
  I § adj (i) 1 sporadic; sparse 2 infrequent 3 rare 4 (Fig) unusual, extraordinary, exceptional
  II § adv 1 far apart; sparsely 2 rarely; infrequently
  ○ **rrallë e kur** now and then
  ○ **rrallë e për mall** only rarely
  ○ **rrallë e tek** 1 very rarely, seldom 2 spaced well apart, sparsely

rrallëherë adv hardly ever

rrallëkund adv hardly anywhere

rrallëkush pron hardly anyone

rrallësi nf (Book) rarity, rareness; sparseness

rrallësim nm ger = rrallim

rrallësinë nf area with sparse plant growth; sparse forest

rrallëso·het vpr = rrallo·het

rrallëso·n vt = rrallo·n

rrallim nm ger 1 < rrallo·n, rrallo·het 2 loose (un-crowded) spacing/distance

rrallishtë nf 1 = rralles·ë 2 sparse grove of trees

rrallo·het vpr 1 to become more sparse, get thinned out; become more infrequent; become rarefied 2 (Fig Colloq) to grow senile/demented: go dotty, lose one's marbles
  ○ **rallohu prej këtej!** (Impol) make yourself scarce! get out of here!

rrallo·n vt 1 to make [] more sparse: thin [] out, space out [], rarefy 2 to cut down consumption of [], reduce frequency of []: cut down on []

rrallojë nf = rralles·ë

rralluar adj (i) thinned out; depleted; rarefied

rrallues
  I § adj used for pruning or thinning out
  II § n [Agr] person engaged in pruning or thinning out

rralluk adj, nm 1 (ear of corn) having few kernels 2 gap-toothed (person)

rram-bam adv (Colloq) somehow, with great difficulty, barely; so-so

*__rrangaj__ adv in a clutter/jumble, in disorder

rrangallë OR **rrangalle** nf, adj (Impol) old, broken-down, and worthless (person/animal/thing)

*__rrangë__ np fem = rrangulla

*__rrangëlle·n__ = rrangullo·n

rrangulla np fem miscellaneous items: household junk, everyday odds and ends

rrangullina np fem = rrangulla

*__rrangullo·n__ vi to jangle, clatter; (of teeth) chatter

rranicë nf (Reg) large piece of food: chunk, hunk, slab

rrap nm [Bot] Oriental plane tree (Platanus orientalis)

*__rrap__ = rrop

rrapaçuk adj = rrapashyt

rrapamë nf = rropamë

rrapanidhe nf [Bot] radish (Raphanus)

*__rrapas__ stem for 1st sg pres, pl pres, 2nd & 3rd sg subj, pind < rrapat·

rrapashyt adj, nm stocky (person)

*__rrapat·__ vt = rropat·

*__rrapat·et__ vpr = rropat·et

*__rrapaticë__ = rrakaticë

rrapatime nf noisy row, brawl

*__rrapatishte__ OR **rrapatishtë** nf = rrapishtë

rrapatos·et vpr to make a lot of noise intentionally, make a racket

rrapçalle nf trifle(s), junk

rrapëlli·n vi to make a loud booming sound: boom

rrapëllimë nf booming sound, boom

rrapëllo·n vi = rrapëlli·n

Rrapli nm Rrapi (male name)

rrapinë nf timber that bears the upright stakes forming a side of a cart

rrapishtë nf grove of plane trees

rrapitoll adv
  ○ **rrapitoll me tokën** level with the ground

Rrapo nf Rrapo (male name)

rrapore nf [Bot] plane tree family Platanaceae

*__rrapsall__ = rapsall

rrapshte·het vpr (of tender plant parts) to shrivel up and get tough

rrapshtenjtë adj (i) (of formerly tender plant parts) shriveled up and tough

rraptimë nf = rrapëllimë

rrapto·n vi = rrapëlli·n

rraqe np fem (Colloq) household stuff, goods and belongings; household junk

rras·
  I § vt 1 to press down on [], press [] down; press [] down flat 2 to fill [] to overflowing: cram 3 (Colloq) to stick/clap/bang [] in
  II § vi to come pouring in from all directions
  ○ [] **rras· brenda** (Colloq) to put [] in jail: throw [] into the slammer
  ○ **<> a rras· me** [] (Colloq) to hit <> hard with []

rras·et vpr 1 to enter [] violently 2 to crouch down 3 (Fig Colloq) to get stuffed (from eating) 4 (of bread) to get stale and hard

rrasallis stem for 1st sg pres, pl pres, 2nd & 3rd sg subj, pind < rrasallit·

rrasallit· vt to make [something soft and loose] more compact: compact

rrasallit·et vpr to become compacted

rrasallitje nf ger 1 < rrasallit·, rrasallit·et 2 compaction

*__rrasanike__ nf seed cabbage

rrasash adv

rrasbuq adv

rrasë nf 1 flat rock; slate; slab; rock slab; flooring tile; flagstone 2 face of a cliff

○ *Ka-*^{3sg} *gjetur*/*gjeti* rrasa vegshin/vorbën. "The slab of rock found its cooking pot." *(Pej)* The devil has found his mate.

○ **rrasa e vegshit** rock slab used to cover a cooking pot

rra·sët *adj (i), pred* tightly knit/woven; densely packed, compressed

rras·ík *adj, nm* flat (stone)

rras·ít *vt* = rrasallít·

rras·ít·*et vpr* = rrasallít·*et*

***rra·sje** *nf* attempt, trial

rras·kap·ís *stem for 1st sg pres, pl pres, 2nd & 3rd sg subj, pind* < **rraskapít**·

rras·kapít· *vt* to tire [ ] out completely, exhaust

rras·kapít·*et vpr* to get very tired, become utterly exhausted

rras·kapítje *nf ger* **1** < **rraskapít**·, **rraskapít**·*et* **2** utter exhaustion **3** *[Med]* prostration

rras·kapítur *adj (i)* **1** utterly tired out: exhausted **2** *(Fig)* very poor, down and out

rra·skë *nf* rennet, rennin

*__rra·skëz__ *nf* = rraskë

*__rras·meni__ *nf* density

rraso·ll *nm (np ~ j)* pickled vegetable, mixed pickles

rras·ór *adj* slab-shaped; formed of slabs

rrash·aták *adj* short and stumpy, squat

*__rrash·ino·__·*n vt* to level

*__rrash·katie·lla__ *nm* vermicelli

*__rrash·nalte__ *nf* upland meadow, mountain pasture = rrafshnaltë

*__rrash·nalto·__·*n vt* to make [ ] level, grade

*__rrash__ *(Reg Gheg)* = rrafsh

rrashqel

  I § *nm* hook of a tapeworm

  II § *adj* gross, coarse

rrasht *nm (Reg)* bone

rrashtë *nf* **1** *(Reg)* bone **2** skull **3** worn or bent utensil used for storage

○ **rrashta e breshkës** turtle shell

○ **rrashta e lugëve** container for keeping spoons

○ **rrashta e rrobave** tub of lye for clothes

rrasht·ín·e *nf* **1** felt skullcap **2** level/flat place

*__rrashtjel__ *nm* grate, grill

*__rrashtjelo·__·*n vt* to rake

*__rrash·tul·te__ *nf* lowland plain

rrath·ë *np* **1** < **rreth 2** reel on a trawling pole used in fishing

○ **rrathët e barkut** "hoops of the belly" roll of fat around the belly, love handles

○ **rrathët e gushës** "hoops of the throat" double chin

○ [ ] **janë liruar rrathët** [ ] *has* flipped (his lid)

rrath·ë-rrath·ë *adv* arranged in circles/circlets one upon another

rrath·je *nf [Bot]* edible mushroom with a light brown cap, circles of white on the stem, and a milky excrescence: saffron milk cup, delicious lactarius *(Lactarius deliciosus)*

*__rrauxha·u__ *adv* in a rowdy-dowdy way, boisterously

rra·vë *nf* path, trail

rra·vëz *nf* furrow

rravg·ím *nm ger* **1** < **rravgo·**·*n* **2** *[Med]* aberration

rravgo··*n vi* **1** to wander all around **2** to lose clarity: fade

rra·xhe

  I § *nf* **1** piece of wood used to level off a heap (of grain, flour) that is higher than the brim of its container **2** *[Ichth]* ray *(Raja)*

  II § *adv* full to the brim

○ **me/në rraxhë** full to the brim

rrazbít·*et vpr* to become weak and emaciated

*__rrazíke__ *nf* = kular

rre *nf* **1** narrow path; trail, snowtrail **2** trail left by a snail or reptile **3** *[Invert]* intestinal worm: threadworm *(Enterobius vermicularis)* **4** *[Invert]* mawworm *(Ascaris lumbricoides)*

rre··*het vpr* < **rre·**·*n (Colloq)* to be deceivable/deceived

rre··*n vt (Colloq)* to lie to [ ]

○ **rre·**·*n* **ashiqare**/**për hava** to be a clumsy liar

○ **<> rre·**·*n*^{3sg} **mendja se __** < > foolishly *thinks* that __

○ **rre·**·*n* **përtokë/shtruar** to be a clever and convincing liar

rre·*stem for pdef, opt* < **rry·e·**·*n*

rreb·án *adj* given to acting on whim: impulsive, capricious

rreb·áq *adj (Impol)* **1** = rrebán **2** thin and sickly

rre·be *nf* momentary feeling: caprice, whim; temper

rre·be·mádh *adj, n* overly impulsive: capricious (person)

rrebe·mírë *adj* **1** in a good mood/humor **2** cool-tempered

rre·bésh *nm* **1** outburst of rain: rainstorm, cloudburst **2** *(Fig)* outburst, outpouring **3** *(Fig)* catastrophe, disaster

*__rrebesh·ësi__ *nf* tempest, hurricane

*__rrebesh·ím__ *nm* **1** catastrophe, disaster **2** assault, attack

*__rrebesh·o·__·*n vt* **1** to wreck, destroy **2** to assault, attack

*__rrebesh·tar__ *adj* catastrophic, disastrous

rrebesh·të *adj (i)* in a sudden outburst

*__rrebesh·tor__ *adj* causing destruction, destructive

*__rrebesh·ues__ *nm* destroyer

*__rre·btë__ = rreptë

rre·bull *nm* **1** *[Med]* impetigo **2** *(Fig)* bad temper *3 [Bot]* maple = **panjë**

*__rre·bull·të__ *adj (i)* of maple

*__rre·cë__ *nf* lining/wall of the stomach

rreck·amán *adj, n* **1** (person) dressed in tattered clothes **2** *(Fig)* very poor (person)

rreck·aman·o·s· *vt* to tatter

rreck·aník *adj* tattered, raggedy

rre·cka-rre·cka *adj, adv* in tatters and shreds, raggedy; hanging in tatters

rre·ck·ë *nf* old and worn out piece of cloth or clothing: rag

rreck·o·s· *vt* = lecko·s·

rreck·o·s·*et vpr* = lecko·s·*et*

rreck·o·s·ur *adj (i)* = lecko·s·ur

*__rredh__ = rreth

*__rref__ = rreh

*__rref·a·s__ *stem for 1st sg pres, pl pres, 2nd & 3rd sg subj, pind* < **rrefa**·t·

*__rref·at·__ *I §* *vi* OR **rref·a·t**·*et II §* *vpr* = rrembo·*het*

*__rref·a·të__ *nf* branch, twig

*__rref·ë·go·__·*het* = rrefkëto·*het*

*rrefkë *nf (Reg Tosk)* pulse, throb

*rrefkësi *nf* violence; rage; temper

rrefkët
I § *adj (i)* **1** harsh, rough **2** savage, furious, violent, fierce
II § *adv* harshly, roughly

rrefkëto·het *vpr* to get furious/violent, lose one's temper

rrefkëto·n *vt* to make [] furious/violent

rregë *nf* **1** formerly arable land ruined by erosion or flood **2** narrow strip of ground running through a rocky area on a mountainside

rregull
I § *nm* **1** order; regularity; proper order **2** rule, norm
II § *nf* **1** rule, principle **2** regulation
∘ **rregulla e artë e mekanikës** the law of conservation of energy
∘ **rregulla dëftuese** guidelines
∘ **s'ësh-të në rregull** not behave properly; not be in proper order
∘ **rregull e prerë** hard and fast rule

rregulli *nf collec* kin, kinfolk

rregullim *nm ger* **1** <**rregullo·n**, **rregullo·het 2** adjustment

rregullisht *adv* in regular manner, as a rule: regularly, normally; usually

rregullo·het *vpr* **1** to fix up one's appearance: groom oneself **2** *(Colloq)* to become better looking **3** (of weather) to get better **4** *(Colloq)* to get back in good shape, recover **5** to get settled (in a position/job/house) **6** to come to an agreement; patch things up

rregullo·n *vt* **1** to arrange [] in proper order **2** to put [] in order, adjust; put [] back in order, readjust; fix, repair; settle; regulate **3** *(Colloq)* to take care of [a matter]: take [] in hand **4** *(Colloq)* to have [it] fixed (with someone to do something irregular)
∘ <>a **rregullo·n bërroren** to punish <> severely for doing something wrong; give <> the beating that <> deserves
∘ **rregullo·n borxhet me** [] to settle one's loans with []
∘ **rregullo·n gojën** to mind/watch one's language
∘ <>a **rregullo·n hesapin** to settle <>'s hash
∘ <>a **rregullo·n kurrizin** to punish <> severely for doing something wrong; give <> the beating that <> deserves
∘ **rregullo·n llogarinë me** [] to settle one's accounts with []
∘ [] **rregullo·n me mik/anë miku** to get [] arranged through an influential friend, fix [] with the help of a friend with pull
∘ **e rregullo·n pllakën** to arrange matters to one's advantage
∘ <>a **rregullo·n qejfin** to teach <> a lesson, correct <>'s wrongful behavior; give <> the beating that <> deserves
∘ <>a **rregullo·n samarin** to punish <> severely for doing something wrong: give <> the beating that <> deserves
∘ <>a **rregullo·n shpinën** to punish <> severely for doing something wrong; give <> the beating that <> deserves
∘ **e rregullo·n vajzën** *(Colloq)* to marry off one's daughter well

*rregullor
I § *adj* according to rule: regular

II § *n* ruler, regulator, master

rregullore *nf* set of regulations: regulations; book of regulations

rregullsi *nf* regularity, orderliness

rregullsishëm *adj (i)* according to the rules: regular

rregullshëm *adj (i)* = **rregullsishëm**

rregullshmëri *nf* = **rregullsi**

rregullt *adj (i)* **1** regular; standard **2** proper **3** [*Mil*] properly trained

rregulltar
I § *n* **1** [*Relig*] member of a Catholic religious order
*2 regulator
II § *adj* [*Relig*] belonging to a Catholic religious order

rregullues
I § *adj* serving to regulate: regulating, controlling
II § *nm* regulator, control
III § *n* **1** person who directs traffic: traffic controller
*2 monitor ***3** steward of an estate

rregzinë *nf* insole pad in clogs; woolen footwrapping worn instead of stockings

*rregj = **regj**

*rregjëni *nf (Old)* kingdom, realm

*rregjësi *nf (Old)* = **rrezatim**

*rregjo·n *vt* = **rrëgjo·n**

*rregjos *vt* = **regj·**

*rregjtar *n* tanner

*rregjtor *n (Old)* = **rregjtar**

*rregjuar = **rrëgjuar**

rreh·
I § *vt* **1** to beat/pat [] repeatedly: pound, beat, pat, batter, buffet, flail; hammer [metal]; clap [hands]; churn [milk]; hackle [fiber]; flail **2** to beat [] (in a game) **3** to traverse [] frequently **4** *(Fig)* to give [a subject] a good going over, thoroughly explore [a matter] **5** *(Colloq)* to iron **6** *(Euph)* to castrate, geld
II § *vi* **1** to beat (rhythmically); hammer; throb **2** *(Fig)* to strive **3** *(Fig)* to direct steady attention to something, be intent on something: concentrate **4** (of fish) to spawn
∘ **rreh· baltën** to prepare slush/mortar/cement by thorough mixing
∘ **rreh· benë** *(Old)* to make a vow, take an oath
∘ **rreh· brumin** to knead dough
∘ <> **rreh·³ˢᵍ delli** <>'s pulse is beating
∘ **rreh· dyert e botës** "knock on the doors of other people" to go from door to door (begging or looking for work)
∘ <> **rreh·³ˢᵍ dyfeku lart** *(Pej)* <> acts like a big shot
∘ **rreh· dynjanë/dheun 1** to travel everywhere **2** to look everywhere: beat the bushes looking
∘ **rreh· gjoksin** "beat one's breast" **1** to make empty boasts; boast loudly **2** to make a clean breast of it
∘ **rreh· jetën** "beat one's life" **1** to beat the bushes looking, look everywhere **2** to travel everywhere
∘ **rreh· kohën** to beat time (rhythmically)
∘ **rreh· kraharorin** "beat one's chest" **1** to make empty boasts; boast loudly **2** to make a clean breast of it
∘ **rreh· lart** to think too highly of oneself
∘ **rreh· lopatat** to row oars
∘ **rreh·³ˢᵍ maqina** the engine knocks
∘ **rreh· me hekur** *(Colloq)* to iron

○ **rreh· me makinë** *(Colloq)* to type (on a typewriter)

○ **rreh· me mend** to think hard

○ [] **rreh· me mend** to think [] over, consider []

○ **rreh· mendjen** to cudgel one's brains, think hard

○ **i rreh· në atë krah** to touch that subject, bring up that subject

○ [] **rreh· në havan** to examine [] thoroughly; deliberate over <>, digest <> carefully

○ **rreh· nga _** to take the part of [], come down on []'s side

○ **rreh· një rrugë** to frequent a road

○ [] **rreh· paq** to give [] a thorough beating

○ **rreh· qerpikët** to blink

○ **rreh· qumësht** to churn milk

○ **rreh· rëndë** to think too highly of oneself

○ [] **rreh· si qenin në bostan** "beat [] like the dog in the melon patch" to beat [] heavily, beat [] badly

○ <> **rreh· supet** to pat <> on the back

○ <> **rreh·**³ᵖˡ **shumë çekanë në kokë** "many hammers beat <> on the head" <> *has* many things to worry about, <> has many problems

○ **rreh· shuplakat** to clap hands

○ **rreh· një tel** to send a wire (telegram), telegraph

○ **rreh· telefonin** to keep calling on the telephone

○ **rreh· telin/telat** *(Old)* to send a wire (telegraph) = **telegrafo·**·*n*

○ **të rreh·**³ˢᵍˢᵘᵇʲ **çekani** that the major emphasis be placed

○ **rreh· ujë në havan** "beat water in a mortar" **1** to waste one's time/effort **2** to talk in vain: beat one's gums; beat a dead horse

○ **rreh· vendin** to look everywhere: beat the bushes looking.

○ <> **rreh·**³ˢᵍ **zemra për** [] "<>'s heart beats for []" <> *is* deeply concerned for [] out of love

*__**rrej*ë* = rrejm*ë***__

*__**rrejm*ë***__

I § *adj (i)* false = **rrem*ë***

II § *nf (e)* falsehood, lie

*__**rrëj*n*ës**__ *nm (Reg Gheg)* = **rrenës**

rrejsh*ë*m

I § *adj (i)* *(Colloq)* false, fake, fictitious = **gënjeshtërt**

II § *adv* while lying: falsely

rrejt *stem for pdef, opt, adm, part* <**rre·**n

*__**rrejtsh*ë*m = rrejsh*ë*m**__

rrek· *vt* **1** to annoy/weary [] (by beating around the bush): exasperate **2** to amuse, divert **3** *(Reg)* to make [] tardy: delay

rrek·et

I § *vpr* **1** to make every effort, really try, try hard **2** to amuse/divert oneself **3** *(Reg)* to be late/tardy

II § *vp impers* it *is* getting ready to (snow, rain)

*__**rreke** *nf* foppery__

rrek*ë*

I § *nf* **1** tree-ripened dry fig **2** dewlap on a goat **3** tricky move (to outmaneuver an opponent): trick

II § *adj* (of a fig) tree-ripened and dry

*__**rrek*ë*no·het** *vpr* (of a fig) to become ripe and dry on the tree__

rrek*ë*t *adj (i)* (of a fig) tree-ripened and dried; over-ripe

rrek*ë*z *nf* tricky move (to outmaneuver an opponent): quick fake; trick

rrek*ë*zin*ë* *nf* **1** insole in clogs **2** *(Fig)* rag

rrek*ë*zo··*het* *vpr* to dry out in the sun: parch

rrekje *nf ger* <**rrek·**, **rrek·**et

*__**rrekt** = rekët__

*__**rrekto·**·n__

I § *vi* **1** to breathe **2** to weep, sob

II § *vt* to stimulate, rouse, encourage

*__**rrek*un* *adj (i) (Reg Gheg)* = **rrekët**__

rrem *nm* **1** *[Naut]* oar *__**2** branch *__**3** = **rrym*ë***

rremall *adj, n* = **rremash**

*__**rremar** *n* = **rremtar**__

rremash *adj* deceitful (person)

rremb *nm* **1** twig **2** branch, branchlet **3** sub-group divided off from a larger group: band of stragglers **4** *[Anat]* blood vessel **5** mood **6** *(Fig)* family bond/tie; family trait

○ **rrembi i kosës** handle for the auxiliary hand on a scythe

rremba-rremba *adj* branched, branching out: ramate

rrembo··*het* *vpr* to branch out, give off branches

rrembo*s*ur *adj (i)* easily angered: irascible, hot-tempered

rrembth *nm* twig; sprig, sprout

rrem*ë* *nf* **1** millrace, mill stream; irrigation furrow *__**2** epidemic

rrem*ë*

I § *adj (i)* **1** false **2** illusory, deceptive; fake, pseudo

II § *nf (e)* falsehood, lie

*__**rrem*ë*s** *adj, n* = **rrenës**__

rremo··*het* *vpr* = **degëzo·**·*het*

*__**rremo·**·n *vt* = **rremto·**·n__

rremtar *nm* oarsman, rower

*__**rremtlesi** *nf* falsehood, lying__

rremth *nm* = **rrembth**

*__**rren** = **rrën**__

rrenaca*k*

I § *adj (Colloq)* habitually lying: fibbing, deceitful

II § *nm (Colloq)* habitual liar: fibber

rrenak *OR* **rrenavec** *adj, n* = **rrenës**

*__**rrënc** *OR* **rrencar** *adj, n (Reg Gheg)* = **rrenës**__

*__**rrende** *nf* = **rende**__

rren*ë* *nf (Colloq)* fib, lie

○ **rrena në diell** patent lie

rren*ë*s

I § *adj (Colloq)* **1** lying **2** having only the appearance of the real thing: fictitious, pseudo, sham, mock, illusory

II § *n (Colloq)* liar

rreng *nm (np ~ gje)* dirty trick; practical joke

*__**rrengçuer** *adj (fem ~ore) n (Old)* = **rrengshor**__

*__**rreng*ë*** *nf* *[Ichth]* herring__

rrengshor *adj, n* insidious/perfidious (person)

*__**rrënsh*ë*m** *adj (i) (Reg Gheg)* = **rrenës**__

*__**rrenuesh*ë*m** *adj (i)* ruinous, destructive__

rrepak *adj* *[Bot]* shaped like a turnip: *(napiform)*

rrepan *nm* *[Bot]* radish *(Raphanus sativus)*

○ **rrepan sheqeri** *[Bot]* sugar beet = **panxharsheqeri**

*__**rrepe** *np* <**rrap** *[Bot]* Oriental plane trees__

rrep*ë* *nf* *[Bot]* turnip *(Brassica rapa)*

○ **rrep*ë* e kuqe** *[Bot]* = **rrik*ë***

○ **rrep*ë* sheqeri** sugar beet = **panxharsheqeri**

rrepïc*ë* *nf* *[Bot]* rugose rapistrum *(Rapistrum rugosum)*

rrepishte _OR_ **rrepishtë** _nf_ field of turnips

*__rrepkë__ _nf (Reg Tosk)_ [_Bot_] turnip
 ○ **rrepkë e kuqe** carrot

rrepshëm _adj (i)_ = **rreptë**

rreptas _adv_ **1** severely, harshly; sternly **2** strictly, rigorously **3** fiercely, violently

rreptë
 _I §_ _adj (i)_ **1** severe, harsh **2** strict, precise **3** stern **4** fierce, violent
 _II §_ _adv_ **1** severely, harshly; sternly **2** strictly, rigorously **3** fiercely, violently

rreptësi _nf_ **1** severity, harshness **2** strictness; sternness **3** ferocity

rreptësisht _adv_ **1** severely, harshly; sternly **2** strictly; rigorously

rreptëso · _het vpr_ to become fierce/strict/severe/stern/harsh

rreptëso · _n vt_ **1** to make [] more severe/harsh, make [] stricter **2** to infuriate, enrage

rresë _nf (Colloq)_ way of life, life style

rreshk _nm_ **1** [_Dairy_] scorched crust formed on burnt food or milk **2** smell of burnt food **3** _(Fig)_ burning desire: avidity, appetite **4** habit, vice

rreshk · _vt_ **1** to sear/brown [food]; toast **2** to parch, wither; wizen, weather (with heat)

rreshk · _et vpr_ **1** to get toasted: toast **2** to dry up and wither; dry up and wrinkle **3** to become parched (with thirst) **4** to get sunburned

rreshkataq _adj_ wizened, wrinkled with age

rreshkatore _nf_ toaster

rreshkë _nf_ **1** piece of toasted bread: toast; piece of crisply rendered fat/meat: crackling **2** tree-ripened dried fig

rreshkim _nm_ dryness in the mouth (from fever or thirst): thirstiness

rreshko · _het vpr_ to feel famished

rreshko · _n_ = **rreshk** ·

rreshkur _adj (i)_ **1** toasted; sunburned **2** dried up, parched

rreshme _nf_ **1** avalanche of snow **2** slope covered with rock debris, scree

rreshpe _nf_ **1** [_Geol_] stratified rock: slate, schist **2** avalanche of snow **3** slope covered with rock debris, scree

rreshpor _adj_ [_Geol_] containing or consisting of schist: schistose

rresht
 _I §_ _nm_ row, line, column; rank
 _II §_ _adv_ in a row, in succession, one after another; continuously

*__rresht__ _vt_ **1** to let [] rest: fixate, fix **2** _(Old)_ to arrest

*__rreshtar__ = **rreshter**

rreshtazi _adv_ in succession

rreshter _nm_ **1** [_Mil_] sergeant **2** non-commissioned officer *__3__ corporal

rreshtim _nm ger_ **1** < **rreshto** · _n_, **rreshto** · _het_ **2** line-up **3** military formation

*__rreshtna__ _np_ < **rrasht** _(Reg Gheg)_ skeleton

rreshto · _het vpr_ **1** to line up **2** [_Mil_] to line up in ranks **3** _(Fig)_ to join the ranks; take one's proper place

rreshto · _n vt_ **1** to put/arrange [] in rows; line [] up **2** _(Fig)_ to list, enumerate; classify *__3__ to arrest

rreshtor _adj_ **1** [_Ling_] ordinal **2** [_Mil_] pertaining to drill formation

rreshtore _nf (Colloq)_ [_Mil_] parade drill, military drill

*__rret__ = **rrjet**

rretër = **retër**

rreth
 _I §_ _nm (np rrathë)_ **1** circle **2** hoop; ring **3** compass, circle, range, domain **4** circumference, perimeter **5** [_Sport_] race circuit **6** horizon **7** _(Fig Colloq)_ big bunch, flock **8** ammunition belt **9** snowshoe **10** tire (on a wheel)
 _II §_ _nm (np ˜ e)_ **1** largest administrative subdivision in Albania: district **2** environs **3** _(Fig)_ family/social circle; circle of helpful friends **4** line of latitude
 III § _adv_ all around
 _IV §_ _prep (abl)_ around, surrounding; about
 ○ **rreth i hekurt** [_Mil_] tight encirclement; pincers movement
 ○ **rrethi i kosës** metal ring that fastens a scythe blade to its handle
 ○ **rreth i mbyllur** _(Book)_ **1** vicious circle **2** tight spot
 ○ **rreth e okolla** round and around
 ○ **rreth e (për)qark** *__1__ round and about; all around **2** around and around
 ○ **rrethi i qendrës** [_Soccer_] kickoff circle
 ○ **rreth e rreth/rrotull** **1** round and about; all around **2** around and around
 ○ **i vje·n rreth** to go at it by a circuitous route, approach the matter indirectly; speak indirectly

rrethak
 _I §_ _nm_ round fenced enclosure
 _II §_ _adj_ resembling a circle, like a circle

rrethako · _n vt_ = **rretho** · _n_

rrethanë _nf_ circumstance
 ○ **rrethana lehtësuese** [_Law_] mitigating circumstances
 ○ **rrethana rënduese** [_Law_] aggravating circumstances

rrethanik _I §_ _nm OR_ **rrethanike** _II §_ _nf_ [_Food_] walnut-filled pastry snail

rrethanor
 _I §_ _adj_ circumstantial
 _II §_ _nm_ [_Ling_] complement of circumstance

rrethas _adv_ all around; in a circle

*__rrethatar__ _nm (Old)_ rim of a wheel

rrethato · _n vt_ = **rretho** · _n_

rrethator
 _I §_ _adj_ circular, round
 _II §_ _nm_ = **rrethak**

rrethatore _nf_ **1** ammunition belt **2** big pan with a high rim **3** mountaineer's flat-topped skullcap made of white felt **4** = **rrethanik**

*__rrethçe__ _adv_ = **rrethas**

rrethe _np_ **1** environs, outskirts **2** tied-on moccasins with leather soles and uppers crosslaced all around with thongs **3** well-worn shoes

rrethe _nf_ **1** enclosed grazing meadow surrounded by a simple stone wall **2** balustraded balcony around the second story of a house

rrethim _nm ger_ **1** < **rretho** · _n_, **rretho** · _het_ **2** [_Mil_] encirclement, siege **3** [_Ling_] environment, context **4** surrounding wall/fence

rrethimtar _nm_ besieger

rrethinë _nf_ **1** suburb, environs, outskirts **2** uncultivated narrow strip of land surrounding a field

rrethje *nf* copper kettle with an arched handle

rrethkomandant *nm* [*Hist*] district commandant (of the gendarmerie)

rrethkomandë *nf* [*Hist*] district command; district headquarters

rrethlule *nf* [*Bot*] perianth

rretho•het *vpr* to take a position in a circle: gather around

rretho•n *vt* to encircle; surround

rrethojë *nf* **1** fence **2** large round pan **3** enclosure for animals

rrethor *adj* **1** circular; all around **2** [*Tech*] (of a saw) circular

rrethore *nf* **1** loose-hanging skirt worn by women in central Albania **2** playpen for toddlers **3** ammunition belt

rrethosë *nf* enclosure for protected grass

*****rrethpërqarkët** *adj* (i) having a coiled/radiating shape: whorled; rotate

rrethpre *stem for pdef, part, imper sg, adm, opt* <**rrethpret•**

rrethpre̱rë *part* <**rrethpret•**

rrethpre̱rje *nf* (Old) **1** <**rrethpret•** **2** circumcision = **synet**

rrethpres *stem for 1st sg pres, pl pres, 2nd & 3rd sg subj* <**rrethpret•**

rrethpret• *vt* (Book) to circumcise

rrethpris *stem for pind, 2nd pl pres* <**rrethpret•**

rrethprit *stem for pind, imper, vp* <**rrethpret•**

rrethqarkullim *nm* (Book) circulation

rrethsjellës *adj* circulatory

rrethsjellje *nf* [*Astron*] orbit **2** circulation

rrethshkrim *nm ger* [*Math*] <**rrethshkrua•n**

rrethshkrua•n *vt* [*Math*] to circumscribe

rrethshkruar *adj* (i) [*Math*] circumscribed

rrethtar *n* member of the inner circle surrounding a royal person: courtier

rrethuar
I § *adj* (i) **1** surrounded by a fence or wall: enclosed **2** surrounded by enemy forces: besieged
II § *nm* (i) besieged inhabitant

rrethues
I § *adj* **1** surrounding, enclosing **2** besieging
II § *n* besieger

rrethujzë *nf* (Old) island

rrevë *nf* (Reg) lot, chance = **short**

rrexë *nf* **1** lace = **dantellë 2** tulle = **tyl**

rrezak *adj* [*Bot*] radial (RR)

Rrezart *nm* Rrezart (male name)

Rrezarta *nf* Rrezarta (female name)

rrezatim *nm ger* **1** <**rrezato•n**, **rrezato•het 2** radiation

rrezato•het *vpr* **1** to emit rays/radiation **2** (Fig) to radiate in various directions: spread

rrezato•n
I § *vt* to radiate [ ]
II § *vi* to emit rays: shine

rrezatues
I § *adj* radiating; radiant
II § *nm* radiating device/body

rreze *nf* **1** ray **2** field of radiation **3** (Fig) span, scope, range **4** spoke (of a wheel) **5** [*Ichth*] ray of a fish fin **6** (Colloq) horn (of an animal) **7** [*Geom*] radius

8 quality rating (of an agricultural product) **9** (Colloq) sunny spot = **shullë**
○ **ësh•të me rreze** to radiate beauty, be radiantly beautiful
○ **rreze palcore** [*Bot*] medullary rays
○ **rreze vinçi** boom/jib of a crane
○ **rrezet x** [*Phys*] X-rays

rrezear *adj* (Poet) = **rrezearte**

rrezearte *adj* (Poet) golden-rayed

rrezediellore *np* [*Zool*] Heliozoa

rrezekuq *adj* (Poet) tinged with red: rose-fingered

rrezeplote *adj* (Poet) full of light

rrezet = **rrezat**

rrezg *nm* highest point, height, peak

rrezga-bjezga *adv* in pandemonium, in complete disorder: pell-mell

rrezgë *nf* (Reg) grape stem = **rruvan**

*****rrezgull** *nf* = **rriskull**

rrezigall *nm* arsenic; poison

rrezik *nm* (np ~ qe) **1** danger **2** risk, hazard **3** (Colloq) misfortune, accident; person who has suffered a misfortune
○ **rreziku i djathtë/majtë** danger from the right/left (wing)

rrezikim *nm ger* **1** <**rreziko•n**, **rreziko•het 2** endangerment

rreziko•het *vpr* to take a risk

rreziko•n
I § *vt* to put [ ] in danger, put [ ] at risk: endanger, risk
II § *vi* to take a risk

rrezikshëm *adj* (i) dangerous; risky

rrezikshmëri *nf* dangerousness; riskiness

rrezikzezë *nf fem* (Colloq) <**rrezikzi**

rrezikzi
I § *nm* (np ~ nj) (Colloq) person who has suffered a misfortune: poor guy!
II § *adj* *unfortunate

rrezinë *nf* place that basks in the sun: sunny spot

rrezit• *vi, vt* = **rrezo•n**

rrezit•et *vpr* = **rrezo•het**

rrezitje *nf ger* <**rrezit•**, **rrezite•t**

rrezm *nm* (Colloq) height of success, peak

rrezo•het *vpr* to take the sun, bask in the sun

rrezo•n
I § *vi* to give off rays, be radiant; shine
II § *vt* to radiate; expose [ ] to the sun's rays

rrezor *adj* **1** radial, radiating **2** (Fig Poet) radiant, resplendent

rrezore *np fem* [*Bot*] plants of the madder family Rubiaceae

rrezore *np* [*Zool*] Radiolaria

rrezhde *nf* unripe mulberry = **rezhdë**

*****rrezhdë** *nf* **1** walnut blossom **2** cell of a honeycomb

*****rrëbesh** = **rrebesh**

rrëbisht• *vt* to shear [a sheep/goat] around the tail = **bishto•**

*****rrëbishtas** *adv* = **bishtas**

rrëbyth• *vt* to force [ ] backwards: back; push back: repel

rrëbyth•et *vpr* **1** to scoot backwards on the buttocks **2** (Fig) to scoot away in shame, run away secretly

rrëcok *nm* **1** gizzard **2** boil, furuncle; carbuncle **3** (Fig Pet) little kid (child): squeezix *4 roasted tripe

rrëcoke *nf* strip of cloth

rrëfa'në *nf* **1** handle of a vessel/utensil **2** stem of a fruit

rrëfa'ngull *nf* buttonhole

rrëfa't·et *vpr* to divide up into branches, branch off/out

rrëfa'të *nf* loose tree branch; dead branch

rrëfe·het *vpr* **1** to come to light, be revealed **2** *(Fig)* to reveal one's inner self: open up **3** [Relig] to confess one's sins: confess
　∘ **s'rrëfe·het**³ˢᵍ **me gojë** to be shocking and incredible, be not-to-be-believed

rrëfe·n
　I § *vt* **1** to narrate, relate; report; say **2** to tell, confess **3** to indicate; show, display **4** [Relig] to take []'s confession: confess
　II § *vi* to seem, appear to be
　∘ **i rrëfe·n babait arat** *(Iron)* to try to tell someone his own business
　∘ **<> rrëfe·n edhe zorrët e barkut** "tell <> even the intestines and stomach" to tell <> even one's innermost secrets: spill one's guts to <>
　∘ **<>a rrëfe·n**³ʳᵈ **qejfin** to teach <> a good lesson
　∘ **<> rrëfe·n shkopin** "show <> one's stick" to threaten <>
　∘ **<> rrëfe·n udhën/udhët/rrugën** *(Impol)* to kick <> out, show <> the door

rrëfe'jë = **rrëfe'një**

rrëfe'një *nf* short simple narrative: tale

rrëfe'njës
　I § *adj* indicative
　II § *n* = **rrëfyes**

*****rrëfenjësi** *nf (Old)* confession

*****rrëfenjëtar** *n (Old)* storyteller

*****rrëfepri'tës** = **rrufepri'tës**

rrëfe'së *nf* short account of an incident: anecdote

rrëfe'shk *nm* **1** [Bot] thistle *(Silybum)* **2** [Ornit] goldfinch = **kryea'rtëz**

rrëfi'm *nm ger* **1** <**rrëfe·n, rrëfe·het** **2** short narrative: story, tale **3** confession

rrëfye's *nm* **1** storyteller **2** [Relig] priest who hears confessions: confessor **3** indicator

rrëfye'sto're *nf* [Relig] place where confession is heard: confessional

rrëfye'shëm *adj (i)* **1** expressible **2** acceptable for telling, reportable **3** appropriate for confession: confessable

rrëfyeto're = **rrëfyesto're**

rrëga'll·et *vpr* = **rrokulli's·et**

rrëga'llë *nf* rocky ravine

rrëgalli'në *nf* rocky ravine; soil full of washed-down rock and gravel

*****rrëgosa'r** *n (Reg)* = **rrogozta'r**

*****rrëgosta'r** *n (Reg)* = **rrogozta'r**

*****rrëgo'stë** *nf (Reg)* = **rrogo'z**

*****rrëgo'stët** *adj (i)* = **rrogo'ztë**

*****rrëgu'na** *np* lower branches of a tree

rrëgja'k *adj* runty

rrëgja'k·et *vpr* to get thin and feeble; become anemic

rrëgja'kur *adj (i)* anemic

rrëgji'm *nm ger* <**rrëgjo'·n, rrëgjo'·het**

rrëgjo'·het *vpr* **1** to shrivel/shrink up, get thin and weak **2** *(Fig Book)* to become diminished, dwindle **3** to become senile, go dotty
　∘ **rrëgjo·het**³ˢᵍ **dita** daylight *gets* shorter: the days *are getting* shorter

rrëgjo'·n *vt* **1** to shrivel, shrink **2** *(Fig Book)* to oversimplify []; diminish [] in some respect; lessen, reduce, weaken **3** to screw up [the eyes]: squint

rrëgjo'll *nm* sty (in the eye)

rrëgju'a'r *adj (i)* **1** stunted; shrunken, shriveled up; withered **2** weakened, diminished, lessened **3** [Ling] reduced

rrëgju'kull *nf* dwarf; runt

rrëgjy'l *nm* = **rrëgjy're**

*****rrëgjy'n** *nm (Old)* shark

rrëgjy're *nf* **1** abscess on the sole of the foot: foot blister; carbuncle on the foot **2** bunion, callus, corn = **ka'llo**

*****rrëk** *nm* blockhead, boor

rrëka'jë
　I § *nf* gushing stream of water, torrent; mountain stream, brook
　II § *adv* in torrents/gushes

rrëke' *nf* **1** rapid stream of water; spate, freshet; gush **2** *(Fig)* torrent, flood **3** twisting and turning line embroidered on outer garments

*****rrëke'shëm** *adj (i)* torrential

*****rrëke'll** *nf* water jar that is flat on one side for carrying by pack animals

rrëke'lle·het *vpr* **1** to tumble/hurtle/roll down **2** to roll over and over **3** to fall over; fall from power: topple

rrëke'lle·n *vt* **1** to cause [] to tumble/hurtle down; roll [] down/over **2** to gulp [] down, guzzle [] down

rrëke'lli'm *nm ger* **1** <**rrëke'lle·n, rrëke'lle·het** **2** tumble **3** gulp **4** noise made by a tumbling object

*****rrëke'lle'katru've** = **rrëke'll**

rrëke'o'të *nf* something in a round shape: wheel of wax/tallow

rrëku'all *nm* [Bot] Spanish oyster plant *(Scolymus hispanicus)*

rrëku't·et *vpr* to go into hiding

rrëma'ç *adj, n* left-handed (person)

rrëma'ktë *adj (i)* on the left

*****rrëma'zëm** *adj (i)* = **mizo'r**

*****rrëmb** *nm* = **rremb**

rrëmb'aj-kë'mb'aj *adv* in a slapdash manner, recklessly

rrëmbe·het *vpr* **1** to rush, act hastily, get overexcited **2** to be totally caught/wrapped up, be obsessed **3** to get singed; be scorched **4** to hug
　∘ **rrëmbe·het pas <>** to be very excited about <>, get caught up in <>

rrëmbe·n
　I § *vt* **1** to take [] with force: grab, seize **2** to take [] away from <> by force: snatch [] from <> **3** *(Fig)* to attract [] by sheer power: captivate **4** *(Fig)* to gain [] by hard struggle **5** *(Fig Colloq)* to understand instantly: grasp immediately **6** *(Fig Colloq)* to catch [] momentarily **7** to scorch []
　II § *vi* **1** to lean to one side **2** to get scorched **3** to grapple
　∘ **rrëmbe·n armët/pushkët** to grab one's weapons, get ready for battle
　∘ **<>a rrëmbe·n fjalën** "seize the word" to seize the floor from <>, interrupt <> and not allow <> to continue
　∘ **ta rrëmbe·n fjalën nga goja** "snatch the word out of your mouth" to be quick-witted, get what you mean quickly (even before the word is out of your mouth)

○ **<> rrëmbe·n kafshatën nga goja 1** to take the bread from <>'s mouth, take away <>'s last means of support; leave <> in helpless misery **2** ○ *is* too inept to prevent others from taking the food right out of <>'s mouth: <> always lets others get the better of <>
○ **<> rrëmbe·n kohën** "seize <>'s time" to waste <>'s time
○ **[ ] rrëmbe·n me sy** to steal a glance at [ ]
○ **rrëmbe·n nga __** to show favor toward __: favor

rrëmbes *nm* robber, pillager

rrëmbesë *nf* **1** = **rrëmbim 2** strong river current; river rapids

****rrëmbë** *nf* vein

rrëmbim *nm ger* **1** <**rrëmbe·n**, **rrëmbe·het 2** sudden force; vehemence **3** rush, haste; uncontrollable temper

****rrëmbimqar** *OR* **rrëmbimtar** *adj* predaceous; rapacious

rrëmbimthi *adv* with sudden force; vehemently

rrëmbush· *vt* to fill <>'s eyes with tears (from emotion)

rrëmbush·et *vpr* to be overwhelmed by deep emotion
○ **rrëmbush·et me [ ]** to fill up on [ ], ingest a large quantity of [ ]

rrëmbyer
I § *part* <**rrëmbe·n**
II § *adj (i)* **1** taken by force: grabbed, stolen **2** moving with a burst of speed: surging, in a gush, with a rush **3** impetuous, rash, hasty
III § *adv* impetuously, in haste, in a hurry; hastily, hurriedly; rashly

rrëmbyerazi *adv* rashly, impetuously, in haste

****rrëmbyershëm** *adj (i)* rash, hot-tempered; violent

rrëmbyes
I § *adj* **1** predatory, rapacious **2** *(Fig)* captivating
II § *n* **1** predator = **grabites 2** *(Fig)* kidnapper, pillager; captivator

rrëmbyeshëm
I § *adj (i)* **1** moving in an impetuous/violent rush: gushing, dashing **2** hasty, impetuous, rash
II § *adv* in haste, hastily, in a tremendous rush; rashly

rrëmbythje *nf* remains of a crop after harvesting: stubble; worthless tail-ends, rubbish

****rrëme·n** *vt (Reg Gheg)* = **rrëmbe·n**

rrëmejtë *adj (i)* very steep, precipitous

rrëmet
I § *nm* **1** turbulent water, flood of water, bursting downpour **2** crowd of people **3** *(Fig)* massive amount **4** *(Fig)* confused mess
II § *adv* in massive amounts

rrëmeta *np fem* snowshoes woven of bast fiber

rrëmetë *nf* **1** bushy branch used as a broom: besom ****2** clog made of wooden strips

rrëmih· *vt* **1** to excavate; dig [ ] out; dig away at [ ] **2** *(Fig)* to dig around for [ ]

rrëmihës *n* digger
○ **rrëmihës varresh** gravedigger

rrëmijë *nf* digging

****rrëmimtar**
I § *adj* excavating, digging
II § *n* excavator, digger

rrëmiqe *nf* steep incline: cliff, crag

****rrëmitës** = **rrëmihës**

rrëmo·n
I § *vt* **1** to dig away at [ ]; dig [ ] out **2** *(Colloq)* to irritate, provoke
II § *vi* to search carefully: poke around, dig around
○ **<> rrëmo·n barkun** to strike <>'s hidden sore point; discover <>'s deep down personal secret

rrëmojëse = **rrëmuese**

rrëmore *nf* **1** steep incline: cliff, precipice **2** ravine filled with rocks; area covered with slippery rocks

****rrëmp** = **rremb**

rrëmues *adj* digging; probing

rrëmuese *nf* **1** digging machine, digger **2** toothpick

rrëmujaxhi *nm (np ˜ nj) (Colloq Pej)* messy person; creator of disorder and confusion

rrëmujë
I § *nf* **1** disorder, jumble, confusion **2** tumult; hubbub
II § *adv* in disorderly confusion

rrëmujëdashës *adj* = **rrëmujshëm**

rrëmujëmadh *adj, n* **1** *(Colloq Pej)* messy (person) **2** rowdy (person); (person) who causes a tumult

rrëmujos· *vt* to ravage, devastate; mess up [ ], make a mess of [ ]

rrëmujshëm *adj (i)* disorderly, chaotic; tumultuous, roisterous

****rrëmullë** *nf* = **rrëmujë**

****rrën** = **rren**

rrënd *nm* = **rrëndës**

rrëndës *nm* rennet

rrëndo·het *vpr* to dry up and cease to function: wither

rrëndo·n *vt (Reg)* (of a blade) to cause nicks

rrëndos· *vt [Dairy]* to add rennet to [milk] (to make cheese)

****rrënë** *nf* **1** rennet = **rrëndës 2** = **rrenë**

****rrëngallë** *nf* = **rrëgallë**

rrëngje·n *vi* to emit rays of light: shine, sparkle

rrëngjeth *OR* **rrënqeth** = **rrëqeth**

****rrënicë** *nf* chunk of bread

rrënim *nm ger* **1** <**rrëno·n**, **rrëno·het 2** downfall **3** (building) ruin

rrënimë
I § *nf* destructive deluge following a heavy rain
II § *adv* in a deluge

rrënimtar
I § *adj* ruinous, destructive
II § *n* wrecker, ravager, spoiler

rrëno·het *vpr* to fall into ruin; be ruined (economically)

rrëno·n *vt* to turn [ ] into a ruin: ruin

rrënoje *nf* ruinous state: shambles; ruin, ruins

rrënore *nf* **1** land fallen into disuse, abandoned infertile land; wasteland **2** = **rrënojë**

rrënqeth· *vt* = **rrëqeth·**

rrënuar *adj (i)* **1** in ruins **2** *(Fig)* ruined; badly damaged, in terrible shape

rrënues *adj* ruinous, inflicting heavy damage

rrënxak *nm* person suffering a hernia

rrënxi·n *vi* to appear very dark

rrënxim *nm ger* **1** <**rrënxo·n 2** hernia

rrënxo·het *vpr* to get a hernia/rupture

rrënxuar *adj (i)* (of males) having a hernia: ruptured

rrënja'k *adj* [*Bot*] growing directly from the root of a plant: radical

*****rrënje·n** *vi* to emit rays, radiate

rrënje' *nf* **1** root **2** (in counting) agricultural plant/tree **3** [*Bot*] English oak (*Quercus robur*) **4** [*Math*] radix; root

  ○ **rrënja e hundës** bridge of the nose

  ○ **rrënjë më rrënjë** down to the last detail

  ○ **nga e ka· rrënjën** "from where does {} have roots" what <>'s roots (family background) *are*

  ○ **ësh·të pa rrënjë** to have no family left

  ○ **rrënjë pas rrënjë** generation after generation

rrënje'da'lë *adj* **1** (*Colloq*) left without descendants **2** (*Curse*) may he and his kind die out! **3** miserable, wretched

rrënje's

  I § *nm* original inhabitant

  II § *adj* aboriginal

rrënje'si'sht *adv* radically, fundamentally

rrënje'so'r *adj* radical, fundamental

rrënje'shku'lës *nm* [*Tech*] machine that pulls out tree roots: root excavator

rrënje'shku'lur *adj* **1** uprooted from home and not settled elsewhere: homeless **2** immigrated

rrënje'to'r *nm* [*Math*] root sign: radical

rrënje'z *nf* [*Bot*] rootlet; radicle ()

rrënje'zi'm *nm ger* [*Agr*] <**rrënjëzo··n**, **rrënjë-zo··het**

rrënje'zo'·het *vpr* [*Agr*] to issue/sprout roots: root

rrënje'zo'·n

  I § *vt* [*Agr*] to induce [a plant] to issue/sprout roots: root [a plant]

  II § *vi* to issue/sprout roots: root

rrënje'zu'ar *adj* (i) [*Agr*] having issued/sprouted roots: rooted

rrënji'shtë *nf* **1** uprooted tree stump **2** area covered with tree stumps or tree roots **3** (*Fig*) foot of a hill/mountain

rrënjo'më *nf* [*Agr*] thin branch used as a cutting to sprout roots

rrënjo'r

  I § *adj* of or pertaining to roots: radical

  II § *nm* **1** [*Chem Math*] radical **2** [*Ling*] root, stem, theme, radical

rrënjo're *np fem* [*Bot*] bulbous and tuberous plants

rrënjo's· *vt* to implant, instill

rrënjo's·et *vpr* **1** [*Agr*] = **rrënjëzo··het 2** (*Fig*) to take root

rrënjo'sje *nf ger* <**rrënjo's·**, **rrënjo's·et**

rrënjo'sur *adj* (i) rooted, deeply implanted

*****rrëpi'jtë** *adj* (i) = **rrëpi'rët**

*****rrëpi'në** (*Reg Gheg*) = **rrëpi'rë**

rrëpi'rë *nf* **1** steep/precipitous slope; ravine **2** short cloudburst **3** rivulet formed by rain

*****rrëpi'rë'shëm** *adj* (i) = **rrëpi'rët**

rrëpi'rët *adj* (i) steep, precipitous

*****rrëpi'shte** *nf* **1** = **rrapi'shtë 2** plane tree brush/branches used for firewood

*****rrë'pi'të** = **rrëpi'rët**

*****rrë'pje'të** = **rëpje'të**

*****rrë'po'sh'ëm** *adj* (i) lower, nether, low, inferior

*****rrëqa's·** *vi* to bother/annoy <>

rrëqa's·et *vpr* to move back/away, withdraw, retreat

rrëqe'bull *nm* (*np* ˜*j*) [*Zool*] lynx

rrëqe'th· *vt* **1** to shear [sheep] under and behind the muzzle **2** to make [ ]'s flesh crawl, give [ ] the shivers; make [ ] shiver **3** to touch [ ] lightly; lightly take hold of [ ]

rrëqe'th·et *vpr* to shiver, shudder

  ○ <> **rrëqeth·et³ᵖˡ flokët** <>'s hair *stands* on end

  ○ <> **rrëqeth·et³ˢᵍ mishi** <>'s flesh crawls, <> *has* the shivers, <> *feels* creepy

rrëqe'th'ës *adj* causing one to shiver/shudder: blood-chilling, chilling; creepy

rrëqe'thje *nf ger* **1** <**rrëqe'th·**, **rrëqe'th·et 2** shivers; chills

rrëqe'th'shëm *adj* (i) = **rrëqe'thës**

*****rrëqe'th'ur** *adj* (i) (of hair) standing on end, (of feathers) ruffled

*****rrëqu'kull** *nf* little woman/child

rrësk *nm* **1** (*Colloq*) = **risk 2** possession, thing, object *****3** treasure, treasured object

rrësha'jë

  I § *nf* (*Reg*) [*Zool*] chicken-snake, four-lined rat snake (*Elaphe quatuorlineata*)

  II § *np fem* [*Relig*] Whitsuntide, Pentecost

*****rrësha'në** *adv* sliding, slipping, gliding

*****rrësha's·** = **rrëshqa's·**

rrëshe·n *vi* (of bees) to swarm

rrëshej *np* <**rrëshyell**

rrëshe'k *nm* **1** = **rrëshi'q *2** bladder *****3** sac; vesicle

rrëshe'kth *nm* [*Bot*] dry fruit of a monocarpic plant that splits lengthwise as it ripens: (*follicle*)

rrëshe'm *nm* young bee

*****rrëshe't** = **rrëshqe't**

rrëshi'm *nm ger* **1** <**rrësh·et 2** swarm of bees

rrëshini'm *nm ger* <**rrëshino'·n**

rrëshino'·n *vt* to polish [something made of wood] with a resin or wax

*****rrëshi'n** (*Reg Gheg*) = **rrëshi'r**

rrëshino'r *adj* resinous

rrëshi'q *nm* skin bag; bellows = **sha'kull**

rrëshi'rë *nf* resin

rrëshi'rtë *adj* (i) containing resin: resinous

*****rrëshi's** = **rrëshqi's**

*****rrëshi't** = **rrëshqi't**

*****rrëshka'më** *nf* slip, slide

rrëshka'njas *adv* = **rrëshqi'tas**

rrëshka'të *nf* **1** landslide **2** (*Fig*) disaster, calamity

*****rrëshhnja'në** = **rrëshqa'në**

rrëshqa'n·et *vpr* to crawl on the ground, creep along

rrëshqa'nas *adv* = **rrëshqa'në**

rrëshqa'në *adv* crawling (on the ground), creeping

rrëshqa'n'ës *nm, adj* **1** = **rrëshqano'r 2** (*Euph*) snake

rrëshqano'r

  I § *nm* [*Zool*] reptile = **zvarrani'k**

  II § *adj* **1** [*Zool*] reptilian = **zvarrani'k 2** [*Bot*] having a stem that hugs the ground: procumbent

rrëshqa'nthi *adv* = **rrëshqa'në**

rrëshqa's *stem for 1st sg pres, 1st & 3rd pl pres, 2nd & 3rd sg subj* <**rrëshqe't·**

*****rrëshqe'së** *nf* reptile

rrëshqe't· *vi* **1** to slide down; slide; slither **2** to skate; ski; skate/slide/glide along **3** to slide by without notice; slide away **4** to slide down **5** to slip; slip and fall

  ◦ <> **rrëshqet·**^3sg **goja** <>'s tongue *slips*

  ◦ <> **rrëshqet·**^3sg **gjuha** <>'s tongue *slips*

  ◦ <> **rrëshqet·**^3pl **këmbët** "<>'s feet *slip*" <> *slips* and *falls*; <> *makes a mistake and loses* <>'s high position

  ◦ <> **rrëshqet· nga mendja** to slip from <>'s mind

  ◦ **rrëshqet· nga mendja** to go out of one's mind: go crazy

  ◦ **rrëshqet· si ngjalë** to be slippery as an eel

  ◦ <> **rrëshqet·**^3sg **shëndeti** <> is in failing health

rrëshqis *stem for 2nd pl pres, pind* <**rrëshqet·**

rrëshqit *stem for pdef, opt, adm, part, pind, 2nd pl pres, imper, vp* <**rrëshqet·**

rrëshqitas *OR* **rrëshqitazi** *adv* **1** (by) sliding, slipping out/down/away **2** without notice, secretly; incidentally **3** in grazing fashion: lightly, barely **4** superficially, in passing

rrëshqitë *nf* **1** slippery place **2** slide

rrëshqitës

  I § *adj* **1** slippery **2** [*Tech*] sliding **3** (of land) subject to sliding, unstable **4** [*Lit*] dactylic

  II § *n* skater

  III § *nm* [*Tech*] **1** sliding part of a mechanism: slide **2** [*Postal*] chute

rrëshqitëse *nf* **1** sled; sleigh; toboggan **2** skate

rrëshqitje *nf ger* **1** <**rrëshqet·** **2** (*Fig*) unconscious error: slip **3** [*Bot*] edible mushroom with a gray cap with white underside, which feels a bit greasy to the touch

rrëshqitshëm *adj* (i) **1** slippery **2** (of land) subject to sliding, unstable

rrëshqitur *adj* (i) fallen in a landslide

rrëshyell *nm* sow thistle (*Sonchus oleraceus*)

rrëvizgë *nf* crack in the rind of a melon

*****rrëximm** *nm ger* <**rrëxo·**n

*****rrëxo·**n *vt* = **rrëzo·**n

*****rrëxuall** *nm* [*Bot*] groundsel (*Senecio vulgaris*)

*****rrëxhâ(n)** *nm* (*Reg Gheg*) = **rëgjâ**

rrëzaje *np* <**rrëzall** **1** alluvial sediment **2** leavings, dregs

rrëzak *nm* **1** person who sticks in a corner **2** frail and stunted child

rrëzall *nm* (*np ˜ je*) **1** whole plant, including the branches, stalk, and roots **2** debris left by a flood **3** (*Fig Pej*) worthless person from the very dregs of society: no-good bum

rrëzë

  I § *nf* **1** place of juncture between something vertical and something horizontal: base, foot (of a tree/hill/mountain), bank (of a river), edge (of a forest) **2** place where an organ/limb is attached to the body **3** far/dark corner: hidden nook **4** (*Colloq*) root of a plant **5** [*Bot*] blackberry, bramble *Rubus*

  II § *prep* (*abl*) at the base/foot of <>; right at the edge of <>

  ◦ **rrëza e malit** foot of the mountain

rrëzëlle·n *vi* to glitter; sparkle

rrëzëllim *nm ger* **1** <**rrëzëllo·**n **2** = **rrëzëllimë**

rrëzëllimë *nf* glitter, sparkle

rrëzëllor *adj* (*Poet*) = **rrëzëllues**

rrëzëllues *adj* glittering brightly, sparkling

rrëzëmalas *n* villager living at the foot of a mountain

*****rrëzik** = **rrezik**

*****rrëzikçar** *adj* = **rrezikshëm**

rrëzikët *adj* (i) risky, dangerous

rrëzim *nm ger* **1** <**rrëzo·**n, **rrëzo·**het **2** = **rrëzimë** **3** fall, crash; downfall; collapse **4** landslide

rrëzimë *nf* deep gorge, crevasse

rrëzishtë *nf* crevice in rock

rrëzit· *vt* to put [] away into the corner

rrëzit·et *vpr* to shrink up into a narrow space, huddle into a corner

rrëzo·het *vpr* **1** to fall, fall down; collapse; fall out **2** to fall from power; lose vitality/health, get worse **3** to move from a higher to a lower elevation, descend from a higher region to a lower one; slide down

  ◦ **rrëzo·**het **nga fiku** (*Iron*) to lose one's high position

rrëzo·n

  I § *vt* **1** to cause [] to fall: knock/throw/cut down; let [] fall, drop; let [] down **2** to cause [] to fall apart: break, break [] down/up **3** (*Fig*) to overthrow; upset, overturn **4** (*Fig*) to dispute/reject [] **5** (*Colloq*) to give [] a failing grade: fail **6** (*Fig*) to derogate, defame

  II § *vi* [*Naut*] (of a boat) to move off course

  ◦ <> **rrëzo·**n **këmbët** "knock <> off <>'s feet" to make <>'s legs tired

  ◦ **rrëzo·**n **malet** "knock down the mountains" to be strong enough to move mountains

  ◦ [] **rrëzo·**n **me një gisht** "overturn [] with a finger" to knock [] over with a feather

  ◦ [] **rrëzo·**n **në pluhur 1** to reduce [] to dust; destroy [] completely **2** to give [] up, abandon; reject []

  ◦ [] **rrëzo·**n **pykë** to leave/knock [] flat on the ground; leave [] dead on the spot

rrëzomë *nf* **1** foothill area (of a mountain) **2** = **rrëzimë**

rrëzore *np* [*Bot*] madder family *Rubiaceae*

*****rrëzuell** *nm* = **rrëgjoll**

*****rrgja** = **rrozha**

*****rrgjând** (*Reg Gheg*) = **argjënd**

*****rrgjolle** *nf* wasteland, rough ground

rri· *vi* **1** to continue in a particular position or condition for a period of time: stay, stand **2** to sit; sit down **3** to fit well: suit; fit on one's body **4** (*Colloq*) to keep/stick to <>

  ◦ <> **rri·** (*Crude*) it seems to <>

  ◦ <> **rri· çekan/çekiç mbi kokë** "keep a hammer over <>'s head" to keep nagging <>, keep a whip over <>'s head, keep forcing <> on

  ◦ <> **rri· deri** __ (*Colloq*) to reach <>'s __: come/hang down to <>'s __

  ◦ **s'**<> **rri·**^3pl **duart (rehat)** "<>'s hands never *stay still*" <> never let's well enough alone

  ◦ **rri· duke tharë trahan** "stand around drying crackers" to be occupied doing very unimportant/easy work

  ◦ **rri· e mba·**n **murin** "stand and hold up the wall" to wait in vain

  ◦ <> **rri· gatitu** to be obedient to <>

  ◦ <> **rri· gjel** to be insolent toward <>

  ◦ **Nuk rri·**^3sg **gjeli mbi vezë.** "A rooster does not sit on eggs." This *is* not the right person for the job.

  ◦ <> **rri· gjemb** to keep nagging <>; constantly supervise what <> is doing

  ◦ **rri· gjemb** to be sharply dressed, be dressed nattily

  ◦ **nuk** <> **rri·**^3sg **gjuha (rehat)** <> *cannot* keep from talking

○ **Nuk rri iriqi në plis.** "The hedgehog does not stay on a clod of earth." *(Prov)* No one likes to be cooped up all day.

○ **rri· jashtë valles** "stay/be out of the dance" not participate and share responsibility

○ **<> rri· kallkan** to stand bravely against <>, show <> no fear, face <> resolutely

○ **rri· këmbë mbi/përmbi këmbë** to be/act too casual, be complacent

○ **<> rri· kokëmënjanë** to avoid <> out of resentment

○ **<> rri· kokërr** to face <> boldly, stand firm against <>, stand eyeball to eyeball with <>

○ **<> rri· kundër** to stand opposed to <>, oppose <>

○ **<> rri· mashë** to be <>'s lackey

○ **rri· mbi dy karrige** *(Pej)* to profit from two sides by catering opportunistically to both; lack commitment

○ **<> rri· mbi kokë/krye** to stay constantly at <>'s side; keep right on top of <>, check constantly what/ how <> is doing

○ **rri· mbi libra** to keep one's head buried in the books, keep studying

○ **rri· mbi prrush** to be in bad straits, be in a terrible situation

○ **rri· mbi thëngjij** to be in bad straits

○ **rri· mbrapa** to survive

○ **<> rri· me buzë** to feel resentful against <>

○ **rri· me buzë** to have a sad look on one's face: pout, sulk

○ **rri· me dorë në xhep** "stay with hand in pocket" to be a spendthrift, spend money too freely

○ **rri· me dhëmbë jashtë** *(Pej)* to keep baring one's teeth and laughing: keep up a cackle

○ **<> rri· me fyt** to choke with anger toward <>

○ **rri· me gisht në këmbëz** to have/keep one's finger on the trigger, be ready for battle

○ **<> rri· me grushte hundëve** "stay with fists under <>'s nose" *(Pej)* to constantly threaten <>; threaten <> in public; be a bully towards <>

○ **<> rri· me hanxhar në dorë** to threaten <> constantly

○ **<> rri· me hundë/turinj** to maintain an unfriendly demeanor toward <>

○ **rri· me një pëllëmbë hundë** to maintain an unfriendly demeanor

○ **rri· me turiçka** to remain angry, stay sore: have one's nose out of joint

○ **rri· me** [ ] to hang around with [ ], associate with [ ] socially

○ **rri· me mërzi** to look worried

○ **(atje/këtu) <> rri·³ˢᵍ mendja** to be unable to take one's mind off []: keep worrying about <>

○ **<> rri·³ˢᵍ mendja** {} <>'s mind is {*somewhere*}, <> keeps thinking {*about someone/something*}

○ **<> rri· më këmbë** to be at <>'s beck and call

○ **rri· më këmbë 1** to stand ready **2** to stand

○ **rri· mënjanë** to take no part, stand on the sidelines

○ **rri· mriz 1** *(Impol)* to stand around doing nothing: loiter, waste time **2** to stand bewildered, stand in a daze

○ **rri· ndër grepa** to be in big trouble; be on pins and needles

○ **rri· në cingali** to stay at the ready, keep one's finger on the trigger

○ **rri· në fresk** to stay where it's cool

○ **rri· në grepa** to be in big trouble; be on pins and needles

○ **rri· në hije** to remain uninvolved, not participate, stand on the sidelines

○ **<> rri· në kokë/krye** to stay constantly at <>'s side; keep right on top of <>, check constantly what/ how <> is doing

○ **<> rri· në krah** to be right next to <>; <> *stays* close to {}; <> *stands* ready to support {}

○ **rri· në një sofër me** [] to share common interests and goals with []

○ **rri· në prag** to stay close to home

○ **<> rri· në qime** to be constantly at <>'s elbow

○ **Rri në tokë!** "Stay on the ground!" *(Iron)* Come on now, you don't mean it!

○ **rri· në vend** to stay in one place; not move, not change; lag behind

○ **rri· në vend-numëro** to make no progress: spin one's wheels

○ **<> rri· nuse** "stand by <> like a new wife" **1** to stand by to attend to <> needs promptly **2** to submit to <>, obey <> in every way

○ **rri· përdhe** to sit on the ground

○ **<> rri· përsipër** to supervise <>; attend to <>

○ **<> rri· poshtë** "stay low to <>" to kowtow to <>

○ **<> rri· pranë** to look after [] with great care

○ **i rri· punës mbi kokë/krye** to stick to the job

○ **i rri· punës përsipër si vaji mbi uthull** "stay on top of one's work like oil on vinegar" to be absolutely devoted to one's job

○ **<> rri· qiri (me këmbë)** to stand ready to help <> in any way; take good care of <>

○ **rri· (si) qiri** to stand up straight without moving, stand at attention

○ **rri· rehat** to rest easy

○ **rri· si beu në kashtë** *(Tease)* to strut around like a rooster

○ **<> rri· si dadë** to treat <> like a baby, not leave <> alone for a minute

○ **rri· si dhia majë drizës** "stay like a goat atop a bramblebush" to sit uncomfortably

○ **rri· si hu (gardhi) 1** to be dumbfounded **2** not know what to say/do

○ **rri· si i shurdhri në kuvend** "remain like the deaf man in a discussion" to have no idea of what is going on, understand nothing of what is being said

○ **rri· si kërcu** just stand/sit there like a bump on a log

○ **rri· si krushk/krushkë** to behave like a guest expecting to be served; stand (around) without doing anything, stand idly by

○ **<> rri· si lopës pa viç** to always treat <> especially nicely

○ **rri· si mace e lagur** *(Impol)* to stand shamefaced

○ **rri· si macja nën sofër** "stay under the table like a cat" to cringe in fear

○ **rri· si mbi gozhdë** to be sitting on needles and pins

○ **rri· si me qoshe** "stay as if with corners" to look sullen

○ **rri· si mi i lagur** *(Scorn)* to stand shivering with fear and guilt

○ **rri· si murga në linjë** to stand around in a kind of daze without saying anything

○ **rri· si mysafir** "sit like an invited guest" not lift a finger to help

○ **rri· si nën plaf** to stay under cover

○ **rri· si nuse** "stand like a new wife" to stand still and not say anything; remain silent; not do anything, sit on one's hands

○ **rri· si pelë** "sit there like a mare" **1** *(Pej)* to sit on one's ass without working, be lazy **2** not behave like a lady

○ **rri· si plëndës** to sit in a slouched position

○ **rri· si pulë e lagur** *(Scorn)* to be shivering with fear; stand submissively (with head bowed); behave in humbled fashion

○ **rri· si pulë** stay very quiet without moving from one spot; stand submissively/timidly

○ **rri· si qyp** to sit like a lump of clay

○ **rri· si shushunja në hi** "stay like a leech in ashes" not make a move nor a sound, remain silent and motionless

○ **<> rri· sipër** to look after <>; supervise <> carefully

○ **<> rri·³ˢᵍ sofra shtruar** "<>'s table is always set" = *is* very attentive to <>'s guests, <> *is* very hospitable

○ **<> rri· sus** to kowtow to <>

○ **<> rri· shpatë mbi kokë** to keep <> on a tight rein by threat of punishment

rribë *nf* **1** wind force; full force of the wind **2** water force: torrent, waterfall

rric|**a**

I § *np* <**rric**ë **1** lace **2** *(Fig)* straits, difficult position

II § *adv* (of hair) in curls; (of thread) in the form of lace

rric|**a-rric**|**a** *adv* completely in curls

rricë

I § *nf* **1** small curl **2** tendril **3** *(Fig)* desperation

II § *adv* in desperate straits, in distress

○ **ricë me ricë** completely full, to the brim

rri|**dh** *stem for 2nd pl pres, pind, imper, vp* <**rrje·dh·**

*****rrif** = **rrih**

rrigë *nf* = **rig**ë

*****rrigo**|**n** *nm (Reg)* = **rigo**n

*****rrigo**|**s**|**ë** = **rrëgo·st**ë

rri|**h** *stem for 2nd pl pres, pind, imper, vp* <**rreh·**

rri|**he·** *vpr* <**rri·**

○ **s'<> rri·het³ˢᵍ** <> *can't stand still*; <> *is* impatient, <> *can't stand* inaction

○ **s'<> rri·het³ˢᵍ në (një) vend** "for <> there *is no* staying in one place" <> *is* troubled and uneasy; be in an agitated state

○ **pa** [] **s'rri·het³ˢᵍ** one can't live without []

rri|**he·** *vpr* <**rreh·** **1** to fight **2** to gain rich experience **3** (of fish) to spawn **4** to hunt around for a place to settle down in

rrikë *nf* **1** wall cabinet for keeping tableware **2** *[Bot]* radish *(Raphanus sativus)* = **rrep**ë **e kuqe**

○ **<>a bë·n (kokën) rrikë** to give <> a very short haircut

*****rrik**ël *nm* buttermilk

rrikë *nf* *[Bot]* = **rrik**ë

*****rrill** *nm* *[Bot]* = **rry**ell

*****rrill**ë

I § *nf* *[Bot]* pea *(Pisum sativum)*

II § *adj* having tiny fruit

rrime *nf* *[Invert]* earthworm, rainworm

*****rrim**ë *nf* rhyme = **rim**ë

*****rrim**ë|**ta**|**r** *n* rhymester

*****rrim**|**të** *adj (i)* = **rim**të

*****rrim**|**to**·n *vt* to rhyme = **rimo**·n

*****rrinqit** *nm* *[Entom]* vine fretter, vine louse, vine pest

rrip

I § *nm* **1** strip of leather, strip/band of material **2** belt; strap **3** strip of land **4** *(Fig Crude)* stupid/inept person

II § *adj* **1** *(Fig)* very thin and weak **2** *(Fig Crude)* stupid; inept **3** *(Colloq)* = **rripa**k

○ **rrip daullje** empty-headed, stupid; bewildered

○ **rripat e frerit** reins

○ **rrip transmisioni 1** *(Tech)* drivebelt **2** *(HistPK)* use of trade unions to convey the Party's message to the people

○ **rripi me unaza** *[Riding]* standing martingale

○ **rripi i xhaketës** *[Riding]* martingale

rrip·et *vpr* <**rrje·p· 1** to shed bits of the outer layer: (of skin) peel; lose hair/feathers, moult **2** (of clothes) to wear out **3** (of land) to become eroded and barren **4** *(Fig)* to work to the point of exhaustion: work one's fingers to the bone **5** *(Colloq)* to die after a lingering illness

rrip *stem for 2nd pl pres, pind, imper, vp* <**rrje·p·**

rripak *adj* leathery; hard to chew: stringy

rrip|**a**|**qe** *nf* rocky slope

rrip|**a-rrip**|**a**

I § *adv, adj* in strips; in stripes, striped

II § *adj* (of a landscape) broken up by steep slopes

rrip|**as** *adv* (method of wrestling) while holding on to the opponent's belt

rripë

I § *nf* steep slope bordering a precipice; precipice; ravine

II § *adj* very steep, precipitous

rrip|**ë**|**çir**ë *nf* small ravine; small furrow created by rain

rrip|**ë**|**sir**ë *nf* ravine, cliff, precipice; area with many ravines: precipitous area

rrip|**ë**|**tir**ë *nf* thin covering

*****rrip**|**k**ë *nf* **1** *(Dimin)* <**rrip 2** shoelace, thong

rrip|**o·het** *vpr* to get thin and weak: become all skin and bones

rrip|**o·n** *vt* to divide/cut [] into strips

rrip|**onj**ë *nf* **1** thin and narrow strip/slice; narrow strip of land **2** = **rrip**ë

rrip|**or** *adj* *[Geol]* precipitous

rrip|**osk**ë *nf* narrow strip

rrip|**ovin**ë *nf* shale = **grill**

rrip|**oz** *nm* strip of flypaper

rrip|**shte·het** *vpr* to get tough as leather, become leathery

rrip|**shte**|**njt**ë *adj (i)* = **rripa**k

rriqër *nf* *[Entom]* tick = **këpu·sh**ë

○ **ësh·të rriq**ër to be a real leech

○ **rriq**ër **djathi** *[Invert]* flour mite *Acarus siro*

rris *stem for 1st sg pres, pl pres, 2nd & 3rd sg subj, pind* <**rrit·**

rris|**g**ë *nf* stone sliver/chip

*****rris**k = **risk**

rrisk|**a-rrisk**|**a** *adv* into thin slices/strips/shreds

rriskë *nf* **1** thin slice; narrow strip; shred **2** thin stone slab *****3** seam *****4** layer

*****rrisk**ël *nf* sickle

rrisk|**im** *nm ger* <**risko**·n

rrisk|**o·n** *vt* **1** to slice **2** *[Publ]* to trim

rrisk|**ull** *nf* small slice, sliver

rrit· *vt* **1** to bring up [children], grow [plants], breed [domesticated animals]: raise **2** to nourish **3** to let

[] grow; produce large [] **4** to increase **5** *(Fig)* to upgrade [], advance **6** *(Fig)* to overdo, overexert

○ **<>a rrit· fjalën** *(Pej)* to endorse obsequiously anything <> says, just climb on <>'s bandwagon

○ **rrit· gjarprin në gji** to harbor a viper in <>'s bosom

○ [] **rrit· me gji** to feed [] only from the breast: breast-feed

○ **<>[] rrit· mendjen/veshët** to inflate <>'s ego

○ **e rrit· moshën** "lower/raise/change the age" to put down a lower/higher/different age (on a document)

○ **T'u rrittë nderi!** "May your honor grow!" *(Felic)* (in thanks) Bless you!

○ **Rrit sorrën të të nxjerrë sytë.** "You raise a crow so that it can peck out your eyes." That's the gratitude you get!

○ **U rritsh!** *(Colloq)* (said to a child who has just sneezed) Bless you! Gesundheit!

rrit·et *vpr* **1** to grow **2** to grow larger, increase; (of the moon) wax **3** to grow up

○ **rrit·et**^{3sg} **dita** "the day *grows*" the days *are growing* longer

○ **<> rrit·et**^{3sg} **hunda** "<>'s nose swells" <> *becomes* swell-headed, <> *gets* conceited

○ **rrit·et**^{3sg} **lumi** "the river/torrent *grows*" the river *is getting* higher

○ **rrit·et me bishtra preshi** "grow up eating leek stems" to grow up poor

○ **rrit·et me thërrime** "be raised on crumbs" to grow up poor, be raised in poverty

○ **rrit·et me tul simiteje** "be raised on the soft part of chickpea buns" to grow up in luxury

○ **<> rrit·et**^{3sg} **mendja** "<>'s brain swells" <> *becomes* swell-headed, <> *gets* conceited

○ **rrit·et në prehër të nënës** "grow up in one's mother's lap" *(Impol)* to be used to mollycoddling, be overprotected; never have had to face harsh reality

○ **rrit·et**^{3sg} **përroi** "the river/torrent *grows*" the river *is getting* higher

○ **rrit·et si thekra pa bukë** "grow like wild rye" to grow very tall

○ **<> rrit·et**^{3pl} **veshët** <> *gets* conceited: <> *gets* a swelled head

○ **<> rrit·et**^{3sg} **zemra** "<>'s heart swells" <>'s heart *swells* (with delight/pride/), <>'s heart *is* gladdened

rritë *nf* period of growing up: growing years

rrit·ës

I § *adj* **1** growing; producing, productive **2** increasing, rising **3** [*Math*] increasing incrementally: progressive

II § *n* grower

○ **rrit·ës shtazësh** *(Colloq)* stockbreeder

rritje *nf ger* **1** <**rrit·**, **rrit·et** **2** growth

○ **rritje e kafshëve** stockbreeding

○ **rritje e peshkut** fish nursery

rrit·shëm *adj (i)* = **rritur**

rrit·ur

I § *part* <**rrit·**, **rrit·et**

II § *adj (i)* **1** grown; full-grown, adult, big; fully grown **2** grown big; much grown **3** increased, greater

III § *n (i)* adult, grown-up

○ **i rritur me ajkë qumështi** "be raised on milk cream" reared from childhood with the best of everything

○ **ësh·të rritur në pupla** to have been used to a life of ease and comfort, have been raised in a life of ease and comfort, {}'s life has been a bed of roses

*rrizë = **rizë**

rrizhgo·n *OR* **rrizhko·n** *vt* to gobble/gulp [] down, devour = **rrushkullo·n**

rrjedh· *vi* **1** to flow; flow by **2** to leak **3** to flow as a result: follow **4** to pour in/out, stream in/out **5** *(Fig)* to transpire, happen: go off/on, go **6** *(Fig CollogImpolite)* to lose one's good sense: grow senile, go nutty

○ **<> rrjedh·**^{3sg} **goja** <> *speaks* easily/fluently

○ **<> rrjedh·**^{3sg} **goja lëng** <>'s mouth is watering: <> *has* a craving

○ **<> rrjedh·**^{3sg} **goja mjaltë** "<>'s mouth *flows* with honey" <> *speaks* pleasantly; <> *speaks* beautifully

○ **rrjedh·**^{3sg} **gjaku rrëke/lumë** "the blood *flows* like a torrent/river" the blood *flows* like water; the blood *flows* in a torrent

○ **rrjedh· lumë** to stream out, flow in rivers

○ **rrjedh· nga __** to originate/rise from __: stem from __

○ **rrjedh·**^{3pl} **qiejt** "the skies pour out" there *is* a cloudburst, it *begins* to rain in buckets, it *is* raining cats and dogs

○ **<> rrjedh·**^{3pl} **sytë** "<>'s eyes *flow*" **1** tears *flow* from <>'s eyes **2** <>'s eyes *get* tired from being overworked

○ **<> rrjedh·**^{3pl} **trutë** "<>'s brains *have* flowed" <> *becomes* senile/dotty

○ **<> rrjedh·**^{3sg} **zemra gjak** "<>'s heart *drips/flows* blood" <>'s heart *bleeds*

rrjedh·cë *nf* small stream, rivulet

rrjedh·ë *nf* **1** flow; stream **2** river channel, riverbed **3** *(Fig)* source, origin **4** float (in a fishing net)

rrjedh·ës *adj* flowing constantly, running; fluid

rrjedhi *nf* runoff from the mountains

rrjedhim *nm* result

○ **si/për rrjedhim** as a result

rrjedhimisht *adv (Book)* as a result: consequently, therefore

rrjedhimor *adj* [*Ling*] resultative; resultant

rrjedhje *nf ger* **1** <**rrje·dh·** **2** flow; stream **3** leaking liquid: leak **4** *(Fig)* gradual diminution **5** [*Geog*] river channel

rrjedhojë *nf* **1** result **2** *(Neol)* [*Ling*] derived word

rrjedhor *adj, nf* resultant

rrjedhore *adj, nf* [*Ling*] ablative (case)

*rrjedhsim *nm (Reg Gheg)* deduction

*rrjedhso·n *vt (Reg Gheg)* to deduce

rrjedhshëm

I § *adj (i)* **1** flowing, running **2** fluid **3** *(Fig)* fluent

II § *adv* **1** in a flow; fluidly **2** *(Fig)* fluently

rrjedhshmëri *nf* **1** fluidity **2** fluency

*rrjedhti *nf* **1** *(Book)* flow **2** fluency

*rrjedhtim *nm* **1** flow, current **2** consequence, result **3** deduction

rrjedhur

I § *part* <**rrje·dh·**

II § *adj (i)* *(Colloq Pej)* senile, dotty

∘ **Ku ka·**^{3sg} **rrjedhur, do të pikojë.** "Where it *has* flowed, it will drip." There may not be as much as before, but there is still something.

rrjep· *vt* **1** to remove the outer layer: peel [fruit], peel off [bark], skin/fleece [animals]; scale [fish], pluck [fowl] **2** to gouge, gouge out [] **3** *(Fig)* to take unfair advantage of []'s generosity/helplessness: exploit [] mercilessly; pluck [] clean, fleece [someone]; rob
∘ **e rrjep· morrin nga bishti** "peel the louse from the tail" to be too thrifty, pinch pennies
∘ **rrjep· rrëshiq** [] to skin [a sheep/goat] whole (without damaging the hide)
∘ [] **rrjep· të gjallë** "skin [] alive" **1** to beat [] to a pulp, beat [] up badly **2** to take ruthless advantage of []

rrjepaca·k *adj, n* **1** = **rreckama·n 2** (person) who flays/fleeces/skins

rrjepacu·k *nm* = **rrjepaca·k**

rrjepa·rrjepa *adv* scaling/flaking off; coming apart in pieces

rrjepa·s *adv* in a quarrelsome relationship, on bad terms

rrjepë *nf* **1** eroded and barren area **2** sheep or goat with many bare spots **3** bare spot **4** scale, squama; dandruff, flake, flaking

rrjepës *nm* **1** flayer, skinner, fleecer **2** *(Pej)* plunderer **3** [*Med*] pellagra

rrjepët *pple (i)* flayed, skinned

rrjepje *nf ger* **1** < **rrjep·, rrip·et 2** robbery

rrjepur
I § *part* < **rrjep·, rrip·et**
II § *adj (i)* **1** having lost its outer covering: shorn; peeled; plucked; bald; eroded; bare **2** showing the effects of heavy use/wear: worn out; peeling away in spots **3** *(Fig)* worn out by hard work, exhausted **4** = **rrjepët**

rrjepura·k *adj (Insult)* thieving, plundering

*****rrjesht** = **rresht**

*****rrjeshta·r** *n (Old)* poet

rrjeshta·s OR **rrjeshta·zi** *adv* in a row, in succession, one after another; continuously

*****rrjeshto·r** = **rreshto·r**

rrjet *nm* network

rrjetë *nf* **1** net **2** web **3** *(Fig)* finely devised trap **4** = **rrjet 5** netted shopping bag

rrjetëz *nf* **1** [*Optics*] cross-hairs of an optical instrument: reticle **2** [*Anat*] retina

rrjetëza·k *adj* [*Med*] retiform

rrjetëzi·m *nm* *(Book)* reticulation; networking

rrjetëzo·r *adj* [*Med*] retinal

rrjetëzua·r *adj (i)* [*Spec*] reticulated

rrjetinë *nf* [*Anat*] retina = **retinë**

rrjeto·n *vt* to mend [] by weaving across a hole: darn

rrjeto·r *adj* [*Spec*] reticular, web-like

*****rrkut·et** *vpr* = **struk·et**

*****rrno·k** *nm* small island, islet

rro·het *vp impers* < **rro·n** it *is* possible to live/survive

rro·n *vi* **1** to live; stay alive; survive; survive for a long time **2** to reside, live, dwell
∘ **T'ju rrojë e me jetë të gjatë!** "He/She should live and hava long life!" (congratulatory formula to new parent) I wish him/her a long and happy life!
∘ **rro·n kot** to waste one's life
∘ **rro·n me ditë** to live from day to day, live from hand to mouth

∘ **rro·n me një shoshë lakra** to be miserably poor
∘ **rro·n me të vërtetën** to live an honest life, be incapable of not telling the truth
∘ **rro·n (edhe) në rrasë të gjallëk** to be capable of performing miracles, be extremely able
∘ **rro·n pa plëng e pa shtëpi** "live without property and without a home" to live a homeless life
∘ **rro·n si gogla mbi ujë** to have no support or help; be in an insecure situation: live in a house of cards
∘ **rro·n veresie** to live an aimless life
∘ **Të rroni vetë!** "May you yourself live!" *(Felic)* (expressing condolences to a mourner) Chin up! Try to keep going!

rro *stem for 3rd sg pdef, opt* < **rrua·n**

rroba *np* < **rrobë 1** clothes; underclothes **2** *(Colloq)* bedclothes

rrobalarës *adj* used for washing clothes

rrobalarëse *nf* **1** washerwoman, laundress **2** washing machine

rrobaqepës *nm* man who sews clothing: tailor

rrobaqepëse *nf* woman who sews clothing: seamstress

rrobaqepësí *nf* **1** the art and craft of making clothing: clothes-making, tailoring **2** tailor shop

rrobë *nf* **1** cloth **2** piece of clothing **3** robe, dressing gown **4** *(Fig)* clothing
∘ **rroba banje** bathing suit
∘ **rroba kombëtare** ethnic dress, national costume
∘ **rroba për të dalë** dress clothes
∘ **rrobë resmi** formal attire
∘ **rrobat e trupit** the clothes that one is wearing

rrobit·et *vpr* = **rrazbit·et**

rroblo·n *vt* **1** to spread [clothes] in a mess all over the house **2** to ransack [] looking for something hidden; rummage through []

rroboç *nm* [*Bot*] thin sapling that sprouts near a tree trunk = **mënjollë**

rrobull *nm (np ⁓ j)* [*Bot*] Heldreich pine *(Pinus heldreichi)*

rroburína *np fem* personal effects and household goods

rroc *invar* cartilage, gristle

*****rrocomo·k** OR **rrocombo·k** *adj* deformed, hunchbacked

rroç *n* **1** plain white pigeon (without a crest) **2** *(Pet)* healthy little child

rroçe *nf* small item of little importance

*****rroçkë**
I § *nf* **1** water pipe **2** *(Fig Colloq Crude)* penis: prick, cock
II § *adv* gratis

rrodh *stem for pdef* < **rrjedh·**

rrodhe *nf* **1** *(Bot)* burr **2** [*Bot*] burdock *(Arctium)* **3** [*Bot*] spiny cocklebur *(Xanthium italicum)* **4** *(Fig Pej)* annoying person who is difficult to get rid of: pest
∘ **rrodhe e madhe** great burdock *Arctium lappa, Lappa major*

*****rrodhesë** *nf* parting of the hair/mane; tuft of hair at the crown of the head; crown of the head

rrodhës *nm* [*Ornit*] siskin *(Carduelis spinus)*

rrodhëz *nf* [*Bot*] burr, lesser burdock *(Arctium minus)*

*****rrodhík** *nm* waste pipe, drain; gutter

rrodhíshte OR **rrodhíshtë** *nf* area that is full of burdock

*rrodhustan *nm* [*Bot*] damask rose (*Rosa damascena*)

*rrofatë *nf* bush with slender branches

rro·ftë *3rd sg opt* <**rro·**n (interjection expressing approval and encouragement) long live! viva!

rro·gë *nf* **1** salary, wage **2** (*Old*) pay given to a servant or herdsmansmall alpine meadow, mountain lea
  ○ **rrog**ë **baz**ë basic pay; salary
  ○ **rrog**ë **jetike** (*Old*) honorary lifetime stipend
  ○ **rrog**ë **personale** bonus pay

rrogë**tar** *n* **1** (*Old*) indentured servant or herdsman **2** wage-earner **3** (*ColloqImpolite*) mercenary soldier **4** (*Pej*) paid servant

rrogë**tari** *nf* (*Old*) staff (of servants)

rrogë**teshë** *nf* (*Old*) indentured female servant or housemaid

rrogë**to·**n *vt* to pay (an employee)

rrogë**z** *nf* [*Agr*] wooden linchpin securing the handle to the beam of a plow

rrogo·n
  I § *vi* (*Old*) to work for hire; do odd jobs
  II § *vt* * (*Old*) to earn

*rrogominë *adj* shaggy

rrogomis· *vt* to hurl [] down

rrogomis·et *vpr* to hurtle down

rrogoz *nm* **1** woven reed mat, floor mat **2** area of about the size of a floor mat **3** [*Bot*] = shavar **4** (*ImpolFig*) shameless good-for-nothing person

rrogoztar *n* weaver of rush mats, mat maker

rrogoztë *adj* (i) made of rush fiber; made of rush mats

rrogzina *np fem* short breeches made of heavy wool felt

*rrogje *nf* = rogje

*rrojbë = rrolbë

*rrojbëz *nf* tangled knot, tangle

rrojë *nf ger* **1** <**rrua·**n, rru·*het* **2** shaving (with a razor) **3** life; way of life, life style ***4** bribe

rrojës *adj* long-lived

*rrojkë *nf* **1** [*Entom*] queen bee ***2** (*Fig*) worthless drone, lazy good-for-nothing

*rrojme *nf* short story, yarn

*rrojnik *nm* honeycomb

rrojt *stem for pdef, opt, adm, part, vp* <**rro·**n
  ○ **Rrojtën e trashëguan** "They lived and had heirs." (closing formula for folktales) And they lived happily ever after.

rrojtar *OR* **rrojt**ës *nm* **1** (*Old*) = berber ***2** = rojtar

rrojtje *nf ger* **1** <**rro·** **2** way of life

rrojtme *nf* way of life

*rrojtor *nm* barber = rruajtës

rrojtore *nf* barbershop = berber

rrojtur *part* <**rro·**

rrok *adj* not ready for consumption: (of fruit) unripe, (of meat) uncooked

rrok·
  I § *vt* **1** to grip; grasp, grab; seize, apprehend **2** to encompass, take [] in; comprehend **3** to succeed in hitting: hit [] **4** to reach [an age]
  II § *vi* to get blocked/stuck
  ○ **rrok· armë** to grab one's weapons, get ready for battle
  ○ <> **rrok· dorën** to shake hands with <>
  ○ [] **rrok· në grykë** to hug [] around the neck

  ○ **rrok· penën** "grab the pen" to get down to some serious writing
  ○ **nuk <>a rrok·**^{3sg} **pëllëmba** "<>'s palm does not span it" **1** <> *has* no standard by which to measure it **2** there *is* no way for <> to do it
  ○ [] **rrok· për qafe** to hug [] around the neck
  ○ **rrok· pushkët** to grab one's guns, get ready for battle
  ○ **rrok· shenjën** to hit the target

rrok·et *vpr* **1** to embrace **2** to wrestle **3** (*Fig*) to argue, fight **4** to converge **5** (*Colloq*) to get rich

rrokapjekthi *adv* = rrokopujë

rrokaqiell *nm* (*np* ~ *j*) [*Constr*] skyscraper

rrokas *adv* by/around the waist

rroke *nf* [*Invert*] threadworm = rre

rrokë *nf* **1** spiral; spiral staircase **2** piece of wood used to bolt a door: door bolt, door latch ***3** scurf

rrokës *adj, n* predacious/grasping (person)

*rrokësim *nm* [*Ling*] syllabification = rrokjezim

rrokëz *nf* **1** [*Anat*] cochlea ***2** stylus; penholder

*rrokëzim = rrokjezim

rrokëzo·n *vt* **1** to intertwine/embroider strands to form [tufts] **2** to sew ornamental stripes on []

rrokje *nf* [*Ling*] syllable

rrokje *nf ger* **1** <**rrok·**, **rrok·et** ***2** grip, grasp, grab; embrace

rrokjeformues *adj* [*Ling*] forming a syllable: syllabifying, syllabic

rrokjesor *adj* [*Ling*] of or pertaining to syllables: syllabic

rrokjezim *nm ger* **1** (*Book*) <**rrokjezo·**n **2** [*Ling*] syllabification

rrokjezo·n *vt* (*Book*) to articulate [] syllable by syllable; divide a word into syllables: syllabify

rrokme *nf* **1** [*Dairy*] plunger in a milk churn = filiç **2** (*Reg*) task **3** (*Reg*) rash action **4** strong grip/hug

rrokoll *adv* in a mess, in total disorder; all wrong, badly

rrokopujë *adv* **1** head over heels, tumbling down **2** (*Fig*) in a mess, in total disorder; all wrong

rrokotele
  I § *nf* (*Fig*) good-for-nothing (person)
  II § *np* objects of no value: trinkets, trivia

*rrokotjel *nm* [*Dairy*] plunger (of a churn) = rrokme

*rroksim *nm ger* <**rrokso·**n

*rrokso·n *vt* = rrokjezo·n

*rroksor *adj* syllabic = rrokjesor

*rroktabek·et *vpr* to turn a somersault

*rroktabektazi *adv* = rrokopujë

rrokull *adv prep* (*abl*) = rrotull

rrokulle·het *vpr* = rrëkëlle·het

rrokulle·n *vt* = rrëkëlle·n

rrokulli *nf* (*Old*) **1** whole world, universe ***2** = rrukulli

rrokullimë
  I § *nf* **1** hurtling down; crashing down **2** slope too steep to keep rocks from tumbling down: ravine, cliff **3** (*Fig*) veritable flood **4** (*Fig*) path straight down, road to perdition, the way to total ruin
  II § *adv* in a total mess

rrokullimthi *adv* hurtling down, headlong

rrokullis· *vt* **1** to roll [] downhill; cause to tumble down **2** to let loose [a barrage of words] **3** to overturn; topple **4** *(Fig)* to manage somehow to drag through [a period of time]

rrokull i's·*et* *vpr* **1** to hurtle down **2** *(Fig)* to be toppling fast **3** *(Fig)* (of time and events) to tumble on and on, follow one after another without cease

rrokull i's je *nf ger* **1** <**rrokullis**·, **rrokullis**·*et* **2** tumble

rrokull o·*n* *vt* **1** = **rrëkëll**e·*n* **2** = **rrotullo**·*n*

rro'kull të *adj (i)* round, spherical

rrokull u'e s

I § *adj* **1** rolling; hurtling down ***2** precipitous

II § *nm* ***precipice**

rrol

I § *nm* **1** ox that is too old to be worked **2** *(Fig)* frail old man

II § *adj* old and frail

rrolbë *nf* [*Bot*] safflower *(Carthamus tinctorius)*

rro'le *nf* **1** old cow **2** *(Fig)* frail old woman

***rro'lle** *nf* = **rru'**zull

***rrollim**ë *nf* doorlatch

***rroma'nx** OR **rroma'nz** *nm (Reg Gheg)* novel, romance = **roma'**n

***rromb** *nm* **1** [*Geom*] rhombus **2** [*Ichth*] plaice

***rromboid** *nm* [*Geom*] rhomboid = **romboi'd**

rro'me *nf* **1** bare corncob **2** *(Fig)* something said as a joke; comic verse, doggerel

***rrom ull a'k ë t** = **rrumbulla'k**ët

***rromu's** = **romu'z**

rrondoko'p *adj, n (Colloq)* short and plump (person)

***rro'ngull a** = **rra'ngulla**

***rro'nj**ë = **rro'j**ë

***rro'nj**ës = **rru'es**

rro'p *stem for pdef* <**rrje'p·**

rropa'k *nm* room addition

rropa'më *nf* banging/pounding noise; clatter, din

rropa's *stem for 1st sg pres, pl pres, 2nd & 3rd sg subj, pind* <**rropa't**·

rropa't· *vi* to make noise by walking heavily, stamp along

rropa't·*et* *vpr* **1** to smack together, clatter **2** to turn from side to side (in a lying position), writhe **3** *(Fig)* to make strenuous efforts: strive, struggle; wrestle **4** to fight noisily: brawl

***rropa'te** *nf* great effort, struggle

***rropa'tic**ë = **rraka'tic**ë

rropa'timë = **rropa'm**ë

rropa't je *nf ger* **1** <**rropa't**·, **rropa't**·*et* **2** struggle **3** = **rropa'm**ë

rropo's· *vt* **1** to shatter, demolish **2** *(Fig)* to overthrow; conquer

rropo's·*et* *vpr* to fall into shambles; be leveled to the ground

  ◦ **po rropo's**·*et³ˢᵍ* **qielli** "the sky *is falling* apart" it *is raining* very hard

rropull i' *np fem* **1** entrails **2** *(Fig)* unimportant things, junk **3** *(Reg)* grape stems

***rro'sa** *np* = **gjo'll**ë

rroskave'c *nm* **1** cartilage (of the nose or esophagus) **2** hard core of cabbage

***rroso'k** *nm* rag

rrospi' = **rruspi'e**

rrosh *nm* = **rrol**

rro'she *nf* = **rro'le**

rroshpo'një *nf* part of a river bank that has been hollowed out by the erosive action of the river: river hollow

***rro't·**·*et* *vpr* to get drunk

***rrota'r** *adj* rotating, rotary = **rrotullo'r**

***rrotata'r** *adj (Old)* circular = **rretho'r**

rrota'tiv *nm* rotary printing press

rrote' *nf* **1** wheel **2** disk **3** *(Crude Insult)* moron **4** [*Gymnastics*] cartwheel

  ◦ **rrotë e dhëmbëzuar** cogwheel

rro'te's *adj* [*Bot*] whorled: *verticillate*

rro'tëz *nf* **1** [*Text*] small spool (for thread or yarn) ***2** small wheel

rro'tkë *nf (Reg)* = **rro'tëz**

rroto'·*n* *vt* **1** to cut [] into disks **2** to darn [socks] in a circular patch **3** *(Fig)* to sweep [] up

rroto'vile *nf* **1** potter's wheel **2** = **motovi'le** **3** pulley; capstan; windlass

rro'tull

I § *nf* **1** circular/cylindrical object: disk; spool; wheel; paper or wire rolled into a cylinder; ornamental woven/embroidered disk **2** disk on the bottom of the plunger of a churn **3** [*Anat*] ring-shaped bony structure **4** [*Tech*] pulley wheel **5** *(Fig)* indirect satirical remark

II § *adv, prep (abl)* around, about

  ◦ **rrotulla e gjurit** [*Anat*] kneecap

  ◦ **rrotulla e kurrizit** [*Anat*] spinal vertebrae

  ◦ **rrotulla e qafës** [*Anat*] cervical vertebra

  ◦ **i vje·n rrotull** to go at it by a circuitous route, approach the matter indirectly; speak indirectly

rrotulla'k

I § *adj* round, circular

II § *nm* disk at the bottom of the plunger of a churn

rrotulla'k ëz *nf* round upper part of a Moslem priest's turban

rrotulla'me *nf* **1** large disk-shaped form: large disk/wheel/roll; wheel of cheese; disk on the plunger of a churn **2** ring-shaped form: curl (of smoke) **3** amusement ride in the form of a wheel with hanging seats

rrotulla'më *adj* disk-shaped, round

rrotulla'r *adj* **1** round-shaped: round, circular **2** [*Bot*] orbicular

rrotulla're *nf* curled or cylindrical form: curl

rrotulle's *nm (Old)* = **tornito'r**

rrotull i'm *nm ger* **1** <**rrotullo'**·*n*, **rrotullo'**·*het* **2** rotation, revolution, full turn

  ◦ **rrotullim anash** [*Gymnastics*] cartwheel

  ◦ **rrotullim para** [*Gymnastics*] handspring

  ◦ **rrotullim prapa** [*Gymnastics*] backflip

rrotull i'm thi *adv* all the way around, in a full circle

rrotullo'·*het* *vpr* **1** to revolve, rotate; spin (around) **2** to deviate from a straight path, bear to one side; weave from side to side

rrotullo'·*n*

I § *vt* **1** to rotate []; turn [] around/over; spin [] around **2** to wrap [] around **3** to go around [] **4** *(Fig)* to give [] the runaround

II § *vi* to take a turn for the better: get better

  ◦ [] **rrotullo·n në mend** to turn [] over in one's mind, consider [] from various aspects

  ◦ **rrotullo·n sytë** to cast one's eyes about, look all around

  ◦ [] **rrotullo·n teposhtë** to roll [] downhill

  ◦ **rrotullo·n tokën** to turn up/over the soil

rrot͏ull͏o͏̈r *adj* **1** moving in a circular or spiraling path; rotating, rotary **2** = **rrotulla͏̈r**

rrot͏ull͏o͏̈re *nf* variety of round pear

rro͏̈t͏ull͏te͏̈ *adj (i)* disk-shaped

***rrot͏ull͏u͏a͏̈r** *adj (i)* rounded, disk-shaped; concentric

rrot͏ull͏u͏e͏̈s
  I § adj [Tech] rotational; rotary; rotative
  II § n rotator

rrot͏ull͏u͏e͏̈sh͏e͏̈m *adj (i)* rotatable

***rroth** *nm* [Bot] dodder (Cuscuta)

rrov *stem for 1st & 2nd sg pdef* <**rru͏a·n**

***rroz** *nm* corn (on the foot)

rrozg
  I § nm (Impol) frail old man
  II § adj too old and frail to work

rro͏̈zg͏a *np* <**rro͏̈zg͏e͏̈** driftwood and other river debris: debris

rrozg͏a͏n
  I § adj (Impol) too old and frail to work
  II § n frail old person

rro͏̈zg͏e͏̈ *nf* **1** dry branch (of a tree or bush): dry brush, brushwood **2** scrub, thicket ***3** old hag old crone

***rrozha(n)** *nm* branch of a river near its mouth: distributary

***rrshim** *nm* cloudburst, downpour

rru͏·het *vpr* <**rru͏a·n** to shave; not wear a beard or mustache

***rru͏a** *nm (obl ~o͏̈i)* stream; flow

rru͏a·n *vt, vi* **1** to shave [] with a razor **2** to scrape [] clean **3** (FigImpolite) to eat [] up completely, scrape/lick [the plate] clean
  ○ **e rrua·n boje͏̈n** "keep one's color" to be well-preserved for one's age
  ○ <**rrua·n mjekre͏̈n** (Fig Crude) to take everything <> has: take <> to the cleaners
  ○ <**a rrua·n** [] (Fig Crude) to take all <>'s []: clean <> out of []

***rru͏a͏jt͏e͏̈s** OR **rru͏a͏nj͏e͏̈s** *nm* barber

rru͏a͏r
  I § part <**rru͏a·n, rru͏·het**
  II § adj (i) **1** shaved **2** depleted of plant life: barren
  III § nn (te͏̈) the act/action of shaving

rru͏a͏z͏a *np* <**rru͏a͏ze͏̈ 1** string of beads; necklace **2** dewlaps on a goat

rru͏a͏z͏e͏̈
  I § nf **1** bead **2** [Anat] vertebra **3** [Physiol] blood corpuscle **4** spinal column; back **5** neck **6** (Colloq) small slice of meat: cutlet
  II § adj round and shiny: pearly
  ○ **rruazat e bardhe͏̈** [Physiol] white blood corpuscles
  ○ **rruaze͏̈ e gjurit** [Anat] kneecap
  ○ **rruazat e kuqe** [Physiol] red blood corpuscles
  ○ **rruaze͏̈ e kurrizit** [Anat] spinal vertebrae
  ○ **rruaze͏̈ e qafe͏̈s** [Anat] cervical vertebra
  ○ **rruaze͏̈ e zverkut** [Anat] cervical vertebra

rruaz͏o͏r *adj* [Med] vertebral

rruaz͏o͏r͏e *np* [Zool] vertebrata

rru͏ç͏e͏̈ *nf* (Bot) turpentine tree, terebinth (Pistacia terebinthus) = **ba͏̈fe͏̈r**

rrudh· *vt* **1** to cause [] to wrinkle: wrinkle; pucker **2** (Fig) to shrink/squeeze [] down, constrict, reduce
  ○ **rrudh· ballin** to frown sadly, look glum
  ○ **rrudh· buze͏̈t** to turn up one's nose

○ **e rrudh· dore͏̈n** "squeeze one's hand" **1** to tighten up on spending, become more thrifty **2** to be tight-fisted
  ○ **e rrudh· goje͏̈n** to hold one's tongue; watch what one says
  ○ **rrudhe gjuhe͏̈n!** you should watch your tongue!; hold your tongue!
  ○ **rrudh· hunde͏̈t** to turn up one's nose
  ○ **rrudh· krahe͏̈t** to shrug one's shoulders
  ○ <**i rrudh· penje͏̈t** to keep tight rein on <>
  ○ **rrudh· supet 1** to shrug one's shoulders **2** to answer with a shrug of the shoulders: how should I know!?
  ○ **rrudh· syte͏̈** to screw up one's eyes, squint
  ○ **rrudh· turinjte͏̈** to turn up one's nose
  ○ **rrudh· vetullat** to frown sadly, look glum
  ○ <**a rrudh· zemre͏̈n 1** to make <> dispirited, demoralize <> **2** to afflict <> with disappointment, deeply disappoint <>

rru͏dh·et *vpr* **1** to wrinkle up, get wrinkled **2** to pucker up **3** to shrivel up, shrink; hunch up **4** (Fig) to speak hesitantly/haltingly out of apprehension
  ○ <> **rrudh·et³ᵖˡ syte͏̈** <> screws up <>'s eyes, <> squints
  ○ <> **rrudh·et³ᵖˡ trute͏̈** <> goes dotty, <>'s brains get scrambled, <> becomes senile

rrudh͏a͏c *adj, n* (person) with wrinkled face/skin

rrudh͏ac͏a͏k *adj* heavily wrinkled

***rrudh͏a͏ç** = **rrudha͏c**

rru͏dh͏a-rru͏dh͏a *adj* full of wrinkles

***rru͏dh͏e** *nf* [Bot] great burdock (Arctium lappa)

rru͏dh͏e͏̈ *nf* **1** wrinkle; crease, crinkle **2** rough and uneven surface; wavy surface
  ○ **rrudhat e trurit** [Anat] folds in the brain, convolutions of the brain: gyri

rru͏dh͏e͏̈s *adj* **1** causing the mouth and tongue to pucker: astringent **2** [Geol] plicative

rru͏dh͏e͏̈t *adj (i)* = **rru͏dhur**

rrudh͏i͏sht͏e͏̈ *nf* area broken up by steep hills and ravines

rru͏dh͏je *nf ger* **1** <**rru͏dh·, rru͏dh·et 2** rough/uneven terrain

rrudh͏o͏s· *vt* = **rrudh·**

rrudh͏o͏s·et *vpr* = **rru͏dh·et**

rrudh͏o͏sje *nf ger* = **rru͏dh͏je**

rrudh͏o͏s͏ur *adj (i)* = **rru͏dhur**

rru͏dh͏sh͏e͏̈m *adj (i)* easily wrinkled, wrinkly

rru͏dh͏ur
  I § part <**rrudh·, rru͏dh·et**
  II § adj (i) **1** wrinkled **2** (Fig) senile, dotty
  ○ <> **e͏̈sh·te͏̈³ᵖˡ rrudhur trute͏̈** "<>'s brains have wrinkled" (Contempt) <> has become senile/dotty

rr͏u͏e͏̈s
  I § adj (used for) shaving
  II § n **1** barber **2** (Pej) gluttonous eater

***rr͏u͏e͏̈z** *nf* = **rruaze͏̈**

rruf· *vt* (Colloq) to gulp down

rrufa͏k *adj* dried up and wrinkled; old and tough

***rrufa͏n** *adj* half-dried grape

rrufç *adj* (of hair) curly

rrufço·n *vt* to curl [hair]
  ○ **rrufço·n mustaqet** to twist one's mustache

rrufe
  I § nf **1** lightning bolt, thunderbolt **2** (Fig) terrible threat; heavy curse

II § adj very quick; short and quick
III § adv quick as lightning, like lightning

rrufe ma dh
   I § adj *(Curse)* may-lightning/disaster-strike (him)!
   II § n person struck by lightning/disaster

rrufe prit ës nm lightning rod

rrufe prit ëse nf = **rrufeprītës**

rrufe shëm adj (i) lightning-quick, like lightning

*****rrufe zë** nf dimin small flash of lightning

*****rrufe zo •**n vt to unleash lightning

rru fë nf 1 runny nose accompanied by sneezing: cold in the nose, catarrh 2 [*Med*] coryza, rhinitis

*****rrufgu e shëm** adj (i) overhasty

rrufīs stem for 1st sg pres, pl pres, 2nd & 3rd sg subj, pind < rrufit·

rrufīt· vt 1 to sip; slurp 2 to suck [] in forcibly; suck/ swallow up [], gobble up []

rrufīt·et vpr 1 to exert force from within: pull/suck/ draw in 2 to become emaciated

rrufītje nf ger < rrufit·, rrufit·et

rrufītur adj (i) pulled/sucked/drawn in; emaciated

rrufja n nm 1 *(Pej)* panderer, pimp 2 dirty bastard

rru fka np < rru fkë [*Food*] pancakes fried in oil and seared with sugar syrup

rru fkë nf 1 soft-boiled egg 2 *(Fig)* chubby woman

rrufsh adj (of hair) in curls, curly

rrufsh a k adj, n (person) with curly hair

rrufsho •n vt 1 to curl/twist [hair] 2 to nibble [] (with the teeth)

rru full nf 1 eddy, whirlpool 2 *(Fig)* noisy hubbub

rrug aca k = **rrugaç**

*****rrug ac ë** nf = **rrugi cë**

rrug aç
   I § adj *(Pej)* (of a young person) ill-bred and ill-behaved, foul-mouthed; having loose morals
   II § n *(Pej)* young hooligan/bum, street tough

rrug aç ēri nf 1 bad behavior; delinquency 2 *(Collec)* badly-behaved people taken as a collective whole, (juvenile) delinquents

*****rruge** nf brushwood

rru gë nf 1 road; street; route, path; passageway 2 trip, journey 3 long narrow carpet covering a passageway: runner 4 [*Anat*] tract 5 [*Bot*] gromwell (*Lithospermum officinale*) = **kokërrujë** 6 *(Colloq)* delivery route
   ○ **rrugët ajrore** respiratory tract
   ○ **rrugë e drejtë** proper path, right track
   ○ **rrugë dheu** dirt road
   ○ **rrugë hekurore** railroad
   ○ **rrugë e hekurt** *(Book)* railroad
   ○ **Rruga e mbarë <> qoftë!** "May <>'s road be successful!" *(Felic)* May <> have a good trip!
   ○ **Rrugë e mbarë!** *(Felic)* Have a good trip! Bon voyage!
   ○ **rrugë e mbathur** cobblestone street
   ○ **rrugë e mesme** middle road
   ○ **rrugë pa krye** road leading nowhere, street that comes to a dead end
   ○ **rrugë (e) pa rrugë** road or no road
   ○ [] **pafsha në rrugë të madhe!** "May I see [] out on the street!" *(Curse)* I wish [] the worst of luck!
   ○ **ësh·të për rrugë** to be about to set off (on a trip/ journey)
   ○ **rrugë qerresh** unpaved road

   ○ **rrugë e qorre 1** road that comes to a dead end; blind alley 2 narrow path
   ○ **Rruga e Qumështit** [*Astron*] The Milky Way
   ○ **Rruga Qumështore** [*Astron*] The Milky Way
   ○ **rrugë e rrahur** much-traveled road; beaten path
   ○ **Rruga vade s'ka.** "The road has no limit." *(Prov)* You never know what might happen.
   ○ **rrugë e verbër 1** road that comes to a dead end; blind alley 2 narrow path

rrugë da lje nf 1 exit road/path: egress, exit; way out 2 *(Fig)* escape route; solution to a difficult problem

rrugë ka lim nm route

rrugë kry q nm = **udhëkry q**

rrugë na jë nf wide road for pedestrians

rrugë rrëfy e s nm = **udhërrëfy es**

rru gë s
   I § nm ram that other sheep follow: bellwether
   II § adv *on the way, along the road

rrugë ta r
   I § n foot-traveler; traveler
   II § adj traveling, on the road

rrugë tim nm ger 1 < rrugëto •n 2 travel plan/route: itinerary; journey

rrugë to •n vi = udhëto •n

rrugë tregu e s nm = udhërrëfy es

rru gë z nf 1 = rrugi cë 2 space between honeycombs in a beehive; bees in that space

rrugë zgji dhje nf method for solving a problem

rrug i cë nf 1 narrow street; alley; lane 2 neighborhood street; neighborhood around a small street 3 foot path, garden path 4 corridor 5 long narrow carpet covering a passageway: runner

*****rrug im** nm *(Old)* communication

rrug i në nf 1 corridor 2 aisle 3 small street; alley 4 neighborhood street; neighborhood around a small streetpassage; path

rrug o •het vpr 1 to take to the road, travel 2 *(Fig)* to along with a proposed solution to a controversy/ difficulty

rrug o •n
   I § vi = udhëto •n
   II § vt 1 to show [] the way, guide 2 *(Fig)* to resolve a controversy/difficulty for []

rrug o r adj 1 of or pertaining to streets/roads 2 involved with street/road repair; involved with street/ road traffic

*****rruk** adv in a rolling movement, rolling

rruk· vt *(Colloq)* = rruko •n

rru kë
   I § nf, adj (walnut) stripped of its outer green husk
   II § adj stripped bare

rruk o •het vpr *(Colloq)* to shave (oneself) extra close

rruk o •n vt to strip off the outer husk of []

*****rrukull e •het** vpr = rrëk elle •het

*****rrukull e •**n vt = rrëk elle •n

*****rrukull i** nf precipice

*****rrukull im** nf = rrëk ellim

*****rrukull imë** = rrokulli më

*****rrukull im thi** = rrokulli mthi

*****rrukull i në** nf = rrokulli në

*****rrukull i s·** vt = rrëk elle •n

*****rrukull u e s** = rrokullu es

*****rrum** nm 1 stalk, cornstalk *2 bell clapper *3 plunger, ramrod

rrumaduc *adj, n (Colloq)* **1** short and plump (person) **2** low and squat (house)

rrumb *nm* **1** ball-shaped clapper on a bell **2** empty corncob **3** corncob or clay plug used to stop up a jug **4** small round stone that children play with **5** [*Agr*] wooden linchpin securing the beam to the frame of a plow *6 zero, naught

rrumbull

   I § nm (np ˉj) ball-shaped object
   II § adv into a ball, in a wad
   III § adv fully

rrumbullak

   I § adj round, spherical
   II § adv **1** ball-shaped = **rrumbullakët 2** *(Colloq)* round, circular **3** (with expressions of quantity) in full measure, no more and no less: exactly, to the dot **4** *(Fig)* right out, plainly

rrumbullake *nf* **1** round skullcap **2** *(Colloq)* circular line: circle **3** *(Old)* houses and shops built around a circle: town circle

rrumbullakësi *nf* sphericity, globularity; roundness

rrumbullakët *adj (i)* **1** spherical, globular **2** arched, round; circular **3** (of numbers) round

rrumbullakim *nm ger* <**rrumbullako**·*n*, **rrumbullako**·*het*

rrumbullako·*het vpr* **1** to become round **2** to fill out, get plump

rrumbullako·*n vt* to make [] round; round (off) [a number]; round/fill out []

rrumbullakos· *vt* **1** = **rrumbullako**·*n* **2** *(Pej)* to present [a matter] in terms that smooth over the problems **3** *(Colloq)* to make [an age], complete [a period of time] **4** to plump [] up

rrumbullakos·*et vpr* = **rrumbullako**·*het*

rrumbullakosje *nf ger* <**rrumbullakos**·, **rrumbullakos**·*et*

rrumbullakthi *adv* rounding off the jagged edges

rrumbullakuar *adj (i)* rounded/smoothed out, with jagged edges rounded off; (of numbers) rounded off

rrumbullakur *adj (i)* **1** = **rrumbullakuar 2** *(Pej)* smoothing over the problems

*rrumbullësi *nf* = **rrumbullakësi**

rrumbullo·*het vpr* **1** to become round; become round as a ball **2** *(Fig Colloq)* to get completely full (of food or drink); drink oneself silly

rrumbullo·*n vt* **1** to round off [] **2** to rotate [] **3** *(Fig Colloq)* to polish [] off, gobble/guzzle down []

rrumbullos· *vt* **1** to round off [] **2** to make [] dead drunk

rrumbullos·*et vpr* to become dead drunk

rrumbullt *adj (i)* = **rrumbullakët**

*rrume *nf* bottle

*rrump *nm* zero, naught = **rrumb**

*rrumull *adv* resolutely, firmly; directly, straight away

rrunak *nm, adj* male yearling (lamb), yearling (ram)

rrunë *nf* female yearling (lamb), yearling (ewe)

rrunëz *nf* = **rrunë**

rrunëzak

   I § nm, adj = **rrunak**
   II § adj (of children) having a well-proportioned body

rrunga *nf* = **rrungajë**

rrungajë

   I § nf **1** avalanche (of snow) **2** fallen tree that is dried out and rotting; debris in a river that has fallen from a mountain **3** = **rrëgallinë 4** turbulent stream carrying tree and rock debris **5** *(Fig)* stampede **6** *(Fig Pej)* blockhead, simpleton *7 breakwater
   II § adv in a stampede; in total disarray, strung out in disorder

rrungall *I § nm OR* **rrungallë** *II § nf* avalanche

rrungë *nf* avalanche

rrungice *nf* chunk cut from a larger piece of hard material; raw chunk of wood

*rrungull = **rrokull**

*rrungulli·*n vi, vt* to roll/bowl [] down; hurl [] down

*rrungullimë *nf ger* <**rrungulli**·*n*

*rrungullis· = **rrungulli**·*n*

*rrunicë *nf (Reg)* = **rranicë**

*rrunzak *nm* male lamb

*rrunzë *nf* female lamb

rrunjë *nf* [*Bot*] turpentine tree, terebinth (*Pistacia terebinthus*) = **bafër**

*rrupë *nf* cushion, pad

*rrupice *nf* stripe; edging

rrurëz *nf* **1** = **rrunë 2** *(Fig)* something said in fun; joke **3** *(Fig)* impediment, muddle, tangle

rrus·*et vpr* to descend

*rruskulli *nf* foul/profane language

rruspi *OR* **rruspie** *nf (Pej)* whore

rrush *nm* **1** [*Bot*] grape **2** *(Child)* (child's word for penis) weenie

   ○ **rrush arushe** [*Bot*] = **rrusharushë**
   ○ **rrush arre** large sweet green grape
   ○ **rrush i bardhë** [*Bot*] green grape
   ○ **i bë**·*n (paratë/të hollat)* **rrush e kumbulla** "treat money like grapes and plums" to spend money wastefully: spend money like water, throw one's money away
   ○ **rrush bishtdhelpre** grape having sparse clusters of slightly sour oblong green fruit
   ○ **rrush çaush** variety of grape with large light-colored fruit
   ○ **rrush çilek** grape with a smell like wild strawberries
   ○ **rrush i egër** = **larushk**
   ○ **rrush frëngu** [*Bot*] European gooseberry *Ribes reclinatum, Ribes grossularia*
   ○ **rrush gardhi** [*Bot*] wild grape *Vitis sylvestris* = **larushk**
   ○ **rrush gjarpri** [*Bot*] black borony *Tamus communis* = **pejzë**
   ○ **rrush lepuri** [*Bot*] wild grape *Vitis sylvestri* = **larushk**
   ○ **rrush mace** [*Bot*] rock currant *Ribes petraeum Wulf.*
   ○ **rrush mali** [*Bot*] whortleberry, bilberry *Vaccinum myrtillus* = **boronicë, qershízë, thrashegër**
   ○ **rrush mandakuq** [*Bot*] fox grape *Vitis labrusca*
   ○ **rrush me erë** [*Bot*] fox grape *(Vitis labrusca)*
   ○ **rrush miskodel** *(Old)* muscatel grape
   ○ **rrush pule** "chicken grape" [*Bot*] wild strawberry *Fragaria vesca*
   ○ **rrush pulëz** early-ripening white grape with small fruit
   ○ **rrush qelbës** [*Bot*] fox grape *Vitis labrusca*
   ○ **rrush qeni** [*Bot*] whitebeam mountain ash *Sorbus aria*

○ **rrushi i qyqes** [*Bot*] *= rrushqyqe
○ **rrush Serrezi** [*Bot*] European gooseberry *Ribes reclinatum, Ribes grossularia*
○ **rrush tajkë** [*Bot*] *= korith
○ **rrush toke** [*Bot*] European gooseberry *Ribes reclinatum, Ribes grossularia*
○ **rrush i thatë** raisin
○ **rrush thëllëze** [*Bot*] daphne *Daphne oleoides*
● **rrush vajguri** late-ripening grape with a kerosene-like odor: fox grape *Vitis labrusca*
○ **rrush venetiku** [*Bot*] European gooseberry *Ribes reclinatum, Ribes grossularia*
○ **rrush i zi** [*Bot*] purple grape

rrusharushë [*Bot*] bearberry (*Arctostaphylos uva ursi*)

rrushatake *adj* type of sweet juicy pear with round fruit that ripens at the time of grape harvest

rrushe *nf* plump goat

rrushe *nf* [*Bot*] rock rose (*Cistus*)

rrushemë *adj (i)* (of wood) not yet seasoned

rrushk *nm (np ˜ qe)* [*Bot*] berry

rrushkull *nm (np ˜ j)* 1 [*Bot*] butcher's-broom (*Ruscus aculeatus*) 2 [*Bot*] silk vine (*Periploca graeca*) 3 [*Ornit*] nightingale

rrushkulli *nf* 1 sorrow, sadness 2 filthy language

rrushkullo ·*het vpr* 1 to get a bad/bitter taste in one's mouth 2 (*Fig*) to feel saddened, feel sorrow 3 (*Colloq*) to stuff oneself full

rrushkullo ·*n vt* 1 to taste bad to [] 2 to sadden [] 3 (*Colloq*) to gobble/guzzle [] down in one gulp

rrushkullues *adj* [*Geog*]

rrushkuq *nm* [*Bot*] Judas tree (*Cercis siliquastrum*)

rrushkuqe *nf* 1 [*Bot*] goldmoss stonecrop, goldmoss (*Sedum acre*) 2 Judas tree (*Cercis siliquastrum*) = lofatë

*****rrushp** *nm (Old)* small gold coin = ruspë

*****rrushpule** *nf* [*Bot*] wild strawberry (*Fragaria vesca*)

rrushqyqe *nf* [*Bot*] goldmoss stonecrop, goldmoss (*Sedum acre*)

rrushzeze *nf* [*Bot*] = thanukël

*****rrutull** = rrotull

*****rrutullamë** = rrotullamë

rruvan *nm* grape stem

rruvijash *adv*

rruvijë *nf* line drawn on or slightly into a surface; engraved line, shallow groove

*****rruvijtun** *adj (i) (Reg Gheg)* striped, lined

rruvizë *nf* = rruvijë

rruvjeshkull *nf* = rruvijë

*****rruxe** *nf* ewe with only one birth to her credit

*****rruxull** = rruzull

*****Rruzalem** *nm (Old)* Jerusalem

rruzare *nf (Old)* [*Relig*] 1 rosary 2 prayer said while telling beads of a rosary

*****rruzë** *nf* bead = ruazë

rruzull *nm (np ˜ j)* 1 orb, globe; ball, sphere 2 globule

rruzullim *nm* universe

rruzullor *adj* [*Spec*] spherical

rry·*het vpr* < rrye·n to gain experience; become inured

rrye·*n*
I § *vi* 1 to suffer greatly on account of someone: get tired, suffer 2 to become inured; get toughened
by experience 3 to practice, get trained 4 to grow slowly, barely grow
II § *vt* to train [] through laborious exercise

rryell
I § *nm (np ˜ j)* [*Bot*] euphorbia (*Euphorphia L.*)
II § *adj* having an acrid taste

rryem *adj (i)* highly experienced, well-trained; having gone through the mill

rryeshëm
I § *adv* slowly and with difficulty; laboriously, ploddingly
II § *adj* urgent

*****rryeshmeni** *nf (Reg Gheg)* urge, drive

rryetas *adv* = rryeshëm

*****rrykël** *nf* bolt, nail, peg

rryl *nm* 1 [*Anat*] windpipe, trachea 2 neck tendon 3 throat; neck (of a bottle/pot) 4 large and full ear of corn 5 (*Fig*) big oaf

rryla *np* < rryl elbow macaroni

rrylë *nf* [*Bot*] lentil

*****rryll** = rryl

rrym *nm* wake (of a ship)

*****rrymbë** = rrymë

rrymë *nf* current; flow, stream; freshet
○ **rrymë mendore** train of thought
○ **rrymë e ndryshueshme** [*Electr*] alternating current

rrymëpërndarës *nm* (*Book*) [*Electr*] distributor

*****rrymësi** *nf* flow

rrymo·*n vi* to flow in a current/stream

rrymtas *adv* in a torrential stream

*****rryp** = rrip
○ **rrypë e pjetjes** truss for a hernia

*****rrypak** *adj* = rripak

*****rryple** *nf* strip of fabric torn from a larger piece

rrypinë *nf* strip of land

*****rrypshtejshëm** *adj (i)* (of fruit) ropy and hard to swallow

rryqe *nf* 1 small clay jug without handles 2 (*Fig*) frail old man

*****rryshëm** = rryeshëm

*****rryshkët** = rreshkët, fishkur

s [së] *nf* **1** the consonant letter "s" **2** the voiceless apical sibilant represented by the letter "s"

s' *pcl* negative particle before verbs: not = **nuk**

S *abbrev* < **Sulmues** (used as a mark of honor in imitation of use by military brigades): attack (force)

sa

I § *interrog quant pron/determiner* how much, how many

II § *interrog adv* to what extent/degree: how much, how many

III § *conj* **1** to the extent/degree that: as much (as), as many (as); as soon as, as long as, so long as; so much, so much that; however much, however many; up the point that; enough so that **2** rather than

IV § *exclamatory pcl* expresses amazement: how (many/much) __!, what (a) __! **sa u habita.** how amazed I was! what (a) __! **sa ditë e bukur!** what a beautiful day

V § *pronoun* **1** *(Colloq)* a certain amount, some **2** of the size of, as big as

∘ **sa** {*past tense verb*} just (recently) {}

∘ **sa __ aq__** the more __ the more __

∘ **sa <> arri·**n^{3sg} **dora** as much as <> can, with all <>'s might

∘ **sa bë·**n^{3rd} {} how much *does* {} cost

∘ **sa <> del·**^{3sg} **kurrizi** until <> can no longer hold <>self straight

∘ **Sa <> di·**^{3sg} **lëkura/koka!** How clever {} *is*! That's smart of {}!

∘ {*number*} **e sa** a little more than {}, something more than {}

∘ **sa <> ha·**^{3pl} **këmbët** as fast as <>'s legs *will take* <>

∘ **sa <> ha·**^{3sg} **goja** "as many as <>'s mouth *can* hold" with as many invectives as <> *can* think of

∘ **sa <> ha·**^{3sg} **krahu** with all <>'s might

∘ **sa <> ha·**^{3sg} **palla** with all <>'s force: as hard as <> *can*

∘ **sa më s'bë·**het^{3sg} it couldn't be more/better, it couldn't get better

∘ **është sa një shurdhjesë** *(Impol)* (of a person) to be of very small stature: be very short

∘ **sa para <> bë·**n^{3sg}/**vle·**n^{3sg} **lëkura** "how much money <>'s skin is worth" *(Iron)* just how much <> *is* worth: just how good <> *is*

∘ **sa <> puno·**n^{3sg} **zëri** "as much as <>'s voice *works*" at the top of <>'s voice

∘ **sa s'bë·**het^{3sg} **hesap** who *knows* how many/much: uncountable, abundant

∘ {*adjective*} **sa s'ka** the most {}, extremely {}

∘ **sa s'thu·**het^{3sg} more than one *can* say: innumerable, immeasurable

∘ **sa e sa** {*plural noun*} many many {}, many a {}

∘ **sa shko·**n **e** {*verb*} to keep getting/growing more {}

∘ **sa të ha·**^{3sg}/**përfshi·**n^{3sg}/**rrok·**^{3sg} **syri** as much as the eye can encompass

∘ **sa të zbardh·**et^{3sg} **penda e korbit** until hell freezes over: forever

∘ **sa e zeza e thoit** an amount too small to be useful: not enough to put in your eye

∘ **sa <> zë·**^{3sg} **syri** as far as <>'s eye *can see*

saba'h *nm (Colloq)* morning = **mëngjes**

*****sabe** *nf* = **hobe**

*****sa'bër** *nf(Old)* patience

*****sabit·**et *vpr* to dry out somewhat

sabot|ato'r *n* saboteur

sabot|ím *nm ger* **1** < **saboto'·**n **2** sabotage

saboto'·n *vt* to sabotage

sabot|ue's *adj* with deliberate intention of sabotage

Sabrí *nm* Sabri (male name)

saç *nm* metal dome over which hot ashes are placed to bake the food underneath: baking dome, Dutch oven

∘ **saç pa prush** **1** person who can do nothing to help you; person who spends time without accomplishing anything **2** fruitless activity; something that offers no gain

saçmë *nf* **1** lead pellet, shot pellet, grapeshot; shrapnel **2** shot sinker (on a fishing line) **3** [*Tech*] ball bearing

sa'de *adj (Colloq)* prepared without mixing in anything else: pure, unadulterated, plain, straight

Sade'te *nf* Sadete (female name)

Sadík *nm* Sadik (male name)

sadíst *n* sadist

sadi'zëm *nm* sadism

sado'

I § *exclamatory adv (Colloq)* that's enough!

II § *conj* **1** however much, no matter how much **2** although, however

sado'mo's *pcl* **1** *(Old)* nevertheless **2** at least

sa'do'pa'k *adv* no matter how little/small, however little/few

sa'do'që *conj* even though, notwithstanding that

*****sa'do'shëm** *adj (i)* sufficient

*****safa'q** *nm* [*Bot*] *(Urospermum)*

safë *nf* tankard made of tin

safí *adj, adv (Colloq)* unmixed with anything else: pure, unadulterated, plain, straight

safík *adj* [*Lit*] sapphic

safír *nm* [*Min*] sapphire

safí'zëm *nm* sapphism

*****safra'n** *nm* saffron

saftja'n *nm* dyed and polished soft leather of goatskin/sheepskin: morocco

sa'gë *nf* **1** perforated deep pan for roasting chestnuts **2** [*Lit*] saga

*****sagllá'm** *adj* = **saklla'm**

sagu' *OR* **sago'** *nf* sago

*****sagu'të** *nf* = **sago'**

sa'gje *nf (Reg)* fishing creel made of wicker

saha'n *nm* (copper) bowl; bowlful

saha'në *np* < **saha'n** kitchen vessels

sahan·lëpi·rës *nm (Contempt)* servile parasite: lickspittle, toady

Saha·rë *nf* Sahara

***saha·rkë** *nf* = **bonbo·ne**

saha·t *nm* 1 *(Colloq)* timepiece: clock, watch; clock tower 2 metering device: meter, flow meter 3 *(Colloq)* hour; o'clock = **o·rë** 4 designated time: appointed hour

    ◦ **e sheh· sa ësh·të**^{3sg} **sahati** "see what time it is" *(Iron)* to know the score, see how things stand

sahat·çi *nm (np ~ nj) (Colloq)* clock/watch repairman: watchmaker = **orëndre·qës**

***sahat·xhi** = **sahatçi**

***sahi·të** *nf* knitting needle

SAIDE *abbrev* < **Shoqëria Anonime Industriale e Duhaneve-Elbasan** *[Hist]* Industrial Tobacco Corporation of Elbasan

Saimi·r *nm* Saimir (male name)

saj

    I § enclitic after prepositions that take an ablative object indicates a 3rd sg fem object for the preposition: her

    II § pronominal adj (i) of hers, her; its

    III § n (i) 1 hers; its 2 her folks/people

saj·a *adj (e)* her own way; its own way

sajdi *nf (Colloq)* hospitableness; courteous respect

sajdi·s· *vt (Colloq)* to treat [] hospitably; pay courteous respect to []

sajdi·s·shëm *adj (i)* hospitable

saje *nf*

saje *nf* sledge; sled, sleigh

saji·m *nm ger* 1 < **sajo··n**, **sajo··het** 2 something that has been fashioned/prepared: creation, preparation, contrivance; design 3 *(Pej)* pure fabrication: lie

sajnë *nf* splashing wave; surf

sajo··het *vpr* to be formed, be created

sajo··n *vt* 1 to devise, contrive; form, fashion 2 *(Pej)* to make [] up, fabricate 3 to arrange for [], provide for []

    ◦ **sajo·n me nofulla** to set one's jaw

saju·a·r *adj (i)* fabricated; artificial

saju·e·shëm *adj (i)* feasible

sak *adv (Colloq)* 1 without defect, perfect; intact 2 exactly so; really, certainly; for sure

sak *nm* 1 person who pours raki for guests 2 *(Reg)* long-handled pouch-shaped fishing net with a circular wooden rim

sakana·k *nm* = **kundëre·rë**

sa·ka·q *adv (Colloq)* right away, at once

sa·kaq·he·rë *adv (Colloq)* = **sakaq**

sakari·në *nf* saccharin

saka·t

    I § adj *(Colloq)* crippled

    II § n cripple

    ◦ **sakat nga mendja/trutë** *(Colloq)* lamebrained

sakati·m *nm ger* < **sakato··n**, **sakato··het**

sakat·llë·k *nm (np ~ qe) (Colloq)* crippling defect, infirmity

sakato··het *vpr (Colloq)* to become a cripple, be crippled

sakato··n *vt (Colloq)* to cripple

sakato·s· = **sakato··n**

sakatu·a·r *adj (i)* crippled, maimed

sak·avi·cë *nf* long-handled hatchet: pruning hook, chopper

sa·kë *nf* short-handled axe

sa·këz *nf [Bot]* = **halmu·cë**

sakī·cë *nf* hatchet

sakic·o··n *vt* to cut with a hatchet; chop

saklla·m

    I § adv *(Colloq)* 1 safe and sound, in one piece 2 accurately, bang on

    II § adj *(Colloq)* 1 in good health: fit, sound 2 flawless 3 *(Fig)* reliable

sa·ko *nf* 1 church servant 2 sack coat

***sakomi·le** *nf [Bot]* three-lobed sage *(Salvia triloba)*

sakralgji *nf [Med]* sacral pain: sacralgia

sakresta·n *nm* sacristan

sakrifi·cë *nf* 1 personal sacrifice 2 personal privation, deprivation

sakrifik·i·m *nm ger* < **sakrifiko··n**, **sakrifiko··het**

sakrifik·o··het *vpr* to make personal sacrifices; live with deprivation

sakrifik·o··n *vt* to sacrifice

sakrifik·u·e·s *adj* ready to make personal sacrifices: self-sacrificing

sakrile·gj *nm (Book)* sacrilege

saksi *nf* flowerpot; flower vase

saksofo·n *nm [Mus]* saxophone

saksofon·i·st *n* saxophonist

sakso·n *adj* Saxon

Sakson·i *nf* Saxony

sa·kt·as *adv* = **saktësi·sht**

sa·k·të *adj (i)* 1 flawless, undamaged, perfect 2 exact, accurate; reliable, trustworthy

sakt·ë·si *nf* accuracy, precision

saktë·si·m *nm ger* 1 < **saktëso··n** 2 clarifying detail, specification

saktë·si·sht *adv* precisely, accurately

saktë·s·o··n *vt* 1 to make [] more precise: perfect, refine; revise for accuracy 2 to give/add/correct clarifying details about []

***sa·ku** *conj* 1 instead of, rather than *2 so long as

salama·ndër *nf [Zool]* salamander 2 European fire salamander, spotted salamander *(Salamandra salamandra)*

    ◦ **salamandra e zezë** *[Zool]* Alpine salamander *Salamandra atra*

salbi *nf [Bot]* sage = **sherbe·lë**

sa·lcë *nf [Food]* sauce; tomato sauce

    ◦ **salcë kosi** yogurt that has been strained through cheesecloth

sald·a·to·r *n* welder

sald·a·tri·çe *nf* welding machine

saldi·m *nm ger [Tech]* < **saldo··n**

sa·ldo *nf* 1 *[Fin]* account balance 2 *[Commerc]* balance of payments

saldo··n *vt [Tech]* to weld

sale·p *nm* 1 salep 2 hot thick elixir made of ground up salep tubers diluted with water and sweetened with sugar 3 *[Bot]* orchid *(Orchis)*

salep·çi *nm (Old)* person who make and sells salep elixir 2 *(Pej)* useless person steeped in obsolete ideas and habits

salep·o·re *np [Bot]* orchid family *Orchidaceae*

***sa·lë** = **sa·llë**

Sali *nm* Sali (male name)

*sali**agos** nm [Invert] sea snail

sal**ikim** nm ger (Old) **1** <saliko ∙n **2** Catholic burial rites

sal**iko** ∙n vt (Old) to consecrate [a Catholic grave]

salin**itet** nm (Book) salinity

sal**mon** nm [Ichth] salmon

salmon**elë** nf [Med] salmonella

sa**lpe** nf [Ichth] salema (Sarpa salpa)

salpe**tër** nf saltpeter (potassium nitrate)

sal**siçe** nf [Food] frankfurter, hot dog

SALT abbrev (English) SALT = Strategic Arms Limitation Treaty

salto nf [Gymnastics] somersault

salv**ime** np fem (Book Old) (religious) persecution

sal**vo** ∙n vt (Book Old) to persecute [] (for religious reasons)

sall adv (Reg Old) alone; only = ve**tëm**

*sal**la** adv = **sall**

*sallagj**ak** nm (Old) hammock

*sallaha**ne** nf **1** seesaw ***2** = sallaha**në**

sallaha**në** nf slaughterhouse

sallaʾs∙
   I § vt (Old) to baste (in sewing)
   II § vi (Colloq) to hang around without working: loiter

*salla**kët** adj (i) (Colloq) = sol**lak**

*salla**ks** adj (Colloq) left-handed; left-footed = sol**lak**

salla**m** nm [Food] sausage

sallam**atas** adv (Colloq) childishly and thoughtlessly, silly

sallam**eri** nf **1** plant that makes sausages **2** (Collec) sausage

sallam**ur** nm salt-preserved meat

salla**të** nf **1** salad; salad vegetable **2** (Reg) cucumber
   ∘ sal**latë** deti **1** [Bot] common sea lettuce Ulva lactuca **2** [Invert] green laver Ulva rigida
   ∘ sal**latë** jeshile lettuce; green salad with onions
   ∘ sal**latë** e kuqe [Invert] red laver Porphyra leucosticta
   ∘ sallatë lakër Chinese cabbage
   ∘ sallatë pambukje/pambukore soft-leaved lettuce, tender lettuce: butter(head) lettuce
   ∘ sal**latë** ruse "Russian salad" cold salad made of cooked vegetables mixed together and topped with a mayonnaise dressing and slices of hard-boiled egg

sallatku**a** nm [Bot] spiny broom (Calicotome)

sallat**or** nm (Reg) cucumber, gherkin

*sall**bi** nf [Bot] garden sage (Salvia officinalis)

*sal**llcë** nf [Food] sauce = sal**cë**

sal**llë** nf **1** large room, hall ***2** [Bot] = sul**lë**
   ∘ sal**llë** komandimi control room

sallga**m** OR sallgë**m** nm (Reg) [Bot] = aca**cie**

sallha**ne** nf (Old) = therto**re**

sallma**n** nm (Old) embroidered scarf (worn by women in parts of northern Albania)
   ∘ sal**lman** i bardhë white scarf worn by widows

*salln**is**∙ vi = lëku**nd**∙

sal**llo** nf rendered lard

sallo**n** nm **1** entrance hall; lobby **2** showroom **3** (Pej) salon
   ∘ sallon mode tailor shop selling made-to-order clothes

salltan**et** nm (Pej) extravagant luxury/splendor; ostentation, pomp

sa**m∙et** vpr to go bad and begin to smell: putrefy

sama**r** nm **1** packsaddle **2** straw-filled protective pad worn on the back by a person carrying a heavy load **3** humped part (of something); bridge of the nose; bridge of a stringed instrument **4** turtle shell; snail shell **5** chicken breast

samar**bërës** nm = samarpunu**es**

samar**je** adj fem used for carrying a packsaddle: pack

samar**os**∙ vt (Colloq) to put a packsaddle on []

samar**oskut** nm soft white wool flannel

samar**punues** nm packsaddle maker, saddler

*samar**tar** n = samarpunu**es**

samar**xhi** nm (np ⁻ nj) = samarpunu**es**

*sa**më** nf dog excrement, dog shit

samovar nm (Book) samovar

*samov**illa** np [Folklore] water nymphs who put spells on babies

sam**sa** nf [Food] sweet pastry made like baklava (but with less dough) and served in rhomboid slices

sa**mtë** adj (i) tasteless, bland

sam**tim** nm (of food) smell; funny smell

sam**to**∙het vpr to lose its taste; start to smell funny

sam**to** ∙n vt to make [food] tasteless; cook [a dish] that is flavorless

samu**n** nm **1** [Ichth] = tro**ftë** ***2** = samu**ne**

samu**ne** nf small round bun (eaten during Ramadan)

samura**j** nm samurai

*san**aje** nf collec hay = sa**ne**

sa**natadita** indecl fem period of time when night and day are of equal length: equinox

sanatoriu**m** nm sanatorium

sanda**le** nf open sandal held on by straps

sanda**ll** nm [Naut] small boat propelled by oars or motor; small ferry boat

*Sa**nder** nm Alexander. (nickname for Aleksander)

sander**ma** nf cooking/laundry shed across the courtyard from the house

sandu**iç** nm sandwich

*sa**ne** nf = sa**jë**

*san**esë** nf island = ishu**ll**

sa**në** nf hay

sa**nëz** nf [Bot] yellow gentian (Gentiana lutea)

san**ëzore** np [Bot] gentian family Gentianaceae

sangu**in** adj [Psych] sanguine (temperament)

*san**icë** nf sledge

San**ie** nf Sanie (female name)

sanita**r**
   I § adj hygienic; sanitary
   II § n [Mil] medic

sanita**re** nf **1** <sanita**r** **2** cleaning woman in a hospital

*sanks**ion** = sanks**ion**

sanks**ion** nm sanction

sanksion**im** nm ger <sanksiono∙n

sanksion**o** ∙n vt [Law] to sanction

sanskr**it** adj Sanskrit

sanskrit**isht** adv in Sanskrit (language)

sanskrit**ishte** nf Sanskrit language

*sa**nxë** nf [Bot] great yellow gentian = sa**nëz**

sanxha*k* *nm (np ˜ qe)* [*Hist*] large administrative unit under the Ottoman Empire, province: sanjak

sanxhak|**bej** *nm* [*Hist*] military and civil head of a sanjak

sap
I § *nm* [*Constr*] prefabricated ceiling joist made of component blocks held together by reinforcing rods and concrete
II § *adj* (of a building block) having longitudinal perforations (for insertion of reinforcing rods) and side gutters (into which concrete will be poured)

sape**|**tk*ë *nf* haversack, bag

sapfi*r = **safi*r***

saplla|**ke** *nf* tankard

sa|**po**
I § *adv* just before, just now, just
II § *conj* **1** as soon as, right after; from/since the moment **2** (*Colloq*) since (in the sense of because), inasmuch as
○ **sapo ka· dalë nga shpërgënjtë** (*Impol*) to be hardly out of diapers, be still immature

sa|**poa**|**rdh**|**ur** *adj (i), n* newly arrived (person) = **porsaa**|**rdhur**

sa|**poçe**|**l**|**ur** *adj (i), n* freshly bloomed; just opened; just hatched = **porsaçe**|**lur**

sa|**poçliru**|**ar** *adj (i)* newly liberated = **porsaliru**|**ar**

sa|**poda**|**l*ë*** *adj (i)* newly emerged = **porsada**|**l*ë***

sa|**poemë**|**ru**|**ar** *adj (i)* just named, newly designated = **porsa emë**|**ru**|**ar**

sa|**pofeju**|**ar**
I § *adj (i)* newly betrothed, just engaged
II § *n (i)* new fiancé = **porsafeju**|**ar**

sa|**pofillu**|**ar** *adj (i)* newly begun, recently initiated = **porsafillu**|**ar**

sa|**poformu**|**ar** *adj (i)* newly formed = **porsaformu**|**ar**

sa|**poko**|**rr**|**ur** *adj (i), n* newly reaped = **porsako**|**rr**|**ur**

sa|**pokriju**|**ar** *adj (i)* newly created = **porsakriju**|**ar**

sa|**poli**|**nd**|**ur** *adj (i), n* new-born, newly born = **porsali**|**ndur**

sa|**pomartu**|**ar** *adj (i), n (i)* newly-wed = **porsamartu**|**ar**

sa|**pondërtu**|**ar** *adj (i), n (i)* newly constructed = **porsandërtu**|**ar**

sapu|**n**
I § *nm* soap
II § *adj* (*Colloq*) very fat/plump
○ **sapun mbi gunë** deceptive trick, fraud
○ **sapun myshqe** (*Old*) musk-scented soap
○ **sapun pa shkumë** "soap without suds" useless talk/activity

sapun|**ëzi**|**m** *nm ger* [*Chem*] saponification

sapun|**ëzo ·het** *vpr* [*Chem*] to undergo saponification

sapun|**ëzo ·n** *vt* [*Chem*] to saponify

sapun|**ëzu**|**es** *adj* [*Chem*] used in saponification: saponifying

sapun|**im** *nm ger* < **sapuno ·het**

sapun|**is·** *vt* to apply soap to [ ], soak/rub [ ] with soap: soap

sapun|**is·et** *vpr* to become soapy, get soaped

sapun|**isje** *nf ger* < **sapunis·**, **sapunis·et**

sapun|**o ·het** *vpr* = **sapunis·et**

sapun|**or** *adj* [*Spec*] saponaceous

sapun|**xhi** *nm (np ˜ nj)* (*Old*) soap seller, soap maker

sa|**që** *conj* so (much/many) that

saraç *nm* maker of leather goods: leatherworker, leather craftsman

saraçine|**sk*ë*** *nf* [*Tech*] stopcock

saraf
I § *nm* **1** (*Old*) money changer **2** (*Pej*) stingy miser
II § *adj* (*Pej*) stingy, miserly

saraf|**ll*ë***|**k** *nm* stinginess, miserliness

sara|**g*ë*** *nf* **1** kippered bleak **2** [*Ichth*] = **cera**|**g*ë***

saraho|**sh** = **sarho**|**sh**

saraj *nm* **1** (*Old*) seraglio, palace; women's quarters in a seraglio **2** government headquarters; large administrative building

sara|**ll*ë***|**k** *nm* (*Old*) [*Med*] jaundice

Sara|**nd*ë*** *nf* coastal resort city in southwestern Albania: Saranda

sarand|**jot**
I § *adj* of or pertaining to Saranda
II § *n* native of Saranda

sara|**nxh*ë*** *nf* (*Old*) cistern for water, water tank

Saraqi*n *nm* [*Hist*] Saracen

saraxha *nf* [*Med*] scrofula = **stërku**|**ngull**

sarde|**le** *nf* [*Ichth*] sardine (*Sardinia pilchardus*)
○ **sardele kanali** [*Ichth*] round sardinella *Sardinella aurita*

sardine|**le** *nf* [*Ichth*] round sardinella (*Sardinella aurita*)

sardhoni*k *nm* sardonyx

sarë|**k** I § *nm (np ˜ qe)* OR **sarë**|**k*ë*** II § *nf* (*Old*) turban typically worn by Moslem clergymen

sa|**rg**|**ël** *nf* [*Agr*] grafting tool

sargi *nf* sacking cloth, burlap

sargo|**n** *nm* [*Ichth*] common two-banded sea bream (*Diplodus vulgarus*)

sarho|**sh**
I § *nm* (*Pej*) drunkard, lush
II § *adj* (*Pej*) hard-drinking

sarka**|**dh*e = **sorka**|**dh*e***

sarkast|**ik** *adj* sarcastic

sarka|**z*ë***|**m** *nm* sarcasm

sa|**rk*ë*** *nf* (*Colloq*) **1** physique **2** characteristic external appearance (of a person): cast, physique **3** characteristic clothing, attire

sarkofa|**g** *nm* sarcophagus

sarko|**m*ë*** *nf* [*Med*] sarcoma

***sarko**|**pt** *nm* [*Invert*] ringworm tick

sarma *nf* [*Food*] stuffed grape/cabbage leaves = **japra**|**k**

saru|**sh*ë*** *nf* [*Bot*] woundwort (*Stachys*)

saru|**sht*ë*** *nf* [*Bot*] figwort (*Scrophularia*)

sa|**s*ë*** *nf* (*Reg*) type of marsh reed used to weave straw mats: rush

sasi *nf* quantity

sasi|**or** *adj* quantitative

sa|**t** *adj (i), n (i)* of how many, which one (in a series), in what position (in a ranked order)

SATA *abbrev* (*Italian*) < **Societa Automobilistica Transporto-Albania** [*Hist*] Automobile and Transport Association of Albania (Italian association 1939-43)

sata|**c** *nm* coarse sieve, riddle = **sita**|**c**

Sata|**n** OR **Satana** *nm* Satan

satan|**ik** *adj* satanic

sate *gen/dat/abl* <**jote** thy, your (2nd sg)

satelit
I § *nm, adj* satellite
II § *nm* [*Tech*] planetary gear

saten *nm* satin

saté *nf* bus (originally the brand name of a bus manufacturer)

satër *nm* **1** meat cleaver **2** executioner's axe; battle-
ax **3** tobacco-shredding knife

satërac *nm* harrier's knife for trimming a horse's
hooves

satin *nm* satin

satir *nm* satyr

satirë *nf* satire

satirik *adj* satirical

satirizim *nm ger* <**satirizo** ·*n*

satirizo ·*n* *vt* to satirize

satirizues *adj* using satire to gain an effect: sati-
rizing

satraç *nm* knife for paring hoofs

satrap
I § *nm* satrap
II § *adj* despotic and cruel

satraplak *nm (np satrapleq)* [*Hist*] = **stërplak**

savan *nm* shroud

savanë *nf* [*Geog*] savanna

***savanos·** *vt* to wrap [ ] in a shroud: enshroud

***savat** *nm* marquetry (with black tracery inlaid on
silver)

***savit·** *vt* [*Constr*] to plaster a wall with a float

savurrë *nf* [*Naut*] ballast

saxhak *nm* trivet for supporting a pot on the fire

***saza** *adv* for a little while

Sazan *nm* **1** island at the mouth of the Bay of Vlora
2 Sazan (male name)

saze
I § *nf* [*Mus*] **1** folk instrument with a mandolin-like
body, a long neck, and ten strings divided into three
courses **2** (*Colloq*) mouth organ, harmonica
II § *np* folk band; folk instruments

sazexhi *nm (np ˜ nj) (Colloq)* [*Mus*] musician in a
folk band

se
I § *conj* **1** (following a transitive verb and followed
by a verb in the indicative) that **2** (preceded by a comparative expression and followed by an adverbial or
adjectival expression) than **3** (between two complete
clauses) because **4** (*Colloq*) (between two identical
words or phrases) whether or not _ **5** (between two
contrastive words or phrases) whether _ or _
II § *interrog* (after a preposition) what
III § *pcl* **1** (at the end of a clause) asks for confirmation: hunh? what do you say? **2** (before an interroga-
tive/indefinite pronoun) indicates greater indefiniteness: some_ or other
  ∘ **se s'bë** ·*n³ˢᵍ* no matter what, willy-nilly

seancë *nf* **1** each of the sittings of an assembly of
people: sitting, meeting **2** each of a series of ap-
pointments: session

SEATO *abbrev (English)* SEATP = Southeast Asia
Treaty Organization

sebep *nm (Colloq)* **1** reason = **shkak 2** false excuse
3 important family occasion
  ∘ **Rroftë sebep!** "Long live the occasion!" (*Iron*)
(ironic comment about someone who has taken undeserved advantage of an occasion)

secil *n (definite case forms only)* serving as determiner or pronoun each (one), every (one)
  ∘ **Secili ka hallin e vet, kurse mullisi të ujit.**
"Each has his own trouble, like the miller with the
water." Everyone sees his own problems.
  ∘ **secili sipas gustos** each to his own taste
  ∘ **Secili shikon/këqyr tymin e vet.** "Each one
watches his own smoke." Everyone looks after his
own interests.
  ∘ **Secili të vetën, mullisi të ujit.** "Each his own,
the miller the water." Everyone sees his own problems.

secilido *n (definite case forms only; gender, number, and case suffixes take the place of i as appropriate)* serving as determiner or pronoun = **secil**

seç
I § *pron* some indeterminate thing: something, anything; whatever, what
II § *quant* to some indeterminate extent/degree:
some
III § *pcl used in folk lyrics* indicates that the speaker
is happily pleased with what follows in the sentence:
how nice!: indicates surprise: hey!

***sedan** *nm (Reg)* [*Bot*] parsley = **majdanoz**

sedef *nm* mother-of-pearl: nacre

sedefte *adj (i)* made of mother-of-pearl: pearl

sedër *nf* **1** pride, self-respect, dignity, prestige **2** personal drive to do well: ambition, zeal, spirit

sedërfyer *adj* having wounded pride, with one's
dignity insulted

sedërlenduar *adj* with hurt pride, affronted in dignity

sedërmadh *adj* **1** having easily hurt pride, with a
fragile ego: touchy **2** having an inflated ego, big-
headed **3** having self-pride in one's work

sedërqar *adj (Colloq)* = **sedërmadh**

***sedërti** *nf (Old)* luxury

sedie *nf* [*Tech*]
  ∘ **sedie e valvolës** [*Tech*] valve seat

sedije *nf (Colloq)* ignorance

sedilje *nf* seat (in a vehicle)

sedo *pron (Colloq)* anything whatever, anything at
all

sefergjen *nm* [*Bot*] basil = **borzilok**

seferta *nm* metal containers stacked and fastened
together at the handle for storing several foods
at a time; each of these containers

sefir *nm* [*Bot*] moonwort (*Botrychium lunaria*)

sefkël *nf* [*Bot*] spinach beet (*Beta cicla*)

sefte
I § *nf* **1** (*Colloq*) first sale of the day at a shop **2** first
time; time, instance
II § *adv* **1** (*Colloq*) at first **2** for the first time

segment *nm* segment

segmentor *adj* [*Tech*] segmental

sehir *nm* **1** (*Colloq*) viewing for pleasure, idle observation: looking around, casual looking **2** visual access to a view; view, prospect, vista **3** (*Reg*) surprise
at something unusual

sehirxhi *nm (np ˜ nj)* **1** (*Colloq*) spectator, onlooker
2 (*Pej*) mere spectator, indifferent onlooker

***seicil** = **secil**

Seit *nm* Seit (male name)

***sej** *conj* so long as, while

sejmen *nm* **1** (*Old*) bodyguard, escort **2** (*Pej*) henchman

se·jtë *interrog adj (i)* of what, from what (is something made)?

sek *nm (np ~q)* square winepress

sekante *nf* [*Geom*] secant

*****sekcion = seksion**

sekondant *nm* personal assistant, aide: second (in a duel, in a boxing/chess match)

sekondar *adj* secondary

sekondë *nf* **1** second (of time/angle/pitch) **2** *(Fig)* short period of time: second, moment

sekondëmatës *nm* stopwatch

sekrecion *nm* [*Physiol*] secretion

sekret *nm, adj* secret

sekretar *n* **1** secretary **2** recording stenographer

sekretari *nf* **1** secretary's office **2** *(Collec)* official recorders (of a trial or important meeting)

sekretariat *nm* secretariat

sekretim *nm ger* [*Physiol*] **1** <sekreto·n, sekreto·het **2** secretion

sekreto·het *vpr* [*Physiol*] to be secreted, flow, issue

sekreto·n *vt* [*Physiol*] to secrete [secretions]

seks *nm* sex
  ◦ **seksi i dobët/bukur** "the weak/beautiful sex" females, women
  ◦ **seksi femëror** females, women
  ◦ **seksi i fortë** "the strong sex" males, men
  ◦ **seksi mashkullor** men

seksapil *nm* [*Cine*] sex appeal

sekser *nm* **1** real estate agent **2** *(Reg)* = saraf

sekseri *nf (Old)* **1** real estate business **2** broker's fee *****3** brokerage

seksion *nm* section

seksual *adj* sexual

seksualizëm *nm (Book)* **1** sexual feeling **2** sexualism

sekt *nm* sect

sektar *adj (Pej)* sectarian

sektarizëm *nm (Pej)* sectarianism

sektor *nm* sector

sektorial *adj* **1** sectorial **2** *(Fig Pej)* narrowly reflecting the interest of a single sector: parochial and partisan, sectarian

seku *adverb* somewhere

sekuestër *nf* [*Law*] sequestration (of property)

sekuestrim *nm ger* [*Law*] <sekuestro·n

sekuestro·n *vt* [*Law*] to attach/seize [personal property] by legal means: sequester [property]

sekuestrues *nm* [*Law*] commissioner authorized to sequester a piece of property

sekular = shekullar

sekull *nm* [*Bot*] beet = pazi

*****sekur** *conj, pron* <when

sekush
  I § *pron* someone
  II § *pron* everyone

selam *nm (Colloq Old)* greetings: salaam

selamet *nm (Old)* happy resolution of a bad situation; good outcome

Selami *nm* Selami (male name)

selamllëk *nm (np ~qe) (Old)* room for entertaining male guests, guest parlor in a rich Moslem house

Selanik *nm* Salonika

Selanik *nm* Salonika, Thessalonika

*****selc** *nm* soda water

selekcion = seleksion

seleksion *nm* selection

seleksionim *nm ger* **1** <seleksiono·n **2** selection **3** [*Agr*] eugenic selection

seleksiono·n *vt* to subject [ ] to a selection process: select

seleksionues
  I § *adj* selective
  II § *n* expert employed in a selection process: selector

*****Selenik = Selanik**

selfian *nm* [*Bot*] = borzilok

seli *nf* headquarters, seat

selinë *nf* = selino

selino *I* § *nf OR* **selin** *II* § *nm* [*Bot*] celery (*Apium graveolens*)
  ◦ **selino e egër** [*Bot*] wild celery *Apium graveolens var silvestre* = sherp

seli·s *stem for 1st sg pres, pl pres, 2nd & 3rd sg subj, pind* <seli·t

selishtë *nf* garden plot near the house: kitchen garden

seli·t· *vt* **1** *(Colloq)* to implant and take care of [ ]: cultivate; raise and educate well **2** to install [new settlers] in a place: colonize, settle

seli·t·et *vpr* **1** to take root, get established; settle, settle down; prosper **2** *(Colloq)* to grow up well

selitje *nf ger* **1** <seli·t·, seli·t·et **2** cultivation

selvi *nf* [*Bot*] cypress, funeral cypress (*Cupressus sempervirens*) = qiparis

Selvi *nm* Selvi (female name)

selviore *np* [*Bot*] cypress family *Cupressaceae*

semafor *nm* signal light; traffic light

Seman *nm* Seman (male name)

semantik *adj* semantic

semantikë *nf* [*Ling*] semantics

semasiologji *nf* [*Ling*] semasiology

sembër *np masc (Old)* **1** poor farmers who take turns using a team of oxen to which each contributes one ox **2** herdsmen who merge their small herds for common pasturing

*****sembim = sëmbim**

semestër *nm* semester

semestral *adj* semestral

semiaks *nm* [*Tech*] swing axle, semi-axle

semimaturë *nf (Old)* set of examinations formerly given to students after the fourth year of secondary school

seminar *nm* **1** seminar **2** seminary **3** school for training teachers: normal school

seminarist *n* seminarian, seminarist

semiotikë *nf* semiotics

semit *nm* Semite

semitik *adj* semitic

semolinë *nf* semolina

*****semos** *conj* <se mos lest

*****sempël** *adj* simple = thjeshtë

*****senap** *nm* mustard

senat *nm* senate

senator *n* senator

send *nm* **1** material object, inanimate thing; object, thing **2** thing required: necessity **3** *(Euph)* apoplexy, stroke

*****sendar** *adj (Old)* material, concrete

*se'nd_ë_r = se'd_ë_r

sendër'gji' _nf (Book)_ artifice

sendër'gji'm _nm ger_ **1** <**sendërgjo'·n, sendërgjo'·het 2** complete fabrication, lie

sendër'gjo'·het _vpr_ to be devised, fabricated

sendër'gjo'·n _vt_ **1** to devise, fabricate, invent **2** to fabricate, lie

*sendër'ta'r _adj_ hardworking

sendërti'm _nm ger_ **1** _(Book)_ <**sendërto'·n, sendërto'·het 2** realization, fulfilment

sendër'to'·het _vpr_ to be realized, be fulfilled

sendër'to'·n _vt (Book)_ to bring [] to reality: realize, fulfil

send_ë_zi'm _nm ger_ **1** _(Book)_ <**sendëzo'·n, sendëzo'·het 2** embodiment

send_ë_zo'·het _vpr (Book)_ to take body, become embodied

send_ë_zo'·n _vt (Book)_ to make [] corporeal, incorporate: embody

*sendi's· _vt_ to exacerbate, annoy

sendo'n _nm_ white bed-sheet

sendo'r _adj_ **1** _(Book)_ material, substantive **2** _[Ling]_ concrete

send_th_ _nm_ worthless junk

sene' _nf (Old)_ year

Senega'l _nm_ Senegal

senegale'z
    _I §_ _adj_ Senegalese
    _II §_ _n_ native of Senegal

sene't _nm (Old)_ receipt (for money received), bill of sale
    ∘ **senet bakri** _(Old)_ official document

*senkser' = sekser'

sensacio'n _nm_ sensation

sensacional _adj_ sensational

sensi'b_ë_l _adj_ sensitive, touchy; tender-hearted

sensibili'te't _nm (Book)_ sensibility, sensitivity

sensibili'zo'·n _vt (Book)_ **1** to sensitize **2** _(Fig)_ to make [] aware

sensua'l _adj (Book)_ sensual

sensuali'te't _nm (Book)_ sensuality

sensuali'z_ë_m _nm._ **1** sensualism; sensuality **2** _[Phil]_ sensationalism

sente'nc_ë_ _nf_ **1** epigrammatic sentence, aphorism, epigram **2** _(Law)_ sentence

sentimenta'l
    _I §_ _adj_ sentimental
    _II §_ _n_ sentimentalist

sentimentali'z_ë_m _nm_ sentimentalism

sepa'l _nm [Bot]_ sepal

separati'st _adj, n (Book)_ separatist

separati'z_ë_m _nm (Book)_ separatism

separato'r _nm [Tech]_ separator

sepe'te _nf_ **1** hope chest **2** wicker hamper

sepi' _nf [Zool]_ = **se'pje**

se'pje _nf [Invert]_ cuttlefish

sepjo'l_ë_ _nf [Invert]_ kind of cuttlefish _(Sepietta oweniana)_

se'pse
    _I §_ _conj_ because
    _II §_ _adv_ for some (unknown) reason, the reason why

*seq _np_ <**se'k**

se'ra _np_ hothouses

serasqe'r _nm [Hist]_ commander-in-chief of the army in the Ottoman Empire

*seravi's _stem for 1st sg pres, pl pres, 2nd & 3rd sg subj, pind_ <**seravi't·**

*seravi't· _vt_ to pile up [], stack []

serb _adj, n_ Serbian, Serb

serbato'r _nm [Tech]_ fuel tank, gas tank

serbe's _adv, adj (Colloq)_ with head held high, with great pride and courage, with great bearing

Serbi' _nf_ Serbia

serbi'sht _adv_ in Serbian (language)

serbi'sht|e _nf_ Serbian language

serbokroati'sht _adv_ in Serbo-Croatian (language)

serbokroati'sht|e _nf_ Serbo-Croatian language

serboma'dh _adj, n (Pej)_ (person) believing in Serbian dominance/superiority

serda'r _nm [Hist]_ commander of a Turkish army during the Ottoman Empire

serde'n _nm [Bot]_ = **lulemëlla'g_ë_**

se're _nf_ square block of wood used by a cap maker to pound wool into felt

serena'd_ë_ _nf_ serenade

serena't_ë_ = serena'd_ë_

se'r_ë_ _nf_ **1** bitumen, natural asphalt ***2** hell ***3 = së'r_ë_**
    ∘ **(i zi) sere** pitch black

sergje'n _nm_ wall shelf/rack for kitchen utensils, open cupboard

*sergji' = sergje'n

seri' _nf_ **1** series **2** (movie) serial

seri'c_ë_ _nf [Bot]_ alyssum _(Alyssum)_

*seri'n _pred_ (of weather) cool

seri'n_ë_ _nf_ type of juicy dark grape with large fruit

serio'z _adj_ serious; thoughtful, responsible, weighty

seriozi'sht _adv_ seriously

seriozi'te't _nm_ seriousness

serm _nm_ silver = **argje'nd**

serma' _nf (Old)_ **1** silver; silver coin; silver ornament **2** saved money, accumulated savings, capital

serma'j_ë_ _nf (Old)_ = **serma'**

se'rmt_ë_ _adj (i)_ = **argje'ndt_ë_**

sero'·het _vpr_ **1** _(Colloq)_ to get all dirty, get black with dirt **2** to take on an angry countenance: darken with anger

sero'·n
    _I §_ _vt_ **1** _(Colloq)_ to cover [] with asphalt **2** to darken, blacken **3** _(Fig)_ to shame, dishonor
    _II §_ _vi_ to take on an angry countenance: darken with anger

sero's· = sero'·n

sero'z _adj [Anat]_ serous

serpenti'n _nm [Min]_ serpentine (stone)

se'rt_ë_ _adj (i) (Colloq)_ **1** stiff, inflexible **2** having a strong taste/smell **3** _(Fig)_ surly; (of a draft animal) difficult to manage; (of terrain) rugged, rough; (of weather) inclement, harsh

seru'm _nm [Med Biol]_ serum

servi'l
    _I §_ _adj_ sycophantic
    _II §_ _n_ sycophant

servili'z_ë_m _nm_ sycophancy

servi'r· _vi, vt_ **1** to present food/drink: serve **2** to make a presentation of [], serve up []

servis nm **1** service (of tableware for 6-12 people) **2** [*Sport*] serve, service

serrë nf tall and rugged cliff, high craghothouse

sesa conj than

SESA abbrev < **Shoqëria Elektrike Shqiptare Anonime** [*Hist*] Albanian Electric Association

sesi

I § adv in some way: somehow

II § nf method for accomplishing something: means, way

○ **nuk ka sesi** it is impossible; there's no way

****sesihe** nf = **sesi**

sesion nm each of a series of meetings of a formal assembly; school term: session

****sestim** nm ger < **sesto·n**

****sesto·n** vt to stitch [] loosely as an intermediate step: baste

set nm [*Sport*] part of a match consisting of several games: set

setac nm coarse sieve, riddle = **sitac**

****setë** nf sieve = **sitë**

setër nf **1** jacket (for men); wool jacket **2* (*Old*) hood/bonnet (of a car)

sevap nm **1** (*Old*) gift/act of charity, alms **2** (*Contempt*) unwanted help offered just for show

sevda nf passion, love

○ **ësh-të** {} **për sevda** to be a really wonderful {}

sevdalleshë nf, adj fem = **sevdalli**

sevdalli nm, adj masc (pl ~ nj) (*Colloq*) **1** (person) who falls in love right away: sucker for love **2** (person) who is crazy about something, enthusiast

sevdallis·et vpr to fall in love

së

I § proclitic attributive article **1** marks agreement with a feminine definite non-nominative, non-accusative referent **2 = e**

II § formative introducing ablative-like adverbial expressions from, by

sëfundi adv < **së fundi** at last, finally

sëkëlldi nf (*Colloq*) **1** distress caused by disease or body malfunction: trouble, discomfort, misery **2** (*Fig*) serious worry/problem, terrible anxiety: bad trouble

sëkëlldis· vt (*Colloq*) to cause [] physical or emotional distress: worry, trouble; upset

sëkëlldis·et vpr (*Colloq*) to be troubled: worry; feel upset

sëkëlldisur adj (i) **1** (*Colloq*) troubled, worried, upset **2** in trouble

sëlli nf = **sillë**

sëlli·n vi = **sillo·n**

sëllo·n vt (*Reg*) **1** to strike/hit ◇ hard **2** (*Fig*) to bang on ◇, come down hard on ◇

○ **<>a sëllo·n** to bawl ◇ out; take strong actions against ◇

sëmbar· vt to put [] on the right road, steer [] down the proper path

****sëmbër = sembër**

sëmbim nm **1** sharp pain: twinge, pang **2** feeling of regret

sëmbo·n vi to cause ◇ to feel a twinge; cause ◇ to feel a twinge of regret

sëmbonjës adj [*Med*] causing twinges: shooting

****sëmëdell** nm [*Bot*] wig tree, smoke tree (*Cotinus coggygria*)

****sëmu·het = sëmur·et**

****sëmu·n** vt (*Reg*) = **sëmur·**

****sëmue** (*Reg Gheg*) = **sëmund**, **sëmur**

****sëmundë = sëmundje**

****sëmundëm** adj (i) ill, sick

sëmundje nf **1** illness, disease, ailment **2** (*Fig*) improper penchant: predilection, proclivity

○ **sëmundje e gjëndrës** scrofula

○ **sëmundje e heshtur** latent disease

○ **sëmundje e hënës** (*Colloq*) [*Med*] epilepsy

○ **sëmundje e kërbishtjeve** lumbago

○ **sëmundje e ligë** (*Colloq*) epilepsy

○ **sëmundje e madhe** (*Old Colloq*) epilepsy

○ **sëmundje e qenit** [*Med*] echinococcosis

○ **sëmundje e rrezes** radiation sickness

○ **sëmundje e rritjes** maturation problem, growing pains

○ **sëmundje e sheqerit** [*Med*] diabetes mellitus

○ **sëmundje e tokës** (*Colloq*) epilepsy

sëmundjeprurës adj (*Book*) disease-carrying: pathogenic, morbific

sëmundshmëri nf [*Med*] rate of illness

sëmur· vt **1** to be injurious to []'s health, cause disease in [] **2** to make [] feel ill: make [] sick, ail

sëmur·et vpr to fall ill, get sick; become diseased

sëmurë

I § adj (i) **1** ill, sick, diseased, ailing; sickly; sick-looking **2** (*Fig*) unhealthy

II § n (i) ailing/sick person; the sick; patient

III § adv in an ailing/sick/diseased condition: ill

sëmurëtore nf (*Old*) hospital

****sëmurje = sëmundje**

****sëmutë** adj (i) (*Reg Gheg*) = **sëmundëm**

sëndis· vt **1** (*Colloq*) to cause [] vexation: bother, vex, trouble, worry, grieve **2** to cause [] pain: hurt

sëndis·et vpr (*Colloq*) to be troubled: worry; feel upset

sëndisje nf (*Colloq*) worry; upset feeling; hurt, pain

sëndisur adj (i) troubled, worried, upset, sad

sënduk nm wooden box with a lid: wooden chest

○ **sënduk gjimnastikor** [*Gymnastics*] vaulting box

****sëpari** adv < **së pari** in the first place

sëpatar nm axeman, logger

sëpatë nf axe; hatchet; broadaxe, battle-axe

○ **ësh-të sëpatë me dy presa/tehe** "be a two-edged axe" to be very adept/capable

○ **sëpatë pa bisht** something of no value to anyone

sëprapi = prapi

sëprapthi = prapthi

sërë nf **1** series, row, string **2** turn (in a sequence of opportunities to participate) **3** (*Colloq*) opportunity, chance **4** (*Colloq*) social stratum/class **5** (*Colloq*) close family

****sërëndis** stem for 1st sg pres, pl pres, 2nd & 3rd sg subj, pind < **sërëndit·**

****sërëndit·** vt to line [] up, list

sërish OR **sërishmi** adv anew: another time, again

sërithi adv = **sërish**

sërma nf = **gjymysh**

sërmët adj (i) of silver = **argjendtë**

sëros· vt to string [] together; arrange [] in a series

****sërpkë** nf Serbian woman

sërrek nm new growth on trees

sfakë nf [Bot] Jerusalem sage (Phlomis fruticosa) = bezgë

*****sfejkë** nf [Bot] = sefkël

sferë nf sphere

sferik adj spherical

*****sfëngër** OR **sfëngjer** = sfungjer

sfidë nf (Book) **1** challenge to a duel **2** defiant challenge, challenge

sfido·n vt (Book) **1** to challenge [] to a duel **2** to challenge, challenge defiantly

sfilis stem for 1st sg pres, pl pres, 2nd & 3rd sg subj, pind <sfilit·

sfilit· vt to make [] suffer, inflict pain on []: torment, torture

sfilit·et vpr to toil and suffer to the point of exhaustion; be racked with pain and suffering

sfilitës adj excruciating

sfilitje nf severe suffering, excruciating pain: torment, torture

sfilitur adj (i) tired and exhausted from toil; distraught

sfinë nf **1** wedge (for cleaving wood) **2** = spicë

sfingës nm [Ornit] goldfinch (Carduelis carduelis)

sfinks nm sphinx

sfok· vt to nip at [] with the fingers, pinch [] playfully

sfond nm **1** background ***2** dense growth, thicket

sfrat nm levee, dike; dam, weir

sfungjer nm sponge
  ○ **sfungjer kali** [Invert] horse sponge Hippospongia communis
  ○ **sfungjer tualeti** [Invert] Dalmatian sponge Spongia officinalis

sfungjeror adj (i) spongy

sfungjertë adj (i) made of spongy material, spongy

sfurk nm (np ˜ qe) **1** pitchfork, hayfork **2** [Zool] = sfurkth **3** (Reg) table fork = pirun **4** [Zool] green lizard (Lacerta trilineata)

sfurkth nm **1** [Invert] scorpion = akrep **2** breastbone of a bird

sfurqi nf measure equal to the distance from the tip of the index finger to the tip of the spread thumb = bërxhik

sfytës nm = stërfytës

sfytyri·n vi **1** to snort with anger; (of a horse) whinny nervously ***2** to pant, gasp, puff, sniff ***3** to quiver with anger/fright

*****sfytyrim** nm quiver (with anger/fright)

si
  I § adv conj **1** in what way: how; what **2** in such a way that **3** as; like; as if **4** such as
  II § pcl to some approximate degree/extent: somewhat, somehow, something like
  ○ **si** {time reference point} {number} {measure of time} {number} {periods of time} from {time reference point}; {number} of {} ago counting from {time reference point} **si nesër pesë vjet** five years from tomorrow; five years ago tomorrow
  ○ {number} {measure of time} **si** {time reference point} **1** {number} {periods of time} from {time reference point} **2** {number} of {} ago counting from {time reference point} **pesë vjet si nesër** five years from tomorrow five years ago tomorrow
  ○ **<>u ngjit si bajga pas këpucës** "stick like shit to a shoe" (Crude) to stick to <> like glue; be a nuisance to <>
  ○ **ësh·të si bjeshka** to be plump and pretty

  ○ **ësh·të^{3sg} si bletë e plotë** to be abundantly provided with all the necessities of life
  ○ **ësh·të si bryma para diellit** to be not long for this earth
  ○ **si buka që ha·** without any doubt: absolutely
  ○ **ësh·të si deti me ujë** "be like a sea/lake with water" to be very well off
  ○ **ësh·të si dredhë** to be thin as a rail
  ○ **ësh·të^{pl} si dy pika uji** "be alike as two drops of water" to be alike as two peas in a pod
  ○ **si e do·^{3sg} radha** "as order demands" as required/proper
  ○ **ësh·të si era e malit** "be like the mountain wind" to be immature and fuzzy-minded
  ○ **ësh·të^{pl}/shko·n^{pl}/ve·te^{pl} si eshka me urorin** "{} get along like tinder with flint" sparks fly when {} get together, {} always fight
  ○ **ësh·të^{3sg} si filli i merimangës** "be like spider silk" to be in delicate condition, be very fragile
  ○ **ësh·të si fryma** to be flighty
  ○ **ësh·të si grizhla** to be one's own worst enemy
  ○ **ësh·të si grosha shatë javë** to be immature
  ○ **ësh·të si guri në hobe** to move around from place to place, not stay in one place
  ○ **ësh·të si gjoli me ujë** "be like a sea/lake with water" to be very well off
  ○ **ësh·të si gjuha në gojë** to be very useful, be indispensable
  ○ **ësh·të si gjym i zi** to be ugly as sin
  ○ **ësh·të si harrje** to be a terrible nuisance
  ○ **si hy·n (e) del·** to get nothing out of it
  ○ **s'ësh·të^{pl} si këmbët e dhisë** "not be like the feet of a goat" {} don't all have to be treated the same
  ○ **ësh·të si maja e gjilpërës** to be catty
  ○ **ësh·të^{pl} si mishi me thuan/kockën** to be inseparable (companions)
  ○ {noun} **si mos** {same noun} there couldn't be a better {} **vajzë si mos vajzë** the best of all possible girls
  ○ **ësh·të^{pl} si nata me ditën** to be as different as day and night
  ○ **ësh·të si në ethe** to be feverish and have the chills
  ○ **ësh·të si patë** to be fat as a goose
  ○ **ësh·të si plep** (Colloq) to be tall and straight
  ○ **si qyqja verën** "like the cuckoo treats summer" trying hard to make it last forever
  ○ **ësh·të si sapuni me shparcën** "be like soap with a washcloth" to be always in each other's company: be always together, be inseparable
  ○ **ësh·të si tenjë** to be very thin
  ○ **ësh·të si top** to be chubby
  ○ **<> rrinë rrobat si thes** <>'s clothes fit <> like a sack, the clothes are too big for <>
  ○ **ësh·të si zogjtë e klloçkës** to be small and weak; need special care and protection

si nf [Mus] pitch above la: si, ti; the note "B" in music

Siberi nf Siberia

siberian adj, n Siberian

sibilant nm [Ling] sibilant

sibilë nf sibyl

*****sicil** = secil

Sicili nf Sicily

sicilian adj, n Sicilian

*****sicilis** stem for 1st sg pres, pl pres, 2nd & 3rd sg subj, pind <sicilit·

*sicilít· vt to allot

siç conj as; like; as for example

  ○ **siç duken bathët** as things look

  ○ **siç shi·het^{3sg}** as is obvious, as everyone knows, obviously

  ○ **siç tregojnë bathët** as things look

*siçdo pron something, anything

SIDA

  I § abbrev

  II § nf [Med] AIDS (the disease)

siderurgjí nf iron and steel metallurgy; heavy industry: siderurgy

siderurgjík adj of or pertaining to iron and steel metallurgy: siderurgical

sido adv in any way: anyhow, however, no matter how, in whatever manner

  ○ **sido që __ 1** even though __ **2** whatever

sidokudo

  I § adv **1** no matter how: carelessly, haphazardly **2** no matter what: in any case

  II § adj careless; slipshod

sidomos pcl especially

sidoqë __ conj **1** although, even though __ **2** whatever __

sidoqoftë adv be that as it may, however that may be

sidozot adv (Colloq Old) as for example, let's say

*siell· = sjell·

sifilitík adj [Med] syphilitic

sifilíz nm [Med] syphilis

sifón nm **1** siphon **2** s-shaped air trap (in plumbing) **3** (Colloq) carbonated water, soda water; carbonic acid gas: soda gas

sigël nf (Offic) initial (of a name); acronym

siglím nm ger (Offic) <siglo·n

siglo·n vt to sign [] with one's initials as an indication of approval: initial

sígme nf [Anat] sigmoid colon

*sigur

  I § adj secure, safe

  II § adv securely, safely

*sigurecë = siguresë

siguresë nf **1** [Tech] safety lock, safety catch **2** (electrical) fuse ***3** (Old) safety; security

  ○ **siguresë e shkrishme** [Electr] (electrical) fuse

sigurí nf **1** safety; security **2** certainty; assurance, faithreliability

sigurím nm ger **1** <siguro·n, siguro·het **2** security; safety **3** government agency responsible for state security (secret police) **4** assurance **5** insurance

  ○ **sigurimet shoqërore** social security

sigurísht adv certainly

siguro·het vpr **1** to protect oneself, make oneself secure **2** to assure oneself **3** to get insurance

  ○ **siguro·het me** [] to provide oneself with []

siguro·n vt **1** to make [] secure: secure **2** to assure; ensure **3** to insure

sigurshëm adj (i) = sigurt

sigurt adj (i) **1** secure, safe **2** certain: reliable; sure

*sigurti nf (Old) = siguri

siguruar

  I § adj (i) **1** insured **2** secured, safe

  II § nn (të) insurance

siharíq nm (Colloq) good news, happy message

sihariqtar n (Colloq) bearer of good news

sihír nm (Old) sorcery, magic

sikalaç adj (Colloq) skillful and quick in work

sikalaqe fem = sikalaç

sikërdís· vt to send [] away

siklet nm (Colloq) troubled state: distress, worry; embarrassment

sikter interj (Colloq) expresses abhorrence

sikundër conj as = sikurse

sikundërqë conj as = sikurse

sikundërse conj as = sikurse

sikur

  I § conj **1** as if, as though **2** if only; only if **3** = sikurse

  II § pcl seemingly, apparently; somehow

  ○ **sikur bie₁·^{pdef} në bunar** without leaving a trace

  ○ **sikur <> janë mbytur gjemitë** "as if his ships have sunk" looking gloomy

  ○ **sikur <> ka· ngrënë pula kapsollën** "apparently <>'s chicken has eaten the firing cap" <> is in deep trouble

  ○ **sikur [] ka· nxjerrë/qitur nga hunda/për hundësh** [] is one's spitting image

  ○ **sikur <> ka· prerë kërthizën** as if one owes <> a great favor

  ○ **sikur <> ka· prerë kokën së ëmës/nënës** <> is the spitting image of <>'s mother

  ○ **sikur <> ka· prerë kokën të atit/babajt** <> is the spitting image of <>'s father

  ○ **sikur <> ka·^{3sg} ngrënë gomari bukën** "as if the donkey has eaten <>'s food" <> looks sad: <> looks down in the mouth

  ○ **sikur <> ka·^{3sg} ngrënë macja brumin** "apparently <>'s cat has eaten the dough" **1** <> looks sad: <> looks down in the mouth **2** <> is in deep trouble

  ○ **sikur shkel· mbi gjemba** like walking on eggs

  ○ **sikur vë· telat** "as if {} was putting on bridal ornaments" (said of/to someone who is very tardy)

sikurse conj as

sikush pron everyone

silabë nf [Ling] syllable

silah nm (Old) ornamented wide leather belt (for carrying small arms and ammunition)

silazh nm [Agr] silage

silazhím nm ger **1** <silazho·n **2** ensilage

silazho·n vt to ensile

*síle nf bottle

silíc nm [Chem] silicon (Si)

silícium = silíc

silicor adj [Min] siliceous; highly siliceous

*silíç = silíc

silikat

  I § nm silicate; construction material containing silicates

  II § adj silicic

silikor adj silicate

*siliqokë nf [Ornit] daw = stërqokë

silogjízëm nm [Phil] syllogism

sílos nm silo

siluetë nf silhouette

silur nm [Mil] torpedo

silurhedhëse nf [Mil] torpedo boat

silurím nm ger <siluro·n

siluro·n vt to torpedo

siluru|e|s
  I § adj armed with torpedoes
  II § nm torpedo boat
  III § adj, n (Fig Pej) (one) secretly aiming to destroy

silvi|kultur|ë *nf* [*Agr*] forestry = **pylltari**

sill·*et vpr* <*sje*ll· **1** to turn **2** to run around (doing something or nothing) **3** to make every effort to do something **4** *(Fig)* to conduct oneself (in a particular way): behave
  ◦ <> **sill**·*et³⁸⁹* **festja/takija/mendja/koka vër-dallë/rrotull** "<>'s fez *spins* around" <>'s head is spinning with all the things <> has to worry about
  ◦ **Sillet nga sillet, bie në kunj e lidhet.** "Round and around, but tied to a stake." (said of/to someone who thinks of getting away) You/He will never make it.
  ◦ <> **sill**·*et* **përqark** to keep hanging around <> (with bad intentions)
  ◦ **sill**·*et* **përqark 1** to spin **2** to spend one's time idly going from place to place: run around
  ◦ <> **sill**·*et* **rrotull/rreth/vërdallë 1** to revolve around <> **2** *(Fig)* to see to <>'s needs, look after <> **3** to try to get on <>'s good side, play up to <>: woo <> **4** *(Fig)* to cajole <> **5** to hang over <>'s head, be a constant danger to <>
  ◦ **sill**·*et* **rrotull/rreth/vërdallë 1** to revolve, rotate; spin (around) **2** *(Fig)* to run around without accomplishing anything, waste time running around
  ◦ **sill**·*et* **si arkond** to act like a big shot, try to throw one's weight around
  ◦ **sill**·*et* **si bishti i pelës** "turn around like the tail of a mare" to run around all day doing nothing
  ◦ **sill**·*et* **si kali në lëmë** *(Impol)* to roam around idly
  ◦ **sill**·*et* **si lëmshi në shoshë** "behave like a lump in a sieve" move around without doing anything useful
  ◦ **sill**·*et* **si njerkë** to be vicious, mean (to children)
  ◦ **sill**·*et* **si pordha nëpër brekë** "conduct oneself like a fart through underwear" *(Crude)* to fart around

sill *stem for 2nd pl pres, pind, imper, vp* <*sje*ll·

sillë *nf* **1** *(Old)* food brought in the morning to a farmer woring in the fields **2** breakfast

sillo·*n vi* to eat breakfast

SIM *abbrev (Italian)* <**Servizio Informazioni Militari** Military Intelligence Service

simahor *n (Reg)* partner in crime: accomplice, crony

simbas *prep (abl)* = **sipas**

simbioz|ë *nf* symbiosis

simbol *nm* symbol

simbolik *adj* symbolic

simbolik|ë *nf* **1** *(Book)* symbolic meaning: symbolism **2** symbolic system: symbolism

simbolist *n* symbolist

simboliz|ëm *nm* symbolism

simbolizo·*n vt* to symbolize

si|m|e *gen/dat/abl* <**i**me my

simetri *adj* symmetry

simetrik *adj* symmetrical

simetrikisht *adv* symmetrically

simfoni *nf* symphony

simfonik *adj* symphonic

simitçi *nm (Old)* baker of chickpea buns; chickpea-bun vendor

simite *nf* soft bun made with chickpea dough

*****simje**t| = **sivje**t|

*****simko**·*n vt* to nip, pinch

Simon *nm* Simon (male name)

si|mo|t|ër *nf* organization engaged in the same kind of activity: sister enterprise

simpati *nf* sympathy

simpatik *adj* **1** sympathetic **2** nice, likable; attractive

simpatiza|nt *nm* = **simpatizu**es

simpatizo·*n vt* to sympathize

simpatizu|e|s *nm* sympathizer

*****simpath** = **simpat**

simposium *nm* symposium

simptomatik *adj (Book)* symptomatic

simptom|ë *nf (Book)* symptom

simulant *nm* **1** [*Med*] malingerer **2** *(Book)* pretender, faker, fraud

simulim *nm ger (Book)* <**simulo**·*n*

simulo·*n*
  I § vi (Book) [*Med*] to malinger
  II § vt **1** to fake **2** [*Law*] to fabricate

sinagog|ë *nf* synagogue

sinap *nm* [*Bot*] mustard *(Sinapis)*

sinapiz|ëm *nm* mustard plaster

*****sinda**ks *nm (Old)* [*Ling*] syntax

*****sindaks**or *adj* [*Ling*] syntactic = **sintakso**r

*****sindë**kur *conj* as when, as

sindikal *adj* pertaining to trade unions or syndicates

sindikalist *n, adj* **1** trade unionist **2** syndicalist

sindikaliz|ëm *nm* syndicalism

sindikatë *nf* **1** trade union, labor union **2** syndicate

*****sindik**u|a|r *n (i)* member of a trade/labor union

*****si**ndo|nja *adv (followed by a number) (Colloq)* approximately, something like, some

*****si**ndo|zo|t *adv* by the same token, in the same way, just as

sinekdok|ë *nf* [*Lit*] synecdoche

*****sinema** *nf* cinema

*****sineri** *nf* envy, jealousy

*****si**ng|ër *nf (Old)* concubine

singular *nm* [*Ling*] singular

sini *nf* **1** large copper tray **2** [*Ethnog*] gift of clothing sent by the bridegroom to his prospective bride

si|nisi *nf* peninsula = **gadi**shull

sinitar *nm* [*Ethnog*] member of the bridegroom's party who delivers a gift of clothing to the prospective bride

sinkop|ë *nf* syncope

sinkroni *nf* synchrony

sinkronik *adj* synchronic

sinkroniz|ëm *nm* synchronism

sinkronizim *nm ger* **1** [*Spec*] <**sinkronizo**·*n* **2** synchronization

sinkronizo·*n vt* to synchronize

sinod *nm* [*Relig*] synod

*****sino**dh *nm* synod

sinonim
  I § nm [*Ling*] synonym
  II § adj synonymic

sinonimi *nm* [*Ling*] synonymy

sinonimik *adj* synonymous

sinoptik *adj (Book)* of or pertaining to weather: synoptic

sinoptikë *nf* **1** [*Meteor*] synoptic meteorology, study of the weather **2** weather bureau/service **3** (*Book*) synopsis

sino'r *nm* (*Old*) **1** field/village boundary **2** region, land **3** (*Colloq*) boundary

sinozi't *nm* = sinusi't

singeri'sht *adv* sincerely

singeri'tet *nm* sincerity

singer'të *adj (i)* sincere

sintaksë *nf* [*Ling*] syntax

sintakso'r *adj* [*Ling*] syntactic

sinteti'k *adj* synthetic

sintetizi'm *nm ger* **1** <sintetizo'·n, sintetizo'·het **2** synthesis

sintetizi'sht *adv* synthetically

sintetizo'·het *vpr* [*Chem*] to be produced synthetically

sintetizo'·n *vt* **1** to make a synthesis of [ ] **2** to synthesize

sintetizu'es *adj* synthesizing; synthetic

sinte'zë *nf* synthesis

sinu's *nm* **1** [*Geom*] sine **2** [*Med*] sinus

sinusi't *nm* [*Med*] sinusitis

sinusoi'dë *nf* [*Math*] sine curve

*****sinxhi'r** = zinxhi'r

sinja'l *nm* signal

sinjalizi'm *nm ger* <sinjalizo'·n

sinjalizo'·n *vt, vi* **1** to signal **2** to signalize

sinjalizu'es
   I § *nm* signalman, signaller
   II § *adj* serving to signal: signalling

*****sipa'r** *nm* (theater) curtain

sipa's *prep (abl)* according to; in accordance with

sipër
   I § *adv* **1** above, higher; up above **2** on the upper side
   II § *prep (abl)* **1** over, above **2** over and above, beyond expectations of **3** involved with
   ∘ **në** [ ] **e sipër** in the course of [ ], while [ ]ing, during [ ]
   ∘ **sipër e sipër** very superficially

*****sipëra'n** *nm* sovereign

*****sipëra'ni** *nf* sovereignty

*****sipërfa'qas** *adv* superficially

sipërfa'qe *nf* **1** surface **2** surface area **3** [*Math*] area

sipërfaqëso'r *adj* **1** on the surface: surface **2** superficial

sipërfaqshëm *adj (i)* superficial

sipërfiti'm *nm* surplus profit

sipëri' *nf* superiority; superlativeness

sipërliqe'nas *n* inhabitant of a lakeside area

sipërlu'mas *n* inhabitant of the hills overlooking a river

sipërm *adj (i)* **1** upper; uppermost, top **2** northern **3** above-mentioned

sipërma'rrës
   I § *n* entrepreneur; contractor
   II § *adj* entrepreneurial

sipërma'rrje *nf* **1** enterprise, business firm, business **2** (*Fig*) (risky) undertaking

sipërmi *adv (së)* from above

*****sipërndie'shëm** *adj (i)* supersensitive

*****sipëro'r** *adj* superior

sipëro're *nf* [*Ling*] superlative (degree)

sipërpërme'ndur *adj (i)* (*Book*) mentioned above

*****sipërqy'rje** *nf* supervision = mbikëqy'rje.

*****sipër'si** *nf* superiority

sipërshënu'ar *adj (i)* (*Book*) noted above, above-mentioned

*****sipërshkri'm** *nm* inscription = mbishkri'm

sipërtregu'ar *adj (i)* (*Book*) indicated above

sipërthë'në *adj (i)* aforesaid

sipërvendo'sje *nf* (*Book*) superposition

*****sipi** *nf* (*Reg Gk*) = se'pje

*****sipra'ni** *nf* **1** superiority **2** sovereignty = sovranite't

*****si'prazi** *adv* from above

*****sipri'** *nf* surface

*****sipri'në** *nf* top part

*****sipro'r** *adj* superior

sipsi *nf* pipe bowl

*****Siqeli'** = Sicili'

*****si'r** *nm* = sihi'r

sira
   I § *nf* sequence, order
   II § *adv* in sequence, in a row, in succession

sire'në *nf* siren

Siri' *nf* Syria

siria'n *adj, n* Syrian

*****siri'ngë** *nf* syringe

*****sirja'n** = siria'n

*****si'rk** *nm* [*Invert*] silkworm

*****si'rme** *nf* ear of corn

*****siro'nkë** *nf* [*Ichth*] = ciro'nkë

sirt *nm* **1** beam of a plow **2** door bolt **3** steel die with graduated holes used as a drawplate for gold wire

sirta'r *nm* drawer (in furniture)

SIS *abbrev (English)* (British) Secret Intelligence Service

si's *stem for 1st sg pres, pl pres, 2nd & 3rd sg subj, pind* <si't·

sisa'k *adj* [*Zool*] = siso'r

*****sisa'm** = susa'm

*****sisara'k** *adj* [*Zool*] = siso'r

si'së *nf* **1** teat; nipple **2** (*Colloq*) breast milk

sisëdhë'nës *adj* "breast-giving" **1** nursing **2** [*Zool*] = siso'r

siso'r *nm* [*Zool*] mammal = gjita'r

siste'm *nm* system

sistemati'k *adj* systematic

sistemati'kë *nf* [*Biol*] systematics, taxonomy

sistematiki'sht *adv* systematically

sistematizi'm *nm ger* **1** <sistematizo'·n **2** systematization

sistematizo'·n *vt* **1** to systematize **2** [*Spec*] to classify [ ] in a taxonomy

sistemi'm *nm ger* **1** <sisto'·n, sisto'·het **2** [*Agr*] system aimed at controlling erosion and increasing productivity: land/soil management

sistemo'·het *vpr* to settle down

sistemo'·n *vt* **1** to put [ ] into proper place; systemize **2** to settle [ ]

siste'mor *adj* (*Book*) of a systematic nature, inherently systematic; systematic

si'f· *vt* to sift

SITA *abbrev* <**Shoqëria Industriale Tregtare Anonime** [*Hist*] Industry and Commerce Corporation

sita'c
   I § *nm* coarse sieve, riddle

II § *adv (Fig)* riddled with holes

sitë *nf* 1 sieve 2 [*Tech*] sifting screen

sitës *adj* sifting, straining

sitëthuash = si të thuash so to speak, as they say

sitje *nf ger* <sit·, sit·et

sitka *np fem* chaff and bran left in grain sieve

sitkë *nf* 1 [*Bot*] bulrush *(Scirpus)* 2 *(Reg)* = sitëS
  ∘ **sitka liqeni** club rush, great bulrush *Scirpus lacustris*

sitor *adj* sieve-like

***sitos·** *vt* = sit·

situatë *nf* situation

situr *adj (i)* 1 sifted 2 made with sifted flour

siujdhesë OR **siujdhezë** *nf (Old)* peninsula = gadishull

***sivakë** *nf* tunic, jacket

sivë
  I § *adj* = sivër
  II § *nf* * = sivakë

sivëlla *nm (np* sivëllezër*)* 1 colleague, fellow
  2 *(Old)* sister publishing house = simotër

sivër *adj (i)* (of an animal) gray-haired, silver-gray

***sivjeçëm** *adj (i)* = sivjetshëm

sivjemë = sivjetmë

sivjet *adv* this year

sivjetmë *adj (i)* = sivjetshëm

sivjetshëm *adj (i)* of the current year: this year's

sixhade *nm* tightly-woven smooth rug/tapestry: Persian rug, knotted rug, pile rug; prayer rug

sixhim *nm (Old)* thick cord; strong cord

***sizar** *nm* caraway

sizmik *adj* seismic

sizmograf *nm* seismograph

sizmolog *n* seismologist

sizmologji *nf* seismology

sizmologjik *adj* seismological

***sjap** *nm* = cjap

sjell· *vt* 1 to bring, bear; bring/take [] along; convey, conduct 2 to bring forward/out/up/about 3 to turn [] around; turn over [] 4 to take a turn/stroll around [a place] 5 *(Fig Colloq)* to give [] the runaround
  ∘ <> **sjell·** to strike/fell <>
  ∘ [] **sjell· anepërqark** to give [] the runaround
  ∘ <>a **sjell· diellin dy gisht mbi kokë/krye** "bring the sun two inches over <>'s head" to bring <> to near disaster
  ∘ [] **sjell· dokërr** to give [] the runaround
  ∘ [] **sjell·-³ˢᵍ era** "the wind *brings* []" [] *comes* out of nowhere
  ∘ **sjell· faqet** to turn over the pages
  ∘ <>a **sjell· fjalën rrotull/vërdallë/larg e larg** to beat around the bush with <>
  ∘ e **sjell· gajtan muhabetin** to be in control of the situation
  ∘ <>a **sjell· gjakun në vend** to take a load off <>'s mind, calm <> down
  ∘ e **sjell· kokën/kryet** *(Impol)* (expressing displeasure at an arrival) to get one's damn self here: arrive
  ∘ <> **sjell· krahët/kurrizin/shpatullat/shpinën** to turn one's back on <>; leave <> in the lurch
  ∘ [] **sjell· mbrapsht** to turn [] upside down, make a mess of []
  ∘ <>a **sjell· mendjen rrotull/vërdallë/përqark** to totally confuse <>, <>'s mind *gets* bewildered by {}

∘ [] **sjell· më bisht** to put [] back on one's feet, bring [] round
  ∘ <>[] **sjell· ndër mend** to remind <> of []
  ∘ [] **sjell· ndërmend** to bring [] to mind
  ∘ <> **sjell· në biçim** to put <> right, put <> in order
  ∘ [] **sjell· në fije** to put [] in order, make [] go well
  ∘ [] **sjell· në gojë** to talk/gossip about []
  ∘ <>[] **sjell· në grykë të pushkës** "lead [] to the muzzle of the gun" "bring [] to the muzzle of <>'s gun" 1 [*Hunting*] to drive [] into an ambush where <> is waiting 2 to prepare everything necessary for <>'s []
  ∘ [] **sjell· në hulli** to get [] to behave properly
  ∘ [] **sjell· në jetë** 1 to save [] 's life; show [] how to live 2 to bring [] to light
  ∘ [] **sjell· në majë të gishtit** to have [] wrapped around one's little finger
  ∘ [] **sjell· në rreth** to put/set [] right
  ∘ [] **sjell· në rrugë të mbarë** to set [] on the proper path
  ∘ [] **sjell· nga jashtë** to bring [] from abroad; import
  ∘ [] **sjell· për veshi** "take [] by the ear" to drag [] kicking and screaming, pull [] by the ear
  ∘ [] **sjell· rrotull** to give [] the runaround
  ∘ [] **sjell· rrufull** 1 to lead [] all around the mulberry bush 2 to cause a mess for [], make things a mess for []
  ∘ <>a **sjell· shpirtin në fyt/ndër dhëmb** "bring <>'s soul *in* <> 's throat/*between* <> 's *teeth*" to cause <> torment, be a pain in the neck to <>
  ∘ <>a **sjell· shpirtin në majë të hundës** to bring <> to the end of <>'s endurance
  ∘ <>a **sjell· shpirtin në vend** to make <> feel refreshed/revived, pep [] up
  ∘ **sjell· vallen** to dance
  ∘ [] **sjell· vërdallë** to give [] the runaround
  ∘ **sjell· zjarrin (në shtëpi)** to introduce discord/dissension into the family

***sjella** *nn (të)* manners, deportment, behavior

sjellë
  I § *part* <sjell·
  II § *adv (Colloq)* late
  III § *adj (i)* *1 = sjellshëm 2 water level (of a river)

sjellës *adj* bearing, bringing; yielding, supplying

sjellje
  I § *nf ger* 1 <sjell·, sill·et 2 conduct, deportment, demeanor; proper behavior, decorum 3 whirlwind, twister
  II § *np fem* materials carried by a flow: load, charge, discharge

sjellshëm *adj (i)* well-behaved, well-mannered

***sjep** *np* = cjep

***sjepar** = sqepar

sjerushë *nf* [*Bot*] 1 water mint *(Mentha aquatica)* 2 Jacob's rod *(Asphodeline)*

***sjestë** *nf* 1 case; occasion; circumstance 2 accidental circumstance: accident, chance 3 opportunity, chance

***sjetullë** *nf* = sqetull

***sjoll** *nm* = sqoll

skabiolë *nf* [*Fencing*] saber

skadim *nm ger* 1 <skado·n 2 expiration 3 [*Fin*] maturation

skado·n *vi* 1 to come to an end: expire 2 to become due, become payable 3 [*Fin*] to mature

skadua'r *adj (i)* **1** expired; **2** now payable: due; mature

skadhinë *nf* [*Ichth*] angel shark *(Squatina squatina)*
  ∘ **skadhin**ë **pendëzezë** [*Ichth*] flapper skate *Raja batis*

*****skaf** *nm* hull (of a boat)

skafa'ndër *nm* protective clothing for surviving under water or in outer space: deep-sea diving suit, space suit

*****skafto'r** *n* diver (underwater) = **zhy'tës**

skaj *nm* **1** edge; hem, rim, margin, border; limit, end **2** corner **3** place furthest from the center: extremity; outer limit **4** *(Old)* = **term**
  ∘ **nuk ia di· skajin mallit/pasurisë** "not know the limit to one's wealth" <> *is* swimming in money
  ∘ **skaj më skaj** from one end to the other, everywhere

*****skaj**ë *nf* grapeshot

skaji'm *nm ger* **1** <**skajo'·n 2** limit

skajo'·n *vt* **1** to set [] aside; place [] further away **2** to put a border/rim/hem/edge on [] **3** to attach **4** *(Old)* [*Ling*] to inflect [] for definiteness: put [] in its definite form, make [] definite

skajo'r *adj* **1** *(Book)* on the outer border: marginal **2** *(Fig)* extreme

skaj'shëm *adj (i)* extreme

skaj'shmëri *nf (Book)* extreme position; extremity

*****skajto'r** = **skajo'r**

skajua'r *adj (i)* **1** put aside; apart **2** *(Old)* [*Ling*] = **shqua'r**

*****skajue'm** *adj (i) (Reg Gheg Old)* [*Ling*] definite

skajullo're *nf* bed table

*****skaki** *nf (Reg Gk)* chess = **shah**

*****skakita'r** *n (Reg Gk)* chess player = **shahi'st**

skalabë OR **skala'p**ë *nf* = **skllotin**ë

*****skalapurri'** *adv* amiss

*****skalava'run** *adj (i)* hanged, hung

*****skali'** *nf* carving, engraving; sculpture = **skali'tj**e

skalio'n *nm* [*Mil*] echelon

*****skalioni'm** *nm* [*Mil*] disposition of troops in echelon: echelonment

skali's *stem for 1st sg pres, pl pres & 2nd & 3rd sg subj, pind* <**skali't·**

skalisti'r *nm* two-pronged hoe

skali't· *vt* **1** to chisel, carve; incise, engrave **2** *(Reg)* to hoe, cultivate

skali't·et *vpr* to become deeply etched/engraved

skali'tës *nm* **1** stonemason, stone carver **2** sculptor **3** [*Spec*] engraver; printmaker

skali'tje *nf ger* **1** <**skali't·**, **skali't·et 2** chiseled/carved/incised/engraved image: sculpture, relief, carving, inscription

skali'tur *adj (i)* chiseled, carved; incised, engraved

skalm *nm* oarlock, rowlock

skallangu'r *nm* unripe grape

skallo'më *nf* quay, dock

skallu'a *nm (obl ~o'i, np ~o'nj)* bud, sprout

skam *nm* = **ska'mj**e

*****skambi'l** *nm* checkers (the game), draughts

ska'mës *adj, n* (person) who has nothing, (person) in extreme poverty, destitute (person)

ska'mët *adj (i)* = **ska'mur**

ska'mje *nf* poverty

ska'mno'r
  I § *n* destitute person
  II § *adj* * = **ska'mur**

Ska'mpa *nf* [*Hist*] name of Elbasan in ancient times

skamta'r *adj* = **ska'mur**

ska'mur *adj (i)* destitute, poor

skanda'l *nm* **1** scandal; outrage **2** scandalous behavior; outrageous behavior

*****skandali's·et** *vpr* = **skandalizo'·het**

skandalizo'·het *vpr* to feel scandalized/shocked; be outraged

skandalo'z *adj* scandalous; outrageous

*****Skande'ri** *nf (Old)* Alexandria = **Aleksandri'**

skandina'v *adj, n* Scandinavian

skapame'nto *nf* [*Tech*] muffler (on a motor vehicle)

skapa'n *nm (Impol)* big good-for-nothing oaf

*****skapa's** *stem for 1st sg pres, pl pres, 2nd & 3rd sg subj, pind* <**skapa't·**

*****skapa't·** *vt* to castrate

ska'pe *interj* (said to a dog) sic 'im!

ska'pë *nf* **1** *(Colloq)* mountain peak **2** *(Fig)* peak

*****skapërdhi'ks** *nm* to curvet

*****skapto'·n** *vi* **1** to chatter one's teeth from the cold **2** to show one's teeth: snarl

skapulli'm *nm ger* <**skapullo'·n**, **skapullo'·het**

skapullo'·het *vpr* to get out of a difficult situation: escape

skapullo'·n *vt* to pull [] out of a difficult situation: rescue, extricate

*****skarama'gje** *nf* type of raincoat

ska'rco *nf* (factory) reject

ska'rë *nf* **1** kitchen grill, broiler **2** metal grate; metal grid **3** carrying rack for the rear wheel of a bicycle

skarlati'në *nf* [*Med*] scarlatina, scarlet fever

skarpa't *nm* escarpment

skarto'·n *vt* **1** to reject [] (as defective) *****2** to slaughter

*****skarrina'me** *np* = **naze**

skatha'r *nm* [*Entom*] winged vine louse

skeç *nm* vaudeville sketch: skit

skeda'r *nm* file box/drawer of index/note cards

ske'dë *nf* index card, note card

skedi'm *nm ger* <**skedo'·n**

skedo'·n *vt* to note [] down on an index card

*****skef** *nm* = **skote'**

skela'ri *nf* [*Constr*] scaffolding

skele'ri = **skela'ri**

skele't *nm* **1** skeleton **2** frame, framework
  ∘ **skeleti i tokës** [*Agr*] soil fraction composed of rock and gravel

skeleto'r *adj* [*Spec*] skeletal

skelë *nf* **1** pier, wharf, dock **2** port city; wharf district; port **3** [*Constr*] scaffold **4** support frame for construction or repair work: armature, sawhorse **5** windlass for hoisting water from a well

skemati'k *adj* schematic

skematiki'sht *adv* schematically

skemati'zëm *nm* schematism

skematizo'·n *vt* to schematize

ske'më *nf* **1** schematic drawing/plan, schema **2** oversimplified representation; rigid scheme

skena'r *nm* [*Theat Cine*] **1** script, scenario **2** stage scenery, decor

***sken·ari** nf[*Theat Cine*] scenario

sken·arist n[*Theat Cine*] script writer: scenarist

***ske·ncë** = shke·ncë

ske·në nf [*Theat Cine*] **1** stage **2** stage scenery **3** scene

sken·ik adj [*Theat*] of appropriate for or pertaining to the stage: theatrical

sken·o·graf nm [*Theat Cine*] scenographer

sken·o·grafi nf[*Theat Cine*] **1** set/scenery design **2** scenery used in a theatrical production: set

sken·o·grafik adj[*Theat Cine*] pertaining to theatrical scenery

***skep** nm **1** corner = cep *2 beak = sqep

ske·ptër nm scepter

skeptic·izëm nm scepticism

skept·ik
    I § nm sceptic
    II § adj sceptical

***skep·to·re** nf = sqepto·re

***skep·tra·shë** nf = sqeptra·shë

***skep·ve·rdhë** nf = sqepve·rdhë

s·ke·q·et vpr to get angry, take offense

skerbull nm [*Bot*] false indigo *(Amorpha fruticosa)*

skerc nm [*Veter*] **1** laming disease that affects goats in the knees **2** = shke·pëz

ske·rco nf [*Mus*] scherzo

ske·rmë nf [*Sport*] fencing

*ske·rre** nf worm

*ske·dej·më** adj (i) = dej·më

Skënde·r nm Skënder (male name), Alexander

skënderbeg·as nm student at the Skanderbeg military school in Tirana: cadet

skërc nm [*Veter*] caprine arthritis

skër·deh· vt to make [ ] very drunk

skër·deh·et vpr to get dead drunk

skër·dehur adj (i) very drunk, dead drunk

*skërfell** = skërfyell

*skërfëndell** nm [*Ornit*] buzzard *(Buteo buteo)*

skërfit· vt **1** to scrape off the crust of [ ] in little pieces **2** to scratch [soil] to a shallow depth, plow/hoe/cultivate lightly **3** *(Fig)* to make [ ] sore, chafe, irritate **4** *(Fig)* to open [one's eyes] wide

skërfit·et vpr **1** to flake off **2** (of a plant with compact leaves/petals) to open out fully **3** to open one's eyes wide: goggle

skërfit·je nf ger <skërfit·, skërfit·et

skër·fyell nm **1** [*Anat*] trachea, windpipe **2** *(Fig)* very tall and thin person: beanpole **3** (plant) shoot

skër·kë nf **1** crag; rocky/craggy mountainous area **2** hollow ravine amidst steep crags

skër·le·pë nf = skle·pë

*skër·le·pkë** nf = skle·pë

skër·lutë nf = skle·pë

skërmis· stem for 1st sg pres, pl pres, 2nd & 3rd sg subj, pind <skërmit·

skër·mit· vt **1** to scratch/tear off the covering layer of [ ]: tear **2** to nibble/claw [ ] apart/away **3** to gnash [one's teeth]
    ∘ <> **skërmit· dhëmbët** to bare one's teeth at <>, threaten <>

skër·mit·et vpr **1** to get scratched (by something sharp) **2** to gnash one's teeth **3** to bare one's teeth in a menacing manner

skërm·it·ës adj menacing = kërcënu·es

skërm·it·je nf ger **1** <skërmit·, skërmit·et **2** grimace expressing scorn

skërpi·cje nf wooden framework enclosing the wheels that raise or lower the harness of a loom

skëte·rrë
    I § nf **1** [*Relig*] Hell **2** *(Fig)* living hell **3** *(Fig)* very hot place; battlefield area with intense fire **4** total darkness
    II § adj *(Fig)* very dark, black

skëte·rr·shëm adj (i) **1** hellish, infernal **2** without a ray of light: pitch dark

skëte·rr·të adj (i) = skëte·rrshëm

ski nf **1** ski **2** the sport of skiing

ski·ator n = skita·r

ski·cë nf sketch

skic·o·het vpr to take shape in outline form

skic·o··n vt to make a sketch of [ ]; sketch out [ ]

skic·o·graf nm draftsman

skiç
    I § nm **1** edge, border **2** *(Fig)* pride; big-headedness
    II § adv on a slant, leaning to one side

skifter nm **1** [*Ornit*] falcon **2** *(Fig)* courageous and fierce fighter
    ∘ **skifteri i drurëve** [*Ornit*] hobby *Falco subbuteo L.*
    ∘ **skifteri i gjuetisë** [*Ornit*] saker falcon *Falco cherrug*
    ∘ **skifteri kthetrazi** [*Ornit*] kestrel *Falco tinnunculus L.*

ski·lak nm [*Zool*] male fox

ski·le nf **1** [*Zool*] fox = dhe·lp·ër **2** *(Fig)* wily person

ski·li nf wiliness

ski·li·fa·cë nf facial gesture expressing dissatisfaction/scorn: grimace, scowl, look of disgust

*skili·fa·qe** = skili·fa·cë

*ski·në** nf infirmity

skirfi·cë nf [*Entom*] = do·sëz

skirr nm [*Med*] scirrhus

skirr·oz adj [*Med*] scirrhous

*skit** = skith

skita·r n [*Sport*] skier

*ski·të** nf [*Colloq*] diarrhea: the runs

*skitl·o··n** vt to scribble on [ ]; smear, smudge

skith adj, n [*Hist*] Scythian

Skithi nf [*Hist*] Scythia

skizma·tik adj, n schismatic

ski·zmë nf schism

skizofre·n nm [*Med*] schizophrenic person

skizofreni nf [*Med*] schizophrenia

*skj** = sq

*skja·r·et** vpr = sqaro·het

skle·pë nf yellow mucus discharged from the eyes

sklepo·s·et vpr (of the eyes) to discharge yellow mucus

sklepo·sur adj (i) full of yellow mucus

skle·rë nf [*Anat*] sclera

sklerotik adj [*Med*] sclerotic

sklerot·izim nm ger <sklerotizo··n, sklerotizo··het

sklerotizo··het vpr **1** [*Med*] to become sclerotic **2** *(Fig)* to become fossilized by obsolescent methods

sklerotizo··n vt **1** [*Med*] to cause sclerosis **2** *(Fig)* to cause [ ] to fossilize in obsolescence

sklero·zë nf [*Med*] sclerosis

*sklu·bë** = skle·pë

skllaf *nm* surf

skllapë *nf* **1** wooden bar that swivels down into brackets to block a door from opening: door bar **2** mouthpiece (of a reed instrument used for folk music) ***3** snow falling in big flakes

skllav *n* slave

skllavëri *nf* slavery

skllavërim *nm ger* **1** <skllavëro·*n* **2** enslavement

skllavëro·*n vt* to enslave

skllavërues *nm* of enslavement, enslaving

skllavopronar

I § *nm* [*Hist*] slave owner

II § *adj* slave-owning

skllavopronari *nf* slave ownership

*skllavos· *(Old)* = skllavëro·*n*

skllevër *np masc* <skllav

sklloçis *stem for 1st sg pres, pl pres, 2nd & 3rd sg subj, pind* <sklloçit·

sklloçit· *vt* to get [ ] all dirty/muddy

skllop *nm* **1** muddy slush; thin mud; slough **2** [*Ornit*] herring gull *(Larus argentatus)*

skllotë *nf* = shqotë

skllotinë *nf* rain and snow falling together: sleet

∘ **skllot**inë **bore** melting snow

skllup· *vt* **1** to swallow [ ] without chewing: gulp down [ ] **2** to eat gluttonously

skllupe *nf* thick branch growing directly from the trunk of the tree: main branch

skobuz *nm* [*Ichth*] Lake Ohrid nase = njilë

skocez

I § *adj* Scottish

II § *nm* Scotsman

Skoci *nf* Scotland

skocisht *adv* in Scottish (language)

*skodhe *nf* [*Agr*] board dragged over ground to level it: drag harrow, board harrow

*skofet *nm* low-lying ground

skofi *nf* courtesy, good manners

skofiar *adj* courteous, well-mannered

skolastik *nm, adj* scholastic

skolastikë *nf* scholasticism

*skomolis· *vi (Reg Gk)* to confess

skonto *nf* discount

*skopac OR **skopa**n *nm* eunuch

skopas *stem for 1st sg pres, pl pres, 2nd & 3rd sg subj, pind* <skopat·

skopat· *vt* to castrate

skopec *adj, nm* castrated (bull, ram, billy goat) = tredhak

skopis *stem for 1st sg pres, pl pres, 2nd & 3rd sg subj, pind* <skopit·

skopit· *vt* **1** to castrate **2** to lance [a wound, a snakebite]

*skopitje *nf* castration, gelding

skorbus *nm* [*Ichth*] tench = njilë

skorbut *nm* [*Med*] scorbutus, scurvy

skorec *nm* wooden trough in a water-powered gristmill through which grain goes from the hopper into the millstones

skorfan *nm* red scorpionfish *(Scorpaena scrofa)*

skorie *nf* **1** scoria **2** *(Fig)* foreign impurity remaining from the old days

*skorpis· *vt* to dissipate, disperse

skort *nm* [*Ichth*] roach *(Cyprinidae)*

∘ **skort i bardhë** [*Ichth*] white roach *Rutilus rubilio ohridanus Kar., Leucos aula var. ohridanus* = gurnec

∘ **skort bari** [*Ichth*] = skort i verdhë

∘ **skort me vizë** [*Ichth*] **1** schneider (of Lake Ohrid) *Alburnoides bipunctatus ohridanus Kar.* = barkgjerë **2** soufie *Leuciscus souffia montenegrinus*

∘ **skort i verdhë** [*Ichth*] Lake Ohrid Italian roach *Rutilus rubilio Ohridanus*

∘ **skort i zi** black roach *Pachychilon pictum Heck et Kner.* = mërunë

skorran *adj* emaciated

skorratinë *nf* snow storm

skorrë *adj* = skorran

skotë *nf* **1** set of descendants from a common ancestor: breed/stock (of animals), race/family (of people), strain **2** *(Pej)* poor stock

*Skoti = Skoci

skra *nf* [*Invert*] worm; fishing worm, earthworm

*skrajë *nf* = skra

skrap *nm* [*Zool*] European fire salamander, spotted salamander *(Salamandra salamandra)*

Skrapar *nm* district in southern Albania: Skrapari

*skraparas *adj, n* = skraparlli

skraparlli

I § *adj* of/from Skrapari

II § *n* native of Skrapari

skrapth *nm* [*Zool*] **1** European whip snake *(Coluber jugularis)* **2** poisonous black beetle (similar to the dung beetle)

skremo·*n vt* [*Dairy*] to skim the cream off [milk]

skremuar *adj (i)* skimmed

skrepatar *adj* thin, lean

skreper *nm* [*Tech*] scraper, power shovel

skrimtë *adj (i)* = përkorë

skrips *nm* wisp of grass in a wet area

*skrob *nm (Old)* chest, breast = kraharor

skrodh *nm* freeloader, sponger

skrofull *nf* [*Med*] scrofula = stërkungull

*skrofurë *nf* = skrofull

skrop *nm* **1** [*Food*] cornmeal mush served with milk ***2** body (of an animal/human)

*skroth *nm* sponger, parasite

skrupë *nf* [*Text*] defective fabric/cloth

skrupull *nm (Book)* scruple

skrutë *nf* empty swagger; conceit, arrogance

*skrrajë

I § *nf* **1** [*Invert*] = skra **2** = skrrile

II § *adj* thin and lean

*skrrile *nf* woman who is thin and lean, skinny beanpole

*skrrutë *nf (Pej)* = skrrile

skuadër *nf* **1** [*Mil Sport*] squad, team **2** try square

∘ **skuadra përfaqësuese** [*Sport*] all-star team; representative team

skuadërkomandant *nm* [*Mil*] squad/team captain/leader

skuadrilje *nf* [*Mil*] squadron (of airplanes): escadrille

skuadron *nm* [*Mil*] squadron (of cavalry)

*skud *nm* udder

*skudër *nf* shed, stall, stable

*skudëri *nf* stables

skufje *nf* **1** round cap attached firmly to the head and reaching to the nape of the neck **2** hair snood **3** [*Med*] capeline bandage

*skujmë *adj (i)* dark red, maroon

*skulíc *adj* low-down, good-for-nothing

*skulifaqe *nf* wry face, grimace

*skulíth *nm* = skulot

*skulot *nm* scoundrel, rogue

skulptor *n* sculptor

skulptural *adj* = skulpturor

skulpturë *nf* sculpture

skulpturor *adj (Book)* **1** sculptural **2** *(Fig)* of the quality of fine sculpture: finely-chiseled

skumbri *nf* [*Ichth*] chub mackerel *(Scomber scomber)*

○ **skumbri e madhe** [*Ichth*] bullet tuna *Auxis rochei*

skundër *nf* wind blowing directly toward the bow: facing wind

skundill *nm (np ˜j)* hem (of a garment)

*skunë *nf* schooner

skupë *nf* chisel with a concave blade: scoop, gouge

skupës *nm* adze with a concave blade: spout adze

skupira *np* rubbish, trash, sweepings

skuq·
I § *vt* **1** to make [] red, color [] red **2** to fry **3** to heat [] until red-hot **4** *(Fig Colloq)* to make []: blush: embarrass [] **5** *(Fig Colloq)* to teach [] a good lesson (by beating [] in a game); give [] a scathing rebuke
II § *vi* to get red
○ <>*i* skuq· veshët to box/twist <>'s ears; punish <>; lambaste

skuq·et *vpr* **1** to get red/reddish, become red: redden; blush **2** to get ruddish ripe **3** to turn brown (during frying) **4** to get red-hot **5** to feel embarrassed: blush with embarrassment
○ as skuq·et as zverdh·et to be shameless
○ skuq·et e merr· flakë to have a hot temper; lose one's temper
○ s'<> skuq·et³ˢᵍ faqja/fytyra "<>'s face *doesn't* blush" <> *has* no sense of shame, <> *is* shameless
○ skuq·et gjer te veshët **1** to get red in the face **2** to blush with joy, grin from ear to ear
○ skuq·et me dhjamin e {*pronominal adj*} to do everything on {*one's*} own, get by on {*one's*} own
○ skuq·et si lafsha e gjelit to get red in the face with anger

skuqje *nf ger* <skuq·, skuq·et

skuqur *adj (i)* **1** ruddish ripe **2** golden brown (from frying) **3** red-hot **4** blushing **5** *(Fig Colloq)* easily embarrassed, very modest: bashful

*skuranë *nf* waterfall

*skuri *nf* rust

skuriq *adj, n* **1** untidy and dirty (person) **2** *(Fig)* worthless (person)

skurte·het *vpr* to lose all strength, grow completely weak

skurrjalë *nf* rotting bones, skeleton

skut·et *vpr* **1** to huddle in a dark and secluded place; hide out **2** (of a male livestock animal) to follow behind <*a female in heat*> *3 to waddle

*skutelë *nf* dome

skuter *nm (Old)* owner of sheep who keeps them in a mountain sheepcote with a shepherd in charge

skutë *nf* **1** hidden out-of-the-way place: nook; den, lair; hideout **2** woolen apron/pinafore; square piece of wool cloth used as a covering

skutëliq *nm* hidden cranny, crevice, nook

skutëlo·n *vt* to stash [] away for safe keeping

skutinë *nf* **1** diaper **2** rag

*skutliq *nm* crevice, cranny

skuto·n *vt* to plug holes in [a wall/window]

*Skutonë *nf* Illyrian goddess of health

skutuliq = skutëliq

skuth *nm (Pej)* sneaky person, sneak: wolf in sheep's clothing, snake in the grass

skuthni *nf* sneakiness

*skyfer *nm* [*Ornit*] falcon = skifter

slab *nm* [*Tech*] slab

*slargu *(Colloq)* <së largu

slitë *nf* **1** [*Tech*] sled, sledge **2** sliding carriage on a machine = karel

slogan *nm (Book Pej)* slogan

*slugoos· *vt* to wrench [] out of its socket: dislocate

sllallom *nm* [*Sport*] slalom

sllav
I § *nm* Slav
II § *adj* Slavic

sllavisht *adv* in a Slavic language, in Slavic

sllavishte *nf* **1** Slavic (language) **2** *(Colloq)* Serbo-Croatian (language)

sllavizëm *nm* [*Ling*] borrowing from a Slavic language

sllavomadh *adj (Pej)* pertaining to or serving Slavic aspirations to dominate non-Slavs

*sllobë *nf* character, letter

*sllog *nm* piece of farmland

sllovak *adj* Slovak, Slovakian

Sllovaki *nf* Slovakia

sllovakisht *adv* in Slovak (language)

sllovakishte *nf* Slovak (language)

slloven *adj, n* Slovenian, Slovene

Slloveni *nf* Slovenia

sllovenisht *adv* in Slovene (language)

sllovenishte *nf* Slovene (language)

smag *nm* **1** wooden peg; wooden hook **2** small nail **3** stinger (of a bee/wasp) **4** = smat

*smakth *nm* afterbirth (of an animal)

smalt *nm* **1** tooth enamel **2** enamel (on metal) = emal

smaltim *nm ger* <smalto·n

smalto·n *vt* [*Tech*] to enamel = emalo·n

smaltuar *adj (i)* = emaluar

*smar *nm* [*Bot*] rosemary = rozmarinë

smat *nm* **1** seed sprout, new seedling **2** = smag **3** thin peg used as an awl

smatos·
I § *vi* to sprout
II § *vt* to pierce [] with an awl (in preparation for stitching)

smerald *nm* emerald

smeril
I § *nm* emery, emery paper, sandpaper; emery stone
II § *adj* containing emery

smerilim *nm ger* [*Tech*] <smerilo·n

smerilo·n *vt* [*Tech*] to rub [] with emery

smilar *nm* stone chisel; wood-handled chisel

smilat· *vt* to play up to [], flatter, pamper; fawn on []

smil|**at**|ës *nm* flatterer; pamperer

smil|**o**·*n* = smila·t·

smir|**ak** *adj, n* = smir**ë**zi

smir|**ë** *nf* malice induced by envy; spiteful jealousy

smir|**ë**|**keq** *adj* envious, jealous; spiteful

smir|**ës** *adj, n* = smir**ë**zi

smir|**ë**z|i *adj, n (fem sg ˜ez, masc pl ˜inj, fem pl ˜eza)* spitefully envious (person); malicious (person)

smi|**rn**|ë *nf* [*Bot*] celery-like plant *(Smyrnium perfoliatum)*

smir|**o**·*het vpr* to be envious/jealous

smir|**o**·*n vt* to envy

smir|**or**

  I § *n* envious person
  II § *adj* envious

smir|**tar** *n* = smir**ë**zi

smoking *nm* tuxedo, dinner jacket

***smoll**|ë *nf* rosin

SMT [*së-më-të*] *nf abbrev* <**Stacioni i makinave dhe i traktorëve** workshop for repairing tractors and other other agricultural machinery for agricultural cooperatives

***smuj**|**kë** *nf* chyme

smuq|**th** *nm collec* entrails

snajper *nm* **1** sniper **2** sharpshooter, marksman

***snaq** *adj* despicable

snob *nm* snob

snob|**izëm** *nm* snobbery

sob|**axhi** *nm (np ˜nj) (Colloq)* person who makes and repairs stoves and heating ducts

so|**b**|ë *nf* **1** stove: heating stove, cooking stove **2** *(Reg)* first-floor room that is kept heated in winter
  ∘ **sob**ë **ekonomike** large commercial-size stove with both a cooking range and an oven

***sob**|ë|**tar** *nm* stove-fitter

social *adj* social = shoqëro·r

social|**demokrac**|í *nf* social democracy

social|**demokrat**

  I § *nm* social democrat
  II § *adj* social democratic

social|**imperialist** *n* socialist imperialist

social|**imperial**|**izëm** *nm* imperialism as practiced by a socialist country

social|**ist** *adj, n* socialist

social|**izëm** *nm* socialist

social|**izim** *nm ger* <socializo·*n*

social|**izo**·*n vt* to socialize

sociolog *n* sociologist

socio|**logjí** *nf* sociology

socio|**logjík** *adj* sociological

***so**|**ç**|ëm *adj (i) (Colloq)* = sotsh**ë**m

so|**dë** *nf* **1** soda *(sodium bicarbonate)* **2** baking soda *(sodium carbonate)*
  ∘ **sod**ë **kaustik** caustic soda *sodium hydoxide*

sodís| *stem for 1st sg pres, pl pres, 2nd & 3rd sg subj, pind* <sodí·t·

sodí·t·

  I § *vt* to observe
  II § *vi* to stand by and watch

sodít|ës

  I § *adj* **1** studiously watching, observant **2** merely watching, watching from the sidelines
  II § *n* observer, watcher; idle spectator

sodít|**je** *nf ger* **1** <sodí·t· **2** observation **3** [*Philos*] direct observation

sodium *nm* [*Chem*] sodium *(Na)*

sodóm· *vt (Old)* to raze [the property] of a fugitive from canonic justice

SOE *abbrev (English)* British office of secret intelligence

sofa *nf* **1** upholstered sofa **2** = sofa·t

sofa·t *nm* **1** stone bench outside the entrance door: front stoop **2** ledge **3** upholstered sofa

so|**fër** *nf* **1** low round wooden table around which people sit (on the floor) to eat; dining table **2** *(Collec)* group of people sitting at one table **3** *(Fig Pej)* set of interests and goals shared by a group of people
  ∘ **Sofrën shtroje edhe me bukë e kripë (e qepë)!** "Set the table even with bread and salt (and onions)!" *(Prov)* You must be hospitable even if you have little yourself!

Sofík|a *nf* Sofika (female name)

sofíst *nm* sophist

sofistík *adj* sophistical

sofistík|ë *nf* sophistry

sof|**izëm** *nm* sophism

So|**fje** *nf* Sofia

sofr|**abez** *nm* tablecloth

soft *nm* windowsill, window ledge = sofa·t

***sogar** *nm* rogue, scoundrel

***sogarí** *nf* roguery

sogje *nf* **1** *(Poet Old)* guard, watchman; patrol **2** watchtower

sogje|**tar** *nm (Poet Old)* sentry

***sogjo**·*n vi* to mount guard

sohi *nf* sunless/shady place

soh|**íshtë** *nf* shady area (in the mountains)

***soh**|**ít**·*et vp reflex* to shade oneself

***sohu**|**ne** *np fem*
  ∘ **me (tërë) sohune** with a cold look

soj *nm* **1** sort, kind **2** lineage, stock **3** *(Old)* family of good repute: good family **4** [*Biol*] variety
  ∘ **soji e sorollopi** *(Impol Colloq)* whole damn family

sojak *nm* pocket knife; penknifepruning-knife

***soje** *enclitic after prepositions that take an ablative object* indicates a 3rd sg fem object for the preposition: her = sa·j

soj|ë *nf* [*Bot*] soybean *(Soja max, Glycine hispide)*

soj|ë|**trashë** *adj* coarse, vulgar

sojk|ë *nf* = soja·k

soj|**lesh**|ë *nf, adj fem* = sojli

sojl|í *nm, adj masc (pl ˜nj) (Colloq Old)* (person) of highly-regarded/good family; (animal) of good stock, pure-blooded (animal)

soj|**ník** *adj (Colloq Old)* = sojli

soj|**sëz** *adj, n (Colloq Insult)* (person) of a low-regarded family: (person) of poor stock

soj|**shëm** *adj (i) (Colloq)* of good stock; from a good family

***soj**|**tar** *nm* juggler

***soj**|**tarí** *nf* juggling

sokak *nm* narrow alley paved with cobblestone

sokëll|**as**| *stem for 1st sg pres, 1st & 3rd pl pres, 2nd & 3rd sg subj* <sokëllit·

sokëll|**et**· = sokëlli·*n*

sokëll|**í·n** *vi* to yell loudly: shout, bellow

sokëllimë nf **1** loud yell: shout, bellow **2** loud resonant sound: boom; loud sharp noise: screech, clang

sokëllis stem for 2nd pl pres, pind <**sokëllit**·

sokëllit· vt = **sokëlli**·n

sokëllitje nf ger **1** <**sokëllit**· **2** =**sokëllimë**

sokol nm [Ornit] **1** peregrine falcon (Falco peregrinus L.) = **petrit 2** (Fig) handsome, brave, and capable boy/man
  ○ **sokoli kthetrazi** [Ornit] kestrel Falco tinnunculus

Sokol nm Sokol (male name)

sokoleshë nf (Fig) attractive, capable and brave girl/woman

Sokrat nm Sokrat (male name), Socrates

sol nm [Mus] pitch name of the note above mi: sol; the musical note G

solanace np [Bot] = **solanore**

solanore np [Bot] nightshade family Solanaceae

solar nm fuel oil

solecizëm nm solecism

solemn adj **1** celebrated in a formal and grand manner: grand **2** solemn

solemnisht adv solemnly; in a formal and grand manner

solemnitet nm (Book) solemnity; grandeur

soletë nf [Constr] slab of a reinforced concrete floor between the storeys of a building

solfezh nm [Mus] solfeggio, solfège

solid adj solid

solidar adj **1** being in sympathetic agreement: having solidarity **2** [Law] jointly responsible

solidarësi nf **1** (Book) solidarity **2** [Law] joint liability

solidaritet nm (Book) = **solidarësi**

solidarizim nm ger <**solidarizo**·het

solidarizo·het vpr to express one's solidarity

solist n soloist

solo
  I § nf [Mus] solo
  II § adv as a solo

solstic nm [Astron] solstice

solucion nm [Chem] solution = **tretësirë**

solvent nm [Chem] solvent

soll stem for pdef <**sjell**·

sollak adj (Colloq) left-handed; left-footed

sollake nf (Colloq) the left hand

som nm [Ichth] black bullhead (Ictahurus melas)

somalez adj, n Somalian

Somali nf Somalia

somnambul nm [Med] somnambulist, sleepwalker

somnambulizëm nm [Med] somnambulism, sleepwalking

***somsa** nf baklava with walnut layers

somune nf (Old) flat round bun made with fine wheat flour

sonatë nf [Mus] sonata

sondazh nm **1** (Book) = **sondim 2** test probe: sounding

***sonde** = **sonte**

sondë nf(Colloq) **1** drilling rig **2** [Med] sound, probe ()

sondim nm ger (Book) <**sondo**·n, **sondo**·het

sondist n [Spec] operator of a drilling rig: driller

sondo·n vt **1** [Spec] to do a test boring of []: drill, probe **2** (Fig Book) to explore in a preliminary way: take a sounding

sonet nm [Lit] sonnet

sone gen/dat/abl <**jonë** our

sonte adv this evening, tonight; this past night

sop nm **1** hummock, mound, hillock, knoll; ridge **2** spout through which the water comes from the millrace against the vanes of the millwheel **3** barrel tap; stopper/bung made of wood or corncob
  ○ **sopa (e) gropa** hills and hollows

sopal nm small embankment, hillock

sopatë nf = **sëpatë**

sopojak nm [Bot] European hornbeam (Carpinus betulus) = **shkozëbardhë**

soprano nf [Mus] soprano

***soreg** nf [Zool] field mouse

sorgum nm [Bot] broomcorn, sorghum (Sorghum vulgare) = **melekuqe**

sorkadh nm **1** [Zool] roebuck = **kaproll 2** (Fig) lithe and handsome boy

sorkadhe nf **1** [Zool] roe doe = **kaprolle 2** (Fig) lithe and pretty girl

sorkë nf, adj (sheep) with black spots on the muzzle or around the eyes

***sormë** adj (i) (Reg) = **sotëm**

sorogat nm surrogate

sorolang nm = **spirileng**

sorollas stem for 1st sg pres, pl pres, 2nd & 3rd sg subj, pind <**sorollat**·

sorollat· vt **1** (Colloq) to rotate, wind, spin, turn **2** (Fig) to give [] the runaround; deliberately delay [], put [] off on purpose

sorollat·et vpr (Colloq) **1** to spin one's wheels, make no progress **2** to stand around without working: procrastinate **3** to wander around aimlessly, perambulate

***sorollatë** nf somersault

sorollatje nf ger (Colloq) <**sorollat**·, **sorollat**·et

sorollimthi adv around and around

sorollop nm (ColloqImpolite) distant relatives, one's remote kin

***sortiment** nm [Econ] = **asortiment**

sorrak
  I § nm [Ornit] male crow; jackdaw
  II § adj **1** (of domestic animals) black as a crow **2** (Fig Insult) shameless, base

sorrë nf[Ornit] **1** hooded crow (Corvus cornix L.) **2** daw = **stërqokës**
  ○ **Sorra sorrës s'ia nxjerr sytë.** "A crow does not peck out the eyes of another crow." A bad person is safe from harm from other bad people.
  ○ **sorrë sqepbardhë** [Ornit] rook Corvus frugilegus L.

sorrëshkinë nf [Ornit] swift (Apus apus)

sorrëz nf small wooden peg that secures the iron rings attaching the tongue of the plough or cart to the oxyoke

sorrmë adj (i) **1** (of livestock) with black and white spots on the muzzle **2** having a dark complexion; having dark eyes and eyebrows

sorrush adj, n **1** (Pet) (person) with dark eyes and eyebrows **2** (livestock) with dark patches (around the eyes)

sos pcl (Colloq) expresses incredulity

sos·

_I §_ vt (Colloq) **1** to finish/use up [] **2** to bring to a successful conclusion: complete, conclude; fulfil
_II §_ vi **1** to suffice, succeed **2** to arrive

○ **sos· fjalën** _(Colloq)_ to finish what one is saying

sos·et vpr **1** (Colloq) to be finished/used up, be all gone **2** (Fig) to be fulfilled **3** to arrive

○ **Nuk soset deti me lugë.** "The sea cannot be exhausted with a spoon." _(Prov)_ The sea can't be emptied with a teaspoon.

○ <> **sos·**_et³ˢᵍ_ **fryma 1** <> _is_ out of breath; <> _can_ barely breathe **2** <>'s life _comes_ to an end

○ <> **sos·**_et³ˢᵍ_ **jeta** <>'s life _comes_ to an end

SOS [_sos_] nm SOS (distress signal)

sosë nf end, finish; death

sosje nf ger **1** (Colloq) <**sos·**, **sos·et 2** = **sosë**

*__**sosmi**__ adv (sē) at last, finally

sosur nm ger (të) (Colloq) <**sos·**, **sos·et**

sosh pl fem abl (Old) those = **asosh**

sot adv today

○ **Sot i bën hunjtë, nesër i djeg.** He/she says one thing today, another thing tomorrow. You can't trust him/her.

○ **sot e mot** now and forever, for all time

○ **sot e kësaj dite** up till now

○ **sot e gjithë ditën** without interruption until now, continually

○ **Sot është, nesër s'është. 1** It's available today, but may not be tomorrow. **2** Here today, gone tomorrow.

○ **sot ka·, sot ha·** to spend everything one earns, live from hand to mouth

○ **ësh·të sot për nesër** to be nearing the end of one's life

○ **sot për sot** for the present, as for now; at the present time

sotëm adj (i) **1** of today, today's **2** present-day; of modern times

sotinë nf empty honeycomb; wasp nest

sotme nf (e) the present day: the present

sotpërsotshëm adj (i) of right now, of the present, of the present day

sotshëm adj (i) = **sotëm**

sovajkë nf shuttle (of a loom or sewing machine)

soval nm = **kastriq**

sovjet nm soviet

sovjetik adj **1** of or pertaining to a soviet **2** of or pertaining to the Soviet Union: soviet

sovkoz nm national agricultural enterprise in the Soviet Union

sovran nm, adj sovereign

sovranitet nm sovereignty

spagë nf = **spango**

spahi nm [Hist] cavalryman given territory and feudal rights, including the right to collect tithes, by the Ottoman Empire in exchange for military service: spahi

spahillëk nm (np ~qe) **1** [Hist] office and function of a spahi **2** tithe collected by a spahi **3** territory under the control of a spahi

spajk nm decoration on the side of a stocking: clock

spakatë nf [Gymnastics] split

spalcë nf [Ichth] gilt-head sea bream (Sparus aurata)

○ **spalcë e egër** [Ichth] blue-spotted sea bream Pagrus coeruleostictus

○ **spalcë e kuqe** [Ichth] = **gjanës**

○ **spalcë nate** [Ichth] white sea bream Diplodus sargus sargus

○ **spalcë pullalie** [Ichth] red sea bream Pagellus bogaraveo

○ **spalcë rëre** [Ichth] striped sea bream Lithognathus mormyrus

spaletë nf [Mil] epaulet

*__**spanak**__ nm spinach = **spinaq**

*__**spanaq**__ nm (Reg Kos) = **spinaq**

spango nf **1** heavy twine **2** string holding a plumb bob

*__**spanisht**__ = **spanjisht**

*__**spanoj**__ adj (Reg Gk) beardless

Spanjë nf Spain

spanjisht adv in Spanish (language)

spanjishte nf Spanish language

spanjoll
_I §_ adj Spanish
_II §_ n Spaniard

*__**sparagë**__ nf asparagus

*__**sparmacetë**__ nf spermaceti; candle (made of spermaceti)

sparo nf

○ **sparo bishtzezë** [Ichth] annular sea bream Diplodus annularis

○ **sparo e zezë** [Ichth] zebra sea bream Diplodus cervinus cervinus

sparqe nf [Bot] broomrape (Orobanche)

sparqore np [Bot] broomrape family Orobanchaceae

spartakiadë nf sports meet

spartan adj, n Spartan

spastrim nm ger <**spastro·**n, **spastro·**het

spastro·het vpr to become purified; get cleaned up/out

spastro·n vt to clean up/out [], purge

spastrues adj serving to clean up/out, cleaning; purging of undesirable elements

spat nm [Min] foliated mineral with a vitreous luster: spar, spath

○ **spat i fushës** feldspar

spathi
_I §_ nm (np ~nj) club (in card games)
_II §_ adj of clubs

spathinjsh adv

spathok nm (Reg) **1** rag, tatter **2** (Contempt) person dressed in rags, raggedy bum

spazmë nf [Med] spasm

spec nm **1** red/Cayenne pepper, Spanish pepper (Capiscum annuum) **2** ground red pepper **3** (Fig Colloq) highly excitable person **4** (Reg Kos) bell pepper, green pepper

special adj special

specialist n specialist

specialitet nm specialty

specializim nm ger **1** <**specializo·**n, **specializo·**het **2** specialization

specializo·het vpr **1** to study a specialty **2** to specialize

○ **specializo·**het **për** [] to get specialized training in []

specializo·n *vt* **1** to train [] in a specialty **2** to focus [a field of endeavor] on a specialty
○ **specializo·n për** [] to give specialized training in []

specializuar *adj (i)* specialized

specie *nf [Biol]* species

specifik *adj* **1** *(Book)* special; distinctive, specially characteristic **2** specific

specifikí *nf (Book)* distinctive nature

specifikím *nm ger (Book)* **1** < **specifiko·n** **2** specification **3** list of specifications

specifiko·n *vt* **1** *(Book)* to specify **2** *(Spec)* to sort []

****spejz** *nm* tendril

spektakël *nm* spectacular performance; spectacle

spektakular *adj* spectacular

spektator *n* **1** spectator **2** *(Fig Pej)* idle spectator

spektër *nm* spectrum

spektror *adj [Phys]* of the spectrum: spectral

spektroskop *nm [Phys]* spectroscope

spekulator *n* speculator

spekulím *nm ger* **1** < **spekulo·n, spekulo·het** **2** speculation

spekulo·n *vi* **1** to take advantage of the market: speculate **2** *(Fig)* to play with the truth to gain one's ends

spekulues
I § *adj* taking advantage of the market: speculative
II § *n* speculator

spermatofite *np [Bot]* Spermatophyta

spermë *nf [Physiol]* sperm

spesor *nm [Tech]* **1** spacer **2** shim

spërdredh· *vt* to twist/twirl/wag []; hard; twist/ twirl/wag [] again and again

spërdredhje *nf ger* < **spërdredh·, spërdridh·et**

spërdridh·et *vpr* **1** to twist hard from the waist; walk in a widely weaving line **2** to twist and turn sharply; twirl/curl all around **3** *(Pej)* to stand/walk with abnormally swiveling hips

spërdridh *stem for 2nd pl pres, pind, imper, vp* < **spërdredh·**

spërdrodh *stem for pdef* < **spërdredh·**

spërëngë *nf [Bot]* asparagus *(Asparagus)* = **shpar-gull**

****spërhell·** *vt* to sharpen the point of [], put a sharp point on []

spërk *nm (Reg)* = **qose**

spërkas *stem for 1st sg pres, pl pres, 2nd & 3rd sg subj, pind* < **spërkat·**

spërkat· *vt* **1** to sprinkle; spray **2** to spatter [] (with something dirty)

spërkat·et *vpr* to get spattered (with something dirty)

spërkates
I § *adj* used for spraying; involved with spraying
II § *n* person engaged in spraying: sprayer

spërkatëse *nf* spray pump

spërkatje *nf ger* < **spërkat·, spërkat·et**

spërket· *vp* < **spërkat·**

spërkë *nf* **1** spattered drop **2** polka dot

spërkël *nf* small drop of spray

spërkís *stem for 2nd pl pres, pind* < **spërkat·**

spërkít *stem for pdef, opt, adm, part, pind, 2nd pl pres, imper, vp* < **spërkat·**

spërndrís *stem for 1st sg pres, pl pres, 2nd & 3rd sg subj, pind* < **spërndrít·**

spërndrít·
I § *vt* to make [] shine with cleanliness
II § *vi* to shine

****spërthikët** *adj (i)* brisk, lively

spi *nf* gusset for the armpit of a jerkin

spic *adv (Colloq)* in spiffy shoes and clothes

spica *np* < **spicë** thin branches used as kindling wood

spicak
I § *adj* provoking, provocative
II § *nm* provoker

spicer *nm (Old)* druggist

spicerane OR **spicerane** *nf (Old)* apothecary

spicë
I § *nf* **1** splinter; small chip **2** *(Fig)* provocative word, barb **3** spoke of a wheel **4** cotter pin
II § *adj* having a sharp tip
III § *adv* sharply dressed: dressed nattily

spicëtar
I § *n (Pej)* plotter, intriguer; agitator, provocateur
II § *adj* crafty

spicos· *vt* to splinter [wood], chop up [wood]

spicos·et *vpr* to splinter apart

****spidhë** *nf* whore = **kurvë**

****spieg** = **shpjeg**

****spihat·** *vi impers (Reg)* it snows in fine flakes

spik *nm* **1** thick cord made of twisted wool **2** ornamental dark wool braid used to decorate an ethnic costume

spikamë *nf* **1** elevation in an otherwise relatively flat land surface: rise **2** uneven land surface

spikas *stem for 1st sg pres, pl pres, 2nd & 3rd sg subj, pind* < **spikat·**

spikat· *vi* to stand out, be distinguished/conspicuous

spikat·et *vpr* to be distinguished

spikatëm *adj (i)* prominent, distinguished; conspicuous, striking

spikatës *adj* distinguished; obvious, conspicuous

spikatje *nf ger* < **spikat·**

spikatshëm *adj (i)* = **spikatës**

spiker *n* news broadcaster; program announcer

spikth *nm* **1** = **spik 2** final row of a knitted stocking **3** young shoot, sprout **4** *[Ornit]* woodpecker

spilar *nm* **1** fish trap with a net at the end **2** dead-fall trap

spilc *nm* **1** spoke of a wheel **2** supporting stick used to prop up the slab in a dead-fall bird-trap
○ **ësh-të në spilca 1** to be so tired that one can hardly stand up, be about to fall over **2** on pins and needles

****spilcë** *nf [Agr]* linchpin securing the beam of the plow to the yoke

spillo·het *vpr* to get all dressed up for a special occasion: get spruced up

spinaq *nm [Bot]* spinach: prickly-seeded spinach *(Spinacia oleracea)*

spinë *nf* **1** *[Electr]* electric plug **2 (Old)* fork

****spinër** *nf [Bot]* monkshood *(Aconitum napellus)*

****spinok** = **spinaq**

spinot *nm [Tech]* metal pin

****spipllore** *nf (Old)* woman who gossips a lot

****spir** *nm* = **mamuz**

spirale *nf* spiral

spirancë *nf* anchor

spirë *nf* 1 (*Colloq*) [*Med*] diarrhea: loose bowels 2 (*Pej*) watery and tasteless soup/food 3 [*Spec*] turn of wire in a coil *4 (*Reg Colloq*) mucal discharge from the nose: snot

spirëgjake *nf* (*Colloq*) [*Med*] dysentery

*spirilang = spirilëng

spirilëng *nm* (*np* gje) watery and tasteless food

*spirillose *nf* disease that affects hens

spiritizëm *nm* belief in ghosts and spirits: spiritualism

spiro·*het vpr* to have diarrhea; suffer from dysentery

Spiro *nf with masc agreement* Spiro (male name)

*spirue *nm* (*obl* ˜oi) (*Reg Gheg*) = mamuz

spiruq *nm* [*Food*] light-textured large round pastry made with milk

spital *nm* hospital

spitalor *adj* (*Book*) pertaining to or located in a hospital

spitullaq
  I § *adj* (*Pej*) dressing up like a dandy: overdressing, foppish
  II § *n* person who overdresses: dandy, fop

spitullim *nm ger* 1 (*Pej*) <spitullo·het 2 overconcern with one's outward appearance: foppishness

spitullo·*het vpr* 1 to overdress (in order to attract attention) 2 to behave in an affected manner

spith *nm* [*Med*] dropsy

spiun
  I § *nm* spy
  II § *adj* equipped for spying

spiunazh *nm* espionage

spiunim *nm ger* <spiuno·n

spiunllëk *nm* (*np* ˜qe) (*Colloq Contempt*) spy business

spiuno·*n vt* (*Contempt*) 1 to spy on [] 2 to report another's behavior to a superior/adult: tattle/tell on []

spjeg = shpjeg

*splon *nm* animal pen with a roof

spol *nm* 1 scoop for bailing out a boat: bail *2 (*Old*) board used for counting money: counter

*sponde *nm* [*Lit*] spondee

spontan *adj* (*Book*) spontaneous

*spontaneisht = spontanisht

*spontaneitet *nm* spontaneity

spontanisht *adv* spontaneously

sporadik *adj* (*Book*) sporadic

sporadikisht *adv* (*Book*) sporadically

spore *nf* [*Biol*] spore

*sporëng *nm* [*Bot*] sharp-leaved asparagus (*Asparagus acutifolius*)

sporofite *np* [*Bot*] sporophytes

sport *nm* sport
  ◦ (sa) për sport just for fun

sportdashës
  I § *adj* sports-loving
  II § *n* sports-lover

sportel *nm* ticket window; small window for dealing with the public: counter window, wicket

sportelist *n* person who works behind a counter window: cashier, ticket-seller

sportist *n* participant in sports

sportiv *adj* pertaining to, characteristic of, or used in sports

spraps· *vt* to push [] backward, back [] up

spraps·*et vpr* to back up, move backward; go back, recoil, retreat

sprapsje *nf ger* 1 <spraps·, spraps·et 2 retreat

sprasëm *adj* (*i*) toward the end, in the latter part; rear

spreth *nm* 1 eaves 2 hat brim

*sprihë = sprijë

sprijë *nf* 1 [*Myth*] harpy 2 (*Fig Insult*) mean woman: harpy

sprintier *nm* [*Track*] sprinter

sprovë *nf* 1 trying experience, test of character; experience 2 experiment; preliminary study 3 = provë

sprovim *nm ger* <sprovo·n, sprovo·het

sprovo·*het vpr* 1 to put oneself to the test 2 to pass a test; prove oneself, come through

sprovo·*n*
  I § *vt* 1 to put [] to the real test: test/try out [] 2 to suffer [a bad experience], undergo []
  II § *vi* to try hard

sprovuar *adj* (*i*) tested by experience, proven by trial: tried and true, experienced, reliable

sprucator *nm* [*Tech*] sprayer, atomizer

sprucim *nm* [*Tech*] spray

spuntim *nm ger* 1 <spunto·n 2 tick mark

spunto·*n vt* to mark [] with a tick

spurdhiq *nm* [*Ornit*] = spurdhjak

spurdhis· *vi* to use foul language, talk dirty

spurdhjak *nm* 1 [*Ornit*] small bird: wren, sparrow 2 (*FigImpolite*) worthless small and inexperienced child: shitty little runt, snot-nose kid

spurdhjakës *nm* (*Impol*) = spurdhjak

sqap *nm* (*np* sqep) = cjap

sqapth *nm* 1 [*Agr*] wooden linchpin securing the handle to the beam of a plow 2 [*Bot*] snowy mespilus (*Amelanchier ovalis*)

sqaq· *vt* 1 to make [] soft and mushy by soaking: macerate, ret [flax/ hemp]; stew [meat] 2 to debilitate [] and make limp with weakness; tire [] out completely

sqaq·*et vpr* 1 to become soft and mushy 2 to become debilitated and limp with weakness; get completely tired out

sqarim *nm ger* 1 <sqaro·n, sqaro·het 2 clarification

sqaro·*het vpr* 1 to become clear, clear up 2 to gain a clear understanding; get a clear explanation

sqaro·*n vt* 1 to clear up []; make [] clear, clarify 2 to clarify matters for [], make matters clear for []

sqarues *adj* clarifying, elucidating; illustrative

sqarueshëm *adj* (*i*) explicable

*sqelë *nf* = skelë

*sqenë *nf* scene, scenery

*sqenëtar *n* scenery maker

sqep
  I § *nm* 1 beak 2 [*Mus*] mouthpiece of a single-reed instrument 3 corner = cep 4 pointed projecting piece/part
  II § *np* <sqap
  ◦ sqep çafke [*Bot*] common storksbill *Erodium cicutarium*

sqep·*et vpr* to pick at one's food

sqapadruth *nm* [*Ornit*] woodpecker = qukapik

sqepak *adj* tapering to a point: beak-shaped

sqep·a|lu'gë *nf* [*Ichth*] Atlantic saury (*Scomberesox saurus*)

sqep·a'r *nm* **1** adze **2** small hoe with a mattock-like blade

sqep·ato'r *nm* [*Ornit*] woodpecker = **qukapík**

sqep·bízë [*Ornit*] avocet (*Recurvirostra avosetta L.*)

sqep·ça'fkë *nf* [*Bot*] common storksbill (*Erodium cicutarium*)

sqep·gja'të
I § *adj* **1** long-beaked **2** (*Fig*) jabberer, chatterbox
II § *nf* **1** [*Ornit*] oystercatcher (*Haematopodidae ostralegus*) **2** [*Ornit*] = **shapto're**

sqep·gjilpë'rë *adj* (*Poet*) sharp-beaked

sqep·ho'llë *adj* thin-beaked
∘ **sqepholli i xunktheve** [*Ornit*] fan-tailed warbler *Cisticola juncidis*

sqep·kry'q *nm* [*Ornit*] red crossbill (*Loxia curvirostra*)

sqep·kthy'er *adj* having a curved beak

sqep·lu'gë *nf* [*Ornit*] shoveler (*Anas clypeata*)

sqepo't *nm* [*Ichth*] snipe/trumpet fish (*Macroramphosus scolopax*)

sqep·to'·n *vt* to peck [] with the beak

sqep·to're *nf* [*Ornit*] woodcock = **shapto're**

sqep·trashë
I § *adj* having a big beak
II § *nm* [*Ornit*] hawfinch, grosbeak (*Coccothraustes coccothraustes*)

sqep·tha'të *nm* [*Ornit*] woodpecker = **qukapík**

sqep·ve'rdhë
I § *adj* [*Ornit*] yellow-billed
II § *nf* (yellow-billed) blackbird = **mëlle'një**

*****sqe·rmë** *nf* [*Sport*] = **ske'rmë**

*****sqe'rmo··n** *vi* [*Sport*] to fence

sqe'tull *nm* **1** underarm, armpit **2** rock/mountain hollow **3** [*Bot*] axil
∘ **nën sqetull** under the wing, under protection

sqetull·a'r *nm* armpit gusset

sqetull·o'r *adj* [*Bot Med*] axillary

sqetull·o're *nf* axillary sprout

*****sqifte'r** = **skifte'r**

sqim·a *np* < **sqimë** whims

sqim·atar *adj, n* **1** (person) who is overly fastidious in dress and personal appearance: vain/foppish (person) **2** (person) who puts on airs; affected/conceited (person)

sqim·ë *nf* **1** ostentatious dress; excessive attention paid to one's personal appearance **2** vanity; conceit, conceitedness **3** fussiness, finickiness

sqim·ë't *adj* (i) = **sqimatar**

*****sqim·shë'm** *adj* (i) ostentatious, flashy; vain

*****sqipa'r** *nm* (narrow) passage, path

*****sqjo'·het** *vpr* = **zgjo'·het**

*****sqjo'·n** *vt* = **zgjo'·n**

sqoh *nm* [*Ichth*] dusky grouper (*Epinephelus guaza*)

*****sqo'kë** = **squkë**

sqoll *nm* **1** washbasin, sink; drainboard **2** drain, drainpipe

sqo'të *nf* = **shqo'të**

*****squ'a'r** *adj* (i) = **zgju'ar**

*****squa'|rësí** *nf* = **zgjuarsí**

*****squ'et** *adj* (i) (*Reg*) **1** = **zgju'ar 2** [*Ling*] definite

*****sque'ti** *OR* **sque'tsi** *nf* (*Reg*) = **zgjuarsí**

squ'fur *nm* [*Chem*] sulfur ((S))

squfur·ím *nm ger* < **squfuro'·n**

squfuro'·n *vt* to dust [fruit trees, grapevines] with sulfur or sulfur dioxide: sulfurize

squfur·o'r *adj* [*Spec*] containing sulfur: sulfurous

squfuro's· *vt* = **squfuro'·n**

squfur·o'sje *nf ger* = **squfurím**

*****squfur·o'sh** *adj* = **squfuro'r**

squ'furt *adj* (i) made of sulfur; containing sulfur

*****squ'hë** *nf* catapult

squk· *vi* **1** (of a hen) to cluck while brooding **2** (of a hen) to brood (over eggs)

squ'kë
I § *nf* brood hen
II § *adj* rotten egg

s|qu'll· *vt* **1** to soak [] thoroughly **2** to make [] soft and mushy

s|qu'll·et *vpr* **1** to get soaked **2** to get soft and mushy; get overripe **3** (*Fig*) to become sluggish; become debilitated **4** (*Fig*) to get tearful

s|qu'll·ët *adj* (i) **1** soft and mushy **2** flaccid, limp **3** (*Fig*) lethargic, sluggish

*****squp** (*Colloq*) = **sqep**

*****squp·tra'shë** *nm* [*Ornit*] = **sqeptra'shë**

*****squp·ve'rdhe** *nf* [*Ornit*] = **sqepve'rdhe**

sqyre *nf* deep clay dish

*****sqyt** *nm* shield = **shqyt**

stabil·ime'nt *nm* industrial building and its equipment: plant, works, factory

stabil·ite't *nm* stability = **qëndrueshm|e'rí**

stabil·izato'r *nm* [*Spec*] stabilizer; power conditioner

stabil·izím *nm ger* **1** < **stabilizo'·n, stabilizo'·het 2** stabilization

stabil·izo'·het *vpr* **1** (*Book*) to stabilize **2** to settle down (in a permanent job/home)

stabil·izo'·n *vt* **1** to stabilize [] **2** to settle [someone] (in a permanent job/home)

stacio'n *nm* **1** station **2** temporary stopping place
∘ **stacion autobuzi** bus stop

stad *nm* stage, step

stadiu'm *nm* stadium

stafe'të *nf* **1** [*Sport*] relay race **2** baton/staff or flag handed off in a relay race

stafídhe *nf* raisin

stafiloko'k *nm* staphylococcus

stago'n *nm* **1** poultry gizzard **2** (*Old*) large copper bowl; font for holy water

*****staja'n** *nm* (*Old*) household steward, butler

*****stajan·íce** *nf* (*Old*) housekeeper

*****staje** *nf* gang, band

stakanovíst *n* worker who far exceeds expectations in terms of both productivity and creativity: Stakhanovite

stakanov·ízëm *nm* initiative to exceed expectations in terms of both productivity and creativity: Stakhanovism

stalagmít *nm* stalagmite

stalaktít *nm* stalactite

*****sta'lë** *nf* (*Old*) herd, flock

sta'llë *nf* stable (for livestock)

stall·ier *n* stableman

stall·o'r *adj* of or pertaining to livestock stables

*****stambë** *nf* = **stampë**

Stamboll *nm* Istanbul

*__stambos·__ *vt* = stampo·*n*

STAMLES *abbrev* <**Shoqëria Tregtare Anonime për Monopolin e Letrave dhe të Shkrepëseve** [*Hist*] Incorporated Commercial Monopoly for Paper and Matches

stampë *nf* **1** [*Spec*] die/stamp/mold for producing multiple copies **2** (*Colloq*) die press **3** printing press **4** [*Cine*] print (of a film)

stampim *nm ger* [*Spec*] <**stampo·**n, **stampo·het**

stampo·n *vt* **1** to produce [multiple copies] by using a die/stamp/mold **2** to print [a photograph] **3** to imprint [] with a stamp

stan *nm* **1** herdsman's camp for dairy animals **2** flock of sheep **3** (*Fig Contempt*) dirty gang/camp

  ∘ **stan me lepuj** "herdsman's camp with rabbits" something ridiculously impossible

  ∘ **stan pa qen** (*Pej*) place that lets anybody come and go as they like, improperly controlled place

  ∘ **stan vorbash** (*Impol*) unproductive organization

stanar *n* herdsman in a herdsman's camp for dairy animals

standard *nm, adj* standard

  ∘ **standardi i jetesës** standard of living

standardizim *nm ger* **1** <**standardizo·**n **2** standardization

standardizo·n *vt* **1** to standardize **2** (*FigImpolite*) to produce [] by mechanical formula: grind out []

stanok *nm* [*Mil*] sighting device used for target training

stanore *nf* dairywoman working in a mountain camp of herdsmen

stap *nm* (*np ~ inj*) **1** stick (of wood), staff **2** club, cudgel

stapis *stem for 1st sg pres, pl pres, 2nd & 3rd sg subj, pind* <**stapit·**

stapit· *vt* **1** to hit/beat [] with a stick: thrash, flog **2** (*Colloq*) to freeze [] in place (with fear/surprise): stop [] short

stapit·et *vpr* **1** to stop in one's tracks, freeze in place **2** to show up suddenly, appear suddenly to <>

stapitje *nf ger* <**stapit·**

starë *nf* (*Old*) unit of measurement (of oil) approximately equal to twenty-eight kilograms

*__starifat__ *nm* [*Ethnog*] leader of the escort group from the groom's family that come to fetch the bride = **krushkaparë**

start *nm* **1** [*Sport*] start; starting line **2** line behind which an airplane waits for take-off **3** (*Fig Book*) start of something significant: the beginning

Stas *nm* Stas (male name)

*__stasion__ OR **stasjon** = stacion

statik *adj* static

statikë *nf* [*Phys*] statics

statistik *n* statistician

statistikë *nf* statistics

statistikor *adj* statistical

stativ *nm* [*Cine*] tripod

  ∘ **stativ bretkocë** [*Cine*] high hat, baby tripod

stator *nm* [*Spec*] stator

statujë *nf* statue

statukuo *nf* status quo

status *nm* status

  ∘ **status aktual** status quo

statut *nm* **1** set of regulations governing a political/social organization: ordinance **2** (*Old*) ordinance regulating a craft guild

  ∘ **statuti themeltar** bylaws

*__stavar__ *nm* (*Reg Gk*) beam of a plow

stavë *nf* stack, pile, heap = **stivë**

stavis· *vt* to pile/heap [] up

*__stavnik__ *nm* kind of net

Stavri *nm* Stavri (male name)

stavridh *nm* [*Ichth*] Atlantic horse-mackerel (*Trachurus trachurus*)

  ∘ **stavridh kanali** [*Ichth*] blue jack mackerel *Trachurus picturatus*

  ∘ **stavridh mesjetar** [*Ichth*] Mediterranean horse-mackerel *Trachurus mediterraneus*

staxhionim *nm ger* <**staxhiono·**n, **staxhiono·het**

staxhiono·het *vpr* [*Spec*] to become seasoned

staxhiono·n *vt* [*Spec*] to keep [] in a special temperature and humidity environment for a period of time: season []

stazë *nf* [*Med*] stagnation, stasis

stazh *nm* practical training; probationary period in a job/organization; period of practical labor required of students before beginning higher education

stazhier *n* person in probationary status; prospective student doing required practical labor

stearinë *nf* stearine

Stefan *nm* Stefan (male name)

stegë *nf* cartridge clip

stejë *nf* **1** wick **2** saddle pad

stekë *nf* **1** billiard stick: cue **2** [*Sport*] crossbar (in high-jumping) **3** [*Sport*] ski pole **4** [*Med*] splint **5** type of hairpin

  ∘ **stekë bilardoje 1** pool cue, billiard stick **2** (*Joke*) tall lanky person: beanpole

stela *np* <**stelë** (*Reg*) **1** bed linen and covering **2** (*Impol*) worn out old clothes; old rags

stelë *nf* **1** piece of old clothing: rag **2** rag used as a bed for a dog; doghouselair, den **3** (*FigImpolite*) small, ill-kept hut/room **4** saddle pad **5** (*Impol*) poor tobacco made from leftover leaves; autumn-ripening tobacco **6** [*Archeol*] stele

stemë *nf* heraldic coat of arms; emblem, emblematic seal; logo

stendë *nf* **1** public bulletin board **2** display stand

stenë *nf* (*Reg*) **1** rocky mass with deep crevasses; hollow in a river bank **2** thin partition wall

*__stenicë__ *nf* [*Entom*] bedbug

stenograf *n* stenographer

stenografi *nf* stenography

stenografik *adj* stenographic

stenografim *nm ger* <**stenografo·**n

stenografist *n* = **stenograf**

stenografo·n *vt* to record [] stenographically

stenogram *nm* stenographic text

stenokardi *nf* [*Med*] chest pain

stenozë *nf* [*Med*] stenosis

step *nm* pointed tip

step·et *vpr* **1** to step aside, give way **2** (*Fig*) to hold/hang back: falter, hesitate

stepë *nf* [*Geog*] steppe

stepje *nf ger* **1** <**step·et 2** withdrawal, retreat

stepor *adj* [*Geog*] of or pertaining to the steppes

stere *nf* dry land, terra firma

stereometrí *nf* 1 stereometry; solid geometry 2 *(Colloq)* textbook on solid geometry

stereometrík *nf* stereometric

stereotíp
 I § *nm* stereotype
 II § *adj* stereotypical

ste rë *nf (Reg)* = **sternë**

steríl *adj* sterile

steriliz im *nm ger* 1 [*Med Biol*] <**sterilizo ·n** 2 sterilization

steriliz o ·n *vt* to sterilize

sterlinë *nf* sterling

sternë *nf* underground cistern; tank for holding large amounts of a liquid

*****ster os·** = **sterro ·n**

*****sterpídhë** *nf* roof gutter = **ullu**k

*****sterpos·et** *vpr* to turn twilight, grow dusk

sterrë *adj* 1 pitch dark; jet black 2 *(Fig)* evil, dirty ○ **sterrë i zi** pitch black

sterrím *nm ger (Old)* 1 <**sterro ·n, sterro ·het** 2 blackout

sterro ·het *vpr* 1 to become very dark, turn dark; get black; undergo a blackout 2 *(Fig)* to be covered with shame; feel humiliated

sterro ·n
 I § *vt* 1 to make [] very dark: darken, blacken; black out 2 *(Fig Colloq)* to wreck []; mess [] up badly
 II § *vi* 1 to look black 2 *(Fig)* to look very gloomy; get dark with emotion

sterros· = **sterro ·n**

stetoskóp *nm* [*Med*] stethoscope

stër *formative prefix* 1 expresses semantic enlargement or excess: ultra-, super-, over- 2 (with kinship terms) great-

stërbuja r *adj* too generous

*****stërda ·het** *vpr* = **stërnda ·het**

stërdit·et *vpr* 1 to have an unexpected encounter 2 to appear suddenly to <>

*****stërdhámb** *OR* **stërdhámb** ës *(Reg Gheg)* = **stërdhë mb**

stërdhë mb *nm* snaggletooth; canine tooth, eyetooth

stërfal·et *vpr* to greet one another and embrace warmly

stërfalur *adj (i)* hypocritical religious zealot

stërfar· *vt* to annihilate, wipe out completely

stërflok *nm* newly hatched louse, nit

stërflok· *vt* 1 to muss up [the hair] 2 *(Fig)* to make a mess of []

*****stërflok** ës *n* troublemaker

*****stërfllo ·n** *vi (Colloq)* 1 to cuss with outrage 2 = **turfullo ·n**

stërfok *nm* (of animals) lair, den

*****stërform im** *nm* transformation

*****stërform o ·n** *vt* to transform

stërfyc *nm* = **stërfyt**ës

stërfyt *nm* conduit for water, water pipe

stërfyt ës *nm* 1 popgun *(Old)* *2 syringe; sprayer

*****stërg** *nm (np ~gje)* [*Ornit*] stork

stërgi *nf* [*Med*] = **rodhje**

stërgjate *adj (i)* 1 too long/tall 2 oblong; elongated

stërgja tshem *adj (i)* = **stërgjat**ë

stërgji *nf* [*Bot*] dragon arum *(Drancunculus vulgaris)*

stërgjysh *nm (np ~ër)* 1 great grandfather 2 *(Fig)* originator, founder: father

stërgjysh e *nf* great grandmother

stërgjysh er *np* <**stërgjysh** forefathers

stërgjysh or *adj (Elev)* ancestral

stërhell *nm* extremely tall and thin man

stërhollë *adj (i)* 1 extremely thin; subtle 2 shrewd

stërhollës *n* excessively meticulous person, hairsplitter

stërholli *nf* 1 excessive meticulousness, hairsplitting 2 excessive detail

stërholl im *nm ger* 1 <**stërhollo ·n, stërhollo ·het** 2 refinement

stërhollo ·het *vpr* to become finely refined

stërhollo ·n *vt* 1 to refine 2 to go into excessive detail with []: draw out [discourse] excessively

stërhollu ar *adj (i)* 1 excessively refined: affected 2 overly detailed and confused 3 too complicated 4 wily; sophistical

stërkalë *nf* 1 drop of spray from a dashing wave 2 spatter

stërkandr·et *vpr* (of wood) to become worm-eaten, go to rot

stërkas *stem for 1st sg pres, 1st & 3rd pl pres, 2nd & 3rd sg subj* <**stërket·**

stërkeq·et *vpr* to become emaciated and sicklooking

stërkeqët *adj (i)* emaciated and sick-looking

stërket· *vt* to spray, sprinkle, spatter

*****stërkë** *nf* track, trail

stërkëmb ës *nm* leg stuck out to trip someone

stërkis *stem for 2nd pl pres, pind* <**stërket·**

stërkit *stem for pdef, opt, adm, part, pind, 2nd pl pres, imper, vp* <**stërket·**

stërkitë *nf* 1 spattered drop, spot (on fabric caused by liquid) 2 salty water = **shëlli**rë

stërkitje *nf* <**stërket·**

stërklas· *vt* = **stërkas·**

stërklet· *vt* = **stërket·**

stërklit *vt* = **stërkit**

stërko ·n *vt* = **stërka** s·

stërkungull *nm* 1 redberry bryony *(Bryonia dioica)* 2 [*Med*] scrofula = **saraxha**

stërlag ës *nm* toy squirt gun

stërlashtë *adj (i)* 1 ancient 2 extremely/too old (person) 3 *(Impol)* timeworn, old-fashioned

stërlëng *nm (Tease)* weak and watery food with no nutritional value

stërlodhje *nf* state of complete fatigue: utter exhaustion

stërmadh *adj (i)* enormous

stërmadhim *nm ger* 1 <**stërmadho ·n** 2 exaggeration

stërmadho ·n *vt* to exaggerate

*****stërmak** *adj* clumsy, awkward

*****stërma** s *stem for 1st sg pres, pl pres, 2nd & 3rd sg subj, pind* <**stërma** t·

stërmat· *vt* 1 to remeasure [] again and again 2 to estimate the size of []

stërmbe së *nf* 1 great granddaughter; grand niece 2 *(Fig)* female descendant with characteristics inherited from an ancestor

stërmund im *nm ger* 1 <**stërmundo ·n, stërmundo ·het** 2 exhaustion 3 extraordinary effort

stër**mund**o· *het vpr* **1** to get extremely tired: become exhausted **2** to use up all one's energy in an attempt

stër**mund**o· *n vt* to exhaust [someone]

stër**nda**· *het vpr* to be divided into smaller and smaller pieces

stër**ngop**· *vt* **1** to overstuff [] (with food/drink) **2** to oversaturate

stër**ngop**·*et vpr* **1** to get overstuffed (with food/drink) **2** to get oversaturated

stër**ngo**'**pje** *nf ger* <stër**ngop**·, stër**ngop**·*et*

stër**ngo**'**pur** *adj (i)* overstuffed (with food/drink); oversaturated

stër**nip** *nm (np ~ër)* **1** great grandson; grand nephew **2** *(Fig)* descendant with characteristics inherited from an ancestor

stër**nip**'**ëri** *nf* lineage, descent

stër**nishtë** *nf* harvested field reused as pasture or for replanting with a different crop

stër**nxeh**· *vt* to make [] extremely hot; overheat

*stër**pa**'**pë** *nf* antipope

*stër**pic**ë *nf* mousetrap; trap

*stër**pidh**ë *nf* drain, drain pipe, sewer

stër**pik** *nm* sapling that sprouts from the base of the trunk of the tree or vine

stër**pik**·

  I § vt **1** to sprinkle, spray; spatter **2** to propagate [grapevines] by layering: layer = **përpajno**·*n*
  II § vi to sprout from the base of the trunk of the tree or vine

stër**pik**·*et vpr* to get all spattered (and dirty)

stër**pik**ë *nf* spattered drop

  ∘ **Pifsh stërpikën** *(Curse)* May you drink poison!

stër**pik**ës *n* sprinkler, sprayer

stër**pik**je *nf ger* **1** <stër**pik**·, stër**pik**·*et* **2** spray

stër**plak** *nm (np stërple'q)* *[Hist]* elder called in by council of elders to help adjudicate a dispute under canonic law

*stër**prind**ë *np* ancestors

stër**puj**ë *nf [Bot]* **1** parsnip *(Pastinaca sativa)* *2 anthriscus

stër**qit**ur *adj (i)* irksome, bothersome, vexatious

stër**qok** *nm [Ornit]* jackdaw *(Corvus monedula)*

stër**qok**ë *nf [Ornit]* daw *(Corvus monedula)*

  ∘ stër**qok**ë e malit alpine chough *Pyrrhocorax graculus* = gali·c*ë*

stër**shit**·*et vpr* **1** to sell everything that one has **2** *(Pej)* to sell out (for personal gain)

stër**sho**'**sh**· *vt* to sift [] over carefully (in one's mind), consider [a matter] from every angle

stër**tha**' stem for pdef <stërtho·të

stër**tha**'**shë** *1st sg pdef* <stërtho·të

stër**the**' *2nd sg pdef* <stërtho·të

stër**the**'**m** *1st sg pres & subj* <stërtho·të

stër**the**'**mi** *1st pl pres* <stërtho·të

stër**the**'**n** *stem for part, opt, adm* <stërtho·të

stër**the**'**në** *part* <stërtho·të

stër**tho**·**të** *vt* to say [] again and again, say many times

*stër**tho**'**m** *1st sg subj* = stërthem

*stër**tho**'**mi** *1st pl pres* = stërthemi

stër**tho**'**në** *3rd pl pres & subj* <stërtho·të

stër**tho**'**ni** *2nd pl pres* <stërtho·të

stër**tho**'**sh** *stem for pind* <stërtho·të

stër**thu**' *stem for vp* <stërtho·të

stër**thu**'**a**

  I § 2nd sg pres <stërtho·të
  II § 2nd sg pres & imper = stërthu'aj

stër**thu**'**aj** *2nd sg imper* <stërtho·të

stër**thu**'**ash** *2nd sg subj* <stërtho·të

stër**va**'**l**·*et vpr* to fall to the ground one after another, pile up on the ground; fall flat on the ground

stër**vec** *nm* rain falling at an angle

stër**vin**ë *nf* animal carcass, carrion

stër**vit**· *vt* to train/teach [] by means of drill

stër**vit**·*et vpr* **1** to undergo training **2** to exercise, practice, drill

stër**vit**ës *nm* trainer

stër**vit**je *nf ger* **1** <stër**vit**·, stër**vit**·*et* **2** drill, training, exercise, practice

stër**vit**or *adj* pertaining to or useful for drill/training/exercise/practice

stër**vit**ur

  I § part <stër**vit**·, stër**vit**·*et*
  II § adj (i) trained, well-trained

stër**vjedh**ës *n* one who steals something stolen earlier

stër**vjet**ër *adj (i)* extremely old; timeworn

*stër**xe**·*n vt* = stërnxeh·

*stër**rall** *nm* flint = strall

*stif *nm* = stivë

*stif**o**·*n vt* = stivo·*n*

*stig**mat**ë *nf [Bot]* stigma

stig**mat**i**zim** *nm ger* **1** *(Book)* <stigmatizo·*n* **2** denunciation

stig**mat**i**zo**·*n vt (Book)* to censure forcibly: denounce, decry

stig**mat**i**zue**s *adj (Book)* with forcible censure: damning, denunciatory

stihi' *nf* **1** *[Myth]* fire-breathing winged fury; serpent who guards a netherworld treasure **2** *(Fig Book)* uncontrollable violent force: fury **3** overgrown monster

*stih**o**·*n vt* = nguc·

stik**ë** *nf [Bot]* = fëstek

stil *nm* style

  ∘ **stil bretkose** *[Sport]* swimming frog-style: breaststroke

  ∘ **stil flutur** *[Swimming]* butterfly stroke

  ∘ **stil i lartë** *[Ling]* elevated style

  ∘ **stil në ijë** *[Sport]* sidestroke in swimming

stil**ist** *n* **1** stylist **2** person who studies stylistics

stil**ist**ik *adj* stylistic

stil**ist**ikë *nf* stylistics

stil**ist**iki**sht** *adv* stylistically

stil**ist**ikor *adj* = stilistik

stil**izim** *nm ger* **1** <stilizo·*n* **2** stylization

stil**izo**·*n vt* to stylize

stilo**graf** *nm* **1** fountain pen *2 = stilolaps

stilo**kalem** *nm* = stilolaps

stilo**laps** *nm* ball-point pen

*stim**ë** *nf* esteem, high regard

stim**ul** *nm (np ~ij)* **1** stimulant, stimulus **2** incentive

  ∘ **stimul moral** moral incentive

stim**ulim** *nm ger* **1** <stimulo·*n*, stimulo·*het* **2** stimulation

stim**ulo**·*n vt* to stimulate; give an incentive to []

stimulu|es nm **1** stimulating; giving an incentive **2** [Biol] stimulant

stinë nf season (of the year)

stin|**im** nm ger = **staxhioni**m

stin|**o**·het vpr = **staxhiono**·het

stin|**o**·n vt = **staxhiono**·n

stin|**o**r adj seasonal

stipë**s** nm [Min] alum

*__stip__|**k**ë nf [Ornit] small lake-bird

stis· vt (Colloq) **1** to build/make [] extemporaneously: make up [] on the spot, improvise; build. make **2** to make up [something untrue], devise [something bad]

stis·et vpr (Colloq) **1** to get all dressed up **2** to come into being, be generated/created

stis|**ës** n (Colloq) builder/maker (of something informal); improviser, deviser

stis|**je** nf (Colloq) informal construction/building; improvisation

stivë = **stivo**·n

stiv|**im** nm ger < **stivo**·n

stiv|**o**·n vt to place [] in a stack: stack

s|**tjegull** nf part of the roof from which the water drips: edge of the eaves

*__stoçe__n nm (Reg Tosk) cold east wind; gale

stof nm (np ˜ra) wool fabric

*__stof__ë = **stuf**ë

stog nm (np ˜gje) haystack, hayrick

stoic|**izë**m nm stoicism

stoik adj, n stoic

stok nm (np ˜qe) supply of material/goods: stock

stokatriç**e** nf [Tech] slotting machine

stol nm **1** stool (for sitting) **2** bench (for sitting)

stolë nf [Relig] (ecclesiastical vestment) stole

stoli nf adornment; decoration

stoli|**s**· vt to adorn; decorate

stoli|**s**·et vpr to adorn oneself, dress up

stoli|**s**|**je** nf ger **1** < **stoli**s·, **stoli**s·et **2** = **stoli**

stoli|**sur** adj (i) adorned, decorated

stolon nm [Bot] stolon

stom·n nm embankment; ridge

stomak nm [Anat] stomach

stomato|**lo**g n [Med] stomatologist ()

stomato|**logji** nf [Med] stomatology ()

*__stom__n ë nf= **shtamb**ë

stom|**o**·n vt to bank [] up, embank

ston|**im** nm dissonance, discord, discordance

ston|**o**·n vi to be out of tune, be dissonant

ston|**ue**s adj dissonant, discordant, discordant

stop interj (Colloq) command given to halt: stop! halt!

stopan nm = **stana**r

stopan|**e**|**sh**ë nf < **stopa**n

*__stop__|**is** = **stapi**s

*__stop__|**it** = **stapi**t·

stop|**o**·n vt [Soccer] to trap [a ball]

*__stor__|**as** = **stora**zi

*__stora__s· vt to erect

*__stora__s·et vpr to stand up/erect; rear up

*__stora__s|je nf ger < **stora**s·, **stora**s·et

*__stora__|**sur** adj (i) standing, erect

*__stor__|**azi** adv standing on end, upright, erect

strabi|**z**ë**m** nm [Med] strabismus, squint

stra|**g**ë nf [Ichth] Twaite shad from a year old to sexual maturity

*__stra__|**h**ë nf slab (of rock); flagstone

stra|**jc**ë nf= **tra**st**ë**

*__strako__l nm leash

*__strakulshe__|**d**ë**r** nf dragon = **kuçe**d**ë**r

strall

  I § nm (np ˜je) flint

  II § adj hard as flint

stra|**ll**t**ë** adj (i) **1** made of flint **2** (Fig) hard as flint

stramastik

  I § adj [Bot Zool] hybrid

  II § nm child of mixed parentage

*__stramulla__r = **strumbulla**r

stran|**ic**ë nf **1** (Reg) sidebeam of a rackwagon bed to which the railings are fixed = **përbrij**ë**s**e **2** board placed over the corpse in the grave before covering with dirt **3** gravestone

strapac nm (Reg) extreme exertion, strain

strapac|**o**·n vt (Reg) to put great strain on [], be hard on []: strain, wear [] out

*__strapc__ nm [Ornit] sparrow

strateg nm **1** military strategist **2** (Fig) skillful military commander **3** (FigElevated) great political leader **4** [Hist] commanding military officer in ancient Greece and in the Byzantine Empire: strategus

strategj|**i** nf strategy

strategj|**i**k adj strategic

stratifik|**im** nm [Geol] stratification = **shtresi**m

stratigrafi nf stratigraphy

stratosfer**ë** nf stratosphere

strave|**c**ë nf short embroidered apron with long fringes hanging from the bottom, which is worn by women in parts of northern Albania as part of their ethnic costume

*__str__ê**(n)** nm (np ˜j) (Reg Gheg) hen roost, chicken coop

*__stred__|**it**·et vpr to loom up, suddenly appear

*__stre__dh· vt = **zhdre**dh·

stre|**g**ë nf **1** stacked sheaves of grain: shock of grain **2** stack, pile, heap = **stiv**ë

streh|**aca**k adj, n (person) wandering around aimlessly

strehë nf **1** eaves, overhang **2** shelter; housing **3** (Fig) refuge, asylum **4** hat brim **5** shed

  ○ **streh**ë **vorfë**nore "shelter for the poor" orphanage

streh|**im** nm ger **1** < **streho**·n, **streho**·het **2** shed **3** shelter; housing **4** temporary refuge, asylum **5** [Mil] bomb shelter

  ○ **strehim politik** political asylum

streh|**o**·het vpr **1** to find shelter, take shelter **2** to take refuge

streh|**o**·n vt **1** to give [] shelter to []: shelter **2** to give refuge to []

streh|**ore** nf [Hist] broad wicker shield against arrows and stones

streh|**ue**s nm person who gives refuge: harborer

stre|**l**ë nf doghouse

strem nm (covered) wagon; military wagon of earlier times

strem**ë** nf (Old) land measure equal to about a third of an acre

streptokok nm [Med] streptococcus

streptomicinë nf [Pharm] streptomycin

*strëk-strëk *onomat* (of cowbells) tinkle tinkle

stricë *nf* **1** game in which two opponents each play their three stones into a square divided into four smaller squares = **tresh 2** [*Ornit*] gray wagtail (*Motacilla cinerea*)

*stridh *stem for 2nd pl pres, pind, imper, vp* < **stre dh·**

stridhe-lugë *nf* [*Invert*] fan shell (*Neopycnodonte cochlear*)

stridhë *nf* oyster (*Ostrea edulis*)

striknínë *nf* strychnine

strikt *adj* strict

stringë = **stringël**

stringël *nf* **1** small metal ornament worn by women on the chest/waist **2** small trinket, knick-knack

*strodh *stem for pdef* < **stre dh·**

strofak *nm* = **strofkë**

strofë *nf* [*Lit*] strophe, stanza
  ○ **strofë dyshe** [*Lit*] couplet
  ○ **strofë gjashtëshe** six-line stanza
  ○ **strofë katërshe** [*Lit*] four-line stanza, quatrain

strofkë *nf* den, lair

strofull *nm* (¯ *j*) **1** = **strofkë 2** [*Med*] strophulus, red gum

strok· *vt* to infect [] with scabies/mange

strok·et *vpr* to become infected with scabies/mange

strokaq *adj* **1** having scabies: mangy, scabious **2** (*Impol Insult*) feeble, weakling

strokë *nf* **1** mange, scabies **2** unshorn wool left on the forequarters of the belwether

stromë
  I § *nf* **1** bed pad, mattress **2** saddle pad = **stelë 3** garden plot, garden bed **4** [*Biol*] tissue framework supporting an organ: stroma
  II § *np* bedding

strongilozë *nf* [*Veter*] strongylosis

*strongjílos = **strongilozë**

struc *nm* ostrich

*strudh *nm* [*Ornit*] ostrich = **struth**

*strufë *nf* tin = **teneqe**
  ○ **strufë shale** stirrup

strug *nm* (*np* ¯ *gje*) (carpenter's) plane = **zdrukth**

strugë
  I § *nf* woolen blanket used as a cloak; white woolen cloak worn by livestock herders in parts of northern Albania
  II § *nf* **1** wetlands with marshland shrubs; swamp, pond **2** stream of water

*strugo·n *vt* = **zdruktho·n**

strujak *nm* **1** petty thief; pickpocket **2** (*Old Contempt*) smalltime village thief: local pilferer

strujni *nf* pilferage

struk·et *vpr* **1** to cringe, cower; huddle up; huddle together **2** to go into hiding, take refuge

strukë *nf* **1** refuge, hideout, lair **2** scarf

strukët *adj* (*i*) huddled up; cringing

strukje *nf ger* < **struk·et**

strukturalíst *adj* structuralist

strukturalízëm *nm* structuralism

strukturë *nf* structure

strukturor *adj* [*Spec*] structural

strukull *nm* (*np* ¯ *j*) chicken coop

strum *nm* **1** deep pool in a river; deep pond under a waterfall **2** drainage line **3** marshy land, swampland

strumbull *nm* (*np* ¯ *j*) **1** site of habitation **2** = **strumbullar 3** [*Tech*] axle **4** haycock

strumbullar *nm* **1** center post in a threshing floor to which a horse is tied and then driven in ever smaller circles to trample the sheaves of grain **2** (*Fig*) pivotal figure/object **3** pole at the center of a haycock **4** haycock **5** (*Reg*) goad, prod = **hosten 6** (*Old Colloq*) cylindrical object, roller

strumbullo·n *vi* [*Tech*] to revolve around an axis

strumë *nf* [*Med*] **1** goiter **2** exophthalmic goiter (*Basedow's disease*)

strung *nm* (*np* ¯ *gj*) wattled hurdle used to control the movements of sheep = **shtrungë**

strunxë *nf* hard shove (with the hand); slap

strup *nm* (*Reg*) **1** grime on a baby's head **2** = **rrebull**

*strupull *nm* bunch, tuft; heap

*struth *nm* [*Ornit*] ostrich (*Struthio camelus*)

student *n* student (in an institution of higher education)
  ○ **student i mbrëmjes** night-school student

studentesk *adj* = **studentor**

studentor *adj* of or pertaining to students

studim *nm ger* **1** < **studo·n, studo·het 2** study

studimor *adj* associated with or devoted to serious/scientific study

studio *nf* studio

studio·n *vt, vi* to study

studioz *adj* studious

studiues *nm* person who studies a subject: student, scholar, researcher

stufë *nf* stove (for heating/cooking)

stuhí *nf* **1** long storm with wind and rain/snow: storm **2** (*Fig*) protracted outburst **3** (*Fig*) unexpected tribulation

stuhíshëm *adj* (*i*) **1** stormy **2** (*Fig*) sudden and with great force

stukim *nm ger* < **stuko·n, stuko·het**

stuko *nf* **1** putty **2** stucco

stuko·n *vt* to apply putty to []: putty, lute

stumbo *nf* with *masc agreement* potbellied man

*sturë *nf* floor mat made of woven reeds

suadhe *nf* **1** bulbous end of the body of a killed and plucked fowl: tail **2** hemorrhoids, piles = **majasëll**

suaj *fem gen dat abl* < **juaj** your

suall *stem for pl pdef* < **sjell·**

suazë *nf* **1** frame (for pictures/eyeglasses) **2** (*Fig*) limiting framework, framework

suber *nm* [*Bot*] cork oak (*Quercus suber*)

subjekt *nm* **1** subject **2** [*Lit*] plot
  ○ **subjekt i krimit** [*Law*] criminal suspect

subjektiv *adj* subjective

subjektivíst *adj* subjectivist, subjectivistic

subjektivísht *adv* subjectively

subjektivízëm *nm* subjectivism

substancë *nf* substance

subtitër *nm* [*Cine*] subtitle

subtitrim *nm* [*Cine*] adding subtitles: subtitling

subvencion *nm* [*Fin*] subvention, subsidy

subvencionim *nm ger* [*Fin*] **1** < **subvenciono·n 2** subsidization **3** = **subvencion**

subvenciono·n *vt* [*Fin*] to give a subvention to []; support [] with a subvention: subsidize

subversiv *adj* (*Book Pej*) subversive

Sudan *nf* Sudan

sudan|ez *adj, n* Sudanese

suede|z
I § *adj* Swedish
II § *n* Swede

Suedi *nf* Sweden

suedi|sht *adv* in Swedish (language)

suedi|shte *nf* Swedish language

suferinë *nf* strong, cold and wet wind

*****sufër** *nf* 1 [*Bot*] brier *(Erica arborea)* *2 = sofër

suficit *nm* [*Fin*] surplus

suficitar *adj* [*Fin*] showing a surplus

sufiks *nm* [*Ling*] suffix

sufiksim *nm* [*Ling*] suffixation

sufler *nm* 1 prompter (in a theater) 2 *(Fig)* person (pupil) who whispers the answer to another person; person who suggests a response

*****sufluk** *nm* span between the stretched thumb and forefinger

sufrim *nm ger* <sufro·*n*

sufro·n *vt* to whisper to []

*****sufros·** *vt* to inflate, swell

*****sufros·et** *vpr* to swell up

*****sufrues** *n* = sufler

sugar *nm (Reg)* 1 suckling lamb, late-born lamb separated from its mother 2 *(Fig Pet)* youngest child; darling little boy, pet/favorite child

*****sugur** = sigur

sugjerim *nm ger* <sugjero·*n* 2 suggestion

sugjero·n *vt* to suggest

sugjestion *nm* suggestion

sugjestionim *nm ger* <sugjestiono·*n*, sugjestiono·*het*

sugjestiono·het *vpr* to be influenced by suggestion

sugjestiono·n *vt* to influence [] by suggestion

sugjestiv *adj (Book)* suggestive

*****suha|dhe** *nf* piles, hemorrhoids

suitë *nf* 1 *(Book)* entourage 2 [*Mus*] suite 3 [*Geol*] rock series

sukale *nf* land at the foot of a mountain

sukë *nf* hump of land, hillock, small hill

sukore *nf* hummock

sukses *nm* success

sukses|shëm *adj (i)* successful

sukull *nm (np ~j)* 1 wadded-up cleaning rag 2 *(Fig)* old clothes, worthless rags 3 globular mass: wad, clump 4 long tubular fishing net with a series of wooden hoops: eel trap, eel pot, eel basket

sukullar *adj* dressed in rags

sukullo·n *vt* 1 to wad up []; wrap up [] carelessly 2 to tear [] to rags 3 *(Fig)* to abuse, maltreat

sul *nm* tree trunk hollowed out to make a boat: dugout

sul·et *vpr* 1 to rush/dash/charge forward 2 *(Fig)* to throw oneself into <*a task*> 3 *(Colloq)* to attack <> with words: lambaste <>, chew <> out

Sul *nm* ethnographic region in northern Greece: Suli

sule *nf* small, long and narrow, flat-bottomed rowboat: skiff

Sulejman *nm* Sulejman (male name)

sulë *nf* [*Ornit*] gannet *(Sulidae)*

sulfamid *nm* [*Pharm*] sulfanilamide

sulfat *nm* [*Chem*] sulfate

sulfur *nm* [*Chem*] 1 sulfurous mineral 2 sulfur = squfur

sulfurik *adj* [*Chem*] sulfuric

sulfurim *nm ger* 1 [*Chem*] <sulfuro·*n* 2 = squfurim

sulfuro·n *vt* [*Chem*] to sulfurate

sulfuror *adj* [*Chem*] sulfurous

sulinë *nf* narrow metal pipeline; water conduit/pipe

suljot
I § *adj* of or pertaining to Sul
II § *n* native of Sul

sulm *nm* aggressive act of violence: attack, assault
∘ *{period of time}* **sulmi** *{}* of concentrated attack on a problem
∘ **Në sulm!** [*Mil*] Attack!
∘ **sulm i tërbuar** violent onslaught

sulmim *nm ger* <sulmo·*n*

sulmo·n *vt* to attack

sulmues
I § *adj* 1 used for or engaged in attacking 2 aggressive, vigorous, energetic; distinguished by efforts to surpass norms
II § *n* 1 person on the attack: attacker, aggressor 2 energetic worker
∘ **sulmues krahu** [*Soccer*] wing forward

sulur *nn (të)* sudden dash; sudden onslaught

sullë *nf* [*Bot*] Italian sainfoin, French honeysuckle *(Hedysarum coronarium)*

sultan *nm* sultan

sultanat *nm* sultanate

sultane|shë *nf* mother or wife of the sultan: sultana, sultaness

sultankë *nf* [*Ichth*] = kubël

*****sullupje|së** *nf* [*Bot*] wood-sorrel *(Oxalis acetosella)*

*****sumak** *nm* [*Bot*] = shqeme

*****sumaro·n** *vi* to become verdant, turn green

*****sumbë** *nf* = sumë

sumbull *nf* 1 small round button: knob 2 [*Bot*] leaf bud 3 small metal ball used as an ornament 4 globular drop of liquid: drop

sumbullare *nf* 1 [*Bot*] common hop *(Humulus lupulus)* 2 traveller's joy, old man's beard *(Clematis vitalba)*

sumbullo·n *vi* (of a tree) to come into bud: bud

sumbullore *nf* barren strip running up the slope of a mountain

sumë *nf* 1 *(Crude)* ass, arse, butt *2 sum

sundim *nm ger* 1 <sundo·*n* 2 domination, rule 3 period of rule, reign 4 ruled domain

sundimtar *nm* 1 sovereign, ruler 2 [*Hist*] district regent

sundo·n
I § *vi* to reign, rule; be dominant
II § *vt* 1 to rule over [] 2 to dominate; control
∘ **e sundo·n veten** to have self-control

sundues
I § *adj* dominant; ruling
II § *n* dominator; ruler

sunduk *nm* storage chest

*****sungë** = sumbë

*****sungjer** = sfungjer

*****sungji** = syngji

*****suni** *np masc* Sunni Moslems

sup *nm* upper surface of the shoulder: shoulder
∘ **Sup-armë!** [*Mil*] Shoulder arms!

○ **sup më sup** shoulder to shoulder

*supa·të = sëpatë

super formative prefix super-

super automatík adj completely automatic

super fosfat nm superphosphate (chemical fertilizer)

super fuqí nf superpower

superio·r
 I § adj higher, upper
 II § adj, n superior

superioritet nm (Book) superiority

superlatív nm superlative

superme·n nm superman

super merkatë nf supermarket

super prodhím nm [Econ] overproduction = mbiprodhím

super soník adj [Spec] supersonic

supersticio·n nm superstition

supersticio·z adj superstitious

super struktu·rë nf superstructure

super struktur o·r adj superstructural

supë nf 1 soup; broth 2 bowlful of soup/broth

supëz nf shoulder strap

supie·rë = supje·rë

*supje nf [Ichth] = se·pje

supje·rë nf soup tureen

suplementa·r adj (Book) supplementary

sup o·r adj of the shoulder

sup o·re nf (Colloq) epaulet = spale·të

supo·rt nm [Tech] tool carriage/saddle

supozím nm ger (Book) 1 <supozo·n, supozo·het 2 assumption 3 supposition

supozo·het vpr 1 (Book) to be assumed 2 to be supposed

supozo·n vt, vi (Book) 1 to assume 2 to suppose

*suprav = soprav

supre·m adj (OfficElevated) supreme

suprem ací nf (OfficElevated) supremacy

suprimím nm ger 1 (OfficElevated) <suprimo·n 2 suppression

suprimo·n vt (OfficElevated) to suppress; discontinue, suspend

sur nm facial feature

*sura·t nm = surra·t

surb· vt to sip; slurp

*surbelë nf [Bot] sage (Salvia officinalis)

surb o·n vt = surb·

su·rbull adj (of eggs) soft-boiled

*surdís·et vpr to have diarrhea

su·re nf [Relig] chapter of the Koran: sura

*surfull = shqufur

*sur gja·të nf having a long face

su·rle nf [Mus] folk shawm

surmë adj (i) dark gray

surprízë nf surprise

*su·rup nm roof gutter = ulluk

su·rvë nf [Bot] mountain ash = va·dhë

surra·t nm (Colloq) 1 face 2 (Pej) ugly/dirty face; snout-face; evil person 3 scarecrow = dordole·c

surrealíst adj, n [Art] surrealist

surrealízëm nm [Art] surrealism

surre·tër OR surre·ta np = surra·t (Old) celebration at carnival time with masks and colorful costumes

surrík nm chicken coop

*surríl = curríl

surroga·t nm 1 ersatz substitute 2 (Fig) pale imitation

*surrulla = soro·lla

su·rrzël nf [Anat] mucous membrane

sus
 I § adv 1 (of a dog) standing on its hind legs 2 (Fig) keeping quiet and well-behaved (under pressure by an authority)
 II § interj quiet!, sh!

susa·k nm 1 [Bot] bottle gourd, calabash (Lagenaria vulgaris) = kungulli gjës 2 gourd made into a bottle: gourd bottle

susa·m nm [Bot] sesame (Sesamum indica)

su·sme nf woven/embroidered/carved floral figure

su·stë nf 1 (elastic) spring 2 bed frame with interwoven bedsprings 3 push button 4 snap fastener 5 (Fig Pej) motivating force

suta·k nm (Reg) skull

su·të nf 1 [Zool] doe 2 (Fig) pretty and graceful girl; nice girl 3 [Folklore] character in folktales that appears with a cow-like form

sutu·rë nf [Med] suture

suva nf coat of plaster (on walls/ceilings)

*suvajkë = sovajkë

suva·l nm big snake believed to kill its prey by strangling

suva·lë nf billowing/raging wave

suvarí nm (np ~ nj) (Old) Ottoman cavalryman; cavalryman used as a rear bodyguard by a bey

suvatím nm ger <suvato·n

suvato·n vt to apply (a coat of) plaster to [ ]

suvato·r n plasterer

suvatu·es
 I § adj used for plastering
 II § n plasterer

suva·xhi nm (np ~ nj) = suvato·r

*su·vër nm [Bot] service tree (Sorbus domestica)

suxhu·k nm 1 [Food] liver sausage 2 Turkish delight filled with walnuts and shaped like a sausage

Suza·na nf Suzana (female name)

su·zhë nf dryness, aridity

SVEA abbrev (Italian) <Societa Svilupo Economico dell'Albania [Hist] Association for the Economic Development of Albania (1925-1944)

*Sve·ce OR Sve·cje nf (Old) Sweden = Suedí

*svede·z = suede·z

*Svedí = Suedí

*s verdh = zverdh

*Svicër = Zvicër

*svicëra·n adj, n = zvicëra·n

s vi·rdh stem for 2nd pl pres, pind, imper, vp <svjer dh·

*s vje·rdh· = zvjer dh·

*s vo·rdh stem for pdef <svjer dh·

sy(r)
 I § nm 1 eye 2 eyesight 3 expression conveyed by the eyes 4 (Colloq) good appearance 5 (Fig) good position for observation: good view 6 loop in the end of a thread or rope 7 [Tech] round hole for inserting something 8 [Anat] (bone) joint 9 [Publ] face of a raised character on a piece of type

II § *np (Colloq)* face

○ **s'ka· sy e faqe** to be ashamed to show oneself, be ashamed to face the world

○ **s'ka· sy** not look like much, not be presentable

○ **s'mbyll· sy** not close one's eyes (all night): not get any sleep

syártë *nf [Invert]* lacewing fly

sybajáme *adj* almond-eyed

sybárdhë
I § *adj, n* (person) with light gray eyes
II § *nm [Bot]* spiny clotbur, spiny cocklebur *(Xanthium spinosum)*

syblértër *nf [Entom]* kind of cereal pest *(Chlorops pumilionis Bjen.)*

syç *nm* fear of saying the wrong thing: shyness

syçakërr *adj (Pej)* cross-eyed, cockeyed

syçelë
I § *adj* = **syhápur**
II § *adv* with eyes open

syçelët *adj* = **syhápur**

syçkë *nf* **1** *(Pet)* pretty little eye **2** eyelet **3** *[Entom]* (of an insect) stigma *()* **4** bud **5** small hole (in a stocking)

sydrejtë *adj* having a sharpshooter's eye, straight-shooting

sydhelpër *adj* wily, sly

syegër *adj* fierce, wild-eyed

*syenë *nf* deep pool in a body of water; fishing area

syfýr *nm [Relig]* pre-dawn food eaten by observant Moslems during Ramadan

sygacë *adj* = **syshkëndijë**

sygështenjë *adj* having dark brown eyes

sygrifshë *adj* having light-colored eyes with vari-colored specks

sygjallë *adj* having lively eyes

sygjarpër *nm* **1** *[Bot]* prickly poppy *(Papaver argemone)* **2** yellow vetchling *(Lathyrus aphaca)*

syhapët *adj* = **syhápur**

syhaptësi *nf* vigilance

syhápur *adj* **1** open-eyed **2** *(Fig)* vigilant

syjeshíle *nf [Ichth]* shortnose greeneye *(Chlorophthalmus agassizii)*

syka *nm (obl ˉu) [Bot]* **1** garden anemone *(Anemone stellata)* **2** common dandelion *(Taraxacum officinale)*

sykaçkë *adj (i)* = **syrrúsh**

sykaltër
I § *adj* blue-eyed
II § *nf [Entom]* = **syblertër**

sykán *nm, adj* (white ram) with dark rings around the eyes or dark blotches on the muzzle

sykáth *nm* sty on the eyelid

sykéq *adj, n* **1** (person) with the evil eye **2** envious (person)

sykë *nf, adj* (white ewe) with dark patches on the face

sykëm *adj (i)* (of livestock) with dark patches on the face: motley colored, piebald

syko *nf, adj* (cow/calf) with dark markings around the eyes

sykúq
I § *adj* (of livestock) having brown rings around the eyes
II § *nf [Ichth]* Italian roach *(Rutilus rutilus rubilio Bonaparte)*

sylárë *adj* = **sylarúsh**

sylármë *adj* = **sylarúsh**

sylarósh = **sylarúsh**

sylarúsh *adj* having light-colored eyes with dark specks

sylarúshle *nf (Poet)* girl with speckled blue eyes

sylésh *adj, n* (person) who is blind to what is going on, easily duped/confused: wooly-minded

syltepríç *nm [Food]* rice pudding = **sytliaç**

syltiaç *[Food]* rice pudding

syluga̋t *adj (Insult)* eyes wide with greed, insatiable

sylynjar *nm* spout at a spring

sylýqe *nf [Zool]* tadpole

syll *adj* cross-eyed, cockeyed

syllambyllthi *adv* blindfolded; playing while blindfolded

syllít· *vt (Pej)* to watch [] out of the corner of the eye

symáce *adj (Pej)* having shiny light-colored eyes like a cat's

symádh *adj (i), masc sg* having large eyes: big-eyed

symádhe *adj (e) fem sg* = **symádh**

symanusháqe *adj* blue-eyed

symátje *nf* measurement/estimate made by the unassisted eye: eyeball measurement

*symbol *nm* symbol

symbyllas *OR* **symbyllazi** *adv* **1** with one's eyes shut **2** *(Fig)* without needing to look, with thorough familiarity **3** *(Fig)* without due consideration: blindly, rashly

symbylltas = **symbyllas**

symbyllthi *adv* **1** *(Fig)* without needing to look, with thorough familiarity **2** *(Fig)* without due consideration: rashly

symbyllurazi = **symbyllas**

symëdha *adj (të) fem pl* = **symádh**

symëdhenj *adj (të) masc pl* = **symádh**

symëshqerrë *adj (Pet)* having big soft eyes (like a lamb's)

symízë *adj* having small dark eyes

*sympath = **simpat**

symprehtë *adj* sharp-eyed, sharp-sighted

symprehtësi *nf* sharp-sightedness

synét *nm* ritual circumcision

synetllëk *nm (np ˉ qe)* Moslem ceremony for a circumcision

syneto̊·n *vt* to circumcise

*syngjer = **sfungjer**

syngjí *nf (Old)* bayonet

syním *nm* **1** intention **2** *(Pej)* evil intention

syno̊·n
I § *vt* to intend
II § *vi* to aim (with a weapon)

synór *nm [Spec]* eyepiece, ocular

sypafjétur *adj* ever-vigilant

sypallúa *nm (obl ˉoi) [Agr]* olive scab *(Cyclocomium oleaginum)*

*sypámës *n (Old)* eyewitness

sypanginjur *adj (i)* insatiable, greedy

sypatrémbur *adj (Elev)* unflinching, dauntless

sypetrít *adj (Elev)* **1** sharp-sighted, eagle-eyed **2** *(Fig)* stouthearted, courageous

sypërdhe *adv* with downcast eyes

sy|për·gja|kun *adj (i) (Old Regional Gheg)* bloodshot

sy|përmby's *adv, adj* = sypërmby'sur

sy|përmby's|ur
I § *adv* with lowered head and gloomy face; with glance averted
II § *adj* furtive

sy|pish|ë *adj (i)* watchful, vigilant

sy|pla's|ët *adj (i)* 1 = sypla'sur *2 callous

sy|pla's|ur *adj* 1 *(Pej)* blind, as if blind; careless; easily deceived 2 *(Curse)* may his eyes go blind! 3 evil-eyed (person)

*sypra'n *adj (Old)* sovereign

*sypra'ni *nf (Old)* sovereignty

syprin|ë *nf* 1 upper surface, surface 2 upper part of shoes: uppers 3 *[Geom]* plane surface

*sypro'r *adj* superior

*sypro'ri *nf* superiority

sy|qe'n|ëz *nf [Folklore]* malevolent old woman with two eyes in front and two behind who appears in Albanian folktales

sy|qershi *adj* having beautiful eyes

sy|qe'sh|ur *adj* with laughing eyes, with a happy countenance

*sy|qo'k *nm [Ornit]* rook = stërqo'k

syrdis· *vt* = syrgjyno's·

sy're'sh *3rd pl pron abl (Old Poet)* of them

*sy're'sh shelf

sy'rëz *np masc* small bubbles that form in a liquid; cluster/line of bubbles

syrgjy'n
I § *nm (Colloq)* 1 banishment, exile 2 exiled person: exile
II § *adj* in exile

syrgjyno's· *vt (Colloq)* to banish, exile

syrgjyno's|je *nf ger (Colloq)* <syrgjyno's·, syrgjyno's·*et*

syrgjyno's|ur *adj (i), n (i)* banished/exiled (person) in exile

sy'r|i *obl* <sy(r)
○ Syri i bardhë si një kokërr dardhë. "The white eye like a pear fruit." *(Prov)* Judging from { }'s looks, { } seems very nice.
○ syri i gjurit *[Anat]* kneecap
○ syri i keq/lig 1 evil eye 2 evil spell
○ syri i këmbës ankle
○ syri i padovës *[Entom]* giant silkworm moth, large emperor moth, giant peacock moth *Saturnia pyri*
○ syri i palloit *[Agr]* = sypallu*a*
○ Syri plot e dora thatë. "Full eye and empty hand." *(Prov)* Plenty around, but it's impossible to get any. Water water everywhere and not a drop to drink.

*sy'rm|ë *nf* silver thread/wire; metal filament

*syrta'r = sirta'r

*sy|rrëm|a'kt|ë *adj* squinting

sy|rrëm|u'e's *adj* having piercing eyes

sy|rru'sh *adj* pop-eyed

sysk *adj* (of a livestock animal) having markings around the eyes

sy'sk|ë *nf* livestock animal with markings around the eyes

*syste'm = siste'm

sy|shkëndi'j|ë *adj* having sparkling/flashing eyes

sy|shkru'a'r *adj (Poet)* speckled blue eyes

sy|shqipo'nj|ë *adj* sharp-sighted: eagle-eyed

sy|shtrë'mb|ër *adj* cross-eyed, cockeyed

sy|shtrë'mb|ët = syshtrë'mb|ër

sy'ta'r *adj* sharpshooter, marksman

*sytja'sh = sytlia'ç

sytje'n|ë *nf* brassiere, bra

sytlia'ç *nm [Food]* = sytlia'ç

sy|to'kas *adv* 1 with eyes looking at the ground 2 *(Fig)* looking down ashamedly

sy'th
I § *nm* 1 *[Bot]* leafbud 2 eyelet; buttonhole; small hole in fabric/leather 3 knitted/tied/crocheted loop 4 eyehole in a door 5 each pouch in a double saddle-bag; drawer (in furniture) 6 marginal note (in a book or newspaper) 7 *(Fig)* bubble in a surface
II § *adv* with one's own eyes, for certain
○ syth i fjetur leafbud that never opens

sy'th· *vt* to make a loop in [ ] and tighten it; tighten [a loop]

*sy|the'll|ë *adj* having deep-set eyes; hollow-eyed

*sy|thje'rm|ë *adj* hazel-eyed

sy'u = syri

sy|ulli *adj* dark-eyed

sy|vë'ng|ër *adj* cross-eyed, cockeyed

sy|vi'çe *nf [Bot]* corn chamomile *(Anthemis arvendsis)*

sy|xi'x|ë *adj* = syshkëndi'j|ë

syz *nm (Colloq)* star (in the sky)

sy'|za *np* = sy'ze

sy'|ze *np fem* eyeglasses, glasses, spectacles
○ syze mbrojtëse protective goggles

sy'ze *adj* eye-like: oval in shape

sy|ze'z|ë *fem* <syzi

sy'|zë *nf* 1 drawer (in furniture) 2 cell in a honeycomb 3 leafbud 4 knitted/tied/crocheted loop 5 *(Fig)* bubble in a surface

sy|zë'n|ë *adj* ashamed to show one's face

sy|zi *adj, n (fem sg ~ëz, masc pl ~inj, fem pl ~eza)* dark-eyed (one)

sy'z|kë *nf* = sy'sk|ë

sy|zo·*het vpr* to encounter/confront someone

sy|zo·*n vt* 1 to bring [ ] forth as evidence (before <>'s very eyes); propose, proffer; confront <> with [ ] 2 to figure out [ ]

sh [*shë*] *nf* **1** the consonant digraph "sh" **2** the voiceless lamino-palatal sibilant represented by the digraph "sh"

sh
  I § formative prefix (only before a voiceless obstruent) indicating the opposite or reverse of the meaning of the stem to which it is attached un-, de-, dis-
  II § causative pref en-

sha = pa**sha**

sha·het *vpr* <**sha·n** **1** to trade insults; speak abusively, yell at each other **2** to complain loudly

sha·n
  I § *vt* **1** to abuse [] with language: cuss at; scold, upbraid **2** to find fault with []
  II § *vi* to complain loudly
  ○ [] **sha·n me rrënjë (e me degë)** "upbraid [] by root and by root/branch" to heap verbal abuse on [], cuss [] out harshly
  ○ [] **sha·n me rroc e me koc** to abuse [] severely with language: cuss [] out nastily
  ○ **Sha·**³*ˢᵍ* **shtamba të zotin** "the pot *maligns* the master" (*Iron*) (said of someone who speaks ill of the person who made him what he is)

*__*shaba*__ *nf* tripe

shabak|im *nm ger* <**shabako·het**

shabako·het *vpr* to revel in overeating and drinking: carouse

*__*shabi*__ *nf* [*Bot*] garden sage (*Salvia officinalis*)

shabllon
  I § *nm* **1** pattern; template **2** (*Fig*) mechanical copy: cliché
  II § *adv* (*Pej*) in a mechanical way, without any creativity

shabllon|ist
  I § *n* **1** worker who operates from a pattern/die/mold **2** person who is imitative in a mechanical way: copycat, slavish imitator, cliché artist
  II § *adj* (*Fig Pej*) imitative in a mechanical way: copy-cat

shabllon|izëm *nm* (*Pej*) mechanical/slavish imitation

*__*shaboj*__**ë** *nf* = sheboj**ë**

shadok *nm* [*Bot*] shaddock, pomelo *Citrus grandis*

shafia|n *nm* sheepskin leather

*__*shafis*__| *stem for 1st sg pres, pl pres, 2nd & 3rd sg subj, pind* <**shafi|t·**

*__*shafi|t·*__ *vt* to palliate

*__*shafi|t|ës*__ *adj, nm* palliative

shafra|n
  I § *nm* **1** saffron **2** [*Bot*] saffron crocus (*Crocus sativa*)
  II § *adj* saffron-colored; having a saffron taste

shag *nm* heavy coarse cloth made of flax or hemp and used as simple floor/body covering or as sacking: sackcloth; object made of sackcloth

shaga|s| *stem for 1st sg pres, pl pres, 2nd & 3rd sg subj, pind* <**shaga|t·**

shaga|t· *vt* (*Reg*) to needle; mock

*__*shaga|t*__**ë** *nf* mockery

sha|ge *nf* (*Reg*) **1** heavy coarse cloth made of flax or hemp and used as simple floor/body covering or as sacking: sackcloth; object made of sackcloth = zha**k**ë **2** woman's skirt made of sackcloth **3** potholder, hot pad

shag|it· *vi* to crawl on one's belly

shah
  I § *nm* **1** chess **2** check (in chess) **3** shah
  II § *adv* **1** standing on the hind legs: rearing up **2** frozen in place: petrified = **shtang** **3** alone and abandoned, wretched
  ○ **nuk shah·et**³*ˢᵍ* it's not so bad
  ○ **shah·et**ᵖˡ **e përshah·et**ᵖˡ to outdo one another in exchanging insults

shaha|rr *nm* pockmark = muli**çk**ë

*__*shah|ërak*__ *adj, n* abusive/foul-mouthed (person)

*__*sha·h|ës*__ *adj, n* = shah**ërak**

shahi *nf* (*Old*) musket

shahi|n *nm* falcon, hawk

*__*shahi|në*__ *nf* = shahi

*__*shahi|rë*__ *nf* (*Old*) harmonica, mouth organ

shah|ist *n* chess player

shah|it *n* (*Old*) witness
  ○ **shahit syri** eyewitness

sha·h|thi *adv* standing on the hind legs: rearing up

shai|r *nm* (*Old*) musician in a folk band = sajexhi**n**

shaja|k *nm* **1** homespun wool flannel used for outer garments **2** woolen cloak

shaja|k|të *adj* (*i*) made of coarse woven and felted homespun wool fabric

shaj|ë *nf* [*Bot*] borage (*Borago officinalis*)

*__*shâj|ë*__ *nf* (*Old Regional Gheg*) compression, pressure

*__*shajk*__ *nm* (*pl ~ qe*) = shka**k**

sha|jkë *nf* **1** small sharp nail: tack **2** rivet

shajni *nf* apparition, mirage, vision = vegi**m**

shajni|tur *adj* (*i*) tacked down; nailed in place

shajt|im *nm* **1** fainting spell; attack of apoplexy **2** bitter thing, poison

shajto·het *vpr* to get/be badly hurt

shajto·n *vt* **1** to bruise [a body part] badly: bludgeon, maim **2** (*Fig*) to inflict emotional distress on []: wound [] (emotionally), hurt **3** to destroy/ruin []
  ○ **shajto·n nga mendtë** to lose one's mind, go out of one's mind

shajt|uar *adj* (*i*) **1** accursed, damned **2** (*Curse*) may-he-be-struck-by-apoplexy

shaka *nf* joke
  ○ **shaka me spec** dangerous joke
  ○ **shaka me thepa** biting humor
  ○ **shaka me zarar** malicious humor
  ○ [] **merr· me shaka** not take [] seriously

shaka|tar *adj, n* (*Book*) = shakaxhi** n**

shakaxhi *nm* (*np ~ nj*) *adj* **1** (person) who likes jokes or likes to joke **2** comical, funny; joking

sha|kë *nf* = bu**sht**ër

shakllaban *adj (Colloq)* **1** *(Pej)* excessively talkative, garrulous: gabby **2** *(Reg)* lethargic, sluggish; aloof, withdrawn

shakmis· *vt* to tear up and shred [ ]

shakmisur *adj (i)* **1** torn up and shredded **2** (of hair) standing on end, mussy; having mussy hair

shakmizë *nf* multitude, horde

*shakshi *adj* cross-eyed/cockeyed

shaktis· *vt* to bewilder, confuse = **çakërdis·**

shakull
I § *nm (np ~ j)* **1** heavy leather bag made of a sheep-skin or goatskin: skinbag **2** bellows (of a forge) = **gjyryk 3** = **shakullinë 4** [*Med*] follicle
II § *adj* distended, inflated
III § *adv* collapsed and lifeless on the ground

shakullinë *nf* whirlwind

shakullis· *vt* to tumble/roll [ ] down; knock [ ] down, knock [ ] flat

shakullis·et *vpr* **1** to tumble down; collapse like a bag of wind: fall down flat **2** to lie down/out flat; bask **3** to lie down and roll: wallow

shakullo·n *vt* = **shakullis·**

shakullor *adj* **1** [*Spec*] shaped like a whirlwind **2** rotary

shakullore *nf* **1** leather pouch for tobacco or dairy products **2** = **shakullinë**

*shalaga *nf* [*Bot*] globe artichoke *(Cynara scolymus)*

shalahipas *adv*

shalakat· *vt* to sway [ ] from side to side

shalakat·et *vpr* to sway from side to side, weave; waddle

shalakuq· *vt* to warm/toast [ ] by the fire

shalakuq·et *vpr* to get warm and dry by the fire, warm up and dry out near the fire

*shalaq *nm* pole used for scaling a wall; stilt

shalaqe *nf* passage opening through a garden hedge/fence; stile over a hedge/fence

shalare *nf* **1** stile over a hedge/fence **2** *(Fig)* person who helps another surmount a difficulty

shalator *nm* tree with a branch stump for hanging something

shalavriq
I § *adj, n* **1** *(Impol)* (person) who walks clumsily with misshapen upper legs: bandy, bowlegged **2** *(Fig)* clumsy; thickheaded
II § *adv* sluggishly and unsteadily

shalaxhi *nm (np ~ nj)* saddler

shalcë *nf* yogurt salted and kept in a closed container for use in winter

shalë *nf* **1** saddle **2** inner side of upper leg, inner thigh; upper leg, thigh; thigh bone **3** leg (from hip to ankle)
∘ **shalë femërore** [*Riding*] sidesaddle
∘ **shalë mbi samar** "saddle upon packsaddle" yet one more burden on top of all the others
∘ **shalë turke** [*Med*] pituitary fossa *sella turcica*

Shalë *nf* mountainous sub-region and town in north-western Albania: Shala

shalëgjatë *adj, n* long-legged/leggy (person)

shalëhapur *adv* with legs apart

shalëpërkulje *nf* [*Sport*] knee-bend exercise

shalës *nm* wooden trough used in beating flax

shalësinë *nf* infertile soil

shalëshkurtër *adj, n* short-legged (person)

shalështrembër *adj* bandy-legged, bowlegged

shalështrembët = **shalështrembër**

shalim *nm ger* <**shalo·n**

shaljan
I § *adj* of/from Shala
II § *n* native of Shala

shalo·n *vt* to saddle; break [ ] to the saddle

shalok *nm* bipod with legs two meters apart that is used as a compass to measure the amount of land that has been worked during a period of time

shaloke *np fem* knee-length women's underwear

shalor *nm* = **shalare**

shalqi(r) *nm (np ~ nj)* watermelon *(Citrullus vulgaris)*

*shaltar *n* = **shalaxhi**

shaluar *adv* astride

*shalzë *nf(Old)* swing

shall *nm* scarf

shallagonë *nf* [*Bot*] Jerusalem artichoke *(Helianthus tuberosus)*

shallvare *np fem* heavy pantaloons worn by both men and women in some regions of Albania: loose trousers with tapered legs

shallvaregjerë *adj (Impol)* having baggy pants

shamatar *n, adj* (person) who constantly and loudly complains

shamatatel *nm* zinc and copper alloy used to make tinsel

shamataxhi *nm (np ~ nj)* boisterous person

shamatë *nf* noisy argument; clamor, tumult, hubbub, rumpus

shamatim *nm* noisy quarrel, brawl

shamato·het *vpr* to quarrel noisily, argue loudly, squabble

shamato·n *vi* to cause <> to quarrel

*shamb·et *vpr (Reg)* = **shemb·et**

*shamblak *adj* awkward

shamërdan *nm* [*Constr*] pile driver

shami *nf* handkerchief; kerchief

shamibardhë *adj* wearing a white kerchief on her head

shamikuqe *adj* wearing a red kerchief on her head

shamiverdhë *adj* wearing a yellow kerchief on her head

shamizezë *nf* wearing a black head kerchief as a sign of mourning

shamizë *adj* small kerchief

*shamje *nf (Reg Gheg)* = **sharje**

shamot *nm* fireclay

shampanjë *nf* champagne

shampo *nf* shampoo

shamti·n *vi (Reg)* to sigh; moan = **psheretï·n**

shamtinë *nf(Reg)* **1** sigh; moan = **psheretïmë**, **aht 2** heavy curse, imprecation = **nëmë**

shanc *nm* chance, lucky chance, luck; good luck

shandan *nm* candle holder: chandelier, candlestick

shaneshin *nm* **1** *(Old)* low wooden sofa-bed; covering of a low wooden sofa-bed **2** ground-floor room with a low wooden bench along one wall **3** = **sharapoll 4** outdoor balcony with a wooden balustrade

Shangaj *nm* Shanghai

shans *nm* chance

shantazh *nm* extortion, blackmail

shap *nm* **1** [*Min Chem*] alum **2** [*Veter*] foot-and-mouth disease

shapako̱t *adj, n* demented/dotty (person)

shapako̱t·et *vpr* to become demented, go dotty

shape̱të *nf* **1** *(Reg)* old caved-in skullcap **2** small slab of earth/stone **3** *(Fig)* slovenly person; dull-witted and slow person: oaf

shapërto̱·het *vpr* to plunge into mud; walk through mud

shapka̱t *nm* [*Food*] cornmeal pasty (particularly if made with a green vegetable) = **pispili̱**

sha̱p|kë *nf* **1** cap (with a brim in front) worn by men **2** open-heeled house slipper; old shoe with broken-down heel, worn-out old shoe **3** [*Ornit*] woodcock = **shapto̱re**
  ○ **shapka e ujit** [*Ornit*] snipe *(Gallinago gallinago)*

shapkë̱to̱r *adj* (of a kitchen vessel) very shallow, flat

shapkë̱to̱re *nf* **1** [*Ornit*] = **shapto̱re 2** (*Pej*) slut

*****sha̱p|këzë** *nf* [*Bot*] **1** maidenhair fern *(Adianthum capillus-veneris)* **2** navelwort *(Cotyledon umbilicus)*

shaplo̱·n *vt* to break up [clods of soil] = **capo̱·n**

shapo̱·n *vt* to polish (after applying a polishing substance)

shapo̱nj *nf* [*Bot*] wallflower, gillyflower *(Cheiranthus cheiri)*

shaptilogra̱f *nm* [*Publ*] mimeograph machine

shaptilografi̱m *nm ger* [*Publ*] < **shaptilografo̱·n**

shaptilografi̱st *n* [*Publ*] operator of a duplicating machine

shaptilografo̱·n *vt* [*Publ*] to mimeograph, duplicate

shaptilografua̱r *adj (i)* [*Publ*] mimeographed, duplicated

shapto̱re *nf* [*Ornit*] woodcock *(Scolopax rusticola)*

shap|th *nm* [*Veter*] foot-and-mouth disease

shapuli̱cë *nf* [*Zool*] common toad *(Bufo bufo)*
  ○ **shapulicë barkbardhë** [*Zool*] green/water frog *Rana ridibunda*

sha̱|ra *np (të)* abusive words, insults, invective

sharabaj̱kë *nf* (*Old*) large four-wheeled carriage/coach: charabanc

sha̱|rak *nm* foul-mouthed person

sharamandu̱k· *vt* (*Reg*) = **sharandu̱k·**

sharamandu̱k·et *vpr* (*Reg*) = **sharandu̱k·et**

shar|a̱n *adj, nm* **1** (livestock) marked by dark spots: spotted, speckled **2** (corn) with mixed dark and light kernels **3** [*Ichth*] sharpsnout sea bream *(Diplodus puntazzo)*

sharandu̱k· *vt* **1** to pull at [] playfully; tug on [] one way and another **2** to beat [] hard

sharandu̱k·et *vpr* to pull at one another playfully, wrestle playfully, play around: tussle

shara̱në *nf* ravine into which rocks have rolled down; pile of rocks

sharapi̱q·et *vpr* < **sharapj̱ek·** to tussle and roll over on the ground

sharapi̱q *stem for 2nd pl pres, pind, imper, vp* < **sharapj̱ek·**

sharapj̱ek· *vt* to tussle with []; hurl/plunk [] down hard on the ground

sharapj̱eku̱r *part* < **sharapj̱ek·**, **sharapi̱q·et**

*****sharapo̱f** = **sharapo̱ll**

sharapo̱ll *nm* oriel with slit windows used as a watchpost: turret

sharapo̱q *stem for pdef* < **sharapj̱ek·**

shara|va̱zë *nf* weed

shara|vi̱dhe *nf* (*Reg*) [*Invert*] mollusk, oyster, cockle; seashell

sha̱rde *nf* [*Zool*] = **bollësha̱rde**

sha̱|rë
  I § *part* < **sha̱·n**
  II § *nf* = **sha̱rkë**
  III § *nf (e)* insult; reproach
  IV § *nn (të)* = **sha̱rje**
  ○ **s'ësh·të[3rd] për t'u sharë, as për t'u lavdëruar** "not be for complaining about nor for praising" it's nothing special one way or another

sha̱rës *adj* scolding, insulting

*****sha̱rgë** *adv* = **zva̱rrë**

sha̱rgo̱·het *vpr* (*Reg*) to leave, flee, scat

sha̱rgo̱·n *vt* (*Reg*) **1** to force/drive out, eject **2** (*Fig*) to hurt [] emotionally; mix [] up, bewilder

sha̱rje *nf ger* **1** < **sha̱·n**, **sha̱·het 2** verbal abuse, invective

shark *nm (np ~ qe)* **1** green outer hull of certain nuts **2** [*Bot*] pulp surrounding the seed of a fruit **3** snakeskin **4** = **bërru̱c**

sha̱rkë
  I § *nf* (pleated) woolen cloak worn by women; long felt jerkin for women
  II § *nf, adj* (sheep) marked by dark spots

sharki̱ *nf* [*Mus*] long-necked stringed instrument with 5-12 strings in three courses and 12-22 frets

sharlata̱n
  I § *nm* charlatan
  II § *adj* deceptive and dishonorable

sharlatani̱zëm *nm* charlatanism

*****sharmashi̱k** *nm* [*Bot*] = **shermashe̱k**

sharme̱nd = **sherme̱nd**

sha̱rmë *adj (i)* (of livestock) marked by spots: spotted, speckled

sharmo̱·n *vt* to prune [a grapevine]

sharni̱r *nm* [*Tech*] = **çernie̱rë**

*****sha̱rnje·n** *vt* to water [flowers]

sha̱rov *nm* (*Reg*) big sheepdog with dark/darkly-spotted fur

sha̱rpë *nf* long black silk scarf hanging in back from the head to the waist by women in mourning

*****sharqi̱(n)** *nm (np ~ nj)* (*Reg Gheg*) = **shalqi̱**

shart *nm* (*Old*) **1** condition specified in an agreement: stipulation, provision **2** [*Relig*] precept; rite

sharta̱k *nm* = **sharte̱së**

sharte̱së *nf* **1** graft on a fruit tree; scion used in a graft; host plant in a graft **2** (*Fig*) artificial appendage

sharteso̱re *nf* [*Agr*] plant nursery

sharti̱m *nm ger* < **sharto̱·n**

sharto̱·n *vt* **1** [*Agr*] to graft **2** (*Old*) to crossbreed [animals] **3** (*Fig Pej*) to patch [] together artificially **4** (*Old*) to vaccinate []; vaccinate <> against [] **5** (*Colloq*) to repair with a patch: patch **6** (*Fig Old*) to plant/instill [an idea, a doctrine]

sharto̱re *nf* host plant of a graft

shartua̱r *adj (i)* **1** grafted; improved by grafting **2** (*Fig*) artificially grafted together
  ○ **i shartuar në degë** bad-mannered; cantankerous, hard to deal with

shart'ues n specialist in plant grafting

sharra'k nm small grove of trees: copse

*__sharra'r__ n (Old) = sharrëta'r

sha'rras np [Med] lockjaw, tetanus

*__sharra'tor__ n (Old) = sharrëta'r

sharrë
I § nf 1 saw; saw blade 2 saw mill 3 saw-toothed ridge: (steep) mountain range, hidden reef (in the ocean); spinal column, spine; back (of cattle/horses) 4 scorched corncob used to shell corn 5 [Med] lockjaw, tetanus
II § adj 1 sawtooth; wavy 2 (of teeth) very sharp; (of a knife) dulled with an irregular edge: blunt *3 = stërqok

sharrëta'r nm lumberjack; sawyer

sharrëxhi nm (np ˉnj) (Colloq) = sharrëta'r

sharrëz nf 1 [Anat] sagittal suture joining the bones of the skull 2 sagittal·fin 3 [Med Veter] lockjaw, tetanus 4 [Veter] disease of cattle/horses in which small pustules appear on the cheeks and tongue causing swelling and difficulty in eating 5 [Anat] papilla

sharri'm nm ger < sharro·n

*__sharro'·het__ vpr to perish

sharro'·n
I § vt to saw
II § vi 1 to lose oneself (in something), sink down (in something) 2 to perish
   ◦ **sharro·n nga** [] to be dying of []
   ◦ **sharro·n për** [] to be dying for [], want [] badly
   ◦ [] **sharroftë sharra!** "May the saw saw []!" (Curse) Death to []!

sharro'k nm = sharrëta'r

sharru'ar adj (i) 1 sawn 2 sawtoothed

sharru'es n sawyer
   ◦ **sharruesi i drithërave** [Entom] wheat stem sawfly Cephus pygmaeus L.

shasi nf [Tech] chassis

*__sha'sme__ np shot pellets (for a shotgun): shot, grapeshot

shasti nf bewilderment

shastima'dh adj, n (Reg) bewildering (person)

shasti's·
I § vt to bewilder, daze
II § vi = shastis·et
   ◦ <> **shastis· kokën/kryet** (Colloq) to annoy <> badly by a displeasing repeated action: give <> a splitting headache, drive <> crazy with that stuff
   ◦ <> **shastis· trutë** to annoy <> past endurance

shasti's·et vpr to be bewildered

shasti'sje nf ger 1 < shastis·, shastis·et 2 bewilderment

shasti'sur adj (i), n (i) bewildered, dazed; slow-witted/scatterbrained (person)

*__shashi__ adj = shakshi

shat I § nm OR **sha'të** II § nf 1 hoe 2 (Colloq) cultivation by hoe: hoeing
   ◦ **shat rrotullues** rotary hoe
   ◦ **Shati tërheq nga vetja.** "The hoe pulls toward itself." (Prov) A person looks after his own interests first.

shatër
I § nm [Hist] boy who serves as a domestic or garden servant in a feudal court: page, gardener

II § nf (Reg) old house slipper; old shoe used as house slipper

shatërka'z nm scuffle hoe, Dutch hoe, push/thrust hoe

shatërva'n nm gushing well/spring; sudden outpour, gush

shatëta'r n (Old) seasonal agricultural worker used to cultivate crops with a hoe

*__shati'n__ nm [Ornit] young gander

shato'·n vt (Old) to cultivate [] with a hoe: hoe

shato'r n (Old) = shatëta'r

shato'rr
I § adj having tent-like appressed branches
II § nm strong and stocky person

shato'rre nf 1 tent; large umbrella 2 (Colloq) outer ear, ear

*__shato'rrëz__ nf (Old Colloq) outer ear, ear

*__shato'rrth__ nf dimin (Old) little umbrella

shato'rrthi adv in a tent shape: tent-like

sha't-pa't adv (Colloq) = shatra-pa'tra

sha'tra-pa'tra adv (Colloq) 1 in a jumble, in gibberish: higgledy-piggledy 2 hastily and superficially: slapdash 3 dragging the legs and weaving from side to side

shatriva'n = shatërva'n

shau'll nm (Reg) plumb line (used by a mason) = plumbçe

*__shaure't__ nm 1 ghost 2 = luga't

shava'r nm [Bot] 1 rush, reed 2 cattail, reedmace (Typha) 3 bulrush, great reedmace (Typha latifolia) 4 Mediterranean needlegrass (Stipa mediterranea SH)

shavaro're np fem [Bot] plants of the cattail family Typhaceae

shaz adv (Old) full to the brim, brimful

ShBA abbrev < Shtetet e Bashkuara të Amerikës
USA = United States of America

*__shbati'cë__ = zbati'ce

*__shdoga'n__ < shdogan

*__shdre'dh·__ = zhdre'dh·

*__shdrejt'azi__ = zhdrejtazi

*__shdrejti'm__ nm ger 1 < shdrejto·n 2 misguidance, misdirection

*__shdrejto'·n__ vt to mislead, misguide, misdirect

*__shdrejto'njës__ adj misleading

*__shdrint·__ vt to unravel

*__shdri's__ = zdris

*__shdri't·__ = zdri't·

*__shdrivilli'm__ nm evolution, development

*__shdrivillo'·n__ vt to evolve, develop

*__shdrivillu'es__ adj evolutionary, developmental

she nm torrential stream that flows from the mountains year-round

shebe'k nm 1 (Old) poor/orphaned boy who becomes a menial servant; servant who attends the rich or powerful 2 person with a dwarfish body: dwarf 3 little boy who never sits still: frisky little scamp

sheboje nf [Bot] wallflower, gillyflower (Cheiranthus cheiri)

shef nm chief
   ◦ **shef kontabël** chief bookkeeper

*__she'fi__ nf = kufi

*__shefita'r__ adj, n = kufitar

shefteli nf [Bot] (variety of) small peach

She'ga nf Shega (female name)

shegan *adj, n* **1** roan (horse/cattle) **2** (person) with rosy cheeks, flush with health

shegas *stem for 1st sg pres, pl pres, 2nd & 3rd sg subj, pind* <**shegat**·

shegat· *vt (Reg)* = shagat·

shegert *nm* shopkeeper's apprentice = **çirak**
  ○ **shegerti i madh/defterit** apprentice entrusted with the account book, chief apprentice

shegerte/shë *nf* <**shegert**

shegerti *nf* **1** apprenticeship **2** *(Collec)* apprentices as a collective

shegë *nf* [Bot] pomegranate *(Punica granatum)*

shegore *np fem* [Bot] pomegranate family *Punicaceae*

shegune *nf* coarse woolen cloak

*****shegj** *np* <**shag**

sheh *nm (np ~ lerë)* [Relig] head of a Moslem religious group

sheh· *vt* **1** to see; look at [] **2** to have a view of [], look out on [] **3** *(Colloq)* to see/attend to [] (in order to take care of a problem)
  ○ **nuk sheh· buallin para sysh/syve** to miss the obvious: not see the nose in front of one's face
  ○ **sheh· dritën** "see the light" *(Book)* (of something written) to get published
  ○ <> **sheh·**[3sg] **edhe shpina** "even <>'s back can see" <> *is* very smart
  ○ **Sheh fiku fikun e piqet.** "One grape sees another grape and ripens." *(Prov)* One follows the lead of the other.
  ○ <> **sheh· gjasën** to see the possibility of <>, see that <> is possible
  ○ **sheh· gjasën** to see one's chance/opportunity
  ○ <> **sheh· hairin** to make a profit from <>; use <> to advantage; get useful help from <>
  ○ **sheh· kiametin me sy** to know horror/terror at first hand, have seen/experienced the worst
  ○ **sheh· larg** to think ahead, have foresight
  ○ **nuk** [] **sheh· mbroth** to feel that something *is* wrong with []: [] *does* not look quite right to one
  ○ [] **sheh· me bishtin e syrit 1** to see [] out of the corner of the eye **2** to disparage [], undervalue []
  ○ [] **sheh· me një sy tjetër** to look at [] quite differently, see [] quite differently
  ○ [] **sheh· me sy të mirë** to look at [] with a kind eye
  ○ [] **sheh· me sy të shtrembër/keq/lig 1** to have a low regard for []; look at/on [] with disfavor **2** to have no interest in []'s welfare
  ○ [] **sheh· me sytë e ballit** to see [] with one's own eyes
  ○ [] **sheh· me syze të errëta** to make [] seem worse than [] really is: see/present [] in a bad light
  ○ <> **sheh· mendjen** to figure out what <> thinks; read <>'s mind; read <>'s mind, figure out <>'s intentions
  ○ **nuk sheh· më larg/tutje se hunda e** {*pronominal adj*} to be able to see no further than the end of {*one's*} nose; be not very smart
  ○ [] **sheh· në bebe të syrit 1** to look [] in the eye, show no fear of [] **2** to keep a constant eye on [] (usually a child)
  ○ [] **sheh· nën hundë** to look down one's nose at []
  ○ **Sheh pema pemën e piqet.** "The fruit sees the fruit and gets ripe." *(Prov)* People do what they see others do.

  ○ **sheh· përtej bjeshke 1** to see far, see far ahead **2** to be farsighted, have foresight
  ○ **nuk sheh· përtej hundës së vet** not be able to see beyond the end of one's nose; has a limited outlook
  ○ **e sheh· (punën/veten) pisk** to get into a tight spot, be in a bad way
  ○ <> **sheh· pulsin 1** to take <>'s pulse **2** to try <*a candidate*> out
  ○ **sheh puna punën** "the work sees the work" let's see how it goes
  ○ **Sheh qimen në syrin e tjetrit dhe nuk shikon/sheh trarin në syrin e vet.** "You see the hair in someone else's eye but don't see the wooden beam in your own eye." You see someone else's slightest fault but miss your own glaring faults.
  ○ **Sheh rrushi rrushin e piqet.** "One grape sees another grape and ripens." *(Prov)* One follows the lead of the other.
  ○ **Nuk sheh syri, sheh mendja.** "The eye *doesn't see*, the mind *sees*." You don't see if your mind is elsewhere.
  ○ **s'do· t'**<>**i shoh sytë** "not want one's eyes to see <>" not want to see <> ever again
  ○ <>**a sheh· sherrin** to experience trouble from <>: <> *gives* one a lot of trouble
  ○ [] **sheh· shtrembër 1** to have a low regard for []; look at/on [] with disfavor **2** to have no interest in []'s welfare **3** to look daggers at []
  ○ [] **sheh· të udhës** to deem [] to be quite proper, consider [] to be all right
  ○ **Sheh** [] **tym e bë·**n **konak.** "{} *sees* smoke and *makes* {}self at home." {} spends {}'s time going around and making idle conversation instead of working.
  ○ **e sheh· veten si në pasqyrë** "see oneself as in a mirror" to be conscious of one's own mistakes
  ○ [] **sheh· vëngër 1** to have a low regard for []; look at/on [] with disfavor **2** to have no interest in []'s welfare **3** to look daggers at []
  ○ **Sheh· yllin e merr· pyllin.** "{} *sees* the star and *takes* to the forest." {} *acts* without thinking carefully
  ○ **sheh· zi** to look only on the dark side, see only what is bad

*****shehër** *nm (Old)* = qytet

sheik *nm* leader of an Arabian clan: sheik

shejmirë *nf* [Entom] cricket

*****shejni** *nf* = shenjë

*****shejno·**n = shënjo·n

*****shêjo·** = shenjo·n

shejtan
  I § *nm* Satan; devil, demon; imp
  II § *adj, nm (Crude)* devilishly clever (person)
  ○ **ësh-të i shejtanit e i mejdanit** "be of the devil and of the duelling ground" to be capable of both bad and good

shejtanbudalla *nm (np ~ enj) (Colloq)* devilishly crafty person pretending to be a fool

shejtane OR **shejtankë** *nf, adj (Pet)* devilish/impish female

shejtani *nf* = shejtanllëk

shejtanllëk *nm (np ~ qe)* devilishness

*****shêjtar** = shenjëtar

*****shêjtëm** *adj (i) (Reg Gheg)* (Reg Gheg) saintly, holy

*****shêjtneshë** = shenjtëreshë

*****shêjtni** = shenjtëri

*shêjtnim = shenjtërím
*shêjtnisht = shenjtërísht
*shêjtnore = shenjtërore
*shêjtnueshëm adj (i) (Reg Gheg) (Reg Gheg) = shenjtëruar
*shêjto·n (Reg Gheg) = shenjtëro'·n
*shêjtore nf (Reg Gheg) = shenjtëreshë
*shejth nm birthmark mole
sheke nf **1** wooden cask/tub/bucket **2** covered wooden bowl used by herdsmen for dairy uses **3** (Old) grain measure regionally varying in quantity from fifty to a hundred kilograms
*shekëll nf shekel
shekspirian adj, n Shakespearean
shekull nm (np ˜ j) **1** century **2** (Old) secular world
shekullar
  I § adj (Book) secular, lay
  II § nm **1** [Relig] secular Catholic ecclesiastic **2** (Old) layman
shekullarizim nm ger (Book) < shekullarizo'·n
shekullarizo·n vt (Book) to secularize
shekulli nf general public, laity
shekullor adj of the century: century-old; century-long
sheleg n yearling lamb
shelegar n shepherd who tends lambs after weaning
shelg nm (np ˜ gje) [Bot] willow (Salix L.)
  ○ **shelg i bardhë** [Bot] white willow (Salix alba)
  ○ **shelg i butë** [Bot] weeping willow (Salix babylonica)
  ○ **shelg i egër** [Bot] goat willow, common willow (Salix caprea) = morinë
  ○ **shelg industrial** = shelgjishtër
  ○ **shelg i kuq** = shelgjishtër
  ○ **shelg lotues/vajtues** [Bot] weeping willow (Salix babylonica)
  ○ **shelg i mbylltë** [Bot] almond-leaved willow Salix triandra
  ○ **shelg i verdhë** [Bot] yellow-stem white willow Salix vitellina
shelgore np fem [Bot] trees and shrubs of the willow family Salicaceae
shelgjishtë OR **shelgjishte** nf **1** willow grove **2** [Bot] = shelgjishtër
shelgjishtër nf [Bot] purple osier willow (Salix purpurea)
*shelikademe nf
shelkë nf **1** lid, cover ***2** small wooden box
*shelnje nf [Bot] = shelg
shelqe nf **1** wooden wall-rack for tableware and salt **2** shepherd's food bowl ***3** = shelg
*shelqet nm = shelqishte
shelqëror nm tree trunk with branches broken-off to hang up vessels in a mountain dairy camp
*shelqi(n) nm (np ˜) (Reg Gheg) = shalqi(r)
shelqishte nf watermelon patch/field
shemb· vt **1** to cause [] to crumple to the ground; demolish **2** to batter **3** to hurt [] badly **4** (Fig Colloq) to stuff [] full
  ○ **shemb· malet** "knock down the mountains" to be strong enough to move mountains
  ○ [] **shemb· me katra** "fill [] full of fours" to give [] many failing grades
  ○ [] **shemb· me** [] (Pej) to give [] an abundance of [], smother [] with []

shemb·et vpr **1** to fall to the ground, fall down, collapse; crumble to the ground **2** (of ground) to sink/slide down **3** (Fig) to die/fade out, disappear **4** to get badly hurt (but not cut) **5** (Colloq) to get a hernia/rupture = rrënxo·het **6** (Colloq) to miscarry, have a miscarriage
  ○ **shemb·et me katra** (Colloq) to get a lot of failing grades
  ○ **shemb·et me** [] (Colloq) to stuff oneself with []
  ○ **shemb·et në punë** to smother oneself in work
  ○ **shemb·et qielli** "the sky falls down" it starts to rain in buckets, it is raining cats and dogs
shembë nf **1** = shembëtirë **2** utter ruin
*shembëll = shembull
shembëlle·n
  I § vi to be similar to <>, resemble <>
  II § vt to tell [] apart, identify, distinguish
shembëllesë nf = shembëllim
shembëllim nm **1** resemblance, similarity **2** [Optics] mirror image
shembëllor = shembullor
shembëlltyrë nf = shëmbëlltyrë
*shembër = shemër
*shembëro·n vt to rival
shembëtirë nf sunken ground; crevasse/gorge left by landslides; mountain gorge
shembje nf ger **1** < shemb·, shemb·et **2** rock-slide, landslide **3** bruise
shembull nm (np ˜ j) **1** example **2** comparable example: likeness, counterpart
shembullor adj serving as an example, exemplary
shembur adj (i) **1** fallen down, in ruins **2** (Fig) in ruin, ruined **3** (of land) subsided, downfallen **4** badly bruised
shemë nf **1** hive of young bees; bee swarm **2** hive of bees with a queen **3** (Fig) large number (of animate things): swarm, bevy
shemër
  I § nf (in polygamous marriages) second wife, other wife: concubine
  II § nm (Fig) rival, antagonist, opponent
shemëri nf rivalry
shemërto·het vpr to heal up, recover, close over (of a wound)
shemërto·n vt (Reg) to replace [an unproductive plant] with a healthy sprout = ko·n
shemtyrë nf= shëmbëlltyrë
shend nm great joy, delight
shendim nm feeling of great joy/delight
shendo·het vpr to rejoice
shendo·n vt, vi to fill [] with joy
shenishan nm fortified window projecting from the side of a tower
shenj· vt to cause [fruit] to show signs of ripening: ripen [fruit]
shenj·et vpr (of fruit) to start to show signs of ripening: ripen
shenjas adv
shenjestër nf = shënjestër
shenjë nf **1** sign **2** scar; brand (on an animal), identifying mark; birthmark mole; distinguishing characteristic; trace, mark **3** target (aimed at in shooting) **4** medal (awarded as an honor) **5** symbol; signal; gesture; indication; omen **6** choice bit/slice of roasted

meat offered a sign of honor **7** [*Ethnog*] ceremonial gift exchanged to confirm an engagement of marriage
  ○ **shenjat e bardha** white stripes marking a crosswalk for pedestrians: zebra crossing
  ○ **i bie**₁· **në shenjë/shenjës** to hit the target, be right on target; find just what one is looking for; get to the nub of the matter; hit the nail on the head
  ○ **shenjë e madhe** gift exchanged as a token of betrothal at the final betrothal ceremony
  ○ **shenjë personale** [*Mil*] identification number/tag: dog tag
  ○ **shenjë qiellore** zodiac sign
  ○ **shenjë e vogël** gift exchanged as a token of betrothal at the preliminary betrothal ceremony

shenjëdhënës
  I § *nm, adj* [*Mil*] used to give a signal: signalling
  II § *nm* signalman, signaller; signal

shenjëshkurtër *adj* [*Mil*] short of the target/mark

shenjëtar
  I § *nm* marksman
  II § *adj* sharpshooting, accurate

shenjëtari *nf* marksmanship

shenjëz *nf* (*Dimin*) tiny sign/mark

Shenjëza *np* [*Astron*] Pleiades

shenjim *nm* <shenjo·n

shenjo·n *vt* **1** to point to [], designate; indicate, mean, signal; determine **2** [*Tech*] to scribe

shenjt *nm* (*np* ˜ ër) saint

shenjtë *adj* (*i*) **1** saintly **2** holy, sacred

shenjtëreshë *nf* <shenjt

shenjtëri *nf* [*Relig*] holiness (also used as a high religious title)

shenjtërim *nm ger* <shenjtëro·n, shenjtëro·het

shenjtërisht *adv* in saintly manner, like a saint

shenjtëro·het *vpr* **1** [*Relig*] to behave/live like a saint; become holy **2** (*Fig*) to become sacrosanct/sanctified

shenjtëro·n
  I § *vt* **1** to sanctify, hallow **2** to honor/consider/treat [] as sacred; take [] as sacrosanct
  II § *vi* (*Colloq*) to stand silent and unmoving

shenjtëror *adj* [*Relig*] holy; saintly

shenjtërore *nf* [*Relig*] holy place: shrine

shenjtëruar *adj* (*i*) **1** sanctified **2** (*Fig*) sacred

shenjtor *n* [*Relig*] = shenjt

*shepkë *nf* [*Ornit*] = shapkë

sheputkë *nf* pod (of a pulse plant)

sheqe *nf* = sheke

sheqer *nm* sugar
  ○ **sheqer frutash** [*Chem*] levulose
  ○ **ësh·të sheqer i gjallë** to be pleasant in speech
  ○ **sheqer petak** lump sugar
  ○ **sheqer toz** powdered sugar

sheqere
  I § *nf* **1** = sheqerkë **2** (*Pet*) sweet girl
  II § *adj* **1** (of a variety of pear) very sweet **2** light pink (color)

sheqerim *nm ger* <sheqero·n, sheqero·het

sheqerizim *nm* [*Chem*] saccharification

sheqerkë *nf* (*Reg*) candy
  ○ **sheqerkë me helm** "candy with poison" something attractive in appearance but dangerous in fact: poisoned apple

sheqermbajtës *adj* [*Chem*] containing sugars: (*sacchariferous*)

sheqermbajtëse *nf* sugar container (for serving sugar at the table)

sheqerna *np masc* **1** [*Chem*] organic sugars **2** candies

sheqero·het *vpr* [*Chem*] to turn to sugar; increase in sugar content

sheqero·n *vt* **1** to add sugar to []; cover [] with sugar **2** [*Chem*] to convert [] into sugar; increase the sugar content of []

sheqeror *adj* **1** containing/yielding sugar **2** [*Geol*] saccharoidal

sheqeros· *vt* **1** to thicken/cover [] with sugar; add sugar to [] **2** (*Fig Pej*) to cover up [] with a sugar coating, mask [faults, defects] by using honeyed words

sheqeros·et *vpr* to become crystallized into sugar

sheqerosje *nf ger* <sheqeros·, sheqeros·et

sheqerosur *adj* (*i*) **1** sweetened; sugared **2** (of sugary substances) crystallized **3** (*Fig Pej*) covered with a sugar coating, masked by honeyed words

sheqerpare *nf* [*Food*] kind of cake served with syrup

sheqertar = sheqerxhi

sheqertë *adj* (*i*) **1** containing or made of sugar; sugary **2** sweet

sheqerxhi *nm* (*np* ˜ nj) (*Old*) candy maker/seller: candyman, confectioner

sheqëz *nf dimin* <sheke small wooden bucket

sherbelë *nf* [*Bot*] sage (*Salvia L.*)

sherbet *nm* **1** sugar syrup **2** flavored sweet beverage **3** whitewash, whiting
  ○ **sherbet gëlqereje** whitewash, limewater, hydrate of lime

sherbetim *nm ger* <sherbeto·n

sherbeto·n *vt* **1** to pour sugar syrup on [a dessert] **2** to apply whitewash to [a wall/building]: whitewash

shere *nf* [*Bot*] **1** spiny bear's breech (*Acanthus spinosus*) **2** thistle (*Silybum*) *3** head of lettuce/cabbage

sheriat *nm* [*Relig*] Islamic law, Sheriat

sherif *nm* sheriff

*sherit *nm* = shirit

shermashek *nm* [*Bot*] ivy = urth

shermend *nm* branch pruned from a grapevine; cutting from a grapevine

sherp *nm* [*Bot*] wild celery (*Apium graveolens var silvestre*)

sherr
  I § *nm* **1** loud quarrel, squabbling; discord, dispute, argument **2** (*Colloq*) mischief **3** (*Colloq*) envy
  II § *adj* argumentative, quarrelsome; mischievous; envious

*sherr· *vt* to castrate

sherr·et *vpr* (of a baby) to be in an agitated state: fuss

sherrac *adj* **1** = sherrak **2** wicked

sherrak
  I § *adj, n* squabbling/quarrelsome (person)
  II § *nm* castrated goat

sherrbudalla *nm* (*np* ˜ enj) (*Colloq*) person who causes mischief either out of stupidity or pretended innocence

sherret
  I § *adj* quarrelsome; mischievous
  II § *n* squabbler; mischief-maker

sherri *nf* cunning, deceit, deception, fraud; mischief

sherr|madh
I § adj mischievous
II § n mischief-maker

sherr|tar adj 1 = sherrak 2 fraudulent, wily; wicked

sherr|xhe'shë nf < sherrxhi

sherr|xhi nm (np ˜ nj) 1 mischief-maker 2 crafty rogue: sneak, cheat

shes| stem for 1st sg pres, 1st & 3rd pl pres, 2nd & 3rd sg subj <shet·

she'stë nf 1 (Colloq) pair of compasses, dividers 2 proposal, plan *3 (Reg Gheg) quality

shesti nf system, plan

shestim nm ger 1 <shesto'·n 2 arrangement, plan *3 settlement

***shest|is·** vt to disturb, trouble

***she'stje** nf purpose, object

shesto'·n vt to lay out [ ]; plan out [ ], devise
  ○ shesto·n çarqe to lay traps

shestu|es adj arranging

shesh
I § nm 1 level ground, flat and open area; ground, ground level 2 plain; plaza; clearing, glade; playing field, arena; platform 3 flat surface
II § adj flat, level; flat and open
III § adv 1 on the ground 2 (Fig) casually
  ○ shesh armësh field of battle
  ○ shesh i burrave 1 plaza where the men of a village gather 2 place for settling disputes by fighting
  ○ shesh ditor playground in a summer camp
  ○ shesh gjeografik schoolyard area set aside for the study of geography
  ○ shesh i këmbës sole of the foot
  ○ shesh i kokës top of the head
  ○ shesh me lule 1 something made to appear rosier than it is 2 (Fig) easy life without problems: bed of roses
  ○ shesh montimi [Constr] area next to a construction site where prefabricated parts are assembled: assembly area
  ○ shesh ndërtimi [Constr] construction site
  ○ s'ësh-të në shesh, po në thes not be out in the open, not be obvious
  ○ shesh për shesh openly, straight out, boldly
  ○ shesh prodhimi [Constr] preparation area next to a construction site
  ○ shesh pushimi [Constr] staircase landing
  ○ shesh qitjeje [Mil] field of fire
  ○ shesh i shpatës flat of the sword
  ○ shesh veprimi range of action: scope
  ○ shesh veror playground in a summer camp

she'sh|as OR **she'sh|azi** adv plainly, openly

she'sh|e nf flat skullcap worn by men in northern Albanian

***she'sh|ël|a** np fem = she'shje

shesh|gro'pë nf level ground in a pitted area

sheshim nm ger <shesho'·n, shesho'·het

shesh|inë nf flat terrain

she'sh|it adv 1 out in the open: plainly, openly 2 (Fig) desolate, helpless

she'sh|je nf "flat shoe" house slipper

she'sh|më adj (i) = she'shtë

shesh|naj|a nf broad open and level area

shesho'·het vpr 1 to stretch (oneself) out, stretch out flat 2 (of differences) to diminish, moderate; become conciliated, even out

shesh|o'·n vt 1 to make [ ] level/flat/even/smooth 2 to level [ ] to the ground: raze 3 to put [ ] right, fix 4 (Fig) to iron out [differences]
  ○ <> shesho·n udhën to clear the way for <>, reduce the obstacles in <>'s path, prepare the ground for <>

shesh|o're nf 1 small flat area, piece of level ground; plateau 2 [Constr] stair landing 3 [Mil] gun emplacement

shesh|pa'mje nf (Book) field of vision = fushëpamje

shesh|qitje nf [Mil] field of fire, firing range

she'sh|të adj (i) 1 level, flat; smooth, even 2 shallow, flat 3 flat-bottomed; (of shoes) without heels 4 without impediment: clear, open

***shesh|tim** = shestim

***shesh|tirë** nf plain

shesh|to'·n = shesho'·n

shesh|ua'r adj (i) leveled; made even; stretched out; razed

shet· vt 1 to sell 2 (Pej) to sell out [ ]: betray 3 (Fig Pej) to try to pass [ ] off (as something other than what it is)
  ○ shet· dëngla to brag about one's exploits
  ○ shet· dije to brag pretentiously (about what one knows), pretend to know
  ○ shet· dokrra to brag about one's exploits
  ○ shet· e nuk ble·n "sell and not buy" to speak pretentiously and not listen to others
  ○ e shet· lart to be snooty, be a snob
  ○ e shet· lëkurën shtrenjt to sell one's life (skin) dearly
  ○ shet· me dëm to be poor at business, constantly sell at a loss
  ○ [ ] shet· me dëm to sell [ ] at a loss
  ○ shet· mend to brag pretentiously
  ○ shet· nga nënbanaku (Pej) to sell under the counter (unofficially and as a personal favor)
  ○ shet· pallavra to brag about one's exploits
  ○ [ ] shet· për pesë para "sell [ ] for five cents" to sell/buy [ ] at a very low price: sell/buy [ ] for a song
  ○ shet· përalla to brag about one's exploits
  ○ <> shet· profka "sell twaddle to <>" to puff oneself up in the eyes of <>; tell <> a bunch of lies
  ○ shet· rrobat dhe lëkurën to sell oneself body and soul, sell out
  ○ e shet· sapunin për djathë "sell soap as cheese" to be a swindler
  ○ e shet·³sg shkumën për ajkë "sell foam as cream" to represent things as being much better than they really are
  ○ shet· të trasha/rënda 1 to boast, brag 2 to show off by using big words

she'te np fem bran

***she'tër** np <shat

***sheti's** = shëtis

***shetit** = shëtit

she'tk|ë nf horse's mane, mane

shevro nf soft thin leather made of goat or sheep skin

shevro'n adj [Tech] in the form of a chevron, double helical

shezlo'ng nm chaise longue, reclining chair

***shëgje'ta|r** = shigjetar

***shëgje't|ull** nf 1 arrow, dart 2 = shigjetull

***shëk|im** = shikim

***shëlar** = shilar

shëlbese *nf* [*Relig*] = shëlbim

shëlbim *nm* 1 [*Relig*] salvation, redemption 2 *(Old)* rescue, liberation

shëlbo·het *vpr* [*Relig*] to achieve salvation, be saved

shëlbo·n *vt* 1 [*Relig*] to redeem [a person] spiritually: save 2 *(Old)* to rescue, liberate

shëlbues *nm* 1 [*Relig*] savior 2 *(Old)* rescuer, liberator

shëlinok *nm* [*Bot*] balm = pshelinok

shëllí·n *vt* to salt; preserve [] by salting; put [] in brine; pickle

***shëllinshëm** *adj (i) (Reg Gheg)* = shëllirshëm

shëllirë
I § *nf* 1 brine; pickling brine 2 salty sea water (from which salts are extracted); saline solution 3 barren alkaline soil 4 oversalted dairy product
II § *adj* very salty

shëllirshëm *adj (i)* briny, salty, saline

shëllirtë *adj (i)* heavily salted, briny; saline

shëmb = shemb

shëmbëll = shembull

shëmbëlle·het *vpr* 1 to bear a resemblance, come to look alike 2 to come to mind, be imagined

shëmbëlle·n
I § *vi* to resemble
II § *vt* 1 to discern; find [] comparable 2 to call [] to mind, recall

shëmbëllese *nf* 1 = shëmbëllim 2 = shëmbëlltyrë

shëmbëllim *nm* 1 optical imaging 2 resemblance; exact resemblance: spitting image; image 3 = shëmbëlltyrë 4 *(Old)* example = shembull

shëmbëllor = shembullor

shëmbëlltyrë *nf* 1 image (of a model); copy 2 example, sample 3 parable

***shëmbim** *nm* = shembje

shëmbje = shembje

***shëmbos** *vt* = shemb·

***shëmbull** *nm (np ˜j)* = shembull

shëmëhill *nm (Old)* November = nëntor

shëmim *nm ger* 1 <shëmo·n 2 wheezing; sobbing

shëmitër *nm (Old)* October = tetor

shëmo·n *vi* 1 to wheeze; sob 2 to groan

shëmtak *adj (Contempt)*

shëmtarak *adj (Contempt)* ugly; repulsive

shëmti *nf* 1 ugliness; repulsiveness 2 = shëmtirë 3 [*Med*] teratosis

shëmtim *nm ger* 1 <shëmto·n, shëmto·het 2 = shëmtirë

***shëmtinë** *nf (Reg Gheg)* = shëmtirë

shëmtirë *nf* 1 ugly/repulsive person/thing; horrible sight 2 ugliness; repulsiveness

shëmto·het *vpr* 1 to grow ugly; become repulsive 2 to make an ugly grimace

shëmto·n *vt* 1 to make ugly, deface, disfigure; spoil; contort [one's face] in a grimace 2 *(Fig)* to make [] joyless

shëmtuar
I § *adj (i)* 1 ugly; repulsive 2 *(Fig)* grisly, gruesome, hideous; horrid
II § *nf (e)* [*Philos*] ugliness; repulsiveness
III § *adv* repulsively, horribly

***shëmtyrë** = shymtyrë

shën *adj* saint, holy

○ **Shën Triadhë** Holy Trinity

shënak *nm* [*Food*] kind of bread made with wheat flour, buttermilk, and butter

shënaq *nm (Colloq)* = vaksinues

***shëndan** = shandan

***shëndenë** *fossilized accusative form* <shëndet *(Reg Tosk)*

shëndet *nm* 1 health 2 toast (wishing someone good health before drinking) 3 *(Colloq)* good wishes; greetings
○ **Shëndet!** *(Felic)* 1 Gesundheit!, Bless you! 2 *(Colloq)* Goodbye!, Stay well!
○ **Rri/Rrini me shëndet!** *(Felic)* Stay well! Goodbye!

shëndetdobët *adj* = shëndetlig

shëndetdhënës *adj (Book)* healthful

shëndetësi *nf* public health

shëndetësim *nm ger (Book)* <shëndetëso·n, shëndetëso·het

shëndetëso·het *vpr (Book)* to regain health: recuperate

shëndetëso·n *vt* 1 *(Book)* to treat [plants, animals] (for a disease); restore [plants, animals] to health; make [] healthy/well 2 to clear [] of unhealthful conditions, make [] safe (in terms of health)

shëndetësor *adj* 1 pertaining to health and its maintenance; hygienic 2 sanitary

shëndetlig *adj* poor in health: sickly

shëndetpakë *adj (i)* in poor health

shëndetplotë *adj (i)* in robust health, healthy

shëndetshëm *adj (i)* 1 healthy, well 2 healthful

***shëndërtat** *nm* Orthodox religious holiday on August 6

***shëndí·n**
I § *vi* = shëtit·
II § *vi, vt* = shndrit·

***shëndis** *stem for 1st sg pres, pl pres, 2nd & 3rd sg subj, pind* <shëndí·

***shëndit·** *vi* = shëtit·

shëndosh· *vt* 1 to make [] healthy/well; heal []; make [] stronger 2 to cause [] to gain weight; fatten [livestock] 3 to make [soil] more fertile: enrich [soil]
○ <> **shëndosh· kryet** to pay a condolence visit to <>
○ <> **shëndosh· zemrën** to console <>, comfort <>; cheer <> up

shëndo·sh·et *vpr* 1 to get healthy 2 to regain health: recuperate, heal 3 to gain weight; get plump; become robust 4 (of soil) to become more fertile: get enriched
○ **S'shëndoshet kau ditën që theret.** "The ox cannot be fattened on the day that it is slaughtered." *(Prov)* There's no use trying to do everything at the last moment.

shëndoshë
I § *adj (i)* 1 robust: healthy; sturdy; solid; firm, sound 2 stout, plump, chubby
II § *adv* 1 in good health, well; safely 2 expression of good wishes towards __: here's to __!
○ **shëndoshë me grosh** *(Old)* it does no good to be healthy if you have no money: health by wealth
○ **i shëndoshë si shuk** plump as a peach, the picture of health
○ **Vafsh shëndoshë!** "May you go healthy" *(Felic)* Arrive safely!

shëndoshje *nf ger* <shëndo·sh·, shëndo·sh·et

***shëndr** = shndr

*__shëndre__ = shënëndre

shën·e·s ë *nf* **1** token **2** place marker

shën·ëndre *nm* **1** *(Old)* December **2** St. Andrew *3** in Albanian popular belief a figure dressed in iron who appears at night during December and shakes doors

Shëngjergj *nm* **1** region east of Tirana **2** *(Old)* St. George

shëngjergj·as
I § *n* native of Shëngjergj
II § *adj* of or pertaining to Shëngjergj

shëngjetë *nf* **1** *(Old)* prize part of the kill taken by the hunter who has made the first hit *2 = shigjetë*

Shëngjin *nm* **1** northernmost Adriatic port city in Albania **2** *(Old)* St. John

shëngjin·as
I § *n* native of Shëngjin
II § *adj* of or pertaining to Shëngjin

shëngjin·ës *adj*

*__shënik__ *nm* = shinik

shën·im *nm ger* **1** <shëno′·n **2** annotation, note; footnote; marginal note; black mark **3** [*Mil*] = shënjim **4** *(Old)* = shenjë

shëno·n
I § *vt* **1** to mark [] (for identification/treatment): label; designate; mark [] down **2** to take note of [: note (down), remark, record **3** [*Sport*] to score **4** [*Tech*] to scribe **5** to vaccinate; administer [a disease] vaccine
II § *vi* (of fruit) to start to show signs of ripening: ripen; begin to form fruit: fruit
III § *vi, vt* = shënjo′·n
  ○ **shëno·n** [{number between 0 and 9}] **e** [{number between 0 and 9}] **në dorë/mend** "score [] and [] in the hand/mind" (in doing addition or multiplication) to put down [] and carry the [] **shëno·n zero e dy në mend/dorë** "score zero and two in the mind/hand" to put down zero and carry the two

*__shënt__ = shenjt

shën·uar *adj (i)* **1** marked, designated, labeled **2** *(Fig)* of significance, significant

shën·ue·s *nm* **1** [*Sport*] scoring player, scorer **2** [*Tech*] scriber

shën·ue·shëm *adj (i)* **1** significant **2** notable, distinctive

shënjestër *nf* [*Mil*] rearsight (on the barrel of a gun): gunsight

shënj·ë = shenjë

shënj·ërak *adj, n* hideous (person)

shënj·im *nm ger* [*Mil*] <shënjo′·n

shënjo·n *vt, vi* [*Mil*] to take aim (at []), aim (at [])

*__shënjtë__ *adj (i)* = shenjtë

*__shënjtër__ *adj* = shenjtë

shënjt·ëro·n = shenjtëro′·n

*__shënjt·ëro·re__ *nf* = shenjtëro′re

shënju·e·s *nm* [*Mil*] artilleryman whose task is to aim the weapon: *(layer)*

shëpullë *nf* slap in the face, box on the ears

shërbe·het *vp reflex* to serve oneself (to food and drink)

shërbe·n
I § *vi, vt* to serve
II § *vi* **1** to do military service **2** *(Old)* to work as a servant

*__shërbelë__ = sherbelë

shërbe·s·ë *nf* **1** *(Reg)* chore **2** [*Relig*] service **3** *(Old)* = shërbim

shërbëtor *n* **1** servant **2** *(Old)* janitor

shërbim *nm ger* **1** <shërbe·n, shërbe·het **2** service **3** job, duty **4** task serving plant/animal husbandry, farming chore
  ○ **shërbim i lartë** [*Volleyball*] overhand service
  ○ **shërbim me hark** [*Volleyball*] hook service
  ○ **shërbim tenis** [*Volleyball*] overhead service

*__shërbimtar__ *n* of assistance, obliging, helpful

shërby·e·s
I § *adj* **1** pertaining to or involved in service **2** [*Ling*] auxiliary
II § *n* **1** attendant, servant **2** janitor

shër·e·s·ë *nf* cure

shër·im *nm ger* **1** <shëro′·n, shëro′·het **2** medical treatment; cure

*__shërmil__ *nm* *(Old)* hangman

shëro·het *vpr* **1** to get over an illness/pain: get better, get well **2** to become healed: heal up

shëro·n *vt* **1** to heal, cure **2** *(Fig)* to straighten [someone with a serious fault] out, put [] on the right path

shëronj·ë·s *adj, n* = shërue·s

shërue·s
I § *adj* having power to heal: curative, healing; medicinal
II § *n* *(Old)* healer, doctor

shërue·shëm *adj (i)* curable, remediable

shëshërit *vi* (of a snake) to hiss

shët *onomat* command to someone else to make less noise: shush!

shëtis *stem for 1st sg pres, pl pres, 2nd & 3rd sg subj, pind* <shëti′t·

shëtit·
I § *vi* to go on a stroll/outing: stroll around, amble; go on a tour; travel around
II § *vt* **1** to tour **2** to take [someone] on a stroll/tour
  ○ **shëtit· dynjanë** to travel everywhere
  ○ **shëtit· lule me lule** "go from flower to flower" *(Pej)* to run around with one girlfriend after another (but have no permanent attachment to any)
  ○ **shëtit· me pëllëmbë** to wander over every inch of the ground
  ○ **shëtit· sytë/vështrimin** to let one's eyes wander, look around

shëtit·ë·s
I § *adj* **1** itinerant, traveling **2** [*Med*] ambulatory
II § *n* traveler

shëtitje *nf ger* **1** <shëti′t· **2** stroll, outing, amble; casual tour

shëtit·ore *nf* boulevard designed for pleasant strolling: promenade

shëtit·ur
I § *part* <shëti′t·
II § *adj (i)* well-traveled, worldly

shfajësim *nm ger* **1** <shfajëso′·n, shfajëso′·het **2** excuse; justification, vindication

shfajëso·het *vpr* to make excuses; attempt to prove one's innocence; vindicate oneself

shfajëso·n *vt* to exculpate, exonerate, excuse; vindicate

shfaq· *vt* **1** to reveal, display, manifest **2** to express **3** to present, show; perform

shfaq·et
I § *vpr* to appear

II § *vp reflex* to express oneself

***shfaqës** *n* performer, player; displayer

***shfaqësinë** *nf (Old Regional Gheg)* display, performance, exhibition; demonstration; presentation; show

***shfaqët** *adj (i)* obvious, evident, manifest

shfaqje *nf ger* 1 <shfaq·, shfaq·et 2 display, exhibition; demonstration; presentation; show, showing 3 [Phil] external appearance, manifest form

***shfaqto·** *n vt (Old)* to present, introduce

shfaqur *adj (i)* 1 overt; exhibited, shown 2 obvious, evident, manifest

shfarim *nm ger (Old)* = shfarosje

shfaro· *n vt (Old)* = shfaros·

shfaros· *vt* to exterminate, annihilate, eradicate

shfaros·et *vpr* to disappear completely: vanish

shfarosës *adj* devastating, annihilating

shfarosje *nf ger* 1 <shfaros·, shfaros·et 2 extermination, annihilation, eradication

shfarosur *adj (i)* exterminated, annihilated

shfecun *nm* [Bot] false indigo *(Amorpha fruticosa)*

shfejim *nm ger* <shfejo·n

shfejo·et *vpr* to break off one's engagement

shfejo· *vi* to break off []'s betrothal/engagement

shfletim *nm ger* <shfleto·n, shfleto·het

shfleto· *n vt* to leaf through []

shfletos· *vt* to sort [tobacco leaves] (by quality)

shfletosje *nf ger* <shfletos·, shfletos·et

shfletues *n* sorter of tobacco leaves

shflukët *adj (i) (Reg)* feeble, weak

shformim *nm ger* 1 <shformo·n, shformo·het 2 deformation; deformity

shformo·het *vpr* to become deformed

shformo· *n vt* to deform

shfre·n

I § *vi* 1 to expel air/vapor: blow off steam 2 to express pent-up feelings forcibly: blow off steam; blow up; unburden one's heart, speak openly 3 to get out of a closed vehicle and roam around: take a breather

II § *vt* to express [an emotion], unleash

***shfrejtje** *nf ger* <shfr·et

***shfreni** *f (Pej)* licentiousness, wantonness

shfrenim *nm ger* 1 <shfreno·n, shfreno·het 2 *(Pej)* licentiousness, wantonness

shfreno·het *vpr* 1 to burst out in fury 2 *(Pej)* to become licentious

shfreno· *n vt* 1 to release the braking mechanism of [] 2 *(Fig)* to allow [] to be uncontrolled, give [] too much freedom; make [] licentious

shfrenuar *adj (i)* unbridled, unrestrained; licentious, wanton

shfrim *nm ger* 1 <shfr·et 2 unrestrained expression of thoughts/feelings

shfronësim *nm ger* 1 <shfronëso·n 2 dethronement

shfronëso· *n vt* to dethrone; unseat, overthrow

shfronëzo· *n* = shfronëso·n

shfronim *nm* dethronement

shfry·het *vpr* 1 to become deflated: deflate 2 to become less swollen

   ◦ <> **shfry·het** to vent one's rage/anger on <>: blow off steam at <>, blow up at <>

shfry·n

I § *vi* 1 to expel air/vapor forcibly and noisily: snort, blow hard 2 to burst, burst out, erupt 3 to well up, overflow

II § *vt* 1 to clear [] by blowing; blow [one's nose] 2 to spit out [], spew 3 to burst/explode [] 4 *(Fig)* to deflate [something that is overinflated]: reduce [] to essentials

III § *vi, vt* to express [pent-up feelings] forcibly: blow up in a rage

   ◦ **shfry·n hundët** to blow one's nose

***shfryeme** *nf (e) (Reg)* 1 releasing air from a container 2 outburst of temper: blowup

***shfryjtje** *nf ger* <shfry·n

shfryrë *nf (e)* emotional outburst

shfryrës *nm* [Tech] exhaust opening

shfryrje *nf ger* 1 <shfry·n, shfry·het 2 = shfryrë

shfrytëzim *nm ger* 1 <shfrytëzo·n 2 exploitation

shfrytëzo· *n vt* 1 to exploit 2 to make use of []: employ; take advantage of []

shfrytëzuar *adj (i)* exploited

shfrytëzues

I § *adj* exploiting, exploitive

II § *n* exploiter

shfrytëzueshëm *adj (i)* exploitable

***shfryto·** *n* = shfrytëzo·n

***shfrytues** = shfrytëzues

***shfundos·** *vt* 1 to send [] to the bottom 2 *(Fig)* to wreck

shfuqizim *nm ger* 1 [Law] <shfuqizo·n, shfuqizo·het 2 nullification

shfuqizo· *n vt* [Law] to declare [] null and void, nullify, abrogate

shfuqizuar *adj (i)* [Law] null and void, abrogated

shfuqizues *adj* [Law] nullifying, voiding, abrogating

***shfurk** = sfurk

shfytyrim *nm ger* = shpërfytyrim

shfytyro·het *vpr* = shpërfytyro·het

shfytyro· *n vt* = shpërfytyro·n

shfytyrues *adj* = shpërfytyrues

***shgënje·** *n* = zhgënje·

***shgjakës** = zhgjakës

***shgjakos·** *vt* = zhgjakëso·n

***shgjet** CF= shigjet

***shgjymt** = zhgjymt

***shgjymtyrim** *nm ger* 1 <shgjymtyro·n 2 mutilation

***shgjymtyro·** *n vt* to mutilate

shi·het

I § *vpr* <she·h 1 to be evident 2 to meet together 3 to show up somewhere

II § *vpr* <shi·n to crumble

shi·n

I § *vt* 1 to thresh [grain]; shell [corn] by beating with a stick the dried ears lying on a wicker screen; shell [beans] by striking the dried pods with a flail 2 *(Reg)* to crush/crumble [] by pounding

II § *vi (Fig Pej)* to do just as one likes without regard to others

   ◦ **shi·n si kali në lëmë** *(Pej)* to do whatever one wants

shi

I § *nm* rain

II § *pcl (Reg)* right then/there, exactly, right

   ◦ **shiu i budallait** soft drizzle

○ **shi e diell** changeable weather: sometimes raining, sometimes sunny
○ **shi i hollë** drizzle
○ **shi i imët** fine rain, drizzle
○ **shi pjesnik** *(Old)* local shower
○ **shi i rëndë** heavy rainstorm
○ **shi yjor** [*Astron*] meteor shower

***shi(n)** *nm (pl ‾ na)* nape = **zverk**

shiatik
 I § *adj* [*Anat*] sciatic
 II § *nm* **1** sciatic nerve **2** [*Med*] sciatica

shibë *nf* catarrh (in both humans and animals) = **rrufë**

shibël *nf* breadcrumb, crumb

shibëllo·n *vi* to fritter away one's energies

***shibi** *nf* trifle

shifër *nf* **1** numeral **2** number **3** cipher, code

shifon *nm* sheer silk/cotton fabric: chiffon; head kerchief made of black chiffon

shifrant *nm* cipher clerk

shifrar *nm* register of ciphers: code book

shifrim *nm ger* **1** <**shifro·n** **2** encipherment

shifro·n *vt* **1** to encipher, encode **2** [*Fin*] to assign [] a numerical value

shifruar *adj (i)* **1** enciphered, encoded **2** [*Fin*] designated by a numeral: numbered

***shigëllimë** *nf ger* <**shigëllo·n**

***shigëllo·n** *vt, vi* = **shungullo·n**

shigjetak *adj* [*Bot*] sagittate *(SH)*

shigjetar *n* archer, bowman

shigjetë
 I § *nf* **1** arrow **2** something with a long, thin, and pointed shape **3** pointer on a dial: needle **4** *(Fig)* spoken barb **5** [*Zool*] = **shigjetull 6** shuttle (of a loom) **7** *(Old)* prize part of the kill taken by the hunter who has made the first hit
 II § *adv* **1** quick as an arrow ***2** [*Invert*] wireworm used as a bait
 ○ **shigjetë** *bregdetare* [*Geog*] bayhead bar, sandspit
 ○ **shigjeta e gjatë** [*Zool*] whip snake *Coluber jugularis*
 ○ **shigjeta e hollë** [*Zool*] Dahl's whip snake *Coluber najadum*
 ○ **shigjeta e shkurtër** [*Zool*] Balkan racer *Coluber gemonensis*

shigjetim *nm ger* <**shigjetio·n**, **shigjetio·het**

shigjeto·het *vp recip* to exchange barbed looks

shigjeto·n *vt, vi* **1** to shoot arrows (at []) **2** *(Fig)* to cast a menacing glance; attack [] with barbed words

shigjetor *adj* [*Med*] sagittal

shigjetull *nf* [*Zool*] European whip snake (mistakenly believed to be poisonous) *(Coluber jugularis)*

shih *stem for 2nd pl pres, pind, imper, vp* <**sheh·**
 ○ **Shih me sy e s'është për ty.** "See with the eye and it isn't for you!" You may look at it, but you can't have it.
 ○ **Shih me sy e plas me zemër.** "See with the eye and eat your heart out!" You may look at it, but you can't have it.
 ○ **Shih qesen tëndе!** "See to your own purse!" Mind your own business!
 ○ **shih·et^3rd si në pëllëmbë të dorës** to be as visible as if {} were in the palm of one's hand
 ○ **Shih e shkruaj!** "Look and write!" It's self-explanatory.

***shii** *np* Shiite Moslems

shije *nf* **1** taste; flavor **2** pleasure enjoyed in eating

shije'së *nf* taste; fragrance

shijim *nm ger* <**shijo·n**

shijo·n *vt* **1** to sample [food, drink]: taste **2** *(Fig)* to enjoy, like, esteem
 ○ <> **shijo·n** to taste good to <>

shijor *adj (Book)* pertaining to taste

shijosh *adj* = **shijshëm**

shijshëm *adj (i)* **1** (of food) tasty, good-tasting **2** (of people) sweet, nice

shijuar *nn (të)* sense of taste

SHIK [*shik*] *abbrev nm* <**Shërbimi Informativ Kombëtar** National Information Service (= FBI)

shik *adv (Colloq)* in/with elegant taste: chic

***shik·** *vt* = **fshik·**

shikakuq *nm* [*Bot*] **1** European spindle tree = **fshikakuq 2** cotoneaster *(Cotoneaster integerrimus)*

shikarth *nm* [*Bot*] bladder senna = **fshikartë**

shikëll *nf* oak gall, oak apple

shikim *nm ger* **1** <**shiko·n**, **shiko·het 2** look, glance **3** expression conveyed by the eyes: look **4** vision **5** *(Fig)* aspect, regard; outlook

shiko·het *vpr* to see one another: meet

shiko·n
 I § *vt* **1** to look at []; observe **2** to examine [] carefully **3** to take care of []; look after []; see to []
 II § *vi* **1** to look **2** to take heed, take care: look out **3** to see
 ○ **shiko·n derën** to keep looking at the door, wait impatiently for someone's arrival
 ○ <**a shiko·n gojën** "look at <>'s mouth (in order to make sure <> has enough to eat)" to keep <> well-fed
 ○ [] **shiko·n me bishtin e syrit 1** to see [] out of the corner of the eye **2** to disparage [], undervalue []
 ○ **shiko·n me ngulm** to watch <> constantly, not take one's eyes off <>
 ○ [] **shiko·n me sy të shtrembër/keq/lig 1** to have a low regard for []; look at/on [] with disfavor **2** to have no interest in []'s welfare
 ○ [] **shiko·n me syrin e njerkës** [] gets treated unfairly
 ○ [] **shiko·n me syrin plot 1** to view [] with envy **2** to examine [] carefully; look [] over from head to toe
 ○ [] **shiko·n me syze të errëta** to make [] seem worse than [] really is: see/present [] in a bad light
 ○ [] **shiko·n me vetulla** to scowl at []
 ○ [] **shiko·n në bebe të syrit 1** to look [] in the eye, show no fear of [] **2** to keep a constant eye on [] (usually a child)
 ○ [] **shiko·n në sy 1** to look [] in the eye **2** to face up to []
 ○ **shiko·n nën ballë** to have a look of anger/hatred on one's face
 ○ [] **shiko·n nën qepalla** "look at [] under the eyelids" not look at [] in the eye
 ○ [] **shiko·n nën vetulla** to scowl at []
 ○ **shiko·n nga qofkat** "look at the blackbirds" to keep shifting one's gaze, let one's attention wander
 ○ [] **shiko·n për fill e për fërkem** to examine [] in great detail: go over [] with a fine-toothed comb
 ○ **shiko·n për sherr** to look for a fight, ask for trouble
 ○ **shiko·n portën** to keep looking at the outer door, wait impatiently for someone's arrival

○ **Shiko punën/punëzën tënde!** Mind your own business!

○ **Shikon qimen në syrin e tjetrit dhe nuk shikon/sheh trarin në syrin e vet.** "You see the hair in someone else's eye but don't see the wooden beam in your own eye." You see someone else's slightest fault but miss your own glaring faults.

○ **shiko·***n* **qimen në vezë/të bardhën e vezës** "see the hair in (the white of) an egg" to try to find fault, pick at details

○ **Shiko rrugën tënde!** Mind your own business!

○ [] **shiko·***n* **si ujku hënën** "look at [] like the wolf at the moon" to give [] an angry stare, look at [] with anger

○ [] **shiko·***n* **shtrembër 1** to have a low regard for []; look at/on [] with disfavor **2** to have no interest in []'s welfare **3** to look daggers at []

○ **e shiko·***n* **shumë gojën** to be perfectly capable of getting oneself fed

○ **e shiko·***n* **të vërtetën në sy** "look at the truth in the eye" to face facts, face the truth squarely

○ [] **shiko·***n* **vëngër 1** to have a low regard for []; look at/on [] with disfavor **2** to have no interest in []'s welfare **3** to look daggers at []

shiku'es *nm* **1** observer **2** spectator

shil *nm* **1** (*Reg*) desire, wish; craving, lust **2** suspicion, doubt

shila'r· *vi* to swing, dangle

shila'r·et *vpr* to swing (back and forth), dangle, sway = **kolovi't·et**

shila'r ës *nm* **1** children's swing **2** seesaw

shila'rth *nm* = **shila'rës**

shila'rthi *adv* swinging back and forth

shili'ngë *nf* shilling

*****shilo'·***n* *vt* = **shalo'·***n*

shilo'r *nm* **1** crossmember connecting the support forks of a grape arbor; yoke worn on the shoulders for carrying cumbersome loads **2** fence stile **3** children's swing

shilo'rth *nm* crossmember connecting the support forks of a grape arbor; yoke worn on the shoulders for carrying cumbersome loads

shi'lte *OR* **shilte** *nf* foam pad for a bench, bench cushion

*****shilu'r** = **shilo'r**

*****shilu'r·** *vt* = **shila'r·**

*****shilu'r·et** *vpr* = **shila'r·et**

*****shilu'rth** *nm* = **shila'rës**

*****shilu'rth a** *np* (*Old*) **1** <**shilu'rth 2** vicissitudes of life, ups and downs

shi'mat ës *adj* [*Meteor*] rain gauge

shi'mba jt ës *nm* rain cistern

shi'mble dh ës *adj* [*Geog*] in which rain collects: rain-collecting

shimpanze *nf* [*Zool*] chimpanzee

shimshi'r *nm* [*Bot*] boxwood (*Buxus sempervirens*) = **bush**

shina ko't
  I § *adj* capricious, queer = **tekanjo'z**
  II § *n* queer/odd person

shina ko't ë *nf* caprice, whim

shina ndërru'e s *nm* railroad worker who repairs the rails

shina shtru'e s *nm* worker who lays steel rails

shi'ndër *nf* [*Bot*] resin = **rrëshi'rë**

shi'në *nf* **1** steel rail (on a railroad track) **2** iron rim on a wooden wheel

*****shi'ni** *obl* <**shi**(*n*)

shini'k *nm* dry measure of grain varying by region from 35 to 150 kilograms: bushel

shi'no'·*n* *vi* to rain

shinobu's *nm* rail bus, rail diesel car

*****shinja'll** *nm* devil, demon

shi'o's ë *nf* (*Reg*) red soil/clay/earth

*****ship** *pred* full

*****shi'pkë** *nf* = **shupla'kë**

*****shiq i'm** = **shiki'm**

*****shiqu'e s** = **shiku'es**

shi'r a *np* (*të*) *fem* **1** threshing; threshing time/season **2** grain brought to the threshing floor

shi'ra *np* <**shi** rains, raining

shi'r ë *adj* (*i*) threshed, for threshing

shi'r ë *nf* **1** resin = **rrëshi'rë** ***2** must of grapes/pears

shi'r ës
  I § *adj* for threshing
  II § *n* thresher

shi'r ëse *nf* threshing machine

shiri'ngë *nf* [*Med*] syringe

shiri't
  I § *nm* **1** ribbon; strip; stripe; tape **2** [*Mil*] officer's stripe (worn on the uniform) **3** [*Invert*] tapeworm
  II § *adj* formed like a long narrow strip; ribbon-like

○ **shirit bigëzor** [*Bot*] kind of brown alga *Dictyota dichotoma*

○ **shirit filmi** strip of photographic film

○ **shirit i kuq** red sash (worn around the arm to indicate that one is on official business)

○ **shirit i librit** silk ribbon attached to a book to serve as a bookmark

○ **shirit makine** typewriter ribbon

○ **shirit i mbërritjes** [*Sport*] ribbon marking the finish line of a race: finish ribbon

○ **shirit mitralozi** [*Mil*] ammunition belt for a machine gun

○ **shirit shërbimi** [*Mil*] red sash (worn around the arm to indicate that one is on military duty)

○ **shirit i telegramit** ticker tape

○ **shirit i zi** black ribbon (worn to indicate mourning)

shi'r je *nf ger* **1** <**shi'·***n*, **shi'·het 2** crops involved in threshing

shir k *nm* (*np* ˜ *qe*) leather/skin bag, pouch

shiro'k *nm* [*Meteor*] humid, rain-bearing wind: sirocco

*****shiru'p** = **shuru'p**

shis *stem for pind, 2nd pl pres, imper* <**she't·**

*****shi'se** *nf* = **shqi'së**

shist *nm* [*Geol*] schist = **rre shpe**

shisto'r *adj* [*Geol*] schistose = **rreshpo'r**

shish *nm* **1** spit (for broiling meat): brochette, skewer **2** double-edged dagger; short spear

shisha'ne *nf* [*Hist*] musket

shi'she *nf* bottle

○ **shishe gjimnastikore** [*Gymnastics*] Indian club, club

*****shi'sh ko** *nf with masc agreement* = **shishma'n**

shishma'n *nm* man with a big paunch, fat man

shish qeba'p *nm* [*Food*] skewered chunks of meat roasted over a fire: shish kebab

shit·et *vpr* <**shet·** 1 to be for sale 2 *(Pej)* to sell out (one's principles/country) for personal profit 3 *(Pej)* to put on an act, pretend to be something
∘ **shit·et për tridhjetë aspra** to sell out for thirty pieces of silver

shit *stem for part, pdef, pind, 2nd pl pres, imper, vp* <**shet·**
∘ **Shiti gjetkë∥ Shitja tjetërkujt këto!** Go peddle your wares somewhere else! Try to find some other sucker to believe these things!.

shit ble'r *ës nm (Old)* commercial trader: merchant

shit ble'rje *nf* commerce

shit e *nf* 1 *[Folklore]* punishment inflicted by mountain spirits on a person who happens to interrupt their dancing or eating 2 *[Veter]* disease that lames sheep/goats = **shqe pëz** 3 *(Reg)* slap/cuff/box with the hand

shit ës
I § *adj* involved in selling
II § *n* salesperson; vendor
∘ **shitës ambulant** peddler

*__shit__ësi *nf (Old)* salability

shit im *nm ger* <**shitio** ·*n*, **shito**·*het*

shit je *nf ger* <**shet·**, **shit·et**

shit o·het *vpr [Folklore]* to be paralyzed or struck dumb by mountain/forest fairies; be bewitched

shit o·n *vt* 1 to punish [ ] by casting a spell, put a curse on [ ] 2 *(Reg)* to strike [ ] down; strike [ ] hard

shit ua'r *adj (i)* 1 *[Folklore]* paralyzed/dumbstruck (by mountain/forest fairies) 2 *(Reg)* wounded

shit u es
I § *n* one who strikes/wounds another
II § *adj (Reg) (Fig)* penetrating, striking

shi tur
I § *adj (i)* 1 sold 2 *(Pej)* venal, mercenary
II § *n (i) (Pej)* mercenary, lackey

*__sh ka__ = çka

shka' *stem for pdef, opt, adm, part, imper* <**shket·**
∘ <> **shkau shëndeti** <> is in failing health

shka b *ë nf [Ornit]* 1 griffon vulture *(Gyps fulvus Habl.)* 2 eagle = **shqipo'nj** *ë*
∘ **shkaba mjekroshe** *[Ornit]* bearded vulture, lammergeier *Gypaetus barbatus L.*

*__shkab o'nj__ë *nf [Ornit]* = **shqipo'nj** *ë*

shkadhe'c *nm [Agr]* broad wooden plank used as a drag harrow on small plots of ground

shkadhe's *ë nf [Agr]* bed of planting soil; agricultural terrace covered with planting soil

shkadh i's *stem for 1st sg pres, pl pres, 2nd & 3rd sg subj, pind* <**shkadh** *í·*

shkadh i't· *vt* 1 *[Agr]* to prune [a tree] 2 to clear away the underbrush under [a tree] *__3__ = çkal** *í·*

shkadh i'tje *nf ger [Agr]* <**shkadh** *í·*

*__shkaf__ = shkëf

shkafanj i's *stem for 1st sg pres, pl pres, 2nd & 3rd sg subj, pind* <**shkafanj** *í·*

shkafanj i't· *vt* 1 *(Reg)* to wreck, ruin; squash, bash in [ ] 2 to tear/rip [ ] to pieces: shred

*__shkaf i's__ *stem for 1st sg pres, pl pres, 2nd & 3rd sg subj, pind* <**shkaf** *í·*

*__shkaf i't·__ *vt* to gulp [ ] down

*__shkaf n o'r__ *adj* intestinal

shkag im *nm ger (Reg)* <**shkago**·*n*

shkag o·n *vt (Reg)* to reject

shka jt *stem for pdef* <**shket·**

*__shka jt sh ëm__ *adj (i)* slippery

shka k *nm (np ~ qe)* 1 cause 2 reason; pretext *__3__ trap

shkak *ësi nf [Philos]* causality; causation

shkak *ëso'r adj [Philos]* causal

shkak o'r *adj [Ling]* 1 causative 2 causal

shkak ta'r *n* causal agent: causer, cause

shkak t im *nm ger* <**shkakto**·*n*, **shkakto**·*het*

shkak t o·n *vt* to cause, bring about [ ]; create

shkak t ues *nm* = shkakta'r

shkal *nm* heavy rain, cloudburst

shkal· *vt* 1 to beat [wool] (in a fulling mill) 2 to bewitch; stupefy

shka l·et *vpr* 1 to be under a spell, be bewitched 2 to lose one's mind, go crazy

shkalafe'nd·et *vpr (Colloq)* to get exhausted by fatigue, become utterly worn out

shkalaf i's *stem for 1st sg pres, pl pres, 2nd & 3rd sg subj, pind* <**shkalaf** *í·(Colloq)*

shkalaf i't· *vt (Colloq)* to rip/tear [ ] to pieces: shred

shkalaf i't·et *vpr* 1 *(Colloq)* to rip, get torn/shredded 2 to get exhausted by fatigue, become utterly worn out

shkalaf i'tur *adj (i)* 1 *(Colloq)* ripped up, all torn, shredded 2 exhausted by fatigue, utterly worn out

shkala r i's· *vt* to knead [fermented wheat flour] in order to extract starch

shkalave'sh· *vt (Reg)* to contort, disfigure 2 = **shkalafi** *t·* 3 to beat [ ] up, bash

shkalave'sh·et *vpr* 1 *(Reg)* to become contorted, be disfigured 2 = **shkalafi** *t·et*

shkalave'sh ur *adj (i)* 1 contorted, disfigured 2 = **shkalafi** *tur*

*__shkalavi q·__ *vt* to beat [ ] down, quash; squash

*__shkal ba l'të__ *nf* thrall, slave

shkalb ëz i'm *nm ger [Agr]* <**shkalbëzo**·*n*

shkalb ëzo·n *vt [Agr]* to clear [ ] of [dead branches/trees: deadwood]

shkalc *nm (Reg)* 1 wooden handbarrow for carrying dirt/manure, handbarrow with a wooden frame and a wickerwork bed; litter, stretcher, bier 2 trough with a wickerwork bed for shelling corn; trough for pressing grapes/olives

shkal e *nf* problem, difficulty, impediment

sh kali's *stem for 1st sg pres, pl pres, 2nd & 3rd sg subj, pind* <**shkal** *í·*

sh kal i't·
I § *vt* 1 *[Tech]* to cause [something made of steel] to lose its temper, spoil the temper of [metal] 2 to pamper/spoil 3 to debilitate/enfeeble 4 to unload, disembark [cargo]
II § *vi (Old)* to dismount, disembark; alight; arrive for an overnight stay

sh kal i't·et *vpr* to become debilitated/enfeebled

sh kali ta'r *adj, n* pampered/spoiled (child)

sh kal i'tje *nf ger* 1 *[Tech]* <**shkalí** *t·*, **shkalí** *t·et* 2 debilitation; debility *__3__ craziness, lunacy

sh kal i'tur *adj (i)* 1 debilitated, enfeebled; (of steel) having lost its temper: untempered *__2__ (of a child) spoiled

shkalo j *ë nf [Bot]* false indigo *(Amorpha fruticosa)*

shkalo's·
I § *vt* to unload, disembark [cargo]
II § *vi (Old)* to dismount, disembark; alight; arrive for an overnight stay

shka'lur *adj (i)* **1** bewitched, under a spell **2** *(Fig)* out of one's mind, crazed **3** fulled

shkallaq
I § *adj (Impol)* crazy; nutty, loony, silly
II § *n (Impol)* crazy person: nut

shkalla're *nf* **1** stairstep, step; foothold **2** row of seats (in a banked auditorium/arena)

shka'lle *nf* rope loop hanging from a saddle to act as a stirrup for mounting

shka'llë
I § *nf* **1** ladder, stepladder **2** stairway, staircase; stairway entrance **3** = **shkalla're 4** *[Geog]* steep and narrow stepped path in a mountain gorge; step-like series of boulders on the face of a mountain **5** scale **6** *(Fig)* scale (of magnitude); range, series; extent **7** degree **8** *(Fig)* level, rank; class, order **9** *(Fig Old)* social class **10** gouge mark; nick, notch **11** = **shka'lle 12** forked prop used as an aid to load a pack saddle with something heavy
II § *np* rows of seats in a stadium: bleachers
∘ **shkallët e krahasimit** *[Ling]* degrees of (grammatical) comparison
∘ **shkalla krahasore e sipërisë** *[Ling]* superlative degree of comparison
∘ **shkalla krahasore e ultësisë** *[Ling]* inferior degree (in comparisons)
∘ **shkalla krahasore** the comparative degree
∘ **Shkalla e lartë do/kërkon këmbë të fortë.** "A tall ladder demands strong legs." *(Prov)* An ambitious undertaking requires a strong will.
∘ **shkallë ngjitëse** *[Mus]* ascending scale
∘ **shkallë njerëzish** people of the same generation
∘ **shkalla e skelës** *(Old)* harbor dock, jetty
∘ **shkallë suedeze** parallel wall bars used in gymnastic exercises: Swedish bars, wall ladder
∘ **shkallë superiore** *[Ling]* superlative degree
∘ **shkallë e thyer** *(Impol)* piece of useless junk; worthless person

shka'llë-shka'llë
I § *adv, adj* stepped, step-like: terraced; wavy (hair)
II § *adv* gradually

shka'llëz *nf* **1** = **shkalla're 2** *(Dimin)* < **shka'llë**

shkallëzi'm *nm ger* **1** < **shkallëzo'·n 2** gradation **3** escalation

shkallëzo'·n *vt* **1** to form [] into steps **2** to mark divisions [] by scaled lines: graduate **3** to increase [] in scale; increase [] gradually; escalate **4** to sort [] into a particular order

shkallëzo'r *adj (Book)* gradual

shkallëzua'r *adj (i)* **1** stepped; terraced **2** graduated, scaled **3** increasing stepwise, growing gradually

shkalli'në *nf* = **shkalla're**

*****shkallka** *adv* = **rrokopujë**

shka'llmë *nf* sword, saber

shkallmi'm *nm ger* < **shkallmo'·n, shkallmo'·het**

shkallmo'·het *vpr* **1** to break/tear down/up/apart completely **2** *(Fig)* to become completely fatigued

shkallmo'·n *vt* **1** to dislocate [] from its base, break/tear [] down/up/apart completely **2** *(Fig)* to tire [] out completely, exhaust

shkallmua'r *adj (i)* **1** completely broken/torn down/up/apart: devastated **2** *(Fig)* completely fatigued, utterly exhausted

shkallmu'es
I § *adj* devastating
II § *n* devastator, despoiler

shkallo'·n
I § *vi* to go crazy/mad
II § *vt* to drive [] crazy/mad

shkallo'më *nf* = **shkalla're**

shkallo'r *adj* **1** *[Spec]* graduated, scaled **2** scalar *****3** = **shkallëzo'r**

*****shkalli'sisht** *adv (Old)* gradually

*****shkalli'tore** *nf (Old)* escalator

shkallua'r *adj (i), n (i)* crazy/insane/mad (person)

*****shkamb** *nm (Reg Gheg)* = **shkëmb**

shkanco'·n *vt* to draw [one's knife] (out of its sheath)

shka'ndull *nm (np ~ j)* **1** curse, foul language; obscenity; obscene behavior **2** bad model/example

shkandulli *nf* wickedness, wrongdoing

shkandullo'·n *vt* to lead into wickedness/sin

shkape's *stem for 1st sg pres, pl pres, 2nd & 3rd sg subj, pind* < **shkape't·**

shkape't· *vt* **1** to smack, slam, bang *****2** *(Reg Gheg)* to pour [] out, pour
∘ **shkapet· mendtë** to rack one's brain

shkape't·et *vpr* **1** = **përpla's·et** *****2** *(Reg Gheg)* to pour down

*****shkape'tje** *nf ger* **1** < **shkape't·, shkapet·et** *****2** *(Reg Gheg)* downpour, outpour

shkapërce'·n *vt* = **kapërce'·n**

shkapërci'm *nm ger* **1** = **kapërci'm 2** *(Fig Old)* minor transgression: misdeed

shkapërda'·het *vpr* to become scattered, scatter out; disperse

shkapërda'·n *vt* to strew, scatter; disperse

*****shkapërda'më** *adj (i)* scattered, dispersed

shkapërda'r
I § *adj* squandering, extravagant; wasteful
II § *n* spendthrift, wastrel, squanderer

shkapërde'rdh· *vt* **1** to distribute [] randomly: disperse, scatter, spill **2** to squander, waste

shkapërde'rdh·et *vpr* **1** to disperse **2** to dissipate

shkapërde'rdh es *adj* = **shkapërda'r**

shkapërde'rdhje *nf ger* **1** < **shkapërderdh·, shkapërderdh·et 2** extravagance, waste

shkapërde'rdhur *adj (i)* **1** broadly dispersed/disseminated; scattered **2** dissipated, disjointed

shkapërdhi *nf* child who is always climbing around and getting into mischief; nimble child

shkapërthe·n *vt* **1** to unfasten; dismantle; open [] up **2** to break/bust [] open; destroy; crush

shkapërthi'm *nm ger* < **shkapërthe·n**

shkapërvi'l·et *vpr* to clamber about

*****shkapërx** = **shkapërc**

*****shkapërxye's** *adj* passing, exceeding; excelling; excessive

shkapula'r *nm (Reg)* shoulder
∘ [] **heq· (për/prej) shkapularësh** to pull [] with []'s shoulders dragging on the ground

shka'qe *np* < **shkak**

shkara'ngjit·et *vpr* to clamber up (while holding on with arms and legs)

shkara'nik *adj* slippery

*****shkarave'sh·** *vt* to make [] shapeless, maul

*****shkaravi'në** *nf* = **shkarravi'në**

*****shkaravi'is** *stem for 1st sg pres, pl pres, 2nd & 3rd sg subj, pind* < **shkaravi't·**

*****shkaravi't·** *vi, vt* = **shkarravi't·**

shka'razi OR **shka'ras** adv **1** obliquely, superficially; grazingly **2** indirectly, incidentally

sh|karbon|izím nm ger <**shkarbonizo·**n

sh|karbon|izo·n vt [Tech] to decarbonize

shka'rdhë nf **1** long stick attached to a chain around a dog's neck to keep him from biting the person leading him **2** (Reg) wicker gate in a fence

shka'rdh|ínë nf ramshackle house, shanty

shka'rë part <**shket·**

shkarë**ze·**het vpr to wallow in the mud

shkarë**ze·**n vt **1** to drag [] through mud; ruin, destroy **2** (Fig) to disparage, derogate

shkarë**zím** nm ger **1** <**shkarëze·**n, **shkarëze·**het **2** (Fig) disparagement, scorn

shkarë**zím**ë nf **1** sliding ground: slide; talus **2** slippery ground, sliding place

shkarë**zít·**et vpr to go sliding, slide

shka'rje nf ger **1** <**shket· 2** landslide; slippage, slip; slide **3** unwitting error: slip

sh|karke'së nf **1** electrical discharge **2** disburdenment

sh|karkí nf (Colloq) justification, excuse

sh|karkím nm ger **1** <**shkarko·**n, **shkarko·**het **2** discharge

  ◦ **shkarkim atmosferik** bolt of lightning or thunder

sh|karko·het

  I § vpr to let loose one's feelings, unloose something pent up inside

  II § vp reflex to exonerate oneself

sh|karko·n

  I § vt **1** to unload **2** to relieve of [a responsibility/burden], release

  II § vi, vt **1** to discharge **2** (Old) to disembark

sh|karku'es

  I § adj serving or pertaining to a discharge

  II § n worker responsible for unloading: unloader

  III § nm **1** outlet for surplus liquid: overflow **2** [Electr] overvoltage suppressor; lightning arrester

shkar|me'nd nm poor soul, unfortunate wretch

shkarmís stem for 1st sg pres, pl pres, 2nd & 3rd sg subj, pind <**shkarmít·**

shkarmít· vt tear [] up/apart, rip [] to pieces; dismember

shka'rpe nf **1** kindling, brushwood **2** (Reg) old shoe; worn out shoe **3** empty honeycomb **4** (Reg) [Bot] mastic tree = **xín**ë

shka'rpë**za** np = **shkarpurína**

shkarp|urína np fem kindling wood, brush

*****shkartím** nm ger **1** <**shkarto·**n **2** removal

shkartínë nf **1** worm-eaten wood **2** ramshackle house, shanty

shkartís· vt **1** (Colloq) to mix [] together, mingle *****2** to get rid of [], remove

shkartís·et vpr (Colloq)

  ◦ **shkartis·**et **me** [] **1** to get mixed up with [], mingle with [] **2** (Fig) to get into trouble with []

shkartís|je nf ger (Colloq) **1** <**shkartís·**, **shkartís·**et **2** mixture = **përzie'rje**

shkartís|ur adj (i) (Colloq) mixed, mixed together

shkart|o·n vt **1** (of larvae) to eat [] away to cull out [] **2** to get rid of [], remove

shkarth nm **1** [Zool] squirrel **2** (Old) paid servant boy **3** twig, straw

  ◦ **shkarth dyqani** shopkeeper's apprentice

shka'rth|a np **1** <**shkarth 2** brushwood, undergrowth

*****shka'rth|azi** adv **1** sliding, gliding **2** askew

shka'rthi adv obliquely

shkarthí nf (Colloq) brute force, violence

shkarze'·het vpr to roll around in the dust

shkarze·n vt to treat [] with contempt: abase

shkarrave'sh· vt to divide [] into pieces by forcible action: cut/chop/break/tear [] to pieces

shkarraví|në nf **1** scrawl, scribble **2** (FigImpolite) worthless literary work, drivelsmudge

shkarraví|s stem for 1st sg pres, pl pres, 2nd & 3rd sg subj, pind <**shkarraví·**t·

shkarraví·t· vi, vt **1** to scribble, scrawl out [] **2** (FigImpolite) to write [drivel, poor poetry] *****3** to smudge *****4** to drag along; slouch, slink

shkarraví|të**s** n (Impol) scribbler

shkarraví|tje nf ger **1** <**shkarraví·**t· **2** = **shkarraví**në

shkas nm motivating cause: reason; impetus, impulse, drive, motive

shka's stem for 1st sg pres, 1si & 3rd pl pres, 2nd & 3rd sg subj <**shket·**

shka's|ës adj sliding

shkatarra'q

  I § adj (Impol) in shambles, in ruin, broken-down **2** slovenly, sloppy, slipshod; destructive, ruinous

  II § n slipshod worker, slovenly/sloppy person

shka'tërr adv in a devastated/demolished condition; in disorder, in a mess

shka'tërr nf [Ichth] sting ray Dasyatis pastinaca

  ◦ **shkatërr bishtgjatë** [Ichth] roughtail stingray Dasyatis centroura

  ◦ **shkatërr manushaqe** [Ichth] violet stingray Dasyatis violacea

shkatërre'së nf **1** devastation *****2** = **shkat**ë**rrí**në

shkatërrím nm ger **1** <**shkatërro·**n, **shkatërro·**het **2** devastation; dilapidation

shkatërrimta'r

  I § adj devastating

  II § n devastator, demolisher

shkatërrínë nf dilapidated old building

shkatërro·het vpr **1** to fall into ruin, become dilapidated; break down **2** to grow feeble

shkatërro·n vt **1** to ruin [] completely: devastate, demolish **2** to untangle

shkatërru|ar adj (i) **1** devastated; broken down **2** (Impol) = **shkatarra'q**

shkatërru'e|s adj, n = **shkatërrimta'r**

shkath· vt to rouse [] from numbness: thaw out []

shka'th·et vpr to become more energetic/alert; brighten up

shkath|ësí nf = **shkathtësí**

shka'th|ët

  I § adj (i) mentally/physically quick: adroit, agile, deft; clever, smart

  II § adv with agility: adroitly, deftly; cleverly

shkath|ëto·n vt = **shkathtëso·**n

shkath|o·n vt = **shkath·**

shkath|t|ësí nf agility, adroitness, nimbleness; smart, mental quickness, cleverness

shkath|t|ësím nm ger <**shkathtëso·**n, **shkathtë-so·**het

shkath|t|ë|so·het vpr to gain adroitness/agility

shkath|të**s|o·n** *vt* to make [] more adroit/agile: train

***shkath|t**í *OR* **shkath|t|í**n*ë* *nf* = **shkathtësí**

shka|u *3rd sg pdef* < **shket·**

shka|zmë *nf* slippery muddy ground

***shkec·** *vt* = **shqal**t·

shkel·

I § *vt* **1** to step on [], tread; trample; stamp **2** *(Fig)* to set foot on/in [] **3** *(Fig Colloq)* to trip on [], slip carelessly on [] **4** to exert pressure on [something that offers resistance]: press; full [cloth] **5** *(Colloq)* to iron, press **6** *(Fig)* to subjugate, suppress **7** *(Fig)* to violate **8** to cast a spell over [], put a charm/curse on []: hex **9** *(Colloq)* to afflict **10** to mount (sexually) [a hen] **11** *(Colloq)* to massage [] with one's foot **12** *(Fig Colloq)* to begin [a period of time]

II § *vi* **1** to stomp, tromp, tramp, trample, tread; practice repression **2** *(Fig)* to set foot; enter **3** *(Fig Colloq)* (of a period of time) to arrive, begin

∘ **ia shkel·** (gazin) **1** *(Colloq)* to step on the gas, step on it: hurry up **2** to do something in haste

∘ **shkel· betimin** to betray one's solemn oath

∘ <> **shkel· bishtin** "step on <>'s tail" **1** to infringe on <>'s rights **2** to put [] in a predicament

∘ <> **shkel· brezin** "step on <>'s sash" to give <> cause for a quarrel, step on <>'s toes

∘ <> **shkel· bukën (me këmbë)** to show ingratitude to <>

∘ **shkel· e shko** sloppy

∘ **të shkel· hijen (prapa)** "steps on your shadow (from behind)" {} is quick to take advantage of opportunities; {} is masterful/adept

∘ **shkel· keq** to make a misstep/mistake

∘ <> **shkel·**[3sg] **këmba shesh/dyst** "<>'s foot steps flat on the ground" <> has had an easy time of it; <> feels confident/easy

∘ **shkel· këmbë** *(Old)* to put one's foot down: be stubborn, insist

∘ **shkel· kurorën** to break one's marriage vows, commit adultery

∘ **shkel· mbi gjarpërinj** to get into a big mess, fall into a snakepit

∘ [] **shkel· me këmbë 1** to trample on [] **2** to reject []

∘ [] **shkel·**[3sg] **me para/ryshfete** "step on [] with money/bribes" to get to [] with a bribe, bribe []

∘ **e shkel· me të dy/dyja këmbët** to make a big blunder

∘ **shkel· në erë** to run fleetingly, barely touch the ground in running

∘ **shkel· në gjurmët e** <> to follow in <>'s footsteps

∘ [] **shkel· në kallo/lyth** to touch []'s most sensitive spot

∘ **shkel· në pambuk** to have a soft life

∘ **nuk** <>**a shkel·**[3sg] **njeri hijen prapa** <> *is* so fast that nobody *can* catch <>

∘ <> **shkel· syrin** to give <> the eye, wink at <>

∘ <>**a shkel· vrapit** to take to one's heels, speed away

shkel·et

I § *vp reflex* to shove one another

II § *vpr* (of poultry) to copulate with a male: mate

shkel|ba|të**s** *n (Old)* marriage broker, go-between, matchmaker = **lajmës**

shkel|c *nm* stairstep: step

shke|l|ës

I § *n* **1** violator; trespasser, transgressor; oppressor **2** apparatus for exerting pressure: press, ram; winepress **3** *(Old)* = **shkelba|t**ë**s**

II § *adj* oppressive; trespassing, invading

shke|l|ët *adj (i)* **1** downtrodden **2** trodden

shke|l|ë|z *nf* = **shkalla**re

shke|l|je *nf ger* < **shkel·**, **shkel·et**

shkel|m *nm* kick

∘ **i bie**₁· **së mirës//bukës me shkelm** "kick away something good//food" to throw it all away, throw away a good opportunity

∘ **shkelm dënimi** *(Old)* [*Sport*] penalty kick

∘ **shkelmi i parë** [*Soccer*] kickoff

∘ **shkelm ridërgimi** [*Soccer*] goal kick

∘ **shkelmi i vdekjes** deathblow

shkelm|ím *nm ger* < **shkelmo·n**

shkelm|o·n

I § *vt, vi* to kickD to trample

II § *vt (Fig)* to reject [] curtly and decisively: spurn sharply

shkel|tar *n (Old)* trampler; transgressor

shke|l|ur

I § *part* < **shkel·**, **shkel·et**

II § *adj (i)* **1** stepped-on; trodden; (of shoes) well-worn **2** fulled **3** *(Fig)* downtrodden, oppressed

∘ **nuk ka shkelur kurrë këmba e** <> {*place adverbial*} <> has never set foot {*somewhere*}

shke|l|ur|a *np (të) fem* [*Ethnog*] exchange visits by the bridegroom's party and the bride's party to exchange engagement tokens

shke|l|ë|z *nf* [*Bot*] = **shkozëze|z**ë

shkem|o·n *vi* (of a tree) to sprout new leaves and branches

shkenc|ë *nf* science

shkenc|ë|rísht *adv* scientifically

shkenc|ë|tar *n* scientist; scholar

∘ **shkencëtar kabineti** *(Book Pej)* ivory tower scientist

shkenc|or *adj* scientific

shkenc|o|ro-popull|or *adj* presented in popular scientific terms

shkep· *vt* = **shqep·**

***sh|ke|p|ë** *nf* rip (in clothing), tear = **shqe|pj**e

shke|p|ëz *nf* [*Veter*] = **shqe|pëz**

***shkep|o·n** *vi* = **shqepo·n**

***shkept|í·n** = **shkrepti·n**

***shkept|í|m**ë *OR* **shkept|í|n**ë *nf* = **shkrepti|m**ë

***shkept|ít·** = **shkrepti·n**

***shkept|o·n** = **shkrepti·n**

shkep|ty|r|ëz *nf* [*Veter*] = **shqe|pëz**

shkerp *nm* [*Ichth*] black scorpionfish *(Scorpaena porcus)*

∘ **shkerp i kuq** [*Ichth*] *Scorpaena elongata*

∘ **shkerp kuqalosh** [*Ichth*] swallowtail sea perch *Anthias anthias*

∘ **shkerp i madh** [*Ichth*] red scorpionfish *Scorpaena scrofa*

∘ **shkerp thellësie** [*Ichth*] rockfish *Helicolenus dactylopterus dactylopterus*

∘ **shkerp i vogël** [*Ichth*] *Scorpaena notata*

***shke|rr·** = **shqe|rr·**

shkes *nm* [*Ethnog*] = **shku|es**

shke·së *nf* [*Ethnog*] = **shkuesi** 2 matchmaker (female) = **shkue**se 3 herd of livestock en route 4 sudden short burst of rain

shkesi *nf* [*Ethnog*] = **shkuesi**

shket· *vi* 1 to slip; slip and fall 2 to skate; ski; skate/ glide along, slide 3 to slide by without notice; slide away; slip away, evade 4 to slide down 5 (*Fig*) to make a slip: slip up/out, slip

  ◦ <> **shket·**³ᵖˡ **burgjitë** "<>'s screws slip" (*Colloq*) <> loses <>'s good sense

  ◦ <> **shket·**³ˢᵍ **goja** <>'s tongue *slips*

  ◦ <> **shket·**³ˢᵍ **gjuha** <>'s tongue *slips*

  ◦ <> **shket·**³ˢᵍ **këmba** "<>'s foot *slips*" <> *slips* and *falls*; <> *makes* a mistake and *loses* <>'s high position

  ◦ <> **shket·**³ᵖˡ **këmbët** "<>'s feet *slip*" <> *slips* and *falls*; <> *makes* a mistake and *loses* <>'s high position

  ◦ <> **shket· nga duart/dora** to slip out of <>'s hands; escape from <>'s control; <> *loses* control of {}

  ◦ <> **shket·**³ˢᵍ **pena** "<>'s pen *glides* along" <> *writes* easily, words *pour* out of <>'s pen easily

  ◦ **shket· si ngjalë** to be slippery as an eel

  ◦ <> **shket·**³ᵖˡ **trutë** "<>'s brains *slip*" (*Colloq*) <> becomes dotty, <> slips a cog

  ◦ <> **shket·**³ᵖˡ **themelet** "<>'s foundations *slip*" <> loses <>'s basic support: the bottom *slips* out from under <>

  ◦ <> **shket·**³ᵖˡ **vidhat** "<>'s screws slip" (*Colloq*) <> *loses* <>'s good sense

shke·zë *nf* large chip/sliver

*****shkëbith·** *vt* to wipe out, destroy

shkëf *nm* 1 (*Colloq*) belly cavity; guts; caul 2 heart and soul *3 womb, uterus; (cow's) vagina; rectum

shkëlba·z-*et vpr* to expectorate phlegm, spit out phlegm

shkëlbo·zë *nf* tree bark

shkëlfit· *vt* 1 to peel off the outer layer of []: skin, peel 2 (*Fig*) to irritate: get under []'s skin

shkëlfit·-*et vpr* (of skin and flesh) to rot and fall off; (of paint) peel off

shkëlnje·t *nm* (*Reg*) [*Bot*] = **krifsh**ë

shkëlqa·r· *vt* to polish

shkëlqa·r·-*et vpr* 1 (of weather) to clear up 2 (*Fig*) to shine

shkëlqa·rmë *adj* (*i*) = **kthje·llët**

shkëlqe·n *vi* to shine

shkëlqe·së *nf* 1 (*Old Offic*) = **shkëlqesi** 2 brilliance, shine, polish

shkëlqesi *nf* (*Offic*) Excellency (as an honorific term of address)

shkëlqi·m *nm ger* 1 <**shkëlqe·**n 2 blaze/flash of light 3 reflected light, reflection 4 luster 5 (*Fig*) apparent magnificence 6 (*Fig*) pinnacle of fame, flowering; illustriousness, glory 7 [*Phys*] luminance

Shkëlqi·m *nm* Shkëlqim (male name)

shkëlqim·plo·të *adj* (*Poet*) full of light: lambent, lucent

shkëlqim·ta·r *adj* (*Poet*) gleaming, lustrous; shining

shkëlqy·er *adj* (*i*) 1 shiny, gleaming 2 (*Fig*) exemplary, outstanding; brilliant

shkëlqy·es *adj* shiny, shining, glossy

shkëlqy·esh·ëm *I* § *adj* (*i*) 1 emitting a strong light: bright, glaring 2 brilliant, bright; shiny 3 (*Fig*) exemplary, outstanding
II § *adv* very well: brilliantly, wonderfully

shkël·ve·sh· *vt* 1 to lacerate [skin/flesh] 2 to strip [a tree] of leaves 3 to beat the living daylights out of []

*****shkëlze·**n *vi* = **shkëlqe·**n

Shkëlze·n *nm* Shkëlzen (male name)

*****shkëlzi·m** *nm ger* <**shkëlze·**n = **shkëlqi·m**

shkëmb
  I § *nm* (*np* ˜ *inj*) 1 rock mass: boulder, rocky crag/ cliff 2 [*Geol*] rock (as a substance) 3 [*Agr*] sole of a wooden plow 4 stool; crude wooden chair
  II § *adj* rocky; hard as rock; tough as a rock

  ◦ **shkëmb amënor** [*Geol*] *= **shkëmb mëmë**

  ◦ **shkëmb mëmë** [*Geol*] mother rock, source rock, parental rock

shkë·mb·a *np* <**shkëmb** stools; crude wooden chairs

*****shkëmba·r** *adj* (*Old*) = **shkëmbo·r**

shkëmbe··het *vp recip* to pass each other going in opposite directions: trade directions (after meeting)

shkëmbe··n *vt* 1 to exchange 2 to replace 3 to mistake [one person for another] 4 (*Fig*) to alter, change

  ◦ **shkëmbe··n fjal**ë to exchange words; exchange bitter words

  ◦ **shkëmbe··n hiçin me pluhur** "trade something of no value for dust" to make absolutely no profit, gain absolutely nothing

shkëmbe·së *nf* (*Old*) ransom

shkëmbët *adj* (*i*) = **shkëmbo·r**

shkëmbi·m *nm ger* 1 <**shkëmbe··**n, **shkëmbe··het** 2 exchange; trade

shkëmbi·nj *np* <**shkëmb**

shkëmbi·shtë *nf* rocky area; bedrock, stony ground

shkëmbo·r *adj* of rock/stone: rocky, stony

shkëmbo·re *nf* = **shkëmbi·sht**ë

shkëmbtë *adj* (*i*) 1 = **shkëmbo·r** 2 solid as rock

shkëmb·th *nm* (*Reg*) [*Mus*] bridge (of a stringed instrument) = **sama·r**

shkëmby·er *adj* (*i*) = **këmby·er**

shkëmby·erazi *adv* 1 alternately, reciprocally 2 (traded) even, one for one: in a straight barter

shkëmby·esh·ëm *adj* (*i*) exchangeable, convertible

shkëme·s· *vt* 1 to clear [scrub vegetation, brush] with a billhook 2 (*Fig*) to mow [] down, lay [] low; deprive [] of all rights

shkëme·së *nf* discharge/settlement (of a debt); absolution

shkëndijë
  I § *nf* 1 spark 2 sparkle 3 [*Zool*] firefly 4 [*Zool*] long-legged dark insect with big wings that damages the flowers of fruit
  II § *adj* 1 sparkling bright, bright and shiny 2 (*Fig*) quick and clever

  ◦ **Shkëndijat dalin në maj.** "Fireflies come out in May." (*Prov*) Things must be done in their proper time.

shkëndij·ëz *nf* 1 [*Entom*] firefly 2 (*Dimin*) = **shkëndij**ë

  ◦ **Shkëndijëzat dalin në maj.** "Fireflies come out in May." (*Prov*) Things must be done in their proper time.

shkëndiji·m *nm* (*Book*) glistening, sparkle, glitter; gleam, twinkle

shkëndijo·*n vi* **1** to give off sparks **2** to sparkle; glitter

shkëndi|**s** *stem for 1st sg pres, pl pres, 2nd & 3rd sg subj, pind* <**shkëndí***t*·

shkëndí|*t*· *vi* to scintillate with light: sparkle, glitter, glint, flash; gleam, glisten

***shkëndí**|**zë** *nf* **1** [*Invert*] firefly **2** sparkle, spark, flash

shkëndo|·*n vi* to sparkle

***shkëndri**|**s** = **shkëndis**|

shkëndri**|*t*· = **shkëndít*·

***shkëndri**|**tje** *nf* = **shkëndijím**

shkëpu̇rdh·

  I § vi (Colloq) to paw/scratch at the ground
  II § vt **1** to poke [a fire], stir up [live coals/embers] **2** = **shpí**·*n*

shkëpu̇rdh·*et vpr* **1** (*Reg*) to thrash around, writhe **2** (*Fig*) to struggle/strive hard

shkëpu|**s** *stem for 1st sg pres, pl pres, 2nd & 3rd sg subj, pind* <**shkëpú***t*·

sh|**këpu**|*t*· *vt* **1** to break off [] **2** to yank [] off/apart/ away/out: detach, pluck, pick, wrest **3** to get [] by force or artifice **4** to wean **5** [*Offic*] to shunt [a village] from one administrative domain to another ∘ **shkëput**· **hesapin me** [] "break off one's account with []" to close accounts with [], break off completely with []

sh|**këput**·*et vpr* **1** to break away/off/out **2** to break/ come apart/away; get away; separate **3** to have/take a break

sh|**këpu̇t**|**je** *nf ger* **1** <**shkëpú***t*·, **shkëput**·*et* **2** detachment, separation; break

sh|**këpu̇t**|**ur**

  I § adj (i) **1** detached, broken away/off **2** exceptional
  II § adv = **shkëpu̇turazi**

sh|**këpu̇t**|**ur**|**azi** *adv* separately; out of context

shkërba' *nf* monstrous beast, monster

shkërba'**dër** *nf* = **shkërba**

shkërbe' *nf* **1** (*Reg*) savage beast, wild animal; large bird of prey **2** monstrous beast, monster

shkërb|**e**·*n* = **shkërbo**'·*n*

shkërb|**im** *nm ger* **1** <**shkërbo**'·*n* **2** imitation

shkërb|**o**·*n vt* to mimic, imitate

***shkërb**|**ye**|**s**

  I § adj imitative
  II § n imitator

***shkërb**|**ye**|**shëm** *adj (i)* imitable

shkërdh|**a**|**të** *nf (Crude Colloq)* = **shkërdhe̊s**e

shkërdh|**e**·*n vt (Crude Colloq)* **1** to fuck **2** to fuck [] up

shkërdh|**e**'**c** *nm (Reg)* [*Dairy*] milk churn

shkërdh|**e**'**së** *nf (Crude Colloq)* **1** fucker **2** fucking

shkërdh|**im** *nm ger (Crude Colloq)* <**shkërdhe**·*n*

shkërdh|**ye**'**r** *adj (i) (Crude Colloq)* sexually loose, promiscuous: slutty

***shkërfit** (*Reg*) = **skërfit**|

shkërm|**o**·*n*

  I § vt **1** to clean [] well by rubbing/scraping: scrub **2** (*Fig Pej*) to take everything of value in <>'s []: clean out []
  II § vi (of pigs) to root around in the ground; (of chickens) scratch the ground

shkërmo̊q· *vt* **1** to reduce [] to small bits, fragmentize: crumble, crush, crunch; demolish **2** to detach

the small edible parts from the whole: shell [corn], split up [garlic] (*Colloq*) to break [money] (into small coins), change [money]

shkërmo̊q·*et vpr* to break apart into component parts: crumble; fall apart, disintegrate

shkërmo̊q|**je** *nf ger* <**shkërmo̊q**·, **shkërmo̊q**·*et*

shkërmo̊q|**ur** *adj (i)* broken into particles, crumbled

shkërpi̇c|**ë** *nf* **1** (*Colloq*) spark **2** (*Fig*) excuse, pretext

sh|**këshill**|**o**·*n vt* to advise [] against doing something; dissuade

shkill· *vi* to whisper

***shki̇m** *nm* seeing one other socially, warm social relationship
  ∘ **shkim i de̊rës** threshold, doorsill
  ∘ **shkim i syrit** eye socket

shki̇m|**ëz** *nf* piece of paper

***shki̇ne** *nf* Serbian girl/woman

***shki̇n**|**isht** *adv* in Serbian fashion

shki̇|**s**

  I § stem for 2nd pl pres, pind <**shket**·
  II § stem for 1st sg pres, pl pres, 2nd & 3rd sg subj, pind * <**shqi̇t**·

sh|**kishërim** *nm ger* **1** [*Relig*] <**shkishëro**'·*n* **2** excommunication

sh|**kishëro**·*n vt* [*Relig*] to excommunicate

sh|**kishërua**|**r** *adj (i)* [*Relig*] excommunicated

shki̇t|

  I § stem for pdef, opt, adm, part, pind, 2nd pl pres, imper, vp <**shket**·
  II § vt * = **shqi̇t**·

shki̇t|**ës** *adj* slippery = **rrëshqi̇tës**

shki̇t|**ëse** *nf* sledge

shki̇th·*et vpr* to cry without tears: sob, whimper

***shkja** *nm (Crude)* Slav

***shkje** *np* <**shkja**

***sh**|**kje**|**pët** *adj (i)* = **shqe̊pët**

***sh**|**kjep**|**o**·*n* = **shqepo**'·*n*

***sh**|**kje**|**pul** = **shqepul**

***shkla**|**s** *stem for 1st sg pres, 1st & 3rd pl pres, 2nd & 3rd sg subj* <**shklet**·

shklebu|**a** *nm (obl˜o'i, np ˜onj) (Reg)* unripe melon

***shkle**|**pë** = **skle̊pë**

shklese *adj* freestone = **çȧhje**

shkle|**s**|**ë** *nf* roof sheathing, roof lath

***shkl**|**et**· *vt* = **shkel**

***shkli**|**s** *stem for 2nd pl pres, pind* <**shklet**·

***shkli̇t** *stem for pind, 2nd pl pres, imper, vp* <**shklet**·

shkllop *nm* mud puddle

***shklluk**|**o**'·*n vi* to lay a rotten egg

shklluq· *vt* to drink [] down in one gulp

***sh**|**kmes**· *vt* to prune, trim

shko ·*het vp impers* it is capable of being traveled, it is passable: one may go/pass through
  ∘ **nuk shkohet më gjatë kështu** it's not good to go on any longer like this

shko|·*n*

  I § vi **1** to go **2** to go away/off; go off to become __ **3** to change residence/job: move **4** to fare, prosper; (of money) to be worth **5** (*Colloq*) to surpass <> **6** to pass/spend (a length of time) **7** (*Colloq*) to pass on: die **8** to pass over/through <> **9** (*Colloq*) to be spent/ exhausted **10** to be headed straight, be on the way **11** to extend, reach **12** to be suitable, fit, comport; get along together **13** (of something swallowed) to go down **14** (*Fig*) to go into <>, examine <> **15** to make

an involuntarily movement **16** to overflow, flow out **17** *(Colloq)* to function, operate; get along
II § *vt* **1** *(Colloq)* to pass/get over [an obstacle/illness] **2** to slip [] **3** to pass/spend [a period of time] **4** *(Colloq)* to surpass **5** to bring [some means] to bear, use [an implement] on ⬦; apply [] to ⬦

○ ⬦ **shko**·*n*^{3rd} {} *don't* work out for ⬦, ⬦'s {} go for naught; ⬦'s {} *miss*

○ **s'**⬦ **shko**·*n* **as në vesh** "not even get to ⬦'s ear (let alone ⬦'s stomach)" not be enough food to fill ⬦ up

○ **nuk** ⬦ **shko**·*n*^{3sg} **as buka, as uji** ⬦ no longer has any interest in food nor drink, ⬦ has lost all appetite for eating or drinking

○ ⬦ **shko**·*n*^{3sg} **bark** ⬦ *has* diarrhea

○ ⬦ **shko**·*n*^{3sg} **barku pizgë** to have a bad case of the runs (diarrhea)

○ ⬦ **shko**·*n*^{3sg} **barra** *(Colloq)* ⬦'s fetus/baby is stillborn, ⬦ *has* a miscarriage

○ ⬦ **shko**·*n*^{3sg} **bizgë** ⬦ *has* the runs, ⬦ *has* diarrhea

○ ⬦ **shko**·*n*^{3sg} **bokë (puna)** things *go* badly for ⬦

○ **shko**·*n* **bredhë** to romp, gambol, frisk

○ **shko**·*n*^{pl} **brisk e thua** to be at dagger points, stand toenail to toenail

○ **shko**·*n* **brue** to pace up and down, amble around

○ ⬦ **shko**·*n*^{3sg} **buza vesh më vesh** "⬦'s lip *goes* from ear to ear" ⬦ *laughs* heartily; ⬦ *lights* up with happiness

○ **shko**·*n* **çap e jakë** *1 to walk back and forth **2** *(Fig)* to keep busy doing nothing

○ **shko**·*n* **dëm** to come to nothing, go for naught

○ ⬦ **shko**·*n*^{3pl} **djersë të ftohta** ⬦ *breaks* out in a cold sweat

○ **shko**·*n* **duke** {*participle*} to keep growing/getting more {}

○ **shko**·*n* **dushk për gogla** to go to waste

○ **shko**·*n*^{3sg} **edhe i njomi (bashkë) me të thatin** "the wet also *burns* (together) with the dry" the innocent *pay* (together) with the guilty

○ ⬦ **shko**·*n* **edhe një dorë** "run one more hand over ⬦" to give ⬦ an additional treatment of a process done by hand

○ ⬦ **shko**·*n*^{3sg} **fëmija** *(Colloq)* ⬦'s fetus/baby is stillborn

○ **shko**·*n* **firë** to come to nothing, go for naught

○ ⬦ **shko**·*n*^{3sg} **fjala** "⬦'s word *goes*" what ⬦ says *carries* a lot of weight, ⬦ *has* a lot of influence

○ ⬦ **shko**·*n*^{3rd} **gand** to be all for nothing for ⬦

○ ⬦ **shko**·*n*^{3sg} **goja lëng** ⬦'s mouth is watering: ⬦ *has* a craving

○ ⬦ **shko**·*n*^{3sg} **goja prapa** to get tired of saying the same thing over and over, get tired of repeating oneself

○ ⬦ **shko**·*n*^{3sg} **goja vesh më vesh** "⬦'s mouth *goes* from ear to ear" ⬦ *laughs* heartily; ⬦ *lights* up with happiness

○ **nuk** ⬦ **shko**·*n*^{3sg} **gomari në udhë/urë** "⬦'s donkey won't go on the path/bridge" **1** things *don't* work out the way ⬦ *intends/expects* **2** ⬦'s attempt to pull a fast one *fails*

○ ⬦ **shko**·*n*^{3sg} **(puna) grurë** it (the matter) *is going* very well for ⬦

○ **shko**·*n* **gjak e lak** (of people) to get along together very badly, mix like oil and water

○ **shko**·*n*^{3sg} **gjaku deri në bark/shalë të kalit** "blood *comes* up to the horse's belly/saddle" the place *is* knee-deep in blood

○ **shko**·*n*^{3sg} **gjaku deri në tra** "blood *comes* up to the rafter" the place *is swimming* with blood

○ **shko**·*n*^{3sg} **gjaku rrëke/lumë** "the blood *flows* like a torrent/river" the blood *flows* like water; the blood *flows* in a torrent

○ ⬦ **shko**·*n*^{3sg} **gjaku te këmbët 1** ⬦ *gets* numb (from too much walking/standing) **2** ⬦ *gets* terrified

○ **shko**·*n* **gjatë** to last/take a long time

○ **Nuk shkon gjithmonë kungulli mbi ujë.** "Squash does not float forever." *(Prov)* Deception cannot stay hidden forever: Truth will out.

○ ⬦ **shko**·*n*^{3sg} **gjuha prapa** to get tired of saying the same thing over and over, get tired of repeating oneself

○ **shko**·*n* **gjym** (of an activity) to go very well/pleasantly

○ **shko**·*n* **jetë** to have a good life

○ **e shko**·*n* **jetën** to spend one's life

○ **nuk** ⬦ **shko**·*n*^{3sg} **kali në udhë/urë** "⬦'s horse won't go on the path/bridge" **1** things *don't* work out the way ⬦ *intends/expects* **2** ⬦'s attempt to pull a fast one *fails*

○ **shko**·*n* **keq** to be on bad terms

○ ⬦ **shko**·*n*^{3pl} **këmbët shul e shul** ⬦ *staggers*

○ **Shkoftë kohë e shkoftë mot, e vërteta del më not.** "Let time pass and weather pass, the truth *comes* out swimming." *(Prov)* Truth will out.

○ ⬦ **shko**·*n*^{3sg} **koka** ⬦ *gets* killed

○ **shko**·*n* **kot së koti** to go to waste

○ **shko**·*n* **ku sytë këmbët** to take to one's heels.

○ **shko**·*n* **ku** [] **shpinin këmbët** to go without thinking/knowing about where [one] is going

○ **shko**·*n* **kurban** to die for nothing

○ ⬦ **shko**·*n*^{3sg} **lak** ⬦ *is having* some trouble

○ **shko**·*n* **larg** to go to excess, go too far, carry things too far

○ **shko**·*n* **lule me lule** "go from flower to flower" *(Pej)* to run around with one girlfriend after another (but have no permanent attachment to any)

○ **shko**·*n* **(për) lyrë leshi** to go to waste

○ [] **shko**·*n* **llavesh** to neglect []

○ ⬦ **shko**·*n* **makinën** "run the machine over ⬦" to give ⬦ a close haircut

○ **shko**·*n* **me duar në xhepa** "go with hands in pockets" to come/go empty-handed; come/go unprepared

○ **shko**·*n* **me këmbë plumbi** "walk with leaden foot" to walk slowly and cautiously

○ **shko**·*n* **me shoshë për ujë** "go for water with a screen" to do useless work

○ **shko**·*n* **me të shumtët** "go with the majority" *(Impol)* (of a person) to die

○ **shko**·*n* **me** [] to get along with []; go around with []

○ ⬦ **shko**·*n*^{3sg} **mendja** it crosses ⬦'s mind

○ ⬦ **shko**·*n*^{3sg} **mendja për peshk** ⬦ *has* a sudden desire/yen for something hard to find

○ ⬦ **shko**·*n*^{3sg} **mendja për** [] ⬦ *gets* a sudden desire for [], have a hankering for []

○ <> **shko·**n **mendja te** {} <> starts to think about {}

○ <> **shko·**n^{3sg} **moda** <> *goes* out of fashion

○ <> **shko·**n^{3pl} **mornica nëpër trup** <> *is shivering* from the cold

○ **shko·**n^{pl} **mykë e pykë** "go like sledge and wedge" to get along badly, neither side will give in

○ <> **shko·**n^{3sg} **nata në gjunjë** *is* up all night, <> *does* not sleep all night

○ <> **shko·**n **ndër mend** to enter <>'s mind

○ [] **shko·**n **ndër mend** "put [] through one's mind" to think of [], consider []

○ **shko·**n **në Berat për një masat** "go all the way to Berat for a flintstone" to put out a lot of effort to accomplish something of no importance, go to a lot of trouble for nothing

○ **shko·**n^{3pl} **në majë e në bisht** to get along badly

○ **shko·**n **në bukë të** {*pronominal adj*} to grow up and start {*one's own*} life; get married

○ **shko·**n **në djall *1** to move very far away: move to the end of the earth **2** to get totally wrecked; get it in the neck

○ **shko·**n **në dhé të huaj** "go to foreign land" to emigrate

○ **shko·**n **në fill të vdekjes** to be almost dead, be as good as dead

○ [] **shko·**n **në hell** to put [] on a spit, skewer

○ **shko·**n **në majë të briskut** to barely avert disaster: escape by a hair

○ <> **shko·**n **në mendje** to come to <>'s mind, occur to <>

○ [] **shko·**n **në mendje** "put [] in one's mind" to think of [], consider []

○ **shko·**n **në pikë të fundit** "go to the final point" to suffer a complete decline in fortune

○ <> **shko·**n **në satër** to chop off <>'s head; kill off <>

○ <> **shko·**n **në taban** to investigate <> to the very core, delve into <> deeply

○ <> **shko·**n **në thikë** to put <> to the sword, massacre <>

○ **shko·**n^{3sg} **në vend (fjala)** (the express wishes) *are* fulfilled, (what has been said) *is* complied with

○ <> **shko·**n **në vesh që/se** __ <> *hears* accidentally that __, <> *happens* to hear that __

○ **shko·**n **në vesh të shurdhër** "go into a deaf ear" to fall on deaf ears

○ **të shko·**n **në vrimë të gjilpërës** "put you through the eye of a needle" to be extraordinarily adept

○ [] **shko·**n **në vrimë të gjilpërës 1** to reprimand [] severely **2** to make [] do something, force **3** to examine [] carefully and in detail

○ [] **shko·**n **nëpër duar** to look over []

○ **shko·**n **nga sytë këmbët** to take to one's heels

○ **shko·**n **nga të fryjë era** to swing whichever way the wind is blowing

○ **shko·**n **nga [] shpinin këmbët** to go without thinking/knowing about where [one] is going

○ **shko·**n **nuse** (of a girl) to get married, become a bride

○ **shko·**n^{3sg} **i njomi për të thatin** "the wet *burns* in place of the dry" the innocent pay for the sins of the guilty

○ **Shkoftë ora e dëgjoftë!** "May the fairy go and listen!" *(Felic)* Let's wish for luck!

○ **shko·**n **pa hoxhë** *(Iron)* to end up as nothing; go to waste, go for naught

○ <> **shko·**n **pas** <> **1** to go after <>, chase <>; chase after <> **2** to follow <> **3** to court <>

○ <> **shko·**n **pas bishtit** to flatter and support <>, be <>'s toady

○ <> **shko·**n **pas fijes/fillit** to try to please <>; speak and act according to <>'s wishes

○ <> **shko·**n **pas fyellit** to do whatever will please <>, agree with anything <> says

○ **shko·**n **pas gjurmëve** to follow the tracks/trail

○ **shko·**n **pas qerres së** <> to jump on <>'s band-wagon, join <>'s camp, follow <>'s lead

○ **shko·**n **pas rrymës** to go with the flow; go along with the crowd

○ <> **shko·**n **pas ujërave** to just do what will please <>

○ **shko·**n **pas valles (së** <>) *(Pej)* to do whatever <> wants: just take one's lead from <>

○ **shko·**n **për aheng** to go off to have a good time

○ <> **shko·**n **për dorë** to come easy to <>; suit <> fine

○ **shko·**n **për dhjamë qeni** to end up as nothing; go to waste, go for naught

○ <> **shko·**n^{3sg} **për farë** <> *gets* it from <>'s family

○ <> **shko·**n^{3sg} **për gjak** it's in <>'s blood (there's nothing that can be done about it)

○ <> **shko·**n **për hullie** to just go along with whatever <> wants? just do whatever <> wants

○ **shko·**n **për kryeshëndoshë** to pay one's condolences

○ **shko·**n **për lesh e del·**/**vje·**n/**kthe·**het **i qethur** "go for wool and come back sheared" *(Prov Iron)* to try to make things better but only make them worse

○ **shko·**n **për mort** to go on a consolation visit (to the survivors of the deceased)

○ **shko·**n **për peshk** to go fishing

○ **shko·**n^{3sg} **për piri** <> *has* the perverse habit of {}

○ <> **shko·**n **për plak** "go to <> as an elder" to seek sage advice from <>

○ <> **shko·**n **për shtat** "not go for <>'s body" **1** to be suitable for <> **2** (of clothes) to fit <>, look nice on <>

○ **shko·**n **për**//**për të bërë vorba/vegsha** "go for // to make pots" *(Iron)* to buy the farm: die

○ **shko·**n **përpjetë** to grow bigger and better, make good progress

○ **shko·**n **plep** *(Colloq)* (of a conversation/discussion) to go well

○ **shko·**n **poshtë** to take a downward direction: descend, go down

○ <> **shko·**n **prapa** to follow <>'s lead; follow the path take by <>

○ **shko·**n **prapa diellit** to go into the hinterlands; go with little chance of ever returning

○ <> **shko·**n^{3sg} **puna fjollë** things *are going* very well for <>, <> *is doing* fine

○ <> **shko·**n^{3sg} **puna kryq** things go badly/wrong for <>

○ <> **shko·**n **radha** <> has <>'s turn

○ **shko·**n **rrobat në** [] to rinse off the clothes in [a body of water]

○ **shko·**n^{3sg} **(puna) sahat** to go like clockwork, work perfectly

○ **shko·n si cjapi te kasapi** "go like a goat to the butcher" to walk into trouble with one's eyes closed: go like a sheep to the slaughter

○ **shko·n si dash kurbani** to die for nothing

○ **shko·n si guri në ujë/pellg/lumë** to be all for nothing, get nowhere

○ **shko·n si macja me miun** "go like the cat with the mouse" to be constantly at odds (with one another): get along like cats and dogs

○ **shko·n si miza pa kokë/krye** to wander aimlessly; go blindly

○ **shko·n si në dasmë** "go as if to a wedding" to go unprepared

○ **shko·n si në vaj** to go very smoothly

○ **shko·n^pl si qeni me macen** to go at each other like cats and dogs

○ **shko·n si qeni në vresht/rrush** "die like the dog in the vineyard/grapes" to die by pure happenstance

○ **shko·n si sëpata pa bisht** to be a total waste

○ **<> shko·n^{3sg} si shala gomarit** "fit <> like a saddle on a donkey" (Iron) to fit <> badly: fit like a glove on a foot

○ **shko·n^pl si shemër** to be constantly bickering

○ **shko·n si vetëtima e beharit** "leave like the lightning of summer" to leave very quickly

○ **shko·n sipas avazit të <>** to do whatever will please <>, agree with anything <> says

○ **shko·n shpejt ne shtrat** to go to bed early

○ **<> shko·n^{3pl} shtatë palë djersë** "seven sets of sweat pass through <>" <> breaks out in a cold sweat

○ **<> shko·n^{3pl} shtatë** (Crude) <> is scared out of <>'s wits: <> is shitting in <>'s pants from fear

○ **<> shko·n^{3pl} shtatë në qase** (Crude) <> is scared out of <>'s pants: <> is scared shitless

○ **shko·n shul e del·/vje·n lloz** "come in as a rod and go out as a bar" to gain nothing (from a lesson/experience)

○ **Shkoi shyta të kërkojë brirët, la edhe veshët.** "The hornless ewe/nanny went looking for horns, also lost her ears." (Prov Iron) Try to get more and end up getting less.

○ **shko·n tatëpjetë** to go downhill; go into decline, keep getting worse and worse

○ **[ ] shko·n tatëpjetë** to swallow [ ]: down [ ]

○ **shko·n tek teshat** to go to one's grave: die

○ **<> shko·n^{3pl} tetë në qase** (Crude) <> is scared out of <>'s pants: <> is scared shitless

○ **shko·n trapa-trapa** to wobble along unsteadily

○ **<> shko·n^{3sg} tymi drejt/gjyryk** things are going well for <>

○ **<> shkon tymi oxhak** everything goes smoothly for <>

○ **shko·n^pl thikë e brisk** to be at dagger points, stand toenail to toenail

○ **shko·n^pl thikë e sëpatë** to be at loggerheads; go at each other hammer and tongs

○ **ta shko·n^{3sg} ujët/ujin nën rrogoz/hasër/vete** "put water under your floor mat" to always be doing things behind your back

○ **<> shko·n^{3pl} urov** (Crude) <> is scared out of <>'s wits: <> is shitting in <>'s pants (from fear)

○ **shko·n ushtar** to enter military service, join the army

○ **shko·n va pa va 1** to go out without any particular destination **2** to come out all right despite the problems

○ **{} shkoi e vajti** "{} passed and went" **1** {}'s time is over and gone **2** {} is over and done with

○ **shko·n vapë** to take a break during the hot time of the day: take a siesta

○ **nuk <> shko·n^{3sg} vula** "<>'s stamp *doesn't go*" no one listens to <>, <> *has* no influence

○ **<> shko·n^{3sg} zemra te thembra** "<>'s heart goes/sinks to <>'s heels" <>'s heart sinks (to <>'s toes): <> *gets* fearful; <> *gets* demoralized/disappointed

Shkodër nf city in northwestern Albanian: Shkodra, Scutari

shkodra·n

  I § *adj* of/from Shkodra

  II § *n* native of Shkodra

shkodra·nçe *adv* in the manner/language of people from Shkodra

shkodra·nishte *nf* the Shkodra subdialect of Albanian

shkoftëla·rg *nm* (Euph) = **qoftëla·rg**

*★**shko·jë** *nf* (Old) going, leaving

shko·jëz *nf* small hole in the skin: pore

shko·kël *nf* corncob

shko·këllim *nm ger* <**shkokëlo·n**, **shkokëlo·het**

shko·këllo·het *vpr* **1** (of fruit/grain) to come/fall off from the cluster/head **2** (Fig Colloq) to split one's sides laughing

shko·këllo·n *vt* **1** to separate [the kernels] from a head of grain: shell [corn] **2** (Fig) to figure out [ ], untangle **3** (Fig Colloq) to cause [ ] to break up in laughter: lay [ ] in the aisles, make [ ] die laughing

shko·këlluar *adj* (i) separated from the husk/pod/cluster: shelled

shkokërdho·het *vpr* (Reg) to double over from bearing a heavy load on one's back; be exhausted from hard work

shkokërdho·n *vt* (Reg) to hurt [ ] so badly as to make [him] feel [his] back is broken

shkokërdhuar *adj* (i) hurt so badly as to feel one's back is broken

shkokërro·het *vpr* (Reg) = **shkokëlo·het**

shkokërro·n *vt* (Reg) = **shkokëlo·n**

shkoklavi·s *stem for 1st sg pres, pl pres, 2nd & 3rd sg subj, pind* <**shkoklavit·**

shkoklavit· *vt* to disentangle, untangle

shkoklavit·et *vpr* **1** to get untangled; get straightened out, get resolved **2** (Fig) to escape (from of an entanglement), get out of a mess

shkoklavitje *nf ger* <**shkoklavit·**, **shkoklavit·et**

shkoli·s *stem for 1st sg pres, pl pres, 2nd & 3rd sg subj, pind* <**shkolit·**

shkolit· *vt* **1** to unfasten, peel [ ] apart; unsolder **2** (Colloq) to pull [a building/wall] down **3** (Fig Colloq) to figure [ ] all out

shkolit·et *vpr* **1** to come unfastened/apart; get unstuck **2** (Fig Colloq) to become detached, separate; depart **3** (Fig Colloq) to get untangled; get straightened out, get worked out

shkolitje *nf ger* <**shkolit·**, **shkolit·et**

shkolonizi·m *nm ger* **1** <**shkolonizo·n**, **shkolonizo·het 2** decolonization

shkolonizo·n *vt* to decolonize

shkolla'r
I § adj educated; well educated, knowledgeable *II §* n **1** elementary or secondary school student **2** (Colloq) educated person; well-educated/knowledgeable person **3** (Reg) teacher

sh|koll|ari's· vt to remove the starch from [cloth]

sh|koll|ari's|je nf ger <**shkollaris·**

shkollari'zëm adj (Pej) typical of grade school, with a schoolbook mentality: oversimplified and abridged, lacking originality; pedantic/academic/scholastic

shkollari'zëm nm (Pej) grade-school mentality/ treatment, grade-school level

shkollë nf **1** school **2** school system **3** education **4** [Mil] training
  ○ **shkolla e mesme** secondary school: grades nine through twelve
  ○ **shkollë pesëvjeçare** (Old) elementary school for grades one through five
  ○ **shkollë pune** technical school
  ○ **shkollë qytetëse** (Old) grammar and secondary school offering general education
  ○ **shkollë shënjimi** [Mil] target training school for civilian reservists
  ○ **shkollë unike** (Old) required seven-years of elementary education

shkoll|i'm nm ger <**shkollo'·n, shkollo'·het**

shkoll|o'·het vpr to go to school: study, be schooled

shkoll|o'·n vt to send [] to school: educate, school

shkoll|o'r adj pertaining to (elementary and high) school: scholastic, school

shkoll|ua'r adj (i) schooled, educated

sh|komb|ëtar|iz|i'm nm ger <**shkombëtarizo'·n, shkombëtarizo'·het**

sh|komb|ëtar|iz|o'·het vpr to lose national/ethnic identity

sh|komb|ëtar|iz|o'·n vt to strip [] of national/ethnic identity

sh|komb|ëtar|iz|ua'r adj (i) deprived of national/ethnic identity

shkop
I § nm (np ~ i'nj) **1** wooden stick; rod; cane **2** [Agr] wooden linchpin securing the moldboard to the beam of a wooden hand plow **3** chopstick **4** (Colloq) blow/beating delivered with a club or stick; heavy scolding; violence or threat of violence **5** (Fig Pej) blockhead *6 wood rail
II § adj thin as a rail
  ○ **shkop bilarde** cue stick
  ○ **shkop e cingël** tipcat = **cingëlthi**
  ○ **shkop kërcimi** [Track] pole used in pole-vaulting
  ○ **Shkopin, po e ndyve të tërë, s'ke ku e kap.** "If you got the stick dirty all over, you have nowhere to grasp it." (Prov) Since you really ruined it, there's no way fix it. With all that you have done, there is nothing that can be done to help.
  ○ **shkop stafete** [Track] (relay) baton

shkop|a|ci'ng|thi OR **shkop|a|xi'ng|ël** OR **shkop|a|xi'ng|l|ash** adv

shkop|e|ci'ng|ël nm stick used in children's game of tipcat

shkop|ijo'rë np [Entom] stick insects

shkopi's| stem for 1st sg pres, pl pres, 2nd & 3rd sg subj, pind <**shkopi't·**

shkopi't· vt to beat [someone] with a stick/rod/club: flog, thrashto castrate

shkop|i'tur adj (i) castrated

shkop|ku'qe nf [Bot] = **mëlla'gjër**

sh|kopsi's| stem for 1st sg pres, pl pres, 2nd & 3rd sg subj, pind <**shkopsi't·**

sh|kopsi't· vt to unbutton

sh|kopsi't·et vpr to get unbuttoned

sh|kopsi't|je nf ger <**shkopsi't·, shkopsi't·et**

sh|kopsi't|ur adj (i) unbuttoned

shkop|th nm **1** (Dimin) small stick; rod **2** [Agr] wooden linchpin (used to secure the moldboard to the beam of a wooden hand plow)
  ○ **shkopthat e tuberkulozit** (Old) [Med] rod-shaped tuberculosis bacilli

shkoq· vt **1** to separate similar small elements from [an encompassing whole]: shell [beans, peas, corn]; hull [grain]; detach [cartridges] (from a gunbelt); disperse [a military force] **2** to crumble [] into small pieces **3** (Colloq) to make change for [money]: break [a piece of money] **4** (Colloq) to separate [] **5** (Colloq) to make [] explicit; analyze, explain

shko·q·et vpr **1** to come apart: separate; disperse; be crumbly, crumble **2** to be cleared up, be resolved **3** (Colloq) to become emaciated **4** (Fig Colloq) to take great delight, revel **5** (Fig) to come into focus in the distance gradually *6 to stand out as distinct, become distinctive

shko'q|ës adj used for shelling/hulling (grain)

shkoqi's| stem for 1st sg pres, pl pres, 2nd & 3rd sg subj, pind <**shkoqi't·**

shkoqi't· vt **1** to clarify [] in detail, set [] out in detail: make [] explicitto analyze **2** (Colloq) to make out [], discern

shkoqi't·et vpr to settle accounts

shkoqi't|ës adj providing a detailed explanation: clear and detailed, explanatory

shkoqi't|je nf ger **1** <**shkoqi't·, shkoqi't·et 2** clarification, explanation **3** (Colloq) analysis

shkoqi't|sh|ëm adj (i) explicable

shkoqi't|ur adj (i) detailed; distinct, clear

shko'q|je nf ger <**shko'q·, shko'q·et**

shko'q|ur
I § adj (i) **1** separated from a containing cover: (of beans, peas, corn) shelled; (of grain) hulled; (of cartridges) detached (from a gunbelt); (of solid material) crumbled **2** dispersed **3** (Colloq) = **shkoqi'tur 4** (Colloq) (of money) in small bills, in change
II § adv **1** distinctly **2** explicitly

shko'q|ur|a np (të) small bills, small change, change

shkordh· vt to release [something exerting pressure]: vent; spew out []

shko'rdh·et vpr **1** to become less swollen; become deflated; lose weight **2** to become emaciated, waste away

shko'rdh|ët adj (i) **1** deflated, reduced **2** enervated, exhausted, weak

shkordh|o'qe np (Colloq) balderdash, nonsense

shko'rdh|ur adj (i) = **shko'rdhët**

shko'rs|ë nf **1** coarse rug woven of goat hair; bedcover; plain cloth covering **2** hood made of wicker and clay and used over an open fireplace in a room to prevent sparks from burning the ceiling beams

shkorre' nf **1** = **shkorre't 2** = **shku'rre**

shkorre't nm **1** bramble thicket **2** undergrowth, brushwood

shko'ta np fem (Reg) innards, guts

shkoze't nm = **shkozi'shtë**

shko·zë *nf* [*Bot*] hornbeam (*Carpinus*)

○ **shkozë e bardhë = shkozëbardhë**

○ **shkozë e keqe** [*Bot*] **= shkozëzezë**

○ **shkozë e zezë = shkozëzezë**

shkozëbardhë *nf* [*Bot*] European hornbeam (*Carpinus betulus*)

shkozëzezë *nf* [*Bot*] Oriental hornbeam (*Carpinus orientalis Mill.*)

shkozishtë *nf* hornbeam forest

shkrabë *nf* scrawl, scribbling

*__*shkrahis__* | *stem for 1st sg pres, pl pres, 2nd & 3rd sg subj, pind* < **shkrahit·**

*__*shkrahit·__* *vt* (*Old*) to expand

shkrap

I § *nm* (*Reg*) [*Invert*] scorpion **= akrep**

II § *onomat* snapping sound made by a gunbolt when the gun fires

○ **nuk ia bë·n shkrap** (*Colloq*) to prove to be totally incompetent

*__*shkrar__* *nm* [*Zool*] squirrel

shkredh *stem for opt, adm, part* < **shkridh·et**

*__*shkref = shkreh__*

shkrefëti·n *vi* (of a horse) to neigh

shkreh·

I § *vt* **1** to release [] from a readied condition: fire [a gun]; unset [a trap], uncork [a bottle], disassemble [] a plow, strike [a tent], dismount [a still], unyoke [oxen] from a plow, disconnect the utilities from [a house] **2** (*Fig*) to break off [], call [] quits **3** (*Fig*) to exhaust; run [] into the ground

II § *vi* (*Colloq*) to take to one's heels, run away

○ **ia shkreh·** <> to burst out in <>

○ **s'e shkreh· ndonjëherë (pushkën)** to have no battle experience: never have fired one's gun; never have to struggle

shkreh·et *vpr* **1** to undergo a release of tension/energy: be released, fired, set off, sprung **2** (*Fig*) to burst out, gush; explode at <> **3** (*Fig*) to vent one's anger/spleen on <> **4** (*Fig*) to be exhausted; wind down, come to an end; be thoroughly defeated

shkrehës

I § *adj* serving to spring/release a mechanism: triggering

II § *nm* **1** bird snare **2** [*Tech*] release mechanism **3** [*Electr*] switch **4** [*Mil*] detonating fuse, mine fuse

shkrehje *nf ger* **1** < **shkreh·, shkreh·et 2** gunshot

shkrehur

I § *adj* (i) **1** released, unleashed; (of a gun) fired; (of a trap) sprung; (of a house) let go, left in disorder **2** (*Fig*) exhausted, at the end of one's strength **3** (*Fig*) morally unrestrained: dissolute

II § *nf* (e) **1** firing, shooting **2** burst

shkrelë *nf* (*Reg*) large leaf of corn

shkrep *nm* **1** pointed crag; barren peak, rocky crag **2** [*Med*] muscle spasm, cramp **= ngërç**

shkrep·

I § *vt* **1** to strike [a match, flint] (in order to start a fire), attempt to ignite [] **2** to trigger [a gun/camera], fire (off) [] **3** (*Colloq*) to slam **4** to parch

II § *vi* **1** to shoot **2** to begin to shine: glimmer, (of the sun) dawn **3** to flash suddenly (like lightning): sparkle **4** <> suddenly *gets* a whim **5** to begin suddenly: gush out **6** (*Colloq*) to bear a resemblance to <> **7** to provoke a battle/argument

○ **nuk ia shkrep·** (*Fig ColloqImpolite*) not get the hang of it, not figure it out

○ **shkrep· fitilin** to trim the wick (so that it burns better)

○ **shkrep· këmbët** to stamp one's feet

○ **<>a shkrep· me sëpatë** to say it right to <>'s face

○ **s'<> shkrep·³ˢᵍ me** [] (*Fig Colloq*) <> *does not hit* it off with []

○ **<>a shkrep· në fytyrë/hundë/turi** to say it right to <>'s face

○ **<> shkrep·³ˢᵍ një xixë** a sudden thought *pops* into <>'s head, <> suddenly *gets* a new idea

○ **shkrep· syrin** to wink

○ **i shkrep· sytë** {}'s eyes sparkle

shkrep·et *vpr* **1** to be triggered/released; (of a weapon) fire automatically **2** (*Reg*) to collide **3** to affect <> with an urge

○ **<> shkrep·et³ˢᵍ** {} **1** <> gets the hang of {} **2** (*Fig Colloq*) <> gets a whim, <> gets a sudden urge

○ **<> u shkrep +** {*neuter deverbal noun*} <> burst out {} **asaj iu shkrep të qarët** she burst out crying **m'u shkrep të qeshurit** I burst out laughing

shkrepa *np fem* coarse flour left after sifting

*__*shkrepcë__* *nf* **= shkrepëse**

shkrepës

I § *adj* serving to strike a spark; serving to fire a gun

II § *nm* **1** flintstone; firing mechanism **2** (*Reg*) cigarette lighter **= çakmak** *__*3__* match

shkrepëse *nf* match (for lighting a fire); box of matches

shkrepët *adj* (i) difficult to traverse: steep; rugged

shkrepje *nf ger* **1** < **shkrep·, shkrep·et 2** (sound of) gunfire **3** (*Colloq*) sudden urge/hankering

shkrepor *adj* (of an area) full of steep crags: craggy, rocky, rugged

shkrepshëm *adj* (i) (*Reg*) nimble and smart

shkreptí·n *vi* (of lightning) to flash; shine with a bright light: flare, glisten

shkreptimë *nf* **1** flash of lightning **2** glare of the eyes

shkreptimtar *adj* (*Poet*) flashing, dazzling

shkreptírë *nf* flash

shkreptízë *nf* pimple from which smaller pimples seem to radiate

shkreptó·n *vt* (of lightning) to flash

shkrepur

I § *part* < **shkrep·, shkrep·et**

II § *adj* (i) **1** parched **2** (*Fig*) in very bad shape: badly off, very poor

III § *nf ger* (e) **= shkrepje**

IV § *nn ger* (të) < **shkrep·, shkrep·et**

shkresar *nm* (*Old*) keeper of a public register: registration clerk, registrar

shkresaxhi *nm* (np ˜ nj) (*Pej*) pencil pusher

shkresë *nf* **1** official memorandum **2** (*Reg*) something written: writing **3** (*Old*) ability to read and write: literacy

shkresína *np* **= shkresurinë**

shkresomani *nf* (*Pej*) mania for writing memoranda

shkresori *nf* material used for writing: writing implements, stationery

shkresurinë *nf* **1** (*Impol*) worthless and unnecessary writing: silly scribbling **2 = shkresori**

shkret· *vt* to abandon, forsake, desert

shkre't·*et vpr* to be left all alone in the world: be forsaken

shkreta'n *adj, n* (person) forced to live on one's own; (person) left all alone in the world

shkre'të
I §   *adj (i)* **1** abandoned, forsaken **2** alone and miserable, wretched, forlorn **3** dead, late **4** (as a disparaging epithet) damned, damn **5** (as a pitying epithet or ironically as a derisive epithet) poor
II §   *nm* (expressing compassion) poor fellow/guy
III §   *nf (e)* **1** (expressing compassion) poor thing! **2** *(Colloq)* the damn thing!
IV §   *adv* **1** abandoned, forsaken; in a bad way, helpless **2** fallow **3** *(Reg)* wastefully, in vain, idly
∘ **të shkretën** the damn thing!

shkret'ëro'·*n vt (Reg Tosk)* = **shkreto'·***n*

shkret'ëti'rë *nf* desert; wasteland, wilderness

shkreti' *nf* **1** = **shkretëti'rë 2** desolation, desertedness

shkreti'm *nm ger* <**shkreto'·***n*, **shkreto'·***het*

shkretino'r *adj (Book)* of or pertaining to a desert; desert-like

*** shkretn|o'·***n vt (Reg Gheg)* = **shkreto'·***n*

shkreto'·*het vpr* **1** to become deserted; fall into ruin **2** to be desolate

shkreto'·*n vt* **1** to lay waste to [ ]: devastate; depopulate; annihilate, wipe out **2** to leave [ ] desolate, desert

shkretua'r *adj (i)* deserted; desolate

shkrënd· *vt [Dairy]* to strip the udders of [a milk animal] completely dry **2** to empty out [ ], evacuate; leave [ ] empty **3** *(Fig)* to take everything of value from [ ]: impoverish

shkrënd·*et vpr* **1** to dry up completely **2** to have an empty stomach **3** to become bare/barren **4** *(Fig)* to become impoverished

shkrënd'ur *adj (i)* **1** completely dried up **2** empty (in the stomach) **3** *(Fig)* impoverished
∘ **i shkrëndur nga trutë** *(Colloq)* brainless, empty-headed, stupid, pea-brained

shkri·*n*
I §   *vt* **1** to melt **2** to fuse [ ] together **3** *(Fig)* to dissolve/liquidate [an organization] **4** *(Fig)* to spend [ ] entirely, expend every ounce of [ ] **5** to restore feeling in [one's limbs], limber up [one's limbs] **6** *(Fig Colloq)* to cause to melt with laughter/joy: crack/break [ ] up **7** *(Fig Colloq)* to make [ ] to exquisite perfection
II §   *vi* **1** *(Fig)* to sweat heavily because of hot weather: be melting from the heat **2** *(Colloq)* to quiet/calm down; feel comforted
∘ **shkri·***n*[3sg] **akulli** "the ice *melts*" conditions *improve*
∘ **shkri·***n* **jetën për** [ ] to work body and soul all one's life for [ ]
∘ **shkri·***n* **si vesa e mëngjesit / në diell** "disappear like the dew of *morning // in the sun*" to disappear fast, vanish quickly without a trace

sh|kri'dh·*et vpr* to emerge from the water

shkrif· *vt* **1** to separate [ ] into component parts: loosen, disentangle; break up, crumble; teasel, card [wool], comb out [flax] **2** to restore feeling in [one's limbs], limber up [one's limbs] **3** to clear [one's throat/voice]

shkri'f·*et vpr* to regain feeling in one's limbs = **shpi'·***het*

shkrif'ëri'm *nm ger* **1** <**shkrifëro'·***n*, **shkrifëro'·***het* **2** *[Geol]* alluvial deposit containing valuable minerals: *(placer)*

shkrif'ëro'·*het vpr* **1** (of soil) to become broken up, break up **2** to cheer up; become exhilarated

shkrif'ëro'·*n vt* **1** to break up [soil] **2** to cheer [ ] up; exhilarate

shkrif'ërua'r *adj (i)* **1** (of soil) broken up **2** cheered up; exhilarated

shkrif'ërue's *adj* serving to make loose

shkrif'ës
I §   *adj* serving to loosen up
II §   *nm* machine that performs a loosening function: carding machine (for separating cotton fibers); shaker (for loosening soil from molds in a foundry); scarifier, ripper (for loosening agricultural soil)
III §   *n* carding machine operator

shkri'fët *adj (i)* **1** loose, uncompacted; mushy **2** light and spongy; puffy **3** *[Publ]* spaced (type) **4** (of body limbs) restored to feeling: limber **5** *(Fig)* cheerful; calm and relaxed

shkri'fje *nf ger* <**shkrif·**, **shkrif·***et*

shkrift'im *nm ger* <**shkrifto'·***n*, **shkrifto'·***het*

shkrift'o·*het vpr* = **shkrif·***et*, **shkrifëro'·***het*

shkrift'o·*n vt* = **shkrif·**, **shkrifëro'·***n*

shkrift'ua'r *adj (i)* = **shkrifua'r**, **shkrifërua'r**

shkrift'ue's
I §   *adj* = **shkrif'ës**
II §   *nm [Agr]* attachment to a plow frame for breaking up the clods: subsoiler

shkri'fur *adj (i)* **1** separated into component parts: loosened, disentangled; broken up, crumbled; teaseled, (of wool) carded, (of flax) combed **2** limbered up **3** *(Fig)* (of the voice) clear and mellow **4** *(Fig)* cheerful, carefree; calm

shkri'|he· *vpr* <**shkri·***n* **1** to melt; dissolve **2** to become spent; get completely spent **3** *(Fig)* to waste away **4** to become limber **5** *(Fig)* to become unified, show solidarity **6** *(Fig Colloq)* to feel relieved **7** *(Fig Colloq)* to crack/break up (in laughter)
∘ **<> shkri·***het*[3sg] **gjaku** <>'s blood *calms* down (after a fright/shock)
∘ **shkri·***het* **pas <>** to be wild about <>
∘ **shkrih·***et* **si kripa në ujë** "dissolve like salt in water" to waste away (from an illness), become all skin and bones, become emaciated; lose a lot of weight in a short length of time

shkri'he· *vpr* <**shkreh·**> (of braids) to become unplaited; (of hair) to become disheveled/tousled

shkri'm *nm ger* **1** <**shkrua·***n*, **shkru·***het* **2** piece of writing, writing **3** ability to write, handwriting; schooling **4** writing system, orthography
∘ **shkrim rrokjesor** *[Ling]* syllabic orthography, syllabary
∘ **shkrimi i shenjtë** holy writ, scripture

sh|krimb· *vt* **1** to free [ ] from worms or other parasites: worm, delouse **2** to clean [ ] out thoroughly **3** *(Reg)* to disinfect

shkrimo'r *adj (Book)* of or pertaining to writing; in writing, written

shkrim'ta'r *n* writer, author

shkrim'taru'c *nm (Scorn)* hack writer

*** shkri'nj|ë** *nf (Old Regional Gheg)* = **shkrito're**

sh|krip'ëso'·*n* = **shkripëzo'·***n*

sh|krip'ëzi'm *nm ger* **1** <**shkripëzo'·***n*, **shkripëzo'·***het* **2** desalinization

sh|krip'ëzo'·*het vpr* to lose salinity

sh|krip'ëzo'·*n vt* to desalinize, desalinate

shkrips *nm [Bot]* field horsetail *(Equisetum arvense)*

shkri'rë *adj (i)* **1** melted; thawed; molten **2** processed by solidification from a molten state

shkri'rës
I § *adj* used for melting/smelting
II § *nm* **1** smelter, melter **2** [*Tech*] flux, fusing agent

shkri'rëz *nf* [*Electr*] (electrical) fuse

shkri'rje *nf ger* **1** <shkri•n, shkri•het **2** fusion

*shkri'sinë** *nf (Old Regional Gheg)* solution (dissolved mixture), fusion

shkri'shëm *adj (i)* easily meltable, fusible

shkri'shm|ëri *nf* fusibility, meltability

shkritar *n* metal caster, foundryman

*shkri'të** *adj (i)* = shkri'rë

shkritore *nf* foundry = fonderi

shkro'•*n* *vt* = shkrua•n

shkro'dh *stem for pdef* <shkri'dh•et

shkrofëti'•*n* *vi* to snort

shkrofëti'më *nf ger* **1** <shkrofëti•n **2** snort

shkrolc *nm* = shkrolës

shkrolë *nf* **1** = shkro'një *2** piece of writing: document **3** *(Reg)* floral ornamentation

shkrol'ës *nm (Old)* **1** wooden shelf/rack on the wall **2** wooden seal used to stamp an ornamental symbol on bread

shkro'një *nf* **1** letter (of an alphabet) **2** *(Old)* what is written: destiny
  ∘ **shkronja të hapura** [*Publ*] spaced out letters/characters

shkro'një'ba'rdhë *adj (Colloq)* lucky

shkro'njës
I § *nm (Old)* = patëllxha'nës
II § *n (Old)* *writer, author

shkro'një'tore *nf (Old)* grammar book

shkro'një'z *nf* **1** letter (of an alphabet) **2** carved floral ornament

shkro'një'zi *adj (fem sg ~ëz, masc pl ~ inj, fem pl ~eza) (Colloq)* ill-fated: unlucky

shkro'njor *adj (Book)* of, pertaining to, or expressed in letters of the alphabet: literal

shkru'•*het* *vpr* <shkrua•n *(Colloq)* to enroll, join up

shkrua'•*n*
I § *vi, vt* to write
II § *vt* **1** *(Colloq)* to make a record of [], register **2** *(Colloq)* to embroider; draw decorative designs **3** *(Colloq)* to vaccinate <> against []
  ∘ [] **shkrua•n në akull** to consider [] as lost
  ∘ **shkrua•n një faqe të lavdishme/ndritur** "write a glorious/shining page" to write a glorious page of history, perform a heroic act
  ∘ **shkrua•n rrallë** to write with widely spaced letters/lines
  ∘ **shkrua•n si me këmbët e pulës** to have terrible handwriting/penmanship, scrawl: make chicken scratches

shkru'ar
I § *part* <shkrua•n, shkru•het
II § *adj (i)* **1** written **2** embroidered; decorated with a drawn design; very good-looking, beautiful **3** fated
III § *nf (e)* fate
IV § *nn ger (të)* **1** <shkrua•n, shkru•het **2** *(Old)* = shkrim

shkru'arje *nf* writing

shkru'es *nm* **1** writer; author **2** *(Old)* scribe **3** carpenter's tool for scribing lines: marking gauge, scriber
  ∘ **shkrues i kompanisë** *(Old)* [*Mil*] company clerk

shkru'e'shëm *adj (i)* writable

shkrumb *nm* carbonized residue from burning; smelly residue of scorched food stuck to the bottom of a pan

shkru'mbët *adj (i)* **1** charred, burned *2** *(Old)* (of horses) having black patches/spots

shkrumb|ëzi'm *nm ger* <shkrumbëzo•n, shkrumbëzo•het

shkrumb|ëzo'•*het* *vpr* = shkrumbo•het

shkrumb|ëzo'•*n* *vt* = shkrumbo•n

shkrumb|ëzu'ar *adj (i)* = shkrumbu'ar

shkrumbi'm *nm ger* **1** <shkrumbo•n, shkrumbo•het **2** incineration

shkrumbi's *stem for 1st sg pres, pl pres, 2nd & 3rd sg subj, pind* <shkrumbi't•

shkrumbi't• *vt* = shkrumbo•n

shkrumbo'•*het* *vpr* to burn to a crisp, burn up completely

shkrumbo'•*n* *vt* to burn [] to a crisp, incinerate; cremate

shkrumbo's• *vt* = shkrumbo•n

shkrumbo'sje *nf ger* **1** <shkrumbos•, shkrumbos•et **2** incineration; cremation

shkrumbu'ar *adj (i)* **1** incinerated; burnt; cremated **2** cooked to a crisp; parched

shkrydh• *vt* **1** to make less compressed: loosen/break/soften [] up **2** to restore feeling in [one's limbs]; limber up [one's limbs], stretch [one's limbs] **3** *(Fig)* to waste [money]

shkrydh•*et* *vpr* **1** to become less hard/dense: loosen/soften up **2** to regain feeling in one's limbs

shkry'dhët *adj (i)* soft and crumbly **2** *(Fig)* agile and skillful *3** (of bones) still soft; (of fruit) overripe

shkry'dhje *nf ger* <shkry'dh•, shkry'dh•et

shkrydhtë'si *nf* looseness

shkrymb• *vt* = shkrimb•

*shkrre•*n = shkrrye•n

shkrry'•het *vpr* = zhgë'rry•het

*shkrry'e•*n *vt* = zhgë'rrye•n

shkualifiki'm *nm ger* **1** <shkualifiko•n, shkualifiko•het **2** [*Sport*] disqualification

shkualifiko'•*het* *vpr* to lose one's certification/license, be demoted/fired

shkualifiko'•*n* *vt* [*Sport*] to disqualify

shkualifiku'ar *adj (i)* **1** having lost one's certification/license: disbarred **2** [*Sport*] disqualified

shku'ar
I § *adj (i)* **1** past; previous, earlier: last **2** of advanced age: past one's/its prime **3** *(Colloq)* (of clothes) worn out **4** = shku'e'shëm
II § *nf (e)* **1** the past **2** [*Ling*] past tense **3** *(Colloq)* slight illness that spreads to many people and then passes quickly: a touch of something going around
III § *nn (të)* = shku'arje
IV § *prep (abl)* surpassing all other <>s, more than a <>

shku'arje *nf ger* **1** <shko'•n **2** peace and harmony, mutual understanding

shku'eri *nf (Reg)* nomadic life

shku'es *n* [*Ethnog*] matchmaker

shk|ues|í *nf* [*Ethnog*] marriage brokerage: match-making

shk|u'e|shëm *adj (i)* easy to get along with: companionable, sociable

shkuj *nm (Reg)* air current: draft

sh|kuj *vt* **1** to neglect **2** to free [] of worry, offer relief to []: relieve

sh|kujde's·et *vpr* **1** to be neglectful; show no concern, be indifferent **2** to put aside one's troubles; become carefree/casual

sh|kujdes|í *nf (Book)* = shkujde'sje

sh|kujde'sje *nf* **1** neglect, carelessness; indifference, heedlessness **2** nonchalance, casualness; relaxation

sh|kujde's|ur *adj (i)* negligent, careless; casual, nonchalant

shkul
I § **nm 1** skein of yarn **2** *(Fig)* wisp; tuft **3** = shkulm **4** swig
II § *adj, adv* boiling hot

shkul· *vt* **1** to yank [] up/out/away/off; yank on [], yank **2** to force [] out/away, drive [] out; root [] out, uproot **3** to overwhelm, overcome
∘ **ia shkul·** *(Colloq)* to sing/play (music) beautifully: sing/play up a storm
∘ **e shkul· barkun** to waste one's breath trying to be heard
∘ <> **shkul· dhëmballët/dhëmbët** "yank/twist <>'s molars/teeth" to punish <> severely
∘ [] **shkul· me rrënjë e me degë** "pull [] up by root and by branch" to expel [] together with []'s entire family
∘ **Shkul një gur nga një mur.** "Yank a rock from a wall" (said of someone who is very stingy) Try to borrow a dime from him and he acts as if you are trying to ruin him by pulling a rock out of his wall.
∘ [] **shkul· nga rrënjët/me rrënjë** "pull out by the root(s)" to eradicate []
∘ <> **shkul· veshin/veshët** to chastise/scold <>
∘ <> **shkul· zorrët** to turn <>'s stomach; make <> puke

shku'l·et *vpr* **1** to change position/residence: move **2** to be overwhelmed (by joy/laughter)

shkul|ara'k
I § *adj* **1** orphaned **2** displaced and feeling alone
II § *n* orphan; displaced person

shku'le-shku'le *adv* in waves/torrents

shku'lë *nf (Colloq)* diarrhea

shku'l|ës *adj* serving to uproot: uprooting

shku'l|ëse *nf* [*Agr*] grubbing hoe, grubber

shku'l|je *nf ger* < shku'l·, shku'l·et

shku'l|kë *nf* **1** forked pole over which fishing nets are spread to dry **2** bare branch stuck in the ground to indicate an area temporarily off limits for grazing **3** water in a rolling boil

shkulm *nm* surge

shkulm|ím *nm* impulse, urge

shkulm|o'·n *vi* to come to a rolling boil; make waves; get foamy, foam up

shkulo're *nf* warm round bun

sh|kull|o'·het *vpr* **1** to become clear, clear up **2** to get cleaned up

shkull|o'·n *vt* to empty [] to the last drop; drink [] all up

shkullo'je *nf* iron poker with a hook at the end for moving objects in the fire; fire tongs

*shkullo're** *nf* = shkullo'je

shkuma'k *adj* covered with foam; foaming

shkuma're *nf* **1** cuttlebone **2** [*Dairy*] wooden spoon used by shepherds to drink the foam of freshly drawn milk

shkumbavi's *stem for 1st sg pres, pl pres, 2nd & 3rd sg subj, pind* < shkumbavi't·

shkumbavi't· *vi* to foam

shkumbavi't·et *vpr* to boil with rage; foam at the mouth

*shku'mbë** = shku'më

Shkumbi'n *nm* Shkumbin River (dividing northern from southern Albania)

shkumbull|o'·n *vi* to foam at the mouth

shkumbz|o'nje's *adj* = shkumëzo'r

shku'më
I § *nf* **1** foam; suds **2** drool **3** *(Colloq)* epilepsy
II § *adj* spongy, foamy
∘ **shkumë deti** meerschaum
∘ **shkumë pastash** [*Food*] beaten egg whites with sugar (used in making pastry)

shkumë|ba'rdhë *adj (Poet)* white with foam, white-flecked

shkumë|da'lë *adj* = shkumënga're

shkumë|ma'dh *adj* = shkumënga're

shkumënga're *adj, n* **1** epileptic **2** *(Curse)* may he be struck by epilepsy!

shku'm|ës *nm* chalk

shku'm|ët *adj (i)* foamy

shku'mëz *nf* **1** [*Bot*] soapwort *(Saponaria)* *2** = shku'mës

shkumëz|i'm *nm ger* **1** < shkumëzo'·n, shkumëzo'·het **2** piece/fleck of foam, suds

shkumëz|o'·het *vpr* **1** to be covered with foam: foam up **2** *(Fig)* to foam at the mouth: boil with anger, rage **3** *(Fig)* to exert oneself mightily in strenuous physical labor: knock oneself out working

shkumëz|o'·n
I § *vi* **1** to form foam: foam, lather **2** to foam at the mouth: froth, drool
II § *vt* to apply foam/suds to []

shkumëz|o'r *adj (Poet)* foamy, foaming, frothy

shkumëz|ua'r *adj (i)* **1** covered/flecked with foam, foamy **2** foaming at the mouth: drooling; in a rage

shkumëz|ue's *adj* foaming, foamy

shkum|o'·het *vpr* = shkumëzo'·het

shkum|o'·n *vi, vt* = shkumëzo'·n
∘ **Shkumo-n^{opt}** I May {} have a fit!

shkum|o'r *adj (Poet)* = shkumëzo'r

shkum|o're *nf* beverage that foams when poured: sparkling/gaseous/carbonated drink

shku'm|të *nn (të)* epilepsy

shkum|ua'r *adj (i)* = shkumëzua'r

shkum|ue's *adj* = shkumëzue's

shkum|ue'shëm *adj (i)* sudsy

shkund· *vt* **1** to shake **2** to shake [] off/out **3** *(Fig)* to shake up []: rouse [] to action, wake up [] **4** to drink [a bottle/glass] bottoms up, drink [] down in one swig **5** *(Fig Colloq)* to empty out [], spend the whole []
∘ **e shkund· arrën në korrik** "shake the walnut tree in July" **1** to lack patience **2** to be hasty **3** to be immature
∘ **i shkund· dyqanet** "shake up the shops" to go on a buying spree

○ **ësh·të shkund e ha** "be shake and eat" to live for the moment

○ **e shkund· kuletën** to spend all one's money

○ **e shkund· manin në prill** "shake the mulberry tree in April" **1** to lack patience **2** to be hasty **3** to be immature

○ **shkund· me duar e shtyp· me këmbë** "shake down with one's hands and squash with one's feet" to do something well and then go and ruin it

○ **shkund· pemët e të tjerëve** "shake other people's fruit trees" to live off of other people

○ **e shkund· qesen** "shake the purse" **1** to spend too much; spend all one's money **2** to list every fault

○ **e shkund· tërë thesin** "shake the whole bag" to tell absolutely everything one knows, blab every detail

○ **e shkund· thesin** "shake the bag" to spend everything one has

○ **shkund· urët** "poke the burning logs" to try to speed things up, pour some oil on the fire

shku`nd·*et vpr* **1** to tremble, shake **2** to become bare from shaking **3** to shake oneself off (trying to get clean) **4** *(Fig)* to be roused to action, wake up **5** *(Fig)* to waste all that one has: spend oneself dry, go broke **6** *(Fig)* to go dotty

○ **<> shkund·**³ᵖˡ **zorrët** "<>'s intestines *shake*" <>'s stomach *is rumbling*, <> *is hungry*

shkund|**a**|**dimë**r *nm* period of three days between March and April personified as the transition from winter to spring

shkund|**ëll**|**ímë** *nf* earthquake, tremor

shkund|**ëll**|**o`** ·*n vt* to shake [] hard, rattle, jolt

sh|**kundërm**|**o`** ·*n vt* to deodorize

*sh|**kundërm**|**u**|**e`s** *adj, nm (Old)* deodorant

shku`nd|**ës**

I §ʃ adj used for shaking

II §ʃ n **1** person who shakes olives down: shaker **2** [*Ornit*] white/pied wagtail (*Motacilla alba*)

**shku`nd**|**je** *nf ger* <shku`nd·, shku`nd·*et*

shkund|**ull**|**ímë** *nf* loud quaking, thunderous quake; temblor, earthquake

shkund|**ull**|**ít·** *vt* = shkundullo` ·*n*

shkund|**ull**|**o`** ·*het vpr* to shake oneself strongly, shake oneself awake

shkund|**ull**|**o`** ·*n vt* to shake [] forcefully

shku`nd|**ur** *adj (i)* **1** shaken down/off **2** *(Fig)* impoverished, broke **3** *(Fig)* senile, dotty

○ **ësh·të i shkundur puplash** "have one's feathers shaken off" **1** to be utterly poor, not have a penny to one's name **2** *(Pej)* not have a brain in one's head

Shkup *nm* city in Macedonia with a large Albanian population: Shkup, Skopje

shku`p|**ë** *nf* warm wind that melts the snow

shkup|**ja`n**

I §ʃ adj of/from Skopje

II §ʃ nm native of Skopje

sh|**kuraj**|**ím** *nm ger* **1** <shkurajo` ·*n* **2** discouragement = dekuraj**ím**

sh|**kuraj**|**o`** ·*n vt* to discourage = dekurajo` ·*n*

*shkurat|**í**|**në** *nf* **1** = skorratí**në** **2** squall

*shku`rc *nm* [*Ornit*] quail (*Coturnix coturnix coturnix*)

sh|**kurdí**s· *vt* to unwind []; make [a stringed instrument] go out of tune

sh|**kurdí**s·*et vpr* to unwind; (of a stringed instrument) go out of tune

sh|**kurdís**|**je** *nf ger* <shkurdís·, shkurdís·*et*

sh|**kurdís**|**ur** *adj (i)* **1** unwound; (of a stringed instrument) out of tune **2** *(Fig)* not acting normal, out of sorts

sh|**kuror**|**ëz**|**ím** *nm ger* **1** <shkurorëzo` ·*n*, shkurorëzo` ·*het* **2** [*Law*] divorce

sh|**kuror**|**ëz**|**o`** ·*het vpr* **1** [*Law*] to get divorced **2** *(Book)* to discredit

sh|**kuror**|**ëz**|**o`** ·*n vt* [*Law*] to divorce

sh|**kuror**|**ëz**|**u**|**ar** *adj (i)* divorced

shkurt

I §ʃ adv **1** briefly; in short, in brief **2** in a short/shallow manner

II §ʃ nm short male

○ **shkurt hesapi** in short, to make the story short

○ **Shkurti shkurton urët.** "February shortens the burning logs." *(Prov)* The cold in February makes one burn a lot of wood. In winter expenses for fuel are greater.

Shkurt *nm* February

shkurt|**abíq** *adj, n (Impol)* short (person): midget, shorty

shkurt|**a**|**biq**|**ësí** *nf* [*Med*] dwarfishness, dwarfness

shkurt|**ala`c** OR **shkurt**|**ala`k** = shkurtala`q

shkurt|**ala`q** *adj (Impol)* = shkurtabíq

shkurt|**ale`c** = shkurtala`q

shkurt|**a`qe** *nf* **1** *(Colloq)* final offer/price (in bargaining) **2** = shku`rtje **3** short woman

shku`rt**|**as** OR **shku`rt|**azi** *adv* succinctly

shku`rt|**e** *nf* **1** *(Colloq)* open shirt-like garment; short quilted jacket worn by women **2** final offer (in bargaining)

shkurt|**es**|**í** *nf* **1** [*Ling*] acronym *2 abridgement, digest

shku`rt|**ë** *nf* **1** short woman **2** open shirt-like garment; short quilted jacket worn by women **3** casting lots by drawing straws **4** [*Ornit*] quail (*Coturnix coturnix*)

shku`rt|**ër** *adj (i)* short

shku`rt|**ësí** *nf* shortness

shku`rt|**ëz** *nf* **1** casting lots by drawing straws **2** [*Ornit*] quail (*Coturnix coturnix coturnix*)

*shku`rt|**ic**|**ë** *nf(Old)* shortness

shkurt|**ím** *nm ger* **1** <shkurto` ·*n*, shkurto` ·*het* **2** abridgment **3** *(Old)* summary **4** abbreviation

shkurt|**im**|**ísht** *adv (Book)* briefly; in short, in brief; succinctly

shku`rt|**je** *nf (Colloq)* final days of life: the end

shkurto` ·*het vpr* **1** to get shorter; shrink **2** to decrease

○ **<> shkurto·**·*het*³ˢᵍ **drita e syve** "<>'s eyesight *is shortened*" <>'s eyesight *weakens*

○ **<> shkurto·**·*het*³ᵖˡ **këmbët** "<>'s legs *are shortened*" <> *feels* unsteady on <>'s legs, <> *is* unable to walk

○ **<> shkurto·**·*het*³ˢᵍ **laku/litari** "<>'s rope/noose *is getting tighter*" <> *is* coming to the end of <>'s rope; <> *is nearing* the end (of life), <> *is dying*

shkurto` ·*n*

I §ʃ vt **1** to shorten **2** to reduce, lessen **3** to cut []; cut down [the enemy], kill **4** (of something cold) to cut [] through, bite **5** *(Colloq)* to cut down on [redundant employees], cut out/back []

II §ʃ vi to save time by taking a short cut

○ **<>a shkurto·**·*n* **dorën** to put a stop to <>'s wrongful use of <>'s hands

○ <> **shkurto**·*n* **duart** to deprive <> of <>'s main source of strength: cut off <>'s right arm

○ **Shkurtoje gjuhën!** Don't talk so much! You've talked long enough!

○ <>*i* **shkurto**·*n* **këmbët** "shorten <>'s legs" to punish <> severely (in order to prevent repetition of the crime)

○ <> **shkurto**·*n* **kokën/kryet** to cut off <>'s head

shkurto're *nf* **1** short cut **2** abridgement, digest

shkurt|u'a|r *adj (i)* shortened; abridged

shkurr|a'jë *nf* = **shkorre't**

shkurr|a'k *adj* [*Bot*] having a shrub form: bushy, shrubby

shku'rre *nf* **1** [*Bot*] shrub, bush **2** scrubland, brush

*****shkurre't** *nf* = **shkorre't**

shkurr|i's *stem for 1st sg pres, pl pres, 2nd & 3rd sg subj, pind* < **shkurrit**·

shkurr|i'shtë *nf* = **shkorre't**

shkurr|i't· *vt* to clear scrubland, cut the underbrush

shkurr|na'jë *nf* = **shkorre't**

shkurr|o'·*n vt, vi* **1** to empty [] to the last drop; drink up [] **2** = **shkurrit**·

*****sh|kushull|i'm** *nm ger* **1** < **shkushëllo'**·*n* **2** discouragement, despondency

*****sh|kushull|o'**·*n vt* to discourage

*****sh|kushull|u'e|m** *adj (i) (Reg Gheg)* despondent, disconsolate

sh|ky'ç· *vt* **1** to unlock **2** [*Electr*] to switch off []

sh|ky'ç·*et vpr* [*Electr*] to switch off

sh|ky'ç|ës *adj* [*Electr*] serving as a switch

sh|ky'ç|je *nf ger* [*Electr*] < **shky'ç**·, **shky'ç**·*et*

sh|ky'ç|ur *adj (i)* [*Electr*] switched off

shky'es *n* clever and competent person

shle' *stem for pdef, opt* < **shly'e**·*n*

shli'cë *nf* [*Tech*] = **shli'zë**

*****shli'rë** *nf* = **cli'rë**

shli'vë *nf* slivovitz, plum brandy

shli'zë *nf* **1** mortise **2** [*Tech*] spline

shliz|o'·*n vt, vi* to make a mortise/spline in []

*****shl|o'**·*n vt, vi* = **lësho'**·*n*

*****sh|lodh**· = **çlodh**·

ShLU *abbrev* < **Shkolla e lirë ushtarake** military school for non-military people

shluk *nm (np ˜ qe)* skin blister caused by burning/ scalding

shluk|ëz|o'·*n vt* to blister skin by burning/scalding

*****sh|lu'l|z** = **çlul'ëz**

*****sh|lu'q**·*et vpr* to make faces, grimace, scowl

shly'·*het vpr* **1** to vanish; fade **2** (*Fig*) to settle up (mutual obligations/debts); get absolved

shl|y'e·*n vt* **1** to wipe out []: expunge, erase **2** (*Fig*) to absolve of [a misdeed/debt/obligation]; remit [a sentence]

shl|y'er
  I § *part* < **shly'e**·*n*
  II § *adj (i)* absolved

shl|y'er|je *nf ger* < **shly'e**·*n*, **shly'**·*het*

shl|y'er|shëm *adj (i)* absolvable, expungeable, clearable

shl|yr|ës|o'·*n vt* to remove the fat from [], scour

*****shlle'gë** *nf* [*Zool*] = **nepë'rkë**

shlli'gë *nf* **1** [*Zool*] viper = **nepë'rkë 2** (*Folklore*) offspring of a dragon **3** (*Fig*) spiteful and talkative woman

---

○ **shlli'gë shullëri 1** poisonous snake basking in the sun **2** very clever woman/girl with a sharp and biting tongue

shllim *nm* image, notion, idea

*****shllu'ngë** *nf* = **shtëllu'ngë**

*****shllup**· *vt* to gulp [] down = **shklluq**·

*****sh|ma'jtë** *adj (i)* = **majtë**

*****sh|mall**· = **çmall**·

*****sh|mall|o'**·*het vpr* = **çma'll**·*et*

*****sh|mall|o's**·*et vpr* = **çma'll**·*et*

sh|mang· *vt* **1** to divert [] from a path, deflect **2** (*Fig*) to shun; avoid, avert, prevent

sh|ma'ng·*et vpr* **1** to shy away; stay away; avoid <> **2** to deviate from the path **3** [*Sport*] to duck/get away from <>

*****sh|ma'ng|cë** *nf* railroad switch

sh|ma'ngë *nf* [*Bot*] hawksbeard (*Crepis*)

sh|ma'ng|ie *nf ger* **1** < **shmang**·, **shma'ng**·*et* **2** deviation **3** avoidance

sh|ma'ng|shëm *adj (i)* avoidable, avertable, preventable

sh|ma'ng|ur *adj (i)* off the beaten path, unfrequented, out of the way

*****sh|mashkull** = **çmashkull**

*****sh|ma't**·*et* = **çma't**·*et*

*****sh|mbreh**· = **çmbreh**·

*****sh|mbush**· *vt* to empty = **çmbush**·

*****sh|mend|o'**·*n vi*

*****shmëri'm** *nm* = **shëmti'rë**

*****sh|mërz|i't**·*et vpr* to overcome boredom, kill time

*****sh|mirë'z|o'**·*het vpr* to get worse

*****sh|mobil|iz|i'm** *nm ger* < **shmobilizo'**·*n*

*****sh|mobil|iz|o'**·*n vt* = **çmobilizo'**·*n*

*****shmria'k** *nm (i)* = përzi'tës

*****sh|nder** = **çnder**

sh|nderr|i'm *nm ger* **1** < **shndërro'**·*n*, **shndërro'**·*het* **2** radical transformation

sh|ndërr|o'·*het vpr* to undergo radical transformation

sh|ndërr|o'·*n vt* **1** to transform [] radically **2** (*Colloq*) to interchange

sh|ndërr|u'e|shëm *adj (i)* transformable

sh|ndri·*n vi* to shine, shine brightly

sh|ndri's| *stem for 1st sg pres, pl pres, 2nd & 3rd sg subj, pind* < **shndrit**·

sh|ndrit·
  I § *vi* **1** to shine brightly; shine with cleanliness/ purity **2** (*Fig*) to stand out
  II § *vt* (*Fig*) to enlighten

○ **shndrit**· **si meteor** (*Book*) to flash for a moment and then disappear; be a flash in the pan

sh|ndrit|ës *adj* shining, shiny

sh|ndrit|je *nf ger* **1** < **shndrit**· **2** shine, sparkle

sh|ndrit|shëm *adj (i)* **1** shining brightly: bright, shiny **2** (*Fig Book*) illustrious, of great renown

sh|ndri'zë *nf* sparkler, sparkling thing; precious stone

shne'gull *nf* **1** multicolored braided woolen cradle strap; decorative ribbon/braid **2** woman's backpack that is embroidered and decorated with ribbon **3**

*****sh|nej|shëm** *adj (i) (Old)* [*Ling*] = **panyjshëm**

*****sh|ngul**· = **shkul**·

shno's| *stem for 1st sg pres, pl pres, 2nd & 3rd sg subj, pind* < **shno't**· (*Reg*)

shno't· *vi* (*Reg*) to fail to keep [one's word/promise]

shno't·*et vpr* (*Reg*) to go back on one's word, break one's word

*****sh|njer|ëz|i'm** = **çnjer|ëzi'm**

sho| *stem for 3rd sg pdef* <**shua**•*n,* **shu**•*het*

shodol *adj, n* lanky (oaf); weak and plodding (person)

shofer *n* driver, chauffeur

shofke *nf (Reg)* mirror = **pasqyrë**

shofsh| *stem for opt* <**shua**•*n,* **shu**•*het*

shofte *3rd sg opt* <**shua**•*n,* **shu**•*het*
  ○ <>**u shoftë/harroftë emri!** "May <>'s name be forgotten!" *(Curse)* May <> drop dead and be forgotten!
  ○ <>**u shoftë pisha!** "May <>'s torch be extinguished!" *(Curse)* I hope <> dies! <> can drop dead for all I care!
  ○ <>**u shoftë ymri!** "May <>'s life be extinguished!" *(Curse)* May <> die!

shog *nm* bald man = **tullac**

shog•*et vpr* **1** to go bald; lose hair **2** *(Fig)* to lose interest, cool off

shogan *adj, nm* bald (man)

shogë *nf* bald spot

shogëlinë *nf* small barren area: bare spot; small clearing in the woods

shogët *adj (i)* **1** bald, hairless **2** [*Bot*] glabrous **3** *(Reg)* = **plogët**

shogur *adj (i)* hairless

shoh| *stem for 1st sg pres, 1st & 3rd pl pres, 2nd & 3rd sg subj* <**sheh**•
  ○ **shohim e bëjmë** "we see and we do" let's see how it goes (before we act)
  ○ **nuk** [] **shoh dot me sy** "I don't ever see <> by eye" I never want to see [] again
  ○ **nuk** <> **shohin sytë këtej** "<>'s eyes *do not* look around here" <> *doesn't* dare to show <>'s face around here, <> *doesn't* dare to come this way

shoje *np* <**shuall**

shojnicë *nf* granary

*****shojtje** *nf ger (Reg)* = **shuarje**

shojzë *nf* **1** [*Ichth*] flounder *(Platichthys flesus luscus)* **2** [*Bot*] winged seed: samara
  ○ **shojzë deti** [*Ichth*] megrim *Lepidorhombus whiffiagonis*
  ○ **shojzë laroshe** [*Ichth*] Bloch's topknot *Phrynorhombus regius*
  ○ **shojzë pikaloshe** [*Ichth*] plaice *Pleuronectes platessa*

shok
  I § *nm* **1** mate, (male) spouse, husband; teammate **2** comrade, companion, fellow; male friend; male person **3** *(Colloq)* partner **4** (in a comparison): equal: peer
  II § *adj* [*Law*] associateheavy blow: shock
  ○ **shok armësh** comrade-in-arms
  ○ **shok dhome** roommate
  ○ **shoku i jetës** life companion: husband
  ○ **shok ka**• **veten** to have no equal, be unique
  ○ **shok lufte** war comrade
  ○ **shok mali** comrade in a mountain guerilla army: fellow partisan
  ○ **ësh-të shok me para** "be a friend with money" to be a fair-weather friend
  ○ **shok me shok** with one another
  ○ **shok pjesëmarrës** [*Law*] accomplice; partner
  ○ **shok rruge** travel companion, fellow traveler

shoke *nf* **1** broad multicolored woolen sash wrapped around the waist; multicolored cradle strap **2** *(Fig)* belt, strip

○ **shoka e kumbarës** "godparent's waistband" *(Reg)* rainbow

shokëz *nf* narrow belt

shoku-shoku *reciprocal noun* each other

shollar *n* cobbler

shollë *nf* **1** leather for shoe soles; shoe sole **2** sole of the foot **3** *(Reg)* short heavy wool sock worn indoors over regular stockings: wool slipper; slipper sole **4** *(Reg)* moccasin, shoe
  ○ <> **ësh-të bërë faqja shollë** <> *has* lost all sense of shame
  ○ **sholla me hundë** moccasin with a turned-up pointed tip

shollëz *nf dimin* <**shollë**

shollomotkë *nf (Reg)* weak raki or wine with a cloudy appearance: bad raki, poor wine

shollondur *nm (Reg)* livestock remains left by a predator

*****shollxhi** *nm (np ~nj)* moccasin maker

*****shondolem** *adj* awkward, foolish

*****shoner** *nm (Old)* schooner

shop *nm (Reg)* blockhead, idiot

shoq
  I § *nm* **1** husband **2** *(Colloq)* = **shok**
  II § *nm (i)* her spouse/husband
  ○ **shoq me shoq** with one another

shoqatë *nf* organization of people with a common purpose or interest: association, society

shoqe
  I § *nf* <**shok 1** female companion/friend/fellow/peer **2** wife **3** female person
  II § *adj* <**shok** [*Law*] associate
  III § *nf (e)* his spouse/wife
  ○ **shoqja e jetës** life companion: wife

shoqëri *nf* **1** society **2** friendly social relationship; friendly association; social circle **3** organization of people with a common purpose or interest: association **4** clique **5** corporation
  ○ **shoqëri anonime** corporation

shoqërim *nm ger* **1** <**shoqëro**•*n,* **shoqëro**•*het* **2** accompaniment **3** association **4** [*Bot*] community

shoqërisht *adv* **1** in a friendly manner; together **2** *(Book)* socially

shoqërizim *nm ger* **1** <**shoqërizo**•*n,* **shoqërizo**•*het* **2** socialization

shoqërizo•*het vpr* **1** to become socialized **2** to take on public responsibility for a previously private responsibility **3** [*Econ*] to become public property

shoqërizo•*n vt* **1** to socialize **2** to shift responsibility for [] from the private to the public sector **3** [*Econ*] to appropriate [property] to public ownership

shoqërizuar *adj (i)* [*Econ*] socialized

shoqëro•*het vpr* to have a friendly relationship/association
  ○ **shoqëro**•*het* **me** [] **1** to keep company with [] **2** to be concomitant with [] **3** *(Book)* to be provided with []

shoqëro•*n vt* **1** to accompany; escort; see [] off **2** [*Agr*] = **bashkëshoqëro**•*n*
  ○ **shoqëro**•*n* **me artileri** [*Mil*] to provide artillery support
  ○ [] **shoqëro**•*n* **me sy** to follow [] with one's eyes

shoqëror *adj* **1** social **2** belonging to the public: public **3** friendly

shoqëroro-kulturor *adj* sociocultural

shoq|**ër**|**u**|**a**|**r** *adj (i)* **1** = shoqëru'eshëm **2** accompanied

shoq|**ër**|**u**|**e**|**s**

I §ʃ adj **1** accompanying; escorting; associated; concomitant, co-occurrent **2** [*Agr*] grown together with another crop **3** [*Psych*] associative, associational

II §ʃ n **1** escort, guide; chaperone **2** conductor (on a train or bus) **3** [*Mus*] accompanist

shoq|**ër**|**u**|**e**|**shëm** *adj (i)* sociable, gregarious; friendly

sho'qi-sho'qëm *adj (i) (Colloq)* reciprocal; mutual

sho'qi-sho'qin *nm recip acc (Colloq)* each other = njëri-tjetrin

sho'qi-sho'qit *nm recip dat (Colloq)* each other = njëri-tjetrit

sho'qja-sho'qen *nf recip acc (Colloq)* each other = njëra-tjetrën

sho'qja-sho'qes *nf recip dat (Colloq)* each other = njëra-tjetrës

****shoq**|**n**|**u**|**e**|**shëm** *adj (i)* = shoqëru'eshëm

****shoqollogjí** *(Old)* = sociologjí

****shor** *nm* [*Ichth*] electric ray, crampfish

sho'rde *nf* [*Zool*] blotched gray snake that grows up two and a half meters long

****sho're** *nf* skin eruption: rash

short *nm* **1** casting lots, lottery; sortilege; marked counter used in sortilege **2** *(Colloq)* share that falls to one by lot: lot, luck of the draw; luck **3** *(Colloq)* spouse = bashkëshort

short|**a**|**r** *n* fortuneteller = falltar

short|**ar**|**í** *nf* fortunetelling

short|**as** *adv* by chance

sho'rt|**ë** *nf* **1** lot, luck **2** share, portion

short|**í** *nf* witchcraft; superstition

short|**o**·*n* *vt (Colloq)* **1** to decide, determine **2** to foretell ***3** = sharto·*n*

****short**|**thën**|**ës** *n* fortuneteller

short|**z**|**í** *adj, n (fem sg ~ëz, masc pl ~ínj, fem pl ~eza)* = fatzí

shorr· *vt (Reg)* to put pressure on []: squeeze; force, oblige

shosh· *vt* **1** to put [] through a screen: screen [], winnow [] **2** *(Fig)* to sift through [a matter] carefully, examine [a topic] thoroughly

○ **Shosh e sit e mos gatuaj.** "Sieve and sift and not cook." A lot of effort goes into it, but nothing comes out.

sho'sh·*et* *vpr* to sift down

shosh|**a**|**r** *n* winnower, sifter

shosh|**a**|**re** *nf* **1** perforated ladle **2** tea filter **3** sieve

sho'sh|**ë**

I §ʃ nf **1** screen used for grading/separating: winnowing screen, winnow; riddle **2** *(Fig)* screening/filtering device **3** sprinkler **4** *(Fig)* small place, patch, little bit **5** [*Bot*] carline thistle *(Carlina acaulis)*

II §ʃ adj riddled with holes

○ **të jep ujë me shoshë** "gives you water with a winnowing screen" fg *is* extraordinarily skillful

○ **të nis me shoshë për ujë** "sends you off for water with a screen" fg lures you with false hopes

○ **ësh**·*të* **shoshë pa rreth** "be a screen without a frame" to be useless because of an essential defect

○ **shoshë e prishur** "broken sieve" very talkative person

○ **Shosha shosh, sita sit.** "The screen screens, the sieve sifts." *(Prov)* What one does the other cannot do.

○ **ësh**·*të* **shoshë e shpuar** *(Impol)* to be good for nothing, be useless

shosh|**ë**|**lím** *nm ger* < shoshëlo·*n*

shosh|**ë**|**lo**·*n* *vt* **1** to sift through [a matter] carefully, examine [a topic] thoroughly **2** to gossip about []

sho'sh|**ës** *adj* used for sifting

shosh|**ís** *stem for 1st sg pres, pl pres, 2nd & 3rd sg subj, pind* < shoshít·

shosh|**ít**· *vt* **1** to sift, sieve; screen; winnow **2** *(Fig)* to examine [a topic] thoroughly, scan [] carefully: sift through [a matter]

shosh|**ít**|**ës**

I §ʃ adj used for sifting

II §ʃ n sifter, winnower

shosh|**ít**|**je** *nf ger* < shoshít·

shosh|**ít**|**ur**

I §ʃ part < shoshít·

II §ʃ adj (i) = sho'shur

sho'shje *nf ger* < shosh·, sho'sh·*et*

shosho'ne *np fem* women's galoshes

shosho'r *adj* sieve-like

sho'sh|**ur** *adj (i)* passed through a winnowing screen: winnowed

shota'n *nm (Reg)* [*Ornit*] sheldrake

sho'të *nf (Reg)* [*Ornit*] shelduck *(Tadorna tadorna)*

sho'v| *stem for 1st & 2nd sg pdef* < shu'a·*n*

shovin|**íst** *adj, n* chauvinist

shovin|**íz**|**ëm** *nm* chauvinism

****shpâ(n)** *nm (Reg Gheg)* = shpan

shpa|**be's**·*et* *vpr* to be faithless/perfidious: break one's word

shp|**ag**|**e's** *nf* **1** *(Old)* amount paid in recompensation for harm/injury: damages **2** revenge, vengeance

shp|**ag**|**es**|**ta'r** *n (Old)* = shpagimta'r

shp|**ag**|**ë** *nf* revenge, vengeance

shp|**ag**|**ë**|**ma'rr**|**ës** *adj, n* = shpagimta'r

shp|**ag**|**ëzo**·*het vpr* [*Relig*] to renounce one's Christian faith and change one's baptismal name: become unchristened

shp|**ag**|**ëzo**·*n* *vt* **1** [*Relig*] to annul the christening and baptism of: unchristen **2** *(Book)* to expunge []'s name (from a public place)

shp|**ag**|**ëz**|**u**|**a**|**r** *adj (i)* **1** [*Relig*] unchristened **2** with the name expunged

shp|**ag**|**ím** *nm ger* **1** < shpagu'a·*n*, shpagu·*het* **2** recompensation for harm/injury: damages **3** revenge, vengeance

shp|**ag**|**im**|**ta'r**

I §ʃ adj avenging

II §ʃ n avenger

shp|**ag**|**u**·*het vpr* to take revenge

shp|**ag**|**u**|**a**·*n* *vt* **1** to pay for [damage/injury]: indemnify, recompensate **2** *(Fig)* to pay <> back for []: avenge []

shp|**aketo**·*n* *vt* to take [] out of its package: unpack, unwrap

****shp**|**alc**|**ë** *nf* = shpa'rcë

****shp**|**al**|**ís**· = shpalo's·

****shp**|**al**|**ís**·*et* = shpalo's·*et*

shp|**al**|**o**·*het vpr* = shpalo's·*et*

shpalo·*n*
I § *vt* = shpalo's·
II § *vi (Reg)* (of leaves) to open up, unfold

shpalo's· *vt* **1** to unfold [], unfurl [] **2** to leaf through [] **3** *(Fig)* to reveal/present [] in a piecemeal and gradual way
　◦ **shpalos· flamurin** to raise the flag, take the lead in speaking up

shpalo's·*et vpr* **1** to unfurl, unfold **2** *(Fig)* to come into view in a piecemeal and gradual way: gradually come to light, be revealed bit by bit

shpalo'sje *nf ger* <shpalo's·, shpalo's·*et*

shpalo'su'r *adj (i)* unfolded, unfurled

shpall· *vt* to give official notice of []: declare, proclaim, announce
　◦ <> **shpall·** *(Colloq)* to scare <> stiff, terrify <>
　◦ <> **shpall· luftë** to declare war against <>

shpall·*et vpr*
　◦ <> **shpall·***et (Colloq)* to get terribly frightened: get scared stiff

shpall·ës *n* declarer, announcer, proclaimer

shpall'ët *adj (i)* **1** = shpa'llur **2** obvious

shpall'je *nf ger* **1** <shpall·, shpall·*et* **2** declaration, announcement, proclamation, notice

shpall'ur *adj (i)* declared

shpan *nm* **1** lime (calcium oxide) material used in building construction, porous limestone **2** calcification left in a vessel by boiling water

shpandko'·*het vpr (Fig)* to get completely tired out, become exhausted

shpandko'·*n vt (Reg)* **1** to eviscerate **2** to batter, shatter **3** *(Fig)* to tire [] out utterly, exhaust

shpa'rcë *nf* washcloth, wash rag

shpardh *nm* [*Bot*] Hungarian oak, Italian oak *(Quercus frainetto)*

shpardh'isht*ë* *nf* forest of Hungarian oak

shpa're'ë* adv* = qëpa'rë

shparg *nm (np ˜gje)* [*Bot*] **1** asparagus *(Asparagus)* **2** sharp-leaved asparagus *(Asparagus acutifolius)* **3** asparagus fern *(Asparagus plumosus)*

shparg'e*r* nm* = pele'n*ë*

shpa'rgull *nm (np ˜j)* [*Bot*] sharp-leaved asparagus *(Asparagus acutifolius)*

shpari's *stem for 1st sg pres, pl pres, 2nd & 3rd sg subj, pind* <shpari't·

shpari't· *vt (Reg)* to tire [] out greatly

shpari't·*et vpr (Reg)* to get very tired, become exhausted

***shpa'rsh*ë*m** *adj (i)* = qëpa'rsh*ë*m

shparta'll *adv* in a disorderly mess

shpartall'i'm *nm ger* **1** <shpartallo'·*n*, shpartallo'·*het* **2** utter defeat

***shpartall'i'na** *np* <shpartalli'n*ë (Colloq)* ruins, rubble, debris: a dump

shpartall'i'n*ë* *nf* dilapidated old structure, ramshackle building; wreck

shpartall'i's· = shpartallo'·*n*

shpartallo'·*het vpr* to become disheveled; let oneself go (out of sheer exhaustion)

shpartallo'·*n vt* to put [] into disarray, wreak disorder on []: beat badly; wreck; disarrange, jumble, dishevel

shpartall'ua'r *adj (i)* **1** disheveled; utterly exhausted, completely worn out **2** in utter disorder, soundly defeated

shpart*ë* *nf* [*Bot*] = gjine'sht*ë*r

***shparth** = shpardh

shparr *nm* [*Bot*] = shpardh

shparr'isht*ë* *nf* = shpardhi'sht*ë*

shpat *nm* mountain/hill slope

Shpat *nm* **1** highland ethnographic region in central Albania **2** Shpat (male name)

shpata'r *nm* **1** [*Hist*] swordsman **2** [*Fencing*] épéeist

shpata'ra'k
I § *adj* of or pertaining to Shpat
II § *nm* native of Shpat

shpa't*ë* *nf* **1** sword **2** [*Fencing*] épée **3** reed (on a loom) **4** [*Text*] fabric of the width of the reed: full-width fabric **5** rib of a pack-saddle **6** cross-plank of a cart bed **7** [*Agr*] simple mechanism that joins the sole to the beam of a wooden plow and controls the depth of the furrow made **8** [*Bot*] century plant *(Agave americana)* **9** [*Ichth*] = peshk-shpat*ë*
　◦ **ësh·të shpatë e gjallë** to be brave in battle, be a courageous fighter
　◦ **ësh·të shpatë nga goja 1** to be an eloquent and persuasive speaker **2** to have a sharp/biting tongue
　◦ **ësh·të**³ˢᵍ **shpatë e thyer** to be powerless; be of no further use/value

***shpa't*ë*ll** *nf* = shpatull

shpat*ë*mba'jt*ë*s *nm* [*Hist*] sword carrying for a mounted knight

shpat*ë*z *nf* **1** [*Agr*] vertical brace between the sole and beam of a wooden plow which also serves to control the angle at which the plowshare enters the soil **2** splint (for a broken limb) **3** reed (on a loom) **4** fabric of the width of the reed: full-width fabric **5** side rib of a packsaddle **6** cross-plank of a cart bed **7** [*Bot*] gladiolus *(Gladiolus)* **8** [*Bot*] iris = shpato're
　◦ **shpatëz kadife** [*Bot*] snake's head iris, widow iris *Hermadactylis tuberosus* = karaka'fte
　◦ **shpatëz e kuqe** [*Bot*] corn flag gladiolus *Gladiolus segetum*

shpat*ë*zh've'sh'ur *adj (Poet)* sword unsheathed: ready to fight

shpati'n*ë* *nf* slope on a small hill; small hill

shpato'r *adj* sword-like, ensiform

shpato're *nf* [*Bot*] **1** iris *(Iris germanica)* **2** iris family *Iridaceae* **3** = shpati'n*ë*

shpatu'k *adj* flat on both sides, squat

shpa'tull *nf* **1** part of the back that covers the shoulderblade **2** [*Anat*] shoulderblade *scapula* **3** side rib of a packsaddle **4** cross-plank of a cart bed **5** [*Agr*] vertical part of the frame at which the plow sole is joined to the plow beam **6** splint (for a broken limb) **7** trowel **8** splint **9** mountain slope, hillside **10** [*Bot*] sprout from a fruit tree that grows out near the base of the trunk
　◦ **Shpatullat duan këmbë.** "Shoulders need legs." *(Prov)* No matter how strong you are, you need the support of others.
　◦ **s'ka· shpatulla për** [] to lack the ability/backbone required for []: not have what it takes for []
　◦ **Shpatullat me zemrën s'janë motra.** "Shoulders and heart are not sisters." *(Prov)* Courage does not always go with strength.
　◦ **Shpatullat s'bëhen tri.** "One doesn't have three shoulders." *(Prov)* There is a limit on how much one can handle.

shpatull'a'k *adj* = shpatu'k

shpatull'a'n *adj, n* broad-shouldered (person)

shpatull|ar *n* *(Old)* person who foretells the future by studying the scapula of livestock: scapulomancer

shpa'tull|ash *adv*

shpatull|gjer|ë *adj* broad-shouldered

shpatull|in|ë *nf* = **shpatin|ë**

shpatull|ngusht|ë *adj* narrow-shouldered

shpatull|or *adj* 1 [*Anat*] scapular 2 = **shpatulla|n**

shpatull|ore *nf* 1 [*Sport*] parallel wall bars used in gymnastic exercises: Swedish bars, wall ladder 2 [*Hist*] piece of armor that protects the shoulders

*****shpe|je** *nf* [*Bot*] = **shpel**

shpejt *adv* 1 quickly, rapidly 2 soon 3 early 4 *(Colloq)* a long time ago; for a long time
  ○ **shpejt a/ose vonë** sooner or later
  ○ **shpejt e shpejt** 1 within a very short time 2 *(Pej)* hastily

shpejt|as *OR* **shpejt|azi** *adv* speedily, quickly; in a hurry; immediately, right away

shpejt|ë *adj (i)* 1 fast, fleet; rapid; quick 2 bright, apt 3 *(Reg)* early; old, ancient

shpejt|ëm *adj (i)* speedy

shpejt|ës|i *nf* 1 speed; quickness; rapidity 2 [*Phys*] velocity 3 [*Tech*] (first/second/third/reverse) gear

shpejt|ës|o·*n* *vt* = **shpejto**'·*n*

shpejt|i *adv (së)* right away, very soon, in a short while

shpejt|i *nf* = **shpejtësi**

shpejt|im *nm ger* 1 < **shpejto**'·*n*, **shpejto**'·*het* 2 (high) speed; hurry 3 haste, rush *4 *(Reg)* = **shpëtim**

shpejt|o·*het* *vpr* 1 to increase in speed/frequency: speed up 2 to act in haste

shpejt|o·*n*
  I § *vt* 1 to increase the speed of []: speed [] up, accelerate 2 to bring [] about sooner: hasten 3 to induce [] to hurry
  II § *vi* to go fast, speed; hurry

shpejt|u|ar *adj (i)* 1 increased in speed/frequency: speeded up 2 done in haste: hasty

shpejt|u|es
  I § *adj* speeding up, hastening; accelerating
  II § *nm* [*Chem*] substance that accelerates a reaction: accelerant

shpel *nm* [*Bot*] black poplar *(Populus nigra)*

*****shpelino'k** *nm* [*Bot*] balm *(Melissa officinalis)*

shpell|ar
  I § *adj* cavernous
  II § *n* cave dweller; caveman

shpell|ë
  I § *nf* 1 mountain cavern, cave 2 boulder, large rock
  II § *adj (Colloq)* loud and high; hard and strong
  ○ **ësh-të shpellë e madhe** to be big troublemaker

shpell|in|ë *nf* 1 small cave, grotto 2 area with many caves

shpell|o·*n* *vt, vi* 1 to dig [a big cavity] under ground, burrow in [] 2 *(Fig)* to send [] to []'s grave

shpell|or *adj (Book)* of or pertaining to a cave; cave-dwelling

shpend *nm* 1 [*Ornit*] fowl; poultry animal 2 *(Reg)* game animal/fowl: game
  ○ **shpend gëzofi** *(Reg)* animal hunted for its pelt: fur animal
  ○ **ësh-të shpend i gjallë** (of a person) to be fast moving, be fast
  ○ **shpend puplash** *(Reg)* bird with feathers used by humans: feathered bird

Shpend *nm* Shpend (male name)

shpend|ar|i *nf* poultry farming; poultry house, poultry division

shpe'nd|ël *nf* pinfeather, down

shpe'nd|ër *nf* 1 [*Bot*] hellebore *(Helleborus)* = **taçe** 2 *(Reg)* bramble bush 3 danewort *(Sambucus ebulus)* = **qingël**

shpênd|ër|i *nf collec (Reg Gheg)* = **shpendi**

shpend|ërrit|ës *n* poultry raiser/grower

shpend|i *nf collec* fowl, poultry = **shpesëri**

shpend|keq *nm (Colloq)* [*Ornit*] owl

shpend|lo·*n* *vt* to pluck feathers/pinfeathers from []

shpe'nd|thi *adv*

shpe'ne *nf* [*Bot*] common snowdrop *(Galanthus nivalis)*

shpe'ngël *nf* [*Bot*] bear's-foot *(Helleborus foetidus)*

shpeng|im *nm ger* 1 < **shpengo**'·*n*, **shpengo**'·*het* 2 payment to redeem collateral

shpeng|o·*het* *vpr* to slip out of hobbles, get out of being tied up; become unfettered; get free

shpeng|o·*n* *vt* 1 to redeem [something given as collateral] 2 to free up [] 3 to remove hobbles from []

shpeng|u|ar
  I § *adj (i)* unfettered; unconstrained
  II § *adv* in an unconstrained manner: freely, unhesitatingly

shpenk|o·*n* *vt* to disembowel/draw [poultry]

shpenz|im *nm ger* 1 < **shpenzo**'·*n*, **shpenzo**'·*het* 2 expenditure, expense

shpenz|o·*het* *vpr* to spend money, incur expenses

shpenz|o·*n* *vt, vi* 1 to spend 2 to consume, use up []; cause [] to spend money 3 to cause expense: cost
  ○ **shpenzo**·*n* **me zgrip** to be very thrifty in spending

shperr· *vt* 1 to win all [the money/chips] 2 *(Fig)* to exhaust

shperr·*et* *vpr* 1 to lose it all 2 *(Fig)* to become exhausted

shpes|ë *nf* [*Ornit*] = **shpend**

shpes|ër|i *nf collec* fowl

shpes|ur|ina *np fem* large variety of fowl, kinds of fowl

shpesh *adv* 1 with short intervals: often, frequently 2 at close intervals: densely
  ○ **shpesh e më shpesh** ever more frequently, more and more

shpe'sh|ë *adj (i)* = **shpeshtë**

shpesh|he'rë *adv* many times, often

shpesh|o·*n* = **shpeshto**'·*n*

shpesh|ta'k *nm (Reg)* dense forest

shpesh|të *adj (i)* 1 closely spaced: frequent; crowded, dense; heavy (snow/rain) 2 tightly woven

shpesh|të|si *nf (Book)* frequency; density

shpesh|t|i *nf* = **shpeshtësi**

shpesht|im *nm ger* 1 < **shpeshto**'·*n*, **shpeshto**'·*het* 2 = **shpeshtësi**

shpesht|in|ë *nf* dense grove/copse

shpesht|o·*het* *vpr* to become more frequent; become more densely packed

shpesht|o·*n* *vt* 1 to increase the frequency of []: intensify [] in frequency, speed up [] 2 to increase the density of []: compact o **shpeshto**·*n*³ᵖˡ **gjelat** the rooster crowing *gets* more frequent (dawn *is approaching*)

shpeshtua|r *adj (i)* shortly spaced: rapid

shpet *nm (Reg)* = **pahí**

sh|**pet**ë|**zim** *nm* [*Min Geol*] cleavage

shpe'zë *nf* = **shpend**

o **shpezë uji** waterfowl

shpezë'ri

I § *nf collec*

II § *adj* = **shpesë'ri**

shpezë'to're *nf* aviary, birdcage

shpëla·**het**

I § *vp reflex* to rinse oneself off

II § *vp recip* to clear mutual debts: become all square

shpëla·*n* *vt* **1** to wash away [ ]; wash [ ] clean; rinse, rinse off/out/away [ ] **2** *(Iron)* to consume the entire contents of a food/drink container: eat [ ] clean, drink [ ] dry **3** *(Fig)* to pay off one's obligation in respect to [ ], discharge [a debt/duty] **4** (of moving bowels) to purge, clean out [ ]

o **i shpël**a·*n* **duart nga** { } to have nothing more to do with {*a person*}: wash one's hands of { }

o <> **shpël**a·*n* **hambarët/kazanët** "clean out <>'s granary/cauldron" to eat <> out of house and home

o <>**a shpël**a·*n* **kokën** "rinse out <>'s head" to rid <> of the crazy ideas <> in <>'s head

o [ ] **shpëlaftë mortja/kolera!** "May death/plague wash [ ] away!" *(Curse)* I hope [ ] dies!

shpëla|**k**|ë**s** *nm* wooden bat for beating clothes during washing: wash paddle

****shpël**a**q**ët *adj (i)* = **shpëla'rë**

shpëla**ra** *np* (të) *fem* **1** dirty dishwater **2** *(Euph)* menstrual flow, menses

shpëla**rë** *adj (i)* **1** rinsed; washed off **2** *(Fig)* washed out; faded, weak **3** *(Impol)* bland, dull, vapid, wishy-washy **4** *(Impol)* shameless

shpëla**rë**s *adj* used for rinsing

shpëla**rje** *nf ger* < **shpël**a·*n*, **shpël**a·**het**

sh|**pëlq**e·*n* *vt* to stop liking [ ], take a dislike to [ ]

****sh**|**pëlq**im *nm* displeasure

shpëndër *nf* [*Bot*] = **shpendër**

shpënë *part* < **shpí**e·

shpën|ë**s**

I § *n* one who takes someone/something somewhere: bearer

II § *adj* propelling, driving

shpën|**ie** *nf ger* **1** < **shpí**e·, **shpí**·**het** **2** propulsion, drive *(Old)* **3** conveyance, transportation

shpër *formative prefix* typically indicates action that intensely distributes energy or material or that counters a given condition: de-, dis-, re-

shpër|**ball**·**et** *vpr* to face up to <> openly, have a confrontation

shpër|**bashkim** *nm ger* [*Chem*] < **shpërbashko'**·*n*, **shpërbashko'**·**het**

shpër|**bashk**o'·**het** *vpr* [*Chem*] to dissociate

shpër|**bashk**o'·*n* *vt* [*Chem*] to cause dissociation of [ ]

shpër|**be**·**het** *vpr* to perjure oneself: falsely take an oath

shpër|**be**·*n vi* to make a false vow: falsely swear

shpër|**be**|**më** *adj (i)* perjuring = **berrejsh**ë**m**

shpërbetar

I § *adj* perjurious

II § *n* perjurer

shpër|**bet**o'·**het** *vpr* = **shpërbe**·**het**

shpër|**bë**·**het** *vpr* to decompose

shpër|**bë**·*n vt* [*Spec*] to cause a decomposition

shpër|**bë**|**rë** *adj (i)* decomposed

shpër|**bë**|**rje** *nf ger* **1** < **shpërbë**·*n*, **shpërbë**·**het** **2** decomposition **3** [*Phys*] diffraction

shpër|**ble**·*n vt* **1** to repay/reward <> for [ ]; recompensate **2** to pay ransom for [ ]: ransom

o <>**a shpërble**·*n* **me të njëjtën monedhë** *(Book)* to pay <> back in kind, respond to <> in kind; pay <> back in <>'s own coin

shpër|**ble**|**së** *nf* **1** ransom **2** = **shpërblim**

shpër|**ble**|**star** *n* = **shpërblimtar**

shpër|**blim** *nm ger* **1** < **shpërblo**·*n* **2** repayment **3** payment for services rendered: compensation, wage **4** reward, award **5** payment for damages: recompensation **6** revenge, vengeance **7** redemption

shpër|**blimtar** *n* **1** *(Old)* payer of ransom **2** redeemer

shpër|**bl**u·*n vt* *(Intens)* to turn [ ] over and over in one's mind; consider [ ] carefully for a long time

shpër|**blyer** *adj (i)* having won an award: award-winning, rewarded

shpër|**bl**|**yes**

I § *n* **1** one who pays a compensation **2** redeemer

II § *adj* *compensatory

shpër|**byth**· *vt* *(Scorn)* to abuse [ ] badly

shpër|**byth**·**et** *vpr* *(Reg)* to turn tail, run away

shpër|**dal**ë *adj (e) fem* *(Pej)* totally wanton = **përdal**ë

shpër|**derdh**· *vt* *(Intens)* to spill [ ] out all over

shpër|**derdh**·**et** *vpr* *(Intens)* to spill out all over

shpër|**dirr**·**et** *vpr* < **shpërdjerr**· *(Reg Intens)* to disappear, vanish

shpër|**djerr**· *vt* *(Reg Intens)* to make [ ] disappear, cause [ ] to vanish

shpër|**djerr**|ë *part* < **shpërdjerr**·

shpër|**dor**· *vt* = **shpërdoro'**·*n*

shpër|**dor**| *stem for pdef* < **shpërdjerr**·

shpër|**dorim** *nm ger* **1** < **shpërdoro'**·*n* **2** abuse; misuse

shpër|**doro'**·*n vt* to abuse; misuse

shpër|**doru**a**r** *adj (i)* misused; abused

shpër|**doru**|**es**

I § *nm* abuser

II § *adj* abusive

shpër|**dor**u**r** *adj (i)* = **shpërdoru**a**r**

shpër|**dredh**· *vt* **1** to untwist [ ], unravel [ ]; straighten [ ] out **2** = **çmbështj**e**ll**·

shpër|**dredh**|**je** *nf ger* **1** < **shpërdredh**·, **shpërdridh**·**et** **2** sinuous body movement

shpër|**dredh**|**ur** *adj (i)* untwisted, unraveled; straightened out

shpër|**dridh**·**et** *vpr* **1** to untwist, unravel; straighten out **2** *(Colloq)* to twist and turn in a sinuous manner

o <> **shpërdridh**·**et**³ˢᵍ **kërthiza** "<>'s navel *untwists*" <>'s belly knots up with disgust

shpër|**dridh**| *stem for 2nd pl pres, pind, imper, vp* < **shpërdredh**·

shpër|**drodh**| *stem for pdef* < **shpërdredh**·

shpër|**dh**|**et** *nm* = **shpardhisht**ë

shpër|**dhi**|**të** *adj (i)* *(Reg)* nimble, agile

shpërdho's· *vt* *(Reg)* to make [ ] dirty, soil

*shpërë**ng** *nm* = shpar**gull**

shpër**faq·** *vt (Colloq)* to reveal, disclose; reveal [ ]'s true nature/character/colors
◦ <>a shpërfaq· *(Reg)* 1 to terrify <> 2 to disgust <>

shpër**faq·** *et vpr (Colloq)* 1 to reveal oneself; come out into the open 2 to appear (in a dream)

shpër**faq**je *nf ger* 1 <shpërfaq·, shpërfaq·et 2 revelation

shpër**fik·** *vt (Intens)* to bring [ ] to total ruin, ruin [someone], impoverish

shpër**fik·** *et vpr (Intens)* to be done for, be finished, be at the end of one's rope; be impoverished

shpër**fill·** *vt* to have disdain for: disdain

shpër**fill**ës *adj* disdainful, disrespectful; scornful

shpër**fill**je *nf ger* 1 <shpërfill· 2 disdain, disparagement, depreciation

shpër**fill**shëm *adj (i)* unworthy of respect, worthless

shpër**form**im *nm ger* = shpërfytyr**im**

shpër**form**o·*het vpr* to metamorphose

shpër**form**o·*n vt* to change [ ]'s form, transform

shpër**fytyr**im *nm ger* 1 <shpërfytyro·*n*, shpërfytyro·*het* 2 change in appearance: transformation; distortion

shpër**fytyr**o·*het vpr* to change in appearance: become transformed/distorted

shpër**fytyr**o·*n vt* to transform [ ] in appearance: distort

shpër**fytyr**uar *adj (i)* changed in appearance: transformed; distorted

shpër**fytyr**ues *adj* changing in appearance: transforming; distorting

shpër**gjënj** *np* <shpargër
◦ ësh·të ende në shpërgënjtë to be still in diapers, be wet behind the ears

shpër**gjëti** *nf* 1 [*Bot*] lichen = liken 2 [*Med*] = urdhje

shpër**gjum·** *vt* 1 to dispel [ ]'s sleepiness, wake [ ] up 2 *(Fig)* to make [ ] aware/alert

shpër**gjum·**et *vpr* 1 to come awake 2 *(Fig)* to become aware/alert

shpër**gjum**ur *adj (i)* awake

shpër**hap·** *vt (Intens)* to scatter [ ] in all directions; diffuse [ ]

shpër**hap·**et *vpr* to scatter in all directions; diffuse

shpër**hap**je *nf* diffusion

shpër**jer·** *vt (Reg)* to reseed [ ] after the first seed has failed to sprout

shpër**jer**je *nf ger (Reg)* <shpërjer·

shpër**ka**s = spërka**s**

shpër**ka**t· = spërka**t·**

shpër**ke**t· = spërke**t·**

shpër**kënd**e·*n vt (Intens)* to misdirect [ ], lead [ ] astray, mislead

shpër**kënd**is *stem for 1st sg pres, pl pres, 2nd & 3rd sg subj, pind* <shpërkëndi**t·**

shpër**kënd**it· *vpr* = përshkëndi**t·**

shpër**kënd**it·*et vpr* = përshkëndit·*et*

shpër**kis** = spërki**s**

shpër**kit** = spërki**t**

shpër**ko**q· *vt* 1 *(Intens)* to scatter [seed] widely, broadcast [seed], disperse 2 *(Reg)* to get change for [money], break [a piece of paper money] 3 *(Fig)* to scatter [ ] to the four winds

shpër**ko**q·*et vpr (Intens)* to become widely dispersed, spread all over

shpër**ko**qje *nf ger (Intens)* <shpërkoq·, shpërkoq·*et*

shpër**la**·*het vpr* = shpëla·*het*

shpër**la**·*n vt* = shpëla·*n*

*shpër**la**fë *nf* [*Bot*] spiny broom (*Calicotome villosa*)

shpër**lak**ës *nm* = shpëlakës

*shpër**la**mje *nf ger (Reg Gheg)* = shpërlarje

shpër**la**rë *part* <shpërla·*n*

shpër**la**rje *nf ger* <shpërla·*n*, shpërla·*het*

shpër**la**sina *np fem* dirty debris carried in a flow of water; sediments carried along in water

*shpër**la**sinë *nf* torrent of water, downpour

shpër**mall**o·*het vpr* = çmall·*et*

shpër**men**d· *vt* to addle

shpër**men**d·*et vpr* to become addled, go crazy

shpër**mirat**im *nm ger* 1 *(Book)* <shpërmirato·*n* 2 disapproval, rejection

shpër**mirat**o·*n vt (Book)* to disapprove, reject

shpër**nda**·*het vpr* 1 to become dispersed: scatter 2 *(Fig)* to be involved in too many things: be spread too thin
◦ shpërnda·*het*pl si zogjtë e korbit to scatter like flies

shpër**nda**·*n vt* 1 to divide [ ] into shares 2 to distribute; disseminate 3 to scatter 4 [*Phys*] to diffract 5 to dissolve [a social/political organization] 6 *(Fig)* to cast away [ ], remove

shpër**nda**ras *OR* shpërnda**r**azi *adv* in scattered fashion, separately

shpër**nda**rë *adj (i)* 1 scattered, unconcentrated 2 disunited 3 spread thin, unconcentrated

shpër**nda**rës
I § *n* 1 distributor 2 mail/newspaper deliverer
II § *adj* distributive

shpër**nda**rëse *nf* (manure) spreader

shpër**nda**rje *nf ger* 1 <shpërnda·*n*, shpërnda·*het* 2 distribution 3 [*Phys*] diffraction

shpër**nda**s *n* = shpërndar**ës**

*shpër**nde**rët *adj (i)* = çndershëm

shpër**nde**rim *nm ger (Old)* = çnderim

shpër**nde**ro·*n vt (Old)* to dishonor = çndero·*n*

shpër**ngo**·*n vt* to fail to acknowledge/appreciate [a favor]; be ungrateful to <> for [ ]

shpër**ngul·** *vt* 1 to resettle [ ] in a new place: displace 2 to move [ ] elsewhere 3 [*Agr*] to transplant = artis·

shpër**ngul·**et *vpr* to resettle; become displaced

shpër**ngul**im *nf ger* 1 <shpërngul·, shpërngul·*et* 2 official change of residence 3 *(Colloq)* academic transcript given when a student changes schools in the middle of the year

shpër**ngul**tore *nf* [*Agr*] tree nursery, seedling nursery

shpër**ngul**ur *adj (i), n (i)* displaced (person)

shpër**ngja**si *nf* = shpërngjashm**im**

shpër**ngjashm**im *nm* [*Ling*] dissimilation

shpër**njeh** *stem for 2nd & 3rd sg pres* <shpërnjoh·

shpër**njih** *stem for 2nd pl pres, pind, imper, vp* <shpërnjoh·

*shpër**njof**ës *adj* = shpërnjohës

shpër'njoh· *vt* to be unwilling to acknowledge [], fail to acknowledge; be ungrateful to <> for [a favor]

shpër'njoh'ës
 I § *adj* ungrateful
 II § *n* ingrate

shpër'njoh'je *nf ger* <**shpërnjoh·**

shpëro'·*n* *vt, vi* *(Old)* = **shpreso'·***n*

shpër'pall· *vt (Intens)* to spread [a rumor] broadly

shpër'pall·et *vpr (Intens)* (of a rumor) to get around to the whole world

shpër'pjesë'tim *nm* lack of proportion: disproportion, imbalance

shpër'pjesë'timo'r *adj (Book)* out of proportion: disproportional, disproportioned, imbalanced

shpër'pjesë'tua'r *adj (i) (Book)* ill-proportioned; disproportioned, unbalanced

shpër'pje'stë *adj (i)* = **shpërpjesë'timo'r**

shpër'push· *vt* = **përpush·**

shpër'push·et *vpr* = **përpush·et**

shpër'qendri'm *nm ger* <**shpërqendro'·***n*, **shpërqendro'·***het*

shpër'qendro'·*het* *vpr* **1** to become fragmented and dispersed; be deployed **2** (of concentration/attention) to shift; become distracted

shpër'qendro'·*n* *vt* **1** to fragmentize and disperse []: scatter; deploy **2** to shift [concentration/attention]

shpër'qendrua'r *adj (i)* **1** fragmented and dispersed: scattered **2** lacking concentration/focus: wool-gathering, abstracted, absent-minded

shpër'rendo'·*n* [*shpër-re-ndo'*] *vt* to throw [] into disorder

shpër'shi'je *nf (Book)* **1** unpleasant taste in the mouth **2** disparagement, scorn; disgust; disrespect

shpër'the·*n*
 I § *vt* **1** to make a breach in [], burst/break through [] **2** to initiate [] suddenly and with force: set off, launch
 II § *vi* **1** to break out **2** to burst out, erupt
 ○ **shpërthe·***n* **një derë/portë të hapur** to put forward something that is already known; reinvent the wheel
 ○ **shpërthe·***n*^{3pl} **retë** the clouds *burst* and let the rain fall in floods

shpër'theko'·*het* *vpr* to become unbuttoned

shpër'theko'·*n* *vt* **1** *(Reg)* to unbutton **2** to detach

shpër'thi'm *nm ger* **1** <**shpërthe·***n* <**shpërthe·** **2** explosion **3** (volcanic) eruption **4** [*Ling*] plosion

shpër'thimo'r *adj [Geol]* of volcanic origin, eruptive

shpër'thiq· *vt* to squash

shpër'thiq·et *vpr* **1** to squirt out **2** to have diarrhea

shpër'thi'thje *nf [Chem]* desorption

shpër'thu'q· *vt (Reg)* = **shkoq·**

shpër'thu'r· *vt (Intens)* = **shthur·**

shpër'thu'r·et *vpr (Intens)* = **shthur·et**
 ○ **shpërthur·**et^{3sg} **vendi** the country *loses* all semblance of order, the whole place *comes* apart

shpër'thy'es *adj* **1** explosive **2** [*Ling*] plosive

shpër'va'r·et *vpr* **1** = **kacava'r·**et **2** to bend over and hang down; bend down (from the weight of fruit/ snow) **3** to hang down

shpër'va'rur *adj (i)* hanging down heavily (from the weight of fruit/snow)

shpër've'sh· *vt* **1** *(Intens)* = **përve'sh·** **2** to turn [one's lips] out (in a gesture of distaste/scorn) **3** to turn [one's pocket] inside out **4** to unsheath

shpër've'shur *adj (i)* **1** *(Intens)* = **përve'shur 2** uncovered

shpër'vetim *nm* [*Biol*] disassimilation

shpër'vi'l·et *vpr* = **shpërvish·et**

shpër'vi'l *stem for 2nd pl pres, pind, imper, vp* <**shpërvje'l·**

shpër'vi'sh·et *vpr* **1** (of the lips) to roll up, curl **2** *(Fig)* to roll up one's sleeves and get down to <>, really have a go at <>

shpër'vje'l· *vt* **1** to roll/tuck up [one's sleeves/pants]; lay [] bare, expose, uncover **2** to make a face by curling [one's lower lip] down and out in a gesture of disapproval

shpër'vjelë *adj (i) (Intens)* (of sleeves/pants) really turned/tucked up (and ready to go at it)
 ○ **shpërvjelë në punë** hard at work, deeply engaged in work

shpër'vje'lje *nf* indentation in the lip of a vessel (for pouring)

*****shpër'vje'lur** *adj (i)* busily engaged, busy

shpër'vo'l *stem for pdef* <**shpërvje'l·**

shpër'zjeshto'·*n* *vi, vt (Reg)* = **shpërrendo'·***n*

shp'ërral'ës *n* person who tells embroidered stories; spreader of false gossip

shp'ërral'im *nm ger* **1** <**shpërralo'·***n* **2** embroidered story; false gossip

shp'ërrallo'·*n* *vi, vt* to tell [an embroidered story]; spread false gossip (about [])

shpët'e'së *nf* [*Relig*] redemption, salvation

shpët'im *nm ger* **1** <**shpëto'·***n* **2** rescue, relief; salvation, deliverance

Shpët'im *nm* Shpëtim (male name)

shpët'im'pru'rës *adj* bringing relief, offering escape/rescue

shpët'im'ta'r
 I § *adj* offering relief, saving from harm: relieving, rescuing
 II § *n* rescuer, deliverer; savior, redeemer
 ○ **shpëtimtar i gjendjes** hero of the hour

shpët'o'·*n*
 I § *vt* **1** to rescue, save **2** *(Colloq)* to bring [] to an end: conclude
 II § *vi* **1** to escape; get away **2** to slip out/away **3** to get relief
 ○ <> **shpëto·***n* to escape from <>; gain relief from <>
 ○ **shpëto·***n* **gjallë me krye** to escape with one's life
 ○ <> **shpëto·***n* **nga dora/duart 1** to get away from <>; escape from <> **2** <> *loses* a good opportunity in {}
 ○ **shpëto·***n* **nga lumi e bie**₁**· në det** to jump out of the frying pan and into the fire
 ○ **shpëto·***n* **për lik** to escape by a hair, barely/narrowly escape
 ○ **shpëto·***n* **për një fije floku** to escape by a hair
 ○ **shpëto·***n* **për majë të gjilpërës** to have a close call/shave, make a narrow escape
 ○ <> **shpëto·***n*^{3sg} **shparca nga duart** "the washcloth *slips* out of <>'s hands" <> *is* very weak/feeble
 ○ <> **shpëto·***n*^{3sg} **shurra** "<>'s piss *leaks* out" **1** *(Crude)* <> *feels* the urge to urinate: <> feels like

taking a leak 2 *(Crude Contempt)* ◇ *is pissing* in
◇'s pants (with fear)
○ **shpëto**·*n³ˢᵍ* **zogu nga dora** "the bird *escapes* from ◇'s hand" ◇ *lets the opportunity slip
away*

shpëtu|ar
I § *adj (i)* saved, rescued
II § *n (i)* rescued/saved person

shpëtu|es *adj* serving to rescue: saving, lifesaving

shpi·*het* *vpr* **1** (of one's limbs) to regain feeling, lose
numbness **2** *(Fig)* to get refreshed

shpi·*n* *vt* to restore feeling in [one's limbs], get rid of
numbness in [one's limbs]; limber up [one's limbs],
stretch [one's limbs]
○ **shpi·***n* **kockat** to pull oneself together (after being
exhausted): rest up

***shpi|** *nf (Colloq)* = **shtëpi**

***shpia'r** = **shtëpiar**

shpie· *vt* **1** to take [] (somewhere); carry, convey,
transport **2** to steer, direct **3** *(Colloq)* to take one's
time with []
○ **ia shpie·** to be getting along
○ **shpie· buzën në gaz** "put one's lips into a smile"
to smile
○ **e shpie· buzën vesh më vesh** "convey the lip
ear to ear" to light up with happiness
○ [] **shpie· dëm** to ruin []; [] *goes* for nothing, []
comes to naught
○ **e shpie· fjalën për** [] to bring up the subject of
[]
○ ◇**a shpie· gojën te veshi** to wear out one's
voice asking in vain for ◇
○ **shpie· keq me** [] to get along badly with []
○ [] **shpie· në litarë** to send [] to the gallows
○ **shpie· në vend** to comply with [], fulfil []
○ **s'◇ shpie·³ˢᵍ puna atje** there *is* nothing there
of of interest to ◇
○ **shpie· ujë në mullirin e** ◇ "carry water to ◇'s
mill" to be beneficial to ◇'s *opponent*

***shpieg|** = **shpjeg**

***shpif** *nm (Reg)* poplar

shpif· *vt, vi* **1** to slander, defame **2** to embroider the
truth, say false things, lie **3** *(Colloq)* to make up [];
create, fabricate
○ ◇ **shpif·** **1** to terrify ◇ **2** to disgust ◇

shpif·*et* *vpr* to appear out of nowhere, arise mysteriously
○ ◇ **shpif·***et* **1** ◇ *gets* terrified **2** ◇ *gets* disgusted
○ ◇ **shpif·***et³ˢᵍ* **mortja** ◇ *is* absolutely terrified

shpifaca|k *n (Scorn)* = **shpifës**

shpifama|n *nm (Scorn)* = **shpifës**

shpifara|k *adj, n (Scorn)* = **shpifës**

shpifarra|q *adj* slanderous

shpife| *nf* **1** scarecrow **2** false story

***shpifër** *adj* = **shpifës**

***shpifërisht** *adv* slanderously

shpif|ës
I § *adj* slanderous
II § *n (Scorn)* slanderer, fabricator, liar

shpifje *nf* slander; fabrication

shpiftar *adj, n* = **shpifës**

shpif|ur *adj (i)* made up, fabricated, false **2** *(Col-
loq)* artificial, fake **3** *(Impol)* scraggly, unkempt
4 *(Impol)* disgusting

shpik· *vt* **1** to invent **2** *(Colloq)* to make [] up, fabricate

sh|pik· *vt* **1** to drink [] to the last drop: drink [] up
2 to drain [] completely, use [] up, exhaust **3** to draw
[] from a well **4** *(Colloq)* to win all of []'s money/
chips (in a game)

shpik·*et* *vpr (Colloq)* to come about, appear

sh|pik·*et* *vpr* **1** to spring a leak: leak **2** *(Colloq)* to
lose/spend all one's money

***shpik|atar**
I § *adj (Old)* inventive
II § *n (Old)* inventor

shpik|ës *n* inventor

shpik|ëzi|m *nm ger* <**shpikëzo·**·*n*

shpik|ëzo· *n* *vt* [*Dairy*] to strip [an udder] (of all its
milk)

shpik|je *nf ger* **1** <**shpik·, shpik·***et* **2** invention

shpik|ur *adj (i)* invented, made up, imagined; imag-
inary

shpi|m *nm ger* <**shpo·**·*n*, **shpo·**·*het*
○ **shpim me gjilpërë** [*Med*] acupuncture

shpim-kërki|m *nm* [*Min*] prospection/exploratory
drilling

shpim-shfrytëzi|m *nm* [*Min*] drilling for ex-
ploitation of a natural resource

shpina|ke *nf* cloth used by women for carrying loads
on the back: back sling

shpin|as *nm* place that gets no sun

shpindel *nm* [*Tech*] spindle

shpinë *nf* **1** back (of a person, animal, building, piece
of furniture/clothing); back of the hand, instep (of a
foot), dorsum (of the tongue); back (top) of a ridge;
back (dull side) of a knife/sword/saw **2** spine (of a
book) **3** [*Mil*] rear; rear guard **4** *(Colloq)* top surface

shpin|ëmarr|ës *adj* [*Mil*] attacking the rear; trained
for rear guard attack

shpin|ëmarr|je *nf* [*Mil*] attack from the rear

shpin|ëz *nf dimin* <**shpinë**

shpin|o· *n* *vt* to turn one's back on []: reject, neglect,
disregard, ignore

shpin|or *adj* dorsal

shpin|ore *nf* **1** chairback **2** [*Sport*] parallel wall bars
used in gymnastic exercises: Swedish bars, wall lad-
der **3** wool protector worn by women carrying water
jugs on their backs

shpin|zë *nf* back support, backrest

shpiq·*et* *vpr* to become dessicated, dry up

***shpir** *imper* <**shpi·**e·

Shpira|g *nm* mountain and ethnographic region west
of Berat

shpirag|aj *nm* native of Shpirag

***shpirce** *nf (Old)* = **shkrepëse**

shpirë *nf* **1** lung **2** asthma

shpir|rje *nf ger* <**shpi·***n*, **shpi·***het*

shpirt *nm (np ~ ra)* **1** spirit **2** that which is most
precious to one: soul; essence, character **3** *(Colloq)*
life **4** *(Colloq)* a person **5** *(Pet)* darling, sweetheart
○ **të ka·³ˢᵍ lezet shpirti** "your soul has delight"
(Colloq) it *gives* you a big kick, it *makes* you feel
wonderful
○ **me (gjithë) shpirt** energetically, with enthusiasm,
wholeheartedly
○ **ësh·të shpirt njeriu** to be a real human being,
have human feelings; be sympathetic
○ **shpirt njerke** vicious, mean (to children)
○ **shpirti praktik** ability to get things done quickly
and well: practical nature

shpirta'r *adj* pure in spirit, incapable of deception: totally honest

shpirt|ba'rdhë *adj* charitable in nature, generous

shpirt|bardhë'si *nf* generosity of character, altruism

shpirt|brengo's|ur *adj* with a heavy spirit, sad

shpirt|buja'r *adj* of a generous nature

shpirt|bu'të *adj* of a compassionate nature: tender-spirited

shpirt|butë'si *nf* inherent compassion, natural empathy

shpirt|çi'lt|ër *adj* having a sincere/frank character = **shpirtdëli'rë**

shpirt|dëli'rë *adj* pure in character

shpirt|dëlirë'si *nf* purity of character

shpirt|do'bët *adj* **1** weak in character, weak-willed **2** mean-spirited

shpirt|dhe'mb|sh|ur *adj* of a sympathetic/empathetic/compassionate nature

shpirt|e *nf (Pet)* darling, dear

shpirt|e'g|ër *adj* bestial in character: inhumane, ruthless, merciless

shpirt|ëri'm *nm ger* <**shpirtëro' •n**, **shpirtëro' •het**

shpirt|ëri'sht *adv* in spirit, spiritually; psychologically; morally

shpirt|ëro' •het *vpr* to become spirited/animated, become inspired

shpirt|ëro' •n *vt* to uplift the spirits of []: exhilarate, animate, inspire; elate

shpirt|ëro'r *adj* psychic, mental; spiritual

shpirt|ëso' •n *vt* to animate

shpirt|ëzi'm *nm ger* **1** *(Book)* <**shpirtëzo' •n 2** inspiration

shpirt|ëzo' •n *vt* **1** *(Book)* to ascribe human thoughts and feelings to [animals, natural phenomena] **2** *(Fig Old)* to lift []'s spirits; inspire

shpirt|ëzu'e|s *nm (Old)* person who inspires others: inspirer

shpirt|fe'rrë *adj* of devilish character: malevolent

shpirt|fëlli'q|ur *adj* of low character that corrupts others

shpirt|fo'shnjë *adj* having a childlike nature: ingenuous, innocent and pure

shpirt|gry'm|ët *adj* of rotten character: damned

shpirt|gry'm|ur *adj* = **shpirtgry'mët**

shpirt|gu'r *adj* having a heart of stone: merciless, cruel

shpirt|gje'rë *adj* having a tolerant disposition: generous, patient

shpirt|gjerë'si *nf* kind-heartedness, broad-mindedness, generosity

shpirt|helm|u'ar [*shpirt-hel-mu'ar*] *adj* deeply saddened, greatly troubled

shpirt|hu'mb|ur [*shpirt-hu-mbur*] *adj, n (Curse)* damned (person)

shpirt|katra'n *adj (Pej)* of a malicious nature: black-hearted, vicious

shpirt|ka'zmë *adj* "soul of a pickaxe" *(Pej)* with a heart of flint: merciless, vicious, cruel

shpirt|ke'q *adj, n* malevolent/unscrupulous (person)

shpirt|keq|ë'si *nf* = **shpirtligë'si**

shpirt|këlli'rë *adj* = **shpirtfëlli'qur**

shpirt|këpu't|ur *adj* broken in spirit: dispirited, demoralized

shpirt|kri'mb|ur *adj (Pej)* rotten to the core

shpirt|kull|u'ar *adj* with a pure heart

shpirt|le'pur *adj* timorous in character: chicken-hearted, timid

shpirt|li'g *adj* = **shpirtke'q**

shpirt|lig|ë'si *nf* malevolence

shpirt|ma'dh *adj* of magnanimous nature; generous

shpirt|madh|ë'si *nf* magnanimousness; generosity

shpirt|mëdha *fem pl* <**shpirtma'dh**

shpirt|mëdhe'nj *masc pl* <**shpirtma'dh**

shpirt|mi'rë *adj* goodhearted: kind, benevolent

shpirt|mirë'si *nf* goodheartedness: kindness, benevolence

shpirt|mizo'r *adj* of a cruel nature: heartless, vicious

shpirt|nde'zur *adj* of blazing spirit, with spirit aflame

shpirt|ndri't|ur *adj, n* **1** (person) of pure and noble spirit **2** [*Relig*] (said of someone dead or wounded) blessed, God bless him!

shpirt|ngu'shtë *adj* mean-spirited: niggardly; stingy

shpirt|ngushtë'si *nf* meanness, miserliness, stinginess

shpirt|o
I § *nf* **1** *(Reg)* = **shkre'pse 2** *(Colloq)* alcohol, spirits
II § *adj* very clever and nimble-minded

shpirt|pa'k|të *adj (Pej)* of weak character: namby-pamby, cowardly; selfish

shpirt|pango'p|ur *adj* of insatiable character: avaricious, greedy

shpirt|pa'stër *adj* sincere, open

shpirt|plago's|ur *adj* wounded in spirit: much saddened, heavyhearted

shpirt|pla'sur *adj* heartbroken, badly disappointed

shpirt|qe'n *adj* "dog-hearted" *(Pej)* cruel, heartless, merciless

shpirt|ro'b *adj, n (Scorn)* (person) of servile nature

shpirt|sklla'v *adj (Scorn)* = **shpirtro'b**

shpirt|shi't|ur *adj, n (Scorn)* of treacherous character: base

shpirt|trazu|a'r *adj* disturbed in spirit: perturbed

shpirt|tha'rë *adj* = **shpirttha'të**

shpirt|tha'të *adj* lacking human feelings, inhumane, cold-blooded

shpirt|u'jk *adj* = **shpirtqe'n**

shpirt|u'lët *adj* of base character: ignoble, low

shpirt|ve'gjël *adj pl* = **shpirtvo'gël**

shpirt|vo'gël *adj (Pej)* small-minded: petty, mean; niggardly, miserly, selfish

shpirt|vogël|si *nf* small-mindedness: pettiness, meanness; niggardliness, miserliness, selfishness

shpirt|vra'rë *adj* wounded in spirit: saddened, downhearted

shpirt|zbra'z|ur *adj* feeling an inner void: spiritually empty, emotionally drained

shpirt|zi *adj, n (fem sg ~ ëz, masc pl ~ inj, fem pl ~ eza)* (person) with a spiteful/malicious/vicious temperament, cruel (person)

shpirra'q
I § *adj* **1** asthmatic **2** speaking with a nasal voice **3** sickly
II § *n* [*Veter*] person/animal with an asthmatic condition: broken-winded (of horses)

shpirrë *nf (Colloq)* **1** [*Med*] asthma **2** [*Veter*] respiratory catarrh in livestock and poultry: heaves (in horses)

shpirro·s·*et vpr* to get an asthmatic attack

***shpis**|**ak** *adj* domestic = **shtëpiak**

shpit|**ë** *adj (i)* quick, clever

shpjeg|**ím** *nm ger* **1** < **shpjego** ·*n*, **shpjego** ·*het* **2** explanation

shpjego·*het vpr* to come to an understanding

shpjego·*n vt* to explain

shpjeg|**ue**|**s**

I § *adj* explanatory

II § *n* one that explains: explainer, guide, docent (in a museum)

shpjeg|**ue**|**se** *nf (Book)* **1** explanatory guide: legend (with a map/chart) **2** inscription

shpjek|**ur** *part* < **shpiq**·

shpjer| *stem for imper, 3rd sg subj* < **shpí**·e·
  ∘ **Shpjer gojën te buka e jo bukën te goja.** "Bring your mouth to the bread and not the bread to your mouth." *(Prov)* Nothing comes without a little effort. You've got to sweat a little to get what you want.

shplaka|**n** *adj, n* wretched (person)

***shpla**|**kë** *nf* = **shuplak**·

***shplak**|**ím** *nm ger* < **shplako**·*n*

***shplak**|**o**·*n vt* = **shuplak**·

***shpla**|**sje** *nf* outburst

shpleks· *vt* to untwist; unravel; untangle

shple|**ks**·*et vpr* **1** to become unraveled/untwisted/untangled **2** to unbraid and let down one's hair **3** to become separated from one's group

shple|**ksje** *nf ger* < **shpleks**·, **shpleks**·*et*

shple|**ks**|**ur** *adj (i)* unraveled, untwisted, untangled

***shplodh** = **çlodh**

shpluhuro·*n vt* **1** to remove the dust from [ ]: dust, dust[ ] off **2** to spread [fine particles] through the air: dust

shpluhuro|**s**· *vt* = **shpluhuro**·*n*

***shplla**·*het vpr* to vent one's anger

***shpnes**|**ë** *nf (Reg Gheg)* = **shpres**|**ë**

***shpnetkë** *nf [Anat]* = **shpretkë**

shpo|**het**

I § *vpr* **1** to develop a hole; spring a leak; (of a wound) to open and begin to run **2** *(Colloq)* to undergo acupuncture

II § *vp reflex* to prick/stick oneself

  ∘ <> **shpo**·*het* **kazani** "<>'s boiler *springs* a leak" things turn out worse than expected by <>

  ∘ **shpo**·*het* **në hundë** to bet one's life on it

shpo·*n*

I § *vt* **1** to make a hole in [ ] with a sharp point: puncture, pierce; bore, drill; prick, sting; stab **2** *(Fig Colloq)* to spur/goad/prod [ ]; provoke; instigate **3** *(Fig Colloq)* to prod [ ] to remember **4** *(Fig)* to tell on [ ]: tattle **5** *(Fig Colloq)* to investigate [ ] in detail

II § *vi* **1** to have a sharp point **2** to be the source of sharp pain to <>: hurt <> terribly, give <> a sharp pain **3** *(Fig)* to tattle

  ∘ **t'i shposh/shpoje buzët** "you may pierce your lips" you can/could stand there and talk all day and night (it won't/wouldn't change somebody's mind)

  ∘ <> **shpo**·*n*[superscript]^{3sg} **hundën** "it *penetrates* <>'s nose" (the smell *is* so strong/bad/piercing that) it *hurts* <>'s nose

  ∘ [ ] **shpo**·*n* **me bodec** to spur [ ] to action

  ∘ **shpo**·*n*^{3pl} **qiejt** "the skies are *cut open*//*pierced*" there *is* a cloudburst, it *begins* to rain in buckets, it *is* raining cats and dogs

  ∘ <> **shpo**·*n*^{3sg} **veshët/veshin** "pierce <>'s ears/ear" (the sound *is* so loud/piercing that) it *hurts* <>'s ears

  ∘ <> **shpo**·*n*^{3sg} **zemrën** "pierce <>'s heart" to touch <> deeply; wound <> to the heart

shpo|**jë** *nf* animal burrow: foxhole

sh|**polariz**|**ím** *nm ger* **1** *[Phys]* < **shpolarizo**·*n*, **sh-polarizo**·*het* **2** depolarization

sh|**polariz**|**o**·*het vpr* *[Phys]* to lose polarization

sh|**polariz**|**o**·*n vt* *[Phys]* to depolarize

shpo|**një** *nf* provocation, irritant

shpo|**një**|**s**

I § *adj* = **shpues**

II § *nm* = **shpuese**

sh|**popull**|**ím** *nm ger* **1** < **shpopullo**·*n*, **shpopullo**·*het* **2** depopulation

sh|**popull**|**o**·*het vpr* to become depopulated

sh|**popull**|**o**·*n vt* to depopulate

sh|**popull**|**uar** *adj (i)* depopulated

sh|**popull**|**zím** *nm ger* = **shpopullím**

sh|**popull**|**zo**·*het vpr* = **shpopullo**·*het*

sh|**popull**|**zo**·*n vt* = **shpopullo**·*n*

sh|**popull**|**zuar** *adj (i)* = **shpopulluar**

shpoq| *stem for pdef* < **shpiq**·*et*

shpor *nm* **1** (of an animal) breastbone *(Old)* **2** sternum

shpor *nm* **1** spur = **mamuz 2** *[Bot]* spur **3** = **lehe 4** measure of width of a plot of land that can be sown in one pass by hand broadcasting **5** small ditch dividing strips of land; irrigation furrow in a field

***shpo**|**re** *nf* brook, creek

shporet *nm* kitchen stove, cooking range

shpori|**z** *nm [Bot]* vervain *(Verbena)*

shporo·*het vpr* = **shpo**·*het*

shporo·*n vt* **1** to pierce; bore **2** to spur, goad

shport|**ar** *n* basket-maker

shport|**arí** *nf* basket-making

shport|**ë** *nf* **1** basket **2** woven muzzle for oxen

  ∘ **shportë karavidhesh** "basket of lobsters" squabbling bunch of people

  ∘ **shportë pa fund** *(Colloq)* person who can't keep a secret: blabbermouth

shport|**ëz** *nf dimin* < **shportë**

shporr· *vt* **1** to force [ ] out/away: force [ ] to leave, remove [ ] forcibly, get rid of [ ], chase [ ] out/away ***2** to cast [ ] off, discard

  ∘ **Shporrmu sysh!** Get out of my sight!

shporr·*et vpr* to get away/out, clear out, be off

shpo|**rrje** *nf ger* < **shporr**·, **shporr**·*et*

shpot|**ar**

I § *adj* mocking, derisive

II § *n* person who mocks others: mocker, scoffer

shpot|**ë** *nf* = **shpotí**

shpot|**í** *nf* mockery, derision

shpot|**ís** *stem for 1st sg pres, pl pres, 2nd & 3rd sg subj, pind* < **shpotít**·

shpotít· *vt* to treat [ ] with sarcasm, make fun of [ ], mock

shpotít·*et vpr* to be sarcastic/derisive

  ∘ **shpotit**·*et* **me** [ ] to treat [ ] with sarcasm, make fun of [ ], mock [ ]

shpotitës
I § *adj* mocking, scornful, sarcastic
II § *n* mocker

shpotiʻtje *nf =* shpoti

*shpovaʻrʌes *n* troublemaker

*shpoz = shpuz

shpraʻjʌe *nf* disinfection

shpraʻjʌes *nm* disinfectant

*shpraʻll = shprrall

*shpralliʻm *nm* talebearing, gossip

*shpraʻps·et *vpr* = spraʻps·et

*shpraʻpsi *OR* shpraʻpsje *nf* retreat

*shpraz = zbraz

shprehʻ· *vt* to express

shpreʻh·et *vpr* to express oneself; find expression; be expressed

shpreʻh·et *vpr* to rest up, relax

shpreʻhʌes
I § *adj* expressive
II § *n* spokesman, spokesperson, representative

shprehʌesi *nf (Book)* expressiveness

shprehiʻ *nf* 1 ability gained by practice: skill 2 habit

shprehiʻmʌisht *adv* expressively

shpreʻhʌje *nf ger* 1 *<*shpreʻh·, shpreʻh·et 2 expression

shpreʻhʌur *nn (të)* expressing, expression

Shpreʻsʌa *nf* Shpresa (female name)

shpreʻsʌe *nf* hope

shpresʌedhëʻnʌes *adj* hope-giving, hopeful

shpresʌehuʻmbur *adj* having lost all hope: without hope, dejected

shpresʌeploʻtë *adj* full of hope: hopeful, optimistic; very promising

shpresʌepreʻrë *adj* devoid of hope: in despair

shpresʌeshuʻar *adj* without a flicker of hope: in great despair, greatly disappointed

shpresʌetaʻr
I § *adj* 1 *(Book)* hopeful, aspiring 2 optimistic
II § *n* 1 *(religious)* aspirant 2 optimist

shpresoʻ·n *vt, vi* to hope; have high hopes
∘ shpresoʻ·n **në** [] to hope for []

shpreʻtkʌe *nf* 1 *[Anat]* spleen 2 *(Colloq)* thin layer of microorganisms that form at the bottom of a vinegar container 3 = shpreʻtkʌez

shpreʻtkʌez *nf [Veter]* disease in livestock characterized by a swelling of the spleen

shpriftëʻroʻ·n *vt [Relig]* to deprive [] of priestly functions/offices: unfrock, defrock

*shpriʻhʌe *nf =* shproʻhʌe

shpriʻsh·
I § *vt* 1 to disentangle, untangle, loosen 2 to muss up [], ruffle, crumple 3 to break up the surface of [soil]; break [new ground] 4 *(Reg)* to feed [livestock] in the morning
II § *vi (Reg)* to have a bite to eat (on an empty stomach): snack

shpriʻsh·et *vpr* 1 to spread all over, become dispersed; come apart completely, break up into pieces 2 to tear one's hair and clothes in grief 3 to toil to the point of exhaustion, work to the breaking point
∘ shpriʻsh·et **si liri/leshi** to be completely exhausted (by hard work)

shpriʻshʌaleʻsh *nm* comb for disentangling wool/flax

shpriʻshʌe *nf* light breakfast (eaten early in the morning just to put something into the stomach): breakfast snack

shpriʻshʌet *adj (i) (Reg)* bareheaded

shpriʻshʌje *nf ger <*shprish·

shpriʻshʌur *adj (i)* 1 *[Text]* (of wool) disentangled and ready for spinning: teased and dressed 2 unkempt and mussy 3 widely dispersed 4 contorted, crooked, awry

*shproʻbatinʌo·het *vpr* to break one's pledge of blood fellowship

shproʻhʌe *nf* 1 *[Bot]* belladonna, deadly nightshade (*Atropo belladonna*) = helmariʻnʌe 2 dragon

shproletariʻzʌim *nm ger <*shproletarizoʻ·n, shproletarizoʻ·het

shproletarizoʻ·het *vpr* to diminish in proletarian content

shproletarizoʻ·n *vt* to decrease the proletarian component of [ ], diminish [ ] in percentage of workers

shproletariʻzʌuar *adj (i)* diminished in terms of percentage of workers; having lost its proletarian base

shpronʌesiʻm *nm ger* 1 *<*shpronʌesoʻ·n 2 expropriation; dispossession

shpronʌesoʻ·n *vt* to expropriate; dispossess

shpronʌesuʻar *adj (i)* 1 expropriated 2 dispossessed

shpronʌesuʻes *nm* expropriator

*shproʻv = sprov

*shproviʻmʌtar
I § *n* experimenter, tester
II § *adj* experimental

*shprovoʻ·n *vt* to experience, test, try

*shprovuʻar *adj (i)* tested, tried

shpruʻsh· *vt* 1 to poke [a fire], stir up [live coals/ embers] 2 (of chickens) to scratch [the ground] for bits of rock

shpruʻshʌis = shpuzʻis

shpruʻshʌit = shpuzʻit

shpraʻllʌes *n* scandalmonger, gossip

*shpraʻllʌis *stem for 1st sg pres, pl pres, 2nd & 3rd sg subj, pind <*shprralliʻt·

*shpraʻllʌit· *vt =* pʌerralliʻs·

*shpraʻllʌo·n *vt* 1 to make [] into a story 2 to tell tales, spread scandal, gossip

*shpraʻllʌues
I § *adj* talebearing
II § *n* talebearer

shpuʻar
I § *part <*shpoʻ·n
II § *adv* amiss, badly, wrong, unsuccessfully
III § *adj (i)* pierced with holes: perforated; leaky
IV § *nf (e)* 1 puncture; small wound, prick; leaky hole, leak 2 piercing feeling: twinge, prick
∘ <> **ësh·të** ³ˢᵍ **shpuar kuleta/xhepi** "<>'s wallet/pocket has sprung a leak." *(Iron)* <> has no money; <> has spent <>'s money wastefully; <> has a hole in <>'s pocket

shpuʻarje *nf =* shpiʻm

*shpuʻe *adv (Reg Gheg)* amiss, badly, wrong, unsuccessfully

shpuʻes
I § *adj* 1 serving to pierce/drill/bore holes; of or pertaining to boring 2 piercing, penetrating 3 nosy, inquisitive, prying
II § *n [Min]* driller

III § *nm* [*Tech*] = **shpuese**

○ **shpuesi i frutave** [*Entom*] small insect (dark blue with sparse short hairs on the body) that is destructive to fruit

shpuese *nf* [*Tech*] gimlet, drill, auger

shpulpo ·*n vt* to strip meat from bones

shpulpuar *adj* (i) (of bones) stripped of meat

shpullë *nf* **1** flat/palm of the hand **2** slap of the hand: hand slap, slap

shpundër *nf* hand with six fingers

shpundrak *adj, n* six-fingered (person)

shpuplim *nm* <**shpuplo** ·n, **shpuplo** ·het

shpuplo ·het *vpr* to lose feathers: molt

shpuplo ·*n vt* **1** to pluck (the feathers of) [fowl] **2** (*Fig*) to rob [] blind, clean [] out, leave [] bare

shpupluar *adj* (i) having lost its feathers: plucked, molted

shpupuris *stem for 1st sg pres, pl pres, 2nd & 3rd sg subj, pind* <**shpupurit** ·

shpupurish · *vt* **1** to poke [a fire] **2** (of fowl) to scratch and peck at [] **3** to tousle, tussle; ruffle

shpupurish ·*et vpr* **1** to ruffle one's hair/feathers **2** = **përpush** ·*et* **3** (*Fig*) to move around busily/restlessly

shpupurishje *nf ger* **1** <**shpupurish** ·, **shpupurish** ·*et* **2** ruffling sound

shpupurishur *adj* (i) dishevelled, ruffled, tousled

shpupurit · *vt* = **shpupurish** ·

shpur *stem for pdef* <**shpi** e·

shpurdh ·

I § *vt* (*Reg*) to scratch at [dirt]

II § *vi* to wriggle; writhe

shpurdh ·*et vpr* (*Reg*) to wriggle around impatiently

shpurë *nf* entourage

shpurris *stem for 1st sg pres, pl pres, 2nd & 3rd sg subj, pind* <**shpurrit** ·

shpurrit · *vt* **1** to poke [a fire] **2** (of fowl) to scratch and peck at [] **3** (*Fig*) to dig out what [] thinks, try to read []'s mind, divine []'s intentions

shputë *nf* **1** sole (of the foot), foot; (bottom of the) paw **2** palm of the hand **3** hand slap, smack **4** foot sock worn indoors over regular stockings **5** part of a stocking below the ankle

shputëmadh *adj* big-footed

shputo ·*n vt* to strike with the paw

shputor *adj* [*Zool*] plantigrade

shpuzak *adj* **1** very quick and clever, skittering quickly **2** (*Fig Pej*) sneaky, deceptive

shpuzanik *nm* round wafer baked in hot ashes

shpuzë

I § *nf* tiny ember still burning among the hot ashes; cigarette ashsponge

II § *adj* *1** flaming red **2** having a sparkling personality/mind

shpuzis *stem for 1st sg pres, pl pres, 2nd & 3rd sg subj, pind* <**shpuzit** ·

shpuzit · *vt* to poke [a fire], stir [hot ashes]

shpuzit ·*et vpr* to get burned by hot ashes

shpuzore *nf* **1** small scoop used to shovel cinders and ashes onto a Dutch oven **2** ashtray

shpyllëzim *nm ger* **1** <**shpyllëzo** ·n **2** deforestation

shpyllëzo ·*n vt* to clear [] of trees; deforest

shpyllëzuar *adj* (i) cleared of trees (and ready to be used for agriculture)

shpyrt *nm* = **shpirt**

shqa *stem for pdef, opt, adm, part, imper* <**shqet** ·

shqar = **sqar**

shqarth *nm* [*Zool*] stone marten, beech marten (*Martes foina*)

shqarr *nm* [*Zool*] = **shqarth**

shqas *stem for 1st sg pres, 1st & 3rd pl pres, 2nd & 3rd sg subj* <**shqet** ·

shqaz *adj, n* (sheep) with a dark nose and feet

shqe *stem for pdef, opt* <**shqye** ·n

shqekë *nf* = **shtjekëz**

shqekëz *nf* = **shtjekëz**

shqelm *nm* kick = **shkelm**

shqelmo ·*n vt* to kick = **shkelmo** ·

shqelmonjës *adj* kicking, trampling

shqem *nm* raised door sill, threshold

shqembe *np* <**shkamb**

shqeme *nf* [*Bot*] Sicilian sumac (*Rhus coraria*)

shqemëz *nf* [*Bot*] = **shqeme**

shqemore *np fem* [*Bot*] sumac family Anacardiaceae

shqende *np* underwear

shqendërsim *nm ger* = **decentralizim**

shqendërso ·*n vt* = **decentralizo** ·n

shqeni *nf* (*Old*) = **shqeri**

shqenisht *adv* (*Old*) = **shqerisht**

shqep · *vt* **1** to unsew; undo/rip a seam of [a piece of clothing] **2** to rip [] out/apart/off **3** (*Colloq Intens*) to shred [] to pieces with the teeth; eat [] up **4** (*Fig Crude*) to beat [] badly: wallop **5** (*Fig Crude*) to stuff, gorge, cram

shqep ·*et vpr* **1** to become unstitched; come apart at the seams; come apart, fall apart **2** (*Fig*) to become unattached from <> **3** (*Crude*) to gorge oneself; get stuffed, fill up; wallow **4** (*Reg*) to go off in different directions: become widely dispersed

shqepadru (*r*) *nm* (*np* ~ *nj*) [*Ornit*] woodpecker = **qukapik**

shqepët *adj* (i) **1** lame, crippled **2** = **shqepur**

shqepëz *nf* [*Veter*] disease that lames sheep/goats (*pododermatitis*)

shqepje *nf ger* **1** <**shqep** ·, **shqep** ·*et* **2** rip (in clothing), tear

shqepo ·n

I § *vi* **1** to limp, hobble **2** (*Fig*) to slip up, make a mistake **3** (*Fig*) to stammer, stutter **4** (*Fig Colloq*) to break one's word

II § *vt* to lame

shqepsë = **shqepëz**

shqeptas OR **shqeptazi** *adv* apart, separately

shqeptore *nf* [*Ornit*] woodcock

shqeptyrëz *nf* [*Veter*] = **shqepëz**

shqepul *adj* = **shqepët**

shqepur *adj* (i) apart/open at the seams

shqerak *adj* **1** (of chickens) domestic, local, ordinary, common **2** (of a type of plum) small, green-tinged-with-red, and slightly sour

shqerëz *nf* rip, tear; scratch

shqeri *nf* (*Old Collec*) Slavic people

shqerisht *adv* (*Old*) in a Slavic language

shqerishte *nf* (*Old*) Slavic language

shqerkë *nf dimin* lambkin

shqe·rr·
  I § *vt* **1** to rip, tear **2** to scratch
  II § *vi* to feel a piercing pain

shqerra·k *adj* = shqera·k

shqerra·sh *nm* [*Bot*] field daisy; camomile

shqe·rre *nf* embroidered trimming on traditional Albanian trousers

shqe·rrë
  I § *nf* lamb = shtje·rrë
  II § *part* <shqerr·
  III § *adj* (i) hoarse·

shqe·rrëz *nf dimin* lambkin

shqe·t *vt* = shke·t

shqetë *adj* (i) disquieted, perturbed, disturbed

shqetësí *nf* unrest

shqetësím *nm ger* **1** <shqetëso·n, shqetëso·het
  2 <shqetëso·n, shqetëso·het **3** disquiet, anxiety, uneasiness

shqetëso·het *vpr* to feel disquieted/anxious/uneasy/uncomfortable, worry

shqetëso·n *vt* to disquiet; disturb, perturb, disrupt

shqetësuar *adj* (i) **1** uneasy, ill at ease; restless **2** worried, disturbed; agitated

shqetësue·s *adj* disquieting; disturbing

shqetí *nf* disquiet, unrest

shqe·to
  I § *adj* (*Colloq*) without additional ingredients: plain, straight, neat, pure
  II § *adv* frankly, plainly
  III § *nf* [*Food*] meat stew without vegetables

shqe·v *stem for 1st & 2nd sg pdef* <shqye·n

shqe·zë *nf* harrow

shqezo··n *vt* to level out [] with a harrow: harrow

shqicë *nf* [*Ornit*] swan (*Cygnus*)

shqifte·r *nm* [*Ornit*] = sqifte·r

shqilcë *nf* (*Reg*) [*Dairy*] rennet

shqilë *nf* (*Reg*) **1** [*Dairy*] rennet; cheese starter; type of cheese **2** belly, stomach

shqilo·k *nm* wooden bowl in which rennet is kept

shqi·m *nm ger* **1** <shqua·n, shqu·het **2** (*Old*) distinction (*Old*) *3 ruin, destruction

shqim·
  I § *vt* **1** to extinguish **2** (*Fig*) to destroy completely: wipe [] out totally; annihilate, eradicate
  II § *adv* completely, totally
  ∘ <>a shqim·derën to bring <>'s family line to an end

shqim·et *vpr* to die out, perish; disappear
  ∘ <> shqim·et[3sg] hisja there remain no males left to carry on <>'s family

shqi·mët *adj* (i), *n* (i) pitiful/forlorn/miserable (person)

shqi·mëz *nf* small fragment; piece of paper

shqi·mth *nm* **1** (*Reg*) dandruff = zbokth *2 = shqem

shqi·nd *nm* [*Bot*] = xí·në

shqi·në·s *nm* [*Bot*] pepper tree (*Schinus molle*)

shqi·p *adv* **1** in Albanian **2** comprehensibly, clearly, plainly; forthrightly

shqi·pe *nf, adj* Albanian (language)

shqi·pe
  I § *nf* eagle = shqiponjë
  II § *adj* deft and quick, adept, very capable
  ∘ shqipe fushe [*Ornit*] hen-harrier *Circus cyaneus L.*

∘ shqipe e zezë [*Ornit*] osprey *Pandion haliaetus L.*

Shqi·pe *nf* Shqipe (female name)

shqipëllo··n *vt* to explain [] clearly

Shqipërí *nf* Albania

shqipërím *nm ger* <shqipëro·n

shqipërísht *adv* = shqiptarísht

shqipëro··n *vt* to translate [] into Albanian, render [] in Albanian; convert [a foreign word/name] into an Albanian form

shqipëruar *adj* (i) translated into an Albanian version; (of a foreign word/name) converted into Albanian form

shqipërue·s *nm* translator into Albanian

shqipfolë·s *adj, n* (*Book*) Albanian-speaking (person)

shqipo *nf with masc agreement* (*Colloq*) prototypical Albanian man who embodies the highest virtues of the Albanian ethnic character

shqipo··n *vt* to say/pronounce [] clearly

shqiponjë *nf* **1** eagle **2** golden eagle (*Aquila chrysaetos*) **3** (*Fig*) proud and brave person; skillful person **4** [*Bot*] monstera (with leaves like those of an eagle) = luleshqiponjë
  ∘ shqiponja e detit **1** [*Ornit*] sea eagle, white-tailed eagle (*Haliaetus albicilla L.*) **2** [*Ichth*] eagle ray (*Myliobatis aquila*) = flutura·skë
  ∘ shqiponja dykrenore double-headed eagle (used as a symbol of Albania)
  ∘ shqiponja gjarpërngrënëse [*Ornit*] snake eagle, short-toed eagle *Circaetus gallicus*
  ∘ shqiponja gjype [*Ornit*] griffon vulture *Gyps fulvus*
  ∘ shqiponja e maleve [*Ornit*] golden eagle (*Aquila chrysaetos L.*) = lara·sh
  ∘ shqiponja me kurriz [*Ornit*] = shqiponjë gjype
  ∘ Shqiponja nuk ha miza. "The eagle does not eat flies." (*Prov*) An important person does not deal with trifles.
  ∘ shqiponja e zezë [*Ornit*] black vulture (*Aegypius monachus*)

shqiponjkë *nf dimin* (*Reg*) eaglet

shqiptar *adj, n* Albanian

shqiptarçe *adv* (*Colloq*) in Albanian fashion, in a traditional Albanian way = shqiptarísht

shqiptarësí *nf* **1** (*Book*) Albanian character/origin/spirit **2** (*Old*) = shqiptarí

shqiptarí *nf* **1** the Albanian people as a collective whole **2** sense of being Albanian, Albanian consciousness, Albanian patriotism: Albanicism

shqiptarísht *adv* in an Albanian way, Albanian-style

shqiptarízëm *nm* sense of being Albanian, Albanian consciousness, Albanian patriotism: Albanicism

shqiptarizím *nm ger* <shqiptarizo·n, shqiptarizo·het

shqiptarizo·het *vpr* to take on an Albanian character/form: become Albanicized

shqiptarizo··n *vt* to instill Albanian character in [], give [] an Albanian form: Albanicize

shqiptarkë *nf* (*Reg Pet*) Albanian girl/woman

shqiptarofíl *nm* foreigner who admires Albania or things Albanian, friend of Albania: Albanophile

shqipti'm *nm ger* **1** <shqipto'·*n*, shqipto'·*het* **2** pronunciation, articulation

shqiptimo'r *adj* [*Ling*] pertaining to pronunciation: articulatory

shqipto'·*het vpr* to express one's opinion

shqipto'·*n vt* to pronounce, articulate

shqiptue'shëm *adj* (*i*) pronounceable, articulable

*****shqipzo'**·*n vt* = shqipёro'·*n*

shqir'·*et vpr* to screech

*****shqir'** *stem for 2nd pl pres, pind, imper, vp* <shqjerr·

shqi'rёz *nf* [*Ornit*] gray partridge (*Perdix perdix*)

shqirr' *stem for 2nd pl pres, pind, imper, vp* <shqjerr·

*****shqi'rre** *nf* [*Ornit*] woodcock (*Scolopax rusticola*)

shqirrё *nf* [*Bot*] **1** = plish **2** woodland bulrush (*Scirpus sylvaticus*) *****3** = shte'rpё

shqi's
I § *stem for 1st sg pres, pl pres, 2nd & 3rd sg subj, pind* <shqit·
II § *stem for 2nd pl pres, pind* *****<shqet·

shqi'sё *nf* **1** sensory faculty: sense; sense organ **2** (*Old*) mental ability, judgmental sense

shqiso'r *adj* sensory

shqi't· *vt* **1** to detach, unstick; separate from [ ], leave [ ] **2** (*Reg*) to tear, tear [ ] up **3** (*Fig*) to rip [ ] off from <> **4** (*Reg*) to disentangle [wool] **5** (*Fig*) to resolve [a problematic matter], puzzle out [ ]

shqi't·*et vpr* **1** to become detached, come off; become separated, go away **2** (*Fig Colloq*) to get very tired, fall apart (from fatigue)

shqi't *stem for pind, 2nd pl pres, imper, vp* <shqet·

shqi'tё *nf* = rrёshqi'tё

shqi't'ёs
I § *nm* **1** wide-toothed comb used for disentangling women's hair **2** person who breaks up a fight
II § *adj* = rrёshqi'tёs

shqi'tёz *nf* **1** merganser (*Mergys merganser*) **2** (*Reg Arb*) [*Ornit*] mute swan = mje'llmё

shqi'tje *nf ger* <shqi't·, shqit·*et*

shqi'tur *adj* (*i*) **1** torn, torn off/up **2** very tired, worn-out (from fatigue)

shqo'fto *nf with masc agreement* (*Reg*) the devil, Satan

shqo'lle *np* <shqu'all

shqo'pё *nf* [*Bot*] **1** heath, heather (*Erica*) **2** (*Colloq*) broom made of heather **3** briar
○ **shqo'pё e bu'tё** tree heath (*Erica arborea*)
○ **shqo'pё e egёr** [*Bot*] type of heath (*Erica manipliflora Salisb*. (*Erica verticillata*))

shqopi'shtё *nf* thicket of heath, heath

shqopo're *np fem* [*Bot*] heath family *Ericaceae*

shqo'ptё *adj* (*i*) made of heather wood

*****shqor'** *stem for pdef* <shqerr·

shqo'tё *nf* **1** rain falling with snow: sleet **2** wet snow: slush **3** rainstorm; cloudburst **4** (*Fig*) tribulation, calamity

shqo'v *stem for 1st & 2nd sg pdef* <shqu'a·*n*

shqu·*het vpr* **1** to become distinguishable: loom, appear **2** to gain distinction, stand out

shqu'a·*n*
I § *vt* **1** to distinguish [ ] with the eye, make [ ] out: discern **2** to bring [ ] into prominence; make [ ] distinctive, distinguish **3** [*Ling*] to put [a noun] into a definite case form

II § *vi* **1** to gain distinction, stand out **2** to become distinguishable: loom, appear

*****shqu'a'jtje** *nf* **1** distinction **2** (*Old*) [*Ling*] definiteness

shqu'all *nm* thong made of the bark of the linden tree

shqu'a'r *adj* (*i*) **1** distinguished; distinctive **2** [*Ling*] (of a nominal case form) definite

shqu'a'rje *nf ger* <shqua·*n*, shqu·*het*

shqua'rsi' *nf* **1** [*Ling*] definiteness **2** (*Old Offic*) Excellency (as an honorific term of address) = shkёlqesi'

shqu'ell *nm* = shqu'all

shqu'e's *adj* **1** distinctive, distinguishing **2** [*Ling*] marking definiteness: definite

shqy'·*het vpr* **1** to get torn, tear; get torn off/up; become disheveled **2** (*Fig*) to quarrel bitterly, have a serious fight **3** (*Fig*) to become exhausted by exertion
○ **shqy·*het*^{3sg} daullja** "the drum *gets* torn (from being beaten so loudly and long)" **1** they *are beating* the drum loudly (in order to make an important public announcement) **2** it is a bang-up party
○ **shqy·*het* gazit** to split one's sides laughing
○ <> **shqy·*het*^{3sg} gurmazi** "<>'s throat gets torn" <> *strains* <>'s throat, <> *gets* hoarse (from yelling)
○ **shqy·*het* sё qeshuri** to split one's sides laughing
○ <> **shqy·*het*^{3sg} zemra** "<>'s heart gets torn" <> *gets* heartbroken
○ <> **shqy·*het*^{3sg} zёri** <> *strains* <>'s voice, <> *makes* <>self hoarse

shqye'·*n vt* **1** to tear [ ] off/up/apart; rip, shred, tear; dismember **2** to open [ ] wide **3** (*Colloq*) to split [ ]'s sides (with laughter), break [ ] up (with joy)
○ **shqye·*n* gurmazin** "tear one's throat" to get hoarse from yelling
○ <> **shqye·*n*^{3sg} kolla** <> *has* a racking cough
○ **shqye·*n* sytё** to pop out one's eye's in amazement

shqye'r *adj* (*i*) **1** tattered, torn **2** (*Fig*) opened wide in amazement **3** (*Fig*) (of eyes) bulging **4** (*Fig*) hoarse

shqye'rje *nf ger* **1** <shqye·*n*, shqy·*het* **2** torn place, tear

*****shqym**· *vt* **1** to tear, rip, rend **2** to extinguish, destroy

*****shqymb**· *vt* = shu'a·*n*

*****shqy'm'ёs** *n* apostrophe (punctuation mark) = apos-tro'f

*****shqy'p** = shqip

*****shqyra'k** *adj* = shqera'k

shqyrti'm *nm ger* <shqyrto'·*n*

shqyrto'·*n vt* to conduct an inquiry/investigation into [ ]; examine [ ] thoroughly
○ [ ] **shqyrto·*n* degё mё degё** to investigate [ ] in great detail

shqyrtu'e's *adj* investigatory; inquisitory

shqyt
I § *nm* **1** shield **2** (*Reg*) hunk of bread
II § *adv* (*Reg*) in a blocking position

shqyta'r *nm* [*Hist*] **1** shield-bearer **2** title of minor nobility

*****shqy'tё** *nf* bit, piece

*****shr-** = çr-

*****shra'nd**·*et vpr* (*Reg*) to get a hernia from lifting things that are too heavy

*****shra'ndё** *nf* (*Reg*) weight that is too heavy

shrapne'l *nm* [*Mil*] shrapnel bomb

shre'gull *nf* **1** children's swing **2** seesaw **3** woolen rope used by a woman to secure a cradle on her back shrr- = çrr-

*shrregullò •n vt = çrregullò •n

*shrregullshëm adj (i) = çrregullshëm

*shrregulltë adj (i) = çrregullt

*shrrod = çorod

shtab nm executive staff; headquarters

shtagë nf 1 long stick, pole; staff 2 (Reg) rolling pin = petës 3 [Tech] piston rod *4 shaft
  ○ shtagë arrash "walnut pole" tall thin person: bean pole

shtalb nm = shtalp

*shtalbabutë nm [Bot] = shtalbës

shtalbër nm [Bot] = shtalbës

shtalbës nm [Bot] silk vine (Periploca)
  ○ shtalbës i egër [Bot] queen of the meadow Filipendula ulmaria

shtalkë nf 1 door/window frame; door/window jamb 2 upright support of wood: wooden prop 3 (Colloq) crutch = patericë

shtalkò •n vt to square up [], make [] square

shtalp
  I § nm 1 corn/wheat whose grain is still milky 2 rennet 3 (Colloq) semen
  II § adj 1 still soft and moist 2 (Fig) unripe, immature

shtalpak adj = shtalpët

shtalpë nf 1 [Dairy] curdled cream; sauce made of creamy yogurt 2 freshly made cheese; milk which has just been curdled by rennet

*shtalpër nm [Bot] = shtalbës

shtalpët adj (i) [Dairy] (of grain) still soft and milky inside; soft

*shtallë nf stall (for livestock)

shtambar n potter

shtambaxhi nm (np ˜ nj) = shtambar

shtambë nf 1 potbellied clay water ewer with one or two handles 2 (Reg) [Dairy] shepherd's wooden flask for milk or buttermilk

*shtamin nm [Bot] stamen = thek

shtampë nf 1 [Tech] = stampë 2 (Fig) mechanical copy; cliché

*shtampos• vt = stampo •n

*shtamposje nf ger <shtampos•

shtand nm = stendë

shtang
  I § nm 1 arrowhead; spear head 2 (Old) (of an object at a market) fixed price
  II § adv as if paralyzed (by fear/astonishment): rigid

shtang•
  I § vt to make [] rigid (with astonishment/fear); take [] aback; stupefy
  II § vi to go rigid (with astonishment/fear), grow stiff

shtang•et vpr to become immobilized (by astonishment/fear): become rigid

shtangë nf 1 [Tech] drill pipe, drill rod 2 [Sport] dumbbell used in weight lifting

*shtangër adj (i) (Reg Gheg) = vëngër

shtangës adj astounding, astonishing

shtangësi nf 1 rigidity; stiffness 2 (Book) emotionally/mentally induced rigidity: trance, dumbfoundedness, astonishment, paralysis

shtangësim nm rigidity

shtangëso •het vpr to become rigid

shtangëso •n vt to make rigid, stiffen; solidify

shtangët adj (i) rigid

shtangie nf ger <shtang•, shtang•et

shtangim nm ger = shtangie

shtangist n [Sport] weight lifter

shtango •het vpr = shtang•et

shtango •n vt, vi = shtang•

shtanguar adj (i) = shtangur

shtangur adj (i) stupefied

shtapos• vt to uncork

shtarcë nf [Bot] herb paris (Paris quadriifolia)

shtarë
  I § nf 1 [Bot] white false hellebore (poisonous) (Veratrum album) 2 (Fig) poison 3 (Fig Colloq) harm, grief
  II § adj (Colloq) too salty; poisonous
  III § adv amiss, badly

shtarët adj (i) bitter

shtaro •het vpr to become embittered

shtaro •n vt 1 to sadden, grieve, embitter 2 (Colloq) to choke down [food] (in emotional distress)

*shtarpë nf [Bot] setaria, foxtail millet (Setaria)

shtat nm 1 (human) body 2 body height; height 3 stature
  ○ shtati pyll e mendja fyell "body like a forest and mind like a flute" tall and handsome but brainless person

shtatanik
  I § adj, n "seven-monther" prematurely born (person)
  II § adj premature; weak and immature
  ○ shtatanik (në bark) person who can't wait his turn, impatient person

shtatat np fem (të) (Old) [Relig] the seventh day memorial for someone who has died; the memorial meal served on the seventh day after death

shtatbilonjë adj, nf (girl) with a tall and slender body

shtatbukur adj (of a girl) with a nice body

shtatçetinë adj (of a girl) with a body like a black spruce: tall and straight

shtatderdhur adj (of a boy or girl) with a nicely formed body

shtatdrejtë adj having a straight body

shtatë
  I § num seven; number seven
  II § adj (i), n (i) seventh
  III § nf the number seven; the grade seven (where ten is the highest possible grade)
  IV § nf (e) 1 (fraction) a seventh 2 seventh grade (in elementary school); seventh grade class/classroom
  V § np (të) a group of seven, seven at one time; all seven
  ○ [] pafsha shtatë pashë nën dhé! "May I see [] seven fathoms below ground!" (Curse) I hope to see [] dead and buried!
  ○ shtatë pashë nën dhé "seven fathoms below ground" very deep
  ○ të vrasësh/vrisje shtatë (e) nuk __ "you may/ might kill seven and still not __" try as you like, you can't __

shtatballësh adj [Spec] (of earthquakes) with a magnitude of seven

shtatëdhjetë
  I § cardinal number seventy
  II § adj (i), n (i) seventieth

shtatëdhjetëvjeçar
I § *adj* seventy years long, lasting seventy years; seventy years old
II § *n* septuagenarian

shtatëmbëdhjetë
I § *num* seventeen; number seventeen
II § *nf* **1** the number seventeen **2** *(Colloq)* loony bin **3** lunacy
III § *adj (i), n (i)* seventeenth

shtatëmuajsh *adj* seven-month old

shtatëmujor *adj* seven-month

shtatëngjyrësh *nm* having seven colors, seven-colored

shtatëpëllëmbëmjekër *nm* [Folklore] old dwarf with a seven-inch wide beard and extraordinary powers who appears in Albanian folktales

shtatëqind
I § *num* seven hundred; number seven hundred
II § *nf* the number seven hundred

shtatëqindtë *adj (i), n (i)* seven hundredth

shtatërrokësh
I § *adj* [Lit] composed of seven syllables
II § *nm* [Lit] seven-syllable line of verse

shtatëvjeçar *adj* seven-year long, lasting seven years; seven years old

shtatëvjeçare *nf (Old Colloq)* seven-year long elementary school: primary school

shtatfiliz *adj* = shtatbilonjë

shtatgjatë *adj* tall in stature: tall

shtatgjatësi *nf* height

shtathedhur [shtat-hedh-ur] *adj* having a well-developed, tall, and graceful body

shtathijshëm [shtat-híj-shëm] *adj (i)* having a well-formed, good-looking and tall body: lithe, slim

*shtathjedhun *adj (i)* (Reg Gheg) = shtathedhur

shtathollë [shtat-hollë] *adj (i)* having a tall, slender body: svelte

shtatkunaçe *nf* [Anat] reticulum (of ruminant animals)

shtatlartë *adj* having a tall body: tall

shtatmadh *adj* portly, stout

shtatmadhori *nf* [Mil] general staff (headquarters)

shtatmesatar *adj* of medium stature

shtator *nm* September

shtatore *nf* statue

shtatorë *np masc* [Ethnog] bride's relatives who visit her in her new husband's home seven days after the wedding

shtatpaktë *adj* small and thin in stature

shtatselvi *adj* "with a body like an Italian cypress" tall and stately

shtatshëm *adj (i)* robust and good-looking, well built

shtatshkurtër *adj* short in stature

shtatujë *nf* = shtatore

shtatullët *adj (i)* = shtatshkurtër

shtatvigan *adj* of gigantic stature: huge

shtatvogël *adj* small/slight in stature, small-bodied: little, short

shtatzan *adj* = shtatzën

shtatzënë
I § *adj* pregnant, with child
II § *nf* pregnant woman

shtatzënësi *nf* pregnancy

shtatzëni *nf* = shtatzënësi

*shtavillë *nf* leather

shtazan *nm (Reg)* moist condition of soil most appropriate for plowing and sowing

shtazarak *adj* **1** bestial, animal; brutal, savage **2** unrestrained, uncontrollable

shtazë *nf* **1** animal, beast = kafshë **2** (Fig Pejorative Insult) burly and ill-mannered person; brutal and cruel person: brute

shtazëri *nf* **1** (Collec) animals as a collective whole: fauna, the brutes **2** brutality, bestiality **3** foolish behavior, stupid mistake

shtazërim *nm ger* <shtazëro·n, shtazëro·het

shtazërisht *adv* brutally; bestially

shtazëro·het *vpr* to become animal-like in appearance or behavior

shtazëro·n *vt* to cause to behave like an animal: bestialize

shtazëruar *adj (i)* having become animal-like in appearance or behavior

*shtazëz *nf* animalcule

shtazor *adj* **1** of or pertaining to animals; having an animal origin **2** bestial, brutal; savage, cruel

shteg *nm* **1** narrow passage through a barrier: path, gap, pass **2** rough/wild trail (in a mountain/forest); narrow path **3** (Fig) difficult path to reach a goal: hard way out **4** (Fig) opening, opportunity; opportune moment **5** part (in the hair created by combing); part of the forehead between the eyebrows **6** (Reg) trip, journey
○ <>a bie₂· (fjalën) në shteg "bring <>'s opportunity to speak to the path" to give <> the opening to speak that <> has been waiting for
○ shteg më shteg wherever the path leads

shtegdalje *nf* **1** escape path, way out (of a difficult situation) **2** (Fig) difficult path to reach a goal: hard way out

shtegjës *nm* hunter lying in wait

shtego·n *vi* to set out on the way, take to the road
○ <> shtego·n³ˢᵍ mendja <>'s mind wanders, <> thoughts *are* elsewhere

shtegtar
I § *adj* migratory; nomadic; traveling, roving
II § *n* **1** migrant; nomad; constant traveler **2** (Old) traveling merchant

shtegtari *nf collec* nomadic/migratory group; migration

shtegti *nf* **1** migration **2** pilgrimage

shtegtim *nm ger* **1** <shtegto·n **2** migration

shtegto·n
I § *vi* **1** to journey; travel abroad **2** to migrate **3** to live a nomadic life
II § *vt* to move [livestock, bees] to better pasture

shtegtuar *adj (i)* having traveled far; far from home; migrated

shtegtues *adj* = shtegtar

shtegth *nm* part (in the hair created by combing)

shtehëzim *nm ger* [Tech] <shtehëzo·n

shtehëzo·n *vt* [Tech] to round off the sharp edges/point of []

*shtek| = shteg|

shtemët
I § *adv* without a sound, mutely, silently
II § *adj (i)* deaf and dumb; mute; silent

shtendos· *vt* to release [] from tension/strain; relieve [nervous tension]

shtendos·et *vpr* to relax

shtendosje *nf ger* 1 <shtendos·, shtendos·et 2 relaxation

shtendosur *adj (i)* 1 released from tension: slack 2 *(Fig)* relaxed, relieved

shter·
I § *vi, vt* 1 to stop flowing: dry [] up 2 *(Fig)* to come/ bring to an end
II § *vt (Fig)* to tire [] out, use [] up: exhaust

shter·et *vpr* 1 to run dry, come to an end: dry up, cease 2 to lose moisture by evaporation: dry out 3 *(Fig)* to weaken, decline, fade out

***shterbët** *adj (i)* = shterp

shterc *nf* nasty old man

***shtercë** *nf* old crone

shterë *nf (Reg)* large stone mortar

shterim *nm ger* <shtero·n, shtero·het

shterje *nf ger* <shter·, shter·et

shtero·het *vpr* = shter·et

shtero·n *vi* = shter·

shterp *adj* infertile, barren; sterile; unproductive

shterpake *adj, nf* = shterpë

shterpan *nm* female fish without roe

shterpar *n* shepherd who looks after barren ewes

shterpe *OR* **shterp** *ë nf* female livestock animal that has not achieved pregnancy in a year; sterile female

shterpëri *nf collec* 1 infertile livestock 2 infertility, sterility

shterpërim *nm ger* <shterpëro·n

shterpëro·n
I § *vi* (of animate beings) to become infertile
II § *vt* to decrease the fertility of [], make [] infertile

***shterpës** = shterpëz

shterpësi *nf* 1 barrenness, infertility, sterility 2 *[Med]* agenesis

shterpësirë *nf* barrenness, infertility, sterility

shterpët *adj (i)* = shterp

shterpëzim *nm ger* <shterpëzo·n, shterpëzo·het

shterpëzo·het *vpr* to become infertile/sterile; lose one's creativity

shterpëzo·n *vt* to make [] infertile; sterilize

shterpim *nm ger* 1 <shterpo·n 2 *(Reg)* = shterpëri

shterpo·n *vi* 1 (of living things) to become infertile 2 to stop flowing, dry up; (of milk animals) go dry

shterpor *nm* two-year old male sheep or goat

shterpore *nf* 1 infertile young ewe or nanny goat; ewe/nanny with no offspring for the year 2 two-year old female sheep or goat 3 shed in which infertile livestock are segregated

shteruar *adj (i)* 1 = shterur 2 carried through to the end: thorough

shterues *adj (Book)* exhaustive, thoroughgoing

shterueshëm *adv* exhaustively, thoroughly

shterur *adj (i)* dried up

***shterzuer** *adj (i) (Reg Gheg)* infertile

***shterr·** *vi* = shter·

***shterr** *stem for pdef. opt. adm. part. imper* <shterret·

***shterrë** *nf* heifer

***shterrëni** *nf* = shterpësi

***shterrim** *nm* 1 running dry 2 infertility, sterilization

***shterrje** *nf (Old)* drainage

shtesë *nf* 1 supplement 2 increase, increment, augmentation, addition, extension 3 *[Soccer]* time extension; overtime period; injury time

shtesor *adj [Ling]*

shtet *nm* state

shtetar *n (Book)* statesman

shtetas *n* citizen

shtetëror *adj* of or pertaining to the state; under the control of the state, operated by the state: national

shtetësi *nf* citizenship

shtetëzim *nm ger* 1 <shtetëzo·n 2 nationalization

shtetëzo·n *vt* to make [] the property of the state: nationalize

shtetëzuar *adj (i)* taken over by the state: nationalized

shtetmadh *adj* of or by large nations

shtetnor *(Reg Gheg)* = shtetëror

shtetrrethim *nm* martial lawcurfew

***shtëkur·** *vt* = shtri·n

shtëlli·n *vi* = shtëllit·

shtëllis *stem for 1st sg pres, pl pres, 2nd & 3rd sg subj. pind* <shtëllit·

shtëllit· *vt* 1 to spread [] out 2 to loosen [] from a fixed condition: uncurl, unbraid; hackle/comb [wool] 3 *(Fig)* to disperse [] 4 *(Fig)* to lay [] out in detail

shtëllit·et *vpr* 1 to spread out; become dispersed; uncurl 2 *(Fig)* to unfold, develop, elaborate

shtëllitje *nf ger* <shtëllit·, shtëllit·et

shtëllo·n *vt* 1 to hackle/comb [wool] 2 *(Reg Arb)* to throw, toss

shtëllung·et *vpr* to rise in spreading curls: uncurl upward

shtëllunga-shtëllunga *adv* in spreading curls, uncurling

shtëllungë *nf* 1 hank of fiber to be spun into yarn 2 cluster of vapor rising in spreading curls: curling smoke, billowing cloud

shtëllungor *adj* (of clouds) billowing

***shtëmâng·** *vt (Reg Gheg)* = shtëmëng·

***shtëmbar** = shtambar

***shtëmbë** = shtambë

shtëmëng· *vt* = shmang·

shtëmëngët *adj (i)* 1 standing apart 2 on the left

shtënë
I § *part* <shti·e·
II § *nf (e)* discharge of a firearm: shot, gunshot, shooting
∘ **nuk ka shtënë gjë në gojë** "not have put anything in one's mouth" not have eaten a thing all day

shtënë *adj (i)* 1 stillborn 2 feigned, phony, insincere

shtëng
I § *nm* hard object/ground/bread
II § *adj* 1 hard 2 = vëngër
III § *adv* in a hard lump

shtëng·et *vpr* = shtang·et

shtëngezë *nf* pillar, support

shtëngër *adj (i) (Reg)* = vëngër

shtënie *nf ger* <shti·e·

shtëno·n *vi* to avoid work, dawdle at work: dawdle

***shtëpâ(n)** *nm (pl ˜ j) (Reg Gheg)* = stanar

shtëpí *nf* **1** house; home **2** household; family; dynasty **3** *(Fig Colloq)* homeland **4** institution, firm **5** room in a house **6** *(Colloq)* building = **ndërte·s**ë **7** *(Colloq)* receptacle that holds something firmly: socket (for a tool handle), gem socket (in a ring)
　○ **shtëpi muze** house dedicated as a museum
　○ **shtëpi buke** hospitable
　○ **nuk e di· se ku rri· me shtëpi** "not know where one lives" not know what kind of person {*someone*} is
　○ **shtëpia e fëmijës** "children's home" orphanage for older children
　○ **shtëpia e foshnjës** "baby's home" orphanage for babies and young children
　○ **Nuk ka shtëpi pa derë.** "There is no house without a door." *(Prov)* Every problem has a solution.
　○ **shtëpi korrektimi** reformatory
　○ **shtëpia e madhe** one's extended family
　○ **shtëpi me prik** house with a steep roof
　○ **shtëpi me taban** house with a dirt floor
　○ **ësh·të**³ˢᵍ **shtëpi me themel** to be economically sound
　○ **shtëpi e ndotë** brothel
　○ **shtëpi e oficerave** *(Old)* officers' club (in a town)
　○ **shtëpi pa fjalë** harmonious family (without arguments)
　○ **shtëpi pa qira** *(Colloq)* jail
　○ **shtëpi përdhese** one-storey house
　○ **shtëpi përtrojce** one-storey house: bungalow
　○ **shtëpi publike** brothel
　○ **shtëpi pushke** "house of the gun" family known for its brave fighters
　○ **shtëpi qortimi** reformatory
　○ **Shtëpinë shite, shokun mbaje!** "Sell your house, keep your friend!" *(Prov)* A faithful friend is better than gold. Whatever else you do, hold on to your friends. A good friend is more precious than gold.
　○ **shtëpi e shurdhët** childless home
　○ **U thurtë ajo shtëpi!** "May that house be fenced up!" *(Curse)* May that whole family be damned!
　○ **shtëpi ushtarake** *(Old)* barracks
　○ **shtëpia e zjarrit** cookhouse

shtëpia͕k
I § *adj* **1** of or pertaining to the home: domestic **2** home-loving, stay-at-home
II § *nm* *(Reg)* head of the family, master of the house

shtëpia͕ke *adj, nf* (girl/woman) involved in housekeeping/homemaking

shtëpia͕k͕ës
I § *n* **1** household member **2** *(Old)* inhabitant
II § *adj* home-loving, stay-at-home

shtëpia͕r
I § *n* member of the household
II § *adj* **1** home-loving, stay-at-home **2** involved in housekeeping/homemaking

shtëpia͕sh *adv*

shtëpini *nf* *(Colloq)* housework

shtëpipri͕sh͕ës *n* profligate (to the point of bringing ruin on one's family): prodigal

shtëpipri͕sh͕ur *adj, n* **1** (person) without home and without belongings: homeless, very poor **2** home-neglecting/profligate (person)

shtëpi͕zë *nf* little house

*shtëpizo·n *vt* to house, domesticate

*shtëpo·n = **shpëto·n**

*shtëpre͕së
I § *nf* dairymaid; good housekeeper
II § *adj* of or pertaining to housekeeping: domestic

*shtëpre͕shë *nf* housekeeper

shtërg *nm (np ~ gje)* [*Ornit*] stork
　○ **shtërg misiri** [*Ornit*] curlew *genus Numenius*

*shtërga͕të = **shtrënga͕të**

*shtërk *nm (np ~ qe)* [*Ornit*] = **shtërg**

*shtërma͕jtë *adj (i)* = **majtë**

shtërme͕n *nm* [*Bot*] winter savory *(Satureia montana)* = **trumz**ë

*shtërngi͕cë *nf* = **shtrënge͕s**ë

shtërngo·n = **shtrëngo·n**

*shtërngue͕shëm *adj (i)* cramped; constrained, restricted

*shtërngu͕të *adv* tightly; strictly

*shtëro·n *vt, vi* = **shter·**

shtërpí *nm (np ~ nj)* [*Zool*] reptile = **zvarraník**

*shtërpo·n *vt, vi* = **shterpëzo·n**

*shtërpo͕r *adj* = **shterp**

shtërzi͕m *nm ger* < **shtërzo·n, shtërzo·het**

shtërzo·n *vi* **1** to strain hard (trying to defecate or give birth) **2** *(FigImpolite)* to bust one's gut trying

shtërra͕s *stem for 1st sg pres, 1st & 3rd pl pres, 2nd & 3rd sg subj* < **shtërret·**

shtërret· *vi* = **shtërro·n**

shtërri͕s *stem for 2nd pl pres, pind* < **shtërret·**

shtërri͕t *stem for pind, 2nd pl pres, imper, vp* < **shtërret·**

*shtërro·n *vt* **1** to shrivel/shrink ***2** to run dry

*shtëzo·n = **shtozo·n**

shti·het *vpr* **1** to appear to ◇ (in a phantasmagoric vision) **2** = **shtir·et**
　○ **shti·het pas** ◇ to be enthusiastic/wild about ◇, be devoted to ◇
　○ **◇ shti·het për** [] ◇ has a craving for [], ◇ just loves [a certain food]

shti͕ *stem for pdef, opt* < **shti/e·**

shtia͕k *adj, n* **1** sham, fake **2** aborted (fetus), stillborn

*shti͕az *np fem* sparks

shti/e·
I § *vt* **1** to put [] inside an enclosed space: stick [] inside, put [] in, insert **2** to put [food, liquid] into a vessel, add **3** to stick [] on; attach; assign [guilt] **4** to thrust **5** to give ◇ [food]: feed **6** to put out []: sprout **7** to put [] aside (in storage): save **8** to put [] to work **9** to entrust responsibility for []: engage **10** to afflict ◇ with [] **11** to drop [] to the ground, throw [] down; miscarry, abort, lose **12** *(Colloq)* to pull apart [wool]; puff up [a pillow/pad] **13** to cast [] (for purposes of divination or for reaching a decision), toss [a coin]; forecast [destiny]
II § *vi* **1** to shoot; strike **2** to miscarry, abort **3** *(Colloq)* to bear a resemblance **4** *(Reg)* (of bees) to swarm **5** to coerce [] to do something
　○ **aq ◇a shti/e·** ◇ *doesn't* know any better
　○ **◇ shti/e· botën** to instill ◇ with terror, terrify ◇
　○ **shti/e· brinjët** to break one's back (working), work one's tail off
　○ **po i shti/e· bukët të mirë** (of a newly married woman) she's doing a very good job
　○ **shti/e· cita** to sow discord, provoke a quarrel
　○ **shti/e· çakthi mbi të tjerët** to be overpowering, stand out among others

○ **<> sht*i*e·**.^{3sg} **çatia shi** <>'s roof *leaks* when it rains

○ **po i sht*i*e· çyrekët të mirë** (of a newly married woman) she's doing a very good job

○ **sht*i*e· dashuri** to fall in love

○ **e sht*i*e· shejtanin/dreqin/djallin në shishe** "stick the devil in the bottle" *(Joke)* to be devilishly clever

○ **sht*i*e· fall** to tell someone's fortune, divine

○ **sht*i*e· fite** to sow discord, provoke a quarrel

○ **sht*i*e· fitil** to sow discord, provoke a quarrel

○ **sht*i*e· gverë/gverrë** to sow discord

○ **nuk sht*i*e· gjë në thes** not get a thing out of it for oneself

○ **nuk sht*i*e· gjumë në sy** "not put sleep in the eye" not get a wink of sleep

○ **i sht*i*e· hile punës** to fake work

○ **sht*i*e· hollë** to be a good shooter/shot

○ **<> sht*i*e· iletin** to give <> a fit: bother terribly; terrify

○ **<> sht*i*e· kalla** to provoke <> to do something (wrong); cause <> to quarrel

○ **sht*i*e· keq** to sow discord, provoke a quarrel

○ **<> sht*i*e· këmbët** to work <>'s tail off

○ **<>i sht*i*e· (të dy) këmbët në një këpucë/opingë *1** to put <> into a difficult position **2** to make <> do one's bidding **3** to give <> a good lesson (in proper behavior)

○ **sht*i*e· kokën në strajcën e tjetrit** to stick one's nose into other people's business

○ **i sht*i*e· krahët derës/murit** to put one's shoulder to the wheel

○ **sht*i*e· kryet në strajcën e tjetrit** to stick one's nose into other people's business

○ **sht*i*e· kunja** to sow discord, provoke a quarrel

○ **sht*i*e· kurorë** to get married

○ **sht*i*e· me bathë** *(Joke)* to make a guess, read the tea leaves

○ **[] sht*i*e· në kokë** to plant [] firmly in one's mind, stick [] into one's head

○ **[] sht*i*e· ndër/në mend** to plant [] firmly in one's mind, stick [] into one's head

○ **[] sht*i*e· në mendje** to plant [] firmly in one's mind

○ **e sht*i*e· morrin në hell** to be very stingy

○ **<>a sht*i*e·**.^{3sg} **ndër mend/mendje** to call [] to <>'s mind

○ **[] sht*i*e· në amë** to put [] back on the right track

○ **[] sht*i*e· në be** to put [] under oath; force [] to take an oath, make [] swear

○ **[] sht*i*e· në bigë** to put [] into a difficult position

○ **[] sht*i*e· në dhe** "stick [] into ground" to bury in the ground

○ **[] sht*i*e· në grackë** "stick [] into a trap" **1** to play [] for a sucker, lure [] in, inveigle [] into a trap: sucker **2** to succeed in catching [] **3** to have [] in the palm of one's hand, have [] where one wants []

○ **sht*i*e· në harresë** "stick [] into oblivion" to put [] in the back of one's mind, neglect []

○ **sht*i*e· në hi** to be a coward

○ **[] sht*i*e· në kllapë** "stick [] into a trap" **1** to play [] for a sucker, lure [] in, inveigle [] into a trap: sucker **2** to succeed in catching [] **3** to have [] in the palm of one's hand, have [] where one wants []

○ **[] sht*i*e· në kurth** "stick [] into a trap" **1** to play [] for a sucker, lure [] in, inveigle [] into a trap: sucker **2** to succeed in catching [] **3** to have [] in the palm of one's hand, have [] where one wants []

○ **[] sht*i*e· në lak** "stick [] into a snare" **1** to play [] for a sucker, lure [] in, inveigle [] into a trap: sucker **2** to succeed in catching [] **3** to have [] in the palm of one's hand, have [] where one wants []

○ **[] sht*i*e· në leqendi** to afflict [] deeply, hurt deeply

○ **<>a sht*i*e·**.^{3sg} **në mend/mendje** to call [] to <>'s mind

○ **[] sht*i*e· në ngasje** to tempt [] into sin, seduce

○ **s'[] sht*i*e· në numër** not (even) count [], not consider []

○ **[] sht*i*e· në rreth 1** to encircle; surround **2** to find a plan to exert pressure on []: hit on the way to put the screws to []

○ **[] sht*i*e· në thes** "stick [] into a sack" **1** to play [] for a sucker, lure [] in, inveigle [] into a trap: sucker **2** to succeed in catching [] **3** to have [] in the palm of one's hand, have [] where one wants []

○ **[] sht*i*e· në varr/dhé për së gjalli/të gjallë** "put [] in the grave alive: bury [] alive" to bring [] to an early grave

○ **<>[] sht*i*e· në vesh** "put [] into <>'s ear" to teli [] to <>; whisper [] into <>'s ear; plant [] in <>'s ear

○ **[] sht*i*e· nën kontroll** to get [] under control

○ **<> sht*i*e· pishat** "poke torches into <>" to stir <> up, incite <> to fight

○ **<>i sht*i*e· pleshtat në vesh** "put fleas into <>'s ear" to make an innuendo: put a bug in <>'s ear, put a bee in <>'s bonnet

○ **<> sht*i*e· prush në shalë** "stick a bed of hot coals in <>'s saddle" to incite hatred/anger in <>

○ **sht*i*e· rrënjë** to take root; settle down, take up permanent residence: become implanted

○ **sht*i*e·**.^{3sg} **rruaza në pe** "string beads on a thread" **1** to work slowly and painstakingly **2** to do wasted work

○ **si ia sht*i*e·** as {} *sees* it, in {}'s opinion

○ **sht*i*e· spica** to sow discord, provoke a quarrel

○ **<>a sht*i*e· syrin** "one's eye *lands* on <>" **1** to choose <> for the task **2** to take a liking to <>

○ **nuk <>i sht*i*e· sytë** to pay no attention to <> out of disrespect

○ **e sht*i*e· shejtanin në shishe** "stick the devil in the bottle" *(Joke)* to be devilishly clever

○ **sht*i*e· shkelma 1** to let kicks fly: kick **2** to make unreasonable objections: kick

○ **sht*i*e· short** to cast lots, draw straws

○ **<> sht*i*e· shpirt** to inspire courage in <>

○ **<> sht*i*e· shurdhat** to turn a deaf ear

○ **sht*i*e· shurdhat** to pretend to be deaf

○ **sht*i*e· tehri** to sow discord, provoke a quarrel

○ **sht*i*e· tek e çift** to cast lots by simultaneously holding up some number of fingers and then counting whether the sum of fingers held up is odd or even

○ **Të shtie miza e s'të nxjerr bualli.** "The ant pushes you in and your ox can't pull you out." It's easy to get into trouble and hard to get out of it.

○ **<> sht*i*e· trutë e gomarit** "they have stuck him with the brain of the donkey" they have brainwashed <>, <> doesn't think with an independent mind any more

○ **<> sht*i*e· veremin** to drive <> to despair; make <> despondent

○ **<> sht*i*e· veshët në lesh** "stick one's ears in wool" to refuse to listen, stop up one's ears, turn a deaf ear to <>; not give a thought to <>, not think about <>

○ <> shti·e· **veshët në tul** "stick the ears in soft flesh" to pretend not to hear; be lenient
○ <> shti·e· **zekthin** to give <> an incentive, arouse <>'s interest
○ shti·e· **zinë** *(Colloq)* to create a shortage
○ shti·e· **zjarrin në shtëpi** to cause bickering/trouble in the family

shtie·ke·q
I § *adj* bad-mouthing; provocatory
II § *n* bad-mouther, provocateur

*shtiell = shtjell

shtie·s
I § *nm* (*Old*) killer
II § *n* fortuneteller

shti·gje *np = shteg*

*shtija·k = shtia·k

shti·je *nf* 1 knitting needle 2 tongue of a cart; beam of a plow 3 flagpole 4 [*Text*] lease stick 5 (*Fig Colloq*) sun ray; reflected sun ray 6 stern mast on a small boat 7 [*Bot*] leafless flower-bearing stalk growing directly out of a root: *(scape)*

*shtijke·q *adj* defamatory, provocative, slanderous

*shtill *nm* axletree, axle

shti·ll·et *vpr* 1 to open out: uncoil, unfurl, unfold, unwrap 2 to swirl 3 (*Fig*) to develop gradually: unfold, fan out, swell

shti·ll *stem for 2nd pl pres, pind, imper, vp* <shtje·ll·

*shti·llë *nf = shtjellës*

*shtillzo·n *vt = shtjello·n*

shti·m *nm ger* <shto·n, shto·het

shti·nja·k *adj, n* fake, sham, phony

shti·nja·t·et *vpr* to pretend to be something other than what one is: pretend, fake, pose

*shti·qe *np* <shtek

shtir· *vt* 1 (*Colloq*) to ford [a stream] 2 (*Fig*) to overcome [an impediment, a difficulty]
○ e shtir· **lumin** to put a past problem/difficulty behind one

shti·r·et *vpr* to put on a sham: pretend, fake

shtir *stem for pdef* <shti·e·

shtira·ca·k
I § *adj* fake, sham, phony
II § *n* poser, pretender, hypocrite

shtira·k *adj* fake, sham, phony

shti·rë *nf* 1 tremendous greed *2 envy

shti·rë
I § *part* <shti·e·
II § *adj* (*i*) 1 feigned, put-on, phony, insincere 2 stillborn, aborted; having given birth to stillborn offspring 3 emaciated and weak

shti·rë·si *nf* pretense, hypocrisy; artificiality

shti·rje *nf* hypocritical behavior; phony manner

shti·rr *stem for 2nd pl pres, pind, imper, vp* <shtjerr·

shtiza·r *nm* [*Hist*] fighter armed with a lance/spear: spearman, (cavalry) lancer

shtizë *nf* 1 lance, spear; javelin 2 shaft: tongue of a cart; beam of a plow 3 knitting needle 4 [*Text*] lease stick 5 shuttle (of a loom) 6 flagpole 7 one of a pair of poles used to carry sheaves of grain 8 game played by shepherds throwing their crooks as far as possible and still land with their points sticking in the ground 9 arm of a weighing scale along which metal ball is moved 10 (*Fig Colloq*) sun ray; reflected sun ray 11 [*Ornit*] owl 12 [*Ichth*] garfish *Belone belone* 13 [*Ichth*] Atlantic saury *Scombresox saurus* 14 [*Biol*] style, stylet

shtizë·mba·jt·ës *nm* [*Hist*] spearman; lancer

shtizo·n *vt* 1 to run [] through with a spear; fight with a spear 2 to chop up [wood] into thin pieces

shtizo·r
I § *adj* thin and pointed
II § *nm = shtiza·r*

shtje·gë·z *nf* 1 = shtje·kë·z *2 pocket slit in trousers

shtje·gullë *nf* rain gutter on a roof, eaves

shtje·kë *nf* 1 pocket (in white-flannel breeches) without a lining 2 buttonhole 3 small loop; slipknot 4 receding hair line above the temples 5 (*Reg*) small irrigation furrow

shtje·kë·z *nf* 1 (*Dimin*) <shtje·kë 2 notch in a gunsight 3 notch for the bowstring in the end of an arrow shaft 4 loop

*shtjelm *nm (Reg Gheg)* kick = shkelm

shtje·ll· *vt* 1 to throw [] hard: hurl 2 to pull [fibrous material] apart 3 to unfold, unfurl, unwind; unwind [thread] (onto reels) 4 to lay out [], discourse upon []: explain, expatiate

*shtjelle·së *nf* explanation = shtjellim

shtjellë
I § *part* <shtje·ll·
II § *nf* 1 swirl, eddy, maelstrom: (of water) whirlpool, waterspout; (of wind) whirlwind, cyclone 2 = shtje·llë·s

shtjellë·s *nm* [*Text*] barrel-like reel for winding yarn or thread into skeins: skein winder

shtjellë·z = shtje·llë·s

shtjellim *nm ger* 1 <shtjello·n, shtjello·het 2 explanation, elaboration

*shtjellisje *nf ger = shtjellim*

shtje·llje *nf ger* 1 <shtje·ll·, shti·ll·et 2 = shtje·llë

shtjello·het *vpr* 1 = shti·ll·et 2 to unfold, evolve, develop

shtjello·n *vt* 1 to lay out []: explain; expand upon [], elaborate 2 to unfold, unfurl, unwind 3 (*Old*) to develop, broaden

shtjello·r *adj* swirling, whirling

shtjellua·r *adj* (*i*) 1 elaborate 2 [*Ling*] (of verbs) finite

shtje·r *imper* <shti·e·

shtje·r *stem for imper, 3rd sg subj* <shti·e·

shtjera·ke·q *adj = shtijke·q*

shtjerë *nf* defamatory/provocative language: slander

shtjerr· *vt* 1 to unravel; unwind [yarn/thread] 2 to disentangle, clarify, resolve

shtjerrë
I § *nf* lamb
II § *adj* well-behaved, docile, obedient

shtje·rrë *part* <shtjerr·

shtjerri *nf collec* 1 lambs and kids as a collective class; flock of lambs and kids 2 flock of heifers

shto·het *vpr* to get bigger/greater, get more numerous: increase
○ shto·het **si farë e hithrës/sinapit/lirit** to multiply like rabbits, grow like weeds

shto·n
I § *vt* to augment; increase; add; add on [], supplement
II § *vi* to get bigger: gain weight; increase
○ **nuk shto·n as mungo·n gjë** not add or subtract anything (to one's account), not embellish nor leave out anything (in telling something)

◦ [ ] **shto**·*n* **nga xhepi** to add [something personal] to a narrative account

◦ **Shto ujë e shto miell.** "Add water and add flour." *(Impol)* The more you add, the more you need.

*shtof = stof

shtog *nm (np ˜ gje)* [*Bot*] elderberry tree/bush, European elder *(Sambacus nigra)*

◦ **shtog i egër** [*Bot*] bladdernut tree/bush *(Staphylea)*

shto'**gër** *nf* [*Bot*] **1** bladdernut tree/bush *(Staphylea)* **2** forsythia = **boshtër**

shtog i shtë *nf* area with elderberry trees/bushes

shtogro'**re** *np* [*Bot*] bladdernut family *Staphyleaceae*

shtog të *adj (i)* **1** made of elderberry wood **2** *(Fig)* frail

shto jcë

I § *nf* secondary/small addition: appendage, supplement, addendum; annex; codicil, appendix

II § *adj* additional; supplementary

shto jë *nf* increase, growth

shto jë'**s** *adj* **1** capable of expansion, expanding when boiled **2** prolific

*shto jzava lle = shtojzovalle

shto jzorre shta *np fem* [*Folklore*] fairies = **shtojzovalle**

shto jzova lle *nf* **1** oread, dryad, fairy **2** *(Fig)* beautiful girl

shtoll *stem for pdef* < **shtjell**·

shto'**në** *nf* **1** sewer; cesspool, catchment **2** water channel, canal **3** pond from a spring **4** *(Reg)* kitchen sink = **sqoll**

shtopi s· *vt* to blunt, dull

shto pje *nf* = **mëllagjër**

shto r *stem for pdef* < **shtjerr**·

shtozo'·*n* *vi (Reg Old)* to say grace after a meal; finish eating a meal; eat

shtradh *nm* residue left by melting wax: wax drippings

*sh trajti m *nm* **1** < **shtrajto**'·*n* **2** transformation, deformation

*sh trajto'·*n* *vt* to transform, deform

shtra k *nm* **1** thin outer skin; membrane; filmy layer that forms on liquids: scum **2** [*Anat*] placenta **3** hall corridor **4** partitioning wall: partition, curtain, fence; partition board **5** isolation shed for sick animals

shtrall *nm* sediment left by molten wax

shtrap *nm* **1** filmy layer that forms on liquids: scum; pond scum **2** spiderweb, cobweb

shtra për *nm* [*Bot*] shepherd's purse *(Capsella bursa pastoris)*

shtrap ëzo'·*het vpr* **1** to lie loosely along the surface of the ground: be procumbent **2** (of a plant) to put out roots/branches

shtrap ëzua r *adj (i)* (of a plant) lying loosely along the surface of the ground: procumbent

shtrapnje·*n* *vi* **1** (of a plant) to grow new saplings near the stump **2** (of a stream of water) to diverge into many branches

shtra qe *np* < **shtrak**

*sh trashgi m *nm ger* < **shtrashgo**'·*n*

*sh trashgo'·*n* *vt* to disinherit

shtrat *nm* **1** bed; cart/wagon/carriage bed; roadbed, riverbed; seedbed; hotbed **2** supporting stratum, bed layer; layer of snow/sleet **3** supporting platform; platform for a watchman/fisherman; gun platform **4** arbor-like structure for supporting vine plants or for drying tobacco **5** [*Bot*] receptacle (for the floral

organs at the end of a flower stalk) **6** gelatinous layer of microorganisms that forms in vinegar; scab that forms in a wound/sore **7** crotch (in pants/underwear) ***8** perineum **9** [*Anat*] placenta **10** spiderweb, cobweb **11** *(Fig Colloq)* man and wife, married couple **12** termite nest in wood: bed of termites

◦ **shtrat i fëmijës** [*Anat*] placenta

◦ **shtrat i ftohtë** [*Hort*] forcing frame

◦ **shtrati i lëshimit të raketës** rocket launch pad

◦ **shtrat i ngrohtë/nxehtë** hotbed

shtrat ëzi m *nm ger* [*Agr*] < **shtratëzo**'·*n*

shtrat ëzo'·*n* *vt* [*Agr*] to force [a plant] in a hotbed

shtrat ëzua r *adj (i)* [*Agr*] (of a plant) forced in a hotbed

shtrat gje rë *adj* having a broad streambed

shtrat im *nm* [*Min*] bearing stratum, deposit

shtrato re *nf* grape trellis = **pjergullo re**

*shtravi s *stem for 1st sg pres, pl pres, 2nd & 3rd sg subj, pind* < **bubi t**·

*shtravi t· *vt* to cause [ ] to shudder

shtra zë *nf (Reg)* **1** platform for a haystack (to keep it dry); haystack erected on a platform **2** arbor-like structure for supporting vine plants or for drying tobacco **3** thin layer of microorganisms that forms at the bottom of a vinegar container **4** scab formed over a wound/sore ***5** *(Old)* watchman, guard

*shtraz ta r

I § *n* watchman, guard; sentry

II § *adj* watchful, vigilant

shtreb· *vi* (of a fly) to deposit eggs, flyblow

shtre bë *nf* = **shtrep**

shtre gë *nf* **1** stack of hay or corn sheaves **2** stack of wood, woodpile

*shtrejt = shtre njt

*shtrejt sinë *nf* = **shtrenjtësire**

shtrejt sirë *nf* **1** expensive thing, costly object **2** = **shtrenjt ësi**

shtrek *nm (Reg)* = **kërmë**

shtremb *nm (Impol)* deformed person

shtre mb·*et vpr* to become crooked/lopsided; go awry/aslant; become distorted

shtremb a k *adj (Impol)* = **shtrembalu q**

shtremb alu q

I § *adj (Impol)* deformed, misshapen, crooked

II § *adj, n* (person) with a deformity

shtremb ani k *adj (Impol)* = **shtrembalu q**

shtremb ara k *adj, n* = **shtrembalu q**

shtre mb a-shtre mb a *adv, adj pred* not straight: crooked, awry; (of a road) full of curves, windy

shtre mb azi *adv* crookedly, awry

shtre mb ër

I § *adv* **1** not straight: crooked, awry **2** *(Fig)* improperly, wrongly

II § *adj (i)* **1** crooked, lopsided; distorted **2** *(Fig)* inaccurate, mistaken, wrong; dishonest

III § *nf (e)* wrongful thing, wrong; dishonesty

◦ **Të rrimë shtrembër e të flasim drejt!** "Let us stand crooked and talk straight." *(Prov)* Even if we don't like it, we have to say what's true!

◦ **<> shko**·*n*[3rd] {*food*} **shtrembër** { } *goes down* (<>'s windpipe) the wrong way

◦ **<> ve**·**te**[3rd] {*food*} **shtrembër** { } *goes down* (<>'s windpipe) the wrong way

shtremb ëri *nf* **1** dishonesty **2** crooked business, dishonest act, cheating

shtremb|ër|**ïm** *nm ger* 1 <**shtrembëro**'·*n*, **shtremb**-*ëro*·*het* 2 deformity, distortion 3 deviation, aberration, defect

shtremb|*ër*o·*het vpr* to get bent out of shape, become/go crooked; become contorted

shtremb|*ër*o·*n vt* 1 to make [] crooked 2 to bend [] out of shape, contort 3 *(Fig)* to get [] wrong, screw [] up 4 to distort
∘ **shtrembëro**·*n* **fytyrën/buzët/turinjtë** to make a wry face to express disappointment/disapproval
∘ **shtrembëro**·*n* **sytë** 1 to cross one's eyes 2 to squint

shtremb|ër|**u'a'r** *adj* (i) bent out of shape, crooked; leaning to one side; distorted

shtremb|ër|**u'e's** *nm* distorter

shtremb|ë|**sï** *nf* = **shtrembëri**

shtremb|ë|**sï'r'ë** *nf* 1 *(Impol)* deformity, defect 2 = **shtrembëri** 3 *(Colloq)* deformed and ugly person

shtre'mb|ët *adv, adj* (i) = **shtrembër**

*__shtremb__|ë|**to**·*n vt* = **shtrembëro**'·*n*

shtre'mb|ë*z* *nf* [*Veter*] sheeprot

*__shtremb__|no'·*n vt* (*Reg Gheg*) = **shtrembëro**'·*n*

*__shtremb__|si'në *nf(Old)* turning handle: crank

shtre'mb|tas *adv* = **shtre'mbër**

shtre'njtë
I § *adj* (i) expensive; precious, dear
II § *adj* (i), *n* (i) 1 dear, precious; darling 2 *(Colloq)* stingy, miserly
III § *adv* at high cost: costly, dear(ly)
∘ **I shtrenjtë në hime, i lirë në miell.** *(Prov)* Penny-wise and pound-foolish.

shtrenjt|ë|**sï** *nf* high cost: expensiveness, costliness; expense level

shtrenjt|ë|**si'm** *nm ger* = **shtrenjtim**

shtrenjt|ë|**so**·*het vpr* = **shtrenjto**·*het*

shtrenjt|ë|**so**·*n vt* = **shtrenjto**'·*n*

shtrenjt|**im** *nm ger* <**shtrenjto**·*n*, **shtrenjto**·*het*

shtrenjt|o·*het vpr* to become more expensive

shtrenjt|o·*n vt* to raise the price of [], make [] more expensive

shtrep *nm* [*Entom*] cheese mite *(Acarus siro)*

shtre's'a-**shtre's'a** *adj, adv* arranged in layers; in multiple layers

shtre's'ë *nf* 1 layer; stratum 2 pad laid out for sleeping or sitting; mat; rug 3 bedding of leaves/straw laid out for animals

shtres|ë|**ho'llë** *adj* [*Geol*] in a thin stratum: thin-bedded

*__shtres__|ë|**ta'r** *adj* stratified

shtres|ë|**tra'shë** *adj* [*Geol*] in a thick stratum: thick-bedded

shtres|ë|**zi'm** *nm ger* 1 = **shtresim** 2 [*Spec*] stratification

shtres|ë|**zo**·*het vpr* = **shtreso**·*het*

shtres|ë|**zo**·*n vt* = **shtreso**·*n*

shtres|ë|**zu'a'r** *adj* (i) [*Geol*] stratified

shtres|**im** *nm ger* 1 <**shtreso**·*n*, **shtreso**·*het* 2 stratification

shtres|**i'në** *nf* foundation layer, foundation

shtres|**na'jë** *nf* [*Geol*] stratum

shtres|o·*het vpr* to settle in layers; stratify, be stratified

shtres|o·*n vt* to lay [] out in layers: stratify

shtres|o'r *adj* (*Book*) stratified, stratiform

shtre'tër *np* <**shtrat**

shtreth *nm* 1 kitchen shelf 2 tent-like shelter constructed of branches by shepherds in highland camps

shtre'ze *nf* bilge (of a ship's hull)

shtre'zë *nf* snow frozen on tree branches; hoarfrost

*__shtrëmb__ = **shtremb**

*__shtrënga'c__
I § *adj* miserly, tight
II § *n* miser, tightwad

shtrënga'të *nf* 1 thunderstorm 2 *(Fig)* outburst, sudden outburst 3 difficult situation, tight straits

shtrëng|**e's'ë** *nf* 1 duress, coercion 2 severe constraint; difficult situation, tight straits 3 tight squeeze 4 vise-like wooden mechanism used to mold felt skullcaps 5 cinch strap to secure a saddle = **nënba'rkëz**

shtrëng|**i'c'ë** *nf* 1 duress, coercion 2 severe constraint; difficult situation, tight straits

shtrëng|**im** *nm ger* 1 <**shtrëngo**'·*n*, **shtrëngo**'·*het* 2 duress, coercion 3 [*Law*] legal coercion 4 severe constraint; difficult situation, tight straits 5 strict discipline, tight restraint
∘ **shtrëngim i dorës** handshake

shtrëng|o·*het vpr* 1 to stick tight/close; hold tight, stay firm 2 to be under constraint 3 to restrain one's living expenses: tighten one's belt 4 to strain oneself 5 to act under coercion: be compelled 6 to act with urgency 7 *(Colloq)* to get dressed; arm for combat: don arms
∘ <> **shtrëngo**·*het*[3sg] **litari në fyt/për gryke** "the rope *is tightening* around <>'s neck" <> *is nearing* <>'s end: <> is at the end of <>'s rope
∘ **shtrëngo**·*het* **me** [] to tighten [] around one's body
∘ **shtrëngo**·*het*[3sgpast] **puna** the matter *has gotten* more difficult, it *is* hard
∘ <> **shtrëngo**·*het*[3sg] **zemra/shpirti/kraharori** <> *feels* just terrible (about something)

shtrëng|o·*n*
I § *vt* 1 to clench; squeeze; constrain 2 to fasten, fasten [] tight; tighten 3 to cause [] a cramping pain; strain 4 to compel, coerce 5 to crowd [] (by sitting too close) 6 *(Fig)* to subject [] to discipline: restrain
II § *vi* to grow more and more intense
∘ <> **shtrëngo**·*n* **burgjitë** "tighten the screws on <>" to make <> do what one wants: put the screws to <>
∘ <> **shtrëngo**·*n* **çivitë** "tighten the screws on <>" to make <> do what one wants: put the screws to <>
∘ <>*i* **shtrëngo**·*n* **darët** "tighten the pincers on <>" 1 to make <> do what one wants: put the screws to <> 2 to put under greater control: tighten the reins on <>
∘ <>*i* **shtrëngo**·*n* **dizgjinët** to put under greater control: tighten the reins on <>
∘ **e shtrëngo**·*n* **dorën** "squeeze one's hand" 1 to tighten up on one's spending, become more thrifty, start to scrimp 2 to be tightfisted
∘ <> **shtrëngo**·*n* **dorën** "squeeze <>'s hand" to shake <>'s hand: congratulate <>
∘ <>*i* **shtrëngo**·*n* **dhëmbët nganjëherë** "tighten <>'s teeth occasionally" to give <> a good taste of discipline from time to time
∘ **shtrëngo**·*n* **dhëmbët** to grit one's teeth, gather up all one's strength
∘ <> **shtrëngo**·*n* **frerin** to tighten the reins on <>
∘ **ia shtrëngo**·*n* **frerin gjuhës** to weigh one's words carefully before speaking

○ **shtrëngo·n grushtet** "clench the fists" to prepare to make a great effort

○ **shtrëngoje gjuhën pas/prapa dhëmbëve!** "keep your tongue behind your teeth" don't speak!

○ **shtrëngo·n këmbët** to hurry: shake a leg

○ **nuk <>a shtrëngo·n³ˢᵍ këpuca këmbën** "<>'s shoe *doesn't* pinch (hurt/squeeze) <>'s foot" <> *is* not desperately short of money

○ **<>a shtrëngo·n lakun** to tighten one's control on <>, pull the reins in on <>

○ **shtrëngo·n në gji** to clasp to one's bosom

○ **<> shtrëngo·n në zemër** to weigh heavily on <>'s mind

○ **shtrëngoi puna** it has become an urgent matter, time has run out

○ **shtrëngo·n radhët** to join ranks, unite forces

○ **shtrëngo·n retrat** "tighten the thongs" **1** to tie up one's moccasin laces **2** to practice greater thrift: tighten one's belt,

○ **<> shtrëngo·n rripat** to tighten the reins on <>

○ **shtrëngo·n rripat** "tighten the straps" **1** to tie up one's moccasin laces **2** to practice greater thrift: tighten one's belt

○ **Shtrëngo rripat!** Prepare for action!

○ **shtrëngo·n rripin** to tighten one's belt

○ [] **shtrëngo·n³ˢᵍ ujët e hollë** []'s bladder is putting on pressure, [] needs to urinate: [] *has* to go to the bathroom

○ [] **shtrëngo·n³ˢᵍ veza** "the egg *puts* a strain on []" [] *is* under urgent pressure

○ **<> shtrëngo·n vidhat** "tighten the hinge on <>" to make <> do what one wants: put the screws to <>

shtrëngojë *nf* tightening device: clamp, turnbuckle, vise

shtrënguar
I § adj (i), adv **1** squeezed together **2** fastened tight
II § adj (i) **1** (Fig) urgent **2** (Fig) tight-fisted, stingy; stingy with praise, slow to give credit **3** (Fig) (of competitive scores) with a narrow margin of difference
III § adv **1** very frugally **2** in tight straits, in a tight squeeze (economically)

shtrëngues adj **1** serving to fasten strongly: fastening **2** causing a cramp: cramping **3** coercive

shtrënguese *nf* clamp

shtrëngueshëm
I § adj (i) **1** stingy **2** (Old) strict **3** urgent
II § adv squeezing/fastening tightly

shtri·n
I § vt **1** to stretch; stretch [] out; spread, extend **2** to lay out [], lay; bring to the ground, kill **3** to lay out [] for the grave
II § vi (Reg) to run fast

○ **<> shtrifshin!** "May they lay <> out (for burial)!" (Curse) I hope <> *drops* dead!

○ **shtri·n dorën/duart mbi/në** [] **1** to make a grab for [] **2** to stick one's nose into [] (where it doesn't belong)

○ **<> shtri·n dorën 1** to lend <> a hand, help <> out **2** to request <>'s help: put one's hand out to <> **3** to extend one's hand to <> for a conciliatory handshake

○ **e shtri·n gojën** to start vicious rumors

○ **Shtriji këmbët sa ke jorganin/plafin/shtratin.** "Stretch your legs according to your coverlet." (Prov) Cut your coat according to your cloth. Know your own limits!

○ **i shtri·n kthetrat** "extend one's talons" (Pej) to make a power grab

○ **Më shtrifsh!** "May you lay me out (for burial)!" (Colloq) (used in making an urgent but friendly request) Please help me!

○ **<> shtri·n qafën** "stretch one's neck to <>" (Contempt) to surrender abjectly: knuckle under

shtrig
I § nm (np ~ gj) **1** man-eating ugly sorcerer: wizard **2** (Pej) solitary misanthropic old man; dirty old man; mean and stingy man
II § adj (Pej) mean and stingy

shtrigan nm = shtrig

shtriganë nf = shtrigë

shtrigë nf **1** man-eating ugly sorcerer: harpy, witch **2** (Pej) solitary misanthropic old woman; old crone/hag; mean and stingy woman **3** [Entom] moth

shtrigëri nf sorcery, witchcraft, wizardry

shtrihe·t vpr **1** to stretch; stretch out **2** to extend, lie **3** to lie dead

shtrim nm ger <shtro·n, shtro·het

shtriq· vt to stretch [one's limbs]

shtriq·et vpr to stretch one's limbs

shtriqe np <shtrek

shtrirazi adv level with a surface, along a surface

shtrirë
I § adj (i), adv **1** stretched out; outstretched, extended **2** spread out **3** (Colloq) flat, low
II § nf(e) desire to stretch one's limbs felt at the onset of a fever

shtrirje nf ger **1** <shtri·n, shtriri·het **2** extension **3** surface area, area; expanse, extent

shtriskim nmact <shtrisko·n

shtrisko·n vt to prune, trim

shtrishëm adj (i) (Book) ductile

shtrishmëri nf (Book) ductility

*****shtrit·et** = shtri·het

shtro·het vpr **1** to become flat/level, lie down; become calm **2** to be seated (in a casual way for an enjoyable purpose) **3** to have a stay in a medical facility: be an inpatient **4** (of precipitation from the sky) to be of sufficient quantity to remain for a while **5** (of a hen) to sit on eggs: brood **6** (Fig) to get down to work on <> **7** to submit; calm down and behave properly; (of animals) be broken/tamed; (of motors) be broken in **8** to present itself

○ **shtro·het³ᵖˡ gjakrat** tempers cool

○ **shtro·het këmbëkryq** "sit cross-legged" **1** to have an extended face-to-face discussion **2** to make oneself at home; take over completely

○ **shtro·het në kuvend** to start extensive face-to-face discussion

○ **shtro·het në një sofër me** [] to share common interests and goals with []

○ **shtro·het rrafsh me** [] to sit down and talk things over with [] personally

○ **shtro·het vendçe** to have an extended face-to-face discussion

shtro·n
I § vt **1** to lay; lay [] down/out; set out **2** to hospitalize **3** to flatten [] out **4** to lay/put up [vegetables] for the winter: pickle **5** to force [] to submit/obey, subjugate, allay; make [] behave properly **6** to break [an animal] to the saddle; break [a new machine] in **7** (Fig) to calm
II § vi **1** (of precipitation from the sky) to be of sufficient quantity to remain for a while **2** (Fig) to calm down

○ **<>a shtro**·*n* to put out nice things for <> to eat and drink

○ **shtro**·*n* **çipat me** [] to smooth things over with [], make up with []

○ **<>a shtro**·*n* **deri në gju** to serve a bounteous meal to <>

○ **shtro**·*n* **dhomën** to put the room back in order and lay out the good floor and furniture coverings

○ **shtro**·*n* **gunën** to settle in for a long stay

○ **shtro**·*n* **kloçkën** to put eggs (for warming) under a brood hen

○ **e shtro**·*n* **kurrizin** "lower one's back" (*Contempt*) to surrender abjectly: knuckle under

○ **shtro**·*n* **kuvend me** [] to start extensive face-to-face discussion with []

○ **shtro**·*n* **linjën** to install a telephone line

○ **<>a shtro**·*n* **me lule** "bestrew <>'s path with flowers" to depict [] to <> as being a paradise

○ **e shtro**·*n* **mendjen** to finally make up one's mind

○ **shtro**·*n* **motorin** to break in the motor

○ [] **shtro**·*n* **në dru/dajak** to give [] a severe beating/drubbing

○ [] **shtro**·*n* **në havan** to make [] behave properly; make [] get in line, make [] toe the mark; force [] into submission

○ **e shtro**·*n* **qafën** "lower one's neck" (*Contempt*) to surrender abjectly: knuckle under

○ **shtro**·*n* **shtëpinë** to put the house back in order and lay out the good floor and furniture coverings

○ **shtro**·*n* **tryezën** to set the table

○ **shtro**·*n* **vrahun** to lay out the sheaves of grain on the threshing floor

shtrofa'k *nm* = **stro'fkë**

shtro'fkë *nf* = **stro'fkë**

** **shtro'fk|ull** *nf* = **stro'fkë**

shtro'full *nf* = **stro'fkë**

** **shtroh**· *vi* = **shter**·

shtro'hë *nf* dog kennel, doghouse

shtro'||i *obl* <**shtru'a**

shtroje'rë *nf* place sheltered from the wind: lee

shtro'jë *nf* **1** covering, pad **2** bed cover: sleeping mat **3** bedding of leaves/straw laid out for livestock **4** floor covered by wood or tile: flooring **5** shoe pad; stocking sole; foot warmer **6** bottom surface, bed

shtro'jsë *nf* **1** = **posti'qe 2** doormat **3** roof tile laid with its convex side down **4** beam used in subfloor

shtro'më *nf* saddle pad

** **shtro'nj** *np* <**shtru'a**

shtro'njar *adj* lying along the ground: procumbent

shtro'njare *nf* **1** pad **2** low-lying brambles

shtro'së *nf* goatskin mat = **posti'qe**

** **shtru'a** *nm* (*obl* ˜ **o'i**, *np* ˜ **o'nj**) kennel

shtru'ar

I § *part* <**shtro**·*n*

II § *adv* **1** lying down/flat **2** all set/ready **3** calmly; gently; without impediment

III § *adj (i)* **1** flat, level; gentle **2** (of rain) gentle and steady **3** (*Fig*) quiet and relaxed, moderated **4** (*Fig*) well-behaved; calm; patient; diligent **5** paved **6** (of a table/room/house) all set up and ready (for company) **7** (of a hen) sitting on eggs: brooding **8** (*Reg*) pickled, cured

IV § *nm (i)* inpatient

V § *nf (e)* **1** (*Colloq*) bedding **2** (*Reg*) pickled vegetable

shtru'ara'zi *adv* **1** stretched out on the ground **2** in an unhurried manner

shtru'arje *nf ger* <**shtro**·*n*, **shtro**·*het*

shtru'arshëm *adj (i)* docile

** **shtru'e|m** *part* (*Reg Gheg*) = **shtru'ar**

** **shtru'e|m|as** *adv* (*Reg Gheg*) = **shtru'ar**

** **shtru'e|me** *nf (e)* mattress, bed

shtru'e|s

I § *adj* serving to lay: laying, paving

II § *n* person who lays something: layer

shtru'e|s|e *nf* machine used to lay something: layer

shtruf *nm* **1** (*Old*) ring that hold the barrel and stock together in old guns **2** (*Reg*) goatskin thong used to tie up animals

shtru'ge *nf* wooden milk bucket

** **shtru'g|un** *adj (i)* (*Reg Gheg*) = **stru'kë**t

** **shtru'k**·*et* = **stru'k**·*et*

shtru'ngë *nf* **1** narrow runway in a goat/sheep pen into which animals are guided for individual handling **2** goat/sheep pen = **va'thë 3** small shallow channel dug from the irrigation canal into the irrigation ditch of a field **4** (*Colloq*) = **shtru'ngël**

shtru'ngël *nf* [*Dairy*] wooden pail used for milking

shtrungë'tar *n* [*Dairy*] person who milks animals in a milking enclosure: milker

** **sh|trups|o**·*n vt* to maim, deform, disfigure

** **shtrush** *nm* rush (of water); rustle (of leaves)

shtruthu'llë *nf* [*Bot*] an Iranian plant that produces edible rice-like seeds (*Morina persica*)

shtrydh· *vt* **1** to squeeze out []: squeeze; squeeze [] dry **2** (*Fig*) to grab and squeeze [someone] **3** (*Fig*) to squeeze [] down to the essentials

○ **e shtrydh**· **lopën** to squeeze the last drop out of the cow

○ **(e) shtrydh**· **(mirë) mendjen** "squeeze one's mind" to think hard: rack one's brains

○ **shtrydh**· **sytë** to make a pretense of crying

○ **shtrydh**· **trutë** "squeeze one's brains" to think hard: rack one's brains

○ **i shtrydh**· **xhepat** "squeeze <>'s pockets" to squeeze the last cent out of <>

○ **<> shtrydh**· **zëmrën** to tear at <>'s heart, tug at <>'s heartstrings

shtry'dh·*et vpr* **1** (*Colloq*) to hold back in talking, keep something back **2** (*Fig*) (of clouds) to release rain

** **shtrydh|a'k**

I § *adj* = **shtry'dhës**

II § *nm* squeezer

shtry'dh|c *nm* press = **shtry'dhëse**

** **shtry'dh|c|a** *np* **1** <**shtrydhc 2** mangle

shtry'dh|ës *adj* serving to squeeze: squeezing

shtry'dh|ëse *nf* squeezer; mangle

shtrydhë'tar

I § *adj* (*Pej*) exploitative

II § *n* exploiter

shtry'dh|ëz *nf* [*Bot*] wild strawberry (*Fragaria vesca*)

shtry'dh|je *nf ger* <**shtry'dh**·, **shtry'dh**·*et*

shtrydh|o're *nf* = **shtry'dhëse**

shtry'dh|ur *adj (i)* squeezed dry/out

shtry'dh|ur|a *np (të) fem* pressings, squeezings

** **shtrrâ|j** *nf* (*Reg Gheg*) [*Bot*] plant runner

** **shtrra'k** *nm (np ˜ qe)* **1** partition wall **2** [*Anat*] caul: amnion () **3** sloughed skin (of a reptile): slough

** **shtrri** *nf collec* young livestock: lambs and kids

** **shtrri'|a** *OR* **shtrria'kë** *np fem* = **shtrri**

shtu·ar
I § *nf (e)* supplement, appendage
II § *nn (të)* breeding, propagation

shtu·ara *adv (Reg)* on/to one's feet: standing up

shtu|e·shëm *adj (i)* **1** capable of expansion; expanding when boiled **2** prolific

shtuf
I § *nm* **1** pumice **2** sandstone **3** [*Anat*] upper-arm bone: humerus
II § *adj* of pumice; of sandstone

shtufa·k *adj* = **shtufo·r**

shtufishtë *nf* area with pumice stone; soil of crumbled pumice; poor soil

shtu·fje *adj* August-ripening pear with large, very sweet, mushy fruit

shtufo·r *adj* composed of pumice; pumice-like

shtuftinë *nf* = **shtufishtë**

shtuk *nm* putty, mastic, spackle

shtuni·ak *nm (Reg)* overnight guest coming on business or encountered by chance

shtu·në *nf (e)* Saturday

shtupe·llë *nf (Old)* heavy wrapping paper for groceries

shtu·pë
I § *nf* **1** tow, oakum **2** plug (usually made of wadded-up rag); washrag **3** food chewed up into a hard-to-swallow wad; tough and dry wad **4** [*Bot*] kind of grass (*Diplachne serotina*)
II § *adj* dry and hard to chew

***shtu·pës** *nm* sandstone

shtupi·m *nm ger* < **shtupo··n**

shtupo··n *vt* to stop up [] with a plug: plug

shtupo·s· *vt* = **shtupo··n**

shtupo·sje *nf ger* = **shtupi·m**

shtupo·sur *adj (i)* sealed by a plug: plugged

shtupu·es *nm* person who seals leaks on a boat

shtu·r *stem for pdef* < **shti·e·**

shtu·rë *nf* [*Ornit*] starling (*Sturnus vulgaris L.*)

shturma·n
I § *nm* navigator
II § *adj* *navigational

shty·het *vpr* **1** to push and shove; shove each another **2** to move away a little to make room: shove down **3** *(Fig)* to push on: advance
∘ **nuk shty·het më gjatë/tutje** not extend/go any further

shty·n *vt* **1** to push; push back [] **2** to poke [] lightly (in order to attract []'s attention); impel, induce, instigate; provoke, irritate **3** to push/force [] back: repel **4** to put off [] until later: delay, postpone **5** to swallow [] down **6** to manage to get through [a period of time], make it through []: pull through []
∘ **shty·n gardhin** "push the wicker fence" to move a boundary marker (in order to extend one's property)
∘ **shty·n gjylen** [*Sport*] to put the shot; be a shotputter
∘ **shty·n kufirin** "push the boundary" to move a boundary marker (in order to extend one's property)
∘ [] **shty·n me gjoks** to accomplish [] by insistent/persistent pushing
∘ [] **shty·n me hosten** to force [] to do something against []'s will
∘ **shty·n mezhdën** "push the embankment" to move a boundary marker (in order to extend one's property)

∘ [] **shty·n për ditën e moskurrit** *(Iron)* to put [] off to some indefinite time in the future
∘ **shty·n urët** "poke/disturb the burning embers" to exacerbate bad feelings: stir the pot

***shtyllajë** *nf* colonnade = **shtyllnajë**

shtylla·k
I § *nm* doorjamb
II § *adj* **1** tall and strong (like a post) **2** *(Fig)* reliable, trustworthy

shtylla·r *nm* supporting pillar

shtyllë
I § *nf* **1** column; pillar, post **2** [*Soccer*] bar in the frame of the goalpost **3** *(Fig)* main support, bearer of the major burden: pillar (of society), breadwinner (of the family)
II § *adj* holding firm: unshakable, steadfast, staunch
∘ **shtyllë çeliku** pillar of steel, unbreakable and unyielding, tower of strength
∘ **shtyllë feneri** lamppost
∘ **shtylla kurrizore/e kurrizit** [*Anat*] spinal column
∘ **shtyllë shpinore** spinal column

shtyllëngu·lë *nf* piling; paling, palisade

shtyllërrah·ës *nm* [*Tech*] pile driver
∘ **shtyllërrahës lundrues** [*Tech*] floating pile driver

shtyllëz *nf* **1** [*Bot*] style (bearing the stigma of the ovary) **2** *(Dimin)* = **shty·llë**

shtyllnajë *nf* [*Arch*] colonnade, arcade

***shtyllo··n** *vt* to prop/shore [] up

***shtyllo·s·** *vt* = **shtyllo··n**

***shtyllo·sur** *adj (i)* **1** pillar-like **2** pillared

***shty·m** *part (Reg Gheg)* < **shty·n**

shty·më *nf* push, shove

shtyp *nm* **1** publishing by means of a press: printing, print **2** printed journalism: the press
∘ **shtyp i lartë** **1** [*Publ*] letterpress printing; object produced by letterpress **2** raised type
∘ **shtyp i rrafshët/sheshtë** [*Publ*] flatbed/planographic printing
∘ **shtyp i thellë** [*Publ*] letterpress printing; object produced by letterpress; intaglio printing
∘ **shtyp i ulët** [*Publ*] duplication by stencil; stencil duplicate

shtyp· *vt* **1** to press down hard on []: crush **2** to massage **3** *(Fig)* to suppress **4** to print [] (in a press), publish
∘ [] **shtyp·**^3pl **ethet** [] *feels* feverish, [] *has* a slight fever
∘ <>a **shtyp· kokën** **1** to make <> behave: tame <>'s orneriness, break <> **2** to take care of <> for good; kill <>
∘ <> **shtyp· kripë mbi kokë** "crush salt on <>'s head" to make <> suffer greatly, become a big headache to <>
∘ **shtyp· pleshta** "squash fleas" to spend one's time doing useless work; twiddle one's thumbs
∘ **shtyp· ujë në havan** "pound water in a mortar" to waste one's time/effort
∘ <>a **shtyp· zemrën** to tug at <>'s heartstrings

shty·p·et *vpr* **1** to get crushed; crowd together closely **2** *(Fig Colloq)* to shrink from doing something, be reluctant/hesitant about doing something

shtypa·r *nm (Reg)* wooden mortar

shtyp·c *nm* = **shty·pës**

shtype·c *nm* pestle

shty|**p**|**ël** *nf* perceptible trace left by pressure: impression, imprint; stamp; dent

***shty**|**p**|**ëm** *adj (i)* imprinted; printed

shty|**p**|**ës**
   I § *adj* **1** exerting heavy pressure **2** serving to crush: crushing **3** oppressive, repressive, suppressive
   II § *nm* device/tool for exerting pressure: pestle; press; roller; rammer; plunger of a churn
   III § *n (Fig)* oppressor; suppressor

shty|**p**|**ëse** *nf* **1** mortar (used with a pestle) **2** press

shty|**p**|**ët** *adj (i)* pressed down, flattened

shty|**p**|**je** *nf ger* **1** <**shty**·p·, **shty**·p·*et* **2** pressure = **trysn**|**i** **3** dent

shty|**p**|**kë** *nf* **1** interior angle between two walls: corner **2** wooden gusset reinforcing each corner of a door

shtyp|**shkr**|**im** *nm (Book)* printing, publishing

shtyp|**shkr**|**o**|**një** *nf* printing establishment: printer

shtyp|**shkr**|**u**|**a**·*n* *vt (Old)* to print, publish

shtyp|**shkr**|**u**|**ar** *adj (i) (Old)* printed, published

shtyp|**shkr**|**u**|**es** *nm (Old)* **1** printer (in the printing trade) **2** publisher

shtyp|**to**|**re** *nf (Old)* = shtypshkro|n*ë*

shty|**pur**
   I § *adj* **1** crushed; crushed flat; flat **2** severely oppressed, suppressed **3** printed, published; typed
   II § *n (i)* oppressed person
   III § *nf (e)* dent
   ∘ **i shtypur me këmbë bibash** dim-witted

***shty**|**r** *vt* **1** = shty·*n* **2** to cross [a river]

shty|**r** *stem for sg pdef, part* <shti·e·

shtyr|**ana**|**k** *OR* **shtyr**|**ani**|**k** *nm* premature baby; stillborn baby

shty|**rë**
   I § *part* <shti·e·
   II § *part* <**shty**·n, **shty**·*het*
   III § *adj (i)* **1** put up to it by someone else: pushed into it **2** *(Fig)* postponed, put off **3** aged, old
   IV § *nf (e)* push, shove
   ∘ **ësh·të shtyrë në moshë** (of a person) to have become of advanced age, have gotten old
   ∘ **i shtyrë në mot** of advanced years: elderly
   ∘ **ësh·të shtyrë në pije** to have become a real drunk

shty|**r**|**ës** *n* **1** instigator, inciter **2** cattle prod, goad

shty|**r**|**je** *nf ger* **1** <**shty**·*n*, **shty**·*het* **2** push, shove

shty|**së** *nf* push, shove; motive, impetus

***shty**|**t** *stem for imper, pdef, opt, adm, part* <**shty**·n

shty|**t**|**ës**
   I § *adj* **1** providing the driving power: driving, propellant **2** instigating, instigative
   II § *nm* **1** [*Tech*] propelling device: driver, impeller **2** = **shty**'s*ë*
   III § *n* **1** instigator, inciter **2** worker whose job requires pushing: pusher **3** [*Sport*] shotputter

shty|**t**|**ëse** *nf* [*Tech*] propelling device: driver, impeller

shty|**t**|**je** *nf ger* **1** = shty|r**je 2** [*Sport*] press (in weight lifting)

shty|**t**|**kë** *nf* **1** protective waterproof diaper cloth **2** a little push: impetus, incentive

shty|**t**|**ur** *nf (e)* push, shove

sh|**tha** *stem for pdef* <shtho·të

sh|**tha**|**shë** *1st sg pdef* <shtho·të

sh|**the** *2nd sg pdef* <shtho·të

sh|**the**|**m** *1st sg pres & subj* <shtho·të

sh|**the**|**mi** *1st pl pres* <shtho·të

sh|**thë**|**n** *stem for part, opt, adm* <shtho·të

sh|**thë**|**n** *ë part* <shtho·të

sh|**thë**|**rr**|**e**|**s** *stem for 1st sg pres, 1st & 3rd pl pres, 2nd & 3rd* <**shthërr**e·t

sh|**thërr**|**et**· *vt* to notify [guests] that the wedding has been called off

sh|**thërr**|**is** *stem for 2nd pl pres, pind* <shthërre·t·

sh|**thërr**|**it** *stem for pdef, opt, adm, part, pind, 2nd pl pres, imper, vp* <**shthërr**e·t·

sh|**thirr** *stem for pdef, opt, adm, part, imper, vp* <**shthërr**e·t·

sh|**thi**|**rr**|**ës** *nm* messenger notifying guests that the wedding has been called off

sh|**thirr**|**je** *nf ger* <shthërre·t·

shtho·**të** *vi* to take back what one says: unsay

sh|**tho**|**në** *3rd pl pres & subj* <shtho·të

sh|**tho**|**ni** *2nd pl pres* <shtho·të

sh|**tho**|**sh** *stem for pind* <shtho·të

sh|**thu** *stem for vp* <shtho·të

sh|**thu**|**a** *2nd sg pres* <shtho·të

sh|**thu**|**aj** *2nd sg imper* <shtho·të

sh|**thu**|**ash** *2nd sg subj* <shtho·të

sh|**thur**· *vt* **1** to undo [something woven/braided]: unravel, unbraid **2** *(Fig)* to ease up on [ ], slacken **3** *(Fig)* to free [ ] from moral constraint: corrupt, unleash
   ∘ **e shthur· gojën 1** *(Pej)* to use dirty language **2** to talk back
   ∘ <>**i shthur· mendimet** to disorder <>'s thoughts, disrupt train of thought

sh|**thur**·*et vpr* **1** to become unwoven: unravel **2** *(Fig)* to become loose and disorganized: fall apart, unravel; ease up, become slack; become undisciplined/dissolute
   ∘ <> **shthur**·*et*³ᵖˡ **mendimet** <> loses <>'s train of thought

sh|**thur**|**ës** *adj* leading to degeneration/breakdown

sh|**thur**|**je** *nf ger* **1** <shthur·, shthur·*et* **2** lack of organization/discipline; decomposition, breakdown; dissoluteness, degeneration, degeneracy

sh|**thur**|**ur** *adj (i)* **1** unplaited, unwoven, unknitted **2** *(Fig)* disjointed, disorganized; slack **3** intemperate, dissolute

sh|**thurr** = shthur|

shu·**het** *vpr* to come to a gradual end: (of a sound) fade out, die down; (of a fire/light) go out; (of an electrical apparatus) go off; (of a person) become exhausted, die; (of a family/people) die out; (of a motor) stop, die; (of writing) become faint and illegible; (of a habitation) go into ruin, be abandoned; (of a duty/privilege/punishment) expire, terminate; (of a desire/need) to be satisfied/relieved; (of liquids) get diluted; (of food) get basted; (of quicklime) become hydrated
   ∘ <> **shu**·*het*³ˢᵍ **fara** "<>'s seed *disappears*" <> completely *disappears*
   ∘ **shu**·*het*³ᵖˡ **gjakrat** tempers *cool*
   ∘ **Nuk shuhet pazari për gjilpëra.** "The market never runs out of needles." *(Prov)* There are plenty more fish in the sea.
   ∘ <> **shu**·*het*³ˢᵍ **pragu** <> has no family anymore: <> *is* all alone in the world
   ∘ **shu**·**het si shkëndijë** to die suddenly, be gone in an instant

○ <> **shu·***het*[3pl] **sytë** (Elev) <>'s eyes stop seeing: <> *dies*

○ <> **shu·***het*[3sg] **ylli** "the star has gone out" <> *is all gone, there is absolutely no more* <>

shu·*n vi* to be silent/quiet, say nothing

shua·*n*

I § *vt* **1** to extinguish: quench [something burning]; satisfy [a desire]; turn/switch off [something operating] **2** (Fig) to cause [] to disappear gradually: obliterate, erase; fade [] out **3** (Colloq) to wipe [] out; spend [] all, completely tire [out]: exhaust; beat up [] **4** to cool/dilute [] by adding liquid

II § *vi* (Colloq) to cease; die

○ **shua·***n* **etjen** to quench/satisfy/slake one's thirst

○ <>**a shua·***n* **farën** to get rid of <> completely, make <> disappear completely, wipe out every last trace of <>

○ **shua·***n* **gëlqeren** to slake lime

○ [] **shua·***n* **me** {} (Pej) to smother/pelt [] with {}

○ <>**a shua·***n* **oxhakun** to wipe out all the members of <>'s family; bring <>'s family line to a close

○ **shua·***n* **uri** to appease/slake one's hunger

○ **e shua·***n* **zjarrin** "put out the fire" to calm down the situation, pour water on the fire: calm the raging waters

shu|**all** *nm (np ˜ j)* **1** leather for shoe soles; shoe sole **2** sole of the foot **3** (Reg) short heavy wool sock worn indoors over regular stockings: wool slipper; slipper sole

shu|**ar** *adj (i)* **1** extinguished **2** turned off, not in operation **3** (Fig Colloq) wiped out **4** (Euph) dead, deceased **5** (Fig Colloq) orphaned and alone; childless **6** forlorn, wretched **7** weak, faint; dim **8** (of liquor) diluted; (of lime) slaked

○ **i shuari me bojë** the poor thing!

shu|**a'r|ës** *nm* **1** [Tech] quicklime hydrator (for making slaked lime) **2** rubber eraser

shu|**a'rje** *nf ger* **1** < **shua·***n*, **shu·***het* **2** extinction

*⃰**shu**|**ell** = **shu**|**all**

shufala'k *adj* (Pej) slovenly in dress: dowdy

shu|**fël** *nf* **1** old rag **2** debris carried into the air by flames

shu|**fër** *nf* **1** thin bare stick, withe **2** rod, bar; pole, picket **3** flailing blow **4** metal coil used to heat water

shu|**fkë** *adj, nf* (vegetable) that seems ripe on the outside but is empty inside

shufl|**ak** *adj* dressed in rags, tattered

shufr|**im** *nm* < **shufro·***n*

shufro|**·***n vt* **1** to weave [] with withes **2** to beat [] with a thin stick: flog, thrash; lambaste

*⃰**shufull**|**i·***n vi* to murmur

shuga|**s** *stem for 1st sg pres, pl pres, 2nd & 3rd sg subj, pind* < **shuga·***t*·

shuga·*t*· *vt* to put an end to []: extinguish, quell

shuga·*t*·*et vpr* to wane; fade out

shuga|**tur** *adj (i)* faded, dim

*⃰**shug**|**ëll|aq** *adj* trembling

*⃰**shug**|**ëll|o·***n vi* to tremble; (of leaves) rustle, quake

shugur|**im** *nm ger* **1** < **shuguro·***n*, **shuguro·***het* **2** consecration

shuguro|**·***het vpr* [Relig] to receive consecration/ordination

shuguro|**·***n vt* [Relig] **1** to consecrate **2** to ordain

shuguru|**ar** *adj (i).* consecrated

shuj *imper* < **shu·***n* be quiet! hush!

shu|**jt** *stem for pdef, opt, adm, part, vp* < **shu·***n*

*⃰**shujt**|**ar** *adj* nutritive

shujt|**ë** *nf* feed, food, foodstuff

shujt|**o·***het vpr* to take food: feed, eat

shujt|**o·***n vt* to give [] food: feed []

shujt|**uar** *adj (i)* fed, well-fed

*⃰**shujt**|**ues** *adj* nutritious

shuk

I § *nm* wadded-up mass of a soft substance: lump, ball, wad

II § *adv* **1** in a wad/lump, lumped into a little ball **2** dead on the spot

○ **shuka gjeli** little balls of dough fed to turkeys to fatten them

○ **shuk e puk** in a huddled heap

shuk· *vt* **1** to wad up [], lump [] into a little ball **2** to beat/hit [] hard, slug; slam; knock down **3** to shake

○ [] **shuk·** **me dru** to give [] a bad beating: beat [] to a pulp

○ **shuk·** **zërin** "wad up the voice" (Impol) to stop talking: put a sock in it, shut up

shu|**k·***et vpr* **1** to crouch, squat **2** to fall down lifelessly; fall dead on the spot **3** to shake apart, bump along **4** to wrestle each other to the ground

shuka|**s** *stem for 1st sg pres, pl pres, 2nd & 3rd sg subj, pind* < **shuka·***t*·

shuka·*t*· *vt* to wad up [], lump [] into a little ball

○ **Shukat!** Shut up! Put a sock in it!

shuka·*t*·*et vpr* to crouch, squat

shu|**k|je** *nf ger* **1** < **shuk·**, **shu·k·***et* **2** sharp hit: jolt, shake

shuk|**o·***s· vt* to wad up [], lump [] into a little ball

shuk|**o·***s·et vpr* to crouch, squat

shukre|**të** *nf* slap

shu|**k|thi** *adv* in a ball = **to'pthi**

shu|**kull** *nm (np ˜ j)* [Bot] pepperwort, peppergrass, pepper cress (Lepidium) = **dje'gës 2** upright mignonette (Reseda alba)

shukull|**o're** *np* [Bot] mignonette family Resedaceae

shul

I § *nm* **1** wooden pole **2** gate bar; door bolt **3** gun bolt **4** roller bar; cylinder **5** (Colloq) boatmast **6** tie beam in a roof truss **7** = **tredh**|**ës 8** (Reg) = **vig 9** (Fig Colloq) brawny person; tall dolt

II § *adv* **1** crosswise, sideways; aslant, obliquely; askew, awry, lopsided **2** in the wrong direction: backwards **3** frankly **4** henceforth, from then on

○ **shul gardhi** "fence post" (Impol) blockhead, idiot

○ **shul mullari** wooden pole at the center of a haycock

○ **shul e tërthor** crisscross

shu|**l·***et vpr* **1** to hang askew; turn (oneself) askew **2** = **shular·***et*

shul|**ajkë** *nf* = **shula'rkë**

shula'k *adj, n* stout/brawny (person)

shul|**ama'q** *adj, n* (Pej) bowlegged (person) with a waddling gait

shul|**ana'k** *nm* **1** tie beam in a roof truss **2** roller (on a loom)

shula'q *adj* (Pej) = **shulama'q**

shul|**a'r** *nm* long straight piece of wood: wooden bar

shular·*et vpr* to lie askew

shul|**a're** *nf* side beam of a cart

shula'rkë *nf* short piece of wood: rod

shulas adv **1** crosswise, sideways; sidesaddle *2 lying on the ground

shulc nm = **shulës**

shulës nm **1** gate/door bar, door bolt **2** roller (on a loom)

shulët adj (i) **1** lopsided, slanting, crooked **2** = **shulmë**

shulicë nf **1** [Naut] sailyard **2** (Reg) gate/door bar **3** mast

shulk nm (np ˜q) [Hist] servant = **shkarth**

shulmë adj (i) level, flat, smooth

shulnajë nf = **pjerrësirë**

shulo ·het vpr to get bent over; become stooped

shulo ·n vt **1** to set [] on a slant, place/bend [] askew **2** to cut [] down **3** to bar/bolt [a door/gate] **4** (Colloq) to hit [] with a stick: cane

shulor adj long and crooked

shulore nf **1** road that goes up a hill/mountainside on a slant *2 taproot

shulq np = **shulk**

shultinë nf (Reg) particular time; season; proximate time

shulthi adv crosswise, transversely; aslant, obliquely; askew, awry, lopsided

shullan nm [Zool] sand viper, nose-horned viper (Vipera ammodytes)

shullâ(n) (Reg Gheg) = **shullë**(r)

shullatë nf (Reg) spout through which water comes with force

shullë(r) nm (np ˜re) **1** sunny place out of the wind, sunbathed area **2** sunbathing **3** (Fig) to lie around idly

shullë ·het vpr to bask in the sun, sunbathe

shullë ·n vt (of the sun) to warm; tan

shullër sg pdef, part <**shullë ·n**

shullërë part <**shullë ·n**

shullëri
  I § obl <**shullë**
  II § sg pdef, part <**shullë**(r)

*****shulltore** nf pear tree with grafts: grafted pear tree

shuma nf (e) = **shumta**

shumanësi nf = **shumanshmëri**

shumanshëm adj (i) **1** many-sided; from multiple points of view **2** broadly knowledgeable, polymathic, versatile; broad-ranging **3** = **shumëpalësh**

shumanshmëri nf **1** many-sidedness **2** multifariousness, diversity

shumatomik adj [Chem] poly-atomic

*****shumbricë** nf [Bot] = **zhumbricë**

shumë
  I § quant (followed by a noun) much, many, a lot of
  II § pcl (followed by an adjective/adverb) very, quite
  III § adv **1** very much, a lot; to a great degree/extent **2** too much **3** for a long time
  IV § adj (i) = **shumtë**
  ○ **ësh-të**[pl] **shumë shokë/miq** to be close friends
  ○ **shumë babo e mbytin fëmijën** too many cooks spoil the broth
  ○ **shumë hollë** in straightened circumstances
  ○ **shumë kush** many a one
  ○ **shumë më __** much more __, much __er
  ○ **shumë i nderuar** right honorable
  ○ **Shumë pula e pak vezë.** "Many chickens and few eggs." It's a lot of big talk but not much action. Talk is cheap.

○ **Shumë pupla e pak mish.** "Many feathers and little meat." (Prov) Much smoke and little fire. Plenty of talk but little action.
  ○ **shumë e shumë** in abundance
  ○ **shumë shumë 1** at most *2 on the whole

shumë nf **1** sum **2** amount, quantity; sum/amount of money
  ○ **shumë e përgjithshme** grand total

shumë formativ mult-, poly-, many-

shumëbarrëshe adj [Med] multigravida, multipara

shumëbazik adj [Chem] polybasic

shumëbërthamor adj [Biol Med] multinucleate

shumëdashur adj (i) much-loved, beloved

shumëdegësh adj having many branches: multibranched

shumëdëshiruar adj (i) much-desired, eagerly-awaited

shumëditësh adj = **shumëditor**

shumëditor adj of many days' duration

shumëfaqësh adj [Geom] polyhedral

shumëfarësh adj = **shumëllojshëm**

shumëfazësh adj multiphasic

shumëfazor adj [Electr] polyphase

shumëfijësh adv composed of many strands

shumëfish
  I § nm, adj multiple
  II § adj, adv many times greater/larger/more; manyfold

shumëfishim nm ger <**shumëfisho ·n**, **shumëfisho ·het**

shumëfisho ·het vpr to increase manyfold: multiply

shumëfisho ·n vt **1** to increase [] manyfold: multiply **2** to make many copies of []: duplicate [] in multiple copies **3** [Text] to combine multiple strands into one

shumëfishtë adj (i) **1** composed of multiple parts/entities **2** manyfold **3** [Math] divisible with no remainder: simply multiple, evenly factorable, integrally divisible

shumëfishuar adj (i) **1** increased by many times **2** [Text] composed of multiple strands: multiply

shumëfishues
  I § adj serving to duplicate/increase manyfold
  II § nm multiplying device: multiplier

shumëfjalësh adj [Ling] consisting of many words: multi-word

shumëfletësh adj (of plywood) multi-ply; multileafed

shumëformësi nf (Book) multiformity

shumëformësh adj multiform

shumëfrymësh adj composed of many individuals, having many members

shumëgarësh nm [Sport] contest in which performance in multiple events is scored: multiple-event meet

shumëgarist n [Sport] athlete trained for or participating in a multiple-event meet

shumëgjuhëshëm adj (i) multilingual, polyglot

shumëgjymtyrësh adj [Ling] having multiple constituents, multiplex

shumëhamës
  I § adj (Reg Gheg) greedy
  II § n glutton

shum**ë**he'ra *adv* frequently, often

shum**ë**her'sh**ë**m *adj (i)* frequent

shum**ë**kanal|**ë**sh *adj* [*Brdcast*] multichannel

shum**ë**kat|**ë**sh *adj* multistoried

shum**ë**k**ë**mb|**ë**sh *nm* [*Invert*] millipede *(Myriapoda)*

shum**ë**k**ë**'nd *acc* <shum**ë**ku'sh

shum**ë**k**ë**nd|**ë**sh
  I § *adj* polygonal
  II § *nm* polygon

shum**ë**ko'k|**ë**sh *adj* many-headed

shum**ë**ko'mb|**ë**sh *adj* multinational

shum**ë**kre'r|**ë**sh *adj* = shum**ë**ko'k**ë**sh

shum**ë**ku'jt *dat/abl* <shum**ë**ku'sh

shum**ë**ku'nd *adv* in many places

shum**ë**kuptim|**ë**si *nf* [*Ling*] polysemy

shum**ë**kuptim'sh**ë**m *adj (i)* [*Ling*] polysemantic

shum**ë**kuro'r**ë**sh|e *adj* [*Law*]

shum**ë**ku'sh *pron* many people, many

shum**ë**lloj|**ë**si *nf (Book)* = shum**ë**llojshm|**ë**ri

shum**ë**llo'jsh**ë**m *adj (i)* of various/diverse kinds; highly variegated; diverse

shum**ë**llojshm|**ë**ri *nf (Book)* great diversity/variety

shum**ë**llo'jt**ë** *adj (i)* = shum**ë**llo'jsh**ë**m

shum**ë**mi'j|**ë**sh *adj* numbering many thousands

shum**ë**milia'rd|**ë**sh *adj* numbering in the billions; worth billions

shum**ë**milio'n|**ë**sh *adj* numbering in the millions; worth millions

shum**ë**ndera'r *adj (i)* highly honored, revered

shum**ë**ndri'tur *adj (i)* illustrious

shum**ë**ndu'arsh**ë**m *adj (i)* of diverse kinds

*shum**ë**ngr**ë**n|**ë**s *adj* having a big appetite; voracious

shum**ë**ngjyr**ë**'sh *adj* 1 multicolored 2 *(Fig Book)* of various political stripes

shum**ë**ngjy'r**ë**t *adj (i)* = shum**ë**ngjy'r**ë**sh

shum**ë**ngjy'rsh**ë**m *adj (i)* 1 multicolored 2 *(Fig)* various, diverse

shum**ë**pa'l|**ë**sh *adj* involving multiple parties: multipartite, multilateral

shum**ë**pe't|**ë**sh *adj* having multiple thin layers: multilayered, multifoliate

shum**ë**pi'k|**ë**sh *nm* [*Ling*] ellipsis (punctuation mark)

*shum**ë**pje'll|**ë**s *adj* prolific

shum**ë**pje'll|**ë**sh|e *adj fem* [*Biol*] multiparous

shum**ë**pje's|**ë**sh *adj* consisting of multiple parts: multipartite

shum**ë**po'l|**ë**sh *adj* multipolar

shum**ë**pri'tur *adj (i)* long-awaited; eagerly-awaited

*shum**ë**qeliza'r = shum**ë**qelizo'r

shum**ë**qelizo'r *adj, n* [*Biol*] multicellular (organism)

shum**ë**rro'k|**ë**sh *adj* [*Ling*] polysyllabic

shu'm**ë**s *adj, nm* [*Ling*] plural

shum**ë**sekto'r|**ë**sh *adj* [*Econ*]

shum**ë**si' *nf* 1 multiplicity; large quantity/amount 2 *(Old)* largest part: majority, bulk *3 crowd

shum**ë**shekull|o'r *adj* of many centuries, centuries-long

shum**ë**shka'll|**ë**sh *adj* conducted in indirect stages: multistage

shum**ë**shtre's|**ë**sh *adj* multilayered

shum**ë**-shum**ë** *adv* 1 at most; more or less 2 the most possible; to the greatest extent

shum**ë**to'n|**ë**sh *adj* weighing many tons; capable of bearing tons of weight

shum**ë**trajt|**ë**sh *adj* polymorphic

shum**ë**trajtsh**ë**m *adj (i)* = shum**ë**tra'jt**ë**sh

shum**ë**vale'nt *adj* 1 [*Chem*] polyvalent 2 *(Book)* multivalent

shum**ë**varia'nt|**ë**sh *adj (Book)* having many variants

shum**ë**ve'nd|**ë**sh *adj* having room for many people: large-capacity

shum**ë**v**ë**lli'm|**ë**sh *adj* multivolume

shum**ë**vjeça'r *adj* 1 of many years; long-term 2 [*Bot*] perennial

*shum**ë**vo'jtur *(Reg)* = shum**ë**vu'ajtur

shum**ë**vu'ajtur *adj (i)* long-suffering

shum**ë**z**ë**'r|**ë**sh
  I § *adj* 1 composed of many voices 2 [*Mus*] polyphonic
  II § *nm* [*Mus*] polyphony

shum**ë**zi'm *nm ger* 1 <shum**ë**zo' •n, shum**ë**zo' •het 2 [*Math*] multiplication

shum**ë**zo' •het *vpr* 1 to reproduce, multiply; propagate 2 to increase

shum**ë**zo' •n *vt* 1 to duplicate 2 to multiply 3 to increase []

shum**ë**zo'r *adj* [*Ling*]

shum**ë**zu'ar *adj (i)* [*Math*] = shum**ë**zu'esh**ë**m
  ∘ shum**ë**zuar me [] multiplied by []

shum**ë**zu'es
  I § *adj* 1 reproductive 2 [*Tech*] serving to multiply
  II § *nm* 1 [*Math*] multiplier 2 device that indicates multiples

shum**ë**zu'esh**ë**m *nm (i)* [*Math*] multiplicand

shumi'c**ë** *nf* 1 multitude; large quantity 2 majority
  ∘ shumica d**ë**rrmuese the overwhelming majority

shumi'm *nm ger* 1 <shumo' •n, shumo' •het 2 = shum**ë**zim

shumo' •het *vpr* 1 to increase 2 to reproduce, multiply

shumo' •n *vt* to increase [] in number/amount

shumo'r *adj* 1 *(Book)* cumulative; in total *2 multiple

shu'mta
  I § *nf (e)* greatest part: bulk, majority, most of it/ them
  II § *adv* at most

shu'mt**ë**
  I § *adj (i)* in large quantity; many, numerous
  II § *np (t**ë**)* 1 large number, the many: legion 2 the majority

shungull'im**ë** *nf* loud rumble

shungullo' •n
  I § *vi* 1 to rumble loudly, reverberate 2 to shake violently
  II § *vt* to shake/rock [] with force

*shungull|u'e's *adj* rumbling, reverberate

*shungull|u'e'sh**ë**m *adj (i)* = shungullu'es

*shu'nj**ë**z *nf (Old)* vegetable

*shu·pkë *nf* fruit without flesh inside: empty fruit, hollow nut

shupla·k· *vt* **1** to slap **2** to strike [] with a spell: bewitch

shupla·k·et *vpr* to become weak under the influence of a spell

shupla·kë *nf* **1** palm of the hand **2** slap; slap in the face **3** measure across the four fingers of one hand: handwidth **4** axe blade (without the heel)

shupla·kje *nf ger* <**shupla·k·, shupla·k·et**

shupla·kur *adj (i), n (i)* (person) languishing under a spell

shu·prag *nm* **1** left completely alone in the world, without close family = **pragshuar 2** *(Pej)* person who shows no concern for his family; incompetent/bootless person

*shu·pullë *nf* smack, slap

shur *nm* = **zhur**

shu·rbë *nf* [*Bot*] service tree *(Sorbus domestica)*

shurdh
  I § *adj, n* deaf (person)
  II § *adv (Fig)* still and deserted; without the sounds of someone who brought joy: joyless

shu·rdh·et *vpr* = **shurdho··het**

shurdha·c
  I § *nm* [*Bot*] great reed mace, broadleafed bulrush *(Typha latifolia)*
  II § *adj (Impol)* = **shurdha·q**

shurdha·k *adj (Impol)* stone deaf

shurdha·man *adj, n (Impol)* = **shurdha·q**

shurdha·q *adj, n (Impol)* stone deaf (person)

shurdha·vel *adj, n* = **shurdha·q**

shurdhe·së *nf* **1** animal's lair **2** = **shurrëqe·nëz**

shu·rdhër
  I § *adj (i), n (i)* deaf (person)
  II § *adj (i)* muted, muffled, dull; quiet, silent
  III § *adv* **1** with a muffled/muted sound **2** *(Fig)* soundless and deserted; without the sounds of someone who brought joy: joyless

shurdhe·si *nf* **1** deafness **2** *(Fig)* deep silence

shu·rdhët
  I § *adj (i)* **1** deaf **2** *(Fig)* muffled, muted; (of a pain) dull **3** [*Ling*] voiceless
  II § *adv* with a muffled/muted sound

shurdhi *nf* [*Bot*] Hispania oak *(Quercus hispanica)*

shurdhi·je *nf* [*Bot*] kind of cork oak *(Quercus pseudosuber)*

shurdhi·m *nm ger* <**shurdho··n, shurdho··het**

shurdhi·jes *nf* **1** placenta **2** pus **3** *(Impol)* small and ugly person; socially worthless and immature person

shurdh|meme·c
  I § *adj* deaf and mute
  II § *n* deafmute

shurdho··het *vpr* **1** to go/become deaf **2** *(Fig)* to go silent, feel abandoned and lonely **3** (of damp powder or sterile seed) to become useless **4** [*Ling*] to lose its voicing: become voiceless

shurdho··n *vt* **1** to deafen **2** *(Fig Pej)* to tire [] out with constant noise/talking
  ∘ **<> shurdho··n veshët** "deafen/remove <>'s ears" to bore <*a listener*> to death; hammer constantly at <>

shurdh|uar *adj (i)* **1** deafened **2** (of damp powder or sterile seed) made useless

shurdh|ue·s *adj* deafening

shuri·shtë *nf* = **zhuri·shtë**

*shu·rkë *nf* stagnant pond

shurqe·l *nm* = **uje·varë**

shuruka·më *nf (Colloq)* din
  ∘ **do t'<> dëgjo··het[3sg] shurukama** there will be a big stink made about <>

shuruko··n *vi* to make a din

shuru·p *nm* **1** fruit syrup **2** [*Pharm*] medicinal syrup

shurr· *vi* to piss

shurra·k
  I § *adj (Impol)* bed-wetting
  II § *n (Impol)* bed wetter

shurra·man *n (Impol)* bed wetter

*shurra·q = **shurra·k**

shu·rrcë *nf* [*Anat*] = **shu·rrëz**

shu·rrë *nf* piss, urine

shurrë|gja·ke *nf* [*Veter*] = **shurrëku·qe**

shurrë|ku·qe *nf* [*Veter*] disease in livestock caused by a parasite that destroys red blood corpuscles and reddens the urine *(pyroplasmosis, haemasporidiosis)*

shurrë|pe·lë *nf* [*Bot*] Alpine buckthorn *(Rhamnus fallax)* = **arrç**

shurrë|pu·lë *nf* = **shurrëqe·nëz**

shurrë|qe·nëz *nf* **1** blood and pus oozing from a wound **2** blister on the heel

shu·rrëse *nf (Reg)* = **shty·tkë**

shurrë·tore *nf (Old)* public street urinal: pissoir

shu·rrëz *nf* [*Anat*] urethra

shurrë|zë·në *adj, n* **1** (person) who holds urine in and does not urinate **2** *(FigImpolite)* incompetent (ninny)

shurro··het *vpr (Crude)* to piss in one's pants; wet one's bed

shurro··n
  I § *vi (Crude)* to piss
  II § *vt (Crude)* to piss on []

shu·sh·et *vpr* = **shusha·t·et**

shusha·llë *nf* (shelled) corncob

shusha·q *adj (Impol)* = **shusha·tur**

shusha·s *stem for 1st sg pres, pl pres, 2nd & 3rd sg subj, pind* <**shusha·t·**

shusha·t· *vt* to drive [] daft/nuts; bewilder

shusha·t·et *vpr* **1** to go daft/nuts; become bewildered **2** to become senile

shusha·tje *nf ger* **1** <**shusha·t·, shusha·t·et 2** bewilderment

shusha·tur *adj (i)* **1** bewildered **2** daft; senile, dotty

shusha·vel *adj (Impol)* = **shushk**

shusha·vë *nf (Colloq)* aimless dispersal

*shusha·vis *stem for 1st sg pres, pl pres, 2nd & 3rd sg subj, pind* <**shushavit·**

*shushavi·t· *vt* to scatter, disperse

*shushavi·t·et *vpr* to lounge around, loiter

*shushavi·tur *adj (i)* **1** scattered, dispersed **2** loitering, time-wasting

shu·shël *nf (Reg)* covering of a seed food: (bean) pod, (corn) husk, chaff

shu·shk
  I § *adj (Impol)* hopelessly bewildered: nuts, daffy
  II § *n* nut, ninny, fool

shu·shkël = **shu·shël**

shu·shull *nf* **1** wood debris left by rushing mountain water **2** debris, trash, sweepings **3** *(Fig Pej)* dirty trash, dregs of society
  ∘ **shushull në sy** speck in the eye

shush|ulla·t·*et vpr* = **shusha·t**·*et*

shushu·një *nf* **1** leech **2** *(Fig Pej)* bloodsucker
∘ **shushunja e dardhës** [*Entom*] shiny fruit-damaging black insect with transparent wings
∘ **shushunja e të lashtave** [*Entom*] shiny blue-green bug that damages crops

shushu·q *adj, n* (person) who pronounces sibilants (hissing consonants) as shibilants (hushing consonants)

shush|uri·n *vi* **1** to make a continual susurrous sound **2** to whisper; rustle; sough

shush|urimë *nf* continual susurrous sound: rustle, whisper, sough

shush|uris *stem for 1st sg pres, pl pres, 2nd & 3rd sg subj, pind* < **shushurit**·

shush|urit· *vi* = **shushuri**·*n*

shush|uritës *adj* making a continual susurrous sound; whispering

shush|uritje *nf ger* = **shushurimë**

*__shush|uro·n__ *vi* = **shushuri**·*n*

shut|ër *nf* [*Med*] typhoid fever

*__shut|is__ *stem for 1st sg pres, pl pres, 2nd & 3rd sg subj, pind* < **shutit**·

*__shut|it·__ *vi* to hush, quiet; subdue

*__shut|itur__ *adj (i)* hushed, muffled; subdued

*__shut|o·n__ *= **shyto**·*n*

shu·tra *np fem* carding comb for wool; hackle board for flax

*__shutra·k__ *adj* [*Med*] typhous

shutr|o·*n vt* to card wool; hackle flax

shu·tull *adj, nf (Impol)* stupid/silly/crazy (woman)

*__shva·l__·*et vpr* to sink down

*__shval|inë__ *nf* **1** sunken area **2** place full of fallen debris

shvenk *nm* [*Cine*] Swiss-pan, flash-pan

*__sh|vërgjër__ = **zhvirgjër**

*__sh|vërgjin__ = **zhvirgjër**

*__shy|lazi__ *adv* = **shu·las**

shyl|o·s· *vt* to bar/bolt [a door/gate]

*__shymty·rë__ *nf* = **shëmti·rë**

shyqy·r
I § *interj (Colloq)* expresses pleasure at an outcome: that's lucky! good for __!
II § *nm (Old Colloq)* congratulations

shyt
I § *adj* **1** (of horned animals) missing horns **2** (of a vessel) missing its handle/spout/neck **3** blunt on top
II § *n* livestock animal missing its horns
III § *pred* **1** with a flat/even surface; blunt on top **2** half done, interrupted in the middle **3** *(Fig)* collapsed like an empty sack: limp

shy·ta *np fem* [*Med*] mumps *(epidemic parotitis)*

shyta·n *adj* (of an animal) missing its horns, polled

shy·të *nf, adj (Colloq)* flat-nosed (truck/lorry)

shyt|im *nm ger* < **shyto**·*n*, **shyto**·*het*

shyt|o·n *vt* **1** to break off the handle/spout/neck of [a vessel] **2** to trim/prune [a plant/tree] **3** to maim, amputate; truncate

t [të] nf **1** the consonant letter "t" **2** the voiceless postdental or alveolar apical stop represented by the letter "t"

t'et gen/abl/dat < i **ati** his/her/its/their father

t'i sequence of proclitics **1** conjunctive proclitic + 3rd sg referent **2** nd sg referent + 3rd sg referent **3** nd sg referent + 3rd pl object

○ **t'i lë· këmbët e arushës në dorë** {} would leave you in the lurch; {} would cheat you

t'ia sequence of proclitics conjunctive proclitic + 2nd sg referent + 3rd sg object

t'iu sequence of proclitics **1** conjunctive proclitic + 3rd sg referent + reflexive clitic **2** (Colloq) 2nd sg referent + 3rd sg referent + reflexive clitic

t'jau sequence of proclitics (Reg Colloq) **1** conjunctive proclitic + 3rd pl referent + 3rd sg object **2** conjunctive proclitic + 3rd pl referent 3rd pl object **3** conjunctive proclitic + 2nd pl referent + 3rd sg object **4** conjunctive proclitic + 2nd pl referent + 3rd pl object

t'ju sequence of proclitics conjunctive proclitic + 2nd pl

t'jua sequence of proclitics conjunctive proclitic + 2nd pl referent + 3rd object

*****t'onë** masc pl (Reg) our, of ours = **tanë**

t'u sequence of proclitics **1** conjunctive proclitic + reflexive clitic **2** conjunctive proclitic + 3rd pl referent 3 nd sg referent + reflexive **4** nd sg referent + 3rd pl referent **5** (Colloq) conjunctive proclitic + 2nd pl referent

t'ua sequence of proclitics conjunctive proclitic + 3rd pl referent + 3rd sg object

t'a sequence of clitics conjunctive proclitic + 3rd sg object

ta accus enclitic used directly after a preposition < **ata** them

tabaçinë nf **1** poor quality wool/goathair **2** hair removed from leather before tanning

tabak nm **1** large sheet (of paper, sheet metal); cigarette paper **2** (Old) tanner

tabakia nf **1** serving tray **2** box of tobacco

tabake nf serving tray

*****tabakhane** nf (Old) **1** tannery **2** tanners' neighborhood

tabako nf snuff

taban nm **1** sole (of the foot/shoe); insole of a shoe **2** hard foundation layer: hard stratum lying under cultivated ground, bedrock, bed (of a river); native soil **3** thick supporting beam: roof beam **4** crown of the head: pate **5** (Colloq) = **butt of a rifle**

tabare nf long heavy overcoat

tabelë nf **1** systematic arrangement of data: table; schedule **2** public bulletin board: advertising sign, plaque, poster

○ **tabelë e basketbollit** [Sport] backboard (in basketball)

○ **tabelë e zezë** blackboard

*****tabellë** = **tabelë**

tabiat nm (Colloq) particular manner: custom, nature, habit

tabje nf (Old) [Mil] entrenchment, trench

tabletë nf [Med] tablet, pill = **hape**

tablo nf **1** tableau **2** (Book) general outlook, broad picture

tabllo = **tablo**

tabor nm **1** [Hist] old Ottoman military unit of a thousand men = **batalion 2** (Fig Colloq) big gang of people

tabu nf taboo

tabut nm (Old) coffin; bier = **arkivol**

taç nm **1** last-born piglet in a litter; smallest piglet in a litter **2** youngest and favorite child: baby of the family **3** (Old) white fez with a green band marking the wearer as a sheikh, dervish, or Bektashi leader

taçe nf [Bot] hellebore (Helleborus)

*****taf** n [Ornit] kestrel

Tafil nm Tafil (male name)

taft nm (Colloq) **1** stink **2** emanation wafting from something very hot/cold **3** (Old) royal throne; position of high rank

○ **Tafti-bafti!** Let's take a chance! However it turns out! Whatever happens!

tafta nf taffeta

*****taftim** nm astonishment, shock

taftis· vt **1** to enthrall, enchant *****2** to enthrone

○ **taftis· mbas/pas <>** to be dazzled/spellbound by <>, be crazy about <>

taftis·et vpr to become enthralled/enchanted, be smitten

○ **taftis·et mbas/pas <>** to become crazy about <>

*****tagan** nm yataghan = **jatagan**

tagar nm (Old) **1** = **tangar 2** measure of approximately 6 kilograms

tagër nm **1** [Hist] tariff, tax **2** (Old) prerogative, right, entitlement *****3** (Old) copyright

tagrambledhës nm [Hist] tax collector, tax gatherer

tagrapagues nm [Hist] tax payer

tagrim nm [Hist] taxation

tagji nf fodder, horsefeed; feed grain

tagjis stem for 1st sg pres, pl pres, 2nd & 3rd sg subj, pind < **tagjit·**

tagjit· vt **1** to feed [an animal] fodder: fodder **2** (Fig Colloq) to feed [] well

tagjit·et vpr **1** to eat fodder **2** (Fig) to eat well

tahin nm (Old Colloq) allotted amount: ration

tahma = **tamah**

tahmin invar (Colloq Old)

tahsildar n (Old) [Hist] tax collector

*****tairë** nf = **tajer**

tajar n operator of a tool that operates with a revolving motion: lathe worker

tajer nm **1** long-handled paddle for moving bread in and out of the oven **2** breadboard, pastry board = **qer**

tajë nf **1** wet nurse **2** [Spec] screw **3** (Colloq) tool that operates with a revolving motion: vise, brace, lathe

*****tajfë** nf **1** = **taraf 2** crew **3** (Pej) clique

tajfu'n *nm* **1** typhoon **2** *(Fig)* powerful force/storm

ta'jgë *nf* [*Geog*] taiga

tajĩs | *stem for 1st sg pres, pl pres, 2nd & 3rd sg subj, pind* < **tajĩt·**

tajĩt·
  I § vt to breastfeed [someone else's baby], suckle [ ]
  II § vi to exude moisture: ooze, drip

ta'jkë *nf* [*Bot*] large thick-skinned grape with a long, tapering shape

Tajla'ndë *nf* Thailand

Tajva'n *nm* Taiwan

takamĩs· *vt* to equip: provide [a house] with furniture, furnish, outfit [a laboratory/workshop]

taka't *nm (Colloq)* strength, ability

ta'ke *nf* rowboat

taketu'ke *nf* ashtray

ta'kë *nf* **1** shoe heel; shoe cleat **2** [*Sport*] foul in soccer incurred by kicking an opponent with one's cleats

takëm *nm (Colloq)* set of things serving a particular function: furnishings, trappings, tack, utensils; harness
  ○ **takëm i kafes** coffee set/service
  ○ **takëm i ngrënies** eating utensils
  ○ **takëm i shalës** tackle (saddle and harness)
  ○ **takëm i shtëpisë** home furnishings; furniture

*****takëmĩs·** *vt* to fit [ ] out: equip, rig, harness

*****takëmĩsje** *nf ger* **1** < **takëmĩs·** **2** equipment, rigging, harness

ta'kër *nf* [*Bot*] marshmallow *(Althaea officinalis)*

taki'je *nf* **1** narrow peaked cap made of stitched double-ply cloth and worn characteristically by villagers in Myzeqe **2** quilted red fez worn by people in northern Albania

takikardĩ *nf* [*Med*] tachycardia

takĩm *nm ger* **1** < **takó·n, takó·het 2** arranged meeting: conference; appointment, date **3** hearing (held to hear complaints/petitions) **4** [*Sport*] encounter

takllĩmë *nf* **1** wooden clapper in a grain mill = **çaka'lle 2** large, long-necked, two-stringed mandolin

takllĩmëz *nf* **1** [*Anat*] eardrum **2** clapper on a mill hopper

takllo'·n *vi, vt* to rap, tap

*****ta'kma'k** *nm* = **tokma'k**

takó·het *vpr* **1** to come together: meet; have a meeting **2** to greet one another (by shaking hands) **3** to be encountered: come up, occur

takó·n
  I § vt **1** to bump/run into [ ]: encounter **2** to have a meeting with [ ]: meet **3** to touch [ ] (with a part of one's body); cause [ ] to touch
  II § vi **1** to touch/concern ◇ **2** to belong to ◇ **3** to happen
  ○ **tako·n në** [ ] to happen upon [ ], meet [ ] by chance, come across [ ]; strike [a mineral find]

*****takrava'te** *np* household utensils

taks· *vt (Colloq)* **1** to promise [something] to < *someone* > **2** [*Relig*] to pledge **3** to make a decision to do something: decide [something]
  ○ **taks· se** __ to suppose that __

ta'ks·et *vpr (Colloq)* to make a vow; take vows

taksamble'dhës *nm* tax collector

taksapague's *nm* taxpayer

*****taksa'të** *nf* taxation

ta'ksë *nf* tax, impost

taksĩ *nf* taxi

taksĩda'r *nm (Colloq)* tax collector

taksĩm *nm (Old)* [*Mus*] piece in free meter played by a solo instrument in a folk band

taksĩm *nm ger* **1** < **takso'·n 2** taxation

taksira't *nm (Colloq)* **1** piece of bad luck: misfortune, trouble **2** bad act: wrong, sin

taksira'tma'dh *adj, n (Colloq)* (person) constantly visited by misfortune: really unlucky (guy)

takso'·n *vt* to impose a tax on [ ]: tax

ta'ksur *nf(e) (Old)* promise

takt *nm* **1** tact **2** [*Mus*] tactus, beat; time signature **3** [*Ling*] part of the phrase that bears the phrasal stress: phrase head **4** [*Spec*] full cycle

tak-ta'k *onomat* tick-tock

taktĩk *adj* tactical

taktĩkë *nf* tactics
  ○ **taktika e tokës së djegur** scorched-earth tactics

takue's
  I § adj **1** [*Electr*] interrupting **2** [*Spec*] in contact: contacting
  II § nm [*Electr*] interrupter

tale'nt *n* **1** talent **2** talented person **3** [*Hist*] talent (unit of weight)

talentua'r *adj (i)* talented

ta'lë *nf (Colloq)* permitted/allocated amount; limit
  ○ **ve·te në talë** to eat one's fill, get full

ta'lër *nm* open vat

talĩkë *nf* small four-wheeled cart; four-wheeled wagon pulled by horses

talk *nm* talc

talmu'd *nm* Talmud

talmudĩst
  I § n (Book) **1** talmudist, Talmud scholar **2** scholiast; pedant
  II § adj (Book) talmudic, scholastic; pedantic

talmudĩzëm *nm (Book)* talmudism; scholasticism; pedantry

talu're *nf* large platter; large shallow bowl

*****ta'lvë** *nf* shelf; mantelpiece

tall· *vt* **1** to make fun of [ ]; ridicule; deride; taunt **2** to deceive [ ] with false hopes/promises, lead [ ] on: delude

ta'll·et *vpr* **1** to fiddle around, dawdle, dillydally **2** to be fooling: raise false hopes, make false promises, lead people on
  ○ **tall·et me** [ ] to make fun of [ ]; carry on insulting banter with [ ]

tallaba'k
  I § nm alluvial silt left on fields that gets hard when it dries
  II § adj (of soil) packed hard

tallaga'n *nm* **1** man's plain woolen cloak with a collar and short sleeves allowed to dangle empty **2** man's long overcoat that is either sleeveless or has false sleeves

*****tallallĩs** | *stem for 1st sg pres, pl pres & 3rd sg subj, pind* < **tallallĩt·**

*****tallallĩt·** *vt* = **tellallĩs·**

*****talla'nd** *nm (Old)* talent (unit of weight)

talla'sh *nm* residue/scraps left from sawing/planing/cutting a hard material: sawdust, shavings, chips

talla'z *nm* **1** large/violent ocean wave: heavy sea **2** *(Fig)* strong impulse, energetic force **3** *(Fig)* sea of troubles, terrible difficulties **4** wavy sheen

talla′ze-talla′ze *adv* in big waves

tallaz′ma′dh *OR* **tallaze′ma′dh|e** *adj* with heavy seas, having big waves

tallaz′o ·*het vpr* **1** to have big waves **2** to rock/shake back and forth, come in big waves
  ◦ <> **tallazo**·*het³ˢᵍ* **zemra** <> *gets very upset/worried*, <> *is shaken*

tallaz′o·*n vi* to have big waves

ta′llë *nf* **1** corncob **2** cornstalk; cornstraw **3** [*Bot*] Johnsongrass = **vu′l**ë**r** *4 cornhusk

ta′ll|ës
  I § adj derisive, mocking
  II § n derider, mocker

tall′ishtë *nf* **1** field with much Johnsongrass **2** field of corn stubble

ta′ll|je *nf ger* **1** <**ta′ll**·, **ta′ll**·*et* **2** ridicule, mockery

tallo′n *nm* ration card

tall′o′s *nm* straw waste left from threshing; chaff

*tall′o′z = tall′o′s

tama′h *nm* (*Colloq*) **1** voracious desire: greed, avarice **2** spiteful envy, jealousy

tamah′qar *adj, n* (*Colloq*) avaricious/greedy/envious (person)

tamah′qar|lë′k *nm* (*np ˜ qe*) (*Colloq*) **1** greediness, avariciousness **2** jealousy

tama′m
  I § pcl (*Colloq*) exactly, precisely; fully
  II § adv (*Colloq*) **1** exactly right **2** exactly alike
  ◦ **s′ësh·të tamam (nga koka)** not be right in the head

tama′m|të *adj (i)* exact; exactly alike

ta′mb|ël *nm* (*Reg*) milk = **qu′mësht**

tamb′ël′to′re *nf* [*Bot*] common dandelion (*Taraxacum officinale*) = **qumështo′re**

tamblaˈgja′k *nm* [*Bot*] greater celandine (*Chelidonium majus*)

tambla′k *adj, nm* (*Reg*) suckling (lamb/kid/calf)

tambla′to′re
  I § nf (*Reg*) **1** cow that gives a high yield of milk: milk cow **2** [*Bot*] = **tamb′ël′to′re**
  II § adj (*Reg*) high in milk yield

tamblo′re *nf(Reg)* = **tamblato′re**

tamblu′c *nm* [*Zool*] small rock-dwelling lizard with a big head, large eyes, and short legs

tambu′r *nm* **1** tambour (drum) **2** [*Archit*] tambour (column) **3** [*Spec*] drum

tambura′ *nf* [*Mus*] mandolin with two strings tuned a fourth apart: tambura

tambur′ist *n* [*Mus*] player of a tambour: drummer

*Ta′mes *nm* = Tamiz

ta′më *nf* fountainhead

ta′m′ërr *nf* [*Mus*] = **tambura′**

Tamiz *nm* Thames

tamta′m *nm* **1** tomtom **2** drumbeat **3** (*Fig*) signal drumming **4** (*Fig Pej*) noisy commotion: hullabaloo

*ta′mth *I § nm* OR **ta′mz**ë *II § nf (Reg Gheg)* = **të′mbl**ë

Ta′n|a *nf* Tana (female name)

*ta′nd*ë *(Reg Gheg)* = **te′nd**ë

ta′në *masc pl* <**y′n**ë our, of ours

*tâ′n*ë *nf(Reg Gheg)* tannin

*tane′si *(Reg Gheg)* = **tërësi**

ta′në**t** *pl masc* <**y′n**ë **1** ours **2** our male relatives/friends

ta′në**za** *np fem* coma preceding death

tanga′llë *nf* dense virgin forest

tanga′r *nm* (*Reg*) brazier for holding burning coals or charcoal = **manga′ll**

tange′nt = **tangje′nt**

ta′ngë *nf* **1** feeling of regret (left from not having done something) *2 grievance

ta′ngo *nf* tango

tangje′nte *nf* [*Geom*] tangent

tangjent′or *adj* [*Geom*] tangential

tani′ *adv* now, presently
  ◦ **tani e pak** in a little while

Ta′n|i *nm* Tani (male name, nickname for Artan)

tani′k *adj* tannic

tani′më *adv* = **ta′shm**ë

tani′n *nm* tannin

tani′për′tani′sh|ëm *adj (i)* **1** = **tani′sh**ë**m** **2** just for now, for the time being: temporary

tani′sh|ëm *adj (i)* present, current

tani′shm|e *nf (e)* present times, the present

tani′thi *adv* = **tani′**

TANJUG *abbrev* (*Serbian*) <Telegrafska agencija nove Jugoslavije TANJUG (Yugoslavian news agency)

tank *OR* **tanks** *nm* [*Mil*] armored tank

tank′ist *n* [*Mil*] tank driver; member of a tank crew: (tanker, tankman)

tank′o′dro′m *nm* [*Mil*] area used for tank training and exercises

tan′o ·*het vpr* to be upset/worried

tan′o·*n vt* **1** to avert **2** to pester; bother *3 to remove

tano′r *nm* bread paddle = **qe′h**ë**n**

tante′llë *nf* lace = **dante′ll**ë

Tanu′sh *nm* Tanush (male name)

Tanzani′ *nf* Tanzania

Tanzima′t *nm* period of moderate reform in the 19th-century Ottoman Empire

*tapa′ll = topa′ll

tapa′nxhë *nf* = **topa′nxh**ë

*tape′t *nm* **1** rug/carpet made of synthetic material **2** [*Sport*] mat (in wrestling); canvas (in boxing)

ta′pë
  I § nf **1** cork **2** packing material (to restrict risky movement) **3** life belt made of cork
  II § adj (*Fig Colloq*) falling-down drunk, stone drunk
  ◦ **ësh·të tap**ë **(topi) 1** to be a dimwit **2** to be completely ignorant in an area

tapë′nxjerr′|ëse *nf* corkscrew

tapi′ *nf* registered title to a piece of real estate: deed

*tapicar′i = tapiceri′

tapiceri′ *nf* decorative material on furniture, walls, or doors: upholstery, tapestry, wallpaper

tapicie′r *n* upholsterer

*tapino′s· *vt* to mortify, humble

*tapino′s′ur *adj (i)* mortified, humbled

tapi′r *nm* [*Zool*] tapir

tap′o′s· *vt* **1** to plug [] with a cork: bung **2** to seal up []

tap′o′s·et *vpr* to be sealed tight

tap′o′s′je *nf ger* <**tap′o′s·**, **tap′o′s·***et*

tar *nm* (*Colloq*) opportunity, chance

taraba *nf* wooden shutter (for a store or house); wooden crossbar over the outside of a door serving to lock the door

tarabac *nm* little boy

tarabe *nf* **1** wooden shutter (for a store or house); wooden crossbar over the outside of a door serving to lock the door **2** wooden barricade (to be climbed over as a strenuous physical exercise)

tarabuk *nm* [*Mus*] = darabuk

tarace = tarracë

taraf *nm* **1** (*Colloq*) faction **2** (*Pej*) bunch of cronies

tarafllëk *nm* (*np ˜ qe*) (*Colloq*) favoritism shown to one's friends and relatives, cronyism

tarale *adv* without a firm foundation, dangling in the air

tarallak *nm* simpleton, idiot

tarantelë *nf* [*Mus*] tarantella

tarator *nm* [*Food*] sour yogurt mixed with chopped cucumbers, olive oil, garlic, and salt and eaten as an appetizer

taravol *adj* (*Colloq*) audacious, fearless: spunky

taraxhile *nf* cart wheel, wheel

tarbe *adj* (*Colloq*) **1** emaciated **2** penniless, broke

tarbos *vt* (*Colloq*) to take all [ ]'s money (in a game): break [ ], clean [ ] out

tarçuk *nm* = tarkaçe

tarde *nf* [*Ornit*] great bustard (*Otis tarda L.*)

tarentulë *nf* [*Zool*] **1** tarantula **2** wolf spider (*Lycosa tarentulla*)

tarë *nf* tare (weight)

targe *nf* identification plaque: license plate

tarifë *nf* [*Fin*] **1** tariff; tariff rate; list of tariff rates **2** salary; salary rate; list of salary rates
  ◦ **tarifë e dorëzimit** [*Postal*] delivery charge
  ◦ **tarifë e komisionit** [*Postal*] commission fee

tarifor *adj* [*Fin*] of or pertaining to tariffs/salaries

tarikat *nm* **1** [*Relig*] brotherhood of Moslem religious mystics, Moslem sect: tariqat () **2** (*Colloq*) bunch of act-alikes: tight clique

tarim *nm ger* <taro·n

tarkaçe *nf* leather pouch for food carried by livestock herders

taro·n *vt* [*Spec*] **1** to tare **2** to adjust [ ] according to a standard: calibrate

taroç *nm* young bull = mëzat

tarogzë *nf* = parzmore

tarok = taroç

tars *nm* [*Anat*] ankle

tartabiq *nm* = tartabiqe

tartabiqe *nf* **1** [*Entom*] bedbug (*Cimex lectularius*) = çimkë **2** [*Entom*] aphid **3** (*Impol*) scrawny little girl/woman **4** (*Impol Insult*) shameless pest who intrudes in personal matters

tartakut *nm* **1** [*Veter*] equine pneumonia with severe shaking (*pleuropneumonia contagiosa equum*) **2** (*Colloq*) bad cold with severe chills and shaking **3** (*Insult*) scoundrel: rat

tartallis· *vi* (*Reg*) = përpëllit·et

tartar
  I § *adj, nm* Tartar
  II § *nm* (*Old*) rider carrying postal mail during the Ottoman occupation: pony express rider
  ◦ **Tartari e merr.**[3sg] **vesh (se ç'bë·**het[3sg]**).** "The Tartar *understands* (what *is going* on)." The

devil only *knows* what *is going* on. It *is* total confusion.

tartaros·
  I § *vt* (*Colloq*) to make [ ] sour: sour
  II § *vi* (*Colloq*) to get numb with cold

tartaros·et *vpr* **1** (*Colloq*) to become fermented/ leavened: get sour **2** to shiver with cold, freeze to death from the cold **3** (*Fig*) to turn pale with displeasure

tartrik *adj* [*Chem*] tartaric

tarr· *vt* = harr·, tëharr·

tarrabec *nm* (*Reg*) young adolescent boy: young lad

tarracë *nf* terrace

tas *nm* **1** bowl-shaped container: cup, mug; bowl **2** cupful, bowlful **3** crested pigeon

taskë *nf dimin* (*Reg*) little cup/bowl

tasllan *nm* [*Bot*] cherry-laurel (*Prunus laurocerasus*)

tasma *nf* razor strop

tasqebap *nm* [*Food*] meat stew, fricassee

TASS *abbrev* (*Russian*) <**Telegrafnoe Agenstvo Sovjetskogo Sojuza** TASS (News Agency of the Soviet Union)

tast *nm* **1** [*Mus*] fret on a stringed instrument **2** actuating lever operated by touch: key (on a keyboard); sending key (on a telegraph)

tastierë *nf* keyboard; set of pushbuttons

tasuk *nm* small cup

tash *adv* = tani
  ◦ **tash** {*expression of time*} {} ago; {} from now
  tash një ditë one day ago; a day from now
  ◦ **tash e mbrapa** from now on

tashëm *adj (i)* = tanishëm

tashma *adv* nowadays

tashme *nf (e)* **1** the present **2** [*Ling*] the present tense

tashmë *adv* by now; already

tashti *adv* now = tani

tashtishëm *adj (i)* = tanishëm

tatalosh = tatëlosh

tatarec *nm* (*Old*) conical cap formerly worn by women

tatareq *nm* [*Bot*] European spindle tree (*Euonymus europaeus*) = fshikakuq

tatë *nf with masc agreement* (*Colloq*) papa

tatëlosh
  I § *nm* (*Colloq*) **1** gran'pa = tatëmadh **2** nice old guy; kindly, good-natured person
  II § *adj* kindly, nice

tatëmadh *nm* (*Colloq*) endearing and respectful family term for one's grandfather or other elderly person: gran'pa, gramps

tatëpjes *stem for 1st sg pres, pl pres, 2nd & 3rd sg subj, pind* <tatëpjet·

tatëpjet· *vi* to slope, tilt

tatëpjetë
  I § *adv* downhill; downward
  II § *prep (abl)* down
  III § *adj (i)* downhill, sloping downward
  IV § *nf (e)* downhill slope; decline; decrease
  V § *nf* **1** downhill slope, downslope, drop, declivity **2** (*Fig*) decrease of intensity /degree; worsening situation; decline, slump
  ◦ **e tatëpjetë e ëmbël/butë** gentle downward slope, gradual downslope

tatë·pjetëm adj (i) sloping down, downhill

tatë·poshtë adv = tërposhtë

tatë·zot nm 1 (Colloq) grandfather 2 [Ethnog] patriarchal head of a large family = babëzot

tatim nm ger 1 <tato· ·n 2 tax, tariff
 ∘ **tatime në natyrë** tax payment in kind

tatimfitim nm income tax

tatimor adj (Offic) pertaining to taxes; derived from taxes

tatimpagues nm taxpayer

Tatjana nf Tatjana (female name)

tato· ·n vt to levy a fee/tax on [someone]: charge [], tax []

tatuazh nm tattooing; tattoo

tatueshëm adj (i) (Offic) subject to tax: taxable

*__tatule__ nf = tatull

tatull nf [Bot] 1 jimsonweed (Datura stramomium, thorn-apple) (Datura stramomium) 2 venuscup teasel (Dipsacus sylvestris)

taulant
 I § nm [Hist] member of one of the Illyrian tribes that formerly inhabited the coastal lowlands of central Albania
 II § adj of or pertaining to these people

Taulant nm Taulant (male name)

tautologji nf [Spec] tautology

tautologjik adj [Spec] tautologic, tautological

tavan nm 1 ceiling 2 [Min] rock/layer immediately above the seam of a mineral deposit: roof (SH)
 ∘ **s'ka· tavan** to be without limit, have no set limits

tavanim nm ger [Constr] <tavano· ·n

*__tavanis·__ vt = tavano·n

*__tavanisje__ nf ger 1 [Constr] <tavanis· 2 ceiling material

tavano· ·n vt [Constr] to install a ceiling in []

tavanpunues nm ceiling installer

tavanxhi nm 1 = tavanpunues 2 (Old) carpenter = marangoz

tavapjekës nm baker of roasted foods

tavernë nf basement tavern, small rathskeller

tavë nf roasting pan; food cooked in a roasting pan; amount that fills a roasting pan

tavlla nf container for solder (used by a coppersmith)

tavllë nf 1 ashtray 2 backgammon board; backgammon

tavolinë nf table

tavullë nf = tavllë

taze
 I § adj (Colloq) fresh; newly picked, freshly cooked
 II § adv (Colloq) just a little while ago: freshly

te
 I § prep (nom) at/to the location of {}: at/to {}'s place, at {}
 II § conj 1 in the place/time/way that: where; while; as; since 2 in what way: how

teatër nm theater
 ∘ **teatër veror** open air theater used in summer to present plays

teatral adj theatrical

teatro
 I § np <teatër
 II § nf (Colloq) = teatër

teatror adj (Book) of or pertaining to the theater: theatrical

tebaizëm nm [Med] addiction to opium

tebdil adv (Colloq) in disguise

tebeshir nm (Old Reg) chalk = shkumës

TEC abbrev <Termoelektrocentral Thermoelectric Power Plant

*__tef__ nm = teh

tefe nf = bërdilë

teferiç nm (Colloq Old) 1 relaxing stroll 2 shady place near the water (for a pleasant and cool stroll) 3 cool breeze

*__teferike__ nf change (money)

Tefik nm Tefik (male name)

Tefta nf Tefta (female name)

*__tefter__ nm = defter

teftik nm (Colloq) = vrull

tegel nm stitched seam; seam

teh nm 1 sharp edge; blade 2 (Fig) crucial/focal point

tehemteh adv from one end to the other: everywhere

tehmprehtë adj 1 sharp-edged, keen 2 (Fig) strong, sharp; with a fine edge, ready and able to take on anyone

tehndryshkur adj 1 having a rusty blade: dull 2 (Fig) weak, feeble

tehri nf embroidery floss used in decorative braid

teinë nf caffeine component of tea: theine

tej
 I § adv yonder; far away
 II § prep (abl) 1 beyond 2 over and above <>, more than <>, surpassing <>
 ∘ **tej për tej** 1 from one end to the other; all the way through 2 completely, thoroughly, through and through
 ∘ **tej së tejme** extreme
 ∘ **tej e tej** *= tejetej
 ∘ **tej e tëhu/tutje** here and there, all over the place

tejbart· vt to convey, transport

tejbartës
 I § adj used for conveying
 II § nm device used for conveying: conveyor

tejbartje nf ger <tejbart·

tejçim nm ger 1 [Spec] <tejço· ·n, tejço· ·het 2 transmission

tejço· ·het vpr [Spec] to be conducted, get transmitted

tejço· ·n vt to conduct, transmit

tejçues nm [Electr] conductor

tejdet nm territory across the sea; lands beyond the sea, overseas

tejdetas
 I § adj pertaining to territory across the sea or to its inhabitants
 II § n inhabitant of territory across the sea

tejduk·et vpr to show through

tejdukje nf = tejdukshmëri

tejdukshëm adj (i) (Book) transparent

tejdukshmëri nf (Book) transparency

teje pron 2nd sg abl <ti

tejefund adv = tejendanë

tejembanë adv, prep (abl) = tejendanë

tejendanë
 I § adv 1 far and wide, everywhere 2 completely, thoroughly
 II § prep (abl) throughout

tejet adv extraordinarily, enormously

tej·e·tej *adv* all the way through; from one end to the other

tej·fund·or *adj* [*Ling*] **1** antepenultimate **2** having the stress on the antepenult

tej·kal·im *nm ger* **1** <tejkalo·*n* **2** overproduction

tej·kalo··*n vt* **1** to exceed [the amount expected] **2** to pass [another vehicle]

tej·lu·mas
I § *adj* pertaining to territory across the river or to its inhabitants
II § *n* inhabitant of territory across the river

tej·lu·më *nm* territory across the river

tej·mal *nm* territory on the other side of the mountain

tej·mal·as *adj* **1** on the other side of the mountain: ultramontane **2** inhabitant of territory on the other side of the mountain

tej·mata·në *adv* **1** from one end/side to the other, completely **2** yonder over there, far away

tej·mbu·shje *nf* [*Veter*] bloating in animals *dilatatio acuta ruminis ab ingestis*

tej·m·ë *adj* (*i*) located beyond/across: on the other side; far distant = përtejm·ë

tej·ngi·m·ë *adj* (*i*) surfeited, sated; oversaturated

tej·ngo·p· *vt* [*Spec*] = mbingo·p·

tej·ngo·pje *nf ger* [*Spec*] = mbingo·pje

tej·ngo·p·ur *adj* (*i*) [*Spec*] = mbingo·pur

tej·ngro·h· *vt* to overheat

tej·nxe·h· *vt* [*Spec*] = mbinxe·h·

tej·nxe·h·et *vpr* [*Spec*] = mbinxe·h·*et*

tej·nxe·hje *nf* [*Spec*] = mbinxe·hje

tej·pa·m·ës *adj, n* = largpamës

tej·pam·ësi *nf* = largpamësi

tej·pa·mje *nf* **1** = largpa·mje **2** = tejdu·kshm·ëri

tej·pa·shëm *adj* (*i*) = tejdu·kshëm

tej·pa·shm·ëri *nf* (*Book*) = tejdu·kshm·ëri

tej·përcjell·shm·ëri *nf* [*Phys*] superconductivity

tej·përtej
I § *adv* **1** from one end to the other; all the way through **2** completely, thoroughly, through and through
II § *adv, prep* (*abl*) throughout

tej·pi·q·*et vpr* to become overripe

tej·pjekje *nf ger* <tejpi·q·*et*

tej·pje·kur *adj* (*i*) overripe

tej·po·q *stem for pdef* <tejpi·q·*et*

tej·qyr·ë *nf* (*Colloq*) telescope; field glasses

tej·reaksion·ar *adj* ultra-reactionary

tej·shëm *adj* (*i*) over there/yonder, further/furthest away

tej·shik·im *nm* foresight

tej·shik·o·nj·ës *adj* = tejshiku·es

tej·shiku·es *adj* having foresight, forward-looking, foresighted; able to see at a distance, farsighted

tej·shiku·e·shëm *adj* (*i*) transparent

tej·shkr·im *nm ger nm* [*Ling*] transcription = transkriptim

tej·shku·ar *adj* (*i*) (*Book*) in the distant past

tej·shpejt·ë *adj* (*i*) (*Book*) super fast, very fast

tej·shp·im *nm ger* **1** <tejshpo·*n* **2** hole that goes completely through

tej·shp·o··*n vt* to pierce [] through to the other side

tej·shpu·ar *adj* (*i*) pierced all the way through

tej·shtri··*het vpr* to extend broadly, exceed its usual limits

tej·shtri··*n vt* (*Book*) to extend beyond the limits of [], overextend

tej·shtri·r·ësi *nf* [*Geol*] transgression

tej·shtri·rje *nf ger* <tejshtri··*n*, tejshtri·*het*

tej·uj·as *n* person who lives on the other side of the water

tej·vështr·im *nm* foresight

tej·vështr·o·nj·ës *adj* foresighted, foresighted

te·jz·ë *nf* **1** [*Anat*] body sinew: tendon, ligament, muscle fiber **2** buzuk string **3** thin woolen yarn
∘ **tejzat e zërit** vocal cords

tek
I § *prep* (*nom*) *conj* = te
II § *adv* singly; alone
III § *adj* **1** for only one; single; alone, apart **2** odd (as opposed to even); odd-numbered
IV § *n* single/separate one
∘ **tek andej** further on, ahead
∘ **tek e fundit** when it comes right down to it, after all, in the final analysis
∘ **tek ish gardh s'u bë shteg** things haven't changed
∘ **tek e mbramja** = tekefundit
∘ **tek e tek** one by one
∘ **ësh·të akoma/ende/hala tek ura** "still be at the bridge" to be behind the times, not be up on the latest

te·k·et *vp impers* <> *feels* like having/doing something: <> *has* a whim/hankering, <> *gets* an urge

tek·a·ma·dh *adj* full of whims: capricious

tek·andej *adv* (*Colloq*) **1** over yonder **2** later on

tek·a·njo·s *adj* = tekanjo·z

tek·a·njo·z
I § *adj* **1** given to acting on whim: impulsive, capricious **2** (*Fig*) causing unexpected trouble; behaving/appearing unexpectedly
II § *n* person who acts on whim

tek·do
I § *adv* anywhere; everywhere
II § *conj* wherever

te·ke *nf* **1** single-barreled shotgun **2** (*Colloq*) shot glass; (quantity) shotglassful, shot **3** (*Old*) single-barreled pistol carried on the belt

tek·e·fu·nd·it *adv* when it comes/came right down to it, after all is/was said and done: in the final analysis, in the end

tek·e·mbra·mja *adv* = tekefundit

te·k·ë *nf* **1** whim; insistent whim, wheedling **2** (*Fig*) capricious behavior: vagary, caprice

te·kë·ndej *adv* **1** (*Reg*) around here somewhere, hereabouts; around about this time **2** from here on out; from now on, henceforth

teklif *nm* (*Colloq*) inhibition

tek·nefe·s
I § *nm* (*Old*) **1** = shpirr·ë **2** = shpirra·q
II § *adj* = shpifarra·q

tek·nik
I § *adj* technical
II § *n* technician, specialist

tek·ni·ke *nf* (*i*) = tekniku·m

tek·nik·ë *nf* technology; technique

tek·nik·isht *adv* in technical matters: technically

tek·nik·o-shkenc·or *adj* technical and scientific

tek·nik·o-taktik *adj* technical and tactical

tekn|ik|u'm *nm* technical secondary school

tekn|o|kraci' *nf* technocracy

tekn|o|kra't
I § *nm* technocrat
II § *adj* technocratic

tekn|o|krati'k *adj* technocratic

tekn|o|krat|iz̈ëm *nm* technocratism

tekn|o|lo'g
I § *n* technologist
II § *adj* industrial

tekn|o|logji' *nf* technology

tekn|o|logji'k *adj* technological, technical

tek|që *conj* while; whereas = **ndërsa'**

tek|sa' *conj* 1 as soon as; just as 2 while

tekst *nm* 1 text 2 textbook

teksti'l
I § *nm* textile
II § *adj* involved in or pertaining to the production of textiles

tekstil|i'st *n* textile worker

tekstual|i'sht *adv* word-for-word

tekta'l *adj* [*Ling*] tectal

tektoni'k *adj* [*Geol*] tectonic

tektoni'kë *nf* [*Geol*] tectonics

tek-tu'k *adv* 1 here and there; every now and then 2 seldom; once in a while, occasionally

te'k|ur
I § *nf(e)* whim
II § *nn ger (të)* <**te'k**·*et*

te'k|ur|a *np (të)* <**te'kur** balderdash, nonsense

tel *nm* 1 wire 2 string (for a stringed musical instrument) 3 gold/silver thread
◦ **tel dreqi** [*Bot*] dodder = **kusku'të**
◦ **tel gjashtësh** six-ply wire
◦ **tel katërsh** four-stranded wire
◦ **tel me thumba/gjemba** barbed wire
◦ **tel rrobash** clothesline

te'l|a *np masc (Old)* strands of gilt wire decorating a bride

tel|a'ke *nf* woman who adorns the bride with a decorative veil of metallic strands

tel|a|pre'r|ës *adj* = **telpre'rës**

tela'sh *nm (Colloq)* tough problem: predicament, trouble, worry

telati'n *I § nm* OR **telati'në** *II § nf* 1 soft patent leather 2 *(Old)* brown leather with stripes that is used for moccasin uppers

tel|a|to're *nf* bride adorned with a decorative veil of metallic strands

te'l|içë *nf* wire

tel|dre'q *nm* [*Bot*] dodder *(Cuscuta)*

tele'f *invar (Crude)*

teleferi'k *nm* aerial tramway: telpher

tele|fo'n *nm* telephone

tele|foni'k *adj* telephonic

tele|fon|i'm *nm ger* 1 <**telefono'**·*n* 2 telephone conversation

tele|fon|i's· *vt, vi* = **telefono'**·*n*

tele|fon|i'st *n* 1 telephone switchboard operator, central, operator 2 [*Mil*] telephone line installer 3 = **fillrojtës**

tele|fon|iz|i'm *nm ger* <**telefonizo'**·*n*

tele|fon|iz|o'·*n vt* to provide [] with telephone communication

tele|fon|o'·*n vt, vi* to telephone

tele|gra'f *nm* 1 telegraph 2 telegraph office

tele|graf|ha'ne *nf(Old)* telegraph office

tele|grafi' *nf* telegraphy

tele|grafi'k *adj* telegraphic

tele|graf|i'st *n* 1 telegraph operator 2 worker in a telegraph office

tele|graf|i'sht *adv* telegraphically

tele|grafo'·*n vt, vi* to telegraph

tele|gra'm *nm* telegram

tele|koma'ndë *nf* remote control device

tele|komand|i'm *nm ger* 1 [*Spec*] <**telekomando'**·*n* 2 remote control

tele|komand|o'·*n vt* [*Spec*] to operate [] by remote control .

tele|komand|u'a|r *adj (i)* [*Spec*] remotely controlled

tele|komunikacio'n *nm* telecommunication

tele|me'tër *nm* telemeter; range finder

tele|metri' *nf* telemetry

tele|metri'k *adj* telemetric

telendi' *nf(Colloq)* 1 shameful behavior 2 humiliating insult

telend|i's· *vt* 1 *(Colloq)* to shame, humiliate, abase; badmouth 2 to insult seriously *3 to suffocate

telend|i's·*et vpr (Colloq)* to feel humiliation, be publicly humiliated

telend|i'sje *nf ger* 1 *(Colloq)* <**telendi's**·, **telendi's**·*et* 2 humiliation 3 *(Colloq)* = **telendi'**

telend|i'sur *adj (i) (Colloq)* humiliated, publicly shamed; slandered

tele|objekti'v *nm* [*Tech*] telescopic lens, telephoto lens

tele|pati' *nf* telepathy

tele|sko'p *nm* telescope

tele|spektato'r *n* person who watches a television program: television viewer

teleshma'n *adj, n (Colloq)* (person) not right in the head: wacky (person)

tele|ta'jp *nm* teletype

tele|ti's· *vt* 1 to adorn [the bride] with a decorative veil of metallic strands 2 to doll [] up (like a bride), put makeup and ornaments on []

tele|ti's·*et vpr* 1 to don the bridal veil 2 to get all dolled up (like a bride)

tele|vizio'n *nm* television

tele|vizion|i'k *adj* = **televizi'v**

tele|vizi'v *adj* on/for television; characteristic of or pertaining to television

tele|vizo'r *nm* television set

te'l|ët *adj (i)* of wire

tel|ëzi'm *nm ger* [*Tech*] <**telëzo'**·*n*

tel|ëzo'·*n vt* [*Tech*] to draw [] into wire: wiredraw

tel|ëzu'es
I § *adj* [*Tech*] serving to draw wire
II § *n* [*Tech*] worker at a wire-drawing machine

tel|ëzu'e|se *nf* [*Tech*] wire-drawing machine

tel|ëzu'e|sh|ëm *adj (i)* ductile (into wire)

telfe'r *nm* [*Tech*] telpher

teli'g *nm* horsecollar

teliko's· *vt (Colloq)* to weaken [] to the point of exhaustion: run [] down completely, knock [] out

teliko's·*et vpr (Colloq)* to be incapacitated by weakness/exhaustion: be completely run down, be out on one's feet

teliko'sur *adj (i) (Colloq)* incapacitated by weakness/exhaustion: completely run down, out on one's feet

tel'is· *vt (Old)* to adorn the forehead and face of [the bride] with pieces of wire

tel'is·et *vpr (Old)* to don the bridal facial ornaments of wire

tel'ish *nm* 1 filigree 2 [*Bot*] cocksfoot, orchard grass (*Dactylis glomerata*)

*telisht** *nm* filigree

tel'ishtë *nf* 1 tack, small nail 2 knitting needle

tel'je *adj* = **te'lt**ë

Te'lo *nf with masc agreement* (male name)

telo'znë *nf* [*Hist*] = **hara'ç**

tel'pre'r'ës *adj* used for cutting wire: wire-cutting

tel'të *adj (i)* of wire, made of wire

telve' *nf (Old)* coffee dregs

tella'll *nm* 1 *(Old)* town-crier 2 *(Old)* hawker (in a market) 3 *(Pej)* propagandist, promoter

tellall'is· *vt (Colloq)* 1 to give [] the news, inform [] 2 to spread [the news/dirt] all around; make a big to-do/hullabaloo about []

te'ma'las *n (i)* one who dwells on the other side of the mountain

temati'k *adj* thematic

temati'kë *nf* set of themes/subjects

*temel** = **theme'l**

temena' *nf (Colloq)* 1 elaborate salute in Turkish manner in which a bow accompanies a flowery hand gesture going from the heart to the forehead to indicate one's humble respect 2 *(Pej)* bowing down as a token of subservience

te'më *nf* 1 theme 2 subject 3 [*Ling*] stem, theme

temi'n *nm* = **xhi'xh**ë

temja'n *nm* incense

temjani'cë *nf* [*Relig*] censer, thurible

temjani's· *vt* [*Relig*] to cense

temjano's· = **temjani's·**

Te'mo *nf with masc agreement* Temo (male name)

temp *nm* tempo

temperame'nt *nm* 1 temperament 2 gusto, zest

temperatu'rë *nf* temperature

te'mpo *nf* [*Mus*] tempo

te'mpull *nm (np ~ j)* temple

tempulla'r *nm* [*Hist*] Templar

tena'r *nm* [*Anat*] thenar

tende'ncë *nf* tendency; predilection, penchant; bias

tendenci'oz *adj* tendentious, biased

tendenci'ozite't *nm* tendentiousness, bias

tendë *nf* 1 tent 2 place sheltered from above: canopy; awning; shaded spot for livestock to escape the heat; shaded pen for livestock
  ◦ **tend**ë **rrushi** grape arbor

tendo's· *vt* to put [] under tension, make [] tense: stretch [] out, stretch; tighten; strain

tendo's·et *vpr* 1 to stretch out, open up/out; become taut, tense up 2 *(Fig)* to get tense; tense oneself

tendo'sje *nf ger* 1 <**tendo's·**, **tendo's·et** 2 tension

tendo'sur *adj (i)* 1 stretched out; under tension, stretched taut 2 *(Fig)* taut and ready for action

te'ne *nf* panel of a rug

tene' *nf(Reg)* 1 = **qeshqe'k** 2 cracked wheat, bulgur

*tene'c** *nm* = **gane'c**

*tene'l** *nm* [*Bot*] basil = **borzilo'k**

teneqe' *OR* **tene'qe** *nf* 1 tin-plated iron: tin plate, tin 2 *(Colloq)* tin container: tin can, tin box
  ◦ **ësh·të teneqe** to have nothing left, be flat broke
  ◦ **teneqe e shpuar** "leaky tin can" *(Impol)* intolerable prattler/blabbermouth

teneqe'punu'e's *nm* tinsmith

teneqexhi' *nm (np ~ nj)* = **teneqepunu'es**

*teni** *nf* [*Invert*] tapeworm, taenia

tenia'zë *nf* [*Med*] taeniasis

tenido'zë *nf* [*Med*] taeniasis

te'nie *nf* [*Med*] taenia

teni's *nm* [*Sport*] tennis

teni'st *n* [*Sport*] tennis player

*te'nk**ë *nf* [*Ichth*] tench = **ti'ng**ë

teno'r *nm* [*Mus*] tenor

tensio'n *nm* 1 [*Phys*] pressure 2 [*Electr*] voltage 3 [*Med*] blood pressure; high blood pressure 4 *(Fig)* tension, stress
  ◦ **tensioni i avullit/gazit** [*Phys*] vapor pressure
  ◦ **tensioni i gjakut** blood pressure

tentativë *nf* 1 attempt, endeavor, try, trial 2 [*Law*] unsuccessful attempt

tenti'm *nm ger* 1 <**tento'·n** 2 attempt, try

tento'·het *vpr* to have a tendency, lean, incline

tento'·n *vi* to make an attempt: attempt, try

tenxhe're *nf* 1 metal cooking utensil with a lid: pot, cooker, stewing pot; kettle 2 potful, kettleful
  ◦ **tenxhere me presion** high-pressure cooker

te'një *nf* 1 [*Entom*] moth whose larva is a destructive pest, clothes moth 2 [*Entom*] greater wax moth *(Galleria mellonella)* 3 tapeworm
  ◦ **tenja e bizeles** [*Entom*] pea moth *Cydia nigricana* Steph.
  ◦ **tenja e çepallave** [*Entom*] almond moth, warehouse moth, fig moth *Ephestia cautella* Nalk
  ◦ **tenja e drithërave** [*Entom*] cereal moth *Sitotroga cerealella* L.
  ◦ **tenja e fikut** [*Entom*] fig moth *Simaethis nemorana*
  ◦ **tenja e grurit** [*Entom*] = **mola e grurit**
  ◦ **tenja e mollës** [*Entom*] Adkin's apple ermel, apple moth, ermine moth *Hyponomeuta malinellus* Zell.
  ◦ **tenja e patates** [*Entom*] potato tuberworm *Phthorimaea operculella* Zell.
  ◦ **tenja e qepës** [*Entom*] leek smudge *Acrolepsis assectella*
  ◦ **tenja e rrushit** [*Entom*] 1 moth larva found on grapes *Polychrosis botrana* Poda 2 small brown-barred conch, grapeberry moth *Eupoecilia (Clysia) ambiguella* Hb.
  ◦ **tenja e ullirit** [*Entom*] olive-moth *Prays oleae*

tenjo's· *vt* to eat away (like the larva of a moth)

tenjo's·et *vpr* to be eaten away from the inside; decay; eaten away by disease

tenjo'sur *adj (i)* 1 moth-eaten 2 diseased, infected; not healing

teodoli't *nm* [*Spec*] theodolite

teokraci' *nf* theocracy

teokrati'k *adj* theocratic

teolo'g *n* theologist; theologian

teologji' *nf* theology

teologji'k *adj* theological

teore'më *nf* [*Math*] theorem

teori' *nf* 1 theory 2 *(Pej)* abstract/impractical theory

teorici'e'n *nm* theoretician

teorik *adj* theoretical

teorikisht *adv* theoretically

*****teorisien** = teoricie**n**

teorizim *nm ger* <**teorizo**·*n*

teorizo·*n* *vt* **1** to theorize; generalize **2** *(Pej)* to make up abstract/impractical theories about []

teorizues *nm* **1** theoretician **2** *(Pej)* impractical theorist

teozofi *nf (Book)* theosophy

tepe *nf* **1** *(Colloq)* small hill, hillock; hilltop **2** top of the head: pate *****3** [*Bot*] = **tep**ë

tepelek *nm (Colloq)* top of the head: pate, cranium

tepelenas
 I § *adj* of or pertaining to Tepelena or its inhabitants
 II § *n* native of Tepelena

Tepelenë *nf* city and district in southern Albania: Tepelena

tepë *nf* [*Bot*] einkorn *(Triticum monococcum)*

tepër
 I § *adv* **1** excessively: too much/many **2** more than enough: extra
 II § *pcl (before an adjective or adverb)* too

tepërm *adj (i)* = **tepërt**

tepërmi *adv (së)* **1** to an excessive or exceptional degree: too much, excessively, in excess **2** to a high degree: greatly, very much

tepërsi *nf* excess = **tepri**

tepërshëm *adj (i)* = **tepërt**

tepërt
 I § *adj (i)* **1** exceeding normal limits: extreme, extraordinary, exceptional **2** exceeding necessary/useful limits: in excess, excessive; superfluous, extra
 II § *nn (të)* extremely large amount/degree

tepër-tepër *adv* to the highest possible degree: infinitely; exceedingly, enormously

tepishtë *nf* = **tepore**

tepore *nf* land sown in einkorn; field of einkorn

teposhtë
 I § *nf* down slope; decline
 II § *adv* downhill, downward; down
 III § *prep (abl)* down

tepri *nf* excess; extremely large amount

tepricë *nf* **1** surplus; remainder **2** = **tepri**

teprim *nm ger* <**tepro**·*n*, **tepro**·*het* **2** excess

tepro·*het* *vp impers* it *is* more than necessary, it *is* excessive

tepro·*n*
 I § *vt* to overdo []
 II § *vi* to remain as excess/surplus: be extra, be left over
 ○ **s'<> tepro**·*n^{3sg}* **koha** <> *has* no (free) time left

tepruar *adj (i)* remaining as excess: extra, left over, surplus

tepsi *nf* large round baking sheet
 ○ **tepsi bakllavaje** large pie pan
 ○ **tepsia e bukës** round baking tray placed on a stool to serve as a low dining table

teptis· *vi (Colloq)* **1** to appear suddenly/unexpectedly/forcibly: burst forth, burst out; (of a liquid) gush out **2** *(Fig)* to lose self-control: erupt **3** (of a gun) to recoil

teptis·*et vpr (Colloq)* to lose self-control: erupt

teptisje *nf ger (Colloq)* <**teptis**·, **teptis**·*et*
 ○ **teptisje gjaku** *(Colloq)* blood hemorrhage

teqe *nf* **1** religious center for members of Bektashi faith: tekke **2** *(Fig)* sacred place

ter
 I § *nm* young bull = **dem**
 II § *adj* uncastrated

ter· *vt* to dry [] out/off: dry
 ○ **<>i ter**· **këmbët/opingat** *(Impol)* to do <> in: kill <>

ter·*et vpr* <**ter**· **1** to dry out/off: get dry **2** to go away, leave quickly, disappear **3** *(Fig)* to die down, come to a halt: cease
 ○ **ter**·*et* **në fytyr**ë to grow pale from fear/shock

*****terace** *nf* blotting paper, blotter

*****terac**ë *nf* terrace = **tarrac**ë

terak
 I § *nm* uncastrated bull
 II § *adj* **1** uncastrated **2** dried out/off, dry

teran *adj* emaciated

terapeutik *adj* [*Med*] therapeutic

terapeutikë *nf* [*Med*] therapeutics

terapi *nf* [*Med*] therapy

terapist *nm* [*Med*] therapist

terciar *nm* tertiary

tercinë *nf* [*Lit*] **1** terza rima **2** terzina

*****terebentin**ë = **terpentin**ë

*****terebinthin**ë = **terpentin**ë

terelike *nf* house slipper(s)

*****teren** = **terre**n

terezi *nf (Colloq)* **1** balance scale **2** carpenter's level **3** balance, equipoise **4** *(Fig)* proper condition/state; propriety **5** good sense, proper mind
 ○ **s'ka· terezi** _ not have in mind to _, not be about to _
 ○ **s'e mat· fjalën në terezi** not consider one's words carefully: not think before one talks

terezis stem for *1st sg pres, pl pres, 2nd & 3rd sg subj, pind* <**terezit**·

terezit· *vt* **1** *(Colloq)* to balance; weigh **2** to aim [] straight at <> **3** to measure out [] properly **4** *(Fig)* to think [] through carefully

terezit·*et vpr (Colloq)* to think before acting, think it through first; plan one's actions; concentrate on one is doing and not rush

terë *nf* **1** dry land, terra firma **2** dry side (of the flipped hard disk in a children's game of "wet or dry")

terës *adj* *****1** causing drying **2** [*Med*] siccative

teri *nf* estrus period (in cattle): rut, rutting, heat

terig *nm* = **terik**

terik *nm (np ~ qe)* **1** dry land, terra firma **2** arid ground, dry soil **3** cool breeze

terinë *nf* **1** soil incapable of retaining moisture: arid land, dry soil **2** sunny place in the wind for drying clothes **3** temporary shelter made of leaves and straw; sheep enclosure sheltered by straw and surrounded by a wicker fence

terital *nm* [*Text*] polyester fiber; heavy polyester fabric; clothing made of polyester material

terjak *adv (Colloq)* exactly right: precisely, correctly

terjaqi *nm (np ~ nj) (Colloq)* man whose lifetime of drinking or smoking has made him an expert in the subject

terjas·
 I § *vi (Colloq)* to make an attempt: attempt, try
 II § *vt (Colloq)* to try [] out

terjasje *nf* **1** <**terjas**· **2** attempt, try, trial

te'rje *nf ger* <**ter-, ter-***et* = **tharje**

terk *adj* (of a horse) having difficulty in breathing, asthmatic

te'rlë *nf* group of shepherd's huts in a mountain camp

terliqe *nf* house slipper made of thin leather

term *nm* term

term'al *adj* of heat generated by hot springs: thermal

termale = **tërmale**

te'rmë *adj (i)* arid, dry; dried out

term'ëzat *nm* uncastrated bull calf

term'ik *adj* thermal

terminologji *nf* [*Ling*] terminology

termino'logjik *adj* [*Ling*] terminological

termite *np fem* [*Entom*] termite

te'rmo *formativ* thermo-

termobërtham'or *adj* thermonuclear

termocentral *nm* thermoelectric plant

termoçift *nm* [*Phys*] thermocouple

termodinamikë *nf* [*Phys*] thermodynamics

termoizol'im *nm* [*Phys*] heat insulation

termometër *nm* thermometer

termoplast *nm* [*Chem*] thermoplast

termos *nm* thermos bottle, vacuum flask

termosifon *nm* [*Tech*] thermosiphon

terpentinë *nf* turpentine

terplotë *nf* **1** large wooden scoop used for winnowing grain: grain scoop **2** scoop used for dipping dry granular substances out of sacks: small scoop, coffee/sugar scoop

terpo = **tërposhtë

terpo'sinë *nf* top layer; topsoil

ters

I § *adj (Colloq)* **1** unlucky **2** wrong, bad **3** ornery, contrary, perverse

II § *n (Colloq)* **1** jinx **2** ornery person

III § *adv (Colloq)* **1** badly, wrongly **2** perversely, peevishly

○ **Tersi i Pojanit** *(Crude)* a terrible jinx

ters'llëk *nm (np ˜ qe)* **1** *(Colloq)* bad humor, irritable disposition; wickedness **2** bad luck, misfortune; adversity **3** nasty language

tertë *adj (i)* dry; (of weather) not raining

tertip *nm (Old)* **1** orderliness, good order **2** plan

terzi *nm (np ˜ nj) (Old)* tailor (for traditional costume)

terr *nm* pitch darkness, darkness, dark

terr- *vt* to darken

terr-*et* *vp impers* it *gets* dark

terrat'is- *vt* to make [] dark: darken; cloud, obscure

terrat'is-*et* *vp* to get dark, darken

terre'n *nm* **1** terrain **2** field site (as opposed to the home office) **3** site where political work is done with a local population: grass roots location

te'rrët *adj (i)* dark

terrinë *nf* darkness

territor *nm* territory

territorial *adj* territorial

terrn'o- *n vt, vi* = **ndërro-**·*n*

terro'-*het* *vpr* to get dark

terro'-·*n vt, vi* to darken

terror *nm* terror

○ **terror i bardhë** "white terror" *(HistPK)* violent acts perpetrated by counterrevolutionaries

terror'ist *n, adj* terrorist

terrorist'ik *adj* terroristic

terror'izëm *nm* **1** terrorism **2** terror

terror'izo-·*n vt* terrorize

terr'sinë *nf* = **terrinë**

terrs'o-*het** *vpr* = **terro** ·*het*

terrs'o-·*n vt, vi* = **terro** ·*n*

te'rrshëm *adj (i)* dark

terr'to-*het* *vpr* to get/grow dark; grow sullen, glower

te'serë *nf* **1** document proving an individual's membership in a political/social organization: membership card **2** *(Old)* passbook; ration card/book

te'skë *nf* adze

tesl'icë *nf* carpenter's adze

tesl'im

I § *adv* **1** *(Colloq)* in safekeeping; in trust, in charge, under protection **2** into another's control **3** very ill, almost dead

II § *interj* here, take it, do what you like with it!

tespi *np fem* = **tespi'he**

tespiçe *nf* [*Food*] cake served with hot sugar syrup

tespie *nf* [*Bot*] Persian lilac, Indian bead tree *(Melia azedarach)*

tespi'he *np fem* string of Moslem prayer beads; worry beads

tespije *np fem* = **tespi'he**

tespi'xhe *np fem* sweet noodle pudding

tesprot *n* [*Hist*] member of one of the Illyrian tribes that formerly inhabited the region of southern Albania bordering the Ionian Sea

tesqere *nf (Old)* **1** discharge document given to a soldier finishing his military service during the Ottoman occupation of Albania **2** card announcing a wedding/death

testament *nm* **1** [*Law*] testamentary document: will **2** *(Fig)* last wishes before death: legacy **3** [*Relig*] Testament **4** expression of important convictions: testament

testament'ar *adj* testamentary

te'ste *nf* **1** (of tableware utensils all of the same category) set of ten **2** *(Colloq)* set of people of the same age: age group, generation **3** *(Colloq)* set of people with the same kind/level of position **4** *(Colloq)* (of beverages and foodstuffs) quality, category **5** small cup that covers the hidden object in a game of thimblerig **6** *(Reg)* garlic press; pestle for mashing coffee beans **7** test

testembel *nm* *(Colloq)* animal knucklebone used in playing a children's game

testër'o-·*n vt* to investigate [] thoroughly: scrutinize []

testikulë *nf* [*Anat*] testicle

test'im <**testo**·*n*

testo'-·*n vt (Book)* to test

tesh *nm* **1** [*Med*] syphilis **2 good-for-nothing **3 now = **tash**

tesh- *vi* to sneeze

tesh-*et** *vpr* = **teshti-**·*n*

tesh'ia *np fem* <**teshe** **1** clothes; underclothes **2** household goods **3** [*Hist*] funerary pottery

teshalar'ëse *nf* = **rrobalar'ëse**

tesha'shit'ës *nm* = **rrobashi'tës**

teshato're *nf* = **gardëro'bë**

tesherit-*et** *vpr* to swagger, show off

te'shë *nf* **1** particle that gets in the eye **2** *(Reg)* whorl (on a spindle) = **agërsha'k**

te'shëz *nf* [*Veter*] anthrax = **plasje**

teshti·*n vi* to sneeze

teshtî|më *nf* sneeze

teshti|tje *nf ger* 1 <**teshti**·*n* 2 = **teshtî|m**ë

teshtî|tur *nf (e)* sneezing

*****tet** *nm* the sea at dawn

tet|anî|k *adj, n* (baby) born prematurely (in the eighth month)

tetano's *nm* [*Med*] tetanus = **sha'rrëz**

tet|a'r *n* 1 [*Mil*] corporal *****2** private first class

te'të

  I § *num* eight; number eight

  II § *adj (i), n (i)* eighth

  III § *nf* the number eight; the grade of eight (where ten is the highest possible grade)

  IV § *nf (e)* **1** (fraction) an eighth **2** eighth grade (in elementary school); eighth grade class/classroom

  V § *np (të)* a group of eight, eight at one time; all eight

tetë|dhje'të

  I § *num* eighty

  II § *adj (i), n (i)* eightieth

tetë|fa'q|ësh *nm* [*Geom*] octahedron

tetë|fisho|·*n vt* to multiply [] by eight, increase [] eightfold

*****te|tëhu**· = **tëhu'**

tetë|kë'mb|ësh *nm* [*Invert*] octopod; octopus

*****tetë|kë'nd|**ës = **tetëkë'nd|ësh**

tetë|kë'nd|ësh

  I § *nm* [*Geom*] octagon

  II § *adj* octagonal

tetë|mbë|dhje'të

  I § *num* eighteen; number eighteen

  II § *nf* the number eighteen

  III § *adj (i), n (i)* eighteenth

tetë|mu'aj|sh *adj* having completed eight months: eight-month, eight-month old

tetë|mu'jo'r *adj* = **tetëmu'ajsh**

tetë|qî'nd

  I § *num* eight hundred; number eight hundred

  II § *nf* the number eight hundred

tetë|qî'nd|të *adj (i)* eight-hundredth

tetë|rro'kë|sh

  I § *adj* composed of eight syllables: octasyllabic

  II § *nm* [*Lit*] octasyllabic line

tetë|rro'kë|she *nf* **1** [*Mus*] octet **2** [*Mus*] octave **3** [*Mil*] eight-man squad

tetë|sh *adj (Colloq)* in eight parts; measuring eight units in value

tetë|she *nf* **1** group of eight **2** *(Old)* = **teta're**

tetë|vjeç|a'r

  I § *adj* eight years old; eight years long; lasting eight years

  II § *nm* eight-year period

  III § *n* eight-year old child

tetë|vjeç|a're *nf* eight-year elementary school, grade school

te'to *nf* **1** aunt **2** *(Child)* title of respectful address for an older woman: Auntie

tet|o'r *nm* October

tet|o'rë|sh

  I § *adj* lasting for eight hours

  II § *nm* eight-hour period; eight-hour workday

*****tetovî|m** *nm (Reg)* tattoo(ing)

*****tet|po'sht**ë *adv* = **tërpo'sht**ë

tetraciklî'në *nf* [*Med*] tetracycline

tetrae'd|ër *nf* [*Geom*] tetrahedon

te't|she *nf* **1** the number eight **2** eight-shot revolver

*****te|u'j|as** *nm* = **matanu'jas**

Teu't|a *nf* Teuta (female name)

*****tevabî** *nf (Old)* flunky, lackey

tevatu'r *nm (Old)* **1** public clamor, brouhaha, babel **2** [*Law*] hearsay testimony

*****tevatu'r**ë *nf* rumor

teveqe'l

  I § *adj (Colloq)* slow-witted, slow, retarded; stupid

  II § *n* dimwit; moron

tevlî'g *nm (np ~ gje)* = **tevlî'k**

tevlî'k *nm* bow of a yoke, oxbow

*****te|vo'n|a** *adv (Colloq)* **1** afterwards **2** toward evening **3** = **tekefu'ndit**.

tez|a'k *nm* son of mother's sister: cousin

te'ze *nf* mother's sister, aunt *(collateral female relative ascending or descending in mother's matriline or patriline)*

teze|ma'dhe *nf* great aunt

te'zë *nf* **1** thesis **2** set of final examination questions

te'zgë *nf* **1** sales counter, sales booth/stand; peddler's cart **2** handbarrow **3** body litter: stretcher

tezgja'h *nm* **1** weaving machine: textile loom, industrial loom **2** work table **3** mandolin pick made of cherry bark **4** large anvil used by blacksmiths **5** *(Reg)* wooden bottle for keeping roasted coffee beans

tezgjah|î'st|e *nf* woman who operates a textile loom

tezgje're *nf* handbarrow used in construction work

t·ë *conjunctive proclitic marking a verb in the subjunctive mood* that, to

  ◦ {*imper sg verb*} **të** {*imper 1st pl same verb*}! let's {*verb*} quick! **ik të ikim!** let's get out of here!

t·ë *2nd sg object pronominal proclitic indicates that the following verb has a 2nd sg object or referent: thee/thy/you/your*

  ◦ **të bë·n të dalësh prej lëkure** "{} *makes* you want to jump out of your skin" {} annoys you so much that you can't stand it any more

  ◦ **tharto·**n^{3sg} "{} *puckers* your lips" {} can run rings around you

  ◦ **të ça·n hundët** {} *makes* your nose smart, have a pungent smell

  ◦ **të ça·**n^{3pl} **mushkonjat** *(Colloq)* the mosquitoes *eat* you up

  ◦ **të ça·**n^{3sg} **në ballë** "{} *hits* you in the forehead" {} *hits* the spot (said of a very cold or very strong drink)

  ◦ **të ço·**n^{pres} **në njëqind/dyzet/shtatë çezma/ kroje/burime e s'të jep ujë** "{} *takes* one to a hundred fountains and never *gives* you water" {} gives one much hope but never *comes* through: {} *leads* you on

  ◦ **të ha· dheun nën këmbë** "{} *eats* the ground under your feet" {} *is* a treacherous/rotten person

  ◦ **të ha· në dritë të syrit 1** {} *is* fearless **2** you *cannot* pull the wool over {}'s eyes, {} *is* very shrewd

  ◦ **të ha· të bardhën e syrit** "{} *eats* the white of your eye" **1** {} would rob you blind **2** {} *is* very clever/adept

  ◦ **të ha·**^{3rd} **kokërdhokun e syrit** "{} *eats* your eyeball" **1** {} *keeps* after you to get what {} *wants*, {} *pesters* you constantly, {} *is* annoyingly persistent **2** {} *is* a pest **3** {} *is* very shrewd

teshti·*n vi* to sneeze

teshti'më *nf* sneeze

teshti'tje *nf ger* 1 <**teshti·***n* 2 = **teshti'më**

teshti'tur *nf (e)* sneezing

*****tet** *nm* the sea at dawn

tet'ani'k *adj, n* (baby) born prematurely (in the eighth month)

tetano's *nm* [*Med*] tetanus = **sharrëz**

teta'r *n* 1 [*Mil*] corporal *2 private first class

te'të
I § *num* eight; number eight
II § *adj (i), n (i)* eighth
III § *nf* the number eight; the grade of eight (where ten is the highest possible grade)
IV § *nf (e)* 1 (fraction) an eighth 2 eighth grade (in elementary school); eighth grade class/classroom
V § *np (të)* a group of eight, eight at one time; all eight

tetë'dhje'të
I § *num* eighty
II § *adj (i), n (i)* eightieth

tetë'fa'q'ësh *nm* [*Geom*] octahedron

tetë'fisho·o·*n vt* to multiply [] by eight, increase [] eightfold

*****tetë'hu** = **tëhu'**

tetë'kë'mb'ësh *nm* [*Invert*] octopod; octopus

*****tetë'kë'nd'ës** = **tetë'kë'nd'ësh**

tetë'kë'nd'ësh
I § *nm* [*Geom*] octagon
II § *adj* octagonal

tetë'mbë'dhje'të
I § *num* eighteen; number eighteen
II § *nf* the number eighteen
III § *adj (i), n (i)* eighteenth

tetë'mua'jsh *adj* having completed eight months: eight-month, eight-month old

tetë'mujo'r *adj* = **tetë'mua'jsh**

tetë'qi'nd
I § *num* eight hundred; number eight hundred
II § *nf* the number eight hundred

tetë'qi'nd't'ë *adj (i)* eight-hundredth

tetë'rro'kë'sh
I § *adj* composed of eight syllables: octasyllabic
II § *nm* [*Lit*] octasyllabic line

tetë'rro'kë'she *nf* 1 [*Mus*] octet 2 [*Mus*] octave 3 [*Mil*] eight-man squad

te'të'sh *adj (Colloq)* in eight parts; measuring eight units in value

te'të'she *nf* 1 group of eight 2 *(Old)* = **teta're**

tetë'vjeça'r
I § *adj* eight years old; eight years long; lasting eight years
II § *nm* eight-year period
III § *n* eight-year old child

tetë'vjeça're *nf* eight-year elementary school, grade school

te'to *nf* 1 aunt 2 *(Child)* title of respectful address for an older woman: Auntie

teto'r *nm* October

teto'rë'sh
I § *adj* lasting for eight hours
II § *nm* eight-hour period; eight-hour workday

*****tetovi'm** *nm (Reg)* tattoo(ing)

*****tet'po'shtë** *adv* = **tërpo'shtë**

tetraciklí'në *nf* [*Med*] tetracycline

tetrae'd'ër *nf* [*Geom*] tetrahedon

te'tshe *nf* 1 the number eight 2 eight-shot revolver

*****te'u'jas** *nm* = **matanujas**

Teu't|a *nf* Teuta (female name)

*****tevabi'** *nf (Old)* flunky, lackey

tevatu'r *nm (Old)* 1 public clamor, brouhaha, babel 2 [*Law*] hearsay testimony

*****tevatu'rë** *nf* rumor

teveqe'l
I § *adj (Colloq)* slow-witted, slow, retarded; stupid
II § *n* dimwit; moron

tevlí'g *nm (np ˜ gje)* = **tevlí'k**

tevlí'k *nm* bow of a yoke, oxbow

*****te'vo'n|a** *adv (Colloq)* 1 afterwards 2 toward evening 3 = **tekefu'ndit**.

teza'k *nm* son of mother's sister: cousin

te'ze *nf* mother's sister, aunt *(collateral female relative ascending or descending in mother's matriline or patriline)*

teze'ma'dhe *nf* great aunt

te'zë *nf* 1 thesis 2 set of final examination questions

te'zgë *nf* 1 sales counter, sales booth/stand; peddler's cart 2 handbarrow 3 body litter: stretcher

tezgja'h *nm* 1 weaving machine: textile loom, industrial loom 2 work table 3 mandolin pick made of cherry bark 4 large anvil used by blacksmiths 5 *(Reg)* wooden bottle for keeping roasted coffee beans

tezgjah'ist'e *nf* woman who operates a textile loom

tezgje're *nf* handbarrow used in construction work

të *conjunctive proclitic marking a verb in the subjunctive mood* that, to
○ *{imper sg verb}* **të** *{imper 1st pl same verb}*! let's *{verb}* quick! **ik të ikim!** let's get out of here!

të *2nd sg object pronominal proclitic* indicates that the following verb has a 2nd sg object or referent: thee/thy/you/your
○ **të bë·***n* **të dalësh prej lëkure** "{} *makes* you want to jump out of your skin" {} annoys you so much that you can't stand it any more
○ **tharto·***n[3sg]* "{} *puckers* your lips" {} can run rings around you
○ **të ça·***n* **hundët** {} *makes* your nose smart, have a pungent smell
○ **të ça·***n[3pl]* **mushkonjat** *(Colloq)* the mosquitoes *eat* you up
○ **të ça·***n[3sg]* **në ballë** "{} *hits* you in the forehead" {} *hits* the spot (said of a very cold or very strong drink)
○ **të ço·***n[pres]* **në njëqind/dyzet/shtatë cezma/ kroje/burime e s'të jep ujë** "{} *takes* one to a hundred fountains and never *gives* you water" {} *gives* one much hope but never *comes* through: {} *leads* you on
○ **të ha· dheun nën këmbë** "{} *eats* the ground under your feet" {} *is* a treacherous/rotten person
○ **të ha· në dritë të syrit** 1 {} *is* fearless 2 you *cannot* pull the wool over {}'s eyes, {} is very shrewd
○ **të ha· të bardhën e syrit** "{} *eats* the white of your eye" 1 {} would rob you blind 2 {} *is* very clever/adept
○ **të ha·***[3rd]* **kokërdhokun e syrit** "{} *eats* your eyeball" 1 {} *keeps* after you to get what {} *wants*, {} *pesters* you constantly, {} is annoyingly persistent 2 {} *is* a pest 3 {} *is* very shrewd

të|ho'll|ës *nm* rolling pin = **petës**

të|holl|im *nm ger* <**tëhollo·**n, **tëhollo·**het

të|hollo'·het *vpr* = **hollo·**het

të|hollo'·n *vt* = **hollo·**n

të|holl|ua'r *adj (i)* = **hollua'r**

***të|ho'q**| *stem for pdef* <**tëh**jek·

tëhu' *adv* **1** *(Colloq)* over here, this way **2** up to now, until now

○ {*quantifier + unit of time*} **e tëhu** for the past { }

të|hu'a·n *vt* **1** to alienate, estrange; treat [ ] like a stranger, behave coldly toward [ ] **2** to remove, take away

***të|hu'e·**n = **tëhua·**n

***të|hu'll·** = **tëho'll·**

***të|hu'mb·** *vi* **1** to lose oneself, get totally absorbed **2** to get lost, go astray, stray **3** to disappear

***të|hu'mb·**et *vpr* to sink down

të|la'r|ët *nf* tied-up bundle

të|la'r|a *np fem* dirty wash water, dishwater

të|lasht|o're *nf* land sown with crops

të|ly'e|n *nm (Colloq)* [*Dairy*] butter

***të|ly'e|r** *(Colloq)* = **tëlye·n**

të|ly'|n = **tëlye·n**

***të|ma'll|ë** *nf* molar (tooth) = **dhëmballë**

të|mbë'l
I § *nf* = **ëmbëlsi'rë**
II § *nm* gall bladder; gall
III § *adj* very bitter

të|mbël|pla's|ur *adj (i)* in a rage, raging

të|mbë'l|th = **tëmth**

të|mbl|agja'k = **tamblagja'k**

të|mbl|ë *nf* [*Anat*] temple (on the side of the forehead)

të|mo'tje *np fem* = **zahire'**

të|mth *nm* [*Anat*] **1** temple (of the skull) ***2** gall bladder

të|nd *pronominal adj masc sg gen dat abl acc* <**yt**

të|nd|e *pronominal adj fem sg gen dat abl acc* <**jote**

***të|ndë** = **tendë**

të|ngë *nf* = **peng**

të|pkë *adv (Reg Colloq)* exactly, exactly like

të|po'shte *nf* downslope, drop, declivity

të|po'shtë *adv* = **tërpo'shtë**

***të|poshtî|zë** *nf* = **tëpo'shte**

tër|bi'm *nm ger* **1** <**tërbo·**n, **tërbo·**het **2** raging anger; fury **3** furious speed/drive **4** [*Veter Med*] rabies

***tër|bne'sh** *nm* brushwood, undergrowth, scrub

tër|bo'·het *vpr* **1** to become rabid **2** to become enraged: go into a rage **3** *(Fig)* to explode with fury: rage **4** to be subject to uncontrollable desires; go wild **5** to behave like a spoiled brat **6** to grow rampant; grow in profusion; (of plants) grow exuberant

tër|bo'·n
I § *vt* **1** to make [ ] rabid; drive [ ] crazy **2** to enrage **3** *(Fig)* to spoil (by overpampering) **4** to irritate [ ] beyond endurance, drive [ ] crazy
II § *vi* **1** to become rabid **2** *(Fig)* to go out of control (from overpampering); go wild, run rampant

tër|bo'|rë *nf (Reg)* rabies

tër|bu'a|r *adj (i)* **1** rabid **2** enraged, furious **3** *(Fig)* raging; out of control, uncontrollable

***të're** *nf* **1** axletree **2** roller

të|rë
I § *determiner* **1** (followed by a noun in definite form) the entire, the whole **2** (followed by a deictic determiner) all that/those **3** (followed by a kinship noun in definite form) just like ___ **4** (followed by a noun in indefinite form) full of___
II § *adj (i)* in entirety: whole, entire
III § *nm (i)* everyone
IV § *nf (e)* whole; whole thing
○ **tërë ditën e ditës** the whole livelong day
○ **tërë hundë (e buzë)** with a cold look
○ **tërë sy e veshë** all eyes and ears

të|rë|fuqi'|shëm *adj (i)* all-powerful, omnipotent, almighty

***të|rë|një** *adv* always; forever

të|rë|se'j *adv (Colloq)* in all; in its entirety

të|rë|si' *nf* **1** whole set; entirety **2** wholeness, integrity; indivisibility

të|rë|si|shë'm *adj (i)* = **tërëso'r**

të|rë|si'sht *adv* entirely, wholly

të|rë|so'r *adj* entire, whole

tër|fi'l *nm* [*Bot*] clover *(Trifolium)*
○ **tërfil plage/plagësh** [*Bot*] woundwort, kidney vetch anthyllis *(Anthyllis vulneraria)* = **lulele'she**

tër|fil|i'sht|ë *OR* **tër|fil|i'shte** *nf* field/patch of clover

tër|fil|o're *nf* small field/patch of clover

***tër|fuk|o'r**
I § *adj* [*Ornit*] grallatorial
II § *np* [*Ornit*] grallae

tër|fu'r|cë *nf* crutch

tër|fu'r|k *nm (np ~q)* hayfork, pitchfork

tër|furk|o'·n *vt* to pick up [ ] with a hayfork

***tër|furk|o'r** *adj* [*Ornit*] of the order of wading birds (grallatorial)

***tër|furk|o're** *nf* [*Ornit*] wading bird *(Grallatores)*

***tër|fu'rk|th** *nm* scorpion

tër|fy't|ës *nm* popgun = **stërfy'tës**

***tër|gjo'·**n *vt* **1** to reprimand, scold **2** to bully

tër|hani'k *nm* sour porridge made with buttermilk

tër|ha'p·et *vpr (Intens)* to spread broadly

tër|he'dh· *vt (Intens)* to throw [ ] all around: toss [ ] helter-skelter

tër|he'q· *vt* **1** to pull **2** to draw **3** to pull/draw [ ] out; withdraw **4** to pull/draw in [ ]; suck in/on [ ] **5** *(Fig)* to attract **6** to stretch [ ] out, straighten [ ] out
○ **e tërheq· fjalën 1** to go back on one's word **2** to take back what one has said
○ **i tërheq· fjalët zvarrë 1** to drag out one's words: drawl **2** to drag out an action: drag along, malinger
○ **Tërheq·**[3sg] **gota gotën.** "The glass attracts another glass." One drink leads to another.
○ **tërheq· këmbën zvarrë/rrëshqanë** "drag one's foot" **1** to want others to follow one's lead **2** to bring good luck **3** to attract others by one's example
○ <> **tërheq·**[3sg] **kërraba nga vetja** *(Pej)* <> looks out only for <>self, <> is completely selfish: <> always looks out for number one
○ [ ] **tërheq· në baltë** to lead [ ] down the wrong path
○ **e tërheq· pas derën** to close the door after one
○ [ ] **tërheq· për hunde/hundësh** to lead/have [ ] by the nose
○ [ ] **tërheq· për kapistalli/kapistre** to make [ ] do what one wants; lead by the nose

∘ [] **tërheq· për veshi** "pull [] by the ear" to lead/have [] by the nose

∘ [] **tërheq· prej gjuhe** to force [] to speak unwillingly

∘ [] **tërheq· prej hunde/hundësh** to lead/have [] by the nose

∘ <>a **tërheq·**^{3sg} **rrënja për** [] "<>'s root pulls for []" <> *itches* for []

∘ <> **tërheq· veshin/veshët** to chastise/scold <>

∘ <> **tërheq· vëmendjen** to draw/hold <>'s attention

∘ <> **tërheq· vërejtje(n) 1** to deliver a disciplinary warning to <>, scold, criticize <> **2** to draw <>'s attention; make a strong impression

∘ [] **tërheq· zvarrë 1** to drag [] along the ground; drag [] out **2** to keep [] from coming into []'s own

tërhe'qës
I § *adj* **1** serving to pull/draw; used for draft purposes **2** *(Fig)* attractive
II § *nm* pulling device/vehicle/mechanism: belttread tractor for pulling heavy artillery or armored troop carriers

tërheq'ësi *nf* attractiveness

tërhe'qje *nf ger* **1** <**tërhe'q·, tërhi'q·et 2** attraction

tërhe'qur *part* <**tërheq·, tërhi'q·et**

tërhi'dh·et *vpr (Intens)* to jump up and down (with joy/rage)

tërhi'dh| *stem for 2nd pl pres, pind, imper, vp (Intens)* <**tërhe'dh·**

tërhi'q·et *vpr* **1** to pull back; withdraw; retreat **2** to crawl backwards **3** to creep **4** to be strongly attracted, be much taken: be a devotee

tërhi'q| *stem for 2nd pl pres, pind, imper, vp* <**tërheq·**
∘ **Tërhiq e mos këput.** "Pull and don't break." **1** Getting by, but just barely. Making some progress, but very slowly **2** painfully slow

****tërhje'k·** = tërhe'q·

tërho'dh| *stem for pdef* <**tërhe'dh· (Intens)**

tërho'll· *vt* to make [] thin/thinner

tërho'll·et *vpr* to get thin/thinner

tërho'llës *n* rolling pin

tërho'q| *stem for pdef* <**tërheq·**

tërho'z· = tëhu'z·

tërho'zët *adj (i)* = tërhu'zur

tërhu' = tëhu'

tërhu'z· *vt* to make [a horse] shy: spook

tërhu'z·et *vpr* **1** (of a horse) to shy; shy away from being saddled/ridden; be skittish **2** *(Fig)* to snort with rage; become incensed

tërhu'zur *adj (i)* **1** (of a horse) spooked, skittish **2** *(Fig)* snorting with rage; incensed

****tërku'l** *nm* pitchfork

tërkuz'a'r *n* ropemaker

tërku'z'as *adv* = lita'rthi

tërku'zë *nf* **1** rope (usually made of goathair); cable **2** *(Reg)* halter (for horses)

tërkuz'o're *nf (Colloq)* telpher = telefe'rik

tërli'k *nm* [*Ethnog*] long, pleated, black woolen cloak worn by women of northeastern Albania

****tërma'** *adv* = tërma'l

tërma'l *adv* uphill = përpje'të

tërma'le *nf* uphill slope

tërma'ltë *adj (i)* steeply rising, steep

****tërma'sinë** *nf* = tërma'le

tërme'g·et *vpr* = tërmek·et

****tërme'gët** *adj (i)* = tërmekët

****tërme'gshëm** *adv* horribly

****tërme'k** *nm (pl ˜ qe)* = tërme't

tërme'k·et *vpr* to shake with fury, fly into a rage

tërme'kët *adj (i)* shaking with fury, enraged

tërme't *nm* earthquake

****tërmo'në** *adv* always, constantly

****tërn|** = altern|

****tërnago'p** *nm* = ka'zmë

****tërna'ltë** = tërma'l

****tërn'ue'razi** *adv* in alternation

tërpa'sme *nf* uphill slope already traversed (in climbing)

tërpi' *nf* [*Med*] consumption, phthisis

tërpje'të *adv* = përpje'të

****tërpos'i'në** *nf* = tatëpje'të

tërpo'shtë *adv* downhill, downward; down

tërqe'th·et *vpr* = rrëqe'th·et

tërsëllë'm *nm (Colloq)* **1** great force: slam, bang **2** anger, ferocity; hostility

tërsi're *nf* rope

****tërsha'në** *(Reg Gheg)* = tërshë're

tërshano're *nf* = tërshër'ishtë

tërshë'rë *nf* [*Bot*] oats *(Avena sativa)*
∘ **s'di·sa/ku shko·n**^{3sg} **tërshëra** "not know how much // where oats go" there is utter chaos
∘ **tërshërë e çmendur** [*Bot*] = tërshërë e egër
∘ **tërshërë e egër** [*Bot*] wild oat *Avena fatua*

tërshë'rët *adj (i)* of oats, oaten

tërshë'rëz *nf* [*Bot*] meadow oat grass *(Avena pratensis)*

tërshër'ishtë *nf* **1** field of oats **2** oat straw

tërtë'r = tirti'rnm gold or silver thread used in embroidery

tërtho'r
I § *adj* = tërtho'rtë
II § *adv* **1** diagonally; slantwise: oblique **2** indirectly **3** awry
∘ **tërthorja e barkut** [*Anat*] the diaphragm

tërtho'rak *nm* **1** [*Constr*] perpend stone, through stone **2** *(Book)* [*Geom*] diameter

tërtho'razi OR **tërtho'ras** *adv* **1** diagonally, with a slant **2** indirectly, obliquely

tërtho'rce *nf* crossbar, crosstie

tërtho're *nf* **1** town periphery **2** winding road; convoluted pathway **3** = tërtho'rëse **4** *(Colloq)* arc in the sky to the zenith **5** crossroad **6** barrier

tërtho'rëse *nf* crosstie on railroad track: sleeper

tërtho'ri *adv* = tërtho'razi

tërtho'rtë *adj (i)* oblique

tërthor'zo·n *vt* to transverse [] obliquely: cross [] on a slant

****tërthu'r·** = tërthor·

****tërthu'rshëm** *adj (i)* = tërtho'rtë

****tërvi'lmë** *adj (i)* = tërvitshëm

tërvi't *adv* year-before-last = parvje't

tërvi'tshëm *adj (i)* of the year before last = parvje'tshëm

****tërvje'më** *adj (i)* = tërvitshëm

tërr *adv* not in the slightest
∘ **nuk i bën syri tërr** not be fazed for a moment, not blink an eye

∘ **nuk i bën veshi tërr** not pay any heed

tërrkat· *vi* [*Mus*](of a musical instrument) to hit the wrong note, sound a sour note

***tështi·**·*n vi* = **teshti·**·*n*

*****tështi|tje** *nf* = **teshti·**m*ë*

tët *pronominal adj masc acc* <**yt**

ti *pron 2nd sg* thou, you

∘ **Ti lypës e unë përderës.** "You a beggar and I a mendicant." You and I are equally poor.

∘ **Ti zot, unë zot, po gomarin kush e kullot?** "I am the master and you are the master, so who pastures the donkey?" Somebody's got to do the work. Too many chiefs and not enough Indians.

ti|bie *nf* [*Anat*] tibia

*****tierr** = **tjerr**

ti|fo *nf* [*Med Veter*] typhoid fever

∘ **tifo e morrit** [*Med*] epidemic typhus

∘ **tifo e zorrëve** [*Med*] typhoid fever

tifo|z

I § *n* (sports) fan, enthusiast

II § *adj* enthusiastic, fervent

tifti|k *nm* (*np ˜ qe*) angora wool; mohair

tiga|n *nm* long-handled pan: skillet, frying pan

tigani|s· *vt* to fry [] (in a pan)

tigani|s··*et vpr* **1** to fry **2** (*Fig*) to get/feel very hot

∘ **tiganis·***et* **me dhjamin e** {*pronominal adj*} to do everything on {*one's*} own, get by on {*one's*} own

tigani|s|je *nf ger* <**tiganis·**, **tiganis·**·*et*

tigani|s|ur *adj* (*i*) pan-fried

ti|gër *nm* **1** [*Zool*] tiger **2** (*Fig Pej*) fierce and cruel person

ti|j

I § *pronominal adj* (*i*) of his, his; its

II § *n* (*i*) **1** his; its **2** his folks/people

III § *enclitic after prepositions that take an ablative object* indicates a 3rd sg masc object for the preposition: him, it

ti|ja *adj* (*e*) his own way; its own way

tik-ta|k *onomat* tick-tock

tikta|k *nm* ticking sound

tik-tik-ti|k *imper interj* call to attract chickens: here chick-chick-chick!

ti|llë *adj* (*i*) such, such a

ti|m *masc gen dat abl acc* <**im**

ti|me *fem acc* <**im**

*****timja|n** = **temjan**

timo|n *nm* **1** rudder, helm; steering mechanism; steering wheel **2** (*Fig Book*) steering/guiding force

timon|ie|r *n* **1** helmsman, steersman **2** (*Fig Book*) leader, director

*****tim|os** = **tymos**

timpa|n *nm* [*Anat*] eardrum (*tympanum*)

Ti|na *nf* Tina (female name)

*****ti|naj** *adj* (*i*) his; its = **tij**

tina|r *nm* large wooden container with a wide bottom and narrower top: pickle barrel, cheese vat, butter cask

ti|në

I § *nf* alluvial sediment, mud

II § *adj* (*i*) **1** clouded with mud: muddy *****2** = **tina|r**

tin|ëz *adv* furtively, sneakily; secretly, on the quiet; imperceptibly

tin|ëz|a|k *adj, n* (*Pej*) = **tinëza|r**

tin|ëza|r *adj, n* (*Pej*) sneaky/sly (person)

tin|ëz|i *nf* (*Pej*) sneakiness, slyness, insidiousness, furtiveness; secrecy

tin|ëz|i|sht *adv* (*Pej*) sneakily, slyly

tin|ëz|o··*het vpr* **1** to leave secretly: steal away **2** (*Pej*) to sneak out/away; sneak

*****tin|ëz|o·**·*n vt* to conceal, cloak

ti|ngë *nf* [*Ichth*] tench (*Tinca tinca*)

*****tingëll** = **tingull**

tingëll|a *np fem* earrings with spangles

tingëll|i|m *nm ger* **1** <**tingëllo·**·*n* **2** ringing sound resulting from striking a resonant object: clang, twang **3** [*Ling*] pronunciation

tingëll|i|më *nf* **1** ringing sound resulting from striking a resonant object: clang, twang **2** [*Lit*] sonnet two quatrains followed by two tercets of eleven-syllable lines

tingëll|o··*n vi* **1** to make a resonant metallic sound: clang, twang; ring, peal **2** [*Ling*] to be pronounced: sound **3** (*Fig*) to voice; sound, resound

tingëll|o|r *adj* = **tingëllu|es**

*****tingëll|t** *adj* (*i*) [*Ling*] = **tingullt**

tingëll|u|es *adj* making a sound, sonorous; resounding, echoing

tingëll|u|e|shëm *adj* (*i*) resounding, echoing

ti|ng|ëz *nf* finger cymbals

tingtin|gë *nf* (*Colloq*) down/downhill slope

ti|ng|thi *adv* hopping on one foot

ti|ngull *nm* (*np ˜ j*) **1** sound; resonant sound **2** [*Mus*] musical sound: tone **3** [*Ling*] speech sound, sound segment

tingull|imit|i|m *nm* **1** [*Spec*] sound imitation **2** [*Ling*] onomatopoeia = **onomatope**

tingull|imit|u|es *adj* **1** sound-imitating **2** [*Ling*] onomatopoeic = **onomatope|k**

tingull|o|r *adj* **1** [*Ling*] of or pertaining to speech sounds: phonetic: phonetic, phonic **2** pronounced, vocalized

tingull|t *adj* (*i*) [*Ling*] voiced

*****ti|nkë** *nf* [*Ichth*] tench = **tingë**

tip

I § *nm* **1** set sharing a distinctive characteristic: type **2** model, prototype **3** [*Lit Art*] embodiment of a type: quintessence

II § *adj* serving as a model

tipa|r *nm* feature: facial feature; distinguishing feature, characteristic

tip|ës|o|r *adj* typifying

tipi|k *adj* **1** typical; distinctive, characteristic **2** [*Lit Art*] embodying a type: quintessential

tipi|ke *nf* (*Book*) that which is typical: typification, quintessence

tip|iz|i|m *nm ger* <**tipizo·**·*n*

tip|iz|o··*n vt* **1** [*Lit Art*] to capture the quintessential character of []; typify **2** [*Tech*] to follow a model

tip|iz|u|es *adj* [*Lit Art*] distinctive, characterizing, typifying

tip|ogra|f *nm* typesetter

tip|ografí *nf* = **shtypshkro|nj**ë

tip|ografïk adj [Publ] of or pertaining to printing/publishing

tip|o|logjï nf (Book) typology

tip|o|logjïk adj (Book) typological

tip|o's· vt (Colloq) to imprint [] in the mind

tip|o's·et vpr (Colloq) to make a deep/long-lasting impression: become imprinted

TIR abbrev (French) <**Transports Internationals Routiers** International Road Transport

tir| stem = **tirr**

tira'n nm tyrant

tira'n|as
 I § n inhabitant of Tirana
 II § adj of/from Tirana

tira'nd|ë nf strap over the shoulders that holds up clothing: suspenders, braces; shoulder strap

Tira'në nf Tirana (capital city of Albania); district in central Albania

tiran|ï nf tyranny

tiran|ïk adj tyrannical

tiran|iz|ïm nm ger <**tiranizo'·n**

tiran|izo'·n vt to tyrannize

tiran|të nf = **tirandë**

tira'zh nm [Publ] number of copies printed from a single setting of type: edition size

tï're nf 1 coarse cotton thread 2 long towel worn over hair by country women 3 womens' long white stocking

tï'rë nf wooden wine vatskein/hank (of yarn)

tiristo'r nm [Phys] thyristor

***tirjaqï** adj = **terjaqï**

tïrk nm (np ˜ q) 1 white flannel or felt 2 men's long white gaiter, legging

tiroi'd nm 1 [Anat] thyroid gland 2 [Med] swollen thyroid glands: thyroid condition

tirq np <**tïrk** 1 tight-fitting embroidered white-flannel breeches with decorative braid at the bottom of the legs and on the pockets: white flannels; traditional trousers with narrow legs 2 = **tïrk**

tïrr stem for 2nd pl pres, pind, imper, vp <**tjerr·**

tis nm 1 veil 2 [Med] conjunctivitis 3 [Bot] yew = **bërshe'n**

tisa'zh nm 1 weaving/textile industry 2 (Colloq) textile mill

***tïsk|ë** nf fear, dread

tis|o're np [Bot] yew family Taxaceae

tita'n nm 1 titan 2 [Chem] titanium (Ti)

titan|ïk adj titanic

tïtu'll nm (np ˜ j) title

titulla'r n 1 head of an official institution: titular 2 (Book) title-bearer

titull|o'·n vt to assign a title to []: entitle

tï'zg|e nf 1 = **dïzg·e** 2 slingshot, sling = **hobe'**

***tjatro'·n** vi to be different, differ

tje'gull nf roof tile
 ∘ **s'ka· tjegull mbi kokë/krye** not have a roof over one's head, not even have a hole to call home
 ∘ **tjegull e kthyer/zhubravitur** pantile

tjegulla'r n 1 tile maker 2 roof tiler

tjegull|o're nf [Bot] hart's tongue fern (Scolopendrium vulgare, Phyllitis scolopendrium)

tje're pl (të) <**tjetër**

tjerr nm spun yarn

tjerr· vt 1 to spin [yarn, thread] 2 (Fig) to prolong [] needlessly: spin out [] 3 (Fig) to make [] up, fabricate
 ∘ **i tjerr· fjalët** 1 to drag out what one is saying 2 to spin out one's words with care
 ∘ **tjerr· hollë** to be very smart/clever, be quick-minded; speak in clever and suggestive/allusive language
 ∘ **tjerr· lëmshe kundër** <> to make up stories in order to defame <>; weave a plot against <>
 ∘ [] **tjerr· tortë** to drag [] out needlessly, go too slowly with []
 ∘ **ia tjerr· thekun bisedës** to be good at carrying on friendly conversation

tjerr|ato're nf spinner (female) of wool

tje'rr|e nf [Text] forked distaff

tje'rr|ë
 I § part <**tjerr·**
 II § nf [Text] homespun cloth
 III § adj (i) *spun

tje'rr|ës
 I § adj [Text] used in spinning
 II § n operator of a spinning machine/wheel: spinner

tje'rr|je nf ger <**tjerr·**

tje'rr|më adj (i) having a drawn face: sunken-cheeked

tje'rr|shëm adj (i) capable of being spun (into thread/yarn): spinnable

tjerr|ta'r n (Old) = **tjerrës**

tjerr|to're nf spinning section of a textile mill), spinning mill

tje'tër adj, n, determiner 1 other; another 2 next (in sequence)
 ∘ **Tjetrit i digjet mjekra, ai kërkon të ndezë cigaren.** "The other one's beard is burning, and he tries to get his cigarette lit from it." He is completely insensitive to other people's serious problems
 ∘ **tjetër gjë** something else; something quite different
 ∘ **tjetër për tjetër** (something) quite/completely different, quite another thing; in a completely other way

tjetër|an|shëm adj (i) [Geom] (of angles) opposite

***tjetër|da'sh|ës** adj altruistic

tjetër|ka'h adv in/to/from a different place, some other place; in a different direction; elsewhere

tjetër|kënd acc <**tjetërkush**

tjetër|kujt gen (i) dat abl <**tjetërku'sh**

tjetër|ku'nd adv somewhere other than here: elsewhere

tjetër|ku'sh pron someone else

***tjetër|lloj|shëm** adj (i) heterogeneous

tjetër|o'r adj [Electr] alternating (current)

tjetër|pa'rdje adv day before the day before yesterday: three days ago

tjetër|pas|ne'sër adv day after the day after tomorrow, three days from today

tjetër|qy'sh adv in another way, differently: otherwise

***tjetër|sï** adv otherwise

tjetër|sï'm nm ger (Book) <**tjetërso'·n**, **tjetërso'·het**

tjetër|so'·het vpr (Book) to become someone else's property: change ownership

tjetër|so'·n vt 1 (Book) to transfer ownership of [], alienate [property]; sell 2 to alter, change

tjetër|so'j adv (Colloq) in another manner, otherwise: somehow else

tjetër·su·a·r *adj (i)* *(Book)* transferred in ownership, alienated; sold

tjetër·su·e·sh·ëm *adj (i)* *(Book)* (of property) transferrable: alienable; capable of being bought or sold

tjetr·azi *adv* otherwise

tkurr· *vt* to shrink; contract

tku·rr·et *vpr* to shrink (up); contract

tku·rr·ës *adj* **1** shrinking, contracting **2** *[Phys]* contractive **3** *[Med]* astringent

tku·rr·je *nf ger* **1** <**tkurr·, tku·rr·et 2** contraction

tku·rr·sh·ëm *adj (i)* contractable, contractile

tku·rr·shm|ëri *nf* *[Phys]* contractility

tku·rr·ur *adj (i)* compacted, contracted

***tla·nd·ër** *nf* bundle = **tëla·nd·ër**

***tiloftar** *nm* glutton

tmerr

I § *nm* **1** great fear: terror, dread; fright **2** cause of great fear: horror, terror
II § *pred* terrible

tme·rr|ës·isht *adv* terribly, extremely

tme·rr·ët *adj (i)* terrified

***tme·rr·ik** *adj (i)* terrifying

tmerr·im *nm* = **tmerr**

tme·rr·isht *adv* terribly, horribly

tmerr·o·het *vpr* to be/become terrified

tmerr·o·n *vt* to terrify

tmerr·onj·ës *adj* = **tme·rrsh·ëm**

tme·rr·sh·ëm *adj (i)* **1** terrifying; terrible, horrible **2** formidable, huge

***tme·rr·ta·r** *adj* = **tme·rrsh·ëm**

tmerr·ua·r *adj (i)* **1** terrified **2** fearsome, horrible, gruesome

to *accus form used directly after a preposition* <**ato** them

***to·be** *invar*

toç

I § *nm* **1** small ear of corn; small melon; small head of lettuce/cabbage **2** *(Pet)* (child's) head **3** *(Colloq)* bald spot on the head
II § *pred* bald
III § *adj* *(Fig)* dim-witted, stupid

toçile = **toçilë**

toçillë *nf* **1** potter's wheel **2** pedal-operated grindstone/whetstone for sharpening tools = **qostër**

toçis *stem for 1st sg pres, pl pres, 2nd & 3rd sg subj, pind* <**toçit·**

toçit· *vt* to decant; empty [] by pouring; pour [] out

toçit·je *nf ger* **1** <**toçit· 2** decantation

tog *nm (np ~ gje)* **1** pile, heap **2** small group of people: bunch, cluster **3** *[Ling]* cluster

toger *nm* *[Mil]* lieutenant

togë *nf* **1** *[Mil]* platoon **2** *[Hist]* toga **3** *(Fig Bookish Pej)* cloak that hides the real intent/content
○ **togë gjurmuese/gjurmuesish** *[Mil]* scouting patrol

togë|komandant *nm* *[Mil]* platoon commander

togëz *nf* = **to·këz**

togëzo·n *vt* to pile up [], put [] into a heap

tog|fjal·ësh *nm* *[Ling]* word group, phrase

to·gje-to·gje *adv* in clusters/piles/groups

toj·ë *nf* **1** thong/cord made of twisted fibers **2** wick of an oil lamp **3** coarse/unusable fiber drawn from the the first stages of unwinding a silk cocoon; left-over/unused silk cocoon **4** fishing line **5** grapevine scion; grapevine cutting planted in the ground **6** *[Ornit]* crane = **kurr·ilë**

tok *adv* together in a group/pile/mixture; together as a group

tok· *vt, vi* **1** to chop up [meat]: hack **2** to hammer [a blade] in order to sharpen it; dress [a millstone] **3** to bring [] together in a gesture: shake/clasp [hands]; click [glasses] when toasting **4** to mix [] together **5** to knock (on [a door])

to·k·et *vpr* to shake hands

to·k|a *invar*

to·ka *nf* = **to·këz**

to·kë *nf* **1** earth; soil; ground; land; territory **2** *(Elev)* homeland **3** signal bell/gong ***4** *(Old)* cluster, bundle, bunch
○ **to·kë buke** land used to produce grain
○ **nuk ësh·të ende në to·kë të bukës** not yet start making one's own living
○ **to·kë e cekët** thin soil, soil with a thin layer of workable ground
○ **to·kë e lehtë** light and friable soil
○ **to·kë mbi ujë** land without natural irrigation; land not under irrigation
○ **to·kë nën ujë** land under (natural) irrigation
○ **ësh·të për to·kë** *(Colloq)* **1** to be in terrible condition, be for the birds **2** to be good for nothing
○ **to·kë e re** land being plowed for the first time
○ **to·kë e rëndë** hard ground
○ **to·kë skeletore** *[Agr]* skeletal soil
○ **to·kë e tavan** "floor and ceiling" in/into disarray, in/into a hodgepodge: topsy-turvy
○ **to·ka të kafenjta** *[Agr]* rich organic soil

to·kël *nf* chunk

to·këll·im·e *nf* bare ground/land

to·kë·s

I § *nm* "dweller in the earth" *(Euph)* snake
II § *adj* dwelling on dry land: terrestrial

to·kë·so·r *adj* **1** of or pertaining to the Earth; of or pertaining to earth; made of earth, earthen; of or pertaining to the real world, earthly **2** of or pertaining to land/ground/soil **3** of or pertaining to a particular area/place: local; territorial

to·kë·t *adj (i)* dwelling on dry land: terrestrial

to·kë·z *nf* buckle; clasp

tokë·zim *nm ger* **1** *[Phys Tech]* <**tokë·zo·n 2** electrical grounding connection: ground

tokë·zo·n *vt* *[Phys Tech]* to ground (electrically)

tokë·zu·a·r *adj (i)* *[Phys Tech]* (electrically) grounded

tokë·zu·e·s

I § *adj* *[Phys Tech]* serving to ground electrically: grounding
II § *nm* *[Phys Tech]* grounding device/element: ground

tok|ic·e *nf* group, bunch, cluster

tokma·k *nm* **1** heavy wooden device used as a soil compactor: soil rammer **2** heavy wooden mallet; sledgehammer; maul **3** door knocker **4** mortar for crushing condiments

***tok|or** *adj* dwelling on dry land: terrestrial

toksin·ë *nf* *[Biol Med]* toxin

to·k|thi *adv* **1** = **tok** ***2** *(Old)* in mass, wholesale

to·ku *adv (së)* together = **ba·shku**

toku·r·ë *nf* *[Geog]* isthmus = **istëm**

tolera·nc·ë *nf* tolerance

tolera·nt *adj* tolerant

toler|o· *·n vt* to tolerate

*__**tolimo·li** *adv* higgledy-piggledy, helter-skelter, topsy-turvy

*__**toll|a·c** = **tulla·c**

to·llë *nf* **1** bald pate, bald spot **2** drumhead of a tambourine

tollomba·z
   I § *nm* [*Mus*] = **dumale·k**
   II § *adj* (*Fig Colloq*) empty-headed, stupid

tollov|í *nf* (*Colloq*) chaotic mess, big jumble

tollov|ís *stem for 1st sg pres, pl pres, 2nd & 3rd sg subj, pind* < **tollovi·t·**

tollov|í·t· *vt* (*Colloq*) to give [ ] the runaround

tollov|í·t·et *vpr* (*Colloq*) to get all confused; get upset

*__**tollumba·c** *nm* toy balloon = **tullumba·c**

tollu·mbë *nf* **1** clog/shoe with a flat sole and no heel **2** = **caru·qe**

tom *nm* **1** [*Publ*] numbered volume (of a series) *2 ear of corn/maize

to·mbol *nf* game like lotto: tombola

to·m|ës *nm* [*Ornit*] type of finch

Tomo·r *nm* Tomor (male name)

ton *nm* **1** tone **2** ton **3** [*Ichth*] tuna, tunny **4** [*Mus*] pitch (of a tone, of the voice); key (of a piece of music)
   ○ **ton i kuq** [*Ichth*] Atlantic bluefin tuna *Thunnus thynnus thynnus*
   ○ **ton pendëgjatë** [*Ichth*] albacore *Thunnus alalunga*
   ○ **ton vizak** [*Ichth*] skipjack tuna *Katsuwonus pelamis*
   ○ **ton i vogël** [*Ichth*] little tunny *Euthynnus alletteratus*

to·n|a
   I § *fem pl* < **jo·n**ë our, of ours
   II § *pl fem* **1** ours **2** our female relatives/friends

ton|a·zh *nm* tonnage

tonela·të *nf* ton

*__**ton|ela·zh** = **tona·zh**

to·në *gen/dat/abl/acc* < **y·n**ë our

toni·k *adj, nm* tonic

*__**toní·t·et** *vp impers* it *hurts* ◇, ◇ *aches*

top
   I § *nm* **1** ball **2** [*Mil*] cannon **3** bale **4** [*Text*] broad color stripe on thin cloth
   II § *adv* **1** all together in one group/clump/bunch: in a ball/bale/clump **2** (*Colloq*) with finality, totally: absolutely, right
   ○ **top basketbolli** ball used in basketball: basketball
   ○ **top deti** [*Bot*] kind of green alga *Codium bursa*
   ○ **top i diskutueshëm** [*Soccer*] drop ball
   ○ **top i gjatë** [*Tennis*] forward spin
   ○ **top jashtë loje** [*Volleyball*] dead ball
   ○ **top i këputur** [*Tennis*] drop shot
   ○ **top i lehtë** [*Tennis*] lob
   ○ **top i lojës** [*Tennis*] game ball
   ○ **top i mbushur** [*Gymnastics*] medicine ball
   ○ **top me të prerë** [*Tennis*] chopped ball
   ○ **topi s'[] nda·n**^{3sg} "a cannon couldn't separate [ ]" [ ] *have* an unbreakable friendship
   ○ **ësh·të top sheqeri** (of a girl) to be healthy and comely
   ○ **top i zbortë** snowball

*__**topa·c** = **topa·z**

topa|gro·p|thi = **topgro·pthi**

topa|hí|p|as *adv*

topa·ll *adj* (*Colloq*) lame: gimpy

*__**topalla·k** *adj* bunch, cluster, bundle

topall|o· *·n vi* = **çal|o·** *·n*

*__**topa·n** *nm* drum

topa·nxhë *nf* (*Old*) muzzle-loading flintlock pistol; pistol

topa·r *n* [*Hist*] cannoneer, gunner

*__**to·p|ash** = **to·pthi**

topa·z *nm* [*Min*] topaz

*__**top|bo·rë** *nf* [*Bot*] snowball, guelder rose (*Viburnum opulus*)

to·p|çe
   I § *adj* **1** (*Colloq*) chubby **2** (of flowers) having a ball-like form
   II § *adv* (of health) in good shape, very well

top|çí *nm* (*np ̄ nj*) (*Old*) [*Mil*] cannoneer, gunner

to·pe *nf* chubby sheep/goat

to·pe *np* (*Crude Colloq*) testicles: balls

to·për *nf* hatchet

top|gro·p|thi *adv*

topí *nm* **1** (*Colloq*) reservoir of water for irrigation in dry weather **2** (*Reg*) pile, heap; stack

top|ís *stem for 1st sg pres, pl pres, 2nd & 3rd sg subj, pind* < **topí·t·**

top|í·t· *vt* **1** to blunt, dull **2** to daunt, intimidate, dismay; cause [ ] to back off, restrain **3** to tire [ ] out

top|í·t·et *vpr* **1** to become blunt, get dull, lose its edge **2** to be daunted/intimidated/dismayed; back off; freeze up **3** to get lethargic; become exhausted

top|ít|ës *adj* **1** daunting, dismaying **2** causing lethargy; tiring, exhausting

top|í·tje *nf ger* **1** < **topí·t·**, **topí·t·et** **2** dullness of sensitivity, obtuseness

top|í·tur *adj (i)* **1** in consternation: daunted, dismayed **2** exhausted, tired out

topja·k *nm* [*Hist*] tax imposed in early times for grazing livestock

top|kalo·r|th|azi *adv*

to·p|kë *nf* [*Bot*] stigma (of a flower)

topogra·f *nm* topographer

topografí *nf* [*Geod*] topography

topografí·k *adj* [*Geod*] topographical

top|ola·k *adj* chubby, pudgy; plump

toponí·m *nm* [*Ling*] toponym

toponimí *nf* [*Ling*] toponymy

toponomastí·kë *nf* [*Ling*] toponomastics

*__**toprr|o·** *·n vt* to daze, stupefy

*__**toprr|ua·r** *adj (i)* dazed, numbed, stupefied

top|sheqe·r *adj, n* (child or young woman) having a rotund face with fair skin

topta·n *adv* (*Colloq*) in wholesale lots, all together, as is

to·p|thi *adv* in a ball

top|u·rre *nf* club with a knob at one end: cudgel

top|urru·k *adj, n* (*Pet*) chubby (child)

top|u·z
   I § *nm* **1** (*Old*) spiked cudgel: mace **2** drumstick (for beating a drum) **3** [*Invert*] straight-spine murex (*Bolinus brandaris*)
   II § *adv* gathered into a bun (of hair)

tor *nm* [*Math*] torus

to·r *stem for pdef* < **tjerr·**

*torallak = torollak

torbë nf **1** sack, pouch, bag **2** bale of cotton yarn weighing about nine kilograms

*torël nf = trokull

torfë nf **1** peat **2** turf

torishtë nf(Reg) **1** fenced sheep pen that is periodically moved in order to distribute the manure evenly over a field **2** commons land used for grazing

*torit·et vpr **1** to scatter, disperse **2** to be distraught

tork nm (np ˜ qe) **1** (Reg) heavy wooden beam used to exert pressure on an olive press **2** trough used for crushing grapes **3** = trokull

torkë nf **1** skein **2** bundle of four or five strings of tobacco **3** knotted towel or cloth used in children's games ***4** tails (in heads or tails)

torkulle nf = trokull

torlar adj clever

torllak nm (Old) tax imposed in early times for grazing livestock in mountain pastures = topjak

tornim nm ger [Tech] < torno·n

tornitor n lathe worker

torno nf [Tech] lathe

torno·n vt [Tech] to turn [] (on a lathe)

toroli alternate stem for oblique sg (pl ˜ nj) < torua

torolec nm [Entom] = torrkaç

torolingë
I § nf children's whistle made of reed or straw
II § adj (Fig Pej) feather-brained, empty-headed

torolis stem for 1st sg pres, pl pres, 2nd & 3rd sg subj, pind < torolit·

torolit· vt to fondle, pet, caress, cuddle

torollak adj, n (Colloq Pej) stupid/simple-minded (person)

*torollaqe fem < torollak

toroman adj, n (Colloq Pej) = torollak

tororis· vt (Colloq) **1** to play with [] by throwing it up into the air and catching it; soothe by rocking [] in one's arms **2** to lull and rock [] to sleep **3** (Fig) to give [] the runaround; make excuses for putting [] off

tororis·et vpr to loiter

toroshosh· vt (Colloq) to think [] over carefully, turn [] over in the mind

torpedinierë nf [Mil] torpedo boat

torpilë nf [Mil] torpedo = silur

torpilim nm ger [Mil] < torpilo·n

torpillo·n vt [Mil] to torpedo = siluro·n

torpillë nf [Ichth] torpedo (Torpedo torpedo)

*torpillo·n vt to torpedo

*torpillore nf [Naut] torpedo boat

tortë nf **1** torte **2** strong, thick rope made of flax

torturë nf torture

torturim nm ger < torturo·n, torturo·het

torturo·het vpr to be racked with pain and suffering: suffer agony

torturo·n vt to torture; agonize

torturues adj causing torture: agonizing

torthi adv around and around, in circles

torua nm (obl ˜ oi) **1** track made by walking: footprint, trail, spoor **2** hidden path **3** careful attention; presence of mind

*torrë nf tour, circuit, circle

torrkaç nm [Entom] **1** cricket (Gryllus) **2** woodpecker = qukapik

torrlë nf **1** (Old) small screw **2** oil lamp wick-holder with an adjusting thumb screw **3** (Fig) mess, muddle = ngatërresë

torrlo·n vt to confuse/deceive/mislead [someone]

torrolloc
I § adj foolish
II § n fool

torrovan nm [Entom] = torrkaç

torroveshkë nf animal's mouth: muzzle, snout

torrovile nf skein winder

toskë
I § adj [Ethnog] of or pertaining to Toskëria or its inhabitants
II § n Albanian from Toskëria: Tosk

Toskëri nf ethnographic region encompassing southern Albania

toskërisht adv [Ling] in a Tosk variety of Albanian (language)

toskërishte nf [Ling] Tosk (dialect)

*tostongale nf bonfire

total adj, nm total

totem nm totem

totemizëm nm totemism

*totkë nf nickname

*toto nf with masc agreement Orthodox priest

totolesh adj, n gullible (person)

*tovër nf old woman

toz nm (Colloq) pulverized material: powder, dust

*tozlimon nm = limontoz

*tozlluk nm white-flannel legging

TPE abbrev < Tregu i përbashkët Evropian European Common Market

*tpi nm (pl ˜ ni) milk churn

tra(r)
I § nm **1** wooden beam; roof beam **2** [Ethnog] separate household: family
II § adj (Fig) dull-witted, thick in the head
◦ ësh-të (si) tra i pagdhendur/palatuar "be like rough lumber" **1** (of a man) to look like a fat pig **2** to be a blockhead/numskull

trabadar nm thole

*trabokull nm yearling kid

*trackë nf [Ornit] wren = cinxami

tradicional adj traditional

traditë nf tradition

tradhët = tradht

tradhmend adv unawares, unexpectedly

tradhtar
I § n traitor; person who breaks his word, faithless/unfaithful/disloyal person
II § adj treasonable; treacherous; faithless, unfaithful

tradhti nf **1** treason; treachery **2** breaking one's word, faithlessness **3** infidelity, betrayal

tradhtisht adv treacherously, perfidiously

tradhto·n vt **1** to betray **2** to be disloyal/unfaithful to []; break [one's word]; break one's word to []

tradhtor = tradhtar

trafik nm traffic

traget nm ferryboat

tragë nf **1** track; trace; mountain trail **2** (Fig) direction in which something is going **3** intellect, mind

○ tragë e verbër "blind trail" trail that is so narrow and lightly marked as to disappear completely in places

tragëzo ·n vt to follow [a trail/trace]: track, trace

tragzë nf = çakalle

tragjedi nf tragedy

tragjik adj tragic

tragjike nf [Lit Art] that which is tragic: the tragic, tragic nature

tragjikomedi nf tragicomedy

tragjikomik adj tragicomic, tragicomical

tragjizëm nm tragic element/characteristic

trahan nm = trahana

trahana nf 1 [Food] sourdough mixed with yogurt or milk, dried in the sun, and then crumbled into small pieces; porridge 2 bulgur, cracked grain, groats

trainer = trajner

*trajce nf = trastë

trajektore nf trajectory

trajner nm [Sport] coach, trainer

*trajstar n bag maker

trajstë nf = trastë

*trajstëz nf dimin small bag: pouch; vesicle, sac

trajtesë nf 1 treatise 2 (Old) treatment

trajtë nf 1 form, shape, figure; appearance 2 [Ling] form; morph

trajtëformim nm [Ling] inflection

trajtëformues adj [Ling] inflectional

trajtësim nm ger < trajtëso·n, trajtëso·het

trajtëso·het vpr to take on a particular form, take shape

trajtëso·n vt to give [] a particular form: shape

trajtim nm ger 1 < trajto·n 2 treatment *3 (Reg) building

trajto·n vt 1 to give [] a treatment: treat 2 (Reg) to form, construct *3 to repair

trak adj, n [Hist] Thracian

trakaliç adj, nm unripe (fig)

trakalle nf clapper, knocker = trakullore?

trakas adj, n [Hist] = trak

trakaxhike nf small leather pouch for food carried by livestock herders

trake nf [Anat] trachea

trakeit nm [Med] tracheitis

traki nf Thrace

trakie nf [Invert] kind of clam Thracia papyracea

trakisht adv in Thracian (language)

trakishte nf Thracian language

trakje nf bell

trakt nm secretly distributed political leaflet/tract

trakta't nm 1 treaty 2 treatise

traktor nm tractor

traktorist n tractor driver

trakull nm device for applying pressure: press

trakulli·n vi to knock/rap (on a door/window)

trakullimë nf sound of knocking/rapping; clatter

trakullo·n vi to make a knocking sound, knock; clatter

trakullore nf door knocker; ratcheting noisemaker

trakullues
I § adj knocking
II § n incessant talker: chatterbox

trakzë nf = çakalle

*tralis = trallis

trallis· vt to put [] into a stupor

trallis·et vpr to go into a stupor

trallisur adj (i) in a stupor

tramak nm 1 cornstalk 2 ear of corn

trambë nf (Colloq) barter

*tramëzim nm ger < tramëzo·n

*tramëzine nf = trazire

*tramëzo·n vt = trazo·n

*trampline = trampoline

trampoline nf 1 diving board, jumpboard 2 (Fig Book) jumping off point

*tramtë = trambë

tramvaj nm tramway, tramline; tram

trand· vt to cause to quake: shake

trand·et vpr to quake

*trandafil (Reg Gheg) = trëndafil

*trandës adj = trandshëm

*trandshëm adj (i) quaking, shaking

trangull nm (np ~ j) [Bot] cucumber (Cucumis sativus) = kastravec

○ trangull pa fara (ColloqImpolite) completely brainless, really stupid

*trano adv downward, below

transaksion nm transaction

transatlantik adj transatlantic

transferim nm ger 1 < transfero·n, transfero·het 2 job transfer

transfero·het vpr to transfer officially from one position to another

transfero·n vt to transfer [] officially (from one position to another)

transferueshëm adj (i) transferrable

transformator nm [Phys] transformer

transformim nm ger < transformo·n

transformo·n vt to transform

transfuzion nm transfusion

transistor nm 1 [Phys Electr] transistor 2 (Colloq) small portable transistor radio

transit
I § nm transit
II § adv in transit, passing through

transitiv adj [Ling] transitive

transitor adj (Book) transitional = tranzitor

transkriptim nm ger 1 < transkripto·n 2 transcribed copy: transcription

transkripto·n vt to transcribe

translat nm figurative expression

transliterim nm transliteration

translitero·n vt to transliterate

transmetim nm ger 1 < transmeto·n 2 broadcast, transmission

transmeto·n vt (Book) to transmit

transmetues adj transmitting

transmision nm [Tech] (in a motor vehicle) transmission; gearbox

transoqeanik adj transoceanic

transparent adj transparent

transport nm transport; transportation

transportim nm ger 1 < transporto·n 2 transportation

transportjer nm [Tech] conveyer

transporto·n vt to transport

transport|ue̱s nm carrier, transporter; conveyor (belt)
  ○ **transportues i blinduar** armored vehicle
transport|ue̱|she̱m adj (i) transportable
TRANSSHQIP (abbrev) Albanian transportation agency for foreign commerce
TRANSTREG abbrev <**Ndërmarrja e transportit e tregëtisë** Agency for Commercial Transport
transversa̱l adj transverse
transversa̱l|isht adv transversely
transhe̱ [tran-she̱] nf trench
tra̱nxh|ë nf [Tech] shearing machine, shear
  ○ **tranxhë̱ pre̱rëse** [Tech] shearing machine
tranzi̱t = transi̱t
tranziti̱v adj [Ling] transitive
tranzito̱r adj (Book) transitional
trap nm 1 furrow; ditch 2 deep gully 3 deep hole in the ground (in which potatoes are stored for the winter) 4 embankment, levee; uncultivated strip of land bordering a field 5 raised footwalk along a ditch 6 (Reg) cultivated strip of land 7 narrow trail (in woods or mountains) 8 dense copse of short trees 9 raft; pontoon raft used as a ferry
trapa̱n nm = **trapano̱**
trapa̱no̱ nr [Tech] drilling machine: drill
trapa̱r n bargeman, raftsman
trapa̱-tra̱pa adv staggering from side to side
trapa̱xhi nm (np ~ nj) ferryman
trapaza̱n nm 1 (Old) high recess with a railing above a guest parlor enabling women to look down without being looked at by men 2 room lit by a dormer window, attic room 3 (Old) platform for little children at one end of the guest parlor 4 kitchen sink = **sqo̱ll**
trape̱s|kë nf dimin (Reg) small table
trape̱z nm [Geom] 1 trapezoid 2 [Gymnastics] trapeze
trapeza̱ri nf (Old) 1 dining room 2 large dining table
trapeze̱ri = trapeza̱ri
trape̱z|ë nf table = **trye̱zë**
trape̱zo̱id nm [Geom] trapezium
trapezo̱id|a̱l adj [Geom] trapezoidal
***trapi̱** nf schematic plan: diagram, outline
trapi̱s stem for 1st sg pres, pl pres, 2nd & 3rd sg subj, pind <**trapi̱t·**
***trapi̱s|je** nf = **trapi̱**
trapi̱t·
  I § vi 1 to pick one's way along narrow trails 2 to take short cuts 3 to wander around
  II § vt 1 to search all around for [] 2 to give preliminary shape to [], make a mock-up/model of []
***trapiza̱n** nm banister
tra̱r|ë np <**tra̱(r)**
tra̱r|i obl <**tra̱(r)**
tra̱se̱ nf road bed, track bed; canal bed
trasi̱m nm ger <**traso̱ ·n**
***tra̱s|je** nf = **tra̱stë**
traso̱ ·n vt to specify, determine
trasta̱r n (Colloq) purse-snatcher, thief = **vje̱dhës**
tra̱stë nf shopping bag; shoulder bag
  ○ **trasta e herdha̱ve** [Anat] scrotum
trasversa̱l adj transverse
trash· vt 1 to increase [] in thickness: thicken 2 (Fig Colloq) to increase [] in density/intensity: deepen;

intensify; make more serious; strengthen 3 (Fig Colloq) to exaggerate; overdo
  ○ **i trash·**^{pl} **fjalët** to exchange bitter words, start to quarrel
  ○ <> **trash· mendjen** to fill up <>'s mind with lies: confuse <> thoroughly
tra̱sh·et vpr 1 to get thicker 2 to thicken; become more dense 3 to put on weight, get fat 4 (of a voice) to get deeper 5 (of a cutting tool) to become dull/blunt 6 (Fig Colloq) to increase in strength/size/depth/weight; get too large
  ○ <> **trash·et**^{3sg} **gjuha** "<>'s tongue thickens" (Impol) <>'s speech becomes slurred from drinking too much
  ○ <> **trash·et**^{3pl} **gjunjët** "<>'s knees thicken" is very tired, <> is so tired that <>'s knees can hardly move
  ○ <> **trash·et**^{3sg} **koka/truri/mendja** "<>'s mind dulls" (Impol) <>'s head/brain gets rusty; <> becomes senile, <> becomes dotty in the head
  ○ <> **trash·et**^{3sg} **lëkura** "<>'s skin gets thick" 1 <> becomes toughened by experience 2 <> become thick-skinned (and impervious to criticism)
  ○ <> **trash·et**^{3sg} **qafa** (Pej) "<>'s neck gets thick" 1 <> gets fat 2 <> gets wealthy
  ○ <> **trash·et**^{3pl} **veshët** "<>'s ears get thick" <> gets hard of hearing
trashalu̱q adj, n (Pej) fatso
trashama̱n adj, n (Pej) 1 = **trashalu̱q** 2 fathead(ed)
trashama̱n|çe adv in a fatheaded way, boorishly
trashaman|ë̱si nf fatheadedness, boorishness
trashamani̱ nf 1 obesity, fatness 2 coarseness, boorishness
trashani̱k adj 1 (Pej) (of a person) coarse, crude, gross 2 conspicuous, obvious
trashanik|ë̱si nf (of a person) coarseness, crudeness
tra̱she nf fat cow/goat
tra̱shë
  I § adj (i) 1 thick; stocky, plump; dense; broad 2 coarse; (of air) thick with impurities/moisture 3 (of voices/sounds) deep 4 of or pertaining to cattle: bovine 5 (Colloq) fat; (of soil) fertile 6 (Fig) slow-witted, dense
  II § nf (e) thick part; thick thing
  III § adv in thick pieces; coarsely
  ○ **e trasha e kofshë̱s = trash|ë̱kofshë̱**
  ○ **trashë e gje̱rë** spread out flat
trash|ë̱go̱ nm ger 1 <**trash|ë̱go̱ ·n, trash|ë̱go̱ ·het** 2 heritage; inherited quality; inheritance 3 (Colloq Felic) long life and many heirs!
trash|ë̱gimi̱ nf inheritance
***trash|ë̱gim|lâ̱n|ës = trash|ë̱gim|lë̱nës**
trash|ë̱gim|lë̱n|ës n [Law] person who leaves an inheritance: testator
trash|ë̱gim|o̱r adj [Law] pertaining to an inheritance: heir
trash|ë̱gim|ta̱r n 1 inheritor, heir 2 (Colloq) child, descendant
trash|ë̱go̱ ·het vpr 1 to enjoy a happy life with one's family; enjoy a long and happy life, live happily ever after 2 to be passed along as a heritage
trash|ë̱go̱ ·n
  I § vt to inherit
  II § vi (Colloq) to enjoy a happy life (with one's family)

trashëgo·r _adj (Old)_ [_Ling_] possessive

trashëgo·re _np fem_ [_Ethnog_] congratulatory visits exchanged during the first week of betrothal

trashëgua·r _adj (i)_ inherited

trashëgue·s _nm_ heir

trashëgue·shëm _adj (i)_ inheritable, hereditary

trashëgue·shmëri _nf_ inheritability

trashëko·fshë _nf_ thigh (of a cut-up fowl); plump part of the thigh

trashësi _nf_ 1 thickness 2 stockiness, plumpness; coarseness; heaviness; (of voices/sounds) depth, low register

trashëso·_het_ _vpr_ = tra·sh·et

trashi _nf_ rich/fertile soil

trashje _nf ger_ 1 <trash·, trash·et 2 thick part; thick thing 3 thigh

trashkël _nf_ crumb, fragment

trasho·_het_ _vpr_ = trash·et

trasho·n _vt_ = trash·

trashtinë _nf_ 1 [_Bot_] henbane (Hyoscyamus niger) 2 (Fig) fat-headedness, oafishness, ignorance; stupid person

trashuke _nf_ fat goat

trashullak _adj_ = trashaluq

trate _nf_ [_Fish_] large fishing net with cork floats and lead sinkers

tratkë = tratë

trath _nm_ roof lath

***tratht** = tradht

traumatizo·n _vt_ [_Med_] to traumatize

traumatologji _nf_ [_Med_] traumatology

traumë _nf_ trauma

travajë _nf_ (Book) travail

travajo·_het_ _vpr_ (Book) to fret, worry

travajo·n _vt_ (Book) to torment, afflict

traversë _nf_ 1 [_Const_] cross-piece, transom 2 crosstie on railroad track: sleeper = tërthorëse 3 [_Sport_] (soccer) cross-bar above the goal net

***travis** _stem for 1st sg pres, pl pres, 2nd & 3rd sg subj, pind_ <travit·

***travit·** _vt_ = trallis·

***travit·et** _vpr_ = trallis·et

***travitur** _adj (i)_ = trallisur

traze _nf_ 1 wicker rack holding the meat to be smoked over a chimney 2 (Old) piece of mesh on a small metal stand over a fire to catch flying sparks

trazim _nm ger_ <trazo·n, trazo·het

trazirë _nf_ demonstration by a mob of people, riot; disorderly confusion, turmoil, tumult

trazo·_het_ _vpr_ 1 to get fouled/tangled/mixed up: get all confused 2 to get worried, worry 3 to take a turn for the worse; change for the worse, worsen

trazo·n
   _I §_ _vt_ 1 to stir; stir up [] 2 (Fig) to make [] complicated/murky/confused; disturb 3 (Colloq) to hoe [the soil] around a crop: cultivate
   _II §_ _vi_ to make <> feel dizzy
   ∘ **trazo·n fjalë me** [] to have a quarrel with []
   ∘ <> **trazo·n gjakun** to upset <> terribly
   ∘ **trazo·n urët** "poke/disturb the burning embers" to exacerbate bad feelings: stir the pot

trazore _nf_ 1 [_Food_] cornbread made with butter and cheese and served piping hot 2 long-handled wooden mixing spoon

trazovaç _adj, n_ (child) who gets into everything, mischief-maker

trazua·r _adj (i)_ = përzier

trazue·s
   _I §_ _adj_ 1 stirring, mixing 2 disturbing
   _II §_ _n_ disturber
   III § _n_ 1 stirrer, mixer 2 disturber

tre
   _I §_ _num masc_ three
   _II §_ _np (të) masc_ a group of three, the three of them, all three
   ∘ **tre hunj e një thupër** (Pej) carelessly, superficially
   ∘ **ësh·të tre mel e dy grurë** (Impol Colloq) to be stupid: have nothing much upstairs

***trecepsh** _nm (Old)_ triangle

***trecklë** _nf_ [_Ornit_] = trishtil

treçerek _nm_ three-fourths

treçerekëshe
   _I §_ _nf_ 1 three-quarter-length coat for women 2 container with a capacity of three-fourths of the standard amount
   _II §_ _adj_ three-quarter

treditësh _adj_ three-day old; three-day long

treditor _adj_ lasting/taking three days; three-day long

tredh· _vt_ to castrate

tredhak
   _I §_ _nm_ castrated livestock animal
   _II §_ _adj_ castrated

tredhëmbësh
   _I §_ _adj_ three-pronged
   _II §_ _nm_ pitchfork with three tines

tredhës _nm_ castration/gelding tool

tredhje _nf ger_ 1 <tredh· 2 castration

tredhur _adj (i)_ castrated

trefazor _adj_ [_Electr_] three-phase

trefish
   _I §_ _adj, nm_ triple
   _II §_ _adv_ thrice, three-fold

trefisho·_het_ _vpr_ to increase three-fold: triple

trefisho·n _vt_ to triple []

trefishtë _adj (i)_ triple; three-part, tripartite, three-fold

trefletësh
   _I §_ _adj_ 1 (of textiles) in three panels: three-paneled 2 (of plywood) three-ply 3 [_Tech_] having three blades, triple-bladed
   _II §_ _nm_ [_Bot_] clover = tërfil

treg _nm (np ~gje)_ market
   ∘ **tregu i punës** labor market

tregarësh _nm_ [_Sport_] athletic contest requiring participation of each contestant in three different events

tregim _nm ger_ 1 <trego·n, trego·het 2 [_Lit_] narrative; short story, tale

tregimtar
   _I §_ _n_ story teller/writer
   _II §_ _adj_ narrative

trego· _vpr_ 1 to reveal oneself to be _: prove to be _ 2 to pretend, pretend to be _; act like _
   ∘ **nuk trego·**_het_^{3rd} **me gojë** "not to able to be told by words" to be inexpressible, words _cannot_ express {}

trego·*n*

I § *vt* **1** to indicate; show; exhibit, display **2** to attest to [ ], demonstrate **3** to tell; say **4** *(Colloq)* to tell/inform on [ ], expose; denounce

II § *vi* to seem to be, seem: look

○ **i trego·***n* **babait arat** *(Iron)* to try to tell someone his own business

○ **<> trego·***n* **bërrylin** "show <> one's elbow" to turn one's back on <>, turn <> down

○ **<> trego·***n* **cepin** to remind <> of <>'s inferior position: put <> in <>'s place

○ **<> trego·***n* **dhëmbët 1** to bare one's teeth at <>, threaten <> **2** to reveal one's evil intentions

○ **trego·***n* **edhe qumështin e nënës** "tell even about one's mother's milk" to tell everything

○ **trego·***n* **fije (e) për pe** to tell in utmost detail

○ **<> trego·***n* **gjoksin** to stand up to <>, meet <> head on, confront <> courageously

○ **trego·***n* **kujdes për** [ ] to look after [ ]

○ **<> trego·***n* **lëkurën e ujkut** "show <> the skin of the wolf" to menace <>

○ **<>a trego·***n*^{3sg} **qejfin** to teach <> a good lesson

○ **<> trego·***n* **rrugën** *(Impol)* to kick <> out, show <> the door

○ **<> trego·***n* **se nga lind dielli** "show <> from which direction the sun rises" *(Iron)* to give <> a severe beating/scolding

○ **<> trego·***n* **strajcën me tagji** "show <> the bag with fodder" to tell <> only the good part, show <> only the good side

○ **<> trego·***n* **shkopin** "show <> one's stick" to threaten <>

○ **<> trego·***n* **udhën/udhët** *(Impol)* to kick <> out, show <> the door

○ **<> trego·***n* **vendin** to give <> deserved punishment, teach <> a good lesson

○ **<> trego·***n* **zorrët e barkut** "show <> one's entrails" to tell <> even the most intimate details: air one's dirty linen in public to <>

tregˈtar

I § *n* merchant, tradesman, businessman

II § *adj* of or pertaining to commerce/business: commercial

○ **tregtar flamurësh** "flag merchant" *(Book)* person of weak character; person without principles

tregˈtarˈisht *adv* *(Book)* commercially

tregˈtarˈuˈc *nm* *(Pej)* small-time tradesman, petty shopkeeper

tregˈtiˈ *nf* commerce, business

tregˈtiˈm *nm ger* <**tregto·***n*

tregˈtiˈsht *adv* commercially

tregˈtiˈzë *nf* small business: shop/store, market stall

tregto·*n* *vi, vt* to be in business: do business, deal/trade in [ ]

tregˈtoˈre *nf* place of business: shop, store

tregˈtuˈes

I § *adj* commercial

II § *n* merchant, dealer

tregˈtuˈeˈshëm *adj (i)* marketable

tregˈuˈes

I § *adj* indicatory, indicative

II § *nm* **1** indicator **2** index **3** informational road sign: signpost, milestone **4** [*Math*] exponent

treˈgjyˈsh *nm* = **stërgjyˈsh**

treˈhaˈpësh

I § *adj* performed in three steps

II § *nm* **1** [*Sport*] triple jump **2** taking three steps without bouncing the basketball: traveling

*****trek** *nm* fragment, bit

treˈkaˈtësh *nm* having three storeys, three-storey

treˈkëmbësh *nm* **1** tripodic gallows tree **2** tripod; trivet

treˈkëndësh

I § *adj* triangular

II § *nm* triangle

○ **trekëndëshi revolucionar** "revolutionary triangle" *(HistPK)* tripartite system of education: academic study, productive work, and military training

○ **trekëndësh rezistencash** [*Electr*] impedance triangle

treˈkëndoˈr *adj* **1** triangular **2** three-faceted

treˈleˈkësh *adj* worth/costing three leks

treˈleˈkˈshˈle *nf* three-lek bill

tremb· *vt* **1** to frighten [ ] suddenly: scare **2** to intimidate **3** *(Colloq)* to shoo off [ ] **4** *(Fig)* to interrupt, bring [ ] to an end

○ **s'e tremb· (fare) qimen** to be totally undaunted: not blink an eye, be unflinching

treˈmbˈet *vpr* **1** to be scared **2** to be worried; become anxious

○ **Nuk trembet ariu/arusha me shoshë.** "The bear is not frightened off with a screen." **1** *(Prov)* You need the right tools to do an important job. **2** *(Pej)* You can't fight your enemies with a popgun.

○ **<> tremb·***et*^{3sg} **gjaku** <>'s blood *freezes* with fear

○ **tremb·***et* **nga një albër** to be frightened by some tiny thing, be afraid for nothing

○ **s'<> tremb·***et*^{3sg} **syri** <> is not fazed for a moment, <> *does* not blink an eye

○ **S'trembet ujku nga mushkonjat.** "The wolf is not frightened by mosquitoes." *(Prov)* The strong are not going to be intimidated by the weak.

treˈmbë *nf* sudden fright: scare; uneasy fear, dread

treˈmbˈëˈdhjeˈtë

I § *num* thirteen; number thirteen

II § *nf* the number thirteen

III § *adj (i), n (i)* thirteenth

trembˈëlˈaˈk *adj, n* timid/timorous (person)

treˈmbˈës

I § *adj* **1** timid; timorous **2** frightening, intimidating

II § *n* intimidator, bully

treˈmbˈje *nf ger* (<**tremb·**, **tremb·***et* **2** intimidation

treˈmbˈshëm *adj (i)* easily frightened: fearful

treˈmbˈur *adj (i)* scared, frightened, afraid

treˈme *nf* **1** = **hajaˈt 2** [*Anat*] atrium *****3** blacksmith's forge

treˈmˈëˈzaj *adv* in/into three parts

*****treˈmˈëˈzo·***n* *vt* to increase [ ] threefold, triple

*****trêmˈje** *nf (Reg Gheg)* = **trembˈje**

*****treˈmuajoˈr** = **tremujoˈr**

treˈmuaˈjˈsh

I § *adj* three months old/long; trimonthly

II § *nm* three-month period

treˈmujoˈr

I § *adj* trimonthly, quarterly

II § *nm* three-month period, quarter (of a year)

tren *nm* (railroad) train

*****trendeliˈnë** = **trëndeliˈnë**

treˈnˈëz *nf* support beam

treˈngjyˈrësh *adj* tri-colored

tren|i *nf* madness, insanity

tren|im *nm ger* **1** <*treno·n*, *treno·het* **2** insanity, madness

tren|o·het *vpr* **1** to go mad/crazy **2** to rage with anger

tren|o·n *vt* to drive [] mad; make [] very mad
○ **treno·n pas** <> to be crazy about <>

tre·ntë *adj (i)* **1** mad **2** wild, uncontrollable

*trenj *np (Reg)* <tra

tre|pa|lësh *adj* tripartite

*tre|ple *np* <trap

*trepet|is· *vt* to cause [] to vanish/disappear

*trepet|is·et *vpr* to cease to exist; vanish, disappear

tre|qe|ni|ke *nf* yoke connecting three oxen: triple yoke

tre|qind *num* three hundred; number three hundred

tre|qind|të *adj (i), n (i)* three hundredth

tre|qind|vjeç|ar *nm, adj* tri-centennial

*trer|ë *np* <tra

tre|rrok|ësh
  I § *adj* [*Ling Lit*] trisyllabic
  II § *nm* [*Ling*] trisyllable

tres *stem for 1st sg pres, pl pres, 2nd & 3rd sg subj, pind* <tret·

tre|skë *nf* lump of hard stone

*tre|skll|a *nf* fragments

tre|sh
  I § *adv* in three parts; three times
  II § *adj* **1** composed of three members: triadic, triple **2** with a capacity of three of the units measured
  III § *nm* number three
  IV § *nm* **1** the number three **2** trey, playing card with three pips **3** game in which two opponents each play their three stones into a square divided into four smaller squares; morris

tre|she *nf* **1** group of three: trio **2** pot holding three cups of coffee

tret·
  I § *vt* **1** to melt; dissolve **2** to digest, absorb; erode; rot **3** to waste; waste away [], emaciate **4** to lose **5** to toss [something worthless] away **6** to send [] away, expel **7** (*Fig*) to put up with [], stomach
  II § *vi* **1** to get lost **2** to go far away, go into exile
  ○ <> **tret·**³ˢᵍ **boja** there *is* not a trace of <>, <> *disappears*
  ○ **s'**[] **tret· dheu** "the earth *does not lose* []" [] will never disappear, [] will never be forgotten
  ○ <>**a tret· farën** to get rid of <> completely, make <> disappear completely
  ○ **nuk** [] **tret·**³ˢᵍ **mideja** [] *is* not easily believable: [] *is* hard to swallow
  ○ **tret· si re** to disappear/vanish like a cloud
  ○ **tret· shikimin/vështrimin larg** to stare far off into space, stare absentmindedly

tre·t·et *vpr* **1** to melt away; dissolve **2** to get digested/absorbed; erode; rot **3** to get wasted; waste away, become emaciated **4** to disappear, get lost
  ○ <> **tret·et**³ˢᵍ **fara** "<>'s seed *disappears*" <> completely *disappears*
  ○ **tret·et në mendime** to get lost in thought
  ○ **tret· si kripa në ujë** "dissolve like salt in water" to waste away (from an illness), become all skin and bones, become emaciated; lose a lot of weight in a short length of time

tre|tar *n* **1** [*Hist*] sharecropper who pays a third of his produce for the use of land/livestock; person receiving such a third **2** triplet = **trinja|k**

tret|dhe *nm* place of exile

tre|të
  I § *adj (i), n (i)* third
  II § *nf (e)* **1** third grade (in elementary school); third grade class/classroom **2** [*Hist*] levy of one third of his produce paid by a tenant farmer to his landlord **3** (*Old*) [*Relig*] commemoration of a death three days later by the relatives; commemorative meal on the third day after a death

tre|të|nat|ë *nf* [*Ethnog*] family celebration on the third night after a birth during which the infant is given a name

tret|ës *adj, nm* solvent

tret|ësi|rë *nf* [*Chem*] solution

tret|je *nf ger* **1** <tret·, tret·et **2** digestion **3** = **tretësi|rë**

tret|o·n *vt* to till [] for the third time in a year; rework [the soil]

tre|ton|ësh *adj* weighing three tons; with a capacity of three tons

tret|shëm *adj (i)* soluble; digestible

tret|shm|ëri *nf* solubility; digestibility

tre|tur
  I § *part* <tret·, tret·et
  II § *adj (i)* **1** molten **2** thin and weak, emaciated
  ○ **ësh·të tretur e kulluar** to be completely emaciated, have become all skin and bones

tre|vend|ësh *adj* with a capacity of three places; for three people

tre|v|ë *nf* **1** territory, province **2** patch of pasture

tre|vjeç|ar *adj* lasting three years, for three years; triannual; three years old

tre|vjet|or *nm* three-year period; third anniversary

trev|o·n *vi* to do/go well, flourish

tre|zo|nj|ë *nf* **1** thorn **2** bloody bump

trëmb|ër|ak *adj* = **trembëla|k**

*trëmb|ës = **trembës**|

trëndafi|l
  I § *nm* **1** [*Bot*] rose (*Rosa*) **2** (*Fig Pet*) girl/boy in the flower of youth
  II § *adj* rose-colored, rose (in color), pink
  ○ **trëndafil breshke** [*Bot*] evergreen rose = **balkroc|ë**
  ○ **trëndafil deti** [*Zool*] sea anemone (*Actinia*)
  ○ **trëndafil i egër** [*Bot*] dog rose (*Rosa canina*)

trëndafil|isht|ë *nf* rose garden

trëndafil|ore *np fem* [*Bot*] rose family *Rosaceae*

trëndafi|l|të *adj (i)* rose-colored, pink; rosy

trëndeli|n|ë *nf* **1** [*Bot*] sickle-fruited fenugreek (*Trigonella corniculata*) **2** (*Fig*) pleasant and pretty girl
  ○ **ësh·të trëndelin|ë (nga mendja)** (*Impol*) to lack good sense, have no brains
  ○ **trëndelin|ë yzerlike** fenugreek *Trigonella foenum-graecum*

tri
  I § *num fem* three; number three
  II § *nf* the number three
  III § *np (të) fem* the three of them, all three
  ○ **ësh·të**³ʳᵈ **tri në degë e dy në majë** {} *is* foolish and immature
  ○ **tri plakat** [*Myth*] = **shkundadi|mër**

tria|dë *nf* (*Book*) triad

tria|dhë nf trinity

tria|kë nf (Old) = **tri|kë**

tria|re adj (of a bell) composed of three superimposed bells (with a single clapper)

tribu|n nm 1 [Hist] Roman tribune 2 (Elev) ardent and eloquent protector of the people: tribune

tribu|në nf 1 dais, tribune, podium; review platform 2 stadium box

tri|çi|kël nm three-wheeled motor vehicle: tri-wheel motorcycle

*****tri|çkë** nf threesome, trio

tri|dh stem for 2nd pl pres, pind, imper, vp < **tre|dh•**

tridh|ë|bo|të nf [Bot] martagon lily (Lilium martagon)

*****tri|dhëmb|sh** nm trident

tri|dhjetë
 I § num thirty; number thirty
 II § nf the number thirty
 III § adj (i), n (i) thirtieth

tri|dhjetë|le|k|ësh
 I § adj (Offic) worth thirty leks; costing thirty leks
 II § adj, nm (Colloq) (bill) worth three leks

tri|dhjetë|le|k|ëshe nf three-lek bill

tri|dhjetë|vjeça|r adj 1 thirty-year old 2 lasting thirty years

tri|dhjetë|vjeto|r adj thirtieth anniversary

tri|fazo|r adj triphasic

*****tri|fi|l** = **tër|fi|l**

trig|ël nm [Ichth] striped mullet, long-snouted mullet (Mullus surmuletus) = **barbun guri**

trigonometri| nf [Math] trigonometry

trigonometri|k adj [Math] trigonometric

trija|re = **tria|re**

tri|kë nf 1 centaury; drug centaurium used in herb medicine to reduce fever (Centaurium umbellatum) 2 antidote for poisonous bites/stings 3 thin branch, switch; twig

*****tri|këmbë|s** nm (Reg) = **trekëmbë|sh**

tri|ko nf sweater, pullover
 ○ **triko golf** turtle-neck sweater

trikota|zh nm 1 knitting; knitting industry 2 knitwear

triko|zë nf [Med] trichosis

tri|ku|l nm three-tined hayfork

trilio|n nm trillion (1,000,000,000,000)

trilogji| nf [Lit] trilogy

trill nm 1 sudden whim, caprice 2 sudden flutter of wings

trill|a|n adj, n = **tekanjo|z**

trill|i|m nm ger 1 < **trillo|•n**, **trillo|•het** 2 fiction, phantasy

trillo|•n vt to make up [ ] (from the imagination): invent, devise

trill|ua|r adj (i) made up (from the imagination): fictitious; trumped-up

trill|ue|s nm 1 fabricator, slanderer 2 schemer, plotter

trim
 I § nm 1 (Old) armed guard; warrior 2 heroic/brave/valorous man: hero 3 grown man
 II § adj brave (in battle); courageous, stalwart
 ○ **trim i dheut** (Poet) strong and brave person
 ○ **Trim është ai që mund veten.** (Prov) The real master is the person who masters himself.
 ○ **trim i marrë** crazy fool
 ○ **trim mbi trima** particularly brave person: real hero, bravest of the brave
 ○ **trim me fletë** "winged hero" particularly brave person: real hero
 ○ **trim për vdekje e për tokë** (Elev) person who is fearless even in the face of death
 ○ **trim rrufe** "lightning-bolt hero" (Poet) quick-striking warrior

trim|a|ç nm (Contempt) coward who puts on false show of bravery; pompous hero

trim|alo|ç adj = **trima|ç**

trime|stër nf quarter (of a year): trimester

trim|ë|re|s|ë nf heroic/brave/valorous act, heroism

trim|ë|re|shë nf < **trim** heroic/brave/valorous woman: heroine

trim|ë|ri| nf (np ˜ra) 1 bravery, valor 2 brave/valorous act, heroic deed

trim|ë|ri|sht
 I § adv bravely, valorously, heroically
 II § adj of or pertaining to heroic valor

trim|ë|ro|•het vpr 1 to become full of courage: take heart 2 to make a pretense of bravery; try to frighten <>

trim|ë|ro|•n
 I § vt to instill [ ] with courage: encourage, brace
 II § vi to be valorous, become courageous

trim|ë|ro|r adj heroic

trim|ë|rue|s adj instilling courage, encouraging, heartening

*****trim|ni|na** np = **trim|ë|ri|ra**

*****trim|no|sh** = **trimo|sh**

trim|o|ç = **trimo|sh**

trim|o|sh
 I § nm (Reg Gheg) (Pet) young boy; audacious boy
 II § adj stouthearted

tri|moto|r adj, nm trimotor (airplane)

trim|sho|r nm = **trimo|sh**

trim|th nm dimin (Pet) [Ethnog] endearing term for a mourning widow's dead husband: dear little hero

tri|na|k n triplet

*****tri|n|cë** nf [Ornit] sandpiper, shank (Tringa)

tri|në nf 1 wattled screen/partition; wattled gate for a sheep pen; wattled fence surrounding a sheep fold 2 harrow 3 crude raft 4 back of the hand, metacarpus; instep, metatarsus *5 wickerwork, wattle

tringe|c nm [Ornit] greater titmouse = **trishti|l**

tri|ng|ë nf [Ornit] bullfinch, finch

tring|ëll|i|•n vi, vt to tinkle; clink, clank; knock

tring|ëll|i|m nm ger < **tring|ëllo|•n**

tring|ëll|i|më nf ger 1 < **tring|ëll|i|•n** 2 tinkle; clink, clank; knock

tring|ëllo|•n vi, vt = **ting|ëllo|•n**

tri|ngjy|r|ësh = **trengjy|rësh**

trini| nf 1 [Relig] trinity 2 triad

trin|i|m nm ger < **trino|•n**

*****tri|nko** adj = **fri|ngo**

trin|o|•n vt to run a harrow over [ ]: harrow

tri|no|m nm 1 [Math] trinomial 2 triad

trino|r adj [Anat] tarsal

tri|nja|k n, adj triplet

trio nf [Mus] trio

trio|dë nf [Spec] triode

tri|pa|l|ësh adj three-sided

tripa|re nf [Med] tripara

tri|pje|s|ësh adj tripartite, three-part

trips nm [Entom] thrips (Thripidae)

○ **tripsi i duhanit** [*Entom*] tobacco thrips *Thrips tabaci Lind.*

○ **tripsi i grurit** [*Entom*] European grain thrips *Limothrips cerealium Hal.*

○ **tripsi i hardhisë** [*Entom*] grape leafhopper *Drepanothrips Reuteri Uzel.*

○ **tripsi i serrave** [*Entom*] greenhouse thrips *Heliothrips haemorrhoidalis*

triqo'she
I § *adj* triangular
II § *nf (Old)* triangle

triqo'sh*ës adj, nm* = **triqo'she**

trisk *nm (np ~qe)* = **sherme'nd**

trisk*ë nf* **1** ration card **2** *(Old)* membership card

trisket'im *nm* rationing system

triskull *nm (np ~j)* **1** young sprout **2** thin sliver

trisqe *np* <**trisk**

*****trist** = **trisht**

trish *adv* in three parts; three times

trishe *nf* = **triskull**

*****trishku***ll* = **triskull**

trishtil *nm* [*Ornit*] titmouse, tit *(Parus)*

○ **trishtili i kaltër** [*Ornit*] blue tit *Parus caeruleus L.*

○ **trishtili kokëzi** [*Ornit*] black-capped chickadee *Parus atricapillus L.*

○ **trishtili me çafkë** [*Ornit*] crested tit *Parus cristatus L.*

○ **trishtili me mustaqe** [*Ornit*] bearded tit *Panurus biarmicus*

○ **trishtili i vogël i murmë** [*Ornit*] marsh tit *Parus palustris L.*

○ **trishtili i zi** [*Ornit*] coal tit *Parus ater L.*

trisht'im *nm* melancholy, deep sadness

trishto'·*het vpr* to fall into melancholy

trishto'·*n vt* to make [] melancholic, sadden [] deeply

trishtu'ar *adj (i)* melancholic, deeply sad

trishtu'es *adj* causing deep sadness, saddening

trishtu'e'sh'ëm *adj (i)* causing deep sadness, sad

*****trishu'lët** *adj (i) (Old)* three-masted

trishull *nm (np ~j)* [*Bot*] bladdernut *(Staphylea)*

Trita'n *nm* Tritan (male name)

*****trita'r** *nm* triose

trito'l *nm* [*Chem*] trinitrotoluene, TNT

trito'n *nm* **1** [*Zool*] newt **2** smooth newt *(Triturus vulgaris)*

○ **triton me kreshtë** [*Zool*] crested newt, warty newt, great warty newt *Triturus cristatus*

○ **tritoni me pika** [*Zool*] spotted smooth newt *Triturus vulgaris*

triu'mf *nm* triumph

triumfa'l *adj* **1** *(Book)* triumphal **2** triumphant

triumfal'isht *adv (Book)* triumphally; triumphantly

triumfato'r *adj (Book)* triumphant

triumfo'·*n vi* to triumph

triumfu'e's
I § *adj* triumphant
II § *n* victor

triumvira't *nm (Book)* triumvirate

triv*ë nf (Reg)* spoor = **fërke'm**

○ **s'ësh·të në trivë** not be in one's right mind, be out of one's mind

tri'z*ë nf* **1** group of three: threesome **2** children's game played by hopping three times on one leg

tro *stem for pdef, opt, adm* <**tru'a·***n*

troboli'c*ë nf* = **tu'nd***ës*

*****tro'ce** *np fem* woes, troubles

trock'ist *n* Trotskyite

trock'ize'm *nm* Trotskyism

troç *adv (Colloq)* (say) right out, outright

○ **troç e mroç** fairly well

tro'dh *stem for pdef* <**tre dh·**

trofe' *nm* trophy

troft*ë nf* [*Ichth*] freshwater trout *(Salmo trutta)*

○ **troftë e argjendtë** [*Ichth*] argentine *Argentina sphyraena*

○ **troftë deti** [*Ichth*] whiting *(Merlangus merlangus)*

○ **troftë e egër** "wild trout" [*Ichth*] sea trout *Salmo trutta paparisto*

○ **troftë gjuce** [*Ichth*] Albanian lake trout *(Salmo trutta macrostigma)*

○ **troftë liqeni** [*Ichth*] lake trout *(Salmo trutta lacustris)*

○ **troftë mali** [*Ichth*] brown trout *(Salmo trutta fario)*

○ **troftë e mermertë** [*Ichth*] kind of lake trout *Salmo trutta marmorata*

○ **troftë qeni** "dog trout" [*Zool*] tadpole, pollywog = **fulte'rëz**

○ **troftë race** [*Ichth*] rainbow trout *Salmo gairdnieri Franc*

troglodi't *nm* troglodyte

troha'll*ë nf* ground eroded by water

troha's·*et* = **thërrmo'·***het*

troha's *stem for 1st sg pres, 1st & 3rd pl pres, 2nd & 3rd sg subj, vp* <**trohi't·**

trohi's *stem for 2nd pl pres, pind* <**trohi't·**

trohi't· *vt* = **thërrmo'·***n*

*****tro'ik***ë* = **trojk***ë*

troje *np* <**tru'all**

trojk*ë nf* troika

trok *nm* **1** trot **2** sound of steps: hoofbeat, footstep

trokaik *adj* [*Lit*] trochaic

troka'le *nf* = **tro'ke**

troka's *stem for 1st sg pres, 1st & 3rd pl pres, 2nd & 3rd sg subj* <**troket·**

trokashk*ë nf* wooden beater (regulating the flow of grain to the grindstone in a mill): clapper = **çaka'll***e*

tro'kje *nf* **1** small squat bell worn by livestock, cowbell; small bell **2** door knocker; mill clapper

troke' *nm* [*Lit*] trochee

troket·
I § *vi* **1** to knock **2** to beat **3** to clatter **4** *(Fig)* to resound in <>'s head
II § *vt* to strike [a hard substance] lightly: tap, clap
○ <>[] **troket·** to hit <> with [the plain facts/truth], tell <> [] right out
○ **troket· në derë/portë të hapur** to put forward something that is already known; reinvent the wheel
○ **troket· në derë** to be knocking at the door; be just around the corner, be almost here, be at hand
○ **troket· në derën/portën e shurdhit** "knock at the door/gate of the deaf man" to be wasting one's breath, be talking to the wall

tro'k*ë*
I § *nf* ground, earth; bare ground (with packed dirt)
II § *adj* **1** completely dry, bone dry **2** *(Fig)* dirt poor **3** filthy with dust/dirt **4** in rags, tattered **5** *(Fig)* dead drunk
○ **ësh·të trokë nga mendja** *(Pej)* to have nothing in one's head, be totally empty-headed, be a dimwit

trok'ëlli·*n vi, vt* **1** = **troket·** **2** to make a resonant metallic sound: clang, twang; ring, peal

trok·ëllim·ë nf **1** sharp noise heard when something hard is struck lightly: knocking, tapping, rapping **2** sound of steps: hoofbeat, footstep

trok·ëll·is stem for 1st sg pres, pl pres, 2nd & 3rd sg subj, pind <trokëllit·

trok·ëll·it· vi = troket·

trok·is stem for 2nd pl pres, pind <troket·

trok·it stem for pdef, opt, adm, part, pind, 2nd pl pres, imper, vp <troket·

trok·itje nf ger **1** <troket· **2** sound heard when something hard is struck lightly

troko·n
I § vt **1** to get [] all filthy **2** to wear to shreds, tatter **3** to ruin
II § vi to trot

*trokola·r nm person who is dirt poor

trok·th nm **1** = trok *2 middle finger

trok·thi adv **1** at a trot **2** (Colloq) on the double, in a hurry, quickly

trok·ull nf wooden olive press

trok·ull·im nm = trokëllimë

trolejbus nm trolleybus

troll = truall

*troll·im nm fatigue, exhaustion

tromaks· vt (Colloq) to terrify, scare badly

tromaks·et vpr (Colloq) to feel terror, get terribly scared

tromb nf [Med] thrombus
∘ tromb gjaku [Med] blood clot

tromb·ë nf [Mus] trumpet =

trombocit nm [Med] thrombocyte

tromboflebit nm [Med] thrombophlebitis

trombon nm [Mus] trombone

trombonist n [Mus] trombonist

trombozë nf [Med] thrombosis

*tromolluz adj corpulent, stout

trond·is stem for 1st sg pres, pl pres, 2nd & 3rd sg subj, pind <trondit·

trond·it· vt **1** to cause [] to shake [] from the foundations; shake [] up badly **2** to shock

trond·it·et vpr **1** to shake from the foundations **2** (Fig) to collapse, deteriorate

trond·itje nf ger **1** <trondit·, trondit·et **2** severe shaking; jolt **3** (Fig) shock **4** [Med] concussion **5** (Fig) shakiness, fundamental instability

trond·itsh·ëm adj (i) severely shaking: jolting; shocking

trond·itur adj (i) **1** shaken from the very foundations; badly shaken; badly damaged **2** in shock

*trongull (Reg Gheg) = trangull

trop nm **1** crushed wine grape left to ferment **2** [Agr] residue of grape skins, seeds and stems after pressing of wine grapes: pomace () **3** [Lit] trope

tropal nm [Lit] boulder

tropa·r nm [Relig] chanted prayer, hymn

tropik nm [Geog] tropics
∘ Tropiku i Bricjapit [Geog] Tropic of Capricorn
∘ Tropiku i Gaforres Tropic of Cancer

tropikal adj tropical

*troskë nf razorblade, knife blade

trosh·it· vt **1** to jolt, jerk **2** to crush [] to bits, break [] down

trosh·it·et vpr **1** to be shaken apart, bump along **2** to break up into bits, break apart, crumble

trosh·itje nf ger <troshit·, troshit·et

*trosh·itur adj (i) **1** crumbled **2** broken, dejected, downcast

troshk·ë nf crumb, bit, fragment

trotil nm [Chem] trinitrotoluene = tritol

trotua·r nm sidewalk

tru(r) nm brain
∘ s'ka· tru "not have a brain" not be smart
∘ tru i mesmë [Anat] midbrain
∘ tru i pasmë [Anat] metencephalon

tru·het vpr <trua·n **1** = përgjëro·het **2** to make a deep personal commitment, dedicate oneself

trua·n vt **1** to dedicate [] to <> **2** to invoke the devil in cursing []

truall nm **1** piece of ground on which something is built: lot, land **2** packed earth serving as the ground floor of a house; ground **3** arable plot of earth **4** country, land; motherland **5** background textile for embroidery **6** (Fig) arena of activity, fertile field of action

trua·r adj (i) damned, cursed

*tru·bull = turbull

truc adv tamped down, packed hard, compact, dense

truc· vt to tamp/pack [earth] down

truç
I § nm bunch, group
II § adv = tok

trudal·ë adj, n (Pej) brainless/stupid (person)

*true·n vt (Reg Gheg) = trua·n

*tru·ell = truall

*true·z·ë = tryezë

truho·llë adj shrewd, smart, sharp: brainy

*truj·ë nf fortress

truk nm practical joke, trick

*trulla·k = torollak

*trullo·het vpr = trullos·et

*trullo·n·v = trullos·

trullos· vt **1** to make [] dizzy/confused: stun, daze **2** to deafen; bewilder, confuse

trullos·et vpr **1** to become dizzy/dazed **2** to become bewildered/confused

trullosje nf ger **1** <trullos·, trullos·et **2** daze

trullosur adj (i) dazed, dizzy; bewildered, confused

trumbeta·r nm trumpeter

trumbet·ë nf bugle; trumpet

trumbet·im nm ger <trumbeto·n

trumbeto·n
I § vt **1** to trumpet out []; play [] on the trumpet/bugle **2** (Fig) to blare out [an announcement]
II § vi **1** to play the trumpet/bugle **2** to trumpet out an alarm

*trumbeto·r adj blaring

trumb·ë nf **1** crowd, troop, bunch, flock **2** manually-operated water pump *3 (Old) bugle, trumpet **4** domed vault, catacomb
∘ trumb·ë ere whirlwind

trumc = trumcak

trumcak nm [Ornit] sparrow, house sparrow (Passer domesticus)

trum·ë
I § nf = trumbë
II § adv in a group, together

trumha·s· vt to scare [] away, shoo [] off; scatter

trumha·s·et vpr **1** to scatter away **2** (Fig) to lose one's head (in anger)

trumha'sur _adj (i)_ **1** scared, frightened **2** _(Fig)_ distraught, bewildered

tru'mzë _nf_ **1** [_Bot_] winter savory _(Satureia montana)_ **2** [_Anat_] thymus

tru'ndry'shkët = **trundry'shkur**

tru'ndry'shk|ur _adj_ **1** _(Pej)_ slow-witted, soft in the head **2** outmoded in thinking, out of date

trung _nm (np ˜ gje)_ **1** trunk; unprocessed tree log **2** block of wood **3** shaft **4** main shaft (of a mine); torso **5** _(Fig Insult)_ dolt, fool
  ∘ **trung koni** [_Math_] frustum of a cone
  ∘ **trung piramide** [_Math_] frustum of a pyramid
  ∘ **trung i trurit** [_Anat_] brainstem

trung|gja'të _adj_ (of trees) having a tall trunk

trung|kon _nm_ [_Math_] frustum of a cone

trung|o'·_n_ _vt_ to cut off the branches of [a tree], strip [] down to the trunk

trung|piramidë _nf_ [_Math_] frustum of a pyramid

trung'th _nm_ **1** _(Dimin)_ <**trung 2** stem

trun|o'r _adj_ of or pertaining to the brain: cerebral

trunt _nm (Reg)_ warm nook by the fireplace

*__trunxh__ _nm_ = **tunxh**

trunj|ëz·o·_het_ _vpr_ to get all tired out, become exhausted

trunj|ëz·o·_n_ _vt_ to tire [] out, exhaust

trup
  _I §_ _nm_ **1** body **2** main body: trunk (of a tree), shaft (of a screw), fuselage (of a plane), frame (of bicycle), stem (of a word) **3** [_Geom_] solid **4** _(Collec)_ corps, troop, group **5** [_Tech_] frame/box around a mechanical part: housing
  _II §_ _adv_ **1** in one body: all together, as one **2** straight across **3** right out, plainly: point-blank
  ∘ **trupi boçkë e mendja lomçkë** _(Impol)_ a child's mind in an adult's body
  ∘ **trupi diplomatik** the diplomatic corps
  ∘ **trup i huaj** foreign body
  ∘ **trupi konsullor** the consular corps
  ∘ **trup i lidhur** well-built body
  ∘ **trupi mësimor/pedagogjik** _(Collec)_ the teaching staff (of an educational institution)
  ∘ **trup i prerë** having a nice-looking body
  ∘ **trupi pyll e mendja fyell** "body like a forest and mind like a flute" tall and handsome but brainless person

trup|a'k
  _I §_ _nm_ log for the fire; small body
  _II §_ _adj_ solid, dense, packed

trup|arma'të _nf_ **1** military corps composed of two or more divisions **2** = **korparmat**ë

trup|a'zi _nf_ [_Med_] dropsy, edema

trup|a'zi _adv_ (fighting) hand-to-hand; grappling

trup|brï'shtë _adj_ having a frail body

trup|de'rdh|ur _adj_ slender and good-looking

trup|do'bët _adj_ having a thin and frail body; feeling tired and weak

trup|dre'jtë _adj_ having a well-formed and healthy body; having good/erect posture

tru'pë _nf_ troop; troupe

trup|ër'ï'sht _adv_ _(Book)_ with/in the body, physically

trup|ës _nm_ block of wood

*__trup|ës'o·_n_ = trupëz·o·_n_

trup|ëz'ï'm _nm ger_ **1** <**trupëz·o·_n_, trupëz·o·_het_ **2** embodiment

trup|ëz'o·_het_ _vpr_ **1** to take concrete form, become embodied **2** [_Chem_] to become solidified

---

trup|ëz'o·_n_ _vt_ **1** to embody; incorporate **2** = **trung|o·_n_ 3** [_Chem_] to solidify

trup|gja'të _adj_ tall in stature, tall-bodied

trup|he'dh|ur _adj_ = **shtathe'dhur**

trup|ho'llë _adj_ tall and thin, lanky

trup|ïcë _nf_ block of wood used as a stool

trup|ïm _nm ger_ <**trupo'·_n_

trup|lï'dh|ur _adj_ having a nice figure, well-built

trup|ma'dh _adj_ "large-bodied" big (in stature)

trup|mbu'sh|ur _adj_ having a plump body: chubby, pudgy

trup|o'·_n_ _vt_ **1** to trim [a tree] of all branches and roots: make [a tree] into a log **2** to take a short cut across [], cut straight through [] *__3__ to amputate

trup|o'r _adj_ corporeal, bodily, physical

trup|o're _nf (Book)_ statue

trup|pa'k|ët _adj_ having a thin build, skinny

trup|rojë _nf_ **1** [_Mil_] military guard, guard troops: guard unit **2** guard post, guard position

trups _nm_ chopping block

trup|shëndo'sh _adj_ corpulent, portly, stout

trup|shku'rtër _adj_ = **shtatshku'rt**ër

trup'th _nm dimin_ **1** [_Med_] corpuscle **2** small body, particle

tru'p'thi _adv_ (lifted) into the air, bodily

tru'p|ull _nm (np ˜ j)_ wool fleece

trup|vo'gël _adj_ "small-bodied" small (in stature), little

trup|ze'za _np_ [_Entom_] darkling beetles _(Tenebrionidae)_

tru·r||i _obl_ <**tru(r)**

trus· _vt_ = **trys·**

tru'skë _nf_ [_Bot_] coco-grass, nut grass (used as bedding straw for livestock) _(Cyperus rotundus)_

trus|nï = **trysnï**

trust _nm_ [_Econ_] association of companies sharing pooled capital: trust

tru'|shëm _adj (i)_ brainy, intelligent

trushk|e _stem for pdef, opt_ <**trushky'e·_n (Old)_

trushk|ïm _nm ger (Old)_ <**trushky'e·_n_

trushky'e·_n_ _vt (Old)_ to steal [] from a holy place, **tru'th** _nm_ [_Anat_] cerebellum

tru|tha'rë _adj._ _n_ **1** _(Pej)_ lame-brained (person) **2** _(Curse)_ may his brain dry up in his head!

*__tru'th|o'r__ _adj_ [_Anat_] cerebellar

*__truveza'r__ _nm (Old)_ = **tryeza'r**

*__tryel'l__ë _nf_ = **turjel**ë

tryeza'r _n_ money lender

trye'zë
  _I §_ _nf_ **1** table **2** _(Colloq)_ party thrown to honor a special occasion
  _II §_ _adj_ suitable to eat/drink: fit for the table
  ∘ **tryeza e gjelbër** _(Old)_ table around which diplomatic discussions are conducted
  ∘ **tryezë e pazarllëqeve** bargaining table

trys· _vt_ **1** to press down on [] (with hand or foot); push [] down hard **2** to compress

try'sa _np fem_ tissue in which the teeth are embedded: gums

trys|nï _nf_ pressure

*__trratk__ _nm (Old)_ in-kind tax or tithe assessed against farmers during the Ottoman occupation

*__trratk|o·_n_ _vt (Old)_ to assess a farmer's [fields] a tax/tithe in kind

tu *pronominal adj masc pl (të)* <**yt** thy

tu|**a** *pronominal adj fem pl (të)* <**jot**e thy

*tu**a**´**f** *adj* = tuha´f

tu|**aj** *pronominal adj sg gen/dat/abl/acc, masc pl* <**juaj**

tu|**aj**|**a** *pronominal adj fem pl* <**juaj**

tuale´**t** *nm* makeup, cosmetics

tub *nm* tube, duct, pipe
  ○ **tubi i shikimit** "the tube of vision" the barrel of a microscope
  ○ **tubi i tymsit** *(Old)* the exhaust pipe (on a motor vehicle)

tub|**acio**´**n** *nm* system of pipes and ducts: piping, ducting, mains

tub|**ani**´**k** *nm* **1** *(Reg)* herdsman with responsibility for several flocks/herds; town herdsman **2** *(Old)* person who has much livestock

tuberkul|**a**´**r** *adj* [*Med*] tubercular, tuberculous

tuberkul|**oz**
  I § *adj* [*Med Veter*] tubercular
  II § *nm* **1** [*Med Veter*] tuberculosis **2** person with tuberculosis

tu|**bë** *nf* **1** bunch, group, herd, flock *2 tube, pipe
  ○ **tuba tuba** in bunches/groups/herds/flocks

tu|**bë**´**z** *nf dimin* <**tu**´**bë**

tub|**ë**´**zi**´**m** *nm ger* = tubi´m

tub|**ë**´**zo**´•**het** *vpr* = tubo´•het

tub|**ë**´**zo**´•**n** *vt* = tubo´•n

tub|**i**´**m** *nm ger* **1** <**tubo**´•**n**, tubo´•het **2** gathering of people for a common purpose: assembly, conference

tub|**o**´•**het** *vpr* to gather together in a group, assemble

tub|**o**´•**n** *vt, vi* to gather [] together, assemble

tub|**ola**´**r** *adj* [*Spec*] shaped like a tube: tubular

tuç *nm* **1** [*Wrestling*] touch *(Old)* *2 = tunxh

*tud**i**´(n) *nm* necklace

*tu**´e** *(Reg Gheg)* = du´ke

tufa´**n** *nm* storm
  ○ **ësh-të tufan** to have nothing to one's name, be destitute

tu|**fa-tu**´**fa** *adv* grouped together in clusters: in bunches/droves/flocks

tu´**fë**
  I § *nf* **1** crowd, flock; group; cluster **2** tuft; tassel; bunch; flower bouquet **3** large number, big bunch
  II § *adv* together in a group
  ○ **tufë misri** corn tassel

tuf|**ë**´**ku**´**qe** *nf* [*Bot*] plant with clusters of red flowers

tuf|**ë**´**l** *nf* small bunch/cluster

tuf|**ë**´**s** *adj* forming a cluster, in a tuft, tufted

tuf|**ë-tu**´**fë** = tu´fa-tu´fa

tuf|**ë**´**z** *nf (Dimin)* <**tuf**ë

tuf|**ë**´**zi**´**m** *nm ger* <**tuf**ë**zo**´•**n**

tuf|**ë**´**zo**´•**n** *vt* to gather [] into a bunch

tuf|**ë**´**zu**´**a**´**r** *adj (i)* **1** bunched, clustered **2** tufted, tasseled

tufk *nm* [*Bot*] pollen

tu´**f**|**kë** *nf dimin (Reg)* = tu´fëz

tuf|**o**´•**n**
  I § *vt* = tufëzo´•n
  II § *vi* to sprout tassels

tuf|**sha**´**k** *adj* tufted, tasseled; in a tuft

tu´**g**|**ë** *nf* **1** [*Hist*] status-marking tassel worn on a fez **2** body discomfort caused by disease or malfunction

*tug|o´•**het** *vpr* to feel discomfort (from disease or body malfunction)

tuha´**f**
  I § *adj (Colloq)* eccentric, odd, peculiar
  II § *n, interj (Pej)* head-in-the-sky dreamer

tuhaf|**llë**´**k** *nm (np ~ qe)* eccentricity, peculiarity

tuhari´**t** = tuha´t•

*tuhari´s| = tuha´s

tuha´**s** *stem for 1st sg pres, pl pres, 2nd & 3rd sg subj, pind* <**tuha**´**t**•

tuha´**t**•
  I § *vt (Colloq)* to break up [], disperse [], scatter []
  II § *vi (Colloq)* **1** to boil over **2** to smoke (tobacco)

tuha´**t**-*et* *vpr (Colloq)* **1** to break up, disperse, scatter **2** to run around doing nothing

*tu**´he** *adv* = tëhu´
  ○ **tuhe e tutje** here and there

tu´**d** *nm* tweed

tu´**je** *np fem (Colloq)* high spirits; joys, delights
  ○ **tujet e dheut** all the joys/pleasures/delights of the world

tuj|**ë** *nf* = tug**ë**

*tuk *adv*

tu´**ke** = du´ke

tukej|**më** *adj (i)* in poor health

tuke´**q** *adv* in poor straits, in a bad situation

tuke´**q**-*et* *vpr* **1** to deteriorate in health, grow worse **2** to feel sad

tuke´**q**|**më** *adj (i)* in poor health, frail; sickly

tuke´**q**|**ur** *adj (i)* gaunt, emaciated; feeble

tul
  I § *nm* **1** soft meaty part: flesh **2** pith, pulp
  II § *adj* **1** (of soil) soft and fertile **2** = tu´ltë
  ○ **tuli i këmbës** calf of the leg
  ○ **tul e lëng** (of soil) rich and fertile
  ○ **tul me dy sy** "flesh with two eyes" **1** imbecile, moron: dodo **2** person with no sense of morality, shameless person

tul|**a**´**s** *stem for 1st sg pres, pl pres, 2nd & 3rd sg subj, pind* <**tula**´**t**•

tula´**t**• *vt* **1** to press down (on) [] **2** = tund•

tula´**t**-*et* *vpr* **1** to curl/hunch up; crouch down; huddle up, huddle together **2** to shrivel up **3** (of soil) to get hard and compacted **4** to lose force, die down *5 = tund•et

tu´**le** *np* <**tul** *(Colloq)* buttocks

tul|**ë**´**s** *adj* full of meat (without much bone); fleshy, meaty

tul|**i**´**cë** *nf (Colloq)* tender meat; soft flesh

tul|**i**´**në** *nf* soft and fertile piece of ground

tulipa´**n** *nm* [*Bot*] tulip (Tulipan)

*tul|i´s| *stem for 1st sg pres, pl pres, 2nd & 3rd sg subj, pind* <**tul**i´t•

*tul|i´t• *vt* to quell, stifle

tuli´**t**-*et* *vpr* = tula´t•et

tul|**ku**´**q**
  I § *adj* = mishku´q
  II § *nm* [*Bot*] alder buckthorn (Frangula alnus)

tul|**o**´**r** *adj* [*Bot*] succulent

tul|**ta**´**k** *adj* fleshy, thickset

tu´**l**|**të** *adj (i)* meaty, fleshy: succulent

*tul|ti´në *nf* fertile land; land ready for sowing

tull|**a**´**c** *adj, n* bald/bald-pated (person)

tullár n 1 brick-maker 2 hand loom *3 horse with white feet

tullë
I § nf 1 brick 2 (ColloqImpolite) bald pate 3 (Colloq Impol) bald person: baldy
II § adj bald

tullúmb nm water pump (with a handle)

tullumbác nm toy balloon

tullumbáce nf 1 [Anat] bladder 2 fish bladder 3 toy balloon 4 (Fig) (soap) bubble

tullúmbë nf 1 [Food] sweet made of molded egg dough that has been fried in butter and immersed in syrup 2 = tullúmb

tullupán nm white head scarf worn by women

tumanár nm [Ornit] Dalmatian pelican (Pelicanus crispus)

tumáne np fem = çitjáne

tumbák nm = tunxh

tumbár vt to put [] right, fix

tumbë nf 1 tuft 2 tassel 3 cluster, bunch; clump (of trees) 4 four or five strings of tobacco baled together 5 peak; treeless hilltop, bare mountain top 6 (Reg) [Archeol] = tumë

tume nf treeless hilltop, bare mountain top

tumë nf 1 [Archeol] burial mound: tumulus () = kodërvarr *2 = tume

tumël nf back of the head

tumír· vt to accept [] as settled: concur, agree

tumír·et vpr to settle in, get used to a place

tumírë adv healthy and well-off, well

tumírëmbeç interj stay well!

tumór nm [Med] tumor

tumrrúk nm sledgehammer

tumúl nf [Archeol] small burial mound: (small barrow)

***tumulláce** nm = tullumbáce

tun nm 1 blunt side of a bladed tool 2 butt of a gun

***tunc** nm = tunxh

tund· vt 1 to shake; rock 2 to churn 3 to cause [] to change position; cause [] to move back and forth
  ○ <> tund· bishtin (Pej) to lead <> on; flirt
  ○ tund· degën e ullirit "wave the olive branch" (Iron) to pretend to be peaceloving in order to conceal one's belligerent intentions
  ○ tund· derën "swing the door back and forth" (Impol) to sit around doing nothing, twiddle one's thumbs, waste time on trivia
  ○ <> tund· dorën to shake hands with <>
  ○ <> tund· dhëmballët/dhëmbët "yank/twist <>'s molars/teeth" to punish <> severely
  ○ tund· këmbën (Impol) to kick the bucket: die
  ○ tund· këmbët në diell "rock one's feet in the sun" (Impol) to hang around doing nothing
  ○ tund· këmbët 1 to stamp one's feet 2 to put on an emotional display of displeasure: carry on 3 to insist strongly 4 to keep on trying and trying, try mightily
  ○ tund· kokën to nod one's head (in agreement); shake one's head (in disagreement); nod one's head (in greeting)
  ○ ësh·të^{3sg} tund e mos (u) shkund "be shake (the fruit tree) but not (no fruit) is shaken down" (of a person) to be all work and no result, be someone who works hard and produces nothing
  ○ <> tund· pallën to shake one's sword at <>: menace <> with a weapon, try to threaten/frighten <>
  ○ tund· paratë to pay immediately in cash: pay up

  ○ tund· rrjetën "shake the net" (Colloq) [Soccer] to score a goal with a hard-hit shot
  ○ <> tund· shkopin to threaten <>, shake one's fist at <>
  ○ <> tund· shpatën to shake one's sword at <>: menace <> with a weapon, try to threaten/frighten <>
  ○ tund· tespihet "turn the beads" to waste time idly, twiddle one's thumbs
  ○ s'[] tund·^{3sg} (as) topi "not (even) a cannon can shake []" 1 [] is absolutely definite 2 [] can't be budged
  ○ tund· zinxhirin "turn the chain" to waste time idly, twiddle one's thumbs

tund·et vpr 1 to rock back and forth or up and down 2 to shake; stir, wave 3 to change position 4 to stagger
  ○ tund·et e shkund·et to strut around, show off; swagger around bragging
  ○ nuk tund·et nga vendi not worry about anything
  ○ tund·et^{3sg} vendi 1 the whole place gets stirred up 2 the whole place is talking about it

tundáç nm = tundës

tundállë nf [Dairy] plunger in a milk churn

tundbíshtje nf = bishtatundës

tundéllo·n vt [Ornit] = tundulló·n

tundër nf [Geog] tundra

tundës nm [Dairy] 1 milk churn 2 plunger in a milk churn

tundím nm ger 1 <tundo·n, tundo·het 2 temptation (into sin)

tundje nf ger 1 <tund·, tund·et 2 shaking, tremor 3 (Reg) = tundës

tundo·het vpr 1 to give in to temptation; fall into sin 2 to become disturbed/annoyed

tundo·n vt 1 to tempt [] to do something bad; lead [] into sin; seduce 2 to bother, annoy

***tundór** adj (Old) shaking

tundshëm adj (i) 1 [Law] movable 2 shaky

tundubíshtje nf ger [Ornit] wagtail = bishtatundës

tundúes adj 1 seductive, tempting 2 annoying, bothersome

tundullím nf 1 shaking *2 (of waves) breaking

tundulló·n vt to shake [] with force, rattle

tunél nm 1 tunnel 2 underground shelter: bomb shelter 3 (Fig) road bordered on both sides by dense trees

tunelizím nm building of underground shelters; sheltering underground

tunë nf 1 [Ichth] tuna, tunny *2 = tungë

***tung** abbrev interj (Colloq Reg) <tungjatjeta

***tungë** nf heavy end of a tool; butt of a gun

tungjatjéta interj <t'u ngjattë jeta expresses friendly greeting or leave-taking, long life to you!: hello, goodbye
  ○ mor tungjatjeta marks a change into a familiar, intimate relationship with one's audience: (hey) buddy; let me tell you!
  ○ or tungjatjeta marks a change into a familiar, intimate relationship with one's audience: (hey) buddy; let me tell you!

tungjatjétani pl <tungjatjeta

tuníkë nf 1 [Hist] tunic (as worn in Rome) 2 [Anat Bot] covering membrane = vemesë

Tunizí nf Tunisia

tunizia'n *adj, n* Tunisian

tunxh *nm* [*Min*] brass

tu'nxh|të *adj (i)* made of brass

tupa'k *nm* garlic press

tupa'n *nm (Old)* big drum, bass drum
○ **e hedh· vallen/kërce·n si të bjerë tupani** "dance as the drum beats, dance to the rhythm of the drum" *(Pej)* to adapt one's actions to fit the circumstances; change one's opinions to suit the circumstances

tur *nm* [*Cycling*] lap, circuit

turani'k *adj* [*Ling*] Turkic (language family)

tu'rbë *nf* peat = to'rfë

turbi'në *nf* [*Tech*] turbine

tu'rbull *adv* **1** mixing in impurities; with turbid water; with overcast/cloudy skies **2** unclearly **3** *(Fig)* not feeling well; not in good spirits

turbull|i'm *nm ger* **1** <turbullo'·n, turbullo·het **2** = turbulli'rë

*****turbull|i'në** *(Reg Gheg)* = turbulli'rë

turbull|i'rë *nf* **1** turbidity; turbid liquid **2** overcast weather **3** something indistinct/unclear **4** *(Fig)* feeling of disquiet: queasiness, discomfort, uneasiness

turbullo'·het *vpr* **1** to become turbid/murky; cloud up **2** *(Fig)* to become confused and unclear; get tangled up and obscure **3** *(Fig)* to become troubled, get upset

○ <> **turbullo·het**[3sg] **gjaku** <> gets very upset/frightened

turbull|o'·n *vt* **1** to roil **2** *(Fig)* to create turmoil/disorder in [], stir up [] **3** *(Fig)* to cloud/becloud <>'s [mind, judgment]; put [] in a daze: bewilder **4** *(Fig)* to upset [] greatly
○ **nuk turbullo·n ujë** not rock the boat, not cause any trouble
○ **turbullo·n ujërat/ujin** to muddy the waters, confuse matters

tu'rbull|t *adj (i)* **1** turbid; murky, unclear; cloudy, clouded; obscure, dark **2** full of turmoil and disorderly confusion: unsettled, troubled

turbull|ua'r *adj (i)* **1** turbid, muddy **2** *(Fig)* confused; troubled

turbull|ue's *adj* **1** troubling, troublesome **2** *(Fig)* causing turmoil

*****tu'rçe**
  I § *nf* = turqi'shte
  II § *adv* **1** in the Turkish manner **2** = turqi'sht

ture'çk = turi'çk

turfull|i'm *nm ger* **1** <turfullo'·n **2** = turfulli'më

turfull|i'më *nf* snorting sound, snort

turfull|o'·n *vi* **1** to make a snorting sound: snort **2** *(Fig Colloq)* to snort with anger; become indignant **3** (of a motor) to roar

turi' *nm* **1** projecting front part of an animal head: muzzle; snout; trunk (of an elephant) **2** projecting front part of a motor vehicle **3** *(Pej Insult)* person's face

turi|ba'rdhë *adj* having a white muzzle, white-muzzled

turi|bo'llë *adj, n (Insult)* puffy-faced

turi'çk|a *np (Colloq Scorn)* snout

turi'çk|ë *nf (Pej Colloq)* **1** ugly/dirty face; snout-face **2** snout-faced woman

turi|de'rr
  I § *adj (Insult)* pig-faced

  II § *n* pig-snout

turigja't|ë *nm* **1** [*Entom*] weevil **2** clover seed weevil *(Apion assimile)*
  ○ **turigjati i artë** "golden weevil" [*Entom*] *Otiorhynchus aurosparus*
  ○ **turigjati i frutave** "fruit weevil" [*Entom*] *Rhynchites bacchus L.*
  ○ **turigjati i grurit** [*Entom*] grain/granary weevil, corn weevil *Calandra granaria L..*
  ○ **turigjati i jonxhës** [*Entom*] alfalfa weevil, lucerne weevil *Phytonomus variabilis*
  ○ **turigjati i lakrës** [*Entom*] kind of weevil *Baris coerulescens Scop.*
  ○ **turigjati i lëvorës** [*Entom*] kind of weevil *Magdalis armigera Geoff.*
  ○ **turigjati lulengrënës** "blossom-eating weevil" [*Entom*] *Phyllobius viridicollis*
  ○ **turigjati i luleve** "flower weevil" [*Entom*] *Rhynchites bacchus L.*
  ○ **turigjati i orizit** [*Entom*] rice weevil *Calandra oryzae L.*
  ○ **turigjati i panxharit** [*Entom*] weevil found on sugar beets *Cleonus mendicus Gull.*

turi'ku'q
  I § *adj* ruddy-faced; flushed, red in the face
  II § *n* brown-faced goat/sheep

turima'ce *adj, n* "cat-face" *(Insult)* (person) with delicate features and a small face

turi|majmu'n *adj, n* "monkey-face" *(Insult)* (person) with an ugly face

turi|mi' *adj* "mouse-face" *(Insult)* (person) with a tiny drawn face

turi'|nj *np* <turi'
  ○ **me (tërë) turinj** with a cold look

turiqe'n *adj* "dog-face" *(Insult)* (person) with a big projecting jaw

turi'r|i *obl* <turi'

turi's| *stem for 1st sg pres, pl pres, 2nd & 3rd sg subj, pind* <turi't·

turi'së'z *adj* sullen, surly

turi|spe'c *adj (Pej Insult)* "pepper-face" **1** (person) with a long thin face; (person) with a ruddy complexion **2** *(Fig)* hot-tempered (person)

turi'st *n* tourist

turisti'k *adj* touristic; attractive to tourists

turi't· *vt* to shoo [] away

turiva'r|ur *adj, adv (Pej)* scowling, in a scowl

turi|vra'rë *adj (Pej)* glum, morose

turize'zë *fem* <turizi'

turi'z|ë *nf* muzzle (placed over an animal's snout)

turi'zëm *nm* tourism

turi'zi *adj, n (fem sg ˜ez, masc pl ˜inj, fem pl ˜eza)* **1** *(Pej)* dark-faced/swarthy (person) **2** *(Fig)* gloomy-faced/dour (person)

turje'lë *nf* **1** drill, auger, bit **2** corkscrew **3** *(Fig Pej)* snoop

turjel|i'm *nm ger* <turjelo'·n

turjel|o'·n *vt* to drill, bore

turk
  I § *adj* Turkish
  II § *nm (np ˜q)* **1** Turk **2** *(Old)* Moslem

turke'shë *nf* <turk Turkish woman

turko'sh = turkosha'k

turk|osha'k *adj, n (Pej)* **1** dirty Turk(ish) **2** reactionary and cruel; old-fashioned and crude

turli
I § nf [*Food*] mixture of vegetables
II § determiner (followed by abl pl case) a whole variety of

turmë OR **turme** nf **1** herd, flock **2** mob; throng, crowd; common people, hoi polloi

turn nm duty period for alternating groups: (for workers) workshift, shift; (for military or naval personnel) watch

turne nm **1** tour **2** [*Sport*] tourney, tournament

turp nm **1** shame **2** bashfulness, shyness; embarrassment **3** sense of shame **4** disgrace **5** disgraced person

turpe|ma'dh adj (Pej) stained with dishonor, in disgrace

turp|ëm adj (i) = **turpshëm**

turp|ëri nf shameful thing/act: disgrace

turp|ërim nm ger <**turpëro**·n, **turpëro**·het

turp|ërisht adv with shame, ashamedly, shamefacedly

turp|ëro'·het vpr to be ashamed; be bashful/shy

turp|ëro·n vt **1** to disgrace; shame; make [] ashamed/bashful **2** to dishonor, rape

turp|ërua'r adj (i) ashamed

turp|ma'dh adj **1** = **turpshëm 2** = **turpemadh**

tu'rp|shëm adj (i) **1** shameful, disgraceful **2** bashful **3** obscene

turq masc pl <**turk**

turq|ëri nf **1** (Colloq) Turks as a collective whole: Turkdom **2** (Pej) backward outlook, social backwardness

Turq|i nf Turkey

turq|isht adv in Turkish (language)

turq|ishtje nf Turkish language

turq|izëm nm [*Ling*] Turkism

turshe·n vt to break [] into fragments: crush, crumble: utterly destroy

turshi nf [*Food*] pickled vegetable, pickle: pickled cucumber/cabbage/eggplant/pepper

*****turtë** nf torte = **tortë**

tu'rtull nm (np ~ j) [*Ornit*] turtledove (Streptopelia turtur)

turtull|e'shë nf <**turtull**

turtull|is stem for 1st sg pres, pl pres, 2nd & 3rd sg subj, pind <**turtullit**·

turtull|it· vi (Colloq) to prattle on and on

*****turul|is** stem for 1st sg pres, pl pres, 2nd & 3rd sg subj, pind <**turulit**·

*****turul|it**· = **turtullit**·

*****turull|a'k** adj = **torollak**

*****turull|u'qe** nf foolish girl/woman

turu'nxh nm [*Bot*] bigarade, seville orange, sour orange (Citrus aurantium)

turr nm burst of energy: rush, flurry, turbulence

tu'rr·et vpr **1** to rush, attack **2** to present a great menace

turra' nf twisted and knotted cloth used in playing games

turrahi nf **1** (Colloq) evasive language: deviousness **2** raucous commotion made by an angry person

turrah|is stem for 1st sg pres, pl pres, 2nd & 3rd sg subj, pind <**turrahi**·

turrah|it· vt (Colloq) to be evasive (in language)

tu'rr|as adv = **turravra'p**

turr|a|vra'p adv in a big hurry, at high speed, pellmell

turr|a|vra'p|thi adv = **turravra'p**

turre'c nm [*Ornit*] = **turtull**

*****turre'zë** nf [*Hist*] small coin; money

tu'rrë nf **1** wood piled in cords; woodpile: pile **2** flock, group **3** = **torkë 4** food patty (for children) made of crumbled bread, cheese, and butter; large pellet of soaked bread force-fed to fowl **5** twisted and knotted cloth used in playing games **6** [*Hist*] Sultan's seal
○ **turrë kashte** bundle of sheaves

*****tu'rr|je** nf sortie, sally, charge

*****tu'rr|me** nf (e) = **turrje**

turrna'k vi (of the turtledove) to warble

*****tu'rro** nf [*Ornit*] = **turtull**

tu'rr|shëm adj (i) surging

tu'rr|thi adv in a surge

tus stem for 1st sg pres, pl pres, 2nd & 3rd sg subj, pind <**tut**·

*****tush** nm = **dush**

Tush nm Tush (male name)

tu'shë nf [*Ornit*] fieldfare (Turdus pilaris)
○ **tusha këngëtare** [*Ornit*] song thrush Turdus philomelos ericetorum
○ **tushë mali** mistle thrush Turdus viscivorus L. *= cëre
○ **tusha vetullbardhë** [*Ornit*] continental song thrush, whistling thrush, throstle, mavis Turdus philomelos (musicus)

tut· vt to frighten, scare; cause [] to hesitate out of fear: intimidate

tut·et vpr to get a scare; be afraid
○ **tut**·et **nga hija e** {pronominal adj} to be afraid of {one's} own shadow

tu'ta np fem sweat suit

tut|ara'k
I § nm **1** sudden fear: scare **2** ire; burst of temper
II § adj *timid, anxious

tut|e'c adj timorous, cowardly

tutel|ë nf (Book) strict supervision, tutelage

tu|të np (të) <**yt**

tu'të nf fright, fear

tu'tël nf **1** wrinkle; crease, fold; pleat **2** tassel

tutël|o'·het vpr **1** to get crumpled/wrinkled **2** to get mussed/tangled up

tutël|o'·n vt **1** to wrinkle, crumple; crease, fold **2** to muss up [] **3** to make [] soft by squeezing: knead, crumple **4** (Fig) to pound [] into a soft mass **5** to cover [] in order to suppress activity: smother, stifle

tut|ër adj deviousness

tut|ës
I § adj **1** easily frightened: timorous **2** expressing fear: frightened
II § n coward

tu'tje
I § adv **1** far away; far; away **2** farther, further **3** over there; yonder **4** later; afterwards
II § prep (abl) beyond
○ **s'ësh-të as për tutje as për tëhu** (of a person) not be worth a dime; be incapable of doing anything
○ **tutje tëhu 1** back and forth; all over the place **2** then and now, all through time **3** from time to time, once in a while

tutje|më adj (i) farther, further; distant, remote

tu·tje-tëhu
I § *adv* **1** back and forth; all over the place **2** then and now, all through time **3** from time to time, once in a while
II § *prep (abl)* throughout

tutka·ll *nm* glue

tu·tkë *nf (ColloqImpolite)* head, mind: noodle

tutku·n
I § *adj, n (Pej Insult)* noodle-brained (person), nitwit
II § *nm* [*Ornit*] jay *(Garrulus glandarius)*

tuto·r *n* **1** tutor **2** [*Law*] legal guardian **3** *(Pej)* overzealous guardian, overprotective custodian

tutori· *nf* **1** tutelage **2** tutorship **3** [*Law*] legal guardianship **4** *(Pej)* overzealous guardianship, over-protectiveness

tu·tshëm *adj (i)* frightening, fearful; expressing fear: frightened

tutula·t-*et vpr (Colloq)* to find respite

tuturi·t· *vi* (of swallows) to twitter

tuxha·r *n (Old)* dealer, trader

TVSh *abbrev* < **Televizioni Shqiptar** Albanian Television

ty
I § *pron 2nd sg acc/dat* < **ti** thee, you
II § *pron 2nd sg nom (Colloq)* (used after prepositions that take the nominative case)

tyf· *vi (Colloq)* to give off a strong odor = **kundërmo·**

*****tyfe·k** *nm (np ~ qe)* = **dyfe·k**

tyfta·jë *nf (Colloq)* smell, odor

*****ty·kë** *nf* = **qy·të**

tyl *nm* **1** tulle **2** *(Fig Book)* veil

*****tyly·m** *nm* [*Ichth*] tuna, tunny

tym *nm* **1** smoke **2** *(Colloq)* dust **3** *(Colloq)* mist **4** *(Old)* [*Ethnog*] household **5** [*Hist*] = **tymja·ke**
∘ **tym i agushtë** stifling smoke
∘ **tym dynjaja** utter chaos
∘ **tym e mjegull** in a rage/fury
∘ **tym për krye** utter disaster, disastrous situation
∘ **Tym të bëhet!** Whatever happens, happens! Let the worst happen!
∘ **Tym të dalë!** Whatever happens, happens! Let the worst happen!
∘ **Tymi të shkojë drejt, pa le të jetë oxhaku i shtrëmbër!** "May your smoke go straight, even though your chimney is crooked!" *(Prov)* It doesn't matter what others think if one is doing right!

tyma·k
I § *adj* smoking, smoky
II § *nm (Reg)* chimney

tyma·r *nm* chimney, smokestack

tyme·k *nm* strong tobacco

tymë·n *nm* woof (of a weave)

*****tyme·s** *(Old)* exhaust (of a motor vehicle)

tyme·se *nf* smoke-bellows used for smoking out bees

tymëz *nf dim* < **tym**

tymi·s *stem for 1st sg pres, pl pres, 2nd & 3rd sg subj, pind* < **tymi·**·

tymi·t· *vt* to cure [food] with smoke: smoke

tymi·tje *nf* smoking; fumigation

tymi·tur *adj (i)* smoked; smoky

tymja·ke *nf* [*Hist*] tax imposed on each household under the Ottoman occupation

tymna·jë *nf* = **tymta·jë**

tymna·r *nm* = **tyma·r**

tymo··*n vt, vi* = **tymo·s**·

tymo·re *nf* smoke funnel, chimney

tymo·s· *vt, vi* **1** to make [] smoky: smoke up [] **2** to cure [food] with smoke: smoke ***3** to fumigate

tymo·s-*et vpr* to become saturated with smoke; (of food) get cured with smoke: be smoked

tymo·sje *nf ger* < **tymo·s·, tymo·s·et**

tymo·sur *adj (i)* saturated with smoke; preserved by smoking: smoked

tymta·jë *nf* **1** cloud of thick smoke **2** thick fog; thin cloud

tymta·r *nm* smokestack, chimney

tymtë *adj (i)* **1** covered with smoke; murky **2** full of smoke **3** *(Colloq)* gaseous

tymto··*n vi* to vanish like a puff of smoke: disappear suddenly

tymto·re *nf* **1** *(Old)* censer = **temjani·cë** **2** chimney

tymth *nm* [*Agr*] smut

tymthi·th·*es* *nm* **1** air purifier **2** pipe (for smoking tobacco)

tymue·s *adj* serving to produce a cloud/screen of smoke

typth *nm* small hammer

ty·r *n (i)* **1** theirs **2** relative/friend of theirs

ty·rbe *nf* mausoleum over a Moslem grave

ty·re
I § *enclitic after prepositions that take an ablative object* (indicates a 3rd pl object of the preposition) them
II § *pronominal adj (i)* of theirs, their

*****tyrli·** = **turli·**

tyt *interj* **1** shame on you! shut your mouth! **2** scram!; shoo!

ty·t *pronominal adj masc gen dat abl* < **yt**

ty·ta *pronominal adj fem pl* < **jo·te**

ty·të
I § *nf* **1** gun barrel **2** long and hollow space; tubular part **3** *(Fig)* empty-headed featherbrain: fool **4** *(Crude)* mouth: trap
II § *adv* empty, hollow

tytka·th *nm (Colloq)* [*Med*] sty on the eyelid

tyto·sh *adj, n* worthless (person)

ty-ty *onomat* sound of a bugle

*****tytyka·th** *nm (Reg Tosk Colloq)* = **tytka·th**

tyzha·r *nm (Old)* rich merchant

THth

th [*thë*] *nf* **1** the digraph "th" considered to be a single letter in the Albanian alphabet **2** the voiceless inter-dental fricative consonant represented by that letter

tha *3rd sg pdef* <**tho·të**

tha·*het vpr* **1** to dry up; go dry **2** to wither, wither away; become emaciated **3** *(Intens)* to become rigid/numb with cold; freeze

○ <> **tha**·*het*^{3sg} **barku** "<>'s belly *shrivels*" **1** <> gets hungry **2** (of a woman) <> can no longer bear children, *becomes* infertile

○ <> **tha**·*het*^{3sg} **buza/goja/gryka/gurmazi** <>'s gets thirsty; <> gets famished

○ <> **tha**·*het*^{3pl} **duart** "<>'s hands *go* numb" <> *becomes* too shocked to do any more work

○ <> **tha**·*het*^{3pl} **këmbët** <>'s feet *go* numb (from walking), <>'s feet *are* dog tired

○ **s'**<> **tha**·*het*^{3sg} **luga** "<>'s spoon *doesn't go* dry" <> *is* capable of feeding <>self; <> *is* capable of supporting <>self (and <>'s family)

○ <> **tha**·*het*^{3sg} **pështyma në grykë** "<>'s saliva *dries* up in the throat" <>'s words *freeze* in <>'s throat; <> *can speak* no longer

○ <> **tha**·*het*^{3sg} **pështyma** "<>'s saliva *gets* dry" <> *is* very thirsty

○ <> **tha**·*het*^{3sg} **plaga** <>'s wound forms a scab

○ <> **tha**·*het*^{3sg} **syri për** [] <> *has not seen* [] for a long time

○ <> **tha**·*het*^{3pl} **vezët** "<>'s eggs *dry* up" <> cannot have any more offspring

○ <> **tha**·*het*^{3sg} **zorra** "<>'s gut *dries* up" <> *has* not eaten for a long time, <> *is* almost starving

tha·n

I § vt **1** to make [] dry: dry, dry up [], suck [] dry **2** to cause [] to wither: wither, emaciate **3** to freeze/numb [] with cold **4** *(Fig Colloq)* to master [] completely: have [] down cold

II § *vi* to freeze from the cold, go numb from cold

○ <>*a* **tha·n barkun** to deprive <> of food, let <> go hungry

○ **e tha·n barkun** to deprive oneself of food, go without eating

○ <> **tha·n derën** to deprive <> of <>'s family

○ <> **tha·n duart** to deprive <> of <>'s main source of strength: cut off <>'s right arm

○ **Si** <>**u tha goja që nuk foli/tregoi** "How did <>'s mouth dry up since <> did not speak up" <> should have spoken up about [].

○ **Si** <>**u tha goja që nuk** [] **tha.** "How did <>'s mouth dry up since <> did not say []." <> should have spoken up about [].

○ **Si** <>**u tha goja, po/kur/që** [] *tha/foli/tregoi* "How did <>'s mouth dry up since <> said []" <> should not have spoken up about [].

○ **Si s'**<>**u tha goja, po/kur/që** [] *tha/foli/tregoi* "How did <>'s mouth not dry up since <> said []" <> should not have spoken up about [].

○ <>*a* **tha·n gojën** to deprive <> of food, let <> go hungry

○ **e tha·n gojën** to deprive oneself of food, go without eating

○ <> **tha·n kupën** to leave <> in total poverty

○ <>*a* **tha·n lugën** to take the bread from <>'s mouth, take away <>'s last means of support; leave <> in helpless misery

○ <>*a* **tha·n prehrin** "dry <>'s lap" (of a child) to die and leave an empty space in <>'s heart

○ **ta tha·n qoshen** to do things to perfection for you, do excellent work for you

○ <> **tha·n sytë** "dry <>'s eyes" to deprive <> of the pleasure of seeing one, make <> miss one

○ <>*i* **tha·n trutë** to exhaust <>'s brains completely: drain <>'s mind

○ <> **tha·n vatrën** (of a woman) not bear <> any children

○ <>*a* **tha·n zemrën** to cause <> terrible grief; leave <> in lonely grief

tha| *stem for pdef* <**tho·të**

○ **a i tha**^{pdef} **a s'i tha**^{pdef} **dy fjalë** {} spoke very little

*****tha'an|as** *np masc* cornelian cherry copse

tha'dër
I § *nf* adze
II § *adj* *(Fig)* wiry

thadër'ta'r *n* person who works with an adze

thadr'im *nm ger* <**thadro·n, thadro·het**

thadr'o ·*het vpr* to be incised permanently

thadr'o·n *vt* **1** to work [] with an adze: carve [], rout out [] **2** *(Fig)* to implant [] deeply; make an unforgettable impression on []; instill moral training in []

tha'gmë *nf* miracle, marvel

*****thak** *nm* = **thek**

*****tha'lb** *nm* = **thelb**

*****tha'mje** *nf ger* *(Reg Gheg)* = **tharje**

than|ak *adj* = **thanës**

than|a'kë *nf* syrup or preserve made of cornelian cherries

than'e'c *nm* grape resembling a cornelian cherry

tha'në *nf* **1** *[Bot]* cornel, cornelian cherry *(Cornus mas)* *****2** winter stall for sheep

○ **than**ë **e egër** *[Bot]* = **thanuk**ë**l**

○ **than**ë **e kuqe** dogberry-red in color

○ **Thanat nuk numërohen.** *(Prov)* Minor details don't matter.

○ **than**ë **qere** *(Old)* *[Bot]* cornelian cherry

○ **than**ë **ujku** *[Bot]* = **thanuk**ë**l**

thanë**|ke'qe** *nf [Bot]* = **thanuk**ë**l**

thanë**|ku'qe** *nf [Bot]* = **tha'n**ë

thanë**|qe're** *nf [Bot]* = **thanuk**ë**l**

tha'n|ës *adj* shaped like a cornelian cherry

thanë**s|ba'rdh**ë *adj* (of grapes) green and shaped like a cornelian cherry

thanë**s|ku'q** *adj* (of grapes) red and shaped like a cornelian cherry

tha'në'z *nf* fruit of the cornel: cornelian cherry

thani'shtë *nf* **1** cornelian cherry copse **2** = **thanu'kël** **3** cornel branch

thano're
I § *nf* cornelian cherry copse
II § *np* [*Bot*] dogwood family *Carnaceae*

thano's· *vt* to beat [ ] with a stick of cornel: give [ ] a good beating

tha'ntë *adj (i)* of cornelian cherry

thanu'kël *nf* [*Bot*] red dogwood, blood-twig dogwood (*Cornus sanguinea*)

thanu'lë *nf* [*Bot*] dogberry, wild cornel = **thanu'kël**

tha'nzë *nf* = **tha'në**

thar· *vt* [*Dairy*] to add a fermenting/souring agent to [milk]

tha'r·et *vpr* [*Dairy*] (of milk) to turn sour and curdle; spoil

*****thara'c** *nm* [*Agr*] = **taraka'c**

taraka'c *nm* [*Agr*] farmer's weeding hoe

tharb *nm* fermenting/souring/leavening agent

tharb· *vt* to ferment/sour/leaven [ ] with a starter

tha'rb·et *vpr* **1** to turn sour, ferment **2** (*Fig*) to go crazy

tha'rbët *adj (i)* sour

*****tharbëti'cë** *nf* [*Bot*] = **tharbëtu'shë**

tharb|ëti'm *nm ger* <**tharbëto'·n**, **tharbëto'·het**

tharb|ëto'·het *vpr* **1** = **tharmëto'·het 2** to go sour

tharb|ëto'·n
I § *vt* **1** = **tharmëto'·n 2** (*Fig*) to sour, rankle
II § *vi* = **tharmëto'·het**

*****tharbë'to're** *nf* [*Bot*] = **tharbëtu'shë**

tharb|ëtu'es *adj* = **tharmëtu'es**

tharbëtu'shë *nf* [*Bot*] wood-sorrel (*Oxalis acetosella*)

tharbo're *nf* [*Dairy*] dairy products made of soured milk

tha'rë
I § *part* <**tha·n**, **tha'·het**
II § *adj (i)* **1** dried; dried out/up **2** withered; emaciated **3** numb, dead

   ○ **nuk** <> **ësh·të**[3pl] **tharë (akoma/ende) lotët** "<>'s tears have not (yet) dried" <> is still in mourning

   ○ <> **ësh·të**[3pl] **tharë trutë** "<>'s brains have withered" (*Contempt*) <> has become senile/dotty

tha'rës
I § *adj* serving to dry/dehumidify
II § *nm* **1** = **tha'rëse 2** [*Med*] siccative

tha'rëse *nf* drying device: dryer, dehumidifier

tharësi'rë = **tharti'rë**

thari'shtë *nf* mown field

tha'rje *nf ger* **1** <**tha·n 2** drainage (of soil)

thar|k *nm* (*np* ~**qe**) **1** weaning pen for young livestock; livestock pen **2** storage crib/shed/chest loosely enclosed to allow ventilation **3** large basket for carrying hay/straw **4** (*Colloq Collec*) offspring of a particular birth period: litter, generation; children of a particular wife

tharm *nm* **1** fermenting/leavening agent: starter culture, starter; yeast; barm **2** sour taste; souring agent **3** (*Fig*) fomenting agent: stimulus, wellspring

tharm|ëti'm *nm ger* **1** [*Spec*] <**tharmëto'·n**, **tharmëto'·het 2** fermentation

tharm|ëto'·het *vpr* [*Spec*] to ferment

tharm|ëto'·n
I § *vt* [*Spec*] to add yeast to [ ] as a fermenting agent: leaven
II § *vi* = **tharmëto'·het**

tharm|ëtu'es *adj* = **tharbëtu'es**

tharm|ëz *nf* [*Spec*] fermenting agent

tharm|i'm *nm ger* = **tharmëti'm**

tharm|o'·n *vt* = **tharmëto'·n**

tharta'nik
I § *adj* sour-tasting, tart
II § *nm* = **tharbo're**

tha'rtë
I § *adj (i)* **1** sour **2** [*Chem*] acidic **3** (*Fig*) painful **4** (*Fig*) nasty
II § *adv* **1** sourly; nastily; unpleasantly **2** causing one to smart

thartësi'rë = **tharti'rë**

tharti' *nf* **1** sourness; tartness **2** [*Chem*] acidity

tharti'çkë *nf* **1** (*Colloq*) sour piece of fruit **2** (*Fig Pej*) gossipy woman who speaks with malice and spite: catty woman, old witch

tharti'm *nm ger* **1** <**tharto'·n**, **tharto'·het 2** sourness; tartness

tharti'rë *nf* sourness, acidity; sour taste/flavor; sour flavoring

tharto'·het *vpr* **1** to turn sour; spoil **2** to ferment **3** to become acidic **4** (*Fig*) to put on a sour face

tharto'·n *vt* **1** to make [ ] sour: sour **2** to start fermentation process in [ ]: curdle **3** [*Chem*] to acidify, acidulate **4** (*Fig*) to put a sour expression on [the face] **5** (*Fig*) to exacerbate, make [ ] worse

   ○ **tharto·n buzët** to make a wry face to express disappointment/disapproval

   ○ **i tharto·n**[pl] **fjalët** to exchange bitter words

   ○ <> **tharto·n trutë** to annoy <> past endurance

   ○ <>**i tharto·n trutë** to addle <>'s brain; totally confuse <>; tire <>'s brain out (so that <> *is* too tired to think)

tharto'r
I § *adj* **1** sourish, sour **2** [*Chem*] acidic
II § *nm* **1** [*Dairy*] cold drink made of milk mixed with whey **2** pastry made with whey rather than milk in the filling **3** [*Chem*] acid

tharto're *nf* **1** [*Bot*] garden sorrel (*Rumex acetosa*) **2** [*Bot*] sheep sorrel (*Rumex acetosella*) = **uthulli'shte 3** whey to which yogurt starter has been added

tharto'sh *adj* tart, sourish: acidulous

thartu'ar
I § *part* <**tharto'·n**, **tharto'·het**
II § *adj (i)* turned sour; spoiled

   ○ <> **ësh·të**[3pl] **thartuar trutë** "<>'s brains have been fermented" (*Impol*) <>'s brain *has* become senile, <>'s brain *is* fried

thartu'es *adj* **1** causing sourness: souring **2** [*Chem*] acidizing; acidifying ()

thartu'shë *nf* [*Bot*] **1** garden sorrel (*Rumex acetosa*) **2** pale persicaria (*Polygonum lapathifolium*)

tha'së *np* <**thes**

thashe'the'me *np fem* tattle of a gossip, idle talk: rumor, gossip, hearsay

thashe'theme'xhi *nm* person who spreads gossip/rumors: gossip, rumor-monger

tha'shë *1st sg pdef* <**tho'·të**

tha'shë *1st sg pdef* <**tho'·të**

tha'shëm
I § *adj (i)* not having eaten a thing
II § *adv* on an empty stomach

that'a'k *adj* very thin and drawn: skinny, emaciated; gaunt, haggard

that'a'ni'k *adj, n* wizened/emaciated (person) = **thati'm**

tha'të
I § *adj* **1** dry **2** dried up; arid; bare; empty **3** thin, emaciated, skinny **4** *(Fig)* without appeal to the senses/emotions
II § *nn (i)* abscess in the skin: boil, furuncle
III § *nn (të)* **1** dryness, aridity; drought **2** dry land; shore
IV § *adv* **1** in dry condition **2** without precipitation: rainless **3** empty, bare **4** without appeal to the senses/emotions
V § *nf (e)* dryness, aridity; drought
 ○ **në/më të thatë** without any reason

that'ë'si *nf* **1** dryness; lack of water: aridity **2** = **thatësi're**

that'ë'si're *nf* **1** drought; dry spell **2** dryness, aridity

thati'k *adj* = **thata'ni'k**

thati'm *adj, n* thin/lean/skinny (person)

thati'n *nf* **1** arid and infertile land **2** dryness, aridity *3 drought; dry spell

thati'q *adj, n (Tease)* skinny

thatu'sh *adj, n* = **thata'ni'k**

the *2nd sg pdef* <**tho·të** you said

the | *stem for pdef, opt* <**thy'e·n**

***thea'tër** *I* § *nm* OR **thea'tro** *II* § *nf (Colloq)* = **tea'tër**

thec'a'k *nm* [*Bot*] fragile plant that grows in mountainous areas

the'ç *adj* breakable, friable: fragile, brittle

thefqa'fë *nf* **1** place fraught with danger: dangerous precipice **2** waterfall

thek *nm* [*Bot*] **1** tuft, tassel **2** beard (of grain) **3** stamen **4** [*Bot*] = **teli'sh**

thek· *vt* **1** to pierce, pierce through [ ] **2** to strike/hit [ ] suddenly **3** to speed up [ ] **4** to move [ ] deeply (emotionally): touch **5** to toast [ ] (in the fire)
 ○ **të thek·** *(Colloq)* to be very capable, be topnotch

the'k·et *vpr* **1** to feel emotionally moved, be touched **2** to bask

the'ke *np fem* deceptive tricks

the'kë *nf* **1** tasseled fringe **2** [*Bot*] stamen **3** [*Optics*] fringe
 ○ **thekë e degë** all torn up, in little pieces

thek'ë'ku'q *nm* [*Bot*] small-grained wheat with reddish awns

thek'ër *nf* [*Bot*] rye *(Secale cereale)*

thek'ër'i'shtë OR **thek'ër'i'shte** *nf* **1** = **thekëro're** **2** rye straw

thek'ëro're *nf* field of rye

the'kër't *adj (i)* of or pertaining to rye; made of rye flour

thek'ërri'cë *nf* piece of toast: toast

***thek'ërri's** *vt* = **thekërro'·n**

thek'ërr'o·het *vpr* (of bread) to get toasted

thek'ërr'o·n *vt* to toast [bread]

***thek'ërro're** *nf* field sown in rye

the'k'ës *nm* **1** toaster *2 = **theks**

the'k'ët *adj (i)* **1** piercing *2 toasted

the'kë-the'kë *adj* **1** fringed in tassels **2** worn out and falling apart: hanging in threads

thek'ë'zi *nm* [*Bot*] large-grained wheat with dark awns

thek'o· *vi* to snow in large, fleecy flakes

thek'o're *nf* garment/rug with a tasseled fringe

theks *nm* **1** accent; emphasis **2** [*Ling*] stress, accent

theks'i'm *nm ger* **1** <**thekso·** *n* **2** emphasis **3** accent, accentuation

thekso'·n *vt* **1** to emphasize, stress; accentuate **2** [*Ling*] to stress, accent

theks'o'r *adj* [*Ling*] of or pertaining to stress, accentual

theks'u'a'r *adj (i)* **1** emphatic; intense; (of a slope) steep **2** [*Ling*] stressed, accented; emphasized

the'k'shëm *adj (i), adv* with piercing effect, in a piercing manner: piercing

the'k'ur *adj (i)* **1** toasted; scorched **2** *(Fig)* laid away for a long time **3** *(Fig)* seasoned, experienced

the'k'ura *np (të)* *(Fig)* sage words

thek'uri'në *nf* crumb

thel *nm* **1** big nail: spike **2** iron bar from which bells hang in a belfry

the'la-the'la *adv* in slices, sliced up; diced

thelb *nm* **1** innermost edible part, meaty part: kernel; nutmeat; clove (of garlic) **2** [*Bot*] cotyledon **3** *(Fig)* most central/essential part: heart, core; essence, nub
 ○ **ushqyer/rritur me thelbinj arre** "nourished/raised on walnut nutmeats" reared having the best of everything, reared in luxury

thelb'ës'o'r *adj* constituting the basic core: fundamental, central, elemental

thelb'o'r *adj* **1** pertaining to the innermost edible part **2** [*Bot*] cotyledonary **3** = **thelbëso'r**

the'lë *nf* **1** part that has been cut off from a whole: slice; cut **2** segment (of a segmented fruit) **3** gash
 ○ **Thela e madhe të ngec në fyt.** "The big slice sticks in your throat." *(Prov)* Try for too much and you get nothing. Don't be greedy, take what you can get.
 ○ **thelë mbi bisht** asking too many privileges on top of one another

thel'ëm'o·n *vt* to slice

the'l'më *nf* scrap of cloth

thelm'o·n *vt* = **thelëmo'·n**

***thelp** = **thelb**

thelp'i'nj *np* <**thelb**

the'l'la *np (të) fem (Colloq)* deep matters; profundities

the'l'lë
I § *adj (i), adv* deep, deeply; profoundly, seriously
II § *nf (e)* deep pool (in a channel/body of water), depths
 ○ **thellë një bel** to spade depth, deep as the length of a spade blade

thell'ë'si *nf* **1** depth **2** profundity

***thell'ë'si'në** = **thellësi're**

thell'ë'si're *nf* deep place, abyss, depths

thell'ë'si'sht *adv* deeply, profoundly

thell'ë'thy'er'je *nf* [*Sport*] lunge

thel'li *nf* depth; deep place

the'l'li *adv (së)* deeply, deep down

thell'i'm *nm ger* **1** <**thello'·n**, **thello'·het** **2** depression, hollow; deep place

thell'i'në *nf* **1** = **thellësi're** **2** artificial pond

thellö·*het vpr* **1** to become deeper; become hollowed out **2** *(Fig)* to enter deeply, delve

thellö·*n vt* **1** to deepen; intensify, amplify, develop *2 (Old)* to bury
  ○ **thello**·*n* **rezultatin** [*Sport*] to widen the score

thellomë *nf* deep part (of a channel/body of water); depths

thelluar *nf (e)* deep part (of an object): groove, pit, furrow

them *1st sg pres* <**tho·të**

thembër *nf* heel
  ○ **Thembra e Akilit** *(Book)* Achilles' heel

thembërzo·*n vt* to carve [] into a heel-like shape

thembros· *vt* to fill [someone] up of bread crusts

thembros·*et vpr* to fill up on bread crust

themel *nm* foundation, base; basis
  ○ **Themeli çati le të bëhet!** "Let the foundation become the roof!" It can all go to Hell for all I care.

themeldalë *adj* **1** (of a building) whose foundation has shifted: ruined, broken-down **2** (of a person) left with nothing and no one: totally wretched

themelfortë *adj* having a strong foundation, well established

themeli *nf* = **themel**

themelim *nm ger* **1** <**themelo**·*n* **2** establishment

themelo·*n vt* to lay the foundation of []: establish, found

themelor *adj* forming the foundation: basic, fundamental

themeltar *adj* **1** *(Book)* = **themelor 2** *(Book)* principal, main **3** *(Old)* = **themelues**

themeltë *adj (i)* having a solid basis, well established/founded

themelues
  I § *nm* founder
  II § *adj* founding

themelvën|ës
  I § *adj* participating in establishing a foundation: foundational, constitutional
  II § *n* participant in establishing fundamentals

themethashe *np* = **thashetheme**

themi *1st pl pres* <**tho·të**
  ○ **ta themi në mes tonë** let's just keep it between ourselves

*****theori** *nf* theory

thep
  I § *nm* **1** sharp peak; sharp point/protrusion **2** [*Mil*] sighting pin at the end of a gun barrel: foresight, frontsight *()*
  II § *adj* **1** sharp-tongued: acerb, caustic; ready with answers **2** fidgety, overactive; constantly pestering, vexatious

thepajë *nf* land with many sharp peaks, craggy cliff

thepak
  I § *nm* sharp peak of a mountain; rocky crag
  II § *adj* strong and indomitable

thepan *adj, n* **1** adept/skillful (person) **2** persistent (person)

thepa-thepa *adv* with many sharp peaks

thepël *nf* sharp fragment: splinter

thepët *adj (i)* **1** jagged **2** thin and pointed, tapered

thepis· *vt* **1** to put a sharp tip on []; sharpen, point **2** to cast [] down from a steep height **3** *(Fig)* to put [] into a rapid decline; bring [] into sudden ruin

thepis·*et vpr* **1** to fall from a high peak **2** *(Fig)* to suffer a rapid decline; fall into sudden ruin

thepisje *nf ger* **1** <**thepis**·, **thepis**·*et* **2** = **thepore**

thepisur *adj (i)* **1** pointed, sharp-edged; sharply peaked, jagged; craggy **2** very steep, with sharp drops

thepje *nf* = **thepël**

thepor *adj* = **thepët**

thepore *nf* land with sharp peaks; land with steep cliffs

theqafje *nf* **1** steep cliff **2** *(Fig)* downfall, collapse

ther·
  I § *vt* **1** to cut the head of []; slaughter **2** to pierce the skin of []: stab; prick, sting **3** to sew [quilted fabric] with a stitch going all the way through
  II § *vi* **1** to be the source of stabbing pain to <>: hurt <> terribly, give <> a stabbing pain **2** *(Colloq)* to go away very fast: tear off at a gallop
  ○ **ësh-të ther e mos e rrip** "it *is* kill (an animal) and not skin it" to be someone who never finishes what he begins
  ○ [] **ther· në grykë** "stab [] in the throat" to do [] a lot of harm, do serious damage to [], do [] in
  ○ <> **ther·**^{3pl} **sytë** "<>'s eyes feel a sharp pain (when they see the person discussed)" <> can't stand the sight (of the person discussed)
  ○ <> **ther·**^{3sg} **shpirti (për** [])" "<>'s soul *pains* (for [])" <> *feels* very sad (about [])
  ○ <> **ther·**^{3pl} **veshët (kur** [] **dëgjo·**n)" "<>'s ears *pain* <> (when <> *hears* [])" it hurts <>'s ears (to hear []); <> gets a real pain (when listening to [])
  ○ <> **ther·**^{3sg} **veshi (kur** [] **dëgjo·**n)" "<>'s ear *pains* <> (when <> *hears* [])" it hurts <>'s ears (to hear []); <> gets a real pain (when listening to [])
  ○ **ther· vrapin** to break into a run
  ○ <> **ther·**^{3sg} **zemra (për** [])" "<>'s heart *pains* (for [])" <> *feels* very sad (about [])

ther·*et vpr* **1** to engage in mutual slaughter: have a bloody battle; have a terrible argument **2** to cut/prick oneself
  ○ **ther·et po s'qe kështu** "kill oneself if it was not so" to swear that it was so

therekal *nm* [*Bot*] carline thistle (*Carlina vulgaris*)

ther|ës
  I § *adj* **1** piercing, stabbing; stinging, biting **2** *(Book)* of critical importance: crucial, urgent
  II § *n* slaughterer, butcher

theribujkë *nf* [*Bot*] = **ferrënuse**

therimi *nm* [*Bot*] = **rrushkull**

therishte *nf* infant, baby

therje *nf ger* **1** <**ther·**, **ther·**et **2** sharp pain; twinge

therkë *nf* **1** large trough **2** dugout boat = **sul**

thermë *nf* sharp/stabbing pain

*****thermometër** *nf* thermometer

thero·*n vi* to be the source of stabbing pain to <>: pain <> terribly, give <> a stabbing pain, hurt <> badly

theroke *nf* [*Bot*] small shrub with sharp-pointed leaves (*Thymelaea hirsuta*)

theror *n* **1** sacrificial animal, person sacrificed **2** *(Poet)* martyr

therore *nf* (sacrificial) altar

therori *nf* sacrifice

therorizo·*het vpr* to practice self-sacrifice

therori**zo** ·*n vt* to sacrifice

therpele *nf* [*Bot*] **1** butcher's-broom *(Ruscus aculeatus)* **2** silk vine *(Periploca graeca)*

ther**shëm**
  I § *adv* in a sharp manner: harshly, bitingly
  II § *adj (i)* = **the**rës

thertore *nf* place where butchering is done: slaughterhouse, slaughter yard

ther**ur** *adj (i)* slaughtered (by cutting off the head); butchered; in carcass form

*****the**rr**ë *nf* = **fe**rrë
  ○ **therr**ë **e kuqe** [*Bot*] dog rose *Rosa canina*

therroko**re** *np fem* [*Bot*] = **thërrok**o**re**

thes *nm* sack, bag
  ○ **Thesi bosh s'qëndron/rri më këmbë.** "An empty sack cannot stand up." *(Prov)* A person can't go without eating.
  ○ **ësh·të thes fjalësh/llafesh/përrallash** to be too talkative; gossip too much
  ○ **thes i grisur/shpuar 1** person who owns nothing, poor man **2** person who can't hold on to money: spendthrift, compulsive spender **3** person who can't keep a secret: blabbermouth
  ○ **thes me pleshta** "sack of fleas" something ridiculously impossible
  ○ **thesi i rërës** "sandbag" [*Boxing*] heavy punching bag

thesar *nm* treasure; treasury

thesarm**ba**j**t**ës *nm (Book)* guardian of a treasure

Thëllëza *nf* Thëllëza (female name)

thëllëzë *nf* **1** [*Ornit*] partridge **2** *(Fig Pet)* pretty girl
  ○ **thëllëz**ë **fushe** [*Ornit*] gray partridge *(Perdix perdix)*
  ○ **thëllëz**ë **mali** [*Ornit*] rock partridge *(Alectoris graeca)*

thëllim *nm* bitterly cold wind/weather

thëllo ·*n vi* (of weather/wind) to be bitterly cold
  ○ <> **thëllo**·*n* **në zemër** to cause <> anguish

thën stem for part, opt, adm <**tho**·**të**

thën**ç** stem for opt <**tho**·**të**
  ○ {*indefinite noun*} <> **thënçin** "They call it {}" *(Iron)* You call this {} **Jetesë i thënçin** You call this living!? **Ilaçe u thënçin** You call these medicines!?

thën**i**e part <**tho**·**të**

thën**i**e
  I § *nf (e)* **1** saying, adage, maxim **2** *(Old)* what is foretold: fate, destiny
  II § *nn ger (të)* <**tho**·**të**, **thu**·*het*
  ○ **nuk ësh·të**^{3sg} **e thënë (që)** _ **1** there *is* no requirement that _, it *is* not written anywhere that _ **2** it never works out that _, it just never seems to happen that _
  ○ **nuk ësh·të**^{3sg} **e thënë** not meant to be, not be in the cards
  ○ **ashtu ësh·të**^{3sg} **(e) thënë** "so it *is* said (written)" that's how the cookie crumbles, that's the way it goes

thëngjill *nm (np ~ j)* **1** glowing ember, hot coal **2** coal; charcoal **3** [*Chem*] carbon
  ○ **thëngjill druri** charcoal
  ○ **thëngjill guri** (rock) coal
  ○ **thëngjill i gurtë** (rock) coal
  ○ **thëngjill i mbuluar** "covered burning ember" sneaky person

thëngjilla**k** *adj* = **thëngjillo**r

*****thëngjilla**r = **thëngjillta**r

thëngjillë**s** *nm* carbuncle

thëngjillë**z**i**m** *nm* [*Geol*] coking, carbonization

thëngjillgu**r** *nm* bituminous coal, coal

thëngjillim *nm ger* **1** <**thëngjillo**·*n* **2** carbonization

thëngjillo·*n vt* to carbonize

thëngjillor *adj (Book)* **1** of or pertaining to coal/charcoal; containing coal **2** [*Chem*] carbonic

*****thëngjill**o**s**· *vt* = **thëngjillo**·*n*

thëngjillta**r** *n* maker of charcoal (from wood)

thëngjillto**re** *nf* charcoal pit

*****thë**n**i** = **thëri**jë

thën**i**e *nf ger* **1** <**tho**·**të**, **thu**·*het* **2** what is said: opinion, expression; declaration **3** [*Ling*] phrasal expression: phrase

thën**të** *3sg opt* <**tho**·**të**
  ○ <> **a thëntë prifti/hoxha në vesh** "May the priest say it in <>'s ear!" *(Curse)* May <> die!

*****thënu**k**ël** = **thanu**kël

*****thë**r**b**ël *adj* (of a nut containing no nutmeat) empty

thëri = **thëri**jë

thërijë *nf* nit

*****thërma**q**e** *np fem* = **thërrmo**qe

thërmi OR **thërm**i**j**ë *nf (Old)* atom

*****thërm**i**q**e *np fem* = **thërrmo**qe

*****thërm**o ·*n* = **thërm**o·*n*

thërpe·*het vpr* = **përçit**·*et*

*****thërpe**l**e** *nf* = **therpel**e

thërra**s**· *stem for 1st sg pres, 1st & 3rd pl pres, 2nd & 3rd sg subj* <**thërret**·

thërre**ck**ë *nf* [*Bot*] thistle *(Silybum)* = **gjembaç**

thërre**s**· *stem for 1st sg pres, 1st & 3rd pl pres, 2nd & 3rd* <**thërret**·

thërre**t**·
  I § *vt* **1** to call (to) [] **2** to yell at [], scold **3** to invite; summon
  II § *vi* to cry out in a loud voice, scream
  ○ **thërret**· **beriha** to sound the alarm, raise a hue and cry
  ○ **thërret**· **me sa ka**· **në kokë** to bellow/yell with all one's might, cry out at the top of one's
  ○ <> **thërret**· **mendjes** to think about what one *is* doing
  ○ [] **thërret**· **në bejleg** to challenge [] to a duel
  ○ **thërret**· **në kupë të qiellit** "yell to the dome of the sky" to yell at the top of one's voice; cry out to the high heavens
  ○ [] **thërret**· **në kushtrim** to sound the alarm to []
  ○ [] **thërret**· **në raport** to call [] to account
  ○ [] **thërret**· **në ushtri** to call [] up for military service
  ○ [] **thërret**· **nën armë** to call [] up for military service

thërri**me** *nf* **1** crumb **2** tiny rice-like pasta **3** little piece of something: particle **4** *(Fig)* very small amount: tiny bit

thërri**s**· *stem for 2nd pl pres, pind* <**thërret**·

thërri**t**· *stem for pdef, opt, adm, part, pind, 2nd pl pres, imper, vp* <**thërret**·

thërri**t**ë**s** *nm* [*Ethnog*] = **thi**rrës

thërrm**i**j**ë** *nf* **1** particle; grain, granule **2** crumb **3** very small part, little bit

thërrm**i**j**ë**z *nf* tiny particle

thërrm|im *nm ger* 1 <**thërrmo**´·*n*, **thërrmo**´·*het* 2 fragmentation

thërrmo´·*het vpr* to become fragmented and disorganized; crumble, crumble apart

thërrmo´·*n vt* 1 to break/fragment [] into small bits 2 to hurt [] badly: crush; destroy
  ○ <>**a thërrmo**·*n* **zemrën** to break <>'s heart

thërrm|ok *nm* = **cërmok**

thërrm|ok|ull *nf* left-over crumb

thërrm|oqe *np fem* 1 coarsely ground grain 2 bread/cheese crumbs

thërrm|ues *adj* serving for fragmentation

thërrm|ues|hëm *adj (i)* capable of being broken into fragments, easily crumbled: crumbly, friable

thërro|ke *nf* daphne *(Daphne mezereum)*

thërrok|ore *np fem* [*Bot*] daphne family *Thymelaeaceae*

thëth|i´·n *vt* = **thith**·

*****thëth|im** *nm* suction

*****thëth|i|njës** OR **thëth|i|tës** *adj* sucking; absorbent

thëth|itje *nf ger* = **thithje**

thi *nm* 1 boar 2 *(Fig)* person who is strong, tough, and unyielding: bull
  ○ **mish derri/thiu** pork

thi|as *adv* courageously, bravely, steadfastly

*****thij|osh** *adj* = **thinjosh**

thika|ç *nm* large double-edged knife (for carving wood)

thika|r *n (Old)* cruel and bloodthirsty person

thika|re *nf* 1 broadsword 2 *(Fig)* sharp pain

thi|kas OR **thi|kazi**

thik|ë
  I § *nf* 1 knife 2 blade 3 *(Fig)* very steep place, cliff 4 *(Fig)* sharp pain
  II § *adj* very steep
  III § *adv* straight up
  ○ **ësh·të thikë me dy presa/tehe** 1 to cut both ways, have advantages and disadvantages 2 to require very careful handling
  ○ **ësh·të**^*pl* **thikë më thikë** to be at dagger points, stand toenail to toenail
  ○ **Pret thika në mish të botës.** "The knife cuts into someone else's flesh." It's someone else's ox that gets gored.
  ○ **thikë në zemër** bitter blow
  ○ **thikë pas shpine** "knife behind the back" *(Pej)* hiding one's murderous intent
  ○ **thikë plori** [*Agr*] knife coulter

thik|ë|bër|ës *nm* cutler

thik|ë|mba|jt|ëse *nf* [*Tech*] (on a lathe) tool-post; tool-holder

thik|ëz *nf dimin* 1 small knife 2 [*Agr*] linchpin securing the handle to the beam of the plow 3 [*Constr*] wedge-shaped stone (used to form an arched ceiling): voussoir () *4 potter's modeling tool: pallet

thik|tar *n (Old)* = **thikëbërës**

thik|të *adj (i)* very steep, precipitous, sharp

thile *nf* 1 buttonhole = **filiqe** 2 loop in a mesh; hole in a woven textile = **iliqe**

*****thil|iqe** *nf* buttonhole = **filiqe**

thima|ç OR **thima|n** = **thimash**

thima|r [*Bot*] conehead thyme *(Thymbra capitata)* = **thrumbe**
  ○ **thimar i kalit** [*Bot*] kidney-vetch *Anthyllis hermanniae*

thim|ash *adj* (of animals) having gray hair

thim|ë *adj (i)* grayish, gray

Thim|i *nm* Thimi (male name)

*****thimja|më** *nf* incense = **temjan**

*****thimjat|is·** *vt* to cense = **temjanis·**

*****thimjat|on** *nm* [*Relig*] censer, thurible = **temjanicë**

thimth *nm* 1 stinger (of an insect) 2 [*Tech*] narrow end of a cart/wagon axle that goes through the hub: journal () 3 teat, nipple 4 *(Fig)* caustic remark; sarcasm

thimth|ak *adj* stinging, prickly

*****thimth|im** *nm ger* <**thimtho**´·*n*

*****thimtho|´·n** *vt* to sting, prick

thin|a|ç = **thimash**

*****thind** *nm* 1 beak, bill (of a bird) 2 nipple (of a breast) = **thithë**

thin|eshë *nf* 1 (swine) sow 2 *(Fig)* capable girl/woman who is tough and stands her ground: doughty girl/woman

*****thingji|ll** *nm (np ˜j)* = **thëngjill**

thin|isht *adv* courageously, bravely, stalwartly

*****thinx** *nm* hinge pin of a door/window, hinge

thinj· *vt* 1 to give [] gray hair, cause [] to get gray 2 *(Fig)* to cause [] to suffer

thinj·et *vpr* 1 to get gray hair 2 *(Fig)* to age prematurely; suffer/tire badly

thinj|ak
  I § *adj* with some gray hairs: slightly grizzled
  II § *n* person starting to get gray

thinj|ë *nf* gray hair

thinj|osh *adj, n* (one) having gray hair

thinj|të *adj (i)* gray-haired

thinj|ur *adj (i)* gray-haired, grizzled

thir = **thirr**

*****thirimí** *nf* [*Bot*] = **therpelë**

*****thir|qe** *nf* [*Bot*] chickpea *(Cicer arietinum)*

thirr *nm (Reg)* soot = **blozë**

thirr *stem for pdef, opt, adm, part, imper, vp* <**thërret**·
  ○ **Thirri mendjes!** Come to your senses!

thirr|a|va|jë *nf (Old)* (legal) complaint

*****thirr|c** = **thirrës**

thirr|ë *part* <**thërret**·

thirr|ës *nm* [*Ethnog*] caller who announces news, particularly of marriage or a death; person who issues invitations to a wedding

thirr|ëse *nf (Old)* wedding invitation

thirr|je *nf ger* 1 <**thërret**·, **thirr·et** 2 call; announcement; notification 3 [*Mil*] roll call 4 *(Fig)* clamor made by yelling 5 [*Lit*] vocative address: *(apostrophe)*

thirr|më *nf* 1 loud call: shout, yell; bellow, roar, screech, howl 2 exclamation 3 *(Old)* [*Ling*] interjection

thirr|mor *adj* [*Ling*] exclamatory; vocative

thirr|or
  I § *adj* [*Ling*] vocative
  II § *n* [*Ling*] addressee

thirr|ore *nf* vocative case

thirr|ur
  I § *adj (i), n (i)* (person) called/summoned/invited
  II § *nf (e)* yelling, shouting

*****thi|tak** *nm (Reg Gheg)* pork

thith *nm* **1** teat, nipple **2** [*Bot*] parasitic root **3** hinge **4** whirlpool, eddy **5** [*Zool*] = **thithëlopё**

thith·
I § *vt* **1** to suck, suck [] in; inhale **2** to absorb **3** to siphon/drain [liquid]
II § *vi* (of a pipe/flue/chimney) to provide a draft: draw
◦ <> **thith· gjakun** "drink/suck <>'s blood" **1** to exploit <> mercilessly: make <> sweat blood **2** to inflict terrible pain on <>, torture <> to death
◦ **thith· me hundë** to sniff
◦ <>a **thith· vlagën 1** to know <*someone*> very well **2** to learn from experience that <> is not to be feared, learn from experience that <> *is* just a paper tiger

thith·et *vpr* to become thin and drawn, become pinched

thithak
I § *nm* **1** [*Bot*] sucker () **2** [*Zool*] insect's stinger
II § *adj* [*Med*] mammillary

thithator *n* suckling lamb/kid

thithë *nf* nipple

thithëlopё *nf* **1** [*Zool*] large toad once believed to suck milk from cows: common toad *(Bufo bufo)* **2** (*Fig*) fat and disgusting woman

thithës
I § *adj* capable of absorbing: absorptive
II § *nm* suction device; absorptive material/substance

thithëse *nf* **1** blotting paper; blotter **2** [*Hydrol*] suction pump **3** whirlpool, eddy

thithje *nf ger* **1** <**thith·**, **thith·**et **2** suction **3** inhalation **4** absorption **5** quantity drawn in/up in one suck: draft

thithkë *nf* **1** [*Anat*] teat **2** pacifier (for a baby to suck on)

thithshmëri *nf* absorbability

thithur *adj* (*i*) thin and drawn, pinched

thiul *nf* [*Ornit*] type of wild duck with a large head and thick neck

*****thjajë** *nf* aunt

*****thjermë** *adj* light gray = **përhimё**

thjerrë *nf* **1** [*Phys*] lens **2** [*Bot*] = **thjerrëz**

thjerrëz *nf* [*Bot*] common lentil *(Lens culinaris)* = **thjerrë**
◦ **thjerrëz e syrit** [*Med*] crystalline lens

thjerrëzak *adj* [*Spec*] = **thjerrëzor**

thjerrëzor *adj* [*Spec*] lenticular

thjerrishtë *nf* field of lentils

*****thjeshlëm** *adj* (*i*) = **thjeshtë**

thjesht *adv* simply; purely; plainly; clearly; in an open and friendly manner; in an unsophisticated manner

thjeshtazi *adv* simply, purely

thjeshtë *adj* (*i*) simple, elementary; pure; plain; clear; open and friendly; unsophisticated

thjeshtër
I § *nm* stepson
II § *nf* stepdaughter

thjeshtëri *nf collec* stepchildren

thjeshtësi *nf* simplicity; purity; clarity; plainness; modesty; absence of sophistication

thjeshtësim *nm ger* **1** simplification **2** oversimplification

thjeshtësisht *adv* (*Book*) = **thjesht**

thjeshtëso·het *vpr* = **thjeshto·het**

thjeshtëso·n *vt* **1** to simplify **2** to oversimplify

thjeshtëzim *nm ger* **1** <**thjeshtëzo·n 2** oversimplification

thjeshtëzo·n *vt* to oversimplify

thjeshtëzues *nm* one who oversimplifies: oversimplifier

thjeshti *nf* = **thjeshtësi**

thjeshtim *nm ger* **1** <**thjeshto·n**, **thjeshto·het 2** simplification **3** oversimplification

thjeshtligjërim *nm* [*Ling*] vulgar/crude level of language, low register

thjeshtligjërimor *adj* [*Ling*] vulgar; crude

thjeshto·het *vpr* to become simplified/reduced

thjeshto·n *vt* **1** to simplify; reduce **2** to oversimplify

thjeshtueshëm *adj* (*i*) [*Math*] reducible

thnegël *nf* [*Entom*] ant

tho·të *vi*, *vt* **1** to say; tell **2** to opine, think **3** to mean **4** to suggest, propose **5** (*Colloq*) to give [a name] to <>; call <> (by a name)
◦ ia tho·të³ˢᵍ (për/në []) to be adept, be really good at []
◦ ia tho·të a s'ia tho·të to sing/play music very well: is that or is that not great singing/playing by {}!
◦ nuk tho·të asnjë gjysmë fjale not say a single word
◦ tho·të atë që është to only say what is true
◦ <>a tho·të copë (*Colloq*) to say it to <> straight out; tell <> the God's honest truth
◦ i tho·të derrit dajë (*Crude*) to have to be friendly/ nice to someone one dislikes
◦ tho·të fill e flakë to blurt out everything at one time
◦ <>[] tho·të me thepa to say [] to <> with deliberate malice, tell it to <> maliciously
◦ tho·të me vete to say to oneself
◦ [] tho·të me mend to rehearse [] in one's mind
◦ <> tho·të³ˢᵍ mendja se _ it is just in <>'s mind that _: <> only *thinks* that _
◦ <> tho·të ndal to say "Halt!" to <>, succeed in stopping <>
◦ <>a tho·të në fytyrë to say it right to <>'s face
◦ <>a tho·të³ˢᵍ në sy to say it right to <>'s face
◦ <>[] tho·të në vesh to tell [] to <> in a low voice: whisper [] in <>'s ear
◦ <>a tho·të në vesh to gossip to <> with malicious intent
◦ tho·të nëpër dhëmbë "talk through one's teeth" to mumble
◦ i tho·të qenit qen "call a dog a dog" to call a spade a spade
◦ <>a tho·të rrumbull to speak frankly to <>
◦ <>i tho·të të katër të vërtetat në sy "say the four truths to <> in the eye" to speak the truth right to <>'s face
◦ i tho·të vetes burrë to consider oneself grown up
◦ <>a tho·të³ˢᵍ zemra <> has a feeling in <>'s heart, <> has a premonition

tholi *obl* <**thua**

*****thojcë** *nf* wood sliver/chip/shaving

thom *1st sg subj* (*Reg*) = **them**

thomi *1st pl pres* (*Reg*) = **themi**

thonë *3rd pl pres* <**tho·të**

thoˈni
I § 2nd pl pres <**thoˈ·të**
II § obl <**thuˈa**

thoˈnj *np* <**thuˈa**
○ Të jep/jepte thonjtë e bufit për të të nxjerrë sytë. "{} gives/gave you owl's talons in order to pull out your eyes." *(Pej)* {} is/was nice to you just to use you for {}'s evil purposes.
○ **sˈka· thonj** *(Impol)* to have no more ability to do harm, have no teeth
○ **që/sa të lësh thonjtë** "so that you leave your fingernails (in the food)" finger-licking delicious
○ **ësh·të me thonj 1** *(Pej)* to have claws; be dangerous **2** to be light-fingered, be given to stealing
○ <> **ësh·të**³ᵖˡ **rritur thonjtë** "<>'s claws *have* grown" *(Pej)* <> *has* become a menace
○ <> **ësh·të**³ᵖˡ **zgjatur thonjtë** "<>'s claws *have* lengthened" *(Pej)* <> *has* become a menace

thoˈnjˌas OR **thoˈnjˌaz** *adv* tooth and nail, (fighting) like cats and dogs

thoˈnjˌëz *nf*[*Bot*] **1** hen-and-chickens, roof houseleek (*Sempervivum tectorum*) **2** claw-like end of a petal: (*unguis*)

thoˈnjˌëza *np fem* [*Ling*] quotation marks, inverted commas

thonjˈëzaˈk *adj* [*Bot*] claw-like

thonjˈgjaˈtë *adj* **1** having long claws/talons/nails **2** *(Fig Pej)* greedy and grasping; predatory, thieving

thoˈnjˌtë *adj (i)* **1** having claws/talons/nails: clawed **2** (of skin) horny, corneous

thopç = **thoˈpërç**

thoˈpërç *nm* [*Folklore*] wicked small jinni

thoˈsh *stem for pind* <**thoˈ·të**
○ **do të thotë** it means
○ **ta thotë në sy** "{} says it straight to your face" {} is completely up front, {} is a straightforward person

***thraˈpse** *nf* broken-off tree branch with dried-out leaves

thrasheˈgjër *nf* [*Bot*] bilberry, whortleberry (*Vaccinium myrtillus*)

thruˈmbe OR **thruˈme** *nf* [*Bot*] conehead thyme (*Thymus capitatus*)

thrumbiˈshtë *nf* [*Bot*] = **thruˈmbe**

thuˈ·het *vp impers* <**thoˈ·të** it is said, they *say*

thuˈ *stem for vp* <**thoˈ·të**

thuˈa *nm* **1** nail (fingernail, toenail); claw; talon **2** *(Colloq)* hoof
○ **thua pule** "chicken talon" [*Bot*] birdsfoot-trefoil = **thuapuˈlë**

thuˈa
I § 2nd sg pres <**thoˈ·të**
II § pcl (*in questions*) by any chance? what do you say? do you think so?
III § 2nd sg pres, imper = **thuˈaj**
○ **sˈke çˈ<> thua** "you don't have anything to say against <>" <> *is* perfect/marvelous

thuˈaj 2nd sg imper <**thoˈ·të**

thuˈajse *pcl* "might-as-well-say" almost, nearly: practically

thuamaˈce *nf* [*Bot*] common portulaca = **thoˈnjëz**

thuapuˈlë *nf* [*Bot*] birdsfoot-trefoil (*Lotus corniculatus*)

thuˈash 2nd sg subj <**thoˈ·të**

thuˈath *nm* [*Med Veter*] **1** whitlow, felon **2** ophthalmia; conjunctivitis

***thuˈe** = **thuˈa**

thuk
I § nm **1** mortar (used for pounding) **2** lisper
II § adj **1** sturdy **2** lisping

thuk· *vt* to pound; compact

thuk·et *vpr* to become compacted

thuˈkët *adj (i)* **1** compact; dense **2** plump **3** *(Fig)* concise

thukˈetˈi *nf* (*Book*) compactness; density

***thukˈmeni** = **thukˌeti**

thumb *nm* **1** stinger; thorn, prick **2** shoe tack/spike **3** teat, nipple **4** bell clapper **5** sharply pointed device/object: goad; firing pin, arrow point **6** [*Agr*] = **thumbrˈizë 7** *(Fig)* caustic remark; sarcasm
○ **thumb gjiri** [*Anat*] nipple (of the breast)

thumbaˈc *nm* metal tip of a goad

thumbaˈt *nm* **1** sharply pointed rod used to shuck corn **2** wooden pin used to fasten a full sack

thumbeˈc = **thumbaˈc**

thuˈmbˌër *nf* (*Old*) headrest

thuˈmbˌëz *nf dimin* small spike, tack

thumbˈim *nm ger* **1** <**thumboˈ·n, thumboˈ·het 2** pain from a sting

thumboˈ·het *vpr* to exchange provocative/sarcastic remarks

thumboˈ·n *vt, vi* **1** to sting, prick **2** *(Fig)* to aim provocative/sarcastic remarks at [ ], provoke <>; be sarcastic: needle

thumboˈs· = **thumboˈ·n**

thumbrˈizë *nf* [*Agr*] wooden linchpin joining the beam to the rest of a wooden plow

***thumbˌsëpaˈtë** *nf* [*Ornit*] woodpecker (*Picus, Dryocopus*)

thumbuˈes
I § adj, nm **1** stinging **2** *(Fig)* piercing (glance/smile); trenchant (remark)
II § nm [*Entom*] stinging insect

***thuˈmbull** *nf* button, round button = **suˈmbull**

***thumbulloˈ·n** *vi* (of a tree) to come into bud: bud = **sumbulloˈ·n**

thumbverˈdhe
I § nf [*Ornit*] yellow-billed blackbird = **mëlleˈnjë**
II § adj = **sqepveˈrdhë**

thuˈndër *nf* **1** hoof **2** [*Spec*] solid base **3** *(Fig)* heel of oppression ***4** heel (of a shoe)
○ **thundër mushke** [*Bot*] = **thundërmuˈshkë**

***thundërˈbuˈlk** *nm* [*Bot*] (*Ononis vulgaris*)

thundërmuˈshkë *nf*[*Bot*] common coltsfoot (*Tussilago farfara*)

thuˈndërˌz *nf* [*Bot*] = **thundërmuˈshkë**

thundraˈc *nm* farrier's long-handled knife with a concave shape adapted to trimming a horse's hoof before nailing on the horseshoe

thundraˈk *adj* [*Zool*] hooved, ungulate

thundroˈ·n *vt* **1** to trample [ ] with the hoof ***2** to trample

thundroˈr *adj* [*Zool*] = **thundraˈk**

thundroˈre *np* [*Zool*] ungulates

thuˈpër *nf* **1** thin flexible stick: switch, withe **2** cleaning rod **3** bow (for a stringed instrument)

thuˈpërz *nf* (conductor's) baton

thupraˈk *adj* (of a person) lithe; wiry

thuprˈim *nm ger* <**thuproˈ·n**

thuproˈ·n *vt* to thrash, flog

thuq|ëro·n *vi* to speak indistinctly: mumble, lisp; barely speak

thur· *vt* **1** to make [] by interlacing components: braid; interweave; knit; wattle **2** to surround [] with a fence **3** to devise; make up, create
  ∘ **e thur gardhin e hap shtegun** "you weave the fence, you open the path" working without a plan
  ∘ **e thur· gojën/grykën** *(Colloq Scorn)* to shut one's trap, button one's lip, shut up
  ∘ ⟨⟩ **thur· lavde** to praise ⟨⟩ to the skies
  ∘ ⟨⟩ **thur· lesa** to weave snares for ⟨⟩, lay a trap for ⟨⟩
  ∘ **Thur livadhin e lë shtegun hapur.** "Fence the meadow and leave the gate open." Does part of a job, but leaves a crucial part unfinished.
  ∘ **thur· një cigare** to roll a cigarette
  ∘ **thur e shthur** do-and-undo-and-never-get-finished

thu'r·et *vpr* **1** to become close-knit; become interwoven **2** *(Fig)* to become inextricably interrelated

thura'k *nm* [*Hist*] coat of mail: hauberk

thur|i'm|ë *nf* **1** thing made of interlaced components: mesh, knitting, braid, wattle, wickerwork **2** wattled fence

thu'r|je *nf ger* **1** <**thur·**, **thu'r·et** **2** interlacing (as a method of joining or making things) **3** interlaced thing **4** fenced enclosure

thu'r|ur *adj (i)* **1** enclosed by a wattled fence: fenced **2** made of interlaced components: knitted; braided; wattled

thutha'k = **thuthu'q**

thutha'q = **thuthu'q**

***thu'thë** *nf(Old)* lisp

thuthlo·n *vi* to lisp

thuthu'q [*thu-thu'q*]
  I § *adj* **1** lisping **2** tongue-tied
  II § *n* lisper

thuthuq|ësi [*thu-thuq-si*] *nf(Book)* lisp, lisping

thy·het *vpr* <**thye·n** **1** to break up, become fragmented **2** to bend, bend over **3** to change direction abruptly **4** [*Phys*] to become refracted **5** to become broken in health/spirit/strength/intensity: break
  ∘ ⟨⟩ **thy·het**^{3pl} **gjunjët** "⟨⟩'s knees *bend*" ⟨⟩'s knees *buckle*
  ∘ **nuk** ⟨⟩ **thy·het**^{3sg} **pupla në dorë** "the feather on ⟨⟩'s hand does not break" ⟨⟩ is very clever; ⟨⟩ is nobody's fool

***thy'ç** *adj* breakable, friable: fragile, brittle = **theç**

thye·n
  I § *vt* **1** to break [] (into parts), break [] into parts; fracture **2** *(Fig)* to renounce; reject; violate; disobey [a command] **3** *(Fig)* to break [] down: overcome, beat **4** to change/convert [money] **5** to bend; fold **6** [*Phys*] to refract
  II § *vi* *(Fig)* (of day/night) to be coming to an end
  ∘ **thye·n akullin** *(Book)* to break the ice
  ∘ **thye·n arra kot** to talk foolishness
  ∘ **thye·n arrëzën 1** to fall and get badly hurt, break one's neck **2** to leave at last
  ∘ **Thyej arrëzën!** "Break your neck!" *(Pej)* Get the hell ere! To Hell with you!
  ∘ ⟨⟩ **thye·n brinjët** *(Scorn)* to beat ⟨⟩ to a pulp; teach ⟨⟩ a good lesson; make ⟨⟩ swallow ⟨⟩'s boasts; make ⟨⟩ eat ⟨⟩'s words
  ∘ ⟨⟩**a thye·n bririn** to break ⟨⟩'s rebellious spirit
  ∘ **thye·n dorën** "break one's hand" to acquire requisite skills by practice: get broken in (on a task)

  ∘ ⟨⟩ **thye·n dhëmbët** *(Scorn)* to beat ⟨⟩ to a pulp; teach ⟨⟩ a good lesson; make ⟨⟩ swallow ⟨⟩'s boasts; make ⟨⟩ eat ⟨⟩'s words
  ∘ **thye·n dhëmbët** to suffer a bad loss, take a beating
  ∘ **i thye·n**^{pl} **fjalët** to exchange bitter words, have a terrible argument, quarrel
  ∘ ⟨⟩ **thye·n fulqinjtë** *(Scorn)* to beat ⟨⟩ to a pulp; teach ⟨⟩ a good lesson; make ⟨⟩ swallow ⟨⟩'s boasts; make ⟨⟩ eat ⟨⟩'s words
  ∘ **thye·n gërmicën** "break one's neck" *(Impol)* to kick the bucket, die
  ∘ **thye·n gjuhën** to begin to feel comfortable in speaking [a foreign language/dialect]
  ∘ ⟨⟩ **thye·n hundët** *(Scorn)* to beat ⟨⟩ to a pulp; teach ⟨⟩ a good lesson; make ⟨⟩ swallow ⟨⟩'s boasts; make ⟨⟩ eat ⟨⟩'s words
  ∘ **thye·n hundët** to fall and get badly hurt, break one's neck
  ∘ **thye·n këmbën** to sprain/turn an ankle
  ∘ **e thye·n këmbën** to leave at last
  ∘ ⟨⟩**i thye·n kockat** to beat ⟨⟩ up badly
  ∘ ⟨⟩**a thye·n kokën** to take care of ⟨⟩ for good; kill ⟨⟩
  ∘ **thye·n kokën** to break one's neck, get hurt badly
  ∘ **thye·n kurorën** to break one's marriage vows, commit adultery
  ∘ **[] thye·n në mes 1** to cause [] a lot of harm, hurt [] badly **2** to cause [] despair, demoralize **3** to beat the living daylights out of []
  ∘ ⟨⟩ **thye·n nofullat** *(Scorn)* to beat ⟨⟩ to a pulp; teach ⟨⟩ a good lesson; make ⟨⟩ swallow ⟨⟩'s boasts; make ⟨⟩ eat ⟨⟩'s words
  ∘ **thye·n qafën 1** to fall and get badly hurt, break one's neck **2** to leave at last
  ∘ **Thyej qafën!** "Break your neck!" *(Pej)* Get the hell ere! To Hell with you!
  ∘ **thye·n rruazën** to bow down; submit
  ∘ ⟨⟩ **thye·n**^{pl} **shtambat** (of women/girls) ⟨⟩ *break* off friendship
  ∘ **Të thye arrën në dorë.** "{} breaks your walnuts by hand" **1** {} is very shrewd/astute **2** *(Pej)* {} is very tricky
  ∘ ⟨⟩ **thye·n turinjtë** *(Scorn)* to beat ⟨⟩ to a pulp; teach ⟨⟩ a good lesson; make ⟨⟩ swallow ⟨⟩'s boasts; make ⟨⟩ eat ⟨⟩'s words
  ∘ **thye·n turinjtë** to fall and get badly hurt, break one's neck
  ∘ **thye·n urinë** to appease/slake one's hunger
  ∘ **thye·n veshin** to break in one's ears, get used to listening (to a foreign language/dialect)
  ∘ ⟨⟩**a thye·n zemrën 1** to disappoint ⟨ **2** to grieve ⟨⟩
  ∘ **thye·n zverkun 1** to fall and get badly hurt, break one's neck **2** to leave at last

thye'r
  I § *part* <**thy'e·n**
  II § *adj (i)* **1** broken **2** hilly
  ∘ **thyer më dysh** bent over double from old age, sickness, or hard work

thye'r|ës
  I § *nm* **1** breaker **2** = **thyerëse**
  II § *adj* **1** capable of or serving to break something into pieces: breaking, fragmenting **2** [*Phys*] refractive

thye'r|ëse *nf* **1** [*Spec*] device for breaking something into pieces: breaker, cracker **2**[*Phys*] refractor
  ∘ **thyerëse arrash/lajthish** nutcracker

thye|rje *nf ger* **1** <thy'e •*n* **2** fracture, crack, break

thye|s *nm* **1** trespasser **2** [*Spec*] = **thye'rës**e

thye|së *nf* **1** [*Math*] fraction **2** loop
○ **thyes**ë **e pathjeshtë** [*Math*] improper fraction

thye|s|ím *nm ger* **1** [*Spec*] <thyeso' •*n* **2** product of fractionation: fraction

thye|s|o' •*n* *vt* [*Spec*] to fractionate

thye|s|o'r *adj* [*Math*] fractional

thye|s|u|a'r *adj (i)* [*Tech*] fractionated

thye|shëm *adj (i)* **1** breakable; fragile **2** bendable, flexible **3** jagged

thye|shm|ëri *nf (Book)* frangibility

thye|z *nf* fragment, chip

thye|z|ím *nm ger* **1** <thyezo' •*n* **2** mosaic

thye|z|o' •*n* *vt* to adorn [] with rock pieces: cover [] with mosaic stone

thy|skë *nf (Reg)* rugged country, broken up by jagged mountains and steep ravines

Uu

u *nf* **1** the letter "u" in the alphabet **2** the rounded high back vowel represented by that letter

u
  I § *pronominal clitic preceding a verb, or suffixed to a verb stem in the imper* indicates that the verb has a 3rd pl referent: to/for/of them
  II § *reflexive dative clitic* marks as reflexive the immediately following past definite, participial, optative, or admirative verb form

u *interj* **1** announces that what follows has just come to the speaker's notice: hey! **2** expresses the speaker's displeasure with what follows: oh!

u'a *sequence of clitics* rd sg referent + 3rd sg/pl object

ua *interj* (*Colloq*) expresses the speaker's surprise: well now! oops!

*u'a·s *n* = hu**a**s

u'bël *nf* waterhole opened in the mountains for livestock pastured there

ububu
  I § *interj* expresses pain or unhappiness: oh me oh my!, alas!
  II § *nf* utterance of this expression to express pain or unhappiness

UDB *abbrev (Serbian)* <*Uprava Drzavne Bezbednosti* National Security Administration (secret police)

*udo'b *OR* **udobi'sht** *adv* without much effort, easily

udh·a'k *nm* **1** traveller; explorer **2** guide

udh·aki'm *nm ger* <**udhako·**n

udh·ako· *n vi* to go often

udh·emba'rë *nf* farewell wishing to someone about to leave: have a good trip!

u'dhë *nf* **1** path; pathway, way; road **2** trip, journey **3** long narrow carpet covering a passageway: runner
  ∘ **ësh·të³ʳᵈ e udhës** to be proper/right
  ∘ **Udha (e) mbarë!** (*Felic*) Have a nice trip! Pleasant trip! Bon voyage!
  ∘ <> **duk·et³ʳᵈ e/të udhës** to seem proper/right to <>
  ∘ **(gjatë) udhës** along the way, during the trip
  ∘ **udhë e hekurt/hekuri** (*Old Book*) railroad = **hekurudhë**
  ∘ **udhë hekurore** railroad
  ∘ **udhë kryq** = u'dhëkryq
  ∘ **udha e mbarë** (<> **qoftë**)! "successful road!" (may <>) have a good trip!
  ∘ **udhë e mesme** middle road
  ∘ **udhë pa krye** road leading nowhere, street that comes to a dead end
  ∘ **udhë pa udhë** "with or without a path" road or no road
  ∘ **ësh·të për udhë** to be about to set off (on a trip/journey)
  ∘ **udhë qorre 1** road that comes to a dead end; blind alley **2** narrow path
  ∘ **Udha e Qumështit** [*Astron*] The Milky Way
  ∘ **udhë trimash** dangerous but glorious path, path of heroes

∘ **udhë e verbër 1** road that comes to a dead end; blind alley **2** narrow path

udhë·çe'l·ës *n* (*Book*) pathfinder, trailblazer: pioneer

udhë·da'lje *nf* **1** passageway **2** (*Fig*) way to solve a problem

udhë·dëftu'e·s *nm* trailblazer, guide

udhë·ha'p·ës *n* (*Book*) trailblazer, pioneer

udhë·he'q·
  I § *vt* to lead; guide; direct
  II § *vi* to lead the way

udhë·he'q·ës
  I § *adj* **1** leading; guiding **2** directorial, administrative
  II § *n* **1** leader; guide **2** administrative head: director, head ***3** air traffic controller

udhë·he'qje *nf ger* **1** <**udhëheq·**, **udhëhiq·**et **2** leadership, direction; guidance **3** (*Collec*) members of the directive staff: directorship, board of directors, directive council

udhë·he'qur *part* <**udhëheq·**, **udhëhiq·**et

udhë·hi'q·et *vpr* <**udhëheq·** to act under guidance/influence: follow directives, be led

udhë·hi'q *stem for 2nd pl pres, pind, imper, vp* <**udhëheq·**

udhë·ho'q *stem for pdef* <**udhëheq·**

udhë·kry'q *nm* crossroad

udhë·mba'rë *nm* person on the right path, straightforward and honest person

udhë·pastro'njës *nm* (*Old*) streetsweeper

udhë·përshkru'e·s *nm* (*Book*) travel writer

udhë·pri'jës *n* guide

udhë·pu'kë *nf* (*Old*) highway

udhë·rrëfi'm *nm* signpost, road sign

udhë·rrëfye's
  I § *adj* indicating the route, road-marking
  II § *n* guide
  III § *nm* guidebook; road guide; travel guide; signpost, road sign

u'dhë·shëm *adj* (*i*) appropriate

udhë·ta'r *n* traveler, wayfarer; passenger

udhë·ta'rçe *adv* hastily, while busy with something else: on the go

udhë·ti'm *nm ger* **1** <**udhëto·**n **2** journey, trip; travel; travel route; travel time
  ∘ **udhëtimi i fundit** (*Book*) the final journey: the funeral

udhë·to'· *n vi* to travel, journey

udhë·to're *nf* **1** stocking carried along by the person taking his turn in the game = **kapu'ças *2** timetable

udhë·tregu'e·s *adj, n nm* = udhë'rrëfye·s

udhë·tu'e·s
  I § *adj* **1** traveling **2** (*Old*) in progress, present
  II § *n* traveller

u'dhë·z *nf* **1** (*Dimin*) <**u'dhë 2** long narrow carpet covering a passageway: runner **3** part (in the hair created by combing)

udhë·ze'zë *fem* <**udhëzi'**

udhëzgjídhje *nf* method for solving a problem = **rrugëzgjídhje**

udhëzi *adj, n (fem sg ˜ëz, masc pl ˜ínj, fem pl ˜eza) (Colloq)* **1** (one) on the wrong path, that has gone astray **2** *(Curse)* bad-luck-to-him/her!

udhëzím *nm ger* **1** <**udhëzo·n 2** guidance; instruction, direction

udhëzo·n *vt* to guide, direct, instruct

udhëzues
I § adj **1** instructional, guiding **2** [*Spec*] transmitting power: drive, driving
II § n guide

udhëzúese *nf* [*Tech*] guideway, guide

udhícë *nf* alley

udhíshtë *nf* **1** narrow path **2** long narrow carpet covering a passageway: runner

udho·het *vpr* to get on the right path, find the way

udho·n *vt* to put [] on the right path

udhóre *nf* [*Ichth*] = **kocë**

UEFA *abbrev (English)* Union of European Football (Soccer) Associations

UEM *abbrev* <**Uzina elektro-mekanike** electromechanical factory

uf *interj* expression of unhappiness: ah me!

UFD *abbrev* <**Uzina e fermentimit të duhanit** Tobacco Fermentation Plant

ufëm *nf* sultry heat, sultriness; sultry weather

UFO *abbrev (English)* UFO = Unidentified Flying Object

***u'full** *OR* **u'fullë** *nf (Colloq)* = **u'thull**

uga'ndas *adj, n* Ugandan

Uga'ndë *nf* Uganda

uga'r
I § adj, nm plowed (land) and ready for planting; plowed (field), but not yet planted; arable (land), but left fallow for a year or two
II § nm initial plowing
∘ **ugar i bardhë** [*Agr*] farmland left fallow for a number of years
∘ **ugar i zi** [*Agr*] farmland left fallow for a year

UGB *abbrev* <**Uzina e gozhdëve dhe e bulonave** nail and bolt factory

***ugíç** *nm* = **ogíç**

ugrofín *adj* [*Ling*] Finno-Ugric

ugu' *nf (Old)* payment for the use of a horse for threshing

***ugu'r** *nm* augury, omen = **ogu'r**

ugu'rshëm *adj (i)* of good augury, boding well = **ogu'r**

uh *interj, nm* **1** exclamation of sudden pleasure or displeasure: ooh! **2** exclamation of sudden realization: oh!

***u'·het** *vpr* = **hu·het**

ui'ski *indecl masc* whiskey

uj· *vt* to make [] watery, dilute

uja'cë *nf* = **ujerë**

***uja'ks** = **huja'ks**

uja'n *nm* broad expanse of water

uja'r *n* person who distributes water: water carrier/pourer, water sprayer, water boy

ujato're *nf* woman who fetches water

ujca'k *adj* (of grapes) watery (suited for making raki)

ujco·n *vi* (of a wound/sore) to ooze

ujdí *nf (Colloq)* accord, agreement: deal; good relations, harmony

ujdís·
I § vt (Colloq) **1** to put [] back in order: fix, repair **2** *(Fig)* to put [] in good order **3** to fix up [a bride], adorn **4** [*Food*] to add flavoring to []: flavor
II § vi **1** *(Fig)* to fix things up with someone, come to an agreement **2** to be well suited; be suitable, suit; go together well
∘ <>**a ujdís· bërroren/kurrizin/samarin/shpínën** to punish <> severely for doing something wrong: give <> the beating that <> deserves
∘ <>**a ujdís· qejfin** <> a lesson, correct <>'s wrongful behavior; give <> the beating that <> deserves

ujdís·et *vpr (Colloq)* **1** to get into good shape: get all dolled up; get all plump and pretty; be sitting pretty **2** *(Fig)* to come to a meeting of minds; make peace

ujdísje *nf ger (Colloq)* <**ujdís·, ujdís·et**

ujdís·ur *adj (i)* in good order, fixed; accomplished; achieved; suitable

ujdhes·ar *n* islander

ujdhesë *nf* [*Geog*] island

ujë'm
I § nm (Old) **1** [*Agr*] portion of grain/flour given in payment to the miller for milling grain; payment in kind **2** grain/flour of different kinds that have been mixed together; hodgepodge, jumble
II § adj, adv all mixed together, in a hodgepodge

ujë'mës *n (Old)* [*Agr*] person responsible for getting or keeping the grain/flour given in payment to the miller

ujë'mse *nf (Old)* [*Agr*] wooden measure holding approximately twenty kilograms of grain

ujë'mtë *adj (i)* made with multigrained flour

ujerë *nf* land that is always wet

uje'rk *nm* watery pus that drains from a wound

ujëzë *nf* [*Agr*] wooden or wire bit placed in a calf's mouth to keep it from sucking milk from a cow

ujë
I § nm **1** water **2** watery substance; watery solution; dilutant **3** urine
II § nn **1** water **2** *(Euph)* human excrement **3** liquid used in tempering metal
III § adj **1** soaking/dripping wet **2** *(Fig)* still wet behind the ears: immature
IV § adv (Colloq) thoroughly
∘ **ujë i ashpër** hard water
∘ **ujë i bekuar** *(Joke Crude)* raki
∘ **ujë i embël** water without salt: fresh water
∘ **ujë i fjetës** still water; stagnant water
∘ **ujë i rëndë/fortë** water with a high content of lime
∘ **ujë i gazuar** carbonated water
∘ **ujë gjirizi** sewage
∘ **ujët e hollë** *(Euph)* urine: number one
∘ **s'ka· ujë në sy** "have no water in one's eye" **1** to have no sense of shame: be shameless **2** to be penniless
∘ **ujë i kripur** salt water, brine
∘ **ujë i lehtë** water without a low content of lime
∘ **ujët e madh** *(Euph)* bowel movement: number two, stool
∘ **ujë i madh** *(Euph)* = **ujët e madh**
∘ **ësh·të mbi ujë** to be in an uncertain situation, be in an insecure position
∘ **ujë mbretëror** "royal water" [*Chem*] aqua regia *nitrohydrochloric acid*
∘ **ujë i oksigjenuar** [*Chem*] hydrogen peroxide

○ **ujë i pafolur** [*Ethnog*] water that will have magical powers if carried to an afflicted person's house from a spring by someone who remains mute along the way

○ **ësh·të ujë që s'ec·ën**³ˢᵍ "be (like) water that *does* not move" to be slow-moving and clumsy

○ **ujë i rëndë 1** water with high mineral (lime) content (that weighs heavy on the stomach) **2** [*Phys*] heavy water

○ **ujë i shkumueshëm** water in which soap suds easily: soft water

○ **ujë i tërbuar** (*Joke*) raki

○ **ujët e trashë** (*Euph*) bowel movement: number two, stool

○ **uji i trashë** (*Euph*) = ujët e trashë

○ **ujë vrotomi** water from melted snow

ujëgrumbullúes *nm* [*Hydrol*] = ujëmbledhës

ujëhollënxjerrës *nm* [*Anat*] urethra

ujëhollërrjedhës *nm* [*Anat*] ureter

ujëlëshúes *nm* [*Hydrol*] sluice

ujëmatës
  I § *nm* water meter; water-level meter
  II § *adj* used for measuring water use/level

ujëmbajtës *adj* [*Geol*] containing water, water-bearing: (*aquiferous*)

ujëmbartës *adj* water carrier = ujar

ujëmbledhës
  I § *nm* [*Hydrol*] irrigation reservoir
  II § *adj* serving to collect water for irrigation

ujëmjaltë *nm* nectar

ujëmore *nf* **1** (*Reg*) spring, fountainhead **2** head/source of a river or stream

ujëndarës *adj* [*Geog*] separating/dividing two bodies/streams of water

ujëndarëse *nf* [*Geog*] elevated land separating two bodies/streams of water: land divide, watershed

ujëndenjëse *nf* pond

ujëngrohës *nm* water heater

ujëpakë *adj* with little water flow

ujëplotë *adj* with water up to the brim

ujëpritës *adj* serving to restrain the flow of water

ujëra *np* < ujë **1** waters **2** tides

○ **ujërat e bardha** "white waters" rainwater

○ **s'bie₁ · në ato ujëra** not get involved in something bad; not get trapped into that kind of thinking/acting

○ **ujërat e gruas** [*Physiol*] amniotic fluid

○ **ujërat e liga** "bad waters" sewage

○ **ujërat e verdha** "yellow waters" stagnant water

○ **ujëra të zeza** sewage

ujëra-ujëra *adv* **1** in varying shades of a color; color-streaked **2** [*Text*] striped

ujës
  I § *adj* **1** aquatic **2** juicy
  II § *nm* **1** wooden sluice-gate **2** carpenter's level

ujëse *np fem* [*Text*] thin interwoven stripes of color in cloth

ujëse *nf* **1** water vessel **2** water blister

ujësi·n *vi* (of foods) to become watery; undergo water separation/condensation

ujësim *nm ger* **1** < ujëso·n, ujëso·het **2** liquefaction

ujësirë *nf* **1** place that stays moist/wet **2** swamp = moçal

ujësjellës *nm* **1** system of utilities for bringing and distributing water **2** watermain; aqueduct

ujëso·het *vpr* (*Book*) **1** to become liquefied, turn into liquid **2** to become full of juice, get juicy **3** to become full of water and ooze out

ujëso·n
  I § *vt* (*Book*) to liquefy
  II § *vi* to ooze/leak water

ujësuar *adj* (*i*) (*Book*) **1** liquefied **2** saturated with water

ujëshkarkúes *nm* [*Hydrol*] overflow sluice

ujëshumë *adj* overflowing with water, with heavy waterflow; water-rich

ujëturbull *adj* having turbulent and turbid water

ujëvarë *nf* waterfall, cataract

ujëz *nf* water blister

ujëzezë *fem* < ujëzi

ujëzi *adj*, *n* (*fem sg ˜ez, masc pl ˜inj, fem pl ˜eza*) miserly (person)

ujis *stem for 1st sg pres, pl pres, 2nd & 3rd sg subj, pind* < ujit·

ujit· *vt* **1** to water; sprinkle **2** to irrigate

ujitës
  I § *adj* providing water, irrigating
  II § *n* irrigation worker

ujitëse *nf* watering can

ujitje *nf ger* **1** < ujit· **2** irrigation

○ **ujitje e bardhë** irrigation with water alone (without added fertilizer)

○ **ujitje me përmbytje** [*Agr*] method of irrigation by flooding the field: submersion irrigation

○ **ujitje me valë** [*Agr*] irrigation by swamping fields with water: flood irrigation

ujitshëm *adj* (*i*) capable of being irrigated: irrigable

ujitur *adj* (*i*) irrigated

ujk *nm* (*np ˜q*) **1** wolf (*Canis lupus*) **2** (*Fig*) cruel and voracious person **3** (*Fig Colloq*) very strong person; extremely able person **4** roof-support post, truss

○ **ujk deti** "sea wolf" sailor toughened by hard experience: old salt

○ **ujk me brirë 1** (*Crude*) ornery guy **2** ugly guy; horrible thing **3** something that badly impedes progress: terrible stumbling block

○ **ujk me lëkurë qengji** wolf in sheep's clothing

○ **ujk plak** person toughened by the hardships of life; person with a great deal of experience

○ **Ujku qimen ndërron, por zakonin s'e harron.** "The wolf changes its coat, but does not forget its habits." The leopard cannot change its spots.

○ **ujk i vjetër** person toughened by the hardships of life; person with a great deal of experience

ujkeshë *nf* = ujkonjë

ujkonjë *nf* female wolf, wolf bitch

ujkth *nm* wolf skin

ujnajë *nf* broad expanse of water: sheet of water, ocean

ujo·n *vt* = ujit·

ujor *adj* **1** of or pertaining to water; watery, aqueous **2** of, for, or pertaining to irrigation **3** living in water: aquatic, marine

ujore *nf* watering site for livestock: horse-pond, water hole; water trough

ujq *np* < ujk

ujqër *np* < ujk

ujqëri *nf collec* **1** wolves as a collective whole **2** roof trussing; roof-support posts

ujqërïsht *adv* wolf-like: wolfishly, voraciously

u·jshëm *adj (i)* **1** water-soaked, wet; aqueous **2** watery, thin **3** juicy

*ujta·k *adj* = ujo·r

ujti· *nf (Reg)* iron (for ironing clothes)

ujti·s·
I § *vi* to bleed/bubble with moisture
II § *vt (Reg)* to iron [clothes]

*ujto·re *nf* = ujo·re

ujth *nm* **1** fluid that oozes from a wound/blister: pus **2** [*Bot*] plant fluid, sap **3** [*Anat*] urinary bladder; bladder disease **4* urinevesica **5* [*Veter*] vesicular disease on the feet of afflicted animals **6** soft spot in the top of an infant's head **7** (*Colloq*) basting stitch = ildí

*uk *nm (np ~ q) (Reg)* = ujk

*u·këm *nf(Reg)* = ufëm

ukrai·n·as *adj, n* Ukrainian

Ukrai·në *nf* the Ukraine

ukra·jë *nf* small forest, woods, wood

ukube·t *nm* great suffering

ul· *vt* **1** to lower **2** to bend/tilt [] down **3** to seat; land [an airplane] **4** to decrease, reduce, diminish **5** *(Fig)* to demote; degrade, debase
∘ **ul· armët** to lay down one's arms: stop fighting, stop resisting, surrender
∘ **e ul· bishtin** "lower one's tail" *(Pej)* to crawl away with one's tail between one's legs
∘ [] **ul·e ço·n/ngre·** to keep touting [], keep talking about []
∘ **e ul· flamurin** to lower the flag, give up, surrender
∘ **e ul· hundën 1** *(Iron)* to come down from one's high horse **2** to become more subdued, become better behaved
∘ **ul· kokën/kryet** "lower one's head" **1** to bow one's head in submission, humble oneself; bow one's head in shame **2** to obey humbly; be humble **3** to come down from one's high horse
∘ <>**a ul· kurrizin** to subjugate <>
∘ **e ul· kurrizin** "lower one's neck/back" *(Contempt)* to surrender abjectly: knuckle under
∘ **ul· kurrizin 1** to hunch over **2** to stop resisting **3** to subjugate
∘ **ul·²ⁿᵈ mesin** "bend your back (to the task)" get down to work
∘ **e ul· moshën** "lower/raise/change the age" to put down a lower/higher/different age (on a document)
∘ **ulu nga fiku** *(Iron)* stop showing off! get down off your high horse!
∘ <> **ul·³ᵖˡ pendët/puplat 1** <>'s feathers settle down **2** *(Fig)* <>'s anger abates, <> *calms* down **3** *(Impol Fig)* <> *loses* <>'s former power/influence; <> *comes* down off <>'s high horse
∘ **e ul· qafën** "lower one's neck/back" *(Contempt)* to surrender abjectly: knuckle under
∘ **Ulu (poshtë) se të panë!** "Sit (down) for they see you!" *(Iron!)* (you can sit down now, they see you) Stop acting so high and mighty! You can stop showing off now!
∘ <> **ul· veshët** "lower one's ears" **1** to have a sullen expression on one's face; have a gloomy look; look offended **2** to feel disappointed and resentful **3** <> *loses* <>'s former power/influence; <> *comes* down off <>'s high horse
∘ <>**a ul· zërin** "lower <>'s voice" to make <> more lenient

∘ **ul· zërin** "lower one's voice" to reduce the intensity of one's complaints

u·l·et *vpr* **1** to descend, go/come down; go/come south **2** to sit down; settle; set down, come to earth **3** to bend over/down **4** to get lower (in magnitude/intensity): decrease; fade; calm down **5** to lose status
∘ **Ulu/uluni ca!** Come down (in price) a little! Stop asking for so much! Be a bit more reasonable! Lower your expectations!
∘ **ul·et³ᵖˡ gjakrat** tempers *cool*
∘ **ul·et këmbëkryq 1** to sit cross-legged **2** to have an extended face-to-face discussion **3** to make oneself completely at home; settle in; take over completely
∘ **ul·et në bisht** to squat
∘ **ul·et në gjunjë** to kneel; sit on one's knees
∘ **ul·et nga shala e hip-ën në samar** "get off the saddle and on a packsaddle" *(Iron)* to suffer a loss in rank: come down a notch
∘ **ul·et shtruar** to settle down calmly and carefully to work

u·las *adv* = ultas

u·lcer·ë *nf* [*Med*] ulcer

ulëra·k *nm* **1** whiner, complainer **2** sufferer of a great loss who is about to wail

ulëri·n *vi* **1** to howl; wail **2** to make a loud fuss; scream

ulëri·më *nf* **1** howl; wail **2** loud fuss; scream
∘ **ulërimë me thes në kokë** "wailing with a sack on one's head" horrible enough to make one scream, so terrible you want to scream

ulëri·t·ës *adj* howling, wailing; screaming

ulëri·t·ur *nn (të)* howling; wailing

u·l·ës *nm* **1** wooden beam that raises and lowers the upper millstone to regulate the fineness of the grind = çu·es, ngre·hës **2** [*Spec*] substance/device that lowers activity/intensity: depressant, depressant

u·l·ët
I § *adv* **1** at/to a low position/level **2** in a base/vile manner
II § *adj (i)* **1** low, lower; lowest **2** base, vile

u·lëz *nf* [*Bot*] = u·lzë

****ulíc·ë** *nf(Old)* lane, alley, street

ul·isht·ë *nf* small tub of lye in which clothes are soaked before washing

u·lje *nf ger* **1** <ul·, u·l·et **2** reduction, decrease; diminution
∘ **ulje në pozitë** demotion

*ulk *nm (np ~ q)* = ujk

ulk·on·jë *nf (Old)* = ujko·një

****ulme·-n** *vt* to make [] wet

****ulme·t·et** *vpr* to get wet

ulo·-n *vi* to sag

ulo·k *adj, n (Colloq)* paralyzed (person), paralytic

ulok·ësí *nf* paralysis

ulpëtí *nm (np ~ nj)* [*Bot*] wych elm, Scotch elm = hí·thës

Ulqín *nm* coastal city in southwestern Montenegro: Ulqin, Ulcinj

ulqi·n·as
I § *adj* of/from Ulcinj
II § *n* native of Ulcinj

****ulta·re** *nf(Old)* chair

u·ltas *OR* **u·ltazi** *adv* at a low level; close to the ground

ult|ë'si *nf* low level, lowness

ult|ë'si|rë *nf* [*Geog*] lowland, depression

ultimatum *nm* ultimatum

ultra| *formativ (Book)* ultra-

ultra|tin'gull *nm (np ~j)* [*Phys*] ultrasound

ultra|violet *adj* = ultravjo'llcë

ultra|vjo'llcë *adj* [*Phys*] ultraviolet

u'lur

I § *part* <ul•, ul•et

II § *adv* **1** seated **2** tilted to one side

III § *nf (e)* depression in a surface, low place

u'lzë *nf* [*Bot*] Tartarian maple (*Acer tartaricum*)

***ulla'r** *nm* halter, bridle = julla'r

ulla'stër *nf* [*Bot*] wild olive (*Olea oleaster*)

ulli(r) *nm (np ~nj)* common olive (*Olea europaea*)
  ○ **ulli i egër** [*Bot*] = ullastër
  ○ **ulli kripës** large olive that has been marinated in brine

ulli|njo're *np fem* [*Bot*] trees of the olive family Oleaceae

ulli|'njtë *adj (i)* of olives, of olive wood

ullir *sg def, sg abl indef* <ulli

ulli|rri'tës *n* specialist in olive growing: olive grower

ulli|sht'a'r *n* **1** person who works in an olive grove
  2 = ullirritës

ulli|shtari *nf* [*Agr*] olive husbandry

ulli|shtë *OR* **ulli|shte** *nf* field of olives

ulli|sht'o'r *adj* planted in olives

ulli|sht'o're *nf* olive grove

ull'o're *nf* [*Ichth*] = ko'cë

ullu'k *nm (np ~qe)* **1** roof gutter, eaves gutter **2** groove into which another piece slips or fits: slot, mortise **3** (*Colloq*) small stream of water ***4** gutter, trough, duct

ulluk|u'a'r *adj (i)* grooved, channeled

ullulla' *nf (Colloq)* lullaby

ulluve'gë *nf* [*Ornit*] **1** (*Reg*) owl = kukuva'jkë **2** barn owl (*Tyto alba*)

umb *nm* [*Agr*] small plowshare on a wooden plow

UMB *abbrev* <Uzina mekanike bujqësore agricultural machinery factory

***umbre'llë** *nf* umbrella = ombre'llë

UMGj *abbrev* <Uzina mekanike e gjeologjisë factory for making mining machinery

UMN *abbrev* <Uzina mekanike e naftës petroleum machinery factory

una'k *nm* stone firedog

unani'm *adj* unanimous

unanimi'sht *adv* unanimously

unanim|ite't *nm (Book)* unanimity

una'zash *adv*

una'za-una'za *adv, adj* in/with a ring-like form; in ringlets, in curls

una'zë *nf* **1** ring **2** [*Zool*] segment (of an annelid body)
  ○ **unazë gjarpër** ring in the form of a coiled snake
  ○ **ësh•të në unazë** to be engaged (for marriage)

unaz'i'm *nm ger* <unazo •n

unaz'o' •n *vt* **1** to remove a ring of bark from [ ] **2** to band [a bird] for identification

unaz'o'r *adj* **1** ring-like, circular; consisting of rings **2** [*Zool*] having an annulated body: *annulate*

unaz'o're *nf* [*Zool*] tent caterpillar (*Malacosoma neustria*)

unaz'o'rë *np masc* [*Zool*] annelids (*Annelida*)

UNÇSh *abbrev* <Ushtria Nacionalçlirimtare Shqip-tare [*Hist*] Albanian National Liberation Army

und *nm* **1** [*Zool*] food in a ruminant's crop: cud **2** squashed/crumbled remains

***undy'r| = yndy'r**

undy'r|të *adj (i)* = yndy'rshëm

UNESKO *abbrev (English)* UNESCO = United Nations Education, Scientific, and Cultural Organization

u'në

I § *pron 1st sg nom* I

II § *nm* the "I", ego
  ○ **Unë me bukë e ai me gurë** I do something nice for him and see what it gets me!
  ○ **Unë për lisa, ti për fshesa.** Obviously there has been a complete misunderstanding. We went off in two completely different directions.
  ○ **Unë them "ja ujku!", ti kërkon gjurmët.** "I say 'there's a wolf!', you look for his tracks." (*Prov*) (said to someone wasting time looking in the wrong place for something quite obvious)

***u'ngër** *nm* [*Zool*] = ujk

***ungri'më** *nf* (of a dog/wolf) howl; (of a pig) squeal

***ungro' •n** *vi* (of a dog/wolf) to howl; (of a pig) squeal

ungj *nm* uncle

***ungji** *adv (Reg)* in entirety

ungji'll *nm (np ~j)* **1** gospel **2** evangelist

ungjill|ëz'i'm *nm ger* [*Relig*] <ungjillëzo' •n

ungjill|ëz'o' •n *vt* [*Relig*] to evangelize

ungjill'o'r

I § *n* [*Relig*] evangelist

II § *adj* [*Relig*] evangelical

ungjill|ta'r *n* [*Relig*] evangelist

***ungj|** (*Reg*) = ul

unifik|i'm *nm ger (Book)* **1** <unifiko •n **2** unification

unifik'o' •n *vt (Book)* to unify; unite

unifik|u'a'r *adj (i) (Book)* unified; united

unifo'rm *adj (Book)* uniform = njëtrajtsh'ëm

unifo'rmë *nf* uniform (clothing)

uni'k *adj* **1** unique **2** same for all, standard **3** undivided, united; single

unipa're *nf* [*Med*] unipara

unite't *nm* **1** unity **2** unit

unive'rs *nm (Book)* universe

univers|a'l *adj* **1** universal **2** general; general-purpose

univers|ali'z'i'm *nm ger* **1** (*Book*) <universalizo' •n, universalizo •het **2** generalization

univers|ali'z'o •het *vpr (Book)* to become universalized/generalized

univers|ali'z'o' •n *vt (Book)* to universalize, generalize

univers|ia'dë *nf* sports contest involving college students

univers|ita'r

I § *adj* of or pertaining to universities or university students

II § *n* university student

univers|ite't *nm* university

UNO *abbrev (English)* U.N. = United Nations Organization

***uno'r** *nm (Reg Gheg)* = uro'r

UNRRA *abbrev (English)* [*Hist*] UNRRA = United Nations Relief and Rehabilitation Administration

***u'nsh|ëm** *adj (i) (Reg Gheg)* = u'rshëm

unshim *nm* hunger

unsho' ·*n vt* to allow to die of hunger

***unto'** ·*het vpr* to get hungry

u'nzë *nf* **1** [*Agr*] fungus disease of cereal grasses: smut *2 pen point

unzo' ·*het vpr* [*Agr*] to become affected with smut

***unji** *(Reg Gheg)* = **ul|**

***unji** = **ungji**

***unj|t** *adj (i) (Reg Gheg)* = **u'rshëm**

Uoll-Strit *nm* Wall Street

UPI *abbrev (English)* UPI = United Press International

UPN *abbrev* <**Uzina e përpunimit të naftës** petroleum refining plant

UPNÇLSh *abbrev* <**Ushtria Partizane Nacionalçlirimtare Shqiptare** [*Hist*] Albanian Partisan Army for National Liberation

UPO *abbrev (French)* <**Union Postale Universelle** UPO = Universal Postal Union

upri *nf*[*Hist*] group of villagers who come together to give free help to a neighbor; help given by this group

uragan *nm* **1** [*Meteor*] hurricane **2** *(Fig)* powerful social movement

uran *nm* [*Chem*] = **uranium**

uranium *nm* [*Chem*] uranium

uranor *adj* [*Chem*] of or containing uranium

u'ras *adv*

ura'ta *np* <**uratë** [*Relig*] rosary beads, rosary

uratar *nm (Old)* [*Relig*] priest

uratë *nf* **1** [*Relig*] prayer **2** blessing **3** *(Colloq)* [*Relig*] priest
   ∘<> **pastë lënë uratën!** "May {} have left <> {}'s blessing!" (said as consolation to children upon the death of an aged parent)

uratim *nm ger* blessing = **bekim**

urato' ·*n vt* to bless

uratore *nf*[*Relig*] **1** prayer book **2** place where a priest say prayers: oratory

urban *adj* urban

urban|ist *n* urbanologist

urban|istik *adj* urbanologistic

urban|istikë *nf* urbanology

urban|izëm *nm* = **urbanistikë**

urban|iz|im *nm ger* **1** <**urbanizo'** ·*n* **2** urbanization

urban|izo' ·*n vt* to urbanize

***urc** *nm* = **urës**

***urd|i** *nf(Old)* = **ushtri**

u'rdhë *nf* [*Bot*] = **urth**

***urdhënar** *adj* ordinary, usual; for everyday use

u'rdhër *nm* **1** order; command **2** religious order **3** [*Hist*] feudal order **4** medal of honor
   ∘ **urdhër ekzekutimi** "execution order" death warrant
   ∘ **urdhër kontrolli** search warrant

urdhërate *nf (Colloq)* **1** assignment to perform a chore **2** servant = **urdhëratës**

urdhëratës *n* **1** *(Old)* youngest person assigned to do chores; servant **2** person who has no say and must do what someone else says

urdhërderdhje *nf* [*Fin*] receipt for delivery of cash: cash receipt

urdhërdorëzim *nm* [*Fin*] delivery receipt

urdhërdhënës
   I § adj [*Law*] having the right to give/issue orders: having executive authority

II § n **1** person who gives/issues an order **2** *(Pej)* autocratic bureaucrat

urdhërësë *nf* ordinance, executive order

urdhërim *nm ger* **1** <**urdhëro'** ·*n* **2** order, command

urdhërngarkim *nm* [*Fin*] bill of lading, shipping bill, packing slip

urdhëro' ·*n*
   I § vt **1** to order, command **2** *(Colloq)* to manage to control/move [ ]
   II § vi **1** to give an order **2** to invite <> politely to come
   III § 2nd person forms only (Colloq) you wish/want/desire
   IV § imper forms only **1** indicates respectful attention to another person's needs or requests: yes? **2** requests repetition of something just said, but not heard well: excuse me? **3** indicates a polite request: please! **4** *(Iron)* I hope you're pleased now! Now you've done it!

urdhëror *adj* **1** expressing/constituting a command: imperative **2** [*Ling*] imperative

urdhërore *nf* [*Ling*] imperative mood

urdhërpagesë *nf* [*Fin*] money order

urdhërporosi *nf* [*Econ*] request for merchandise: order; order form

urdhërqind|ës *n* centurion

urdhërshërbim *nm* [*Fin*] authorization document and expense record for a person on official business outside his regular place of work/residence

***urdhërtar** *n (Old)* ruler, commander

urdhëru'ar *adj (i)* **1** under orders, commanded **2** receptive to orders/requests: ready to serve, obedient

urdhëru'es
   I § adj **1** containing/giving an order **2** imperative; imperious
   II § n person who gives/issues an order

urdhërxhirim *nm* [*Fin*] transfer order on a giro account

u'rdhje *nf* [*Med*] impetigo

***urdhnar** *adj (Old)* domineering

ure' *nf* urea

ure'kth *nm* [*Veter*] disease of animals in which body cavities fill up with pus *(empyema)*

urelë *nf* narrow ditch of water

urenjë *nf* [*Bot*] yew = **bërshen**

ureter *nm* [*Med*] ureter

uretër *nm* [*Med*] urethra

ure'zë *nf* [*Agr*] wooden piece forming the underpart of the an ox-yoke frame

u'rë *nf* **1** bridge **2** [*Tech*] axletree **3** [*Agr*] wooden piece forming the underpart of the an ox-yoke frame **4** [*Agr*] sole of a wooden plow **5** [*Archit*] = **kulmar 6** piece of burning wood used to provide light or fire
   ∘ **urë dhëmbësh** bridge (for false teeth)
   ∘ **ura e këmbës** [*Anat*] the arch of the foot
   ∘ **urë ngritëse** drawbridge
   ∘ **urë pa qemer** something unstable/weak
   ∘ **ësh·të urë e pashuar** "be an unextinguished ember" to be a secretive/sneaky person
   ∘ **ura e supit** [*Anat*] collarbone, clavicle

urëkalim *nm* transition link/bridge

u'rës *nm* triangular metal frame that supports fire logs in a hearth; rock against which fire logs in a hearth lean

u'rët *adj (i)* = **uritur**

urëti nf hunger

urëto -het vpr to feel hungry

urëto -n vi to hunger

urëtuar adj (i) hungry

urëz nf 1 [Agr] wooden underpart of an ox-yoke frame 2 bow of the yoke that goes under each ox: oxbow 3 forked end of the tongue (of a cart) to which the ox-yoke is attached 4 [Agr] sole of a wooden plow 5 bridge of a stringed instrument = **magjar** 6 gangplank 7 (Old) firing pan in an old gunlock

urëzak nm stone or metal support for logs burning in a fireplace

urëzo -het vpr to bow down in submission, let people walk all over one: be submissive

urgus vt 1 (Colloq) to bloat []'s belly 2 to beat [] hard 3 (Fig) to exasperate

urgus-et vpr (Colloq) 1 to feel/become bloated 2 (Fig) to become exasperated

urgusje nf ger < **urgus**-, **urgus**-et

urgjencë nf 1 urgency 2 emergency 3 (Colloq) emergency room

urgjent adj urgent; as an emergency

urgjentisht adv urgently

uri nf 1 hunger 2 famine

urim nm ger 1 < **uro**-n, **uro**-het 2 expression of good will for another's well-being: well wishing, good-luck wish, well wishes, congratulations

Urime nf Urime (female name)

urinar adj [Med] urinary

urinë nf urine

urinim nm 1 < **urino**-n 2 urination

urino-n vi to urinate

urinoz adj [Med] urinous

uriq nm [Med] cancer = **irizë**

urishtë nf mound of earth created by a burrowing mole

urit-et vpr to be/get hungry

uritur
I § adj (i) hungry; famished; insatiable
II § n (i) hungry person

urith nm 1 [Zool] mole (burrowing insectivore) 2 (Fig Insult) short, skinny person: runt

*_**urith-burgth**_ nm [Entom] mole cricket

urithe nf [Bot] tragacanth, goat's thorn (Astragalus)

urjezë nf embroidered or knitted eyelet

urlë nf 1 [Dairy] boiled milk or yogurt that are salted and stored in a leather/cheesecloth bag 2 cheese made in a leather bag and periodically laced with milk

*_**urmë**_ = **hurmë**

urnë nf funerary urn

uro -het vpr to exchange good luck wishes

uro-n vt to express good will for another's well-being: wish [] well, wish [] good luck, congratulate

urogjen adj urogenital

urojmë nf pillar, prop

*_**urok**_ nm (Old) aim, purpose, objective; intention

urolog n urologist

urologji nf urology

uror nm piece of steel used to strike sparks from a flintstone

urov nm 1 [Bot] common vetch (Vicia sativa) 2 bitter vetch (Vicia ervilia)

urovishtë nf 1 field planted in vetch 2 vetch hay

urshëm adj (i) hungry
○ **ësh-të urshëm** to be hungry

URT abbrev < **Uzina e radio-televizorëve** factory for making television and radio sets

urtar nm (Old) [Ethnog] wise elder who arbitrates disputes according to mountain customs

urtë
I § adj (i) 1 well-behaved; gentle, calm, quiet 2 compliant, tractable, obedient 3 sage; prudent
II § adv 1 calmly, quietly 2 obediently 3 sagely; prudently
○ **Urtë e butë e plot tigani.** "Calmly and gently and with a full skillet." (Iron) (said of someone who refuses to get emotionally stirred up)
○ **urtë e butë** 1 by gentle persuasion 2 quietly and calmly, gently; calmly, without haste

*_**urtërisht**_ = **urtësisht**

urtësi nf 1 calmness, sobriety; gentleness 2 sagacity, wisdom; prudence

urtësimor adj disciplinary, correctional

urtësisht adv gently, nicely, calmly; wisely, prudently

urtëso -het vpr 1 to become calm and quiet: calm/settle down, come to one's senses, behave 2 to gain wisdom, become sagacious, learn prudence; become mature

urtëso -n vt to calm/quiet [] down; make [] behave

urtësuar adj (i) 1 well-disciplined 2 sane, reasonable

urti nf 1 calmness 2 prudence, wisdom, common sense 3 (Old) [Ethnog] council of elders/sages that arbitrates disputes according to mountain customs

urtikace nf [Bot] Urticaceae

urtiplotë adj full of wisdom: sagacious

urtisht adv = **urtësisht**

urtishte nf unripe plum

urto -het vpr = **urtëso** -het

urto -n vt = **urtëso** -n

urtuar adj (i) famished, hungry

urtytë nf [Bot] wild strawberry = **luleshtrydhe**

urth nm 1 [Bot] English ivy (Hedera helix) 2 [Agr] black rot 3 [Med] impetigo 4 [Med] heartburn *5 tubercle

urthore np fem [Bot] ginseng/ivy family Araliaceae

uruar adj (i) 1 well-behaved, gracious 2 blessed; well-blessed 3 (Euph) darn, damned, blessèd

Uruguai nm Uruguay

*_**urup**_ nm = **rup**

urra interj, nf 1 hurrah, hooray 2 [Mil] used as rallying cry in battle to start an attack: mount up! let's go!

urre-het vpr to hate/despise one another

urre-n vt to hate, despise

urrejtës adj filled with hate

urrejtje nf hate, detestation

urrejtshëm adj (i) hateful, detestable

urrejtur adj (i) hated, despised

urrë nf sapwood, alburnum

urryer adj (i) hated, despised

urryes adj = **urrejtës**

USA abbrev (American) USA = United States of America

USD abbrev United States dollars

USHT *abbrev* <**Universiteti Shtetëror i Tiranës** [*Hist*] State University of Tirana

usi *nf* bad smell: stink

*****ust** *interj* (used to urge on an ox) giddyup!

usta *nm (np ˜ llarë) (Colloq)* **1** man who has achieved mastery of a craft/skill: master; master craftsman **2** title of address used by an apprentice toward his teacher: master **3** mason = **murator 4** crafty/cunning person
  ○ **usta pa mistri** "master mason without a trowel" to have the knowledge but not the means and organizational skills needed

ustalleshë *nf* <**usta** *(Colloq)* **1** woman who has achieved mastery of a craft/skill: mistress of her trade **2** crafty/cunning woman

ustallëk *nm (Colloq)* **1** craft, trade **2** mastery, skill **3** craft, cunning

*****uste(n)** *nm* = **hosten**

*****usteshë** *nf* = **ustalleshë**

ush *interj* command to a donkey to go forward or change direction: gee!

ushe *nf* **1** blind made of branches and leaves to camouflage a hunter **2** sluice gate made of wattle

ushejzë *nf* [*Bot*] carline thistle = **ushonjëz**

ushezë *nf* **1** = **ushe 2** funnel-shaped fish weir

ushinth *nm* [*Bot*] firethorn *(Pyracantha coccinea)*

ushkur *nm* waistband used to tie up underpants/pantaloons

ushojzë *nf* [*Ichth*] = **shojzë**

ushonjëz *nf* [*Bot*] carline thistle *(Carlina)*

ushqe *·het vpr* to take sustenance
  ○ **ushqe** *·het* **me** [] to feed on []; intake [] as raw material; have [] as its energy source

ushqe *·n vt* **1** to feed; nourish, sustain **2** to serve as energy source for []
  ○ <**>a ushqe** *·n* **fjalën/bisedën/mendimin 1** to support what <> says/thinks **2** *(Pej)* to chime in to agree with and support anything <> says
  ○ [] **ushqe** *·n* **me duar plot** to pamper [], spoil []
  ○ <**> ushqe** *·n* **me** [] to provide <> with [], supply [] to <>

ushqerë *nf* [*Bot*] viper's bugloss *(Echium vulgare)*

ushqerëz *nf* [*Bot*] = **ushqerë**

ushqim *nm ger* **1** <**ushqe** *·n*, **ushqe** *·het* **2** nourishment, nutrition; food; sustenance **3** [*Spec*] energy supply
  ○ **ushqim i njomë/gjelbër** "wet/green food" [*Agr*] fresh hay, green fodder; fodder consisting of fresh hay mixed with food by-products
  ○ **ushqime rrënjore** fodder composed of tuberous plants
  ○ **ushqimi social** *(Collec)* public eateries
  ○ **ushqim i thatë/trashë/ashpër** [*Agr*] dry hay/fodder

ushqimor *adj* **1** pertaining to or providing nourishment/sustenance/energy: nutritional **2** [*Med*] alimentary **3** [*Law*] providing the necessities of life

ushqimore *nf* grocery store

*****ushqimtar** *adj* alimentary, nutritive

*****ushqimtore** *nf* communal dining room

ushqyer
  I §ipart <**ushqe** *·n*, **ushqe** *·het*
  II § *adj (i)* fattened; well-fed
  ○ **i ushqyer me thelpinj arre** reared from childhood with the best of everything

ushqyerit *nn (të)* feeding

---

ushqyerje *nf* [*Med*] nutrition

ushqyes
  I § *adj* nutritious; nutritional; nourishing
  II § *nm* (device/means) that feeds/supplies: feeder

ushqyeshëm *adj (i)* nutritious, nourishing, wholesome

usht *nm (np ˜ re)* = **ushtër**

ushtar
  I § *n* **1** soldier **2** private (military rank) **3** *(Elev)* champion/defender (of a cause)
  II § *nm* [*Chess*] pawn

ushtarak
  I § *adj* military
  II § *n* member of the military forces

ushtarakisht *adv* **1** militarily **2** in a military manner

ushtë *nf* **1** [*Hist*] spear, lance **2** unripe spike of grain = **ushtër**

ushtëmbajtës *nm* [*Hist*] soldier armed with a spear/lance

ushtër
  I § *nf* unripe spike of grain
  II § *adj* unripe; immature

ushtëresë *nf (Old)* military encampment

ushtëtar *n* [*Hist*] = **ushtëmbajtës**

ushtëti *·n* = **ushto** *·n*

ushtimë *nf* muffled loud noise from a distant source: rumble/roar; reverberation

ushto *·het vpr* **1** = **staxhiono** *·het* **2** *(Fig)* to become seasoned by experience

ushto *·n*
  I § *vi* **1** to make a heavy rolling noise from a distance: rumble, roar **2** to make a loud reverberating sound: resound, peal, ring out
  II § *vt (Colloq)* **1** = **staxhiono** *·n* **2** to harden [pottery/tools] by coating with grease and heating in an oven **3** to put [] to the test: try [] out; try, test
  ○ <**> ushto** *·n³ᵖˡ* **sheket/kadet/hambarët** "<>'s storage containers *are rumbling*" <>'s larders are empty; <> *is* destitute: <>'s cupboard *is* bare

ushtor *nm* = **bekçi**

*****ushtratë** *nf (Old)* military campaign

ushtre *nf* unripe fruit

ushtri *nf* **1** army **2** *(Colloq)* military service
  ○ **ushtri e kazermës** *(Pej Npc)* professional army trained to ignore the support of the common people

ushtrim *nm ger* **1** <**ushtro** *·n*, **ushtro** *·het* **2** exercise

ushtrimor *adj* pertaining to or used for doing exercises

ushtrimore *nf* **1** preparatory school for teachers; practicum **2** drillyard, drill field

ushtro *·het vpr* **1** to do exercises: train, exercise, practice **2** to become practiced

ushtro *·n vt* **1** to exercise **2** to practice

ushtrues *nm* **1** person who practices **2** person in training, exerciser

ushtuar *adj (i)* **1** (of wood/people) seasoned **2** *(Reg)* (of clothes) worn for some time

ushuj *I §* *nm* OR **ushujë** *II §* *nf* pork fat, lard

ushunjëz *nf* [*Zool*] leech = **shushunjë**
  ○ **ushunjëza e drithërave** [*Entom*] leaf beetle *Lema melanopus L.*
  ○ **ushunjëza e gjetheve** [*Entom*] cherry slug *Caliroa limacina Red.*

ut *nm* **1** [*Mus*] large mandolin-like instrument with four strings: oud **2** [*Ornit*] hoot owl

UT *abbrev* <**Universiteti i Tiranës** University of Tirana

UTEL *abbrev* <**Uzina e telave** wire factory

utilitár *adj (Book)* based on practical motives: utilitarian

utilitaríst *adj (Book)* based on utilitarianism: utilitarian

utilitarizëm *nm (Book)* utilitarianism

utopí *nf* **1** utopia **2** utopianism

utopík *adj* reflecting utopian principles: utopian

utopíst *n* supporter/promoter of utopianism: utopian

utopizëm *nm* utopianism

utri·*n vi* (of a sow) to come into heat: rut

utrítje *nf* estrus (of a sow)

uturí·*n vi* to roar

   ○ <> **uturi**·*n*[3pl] **veshët** <>'s ears *are ringing*

uturímë *nf* roaring, roar; buzzing, buzz

uth *nm* [*Med*] **1** heartburn **2** impetigo

****uthët** *adj (i)* = **athët**

****uthto**·*n vt* to sour = **atheto**·*n*

uthull
   I § *nf* vinegar
   II § *adj* very sour
   ○ **Uthulla e fortë prish enën e vet.** "Strong vinegar breaks its own container." *(Prov)* {}'s hot temper will be {}'s undoing.
   ○ **Pi/Pini uthull!** "Drink vinegar!" *(Tease)* Calm down!

uthullaç
   I § *nm* [*Bot*] = **uthullíshtë**
   II § *adj* sour as vinegar

****uthullake** *nf* [*Bot*] curled dock (*Rumex crispus*)

uthullare *nf* [*Bot*] = **uthullíshtë**

uthullícë *nf* [*Bot*] = **uthullíshtë**

uthullím *nm ger* **1** <**uthullo**·*n*, **uthullo**·*het* **2** sour flavor, sourness

uthullírë *nf* **1** sour/vinegary thing = **uthullíshtë** **2** *(Fig)* [*Bot*] spiteful and talkative woman

uthullíshtë *I §* *nf OR* **uthullíshte** *II §* *nf* [*Bot*] sheep sorrel, sour dock (*Rumex acetosella*)

uthullník *nm* = **uthullóre**

uthullníke *nf* [*Bot*] = **uthullíshtë**

uthulló·*het vpr* **1** to turn into vinegar; become sour as vinegar, become very sour **2** *(Fig Colloq)* to go sour, get messed up

   ○ <> **uthullo**·*het*[3pl] **trutë** "<>'s brains *becomes* messed up" <> *becomes* unable to think coherently: <> *goes* dotty

uthulló·*n vt* **1** to make [] into vinegar, make [] very sour **2** to add vinegar to []

uthullór *adj* acetic

uthullóre *nf* vinegar container

uthullósh *adj* slightly sour, sourish, a bit sour

uthullt *adj (i)* **1** sour as vinegar, very sour **2** vinegary in color

uthulluar
   I § *part* <**uthullo**·*n*, **uthullo**·*het*
   II § *adj (i)* **1** turned to vinegar; vinegary **2** pickled in vinegar; made with vinegar
   ○ <> **ësh-të**[3pl] **uthulluar trutë** "<>'s brains have turned to vinegar" *(Impol)* <>'s brain *has* become senile, <>'s brain *is* fried

****uve** *nf* egg

uverturë *nf* overture

****uvíll** *nm (pl ~ j)* = **yll**

u'vje *nf* **1** edge of a piece of cloth **2** woolen cradle strap

u'xhë *nf* grotto, cave

uzdajë *nf (Reg)* hope = **shpresë**

****uzdaít**·*et vpr* to take hope/heart

****uzengjí** *nf* stirrup = **yzengjí**

uzínë *nf* manufacturing/refining plant: factory, mill, smelter

u'zo *nf* ouzo

uzúrë *nf (Old)* usury

uzúrpator *n (Book)* = **uzurpúes**

uzurpím *nm ger (Book)* <**uzurpo**·*n* **2** usurpation

uzúrpo·*n vt (Book)* to usurp

uzurpúes *n (Book)* usurper

****uzurtár** *n (Old)* usurer

v [*vë*] *nf* **1** the consonant letter "v" **2** the voiced labiodental fricative represented by the letter "v"

v. *abbrev* <**viti** the year

V.R. *abbrev* <**Vini re!** Notice!

va *nm* **1** ford (over a river) **2** *(Reg)* path through a field/forest **3** *(Fig)* escape route, solution to a difficult problem: way out

***vabë**·**zi** *nf* = **babë**·**zi**

vadaro̱sh *nm* fruit stem = **rrëfa̱në**

va̱de *nf* **1** *(Old)* time limit: deadline, due date = **afat** **2** grace period for late payment

vade̱në·s *nm* [*Bot*] = **vode̱nës**

va̱dë
  I § *nf (Reg)* **1** irrigation system; irrigation line; amount of water needed to irrigate a field **2** irrigation
  II § *adv* in a stream/gush

vad|is *stem for 1st sg pres, pl pres, 2nd & 3rd sg subj, pind* <**vadit·**

vadi̱t· *vt* to irrigate, water = **uji̱t·**

vadi̱t·et *vpr* **1** *(Reg)* to get used to a place: be accustomed, be well-rooted **2** to get irrigated

vadi̱të·s *adj* = **uji̱tës**

vadi̱të·se *nf* = **uji̱tëse**

vadi̱tje *nf ger* **1** = **uji̱tje** **2** irrigation

vadi̱tur *adj (i)* practiced, experienced; trained, skilled

va̱dhë *nf* [*Bot*] **1** mountain ash *(Sorbus)* **2** fruit of the mountain ash: sorb apple
  ○ **va̱dhë e bu̱të** [*Bot*] service tree *Sorbus domestica*
  ○ **va̱dhë e egër** [*Bot*] rowan, mountain ash *Sorbus aucuparia*

vadhë·vi̱çe *nf* [*Bot*] mountain ash, wild service tree *(Sorbus torminalis)*
  ○ **vadhëvi̱çe e bardhë** [*Bot*] whitebeam tree *Sorbus aria Crantz*

va̱dhë·z *nf* [*Bot*] = **va̱dhë**

vaft *nm (Reg)* = **vakt**

vagabo̱nd *n, adj* vagrant

vagabond|a̱zh *nm* vagrancy

vag|ëllim *nm ger* **1** <**vagëllo̱·n**, **vagëllo̱·het** **2** = **vagëllime**

vag|ëllime *nf* **1** faint/dim light, glimmer of light; first faint light of morning; murky light **2** *(Fig)* murky/unclear situation, murkiness; dimness, faintness

vag|ëllim|**thi** *adv* **1** murkily **2** *(Fig)* as if in a dream, dimly

vag|ëllo̱·het *vpr* to grow murky/dark/dim: darken, fade, dim

vag|ëllo̱·n
  I § *vi* **1** to have weak eyesight; see things faintly **2** to glimmer/glow faintly; start to grow light
  II § *vt* **1** to blink **2** to diminish the light given off by []: darken, dim

vag|ëllu̱ar *adj (i)* murky; dim

va̱g|ët *adj (i)* dim, faint; vague, murky

vagi̱në *nf* [*Anat*] vagina

***vagi̱r** *nm* weight (used on a balance scale)

vago̱n *nm* railroad car; hand car
  ○ **vagon cisterṉë** [*Rr*] railroad tank car
  ○ **vagon dekovi̱li** [*Min*] narrow-gauge freight car used in a mine: coal car, tub
  ○ **vagon frigorif̱er** [*Rr*] refrigerator car
  ○ **vagon gju̱mi** [*Rr*] sleeping car, sleeper
  ○ **vagon kafshë̱sh** [*Rr*] cattle car
  ○ **vagon mallra̱sh** [*Rr*] freight car
  ○ **vagon udhëtarë̱sh** [*Rr*] passenger car

vagoni̱st *n* [*Min*] loader of mine trucks: carman

vagon-restora̱nt *nm* dining car

vagon|shty̱r|ë·s *n* = **vagoni̱st**

va̱gull *adj* = **va̱gullt**

vagu̱ll| = **vagë̱ll**

vagu̱ll|e·së *nf* first faint light of morning: daybreak

vagu̱ll|i *nf* = **vagëllim**

vagu̱ll|im *nm* = **vagëllim**

vagu̱ll|o̱·n = **vagëllo̱·n**

va̱gullt *adj (i)* murky, dim, faint

vagjeli̱ *nf (Colloq)* nutritious food; good food

***vaht** *nm* = **vakt**

vais·
  I § *vi (Colloq)* to lean to one side, tilt; sag on one side
  II § *vt* to tilt/bend [] to one side; hang [] over on one side

vais·et *vpr* to lean to one side, be tilted; sag on one side

vais|je *nf ger* **1** <**vais·**, **vais·et 2** tilt

vais|ur *adj (i)* tilted to one side

vaj
  I § *nm* oil
  II § *adj* quite calm; well-behaved
  III § *adv* well, smoothly, easily
  ○ **vaj akre̱pi** herbal folk medicine made with scorpion toxin and oil: scorpion oil
  ○ **vaj bimë̱sh** vegetable oil
  ○ **vaj hi̱ndi** castor oil
  ○ **vaj li̱ri** linseed oil
  ○ **vaj i mi̱rë** *(Colloq)* olive oil
  ○ **vaj pambu̱ku** cottonseed oil
  ○ **vaj reci̱ni** castor oil
  ○ **vaj i tra̱shë** *(Colloq)* resinous oil
  ○ **U derdh vaji, s'mblidhet më.** "The oil spilled, it cannot be gathered back anymore." *(Prov)* There's no use crying over spilt milk. That's water over the dam.
  ○ **vaj e ve̱rë e uthu̱ll** "oil and wine and vinegar" *(Colloq)* like a rainbow

vaj
  I § *nm* **1** wail mourning a death: dirge, lament **2** mournful cry; crying **3** calamity, disaster; bereavement
  II § *interj (Colloq)* (cry of woe) woe is me!
  ○ **Vaj halli!** **1** What a calamity! Oh no! **2** Just think how terrible _! **Vaj halli të ishe drejtor i firmës!** Just imagine how bad it would be if you were chief of the whole firm!

vajanîcë *nf* **1** box containing lubricant for a gun **2** small oil can with a spout

*__*va'jc** *adj* constantly wailing

*__*va'jc** *opt 1st sg* <ve·te

vajdhën·ës *adj* oil-bearing: oleaginous

*__*vaj'ere** *nf* ointment

va'jë *nf (Reg)* wet nurse = **mënde'shë**

vaj'ës
    I § *adj* **1** yielding much oil, highly oleaginous: oily **2** constantly wailing
    II § *nm* highly oleaginous olive

vajgu'r *nm* **1** kerosene **2** *(Old)* petroleum

vajgurmba'jt·ës *adj* containing petroleum: petroleum-bearing, oil-bearing

vajguro'r *adj* **1** = **vajgurmbajt**ës **2** of or involved in petroleum refining: oil-refining

vajgursjel'lës *nm* = **naftesjel'lës**

vaji'm *nm ger* <vajo'·n

vajis· *vt* = vajo'·n

vajmede't *interj (Colloq)* expresses feeling of great sadness and wretchedness: oh what misery!

vajnîk *nm* oil can with a spout

vajo'·n *vt* **1** to coat [] with oil: oil **2** *[Relig]* to anoint [] with oil

vajo'r *adj* oil-bearing: oleaginous

vajos· *vt* = vajo'·n

vajo'sje *nf ger* = vaji'm

vajo'sur *adj (i)* = vaju'ar

vajo'sh *adj* **1** mournful **2** oily

vaj'ra *np* <vaj oils

vajshëm *adj (i)* mournful, sorrowful

va'jt *stem for part, pdef, adm* <ve·te **1** *(Fig Colloq)* passed away: died **2**
    ◦ <> **vajti goja prapa qafës** <>'s words fell on deaf ears, <> spoke in vain
    ◦ <> **vajti koka** <> *gets killed*
    ◦ **vajti te molla e kuqe 1** {*the news*} spread everywhere, spread to the far corners of the earth **2** *(Impol)* {} died: {} got it in the neck, {} bought the farm
    ◦ <> **vajti thika në heqës** <> *comes to the end of* <>'s rope

vajti'm *nm ger* **1** <vajto'·n **2** wailing to mourn the dead; keening

vajtimo'r *adj (Poet)* mournful, dolorous

vajtimo're *nf* = vajto're

vajtimta'r *adj (Poet)* mournful, dolorous, plaintive

vajtim'thi *adv* mournfully

va'jtje *nf ger* <ve·te

va'jtje-a'rdhje *nf* **1** round trip **2** goings and comings: social visits

vajto'·n *vi, vt* **1** to wail out a rhythmic eulogy [for someone dead]: keen; wail in mourning [for someone dead], lament **2** *(Fig)* to grieve, mourn, lament

vajto'jcë *nf [Ethnog]* = vajto're

vajto're *nf [Ethnog]* female keener

*__*va'jtshë** *1st sg pdef* <ve·te I went

vajtu'ar *adj (i)* = vajtu'esh**ëm**.

vajtu'es
    I § *n* *[Ethnog]* mourner who wails out a rhythmic eulogy for the dead person: keener
    II § *adj* mournful, dolorous

vajtu'eshëm *adj (i)* plaintive, doleful; pathetic, pitiful, miserable

va'jtur
    I § *part* <ve·te
    II § *adj (i)* on its/one's last legs, worn-out
    III § *nn (të)* going away, departing

vaju'ar *adj (i)* well-oiled

va'jzë
    I § *nf* **1** girl **2** daughter
    II § *adj* virgin
    ◦ **vajzë e gjetur** stepdaughter
    ◦ **vajzë mashkull** tomboy
    ◦ **vajzë mashkullore** *(Reg)* tomboy
    ◦ **vajzë rrugësh** young slut
    ◦ **vajzë në/për shpirt** adopted son/daughter
    ◦ **vajzë tigani** *(Impol)* pampered/spoiled girl

vajzëri *nf* **1** girlhood **2** virginity **3** the girls (of a place) as a collective whole

vajzërisht *adv* in the manner of a girl; girlishly

vajzëro'r *adj* characteristic of or pertaining to girls; girlish

vajzu'rina *np fem* **1** young girls, little girls **2** *(Impol)* young and foolish girls

vak· *vt* **1** to make [a liquid] tepid **2** *(Fig)* to enfeeble: weaken []

vak·et *vpr* **1** to warm up a bit, get somewhat warm **2** *(Fig)* to lose force/intensity: weaken; wane, dwindle **3** *(Colloq)* to pass away quietly: die

vaka'nt *adj* vacant

vakëf *nm [Hist]* **1** holy ground **2** under the Ottoman empire, land dedicated for supporting religious or educational institutions

vakëmishtë *nf* place that gets plenty of sun, warm place = **shullë**

va'kët *n, adj* (sheep) with dark or dark/spotted feet and muzzle

vakërri'më *nf* bleating

vakërro'·n *vi* to bleat

vakësi *nf* = vaktësi

vakësi're *nf* **1** = vaktësi **2** mild warm weather **3** *(Fig)* vapid/dull thing

va'kët *adj (i)* **1** lukewarm, tepid **2** *(Fig Colloq)* not likely to be productive, just so-so **3** *(Fig Colloq)* vapid, insipid; listless; apathetic

vaki *nf (Colloq)* occurrence, happening

va'kje *nf ger* **1** <vak·, va'k·et **2** feeling of tiredness and weakness: enervation, listlessness

vako'·n *vt* = vak·

vaksi'në *nf [Med]* vaccine

vaksini'm *nm ger* **1** *[Med]* <vaksino'·n **2** vaccination

vaksino'·n *vt [Med]* to vaccinate

vaksino'r *adj* vaccinal

vaksinu'ar *adj (i) [Med]* vaccinated

vaksinu'es *nm [Med]* vaccinator

vakt *nm (Colloq)* **1** right time for something, proper season: due time; time due; mealtime **2** person's financial condition

vaktësi *nf* **1** tepidity **2** *(Fig)* lethargy, torpor, lassitude, languor; apathy

vaku'm *nm [Tech]* vacuum

va'kur *adj (i)* **1** warmed up **2** lukewarm, tepid **3** *(Fig)* lethargic, lifeless, torpid

vakuu'm *nm [Tech]* = vaku'm

*__*valandi's·** *vt (Old)* to arrange

valanîcë *nf [Text]* = dërsti'lë

valanïdh *nm* [*Bot*] Valonia oak (*Quercus macro-lepis*)

va'las *adv* constantly quarrelling

val·a·va·las *adv* = **va'las**

val·a·vít = **valëvít**

*val·bu'ke *nf* gruel of bread and milk = **bukëva'lë**

valc *nm* [*Mus*] = **vals**

*valce'r *nm* [*Mus*] = **vals**

Valdete *nf* Valdete (female name)

vale'ncë *nf* [*Chem*] valence

*valent *nm* [*Chem*] = **valencë**

valeria'në *nf* [*Bot Pharm*] valerian (*Valeriana*)

valerianore *np* [*Bot*] valerian family *Valerianaceae*

va'lë
I § *nf* 1 wave, undulation 2 state of liquid in a rolling boil; boiling-hot liquid 3 (*Colloq*) kettle for boiling water 4 bubble formed during boiling 5 (*Reg*) [*Food*] pap made of bread soaked in boiling water/milk 6 (*Fig*) instance, time, occasion 7 (*Fig*) change that proceeds in increasingly stronger gushes/impulses of intensity 8 (*Fig*) high point: crest, peak
II § *adj* extremely hot: boiling, scalding
III § *adv* boiling (hot)
IV § *adj* (*i*) boiling/scalding hot; torrid
∘ **valë pas vale** occasionally
∘ **vala e shpirtit** death throes

val·bu'ke *nf* 1 steam kettle 2 [*Food*] small pieces of bread boiled in water, mixed with oil or butter and usually cheese; pap made of bread soaked in boiling water/milk

valë·madh
I § *adj* (*Poet*) flowing in mighty waves
II § *n, adj* (*Fig*) (person) who has suffered terrible misfortune in life

valë·prit·ës *nm* [*Naut*] breakwater = **valëthy'es**

*valë·s| = **valëz|**

valë·shpejtë *adj* (*Poet*) flowing in gushing waves, rapidly flowing

valë·shu·më *adj* (*Poet*) rich in waves

va'lët *adj* (*i*) boiling/scalding hot; torrid = **va'lë**

*valë·tím *nm* ger* = **valëzím**

valë·thy'es *nm* [*Naut*] breakwater

va'lë-va'lë *adv* in waves, wavy

valë·vís| stem for 1st sg pres, pl pres, 2nd & 3rd sg subj, pind <**valëvít·**

valë·vít· *vt* to cause [] to move back and forth smoothly: sway/swing/wave

valë·vít·et *vpr* to move back and forth smoothly, move in waves, ripple

valë·vít·ës *adj* swaying, swinging, waving

valë·vítje *nf ger* <**valëvít·**, **valëvít·et**

valë·zím *nm ger* 1 <**valëzo·n**, **valëzo·het** 2 undulation

valë·zo·het *vpr* to take on wave form; move in waves

valë·zo·n
I § *vi* to undulate; billow; surge
II § *vt* to create waves in []

valë·zo'r *adj* (*Poet*) rippling, wavy

valë·zu'es *adj* having waves, with wave movement

vali *nm* (*np ~ nj*) [*Hist*] governor of a vilayet under the Ottoman Empire

Va'li *nm with fem agreement* Vali (female name)

valík *nm* high/prime point: peak, crest = **vlug**

valim *nm ger* <**valo·n**, **valo·het**

valíshtë *nf* (*Reg*) rock slide; avalanche

valíxhe *nf* suitcase, valise

va'lo·het *vpr* to reach its boiling point: boil

va'lo·n
I § *vi* 1 to boil 2 to wave lightly in the breeze
II § *vt* to heat [] to the boiling point: boil []
∘ **valo·n³ˢᵍ druri** fists *are flying* everywhere

valo'më *nf* 1 big wave 2 (*Fig*) current, flow

valo'r *adj* [*Spec*] of or pertaining to wave motion

valo're *nf* steam kettle

vals *nm* [*Mus*] waltz

valu'ar *adj* (*i*) boiled

valu'të *nf* [*Fin Econ*] foreign currency

valuto'r *adj* [*Fin Econ*] pertaining to or involving foreign currency

valvo'l *nm* valve

*vallanïdh = **valanïdh**

valldare *nf* [*Bot*] egg-shaped purple plum (*Prunus domestica L*)

va'lle *nf* 1 dance; folk dance 2 (*Fig*) hard thing to do, tough/complicated/risky business
∘ **valle çalthi** kind of dance with limping steps by person in the lead
∘ **valle malenake** pair dance of central Albania
∘ **valle e rëndë** folk dance that requires energetic movement
∘ **vallja e sinisë** dance at the height of gaiety in a celebration in which the dancer demonstrates his extraordinary ability to do complicated steps without stepping off a large copper tray
∘ **vallja e tepsisë** dance that uses a round baking tray as a drum for rhythmic accompaniment

valle'z *nf dimin* 1 <**valle** 2 series of movements made by spawning fish

va'llë *pcl* tentatively suggests a statement for confirmation; expresses uncertainty or curiosity: I wonder, I suppose; perhaps

vallëto'r *n* = **valltar**

vallë·zím *nm ger* 1 <**vallëzo·n**, **vallëzo·het** 2 ballroom dance

vallë·zo·n *vi, vt* to dance in ballroom style

vallë·zu'es *nm* person who dances: dancer

vallku'a *nm* (obl ~ o'i, np ~ o'nj) 1 [*Fish*] fyke net 2 washing paddle, clothes flail

vallo·n *vi* (*Colloq*) to join the dance, dance

valltar *n* dancer

*vallzo'r *adj* of or pertaining to dancing

vampír *nm* 1 vampire 2 (*Fig*) insatiable eater, glutton 3 [*Zool*] vampire bat
∘ **Vampiri e njeh lugatin.** "The vampire knows the monster man." (*Prov*) One thief will recognize another thief.

Van *nm* Van (male name)

vana'd *nm* [*Chem*] vanadium (*V*)

vanadium *nm* [*Chem*] = **vana'd**

vanda'k
I § *nm* 1 bundle 2 amount small enough to be carried in one's arms or on one side of a horse 3 large amount: big bundle
II § *adv* in a bundle
∘ **vandak me bezga** (*Contempt*) dimwit, blockhead

vanda'l *nm* 1 (*Fig Pej*) vandal; barbarian 2 [*Hist*] Vandal

vandalízëm *nm* vandalism; barbaric behavior

vane'll *nm* (*np ~ j*) [*Ornit*] lapwing *Vanellus vanellus*

vane´së nf [*Entom*] vanessa (butterfly)

vaˈnë nm (np ˜ gje) **1** slot, groove **2** wall built around the mouth of a well

vang nm (np ˜ gje) **1** wheel rim **2** leather thong used to tie up moccasins

vaˈngë nf (*Reg*) [*Agr*] trenching spade (with a narrow sharp blade)

*****vangë́ro** ·*n* = vëngë́ro

*****vaˈngët** adj (i) = vëˈngër

*****vangoˈsh** adj, n = vëngëˈrosh

Vangjel nm Vangjel (male name)

*****vangjelizmo** nm Annunciation Day (March 25)

*****vaníle** = vanílje

vanílje nf **1** [*Bot*] vanilla plant (*Vanilla*) **2** vanilla flavoring

vanoˈr nm [*Constr*] = vetullaˈr

vapeˈm nm [*Chem*] white clay used for its lime (calcium oxide) content = dherruˈsh

vapë́ nf **1** hottest time of the summer: hot spell, hot weather **2** hottest part of a summer day: heat of the day **3** sweltering heat

vapë́he´rë nf hottest part of a summer day: heat of the day

vapë́siˈrë nf oppressive/sweltering heat

vapë́t adj (i) very hot, uncomfortably hot

vapë́to ·*n* vt to cause sweltering heat

vapím nm ger < vapo ·*n*, vapo ·*het*

vaˈpje nf **1** heat rash, heat blister **2** [*Invert*] = haˈrrje

vapo ·*het* vpr **1** to feel the oppressive heat, get hot **2** = vapo ·*n*

vapo ·*n* vi to avoid the heat of the day, stay in the shade, take a siesta

vapoˈr nm steamship; (power-driven) ship

vapoˈre nf **1** small shelter offering shade to agricultural workers trying to get out of the sun **2** heat rash, heat blister

vapulliˈm I § nm OR **vapulliˈm**ë II § nf = vapë́siˈrë

vaqeˈt nf cowhide, tough leather

var· vt **1** to hang; hang [ ] up; hang [ ] down **2** to bring [ ] down **3** (*Fig Colloq*) to let [ ] hang, let [ ] go: neglect **4** (*Fig*) to hang on [ ]: depend on [ ] **5** (*Fig Colloq*) to charge ⟨⟩ with [a task]: stick ⟨⟩ with [a job]

  ○ nuk ⟨⟩a var· not give a hang about ⟨⟩, let ⟨⟩ go hang

  ○ ⟨⟩a var· atë këmborë to charge ⟨⟩ with that (difficult) task

  ○ i var· buzët (një pëllëmbë) "let one's lips/nose/snout hang down (a handbreadth)" **1** to get a sullen expression on one's face: pout **2** to take on a gloomy look **3** to look offended

  ○ nuk ⟨⟩a var· hejbetë to show no respect for ⟨⟩, pay ⟨⟩ no mind

  ○ i var· hundët (një pëllëmbë) "let one's lips/nose/snout hang down (a handbreadth)" **1** to get a sullen expression on one's face: pout **2** to take on a gloomy look **3** to look offended

  ○ i var· kapakët e syve to be unable to keep one's eyes open

  ○ nuk ⟨⟩a var· kapistrën to show no respect for ⟨⟩, pay ⟨⟩ no mind

  ○ ⟨⟩ var· këmborën (prapa/në qafë) to tease and embarrass ⟨⟩ in front of others; humiliate ⟨⟩

  ○ nuk ⟨⟩a var· kapistrën/këmborën to show no respect for ⟨⟩, pay ⟨⟩ no mind

  ○ ⟨⟩a var· këtë këmborë to charge ⟨⟩ with this (difficult) task

  ○ var· kokën/kryet to hang one's head (in shame)

  ○ ⟨⟩[ ] var· në qafë "hang [ ] onto ⟨⟩'s neck" to place [a burden] on ⟨⟩

  ○ ⟨⟩ var· nga fjalë to give ⟨⟩ a piece of news

  ○ e var· plëndësin në qafë "hang the tripe around one's neck" to lose all sense of shame

  ○ ⟨⟩ var· teneqenë (*Impol*) to humiliate ⟨⟩ publicly

  ○ nuk ⟨⟩a var· torbën/trastën to show no respect for ⟨⟩, pay ⟨⟩ no mind

  ○ ⟨⟩ var· turiçkat to get angry/sore: get one's nose out of joint

  ○ i var· turinjtë (një pëllëmbë) "let one's lips/nose/snout hang down (a handbreadth)" **1** to get a sullen expression on one's face: pout **2** to take on a gloomy expression on one's face **3** to look offended

  ○ ⟨⟩ var· ujkut mëlçitë në qafë "hang one's liver on the neck of a wolf" (*Iron*) to ask the fox to guard the chicken coop

  ○ [ ] var· vath në vesh "hang [ ] as an earring in one's ear" to try never to forget [ ]; make a reminder of [ ] for future revenge

  ○ ⟨⟩ var· veshët "lower one's ears" **1** to have a sullen expression on one's face; have a gloomy look; look offended **2** to feel disappointed and resentful **3** ⟨⟩ loses ⟨⟩'s former power/influence; ⟨⟩ comes down off ⟨⟩'s high horse

  ○ nuk ⟨⟩a var· veshin to pay ⟨⟩ no mind

  ○ ⟨⟩ var· vetullat **1** to frown **2** to get angry

  ○ ⟨⟩ var· zilen to egg ⟨⟩ on, incite ⟨⟩: get ⟨⟩ all wound up

var·et vpr **1** to hang down; hang **2** to hang on **3** to hang oneself **4** to go down **5** (*Fig*) to be/become a burden (on ⟨⟩)

  ○ po ⟨⟩ var·et[3sg] koka ⟨⟩'s head *is nodding*: ⟨⟩ *is feeling* drowsy, ⟨⟩ *is falling* asleep

  ○ ⟨⟩ var·et[3pl] mishrat ⟨⟩ *is* very flabby

  ○ ⟨⟩ var·et[3pl] mustaqet "⟨⟩'s mustache *droops*" (*Iron*) ⟨⟩ *loses* his honor as a man, ⟨⟩'s manly honor *is* in question

  ○ var·et në fije të perit to hang by a thread; be in great danger

  ○ ⟨⟩ var·et në qafë "hang on to ⟨⟩'s neck" to honey up to ⟨⟩

  ○ var·et nga **1** to depend on {}; be conditional on {} **2** [*Ling*] to be grammatically dependent on {}

  ○ var·et pas ⟨⟩ to depend on ⟨⟩, pin one's hopes on ⟨⟩

  ○ ⟨⟩ var·et[3sg] samari nën bark "⟨⟩'s packsaddle to *hangs* under the belly" ⟨⟩ *is* in serious trouble

  ○ var·et tek {} to rely on {}

  ○ ⟨⟩ var·et[3pl] tulet ⟨⟩ *is* very fat and flabby

  ○ ⟨⟩ var·et[3sg] zëri ⟨⟩ *strains* ⟨⟩'s voice, ⟨⟩ *makes* ⟨⟩ self hoarse

varaˈk nm **1** [*Spec*] metallic gloss; gold/silver dust **2** metal foil: tinfoil

vaˈrda
  I § interj (*Colloq*) keep it up!
  II § adv incessantly

vardaˈr
  I § nm juncture of two streams of water, river junction
  II § adv one after the other, continually

*****varde´** nf = lavërdaˈn

vardis·et *vpr* **1** to importune ◇, keep after ◇; hound ◇ **2** to be/become a burden (on ◇); stick to ◇

vardisje *nf ger* **1** <vardis·et **2** importunate request: entreaty

vardo·n
  I § *vi (Colloq)* to toil in drudgery
  II § *vt (Colloq)* to beat [] up, work [] over

vardua *nm (obl ˜ oi, np ˜ onj)* [*Ornit*] greenfinch (*Carduelis chloris*)

*vardhar *nm* **1** waterfall **2** = vardar

*vardhë *nf with masc agreement (Old)* sentry, guard.

vare
  I § *nf* **1** [*Spec*] sledgehammer **2** [*Agr*] wooden sodbuster **3** bare mountain slope
  II § *adj* very heavy; very strong
  III § *adv* very (heavy)

varelë *nf* large wooden cask: barrel

varesë *nf* (hanging) chain

varë *adv* in an unresolved state: hanging, pending, up in the air

*varëm *adj (i)* **1** hanging; pendulous **2** dependent

varës
  I § *adj* **1** hanging; pendulous **2** dependent **3** [*Bot*] = kacavarës **4** *(Old)* = vartës
  II § *n* hangman, hanger

varëse *nf* **1** wall rack with pegs/hooks for hanging up clothes; coat hanger, clothes hook **2** necklace

varësi *nf (Book)* dependence

varf *nm (Old)* Bektashi dervish

varfanjak
  I § *adj* **1** pertaining to or characteristic of the poor **2** *(Pej)* miserly, stingy **3** = varfër
  II § *n* person living in poverty: poor man, pauper

varfër
  I § *adj (i)* poor
  II § *n (i)* pitiable person: poor guy

varferi *nf* **1** poverty **2** *(Collec)* the poor, poor people

varferim *nm ger* **1** <varfero·n, varfero·het **2** impoverishment; depletion

varferisht *adv (Book)* in poverty, poorly; badly

varferohet *vpr* **1** to get poorer; become poor **2** to become depleted

varfero·n *vt* **1** to impoverish **2** to deplete

varferor *adj (Book)* pertaining to the poor

varferuar *adj (i)* impoverished; depleted

varg
  I § *nm (np ˜ gje)* **1** string (of objects of the same kind): string; chain; series **2** [*Lit*] verse line **3** *(Fig)* large quantity/number: a whole series
  II § *adv* in sequence, one after another
    ○ **varg i bardhë** [*Lit*] blank verse
    ○ **varg heroik** [*Lit*] heroic verse
    ○ **varg i lirë** [*Lit*] free verse
    ○ **varg pas vargu** one after another
    ○ **varg e varg** one after another
    ○ **varg e vijë/vistër** one after another

vargan
  I § *nm* line of things/animals/people: file, column, procession; line, row
  II § *adv* in a line/row, one after another

vargare *nf* **1** [*Ethnog*] necklace of golden coins **2** bridal trousseau; dowry

vargas OR **vargazi** *adv* (moving) in a line

*vargenj *nm* = vargër

*vargenim *nm (Reg Gheg)* = vargërim

vargër *nm* uncastrated ram or billy goat used for breeding: buck

*vargërim *nm* **1** <vargëto·n **2** versification

*vargëro·n *vt* = vargo·n

vargës *nm* = vargër

*vargëso·n *vt* = vargo·n

vargëtar *n* **1** *(Old)* stringer of verses, versemaker: poet **2** *(Pej)* = vargëzues

vargëtim *nm ger* <vargëto·n, vargëto·het

vargëto·het *vpr* to form a chain

vargëto·n
  I § *vt* to string/chain [] together
  II § *vi* to make/form a chain

vargëzim *nm ger* **1** <vargëzo·n, vargëzo·het **2** [*Lit*] versification

vargëzo·het *vpr* to form a chain/series

vargëzo·n
  I § *vt* **1** to put [] in sequence; arrange [] in series **2** to put [] into verse, versify; set [] to doggerel **3** *(Fig Pej)* to prolong [] unnecessarily: drag [] out
  II § *vi* **1** to form a chain/series **2** to versify; write mere doggerel

vargëzuar *adj (i)* formed into a chain/series

vargëzues *n (Pej)* poetaster, rhymester

vargim *nm ger* **1** <vargo·n, vargo·het **2** procession

vargmal *nm* [*Geog*] mountain range

vargo·het *vpr* to get in line; form a line, line up

vargo·n
  I § *vt* **1** to thread [] on a string/wire: string [] **2** to arrange [] in order: line [] up, put [] in sequence **3** *(Fig Pej)* to prolong [] unnecessarily: drag [] out
  II § *vi, vt (Old)* to versify

vargoi *obl* <vargua

vargonj *np* <vargua imprisoning chains: fetters
  ○ ◇ **ësh-të trashur vargonjsh** "have become thick in the hearth chains" *(Pej)* to have become swellheaded

vargor *nm* heavy chain (to support pothooks) in a fireplace

vargore *nf* cartridge belt

vargos = vargo·n

vargua
  I § *nm (obl ˜ oi, np ˜ onj)* = vargor
  II § *adv* one after the other, in a line/row

varguar *adj (i)* arranged one after another in a line/row

vargje *np* <varg

vargje-vargje *adv* in columns, in rows

variacion *nm* variation; change to relieve monotony, variety; musical variation

variant *nm* variant; version; variation

varice *nf* [*Med*] varix

variete *nf* variety show, vaudeville show

varietet *nm* [*Biol*] variety

varje *nf ger* <var·, var·et

varkar *n* boatman = barkëtar

varkë *nf* boat = barkë

varkëtar *nm* boatman = barkëtar

*varome *nf* faint, swoon

varosh *nm (Old)* **1** part of a medieval town lying outside the castle walls: faubourg **2** part of the town adjacent to the market **3** pastureland = mera

Varshavë *nf* Warsaw

Varshavë *nf* Warsaw

va'rshëm *adj (i)* dependent

va'rt'as *adv* = var ë

va'rt'ës *adj, n* dependent, subordinate

vart'ësi *nf* dependence = varësi

va'rtura *np (të) fem* [*Ethnog*] ornaments hung around the bride's neck or on her chest

va'rur

  I § *adj (i)* **1** hung up, hung **2** hanging down; bent over; in a slump, slumping down **3** sloping steeply down **4** *(Fig)* up in the air, unsettled: hanging **5** dependent; subordinate

  II § *adj (i), n (i)* **1** (person) who has been hung **2** hanging in air

varva't *adj* uncastrated

*varzë *nf* = vajzë

varr

  I § *nm* burial place: grave; tomb

  II § *adj* unbearably difficult; grievous and intolerable

    ○ **varret e fshatit** village graveyard

    ○ **<>u haptë varri/dheu nën këmbë!** *(Curse)* May the ground open up under <>! May <>'s grave open under <>'s feet! I hope <> *dies!*

    ○ **ësh·të varr i mbuluar** to be very close-mouthed/tightlipped

    ○ **Varret nuk flasin.** "Graves don't speak." *(Prov)* Dead men tell no tales.

varraka's *stem for 1st sg pres, pl pres, 2nd & 3rd sg subj, pind* <varraka't·

varraka't· *vt (Colloq)* to delay [] too long: keep putting [] off

varras'li *adj* pockmarked

*varr'e'së *nf* **1** burial **2** = varrezë

varr'e'sht *nm* **1** [*Agr*] swath of hay **2** row of grapevines

varr'e'zë *nf* burial ground, graveyard, cemetery

varrë *nf* **1** wound, gash **2** stripe

varrë'pa'mbyll'ur *adj, n* **1** (person) with open wounds **2** *(Curse)* may he have wounds that never heal!

varrë'z *nf* tomb

varr'gërm'o'njës *n* gravedigger = varrmihës

varr'ha'pur *adj, n* **1** (person) without a grave, unburied (person) **2** (person) with one foot in the grave, (person) near death **3** *(Curse)* may he lie in an open grave!

varr'humb'ur *adj, n* **1** (person) whose grave has been lost **2** *(Curse)* may his grave never be found!

varr'icë

  I § *nf (Reg)* pile of wood

  II § *adv* in a pile/stack

varr'im *nm ger* **1** <varro'·n, varro'·het **2** burial **3** burial ceremony: funeral

varr'im'o'r *adj* pertaining to or used in burials: funeral, funereal

varr'im'ta'r *adj* = varrimo'r

*varr'i'sht'ë *nf (Old)* = varrezë

varr'mi'h'ës *nm* **1** gravedigger **2** *(Fig)* death-dealer, nemesis

varr'o·het *vpr* to become wounded = plago's·et

varr'o·n *vt* **1** to wound = plago's· **2** = varro's·

varr'o's· *vt* **1** to bury **2** *(Fig)* to end [] once and for all; reject [] as totally outmoded

varro's'ës

  I § *adj* used in burials

  II § *nm* undertaker

varr'o's'je *nf ger* **1** <varro's· **2** burial ceremony: funeral

varr'o's'ur

  I § *adj (i)* buried; dead and buried

  II § *n (i)* buried person

varr'o'sh *nm* large tomb; burial plot

varr'pa'gjet'ur *adj, n* = varrhu'mbur

varr'ta'r *nm* = varrmi'hës

varr'vi'th'is'ur *adj, n* **1** (person) whose grave has fallen in **2** *(Curse)* may his grave fall in!

varr'zbul'u'ar *adj, n* = varrha'pur

vasa'l *nm, adj* vassal

vasal'ite't *nm* vassalage

vasie't *nm (Old)* dying wish, last wishes

Vasi'l *nm* Vasil (male name)

va'skë *nf* **1** bathtub **2** [*Spec*] vat

*vasko *nf* [*Bot*] three-lobed sage *(Salvia triloba)*

vasta'k *nm* **1** [*Bot*] flat-topped inflorescence: corymb *()* **2** something hanging down in a spike

vasta'rkë *nf* stake, pole

va'shë *nf (Poet)* young girl, maiden

vash'ëri *nf (Poet)* maidenhood, girlhood

vash'ëro'r *adj (Poet)* maidenly

va'shëz *nf dimin* little girl

Vashingto'n *nm* Washington

*va'sh'o *nf* = vashë

vat *nm* [*Phys*] watt

vata'n *nm (Colloq)* fatherland, motherland; place of birth

va'te *3rd sg pdef* <ve'·te

Vaterlo *nf* Waterloo

vaterpa's *nm* [*Constr*] spirit level

vaterpo'lo *nf* [*Sport*] water polo

va'tër *nf* **1** hearth; fireplace **2** *(Fig)* home **3** small plot of ground **4** [*Spec Geom*] focal point **5** [*Physiol*] nerve center **6** [*Med*] localized/chief site of an infection: focus

    ○ **vatër kulture** cultural/community center (in a small village)

    ○ **vatra moçalizimi** swampy plot of ground

    ○ **vatër zjarri** "fire hearth" potentially explosive place or situation: veritable powderkeg

vatër'prish'ur *adj, n* **1** (person) whose home and family have been destroyed **2** *(Curse)* may everything he has be destroyed!

vatër'shu'ar *adj, n* **1** (person) whose home and family have been wiped out **2** *(Curse)* may everything he has be wiped out!

va'tër'z *nf* **1** *(Dimin)* <va'tër **2** strip of land

vato'r *n* boatman, bargeman, raftsman

vath *nm* **1** earring **2** dewlap on a goat

    ○ **vath i florinjtë në vesh të derrit** "golden earring in a pig's ear" (said of something good but in a bad place or in the wrong hands)

Vath *nm* Vath (male name)

vath'ato'r *adj* = vatho'r

vath'a'to're *nf* bearded goat

va'the *nf* = vatho're

va'thë *nf* **1** fenced-in pen: fold, corral **2** flock kept in a pen: fold **3** apiary; beehives in an apiary

    ○ **vathë për dhen** sheepfold

vathïm *nm ger* <**vatho·** *·n*

vathïna *np fem* field fertilized by a flock kept in a pen for that purpose

vathïnajë *nf* **1** large pens with livestock: stockyard **2** stockyard pens

vatho· *·n vt* **1** to put [livestock] in a pen **2** to fertilize [land] by installing a livestock pen

vathïor *adj* having dewlaps: dewlapped

vathïore *nf* nanny goat with hanging dewlaps

vaz *nm* [*Relig*] sermon by a Moslem priest

vazelïnë *nf* vaseline

va·zo *nf* **1** vase **2** jar used for canning food

vazhdar *nm* = **vargan**

va·zhdazi *adv* = **vazhdimïsht**

va·zhdë *nf* **1** trail (left by a person/animal); trace **2** line along the ground; furrow; rut **3** groove between boards **4** narrow path **5** continuation

vazhdïm *nm ger* **1** <**vazhdo·** *·n*, **vazhdo·** *·het* **2** continuation
∘ **ësh·të në vazhdim** to be still going on, be in progress
∘ **java/muaji/viti në vazhdim** this coming week/ month/year

vazhdïmësï *nf* continuity
∘ **në/me vazhdimësi** (*Book*) continually; constantly

vazhdïmïsht *adv* continually; constantly, steadily, uninterruptedly; perpetually; endlessly

vazhdo· *·het vp impers* it is possible to continue

vazhdo· *·n vt, vi* **1** to continue; follow in the track of [] **2** to attend [school], pursue [education]

vazhdüar *adj (i)* = **vazhdueshëm**

vazhdües
I § *adj* continuing; next
II § *n* follower
III § *nm* next month/year, the coming month/year

vazhdüeshëm *adj (i)* **1** constant; protracted, continual; continuous **2** [*Electr*] direct (current)

vazhdüeshmëri *nf* constancy

VC *abbrev* water closet, toilet

vdar· *vt* = **vdjerr·**

vdek stem for part, opt, adm <**vdes·**

vdekatar *nm* mortal; mortal man

vdekë *nf* = **vdekje**

vdekje *nf* death
∘ **vdekje civile** loss of all civil rights
∘ **vdekje në litar** death by hanging

vdekjeprurës *adj* deadly, lethal, fatal

vdekjesjellës *adj* = **vdekjeprurës**

vdeksor *adj* = **vdekjeprurës**

vdekshëm *adj (i), nm (i)* mortal

vdekshmëri *nf* mortality; mortality/death rate

vdekur
I § *part* <**vdes·**
II § *adj (i)* **1** dead, lifeless; inanimate; dull **2** [*Tech*] idle
III § *n (i)* dead (person)
IV § *adv* lifelessly
∘ **i vdekur e i papambuluar/pakallur** "dead and not covered over" **1** with one foot in the grave **2** totally incompetent
∘ **i vdekur e i pafutur në dhé** "dead and not put in the ground" **1** with one foot in the grave **2** totally incompetent

∘ **i vdekur e i paqarë** "dead and not mourned" **1** with one foot in the grave **2** totally incompetent
∘ **kohë/orë e vdekur** time when there is nothing to do
∘ <*i/u*> **ka vdekur nëna** "<*its/their*> mother has died" **1** (*Crude*) all hope for it/them is gone: it is beyond hope **2** it will happen no matter what, it is a foregone conclusion

vdes·
I § *vi* **1** to die **2** to come to an end; be over and forgotten
II § *vt* **1** to cause []'s death, be the death of [] **2** to beat [] badly, beat [] up **3** to vex/annoy [] terribly
∘ **vdes· me këpucë në këmbë** to die with one's boots on; die suddenly
∘ **vdes· në lemeri** to die a horrible death
∘ **vdes· nga** {} (*Fig*) to be suffering from {}, be dying of {}
∘ **vdes· për** [] (*Fig*) to be dying for [], crave []; need [] badly; love [] deeply
∘ **vdes· së qeshuri** (*Fig*) to die laughing

vdïgë *nf* (*Reg*) epilepsy = **fetigë**

vdinjak = **binjak**

vdïq stem for pdef <**vdes·**
∘ **nuk vdiq, po plasi** "did not die, but burst" (said of someone who dies of heartbreak)

vdir *OR* **vdïrr** stem for 2nd pl pres, pind, imper, vp <**vdjerr·**

vdïrr·et *vpr* **1** (*Reg*) to get lost, vanish **2** to become emaciated; (of the moon) wane **3** (*Fig*) to die out

vdïs stem for 2nd pl pres, pind, imper, vp <**vdes·**

vdjerr· *vt* **1** (*Reg*) to lose = **humb·** **2** (*Fig*) to ruin, corrupt

vdjerrë
I § *part* <**vdjerr·**
II § *adj (i)* **1** eroding away; (of the moon) waning; wasting away **2** deceased; died away, gone, dead **3** (*Fig*) inept; demented
III § *nm* **1** deceased person **2** (*Fig*) inept/demented person

vdor stem for pdef <**vdjerr·**

ve
I § *nf* **1** = **vezë** **2** widow
II § *nm* widower
III § *adj (i)* widowed
∘ **ve fërgesë** fried egg

ve·het *vpr* <**ve·te**

ve·n *vi* **1** to lay an egg **2** (*Reg*) to weave = **vegjo·** *·n*

ve·te *vi* **1** to go; proceed **2** to reach a level/point: arrive (at a destination); get (to an outcome); last (for a period of time) **3** (*Fig Colloq*) to get along **4** (*Fig*) to be suitable/right **5** (*Colloq*) to be in operation: work, go **6** (followed by another verb) to start to __ **7** to spill out **8** (*Fig Colloq*) to cost <*someone*>; get spent
∘ <> **ve·te**[3rd] {} *don't* work out for <>, <>'s {} *go for naught*; <>'s {} *miss*
∘ <> **ve·te**[3sg] **bari sa hanxhari** "the grass costs <> as much as the dagger" it *costs more than what* <> *gets out of it*
∘ <> **ve·te**[3sg] **bark** <> *has diarrhea*
∘ <> **ve·te**[3sg] **barku prapa/në kurriz** <> *gets very hungry*
∘ <> **ve·te buka pas kurrizit** (*Colloq*) <> *is not given a moment to eat in peace*

○ <> **ve·te**^{3sg} **buza vesh më vesh** "<>'s lip *goes* from ear to ear" ○ *laughs* heartily; ○ *lights* up with happiness

○ **ve·te**^{3sg} **dëm koha** time *is* wasted

○ **ve·te dëm** to come to nothing, go for naught

○ **ve·te duke** {*participle*} to keep growing/getting more {}

○ <> **ve·te**^{3sg} **goja prapa/pas (qafës)** "<>'s mouth *goes* behind <>'s neck" ○ *gets* tired of saying the same thing over and over

○ **s'<> ve·te**^{3sg} **goja** "my mouth *doesn't go*" <> *doesn't* want to say it

○ <> **ve·te**^{3sg} **goja te veshi//prapa veshit** "<>'s mouth *goes* to/behind <>'s ear" ○ *wears* <>self out making the same request over and over

○ <> **ve·te**^{3sg} **goja vesh më vesh** "<>'s mouth *goes* from ear to ear" ○ *laughs* heartily; ○ *lights* up with happiness

○ **Ve·te**^{3sg} **gjaku deri në bark/shalë të kalit** "The blood *comes* up to the horse's belly/saddle" There *is* terrible bloodshed.: The place *is* knee-deep in blood.

○ **ve·te**^{3sg} **gjaku deri në tra** "blood *comes* up to the rafter" the place *is* swimming with blood

○ <> **ve·te**^{3sg} **gjaku në fund të këmbëve 1** <> *gets* numb (from too much walking/standing) **2** <> *gets* terrified

○ **ve·te**^{3sg} **gjaku rrëke/lumë** blood *flows* profusely

○ <> **ve·te**^{3sg} **gjaku te këmbët 1** <> *gets* numb (from too much walking/standing) **2** <> *gets* terrified

○ <> **ve·te**^{3sg} **gjuha prapa** to get tired of saying the same thing over and over, get tired of repeating oneself

○ **ve·te gjym** (of an activity) to go very well/pleasantly

○ **ve·te larg** to go to excess, go too far, carry things too far

○ **ve·te me shoshë për ujë** "go for water with a screen" to do useless work

○ **ve·te me** [] to get along with; spend time with []

○ <> **ve·te**^{3sg} **mendja për peshk** <> *has* a sudden desire/yen for something hard to find

○ <> **ve·te**^{3sg} **mendja për** [] <> *gets* a sudden desire for [], have a hankering for []

○ **ve·te në Berat për një masat** "go all the way to Berat for a flintstone" to put out a lot of effort to accomplish something of no importance, go to a lot of trouble for nothing

○ **ve·te në djall 1** to move very far away: move to the end of the earth **2** to get totally wrecked; get it in the neck

○ **ve·te në fill të vdekjes** to be almost dead, be as good as dead

○ **ve·te në gojë të qenit** to place oneself in danger

○ <> **ve·te në mendje** to come to <>'s mind, occur to <>

○ <> **ve·te**^{3sg} **në mykë për** [] "it *goes* to <>'s blunt side" a strong craving for [] suddenly *hits* <>

○ **ve·te në pikë të fundit** "go to the final point" to suffer a complete decline in fortune

○ <> **ve·te**^{3sg} **në vesh** <> *comes* to know {}, <> *learns* of {}

○ <> **ve·te pas ujërave** to just do what will please <>

○ **ve·te për kryeshëndoshë** to pay one's condolences

○ **ve·te për lesh e de·l·/vje·n/kthe·het i qethur** "go for wool and come back sheared" *(Prov Iron)* to try to make things better but only make things worse

○ **ve·te për peshk** to go fishing

○ <> **ve·te për plak** "go to <> as an elder" to seek sage advice from <>

○ <> **ve·te për shtat 1** to be suitable for <> **2** (of clothes) to look nice on <>

○ **ve·te plep** *(Colloq)* (of a conversation/discussion) to go well

○ <> **ve·te**^{3sg} **puna fjollë** things *are going* very well for <>, <> *is doing* fine

○ <> **ve·te**^{3sg} **puna kryq** things go badly/wrong for <>

○ <> **ve·te**^{3pl} **punët në katër rrotë** "<>'s affairs go on four wheels" things *are going* very well for <>

○ **ve·te**^{3sg} **(puna) sahat** to go like clockwork, work perfectly

○ **ve·te si cjapi te kasapi** "go like a goat to the butcher" to walk into trouble with one's eyes closed: go like a sheep to the slaughter

○ **ve·te si guri në ujë/pellg/lumë** to be all for nothing, get nowhere

○ **ve·te si lëkurë dashi** "go like the hide of a ram" to go for naught, come to naught

○ **ve·te si macja me miun** "go like the cat with the mouse" to be constantly at odds (with one another): get along like cats and dogs

○ <> **ve·te**^{3pl} **shtatë** *(Crude)* <> *is* scared out of <>'s wits: <> *is shitting* in <>'s pants from fear

○ **ve·te te burri** *(Colloq)* (of a woman) to get married

○ <> **ve·te te carani 1** to go right into <>'s very home **2** to hug <> warmly

○ **ve·te të merr·**^{subj} **prush** "go to get hot coals" to go for a short while

○ <> **ve·te**^{3sg} **thundra në qafë** "<>'s hoof *goes* to <>'s neck" <> *runs* away at breakneck speed, <> *takes* to <>'s heels

ve| *stem for* pind <**ve·te**

veç
I § *adv* apart; separately
II § *pred* something apart, different
III § *prep (abl)* apart from: besides, except for
IV § *conj* except that, but
V § *pcl* only, just

○ **veç sa nuk/s'** __ barely miss __ing, almost __

○ **Veç shata e lopata do të** [] **ndajë.** "Only the hoe and the shovel will separate []." [] love each other so much that only death can separate [].

○ **veç të tjerave** in addition to others?

○ **veç e veç** each separately

veça·n
I § *adv* apart, separately; aside
II § *pred* something apart, different

veça·n|e *nf* room separated from the rest of the house

veçan|ërisht *adv* **1** particularly, especially; specially *2* separately, singly

veçan|isht *adv* = veçan**ë**risht

veçan|so··n *vt* to separate, isolate

veça·n|tas *adv* **1** = veça·n *2* in addition, besides

veça·n|të *adj (i)* particular, special; distinctive

veça·n|ti *nf* **1** particularity; specialness **2** = veçori

veç|as *adv* **1** separately, apart **2** alone, isolated

veç|azi = veças

veçïm *nm ger* **1** <veço·*n*, veço·*het* **2** isolation, separation **3** [*Ling*] disjunction

veçmas *adv* = veças

veço·het *vpr* to get separated, become isolated

veço·n *vt* **1** to separate, place [] apart; isolate **2** [*Electr Tech*] to insulate

veçor *nm* [*Phys Electr*] insulating material; insulator

veçorï *nf* distinctive characteristic

veçqë *conj* = veçse

veçse *conj pcl* except that, except: only, but

veçuar
    I § *adj (i)* **1** separated; isolated **2** rare **3** [*Ling*] disjoined, disjoint
    II § *n (i)* recluse
      ∘ **I veçuari, i munduari.** "The recluse, the sufferer." *(Prov)* Without friends, one suffers.

veçues
    I § *adj* **1** partitioning, separating **2** distinctive **3** [*Electr*] insulating **4** [*Ling*] disjunctive
    II § *nm* **1** partition **2** [*Electr*] insulator, insulation

*veqd *refl nm* (*Reg Gheg*) = vete

vedër *nf* [*Dairy*] milk bucket/pail

vedërta̱r *n* person who makes and repairs milk buckets/pails

veg *nm* = vegjë

vegë *nf (Reg)* **1** pot handle **2** peg on which to hang something **3** *(Fig)* pretext, excuse **4** *(Colloq)* thigh, leg

vegël *nf* **1** tool; (musical) instrument **2** loom **3** component part of a mechanism/system **4** [*Sport*] gymnastic apparatus **5** *(Colloq)* internal organ **6** *(Reg)* pot handle **7** *(Reg Fig)* pretext, excuse
      ∘ **vegël fryme** [*Mus*] wind instrument
      ∘ **vegël e ndyrë/fëlliqur** person who is used to serve base purposes: dirty tool
      ∘ **vegël e verbër** "blind tool" *(Pej)* flunky, stooge: mere tool

vegïm *nm ger* **1** <vego·*n* **2** faint appearance **3** apparition

vegimor *adj (Poet)* = vegimtar

vegimta̱r *adj (Poet)* phantasmal, apparitional; imaginary

*vegla-çïlës *nm (Old)* master key, skeleton key

veglërï *nf collec* equipment

veglore *np fem* [*Text*] textiles woven on a loom: cloth

vego·n
    I § *vi* to appear faintly; begin to appear; start to get light
    II § *vt* to see [] faintly, barely see []

vegsh *nm* cooking pot, pipkin

vegsha̱r *n* pot maker; potter

vegshata̱r *n* = vegshar

vegta̱r *n* = vegjëtar

vegues *adj* barely visible: faint; (of light) just beginning to shine

vegull *nf* apparition

vegullo·n *vi* = vego·*n*

vegjetacïon *nm* [*Bot*] vegetation

vegjetal *adj* [*Bot*] of vegetable origin: vegetable = bimor

vegjetarian *nm* *(Book)* vegetarian

vegjetatïv *adj* [*Biol Physiol*] involving or promoting plant growth: vegetative

vegjë *nf* **1** four-legged wooden loom; loom **2** = vjegë

vegjël *adj (të) nm (të) masc pl* <vogël

vegjëlï *nf* **1** *(Collec)* common folk **2** childhood = vogëlï **3** *(Collec)* little children, the young

vegjëta̱r *n* person who works at a loom: weaver

vegjo·n
    I § *vi* to work at a loom: weave
    II § *vt* to put the handle on [a pot] = vjego·*n*

vegjore *nf* = vjegore

Vehbï *nm* Vehbi (male name)

*veht *nm* *(Reg Gheg)* = vete

*vehte *nf* self = vete

*vehtesïm = vetësïm

*vehteso·*n* = vetëso·*n*

veja̱n *nm* widower

vejane *nf* = vejushë

vejë *3rd sg subj* <ve·te

vejërï *nf* widowhood, widowerhood

vejëro·het *vpr* to become widowed

vejëro·n
    I § *vi* to remain a widow/widower
    II § *vt* to widow

vejëse *adj, nf* (hen) that is highly productive of eggs

*vejgë *nf (Reg)* = vegë

*vejme *np* wails (of mourning): keening

*vejnï *nf* = vejërï

*vejno·*n* = vejëro·*n*

*vejshëm *adj (i)* widowed

*vejt *stem for part, pdef, opt, adm* <ve·*n*

*vejtës *adj* weaving

*vejtshëm *adj (i)* weavable

*vejtur *adj (i)* *(Reg)* woven tight (in a loom)

*vejuk *adj (i)*

vejush *nm* = vejan

vejushë *nf* widow

vejushkë *nf dimin* young widow

*vek *nm*

*vekës *nm* **1** weaver **2** loom

*vekta̱r *OR* vektor *n* weaver

vektor *nm* [*Math Phys*] vector

*vekutïçkë *nf (Old)* ovary

vel *nm* **1** transparent cloth woven of fine fibers: gauze **2** veil **3** [*Ethnog*] bridal veil **4** sail

vel· *vt* **1** to satiate [] with sweet/greasy food, overstuff [] (with food) **2** *(Fig)* to spoil [] (with overattention); make [] blasé **3** *(Fig)* to make [] sick and tired, bore [] to the point of nausea **4** to nauseate, disgust

vel·et *vpr* **1** to get one's surfeit, get sick (of something/someone) **2** *(Fig)* to get spoiled (by too much of a good thing); become blasé **3** *(Fig)* to make <> sick and tired, bore <> to the point of nausea **4** to get disgusted

*velada̱n = veladon

veladon *nm* [*Relig*] cassock worn by a Roman Catholic priest

velajrore *nf* sailplane, glider

velanï *nf* = vilanï

velarïzo·n *vt* [*Ling*] to velarize

veldro·het *vpr* to wear worn-out clothes, dress in rags

vele *nf* **1** *(Reg)* hinge = menteshë *2* [*Ichth*] fish gill

*velenïs· *vt* to full [woolen material]

velenxë *nf* bed/floor/table woven covering made of thick wool or goat hair

velet adj (Colloq) clever

veletí nf (Colloq) cleverness

*velezo ·n vi to sail

velë nf **1** surfeit (of sweet/greasy food); nausea, disgust **2** sail

*velënxë = **velenxë**

velët adj (i) **1** very sweet/greasy: filling **2** nauseating, disgusting

vel ëz nf [Ichth] fish gill

velim nm [Cine] fogging

velit·et = **vel**·et

*velizo ·n vi to sail

velo nf = **vello**

velodrom nm [Cycling] cycle-racing track; velodrome

velshëm adj (i) nauseating, sickening

*velto ·n vt to nauseate, sicken
  ○ **velto**·n **sytë** to get sleepy/drowsy, drowse

vel uar adj (i) [Cine] fogged

velundrues nm [Ichth] scalloped ribbon fish (Zu cristatus) = **pesh**k-**bishtvel**

vel ur adj (i) **1** feeling stuffed (from eating two many sweets or too much greasy food); overstuffed, satiated: full **2** disgusted **3** (Fig) spoiled by overindulgence

*velzo ·n vt to set sail; hoist sail

vell nm [Bot] yellowish-green shrublet that grows parasitically on juniper (Arceuthobium oxycedri Bieb.)

vello nf **1** [Ethnog] bridal veil **2** (Fig) veil **3** [Text] cotton in a loose skein

*veme nf [Entom] = **vemje**

*vemend = **vëmend**

vemesë nf **1** film formed by boiled milk **2** [Biol] covering membrane: tunic, tunica (V)

vemesor adj [Anat Bot] **1** covered by a membrane **2** membranous

vemesorë np [Biol] tunicates

vem ëz nf [Entom] = **vemje**

velmi 1st pl pres <**ve**·te

vemīzë nf [Entom] = **vemje**

vemje nf **1** [Entom] larva, grub, caterpillar **2** blowfly; flyblow, fly-strike
  ○ **vemja e agrumeve** [Entom] larva of the honeydew moth Cryptoblabes gnidiella Mill
  ○ **vemja e bizeles** [Entom] lima-bean pod borer Etiella zinckenella Tr.
  ○ **vemja e drurit** [Entom] goat moth Cossus cossus L.
  ○ **vemja gjelbëroshe** [Entom] common winter, small winter moth, European winter moth Operophtera brumata L.
  ○ **vemja e gjetheve** [Entom] scarce olive-tree pearl Palpita (Margaronia) unionalis Hb.
  ○ **vemja e kumbullës** [Entom] larva of the plum moth Cydia funebrana Tr.
  ○ **vemja e lakrës** [Entom] cabbage armyworm Mamestra brassicae L.
  ○ **vemja e lastarëve** [Entom] = **vemja e gjetheve**
  ○ **vemja e misrit** [Entom] armyworm Cirphis unipuncta Wik.
  ○ **vemja e panxharit** "beet grub" [Entom] Poeciloscytus cognatus Fieb.

*ven stem for opt, adm, part <**vë**·

*venaro ·n vt to look at [ ], observe

*vencë nf = **vençë**

vençë nf **1** place with a wine press for grapes **2** weak wine made by rinsing water through the grape mash

vend nm **1** place; location **2** populace of a place **3** country; home ground, home country; local area **4** sufficient space: room **5** seat **6** position, job **7** appropriate place/time: right place
  ○ **vend i barutit** field of battle
  ○ **vendi i fëmijës** [Anat] placenta
  ○ **s'gje**·n **vend ku të fut**·et "not find a place to put oneself" to be so upset than one doesn't know what to do
  ○ **vend i hollë** (Euph) male genital area: crotch
  ○ **s'ka**· **vend e trevë prej** <> not have a moment's peace from <>
  ○ **vend i keq/lig** (Euph) lower belly (from the navel to the anus)
  ○ **vend i mirë** (Old) holy place
  ○ **vend i ngrohtë** (Pej) soft job
  ○ **vend i ngushtë** (Book) bottleneck (in a system)
  ○ **vend e pa vend 1** all over the place, whether in the right place or not **2** whether appropriate or not
  ○ **Vendi s'të thotë kurrë ngrihu!** "The place never tells you 'Get up (and go)!'" Don't wait to be asked to leave! Don't overstay your welcome!
  ○ **vend i ujit** (Euph) male genital area: crotch

vendafishim nm poster

vendali nm (np ~ nj) = **vendarak**

vendar adj, n = **vendës**

vendarak nm native, local resident, native inhabitant

vendarritje nf destination

vendas adj, n = **vendës**

vendbanim nm **1** residence **2** center of habitation

vendburim nm **1** source of a stream/river **2** [Min] source of minerals: lode, ore deposit

vendçe adv **1** in the manner of the local natives **2** calmly, quietly **3** intensely: very hard

*vendçor adj **1** = **vendës 2** well-situated

vende-vende adv in several places, here and there

vendës adj, n long-established (resident), local/native/aboriginal (inhabitant)

vendfushim nm [Mil] bivouac area

vendgrumbullim nm assembly location

vendgjetje nf [Archeol] archeological site: find

vendim nm decision

vendimisht adv decisively, resolutely, firmly

vendimtar adj **1** decisive, conclusive, deciding **2** of chief importance

vendkalim nm passageway

vendkëmbim nm [Ling] metathesis = **metatezë**

vendkomandë nf [Mil] = **postkomandë**

vendlindje nf birthplace

vendmbërritje nf = **vendarritje**

vendndalesë nf stopover

vendndalim nm stopping place; bus stop

vendndodhje nf location, position

vendnisje nf point of departure

vendo ·het vpr to settle somewhere; settle in

vendo ·n vt **1** to place [something] **2** to put [something] in an appropriate/secure place **3** to secure a good life for [someone]: settle [someone] comfortably

vendor adj [Ling] locative

vendore nf [Ling] locative case

vendos·
I § *vt* **1** to place; set; put **2** to install; establish **3** to decide

II § *vi* to be determinative, make the decisions: decide

○ [] **vendos· me shpatë** "decide [] by the sword" to decide [] definitively by use of force

vendos··*et* *vpr* to take up residence: settle

vendos·je *nf ger* **1** <vendos·, vendos·*et* **2** *(Colloq)* = vendosmëri ***3** *(Old)* = vendim

vendosmëri *nf* decisiveness, resoluteness, determination

vendosmërisht *adv* *(Book)* resolutely, with determination

vendosur *adj (i)* **1** resolute, determined **2** decided, settled

vendprehje *nf* resting place

vendpushim *nm* resting place
○ **vendpushimi i shkallëve** stair landing

vendqëndrim *nm* place in which something stays, stands or is stationed: station, stand, parking place

vendrojë *nf* [*Mil*] guard post

vendstrehim *nm* **1** bomb shelter **2** [*Agr*] shelter/ shed for machinery and tools, equipment shed

vendtakim *nm* meeting place

venduzë *nf* = ventuzë

vendvarrim *nm* burial place

vendvendosje *nf* (geographic) location

vendverim *nm* summering place

vendvrojtim *nm* [*Mil*] observation point, lookout position

Venecie *nf* Venice

Venedik *nm* Venice, Venetia (especially the Venice of the Venetian Republic)

venedikas *adj, n* Venetian

venerian *adj* [*Med*] venereal

*venetik
I § *nm* Venetian ducat
II § *adj* Venetian

*venetikas = venedikas

venezuellas *adj, n* Venezuelan

Venezuelë *nf* Venezuela

venë *nf* [*Anat*] vein

venë
I § *3rd pl pres* <ve·te
II § *part* <vë·

veni *2nd pl pres* <ve·te

venicë *nf(Reg)* **1** place with a wine press for grapes **2** = dërstilë

venis *stem for 1st sg pres, pl pres, 2nd & 3rd sg subj, pind* <venit·

venit· *vt* to cause [] to lose freshness/force/vitality: wilt, fade; make [] pale and wan

venit··*et* *vpr* **1** to lose freshness/force/vitality: wilt, fade; become pale and wan **2** [*Physiol*] to stop menstruating, enter menopause

venitje *nf ger* <venit·, venit·*et*

venitur *adj (i)* **1** wilted; pale and wan **2** faded, dim

venom *nm* [*Hist*] mores; right granted under the traditional canon of mores

venor *adj* **1** *(Book)* vinous **2** venous

venoz *adj* [*Med*] venous

ventil *nm* air valve

ventilator *nm* **1** electric fan, ventilator **2** [*Tech*] air blower, blow fan

ventuzë *nf* **1** [*Med*] cup used in cupping **2** suction organ/structure for clinging to an object: sucker

venjë *nf* [*Bot*] **1** Greek juniper *(Juniperus excelsa)* ***2** larch
○ **venjë e bardhë** [*Bot*] yew *Juniperus foetidissia*

vepër *nf* **1** deed, act **2** product of extensive activity: work

veprim *nm* **1** action; activity **2** [*Math*] operation **3** [*Lit*] plot (of a novel/drama)

veprimtar
I § *n* active participant = aktivist
II § *adj* working

veprimtari *nf* **1** activity, action **2** active participation; agency

vepro·n *vi* to be active, act
○ **vepro·n me mendje të vet** to make up one's own mind, act according to one's own lights
○ **vepro·n me/më kokën e vet** "act with/on one's own head" to act according to one's own lights, go {}'s own way, do {}'s own thing
○ **vepro·n në tym** to work without a clear plan
○ **vepro·n pas/prapa krahëve 1** to act behind people's back **2** to act unexpectedly
○ **vepro·n prapa shpinës së** <> to use <> as a front; hide behind <>'s skirts

vepror *adj* [*Ling*] active

veprore *nf* [*Ling*] active voice

veprues
I § *adj* active
II § *n* active person; person who is constantly in action
III § *nm* [*Spec*] active ingredient/factor: actuator

veprueshëm *adj (i)* **1** effective **2** doable, practicable

veqil *nm* *(Old)* representative, agent

ver *nm* [*Bot*] hairgrass *(Aira)*
○ **ver kapilar** [*Bot*] annual hairgrass *Aira capillaris*
○ **ver karafilor** [*Bot*] silver hairgrass *Aira caryophyllaea*
○ **ver i vogël** [*Bot*] kind of hairgrass *Aira minuta Loefl.*

*ver *stem for imper* <vë·

Vera *nf* Vera (female name)

Vera *nf* Vera (female name)

verak *adj* = veror

verandë *nf* veranda

verb *nm* **1** blind man **2** [*Ling*] verb

verbal *adj (Book)* verbal

verbalisht *adv (Book)* verbally

verbazi *adv* = verbërisht

verbët *adj (i), n (i)* blind person

verbëri *nf* blindness
○ **verbëri e pulave** [*Veter*] disease that blinds chickens

verbërim *nm ger* = verbim

verbërisht *adv* blindly, rashly

verbëro·het *vpr* = verbo·*het*

verbëro·n *vt* = verbo·*n*

verbësi *nf* = verbëri

verbësir *nf* = verbëri

verbët *adj (i)* blind = verbër

verbim *nm ger* **1** <verbo·*n*, verbo·*het* **2** = verbëri

verbo·het *vpr* to go blind; be blinded

verbo̱·*n vt* to blind

*****ve̱**rb**r**a̱zi *adv* = ve̱rbtas

verbt**a̱s** *adv* blindly

verbu**a̱r** *adj (i)* blinded; blind

verbu**e̱s** *adj* blinding

verca**ll** *nm (np ˜j)* [*Ethnog*] meal served after a death

*****ve̱**rc**ë = ve̱rzë.

verdh· *vt* to give [] a pale yellow/tan color; give [] a pallor, make [] pale
  ∘ <>*i* **verdh· kë̱mbët** "turn <>'s feet pale" *(Impol)* to kill [], knock [] off

ve̱rdh·*et vpr* to turn yellow: turn pale

verdha**c** *adj, n* [*Impol*] = verdhaca̱k

verdhaca̱k *adj, n* [*Impol*] (person) with a pallid/sallow complexion

verdhacu̱k *adj* 1 [*Impol*] = verdhaca̱k 2 pale, dim

verdha̱k *OR* **verdh**ala̱k *adj, n (Impol)* = verdhaca̱k

verdhala̱q *adj, n (Pej)* = verdhaca̱k

verdhala̱sh *adj* = verdhemë̱

verdhama̱n *adj, n (Pej)* = verdhaca̱k

verdha̱n *adj, n* 1 (animal) with a fawn coat 2 = verdhemë̱

verdhani̱ *nf (Colloq)* [*Med*] jaundice

verdhani̱k *adj, n (Impol)* = verdhaca̱k

*****verdh**anja̱k *adj, n (Impol)* = verdhaca̱k

verdha̱sh
  I § *adj* having a slight yellowish tan color; with yellowish tan plumage
  II § *nm* [*Ornit*] golden oriole = beng

verdha̱shkë [*Ornit*] canary *(Serinus canarius)*

*****ve̱rdh**c**ë *nf* mountain woman's brooch

*****verdh**ej**ë *nf* [*Ornit*] golden oriole *(Oriolus oriolus)*

verdhemë̱ *adj (i)* dull yellow, yellow-brown

verdhemë̱t *adj (i)* = verdhemë̱

ve̱rdhë
  I § *adj (i)* 1 color ranging from yellow to tan: yellow, straw-colored, yellowish tan, beige, fawn 2 pallid, pale 3 *(Book Pej)* opportunistic; given to sensationalism; exploiting crime stories to make a profit 4 *(Old)* = gjelbër
  II § *nf (Old)* long-barrelled pistol plated with gold-colored tinplate
  III § *nf (e)* 1 yellow-tan coloring material 2 egg yolk
  IV § *nn (të)* 1 [*Med*] jaundice 2 = fi̱ket

verdhëlle̱më adj (i) somewhat of a yellowish tan tinge; slightly pale

verdhë̱s *adj* (of fruits) yellowish tan

verdhë̱si *nf* yellowness; paleness

verdhësi̱rë *nf* yellow-tan color; pale color

verdhë̱z *nf* [*Med*] 1 epidemic hepatitis 2 jaundice
  ∘ **verdh**ë̱z **pe̱shku** fish gill

verdhë̱za̱k *adj* turned yellowish brown: yellowed

ve̱rdhje *nf ger* < ve̱rdh·, ve̱rdh·et

verdho̱·*het vpr* to be = zve̱rdh·et

verdho̱·*n*
  I § *vt* to give [] a yellowish/brownish color, make [] yellow/tan; (in cooking) brown
  II § *vi* 1 to have a yellowish appearance/sheen, look yellow 2 *(Reg)* to make [] green/verdant

verdho̱sh *adj* yellowish; pale

verdhu̱k *adj, n* 1 yellowish tan (fruit) 2 = verdhaca̱k

verdhu̱l
  I § *adj, n (Impol)* pale in the face = verdhaca̱k
  II § *nm* [*Ornit*] canary

verdhullo̱·*het vpr* to take on a yellowish tinge; have a yellowish gleam/sheen

verdhullo̱·*n*
  I § *vt* to give [] a yellowish color
  II § *vi* to have a yellow gleam/sheen

verdhullo̱r *adj (Poet)* golden-colored

verdhu̱sh
  I § *adj* = verdho̱sh
  II § *nm* [*Ornit*] golden oriole *(Oriolus oriolus)*

verdhu̱she *nf* = verdhu̱shkë

verdhu̱shkë *nf (Colloq)* gold coin

vere̱m *nm* 1 [*Med Old*] consumption (tuberculosis) 2 *(Colloq)* a deadly disease

veremo̱s· *vt* 1 [*Med Old*] to infect [] with tuberculosis 2 *(Fig)* to put [] into terrible despair; annoy [] terribly

veremo̱s·*et vpr* 1 [*Med Old*] to become consumptive (contract tuberculosis) 2 *(Fig)* to fall into terrible despair; become terribly annoyed

veremo̱s**ur**
  I § *adj (i)* 1 [*Med Old*] suffering from tuberculosis: consumptive, tubercular 2 *(Fig)* in terrible despair; terribly annoyed
  II § *n (i)* person with consumption/tuberculosis: consumptive

vereni̱k·et *vpr* to undergo discoloration/darkening of skin: turn livid (from strong emotion), get black and blue, get blue (from cold)

vereni̱kur *adj (i)* livid (from strong emotion), black and blue, blue (from cold)

veresi̱e
  I § *adv (Colloq)* 1 *(Old)* without paying cash, on credit; gratis, free 2 *(Fig Pej)* without thinking: carelessly, thoughtlessly
  II § *nf (Colloq) (Old)* credit purchase
  III § *np* money owed on credit

verevë̱rtë *adv (Colloq)* certainly, surely

ve̱rë *nf* 1 summer 2 wine
  ∘ **ve̱rë dimër** all year long, constantly
  ∘ **verë e hapur** "open wine" wine sold directly from the barrel by the liter
  ∘ **verë myshku** muscatel
  ∘ **ta shet· ujin e pusit për verë** "{} *sells* you water from the well as wine" {} *is* deceitful, you can't trust {}

ve̱rëra *np* < ve̱rë wines

ve̱rë̱z *nf* first day of spring = dita e verës

ve̱rgë *nf* [*Agr*] crosswise floorboard of a cart bed

vergji̱ *nf* [*Hist*] property tax paid to the local fief holder under the Ottoman Empire

ve̱ri *nm* 1 north 2 north wind 3 fan (for fanning oneself)

veria̱k *adj* = verio̱r

verifiki̱m *nm ger* 1 < verifiko̱·*n* 2 verification; verification check

verifiko̱·*n vt* to verify

verigë *nf* 1 link in a chain; chain 2 linchpin securing the yoke to the beam of a plow 3 pot handle; arched handle, bail 4 button hole, button loop; lacing hole in a moccasin 5 slipknot 6 fruit/nuts in a bunch: cluster of grapes

*****verig**o̱r *adj* ring-shaped, annular

veri`lindje *nf* northeast

veri`lind`or *adj* northeastern

ver`im** *nm ger* <**vero`·*n*

veri`or *adj* northern

veri`perënd`im *nm* northwest

veri`perënd`im`or *adj* northwestern

*****veri`skë** *nf* [*Bot*] kind of buckthorn (*Rhamnus fallax*)

veri`shtë *nf* strong wind from the north

ve`rmë *adj (i)* sown in the spring, reaped in the summer

vermu`t *nm* vermouth

vern`ik *nm* glossy finish: varnish, shellac, lacquer, polish, glaze

vero`·*n*
   I § *vi* to spend the summer (somewhere): summer
   II § *vt* to pasture livestock in highlands for the summer

vero`jkë** *nf* [*Ethnog*] = **vero`re

vero`një *nf* [*Bot*] larch

ver`or *adj* of or pertaining to summer; appropriate for or characteristic of summer; ripening in summer

vero`re
   I § *nf* **1** [*Ethnol*] bracelet or necklace of red and white yarn worn by children on the first day of spring **2** fan (for fanning oneself) in summer
   II § *nf* **1** [*Zool*] small green frog that announces the beginning of spring by croaking: European tree frog (*Hyla arborea*) *****2** [*Ichth*] variety of small inedible freshwater fish

version *nm* version

*****ve`rstë** *nf* verst (Russian measure of distance)

verte`bër *nf* [*Anat*] vertebra

vertebra`të** *np masc* [*Zool*] = **vertebro`rë

vertebr`or *adj* [*Anat*] spinal; vertebral; vertebrate

vertebr`or`ë *np masc* [*Zool*] vertebrates

vertika`l *adj* vertical

vertika`le *nf* **1** [*Geom*] vertical line **2** [*Sport*] handstand

vertikal`isht *adv* vertically

*****vertll`o`**·*n* *vi* to prattle

ver`ue`s
   I § *n* summer vacationer/visitor
   II § *adj* spending the summer: summering

ver`uke *nf* small summer-ripening apple

verza`ku`q *nm* [*Ichth*] = **pend`ëku`q**

ve`rzë *nf* **1** [*Ichth*] fish gill **2** [*Agr*] moldboard of a wooden plow **3** [*Agr*] triangular yoke tied around a pig's neck to prevent it from squeezing through narrow spaces

ve`rzën *nf* [*Naut*] bilge

*****verzi`on** = **versi`on**

verzo`më** *nf* = **vërzo`më

verz`or *adj* [*Ichth*] of or pertaining to fish gills

verr *nm* [*Bot*] alder (*Alnus*)
   ○ **verr i bardhë** [*Bot*] speckled/gray/hoary alder *Alnus incana*
   ○ **verr i egër** [*Bot*] kind of buckthorn *Rhamnus fallax*
   ○ **verr kulfini** [*Bot*] Italian alder *Alnus cordata*
   ○ **verr i zi** [*Bot*] European black alder *Alnus glutinosa*

*****ve`rrë** *nf* (*Reg*) = **vri`më**

verri`(r) *nm* (*np ˜ nj*) [*Bot*] = **verr**

verri`shtë
   I § *nf* grove of alders
   II § *adj (i)* of alder wood/trees

ve`rrle *nf* (children's toy) wooden top

ves *nm* **1** vice **2** defect

vesel`i *nf* (*Reg*) abundance

vesel`is** *stem for 1st sg pres, pl pres, 2nd & 3rd sg subj, pind* <**vesel`it·

vesel`it· *vt* **1** (*Reg*) to satiate [] with sweet/greasy food; please [] very much with food **2** to take good care of []; take great pains to care for []

vesel`it·*et vpr* **1** (*Reg*) to become sated with food; enjoy eating very much **2** to grow quickly/profusely, develop well

ve`së *nf* dew; drizzle
   ○ **vesa e mjaltit** plant nectar
   ○ **vesë shiu** drizzle

vesë`to**·*n vi* = **veso`·*n*

vesë`tua`r *adj (i)* = **vesua`r**

ves`im** *nm ger* **1** <**veso`·*n*, **veso`**·*het* **2** thin rain, drizzle

ves`it**· *vi, vt* = **veso`·*n*

ves`it**·*et vpr* = **veso`·*het*

vesk *nm* allure

vesk· *vt* to entice, lure = **josh**·

ve`sk·*et vp impers* it is enticing to <>
   ○ <> **vesk**·*et*[3sg] **për** [] <> finds [] tempting, <> would like to have []

veske`q *adj* having bad vices, having serious defects

*****ves`mi`rë** *adj* moral

*****ves`mi`r`ësi** *adj* morality

veso`·*het vpr* to become covered with dew: get all dewy

veso`·*n vi impers* it dews; it drizzles

vesua`r *adj (i)* wet/covered with dew; wet from a drizzling rain

vesve`s *adj* (*Colloq*) overly worried/suspicious about everything: wary, leery

vesves`eli *nm* (*Colloq*) person who is excessivly and needlessly concerned/suspicious about everything: worrywart

vesh· *vt* **1** to clothe []; put on [clothes] **2** to provide [] with clothes: dress **3** to wear **4** (*Colloq*) to take [] into a job requiring uniform dress **5** (*Fig Colloq*) to stick <> with [responsibility/blame]
   ○ <> **vesh**· (*Colloq*) to talk off the top of one's head
   ○ <>**a vesh**· **1** (*Colloq*) to hit <>, hit <> suddenly: lay one on <>, paste <> one **2** (*Colloq*) to do <> hastily
   ○ [] **vesh**· **dhe** [] **ngjesh**· to dress [] in warm clothes: dress [] warm
   ○ <>**a vesh**· **këmishën me uthull** "dress <> in a shirt wet with vinegar" to give <> a severe beating: beat <> to a pulp, clean the floor with <>
   ○ <>**a vesh**· **me shuplakë** to give <> a slap in the face
   ○ **ia vesh· tjetër për tjetër** to hit on a response that is completely off track

vesh *nm* **1** ear **2** handle **3** bunch (of fruit) **4** moldboard of a plow **5** eye of a needle **6** [*Anat*] (heart) auricle
   ○ **veshi i belit** footrest on a spade handle (used to apply foot pressure for digging)
   ○ **vesh deti** [*Invert*] ormer, abalone *Haliotis tuberculata lamellosa*
   ○ **vesh elefanti** [*Invert*] elephant-ear sponge *Spongia agaricina*
   ○ **vesh gomari** [*Bot*] = **babani`k**

∘ s'merr· vesh not listen, pay no attention; not obey
∘ vesh më vesh ear to ear
∘ nuk e rreh· veshin (për [ ]) not be much concerned (about [ ]): not going to lose any sleep (over [ ])

ve·sh 2nd sg subj (të) <ve·te

vesha'k
I § adj having ears that stick out; (of a cap) having earlaps
II § nm 1 protruding part of something 2 bunch of grapes

vesha'ke nf small clay water pot with a handle

vesha'r nm [Ichth] leaping gray mullet (Liza saliens) = gastu'r

vesh'as adv by the ears; at each other's throat; hand to hand

veshata'k adj eared; long-eared

veshato're nf [Ethnog] woman who dresses and adorns the bride

vesh'bigë adj 1 having perked-up ears 2 (Fig) keeping one's ears cocked, staying alert

vesh'curr adj, n (animal/person) with cropped/small ears

*vesh'ezë nf type of distaff

ve'shë nf copper pail with two side handles

ve'shë np <vesh fish gills

ve'shël adj (i) fertile

ve'shël nf cornhusk

vesh'ëli nf fertility

vesh'ëlis stem for 1st sg pres, pl pres, 2nd & 3rd sg subj, pind <vesh'ëli·

vesh'ëli·t· vt to fertilize

vesh'ëli'tje nf fertilization

ve'shës
I § nm [Spec] person who lines furnaces/ovens with heat-resistant material
II § adj [Spec] used as covering material

ve'shëz nf 1 [Agr] wooden fork running up to the plow beam from the plow tip and functioning as a kind of moldboard on a wooden plow 2 [Entom] earwig = gërshë'rëz 3 little ear; small handle 4 bracket

vesh'flori nm [Ichth] golden gray mullet, long-finned gray mullet (Liza aurata)

*veshg = vëzhg

vesh'goma'r nm 1 [Bot] = babani'k 2 (Insult) donkey-eared

*veshgu'es
I § adj exploratory
II § n explorer

vesh'gjatë
I § adj 1 long-eared 2 (Insult) donkey-eared
II § nm (Euph) donkey

ve'shje nf ger 1 <vesh·, vish·et 2 (Collec) clothing 3 [Spec] covering layer 4 [Constr] wall-covering: paneling, facing, plastering 5 pail with handles on the side
∘ veshje të përmbrendshme underwear

*ve'shk· vt = fishk·

*ve'shk·et = fishk·et

ve'shkë nf [Anat] kidney

*ve'shkët adj (i) = fishkët

*ve'shk·la np kidneys

vesh'ko'r adj [Anat] renal, nephric

*ve'shkull nm [Bot] loranthus (Loranthus europaeus)

*ve'shk·ur adj (i) = fishkët

vesh'le'pur nm [Bot] 1 white campion (Lychnis alba) 2 hare's ear (Bupleurum rotundifolium)

vesh'lopa'të adj (Tease) big-eared, shovel-eared

vesh'llapu'sh adj (Colloq Tease) big-eared

vesh'ma'dh nm 1 big-eared 2 [Zool] long-eared bat

vesh'mba'thje nf collec clothing and footwear

*ve'shme nf (e) garment; coat

vesh'mi'zë nf [Bot] forget-me-not (Myosotis) = lule mosmëharro

vesh'ngre'hur adj (i) = veshbi'gë

vesh'ngri'tur adj = veshbi'gë

vesh'ni'k nm 1 small cluster of grapes 2 baking dome with two side handles 3 container with two handles: vase, pot

vesho'k
I § adj having small ears
II § nm small cluster of grapes

vesho'ke np fem leather blinders for a horse: blinkers

vesho'r adj of or pertaining to the ears; shaped like an ear

vesho're
I § nf 1 earflap 2 copper pail with two side handles
II § np fem = vesho'ke

vesh'pi'pëz adj, n (one) with keen hearing, sharp-eared (one)

vesh'pre're adj, n = veshcurr

*veshqe'të nf [Bot] pea, vetch (Lathyrus) = vingjër

vesh'qi'qër adj 1 = veshbi'gë 2 having good hearing

vesh'qok adj perceptive, mentally keen, quick-witted: clever, smart, sharp

vesh'rëndë adj hard of hearing

vesh'shku'rtër adj short-eared

vesh'shpu'ar adj 1 having pierced ears 2 = veshqok 3 (Pej) oblivious to what others say, impervious to criticism: deaf-eared

*vesht nm (Old) = vresht

*vesht old locative case <vesh "in the ear"

vesh'ta'k adj = veshqok

vesh'ta'r adj 1 keen in hearing; aware of everything going on 2 (Fig) mentally keen, smart

vesh'ta're nf [Ethnog] = veshato're

ve'shtë adj (i) sharp-eared, attentive; mentally sharp

vesh'ti nf attentiveness, care; mental sharpness

vesh'to·n vi to listen, listen carefully; listen attentively, listen close

*veshtr = vështr

*veshtra'k adj attentive, observant

vesh'tu'k adj = veshu'k

ve'shtull nf 1 [Bot] mistletoe (Viscum) 2 [Bot] = veshtullake 3 (Fig) parasite, freeloader
∘ veshtulla e bardhë [Bot] the European mistletoe, white mistletoe Viscum album

vesh'tulla'ke nf 1 [Bot] milkweed 2 sticky gum from this plant

vesh'tulli nf 1 stickiness; viscosity 2 parasitic dependence

vesh'tullo'r adj 1 sticky; viscous 2 clinging (to a plant), parasitic

vesh'u'k adj, n big-eared (person/animal)

vesh'u'l nm cluster/bunch of grapes

ve'shur
I § part <vesh·, vish·et

II § *adj (i)* **1** clothed; dressed **2** *(Colloq)* provided with sufficient clothing **3** covered with a thin layer of something: coated **4** covered by a filmy membrane (over the eye) **5** covered with green growth: verdant **6** covered by clouds: overcast **7** previously worn: used, secondhand
○ **veshur me gëzof** with fur lining
○ **i veshur pingël** all decked out in new clothes
○ **i veshur si kaçup** bundled up in heavy clothing
○ **i veshur si për mik** "dressed as for (receiving) guests" all dressed up in new clothes, dressed for company

veshverdhë *nf* [*Ichth*] leaping gray mullet *(Liza saliens)* = **gastur**

veshvogël *adj* having small ears

vet
I § *reflexive pronominal adj (i)* my/your/his/her/its/our/their own, of my/your/his/her/its/our/their own
II § *n (i)* own relative, own close friend

veta *np* = **vetë** persons, people

vetadministrim *nm ger* **1** <**vetadministro**·*n* **2** self-government

vetadministro·*n vt, vi (Book)* to practice self-government (in respect to [])

vetadministrues *adj* = **vetëqeverisës**

vetadhurim *nm (Book)* self-conceit

vetakuzë *nf (Book)* self-indictment

vetakuzim *nm (Book)* self-accusation

vetasgjësim *nm (Book)* self-destruction

vete *refl nf* **1** self, oneself: myself, yourself, himself, herself, itself, ourselves, yourselves, themselves **2** *(Euph)* groin area of the body: groin
○ **nuk ësh-të në vete** not be in one's right mind
○ **Për vete e bë**-*n*/**ka**-**!** "Does it for {}self (not for me)!" It *serves* {} right!
○ **Për veten e** {*pronominal adj*} **e bë**-*n*/**ka**· "Does it for {}self (not for me)" It *serves* {} right!
○ {} **për vete 1** in {}'s (personal) opinion **2** as for {}

vete *sg pres* <**ve**·**te**

veteclës *adj (Spec)* self-propelled

vetedukim *nm ger* **1** <**veteduko**·*het* **2** self-education

veteduko·*het vpr* to educate oneself

veter. *abbrev* <**veteriner** veterinarian

veteran *n, adj* veteran

veterinar *adj* veterinary

veterinari *nf* veterinary science/medicine; veterinary treatment

veteriner *n* veterinarian

veterrik *nm* [*Hydrol*] diversion channel of an irrigation line to bring water into a field

vetë
I § *nf* person
II § *refl pron* self: myself, yourself, himself, herself, itself, ourselves, yourselves, themselves
III § *adv* without help: by myself/yourself/himself/herself/itself/ourselves/yourselves/themselves
○ **ësh-të dora vetë për** to be uniquely/highly qualified for
○ **vetë i dytë/tretë/.../nëntë** "oneself as a second/third/.../ninth person" together with a second/third/.../ninth other person
○ **vetë flet**·, **vetë dëgjo**·*n* to talk to oneself, no one is paying any attention to what one is saying
○ **vetë ind e vetë majë** all alone

○ **vetë me vete** all by oneself; to oneself
○ **vetë para e vetë pas** (all) alone, by oneself (without anyone else around)
○ **Vetë shëndoshë!** (said in order to console someone who has suffered a great loss) Try to be brave! You'll get through it somehow!
○ **vetë shkrua**-*n*, **vetë vulos**· "write it oneself, stamp it oneself" to be able to act on one's own authority
○ {} **të vetën se/që të vetën** {*verb*} {} just has to have {}'s own way and {*verb*}: {} obstinately {*verb*}:
○ **vetë vali (e) vetë kadi/myfti** "both ruler and judge oneself" so powerful that one can do as one likes
○ **vetë zot, vetë shkop** "both lord and rod oneself" so powerful that one can do as one likes

vetë *formativ* auto-, self-

vetëbartës *adj* [*Tech*] self-propelled

vetëbesim *nm (Book)* self-confidence

vetëbindje *nf (Book)* personal conviction; self-persuasion

vetëdashës
I § *n (Old)* **1** volunteer **2** self-willed person: egoist
II § *adj* **1** voluntary *****2** selfish, egoistic

vetëdashje *nf* **1** willingness, free will "self love" **2** *(Old)* egoism **3** selfishness

vetëdemaskim *nm (Book)* unwitting revelation of one's true colors, self-revelation

vetëdënim *nm (Book)* self-punishment

vetëdije *nf* **1** consciousness; awareness **2** sense of responsibility: conscience

vetëdijshëm *adj (i)* **1** conscious; aware **2** conscientious, responsible

vetëditur *adj (i)* = **vetëdijshëm**

vetëdora *adv* (signed) personally, in person

*****vetëdoras** *adv* by one's own hand

vetëdrejtim *nm ger* **1** <**vetëdrejto**·*n*, **vetëdrejto**·*het (Book)* **2** self direction; self management

vetëdrejto·*het vpr* **1** *(Book)* to be self-governing **2** [*Mil*] to find its target automatically, be self-directional, home in

vetëdrejto·*n vi, vt (Book)* to govern [] oneself

vetëfajësim *nm* [*Law*] self-incrimination

vetëfekondim *nm* self-fertilization

vetëflijim *nm (Book)* self-sacrifice

vetëflijo·*het vpr (Book)* to give oneself in self-sacrifice

vetëgënjim *nm* self-delusion, illusion

vetëgropos·*et vpr* [*Mil*] to dig in

vetëgroposje *nf ger* <**vetëgropos**·*et*

vetëgjykim *nm* **1** [*Law*] = **vetëgjyqësi 2** *(Book)* personal judgment

vetëgjyko·*n vt (Book)* to judge [] for oneself

vetëgjyqësi *nf* [*Law*] taking the law into one's own hands

vetëhelmim *nm (Book)* self-poisoning

vetëheqës *adj* [*Mil*] self-ejecting

vetëjeto·*n vt* to experience [] oneself

vetëjetuar *adj (i)* that has been experienced oneself

vetëkalitje *nf (Book)* getting toughened up

vetëkënaq· *vt (Book)* to give [] self-satisfaction

vetëkënaq·*et vpr* to become self-satisfied

vetëkënaq|ësi *nf* self-satisfaction; self-complacency

vetëkëna'qje *nf ger* 1 *(Book)* <vetëkëna'q·, vetëkëna·q·et 2 = vetëkënaqësi

vetëkontro'll *nm* self-control

vetëkritík *adj* self-critical

vetëkritíkë *nf* self-criticism

vetëkuptímshëm *adj (i)* [*Ling*] semantically independent

vetëkupto'·het *vpr* to be self-evident

vetëkuptu'eshëm *adj (i)* self-evident

vetëkurdís·ës *adj* self-winding

vetëlavdërím *nm (Book)* self-praise

vetëlëku'ndje *nf* [*Phys*] self-excited oscillation

vetëlëvíz·ës *adj* [*Spec*] self-propelled

vetëlëvízje *nf* 1 [*Phil*] mutability 2 [*Spec*] self-propulsion

vetëlídhje *nf* [*Mil*] pinpointing a military target by its grid coordinates on a map

vetëlínd· *vi* 1 [*Biol*] to reproduce by vegetative division 2 to be inborn, be innate

vetëlíndje *nf ger* 1 [*Biol*] <vetëlínd· 2 vegetative division

vetëlíndur *adj (i) (Book)* inborn, inherent

ve'tëm
 I § adj (i) 1 single, lone, only; sole 2 without equal, unique 3 alone; separate, independent 4 unchanging, constant
 II § n (i) one that is all alone in the world
 III § adv 1 only, just; solely, simply 2 alone; all alone in the world; singlehandedly
 IV § pcl if only; just
 V § conj but only/just, except
 ○ **vetëm fill** all alone, quite alone
 ○ **vetëm gjaku** [] **nda·**-*n³ˢᵍ* "only spilling blood will separate/settle []" I won't stop until someone is killed; only vengeance in blood will settle [a blood feud]
 ○ **vetëm për vetëm** 1 completely/quite alone 2 in private
 ○ **ësh-të i vetmi për/në** [] to have no match in regard to [], be incomparable in []
 ○ **vetëm që/se** _ except that _, it's just that _
 ○ **Vetëm qimja e ndan.** Everything is hanging in the balance.
 ○ **vetëm e vetëm** solely, just

vetëmashtrím *nm* self-deception

*vetëmba'jtje *nf* 1 *(Book)* = vetëpërmbajtje 2 self-supporting, self-maintaining

vetëmbje'llje *nf* self-sowing, self-seeding

vetëmbro'·het *vpr* to protect/defend oneself

vetëmbro'jt·ës *adj* self-protective, self-defensive

vetëmbro'jtje *nf* self-protection, self-defense

vetëmbu'rr·et *vpr* to praise oneself, indulge in self-praise

vetëmbu'rrje *nf* self-praise

vetëmbu'sh·ës *adj* [*Mil*] self-loading

*vetëmendím *nm* egoism

vetëmendo'·n *vi, vt (Book)* to express one's own opinion (about [])

vetëmërgím *nm* self-exile

*vetëmí = vetmí

vetëmjaftu'eshëm *adj (i) (Book)* self-sufficient

vetëmjekím *nm* self-medication, self-treatment

---

*vetëmo'·n = vetmo'·n

vetëmohím *nm* self-denial

vetëmohu'es *adj* self-denying

vetënde'z *stem for part, pdef, opt, adm* <vetëndi z·et

vetënde'z·ës *adj* [*Spec*] self-igniting; self-starting (of an engine), having automatic ignition

vetënde'zje *nf ger* 1 [*Spec*] <vetëndi z·et 2 spontaneous combustion

vetëndíz·et *vpr* 1 *(Book)* to self-ignite 2 [*Agr*] to start to rot from excessive moisture; undergo spontaneous combustion

vetëndriçu'es *adj (Book)* self-luminous

vetëngarkím *nm* automatic loading

vetëngarku'es
 I § adj [*Tech*] self-loading
 II § nm [*Tech*] self-loader, power-lift truck

vetëngro'hje *nf* [*Spec*] spontaneous heating

vetëngjíz·et *nf* [*Dairy*] self-clotting, spontaneous curdling

vetëngjízur *adj (i)* [*Dairy*] curdled spontaneously

vetënxítj·et *nf (Book)* inner drive

vetëpadí *nf (Law)* self-accusation

vetëpëlqím *nm (Book)* self-satisfaction; smugness

vetëpërbu'zje *nf (Book)* self-contempt

vetëpërgatít·et *vpr (Book)* to make one's own preparations; self-training

vetëpërgatítj·et *nf (Book)* preparation made on one's own; self-preparation, self-training

vetëpërha'pje *nf* [*Bot*] self-dissemination

vetëpërmba'jtje *nf* self-control; self-composure

*vetëpërmba'nj·ës *adj* = vetëpërmbajtje

vetëpërso'sj·et *nf (Book)* self-improvement

vetëpërtërítje *nf (Book)* self-generation, spontaneous generation

vetëpjalmím *nm* [*Bot*] self-pollination

vetëplago'sj·et *nf (Book)* self-inflicted wound

vetëpllením *nm* [*Biol*] self-fertilization

vetëposhtërím *nm* self-denigration

vetëqe'nie *nf (Book)* ontological independence; independent existence: self-existence

vetëqetësím *nm ger* 1 <vetëqetëso'·het 2 self-complacency

vetëqetëso'·het *vpr* to be/become self-complacent

vetëqeverím *nm ger* = vetëqeverísje

vetëqeverímta'r *adj (Book)* = vetëqeverís·ës

vetëqeverís·
 I § vt to govern one's own []
 II § vi to be self-governing

vetëqeverís·et *vpr (Book)* to be self-governing, govern oneself

vetëqeverís·ës *adj (Book)* self-governing

vetëqeverísje *nf ger* 1 <vetëqeverís·, vetëqeverís·et 2 self-governance

vetëqortím *nm (Book)* self-castigation

vetëqu'·het *vpr (Book)* to be a self-styled ()

vetëqu'·a·n *vt (Book)* to call [] a name/term on one's own authority

vetëqu'ajtur *adj (i) (Book)* self-styled

vetëregjistru'es *adj* [*Tech*] self-recording

vetëreklamím *nm (Book)* self-advertisement

vetëriprodhím *nm (Book)* self-replication

vetëru'ajtje *nf (Book)* self-preservation

vetërrje'dhje *nf* (liquid) discharge, secretion

vetërrotullim *nm ger* **1** *(Spec)* <**vetërrotullo**·*het* **2** rotation

vetërrotullo·*het vpr (Spec)* to rotate on its own axis; rotate automatically

vetërrotullues *adj* [*Spec*] rotating on its own axis; revolving

vetësiguri *nf (Book)* self-assurance

vetësigurim *nm (Book)* personal safety

vetësim *nm ger* **1** <**vetëso**·*n* **2** personification

vetëso·*n vt* to personify = **personifiko**·*n*

vetëstërvitje *nf (Book)* self-training

vetësugjestionim *nm (Book)* autosuggestion

vetësundim *nm (Book)* self-control, self-government

vetësundues *adj* self-controlling, self-governing

vetëshërbim *nm* **1** self-service **2** cafeteria; self-service store

vetëshërbyes *adj* offering self-service

vetëshfajësim *nm (Law)* self-vindication

vetëshkarkim *nm* automatic unloading

vetëshkarkues
I § *adj* self-unloading
II § *nm* self-unloader

vetë-shkrehës *nm* [*Cine*] auto-release, self-timer

vetëshkrues *nm* [*Tech*] self-recording/autographic instrument, recording apparatus

vetëshuarje *nf* [*Phys*] automatic switch-off

vetëshumëzim *nm* [*Biol*] inbreeding; self-fertilization, autogamy

vetëti·*n*
I § *vi impers* lightning *is flashing*
II § *vi* **1** to shine bright; flash **2** to shine/sparkle (with cleanliness) **3** *(Fig)* to come to mind in a flash
III § *vt* to make [] shine/sparkle (with cleanliness)
∘ **nuk** <> **vetëti**·*n³ˢᵍ* **syri** "<>'s eye never *blinks*" <> *is* fearless/intrepid

vetëtimë
I § *nf* lightning, lightning bolt, flash of lightning
II § *adj* **1** *(Fig)* lightning-quick, fast as lightning **2** sparkling-bright; sparkling-clean

vetëtimshëm *adj (i)* = **vetëtimtë**

vetëtimtë *adj (i)* **1** flashing like lightning **2** quick as lightning

vetëtimthi *adv* lightning-fast; in a flash

vetëtis *stem for 1st sg pres, pl pres, 2nd & 3rd sg subj, pind* <**vetëtit**·

vetëtit·*vi* = **vetëti**·*n*

vetëtitës *adj (Book)* **1** brightly shining, radiant **2** shining/sparkling (with purity/cleanliness) **3** (of eyes/face) expressing strong emotion: flashing

vetëto·*n vi* = **vetëti**·*n*

vetëtretje *nf* [*Med*] self-digestion, autolysis

vetëtherori *nf (Book)* self-sacrifice = **vetëflijim**

vetëvajosëse *nf* [*Tech*] self-lubricating

vetëvendos· *vi* **1** to make one's own decisions, settle one's own affairs **2** [*Law*] to be self-determining

vetëvendosje *nf ger* **1** <**vetëvendos**· **2** [*Law*] self-determination

vetëveprim *nm ger* **1** <**vetëvepro**·*n* **2** personal initiative

vetëvepro·*n vi* to act on one's own initiative

vetëveprues *adj* **1** capable of acting on one's own initiative **2** [*Tech*] self-activating, self-actuating

vetëvlerësim *nm (Book)* self-evaluation; self-esteem

vetëvra *stem for pdef, opt, adm, part, imper* <**vetëvrit**·*et*

vetëvrasës
I § *adj* suicidal
II § *n* one who has committed suicide

vetëvrasje *nf* suicide

vetëvrit·*et vpr* to commit suicide

vetëzhvillim *nm (Book)* self-development

veti *nf* property, trait, feature

vetijë *nf* = **veti**

*****vetime** **veti** *adv* within oneself

*****vetimë** = **lightning**

vetinduktim *nm* [*Phys*] self inductance

vetishëm *adj (i)* characteristic

vetiu *adv* without external cause/help: by itself/oneself, spontaneously; by nature

*****vetiut** *(Reg Gheg)* = **vetiu**

vetizolo·*het vpr* to isolate oneself

vetjak *adj* individual, personal, private

*****vetllar** *nm* = **vetullar**

*****vetllim** *nm* = **vetullim**

*****vetllo**·*n vt* = **vetullo**·*n*

vetmas *adv pcl* = **vetëm**

vetmi *nf* being alone, solitude; loneliness

vetmitar
I § *adj (Poet)* solitary
II § *n* solitary person; hermit

vetmo·*het vpr* to stay alone; be isolated

vetmo·*n vt* to make [] live alone; isolate []

vetmor
I § *adj* done alone: individual, single
II § *n* solitary person; hermit

vetmuar *adj (i)* isolated from others: alone; solitary

veto *nf* veto

veto·*n vi (Reg)* = **vetëti**·*n*
∘ **nuk** <> **veto**·*n³ˢᵍ* **ashka e syrit** "<>'s eye *doesn't blink*" <> *is* fearless

*****vetoin**·*et vpr* = **vejëro**·*het*

vetor *adj* **1** [*Ling*] personal **2** [*Med*] inguinal

vetorganizim *nm (Book)* self-organization

vetull *nf* **1** eyebrow; brow **2** overhang **3** arched part of something **4** slice from the heel of the bread; end slice; end piece; strip **5** small curved knife used to scrape the bottom of a wooden vessel **6** groove in a board **7** hem in cloth or carpet; cloth binding **8** = **vetullar**
∘ **vetull buke** heel of a round loaf of bread

vetullabardhë *adj, n* (person) with light-colored eyebrows

vetullak *adj* = **vetullngrysur**

vetullan *adj, n* **1** (person) with bushy eyebrows **2** *(Fig)* (person) of proud and serious mien

vetullar *nm* [*Constr*] grooving plane

vetullarënë *adj* **1** having drooping eyebrows **2** = **vetullngrysur**

vetullasorrë *adj* raven-browed

vetullash *adj* = **vetullan**

vetullfiskajë *adj (Poet)* having thin (sprig-like) eyebrows

vetullgajtan *adj (Poet)* having long delicately shaped eyebrows

vetullgjilpërë *adj* having needle-thin eyebrows

vetullhequr *adj* having plucked eyebrows

vetull⟋hënë adj (Poet) having arched eyebrows like the crescent moon

vetull⟋hollë adj, n (person) with thin eyebrows

vetull⟋im nm ger 1 <**vetullo**'·n, **vetullo**'·het 2 groove/slot in a board: mortise

vetull⟋kale'm adj, n (Poet) (person) with beautiful pencil-thin eyebrows

vetull⟋kale'sh adj, n (person) with dark thick eyebrows

vetull⟋kuro're adj (Poet) having eyebrows arched like a wreath

vetull⟋ngritur adj having high arched eyebrows

vetull⟋ngry'sur adj gloomy-browed

vetullo·het vpr to knit one's eyebrows: frown

vetullo·n
I § vt to make a mortise in [a board]
II § vi to gesture with the eyebrows

vetullo'r adj 1 having thick eyebrows 2 with something of an arch, slightly arched 3 [Med] superciliary

vetullo're nf mound erected around tree roots to retain moisture

vetull⟋o'sh
I § adj, n (person) with thick eyebrows
II § nm [Zool] badger = **baldo'se**

vetull⟋përpje'kur adj having eyebrows that join together

vetull⟋rre'ptur adj having knitted eyebrows

vetull⟋rru'dhur adj 1 having knitted eyebrows 2 = **vetullngry'sur**

vetull⟋shkru'ar adj having beautiful thin eyebrows

vetull⟋tra'shur adj, n (person) with thick eyebrows

vetull⟋u'she nf goat with brown rings around the eyes

vetull⟋va'rur adj = **vetullarë**në

vetull⟋vre'njtur adj having frowning eyebrows

vetull⟋zi adj, n (fem sg ˜ez, masc pl ˜inj, fem pl ˜eza) (person) with very dark eyebrows

***vetun** adv (Reg) = **vetëm**

***vetur** adj (i) densely packed, compressed; dense

veturë nf automobile, car

vetushqye's adj [Biol] capable of manufacturing its own food: (autotrophic)

vetvet'e refl nf self, oneself: myself, yourself, himself, herself, itself, ourselves, yourselves, themselves

vetvet⟋i'shëm adj (i) independent of external influence/cause: self-generated; spontaneous, automatic; independent; personal; natural

vetvet⟋iu adv independently of external influence/cause: spontaneously, automatically, independently; personally; naturally

vetvet⟋o'r adj [Ling] reflexive

vetvet⟋o're nf [Ling] reflexive voice

***vetve't⟋shëm** adj (i) (Old) private

veth nm [Entom] flyblow

***ve'th⟋kë** nf

veza'k adj egg-shaped: oval

vez⟋ara'ke adj, nf egg-laying (hen)

***veze** nf [Invert] dragonfly (Odonata) = **pilive'se**

vezë nf 1 egg 2 [Biol] ovum
  ○ **vezë klluk**ë weak and sickly person
  ○ **vez**ë e **llurbët** soft-boiled egg
  ○ **vez**ë **me dy të verdha/kuq** "like an egg with two yolks" rarity, rare occurrence
  ○ **Vezët në shport**ë e shportën në dorë! "Eggs in the basket and the basket in hand!" (Prov) One must be doubly careful with fragile things.
  ○ **vez**ë e **prishur** "spoiled egg" worthless person
  ○ **U b**ë **veza të mësojë pulën!** "The egg develops far enough to teach the hen!" (Iron) Look who's trying to teach who!
  ○ **vez**ë e **qëruar** "shelled egg" something that is all prepared so as to be easy for the next step
  ○ **vez**ë **syze** egg fried without breaking the yolk: egg sunny-side up

vezë⟋**gjall**ë⟋**pje'll**ës adj [Biol] ovoviviparous

vezë⟋**mbajt**ës adj [Med] oviferous

vezë⟋**ngja'sh**ëm adj ovoid

vezë⟋**pje'll**ës
I § adj [Biol] oviparous
II § nm ovipara

vezë⟋**qeliz**ë nf [Med] ovum, ovulum

vezë⟋**shit**ës n egg-dealer

ve'zë**z** nf [Bot] ovary

vezi'r nm [Hist] vizier

Vezi'r nm Vezir (male name)

ve'zme nf 1 cartridge pouch (worn on the belt) 2 (Old) small box for gunpowder

vezo'r adj = **veza'k**

vezo're nf [Anat Bot] ovary

***vezto**·n vi to form/lay eggs

vezull⟋im nm ger 1 <**vezullo**'·n 2 = **vezullim**ë

vezull⟋imë nf 1 light that is alternately strong and weak: flicker, glitter, glint, flash, glisten, twinkle 2 [Entom] firefly = **xix**ë**llo'nj**ë

vezullo·n vi 1 to shine with alternately strong and weak light: flicker, glitter, glint, flash, glisten, twinkle 2 (Fig) to appear for a brief moment, appear and disappear quickly, flash suddenly

vezull⟋o'jë nf = **vezullo'nj**ë

vezull⟋o'një nf [Entom] firefly = **xix**ë**llo'nj**ë

vezull⟋o'r adj (Poet) = **vezullu'es**

vezull⟋o're nf [Entom] firefly = **xix**ë**llo'nj**ë

vezull⟋u'es adj shining with alternately strong and weak light: flickering, glittering, glinting, flashing, glistening, twinkling

***vezhd**ë nf braid/ribbon used as decorative trim on cloth edges

***vezhd⟋ët** adj (i) trimmed with decorative braid/ribbon

***vezhd⟋o**·n vt to trim with decorative braid braid/ribbon

***ve'zh**ër nf [Entom] earwig

***vezhg** = **vëzhg**

vë· vt 1 to put; place; install 2 to put on: don [clothes]; stage [a play]; affix [ ] to <> 3 to put out [ ] for <>'s use 4 to put [ ] away for later: save 5 to put [ ] forward 6 to use [ ] on <>: put [ ] to <>; push/hit <> with [ ] 7 to set; establish 8 to designate; consider 9 (Colloq) to sow, raise 10 to form [ ] on top
  ○ <> **vë·**³ᵖˡ **ag sytë** 1 <>'s eyes take on a filmy membrane, a filmy membrane forms over the eyes 2 (Fig) <> becomes blind to a danger
  ○ **vë· alarmin** 1 to give the alarm 2 to make a big fuss
  ○ **s'**[ ] **vë· as në majë të gishtit** "not put [ ] even on a fingertip" to consider [ ] to be hopelessly inferior
  ○ <> **vë· balsam** to soothe <>; console <>

○ [] **vë· ballafaqe** to put [] face to face, make [] face each other

○ **vë· ballë për ballë** to put face to face, put into confrontation

○ <> **vë· balluke** to put a cuckold's horns on <*one's husband*>: make <> a cuckold

○ **vë· bark** to get fat; get a potbelly

○ e **vë· barkun në dhé** "put one's belly on the ground" **1** to accept humiliating defeat **2** to grovel

○ e **vë· barkun në ujë** "put one's belly in ujë" to eat nothing

○ e **vë· barrën pas samarit** *(Joke)* to do things backwards, put the cart in front of the horse

○ <> **vë· benzinën** to put <> to the torch; destroy <> completely

○ <> **vë· berihanë** to boo <>

○ **vë· besë kundër <>** to form an alliance against <>

○ <> **vë· besë** to entrust oneself to <>; put one's trust in <>'s hands

○ <> **vë· bërrylin** to give <> the elbow; force <> away/out

○ <> **vë· bina** to fabricate slander against <>

○ u **vë· bojë këpucëve** "put dye on the shoes" to shine shoes with shoe cream

○ <> **vë· brirë** *(Pej)* to put a cuckold's horns on <>: cuckold <>

○ **vë· brumë** to become rich

○ **vë· buç** to swell out on one side

○ **vë· buzën më/në gaz** "put one's lips into a smile" to smile

○ <> **vë· cak** to set limits on <>

○ <> **vë· cipalin** "put the sliver to <>" to force <> out, make [] leave

○ <> **vë· çallmën** to deceive <>

○ <> **vë· çelësin** to lock <> up; close <> up, cease operations of <>

○ i **vë· çelësin shtëpisë 1** to close up the house **2** to bring the family line to a close

○ <> **vë· çullin** to jinx <>, bring bad luck to <>

○ <> **vë· dajakun** "put the cudgel to <>" to use actual force to expel [], kick [] out bodily, run [] out of town

○ **vë· dashuri** to fall in love

○ <> **vë· daullen** to make fun of <> in public

○ ta **vë· dobiçin në prehër** *(Crude)* {} would let you take the blame for something you didn't do

○ **vë· dorashka kadifeje** to feign kindness

○ **vë· dorën në zjarr për** [] "put one's hand in the fire for []" to vouch for [] without reservation

○ **vë· dorën mbi 1** to lend a hand to **2** *(Pej)* to poke/pester; strike, beat **3** *(Pej)* to disturb by touching; filch

○ **vë· dorën në zemër 1** to have pity **2** to sympathize

○ **vë· dorën në plagë 1** to hit a sore spot, touch on a tender subject **2** to find the right remedy

○ **vë· dorën në silah** *(Old)* to get ready to draw one's weapon, put one's hand on one's holster

○ **vë· dorën në zemër për** [] "put one's hand on one's heart for []" to feel compassion for []

○ **vë· dorën në zjarr/prush** "put one's hand/hands in the fire/coals" to be willing to swear to it, be absolutely certain

○ <> **vë· draprin** to reap <> with a sickle; mow <>

○ **vë·**[3sg] **dregëz plaga** the wound forms a scab; the wound/sorrow heals over in time

○ <> **vë· drunë** *(Impol)* to force <> to leave, force <> out; expel <> from an organization: give <> the old heave-ho

○ <> **vë· drynin** to lock <> up; close <> up, cease operations of <>

○ i **vë· drynin gojës** to stop talking

○ i **vë· drynin shtëpisë 1** to close up the house **2** to bring the family line to a close

○ <> **vë· duart në fyt/grykë/gjoks** to put a lot of pressure on <>: hold a knife at <>'s throat?

○ **vë· duart në zjarr/prush** "put one's hand/hands in the fire/coals" to be willing to swear to it, be absolutely certain

○ <> **vë· dyfekun** "put the gun to <>" to fight against <>

○ <> **vë· dyllin** to apply a wax seal to <>, seal <> with wax

○ **vë· dhjamë** "put on fat" **1** to get fat **2** *(Fig)* to get rich

○ **nuk <> vë· faj** not blame; declare <> not guilty

○ <> **vë· ferrën shtëpisë/derës** "put a bramble-bush at the house/door" to destroy a family, bring <>'s family line to an end

○ e **vë· festen mbi sy/mënjanë** "put one's cap over the eyes (and rest)" to have nothing more to worry about, have no more worries, be free of care

○ <> **vë· fitilin** "put the torch/flame/fire/fuse to <>" to put <> to the torch, burn <> up/down; completely destroy <>

○ <> **vë· flakën** "put the torch/flame/fire/fuse to <>" to put <> to the torch, burn <> up/down; completely destroy <>

○ i **vë· fletë gojës (së <>)** "put a sheet in <>'s mouth" to shut <> up, not talk

○ e **vë· foshnjën në tajë** to get a wet nurse for the baby

○ <> **vë· fre** to put a stop/halt to <>; restrain <>

○ i **vë· fre pleshtit** "put a bridle on the flea" to waste time on petty matters; make a fuss about trivia; split hairs

○ <> **vë· fshesën** to get rid of <>

○ <> **vë· fugën** to knock/break <> down, completely ruin <>

○ <> **vë· fund** to put an end to <>

○ <> **vë· gërshërën** "put the scissors to <>" to cut <> with shears, apply the scissors to <>: cut/trim/shear <>, shorten/abridge <>

○ i **vë· gishtin kokës/në kokë** "put one's finger to one's head" to start thinking carefully, do some serious thinking, get one's mind in order

○ **vë· gishtin mbi** to point the finger at

○ **vë· gishtin në plagë 1** to touch a sore point, touch on a tender subject **2** to put one's finger on the problem; find the right remedy

○ i **vë· gojës kanxhën** "put a hook on the mouth" *(Impol)* to keep one's mouth/trap shut, be silent

○ i **vë· gojës lesh** "put wool in the mouth" to put a damper in one's mouth, moderate one's speech; become cautious in one's speech: watch what one says

○ <> **vë· gunën** to hide <> with a cover-up

○ <> **vë· gurët në zemër** "put the rocks on <>'s heart" to use strong coercion on <>

○ <> **vë· gurin e rëndë** "attach a heavy rock to <>" (and throw it in the river) to get rid of <>

○ <> **vë· gurin e varrit** "put the gravestone on <>" to shut the door on <*an issue/problem*> for good: put a lid on <> (so that no one will find out about <>)

○ **vë· gjak** "put blood" to gain weight and become chubby (and thus healthier)

○ <> **vë· gjembin** to pull in the reins on <>, curb <>

○ **nuk vë· gjë në gojë** "not put a thing in the mouth" not eat a thing, not eat

○ **vë· gjilpërat majë më majë** to be at loggerheads

○ **i vë· gjoksin (punës)** to buckle down (to the job), get to work

○ **nuk vë· gjumë në sy** "not put sleep in the eye" not get a wink of sleep

○ <> **vë· gjunët në bark** "put one's heel/knees on <>'s belly" to suppress <> cruelly

○ <> **vë· gjyzlykë** to try to put one over on <>, attempt to fool <>

○ **vë· hardhjen në bisht** "stand a lizard on its tail" to try to do the impossible

○ **vë· inat** to get angry

○ **i vë· jastëk fjalës** to always know what one is talking about

○ **vë· kandidaturën** to run for election

○ <> **vë· kapak** to put a lid on <>: conceal <*a misdeed*>, cover <> up; put an end to <>, bring <> to an end

○ <> **vë· kapakun** to give <> one's stamp of approval

○ **e vë· kapelën** *mbi sy / mënjanë* "put one's cap over the eyes (and rest)" to have nothing more to worry about, have no more worries, be free of care

○ <> **vë· kazmën** to ruin <> completely, make <> a total wreck; damage <> severely

○ <> **vë· këmbën 1** to boot/kick <> out **2** to suppress <>, keep <> under heel **3** to conceal <>; conceal <*a misdeed*>, cover <> up

○ <> **vë· këmbën në fyt/grykë/gjoks** to put a lot of pressure on <>: hold a knife at <>'s throat?

○ **vë· këmbën/këmbët** {*somewhere*} **1** to set foot in/on {} **2** to poke one's nose into {}

○ <>*i* **vë· (të dy) këmbët në një këpucë/opingë 1** to put <> into a difficult position **2** to make <> do one's bidding **3** to give <> a good lesson (in proper behavior)

○ <>*i* **vë· këmbët në rrip të dyfekut** "put <>'s feet <>'s gunstrap" to punish <> severely

○ **e vë· kësulën** *mbi sy / mënjanë* "put one's cap over the eyes (and rest)" to have nothing more to worry about, have no more worries, be free of care

○ [] **vë· klloçkë** to get [] to calm down; get [] to behave

○ **vë· kokën në gërshërë** to put one's head on the line

○ **e vë· kokën në kandar** to put oneself into great danger

○ **e vë· kokën në satër për** [] **1** to swear on one's own head about [] **2** to be willing to stake one's life on []

○ **e vë· kokën në torbë/trastë** to put one's life in great danger, risk one's life

○ **ta vë· kopilin në prehër** (*Crude*) {} would let you take the blame for something you didn't do

○ **vë·**^{3sg} **kore plaga** the wound forms a scab; the wound/sorrow heals over in time

○ <> **vë· kosën** "put the scythe to it" **1** to reap [] with a scythe **2** to cut [] down; obliterate []

○ **i vë· krahët (punës)** to buckle down (to the job), get to work

○ <> **vë· krahët** to wear <> as everyday clothing (instead of on special occasions)

○ **i vë· krahët derës/murit** to put one's shoulder to the wheel

○ **i vë· krahët shtratit** to take to one's bed for a very long time; languish in bed for a long time

○ <> **vë· krusmën 1** to cause <> terrible suffering **2** to exhaust <>; make a shambles of <>

○ **e vë· kryet në torbë/trastë** to put one's life in great danger, risk one's life

○ <> **vë· kryq** to remove <> from a list, remove <> from consideration: cross <> out, cross <> off; have nothing to do with <> any more; give up thinking about <>

○ [] **vë· kryq** to form a cross with []: cross [objects/limbs]

○ <> **vë· kufi** to set limits on <>

○ <>*i* **vë· kufijtë te thana** "set the limits at the cornel tree" to tell <> to keep <>'s nose out of one's business

○ **vë· kujdes për** [] to take (good) care of []; take [] seriously; be careful with []

○ **vë· kujën 1** to yell/bellow angrily **2** to complain loudly and angrily, make a big fuss/to-do

○ **vë· kurorë** to get married

○ <> **vë· kusht** to put a condition on <>

○ <> **vë· kyçin** to lock <> up; close <> up, cease operations of <>

○ **i vë· kyçin gojës** to stop talking

○ **i vë· kyçin shtëpisë 1** to close up the house **2** to bring the family line to a close

○ <> **vë· lakun në fyt/grykë/qafë** "put a noose around <>'s neck" to put heavy pressure on <>: hold a knife to <>'s throat

○ <>*a* **vë· lakun në fyt/grykë/qafë** "put a noose around <>'s neck" to lead <> into a trap, ensnare <>

○ <> **vë· legenin** (*Impol*) to humiliate <> publicly

○ **vë· lemerinë** to howl/wail with terror/grief

○ <> **vë· lerë** to bring <> into dishonor, shame <>

○ <> **vë· lesë** to put an impediment in <>'s way, impede <>

○ <> **vë· lesën** to put an end to <>, shut the door on <>

○ <> **vë· lëkurën e gomarit** "put the donkey skin on <>" to shame <>, humiliate <>

○ <>*a* **vë· lëkurën me** [] to put <> up against [] (in comparison), evaluate <> in comparison with []

○ **vë· lëkurën në rrezik** to put one's life at risk: risk one's skin

○ <> **vë· linjën** to gain supremacy over [], top []

○ <> **vë· litarin në fyt/grykë/qafë** "put a noose around <>'s neck" to put heavy pressure on <>: hold a knife to <>'s throat

○ <>*a* **vë· litarin në fyt/grykë/qafë** "put a noose around <>'s neck" to lead <> into a trap, ensnare <>

○ <> **vë· lulen** to sell <> quickly (out of necessity)

○ <> **vë· majën** "put the tip on <>" to finish [] successfully: pull [] off

○ **ia vë· majën mullarit** "put the top on the haystack" to get the job done, get the problem solved

○ **vë· mall (të madh)** to amass (a lot of) material objects

○ **(nuk) i vë· masë gojës** "(not) put proper limits on one's speech" (not) speak responsibly

○ <> **vë· mbarë e mbarë** to put/arrange <> into proper order

○ **e vë· me bast** to bet

○ [] **vë· me shpatulla** *në mur / pas murit* "put [] with []'s back to the wall" to force [] to admit guilt/defeat

○ e **vë· me inat me** [] to do it to spite []; do it in response to a challenge by []

○ [] **vë· me** [] to put [] on the same level with [], compare [] to []

○ <> **vë· mend** to pay close attention to <>; be careful with <>

○ **vë· mend 1** to learn a (good) lesson, learn from bitter experience **2** to be obedient, listen

○ [] **vë· në/ndër mend/në mendje** to keep [] in mind, make a mental note of []

○ <> **vë· mendjen** to pay close attention to <>; be careful with <>

○ **vë· merak** to feel worried; feel uneasy

○ <> **vë· minat** to blow <> sky high, destroy; undermine <>

○ **vë· mish** "put flesh" to put on weight; get fat

○ <> **vë· mokrat në këmbë** "put millstones on <>'s feet" to hobble/hinder <> badly

○ [] **vë· në ankand 1** to auction off [], put [] up for auction **2** (Fig) to treat [something sacred and precious] as if it something cheap

○ [] **vë· në balancë** to weigh [] carefully = **baraspesh**ë

○ [] **vë· në bazë** [] to make [] one's cornerstone, take [] as fundamental

○ [] **vë· në be** to put [] on/under oath, make [] swear

○ [] **vë· në bigë** to put [] into a difficult position

○ [] **vë· në bisht/grykë të lahutës** to take jabs at []: mock [], make fun of []

○ [] **vë· në bisht** to hold [] in low esteem

○ **vë· në blojë** (Pej) to go ya-ta-ta, ya-ta-ta; begin to talk non-stop, start to grind away like a mill

○ [] **vë· në brazdë** to put [] back on the right track

○ **s'**[] **vë· në brinjë** (Impol) to refuse to marry [], turn [] down as husband or wife

○ e **vë· në çetele** to make a mark as a reminder

○ **s'**[] **vë· në defter 1** to stop caring about []; stop paying attention to [] **2** not take [] into consideration

○ [] **vë· në dijeni (për** []**)** to give [] information (about []), let [] know (about [])

○ [] **vë· në diskutim 1** to put [] up for discussion **2** to question [], dispute []

○ [] **vë· në dorë 1** to succeed in catching []; get [] (into one's possession) **2** to have [] in the palm of one's hand, have [] where one wants []

○ [] **vë· në dritë** to bring [] to light

○ e **vë· në dukje se** __ to emphasize that __; point out that __

○ **vë· në dukje** to mention; emphasize

○ [] **vë· në dyshim** to doubt/question []

○ [] **vë· në dyzen** to tune [a stringed musical instrument]

○ [] **vë· në fije** to put [] in order, make [] go well

○ [] **vë· në funksionim** to put [] into operation; cause/get [] to function properly, get [] to work?

○ **vë· në gaz** to make [] a laughingstock

○ [] **vë· në gaz** to deride/mock []

○ [e] **vë· në gji** "put [a baby] to the breast" to breast-feed []

○ [] **vë· në gjumë *1** to put [] asleep; bore [] to death **2** to make [] unwatchful: lull [] into complacency

○ [] **vë· në gjunjë** to force [] to []'s knees, subjugate []

○ **s'**[] **vë· (fare) në hesap** to give (absolutely) no consideration to [], not (even) to consider [], ignore [] (completely)

○ [] **vë· në hije të hostenit** to take good care of [], put under one's aegis

○ [] **vë· në hije të rigonit** to give unmerited protection to []

○ [] **vë· në hije** to shelter [], take [] in; take care of [], look after []

○ [] **vë· në hulli** to get [] to behave properly

○ **vë· në jetë** to put into effect/practice

○ **s'**[] **vë· në kalem** not take [] into account; pay no attention to [], not even consider []

○ **nuk** [] **vë· në kandar** not give [] due consideration

○ [] **vë· në katror** (Book) to get [someone] into a hopeless predicament; get [someone] hopelessly entangled

○ [] **vë· në komandë 1** to put [] in charge **2** to give [] top priority

○ [] **vë· në korrent** to keep [someone] current

○ [] **vë· në lesë** to lead [] into a trap

○ [] **vë· në lëvizje** to put [] into motion; activate

○ [] **vë· në lidhje** to link [] up

○ [] **vë· në litar** "put [] on a rope" to hang [someone], string [] up

○ [] **vë· në lojë** to play around with []; try to make [] feel foolish

○ e **vë· në lotari** to determine the matter by lot, to decide by drawing straws

○ **s'**[] **vë· në llogari/hesap (fare)** to give (absolutely) no consideration to [], not (even) to consider [], ignore [] (completely)

○ [] **vë· në majë të gjilpërës** "put [] on the tip of a needle" to expose [] to public view

○ [] **vë· në majmëri** to put [a livestock animal] into a fattening pen

○ [] **vë· në mendime** to give [] occasion for thought, give [] something to think about

○ [] **vë· në mengene** to tighten the screws on []

○ [] **vë· në mundim 1** to put [] to a lot of trouble **2** to give [] lot of trouble

○ [] **vë· në nishan** to aim [a weapon] at a target

○ **s'**[] **vë· në numër** not (even) count [], not consider []

○ [] **vë· në një plan** to put [] in the same category, consider [] as equal

○ **vë· në një radhë me** [] to put on the same level as [], consider as equal to []

○ [] **vë· në peshë** "put [] on a scale" to weigh/consider [] carefully

○ [] **vë· në pikëpyetje** to put [] in question, make [] questionable; consider [] questionable/suspicious

○ [] **vë· në plan** to have [] in one's plans, have [] in mind

○ [] **vë· në plumb** to kill [] by shooting: shoot []

○ [] **vë· në provë** to put [] to the test, try [] out

○ [] **vë· në pushkën** "put [] on a gun" to shoot [] down

○ [] **vë· në pyka** to make fun of [], ridicule []

○ <>[] **vë· në qafë** "hang [] onto <>'s neck" to place [a burden] on <>

○ [] **vë· në qendër** [Tech] to center [] (on its axis of rotation)

○ [] **vë· në rabush** to keep [] in mind

○ **nuk** [] **vë· në refene** "not invite [] to the party" not give [] the slightest consideration; not bother to take [] into consideration

○ [] **vë· në rregull** to put [] in order, get [] working, fix []

○ [] **vë· në rrezik** to put [] in danger, put [] at risk

○ [] **vë· në rrugë të mbarë** to set [] on the proper path

○ <> **vë· në satër** to chop off <>'s head; kill off <>

○ [] **vë· në sirtar** "put [] in a drawer" *(Pej)* to file [] away instead of taking care of it

○ [] **vë· në skuadër** to use a try square on []

○ [] **vë· në shënjestër/shenjë** to target [] for criticism; keep [] under constant attack

○ [] **vë· në shfrytëzim** to put [] into utilization

○ [] **vë· në shitje** to put [] up for sale

○ [] **vë· në sitë e në shoshë** to make fun of []

○ [] **vë· në tallje** to make fun of []; ridicule []

○ [] **vë· në tupan 1** to make fun of [] in public **2** to spread the dirt/scandal about []

○ <> **vë· në thikë** to set <> at each other's throats

○ [] **vë· në thua** [] doesn't even enter into {}'s account, {} doesn't consider [] to be in the same league

○ [] **vë· në udhë/rrugë/vijë/binarë** to put [] on the proper/right track; straighten [] out

○ [] **vë· në ujdi** to make sure that [] is done right, arrange [] properly

○ [] **vë· në vaj 1** to put [] in good order: fix [] **2** to soothe [], calm [] down

○ [] **vë· në varr/dhe *për së gjalli / të gjallë*** "put [] in the grave alive: bury [] alive" to bring [] to an early grave

○ [] **vë· në vathë 1** to get [] under complete control **2** to spring a trap on []

○ [] **vë· në vazhdë** to put [] on the right track, get [] to behave properly

○ [] **vë· në vend 1** to pull in the reins on <>, discipline <>, set <> straight **2** to replace [] (with a substitute) **3** to regain []

○ [] **vë· në veprim** to put [] into action; activate

○ [] **vë· në xhep 1** to keep [] in mind **2** to try never to forget []; make a reminder of [] for future revenge

○ [] **vë· në xhepin e pasmë** not worry about [] anymore: put [] all behind one

○ [] **vë· në skenë** to stage [], put on []

○ **vë· nën çizme** to put under the iron heel, oppress, subjugate

○ [] **vë· nën hije të hostenit** to take good care of [], put under one's aegis

○ [] **vë· nën këmbë** to suppress [], subjugate [], dominate []

○ [] **vë· nën komandë** to force [] to obey; subjugate []

○ [] **vë· nën kontroll** to get [] under control; put [] under (one's) control

○ [] **vë· nën ujë** to provide irrigation for [a piece of land]

○ [] **vë· nën vete 1** to put [] under one's own control **2** to force [] to submit, put [] under one's rule: subjugate [] **3** to surpass/outdo []

○ **vë· ngulmin** to keep persisting, persist

○ **vë· nishan** to put up a target

○ **i vë· një gur zemrës** to put aside one's feelings, harden one's heart

○ <> **vë· një pikëpyetje** to put <> in question, make <> questionable; consider <> questionable/suspicious

○ <> **vë· njollë** to stain <>'s reputation; dishonor []

○ <> **vë· ombrellë** "put the umbrella over <>" **1** to do a cover-up on <>, hide <> from the public **2** to impede <>

○ [] **vë· para përgjegjësisë** to call [] to account

○ <> **vë· pehriz gojës** to be more careful about one's language, watch what one says: put a muzzle on one's mouth

○ [] **vë· (si) peng 1** to give [] as hostage **2** to pawn/mortgage []

○ **nuk** [] **vë· për faqe** not give much thought to []

○ [] **vë· për fije** to put [] on the right path

○ [] **vë· përpara 1** to push forward victoriously against [] **2** to put forth the argument that defeats [] **3** to squelch []

○ <> **vë· pikë** to put an end to <> once and for all

○ <> **vë· pishën** "put the torch/flame/fire/fuse to <>" to put <> to the torch, burn <> up/down; completely destroy <>

○ **vë· plaçkë (të madhe)** to amass (a lot of) material objects

○ **i vë· pleshtit zile** "put a bell on the flea" to tell a tall story; make a mountain out of a molehill

○ **e vë· plëndësin në kokë** "put the tripe on one's head" to lose all sense of shame

○ **i vë· plloçën** to put an end to the matter, put a lid on it

○ [] **vë· poshtë 1** to knock [] down **2** to beat/defeat []

○ <> **vë· prangat** to put the handcuffs on <>; arrest <>

○ <> **vë· pritë** "lay an ambush for <>" to put impediments in <>'s path, impede/hinder <>

○ **vë· pulën në zogj** "put the hen on the chicks" to get matters in order, get things arranged properly

○ **e vë· punën nën vete** to get on top of one's work

○ **e vë· punën përpara** to have the work well in hand; have finished the bulk of the work

○ **i vë· punët me rradhë** to put matters in good order

○ **i vë· punët në hulli** to put one's affairs into good shape

○ <> **vë· pushkën** "put the gun to <>" to fight against <>

○ **vë· qafën në zgjedhë** "put one's own neck in the yoke" to take on a very hard task willingly

○ <> **vë· qafolin** to give <> a very tough job to do

○ **e vë· qeleshen *mbi sy / mënjanë*** "put one's cap over the eyes (and rest)" to have nothing more to worry about, have no more worries, be free of care

○ **i vë· qokë fjalës** to speak cautiously

○ <> **vë· qysqinë** to destroy <> utterly

○ **rakia vë·**[3sg] **zinxhir** "the raki forms chains (of bubbles when shaken)" the raki is very strong

○ <> **vë· re** to attach importance to <>; give consideration to <>; pay (too much) attention to <>

○ **vë· re** to notice; observe; pay attention

○ **i vë· rezen derës/shtëpisë** "put the latch on the door/house" to die and bring one's family line to an end

○ <> **vë· rraxhën** to level <> to the ground

○ **vë· rregull** to get everything in order

○ **i vë· rreth kokës** "put a circle around the head" to get oneself into a tight spot

○ <> **vë· saçin** to put <> in a difficult situation: put <> in a tight spot

○ **vë· sedër (me** []) to make a challenge (against [])

○ **vë· sedër** to give one's all, put everything one's got into it

○ <> **vë· sëpatën** "put the axe to it" to chop <> with an axe

○ **vë· sineri me** [] to be envious/jealous of []

○ [] **vë· stavë** to place [] in a stack: stack []

○ <> *a* **vë· syrin** "one's eye *lands* on <>" **1** to choose <> for the task **2** to take a liking to <>

○ <> **vë· syze** to try to put one over on <>, attempt to fool <>

○ <> **vë· sharrën** "put the saw to it" **1** to saw <> **2** to destroy <> completely

○ <> **vë· shenjën** to mark <> for special treatment

○ <> **vë· shiritat** *(Colloq)* to commission <> (as an officer in the military)

○ <> **vë· shkelmin** to let <> go to ruin; squander <>

○ <> **vë· shkelmin në bark** "put one's heel/knees on <>'s belly" to suppress <> cruelly

○ <> **vë· shkelmin në fyt/grykë/gjoks** to put a lot of pressure on <>: hold a knife at <>'s throat?

○ <> **vë· shkopinj në rrota** "put sticks into <>'s wheels" to deliberately cause <> problems, sabotage <>

○ i **vë· shpatullat (punës)** (to buckle down (to the job), get to work

○ **vë· shpresat te** { } to put/pin one's hopes on <>

○ i **vë· shtupën gojës** "put *oakum//a cork* in one's mouth" to keep one's mouth shut, shut up

○ <> **vë· shulin** "use the iron bar on <>" to break/bash <> down; utterly destroy <>

○ e **vë· takijen** *mbi sy/mënjanë* "put one's cap over the eyes (and rest)" to have nothing more to worry about, have no more worries, be free of care

○ **vë· tallën** to stack cornstalks

○ **vë· tamah** to be greedy

○ i **vë· tapën gojës** "put *oakum//a cork* in one's mouth" to keep one's mouth shut; shut up

○ **vë telat** "put on wires (as if adorning a bride)" *(Colloq)* to get all dressed up

○ **vë· tellallin** to make a hullabaloo so that the whole world knows about it; let the whole world in on it

○ <> **vë· teneqenë** *(Impol)* to humiliate <> publicly

○ **vë· termometrin** "put the thermometer" to take someone's temperature

○ **të vë· në bisht të lugës** "put you on the handle of the spoon" to be able to have you dancing on a stick, be able to wrap you around one's little finger

○ <> **vë· torpilë** to torpedo <>, completely wreck <>

○ <> **vë·thembrën në qafë** "put one's heel/foot on <>'s neck" to vanquish/subjugate <>; put <> under one's thumb

○ <> **vë· themelet e <>** to establish the foundations of <>: found <>, establish <>

○ <> **vë· thikën** "put the knife to <>" to cut <> with a knife; butcher/slaughter <> with a knife

○ <> **vë· thonjtë në grykë** to grab <> by the throat; strangle <> with one's bare hands

○ **nuk e vë· ujin në zjarr** "not put water on the fire (to boil)" to be totally unconcerned/indifferent

○ **vë· ujkun bari** "put the wolf as shepherd" to put the fox to guard the chickencoop

○ **vë· ulërimën** to start howling; begin the wailing (for the dead)

○ [ ] **vë· vath në vesh** "put [ ] as an earring in one's ear" to try never to forget [ ]; make a reminder of [ ] for future revenge

○ <> **vë· vegël** "put a tool on <>" *(Pej Reg)* to attach something to <>

○ **vë· vesh/veshin** to try to hear, listen carefully; listen in, try to overhear

○ <> **vë· veshin/veshët** to listen to <>, heed <>, respect what <> says; pay close attention to <>

○ e **vë· veten në lëkurën e <>** "put oneself into <>'s skin" to imagine oneself in <>'s position: put oneself in <>'s shoes/place

○ **vë· veton (në** [ ]) to exercise one's veto (against [ ])

○ **vë·.**[3sg] **veth mishi** "the meat puts flyblow" the meat has become flyblown

○ <> **vë· vigmën** to yell hard at <>, scold <> severely

○ <> **vë· vijë/vizë 1** to draw a line through <>, line <> out **2** to wash one's hands of <>, have nothing more to do with <>

○ <> **vë· vulën** to put one's stamp of approval on <>

○ <> **vë· xixën** to ignite <>

○ **vë·zemrën në dorë** to put oneself totally into <>'s hands

○ i **vë· zile miut** "put a bell on one's mouse" to make up absurd lies, spread false tales

○ <> **vë· zjarr/zjarrin** "put the fire to <>" to set <> on fire; put <> to the torch, burn <> up/down; completely destroy <>

*vëgjïle nf = vigjïlje

*vëjyer adj (i) = vyer

vëlla nm brother

○ vëlla i gjetur stepbrother

○ vëlla pa hise *(Reg)* [Ethnog] male friend who pledges fellowship to another (by drinking a drop of the other's blood): blood brother = vëllam

○ vëlla për babë "brother through father" half brother

○ vëlla për nënë "brother through mother" half brother

○ Vëllai për vëllanë. *(Prov)* Brothers have to help each other out.

○ vëlla prej babait/nënës "brother from the father/mother" half brother

○ vëlla qumështi "milk brother" brother only in the sense of having shared the same wet nurse

○ vëlla shpirti "soul brother" blood brother = vëllam

vëllaçko nf with masc agreement *(Colloq Pet)* = vëlla

*vëllako = vëllaçko

vëllam nm **1** [Ethnog] male friend who pledges fellowship to another (by drinking a drop of the other's blood): blood brother **2** member of bridegroom's party who accompanies the bride at the wedding ceremony; child who stands next to the bride or groom at the wedding ceremony

vëllamërï nf [Ethnog] fellowship/fraternity pledged by blood; blood brotherhood

vëllamï nf [Ethnog] = vëllamërï

vëllath nm *(Pet)* = vëlla

vëllavrasës adj *(Book)* fratricidal

vëllavrasje nf *(Book)* fratricide

vëllazërï nf **1** brotherhood; fraternal fellowship; fraternal group, fraternity **2** [Ethnog] subgroup of families with a recent common ancestor within a patrilineal clan

vëllazërïm nm ger **1** <vëllazëro·n, vëllazëro·het **2** brotherhood

vëllazërïsht adv in brotherly fashion; together as brothers

vëllazëro·n

I § vt to imbue [ ] with brotherly feelings; make fraternal peace between [ ]

II § vi (of multiple stalks) to sprout from a common root

vëllazëro·het vpr **1** to settle into a brotherly relationship, enjoy fraternal peace **2** to fraternize **3** [Ethnog] to pledge blood brotherhood

vëllazëror adj fraternal, brotherly

vëllazëru̇ar adj (i) imbued with brotherly feelings; enjoying fraternal peace

vëlla zi *nm (np ~ nj) (Colloq)* unfortunate brother; brother in name only

vëlle shë *nf* brother's wife, sister-in-law

vëlle zër *np* **1** <*vëlla* **2** [*Bot*] multiple stalks sprouted from a common root
  ◦ **Vëllezër jemi, shok s'jemi.** We may be brothers, but that doesn't mean we are the same.
  ◦ **vëllezër nga dy barqesh** half brothers (with different mothers)
  ◦ **vëllezër nga një bark** half brothers (from the same mother)
  ◦ **vëllezër të një vatre** brothers born and raised in the same house

vëllim *nm* volume

vëllimmat ës *nm* [*Spec*] volumeter

vëllimo r *adj* [*Spec*] pertaining to volume

vëllimshëm *adj (i)* voluminous

*__vëllimtar__ *adj* = vëllimshëm

vëme ndje *nf* mental focus/concentration, attention; special care, consideration
  ◦ **vëmendje e pavullnetshme** [*Psych*] obsession

vëme ndshëm *adj (i)* attentive

vën *stem for opt, adm, part* <*vë*·

vënç *stem for opt* <*vë*·
  ◦ <> **vënçin zilet!** "May they put the bells on <>!" *(Curse)* May <> be publicly shamed! Shame on <>!

*__vënd__ = vend

*__vënd o r__ *adj (Reg)* latch, catch, clasp

vë në
  I § *part* <*vë*·
  II § *adj (i)* **1** artificial **2** brought from elsewhere, imported; grown from a sprout brought in, rather than directly from seed **3** *(Colloq)* put away for later: saved **4** *(Fig)* put up to doing something bad by someone else
  ◦ **sy i vënë** artificial eye, glass eye

vëng *nm (np ~ gje)* **1** wooden rim of a cart/wagon wheel; one section of such a rim: felly **2** hole along the edge of a moccasin for the lacing thong; lacing thong **3** wooden stake (stuck in the ground and tied to something): tether stake, tent stake **4** peg on which to hang something **5** *(Fig)* pretext, excuse **6** *(Reg)* chain **7** *(Reg)* premonition, omen; anxiety

vëngar ash *adj, n* = vëngërosh

vëngër
  I § *adj (i)* **1** having improperly focused/coordinated eyes: cross-eyed, wall-eyed, squint-eyed **2** *(Fig)* complicated, confusing; contumacious, difficult
  II § *adv* **1** cross-eyed; askance **2** *(Fig)* with antipathy; suspiciously
  ◦ **shikim/vështrim i vëngër** "crosseyed look" look that expresses contempt/disrespect/anger/envy/mistrust

vëngëri *nf* **1** cross-eye, squint **2** [*Med*] strabismus *()*

vëngërim *nm ger* <vëngëro·*n*, vëngëro·*het*

vëngërisht *adv* = vëngër

vëngëro ·het *vpr* **1** to become cross-eyed/wall-eyed **2** *(Fig)* to lose one's ability to see things correctly; become perverse in outlook **3** = shtrëmbëro·*het*

vëngëro ·n
  I § *vi* to go awry for <>; (of eyes) look cross-eyed; look askance; squint
  II § *vt* to give [] a scathing look

vëngëro sh *adj, n* cross-eyed/cockeyed (person)

vëngërsi [*Med*] = vëngëri

vëngërt *adj (i)* = vëngër

vëngo ·n
  I § *vt, vi* = vëngëro·*n*
  II § *vi* **1** to go crooked, veer to one side; limp on one foot **2** to resound

vëngo sh *adj, n* = vëngërosh

vëng thi *adv* moving sidewise

vënie *nf ger* <vë·, vi·*het*

vër *stem for imper* <vë·
  ◦ **Vëri majat nga thembrat!** "Put your toes where your heels were!" Turn right around and get ere!.

vërca k *nm* butcher's cleaver

vërda llë
  I § *nf* **1** whirlwind **2** *(Fig)* confused mess
  II § *adv* around and around
  ◦ **i vje·n vërdallë** to go at it by a circuitous route, approach the matter indirectly; speak indirectly

vërda llës
  I § *adj* wandering, roaming
  II § *n* wanderer, roamer

vërdallo s· *vt* to wander, roam

vërda t·et *vpr (Colloq)* to assail <>: let loose on <>

*__vërdo ·n__ *vi* to toil, work hard

vëre·n *vt* **1** to watch [] attentively, look at [] attentively: observe **2** to notice; note **3** to watch out for [] **4** to look after [], take care of []
  ◦ [] **vëre·n me bishtin e syrit 1** to see [] out of the corner of the eye **2** to disparage [], undervalue []

vërejshëm *adj (i)* noticeable, observable

vëre jt *stem for pdef, opt, adm, part* <vëre·*n*

vëre jt ës *n* observer = vëzhgues

vëre jtje *nf ger* **1** <vëre·*n*, vëre·*het* **2** attention **3** critical observation; disciplinary warning; disciplinary/punitive judgment

vërë *nf (Reg)* = vrimë

*__vërgâ(n)__ *nm (pl ~ j) (Reg Gheg)* = vargër

*__vërga ç__ *nm* = vargër

*__vërge nj__ *np* <vargër

*__vërgli m__ *nm ger* <vërglo·*n*

*__vërglo ·n__ *vt* to quiver

*__vërgjill të__ *adj (i)* agile, nimble

*__vërgjiri__ = virgjëri

*__vërke qe__ *nf* owl

*__vërkë__ *nf dimin (Reg)* small hole

vërs ë *nf (Colloq)* age
  ◦ **të një vërsë** of the same age

vërs ník
  I § *adj (Colloq)* of the same age
  II § *n* age-mate

vërsul·et *vpr* **1** to rush forward; rush at/toward <>; dash forward **2** to attack with a rush: assail <>

vërsu lje *nf ger* <vërsul·*et*

vërshëlle·n *vi* to whistle = fishkëlle·*n*

vërshëllim *nm ger* = fishkëllim

vërshëllimë *nf* = fishkëllimë

vërshëllye s *adj* = fishkëllyes

vërshim *nm ger* **1** <vërsho·*n* **2** overflow, flood; cloudburst, downpour; spurt

vërsho·n *vi* **1** to flood, overflow **2** to pour out in a sudden flow: spurt/burst out **3** to rush, pour

vërshue s *adj* flooding out

*__vërte__ *adv, pcl* = vërtet

vërtet· *adv, pcl* truly; really, actually
  ◦ **vërtet që __** while it is true that __: even though __

vërtet· *vt (Colloq)* to confirm

vërtet·et *vpr (Colloq)* to be a witness, testify

vërtet'az *adv* truly, really

vërtete'së *nf (Old)* certificate, affidavit

vërtet'ë
  I § *adj (i)* true
  II § *nf (e)* that which is true, something true: truth
  ∘ **të them/themi të vërtetën** "were I/we to tell the truth" (parenthetical) to tell the truth, actually

vërtet'ësi *nf* = veracity, truth

vërtet'im *nm ger* 1 <**vërteto·n**, **vërteto·het** 2 confirmation 3 certificate

vërteto·het *vpr* to turn out to be true: be confirmed/ substantiated, prove right, be borne out

vërteto·n *vt* 1 to confirm; verify 2 *[Math]* to prove [a theorem]

vërtet'shëm *adj (i)* true = **vërtet'ë**

vërtet'ua'r *adj (i)* proven, proved

vërtet'ue's
  I § *adj* confirming, affirming, certifying
  II § *n* 1 confirmer, affirmer; verifier, certifier 2 *(Old)* customs inspector

vërtet'ue'shëm *adj (i)* verifiable

***vërtëll'im** *nm ger* 1 <**vërtëllo·n** 2 rotation, turn, spin, revolution 3 chatter

***vërtëllo·n** *vt* 1 to rotate, turn, spin, revolve 2 to chatter

***vërtëll'ue's**
  I § *adj* talkative
  II § *n* chatterbox

vërtik *nm* sudden force; rush

vërtik'shëm *adj (i)*, *adv* = **vrikshëm**

vërt'is *stem for 1st sg pres, pl pres, 2nd & 3rd sg subj, pind* <**vërtit·**

vërtit· *vt* 1 to rotate, turn, spin, revolve 2 *(Fig)* to make [] do what one wants: run [] around (by the nose) 3 *(Fig Colloq Pej)* to give [] the runaround; use a dodge to go back on [something said] 4 *(Fig)* to fix up [a matter] by improper means
  ∘ [] **vërtit· nëpër mendje** to turn [] over and over in one's mind

vërtit·et *vpr* 1 to revolve, rotate, spin 2 to turn from one side to another: toss and turn; turn this way and that 3 to wander around 4 to stay close to <>, hang around <> 5 *(Fig)* to keep coming back to the same topic 6 *(Fig Colloq)* to shift sails with every turn of the wind; be evasive in answering; behave in a wily fashion

vërtit'je *nf ger* 1 <**vërtit·**, **vërtit·et** 2 revolution, rotation

***vërty't** *nm* 1 (bodily) strength 2 exertion, strain

***vërty't'shëm** *adj (i)* strong, powerful

vërv'is *stem for 1st sg pres, pl pres, 2nd & 3rd sg subj, pind* <**vërvit·**

vërv'it· *vt* to hurl

vërv'it·et *vp reflex* to hurl oneself

vërv'it'je *nf ger* <**vërvit·**, **vërvit·et**

vërzo'me *nf* 1 *[Fish]* trawlnet, gill net 2 *[Agr]* sacklike net made of rope mesh used to carry hay/straw

vërra's *stem for 1st sg pres, 1st & 3rd pl pres, 2nd & 3rd sg subj* <**vërret·**

vërret· *vi* 1 to bleat 2 *(Pej)* to screech

vërri *nm* 1 sheltered low ground, lee hollow 2 winter pasture 3 *[Bot]* alder *(Alnus)* = **verr** 4 *[Bot]* kind of buckthorn *(Rhamnus fallax)*

vërrim'ë *nf* = **virrmë**

vërri's
  I § *stem for 1st sg pres, pl pres, 2nd & 3rd sg subj, pind* <**vërrit·**
  II § *stem for 2nd pl pres, pind* <**vërret·**

vërri'shte *OR* **vërri'shtë** *nf* winter pasture

vërri't· *vt* to take [livestock] to winter pasture; give fodder to [livestock]

vërrit *stem for pdef, opt, adm, part, pind, 2nd pl pres, imper, vp* <**vërret·**

vërri'ta'r *n* person who takes livestock to winter pasture

***vërrna'l** *adj* huge, massive, gigantic

vërro·n *vi* (of livestock) to spend the winter in winter pasture

***vëshkëll** = **fishkëll**

vëshna'k *nm* 1 = **çurg** *2 ditch

***vëshn'ik** = **vërsnik**

***vësht** *nm* = **vresht**

***vështi'll** = **mbështill**

vështir· *vt* = **pështiro·s·**

vështir·et *vpr* = **pështiro's·et**

vështi'r'a *np (të)* worries, troubles

vështir'ë
  I § *adj (i)* 1 difficult 2 *(Fig)* disgusting, loathsome
  II § *nn (të)* disgust, loathing
  III § *adv* 1 with difficulty 2 it is hard, it would be hard; hardly, hardly ever

vështir'ësi *nf* 1 difficulty; hardship 2 impediment; handicap

vështir'ësim *nm ger* 1 <**vështirëso·n**, **vështirëso·het** 2 = **vështirësi**

vështir'ësi'në *nf* = **vështirësi**

vështir'ëso·het *vpr* to become difficult; become more difficult

vështir'ëso·n *vt* to make [] (more) difficult: impede, hinder; handicap

vështiro·het *vpr* 1 = **vështirëso·het** 2 = **pështiro's·et**

vështiro·n *vt* 1 = **vështirëso·n** 2 = **pështiro's·**

vështiro's· *vt* = **pështiro's·**

vështiro's·et *vpr* = **pështiro's·et**

vështiro'sje *nf ger* <**pështiro's·**, **vështiro's·et**

vështir'shëm *adj (i)* = **vështi'rë**

***vështje'll·** = **mbështjell·**

***vështo·n** = **vështro·n**

***vështo'll** = **mbështoll**

***vështo'r** *nm* = **bekçi'**

vështr'im *nm ger* 1 <**vështro·n**, **vështro·het** 2 look, glance 3 expression conveyed by the eyes: look 4 *(Fig)* point of view, view 5 meaning, sense 6 summary view: survey, summary 7 eyesight
  ∘ **me/në vështrimin e parë** at first sight, right from the start
  ∘ **vështrim i thellë** meaningful look/glance

vështro·het *vp reflex* to look at oneself

vështro·n
  I § *vt* to watch [], look at [] 2 to look after [], see to [] 3 to examine, consider
  II § *vi* to look
  ∘ [] **vështro·n me bishtin e syrit** 1 to see [] out of the corner of the eye 2 to disparage [], undervalue []
  ∘ **vështro·n me ngulm** to watch <> constantly, not take one's eyes off <>

○ [] **vështro·**_n_ **me sy të shtrembër/keq/lig 1** to have a low regard for []; look at/on [] with disfavor **2** to have no interest in []'s welfare

○ [] **vështro·**_n_ **me sytë të mprehtë** to observe [] with a keen eye, watch [] attentively

○ **vështro·**_n_ **nën ballë** to have a look of anger/hatred on one's face

○ [] **vështro·**_n_ **nën qepalla** "look at [] under the eyelids" not look at [] in the eye

○ **vështro·**_n_ **nga qofkat** "look at the blackbirds" to keep shifting one's gaze, let one's attention wander

○ **vështro·**_n_ **nga** {} to have a view of {}, look out on {}

○ **vështro·**_n_ **për** [] to be thinking of [], be considering []

○ [] **vështro·**_n_ **si ujku hënën** "look at [] like the wolf at the moon" to give [] an angry stare, look at [] with anger

○ [] **vështro·**_n_ **shtrembër 1** to have a low regard for []; look at/on [] with disfavor **2** to have no interest in []'s welfare **3** to look daggers at []

○ [] **vështro·**_n_ **vëngër 1** to have a low regard for []; look at/on [] with disfavor **2** to have no interest in []'s welfare **3** to look daggers at []

vështru'a_r_ _nn (të)_ look, glance

vëth _nm_ = vath

vëth'ato_r_ _adj_ = vathato'r

vëth'e _np_ = vatho're

vëz'ëlli·_n_ _vi_ (of insects) to buzz

vëz'ëlli'm_ë_ _nf_ buzzing, buzz, hum

vëzhg'i'm _nm ger_ **1** <vëzhgo'·_n_, vëzhgo'·_het_ **2** observation; inspection; examination **3** care; supervision

vëzhgo'·_het_ _vpr_ to be noted/observed: occur

vëzhgo'·_n_ _vt_ to observe; inspect; examine

vëzhgu'e_s_

_I_ § _adj_ **1** observant **2** [_Mil_] used for observation purposes: scouting, reconnaissance

_II_ § _n_ observer

VFLP _abbrev_ <**Vdekje fashizmit-liri popullit** Death to Fascism – Freedom to the People

vgje(r) _nm (np ~ nj)_ [_Bot_] **1** Austrian pine (_Pinus nigra Arn._) **2** Italian stone pine, umbrella pine (_Pinus pinea_)

vgjer'ishtë _nf_ pine forest

vgje'sht_ë_

_I_ § _nf_ = vgjer'isht_ë_

_II_ § _adj (i)_ made of pine

*****vgjo'll**_ë_ = gjo'll_ë_

vi·_het_ _vpr_ <**vë·** **1** to place oneself **2** to apply oneself to <> **3** to follow <> closely, stick close to <>; keep after <>, importune <>: hound <> **4** (_Colloq_) (followed by a verb in the subjunctive) to begin to __

○ <> **vi·**_het_³ˢ⁹ **futa (një shtëpie)** "the black kerchief is put on <>'s house" <>'s family line is brought to an end by a series of deaths

○ <> **vi·**_het_ **në shpinë** to stay right at <>'s back, follow <> closely behind

○ **vi·**_het_ **në binarë/vijë** to get on the right track/road, take the right path.

○ **vi·**_het_ **në bisht** to lag/remain behind, stay in the rear

○ **vi·**_het_ **në ikje** to take flight, run away

○ **vi·**_het_ **në krye/ballë** to take the lead; take over the leadership

○ **vi·**_het_ **në lojë** to be at stake

○ **vi·**_het_ **në një radhë me** [] to keep up with []

○ **vi·**_het_ **në rrugë** to set off (for a trip/journey)

○ **po vi·**_het_ **në shëndet** to be regaining one's health, be getting better

○ **nuk vi·**_het_ **në xhep** not be worthy of trust: not to be relied on

○ <> **vi·**_het_³ˢ⁹ **njolla me bojë** "be left with dyed spots" <> _is_ stained with shame forever

○ **vi·**_het_ **pas** to tail <>

○ **vi·**_het_ **për rrugë** to set off (for a trip/journey)

○ <> **vi·**_het_³ˢ⁹ **ruba (një shtëpie)** "the black kerchief (sign of mourning) is put on <>'s house" <>'s family line is brought to an end by a series of deaths

○ **vi·**_het_³ˢ⁹ **rresht** to get in line: line up

vi'

_I_ § _stem for pind, 2nd pl pres_ <**ve·te**

_II_ § _stem for 2nd pl pres, pind, imper, vp_ <**vë·**

○ **Vini re!** Notice!

viadu'kt _nm_ [_Constr_] viaduct

via'sk_ë_ = vja'sk_ë_

vibracio'n _nm_ vibration

vibrato'r _nm_ [_Tech_] vibrator

vibro'·_n_

_I_ § _vi_ to vibrate

_II_ § _vt_ to make [] vibrate

vic'a _adv_ plumb full

vick_ë_ _nf_ **1** kick with the hind legs **2** (_Fig Pej_) perverseness, recalcitrance

vick'e_l_ _nf_ = vick_ë_

vickël'o·_n_ _vi_ **1** (of an animal) to kick with the hind legs, buck **2** (_Fig_) to be cantankerous/recalcitrant

viç _n_ **1** calf **2** fawn **3** (_Fig Insult_) naive/inexperienced/immature person

○ **viç i palëpirë** very immature and clumsy person

viç'a_r_ _n_ cowherd for calves

viç'e _nf_ female calf

*****viç'k**_ë_ _nf_ [_Bot_] aromatic plant used in making sweets

viço'k _nm_ **1** yearling bull calf **2** (_Fig Insult_) naive/inexperienced/immature person.

viço'k_e_ _nf_ **1** yearling heifer **2** (_Pet_) healthy and pretty little girl

*****viç'ta**_k_ _nm_ veal

vida'n _nm (pl ~ nj)_ [_Ornit_] male pigeon/dove = pëllu'mb

vide'a'st _nm_ [_Cine_] videomaker

vi'd_ë_ _nf_ **1** [_Ornit_] female pigeon/dove = pëllumbe'sh_ë_ **2** (_Fig Pet_) beautiful woman **3** = vi'dh_ë_

vi'd_ër_ _nf_ **1** [_Zool_] freshwater otter = lu'ndërz **2** stripe/patch in fur/plumage

*****vi'd**_ëz_ _nf_ [_Ornit_] pigeon

vi'dra-vi'dra _adj_ (of animals/birds) with speckled/striped/mottled fur/plumage

*****vidr'u'sh** _adj_ = vi'dra-vi'dra

vi'dul _nf_ (_Colloq Pej_) flattery

vi'dul'a _np_ <vi'dul (_Colloq Pej_) = la'jka

vidul'a'c

_I_ § _adj_ (_Colloq Pej_) flattering

_II_ § _n_ (_Colloq Pej_) flatterer

vidul'o'·_het_ _vpr_ (_Colloq_) to play up, suck up to

vidul'o·_n_ _vt_ (_Colloq_) to cajole

vidu'sh _adj_ = vi'dra-vi'dra

vidh _nm_ [_Bot_] **1** field/English elm, smooth-leaved elm (_Ulmus foliacea_) **2** nettle tree, European hackberry (_Celtis australis_) = cara'c

vidh·et *vpr* **1** to leave secretly; avoid being seen **2** *(Fig)* to avoid/evade <>

vidh *stem for 2nd pl pres, pind, imper, vp* <**vjedh·**

vidh|ez *nf* **1** hackberry **2** [*Bot*] nettle tree, European hackberry *(Celtis australis)*

vidhë *nf* screw
   ◦ **vidhë nënë** [*Tech*] feed screw; lead screw

vidhishtë *nf* hackberry grove

vidho're *np fem* [*Bot*] elm family *Ulmaceae*

vidho's· *vt* to screw [ ] in; put a screw into [ ]

vidho'sje *nf ger* <**vidho's·**

*****vie**·*n* = **vle·***n*

Vietna'm *nf* Vietnam

vietnam|ez *adj, n* Vietnamese

vietnamezojugo'r *adj, n* South Vietnamese

vig *nm (np ˜gje)* **1** beam laid over a stream as a bridge **2** beam of a wooden plow **3** stretcher, bier, barrow **4** chicken coop

viga'n
   I § *nm* giant
   II § *adj* gigantic

vigan|o'r *adj (i)* = **vigan'shëm**

vigan'shëm *adj (i)* gigantic

vi'gël *nf* **1** baby walker **2** cream

vigmba'jt|ës *nm* = **vigta'r**

vi'gmë *nf (Reg)* **1** cry, shriek; bellow, yell **2** reputation

vigta'r *n* stretcher-bearer; pallbearer

vi'gje *np fem* [*Ethnog*] **1** presents/food brought to a celebration of a special occasion **2** meal celebrating the third night of a baby's birth

*****vigjëllo**·*n* = **vigjilo·***n*

vigjëz *nf* [*Bot*] vetch *(Vicia)* = **grashi'në**

vigjile'ncë *nf* vigilance

vigjile'nt *adj* = **vigjilu'es**

vigji'lje *nf* eve (of an event)

vigjilo'·*n vi* to stand vigil

vigjilu'es *adj* vigilant
   ◦ **S'vihen dy gjilpëra majë më majë.** Too many irons in the fire.
   ◦ **s'vihet inat me** [ ] [ ] cannot be challenged
   ◦ **vih·***et* **në/për udhë** to set off (for a trip/journey)

vija|ku'qe *nf (Colloq)* rainbow = **ylbe'r**

vija|no'z *adv* continually

vij|ash *adv* = **pe'tas**

vija-vi'ja *adj* full of lines: heavily lined

vijë
   I § *nf* **1** line; straight line **2** furrow; groove; trace; rut
   II § *adv* in a stream, streaming out
   ◦ **vijat e bardha** white stripes marking pedestrian crossing
   ◦ **vijë fatale** [*Soccer*] goal line
   ◦ **vijë gjarpëruese** wavy line
   ◦ **vijë lufte** battleline, battlefront
   ◦ **ësh·të në vijë 1** to be going smoothly **2** to be on the right path
   ◦ **vija e portës** [*Sport*] goal line
   ◦ **vijë rrushkulluese** line joining points of equal altitude
   ◦ **vija e shënjimit** [*Mil*] sighting line
   ◦ **vijë e trimetërshit** [*Volleyball*] attack line
   ◦ **vijë e thyer** [*Geom*] sharply bent line, line with a sharp break: broken line

◦ **vija e verdhë** "the yellow line" [*Constr*] belt within which building in a village is permitted

vijë|dre'jtë *adj* [*Spec*] rectilinear

vijë|laku'ar *adj* [*Phys*] curvilinear

vijë|përku'lur *adj* [*Phys*] curvilinear

vijë|ro'jt|ës *nm (Old)* [*Sport*] line umpire, linesman

*****vijës** = **vijëz**

vijë|shëni'm *nm* **1** line of sight **2** [*Mil*] aim

vijë|shën|u'es *adj* [*Mil*] (board) used to prop rifle to aid in aiming

vijëz *nf dimin* **1** short thin line; thin trace **2** dash **3** [*Med*] stria

vijëz|i'm *nm ger* **1** <**vijëzo'·***n*, **vijëzo'·***het* **2** sketch; outline

vijëzo'·*het vpr* **1** to take the form of a line get covered with lines **2** *(Fig)* to start to appear in outline form

vijëzo'·*n vt* **1** to make lines on/in [ ]: line, rule, stripe **2** to sketch, draw; sketch out, outline

vijë|zu'ar *adj (i)* made with lines, drawn; outlined; full of lines

vij|i'm *nm ger* **1** <**vijo'·***n*, **vijo'·***het* **2** continuation
   ◦ **{ } në vijim** within this *{time period}*

vijim|ësi *nf (Book)* continuity

vijim|i'sht *adv (Book)* continuously; continually

vijo'·*n*
   I § *vt* **1** to continue; follow **2** to pursue/follow [organized study]
   II § *vi* to continue, keep going

vijo'r *adj* [*Spec*] **1** covered with lines **2** linear

vijo's· *vt* = **vijëzo'·***n*

vijo's·*et vpr* to take the form of a line; get covered with lines

vijo'sës
   I § *adj* for drawing lines
   II § *n* line-drawer; draftsman

vijo'sje *nf ger* **1** <**vijo's·**, **vijo's·***et* **2** sketch

vijo'sur *adj (i)* having lines, lined, (of paper) ruled

vijo'sh *nm* [*Ichth*] striped mullet *(Chelon labrosus)*

viju'es
   I § *adj* following; next
   II § *n* follower

viju'e|shëm *adj (i)* continuous

viju'e|shm|ëri *nf (Book)* continuity; continuousness

vika'më *nf (Reg)* loud cry, shriek; bellow, yell

vika's *stem for 1st sg pres, pl pres, 2nd & 3rd sg subj, pind (Reg)* <**vika't·**

vika't· *vt (Reg)* to cry out loudly: shriek, scream, bellow, yell

vika'tje *nf ger (Reg)* <**vika't·**

vikti'më *nf* victim

vil *stem for 2nd pl pres, pind, imper, vp* <**vje'l·**

vilaje't *nm* [*Hist*] province (in the Ottoman Empire)

vilani' *nf* fainting spell, swoon; queasiness, nausea = **fi'két**

vilani's· *OR* **vilano's·** *vi* = **vilano's·***et*

vilano's·*et vpr* **1** to faint **2** *(Fig)* to grow weak (from laughing or crying)

vilano'sur *adj (i)* in a faint; in a senseless state, without feeling

vila'r
   I § *nm* strip; narrow belt; stripe
   II § *adv* (of cloth) rolled in a bolt

vila's *stem for 1st sg pres, pl pres, 2nd & 3rd sg subj, pind* <**vila't·**

vila·t· *vt (Reg)* **1** to thin out []: prune **2** to shear [sheep] only on the underside and around the neck and tail

*****vila·zë** *nf* wide strip, patch
  ○ **vilazë letre** sheet of paper

*****vi·lcje** *nf* = **vi·le**

vi·le *nf* **1** bunch of grapes **2** [*Bot*] catkin *****3** [*Bot*] wisteria

vi·lez *nf* **1** grapevine; grape arbor **2** (*Dimin*) < **vi·le**

vi·lë *nf* **1** villa **2** cottage *****3** vine tendril

vi·ll·et *vpr* to vomit up food, throw up; feel like vomiting

vill stem for 2nd pl pres, pind, imper, vp < **vje·ll·**

vinç *nm* [*Tech*] hoisting crane

vinçie·r *n* crane operator

vinç-ku·llë *nf* [*Tech*] tower crane

vinç-u·rë *nf* [*Tech*] overhead traveling crane, bridge crane

vingjër *nf* [*Bot*] pea, vetch (*Lathyrus*)

*****vinti·l** *nm* = **venti·l**

vinje·të *nf* [*Postal*] sticker on an envelope

vio·ç *adj* [*Ichth*] thinlip gray mullet (*Liza ramada, Mugil capito*)

viole·ncë *nf* (*Book*) violence

viole·nt *adj* (*Book*) violent

Viole·ta *nf* Violeta (female name)

vio·lë *nf* [*Mus*] viola

violi·në *nf* [*Mus*] violin

violini·st *n* [*Mus*] violinist

violi·st *nm* [*Mus*] violist

violonçe·l *nm* [*Mus*] violoncello, cello

violonçeli·st *n* [*Mus*] cellist

*****vio·së** *nf* < **vio·shë**

vio·shë *nf* [*Ichth*] = **vijo·sh**

vir *nm* **1** (*Reg*) small creek **2** groove made by running water **3** deepest part of a body of water

vira·n
  I § *adj* (*Colloq*) abandoned, deserted
  II § *adj, n* **1** miserable/pitiful (person) **2** (*Fig*) crafty (person)

virano·n *vt* (*Colloq*) to abandon [a place]; leave [] destitute

*****virano·t** *nm* [*Bot*] large dodder (*Cuscuta europaea*)

vi·rdh·et *vpr* < **vje·rdh·** **1** to get in good graces with < >; endear oneself **2** to gain ability (by practice)

vi·rdh stem for 2nd pl pres, pind, imper, vp < **vje·rdh·**

virgjër
  I § *adj (i)* **1** virginal **2** pure, chaste; pristine, natural
  II § *nf (e)* virgin

virgjëre·shë *nf* virgin

virgjëri· *nf* virginity; chastity; purity of spirit

virgjëro·r *adj* (*Poet*) virginal

viro·i *obl* < **virua**

viro·k *nm* **1** skein of yarn **2** hank of cotton or wool

viro·nj *np* < **virua**

virtua·l *adj* (*Book*) virtual

virtualite·t *nm* (*Book*) virtuality

virtuo·z
  I § *n* virtuoso
  II § *adj* virtuosic

*****virtu·t** = **virty·t**

virty·t *nm* virtue

virtytësi· *nf* (*Book*) = **virtytshmëri·**

virty·tshëm *adj (i)* virtuous

virty·tshmëri· *nf* (*Book*) virtuousness

virua *nm* (*obl* ~ *oi, np* ~ *onj*) gushing spring/stream

vi·rus *nm* virus

virusa·l *adj* viral

viruso·r *adj* viral = **virusa·l**

virr
  I § stem for 2nd pl pres, pind, imper, vp < **vje·rr·**
  II § stem for pdef, part < **vërre·t·**

vi·rr
  I § stem for 2nd pl pres, pind, imper, vp < **vje·rr·**
  II § stem for pdef, part < **vërre·t·**

virra·ke *nf* dark stripe on a donkey's shoulder

*****vi·rrë** part < **vërre·t·**

virrmë *nf* (*Reg*) bleating

virrmë·ke·qe *nf* [*Ornit*] owl

*****vi·rrur** part < **vërre·t·**

vis *nm* place, region, territory

visa·r *nm* treasury; treasure

Visa·r *nm* Visar (male name)

*****vise·k** *adj*

vi·se-vi·se *adv* in several places, here and there = **ve·nde-ve·nde**

visk *nm* (*np* ~ *q*) donkey colt = **kërri·ç**

vi·skë *nf* < **visk**

visko·nt *nm* (*Book*) viscount

visko·z *adj* (*Book*) viscous

viskozite·t *nm* (*Book*) [*Phys*] viscosity

viso·re *nf* landscape

visq *np* < **visk**

*****vista·r** = **visa·r**

vi·stër
  I § *nf* **1** things in sequence: series **2** things strung up together: string of fish/fruit/vegetables
  II § *adv* in a string/line/file: one after another, in succession

*****visto··n** *vt* to stamp a visa in [a passport]

vistra·k *nm* = **vi·stër**

vistro··n *vt* to put [] on a string: string [] (one after another)

vi·sh·et *vpr* **1** to put on clothes, get dressed **2** to become covered over by a thin layer of something: mist over, fog up **3** (*Fig Iron*) to clothe oneself in false colors **4** (*Fig*) to become invested in an office **5** (*Colloq*) to take up duty as a member of a uniform-wearing group **6** (*Colloq*) to assail < >
  ○ **vish·et me/në (rroba) të zeza** to dress in black (clothes); be in mourning
  ○ **vish·et me/në hekur/çelik** "be dressed in iron/steel" to be armed to the teeth
  ○ **vish·et me gusto** to dress in good taste
  ○ **vish·et me []** "get dressed with []" to get ready to attack with a []
  ○ **vish·et rëndë 1** to wear heavy clothes: dress warmly **2** to wear a lot of jewelry
  ○ < > **vish·et³ᵖˡ sytë** "< >'s eyes get veiled" **1** < >'s eyes glaze over **2** < > is blind to the truth

vi·sh stem for 2nd pl pres, pind, imper, vp < **ve·sh·**

vishara·k *adj* = **pjello·r**

*****vishina·dhë** = **vishnja·dhë**

*****vishkëllo··n** = **fishkëlle··n**

vishko··n *vt* (*Reg*) to rub; scratch

vishkull

I § nm (np ~ j) straight young sapling with no branches; withe, switch

II § adv naked, bare

vishkullaje nf forest of young oaks; place with young saplings

vishkullar adj thin and straight as a young sapling

vishkullim nm ger < **vishkullo**•n

vishkullo•n vt to whip with a switch; whip

vishnjadhe nf cherry syrup

vishnjak adj of a dark cherry color

vishnje

I § nf 1 morello, dark cherry, sour cherry (Prunus cerasus austera) 2 common cherry (Cerasus vulgaris) 3 cherry syrup

II § adj of a dark cherry color

○ **vishnje e eger** [Bot] sweet cherry Prunus avium

vishta np (te) fem (Reg) = **lashta**

vishte adj (i) (Reg) sown in the autumn; pertaining to or produced by the grain crops sown in autumn

vishtull nf [Bot] mistletoe

vit nm year

○ **vitet** { } the years in the decade {decade number}: the {decade}'s **vitet njezet** the twenties

○ **vit akademik** academic year (in institutions of higher education)

○ **vit i brishte** leap year

○ **vit i mbare** good year

○ **viti ne udhetim** (Book) the year in progress, this year

○ **Viti i Ri** New Year's Day, January 1

○ **vit shkollor/mesimor** school year, instructional year (in primary and secondary schools)

○ **vit visek** leap year

○ **Viti vitit nuk i ngjet.** "A year is not like another year." Times change.

*vitace np fem [Bot] Vitaceae

vital adj (Book) vital

vitalitet nm (Book) vitality

vitamine nf vitamin

vit-drite nm [Astron] light-year

viterk nm stepfather = **njerk**

viterkeshe nf stepmother = **njerke**

vitikulture nf viticulture = **vreshtari**

*vitkur nm = **viterk**

vito nf (obl ~ ua) 1 [Ornit] ring-dove (Columba palumbus) 2 (Fig) beautiful woman

*vitor adj (Old) anniversary

vitore

I § nf 1 [Folklore] lucky snake with golden horns who gives birth to gold; imaginary nonpoisonous short fat snake believed to bring luck and protection to houses whose walls it inhabits 2 (Old) fate 3 woman who is skillful in managing a household; woman who has given birth to many children 4 good cow with a high milk yield

II § adj (of women/girls) skillful in work

○ **Te dalte vitorja perpara!** "May the lucky snake appear in front of you!" (Felic Old) May things go well for you! Good luck!

vitorezi adj (fem sg ~ ez, masc pl ~ inj, fem pl ~ eza) = **fatzi**

vitrine nf 1 display window; display case 2 (Fig Pej) tricked up sample professed to be representative of the whole set

*vitruk nm = **viterk**

vitshem adj (i) yearly, annual

vithaprapa adv = **vithapraptas**

vithanike nf horse blanket = **paravithe**

vithapraptas adv backwards

vithatore nf set of straps securing a pack saddle to the back of a pack animal

vithe np fem 1 rump of a large animal: cruppers 2 buttocks

○ **vithet e kalit** [Gymnastics] croup (of the side-horse)

vithegjere adj broad-rumped

vithemadh adj big-rumped

vithurene adj droopy-rumped

vithetrashe adj fat-rumped

vitheullur adj = **vitherene**

*vithi nf steep bank; precipice

vithis- vt (Colloq) to cause [ ] to sink into the ground; hurl [ ] down

vithis-et vpr 1 (Colloq) to sink down; (of ground) subside, collapse 2 to plunge to the bottom 3 (of a vehicle) to turn/roll over 4 (Fig) to disappear; change radically

vithisje nf ger 1 (Colloq) < **vithis**•, **vithis**•et 2 downfall, collapse

vithisur adj (i) 1 sunken into the earth, swallowed by the earth 2 fallen to the ground; fallen to the bottom of a crevasse; (of a vehicle) turned/rolled over

vithor adj [Anat] gluteal

viu onomat sound of something moving with force through the air rapidly and brushing against something: whoosh

viu-viu onomat = **viu**

vivar nm fish pond

vive nf [Ichth] greater weever (Trachinus draco)

vizak adj lissome

vizals stem for 1st sg pres, pl pres, 2nd & 3rd sg subj, pind < **vizat**•

vizat• vt to draw lines in [ ], fill [ ] with lines; leave line traces in a surface

○ **<>a vizat• shpinen** "draw lines on <>'s back" to leave welts on <>'s back as to leave welts

vizatim nm ger 1 < **vizato**•n, **vizato**•het 2 drawing, sketch 3 (Colloq) drawing notebook, sketch pad

vizatimor adj in cartoon form

vizato•het vpr to appear in outline form; appear in the imagination

vizato•n vt to draw, sketch; sketch out [ ]

vizatues n person who draws/sketches

vize nf 1 line; stripe 2 visa

○ **vize lidhese** hyphen

○ **vize ndarese** [Ling] hyphen at the end of a line

vizgator nm 1 tobacco shredder 2 bloodletting device

vizge nf (Colloq) thin short line; scrawl, scribbling

*vizillim nf [Entom] = **xixellonje**

*vizilloj nf [Entom] = **xixellonje**

vizim nm ger < **vizo**•n, **vizo**•het

vizion nm (Book) apparition = **vegim**

vizite nf visit

vizitim nm ger 1 < **vizito**•n 2 visitation

vizito•n vt to visit

vizitor n visitor

vizitues n = **vizitor**

*vizll**im** *nm ger* <vizllo·*n*

*vizllo·*n vt* = vezullo·*n*

viz**o**·*het vpr* to form a line, extend as a line

viz**o**·*n vt* **1** = vij**e**zo·*n* **2** to enter a visa for <> in [a passport]

vizo**n** *nm* [*Zool*] mink

vizo**r** *adj* ruled with lines: lined

viz**o**re *nf* rule, straightedge, ruler

vizu**a**r *adj* (i) = vizo**r**

vizh**ë** *nf* [*Entom*] goldsmith beetle, rose chafer (*Cetonia aurata*)

*vj**·**et *vi* = vle·*n*

*vjam**çë** *nf* small piece of fat

*vjam**ë** *nf* = dhjam**ë**

*vjam**të** = dhjamt**ë**

vjask**ë** *nf* **1** narrow groove **2** rifling (in a gun barrel) **3** (*Pur*) screw thread **4** thin trail left by something

vjasku**a**r *adj* (i) **1** [*Tech*] having narrow grooves: grooved **2** [*Mil*] (of a gun) rifled

vje·*n vi* **1** to come; arrive **2** to come back; return to original state **3** to come to power **4** to reach a ready state in development **5** (of rivers/bread) to rise **6** to occur to <> by chance: strike <>; happen **7** to fit <>; suit <> **8** to look like <>; have or take on an appearance; be comparable **9** (*Colloq*) to come to (a weight/cost): weigh, cost **10** to begin a continuing process

∘ vje·*n* akolle to go around in circles

∘ <> vje·*n* andrallë **1** <> *gets* dizzy **2** <> *has* some really tough problems: <> *has* a real headache on <>'s hands

∘ <> vje·*n* anës "come to <> on the side" **1** to approach <> indirectly, beat around the bush with <> **2** to scheme to get possession of <>

∘ vje·*n*³ˢᵍ anës për [shi/dëborë] it *is getting* ready to [rain/snow]

∘ <> vje·*n*³ˢᵍ çudi "it *comes* as a surprise to <>" <> *is* surprised/amazed

∘ <> vje·*n*³ˢᵍ dora **1** <> *gets* lucky (in cardplaying) **2** <> *gets* good at it (a skill using <>'s hands)

∘ <> vje·*n*³ˢᵍ dore (për [ ]) <> *has* a knack (for [ ])

∘ <> vje·*n*³ᵖˡ dhentë pa çoban "<>'s sheep *come* even without a shepherd" things *are going* well for <>

∘ <> vje·*n*³ˢᵍ dhoma rrotull/vërdallë "the room *seems* to <> to come around" <> *feels* the house/room spinning around

∘ <> vje·*n*³ˢᵍ era <> *is becoming* publicly known, <> *is being* revealed

∘ <> vje·*n*³ˢᵍ festja vërdallë/rrotull "<>'s fez *spins* around" <>'s head is spinning with all the things <> *has* to worry about

∘ vje·*n*³ˢᵍ fjala the subject *comes* up, the topic *arises*

∘ <> vje·*n*³ˢᵍ fundi me samar to end one's life in great suffering

∘ <> vje·*n*³ˢᵍ fytyra <> *regains* <>'s composure; <> *feels* relieved

∘ <> vje·*n*³ˢᵍ fytyra në vend "<>'s face *comes* in place" <> *regains* <>'s composure; <> *feels* relieved

∘ <> vje·*n*³ˢᵍ gjaku në vend <> *regains* composure; <> *stops* being afraid

∘ <> vje·*n*³ˢᵍ habi "it *comes* as a surprise to <>" <> *is* surprised/amazed

∘ <> vje·*n* hakut to know how to make <> behave

∘ <> vje·*n*³ˢᵍ inat "it *comes* spite to <>" <> *gets* mad/sore

∘ <> vje·*n*³ˢᵍ kaba <> *feels* ashamed

∘ vje·*n*³ˢᵍ kandari në bisht the situation *becomes* intolerable, things have gone too far

∘ vje·*n*³ˢᵍ keq <> *is* sorry

∘ <> vje·*n*³ˢᵍ kocka në fyt "<>'s bone *comes* to <>'s throat" <> *is* in bad straits

∘ <> vje·*n*³ˢᵍ koka vërdallë/rrotull "<>'s head *spins* around" <>'s head is spinning with all the things <> has to worry about

∘ <> vje·*n*³ˢᵍ kripur <> *feels* bitter about {}

∘ <> vje·*n*³ˢᵍ lak <> *gets* nauseous/nauseated, <> *feels* like throwing up

∘ <> vje·*n*³ˢᵍ lepuri në qerre "the hare *comes* to <> in a cart" <> *has* all the luck

∘ <> vje·*n*³ˢᵍ lepuri në shteg "the hare *appears* right in <>'s path" <> *gets* lucky

∘ vje·*n*³ˢᵍ lumi the river rises

∘ <> vje·*n*³ˢᵍ (për) mbarë **1** <> finds {} (more) advantageous **2** <> *is* good with {}, <> *knows* how to deal with {} **3** <> *finds* {} convenient

∘ vje·*n* me bisht prapa to drag along someone who is not invited

∘ vje·*n* me duar në xhepa "come with hands in pockets" to come/go empty-handed; come/go unprepared

∘ vje·*n* me duar plot to show a period of success

∘ vje·*n* me kulaç pas brezi to come in haste; come and stay for only a short time, drop in for a short visit

∘ vje·*n* me urë/pishë në dorë "come with torch in hand" to spread devastation in one's path

∘ <> vje·*n*³ˢᵍ mendja vërdallë/rrotull "<>'s mind *spins* around" <>'s head is spinning with all the things <> has to worry about

∘ <> vje·*n*³ᵖˡ mendtë **1** <> *regains* consciousness: come to; regain one's alertness, come to oneself **2** to learn from bitter experience **3** to be obedient, listen

∘ <> vje·*n*³ˢᵍ mëlçia në grykë "<>'s liver *comes* up to <>'s throat" <> *can't* take it any more, <> *is* fed up

∘ <> vje·*n*³ˢᵍ mirë <> *is* delighted

∘ vje·*n*³ˢᵍ misri në bejleg the corn *is tasseling*

∘ vje·*n* mullarthi me [ ] to play around with [ ] in a torturing way

∘ <> vje·*n*³ˢᵍ ndër mend it occurs to <>

∘ vje·*n* ndër mend to come to one's senses: regain consciousness, come to, wake up to reality; regain one's composure, get a hold on oneself; get oneself back on the right track

∘ vje·*n* në avull to be there when needed badly

∘ vje·*n* në brazdë to get back on the right track; see the light

∘ <> vje·*n*³ˢᵍ në dhëmb to be on the tip of <>'s tongue

∘ vje·*n* në fije to recover from illness or difficult circumstances: get back on track

∘ <> vje·*n*³ˢᵍ në hatër (*Colloq*) to come to <>'s mind

∘ vje·*n* në hulli to follow the right path

∘ <> vje·*n* në mendje to come to <>'s mind, occur to <>

○ <> **vje·***n* **në osh** *(Colloq)* to try to please <>: make <> feel good

○ <> **vje·***n* **në rrugë/binarë/hulli/brazdë** to follow <> slavishly

○ **vje·***n*^{3sg} **në shat** to be ready to be hoed

○ <> **vje·***n* **në shteg** to fall into <>'s hands/power

○ <> **vje·***n* **në shtrungë** to fall <> into one's hands/power

○ **vje·***n*^{3sg} **në të** to come to one's senses

○ **vje·***n* **në udhë/rrugë/vijë/binarë** to get going on the right track; straighten out, go straight

○ <> **vje·***n* **në vesh që/se** _ <> *hears* accidentally that _, <> *happens* to hear that _

○ **vje·***n* **në vete** to come to one's senses: regain consciousness, come to, wake up to reality; regain one's composure, get a hold on oneself; get oneself back on the right track

○ **vje·***n* **në zigj** "come into balance" to get into good shape

○ <> **vje·***n*^{3sg} **opti** <>'s face *shows* <>'s relief

○ <> **vje·***n*^{3pl} **orët** <> *is* possessed by fairies (said when someone is acting crazy with rage)

○ <> **vje·***n*^{3sg} **osh** *(Colloq)* <> *gets* pleasure

○ **vje·***n* **pas** <> to follow <>

○ <> **vje·***n* **pas fijes/fillit** to try to please <>; speak and act according to <>'s wishes

○ <> **vje·***n* **pas hesapit** to be good for <>, be to <>'s benefit

○ <> **vje·***n* **pas qejfit** to come into <>'s favor, become a favorite of <>

○ <> **vje·***n* **për hak** to know how to make <> behave

○ <> **vje·***n* **për hesap** to be good for <>, be to <>'s benefit

○ <> **vje·***n*^{3sg} **për shat** "it *is* fit for <>'s body" **1** to suit/serve <> well **2** (of clothes) to fit <> well

○ <> **vje·***n*^{3sg} **për të** {*participle*} <> *feels* like {}ing

○ <> **vje·***n* **për trup** (of clothes) to fit <>

○ **vje·***n* **pikë me pikë** to come running at top speed

○ <> **vje·***n*^{3sg} **plasja** *(Fig)* <> *feels* like exploding, <> *comes* to the bursting point, <> *is* about to burst with indignation

○ **vje·***n* **qift** "come to <> like a kite" to circle around <> like a hungry wolf; circle around <> ready to grab it

○ <> **vje·***n*^{3sg} **rehat** <> *feels* good

○ <> **vje·***n*^{3sg} **rëndë 1** <> *feels* offended, <> *takes* offense **2** <> *feels* reluctant **3** <> *feels* terribly embarrassed

○ <> **vje·***n* **rreth 1** to revolve around <> **2** to try to get on <>'s good side, play up to <>: woo <> **3** *(Fig)* to see to <>'s needs, look after <> **4** *(Fig)* to cajole <> **5** to hang over <>'s head, be a constant danger to <>

○ **vje·***n*^{3sg} **rreth/rrotull për [shi/dëborë]** it *is* getting ready to [rain/snow]

○ **i vje·***n* **rreth punës/asaj pune** to attend to one's work until it gets done

○ **vje·***n* **rreth 1** to revolve **2** to get by with what one has, get by somehow

○ <> **vje·***n* **rrotull 1** to revolve around <> **2** *(Fig)* to see to <>'s needs, look after <> **3** *(Fig)* to woo <*a girl/woman*> **4** *(Fig)* to cajole <> **5** to hang over <>'s head, be a constant danger to <>

○ **vje·***n* **rrotull 1** to revolve, rotate; spin (around) **2** *(Fig)* to run around without accomplishing anything, waste time running around

○ **vje·***n* **si reja me breshër/furtunë** "come like a hail/storm cloud" to appear suddenly

○ <> **vje·***n*^{3sg} **shpirti (në vend)** "<>'s soul *comes* in place" <> *recovers* <>'s spirits, <> *cheers* up, *feels* relieved

○ <> **vje·***n*^{3sg} **shtëpia rrotull/vërdallë** "the house *seems* to <> to come around" <> *feels* the house/room spinning around

○ <> **vje·***n*^{3sg} **takija vërdallë/rrotull** "<>'s cap *spins* around" <>'s head is spinning with all the things <> has to worry about

○ <> **vje·***n*^{3rdsg} **të ha·**^{subj} **veten 1** <> *feels* desperate **2** <> *discovers* only too late what a terrible mistake <> has made: <> could kick <>self in the head

○ **vje·***n* **të merr·**^{subj} **prush** "come to get hot coals" to come for a short while

○ <> **vje·***n*^{3sg} **të vështirë** <> feels nauseous/sick

○ <> **vje·***n*^{3sg} **tjegulla përqark/vërdallë** "<>'s roof tile *is spinning* around" <>'s head *is spinning* with all the things <> has to worry about

○ <> **vje·***n*^{3sg} **tmerr** <> *gets* terrified

○ **vje·***n* **torrë** to go/spin/turn around; get dizzy

○ <> **vje·***n*^{3sg} **turp** <> *feels* ashamed

○ **vje·***n* **thikas** to be very steep/sheer

○ **vje·***n* **thikë me thikë** "come knife to knife" to come into direct conflict

○ <> **vje·***n*^{3sg} **uri** "it *comes* hunger to <>" <> *feels* hungry

○ <> **vje·***n*^{3sg} **vera te dera** good luck comes <>'s way

○ <> **vje·***n*^{3pl} **veshët** <> *recovers* <>'s hearing

○ **vje·***n*^{3sg} **vetvetiu/vetiu** to become self-evident, become obvious

○ <> **vje·***n*^{3sg} **veza për të pjellë** "<>'s egg *is* about to hatch" *(Crude)* <> *is* under urgent pressure: <> *is* under the gun

○ <> **vje·***n* **vërdallë *1** to revolve around <> **2** *(Fig)* to see to <>'s needs, look after <> **3** *(Fig)* to woo <*a girl/woman*> **4** *(Fig)* to cajole <> **5** to hang over <>'s head, be a constant danger to <>

○ **i vje·***n* **vërdallë 1** to approach a matter indirectly; speak indirectly **2** to go at things by a circuitous route

○ **vje·***n* **vërdallë** to hang around without doing anything

○ <> **vje·***n*^{3sg} **voli** <> *finds* it easier

○ <> **vje·***n*^{3sg} **zemra në vend** "<>'s heart *comes* in place" <> *feels* relieved

○ **nuk** <> **vje·***n*^{3sg} **zëri** "the sound *doesn't* come to <>" *(Iron)* pretends not to hear

○ <> **vje·***n*^{3pl} **zorrët në grykë/fyt/te goja** "<>'s guts *rise* to <>'s throat/mouth" <> *feels* like throwing up

vjeç *adj* years of age

○ {*number*} **vjeç** (of a person) {} years old

vjeça̱r *adj* (*formative suffix following a number stem*) recurrent after {*number*} years **trevjeçar** triennial of _ years of age **tetëvjeça̱r** eight-year-old **shumëvjeça̱r** of several years of age

*vjeç̱ëm *adj* (*i*) = vjetëm

*vjeço̱r *adj* **1** annual **2** one-year-old

vje̱dull *nf* [*Zool*] = vjedhull*ë*

vjedh· *vt* **1** to steal **2** *(Fig)* to plagiarize

○ [] **vjedh· me bisht të syrit** to see [] out of the corner of one's eye, espy [] by chance

○ [] **vjedh· me sy** to steal a glance at []

vjedhacak
I § *n (Colloq Pejorative Insult)* thief; petty thief
II § *adj (Colloq Pejorative Insult)* thieving, thievish

vjedhani *nf* thievery, brigandage

vjedharak *adj* **1** thieving **2** stealthy, sneaky

vjedharash *adj* thieving

vjedhas OR **vjedhazi** *adv* = vjedhurazi

vjedhcak = vjedhacak

vjedhë *nf* theft

vjedhës
I § *n* thief
II § *adj* **1** thieving **2** stealthy, sneaky **3** [*Entom*] white-marked spider beetle *(Ptinus fur L.)*

vjedhësi *nf* theft; thievery

vjedhje *nf ger* **1** <vjedh·, vidh·*et* **2** theft; thievery

*vjedhme *nf* theft; plagiarism

*vjedhrazi = vjedhurazi

vjedhtas *adv* = vjedhurazi

*vjedhullë *nf* [*Zool*] badger

vjedhur
I § *part* <vjedh·, vidh·*et*
II § *adj (i)* **1** stolen **2** *(Fig)* plagiarized

vjedhurazi *adv* stealthily, furtively; by stealth, surreptitiously

vjedhuri *nf* thievery

vjedhurina *np fem* stolen goods

vjedhurisht
I § *adv* **1** by stealing **2** = vjedhurazi
II § *adj* stealthy, furtive; secret

*vjefshëm *adj (i)* = vlefshëm

vjegë *nf* **1** pot handle **2** peg on which to hang something **3** *(Fig)* pretext, excuse **4** link of a chain **5** slipknot **6** buttonhole; loop in a garment for hanging it up **7** twisted leather thong used to tie up moccasins **8** *(Colloq)* tip of a plowshare

vjegëz
I § *nf* **1** buttonhole; loop in an overgarment used to hang it up **2** slipknot **3** twisted leather thong used to tie up moccasins **4** *(Dimin)* <vjegë
II § *adv* easily loosened/undone/untied/unbuttoned

vjego·n *vt* **1** to put the handle on [a pot] **2** to hang [] on a hook

vjegore *nf* clay pitcher whose graceful handle rises higher than the opening

vjeguar *adj (i)* *(Fin)* on time deposit

vjegjës *nm* [*Bot*] broom *(Cytissus)*

vjehërr
I § *nf* mother-in-law
II § *nf (e)* his, her, their mother-in-law
III § *nm* father-in-law
IV § *nm (i)* his, her, their father-in-law

vjehërri *nf* **1** parent-in-law relationship **2** *(Collec)* parents-in-law

*vjejtur
I § *part* <vj·*et*
II § *adj (i)* = vlefshëm

*vjeksë *nf* **1** appendage **2** pendulum

vjel· *vt* to harvest: reap [grain crops, profits], pick [fruit/cotton], gather [items for an anthology], collect [taxes]

vjela *np (të) fem* fruit harvest

vjelë
I § *part* <vjel·
II § *adj (i)* harvested
III § *nn (të)* = vjelje
IV § *nf* *fruit harvest

vjelës *n* harvester: reaper, gatherer, picker; collector

vjelje *nf ger* **1** <vjel· **2** harvest time

*vjelshëm *adj (i)* nauseating, sickening

vjell· *vt* **1** to vomit up [] **2** to lose [color] when washed
○ **vjell· (helm e) vrer** "vomit (poison and) bile" to pour out one's hatred, speak with unmitigated spite: pour out one's bile

vjellë
I § *part* <vjell·
II § *nf (e)* **1** vomit **2** = vjellje
III § *nn (të)* = vjellje

vjellje *nf ger* <vjell·, vill·*et*

*vjeme = vemje

*vjemë *adj (i)* = vjetëm

*vjemje = vemje

vjen
I § *2nd & 3rd sg pres* <vje·*n*
II § *2nd & 3rd sg pres* <vj·*et*

○ **vjen fjala** let's say, such as, for instance
○ <> **vjen hidhur** <> *is* hurt to the quick
○ <> **vjen ligsht 1** <> *feels* bad/sad **2** <> *feels* faint
○ <> **vjen ndoresh** {} {} comes easy to <>, <> has a special talent for {}, {} is <>'s cup of tea, {} is right up <>'s alley
○ <> **vjen ndot** <> *gets* nauseated, <> *feels* disgust
○ <> **vjen (shpirti) në majë të hundës** <> *comes* to the end of <>'s endurance
○ <> **vjen për dore** <> *feels* a need to {}, <> *wants* to {} i **më vjen për të thirrur** I feel like screaming
○ <> **vjen për të** {*participle*} <> *is* good with <>'s hands

vjenez *adj, n* Viennese

Vjenë *nf* Vienna

vjerdh· *vt* to make <> like [] better; put [] in <>'s good graces; mollify []

*vjerdhull *nm* = vjedhullë

vjerdhur *part* <vjerdh·, virdh·*et*

vjershatar *n* poet, versifier

vjershë *nf* verse, poetry

vjershëri *nf* **1** = vjershërim **2** *(Old)* poetry

vjershërim *nm ger* **1** <vjershëro·n **2** versification

vjershëro·n *vt, vi* to versify, compose verse

vjershëruar *adj (i)* versified

*vjershësi *nf* poetry, verse

vjershëtar OR **vjershëtor** *n* versifier, poet

vjershëto·n = vjershëro·n

vjershëtor *n* = vjershëtar

*vjershor = vjershëtar

*vjerr· *vt* = varr·

*vjerrc *nm* = varëse

*vjerrje *nf* = varje

*vjerrsa *np* suspenders, braces

*vjerrtas *adv* suspended, hanging

vjeshk *nm (np ~q) (Reg)* = vishkull

vjeshtak *adj* of or pertaining to autumn; appearing in autumn

vjeshtakës *adj* = vjeshtar

vjeshtar *adj* ripening in autumn

vjeshtarak *adj* autumnal

vjeshtë *nf* autumn
∘ **vjeshta e dytë** October
∘ **Vjeshtë e lugë** "Autumn and spoon." Summer is about over and it's time for hot food.
∘ **vjeshta e mesme** *(Old)* October
∘ **vjeshta e parë** September
∘ **vjeshta e tretë** November

vjeshtoˆ•n *vi* to spend autumn (somewhere)

vjeshtor *adj* = vjeshtak

vjeshtoruk *nf* autumn-ripening fruit/vegetable

vjeshtuk
I § *adj* 1 late-ripening; not well-ripened 2 = vjeshtak
II § *n* *(Pej)* student who must appear in autumn to retake the examination failed in the spring

vjet
I § *np* < vit years
II § *adv* last year
∘ **vjet brishtnuer** *(Old)* leap year
∘ **vjet për vjet** year by year, perennially

vjetˆ•et *vpr* (of a weather phenomenon) to die down, stop

vjetak *adj* = motak

vjetar *nm* annual publication/report

vjet-dritë *np* < vit-dritë [Astron] light-years

vjetëm *adj (i)* of last year, last year's

vjetër
I § *adj (i)* 1 old; aged 2 senior 3 former
II § *nf (e)* that which is out of date: the old, old-fashioned thing
III § *nm (i)* 1 old person 2 person in ancient times

vjetëri *nf* being old, senility; antiquity

vjetërim *nm* [Tech] ageing

vjetërsi *nf* 1 age 2 antiquity 3 seniority

vjetërsim *nm ger* = vjetrim

vjetërsirë *nf* 1 something used for a long time: second-hand item, old clothes 2 old-fashioned thing

vjetërsoˆ•het *vpr* = vjetroˆ•het

vjetërsoˆ•n *vt* = vjetroˆ•n

vjetoˆ•n *vi* to take all year doing something; take forever

vjetor *adj* annual

vjetrim *nm ger* < vjetroˆ•n, vjetroˆ•het

vjetroˆ•het *vp* 1 to get old: age; become worn/outworn 2 to become outdated

vjetroˆ•n *vt* 1 to cause [] to get old (prematurely): age 2 to use [] for a long time, wear [] out

vjetruar *adj (i)* 1 aged 2 timeworn; outworn, worn out

vjetshëm *adj (i)* of last year

*__**vjetull** *nf* [Zool] = vjedhullë

vjeturinë *nf* = vjetërsirë

vjexhës = vjegjës

*__**vjolë** = violë

vjoli *np* folk music instruments; folk music band

vjolixhi *nm (np ˜ nj)* folk musician

Vjollca *nf* Vjollca (female name)

vjollcë *nf* [Bot] violet (Viola L.)

Vjosa *nf* Vjosa (female name)

Vjosë *nf* longest river in southern Albania, spilling down from the Greek mountains southeast of Albania, to the delta on the Adriatic sea north of Vlora

---

vlagë *nf* soil moisture (required for plant growth)

vlagëso•het *vpr* to become moist

vlagëso•n *vt* to moisten [the soil]

vlagët *adj (i)* moist, wet

vlak *nm* leather bucket

*__**vlasta** *nm* = lasta

vle•n
I § *vi* 1 to be worth 2 to be good for ◇, be of value to ◇
II § *vi impers* 1 it *is* worth the trouble to __, be worthwhile 2 ◇ should __
∘ **nuk vle•n³ˢᵍ asnjë grosh/dysh** not be worth a nickel
∘ **s'vle•n³ˢᵍ asnjë pesësh** not be worth a nickel
∘ **s'e vle•n barra qiranë** to cost more than its worth, not to be worth the effort
∘ **nuk ◇ vle•n³ˢᵍ lëkura një para** "◇'s skin *is* not worth a farthing" → *is* unable to anything useful, ◇ *is* a good-for-nothing
∘ **vle•n si** fg to be worth for fg, be of value as fg

vlefshëm *adj (i)* 1 valuable 2 *(Offic)* valid

vlefshmëri *nf* 1 value, worth 2 validity

vleftë *nf* = vlerë

vleftësim *nm ger* < vleftëso•n

vleftëso•n *n* = vlerëso•n

*__**vleftësues** *adj, n* = vlerësues

*__**vleftje** *nf* = vlefshmëri

*__**vleftshëm** *adj (i)* = vlefshëm

vlejtur *part* < vle•n

*__**vleq** *np* < vlak

vlerë *nf* 1 value 2 thing of value: valuable

vlerësi *nf* value, significance; validity

vlerësim *nm ger* 1 < vlerëso•n, vlerëso•het 2 valuation; evaluation 3 appreciation

vlerëso•n *vt* 1 to evaluate 2 to acknowledge the worth of []: value, appreciate

vlerësues
I § *n* evaluator
II § *adj* 1 evaluative 2 commendatory

vlerësueshëm *adj (i)* capable of being evaluated

*__**vlero•n** *vt* = vlerëso•n

vlershëm *adj (i)* valuable

vlertë *adj (i)* = vlershëm

vlesë *nf* betrothal = fejesë

vlesëri *nf* [Ethnog] = mblesëri

vlesëro•n *vt. (Old)* to betroth

vletur *part* = vle•n

*__**vlezhgë** *nf* = lëvozhgë

vlim
I § *nm ger* = valim
II § *nm* * = vlesë

vlo•het *vpr* = fejo•het

vlo•n
I § *vi* 1 to boil 2 *(Fig)* to bubble (with activity): bustle; bubble over (with emotion)
II § *vt* 1 to boil 2 = fejo•n 3 to put [] away for later: save
∘ ◇ **vlo•n³ˢᵍ gjaku** ◇'s blood is heating up: ◇ *is* very lively and energetic
∘ ◇ **vlo•n³ᵖˡ trutë** ◇'s head is spinning with all the things ◇ *has* to worry about

vlonjat
I § *adj* of/from Vlora
II § *nm* native of Vlora

*vlo're nf sling

Vlo'rë nf city and district in southwestern Albania: Avlona, Vlora

vlu'a'r adj (i), n (i) = feju'ar

vlug nm 1 = vlagë 2 (Fig) high/prime point: peak, crest

*vluko'·n vi to be at its peak, flourish

*vly'e'r part <vle·n

*vlla'çë nf [Agr] harrow

*vlladi'kë nf with masc agreement title of archbishop (in Montenegro)

vllah
  I § nm Vlach
  II § adj of or pertaining to the Vlachs (a pastoral people)

vlla'h·çe adv (Colloq) = vllahi'sht

vllah'inkë nf Vlach female

vllah'isht adv 1 in Vlach (language) 2 in the manner of the Vlachs

vllah'isht'e nf Vlach language (Aromanian)

vlla'jë nf = le'he

vlla'një nf = le'he

vllasta'r nm = lasta'r

*vlla'zn (Reg Gheg) = vëllazër

vlleh np <vllah

VNA abbrev (English) Vietnamese News Agency

*vner nm (Old Regional Gheg) = vrer

*vner'im nm ger (Old Regional Gheg) 1 <vnero'·n 2 contamination 3 embitterment

*vnero'·n vt (Old Regional Gheg) = vreros·

*vner'o'r adj (Old Regional Gheg) = vre'rtë

*vner'o'sh adj (Old Regional Gheg) = vre'rtë

*vner'të adj (i) (Old Regional Gheg) = vre'rtë

*vnesht = vresht

*vnesht'ak nm (Reg Gheg) vineyard

*vo'·n vi (Reg Gheg) to lay eggs

*vobek'e'ri' = vobek'e'si

vobek'e'si nf (Old) poverty = varfe'ri

vobek'e'sish't adv (Old) = varfe'risht

vobek'e'so'·n vt (Old) = varfe'ro·n

vobe'kët adj (i) = vobe'ktë

vobe'ktë adj (i) poor = va'rfër

vobe'ktë'si nf poverty = varfe'ri

*vob'e'si = vobek'e'si

*vob'e'sish't = vobek'e'sish't

*vo'b'të = vobe'ktë

voc nm (Reg) young boy = çun

vo'ce nf (Reg) young girl = vajzë

vo'ce'rr adj (i) (Pet) little

voce'rra'k
  I § adj (Pet) little
  II § nm little boy

voce'rra'ke nf (Pet) little girl

voce'rri' nf = voge'li

voce'rrime nf = voge'lsire

voce'rri'na np fem small wares, notions

voce'rro'·het vpr to become smaller; shrink

voce'rro'·n vt to make [] smaller; shrink []

voce'rru'ar adj (i) made smaller; shrunken

voce'rru'sh adj (Pet) sweet little thing: little darling

*vo'ckë nf drinking bottle, flask

vo'ckël adj (i) <vo'ce'rr 1 (Dimin) tiny 2 petty

*vockora'n n = voge'lush

vode'nës
  I § nm [Bot] winter melon
  II § adj pale (in the face)

vo'dkë nf vodka

vo'dh stem for pdef <vje'dh·

vo'dhë nf [Bot] = va'dhë

vodhëvi'çe nf [Bot] 1 = vadhëvi'çe 2 whitebeam (Sorbus aria)

*vo'e nf (Reg) = vezë

*vo'e'se adj egg-laying

*vo'e'së nf dew; drizzle = ve'së

vo'gël
  I § adj (i) 1 small; little; short 2 young 3 (Colloq) of low rank, of little merit/importance 4 in detail; on a one-to-one basis 5 (Pej) petty
  II § n (i) young child/animal
  ○ I vogël për prehër, i madh për zemër. "Small enough for the lap, but big in the heart." (Prov) Small in stature, but big in courage.

voge'la'k adj (Pet) little

voge'li' nf childhood, infancy

voge'l'im nm ger 1 <voge'lo'·n, voge'lo'·het 2 reduction

voge'lime nf trifle = çikërri'me

voge'li'na np fem <voge'line 1 childrens' clothing 2 small items of clothing: clothing accessories

voge'li'ne nf = voge'lime

voge'lo'·het vpr 1 to become smaller; shrink 2 to get shorter 3 to lose stature

voge'lo'·n vt to make [] smaller; reduce [] in amount

voge'lo'sh adj, n (Pet) = voge'lu'sh

voge'lsi' nf 1 smallness 2 = çikërri'me

voge'l'sire nf = çikërri'me

voge'lso'·n = voge'lo'·n

vo'ge'lth adj (Pet) tiny little

voge'lu'ar adj (i) made smaller; shrunken

voge'lu'sh adj, n (Pet) little/tiny (child)

*voge'rro'·n vt to stunt, dwarf

*vogje'li' nf = vegje'li

*vogje'l'im nm = vegje'li

*voj (Reg Gheg) = vaj
  ○ voj i përlyet (Old) lubricating oil

*vo'jce adj, nf egg-laying (hen) = vezara'ke

*vo'jga'z nm (Reg Gheg) = vajgu'r

*voji'cë nf (Reg) = vajani'cë

Vojsa'v'a nf Vojsava (female name)

*vo'jt'ës n person who suffers: sufferer

*vo'jt'je nf suffering, pain = vu'ajtje

*vo'jt'ur
  I § part <vu'a·n
  II § adj (i) = vu'ajtur

vojvo'dë nf 1 [Hist] Ottoman administrative and military functionary in 19th-century northern Albania; duty of that functionary 2 [Ethnog] chieftain of a large clan brotherhood in mountainous parts of northern Albania

voka'l adj [Mus] vocal

*voka'n adj (Reg) = va'kët

vokati'v nm [Ling] vocative (case)

*vok'e'si'në (Reg Gheg) = vakë'si'rë

*vo'kët (Reg Gheg) = va'kët

*vok (Reg Gheg) = vak

vol *nm* **1** pile of targeted walnuts in a children's game; large walnut thrown at the targeted walnut **2** pile of fruit; small quantity of fruit; small basket for fruit

vol *stem for pdef* <**vjel**•

volant *nm* [*Tech*] flywheel

volejboll *nm* [*Sport*] volleyball

volejbollist *n* volleyball player

*****volë = voltë**

volfram *nm* [*Chem*] tungsten *(W)*

voli *nf* **1** optimal time; suitable moment, opportunity, chance **2** free time

volit•
 I § *vi impers* it *is* most convenient for <>
 II § *vt* to make [] more convenient (for <>)

volitësi *nf (Book)* suitability, appropriateness

volitshëm *adj (i)* most propitious: opportune, appropriate; convenient

volt *nm* [*Phys*] volt

Volta e Sipërme *nf* Upper Volta

voltamatës = voltmatës

voltazh *nm* [*Phys Electr*] voltage

voltë *nf (Colloq)* last breath, death rattle

voltmatës *nm* [*Phys*] voltmeter

voltmetër *nf* [*Phys*] voltmeter

volum *nm* volume (capacity)

voluminoz *adj* voluminous

*****voll** *nm* = **voltë**

voll *stem for pdef* <**vjell**•

*****vollcë** *nf* = **vadhë**

*****vollë** *nf* = **vadhë**

*****vollëz** *nf* [*Bot*] medlar = **mushmollë**

*****vollt** *nf* will, wish, desire

vome *np fem* rhythmic eulogy for the dead spoken in a wailing voice: lament

vona *np (të) fem* crops harvested late in autumn

vonak *adj* hatched late

*****vonashi** *adv (Book)* lastly, finally

*****vone** *nf (Old)* late hour

vonesë *nf* **1** tardiness; lateness; delay **2** time required (to do something) **3** = **vonim**

vonestar *n* tardy person; procrastinator; delayer

vonë
 I § *adj (i)* **1** late, tardy **2** recent **3** late-blooming; late-developing; late-maturing; late-harvested
 II § *adv* **1** late **2** lately, recently
 ○ **i vonë nga mendja** "late in the mind" **1** immature **2** mentally handicapped, retarded
 ○ **i vonë nga veshët** hard of hearing

vonë-vonë *adv* **1** very late **2** late at night

vongorec *nm* [*Invert*] = **koshëz**

voni *adv (së)* lately

vonim *nm ger* **1** <**vono**•**n, vono**•**het 2** delay

vonimtar
 I § *adj* delaying
 II § *n* procrastinator; delayer

vono•**het** *vpr* **1** to be late/tardy; hesitate, procrastinate **2** to appear/ripen late

vono•**n**
 I § *vt* to make [] late/tardy, delay
 II § *vi* **1** to arrive late, be late/tardy **2** to procrastinate

vonshëm *adj (i)* **1** late-planted and late-harvested **2** late, tardy; belated **3** of recent times, recent; modern

vonuar *adj (i)* delayed; delayed-action

vonueshëm *adj (i)* belated

vopë *nf* [*Ichth*] bogue bream *(Boops boops)*

vor *stem for pdef* <**vjerr**•

vorbar *n* potter

vorbare *nf* large two-handled clay pot

vorbë *nf* clay pot used for boiling food

vorbës *nm* potter

vorbëtar *n* potter

vorbëtinë *nf* [*Geog*] narrow basin of land; small valley: hollow

vorbëz *nf* hollowed out rock in which rain water gathers

vorbull *nf* **1** whirlpool, eddy **2** whirlwind **3** *(Fig)* powerful wave that carries one along

vordh *stem for pdef* <**vjerdh**•, **virdh**•**et**

vore *nf* cold wind from the north

*****vorfanjak** *(Reg Gheg)* = **varfanjak**

*****vorfën** *adj (i)* *(Reg Gheg)* = **varfër**

vorfënor *adj (Reg)* = **varfëror**

*****vorfn** *(Reg Gheg)* = **varfër**

vorfnore *nf* orphanage

*****vorr** = **varr**

vorraxhi *nm (np ˜ nj) (Colloq)* gravedigger

*****vorrovesh** *nm* [*Bot*] thistle *(Carduus)*

*****vosk** *nm* [*Invert*] = **guaskë**

Voskopojë *nf* town in southeastern Albania that was formerly (in the seventeenth and eighteenth centuries) as a distinguished city of artistic culture

voshtër *nf* [*Bot*] privet *(Ligustrum vulgare)*

votë *nf* **1** vote; voting **2** *(Colloq)* lottery
 ○ **votë deliberative/vendimore** *(Offic)* tie-breaking vote cast by a presiding officer: casting vote

votëbesim *nm* vote of confidence

*****votër** *nf (Reg)* = **vatër**

votim *nm ger* <**voto**•**n**

voto•**n** *vi* to vote, cast a vote

votues *nm* voter

vovë *nf* imaginary monster used to frighten little children; bugaboo, bugbear

voz *nm* small brook bordered by grass

vozabërës *nm* = **vozëtar**

vozapunues *nm* = **vozëtar**

vozaxhi *nm (np ˜ nj)* = **vozëtar**

vozë *nf* barrel, cask, tun

vozëtar *n* cooper

vozëtari *nf* coopering; cooperage

*****vozgar** *n* = **vozëtar**

vozgë = **vozë**

*****vozgo**•**n** *vt* to put [] in a barrel/cask/tun: barrel

vozis *stem for 1st sg pres, pl pres, 2nd & 3rd sg subj, pind* <**vozit**•

vozit•
 I § *vi* **1** *(Colloq)* to row (a boat) **2** to wander around, roam
 II § *vt* to be very much in control of []

vozitës *n* **1** oarsman, rower **2** *(Colloq)* carrier, transporter

vozitje *nf ger* <**vozit**•

vozitshëm *adj (i)* navigable; (of a road) passable, trafficable

voztar *n* = **vozitës**

voztari *nf* boatsmanship

vra *stem for pdef, opt, adm, part, imper* <**vre**t·, **vrit**·*et*
  ∘ **Vrafsh veten!** "May you kill yourself!" Go ahead and get killed! It's on your own head!

vraç
  I § *nm* = **vranç**
  II § *adj* *black

vra ç i *nf* massacre, slaughter = **kërdi**

vra ç ti·n *vt* to massacre, slaughter

vrag ë *nf* **1** narrow trail/path; cart/wagon track **2** trace; impression **3** distance between a pair of wheels on an axle: wheelbase
  ∘ **vrag** ë **e verbër** faint trail/path

vrago·*het vpr* to be marked with some trace of an earlier presence

vrag sh ëm *adj (i)* impressive; touching, poignant

vrah *nm* **1** *(Collec)* [*Agr*] grain sheaves laid out for each threshing by trampling horses; grain and chaff left on the ground after threshing **2** threshing ground

vra j ë *nf* **1** scar left by a wound; bruise mark on the skin **2** bunghole; bung

vramuz *adj (Colloq)* always frowning, dour

vran ç *nm* black horse

vran ës i *nf* **1** overcast weather, cloudiness; gloom, gloominess **2** *(Fig)* gloominess reflected in one's face, dourness

vran ës i r ë *nf* overcast/gloomy weather; cloudy sky

vra n ët *adj (i)* = **vre njtur**

vra ngull *nf* **1** disk-shaped bottom of a plunger for a churn **2** spool for yarn/thread, bobbin

***vrângull** *adj (Reg Gheg)* = **vre njtur**

***vrângull o**·*n*
  I § *vt (Reg Gheg)* = **vrenjt**·
  II § *vi* = **vrenjt**·

***vrân o**·*het vpr (Reg Gheg)* = **vre njt**·*et*

***vrân o**·*n vt (Reg Gheg)* = **vrenjt**·

vrap
  I § *nm* **1** run, running **2** haste **3** speed; speediness
  II § *adv* rapidly, fast; immediately
  III § *interj* run! go! hurry!

vrap ët a r *n* = **vrapto r**

vrap ët o·*n vi* = **vrapo**·*n*

vrap ët o r *nm* = **vrapto r**

vrap im *nm ger* **1** <**vrapo**·*n* **2** run **3** [*Sport*] running; running race
  ∘ **vrapim me top** [*Soccer*] dribbling
  ∘ **vrapim thellësie** [*Track*] long-distance race

vrapo·*n vi* **1** to go fast: run **2** *(Fig)* to hurry; pass quickly
  ∘ **vrapo**·*n* **me të katra** to run fast; run on all fours
  ∘ **vrapo**·*n* **pa prekur në tokë** to go very fast: run without touching the ground, practically fly

vrapo nj ës *nm* **1** runner **2** [*Ornit*] plover *(Charadriidae)*
  ∘ **vraponjës gushëbardhë** [*Ornit*] Kentish plover *Charadrius alexandrinus L.*
  ∘ **vraponjës i madh** [*Ornit*] ringed plover *Charadrius hiaticula L.*
  ∘ **vraponjës i vogël** [*Ornit*] little ringed plover *Charadrius dubius L.*

vrap o re *nf* [*Sport*] track (for running); racing lane

vrap sh ëm *adj (i)* swift

vrap to r *adj* fast-running; swift, speedy, fast; quick and skillful

vra p thi(t) *adv* in haste, hastily

vrapu e s
  I § *n* **1** [*Sport*] runner **2** [*Tech*] device in a spinning machine that gathers and twists the fibers: traveler
  II § *np* [*Ornit*] ratite birds *(Ratitae)*
  III § *adj* running fast; at a run

vra r ë
  I § *part* <**vre**t·
  II § *adj (i)* **1** wounded; injured; bruised; hurt **2** killed, slain **3** *(Fig)* deeply saddened/hurt; feeling very sad **4** *(Fig)* dead tired
  ∘ **i vrarë lie** scarred by pox: pockmarked

vrar ël ij ë *adj* scarred by smallpox: pock-marked

vra s *stem for 1st sg pres, 1st & 3rd pl pres, 2nd & 3rd sg subj* <**vre**t·

vra s ë *nf* = **vrasje**

vra s ës *n* man-killer, killer; executioner

vra s ëse *nf* flyswatter

vras i *nf* killing; mass killing; sequential killing

vras je *nf ger* **1** <**vre**t·, **vrit**·*et* **2** death by killing; murder **3** *(Colloq)* (in a crowd of people) murderous jostling

vras tar *adj* (of a weapon) powerful, death-dealing

***vra sh** ëm *adj (i)* = **vrazhd** ë

***vra shtë** *adj (i)* = **vrazhd** ë

vrati c ë *nf* = **sohi**

vrati k *nm* [*Bot*] spicknel, meum *(Meum athamanticum)*

vrava shk ë *nf* firebrand; torch

vrazhd ë
  I § *adj (i)* **1** rough; crude **2** *(Fig)* harsh, cruel
  II § *adv* **1** roughly; crudely **2** *(Fig)* harshly, cruelly

vrazhd ës i *nf* **1** roughness; crudity **2** *(Fig)* harshness, cruelty

vrazhd ës o·*het vpr* **1** to become rough **2** *(Fig)* to become harsh/cruel

vrazhd ës o·*n vt* **1** to make [] rough: roughen **2** *(Fig)* to cause [] to behave harshly/cruelly

vrazhd o·*het vpr* = **vrazhdëso**·*het*

vrazhd o·*n vt* = **vrazhdëso**·*n*

vreg ën *nf* **1** whip = **kamxhík 2** barge pole **3** mark left by a whiplash/beating: welt

vregën o·*n vt* to whip

vrejt = **vrenjt**

vre mç ë *nf* [*Ornit*] starling *(Sturnus vulgaris)*

vrenjt· *vt* **1** to make [sky/weather] overcast, darken/cloud [sky] **2** *(Fig)* to make [] downcast/gloomy

vre njt·*et vpr* **1** to become overcast, cloud over **2** *(Fig)* to be surly/sullen, frown, scowl

vrenjt ës i r ë *nf* = **vranësi r** ë

vre njt ur *adj (i)* **1** overcast, cloudy **2** *(Fig)* surly, sullen; morose; frowning

vrer
  I § *nm* **1** bile, gall; choler, rage **2** *(Reg)* sputum **3** venom; bitter-tasting sap from a plant **4** *(Fig)* bitter grief/anger/hatred/spite
  II § *adj (Fig)* bitterly sad/angry/spiteful

vrer ës o·*n vt* = **vrenjt**·

vrer ët *adv* with bitter sorrow; venomously

vrer o·*het vpr* = **vreros**·*et*

vrer o·*n vt* **1** to make [] morose **2** to embitter

vreros· *vt* **1** to grieve [] deeply **2** to embitter **3** = **vrenjt**·

vreros·*et vpr* **1** to become bitterly sad; be in despair, be disheartened/demoralized ***2** *(Old)* to be poisoned ***3** to feel bitter ***4** to become overcast

vrero·sje *nf* affliction, despair

vrero·sur *adj (i)* **1** full of bitter grief **2** *(Fig)* venomous

vrero·sh *adj* = vre·rtë

vre·rtë *adj (i)* **1** poisoned, venomous **2** full of bitter grief, mournful; venomous

vresht *I §* *nm* OR **vre·shtë** *II §* *nf* vineyard

vreshta·r *n* vineyard worker; viniculturist

vreshta·rí *nf* cultivation of grapes; viniculture

vreshto·r *nm* guard of a vineyard, vineyard warden

vret· *vt* **1** to kill, slay **2** to wound, injure **3** to hurt **4** *(Colloq)* to break/pick [] apart: toss [salad, spaghetti], knead [dough], break up [a clod of earth], crush [olives] **5** to modify [a color] (by adding another color)

○ **vret· barkun në hije** "hurt one's belly in the shade (from lying there so long)" to dislike working, be lazy

○ **vret· degë më degë** to act high and mighty

○ **vret· e pret₁·** *(Pej)* "kill and cut" **1** to talk and act mean, be a bully **2** to do whatever one likes, act without restraint

○ **vret·³ˢᵍ gjetkë fjala e tij/saj/tyre** "his/her/their word strikes elsewhere" what he/she/they say actually means something other than what it says; what he/she/they say is intended for a different target, what he/she/they say has something/someone else in mind

○ **vret·³ˢᵍ gjetkë fjala ime/jote/jonë/juaj** "(my/your/our/your word) strikes elsewhere" what I/you/we/you say actually means something else; what I/you/we/you say is intended for a different target, what I/you/we/you say has something/someone else in mind

○ **vret·³ˢᵍ gjetkë** "(what is said) strikes elsewhere" it actually means something other than what it says, that doesn't mean what it seems to say

○ **nuk <>a vret·³ˢᵍ këpuca këmbën** "<>'s shoe doesn't pinch (hurt/squeeze) <>'s foot" <> is not desperately short of money

○ **vret· kohën** "kill time" to waste time; kill time

○ **e vret· kokën për** [] "hurt one's head for []" to cudgel one's brains thinking about []

○ **vret· larg** to have a distant/long-term goal; aim at something further

○ **vret· lart** to start to think too highly of oneself, become swell-headed, get conceited

○ [] **vret· me pusi** to kill [] from ambush

○ **e vret· mendjen për** [] "hurt one's mind for []" to cudgel one's brains thinking about []

○ **vret· mendjen** to rack one's brain, cudgel one's brains

○ **vret· miza (gjithë ditën)** "count/kill/catch flies (all day long)" *(Impol)* to waste time idly: sit around (the whole day) twiddling one's thumbs

○ [] **vret·³ˢᵍ ndërgjegjja** []'s conscience *is hurting/bothering* []

○ [] **vret· në zemër** "wound [] in the heart" to hurt []'s feelings deeply: hurt [] to the quick

○ **vret· rëndë** to think too highly of oneself

○ **po** [] **vret·³ˢᵍ samari** "the saddle *is chafing* []" *(Iron)* [] *is feeling* the rub

○ **<> vret· sytë** "hurt <>'s eyes" to be too ugly for <> even to look at

○ **vret· të trasha/rënda** to boast, brag

○ **Të vret natën e të qan ditën.** "{} kills you at night and mourns for you the next day." {} is deceitful/two-faced.

○ **<> vret· veshin/veshët** to hurt <>'s ears; <> cannot bear hearing {}

○ **vret· veshin** to break in one's ears, get used to listening (to a foreign language/dialect)

○ **vret· veten me dorën** {e tij} "hurt oneself with {}'s own hand" to be hurting {}self

vrete·n *nm (Old)* measure of land area somewhat larger than a dynym

vre·vë *nf* **1** *(Old)* calamity **2** fear; anxiety

*****vrë·n** OR **vrër·** = vrenjt·

*****vrër·et** *vpr* = vre·njt·et

*****vrërë·sírë** *nf* = vranësírë

*****vrë·rët** *adj (i)* = vre·njtur

*****vrëro·n** *vt* = vrenjt·

*****vri** *nf* = vërrí

vrie·skë *nf* [*Bot*] thyme *(Thymus)*

vri·gth *nm* [*Anat*] lobule

vri·gull *nm (np ⁻j)* **1** flap **2** lobe of a leaf **3** torn piece; loose piece of cloth, rag **4** (of meat) flank

○ **vrigull i veshit** earlobe

*****vrigullím** *nm ger* **1** <vrigullo·n **2** buzz, whiz; hum, whir

*****vrigullo·n** *vi* to buzz, whiz; hum, whir

vrigullo·r *adj* [*Anat*] lobar

vri·gullt *adj (i)* **1** shaped in a lobe; divided into lobe-shaped pieces having a flap, flapped **2** [*Bot*] lobate; lobed

vrik *adv (Reg)* = vring

*****vri·kshëm**
  I § *adj (i)* sudden
  II § *adv* suddenly

vri·ma-vri·ma
  I § *adv* full of holes
  II § *adj* perforated

vri·më *nf* hole

○ **vrimë e derës** keyhole

○ **ësh·të vrima e fundit e kavallit** "be the lowest hole on the fife" to be low man on the totem pole

○ **Vrima e miut – pesëqind grosh.** "A mouse hole – five hundred piasters." (indicates a desperate need for a place to hide) Any port in a storm (at any price)

vrimo·n *vt* to make a hole in []: puncture, pierce, bore

vring *adv* suddenly; immediately

vringëllí·n *vt, vi* = vringëllo·n

vringëllím *nm ger* **1** <vringëllo·n **2** = vringëllímë

vringëllímë *nf* clanging sound; rattling sound

vringëllísht *adv* whirling around; in a whipping motion

vringëllo·n
  I § *vt* **1** to brandish **2** *(Fig Pej)* to brandish [] as a threat
  II § *vi* to clang, ring out

vringëllúe·s *adj* clanging, ringing

vri·ngthi *adv* = vring

*****vrío·n** *vi* (of a wellspring) to barely flow

*****vrío·n** *nm* barely flowing wellspring

vri·s *stem for 2nd pl pres, pind* <vret·

vrit·et *vpr* **1** to kill oneself, kill one another **2** to die in battle **3** to fight head-to-head **4** to be wounded/hurt; get banged up **5** *(Fig)* to feel deeply hurt/sad **6** *(Fig)* to knock oneself out by exertion

○ **vrit·et si qeni në vresht/rrush** "be hurt like the dog in the vineyard/grapes" to be killed by being at the wrong place at the wrong time

vrit *stem for pind, 2nd pl pres, imper, vp* <**vret·**

vrithe *np fem (Old)* goat pasture near one's house

vrizëm *nf (Colloq)* drizzle, mist

*__vro·n__ *vt* = **vëre·n, vrojto·n**

vrojtim *nm ger* 1 <**vrojto·n, vrojto·het** 2 observation; object of observation

vrojto·n *vt* to watch [ ] carefully: observe

vrojtore *nf* observation point

vrojtues
I § *n* observer
II § *adj* involved in observing; observational

vrokth *nm* 1 *(Reg)* dandruff = **zbokth** 2 *[Bot] (Cionura)*

*__vrom__ *nm (Reg)* highway

*__vromusë__ *nf [Bot]* upright mignonette *(Reseda alba)*

vrotom *nm* large mountain hollow permanently filled with snow used as a summer watering hole for livestock

vrug *nm* 1 *[Agr]* mildew blight, downy mildew *(Peronospora)* 2 grime on clothes/body
○ **vrug i duhanit** *[Agr]* tobacco mildew *(Peronospora hyoscyami)*
○ **vrug i qepës** *[Agr]* onion mildew *(Peronospora destructor)*

vrug· *vt* = **vrugo·n**

vrug·et *vpr* = **vrugo·het**

vrugët *adj (i)* 1 dark (in color) 2 *(Fig)* gloomy, downcast, frowning

vrugo·het *vpr* 1 *[Agr]* (of plants) to suffer mildew blight 2 to become dark, darken; take on a gloomy appearance 3 to become sullied

vrugo·n *vt* 1 *[Agr]* to cause downy mildew to form on [ ] 2 *(Fig)* to lower [ ] in a frown, make [ ] gloomy 3 *(Fig)* to ruin, destroy 4 to sully [one's honor]

vruguar *adj (i)* 1 *[Agr]* (of plants) afflicted with mildew blight 2 dark and gloomy 3 gloomy-faced

vrugur *adj (i)* = **vruguar**

vrujë *nf* small spring (of water)

vrujim *nm* = **burim**

vrujinë *nf* 1 dampness forming on walls: sweat; dampness in the ground 2 ground that stays wet, wet ground

vrujishtë *nf* snow-filled mountain hollow that melts down little by little during the summer

vrujo·n *vi* = **buro·n**

vrull *nm* 1 surge/burst of energy: rush, dash 2 *(Fig)* fervor

vrull·et *vpr* = **vrullo·n**

vrullët *adj (i)* = **vrullshëm**

vrulli *nf* = **vrull**

vrullimë *nf* = **vrull**

vrullo·n *vi* to charge/surge forward, make a rush, dash forth, dash, swoop

vrullshëm *adj (i), adv* with a burst of energy, surging

vrulltas OR **vrulltazi** *adv* = **vrullshëm**

vrulltë *adj (i)* = **vrullshëm**

*__vrullues__ *adj* = **vrullshëm**

vrumbullimë *nf* 1 roar 2 buzzing of bees 3 gurgling sound of a river hitting against rocks

vrumbullit· *vi* 1 to make a long, low-pitched sound: bellow, roar 2 (of bees) to buzz 3 (of a river) to gurgle

vrumbullitje *nf ger* 1 <**vrumbullit·** 2 = **vrumbullimë**

*__vrumulis·__ *vt* = **vrumbullit·**

vrunduj-vrunduj *adv* = **valë-valë**

vrundull
I § *nm (np ˜j)* 1 burst of energy/force; force, power 2 *(Fig)* powerful wave
II § *adv* in a wave of energy/force

vrundullo·n *vi* = **vrullo·n**

vrungull *nm (np ˜j)* = **vrull, vrundull**

vrungullimë *nf* loud rumbling = **shungullimë**

vrungullit· *vi* = **vrungullo·n**

vrungullo·n *vi* 1 = **shungullo·n** 2 = **vrull·et**

vrushkull
I § *nm (np ˜j), nf* 1 = **fshikull** 2 spurting stream of liquid
II § *adv* in a spurt

vrushkullo·n
I § *vt* = **fshikullo·n**
II § *vi, vt* to spurt forth

vrushkullore *nf [Bot]* greenbrier *(Smilax aspera)* = **ferrac**

vrutë *nf [Ichth]* thicklip gray mullet *(Chelon labrosus)* = **buzoç**

*__vrragë__ = **vragë**

*__vrrietë__ *adj* = **vërri**

vrromë *nf* slut, slattern = **molare**

vu
I § *stem for pl pdef, 3rd sg pdef* <**vë·**
II § *stem for vp* <**vua·n**

vua·n
I § *vi* 1 to feel pain 2 to suffer
II § *vt* to cause suffering
○ **vua·n lëngun e ullirit** to suffer severe hardship
○ **vua·n nga trutë e kokës** "suffer from brains in one's head" to suffer from one's own silliness/stupidity
○ **vua·n për mendtë e kokës** "suffer for the brains in the head" to suffer from a problem of one's own making
○ **vua·n pikën e zezë** to suffer terribly
○ **vua·n të zitë e ullirit** to suffer severe hardship

*__vuajshëm__ *adj (i)* endurable, bearable

vuajt *stem for pdef, opt, adm, part* <**vua·n**

vuajtje *nf ger* 1 <**vuaj·, vu·het** 2 suffering, pain

vuajtur
I § *part* <**vua·n**
II § *adj (i)* 1 long-suffering, suffering 2 experienced, toughened by experience: seasoned

*__vuar__
I § *part* <**vua·n**
II § *adj (i)* = **vuajtur**

*__vuej__ *(Reg)* = **vuaj**

vulak *nm* = **lehe**

*__vulangë__ *nf* = **bullungë**

vula-vula *adv* covered with the marks of stamps; covered with small spots: dotted, heavily scarred

vulë *nf* 1 stamp; seal 2 small spot; bruise mark
○ **vulë datare** stamp indicating the date, date stamp
○ **vulë postale** postage stamp
○ **vulë e thatë** "dry stamp" embossing stamp

vulëgdhendës *n* stamp engraver

vulëharruar *adj, n* = **vulëhumbur**

vulë|hu|mb|ur *adj, n* **1** (person) who has disappeared without a trace **2** *(Curse)* may-he-be-wiped off-the-face-of-the-earth! **3** (person) in a total daze

vul|ë|mba|jt|ës *nm* keeper of the (official) seal

vul|ë|pun|u|e|s *nm* = **vulëgdhendës**

vu'l|ër *nf* [*Bot*] Johnsongrass *(Sorghum halepense)* = **tallë**

vul|ë|zi *adj, n (fem sg ~ ez, masc pl ~ inj, fem pl ~ eza)* **1** = **vulëhumbur 2** (person) who has suffered a calamity; unfortunate (person)

vulga'r *adj* **1** *(Pej)* vulgar **2** *(Book)* common, vulgar

vulgar|iz|im *nm ger* **1** *(Book)* <**vulgarizo·n 2** vulgarization

vulgar|izo·n *vt* *(Book)* **1** *(Pej)* to vulgarize **2** to present [ ] in a simplified form to make it available to a broad public: popularize

vulgar|iz|u|e|s *adj (Book)* **1** *(Pej)* vulgarizing **2** popularizing

vul|o·n *vt* = **vulos·**

vulo'më *nf* wooden bung

vulo's· *vt* **1** to certify [ ] with a stamp; affix a seal on [ ] **2** to mark, scar **3** to seal [ ] tight **4** *(Fig Colloq)* to bring [ ] to a final end, decide []: seal []'s fate **5** *(Fig)* to stain, blemish
  ○ **i vulos· gojën** to seal one's lips, not speak again
  ○ <>**a vulos· gojën me shtupë** "seal <>'s mouth with oakum" to forcibly prevent <> from speaking: shut <> up good
  ○ **vulos· veshët** to stuff one's ears (with cotton) against noise

vul|o's·et *vpr* to close up tight; seal by itself

vul|o's|je *nf ger* <**vulos·, vulos·et**

vul|o's|ur *adj (i)* **1** sealed **2** marked **3** *(Colloq)* permanently resolved/decided, absolutely settled

vu'l|vë *nf* [*Anat*] vulva

vulla(n) *nm* strip of land

vulla|n|i *obl* <**vulla(n)**

vulla|nj *np* <**vulla(n)**

vullka'n *nm* **1** volcano **2** *(Fig)* hidden danger posing a great threat: timebomb; pent-up powerful force ready to burst

vullkan|ik *adj* [*Geol*] volcanic

vullkan|iz|im *nm ger* [*Tech*] **1** <**vullkanizo·n 2** vulcanization

vullkan|izo·n *vt* [*Tech*] to vulcanize

vullkan|iz|u|a'r *adj (i)* vulcanized

vullkan|o'r *adj* [*Geol*] = **vullkanik**

vullne's|ë *nf* *(Old)* will, desire

vullne't *nm* will, will power; willingness; desire
  ○ **vulleti i fundit** last wish (before one dies)

Vullne't *nm* Vullnet (male name)

vullnetar
  I § *n* volunteer
  II § *adj* voluntary

vullnet|ar|isht *adv* voluntarily

vullnet|ar|izëm *nm* *(Book)* volunteerism

vullnet|çelik *adj* steel-willed

vullnet|do|bët *adj* weak-willed

vullnet|fo'rt|ë *adj* strong-willed

vullnet|he'ku'rt [*vull-net-he-kurt*] *adj* iron-willed

vullnet|mirë *adj* of good will; willing; well-intentioned

***vullnet|o'r**
  I § *adj* voluntary
  II § *n* volunteer

vullnet|sh|ëm *adj (i)* **1** willing **2** voluntary

vu'|më *part* *(Reg Gheg)* <**vë·**

vur
  I § *stem for sg pdef* <**vë·**
  II § *sg imper* <**vë·**

***vu'rc|ë** *nf* = **furçë**

vurg *nm (np ~ gje)* **1** muddy lowland; permanently wet ground **2** marc residue from pressing olives

vurkolla'k *nm* [*Folklore*] = **lugat**

vurra't· *vt* to scar

vurra't·et *vpr* to become scarred

vurra't|ë *nf* **1** scar **2** dirty stain

vurra'tur *adj (i)* **1** scarred **2** stained with spots

vu'sh|ë *nf* *(Reg)* [*Entom*] dungbeetle, tumblebug *(Scarabaeus sacer)*

vu'të *adj (i)* **1** *(Reg)* level, flat **2** low **3** *(Fig)* humble, compliant

vuth *nm* small piece of flat ground

vu'|u *OR* **vuu'u** *onomat* = **vu-vu**

vuv *adj, n* *(Colloq)* mute (person)

vuv|o's·et *vpr* to become mute; stop talking, shut up

vu-vu' *onomat* sound of howling wind

***vu'zh|ë** *nf* [*Bot*] danewort *(Sambucus ebulus)*

vye·n *vi* = **vle·n**

vye'r *adj (i)* highly valued, in high esteem

vye'sh|ëm *adj (i)* = **vyer**

vy'shk· *vt* = **fishk·**

vy'shk·et *vpr* = **fishk·et**

vy'shk|ët *adj (i)* = **fishkur**

vy'shk|je *nf ger* = **fishkje**

vy'shk|ur *adj (i)* = **fishkur**

WC *abbrev (English)* WC = Water Closet (toilet)

WFTU *abbrev (English)* WFTU = World Federation of Trade Unions

Xx

x [*dzë*] *nf* **1** the consonant letter "x" **2** the voiced apico-alveolar sibilant affricate represented by the letter "x"

x [*iks*] *nm* [*Math*] the variable "x"

*****xâ·** *vt (Reg Gheg)* = zë·

*****xama′re** *nf* = zama′re

xa′nё *nf* **1** [*Bot*] = gjine′shtёr **2** (*Colloq*) coarse cloth woven from the fibers of weaver's broom and used to make sacks **3** grove of trees with pasture

*****xânёs** *n (Reg Gheg)* = nxёnёs

xanxa′r *adj*, *n (Colloq)* **1** (person/animal) with bad habits; hard-to-handle/kicking (animal) **2** mischievous/naughty (person)

*****xanxa′rё** *nf* [*Entom*] mosquito

xa′nxё *nf(Colloq)* **1** serious defect/fault; vice **2** trouble; internal problem **3** mischief, bad deed

xarbaxu′l *nm (Insult)* shabbilily dressed and dirty person: ragamuffin

*****xa′rbё** = za′rbё

xarnave′l *nm (Insult)* shameless person; unreliable person

*****xё·het** *vpr (Reg Gheg)* = zi′·het

*****xe′·n** *vt* = nxe′h·

xe′gёl *nf* [*Entom*] botfly = zekth

xeh· *vt* = nxeh·

xe′h·et *vpr* to get riled = nxe′h·et

xe′he *nf* **1** mineral **2** mine, pit

xehero′·n *vi* to make into ore

xehero′r

  I § *nm* ore

  II § *adj* containing or pertaining to ore

xehero′rmba′jtёs *adj* ore-bearing

xeheta′r *n (Book)* miner of ore

xeheta′ri *nf (Book)* mining of ore

xe′la *np fem (Colloq Pej)* eyes

*****xele′fkё** *nf* corn tassel

*****xe′ro** *nf* zero = ze′ro

xerxe′le *nf* [*Bot*] daphne (*Daphne oleoides*)

*****xe′tё** *adj (i)*, *nn (tё)* = nxe′htё

*****xetma′sё** *nf(Old)* = nxehtёsima′tёs

xexeri′ca *np fem (Colloq)* claptrap, nonsense

xёc

  I § *nm (Colloq)* pitch darkness

  II § *adj (Colloq)* pitch dark

xёgi′m *nm ger* = xёgi′tje

xёgi′s *stem for 1st sg pres, pl pres, 2nd & 3rd sg subj, pind* <xёgi′t·

xёgi′t· *vt (Colloq)* **1** to prick; poke; pester, needle **2** to taunt; provoke, incite; stir up [ ] **3** to instigate?

xёgi′t·et *vp* to exchange taunts

xёgo′·n *vt* = xёgi′t·

*****xёgo′njёs** *nm* agitator, fomenter; instigator

xёrli′s· *vi (Colloq)* to prattle, talk twaddle = dёrdёlli′t·

xёrli′sje *nf ger* **1** <xёrli′s· **2** twaddle, nonsense = dёrdёlli′tje

xёrmo′·n *vi (Reg)* = zbre′t·

xёrxa′lla *np fem (ColloqImpolite)* eyeglasses, spectacles: glasses = sy′ze

*****xёrro′·n** *vt (Colloq)* = rrёzo′·n

xibё′rr *nf* = xibёrra′kё

xibё′rra′kё *nf* infertile soil, unproductive land

xibёrri′mё *nf* **1** steep ground **2** unproductive land

xibёrri′shtё *nf* = xibёrri′mё

xiga′ne *nf* = zama′re

xigё′li′s· *vt* to tickle

*****ximi′cё** *nf* [*Veter*] a disease of horses

xi′nё *nf* **1** pen point **2** [*Bot*] mastic tree (*Pistacia lentiscus L.*)

xing *nm* **1** card game in which a player puts a card down and the other player tries to match it **2** = zink

xingo′nё *nf* deep and dark abyss, chasm

*****xink** = zink

xinxi′fe *nf* [*Bot*] jujube, buckthorn (*Zizyphus jujuba*) = hi′de

xip *nm* **1** sharp point: quill, thorn, spine, stinger **2** *(Fig)* caustic remark

  ○ **xipat e qenit** spiked dog muzzle

xi′pkё *nf* sharp point of a plowman's ox prod

*****xi′r** *stem for 2nd pl pres, pind, imper, vp* <xjerr·

xite′lё

  I § *nf*

  II § *nf (Pej)* woman that no one will consider for marriage: leftover old maid

xixa′r *nm (Reg)* [*Entom*] drone bee

xixa′re *nf* bunch of sparks struck from a flintstone

xixa-xi′xa *adj* **1** full of sparks; sparkling **2** (of textiles) with shiny dots

xi′xё

  I § *nf* **1** spark **2** sparkle, twinkle **3** shiny dot (on textiles)

  II § *adj* sparkling clean; sparkling

xixё′lli′m *nm ger* **1** <xixё′llo′·n **2** = xixё′lli′mё

xixё′lli′mё *nf* **1** twinkling light; glistening **2** sparkle **3** [*Entom*] = xixё′llo′njё

xixё′llo′·n *vi* **1** to give off sparks **2** to sparkle, twinkle **3** *(Fig)* to flash to <>'s mind

xixё′lloje = xixё′llo′njё

xixё′llo′njё *nf* **1** [*Entom*] firefly, glowworm **2** (*Colloq*) girl/woman who brightens up her surroundings; frivolous girl/woman

xixё′llo′re *nf* sparkling gemstone

xixё′llu′e′s *adj* sparkling, glistening; twinkling

xixё′mi′m *nm* sharp pain

xixё′mo′·n *vi* **1** (of body parts) to feel tingly, cause <> to feel pins and needles **2** to cause <> pain, hurt <> **3** to give off sparks, spark

xixё′ri′·n *vi* (of flames) to spurt and give off sparks

xixё′ri′mё *nf* crackling sound (of wood giving off sparks)

*****xixi** = xix′ё

xixime′rkё *nf* sawtoothed line separating knitted figures in stockings

xixinë *nf* = xhixhë

xix·o·n *vi* to give off sparks: spark

*__xjerr·__ = nxjerr·

*__xjerrë__ *part* <xjerr·

xokol *nf* shim

*__xor__ *stem for pdef* <xjerr·

xugis *stem for 1st sg pres, pl pres, 2nd & 3rd sg subj, pind* <xugit·

xugit· *vt (Colloq)* to bother; provoke, taunt

xugit·et *vpr (Colloq)* to exchange taunts

*__xullufe__ *np* = zylyfe

*__xung__ *nm* [Entom] beetle (Coleoptera)

xunkth *nm* 1 [Bot] marsh plant used for withes: rush (Juncus) 2 withe, wicker *3 gorse, furze

xunkthëri *nf* = xunkthëtari

xunkthëtar *n* wickerworker

xunkthëtari *nf* wickerworking

xunkthore *nf* 1 rush family Juncaceae 2 place where rushes grow

xunkthpunues *nm* = xunkthëtar

xuq *n (Colloq)* shrivelled-up old person who can barely speak; dotard

xurxull *adj (Colloq)* 1 soaked from head to toe 2 stone drunk, soused

*__xvar__ *adv* = zvarrë

*__xvas__ *stem for 1st sg pres, pl pres, 2nd & 3rd sg subj, pind* <xvat·

*__xvat·__ *vt* = zhvat·

*__xverk__ *nm (np ˜ qe)* = zverk

*__xvetosje__ *nf* soreness (in the throat)

*__xvërdhi·n__ *vt* = zvjerdh·

XHxh

xh *nf* **1** the consonant or letter "xh" **2** the voiced palatal affricate represented by the letter "xh"

xha *indecl masc* respectful title used in addressing an older man by his first name

xha'b'a *adv* **1** *(Colloq Pej)* without paying, without pay **2** very cheap, for practically nothing

xhaba'xhi'

I § *nm (np ˜ nj) (Colloq)* = qelepirxhi'

II § *adj* freeloading

xhade'

I § *nf (Colloq)* highway, main road; paved road/ street

II § *adj* level, flat; without hindrance/problems

III § *adv (Colloq)* without problems, smoothly

xhadi' *nf(Colloq Insult)* **1** whore, hooker **2** nasty and talkative trouble-maker: old witch

xhagajdu'r *nm (Colloq)* cocky braggart who goes around looking for a fight: bully; belligerent trouble-maker

　∘ **xhagajdur pa mustaqe** "cocky braggart without a mustache" empty braggart

xhahi'l *nm, adj* **1** *(ColloqImpolite)* (person) who is ignorant, backward, uncultured and thickheaded **2** (person) who is cruel and heartless

xhaje' *nf with masc agreement (Reg)* = xhaxha'

Xhaka'rt'ë *nf* Djakarta, Jakarta

xhake't'ë *nf* suit coat, dress jacket

xhako'n *nm* [*Relig*] Roman Catholic deacon

xhakoni' *nf* [*Relig*] Roman Catholic deaconry/deaconhood

xham

I § *nm* **1** glass **2** sheet glass; pane of glass; piece of glass; glass lens **3** *(Colloq)* window; mirror **4** *(Reg)* drinking glass **5** *(Colloq)* deep cup **6** *(Old)* facial treatment and depilatory made of honey and citric acid

II § *pred (Fig)* clean/clear as glass; shiny

　∘ **xham akulli** "ice glass" frosted glass

　∘ **xham dysh** glass pane 2 millimeters thick

　∘ **xham gjashtësh** six-millimeter thick glass pane/ sheet

　∘ **xham katërsh** four-millimeter thick sheet of glass

　∘ **xham i kthjellët** crystal clear

　∘ **uj'ë/lëng xhami** "glass water/liquid" water glass *a syrupy solution of sodium/potassium silicate used for industrial purposes*

　∘ **xham i marrtë** opaque glass

　∘ **xham i pastër** crystal clear

　∘ **xham pllakë** sheet glass

　∘ **xham i qartë** crystal clear

　∘ **xham qorr** opaque glass; frosted glass

　∘ **xham qumësht** white milk glass

xhamada'n *nm* double-breasted waistcoat

Xhamajk'ë *nf* Jamaica

xham'a'pre'r'ë's *n* glass-cutter (person), glazier

xhama'sh *nm* trough in which leather is placed for tanning: currier's trough

xhama'xhi' *nm (np ˜ nj)* = xhamta'r

xham'ba'z

I § *nm (Old Colloq)* **1** dealer in horses, horsetrader; horsetrainer **2** *(Pej)* swindler, double-dealer, con-artist

II § *adj (Colloq Pej)* double-dealing, tricky

xham'ba'z'llë'k *nm (np ˜ qe) (Old Colloq)* **1** horse dealing **2** *(Colloq Pej)* swindle, flimflam

xham'ëzo'·het *vpr* to become hard and brittle

xhami' *nf* mosque

xham'llë'k *nm (np ˜ qe)* **1** glass partition; large expanse of glass **2** *(Colloq)* glass storefront **3** *(Colloq)* glass-walled store

xham'o'r *adj (Book)* vitreous

xham'pre'r'ë's *nf* glass-cutter (tool)

xham'punu'e's *nm* = qelqpunu'es

xham'ta'r *n* **1** glazier **2** = xhampunu'es

xha'm'të *adj (i)* **1** made of glass **2** having a glass front **3** [*Spec*] brittle as glass **4** *(Fig)* crystal-clear **5** *(Fig)* stiff and lifeless; cold and hard

xham'tin'ë *nf* vitrine, display case

xha'm'thi *adv*

xhan

I § *nm (Colloq)* spirit

II § *n (Pet)* darling (as a term of address)

xhan'a'n *adj, n (Colloq)* loving and kind: sweet (person)

xhanava'r *adj, n (Colloq)* (person) who is careless about clothing and appearance, careless and slovenly (person)

xhanda'r *nm* armed policeman, gendarme

xhandarm'ëri' *nf collec* police, gendarmerie

xha'nëm *interj (Colloq)* expresses speaker's frustration: for God's sake!

xhanfe's *nm (Old)* taffeta = tafta'

xhanga'lle *nf* unripe almond

xha'ng'ë *nf* purse (for carrying money), wallet

xhanxhi'n

I § *determiner, pron (Colloq)* not one (person), nobody

II § *adv* empty of people, with nobody there

　∘ **s'kishte xhanxhin** there wasn't a soul there; there wasn't a sound

***xhap'i** *(n) nm* = zhapi'

xha'r'ë *nf* [*Ornit*] griffon vulture (*Gyps fulvus*)

xha'ul *nm* [*Phys*] joule

xhauni's· *vi (Colloq)* to blabber, prattle

xhaval'it· *vt* to tear [] apart

xha've *nf (Colloq)* stray dog

xha'vë'rr *nf* thin wooden branch; piece of kindling wood

xhavë'rri'n'ë *nf* sparse patch of dry bushes

xha'vrr'a *np fem* = xha'vërr prunings; kindling wood

xhaxh'a' *nm (np ˜ lla'rë)* uncle (father's brother)

xhaxh'e'sh'ë *nf* aunt (wife of father's brother)

xha'xh'i *nm (Child)* title of affectionate respect for a man

xha'xh'k'ë *nf(Reg)* mother's sister: aunt

xha'xh·o *nf with masc agreement* **1** *(Colloq)* respectful term of familiar address to an elderly man **2** elderly/old man

xhaz *nm* **1** [*Mus*] jazz **2** jazz band; drum set

xheç *pron (Colloq)* something

xhe'fkë *nf (Colloq)* cornhusk

xhehenem *nm* **1** [*Relig*] Hell (for Moslems) **2** living hell

xhe'ku *adv (Colloq)* = **çoku'**

****xhe'kull**ë *nf* savoy cabbage = **lakra'm**e

xhela' *nf* shoe polish

xhela't *nm* **1** executioner **2** cruel and bloodthirsty person

xhelatin'ë *nf* gelatin

xhelatino'·n *vt* to gelatinize

xhelatino'r OR **xhelatino'z** *adj* gelatinous

xhele'p *nm* [*Hist*] tax on livestock during the Ottoman occupation

xhelep'çi *nm (np ~ nj)* [*Hist*] collector of tax on livestock during the Ottoman occupation

****xheli'k** *nm* tipcat

xheli'në *nf* short jacket

****xheli't** *nm (Old)* dart, arrow, javelin

xhelo'z *adj, n* jealous/suspicious (person)

xhelo'zi *nf* jealousy, suspicion

Xhema'l *nm* Xhemal (male name)

xhena'ze
  I § *nf (Colloq Old)* **1** human corpse (in a coffin) **2** religious burial ritual
  II § *adj* emaciated

xhenem *nm* hell

xhene't
  I § *nm* **1** [*Relig*] Paradise (for a Moslem) **2** *(Fig Colloq)* paradise
  II § *adj (Colloq)* cheerful and making others cheerful

xhenie'r
  I § *nm* [*Mil*] soldier in the engineering corps; military engineer, sapper
  II § *adj* [*Mil*] of, by, used for, or pertaining to military engineering/engineers

xhe'nio *nf* [*Mil*] engineering corps; military engineering

xhenti'l *adj* **1** kind, polite, courteous **2** genteel

xhentile'së *nf* **1** kindness, politeness, courtesy **2** gentility

xhenxhefi'l *nm* [*Bot*] ginger *(Zingiber officinalis)*

xhep *nm* **1** pocket **2** dead end, blind pass **3** [*Alpinism*] cirque, corrie **4** recess in a narrow passageway to permit passing
  ○ **të fut ndër xhepa** {} will always cheat/deceive you
  ○ **T'i këndon/lexon letrat/kartat në xhep.** "{} reads the cards in your pocket" {} has eyes in the back of his/her head, {} can read your mind, {} can see right through you
  ○ **xhepi i plagës** pustule
  ○ **xhepat e syve** bags under the eyes

xhepa'sh *nm* pickpocket

xhepgri'sur *adj* = **xhepshpu'ar**

xhepha'ne *nf (Old)* **1** munitions depot **2** munitions

xhepo'r *adj* [*Zool*] marsupial

xhepshpu'ar *adj, n* loose-spending (spendthrift)

xhepzbra'zur *adj* with empty pockets, broke

xhera'h *nm (Old)* informally trained medical practitioner who performs minor surgery and treats wounds; circumciser

****xherde'k** *nm (Reg Gheg)* = **gjerde'k**

xheri'me *np fem* fine, penalty = **gjo'b**e

xhe'rkë *nf* [*Bot*] variety of white cabbage used to make sauerkraut

xherr *nm (Old)* money paid to band member for providing wedding music; money given to Moslem priest for a service rendered

****xhet** *nm* clan, lineage, stock
  ○ **xhet pas xheti** for generations; from generation to generation

xhevahir
  I § *nm* **1** diamond; gem, jewel **2** *(Iron)* error, mistake
  II § *adj* **1** very nice; goodhearted **2** precious

xhevahi'r'të *adj (i)* made of/with precious stones: jeweled

xheva'p *nm (Colloq)* answer = **përgji'gj**e
  ○ **ësh·të i xhevapit** to be quick with an answer

xheverda're *nf (Old)* muzzle-loading flintlock gun

****xheverxhi'le** *nf* niter, saltpeter

xhez *nm* jazz = **xhaz**

xheza *nf (Old)* punishment; fine

****xhe'zme** = **xhe'zve**

xhe'zve *nf* **1** small long-handled metal pot (with a narrow neck) used to make Turkish coffee **2** *(Reg)* nozzle of a bellows
  ○ **xhezve dyshe** [*Lit*] pot for brewing two cups of coffee

****xhëlli** *nf* = **xhurdi'**

xhërro'kull *nm (np ~ j)* [*Bot*] autumn crocus *(Colchicum)*
  ○ **xhërrokull vjeshtor** [*Bot*] meadow saffron, common autumn crocus *Colchicum autumnale*

xhiba'l *nm* [*Hist*] nineteenth century judicial council operating in northern Albania

xhibe'r *adj* **1** *(Colloq)* lively and nimble **2** ferocious and cruel **3** (of tobacco) strong

xhibli'k *nm* canopy of mosquito netting; canopy bed

xhidavi' *nf* **1** [*Anat*] hump at the base of the neck of livestock **2** [*Veter*] saddle sore at the base of the neck of a beast of burden

xhige'r *nm* **1** *(Old)* lungs of livestock **2** innards (of humans/livestock)

xhi'kë *nf (Old)* **1** respectful term of address to an elderly Moslem woman **2** woman who accompanies the bride to the bridegroom's house and stays over for the first night

xhi'ko *nf (Old)* respectful term of address to an elderly Moslem woman

xhi'lë *nf* **1** two walnuts placed one on top of the other for a children's game **2** two fruits with a single stem, two fruits joined together; double string of corn/tobacco

****xhimxha'kës** *nm* [*Ornit*] sparrow = **trumca'k**

xhin *nm* gin

xhind *nm* [*Folklore*] evil spirit: wicked jinni; genie

xhind'e *nf* **1** [*Folklore*] female evil jinni **2** *(Colloq)* beautiful girl/woman
  ○ **ësh·të me xhinde** to be raging with anger; be quick to anger, be hot-tempered

xhi'ndër *nm (Colloq)* = **shakulli'n**ë

xhindo's· *vt (Colloq)* to drive [] into a mad rage; drive [] mad

xhindo's·et vpr (Colloq) to go into a mad rage; go mad

xhindo'sur adj (i) **1** (Colloq) in a mad rage; mad, out of one's mind **2** furious

xhi'ngël nf **1** spangle; jingle (on a tambourine); little round bell **2** (Fig) bauble; trifle

xhingëri'ma = xhingërrima

xhingërrima np fem baubles; trifles, trivia

xhi'ngla-mi'ngla np fem **1** trifles, trivia **2** small ornaments, baubles

xhins nm (Old) gens, clan: stock

xhinxhe'rkë nf [Ornit] great tit (Parus major)

xhip nm Jeep

xhips = xhip

xhira'fë nf **1** [Zool] giraffe **2** [Cine] boom (for maneuvering equipment into position)

xhi'rgë nf small spot, dot

xhiri'm nm ger <xhiro·n

xhi'ro nf **1** (of wheels) spinning, rotation **2** [Fin] giro income **3** [Econ] flow of materials necessary for production **4** [Sport] lap **5** (Colloq) stroll, tour = shëtitje

xhiro'·n

I § vt, vi to spin, rotate

II § vt **1** [Fin] to indorse [a transfer] from one's giro account **2** to shoot [a movie film]

xhiru'es

I § nm **1** [Fin] person making a giro transfer from his account **2** cameraman

II § adj **1** of or pertaining to a giro account **2** [Cine] used for shooting film

xhi'xhe'll nf **1** glittering but essentially worthless little thing: bauble, trinket, spangle **2** = xi'xe

xhi'xhe'll nf [Bot] cotton thistle (Onopordum)

∘ **xhixhëll dashtër/rrshylli** [Bot] Scotch cotton thistle Onopordum acanthium

∘ **xhixhëll taurike** [Bot] Taurus cotton thistle Onopordum tauricum

xhixhë'llo·n vi to glitter, glisten

xhixhibano'z nm [Bot] carob tree = çiçibano'z

xhixhillo'jë nf [Entom] firefly, glowworm = xixëllo'një

xhixhi'mës nm [Ornit] sparrow

xhi'xho nf (Colloq) respectful term of familiar address used by a woman to an older woman in the family; aged woman

xhoka'punu'es nm tailor of heavy wool/felt garments

xhoka'xhi nm (np ~ nj) = xhokapunu'es

xho'kë nf **1** mid-thigh-length jerkin made of heavy felt **2** sleeveless vest for women

∘ **ta pret₁· xhokën** "will cut down your jerkin" to teach you discipline

xhokë'gri'sur adj (Old) wearing a worn-out jerkin: poor

xhol nm joker (playing card); card game in which the joker is the key card

xhontu'rk

I § nm [Hist] Young Turk (member of the modernizing Turkish revolution at the turn of the 20th century)

II § adj pertaining to the Young Turk revolution

xhora'ke nf = xho're

xho're nf (Colloq) big club with a knob at one end: cudgel

xhuble'të nf heavy black woolen sleeveless smock belling out at the bottom

xhufka'dre'dh'ur adj having braided tassels

xhu'fka-xhu'fka

I § adv in tufts

II § adj having many tufts/tassels

xhu'fkë nf **1** tuft: tassel; pompon; topknot **2** [Bot] matgrass (Nardus stricta) **3** [Bot] pappus ()

xhufkë'gja'të adj having long tassels; wearing long-tasseled clothes or fez

xhufkë'va'rur adj having hanging tassels on clothes or fez

xhufki'm nm ger <xhufko'·n

xhufko'·n vi (of plants) to tassel

xhufko'r adj [Bot] fibrillate, fringed ()

xhuli' nf hip-length sleeveless upper garment of black wool with red braid and long tassels

xhulli'r nf (Reg) plunger of a milk churn

xhuma' nf (e) (Old) Friday

xhuma'r nm [Text] **1** cloth-stretching bar on a loom **2** shaft of a bobbin

xhuma're nf liquid residue left after extracting oil from olives

xhu'mbë nf **1** bump, lump **2** bunch

xhumbël nf small lump

xhumbu'sh nm (Colloq Old) entertainment by drinking and enjoyment of a folk band

xhu'ngë nf **1** bump, lump; hump **2** bulge, protuberance **3** knot, node **4** hillock

xhungël nf dimin <xhu'ngë

xhungël nf jungle

xhu'ntë nf [Tech] clutch; coupling

xhup nm (sport) jacket (piece of clothing)

xhura' nf short shepherd's pipe

xhurdi' nf short-sleeved dark woolen jacket with a fringed back and tasseled shoulders

xhuri't· vi to run/flow off, drain off

xhuve'le nf small stem heavily loaded with fruit

xhuve'të nf corn tassel

xhuxh

I § nm [Folklore] dwarf in folktales

II § adj, n very short (person)

xhuxhmaxhu'xh nm [Folklore] very short old man with a long beard who lives underground; dwarf

xhuxhuma'k adj, n (Child) dwarfish (person), midget

xhv- = zhv-

*__xh've'sh'ët__ adj (i) = zhve'shur

*__xhve'të__ = xhuve'të

xhy'be nf **1** long, loose-fitting, pleated cloak; long cloak worn by Moslem priests and dervishes; long, woolen, pleated cloak worn by women **2** (Fig Pej) mask

xhygy'm nm **1** kettle **2** = gjym

xhyme'rt adj, n (Colloq) generous (person)

y *nf* **1** the letter "y" in the alphabet **2** the rounded high front vowel represented by that letter

y [*ip-si-lòn*] *nm* [*Math Phys*] the variable "y"

y *interj* **1** (*Colloq*) expresses indifference or contempt **2** expresses surprise at something we have just seen

yç *nm* game in which two opponents each play their three stones into a square divided into four smaller squares = **tresh**

yçkël *nf* **1** false reason given for avoiding/hindering an action/activity; hindrance **2** weakness, failing, fault **3** subtle detail, intricacy, fine point

ye·n *vi* to stay awake all night

yejt *stem for pdef, opt, adm, part* <**ye·n**

yha *interj* expresses displeasure or distaste

***y·het** *vpr* <**ye·n**

yj OR **yje** *np* <**yll**

yjendezur *adj* (*Poet*) laden with bright stars

yjendritur *adj* (*Poet*) shining with stars

yjeplotë *adj* (*Poet*) full of stars, dotted with stars

yjestolisur *adj* (*Poet*) adorned with stars

yjeshuar *adj* (*Poet*) with stars shining no more (at daybreak)

yjësi *nf* [*Astron*] constellation (of stars) = **konstelacion**

yjëzim *nm ger* **1** <**yjëzo·n**, **yjëzo·het 2** = **yjësi**

yjëzo·het *vpr* to be filled with stars, shine with stars

yjëzo·n *vi* to shine like a star, glitter

***yjkë** *nf* **1** small star **2** (*Fig*) speck, spot

yjor *adj* (*Book*) pertaining to stars: stellar

ylber *nm* rainbow

ylbertë *adj* (*i*) iridescent; with all the colors of the rainbow

ylberth *nm* [*Anat*] iris (of the eye)

ylefe *nf* (*Old*) = **rrogë**

***ylti** *nf* (*Reg*) iron (for ironing clothes) = **ujti**

***ylyver** = **ylber**

yll

I § *nm* **1** star **2** (*Colloq*) shooting star **3** (*Fig Old*) fate, luck **4** (*Fig Colloq*) reputation **5** (*Fig*) guiding light **6** [*Publ*] = **yllth 7** (*Colloq*) wart; mole

II § *adj* very pretty, very good-looking

  ○ **ylli i ballit** (in figurative expressions) plumb in the middle of the forehead, right between the eyes

  ○ **yll deti** [*Invert*] starfish, sea star

  ○ **Ylli i Dritës** [*Astron*] the planet Venus, morning star

  ○ **yll me bisht** "star with a tail" comet

  ○ **ylli i mollës** apple blossom; star-shaped heart of an apple (cut crosswise)

  ○ **Ylli si dylli.** "Star like wax." Fortune is fickle.

  ○ **T'u shoftë ylli!** "May your star be extinguished!" (*Curse*) May you disappear forever!

Yll *nm* Yll (popular male name)

yllak *adj* [*Anat*] stellate

***ylldije** *nf* (*Old*) astronomy

***ylldijës** *n* (*Old*) astronomer

yllе *nf* **1** cow/goat with a white or colored blaze on the face **2** star-shaped pasta

yllës *nm* **1** small carnation with five pink petals **2** star-shaped pasta

yllëz *nf dimin* **1** small star **2** [*Tech*] sprocket

Yllka *nf* (proper name) female

yllkë *nf* **1** group of five kindergarten children supervised by a teacher; child in such a group **2** = **ylle 3** small red star sewn on children's clothing as an award of merit

yllshuar

  I § *adj* (*Colloq*) unlucky

  II § *n* dead person; poor unfortunate

yllto·n *vt* to light [] up with loveliness, illuminate

yllth *nm* asterisk

yllzak *nm* [*Ichth*] bramble shark (*Echinorhinus brucus*)

ymër *nm* (*Colloq*) (human) life extent: life

  ○ **I paç me ymër!** "May you have life for them!" (*Felic*) May your children live long!

ymërgjatë *adj* (*Colloq*) long-lived

ymërshkurtër *adj* (*Colloq*) short-lived

yndyrë *nf* **1** grease; fat **2** fatty substance: oil, butter **3** (*Colloq*) plant resin **4** (*Fig Colloq*) good taste

  ○ **yndyra e duhanit** tobacco tars that collect in a pipe

  ○ **yndyra e kakaos** cocoa butter

yndyrësi *nf* = **yndyrshmëri**

yndyrëzim *nm ger* [*Spec*] <**yndyrëzo·n**, **yndyrëzo·het**

yndyrëzo·het *vpr* [*Spec*] to become coated with a greasy/oily substance

yndyrëzo·n *vt* to apply an greasy/oily coating to []

yndyror *adj* [*Spec*] fatty; sebaceous

yndyrshëm *adj* (*i*) fat-rich; fatty, greasy; oily

yndyrshmëri *nf* fat content, fattiness; oiliness

yndyrtë *adj* (*i*) = **yndyrshëm**

ynë

  I § *pronominal adj masc sg* <**ynë** our

  II § *nm* ours

***yogurt** *nm* (*Reg*) kefir

yrnek *nm* (*Colloq Old*) pattern; model, sample

  ○ **një yrnek ësh-të**^*pl* to be of the same mold, be just alike

yrt *nm* (*Reg Colloq*) garden near the house; fenced ground around a house: yard

yrysh *nm* (*Colloq*) sudden surge of energy, rush; sudden assault

yrrja *interj* (*Crude*) step on it! get the lead out!

yrrja-byrrja *adv* (*Colloq*) in disorderly confusion, in a muddle

yst *nm* (*Old*) additional money paid to even out a trade

yshmer *nm* [*Food*] snack made by baking crumbled crusts of pastry leaves mixed with eggs and cream

ysht· *vt* **1** to utter a magic incantation to heal/protect [ ] to cast spells **2** to induce [ ] to obey one's wishes blindly, mesmerize [ ]

yshtar *n* *(Old)* = **yshtës**

yshtari *nf* *(Old)* sorcery

yshtës
I § adj *(Old)* involved/used in sorcery; intended as sorcery
II § nm *(Old)* sorcerer, wizard

yshtëse *nf* old sorceress

yshtje *nf* *ger* **1** *(Old)* <**ysht·** **2** magic formula; magic spell

yshtur
I § adj (i) under a magic spell; under someone else's influence

II § nf (e) *(Old)* magic formula; magic spell

yshyr *nm* **1** [*Hist*] in-kind tax or tithe assessed against farmers during the Ottoman occupation **2** *(Colloq Old)* farm produce; fruit produce; fruit tree

yt
I § pronominal adj masc sg nom thy
II § nm **1** thine **2** male relative/friend of thine

yvell *nm (np ~ j)* [*Bot*] mistletoe *(Viscum)* **2** European mistletoe, white mistletoe *(Viscum album)*

yxhym
I § nm = **yrysh**
II § interj let's move! let's go! onward!

yzengji *nf* **1** stirrup **2** [*Anat*] stirrup bone in the middle ear *(stapes)*

z [zë] *nf* **1** the consonant letter "z" **2** the voiced apical sibilant represented by the letter "z"

z *formativ* **1** un- **2** derives verb stems from adjectives with the meaning: to give [ ] the quality of the adjective: en-

***zâ(n)**
  I § nm (pl ˜ na) = **zë(r)**
  II § vt = **zë**

zabari *nf* [*Bot*] woody-stemmed asparagus used in folk medicine to treat syphilis (*Asparagus aphyllus*)

zabe *nf* **1** (*Reg*) strip of bark used to tie on or wrap a plant graft **2** = **hobe**

zabel *nm* grove, copse; thicket

zabërhan *nm* (*Contempt*) rotten street bum, hooligan

zabit *nm* **1** (*Old*) officer = **oficer 2** (*Pej*) cruel and oppressive officer: petty tyrant

zabua *nm (obl ˜ oi, np ˜ onj)* cotter pin (for securing a cart wheel to the axle)

zabullime *nf* (*Reg*) stifling heat, sultry weather/heat, mugginess, heat wave

zabulline = **zabullimë**

zabullishëm *adj (i)* = **zabullueshëm**

zabullo·het *vpr* (*Reg*) to be suffocating from the heat

zabullueshëm *adj (i)* stifling hot, muggy, sultry

***zabun** *adv*
  ◦ **ësh·të zabun** to be unwell

Zadrimë *nf* coastal plain in northwestern Albania: Plain of Zadrima

zadrimor
  I § adj of or pertaining to the Plain of Zadrima
  II § n native of the Plain of Zadrima

***zadhanies** *n (Reg Gheg)* = **zëdhënës**

***zadhanie** = **zëdhënie**

zagal *nm (np ˜ j)* [*Entom*] horsefly, botfly = **zekth**

zagall *nm (np ˜ j)* (*Reg*) muzzle to keep a horse from eating

zagar *n* **1** hunting dog **2** (*Fig*) very perceptive person **3** (*Fig Scorn*) subservient dog: lackey **4** (*Crude*) tramp, bum; promiscuous good-for-nothing

zagën *nf* **1** strip of land between drainage ditches in a field; crest of earth next to a furrow; furrow **2** ridge ***3** wrinkle

Zagori *nf* mountainous ethnographic region of southern Albania

Zagori *nf* mountainous region north of Gjirokastra in the south of Albania

zagorit
  I § adj of or pertaining to Zagoria
  II § nm native of Zagoria

zagushi *nf* sultry heat, mugginess

***zagushis** *stem for 1st sg pres, pl pres, 2nd & 3rd sg subj, pind* < **zagushit**·

***zagushit·** *vt* to be sultry/muggy

***zagushites** *adj* sultry, muggy

***zagjori** *nf* pack (of animals), crowd, horde

***zaharos·et** *vpr* = **sheqeros·et**

zahire *nf* (*Colloq*) food supplies prepared and stored away for a later time: winter provisions

zahmet *nm* (*Colloq*) effort, exertion, endeavor
  ◦ **Bëj/Bëni zahmet!** (*Colloq*) Make some effort! Do me a favor!

zahmetshëm *adj (i)* requiring great effort: arduous; hard, difficult

zaif *adj* (*Colloq*) slightly ill, indisposed, unwell

zaifllëk *nm (np ˜ qe)* indisposition, discomfort

zaje *np* < **zall**

zakon *nm* **1** habit, usage, common practice; custom: traditional custom **2** [*Hist*] body of traditional law

zakone *np* < **zakon** (*Colloq*) menstruation, monthlies

zakonët *adj (i)* = **zakonshëm**

zakonisht *adv* as usual; usually, customarily

***zakonio·n** *vt* to accustom, habituate

zakonor *adj* (*Book*) customary; by custom

zakonshëm
  I § adj (i) ordinary; regular; usual
  II § n (i) ordinary person

zakontë *adj (i)* ordinary; regular; usual

***zakorekë** *nf* linchpin for a yoke

zakum *nm* (*Reg*) [*Bot*] oleander, rosebay (*Nerium oleander*) = **helmës**

zali *nf* fainting fit

zalis· *vt* to cause to faint

zalis·et *vpr* to faint

zalisje *nf ger* **1** < **zalis·, zalis·et 2** faint

zalisur
  I § adj (i) in a faint
  II § n (i) person in a faint

zall *nm (np ˜ je)* **1** pebble, gravel; gravelly shore **2** shore
  ◦ **zall më zall** on all sides, everywhere; in every direction

zallahi *nf* (*Colloq*) commotion, tumult: hubbub, row, din

zallamahi *nf* (*Colloq*) = **zallahi**

***zalldan** *nm* sadness, sorrow; weariness

***zallëm** = **zullum**

zallët *adj (i)* = **zallor**

zalli *nf* bank of a river composed of soft gravel

zalline *nf* **1** bad soil with many rocks **2** gravel bed, gravel beach

zallishte *nf* **1** gravel bed, gravel beach **2** gravelly soil

zallishtor *adj* **1** in or pertaining to gravel beds **2** = **zallor**

zallor *adj* gravelly, pebbly; consisting of gravel/pebbles

zam *nm* = **zamkë**

***zamadh** (*Reg Gheg*) = **zëmadh**

zaman *nm* (*Old*) epoch, era; olden days, yesteryear

zamare *nf* [*Mus*] shepherd's twin pipes, each with its own reed formed by cutting slits in the pipe

*zamarïs *stem for 1st sg pres, pl pres, 2nd & 3rd sg subj, pind* <**zamarï·**

*zamarït· *vt (Old)* *(Old)* to examine, study

*zamarïtje *nf ger (Old)* **1** <**zamarït· 2** examination, study

zambak *nm* [*Bot*] lily (*Lilium*)
  ○ **zambak deti** [*Zool*] sea lily, feather star
  ○ **zambak i egër** [*Bot*] *Narcissus tazetta* = **zburgjës**
  ○ **zambak shqiptar** [*Bot*] Albanian lily *Lilium albanicum*

zambakët *adj (i)* lily-like

zambakore *np fem* [*Bot*] lily family *Liliaceae*

*zambare = zamare

zamë *nf* awl, punch

*zamër *(Reg Gheg)* = **zëmër**

Zamir *nm* Zamir (male name)

zamkë *nf* glue

zamzane *nf* demijohn

*zâna *np* <**zâ**

Zana *nf* Zana (female name)

zanafillë *nf* origin

zanafillës *adj* original, earliest; initial

zanafillor *adj (Book)* aboriginal, original

zanafilltas *adv* at the beginning: initially

*zanamare = zamare

zanat *nm* **1** craft, skill, trade; profession **2** *(Colloq)* regular responsibility/task **3** custom, tradition
  ○ **ësh·të i zanatit** to be a real craftsman/professional

zanatçi *nm (np ~ nj)* **1** craftsman **2** experienced master, master craftsman

zanatli *nm (np ~ nj)* master craftsman

*zanc *nm (Reg Gheg)* = **zënës**

zanë *nf* **1** [*Folklore*] mountain fairy with power to inspire or if offended, to cast a paralyzing spell **2** muse

*zânli *obl* <**zâ**

zanon· *vt* [*Folklore*] (of mountain fairies) to punish [] by casting a spell, put a curse on []

zanor *adj* **1** *(Book)* of or pertaining to voice sound: vocal, (of film) with a sound track **2** [*Ling*] voiced

zanore
  I § *nf* [*Ling*] voiced sound
  II § *adj* like a mountain fairy: beautiful and powerful; irascible and cruel
  ○ **zanore e prapme** [*Ling*] back vowel

zanxhafil *nm* [*Bot*] ginger = **xhenxhefil**

*zanzar *adj* irascible, irritable = **xanxar**

*zanzari *nf* irascibility, irritability

zap *invar (Colloq)*

*zapana *nf (Old)* special room for receiving male guests

zapar· = zagushi

zaparïs *stem for 1st sg pres, pl pres, 2nd & 3rd sg subj, pind* <**zaparï·**

zaparït· *vt* **1** to wrinkle **2** (of a sore/wound) to become inflamed, get worse

zapëri *nf* wrinkle, crease

*zapt = zap

zaptije *nf with masc agreement* *(Old)* policeman (during the Ottoman occupation)

zaptim *nm ger (Colloq)* <**zapto·** n

*zaptimtar *adj, n (Old)* = **zaptues**

zapto· *n vt* **1** *(Colloq)* to occupy [] (by conquest); take [] over **2** to capture, grab; catch

zaptuar *adj (i)* **1** *(Colloq)* taken by force: captured **2** *(Reg)* pregnant

zaptues
  I § *adj* *(Colloq)* occupying, conquering
  II § *n* occupier, conqueror

zar
  I § *nm* **1** die (one of a pair of dice) **2** good luck
  II § *nm* [*Anat*] anklebone *(talus)*
  ○ **zar i fundit** last chance
  ○ **Zaret u hodhën.** "The dice were thrown." The die is cast.

*zarakï *nf* variety of red grapes

zaranë *nf* [*Bot*] = **rigon**

zarar *nm (Colloq)* damage, harm; loss

zararshëm *adj (i)* harmful, injurious = **dëmshëm**

zarbanik *nm (Colloq Insult)* **1** person dressed in rags: ragamuffin, raggedy tramp **2** *(Insult)* dirty bum, cur

zarbë *nf (Colloq)* **1** old rag **2** *(Impol)* stray dog: mutt **3** *(Insult)* dirty bum, cur

zardaf *nm* [*Zool*] pine marten *(Martes martes)*

zarf *nm* envelope (for letters)

zarigogë *nf* [*Ornit*] = **bregcë**

Zarik *nm* Zarik (male name)

zarzavatçi *nm* = **zarzavateshitës**

zarzavate *nf* vegetable

zarzavateshitës *n* vegetable seller = **perimeshitës**

zaten *pcl (Colloq)* just exactly, just, exactly

zates *stem for 1st sg pres, pl pres, 2nd & 3rd sg subj, pind* <**zatet·**

zatet·
  I § *vt* **1** to meet [] unexpectedly, bump into [] **2** to catch **3** to set
  II § *vi* **1** to take up a (combat) position, take a stand; stand (somewhere) **2** to have an unexpected encounter

zatet· *et vpr* **1** *(Colloq)* to meet up **2** to grapple, fight **3** to take up a position **4** to get covered/filled/stopped up

zavall
  I § *nm (Colloq)* worry, trouble, problem
  II § *n* person who has bad problems: poor guy! poor thing!
  III § *adj* beset by trouble: poor _!

*zavendës *(Reg Gheg)* = **zëvendës**

zavë OR **zavëz** *nf* clasp, buckle; small metal loop, small hook

*zavojë *nf* device for fastening a scythe blade and handle together

*zavrak *n* spoiled child, brat

zavrat *nm* strip of cultivated land: bed

zazë *nf* [*Invert*] small mollusk; shell of a small mollusk

zbalt· *et vpr* **1** to lose its taste **2** to eat just a little bit; taste

zbardh·
  I § *vt* **1** to whiten; brighten **2** to bleach **3** to peel/rub off the outer layer of [] in order to expose the good part **4** to grizzle [] (with gray hair) **5** *(Fig)* to bring honor and glory to []; brighten [] so that it reflects honor and glory on <>; brighten up [] **6** to revise [] (in order to make it cleaner/clearer/better)

II § vi **1** to dawn **2** to stand out in whiteness from its surroundings

○ **zbardh· dhëmbët** "whiten one's teeth" *(Pej)* to snicker

○ **<>a zbardh· faqen 1** to save <>'s honor: save <>'s skin **2** to make <> proud

○ **<> zbardh· jetën** to make <> happy

○ **zbardh· sytë** "whiten one's eyes" to turn up one's eyeballs: die

z|ba'rdh·*et vpr* **1** to get gray hair **2** *(Reg)* to stop (wearing the black clothes of) mourning **3** to dawn

○ **<> zbardh·***et^{3pl}* **buzët** <>'s lips *go* white with fear, <> *is* terrified

z|bardh|ala'q *adj* = zbardhalu'q

z|bardh|alu'q *adj* whitish; with a whitish tinge; starting to fade

****z|bardh|c** *nm* = zbardhuli'në

zbardh|ëll e·*het vpr* = zbardhëllo'·het

z|bardh|ëlle·*n*

I § vi = zbardhëllo'·n
II § vt to bleach

zbardh|ëlle'me *adj (i)* tinged with white, whitish

zbardh|ëlle'm|të *adj (i)* = zbardhëlle'më

z|bardh|ëlli'm *nm* shiny whiteness; brightness, glitter

z|bardh|ëlli'më *nf* = zbardhëlli'm

z|bardh|ëllo'·*het vpr* **1** to fade; turn pale/white, blanch **2** to start to get light, begin to dawn

z|bardh|ëllo'·*n vi* **1** to gleam white, have a white glow **2** to start to get light, begin to dawn

z|bardh|ëll|ua'r *adj (i)* **1** having become all white; (of the sky) having become light **2** somewhat bleached, partly faded

z|ba'rdh|ës

I § nm whitening agent, bleach
II § adj used as a whitening agent

z|ba'rdh|ësh *nm [Bot]* = zbardhuli'në

z|bardh|i'm *nm ger* <zbardho'·n, zbardho'·het

z|bardh|je *nf ger* <zba'rdh·, zbardh·et

z|bardho'·*het vpr* = zba'rdh·et

z|bardho'·*n*

I § vt **1** to whiten; brighten **2** to bleach **3** to peel/rub off the outer layer of [ ] in order to expose the good part **4** to revise [ ] (in order to make it cleaner/clearer/better) **5** *[Publ]* to space out the lines/letters on a page

II § vi **1** to dawn **2** to stand out in whiteness from its surroundings

z|bardh|ua'r *adj (i)* bleached

z|bardh|u'e|s *nm, adj* = zba'rdhës

z|bardh|u'k

I § adj pale white, whitish
II § n albino

z|bardh|u'k|ët *adj (i)* pale white, whitish

z|bardh|u'l· *vt* = zbërdhu'l·

z|bardh|u'l·*et vpr* = zbërdhu'l·et

z|bardh|u'l|ët *adj (i)* = zbërdhu'lët

z|bardh|uli'në *nf [Bot]* cambium

z|bardh|ulo'·*het vi impers* it *dawns*, it *gets* light

z|bardh|ulo'·*n vi impers* = zbardhulo'·het

z|ba'rdh|ur *adj (i)* **1** colored white **2** bleached; polished **3** grown gray, grizzled

zba'rët *adj (i)* **1** (of food) flavorless, tasteless, bland **2** *(Fig)* (of people) dull, tedious; cold and unfriendly

z|bari'qe *np fem* **1** innards **2** *(Fig)* inner thoughts, secrets

z|bari's *stem for 1st sg pres, pl pres, 2nd & 3rd sg subj, pind* <zbari't·

z|bari't· *vt* **1** to cook [ ] so as to make tasteless **2** *(Fig)* to cause <> to be antipathetic/cold toward [ ], put <> off [ ]

z|bari't·*et vpr* **1** to lose its taste, become flavorless **2** *(Fig)* to behave in an uncongenial manner: put off people

z|bari'|tur *adj (i)* **1** having lost its flavor: flavorless **2** *(Fig)* tasteless in behavior, guilty of alienating behavior; estranged from other people because of one's tasteless behavior

z|bark|i'm *nm ger [Mil]* **1** <zbarko'·n **2** debarkation (of troops/armaments)

z|bark|o'·*n*

I § vi [Mil] to get out/off of a ship or airplane: disembark, debark

II § vt [Mil] to debark [troops/armaments] from the air/sea

z|bark|ua'r *adj (i) [Mil]* (of troops/armaments) debarked from the air/sea

z|bark|u'e|s

I § adj [Mil] used for debarking troops/armaments from the air/sea; debarking

II § n [Mil] disembarked soldier

z|baro'·*n vt* to remove the innards from [a fowl/animal]: gut

****z|ba'shk|u** *adv* <së ba'shku together, jointly

z|bati'c|ë *nf* **1** ebb tide, low tide **2** *(Fig)* period of retrenchment: decline

z|bati'm *nm ger* **1** <zbato'·n, zbato'·het **2** implementation, execution

z|bati's *stem for 1st sg pres, pl pres, 2nd & 3rd sg subj, pind* <zbati't·

zbati't· *vt* to ebb

zbato'·*n vt* **1** to put [ ] into effect, carry out [ ]: execute, perform, implement, apply, enforce **2** to complete, accomplish, achieve, fulfill

zbat|ua'r *adj (i)* put into effect, applied, enforced, implemented

zbat|u'e|s

I § adj executive; performing
II § n executor, performer

zbat|u'e|sh|ëm *adj (i)* executable, implementable; realizable, performable: feasible

z|ba'th· *vt* to remove [clothing worn on the legs/feet], take [footwear/pants] off; remove [horseshoes]

z|ba'th·*et vpr* **1** to take off one's shoes or stockings **2** (of horseshoes) to fall off **3** (of something in the ground covered with earth) to become uncovered

z|bath|ani'k *nm* = zbathara'k

z|bath|ara'k

I § nm **1** person who goes barefoot **2** very poor person **3** *(Old Contempt)* shoeless bum, rabble

II § adj **1** barefoot, barefooted **2** very poor **3** *(Old Contempt)* riffraff

z|ba'th|je *nf ger* <zba'th·, zba'th·et

z|ba'th|ur

I § adj (i) **1** without shoes/stockings, barefooted **2** (of horses) unshod

II § adv on barefoot, without shoes/stockings, barefooted

z|bavi's *stem for 1st sg pres, pl pres, 2nd & 3rd sg subj, pind* <zbavi't·

zbavit· vt (Colloq) to entertain; amuse

zbavit·et vpr (Colloq) to enjoy/amuse oneself: have fun

zbavitë**s** adj (Colloq) entertaining, amusing: fun

zbavitje nf ger 1 (Colloq) <zbavit·, zbavit·et 2 entertainment, amusement: fun

zbavitshë**m** adj (i) (Colloq) = zbavitë**s**

zbe·n vt = zbeh·

zbeh· vt 1 to make [] pale 2 to make the colors of [] fade: fade 3 to dim 4 (Fig) to diminish [] in intensity: obscure, weaken, fade

zbeh·et vpr 1 to become pale 2 to become faded: fade 3 to get dim 4 (Fig) to become diminished in intensity: become obscure, weaken, fade

zbehje nf ger 1 <zbeh·, zbeh·et 2 = zbehtësí

zbehtak
  I § adj 1 pallid; getting pale in the face 2 faded; dim
  II § n pale-faced person

zbehtas adv dimly; vaguely

zbehtë
  I § adj (i) 1 pale, pallid 2 (Fig) weak, feeble; lackluster, colorless; obscure, vague
  II § adv dimly; vaguely
  III § nn (të) 1 = zbehtësí 2 [Med] jaundice
  IV § nf (Colloq) [Med] jaundice

zbehtësí nf paleness, pallor

zbehur adj (i) 1 pallid, pale 2 faded; weakened, diminished

zbejt· vt to find out what [] wants/knows by treating [] nicely

zbekth nm [Veter] = hírrëz

zbeq· vt 1 (Colloq) to beat [someone] up, beat [] black and blue: whop [] good 2 (Fig) to chew [] out, give it to [someone] good = zhdëp·

*** zbet** = zbeht

*** zbërdha·**het vpr = zbeh·et

zbërdhul· vt to fade, bleach slightly

zbërdhulët adj (i) 1 faded, slightly bleached 2 grayish white, whitish

zbërthe·het vpr 1 to come apart 2 to become unfastened; unbutton one's clothing 3 to open up, tell all

zbërthe·n vt 1 to take [] apart, break [] down; split [] apart; disintegrate 2 to unfasten 3 to decompose 4 to analyze 5 (Fig) to get [] to tell what [] knows: break [someone] down
  ◦ <> zbërthe·n brinjët "break <>'s ribs" 1 to beat <> up badly, beat <> to a pulp 2 to force <> to reveal every detail
  ◦ <> zbërthe·n gojën/gjuhën/dhëmbët "unleash <>'s mouth/tongue/teeth" to get <> to tell everything, make <> talk

zbërthim nm ger <zbërthe·n, zbërthe·het

zbërthyer adj (i) 1 taken apart, disassembled; split apart 2 unfastened 3 analyzed 4 decomposed into components

zbërthyes adj useful for decomposition/analysis into components

zbërthyeshëm adj (i) capable of being taken apart: unfastenable, demountable; decomposable; analyzable

zbërthyeshmëri nf (Book) ability to be taken apart: demountability, decomposability, analyzability

zbim nm expulsion, eviction, deportation

*** zbír·et** vpr 1 to get lost, go astray, stray 2 to disappear, vanish

*** zbír** stem for 2nd pl pres, pind, imper, vp <zbjerr·

zbírr stem for 2nd pl pres, pind, imper, vp <zbjerr·

zbjerr· vt to lose

zbjerrë
  I § part <zbjerr·
  II § adj (i) left fallow = djerr

zbledh· vt = çmbledh·

zblídh·et vpr = çmblidh·et

zblídh stem for 2nd pl pres, pind, imper, vp <zbledh·

*** zblo·**n vt (Colloq) = zbulo·n

zblodh stem for pdef <zble·dh·

zbloguro·n vt to peel the bark/skin off []

zblok nm (np ~qe) open space: clearing (in a forest), flat place (in the mountains)

*** zblokím** nm ger <zbloko·n

*** zbloko·**n vt to release the blockade of [] = zhblloko·n

*** zbluet** adj (i) (Colloq) = zbuluar

zblo·n vt = dëbo·n

zbokth nm dandruff

zbor nm annual military training for civilians

zbor stem for pdef <zbíer·

zborak OR **zborakës** nm [Ornit] = borës
  ◦ zborakësi i malit [Ornit] brambling Fringilla montifringilla L.

*** zbor**ë nf snow = borë

zboríst n (HistPK) civilian engaged in annual military training

zbortë adj (i) (Reg) made of snow

zbraps·et vpr to move backwards, back up; retreat = spraps·et

zbraz· vt to empty [] (of its contents): empty [] out, pour [] out [], evacuate; unload; discharge/fire [a gun]
  ◦ <> zbraz· barkun to disclose every personal detail to <>; pour out one's feelings to <>
  ◦ e zbraz· barkun to disclose every personal detail; pour out one's feelings: spill one's guts
  ◦ zbraz· frymën (Colloq) to empty one's lungs: breathe out, exhale
  ◦ i zbraz· të gjitha to tell everything, tell all
  ◦ <> zbraz· tërë fishekët "fire all one's cartridges at <>" 1 to lambaste <> thoroughly: let <> have it with both barrels, give <> Hell, unload on <> 2 to use every possible argument/means against <>
  ◦ i zbraz· tërë fishekët "fire all one's cartridges" to use every argument; use all one's powers of persuasion
  ◦ <>i zbraz· trutë (Crude) to spill <>'s brains: shoot <> in the head and kill <>
  ◦ i zbraz· xhepat "empty the pockets" to spend all one's money
  ◦ <> zbraz· zemrën to pour out one's heart to <>, unburden one's heart to <>

zbraz·et vpr 1 to stay empty 2 to empty/pour out, discharge 3 (of a gun/explosive) to go off, fire 4 (Fig) to unload/vent [one's thoughts/feelings]

zbrazë**s** adj, n (person/device) whose function is to empty/pour something out

zbrazë**sí** nf = zbrazë**tí**

*** zbraz**ë**sín**ë = zbrazë**sír**ë

zbrazë**sír**ë nf 1 emptiness 2 empty space, void 3 (Fig) lack; blank space, gap, lacuna; absence

zbra'zët

I § *adj (i)* **1** empty **2** unoccupied **3** *(Fig)* blank, hollow

II § *adv* empty; unoccupied

zbraz'ëti *nf* **1** emptiness, vacuity **2** empty space, void **3** *[Phys]* vacuum **4** *(Fig)* lack; blank space, gap, lacuna; absence

***zbraz'ëtin**ë *nf (Reg)* = zbraz*ësirë*

zbraz'ëtirë *nf* = zbraz*ësirë*

zbra'zje *nf ger* **1** <zbra'z·, zbra'z·*et* **2** evacuation; discharge

zbraz'tësi *nf* = zbraz*ëti*

zbra'zur *adj (i)*, *adv* emptied, empty

z'bre's *stem for 1st sg pres, 1st & 3rd pl pres, 2nd & 3rd sg subj* <zbre**t·**

z'bret·

I § *vi* **1** to descend; go down; reach down **2** to get down from [a horse], get off [a vehicle] **3** *(Fig)* to go down in status, suffer a come-down **4** *(Fig)* (of a time of day/year) to fall

II § *vt* **1** to take/bring [] down **2** to reduce [] in amount **3** *[Math]* to subtract

∘ <> **zbret·**³ˢᵍ **damari** <>'s temper *abates*

∘ <> **zbret·**³ᵖˡ **kacabunjtë** <> *cools* off, <> *calms* down

∘ [] **zbret· në tokë** to bring [] down to earth, set [] straight

∘ **zbret· nga fiku** *(Iron)* to lose one's high position

∘ **zbret· nga fuqia** to fall from power, lose power/authority

∘ **zbret· nga shala e hip·ën në samar** "get off the saddle and on a packsaddle" *(Iron)* to suffer a loss in rank: come down a notch

∘ <> **zbret·**³ᵖˡ **orët** <>'s anger *abates*: <> *calms* down

∘ <> **zbret·**³ᵖˡ **qipujt** "the goblins *come* down from <>" <> *calms* down, <>'s rage *abates*

∘ <> **zbret·**³ᵖˡ **xhindet** "the jinni *come* down from <>" <> *calms* down, <>'s rage *abates*

z'bri's *stem for pind, 2nd pl pres, imper* <zbre**t·**

z'brit *stem for part, pdef, pind, 2nd pl pres, imper, vp* <zbre**t·**

zbrit'ës

I § *adj* **1** descending **2** diminishing

II § *nm* *[Math]* subtrahend

III § *n (Old)* descendant

zbrit'je *nf ger* **1** <zbre**t·** **2** downward slope, decline; descent; reduction **3** *[Math]* subtraction

zbrit'shëm *nm (i)* *[Math]* minuend

zbru'·het *vpr* **1** to become soft/pulpy **2** *(Fig)* to get weak/ill; become softer

zbru·n *vt* **1** to soften [something hard] to the consistency of dough by adding liquid and squeezing: knead **2** to soften [] by soaking **3** *(Fig)* to weaken; soften **4** *(Fig)* to beat [someone] to a pulp; browbeat

zbru'jt *stem for pdef, opt, adm, part, vp* <zbru·n

zbru'jtje *nf ger* **1** <zbru·n, zbru·het **2** *[Med]* maceration

zbru'jtur *adj (i)* **1** doughy; soft, pulpy **2** *(Fig)* bruised; soft, weak

zbrum· *vt* **1** = zbrumo'·n **2** to smash

zbrum'im *nm ger* <zbrumo'·n

zbrumo'·n *vt* to make [] into a doughy/pulpy mass by wetting and pressing

zbru'mur *adj (i)* soft as dough; pulpy, doughy

zbu'ar *part* <zbo'·n

zbu'arje *nf ger* <zbo'·n

zbukur'im *nm ger* **1** <zbukuro'·n, zbukuro'·het **2** beautification **3** decoration; ornament, adornment

zbukuro'·het *vpr* to become (more) beautiful, gain in beauty; adorn oneself

zbukuro'·n *vt* **1** to improve [] in beauty: beautify; adorn **2** to give [] gentility, make [] (too) refined **3** *(Fig)* to paint a pretty picture of []: idealize

zbukur'ua'r *adj (i)* beautified; adorned

zbukuru'es

I § *adj* ornamental

II § *n* decorator

zbule'së *nf* disclosure, discovery; revelation

zbul'im *nm ger* **1** <zbulo'·n, zbulo'·het **2** discovery; detection **3** *[Mil]* intelligence acquisition, reconnaissance **4** *[Mil]* intelligence service

∘ **zbulim zanor** *[Mil]* sound detection

zbul'imta'r

I § *adj* exploratory; pioneering

II § *n* explorer, discoverer; pioneer

zbulo'·het *vpr* **1** to get uncovered **2** to become known, get discovered

∘ **i zbulo·het**³ᵖˡ **lakrat lakrorit** "the vegetables emerge from the vegetable pie" the hidden truth *comes* out: the cat *is* out of the bag

zbulo'·n *vt* **1** to uncover **2** to discover; detect **3** *(Fig)* to come to know/understand/realize [] **4** to reveal; disclose

∘ <>(**a**) **zbulo·n barkun** to disclose every personal detail to <>; pour out one's feelings to <>

∘ **zbulo·n dhëmbët** *(Pej)* to snicker

∘ <> **zbulo·n letrat/kartat** to show one's cards to <>; tell <> what one has been hiding

zbul'o'r *nm* radio detector

zbul'ua'r *adj (i)*, *adv* **1** uncovered **2** *(Fig)* unprotected, undefended; unaided, unsupported

zbulu'es

I § *nm* **1** explorer, discoverer **2** *[Mil]* intelligence clerk/officer

II § *adj* exploratory, pioneering **2** *[Mil]* for intelligence purposes

zbun'im *nm ger* **1** <zbuno'·n, zbuno'·het **2** cajolery

zbuno'·n *vt* to cajole; caress

***zbu'rgj**ës *nm* *[Bot]* kind of narcissus *(Narcissus tazetta)*

zbur'im *nm* noisy argument, loud quarrel

z'burth *nm* **1** *[Veter]* = burth **2** *[Bot]* sowbread *(Cyclamen neapolitanum)* **3** *(Fig)* obstinacy, hardheadedness

z'burr'is *stem for 1st sg pres, pl pres, 2nd & 3rd sg subj, pind* <zburr'i**t·**

z'burr'it· *vt* to raise [] to be a man

z'burr'it·et *vpr* to grow into manhood

z'burr'itur *adj (i)* grown into manhood

z'bus *stem for 1st sg pres, pl pres, 2nd & 3rd sg subj, pind* <zbu**t·**

z'but· *vt* **1** to soften **2** to make [] more mild: tame; calm [] down; make [] more agreeable/manageable; domesticate **3** to lessen [] in strength/intensity/degree; mitigate; abate; level [] down; dilute

∘ <>**a zbut· kurrizin/shpinën/brinjët** "soften <>'s back/ribs" to beat <> to a pulp z|bu't·et vpr 1 to get soft 2 to get milder: become tame; calm down; become more agreeable/manageable 3 to diminish in strength/intensity/degree; abate; level out; become diluted

◦ zbut·et^{3pl} gjakrat tempers cool

◦ <> zbut·et^{3sg} zemra 1 <>'s heart softens; <> is deeply touched 2 <> calms down; <> feels consoled

z|but·ë|s
I § adj softening; calming
II § nm 1 tamer 2 substance/device/person employed for softening: softener

z|but|i'm nm ger <zbuto·n, zbuto·het = zbu'tje

z|bu'tje nf ger 1 <zbut·, zbut·et 2 domestication 3 mitigation

z|buto·het vpr = zbut·et

z|buto·n vt = zbut·

z|bu'tshëm adj (i) capable of being made softer/milder; tamable; placable

*z|bu'tu|e|s adj (Old) softening, attenuating; taming; placating

z|bu'tur adj (i) 1 softened, soft; mild; calmed down; diluted 2 domesticated: tamed, tame; (of plant lines) improved by grafting

z|byll· vt to open [a bottle or any container with a neck]: uncork, uncap

z|byth· vt to force [] backwards: back; push back: repel

z|by'th·et vpr to back up

z|by'thje nf ger <zby'th·, zby'th·et

zdap nm 1 long wooden club: cudgel 2 (Fig) tall, strong, but not good-looking boy/man

zdap· vt (Reg) = zhdëp·

zda'p·et vpr (Reg) = zhdë'p·et

*zdapa'l adj 1 tough, sinewy (of wood) knurled, knotted

zdap|llo·n = zdapullo·n

zdap|ullo·n vt (Reg) to beat [] with a cudgel

*z|da's stem for 1st sg pres, pl pres, 2nd & 3rd sg subj, pind <zda|· (Reg)

z|dat· vt (Reg) 1 to alleviate []'s fear/bashfulness 2 to spoil [] by pampering; give [] too much license

z|da't·et vpr (Reg) 1 to stop being afraid/bashful 2 to become pampered/spoiled

z|dati' nf (Reg) excessive freedom/license: pampering

zdatk nm rough unfinished board; partition wall (made of rough unfinished boards)

zdatko·n vt to partition

z|da'tshëm adv (Reg) unabashedly

z|da'tur adj (i) (Reg) excessively pampered, spoiled; shameless, impudent

*z|da'th· vt = zbath·

*z|da'th·et vp = zba'th·et

*z|da'thë
I § part <zdath·, zda'th·et
II § adv on barefoot, without shoes/stockings, barefooted

*z|desh· = zhvesh·

*z|desh| = zhvesh|

*z|de'shë
I § part < zhvesh·, zhvish·et
II § adv unclothed, undressed, without clothes

zdër|dë'ng adj, n (Colloq) big, strong, but not good-looking (person)

zdër|gja·het vpr to stretch out shamelessly in public (thus showing lack of respect)

zdër|ha'll·et vpr 1 (of plants) to grow profusely, grow rampant 2 (Colloq) to carouse in unbridled manner; get drunk at a party

zdër|ha'llje nf (Colloq) excessive indulgence in drinking; drunken party

zdër|la'q· vt = zgërla'q·

zdër|la'q·et vpr = zgërla'q·et

zdër|la'qur adj (i) = zgërla'qur

*zdër|lavi's stem for 1st sg pres, pl pres, 2nd & 3rd sg subj, pind <zdërlavi't·

*zdër|lavi't· vt to soil; spoil

zdër|lu'g nm (np ~ gje) deep crevice in the rocks, mountain crevasse

zdër|vi·het vpr (Reg) to lose skin/scab/bark by scraping/scratching/peeling

zdër|vi·n vt (Reg) to remove the outside layer of []: skin, peel, shuck; scrape

zdër|ra'ni'k adj, n (Colloq Insult) gabby (person)

zdë'rre nf 1 (Colloq) [Med] diarrhea: the runs 2 (Insult) gabby female, chatterbox 3 (Insult) mouth of a gabby person: big mouth

z|di'rgj·et vpr to descend; flow down

z|di'rgj stem for 2nd pl pres, pind, imper, vp <zdjer|g·

z|di'rgj|ur part <zdi'rgje·t

z|djerg·
I § vt 1 (Reg) to lower 2 to cause [] to crumple to the ground
II § vi (Reg) = zdi'rgj·et

z|djerg stem for opt, adm, part <zdi'rgje·t

z|djerg|ur part <zdjer|g·

z|do'rgj stem for pdef <zdjer|g·, zdi'rgje·t

zdra·het vpr = zhdëp·

zdra·n vt (Reg) = zhdëp·

zdra'le nf [Naut] stay attached to the mainmast

zdra'lë nf dirt on unwashed body or clothes: grime, filth

*zdra'm·et vpr (Reg Gheg) = zdrë'm·et

*zdra'më nf(Reg) 1 = zdrë'më 2 = zdrë'mur

zdra|nglo·n vt (Reg) to tear [] to tatters

zdra'nk|thi adv briskly, quickly; at a fast trot

*z|dredh· vt = zhdredh·

zdrë'm·et vpr to get sores from a chafing burden; have skin/bark peeling away in places; lose plaster/paint in places

zdrë|mu|a'q adj (Pej) = zdrë'mur

zdrë'më nf 1 sore on an animal's skin caused by a chafing burden 2 bare spot on a plant/wall where the covering layer is missing 3 = zdra'lë

zdrë'm|ur adj (i) 1 (of a draft animal) having a sore on the skin 2 having skin/bark peeling away in places: losing plaster/paint in places 3 grimy from body dirt and grime

zdrë'nk
I § nm (of a draft animal) fast lumbering trot
II § adv = zdrë'nkthi

zdrë'nk|thi adv 1 (of a moving draft animal) lumbering along at a fast trot 2 (Fig) hastily

*z|dri'dh stem for 2nd pl pres, pind, imper, vp <zdre'dh·

*z|dri'gj = zdi'rgj

z|dri's stem for 1st sg pres, pl pres, 2nd & 3rd sg subj, pind <zdri't·

z|drit·
I § *vt* to bathe [] with light, illuminate, light up []
II § *vi* to shine

z|drit·et *vpr* **1** to be full of light, be bright, shine bright **2** *(Fig)* to become clear = **sqaro**' ·**het**

z|drit|shëm *adj (i)* **1** bright and shining **2** permeable by light: translucent

*zdri|vill *(Old)* = **zhvill**

*zdri|vill|o's· *vt (Old)* = **zdruktho**' ·**n**

*zdri|vill|ta'r *n (Old)* = **zdrukthëta'r**

*zdri|vill|tari' *nf (Old)* = **zdrukthëtari'**

*zdri|vill|tho' ·**n** *vt (Old)* = **zdruktho**' ·**n**

*z|drodh *stem for pdef* <**zdredh·**

zdroni'ka *np fem [Food]* chunks of a dried porridge used to make a thick soup

zdrug *nm (np ~ gje)* = **zdrukth**

zdrug|i'm *nm ger* <**zdrugo**' ·**n**

zdrug|o' ·**n** *vt* **1** = **zdruktho**' ·**n** **2** *(Fig)* to smack [] and scold him/her with abusive and insulting language; beat [] to a pulp

zdrug|u'a|r *adj (i)* = **zdrukthu'ar**

zdrug|uli'na *np fem* wood shavings

zdruk|th *nm* tool for planing wood: plane
○ **zdrukth qorr** "blind plane" rabbet plane
○ **zdrukth i trashë/tek** "thick plane" plane set for a deep cut
○ **zdrukth ulluk** "groove plane" router plane

zdruk|th|ëta'r *n* woodworker; carpenter

zdruk|th|ëtari' *nf* **1** woodworking; carpentry **2** woodworking/carpentry workshop/department

zdruk|th|i'm *nm ger* <**zdruktho**' ·**n**

zdruk|th|o' ·**n** *vt* to plane [a wooden object]

zdruk|th|u'a|r *adj (i)* smoothed by a plane: planed

zdruk|th|u'e|s *adj* used for planing

zdryp· *vt, vi* = **zbre·t·**

zdryp·et *vpr* to sink; subside

*zdry'p|ës *adj (Reg)* = **zbri't·ës**

zdry'p|je *nf* <**zdryp·**

zeb|a'sh *adj* black-haired

ze'b|ë *adj, n* black-haired/black-bodied (goat/animal)

ze'bër
I § *nf [Zool]* zebra
II § *adj* **1** (of livestock) having white-tinged black hair **2** (of a person) dark-skinned

Zef *nm* Zef (male name)

zefi'r *nm* gentle west wind: zephyr

zega'l *nm [Entom]* = **zekth**

ze'gël *nm [Entom]* = **zekth**

*zeg|th = **zekth**

zehe'r *nm (Colloq)* = **helm**

zeher|o' ·**n** *vi* to poison; embitter

ze'je *nf* craft, trade

zej|shëm *adj (i)* skillful at a craft.

zej|ta'r
I § *n* craftsman, artisan
II § *adj* involved with a trade/craft

zej|tari' *nf* **1** craft; craftsmanship, artisanship, artisanry **2** profession **3** *(Collec)* the crafts

*zek *nm [Entom]* caterpillar

ze'kë
I § *adj, nf* completely black (cow/ewe)
II § *nf (Insult)* woman/girl of dark complexion, brunette

zek|th *nm* **1** *[Entom]* horsefly, botfly *(Tabanus bovinus)* **2** *[Veter]* disease of cattle caused by the larvae of these insects *(hypodermatosis)*
○ **zekthi i dhënve** *[Invert]* sheep botfly *Oestrus ovis* = **borbole'c**

Zela'nd|a e Re *nf* New Zealand

*zelika'dë *nf [Bot]* variety of lily

zell *nm* zeal

zell|ma'dh *adj* exhibiting great zeal

*zell|o' ·**n** *vt* to fire [] with enthusiasm/zeal

ze'll|shëm *adj (i)* zealous

zell|ta'r *adj, n* zealous (person)

zell|tari' *nf* zealousness, zeal

zembere'k *nm* **1** watchspring **2** *(Colloq)* firing mechanism of a gun; trigger **3** *(Fig Colloq)* driving force, impetus **4** *(Reg)* door/window latch

ze'mër *nf* **1** heart **2** *(Reg) [Anat]* abdominal cavity; belly = **lugth 3** *(Colloq)* sweetheart, honey
○ **s'ka· zemër 1** to have no feelings; be merciless **2** to be squeamish; not have the heart to see or hear sad things
○ **zemër e madhe** big-hearted person
○ **zemër njerke** vicious, mean (to children)

zemër|a'k *adj* **1** irascible **2** angry **3** *(Fig)* stormy

zemër|a'kull *adj* **1** with a heart of ice: devoid of feeling **2** = **zemërgu'r**

zemër|a'rtë *adj* with a heart pure as gold: sincere

zemër|a'shp|ër *adj* hard-hearted

zemër|a'të *nf* anger = **zemëri'm**

zemër|a'tshëm *adj (i)* angry; ill-tempered, irascible

zemër|ba'rdhë *adj, n* kind and generous (person)

zemër|ba'rdh|ësi *nf* generous kindness

zemër|bi'shë *adj* cruel

zemër|bo'rë *adj* = **zemërpa'stër**

zemër|breng|o'sur *adj* with a sorrowed heart

zemër|buja'r *adj* with a generous heart

zemër|bu'të *adj* softhearted, compassionate

zemër|but|ësi *nf* softheartedness, compassion

zemër|çeli'k *adj, n* courageous (person)

zemër|çe'l|ur *adj, adv* = **zemërha'pur**

zemër|çje'rr|ës *adj* heartrending

zemër|dëli'rë *adj (Poet)* without guile, sincere, innocent, pure

zemër|dëli'r|ësi *nf (Poet)* guilelessness, innocence

zemër|dje'g|ur *adj, n adv* (person) with a bitterly grieving heart, (person) in bitter grief

zemër|do'bët *adj* easily touched (in the heart): softhearted

zemër|dre'dh|ur *adv* with a quivering heart

zemër|dhe'mb|sh|ur *adj, n* deeply compassionate/sympathetic (person)

zemër|dhe'mb|sh|uri *nf* deep compassion/sympathy

zemër|dhe'n|ës *adj* encouraging

zemër|dhi'mb|shëm *adj (i)* compassionate, sympathetic

zemër|flori' *adj* = **zemëra'rtë**

zemër|fto'htë *adj* coldhearted: incompassionate, unsympathetic

zemër|gu'r *adj, n* stonehearted (person)

zemër|gje'rë *adj* bighearted: tolerant; liberal, generous

zemër|gjer|ësi *nf* magnanimity; liberality

zemër·ha·pur
I § *adj* straightforward, frank; sincere, honest
II § *adv* in a straightforward/frank manner; sincerely, honestly

zemër·he·kur *adj, n* **1** unemotional **2** able to resist hardship/pain: tough/patient **3** = **zemërgur**

zemër·i·m *nm* spite, anger; indignation

zemër·ka *nm* [*Invert*] heart cockle (*Glossus humanus*)

zemër·katra·n *adj (Pej)* = **zemërzi**

zemër·ke·q *adj, n* deeply malicious (person)

zemër·këlli·rë *adj, n* = **zemërkeq**

zemër·krund-e-gërdh·u *OR* **zemër·krund·e-e-gërdh·u** *adj* "heart of chaff and bran" stingy, miserly

zemër·ku·q *adj* (of certain fruits) red on the inside

zemër·le·pur *adj* "rabbit-hearted" chicken-hearted, easily frightened, cowardly

zemër·lësh·u·ar
I § *adj, n* disheartened/discouraged (person); (person) lacking self-confidence
II § *adv* disheartened; without self-confidence

zemër·li·g *adj* = **zemërkeq**

zemër·lig·ësi *nf* deep malice

zemër·lua·n *adj* lion-hearted, courageous

zemër·ma·dh *adj, n* bighearted/generous (person)

zemër·madh·ësi *nf* bigheartedness, generosity

zemër·mi·rë *adj* good-hearted (person)

zemër·mir·ësi *nf* good-heartedness

zemër·nde·zur *adj (Poet)* inspired by noble feelings/intentions, with uplifted heart

zemër·ndry·dh·ur *adj* with an anguished heart

zemër·ndry·shk·ur *adj* = **zemërzi**

zemër·ngri·rë
I § *adj* with an worried heart: anxious
II § *adv* with anxious heart: anxiously

zemër·ngusht·ë *adj* intolerant, impatient; ungenerous, petty

zemër·ngusht·ësi *nf* intolerance, impatience; pettiness

zemër·nxi·rë *adj, n* **1** (person) with a troubled/grieving heart **2** = **zemërzi**

zemër·o··het *vpr* **1** to become angry **2** to take offense

zemër·o··n *vt* **1** to anger **2** to create enmity in [ ]

zemër·o·r *adj (Book)* courageous

zemër·pa·k *adj* cowardly

zemër·pa·stër *adj* pure of heart; chaste, untainted

zemër·përvël·u·ar *adj, n adv* = **zemërdjegur**

zemër·pi·së *adj, n* = **zemërkeq**

zemër·plago·s·ur *adj* with a wounded/grieved heart: in despair

zemër·pla·s·ët *adj* heartbroken, dejected

zemër·pla·s·ur *pred, n* heartbroken/dejected (person)

zemër·prish·ur *pred* brokenhearted

zemër·pul·ë *adj* chicken-hearted, faint-hearted

zemër·qe·n *adj, n* "dog-hearted" *(Pej)* beastly/cruel (person) = **zemërkeq**

zemër·qëru·ar *adj* = **zemërpastër**

zemër·shkëmb *adj* **1** unemotional **2** able to resist hardship/pain: tough/patient

zemër·shkre·të *adj* **1** pitiful, wretched **2** self-sacrificing

zemër·shtri·gë *adj, nf (Pej)* (woman) with the heart of a witch

zemër·shu·ar *adj* despondent

zemër·tha·rë
I § *adj, n* = **zemërgur**
II § *adv* mercilessly

zemër·thy·er *adj, adv* brokenhearted, in despair; disappointed

zemër·ua·r *adj (i)* angered, angry; indignant

***zemër·ul·ët** *adj* softhearted, compassionate, sympathetic

zemër·vo·gël *adj* small-minded: petty, mean; selfish; envious

zemër·vogël·si *nf* small-mindedness: pettiness; selfishness; enviousness

zemër·vra·rë *adj* with a saddened heart: sorrowful, in grief

zemër·zi *adj, n (fem sg ~ e·z, masc pl ~ inj, fem pl ~ eza)* "black-hearted" malicious/vile/evil (person)

zemër·zja·rr·të *adj (Poet)* with a flaming heart, inspired by noble feelings

zemër·zhur·it·ur *adj, adv* with (a) yearning heart

***zemre·k** *nm* = **zemberek**

***ze·m·zë** *nf (Colloq)* sweetheart

***ze·n·ë** = **zë·n·ë**

zengji *nf* stirrup

zengji·n *adj, n (Old)* rich/wealthy (person/thing)

zeni·t *nm* **1** [*Astron*] zenith **2** *(Fig)* highest point: peak

zepeli·n *nm* [*Av*] zeppelin, dirigible, airship

***zeqa·t** *nm* alms for the poor prescribed by Islam as a fraction of one's income

Ze·qo *nf with masc agreement* Zeqo (male name)

zerde *nf* [*Food*] sweet rice pudding

zerdeli *nf* [*Bot*] variety of sweet-smelling apricot with small fruit and a bitter-tasting kernel

ze·ro *nf* zero
  ◦ **ësh·të zero** to be worthless because totally ignorant
  ◦ **zero me bisht/xhufkë** *(Pej)* ignoramus, incompetent, good-for-nothing

zerva *nf (Reg)* [*Food*] = **paluze**

ze·rre *nf (Reg)* tiny piece: grain, crumb

zeshk· *vt* to darken [ ] by heat rays: tan, bronze, brown

ze·shk·et *vpr* to turn brown (from the sun), get suntanned

zeshk·ama·n = **zeshkan**

zeshk·a·n *adj, n* (person) with a dark/sallow complexion

ze·shk·ël *nf (Impol)* girl/woman with a dark/sallow complexion

ze·shk·ët *adj (i)* with a bronzed complexion: tan

zeshk·im *nm ger* <**zeshko··n**, **zeshko··het**

zeshk·o··het *vpr* = **zeshk·et**

zeshk·o··n *vt* = **zeshk·**

zevze·k *adj, n* (person/animal) in restless motion; rambunctious (person)

ze·z *fem* = **zi**

ze·z·a *np fem* **1** <**zi** **2** black clothes worn by old men/women, usually as a sign of mourning

zez·a·k
I § *n* person of a dark-skinned race: black
II § *adj* of or pertaining to blacks

zez·e·li·në *nf* place in the shade, shady spot

zeˈzë

I § adj (e) fem sg <**zi**

II § nf (e) **1** black (the color); black dye **2** *(Fig)* grievous misfortune; terrible suffering; bad thing

zezˈim nm ger <**zezo·n**, **zezo·het**

zeˈzkë nf black cow, ewe or nanny goat

zezoˈ·het vpr **1** to fall into misfortune; be overwhelmed by trouble **2** to fall into shame, suffer shame

zezoˈ·n vt **1** to make [] black (or very dark) **2** *(Fig)* to make [] wretched; cast a blight over [], spoil **3** *(Fig)* to bring shame to [], shame []

zezoˈnë nf terrible misfortune, calamity; catastrophic destruction; misery; ruin

zezuˈar adj (i) darkened

zë(r) nm (np ˜ra) **1** voice **2** characteristic sound made by something **3** *(Fig)* reputation **4** *(Old)* vote **5** item/article (in a list), entry (in a dictionary/ledger)
  ◦ **zë i bardhë** clear pure voice (of women and children)
  ◦ **s'bë·n zë** not make a sound, not be heard; not speak up, make no protest, not object
  ◦ **zë i çjerrë** hoarse voice; harsh voice
  ◦ **me zë të lartë** with insistence, insistently
  ◦ **zë në shkretëtirë** *(Book)* lone voice that no one pays attention to
  ◦ **ësh·të pa zë** "be without voice" to do as one is told, not talk back

zë·

I § vt **1** to take **2** to take hold of []: grab; pinch; capture; occupy **3** to catch; catch up with [] **4** to get **5** to fasten **6** to get covered/encrusted/infested/ with [] **7** to cause [] a sore **8** to take effect on [] **9** *(Colloq)* to break [a draft animal] to the plow/yoke/saddle **10** to enter into a close relationship with []: make [a friend], take [a husband] **11** *(Colloq)* to become engaged to [] **12** to hit; touch **13** to close up/off [] **14** to take in: involve, include, comprise; earn, make **15** to take [] into consideration: count **16** *(Colloq)* to come across []: encounter [] **17** to cause [] to congeal

II § vi **1** to become fastened: stick **2** to take hold; catch; dig in; catch fire **3** to sprout

III § vt, vi to start, begin
  ◦ **nuk** [] **zë·**^{3sg} {time noun + nom sg def} "the {} will not catch []" [] won't last through the {}; [] will be gone within the {}
  ◦ **zë· aj** to take a bite
  ◦ **zë· akull** to form an icy layer: ice up
  ◦ [] **zë·**^{3pl} **andrallat** [] gets into deep trouble
  ◦ **zë· arrëzën** to break one's neck
  ◦ **zë· barkun** to eat just enough to settle one's stomach
  ◦ **zë· be** to take an oath, swear
  ◦ <> **zë· besë** to put faith in <>; believe <>, trust <>
  ◦ <>a **zë· bicen** to block <> at every turn
  ◦ <> **zë·**^{3sg} **bishti dhjamë** "<>'s tail gets fat" <> lives in clover/luxury
  ◦ [] **zë·**^{3sg} **bizga** [] the runs, [] gets diarrhea
  ◦ <> **zë· bosh** <> is caught unprepared, <> is caught short
  ◦ **zë· brinjët me duar** to break up with laughter
  ◦ **zë· brumë** to gain/regain a comfortable economic position, get on one's feet economically
  ◦ **s'<> zë·**^{3sg} **bytha vend** "<>'s ass does not settle down" *(Crude Pej)* <> does not stick to <>'s work

  ◦ **zë· cefël** to completely lose one's temper: fly off the handle
  ◦ **zë· cergë** to gain/regain a comfortable economic position, get on one's feet economically
  ◦ <> **zë·**^{3sg} **çarku kokën** <> gets into big trouble, <> gets into a hopeless mess
  ◦ <> **zë· çelën** to put <> into an impossible situation, get <> into a tight corner
  ◦ [] **zë·**^{3sg} **damari** [] loses <>'s temper, [] flies off the handle
  ◦ <> **zë· derën** to be drop in uninvited; be a frequent and unwelcome visitor
  ◦ <> **zë·**^{3sg} **dora (çdo gjë)** everything comes easy to <>; everything comes out well for <>
  ◦ **zë· dorë** to come to an agreement
  ◦ <> **zë· dorën** to take <>'s hand and kiss it
  ◦ **zë·**^{3sg} **dregëz plaga** the wound forms a scab; the wound/sorrow heals over in time
  ◦ **zë· dyshekun** to take to one's bed with a lingering illness
  ◦ <> **zë·**^{3sg} **dhëmbi** <> has a little bit to eat, <> eats a small bite
  ◦ <> **zë·**^{3sg} **dhëmbi bukë/tagji** <> gets back on <>'s economic feet, <> recovers economically
  ◦ **s'ta zë dhëmbi 1** that's barely enough to taste **2** it shouldn't even be mentioned
  ◦ **zë· dhjamë** "take on fat" **1** to get fat **2** *(Fig)* to get rich
  ◦ **zë· erë** to take on an odor, become spoiled
  ◦ **s'<> zë·**^{3sg} **eshka** <> cannot make a go of it
  ◦ [] **zë· fill** to mention []; remember []
  ◦ <>a **zë· fjalën në gojë** to interrupt <>
  ◦ **zë· fole 1** to settle down **2** to appear, take shape
  ◦ [] **zë·**^{3sg} **fruthi** [] gets the measles
  ◦ <> **zë· frymën** "take <>'s breath" to stifle <>; keep <> from talking; not give <> a chance to breathe
  ◦ **zë· fundin e barkut** to eat very little, only enough to relieve one's hunger
  ◦ <> **zë·**^{3sg} **goja bar** "<>'s mouth grows grass" (be all alone and) have no one to talk to
  ◦ <> **zë·**^{3sg} **goja erë** "<>'s mouth gets a smell" to have no one to talk to
  ◦ <> **zë·**^{3sg} **goja lesh** to get tired of saying the same thing over and over
  ◦ <> **zë·**^{3sg} **goja rreshkim** <>'s throat gets dry
  ◦ <> **zë· gojën** "take <>'s mouth" **1** to keep <> from speaking **2** to quiet <> by granting only a token part of []'s request
  ◦ <>a **zë· gojën me shtupë** "close <>'s mouth with oakum" to forcibly prevent <> from speaking: shut <> up good
  ◦ <> **zë· grykën** "take <>'s throat" to quiet <> by granting only a token part of []'s request
  ◦ **zë· guç** (of a horse) to bite
  ◦ <> **zë·**^{3sg} **guri këmbët** <> has no choice, <> is in a tight spot
  ◦ [] **zë·**^{3sg} **gjaku 1** [] the sight of blood sickens []; the sight of blood (of the murdered person) transfixes [the killer] (in horror) **2** *[Ethnog]* the duty of taking blood revenge falls upon []
  ◦ [] **zë·**^{3sg} **gjarpri** terrible misfortune befalls []
  ◦ <> **zë·**^{3sg} **gjuha lesh** to get tired of saying the same thing over and over

○ **nuk <> zë·**^{3sg} **gjuha vend ndër dhëmbë** <> cannot hold <>'s tongue, <> cannot keep <>'s mouth shut

○ **zë· gjuhën 1** to bite one's tongue: keep silent; be sorry for what one has said **2** *(Contempt)* to kick the bucket, die

○ **zë· gjuhën aj** to hold one's tongue, refrain from speaking

○ **nuk** [] **zë·**^{3sg} **gjumi për __** [] never *stops* worrying about __

○ [] **zë·**^{3sg} **gjumi** [] *falls* asleep

○ **s'**[] **zë·**^{3sg} **halli** "no worry *touches* []" [] *doesn't care*

○ **<> zë·**^{3sg} **hera** <> *happens* to (be)

○ **<>**[] **zë·**^{3sg} **hunda** <> has an inkling about/that []

○ **zë· jatakun** to take to one's bed with a lingering illness

○ **s'**[] **zë·**^{3sg} **java** [] cannot last through the week

○ **<>a zë· jetën (në) gjak** to make <>'s life very hard

○ [] **zë·**^{3sg} **kalemi** [] *is* selected/chosen arbitrarily; good/bad luck *falls* to [] completely by chance

○ **<> zë·**^{3sg} **këmba rrafsh** "<>'s foot *touches* level ground" <> *goes* down to the lowlands

○ **s'e zë·**^{3sg} **këmba** "no foot *touches* it" (of a place/road) to be untrodden

○ **<> zë·**^{3sg} **këmba vend** <> *put* <>'s foot on solid ground; <> *settles* down in one place

○ **zë· këmbën e <>** to take over <>'s position

○ **<> zë· këmbën 1** to kiss <>'s foot; humble oneself to <> **2** to take <>'s place, substitute for <>

○ **nuk <> zë·**^{3pl} **këmbët dhé/tokë/vend 1** <> *keeps* moving around; <> *can't* seem to settle down **2** <> *can't* stay out of trouble **3** <> *runs* very fast

○ **<>i zë· këmbët** "fasten <>'s legs" to hobble <>; make it difficult for <> to move, make it hard for <> to do anything; be a terrible burden on <>

○ **<>i zë· këmbët me derë** "catch <>'s feet in the door" to show <> the door (in an inhospitable manner), practically slam the door on <>

○ **zë· këndin** (of one who is old) to stay all day in one's warm corner nook; (of one who is ill) languish in the corner with a lingering disease, take to bed

○ **<> zë·**^{3pl} **kockat rehat** "<>'s bones *grab* a rest" <> finds a place to put <>'s weary bones

○ **<> zë·**^{3sg} **koka në tavan** "<>'s head reaches to the ceiling" <> *is* very tall

○ [] **zë·**^{3sg} **koka** [] *gets* a headache

○ **<>a zë· kokën me derë** "fasten <>'s head with a door" to be able to get <> to do anything one wants: have <> in one's pocket

○ **zë· kokën me dorë** "take one's head in one's hands" to be shocked and angry at news of a misdeed, shake one's head in shocked disbelief

○ **zë·**^{3sg} **kore plaga** the wound forms a scab; the wound/sorrow heals over in time

○ **zë· krahë** to sprout wings: become fledged

○ **zë· krevatin** to take to one's bed with a lingering illness

○ **zë· krimba 1** to become filthy from failure to clean up for a long time: become a pigsty **2** to remain in one spot without moving for a long time

○ **zë· ledhin** *(Impol)* to kick off, die

○ **e zë· lepurin/dhelprën me qerre** "catches the hare/fox with a cart" to be able to accomplish difficult tasks without wasteful haste: have a quiet but steady competence

○ **e zë· lepurin në lak** to have the matter all finished

○ **<> zë·**^{3sg} **lotaria** the lot *falls* to <>, chance has picked []

○ **<> zë·**^{3sg} **luga ujë** "<>'s spoon *gets* wet" <>'s financial situation *is improving*, <> *is getting* back on <>'s feet

○ **<> zë·**^{3sg} **magjja kokën** "the washtub *takes* <>'s head" <> is in deep trouble

○ **zë· majin** "take the May" *(Old)* [Ethnog] to celebrate the flower season in May

○ [] **zë· mat 1** to checkmate [] **2** to put [] in a tight position, put [] with []'s back against the wall

○ [] **zë· me domate** to heckle []

○ **s'**[] **zë· me dorë** not even touch [], not even get started with []

○ [] **zë· me gojë** to call to mind, mention []

○ [] **zë· me pelë për dore** "catch [] with the mare in hand" to catch [] red-handed

○ [] **zë· me presh në dorë** to catch [] red-handed

○ [] **zë· me yha** to heckle []

○ **zë· mend 1** to learn from bitter experience **2** to be obedient, listen

○ **s'**[] **zë·**^{3sg} **meraku** "no worry *touches* []" [] *doesn't care*

○ **zë· miza (gjithë ditën)** "count/kill/catch flies (all day long)" *(Impol)* to waste time idly: sit around (the whole day) twiddling one's thumbs

○ **zë· mullën** to eat something small just to soothe the appetite: have a small snack

○ **zë·**^{3rd} **myk** to get moldy; show the result of long neglect

○ [] **zë· ndër lakra** to catch [] red-handed

○ **zë·**^{3rd} **ndryshk** to get rusty; show the result of long neglect

○ [] **zë· në cak** to catch [] red-handed

○ [] **zë· në faj** to catch [] in the act, nail [] dead to rights

○ [] **zë· në fjalë** "catch [] in a word" to catch [] out in a mistake

○ **zë· në gojë** [] to mention []

○ [] **zë· në gojë** to call to mind, mention []

○ [] **zë· në gushë** to embrace [] (in a friendly manner)

○ **nuk** [] **zë· (fare) në hesap/numër** to give (absolutely) no consideration to [], not (even) to consider [], ignore [] (completely)

○ **s'**[] **zë· në numër** not (even) count [], not consider []

○ **zë· në thua 1** to stumble **2** to blunder

○ **zë· nga bishti** to start from the wrong end

○ [] **zë· nga bishti** "take [] by the tail" to start [] from the wrong end, do [] backwards

○ [] **zë· nga veshi** "grip [] by the ear" to give [] a severe scolding, chastise [] strongly

○ [] **zë· ngoje 1** to mention [] **2** to gossip about []

○ [] **zë· ngushtë** to catch [] unprepared

○ **i zë· nuse djalit** "get a bride for the boy" to arrange a betrothal

○ **s'**[] **zë· njeri me dorë // për bishti** "no one takes [] by the hand/tail" no one *is* interested in []

○ [] **zë· pa fener** to catch [] in the act, catch [] red-handed

○ **zë· peshk në bar** "catch fish in grass" to be extraordinarily capable, be a miracle worker

○ [] **zë· për fyti/gryke** to put heavy pressure on []

○ [] **zë· për palltoje** "grab [] by the overcoat" to remind [] persistently of one's request, keep pulling at []

○ [] **zë· për veshi** "grip [] by the ear" to give [] a severe scolding, chastise [] strongly

○ <> **zë· për** {*body part in the ablative indefinite case*} to take <> by the {} **më zuri për dore** he took me by the hand

○ **zë· përruan** *(Impol)* to kick off, die

○ [] **zë· pleqëria** old age*comes* upon []

○ **zë· pleshta** "catch fleas" to spend one's time doing useless work; twiddle one's thumbs

○ [] **zë· pluhuri** the dust *takes* [] over: [] *gets* completely forgotten; [] *gathers* dust, [] *is* unused for a long time

○ **e zë· plumbin** *(Colloq)* to get shot: get a taste of lead, eat lead

○ [] **zë· prej jake** to compel/coerce []

○ **zë· pritë** to take up a position of ambush

○ **nuk zë· punë me dorë** "not take work by the hand" not do any work

○ [] **zë· pupa** to deny []

○ <> **zë· pusi** to waylay <>, ambush <>

○ **zë· qafën** *(Impol)* **1** to get badly hurt: break one's neck **2** to kick off, die

○ **nuk** [] **zë·³ˢᵍ qederi** "no worry *touches* []" [] *doesn't care*, [] doesn't give a damn

○ <> **zë·³ˢᵍ qerrja bishtin** <>'s gets trapped (and is now in a hopeless situation)

○ [] **zë·³ᵖˡ qipujt** "the goblins *grab* []" [] *is* possessed by demons; [] *flies* into a rage?

○ **zë· qoshe 1** to get infirm with age and stay indoors **2** to keep to oneself and mind one's own business

○ [] **zë·³ˢᵍ qymyri** "the coal fumes *get* []" [] *falls* in love

○ <> **zë·³ˢᵍ rrasa bishtin** <>'s gets trapped (and is now in a hopeless situation)

○ <> **zë·³ᵖˡ rrebet** <> *bursts* into a rage

○ **zë· rrënjë** to take root; settle down, take up permanent residence: become implanted

○ <> **zë·³ˢᵍ rrota bishtin** <>'s gets trapped (and is now in a hopeless situation)

○ **zë· rruaza** to form bubbles

○ **zë· rruazën** *(Impol)* **1** to get badly hurt: break one's neck **2** to kick off, die

○ **zë· rrugën 1** to take to the road, leave home **2** to set off (on a trip/journey)

○ <> **zë· rrugën** to block <>'s path, impede <>'s progress; get in <>'s way

○ <> [] **zë·³ˢᵍ syri** <>'s eye *catches* sight of [], [] *catches* <>'s eye

○ <> **zë· sytë** to lead <> astray

○ <>**a zë·³ˢᵍ sytë buka/e mira** "the bread/good veils <>'s eyes" the life of plenty *blinds* <> (to impending peril)

○ <> **zë·³ᵖˡ sytë lëmashk** <>'s eyes *become* covered by a film

○ <> **zë·³ˢᵍ sharra në gozhdë** "<>'s saw *hits* a nail" <>'s plan *hits* a snag; <> *runs* into a dead end

○ <>**a zë· shpirtin ngjak** to make <>'s life Hell

○ [] **zë· shtatë palë ethe** "seven sets of fever *beset* []" **1** [] *breaks* out in a bad fever **2** [] *is scared* out of []'s pants

○ [] **zë·³ˢᵍ shtëpia** "the house takes []" [] *gets* terribly embarrassed, [] *wants* to fall through a hole in the floor

○ **zë·³ˢᵍ shtrat dëbora** the snow *settles* in

○ **zë· shtratin** to take to one's bed with a lingering illness

○ <>[] **zë· shul** to make <> pay through the nose for [the favor] by constantly reminding <> of it

○ <>**a zë· shul 1** to throw a monkey wrench into <>'s plans **2** to oppose <> stubbornly on the matter **3** to settle in for a long stay

○ [] **zë·³ˢᵍ taksirati** bad luck *befalls* []; [] *is* in big trouble

○ [] **zë·³ˢᵍ tavani** "the ceiling takes []" [] *gets* terribly embarrassed, [] *wants* to fall through a hole in the floor

○ <> **zë·³ᵖˡ trutë ndryshk/myk 1** <> *is* out of date in <>'s thinking; <> *thinks* in an old-fashioned way **2** <> has lost some of one's mental facility, <>'s mind gets rusty

○ **zë· udhë/udhën 1** to take to the road, leave home **2** to set off (on a trip/journey)

○ <> **zë· udhën** to block <>'s path, impede <>'s progress; get in <>'s way

○ **nuk** <> **zë·³ˢᵍ ujë lopata/shati** "<>'s shovel can't lift much water" **1** <> *has* no influence, <> does not pull much weight **2** <> *does* not succeed

○ **e zë· vaun** to overcome one's past difficulties, get past one's problems

○ <> **zë·³ˢᵍ vend fjala** "<>'s word *settles* in" <>'s words *carry* weight, what <> says is influential

○ s'<> **zë·³ˢᵍ vend gjaku** <> *can't* sit still

○ s'<> **zë·³ʳᵈ vend** not be enough (food) to satisfy <>

○ **zë· vend 1** to take one's place, sit down **2** to settle (down/in); become established, become an integral part **3** to be influential, carry weight, count for something

○ s'<> **zë·³ˢᵍ vendi** <> *can't* stay/sit still

○ <> **zë· vendin** to take <>'s place, substitute for <>

○ <>[] **zë·³ˢᵍ veshi** "<>'s ear *catches* []" <> *hears* [] in passing, <> *happens* to hear [], <> accidentally *hears* []

○ **e zë· veshin 1** to fall asleep **2** to die

○ **zë· viset** to take up a position of ambush

○ **zë· vrimat** "take to one's burrows" to go into hiding

○ [] **zë·³ᵖˡ xhindet** "the jinni *grab* []" [] *is* possessed by demons; [] *flies* into a rage?

○ **zë· zemrën** to eat just enough to settle one's stomach

○ **zë· zverkun** *(Impol)* **1** to get badly hurt: break one's neck **2** to kick off, die

zë·bu·k·ur *adj* having a beautiful voice: sonorous

zë·çje·rr·ë *adj* having a raspy voice; hoarse

zë·dre·dh·ur *adv* in a shaky voice

zë·dhën·ës *nm* spokesman

zë·dhën·ëse *nf* **1** spokeswoman **2** official news agency

zë·dhën·ie *nf (Old)* announcement, report

zë·ëmb·ël *adj* having a pleasant (sweet) sound/voice

zëizolues *adj* sound-insulating

zëmadh *adj* 1 loud 2 *(Fig)* well-known, famous

zëmatës *nm* [*Spec*] sound level meter

zëmbicë *nf* [*Veter*] = zburth

zëmër *nf* 1 time between the mid-day and evening meals; food eaten during that time: mid-afternoon snack 2 = zemër

****zëmër** = zemër

zëmërherë *nf* mid-afternoon

zëmëro •*n vi* to eat a mid-afternoon snack

****zëmrek** *nm* = zemberek

zën *stem for opt, adm, part* <zë•, zi•het

zënç *stem for opt* <zë•, zi•het

zënë
  I § *part* <zë•, zihe•t
  II § *adj (i)* 1 captured 2 occupied, taken; busy 3 obscured, invisible 4 (of plants) sprouted; rooted 5 *(Colloq)* engaged (to be married); pregnant; well off, rich 6 *(Colloq)* closed, shut 7 *(Colloq)* (of colors) dark
  III § *pred* occupied, busy

zënës *nm* wooden device used to control the flow of water from the mill race into a gristmill

zënëse *np fem* cloth potholder

zëngjirur *adj* with a hoarse voice

zënie *nf ger* 1 <zë•, zi•het 2 wrangle, quarrel, fight, strife 3 seizure

zënkë *nf* angry quarrel, scrap

zëntë *3sg opt* <zë•, zi•het
  ◦ <> **zëntë fytin/grykën!** "May <>'s throat be blocked up" *(Curse)* I hope <> *chokes*!
  ◦ <>**u zëntë fyti/gryka!** *(Curse)* I hope <> *chokes and dies*!
  ◦ <>**u zëntë lëfyti** *(Curse)* May <>'s throat block up!: I hope <> *chokes*!
  ◦ <> **zëntë oborri bar** "May <>'s garden be overgrown with grass" *(Curse)* May <> and <>'s whole family disappear from the face of the earth!
  ◦ <> **zëntë sytë buka!** "May bread cover <>'s eyes!" *(Curse)* (said of a person ungrateful for one's long caretaking) May <> go blind!
  ◦ <> **zëntë shtëpia bar** "May <>'s house be overgrown with grass" *(Curse)* May <> and <>'s whole family disappear from the face of the earth!

zër *stem for imper* <zë•, zi•het
  ◦ **Zër në gojë qenin, *rrëmbe/bëj gati* shkopin.** "Mention the dog, grab the stick." *(Prov Pej)* Speak of the devil (and here he is).

zëra *np* <zë(r)

zërë *nf* [*Folklore*] = zanë

zëri *obl* <zë(r)

****zërmurë** *np masc* bonfires

zëro •*n vt* to start, begin

zësjellës *adj* [*Phys*] sound-conductive

zësjellje *nf* [*Phys*] sound-conduction

zëshëm *adj (i)* 1 loud, noisy 2 vocal 3 [*Ling*] voiced

zëshmim *nm* [*Ling*] voicing

zëshmo •*het vpr* [*Ling*] to become voiced

zët *nm (Colloq)* dislike, spite

zëv. *abbrev* <zëvendës

zëvendës *n* second-in-command; person substituting for a chief in performing duties

zëvendës *formativ* substitute-, vice-, deputy-

zëvendësdrejtor *n* deputy-director

zëvendësi *nf (Book)* position of the second-in-command; period during which second-in-command is in power: regency

zëvendësim *nm ger* 1 <zëvendëso•n 2 replacement; substitution

zëvendëskryeredaktor *n* deputy editor-in-chief

zëvendëskryetar *n* deputy-chief

zëvendësministër *n* deputy-minister

zëvendëso •*n vt* to replace; substitute for [ ]

zëvendësprokuror *n* deputy-prosecutor

zëvendëssekretar *n* deputy-secretary

zëvendësues *adj, n* (person/thing) serving as a substitute/replacement

zëvendësueshëm *adj (i)* replaceable, substitutable

zëzëllimë *nf* = zukamë

zëzëllo •*n vi* = zukat•

****zgadâ(n)** *nm (pl ˜j)* part of a river bank that has been hollowed out by the erosive action of the river

zgafelle *nf* large cave in a hill/mountain: cavern

zgafullo •*het vpr* 1 to have one's clothes open and in disarray; strip off one's clothes 2 to open wide, open up; get torn apart

zgafullo •*n vt* 1 to dig/drill/make a hole in [ ] 2 to lay [part of the body] bare, expose [part of the body]

zgajt•*et vpr* to get limp and listless, become enervated; let oneself go completely, have no energy

zgajtur *adj (i)* limp and listless, enervated; without energy

zgal• *vi (Reg)* to dawn, get light

zgal•*et vpr* (of weather/sky) to clear up

zgale *nf (Reg)* hole/crack (in a wall) = borde

zgalem *nm* 1 [*Ornit*] little tern *Sterna albifrons* 2 stormy petrel (*Hydrobates pelagicus*) 3 *(Fig Poet)* precursor/herald of an important event

****zgalit**•*et vp impers* (of the weather) to become clear, clear up

****zgallo** *nf with masc reference* big good-for-nothing oaf

zgallo •*n vi impers* it dawns

zgaq *nm* 1 leftover waste: dregs, rubbish 2 *(Fig)* good-for- nothing bum, shameless scum

zgaq• *vt (Colloq)* to unclothe; uncover; discover

zgaq•*et vpr (Colloq)* to get undressed/uncovered; get disclosed

zgarbë *nf* hollow in a tree trunk

zgarbull *nm (np ˜j)* = zgarbë

zgarbullo •*n vt* to hollow out [the trunk of a tree]

zgardhngjesh•*et vpr (Colloq)* to have the sash/belt (around one's waist) come loose; become disheveled in dress

zgardhno •*het vpr* to spring a rung (of a barrel); break/come apart (of a wattled fence)

zgargull *nm* [*Ornit*] starling (*Sturnus vulgaris*)

zgavelle = zgafelle

zgavër *nf* 1 hollow (in a tree or rock); cavern 2 cavity 3 [*Anat*] body cavity containing organs: (eye) socket, (abdominal/chest) cavity

zgavërt *adj (i)* 1 hollow 2 sunken

****zgavlan** *nm* mantelpiece

****zgavlo** •*n vt* to unearth

zgavrim *nm ger* <zgavro•n, zgavro•het

zgavriq
  I § *adj* hollow
  II § *nm* small cavity

zgavro··*het* *vpr* to become hollow; get a cavity

zgavro··n *vt* to hollow out []

zgavror *adj (Book)* hollow

zgavruar *adj (i)* **1** hollowed out; with a cavity **2** sunken

zgavruq = zgavriq

zgerdhë *nf [Anat]* bronchial tube, bronchus

zgëq *nm* nook, cranny

zgërbis *stem for 1st sg pres, pl pres, 2nd & 3rd sg subj, pind* <**zgërbit·**

zgërbit· *vt* to clean [] by rubbing: scour, scrape, scrub

zgërbonjë *nf* = zgarbë

zgërdhagët *adj (i)* (of stone) deeply fissured; hollowed out

zgërdhelë *nf* cracked opening; gap

zgërdhesh·et *vpr* = zgërdhi·*het*

zgërdheshje *nf* show of scorn with a sneer and a laugh: smirk, snicker

zgërdhi·het *vpr (Pej)* to sneer and laugh with scorn: snicker

zgërdhi·n *vt*
  ○ **zgërdhi·**n **dhëmbët** *(Pej)* = zgërdhi·*het*

zgërdhirje *nf ger* <**zgërdhi·**het

***zgërgërim** *nm ger* <**zgërgëro·**n

***zgërgëro·**n *vt* to bubble, burble

zgërlaq· *vt* **1** to squash **2** *(Fig)* to tire [] out completely, exhaust

zgërlaq·et *vpr* **1** to get mushy inside **2** *(Fig)* to become completely tired out, be exhausted

zgërlaqur *adj (i)* **1** squashed; mushy **2** *(Fig)* weak and limp from exhaustion

***zgërlis** *stem for 1st sg pres, pl pres, 2nd & 3rd sg subj, pind* <**zgërlit·**

***zgërlit·** *vt* to make faces, grimace; pout

***zgërlitës** *adj* pouting, tearful

zgërmis *stem for 1st sg pres, pl pres, 2nd & 3rd sg subj, pind* <**zgërmit·**

zgërmit· *vt* to scrape away at [], scratch, scrape; hollow out

zgërqesh·et *vpr* = zgërdhi·*het*

zgidh = zgjidh

***zgiq** *nm* hidden out-of-the-way place: nook; den, lair; hideout

***zglebur** *adj (i)* bleary-eyed, rheumy

zgobell *adj, n (Pej)* tall and ugly (person)

zgobinalle *nf* area with crags and crevices

***zgobinetë** *nf* **1** deep spot in water **2** mountain hollow filled with snow and used as a watering hole for livestock

zgorç *nm* = zgavër

zgoriq *nm dimin* small hole/cavity/hollow

zgork·et *vpr* = zgrop·*et*

zgorkë *nf* **1** deep hollow in a river bed; empty place **2** *(Colloq)* abdominal cavity: belly

zgorko·n *vt* to hollow out a hole in []

***zgorofaqe** *nf [Bot]* primrose; cowslip

zgorovaje *nf* large wooden tub

***zgorto·**n = zgorko·*n*

zgorre *nf* **1** the bones of a body: skeleton **2** bramble thicket

zgot *nm* bottom hole in the hopper through which grain falls to the millstone

***zgozhdo·**n *vt* to unnail = zhgozhdo·*n*

zgrap· *vt* **1** to munch [grass/leaves] noisily **2** to crack [nuts] with the teeth **3** to bite into [] **4** *(Colloq)* to swipe, filch

zgratho·n *vt* to remove the straw from [flax]: dress [flax]

***zgrebis** = zgërbis

***zgrebit·** *vt* = zgërbit·

zgrep·et *vpr* to become hunched over and emaciated

zgrip
  I § *nm* **1** brink; edge, border **2** *(Fig)* the final point: the end **3** very small amount
  II § *adv* to a shallow depth; superficially
  ○ **ësh·të më zgrip** to be chancy/unsafe; be in perilous/dangerous condition

zgripët *adj (i)* **1** shallow **2** on a tight budget; frugal, thrifty **3** *(Fig)* prudent; reticent

zgriptas *adv* **1** very sparingly; superficially **2** by pure force, forcibly

***zgriptina** *np fem* shallows

zgripto·n
  I § *vt* **1** to cut down on [expenses] for the sake of frugality **2** to move [] to the limit, take/bring [] to the very edge
  II § *vi* to have barely started, have just begun

zgripthi *adv* **1** alongside **2** superficially

zgrof
  I § *nm (Colloq)* stomach; belly
  II § *adj* hollow, empty

***zgroftirë** *nf* foul smell, stench

zgrop *nm (Colloq)* = zgrof

zgrop·et *vpr (Colloq)* to have an empty stomach; have an empty stomach and be very hungry

***zgropëm** *adj (i)* empty-feeling, very hungry

zgropim *nm ger* **1** <**zgropo·**n **2** excavation

zgropo·n *vt* to excavate

zgurdullim *nm ger* <**zgurdullo·**n, zgurdullo·*het*

zgurdullo·het *vpr* (of eyes) to goggle

zgurdullo·n *vt* to open [the eyes] very wide (in fright/anger): pop [] open

zgurdulluar *adj (i)* goggle-eyed

zgurdhë *nf [Anat]* **1** bowels, colon **2** asshole, anus **3** *(Crude)* gullet

zgjas *stem for 1st sg pres, pl pres, 2nd & 3rd sg subj, pind* <**zgjat·**

zgjat·
  I § *vt* **1** to lengthen; prolong **2** to extend; hold [] out to <>
  II § *vi* **1** to grow longer **2** to continue for a length of time: last, extend
  ○ <>[] **zgjat·** to let <>'s [] get long
  ○ <>a **zgjat·** to try to be too nice to <>
  ○ **nuk** <>a **zgjat·** not stretch matters out with <>, not waste time with <>
  ○ <> **zgjat·** **dorën 1** to lend <> a hand, help <> out **2** to request <>'s help: put one's hand out to <> **3** to extend one's hand to <> for a conciliatory handshake
  ○ **e zgjat·** **gjuhën si lëpjetë/lëpushë/lëpushkë** "grow a tongue as long as a sorrel leaf" *(Pej)* to talk too much (and say silly and irrelevant things)
  ○ **zgjat·** **hundët** "grow a long nose" *(Pej)* to stick one's nose into other people's business
  ○ **Zgjati këmbët sa ke jorganin/plafin/shtratin.** "Stretch your legs according to your coverlet." *(Prov)* Cut your coat according to your cloth. Know your own limits!

○ **zgjat· krahët** "grow long arms" to extend one's influence

○ **e zgjat· muhabetin me** [] "prolong the chat with []" to get on friendly terms with []

○ **<> zgjat· qafën** "stretch one's neck to <>" (*Contempt)* to surrender abjectly: knuckle under

○ [] **zgjat· tortë** to drag [] out needlessly, go too slowly with []

○ **<> zgjat· veshët** "lengthen <>'s ears" **1** to make <> wait a long time, leave <> to twiddle <>'s thumbs waiting **2** to chastise/scold <>

○ **<>*i* zgjat· veshët** "lengthen <>'s ears" to praise <> excessively: give <> a swelled head, inflate <>'s ego

○ *i* **zgjat· veshët** "extend one's ears" to try hard to hear; try to listen in

○ **<> zgjat· veshin** "lengthen <>'s ear" to chastise/scold <>

z gja·t·*et vpr* **1** to get longer/taller **2** to extend; extend out; stretch out **3** to take longer than expected; take too long **4** (of a time period) to get longer

z gja·t ës *adj* **1** [*Tech*] serving to lengthen: stretching, prolonging, protracting, extending **2** [*Ling*] lengthening; durative

z gjat·im *nm ger* **1** <zgjato·*n,* zgjato·*het* **2** elongation; continuation **3** [*Tech*] extensibility **4** [*Mus*] length of a note

z gjat·je *nf ger* **1** <zgja·t·, zgja·t·*et* **2** extension; continuation; duration

○ **zgjatje fjalësh** long-windedness, verbosity

z gjato··n *vpr* = zgjat·*et*

z gjato··n *vt, vi* = zgja·t·

z gja·tur *adj (i)* **1** elongated; lengthened **2** extended; prolonged

zgje b··*et vpr* = zgjebo·s·*et*

zgjeb anik *adj* = zgjebara·k

zgjeb ara·k

I § *adj* covered with scabs: scabby, mangy, scurvy

II § *n* (*Scorn*) ill-clad and filthy person; contemptible person

zgjeb a·sh *adj* = zgjebara·k

zgje be *nf* **1** [*Med*] scabies, itch **2** [*Veter*] scabies, mange

zgje b·ëç *nm* [*Bot*] Italian clematis (*Clematis viticella L.)*

zgje b·ët *adj (i)* = zgjebara·k

zgje b·ëz *nf* [*Bot*] bugloss (*Anchusa arvensis)*

zgjeb o·r *adj* [*Med*] scabious

zgjeb o·s· *vt* to infect [] with scabies/mange

zgjeb o·s··*et vpr* to get scabies/mange

zgjeb o·s·ur *adj (i)* **1** afflicted with scabies/mange: mangy **2** *(Fig Scorn)* filthy; worthless

zgje b·ur *adj (i)* = zgjebo·sur

zgjedh· *vt* **1** to select, choose; elect **2** (*Colloq*) to figure out [], solve

○ **<>*a* zgjedh· mendjen** to figure out what <> thinks; read <>'s mind; read <>'s mind, figure out <>'s intentions

zgje dh·ë *nf* ox-yoke, yoke

zgje dh·ës

I § *n* **1** voter, elector **2** person who has first choice; chooser, selector

II § *adj* **1** having the right to vote; voting **2** selective, choosy

zgje dh·ëz *nf dimin* **1** little yoke **2** [*Mus*] bracket (in printed music)

zgjedh·im *nm ger* **1** <zgjedho·n **2** [*Ling*] conjugation

zgje dh·je

I § *nf ger* <zgje dh·, zgji dh·*et*

II § *nf* **1** choice **2** elections

zgjedh je·so·r *adj (Book)* electoral

zgjedh o·n· *vt* **1** to yoke up [oxen], put [] under the yoke **2** [*Ling*] to conjugate [a verb]

zgjedh u·e·shëm *adj (i)* [*Ling*] capable of being conjugated

zgjedh ·ur *adj (i)* **1** selected; of choice quality, select **2** elected

zgje rbe *nf* [*Entom*] moth; moth larva

z gjer·im *nm ger* **1** <zgjero·*n,* zgjero·*het* **2** widest part, width; widened part **3** additional dwelling space: more room to live in

z gjer o··het *vpr* to extend over a broad(er) area, become broader, increase in breadth: widen (out); broaden (out)

z gjer o··n *vt* to extend [] over a broad(er) area, increase [] in breadth: widen; broaden

z gjer u·a·r *adj (i)* extended over a broad(er) area, increased in breadth: widened; broadened

z gjesh· *vt* to loosen/remove [something worn around the waist]

z gje sh·ur

I § *adv* **1** ungirt; unarmed (without a weapon bound to the waist) **2** in an unconstrained manner: freely, unhesitatingly

II § *adj (i)* unrestrained, free

z gji·ç *nm* [*Geog*] small inlet in a body of water: cove

z gjidh· *vt* **1** to untie, unbind; loosen **2** to set [] free, loose: unleash, unyoke **3** to break off [a relationship], break [an agreement, a spell] **4** [*Math*] to solve **5** *(Fig)* to arrive at a solution for []: resolve

○ **e zgjidh· dorën** to begin to spend money freely

○ **<> zgjidh· duart** to untie <>'s hands, give <> a free hand

○ **<>*a* zgjidh· gojën/gjuhën** to loosen <>'s tongue, get <> to talk

○ **e zgjidh· gojën/gjuhën** to tell all (the secrets): spill the beans, let it all out, blab

○ **iu zgjidh gryka thesit** "untie/open the neck of the sack" to disclose everything

○ **e zgjidh· kuletën/qesen/trastën** to begin to spend money more freely: stop being so tight-fisted, open one's pursestrings a bit

○ **zgjidh· martesën** to dissolve the marriage: get divorced

○ [] **zgjidh· me shpatë** "decide [] by the sword" to decide [] definitively by use of force

○ **e zgjidh· thesin 1** to begin to spend money more freely: stop being so tight-fisted, open one's pursestrings a bit **2** to tell all (the secrets): spill the beans, let it all out, blab

z gjidh··*et vpr* to become untied/unbound; lose one's bonds; become released from an obligation; break a spell

○ **<> zgjidh·**·*et*[3sg] **goja/gjuha** "<>'s mouth/tongue *is* unleashed" the words pour out of <>'s mouth

z gjidh *stem for 2nd pl pres, pind, imper, vp* <zgje·dh·

z gjidh·ëm *adj (i)* untied, loose

z gjidh·ës *adj* **1** releasing, freeing **2** contributing to a solution

zgjïdhje *nf ger* **1** <zgjïdh·, zgjïdh·*et* **2** solution **3** resolution (of a difficulty/problem/plot) **4** dissolution, dissociation

zgjïdhshëm *adj (i)* **1** capable of being untied/unbound; dissolvable; non-binding **2** solvable; resolvable

zgjïdhur *adj (i), adv* **1** untied, unbound; unleashed; dissolved, dissociated; resolved, solved **2** released from an obligation

zgjim *nm ger* **1** <zgjo·*n*, zgjo·*het* **2** time of awakening, wake-up time **3** *(Old)* knowledge, education

*****zgjimtar**
 I § *adj* awakening, stirring
 II § *n* person who calls for an awakening

zgjïrë *adj (i)* convex = mysët

zgjïsh·*et* *vpr* to ungird one's arms (unbind the sash that girds arms to one's waist)

zgjïsh *stem for 2nd pl pres, pind, imper, vp* <zgjesh·

zgjïo·*het* *vpr* **1** to wake up, awaken **2** *(Fig)* to come to life; come to mind
 ○ **zgjo·***het* **me tre pashë diell** to wake up when the sun is already high in the sky

zgjïo·*n* *vt* **1** to wake [] up: awaken **2** *(Fig)* to make [] aware

zgjïodh *stem for pdef* <zgjeïdh·

zgjïo'i *obl* <zgju'a

zgjïonobar *nm* [Bot] *(Paronychia)*

zgjïonja *np* <zgjïonjë hangnails

zgjïonjë OR **zgjïonjëz** *nf* [Med Veter] disease that causes inflamed sores next to human nails and in the middle of animal hooves *(onychomycosis)*

zgjïua *nm (obl ~ oï, np ~ oje)* beehive

zgjïuar
 I § *adj (i)* **1** awake, not yet sleeping; unable to sleep **2** *(Fig)* alert; smart, bright, clever **3** [Bot] freshly sprouted
 II § *n (i)* wide-awake/alert/clever person
 III § *adv* wide awake; alert

zgjïuarsi *nf* cleverness, intelligence, brightness

zgjïuath *nm* [Med] whitlow

*****zgjïues** *adj* giving alarm, rousing

*****zgjïuet** *adj (i)* **1** *(Reg)* awake **2** alert; smart, bright, clever

zgjïuetësi = zgjuarsi

zgjïumth *nm (Reg Arb)* = gjumës

zgjïmët *adj (i)* = lugët

zgjïyrajkë *adj, nf (Reg Insult)* slovenly (girl/woman)

zgjïyran *adj, nm (Insult)* slovenly (boy/man)

zgjïyrë
 I § *nf* **1** slag, scoria **2** soot **3** grime on clothing **4** *(Fig)* worthless part/residue; masking layer that hides something of value
 II § *adj* **1** filthy **2** *(Fig)* wretched, miserable
 III § *adv* **1** badly, wretchedly **2** extremely, terribly, very

zgjïyro·*n* *vt* = zgjyros·

zgjïyros· *vt* **1** to rust/tarnish [] **2** to get [] grimy/dirty

zgjïyros·*et* *vpr* **1** to rust/tarnish **2** to get grimy/dirty

zgjïyrosur *adj (i)* **1** rusted, rusty **2** grimy, soiled; dirty

zi·*het* *vpr* **1** to quarrel; fight **2** to hold on **3** *(Fig)* to become friends; become relatives **4** to begin, start **5** to reach the intended fermentation state: congeal, set; (of dough) rise **6** to get pregnant; (of an embryo)

take shape **7** *(Colloq)* to improve (in economic condition); start to shape up **8** to have significance: count **9** to get stopped up, become covered over
 ○ **Nuk zihet dielli me plisa.** "The sun cannot be covered over by clods of earth." *(Prov)* Truth will out. You can't hide the truth.
 ○ <> **zi·***het^{3sg}* **gjuha** "<>'s tongue *stops* up" <> *becomes* tongue-tied
 ○ **zi·***het* **në lëng të** {*pronominal adj*} "stew in one's own juice" to get along on {*one's*} own
 ○ **zi·***het* **për fyti/gryke me** [] to quarrel/fight bitterly with []
 ○ **zi·***het* **për mjekrën e qoses** "quarrel about the beard of the beardless man" to quarrel over nothing
 ○ **zi·***het* **për pesë/dy para spec** "quarrel about five/two farthings worth of pepper" to quarrel about nothing, fight over a trifle
 ○ <> **zi·***het^{3sg}* **shpirti ngjak** <>'s life *becomes* Hell

zi
 I § *adj (i), (fem sg ~ ez, masc pl ~ inj, fem pl ~ eza)* **1** black **2** dark **3** containing/collecting sewage **4** *(Fig)* miserable, wretched **5** *(Fig)* bringing misfortune, fatal, bad
 II § *nm (np ~ eza)* **1** miserable/wretched person **2** dark-skinned person **3** [Chess] person playing the black pieces: black
 ○ **i zi katran/shkrumb/skëterrë** pitch black

zi
 I § *nf* **1** grief; period of mourning **2** something black worn as symbol of mourning: mourning clothes, black ribbon **3** *(Fig)* calamity, disaster; bad times; food shortage **4** greed
 II § *nn (të)* **1** black, blackness **2** mourning; mourning/black clothes **3** *(Fig)* dark shadow/cloud; misery, misfortune
 III § *adv* in black; (dress) in black clothing
 ○ **zi buke** famine
 ○ **të zitë** *(Colloq)* (used after a question word to indicate exasperation) in hell!

zi'3 *stem for 2nd pl pres, pind, imper, vp* <zë·

zïe·n
 I § *vt, vi* to boil; seethe
 II § *vi* **1** to ferment **2** to have a prickly feeling; feel numb **3** to proceed with great energy: bubble (with excitement), bustle (with activity)
 ○ <> **zïe·n** {} "<>'s {} *is boiling*" <> hears a disturbing buzzing/ringing in {} **më ziejnë veshët** my ears are ringing
 ○ <> **zïe·n^{3sg}* **gjaku** "<>'s blood is heating up: <> *is* very lively and energetic
 ○ **zïe·n^{3sg}* **kazani** there *is* a lot of talk going around, the town is abuzz; there is a lot of activity, things are buzzing
 ○ <> **zïe·n^{3sg}* **koka** "<>'s head *is boiling*" <>'s mind is in turmoil
 ○ **zïe·n^{pl}* **në një kazan** "boil in one cauldron" to be all the same
 ○ **zïe·n^{3sg}* **në të katër rrylat** to boil noisily
 ○ **zïe·n^{3sg}* **puna** "the work *is boiling*" work *is* going at breakneck speed
 ○ **zïe·n** **raki** to distill raki
 ○ **zïe·n** **si kazan** to be agitated and restless
 ○ <> **zïe·n^{3sg}* **toka/trualli nën këmbë** "the ground *burns* under <>'s feet" nowhere *is* there safety for <>, there is no respite for <> there

○ <> zie·n³ᵖˡ **trutë** <>'s head is spinning with all the things <> has to worry about

○ <> zie·n³ᵖˡ **veshët 1** <> has a ringing in <>'s ears **2** <> is sick and tired of listening to the same old thing

zi'er
I § part <zie·n
II § adj (i) boiled

zie'rje nf ger **1** <zie·n, zi·het **2** [Tech] welding

zift nm **1** bitumen, asphalt **2** tar

zigu'r nm male yearling lamb; young ram

zigza'g
I § nm zigzag
II § adv with sharp turns, with twists and turns: in zigzags

zigj nm **1** balance with a long scaled beam, ball-shaped counterweight, and hanging chains to hold the object to be weighed: steelyard *2 object used as a weight: weight

*zigj'a·s stem for 1st sg pres, pl pres, 2nd & 3rd sg subj, pind <zigja·t·

*zigj'a'· vt to put [] on a balance: weigh
○ zih·et për një lugë çorbë "quarrel about a spoonful of thick soup" to break off a friendship over a trivial matter, break off a social relationship over nothing
○ zih·et për të bardhat e laraskës to argue about nothing

*zihariqta'r n (Old) messenger = sihariqta'r

*zi'hje nf quarrel, squabble

zijafe't nm (Old) = gosti

zijo's· vt to starve; make [] feel hungry

zijo's·et vpr to be starving, hunger

zijo'sur adj (i) **1** famished, hungry; ravenous **2** (Fig) unconstrainable, impatient

zijo'sh adj, n (person/animal) with a bronze/brown/dark skin; dark-haired, dark-coated

zi'keq adj starved, hungry; insatiable

zila'r adj, n envious/jealous person

zile
I § nf bell
II § np [Mus] finger cymbals
○ zile dyjare double bell (one inside the other)

zile'ps· vt **1** to make [] envious **2** to envy []

zile'ps·et vpr to be envious

zile'pshëm adj (i) enviable

zili' nf envy

*zilinj'a'r = ziliqar

ziliqa'r adj, n envious person

ziliqari'sht adv enviously

zili's· vt to envy

zili's·et vpr = zile'ps·et

zimbi'cë nf [Veter] growth/tumor on a horse's palate

zindjell'ës adj attracting/portenting misfortune

zink nm [Chem Min] zinc (Zn)

zinki'm nm ger [Tech] <zinko'·n

zinko'·n vt [Tech] to coat [] with zinc: galvanize

zinku'ar adj (i) [Tech] coated with zinc: galvanized

zinxhi'r
I § nm **1** chain; chain drive **2** [Mil] chain formation
II § adj, adv in a chain; in chain formation, like a chain
○ zinxhir deti [Bot] kind of calcareous green alga Halimeda tuna

zinxhi'rtë adj (i) **1** made of chain **2** (Fig) one after another, in a chain

zi'nj adj (të) masc pl <zi

*zijo'sur adj (i) = zijo'sur

zijo'sh = zijosh

zi'shëm adv (Colloq) in mourning

*zja'me nf [Entom] firefly, glowworm

*zjamu're np fem = zërmu'rë

*zja'rm = zjarrm

*zjar'mu'r nm bonfire

zjarr
I § nm **1** fire; flame **2** [Ethnog] family; clan **3** high temperature, fever **4** [Mil] gunfire **5** (Fig) passion; ardor
II § adj impassioned, fervent
III § adv aflame, on fire
○ Zjarr! [Mil] Fire! Shoot!
○ zjarr dimri big fire
○ zjarri i egër/duhanit disease of tobacco manifested as dark spots on the leaves
○ zjarr i kryqëzuar [Mil] crossfire
○ zjarr partizan large bonfire commemorating the partisans of World War II; bonfire
○ zjarr për zjarr with immediate retorts back and forth, with an immediate retort, blow for blow; fire for fire
○ zjarr thikë [Mil] raking fire

zjarrduru'es adj **1** fire-resistant; fireproof **2** [Tech] refractory

zjarrdurue'shm'ëri nf [Tech] heat resistance: refractoriness

zjarrfik'ës
I § adj fire-extinguishing; fire fighting
II § n **1** fire fighter **2** (Fig Npc) counterrevolutionary
III § nm fire extinguisher

zjarrfik'ëse nf **1** fire engine **2** fire extinguisher

*zjarri'm nm excitement, passion; temper

zjarri'sht adv fervently, passionately

zjarri'shtë nf **1** fire area in the back of a hearth; fireplace, hearth **2** ashtray

zjarrmato'r adj (Colloq) = zjarrmo'r

zjarrmëta'r nm person who sets and explodes dynamite charges

zjarrmi' nf **1** high temperature of a fever **2** emotional/sexual heat: ardor, passion

zjarrmi'shtë nf room where cooking is done

zjarrmo'·n vt = zjarmo's·

zjarrmo'r adj (Colloq Fig) passionate, zealous: fiery, flaming

zjarrmo's· vt (Fig) to inflame, fire

zjarrmu're np masc wall of fire (lit in a prominent place for a significant occasion or as a signal)

zjarrndez'ës adj incendiary; inflammatory

zjarrni' nf collec [Ethnog] family, clan

zjarro's· vt to set [] on fire, fire []; inflame

zjarro'sur adj (i) inflamed, impassioned, burning

zjarrsi' nf ardor, passion

*zjarrsi'm nf incandescence

zjarrshëm adj (i) fiery

*zjarrsho'jt'ës adj, n nm = zjarrfik'ës

zjarrshu'ar adj **1** left all alone in the world, without close family **2** (Curse) may his household fire be extinguished forever!

zjarrshu'es adj, n nm = zjarrfik'ës

zjarr·ta·r
I § nm fireman (who feeds a fire): stoker
II § adj *fiery

zja·rr·të adj (i) **1** fiery **2** (Fig) impassioned

zjarr·ti·s·et vpr (of grain/flour) to begin to spoil from excessive moisture; ferment

zjarr·to·re nf furnace

zjarr·th nm **1** scarlet fever (Scarlatina) **2** [Bot] plant disease that withers the leaves of tobacco, corn, and grapes: (wildfire)

zjarr·vë·n·ës
I § adj serving to ignite fires; incendiary
II § n arsonist, firebug

zje\ stem for pdef, opt <**zi·**e·n

*zje·rë = zi·er

*zje·rm (Old) = zjarrm

zje·rrçë nf (Reg) long leather thong

zllo·ti nm zloty (Polish money)

z·madh·im nm ger **1** <zmadho·n, zmadho·het **2** enlargement

z·madh·o·het vpr **1** to grow in size/age/height: get bigger **2** to grow in number/strength

z·madh·o·n vt **1** to enlarge; magnify **2** (Fig) to exaggerate

z·madh·ua·r adj (i) enlarged

z·madh·ue·s adj **1** magnifying **2** [Math] increasing

zmalt = smalt

*z·mbrap = zmbraps

z·mbra·ps· vt **1** to push [] backwards, force [] to go back: repel, push [] back **2** (Fig) to revoke []

z·mbra·ps·et vpr **1** to move back(wards): withdraw, fall back; retreat **2** (Fig) to back down

z·mbra·ps·je nf ger <zmbraps·, zmbra·ps·et

*z·mbru = zbru

zmera·ld = smera·ld

zmeri·l = smeri·l

*zme·rne nf [Ichth] = gjarpër deti

zmo·jë nf wool grease

zmus·im nm ger [Tech] <zmuso·n

zmu·so nf [Tech] chamfer

zmus·o·n vt [Tech] to chamfer

zodia·k nm [Astron] zodiac

zog nm (np ⁓gj) **1** bird **2** young of a bird/fowl: chick **3** (Reg) young of an animal **4** (Reg) son **5** [Anat] muscle of a limb
  ○ **zog bari** [Ornit] small green-colored bird
  ○ **zog blete** [Ornit] bee-eater (Merops apiaster) = bregcë
  ○ **zog bore** [Ornit] chaffinch (Fringilla coelebs) = borës
  ○ **zog çaush** [Ornit] crested field bird with a curved beak
  ○ **zogu i deles** [Ornit] = zogde·le
  ○ **zogu dervish.** [Ornit] crested lark (Galerida cristata) = çafkëlo·re
  ○ **zog dimri** [Ornit] chaffinch (Fringilla coelebs) = borës
  ○ **zog dhensh/i dhenve** [Ornit] = zogde·le
  ○ **zog ferre** [Ornit] wren (Troglodytes troglodytes) = cinxami
  ○ **zog fiku** [Ornit] golden oriole (Oriolus oriolus)
  ○ **zog grabitqar** bird of prey
  ○ **zog gjembi** [Ornit] shrike (Laniidae)
  ○ **zog këng**ë**tar** songbird

  ○ **zogu i krishtit** [Ornit] crested lark (Galerida cristata)
  ○ **zog miu** [Ornit] wren (Troglodytes troglodytes) = cinxami
  ○ **zog mizë** [Ornit] hummingbird (Trochilidae) = kolibër
  ○ **zogu i natës** [Zool] bat (Chiroptera)
  ○ **zog nuseje** [Ornit] goldfinch (Carduelis carduelis) = kryea·rtëz
  ○ **zogu i parajsës** [Ornit] red bird of paradise (Paradisea rubra)
  ○ **zog qepës** [Ornit] penduline tit (Remis pendulinus)
  ○ **zog rrëfeshku** [Ornit] goldfinch (Carduelis carduelis) = kryea·rtëz
  ○ **zog shtrige** [Ornit] wren (Troglodytes troglodytes) = cinxami
  ○ **zog vejtës** [Ornit] weaverbird

zogde·le nf [Ornit] pied wagtail (Motacilla alba)

zo·g·ë nf **1** pullet **2** young bee **3** (Pet) pretty girl/woman **4** [Ornit] moorhen (Gallinula chloropus)

zo·g·ël nf **1** [Bot] alder buckthorn (Frangula alnus) = drunaku·q **2** (Pet) little bird, birdie *3 (Old) larva

zo·g·ëz nf **1** (Dimin) little birdie; chick, fledgling **2** = vra·ngull

zog·ist adj, n adherent of former King Zog: Zogist

zogori nf charging pack of wild (and hungry) animals; rampant mob

zog·rrëfe·shk nm [Ornit] goldfinch = kryea·rtëz

zog·th nm **1** [Anat] muscle of a limb **2** fetlock **3** small bird

zogj np = zog

*zoj·ni nf (of women) competence, ability

*zoj·no·re nf woman/mistress of the house

*zoju·she = zonju·she

zokolatu·rë nf [Constr] socle

zok·th nm **1** = zogth **2** [Bot] whitebeam (Sorbus aria)

*zollo·të nf (Old) old Turkish coin worth 30 para

zo·mo·tër nf (Reg) term used by a new wife for her husband's brother's daughter: niece

zona·k adj bearing poor shrunken heads of grain

zona·l adj (Book) zonal, regional

zo·në
I § nf **1** [Geog] zone **2** region
II § adj (i) = zona·k
  ○ **zonë e mbrojtjes** [Volleyball] back-area
  ○ **zona e rreptësisë** [Soccer] penalty area
  ○ **zonë e trimetërshit** [Volleyball] net area
  ○ **zonë e vdekur** [Mil] blind spot

zon·isht nm corn sown late in the season (in the stubble of a previous grain crop)

zo·nj·a
I § adj (e) <zo·ti **1** (of a woman/girl) masterful; capable/skillful; clever **2** (Pej) masterly in doing something bad: cunning
II § nf (e) **1** proprietress, owner **2** mistress of the household, lady of the house; boss

zo·nj·ë
I § nf **1** lady in a wealthy family with servants: madam **2** (Old) term of address used by a new wife for her mother-in-law and older sisters-in-law: ma'am **3** term of respectful address for a married woman or a respected older woman (but during the period 1947-91, the term was used mostly for foreign women): Mrs., ma'am **4** (Impol) woman who puts on airs and

considers herself too good to work **5** *(Fig)* something that deserves respect

II § adj ladylike, respectable

◦ **zonjë e bukur** *[Bot]* belladonna = **helmarinë**

◦ **zonjë e mirë** *(Euph)* smallpox

zonju·shë *nf* **1** girl in a wealthy family with servants: miss **2** term of respectful address for a young unmarried woman; term of respectful address used by a pupil toward a female teacher: Miss **3** *(Impol)* pampered girl who puts on airs and considers herself too good to work

zoo·gjeografi *nf* zoogeography

zoo·log *n* zoologist

zoo·logji *nf* **1** zoology **2** *(Colloq)* textbook on zoology

zoo·logjik *adj* zoological

zoo·tekni *nf* zootechny

zoo·teknik

I § adj zootechnical

II § nm zootechnician

zoo·teknikë *nf* zootechnics = **zootekni**

zoo·veteriner *nm* specialist in veterinary and zootechnical matters

zor

I § nm *(Colloq)* **1** brute force, coercion **2** hard effort; difficulty **3** difficult situation, great need **4** bashfulness, shyness

II § adv hard, difficult

◦ **zor se/të** _ it is hard to believe that _

zor·im *nm (Colloq)* brute force, coercion

zor·is *stem for 1st sg pres, pl pres, 2nd & 3rd sg subj, pind* <**zorit**

zor·it· *vt (Colloq)* to make things tough for [ ]; put [ ] in a bad way

zor·it·et *vpr (Colloq)* to get into a tough situation; go to a lot of trouble

***zorkadh** = **sorkadh**

zor·shëm *adj (i) (Colloq)* hard to do, difficult; troublesome

zorraxhi *nm (np ˜ nj) (Pej)* toady, sycophant

zorrë

I § nf **1** *[Anat]* intestine **2** hose (for conveying liquids)

II § np **1** abdominal organs, guts **2** seeds and associated membranous tissue inside a melon/gourd/squash

◦ **zorrë çapokore** *[Anat]* ileum

◦ **zorrë e drejtë** *[Anat]* rectum

◦ **zorrë e hollë** *[Anat]* small intestine

◦ **zorrë e kuqe** *[Anat]* gullet, esophagus

◦ **zorra e majme** *(Colloq)* large intestine

◦ **zorrë e përparme** *[Biol]* fore-gut

◦ **zorrë e prapme** *[Biol]* hind gut

◦ **zorrë qorre** *[Anat]* = **zorrë e verbër**

◦ **zorrë e trashë** *[Anat]* large intestine, colon

◦ **zorrë e verbër/verbët** *[Anat]* blind gut, cecum

◦ **zorrë e zbrazët** *[Anat]* jejunum

zorrë·bosh *adj* with an empty belly, not having eaten: hungry

zorrë·cë *nf [Bot]* cinquefoil *(Potentilla)*

zorrë·hollë *adj* unable to keep much in the stomach; in poor health

zorrë·ngushtë *adj* irascible; intractable, rowdy; intolerant, impatient; petty

zorrë·pulë *nf [Bot]* dodder *(Cuscuta)* = **helmëz**

zorrë·shpuar *adj* having a bottomless appetite, never full, insatiable

zorrë-shtojcë *nf [Anat]* vermiform appendage

zorrë·tharë *adj* having not had enough to eat: famished

zorrë·thatë *adj* having had nothing to eat: famished

zorrëz *nf [Veter]* necrosis of the large intestine in livestock caused by torsion

zorr·ovina *nf (ColloqImpolite)* guts, entrails

zorr·ovinë *nf (ColloqImpolite)* intestine-like thing; something long (like an intestine)

***zorr·ovin·or** *adj* intestinal

zot *nm (np ˜ ërinj)* **1** master; headman **2** boss, head **3** *[Relig]* Lord, God **4** term of respectful address for a man (during the period 1947-91, the term in Albania and Kosovo was mostly reserved for foreign men): Mr., mister; sir

◦ **zoti i shtëpisë** pater familias, head of the family

zot·et *vpr (Colloq)* to take it upon oneself, accept a responsibility

zot·ër *np* <**zot**

zot·ëri

I § nf with masc agreement **1** *(Old)* lord of an estate; rich/powerful person **2** *(Old)* term of respectful address for a man of substance: your lordship, lord **3** *(Book)* sir, gentleman (during the period 1947-91 in Albania and Kosovo, the term was restricted mostly to formal and official address to foreigners) **4** *(Contempt)* man who acts like a big shot too high up to work

II § adj gentlemanly

zot·ërim *nm ger* **1** <**zotëro·n**, **zotëro·het 2** mastery; dominion; ownership, possession

zot·ërisht *adv (Book)* in lordly fashion

zot·ëro·n

I § vt **1** to be the master of [ ]: own, possess **2** to master **3** to dominate; rule **4** to have a commanding view over [ ]

II § vi **1** to have a commanding view **2** to be predominant: predominate

***zot·ëror** *adj* dominant, dominating

zot·ërues

I § adj **1** dominant, ruling; proprietary **2** (of a position) commanding, dominating **3** masterful

II § n master

zot·ësi *nf* capability, ability, competence, skill

zot·i

I § adj (i) (of a male) masterful; capable/skillful; clever

II § nm (i) **1** proprietor, owner **2** head of the household, person in charge; boss

◦ **I zoti e shet, tellalli s'e jep.** "The owner sells it, the hawker does not give it." *(Prov)* (said when a person without authority contradicts one with authority)

◦ **I zoti e nxjerr gomarin nga balta.** "The owner gets the donkey out of the mud." *(Prov)* If you want a thing done right you have to do it yourself.

◦ **I zoti e di ku i pikon çatia/shtëpia.** "The head of the house knows where the roof/house leaks." *(Prov)* Only you can know what your problems are: Only you can know where your own shoe pinches.

◦ **i zoti i besë** *[Ethnog]* accused person (at a trial held by a council of elders)

zot·im *nm* pledge of performance

***zot·n** = **zotëri**

zoto·het *vpr* **1** to take it upon oneself, accept a responsibility **2** to become guarantor; make a pledge, promise

zoto·n *vt (Colloq)* **1** to have [] under control: run, command **2** to take possession of []; take [] over by force

zotrote *invar (Colloq)* **1** term of respectful address for an elderly person of substance: sir **2** *(Iron)* derisive term directed at someone putting on airs: big shot

zu *stem for pl pdef, 3rd sg pdef vp* <zë·

*zubë *nf [Bot]* kind of sedge *(Scirpus holoschoenus L., Holoschoenus Link)*

zubëz *nf [Bot]* kind of sedge *(Fimbristyllis)*

*zucë *nf* dregs, sediment

*zuç *nm* fever, passion, ardor

*zuço·n *vi* to have a fever

*zuguli·n *vt* **1** to tickle = gudulis· **2** to disturb, mess [] up

*zuhadhe *np* hemorrhoids = suadhe

zukamë *nf* buzzing/whirring sound: buzz, whir, hum

zukas *stem for 1st sg pres, pl pres, 2nd & 3rd sg subj, pind* <zukat·

zuka·t· *vi* to buzz, whir, hum

zukatje *nf ger* **1** <zukat· **2** = zukamë

*zulmar *adj, n* (person) who seeks glory, ambitious (person)

zulmë *nf* glory; praise, honor

zulmëmadh *adj* highly praiseworthy: glorious

zullap *nm* **1** *(Old)* ferocious carnivorous animal; wild beast **2** *(Crude Insult)* nitwit; ugly bum

zullum
 I § nm **1** *(Colloq)* damage **2** abusive treatment: abuse
 II § n abusive/mean person; naughty/bad person

zullumqar *adj (Colloq)* damaging; abusive

zumare *nf [Mus]* = zamare

*zumber *nm [Ichth]* flathead gray mullet *(Mugil cephalus)*

zumpara OR **zumpare** *nf* sandpaper; emerycloth

zungal *nm* clump of rushes

*zunkth = xunkth

zur *stem for sg pdef, sg imper* <zë·
 ○ **Zure bollën, shtypi kokën.** "You got the snake, now crush its head." *(Prov)* Show the enemy no mercy.
 ○ {} **e zuri buzën** *(Impol)* {} kicked off, {} died
 ○ <>a **zuri cepi i veshit** heard out of the corner of <>'s ear, caught some of it
 ○ <> **zuri guri këmbët** <> is in a tight spot now

zurkajë *nf* waterfall; cataract

zurlë *nf [Mus]* = cyle

zurna *nf [Mus]* = cyle

zuskë *nf (Insult)* woman of loose morals: slut, bitch

*zustra *np fem*

zushë *nf* suffocating heat; thick of the heat, heat of the day

zuzar *n (Insult)* hooligan; bum; nosy pest

zuzarkë = zuskë

zuzëri *nf* hooliganism

zuzëro·n *vi* **1** *(Pej)* to behave like a hooligan **2** *(Reg)* to do hard chores

*zvar = zvarr

zvarg· *vt* to drag out [], prolong

zvarg·et *vpr* to go on and on, drag out, stretch on

*zvargur *adv* = zvarrë

*zvarris = zvarris

*zvarrit· = zvarrit·

zvarranik
 I § adj **1** creeping; decumbent **2** *(Fig)* dragging along slowly, trailing; slow and monotonous **3** *[Zool]* reptilian
 II § nm **1** *[Zool]* reptile **2** *(Reg) [Agr]* heavy wooden beam forming the front/back of a drag harrow **3** *(FigImpolite)* slowpoke **4** *(Fig Contempt)* lickspittle, brownnoser

zvarranike *nf* **1** drag harrow, field harrow **2** *[Bot]* creeping cinquefoil *(Potentilla reptans)*

zvarras *adv* = zvarrazi

zvarrazi *adv* = zvarrë

zvarrë
 I § adv **1** dragging, dragging along; (crawling) along the ground **2** *(Fig)* with difficulty; by force, unwillingly **3** *(Fig)* done late and in a dilatory manner **4** *(Fig)* slowly and in dragging fashion; dragging on and on (monotonously)
 II § nf (Reg) drag harrow, field harrow = zvarranike

zvarrës *adj* dragging; used in a dragging manner

zvarris *stem for 1st sg pres, pl pres, 2nd & 3rd sg subj, pind* <zvarrit·

zvarrit· *vt* **1** to drag **2** to drag [] out, protract, prolong

zvarrit·et OR **zvarris·et** *vpr* **1** to creep, crawl **2** to drag on/along, trail; slide slowly to linger **3** *(Fig)* to have a tough time in life, barely get by

zvarritës *adj* **1** dragging along the ground: creeping, crawling; trailing; procumbent **2** *(Fig)* dragging on monotonously; protractive
 ○ **zvarritës krahëkuq** *[Ornit]* nuthatch *Sitta europaea L.*
 ○ **zvarritës i shkrepave** *[Ornit]* rock nuthatch *Sitta neumayer Mich.*
 ○ **zvarritës i zakonshëm** *[Ornit]* wallcreeper *Tichodroma muraria*

zvarritje *nf ger* **1** <zvarrit·, zvarrit·et **2** crawl

*zvarrnis = zvarris, zvarrit

zvarros· *vt* = zvarrit·

zvarros·et *vpr* = zvarrit·et

zverdh· *vt* to make [] yellow/brown; give [] a yellow/brown cover/coating

zverdh·et *vpr* **1** to turn yellow/brown **2** to grow pale
 ○ <> **zverdh·et**[3sg] **hunda** <> grows pale with fear/anger

zverdhak *nm* **1** yellowed, yellowish **2** having a pallid complexion: pale

zverdhemë *adj (i)* **1** yellowish/brownish **2** pallid, pale

zverdhemtë *adj (i)* = zverdhemë

zverdhë *I § nf* OR **zverdhës** *II § nm [Med]* jaundice = verdhëz

zverdhim *nm ger* = zverdho·n

zverdhje *nf ger* = zverdhim

zverdho·n
 I § vt to give [] a yellow(ish)/brown(ish) color, make [] yellow; (in cooking) brown
 II § vi to yellow; have a yellow appearance/sheen, shine yellow

zverdhosh *adj* tawny

zverdhuk *adj (i)* = zverdhak

zverdhul *adj* pale yellow

zve·rdh·ur *adj (i)* **1** turned yellow/brown: yellowed; (in cooking) browned **2** grown pale

zver·ëti·rë *part* <**zver·ëtit·**

zver·ëti·t· *vt* to make [] sick, disgust

zver·ëti·t··et *vpr* to go out of favor with <>; become alienated from <>

zver·ëti·tje *nf ger* **1** <**zver·ëtit··**, **zver·ëtit··et 2** disgust

zverk *nm (np ~ qe)* back of the neck: nape

zverk·de·rr *adj (Insult)* fat-necked, bullnecked

zverk·o·r *adj [Anat]* occipital

zverk·tra·shë *adj* having a thick neck

zvetë·n·im *nm ger* **1** <**zvetë·no·n, zvetë·no··het 2** perversion, corruption

zvetë·no··het *vpr* to lose good qualities/character: become perverted/corrupt/spoiled

zvetë·no··n *vt* to impair [] in character/quality: pervert, corrupt, spoil

zvetë·n·ua·r *adj (i)* perverted, corrupt, spoiled

***zvë·rdhi··n** *vt* = **zvje·rdh·**

zvicera·n *OR* **zviceria·n** *adj, n* Swiss

Zvi·cër *nf* Switzerland

***zvila·t··et** *vp impers* (of weather) it *clears* up

zvilo··n *vt* to prune away excessive foliage/branches from []; remove the bark from []; clear away the underbrush around []

zvi·rdh··et *vpr* <**zvje·rdh· 1** to lose favor in <>'s eyes, go down in <>'s opinion **2** *(Reg)* (of plants about to bear fruit) to begin to lose flowers
∘ **zvirdh··et nga** {} to be alienated from {}

zvi·rdh· *stem for 2nd pl pres, pind, imper, vp* <**zvje·rdh·**

***zvje·ll·ët** *adj (i)* = **zhdërvjellët**

zvje·rdh· *vt* **1** to wean [a baby] **2** *(Fig)* to chill <>'s feelings toward []; chill <>'s desire for []; alienate <> from [] **3** to prune extra roots and sprouts from [a grafted plant]
∘ **zvjerdh· nga gjiri** to wean

zvje·rdh·ë
I § part <**vjer·dh·**
II § adj (i)

zvje·rdh·je *nf ger* **1** <**zvje·rdh·**, **zvi·rdh··et 2** *[Med]* ablactation

zvje·rdh·ur *adj (i)* **1** weaned **2** gone out of favor, cloying; alienated, estranged **3** *(Reg)* (of a plant) having shed its flowers and about to bear fruit **4** pruned **5** abominable

zvogël·im *nm ger* **1** <**zvogëlo··n, zvogëlo··het 2** diminishment, diminution

zvogëlo··het *vpr* to become smaller: diminish, get shorter/lower, decrease, shrink

∘ <> **zvogëlo·**het³ᵖˡ **sytë** <> *can* hardly keep <>'s eyes open, <> *is falling* asleep

zvogël·o··n *vt* to make [] smaller: diminish, reduce, shorten

zvogël·ua·r *adj (i)* diminished, reduced: smaller, shorter, lower

zvogël·ue·s *adj* **1** *[Ling]* diminutive **2** *[Math]* diminishing, decreasing

zvogël·ue·shëm *adj (i)* capable of being made smaller, capable of being reduced/decreased

zvol *nm* clod of earth

zvo·rdh *stem for pdef* <**zvjer·dh·**

zy·bë *nf with masc agreement (Insult)* incompetent clod

***zyft** *nm* = **zift**

***zy·le** *nf* = **zi·le**

Zy·lo *nf with masc agreement* Zylo (male name)

zyly·fe *nf* **1** lock of hair cut short over the temple: side-bangs **2** tuft of hair

***zymbç** *nm* awl, punch = **za·më**

zymby·l *nm [Bot]* **1** hyacinth *(Hyacinthus)* **2** common hyacinth *(Hyacinthus orientalis)*

Zymby·l *nm* Zymbyl (male name)

zymby·le *nf* two-handled basket

zymne··het *vpr (Reg Gheg)* = **zymto··het**

***zymne··n** *vt (Reg Gheg)* = **zymto··n**

***zymn·im** *nm ger* <**zymne··n, zymne··het**

zy·mt·as *adv* gloomily; somberly

zy·mt·ë *adj (i)* gloomy; somber

zymt·ësi *nf* gloominess, gloom; somberness

zymt·i *nf* = **zymtësi**

zymt·im *nm ger* **1** <**zymto··n, zymto··het 2** gloom

zymto··het *vpr* to become dark and gloomy; become gloomy

zymto··n *vt* **1** to make [] look gloomy/somber/dark **2** *(Fig)* to make [] gloomy

***zyqa·m** *nm* = **rrufë**

zy·rë *nf* **1** office **2** employment as an office-worker **3** *(Old)* difficulty, trouble, need
∘ **Zyra e Radhorit** *(Old)* Records Office

zyrta·r
I § adj **1** official **2** bureaucratic
II § n **1** official **2** bureaucrat

zyrtari *nf (Old)* officialdom, bureaucracy

zyrtar·i·sht *adv* officially

zyrtar·i·zëm *nm (Pej)* bureaucratic red tape

zy·shë *nf (Colloq)* abbreviated form of address used by a pupil toward a female teacher: Missy = **zonju·shë**

zh [*zhë*] *nf* **1** the consonant digraph "zh" **2** the voiced lamino-palatal sibilant represented by the digraph "zh"

zh

I § *formative prefix (only before a voiced obstruent) indicating the opposite or reverse of the meaning of the stem to which it is attached* un-, de-, dis-
II § *causative formative prefix* en-

zhab·*et vpr* to shrivel up, get skin like a toad's; become weak and frail

*****zhab**a**k** *nm* = zhaban

zhaba**lok** *adj* = barkma**dh**

zhaba**n** *nm* male toad

zhabari**s** *stem for 1st sg pres, pl pres, 2nd & 3rd sg subj, pind* <zhabar**i**t·

zhabari**t·**

I § *vt* to shake [a liquid] (in a container) vigorously; dunk [] in water and swish around
II § *vi* = llapashit·*et*

zhabari**t**·*et vpr* to splash around in the water

zhabari**tje** *nf ger* <zhabar**i**t·, zhabar**i**t·*et*

zhabë *nf* **1** [*Zool*] frog, toad **2** [*Zool*] green/water frog (*Rana ridibunda*) **3** edible green/water frog (*Rana esculeuta*) **4** [*Ichth*] angelshark (*Squatina squatina*)
  ○ **zhab**ë **deti** [*Ichth*] angelfish *Lophius budegassa*

zhabërdinë *nf* (*Colloq*) baggy clothes (that hang loose and wiggle when one moves); loose-fitting shoes (so big that they fall off when one walks)

zhabë**rzhye**·*n vt* to get [] completely filthy, soil [] badly

zhabë**s** *nm* (*Old*) leather pouch for carrying the flints for a flintlock gun

zhabi**l** *nm* **1** = zhabin**ë** **2** wheat straw left in the field after reaping **3** [*Ichth*] green wrasse (*Labrus viridis*)

zhabinë *nf* [*Bot*] buttercup, crowfoot (*Ranunculus*)
  ○ **zhabin**ë **flak**ë [*Bot*] spearwort, lesser spearwort *Ranunculus flammula*
  ○ **zhabin**ë **gjuhe** [*Bot*] great spearwort *Ranunculus lingua*
  ○ **zhabin**ë **e pyllit** [*Bot*] wildwood buttercup *Ranunculus nemorosus*
  ○ **zhabin**ë **qepore** [*Bot*] bulb buttercup *Ranunculus bulbosus*
  ○ **zhabin**ë **rrëshqanore** [*Bot*] creeping buttercup *Ranunculus repens*
  ○ **zhabin**ë **e zakonshme** [*Bot*] tall buttercup *Ranunculus acris*

zhabino**k** *nm* [*Bot*] = zhabin**ë**

zhabino**re** *np fem* [*Bot*] buttercup family *Ranunculaceae*

zhabjak** *nm* [*Zool*] **1** = zhap**i** **2** = thithëlop**ë**

zhablla**qe** *np fem* (*Colloq*) old shoes that are so big and ill-fitting that they fall off when one walks

zhabl**lim**ë *nf* shuffling/crunching noise produced by walking on and through dry leaves

zhabl**lo**·*n vi* to make a shuffling/crunching noise (in walking on and through dry leaves)

zhabzhy**rr** *nm* (*Impol*) person dressed in torn and dirty clothes; slovenly person

zhagala**n** *nm* large crackling fire

*****zhag**a**s** *adv* draggingly, by dragging, in a dragging manner

*****zhag**i**tun** *nn* (*të*) (*Reg Gheg*) = fi**k**ë**t

zhagmi**s** *stem for 1st sg pres, pl pres, 2nd & 3rd sg subj, pind* <zhagm**i**t·

zhagmi**t·** *vt* **1** to tug [] apart; tear [] to pieces **2** (*Fig*) to beat [] up badly

zhagmi**tur** *adj* (*i*) torn to pieces

zhagmo·*n vt* = zhagm**i**t·

zhagravi**s** *stem for 1st sg pres, pl pres, 2nd & 3rd sg subj, pind* <zhagrav**i**t·

*****zhagrav**i**t·** *vt* **1** to scribble, scrawl **2** to make [] dirty: soil

zhajkë *nf* **1** [*Text*] refuse from reeling silk from silkworm cocoons **2** hollow walnut

zhajol**lë** *nf* rip in a plant leaf caused by a sharp blow

zhak**e** *nf* **1** loggers' long two-handled saw *****2** = zha**k**ë

zhak**ë**

I § *nf* pond of stagnant water
II § *nf* heavy coarse cloth made of flax or hemp and used as simple floor/body covering or as sacking: sackcloth; object made of sackcloth: canvas bag, rain-cape

zhakëmbe·*het vpr* to dry up and wither; fail to develop properly; get weak and shrivel up

zhakëmbe·*n vt* **1** to crumple; wrinkle **2** to dry up and wither []; impede the growth of []; weaken [] badly, debilitate

*****zhakm**i**s·** = shakm**i**s·

zhak**ra** *np fem* debris carried along by a raging flood

zhalo**n** *nm* [*Spec*] **1** surveyor's stake, leveling rod **2** = shal**o**k

zhaluz**i** *nf* venetian blind; rolling shutter (for a window)

zhal**lo**g**ë** *nf* **1** insole pad; leather patch for shoes **2** thin piece of meat **3** worn out clothing **4** (*Fig*) outworn worthless thing

zhamel *nm* boulder, large rock

zhan**ër** *nm* [*Lit Art*] genre

zhan**g**ë**l** *nf* **1** (*Reg*) thin piece of tough, stringy meat **2** udder

zhangë**ll**i**c**ë *nf* **1** bell that makes a jangling sound **2** (*Insult*) talkative woman

zhangë**ll**i**m**ë *nf* jangling sound

zhangë**ll**o·*n vi* to jangle

zhangë**ll**u**es** *adj* jangling

zhap· *vt* (*Colloq*) **1** to drain [] and leave flabby; wither **2** to stick [] in (with force) **3** to stuff/gorge [] with food **4** (*Fig*) to drain [] of strength, tire [] out completely

zhap·*et vpr* (*Colloq*) **1** to get weak and flabby (from illness) **2** (*Fig*) to feel totally drained, be exhausted **3** to get stuck inside (with force) **4** to stuff/gorge oneself with food, get stuffed

zha·pa *np* <*zha·pë* crude moccasins made of cowhide/horsehide

zhaparis *stem for 1st sg pres, pl pres, 2nd & 3rd sg subj, pind* <*zhaparit·*

zhaparit· *vt (Colloq)* **1** to sear/burn/scald [skin] to the point of raising blisters; wither [a plant] with dry heat **2** to wrinkle [skin] **3** to peel [a fruit/vegetable]

zhaparit·et *vpr (Colloq)* **1** to get dried up and wrinkled skin **2** to dry up and wither

zhapatrinë *nf [Bot]* herbaceous plant whose roots are used as a folk remedy for fever

zha·pë *nf* removable outer layer of a plant or fruit

zhapëhollë *adj* (of fruit/melons) having a thin skin/rind

zhapëkuq *adj* (of fruit/plants) having a red outer layer/skin/bark

zhapëlojë *nf* dried fig

zhapëllimë *nf* sound of (noisy) footsteps/hoofbeats: shuffling, patter, tramp tramp (of feet), clatter (of hoofs)

zhapëllinë = zhapëllimë

zhapëllo·n *vi* to tread noisily (making sharply crackling sounds)

zhapëtrashë *adj* (of fruit/melons) having a thick skin/rind

zhapëverdhë *adj (Impol)* (of people) yellow-skinned; pale and wan, looking sick

zhapëzi *adj, n (fem sg ˜ez, masc pl ˜inj, fem pl ˜eza) (Impol)* (of fruit) having a black skin/rind

zhapí *nm (˜nj)* **1** *[Zool]* lizard **2** green lizard (*Lacerta viridis*)
  ○ **zhapi gomari** *[Zool]* green lizard *Lacerta viridis*
  ○ **zhapi i gjelbër** *[Zool]* green lizard *Lacerta viridis*
  ○ **zhapiu me lara** *[Zool]* spotted leaf-fingered gecko *Gymnodactylus kotschyi*
  ○ **zhapi i ngathët** *[Zool]* sand lizard *Lacerta agilis*
  ○ **zhapi i shtëpisë** *[Zool]* Mediterranean gecko *Hemidactylus turcicus*
  ○ **zhapi i verdhë** *[Zool]* green lizard *Lacerta viridis*

zhapík *nm [Zool]* = zhapí

zhapít·et *vpr (Colloq)* = zhapos·et

*****zhapjak** *nm [Zool]* green lizard (*Lacerta viridis*)

zha·pkë *nf dimin (Reg)* small frog

zhapos·et *vpr (Colloq)* **1** to get weak and flabby (from illness) **2** *(Fig)* to feel totally drained, be exhausted

zhaposur *adj (i)* reduced (by illness) to skin and bones

*****zhaptírë** *nf* marsh, fen

zharavis *stem for 1st sg pres, pl pres, 2nd & 3rd sg subj, pind* <*zharavit·*

zharavit· *vt* to make a mess of []

zharavitje *nf ger* **1** <*zharavit·* **2** mess

zhardhec *nm* snake venom

zhardhok *nm [Bot]* tuber

zhardhokëzim *nm ger [Bot]* <*zhardhokëzo·n*

zhardhokëzo·n *vi [Bot]* (of a tuberous plant) to develop a tuber

zhardhokor *adj [Bot]* tuberous

zhateterë *nf* garter

zharg
  I § *nm* **1** molted skin shed by a snake **2** skin stretched over the body of a bowed lute **3** tree bark **4** *(Impol)* outer garment, coat
  II § *adv* = zvarrë

zharg·et *vpr* **1** to creep, crawl **2** to drag on/along; slide slowly **3** *(Fig)* to have a tough time in life, barely get by

zhargas *adv* = zvarrë

zhargavinë *nf (Reg Pej)* dilapidated old vehicle that barely runs

zhargavit·et *vpr (Reg Pej)* **1** (of a vehicle) to become old and dilapidated and barely running **2** *(Fig)* to get ill and too feeble to work; go to pot

zhargavitur *adj (i) (Reg Pej)* **1** (of a vehicle) dilapidated and old and barely running **2** *(Fig)* ill and too feeble to work; gone to pot

zhargë *nf* **1** old worn-out shoe that keeps falling off and dragging along the ground **2** *(Insult)* foul-mouthed slut

zhargës *nm* bed of a cart that has lost its wheels and that is dragged along the ground as a sledge

zhargët *adj (i)* slovenly/sloppy in dress

zharginë *nf* soggy ground subject to sinking or sliding

zhargit· *vt* = zvarrit

zhargit·et *vpr* = zvarrit·et

zhargo·het *vpr (Colloq)* to creep, crawl = zvarrit·et

zhargo·n *vt (Colloq)* to drag = zvarrit·

zhargon *nm [Ling]* jargon

zharis *stem for 1st sg pres, pl pres, 2nd & 3rd sg subj, pind* <*zharit·*

zharit· *vt* to scorch, burn

zharit·et *vpr* **1** to get scorched **2** to shrivel up

zharitje *nf ger* <*zharit·*, zharit·et

zharrë *nf (Reg)* mountain area covered with grass and tall trees

zhauri·n *vi* to make a booming/roaring sound

zhaurimë *nf* booming sound, roar

zhaurrimë = zhaurimë

*****zhavarí** OR **zhavarinë** *nf* overgrown grass, weed

zhavellë *nf* **1** *[Med]* dysentery **2** *[Hist]* short spear, javelin

zhavorr *nm* **1** aggregate of coarse sand and gravel; gravel **2** *[Geol]* gravelly soil **3** ballast **4** *(Fig)* just so much excess baggage, useless thing

zhavorrim *nm ger* <*zhavorro·n*

zhavorrishte OR **zhavorrishtë**
  I § *nf* gravel bed (from which gravel is mined)
  II § *adj, nf* poor and gravelly (soil)

zhavorro·n *vt* to apply a layer of gravel to []

zhavorruar *adj (i)* covered with gravel

zhbalancim *nm ger (Book)* <*zhbalanco·n*

zhbalanco·n *vt* **1** *(Book)* to unbalance **2** *[Fin]* to throw [] out of balance

zhbart· *vt* to unload

zhbartje *nf ger* <*zhbart·*

zhbë·het *vpr* to come undone

zhbë·n *vt* **1** to undo **2** *(Fig)* to discard; eliminate **3** *(Reg)* to shell [corn]

zhbër *stem for sg pdef, part* <*zhbë·n*

zhbërë *adj (i)* **1** undone: come apart, unraveled, untied **2** *(Reg)* (of corn) shelled

zhbi·n *vt* **1** to yank out [] by the roots **2** to eradicate

zhbiramel *nm (Reg)* = biramel

zhbirim *nm ger* <*zhbiro·n*

zhbiro·n *vt* **1** to make a hole in/through []; pierce **2** *(Fig)* to probe deeply into []

zh|biru|es *adj* **1** piercing; used for boring/drilling **2** *(Fig)* deeply probing

zh|bllok|im *nm ger* <**zhblloko**·*n*, **zhbllokó**·*het*

zh|blloko·*het* *vpr* to become unblocked, regain function

zh|blloko·*n* *vt* **1** to unblock **2** [*Mil*] to break through [a blockade, an encirclement], lift [a siege]

zh|boj|atis· *vt* to make [] colorless: bleach, bleach [] out; decolorize

zh|bo|rde *nf* = **borde**

zh|bord|o·*n* *vt* to make cracks/holes in []; tear, rip

zh|bre·*n* *vt* to unyoke = **çmbreh·**

zh|bre|hur *part* <**zhbre·*n***

zh|brejt *stem for pdef part* <**zhbre·*n***

zh|brengo|s· *vt* to relieve [] of worry/troubles

zh|brengo|s·*et* *vpr* to become relieved of worry/troubles

zh|burg|im *nm ger* <**zhburgo·*n***

zh|burg|o·*n* *vt* = **zhburgo|s·**

zh|burgo|s· *vt* to release [] from prison/jail

zh|burgo|s|ur *adj (i), n (i)* (person) released from imprisonment

zh|burokrat|iz|im *nm ger* <**zhburokratizo·*n*, zhburokratizó·*het***

zh|burokrat|izó·*het* *vpr* to become de-bureaucratized

zh|burokrat|iz|o·*n* *vt* to de-bureaucratize

zh|burrn|im *nm ger* <**zhburrno·*n*, zhburrnó·*het***

zh|burrn|o·*het* *vpr* to lose one's manly virtues/honor

zh|burrn|o·*n* *vt* to unman; deprive [] of manly honor

zh|davar|is *stem for 1st sg pres, pl pres, 2nd & 3rd sg subj, pind* <**zhdavari·t·**

zh|davar|i·t· *vt* **1** to scatter [] far and wide, disperse [] completely **2** *(Fig)* to dispel

zh|davar|i·t·*et* *vpr* **1** to scatter far and wide, disperse completely **2** *(Fig)* to be dispelled, vanish

zh|deh· *vt* to make [] sober

zh|deh·*et* *vpr* to get sober

zh|de|hje *nf ger* <**zhdeh·**, **zhdeh·*et***

zh|de|hur *adj (i)* sobered up

*****zh|dem·** *vt* = **shemb·**

*****zh|dem·*et*** *vpr* = **shemb·*et***

zh|dergj *stem for opt, adm* <**zhdirgj·*et***

zh|detyr|im *nm ger* <**zhdetyró·*n***

zh|detyr|o·*n* *vt* **1** to release [] from a duty; exempt **2** to dismiss from a position

zhdë|fre·*het* *vpr* to release pent-up feelings, blow up at someone

zhdë|fre·*n* *vi, vt* to vent [pent-up feelings]

zhdë|fr|im *nm ger* <**zhdëfre·*n***

zh|dëm|t|im *nm ger* **1** <**zhdëmto·*n*** **2** indemnification **3** indemnity

zh|dëm|t|o·*n* *vt* to pay [] for damages, indemnify

zhdëp· *vt (Colloq)* **1** to beat [someone] up, beat [] black and blue **2** to stuff/gorge with food

zhdëp·*et* *vpr (Colloq)* to get stuffed with food, gorge oneself

zh|dër|ha|ll·*et* *vpr* = **zdërha|ll·*et***

zh|dër|je|nd· *vt* to undo [something woven]

zh|dër|je|nd·*et* *vpr* to come undone, unravel

zh|dër|je|nd|ur *adj (i)* **1** unraveled **2** *(Fig)* slovenly in dress, disheveled; disorganized, dissolute

zh|dër|vi|ll·*et* *vpr* **1** to come unwound/untangled; become untwisted **2** to move sinuously **3** to develop (mentally/physically); become more agile/skillful

zh|dër|vi|ll *stem for 2nd pl pres, pind, imper, vp* <**zhdërvje|ll·**

zh|dër|vje|ll· *vt* **1** to unwind; untangle; untwist **2** to develop [] (mentally/physically); make [] more nimble/agile/quick

zh|dër|vje|ll|ë *part* <**zhdërvje|ll·**

zh|dër|vje|ll|ës|o·*het* *vpr* = **zhdërvi|ll·*et***

zh|dër|vje|ll|ës|o·*n* *vt* = **zhdërvje|ll·**

zh|dër|vje|ll|ët *adj (i)* **1** nimble; agile **2** quick; clever **3** sinuous, windy; with nice curves; curvy; wavy **4** *(Fig)* energetic and lively; fast developing; expressive

zh|dër|vje|ll|je *nf ger* **1** <**zhdërvje|ll·**, **zhdërvi|ll·*et*** **2** = **zhdërvjelltësi**

zh|dër|vje|ll|t|ësí *nf* agility, adroitness; quickness; cleverness; liveliness; expressiveness

zh|dër|vje|ll|t|ëtí = **zhdërvjelltësí**

zh|dër|vo|ll *stem for pdef* <**zhdërvje|ll·**

zh|dirgj *stem for vpr* = **zdirgj·*et***

zh|djerga *np fem* festivities celebrating the descent of the shepherds from their summer mountain pastures

zh|djerg|ur *part* <**zhdirgj·*et***

zh|dogan|im *nm ger* **1** <**zhdogano·*n*** **2** customs clearance

zh|dogan|o·*n* *vt* to clear [] through customs (by paying duties)

zh|dogan|u|ar *adj (i)* cleared through customs

zh|do|rgj *stem for pdef* <**zhdi|rgj·*et***

zh|dredh· *vt* **1** to untwist; unravel **2** to turn [] suddenly toward <>, give [] a sudden twist *****3** to unwrap; unfurl; unfold

zh|dre|dhje *nf ger* <**zhdre|dh·**, **zhdri|dh·*et***

zh|dre|dh|ur *adj (i)* untwisted; unraveled

zh|drejt|azi *adv* indirectly

zh|drejt|ë *adj (i)* **1** indirect **2** [*Math*] inverse (proportion)

zh|dri|dh·*et* *vpr* **1** to become untwisted; unravel **2** to turn suddenly with a twist, twist around; turn toward <> **3** *(Fig)* to take a bad turn

zh|dri|dh *stem for 2nd pl pres, pind, imper, vp* <**zhdre|dh·**

*****zh|dr|im** *nm* conversion

zh|dri|vill|im *nm ger* <**zhdrivillo·*n*, zhdrivilló·*het***

zh|dri|vill|o·*het* *vpr* = **zhdri|vi|ll·*et***

zh|dri|vill|o·*n* *vt* **1** = **zhdërvje|ll·** **2** to expand upon [], elaborate

zh|dro|dh *stem for pdef* <**zhdre|dh·**

zh|dry·*n* *vt* to unlock

*****zh|dryp·** *vt* = **zbre·*t*, zdryp·**

zh|duk· *vt* to cause [] to vanish/disappear
  ◦ [] **zhduk· me një *vijë//të rënë* pene** *(Book)* to make [] disappear with a stroke ("line") of the pen

zh|du|k·*et* *vpr* to cease to exist; vanish, disappear
  ◦ **zhduk·*et* si vesa e *mëngjesit//në diell*** "disappear like the dew *of morning//in the sun*" to disappear fast, vanish quickly without a trace

zh|du|kje *nf ger* **1** <**zhduk·**, **zhdu|k·*et*** **2** disappearance

zh|du|kur
  I § *adj (i)* **1** vanished; extinct **2** [*Law*] missing
  II § *n (i)* **1** person no longer living **2** missing person

zh|dyllo's· *vt* to unseal

zh|dymëzo'·n *vt* to divide [] in two

zh|dhjamo's· *vt* to take the (excessive) fat off of []

zh|dhjamo'sje *nf ger* <**zhdhjamo's·**

zhe'| *stem for pdef, opt* <**zhy'e·n**

zheg *nm* suffocating heat, heat wave; thick of the heat, heat of the day

zhegël|i'në *nf* **1** = **zhegë'r** **2** each of a pair of vertical rods that hold a draft animals head in place under a yoke

zhe'gër *nf* bow of a yoke, collar, oxbow

zheg|i'në *nf* neck-pad under the yoke

zheg|i's| *stem for 1st sg pres, pl pres, 2nd & 3rd sg subj, pind* <**zhegi't·**

zheg|i't· *vi* to rest during the heat of the day: take a siesta

zheg|i't·et *vpr* **1** to rest during the heat of the day: take a siesta **2** to suffer from the heat, feel terribly hot **3** (of plants) to suffer hot-weather burn

zheg|o'·n
I § *vt* **1** to make [] hot *2 to fire [] up, rouse; stir [] to anger?
II § *vi, vt* = **zhegi't·**

zheg|u'li *nf* group of small children being moved as a bunch

zhel|ama'n *adj, n* = **zhela'n**

zhel|a'n *adj, n* tatterdemalion

zhe'le
I § *nf* **1** tattered cloth, rag **2** *(Fig Colloq Pej)* riffraff
II § *np* dirty and tattered old clothes
III § *adj* dirty, old, and tattered

zhele|ma'dh *adj (Insult)* = **zhela'n**

zhele|me'l *adj (Pej)* = **zhela'n**

zhe'le|ndy'rë *adj (Pej)* dressed in filthy rags, shabby and filthy

zhe'le-zhe'le
I § *adj* hanging in rags, completely tattered
II § *adv* in tattered old clothes, all in rags, raggedy

zhel|i'në *nf* old rag

zhel|o'·het *vpr* to get all tattered

zhel|o'·n *vt* to wear [] out all over; reduce [] to tatters, tear [] to rags

zhel|u'a'r *adj (i)* raggedy, tattered

zheng *nm* beestings, foremilk

zhet|i'në *nf [Bot]* prickly thrift *(Acantholimon echinus)*

*****zhevo'l** *nm* = **zhavo'rr**

zhezhi' *nf* **1** smelly residue of scorched food stuck to the bottom of a pot **2** terrible stench (of someone/ something not washed for a long time), dirty stink (of a billy goat)

zhezhi'·n *vi* to give off a bad stench, stink

zhezhi's| *stem for 1st sg pres, pl pres, 2nd & 3rd sg subj, pind* <**zhezhi't·**

zhezhi't· *vt* to overcook [food] so that it sticks to the bottom of the pan

zhezhi't·et *vpr* **1** to get scorched and stick to the bottom of the pan **2** to undergo spoilage (from lack of proper ventilation)

zhezhi'të *nf* smelly residue of food scorched and stuck to the bottom of a pan

zhezhi'tje *nf ger* <**zhezhi't·**, **zhezhi't·et**

zhezhi'tur *adj (i)* **1** scorched to the point of smelling and tasting burned and sticking to the bottom of the

pan **2** stinking badly (from not being kept clean for a long time), having a bad stench **3** spoiled from lack of proper ventilation

zhë'ngë *nf* **1** udder **2** colostrum (from a milk animal)

*****zhë'nicë** *nf* rubbish, waste

*****zhë'rma'k** *nm [Ornit]* = **shka'bë**

zhga'l·et *vpr* to get tired/fatigued, become exhausted

*****zhga'l'ë** *adv* in an unfinished state, uncompleted

zhga'l|i's| *stem for 1st sg pres, pl pres, 2nd & 3rd sg subj, pind* <**zhgali't·**

zhga'l|i't· *vt* to tear [] down, demolish

zhga'l|i't·et *vpr* to collapse

zhgan *nm* **1** pack of wild (and hungry) animals; rampant mob **2** mob, throng; string/column of people

zhga'përre·het *vpr* to open the eyes very wide (in fright/anger); make a face/grimace

zhga'përre·n *vt* to open [the eyes] very wide (in fright/anger)
∘ **zhgapërre·n fytyrën** to make a grimace

zh|gardhi'm *nm ger* <**zhgardho'·n**, **zhgardho'·het**

zh|gardhi'në *nf* **1** rotten wood eaten away by wood-worms **2** broken-down shell of an old house, old hovel

zh|gardhno'·het *vpr* **1** (of something woven/wattled) to come apart, unravel **2** to become weak and flabby

zh|gardhno'·n *vt* **1** to take apart [something woven/ wattled]; unravel [] **2** to make [] soft and weak, squash [] into mush; beat [someone] badly

zh|gardho'·het *vpr* to come apart (with loss of parts of the framework); break down

zh|gardho'·n *vt* to take apart/away the (wattled) fence around []

zh|gardhu'a'r *adj (i)* missing an intact fence

*****zh|gark|** = **shkark**

*****zhgaurre'të** *nf (Reg)* gnarled tree

zh|gëlqer|ëzi'm *nm ger [Spec]* <**zhgëlqerëzo'·n**

zh|gëlqer|ëzo'·n *vt [Spec]* to clean away the lime (used in treating something)

zh|gënje'·het *vpr* to become disillusioned

zh|gënje'·n *vt* **1** to disillusion **2** to overturn, turn [] around

zh|gënji'm *nm ger* **1** <**zhgënje'·n**, **zhgënje'·het 2** disillusionment **3** disappointment

zh|gënjy'er *adj (i)* disillusioned; disappointed

zh|gënjy'es *adj* deceptive

zh|gërshë'to'·n *vt* to unbraid

zh|gërry'·het *vpr* **1** to wallow (in dirt) **2** to lean against something to scratch one's back **3** to get all dirty, become filthy **4** *(Fig)* to work like a slave/ drudge

zh|gërry'e·n *vt* **1** to dig away at [] **2** to drag/roll [] through filth **3** *(Fig)* to spend [] extravagantly, waste, squander **4** *(Fig)* to treat [] like dirt **5** to soil [one's clothes]

zh|gojo'·n *vt* to take [] apart by exerting pressure

zh|go'le *nf* snail shell

zh|go'lkë *nf* acorn cup

zh|gozhdo'·n *vt* to unnail

zh|gradi'm *nm ger* **1** <**zhgrado'·n 2** demotion; notice of demotion

zh|grado'·n *vt* to demote [] in rank/position

zh|gradu'a'r *adj (i)* demoted in rank/position

zh|grap· *vt, vi* **1** *(Colloq)* to scribble **2** = **shkrep·**

*****zh|greh·** *vt* = **shkreh·**

*zh**greh·**et *vpr* **1** = shkre·*het* *2* to collapse; fall apart, wilt, droop

*zh**greḧët** *adj (i)* limp, weak, lax, soft, broken down

*zh**greh'ur** *adj (i)* = zgreheht

zh**gropo's·** *vt* to take [] out of a hole in the ground: dig [] out of the ground, dig [] up; disinter

zh**gropo'sje** *nf ger* **1** <zhgropo's· **2** disinterment

zh**gropo'sur** *adj (i)* taken out of a hole in the ground: dug up; disinterred

*zh**grrys** *stem for 1st sg pres, pl pres, 2nd & 3rd sg subj, pind* <zhgrryt·

*zh**grryt·** *vt* to scratch, claw; scrape
○ zhgrryt· në [] to delve into []

zh**gua'll** *nm (np ~j)* tough outer covering

*zh**gul** = shkul

zh**gun** *nm* heavy white wool fabric woven on two harnesses and fulled; cloak made of this fabric; Franciscan monk's gown made of this fabric

zh**gunaqep'ës** *nm* tailor of heavy white wool clothing

zh**gunta'r** *n* **1** = zhgunaqep'ës **2** weaver of heavy white wool cloth

zh**gun'të** *adj (i)* made of heavy white wool cloth

zh**guri's** *stem for 1st sg pres, pl pres, 2nd & 3rd sg subj, pind* <zhgurit·

zh**guri't·** *vt* **1** (of chickens) to scratch [the ground] for bits of rock **2** to pick [teeth] (with a toothpick)

zh**guri't·**et *vpr* **1** (of chickens) to scratch the ground **2** = zhgërry·het

zh**gjak'ësim** *nm ger* **1** <zhgjakëso'·n, zhgjakëso'·het **2** blood vengeance; act of blood revenge

zh**gjak'ëso·**het *vpr* **1** to take blood revenge); get revenge; be avenged **2** (a slaughtered animal) to be drained of blood

zh**gjak'ëso·**n *vt* **1** to avenge the blood of []; avenge [a wrong] **2** to drain or clean away the blood of [a slaughtered animal]

*zh**gja'ndërr** *adv* daydreaming

zh**gjesh·** *vt* = zgjesh·

zh**gje'sh'ur** *adj (i)* = zgjeshur

zh**gje'tull** *nf* = qep'er

zh**gjeth'ësim** *nm* [Bot] shedding of leaves; defoliation

zh**gjë'ndërr** *nf* **1** waking state after dreaming **2** real-world reality (in contrast to the world of dreams) **3** (Fig) illusion

zh**gjymti'm** *nm ger* **1** <zhgjymto'·n **2** dismemberment

zh**gjymto'·**n *vt* **1** to cripple, maim **2** to dismember, destroy

zh**gjymtyro'·**n = zhgjymto'·n

zh**gjyrç** *nm (Reg)* green outer husk of walnuts

zh**gi'bël** *nf* **1** sliver of wood **2** speck, mote **3** skin blemish: mole **4** (Fig) moral defect: vice

zh**gig** *nm* **1** scorched residue stuck to the bottom of a cooking pot **2** blemish, stain, spot

*zh**giga's** *stem for 1st sg pres, pl pres, 2nd & 3rd sg subj, pind* <zhgiga't·

*zh**giga't·** *vt* to annoy, bother; tease

*zh**gi'gë** *nf* dross

zh**gi'gël**

I § *nf (Reg)* **1** = cingari'dhe **2** piece of nonsense, trifle **3** hanky-panky, monkey business

II § *adj* (of a walnut) without nutmeat

zh**gi'gler** *nm* device for producing a jet

---

zh**gi'gmi'o·**het *vpr* to lose favor in <>'s eyes, go down in <>'s opinion

zh**gi'go'·**n *vt* **1** to cover [] with soot, blacken [] with smoke; to dirty [] with dark spots **2** (Fig) to denigrate, defame, smear

zh**ile'** *nf* waistcoat, vest

*zh**ing'ël** *nf* = xhing'ël

zh**ir** *nm* **1** dross **2** residue of burned grease

zh**irue'të** *nf* weathervane

zh**i'vë**

I § *nf* [Chem] mercury, quicksilver ((Hg))

II § *adj* **1** (Colloq) astringent; too salty; bitter **2** (Fig Colloq) quick and lively; in constant motion

III § *adv* (Colloq) very much; very well

zh**ivo'r** *adj* [Chem] mercurial; mercuric

*zh**izh-bu'bazi** *adv*

*zh**i'zhë** *nf* = xhi'xhë

zh**oke'r** *nm* [Riding] jockey

zh**o'kël** *nf (Reg)* shell, pod, hull, husk

zh**ol** *nm* **1** = zhul **2** (Reg) [Bot] moss = myshk **3** (Reg Fig) worry

zh**ongle'r** *nm* **1** juggler **2** (Fig Pej) sly trickster, clever charlatan; opportunist

*zh**o'rbë** *nf* empty walnut

zh**u'bël**

I § *nf* = zhu'bër

II § *adv* all crinkled and crumpled

zh**u'bër** *nf* **1** wrinkle **2** ripple

*zh**u'blo·**n *vt* = zhubro's·

zh**ubra'vi's** *stem for 1st sg pres, pl pres, 2nd & 3rd sg subj, pind* <zhubravi't·

zh**ubra'vi't·** *vt* = zhubro's·

zh**ubra'vi't·**et *vpr* = zhubro's·et

zh**ubra'vi'tje** *nf ger* = zhubro'sje

zh**ubra'vi'tur** *adj (i)* = zhubro'sur

zh**u'bra-zhu'bra** *adj* full of wrinkles

zh**u'bro·**n *vt* = zhubro's·

zh**u'bro's·** *vt* **1** to wrinkle; crumple **2** to cause ripples in []

zh**ubro's·**et *vpr* to get wrinkled

zh**ubro'sje** *nf ger* <zhubro's·, zhubro's·et

zh**ubro'sur** *adj (i)* **1** wrinkled, crumpled **2** withered

zh**uga'n** *adj (Reg)* = zgjebara'k

zh**u'gë** OR zh**u'gëz** *nf (Reg)* **1** [Med Veter] = zgjebe **2** (Fig Insult) filthy/scurrilous person

zh**u'gull** *nm (Reg)* = zheg

zh**u'kë** *nf* **1** [Bot] rush (Juncus) **2** rush fiber **3** underground spring that makes ground all wet; wet ground; marsh

zh**uki'shte** *nf* marsh of rushes

zh**uko're** *nf* [Bot] rush family Juncaceae

zh**u'kte** *adj (i)* **1** made of rush fiber **2** (Fig) weak and in poor health, thin and sickly

zh**ul** *nm* **1** dirt on unwashed body or clothes: grime, smut **2** joule

zh**ula'n** *adj* **1** = zhulanjo's **2** (Fig) miserable

zh**ulanjo's** *adj (Insult)* grimy, filthy, smutty

zh**ula's** *stem for 1st sg pres, pl pres, 2nd & 3rd sg subj, pind* <zhula't·

zh**ula't·** *vt* **1** to pound [] into flexibility **2** to push/plunge [] under water; steep [] (in liquid) **3** (Colloq) to stuff/gorge [] with food **4** (Fig Colloq) to beat [] up badly, beat [] to a pulp

zhula't·et *vpr* **1** to crouch down **2** *(Colloq)* to get stuffed (with food), gorge oneself

zhula'të *nf* **1** pounding **2** plunge (into liquid), dunk

zhula'tur *adj (i)* **1** (of plant fiber) made pliant by soaking and beating **2** pressed down and kept in one position

zhu'lgë *adj* = **zhu'ngur**

zhuli'cë *nf* [*Bot*] variety of wheat whose flour is good for making pastry dough
  ○ **zhulica e bardhë** easy-to-thresh wheat with short awns
  ○ **zhulica e kuqe** awnless wheat sown in hilly country

zhulo's· *vt* to make [] grimy

zhulo's·et *vpr* to become grimy, get soiled

zhuma're *nf* dregs left after extracting the oil from olives

zhumbi'në *nf (Reg)* **1** baby tooth newly broken through the gums **2** newly formed kernel of corn **3** tooth gum = **try'sa**

zhumbri'cë *nf* [*Bot*] thyme *(Thymus)*

zhumhu'r *nm* muffled noise/roar; din

zhumi'le *np fem* **1** dry stalks and leaves; bedding straw for livestock **2** chaff, trash, sweepings

*****zhung** *nm* round mass, lump

zhu'ng·et *vpr* (of fruit) to get soft and mushy, become overripe

zhu'ngë *adj* (of fruit) soft and mushy, overripe

zhu'ngur *adj (i)* (of fruit) allowed to get soft and mushy, overripened

zhup· *vi* to be noisy, make a racket: bang, clatter

*****zhupllim** *nm* **1** <**zhupllo'·n 2** noisy racket: bang, clatter

*****zhupllo'·n** *vt* = **zhup·**

zhupo'n *nm* petticoat, white slip

zhur *nm* coarse sand

zhuri' *nf* jury = **juri'**

zhuri'në *nf* **1** bed of coarse sand and gravel **2** = **zhuri'shtë**

zhuri's stem for 1st sg pres, pl pres, 2nd & 3rd sg subj, pind <**zhuri't·**

zhuri'shtë
  I § *nf* poor soil composed of coarse sand and gravel; area with such soil
  II § *adj* composed of coarse sand and gravel

zhuri't·
  I § *vt* **1** to cause [] to burn: burn [] to a crisp, burn [] to ashes; char; scorch, scald **2** to parch
  II § *vi* to get charred: char
  ○ **<>a zhuri't· zemrën** *(Fig)* to create a deep longing/yearning in <>'s heart

zhuri't·et *vpr* **1** to get badly burned; get burned to a crisp; get scalded/seared **2** (of plants) to wither from heat; (of soil) crack open with dryness **3** to have a high temperature
  ○ **<> zhuri't·et³ˢᵍ zemra/shpirti (për** [])** "<>'s heart *burns* (for [])" **1** <> *is yearning* (for []), <> has <>'s heart set on []) **2** <>'s heart *is suffering*

zhuri't·es *adj* **1** burning hot, scorching **2** causing a burning pain

zhuri'tje *nf ger* **1** <**zhuri't·**, **zhuri't·et 2** burning thirst; burning desire; intense nostalgia/longing

zhuri'tur *adj (i)* **1** burned to a crisp **2** (of plants) parched from heat; (of soil) cracked open with dryness **3** burning for a drop of water **4** *(Fig)* burning with nostalgia/longing, afflicted by a deep yearning

zhurk *nm (np ˜qe)* area with poor soil composed of coarse sand and gravel

zhu'rmë *nf* **1** noise **2** [*Med*] murmur

zhurmëbë'rës *adj* making noise

zhurmëdhë'nës *adj* producing noise

zhurmëko'të *adj* uselessly/unnecessarily noisy

zhurmëma'dh *adj* very noisy, strident; loud and noisy

zhurmëma't·ës *n* [*Phys*] sound-level meter

zhurmëmby't·es
  I § *adj* [*Spec*] muffling
  II § *nm* [*Spec*] silencer; muffler

zhurmëplo'të
  I § *adj* full of noises
  II § *adv* turbulently, boisterously

zhurmëri' *nf* monotonous din

zhurmëri'm *nm ger* **1** <**zhurmëro'·n 2** = **zhurmërimë**

zhurmëri'më *nf* soft and continuous murmuring/whispering sound

zhurmëro'·n *vi* **1** to make a prolonged muffled sound: murmur **2** to make the sound of complex activity

zhurmëru'es *adj* making a prolonged muffled sound

zhu'rmëshëm *adj (i)* noisy

zhurmëshu'më *adj* **1** moving noisily; bustling with noise **2** *(Pej)* making noise to attract attention

zhu'rmët *adj (i)* **1** full of noise, noisy **2** [*Ling*] obstruent

zhurmëta'r *adj, n* loud-voiced/noisy (person)

zhurmëthi'th·es *adj, nm* [*Spec*] sound absorbent

zhurmi'm *nm ger* **1** <**zhurmo'·n 2** noise

zhurmo'·n *vi* **1** to make noise, be noisy **2** to call out sporadically **3** to resound, echo

zhu'rmshëm *adj (i)* noisy

zhurmu'es
  I § *adj* = **zhu'rmshëm**
  II § *nm* [*Spec*] noise generator

zhurra'k *nm* = **zhuri'në**

zhurre'lë *nf* = **zhuri'shtë**

zhu'shka *np fem (Colloq)* [*Med*] mumps = **shy'ta**

zhuzha'k *nm* **1** [*Entom*] beetle *(Coleoptera)* **2** = **zhuzhi'ngë**
  ○ **zhuzhaku i artë** [*Entom*] rose beetle *Cetonia aurata*
  ○ **zhuzhaku i drithërave** [*Entom*] grain beetle *Zabrus tenebrioides*
  ○ **zhuzhaku i hardhisë** [*Entom*] vine chafer *Anomala vitis*
  ○ **zhuzhaku lëvorengrënës** [*Entom*] sinuate pear borer, flatheaded pear borer, pear borer *Agrilus sinuatus*
  ○ **zhuzhaku i majit** [*Entom*] June beetle *Melolontha melolontha*
  ○ **zhuzhaku me bri** [*Entom*] rhinoceros beetle *Oryctes nasicornis*
  ○ **zhuzhaku i misrit** "corn beetle" [*Entom*] *Pentodon punctatus Vill.*

zhuzha'kë *np* [*Entom*] lamellicorn beetles *(Scarabaeidae)*

zhuzha's stem for 3rd pl pres, 3rd sg subj <**zhuzhe't·**

zhuzhe *nf* = zhuzhak

zhuzhet· *vi* **1** to make a buzzing sound, buzz **2** (of fire) to crackle **3** *(Fig)* = gumëzhi·*n*

zhuzhingë *nf* [*Entom*] goldsmith beetle, rose chafer *(Cetonia aurata)*

zhuzhit· *vt* to toast/roast [food]

zhuzhit stem for pdef, opt, adm, part, pind, vp < zhuzhet·

zhuzhitë *nf* burnt food

zhuzhitje *nf ger* **1** < zhuzhet· **2** = zhuzhurimë

zhuzhull *nm* (np ~ j) [*Entom*] hard-back beetle *(Pentodon idiota)*

zhuzhullim *nm ger* **1** < zhuzhullo·*n* **2** buzz, whir, hum

zhuzhullo·*n* *vi* to buzz, whir, hum

zhuzhunë *nf* [*Entom*] weevil

zhuzhurimë *nf* **1** sound of a burning fire, crackling **2** buzz, whir, hum

zhuzhurit· *vi* = zhuzhet·

zhuzhuritës *adj* annoying monotonous sound

zhuzhuritje *nf ger* = zhuzhitje

zhvar· *vt* to take []down/off from where it is hanging

zhvarrim *nm ger* = zhvarrosje

zhvarros· *vt* **1** to exhume **2** to recover [] from a hiding place, uncover [a hidden object] **3** *(Fig)* to bring []back from the forgotten past

zhvarrosje *nf ger* **1** < zhvarros· **2** exhumation

zhvas stem for 1st sg pres, pl pres, 2nd & 3rd sg subj, pind < zhvat·

zhvat· *vt* **1** to tear off a piece of []; tear [] to pieces, lacerate, shred; tear []away/off/out; take []away by force **2** to take unfair advantage of []'s generosity/helplessness

zhvat·et *vpr* to get scratched up and torn; get one's clothes torn

zhvatarak
  I § *adj* **1** = zhvatës **2** *(Impol)* dressed in tattered clothes
  II § *n* **1** thief **2** badly dressed person

zhvatës *adj, n* predaceous (person)

zhvatje *nf ger* < zhvat·, zhvat·et

zhvatur *adj (i)* **1** torn **2** stolen

zhvendos·
  I § *vt* **1** to move []; displace, deport; shift *2 to extradite
  II § *vi* to change/revoke a previous decision

zhvendos·et *vpr* to change residence/position/location

zhvendosje *nf ger* **1** < zhvendos·, zhvendos·et **2** shift

zhvesh· *vt* **1** to take off [a piece of clothing] **2** to strip [] of outer covering, lay [] bare, denude: undress/unclothe [a person], peel [fruit], skin [an animal], husk [vegetables], gin [cotton], hull [kernels], remove the bark from [a tree], defoliate [plants], bare/unsheathe [a weapon] **3** to thin out [plants], prune **4** *(Colloq)* to take away ◇'s right to wear [the uniform] (characteristic of a profession); dismiss []from the army; dismiss [] from a position/job **5** *(Colloq)* to rob, swindle
  ∘ **e zhvesh· pallën** "unsheathe one's sword" to take off one's kid gloves
  ∘ **zhvesh· shpatën** "unsheathe the sword" to prepare for war, get ready to fight

zhveshës *adj* used for removing the outer covering

∘ **zhveshëse pambuku** cotton gin

zhveshëse *nf* machine for removing grain husks/hulls: husking machine

zhveshje *nf ger* **1** < zhvesh·, zhvish·et **2** [*Geol*] land surface worn away by erosion: *(degradation)*

zhveshur
  I § *adj (i), n (i) adv* undressed/disrobed/naked (person); (person) not properly attired
  II § *adj* stripped

zhvidhos· *vt* to unscrew

zhvidhosur *adj (i)* taken apart by unscrewing

zhvill stem for 2nd pl pres, pind, imper, vp < zhvjell·

zhvillim *nm ger* **1** < zhvillo·*n*, zhvillo·*het* **2** development, evolution

zhvillimor *adj* *(Book)* developmental

zhvillo·*het* *vpr* to develop, evolve

zhvillo·*n* *vt* to develop/evolve []

zhvilluar *adj (i)* well developed, evolved

zhvillues
  I § *adj* stimulating/aiding development
  II § *n* person who develops a theory/idea/science: developer
  III § *nm* [*Photog*] developing fluid

zhvirgjërim *nm ger* **1** < zhvirgjëro·*n* **2** defloration

zhvirgjëro·*n* *vt* to deprive [] of virginity, rupture the hymen of []: deflower

zhvish·et *vpr* **1** to get undressed; become naked **2** to shed leaves; become bare
  ∘ **zhvish·et nga** *fg* to rid oneself of [a vice/prejudice/impediment]

zhvish stem for 2nd pl pres, pind, imper, vp < zhvesh·

zhvjell· *vt* to open up [something in a bundle]

zhvleftësim *nm ger* = zhvlerësim

zhvleftëso·*het* *vpr* = zhvlerëso·het

zhvleftëso·*n* *vt* = zhvlerëso·*n*

zhvleftësues *adj* = zhvlerësues

zhvlerësim *nm ger* **1** < zhvlerëso·*n*, zhvlerëso·het **2** depreciation, devaluation **3** invalidation

zhvlerëso·*het* *vpr* to decrease in value: depreciate

zhvlerëso·*n* *vt* **1** to devalue/devaluate [money] **2** to invalidate; vitiate

zhvlerësuar *adj (i)* **1** devalued; worthless **2** depreciated; lowered in price

zhvlerësues *adj* **1** causing devaluation **2** invalidating

zhvoll stem for pdef < zhvjell·

zhvoshk· *vt* to remove the outer layer of []: decorticate

zhvoshk·et *vpr* to lose pieces of the outer layer of []

zhvoshkje *nf ger* **1** < zhvoshk·, zhvoshk·et **2** decortication

zhvoshkur *adj (i)* with the outer layer removed: decorticated

zhvulos· *vt* **1** to unseal **2** to take off the seal of wax of [a honeycomb]

zhvulosje *nf ger* < zhvulos·

zhvulosur *adj (i)* **1** unsealed **2** (of a honeycomb) without its seal of wax

zhvullnet·et *vpr* to suffer a loss of will/willpower; become apathetic/dispirited

zhvullnetur *adj (i)* suffering a loss of will/willpower; apathetic/dispirited

zhy·het *vpr* **1** to get very dirty **2** *(Fig)* to become sullied by involvement in dirty business **3** (of children) to dirty one's pants (defecate in one's clothes)
  ○ <> **zhy·**het **faqja** to become covered with shame

zhye·n *vt* **1** to make [ ] very dirty, soil [ ] badly **2** *(Fig)* to sully [ ] by involving [ ] in dirty business
  ○ <>**a zhye·**n **faqen** to cover <> with shame

zhyer
  I § part <**zhy**e·n
  II § adj (i) **1** badly soiled **2** *(Fig)* sullied by involvement in dirty business

zhyerje *nf ger* <**zhy**e·n, **zhy**het·

zhyl *nm (Reg)* **1** millrace **2** *(Colloq)* = **zhul**

zhylas| *stem for 1st sg pres, pl pres, 2nd & 3rd sg subj, pind* <**zhyla**t·

zhylat· *vt (Reg Gheg)* to soil

zhylatur *adj (i)* dirty; filthy

zhym *nm* **1** cigarette ash **2** soot = **blozë**

zhymë *nf* swampland, bog

zhymore *nf* swampy soil; swampland, bog = **moçalishte**

zhymtë *nf* swampy

zhyrë = **zhy**er

zhys| *stem for 1st sg pres, pl pres, 2nd & 3rd sg subj, pind* <**zhyt**·

zhyt
  I § nm = **zhy**tje
  II § adv completely submerged, under water

zhyt· *vt* **1** to plunge/immerse [ ] in liquid **2** *(Fig)* to get [ ] into hot water, put [ ] into a difficult situation **3** [Sport] to spike [a volleyball]

zhyt·et *vpr* to submerge; dive

zhytar *n* underwater diver

zhytarak *nm* [Ornit] little grebe, dabchick *(Tachybaptus ruficolis)*

zhytas *adv* under water, submerged, immersed

zhytër *nf* [Ornit] grebe *(Podiceps)*
  ○ **zhyt**ër **e madhe** great crested grebe *Podiceps cristatus*

zhytës
  I § adj connected with or used for underwater diving
  II § n **1** underwater diver **2** [Sport] good underwater swimmer
  ○ **zhyt**ës **i madh** [Ornit] goosander *Mergus merganser L.*
  ○ **zhyt**ës **i vogël laraman** [Ornit] smew *Mergus albellus L.*

zhytje *nf ger* **1** <**zhy**t·, **zhy**t·et **2** immersion **3** underwater swimming

zhytkryekuqe *nf* [Ornit] great crested grebe *(Podiceps cristatus)*

zhytore *nf* diving bell

*****zhy**tr̈ës *n* [Ornit] diver = **nor**

zhytthi *adv* = **zhy**tas

zhytur *adj (i)* submerged; immersed; sunk

*****zhyve**lgë *nf* dead/dried leaves